CW01496080

1999 UNITED KINGDOM AND IRELAND CIVIL AIRCRAFT REGISTERS

Thirty Fifth Year of Publication

Compiled and Edited by Barrie Womersley

CONTENTS

c   Air-Britain (Historians) Limited 1999

Published by: Air-Britain (Historians) Limited

Registered Office: 12 Lonsdale Gardens, Tunbridge Wells, Kent TN1 1PA

Sales Department: 19 Kent Road, Grays, Essex RM17 6DE

Membership Enquiries: (ABN) 1 Rose Cottages, 179 Penn Road, Hazlemere, Bucks HP15 7NE

Front Cover Photograph

Love Air's Jetstream G-LOVA at Biggin Hill in June 1998 and now on a fourth set of UK marks.
(Leslie Dickson)

Rear Cover Photographs

Piper Apache G-BICY at Elmsett in February this year. (Stewart Lanham)

Rotary Air Force RAF 2000 GTX-SE G-BWTK at North Weald. (Ian Burnett)

ISBN 0 85130 276 9
ISSN 0264 - 5270

INTRODUCTION AND EDITORIAL

The first edition of this volume appeared in 1964 with Phil Butler at the helm. By 1968, the fourth edition was being edited by Bernard Martin with assistance from myself and Dennis Fox, then editor Air-Britain's fortnightly "British Civil Aviation News" forebear of the "United Kingdom Register" now contained in "Air-Britain News". The publication consumed just over a comfortable 100 pages. Bernard eventually passed on production of the eighteenth edition to Malcolm Fillmore in 1982. I could not foresee that 30 years after my initial commitment I would become involved once again in the production of Air-Britain's premier monograph. Such is the nature of the beast that "once committed - always involved" seems to be the watchword as all three former editors have made major contributions to my first edition for which I am very grateful. Phil has been instrumental in producing the British Glider Association information, Bernard has been acting as my electronic-mail arm and Malcolm has been passing on copious information to me.

In last year's editorial Malcolm made the point very eloquently that he was retiring in order to make way for an older man. I do not intend to challenge the previous two editors' longevity - Bernard edited from 1968 to 1981 (14) and Malcolm from 1982 to 1998 (17) even though a regenerated National Health Service might allow me to do this. The next editor must already be out there ready to take over in a few years time !

Under Malcolm's stewardship, and supported by Air-Britain's Monograph's Committee, the UK Register has expanded greatly to become an excellent reference volume. I will continue to support the general direction which has encouraged development of the volume around the official UK and Irish Registers. As such I believe the register should concentrate on core activities reflecting individual civil aircraft. For this reason I have decided to discontinue those sections which list airfields and radio frequencies - this area is already well served by a number of excellent guides. I can understand why RAF, RN & AAC historical flights were originally listed but consider the reason is no longer valid. However, the former UK specimens are now listed elsewhere in the book.

During 1998 I spent considerable time discussing the proposed content of this edition with regular readers - there were several pleas for a location index, inclusion of date & place of manufacture data, and the revival of the balloon name listing which featured several years ago. These will be considered for further years. For the future I would like to include a full listing of the PFA project numbering system and there is also now a discrete British Microlight Aircraft Association (BMAA) system to consider. If there is any one who can assist with these projects please make yourself known as soon as possible !   As both these areas now tend to dominate the UK register I would like also to include details of first flights and to this end the PFA's own magazine is a good source of information.

There are some substantial changes in both style and content this year. I am particularly pleased that the CAA has abandoned the special microlight series of registrations - perhaps the aeronautical apartheid to these craft will now die away and they will now be accepted as "a good thing" designed to get people in the air inexpensively and now, safely. As such there will no longer be a separate section for microlights. I have also forsaken the need to identify out of sequence registrations - since this facility commenced in the late 1970s, give or take the occasional pre and post war special set of markings, many out of sequence markings have been subsumed and are now well in sequence. All such registrations are now established within a new Section 1 although there is still a discrete spot for the remnants of the first pre 1928 registration series. Elsewhere both UK and Irish glider registers are joined together in a new Section 3. The former Kilroy section is heavily truncated, somewhat due to time constraints, and now appears as Section 6. Most of this retrospective information should appear in Alan Johnson's monthly UK Register section in "Air-Britain News". Finally the previous type indices have been defragmented and then partially fragmented into UK and non UK areas. The decode register of civil aircraft carrying service markings and the glider index are also included within this section. Regrettably, there is no CAA statistical information this year - I hope this can be re-introduced in the next edition.

Many thanks to this year's contributors and to the continued support from the regular stalwarts, many of whom assisted me as "Display Diary" editor some time ago. For this edition, I would like to thank the following correspondents [as always in alphabetical order]: Barry Abraham, Robert Belcher, Jeff Bell, Peter Budden, B J Burt, Phil Butler, Mike Cain, Ian Callier, Peter Campbell/Cirrus Associates, Richard Cawsey, Chris Chatfield, Noel Collier, Andy Cook, Paul Cunniffe, Tony Doyle, Steve Dudley, Graham Duke, Phil Dunnington, Don Eaves, Ken Ellis, Malcolm Fillmore, Ray Fitton, David Fogwill, Mike Fresh, Wal Gandy, Mike Glazer, Dave Haines, Douglas Hepburn, Coen van den Heuvel, Paul Hewins, Graham Heysett, Nigel Hitchman, Graham Hocquard, Andy Hutchings, Phil Jones, Ian Judge, Bob Kent, Roger Kunert, Steve Laskey, Roger Light, Stuart McDiarmid, Bernard Martin, Pete Mather, Brian Matthews, Peter Miriams, Tony Morris, Ken Parfitt, Jeremy Parkin, Martin Perkins, Stephen Reglar, Steve Roake, Trevor Sexton, Mark Shortman, Mark Simmons, Graham Slack, Colin M Smith, Warren Smith, Steve Sowter, Jeff Spiers, Martyn Steggalls, Mike Stevenson, Mervyn Thomas, Steve Thompson, Nigel Webb & Robert Woodhams .... and, finally, to Angela for her forbearance.

Thanks are also due to those who send in reports and material direct to A-B News editors. The deadline for the 2000 edition is the end of January 2000. I hope to have acquired an e-mail address by then. Meantime, special thanks to Bernard Martin who has continued to drip feed such material all winter plus his own valued contributions. Appreciation is owed to Alan Johnson - editor of the afore-mentioned "UK Register" and for his liaison with the Civil Aviation Authority in London and, also, to Paul Cunniffe for similar duties in Ireland. Much of the glider material comes direct from the BGA through the continued efforts of Phil Butler and Wal Gandy.

APRIL 1999   BARRIE WOMERSLEY
                                                                                        19 The Pastures
                                                                                        Westwood
                                                                                        Bradford on Avon
                                                                                        Wilts BA15 2BH

There are several purposes to this annual volume. The primary one is to list all aircraft on the current civil aircraft registers, giving full details of types and previous identities, registered ownership and/or operator, probable home base and certification of airworthiness status. This information reproduces, expands upon and amplifies the official country registers. However, we go well beyond that; included in the main text are all other known but no longer currently registered UK and Irish aircraft which, no matter where located, remain in a reasonably identifiable condition either under or pending rebuild, in museum or store, even if merely for spares use, or perhaps held for instructional, fire service or similar use. In addition, all other civilian owned, but foreign registered, aircraft believed to be based in the British Isles are also included, so that there is a fully comprehensive guide to the British and Irish civil aviation scene.

On a secondary level we cater for the aviation specialist or historian, who wants to know more about particular aircraft - detailed information such as non-standard engine power, reasons for the aircraft's non-airworthy state and so on. As this book has developed over the years, we have included more and more information - to the extent that we now also give details of significant happenings during the year to support the snapshot at the year end.

A guide to the main text is as follows:-

Registration (Regn)
    Registrations are set out in alphabetic order, other than for the initial 1919/28 "G-E" register which comes first. Aircraft no longer currently registered are marked "*". A few aircraft, either real or static reproductions, are identified in British civil marks for display purposes and are shown as "G-xxxx". Where the same marks have been re-issued or re-allotted, particularly if the first holder or allottee did not use the marks, these are shown with the suffix (2) after the registration.

Type
    We adopt the official type description as set down by the manufacturer or designer. Where there is doubt, reference is usually made to the relevant issue of "Jane's All the Worlds Aircraft". Indication is given if the manufacturer is a successor company or a licence builder - although not always if it is merely a sub-contractor. Under this column, we show engine types in parenthesis if the engine is non-standard and for all home-builds and microlights and for those vintage/classic aircraft where engines can vary. Additional explanatory notes show details of any unrepaired accidents and comments on the airframe's identity and where the true position is at variance with the official records.

Constructor's Number (C/N)
    This is the manufacturer's serial number, which may or not be quoted in the official register. Some aircraft may have more than one number - for example homebuilds can have the builder's own number, as well as the official sequential number allotted by the PFA and on occasion a plan or kit number. All are given where known. Some homebuilds and microlights were registered without any proper c/n - in this case the CAA generally used the owner's initials following by "01" etc. These numbers are replaced if the correct serial is subsequently identified. Many weightshift microlights are given separate c/n's for the trike unit and for the wing by the manufacturer. In many cases, the CAA only registers the wing c/n (although builders such as Hornet, Mainair and Medway issue a composite c/n comprising both units). Wherever known, both c/n's are shown - with the trike unit preceding the wing c/n.

Previous Identities (P/I)
    These are set out in reverse order, with the most recent identity first. Registrations shown in parenthesis were allotted but believed never officially used. The nationality of foreign military serials is indicated only where it may not be apparent. Manufacturers test marks are given, where known, except in respect of where a standard generic mark has been used, such as for Pipers in the 1960s and German motorgliders more recently.

Registration Date (Date)
    This is the date of the original registration for those particular marks, even where subsequently removed and restored.

Owner/Operator
    For current aircraft this is the registered owner. Where the operator is known to be different this is shown in parenthesis. Included under this column are details of status, at the latest reported date, if the C of A is not current or the aircraft is known to be under repair as well as details of any names and, in particular, military colour schemes worn. Some aircraft are shown as temporary un-registered ("Temp unregd"); this is where the CAA has not received an application from a new owner following a sale. A period of discretion is given by the CAA but if no response is received the certificate is cancelled and the aircraft is not permitted to fly. This action usually stimulates the new owner to produce the relevant documentation.

Probable Base
    Information in the column is not guaranteed: there is no official information. Reports by readers visiting airfields and strips are perused to compile this column. When the location is uncertain the owner's home town is shown in parenthesis. Aircraft change base frequently. Readers are reminded that the identification of a base, and particularly if it is a private strip, is not an invitation to visit and in a number of cases, visiting is actively discouraged because of previous abuses. Balloons, microlights, helicopters and gyrocopters are generally shown as being based at the owner's registered address unless an alternative is known. We recognise the need for privacy in this area and consequently not all information is published.

C of A Expiry
    This date indicates the currency of the aircraft and details on the suffix letters are set out on page 5. Where the C of A has expired or lapsed and the aircraft has been reported since that date, a note is given. C of A information is taken from the quarterly register supplements published by the CAA. Some expired, or absent, C of A dates are clearly wrong - a case undoubtedly of paperwork delays within the CAA. C of A's shown in parenthesis are the expiry dates prior to sale overseas for restored aircraft. They are officially quoted by the CAA but have little current relevance.

4

EDITORIAL NOTE

The UK & Ireland Register is correct to 31st December 1998 with new additions and notes incorporated to early April 1999. Information regarding the issue and status of UK Certificates of Airworthiness is correct to 31st December 1998.

ABBREVIATIONS

A/C	-	Aero Club	F/C	-	Flying Club	RTS	-	Reduced to spares
A/c	-	Aircraft	F/Grp	-	Flying Group	Svs	-	Services
Avn	-	Aviation	GC	-	Gliding Club	t/a	-	Trustees of the Assets of
BBM & L	-	British Balloon	HAFB	-	(Hot-Air) Free Balloon			OR Trading As - depending
		Museum & Library	Intl	-	International			on whether a group of
BMAA	-	Britsh Microlight	NTU	-	Not taken up			private owners or a
		Aircraft Association	PFA	-	Popular Flying Association			company
C of A	-	Certificate of	Pwfu	-	Permanently (Withdrawn)	t/s	-	Tail scheme
		Airworthiness			from use			
c/s	-	Colour scheme	R	-	Reservation			
Dbf	-	Destroyed by fire	RAFGSA	-	Royal Air Force Gliding			
Eng	-	Engineering			and Soaring Association			

CERTIFICATES OF AIRWORTHINESS (C OF A) STATUS

The C of A category is indicated by the coding after the date of expiry. No code letter indicates a Private category C of A of one or three year duration. Others are:-

A   Aerial Work: normally indicating crop-spraying, or banner towing/aerial advertising.

AC   Awaiting Certification

E   Exemption: applicable only to microlights not subject to permit to fly status, no new issues are being made.

Exp   Export: issued for limited period solely to facilitate delivery overseas.

F   Ferry: normally issued for two months, and commonly for overseas sale, or an unlicensed aircraft being flown to another airfield for overhaul.

N/E   Non-Expiring: Hot-Air balloons were, until recently, usually certified as such. The suffix in parenthesis indicates whether it is an Aerial Work, Private or Transport certificate. Non-Expiring exemptions were also given a few years ago to certain early microlights. These are being progressively upgraded. Any without a date should, in reality, be considered to have lapsed. A few other N/E certificates are used for exports.

P   Permit to Fly: Introduced in 1950 covering homebuilds, microlights and vintage aircraft - normally issued for one year

PF   Permit to Fly (Ferry): Issued for one specific flight only - the aircraft need not be of a type that normally operates under a permit to fly.

P*   Permit to Fly (Test): Issued for varying periods of one, two or three months for test purposes leading usually to the issue of a full one year permit to fly. Only a few now seem to be issued.

S   Special/l Mainly lapsed now and replaced by permits to fly but sometimes still used for manufacturers trials aircraft, particularly for overseas demonstration.

T   Transport (Passenger): Issued to any aircraft operated for hire or reward, usually for either one or three years.

TC   Transport (Cargo): As above, but aircraft restricted to carrying cargo for hire or reward. Few aircraft fall into this category.

SECTION 1 - UNITED KINGDOM REGISTER

The first permanent United Kingdom Register of Civil Aircraft was inaugurated on 31st July 1919 and ran until 29th July 1928 when the marks G-EBZZ had been issued. With the growth of international civil aviation new regulations were due to come into effect from 1st January 1929. Nonetheless the transition to a second series of registrations commencing from G-AAAA onwards was made with effect from 30th July 1928. Registrations were usually allocated in alphabetical sequence until the late 1970s although there were several exceptions to this rule even in the early years.

The G-AAAA-AZZZ series were all allocated by mid 1972 when a new series G-BAAA commenced. This is still in use in conjunction with registrations allotted from other series extending from G-C.. to G-Z... Many of the G-B... registrations which were issued ahead of the alphabetical sequence have now been subsumed within their proper series. In addition several special registration series have been used covering a) Alphanumeric marks for Concordes in 1979 & 1980, b) Balloons and Airships (G-FAAA-FAAZ) from 1920 to 1928, c) Model balloons from 1982 to date (G-FYAA-FYZZ) and d) Microlights from 1981 to 1998 (G-MBAA-MBZZ, MGAA-MGZZ, MJAA-MJZZ, MMAA-MNZZ, MTAA-MTZZ & MYAA-MZZZ). All UK registrations, including those still valid from the model balloon and microlight series, are now incorporated within this Section.

G-EAAA-EBZZ

Regn	Type	C/n	P/I	Date	Owner/operator	Probable Base	CA Expy
G-EACN*	BAT FK.23 Bantam 1	FK23/15	K-123	29. 5.19	Aviodome/Early Birds Foundation		
	(ABC Wasp)		F1654		(On rebuild 1992) Lelystad, Netherlands		
G-EACQ*	Avro 534 Baby	534/1	VH-UCQ	29. 5.19	Queensland Cultural Centre		
			G-AUCQ/G-EACQ/K-131			Brisbane, Australia	
G-EAML*	Airco DH.6	-	C9449	8. 9.19	South African Air Force Museum		
					(Components only) Pretoria, South Africa		18. 9.20
G-EAOU*	Vickers FB.27A Vimy IV	-	(A5-1)	23.10.19	Not known	Adelaide, Australia	31.10.20
			G-EAOU/F8630		(On display Airport Museum)		
G-EAQM*	Airco DH.9	-	F1278	31.12.19	Australian War Memorial		
	(AS Puma)					Canberra, Australia	1. 1.21
G-EASD	Avro 504L floatplane	E.5	S-AHAA	26. 3.20	AJD Engineering Ltd	Moat Farm, Milden	--
	(Le Clerget 130hp)		S-AAP/G-EASD/(RAF)		(Stored 8.93 pending rebuild)		
G-EAVX	Sopwith Pup	PFA/101-10523	B1807	2.11.20	K.A.M.Baker	(Winscombe, Avon)	--
					(To be "B1807/A7" in RFC c/s)		
	(Claimed to be rebuild of original aircraft which was written-off at Hendon 21.7.21; status uncertain)						
G-EBHX	DH.53 Humming Bird	98	No.8	22. 9.23	The Shuttleworth Trust	Old Warden	2. 7.95P
	(ABC Scorpion II)		(Lympne 1923)		"L'Oiseau-Mouche"		
G-EBIA	R.A.F. SE-5A	654/2404	F904	26. 9.23	The Shuttleworth Trust	Old Warden	14. 5.99P
	(Wolseley Viper 200hp)		"D7000"/G-EBIA/F904		(As F904 "H"in 56 Sqdn RFC c/s)		
G-EBIB*	R.A.F. SE-5A	687/2404	"F939"	26. 9.23	The Science Museum (Flight Gallery)		
	(Regd with c/n 688/2404)		G-EBIB/F937			South Kensington, London	6. 6.35
G-EBIC*	R.A.F. SE-5A	688/2404	"B4563"	26. 9.23	RAF Museum (As "F938")	Hendon	3. 9.30
	(Wolseley Viper 200hp)		G-EBIC/F938		(Regd with c/n 687/2404; allocated 9208M)		
G-EBIR	DH.51	102	VP-KAA	22. 1.24	The Shuttleworth Trust "Miss Kenya"		
	(ADC Renault 120hp)		G-KAA/G-EBIR			Old Warden	18. 7.99P
G-EBJE*	Avro 504K	927	?. 6.24		RAF Museum (As "E449")	Hendon	29. 9.34
	(Includes components of Avro 548A G-EBKN ex E449; allocated 9205M 1994)						
G-EBJG*	Parnall Pixie III	- No.17/No.18	?.7.24		Midland Air Museum	Baginton	2.10.36
			(Lympne 1924)		(Components only remain for long term rebuild 4.96)		
G-EBJO	ANEC II	2	No.7	17.7.24	The Shuttleworth Trust	Old Warden	30.11.35
			(Lympne 1924)		(On rebuild 10.97)		
G-EBKY	Sopwith Dove	w/o 3004/14	"N5180"	27. 3.25	The Shuttleworth Trust	Old Warden	9. 5.99P
	(Le Rhone 80hp)(Converted to Sopwith Pup)		"N5184"/G-EBKY		(As "N6181" in 3 Sqdn RNAS c/s) "Happy"		
G-EBLV	DH.60 Moth	188		22. 6.25	British Aerospace (Ops) Ltd	Old Warden	28. 4.99P
	(Cirrus III)				(On loan to The Shuttleworth Trust)		
G-EBMB*	Hawker Cygnet I	1	No.14	29. 7.25	RAF Museum	Hendon	30.11.61
	(Bristol Cherub III)		(Lympne 1924)				
G-EBNV	English Electric S.1 Wren	4	(BAPC11)	9. 4.26	The Shuttleworth Trust	Old Warden	23.6.87P*
	(ABC 398cc) (Composite aircraft - principally c/n 3 rebuilt 1955/56; as "No.4")						
G-EBOV*	Avro 581E Avian	5116	No 9	7. 7.26	Queensland Cultural Centre		
			(Lympne 1926)			Brisbane, Australia	30. 1.29
G-EBQP	DH.53 Humming Bird	114	J7326	?. 4.27	M.C.Russell	Audley End	AC
			(On rebuild 3.97 based on wings ex Martin Monoplane G-AEYY; to be as "J7326")				
G-EBWD	DH.60X Moth	552		2. 3.28	The Shuttleworth Trust	Old Warden	10. 4.99P
	(Cirrus Hermes 2)						
G-EBXU	DH.60X Moth Seaplane	627		2. 5.28	D.E.Cooper-Maguire	Findon, Worthing	13.12.99P
			(Crashed nr Rio De Janeiro 1930; provenance unconfirmed: restored 1998)				
G-EBYY*	Avro 617 Cierva C.8L Mk.2	-		21. 6.28	Musee de l'Air et de l'Espace		
	(AS Lynx 180hp)					Le Bourget, Paris	13. 7.29
G-EBZM*	Avro 594A Avian IIIA	R3/CN/160		?. 7.28	The Aeroplane Collection Ltd	Manchester	20. 1.38
	(Cirrus)				(On loan to Manchester Museum of Science & Industry)		

G-AAAA-AAZZ

Regn	Type	C/n	P/I	Date	Owner/operator	Probable Base	CA Expy
G-AAAH*	DH.60G Moth	804		30. 8.28	The Science Museum (Flight Gallery)		
					"Jason"	South Kensington, London	23.12.30
	(A replica, allocated BAPC168, is displayed at the Gatwick Hilton Hotel - see SECTION 4)						
G-AACD*	DH.60M Moth	340		16.10.28		St.Ives, Huntingdon	8. 4.38
	(Gipsy I)			(Crashed Fen Ditton, Cambridge 24.6.37, rebuilt but stored in 1989)			
G-AACN*	Handley Page HP.39 Gugnunc	1	K1908	2.11.28	The Science Museum	Wroughton	(19.9.30)
			G-AACN				
G-AADR	Moth Corpn DH.60GM Moth	138	NC939M	2. 6.86	H.F.Moffatt	Woodlow Farm, Bosbury	16. 8.99P
	(Gipsy I)						
G-AAEG	DH.60G Moth	1027	D-EUPI	4. 2.29	J.Dixon	(Brensbach, Germany)	
			D-1599/G-AAEG		(On rebuild 1994 - provenance unconfirmed)		
G-AAHI	DH.60G Moth	1082		?. 5.29	N.J.W.Reid	Lee-on-Solent	30. 6.99P
	(Gipsy I)			(Rebuilt from components remaining from G-AAWO rebuild)			
G-AAHY	DH.60M Moth	1362	HB-AFI	?. 5.29	D.J.Elliott	Thruxton	12. 8.99P
	(Gipsy I)		(CH-480)/G-AAHY		(Brooklands Flying Club c/s)		
G-AAIN	Parnall Elf II	2 & J.6		11. 6.29	The Shuttleworth Trust	Old Warden	30. 4.99P
	(ADC Cirrus Hermes 2)						
G-AALP*	Surrey Flying Svs AL-1	AL-1		29. 8.29	Arden Family Trust (Stored 1.98)		
						Thorncross Farm, Caudleigh	17. 5.40
G-AAMX*	Moth Corpn DH.60GM Moth	125	NC926M	11. 9.86	RAF Museum	RAF Cosford	7. 5.94P
	(Gipsy II)						
G-AAMY	Moth Corpn DH.60GMW Moth	86	N585M	2. 5.80	Totalsure Ltd	(Netherlands)	1. 6.99P
	(Wright Gipsy L320)		NC585M				
G-AANF*	Moth Corpn DH.60GMW Moth	49	N298M	3. 2.87	C.Smith	Mandeville, New Zealand	17. 4.90P
	(Wright Gipsy 1)		N237K/NC237K		(Damaged nr Popham 8.8.89 and on rebuild 2.91)		
G-AANG	Bleriot Type XI	14	(BAPC3)	29.11.81	The Shuttleworth Trust	Old Warden	
	(Anzani 25hp) (1910 original; no external marks)						
G-AANH	Deperdussin Monoplane	43	(BAPC4)	29.10.81	The Shuttleworth Trust	Old Warden	14. 5.83P
	(Anzani Y 35hp) (Possibly c/n 143; no external marks)						
G-AANI	Blackburn 1912 Monoplane No.9	725	(BAPC5)	29.10.81	The Shuttleworth Trust	Old Warden	18. 7.99P
	(Gnome 683 50hp)				(No external marks)		
G-AANJ	LVG C.VI 4503	C7198/18		29.10.81	The Shuttleworth Trust	Old Warden	10. 4.99P
	(Benz 230hp)		"1594"/C7198/18				
	(As "7198/18" in German Air Force c/s; composite aircraft including parts from LVG 1594: captured 1916/17 and allotted RFC serial "XG7")						
G-AANL	DH.60M Moth	1446	OY-DEH	26. 6.87	P.L.Allwork	Hildon-le-Noble, Hants	23. 6.99P
	(Gipsy I)		RDAF S-357/S-107		(In National F/Svs c/s; composite rebuild)		
G-AANM	Bristol F2B Fighter	"67626"	BAPC166	16. 7.87	Aero Vintage Ltd	St.Leonards-on-Sea	
	(RR Falcon)				(On rebuild 8.95 - to carry marks "D7889")		
G-AANO	Moth Corpn DH.60GMW Moth	165	N590N	3. 3.88	A.W. & M.E.Jenkins	Comberton, Cambridge	
			NC590N		(Composite rebuild 11.91)		
G-AANV	Morane Saulnier DH.60M Moth	13	HB-OBU	8. 3.84	R.I.Souch	Hill Farm, Durley	8. 8.97P
			CH-349/F-AJNY				
G-AAOK	Curtiss-Wright	12Q-2026	N370N	18.11.81	Shipping & Airlines Ltd	Biggin Hill	18. 1.84P
	Travel Air CW-12Q (Warner Scarab 145)		NC370N/NC352M				
	(Damaged in gales Rijeka, Yugoslavia 21.10.83 - on rebuild 8.97)						
G-AAOR	DH.60G Moth	1075	EC-AAO	15. 4.85	V.S.E.Norman	Rendcomb	4.10.99P
	(Gipsy I)		(Original identity uncertain and probably composite)				
G-AAPZ	Desoutter I	D.25		?.?.31	The Shuttleworth Trust	Old Warden	3. 3.39
	(Cirrus Hermes)				(National Flying Svs c/s) (Post restoration flight 26.1.99)		
G-AAUP	Klemm L 25aI	145		19. 2.30	Janice I.Cooper t/a Newbury Aeroplane Co		21.11.84P
	(Salmson AD9)				(Stored 6.95)	Denford Manor, Hungerford	
G-AAWO	DH.60G Moth (Gipsy 1)	1235		2. 5.30	N.J.W.Reid & L.A.Fenwick	Lee-on-Solent	20. 1.98P
	(Composite 1953 rebuild including parts of G-AAHI c/n 1082)						
G-AAXK*	Klemm L 25aI	182		?. 5.30	C.C.Russell-Vick	Orpington	29.11.60
					(Damaged White Waltham 3.62; stored 3.96)		
G-AAYX	Southern Martlet	202		14. 5.30	The Shuttleworth Trust	Old Warden	12. 4.49
	(Genet Major 1A)				(On long term rebuild 3.96)		
G-AAZP	DH.80A Puss Moth	2047	HL537	4. 6.30	R.P.Williams	Denford Manor, Hungerford	30. 9.99
	(Gipsy Major)		G-AAZP/SU-AAC/G-AAZP "British Heritage"				

G-ABAA-ABZZ

Regn	Type	C/n	P/I	Date	Owner/operator	Probable Base	CA Expy
G-ABAA*	Avro 504K	-	"H2311" G-ABAA	?. 5.30	RAF Museum	Manchester	11. 4.39
					(On loan to Manchester Museum of Science & Industry)		
G-ABAG	DH.60G Moth (Gipsy I)	1259		23. 6.30	The Shuttleworth Trust	Old Warden	30. 4.99P
G-ABBB*	Bristol 105A Bulldog IIA	7446	"K2227" G-ABBB/R-11/G-ABBB	12. 6.30	RAF Museum	Rotary Farm, Hatch	
					(Damaged Farnborough 13.9.64 & on rebuild by Skysport Engineering 7.97)		
G-ABDX	DH.60G Moth (Gipsy I)	1294	HB-UAS (CH-405)/G-ABDX	?. 8.30	M.D.Souch	Hill Farm, Durley	28. 7.99P
G-ABEV(2)	DH.60G Moth (Gipsy I)	1823	N4203E G-ABEV/HB-OKI/CH-217	10. 3.77	Wessex Avn & Transport Ltd	Chalmington	9.10.97P
G-ABLM*	Cierva C.24 (Gipsy III)	710		22. 4.31	The Science Museum	Salisbury Hall, London Colney	16. 1.35
G-ABLS	DH.80A Puss Moth (Gipsy Major)	2164		7. 5.31	R.C.F.Bailey	Ludlow	2. 8.99P
G-ABMR*	Hawker Hart	H.H-1	"J9933" G-ABMR	28. 5.31	RAF Museum	Hendon	11. 6.57
					(As "J9941" in 57 Sqn c/s)		
G-ABNT	Civilian CAC.1 Coupe (Genet Major 1A) (C/n also quoted as O.3)	O.2.3		?. 6.31	Shipping & Airlines Ltd	Biggin Hill	30. 9.99P
G-ABNX	Robinson Redwing 2 (Genet)	9		2. 7.31	J.A.Pothecary	Newton Toney, Salisbury	21. 6.94P
					(Stored 8.97)		
G-ABOI*	Wheeler Slymph	AHW.1		17. 7.31	A.H.Wheeler	Coventry	
					(Loaned to Midland Air Museum & dismantled components stored 4.96)		
G-ABOX	Sopwith Pup (80 hp Le Rhone)	-	N5195	12. 9.84	C.M.D. & A.P. St.Cyrien		
					(As "N5195" in Museum of Army Flying)	AAC Middle Wallop	22. 4.93P
G-ABSD	DH.60G Moth	1883	A7-96 VH-UTN/G-ABSD	21.11.31	M.E.Vaisey	Hemel Hempstead	
					(On rebuild following import from USA in 1985 as basket case; identity unconfirmed)		
G-ABTC*	Comper CLA.7 Swift (Pobjoy Niagara)	S.32/1		1. 1.32	P.Channon "Spirit of Butler"	Lelant, Cornwall	18. 7.84P
					(Cancelled by CAA 22.2.99; stored since 7.84)		
G-ABUS	Comper CLA.7 Swift (Pobjoy Niagara 3)	S.32/4		27. 2.32	R.C.F.Bailey	Ludlow	19. 6.79P
					(On rebuild 1989)		
G-ABVE	Arrow Active 2 (Gipsy III)	2		19. 3.32	J.D.Penrose	Old Warden	15. 4.99P
					(On loan to The Shuttleworth Trust)		
G-ABWP	Spartan Arrow 1 (Cirrus Hermes 2)	78		4.32	R.E.Blain	Redhill	4. 9.99P
G-ABXL	Granger Archeopteryx (Cherub III)	3A		3. 6.32	The Shuttleworth Trust	Old Warden	22. 9.82P
G-ABYA*	DH.60G Moth (Gipsy I)	1906		6.32	J.F.Moore	Biggin Hill	21. 5.73
					(Crashed Biggin Hill 21.5.72 & stored 2.95)		
G-ABYN	Spartan Three-Seater II	102	EI-ABU G-ABYN	7.32	Julie D Souch	Mandeville, New Zealand	
					(On rebuild by Croydon Avn Co 1995)		
G-ABZB	DH.60GIII Moth Major	5011	SE-AIA G-ABZB	30. 8.32	R.Earl & B.Morris	Foley Farm, Berks	12. 8.99P
					(First post restoration flight 10.8.98)		

G-ACAA-ACZZ

Regn	Type	C/n	P/I	Date	Owner/operator	Probable Base	CA Expy
G-ACAA(2)	Bristol F.2B Fighter - (RR Falcon)			25.10.91	Patina Ltd (Op The Fighter Collection)	Duxford	AC

(Regd as "original" G-ACAA with c/n 7434 ex F4516 but in fact on rebuild 7.97 from various components including ex Weston-on-the-Green fuselage frame/to be "D8084/S")

Regn	Type	C/n	P/I	Date	Owner/operator	Probable Base	CA Expy
G-ACBH*	Blackburn B.2	4700/3	(2895M) G-ACBH	1.12.32	R.Coles t/a Coles Auto Supplies Temple Farm, West Hanningfield, Essex		27.11.41

(Stored 1.96 for possible refurbishment/probably to be composite with G-ADFO c/n 5920/2 written off in 1940)

Regn	Type	C/n	P/I	Date	Owner/operator	Probable Base	CA Expy
G-ACCB	DH.83 Fox Moth	4042		24. 1.33	E.A.Gautrey (Crashed off Southport 25.9.56 & on rebuild 10.95)	Nuneaton	20. 7.57
G-ACDA	DH.82A Tiger Moth	3175	BB724 G-ACDA	6. 2.33	B.D.Hughes	Rotary Farm, Hatch	26. 6.82

(Crashed & burned out nr Cirencester 27.6.79 - rebuild probably composite with G-ANOR by Skysport 1.96)
(Toger Moth N3529, based Old Rhinebeck, New York is marked as "G-ACDA")

Regn	Type	C/n	P/I	Date	Owner/operator	Probable Base	CA Expy
G-ACDC	DH.82A Tiger Moth	3177	BB726 G-ACDC	6. 2.33	The Tiger Club (1990) Ltd (Composite airframe after several major rebuilds)	Headcorn	26. 3.99T
G-ACDI	DH.82A Tiger Moth (Composite rebuild)	3182	BB742 G-ACDI	6. 2.33	J.A.Pothecary Newton Toney, Salisbury		AC
G-ACDJ	DH.82A Tiger Moth	3183	BB729 G-ACDJ	6. 2.33	P.Henley Brickhouse Farm, Frogland Cross		8. 6.01
G-ACEJ	DH.83 Fox Moth	4069		21. 4.33	Janice I.Cooper (Scottish Motor Traction c/s) t/a Newbury Aeroplane Co	Rendcomb	3.11.00
G-ACET	DH.84 Dragon	6021	2779M AW171/G-ACET	21. 4.33	M.D.Souch (Hedge End, Southampton) (On rebuild 1995/Composite based on original wings)		
G-ACGR*	Percival Gull Four IIA (Gipsy Major I)	D.29		11. 5.33	Musee Royal de l'Armee Brussels, Belgium		20. 6.35
G-ACGT*	Avro 594B Avian IIIA	R3/CN/171	EI-AAB	5.33	Yorkshire Light Acft Ltd Leeds-Bradford (On long term rebuild 1.97)		21. 7.39
G-ACIT	DH.84 Dragon 1	6039		24. 7.33	The Science Museum (Highland Airways c/s) "Aberdeen"	Wroughton	25. 5.74
G-ACLL	DH.85 Leopard Moth	7028	AW165 G-ACLL	16. 1.34	D.C.M. & V.M.Stiles (Stored 10.96)	Jurby, IOM	6.12.95P
G-ACMA	DH.85 Leopard Moth	7042	BD148 G-ACMA	14. 3.34	S.J.Filhol (Stored 2.95)	Headcorn	3. 2.94P
G-ACMD(2)	DH.82A Tiger Moth	3195	N182DH EC-AGB/Sp AF 33-5	20. 1.88	M.J.Bonnick Rectory Farm, Abbotsley		18. 4.99
G-ACMN	DH.85 Leopard Moth	7050	X9381 G-ACMN	4.34	Carolyn S.Grace	Duxford	18. 2.00
G-ACOJ(2)	DH.85 Leopard Moth (Composite with wings from HB-OXO)	7035	F-AMXP	5. 6.87	A.J.Norman t/a Norman Aeroplane Trust	Rendcomb	3. 9.01
G-ACSP	DH.88 Comet	1994	CS-AAJ G-ACSP/E-1	21. 8.34	K.Fern (On rebuild 10.96 based on some original components)	Stoke-on-Trent	
G-ACSS	DH.88 Comet (Gipsy Queen 2)	1996	K5084 G-ACSS	4. 9.34	The Shuttleworth Trust "Grosvenor House"	Old Warden	2. 6.94P

(a) Static rep built Australia for film purposes is owned by G Gaywood - see BAPC216 in SECTION 4)
(b) Second flying rep built in 1993 by Repeat Aircraft, Riverside CA, USA for Tom Wathen regd N88XD)

Regn	Type	C/n	P/I	Date	Owner/operator	Probable Base	CA Expy
G-ACTF	Comper CLA.7 Swift (Pobjoy Niagara 2)	S.32/9	VT-ADO	24. 5.34	The Shuttleworth Trust "The Scarlet Angel"	Old Warden	29. 4.99P
G-ACUS	DH.85 Leopard Moth	7082	HB-OXA (G-ACUS)	17.11.77	A.J.Norman t/a Norman Aeroplane Trust	Rendcomb	30. 1.99

(Composite including parts from HB-OXO (G-ACUS) c/n 7045)

Regn	Type	C/n	P/I	Date	Owner/operator	Probable Base	CA Expy
G-ACUU*	Avro 671 Cierva C.30A Autogiro (AS Civet)	726	(G-AIXE) HM580/G-ACUU	26. 6.34	Imperial War Museum - Skyfame Collection (As "HM580")	Duxford	30. 4.60
G-ACUX*	Short S.16 Scion 1	S.776	VH-UUP G-ACUX	26. 6.34	Ulster Folk & Transport Museum (As "VH-UUP")	Holywood, Belfast	-
G-ACVA*	Kay Gyroplane 33/1 (75hp Pobjoy R)	1002		26. 6.34	Glasgow Museum of Transport	Kelvin Hall, Glasgow	
G-ACWM*	Avro 671 Cierva C.30A Autogiro	715	(G-AHMK) AP506/G-ACWM	24. 7.34	E.D. Ap Rees Weston-super-Mare t/a The Helicopter Museum		13. 7.40
G-ACWP*	Avro 671 Cierva C.30A Autogiro	728	AP507 G-ACWP	24. 7.34	The Science Museum (Flight Gallery) South Kensington, London (As "AP507/KX-P" in 529 Sqn c/s)		6. 3.41
G-ACXB(2)	DH.60GIII Moth Major	5098	EC-ABY EC-BAX/Sp AF 30-53/EC-YAY	24. 1.89	D.F.Hodgkinson (Gravesend) (On rebuild)		
G-ACXE	British Klemm L 25c1 Swallow	21		29.10.34	J.G.Wakeford (On rebuild since 1989)	Bexhill-on-Sea	7. 4.40
G-ACYK*	Spartan Cruiser III	101		2. 5.35	Royal Museum of Scotland (Crashed Largs, Ayrshire 14.1.38 & remains recovered 7.73)	East Fortune	2. 6.38
G-ACYR*	DH.89 Dragon Rapide	6261		15.10.34	Museo del Air	Cuatro Vientos, Spain	23. 8.47
G-ACZE	DH.89A Dragon Rapide	6264	G-AJGS G-ACZE/Z7266/G-ACZE	20.11.34	Wessex Avn & Transport Ltd (Stored 8.97)	Henstridge	11. 8.95

G-ADAA-ADZZ

Regn	Type	C/n	P/I	Date	Owner/operator	Probable Base	CA Expy
G-ADAH*	DH.89 Dragon Rapide	6278		30. 1.35	The Aeroplane Collection Ltd	Manchester	9. 6.47
	(On loan to Manchester Museum of Science & Industry; Allied Airways (Gandar Dower) c/s) "Pioneer"						
G-ADEV(2)	Avro 504K	R3/LE/61400	G-ACNB	18. 4.84	The Shuttleworth Trust	Old Warden	10. 4.99P
	(110hp Le Rhone)	"E3404"			(As "H5199")		
	(The p/i is not confirmed but, if correct, the full p/i is 3118M/BK892/G-ADEV/H5199)						
G-ADFV*	Blackburn B.2	5920/8	2893M	3. 4.35	J.Chillingworth	St.Ives, Huntingdon	26. 6.41
			G-ADFV		(Forward fuselage for rebuild 4.96)		
G-ADGP	Miles M.2L Hawk Speed Six	160		20. 5.35	R.I.Souch	Old Warden	24. 4.99P
					(On loan to The Shuttleworth Trust)		
G-ADGT	DH.82A Tiger Moth	3338	BB697	23. 5.35	D.R. & Mrs M.Wood		
			G-ADGT			Fowle Hall Farm, Paddock Wood, Kent	18. 8.97
G-ADGV	DH.82A Tiger Moth	3340	(D-E)	23. 5.35	K.J. & P.J.Whitehead		
			G-ADGV/(G-BACW)/BB694/G-ADGV			Whitchurch Hill, Reading	18. 5.99
G-ADHD(2)	DH.60GIII Moth Major	5105	EC-...	17. 2.88	M.E.Vaisey	Henlow	
			Sp AF 34-5/EC-W32		(Rebuild of ex Spanish components acquired from USA)		
G-ADIA	DH.82A Tiger Moth	3368	BB747	13. 8.35	S.J. Beaty	Wold Lodge	21. 7.99
			G-ADIA				
G-ADJJ	DH.82A Tiger Moth	3386	BB819	29. 8.35	J.M.Presto	Great Eversden	20. 3.75
			G-ADJJ		(Stored 4.95)		
G-ADKC	DH.87B Hornet Moth	8064	X9445	27. 3.36	A.J.Davy	Redhill	30.11.01
			G-ADKC				
G-ADKK	DH.87B Hornet Moth	8033	W5749	9.11.35	R.G.Anniss	(Horsham)	7. 8.00
G-ADKL	DH.87B Hornet Moth	8035	F-BCJO	?.11.35	A. de Cadenet	Perigeux, France	29. 5.95
			G-ADKL/W5750/G-ADKL				
G-ADKM	DH.87B Hornet Moth	8037	W5751	12.11.35	L.V.Mayhead	Hedge End, Durley	6. 7.01
			G-ADKM				
G-ADLY	DH.87B Hornet Moth	8020	W9388	5.10.35	Totalsure Ltd	(Netherlands)	15. 4.99P
			G-ADLY				
G-ADMT	DH.87B Hornet Moth	8093		8. 5.36	P.A.D.Swoffer "Curlew"	White Waltham	19. 5.01
G-ADMW*	Miles M.2H Hawk Major	177	DG590	30. 7.35	RAF Museum	Cardington	30. 7.65
			G-ADMW		(Allotted 8379M; as "DG590"; stored 1.96)		
G-ADND	DH.87B Hornet Moth	8097	W9385	4. 8.36	The Shuttleworth Trust	Old Warden	21. 7.99P
			G-ADND		(As "W9385/YG-L/3" of 502 Sqn)		
G-ADNE	DH.87B Hornet Moth	8089	X9325	10. 3.36	G-ADNE Ltd "Ariadne"	Oaksey Park	17. 3.00
			G-ADNE				
G-ADNL	Miles M.5 Sparrowhawk	239		12. 8.35	A.G.Dunkerley	(Bury, Lancs)	13. 5.58S
		(On rebuild from components discarded from reconstruction 1953 as M.77 Sparrowjet)						
G-ADNZ(2)	DH.82A Tiger Moth	85614	6948M	10.10.74	D.C.Wall	Swanton Morley	16. 7.00
			DE673		(As "DE673")		
G-ADOT*	DH.87B Hornet Moth	8027	X9326	?. 11.35	De Havilland Aircraft Museum		
			G-ADOT			Salisbury Hall, London Colney	15.10.59
G-ADPC	DH.82A Tiger Moth	3393	BB852	24. 9.35	T.Groves t/a G-ADPC Group	(Fareham)	22. 5.99
			G-ADPC		(Composite rebuild)		
G-ADPJ	BAC Drone 2	7		21. 8.35	N.H.Ponsford	Breighton	17. 5.55
	(Douglas Sprite) (Crashed Leicester 3.4.55 and on rebuild 4.96 using parts from G-AEJR c/n 22 & G-AEKU c/n 29)						
G-ADPS	BA Swallow 2	410		4. 9.35	J.F.Hopkins	Watchford Farm, Yarcombe	8. 9.99P
	(Pobjoy Cataract 2)				(On overhaul 10.97)		
G-ADRA	Pietenpol Air Camper	PFA/1514		10. 4.78	A.J.Mason	Hinton-in-the-Hedges	3. 4.98P
	(Cont A65)				"Edna May"		
G-ADRH	DH.87B Hornet Moth	8038	F-AQBY	6. 8.82	I.M.Callier	(Windsor)	
			HB-OBE		(Shipped to Gore, New Zealand for rebuild 5.91)		
G-ADRR	Aeronca C.3	A.734	N17423	6. 9.88	S.J.Rudkin	(Westmoor Farm, Langham)	
			NC17423		(Stored Roughay Farm, Bishops Waltham 1992)		
G-ADSK	DH.87B Hornet Moth	8091	D-EJOM	3.36	R.G.Grocott	(Banbury)	14. 3.70
			AP-AES/G-ADSK/AV952/G-ADSK		(On rebuild Gore, New Zealand 1993 from components)		
G-ADUR	DH.87B Hornet Moth	8085		10. 3.36	Wessex Avn & Transport Ltd	Chalmington	7. 9.93
					(Stored 4.94)		
G-ADWJ	DH.82A Tiger Moth	3450	BB803	9.12.35	C.Adams	Shobdon	
			G-ADWJ		(On rebuild 3.96)		
G-ADWO*	DH.82A Tiger Moth	3455	BB807	9.12.35	Southampton Hall of Aviation	Southampton	
			G-ADWO		(As "BB807")		
		(Composite rebuild including components from G-AOAC & G-AOJJ)						
G-ADXS*	Mignet HM.14 Pou-Du-Ciel	CLS.1		18.11.35	Storey Family	Shoreham	1.12.36
	(Scott Squirrel A2S)				"The Fleeing Fly" (On rebuild at Winthorpe 9.97)		
G-ADXT	DH.82A Tiger Moth	3436		9.12.35	J.R.Hanauer	Goodwood	3. 8.00T
	(Officially restored but is mainly a rebuild of various components)						
G-ADYS	Aeronca C.3 (Aeronca E113C)	A.600		1.36	Janice I.Cooper	Rendcomb	18. 9.99P
					(London Air Park F/C c/s)		

G-AEAA-AEZZ

Regn	Type	C/n	P/I	Date	Owner/operator	Probable Base	CA Expy
G-AEBB	Mignet HM.14 Pou-Du-Ciel	KWO.1		24. 1.36	The Shuttleworth Trust	Old Warden	31. 5.39
G-AEBJ	Blackburn B.2	6300/8		4. 2.36	British Aerospace (Operations) Ltd		
	(Gipsy Major)					Brough	3. 7.00
G-AEDB	BAC Drone 2	13		18. 3.36	M.C.Russell & P.L.Kirk Top Farm, Tadlow		26. 5.87P
	(Cherub III) (Composite with wings of G-AEJH & tail end of G-AEEN; stored 7.96; registered as BGA2731 3.81)						
G-AEDU(2)	DH.90A Dragonfly	7526	N190DH	4. 6.79	A.J.Norman	Langham	10. 6.99
			G-AEDU/ZS-CTR/CR-AAB		t/a Norman Aeroplane Trust		
G-AEEG	Miles M.3A Falcon Major	216	SE-AFN	14. 3.36	G.E.J.Spooner	(Colchester)	2. 7.00
			Fv913/SE-AFN/G-AEEG/U-20				
G-AEEH*	Mignet HM.14 Pou-Du-Ciel	EGD.1		13. 3.36	Cosford Aerospace Museum	RAF Cosford	15. 5.38
G-AEFG*	Mignet HM.14 Pou-Du-Ciel	JN.1	BAPC75	27. 3.36	N.H.Ponsford	Breighton	31. 3.38
	(Scott Flying Squirrel)				(On rebuild 7.96)		
G-AEFT	Aeronca C.3	A.610		17. 4.36	N.C.Chittenden	Kineton	27.10.99P
	(JAP J.99)						
G-AEGV*	Mignet HM.14 Pou-Du-Ciel	EMAC.1		22. 4.36	Midland Air Museum	Coventry	26. 5.37
					(Rebuild with some original components)		
G-AEHM*	Mignet HM.14 Pou-Du-Ciel	HJD.1		30. 4.36	The Science Museum	Wroughton	
	(35 hp ABC Scorpion)				"Blue Finch"		
G-AEJZ*	Mignet HM.14 Pou-Du-Ciel	TLC.1	BAPC120	9. 6.36	Bomber County Avn Museum	Hemswell	
					(Stored 4.97)		
G-AEKR*	Mignet HM.14 Pou-Du-Ciel	CAC.1	BAPC121	26. 6.36	G.Claybourn	Doncaster Museum	22. 6.37
	(Rebuilt using some original components after damaged by fire at RAF Finningley 4.9.70)						
G-AEKV*	Kronfeld (BAC) Drone de luxe	30		13. 1.37	M.L.Beach	Brooklands Museum	6.10.60P
	(Allocated BGA.2510 5.79)				(WFU 14.1.99)		
G-AEKW*	Miles M.12 Mohawk	298	HM503	14. 7.36	L.Casey	Fort Union, Virginia, USA	1. 3.50
			G-AEKW/"G-AEKN"		(Crashed Spain 1.1.50, stored & now on rebuild)		
G-AELO	DH.87B Hornet Moth	8105	AW118	30. 7.36	M.J.Miller	Little Gransden	1. 5.00
			G-AELO				
G-AEML	DH.89 Dragon Rapide	6337	X9450	1. 9.36	Amanda Investments Ltd	Rendcomb	22. 5.99
			G-AEML		"Proteus"		
G-AEMY*	Mignet HM.14 Pou-Du-Ciel	NMB.1		25. 8.36	N.Ponsford	Leeds	
					(Major parts stored 3.96)		
G-AENP	Hawker Afghan Hind	41H/81902	(BAPC78)	29.10.81	The Shuttleworth Trust	Old Warden	30. 9.99P
	(Kestrel V)		R.Afghan AF		(As "K5414 "in 15 Sqdn c/s)		
G-AEOA	DH.80A Puss Moth	2184	ES921	1.10.36	A. & P.A.Wood t/a P & A Wood	Audley End	27. 6.95P
	(Gipsy Major)		G-AEOA/YU-PAX/UN-PAX				
G-AEOF(2)	Rearwin 8500 Sportster	462	N15863	1.12.81	Shipping & Airlines Ltd	Biggin Hill	29. 4.97P
	(85hp Le Blond 5DF)		NC15863		(Stored 8.97)		
G-AEOH*	Mignet HM.14 Pou-Du-Ciel	RCS.1		15.10.36	Billy Dulles	Dieme, France	4.10.37
	(40hp Praga B)		(Reproduction using original wings/extant 1995)				
G-AEPH	Bristol F.2B Fighter	7575	D8096	13.11.36	The Shuttleworth Trust	Old Warden	2. 8.98P
	(RR Falcon 3)		G-AEPH/D8096		(Original c/n 3746, rebuilt c.1931/as "D8096/D")		
G-AERV*	Miles M.11A Whitney Straight	307	EM999	30.12.36	Not known (On rebuild 4.96)		9. 4.66
			G-AERV		Upper Ballinderry, Lisburn, Co.Antrim		
G-AESB	Aeronca C.3	A.638	N15742	5. 8.88	R.J.M.Turnbull (On rebuild 1997)		
			NC15742		Rydinghurst Farm, Cranleigh		
G-AESE	DH.87B Hornet Moth	8108	W5775	13. 1.37	J.G.Green	White Ox Mead, Bath	4.10.01
			G-AESE		"Sheena"		
G-AESZ	Chilton DW.1	DW.1/1		?. 1.37	R.E.Nerou	Coventry	4. 8.53
	(Carden Ford 32hp)				(Long term rebuild project using some original components)		
G-AETA*	Caudron G.III	7487	OO-ELA	29. 1.37	RAF Museum	Hendon	
	(Anzani 90hp)		O-BELA				
	(Also reported as c/n 5019 or 5021; allotted "9203M" 1994; as "(N)3066" in RNAS c/s)						
G-AETG*	Aeronca 100	AB.110		' 2.37	Not known	?	9. 4.68
					(Crashed Booker 7.4.69 & on rebuild with parts from G-AEWV 4.96)		
G-AEUJ	Miles M.11A Whitney Straight	313		19. 2.37	R.E.Mitchell	RAF Cosford	4. 6.70
					(Stored 6.92)		
G-AEVS	Aeronca 100	AB.114		3.37	A.M.Lindsay & N.H.Ponsford	Breighton	24. 2.99P
	(JAP J.99)				(Composite including parts of original G-AEXD)		
G-AEVZ	BA L.25c Swallow II	475		19. 3.37	B.R.Cox Brickhouse Farm, Frogland Cross		8. 6.99P
	(Cirrus Minor)						
G-AEWV*	Aeronca 100	AB.117		5. 8.38	Not Known (Fuselage at Clothall Common 1998)		
G-AEXD	Aeronca 100	AB.124		1. 4.37	Mrs M.A. & R.W.Mills	Hanwell	20. 4.70P
	(JAP J.99)			(Mostly comprises parts of G-AESP after rebuild in 1958: on rebuild 1.91: sold 1997)			
G-AEXF	Percival P.6 Mew Gull	E.22	ZS-AHM	18. 5.37	J.D.Penrose	Old Warden	26. 1.98P
			(Rebuild with c/n PFA/13-10020)				
G-AEXT	Dart Kitten II	123		4.37	A.J.Hartfield Marsh Hill Farm, Aylesbury		3. 5.98P
	(JAP J.99)						
G-AEXZ	Piper J/2 Cub	997		5. 2.38	J.R. & Mrs M.Dowson	Leicester	2.11.78S
	(Cont A75)				(On rebuild)		
G-AEYY*	Martin Monoplane	1	G-AAJK	6. 7.37	R.W.E.Lake, A.D.Raby & D.W.Brabham		3.11.39
	(See comments on G-EBQP; on long term rebuild 1989)				t/a Martin Monoplane Syndicate Hitchin		
G-AEZF*	Short S.16 Scion 2	PA.1008	M-5	18. 6.37	R.Jackson/Acebell Aviation Ltd	Redhill	5. 5.54
			G-AEZF		(On rebuild to static condition 10.96)		
G-AEZJ	Percival P.10 Vega Gull	K.65	SE-ALA	2. 7.37	R.A.J.Spurrell	White Waltham	10. 6.01
			D-IXWD/PH-ATH/G-AEZJ				
G-AEZX(2)	Bucker Bu.133C Jungmeister	1018	N5A	10. 5.88	A.J.E.Ditheridge	Moat Farm, Milden	17. 9.98P
			PP-TDP		(As "LG+03 in Luftwaffe c/s)		

G-AFAA-AFZZ

Regn	Type	C/n	P/I	Date	Owner/operator	Probable Base	CA Expy
G-AFAX	BA Eagle 2 (Gipsy Major)	138	VH-ACN G-AFAX	26.10.37	J.G.Green White Ox Mead, Bath		4. 8.00
G-AFBS*	Miles M.14A Hawk Trainer 3	539	(G-AKKU) BB661/G-AFBS	17. 9.37	Imperial War Museum Duxford (On rebuild 1.99 - unmarked)		25. 2.63
G-AFCL	BA L.25c Swallow II (Pobjoy Niagara 3)	462		3.11.37	A.M.Dowson Old Warden (On loan to The Shuttleworth Trust)		30. 4.99P
G-AFDO	Piper J3C-65 Cub (Frame no.2633)	2593	N21697 NC21697	7. 6.88	R.Wald Le Plessis-Belleville, France "Butter Cub"		27. 7.99P
G-AFEL	Monocoupe 90A (Lambert R266)	A.782	N19432 NC19432	7. 6.82	M.Rieser (Germany)		10. 7.99P
G-AFFD	Percival P.16A Q-Six	Q.21	(G-AIEY) X9407/G-AFFD	12. 2.38	B.D.Greenwood Ronaldsway (On rebuild by Aeroservice IOM Ltd 6.96)		31. 8.56
G-AFFH	Piper J/2 Cub (Cont A40)	1166	EC-ALA G-AFFH	26. 3.38	M.J.Honeychurch Devizes (On rebuild 1997)		(29. 8.53)
G-AFGC	BA L.25c Swallow II (Pobjoy Niagara 3)	467	BK893 G-AFGC	4. 4.38	Glenda E.Arden (Stored 1.98) Thorns Cross Farm, Chudleigh		20. 3.51
G-AFGD	BA L.25c Swallow II (Pobjoy Cataract 3)	469	BK897 G-AFGD	4. 4.38	A.T.Williams, B.Arden, C.A.Cook, J.Hughes & M.Barmby t/a South Wales Swallow Grp Shobdon		22. 9.98P
G-AFGE	BA L.25c Swallow II (Pobjoy Niagara 2)	470	BK894 G-AFGE	4. 4.38	G.R.French Bensons Farm, Laindon "Maggie"		27. 7.98P
G-AFGH	Chilton DW.1 (Lyc O-145-A2) (To be re-engined with Carden-Ford)	DW.1/2		20. 3.38	M.L. & G.L.Joseph Denford Manor, Hungerford (On rebuild by Newbury Aeroplane Co 6.95)		7. 7.83P
G-AFGI	Chilton DW.1 (Walter Mikron 2)	DW.1/3		30. 3.38	J.E. & K.A.A. McDonald White Waltham		8. 4.98P
G-AFGM(2)	Piper J/4A Cub Coupe	4-943	N26895 NC26895	30.12.81	A.J.P.Marshall Carlisle		9. 1.99P
G-AFGZ	DH.82A Tiger Moth	3700	G-AMHI BB759/G-AFGZ	9. 5.38	M.R.Paul & P.A.Shaw Lee-on-Solent		23. 1.00
G-AFHA	Mosscraft MA.1	MA.1/2		27. 2.67	C.V.Butler (Allesley, Coventry) (Small components only stored)		
G-AFHC*	BA L.25c Swallow II (Cirrus Minor)	486		17. 5.38	Arden Family Trust (Stored 1.98) Thorn Cross Farm, Chudleigh		20. 3.51
G-AFIN*	Chrislea LC.1 Airguard	LC.1		7. 7.38	N.H.Ponsford Wigan (New fuselage built by K.Fern combined with original wings/tail; stored 3.96)		
G-AFIR	Luton LA-4 Minor (JAP J-99)	JSS.2		7. 7.38	A.J.Mason (Finmere) (Damaged in forced landing nr Cobham 14.3.71 & on rebuild 1993)		30. 7.71
G-AFIU	Parker CA-4 Parasol	CA-4		19.10.82	S.P.Connatty Wigan (A Luton Minor variant with reserved marks from 1938; stored 3.96)		
G-AFJA	Taylor-Watkinson Dingbat (32hp Carden-Ford)	DB.100		2. 8.38	K.Woolley (Berkswell, Coventry) (Damaged Headcorn 19.5.75 and partially rebuilt; stored 4.94)		23. 6.75S
G-AFJB	Foster-Wikner GM.1 Wicko (Gipsy Major 1)	5	DR613 G-AFJB	15. 8.38	J.Dibble Dublin (As "DR613")		12. 7.63
G-AFJR*	Tipsy Trainer 1	2		20. 8.38	Musee Royal de L'Armee Brussels (Stored 1992 for static rebuild with remains of G-AFRV)		10. 9.64
G-AFJU*	Miles M.17 Monarch	789	X9306 G-AFJU	25. 8.38	Acft Preservation Society of Scotland East Fortune		18. 5.64
G-AFJV	Mosscraft MA.2	MA.2/2		27. 2.67	C.V.Butler (Allesley, Coventry) (Small components only stored)		
G-AFLW	Miles M.17 Monarch	792		2.11.38	N.I.Dalziel White Waltham		30. 7.98
G-AFNG	DH.94 Moth Minor	94014	AW112 G-AFNG	2. 5.39	D.Saunders Galway, Ireland t/a The Gullwing Trust		21.10.98P
G-AFNI	DH.94 Moth Minor (Cabin)	94035	W7972 G-AFNI	11. 5.39	B.N.C. & C.M.Mogg Bibberne Farm, Stalbridge (On rebuild 6.94)		26. 5.67
G-AFOB	DH.94 Moth Minor	94018	X5117 G-AFOB	16. 5.39	Wessex Avn & Transport Ltd Chalmington (Stored 6.94)		11. 5.93P
G-AFOJ	DH.94 Moth Minor (Cabin)	9407	E-1 E-0236/G-AFOJ	21. 7.39	R.M.Long Salisbury Hall, London Colney (In De Havilland Acft Museum)		27. 8.69P
G-AFPN	DH.94 Moth Minor (Now regd with c/n 94016)	94044	X9297 G-AFPN	23. 5.39	J.W. & A.R.Davy Redhill		9. 5.99
G-AFPR	DH.94 Moth Minor	94031	X5122 G-AFPR	16. 5.39	M.D.Souch Gore, New Zealand (Small original components only; on rebuild 1997)		15. 4.56
G-AFRZ	Miles M.17 Monarch	793	G-AIDE W6463/G-AFRZ	24. 3.39	R.E.Mitchell RAF Cosford (Stored 6.92)		29. 6.70
G-AFSC	Tipsy Trainer 1 (Walter Mikron 2)	11		15. 7.39	G.A.Cull Cheddington		21. 9.99P
G-AFSV	Chilton DW.1A (45hp Train)	DW.1A/1		5. 4.39	R.E.Nerou Coventry (On rebuild 12.93)		12. 7.72S
G-AFSW*	Chilton DW.2	DW.2/1		6. 4.39	R.I.Souch Durley, Southampton (Fuselage box in poor condition - possibly beyond rebuild)		
G-AFTA	Hawker Tomtit (Mongoose 3C)	30380	K1786 G-AFTA/K1786	26. 4.39	The Shuttleworth Trust Old Warden (As "K1786")		16. 7.99P
G-AFTN*	Taylorcraft Plus C2	102	HL535 G-AFTN	2. 5.39	Leicestershire C.C.Museums Coalville (On rebuild 10.97) (Cancelled by CAA 13.1.99)		1.11.57
G-AFUP	Luscombe 8A Master (Cont A65)	1246	N25370 NC25370	7. 6.88	R.Dispain Chilbolton		12. 3.97P

Regn	Type	C/n	P/I	Date	Owner/operator	Probable Base	CA Expy
G-AFVE(2)	DH.82A Tiger Moth	83720	T7230	1. 2.78	P.A.Shaw & M.R.Paul (As "T7230")	Lee-on-Solent	15. 4.01T
G-AFVN	Tipsy Trainer 1 (Walter Mikron 2)	12		15. 7.39	D.F.Lingard (Stored 8.97)	Fenland	7. 6.97P
G-AFWH	Piper J/4A Cub Coupe (Cont A65)	4-1341	N33093 NC33093	14. 1.82	O.T.Taylor	(Newark)	10. 4.99P
G-AFWI	DH.82A Tiger Moth	82187	BB814 G-AFWI	19. 7.39	E.Newbigin	Westbury-sub-Mendip	12. 8.00
G-AFWT	Tipsy Trainer 1 (Walter Mikron 2)	13		1. 8.39	J.M.Lovell	(Winchester)	26. 8.98P
G-AFYD(2)	Luscombe 8AF Silvaire (Cont C90)	1044	N25120 NC25120	29. 7.75	J.D.Iliffe	Hampstead Norreys	13. 5.00
G-AFYO(2)	Stinson HW-75 Model 105 (Cont C90)	7039	F-BGQP NC22586	25. 4.77	R.N.Wright Red House Farm, Gedney Marsh, Holbeach		27. 8.99P
	(Probably ex Fr.Mil with identity "22586")						
G-AFZA(2)	Piper J/4A Cub Coupe (Cont A65)	4-873	N26198 NC26198	27. 6.84	J.R.Hope Belle Vue Farm, Yarnscombe t/a G-AFZA Group (Wingnuts Flying Club)		3. 6.99P
G-AFZE*	Heath Parasol (Bristol Cherub III)	PA.1		25. 8.39	Estate of K.C.D.St.Cyrien (Stored 11.93) Horley, Surrey		10. 5.64P
G-AFZK(2)	Luscombe 8A Master (Cont A65)	1042	N25118 NC25118	24.10.88	M.G.Byrnes Walkeridge Farm, Overton		29. 5.97P
G-AFZL(2)	Porterfield CP-50 (Cont A50)	581	N25401 NC25401	18. 3.82	P.G.Lucas & S.H.Sharpe White Waltham t/a The Skinny Bird Flyers		29. 6.99P
G-AFZN(2)	Luscombe 8A Master (Cont A65)	1186	N25279 NC25279	5.10.81	A.L.Young	Henstridge	5. 5.99P

G-AGAA-AGZZ

Regn	Type	C/n	P/I	Date	Owner/operator	Probable Base	CA Expy
G-AGAT	Piper J3F-50 Cub (Franklin 4AC-150)	4062	N26126 NC26126	17. 7.87	G.S.Williams Eastbach Farm, English Bicknor		13. 6.99P
G-AGBN*	GAL.42 Cygnet 2	111	ES915 G-AGBN	4.10.40	Royal Museum of Scotland East Fortune		28.11.80P
G-AGEG	DH.82A Tiger Moth	82710	N9146 D-EDIL/R.Neth AF A-32/PH-UFK/A-32/R4769	16. 8.82	A.J.Norman t/a Norman Aeroplane Trust Rendcomb		2. 5.01
G-AGFT(2)	Avia FL.3 (CNA D4S)	176	I-TOLB MM.....	21. 8.84	P.A.Smith Leicester (As "W7" in Italian Co-Belligerent AF c/s)		5.10.98P
G-AGHB(2)*	Hawker Sea Fury FB.XI	41H-636336	CF-CHB RAN WH589/WH58	9. 5.74	C.Charleston Colchester		22. 5.79P
	(Damaged Munster, Germany 24.6.79; parts sold to USA & incorporated into rebuild as N4434P, using the identity of WH589, further rebuild 3.94 using major sections of wreck plus original centre section of TF956, rear fuselage of R Neth Navy 10-14, ex 6-14/VX715 and parts from G-FURY/WJ244)						
G-AGHY	DH.82A Tiger Moth	82292	N9181	17. 2.88	P.Groves Stubbington		AC
	(Composite rebuild from ex Rollason airframe/components; now on further rebuild)						
G-AGIV	Piper J3C-65 Cub (L-4J-PI) (Frame No.12506)	12676	OO-AFI OO-GBA/44-80380	13. 8.82	P.C. & F.M.Gill Waits Farm, Belchamp Walter		13.12.99P
G-AGJG	DH.89A Dragon Rapide	6517	X7344	25.10.43	M.J. & D.J.T.Miller Duxford (Long term rebuild 1.99 - unmarked)		15.11.74
G-AGLK	Auster 5D	1137	RT475	25. 8.44	Goldhawk Print Services Ltd Biggin Hill		12. 2.01
G-AGMI	Luscombe 8A Master (Cont A65)	1569	N28827 NC28827	15.11.88	P.R.Bush RAF Kinloss (Damaged Biggin Hill 26.3.94; on rebuild 5.95)		5. 4.94P
G-AGNJ(2)	DH(Aust)82A Tiger Moth	660	VP-YOJ ZS-BGF/SAAF 2366	21. 2.89	B.P., A.J. & P.J.Borsberry (On rebuild) Kidmore End, Reading		
G-AGNV*	Avro 685 York C.1	1223	"MW100" "LV633"/G-AGNV/TS798	20. 8.45	RAF Museum RAF Cosford (As "TS798")		6. 3.65
G-AGOH*	Auster 5 J/1 Autocrat	1442		19. 4.45	Leicestershire County Council Museums (On loan to Newark Air Museum) Winthorpe (Cancelled by CAA 18.1.99)		24. 8.95
G-AGOS*	Reid & Sigrist RS.4 Desford Tnr (As Bobsleigh "VZ728"; stored 4.96)	3	VZ728 G-AGOS	?. 5.45	Leicester Museum of Science & Industry Coalville, Leicester		28.11.80P
G-AGOY	Miles M.48 Messenger 3	4690	EI-AGE G-AGOY/HB-EIP/G-AGOY/U-0247	5. 6.45	P.A.Brook West Chiltington, Pulborough (On rebuild 4.92; to be marked as "U-0247")		25.11.53
G-AGPG*	Avro 19 Srs.2	1212		15. 6.45	Manchester Museum of Science & Industry (Stored 3.97) Chadderton		13. 2.71
G-AGPK(2)	DH.82A Tiger Moth	86566	N657DH F-BGDN/Fr AF/PG657	27.10.88	Delta Aviation Ltd. Sywell		21.12.01
G-AGRU*	Vickers V.657 Viking 1	112	VP-TAX G-AGRU	8. 5.46	British Airways plc Brooklands Museum (BEA c/s) "Vagrant"		9. 1.64
G-AGRW*	Vickers V.639 Viking 1	115		8. 5.46	Vienna Airport) Vienna-Schwechat Airport		9. 7.68
G-AGSH	DH.89A Dragon Rapide 6	6884	EI-AJO G-AGSH/NR808	25. 7.45	Venom Jet Promotions Ltd (Philip Meeson) (BEA c/s) "Jemma Meeson" Bournemouth		19. 6.01
G-AGTM	DH.89A Dragon Rapide 6 (Fuselage No.BCL89397)	6746	JY-ACL OD-ABP/G-AGTM/NF875	19. 9.45	Aviation Heritage Ltd Coventry (Dave Geddes)		14.11.99T
G-AGTO	Auster 5 J/1 Autocrat	1822		2.10.45	M.J.Barnett & D.J.T.Miller Duxford (Frame 1.99 - unmarked)		6. 9.97
G-AGTT	Auster 5 J/1 Autocrat	1826		2.10.45	R.Farrer (Bromham, Bedford) (Status uncertain)		11. 2.93
G-AGVG	Auster J/1U Workmaster	1858		7.12.45	S.J.Riddington Leicester (On overhaul 11.95)		25. 4.76
G-AGVN	Auster 5 J/1 Autocrat	1873	EI-CKC G-AGVN	18. 1.46	G.H.Farrar Abbeyshrule		16. 7.98
G-AGVV	Piper J3C-65 Cub (L-4H-PI)	11163	F-BCZK Fr.AF/43-29872	19. 2.81	M.Molina-Ruano (Malaga, Spain)		20. 7.99P
G-AGWE*	Avro 19 Srs.2	1286	TX201	28.12.45	Valiant Air Command Museum (Stored 6.94) Tico, Florida, USA		5. 3.73
G-AGXN	Auster J/1N Alpha	1963		22. 1.46	Gentleman's Aerial Touring Carriage Syndicate Ltd Popham		31. 5.98
G-AGXU	Auster J/1N Alpha	1969		24. 1.46	G.T.Fisher North Side, Thorney		11. 4.99
G-AGXV	Auster 5 J/1 Autocrat	1970		1. 2.46	B.S.Dowsett Little Gransden "Pamela IV"		28. 8.00
G-AGYD	Auster J/1N Alpha	1985		4. 2.46	P.R.Hodson Little Gransden (Damaged nr Felthorpe 25.11.90; on rebuild 4.94)		24.11.90
G-AGYH	Auster J/1N Alpha	1989		4. 2.46	W.R.V.Marklew (Barrow-in-Furness) (On rebuild)		10.10.72S
G-AGYK	Auster 5 J/1 Autocrat	2002		4. 2.46	M.C.Hayes t/a Autocrat Syndicate Bidford (Stored 10.97)		25. 5.96
G-AGYT	Auster J/1N Alpha	1862		18. 1.46	P.J.Barrett Lightwater, Surrey (On overhaul 6.94)		27. 2.91
G-AGYU	DH.82A Tiger Moth	85265	DE208	10. 1.46	P.L.Jones Ronaldsway (As "DE208") (Stored 10.96)		11. 8.01
G-AGYY	Ryan ST3KR (PT-21-RY) (Kinner R56)	1167	N56792 41-1942	15. 6.83	J.J.van Egmond t/a Nostalgic Flying (As "27" in USAAC c/s) (Nijverdal, Netherlands)		14. 7.99P
G-AGZZ	DH.82A(Aust)Tiger Moth	T256 & 926	N3862 VH-BTU/VH-RNM/VH-BMY/A17-503	14. 5.82	G.C.P.Shea-Simonds (Netheravon) (Olympus Cameras c/s)		23. 4.01

G-AHAA-AHZZ

Regn	Type	C/n	P/I	Date	Owner/operator	Probable Base	CA Expy
G-AHAG	DH.89A Dragon Rapide	6926	RL944	31. 1.46	R.Jones t/a Southern Sailplanes (Stored 9.97)	Membury	15. 7.73
G-AHAL	Auster J/1N Alpha	1870		31. 1.46	Wickenby F/C Ltd	Wickenby	7. 6.01T
G-AHAM	Auster 5 J/1 Autocrat	1885		21. 1.46	A.J.Twemlow	Goodwood	24.11.99
G-AHAN	DH.82A Tiger Moth	86553	N90406 F-BGDG/Fr.AF/PG644	31. 5.85	Tiger Associates Ltd	White Waltham	1. 6.99T
G-AHAP	Auster 5 J/1 Autocrat (Rover V-8 conversion)	1887		8. 2.46	V.H.Bellamy (Being modified Aylesbury 8.91; at Farley Farm, Romsey 1.97)	St.Just	20.2.91P*
G-AHAR*	Auster 5 J/1 Autocrat (Frame No.TAY347E/EJA304)	1888	F-BGRZ	?. 2.46	W.P.Miller (Fuselage frame for rebuild 8.98)	Mavis Enderby	
G-AHAT*	Auster J/1N Alpha	1849	(HB-EOK)	11. 2.46	D.Burke (Crashed Old Sarum 31.8.74; open store 6.98)	Dumfries	6. 2.75
G-AHAU	Auster 5 J/1-160 Autocrat (Lyc O-320)	1850	(HB-EOL)	11. 2.46	A.C.Webber, T.P.H.Wiseman & A.B.J.Young	Andreas, IoM	13. 4.00
G-AHAV*	Auster 5 J/1 Autocrat	1863	(HB-EOM)	13. 2.46	C.J.Freeman (Cancelled by CAA 22.2.99; last known stored 4.96)	Headcorn	21. 6.75
G-AHBL	DH.87B Hornet Moth	8135	P6786 CF-BFN	6. 2.46	H.D.Labouchere	Blue Tile Farm, Langham	26.11.99
G-AHBM	DH.87B Hornet Moth	8126	P6785 CF-BFJ/(CF-BFO)/CF-BFJ	6. 2.46	P.A. & E.P.Gliddon	Redhill	18. 3.99
G-AHCK*	Auster J/1N Alpha	1973		25. 3.46	Not known (Damaged Ingoldmells 14.9.91 stored 5.93)	Mavis Enderby	7. 5.94T
G-AHCL	Auster J/1N Alpha	1977	G-OJVC G-AHCL	13. 5.46	Electronic Precision Ltd (On rebuild 8.92 with Lyc O-320)	RAF Mona	10.10.91
G-AHCR	Gould-Taylorcraft Plus D Special (Cont C90)	211	LB352	15. 4.46	D.E.H.Balmford & D.R.Shepherd t/a Wagtail F/Grp	Dunkeswell	2. 9.99P
G-AHEC	Luscombe 8A Silvaire (Cont A65)	3428	N72001 NC72001	28.10.88	S.P.Parsons	Rush Green	27. 1.00P
G-AHED*	DH.89A Dragon Rapide 6	6944	RL962	27. 2.46	RAF Museum (In store 10.95)	RAF Cardington	17. 4.68
G-AHGD	DH.89A Dragon Rapide	6862	NR786	1. 4.46	R.Jones t/a Southern Sailplanes (Destroyed nr.Audley End 30.6.91; components for possible rebuild 1.92)	Membury	20. 9.92
G-AHGW	Taylorcraft Plus D	222	LB375	2. 9.46	C.V.Butler (Op Military Auster Flt) (As "LB375")	Shenington	3. 5.96P
G-AHGZ	Taylorcraft Plus D	214	LB367	24. 4.46	M.Pocock (On overhaul 1992)	(Melksham)	2. 6.71
G-AHHH	Auster J/1N Alpha	2011	F-BAVR G-AHHH	11. 5.46	H.A.Jones	Brampton	31.7.98P
G-AHHP*	Auster J/1N Alpha	2019	G-SIME G-AHHP	11. 5.46	M.J.Bonnick Standalone Farm, Meppershall (Cancelled by CAA 22.2.99; last known on rebuild at Meppershall 1992 following damage in gales in mid-1980s)		8. 3.86
G-AHHT	Auster J/1N Alpha	2022		11. 5.46	A.C.Barber & N.J.Hudson t/a Southdowns Auster Grp Durleighmarsh Farm, Rogate, Petersfield		7. 5.01
G-AHHU*	Auster J/1N Alpha	2023		11. 5.46	L.A.Groves & I.R.F.Hammond t/a Crofton Aeroplane Svs (Crashed at Soria, Spain 10.6.63 & on rebuild 12.91)	Stubbington	12. 6.63
G-AHIP	Piper J3C-65 Cub (L-4H-PI)	12122	OO-GEJ(2) OO-ALY/44-79826	3. 7.85	Veronica L.Tanner & K.F.Spragg (Frame No.11950; official c/n is 12008 - see G-AJAD)	Wellesbourne Mountford	13. 5 99P
G-AHIZ	DH.82A Tiger Moth (Regd with fuselage no.4610)	86533	PG624	23. 4.46	CFG Flying Ltd	Cambridge	1. 6.00T
G-AHKX	Avro 19 Srs.2	1333		18. 5.46	British Aerospace (Operations) Ltd (On rebuild 4.97 by Avro Heritage Society)	Woodford	AC
G-AHKY*	Miles M.18 Srs.2	4426	HM545 U-0224/U-8	26. 4.46	Royal Scottish Museum/Museum of Flight	East Fortune	20. 9.89P
G-AHLI*	Taylorcraft Auster III	540	NJ911	21. 5.46	G.A.Leathers (Cancelled by CAA 23.2.99; status unknown as owner emigrated to New Zealand)	(Orpington)	26. 4.73
G-AHLK	Taylorcraft Auster III	700	NJ889	1. 5.46	E.T.Brackenbury	Leicester	21. 9.97
G-AHLT	DH.82A Tiger Moth	82247	N9128	2. 5.46	K.J.Jarvis	(Wheathampstead)	9. 4.00
G-AHMN	DH.82A Tiger Moth	82223	N6985	8. 5.46	The Museum of Army Flying (As "N6985")	AAC Middle Wallop	14. 4.98P
G-AHNR(2)	Taylorcraft BC-12D (Cont A65)	7204	N43545 NC43545	15.11.88	P.E.Hinkley	Downland Farm, Redhill	2. 6.99P
G-AHOO	DH.82A Tiger Moth (Regd with c/n 86149)	86150	6940M EM967	6. 6.85	J.T. & A.D.Milsom	(Marlborough/Crediton)	
G-AHRI*	DH.104 Dove 1B	04008	4X-ARI G-AHRI	11. 7.46	Newark Air Museum	Winthorpe	
G-AHRO	Cessna 140	8069	N89065 NC89065	25. 1.82	R.H.Screen	Manchester	14. 7.00
G-AHSA	Avro 621 Tutor (Lynx IVM)	-	K3215 G-AHSA/K3215	21. 6.46	The Shuttleworth Trust (As "K3215")	Old Warden	1. 5.99P
G-AHSD	Taylorcraft Plus D	182	LB323	1. 7.46	A.L.Hall-Carpenter (On rebuild 8.95)	(Thetford)	10. 9.62
G-AHSO	Auster J/1N Alpha	2123		8. 8.46	W.P.Miller (On rebuild 8.98)	Mavis Enderby	6. 4.95T
G-AHSP	Auster 5 J/1 Autocrat	2134	F-BGRO G-AHSP	8. 8.46	R.M.Weeks	Stapleford	21. 5.00
G-AHSS	Auster J/1N Alpha	2136		8. 8.46	A.M.Roche	Swanton Morley	10. 3.00

Regn	Type	C/n	P/I	Date	Owner/operator	Probable Base	CA Expy
G-AHST	Auster J/1N Alpha	2137		8. 8.46	A.C.Frost Standalone Farm, Meppershall		3. 7.00
G-AHTE	Percival P.44 Proctor 5	Ae58		26. 6.46	D.K.Tregilgas Hill Farm, Nayland		10. 8.61
					(On rebuild 1.97)		
G-AHTW*	Airspeed AS.40 Oxford 1	3083	V3388	6. 6.46	Imperial War Museum - Skyfame Collection		
					(As "V3388")	Duxford	15.12.60
G-AHUF	DH.82A Tiger Moth	86221	A2123	26. 2.85	First County Finance (UK) Ltd Headcorn		10.12.99
			NL750		(As "T7997") (See G-AOBH)		
G-AHUG	Taylorcraft Plus D	153	LB282	5. 6.46	D.Nieman	(Thame)	12. 7.70
G-AHUI*	Miles M.38 Messenger 2A	6335		19. 7.46	Royal Berkshire Avn Society Woodley		4. 9.60
					(Fuselage stored off-site 11.93)		
G-AHUJ	Miles M.14A Hawk Trainer 3	1900	R1914	6. 6.46	Sir W.J.D.Roberts Strathallan		9. 7.98P
					t/a Strathallan Acft Collection (As "R1914")		
G-AHUN(2)	Temco Globe GC-1B Swift	3536	EC-AJK	24. 7.86	R.J.Hamlett North Weald		4. 8.95P
	(Lyc IO-360)		OO-KAY/NC77764				
G-AHUV	DH.82A Tiger Moth	3894	N6593	24. 6.46	J.D.Gordon Blair Atholl		10. 7.00
G-AHVG*	Percival P.28B Proctor 1	H.224	VH-AVG	17. 6.46	Warbirds Museum Mildura, Australia		
			G-AHVG/BV658				
G-AHVU	DH.82A Tiger Moth	84728	T6313	14. 8.46	R.A.L.Hubbard (As "T6313") Meon		17. 3.00
G-AHVV	DH.82A Tiger Moth	86123	EM929	24. 6.46	R.Jones t/a Southern Sailplanes Membury		2.11.73
					(Crashed Lympne 12.12.71 & on rebuild 1.94)		
G-AHWJ	Taylorcraft Plus D	165	LB294	20. 6.46	M.D.Pitcher & S.D.Lee Ferndown, Hants		30. 6.71
					(On rebuild 1.97)		
G-AHWO*	Percival P.44 Proctor 5	Ae72	(EI-ALY)	22. 7.46	P.Bedford Celbridge, Co.Kildare		11. 3.61
			G-AHWO		(Crashed Collinstown, Dublin 5.5.59 & stored 4.96)		
G-AHXE	Taylorcraft Plus D	171	LB312	9. 7.46	Jenny M.C.Pothecary Old Sarum		14. 7.99P
					(As "LB312")		

G-AIAA-AIZZ

Regn	Type	C/n	P/I	Date	Owner/operator	Probable Base	CA Expy
G-AIBE*	Fairey Fulmar 2	F.3707	N1854 G-AIBE/N1854	29. 7.46	Fleet Air Arm Museum (As "N1854")	RNAS Yeovilton	6. 7.59
G-AIBH	Auster J/1N Alpha	2113		19. 8.46	M.J.Bonnick tandalone Farm, Meppershall		18. 4.98
G-AIBM	Auster 5 J/1 Autocrat	2148		2. 9.46	D.G.Greatrex	Thatcham	9.11.01
G-AIBR	Auster 5 J/1 Autocrat	2151		2. 9.46	R.H. & J.A.Cooper (Stow, Lincoln) (Crashed Gamston 5.9.70 & on rebuild Sandtoft 6.96)		14. 1.70
G-AIBW	Auster J/1N Alpha	2158		2. 9.46	W.B.Bateson	Blackpool	4. 5.97T
G-AIBX	Auster 5 J/1 Autocrat	2159		2. 9.46	B.H.Beeston Little Gransden t/a The Wasp F/Grp		27. 7.98
G-AIBY	Auster 5 J/1 Autocrat	2160		2. 9.46	D.Morris (Stored 6.97)	Sherburn	13. 4.81
G-AICX(2)	Luscombe 8A Silvaire (Cont A65)	2568	N71141 NC71141	27. 1.88	R.V.Smith "Easy Grace"	Henstridge	6. 6.99P
G-AIDL	DH.89A Dragon Rapide 6	6968	TX310	23. 8.46	Atlantic Air Transport Ltd Caernarfon (Op Air Caernarfon)		25. 4.99T
G-AIDS	DH.82A Tiger Moth	84546	T6055	22. 8.46	K.D.Pogmore & T.Dann "The Sorcerer" Bensons Farm, Laindon		16. 7.00
G-AIEK	Miles M.38 Messenger 2A	6339	U-9	27. 8.46	J.Buckingham New Farm, Felton, Bristol (As "RG333" in 2 TAF Comm Sqn c/s)		13. 5.00
G-AIFZ	Auster J/1N Alpha	2182		2.11.46	M.D.Anstey Rushett Farm, Chessington		20. 8.01
G-AIGD	Auster 5 J/1 Autocrat	2186		2.11.46	R.B.Webber Hayrish Farm, Okehampton		31. 8.99P
	(Officially regd incorrectly as J/1N Alpha)						
G-AIGF	Auster J/1N Alpha	2188		5.11.46	A.R.C.Mathie (On overhaul 9.96) Wrexham		19. 5.85
G-AIGP*	Auster 5 J/1 Autocrat (Lyc O-320)	2165		12.10.46	W.P.Miller Mavis Enderby (On rebuild 8.98)		19. 6.72
G-AIGR*	Auster J/1N Alpha	2172		12.10.46	C.J. & D.J.Baker Carr Farm, Newark (Rebuilt 1953 with spare fuselage no. TAY/R/308G; damaged Cranfield 3.86; original frame stored 9.96)		25. 4.88T
G-AIGT*	Auster J/1N Alpha	2176		12.10.46	P.R. & J.S.Johnson (Bury St.Edmunds) (Cancelled by CAA 23.2.99; status unknown)		22.10.76S
G-AIGU*	Auster J/1N Alpha	2180		12.10.46	Not known (On rebuild 3.96) (Selby)		5. 9.74S
G-AIIH	Piper J3C-65 Cub (L-4H-PI)	11945	44-79649	14. 9.46	J.A.de Salis	Oxford	25. 5.99P
G-AIJI*	Auster J/1N Alpha	2307		15. 4.47	C.J.Baker Carr Farm, Newark (Damaged Humberside 12.1.75; frame only for spares use 9.96)		30. 4.76
G-AIJK*	Auster 5 J/4	2067		13.11.46	Leicester Museum of Science & Industry (On rebuild off-site 4.96) Coalville, Leicester		24. 8.68
G-AIJM	Auster 5 J/4	2069	EI-BEU G-AIJM	13.11.46	N.Huxtable Cheddington, Bucks "Priscilla" (Damaged nr.Tring 5.1.97 & stored pending overhaul/repairs)		28. 3.97
G-AIJS*	Auster 5 J/4	2074		13.11.46	R.W.Brown Clothall Farm, Clothall Common (Stored 5.96)		14.12.71
G-AIJT	Auster 5 J/4 Srs.100 (Cont O-200-A)	2075		13.11.46	J.L.Thorogood Insch t/a The Aberdeen Auster F/Grp		31. 3.99
G-AIJZ*	Auster 5 J/1 Autocrat	2195		5.11.46	A.A.Marshall Yeatsall Farm, Abbots Bromley (Crashed Kingsland, Hereford 25.10.70 & frame stored 11.95)		17. 6.71
G-AIKE	Auster 5 (Frame No.TAY 2450)	1097	NJ728	15.11.46	C.J.Baker Carr Farm, Newark (Crashed Luton 1.9.65 & on rebuild 9.96)		3. 2.66
G-AIKR*	Airspeed AS.65 Consul	4338	PK286	25. 9.46	Canadian National Aeronautical Collection Rockcliffe, Canada		14. 5.65
G-AILL*	Miles M.38 Messenger 2A	6341		14.11.46	Miles Acft Collection Woodley (Major components stored off-site 3.96)		11. 4.73
G-AIPR	Auster 5 J/4	2084		9. 1.47	R.W. & Mrs M.A.Mills t/a The MPM F/Grp Church Farm, North Moreton, Wallingford		27. 5.98P
G-AIPV	Auster 5 J/1 Autocrat	2203		9. 1.47	W.P.Miller "Buttercup" Mavis Enderby		8.12.01
G-AIRC	Auster 5 J/1 Autocrat	2215		13. 1.47	R.C.Tebbett	Shobdon	16. 2.01
G-AIRI*	DH.82A Tiger Moth	3761	N5488	22.10.46	E.R.Goodwin Little Gransden (Stored 3.97)		9.11.81
G-AIRK	DH.82A Tiger Moth	82336	N9241	22.10.46	R.C.Teverson, R.W.Marshall & C.E.McKinney Waits Farm, Belchamp Walter		28. 5.01
G-AISA	Tipsy B Srs.1	17		24. 4.47	G.A.Cull	Cheddington	16.12.98P
G-AISC	Tipsy B Srs.1	19		24. 4.47	D.R.Shepherd Cumbernauld t/a Wagtail F/Grp (Stored 6.98)		23. 5.79P
G-AISS	Piper J3C-65 Cub (L-4H-PI) (Frame No.11904)	12077	D-ECAV SL-AAA/44-79781	3. 9.85	K.W.Wood & F.Watson	Insch	25.6.97P
G-AIST	VS.300 Spitfire IA	WASP/20/2	AR213	25.10.46	Sheringham Aviation UK Ltd Booker (As "AR213/PR-D" in 609 Sqdn c/s & "K9853/QV-H" in 19 Sqdn c/s)		7.11.97P
G-AISU*	VS.349 Spitfire LF.VB	CBAF.1061	AB910	25.10.46	Battle of Britain Mem Flt RAF Coningsby (As "AB910/ZD-C" in 222 Sqn) "President Roosevelt"		
G-AISX	Piper J3C-85 Cub (L-4H-PI) (Frame No.11489)	11663	43-30372	28.10.46	V.Luck t/a Cubfly Booker (Rebuilt with ex Spanish airframe)		20. 5.99P
G-AITB*	Airspeed AS.40 Oxford 1	-	MP425	1.11.46	RAF Museum Hendon (As "MP425" in 1536 BATF c/s)		24. 5.61
G-AITF*	Airspeed AS.40 Oxford 1	-	ED290	1.11.46	SAAF Museum Port Elizabeth, S.Africa (On rebuild to flying condition 3.92)		8. 6.60
G-AIUA	Miles M.14A Hawk Trainer 3	2035	T9768	11.11.46	P.A.Brook West Chiltington, Pulborough (Crashed Roborough 26.9.65 & stored 1995 with parts from G-ANWO)		13. 7.67

Regn	Type	C/n	P/I	Date	Owner/operator	Probable Base	CA Expy
G-AIUL*	DH.89A Dragon Rapide 6	6837	NR749	8.11.46	I.Jones	Ley Farm, Chirk	29. 9.67
	(On rebuild 7.97 with parts from G-AEMH/G-AKRN; parts possibly consumed since in rebuild						
	of G-AJBJ: fuselage still present 3.98)						
G-AIVG*	Vickers V.610 Viking 1B	220		18.11.46	Musee National de l'Automobile		
	(Crashed Le Bourget 12.8.53 & fuselage stored 4.95) Mulhouse, France						12. 2.54
G-AIVW*	DH.82A Tiger Moth	83135	T5370	14.11.46	Robertsbridge Avn Society	Robertsbridge	20. 7.85
	(On long term rebuild 3.96 following write off nr Camber 27.8.82;						
	mainly comprises airframe of G-ANLR (82111) ex N6856)						
G-AIXA	Taylorcraft Plus D	134	LB264	13. 1.47	C.W.Udale	Leicester	11. 2.99P
G-AIXJ	DH.82A Tiger Moth	85434	DE426	28.11.46	D.Green	Goodwood	13. 8.00
	(Probably composite airframe rebuilt by Newbury Aeroplane Co 1991)						
G-AIXN	Benes-Mraz M.1C Sokol	112	OK-BHA	22. 4.47	C.M.Howells	Stoke-on-Trent	13. 4.77S
					(On rebuild by Ken Fern 10.96)		
G-AIYG(2)	SNCAN Stampe SV-4B	21	OO-CKZ	31. 8.89	L.Casteleyn	Antwerp-Deurne, Belgium	12. 7.99
	(Gipsy Major)		F-BCKZ/Fr Mil				
G-AIYR	DH.89A Dragon Rapide	6676	HG691	11.12.46	Clacton Aero Club (1988) Ltd "Classic Lady"		
					(Op by Classic Wings)	Clacton/Duxford	29. 4.99T
G-AIYS	DH.85 Leopard Moth	7089	YI-ABI	16.12.46	Wessex Avn & Transport Ltd	Chalmington	7. 5.00
			SU-ABM				
G-AIZE*	Fairchild F.24W-41A Argus 2	565	N9996F	18.12.46	RAF Museum	RAF Cosford	6. 8.66
					(On rebuild by Medway Aircraft Preservation Group of Rochester 11.97)		
G-AIZG*	VS.236 Walrus 1	6S/21840	EI-ACC	20.12.46	Fleet Air Arm Museum	RNAS Yeovilton	
			IAC N-18/L2301		(As "L2301")		
G-AIZU	Auster 5 J/1 Autocrat	2228		31. 1.47	C.J. & J.G.B.Morley	Popham	19. 6.00
G-AIZY	Auster 5 J/1 Autocrat	2233		31. 1.47	B.J.Richards	(Portskewett, Gwent)	20. 9.78S
	(Damaged Portskewett 8.89; on rebuild at Brunel Technical College, Ashley Down, Bristol 6.91)						

G-AJAA-AJZZ

Regn	Type	C/n	P/I	Date	Owner/operator	Probable Base	CA Expy
G-AJAC*	Auster J/1N Alpha	2236		4. 2.47	N.J.Mortimore & H.A.Bridgman	Watchford Farm, Yarcombe	8. 3.79
					(Crashed 14.5.78 & on rebuild 6.94; cancelled as wfu 28.1.99)		
G-AJAD	Piper J3C-65 Cub (L-4H-PI)	12008	OO-GEJ(1)	26. 6.84	N.A.Rooney	(Wymondham)	30.10.98P
	(Frame No.11835) (Regd with c/n 11700)		44-79712				
	(The airframe has the original fuselage of OO-GEJ discarded in a rebuild in 1970s; OO-GEJ was rebuilt using						
	Frame No. 11950 (c/n 12122) ex OO-ALY/44-79826 and is now G-AHIP; OO-ALY was then rebuilt from c/n 11700						
	ex OO-TON/43-30409)						
G-AJAE	Auster J/1N Alpha	2237		4. 2.47	A.C.Ladd	(West Malling)	20. 5.00
G-AJAJ	Auster J/1N Alpha	2243		4. 2.47	R.B.Lawrence (Stored 5.97)	Dunkeswell	18. 4.94
G-AJAM	Auster 5 J/2 Arrow	2371		8. 2.47	D.A.Porter Griffins Farm, Temple Bruer		28. 5.99P
G-AJAO	Piper J3C-65 Cub (L-4H-PI)	12162	OO-RAM	17. 5.85	M.Stow	Kearsley Farm, Peterlee	20.10.99P
	(Frame No.11990)		ALAT/44-79866				
G-AJAP	Luscombe 8A Silvaire	2305	N45778	26.1.89	R J Thomas	Hamilton Farm, Bilsington	25. 5.99P
	(Cont A65)		NC45778				
G-AJAS	Auster J/1N Alpha	2319		14. 3.47	C.J.Baker	Carr Farm, Newark	11. 4.90
					(On rebuild 9.96)		
G-AJBJ*	DH.89A Dragon Rapide	6765	NF894	20. 1.47	John Pierce Avn Ltd	Ley Farm, Chirk	14 .9.61T
					(Under rebuild 3.98)		
G-AJCP(2)	Rollason-Druine D.31 Turbulent	PFA/512		9. 2.59	B.R.Pearson t/a Turbulent Grp Eaglescott		4. 9.78S
	(Ardem 4C02)				(Stored 10.95)		
G-AJDW*	Auster 5 J/1 Autocrat	2320		14. 3.47	D.R.Hunt	Mavis Enderby	17.11.77
					(Being restored to Husky configuration 8.98 with wings of G-AVOD)		
G-AJDY*	Auster 5 J/1 Autocrat	2322		14. 3.47	Truck Panels Ltd	Sywell	9. 7.71
					(On rebuild 7.95) (Cancelled by CAA 13.1.99)		
G-AJEB*	Auster J/1N Alpha	2325		14. 3.47	The Aeroplane Collection	Manchester	27. 3.69
					(On rebuild 11.96 at Manchester Museum of Science & Industry)		
G-AJEE	Auster 5 J/1 Autocrat	2309		14. 3.47	A.R.Carillo De Albornoz	Ronaldsway	10. 7.89
					(Stored 8.92)		
G-AJEH	Auster J/1N Alpha	2312		14. 3.47	J.T.Powell-Tuck	(Pontypool)	28. 5.90
					(Status uncertain)		
G-AJEI	Auster J/1N Alpha	2313		14. 3.47	W.P.Miller	Mavis Enderby	13. 8.94T
	(Composite, rebuilt in 1976, including fuselage of F-BFUT c/n 3357; original fuselage stored by						
	Crofton Aeroplane Svs, Stubbington 1.95: stored 1.97)						
G-AJEM	Auster 5 J/1 Autocrat	2317	F-BFPB	14. 3.47	K.A.Jones (On rebuild 1994)	(Swansea)	18. 2.72
			G-AJEM				
G-AJES(2)	Piper J3C-65 Cub (L-4H-PI)	11776	OO-ACB	21. 9.84	G.W.Jarvis	(Penn, Wolverhampton)	24. 7.99P
	(Frame No.11602)		43-30485		(As "330485/44/C" in USAAC c/s)		
G-AJGJ	Auster 5	1147	RT486	31. 1.47	D.Gotts & E.J.Downing	Old Sarum	30. 6.99
					t/a Auster RT486 F/Grp (As "RT486/PF-A")		
G-AJHJ*	Auster 5	1067	NJ676	10. 2.47	Arden Family Trust		
					(Stored 1.98) Thorncross Farm, Chudleigh		27. 6.49
G-AJHS	DH.82A Tiger Moth	82121	N6866	12. 2.47	J.M.Voeten & H.Van Der Paauw (Op Vliegend Museum)		
						Seppe, Netherlands	18. 6.00
G-AJHU	DH.82A Tiger Moth	83900	T7471	12. 2.47	G.Valenti (As "T7471")	(Parma, Italy)	23. 8.98T
G-AJIH	Auster 5 J/1 Autocrat	2318		2. 4.47	A.H.Diver (Stored 6.97)	Newtownards	19.11.94
G-AJIS	Auster J/1N Alpha	2336		30. 4.47	J.D.Smith & J.M.Hodgson t/a Husthwaite Auster Grp		
						Baxby Manor, Husthwaite	3.12.99
G-AJIT	Auster J/1 Kingsland	2337		30. 4.47	A.J.Kay t/a G-AJIT Group	Netherthorpe	14. 6.99P
	(Cont O-200-A)						
G-AJIU	Auster 5 J/1 Autocrat	2338		30. 4.47	M.D.Greenhalgh	Netherthorpe	25. 6.99
G-AJIW	Auster J/1N Alpha	2340		30. 4.47	Truman Aviation Ltd	Nottingham	16.10.82
G-AJJS(2)	Cessna 120	13047	8R-GBO	7. 1.87	R.W.Marchant, I.D.Ranger	Headcorn	21.10.97P
	(Cont O-200-A) VP-GBO/VP-TBO/N1106M/YV-T-CTA/NC2786N			& S.C.Parsons t/a Robhurst F/Grp			
G-AJJT(2)	Cessna 120	12881	N2621N	27. 1.88	J.S.Robson		
	(Cont C85)		NC2621N			Franklyns Field, Chewton Mendip	27. 7.97P
G-AJJU(2)	Luscombe 8E Silvaire	2295	N45768	10. 1.89	L.C.Moon	White Waltham	23. 7.99P
	(Cont C85)		NC45768				
G-AJKB(2)	Luscombe 8E Silvaire	3058	N71631	4. 1.89	A.F.Hall & P.S.Hatwell		
	(Cont C85)		NC71631			Priory Farm, Tibenham	23. 8.99P
G-AJLR*	Airspeed AS.65 Consul	5136	R6029	21. 5.47	Singapore Airlines	Singapore	23. 4.63
					(As "VR-SCD")		
G-AJOA	DH.82A Tiger Moth	83167	T5424	29. 4.47	F.P.Le Coyte (As "T5424")		
						Lotmead Farm, Wanborough, Swindon	22. 5.00
G-AJOC*	Miles M.38 Messenger 2A	6370		23. 4.47	Ulster Folk & Transport Museum (Stored 4.96)		
						Cultra Manor, Holywood	18. 5.72
G-AJOE	Miles M.38 Messenger 2A	6367		28. 4.47	J.Eagles & P.C.Kirby	Kemble	AC
					t/a Classic Messenger (F/f post restoration 22.11.97)		
G-AJON(2)	Aeronca 7AC Champion	7AC-2633	OO-TWH	3. 1.86	A.Biggs & J.L.Broad	Edge Hill	30. 6.99P
					t/a Oscar November 92 Syndicate		
G-AJOZ*	Fairchild F.24W-41A Argus 1	347	FK338	21. 4.47	The Aeroplane Collection Ltd		
	(UC-61-FA)		42-32142			Woodhall Spa	15.12.63
	(Crashed Rennes, France 16.8.62; on loan to The Thorpe Camp Preservation Group; stored 3.96)						
G-AJPI	Fairchild F.24R-46A Argus 3	851	HB614	26. 4.47	T.H.Bishop	Horsford, Norwich	30. 1.01
	(UC-61A-FA)		43-14887		(As "314887" in USAAF c/s)		

Regn	Type	C/n	P/I	Date	Owner/operator	Probable Base	CA Expy
G-AJPZ*	Auster 5 J/1 Autocrat	2348	F-BFPE G-AJPZ	12. 5.47	W.Hamblen Sopley, Hants		14. 6.85
					(Damaged Thruxton 2.3.84 & on rebuild 2.96)		
G-AJRB	Auster 5 J/1 Autocrat	2350		12. 5.47	N.Ravine	Sywell	29. 1.01
G-AJRC	Auster 5 J/1 Autocrat	2601		12. 5.47	Moira Barker Willyhow Farm, Scarborough		25. 6.99
G-AJRE	Auster 5 J/1 Autocrat	2603		12. 5.47	C,W.N. & A.A.M.Huke	Ince Blundell	5. 8.01
G-AJRH*	Auster J/1N Alpha	2606		12. 5.47	Leicestershire County Council Museums		
					Charnwood Museum, Loughborough		5. 6.69
					(Displayed wef 5.99; cancelled by CAA 18.1.99)		
G-AJRS	Miles M.14A Hawk Trainer 3	1750	P6382 G-AJDR/G-AJRS/P6382	30. 4.47	The Shuttleworth Trust Old Warden		21. 7.99P
					(As "P6382/C" in 16 EFTS c/s)		
					(Composite aircraft which flew as "G-AJDR" 1.54/3.71)		
G-AJSN*	Fairchild F.24W-41A Argus 2	849	HB612 43-14885	8. 5.47	V.Trimble Banbridge, Co.Down		9. 5.69T
					(Damaged Cork 10.6.67 & stored 2.95)		
G-AJTW	DH.82A Tiger Moth	82203	N6965	21. 5.47	J.A.Barker (As "N6965/FL-J") Tibenham		9. 9.00
G-AJUD	Auster 5 J/1 Autocrat	2614		5. 6.47	C.L.Sawyer (On rebuild 8.92) Camberley		18. 5.74
G-AJUE	Auster 5 J/1 Autocrat	2616		5. 6.47	P.H.B.Cole Lavington, Devizes		31.10.99
G-AJUL	Auster J/1N Alpha	2624		18. 6.47	M.J.Crees Halstead, Essex		11. 9.81
					(On rebuild 12.90)		
G-AJVE	DH.82A Tiger Moth	85814	DE943	28. 5.47	R.A.Gammons (Letchworth)		10. 7.00
					(Composite 1981 rebuild including substantial parts of G-APGL c/n 86460/NM140)		
G-AJVH*	Fairey Swordfish II	-	LS326		RN Historic Flight RNAS Yeovilton		
					(As "LS326/L2" in 836 Sqdn c/s)		
G-AJVT*	Auster 5	1495	TJ478	4. 6.47	S.Craggs (Frame/wings stored 5.86)		25. 8.70
					Lane House Farm, Burneston, Bedale		
G-AJWB	Miles M.38 Messenger 2A	6699		17. 6.47	G.E.J.Spooner (Colchester)		13.11.69
					(Crashed Doncaster, Yorks 23.3.70 & on rebuild 1996)		
G-AJXC*	Auster 5	1409	TJ343	11. 6.47	J.Graves Scotland Farm, Hook		2. 8.82
					(Damaged 16.10.87; stored 9.94; current status uncertain)		
G-AJXV	Auster 4	1065	F-BEEJ G-AJXV/NJ695	8. 9.47	Barbara A.Farries Carr Farm, Newark		17.11.99
					(As "NJ695")		
G-AJXY	Auster 4	792	MT243	4. 5.48	P.D.Lowdon (Farnborough)		10.11.70
					(On rebuild 1993)		
G-AJYB	Auster J/1N Alpha	847	MS974	3. 2.49	P.J.Shotbolt		
					Ingthorpe Farm, Great Casterton, Lincs		25. 7.98

G-AKAA-AKZZ

Regn	Type	C/n	P/I	Date	Owner/operator	Probable Base	CA Expy
G-AKAT	Miles M.14A Hawk Trainer 3	2005	F-AZOR G-AKAT/T9738	2. 7.47	J.D.Haslam (As "T9738") Breighton		29. 6.99
G-AKAZ	Piper J3C-65 Cub AN.1 & 8499 (L-4A-PI) (Frame No.8616)		F-BFYL Fr Mil/42-36375	19. 4.82	Jeanne R.Frazer Duxford (As "H/57" in 83rd FS/78th FG USAAF c/s)		31. 8.98P
G-AKBO	Miles M.38 Messenger 2A	6378		15. 7.47	B. du Cros RAF Keevil		24. 5.00
G-AKDK*	Miles M.65 Gemini 1A	6469		22. 8.47	Danmarks Flyvemuseum		
	(For rebuild with parts from G-AJWA c/n 6290; stored 1992)				Kongelunden, Billund, Denmark		27. 3.70
G-AKDN	DHC.1A Chipmunk 10	11		14. 8.47	D.S.Backhouse Old Buckenham		15.10.99
G-AKDW	DH.89A Dragon Rapide	6897	F-BCDB G-AKDW YI-ABD/NR833	25. 8.47	De Havilland Aircraft Museum Trust Ltd "City of Winchester" (On rebuild 3.96) Salisbury Hall, London Colney		AC
G-AKEK*	Miles M.65 Gemini 3A	6483		8. 9.47	M.Vaisey & T.Moore t/a Gemini Wanderers (On long term rebuild 12.94) Rotary Farm, Hatch		22. 9.72
G-AKEL*	Miles M.65 Gemini 1A	6484		8. 9.47	Ulster Folk & Transport Museum (Components only 4.96 - for rebuild with G-AKGE) Holywood, Dublin		29. 4.72
G-AKEZ	Miles M.38 Messenger 2A	6707		27. 8.47	P.G.Lee (As "RG333") (Sold 1997) (New Zealand)		15.11.68
G-AKGD*	Miles M.65 Gemini 1A	6492		11. 9.47	Royal Berkshire Avn Society Woodley (Parts only stored off-site 3.96)		14.11.66
G-AKGE*	Miles M.65 Gemini 3C	6488	EI-ALM G-AKGE	18.10.47	Ulster Folk & Transport Museum (Stored 4.96) Holywood, Dublin		7. 6.74
G-AKHP	Miles M.65 Gemini 1A	6519		3.10.47	P.G.Lee Earls Colne		28.10.99
G-AKHZ*	Miles M.65 Gemini 7	6527		21.10.47	Royal Berkshire Avn Society Woodley		8. 1.64
	(Composite airframe with parts from G-ALMU, G-ALUG & G-AMME; on rebuild by Miles Aircraft Collection for Museum of Berkshire Avn 3.96)						
G-AKIB(2)	Piper J3C-90 Cub (L-4H-PI) (Frame No.12139)	12311	OO-RAY 44-80015	18. 4.84	M.C.Bennett Bodmin (As "480015/M/44" in USAAC c/s)		21. 7.99P
G-AKIF	DH.89A Dragon Rapide	6838	LN-BEZ G-AKIF/NR750	24. 9.47	Airborne Taxi Svs Ltd Duxford/Booker		19. 8.00T
G-AKIN	Miles M.38 Messenger 2A	6728		19. 9.47	R.Spiller & Sons Ltd Sywell		3. 5.99
G-AKIS*	Miles M.38 Messenger 2A	6725		19. 9.47	Musee Royal de L'Armee Brussels (Stored 1992)		5. 8.70
G-AKIU	Percival P.44 Proctor 5	Ae129		20. 2.48	Air Atlantique Ltd Coventry		24. 1.65
G-AKKB	Miles M.65 Gemini 1A	6537		28.10.47	J.Buckingham New Farm, Felton, Bristol (Air Total c/s)		19. 9.98
G-AKKH	Miles M.65 Gemini 1A	6479	OO-CDO	23. 7.48	M.C.Russell Top Farm, Tadlow (Stored 7.96)		21. 9.89T
G-AKKR*	Miles M.14A Hawk Trainer 3	1995	"T9967" G-AKKR/T9708	23. 6.48	Manchester Museum of Science & Industry (Allocated "8378M"; as "T9707") Manchester		10. 4.65
	(P/I could be T9967 from 1943 rebuild)						
G-AKKY*	Miles M.14A Hawk Trainer 3	2078	T9841	23. 6.48	G.H.Johnson/Royal Berkshire Avn Society (As "L6906") Woodley		6.11.64
	(Allocated BAPC44 to reflect rebuild status from various parts)						
G-AKLW*	Short SA.6 Sealand 1	SH.1571	(USA) R Saudi AF/SU-AHY/G-AKLW	26.11.47	Ulster Folk & Transport Museum (Stored 4.98) Holywood, Dublin		
G-AKOE	DH.89A Dragon Rapide 4	6601	X7484	3.12.47	J.E.Pierce Ley Farm, Chirk (British Airways c/s; stored 3.98)		25. 7.82
G-AKOW*	Auster 5	1579	PH-NAD	23.12.47	The Museum of Army Flying		26. 6.82
	(Regd with c/n TJ569A following Dutch rebuild) PH-NEG/G-AKOW/TJ569 (As "TJ569") AAC Middle Wallop						
G-AKPF	Miles M.14A Hawk Trainer 3 (Magister I)	2228	V1075	27. 1.48	P.A.Brook Sandown (As "V1075" in RAF c/s)		30. 8.96P
	(Composite with fuselage of N3788/G-ANLT c/n 836 from 1955 rebuild)						
G-AKPI	Auster 5	1088	NJ703	27. 1.48	B.H.Hargrave Croft, Skegness (To J.Allen 1.91 and stored 5.93; as "NJ703")		1.12.85
G-AKRA(2)	Piper J3C-65 Cub (L-4H-PI) (Frame No.11080)	11255	I-FIVI 43-29964	15. 6.84	W.R.Savin (Cambridge) (On rebuild 8.97)		
G-AKSY*	Auster 5D	1567	F-BGOO G-AKSY/TJ534	10. 2.48	A.Brier Ellerton, Yorks (On rebuild 1992)		
G-AKSZ	Auster 5C (Gipsy Major 1)	1503	F-BGPQ G-AKSZ/TJ457	10. 2.48	A.R.C.Mathie Wrexham		11. 1.99
G-AKTH(2)	Piper J3C-65 Cub (L-4J-PI) (Frame No.13041) (Regd with incorrect c/n 13047)	13211	OO-AGL PH-UCR/45-4471	14. 7.86	G.J.Harry, The Viscount Goschen White Waltham		19. 3.99P
G-AKTI(2)	Luscombe 8A Silvaire (Cont A65)	4101	N1374K NC1374K	27. 5.87	M.W.Olliver Old Sarum		20. 4.99P
G-AKTK(2)	Aeronca 11AC Chief (Cont A65)	11AC-1017	N9379E NC9379E	13. 3.89	R.W.Marshall, G.C.Jones & C.E.McKinney Waits Farm, Belchamp Walter		3. 2.99P
G-AKTN(2)	Luscombe 8A Silvaire (Cont A65)	3540	N77813 NC77813	22. 7.88	M.G.Rummey Goodwood		22.10.98P
G-AKTO(2)	Aeronca 7BCM Champion (Cont A75) (Modified from 7AC standard 8.50)	7AC-940	N8515X N82311/NC82311	19. 5.88	D.C.Murray Lee-on-Solent		22. 9.99P
G-AKTP(2)	PA-17 Vagabond (Cont C85)	17-82	N4683H NC4683H	24. 6.88	G.Campbell Old Sarum t/a G-AKTP Flying Group		27. 5.98P
G-AKTR(2)	Aeronca 7AC Champion	7AC-3017	N58312 NC58312	19. 6.89	C.Fielder "Eddie" New Farm, Felton		27. 7.96P
G-AKTS(2)	Cessna 120	11875	N77434 NC77434	26. 5.88	J.J.Boon "Southern Belle" Popham		25. 6.99P

Regn	Type	C/n	P/I	Date	Owner/operator	Probable Base	CA Expy
G-AKTT(2)	Luscombe 8A Silvaire (Cont A65)	3279	N71852 NC71852	21. 7.88	S.J.Charters (Damaged Chelford,	Orton Grange, Carlisle Cheshire 6.7.91 & on repair 1.96)	23. 6.92P
G-AKUE(2)	DH.82A [OGMA] Tiger Moth	P.68	ZS-FZL CR-AGM/FAP...	12. 2.86	D.F.Hodgkinson (Damaged Bryngwyn Bach 2.1.89 & on rebuild	(Gravesend) Kemble 6.97)	6. 6.91
G-AKUF(2)	Luscombe 8F Silvaire (Cont C90)	4794	N2067K NC2067K	1. 8.88	A.G.Palmer	Wellesbourne Mountford	12. 7.99P
G-AKUG(2)	Luscombe 8A Silvaire (Cont A65)	3689	N77962 NC77962	21. 7.88	P. & L.A.Groves	Exton, Hants	8. 9.99P
G-AKUH(2)	Luscombe 8E Silvaire (Cont O-200-A)	4644	N1917K NC1917K	24.10.88	I.M.Bower "Lucy Too"	Leicester	28. 4.99P
G-AKUI(2)	Luscombe 8E Silvaire (Cont O-200-A)	2464	N45937 NC45937	24.10.88	J.A.Pothecary (Damaged Old Sarum 26.3.89 & on	Newton Toney, Salisbury rebuild 11.96)	17. 1.90P
G-AKUJ(2)	Luscombe 8E Silvaire (Cont C85)	5282	N2555K NC2555K	4. 8.88	R.Fraser & R.Carlton-Green	Coventry	19. 1.99P
G-AKUK(2)	Luscombe 8A Silvaire (Cont A65)	5793	N1166B NC1166B	28.10.88	N.B.Brown t/a Leckhampstead F/Grp	Leckhampstead Farm, Newbury	30. 6.98P
G-AKUL(2)	Luscombe 8A Silvaire (Cont A65)	4189	N1462K NC1462K	9. 2.89	E.A.Taylor (Rebuild nearing completion 3.99)	Southend	21. 5.90P
G-AKUM(2)	Luscombe 8F Silvaire (Cont C90)	6452	N2025B	17. 2.88	Melanie J.Willies Honeydon Farm, Colmworth, Bedford		2. 9.99P
G-AKUN(2)	Piper J3C-85 Cub	6914	N38304 NC38304	13. 1.89	W.R.Savin	Willingham	13. 1.99P
G-AKUO(2)	Aeronca 11AC Chief	11AC-1376	N9730E NC9730E	16. 1.89	S.Longstaff & K.Latham t/a KUO F/Grp	White Waltham	15. 6.99P
G-AKUP(2)	Luscombe 8E Silvaire (Lyc O-320) (To be a floatplane)	5501	N2774K NC2774K	9. 5.89	Melanie J.Willies (Stored 12.96) Honeydon Farm, Colmworth, Bedford		
G-AKUR(2)	Cessna 140	13819	N1647V NC1647V	26. 1.89	J.Greenaway & C.A.Davis	Popham	21. 9.95
G-AKUW	Chrislea CH.3 Srs.2 Super Ace	105		8. 3.48	D.R.Bean	Old Manor Farm, Anwick	29. 5.99P
G-AKVF	Chrislea CH.3 Srs.2 Super Ace	114	AP-ADT G-AKVF	8. 3.48	T.Pate (Stored 4.97)	Kilkerran	17. 7.95P
G-AKVM(2)	Cessna 120	13431	N3173N NC3173N	10. 1.89	N.Wise & S.Walker	Croft-on-Tees, Darlington	11. 5.99P
G-AKVN(2)	Aeronca 11AC Chief	11AC-469	N3742B NC3742B	13. 1.89	C.E.Ellis t/a Breckland Aeronca Grp	Priory Farm, Tibenham	15. 3.99P
G-AKVO(2)	Taylorcraft BC-12D (Cont A65)	9845	N44045 NC44045	10. 1.89	R.J.Whybrow & M.J.Steward t/a Albion Flyers	Priory Farm, Tibenham	28. 9.99P
G-AKVP(2)	Luscombe 8A Silvaire (Cont A65)	5549	N2822K NC2822K	21. 7.88	J.M.Edis	Henlow	25. 2.99P
G-AKVR	Chrislea CH3 Srs.4 Skyjeep	125	VH-OLD VH-RCD/VH-BRP/G-AKVR	8. 3.48	D.R.Bean	Old Manor Farm, Alnwick	
G-AKVZ	Miles M.38 Messenger 4B	6352	RH427	25. 6.48	Shipping & Airlines Ltd	Biggin Hill	24. 9.00
G-AKWS	Auster 5A-160 (Lyc O-320)	1237	RT610	1. 4.48	G.R.Lacey (As "RT610")	Bournemouth	26. 4.00
G-AKWT*	Auster 5	998	MT360	1. 4.48	C.J.Baker (Crashed Nottingham 7.8.48 & stored 9.96)	Carr Farm, Newark	22. 7.49
G-AKXP	Auster 5	1017	NJ633	13. 4.48	M.Pocock (Crashed St.Mary's, Isles of Scilly 9.4.70: on long term rebuild by Classic Vintage Acft Svs 6.95)	Hedge End, Southampton	19.12.70
G-AKXS	DH.82A Tiger Moth	83512	T7105	13. 4.48	P.A.Colman Luxters Farm, Hambleden, Henley-on-Thames		23.10.99
G-AKZN*	Percival P.34A Proctor 3	K.386	Z7197	24. 5.48	RAF Museum (As "Z7197"; also allocated 8380M)	Hendon	29.11.63

G-ALAA-ALZZ

Regn	Type	C/n	P/I	Date	Owner/operator	Probable Base	CA Expy
G-ALAH*	Miles M.38 Messenger 4A	-	RH377	28. 5.48	Not known Sabadella, Barcelona, Spain		18. 4.65
					(Stored 3.95)		
G-ALAX*	DH.89A Dragon Rapide	6930	RL948	27. 5.48	Durney Aeronautical Collection/D.Johnson		
	(Fuselage stored 1994 with components from G-AFRK, G-AHGC, G-AHJS & G-ASRJ) Andover						8. 3.67
G-ALBD	DH.82A Tiger Moth	84130	T7748	27. 5.48	C.H.Schoonbeek (Netherlands)		31.10.81
					(Damaged Leopoldsburg, Belgium 24.5.81 and stored pending rebuild)		
G-ALBJ	Auster 5	1831	TW501	3. 6.48	P.N.Elkington Bloxholm, Sleaford		5. 8.00
G-ALBK	Auster 5	1273	RT644	3. 6.48	S.J.Wright & Co (Farmers) Ltd		
						Ropsley Heath Farm, Grantham	23.10.99
G-ALCK*	Percival P.34A Proctor 3	H.536	LZ766	18. 6.48	Imperial War Museum - Skyfame Collection		
					(As "LZ766")	Duxford	19. 6.63
G-ALCU*	DH.104 Dove 2B	04022	VT-CEH	3. 8.48	Midland Air Museum	Coventry	16. 3.73
G-ALDG*	Handley Page HP.81 Hermes 4	HP.81/8		27.10.49	Duxford Aviation Society	Duxford	9. 1.63
					(Fuselage only) (BOAC c/s) "Horsa"		
G-ALEH	PA-17 Vagabond	17-87	N4689H	17. 8.81	A.D.Pearce White Waltham		11. 3.99P
	(Cont A65)		NC4689H				
G-ALFA	Auster 5	1236	RT607	20.10.48	S.P.Barrett Sturgate		24.11.01
					t/a Golf Alfa Auster Grp		
	(P/i uncertain as c/n 1236 considered sold as HB-EOC 4.48; reported as c/n 826 (MS958) but doubtful)						
G-ALFT*	DH.104 Dove 6	04233		14.12.48	Caernarfon Air World Caernarfon		13. 6.73
G-ALFU*	DH.104 Dove 6	04234		14.12.48	Duxford Aviation Society Duxford		4. 6.71
G-ALGA(2)	PA-15 Vagabond	15-348	N4575H	3.12.86	D.A.Lord Herrings Farm, Sussex		16. 2.99P
	(Lyc O-145)		NC4575H				
G-ALIJ(2)	PA-17 Vagabond	17-166	N4866H	13. 2.87	A.S.Cowan t/a Popham F/Grp G-ALIJ Popham		19. 3.99P
	(Cont A65)		NC4866H			(Damaged at Brimpton 4.5.98)		
G-ALIW	DH.82A Tiger Moth	82901	N27WB	17. 8.81	D.I.M.Geddes & F.R.Curry White Waltham		14. 8.00
			ZK-ATI/NZ899/R5006				
G-ALJF	Percival P.34A Proctor 3	K.427	Z7252	3. 3.49	J.F.Moore Biggin Hill		26. 8.01
G-ALJL	DH.82A Tiger Moth	84726	T6311	7. 3.49	C.G.Clarke Bursledon, Southampton		28. 9.50
					(On long term rebuild from components 11.92)		
G-ALLF	Slingsby T.30A Prefect	548	BGA.599	29. 3.49	J.F.Hopkins & K.M.Fresson Parham Park		
			PH-1/BGA.599/G-ALLF/BGA.599				
G-ALNA	DH.82A Tiger Moth	85061	T6774	11. 4.49	R.J.Doughton Dunkeswell		11.11.01T
					(Brooklands Aviation c/s)		
G-ALND	DH.82A Tiger Moth	82308	N9191	12. 4.49	J.T.Powell-Tuck Abergavenny		11. 4.82
					(Crashed Panshanger 8.3.81 & on rebuild 3.96) (As "N9191" in RN c/s)		
G-ALNV*	Auster 5	1216	RT578	21. 4.49	C.J.Baker(Stored 9.96) Carr Farm, Newark		4. 7.50
G-ALOD	Cessna 140	14691	N2440V	14.10.83	J.R.Stainer Bennington		11. 1.02
G-ALRH	EoN AP.8 Baby	EoN/B/005	BGA629	25. 5.49	P.D.Moran Chipping		
			G-ALRH/BGA629			(Op by EoN Baby Syndicate on BGA CA)		
G-ALRI	DH.82A Tiger Moth	83350	ZK-BAB	2. 5.51	Wessex Avn & Transport Ltd Chalmington		19. 8.94
			G-ALRI/T5672			(As "T5672" in RAF c/s)		
G-ALSX*	Bristol 171 Sycamore 3	12892	G-48/1	17.11.50	E.D.Ap Rees Weston-super-Mare		24. 9.65
			G-ALSX/VR-TBS/G-ALSX t/a The Helicopter Museum				
G-ALTO	Cessna 140	14253	N2040V	19. 1.82	J.P.Bell Eshott		25. 5.98
	(Cont C85)						
G-ALTW*	DH.82A Tiger Moth	84177	T7799	13. 6.49	A.Mangham Hounslow Green, Essex		8. 6.70
					(Crashed Panshanger 5.11.69 & on rebuild 10.91)		
G-ALUC	DH.82A Tiger Moth	83094	R5219	28. 6.49	D.R. & Mrs M.Wood		
					Fowle Hall Farm, Paddock Wood, Kent		21. 9.01
G-ALVP*	DH.82A Tiger Moth	82711	R4770	26. 9.49	V. & R.Wheele (Shoreham)		15. 2.61
					(Stored for rebuild)		
G-ALWB	DHC.1 Chipmunk 22A	C1/0100	OE-ABC	28.12.49	M.L. & J.M.Soper Perth		18. 5.00
			G-ALWB				
G-ALWC*	Douglas C-47A-25DK Dakota 4	13590	KG723	10. 1.50	Ailes Anciennes Toulouse (Open storage 6.95)		
	(Allocated F-GBOL but NTU)		42-93654			Toulouse-Blagnac		6. 2.83A
G-ALWF*	V.701 Viscount	5		2. 1.50	Duxford Aviation Society Duxford		16. 4.72
					(BEA c/s) "RMA Sir John Franklin"		
G-ALWS	DH.82A Tiger Moth	82415	N9328	24. 1.50	A.P.Beynon Welshpool		
	(Regd with c/n 82413)				(On rebuild 5.98)		
G-ALWW	DH.82A Tiger Moth	86366	NL923	24. 1.50	D.E.Findon Bidford		11. 3.00
					t/a Stratford-upon-Avon Tiger Moth Grp		
G-ALXT*	DH.89A Dragon Rapide	6736	4R-AAI	24. 1.50	The Science Museum Wroughton		
			CY-AAI/G-ALXT/NF865 (Railway A/S c/s) "Star of Scotia"				
G-ALXZ	Auster 5-150	1082	D-EGOF	1. 2.50	M.F.Cuming Kemble		18. 7.99
	(Lycoming O-320) (Frame No.TAY24070)		PH-NER/G-ALXZ/NJ689				
G-ALYB*	Auster 5	1173	RT520	3. 2.50	South Yorkshire Aviation Museum		
					(On rebuild 5.97) Home Farm, Firbeck		26. 5.63
G-ALYG	Auster 5D	835	MS968	14. 3.50	A.L.Young Henstridge		19. 1.70
	(Regd with incorrect identity MT968; frame stored 9.95; for rebuild as Auster 5)						
G-ALYW*	DH.106 Comet 1	06009		18. 9.51	RAF Exhibition Unit RAF St.Athan		14. 6.54
					(Fuselage converted to "Nimrod" exhibition airframe as "XV238")		
G-ALYX*	DH.106 Comet 1	06010		18. 9.51	Not known Lasham		21. 7.54
					(Fuselage centre-section stored by DRA 3.93; possibly scrapped)		
G-ALZE*	Britten-Norman BN-1F	1		16. 3.50	Southampton Hall of Aviation Southampton		
G-ALZO*	Airspeed AS.57 Ambassador 2	5226	RJAF-108	5. 4.50	Duxford Aviation Society Duxford		14. 5.72
			G-ALZO/(G-AMAD)			(On rebuild 1.99)		

G-AMAA-AMZZ

Regn	Type	C/n	P/I	Date	Owner/operator	Probable Base	CA Expy
G-AMAI	DH.89A Dragon Rapide	6879	D-ILIT	4. 4.50	J.M.Koch	Sandown	7.11.99T
			EC-AGP/G-AMAI/NR803		t/a The Island Aeroplane Co		
G-AMAU*	Hawker Hurricane IIc	-	PZ865	1. 5.50	Battle of Britain Mem Flt RAF Coningsby		
					(As "PZ865/Q" in RAFSEAC c/s)		
G-AMAW	Luton LA-4 Minor	JRC.1 & SA.I		29. 4.50	R.H.Coates	Hitchin	6. 8.88P
	(Cherub III) (Known as Swalesong SA.I)				(Stored 7.96)		
G-AMBB	DH.82A Tiger Moth	85070	T6801	1. 5.50	J.Eagles	Oaksey Park	
	(Composite rebuild - parts to "G-MAZY" ? - see SECTION XXX; on rebuild 6.95)						
G-AMCA	Douglas C-47B-30DK Dakota 3	KN487		1. 6.50	Atlantic Air Transport Ltd	Coventry	10.12.99A
		16218/32966	44-76634		(Op Air Atlantique) (Pollution Control c/s)		
G-AMCK	DH.82A Tiger Moth	84641	N65N	15. 6.50	D.L.Frankel	Langham	8. 7.01
			C-GBBF/SLN-05/D-EGXY/HB-UAC/G-AMCK/T6193 (On overhaul Swanton Morley 5.97)				
G-AMCM	DH.82A Tiger Moth	85295	DE249	14.12.50	B.C., J.I. & A.K.Cooper		
	(Regd with c/n "89259")					Denford Manor, Hungerford	28. 5.56
	(Crashed nr Somerton 25.9.55 & on long term rebuild from components)						
G-AMDA*	Avro 652A Anson 1	-	N4877	20. 7.50	Imperial War Museum - Skyfame Collection		
					(Unmarked)	Duxford	14.12.62
G-AMEN	PA-18-95 Super Cub	18-1998	(G-BJTR)	29.12.81	A.Lovejoy & W.Cook	Popham	10. 1.00P
	(L-18C-PI)	MM52-2398 "EI.71"/I-EIAM/MM52-2398/52-2398			t/a Sierra Golf F/Grp		
	(Frame No.18-1963; Italian rebuild c/n OMA.71-08)						
G-AMHF	DH.82A Tiger Moth	83026	R5144	6. 2.51	Wavendon Social Housing Ltd	Sywell	22. 8.00
	(Rebuilt with components from G-BABA c/n 86584 ex F-BGDT/PG687) (Anthony West)						
G-AMHJ	Douglas C-47A-25DK Dakota 6	13468	SU-AZI	6. 2.51	Atlantic Air Transport Ltd	Coventry	5.12.99A
		G-AMHJ/ZS-BRW/KG651/42-108962			(Op Air Atlantique) (Pollution Control c/s)		
G-AMIU	DH.82A Tiger Moth	83228	T5495	9. 4.51	R. & Mrs J.L.Jones	Membury	9. 9.71
	(Crashed Booker 15.10.69 & stored 1.92)				t/a Southern Sailplanes		
G-AMKU	Auster 5 J/1B Aiglet	2721	ST-ABD	10. 7.51	P.G.Lipman Romney Street Farm, Sevenoaks		2. 7.00
			SN-ABD/G-AMKU				
G-AMLZ*	Percival P.50 Prince 6E	P.46	(VR-TBN)	23.11.51	Air Atlantique Ltd	Caernarfon	18. 6.71
			G-AMLZ				
G-AMMS	Auster J/5K Aiglet Trainer	2745		11.10.51	A.J.Large	Gloucestershire	19.10.98
G-AMNN	DH.82A Tiger Moth	86457	NM137	24.12.51	M.Thrower "Spirit of Pashley"	Shoreham	25. 6.00
					t/a Northbrook College of Aeronautical Engineering		
	(Composite from unidentified airframe; the original G-AMNN may have been absorbed into G-BPAJ)						
G-AMOG*	Vickers Viscount 701	7	(G-AMNZ)	23. 5.52	RAF Museum	RAF Cosford	14. 6.77
					(BEA c/s) "RMA Robert Falcon Scott"		
G-AMPG(2)	PA-12 Super Cruiser	12-985	N2647M	25. 3.85	R.Simpson	Preston Court, Ledbury	3.12.98P
			NC2647M				
G-AMPI(2)	SNCAN Stampe SV-4C	213	N6RA	13. 2.84	M. F Newman	(Wymondham)	
			F-BCFX		(Frame stored Staverton 3.92)		
G-AMPO	Douglas C-47B-30DK Dakota 3	LN-RTO		25. 2.52	Atlantic Air Transport Ltd	Coventry	29. 3.97A
		16437/33185	G-AMPO		(Op Air Atlantique) (Pollution Control c/s)		
	(Regd with c/n 33186/16438)		KN566/44-76853				
G-AMPP*	Douglas C-47B Dakota 3	15272/26717	XF753	4. 3.52	Not known	(France)	7. 2.71
		G-AMPP/KK136/43-49456			(As "G-AMSU" in Dan-Air c/s; to Euro-Disney 1993)		
G-AMPY	Douglas C-47B-15DK Dakota 3	(EI-BKJ)		8. 3.52	Dak Holdings Ltd	Coventry	5. 1.00A
		15124/26569	G-AMPY/N15751/		(Op Air Atlantique/Pollution Control)		
		G-AMPY/TF-FIO/G-AMPY/JY-ABE/G-AMPY/KK116/43-49308					
G-AMPZ	Douglas C-47B-30DK Dakota 4	EI-BDT		8. 3.52	Atlantic Air Transport Ltd	Coventry	29. 4.01T
		16124/32872	G-AMPZ/		(Op Air Atlantique)		
		TF-AIV/G-41-3-66/PH-RIC/G-AMPZ/OD-AEQ/G-AMPZ/KN442/44-76540					
G-AMRA	Douglas C-47B-15DK Dakota 6	XE280		8. 3.52	Dak Holdings Ltd	Coventry	11. 6.00T
		15290/26735	G-AMRA/KK151/43-49474		(Op Air Atlantique)		
G-AMRF	Auster J/5F Aiglet Trainer	2716	VT-DHA	20. 3.52	A.I.Topps	East Midlands	28.11.99
			G-AMRF				
G-AMRK	Gloster Gladiator 1	-	L8032	16. 5.52	The Shuttleworth Trust	Old Warden	16. 7.99P
	(Bristol Mercury XXX)		"K8032"/G-AMRK/L8032		(As "423" in R.Nor AF c/s)		
G-AMSG	SIPA 903	77	OO-VBL	25.11.81	S.W.Markham	Valentine Farm, Odiham	1. 4.99
			F-BGHB				
G-AMSN	Douglas C-47B-35DK Dakota 4	N3455		28. 4.52	Aces High Ltd	North Weald	3. 1.68
		16631/33379	G-AMSN/EI-BSI/SU-BFZ/G-AMSN/KN673/44-77047		(Stored 10.97)		
G-AMSV	Douglas C-47B-25DK Dakota 3			15. 5.52	Dak Holdings Ltd (Op Air Atlantique)		
		16072/32820	G-AMSV/KN397/44-76488		(Pollution Control c/s)	Coventry	1. 7.01A
G-AMTA	Auster J/5F Aiglet Trainer	2780		24. 5.52	N.H.J.Cottrell	Headcorn	17. 7.00
G-AMTD*	Auster J/5F Aiglet Trainer	2783	EI-AVL	24. 5.52	Leicestershire A/C Ltd	Leicester	8.12.93T
			G-AMTD				
	(Damaged Hayrish Farm, Okehampton 7.8.93; wings noted 5.96; cancelled as WFU 15.1.99)						
G-AMTF	DH.82A Tiger Moth	84207	ZK-AVE	11. 6.52	M.W.Zipfell	RAF Marham	19. 7.01
			G-AMTF/T7842		(As "T-7842")		
G-AMTK	DH.82A Tiger Moth	3982	N6709	18. 6.52	S.W.McKay & M.E.Vaisey	(Berkhamsted)	27. 5.66
					(Stored 2.96)		
G-AMTM	Auster 5 J/1 Autocrat	3101	G-AJUJ	3. 7.52	R.J.Stobo & D.A.Clewley		
	(Auster Acft rebuild - originally c/n 2622)				Oaklands Farm, Stonesfield, Oxon	3. 6.99P
G-AMTV	DH.82A Tiger Moth	3858	OO-SOE	5. 8.52	Medalbest Ltd	Old Sarum	1.10.00
			G-AMTV/N6545				

Regn	Type	C/n	P/I	Date	Owner/operator	Probable Base	CA Expy
G-AMUF	DHC.1 Chipmunk 21	C1/0832		2. 9.52	Redhill Tailwheel F/C Ltd	Redhill	24. 1.02
G-AMUI	Auster J/5F Aiglet Trainer	2790		29. 8.52	Deborah Hatelie (On rebuild 7.93)	(Liverpool)	15. 2.66T
G-AMUJ*	Auster J/5F Aiglet Trainer	2791		29. 8.52	C.J.Baker (Crashed nr Sleaford 8.6.60; stored 9.96)	Carr Farm, Newark	5. 4.61
G-AMVD	Auster 5	1565	F-BGTF G-AMVD/TJ565	6.10.52	M.Hammond (As "TJ565")	(Eye, Suffolk)	6. 4.01
G-AMVP	Tipsy Junior (Walter Mikron 2)	J.111	OO-ULA	23.10.52	A.R.Wershat (Damaged Wroughton 4.7.93; under repair 12.95)	Sandown	22. 6.94P
G-AMVS	DH.82A Tiger Moth	82784	OO-SOJ G-AMVS/R4852	12.11.52	J.T.Powell-Tuck (On rebuild Shobdon 8.92)	(Pontypool)	21.12.53
G-AMYA(2)*	Zlin Z.381 Bestmann (Hirth HM504A)	461	OO-AVC OK-AVC	17. 6.87	K.Weeks/Fantasy of Flight Museum (As "AM+YA" in Luftwaffe c/s) Polk City, Florida		21. 2.96P
G-AMYD	Auster J/5L Aiglet Trainer	2773		13. 2.53	G.H.Maskell	Duckend Farm, Wilstead, Bedford	4. 3.01
G-AMYJ	Douglas C-47B-25DK Dakota 6 15968/32716		SU-AZF G-AMYJ XF747/G-AMYJ/KN353/44-76384	23. 2.53	Atlantic Air Transport Ltd (Op Air Atlantique) (In Pollution Control c/s)	Coventry	4. 4.97A
G-AMYL(2)	PA-17 Vagabond (Cont C75)	17-30	N4613H NC4613H	24. 4.87	P.J.Penn-Sayer (Stored 9.97) t/a The Fun Airplane Co "Yankee Lady"	Scaynes Hill, Haywards Heath	20. 6.89P
G-AMZI	Auster J/5F Aiglet Trainer	3104		4. 5.53	J.F.Moore	Biggin Hill	29.12.00
G-AMZT	Auster J/5F Aiglet Trainer	3107		28. 5.53	D.Hyde, J.W.Saull & J.C.Hutchinson	Cranfield	25. 5.01
G-AMZU	Auster J/5F Aiglet Trainer	3108		28. 5.53	J.A.Longworth, A.R.M. & C.B.A.Eagle t/a Flying Flicks	White Waltham	5. 8.99

G-ANAA-ANZZ

Regn	Type	C/n	P/I	Date	Owner/operator	Probable Base	CA Expy
G-ANAF	Douglas C-47B-35DK Dakota 3		N170GP	17. 6.53	Atlantic Air Transport Ltd Coventry		26. 2.01A
		16688/33436	G-ANAF/KP220/44-77104		(Op Air Atlantique for Racal)		
G-ANAP*	DH.104 Dove 6	04433		17. 7.53	Brunel Technical College Bristol/Lulsgate		
					(Instructional airframe 5.97)		
G-ANCF*	Bristol 175 Britannia 308F	12922	5Y-AZP	3. 1.58	R.Hargreaves (Stored 6.97) Kemble		12. 1.81T
	G-ANCF/LV-GJB/LV-PPJ/(G-ANCF)/G-14-1/G-18-4/(N6597C)/G-ANCF				t/a Britannia Acft Preservation Trust		
G-ANCS	DH.82A Tiger Moth	82824	R4907	12. 9.53	M.A.B.Mitchell Wold Farm, Cambridge		14. 8.99
G-ANCX	DH.82A Tiger Moth	83719	T7229	15. 9.53	D.R.Wood Fowle Hall Farm, Paddock Wood		28. 7.99
G-ANDE	DH.82A Tiger Moth	85957	EM726	23. 9.53	Montrose Aviation Ltd Redhill		4. 2.00T
G-ANDM	DH.82A Tiger Moth	3946	EI-AGP	23. 9.53	J.G.Green White Ox Mead, Bath		14. 8.00
			G-ANDM/EI-AGP/G-ANDM/(G-ANDI)/N6642				
G-ANDP	DH.82A Tiger Moth	82868	D-EBEC	22. 9.53	A.H.Diver Newtownards		20. 7.01
			N9920F/G-ANDP/R4960		(Damaged mid 1995)		
G-ANDX*	DH.104 Devon C.2 (Dove 7XC)	04435	XG496	28. 9.53	L.Richards Newcastle		3.4.86P*
			G-ANDX		(Cancelled by CAA 21.1.99; stored Newcastle since 4.86)		
G-ANEH	DH.82A Tiger Moth	82067	N6797	29. 9.53	G.J.Wells (As "N6797")(Henley-on-Thames)		6. 8.01
G-ANEJ*	DH.82A Tiger Moth	85592	DE638	1.10.53	Royal Malaysian Air Force Museum		
					(As "T7245" in RAF c/s) Sungei Besi Air Base, Kuala Lumpur		
G-ANEL	DH.82A Tiger Moth	82333	N9238	1.10.53	Chauffair Ltd Redhill		17. 6.99
G-ANEM	DH.82A Tiger Moth	82943	EI-AGN	1.10.53	P.J.Benest Hamstead Marshall		16. 7.99
			G-ANEM/R5042				
G-ANEN	DH.82A Tiger Moth	85418	OO-ACG	2.10.53	R.J.Jackson Old Sarum		20. 7.98
			G-ANEN/DE410				
G-ANEW	DH.82A Tiger Moth	86458	NM138	6.10.53	A.L.Young (Stored 4.96) Henstridge		18. 6.62T
G-ANEZ	DH.82A Tiger Moth	84218	T7849	20.10.53	T.S.Warren & C.D.J.Bland Sandown		16. 5.99
G-ANFC	DH.82A Tiger Moth	85385	DE363	13.10.53	J.E.Pierce (N Herefordshire)		11.11.99T
G-ANFH*	Westland WS.55 Whirlwind 1	WA.15		27.10.53	E.D. Ap Rees Weston-super-Mare		17. 7.71
					t/a The Helicopter Museum (Open store 8.98)		
G-ANFI	DH.82A Tiger Moth	85577	DE623	16.10.53	G.P.Graham (As "DE623") Shobdon		19.12.99
					(Tiger Moth "DE623" [D-EDON] displayed Auto Und Technik Museum, Sinsheim)		
G-ANFL	DH.82A Tiger Moth	84617	T6169	22.10.53	R.P., D.R. & R.Whitby Swanton Morley		23. 4.01
					(Stored 10.97)		
G-ANFM	DH.82A Tiger Moth	83604	T5888	22.10.53	S.A.Brook, L.S.Mitton & J.Hartill		
					t/a Reading F/Grp White Waltham		5. 8.01
G-ANFP*	DH.82A Tiger Moth	82530	N9503	28.10.53	M.Biggs (Stored 3.96) Fownhope, Hereford		1. 7.63
G-ANFU*	Auster 5	1748	TW385	31.10.53	J.Stelling Newcastle		17. 2.71
					t/a Newcastle Vehicle Museum		
	(On rebuild 5.93 with frame from un-identified Auster 6;						
	to be "NJ719" using identity of starboard wing ex G-AKPH)						
G-ANFV	DH.82A Tiger Moth	85904	DF155	1.12.53	R.A.L.Falconer Shempston Farm, Elgin		4. 2.01
					(As "DF155")		
G-ANFW	DH.82A Tiger Moth	85660	DE730	5.11.53	G.M.K.Fraser Duxford		21.12.01
	(Regd with Fuselage No.3737)				t/a Fraser Avn (Stored 1.99)		
G-ANFY*	Thruxton Jackaroo	86349	NL906	13.11.53	B.Knock Ashford, Kent		25. 5.68
					(Stored in poor condition 1.96)		
G-ANGK(2)	Cessna 140A	15396	N9675A	10. 3.89	D.W.Munday Popham		21. 7.01
G-ANHK	DH.82A Tiger Moth	82442	F-BHIM	4.12.53	J.D.Iliffe Hampstead Norreys		9. 2.00
			G-ANHK/N9372				
G-ANHR	Auster 5	759	MT192	5.12.53	C.G.Winch Rushett Farm, Chessington		20. 7.86
					(On rebuild 6.96)		
G-ANHS	Auster 4	737	MT197	5.12.53	R.G.Tomlinson Spanhoe		9. 9.00
					t/a Tango Uniform Grp		
G-ANHU	Auster 4	799	EC-AXR	5.12.53	D.J.Baker Carr Farm, Newark		22.10.66
			G-ANHU/MT255		(On rebuild 9.96)		
G-ANHW*	Auster 5D	1396	TJ320	5.12.53	C.J.Baker Carr Farm, Newark		9. 3.70
					(On rebuild 9.96)		
G-ANHX	Auster 5D	2064	TW519	5.12.53	D.J.Baker Carr Farm, Newark		2.11.73
					(Stored 9.96)		
G-ANIE	Auster 5	1809	TW467	5.12.53	S.J.Partridge Bassingbourn		8. 9.99
					(Op Military Auster Flt as "TW467/ROD-F" in 664 Sqn c/s)		
G-ANIJ	Auster 5D	1680	TJ672	5.12.53	M.Pocock Whitchurch, Hants		5. 5.71
					t/a Military Auster Flt as "TJ672" in 657 Sqdn c/s; on rebuild 7.93)		
G-ANIS*	Auster 5	1429	TJ375	5.12.53	R.W.Hall t/a Halls Autospares		
					(Stored 6.97) Longford, Ireland		19. 9.76
G-ANIX	DH.82A Tiger Moth	84764	D-EFTF	14. 4.55	J.M.Koch Sandown		2. 7.00T
					(Op Island Aeroplane Co) (As "T6390" in RAF c/s)		
	(Composite rebuild of un-identified Tiger Moth in Germany 1990/92						
	using documentation of D-ELOM, former G-ANIX/T6390)						
G-ANJA	DH.82A Tiger Moth	82459	N9389	7.12.53	P.Aukland (As "N9389") Seething		1.11.98
G-ANJD	DH.82A Tiger Moth	84652	T6226	8.12.53	A.C.Ladd (On rebuild 7.97) Rochester		6. 9.81
G-ANJK*	DH.82A Tiger Moth	84557	T6066	12.12.53	Not known Rhos-Y-Gilwen Farm, Rhos Hill		12. 5.85
					(As "T6066") (Stored 5.94)		
G-ANJV*	Westland WS-55 Whirlwind 3	WA.24	VR-BET	14.12.53	E.D.Ap Rees Weston-super-Mare		
			G-ANJV		t/a The Helicopter Museum (Stored 5.97)		
G-ANKK	DH.82A Tiger Moth	83590	T5854	24.12.53	Patricia A.Cambridge Pool Quay		18. 1.01
					t/a Halfpenny Green Tiger Grp (As "T5854")		

Regn	Type	C/n	P/I	Date	Owner/operator	Probable Base	CA Expy
G-ANKT	DH.82A Tiger Moth	85087	T6818	24.12.53	The Shuttleworth Trust (As "T6818/91")	Old Warden	1. 8.98P
G-ANKV*	DH.82A Tiger Moth	84166	T7793	30.12.53	Westmead Business Group	Croydon Airport	
	(Provenance uncertain; static rebuild by Acebell Avn early 1994) (As "T7793" in RAF c/s at Terminal Building)						
G-ANKZ	DH.82A Tiger Moth	3803	(N) F-BHIO/G-ANKZ/N6466	30.12.53	D.W.Graham (As "N6466")	Sywell	15. 4.99
G-ANLD	DH.82A Tiger Moth	85990	OO-DPA G-ANLD/EM773	30.12.53	K.Peters	Rushett Farm, Chessington	20. 4.98
G-ANLH	DH.82A Tiger Moth	86546	N3744F OO-EVO/G-ANLH/PG637	4. 1.54	T.S.Warren & J.J.Woodhouse (Damaged port wing at Sandown 27.4.98)	Sandown	7. 5.00T
	(Fuselage No. MCO/DH.4623)						
G-ANLS	DH.82A Tiger Moth	85862	DF113	7. 1.54	P.A.Gliddon	Great Fryup, Egton, Whitby	26. 2.00
G-ANLU	Auster 5	1780	TW448	8. 1.54	B.H.Hargrave (Stored by Crofton Aeroplane Svs 1.95)	Stubbington	8. 8.68
G-ANLW	Westland WS.51 Srs.2 Widgeon	WA/H/133	"MD497" G-ANLW	23. 3.54	Sloane Helicopters Ltd (Stored 8.97)	Sywell	27. 5.81A
G-ANLX	DH.82A Tiger Moth	84165	T7792	8. 1.54	B.J., P.B., A.J. & P.J.Borsberry t/a Jack's Tiger F/Grp	Kidmore End, Reading	11. 4.56
	(Crashed nr Luton Airport 31.12.55; minor components held for composite rebuild)						
G-ANMO	DH.82A Tiger Moth	3255	F-BHIU G-ANMO/K4259	22. 1.54	E. & K.M.Lay (As "K4259/71")	White Waltham	10. 8.00
G-ANMV	DH.82A Tiger Moth	83745	F-BHAZ G-ANMV/T7404	22. 1.54	B.P.Sanders t/a Tigerfly (As "T7404/04")	Booker	26. 6.98T
G-ANMY	DH.82A Tiger Moth	85466	OO-SOL "OO-SOC"/G-ANMY/DE470	22. 1.54	R.Earl & B.Morris (As "DE470/16" in RAF c/s)	Oaksey Park	24. 8.01
G-ANNB	DH.82A Tiger Moth	84233	N6037 D-EGYN/G-ANNB/T6037	22. 1.54	G.M.Bradley (On rebuild Rothesay 4.92)	(Colchester)	12. 6.58
G-ANNE(2)	DH.82A Tiger Moth	"83814"		15. 4.94	C.R.Hardiman (On rebuild 3.96)	Shobdon	30. 5.58
	(Composite airframe, not likely to be connected with original G-ANNE, ex T7418, sold as OO-CCI/90-CCI/9Q-CCI)						
G-ANNG	DH.82A Tiger Moth	85504	DE524	22. 1.54	P.F.Walter	Farnborough	18. 5.01
G-ANNI	DH.82A Tiger Moth	85162	T6953	22. 1.54	A.R.Brett (As "T6953)	Hong Kong	27. 8.00
G-ANNK	DH.82A Tiger Moth	83804	F-BFDO G-ANNK/T7290	22. 1.54	Patricia J.Wilcox (On rebuild Cranfield 5.92)	(Northampton)	25. 9.87
G-ANNN	DH.82A Tiger Moth	84073	T5968	2. 2.54	H.C.Cox (On rebuild 1996)	(Bristol)	
G-ANOD	DH.82A Tiger Moth	84588	T6121	16. 2.54	Penelope G.Grafton (Composite rebuild; on long term rebuild 6.94)	Kidmore End, Reading	7. 2.60
G-ANOH	DH.82A Tiger Moth	86040	EM838	22. 2.54	N.Parkhouse	Great Massingham	14. 3.97T
G-ANOK*	SAAB 91C Safir	91311	SE-CAH	22. 4.54	A.F.Galt & Co Ltd (Stored 4.89)	Kirk Yetholm	5. 2.73
G-ANOM	DH.82A Tiger Moth	82086	N6837	2. 3.54	A.L.Creer (Crashed Fairoaks 17.12.61; on rebuild 12.95)	(Bristol)	3. 5.62T
G-ANON	DH.82A Tiger Moth	84270	T7909	4. 3.54	A.C.Mercer (As "T7909")	Sherburn	4. 8.99
G-ANOO	DH.82A Tiger Moth	85409	DE401	11. 3.54	R.K.Packman	Compton Abbas	19. 5.99
G-ANOR	DH.82A Tiger Moth	85635	DE694	4. 3.54	R.Clifford (See G-ACDA) (As "T6991")	(London NW3)	27. 1.01
G-ANOV*	DH.104 Dove 6	04445	G-5-16	11. 3.54	Royal Museum of Scotland/Museum of Flight (Civil Aviation Authority c/s)	East Fortune	31. 5.75
G-ANPC*	DH.82A Tiger Moth	82858	R4950	19. 3.54	Irish Avn Museum (Crashed nr Loch Leven 2.1.67; stored 4.96)	Castlemoate House, Dublin	2. 9.67
G-ANPE	DH.82A Tiger Moth	83738	G-IESH G-ANPE/F-BHAT/G-ANPE/T7397	27. 3.54	I.E.S.Hudleston	(Lymington)	22.12.99
G-ANPK	DH.82A Tiger Moth	3571	L6936	5. 4.54	D.E.Partridge t/a The P & D Grp (Damaged Jaywick Sands, Clacton 18.8.96; stored 1.97)	Great Waltham	10. 7.97T
G-ANRF	DH.82A Tiger Moth	83748	T5850	24. 5.54	C.D.Cyster	Glenrothes	24. 8.01
G-ANRM	DH.82A Tiger Moth	85861	DF112	8. 6.54	Clacton A/C (1988) Ltd (As "DF112")	Clacton/Duxford	28. 7.01T
G-ANRN	DH.82A Tiger Moth	83133	T5368	24. 5.54	J.J.V.Elwes	Rush Green	10. 8.00
G-ANRP	Auster 5	1789	TW439	21. 5.54	A.Brier (As "TW439")	Breighton	20.10.99
G-ANRX*	DH.82A Tiger Moth	3863	N6550	25. 5.54	De Havilland Aircraft Museum "Border City"	Salisbury Hall, London Colney	20. 6.61
G-ANSM	DH.82A Tiger Moth	82909	R5014	3. 6.54	J.L.Bond	Redhill	23. 7.01
G-ANTE	DH.82A Tiger Moth	84891	T6562	20. 9.54	M.R.Keen (Stored 2.97)	Liverpool	10. 6.89T
G-ANTK*	Avro 685 York C1	-	MW232	23. 7.54	Duxford Aviation Society (On rebuild 1.99)	Duxford	29.10.64TC
G-ANUO*	DH.114 Heron 2D	14062		27. 9.54	Westmead Business Centre (As "G-AOXL" in Morton Air Services c/s)	Croydon Airport	12. 9.86T
G-ANUW*	DH.104 Dove 6	04458		16. 5.55	Ross Aviation Services (Stored 2.97)	Fownhope, Hereford	22. 7.81
G-ANVU*	DH.104 Dove 1B	04082	VR-NAP	12.11.54	Flygvapenmuseum Malmen (Stored 1992)	Malmslatt, Linkoping, Sweden	14. 9.77
G-ANWB*	DHC.1 Chipmunk 21	C1/0987	G-5-17	15. 2.55	G.Briggs (Cancelled by CAA 26.2.99; last known on rebuild 6.96)	Blackpool	8. 3.91
G-ANWO	Miles M.14A Hawk Trainer 3	718	L8262	31.12.58	A.G.Dunkerley (Stored West Chiltington, Pulborough 11.92)	(Bury)	18. 4.63
G-ANWX*	Auster J/5L Aiglet Trainer	3131		25.11.54	D.Hodgkinson "Shepherd's Delight" (Damaged Nayland 1.8.93; on rebuild 9.96)	Canterbury	2. 5.94
G-ANXB*	DH.114 Heron 1B	14048	G-5-14	3.12.54	Newark Air Museum (BEA Scottish Airways c/s) "Sir James Young Simpson"	Winthorpe	25. 3.79

Regn	Type	C/n	P/I	Date	Owner/operator	Probable Base	CA Expy
G-ANXC	Auster J/5R Alpine	3135	5Y-UBD	4.12.54	R.B.Webber	Hayrish Farm, Okehampton	2. 8.98
			VP-UBD/G-ANXC/(AP-AHG)/G-ANXC		t/a Alpine Group		
G-ANXR	Percival P.31C Proctor 4	H.803	RM221	14.12.54	L.H.Oakins (As "RM221")	Biggin Hill	8. 6.00
G-ANZT	Thruxton Jackaroo	84176	T7798	4. 3.55	D.J.Neville & P.J.Dear	Rush Green	14. 8.99
G-ANZU	DH.82A Tiger Moth	3583	L6938	9. 3.55	P.A.Jackson (Stored 1994)		17. 3.91
						Brookfield Farm, Great Stukeley	
G-ANZZ	DH.82A Tiger Moth	85834	DE974	14. 3.55	J.I.B.Bennett & P.P.Amershi	(Hatfield)	28. 2.69T

G-AOAA-AOZZ

Regn	Type	C/n	P/I	Date	Owner/operator	Probable Base	CA Expy
G-AOAA	DH.82A Tiger Moth	85908	DF159	14. 3.55	R.C.P.Brookhouse (Redhill)		8.12.91T
					(Damaged Redhill 4.6.89)		
G-AOBG*	Somers-Kendall SK-1	1		30. 3.55	A.J.E.Smith	Breighton	26. 6.58
					(Wfu after engine turbine failure 11.7.57; stored 10.97)		
G-AOBH	DH.82A Tiger Moth	84350	T7997	31. 3.55	P.Nutley (As "NL750")	Thruxton	20. 2.00
	(Regd with c/n 83818 ex T7439; G-AOBH is marked as "NL750" which belongs to						
	G-AHUF marked "T7997"; both a/c are registered to same owner)						
G-AOBO	DH.82A Tiger Moth	3810	N6473	23. 4.55	J.S. & J.V.Shaw	Cubert, Newquay	28. 9.69T
					(On rebuild 10.97)		
G-AOBU	Hunting Percival P.84	P84/6	(XM129)	2. 5.55	T.J.Manna t/a Kennet Avn	Cranfield	23. 4.99P
	Jet Provost T.1		G-AOBU/G-42-1		(As "XD693/Z-Q" in RAF c/s)		
G-AOBV*	Auster J/5P Autocar	3171		9. 5.55	Not known (Stored 10.97) Cheshunt, Bucks		7. 4.71T
G-AOBX	DH.82A Tiger Moth	83653	T7187	26. 4.55	D.G.Ross	Uffley Common, Odiham	5.11.99
G-AOCP*	Auster 5	1800	TW462	25. 5.56	C.J.Baker	Carr Farm, Newark	22. 6.68
					(Damaged 4.70; on rebuild 9.96)		
G-AOCR	Auster 5D	1060	EI-AJS	25. 5.56	G.J.McDill	Park Farm, Eaton Bray	8. 9.01
			G-AOCR/NJ673		(As "NJ673")		
G-AOCU	Auster 5	986	MT349	8. 6.56	S.J.Ball	Leicester	29. 1.01
G-AODA*	Westland WS.55 Whirlwind Srs.3	WA/113	9Y-TDA	13. 5.55	The Helicopter Museum Weston-super-Mare		23. 8.91A
			EP-HAC/G-AODA		(Bristow Helicopters c/s) "Dorado"		
G-AODT	DH.82A Tiger Moth	83109	R5250	4. 8.55	R.A.Harrowven	Tibenham	30. 4.01
G-AOEH	Aeronca 7AC Champion	7AC-2144	N79854	8. 9.55	R.A. & S.P.Smith	Crowfield	20. 9.97P
	(Cont A65)		OO-TWF				
G-AOEI	DH.82A Tiger Moth	82196	N6946	14. 9.55	CFG Flying Ltd	Cambridge	18. 7.99T
	(Regd with fuselage no. MCO/DH3409, which should be c/n 85332 ex DE298, converted at Croydon						
	as N524R 12.65; a/c is probably a composite airframe)						
G-AOEL*	DH.82A Tiger Moth	82537	N9510	27. 9.55	Museum of Flight/Royal Museum of Scotland		
						East Fortune	18. 7.72
G-AOES	DH.82A Tiger Moth	84547	T6056	6.10.55	A.Twemlow & G.A.Cordery		30. 5.99
						Charity Farm, Baxterley	
G-AOET	DH.82A Tiger Moth	85650	DE720	7.10.55	Venom Jet Promotions Ltd (P.Meeson)		11. 9.99
						Oaklands Farm, East Tytherley	
	(Tiger Moth frame quoted as "G-AOET" is stored by A.S.Topen, Cranfield)						
G-AOEX	Thruxton Jackaroo	86483	NM175	10.10.55	A.T.Christian Walkeridge Farm, Overton		3. 2.68T
					(On rebuild 5.90)		
G-AOFE	DHC.1 Chipmunk 22A	C1/0150	WB702	13. 9.56	E.J.F.McEntee Kirdford, Billingshurst		21. 9.01
					(As "WB702")		
G-AOFJ*	Auster Alpha 5	3401		3.10.56	R.Drew (Stored 8.98)	Perth	20. 9.79
G-AOFM	Auster J/5P Autocar	3178		16. 6.55	W.H.Dyozinski	White Waltham	22.10.00
G-AOFS	Auster J/5L Aiglet Trainer	3143	EI-ALN	28.10.55	P.N.A.Whitehead	Leicester	11. 4.01
			G-AOFS				
G-AOGA*	Miles M.75 Aries 1	75/1007	EI-ANB	9.11.55	The Irish Avn Museum		
	(Damaged Cork 8.8.69; stored 4.96)		G-AOGA			Castlemoate House, Dublin	10.10.69
G-AOGE	Percival P.34A Proctor 3	H.210	BV651	24.11.55	N.I.Dalziel	Biggin Hill	21. 5.84
					(Stored 8.97; cancelled by CAA 19.1.99)		
G-AOGI	DH.82A Tiger Moth	85922	(N)	14.12.55	W.J.Taylor	(Boston)	23. 8.91
	(Stored Ingoldmells 10.92)		OO-SOA/G-AOGI/DF186		t/a Lincs Aerial Spraying Co		
G-AOGR	DH.82A Tiger Moth	84566	XL714	20. 1.56	M.I.Edwards	Swanton Morley	16. 9.96T
			G-AOGR/T6099		(As "XL714"; stored 10.97)		
G-AOGV	Auster J/5R Alpine	3302		2. 2.56	R.E.Heading (Stored 3.97)		17. 7.72
						Walnut Tree Farm, Thorney, Whittlesey	
G-AOHD*	Hunting Percival P.84	P84/12	A99-001	26. 3.56	Royal Australian AF Museum (Stored 1995)		
	Jet Provost T.2		G-AOHD			Point Cook, Victoria	10. 4.60
G-AOHL*	Vickers Viscount 802	161		2. 1.56	London-Southend Airport Co Ltd Southend		11. 4.80T
					(Fire Services trainer 3.99)		
G-AOHM	Vickers Viscount 802	162		2. 1.56	British World Airlines Ltd	Southend	2. 7.99T
G-AOHY	DH.82A Tiger Moth	3850	N6537	23. 2.56	M.Somerton-Rayner	AAC Middle Wallop	20. 8.60
					(On rebuild 2.96)	t/a Historic Aircraft Flight Reserve Collection	
G-AOHZ	Auster J/5P Autocar	3252		28. 2.56	A.D.Hodgkinson	Dunkirk, Canterbury	24. 7.00T
G-AOIL	DH.82A Tiger Moth	83673	XL716	20. 8.56	T.C.Lawless	(Chandlers Ford)	4.10.57
			G-AOIL/T7363		(Status uncertain)		
G-AOIM	DH.82A Tiger Moth	83536	T7109	27. 8.56	D.A.Hardiman	Shobdon	16. 8.00
G-AOIR	Thruxton Jackaroo	82882	R4972	13. 1.56	L.H.Smith & I.M.Oliver	Little Gransden	18. 3.99
G-AOIS	DH.82A Tiger Moth	83034	R5172	13. 1.56	J.K.Ellwood	Sherburn	20. 5.01
G-AOIY	Auster J/5V-160 Autocar	3199		1. 3.56	J.B.Nicholson Watchford Farm, Yarncombe		26. 8.90
	(Lyc O-320)				(On rebuild 3.98)		
G-AOJC*	V.802 Viscount	152	(G-AOHC)	2. 1.56	Not known	Enstone	20. 1.77T
					(Fuselage stored 7.96 - BEA c/s)		
G-AOJD*	V.802 Viscount	153	(G-AOHD)	2. 1.56	Jersey Airport Fire Service	Jersey	13. 6.77T
G-AOJH	DH.83C Fox Moth	FM.42	AP-ABO	29. 3.56	A.J.Norman	Rendcomb	14. 3.99
					t/a Norman Aeroplane Trust		
G-AOJJ	DH.82A Tiger Moth	85877	DF128	5. 4.56	E.Lay & T.J.Pegram t/a JJ Flying Group		
					(As "DF128/RCO-U")	White Waltham	24. 7.00

Regn	Type	C/n	P/I	Date	Owner/operator	Probable Base	CA Expy
G-AOJK	DH.82A Tiger Moth	82813	R4896	5. 4.56	D.E.Guck & P.W.Crispe	Halfpenny Green	22. 7.99
G-AOJT*	DH.106 Comet lXB	06020	F-BGNX	11. 5.56	De Havilland Aircraft Museum		
			(Fuselage only as "F-BGNX" in Air France c/s) Salisbury Hall, London Colney					5. 7.56
G-AOJZ*	DHC.1 Chipmunk 21	C1/0181	"G-ASTD"	16.4.56	Air Service Training Ltd	Perth	13.11.66
			G-AOJZ/WB732 (Crashed nr Perth 31.5.66; instructional airframe 12.95)					
G-AOKH*	Percival P.40 Prentice 1	PAC/212	VS251	11. 4.56	J.F.Moore (Stored 8.97)	Biggin Hill	2. 8.73
G-AOKL	Percival P.40 Prentice 1	PAC/208	VS610	13. 4.56	The Shuttleworth Trust	Old Warden	20. 9.96
					(As "VS610/K-L")		
G-AOKO*	Percival P.40 Prentice 1	PAC/234	VS621	13. 4.56	Atlantic Air Transport Ltd	Coventry	23.10.72
					(Stored for spares 5.96)		
G-AOKZ*	Percival P.40 Prentice 1	PAC/238	VS623	20. 4.56	Midland Air Museum (Stored 4.96)Coventry		
G-AOLK	Percival P.40 Prentice 1	PAC/225	VS618	25. 4.56	A.Hilton	Southend	3.12.98
G-AOLU	Percival P.40 Prentice 1		EI-ASP	25. 4.56	N.J.Butler t/a Montrose Air Station Museum		
	(Regd with c/n 5830/3) B3/1A/PAC/283		G-AOLU/VS356		(On rebuild 8.95; as "VS356") Montrose			8. 5.76
G-AORB(2)	Cessna 170B	20767	OO-SIZ	13. 2.84	A.R.Thompson t/a Hawley Farm Grp		
			N2615D			Hawley Farm, Tadley	21. 2.00
G-AORG	DH.114 Heron 2	14101	XR441	1. 5.56	Duchess of Brittany (Jersey) Ltd	Jersey	10. 2.01
			G-AORG/G-5-16		(Jersey Airlines c/s) "Duchess of Brittany"		
G-AORW	DHC.1 Chipmunk 22A	C1/0130	WB682	28. 5.56	Bushfire Investments Ltd	(Jersey)	19. 5.98
G-AOSF	DHC.1 Chipmunk 22	C1/0023	D-EIIZ	25. 6.56	D.Mercer	Porta Westfalica, Germany	25.10.99
			G-AOSF/HB-TUA/G-AOSF/WB571 (As "WB571/34")					
G-AOSK	DHC.1 Chipmunk 22A	C1/0178	WB726	26. 6.56	E.J.Leigh	Audley End	17.10.99
	(Frame No.DHH/F/121)				(As "WB726/E" in Cambridge UAS c/s)		
G-AOSO	DHC.1 Chipmunk 22	C1/0227	WD288	26. 6.56	The Earl of Suffolk & Berkshire & J.Hoerner		
					(As "WD288") Charlton Park, Malmesbury		14. 9.00
G-AOSU	DHC.1 Chipmunk 22	C1/0217	WB766	28. 6.56	T.Holloway	Inverness	29. 4.00
	(Lyc O-360)				t/a RAFGSA (Op Fulmar Gliding Club)		
G-AOSY	DHC.1 Chipmunk 22	C1/0037	WB585	29. 6.56	Propshop Ltd	Duxford	19. 6.98
					(As "WB585/RCU-X" in 22RFS c/s)		
G-AOTD	DHC.1 Chipmunk 22	C1/0040	WB588	30. 6.56	S.Piech	Biggin Hill	7. 9.00
					(As "WB588/D" in Oxford UAS c/s)		
G-AOTF	DHC.1 Chipmunk 23	C1/0015	WB563	2. 7.56	T.Holloway	RAF Dishforth	29. 6.01
	(Lyc O-360)				t/a RAFGSA (Op Clevelands Gliding Club)		
G-AOTI*	DH.114 Heron 2D	14107	G-5-19	25. 7.56	De Havilland Aircraft Museum		
					Salisbury Hall, London Colney		24. 6.87T
G-AOTK	Druine D.53 Turbi	1 & PFA/230		1.11.56	J.I.B.Bennett & R.G.A.Willoughby t/a The TK F/Grp		
	(Walter Mikron 3)				Whitehall Farm, Benington		8.12.99P
G-AOTR	DHC.1 Chipmunk 22	C1/0045	HB-TUH	12. 7.56	M.R.Woodgate	Aldergrove	12.11.99
			D-EGOG/G-AOTR/WB604					
G-AOTY	DHC.1 Chipmunk 22A	C1/0522	WG472	12. 7.56	S.J.Ellis	(Rhyl)	28. 9.00T
					(As "WG472" in RAF c/s)		
G-AOUJ*	Fairey Ultralight Helicopter	F.9424	XJ928	1. 8.56	E.D.Ap Rees	Weston-super-Mare	29. 3.59
					t/a The Helicopter Museum (Stored 8.97)		
G-AOUO	DHC.1 Chipmunk 22	C1/0179	WB730	10. 8.56	T.Holloway	Bicester	5. 8.00
	(Lyc O-360)				t/a RAFGSA		
G-AOUP	DHC.1 Chipmunk 22	C1/0180	WB731	10. 8.56	A.R.Harding	(Milden)	11. 9.99
G-AOUR*	DH.82A Tiger Moth	86341	NL898	14. 8.56	Ulster Folk & Transport Museum		
					(Crashed Newtownards 6.6.65; stored 4.96) Holywood, Dublin		19.11.66
G-AOVF*	Bristol 175 Britannia 312F	13237	9Q-GAS	13. 2.57	RAF Museum	RAF Cosford	
			G-AOVF		(BOAC c/s)		
G-AOVT*	Bristol 175 Britannia 312	13427		23. 6.58	Duxford Aviation Society	Duxford	11. 3.75
					(Monarch c/s)		
G-AOVW	Auster 5 (Modified)	894	MT119	16.11.59	B.Marriott Ropsley Heath Farm, Grantham		28. 9.00
G-AOXG*	DH.82A Tiger Moth	83805	T7291	3.10.56	Fleet Air Arm Museum	RNAS Yeovilton	
					(As "G-ABUL")		
G-AOXN	DH.82A Tiger Moth	85958	EM727	31.10.56	S.L.G.Darch	East Chinnock, Yeovil	21.12.01
G-AOZE*	Westland WS-51/2 Widgeon	WA/H/141	5N-ABW	11. 1.57	E.D. Ap Rees	Weston-super-Mare	
			G-AOZE		t/a The Helicopter Museum (Under restoration 8.98)		
G-AOZH	DH.82A Tiger Moth	86449	NM129	18. 1.57	G.J. & R.G.Wheele (As "K2572")	Shoreham	2. 9.99
G-AOZL	Auster J/5Q Alpine	3202		5. 2.57	E.A.Taylor (Stored dismantled 3.99)		
						Southend	28. 5.88
G-AOZP	DHC.1 Chipmunk 22A	C1/0183	WB734	14. 2.57	H.Darlington	Audley End	23. 4.99

Regn	Type	C/n	P/I	Date	Owner/operator	Probable Base	CA Expy
G-APAF	Auster Alpha 5	3404	G-CMAL G-APAF	25. 3.57	J.E.Allen (As "TW511")	North Coates	8. 2.99
G-APAH	Auster Alpha 5	3402		29. 3.57	R.D.& E.G.N.Morris	Glasgow	8. 4.00
G-APAL	DH.82A Tiger Moth	82102	N6847	3. 4.57	P.S. & R.A.Chapman (As "N6847")	Little Gransden	24. 6.00
G-APAM	DH.82A Tiger Moth	3874	N6580	3. 4.57	R.P.Williams Denford Manor, Hungerford t/a Myth Grp "Myth"		8. 7.01
G-APAO	DH.82A Tiger Moth	82845	R4922	3. 4.57	Clacton A/C (1988) Ltd (Op Classic Wings)	Duxford/Clacton	10. 8.99T
G-APAP	DH.82A Tiger Moth	83018	R5136	3. 4.57	J.Romain (Damaged Kingston Deverill 4.9.94; on rebuild 1.99)	Duxford	27. 6.96
G-APAS*	DH.106 Comet 1A	06022	8351M XM823/G-APAS/G-5-23/F-BGNZ (BOAC c/s)	23. 5.57	RAF Museum	RAF Cosford	
G-APBE	Auster Alpha 5	3403		7. 5.57	J.McCullough	Newtownards	28. 9.99
G-APBI	DH.82A Tiger Moth	86097	EM903	16. 5.57	A.Wood Halstead, Essex (Damaged Audley End 7.7.80; on rebuild 12.90)		19. 4.82
G-APBO	Druine D.53 Turbi (Cont C75)	PFA/229		3. 6.57	R.C.Hibberd	Devizes	27. 9.99P
G-APBW	Auster Alpha 5A	3405		23. 5.57	N.Huxtable	Cheddington, Bucks	26. 5.00
G-APCB	Auster J/5Q Alpine	3204		5. 6.57	A.A.Beswick & I.A.Freeman	Thruxton	2. 4.99
G-APCC	DH.82A Tiger Moth	86549	PG640	11. 6.57	L.J.Rice Bishopstrow Farm, Warminster		12. 5.00
G-APDB*	DH.106 Comet 4	6403	9M-AOB G-APDB	2. 5.57	Duxford Aviation Society (Dan-Air c/s)	Duxford	7.10.74
G-APEK*	V.953C Vanguard Merchantman	714		9. 9.57	Europe Aero Service (Stored 6.95)	Perpignan	16.12.89F
G-APEP*	V.953C Vanguard Merchantman	719		9. 9.57	Brooklands Museum (Hunting Cargo Airlines c/s) "Superb"	Brooklands	1.10.98T
G-APEY	V.806 Viscount	382		15. 8.57	Helilift Ltd (South Africa)		8.12.99T
G-APFA	Druine D.52 Turbi (Cont A65)	PFA/232		5. 2.57	A.Eastelow & F.J.Keitch	Smiths Farm, Brixham	22. 9.92P
G-APFG*	Boeing 707-436 (Fuselage used for fire suppression trials)	17708	N5094K	7. 8.59	Civil Aviation Authority Building Research Establishment, Cardington		24. 5.81T
G-APFJ*	Boeing 707-436	17711		7. 8.59	RAF Museum (British Airtours c/s)	RAF Cosford	16. 2.82T
G-APFU	DH.82A Tiger Moth	86081	EM879	28. 8.57	Leisure Assets Ltd	Goodwood	11. 4.00T
G-APGL	DH.82A Tiger Moth	86460	NM140	6. 9.57	K.A.Broomfield Charity Farm, Baxterley (Not previously converted; on rebuild 3.97 - see G-AJVE)		
G-APHV*	Avro 652A Anson C.19 Srs.2	-	VM360	19. 9.57	Museum of Flight/Royal Museum of Scotland (As "VM360")	East Fortune	15. 6.73
G-APIE	Tipsy Belfair (Walter Mikron 2)	535	(OO-TIE)	22.10.57	D.Beale	Fenland	22. 5.99P
G-APIH	DH.82A Tiger Moth	82981	N111DH OY-DGJ/D-EMEX/G-APIH/R5086	25.10.57	K.Stewering (Borken-Gemen, Germany)		15. 5.00
G-APIK	Auster J/1N Alpha	3375		11.11.57	N.D.Voce t/a G-APIK F/Grp	Leicester	13. 8.99
G-APIM*	Vickers Viscount 806	412		19.11.57	Brooklands Museum (British Air Ferries c/s) "Viscount Stephen Piercey"	Brooklands	19. 7.88T
G-APIT*	Percival P.40 Prentice T.1	PAC/016	VR192	28.11.57	Second World War Aircraft Preservation Soc. (As "VR192")	Lasham	7. 9.67
G-APIU*	Percival P.40 Prentice T.1	PAC/024	VR200	28.11.57	Atlantic Air Transport Ltd (Spares use 5.96)	Coventry	23. 3.67
G-APIY*	Percival P.40 Prentice T.1	PAC/075	VR249	28.11.57	Newark Air Museum (As "VR249/FA-EL" in RAFC c/s)	Winthorpe	18. 3.67
G-APIZ	Rollason-Druine D.31 Turbulent (VW1600)	PFA/478		22.11.57	M.J.Whatley "Witch Lady"	White Waltham	26.11.98P
G-APJB	Percival P.40 Prentice T.1	PAC/086	VR259	28.11.57	Atlantic Air Transport Ltd (As "VR259/M" in 2 ASS c/s)	Coventry	3. 7.99T
G-APJJ*	Fairey Ultralight Helicopter	F.9428		4.12.57	Midland Air Museum	Coventry	1. 4.59
G-APJO	DH.82A Tiger Moth	86446	NM126	23.12.57	D.R. & Mrs M.Wood	Tunbridge Wells	27. 3.59
	(C/n quoted as "17712"; crashed Ross-on-Wye 5.8.58; on rebuild & may includes components from G-APJR)						
G-APJZ	Auster J/1N Alpha	3382	5N-ACY (VR-NDR)/G-APJZ	3. 1.58	P.G.Lipman Romney Street Farm, Sevenoaks (Damaged Thornicombe 10.11.75; on rebuild 8.90)		15. 7.77
G-APKH	DH.85 Leopard Moth	PPS.85/1/DH7131	AX858 G-ACGS/PH-ALM/G-ACGS	23. 1.58	R.G.Grocott	Konstanz, Germany	16. 7.98P
G-APKM*	Auster J/1N Alpha	3385		27. 1.58	D.E.A.Huggins (Meriden, Coventry) (Stored 4.90)		9. 1.89
G-APKN	Auster J/1N Alpha	3387		27. 1.58	P.R.Hodson t/a The Felthorpe Auster Grp	Felthorpe	21. 5.99
G-APKY	Hiller UH-12B	673	PH-NFL	4. 3.58	D.A.George (Sloane Helicopters Ltd) (Stored 5.96)	Sywell	7. 5.74S
G-APLG	Auster J/5L Aiglet Trainer	3148		4. 3.58	G.R.W.Brown	Dumfries	26.10.68
	(On rebuild by Solway Avn.Society for static display; cancelled by CAA 11.02.99)						
G-APLO	DHC.1 Chipmunk 22A	C1/0144	EI-AHU WB696	1. 5.58	Lindholme Acft Ltd (As "WD379/K" in Cambridge UAS c/s)	Jersey	17. 9.00T
G-APLU	DH.82A Tiger Moth	85094	VR-AAY F-OBKK/G-APLU/T6825	2. 4.58	R.A.Bishop & M.E.Vaisey	Rush Green	14. 8.01

Regn	Type	C/n	P/I	Date	Owner/operator	Probable Base	CA Expy
G-APMB*	DH.106 Comet 4B	6422		15. 4.58	Gatwick Handling Ltd (Training airframe 8.98)	Gatwick	18. 5.79
G-APMH	Auster J/1U Workmaster	3502	F-OBOA G-APMH	15. 4.58	J.L.Thorogood	Insch	19. 5.01
G-APML	Douglas C-47B-1DK Dakota 6	14175/25620	KJ836 43-48359	17. 3.58	Dak Holdings Ltd (Op Air Atlantique)	Coventry	27. 7.84T
G-APMX	DH.82A Tiger Moth	85645	DE715	9. 5.58	G.A.Broughton	Popham	18. 2.99
G-APMY*	PA-23-160 Apache	23-1258	EI-AJT	15. 5.58	W.Fern (On loan to South Yorkshire Aviation Museum)	Home Farm, Firbeck	1.11.81
G-APNJ*	Cessna 310	35335	EI-AJY N3635D	2. 6.58	Northbrook College (Instructional Airframe)	Shoreham	28.11.74
G-APNS	Garland-Bianchi Linnet (Cont C90)	001		17. 6.58	Paul Penn-Sayers Model Svs Ltd (Stored 6.95) Scaynes Hill, Haywards Heath		6.10.78S
G-APNT	Bellamy Currie Wot (Cont PC60) (Regd with c/n P.6,399)	HAC/3		18. 6.58	J.W.Salter "Airymouse"	Newtownards	16. 4.99P
G-APNZ	Rollason-Druine D.31 Turbulent (Ardem 4C02)	PFA/482		17. 4.58	J.Knight (Damaged River Rother nr Iden 3.9.95: on rebuild)	Hailsham	13.12.95P
G-APOD	Tipsy Belfair (Walter Mikron 2)	536	(OO-TIF)	16. 7.58	L.F.Potts (On rebuild 4.97)	Dundee	23. 8.88P
G-APOI	Saunders-Roe Skeeter Srs.8	S2/5081		29. 7.58	Maj.F.F.Chamberlain	Otley, Ipswich	2. 8.99
G-APOL	Druine D.31 Turbulent (Ardem 4C02)	PFA/439		31. 7.58	A.Gregori & S.Tinker (Damaged Charterhall 24.7.93; stored 3.94)	Charterhall	18. 6.94P
G-APPA	DHC.1 Chipmunk 22	C1/0792	N5073E G-APPA/WP917	11. 9.58	D.M.Squires (On rebuild 7.97)	Wellesbourne Mountford	14. 7.85
G-APPL	Percival P.40 Prentice 1	PAC/013	VR189	7.10.58	Susan J.Saggers	Biggin Hill	11. 9.00
G-APPM	DHC.1 Chipmunk 22	C1/0159	WB711	14.10.58	Freston Avn Ltd (As "WB711")	Crowfield	26. 6.99
G-APPN	DH.82A Tiger Moth	83839	T7328	17.10.58	E.G.Waite-Roberts (Basingstoke) (Crashed Mendlesham 14.7.64; rebuild provenance unconfirmed; on rebuild 6.96)		9. 6.65A
G-APRF	Auster Alpha 5	3412	VR-LAF G-APRF	8.12.58	W.B.Bateson	Blackpool	14.11.00
G-APRJ	Avro 694 Lincoln B.2	-	RF342 G-36-3/G-29-1/G-APRJ/RF342	29.12.58	Aces High Ltd (As "G-29-1")	North Weald	
G-APRL*	AW.650 Argosy Srs.101	6652	N890U N602Z/N6507R/G-APRL	2. 1.59	Midland Air Museum (Elan c/s) "Edna"	Coventry	23. 3.87T
G-APRO*	Auster 6	(N370WJ ex G-APRO/WJ370 as "G-APRO" noted with John Morris, Marblehead, Massachusetts, USA 1991)					
G-APRR	CZL Super Aero 45 Srs.04	04-014	OK-KFQ	5. 1.59	R.H.Jowett	Ronaldsway	16. 2.96
G-APRS	Scottish Avn Twin Pioneer 3	561	G-BCWF XT610/G-APRS/(PI-C430)	9. 1.59	Bravo Avn Ltd (Op Atlantic Air Transport Ltd) (As "XT610" in RAE c/s)	Coventry	1. 7.99T
G-APRT	Taylor JT.1 Monoplane (Ardem 4C02)	PFA/537		15. 1.59	M.J.Snelling Stoneacre Farm, Farthing Corner		30. 6.98P
G-APSA	Douglas DC-6A	45497	4W-ABQ HZ-ADA/G-APSA/CF-MCK	12. 2.59	Atlantic Air Transport Ltd (Op by Air Atlantique)	Coventry	11. 4.99T
G-APSO	DH.104 Dove 5	04505	(N1046T) G-APSO	16. 2.59	Cormack (Aircraft Svcs) Ltd (On rebuild 6.98)	Cumbernauld	8. 7.78T
G-APSR	Auster J/1U Workmaster	3499	OO-HXA G-APSR/VP-JCD/G-APSR/(F-OBHR)	22. 4.59	D & K Aero Svs Ltd (Op by P. De Liens)	Temploux, Belgium	16. 9.99A
G-APSY*	Bensen B-7Mc	JH/001 & 2		25. 2.59	J.Howell (Crashed Biggin Hill 19.9.59; stored)	Copthorne, Sussex	
G-APSZ*	Cessna 172	46472	N6372E	21. 5.59	Not known (Damaged Barton 2.3.84; stored 4.91)	Ronaldsway	4. 6.84
G-APTP	PA-22-150 Tri-Pacer (Modified to PA-20 Pacer configuration)	22-5009	EI-AJN	20. 3.59	Comunica Industries International Ltd Roughay Farm, Bishops Waltham		20. 7.00
G-APTR	Auster J/1N Alpha	3392		15. 4.59	C.J. & D.J.Baker (On rebuild 9.96)	Carr Farm, Newark	11. 4.87
G-APTU	Auster Alpha 5	3413		20. 4.59	A.J. & J.M.Davis t/a G-APTU F/Grp	Sywell	8. 6.98
G-APTW*	Westland WS-51/2 Widgeon	WA/H/150		27. 4.59	North East Aircraft Museum (On display 5.97)	Usworth	26. 9.75
G-APTY	Beechcraft G35 Bonanza	D-4789	EI-AJG	4. 6.59	G.E.Brennand & N.B.Gibbons	Blackpool	23. 1.99
G-APTZ	Rollason-Druine D.31 Turbulent (VW1600)	PFA/508		18. 3.59	Tiger Club (1990) Ltd Rushett Farm, Chessington		11. 5.99P
G-APUD*	Bensen B-7Mc	1		11. 5.59	The Aeroplane Collection Ltd (Loaned to Manchester Museum of Science & Industry)	Manchester	27. 9.60
G-APUE	Orlican L-40 Meta-Sokol	150708	OK-NMB	2. 6.59	S.E. & M.J.Aherne	Top Farm, Tadlow	13. 5.00
G-APUK*	Auster 5 J/1 Autocrat	1843	5N-ADW VR-NDJ/G-APUK/D-EGEG/SE-ARA	16. 6.59	P.L.Morley (Stored 1995)	(Yateley)	8.10.75
G-APUP*	Sopwith Pup rep (Le Rhone)	B.5292 & PFA/1582	N5182	13. 2.59	RAF Museum (Allocated 9213M 1994; as "N5182")	Hendon	28. 6.78
G-APUR	PA-22-160 Tri-Pacer	22-6711		3. 7.59	P.J.Hewitt	Clontilew Farm, Portadown	20. 8.01
G-APUW	Auster J/5V Srs.160 Autocar	3273		23. 6.59	E.A.J.Hibbard, D.Ball, P.L.Buckley, R.A.Partridge t/a The Anglia Auster Syndicate	Hill Farm, Nayland	22. 5.00
G-APUY	Druine D.31 Turbulent (VW1300)	PFA/509		24. 6.59	C.Jones (On rebuild 1995; wings at Barton 12.97)	(Stockport)	10..6.86P
G-APUZ	PA-24-250 Comanche	24-1094	N6000P	3. 7.59	R.R. & A.L.Stadie	Blackbushe	1.12.00
G-APVF	Putzer Elster B (Cont O-200-A)	006	D-EEQX 97+04/D-EJUH	29.12.83	A.J.Robinson (As "97+04" in Luftwaffe c/s)	Top Farm, Tadlow	1. 7.98P

Regn	Type	C/n	P/I	Date	Owner/operator	Probable Base	CA Expy
G-APVG	Auster J/5L Aiglet Trainer	3306	(ZK-BQW)	10. 7.59	C.M.Daggett	Cranfield	20. 3.00
G-APVN	Druine D.31 Turbulent (VW1600)	PFA/511		24. 7.59	R.Sherwin Swanborough Farm, Lewes (Stored 3.97)		24. 6.94P
G-APVS	Cessna 170B	26156	N2512C	7. 8.59	N.Simpson "Stormin' Norman"	East Kirkby	23. 6.00
G-APVU	Orlican L-40 Meta-Sokol	150706	OK-NMI	21. 8.59	S.A. & M.J.Aherne (St.Albans) (Damaged Manchester 12.9.78; on rebuild 1993)		27. 6.79
G-APVV*	Mooney M.20A	1474	N8164E	30. 7.59	Newark Air Museum Winthorpe (Crashed at Barton 11.1.81; stored 4.97)		19. 9.81
G-APVZ	Rollason-Druine D.31 Turbulent (Ardem 4C02)	PFA/545		23. 7.59	I.D.Daniels	Maypole Farm, Chislet	14. 6.99P
G-APWA*	HPR.7 Dart Herald 100	149	PP-SDM	28. 9.59	Museum of Berkshire Aviation/The Herald Society G-APWA/PP-SDM/PP-ASV/G-APWA (BEA c/s)	Woodley	6. 4.82T
G-APWJ*	HPR.7 Dart Herald 201	158		28. 9.59	Duxford Aviation Society (Air UK c/s)	Duxford	21.12.85
G-APWL	EoN AP.10 460 Srs.1A	EoN/S/001	BGA.1172	2.9.59	A.J.Langdon & R.A.Munday G-APWL/RAFGSA.268/G-APWL	Eaglescott	
G-APWN*	Westland WS-55 Whirlwind 3	WA.298	VR-BER	8. 9.59	The Midland Air Museum Coventry G-APWN/5N-AGI/G-APWN (Bristow Helicopters c/s) "Skerries"		17. 5.78
G-APWP	Druine D.31 Turbulent	PFA/497		14. 9.59	C.F.Rogers (Wheathamstead) (Status uncertain)		27. 6.67
G-APWU*	Thurston Tawney Owl	TA.1		23. 9.59	Thurston Engineering Ltd Stondon Massey (Damaged Stapleford 22.4.60; stored for possible rebuild)		
G-APWY	Piaggio P.166	362		16.12.59	The Science Museum	Wroughton	14. 3.81
G-APWZ	Lancashire A/c EP-9 Prospector	42		5.11.59	G.B.Pearce Washington, West Sussex t/a Prospector F/Grp		8. 6.01
G-APXJ	PA-24-250 Comanche	24-291	VR-NDA	11.12.59	T.Wildsmith	Netherthorpe	10.10.99
G-APXR	PA-22-160 Tri-Pacer	22-7172		29. 1.60	A.Troughton	Armagh Field, Woodview	25.10.01
G-APXT	PA-22-150 Tri-Pacer	22-3854	N4545A	16. 2.60	J.W. & I.Daniels Ashford, Middx (Damaged Southend 26.12.85 & on rebuild to PA-20 Pacer configuration)		5. 7.87T
G-APXU	PA-22-150 Tri-Pacer (Mod)	22-474	N1723A	10. 2.60	K.Hassell Perth "The Cloth Bomber" (On rebuild 6.98)		20. 2.85
G-APXW*	Lancashire Acft EP-9 Prospector	43		22.12.59	Museum of Army Flying AAC Middle Wallop (Composite rebuild from G-APWZ and others; as "XM819" in Army c/s)		22. 5.76
G-APXX*	DHA.3 Drover 2	5014	VH-EAS VH-EAZ	15.12.59	Second World War Acft Preservation Society Lasham (As "VH-FDT")		
G-APXY	Cessna 150	17711	N7911E	15. 1.60	The Merlin Flying Club Ltd	Hucknall	6. 9.98T
G-APXZ*	Knight Twister	BKT-001 & PFA/1307		7. 1.60	N.H.Ponsford Breighton (Identity unconfirmed; incomplete frame stored 4.96))		
G-APYB	Tipsy T.66 Nipper 3 (VW1834)	T66/S/39		28. 1.60	B.O.Smith (Stored 4.97)	Yearby	12. 6.96P
G-APYD*	DH.106 Comet 4B	6438	SX-DAL G-APYD	21. 1.60	The Science Museum Wroughton (Dan-Air c/s)		3. 8.79T
G-APYG	DHC.1 Chipmunk 22	C1/0060	OH-HCB WB619	11.11.60	E.J.I.Musty & P.A.Colman	White Waltham	14. 6.01
G-APYI	PA-22-135 Tri-Pacer	22-2218	N8031C	8. 2.60	B.T. & J.Cullen Ballyboy, Co.Meath (Modified to PA-20 Pacer configuration)		26. 3.99
G-APYN	PA-22-160 Tri-Pacer	22-6797	N2804Z	24. 2.60	S.J.Raw	Morgansfield, Fishburn	1. 2.99
G-APYT	Champion 7FC Tri-Traveler	7FC-387		9. 5.60	B.J.Anning	Watchford Farm, Yarcombe	14. 6.98P
G-APYU*	Champion 7FC Tri-Traveler	7FC-388		12. 5.60	R.W.Brown Clothall Farm, Clothall Common (Crashed Old Warden 23.4.72; stored 5.96)		6. 8.72
G-APZJ	PA-18-150 Super Cub	18-7233		29. 1.60	R.Jones t/a Southern Sailplanes Membury (Rebuilt 1986 after accident 12.6.83 using un-identified new fuselage frame; original frame in open store Membury 1989)		18.11.99
G-APZL	PA-22-160 Tri-Pacer	22-7054	EI-ALF	27. 1.60	R.T.Evans	Bristol/Lulsgate	14. 5.99
G-APZR*	Cessna 150	17861	N6461T	31. 3.60	Avtech Ltd Biggin Hill (Damaged Biggin Hill 14.1.81; front fuselage only used as engine test-bed 2.95)		4. 4.81
G-APZS	Cessna 175A (Lyc O-360)	56677	N7977T	31. 3.60	G.A.Nash Lower Wasing Farm, Brimpton (Damaged Edinburgh 29.6.94)		15. 8.95
G-APZX	PA-22-150 Tri-Pacer (Modified to PA-20 Pacer configuration)	22-5181	N7420D	28. 4.60	Applied Signs Ltd	Tatenhill	10. 6.00

G-ARAA-ARZZ

Regn	Type	C/n	P/I	Date	Owner/operator	Probable Base	CA Expy
G-ARAD	Phoenix Luton LA-5A Major			29. 4.60	D.J.Bone & P.L.Jobes		
	PAL/1204 & PFA/836					(Guisborough/Sunderland)	
	(Completed but not flown; stored Lennox Plunton, Borgue 3.94)						
G-ARAI	PA-22-160 Tri-Pacer	22-7421		17. 5.60	T.Richards & G.C.Winters	Oxenhope	17. 9.01
G-ARAM	PA-18-150 Super Cub	18-7312		17. 5.60	Clacton A/C (1988) Ltd	Clacton	15. 4.99T
G-ARAN	PA-18-150 Super Cub	18-7307		28. 4.60	A.P.Docherty	Redhill	8. 6.01
G-ARAO	PA-18-95 Super Cub	18-7327		17. 5.60	R.G.Manton	(Great Missenden)	2. 4.01
	(As "607327/L/09" in USAAC c/s)						
G-ARAP*	Champion 7EC Traveler	7FC-394		12. 9.60	J.McGonagal	(Londonderry)	26. 6.82P
	(Damaged Eglinton 22. 9.81; on rebuild 12.92)						
G-ARAS	Champion 7FC Tri-Traveler	7FC-396		12. 9.60	G.J.Taylor	(Uttoxeter)	31. 5.99P
					t/a Alpha Sierra F/Grp		
G-ARAT	Cessna 180C	50827	N9327T	18. 5.60	S.Peck	Eaglescott	19. 5.00
G-ARAU*	Cessna 150	17894	N6494T	29. 4.60	Colton Aviation Ltd	Little Staughton	14. 9.84T
	(Stored unmarked 9.96)						
G-ARAW	Cessna 182C Skylane	52843	N8943T	18. 5.60	P.Channon	Bodmin	4. 7.98T
G-ARAX	PA-22-150 Tri-Pacer	22-3830	N4523A	22. 4.60	P.J.Fahie	Old Sarum	14. 3.99
G-ARAY*	Avro 748 Srs.1A/200	1535	OY-DFV	21. 4.60	Not known	Lasham	16. 6.90T
	G-11/G-ARAY/PI-C784/G-ARAY/VP-LIO/G-ARAY/PP-VJQ/G-ARAY/YV-C-AMC/G-ARAY (Wfu 10.89; fuselage with Fire Svs 12.95)						
G-ARAZ	DH.82A Tiger Moth	82867	R4959	25. 3.60	D.A.Porter Griffins Farm, Temple Bruer		13. 5.01
	(As "R4959/59" in RAF c/s)						
G-ARBC*	Cessna 310D	39234	N6934T	5. 9.60	Air Service Training Ltd	Perth	25. 6.77
	(On fire dump 12.95)						
G-ARBE	DH.104 Dove 8	04517		6. 5.60	M.Whale & M.W.A.Lunn	Kemble	22. 8.99
G-ARBG	Tipsy T.66 Nipper 2	ABAC.1 & 57		11. 5.60	J.Horovitz & J.McLeod	Felthorpe	17. 8.84P
	(VW 1834)			t/a The Felthorpe Tipsy Grp (Damaged on landing Felthorpe 6.5.84; on rebuild 5.91)				
G-ARBH*	DH.104 Dove 1	04196	XY-ABS	14. 7.60	Not known (Stored 11.88) Zaragoza, Spain		5. 8.75
	(Unmarked Dove displayed within Malaga Airport Terminal 3.3.96 - the same ?)						
G-ARBM	Auster 5 J/1B Aiglet	2792	EI-AMO	8. 6.60	B.V.Nabbs & C.Chaddock		
			G-ARBM/VP-SZZ/VP-KKR			Scotland Farm, Hook	16. 4.00
G-ARBN*	PA-23-160 Apache	23-1385	EI-AKI	1. 6.60	Busy Bee Avn Ltd	Sibson	25. 8.86T
			(N3421P)		(Damaged Sibson 8.86; on rebuild 10.94)		
G-ARBO	PA-24-250 Comanche	24-2117		15. 6.60	C.Matthews	(Guernsey)	27. 5.84
	(Damaged in forced landing Morecambe Bay 27.4.83)						
G-ARBP	Tipsy T.66S Nipper 2	54		7. 6.60	F.W.Kirk	Seighford	21. 6.99P
	(VW1834)						
G-ARBS	PA-22-160 Tri-Pacer	22-6858	N2868Z	24. 8.60	S.D.Rowell "Greta" Valley Farm, Winwick		2.12.01
	(Modified to PA-20 Pacer configuration)						
G-ARBV	PA-22-160 Tri-Pacer	22-5836	N8633D	29. 6.60	E R O'Hara	Oaksey Park	2. 7.00
	(Rebuilt 1983/84 using fuselage of G-ARDP c/n 22-4254)			t/a G-ARBV Oaksey Pacers Group			
G-ARBZ	Rollason-Druine D.31 Turbulent			6. 5.60	J.Mickleburgh	Headcorn	15.10.99P
	(Ardem 4CO2)	PFA/553					
G-ARCC	PA-22-150 Tri-Pacer	22-4006	N4853A	23. 6.60	A.S.Cowan t/a Popham F/Grp G-ARCC Popham		11. 4.00
G-ARCF	PA-22-150 Tri-Pacer	22-4563	N5902D	28. 6.60	B.Southerland	East Winch	2. 5.99
G-ARCI*	Cessna 310D	39266	N6966T	21.10.60	Not known	Blackpool	25. 4.84
	(Damaged Sandtoft 22.8.86 on first flight after rebuild; open store 7.97)						
G-ARCS	Auster D.6 Srs.180	3703		4. 7.60	E.A.Matty (Status uncertain)	(Bewdley)	9. 8.93
G-ARCT	PA-18-95 Super Cub	18-7375	EI-AVE	6. 7.60	K.A.Kirk & C.M.Goodwin		
			G-ARCT			Dunnyvadden, Ballymena	21. 4.86
	(Damaged Mullaghmore 29.3.87; stored 1996)						
G-ARCV	Cessna 175A Skylark	56757	N8057T	7.11.60	R.Francis & C.Campbell	Sandtoft	1. 5.99
	(Cont O-300D)						
G-ARCW*	PA-23-160 Apache (Mod)	23-796	N2187P	7. 7.60	Not known Water Leisure Park, Skegness		8. 7.93
	(On rebuild 8.99)						
G-ARCX*	Armstrong-Whitworth Meteor NF.14		WM261	8. 9.60	Royal Museum of Scotland/Museum of Flight		
		AW.2163				East Fortune	20. 2.69S
G-ARDB	PA-24-250 Comanche	24-2166	PH-RON	15. 8.60	A.Scrase, C.Phelps & G.W.Simpson Booker		3. 4.01
			G-ARDB/N7019P		t/a Delta Bravo Acft Associates		
G-ARDD	Scintex CP.301C-1 Emeraude	549		4. 7.60	R.M.Shipp	Breighton	29. 6.98P
	(Rebuilt by EMK Aeroplanes with c/n EMK.004)						
G-ARDE	DH.104 Dove 6	04469	I-TONY	15.11.60	T.E.Evans	Wellesbourne Mountford	25. 8.91
					"Sir Geoffrey de Havilland" (Stored 6.98)		
G-ARDG*	Lancashire Acft EP-9 Prospector 2 47			14. 7.60	G.Pearce/Museum of Army Flying		
	(Stored 7.93 with parts from G-APWZ & G-APXW)			Durrington, W.Sussex			
G-ARDJ	Auster D.6 Srs.180	3704		15. 7.60	R.E.Neal t/a RN Avn (Leicester Airport)		
	(Damaged nr Leicester 30.5.86; on rebuild 6.96) Leicester						7. 7.88T
G-ARDK*	Aero Commander 560F	560F-992-6		9. 1.61	Not known	Lisbon Airport	8.10.69
	(Regn CS-AJL NTU 10.72; open storage 3.95)						
G-ARDO	Jodel D.112	146	F-PBTE	22. 8.60	W.R.Prescott	Kilkeel, Co.Down	8. 7.99P
			F-BBTE/F-WBTE		(Composite with fuselage ofG-AYEO c/n 684 ex F-BIGG)		
G-ARDS	PA-22-150 Caribbean	22-7154	N3214Z	4. 9.60	A.C.Donaldson & C.I.Lavery	Newtownards	31. 3.01
G-ARDT	PA-22-160 Tri-Pacer	22-6210	N9158D	15. 9.60	M.Henderson	Netherley, Aberdeen	13. 6.99
G-ARDV	PA-22-160 Tri-Pacer	22-7487	EI-APA	28. 7.60	R.W. Christie	(Ballymena, NI)	2. 1.99
			G-ARDV		(Damaged at Ballymena 10.7.98)		
G-ARDX*	Auster 6A Tugmaster	1905	TW524	2. 8.60	A.A.Marshall		
	(Damaged Lasham 1.1.64; frame stored 3.96)				Yeatsall Farm, Abbots Bromley		29. 8.64A

Regn	Type	C/n	P/I	Date	Owner/operator	Probable Base	CA Expy
G-ARDY	Tipsy T.66 Nipper 2 (VW Martlet)	55		10. 8.60	M.J.A.Trudgill (Clophill, Bedford)		20.10.99P
G-ARDZ*	SAN Jodel D.140A Mousquetaire	49		10.11.60	M.J.Wright Cherry Tree Farm, Monewden (Cancelled by CAA 26.2.99; stored 9.97)		29.11.91
G-AREA	DH.104 Dove 8	04520		3. 8.60	De Havilland Aircraft Museum Trust Ltd (Stored Hatfield 3.96) Salisbury Hall, London Colney		18. 9.87
G-AREB*	Cessna 175B Skylark	56818	N8118T	29.12.60	R.J.& J.Postlethwaite & J.E.Littler Claybrooke Lodge Farm, Lutterworth (Cancelled by CAA 9.3.99; last known in a damaged condition pre 3.90)		6. 4.91
G-AREH	DH.82A Tiger Moth	85287 T6746M/DE241	(G-APYV)	4. 7.60	N.K.Geddes Lochwinnoch (On long-term rebuild 5.94)		19. 4.66
G-AREI	Taylorcraft Auster III	518 VR-RBM/VR-SCJ/MT438	9M-ALB	14.12.60	P.J.Stock Petersfield (Op Military Auster Flt as "MT438" "Akyab" in SEAC c/s)		21. 4.00
G-AREL	PA-22-150 Caribbean	22-7284	N3344Z	14. 9.60	H.H.Cousins t/a Fenland Aerosvcs Fenland		22. 8.98
G-AREO	PA-18-150 Super Cub	18-7407		24. 8.60	DRA (Farnborough) Gliding Club Ltd DRA Farnborough		31. 8.01
G-ARET	PA-22-160 Tri-Pacer	22-7590		2. 9.60	I.S.Runnalls (On rebuild 10.97) Church Farm, North Moreton, Wallingford		20. 5.83T
G-AREV	PA-22-160 Tri-Pacer	22-6540	N9628D	25.10.60	D.J.Ash "Smart Cat" Barton		19.10.00
G-AREX	Aeronca 15AC Sedan	15AC-61	CF-FNM	12. 9.60	R.J.M.Turnbull & P.Lowndes Rydinghurst Farm, Cranleigh		25. 6.01
G-AREZ	Rollason-Druine D.31 Turbulent (Ardem 4C02)	PFA/561		22. 9.60	J.St.Clair-Quentin (Ledbury) (Status uncertain)		19. 9.84P
G-ARFB	PA-22-150 Caribbean	22-7518	N3625Z	8. 9.60	C.T.Woodward, R.W.Hall & T.Lawton Yeatsall Farm, Abbots Bromley		29.12.99
G-ARFD	PA-22-160 Tri-Pacer	22-7565	N3667Z	8. 9.60	J.R.Dunnett Priory Farm, Tibenham		27. 1.01
G-ARFG	Cessna 175AX Skylark (Rebuilt to Cessna 172 standard 1988)	56505	N7005E	15.11.60	P.K.Blair t/a Foxtrot Golf Grp Sibson		22. 1.01
G-ARFH	PA-24-250 Comanche	24-2240	N7087P	13.10.60	L.M.Walton Sibson		13.11.00
G-ARFI	Cessna 150A	150-59100	N41836 G-ARFI/N7000X	1. 2.61	J.H.Fisher Haverfordwest		26. 6.00
G-ARFL	Cessna 175B Skylark	175-56868	N8168T	2. 2.61	D.J.Mason Denham		16. 2.00
G-ARFO	Cessna 150A	150-59174	N7074X	23. 3.61	S.M.Dorrington & M.Arterton Shipdham		21. 4.00T
G-ARFT	SAN Jodel DR.1050 Ambassadeur	170		27.10.60	R.Shaw (Sowerby Bridge) (Damaged Prestwick 15.6.84; status uncertain)		13.10.84
G-ARFV	Tipsy T.66 Nipper 2 (VW 1834)	44		5.10.60	L.S. & K.L.Johnson (Capel, Ipswich)		14. 7.99P
G-ARGB*	Auster 6A	2593	VF635	12.10.60	C.J.Baker Carr Farm, Newark (Frame only stored 9.96)		21. 6.74
G-ARGG	DHC.1 Chipmunk 22	C1/0247	WD305	19.10.60	B.Hook (As "WD305") Coventry		21. 4.96
G-ARGI*	Auster 6A	2299	VF530	8.12.60	C.J.Baker (Stored 9.96)Carr Farm, Newark		4. 7.76
G-ARGO	PA-22-108 Colt	22-8034		18. 1.61	D.J.Hockings (Heathfield)		14. 8.98
G-ARGV	PA-18-180 Super Cub	18-7559	N10F	20.12.60	Deeside Gliding Club (Aberdeenshire) Ltd (Damaged Aboyne 23.8.96) Aboyne		18. 9.98
G-ARGY	PA-22-160 Tri-Pacer (Modified to PA-20 configuration)	22-7620	G-JEST G-ARGY	20.12.60	G.K.Hare Manor Farm, Glatton (Damaged Flecknoe 4.10.91; stored pending rebuild 7.95)		8. 5.91T
G-ARGZ	Rollason-Druine D.31 Turbulent (VW 1600)	PFA/562		7.11.60	The Tiger Club (1990) Ltd Headcorn		24. 9.99P
G-ARHB	Forney F-1A Aircoupe	5733		17. 4.61	A.V.Rash & D.R.Wickes Earls Colne t/a Aircoupe Hotel Bravo		28. 4.99
G-ARHC	Forney F-1A Aircoupe	5734		26. 5.61	A.P.Gardner Little Gransden		28. 5.01
G-ARHF*	Forney F-1A Aircoupe	5737		26. 5.61	Not known (Stored 8.97) Shipdham		10. 5.94
G-ARHI	PA-24-180 Comanche	24-2260		20.12.60	D.D.Smith (Norwich)		31. 5.00
G-ARHL	PA-23-250 Aztec	27-402		3. 3.61	C.J.Freeman (On overhaul 1.96) Headcorn		23.11.79
G-ARHM	Auster 6A	2515	VF557	5. 1.61	D.Hollowell, R.L.Wharmby & P.H.Hollowell Finmere		9.12.01
G-ARHN	PA-22-150 Caribbean (Rebuilt with parts from G-ATXB)	22-7514	N3622Z	10. 1.61	D.B.Furniss & A.Munro Gamston		1.10.99
G-ARHP	PA-22-160 Tri-Pacer	22-7549	N3652Z	10. 1.61	R.N.Morgan Boones Farm, High Garrett, Braintree		22. 5.00
G-ARHR	PA-22-150 Caribbean	22-7576	N3707Z	10. 1.61	A.R.Wyatt (Buntingford)		26.10.01
G-ARHW	DH.104 Dove 8	04512		10. 1.61	Pacelink Ltd Fairoaks		30. 7.99
G-ARHX*	DH.104 Dove 8	04513		11. 1.61	North East Aircraft Museum Usworth		8. 9.78
G-ARHZ	Rollason-Druine D.62A Condor (Cont O-200-A)	PFA/247 & RAE/602		13.12.60	T.J.Goodwin Hill Farm, Nayland (Damaged Damyns Hall, Upminster 4.9.94)		26. 7.95P
G-ARID	Cessna 172B Skyhawk	172-48209	N7709X	2. 2.61	L.M.Edwards Sleap		14. 6.00T
G-ARIE	PA-24-250 Comanche	24-1888	ZS-CNL	25. 5.61	R.C.Nichols t/a G-ARIE Group Stapleford		21.12.01
G-ARIF	Ord-Hume O-H 7 Minor Coupe (Modified Luton LA-4C Minor)	O-H 7 & PAL/1401		22. 8.60	N.H.Ponsford Wigan (Stored incomplete 3.96)		
G-ARIH	Auster 6A	2463	TW591	23. 1.61	R.Tarder & J.J.Fisher t/a India Hotel Grp (As "TW591" in 664 (AOP) Sqdn c/s) Yeatsall Farm, Abbots Bromley		14. 6.01
G-ARIK	PA-22-150 Caribbean	22-7570	N3701Z	26. 1.61	C.J.Berry Booker		26. 3.00
G-ARIL	PA-22-150 Caribbean	22-7574	N3705Z	26. 1.61	K.Knight (Malvern)		21.12.01
G-ARIM	Druine D.31 Turbulent	PFA/510		27. 2.61	A.Gregori Portmoak		
G-ARJB	DH.104 Dove 8	04518		29. 9.60	Cormack (Aircraft Svs) Ltd Cumbernauld (Stored 6.98)		10.12.73T
G-ARJC	PA-22-108 Colt	22-8154		21. 3.61	F.W.H.Dulles (On rebuild) (Stroud, Glos)		28.11.75
G-ARJE	PA-22-108 Colt	22-8184		29. 3.61	Touchdown Avn Ltd (Macclesfield) (On rebuild 1993)		29. 4.73

Regn	Type	C/n	P/I	Date	Owner/operator	Probable Base	CA Expy
G-ARJF*	PA-22-108 Colt	22-8199		23. 3.61	Not known Stockton, Warminster		9. 2.80
					(On rebuild 6.93)		
G-ARJH	PA-22-108 Colt	22-8249		29. 3.61	A.Vine	Goodwood	7. 8.00
G-ARJR*	PA-23-160 Apache G	23-1966	N4447P	1. 3.61	Oxford Air Training School Oxford		24.10.78
					(Instructional airframe 5.95)		
G-ARJS	PA-23-160 Apache G	23-1977		3. 3.61	Bencray Ltd t/a Blackpool & Fylde A/C		
					(Op Blackpool Air Charter)	Blackpool	17.10.00T
G-ARJT	PA-23-160 Apache G	23-1981		3. 3.61	Hiveland Ltd		
						Water Leisure Park, Skegness	29. 1.01T
G-ARJU	PA-23-160 Apache G	23-1984		3. 3.61	G.R.Manley	Andrewsfield	1. 8.99T
G-ARJV	PA-23-160 Apache G	23-1985		3. 3.61	Metham Aviation Ltd	Blackbushe	11.11.01
G-ARJZ	Rollason-Druine D.31 Turbulent			8. 2.61	C.J.Tilson	Great Massingham	4. 9.95P
	(VW1700)	PFA/564			(Stored 9.97)		
G-ARKG	Auster J/5G Cirrus Autocar	3061	AP-AHJ	22. 2.61	G.C.Milborrow		18. 4.01
			VP-KKN			Spanhoe	
G-ARKJ	Beechcraft N35 Bonanza	D-6736		5. 5.61	T.Cust	Sandtoft	2. 6.01
G-ARKK	PA-22-108 Colt	22-8290		12. 4.61	The Rochford Hundred F/Grp Ltd Southend		9. 9.00
G-ARKM	PA-22-108 Colt	22-8313		12. 4.61	B.V. & E.A.Howes	Earls Colne	7.12.98
G-ARKN	PA-22-108 Colt	22-8327	N10F	9. 5.61	G.Hill	(Waterlooville)	29. 9.97
G-ARKP	PA-22-108 Colt	22-8364		19. 5.61	C.J.& J.Freeman	Headcorn	27. 6.82T
					(On overhaul 4.96)		
G-ARKR	PA-22-108 Colt	22-8376		9. 5.61	Barbara J.M.Montegut	Booker	7. 5.99
G-ARKS	PA-22-108 Colt	22-8422		7. 6.61	R.A.Nesbitt-Dufort		
	(Lyc O-320)					Bradleys Lawn, Heathfield	18.10.01
G-ARLG	Auster D.4/108	3606		4. 4.61	R.D.Helliar-Symons Scotland Farm, Hook		26.10.98P
					t/a Auster D4 Grp (Damaged Hook 16.9.98)		
G-ARLK	PA-24-250 Comanche	24-2433	EI-ALW	25. 5.61	Gibad Aviation Ltd	Stapleford	2. 4.99
			G-ARLK/N10F				
G-ARLO*	Beagle A.61 Terrier 1	2500	TW642	11. 4.61	S.C.Challis Hedge End, Southampton		3.11.79
					t/a British Classic Acft Restorations		
					(Damaged off Shoreham 10.7.79; stored 3.96 for rebuild as Auster AOP.6)		
G-ARLP	Beagle A.61 Terrier 1	3724(1)	VX123	11. 4.61	D.R.Whitby t/a Gemini F/Grp	(Fakenham)	31.10.91
	(C/n officially quoted as 2573/VF631 which became G-ARLM(2)/G-ASDK;						
	damaged Truleigh Farm, Edburton 4.8.91; on rebuild 1992)						
G-ARLR	Beagle A.61 Terrier 2	3721 & B.601	VW996	11. 4.61	M. Palfreman	Bagby	9. 9.01
G-ARLU*	Cessna 172B	172-48502	N8002X	14. 6.61	Irish Air Corps	Baldonnel	6.10.78
					(Damaged 30.10.77; instructional airframe 8.93)		
G-ARLW	Cessna 172B Skyhawk	172-48499	N7999X	15. 6.61	South Lancashire Flyers Ltd	Barton	21. 3.91
					(Damaged Barton 20.2.90; open store 1.96; cancelled by CAA 21.1.99)		
G-ARLX	SAN Jodel D.140B Mousquetaire II	66		12. 4.61	M.J.Dunkerly	(Ouessant, France)	21. 6.01T
G-ARLY*	Auster J/5P Autocar	3271		14. 4.61	P.J.Elliott & G.Green	???	6. 6.71
	(On rebuild to D.6/180 standard using parts from Airedale/G-ARNR & J/5R/G-APAA wings;						
	sold in Switzerland 12.87; cancelled by CAA 25.2.99)						
G-ARLZ	Rollason-Druine D.31A Turbulent			7. 4.61	W.J.Hitchcock & R.J.K.Blech	Coventry	2. 6.99P
	(Ardem 4C02)	RAE/578			t/a Turb Grp		
G-ARMA*	PA-23-160 Apache G	23-1967	N4448P	8. 5.61	Oxford Air Training School Oxford		22. 7.77
					(Instructional airframe 9.96)		
G-ARMB	DHC.1 Chipmunk 22A	C1/0099	WB660	26. 4.61	P.A.Layzell Bunns Bank, Norfolk		6. 7.99
	(Fuselage No.DHB/F/25)				(As "WB660")		
G-ARMC	DHC.1 Chipmunk 22A	C1/0151	WB703	26. 4.61	J.T.H.Henderson White Waltham		26. 3.99
					(As "WB703" in RAF c/s)		
G-ARMD	DHC.1 Chipmunk 22A	C1/0237	WD297	26. 4.61	D M Squires	(Stratford-on-Avon)	
G-ARMF	DHC.1 Chipmunk 22A	C1/0394	WG322	26. 4.61	Westwood Portway Ltd	(Twyford)	12.10.98
					(As "WZ868/H")		
G-ARMG	DHC.1 Chipmunk 22A	C1/0575	WK558	26. 4.61	A.D.Cook Wellesbourne Mountford		16.12.00
	(Fuselage No.DHB/F/460)				t/a The MG Group		
G-ARML	Cessna 175B Skylark	175-56995	N8295T	12. 7.61	R.W.Boote	RAF Lyneham	30.11.98
G-ARMN	Cessna 175B Skylark	175-56994	N8294T	18. 8.61	G.A.Nash Lower Wasing Farm, Brimpton		22. 5.99
G-ARMO	Cessna 172B Skyhawk	172-48560	N8060X	12. 6.61	G.M.Jones	Little Staughton	28. 8.98
G-ARMR	Cessna 172B Skyhawk	172-48566	N8066X	12. 6.61	Sunsaver Ltd	Barton	29. 7.00
G-ARMX*	Avro 748 Srs 1A/101	1538	VP-LVN	28. 4.61	Manchester Airport Fire Training Services		
			G-ARMX		(Fuselage on fire dump 4.97) Manchester		18. 3.84T
G-ARMZ	Rollason-Druine D.31 Turbulent			2. 5.61	J.Mickleburgh & D.Clark	Headcorn	13.12.99P
	(VW1500)	PFA/565					
G-ARNA*	Mooney M.20B Mark 21	1806		26. 6.61	Not known Casablanca-Anfa, Morocco		14. 8.81
					(Stored 3.94)		
G-ARNB	Auster J/5G Cirrus Autocar	3169	AP-AHL	18. 5.61	R.F.Tolhurst Lenham, Maidstone		19. 2.77
			VP-KNL		(Status uncertain - possibly on rebuild 1995)		
G-ARND	PA-22-108 Colt	22-8484		6. 6.61	E.J.Clarke	Seighford	4. 8.99
G-ARNE	PA-22-108 Colt	22-8502		15. 6.61	T.D.L.Bowden	Knettishall	7. 7.00
G-ARNG	PA-22-108 Colt	22-8547		26. 6.61	S.S.Delwarte (On rebuild 8.97) Shoreham		12.10.73
G-ARNH*	PA-22-108 Colt	22-8558		5. 9.61	Fenland & West Norfolk A/c Preservation Society		
					(Crashed 1.9.61; fuselage on rebuild 4.96) West Walton, Wisbech		20. 3.73
G-ARNI	PA-22-108 Colt	22-8575		26. 7.61	B.A.Drury	Rochester	15. 6.98T
G-ARNJ	PA-22-108 Colt	22-8587		3. 8.61	R.A.Keech	(Chester)	16. 1.00
G-ARNK	PA-22-108 Colt	22-8622		5. 9.61	N.G. & A.N.M.McDonald	RAF Coltishall	12.12.01
	(Modified to PA-20 configuration with Lyc O-320 as "Super Colt")						
G-ARNL	PA-22-108 Colt	22-8625		3. 8.61	Miss J.A.Dodsworth	White Waltham	24. 7.00

Regn	Type	C/n	P/I	Date	Owner/operator	Probable Base	CA Expy
G-ARNN	Globe GC-1B Swift	1272	VP-YMJ	11. 5.61	K.E.Sword	(Leicester)	11. 7.74
			VP-RDA/ZS-BMX/NC3279K	(Crashed Hucknall 1.9.73)			
G-ARNO*	Beagle A.61 Terrier 1	3722	VX113	8. 5.61	R.Webber	Hayrish Farm, Okehampton	19. 6.81
				(On rebuild 7.97)			
G-ARNP	Beagle A.109 Airedale A109-P1 & B.503			10. 5.61	S.T. & M.Isbister	Elstree/North Weald	13. 3.00
G-ARNY	SAN Jodel D.117	595	F-BHXQ	13. 6.61	P.Jenkins	Inverness	6. 3.99P
G-ARNZ	Rollason-Druine D.31 Turbulent			28. 6.61	The Tiger Club (1990) Ltd	Headcorn	14. 9.99P
	(VW 1600)	PFA/579					
G-AROA	Cessna 172B Skyhawk	172-48628	N8128X	19. 9.61	D.E.Partridge	Rayne Hall Farm, Rayne	30. 7.00T
					t/a The D & P Group		
G-AROC	Cessna 175BX Skylark	175-56997	G-OTOW	2.10.61	A.J.Symms	Ham Street, Somerset	17.12.99
	(Modified to 172 configuration)		G-AROC/N8297T				
G-AROJ*	Beagle A.109 Airedale	B.508	HB-EUC	17. 5.61	C.J.Baker	Carr Farm, Newark	8. 1.76
			G-AROJ		(On rebuild 9.96)		
G-ARON	PA-22-108 Colt	22-8822		23.11.61	R.W.Curtis	(Warminster)	5. 7.01
G-AROO	Forney F.1A Aircoupe	5750	N25B	3.11.61	W.J.McMeekan	Newtownards	7. 6.01
G-AROW	SAN Jodel D.140B Mousquetaire II	71		13. 9.61	Mousquetaire Ltd	Redhill	9. 7.00T
G-AROY	Boeing-Stearman A75N1	75-4775	N56418	6. 6.61	W.A.Jordan	Little Gransden	12. 4.00
	(PT-17) Kaydet (P&W R985)		42-16612				
G-ARPH*	DH.121 Trident 1C	2108		13. 4.61	RAF Museum	RAF Cosford	8. 9.82
					(British Airways c/s)		
G-ARPK*	DH.121 Trident 1C	2111		13. 4.61	Manchester Airport Fire Sve	Manchester	17. 5.82
G-ARPO*	DH.121 Trident 1C	2116		13. 4.61	CAA Intnl Fire Training Centre	Teesside	12. 1.86
G-ARPP*	DH.121 Trident 1C	2117		13. 4.61	BAA Airport Fire Service	Glasgow	16. 2.86
G-ARPZ*	DH.121 Trident 1C	2128		13. 4.61	RFD Ltd (Esc sys test a/frame)	Dunsfold	26. 1.86
G-ARRD	SAN Jodel DR.1051 Ambassadeur	274		20. 7.61	C.M.Fitton	Watchford Farm, Yarcombe	23.11.99P
G-ARRE	SAN Jodel DR.1050 Ambassadeur	275		20. 7.61	A.Luty & M.P.Edwards	Barton	20.12.98
G-ARRG*	Cessna 175B Skylark	175-56999	N8299T	5.10.61	Not known	Little Staughton	4. 5.73
				(Damaged Great Yarmouth 3.11.70; stored unmarked 9.96)			
G-ARRL	Auster J/1N Alpha	2115	VP-KFK	13. 6.61	G.N.Smith & C.Webb	Headcorn	1. 7.99
			VP-KPF/VP-KFK/VP-UAK				
G-ARRM*	Beagle B.206X	B.001		23. 6.61	Bristol Aero Collection	Kemble	23.12.64S
					(Stored 6.97)		
G-ARRS	Menavia Piel CP.301A Emeraude	226	F-BIMA	29. 6.61	Julia P.Drake & N.W.Cawley	Sturgate	2. 6.99P
					t/a ARSSY Aviation		
G-ARRT	Wallis WA-116/Mc	2		28. 6.61	K.H.Wallis (Stored 8.97)	Reymerston Hall	26. 5.83P
	(McC 4318A)						
G-ARRU	Druine D.31 Turbulent	PFA/502		28. 6.61	N.A.Morgan & J.Paget		
	(VW 1600)		(Damaged Lamberhurst, Kent 8.7.96) Stoneacre Farm, Farthing Corner		27. 2.97P			
G-ARRX	Auster 6A	2281	VF512	4. 7.61	J.E.D.Mackie "Peggy Too"	Popham	7. 6.00
				(As "VF512/PF-M" in 43 OTU c/s)			
G-ARRY	SAN Jodel D.140B Mousquetaire II	72		13. 9.61	Fictionview Ltd		
					Shenstone Hall Farm, Shenstone		25.10.01
G-ARRZ	Rollason-Druine D.31 Turbulent			21. 8.61	C.I.Jefferson "Tarzan" Hingham, Norfolk		21.12.90P
	(Ardem 4C02)	PFA/580		(Damaged Horley, Surrey 21.7.90; on rebuild 9.97)			
G-ARSB*	Cessna 150A	150-59337	N7237X	25. 9.61	Not known	Little Staughton	10. 6.88
					(Open storage 9.96)		
G-ARSG	Roe Triplane Type IV replica	HAC.1	(BAPC1)	29.10.81	The Shuttleworth Trust	Old Warden	2. 5.98P
	(ADC Cirrus III) (Also c/n TRI.1)				(No external marks)		
G-ARSJ	Scintex CP.301C-2 Emeraude	581		28. 7.61	R.J.Lewis	Garston Farm, Marshfield	2. 7.93P
					(On overhaul 6.96)		
G-ARSL	Beagle A.61 Terrier 2	2539	VF581	13. 7.61	D.J.Colclough	Hayrish Farm, Okehampton	30. 9.85A
					(As "VF581") (On rebuild 7.97)		
G-ARSU	PA-22-108 Colt	22-8835	EI-AMI	23.11.61	D.P.Owen	Thruxton	15. 5.00
			G-ARSU				
G-ARSW	PA-22-108 Colt	22-8858		23.11.61	M.J.Kirk t/a Entire Flying Group Cardiff		30. 1.97
G-ARSX	PA-22-160 Tri-Pacer	22-6712	N2907Z	8. 8.61	S.Hutchinson	Rathfriland, Co.Down	16. 5.97
					(Stored 6.97)		
G-ARTD	PA-23-160 Apache	23-1530	N4053P	25. 8.61	Caernarfon Aircraft Maintenance Co Ltd		
						Caernarfon	1.12.01T
G-ARTH	PA-12 Super Cruiser	12-3278	EI-ADO	22. 9.61	R.I.Souch & B.J.Dunford		
						Hall Farm, Durley	21. 4.95P
G-ARTJ*	Bensen B.8M	7		22. 9.61	S.Russell	Wilkieston Farm, Cupar	
	(VW 1600)				(Stored 6.95)		
G-ARTL	DH.82A Tiger Moth		"T7281"	22. 9.61	Fiona G.Clacherty		
	(P/i is doubtful- if correct c/n is 83795; as "T7281" in RAF c/s)			Great Fryup, Egton, Whitby		30. 4.00		
G-ARTM*	Beagle A.61 Terrier 1	3723	WE536	9.10.61	C.J.Baker	Carr Farm, Newark	13.11.71
					(Crashed Priory Farm, Turvey, Beds 28.5.70; on rebuild 9.96)		
G-ARTT	Morane MS.880B Rallye Club	8		11.12.61	R.N.Scott (On rebuild 11.96)	Blackpool	29. 5.94
G-ARTY*	Cessna 150B	150-59482	N7382X	23. 2.62	Air Service Training Ltd	Perth	6.10.68
					(Instructional airframe 5.96)		
G-ARTZ(2)	McCandless M.4	M4/1		24.10.61	W.R.Partridge (Extant 10.95)	St.Merryn	13.10.69P
	(VW 1500) (Two Gyrocopters may have worn these marks - the prototype M.2 (650cc Triumph) at the Ulster Folk & Transport Museum, Dublin is on display and un-marked)						
G-ARUG	Auster J/5G Cirrus Autocar	3272		2. 1.62	D.P.H.Hulme	Biggin Hill	2. 3.00
G-ARUH	SAN Jodel DR.1050 Ambassadeur	284		5.12.61	B.A.H.LeGrange & R.C.Laverick (Stored Denham 3.89)		
					t/a PFA F/Grp No.272	(Ashford, Middx)	4. 7.88
G-ARUI	Beagle A.61 Terrier 1	2529	VF571	9. 3.62	T.W.J.Dann	Southend	28.10.01

Regn	Type	C/n	P/I	Date	Owner/operator	Probable Base	CA Expy
G-ARUL	LeVier Cosmic Wind	103	N22C	28.11.61	P.G.Kynsey "Ballerina"	Headcorn	4. 7.99P
	(Cont O-200-A) (Rebuilt 1973 as c/n PFA/1511)				(Original components on rebuild 12.95)		
G-ARUO	PA-24-180 Comanche	24-2427	N7251P	16. 1.62	J.B.W.Dore	White Waltham	22. 8.00
					t/a The Uniform Oscar Grp		
G-ARUR*	PA-28-160 Cherokee	28-133		16. 1.62	M.Jarrett	Crowland	12.10.92
					(Damaged nr Redhill 14.9.92; fuselage stored 8.97)		
G-ARUV	Piel CP.301 Emeraude Srs. 1	PFA/700		2. 2.62	S.T. & J.A.Smoothy "Emma"	Langar	22. 9.99P
	(Cont C90)						
G-ARUY	Auster J/1N Alpha	3394		2. 2.62	K.B.Mace & R.M.Chaplin		
						Wellesbourne Mountford	21. 5.99
G-ARUZ	Cessna 175C Skylark	175-57080	N8380T	23. 2.62	S.R.Page & M.Lowe	Cardiff	25. 3.00
					t/a Cardiff Skylark Grp		
G-ARVF*	Vickers VC-10-1101	808		16. 1.63	Flugausstellung L & P Junior Museum		
						Hermeskeil, Germany	23.7.81
G-ARVM*	Vickers VC-10-1101	815		16. 1.63	RAF Museum	RAF Cosford	5. 8.80
					(British Airways c/s)		
G-ARVN*	Servotec Rotorcraft Grasshopper 1	1		16. 2.63	E.D.Ap Rees	Weston-super-Mare	18. 5.63
					t/a The Helicopter Museum (Stored 8.97)		
	(Two airframes identified as G-ARVN; the other stored by J.Wilkie at Blackpool)						
G-ARVO	PA-18-95 Super Cub	18-7252	D-ENFI	18. 1.83	Deltair Ltd (Op Medway Flight Training Ltd)		
			N3376Z			Stoneacre Farm, Farthing Corner	19.11.01T
G-ARVS	PA-28-160 Cherokee	28-339		12. 3.62	M & K.Harper	Stapleford	7. 9.00
G-ARVT	PA-28-160 Cherokee	28-379		21. 3.62	Red Rose Avn Ltd	Liverpool	27. 4.01
G-ARVU	PA-28-160 Cherokee	28-410	PH-ONY	30. 3.62	P.F.G.Simms,J.Lamb & P.Barrett	Barton	9. 3.01
			G-ARVU		t/a G-ARVU Flying Group		
G-ARVV	PA-28-160 Cherokee	28-451		11. 7.62	G.E.Hopkins	Shobdon	26.10.00
G-ARVZ	Rollason-Druine D.62B Condor	RAE/606		6.12.61	J.D.Jewitt	(Selby)	5. 5.99
G-ARWB	DHC.1 Chipmunk 22A	C1/0621	WK611	2. 1.62	P.G.Alston	Thruxton	23. 6.99
					t/a Thruxton Chipmunk F/Grp (As "WK611")		
G-ARWH*	Cessna 172C Skyhawk	172-49166	N1466Y	18. 4.62	Not known (Stored for spares 3.96)		
						Stoneacre Farm, Farthing Corner	28. 4.86
G-ARWO	Cessna 172C Skyhawk	172-49187	N1487Y	10. 4.62	J.P.Stafford	Ashcroft Farm, Winsford	12.11.99
G-ARWR	Cessna 172C Skyhawk	172-49172	N1472Y	13. 4.62	M.McCann t/a Devanha F/Grp	Insch	18. 3.01
G-ARWS	Cessna 175C Skylark	175-57102	N8502X	12. 4.62	B.A.I.Torrington	(Swansea)	28. 8.01
G-ARXC*	Beagle A.109 Airedale	B.510	EI-ATD	9. 4.62	C.J.Baker	Carr Farm, Newark	27. 6.76
			G-ARXC		(Stored 9.96)		
G-ARXD	Beagle A.109 Airedale	B.511		9. 4.62	D.Howden (Stored 6.95)	Banchory	13. 6.86
G-ARXG	PA-24-250 Comanche	24-3154		21. 2.62	R.F.Corstin,	Fairoaks	12. 4.99
					t/a Fairoaks Comanche		
G-ARXH	Bell 47G	40	N120B	13. 2.62	A.B.Searle	Parklands, Northampton	6. 7.90
			NC120B		(Stored Luton 6.92)		
G-ARXN*	Cobelavia Tipsy T.66 Nipper 2	77		3. 7.62	I.Wood & C.E.Pickton	Hucknall	19. 8.80P
	(VW 1800)				t/a The Griffon F/Grp (Stored 5.96)		
G-ARXP	Phoenix Luton LA-4A Minor			23. 2.62	E.Evans	Bensons Farm, Laindon	17.10.95P
	(Walter Mikron 3) PAL/1119 & PFA/816				(Stored 8.97)		
G-ARXT	SAN Jodel DR.1050 Ambassadeur	355		14. 3.62	M.F.Coy	Wellesbourne Mountford	8.11.01
					t/a CJM F/Grp		
G-ARXU	Auster 6A	2295	VF526	5. 3.62	E.C.Tait & M.Pocock	AAC Middle Wallop	12.9.99
					(As "VF526/T" in Army c/s)		
G-ARXW	Morane MS.885 Super Rallye	100		30. 3.62	A.F.Danton & A.Kennedy		
						Dunnamanagh, Londonderry	4. 5.01
G-ARYB*	DH.125 Srs.1	25002		1. 3.62	Midland Air Museum	Coventry	22. 1.68
					(Stored 4.96)		
G-ARYC*	DH.125 Srs.1	25003		1. 3.62	De Havilland Aircraft Museum (On rebuild 3.96)		
						Salisbury Hall, London Colney	1. 8.73
G-ARYD*	Auster AOP.6	-	WJ358	8. 3.62	The Museum of Army Flying	AAC Middle Wallop	
					(As "WJ358")		
G-ARYF	PA-23-250 Aztec B	27-2065		11. 4.62	I.J.T.Branson	Biggin Hill	18. 6.99
G-ARYH	PA-22-160 Tri-Pacer	22-7039	N3102Z	9. 3.62	C.Watt	Crosland Moor	18. 4.99
G-ARYI	Cessna 172C	172-49260	N1560Y	13. 7.62	Joyce Rhodes	Blackbushe	24. 7.00T
G-ARYK	Cessna 172C	172-49288	N1588Y	13. 7.62	G.W.Goodban	(Canterbury)	3. 7.00
G-ARYR	PA-28-180 Cherokee B	28-770		12. 7.62	R.P.Synge & C.S.Wilkinson	Turweston	27. 6.00
					t/a GARYR F/Grp		
G-ARYS	Cessna 172C Skyhawk	172-49291	N1591Y	13. 7.62	D.J.Squires, C.J & J.Hill	Coventry	13. 8.00
G-ARYV	PA-24-250 Comanche	24-2516	N7337P	17. 4.62	A.L.Hall-Carpenter	(Thetford)	26. 2.01
G-ARYZ	Beagle A.109 Airedale	B.512		9. 4.62	S.Barker t/a Rutland Avn	Spanhoe	16.11.97
G-ARZB	Beagle-Wallis WA-116 Srs.1 Agile		XR943	18. 4.62	K.H.Wallis (Stored 8.97) Reymerston Hall		29. 6.93P
	(McCulloch 4318A)	B.203	G-ARZB		(Another Wallis is displayed as "G-ARZB" in Planet Hollywood,		
	Leicester Square, London W1, owned by D.Worrall, t/a James Bond Collectors Club, but is unidentified)						
G-ARZD*	Cessna 172C	172-49389	N1689Y	22. 6.62	V.H.Bellamy	St.Just	23.10.77
					(Crashed St.Marys 28.5.77; stored 11.93)		
G-ARZE*	Cessna 172C	172-49388	N1688Y	22. 6.62	The Black Knights Parachute Centre		
						Bank End Farm, Cockerham	16. 3.77
	(Damaged Brawdy 11.9.76; training airframe 3.95)						
G-ARZN	Beechcraft N.35 Bonanza	D-6795	N215DM	23. 5.62	D.W.Mickleburgh	RAF Newton	25. 5.01
G-ARZW	Phoenix Currie Wot	1 & HAC/5		25. 5.62	B.R.Pearson	Eaglescott	7. 1.89P
	(Walter Mikron 3)				(Damaged nr Headcorn 12.2.88; on rebuild 10.95 as Pfalz D.VII scale replica)		
G-ARZX*	Cessna 150B	150-59642	N1242Y	13. 7.62	I.B.Osborn t/a Gate Flyers	Manston	5. 9.99
					(Cancelled by CAA 16.9.98)		

Regn	Type	C/n	P/I	Date	Owner/operator	Probable Base	CA Expy
G-ASAA	Phoenix Luton LA-4A Minor (JAP J.99)	O-H/4		19. 4.62	J.W.Cudby	Netherthorpe	10. 2.00P
G-ASAI	Beagle A.109 Airedale	B.516		26. 6.62	K.R. & R.I. & P.Howden (On rebuild 6.95)	Banchory	20. 5.77S
G-ASAJ	Beagle A.61 Terrier 2 (Initially allocated c/n 3732)	B.605	WE569	26. 6.62	R.Skingley t/a G-ASAJ F/Grp Bassingbourn (Op Military Auster Flt as Auster T.7 "WE569")		19. 8.01
G-ASAK	Beagle A.61 Terrier 2	B.604	WE591	26. 6.62	J.H.Oakins	Biggin Hill	7. 6.98
G-ASAL(2)	Scottish Avn Bulldog Srs.120/124	BH120/239	(G-BBHF) G-31-17	5. 9.73	Pioneer Flying Co Ltd	Prestwick	29. 4.99P
G-ASAN	Beagle A.61 Terrier 2	B.608	VX928	26. 6.62	R.J.Bentley (On rebuild 4.97)	Haverfordwest	28. 6.96
G-ASAT	Morane MS.880B Rallye Club	178		21. 6.62	M.Cutovic	Croft Farm, Defford	8. 7.00
G-ASAU	Morane MS.880B Rallye Club	179		21. 6.62	T.C. & R.Edwards	Sibson	24. 4.00
G-ASAX	Beagle A.61 Terrier 2 (Converted from Auster 6 c/n 1911)	B.609	TW533	12. 6.62	P.G. & F.M.Morris "The Jacobite Air Force" Cheyne Farm, Netherley, Aberdeen		1. 9.96
G-ASAZ	Hiller UH-12E-4	2070	N5372V	18. 6.62	Pan Air Ltd (As "XS165/37" in 705 Sqdn RN c/s)	North Weald	18.12.97T
G-ASBA	Phoenix Currie Wot (Cont C90)	AE.1 & PFA/3005		16. 8.62	M.A.Kaye	Presteigne	20. 9.94P
G-ASBB	Beechcraft 23 Musketeer	M-15		21. 6.62	E.J.Hammond t/a Five Musketeers F/Grp	Cambridge	18.12.00
G-ASBH	Beagle A.109 Airedale	B.519		26. 6.62	D.T.Smollett Bratton Clovelly, Okehampton		19. 2.99
G-ASBU*	Beagle A.61 Terrier 2	3733(1) & B.613	WE570	12. 7.62	G.Strathdee Netherley, Aberdeen (Damaged Netherley 12.8.80; stored for spares 12.95)		5. 7.82
G-ASBY	Beagle A.109 Airedale	B.523		23. 7.62	M.R.H.Wheatley & R.K.Wilson (Stored 5.92)	Warboys, Huntingdon	22. 3.80
G-ASCC	Beagle E.3 Mk.11	B.701	(G-25-12) XP254	23. 7.62	P.T.Bolton South Lodge Farm, Widmerpool (As "XP254") (Damaged Long Marston 5.11.95; on rebuild 9.97)		10. 6.99P
G-ASCD*	Beagle A.61 Terrier 2	B.615	PH-SFT G-ASCD/VW993	23. 7.62	Yorkshire Air Museum (As "TJ704/JA" in Royal Navy c/s)	Elvington	26. 9.71
G-ASCM	Isaacs Fury II PFA/2002/1B & 1			1. 8.62	M.M.Ward (Hamburg)		16. 6.98P
	(Lyc O-290) (PFA c/n is probably the builder's membership no.) (As "K2050" in pre-war RAF c/s)						
G-ASCT*	Bensen B.7Mc (McCulloch 4318E)	DC.3		14. 8.62	The Helicopter Museum Weston-super-Mare (Stored dismantled 8.97)		11.11.66P
G-ASCU	PA-18A-150 Super Cub	18-6797	VP-JBL	31. 8.62	Farm Avn Svs Ltd	Stapleford	14. 9.98
G-ASCZ	Menavia Piel CP.301A Emeraude	233	F-BIMG	1.10.62	P.Johnson	(Bognor Regis)	18.10.99P
G-ASDA*	Beechcraft 65-80 Queen Air	LD-64		2.10.62	Biggin Hill Airport Fire Service (Front section only)	Biggin Hill	8.11.79
G-ASDB*	Rollason-Druine D.31 Turbulent (Ardem 4C02)	PFA/1600		23. 8.62	C.I.Jefferson Hingham, Norfolk (Crashed Shoreham 11.8.68; stored 9.97)		11. 9.68P
G-ASDF*	Edwards Helicopter (Modified Adams-Wilson Hobbycopter)	NAFE.1		17.10.62	J.Parkin RAF Innsworth t/a Computair Consultants (On rebuild 3.96)		
G-ASDK	Beagle A.61 Terrier 2 (Converted from Auster AOP.6 c/n 2573)	B.702	G-ARLM(2) G-ARLP(1)/VF631	26.10.62	M.L.Rose	Sibson	5. 8.99
G-ASDL	Beagle A.61 Terrier 2 (Also c/ns 3727(1) & B.632(1))	B.703	G-ARLN(2) WE558	26.10.62	C.E.Mason	Marsh Hill Farm, Aylesbury	30. 5.00
G-ASDO*	Beechcraft 95-A55 Baron	TC-401		5.11.62	RAF Northolt Fire Service	RAF Northolt	16. 4.83
G-ASDY	Beagle-Wallis WA-116/F (Franklin 2A-120-B) (Regd erroneously as c/n B.204)	B.205		9.11.62	K.H.Wallis	Reymerston Hall	28.10.97P
G-ASEA	Phoenix Luton LA-4A Minor (JAP J.99) (Regd with c/n PFA/1154; c/n also quoted as PFA/1319 which is EAA Biplane G-AYFY) (Damaged Mendlesham 8.4.89; wings at Waits Farm, Belchamp Walter 5/93; on rebuild 1.97)	PAL/1154		14.11.62	J.Bradstock	RAF Wyton	16. 8.89P
G-ASEB	Phoenix Luton LA-4A Minor (Lyc O-145)	PAL/1149		26.11.62	S.R.P.Harper Movenis, Co.Londonderry (On overhaul 4.96)		29.10.82P
G-ASEE*	Auster J/1N Alpha	3359	I-AGRI	1. 2.63	R.Harper Spanhoe (Damaged RAE Bedford 9.2.74; stored 8.92)		1. 6.74S
G-ASEF*	Auster 6A	-	VW985	17.12.62	Not known Arncott, Bicester (Damaged Bicester 1966; stored 11.92)		19.12.66
G-ASEG	Beagle A.61 Terrier 1	2506	VF548	17.12.62	M.J.Kirk Llantwit Major (As "VF548") (Damaged Chesil Beach, Weymouth 2.97)		16. 7.98
G-ASEO	PA-24-250 Comanche	24-3367	(G-ASDX)	23. 1.63	Eagle European Airways Ltd Eastleigh (Op Osprey Aviation)		21. 3.99
G-ASEP	PA-23-235 Apache	27-541		28. 1.63	Air Warren Ltd	Denham	14.11.99
G-ASER*	PA-23-250 Aztec B	27-2283		28. 1.63	Not known Smeeth, Kent (Crashed Nigg Bay, Aberdeen 14.9.72; for recreational purposes 2.97)		17. 8.74
G-ASEU	Rollason-Druine D.62A Condor	RAE/607		12. 2.63	W.M.Grant	Inverness	19. 3.98P
G-ASFA	Cessna 172D Skyhawk	172-50182	N2582U	21. 2.63	D.Halfpenny	Maypole Farm,Chislet	3.11.00
G-ASFD	LET L-200A Morava	170808	OK-PHH	26. 2.63	M.Emery (Stored 7.95)	Guildford	12. 7.84T
G-ASFK	Auster J/5G Cirrus Autocar	3276		7. 3.63	T.D.G.Lancaster	Oxford	20. 5.00
G-ASFL	PA-28-180 Cherokee B	28-1170		7. 3.63	J.Simpson & D.Kennedy	Lee-on-Solent	18.12.00
G-ASFR	Bolkow Bo.208C Junior	522	D-EGMO	12. 3.63	S.T.Dauncey (Stored 4.97)	Yearby	29. 3.90P
G-ASFX	Druine D.31 Turbulent (VW1600)	PFA/513		18. 3.63	E.F.Clapham & W.B.S.Dobie Oldbury-on-Severn		8. 7.99P
G-ASGC*	BAC Super VC-10 Srs.1151	853		11. 4.63	Duxford Aviation Society (BOAC c/s)	Duxford	20. 4.80
G-ASHD*	Brantly B.2A	314		2. 4.63	The Helicopter Museum Weston-super-Mare (Crashed off Brightlingsea, Essex 19.2.67; components stored 5.97)		5. 6.67

Regn	Type	C/n	P/I	Date	Owner/operator	Probable Base	CA Expy
G-ASHH*	PA-23-250 Aztec	27-63	N455SL N4557P	25. 3.63	Not known (Stored 4.97)	Sibson	27. 9.85
G-ASHS	SNCAN Stampe SV-4C (G) (Gipsy Major) (Original fuselage used for spares in rebuild of G-AWEF 1980; rebuilt 1984 using fuselage of G-AZIR c/n 452 ex F-BCXR)	265	F-BCFN	23. 4.63	Three Point Flying Ltd	Rochester	9. 5.99T
G-ASHT	Rollason-Druine D.31 Turbulent (VW1600)	PFA/1610		23. 4.63	C.W.N.Huke	RAF Coltishall	27.10.99P
G-ASHU	PA-15 Vagabond (Rotax 912UL)	15-46	N4164H NC4164H	1. 5.63	G.J.Romanes & T.J.Ventham "Calybe"	Little Bredy	30. 4.99P
G-ASHV*	PA-23-250 Aztec B	27-2347	(N5281Y)	1. 5.63	Alderney Airport Fire Service	Alderney	22. 7.85T
G-ASHX	PA-28-180 Cherokee B	28-1266		3. 5.63	Powertheme Ltd	Barton	24. 4.99
G-ASIB	Reims Cessna F.172D Skyhawk (Wichita c/n 50091)	0006	F-WLIR	9. 5.63	R.G.Jones & D.A.Smart t/a G-ASIB F/Grp	RAF Mona	24. 2.01
G-ASII	PA-28-180 Cherokee B	28-1264		21. 5.63	T.R.Hart & Natocars Ltd	Exeter	13. 6.01
G-ASIJ	PA-28-180 Cherokee B	28-1333		21. 5.63	G.R.Moore t/a G-ASIJ Group	Andrewsfield	29.10.00T
G-ASIL	PA-28-180 Cherokee B	28-1350		21. 5.63	J.Dickenson & C.D.Powell	Leicester	17. 7.97
G-ASIP*	Auster 6A	2549	VF608	22. 5.63	Cotswold Acft Restoration Grp (Damaged Nympsfield 7.5.73; stored 6.97)	Kemble	19. 7.73
G-ASIT	Cessna 180	32567	N7670A	24. 5.63	A. & P.A.Wood	Audley End	8.12.00
G-ASIY	PA-25-235 Pawnee (Modified with four blade propeller)	25-2446		30. 5.63	T.Holloway t/a RAFGSA	RAF Bicester	18. 1.02
G-ASJL	Beechcraft H35 Bonanza	D-5132	N5582D	14. 6.63	Carolyn B.Ranald	White Waltham	20. 6.98
G-ASJO	Beechcraft 23 Musketeer	M-518		18. 6.63	S.Boon t/a G-ASJO Syndicate	Sandown	12. 2.98
G-ASJV	VS 361 Spitfire LF.IXB (Op by The Old Flying Machine Co; as "MH434/PK-K" in 316 Sqdn c/s)	CBAF.IX.552	OO-ARA Belgian AF SM-41/Fokker B-13/R Neth H-68/H-105/MH434	3. 7.63	Nalfire Avn Ltd	Duxford	1. 5.99P
G-ASJY	Gardan GY-80-160 Horizon	13		9. 7.63	P.D.Bradbury & S.M.Derbyshire	Sherburn	17. 5.98
G-ASJZ	SAN Jodel D.117A	826	F-BITD	5. 7.63	W.J. Siertsema	North Moreton	24. 3.99P
G-ASKC*	DH.98 Mosquito TT.35		TA719	8. 7.63	Imperial War Museum - Skyfame Collection (As "TA719/6T")	Duxford	18. 1.64S
G-ASKJ	Beagle A.61 Terrier 1 (EI-AMC) on rebuild Gamlingay 1.96; to be restored as T.7 "VX926" in 664 Sqdn c/s)	3730	(EI-AMC) VX926 (Wfu following u/c collapse Redhill 20.6.84;	16. 7.63	C.C.Irvine	(Congleton)	7. 2.85
G-ASKK*	HPR.7 Dart Herald 211	161	PP-ASU G-ASKK/PI-C910/CF-MCK	17. 7.63	City of Norwich Avn Museum	Norwich	19. 5.85T
G-ASKL	SAN Jodel 150 Mascaret	27		18. 7.63	J.M.Graty	Nuthampstead	1. 7.99P
G-ASKP	DH.82A Tiger Moth	3889	N6588	22. 7.63	The Tiger Club (1990) Ltd	Headcorn	3. 3.00T
G-ASKT	PA-28-180 Cherokee B	28-1410		24. 7.63	A.A.Mattacks	Biggin Hill	10. 9.99
G-ASKV	PA-25-235 Pawnee	25-2272	9Q-CHV G-ASKV/ST-ACW/G-ASKV/ST-ACF/G-ASKV/N6700Z	31. 7.63	Southdown Gliding Club Ltd	Parham Park	11. 3.99
G-ASLH	Cessna 182F Skylane	182-54905	N3505U	19. 8.63	J.M.Powell & J.A.Horton	Framlingham	22. 6.01T
G-ASLK	PA-25-235 Pawnee	25-2370	9Q-CFK G-ASLK/ST-ADT/G-ASLK/N6801Z	20. 8.63	Bristol Gliding Club (Pty) Ltd	Nympsfield	14. 1.00
G-ASLL*	Cessna 336 Skymaster	336-0074	N1774Z	23. 8.63	Not known (Fuselage cabin stored 3.92)	Farley Farm, Romsey	6. 1.74
G-ASLP*	Bensen B.7	11		3. 9.63	R Light & T Smith (Dismantled 2.99)	Stockport	
G-ASLV	PA-28-235 Cherokee	28-10048		11. 9.63	I.L.Harding t/a Sackville F/Grp	Sackville Lodge, Riseley	13.12.98
G-ASLX	Menavia Piel CP.301A Emeraude	292	F-BISV	12. 9.63	D.Wallace	Coonagh, Ireland	7.12.99P
G-ASMA	PA-30-160 Twin Comanche (Modified to C/R status)	30-143		17. 9.63	A.J.Mew & M.F.Oliver t/a Mike Alpha Group "Double Trouble"	White Waltham	5. 1.00
G-ASMC*	Hunting-Percival P.56 Provost T.1	PAC/F/417	XF908	19. 9.63	Not known (Stored 5.86)	Moenchengladbach, Germany	14. 2.72S
G-ASME	Bensen B.8M (Arrow GT500R)	12		24. 9.63	R.M.Harris & R.T.Bennett	Melrose Farm, Melbourne	11.12.99P
G-ASMF	Beechcraft D95A Travel Air	TD-565		26. 9.63	M.J.A.Hornblower	Southend	27. 5.99T
G-ASMJ	Reims Cessna F.172E (Wichita c/n 50584)	0029		25.10.63	A.J.G.Crawshaw	Sherburn	20. 5.01T
G-ASML	Phoenix Luton LA-4A Minor (VW1600)	PAL/1148 & PFA/802		28.10.63	R.Stanley	Fenland	20.12.99P
G-ASMM	Rollason-Druine D.31 Turbulent (Ardem 4C02)	PFA/1611		31.10.63	W.J. Browning "Mouche Miel"	(Ashtead)	1. 7.98P
G-ASMO*	PA-23-160 Apache G	23-1995	5N-AAU 5N-ADB/(N4473P)	30.10.63	Not known (Stored 7.96)	Wallington Green	14. 7.99T
G-ASMS	Cessna 150A	150-59204	N7104X	18.11.63	P.P.Connor	Barton	3.11.00
G-ASMT	Fairtravel Linnet 2	004		20.11.63	A.F.Cashin	Maypole Farm, Chislet	13. 7.99P
G-ASMU*	Cessna 150D	150-60252	N4252U	26.11.63	Not known (Damaged in gales Barton 13.2.89; on rebuild 1991)	(Moss-Side, Manchester)	3.11.85T
G-ASMV	Scintex CP.1310-C3 Super Emeraude	919		22.11.63	P.F.D.Waltham (Stored 10.97)	Leicester	7.11.94
G-ASMW	Cessna 150D	150-60247	N4247U	26.11.63	Yorkshire Light Aircraft Ltd	Leeds-Bradford	4. 9.97T
G-ASMY	PA-23-160 Apache H	23-2032	N4309Y	3.12.63	R.D. & E.Forster (Stored 9.97)	Swanton Morley	25.11.95T
G-ASMZ	Beagle A.61 Terrier 2 (Conversion of Auster AOP.10 c/n 2285)	B.629	G-35-11 VF516	4.12.63	R.C.Burden (As "VF516")	Bagby	20. 2.00
G-ASNB	Auster 6A Tugmaster	3725(2)	VX118	6.12.63	S.Alexander (As "VX118")	(Bromsgrove)	14. 1.02

Regn	Type	C/n	P/I	Date	Owner/operator	Probable Base	CA Expy
G-ASNC	Beagle D.5/180 Husky	3678		9.12.63	E.Brooks & R.Sharman Crowland t/a Peterborough & Spalding Gliding Club		16. 9.00
G-ASND	PA-23-250 Aztec	27-134	N4800P	10.12.63	H.C.Nabeel	Shoreham	23. 7.00T
G-ASNF	Ercoupe 415CD	4754	PH-NCF NC94647	11.12.63	C.R.Weldon	Dublin	2. 7.73
G-ASNG*	DH.104 Dove 6	04485	(EI-BJW)	(Crashed Bodmin 15.6.73; on rebuild 1993 with major parts from OO-JPB c/n 4777) 16.12.63 Not known (On fire dump 8.93) Waterford G-ASNG/HB-LFF/G-ASNG/HB-LFF/G-ASNG/PH-IOM		18.11.80P
G-ASNH	PA-23-250 Aztec B	27-2486		17.12.63	The Earl of Suffolk & Berkshire & J.Hoerner Charlton Park, Malmesbury		20. 6.99
G-ASNI	Scintex CP.1310-C3 Super Emeraude	925		20.12.63	D.Chapman	Wickenby	6. 2.99
G-ASNK	Cessna 205	205-0400	N8400Z	27.12.63	Justgold Ltd (Op Blackpool Air Centre)	Blackpool	18. 7.99T
G-ASNN*	Cessna 182F Skylane	182-55012	N3612U	27.12.63	Manchester Free-Fall Parachute Club Tilstock (Damaged nr Whitchurch, Shropshire 5.1.85; para-trainer use 5.97)		3. 5.85
G-ASNU*	HS.125 Srs.1	25005	D-COMA (D-CFKG)/G-ASNU	9. 1.64	Not known Lagos, Nigeria (Impounded at Lagos through ownership dispute)		5. 1.84
G-ASNW	Reims Cessna F.172E (Wichita c/n 50613)	0031		13. 1.64	B.M.Tremain Draycott Farm, Chiseldon t/a G-ASNW Grp		5. 4.01
G-ASNY*	Campbell-Bensen B.8M (McCulloch 4318A)	RCA/203		15. 1.64	R Light & T.Smith (Rebuilt 2.99)	Stockport	16. 3.70P
G-ASOC	Auster 6A Tugmaster	2544	VF603	21. 1.64	D.J.Moore Sandhill Farm, Shrivenham		20.12.97
G-ASOH	Beechcraft 95-B55A Baron	TC-656		31. 1.64	G.S.Goodsir t/a GMD Grp Biggin Hill		26. 2.01
G-ASOI	Beagle A.61 Terrier 2	B.627	G-35-11 WJ404	31. 1.64	N.K. & C.M.Geddes t/a Ranfurly Flying Group South Barnbeth Farm, Bridge of Weir		19. 6.98
G-ASOK	Reims Cessna F.172E	0057		31. 1.64	D.P. Magnus t/a The Okay F/Grp Denham		9. 8.99
G-ASOL*	Bell 47D-1	4	N146B	31. 1.64	The Helicopter Museum Weston-super-Mare (Stored 8.97)		6. 9.71
G-ASOM	Beagle A.61 Terrier 2	B.622	G-JETS G-ASOM/G-35-11/VF505	3. 2.64	S.J.Tootell	Booker	15. 3.99
G-ASON*	PA-30-160 Twin Comanche	30-312	(N7273Y)	4. 2.64	Not known (On rebuild 12.97) Elstree		30.11.91T
G-ASOX	Cessna 205A	205-0556	N4856U	13. 2.64	A.Turnbull (Status uncertain) Newcastle		1. 8.92
G-ASPF	Jodel-Wassmer D.120 Paris-Nice	02	F-BFNP	26. 2.64	T.J.Bates Dairy House Farm, Nantwich		19. 6.99P
G-ASPI	Reims Cessna F.172E	0050		26. 2.64	J.A.M.Anthony t/a Icarus F/Grp Rochester		17. 4.00
G-ASPK	PA-28-140 Cherokee	28-20051		28. 2.64	Westward Airways (Lands End) Ltd St.Just		21. 1.99T
G-ASPP	Bristol Boxkite Replica (Cont O-200-B) (Also c/n BOX.1)	BM.7279	(BAPC2)	29.10.81	The Shuttleworth Trust "No.12A" (No external registration) Old Warden		2. 5.99P
G-ASPS	Piper J3C-90 Cub (Frame No.21971)	22809	N3571N NC3571N	2. 3.64	A.J.Chalkley Rhoshirwaun, Pwllheli		19. 5.99P
G-ASPU	Druine D.31 Turbulent (VW1500)	PFA/1623		4. 3.64	C.R.Steer Spilsted Farm, Sedlescombe (Damaged Hurst Green, E.Sussex 8.10.95)		16. 8.96P
G-ASPV(2)	DH.82A Tiger Moth	84167	T7794	5. 3.64	B.S.Charters Bensons Farm, Laindon (Identity obscure - original G-ASPV sold to Norway 7.75 & rebuilt as LN-MAX)		31. 8.97
G-ASRB	Rollason-Druine D.62B Condor	RAE/608		11. 3.64	T.J.McRae & H.C.Palmer Shoreham		1.11.98
G-ASRC	Rollason-Druine D.62C Condor	RAE/609		11. 3.64	O.R.Pluck Lower Mountpleasant Farm, Chatteris		27.10.98P
G-ASRH	PA-30-160 Twin Comanche	30-368		19. 3.64	Island Avn & Travel Ltd Chester		13. 3.99
G-ASRI*	PA-23-250 Aztec B	27-2352	N5287Y	24. 3.64	Witney Technical College Witney (Instructional airframe 1.96)		30. 8.87A
G-ASRK	Beagle A.109 Airedale	B.538		26. 3.64	R.K.Wilson & M.R.H.Wheatley Warboys, Huntingdon		2. 6.01
G-ASRO	PA-30-160 Twin Comanche	30-395		31. 3.64	D.W.Blake Halfpenny Green t/a Five Star F/Grp		5. 6.99
G-ASRP*	SAN Jodel DR.1050 Ambassadeur	64	F-BITI	1. 4.64	S.Bichan Aboyne (Ditched in Swanbister Bay, Orkney 17.3.86; on rebuild 10.94; cancelled as wfu 20.1.99)		4.11.86
G-ASRR	Cessna 182G Skylane	182-55135	(G-CBIL) EI-ATF/G-ASRR/N3735U	2. 4.64	Mid-Anglia Flying School Ltd Cambridge		4. 8.97T
G-ASRT	SAN Jodel 150 Mascaret	45		6. 4.64	P.Turton (Status uncertain) Welshpool		3. 6.94P
G-ASRW	PA-28-180 Cherokee B	28-1606		21. 4.64	MK Aero Support Ltd Andrewsfield		8. 6.00T
G-ASSB*	PA-30-160 Twin Comanche	30-432		22. 4.64	Brooklands Technical College Brooklands (Instructional airframe 3.94)		11. 3.93T
G-ASSE	PA-22-108 Colt	22-9832	(N5961Z)	28. 4.64	A.Ingold (Birmingham) t/a G-ASSE Flying Group		12. 6.00
G-ASSF	Cessna 182G Skylane	182-55593	N2493R	5. 5.64	B.W.Wells Baxterley		5. 3.01
G-ASSM*	HS.125 Srs 1/522	25010	5N-AMK G-ASSM	5. 5.64	The Science Museum (Flight Gallery) South Kensington, London		
G-ASSP	PA-30-160 Twin Comanche	30-458		7. 5.64	P.H.Tavener Redhill		6. 1.00
G-ASSS	Cessna 172E	172-51467	N5567T	7. 5.64	D.H.N.Squires & P.R.March Bristol/Lulsgate		27. 5.00
G-ASST	Cessna 150D	150-60630	N5930T	7. 5.64	F.R.H.Parker Pear Tree Farm, Marsh Gibbon, Bicester		15. 7.01
G-ASSV	Kensinger KF (Cont C85)	02	N23S	11. 5.64	C.I.Jefferson Hingham, Norfolk (Crashed Halfpenny Green 2.7.69; on rebuild 9.97)		30. 7.69P
G-ASSW	PA-28-140 Cherokee	28-20055		11. 5.64	W.G.R.Wunderlich Biggin Hill		7. 5.01
G-ASSY	Druine D.31 Turbulent (VW1500)	PFA/586		12. 5.64	D.Silsbury (Ivybridge)		20. 4.84P

Regn	Type	C/n	P/I	Date	Owner/operator	Probable Base	CA Expy
G-ASTA	Druine D.31 Turbulent (Ardem 4C02)	152	F-PJGH	12. 5.64	P.A.Cooke	RAF Brize Norton	13.11.97P
G-ASTG	Nord 1002 Pingouin II	183	F-BGKI Fr.AF 183	21. 5.64	L.M.Walton (On rebuild by The Aircraft Restoration Co 1.99)	Duxford	26.10.73S
G-ASTI	Auster 6A Tugmaster	3745	WJ359	27. 5.64	R.B.Webber (To revert to AOP.6 c/s as "WJ359" in 1999)	Tatenhill	21. 7.99P
G-ASTL*	Fairey Firefly 1	F.5607	SE-BRD Z2033	1. 6.64	Imperial War Museum - Skyfame Collection "Evelyn Tentions" (As "Z2033/275/N" in 1771 Sqn RN c/s)	Duxford	
G-ASTP*	Hiller UH-12C	1045	N9750C	4. 6.64	The Helicopter Museum Weston-super-Mare (Under restoration 8.98)		3. 7.82
G-ASUA*	Nord 1002 Pingouin	248	F-BFDY	23. 6.64	L.M.Walton Long Sutton, Kings Lynn (Crashed Elstree 30.7.64; in store)		28. 7.65
G-ASUB	Mooney M.20E Super 21	397	N7158U	24. 6.64	S.C.Coulbeck	North Coates	17.11.00
G-ASUD	PA-28-180 Cherokee B	28-1654		29. 6.64	S.J.Rogers & M.N.Petchey	Andrewsfield	23. 7.00
G-ASUE	Cessna 150D	150-60718	N6018T	30. 6.64	D.Huckle (Stored 6.94)	West Thurrock	1. 8.90
G-ASUG*	Beechcraft E18S-9700	BA-111	N575C N555CB/N24R	3. 7.64	Royal Museum of Scotland, Museum of Flight (Loganair c/s)	East Fortune	23. 7.75
G-ASUH*	Reims Cessna F.172E	0070		6. 7.64	Not known (Fuselage in open store 7.95)	Clacton	14. 4.78
G-ASUI	Beagle A.61 Terrier 2 (Conversion of Auster AOP.10 c/n 2570)	B.641	VF628	6. 7.64	R.J.Bentley (Nenagh, Co Tipperary)		25.7.99
G-ASUL	Cessna 182G Skylane	182-55077	N3677U	9. 7.64	Blackpool & Fylde A/C Ltd	Blackpool	27. 1.01
G-ASUP	Reims Cessna F.172E	0071		22. 7.64	P.T. & L.E.Trivett t/a G-ASUP Air	Cardiff	8. 6.00
G-ASUR	Dornier Do.28A-1	3051	D-IBOM	28. 7.64	P.R.Dyson (Sold 5.97)	Thruxton	13. 4.00
G-ASUS	Jurca MJ.2E Tempete (Cont O-200-A)	PFA/2001		28. 7.64	D.G.Jones	Coventry	2. 8.99P
G-ASVG	Rousseau Piel CP.301B Emeraude	109	F-BILV	7. 8.64	K.S.Woodard Priory Farm, Tibenham "Emma II"		7. 4.98P
G-ASVM	Reims Cessna F.172E	0077		11. 8.64	J.F.Henderson (Uckfield) t/a Golf Victor Mike F/Grp		30.12.99
G-ASVN	Cessna 206 Super Skywagon	206-0275	N5275U	12. 8.64	L.Rawson	Langar	21. 2.00
G-ASVO	HPR.7 Dart Herald 214	185	PP-SDG G-ASVO/G-8-3	13. 8.64	Dart Group plc Bournemouth t/a Channel Express (Stored 6.97)		14. 1.00T
G-ASVP	PA-25-235 Pawnee	25-2978		17. 8.64	Aquila Gliding Club Ltd Hinton-in-the-Hedges		23. 5.99
G-ASVZ	PA-28-140 Cherokee	28-20357		24. 8.64	J.S.Garvey	(Telford)	3. 7.00
G-ASWB*	Beagle A.109 Airedale	B.543		25. 8.64	A.E.F.Bryant (Nottingham) (Cancelled by CAA 10.6.98 with CofA expired)		27. 6.97
G-ASWH	Phoenix Luton LA.5A Major (Walter Mikron 2)	PAL/1225		31. 8.64	J.T.Powell-Tuck (Pontypool) (Damaged nr Turnworth, Dorset 3.7.77; on rebuild 1991)		22. 6.78S
G-ASWJ*	Beagle B.206 Srs.1	B.009	8449M G-ASWJ	9. 9.64	Midland Air Museum Ashley Down, Bristol (On loan to Brunel Technical College 11.95)		30. 1.75
G-ASWL	Reims Cessna F.172F	0087		10. 9.64	J.A.Clegg	(Swansea)	2. 7.00
G-ASWN	Bensen B.8M	14		15. 9.64	D.R.Shepherd (Not constructed)	(Prestwick)	
G-ASWP	Beechcraft A23 Musketeer II	M-587		22. 9.64	J.Holden & G.Benet (Hastings) (Damaged Sedlescombe 5.3.94; status uncertain)		27. 4.95
G-ASWW	PA-30-160 Twin Comanche	30-556	N7531Y	1.10.64	R.Jenkins t/a RJ Motors	Bournemouth	1. 7.00
G-ASWX	PA-28-180 Cherokee C	28-1932		1.10.64	A.F.Dadds	Biggin Hill	16. 4.00
G-ASXC	SIPA 903 (Cont C90)	8	F-BEYK	6.10.64	M.K.Dartford & M.Cookson Andrewsfield (Stored 4.95)		28. 7.94P
G-ASXD	Brantly B.2B	435		7.10.64	Lousada plc Crawley Park, Husborne Crawley, Bedford (Stored 7.98)		28. 9.99
G-ASXF*	Brantly 305	1014		7.10.64	Binfield, Bracknell		
G-ASXI	Cobelavia Tipsy T.66 Nipper 3 (Jabiru 2200A)	56	VH-CGH OO-KOC/(VH-CGC)	13.10.64	S.C.M.Defries Stapleford t/a Stapleford Nipper Group		21. 8.98P
G-ASXJ	Phoenix Luton LA-4A Minor (Lyc O-145)	PFA/801		14.10.64	M.R.Sallows Damyns Hall, Upminster "Pride & Joy"		10. 2.99P
G-ASXR	Cessna 210 Centurion	57532	5Y-KPW VP-KPW/N6532X	16.10.64	A.Schofield (On rebuild 12.97)	Barton	3. 1.93
G-ASXS	SAN Jodel DR.1050 Ambassadeur	133	F-BJNG	19.10.64	R.A.Hunter	Finmere	30. 6.00
G-ASXU	Jodel Wassmer D.120A Paris-Nice	196	F-BKAG	19.10.64	D.M.Garrett t/a The Jodel Group	Defford	16.11.98P
G-ASXX*	Avro 683 Lancaster B.VII	-	WU-15 Fr.Navy/NX611	22.10.64	F.Panton/Lincolnshire Avn Heritage Centre (Allocated 8375M)	East Kirkby	

("NX611/LE-C" in 630 Sqdn c/s "City of Sheffield" stbd side and "NX611/DX-C" in 57 Sqdn c/s "Just Jane" port side)

Regn	Type	C/n	P/I	Date	Owner/operator	Probable Base	CA Expy
G-ASXY	SAN Jodel D.117A	914	F-BIVA	27.10.64	P.A., R.A.Davies & D.G.Claxton	Cardiff	21.12.99P
G-ASXZ	Cessna 182G Skylane	182-55738	N3238S	28.10.64	P.M.Robertson	Perth	14. 4.00
G-ASYD*	BAC One-Eleven 475AM	BAC.053		9.11.64	Brooklands Museum	Brooklands	13. 7.94
G-ASYG	Beagle A.61 Terrier 2	B.637	VX927	3.11.64	G.Rea (On rebuild 1.95)	Turweston	19. 2.70T
G-ASYJ	Beechcraft D95A Travel Air	TD-595	N8675Q	6.11.64	Crosby Avn (Jersey) Ltd	Jersey	20. 9.01
G-ASYN*	Beagle A.61 Terrier 2	2288 & B.634	VF519	16.11.64	A.A.Marshall (Damaged Netherthorpe 2.1.76; stored 2.96) Yeatsall Farm, Abbots Bromley		28. 3.76
G-ASYP	Cessna 150E	150-60794	N6094T	23.11.64	A.C.Melmore t/a Henlow F/Grp	RAF Henlow	28. 8.00
G-ASZB	Cessna 150E	150-61113	N3013J	16.12.64	T.W.R.Case	Blackbushe	1. 4.01
G-ASZD	Bolkow Bo.208A2 Junior	563	D-ENKI	16.12.64	M.J.Ayres	(York)	23. 6.98P

Regn	Type	C/n	P/I	Date	Owner/operator	Probable Base	CA Expy
G-ASZE	Beagle A.61 Terrier 2	B.636	VF552	17.12.64	P.J.Moore	RAF Leuchars	11. 8.99
	(Conversion of Auster 6 c/n 2510)						
G-ASZJ	Short SC.7 Skyvan 3A Var.100	SH.1831		31.12.64	Trygon Ltd	Weston-on-the-Green	18.12.98A
G-ASZR	Fairtravel Linnet 2	005		5. 1.65	K.H.Bunt & R.Palmer		
						Swanborough Farm, Lewes	29. 3.99P
G-ASZS	Gardan GY-80-160 Horizon	70		6. 1.65	L.R.Burton t/a ZS Group		
						Wellesbourne Mountford	5.11.01
G-ASZU	Cessna 150E	150-61152	N3052J	13. 1.65	T.H.Milburn	Cranfield	13. 3.99
G-ASZV	Tipsy T.66 Nipper 2	45	5N-ADE	14. 1.65	R.L.Mitcham	Little Gransden	23. 5.90P
	(VW1835)		5N-ADY/VR-NDD		(Stored 3.97)		
G-ASZX	Beagle A.61 Terrier 1	3742	(SE-ELO)	18. 1.65	C.A.Bailey	Hayrish Farm, Okehampton	24. 2.90
			WJ368		(Damaged Verdun, France c.6.89; on rebuild 7.97)		

G-ATAA-ATZZ

Regn	Type	C/n	P/I	Date	Owner/operator	Probable Base	CA Expy
G-ATAF	Reims Cessna F.172F	0135		25. 1.65	P.J. Thirtle	(Beverley)	6. 5.01
G-ATAG	CEA Jodel DR.1050 Ambassadeur	226	F-BKGG	25. 1.65	T.M.Dawes-Gamble	Oxford	16. 6.99
G-ATAH*	Cessna 336 Skymaster	336-0007	N1707Z	26. 1.65	Not known	Farley Farm, Romsey	5.12.76
					(Open storage 3.92)		
G-ATAS	PA-28-180 Cherokee C	28-2137		4. 2.65	C.L.Hawkins	(Woodford Green)	30. 7.00
G-ATAU	Rollason-Druine D.62B Condor	RAE/610		10. 2.65	M.A.Peare	White Waltham	19. 8.99
					t/a Golf Alpha Uniform Group		
G-ATAV	Rollason-Druine D.62C Condor	RAE/611		10. 2.65	R.W.H.Watson (Stored 4.97)	Kilkerran	6. 8.94
G-ATBG	Nord 1002 Pingouin II	121	F-BGVX	24. 2.65	L.M.Walton		3. 6.98P
			F-OTAN-5/Fr.Mil		(As "NJ+C11" in Luftwaffe c/s)		
G-ATBH	CZL Aero 145	172015		24. 2.65	P.D.Aviram	Kingston-upon-Thames	26.10.81
					(On rebuild 1997)		
G-ATBI	Beechcraft A23 Musketeer II	M-696		26. 2.65	R.F.C.Dent	Gloucestershire	2. 6.00
G-ATBJ	Sikorsky S-61N	61-269		12. 3.65	Brintel Helicopters Ltd	Sumburgh	2. 6.00T
		(Possibly ex N10043)			t/a British International Helicopters		
G-ATBL	DH.60G Moth	1917	HB-OBA	2. 3.65	J.M.Greenland		
	(Gipsy I)		CH-353			Blackacre Farm, Holt, Wilts	23. 7.98P
G-ATBP	Alpavia Fournier RF3	59		11. 3.65	D.McNicholl	Inverness	8. 7.99
G-ATBS	Druine D.31 Turbulent	PFA/1620		16. 3.65	D.R.Keene & J.A.Lear	Wheatley, Oxon	21.10.99P
	(VW1500)				"Fly Baby Fly"		
G-ATBU	Beagle A.61 Terrier 2	B.635	VF611	17. 3.65	D.M.Snape t/a K9 Flying Group	(Derby)	2. 6.99
	(Conversion of Auster 6 c/n 2552)						
G-ATBW	Cobelavia Tipsy T.66 Nipper 2	52	OO-MAG	19. 3.65	S.C.M.Defries	Stapleford	14. 7.99P
	(VW1834/ACRO)				t/a Stapleford Nipper Grp		
G-ATBX	PA-20-135 Pacer	20-904	VP-KRX	19. 3.65	G.D. & P.M.Thomson	Coventry	13. 6.91
			VR-TCH/VP-KKE		(Stored 5.92)		
G-ATBZ*	Westland Wessex 60 Srs.1	WA/461	G-17-4	22. 3.65	The Helicopter Museum	Weston-super-Mare	5.12.81
			G-ATBZ				
G-ATCC	Beagle A.109 Airedale	B.542		25. 3.65	J.R.Bowden	Biggin Hill	13.10.01
G-ATCD	Beagle D.5/180 Husky	3683		25. 3.65	D.J.O'Gorman	Enstone	12. 3.00
G-ATCE	Cessna U206 Super Skywagon	U206-0380	N2180F	25. 3.65	D.Turner & D.T.Hickling	Langar	22. 5.99
					t/a British Parachute Schools		
G-ATCJ	Phoenix Luton LA-4A Minor	PAL/1163 & PFA/812		5. 4.65	T.N.Farley	(Malvern)	18. 2.99P
	(VW1600)						
G-ATCL	Victa Airtourer 100	93		5. 4.65	A.D.Goodall	Cardiff	23. 4.99
G-ATCN	Phoenix Luton LA-4A Minor	PAL/1118		7. 4.65	J.C.Gates & C.Neilson		
	(Lyc O-145)				Comarques Farm, Thorpe-Le-Soken	26. 6.99P
G-ATCU	Cessna 337 Super Skymaster	337-0133	N2233X	22. 4.65	The Committee for Aerial Photography,		
					University of Cambridge	Cambridge	25. 4.99A
G-ATCX	Cessna 182H Skylane	182-55848	N3448S	26. 4.65	K.J.Fisher (See G-OLSC)	St.Merryn	14. 8.00
G-ATDA	PA-28-160 Cherokee	28-206	EI-AME	27. 4.65	J.Gosling t/a Portway Avn	(Hereford)	15. 5.99
			(G-ARUV)				
G-ATDB	SNCAN 1101 Noralpha	186	F-OTAN-6	27. 4.65	J.W.Hardie	Skelmorlie, Largs	22.11.78S
			Fr.Mil		(On rebuild 8.93)		
			(Nord 1101 as "F-OTAN-6" reported Barton 8.96 but believed to be G-BAYV)				
G-ATDN	Beagle A.61 Terrier 2	B.638	TW641	7. 5.65	Susan J.Saggers (As "TW641") Biggin Hill		8. 7.01T
	(Conversion of Auster 6 c/n 2499)						
G-ATDO	Bolkow Bo.208C Junior	576	D-EGZU	10. 5.65	H.Swift	Hill Farm, Marton, Hull	28. 3.99P
G-ATEF	Cessna 150E	150-61378	N3978U	25. 5.65	K.J.Scamp & A.J.White	Blackbushe	27.10.99
					t/a Swans Avn		
G-ATEM	PA-28-180 Cherokee C	28-2329		26. 5.65	Chiltern Valley Avn Ltd	Bovingdon	4. 2.01
G-ATEP*	EAA Biplane	PFA/1301		28. 5.65	E.L.Martin	Castle Farm, Guernsey	18. 6.73
	(Cont C75)				(Stored in poor condition 8.96)		
G-ATES*	PA-32-260 Cherokee Six	32-20		31. 5.65	Stirling Parachute Centre	??	11. 6.83
			(Crashed nr Kinglassie 8.2.81; front fuselage used as para-trainer 9.92)				
G-ATET	PA-30-160 Twin Comanche	30-770	N230ET	31. 5.65	S.J.Gaveston	Biggin Hill	27. 2.00
			G-ATET/N7749Y				
G-ATEV	CEA Jodel DR.1050 Ambassadeur	18	F-BJHL	31. 5.65	M.G.Cookson (On rebuild 1997)	(Epping)	13. 8.71
G-ATEW	PA-30-160 Twin Comanche	30-719	N7640Y	3. 6.65	J.C.White	Newcastle	9. 6.01
					t/a Air Northumbria Grp		
G-ATEX	Victa Airtourer 100	110	(VH-MTU)	3. 6.65	M.Dale	Rochester	30. 5.99
					t/a The Medway Victa Group		
G-ATEZ	PA-28-140 Cherokee	28-21044		8. 6.65	Lorch Airways (UK) Ltd	Norwich	3.12.99T
G-ATFD	CEA Jodel DR.1050 Ambassadeur	311	F-BKIM	14. 6.65	V.Usher	Carr Farm, Newark	1. 3.97
G-ATFF	PA-23-250 Aztec C	27-2898	N5769Y	16. 6.65	Neatspin Ltd	Tatenhill	10. 8.98
G-ATFG*	Brantly B.2B	448		16. 6.65	Acft Preservation Society of Scotland		
	(Composite with parts from G-ASLO/G-AXSR; displayed Museum of Flight 3.96)					East Fortune	25. 3.85
G-ATFM	Sikorsky S-61N Mk.II	61-270	CF-OKY	21. 6.65	Brintel Helicopters Ltd	Sumburgh	1.10.00T
		(Possibly initially N10052)			t/a British International Helicopters		
G-ATFR	PA-25-150 Pawnee	25-135	OY-ADJ	28. 6.65	Borders (Milfield) Gliding Club Ltd		
					Galewood Farm, Milfield	17. 4.00
G-ATFV*	Agusta-Bell 47J-2A Ranger	2093	9J-ACX	1. 7.65	Not known (Stored 9.93)	Caernarfon	8. 8.92T
			G-ATFV/MM80417				
G-ATFW	Phoenix Luton LA-4A Minor	PFA/811		2. 7.65	P.A.Rose	(Walney)	2.12.97P
	(Lyc O-145)						

Regn	Type	C/n	P/I	Date	Owner/operator	Probable Base	CA Expy
G-ATFX*	Reims Cessna F.172G	0196		8. 7.65	Not known		12. 2.92
	(Damaged Booker 25.1.90; displayed Redhill centre 7.97 - all-red/no marks for "Leprosy Awareness/Flight Aid")						
G-ATFY	Reims Cessna F.172G	0199		8. 7.65	H.Cowan	Kilkeel, Co.Down	25. 5.01
G-ATGE	SAN Jodel DR.1050 Ambassadeur	114	F-BJJF	9. 7.65	J.R.Roberts	Sherburn-in-Elmet	17. 2.01
G-ATGN*	Thorn K-800 Coal Gas Balloon	2		12. 7.65	British Balloon Museum "Eccles" (Stored)	Newbury	
G-ATGO	Reims Cessna F.172G	0181		12. 7.65	W.J.Baker	Bristol/Lulsgate	5. 5.01
G-ATGP	SAN Jodel DR.1050 Ambassadeur	122	F-BJNB	14. 7.65	G.W.Anderson & R.T.Bowden t/a Madley F/Grp	Shobdon	4. 2.01
G-ATGY	Gardan GY-80-160 Horizon	121		20. 7.65	P.W.Gibberson	Birmingham	21. 8.99
G-ATGZ	Griffiths GH-4 Gyroplane	G.1		20. 7.65	R.W.J.Cripps (Stored Shardlow,Derby 7.91)	Spondon, Derby	
G-ATHA*	PA-23-235 Apache	27-610	N4326Y	21. 7.65	Brunel Technical College (Instructional airframe 6.91)	Ashley Down, Bristol	7. 6.86
G-ATHD	DHC.1 Chipmunk 22	C1/0837	WP971 G-ATHD/WP971	26. 7.65	O.L.Cubitt & K.P.A.Lewis t/a Spartan F/Grp (As "WP971")	Denham	30.6.00
G-ATHI*	PA-28-180 Cherokee C	28-2545		2. 8.65	Dublin Institute of Technology	Bolton St, Dublin	
	(Crashed Castlebar, Co.Mayo 9.5.74; Instructional airframe 5.92)						
G-ATHK	Aeronca 7AC Champion (Cont A75)	7AC-971	N82339 NC82339	2. 8.65	T.P.McDonald, T.Crawley & E.Walker	Liverpool	26.10.74 3.11.98P
G-ATHM	Wallis WA-116/F (C/n 213 quoted)	402 & 211	4R-ACK G-ATHM	3. 8.65	Wallis Autogyros Ltd (Stored 8.97)	Reymerston Hall	23. 5.93P
G-ATHN*	SNCAN 1101 Noralpha	84	F-BFUZ Fr.Mil	5. 8.65	E.L.Martin (Stored 8.96)	St.Peter Port, Guernsey	27. 6.75S
G-ATHR	PA-28-180 Cherokee C	28-2343	EI-AOT	11. 8.65	Britannia Airways Ltd	Luton	10. 8.01T
G-ATHT	Victa Airtourer 115	120		16. 8.65	D.A.Beese	Badminton	7.10.99
G-ATHU	Beagle A.61 Terrier 1	AUS/127/FM	7435M WE539	16. 8.65	J.A.L.Irwin	Park Farm, Eaton Bray	7. 9.01
G-ATHV	Cessna 150F	150-62019	N8719S	16. 8.65	D.Hutchinson	Sherburn	2. 2.00
G-ATHX	SAN Jodel DR.100A Ambassadeur	74	F-OBMM	17. 8.65	W.R.Prescott t/a Mourne F/C	Kilkeel, Co.Down	2. 6.99
G-ATHZ	Cessna 150F	150-61586	(EI-AOP) N6286R	20. 8.65	E. & R.D.Forster (Op Norfolk & Norwich A/C)	Beccles	27.3.98T
G-ATIA	PA-24-260 Comanche	24-4049	N8650P	20. 8.65	L.A.Brown t/a The India Alpha Partnership	Leicester	16. 6.01
G-ATIC	CEA Jodel DR.1050 Ambassadeur	6	F-BJCJ	23. 8.65	R.E.Major (St.Agnes, Cornwall) (On overhaul 1993)		1. 6.81
G-ATID	Cessna 337 Super Skymaster	337-0239	N6239F	24. 8.65	Not known (Caldas Da Rainha, Portugal) (Temp unregd 7.7.97)		6. 1.97
G-ATIE*	Cessna 150F	150-61591	N6291R	24. 8.65	Staffordshire Sports Skydiving Club	Chetwynd, Shropshire	7 .9.81
	(Crashed nr Shobdon 28.7.79; fuselage as para-trainer 4.97; abandoned ?)						
G-ATIG*	HPR.7 Dart Herald 214	177	PP-SDI G-ATIG	25. 8.65	Nordic Oil Services Ltd (Stored 7.97)	Norwich	14.10.97T
G-ATIN	SAN Jodel D.117	437	F-BHNV	8. 9.65	G.G.Simpson (Stored 4.97)	Muirhouses Farm, Errol	18. 4.96P
G-ATIR	AIA Stampe SV-4C	1047	F-BNMC	9. 9.65	N.M.Bloom	Abbots Hill Farm, Hemel Hempstead	29. 6.00
	G-ATIR/F-BMKQ/Aeronavale/F-BCDM/Aeronavale						
G-ATIS	PA-28-160 Cherokee C	28-2713		9. 9.65	R.M.Jenner & J.H.Peploe	Draycott Farm, Chiseldon	8. 1.00
G-ATIZ	SAN Jodel D.117	636	F-BIBR	15. 9.65	D.K.Shipton (Peterborough) (Damaged Leicester 30.6.95; sold as "wreck" 5.96)		13. 6.96P
G-ATJA	SAN Jodel DR.1050 Ambassadeur	378	F-BKHL	15. 9.65	D.A.Head & G.W.Cunningham t/a Bicester F/Grp	RAF Bicester	14. 9.99
G-ATJC	Victa Airtourer 100	125		16. 9.65	Aviation West Ltd	Cumbernauld	18. 9.00T
G-ATJF*	PA-28-140 Cherokee	28-21283		20. 9.65	Not known (Crashed Corcubion, Spain 29.8.79; fuselage stored 3.89)	Sabadell, Spain	16. 6.82
G-ATJG	PA-28-140 Cherokee	28-21299		20. 9.65	H.M.Wittmann (Ebersdorf, Germany)		4. 7.99
G-ATJL	PA-24-260 Comanche	24-4203	N8752P	23. 9.65	M.J.Berry & T.R.Quinn	Blackbushe	20. 5.00
G-ATJM	Fokker DR.1 Triplane replica (Siemens SH-14A-165)	002	N78001 EI-APY/G-ATJM	23. 9.65	R.J.Lamplough (As DR1 "152/17") (Stored 10.97)	North Weald	10. 9.93P
G-ATJN	Dormois Jodel D.119	863	F-PINZ	23. 9.65	R.F.Bradshaw	Valley Farm, Winwick	27. 5.99P
G-ATJR*	PA-E23-250 Aztec C	27-3033	N5881Y	30. 9.65	Not known (Stored 11.97)	(Manchester)	23. 7.95
G-ATJT	Gardan GY-80-160 Horizon	108		4.10.65	N.Huxtable	Cheddington	21. 5.99
G-ATJV	PA-32-260 Cherokee Six	32-103	TF-GOS G-ATJV	7.10.65	Wingglider Ltd.	Leeds-Bradford	17. 5.95
G-ATKF	Cessna 150F	150-62386	N3586L	20.10.65	C.J.Freeman	Headcorn	10.7.00T
G-ATKG*	Hiller UH-12B	496	Thai AF 103	21.10.65	Not known (Stored 1.96)	Maltby, Cleveland	28.11.69
G-ATKH	Phoenix Luton LA-4A Minor (Lyc O-145)	PFA/809		25.10.65	H.E.Jenner (Stored 1.96)	Brenchley, Kent	24. 6.92P
G-ATKI	Piper J3C-75 Cub	17545	N70536 NC70536	25.10.65	P.H.Wilmot-Allistone (Taunton) (Overturned taxying Enstone 14.11.93; on rebuild 8.97)		29. 4.94P
G-ATKT	Reims Cessna F.172G	0206		9.11.65	P.J.Megson	Goodwood	13. 2.02
G-ATKU	Reims Cessna F.172G	0232		9.11.65	Holdcroft Avn Svs Ltd (On rebuild 1.97)	Popham	31. 1.95T
G-ATKV*	Westland WS-55 Whirlwind 3				See VR-BEU in SECTION 5		

Regn	Type	C/n	P/I	Date	Owner/operator	Probable Base	CA Expy
G-ATKX	SAN Jodel D.140C Mousquetaire III	163		19.11.65	A.J.White & G.A.Piper (Op Acebell Avn)	Redhill	30. 3.01T
G-ATKZ	Cobelavia Tipsy T.66 Nipper 2 (VW1834)	72		24.11.65	M.W.Knights Blue Tile Farm, Hindolveston		3.11.99P
G-ATLA	Cessna 182J Skylane	182-56923	N2823F	24.11.65	Wilsons of Clifton Ltd	Cranfield	20. 8.99
G-ATLB	SAN Jodel DR.1050/M1 Excellence	78	F-BIVG	29.11.65	B.Lumb t/a La Petit Oiseau Syndicate	Breighton	17. 7.99
G-ATLH*	Fewsdale Tigercraft Gyroplane	F.T5		6.12.65	Not known (Under restoration 2.99)	Thornaby-on-Tees	
G-ATLM	Reims Cessna F.172G	0252		6.12.65	Air Fotos Avn Ltd	Newcastle	3. 3.00T
G-ATLP	Bensen B.8M (McCulloch 4318F)	17		9.12.65	C.D.Julian "Chris"	St.Merryn	19. 5.97P
G-ATLT	Cessna U206A Super Skywagon	U206-0523	N4823F	13.12.65	A.I.M & A.J. Guest	Dunkeswell	24. 5.99T
G-ATLV	Jodel Wassmer D.120 Paris-Nice	224	F-BKNQ	15.12.65	L.S.Thorne	Shenstone Hall Farm, Shenstone	8. 7.99P
G-ATLW	PA-28-180 Cherokee C	28-2877		17.12.65	R.D.Masters (Damaged - struck by D.117 G-ATIZ landing Leicester 30.6.95)	Rush Green	13. 7.95
G-ATMC	Reims Cessna F.150F (Wichita c/n 62849)	0020		28.12.65	C.J. & E.J.Leigh	Audley End	5. 1.01
G-ATMH	Beagle D.5/180 Husky	3684		3. 1.66	Dorset Gliding Club Ltd	Gallows Hill	13. 8.00
G-ATMI	HS.748 Srs.2A/225	1592	VP-LIU	4. 1.66	Emerald Airways Ltd (Reed Avn c/s) "Old Ben" G-ATMI/VP-LIU/G-ATMI/VP-LIU/G-ATMI/VP-LIU/G-ATMI	Liverpool	18. 5.00T
G-ATMJ	HS.748 Srs.2A/225	1593	VP-LAJ	4. 1.66	Emerald Airways Ltd G-ATMJ/6Y-JFJ/G-ATMJ	Exeter	7. 9.00T
G-ATML	Reims Cessna F.150F (Wichita c/n 62722)	0014		6. 1.66	G.I.Smith	(York)	28. 9.01
G-ATMM	Reims Cessna F.150F (Wichita c/n 62775)	0016		6. 1.66	C.J.Freeman	Headcorn	9. 6.01T
G-ATMT	PA-30-160 Twin Comanche	30-439	XW938 N7385Y	10. 1.66	Montagu-Smith & Co Ltd	Turweston	11. 7.99
G-ATMU	PA-23-160 Apache G	23-2000	N4478P	11. 1.66	P.K.Martin & R.W.Harris (Stored 10.97)	Beccles	14. 4.90T
G-ATMW	PA-28-140 Cherokee	28-21486		11. 1.66	Bencray Ltd t/a Blackpool & Fylde A/C	Blackpool	27. 1.01T
G-ATMY	Cessna 150F	150-62642	SE-ETD N8542G	13. 1.66	J.A.Starbuck	Crosland Moor	20. 6.01
G-ATNB	PA-28-180 Cherokee C	28-3057		20. 1.66	G.Taylor	Woodford	31. 3.00
G-ATNE	Reims Cessna F.150F (Wichita c/n 63252)	0042		20. 1.66	J. & S.Brew	Leicester	11. 9.00
G-ATNL	Reims Cessna F.150F (Wichita c/n 63652)	0066		25. 1.66	M.Kemp & D.Plant t/a G-ATNL F/Grp	Popham	4. 7.99
G-ATNV	PA-24-260 Comanche	24-4350	N8896P	28. 1.66	B.S.Reynolds & P.R.Fortescue (Stored 5.97)	Bourn	3. 7.93
G-ATOA	PA-23-160 Apache G	23-1954	N4437P	31. 1.66	K.A.Passmore	Stapleford	18.12.98
G-ATOD	Reims Cessna F.150F (Wichita c/n 62342)	0003		1. 2.66	J.H.A.Boyns, E.Watson & G.Bold	St.Just	2. 7.99
G-ATOE	Reims Cessna F.150F (Wichita c/n 63096)	0031		1. 2.66	J.A.Richardson	(London NW10)	25. 8.01
G-ATOF*	Reims Cessna F.150F (Wichita c/n 63582)	0063		1. 2.66	Air Service Training Ltd (Crashed nr Perth 25.11.71; on fire dump 2.96)	Perth	22. 7.73
G-ATOH	Rollason-Druine D.62B Condor RAE/612			3. 2.66	T.A.Bridge t/a Three Spires Flying Group	Lichfield	11. 6.99P
G-ATOI	PA-28-140 Cherokee	28-21556		3. 2.66	R.W.Nash	RAF Brize Norton	27. 3.99
G-ATOJ	PA-28-140 Cherokee	28-21584		3. 2.66	A Flight Avn Ltd	Prestwick	2. 7.00T
G-ATOK	PA-28-140 Cherokee	28-21612		3. 2.66	G.T.S.Done & P.R.Harrison t/a ILC F/Grp	White Waltham	14.12.00
G-ATOL	PA-28-140 Cherokee	28-21626		3. 2.66	L.J.Nation & G.Alford t/a G-ATOL F/Grp	Cardiff	23. 1.98
G-ATOM	PA-28-140 Cherokee	28-21640		3. 2.66	A Flight Avn Ltd	Prestwick	20. 7.01T
G-ATON	PA-28-140 Cherokee	28-21654		3. 2.66	R.G.Walters	Shobdon	10. 8.98
G-ATOO	PA-28-140 Cherokee	28-21668		3. 2.66	I.Wilson (On rebuild 12.92)	(Stanley, Co.Durham)	24. 9.84
G-ATOP	PA-28-140 Cherokee	28-21682		3. 2.66	P.R.Coombs t/a The Aero 80 F/Grp	Popham	16. 5.99
G-ATOR	PA-28-140 Cherokee	28-21696		3. 2.66	D.Palmer & V.G.Whitehead	Shobdon	18. 5.00
G-ATOT	PA-28-180 Cherokee C	28-3061		3. 2.66	Totair Ltd	Shipdham	22. 6.00T
G-ATOU	Mooney M.20E Super 21	961	N5946Q	3. 2.66	A.C. Mate t/a M20 F/Grp	Sherburn	28. 5.00
G-ATOY*	PA-24-260 Comanche B (Crashed nr Elstree 6.3.79; fuselage displayed)	24-4346	N8893P	7. 2.66	Royal Museum of Scotland/Museum of Flight "Myth Too"	East Fortune	
G-ATOZ	Bensen B.8M (Rotax 503)	18		7. 2.66	N.C.White & W.Stark (Substantially rebuilt in 1986, original airframe stored at Wimborne)	Portmoak	6. 7.99P
G-ATPD	HS.125 Srs.1B/522	25085	5N-AGU G-ATPD	11. 2.66	Wessex Air (Holdings) Ltd	Bournemouth	14.10.98T
G-ATPN	PA-28-140 Cherokee	28-21899		18. 2.66	R.W.Harris, M.F.Hatt, P.E.Preston & A.Jahanfar (Op Southend F/C)	Southend	20. 3.99T
G-ATPT	Cessna 182J Skylane	182-57056	N2956F	22. 2.66	G.B.Scholes t/a Papa Tango Grp	Elstree	11. 8.01
G-ATPV	Barritault JB.01 Minicab (Cont C90) (Rebuild of GY-20 F-PHUC c/n A.155)	0T	F-PJKA	22. 2.66	C.F.O'Niell (Stored 6.97)	Newtownards	28. 4.99P

Regn	Type	C/n	P/I	Date	Owner/operator	Probable Base	CA Expy
G-ATRG	PA-18-180 Super Cub	18-7764	5B-CAB N4985Z	1. 3.66	Lasham Gliding Society Ltd	Lasham	31. 5.98
G-ATRI	Bolkow Bo.208C Junior	602	D-ECGY	3. 3.66	A.A.W.Stevens	Cumbernauld	4. 8.97
G-ATRK	Reims Cessna F.150F (Wichita c/n 63381)	0049	(G-ATNC)	4. 3.66	G.G. & J.G.Armstrong t/a Armstrong Aviation	Wigtown Baldoon	11. 9.98
G-ATRL*	Reims Cessna F.150F (Wichita c/n 63382)	0050		4. 3.66	S.S.Delwarte t/a G-ATRL F/Grp (Wfu and stored 10.97 - see G-AVHM)	Shoreham	21. 2.98
G-ATRM	Reims Cessna F.150F (Wichita c/n 63454)	0053	(G-ATNJ)	4. 3.66	J.Redfearn	(Bishop Auckland)	29.11.00T
G-ATRO	PA-28-140 Cherokee	28-21871		4. 3.66	F.E.Ward t/a 390th F/Grp	Framlingham	7. 7.00
G-ATRP*	PA-28-140 Cherokee	28-21885		4. 3.66	JRB Avn Ltd (Damaged Boughton Monchelsea 16.10.81; wreck stored 10.98)	Southend	20. 9.84
G-ATRR	PA-28-140 Cherokee	28-21892		4. 3.66	Marnham Investments Ltd (Op Manx Flyers AeroClub)	Ronaldsway	5.10.00T
G-ATRW	PA-32-260 Cherokee Six	32-360	N11C	8. 3.66	Moxley & Frankl Ltd & J.Pringle	Biggin Hill	21. 6.98
G-ATRX	PA-32-260 Cherokee Six	32-390		8. 3.66	J.W.Stow t/a The Comet F/Grp	Elstree	14. 8.98
G-ATSI	Bolkow Bo.208C Junior	605	D-EFNU	14. 3.66	M.R.Reynolds & R.S.Jordan Little Snoring t/a G-ATSI Group		31. 1.00
G-ATSL	Reims Cessna F.172G	0260		16. 3.66	L.McMullin	Strandhill	8. 6.98
G-ATSM	Cessna 337A Super Skymaster	337-0434	N5334S	23. 3.66	I.J. & H.R.Jones t/a Landscape & Ground Maintenance	Thruxton	10. 7.97T
G-ATSR	Beechcraft M35 Bonanza	D-6236	EI-ALL	29. 3.66	D.G.Lewendon (Damaged at Kingland Church 6.12.98)	Gloucestershire	15. 6.98
G-ATSX	Bolkow Bo.208C Junior	608	D-EJUC	7. 4.66	R.J.Campbell & M.H.Goley	Bristol/Lulsgate	14. 6.98
G-ATSY	Wassmer WA.41 Super Baladou IV	117		12. 4.66	B.Turnbull t/a Baladou F/Grp	Newcastle	23.11.91
G-ATSZ	PA-30-160 Twin Comanche B	30-1002	EI-BPS (EI-BBS)/G-ATSZ/N7912Y	13. 4.66	P.A.Brook	Shoreham	6. 6.99
G-ATTB	Wallis WA-116/F (Franklin 2A) (Rebuild of WA-116 G-ARZC/XR944 c/n 204)	214		19. 4.66	D.A.Wallis (As "XR944")	Reymerston Hall	18. 5.98P
G-ATTD	Cessna 182J Skylane	182-57229	N3129F	19. 4.66	M.Brennan, M.A.Griggs & P.J.Ackerley	Leicester	30. 4.01
G-ATTF	PA-28-140 Cherokee	28-21939		25. 4.66	D.H.Fear	Bembridge	10. 6.00
G-ATTG	PA-28-140 Cherokee	28-21943		25. 4.66	D.E.Spells (Stored 8.97)	Shipdham	3.10.92T
G-ATTI	PA-28-140 Cherokee	28-21951		24. 4.66	R.H.Rathbone t/a G-ATTI Flying Group	Bristol/Lulsgate	14. 9 01T
G-ATTK	PA-28-140 Cherokee	28-21959		25. 4.66	D.J.E.Fairburn t/a The G-ATTK F/Grp	Southend	25. 2.01
G-ATTM	CEA Jodel DR.250 Srs.160	65		26. 4.66	R.W.Tomkinson	Seletar, Singapore	15.12.01
G-ATTN*	Piccard HAFB (62,000 cu ft)	15 & 1352		27. 4.66	The Science Museum "The Red Dragon" (Envelope/basket stored 6.94)	South Kensington, London	
G-ATTR	Bolkow Bo.208C Junior	612	D-EHEH	28. 4.66	S.Luck Rothwell Lodge Farm, Kettering		14. 8.00
G-ATTU*	PA-28-140 Cherokee	28-21987		2. 5.66	Not known (Damaged in collision with AA-5A G-OCPL Elstree 27.6.92; to unknown hotel & displayed in foyer 1993)	Geneva, Switzerland	4.10.93
G-ATTV	PA-28-140 Cherokee	28-21991		2. 5.66	N.E.Leech t/a G-ATTV Grp	Andrewsfield	28. 9.98
G-ATTX	PA-28-180 Cherokee C	28-3390	PH-VDP (G-ATTX)	2. 5.66	IPAC Avn Ltd	Earls Colne/Southend	11.11.99
G-ATUB	PA-28-140 Cherokee	28-21971		2. 5.66	R.H.Partington & M.J.Porter	Wombleton	31. 1.99
G-ATUD	PA-28-140 Cherokee	28-21979		2. 5.66	Heron Air Services Ltd	Bournemouth	19. 8.00T
G-ATUF	Reims Cessna F.150F (Wichita c/n 63229)	0040		4. 5.66	D.P.Williams "Honeysuckle" Hill Farm, Nayland		21. 6.98
G-ATUG	Rollason-Druine D.62B Condor	RAE/614		4. 5.66	R.Crosby Watchford Farm, Yarcombe		17. 6.99P
G-ATUH	Tipsy T.66 Nipper 1 (VW1600)	6	OO-NIF	4. 5.66	D.G.Spruce	Crosland Moor	27. 9.99P
G-ATUI	Bolkow Bo.208C Junior	611	D-EHEF	4. 5.66	A.W.Wakefield (Status uncertain)	(Stamford)	3. 6.94
G-ATUL	PA-28-180 Cherokee C	28-3033	N9007J	6. 5.66	Kirkland Ltd	Ronaldsway	16. 5.99
G-ATVF	DHC.1 Chipmunk 22 (Lyc AEIO-360) (Regd with Fuselage No. DHB/F/147)	C1/0265	WD327	25. 5.66	T.M.Holloway t/a RAFGSA (Op Four Counties Gliding Club)	RAF Syerston	9. 5.01
G-ATVK	PA-28-140 Cherokee	28-22006		27. 5.66	H Hyde	Calais/Southend	6. 7.01T
G-ATVL	PA-28-140 Cherokee	28-22013		27. 5.66	White Waltham Airfield Ltd White Waltham (Op West London Aero Svs)		8. 9.00T
G-ATVO	PA-28-140 Cherokee	28-22020		27. 5.66	G.R.Bright	(Biggleswade)	13. 2.00T
G-ATVP*	Vickers FB.5 Gunbus Replica (Gnome Monosoupape 100 hp)	VAFA-01 & FB.5		31. 5.66	RAF Museum (As "2345/"Bombay(2)" in RFC c/s)	Hendon	6. 5.69P
G-ATVS	PA-28-180 Cherokee C	28-3041	N9014J	1. 6.66	S.M. Patterson	(London SW11)	23. 7.99
G-ATVW	Rollason-Druine D.62B Condor	RAE/615		7. 6.66	J.P.Coulter & J.Chidley t/a Alpha One F/Grp	Nuthampstead	30.10.99
G-ATVX	Bolkow Bo.208C Junior	615	D-EHER	9. 6.66	D.E.Thomas & R.G.Morris t/a D & G Aviation	Swansea	30.10.99P
G-ATWA	SAN Jodel DR.1050 Ambassadeur	296	F-BKHA	10. 6.66	M.G.Binks t/a Jodel Syndicate	Popham	12.11.99
G-ATWB	SAN Jodel D.117	423	F-BHNH	10. 6.66	C.R.Isbell t/a Andrewsfield Whiskey Bravo Grp	Andrewsfield	7. 5.99P
G-ATWE*	GEMS MS.892A Rallye Commodore 150	10634		13. 6.66	D.I.Murray (Damaged nr Taunton 29.3.81; for rebuild 1989; cancelled by CAA 17.02.99)	(Newport, Gwent)	15. 2.82

Regn	Type	C/n	P/I	Date	Owner/operator	Probable Base	CA Expy
G-ATWJ	Reims Cessna F.172F	0095	EI-ANS	21. 6.66	C.J. & J.Freeman t/a Weald Air Svs	Headcorn	30. 4.01T
G-ATWR*	PA-30-160 Twin Comanche B	30-1134	N8025Y	30. 6.66	Not known (Damaged Crosland Moor 14.9.93; stored 8.94)	Wickenby	22.12.94T
G-ATWS*	Phoenix Luton LA-4A Minor PAL/1195 & PFA/818			30. 6.66	(On rebuild 4.97)	Barton	26. 3.69P
G-ATXA	PA-22-150 Tri-Pacer	22-3730	N4403A	8. 7.66	S.Hildrop	Top Farm, Royston	26. 4.01
	(Modified to PA-20 Super Pacer configuration)				(Damaged undercarriage & propeller Top Farm 11.10.98)		
G-ATXD	PA-30-160 Twin Comanche B	30-1166	N8053Y	12. 7.66	Jet Heritage Ltd	Fairoaks	16. 3.00T
G-ATXJ*	HP.137 Jetstream 300	200		15. 7.66	Cardiff-Wales Airport Fire Service		
	(Modified to Jetstream 41 mock-up/display unit)					Cardiff	8. 2.71
G-ATXM	PA-28-180 Cherokee C	28-2759	N8809J	19. 7.66	M.J.Stack t/a G-ATXM F/Grp	Stapleford	15. 8.99
G-ATXN	Mitchell-Procter Kittiwake 1	1 & PFA/1306		19. 7.66	P.A.Dawson	Shenington	24. 7.98P
	(Lyc O-290)						
G-ATXO	SIPA 903	41	F-BGAP	19. 7.66	S.A. & D.C.Whitehead "La Pirouette"		
						Thruxton	2.11.98P
G-ATXX*	McCandless M.4	M4/3		27. 7.66	Ulster Folk & Transport Museum		
	(VW1600)					Holywood, Dublin	
G-ATXZ	Bolkow Bo.208C Junior	624	D-ELNE	28. 7.66	R.Bradbury t/a Bradbury & ptnrs	Tatenhill	23. 5.99P
G-ATYM	Reims Cessna F.150G	0074		15. 8.66	J.F.Perry t/a J.F.Perry & Co (Stored 11.97)	Rochester	28. 9.92
G-ATYN	Reims Cessna F.150G	0076		15. 8.66	J.S.Grant (Damaged Stewton 30.6.95)	North Coates	13.12.97
G-ATYS	PA-28-180 Cherokee C	28-3296	N9226J	19. 8.66	Wendy J.Waite & E.Baker	Headcorn	21. 5.00
G-ATZK	PA-28-180 Cherokee C	28-3128	D-EFUN N9090J	21. 9.66	B.H. & E.F.Austen t/a Austen Associates (Op RAF Brize Norton F/C) RAF Brize Norton		18. 9.99T
G-ATZM	Piper J3C-90 Cub	20868	N2092M NC2092M	26. 9.66	R.W.Davison	Emlyn's Strip, Rhuallt	23. 6.99P
	(Frame No.21310)						
G-ATZO*	Beagle B.206 Srs.1	044	EI-APO G-ATZO	28. 9.66	Not known Coldwater, Michigan, USA (Sold to USA 12.81 but no regn issued; stored 7.91)		
G-ATZS	Wassmer WA.41 Super Baladou IV	128		30. 9.66	G.R.Outwin & D.P.Bennett	Sandtoft	8.10.99
G-ATZY	Reims Cessna F.150G	0135		14.10.66	J.Easson (Op Edinburgh Air Centre)	Edinburgh	1. 7.00T

G-AVAA-AVZZ

Regn	Type	C/n	P/I	Date	Owner/operator	Probable Base	CA Expy
G-AVAR	Reims Cessna F.150G	0122		27.10.66	J.A.Rees & F.Doncaster t/a Poyston Avn	Haverfordwest	7. 8.01T
G-AVAU	PA-30-160 Twin Comanche B	30-1328	N8230Y	8.11.66	Enrico Ermano Ltd	Fairoaks	21. 4.99
G-AVAW	Rollason-Druine D.62C Condor	RAE/617		10.11.66	S.Banyard t/a Condor Acft Grp	Tibenham	6. 5.00
G-AVAX	PA-28-180 Cherokee C	28-3798		11.11.66	J.J.Parkes	Halfpenny Green	30. 5.99
G-AVBG	PA-28-180 Cherokee C	28-3801		11.11.66	R.A.Cayless & R.D.B.Severn White Waltham t/a G-AVBG F/Grp		13. 3.00
G-AVBH	PA-28-180 Cherokee C	28-3802		11.11.66	T.R.Smith (Agricultural Machinery) Ltd	Shipdham	14. 5.00
G-AVBS	PA-28-180 Cherokee C	28-3938		14.11.66	A.G.Arthur	Perranporth	22. 6.01T
G-AVBT	PA-28-180 Cherokee C	28-3945		14.11.66	J.F.Mitchell	Shoreham	26. 4.01T
G-AVBZ	Reims Cessna F.172H	0387		18.11.66	M.Byl	Crosland Moor	10. 4.00
G-AVCM	PA-24-260 Comanche B	24-4520	N9054P	5.12.66	Airbase Aircraft Ltd	Shoreham	4. 5.99
G-AVCS*	Beagle A.61 Terrier 1	-	WJ363	12.12.66	J.May	Ballynahinch, NI	28. 6.82
					(Damaged Finmere 18.10.81; on rebuild 11.95)		
G-AVCV	Cessna 182J Skylane	182-57492	N3492F	15.12.66	The University of Manchester Institute of Science & Technology	Woodford	2. 2.01
G-AVCX	PA-30-160 Twin Comanche B	30-1302	N8185Y	16.12.66	T.Barge	Nottingham	18.11.00
G-AVDA	Cessna 182K Skylane	182-57959	N2759Q	16.12.66	F.W.Ellis & M.C.Burnett	Water Leisure Park, Skegness	15. 5.98
G-AVDB*	Cessna 310L	310L-0079	N2279F	20.12.66	Not known	Popham	8. 7.79
					(Fuselage only stored 7.98)		
G-AVDF*	Beagle B.121 Pup 1	B.121/001		28.12.66	D.Collings & J.Chillingworth	St.Ives, Cambs	22. 5.68
					(On rebuild Cambridge Airport 4.96)		
G-AVDG	Wallis WA-116 Srs.1 Agile (Rotax 447)	215		28.12.66	K.H.Wallis (Stored 8.97)	Reymerston Hall	23. 5.92P
G-AVDR*	Beechcraft 65-B80 Queen Air	LD-339	A40-CR G-AVDR	5. 1.67	Brunel Technical College (Instructional airframe 6.91)	Ashley Down, Bristol	30. 6.86T
G-AVDS*	Beechcraft 65-B80 Queen Air	LD-337	A40-CS G-AVDS	5. 1.67	Brunel Technical College (Instructional airframe 6.91)	Ashley Down, Bristol	26. 8.77
G-AVDT	Aeronca 7AC Champion	7AC-6932	N3594E NC3594E	5. 1.67	D.Cheney & G.Moore	(Newry, NI)	10. 7.90P
G-AVDV	PA-22-150 Tri-Pacer	22-3752	N4423A	5. 1.67	Suzanne C.Brooks	Wellcross Grange, Slinfold	25. 8.00
	(Modifed to PA-20 Super Pacer configuration)						
G-AVDY	Phoenix Luton LA-4A Minor (Lyc O-145)	PAL/1183 & PFA/808		10. 1.67	M.Stoney	Stapleford	1. 7.99P
G-AVEC	Reims Cessna F.172H	0405		13. 1.67	W.H.Ekin (Engineering) Co Ltd	Inverness	11. 5.99
G-AVEF	SAN Jodel 150 Mascaret	16	F-BLDK	19. 1.67	Heavy Install Ltd	Headcorn	27. 5.99T
G-AVEH	SIAI-Marchetti S.205-20R	346		20. 1.67	M.Jarrett, K.Fear & R.L.F.Darby t/a EH Aviation	Crowland	11. 6.99
G-AVEM	Reims Cessna F.150G	0198		23. 1.67	M.D.N.Fisher	Fenland	15. 2.99
G-AVEN	Reims Cessna F.150G	0202		23. 1.67	N.J. Richardson t/a 150 F/Grp	Southampton	3. 9.01
G-AVER	Reims Cessna F.150G	0206		23. 1.67	E.Atherden	Barton	17. 8.01
G-AVEU	Wassmer WA.41 Super Baladou IV	136		27. 1.67	G.J.Richardson	Little Staughton	10.12.01
G-AVEX	Rollason-Druine D.62B Condor	RAE/616		31. 1.67	J.Riley & M.Mordue	Hinton-in-the-Hedges	5.10.99P
G-AVEY	Phoenix Currie Super Wot (Pobjoy "R")	SE.100 & PFA/3006		31. 1.67	B.J.Anning	Watchford Farm, Yarcombe	4. 8.97P
					(Stored 10.97)		
G-AVEZ*	HPR.7 Dart Herald 210	169	PP-ASW G-AVEZ/HB-AAH	31. 1.67	Norwich Airport Fire Service (For rescue training)	Norwich	5. 1.81
G-AVFB*	HS.121 Trident 2E	2141	5B-DAC G-AVFB	1. 2.67	Duxford Aviation Society (BEA c/s)	Duxford	30. 9.82
G-AVFE*	HS.121 Trident 2E	2144		1. 2.67	Belfast Airport Fire Service	Aldergrove	6. 5.85T
G-AVFG*	HS.121 Trident 2E	2146		1. 2.67	BAA Fire Service	Heathrow	2. 7.85T
G-AVFJ*	HS.121 Trident 2E	2149		1. 2.67	CAA International Fire Training Centre	Teesside	18. 9.83T
G-AVFK*	HS.121 Trident 2E	2150		1. 2.67	Not known (For Fire Section use 6.96)	RAF Valley	15. 8.83T
G-AVFM*	HS.121 Trident 2E	2152		1. 2.67	Brunel Technical College (Instructional airframe 8.98)	Bristol/Lulsgate	2. 6.84T
G-AVFP	PA-28-140 Cherokee	28-22652		1. 2.67	Rebecca L.Howells	Barton	23. 4.99
G-AVFR	PA-28-140 Cherokee	28-22747		1. 2.67	J.B.Edgar & J.E.Brown t/a VFR F/Grp	Newtownards	6. 4.99
G-AVFS	PA-32-300 Cherokee Six	32-40038		1. 2.67	Comed Aviation Ltd	Blackpool	12. 7.91
					(Damaged Crosland Moor 28.9.90; on rebuild 1.97)		
G-AVFU	PA-32-300 Cherokee Six	32-40182		1. 2.67	Ashley Gardner F/C Ltd	Ronaldsway	30. 4.00
G-AVFX	PA-28-140 Cherokee	28-22757		1. 2.67	R.A.Irwin t/a Wessex Flyers Grp	Thruxton	7. 7.01
G-AVFZ	PA-28-140 Cherokee	28-22767		1. 2.67	C.J.Law t/a G-AVFZ F/Grp	Yeovil	10. 9.01T
G-AVGA	PA-24-260 Comanche B	24-4489	N9027P	31. 1.67	M.D.Crooks, J.R.Butterworth & V.R.Dennay t/a Conram Avn Grp "C'est Si Bon" RAF Wittering		21. 1.00
G-AVGC	PA-28-140 Cherokee	28-22777		31. 1.67	P.A.Hill	Popham	22. 4.01
G-AVGD	PA-28-140 Cherokee	28-22782		31. 1.67	S. & G.W.Jacobs	Sywell	17.12.98

Regn	Type	C/n	P/I	Date	Owner/operator	Probable Base	CA Expy
G-AVGE	PA-28-140 Cherokee	28-22787		31. 1.67	A.J.Cutler	Bournemouth	5. 4.01
G-AVGG*	PA-28-140 Cherokee	28-22797		31. 1.67	Yorkshire Light Acft Ltd	Duxford	3. 7.71
					(Crashed Papplewick, Notts 10.8.70; wrecked 1.99)		
G-AVGH*	PA-28-140 Cherokee	28-22802		31. 1.67	Not known (Wreck stored 1.97)	Cardiff	5.12.91T
G-AVGI	PA-28-140 Cherokee	28-22822		31. 1.67	D.G.Smith & C.D.Barden	Barton	10. 8.01
					t/a Golf India Grp		
G-AVGJ*	SAN Jodel DR.1050 Ambassadeur	265	F-BJYJ	31. 1.67	Not known	Enstone	22. 4.85
					(Wfu with glue failure 1985; on rebuild off-site 6.95)		
G-AVGK	PA-28-180 Cherokee C	28-3639	N9516J	2. 2.67	N.K.Lamping & S.B.Smith	Liverpool	28. 8.99T
					t/a Golf Kilo F/Grp		
G-AVGU*	Reims Cessna F.150G	0199		8. 2.67	Colton Avn Ltd	Little Staughton	22. 7.84
					(Damaged Southend 25.5.83; stored dismantled 4.97)		
G-AVGY	Cessna 182K Skylane	182-58112	N3112Q	17. 2.67	R.M.C.Sears & R.N.Howgego	Fenland	24. 3.00
G-AVGZ	CEA Jodel DR.1050 Sicile	341	F-BKPR	14. 2.67	D.C.Webb (Stored 4.97)	Bagby	13. 7.97
G-AVHH	Reims Cessna F.172H	0337		20. 2.67	M.Howson (Stored 8.97)	Sywell	10. 8.96
G-AVHL	SAN Jodel DR.105A Ambassadeur	90	F-BIVY	23. 2.67	V.D.Long	Hethel	17. 7.00
G-AVHM	Reims Cessna F.150G	0181		24. 2.67	Thornhill Avn Ltd & G.Baldock	Shoreham	30.11.01T
	(Rebuilt 1997 with fuselage from G-ATRL [0050] - old fuselage dumped Shoreham)					(Op Airbase)	
G-AVHT	Beagle E.3 (Auster AOP.9M)	-	WZ711	1. 3.67	M.Somerton-Raynor	AAC Middle Wallop	29. 4.01
	(Lyc O-360)					(As "WZ711")	
G-AVHY	Sportavia Fournier RF4D	4009		10. 3.67	J.Connolly	Yearby	25. 2.99P
G-AVIA	Reims Cessna F.150G	0184		10. 3.67	Cheshire Air Training Svs Ltd	Liverpool	22.10.00T
G-AVIB	Reims Cessna F.150G	0180		10. 3.67	Club Air Ltd t/a Aberdeen F/C	Aberdeen	2. 4.00T
G-AVIC	Reims Cessna F.172H	0320	N17011	10. 3.67	Leeside Flying Ltd	(Bandon, Eire)	12. 2.01
G-AVID	Cessna 182K	182-57734	N2534Q	10. 3.67	J.Rolston	Bishops Court, Belfast	4. 7.99
G-AVII	Agusta-Bell 206B JetRanger	8011		10. 3.67	Bristow Helicopters Ltd	North Denes	4. 1.01T
					"Brighton Belle"		
G-AVIL	Alon A.2 Aircoupe	A.5	N5471E	14. 3.67	M.J.Close	Headcorn	7. 6.01
					(As "VX147" in RAF c/s)		
G-AVIN	Socata MS.880B Rallye Club	884		14. 3.67	W.Fairney	Kemble	21. 6.99
G-AVIP	Brantly B.2B	471		14. 3.67	N.J.R.Minchin	Hill Top Farm, Hambledon	18.10.01
G-AVIS	Reims Cessna F.172H	0413		14. 3.67	C.J.Freeman	Headcorn	17. 9.01T
					(Op Weald Air Services) (Damaged Sandown 11.11.98)		
G-AVIT	Reims Cessna F.150G	0217		14. 3.67	I.B.Osborn t/a Invicta Flyers	Manston	2. 4.01
G-AVIZ	Scheibe SF-25A Motorfalke	4552	(D-KOFY)	21. 3.67	D.C.Pattison & D.A.Wilson	Brunton	19. 9.91
					(Stored 5.97)		
G-AVJE	Reims Cessna F.150G	0219		29. 3.67	T.F.Fisher	Booker	7. 1.01
					t/a G-AVJE Syndicate		
G-AVJF	Reims Cessna F.172H	0393		31. 3.67	J.A. & G.M.Rees	Haverfordwest	15.12.00
G-AVJH*	Druine D.62 Condor	PFA/603		31. 3.67	J.Tempest	Kings Cliffe, Peterborough	4.11.83P
	(Cont O-200-A)				(Crashed Nefyn, Gwynedd 31.7.83; on rebuild 12.95)		
G-AVJI	Reims Cessna F.172H	0442		31. 3.67	N.P.Bendle t/a G-AVJI Grp	Shoreham	29. 9.98
				(Damaged Croft Farm, Defford 28.10.95; to Northbrook College 2.96)		
G-AVJJ	PA-30-160 Twin Comanche B	30-1420	N8285Y	7. 4.67	A.H.Manser	Gloucestershire	14. 7.01T
G-AVJK	SAN Jodel DR.1050/M1 Excellence	453	F-BLJH	7. 4.67	M.H.Wylde	Sywell	3. 7.99
G-AVJO	Fokker E.III Replica PPS/FOK/1 & PPS/REP/6			12. 4.67	Bianchi Avn Film Svs Ltd	Booker	13. 8.97P
	(Cont C85) (Regd as c/n PPS/FOK/6)			(Op Blue Max Movie Acft Museum) (As "E.III 422/15" in German c/s)		
G-AVJV	Wallis WA-117 Srs.1	K/402/X		12. 4.67	K.H.Wallis	Reymerston Hall	4. 4.89P
					(Used major components of G-ATCV c/n 301; stored 8.97)		
G-AVJW	Wallis WA-118/M Meteorite	K/502/X		12. 4.67	K.H.Wallis	Reymerston Hall	21. 4.83P
	(Used major components of G-ATPW c/n 401; two gyrocopters may have carried marks G-AVJW; stored 8.97)						
G-AVKB	Brochet MB.50 Pipistrelle	02	F-PFAL	17. 4.67	B.H.Pickard	Earls Colne	30.10.96P
	(Walter Mikron 3)						
G-AVKD	Sportavia Fournier RF4D	4024		19. 4.67	R.E.Cross t/a Lasham RF4 Group	Lasham	16. 6.99P
G-AVKE*	Gadfly HDW-1	HDW-1		19. 4.67	E.D.Ap Rees	Weston-super-Mare	
	(Cont IO-340A)					t/a The Helicopter Museum (Stored 8.97)	
G-AVKG	Reims Cessna F.172H	0345		21. 4.67	P.E.P.Sheppard	Breighton	12.10.00
	(Rebuilt with fuselage of G-AVDC c/n 0382 1986)					t/a Goldwing Grp	
G-AVKI	Slingsby Nipper T.66 RA.45 Srs.3	S.102/1586		24. 4.67	J.M.Greenway	(Penkridge)	7. 8.91P
	(Ardem 4C02) (Tipsy c/n 31)						
G-AVKJ	Slingsby Nipper T.66 RA.45 Srs.3	S.103/1587		24. 4.67	T.Dale	Breighton	21. 8.97P
	(VW1834) (Tipsy c/n 32)					t/a G-AVKJ Group	
G-AVKK	Slingsby Nipper T.66 RA.45 Srs.3	S.104/1588	EI-BJH	24. 4.67	C.Watson	Newtownards	6. 4.99P
	(Ardem 4C02) (Tipsy c/n 74)		G-AVKK				
G-AVKL	PA-30-160 Twin Comanche B	30-1418	OY-DHL	25. 4.67	Bravo Aviation Ltd	Jersey	23. 5.99
			G-AVKL/N8284Y				
G-AVKM*	Rollason-Druine D.62B Condor	RAE/620		26. 4.67	M.Hobson	Cruden Bay, Peterhead	30. 6.82
					(Damaged Wilkieston Farm, Cupar 2/3.3.82; stored 2.96)		
G-AVKN	Cessna 401	401-0082	(N3282Q)	26. 4.67	Law Leasing Ltd	Rochester	23. 4.99
G-AVKP	Beagle A.109 Airedale	B.540	SE-EGA	26. 4.67	D.R.Williams	Spanhoe Lodge	28. 5.00
G-AVKR	Bolkow Bo.208C Junior	648	D-EGRA	28. 4.67	C.W.Grant	Old Sarum	8.11.98
G-AVKZ*	PA-23-250 Aztec C	27-3658	N6448Y	3. 5.67	Not known (Stored 5.93)	Little Snoring	29.10.90T
G-AVLB	PA-28-140 Cherokee	28-23158		8. 5.67	M.Wilson	Little Gransden	2.12.00T
G-AVLC	PA-28-140 Cherokee	28-23178		8. 5.67	NE Wales Institute of Higher Education	Welshpool	25. 9.98
G-AVLD	PA-28-140 Cherokee	28-23193		8. 5.67	S.H.A.Petter	White Waltham	5. 4.00
					t/a The West London Strut F/Grp		

Regn	Type	C/n	P/I	Date	Owner/operator	Probable Base	CA Expy
G-AVLE	PA-28-140 Cherokee	28-23223		8. 5.67	G.E.Wright South Lodge Farm, Widnerpool		22.12.01
					t/a Video Security Svs		
G-AVLF	PA-28-140 Cherokee	28-23268		8. 5.67	G.H.Hughesdon	White Waltham	9. 2.01
G-AVLG	PA-28-140 Cherokee	28-23358		8. 5.67	R.Friedlander & D.C.Raymond		
						Grateley, Andover	2. 7.00
G-AVLH	PA-28-140 Cherokee	28-23368		8. 5.67	M.B.Rothschild	Stapleford	18. 8.00
G-AVLI	PA-28-140 Cherokee	28-23388		8. 5.67	I.R.Richmond & C Baxter	Southend	1. 4.01
					t/a Lima India Avn Club		
G-AVLJ	PA-28-140 Cherokee	28-23393	9H-AAZ	8. 5.67	Demeter Avn Ltd	Luton	2. 7.99T
			G-AVLJ				
G-AVLM	Beagle B.121 Pup 2	B121-003		8. 5.67	T.M. & D.A.Jones	Egginton	29. 4.69S
					(On rebuild 4.97)		
G-AVLN	Beagle B.121 Pup 2	B121-004		8. 5.67	C.A.Thorpe	Manston	19. 8.01
G-AVLO	Bolkow Bo.208C Junior	650	D-EGUC	8. 5.67	P.J.Swain Sandford Hall, Knockin		5. 6.98P
G-AVLR	PA-28-140 Cherokee	28-23288		9. 5.67	S.W.Slade t/a Grp 140	Cambridge	19. 2.01
G-AVLT	PA-28-140 Cherokee	28-23328		9. 5.67	D.Jenvey & K.Piper	Southend	16.11.00
G-AVLW	Sportavia Fournier RF4D	4025		9. 5.67	J.W.Scott	(Evesham)	1. 2.01
G-AVLY	Jodel Wassmer D.120A Paris-Nice	331		11. 5.67	N.V. de Candole		
						Boarsbarrow Farm, Bridport	29. 6.98P
G-AVMA	Socata GY-80-180 Horizon	196		12. 5.67	B.R.Hildick		
					Shenstone Hall Farm, Shenstone		8. 1.01
G-AVMB	Rollason-Druine D.62B Condor	RAE/621		12. 5.67	L.J.Dray Watchford Farm, Yarcombe		9. 8.99P
					"Spirit of Silver City"		
G-AVMD	Cessna 150G	150-65504	N2404J	16. 5.67	T.A.White t/a Bagby Avn	Bagby	2. 8.01
G-AVMF	Reims Cessna F.150G	0203		17. 5.67	J.F.Marsh Newton Green, Sudbury		21. 7.00
G-AVMH	BAC One-Eleven 510ED	BAC.136		11. 5.67	European Avn Ltd	Bournemouth	9. 2.01T
G-AVMI	BAC One-Eleven 510ED	BAC.137		11. 5.67	European Avn Ltd	Filton	25. 1.01T
					(Op Air Bristol)		
G-AVMJ	BAC One-Eleven 510ED	BAC.138		11. 5.67	European Avn Ltd	Bournemouth	17.11.94T
					(Wfu 6.94; cabin trainer use 8.96)		
G-AVMK	BAC One-Eleven 510ED	BAC.139		11. 5.67	European Avn Ltd	Stansted	8. 8.00T
					(Op Jersey European Airways)		
G-AVML	BAC One-Eleven 510ED	BAC.140		11. 5.67	European Avn Ltd	Bournemouth	11. 4.01T
G-AVMM	BAC One-Eleven 510ED	BAC.141		11. 5.67	European Avn Ltd	Bournemouth	26. 8.01T
G-AVMN	BAC One-Eleven 510ED	BAC.142		11. 5.67	European Avn Ltd	Filton	21. 6.00T
					(Op Air Bristol)		
G-AVMO*	BAC One-Eleven 510ED	BAC.143		11. 5.67	RAF Museum	RAF Cosford	3. 2.95T
					(British Airways c/s) "Lothian Region"		
G-AVMP	BAC One-Eleven 510ED	BAC.144		11. 5.67	European Avn Ltd	Bournemouth	6. 4.01T
G-AVMR	BAC One-Eleven 510ED	BAC.145		11. 5.67	European Avn Ltd	Bournemouth	23.10.94T
					(Stored 3.96)		
G-AVMS	BAC One-Eleven 510ED	BAC.146		11. 5.67	European Avn Ltd	Bournemouth	26. 2.01T
G-AVMT	BAC One-Eleven 510ED	BAC.147		11. 5.67	European Avn Ltd	Bournemouth	25.11.00T
G-AVMU*	BAC One-Eleven 510ED	BAC.148		11. 5.67	Duxford Aviation Society	Duxford	8. 1.95T
					(British Airways c/s)		
G-AVMV	BAC One-Eleven 510ED	BAC.149		11. 5.67	European Avn Ltd	Bournemouth	5. 4.93T
					(Stored 9.96)		
G-AVMW	BAC One-Eleven 510ED	BAC.150		11. 5.67	European Avn Ltd	Shannon	4.10.00T
					(Op AB Airlines)		
G-AVMX	BAC One-Eleven 510ED	BAC.151	(5N-USE)	11. 5.67	European Avn Ltd	Bournemouth	27.5.93PF
				G-AVMX	(Stored 2.98)		
G-AVMY	BAC One-Eleven 510ED	BAC.152		11. 5.67	European Avn Ltd	Bournemouth	28. 6.01T
G-AVMZ	BAC One-Eleven 510ED	BAC.153	(5N-OSA)	11. 5.67	European Avn Ltd	Bournemouth	17.10.99T
			G-AVMZ				
G-AVNC	Reims Cessna F.150G	0200		18. 5.67	J.Turner	Popham	24. 3.01
G-AVNE*	Westland Wessex 60 Srs.1	WA/561	G-17-3	15. 5.67	The Helicopter Museum Weston-super-Mare		7. 2.83
	G-AVNE/5N-AJL/G-AVNE/9M-ASS/VH-BHC/PK-HBQ/G-AVNE/(G-AVMC) (As "G-17-3")						
G-AVNN	PA-28-180 Cherokee C	28-4049		26. 5.67	C.S.Mitchell Trenchard Farm, Eggesford		2. 3.00
G-AVNO	PA-28-180 Cherokee C	28-4105		26. 5.67	Allister Flight Ltd	Southend	22. 9.01T
G-AVNP	PA-28-180 Cherokee C	28-4113		26. 5.67	R.W.Harris, P.E.Preston, M.F.Hatt &		
					M.Jahanfar (Op Southend F/C)	Southend	21.10.01T
G-AVNR	PA-28-180 Cherokee C	28-4121		26. 5.67	R.R.Livingstone	Biggin Hill	24. 9.01T
G-AVNS	PA-28-180 Cherokee C	28-4129		26. 5.67	E.Alexander	Andrewsfield	10. 6.00T
G-AVNU	PA-28-180 Cherokee C	28-4153		26. 5.67	O.Durrani	Lydd	11. 2.01T
G-AVNW	PA-28-180 Cherokee C	28-4210		26. 5.67	Len Smith's School & Sports Ltd		
						Fairoaks	2. 7.00T
G-AVNX	Sportavia Fournier RF4D	4026		26. 5.67	M.G.Woollard	Little Gransden	21. 1.99P
G-AVNZ	Sportavia Fournier RF4D	4030		26. 5.67	V.S.E.Norman	Rendcomb	9. 7.01
G-AVOA	SAN Jodel DR.1050 Ambassadeur	195	F-BJYY	31. 5.67	D.A.Willies	Sloothby	7. 8.00
G-AVOC	CEA Jodel DR.221 Dauphin	67		2. 6.67	J.M.Graty	(Buntingford, Herts)	27. 1.02
G-AVOD*	Beagle D.5/180 Husky	3688		6. 6.67	W.P.Miller	Mavis Enderby	31. 7.92T
					(Crashed Crosland Moor 31.7.92; wreck stored 6.96)		
G-AVOH	Rollason-Druine D.62B Condor	RAE/622		6. 6.67	Rankart Ltd	Hinton-in-the-Hedges	1.10.99T
G-AVOM	CEA Jodel DR.221 Dauphin	65		6. 6.67	M.A.T.Mountford Maypole Farm, Chislet		29.10.00

Regn	Type	C/n	P/I	Date	Owner/operator	Probable Base	CA Expy
G-AVOO	PA-18-180 Super Cub	18-8511		7. 6.67	London Gliding Club Pty Ltd Dunstable "Terry Mac"		27. 3.00
G-AVOZ	PA-28-180 Cherokee C	28-3711	N9574J	13. 6.67	P.Hoskins & R.Flavell Booker t/a Oscar Zulu Flying Group		6. 7.01
G-AVPC	Druine D.31 Turbulent (VW1500)	PFA/544		15. 6.67	S.A.Sharp	Wigtown Baldoon	28. 9.99P
G-AVPD	Jodel D.9 Bebe 521/MAC.1/PFA/927 (VW1500)			15. 6.67	S.W.McKay (Stored 2.96)	Berkhamsted	6. 6.75S
G-AVPH	Reims Cessna F.150G	0197		20. 6.67	Zero 9 Flight Academy	Norwich	9. 4.86T
G-AVPI	Reims Cessna F.172H	0409		20. 6.67	R.W.Cope	Netherthorpe	30. 5.00
G-AVPJ	DH.82A Tiger Moth	86326	NL879	20. 6.67	Catherine C.Silk Bericote Farm, Blackdown, Leamington Spa		13. 8.01
G-AVPK	Socata MS.892A Rallye Commodore 150	10736		20. 6.67	B.A.Bridgewater (Stored 8.92) Shelsley Beauchamp, Worcester		10. 1.92
G-AVPM	SAN Jodel D.117	593	F-BHXO	20. 6.67	J.C.Haynes	Breighton	13. 1.99P
G-AVPN*	HPR.7 Dart Herald 213	176	I-TIVB G-AVPN/D-BIBI/(HB-AAK)	22. 6.67	Yorkshire Air Museum	Elvington	14.12.99T
	(Flown to Elvington 20.10.97 for preservation with Yorkshire Air Museum)						
G-AVPO	Hindustan HAL-26 Pushpak (Cont C90)	PK-127	9M-AOZ VT-DWL	31. 3.83	J.A.Rimell Cherry Tree Farm, Monewden		28. 7.99P
G-AVPR	PA-30-160 Twin Comanche B	30-1511	N8395Y	27. 6.67	J.O.Coundley	Jersey/Bournemouth	3. 9.99
G-AVPS	PA-30-160 Twin Comanche B	30-1548	N8393Y	27. 6.67	J.M.Bisco	Gloucestershire	9. 5.99
G-AVPV	PA-28-180 Cherokee C	28-2705	9J-RBP	27. 6.67	S.Moore	Stapleford	4. 9.99
G-AVPY	PA-25-235 Pawnee C	25-4330	N4636Y	7. 7.67	Farm Avn Svs Ltd	(Enstone)	14.10.77S
	(Crashed Lower Radbourne Farm, Ladbroke, Warwicks 25.6.76; status uncertain)						
G-AVRK	PA-28-180 Cherokee C	28-4041		11. 7.67	J.Gama	Coventry	27. 2.00
G-AVRP	PA-28-140 Cherokee	28-23153		14. 7.67	M.H.Hoffman t/a Trent-199	(Lichfield)	15. 5.00
G-AVRS	Socata GY-80-180 Horizon	224		14. 7.67	Air Venturas Ltd	Bagby	7. 8.00
G-AVRT	PA-28-140 Cherokee	28-23143		17. 7.67	C.Moore t/a Star Avn Trust Grp	Stapleford	23.11.99
G-AVRU	PA-28-180 Cherokee C	28-4025		17. 7.67	D.J.Rowell t/a G-AVRU Partnership	Clacton	1. 1.99
G-AVRW	Barritault JB-01 Minicab (Cont C90)	OH-1549 & PFA/1800		18. 7.67	D.J.Smith t/a Kestrel F/Grp	Hucknall	19. 8.99P
G-AVRY	PA-28-180 Cherokee C	28-4089		24. 7.67	Brigfast Ltd	Blackbushe	26. 3.00
G-AVRZ	PA-28-180 Cherokee C	28-4137		24. 7.67	Mantavia Grp Ltd	Guernsey	10.10.99
G-AVSA	PA-28-180 Cherokee C	28-4184		24. 7.67	D.J.Royle & W.Beaty t/a G-AVSA F/Grp	Barton	19. 6.99
G-AVSB	PA-28-180 Cherokee C	28-4191		24. 7.67	T.H.Lloyd	Denham	2. 5.99
G-AVSC	PA-28-180 Cherokee C	28-4193		24. 7.67	Medidata Ltd	White Waltham	17. 3.00T
G-AVSD	PA-28-180 Cherokee C	28-4195		24. 7.67	Landmate Ltd	Haverfordwest	18. 5.01
G-AVSE	PA-28-180 Cherokee C	28-4196		24. 7.67	G.Cotrulia	Kemble	30. 4.00T
G-AVSF	PA-28-180 Cherokee C	28-4197		24. 7.67	S.E.Pick & D.A.Rham t/a Monday Club	Blackbushe	6. 4.01
G-AVSI	PA-28-140 Cherokee	28-23148		24. 7.67	J.I.Dawson t/a G-AVSI F/Grp	White Waltham	21. 1.01
G-AVSP	PA-28-180 Cherokee C	28-3952	(PJ-ACT)	8. 8.67	L.J.Jones	Dunkeswell	17. 9.00T
G-AVSR	Beagle D.5/180 Husky	3689		8. 8.67	A.L.Young	Henstridge	28. 8.99A
G-AVSZ	Agusta-Bell 206B JetRanger	8032	VH-BEQ PK-HBZ/VR-BCR/PK-HBD/VR-BCR/G-AVSZ	8. 8.67	Burman Aviation Ltd Newcastle/Cranfield		16. 6.99T
G-AVTJ	PA-32-260 Cherokee Six (Rebuilt using spare Frame No.32-860S)	32-219	N3373W	14. 8.67	B.L.Morgan (Op Airborne School of Flying)	Bournemouth	21. 1.01T
G-AVTL*	Brighton Ax7-65 HAFB	01		17. 8.67	British Balloon Museum "Bristol Belle"	Newbury	
G-AVTP	Reims Cessna F.172H	0458		17. 8.67	R.A.Lee & A.S.Watkins t/a Tango Papa Grp	White Waltham	7. 4.01
G-AVTT	Ercoupe 415D (Cont C85)	4399	SE-BFZ NC3774H	21. 8.67	Wright Farm Eggs Ltd (Stored 9.97) Cherry Tree Farm, Monewden		20. 1.86
G-AVTV	Socata MS.893A Rallye Commodore 180	10725		24. 8.67	D.B.& M.E.Meeks (Bedale, N.Yorkshire)		6. 8.00
G-AVUD	PA-30-160 Twin Comanche B	30-1515	N8422Y	5. 9.67	P.M.Fox t/a FM Avn	Biggin Hill	6. 5.01
G-AVUG	Reims Cessna F.150H	0234		11. 9.67	R.K.Moody & V.J.Larkin t/a Skyways F/Grp	Netherthorpe	25. 4.99
G-AVUH	Reims Cessna F.150H	0244		11. 9.67	C.M.Chinn	North Coates	11. 8.00
G-AVUO	Phoenix Luton LA.4A Minor	PAL/1313		21. 9.67	M.E.Vaisey (Hemel Hempstead)		
	(Not completed and parts used in construction of G-AXKH - possible long-term build project)						
G-AVUS	PA-28-140 Cherokee	28-24065	(G-AVUT)	25. 9.67	D.J.Hunter	Norwich	28.10.01T
G-AVUT	PA-28-140 Cherokee	28-24085		25. 9.67	Bencray Ltd t/a Blackpool & Fylde A/C	Blackpool	16. 4.01T
G-AVUU	PA-28-140 Cherokee	28-24100	(G-AVUS)	25. 9.67	R.W.Harris, A.Jahanfar, P.E.Preston & M.F.Hatt (Op Southend F/C)	Southend	28. 4.00T
G-AVUZ	PA-32-300 Cherokee Six	32-40302		29. 9.67	Ceesix Ltd	Jersey	23. 4.00
G-AVVC	Reims Cessna F.172H	0443		29. 9.67	A.Turnbull	(Bedlington)	21.10.01T
G-AVVF*	DH.104 Dove 8	04541		2.10.67	Not known (Wreck on fire dump 6.97)	Gloucestershire	11. 2.88

Regn	Type	C/n	P/I	Date	Owner/operator	Probable Base	CA Expy
G-AVVI*	PA-30-160 Twin Comanche B	30-1613	EI-AVD G-AVVI/N8454Y	5.10.67	Not known	Shipdham	7. 3.94T
					(Damaged at Shipdham 7.4.91; on rebuild 8.93)		
G-AVVJ	Socata MS.893A Rallye Commodore 180	10752		6.10.67	P.Etherington (Loughborough) t/a AVVJ Group		30. 8.98
G-AVVL	Reims Cessna F.150H	0257		6.10.67	N.E.Sams "Samurai"	Cranfield	11. 3.89T
	(Experimental Wankel MWAE 100R engine under development 7.97) t/a International Aerospace Engineering						
G-AVVO*	Avro 652A Anson C.19 Srs.2	34219	VL348	6.10.67	Newark Air Museum (As "VL348")	Winthorpe	
G-AVVW*	Reims Cessna F.150H	0258		19.10.67	Brunel Technical College (Instructional airframe 6.91)		
						Ashley Down, Bristol	31. 5.82
G-AVWA	PA-28-140 Cherokee	28-23660		19.10.67	SFG Ltd	Shipdham	3.10.99T
G-AVWD	PA-28-140 Cherokee	28-23700		19.10.67	C.Bentley & G.J.Williams t/a Evelyn Air	Leeds-Bradford	6. 8.01T
G-AVWE*	PA-28-140 Cherokee	28-23720		19.10.67	Not known (On rebuild 11.97)	Blackpool	22. 4.82T
G-AVWG	PA-28-140 Cherokee	28-23760		19.10.67	Bencray Ltd t/a Blackpool & Fylde A/C	Blackpool	11. 8.91T
	(Damaged Tal y Fan, Conwy, Gwynedd 11.12.88; status uncertain - only wings remain 6.96)						
G-AVWI	PA-28-140 Cherokee	28-23800		19.10.67	Mrs.L.M.Middleton	Cranfield	23. 1.00
G-AVWJ	PA-28-140 Cherokee	28-23940		19.10.67	F.E.Telling	(Esher)	13. 8.01
G-AVWL	PA-28-140 Cherokee	28-24000		19.10.67	B.W.Griffiths & R.Fraser-Duthie t/a Bobev Aviation	Coventry	6. 9.01
G-AVWM	PA-28-140 Cherokee	28-24005		19.10.67	A.Jahanfar, P.E.Preston, M.F.Hatt & R.W.Harris (Op Southend F/C)	Southend	27. 5.01T
G-AVWN	PA-28R-180 Cherokee Arrow	28R-30170		19.10.67	Vawn Air Ltd	Jersey	10. 4.99
G-AVWO	PA-28R-180 Cherokee Arrow	28R-30205		19.10.67	R.G.Tweddle	White Waltham	9. 9.00
G-AVWR	PA-28R-180 Cherokee Arrow	28R-30242		19.10.67	S.J.French, G.A.Rogers, C.A.Bailey & R.J.Doughton	Dunkeswell	7. 5.00
G-AVWT	PA-28R-180 Cherokee Arrow	28R-30362		19.10.67	Cloudbase Aviation Ltd	Barton	14. 4.00
G-AVWU	PA-28R-180 Cherokee Arrow	28R-30380		19.10.67	Arrow Flyers Ltd	Denham	18. 5.01
G-AVWV	PA-28R-180 Cherokee Arrow	28R-30404		19.10.67	R.V.Thornton & R.Barron t/a Strathtay F/Grp	Perth	18. 6.99
G-AVWY	Sportavia Fournier RF4D	4031		26.10.67	B.Houghton (Stored Biggin Hill 1992)	(St.Helens)	15. 4.90A
G-AVXA	PA-25-235 Pawnee C (Re-built using new frame)	25-4244	N4576Y	26.10.67	South Wales Gliding Club Ltd	Usk	5. 4.00
G-AVXC	Slingsby Nipper T.66 RA.45 Srs.3 (Ardem 4C02)	S.108/1605		26.10.67	D.S.T.Eggleton	Waits Farm, Belchamp Walter	16. 5.99P
G-AVXD	Slingsby Nipper T.66 RA.45 Srs.3 (VW1834 Acro)	S.109/1606		26.10.67	D.A.Davidson	Shenington	31. 8.99P
G-AVXF	PA-28R-180 Cherokee Arrow	28R-30044		26.10.67	J.A.Lunness t/a JDR Arrow Grp	Top Farm, Tadlow	4. 6.01
G-AVXI	HS.748 Srs.2A/238	1623		2.11.67	Emerald Airways Ltd	Liverpool	30. 8.98T
G-AVXJ	HS.748 Srs.2A/238	1624		2.11.67	Emerald Airways Ltd	Liverpool	22. 8.98T
G-AVXV*	Bleriot IX (Anzani 24hp)	225		2.11.67	(To Imperial War Museum 9.86) (Allocated BAPC.104)	Duxford	
G-AVXW	Rollason-Druine D.62B Condor	RAE/625		3.11.67	A.J.Cooper	Rochester	30. 9.01
G-AVXY	Auster AOP.9 (Regd with c/n AUS/120)	B5/10-120	XK417	7.11.67	E.Wright South Lodge Farm, Widmerpool t/a Auster Nine Grp (As "XK417" in Army c/s)		9. 7.99P
G-AVYE*	HS.121 Trident 1E-140	2139		13.11.67	British Aerospace plc (Cabin fire suppression research	Hatfield	13. 7.82
G-AVYK	Beagle A.61 Terrier 3	B.642	WJ357	20.11.67	J.P.Roland (Stored 8.98)	Aboyne	28. 8.93
G-AVYL	PA-28-180 Cherokee D	28-4622		24.11.67	I.Kerr t/a Cherokee G-AVYL F/Grp	Perth	18. 5.99
G-AVYM	PA-28-180 Cherokee D	28-4638		24.11.67	Carlisle Avn (1985) Ltd	Carlisle	14. 5.01T
G-AVYP	PA-28-140 Cherokee	28-24211		24.11.67	T.D.Reid (Braids) Ltd	Newtownards	19.12.97
G-AVYR	PA-28-140 Cherokee	28-24226		24.11.67	DR Flying Club Ltd (Dowty Rotol)	Gloucestershire	18. 6.00
G-AVYS	PA-28R-180 Cherokee Arrow	28R-30456		24.11.67	A.M.Playford Poplar Hall Farm, Elmsett		19. 1.00
G-AVYT	PA-28R-180 Cherokee Arrow	28R-30472		24.11.67	E.J.Booth & B.D.Tipler	Blackpool	13. 5.00
G-AVYV	Jodel Wassmer D.120A Paris-Nice	252	F-BMAM	27.11.67	A.J.Sephton (Stored 4.96)	Brickhouse Farm, Frogland Cross	30. 8.93P
G-AVZB*	LET Z-37 Cmelak	04-08	OK-WKQ	30.11.67	The Science Museum	Wroughton	5. 4.84A
G-AVZI	Bolkow Bo.208C Junior	673	D-EGZF	19.12.67	C.F.Rogers (Status uncertain)	(Wheathampstead)	24. 7.76
G-AVZN	Beagle B.121 Pup 1	B121-006		19.12.67	J.K.Healey t/a Shipdham Aviators F/Grp	Shipdham	28. 7.01
G-AVZP	Beagle B.121 Pup 1	B121-008		19.12.67	T.A.White	Bagby	8. 6.01
G-AVZR	PA-28-180 Cherokee C	28-4114	N4779L	19.12.67	Lincoln A/C Ltd	Sturgate	30. 4.00T
G-AVZU	Reims Cessna F.150H	0283		29.12.67	R.D. & E.Forster (Op Norfolk & Norwich A/C)	Swanton Morley	6.11.99T
G-AVZV	Reims Cessna F.172H	0511		29.12.67	E.L. & D.S.Lightbown	Crosland Moor	6. 6.97T
G-AVZW	EAA Model P Biplane (Lyc O-290)	PFA/1314		29.12.67	R.G.Maidment & G.R.Edmondson	(Billingshurst)	12. 3.86P
	(Damaged Goodwood 26.4.85; status uncertain)						
G-AVZX	Socata MS.880B Rallye Club	1165		29.12.67	T.C.Bayes	Sturgate	19.11.99

G-AWAA-AWZZ

Regn	Type	C/n	P/I	Date	Owner/operator	Probable Base	CA Expy
G-AWAA*	Socata MS.880B Rallye Club	1174		29.12.67	P.A.Cairns	St.Just	4. 8.91
					(Cancelled by CAA 4.3.99; stored 10.95)		
G-AWAC	Socata GY-80-180 Horizon	234		29.12.67	Gardan Party Ltd "Le Fantome"	Popham	11. 6.01
G-AWAH	Beechcraft D55 Baron	TE-540		1. 1.68	B.J.S.Grey	Duxford	4. 7.99
G-AWAJ	Beechcraft D55 Baron	TE-536		1. 1.68	Standard Hose Ltd	Blackpool	12. 3.01
G-AWAS*	Campbell-Bensen B.8Mc	CA/307		5. 1.68	S.Modi (Stored)		
						Borgo San Laurenz, Florence, Italy	27. 4.70
G-AWAT	Rollason-Druine D.62B Condor	RAE/627		8. 1.68	Tamwood Ltd	Shoreham	23. 2.98
G-AWAU*	Vickers FB.27A Vimy Replica	VAFA-02	"H651"	8. 1.68	RAF Museum	Hendon	4. 8.69
					(As "F8614") "Triple First"		
G-AWAW	Reims Cessna F.150F	0037	OY-DKJ	5. 1.68	The Science Museum (Flight Laboratory)		
	(Wichita c/n 63167)					South Kensington, London	8. 6.92T
G-AWAX	Cessna 150D	150-60153	OY-TRJ	5. 1.68	H.H.Cousins	Fenland	23. 7.99T
	(Tail-wheel conversion)		N4153U		(Rebuilt 1994/96 with G-ASTV fuselage; original stored 11.94)		
G-AWAZ	PA-28R-180 Cherokee Arrow	28R-30512		8. 1.68	R.Z.Staniszewski	Barton	21. 4.99
G-AWBA	PA-28R-180 Cherokee Arrow	28R-30528		8. 1.68	A.Taplin & G.A.Dunster	Stapleford	23. 1.00
					t/a March F/Grp		
G-AWBB	PA-28R-180 Cherokee Arrow	28R-30552		8. 1.68	M.D.Parker & J.Lowe	Bourn	20. 6.99
G-AWBC	PA-28R-180 Cherokee Arrow	28R-30572		8. 1.68	Anglo Avn (UK) Ltd	Bournemouth	28.12.00
G-AWBE	PA-28-140 Cherokee	28-24266		8. 1.68	B.E.Boyle	Edge Hill	8. 3.99
G-AWBG	PA-28-140 Cherokee	28-24286		8. 1.68	Westward Airways (Lands End) Ltd	St.Just	23. 2.01T
G-AWBH	PA-28-140 Cherokee	28-24306		8. 1.68	Transport Command Ltd	Shoreham	16.10.01
G-AWBJ	Sportavia Fournier RF4D	4055		12. 1.68	J.M.Adams	RAF Syerston	14. 4.99P
G-AWBM	Druine D.31A Turbulent	PFA/1647		17. 1.68	A.D.Pratt	North Coates	20. 7.95P
	(VW1700)						
G-AWBN	PA-30-160 Twin Comanche B	30-1472	N8517Y	18. 1.68	Stourfield Investments Ltd	Jersey	14.11.99
G-AWBS	PA-28-140 Cherokee	28-24331		22. 1.68	M.A.English & T.M.Brown	Little Snoring	25.10.01
G-AWBT*	PA-30-160 Twin Comanche B	30-1668	N8508Y	22. 1.68	Cranfield University	Cranfield	25. 3.89
					(Damaged Humberside 10.3.88; instructional airframe 7.97)		
G-AWBU	Morane-Saulnier Type N Replica			22. 1.68	Personal Plane Svs Ltd	Booker	29. 7.97P
	(Cont C90)	PPS/REP/7			(Blue Max Movie A/C Museum; as "MS824" in French AF c/s)		
G-AWBW*	Reims Cessna F.172H	0486		22. 1.68	Brunel Technical College		
				(Crashed Compton Abbas 20.5.73; instructional airframe 6.91)	Ashley Down, Bristol	15. 5.75
G-AWBX	Reims Cessna F.150H	0286		22. 1.68	J.Meddings	Tatenhill	10.10.99
G-AWCM	Reims Cessna F.150H	0281		25. 1.68	R.Garbett	Halfpenny Green	14. 8.99T
G-AWCN	Reims Cessna FR.172E Rocket	0020		25. 1.68	Y.F.Herdman	(Romford)	12. 7.01T
G-AWCO*	Reims Cessna F.150H	0338		29. 1.68	Not known	Biggin Hill	29. 8.75
					(Wreck in open storage 2.95)		
G-AWCP	Reims Cessna F.150H	0354		29. 1.68	C.E.Mason	Shobdon	12. 2.00
	(Tail-wheel conversion)						
G-AWCR*	Piccard Ax6 HAFB	6204		29. 1.68	British Balloon Museum & Library		
					"London Pride 1"	Newbury	
G-AWDA	Slingsby Nipper T.66 RA.45 Srs.3			7. 2.68	J.A.Cheesbrough	Hill Farm, Marton, Hull	24.11.98P
	(Acro/VW1834)	S.117/1624					
G-AWDE	Glos-Air Airtourer T.2	504		9. 2.68	Not known	St.Just	6. 8.76
					(Crashed Stapleford 23.3.75; fuselage in open store 8.96)		
G-AWDI*	PA-23-250 Aztec C	27-3811	N6520Y	15. 2.68	"Crown" or "Queens Head" Public House		
					(Stored 2.97)	Willington, Cardington	30. 6.88T
G-AWDO	Druine D.31 Turbulent	PFA/1649		21. 2.68	R.N.Crosland	Deanland, Hailsham	23.12.97P
	(VW1600)						
G-AWDP	PA-28-180 Cherokee D	28-4870		21. 2.68	B.H. & P.M.Illston	Norwich	7.12.01T
					(Op Norwich School of Flying)		
G-AWDR	Reims Cessna FR.172E Rocket	0004		21. 2.68	B.A.Wallace	Nuthampstead	2. 4.01
G-AWDU	Brantly B.2B	481		23. 2.68	B.M.Freeman	(Stourport-on-Severn)	22. 7.01
G-AWDW	Campbell-Bensen CB.8MS	DS.1330		26. 2.68	M.R.Langton	Berkhamsted	7.10.71P
	(McC.4318C)				(Stored - status uncertain)		
G-AWEF	SNCAN Stampe SV-4C	549	F-BDCT	29. 3.68	The Tiger Club (1990) Ltd	Headcorn	19.12.01T
	(Gipsy Major)						
G-AWEI	Rollason-Druine D.62B Condor	RAE/628		6. 3.68	M.J.Steer	Rushett Farm, Chessington	10.11.98T
G-AWEK	Sportavia Fournier RF4D	4071		6. 3.68	P.Barrett	(Lightwater)	23. 8.74
					(Crashed nr Chelsfield, Kent 25.10.72; stored Rendcomb 12.93)		
G-AWEL	Sportavia Fournier RF4D	4077		7. 3.68	A.B.Clymo	Halfpenny Green	3. 9.99P
G-AWEM	Sportavia Fournier RF4D	4078		7. 3.68	B.J.Griffin	Wickenby	11. 6.99P
G-AWEN*	SAN Jodel DR.1050 Ambassadeur	67	F-BIVD	8. 3.68	Not known	Crosland Moor	8.11.85
					(Crashed Crosland Moor 11.8.83; stored 3.93)		
G-AWEO*	Reims Cessna F.150H	0342		11. 3.68	Shobdon Acft Maintenance Ltd	Shobdon	30. 9.90T
					(Damaged Baginton 22.11.89; on rebuild 3.96)		
G-AWEP	Barritault JB-01 Minicab	PFA/1801		12. 3.68	J.A.Stewart & J.Taylor		
	(Cont C90)					Griffins Farm, Temple Bruer	19. 5.99P
G-AWES*	Cessna 150H	150-68626	N22933	20. 3.68	Yorkshire Light Aircraft Ltd		
			(WFU after gale damage Glenrothes 2.10.81; on rebuild 1.97)			Leeds-Bradford	5. 8.84
G-AWET	PA-28-180 Cherokee D	28-4871		21. 3.68	Broadland F/Grp Ltd	Old Buckenham	30. 4.00
G-AWEV	PA-28-140 Cherokee	28-24460		21. 3.68	Norflight Ltd	Ludham	6. 1.01
G-AWEX	PA-28-140 Cherokee	28-24472		21. 3.68	R.A.Page	Coventry	16. 4.01
					t/a Sir W.G.Armstrong-Whitworth F/Grp		

Regn	Type	C/n	P/I	Date	Owner/operator	Probable Base	CA Expy
G-AWEZ	PA-28R-180 Cherokee Arrow	28R-30592		21. 3.68	T.R.Leighton, R.G.E.Simpson & D.A.C.Clissett	Stapleford	14.11.99
G-AWFB	PA-28R-180 Cherokee Arrow	28R-30689		21. 3.68	Luke Avn Ltd	Bristol/Lulsgate	19.11.01
G-AWFC	PA-28R-180 Cherokee Arrow	28R-30670		21. 3.68	B.J.Hines	Bristol/Lulsgate	16. 7.01
G-AWFD	PA-28R-180 Cherokee Arrow	28R-30669		21. 3.68	D.J.Hill	Andrewsfield	9. 1.99
G-AWFF	Reims Cessna F.150H	0280		25. 3.68	J.A.Hardiman	Shobdon	28. 2.99T
G-AWFH*	Reims Cessna F.150H	0274		25. 3.68	Cheshire Fire Brigade Training School	Winsford	17.12.81
	(Crashed Swanton Morley 16.12.79; now fitted with tail from G-AWTX; stored 12.93)						
G-AWFJ	PA-28R-180 Cherokee Arrow	28R-30688		26. 3.68	Parplon Ltd	Barton	7. 5.99
G-AWFN	Rollason-Druine D.62B Condor	RAE/629		27. 3.68	R.James	Shobdon	26. 6.99P
G-AWFO	Rollason-Druine D.62B Condor	RAE/630		27. 3.68	R.E.Major	Porthtowan, Cornwall	1. 9.99P
G-AWFP	Rollason-Druine D.62B Condor	RAE/631		27. 3.68	E.Davies	White Waltham	22. 5.01
G-AWFR	Druine D.31 Turbulent	SU.001 & PFA/1652		27. 3.68	J.R.Froud	(Edenbridge, Kent)	
					(Under construction 1993)		
G-AWFT	Jodel D.9 Bebe	PFA/932		29. 3.68	W.H.Cole	Spilsted Farm, Sedlescombe	22. 7.69P
	(VW1200)				(Stored 8.94)		
G-AWFW	SAN Jodel D.117	599	PH-VRE F-BHXU	2. 4.68	F.H.Greenwell	Bishopton, Durham	28. 9.98P
G-AWFZ	Beechcraft 19A Musketeer Sport	MB-323	N2811B	3. 4.68	R.Sweet & B.D.Corbett	Booker	12. 5.94
					(Stored 9.97)		
G-AWGA*	Beagle A.109 Airedale	B.535	EI-ATA G-AWGA/D-ENRU	3. 4.68	Not known	(Greater Manchester)	3. 7.86
G-AWGD	Reims Cessna F.172H	0503		5. 4.68	D.Whitton & P.Storey	Sywell	18. 7.00T
G-AWGJ	Reims Cessna F.172H	0531		8. 4.68	J. & C.J.Freeman	Headcorn	7. 7.90T
					(Damaged Headcorn 16.10.87; wreck stored 1.96)		
G-AWGK	Reims Cessna F.150H	0347		8. 4.68	J.S.Melville	Kemble	30. 4.01
G-AWGM*	Mitchell Kittiwake II	002 & PFA/1329		9. 4.68	M.K.Field	Astley, Shrewsbury	13.10.86P
	(Cont O-240-A)				(Cancelled by CAA 4.3.99; damaged Halton 18.1.86; open store 9.95)		
G-AWGN	Sportavia Fournier RF4D	4084		9. 4.68	R.H.Ashforth	Gloucestershire	9. 6.99
					t/a The Gloster Aero Grp		
G-AWGR	Reims Cessna F.172H	0484		9. 4.68	Pauline A.Hallam	Barton	27. 5.01
G-AWGZ	Taylor JT.1 Monoplane	M.1 & PFA/1406		17. 4.68	R.L.Sambell	(Hinckley)	21. 6.93P
	(Ardem 4C02)				(Damaged Sleap 14.7.92)		
G-AWHB	CASA C.2111D (He.111H-16)	049	B21-57	14. 5.68	Aces High Ltd	North Weald	
	(Officially quoted as c/n 167 - ex B21-37)				(As "6J+PR"; on rebuild 10.97)		
G-AWHS*	Hispano HA.1112-Mil	228	C4K-170	14. 5.68	Auto n Technik Museum Sinsheim, Germany		
	(DB.605D)				(As "4+-" in Luftwaffe c/s)		
G-AWHX	Rollason Beta B.2	RAE/04	(G-ATEE)	17. 4.68	S.G.Jones "Vertigo"	Membury	14. 6.87P
					(On rebuild 3.91)		
G-AWHY	Falconar F-11-3 (Cont C90)	PFA/1322	G-BDPB (G-AWHY)	17. 4.68	B.E.Smith	Wellcross Grange, Slinford	11. 6.98P
G-AWIF*	Brookland Mosquito	3 & LC.1		17. 4.68	Not known	St.Merryn	7. 1.82P
G-AWII	VS.349 Spitfire LF.Vc	WASP/20/223	AR501	25. 4.68	The Shuttleworth Trust	Old Warden	31. 8.96P
					(As "AR501/NN-A" in 310 Sqn c/s)		
G-AWIJ*	VS.329 Spitfire F.IIA	CBAF.14	P7350	25.4.68	Battle of Britain Mem Flt RAF Coningsby		
					(As "P7350/BA-Y" in 277 Sqdn c/s)		
G-AWIO*	Brantly B.2B	483	G-OBPG G-AWIO	30. 4.68	Not known (Temp unregd 29.11.95)	Rhyl	5. 8.95
G-AWIP	Phoenix Luton LA-4A Minor			30. 4.68	J.Houghton	Sproatley	8. 5.89P
	(Cont A65)	PAL/1308 & PFA/830			(Damaged nr Holme-on-Spalding Moor 20.7.88; status uncertain)		
G-AWIR	Bushby-Long Midget Mustang	PFA/1315		30. 4.68	K.E.Sword	Leicester	6. 3.90P
	(Cont O-200-A)				(On overhaul 1991)		
G-AWIT	PA-28-180 Cherokee D	28-4987		30. 4.68	Cherry Orchard Aparthotel Ltd		
					(Op Manx Flyers Aero Club)	Ronaldsway	29. 5.99T
G-AWIV	Airmark TSR.3	PFA/1325		30. 4.68	D.J. & F.M.Nunn "Stor" (On overhaul)		
	(Cont PC60)					(Penrhyn, Cornwall)	31. 1.00P
G-AWIW	SNCAN Stampe SV-4B	532	F-BDCC	2. 5.68	R.E.Mitchell	RAF Cosford	6. 5.73
					(On rebuild 3.95)		
G-AWJE	Slingsby Nipper T.66 RA.45 Srs.3	S.121/1628		8. 5.68	T.S.Mosedale	Barton	6. 7.98P
	(VW1834)						
G-AWJF*	Slingsby Nipper T.66 RA.45 Srs.3	S.122/1629		8. 5.68	S.Maric	(Glasgow)	7. 6.88P
					(Stored 6.95)		
G-AWJV*	DH.98 Mosquito TT.35		TA634	21. 5.68	De Havilland Aircraft Museum		
	(As "TA634/8K-K" in 571 Sqdn c/s)					Salisbury Hall, London Colney	
G-AWJX	Moravan Zlin Z.526 Trener Master	1049		22. 5.68	Aerobatics Intl Ltd (On rebuild 12.93)	Rushett Farm, Chessington	29. 5.85A
G-AWJY	Moravan Zlin Z.526 Trener Master	1050		22. 5.68	M.Gainza	White Waltham	29. 8.99
G-AWKB	Jurca MJ.5 Sirocco Type F2 Srs.39	PFA/2204		24. 5.68	G.D.Claxton	(Pontyclun, Glamorgan)	
G-AWKD	PA-17 Vagabond	17-192	F-BFMZ N4892H/NC4892H	27. 5.68	A.T. & Mrs.M.R.Dowie Scotland Farm, Hook		30. 8.98P
	(Cont A65)						
G-AWKM	Beagle B.121 Pup 1	B121-017		11. 6.68	D.M.G.Jenkins Hurstbourne Tarrant, Hants		29..6.84
					(Damaged Swansea 7.91; stored 1.97)		
G-AWKO	Beagle B.121 Pup 1	B121-019		11. 6.68	M.N.Bowman	Old Sarum	23. 6.00T
G-AWKP*	CEA Jodel DR.253 Regent	130		14. 6.68	G.R.W.Wright	Little Gransden	1.10.98
					t/a G-AWKP Grp (Cancelled by CAA 13.10.98)		
G-AWKT	Socata MS.880B Rallye Club	1235		17. 6.68	D.G.Cochrane	Enniskillen	15.10.99

Regn	Type	C/n	P/I	Date	Owner/operator	Probable Base	CA Expy
G-AWKX*	Beechcraft A65 Queen Air	LC-303		21. 6.68	Northbrook College (Instructional airframe 8.97)	Shoreham	25.10.89T
G-AWLA	Reims Cessna F.150H	0269	N13175	27. 6.68	T.A.White t/a Bagby Aviation	Bagby	19. 6.98
G-AWLF	Reims Cessna F.172H	0536		27. 6.68	Gannet Avn Ltd	Aldergrove	25.11.99T
G-AWLG	SIPA 903	82	F-BGHG	27. 6.68	S.W.Markham (Stored 1997)	Valentine Farm, Odiham	22. 8.79P
G-AWLI	PA-22-150 Tri-Pacer	22-5083	N7256D	1. 7.68	J.S.Lewery "Little Peach"	Shoreham	5. 6.99
G-AWLM*	Campbell-Bensen B.8MS (McCulloch 4318A)	CA/311	EI-ATE / G-AWLM	8. 7.68	Not known (Stored 1992)	Haslemere, Surrey	20. 3.80P
G-AWLO	Boeing Stearman E75 (PT-13D) Kaydet (P&W R985) (Modified)	75-5563	5Y-KRR / VP-KRR/42-17400	9. 7.68	N.D.Pickard	Panshanger	7.10.01
G-AWLP	Mooney M.20F Executive 21	680200		9. 7.68	I.C.Lomax	Ottringham	7. 7.00
G-AWLR	Slingsby Nipper T.66 RA.45 Srs.3	S.125/1662		9. 7.68	T.D.Reid	Newtownards	17. 2.99P
G-AWLS	Slingsby Nipper T.66 RA.45 Srs.3	S.126/1663		9. 7.68	G.A.Dunster & B.Gallagher (Damaged Stapleford 14.1.88; on rebuild 1995)	(Loughton, Essex)	25. 3.88P
G-AWLX*	Auster 5 J/2 Arrow	2378	F-BGJQ / OO-ABZ	10. 7.68	W.J.Taylor (On rebuild 11.93)	RAF West Raynham	23. 4.70
G-AWLZ	Sportavia Fournier RF4D	4099		12. 7.68	J.H.Taylor t/a Nympsfield RF4 Group	Nympsfield	31. 1.99P
G-AWMD	Jodel D.11 (Cont C90)	PFA/904		19. 7.68	D.A.Barr-Hamilton t/a Moby Dick F/Grp "Moby Dick"	Shobdon	6. 4.99P
G-AWMF	PA-18-180 Super Cub	18-8674	N4356Z	23. 7.68	Booker Gliding Club Ltd	Booker	26. 8.00
G-AWMI	AESL Airtourer T.2 (115)	505		24. 7.68	W.G.Jones t/a Airtourer Grp	Cardiff	15.12.00
G-AWMK	Agusta-Bell 206B JetRanger	8073	9Y-TFC / G-AWMK/(VR-BCV)/G-AWMK	25. 7.68	M.D.Souster "Liberty Bell"	Redhill	5. 6.00T
G-AWMN	Phoenix Luton LA-4A Minor (VW1800)	PFA/827		30. 7.68	B.J.Douglas	Newtownards	6. 6.98P
G-AWMP	Reims Cessna F.172H	0488		31. 7.68	R.J.D.Blois	Yoxford, Saxmundham	23.12.99
G-AWMR	Druine D.31 Turbulent (VW1390)	43 & PFA/1661		1. 8.68	T.Pearce "Demelza"	Inverness	4. 5.95P
G-AWMT	Reims Cessna F.150H	0360		1. 8.68	Oilfield Expertise Ltd	Newtownards	24. 6.00
G-AWNC	Boeing 747-136	19763		30. 7.68	European Aviation Ltd	(Ledbury)	28. 2.01T
G-AWNE	Boeing 747-136	19765		30. 7.68	British Airways plc "Derwent Water"	Cardiff	7. 4.01T
G-AWNF	Boeing 747-136	19766		30. 7.68	British Airways plc "Blagdon Lake"	Heathrow	25. 6.99T
G-AWNH	Boeing 747-136	20270		29. 1.69	British Airways plc "Devoke Water"	Heathrow	30.12.01T
G-AWNM	Boeing 747-136	20708		29. 3.73	British Airways plc "Ullswater"	Heathrow	26.10.01T
G-AWNN	Boeing 747-136	20809		13. 8.73	British Airways plc "Loweswater"	Heathrow	12. 2.02T
G-AWNO	Boeing 747-136	20810		13. 8.73	British Airways plc "Grafham Water"	Heathrow	8. 1.02T
G-AWNP	Boeing 747-136	20952		18. 9.74	British Airways plc "Hanningfield Water"	Heathrow	12.12.01T
G-AWNT	BN-2A Islander	32		2. 8.68	Aerofilms Ltd	Cranfield	24. 3.01A
G-AWOA	Socata MS.880B Rallye Club	1258		2. 8.68	J.A.Rimmer	Sturgate	8. 6.99
G-AWOE	Aero Commander 680E	753-41	N3844C	5. 8.68	J.M.Houlder t/a Elstree F/C	Elstree	13. 3.00
G-AWOF	PA-15 Vagabond (Cont C90)	15-227	F-BETF	6. 8.68	C.M.Hicks	Barton	24. 2.99P
G-AWOH	PA-17 Vagabond (Cont C90)	17-191	F-BFMY / N4891H	6. 8.68	W.M.Haley, D.Ridley & R.H.Ryle t/a The High Flatts F/Grp High Flatts Farm, Chester-le-Street		19. 5.99P
G-AWOK*	Sussex Gas (Free) Balloon	SARD.1		7. 8.68	British Balloon Museum "Sardinia" (Stored)	Newbury	
G-AWOT	Reims Cessna F.150H	0389		14. 8.68	J.M.Montgomerie & J.Ferguson (Stored 4.97)	Kilkerran	13. 6.89
G-AWOU	Cessna 170B	25829	VQ-ZJA / ZS-CKY/CR-ADU/N3185A	16. 8.68	S.Billington	White Waltham	27. 5.01
G-AWOX*	Westland Wessex 60 Srs.1	WA/686	G-17-2 / G-AWOX 5N-AJO/G-AWOX/9Y-TFB/G-AWOX/VH-BHE/G-AWOX/VR-BCV/G-AWOX/G-17-1	28. 8.68	Paintball Adventure West Kingswood, Bristol		13. 1.83
G-AWPH	Percival P.56 Provost T.1	PAC/F/003	WV420	6. 9.68	J.A.D.Bradshaw Three Mile Cross, Reading		4. 6.99P
G-AWPJ	Reims Cessna F.150H	0376		9. 9.68	W.J.Greenfield (Op Humberside F/C)	Humberside	24. 4.99T
G-AWPN	Shield Xyla (Cont A65)	2 & PFA/1320		13. 9.68	K.R.Snell (Damaged Finmere 16.8.80; on rebuild 3.96)	(Uckfield)	8. 6.81P
G-AWPP	Reims Cessna F.150H	0348		13. 9.68	K2 Aviation Ltd & R.S.Willcock Cranfield (Op Billins Air Services)		22. 7.01T
G-AWPS	PA-28-140 Cherokee	28-20196	5N-AEK	16. 9.68	A.R.Matthews	Tatenhill	18. 9.00
G-AWPU	Reims Cessna F.150J	0411		18. 9.68	LAC (Enterprises) Ltd t/a Lancashire Aero Club	Barton	19.10.00T
G-AWPW	PA-12 Super Cruiser	12-3947	N78572 / NC78572	23. 9.68	AK Leasing (Jersey) Ltd Rushett Farm, Chessington		5. 4.01

Regn	Type	C/n	P/I	Date	Owner/operator	Probable Base	CA Expy
G-AWPY	Campbell-Bensen B.8M	CA/314		20. 9.68	J.Jordan Melrose Farm, Melbourne		
G-AWPZ	Andreasson BA-4B	1	SE-XBS	24. 9.68	J.M.Vening	Goodwood	13. 8.99P
G-AWRK	Reims Cessna F.150J	0410		8.10.68	Systemroute Ltd	Shoreham	15. 7.00T
G-AWRP*	Cierva Rotorcraft CR.LTH.1 Grasshopper III	GB.1		14.10.68	The Helicopter Museum Weston-super-Mare		12. 5.72P
G-AWRS*	Avro 652A Anson C.19/2	33785	TX213	14.10.68	North East Aircraft Museum (On rebuild 5.97)	Usworth	10. 8.73
G-AWRY	Hunting-Percival P.56 Provost T.1	PAC/F/339	XF836 8043M	29.10.81	Sylmar Avn & Svs Ltd (As "XF836/J-G") Lower Wasing Farm, Brimpton (Damaged nr Newbury 28.7.87; on rebuild 6.94)		22. 8.88P
G-AWSA*	Avro 652A Anson C.19/2	293483	N5054 G-AWSA/VL349	21.10.68	Norfolk & Suffolk Avn Museum (As "VL349")	Flixton	
G-AWSH	Moravan Zlin Z.526 Trener Master	1052	OK-XRH G-AWSH	23.11.68	Aerobatics International Ltd White Waltham		8.10.00
G-AWSL	PA-28-180 Cherokee D	28-4907		30.10.68	Fascia Svs Ltd Kings Farm, Thurrock/Southend		23. 7.00
G-AWSM	PA-28-235 Cherokee C	28-11125		30.10.68	N.A.Wright (London SW20) t/a Aviation Projects		9. 3.01T
G-AWSN	Rollason-Druine D.62B Condor	RAE/632		31.10.68	M.K.A.Blyth	Little Gransden	5. 5.98P
G-AWSP	Rollason-Druine D.62B Condor	RAE/634		31.10.68	R.Q. & A.S.Bond (Stored 10.97)	Enstone	23. 1.95
G-AWSS	Rollason-Druine D.62B Condor	RAE/636		31.10.68	N.J. & D.Butler (Stored 10.95)	Fordoun	19.10.94P
G-AWST	Rollason-Druine D.62B Condor	RAE/637		31.10.68	P.L.Clements Beeches Farm, South Scarle		7. 5.98P
G-AWSV*	Saro Skeeter AOP.12	S2/5107	XM553	31.10.68	Major M.Somerton-Rayner (As "XM553") AAC Middle Wallop		22. 2.95P
G-AWSW	Beagle D.5/180 Husky	3690	XW635 G-AWSW	4.11.68	C.Tyers t/a Windmill Avn (As "XW635") Spanhoe		18. 5.01T
G-AWTJ	Reims Cessna F.150J	0419		8.11.68	D.G.Williams	Headcorn	8.12.01T
G-AWTL	PA-28-180 Cherokee D	28-5068		12.11.68	E.Alexander	Andrewsfield	8. 6.01T
G-AWTS	Beechcraft 19A Musketeer Sport	MB-412	OO-BGN G-AWTS/N2763B	14.11.68	J.Holden & G.Benet	Lydd	24. 7.99T
G-AWTV	Beechcraft 19A Musketeer Sport	MB-424	N2770B	14.11.68	T.D.Cooper & D.F.Hurn	Popham	17. 8.00
G-AWTX	Reims Cessna F.150J	0404		18.11.68	R.D. & E.Forster (Stored 8.97)	Sywell	25. 6.95T
G-AWUA*	Cessna P206D Super Skylane P206-0550		N8750Z	21.11.68	Not known (Damaged Thruxton 16.10.87; stored 6.96)	Blackpool	4.12.87
G-AWUB*	Gardan GY-201 Minicab	A.205	F-PERX	22.11.68	R.A.Yates (Fuselage stored 9.91)	Sibsey	23.10.80P
G-AWUE	SAN Jodel DR.1050 Ambassadeur	299	F-BKHE	22.11.68	K.W. & F.M.Wood (On rebuild 4.97)	Insch	AC
G-AWUG	Reims Cessna F.150H	0299		25.11.68	J.Easson (Op Edinburgh Air Centre)	Edinburgh	12. 9.99T
G-AWUH*	Reims Cessna F.150H	0307		25.11.68	Not known (Stored 9.96)	Bournemouth	16. 7.94T
G-AWUJ	Reims Cessna F.150H	0332		25.11.68	S.R.Hughes	Netherthorpe	3. 2.00
G-AWUK*	Reims Cessna F.150H	0344		25.11.68	Not known (Crashed Shoreham 4.9.71; stored 4.95)	Oaksey Park	3. 9.73
G-AWUL	Reims Cessna F.150H	0346		25.11.68	C.A. & L.P.Green	Drayton St.Leonard	20. 4.99
G-AWUN	Reims Cessna F.150H	0377		25.11.68	S.Martin	Compton Abbas	12.11.01
G-AWUO	Reims Cessna F.150H	0380		25.11.68	S.Stevens Lower Wasing Farm, Brimpton t/a SAS F/Grp		2. 4.01
G-AWUT	Reims Cessna F.150J	0405		25.11.68	S.J.Black	Sherburn	18. 9.00
G-AWUU	Reims Cessna F.150J	0408	EI-BRA G-AWUU	25.11.68	A.L.Grey Armshold Farm, Kingston, Cambs		15. 6.97
G-AWUX	Reims Cessna F.172H	0577		25.11.68	D.K. & K.Brian, A.M.Martin & C.Kelly St.Just		27. 3.01
G-AWUZ	Reims Cessna F.172H	0587		25.11.68	G.F.Burling	Andrewsfield	26.10.01
G-AWVA	Reims Cessna F.172H	0597		25.11.68	Barton Air Ltd	Barton	27. 4.97
G-AWVB	SAN Jodel D.117	604	F-BIBA	26.11.68	H.Davies	Swansea	31. 5.99P
G-AWVC	Beagle B.121 Pup 1	B121-026	(OE-CUP)	27.11.68	J.H.Marshall & J.J.West	Sturgate	2. 7.01
G-AWVE	CEA Jodel DR.1050/M1 Sicile Record	612	F-BMPQ	27.11.68	E.A.Taylor	Southend	18. 5.00
G-AWVF	Hunting-Percival P.56 Provost T.1	PAC/F/375	XF877	28.11.68	Hunter Wing Ltd (As "XF877/J-X")	Sandown	10. 3.99P
G-AWVG	AESL Airtourer T2 (115)	513	OO-WIC G-AWVG	29.11.68	C.J.Scholfield	Top Farm, Tadlow	30. 6.01
G-AWVN	Aeronca 7AC Champion	7AC-6005	N2426E NC2426E	4.12.68	P.K.Brown t/a Champ F/Grp	Rush Green	17. 2.99P
G-AWVZ	Jodel D.112	898	F-PKVL	12.12.68	D.C.Stokes Garston Farm, Marshfield		10. 5.99
G-AWWE	Beagle B.121 Pup 2	B121-032	G-35-032	12.12.68	J.N.Randle	Coventry	20. 7.98
G-AWWI	SAN Jodel D.117	728	F-BIDU	13.12.68	W.J.Evans	Rhigos	27. 4.99P
G-AWWM	Gardan GY-201 Minicab	A.195	F-BFOQ	1. 1.69	J.S.Brayshaw Haddock Stone Farm, Markington		10.12.92P
G-AWWN	SAN Jodel DR.1050 Sicile	398	F-BLJA	8. 1.69	R.B.Tyler (Buntingford, Herts)		11. 6.98
G-AWWO	CEA Jodel DR.1050 Sicile	552	F-BLOI	8. 1.69	A.R.Grimshaw & J.Hodcroft t/a The Whiskey Oscar Grp	Barton	15. 5.00
G-AWWP	Aerosport Woody Pusher Mk.3	WA/163 & PFA/1323		7. 1.69	M.S. & Mrs R.D.Bird Pepperbox, Salisbury (Stored 6.93)		
G-AWWT	Druine D.31 Turbulent (VW1600)	PFA/1653		15. 1.69	E.L.Phillips (Damaged on landing Andrewsfield 7.10.96)	Andrewsfield	23. 4.97P
G-AWWU	Reims Cessna FR.172F Rocket	0111		15. 1.69	Westward Airways (Lands End) Ltd St.Just		16. 3.00T

Regn	Type	C/n	P/I	Date	Owner/operator	Probable Base	CA Expy
G-AWWW	Cessna 401	401-0294	N8446F	19.12.68	Treble Whiskey Avn Ltd (Op Westair F/Svs)	Blackpool	3. 2.00T
G-AWWX*	BAC One-Eleven 509EW				See G-OBWG		
G-AWXR	PA-28-180 Cherokee D	28-5171		24. 1.69	Aero Club de Portugal (Lisbon, Portugal)		14. 4.01
G-AWXS	PA-28-180 Cherokee D	28-5283		24. 1.69	J.A.Hardiman	Shobdon	3. 3.00T
G-AWXY	Morane MS.885 Super Rallye	5097	EI-AMG	29. 1.69	K.Henderson	(Witham, Essex)	1. 2.97
G-AWXZ	SNCAN Stampe SV-4C	360	F-BHMZ Fr.Mil/F-BCOI	30. 1.69	Personal Plane Svs Ltd (Op Blue Max Movie Acft Museum)	Booker	17. 9.98A
G-AWYB	Reims Cessna FR.172F Rocket	0075		30. 1.69	C.W.Larkin Larkins Farm, Laindon North		17. 9.00
G-AWYJ	Beagle B.121 Pup 2	B121-038	G-35-038	10. 2.69	H.C.Taylor	Popham	18. 2.99
G-AWYL	CEA Jodel DR.253B Regent	143		11. 2.69	M.R.Elms	Rochester	9. 4.00
G-AWYO	Beagle B.121 Pup 1	B121-041	G-35-041	11. 2.69	B.R.C.Wild	Popham	29.10.99
G-AWYV	BAC One-Eleven 501EX	BAC.178		11. 2.69	European Avn Ltd (Op Maersk Air)	Birmingham	24. 6.01T
G-AWYX	Socata MS.880B Rallye Club	1311		11. 2.69	Marjorie J.Edwards (Open storage 8.97)	Henstridge	27. 6.86
G-AWYY*	Slingsby T.57 Sopwith Camel F.1 replica (Clerget)	1701	"C1701" N1917H/G-AWYY	14. 2.69	Fleet Air Arm Museum (As "B6401")	RNAS Yeovilton	1.9.85P*
G-AWZI*	HS.121 Trident 3B-101	2310		14. 1.69	Surrey County Fire Brigade HQ (Instructional airframe)	Reigate	5. 8.85T
G-AWZJ*	HS.121 Trident 3B-101	2311		14. 1.69	Prestwick Fire Dept (Noted 6.98)	Prestwick	12. 9.85T
G-AWZK*	HS.121 Trident 3B-101	2312		14. 1.69	British Airways plc (Instructional airframe 1.99) (As "Windsor Collection")	Heathrow	14.10.86T
G-AWZM*	HS.121 Trident 3B-101	2314		14. 1.69	The Science Museum (British Airways c/s)	Wroughton	13.12.85T
G-AWZO*	HS.121 Trident 3B-101	2316		14. 1.69	De Havilland Aircraft Museum (Stored 3.96)	Hatfield	13. 2.86T
G-AWZS*	HS.121 Trident 3B-101	2319		14. 1.69	CAA International Fire Training Centre	Teesside	9. 9.86T
G-AWZU*	HS.121 Trident 3B-101	2321		14. 1.69	CAA Fire Service (Open storage 8.98)	Stansted	3. 7.85T
G-AWZX*	HS.121 Trident 3B-101	2324		14. 1.69	Gatwick Airport Ltd (Fire Services airframe)	Gatwick	30. 4.84T
G-AWZZ*	HS.121 Trident 3B-101	2326		14. 1.69	Birmingham Airport Fire Service (Training airframe 3.97)	Birmingham	21. 5.84T

G-AXAA-AXZZ

Regn	Type	C/n	P/I	Date	Owner/operator	Probable Base	CA Expy
G-AXAB	PA-28-140 Cherokee	28-20238	EI-AOA N6206W	17. 2.69	Bencray Ltd Blackpool t/a Blackpool & Fylde A/C		9.10.00T
G-AXAK	Socata MS.880B Rallye Club	1304		20. 2.69	A.G.Foster	North Coates	23. 1.00
G-AXAN	DH.82A Tiger Moth (Official c/n EM720-85)	85951	F-BDMM Fr.AF/EM720	21. 2.69	M.E.Carrell (As "EM720")	Little Gransden	17. 3.99
G-AXAO*	Omega O-56 HAFB (Rebuilt as Western O-65 c/n 021)	02		25. 2.69	Not known "Alcofribas"	Gerrards Cross	19. 5.75S
G-AXAS	Wallis WA-116-T/Mc (Used major components from G-AVDH c/n 216)	217		25. 2.69	K.H.Wallis	Reymerston Hall	15. 6.99P
G-AXAT	SAN Jodel D.117A	836	F-BITJ	26. 2.69	P.S.Wilkinson	Insch	22.12.99P
G-AXAU	PA-30-160 Twin Comanche C (Stored 2.96)	30-1753	N8613Y	25. 2.69	Bartcourt Ltd	Bournemouth	8. 3.86T
G-AXBF	Beagle D.5/180 Husky	3691	OE-DEW	17.10.84	C.M.Barnes Garden Piece, Basingstoke		23. 6.00
G-AXBG	Bensen B.8M	RC.1		12. 3.69	R.Curtis	(Bury St.Edmunds)	
G-AXBH	Reims Cessna F.172H	0571		12. 3.69	D.F.Ranger	Popham	6. 3.00T
G-AXBJ	Reims Cessna F.172H	0573		12. 3.69	R.H.Bowers t/a Bravo Juliet Grp	Leicester	27.11.00
G-AXBU*	Reims Cessna FR.172F Rocket	0073		12. 3.69	M.Hobson Cruden Bay, Peterhead (Crashed nr Priestland, Darvel 13.10.74; wreck in store 2.96)		23. 8.75
G-AXBW	DH.82A Tiger Moth	83595	6854M T5879	12. 3.69	Hunter Wing Ltd (As "T5879")	Frensham	15. 1.01
G-AXBZ	DH.82A Tiger Moth	86552	F-BGDF Fr.AF/PG643	14. 3.69	D.H.McWhir	Newtownards	6. 9.01
G-AXCA	PA-28R-200 Cherokee Arrow	28R-35053		18. 3.69	R.A.Symmonds	Southend	6. 3.00
G-AXCG	SAN Jodel D.117	510	PH-VRA F-BHXI	19. 3.69	C.A.White t/a The Charlie Golf Grp	Andrewsfield	15. 6.99P
G-AXCI*	Bensen B.8M	CEW.1		20. 3.69	Not known (Stored 9.93)	Lichfield	
G-AXCL	Socata MS.880B Rallye Club	1321		25. 3.69	P.P.Loucas	Seething	9. 7.00
G-AXCM	Socata MS.880B Rallye Club	1322		25. 3.69	D.C.Maniford Draycott Farm, Chiseldon		23. 7.01
G-AXCN	Socata MS.880B Rallye Club	1328		25. 3.69	J.E.Compton (Malmesbury) (Damaged Thruxton 16.10.87: on rebuild 1992)		24. 7.87
G-AXCX	Beagle B.121 Pup 2	B121-046	G-35-046	31. 3.69	L.A.Pink	Old Sarum	10. 7.94
G-AXCY	SAN Jodel D.117A	499	F-BHXB	31. 3.69	R.D.P.Cadle	(Chipping Campden)	23. 8.99P
G-AXDC	PA-23-250 Aztec D	27-4169	N6829Y	8. 4.69	N.J.Lilley	Bodmin	24. 8.98T
G-AXDI	Reims Cessna F.172H	0574		14. 4.69	M.F. & J.R.Leusby Wellesbourne Mountford t/a Jeanair		25.11.99
G-AXDK	CEA DR.315 Petit Prince	378		16. 4.69	M.R.Weatherhead & T.J.Thomas Sywell t/a Delta Kilo F/Grp		10. 4.99
G-AXDM	HS.125 Srs.400B	25194		17. 4.69	GEC - Marconi Avionics (Holdings) Ltd Edinburgh		7. 6.99
G-AXDN*	BAC/Aerospatiale Concorde	13522 & 01		16. 4.69	Duxford Aviation Society	Duxford	30. 9.77
G-AXDV	Beagle B.121 Pup 1	B121-049		18. 4.69	T.A.White	Bagby	7. 4.01
G-AXDW	Beagle B.121 Pup 1	B121-053		18. 4.69	I.Beaty, P.J.Abbott & J.R.A.Stevens t/a Cranfield Delta Whiskey Group Cranfield		28. 1.02
G-AXDY*	Falconar F-11 (Incorporated redundant parts from Jodel D.112 G-AYBR; fuselage stored 9.91)	PFA/906		21. 4.69	R.A.Yates	Sibsey	
G-AXDZ*	Airmark Cassutt Speed One (Cont C90)	PFA/1341		21. 4.69	A.Chadwick "White Lightning" Enstone (Cancelled by CAA 26.2.99)		2. 7.99P
G-AXED	PA-25-235 Pawnee B	25-3586	OH-PIM	24. 4.69	Wolds Gliding Club Ltd	Pocklington	11. 3.00
G-AXEH*	Beagle B.125 Bulldog 1	B.125-001		25. 4.69	The Museum of Flight/Royal Museum of Scotland East Fortune		15. 1.77
G-AXEI*	Ward P.45 Gnome	P.45		25. 4.69	A.J.E.Smith & N.H.Ponsford	Breighton	
G-AXEO	Scheibe SF-25B Falke	4645	D-KEBC	1. 5.69	R.Cassidy & W.P.Stephen	Portmoak	19. 3.01
G-AXEV	Beagle B.121 Pup 2	B121-070		6. 5.69	D.S.Russell & J.Powell-Tuck Gloucestershire		21. 5.00
G-AXFG	Cessna 337D Super Skymaster	337-1070	(EI-) G-AXFG/OY-BVP/G-AXFG/N86081	14. 5.69	Helitechnique Ltd	Cumbernauld	15.11.01T
G-AXFM*	Cierva Rotorcraft CR.LTH.1 Grasshopper III	GB.2		19. 5.69	The Helicopter Museum Weston-super-Mare (Completed as ground-running rig; stored 3.96)		
G-AXFN	Jodel D.119	980	F-PHBU	19. 5.69	D.G.West Kearsley Farm, Durham		10. 2.99P
G-AXGA*	PA-18-95 Super Cub (L-18C-PI) (Frame No. 18-2059)	18-2047	PH-NLE (PH-CUB)/R.Neth.AF R-51/8A-51/52-2447	22. 5.69	R.A.Yates Sibsey (Damaged Felthorpe 26.12.86; stored 8.90)		1. 8.89
G-AXGC	Socata MS.880B Rallye Club	1349		23. 5.69	P.A.Crawford & M.C.Bennett (Stored Elstree 9.95) (Saltash/Redruth)		12. 5.88
G-AXGE	Socata MS.880B Rallye Club	1353		23. 5.69	R.P.Loxton	Henstridge	25. 5.01
G-AXGG	Reims Cessna F.150J	0440		28. 5.69	C.F. & R.F.Clarke Little Staughton t/a CTC Associates		17. 7.00
G-AXGP	Piper J3C-90 Cub (L-4J-PI) Frame No.12374) (Quoted as c/n 9542 ex 43-28251)	12544	F-BGPS F-BDTM/44-80248	2. 6.69	W.K.Butler Whittles Farm, Mapledurham		5. 5.94P
G-AXGR	Phoenix Luton LA-4A Minor (JAP J.99)	PAL/1125		2. 6.69	Barbara A.Schlussler (Bourne) (Stored Eshott 4.94)		10. 4.91P
G-AXGS	Rollason-Druine D.62B Condor	RAE/638		3. 6.69	B.W.Haston Shempston Farm, Elgin		21. 6.99P
G-AXGU*	Rollason-Druine D.62B Condor	RAE/640		3. 6.69	Not known Eshott (Crashed nr Godalming, Surrey 31.3.75; stored 9.94)		22. 5.76

Regn	Type	C/n	P/I	Date	Owner/operator	Probable Base	CA Expy
G-AXGV	Rollason-Druine D.62B Condor	RAE/641		3. 6.69	S.B.Robson	Watchford Farm, Yarcombe	5. 4.99P
G-AXGZ	Rollason-Druine D.62B Condor	RAE/643		3. 6.69	J.Evans	Griffins Farm, Temple Bruer	19. 5.99P
G-AXHA	Cessna 337A Super Skymaster	337-0484	(EI-ATH) N5384S	5. 6.69	G.R.E.Evans	Little Staughton	15. 7.99
G-AXHC	SNCAN Stampe SV-4C	293	F-BCFU	6. 6.69	D.L.Webley	Cranwell	16. 4.99T
G-AXHE*	BN-2A Islander	86	4X-AYV G-AXHE	6. 6.69	Not known	Cumbernauld	15. 4.94
					(Crashed Cark 5.2.94: rear fuselage at Strathallan 8.98)		
G-AXHG*	Socata MS.880B Rallye Club	1371		6. 6.69	A.Smails	Ketton, Darlington	26. 5.85
					(Spares use 4.95)		
G-AXHO	Beagle B.121 Pup 2	B121-077		9. 6.69	L.H.Grundy	Thurrock	6. 5.01
G-AXHP	Piper J3C-65 Cub (L-4J-PI)	12932	F-BETT NC74121/44-80636	9. 6.69	Witham (Specialist) Vehicles Ltd	(Grantham)	11.11.99P
	(Frame No.12762)						
	(Regd with c/n "AF36506" which is a USAAC contract number; as "480636 A-58" in US Army c/s)						
G-AXHR	Piper J3C-65 Cub (L-4H-PI)	10892	F-BETI 43-29601	9. 6.69	K.B.Raven & E.Cundy	Bagby	19. 5.99P
					t/a G-AXHR Cub Grp (As "329601/D-44" in US Army c/s)		
G-AXHS	Socata MS.880B Rallye Club	1357		9. 6.69	B. & A.Swales	Carlisle	1. 7.99
G-AXHT	Socata MS.880B Rallye Club	1358		9. 6.69	D.E.Guck	Wellesbourne Mountford	25. 2.01
G-AXHV	SAN Jodel D.117A	695	F-BIDF	9. 6.69	J.S.Ponsford	Hucknall	9. 3.99P
					t/a Derwent F/Grp		
G-AXIA	Beagle B.121 Pup 1	B121-078		17. 6.69	J.M.Bax	Old Sarum	1. 4.01T
G-AXIE	Beagle B.121 Pup 2	B121-087		17. 6.69	G.A.Ponsford	Goodwood	28. 4.01
G-AXIF	Beagle B.121 Pup 2	B121-088	(SE-FGV)	17. 6.69	Julia A.Holmes "Susie II"	Dunkeswell	24. 7.99
G-AXIG	Scottish Avn Bulldog Srs.100/104	BH120-002		24. 6.69	A.A.Douglas-Hamilton	(Haddington, East Lothian)	5. 4.99
G-AXIO	PA-28-140 Cherokee B	28-25764		26. 6.69	White Waltham Airfield Ltd		
					(Op West London Aero Svs)	White Waltham	18. 1.02T
G-AXIR	PA-28-140 Cherokee B	28-25795		26. 6.69	A.G.Birch	Weston Zoyland	13. 5.00
G-AXIT	Socata MS.893A Rallye Commodore 180	11430		27. 6.69	T.J.Price	Bidford	22. 9.99
					(Op Avon Soaring Centre) (Damaged at Seighford 7.11.98)		
G-AXIW	Scheibe SF-25B Falke	4657	(D-KABJ)	3. 7.69	M.B.Hill	Nympsfield	26. 7.99
G-AXIX	AESL Airtourer T4 (150)	A.527		3. 7.69	J.C.Wood	Oaksey Park	16.12.00
G-AXIY*	Bird Gyrocopter	GB.001		3. 7.69	R Light & T Smith	Stockport	
					(Complete - awaiting restoration 2.99)		
G-AXJB	Omega 84 HAFB	04		9. 7.69	Semajan Ltd	Romsey, Wilts	20. 8.73S
	(Initially flown as G-AXDT)				t/a Southern Balloon Grp "Jester"		
G-AXJH	Beagle B.121 Pup 2	B121-089		11. 7.69	J.S.Chillingworth	Duxford	28. 1.01
G-AXJI	Beagle B.121 Pup 2	B121-090		11. 7.69	D.R.Vale	(Burton-on-Trent)	11. 8.99
G-AXJJ	Beagle B.121 Pup 2	B121-091		11. 7.69	S.N.Chater & B.Ward	Crosland Moor	17. 7.00
					t/a The Bumpf Grp		
G-AXJO	Beagle B.121 Pup 2	B121-094		11. 7.69	J.A.D.Bradshaw "Joey"		
						Three Mile Cross, Reading	7. 8.00
G-AXJR	Scheibe SF-25B Falke	4652	D-KICD	14. 7.69	D.R.Chatterton	Nympsfield	14. 4.00
G-AXJV	PA-28-140 Cherokee B	28-25572	N11C	14. 7.69	N.J.Atherton	Perth	8. 6.01
G-AXJX	PA-28-140 Cherokee B	28-25990		14. 7.69	Patrolwatch Ltd	Barton	24. 8.01
G-AXKH	Phoenix Luton LA-4A Minor (VW1600)	PAL/1316 & PFA/823		21. 7.69	M.E.Vaisey	(Hemel Hempstead)	18. 4.84P
					(Status uncertain)		
G-AXKJ	Jodel D.9 Bebe (VW1600)	SAS/002, PFA/928B & PFA/941		22. 7.69	C.C.Gordon & N.Mowbray "Le Bebe"		
						Eastbach Farm, English Bicknor	11.12.97P
G-AXKN*	Westland Bell 47G-4A	WA/719	EC-EDF	22. 7.69	Nash Group Ltd	(Warwick)	
				(D-H...)/G-AXKN/G-17-4 (Cancelled by CAA 9.2.99)			
G-AXKO	Westland-Bell 47G-4A	WA/720	G-17-5	22. 7.69	G.P.Hinkley	Channons Hall, Tibenham	27. 8.99
G-AXKS*	Westland-Bell 47G-4A	WA/723	G-17-8	22. 7.69	Museum of Army Flying	AAC Middle Wallop	21. 9.82
G-AXKW	Westland-Bell 47G-4A	WA/727	G-17-12	22. 7.69	Eyre Spier Associates Ltd		
					(See G-AYOE)	Richmond, N.Yorks	8. 8.99T
G-AXKX	Westland-Bell 47G-4A	WA/728	G-17-13	22. 7.69	Copley Farms Ltd		
						Copley Hill Farm, Babraham	18. 5.01
G-AXKY	Westland-Bell 47G-4A	WA/729	G-17-14	22. 7.69	G.A.Knight & G.M.Vowles	Gamston	17. 6.99
G-AXLG	Cessna 310K	310K-0204	N3804X	25. 7.69	Smiths (Harlow) Aerospace Ltd		
						Willingale	17. 7.00
G-AXLI	Slingsby Nipper T.66 RA.45 Srs.3	S.131/1707		25. 7.69	R.Bailes-Brown & M.J.D.Probert	Gamston	8.12.99P
G-AXLL	BAC One-Eleven 523FJ	BAC.193	OB-R1173 OB-R1137/PP-SDT/G-AXLL/G-16-8	29. 7.69	European Avn Air Charter Ltd	Bournemouth	20. 7.01T
G-AXLS	SAN Jodel DR.105A Ambassadeur	86	F-BIVR	31. 7.69	J.C.M.Robb	White Waltham	15. 3.01
					t/a Axle Flying Club		
G-AXLZ	PA-18-95 Super Cub (L-18C-PI)	18-2052	PH-NLB R.Neth.AF R-45/8A-45/52-2452	31. 7.69	R.J.Quantrell	Low Farm, South Walsham	23. 4.00
	(Frame No.18-2065)				(Damaged Low Farm 14.8.97)		
G-AXMA	PA-24-180 Comanche	24-3467	N8214P	5. 8.69	J.D.Bingham	Gamston	11. 6.01
G-AXMB*	Slingsby T.7 Motor Cadet Mk.2 (Triumph T.100)	BGA805 VM590		5. 8.69	Not known	(Sussex)	9. 7.82P
					(On rebuild 1992)		
G-AXMD*	Omega O-20 HAFB	06		7. 8.69	British Balloon Museum	Newbury	
	(Has second envelope c/n 07 but not known which BBM holds) "Nimble"						
G-AXMN	Auster J/5B Autocar	2962	F-BGPN	14. 8.69	A.Phillips	Haverfordwest	30..7.01
G-AXMP	PA-28-180 Cherokee D	28-5436		19. 8.69	B.Stewart	(Ware)	23. 1.00
G-AXMT	Dornier Bucker Bu.133C Jungmeister	46	N133SJ G-AXMT/HB-MIY/U-99	19. 8.69	W.R.M.Beesley	Breighton	5. 5.99P
G-AXMW	Beagle B.121 Pup 1	B121-101		19. 8.69	DJP Engineering (Knebworth) Ltd		
					(Damaged late 1997)	Cambridge	22. 1.01

Regn	Type	C/n	P/I	Date	Owner/operator	Probable Base	CA Expy
G-AXMX	Beagle B.121 Pup 2	B121-103	VH-UPT G-AXMX/G-35-103	19. 8.69	Susan A.Jones	Cannes, France	5.10.00
G-AXNJ	Jodel Wassmer D.120 Paris-Nice	52	F-BHYO	29. 8.69	D.R.Groom & Ptnrs t/a Clive F/Grp	Sleap	30. 9.99P
G-AXNL	Beagle B.121 Pup 1	B121-113		3. 9.69	J.Coleman	Sywell	7. 4.01T
G-AXNM	Beagle B.121 Pup 1	B121-114		3. 9.69	F.E.Green "Bertie"	Compton Abbas	27. 5.97
G-AXNN	Beagle B.121 Pup 2	B121-104		3. 9.69	Gabrielle Avn Ltd "Gabrielle"	Shoreham	29. 7.00
G-AXNP	Beagle B.121 Pup 2	B121-106		3. 9.69	J.W.Ellis	Ashcroft Farm, Winsford	1. 7.99
G-AXNR	Beagle B.121 Pup 2	B121-108		3. 9.69	M.H.Wood Brookfield Farm, Great Stukeley t/a November Romeo Group		19.10.98
G-AXNS	Beagle B.121 Pup 2	B121-110		3. 9.69	M.J.D.Probert & A.J.Stone t/a Derwent Aero Grp	Gamston	8. 7.01
G-AXNW	SNCAN Stampe SV-4C (Modified)	381	F-BFZX Fr.Mil	11. 9.69	Carolyn S.Grace Blooms Farm, Sible Hedingham		1. 5.99
G-AXNX	Cessna 182M	182-59322	N70606	16. 9.69	D.B.Harper	Biggin Hill	2. 5.99T
G-AXNZ	Pitts S-1C Special EB.1 & PFA/1383 (Lyc IO-360) (Quoted c/n EB.2)			16. 9.69	W.A.Jordan (Stored 3.97)	Little Gransden	30. 8.91P
G-AXOG	PA-E23-250 Aztec D	27-4330	N6965Y	17. 9.69	G.H.Nolan	Biggin Hill	19.10.00
G-AXOH	Socata MS.894A Rallye Minerva 220	11062	D-EAGU	17. 9.69	Bristol Cars Ltd	White Waltham	18. 5.00
G-AXOJ	Beagle B.121 Pup 2	B121-109	G-35-109	24. 9.69	T.J.Martin t/a Pup F/Grp	Rochester	28. 8.00
G-AXOM*	Penn-Smith Gyroplane DJPS.1 (VW1600)			26. 9.69	Stondon Transport Museum & Garden Centre Lower Stondon, Beds		24.2.71P*
G-AXOR	PA-28-180 Cherokee D	28-5453		30. 9.69	Oscar Romeo Avn Ltd	Redhill	1. 4.99
G-AXOS	Socata MS.894A Rallye Minerva 220	11079		3.10.69	P.Mather	Cambridge	20. 5.00
G-AXOT	Socata MS.893A Rallye Commodore 180	11433		3.10.69	P.Evans & J.C.Graves	Doncaster	26. 3.00
G-AXOZ	Beagle B.121 Pup 1	B121-115	N70290 G-AXOZ/G-35-115	7.10.69	R.J.Ogborn	Chester	11.12.00
G-AXPA	Beagle B.121 Pup 1	B121-116	D-EATL G-AXPA/G-35-116	7.10.69	D.G.Lewendon	Gloucestershire	4.11.87
G-AXPB	Beagle B.121 Pup 1	B121-117	G-35-117	7.10.69	M.J.K.Seary & R.T.Austin	Leicester	11.11.01
G-AXPC	Beagle B.121 Pup 1	B121-119	PH-VRS G-AXPC	7.10.69	T.A.White	Bagby	12. 8.00
G-AXPF	Reims Cessna F.150K	0543		14.10.69	D.R.Marks	Enstone	7. 5.98
G-AXPG	Mignet HM.293 (VW1300)	PFA/1333		14.10.69	W.H.Cole Spilsted Farm, Sedlescombe (Stored 3.97)		20. 1.77P
G-AXPM	Beagle B.121 Pup 1	B121-122	G-35-122	20.10.69	R.G.Hayes	North Weald	8. 4.99T
G-AXPN	Beagle B.121 Pup 2	B121-123	G-35-123	20.10.69	D.J.Elbourn, J.Granger & J.D.Scott (XP Parcels c/s) Top Farm, Tadlow		12. 2.02
G-AXPZ	Campbell Cricket (Rotax 582)	CA/320		3.11.69	W.R.Partridge	St.Merryn	27. 4.99P
G-AXRC	Campbell Cricket (VW1600)	CA/323		3.11.69	E.N.Simmons (Boston) (Damaged Wittering 22.10.77; stored Tattershall Thorpe 7.91)		18. 5.78S
G-AXRK*	Practavia Pilot Sprite 115	15 & PFA/1381		4.11.69	M.Oliver (Under construction 7.95)	Crowborough	
G-AXRP	SNCAN Stampe SV.4C				(See G-BLOL)		
G-AXRO	PA-30-160 Twin Comanche C	30-1978	N8820Y	5.11.69	Comanche Hire Ltd	Gloucestershire	3. 3.01T
G-AXRR	Auster AOP.9 AUS.178 & B5/10/178		XR241 G-AXRR/XR241	7.11.69	R.J.Burgess (Horley) (As "XR241" in Army yellow c/s)		21. 9.99P
G-AXRT	Reims Cessna FA.150K Aerobat (Tail-wheel conversion)	0018		12.11.69	J.K.Horne	Elstree	24. 1.00T
G-AXRU*	Reims Cessna FA.150K Aerobat	0020		12.11.69	Arrival Enterprises Ltd Kemble (Cancelled by CAA 2.3.99; stored 6.97)		10.12.87
G-AXSC	Beagle B.121 Pup 1	B121-138	G-35-138	13.11.69	R.J.MacCarthy	Denham	3. 2.01
G-AXSD	Beagle B.121 Pup 1	B121-139	G-35-139	13.11.69	A.C.Townend	Bagby	2. 9.01
G-AXSF	Nash Petrel PFA/1516 & P.003 (Lyc O-360) (Second allocation of PFA c/n but no connection with G-BACA)			17.11.69	Nash Acft Ltd (Stored 10.95)	Lasham	7.4.94P*
G-AXSG	PA-28-180 Cherokee E	28-5605		17.11.69	Admiral Property Ltd	Southend	5. 7.94T
G-AXSI	Reims Cessna F.172H	0687	G-SNIP G-AXSI	19.11.69	A.J.G.Davis St.Marys, Isles of Scilly t/a St.Mary's F/C		23. 7.01
G-AXSM	CEA Jodel DR.1051 Sicile	512	F-BLRH	20.11.69	K.D.Doyle Maypole Farm, Chislet		3.10.98
G-AXSR	Brantly B.2B	474	G-ROOF G-AXSR/N2237U	24.11.69	A.Murzyn West End Farm, Stevington, Bedford		6. 7.01
G-AXSW	Reims Cessna FA.150K Aerobat	0003		25.11.69	R.Mitchell (Chalfont St.Giles)		2. 3.01
G-AXSZ	PA-28-140 Cherokee B	28-26188		26.11.69	R.Gibson & B.Collins White Waltham t/a The White Wings F/Grp		24. 4.00
G-AXTA	PA-28-140 Cherokee B	28-26301		26.11.69	P.J.Farrell t/a G-AXTA Aircraft Group	Shoreham	25. 5.01
G-AXTC	PA-28-140 Cherokee B	28-26265		26.11.69	B.Mellor & W.J.Knott t/a G-AXTC Grp Beeches Farm, South Scarle		AC
G-AXTJ	PA-28-140 Cherokee B	28-26241		26.11.69	K.Patel	Elstree	1. 2.01T
G-AXTK*	PA-28-140 Cherokee B	28-26235		26.11.69	Not known Southend (Damaged Clacton 6.9.81; wreck stored 1.94)		25. 6.84
G-AXTL	PA-28-140 Cherokee B	28-26247		26.11.69	Pegasus Aviation (Midlands) Ltd Halfpenny Green		14.10.01

Regn	Type	C/n	P/I	Date	Owner/operator	Probable Base	CA Expy
G-AXTO	PA-24-260 Comanche C	24-4900	N9449P	28.11.69	Jean L.Richardson "Betsy Baby"	RAF Wyton	21. 7.00
G-AXTP	PA-28-180 Cherokee C	28-3791	OH-PID	1.12.69	C.W.R.Moore	Elstree	26.11.00
G-AXTX	Wassmer Jodel D.112	1077	F-BKCA	3.12.69	C.Sawford	(Cardiff)	6. 8.99P
G-AXTZ*	Beagle B.121 Pup 1	B121-148	G-35-148	4.12.69	R.S. & A.D.Kent	Shoreham	14. 2.76
	(Crashed Andrewsfield 30.3.75; on rebuild 10.96 for Shoreham Avn Heritage Trust- cancelled by CAA 2.3.99)						
G-AXUA	Beagle B.121 Pup 1	B121-150	G-35-150	4.12.69	D.S. Sweet	Wedmore	28. 4.00
G-AXUB	BN-2A Islander	121	5N-AIJ	4.12.69	Headcorn Parachute Club Ltd	Headcorn	25. 4.99
			G-AXUB/N859JA/G-51-47				
G-AXUC	PA-12 Super Cruiser	12-621	5Y-KFR	5.12.69	J.J.Bunton	Maypole Farm, Chislet	28.10.01
			VP-KFR/ZS-BIN				
G-AXUF	Reims Cessna FA.150K Aerobat	0043		9.12.69	A.D.McLeod	Blackpool	23. 7.99T
G-AXUJ	Auster 5 J/1 Autocrat	1957	PH-OTO	11.12.69	J.W.H.Lee & G.L.Brown	Sibson	1. 4.01
G-AXUK	SAN Jodel DR.1050 Ambassadeur	292	F-BJYU	11.12.69	C.J.Dark t/a The Ambassadeurs F/Grp	Enstone	2. 9.00
G-AXUM*	HP.137 Jetstream 1	245		12.12.69	Cranfield University	Cranfield	11.12.99A
					(Cancelled as wfu 20.1.99)		
G-AXUY*	SAN Jodel DR.100A Ambassadeur	51	F-BIZI	18.12.69	J.J.Mott/162 Sqdn ATC	Stockport	3.11.78
					(Crashed Ash House Farm, Winsford 3.9.78; instructional airframe 1.96)		
G-AXVB	Reims Cessna F.172H	0703		22.12.69	J.E.Compton & R.Turner Charlton Park, Malmesbury		26. 5.01
G-AXVK*	Campbell Cricket	CA/327		1. 1.70	R Light & T Smith	Stockport	
					(Under restoration 2.99)		
G-AXVL*	Campbell Cricket	CA/328		1. 1.70	Syrian Military Museum Tekkiye Mosque, Damascus		
G-AXVM	Campbell Cricket (VW1834)	CA/329		1. 1.70	D.M.Organ Stoke Orchard, Cheltenham		4. 4.99P
G-AXVN	McCandless M.4 (Modified) (VW1700)	M4/6		5. 1.70	W.R.Partridge	St.Merryn	
G-AXVU*	Omega 84 HAFB	09		7. 1.70	British Balloon Museum "Henry VIII"	Newbury	28. 4.77S
G-AXVV	Piper J3C-65 Cub (L-4H-PI)	10863	F-BBQB 43-29572	7. 1.70	J.D.MacCarthy	Rathcoole, Co.Cork	16. 6.73
					(Stored 4.96)		
G-AXWA	Auster AOP.9	B5/10/133	XN437	13. 1.70	M.L. & C.M.Edwards (Welling, Kent)		
					(Status uncertain - possibly exported 1994)		
G-AXWF*	Reims Cessna F.172H	0697		16. 1.70	Not known Starling Green, Clavering, Essex		22. 5.85T
	(Damaged Clacton 26/27.11.83; stored 7.95)						
G-AXWT	Jodel D.11 (Cont C90)	PFA/911		26. 1.70	R.C.Owen	Danehill	2. 6.99P
G-AXWV	CEA DR.253 Regent	104	F-OCKL	2. 2.70	J.R.D.Bygraves	Little Gransden	14. 7.00
G-AXWZ	PA-28R-200 Cherokee Arrow	28R-35605		3. 2.70	P.Walkley	(Insch)	4. 8.99
G-AXXC	Rousseau Piel CP.301B Emeraude	117	F-BJAT	4. 2.70	J.A.Sykes	Stretton	28. 6.99P
G-AXXP*	Bradshaw HAB-76 (Ax7) HAFB	RB.001		20. 2.70	British Balloon Museum "Ignis Volens" (Stored)	Newbury	
G-AXXV	DH.82A Tiger Moth	85852	F-BGJI Fr.AF/DE992	24. 2.70	C.N.Wookey (As "DE992")	France Farm, Upavon	28. 4.01
G-AXXW	SAN Jodel D.117 (mod)	632	F-BIBN	26. 2.70	M.Ward	Sturgate	18. 6.99P
G-AXYK	Taylor JT.1 Monoplane (VW1500)	PFA/1409		2. 3.70	D.J.Hulks & R.W.Davies	Headcorn	3. 7.95P
					(Damaged Couhe,France 30.6.95; on repair 11.95)		
G-AXYU	Jodel D.9 Bebe (VW1600)	547	EI-BVE G-AXYU	5. 3.70	D.J.Laughlin	Eglinton	4. 9.99P
G-AXYX*	WHE Airbuggy (VW1600)	1003		10. 3.70	W.B.Lumb (Moston, Manchester)		15. 4.84S
	(Damaged Melbourne, York 30.7.83 - on rebuild/spares for G-AXYZ 7.94)						
G-AXYZ	WHE Airbuggy (VW1600)	1005		10. 3.70	W.B.Lumb	Melrose Farm, Melbourne	22.12.92P
G-AXZA	WHE Airbuggy (VW1700)	1006		10. 3.70	Not known (Hoofdoorp, Netherlands)		15. 8.96P
G-AXZB*	WHE Airbuggy (VW1834)	1007		10. 3.70	Not known (Temp unregd 19.2.97)	Caersws, Powys	18.11.86P
G-AXZD	PA-28-180 Cherokee E	28-5609		12. 3.70	G.M.Whitmore	High Cross, Ware	6. 9.01T
G-AXZF	PA-28-180 Cherokee E	28-5688		12. 3.70	E.P.C. & W.R.Rabson	Eastleigh	23. 7.01T
G-AXZK	BN-2A-26 Islander	153	V2-LAD VP-LAD/G-AXZK/G-51-153	12. 3.70	Headcorn Parachute Club Ltd	Peterlee	27. 1.00
					(Stored 2.99)		
G-AXZM	Slingsby Nipper T.66 RA.45 Srs.3A (VW1600) (Slingsby kit c/n S.133/1709)	PFA/1378		16. 3.70	G.R.Harlow	Newcastle	24. 8.89P
					(Damaged nr Eshott 21.8.89; possible rebuild 5.90)		
G-AXZO	Cessna 180	31137	N3639C	17. 3.70	Golf Centres Group Ltd	Bridport	8.12.99
G-AXZP	PA-E23-250 Aztec D	27-4464	N13819	17. 3.70	D.D.Saint	Bristol/Lulsgate	19. 7.01T
G-AXZT	SAN Jodel D.117A	607	F-BIBD	17. 3.70	N.Batty Haddock Stone Farm, Markington		27.10.99P
G-AXZU	Cessna 182N Skylane	182-60104	N92233	19. 3.70	Susan E.Bradney	Goodwood	5. 2.99

G-AYAA-AYZZ

Regn	Type	C/n	P/I	Date	Owner/operator	Probable Base	CA Expy
G-AYAA	PA-28-180 Cherokee E	28-5799		24. 3.70	Alpha-Alpha Ltd	Liverpool	27. 9.98T
G-AYAB	PA-28-180 Cherokee E	28-5804		24. 3.70	Films Ltd	Fairoaks	18. 7.00
G-AYAC	PA-28R-200 Cherokee Arrow	28R-35606		24. 3.70	G.A.J.Smith-Bosanquet	Knettishall	23. 4.01
					t/a The Fersfield F/Grp		
G-AYAF*	PA-30-160 Twin Comanche	30-2000	N8842Y	26. 3.70	Arrow Air Centre Ltd	Shipdham	8. 5.77
					(Stored 9.95)		
G-AYAJ*	Cameron O-84 HAFB	11		31. 3.70	British Balloon Museum & Library	Newbury	
					"Flaming Pearl"		
G-AYAL*	Omega 56 HAFB	10		2. 4.70	British Balloon Museum	Newbury	25. 8.76
					"Nimble II"		
G-AYAN	Slingsby Cadet III (VW1600)	003 & PFA/1385	BGA1224 RAFGSA 223	6. 4.70	N.C.Stone "Thermal Hopper"	Brunton	26. 2.93P
					(Converted from T.31B Frame No.SSK/FF776; stored 5.97)		
G-AYAR	PA-28-180 Cherokee E	28-5797		8. 4.70	Seawing F/C	Southend	28. 1 02T
G-AYAT	PA-28-180 Cherokee E	28-5801		8. 4.70	A.J.Foyster & D.F.Sargant	Ludham	7. 3.01T
					t/a AYAT F/Grp		
G-AYAW	PA-28-180 Cherokee E	28-5805		14. 4.70	R.C.Pendle & M.J.Rose	Blackbushe	24.10.98T
G-AYBD	Reims Cessna F.150K	0583		7. 4.70	S.S.Delwarte	Shoreham	26. 5.01T
					t/a Evendy Holdings		
G-AYBG	Scheibe SF-25B Falke	4696	(D-KECJ)	13. 4.70	D.J.Rickman	Gallows Hill	4. 4.97
					(Stored 5.98)		
G-AYBO	PA-23-250 Aztec D	27-4510	N13874	15. 4.70	Twinguard Avn Ltd	Denham	28. 3.00
G-AYBP	Jodel D.112	1131	F-PMEK	16. 4.70	G.J.Langston	Bidford	22. 7.99P
G-AYBR	Wassmer Jodel D.112	1259	F-BMIG	16. 4.70	R.T.Mosforth	Netherthorpe	9. 6.98P
G-AYBV*	Chasle YC-12 Tourbillon	MA.001W & PFA/1335		20. 4.70	B.A.Mills	Great Eversden	
					(Not completed; stored 10.91)		
G-AYBW*	Reims Cessna FA.150K Aerobat	0044		22. 4.70	Not known	Linley Hill, Leven	16. 6.73
					(Crashed nr Perth 8.10.72; stored 5.97)		
G-AYCC	Campbell Cricket (Rotax 582)	CA/336		20. 4.70	D.J.M.Charity	Cranfield	10.12.99P
G-AYCE	Scintex CP.301C1 Emeraude	530	F-BJFH	20. 4.70	S.D.Glover	Roborough	2. 7.98P
G-AYCF	Reims Cessna FA.150K Aerobat	0055		22. 4.70	E.J.Atkins	Thruxton	3. 6.00
G-AYCG	SNCAN Stampe SV-4C	59	F-BOHF F-BBAE/Fr.Mil	24. 4.70	Nancy Bignall	White Waltham	6. 7.01
G-AYCJ	Cessna TP206D Turbo Super Skylane	P206-0552	N8752Z	27. 4.70	G.James Villa Farm, Fordhall, Tern Hill		30. 4.00
G-AYCK	AIA Stampe SV-4C (Gipsy Major)	1139	G-BUNT G-AYCK/F-BANE	28. 4.70	J.F.Graham	Jersey	3. 9.01
G-AYCN	Piper J3C-65 Cub	"13365"	F-BCPO	28. 4.70	W.R. & B.M.Young		27. 1.89P
					Furze Hill Farm, Rosemarket, Milford Haven		
	(The c/n quoted became PH-UCM in 11.46 & p/i is doubtful; stored 4.91)						
G-AYCO	CEA DR.360 Chevalier	362	F-BRFI	29. 4.70	B.N.Stevens	(Brough)	6. 7.00
G-AYCP	Jodel D.112	67	F-BGKO	30. 4.70	D.J.Nunn	St.Just	22. 6.99P
G-AYCT	Reims Cessna F.172H	0724		1. 5.70	Haimoss Ltd & D.C.Scouller	Old Sarum	8.12.01T
					(Op Old Sarum Flying Club)		
G-AYDG	Socata MS.894A Rallye Minerva 220	11620		7. 5.70	Hunt and Partners Ltd	White Waltham	18. 5.00
G-AYDI	DH.82A Tiger Moth	85910	F-BDOE Fr.AF/DF174	7. 5.70	R.B. & E.W.Woods & J.D.M.Barr	Hampstead Norreys	28. 4.98
G-AYDR	SNCAN Stampe SV-4C	307	F-BCLG	13. 5.70	A.J.McLuskie		27. 3.75
					(Damaged 16.6.73; on rebuild 8.93) Bishopstrow Farm, Warminster		
G-AYDW*	Beagle A.61 Terrier 2 (Conversion of Auster 6 c/n 1936)	B.646	G-ARLM(1) TW568	20. 5.70	Stick & Rudder Associates	St.Neots	1. 7.73
					(On rebuild Kings Lynn 12.95)		
G-AYDX	Beagle A.61 Terrier 2	B.647	VX121	20. 5.70	A.L.Tuttle	(Corby)	12. 1.00
G-AYDY	Phoenix Luton LA-4A Minor (VW1600)	PAL/1302 & PFA/817		21. 5.70	T.Littlefair & N.Clark Lymington, Hants		15. 8.97P
G-AYDZ	CEA Jodel DR.200 (Lyc O-235)	01	F-BLKV F-WLKV	21. 5.70	L.J.Cudd & C.A.Bailey	Dunkeswell	4. 2.99
G-AYEB	Wassmer Jodel D.112	586	F-BIQR	26. 5.70	C.H.G.Baulf	RAF Wattisham	24. 7.98P
G-AYEC	Menavia Piel CP.301A Emeraude	249	F-BIMV	26. 5.70	J.J.Shepherd "Antoinette"	Netherthorpe	10. 6.97P
	(Damaged on take-off Netherthorpe 6.3.97)				t/a Red Wing F/Grp		
G-AYED	PA-24-260 Comanche C	24-4923	N9417P	28. 5.70	J.V.Hutchinson	(Frangy, France)	1. 9.99
G-AYEE	PA-28-180 Cherokee E	28-5813		28. 5.70	D.J.Beale Draycott Farm, Chiseldon		6. 6.01
G-AYEF	PA-28-180 Cherokee E	28-5815		28. 5.70	B.Chalcroft & J.C.Rideout	Barton	1.12.01
G-AYEG	Falconar F-9 (VW1600)	PFA/1321		29. 5.70	T.J.Wilkinson Sackville Lodge, Riseley		28. 6.99P
G-AYEH	SAN Jodel DR.1050 Ambassadeur	455	F-BLJB	8. 6.70	J.W.Scott "Jemima"	Bidford	18. 8.99
					t/a John Scott Jodel Grp		
G-AYEI*	PA-31 Turbo Navajo	31-631	N6730L	29. 5.70	Not known (Hulk dumped 1.99)	Southend	11. 5.89
G-AYEJ	SAN Jodel DR.1050 Ambassadeur	253	F-BJYG	1. 6.70	J.M.Newbold	Enstone	20. 7.00
G-AYEN	Piper J3C-65 Cub (L-4H-PI)	12184	F-BGQD (F-BGQA)/Fr.AF/44-79888	4. 6.70	P.J.Warde & C.F.Morris		26. 6.99P
					Grove Farm, Raveningham		
	(Frame No.12012; official identity is c/n 9696/43-835 but fuselages probably exchanged with F-BGQA on conversion in 1952/53)						

Regn	Type	C/n	P/I	Date	Owner/operator	Probable Base	CA Expy
G-AYET*	GEMS MS.892A Rallye Commodore 150	10565	F-BNBR	8. 6.70	Not known (Stored 3.97)	Spanhoe	15. 9.96
G-AYEV	SAN Jodel DR.1050 Ambassadeur	179	F-BERH F-OBTH/F-OBRH	10. 6.70	L.G.Evans	Redhill	15.10.99
G-AYEW	CEA Jodel DR.1050 Sicile	443	F-BLMJ	11. 6.70	A.W.Woodcock t/a The Taildragger Group	Long Marston	13. 8.00
G-AYEY*	Reims Cessna F.150K	0553		15. 6.70	W.J.Moyse	Bournemouth	14.10.89T
				(Damaged nr Exbury 24.6.88; stored 8.95; cancelled by CAA 2.3.99)			
G-AYFC	Rollason-Druine D.62B Condor	RAE/644		19. 6.70	A.G.Stevens Little Battleflats Farm, Ellistown, Coalville		4.12.98P
G-AYFD	Rollason-Druine D.62B Condor	RAE/645		19. 6.70	B.G.Manning Little Down Farm, Milson		13. 5.01
G-AYFE	Rollason-Druine D.62C Condor	RAE/646		19. 6.70	D.I.H.Johnstone & W.T.Barnard	Cumbernauld	6.12.01
G-AYFF	Rollason-Druine D.62B Condor	RAE/647		19. 6.70	D.Ellis t/a Condor Syndicate	Eaton Bray	16. 6.99P
G-AYFG	Rollason-Druine D.62C Condor	RAE/648		19. 6.70	W.A.Braim	Hutton Cranswick	8. 9.99
G-AYFJ	SEEMS MS.880B Rallye Club	333	F-BKZR	19. 6.70	D.G.Tucker t/a Rallye FJ Grp (Stored 6.94)	West Thurrock	18. 5.92
G-AYFO*	Dornier Bucker Bu.133 Jungmeister				See N40BJ		
G-AYFP	SAN Jodel D.140 Mousquetaire	18	F-BMSI F-OBLH/F-WNDO	24. 6.70	F.L.Rivett	Redhill	25. 2.99
G-AYFV	Crosby Andreasson Super BA.4B (Lyc IO-320) 002 & PFA/1359			26. 6.70	A.R.C.Mathie	RAF Coltishall	5. 7.95P
G-AYFX*	American AA-1 Yankee Clipper	AA1-0318	N6118L	26. 6.70	Not known (On rebuild 12.95)	Sherburn	8. 7.84
G-AYFY*	EAA Biplane	PFA/1319		26. 6.70	Not known	Not known	
				(Stored, unfinished Tattershall Thorpe 7.91; since sold to unknown Public House for display)			
G-AYGA	SAN Jodel D.117	436	F-BHNU	30. 6.70	R.L.E.Horrell	Oxenhope	6. 2.99P
G-AYGB*	Cessna 310Q	310Q-0111	N7611Q	2. 7.70	Perth College (Instructional airframe 10.97)	Perth	23.10.87T
G-AYGC	Reims Cessna F.150K	0556		2. 7.70	I.R.Jones t/a Alpha Avn Grp	Barton	21. 5.01
G-AYGD	CEA Jodel DR.1050 Sicile	515	F-BLRE	3. 7.70	D.Street t/a G-AYGD F/Grp	Netherthorpe	4.11.01
G-AYGE	SNCAN Stampe SV-4C	242	F-BCGM	6. 7.70	I.,L.J. & S.Proudfoot (Stored 1.99)	Duxford	8. 5.97
G-AYGG	Jodel Wassmer D.120 Paris-Nice	184	F-BJPH	10. 7.70	J.M.Dean Stoneacre Farm, Farthing Corner		8. 4.99P
G-AYGK	IRMA BN-2A-6 Islander	621	SX-BBS G-AYGK	9. 7.70	Pathcircle Ltd "Kythira" (Op British Parachute Centre)	Langar	1.11.99A
G-AYGX	Reims Cessna FR.172G Rocket	0208		15. 7.70	C.Taylor t/a Reims Rocket Group	Barton	8. 7.00
G-AYHA	American AA-1 Yankee Clipper	AA1-0396	N6196L	21. 7.70	G.E.Shaw & P.Kilby t/a Elstree Emus Flying Group	Elstree	7. 2.99
G-AYHI	Campbell Cricket (VW1600)	CA/341		21. 7.70	J.F.MacKay North Kessock, Inverness		19. 8.86P
G-AYHX	SAN Jodel D.117A	903	F-BIVE	23. 7.70	L.J.E.Goldfinch	Old Sarum	28. 4.99P
G-AYHY	Sportavia Fournier RF4D	4156		24. 7.70	P.J. & S.M.Wells	Booker	23. 6.00
G-AYIA	Hughes 369HS (500)	99-0120S		29. 7.70	G.D.E.Bilton (Damaged S.France 1.6.88; stored for spares 8.97)	Sywell	16. 7.88
G-AYIF	PA-28-140 Cherokee C	28-26877		31. 7.70	R.Jackson-Moore & P.R.Wright t/a The Hare F/Grp	Enstone	30. 6.01
G-AYIG	PA-28-140 Cherokee C	28-26878		31. 7.70	Air Caernarfon Ltd	White Waltham	26.11.99T
G-AYII	PA-28R-200 Cherokee Arrow	28R-35736		4. 8.70	P.W.J. & P.A.S.Gove	Exeter	13. 3.00
G-AYIJ	SNCAN Stampe SV-4B	376	F-BCOM	4. 8.70	E.A.Stevenson-Rouse & T.C.Beadle	Headcorn	16. 6.00
G-AYIM	HS.748 Srs.2A/270	1687	G-11-687 CS-TAG/G-AYIM/G-11-5	11. 8.70	Emerald Airways Ltd	Liverpool	21.12.01T
G-AYIT	DH.82A Tiger Moth	86343	F-BGEZ Fr.AF/NL896	20. 8.70	S.R.Pollitt & H.M.Eassie t/a Ulster Tiger Grp	Newtownards	17. 6.98
G-AYJA	SAN Jodel DR.1050 Ambassadeur	150	F-BJJJ	8. 9.70	G.Connell Navan, Co.Meath		5. 5.99
G-AYJB	SNCAN Stampe SV-4C	560	F-BDDF	8. 9.70	F.J.M. & J.P.Esson "Odette" Bere Farm, Warnford		26. 5.01
G-AYJD	Alpavia Fournier RF3	11	F-BLXA	8. 9.70	E.Shouler Beeches Farm, South Scarle (Stored 9.97)		19. 5.95P
G-AYJP	PA-28-140 Cherokee C	28-26403		15. 9.70	RAF Brize Norton F/Club Ltd	RAF Brize Norton	20. 4.01T
G-AYJR	PA-28-140 Cherokee C	28-26694		15. 9.70	RAF Brize Norton F/Club Ltd	RAF Brize Norton	30.11.00T
G-AYJW	Reims Cessna FR.172G Rocket	0225		17. 9.70	J.D.Kelsall, R.J.Catley & P.Marsden	Netherthorpe	30. 6.00T
G-AYJY	Isaacs Fury II (Cont C90)	PFA/1373		23. 9.70	M.G.Jefferies	Little Gransden	24. 7.98P
G-AYKA*	Beechcraft 95-B55A Baron	TC-523	HB-GEW G-AYKA/D-IKUN/N8683M	30. 9.70	Northbrook College (Damaged Elstree 18. 6.89; instructional airframe 7.97)	Shoreham	15. 9.91
G-AYKD	SAN Jodel DR.1050 Ambassadeur	351	F-BKHR	30. 9.70	S.D.Morris	Deanland, Hailsham	20. 6.00
G-AYKJ	SAN Jodel D.117A	730	F-BIDX	6.10.70	J.M.Alexander	Lichfield	15. 6.98P
G-AYKK	SAN Jodel D.117	378	F-BHGM	6.10.70	D.M.Whitham (On rebuild 1995)	Crosland Moor	22. 5.85S
G-AYKL	Reims Cessna F.150L	0676		6.10.70	M.A.Judge t/a Aero Group 78	Netherthorpe	19.11.99T
G-AYKS	Leopoldoff L.7 Colibri (Cont A65)	125	F-PCZX F-APZQ	8.10.70	W.B.Cooper Walkeridge Farm, Overton		15.10.99P

Regn	Type	C/n	P/I	Date	Owner/operator	Probable Base	CA Expy
G-AYKT	SAN Jodel D.117	507	F-BGYY F-OAYY	9.10.70	D.I.Walker & S.A.Chambers Scotland Farm, Hook		22. 6.99P
G-AYKW	PA-28-140 Cherokee C	28-26931		12.10.70	B.A. Mills	Cambridge	
G-AYKX	PA-28-140 Cherokee C	28-26933		12.10.70	B.Malpas t/a Robin F/Grp	Woodford	9.11.00
G-AYKZ	SAI KZ-VIII (Gipsy Major 7)	202	HB-EPB OY-ACB	13.10.70	R.E.Mitchell (Stored 3.95)	RAF Cosford	17. 7.81P
G-AYLA	AESL Airtourer T2 (115)	524		12.10.70	D.S.P.Disney	Bristol/Lulsgate	2. 7.01
G-AYLB	PA-39-160 Twin Comanche C/R	39-63	N8908Y	12.10.70	G.N.Snell	Biggin Hill	15. 6.01
G-AYLC	CEA Jodel DR.1051 Sicile (Lyc O-235)	536	F-BLZG	12.10.70	E.W.B.Trollope Wing Farm, Longbridge Deverill		3. 8.99P
G-AYLF	CEA Jodel DR.1051 Sicile	547	F-BLZQ	14.10.70	A.Haigh & A.C.Frost t/a Sicile Grp Rectory Farm, Abbotsley		16. 6.00
G-AYLL	CEA Jodel DR.1050 Ambassadeur	11	F-BJHK	27.10.70	C.Joly	Lee-on-Solent	18. 5.01
G-AYLP	American AA-1 Yankee	AA1-0445	EI-AVV G-AYLP	21.10.70	D.Nairn & E.Y.Hawkins	Henstridge	30.11.98
G-AYLV	Jodel Wassmer D.120 Paris-Nice	300	F-BNCG	27.10.70	M.R.Henham (Status uncertain)	(London N2)	13. 9.83P
G-AYLX	Hughes 269C	90-0041		28.10.70	Helisport Ltd	Biggin Hill	5. 5.00
G-AYLZ	SPP CZL Super Aero 45 Srs.04	06-014	9M-AOF F-BILP	2.11.70	M.Emery (Sold 1997) (Damaged Andrewsfield 2.1.76)	(Gatwick)	11. 6.76
G-AYME	Sportavia Fournier RF5	5089		6.11.70	R.D.Goodger	Biggin Hill	5. 8.99P
G-AYMF*	AESL Airtourer T6/24	B.557		10.11.70	Not known (Crashed nr St.Just 9.6.72; wreck stored 4.96)	St.Just	20. 1.73
G-AYMK	PA-28-140 Cherokee C	28-26772	(PT-DPU)	17.11.70	M.Wright t/a The Piper F/Grp	Newcastle	29. 9.01
G-AYMN*	PA-28-140 Cherokee C	28-26754	(PT-DPT)	18.11.70	S.Boylan (Damaged Isle of Wight 18.9.88; stored 3.95)	(Shipdham)	4. 9.89
G-AYMO	PA-23-250 Aztec C	27-2995	5Y-ACX N5845Y	18.11.70	R.W.Hinton	Stapleford	17. 2.01
G-AYMP	Phoenix Currie Wot Special (Walter Mikron 3)	PFA/3014		18.11.70	H.F.Moffatt	Woodlow Farm, Bosbury	4.10.94P
G-AYMR	Lederlin 380L Ladybug (Cont C90)	EAA/55189 & PFA/1513		19.11.70	J.S.Brayshaw (Under construction 1992)	(Harrogate)	
G-AYMU	Wassmer Jodel D.112	1015	F-BJPB	23.11.70	M.R.Baker Bradleys Lawn, Heathfield (Damaged Hailsham, E.Sussex 7.1.92; on rebuild Eastbourne 7.92)		5. 6.92P
G-AYMV	Western 20 HAFB	002		23.11.70	G.F.Turnbull "Tinkerbelle"	Clyro, Hereford	
G-AYMW	Bell 206B JetRanger	587	EI-BJR G-AYMW	25.11.70	PLM Dollar Group Ltd	Cumbernauld	21. 4.01T
G-AYNA	Phoenix Currie Wot (Cont A65)	PFA/3016		25.11.70	J.Evans Griffins Farm, Temple Bruer		13.11.97P
G-AYND	Cessna 310Q	310Q-0110	N7610Q	2.12.70	Source Ltd	Bournemouth	17. 6.01T
G-AYNF	PA-28-140 Cherokee C	28-26778	(PT-DPV)	3.12.70	W.S.Bath, M.H.Jones & G.H.Round Coventry t/a BW Aviation		15. 6.00T
G-AYNJ	PA-28-140 Cherokee C	28-26810		3.12.70	Southern Flight Training Ltd Bournemouth		3. 5.00T
G-AYNN	Cessna 185B Skywagon	0518	8R-GCC VP-GCC/N2518Z	3.12.70	Bencray Ltd t/a Blackpool & Fylde A/C	Blackpool	28. 9.00T
G-AYNP*	Westland WS.55 Whirlwind Srs.3	WA/71	ZS-HCY G-AYNP/XG576	14.12.70	The Helicopter Museum (to Hubschrauber Museum 6.95)	(Germany)	27.10.85T
G-AYOE*	Bell 47G	1515	F-OCBF F-BKQZ/D-HEBO	21.12.70	Grenville Helicopters Boship Barn Farm Hotel, Hailsham (Crashed Exmouth 16.7.77; composite static rebuild as "G-AXKW" and used as heliport marker 3.97)		5. 5.79
G-AYOP	BAC One-Eleven 530FX	BAC.233		4. 1.71	European Avn Ltd (Op European Air Charter)	Bournemouth	8. 5.01T
G-AYOW	Cessna 182N Skylane	182-60481	N8941G	6. 1.71	D.W.Parfrey	.(Warwick)	28. 4.01
G-AYOY	Sikorsky S-61N	61-476		7. 1.71	Brintel Helicopters Ltd t/a British International Helicopters	Inverness	21. 4.00T
G-AYOZ	Reims Cessna FA.150L Aerobat	0085		7. 1.71	T.K.Day	Eglinton	12.10.00
G-AYPD	Beechcraft 95-B55A Baron	TC-1389		8. 1.71	F.Sherwood & Sons (Transport) Ltd 	Tatenhill	23.12.01T
G-AYPE	MBB Bo.209 Monsun 160RV	123	D-EFJA	11. 1.71	Papa Echo Ltd "Buswells Spirit"	Redhill	23. 9.00
G-AYPG	Reims Cessna F.177RG Cardinal (Wichita c/n 00102)	0007		11. 1.71	D.P.McDermott	(Tregaron)	20.12.01
G-AYPH	Reims Cessna F.177RG Cardinal (Wichita c/n 00146)	0018		11. 1.71	M.R. & K.E.Slack	Cambridge	15. 4.01
G-AYPI	Reims Cessna F.177RG Cardinal (Wichita c/n 00177)	0025		11. 1.71	Cardinal Avn Ltd	Guernsey	20. 4.00
G-AYPJ	PA-28-180 Cherokee E	28-5821		12. 1.71	Mona Avn Ltd (Op Mona F/C)	RAF Mona	27. 9.01T
G-AYPM	PA-18-95 Super Cub (L-18C-PI)18-1373 (Frame No.18-1282)		ALAT 18-1373/51-15373	13. 1.71	R.Horner	Dunkeswell	18. 6.99P
G-AYPO	PA-18-95 Super Cub (L-18C-PI)18-1615 (Cont O-200-A)		ALAT 18-1615/51-15615	13. 1.71	A.W.Knowles	Bodmin	19. 6.00
	(Rebuilt 1984 using OO-TSJ c/n 18-1398 (Frame No.18-1325) & ex (LN-TSJ)/OO-HMH/51-15398)						
G-AYPP*	PA-18-95 Super Cub (L-18C-PI)18-1626		ALAT 18-1626/51-15626	13. 1.71	R.W.Sage Priory Farm, Tibenham t/a Blackbarn Avn (Crashed Stoke St.Mary, Norfolk 29.12.83; stored 8.97)		31. 8.85

Regn	Type	C/n	P/I	Date	Owner/operator	Probable Base	CA Expy
G-AYPR	PA-18-95 Super Cub (L-18C-PI)	18-1631	ALAT 18-1631/51-15631	13. 1.71	D.G.Holman & J.E.Burrell	Leicester	14. 9.00T
G-AYPS	PA-18-95 Super Cub (L-18C-PI)	18-2092	ALAT 18-2092/52-2492	13. 1.71	R.J.Hamlett, L.G & D.C.Callow	(Harlow)	11.11.98P
G-AYPT	PA-18-95 Super Cub (L-18C-PI) (Frame No.18-1508)	18-1533	(D-EALX) ALAT 18-1533/51-15533	13. 1.71	B.L.Proctor & T.F.Lyddon	Dunkeswell	30. 4.99
G-AYPU	PA-28R-200 Cherokee Arrow	28R-7135005		13. 1.71	Alpine Ltd	Jersey	18. 3.02
G-AYPV	PA-28-140 Cherokee D	28-7125039		13. 1.71	Ashley Gardner F/C Ltd	Ronaldsway	6. 9.01T
G-AYPZ	Campbell Cricket (VW1600)	CA/343		13. 1.71	A.Melody	Uxbridge	20. 8.87P
G-AYRA	Campbell Cricket (VW1600)	CA/344		13. 1.71	R.C.Thomas Deopham Green, Wymondham		31. 8.83P
G-AYRC*	Campbell Cricket	CA/346		13. 1.71	Not known Broughton, Wroughton (Stored 1.96)		17. 8.77S
					(Damaged nr Great Billingham School, Norfolk 8.3.98)		
G-AYRF	Reims Cessna F.150L	0665		14. 1.71	D.T.A.Rees	Haverfordwest	25.11.00T
G-AYRG	Reims Cessna F.172K	0761		14. 1.71	Comed Avn Ltd	Blackpool	26. 7.00T
G-AYRH	GEMS MS.892A Rallye Commodore 150	10558	F-BNBX	14. 1.71	J.D.Watt Damyns Hall, Upminster		28. 9.95
G-AYRI	PA-28R-200 Cherokee Arrow	28R-7135004		15. 1.71	A.E.Thompson White Waltham & Delta Motor Co (Windsor) Sales Ltd		25. 7.99
G-AYRM	PA-28-140 Cherokee D	28-7125049		19. 1.71	M.J.Saggers	Biggin Hill	7. 8.00T
G-AYRO	Reims Cessna FA.150L Aerobat	0102		21. 1.71	J.J.Woodhouse Hinton-in-the-Hedges t/a Flying Svs (Op Fat Boys Flying Club)		21. 5.01T
G-AYRS	Jodel Wassmer D.120A Paris-Nice	255	F-BMAV	22. 1.71	L.R.H.D'Eath	(Diss)	4. 5.99P
G-AYRT	Reims Cessna F.172K	0777		22. 1.71	P.E.Crees	Cumbernauld	16. 3.01
G-AYRU	BN-2A-6 Islander	181	G-51-181 OH-BNA/G-51-181	22. 1.71	Joint Service Parachute Centre AAC Netheravon		10. 3.00
G-AYSA	PA-23-250 Aztec C	27-3799	N6509Y	1. 2.71	N.Parkinson & W.Smith	Coventry	14. 5.99T
G-AYSB	PA-30-160 Twin Comanche C	30-1916	N8760Y	1. 2.71	D.L.Davies	Shoreham	26. 2.00
G-AYSD	Slingsby T-61A Falke	1726		4. 2.71	P.W.Hextall (Stored 1.95)	Tatenhill	29. 4.94
G-AYSH	Taylor JT.1 Monoplane (VW1600)	PFA/1413		10. 2.71	C.J.Lodge Hill Farm, Nayland		5. 5.99P
G-AYSJ	Dornier Bucker Bu.133C Jungmeister	38	D-EHVP G-AYSJ HB-MIW/Swiss AF U-91	12. 2.71	Patina Ltd (Op The Fighter Collection) (As "LG+01" in Luftwaffe c/s) Duxford		1.12.99P
G-AYSK	Phoenix Luton LA-4A Minor (Cont A65)	PFA/832		17. 2.71	S.R.Smith t/a Luton Minor Grp	Barton	27.10.99P
G-AYSX	Reims Cessna F.177RG Cardinal (Wichita c/n 00175)	0024		17. 2.71	C.P.Heptonstall	Sandtoft	16. 5.99
G-AYSY	Reims Cessna F.177RG Cardinal (Wichita c/n 00180)	0026		17. 2.71	Horizon Flyers Ltd	Denham	6. 6.00
G-AYTA*	Socata MS.880B Rallye Club	1789		19. 2.71	The Aeroplane Collection Manchester (On loan to Manchester Museum of Science & Industry)		7.11.88
G-AYTR	Menavia Piel CP.301A Emeraude	229	F-BIMD	3. 3.71	G.N.Hopcraft Croft Farm, Defford		11. 6.99P
G-AYTT	Phoenix PM-3 Duet (Cont C90) (Regd as Luton Minor III)	PFA/841		4. 3.71	H.E.Jenner	Rochester	9. 8.99P
G-AYTV	Jurca MJ.2D Tempete (Cont C90)	PFA/2002		10. 3.71	A.R.Clark Shoreham t/a Shoestring Flying Group		7. 7.98P
G-AYUA	Auster AOP.9	B5/10-119	7855M XK416	12. 3.71	De Havilland Aviation Ltd (Bridgend) (As "XK416"; stored Bruntingthorpe 3.96)		
G-AYUB	CEA Jodel DR.253B Regent	185		15. 3.71	D.J.Brook Deanland, Hailsham		18. 7.99
G-AYUH	PA-28-180 Cherokee F	28-7105042		17. 3.71	C.S.Sidle	Sherburn	28. 2.99
G-AYUI*	PA-28-180 Cherokee F	28-7105043	N8557 G-AYUI	17. 3.71	Ansair Avn Ltd Andrewsfield (Semi-derelict in open storage Andrewsfield 7.97)		5.11.93T
G-AYUJ	Evans VP-1 (VW1776)	PFA/1538		17. 3.71	T.N.Howard Woodvale "Unforgettable Juliet" (Damaged Ainsdale Beach, Southport 16.6.96)		28. 2.97P
G-AYUM	Slingsby T-61A Falke	1730		19. 3.71	R.Sharman t/a Hereward F/Grp Crowland		10. 6.99
G-AYUN	Slingsby T-61A Falke	1731		19. 3.71	C.W.Vigar & R.J.Watts	Rattlesden	20. 5.99
G-AYUP	Slingsby T-61A Falke	1735	XW983 G-AYUP	19. 3.71	P.R.Williams RAF Bicester (Stored 2.97)		15. 7.96
G-AYUR	Slingsby T-61A Falke	1736		19. 3.71	R.Hannigan & R.Lingard	Strubby	4.11.01
G-AYUS	Taylor JT.1 Monoplane (VW1600)	PFA/1412		19. 3.71	R.R.McKinnon Old Sarum (Damaged Coombe Down, Salisbury 3.11.92)		8.10.93P
G-AYUT	SAN Jodel DR.1050 Ambassadeur	479	F-BLJZ	22. 3.71	R.Norris	Cumbernauld	29. 9.01
G-AYUV	Reims Cessna F.172H	0752		26. 3.71	Justgold Ltd	Blackpool	11. 3.00T
G-AYVA*	Cameron O-84 HAFB	17		30. 3.71	A.Kirk "April Fool" Lancing (Balloon Preservation Group 7.98)		6. 9.76S
G-AYVO	Wallis WA-120 Srs.1	K/602/X		6. 4.71	K.H.Wallis (Stored 8.97) Reymerston Hall		31.12.75P
G-AYVP	Aerosport Woody Pusher	181 & PFA/1344		6. 4.71	J.R.Wraight (Stored incomplete) Chatham		
G-AYVT*	Brochet MB.84	9	F-BGLI	13. 4.71	R.A.Yates Sibsey (Damaged 28.6.77; stored 8.90)		20..7.77
G-AYWA*	Avro 19 Srs.2	1361	OO-VIT OO-DFA/OO-CFA	14. 4.71	N.K.Geddes (Stored 5.95) Lochwinnoch		

Regn	Type	C/n	P/I	Date	Owner/operator	Probable Base	CA Expy
G-AYWD	Cessna 182N Skylane	182-60468	N8928G	15. 4.71	S.I.Zorb t/a Wild Dreams Group	Leicester	21. 8.99T
G-AYWE	PA-28-140 Cherokee C	28-26826	N5910U	16. 4.71	N.Roberson t/a Whiskey Echo Grp	Fenland	28. 2.99
G-AYWH	SAN Jodel D.117A	844	F-BIVO	16. 4.71	D.Kynaston & J.Deakin	Willingham	2. 3.99P
G-AYWM	AESL Airtourer T5 (Super 150)	A.534		16. 4.71	H.E.Collett t/a The Star F/Grp	Gloucestershire	4. 5.00
G-AYWT	AIA Stampe SV-4C (Gipsy Major 10)	1111	F-BLEY F-BAGL	21. 4.71	B.K.Lecomber	Denham	22. 5.99T
G-AYWY*	PA-23-250 Aztec D	27-4069	EI-ATI N6735Y	22. 4.71	Dublin College of Technology (Crashed Castlebridge, Wexford 15.10.75; instructional airframe 5.92)	Dublin	21. 5.77
G-AYXO*	Phoenix Luton LA-5A Major (Walter Minor 65hp)	PFA/1211		27. 4.71	C.H.Bestwick (Flown in 1971 but not certified; stored 1.96)	Brenchley, Kent	
G-AYXP	SAN Jodel D.117A	693	F-BIDD	27. 4.71	G.N.Davies	Vowchurch, Hereford	20.11.97P
G-AYXS	SIAI-Marchetti S.205-18R	4-165	OY-DNG	28. 4.71	M.D.Friend	Denham	20. 6.01
G-AYXT	Westland WS-55 Whirlwind HAS.7 (Srs.2)	WA/167	XK940	28. 4.71	G.P.Hinkley (As "XK940"; on rebuild 3.97)	Channons Hall, Tibenham	4. 2.99P
G-AYXU	Champion 7KCAB Citabria	232-70	N7587F	28. 4.71	Norfolk Gliding Club Ltd	Tibenham	21. 5.98
G-AYXW	Evans VP-1 (Ardem 4C02)	PFA/1544		30. 4.71	M.Howe	North Coates	6. 7.99P
G-AYYF	Reims Cessna F.150L	0716		10. 5.71	D.T.A.Rees (Destroyed in crash Aber Farm, Talybont-on-Usk 27.11.90)		20. 2.92T
G-AYYK	Slingsby T-61A Falke	1737		10. 5.71	Cornish Gliding & F/C Ltd	Perranporth	11. 4.97
G-AYYL	Slingsby T-61A Falke	1738		10. 5.71	C.Wood (On rebuild following gale damage at Manston 15.12.82; on rebuild 7.90)	Challock	2. 6.83
G-AYYO	CEA Jodel DR.1050/M1 Sicile Record	622	EI-BAI G-AYYO/F-BMPZ	11. 5.71	D.J.M.White t/a Bustard Jodel Group	Boscombe Down	20.11.98
G-AYYT	CEA Jodel DR.1050/Ml Sicile Record	587	F-BMGU	13. 5.71	C.J.Turner Garston Farm, Marshfield & S.D.Kent t/a Echo November Flight		30. 5.99
G-AYYU	Beechcraft C23 Musketeer Custom	M-1353		14. 5.71	P.W.Johnson & A.G.Payne t/a Sundowner Avn	Sturgate	28. 4.01
G-AYYW	BN-2A-2 Islander	277	D-IOLA G-AYYW/G-51-277	17. 5.71	A T Usher t/a Royal Navy & Royal Marines Sport Parachute Association "Iron Horse"	Dunkeswell	2. 4.99
G-AYYX	Socata MS.880B Rallye Club	1812		18. 5.71	J.G.MacDonald	Morgansfield, Fishburn	23. 1.02
G-AYZE	PA-39-160 Twin Comanche C/R	39-92	N8934Y	20. 5.71	J.E.Balmer	Gloucestershire	13. 8.00
G-AYZH*	Taylor JT.2 Titch	PFA/1316		21. 5.71	P.J.G.Goddard (Cancelled by CAA 23.2.99; no Permit issued & probably not completed)	(Stratford-upon-Avon)	
G-AYZI	SNCAN Stampe SV-4C	15	(EI-) G-AYZI/F-BBAA/Fr mil	24. 5.71	W.H.Smout	Abbeyshrule	28. 7.95
G-AYZJ*	Westland WS-55 Whirlwind HAS.7	WA/263	XM685	24. 5.71	Newark Air Museum (As "XM685/PO-513")	Winthorpe	
G-AYZK	CEA Jodel DR.1050/M1 Sicile Record	590	F-BMGY	24. 5.71	R.L.Sambell & D.G.Hesketh	Stoke Golding	10. 7.00
G-AYZS	Rollason-Druine D.62B Condor	RAE/650		4. 6.71	P.E.J.Huntley & M.N.Thrush	Manor Farm, Inglesham	25. 9.99P
G-AYZU	Slingsby T-61A Falke	1740		4. 6.71	R.G.Garner t/a The Falcon Gliding Grp	Coventry	4. 6.01
G-AYZW	Slingsby T-61A Falke	1743		4. 6.71	V.D.Blaxill & R.J.Jones t/a Portmoak Falke Syndicate	Portmoak	10. 4.01

G-AZAA-AZZZ

Regn	Type	C/n	P/I	Date	Owner/operator	Probable Base	CA Expy
G-AZAB	PA-30-160 Twin Comanche B	30-1475	5H-MNM 5Y-AGB	8. 6.71	Bickertons Aerodromes Ltd	Denham	19. 8.01
G-AZAD	CEA Jodel DR.1050 Sicile	501	F-BLMX	10. 6.71	J.A.D.Reedie & G.W. Mair t/a Cawdor F/Grp	Inverness	18. 4.00
G-AZAJ	PA-28R-200 Cherokee Arrow	28R-7135116		18. 6.71	J.C.McHugh & P.Woulfe	Stapleford	10. 6.00
G-AZAU*	Cierva Rotorcraft Grasshopper III GB.3			21. 6.71	The Helicopter Museum Weston-super-Mare (Incomplete - only floor pan, panel, power and lift group; stored 3.96)		
G-AZAW	Gardan GY-80-160 Horizon	104	F-BMUL	24. 6.71	T.Brown	Maypole Farm, Chislet	5.12.98
G-AZAZ*	Bensen B-8M	RNEC.1		2. 7.71	Fleet Air Arm Museum (Stored 3.96)	Wroughton	
G-AZBA	Tipsy T.66 Nipper Srs.3B (VW1834) (Slingsby-built kit)	PFA/1390		30. 6.71	L.A. Brown	Swansea	10.12.99P
G-AZBB	MBB Bo 209 Monsun 160FV	137	D-EFJO	1. 7.71	G.N.Richardson t/a GN Richardson Motors Shelsley Beauchamp, Worcester		14.11.99
G-AZBC	PA-39-160 Twin Comanche C/R	39-111	N8951Y	1. 7.71	H.G.Orchin	Bourn	27. 8.99
G-AZBE	AESL Airtourer T5 (Super 150)	A.535		5. 7.71	R.G.Vincent t/a BE F/Grp Gloucestershire		27. 8.99
G-AZBH*	Cameron O-84 HAFB	23		8. 7.71	British Balloon Museum & Library "Serendipity"	Newbury	10. 5.81
G-AZBI	SAN Jodel 150 Mascaret	43	F-BMFB	12. 7.71	F.M.Ward	Dishforth	8. 2.00P
G-AZBL	Jodel D.9 Bebe (VW1500)	PFA/938		12. 7.71	J.Hill (Status uncertain - on rebuild 1993 ?)	(Dudley)	15.10.85P
G-AZBN	Noorduyn AT-16-ND Harvard IIB	14A-1431	PH-HON R.Neth.AF B-97/FT391/43-13132	13. 7.71	Swaygate Ltd (As "FT391")	Shoreham	18. 6.99P
G-AZBT*	Western O-65 HAFB	005		15. 7.71	D Harries "Hermes" (Stored 7.98)	Brighton	9. 4.76S
G-AZBU	Auster AOP.9	AUS.183	7862M XR246	15. 7.71	E.Wright t/a Auster Nine Group (As "XR246" in RAE c/s) South Lodge Farm, Widmerpool		31. 3.99P
G-AZBY*	Westland Wessex 60 Srs.1 (Possibly former G-AWOX)	WA/740	G-17-5 G-AZBY/5N-ALR/G-AZBY (As "EM-16" in USMC c/s; on rebuild 8.98)	21. 7.71	Not known	Honey Crook Farm, Redhill	14.12.82
G-AZCB	SNCAN Stampe SV-4C (Gipsy Major 1C)	140	F-BBCR	21. 7.71	M.L.Martin	Redhill	30. 4.96
G-AZCE	Pitts S.1C Special (Lyc O-235)	373.H & PFA/1527		26. 7.71	Not known (Crashed Eastbach Farm 2.9.75 - on rebuild)		18. 6.76S
G-AZCI*	Cessna 320A Skyknight	320A-0021	CF-PKY N3021R	29. 7.71	Not known (Stored in wrecked condition 7.91)	Kano, Nigeria	29. 6.83A
G-AZCK	Beagle B.121 Pup 2	B121-153		30. 7.71	D.R.Newell	Newtownards	10. 6.00
G-AZCL	Beagle B.121 Pup 2	B121-154		30. 7.71	J.J.Watts & D.Fletcher	Old Sarum	8. 7.01T
G-AZCN	Beagle B.121 Pup 2	B121-156	HB-NAY G-AZCN	30. 7.71	R.C.Antonini	Biggin Hill	15. 6.01
G-AZCP	Beagle B.121 Pup 1	B121-158	(D-EKWA) G-AZCP	30. 7.71	T.J.Watson	Elstree	18. 7.01
G-AZCT	Beagle B.121 Pup 1	B121-161		30. 7.71	J.Coleman	Sywell	17. 7.99T
G-AZCU	Beagle B.121 Pup 1	B121-162		30. 7.71	A.A.Harris	Shobdon	5. 8.01
G-AZCV	Beagle B.121 Pup 2	B121-163	HB-NAR G-AZCV	30. 7.71	N.R.W.Long	Compton Abbas	5. 7.99
G-AZCY	Beagle B.121 Pup 2	B121-166	HB-NAW G-AZCY	30. 7.71	D.J. Deas	(Woodbridge)	5.11.01T
G-AZCZ	Beagle B.121 Pup 2	B121-167		30. 7.71	L. & J.M.Northover	Cardiff	22. 5.01
G-AZDA	Beagle B.121 Pup 2	B121-168		30. 7.71	B.D.Deubelbeiss	Elstree	23.12.99
G-AZDD	MBB Bo.209 Monsun 150FF	143	D-EBJC	3. 8.71	Paul James Knitwear Ltd	Leicester	11. 4.01
G-AZDE	PA-28R-200 Cherokee Arrow	28R-7135141		3. 8.71	Electro-Motion UK (Export) Ltd	Leicester	29. 8.99
G-AZDG	Beagle B.121 Pup 2	B121-145	(G-BLYM) HB-NAM/(VH-EPT)/G-35-145	17. 6.85	J.R.Heaps (DHL c/s)	Elstree	25. 2.01
G-AZDJ	PA-32-300 Cherokee Six D	32-7140068	OY-AJK G-AZDJ/N5273S	23. 8.71	K.J.Mansbridge & D.C.Gibbs	(Barry)	3. 4.00T
G-AZDK	Beechcraft 95-B55 Baron	TC-1406		23. 8.71	C.C.Forrester	Denham	23. 2.01
G-AZDX	PA-28-180 Cherokee F	28-7105186		23. 8.71	M.Cowan	Hundon, Suffolk	9. 1.99
G-AZDY	DH.82A Tiger Moth	86559	F-BGDJ Fr.AF/PG650	25. 8.71	J.B.Mills	Willingham	18. 8.97
G-AZDZ*	Cessna 172K Skyhawk	172-58501	5N-AIH N1647C/N84508	25. 8.71	The Fire Service College (Damaged Delapre GC, Northants 19.9.81 & used for fire training 8.98)	Moreton-in-Marsh	25. 2.83
G-AZEE	Morane MS.880B Rallye Club	74	F-BKKA	1. 9.71	J.Shelton	North Coates	27. 9.98
	(Composite including fuselage of G-AZNJ c/n 5375 in 1980; original fuselage stored in rafters South Scarle 9.94)						
G-AZEF	Jodel Wassmer D.120 Paris-Nice	321	F-BNZS	1. 9.71	J.R.Legge	Lumb-in-Rossendale	21. 7.99P
G-AZEG	PA-28-140 Cherokee D	28-7125530		1. 9.71	The Ashley Gardner F/C Ltd	Ronaldsway	3. 7.01T
G-AZER*	Cameron O-42 HAFB	26		9. 9.71	Not known "Shy-Tot"		15. 5.81A
G-AZEU	Beagle B.121 Pup 2	B121-130	VH-EPL G-35-130	15. 9.71	G.M.Moir	Egginton	13. 2.00
G-AZEV	Beagle B.121 Pup 2	B121-131	VH-EPM G-35-131	15. 9.71	G.P.Martin	Goodwood	22. 8.99
G-AZEW	Beagle B.121 Pup 2	B121-132	VH-EPN G-35-132	15. 9.71	K.Cameron	Headcorn	12. 5.00

Regn	Type	C/n	P/I	Date	Owner/operator	Probable Base	CA Expy
G-AZEY	Beagle B.121 Pup 2	B121-136	HB-NAK G-AZEY/VH-EPP/G-35-136	15. 9.71	M.E.Reynolds	Goodwood	26. 6.00
G-AZFA	Beagle B.121 Pup 2	B121-143	VH-EPR G-35-143	15. 9.71	K.F.Plummer Buttermilk Hall Farm, Blisworth		22. 7.01
G-AZFC	PA-28-140 Cherokee D	28-7125486		16. 9.71	M.L.Hannah	Blackbushe	19. 7.99
G-AZFF	Wassmer Jodel D.112	1175	F-BLFI	17. 9.71	R.Pidcock	Fenland	19. 5.99P
G-AZFI	PA-28R-200 Cherokee Arrow 28R-7135160			21. 9.71	GAZFI Ltd	Sherburn	6. 4.01
G-AZFM	PA-28R-200 Cherokee Arrow 28R-7135218			24. 9.71	T.N.Jenness	Biggin Hill	5. 2 01
G-AZFP	Reims Cessna F.177RG Cardinal (Wichita c/n 00194)	0031		29. 9.71	Middleton Miniature Mouldings Ltd (Barnard Castle)		19. 4.00T
G-AZFR	Cessna 401B	401B-0121	N7981Q	30. 9.71	Westair F/Svs Ltd	Blackpool	30. 8.99T
G-AZGA	Jodel Wassmer D.120 Paris-Nice	144	F-BIXV	30. 9.71	A.F. Vizoso Draycott Farm, Chiseldon		5. 1.99P
G-AZGC	SNCAN Stampe SV-4C	120	F-BCGE	2.10.71	V.Lindsay Kidmore End, Reading		22. 2.91
	(Damaged Folly Farm, Hungerford 28.5.90; stored 5.93) (As "No.120" in French A/F c/s)						
G-AZGE	SNCAN Stampe SV-4C	576	F-BDDV	6.10.71	M.R.L.Astor East Hatley, Tadlow		15. 8.94
	(Stored 3.97)						
G-AZGF	Beagle B.121 Pup 2	B121-076	PH-KUF G-35-076	6.10.71	K.Singh	Barton	2. 5.98
G-AZGI	Socata MS.880B Rallye Club	1896		7.10.71	B.McIntyre Movenis, Co.Londonderry		12.11.01
G-AZGL	Socata MS.894A Rallye Minerva 220 11929			7.10.71	The Cambridge Aero Club Ltd Cambridge		26. 8.99T
G-AZGY	Rousseau CP.301B Emeraude	122	F-BRAA	12.10.71	C.J.R.Gray	(Wrexham)	20. 6.99P
G-AZGZ	DH.82A Tiger Moth	86489	F-BGCF Fr.AF/NM181	13.10.71	F.R.Manning (As "NM181")	Dunkeswell	15. 6.98
G-AZHB	Robin HR.100/200B Royal	118		14.10.71	C. & P.P.Scarlett	Lydd	6. 8.00
G-AZHC	Wassmer Jodel D.112	585	F-BIQQ	18.10.71	S.Kent t/a Aerodel Flying Group	Netherthorpe	15. 5.99P
G-AZHD	Slingsby T-61A Falke	1753		18.10.71	Nicola J.Orchard-Armitage	(Deal)	2. 6.00
G-AZHE*	Slingsby T-61B Falke	1755	N61TB G-AZHE	18.10.71	M.R.Shelton	Tatenhill	AC
	(Damaged 17.6.88 & on rebuild - cancelled by CAA 14.3.99)						
G-AZHH	K & S SA.102.5 Cavalier (Lyc O-290)	PFA/1393		20.10.71	D.W.Buckle Morton Carr Farm, Nunthorpe		20. 1.00P
G-AZHI	AESL Airtourer T5 (Super 150) A.540			20.10.71	H.J.Douglas t/a Airtourer Squadron	Biggin Hill	27. 3.99T
G-AZHJ*	Scottish Avn Twin Pioneer 3	577	G-31-16 XP295	20.10.71	Air Atlantique Ltd (Stored 7.97)	Coventry	23. 8.90S
G-AZHK	Robin HR.100/200B Royal	113	G-ILEG G-AZHK	22.10.71	A.Bendkowski & T.A.Houghton	Rochester	19. 7.99
G-AZHR	Piccard Ax6 HAFB	617	N17US	27.10.71	C.Fisher t/a Halcyon Balloon Grp "Happiness"	Sheffield	
G-AZHT	AESL Airtourer T3	525		29.10.71	Aviation West Ltd	(Glasgow)	29. 1.89T
	(Damaged Glenforsa, Mull 29.4.88; stored 6.95)						
G-AZHU	Phoenix Luton LA-4A Minor (VW1834)	PFA/839		1.11.71	W.Cawrey	Netherthorpe	13. 7.99P
G-AZIB	Socata ST-10 Diplomate	141		4.11.71	G.S.Hibbert & T.M.S.Smith North Moreton t/a Diplomate Grp		6. 2.00
G-AZID	Reims Cessna FA.150L Aerobat	0083	N9447	8.11.71	Ricochet Corporation Ltd Halfpenny Green t/a Academy of Aeronautical Excellence		3.11.99T
G-AZII	SAN Jodel D.117A	848	F-BNDO F-OBFO	12.11.71	J.S.Brayshaw Haddock Stone Farm, Markington		3.12.99P
G-AZIJ	Robin DR.360 Knight	634		15.11.71	Rob Airways Ltd	Guernsey	4. 6.00
G-AZIK	PA-34-200-2 Seneca	34-7250018	N2392T	15.11.71	Walkbury Aviation Ltd	Sibson	19. 3.99T
G-AZIL	Slingsby T-61A Falke	1756		16.11.71	D.W.Savage	Portmoak	19.11.99
G-AZIP	Cameron O-65 HAFB	29		24.11.71	P.G.Dunnington "Dante" Hungerford		5. 5.81A
	t/a Dante Balloon Grp (Non-airworthy - stored 2.97)						
G-AZJC	Sportavia Fournier RF5	5108		30.11.71	W.S.V.Stoney	(Arezzo, Italy)	27. 8.99P
G-AZJE	Barritault JB.01 Minicab (Cont C90) JBE.1 & PFA/1806			1.12.71	J.B.Evans (Stored 12.95) Ventnor, IOW		7. 7.82P
G-AZJI*	Western O-65 HAFB	007		2.12.71	British Balloon Museum "Peek-A-Boo"	Newbury	N/E(A)
G-AZJN	Robin DR.300/140 Major	642		6.12.71	Wright Farm Eggs Ltd Cherry Tree Farm, Monewden		22. 5.99T
G-AZJV	Reims Cessna F.172L	0810		8.12.71	J.A. & A.J.Boyd	Cardiff	11. 2.00
G-AZJY	Reims Cessna FRA.150L Aerobat	0126		8.12.71	R.P.Smith	Barton	21. 5.01
	(Rebuilt officially at Sleap 7.81 after ditching off Isle of Man 18.9.72; true pedigree not confirmed)						
G-AZKC	Socata MS.880B Rallye Club	1914		8.12.71	L.J.Martin	Sandown	2. 7.00
G-AZKE	Socata MS.880B Rallye Club	1950		8.12.71	B.S.Rowden & W.L.Rogers	Exeter	6.10.99
G-AZKK	Cameron O-56 HAFB	32		13.12.71	P.J.Green & C.Bosley t/a Gemini Balloon Group "Gemini"	Newbury	N/E(A)
G-AZKO	Reims Cessna F.337F Super Skymaster (Wichita c/n 01380)	0041		20.12.71	P.W. Crispe Wellesbourne Mountford "Bird Dog"		25. 7.99
G-AZKP	SAN Jodel D.117	419	F-BHND	20.12.71	J.Lowe Griffins Farm, Temple Bruer		4. 6.99P
G-AZKR	PA-24-180 Comanche	24-2192	N7044P	23.12.71	T.E.Groves	Rochester	15. 7.00
G-AZKS	American AA-1A Trainer	0334	N6134L	23.12.71	M.D.Henson	Coventry	3. 6.00

Regn	Type	C/n	P/I	Date	Owner/operator	Probable Base	CA Expy
G-AZKV	Reims Cessna FRA.150L Aerobat	0127		23.12.71	B.Flay & T.C.Hocking t/a The Penguin Flt	Bodmin	31.10.93T
	(Damaged Redlake, Lostwithiel 15.9.91; status uncertain - only small parts and wings stored 8.96)						
G-AZKW	Reims Cessna F.172L	0836		23.12.71	J.C.C.Wright	Hinton-in-the-Hedges	21. 6.99T
G-AZKZ	Reims Cessna F.172L	0814		23.12.71	R.D. & E.Forster (Op Norfolk Flying Club)	Norwich	20. 7.01T
G-AZLE	Boeing-Stearman E75 (N2S-5) Kaydet (Cont W670)	75-8543	CF-XRD N5619N/Bu43449	29.12.71	A.E.Poulsom t/a Air Farm Flyers	Manor Farm, Tongham (As "2"in US Army c/s)	20. 3.01
G-AZLF	Jodel Wassmer D.120 Paris-Nice	230	F-BLFL	30.12.71	M.S.C.Ball	Garston Farm, Marshfield	11.11.99P
G-AZLH	Reims Cessna F.150L	0757		31.12.71	Coulson Flying Services Ltd	North Coates	20.11.00T
G-AZLJ	BN-2A mk.III-1 Trislander	319	G-OREG SX-CBN/G-OREG/G-OAVW/G-AZLJ/G-51-319	31.12.71	Hebridean Air Services Ltd (Op Keenair Charter)	Liverpool	2. 2.00T
G-AZLL	Reims Cessna FRA.150L Aerobat	0135		31.12.71	Rankart Ltd	Hinton-in-the-Hedges	19.11.01T
	(Crashed Turweston 4.2.99 & destroyed)						
G-AZLM*	Reims Cessna F.172L	0842		31.12.71	Norfolk & Suffolk Aviation Mus	Flixton	16. 7.93T
	(Crashed Badminton 23.3.91; fuselage stored 9.97)						
G-AZLN	PA-28-180 Cherokee F	28-7105210		3. 1.72	Liteflite Ltd	Oxford	19. 2.01
G-AZLO*	Reims Cessna F.337F Super Skymaster (Wichita c/n 01347)	0029		4. 1.72	Not known (Rear-end stored 5.97)	Bourn	22. 4.82
G-AZLP*	V.813 Viscount	346	(ZS-SBT) ZS-CDT	4. 1.72	Teeside Airport Fire Services	Teeside	3. 4.82T
G-AZLS*	V.813 Viscount	348	(ZS-SBV) ZS-CDV	4. 1.72	CAA International Fire Training Centre	Teeside	9. 6.83T
G-AZLV	Cessna 172K	172-57908	4X-ALM N79138	10. 1.72	B.L.F.Karthaus	Newcastle	18. 1.01
G-AZLY	Reims Cessna F.150L	0771		10. 1.72	Cleveland Flying School Ltd	Teeside	28.11.99T
G-AZLZ	Reims Cessna F.150L	0772		10. 1.72	A.G.Martlew	(Milford Haven)	16. 7.00
G-AZMC	Slingsby T-61A Falke	1757		12. 1.72	Essex Gliding Club Ltd (Sold - stored 8.90)	Challock	22. 9.86
G-AZMD	Slingsby T-61C Falke	1758		12. 1.72	R.A.Rice	Wellesbourne Mountford	1. 6.01
G-AZMF	BAC One-Eleven 530FX	BAC.240	7Q-YKJ G-AZMF/PT-TYY/G-AZMF	12. 1.72	European Avn Ltd (Op European Aircharter) "The European Express"	Bournemouth	22. 1.01T
G-AZMJ	American AA-5 Traveler	0019		27. 1.72	R.T.Love	St.Merryn	25. 2.01
G-AZMN*	AESL Airtourer T5 (Super 150)	A.550		28. 1.72	Not known	Kemble	7. 5.89
	(Damaged Glasgow 23.6.87; stored 6.97)						
G-AZMX*	PA-28-140 Cherokee	28-24777	SE-FLL LN-LMK	7. 2.72	North East Wales Institute of Higher Education (Instructional airframe 3.96)	Connah's Quay	9. 1.82
G-AZMZ	Socata MS.893A Rallye Commodore 180	11927		8. 2.72	Patricia J.Wilcox	Lyveden	31. 1.97
G-AZNA*	V.813 Viscount	350	(ZS-SBX) ZS-CDX	8. 2.72	Not known	Zomergem, Belgium	24. 8.90T
	(Displayed in car park 7.97)						
G-AZNC*	V.813 Viscount	352	(ZS-SBZ) ZS-CDZ	8. 2.72	CAA Intnl Fire Trng Centre	Teeside	18. 5.83T
	(Green/unmarked and used for non-destructive training 5.97)						
G-AZNK	SNCAN Stampe SV-4A (Gipsy Major 10)	290	F-BKXF F-BCGZ	15. 2.72	P.D.Jackson & R.A.G.Lucas "Globird"	Redhill	11. 8.00
G-AZNL	PA-28R-200 Cherokee Arrow II	28R-7235006		16. 2.72	B.P.Liversidge	Framlingham	27. 7.99T
G-AZNO	Cessna 182P Skylane	182-61005	N7365Q	18. 2.72	T & K.Andrewes	Brunton	10. 4.00
G-AZNT	Cameron O-84 HAFB	34		21. 2.72	N.Tasker "Oberon"	Bristol	5. 6.85
G-AZOA	MBB Bo.209 Monsun 150FF	183	D-EAAY	21. 2.72	M.W.Hurst	Seighford	13. 5.01
G-AZOB	MBB Bo.209 Monsun 150FF	184	D-EAAZ	21. 2.72	G.N.Richardson		9. 7.84
	(Crashed Droitwich 21.8.83; stored 8.92) Shelsley Beauchamp, Worcester						
G-AZOE	AESL Airtourer T2 (115)	528		21. 2.72	B.J.Edmondson & J.K.Smithson t/a G-AZOE 607 Grp	Newcastle	30. 6.00
G-AZOF	AESL Airtourer T5 (Super 150)	A.549		21. 2.72	R.J.W.Bayliff & A.C.Hart t/a Cirrus F/Grp	Booker	17. 2.01
G-AZOG	PA-28R-200 Cherokee Arrow II	28R-7235009		21. 2.72	J.G.Collins	Little Gransden	9. 7.98
G-AZOL	PA-34-200-2 Seneca	34-7250075	N4348T	28. 2.72	P.D.Winborne	(London E11)	30. 1.00
G-AZOO	Western O-65 HAFB	015		1. 3.72	Semajan Ltd t/a Southern Balloon Group "Carousel"	Romsey	6. 6.77S
G-AZOR	MBB Bo.105DB	S.20	EC-DOE G-AZOR/D-HDAC	1. 3.72	Bond Helicopters Ltd (Op Essex Air Ambulance)	Boreham	31. 5.99T
G-AZOS	Jurca MJ.5-H1 Sirocco (Lyc O-320)	001 & PFA/2206		1. 3.72	M.K.Field	Sleap	14. 6.99P
G-AZOT	PA-34-200 Seneca	34-7250073	N4340T	3. 3.72	MK Aero Support Ltd	Andrewsfield	4. 3.98T
G-AZOU	SAN Jodel DR.1050 Sicile	354	F-BJYX	7. 3.72	D.Elliott & D.Holl t/a Horsham F/Grp	Wellcross Grange, Slinfold	29. 5.99
G-AZOZ	Reims Cessna FRA.150L Aerobat	0136		7. 3.72	Seawing F/C Ltd "The Wizard of Oz"	Southend	18. 4.99T
G-AZPA	PA-25-235 Pawnee C	25-5223	N8797L	7. 3.72	Black Mountains Gliding Club Ltd	Talgarth	1. 5.01
G-AZPC	Slingsby T-61C Falke	1767		7. 3.72	Ann-Marie Parker	Feshiebridge	31. 7.01
G-AZPF	Sportavia Fournier RF5	5001	D-KOLT	10. 3.72	R.Pye	Blackpool	29. 1.00P
G-AZPH*	Craft-Pitts S.1S Special (Lyc IO-360)	S1S-001-C	N11CB	13. 3.72	The Science Museum (Flight Gallery)	South Kensington, London	4. 9.91P

Regn	Type	C/n	P/I	Date	Owner/operator	Probable Base	CA Expy
G-AZPV	Phoenix-Luton LA-4A Minor (Lyc O-145)	PFA/833		14. 3.72	J.R.Faulkner (Stored 7.98)	Bicester	18. 9.97P
G-AZPX	Western O-31 HAFB	011		20. 3.72	B.L.King t/a Eugena Rex Balloon Grp "Eugena Rex"	Coulsdon	
G-AZRA	MBB Bo.209 Monsun 150FF	192	D-EAIH	21. 3.72	Alpha Flying Ltd	Panshanger	4. 9.00
G-AZRD	Cessna 401B	401B-0218	N7999Q	22. 3.72	G.Hatton t/a Romeo Delta Group	Blackpool	13. 3.00T
G-AZRG*	PA-23-250 Aztec D	27-4386	N6536Y	23. 3.72	Woodgate Avn (IOM) Ltd (On fire dump 4.97)	Ronaldsway	8. 7.93T
G-AZRH	PA-28-140 Cherokee D	28-7125585		23. 3.72	H.B.Carter t/a Trust Flying Group Jersey		10.12.98
G-AZRI	Payne HAFB (56,500 cu.ft)	GFP.1		21. 3.72	C.A.Butter & J.J.T.Cooke "Shoestring" t/a Aardvark Balloon Co Newbury/Southall		
G-AZRK	Sportavia Fournier RF5	5112		23. 3.72	P.M.Brockington & J.F.Rogers Shennington		21. 6.99P
G-AZRL	PA-18-95 Super Cub (L-18C-PI) (Frame No.18-1213)	18-1331	OO-SBR OO-HML/ALAT 18-1331/51-15331	23. 3.72	M.G.Fountain	Leicester	20. 8.01
G-AZRM	Sportavia Fournier RF5 (VW 1834)	5111		24. 3.72	A.R.Dearden & R.Speer	Upper Broyle Farm, Ringmer	24. 2.99P
G-AZRN	Cameron O-84 HAFB	28		28. 3.72	C.A.Butter & J.J.T.Cooke "Old Money"	Newbury	4. 7.81A
G-AZRP	AESL Airtourer T2 (115)	529		28. 3.72	B.F.Strawford	Shobdon	21. 3.01
G-AZRR	Cessna 310Q	310Q-0490	N9923F	28. 3.72	Routarrow Ltd	Seething	23. 4.01
G-AZRS	PA-22-150 Tri-Pacer	22-5141	XT-AAH F-OCGZ/ALAT 22-5141/"FMKAC"	28. 3.72	J.B.Nicholson t/a Sandpiper Grp "Sandpiper" Watchford Farm, Yarcombe		3. 4.00
G-AZRV	PA-28R-200 Cherokee Arrow	28R-7135191	N2309T	4. 4.72	General Airline Ltd	Blackbushe	28. 5.99T
G-AZRW*	Cessna T337C Turbo Super Skymaster	337-0914	9XR-DB N2614S	4. 4.72	Not known (Stored 7.94)	Standalone Farm, Meppershall	7. 6.82
G-AZRX*	Gardan GY-80-160 Horizon	14	F-BLIJ	4. 4.72	Adventure Island Pleasure Ground Marine Parade, Southend-on-Sea		20.2.92
				(Damaged Sandtoft 14.8.91; on display in Crazy Golf course on sea-front 1.99)			
G-AZRZ	Cessna U206F Stationair	U206-01803	N9603G	4. 4.72	M.R.Browne & R.G.Wood t/a Hinton Skydiving Centre Hinton-in-the-Hedges		26. 5.00
G-AZSA	Stampe et Renard SV-4B (Regd in error as c/n "64")	1203	V-61 Belgian AF	5. 4.72	J.K.Faulkner	Biggin Hill	30. 4.98
G-AZSC	Noorduyn AT-16-ND Harvard IIB	14A-1363	PH-SKK R.Neth AF B-19/FT323/43-13064	7. 4.72	Machine Music Ltd (Gary Numan) Duxford (As "43/SC" in USAAF c/s)		5. 5.99P
G-AZSD	Slingsby T.29B Motor Tutor (Rebuild of Slingsby c/n 561)	RGB 01/72 & PFA/1574		7. 4.72	R.G.Boyton t/a Essex Avn	Halstead, Essex	
G-AZSF	PA-28R-200 Cherokee Arrow II	28R-7235048		10. 4.72	W.T.Northorpe t/a Flight Simulation Air Park	Coventry	1. 8.99
G-AZSP*	Cameron O-84 HAFB	43		18. 4.72	British Balloon Museum "Esso"	Newbury	22. 3.82
G-AZSW	Beagle B.121 Pup 1	B121-140	PH-VRT G-35-140	24. 4.72	I.T.Dall	Sywell	21. 8.99
G-AZSZ	PA-23-250 Aztec D	27-4194	N6851Y	25. 4.72	Industrial Cladding Systems Ltd	Cardiff	2. 6.01T
G-AZTA	MBB Bo.209 Monsun 150FF	190	D-EAIF	25. 4.72	A.I.D.Rich	Elstree	7. 9.01
G-AZTD	PA-32-300 Cherokee Six D	32-7140001	N8611N	26. 4.72	Presshouse Publications Ltd	Enstone	16. 8.98T
G-AZTF	Reims Cessna F.177RG Cardinal	0054		28. 4.72	D.A.Wiggins	Booker	3. 8.01
G-AZTK	Reims Cessna F.172F	0116	PH-CON OO-SIR	27. 4.72	Vascas Ltd	Weston, Ireland	20.10.00
G-AZTN*	AESL Airtourer T2 (115)	A.531		28. 4.72	Not known (Crashed Puriton, Somerset 27.6.77; wreck stored 9.95)	St.Just	24. 6.78
G-AZTR	SNCAN Stampe SV-4C	596	F-BDEQ	28. 4.72	P.G.Palumbo (Stored in Blue Max Movie Acft Museum 3.96)	Booker	15. 7.94
G-AZTS	Reims Cessna F.172L	0866		28. 4.72	C.E.Stringer	Humberside	16. 1.00T
G-AZTV	Stolp SA.500 Starlet (Cont C90)	SSM.2 & PFA/1584		19. 5.72	G.G.Rowland (Christchurch) (Damaged Manor Farm, Grateley, Hants 4.7.92; status uncertain)		19.11.92
G-AZTW	Reims Cessna F.177RG Cardinal	0043		28. 4.72	R.M.Clarke	Leicester	15. 5.00
G-AZUM	Reims Cessna F.172L	0863		11. 5.72	L.R.Sullivan t/a Fowlmere Flyers	Fowlmere	16.11.00
G-AZUP	Cameron O-65 HAFB	36		11. 5.72	R.S.Bailey & A.B.Simpson "Eight of Hearts" Aylesbury/Hemel Hempstead		23.10.77S
G-AZUT	Socata MS.893A Rallye Commodore 180	10963	VH-TCH	12. 5.72	J.Palethorpe Blakedown, Kidderminster t/a Rallye F/Grp		9.10.99
G-AZUV*	Cameron O-65 HAFB	41		12. 5.72	British Balloon Museum "Icarus" Newbury (Stored - no longer airworthy)		23. 6.83
G-AZUX	Western O-56 HAFB	017		15. 5.72	D.M.Sandford "Slow Djinn"	Knutsford	
G-AZUY	Cessna 310L	310L-0012	SE-FEC LN-LMH/N2212F	15. 5.72	George Moss & Sons Ltd (Damaged Liverpool 3.7.98)	Liverpool	1.12.99
G-AZUZ	Reims Cessna FRA.150L Aerobat	0146		16. 5.72	D.J.Parker	Netherthorpe	12. 1.00
G-AZVA	MBB Bo.209 Monsun 150FF	177	(D-EAAQ)	16. 5.72	J.Nivison	Thruxton	8. 9.00
G-AZVB	MBB Bo.209 Monsun 150FF	178	(D-EAAS)	16. 5.72	P.C.Logsdon	Dunkeswell	6. 5.00
G-AZVF	Socata MS.894A Rallye Minerva 220	11099	(F-OCSR)	16. 5.72	Westwing Aviation Ltd	Kemble	27. 8.96
G-AZVG	American AA-5 Traveler	AA5-0075		16. 5.72	R.P.Watkins t/a Grumair F/Grp	Newtownards	26. 7.99

Regn	Type	C/n	P/I	Date	Owner/operator	Probable Base	CA Expy
G-AZVH	Socata MS.894A Rallye Minerva 220	12017		16. 5.72	P.L.Jubb Poplar Hall Farm, Elmsett		17. 6.01
G-AZVI	Socata MS.892A Rallye Commodore 150	12039		16. 5.72	H.R.Dyas & V.S.Bryan Shobdon		5. 2.01
					t/a Shobdon F/Grp		
G-AZVJ	PA-34-200-2 Seneca	34-7250125	N4529T	16. 5.72	Skyfotos Ltd (Op Foto Flite) Headcorn		21. 8.00A
G-AZVL	Jodel D.119	794	F-BILB	19. 5.72	P.T.East t/a Forest F/Grp Stapleford		14. 6.99P
	(Built Valladeau)						
G-AZVM	Hughes 369HS (500C)	61-0326S	N9091F	19. 5.72	Diagnostic Reagents Ltd Thame		7. 8.00
G-AZVP	Reims Cessna F.177RG Cardinal	0057		22. 5.72	Cardinal Flyers Ltd Denham		25. 6.01
G-AZWB	PA-28-140 Cherokee E	28-7225244		5. 6.72	B.N.Rides & L.Connor Kemble		11.12.00
G-AZWD	PA-28-140 Cherokee E	28-7225298		6. 6.72	C.B.Mellor t/a BM Avn Eastleigh		30. 4.99T
					(Damaged Cardiff 15.11.98)		
G-AZWE	PA-28-140 Cherokee E	28-7225303		6. 6.72	P.M.Tucker t/a G-AZWE F/Grp Dunkeswell		28. 2.99T
G-AZWF	SAN Jodel DR.1050 Ambassadeur	130	F-BJJT	7. 6.72	R.J.M.Clement Portmoak		27. 8.01
	(Composite including fuselage of DR.1050M F-BLJX c/n 492)				t/a G-AZWF Jodel Syndicate		
G-AZWS	PA-28R-180 Cherokee Arrow	28R-30749	N4993J	8. 6.72	G.S.Blair & I.Parkinson Newcastle		24. 4.00
					t/a Arrow 88 F/Grp		
G-AZWT	Westland Lysander IIIA	Y1536	RCAF 1582	9. 6.72	The Shuttleworth Trust Old Warden		28. 5.99P
			V9552		(As "V9441/AR-A" in 309 Sqn c/s)		
G-AZWY	PA-24-260 Comanche C	24-4806	N9310P	16. 6.72	Keymer, Son & Co Ltd Biggin Hill		15. 4.00
G-AZXA	Beechcraft 95-C55 Baron	TE-72	SE-EKZ	19. 6.72	Cobham Leasing Ltd Bournemouth		25.11.98A
G-AZXB	Cameron O-65 HAFB	48		20. 6.72	R.J.Mitchener & P.F.Smart Andover		6. 5.81A
					t/a Balloon Collection "London Pride II"		
G-AZXC	Reims Cessna F.150L	0793		20. 6.72	D.C.Bonsall Netherthorpe		28. 4.00T
G-AZXD	Reims Cessna F.172L	0878		20. 6.72	Birdlake Ltd Birmingham		29. 5.00T
					(Op Birdlake Avn)		
G-AZXG*	PA-23-250 Aztec D	27-4328	N6963Y	23. 6.72	Cranfield University Cranfield		18. 9.94
		(Crashed Little Snoring 25.10.91; instructional airframe 7.97)						
G-AZYA	Gardan GY-80-160 Horizon	57	F-BLPT	7. 7.72	T.Twelvetree & M.L.Moore (Holyhead)		20. 3.00
G-AZYB*	Bell 47H-1	1538	LN-OQG	4. 7.72	E.D.Ap Rees Weston-super-Mare		8. 9.84
			SE-HBE/OO-SHW		t/a The Helicopter Museum (On rebuild 5.97)		
G-AZYD	GEMS MS.893A Rallye Commodore 180	10645	F-BNSE	30. 6.72	P.Storey Husbands Bosworth		17. 5.98
					t/a Storey Aviation Services		
G-AZYM	Cessna 310Q	310Q-0507	N4592L	6. 7.72	Offshore Marine Consultants Ltd Gamston		17.10.99
G-AZYS	Scintex CP.301C-1 Emeraude	568	F-BJAY	7. 7.72	F.P.L.Clauson Draycott Farm, Chiseldon		5. 5.99P
G-AZYU	PA-23-250 Aztec E	27-4601	N13983	13. 7.72	L.J.Martin Redhill/Sandown		2.11.98
G-AZYY	Slingsby T-61A Falke	1770		12. 7.72	J.A.Towers Yearby		29. 1.99
G-AZYZ	Wassmer WA.51A Pacific	30	F-OCSE	14. 7.72	J.Ward Norwich		11. 8.00
G-AZZG	Cessna 188 Agwagon 230	188-0279	OY-AHT	12. 7.72	N.C.Kensington (On rebuild 5.92) Lairg		1. 5.81A
			N8029V				
G-AZZH	Practavia Pilot Sprite 115	PFA/1532		13. 7.72	A.Moore (Brentwood)		
					(Stored in back garden Dagenham 1992)		
G-AZZO	PA-28-140 Cherokee	28-22887	N4471J	18. 7.72	R.J.Hind Stapleford		24. 8.97
G-AZZR	Reims Cessna F.150L	0690	LN-LJX	24. 7.72	R.W.Smith t/a G-AZZR F/Grp Exeter		20. 7.01
G-AZZV	Reims Cessna F.172L	0883		18. 7.72	D.J.Hockings Rochester		6. 6.99T
G-AZZX	Reims Cessna FRA.150L Aerobat	0152		27. 7.72	Mary Hewison (Luton)		16. 8.88
					(Damaged Newtownards 28.2.87; on rebuild Maypole Farm, Chislet 12.93)		
G-AZZZ	DH.82A Tiger Moth	86311	F-BGJE	27. 7.72	S.W.McKay Blue Tile Farm, Langham		21.12.01
			Fr.AF/NL864		(Post restoration flight 4.12.98)		

G-BAAA-BAZZ

Regn	Type	C/n	P/I	Date	Owner/operator	Probable Base	CA Expy
G-BAAD	Evans Super VP-1 (VW1600)	PFA/1540		27. 7.72	K.McNaughton	Breighton	25. 8.99P
G-BAAF	Manning-Flanders MF.1 Replica (Cont C75)	PPS/REP/8		27. 7.72	Bianchi Avn Film Svs Ltd (Op Blue Max Movie Acft Museum) (No external marks)	Booker	6. 8.96P
G-BAAI	Socata MS.893A Rallye Commodore 180	10705	F-BOVG	31. 7.72	R.D.Taylor	Thruxton	11. 9.00
G-BAAL	Cessna 172A	47678	PH-KAP D-ELGU/N9878T	31. 7.72	Rochester Avn Ltd	Rochester	1. 3.01T
G-BAAT	Cessna 182P Skylane	182-60835	N399JF G-BAAT/N9295G	10. 8.72	Melrose Pigs Ltd	Melrose Farm, Melbourne	30. 4.00
G-BAAU	Enstrom F-28A-UK	092		10. 8.72	G.Firbank	(Macclesfield)	13. 7.85T
G-BAAW	Jodel D.119 (Built Valladeau)	366	F-BHMY	11. 8.72	P J Newson t/a Alpha Whiskey F/Grp	Cherry Tree Farm, Monewden	13. 5.99P
G-BAAZ	PA-28R-200 Cherokee Arrow	28R-7135146	N2388T (XB-VOC)	15. 8.72	A.W.Rix (Damaged by taxying PA-23 G-ESKY Guernsey 13.9.97)	Guernsey	9. 3.00
G-BABB	Reims Cessna F.150L	0830		15. 8.72	Seawing F/C Ltd	Southend	2. 7.00T
G-BABC	Reims Cessna F.150L	0831		15. 8.72	Fordaire Avn Ltd	Sywell	1. 9.00T
G-BABD	Reims Cessna FRA.150L Aerobat	0153		3. 8.72	Cassandra J.Hopewell	Swanton Morley	11. 2.01T
G-BABE	Taylor JT.2 Titch (Cont O-200-A)	PEB/01 & PFA/1394		3. 8.72	P.D.G.Grist	Sibson	7. 5.98P
G-BABG	PA-28-180 Cherokee C	28-2031	PH-APU N7978W	15. 8.72	C.E.Dodge t/a Mendip F/Grp	Bristol/Lulsgate	11.11.00
G-BABH	Reims Cessna F.150L	0820	EI-CCZ G-BABH	15. 8.72	Sherburn A/Club Ltd	Sherburn-in-Elmet	1. 4.01T
G-BABK	PA-34-200-2 Seneca	34-7250219	PH-DMN G-BABK/N5203T	18. 8.72	D.F.J.Flashman	Biggin Hill	24. 9.01
G-BACB	PA-34-200-2 Seneca	34-7250251	N5354T	25. 8.72	Rankart Ltd	Hinton-in-the-Hedges	12. 6.99T
G-BACC	Reims Cessna FRA.150L Aerobat	0157		16. 8.72	C.M. & J.H.Cooper	Cranfield	13.12.01
G-BACE	Sportavia Fournier RF5	5102	(PT-DVZ) D-KCID	25. 8.72	R.W.K.Stead t/a Clockwork Mouse F/Grp "The Clockwork Mouse"	Perranporth	15. 3.99
G-BACJ	Jodel Wassmer D.120 Paris-Nice	315	F-BNZC	1. 9.72	J.M.Allan t/a Wearside Flying Association	Newcastle	28. 2.98P
G-BACL	SAN Jodel 150 Mascaret	31	F-BSTY CN-TYY	4. 9.72	G.R.French	Bensons Farm, Laindon	8. 9.01
G-BACN	Reims Cessna FRA.150L Aerobat	0161		4. 9.72	Cornwall Flying Club Ltd	Bodmin	27. 5.00T
G-BACO	Reims Cessna FRA.150L Aerobat	0163		4. 9.72	M.M.Pepper	Sibson	14. 5.00
G-BACP	Reims Cessna F.150L Aerobat (Converted from FRA.150L standard)	0164		4. 9.72	Vectair Aviation 1995 Ltd	Goodwood	28. 2.01T
G-BADC	Rollason Beta B.2A (Cont C90)	JJF.1 & PFA/1384		7. 9.72	J.C.Mead (On overhaul Barton 5.95)	(Wrexham)	31. 1.85P
G-BADH	Slingsby T-61A Falke	1774		6. 9.72	D.W.Smart t/a Falke F/Grp	Gallows Hill	11. 3.99
G-BADI	PA-23-250 Aztec D	27-4235	N6885Y	5. 9.72	West London Aero Svs Ltd (Open storage 5.97)	North Weald	29.10.92T
G-BADJ	PA-E23-250 Aztec E	27-4841	N14279	11. 9.72	D.C.Hanss t/a Bell Avn	Elstree	21.12.01T
G-BADM	Rollason-Druine D.62B Condor	RAE/653 & PFA/49-11442		8. 9.72	M.Harris & J.Taylor	Yeldon Farm, Nutley	17. 5.99P
G-BADO	PA-32-300 Cherokee Six E	32-7240011	N8664N	15. 9.72	S.L.McEwan t/a G-BADO Flying Group	Gloucestershire	15.10.01
G-BADU*	Cameron O-56 HAFB	47		18. 4.72	J.Philp t/a Serendipity Balloon Grp "Dream Machine"	Pinner	29. 3.78S
G-BADV*	Brochet MB.50 Pipistrelle (Salmson AD9B)	78	F-PBRJ	13. 9.72	H.F.Moffatt (On rebuild)	Woodlow Farm, Bosbury	9. 5.79P
G-BADW	Aerotek Pitts S-2A Special	2035		21. 9.72	R.E.Mitchell	RAF Cosford	16. 9.95T
G-BADZ	Aerotek Pitts S-2A Special	2038		21. 9.72	A.F.D.Kingdon	Blackpool	5. 6.00T
G-BAEB	Robin DR.400/160 Knight	733		19. 9.72	P.D.W.King	Biggin Hill	3. 2.01T
G-BAEC	Robin HR.100/210 Royal	145	EI-BDG G-BAEC	15. 9.72	Designways (Interior Design) Ltd, J.Marriner & L.Stevens t/a Robin Travel	Elstree	24. 3.00
G-BAED	PA-23-250 Aztec C	27-3864	N6567Y	18. 9.72	K.G.Manktelow & N.Brewitt (Manx Airlines c/s)	Ronaldsway	10. 6.01T
G-BAEE	CEA Jodel DR.1050/M1 Sicile Record	579	F-BMGN	29. 9.72	R.Little	Shoreham	12. 6.00
G-BAEM	Robin DR.400/125 Petit Prince	728		25. 9.72	M.A.Webb	Denham	31. 5.00
G-BAEN	Robin DR.400/180 Regent	736		25. 9.72	European Soaring Club Ltd	Le Blanc, France	3. 5.97
G-BAEO*	Reims Cessna F.172M	0911		14. 9.72	Not known (Crashed Barton 7.5.78; wreck stored 4.91)	Ronaldsway	10. 2.79
G-BAEP	Reims Cessna FRA.150L Aerobat (Converted to F150L standard)	0170		14. 9.72	A.M.Lynn t/a Busy Bee	Fenland	4. 5.01T
G-BAER	LeVier Cosmic Wind (Cont O-200-A)	106 & PFA/1571		14. 9.72	R.S.Voice "Filly"	Rushett Farm, Chessington	14. 9.99P
G-BAET	Piper J3C-65 Cub (L-4H-PI) (Frame No.11430)	11605	OO-AJI 43-30314	26. 9.72	C.J.Rees	Valley Farm, Winwick	30. 4.99P
G-BAEU	Reims Cessna F.150L	0873		26. 9.72	L.W.Scattergood	(Selby)	19. 1.01T
G-BAEV	Reims Cessna FRA.150L Aerobat	0173		27. 9.72	Susan C.Griffin	Sibson	28. 2.01

Regn	Type	C/n	P/I	Date	Owner/operator	Probable Base	CA Expy
G-BAEW*	Reims Cessna F.172M	0914	N12798	27. 9.72	Westley Acft	Cranfield	9. 4.94T
					(Damaged nr Sywell 12.11.93; stored 7.97)		
G-BAEY	Reims Cessna F.172M	0915		28. 9.72	R.Fursman	Plymouth	25. 7.99
G-BAEZ	Reims Cessna FRA.150L Aerobat	0169		28. 9.72	Donair F/C Ltd	East Midlands	16. 5.99T
G-BAFA	American AA-5 Traveler	AA5-0201	N6136A	6.10.72	C.F.Mackley	Sleap	31. 8.01
G-BAFG	DH.82A Tiger Moth	85995	F-BGEL	13.10.72	J.E. & P.E.Shaw	Nottingham	6. 8.99
			Fr.AF/EM778				
G-BAFL	Cessna 182P Skylane	182-61469	N21180	15. 8.72	Farm Avn Svs Ltd	Cranfield	23. 7.01
					"Honey Lingers"		
G-BAFP	Robin DR.400/160 Knight	735		19.10.72	T.A.Pugh	Pool Quay, Breidden	22. 2.01
					t/a Breidden F/Grp		
G-BAFS	PA-18-150 Super Cub	18-5338	ALAT	3. 8.72	N.K.Watts t/a G-BAFS Grp	Bembridge	11.12.98
			18-5338				
G-BAFT	PA-18-150 Super Cub	18-5340	ALAT	3. 8.72	T.J.Wilkinson	Sackville Lodge, Riseley	2. 5.00
			18-5340				
G-BAFU	PA-28-140 Cherokee	28-20759	PH-NLS	11.10.72	M.Kostiuk	Beeches Farm, South Scarle	10. 4.00
G-BAFV	PA-18-95 Super Cub	18-2045	PH-WJK	24.10.72	T.F. & S.J.Thorpe	Willingham	16. 9.01
	(L-18C-PI) (Frame No.18-2055)		R.Neth AF R-40/8A-40/52-2445				
G-BAFX	Robin DR.400/140 Earl	739		30.10.72	K.R.Gough		14. 5.01
						Clutton Hill Farm, High Littleton	
G-BAGB	SIAI-Marchetti SF.260	1-07	LN-BIV	20.10.72	British Midland Airways Ltd		
						East Midlands	16. 6.00
G-BAGC	Robin DR.400/140 Earl	737		13.10.72	W.P.Nutt	(Scarborough)	23. 5.99
G-BAGF	Jodel D.92 Bebe	59	F-PHFC	13.11.72	E.Evans	Fobbing, Stanford-le-Hope	
					(On rebuild 8.97)		
G-BAGG(2)	PA-32-300 Cherokee Six	32-7340186		7.12.73	D.Anthill	Guernsey	16. 2.01
G-BAGI	Cameron O-31 HAFB	56		25.10.72	D.C.Boxall	Bristol	19. 9.76S
					t/a Red Section Balloon Grp "Vital Spark"		
G-BAGJ*	Westland SA.341G Gazelle 1				See G-SFTA		
G-BAGL	Westland SA.341G Gazelle 1	1067		26.10.72	Triangle Computer Services Ltd		
					(Op Bournemouth Helicopters) Bournemouth		11. 3.00T
G-BAGN	Reims Cessna F.177RG Cardinal	0068		24.10.72	R.W.J.Andrews	Halfpenny Green	26. 3.01
G-BAGO	Cessna 421B Golden Eagle	421B-0356	N7613Q	24.10.72	Golden Aviation Ltd	Thruxton	6. 7.00T
G-BAGR	Robin DR.400/140 Petit Prince	753		30.10.72	F.C.Aris & J.D.Last	Caernarfon	8. 4.01
G-BAGS	Robin DR.400/100 2+2	760		30.10.72	J.J.Woodhouse	(Fleet)	17. 4.00
					t/a Flying Services		
G-BAGT	Helio H.295 Super Courier	1288	CR-LJG	31.10.72	B.J.C.Woodall Ltd		
						Rushett Farm, Chessington	24. 6.01
G-BAGV	Cessna U206F Stationair	U206-01867	N9667G	31.10.72	K.Brady	Strathallan	22. 4.98
					t/a The Scottish Parachute Club		
G-BAGX	PA-28-140 Cherokee	28-23633	N3574K	30.10.72	K.F.Harris t/a Golf X-Ray Grp	Conington	5. 9.99
G-BAGY	Cameron O-84 HAFB	54		17.10.72	P.G.Dunnington	Hungerford	16. 6.81A
					"Beatrice" (Stored 2.97)		
G-BAHD	Cessna 182P Skylane	182-61501	N21228	25.10.72	G.G.Ferriman	Jericho Farm, Lambley	22.12.00
					t/a Lambley F/Grp		
G-BAHE	PA-28-140 Cherokee C	28-26494	N5696U	30.10.72	A.H.Evans & A.O.Jones		
					(Stored 5.96)	Pool Quay, Breidden	8. 6.95
G-BAHF	PA-28-140 Fliteliner	28-7125215	N431FL	30.10.72	BJ Services (Midlands) Ltd	Coventry	14. 5.01T
G-BAHG	PA-24-260 Comanche B	24-4306	5Y-AFX	2.11.72	B.Walker & Co (Dursley) Ltd		
			N8831P			Gloucestershire	21. 7.00
G-BAHH	Wallis WA-121/Mc	K/701/X		7.11.72	K.H.Wallis	Reymerston Hall	27. 5.98P
G-BAHI	Reims Cessna F.150H	0330	PH-EHA	6.11.72	P.Wagstaff	(London NW10)	19.11.01
G-BAHJ	PA-24-250 Comanche	24-1863	PH-RED	6.11.72	K.Cooper	Halfpenny Green	21. 5.01
			N6735P				
G-BAHL	Robin DR.400/160 Knight	704	F-OCSR	8.11.72	M.D.Hinge & L.A.Maynard	Old Sarum	24. 3.00
G-BAHO	Beechcraft C23 Sundowner	M-1456		7.11.72	P.H.White & J.A.L.Staig	Bournemouth	7.11.99
G-BAHP	Volmer VJ.22 Sportsman	PFA/1313		9.11.72	G.K.Holloway t/a Seaplane Grp	Aboyne	18.10.93P
	(Cont C90)				(Stored 8.98)		
G-BAHS	PA-28R-200 Cherokee Arrow II	28R-7335017	N15147	9.11.72	J.T.Mirley	(Wolverhampton)	29. 5.00
G-BAHX	Cessna 182P Skylane	182-61588	N21363	16.11.72	A.D.Carr t/a PP Dupost Grp	Blackpool	17. 7.00
G-BAIB	Enstrom F-28A	097		22.11.72	P.M.Froud	Goodwood	12. 2.98
					t/a Farmax Helicopters		
G-BAIG	PA-34-200-2 Seneca	34-7250243	OY-BSU	21.11.72	Mid-Anglia Flying School Ltd	Cambridge	6. 8.00T
			G-BAIG/N5257T				
G-BAIH	PA-28R-200 Cherokee Arrow II	28R-7335011		21.11.72	M.G.West	Kings Farm, Thurrock	9. 2.01
G-BAII	Reims Cessna FRA.150L Aerobat	0178		22.11.72	Cornwall Flying Club Ltd	Bodmin	27. 5.00T
G-BAIK	Reims Cessna F.150L	0903		22.11.72	Wickenby Avn Ltd	Wickenby	9. 4.00T
					(Op Lincoln Flight Centre)		
G-BAIL	Reims Cessna FR.172J Rocket	0370		22.11.72	R.H.Blair	Gloucestershire	7. 7.00
					t/a Gloucestershire F/C		
					(Damaged Farley Farm, Winchester 6.3.99)		
G-BAIN	Reims Cessna FRA.150L Aerobat	0177		23.11.72	Cornwall Flying Club Ltd	Bodmin	3.11.00T
G-BAIP	Reims Cessna F.150L	0898		13.11.72	G. & S.A.Jones	Linley Hill, Leven	28. 9.97T
					(Damaged on landing Linley Hill 30.5.95)		
G-BAIR*	Thunder Ax7-77 HAFB	003		27.11.72	S.Faithfull "Jumping Jack"	Not known	N/E(A)
G-BAIS	Reims Cessna F.177RG Cardinal	0069		13.11.72	R.M.Graham & E.P.Howard	Seething	22. 8.99
					t/a Cardinal Syndicate		

Regn	Type	C/n	P/I	Date	Owner/operator	Probable Base	CA Expy
G-BAIW	Reims Cessna F.172M	0928		14.11.72	W.J.Greenfield	Humberside	4.12.00T
G-BAIX	Reims Cessna F.172M	0931		14.11.72	R.A.Nichols	Elstree	19.12.99
G-BAIZ	Slingsby T-61A Falke	1776		27.11.72	G.C.Rumsey & R.G.Sangster t/a Falke Syndicate	Hinton-in-the-Hedges	7. 7.00
G-BAJA	Reims Cessna F.177RG Cardinal	0078		29.11.72	Don Ward Productions Ltd	Rochester	15.10.99
G-BAJB	Reims Cessna F.177RG Cardinal	0080		29.11.72	C.M.Bain	Inverness	5. 8.00
G-BAJC	Evans VP-1 Srs.2 (VW1834)	PFA/1548		30.11.72	R.C.Crowley (Stored 8.97)	Biggin Hill	22. 3.99P
G-BAJE	Cessna 177 Cardinal	177-00812	N29322	30.11.72	H.Snelson	Blackpool	20. 5.00
G-BAJN	American AA-5 Traveler	AA5-0259		29.11.72	K.Bell & J.C.Robinson t/a Janacrew F/Grp	Sherburn	24. 3.00
G-BAJO	American AA-5 Traveler	AA5-0260		29.11.72	P.J.Kelsall t/a G-BAJO F/Grp	Blackpool	19. 1.01
G-BAJR	PA-28-180 Challenger	28-7305008		1.12.72	D.P.Bannister & D.T.Given t/a Chosen Flew F/Grp	Newtownards	26. 3.00
G-BAJY	Robin DR.400/180 Regent	758		4.12.72	J.H.Fenwick t/a Rolincs Avn	Sturgate	6. 7.01
G-BAJZ	Robin DR.400/125 Petit Prince	759		4.12.72	Rochester Avn Ltd	Rochester	24. 6.00T
G-BAKD	PA-34-200-2 Seneca	34-7350013	N1378T	28.11.72	Andrews Professional Colour Laboratories Ltd (Op Foto Flite)	Lydd	17.12.00A
G-BAKH	PA-28-140 Cherokee F	28-7325014		12.12.72	Marnham Investments Ltd (Op Ulster F/C)	Newtownards	16. 3.00T
G-BAKJ	PA-30-160 Twin Comanche B	30-1232	TJ-AAI TJ-ADH/N8122Y	13.12.72	M.F.Fisher & W.R.Lawes	Biggin Hill	2. 7.00
G-BAKM	Robin DR.400/140 Earl	755		15.12.72	D.V.Pieri	Kirkbride	2.10.00
G-BAKN	SNCAN Stampe SV-4C	348	F-BCOY	15.12.72	M.Holloway Watchford Farm, Yarcombe		3. 1.99
G-BAKO*	Cameron O-84 HAFB	57		18.12.72	A D Kent "Pied Piper" (Balloon Preservation Group 7.98)	Lancing	12. 7.76S
G-BAKR	SAN Jodel D.117	814	F-BIOV	27.12.72	R.W.Brown Stoneacre Farm, Farthing Corner		3. 2.99P
G-BAKS	Agusta-Bell 206B JetRanger II	8339		28.12.72	Stephenson Marine Co Ltd (Crashed at Cocking, West Sussex 14.11.97)	Goodwood	26. 6.00T
G-BAKV	PA-18-150 Super Cub	18-8993		22.12.72	L.J.Hounsome	(Romsey)	6. 5.01
G-BAKW	Beagle B.121 Pup 2	B121-175		15.12.72	H.Beavan	White Waltham	26. 5.00
G-BAKY	Slingsby T-61C Falke	1777		20.12.72	Buckminster Gliding Club Ltd	Saltby	7. 8.98
G-BALD	Cameron O-84 HAFB	58		2. 1.73	C.A.Gould t/a Inter-Varsity Balloon Club "Puffin"	Ipswich	2. 7.78S
	(Wfu after severe damage 25.6.78; basket to G-PUFF)						
G-BALF	Robin DR.400/140 Earl	772		5. 1.73	N.A.Smith	Barton	15. 5.00
G-BALG	Robin DR.400/180 Regent	771		5. 1.73	R.Jones t/a Southern Sailplanes	Membury	5. 8.01
G-BALH	Robin DR.400/140B Earl	766		5. 1.73	C.Johnson t/a G-BALH F/Grp	Fenland	21. 6.01
G-BALI	Robin DR.400 2 + 2	764		5. 1.73	A.Brinkley	(Shefford)	3. 9.88
G-BALJ	Robin DR.400/180 Regent	767		5. 1.73	D.A.Batt & D. de Lacey-Rowe Fridd Farm, Bethersden, Kent		31. 5.00
G-BALK*	SNCAN Stampe SV-4C	387	F-BBAN Fr.Mil	3. 1.73	J.Thorogood (Noted 5.98)	Insch	
G-BALN	Cessna T310Q	310Q-0684	N79800	8. 1.73	O'Brien Properties Ltd	Shoreham	1. 5.00T
G-BALY	Practavia Pilot Sprite 150	PFA/05-10009		10. 1.73	A.L.Young t/a Aly Avn (Project part completed and stored 8.95)	(Henstridge)	
G-BALZ	Bell 212	30542	EC-GCR	10. 1.73	Bristow Helicopters Ltd	Redhill	5.10.00T
	EC-931/G-BALZ/9Y-TIL/G-BALZ/VR-BIB/N8069A/G-BALZ/N99040/G-BALZ/EI-AWK/G-BALZ/VR-BEK/N2961W						
G-BAMB	Slingsby T-61C Falke	1778		9. 1.73	S.P.Wareham t/a G-BAMB Syndicate	Kingston Deverill	18. 5.00
G-BAMC	Reims Cessna F.150L	0892		12. 1.73	S.C.Barry	Slinfold	18. 7.99T
G-BAMF	MBB Bo.105DB	S.36	D-HDAM	10. 1.73	Bond Helicopters Ltd (Pollution Patrol)	Sullom Voe	20. 6.00T
G-BAMG*	Avions Lobet Ganagobie	PFA/1336		11. 1.73	Not known (Complete 4.97 but unflown)	Yearby	
G-BAMJ	Cessna 182P	182-61650	N21469	10. 1.73	A.E.Kedros	Shenington	29. 5.00
G-BAMK	Cameron D-96 Hot-Air Airship	72		11. 1.73	D.W.Liddiard "Isibidbi" (To British Balloon Museum	Newbury	24. 4.90A
G-BAML	Bell 206B JetRanger	36	N7844S	5. 1.73	Heliscott Ltd Walton Wood, Pontefract		9. 8.01T
G-BAMM	PA-28-235 Cherokee	28-10642	SE-EOA	16. 1.73	T.R.Astell Spilsted Farm, Sedlescombe		10. 5.01
G-BAMR	PA-16 Clipper (Lyc O-290)	16-392	F-BFMS CU-P339	12. 1.73	H.Royce Bradleys Lawn, Heathfield		31. 1.98
G-BAMS	Robin DR.400/160 Knight	774		15. 1.73	G-BAMS Ltd	Biggin Hill	29. 5.00T
G-BAMT*	Robin DR.400/160 Knight	775		15. 1.73	Southern Sailplanes (Crashed Cudham 8.1.78; wreck stored 1.92)	Membury	15. 5.79
G-BAMU	Robin DR.400/160 Knight	778		15. 1.73	J.W.L.Otty t/a The Alternative F/Grp	Sywell	15. 6.00
G-BAMV	Robin DR.400/180 Regent	777		15. 1.73	K.Jones & E.A.Anderson	Booker	3. 5.00
G-BAMY	PA-28R-200 Cherokee Arrow II	28R-7335015		9. 1.73	G.R.Gilbert t/a G-BAMY Grp	Birmingham	29. 3.01
G-BANA	CEA Jodel DR.221 Dauphin	73	F-BOZR	22. 1.73	G.T.Pryor	Seething	4. 4.00
G-BANB	Robin DR.400/180 Regent	776		22. 1.73	D.R.L.Jones	(Malmesbury)	27. 1.00
G-BANC	Gardan GY-201 Minicab (Cont C90)	A.203	F-PCZV F-BCZV	22. 1.73	J.T.S.Lewis & J.E.Williams Brickhouse Farm, Frogland Cross		16. 8.99P
G-BANF	Phoenix Luton LA-4A Minor (Cont A65)	PFA/838		22. 1.73	W.J.McCollum		5. 6.92P
	(Damaged Mullaghmore 27.6.92; status uncertain) (Magherafelt, Co.Londonderry)						
G-BANK	PA-34-200-2 Seneca	34-7350081	N15636	23. 1.73	Sue Eastwood	Blackbushe	16. 7.01T

Regn	Type	C/n	P/I	Date	Owner/operator	Probable Base	CA Expy
G-BANU	Jodel Wassmer D.120 Paris-Nice	247	F-BLNZ	31. 1.73	W.M. & C.H.Kilner (Clitheroe/Stamford)		14. 7.99P
G-BANV	Phoenix Currie Wot (Lyc O-290)	PFA/3010		25. 1.73	K.Knight (Malvern) (Damaged nr Leek, Staffs 15.9.83; status uncertain)		26. 6.84P
G-BANW	CAARP CP.1330 Super Emeraude	941	PH-VRF	30. 1.73	P.S.Milner	Scotland Farm, Hook	8. 7.98P
G-BANX	Reims Cessna F.172M	0941		31. 1.73	J.F.Davis	South Cerney	6. 8.00T
G-BANY*	Glos-Air Airtourer 115	A533		31. 1.73	Not known (Crashed nr Wick 10.8.75; fuselage stored 8.96)	St.Just	25. 3.77
G-BAOB	Reims Cessna F.172M	0949		2. 2.73	Rentair Ltd, M.Nicoll & D.Williams-Gardner	Earls Colne	21.12.01T
G-BAOG	Socata MS.880B Rallye Club	2249		6. 2.73	J.Luck	Rochester	16. 1.00
G-BAOH	Socata MS.880B Rallye Club	2250		6. 2.73	R.D.Andrews	Dunkeswell	28. 7.01
G-BAOJ	Socata MS.880B Rallye Club	2252		6. 2.73	R.E.Jones	Emlyns Field, Rhuallt	13. 8.01
G-BAOM	Socata MS.880B Rallye Club	2255		6. 2.73	D.H.Tonkin	Bodmin	13. 4.00
G-BAOP	Reims Cessna FRA.150L Aerobat	0190		5. 2.73	Catherine M.Dixon	Barton	6. 3.99
G-BAOS	Reims Cessna F.172M	0946		6. 2.73	Wingtask 1995 Ltd	Seething	14. 8.00T
G-BAOU	Grumman-American AA-5 Traveler	AA5-0298		8. 2.73	R.C.Mark	(Ludlow)	23. 3.01
G-BAOW	Cameron O-65 HAFB	59		6. 2.73	D P Bushby "Winslow Boy" (Balloon Preservation Group 7.98)	Lancing	9. 5.74S
G-BAPB	DHC.1 Chipmunk 22A	C1/0001	WB549	26. 2.73	G.V.Bunyan	Bidford	31. 5.98
G-BAPF*	Vickers Viscount 814	338	SE-FOY G-BAPF/D-ANUN	12. 2.73	The Fire Servive College Moreton-in-Marsh (Instructional airframe 8.98)		13. 6.90T
G-BAPH*	Reims Cessna FRA.150L Aerobat	0194		8. 2.73	South Yorkshire Aviation Museum (Damaged Bodmin 12.7.81; fuselage on display 5.97) Home Farm, Firbeck		26. 7.82
G-BAPI	Reims Cessna FRA.150L Aerobat	0195		8. 2.73	Industrial Supplies (Peterborough) Ltd Sibson		15. 1.01
G-BAPJ	Reims Cessna FRA.150L Aerobat	0196		8. 2.73	M.D.Page	Manston	10. 6.99
G-BAPL	PA-23-250 Turbo Aztec E	27-7304966	N14377	12. 2.73	Donington Avn Ltd	East Midlands	27. 8.01T
G-BAPP	Evans VP-1 Coupe (VW1834)	PFA/1580		13. 2.73	V.Mitchell	Eglinton	27. 5.98P
G-BAPR	Jodel D.11 (Cont PC60)	5295 & PFA/914		14. 2.73	J.P.Liber & J.F.M.Bartlett	Kemble	1. 4.99P
G-BAPS*	Campbell Cougar Gyroplane (Cont O-240-A)	CA/6000		14. 2.73	A.M.W.Curzon-Howe-Herrick (On loan to The Helicopter Museum) Weston-super-Mare		20. 5.74S
G-BAPV	Robin DR.400/160 Knight	742	F-OCSR	19. 2.73	J.D. & M.Millne (Stored 9.97)	Newcastle	16.12.96
G-BAPW	PA-28R-180 Cherokee Arrow	28R-30697	5Y-AIR N4951J	21. 2.73	P.S.Farren & I.W.Lindsey t/a Papa Whisky F/Grp	Denham	3.12.00
G-BAPX	Robin DR.400/160 Knight	789		21. 2.73	M.A.Musselwhite	Sywell	11. 6.00
G-BAPY	Robin HR.100/210 Royal	153		21. 2.73	D.M.Hansell & G.Loxton	Shipdham	7. 7.01
G-BARC	Reims Cessna FR.172J Rocket	0356	(D-EEDK)	5. 3.73	C.H.Porter Croft Farm, Defford t/a Severn Valley Avn Grp		6. 4.01
G-BARD*	Cessna 337C Super Skymaster	337-0857	SE-FBU N2557S	1. 3.73	Not known North Coates (Damaged North Coates 12.6.94; stored 12.95)		9. 1.97
G-BARF	Wassmer Jodel D.112	1019	F-BJPF	5. 3.73	J.J.Penney	Neath	2.12.99P
G-BARG	Cessna E310Q	310Q-0712	N8237Q	2. 3.73	Anglo American Airmotive Ltd Bournemouth		8.12.99
G-BARH	Beechcraft C23 Sundowner	M-1473		2. 3.73	J.R.Pybus	Sherburn	4. 2.01
G-BARI*	Beechcraft C23 Sundowner	M-1475		2. 3.73	Not known Bushey (Crashed nr Coventry 23.4.75; wreck displayed in car-breaker's yard 5.95)		15. 7.75
G-BARN	Taylor JT.2 Titch (Cont C90)	PFA/60-11136		5. 3.73	R.G.W.Newton (On rebuild)	(Seaford)	2.10.92P
G-BARP	Bell 206B JetRanger II	967	N18092	5. 3.73	South Western Electricity plc Bristol/Lulsgate		9. 5.00T
G-BARS	DHC.1 Chipmunk 22	C1/0557	WK520	26. 2.73	J.Beattie RNAS Yeovilton (As "1377" in Portuguese AF c/s)		11. 7.99
G-BARV	Cessna 310Q	310Q-0774		7. 3.73	Old England Watches Ltd	Elstree	13. 7.01
G-BARZ	Scheibe SF-28A Tandem Falke	5724	(D-KAUK)	8. 3.73	K.Kiely	RAF Dishforth	3.11.95
G-BASG	Grumman-American AA-5 Traveler	AA5-0320	N5420L	12. 3.73	D.Cunningham & D.Barr t/a ASG Avn Grp	Glenrothes	20. 1.00
G-BASH	Grumman-American AA-5 Traveler	AA5-0319	EI-AWV G-BASH/N5419L	12. 3.73	G.Jenkins t/a BASH F/Group	Blackbushe	9. 9.99T
G-BASJ	PA-28-180 Cherokee Challenger	28-7305136		13. 3.73	T.J.McElwee Bristol/Lulsgate t/a Challenger Flying Group		4.11.00T
G-BASL	PA-28-140 Cherokee F	28-7325195		13. 3.73	Air Navigation & Trading Co Ltd Blackpool		16. 6.01T
G-BASM	PA-34-200-2 Seneca	34-7350120	N16272	13. 3.73	M.Gipps & J.R.Whetlor	Denham	14.10.01
G-BASN	Beechcraft C23 Sundowner	M-1476		13. 3.73	M.F.Fisher	Seighford	10. 8.98
G-BASO	Lake LA-4-180 Amphibian	358	N2025L	16. 3.73	C.J.A.Macaulay	(Woking)	14. 6.98
G-BASP	Beagle B.121 Pup 1	B121-149	SE-FOC G-35-149	14. 3.73	B.J.Coutts	Sywell	23. 6.01
G-BAST*	Cameron O-84 HAFB	70		15. 3.73	A D Kent "Honey" Longleat House, Wilts (Balloon Preservation Group & displayed 7.98)		2. 5.84A
G-BASU*	PA-31-350 Navajo Chieftain	31-7305023	N7693L	15. 3.73	Not known Exeter (Damaged Dounreay 12.5.87; fuselage on fire dump 11.93)		3.11.87T

Regn	Type	C/n	P/I	Date	Owner/operator	Probable Base	CA Expy
G-BASX	PA-34-200-2 Seneca	34-7350123	N15781	16. 3.73	London Executive Aviation Ltd	Sheffield-City	26. 4.99T
G-BATC	MBB Bo.105DB	S.45	D-HDAW	9. 3.73	Bond Helicopters Ltd (Op Devon Ambulance Service)	Exeter	22. 6.99T
	(Rebuilt using new MBB pod 1989; original pod to Offshore Petroleum Industry Training Board, Montrose 10.90)						
G-BATD*	Cessna U206F Stationair	U206-02014	N60204	12. 3.73	British Parachute School	Langar	
	(Crashed Shobdon 5.4.80; for para-trainer use 6.97)						
G-BATJ	Jodel D.119	287	F-PIIQ	21. 3.73	D.J. & K.S.Thomas	Fenland	27. 6.99P
	(Cont C90) (Built by Ecole Technique Aeronautique)						
G-BATN	PA-23-250 Aztec E	27-7304987	N14391	26. 3.73	Marshall of Cambridge Aerospace Ltd	Cambridge	21.11.99T
G-BATR	PA-34-200-2 Seneca	34-7250290	9H-ABH G-BATR/LN-BDT	23. 3.73	A.S.Bamrah t/a Falcon F/Svs	Biggin Hill	17. 3.99T
G-BATT	Hughes 269C (300)	122-0175		26. 3.73	G.M.Vowles & S.Lane t/a 47 F/C	(Leeds)	6. 9.00T
G-BATV	PA-28-180 Cherokee F	28-7105022	N5168S	26. 3.73	J.N.Rudsdale t/a The Scoreby F/Grp	Sherburn	12. 9.99
G-BATW	PA-28-140 Cherokee Fliteliner	28-7225587	N742FL	26. 3.73	N.C.Spooner & M.Butterworth t/a Tango Whiskey Flying Partnership	Earls Colne	10.12.99
G-BATX	PA-23-250 Aztec E	27-4832	N14271	27. 3.73	C-Tech Industries Ltd (Op Sky Leisure)	Shoreham	28. 5.01T
G-BAUA	PA-23-250 Aztec D	27-4048	N6718Y	26. 3.73	David Parr & Associates Ltd (Open store 8.96)	Aberporth	27. 7.92
G-BAUC	PA-25-235 Pawnee C	25-5243	N8761L	26. 3.73	Southdown Gliding Club Ltd	Parham Park	20. 4.00
G-BAUH	Dormois Jodel D.112	870	F-BILO	29. 3.73	G.A. & D.Shepherd t/a G-BAUH F/Grp	Seething	28. 6.99P
G-BAUI*	PA-23-250 Aztec D	27-4335	LN-RTS	29. 3.73	Brunel Technical College (Stored 1.97)	Bristol/Lulsgate	5.12.88T
G-BAUJ	PA-23-250 Aztec E	27-7304986	N14390	29. 3.73	S.J. & C.J.Westley (Stored 7.97)	Cranfield	25. 7.94T
G-BAUK	Hughes 269C (300)	23-0184		29. 3.73	Curtis Engineering (Frome) Ltd (Stored 8.97)	Sywell	20. 9.93
G-BAUN	Bell 206B JetRanger	464	5N-BAY G-BAUN/5N-AOU/VR-BIA/G-BAUN/N2261W "Captain Freeson"	2. 4.73	Bristow Helicopters Ltd	Redhill	26. 1.02T
G-BAUR*	Fokker F-27 Friendship 200	10225	PH-FEP 9V-BAP/9M-AMI/(VR-RCZ)/PH-FEP (Stored 2.96)	5. 4.73	Jersey European Airways (UK) Ltd	Exeter	5. 4.96T
G-BAUW	PA-23-250 Aztec E	27-4814	N14253	9. 4.73	R.E.Myson	Jersey/Hardings Farm, Ingatestone	22. 7.00
G-BAUY	Reims Cessna FRA.150L Aerobat	0167	N10633	5. 4.73	A.G. Knight t/a Airlaunch	Old Buckenham	8. 2.99
G-BAVB	Reims Cessna F.172M	0965		10. 4.73	T.J.Nokes & T.V.Phillips	Hinton-in-the-Hedges	27. 2.99
G-BAVH	DHC.1 Chipmunk 22	C1/0841	WP975	10. 4.73	Portsmouth Naval Gliding Club	Lee-on-Solent	24. 3.96
	(On conversion to Lycoming 1995)						
G-BAVL	PA-23-250 Aztec E	27-4671	N14063	10. 4.73	S.P. & A.V.Chilcott	Teesside	8. 6.01T
G-BAVO	Boeing-Stearman A75N-1 Kaydet	-	4X-AIH	13. 4.73	Vallingstone Avn Ltd (Martin Shaw)	Swanton Morley	28. 6.01
	(Cont W670)				(As "26" in US Army c/s)		
	(Regd with c/n "3250-1405" which is a part number; real identity unknown)						
G-BAVR	Grumman-American AA-5 Traveler	AA5-0348		12. 4.73	G.E.Murray	Haverfordwest	20. 7.01
G-BAVS*	Grumman-American AA-5 Traveler	AA5-0349		12. 4.73	Not known (Stored 7.93)	Bournemouth	8.11.94
G-BAVU	Cameron A-105 HAFB	66		11. 4.73	Not known	Oxford	5.10.84A
G-BAVZ	PA-23-250 Aztec E	27-7305045	N40241	18. 4.73	Cheshire F/Svs Ltd t/a Ravenair	Manchester	17. 2.01T
G-BAWG	PA-28R-200 Cherokee Arrow II	28R-7335133		18. 4.73	Solent Air Ltd	Goodwood	3. 2.01
G-BAWI*	Enstrom F-28A-UK	120		9. 4.73	Lodge Road Flying Svs	Tattershall Thorpe	10. 4.94T
	(Crashed Bosworth Hall 26.6.92; stored 10.92)						
G-BAWK	PA-28-140 Cherokee Cruiser	28-7325243		24. 4.73	Newcastle-upon-Tyne Aero Club Ltd (Stored 4.97)	Newcastle	3. 8.01T
G-BAWR	Robin HR.100/210 Royal	156		27. 4.73	T.Taylor	Thruxton	8. 6.00
G-BAWU	PA-30-160 Twin Comanche B	30-1477	(G-BAWV) 9J-RFW/ZS-FAM/N8332Y	30. 4.73	Syndicate Clerical Services Ltd	Exeter	2. 5.99T
G-BAWW*	Thunder Ax7-77 HAFB	004	(PH-AWW) G-BAWW	30. 4.73	S.Faithfull "Taurus"		11. 5.84A
G-BAXE	Hughes 269A-1	113-0313	N8931F	2. 5.73	Reeve Newfields Ltd	Sywell	21.12.93S
G-BAXF*	Cameron O-77 HAFB	74		3. 5.73	British Balloon Museum & Library "Granna"	Newbury	N/E(A)
G-BAXJ	PA-32-300 Cherokee Six B	32-40763	N1362Z G-BAXJ/4X-ANY/N5224S t/a Airlaunch (Op Stirling Parachute Centre)	8. 5.73	A.G.Knight	Thornhill, Stirling	11. 6.00
G-BAXK	Thunder Ax7-77 HAFB	005		9. 5.73	A.R.Snook "Jack O'Newbury"	Newbury	2. 7.91A
G-BAXP	PA-23-250 Aztec E	27-4608	N13990	11. 5.73	Amersham Est Ltd (On fire dump 10.97)	Shoreham	5. 3.92T
G-BAXS	Bell 47G-5	7908	5B-CFB G-BAXS/N4098G	11. 5.73	R.M.Kemp t/a RK Helicopters	Fairoaks	2.12.00T
G-BAXU	Reims Cessna F.150L	0959		14. 5.73	M.A.Wilson	Woodvale	22. 3.01T
G-BAXV	Reims Cessna F.150L	0966		14. 5.73	G. & S.A.Jones	(Hull)	14. 5.01T
G-BAXY	Reims Cessna F.172M	0905	N10636	15. 5.73	R.J.W.Wood	Gregory Farm, Mirfield	16. 7.01T

Regn	Type	C/n	P/I	Date	Owner/operator	Probable Base	CA Expy
G-BAXZ	PA-28-140 Cherokee C	28-26760	PH-NLX	15. 5.73	D.Norris & H.Martin t/a G-BAXZ Syndicate	Turweston	1.10.01T
G-BAYL*	SNCAN Nord 1203 Norecrin VI	161	F-BEQV	18. 5.73	J.E.Pierce (Fuselage only stored outside 3.98)	Ley Farm, Chirk	
G-BAYO	Cessna 150L	150-74435	N19471	18. 5.73	W.J.Barnes & A.J.Fisher	(Durham)	8. 6.01T
G-BAYP	Cessna 150L	150-74017	N18651	18. 5.73	D.I.Thomas t/a Yankee Papa F/Grp	Denham	28. 3.99T
G-BAYR	Robin HR.100/210 Royal	164		18. 5.73	Linda A.Christie	Stapleford	23. 5.00
G-BAYV*	SNCAN 1101 Noralpha	193	F-BLTN Fr.AF	22. 5.73	P.Smith (Crashed Longbridge Deverill 23.2.74)	Barton	2. 8.75
	(Loaned to Macclesfield Historical Avn Society & displayed as "3" in Luftwaffe c/s; see G-ATDB)						
G-BAYZ	Bellanca 7GCBC Citabria	461-73		23. 5.73	Rodger Aircraft Ltd	Old Sarum	14. 8.00T
G-BAZC	Robin DR.400-160 Knight	824		29. 5.73	R.Jones t/a Southern Sailplanes	Membury	24. 6.88
	(Damaged in crash Crosland Moor 21.5.88; stored 9.89)						
G-BAZJ*	HPR.7 Dart Herald 209	183	4X-AHR G-8-1	30. 5.73	Guernsey Airport Fire Service (Open storage 6.97)	Guernsey	24.11.84T
G-BAZM	Jodel D.11 PAL/1416 & PFA/915 (Cont O-200-A)			31. 5.73	A.F.Simpson "L'Oiseau Jaime"	Leeds-Bradford	30. 6.99P
G-BAZS	Reims Cessna F.150L	0954		1. 6.73	L.W.Scattergood	Sherburn	25.10.01T
G-BAZT	Reims Cessna F.172M	0996		1. 6.73	M.Fraser	Exeter	22. 5.00
G-BAZU	PA-28R-200 Cherokee Arrow	28R-7135151	EI-AVH	6. 6.73	S.C.Simmons	White Waltham	11.11.01

G-BBAA-BBZZ

Regn	Type	C/n	P/I	Date	Owner/operator	Probable Base	CA Expy
G-BBAE	Lockheed L.1011-385-1-14 TriStar 100	193N-1083	C-FCXB	6. 6.73	Caledonian Airways Ltd	Gatwick	11. 5.00T
			G-BBAE/C-FCXB/G-BBAE/N64854 "Loch Earn"				
G-BBAF	Lockheed L.1011-385-1-14 TriStar 100	193N-1093		6. 6.73	Caledonian Airways Ltd "Loch Fyne"	Gatwick	9. 1.00T
G-BBAH	Lockheed L.1011-385-1-14 TriStar 100	193N-1101		6. 6.73	Caledonian Airways Ltd "Loch Avon"	Gatwick	8. 2.00T
G-BBAI	Lockheed L.1011-385-1-14 TriStar 100	193N-1102	C-FCXJ	6. 6.73	Caledonian Airways Ltd	Gatwick	4. 5.99T
			G-BBAI/C-FCXJ/G-BBAI "Loch Inver"				
G-BBAJ	Lockheed L.1011-385-1-14 TriStar 100	193N-1106		6. 6.73	Caledonian Airways Ltd "Loch Rannoch"	Gatwick	29. 3.99T
G-BBAK	Socata MS.894A Rallye Minerva 220	12080	(D-ENMK)	6. 6.73	R.B.Hemsworth & C.L.Hill		8. 8.98
					Belle Vue Farm, Yarnscombe		
G-BBAW	Robin HR.100/210 Royal	167		12. 6.73	J.R.Williams	Goodwood	12. 6.00
G-BBAX	Robin DR.400/140 Earl	835		12. 6.73	G.J.Bissex & P.H.Garbutt	(Bristol)	11. 5.00
G-BBAY	Robin DR.400/140 Earl	841		12. 6.73	G.A.Pentelow & D.S.Brown t/a Rothwell Grp		31. 1.02
					Rothwell Lodge Farm, Kettering		
G-BBBB	Taylor JT.1 Monoplane SAM/01 & PFA/1422 (VW1600)			4. 6.73	S.A.MacConnacher	(Northampton)	
G-BBBC	Reims Cessna F.150L	0864	N10635	14. 6.73	W.J.Greenfield	Humberside	15.12.01T
G-BBBI	Grumman-American AA-5 Traveler	AA5-0392		15. 6.73	M.E.J.Smith & S.A.James	(London EC1)	12.12.99
G-BBBK	PA-28-140 Cherokee	28-22572	SE-EYF	18. 6.73	Bencray Ltd	Blackpool	19. 4.01
G-BBBL*	Cessna 337B Super Skymaster	337-0555	EI-AVF 5H-MNL/N5455S	19. 6.73	P.R.Moss (Stored 3.92)	Farley Farm, Romsey	12. 2.77
G-BBBN	PA-28-180 Cherokee Challenger	28-7305365		20. 6.73	Estuary Avn Ltd	Southend	13. 1.00T
G-BBBO	SIPA 903	67	F-BGBQ	16. 1.74	G.K.Brothwood & P.R.Tonks t/a Mersey SIPA Group	Liverpool	5. 5.98P
G-BBBW	Clutton FRED Srs.2 DLW.1 & PFA/1551 (VW1834)			26. 6.73	M.Palfreman	Bagby	1. 2.99P
G-BBBX	Cessna 310L	310L-0134	OY-EGW N3284X	28. 6.73	Atlantic Air Transport Ltd	Jersey/Coventry	23.10.99
G-BBBY	PA-28-140 Cherokee Cruiser	28-7325533		28. 6.73	J.M.Scott	Luqa, Malta	5. 5.00
G-BBCA	Bell 206B JetRanger II	1101	N18091	29. 6.73	Kelly Trucks Ltd	Halfpenny Green	8.10.01T
G-BBCB	Western O-65 HAFB	018		29. 6.73	G.M.Bulmer "Cee Bee"	Hereford	19. 5.76S
G-BBCC	PA-23-250 Aztec D	27-4317	N6953Y	29. 6.73	County Garage (Cheltenham) Ltd.	Gloucestershire	14. 5.01
G-BBCF*	Reims Cessna FRA.150L Aerobat	0209		3. 7.73	Air Service Training Ltd (Damaged nr Harrogate 8.9.84 & dumped 6.98)	Perth	6. 3.86T
G-BBCH	Robin DR.400 2 + 2	850		4. 7.73	A.J.& S.P.Smith	(Oxford)	19. 2.01T
G-BBCI	Cessna 150H	150-69282	N50409	4. 7.73	Domeastral Ltd	Elstree	22. 5.00T
G-BBCN	Robin HR.100/210 Royal	168		11. 7.73	K.T.G.Atkins	Bagby	17. 4.00
G-BBCP	Thunder Ax6-56 HAFB	007		11. 7.73	J.M.Robinson "Jack Frost"	Milton-under-Wychwood	10. 7.81A
G-BBCS	Robin DR.400/140B Earl	851		12. 7.73	J.C.Harvey t/a Westfield F/Grp	Spilsted Farm, Sedlescombe	12. 5.01
G-BBCW	PA-23-250 Aztec E	27-4806	N14251	17. 7.73	Jack Tighe Holdings Ltd (Op Eastern Air Executive)	Sturgate	20.10.00T
G-BBCY	Phoenix Luton LA-4A Minor (VW1600)	PFA/825		17. 7.73	T.G.Solomon	(Lewes)	13. 5.99P
G-BBCZ	Grumman-American AA-5 Traveler	AA5-0382		18. 7.73	Golf Charlie Zulu Ltd	Shoreham	13. 8.01T
G-BBDB*	PA-28-180 Cherokee Challenger	28-7305361		18. 7.73	Not known (Wreck stored 4.96)	Newtownards	7. 6.85
G-BBDC	PA-28-140 Cherokee Cruiser	28-7325437		18. 7.73	P.Doggett & P.A.Gray	Andrewsfield	18. 3.01
G-BBDE	PA-28R-200 Cherokee Arrow II	28R-7335250		18. 7.73	R.L.Coleman & A.E.Stevens	Panshanger	4. 7.99
G-BBDG*	BAC/Aerospatiale Concorde 100	100-002 & 13523		7. 8.73	British Airways plc (Stored for spares 2.96)	Filton	1.3.82P*
G-BBDH	Reims Cessna F.172M	0990		19. 7.73	P.S.C. & B.J.Comina	RAF Wyton	18. 5.01
G-BBDJ*	Thunder Ax6-56 HAFB	006		20. 7.73	D P Bushby "Jack Tar" (Balloon Preservation Group 7.98)	Lancing	
G-BBDL	Grumman-American AA-5 Traveler	AA5-0406		18. 7.73	R.J.Baker & W.Woods t/a Delta Lima F/Grp	Coventry	5.12.98
G-BBDM	Grumman-American AA-5 Traveler	AA5-0407		18. 7.73	P.J.Marchant	Rush Green	28. 9.01
G-BBDN*	Taylor JT.1 Monoplane (VW1600)	PFA/1437		24. 7.73	T.Barnes (Under construction 10.90)	Ely	
G-BBDO	PA-23-250 Turbo Aztec E	27-7305120	N40361	24. 7.73	Anstee & Ware Ltd	Bristol/Lulsgate	1. 5.00T
G-BBDP	Robin DR.400/160 Knight	853		25. 7.73	Robin Lance Avn Associates Ltd	Rochester	14. 7.01T
G-BBDT	Cessna 150H	150-68839	N23272	26. 7.73	J.S.Firth t/a Delta Tango Grp	Sherburn	19. 3.00
G-BBDV	SIPA 903	7/21	F-BEYY	30. 7.73	W.McAndrew	Cardington	11. 6.99P
	(Cont C90) (Originally ex F-BEYJ c/n 7 but rebuilt in 1978 from F-BEYY c/n 21)						

Regn	Type	C/n	P/I	Date	Owner/operator	Probable Base	CA Expy
G-BBEA	Phoenix Luton LA-4A Minor (VW1600)	PFA/843		30. 7.73	P.A.Kirkham (Guildford) t/a Luton Minor Group		2.11.99P
G-BBEB	PA-28R-200 Cherokee Arrow II			31. 7.73	R.D.W.Rippingale Anvil Farm, Hungerford		22. 2.01
G-BBEC	PA-28-180 Cherokee Challenger	28-7305478		30. 7.73	J.B.Conway Blackpool		31. 5.01
G-BBED	Socata MS.894A Rallye Minerva 220	12097		30. 7.73	C.A.Shelley Alcester t/a Vista Products (Stored 9.95)		13. 9.87T
G-BBEF	PA-28-140 Cherokee Cruiser	28-7325527		31. 7.73	Comed Avn Ltd Blackpool		21.10.01T
G-BBEL	PA-28R-180 Cherokee Arrow	28R-30877	SE-FDX	6. 8.73	J.Paulson (Op Merseyside Avn) Liverpool		26. 4.01
G-BBEN	Bellanca 7GCBC Citabria	496-73	(D-EAUT) N36416	7. 8.73	C.A.G.Schofield Harpsden Court, Henley-on-Thames		15. 6.98
G-BBEO	Reims Cessna FRA.150L Aerobat	0205		3. 8.73	Moray F/C (1990) Ltd Inverness		7. 6.01T
G-BBEV	PA-28-140 Cherokee D	28-7125340	LN-MTM	8. 8.73	Comed Avn Ltd Blackpool		9. 9.01T
G-BBEW	PA-23-250 Aztec E	27-7305075	EI-BYK G-BBEW/N40262	9. 8.73	Mano et Mano Ltd (New Malden)		3. 9.01T
G-BBEX	Cessna 185A Skywagon	185-0491	EI-CMC G-BBEX/4X-ALD/N99992/N1691Z	7. 8.73	V.M.McCarthy Weston, N Ireland		31.10.99T
G-BBEY	PA-23-250 Aztec E	27-7305160	LN-FOE G-BBEY/N40396	8. 8.73	M.Hall Cumbernauld		21. 1.01
G-BBFC*	Grumman-American AA-1B Trainer	AA1B-0245	(N9945L)	14. 8.73	Not known Enstone (Damaged Perranporth 9.6.96; temp unregd 14.10.96)		25.12.96
G-BBFD	PA-28R-200 Cherokee Arrow II	28R-7335342		8. 8.73	CR Avn Ltd White Waltham		5. 1.01T
G-BBFL	SRCM Gardan GY-201 Minicab (Cont A65)	21	F-BHCQ	17. 8.73	D.Silsbury Dunkeswell (Damaged Bere Alston, Devon 9.6.93; on rebuild 12.95)		21. 9.93P
G-BBFS*	Van Den Bemden K-460 (Gas) Free Balloon	VDB-16	OO-BGX	10. 8.73	British Balloon Museum Newbury "Le Tomate" (Stored 12.94)		
G-BBFV	PA-32-260 Cherokee Six	32-778	5Y-ADF	13. 8.73	A.G.Knight t/a Airlaunch Old Buckenham		26. 2.00
G-BBGB	PA-E23-250 Aztec E	27-7305004	N40206	16. 8.73	Cheshire F/Svs Ltd Manchester t/a Ravenair		28. 1.00T
G-BBGC	Socata MS.893E Rallye 180GT	12215	F-BUCV	16. 8.73	C.Squibb RNAS Culdrose t/a Seahawk Gliding Club		15. 2.01
G-BBGE*	PA-23-250 Aztec D	27-4373	N6137Y	20. 8.73	Not known (Stored 9.96) Bournemouth		17. 8.92T
G-BBGI	Fuji FA.200-160 Aero Subaru	228		21. 8.73	G.C.B.Weir Hill Farm, Nayland		17. 9.98
G-BBGL	Oldfield Baby Lakes (Cont C90)	7223-B412-B & PFA/1593		22. 8.73	F.Ball Jubilee Farm, Wisbech St.Mary		16.12.99P
G-BBGR	Cameron O-65 HAFB	85		20. 8.73	M.L. & L.P.Willoughby Reading "Jabberwock"		26. 5.81A
G-BBGX	Cessna 182P Skylane	182-62350	N58861	30. 8.73	GX Aviation Ltd Glenrothes		1. 4.01T
G-BBGZ	Cambridge Hot-Air Ballooning Assocn HAFB (42,000 cu.ft)	CHABA 42		31. 8.73	R.A. & G.Laslett & J.L.Hinton Newbury "Phlogiston"(Basket only to British Balloon Museum)		
G-BBHF	PA-23-250 Aztec E	27-7305166	N40453	5. 9.73	G.J.Williams Sherburn		6. 1.99T
G-BBHG*	Cessna 310Q	310Q-0806	N69591	6. 9.73	G.P.Williams Bournemouth (Damaged Manston 19.7.93; on rebuild 10.95)		16. 7.95
G-BBHI	Cessna 177RG Cardinal RG	177RG-0225	5Y-ANX N1825Q	7. 9.73	T.G.W.Bunce Newtownards		6. 8.00
G-BBHJ	Piper J3C-85 Cub (Frame No.16037)	16378	OO-GEC	7. 9.73	J.Stanbridge & R.V.Miller t/a Wellcross F/Grp Wellcross Grange, Slinfold		19. 5.99P
G-BBHK	Noorduyn AT-16-ND Harvard IIB	14-787	PH-PPS (PH-HTC)/R.Neth AF	7. 9.73	R.F.Warner t/a Bob Warner Avn (Malvern) B-158/FH153/42-12540 (As "FH153") (Status uncertain)		7. 5.86
G-BBHL	Sikorsky S-61N Mk.II	61-712	N4032S	7. 9.73	Bristow Helicopters Ltd Portland "Glamis" (Op H.M. Coastguard)		4.12.01T
G-BBHM	Sikorsky S-61N Mk.II	61-713	8Q-HUM G-BBHM/N4033S	7. 9.73	Bristow Helicopters Ltd Aberdeen "Braemar"		1.11.01T
G-BBHX*	Socata MS.893E Rallye 180GT	12211		9. 9.73	Not known Bidford (Wreck in open store 5.96)		7. 4.96
G-BBHY	PA-28-180 Cherokee Challenger	28-7305474	EI-BBS G-BBHY/N9508N	7. 9.73	Air Operations Ltd Guernsey		30. 5.99
G-BBIA	PA-28R-200 Cherokee Arrow II	28R-7335287		7. 9.73	G.H.Kilby Stapleford		14.12.00
G-BBIF	PA-23-250 Aztec E	27-7305234		10. 9.73	Home Doors (GB) Ltd Tatenhill "Flying Miss Daisie"		13. 7.98T
G-BBIH	Enstrom F-28A-UK	026	N4875	12. 9.73	Nunkeeling Ltd Elloughton, Brough		18. 2.93
G-BBII	Fiat G.46-3B	44	I-AEHU MM52801	13. 9.73	Bianchi Aviation Film Services Ltd (As "14+" in Luftwaffe c/s) Booker		19. 7.89P
G-BBIL	PA-28-140 Cherokee	28-22567	SE-FAR N4219J	13. 9.73	M.C.Addison & R.Brierley Andrewsfield t/a India Lima F/Grp		23. 4.01
G-BBIN*	Enstrom F-28A	157		13. 9.73	Southernair Ltd (Stored 10.96) Shoreham		26. 9.94T
G-BBIO	Robin HR.100/210 Royal	178		14. 9.73	R.A.King Headcorn		29.10.00
G-BBIV	Hughes 269C	41-0113	N9690F	14. 9.73	The Hughes Helicopter Co Ltd t/a Biggin Hill Helicopters Biggin Hill		26. 8.98T
G-BBIX	PA-28-140 Cherokee E	28-7225442	LN-AEN N20537	17. 9.73	Sterling Aviation Ltd Elstree		28. 1.02T
G-BBJD*	Cessna 172M	172-61374		17. 9.73	Not known Oaksey Park (Crashed Sywell 30.6.78; fuselage as para-trainer 9.95)		18. 1.80
G-BBJI	Isaacs Spitfire (Cont O-200-A)	2 & PFA/27-10055		18. 9.73	A.N.R.Houghton & C.R.Williamson t/a Ranksborough F/Grp (As "RN218/N") Ranksborough Farm, Langham		4.11.98P
G-BBJU	Robin DR.400/140 Earl	874		19. 9.73	J.C.Lister Valley Farm, Winwick t/a Victor Sierra A/C		25. 5.01

Regn	Type	C/n	P/I	Date	Owner/operator	Probable Base	CA Expy
G-BBJV	Reims Cessna F.177RG Cardinal	0098		20. 9.73	Pilot Publishing Co Ltd Biggin Hill		6. 3.00
					t/a Pilot Magazine		
G-BBJX	Reims Cessna F.150L Commuter	1017		20. 9.73	Yorkshire Flying Svs Ltd Leeds-Bradford		1. 8.99T
G-BBJY	Reims Cessna F.172M Skyhawk II	1075		20. 9.73	J.Lucketti	Gamston	29.11.92
					(Damaged Barton 31.1.93; on repair 8.98)		
G-BBJZ	Reims Cessna F.172M Skyhawk II	1035		20. 9.73	J.K.Green	Wickenby	28. 2.01T
					t/a Burks Green & Ptnrs		
G-BBKA	Reims Cessna F.150L Commuter	1029		20. 9.73	R.Hall	Full Sutton	1. 5.00T
G-BBKB	Reims Cessna F.150L	1030		20. 9.73	Justgold Ltd	Blackpool	21. 7.96T
					t/a Blackpool Air Centre		
G-BBKE	Reims Cessna F.150L Commuter	1026		20. 9.73	J.D.Woodward	Bristol/Lulsgate	2. 7.01T
G-BBKF	Reims Cessna FRA.150L Aerobat	0222		20. 9.73	D.W.Mickleburgh	(Leicester)	13. 6.91T
					(Stored Compton Abbas 6.95)		
G-BBKG	Reims Cessna FR.172J Rocket	0465		20. 9.73	R.Wright	Coventry	22. 2.01
G-BBKI	Reims Cessna F.172M Skyhawk II	1069		20. 9.73	C.W. & S.A.Burman	East Winch	16. 9.01
G-BBKL	Menavia Piel CP.301A Emeraude	237	F-BIMK	21. 9.73	P.J.Griggs	(Huntingdon)	21. 1.92P
					(Damaged Ketton 14.7.91; on rebuild Booker 7.91)		
G-BBKR	Scheibe SF-24A Motorspatz	4018	D-KECA	24. 9.73	P.I.Morgans (Stored 5.95)		
					Furze Hill Farm, Rosemarket, Milford Haven		30. 3.79S
G-BBKU	Reims Cessna FRA.150L Aerobat	0214		26. 9.73	T.C.Hocking & H.G.Fawkes	Bodmin	4. 6.01T
					t/a Penguin Grp		
G-BBKX	PA-28-180 Cherokee Challenger			26. 9.73	RAE Aero Club Ltd	Farnborough	22. 7.01T
		28-7305581					
G-BBKY	Reims Cessna F.150L	0991		26. 9.73	Telesonic Ltd	Barton	24.11.00T
G-BBKZ	Cessna 172M	172-61495	N20694	27. 9.73	R.S.Thomson t/a KZ F/Grp	Exeter	23. 3.00T
G-BBLH	Piper J3C-65 Cub (L-4B-PI)	10006	F-BFQY	24. 9.73	Shipping & Airlines Ltd Biggin Hill		4. 2.02T
	(Frame No.9838) (Regd with c/n 10549)		Fr.Mil/43-1145		(As "31145/26/G" in 183rd Field Battalion US Army c/s)		
G-BBLL*	Cameron O-84 HAFB	84		2.10.73	British Balloon Museum	Newbury	25. 5.81A
					"Boadicea"		
G-BBLM	Socata Rallye 100S	2392		3.10.73	Skillcomps Ltd.	(Stourbridge)	5. 9.01
G-BBLS	Grumman-American AA-5 Traveler		EI-AYM	8.10.73	A.D.Grant	Perth	26. 3.99
		AA5-0440	G-BBLS				
G-BBLU	PA-34-200-2 Seneca	34-7350271	N55984	8.10.73	A.S.Bamrah	Biggin Hill	3. 4.00T
					t/a Falcon Flying Services		
G-BBMB	Robin DR.400/180 Regent	848	5Y-ASB	27. 9.73	D.S.Seex	Thurrock	5. 4.01
					t/a Regent Flying Group		
G-BBMH	EAA Sport Biplane Model P.1 PFA/1348			11.10.73	K.Dawson (Status uncertain) (Billericay)		29. 6.87P
	(Cont C90)						
G-BBMJ	PA-23-250 Aztec E	27-7305150	N40387	12.10.73	Lorch Airways (UK) Ltd	Norwich	9. 6.99T
G-BBMN	DHC.1 Chipmunk 22	C1/0300	WD359	12.10.73	R.Steiner	White Waltham	20.10.00
G-BBMO	DHC.1 Chipmunk 22	C1/0550	WK514	12.10.73	D.M.Squires	Wellesbourne Mountford	23.12.01
G-BBMR	DHC.1 Chipmunk 22	C1/0213	WB763	12.10.73	A.J.Parkhouse	Camberley	
					(As "WB763/14") (Stored 12.93)		
G-BBMT	DHC.1 Chipmunk 22	C1/0712	WP831	12.10.73	J.Evans & D.Withers	Graveley	17. 8.00
G-BBMV	DHC.1 Chipmunk 22	C1/0432	WG348	12.10.73	P.J.Morgan (Aviation) Ltd		
					(As "WG348")	Top Farm, Tadlow	28. 3.97
G-BBMW	DHC.1 Chipmunk 22	C1/0641	WK628	12.10.73	J.A.Challen & B.J.Pook t/a Mike Whiskey Grp		
					(As "WK628")	Shoreham	13. 6.99
G-BBMX	DHC.1 Chipmunk 22	C1/0800	WP924	12.10.73	G.C.Martin	Epse, Netherlands	13. 3.99
					t/a Chipmunk 4 Ever Foundation		
G-BBMZ	DHC.1 Chipmunk 22	C1/0563	WK548	12.10.73	P.C.G.Wyld	Booker	1. 9.00
					t/a The Wycombe Gliding School Syndicate		
G-BBNA	DHC.1 Chipmunk 22	C1/0491	WG417	12.10.73	Coventry Gliding Club Ltd		
	(Lyc O-360)				"Carrie"	Husbands Bosworth	22. 6.00
G-BBNC*	DHC.1 Chipmunk T.10	C1/0682	WP790	12.10.73	De Havilland Aircraft Museum (As "WP790/T")		
					Salisbury Hall, London Colney		
G-BBND	DHC.1 Chipmunk 22	C1/0225	WD286	12.10.73	J.W.Bissett & W.Norton (As "WD286/J")		
					t/a Chipmunk G-BCIW Syndicate 1984		
						Top Farm, Tadlow	17. 8.00
G-BBNG	Bell 206B JetRanger	134	VH-BHX	16.10.73	MB Air Ltd (Op Eagle Helicopters)		
		G-BBNG/VR-BEY/G-BBNG/PK-HBO/N6268N			Winchester Farm, Ouston/Newcastle		1. 5.99T
G-BBNH	PA-34-200-2 Seneca	34-7350339	N56492	16.10.73	M.G.D.Baverstock	Bournemouth	8. 8.92
G-BBNI	PA-34-200-2 Seneca	34-7350312	N56286	16.10.73	Channel Avn Holdings Ltd	Guernsey	26. 3.01T
G-BBNJ	Reims Cessna F.150L Commuter	1038		16.10.73	Sherburn A/C Ltd	Sherburn	9.10.99T
G-BBNO	PA-23-250 Aztec E	27-4656	N964PA	22.10.73	A.S.Bamrah	Biggin Hill	18. 1.92
					t/a Falcon F/Svs (Stored 8.97)		
G-BBNV	Fuji FA.200-160 Aero Subaru	232		23.10.73	Caseright Ltd	Hinton-in-the-Hedges	25. 4.99
G-BBNX	Reims Cessna FRA.150L Aerobat	0219		23.10.73	General Airline Ltd	Blackbushe	8. 4.01T
	(Cont O-200-A) (modified)				t/a European Flyers		
G-BBNY*	Reims Cessna FRA.150L Aerobat	0223		23.10.73	Air Tows Ltd	White Waltham	2. 8.87T
					(Damaged Blackbushe 8.6.86; wreck in open storage 5.96)		
G-BBNZ	Reims Cessna F.172M Skyhawk II	1054		23.10.73	R.E.Nunn	Maypole Farm, Chislet	18. 4.00
G-BBOA	Reims Cessna F.172M Skyhawk II	1066		23.10.73	D.C.Harry	Clacton	9. 5.99
G-BBOC	Cameron O-77 HAFB	86		24.10.73	J.A.B.Gray	Cirencester	6. 1.90A
					t/a Bacchus Balloons "Bacchus"		

Regn	Type	C/n	P/I	Date	Owner/operator	Probable Base	CA Expy
G-BBOD	Thunder O.5 HAFB	013		24.10.73	B.R. & M.Boyle "Little Titch" Newbury		
					(On loan to British Balloon Museum 12.93)		
G-BBOE	Robin HR.200/100	26		24.10.73	T.D.Saveker	Bodmin	7. 7.99
G-BBOH	AJEP Pitts S-1S Special			25.10.73	Venom Jet Promotions Ltd (P.Meeson)		
	(Lyc IO-360) AJEP-PS1-S-1 & PFA/1570				Oaklands Farm, East Tytherley/Popham		8. 9.97P
G-BBOL	PA-18-150 Super Cub	18-7561	D-EMFE	26.10.73	Lakes Gliding Club Ltd Walney Island		11. 9.96
			N3821Z				
G-BBOO	Thunder Ax6-56 HAFB	012		24.10.73	K.Meehan Much Wenlock, Shropshire		22. 9.96A
					"Tiger Jack"		
G-BBOR	Bell 206B JetRanger II	1197	(SE-)	30.10.73	M.J.Easey Town Farm, Hoxne, Eye		8. 7.99T
			G-BBOR				
G-BBOX	Thunder Ax7-77 HAFB	011		24.10.73	R.C.Weyda "Rocinante" Harwich, Essex		N/E(A)
G-BBPK	Evans VP-1	PFA/7013		30.10.73	G.D.E.MacDonald (Stored 10.95) Lasham		8. 6.90P
	(VW1600)						
G-BBPM	Enstrom F-28A-UK	165	PH-DMH	30.10.73	R.Brennan, M.G.Redford & D.M. Arends		
			G-BBPM			Barton	3. 7.98
G-BBPN	Enstrom F-28A-UK	166		30.10.73	J.R.Jeffers Coventry		17. 7.00T
G-BBPO	Enstrom F-28A	176		30.10.73	Southern Air Ltd & Jewelhaven Ltd		
						Shoreham	1. 5.00T
G-BBPS	SAN Jodel D.117	597	F-BHXS	30.10.73	A.Appleby Burtenshaw Farm, Barcombe		20. 5.99P
G-BBPU	Boeing 747-136	20953		18. 9.74	British Airways plc Heathrow		9.10.01T
					"Virginia Water"		
G-BBPW	Robin HR.100/210 Royal	176		7.11.73	S.D.Cole Kemble		13. 4.97
					(Damaged on take-off Kemble 24.8.98)		
G-BBPX	PA-34-200-2 Seneca	34-7250262	N1202T	7.11.73	Richel Investments Ltd Guernsey		15. 9.01
G-BBPY	PA-28-180 Challenger	28-7305590		8.11.73	Sunsaver Ltd Barton		13. 7.99
G-BBRA	PA-23-250 Aztec E	27-7305197	N40479	8.11.73	F.Kratky t/a F.K.Global Aviation Denham		7. 5.00
G-BBRB	DH.82A Tiger Moth	85934	OO-EVB	21.11.73	R.Barham (Biggin Hill)		
			Belgian AF T-8/ETA-8/DF198				
		(Damaged Biggin Hill 16.1.87; sold for long-term rebuild - status uncertain)					
G-BBRC	Fuji FA.200-180 Aero Subaru	235		8.11.73	G-BBRC Ltd Blackbushe		31. 7.99T
G-BBRI	Bell 47G-5A	25158	N18092	8.11.73	Alan Mann Helicopters Ltd Fairoaks		19. 7.99T
	(Composite following several major rebuilds)						
G-BBRJ	PA-E23-250 Turbo Aztec E	27-7305223	EI-BOK	12.11.73	Millennium Air Ltd Heathrow		22. 2.99T
			G-BBRJ/N40493				
G-BBRN	Mitchell-Procter Kittiwake I	XW784	20.11.73	R.D.Dobree-Carey Henstridge			26. 6.99P
	(Cont O-200-A) 02 & PFA/1352				(As "XW784/VL")		
G-BBRV	DHC.1 Chipmunk 22	C1/0284	WD347	13.11.73	ABC Advertising Ltd Biggin Hill		28. 4.99T
G-BBRX	SIAI-Marchetti S.205-18F	342	LN-VYH	13.11.73	R.C. & A.K.West Goodwood		21.10.01
			OO-HAQ				
G-BBRY*	Cessna 210 Centurion	57091	5Y-KRZ	15.11.73	Not known Enstone		13. 4.79
			VP-KRZ/N7391E (Crashed Chessington 2.4.78; open storage, unmarked 10.97)					
G-BBRZ	Grumman-American AA-5 Traveler		(EI-AYV)	15.11.73	C.P.Osborne Mullaghmore		30. 4.99
		AA5-0471	G-BBRZ				
G-BBSA	Grumman-American AA-5 Traveler			15.11.73	Usworth 84 Flying Associates Ltd		
		AA5-0472				Newcastle	31. 1.02
G-BBSB	Beechcraft C23 Sundowner 180	M-1516		15.11.73	Amalmay Ltd Woodford		31. 7.99
					t/a Sundowner Group		
G-BBSC	Beechcraft B24R Sierra 200	MC-217		15.11.73	I.Millar & G.H.Emerson Newtownards		3. 6.99
					t/a The Beechcombers F/Grp		
G-BBSM	PA-32-300 Cherokee Six	32-7440005	N11C	14.11.73	MT Management Ltd (Douglas, IOM)		11. 7.00T
G-BBSS	DHC.1 Chipmunk 22	C1/0520	WG470	21.11.73	Coventry Gliding Club Ltd		
					Husbands Bosworth		1. 4.01
G-BBSW	Pietenpol Air Camper	PFA/1506		21.11.73	J.K.S.Wills (London SE3)		
G-BBTB	Reims Cessna FRA.150L Aerobat	0224		26.11.73	Griffin Marston Ltd Compton Abbas		2. 9.99T
					(Op Abbas Air)		
G-BBTG	Reims Cessna F.172M Skyhawk II	1097		26.11.73	R.W. & V.P.J.Simpson Redhill		15. 5.99
					t/a Tango Golf Flying Group		
G-BBTH	Reims Cessna F.172M Skyhawk II	1089		26.11.73	S.Gilmore Newtownards		4. 7.99
G-BBTJ	PA-23-250 Aztec E	27-7305131	N40369	27.11.73	Cooper Aerial Surveys Ltd Sandtoft		28. 3.01T
G-BBTK	Reims Cessna FRA.150L Aerobat	0230		27.11.73	Cleveland Flying School Ltd Teesside		17.10.99T
G-BBTL	PA-23-250 Aztec C	27-3816	N6525Y	29.11.73	Air Navigation & Trading Co Ltd		
					(Stored 6.96) Blackpool		14. 8.89T
G-BBTS	Beechcraft V35B Bonanza	D-9551	N3051W	29.11.73	Sarah Wenham Cannes-Mandelieu		2. 1.00
					t/a Eastern Air		
G-BBTT*	Reims Cessna F.150L Commuter	1055		30.11.73	Not known Newtownards		12. 3.76
					(Crashed Newtownards 9.3.75; stored 4.96)		
G-BBTU*	Socata ST-10 Diplomate	140	F-BTIO	18.12.73	Not known (Wreck stored 3.94) Coventry		14. 4.88
G-BBTX	Beechcraft C23 Sundowner 180	M-1524	5N-AGJ	29.11.73	K.Harding t/a Sundowner Grp Blackbushe		8. 6.01
			G-BBTX				
G-BBTY	Beechcraft C23 Sundowner 180	M-1525		29.11.73	A.W.Roderick & W.Price Cardiff		23. 2.01
G-BBTZ	Reims Cessna F.150L	1063		30.11.73	Marnham Investments Ltd Aldergrove		16. 1.00T
					(Op Ulster F/C)		
G-BBUE	Grumman-American AA-5 Traveler	0479		6.12.73	Hebog (Mon) Cyf Caernarfon		10. 3.00
G-BBUF	Grumman-American AA-5 Traveler	0480		6.12.73	W.McLaren Dundee		31.10.99T
G-BBUG	PA-16-150 Clipper	16-29	F-BFMC	6.12.73	J.Dolan Enniskillen		15.11.98
G-BBUJ	Cessna 421B Golden Eagle	421B-0335	OY-RYD	7.12.73	Church Green Avn Ltd (London WC2)		17. 9.98
			N6187Q				

Regn	Type	C/n	P/I	Date	Owner/operator	Probable Base	CA Expy
G-BBUL*	Mitchell-Procter Kittiwake 1	RB.1		7.12.73	R.C.Bull	(Yorkshire)	AC
	(Cancelled by CAA 22.2.99; no Permit issued & probably not completed)						
G-BBUT	Western O-65 HAFB	020		11.12.73	G.F.Turnbull "Christabelle II"	Clyro, Hereford	23. 4.97A
G-BBUU	Piper J3C-75 Cub (L-4A-PI) (Frame No.10354)	10529	F-BBSQ F-OAEZ/Fr.AF/43-29238	14. 1.74	O.J.J.Rogers	Hulcote Farm, Salford, Beds	23. 7.98P
G-BBVA	Sikorsky S-61N Mk.II	61-718		12. 2.74	Bristow Helicopters Ltd "Vega"	Lee-on-Solent	24. 2.00T
G-BBVF*	Scottish Avn Twin Pioneer Srs.3	558	7978M XM961	17.12.73	Museum of Flight/Royal Museum of Scotland	East Fortune	14. 5.82
G-BBVG*	PA-23-250 Aztec C	27-2610	ET-AEB 5Y-AAT	20.12.73	Colton Aviation Ltd (Stored 9.96)	Little Staughton	10. 9.88T
G-BBVJ	Beechcraft B24R Sierra 200	MC-230		21.12.73	T.Keely	Gamston	26. 3.00
G-BBVO	Isaacs Fury II (Lyc O-320)	PFA/11-10091		20.12.73	C.M.Barnes & D.A.Wirdnam	Garden Piece, Basingstoke	20. 9.99P
	(As Hawker Nimrod "S1579/571" of 408 Flt FAA, HMS Glorious)						
G-BBVP*	Westland-Bell 47G-3B1 (Line No.WAS/177)	WA/580	S.Yemen AF 401/XT401	3. 1.74	Not known (Stored 5.93)	Barton	3. 6.93T
G-BBWZ	Grumman-American AA-1B Tr 2	AA1B-0334		14. 1.74	P.A.Ellway	Sherburn	24. 7.00T
G-BBXB	Reims Cessna FRA.150L Aerobat	0236		16. 1.74	D.M.Fenton	Breighton	12. 7.98T
G-BBXH	Reims Cessna FR.172F Rocket	0113	SE-FKG	21. 1.74	D.Ridley	Chester-le-Street	7. 8.00
G-BBXJ*	HPR.7 Herald 203	196	I-TIVI	18. 1.74	Jersey Airport Fire Service (Crashed Jersey 24.12.74)	Jersey	30. 5.75T
G-BBXK	PA-34-200-2 Seneca I	34-7450056	N54366	21. 1.74	J.A.Rees t/a Poyston Avn	Haverfordwest	18. 2.99T
G-BBXL	Cessna 310Q II	310Q-1076	EI-CLX G-BBXL/(N1223G)	21. 1.74	Thornhill Aviation Ltd	(London N1)	22. 1.01T
G-BBXO	Enstrom F-28A-UK	181		29. 1.74	Stephenson Marine Co Ltd	Goodwood	29. 9.01T
G-BBXS	Piper J3C-90 Cub (L-4H-PI) (Regd as c/n "9865"; Frame No. 12042)	12214	N9865F G-ALMA/44-79918	25. 1.74	M.J.Butler	Ranksborough Farm, Langham	30. 3.98P
G-BBXU*	Beechcraft B24R Sierra 200	MC-238		30. 1.74	J.Coggins (Stored 11.95)	Coventry	18.11.93T
G-BBXY	Bellanca 7GCBC Citabria	614-74	N57639	1. 2.74	R.R.L.Windus	Truleigh Manor Farm, Edburton	12. 6.99
G-BBXZ	Evans VP-1 (VW1600)	PFA/1562		31. 1.74	R.W.Burrows (Stored 10.97)	Swanton Morley	8. 3.96P
G-BBYB	PA-18-95 Super Cub (L-18C-PI) (Frame No. 18-1628)	18-1627	PH-TMA (D-ENCH)/ALAT 18-1627/51-15627	4. 2.74	The Tiger Club (1990) Ltd	Headcorn	15. 6.01T
G-BBYH	Cessna 182P	182-62814	N52744	6. 2.74	Croftmarsh Ltd	Poplar Farm, Croft, Skegness	7.10.99
G-BBYL*	Cameron O-77 HAFB	89		8. 2.74	R.Warner "Phoenix"		19. 6.77S
G-BBYM	HP.137 Jetstream 200	243	G-AYWR G-8-13	13. 2.74	British Aerospace (Operations) Ltd	Dunsfold	20. 9.98A
G-BBYO*	BN-2A Mk.III-1 Trislander	362	ZS-KMH G-BBYO/G-BBWR	27. 2.74	Aurigny Air Svs Ltd	Guernsey	1. 5.92T
	(Wfu 2.92; stored 6.97; to be rebuilt using fuselage of c/n 1072/N3267J)						
G-BBYP	PA-28-140 Cherokee F	28-7425158		19. 2.74	P.M.Evans	Jersey	17. 8.98T
G-BBYR*	Cameron O-65 HAFB	97		14. 2.74	I M Martin "Phoenix" (Balloon Preservation Grp 7.98)	Lancing	
G-BBYS	Cessna 182P Skylane	182-61520	5Y-ATE N21256	14. 2.74	I.M.Jones	Gamston	1. 5.00
G-BBYU*	Cameron O-56 HAFB	96		19. 2.74	British Balloon Museum & Library "Chieftain"	Newbury	28. 2.82A
G-BBZF	PA-28-140 Cherokee F	28-7425195		19. 2.74	Winchester Associates (95) Ltd	Popham	23. 6.00
G-BBZH	PA-28R-200 Cherokee Arrow II	28R-7435102		22. 2.74	M.J.Sandry t/a Zulu Hotel Club	Exeter	4. 6.01
G-BBZI	PA-31-310 Turbo Navajo	31-7401211	N7590L	22. 2.74	Air Care (South West) Ltd	Plymouth	7. 7.00T
G-BBZJ	PA-34-200-2 Seneca	34-7450088	N40880	26. 2.74	Eurofly Share Ltd (Op European Flyers)	Blackbushe	11. 8.00T
G-BBZN	Fuji FA.200-180 Aero Subaru	230		26. 2.74	J.Westwood & P.D.Wedd	Cambridge	10. 4.00T
G-BBZO	Fuji FA.200-160 Aero Subaru	238		26. 2.74	L.A.N.King & M.J.Herlihy t/a G-BBZO Grp	Redhill	28. 3.99
G-BBZS*	Enstrom F-28A-UK	192		27. 2.74	Not known (Damaged nr Tyldesley 29.4.89; stored 6.93)	Goodwood	30. 9.89T
G-BBZV	PA-28R-200 Cherokee Arrow II			11. 3.74	P.B.Mellor	Top Farm, Tadlow	22. 8.99T

G-BCAA-BCZZ

Regn	Type	C/n	P/I	Date	Owner/operator	Probable Base	CA Expy
G-BCAC*	Socata MS.894A Rallye Minerva 220			4. 3.74	Not known		
		12099			Clarence Way, Westpoint Enterprise Park, Trafford Park		7.12.90
					(Damaged Sandown 6.5.90; on display 1994 by Kamikazee Ken's Kitchens)		
G-BCAH	DHC.1 Chipmunk 22	C1/0372	WG316	6. 5.74	Southern Air Ltd (As "WG316")	Shoreham	2. 5.99T
G-BCAN	Thunder Ax7-77 HAFB	015		5. 3.74	D.D.Owen "Beacon"	Wotton-under-Edge	7. 8.88A
G-BCAP*	Cameron O-56 HAFB	92		5. 3.74	K.Tanner "Honey Child"	Lancing	N/E(A)
					(Balloon Preservation Group 12.98)		
G-BCAR*	Thunder Ax7-77 HAFB	019		5. 3.74	British Balloon Museum	Newbury	N/E(A)
					"Marie Antoinette"		
G-BCAS	Thunder Ax7-77 HAFB	018		5. 3.74	D.P.Busby "Drifter"	Lancing	9. 4.91A
					(Balloon Preservation Group 7.98)		
G-BCAZ	PA-12 Super Cruiser	12-2312	5Y-KGK	12. 3.74	A.D.Williams		
			VP-KGK/ZS-BYJ/ZS-BPH		Rhos-Y-Gilwen Farm, Rhos Hill		10. 8.01
G-BCBG	PA-23-250 Aztec E	27-7305224	VP-BBN	13. 3.74	M.J.L Batt	Booker	29.10.01
			VR-BBN/G-BCBG/N40494				
G-BCBH	Fairchild 24R-46A Argus III	975	(VH-AAQ)	13. 3.74	Ebork Ltd	Biggin Hill	20. 3.00
	(UC-61K-FA)		G-BCBH/ZS-AXH/HB737/43-15011				
G-BCBJ	PA-25-235 Pawnee C	25-2380/R		18. 3.74	Deeside Gliding Club (Aberdeenshire) Ltd		
	(Rebuild of c/n 25-2380/G-ASLA/N6802Z, quoting c/n 25-5544 the new fuselage of G-ASLA !)						2. 9.01
G-BCBL	Fairchild 24R-46A Argus III	989	OO-EKE	19. 3.74	F.J.Cox (As "HB751")	Eaglescott	31. 3.96
	(UC-61K-FA)		D-EKEQ/HB-AEC/HB751/43-15025				
G-BCBM	PA-23-250 Aztec C	27-3006	N5854Y	19. 3.74	Hatton & Westerman Trawlers Douglas, IoM		12. 5.01
G-BCBR	AJEP/Wittman W.8 Tailwind	TW3-380		20. 3.74	R.J.Willies		
	(Cont O-200-A)				Honeydon Farm, Colmworth, Bedford		25. 5.99P
G-BCBX	Reims Cessna F.150L	1001	F-BUEO	25. 3.74	J.Kelly (Stored 6.97)	Aldergrove	19. 2.95T
G-BCBZ	Cessna 337C Super Skymaster	337-0942	SE-FKB	28. 3.74	J.J.Zwetsloot	Bourn	27.11.98
	(Robertson STOL conversion)		N2642S				
G-BCCB*	Robin HR.200/100 Club	29		2. 4.74	M.J.Ellis	(Devizes)	12. 6.89
	(Cancelled by CAA 2.3.99; last known stored at Old Sarum 8.90 after damage by gales 25.01.90)						
G-BCCC	Reims Cessna F.150L Commuter	1041		8. 4.74	Fleeting Moments Ltd	East Midlands	15. 2.01T
G-BCCD	Reims Cessna F.172M Skyhawk II	1144		8. 4.74	R.M.Austin	Biggin Hill	23. 1.01T
					t/a Austin Avn		
G-BCCE	PA-23-250 Aztec E	27-7405282	N40544	3. 4.74	A.S.Bamrah	Lydd	5. 7.99T
					t/a Falcon F/Svs (Op SE College of Air Training)		
G-BCCF	PA-28-180 Cherokee Archer	28-7405069		3. 4.74	Topcat Aviation Ltd	Liverpool	13. 6.00
G-BCCG	Thunder Ax7-65 HAFB	020		4. 4.74	N.H.Ponsford	Leeds	N/E(A)
					t/a Rango Balloon & Kite Co "Zephyr"		
G-BCCH*	Thunder Ax6-56A HAFB	024		4. 4.74	A D Kent "Wrangler"	Lancing	
					(Balloon Preservation Group 7.98)		
G-BCCJ	Grumman-American AA-5 Traveler			8. 4.74	T.Needham	Woodford	21. 4.00
		AA5-0546					
G-BCCK	Grumman-American AA-5 Traveler			8. 4.74	Prospect Air Ltd	Manchester	8. 9.99
		AA5-0547					
G-BCCR	Piel CP.301A Emeraude	PFA/712		8. 4.74	J.H. & C.J.Waterman		
	(Cont O-200-A)				Armshold Farm, Kingston, Cambs		20.11.98P
G-BCCU	BN-2A mk.III-1 Trislander	366	4X-CCK	17. 4.74	Hebridean Air Services Ltd	Liverpool	26. 1.99TC
			G-BCCU/9L-LAR/G-BCCU/(LN-VIV) (Op Keenair)				
G-BCCX	DHC.1 Chipmunk 22	C1/0531	WG481	17. 4.74	T.Holloway	RAF Dishforth	28. 3.00
	(Lyc O-360)				t/a RAFGSA (Op Clevelands Gliding Club)		
G-BCCY	Robin HR.200/100 Club	37		18. 4.74	G.J.Blower & G.Priestley	Filton	31. 1.99
					(Damaged High Littleton nr Bristol 8.12.95; on rebuild 7.97)		
G-BCDB	PA-34-200-2 Seneca	34-7450110	N41346	22. 4.74	Bournemouth F/Club Ltd	Bournemouth	30. 7.01T
G-BCDJ	PA-28-140 Cherokee	28-24276	PH-NLV	29. 4.74	B.F.Graham	Filton	26. 5.01T
			N1841J		t/a Bristol Aero Club		
G-BCDK(2)	Partenavia P.68B	32	A6-ALN	4. 7.75	G.Fleck	Nottingham	17. 7.98
			G-BCDK				
G-BCDL	Cameron O-42 HAFB	115		24. 4.74	D.P. & Mrs B.O.Turner "Chums"	Bath	N/E(A)
					(Balloon Preservation Group 12.98)		
G-BCDN*	Fokker F-27 Friendship 200	10201	PH-OGA	29. 4.74	Air UK Ltd	Norwich	19. 7.96T
			JA8615/(LV-PMR)/PH-FDP (Used as apprentice trainer 1.98)				
G-BCDO*	Fokker F-27 Friendship 200	10234	PH-OGB	29. 4.74	Air UK Ltd	Norwich	20. 6.91T
			JA8621/PH-FEZ		"Friendship Lord Butler"		
					(Damaged Amsterdam 19.7.90; Technical College airframe 10.96)		
G-BCDY	Reims Cessna FRA.150L Aerobat	0237		7. 5.74	Mid-Anglia Flying School Ltd	Cambridge	17. 6.00T
G-BCEA	Sikorsky S-61N Mk.II	61-721		7. 6.74	Brintel Helicopters Ltd	Sumburgh	13. 7.00T
					t/a British International Helicopters		
G-BCEB	Sikorsky S-61N Mk.II	61-454	N4023S	2.10.74	Brintel Helicopters Ltd	Penzance	16.12.99T
					t/a British International Helicopters		
					"The Isles of Scilly"		
G-BCEC	Reims Cessna F.172M Skyhawk II	1082		7. 5.74	A.R. & S.D.Bamber	Barton	18. 5.00
G-BCEE	Grumman-American AA-5 Traveler			7. 5.74	Echo Echo Ltd	Bournemouth	15. 5.00
		AA5-0571					
G-BCEF	Grumman-American AA-5 Traveler			7. 5.74	K.W.Longden	Popham	1. 7.00T
		AA5-0572					
G-BCEN	BN-2A-26 Islander	403	4X-AYG	6. 5.74	Atlantic Air Transport Ltd	Lydd/Coventry	7.11.00A
			SX-BFB/4X-AYG/N90JA/G-BCEN (Coastguard c/s)				

Regn	Type	C/n	P/I	Date	Owner/operator	Probable Base	CA Expy
G-BCEO	Grumman-American AA-5 Traveler	AA5-0575		7. 5.74	D.M.Jenden t/a Echo Oscar Flying Group	Teesside	20.11.99
G-BCEP	Grumman-American AA-5 Traveler	AA5-0576		7. 5.74	C.H.Mitchell & G.Pontin t/a Golf Echo Papa F/Grp	(Hastings)	7. 5.00
G-BCER	CAB GY-201 Minicab	8	F-BGJP	8. 5.74	D.Beaumont	Sherburn	24. 3.99P
G-BCEX	PA-23-250 Aztec E	27-7305024	N40225	13. 5.74	Western Air (Thruxton) Ltd	Thruxton	14. 8.99T
G-BCEY	DHC.1 Chipmunk 22	C1/0515	WG465	14. 5.74	T.C.B.Dehn & C.A.Robey t/a Gopher F/Grp (As "WG465" in RAF c/s)	White Waltham	14. 1.02
G-BCEZ	Cameron O-84 HAFB	107		13. 5.74	P.F.Smart & R.J.Mitchener "Stars & Bars" t/a Balloon Collection	Romsey/Andover	20. 7.82A
G-BCFC	Cameron O-65 HAFB	116		15. 5.74	B.H.Mead "Candy Twist"	Bude	20. 3.88A
G-BCFD*	West Ax3-15 HAFB	JW.1		16. 5.74	British Balloon Museum "Hellfire" (Stored)	Newbury	
G-BCFF	Fuji FA.200-160 Aero Subaru	237		21. 5.74	G.W.Brown & M.R.Gibbons	Popham	2.12.00
G-BCFN	Cameron O-65 HAFB	109		23. 5.74	W.G.Johnston & H.M.Savage "Fireball"	Edinburgh	15. 5.77S
G-BCFO	PA-18-150 Super Cub	18-5335	(D-EIOZ) ALAT 18-5335	29. 5.74	Portsmouth Naval Gliding Club	Lee-on-Solent	13. 4.00
G-BCFR	Reims Cessna FRA.150L Aerobat	0244		30. 5.74	Rentair Ltd (Op Essex F/School)	Earls Colne	3.11.99T
G-BCFW	SAAB 91D Safir (Modified)	91-437	PH-RLZ	29. 5.74	D.R.Williams	Peplow	22. 7.00
G-BCFY	Phoenix Luton LA-4A Minor (Ardem Mk.6)	PAL/1301 & PFA/824		29. 5.74	G.Capes (Stored Sywell 8.92)	(Brough)	17. 1.92P
G-BCGA*	PA-34-200-2 Seneca	34-7450166	N41975	4. 6.74	Not known (Crashed Waddington 18.12.77; wreck stored 4.91)	Ronaldsway	15. 7.78
G-BCGB	Bensen B.8 (Rotax 503)	PCL.14		3. 6.74	J.W.Birkett	Bursledon, Southampton	23. 6.99P
G-BCGC	DHC.1 Chipmunk 22	C1/0776	WP903	13. 3.74	Transport Command Ltd (As "WP903" in Queen's Flt c/s)	Shoreham	16. 7.99T
G-BCGG(2)	CEA Jodel DR.250/160	87	G-ATZL	3.11.81	C.G.Gray	Mere House, Stow, Lincs	11. 8.99
G-BCGH	SNCAN NC.854S	122	F-BAFG	10. 6.74	T.J.N.H.Palmer t/a Nord F/Grp	Hill Farm, Nayland	28. 5.99P
G-BCGI	PA-28-140 Cherokee Cruiser	28-7425283	N9573N	10. 6.74	A.Dodd	Panshanger	8. 6.00T
G-BCGJ	PA-28-140 Cherokee Cruiser	28-7425286	N9574N	10. 6.74	BCT Aircraft Leasing Ltd	Bristol/Lulsgate	11. 2.00T
G-BCGM	Jodel Wassmer D.120 Paris-Nice	50	F-BHQM F-BHYM	15. 7.74	M.H.D.Soltau	Clench Farm, Bury St.Edmonds	6. 1.00P
G-BCGN	PA-28-140 Cherokee F	28-7425323	N9595N	10. 6.74	Golf November Ltd	Oxford	26. 7.99
G-BCGP*	Gazebo Ax6-65 HAFB	1		13. 6.74	British Balloon Museum & Library "Aries"	(Newbury)	
G-BCGS	PA-28R-200 Cherokee Arrow II	28R-7235133	N4893T	13. 6.74	S.Rayne t/a Arrow Avn Grp	Top Farm, Tadlow	26.10.00
G-BCGT	PA-28-140 Cherokee	28-24504	N6779J	17. 6.74	M.Fryer t/a EFS F/Grp (Op Essex School of Flying)	Earls Colne	18. 2.00T
G-BCGW	Chittenden-Jodel D.11 (Lyc O-290)	CC.001 & EAA/61554 & PFA/912		14. 6.74	G.H. & M.D.Chittenden (Stored)	Highwood Hall	30. 1.85P
G-BCHK	Reims Cessna F.172H	0716	9H-AAD	19. 6.74	E.C. & A.K.Shimmin	Bagby	29.10.00
G-BCHL	DHC.1 Chipmunk 22A	C1/0680	WP788	20. 6.74	Shropshire Soaring Ltd (As "WP788")	Sleap	18.10.01
G-BCHM	Westland SA.341G Gazelle 1	WA/1168	G-17-20	14. 6.74	The Auster Aircraft Co Ltd (Damaged Springfield Farm, Melton Mowbray 5.7.97)	Melton Mowbray	23. 8.99
G-BCHP	Scintex CP.1310-C3 Super Emeraude	902	G-JOSI G-BCHP/F-BJVQ	24. 6.74	G.Hughes & A.G.Just	Earls Colne	15. 8.97P
G-BCHT	Schleicher ASK 16	16021	(BGA1996) D-KAMY	25. 6.74	D.E.Cadisch & K.A.Lilleywhite t/a Dunstable K16 Grp	Dunstable	13. 5.01
G-BCHV	DHC.1 Chipmunk 22	C1/0703	WP807	27. 6.74	N.F.Charles	Spanhoe	20. 6.98
G-BCHX	Scheibe SF-23A Sperling	2013	D-EGIZ	28. 6.74	R.L.McLean (Damaged 7.8.82; frame stored 7.97) t/a DG Powered Sailplanes	Rufforth	29. 6.83P
G-BCID	PA-34-200-2 Seneca	34-7250303	N1381T	3. 7.74	C.J.Freeman	Headcorn	21. 7.01T
G-BCIE	PA-28-151 Cherokee Warrior (mod)	28-7415405	N9588N	3. 7.74	Tayside Aviation Ltd	Dundee	19.12.99T
G-BCIH	DHC.1 Chipmunk 22	C1/0304	WD363	3. 7.74	J.M.Hosey (As "WD363")	Andrewsfield	19. 6.99
G-BCIJ	Grumman-American AA-5 Traveler	AA5-0603	N6143A	3. 7.74	R.J.Warne	White Waltham	27. 5.00
G-BCIK	Grumman-American AA-5 Traveler	AA5-0604	N6144A	3. 7.74	Trent Avn Ltd	Tatenhill	5. 6.00
G-BCIL*	Grumman-American AA-1B Trainer	0378 AA1B-0378	N6168A	5. 7.74	M.Hobson (Crashed Auchnagatt, Aberdeen 14.6.86; stored 2.96)	Cruden Bay, Grampian	2.10.88
G-BCIN	Thunder Ax7-77 HAFB	030		5. 7.74	R.A. & P G.Vale t/a Isambard Kingdom Brunel Balloon Group	Kidderminster	5. 5.84A
G-BCIR	PA-28-151 Cherokee Warrior	28-7415401	N9587N	9. 7.74	P.J.Brennan	Southend	12. 6.00
G-BCIW*	DHC.1 Chipmunk 22	C1/0899	WZ868	8. 7.74	M.L.Biggs (Damaged Hulcote Farm, Beds 26.11.91; wreck stored 3.96) (As "WZ868/H" in Cambridge UAS c/s; the replacment a/c, G-ARMF, also carries "WZ868/H")	Fownhope, Hereford	11. 7.94
G-BCJH	Mooney M.20F Executive 21	670126	N9549M	11. 7.74	P.J.Bossard (Stored 5.97)	Bourn	30. 6.91

Regn	Type	C/n	P/I	Date	Owner/operator	Probable Base	CA Expy
G-BCJM	PA-28-140 Cherokee F	28-7425321		17. 7.74	Topcat Avn Ltd (Op Manchester School of Flying)	Manchester	7.11.99T
G-BCJN	PA-28-140 Cherokee Cruiser	28-7425350	N9618N	17. 7.74	Taylor Aviation Ltd.	Elstree	25. 7.99
G-BCJO	PA-28R-200 Cherokee Arrow II	28R-7435272		17. 7.74	R.Ross	Oaksey Park	11. 6.00
G-BCJP	PA-28-140 Cherokee	28-24187	N1766J	15. 8.74	D.J. & D.Pitman t/a Omletair Flying Group	Bournemouth	30. 3.01
G-BCKN	DHC.1 Chipmunk 22 (Lyc O-360)	C1/0707	WP811	5. 8.74	T.Holloway t/a RAFGSA (Op Cranwell Gliding Club)	RAF Cranwell	16. 2.01
G-BCKP	Phoenix Luton LA-5A Major (Cont C90)	PFA/1213		6. 8.74	D. & W.H.Gough	Popham	10. 6.98P
G-BCKS	Fuji FA.200-180AO Aero Subaru	FA200-250		2. 8.74	Kestrel Aviation Ltd	Southampton	30. 4.01T
G-BCKT	Fuji FA.200-180 Aero Subaru	FA200-251		2. 8.74	M.A.Petrie t/a G-BCKT Group	Shoreham	20. 5.99
G-BCKU	Reims Cessna FRA.150L Aerobat	0256		1. 8.74	Cardiff-Wales Flying Club Ltd (Damaged 8m NE Birmingham 1.1.99)	Cardiff	18.10.01T
G-BCKV	Reims Cessna FRA.150L Aerobat	0251		1. 8.74	Cleveland Flying School Ltd	Teesside	19.12.99T
G-BCLC	Sikorsky S-61N Mk.II	61-737		9. 1.75	Bristow Helicopters Ltd "Craigievar" Mount Pleasant, Falkland Islands		12. 1.00T
G-BCLD	Sikorsky S-61N Mk.II	61-739		4. 2.75	Bristow Helicopters Ltd "Slains" (Op HM Coast Guard)	Sumburgh	2. 2.00T
G-BCLI	Grumman-American AA-5 Traveler	AA5-0643		12. 8.74	Hoe Leasing Ltd	Luton	8. 5.00T
G-BCLJ	Grumman-American AA-5 Traveler	AA5-0644		12. 8.74	Effie A.A.Andree-Wiltens	Rotterdam, Netherlands	7.11.99
G-BCLL	PA-28-180 Cherokee C	28-2400	SE-EON	13. 8.74	Scout Centre Ltd	Thruxton	5.10.01
G-BCLS*	Cessna 170B	20946	N8094A	23. 8.74	Teesside Flt Centre Ltd	Teesside	27. 1.83
G-BCLT	Socata MS.894A Rallye Minerva 220	12003	EI-BBW G-BCLT/F-BTRL	1. 8.74	K.M.Hood t/a Rallye Group	Bristol/Lulsgate	15. 2.99
G-BCLU	SAN Jodel D.117	506	F-BHXG	28. 8.74	N.A.Wallace	Knettishall	4. 9.99P
G-BCLW	Grumman-American AA-1B Tr2	AA1B-0463		29. 8.74	B.Robinson	Perth	27. 7.99
G-BCMD	PA-18-95 Super Cub (L-18C-PI) (Frame No. 18-2071)	18-2055	OO-SPF R.Neth AF R-70/52-2455	4. 9.74	J.G.Brooks	Dunkeswell	1. 8.98
G-BCMF*	Levi Go-Plane RL.6 Srs.1	EAA.3678		5. 9.74	R.Levi (Damaged Bembridge 16.11.74; stored 12.95)	Newport, IoW	
G-BCMJ	K & S SA.102.5 Cavalier MJ.1 & PFA/1546 (Cont O-200-A) (Tail-wheel conversion)			9. 9.74	R.G.Sykes (Cancelled by CAA 2.3.99; last known on rebuild 7.94)	Cranfield	8. 8.85P
G-BCMT	Isaacs Fury II (Cont O-200-A)	PFA/1522		9. 9.74	M.H.Turner	(Brixham)	
G-BCNC	Gardan GY-201 Minicab	A.202	F-BICF	9. 9.74	J.R.Wraight	(Chatham)	
G-BCNP	Cameron O-77 HAFB	117		16. 9.74	P.Spellward "Blue Fret"	Bristol	17.12.92A
G-BCNR*	Thunder Ax7-77A HAFB	028		13. 9.74	R.Warner "Howdy"	Cranfield	15. 5.81A
G-BCNX	Piper J3C-65 Cub (L-4H-PI)	"11831"	F-BEGM	17. 9.74	K.J.Lord Cherry Tree Farm, Monewden t/a The Grasshopper F/Grp (As "540" in USAF c/s)		14.12.98P

(Previous French identity of c/n 11831 and p/i 43-30540 are quoted although rebuilt in 1960/61 with
c/n 10993; true origin is thought to be Frame No.10993 with c/n 11168 and ex Fr.AF/43-29877)

Regn	Type	C/n	P/I	Date	Owner/operator	Probable Base	CA Expy
G-BCNZ	Fuji FA-200-160 Aero Subaru	257		16. 9.74	J.Bruton & A.Lincoln	Barton	8. 2.99
G-BCOB	Piper J3C-65 Cub (L-4H-PI) (Frame No.10521)	10696	F-BCPV 43-29405	19. 9.74	R.W. & Mrs.J.Marjoram Low Farm, South Walsham (As "329405/A/23" in USAAC c/s)		2. 5.99P
G-BCOI	DHC.1 Chipmunk 22	C1/0759	WP870	24. 9.74	D.S.McGregor	Rayne Hall Farm, Rayne	14. 4.01
G-BCOJ	Cameron O-56 HAFB	124		25. 9.74	T.J.Knott & M.J.Webber t/a Phoenix Balloon Group "Red Squirrel"	Rickmansworth	12. 7.87A
G-BCOL	Reims Cessna F.172M Skyhawk II	1233		25. 9.74	A.H.Creaser	Old Manor Farm, Anwick	8. 4.00T
G-BCOM	Piper J3C-90 Cub (L-4A-PI)	10478	F-BDTP F-BFQP/OO-ADI/43-29187	27. 9.74	Penelope A.Kidd & D.E.S.Clarke t/a Dougal F/Grp "Dougal"	Shoreham	7. 5.99P

(Frame No.10303 - officially regd as c/n 12040 which is correct identity of G-BGPD;
fuselages probably exchanged in France)

Regn	Type	C/n	P/I	Date	Owner/operator	Probable Base	CA Expy
G-BCOO	DHC.1 Chipmunk 22	C1/0209	WB760	10.10.74	T.G.Fielding & M.S.Morton	Blackpool	10.11.00
G-BCOP	PA-28R-200 Cherokee Arrow II	28R-7435296		8.10.74	Evelyn A.Saunders	Halfpenny Green	26. 2.01
G-BCOR	Socata Rallye 100ST	2544	F-OCZK	7. 1.75	P.R.W.Goslin, P.Nichamin & I.M.Speight	Henstridge	25. 9.01
G-BCOU	DHC.1 Chipmunk 22	C1/0559	WK522	10.10.74	P.J.Loweth "Thunderbird 5" (As "WK522" in RAF c/s) (Stored 4.95)	High Easter	30. 3.95
G-BCOX	Bede BD-5A	HJC.4523		10.10.74	H.J.Cox & B.L.Robinson	Chivenor	27.11.95P*
G-BCOY	DHC.1 Chipmunk 22 (Lyc O-360)	C1/0212	WB762	10.10.74	Coventry Gliding Club Ltd	Husbands Bosworth	23. 1.00
G-BCPD	CAB GY-201 Minicab	18	F-BGKN	24.10.74	A.H.K.Denniss	Leicester	1. 4.98P
G-BCPG	PA-28R-200 Cherokee Arrow	28R-35705	N4985S	16.10.74	A.G.Antoniades t/a Roses F/Grp	Barton	22. 5.01
G-BCPH	Piper J3C-65 Cub (L-4H-PI) (Frame No.11050)	11225	F-BCZA Fr.AF/43-29934	13.12.74	M.J.Janaway (As "329934/B/72" in 25th AOP French Armoured Divn of US 3rd Army c/s)	Thatcham	29. 1.99P
G-BCPJ	Piper J3C-65 Cub (L-4J-PI) (Frame No.13036)	13206	F-BDTJ 45-4466	5.11.74	S.Hollingsworth t/a Piper Cub Grp	Popham	21.10.99P

Regn	Type	C/n	P/I	Date	Owner/operator	Probable Base	CA Expy
G-BCPK	Reims Cessna F.172M Skyhawk II	1194	(D-ELOB)	21.10.74	Tilbrook Industries Ltd	Cranfield	12. 1.01T
G-BCPN	Grumman-American AA-5 Traveler	AA5-0665	N6155A	21.10.74	A.Butterfield	Melrose Farm, Melbourne	11. 9.00
G-BCPO	Partenavia P.68B	27		18.10.74	J.Bowles, J.M.Smith & P.J.Wardle	Sywell	29. 6.01
G-BCPU	DHC.1 Chipmunk 22	C1/0839	WP973	24.10.74	P.Waller	Booker	22. 4.99
G-BCPX	Szep HFC.125 (Lyc O-290)	PFA/12-10019		24.10.74	A.Szep	Netherthorpe	20. 9.97P
G-BCRB	Reims Cessna F.172M Skyhawk II	1259		29.10.74	D.E.Lamb	Fenland	4. 5.01
G-BCRE*	Cameron O-77 HAFB	128		30.10.74	K Tanner "Snapdragon" (Balloon Preservation Group 7.98)	Lancing	6.10.83A
G-BCRH*	Alaparma 75 Baldo	41	I-DONP MM53647	5.11.74	Not known (Stored w/o engine 1997)	(Wiltshire)	
G-BCRI	Cameron O-65 HAFB	135		5.11.74	V.J.Thorne "Joseph"	Bristol	26. 8.81A
G-BCRK	K & S SA.102.5 Cavalier (Lyc O-235)	PFA/01-10049		5.11.74	M.F.Newman	(Norwich)	4. 1.99P
G-BCRL	PA-28-151 Cherokee Warrior	28-7415689		5.11.74	F.N.Garland	Biggin Hill	18. 6.00
G-BCRN	Reims Cessna FRA.150L Aerobat	0261		5.11.74	L.D.Johnston t/a The Country Flying Group	Cumbernauld	3. 7.97
G-BCRP	PA-E23-250 Aztec E	27-7305082	N40269	7.11.74	Airlong Charter Ltd	(Norwich)	25. 9.00T
G-BCRR	Grumman-American AA-5B Tiger	AA5B-0006		7.11.74	R.J.Sivier t/a The Capulet F/Grp	Top Farm, Tadlow	13.11.00
G-BCRT	Reims Cessna F.150M Commuter	1164		18.11.74	G.Matthews t/a Blue Max Flying Group	Coventry	24. 3.01T
G-BCRX	DHC.1 Chipmunk 22	C1/0232	WD292	22.11.74	Tuplin Ltd (As "WD292" in RAF c/s)	White Waltham	1. 8.00
G-BCSA	DHC.1 Chipmunk 22 (Lyc O-360)	C1/0691	WP799	25.11.74	T.Holloway t/a RAFGSA	RAF Bicester	3. 4.00
G-BCSB	DHC.1 Chipmunk 22 (Lyc O-360)	C1/0770	WP899	25.11.74	T.Holloway t/a RAFGSA	RAF Bicester	5. 6.00
G-BCSL	DHC.1 Chipmunk 22	C1/0524	WG474	26.11.74	Jalawain Ltd t/a Barton Chipmunk Flyers	Barton	11. 3.99
G-BCSM	Bellanca 8GCBC Scout	108-74		29.11.74	B.T.Spreckley Le Blanc, France (Damaged Sherburn-in-Elmet 7.1.99)		30. 4.01
G-BCST	Socata MS.893A Rallye Commodore 180	10748	F-BPQD	18.11.74	Patricia J.Wilcox	Cranfield	8. 4.00
G-BCSX	Thunder Ax7-77 HAFB	031		2.12.74	C.Wolstenholme "Woophski"	Macclesfield	5. 7.86A
G-BCSY	Taylor JT.2 Titch (VW 1600)	PFA/1504		5.12.74	I.L.Harding Sackville Lodge, Riseley (Construction abandoned at advanced state; stored 3.97)		
G-BCTF	PA-28-151 Cherokee Warrior	28-7515033		11.12.74	E.Reed t/a The St.George F/C	Teesside	6. 8.99T
	(Rebuilt 1989/90 using major components from G-BFXZ)						
G-BCTI	Schleicher ASK 16	16029	D-KIWA	23.12.74	A.J.Southard t/a Tango India Syndicate	Hinton-in-the-Hedges	19. 7.01
G-BCTJ	Cessna 310Q II	310Q-1072	N1219G	23.12.74	D.Pearce & P.Golding t/a TJ F/Grp	Biggin Hill	5. 6.99T
G-BCTK	Reims Cessna FR.172J Rocket	0546		23.12.74	R.T.Love	Bodmin	11.12.99
G-BCTT	Evans VP-1 (VW1600)	PFA/1543		24.12.74	B.J.Boughton t/a The Fersfield F/Grp	Knettishall	25. 6.99P
G-BCTU	Reims Cessna FRA.150M Aerobat	0268		30.12.74	J.A.Rees t/a Haverfordwest School of Flying	Haverfordwest	25. 2.99T
G-BCTW*	Reims Cessna F.150M	1170		2. 1.75	Wickenby Aviation Ltd	Wickenby	20.12.91T
	(Damaged Strangford Lough, NI 12.4.89 & flooding Newtownards 13.12.91; stored 2.93)						
G-BCUB	Piper J3C-65 Cub (L-4J-PI) (Lippert Reed conversion)	13186	F-BCPC 45-4446	13.12.74	A.L.Brown & G.Attwell	Bourn	15. 6.99P
	(Identity incorrect & may be c/n 13370 (ex F-BFBU/45-4630) which is G-BDOL; possibly frames exchanged)						
G-BCUF	Reims Cessna F.172M Skyhawk II	1279		3. 1.75	John L.R.James & Co Ltd	Croft Farm, Croft, Skegness	5. 5.00
G-BCUH	Reims Cessna F.150M Commuter	1195		7. 1.75	M.G.Montgomerie t/a G-BCUH Grp	Elstree	18.11.00T
G-BCUJ	Reims Cessna F.150M Commuter	1176		9. 1.75	E.M.Peacock & F.White t/a G-BCUJ Syndicate	Eddsfield	13.12.01T
G-BCUL	Socata Rallye 100ST	2545	F-OCZL	27. 1.75	C.A.Ussher & Fountain Estates Ltd New Laithe Farm, Harewood, Leeds		8. 5.00
G-BCUO	Scottish Avn Bulldog 120/122	BH120-371	G-107 Ghana AF/G-BCUO	9. 1.75	Cranfield University	Cranfield	16.10.00T
G-BCUS	Scottish Avn Bulldog 120/122	BH120-373	G-109 Ghana AF/G-BCUS	9. 1.75	S.J. & J.J.Ollier	Egginton	2. 4.99
G-BCUV	Scottish Avn Bulldog 120/122	BH120-376	G-112 Ghana AF/G-BCUV	9. 1.75	Dolphin Property (Management) Ltd Hurstbourne Tarrent, Hants (As "CB733" in RAF c/s)		13. 4.00T
G-BCUW	Reims Cessna F.177RG Cardinal	0119	SE-GKL	10. 1.75	S.J.Westley (Westley Acft)	Cranfield	12. 5.00T
G-BCUY	Reims Cessna FRA.150M Aerobat	0269		14. 1.75	J.C.Carpenter Maypole Farm, Chislet		4. 2.01
G-BCVB	PA-17 Vagabond (Cont A65)	17-190	F-BFMT N4890H	22. 1.75	A.T.Nowak	Popham	17. 6.99P
G-BCVC	Socata Rallye 100ST	2548	F-OCZO	16. 1.75	N.R.Vine	Southampton	25. 1.02
G-BCVE*	Evans VP-2	V2-1015 & PFA/7210		16. 1.75	North Western PFA Strut (Under construction 12.97)	Barton	

Regn	Type	C/n	P/I	Date	Owner/operator	Probable Base	CA Expy
G-BCVF	Practavia Pilot Sprite 115			27. 1.75	D.G.Hammersley	Tatenhill	18. 3.99P
	(Cont C125) GBC.1 & PFA/1362						
G-BCVG	Reims Cessna FRA.150L Aerobat	0245	(I-AFAD)	16. 1.75	I.G.Cooper	Compton Abbas	23.11.00
					t/a G-BCVG Flying Group		
G-BCVH	Reims Cessna FRA.150L Aerobat	0258		16. 1.75	Yorkshire Light Acft Ltd	Leeds-Bradford	21. 7.99T
G-BCVJ	Reims Cessna F.172M Skyhawk II	1305		16. 1.75	Rothland Ltd	Blackpool	23.10.00
G-BCVW	Socata GY-80-180 Horizon	145	D-EHST	23. 1.75	P.M.A.Parrett	High Ham, Somerset	19. 3.99
G-BCVY	PA-34-200T Seneca II	34-7570022	N32447	28. 1.75	Oxford Aviation Services Ltd	Oxford	9. 6.00T
G-BCWB	Cessna 182P Skylane II	182-63566	N5848J	29. 1.75	Skylane Whisky Bravo Ltd	Edinburgh	17.12.01T
G-BCWH	Practavia Pilot Sprite 115	PFA/1366		3. 2.75	R.Tasker	Blackpool	14. 6.99P
	(Cont O-240-A)						
G-BCWK	Alpavia Fournier RF3	24	F-BMDD	7. 2.75	T.J.Hartwell & D.R.Wilkinson	Thurleigh	18. 6.99P
G-BCWL	Westland Lysander IIIA	1244	RCAF	9. 9.75	Wessex Avn & Transport Ltd	Duxford	30. 4.99P
					(Op by The Aircraft Restoration Co) (As "V9545/BA-C" in 277 Sqdn c/s)		
	(Composite: main airframe possibly RCAF 2403 with parts ex RCAF 2341, 2349, 2391)						
G-BCXB	Socata Rallye 100ST	2546	F-OCZM	7. 2.75	A.Smails	Ketton, Darlington	2. 7.97
G-BCXE	Robin DR.400 2 + 2	1015		19. 2.75	C.J.Freeman	Headcorn	11. 7.99T
G-BCXJ	Piper J3C-65 Cub (L-4J-PI)	13048	F-BFFH	21. 2.75	W.F.Stockdale	Old Sarum	8. 5.99P
	(Frame No.12878)		OO-SWA/44-80752		(As "480752/E/39" in USAAC c/s)		
G-BCXN	DHC.1 Chipmunk 22	C1/0692	WP800	7. 3.75	G.M.Turner	RAF Halton	26. 3.00
					(As "WP800/2" in Southampton UAS c/s)		
G-BCXO*	MBB Bo.105D	S.80	D-HDCE	27. 2.75	Lands End Theme Park	Lands End	23. 5.94T
	(Original pod replaced 1992 and rebuilt as a display piece) (As "G-CDBS")						
G-BCXZ*	Cameron O-56 HAFB	154		4. 3.75	Not known "Olive"	?	N/E(A)
G-BCYH	DAW Privateer Mk.3 Motor Glider	BGA.1158	10. 3.75	D.B.Limbert	Crosland Moor	24. 7.98P
	(VW1600)	2 & PFA/1568	RAFGSA.264/XA297				
	(Regd as Cadet III and is a converted Slingsby T-31B c/n 839; marked incorrectly as "RAFGSA.246")						
G-BCYJ	DHC.1 Chipmunk 22	C1/0360	WG307	12. 3.75	R.A.L.Falconer	Shempston Farm, Elgin	12. 7.99
					(As "WG307")		
G-BCYK*	Avro (Canada) CF-100	-	RCAF/18393	18. 3.75	Imperial War Museum	Duxford	
	Canuck Mk.IV				(As "18393" in RCAF c/s)		
G-BCYM	DHC.1 Chipmunk 22	C1/0598	WK577	13. 3.75	C.H.Nicholls t/a G-BCYM Grp	Oaksey Park	13. 7.00
G-BCYR	Reims Cessna F.172M Skyhawk II	1288		20. 3.75	J. & L.Donne	Edinburgh	30. 7.01T
					t/a Donne Enterprise (Op Edinburgh F/C)		
G-BCZH	DHC.1 Chipmunk 22	C1/0635	WK622	19. 3.75	A.C.Byrne Botany Bay, Horsford, Norwich		31. 7.87
					(As "WK622" in RAF c/s) (Crashed Pentney, Norfolk 6.9.87; stored 8.93)		
G-BCZI	Thunder Ax7-77 HAFB	037		24. 3.75	R.G.Griffin & R.Blackwell	Newbury	16. 3.86A
					t/a North Hampshire Balloon Grp "Motorway"		
G-BCZM	Reims Cessna F.172M Skyhawk II	1350		3. 4.75	Cornwall F/C Ltd	Bodmin	20.10.00T
G-BCZN	Reims Cessna F.150M	1149		27. 3.75	Mona Avn Ltd	RAF Mona	10.12.00T
G-BCZO	Cameron O-77 HAFB	158		27. 3.75	W.O.T.Holmes "Leo"	Shrewsbury	11.10.86A

G-BDAA-BDZZ

Regn	Type	C/n	P/I	Date	Owner/operator	Probable Base	CA Expy
G-BDAC*	Cameron O-77 HAFB	146		2. 4.75	Not known "Chocolate Ripple" ?		N/E(A)
G-BDAD	Taylor JT.1 Monoplane (VW1700)	PFA/1453		2. 4.75	J.Gunson t/a G-BDAD Grp (Preston) (Damaged Blackpool 21.7.91; status uncertain)		3. 4.92P
G-BDAG	Taylor JT.1 Monoplane (VW1600)	PFA/1430		1. 4.75	T.K.Gough (Worcester) "Biggles Too"		2. 3.98P
G-BDAH	Evans VP-1 (VW1600)	PFA/7007		2. 4.75	G.H.J.Geurts	Cranfield	26. 5.99
G-BDAI	Reims Cessna FRA.150M Aerobat	0266		21. 4.75	A.Sharma	Popham	10. 5.01T
G-BDAK	Rockwell Commander 112A	252	N1252J	10. 4.75	R.W.Fairless	(Portsmouth)	28. 8.00
G-BDAL	Rockwell 500S Shrike Commander	3226	N57134	25. 4.75	Quantel Ltd	Biggin Hill	17. 7.00
G-BDAM	Noorduyn AT-16-ND Harvard IIB	14-726	LN-MAA Fv16047/FE992/42-12479	10. 4.75	K.D.English & N.A.Lees (As "FE992/K-T" in 5(P)AFU c/s)	Duxford	1. 6.99P
G-BDAO	SIPA 91 (Cont C85)	2	F-BEPT	10. 4.75	J.E.Mead	(Cowbridge)	27. 4.98P
G-BDAP	AJEP/Wittman TW.8 Tailwind (Cont O-200-A) 0387 & PFA/3507			9. 4.75	J.Whiting	Bagby	22. 3.99P
G-BDAR	Evans VP-1 Srs.2 PFA/1537 & PFA/62-10461 (VW1600)			10. 4.75	R.B.Valler	Hill Farm, Durley	20. 7.84P
G-BDAX*	PA-23-250 Aztec C	27-3494	5B-CAO N6399Y	15. 4.75	Barry Technical College (Stored 11.95) Cardiff Airport Industrial Park		12.11.93
G-BDAY	Thunder Ax5-42A HAFB	042		8. 4.75	T.M.Donnelly "Meconium"	Doncaster	16. 1.93A
G-BDBD	Wittman W.8 Tailwind (Cont O-200-A)	133	N1198S	25. 4.75	S.D.Arnold & T.Douglas t/a Tailwind Taildragger Grp	Wellesbourne Mountford	21. 4.99P
G-BDBF	Clutton FRED Srs.II (VW 1600)	PFA/1528		15. 4.75	J.M.Brightwell & A.J.Wright	(Derby)	18. 3.98P
G-BDBH	Bellanca 7GCBC Citabria	758-74	OE-AOL	15. 4.75	R.Dixon	(Leatherhead)	16. 6.99
G-BDBI	Cameron O-77 HAFB	162		15. 4.75	C.A.Butter & J.J.Cooke "Funny Money"	Marsh Benham	11. 7.87A
G-BDBJ	Cessna 182P Skylane II	182-63646	N4644K	18. 4.75	H.C.Wilson	Great Ashfield, Suffolk	18.12.99
G-BDBP	DHC.1 Chipmunk 22	C1/0727	WP843	23. 4.75	F.A.De Munck (Op Pionier Hangaar Collection) (As "WP843/F" in RAF c/s) Lelystad, Netherlands		1. 7.99
G-BDBS*	Short SD.3-30 SH.1935 & SH.3001 G-14-3001			21. 4.75	Ulster Avn Society (Stored 4.96) Langford Lodge, Belfast		28. 9.92S
G-BDBU	Reims Cessna F.150M	1174		30. 4.75	R.Edgar	(Ayr)	27. 6.00
G-BDBV	Aero Jodel D.11A (Cont C90)	V.3	D-EGIB	23. 4.75	G.G.Long t/a Seething Jodel Grp	Seething	27.10.99P
G-BDBZ*	Westland WS.55 Whirlwind 2 (HAR.10) (Regd with c/n WA.386)	WA/62	XJ398 (XD768)	23. 4.75	Oxford Air Training School (Instructional airframe 9.96)	Oxford	
G-BDCC	DHC.1 Chipmunk 22 (Lyc O-360)	C1/0258	WD321	25. 4.75	Coventry Gliding Club Ltd	Husbands Bosworth	19. 2.99
G-BDCD	Piper J3C-90 Cub (L-4J-PI) (Frame No.12257)	12429	OO-AVS 44-80133	28. 4.75	Suzanne C.Brook Wellcross Grange, Slinfold (As "480133/B/44" in US Army c/s)		22. 7.99P
G-BDCE	Reims Cessna F.172H	0704	PH-EHB	5. 5.75	Copperplane Ltd (Damaged in gales Bournemouth 3.1.99)	Bournemouth	26. 4.01T
G-BDCI	Scanor Piel CP.301C Emeraude	503	F-BIRC	25. 4.75	D.L.Sentance Rothwell Lodge Farm, Kettering		13.11.99P
G-BDCL	Grumman-American AA-5 Traveler AA5-0773	EI-CCI	5. 5.75	J.Crowe (Stored 11.95)	Coventry	29.11.93T
	G-BDCL/EI-BGV/G-BDCL/N1373R						
G-BDCO	Beagle B.121 Pup 1	B121-171		6. 5.75	J.K.Healey t/a Shipdham Aviators F/Grp	Old Buckenham	28. 7.97
G-BDCS	Cessna 421B Golden Eagle	421B-0832	N1931G	13. 5.75	British Aerospace (Operations) Ltd	Warton	9.10.00T
G-BDDD	DHC.1 Chipmunk 22	C1/0326	WD387	16. 5.75	RAE Aero Club Ltd	Farnborough	15. 8.99T
G-BDDF	Jodel Wassmer D.120 Paris-Nice	97	F-BIKZ	20. 5.75	H.E.G.Luxton & R.P.Peach t/a The Sywell Skyriders F/Grp	Sywell	12. 7.99P
G-BDDG	Dormois Jodel D.112	855	F-BILM	20. 5.75	D.G.Palmer & S.Robinson t/a Wandering Imp Grp	Sturgate	6. 9.98P
G-BDDS	PA-25-260 Pawnee C	25-4757	CS-AIU	22. 5.75	T.J.Price t/a Vale of Neath Gliding Club	Rhigos	4. 3.99
G-BDDT	PA-25-235 Pawnee C	25-5324	CS-AIX N8820L	22. 5.75	P.W.Sleath & W.D.Clifton	Wyberton	8. 7.99A
G-BDDX*	Whittaker MW.2B Excalibur 001 & PFA/41-10106 (VW 1500)			28. 5.75	Flambards Village Theme Park	Helston	
G-BDDZ	Menavia Piel CP.301A Emeraude	253	F-BIMZ	30. 5.75	V.W.Smith & E.C.Mort (Warrington) (Damaged Cranwell North 3.6.84; on rebuild)		20. 6.84P
G-BDEC	Socata Rallye 100ST	2552	F-OCZS	28. 5.75	M.Mulhall	(Kilkenny, Ireland)	27. 2.00
G-BDEF	PA-34-200T Seneca II	34-7570150	N33695	2. 6.75	Central Aviation Ltd	Nottingham	22. 9.99T
G-BDEH	Jodel Wassmer D.120A Paris-Nice	239	F-BLNE	2. 6.75	E.R.O'Hara t/a EH F/Grp	Oaksey Park	4. 5.99P
G-BDEI	Jodel D.9 Bebe 585 & PFA/936 (VW1600)			2. 6.75	R.Q.T.Newns t/a The Noddy Grp "Noddy"	White Waltham	24. 7.98P
G-BDET	DHC.1 Chipmunk 22	C1/0736	(PH-RTH) G-BDET/WP851	17. 6.75	C.Zoeteman (Op Pionier Hangaar Collection) (As "WP851" in RAF c/s) Lelystad, Netherlands		13. 4.00
G-BDEU	DHC.1 Chipmunk 22	C1/0704	WP808	17. 6.75	A.Taylor (As "WP808")	Manor Farm, Binham	28. 1.02
G-BDEX	Reims Cessna FRA.150M Aerobat	0279		12. 6.75	Griffin Marston Ltd (Op Abbas Air)	Compton Abbas	30.10.99T

Regn	Type	C/n	P/I	Date	Owner/operator	Probable Base	CA Expy
G-BDEY	Piper J3C-65 Cub (L-4J-PI) (Frame No.12366)	12538	OO-AAT OO-GAC/44-80242	17. 6.75	W.J. & Mrs.J.Morecraft t/a Ducksworth F/C Highfield Farm, Empingham		4. 9.99P
G-BDEZ	Piper J3C-65 Cub (L-4J-PI) (Frame No.12211)	12383	OO-SOC OO-EPI/44-80087	17. 6.75	R.J.M.Turnbull Rydinghurst Farm, Cranleigh		21. 5.99P
G-BDFB	Phoenix Currie Wot (Walter Mikron III)	PFA/3008		20. 6.75	J.Jennings	Fenland	4. 6.99P
G-BDFC	Rockwell Commander 112A	273	N1273J	17. 6.75	R.Fletcher	Halfpenny Green	25. 9.97
G-BDFG	Cameron O-65 HAFB	179		24. 6.75	N.A.Robertson Combe Hay Manor, Bath "Golly II"		16. 4.88A
G-BDFH	Auster AOP.9 (Frame No.AUS 177 FM)	B5/10/176	XR240	24. 6.75	R.O.Holden (As "XR240")	Booker	2. 6.99P
G-BDFJ	Reims Cessna F.150M	1182		25. 6.75	Cassandra J.Hopewell	(Huntingdon)	14. 8.99T
G-BDFM	Caudron C.270 Luciole (Salmson 7AC)	6607/32	F-BBPT Fr.AF/F-ALVO	2. 7.75	B.Esposito	Panshanger	28. 4.99P
G-BDFR	Fuji FA.200-160 Aero Subaru	FA200-262		7. 7.75	A.G.Brindle & A.Houghton t/a G-BDFR Group	Blackpool	18. 8.01
G-BDFS	Fuji FA.200-160 Aero Subaru	FA200-263		7. 7.75	B.Lawrence	Goodwood	24. 9.00T
G-BDFU*	Dragonfly MPA Mk.1	01		14. 7.75	R.J.Hardy & R.Churcher East Fortune (On loan to Museum of Flight/Royal Museum of Scotland)		
G-BDFW	Rockwell Commander 112A	308	N1308J	18. 6.75	M.E.& E.G.Reynolds	Blackbushe	25. 7.98T
G-BDFX	Auster 5	2060	F-BGXG TW517	9. 7.75	J.Eagles (Damaged Oaksey Park 10.10.93; on rebuild 6.97)	Kemble	3. 6.94T
G-BDFY	Grumman-American AA-5 Traveler	AA5-0806		10. 7.75	R.L.Bagnall & J.Wishart t/a Grumman Grp (Op Edinburgh F/C)	Edinburgh	5. 3.00
G-BDFZ	Reims Cessna F.150M	1184	(D-EIWB) (F-BXIH)	14. 7.75	A.T.Wright	Aldergrove	28. 4.00T
G-BDGB	Barritault JB-01 Minicab (Cont PC-60)	PFA/1819		23. 6.75	D.G.Burden Armshold Farm, Kingston, Cambs		23. 8.99P
G-BDGH	Thunder Ax7-77 HAFB	049		16. 7.75	R.J.Mitchener & P.F.Smart Andover t/a Balloon Collection "London Pride III"		N/E(A)
G-BDGM	PA-28-151 Cherokee Warrior	28-7415165	N41307	30. 7.75	B.Whiting (Op Comed Aviation)	Blackpool	26. 5.00T
G-BDGO	Thunder Ax7-77 HAFB	048		16. 7.75	Justerini & Brooks Ltd "J&B"	Latimer	2. 2.82A
G-BDGP	Cameron V-65 HAFB	658	(N.....) G-BDGP	2. 9.80	A.Mayes & V.Lawton Leamington Spa t/a Warwick Balloons "Ladbroke Motor Group"		17.11.96A
G-BDGY	PA-28-140 Cherokee	28-23613	N3536K	5. 8.75	S.J.Willcox	Bristol/Lulsgate	9. 8.99T
G-BDHJ	Pazmany PL-1 Laminar (Franklin Sport 4B)	PFA/3604		5. 8.75	L.J.Greenhough	Bodmin	5.11.97P
G-BDHK	Piper J3C-65 Cub (L-4A-PI) (Frame No.9068) (Official c/n quoted as 261 with p/i 42-36414 but this is c/n 8538/N75366)	8969	F-PHFZ 42-38400	24. 7.75	A.Liddiard Eastbach Farm, Coleford (As "329417" in USAAC c/s)		23. 8.99P
G-BDIE	Rockwell Commander 112A	342	N1342J	14. 8.75	R.J.Adams	RAF Brize Norton	13. 5.01
G-BDIG	Cessna 182P Skylane II (Reims-assembled with c/n 0020)	182-63938	N9877E	26. 8.75	State of the Art Ltd t/a Air Group 6	Gamston	6. 7.99
G-BDIH	SAN Jodel D.117 (Regd with incorrect c/n 817)	812	F-BIOT	22. 8.75	N.D.H.Stokes (Bath) (Damaged Rydinghurst Farm, Cranleigh 9.12.84; on rebuild)		4. 7.85P
G-BDIJ	Sikorsky S-61N Mk.II	61-751	9M-AYF G-BDIJ	3.10.75	Bristow Helicopters Ltd Lee-on-Solent "Crathes" (SAR conversion; op for HM Coastguard)		31. 5.01T
G-BDIW*	DH.106 Comet 4C	6470	XR398	1. 9.75	Flugausstellung L & P Junior Museum Hermeskeil, Germany		8. 6.81T
G-BDIX*	DH.106 Comet 4C	6471	XR399	1. 9.75	Royal Museum of Scotland, Museum of Flight (Dan-Air c/s) East Fortune		11.10.81T
G-BDJB*	Taylor JT.1 Monoplane Srs.2 JB.JT.1 001 & PFA/1428			2. 9.75	J.F.Barber	Benfleet	19. 1.79S
	(Cancelled by CAA 2.3.99; last known on rebuild with VW1835 engine after accident at Andrewsfield 25.5.78)						
G-BDJC	AJEP/Wittman W.8 Tailwind (Cont O-200-A) 387AW & PFA/3508			29. 8.75	J.H.Medforth Willy Howe Farm, Wold Newton, Driffield		11. 6.99P
G-BDJD	Jodel D.112 (Cont A65)	PFA/910		3. 9.75	J.E.Sweetman (Basingstoke) "Marianne"		9.11.99P
G-BDJF	Bensen B.8MV RPW.1 & PFA G/01-1075			4. 9.75	R.P.White	(Haslemere)	
G-BDJG	Phoenix Luton LA-4A Minor (VW1835)	PFA/828		3. 9.75	S.C.Barry Booker t/a Very Slow Flying Club		19. 5.99P
G-BDJN	Robin HR.200/100 Club	76		22. 9.75	E.C.Huggett	(Wokingham)	29. 4.01
G-BDJP	Piper J3C-90 Cub (Frame No.21017)	22992	OO-SKZ PH-NCV/NC3908K	11.12.75	Holdcroft Aviation Services Ltd Hinton-in-the-Hedges		19.11.99T
G-BDJR	SNCAN NC.858S	2	F-BFIY	30. 9.75	R.F.M.Marson & P.M.Harmer (On rebuild 10.97) (Farnborough. Hants)		23. 5.92P
G-BDKB*	Socata Rallye 150ST	2631		30. 9.75	N.C.Anderson West Galdenoch Farm, Stranraer		4. 6.82
	(Cancelled by CAA 18.2.99; last known on rebuild 6.90 after accident at Coleraine, NI 5.7.81)						
G-BDKC	Cessna A185F Skywagon	185-02569	N1854R	30. 9.75	Bridge of Tilt Co Ltd	Blair Atholl	23. 4.01
G-BDKD	Enstrom F-28A	319		30. 9.75	Normans (Burton-on-Trent) Ltd Burton-on-Trent		6.12.01T
G-BDKH	Menavia Piel CP.301A Emeraude	241	F-BIMN	15.10.75	P.N.Marshall	Insch	30. 9.98P
G-BDKJ	K & S SA.102.5 Cavalier (Cont O-240-A) 72207 & PFA/1589			14.10.75	D.A.Garner (Swansea) (Damaged Staverton 14.9.97)		5. 6.95P

Regn	Type	C/n	P/I	Date	Owner/operator	Probable Base	CA Expy
G-BDKM	SIPA 903	98	F-BGHX	17.11.75	S.W.Markham Valentine Farm, Odiham		17. 6.99P
G-BDKU	Taylor JT.1 Monoplane PFA/1456			22.10.75	C.M.Harding & J.Ball		
	(VW1500) (Possibly incorporates PFA/55-10301)					Downland Farm, Redhill	6. 7.98P
G-BDKW	Rockwell Commander 112	106	N1277J	3.11.75	R.W.Denny Poplar Hall Farm, Elmsett		15. 7.00T
			ZS-MIB/N1106J				
G-BDLO	Grumman-American AA-5A Cheetah		N6154A	3.11.75	S. & J.Dolan	Elstree	25. 6.01T
		AA5A-0026					
G-BDLR	Grumman-American AA-5B Tiger			3.11.75	Magec Avn Ltd	Luton	22. 7.01T
		AA5B-0128					
G-BDLS	Grumman-American AA-1B Tr.2		N6153A	3.11.75	A.L. Hall-Carpenter	Shipdham	28.10.01
		AA1B-0564					
G-BDLT	Rockwell Commander 112A	363	N1363J	4.11.75	D.L.Churchward	Exeter	9. 5.99
G-BDLY	K & S SA.102.5 Cavalier			14.11.75	P.R.Stevens	Thruxton	21. 7.99P
	(Lyc O-290) PFA/01-10011						
G-BDMM*	Jodel D.11	PFA/901		5.11.75	P.N.Marshall	Aboyne	
					(Stored unfinished 6.98)		
G-BDMO	Thunder Ax7-77	053	(EC-)	25.11.75	Balloon Preservation Group	Lancing	
			G-BDMO		"Flash Harry" (Noted 12.98)		
G-BDMS	Piper J3C-65 Cub (L-4J-PI)	13049	F-BEGZ	4.11.75	A.T.H.Martin	Old Sarum	30.11.98P
			44-80753		(As "FR886" in RAF c/s)		
G-BDMW	SAN Jodel DR.100A Ambassadeur	79	F-BIVM	2.12.75	R.O.F.Harper Yew Tree Farm, Lymm Dam		3. 6.99
					t/a G-BDMW F/Grp		
G-BDNC	Taylor JT.1 Monoplane PFA/1454			8.12.75	A.W.Wright & P.Gaskell	Barton	11. 9.98P
	(Walter Mikron III)						
G-BDNG	Taylor JT.1 Monoplane PFA/1405			12.12.75	S.B.Churchill	(Coleford)	26. 2.99P
	(VW 1834)				"The Red Sparrow"		
G-BDNO	Taylor JT.1 Monoplane PFA/1431			15.12.75	S.D.Glover	(Gunnislake)	2. 5.96P
	(VW1600)						
G-BDNR*	Reims Cessna FRA.150M Aerobat	0284		18.12.75	Busy Bee Avn Ltd	Sibson	26. 7.92T
					(Damaged Liverpool 22.1.92; stored 8.97)		
G-BDNT	Jodel D.92	397	F-PINL	2. 1.76	R.F.Morton Manor Farm, Inglesham		8.10.97P
	(VW1600)						
G-BDNU	Reims Cessna F.172M Skyhawk II	1405		2. 1.76	J. & K.G.McVicar	Elstree	31. 3.00T
G-BDNW	Grumman-American AA-1B Trainer			8. 1.76	P.Mitchell	Coal Aston	5. 3.00
		AA1B-0588					
G-BDNX	Grumman-American AA-1B Trainer			8. 1.76	R.M.North	Kimbolton	25. 5.01
		AA1B-0590					
G-BDNZ*	Cameron O-77 HAFB	203		8. 1.76	I.L.McHale Sutton, Surrey		28. 7.81A
					"Winston Churchill"		
G-BDOC	Sikorsky S-61N Mk.II	61-765		20. 3.76	Bristow Helicopters Ltd	Sumburgh	28.12.01T
					"Tolquhoun" (SAR conversion)		
G-BDOD	Reims Cessna F.150M Commuter	1266		20. 1.76	D.M.Moreau	Booker	2. 7.00
G-BDOE	Reims Cessna FR.172J Rocket	0559		20. 1.76	D. & P.A.Sansome		
					Little Chase Farm, Honiley		9.10.99
G-BDOG	Scottish Avn Bulldog Srs.200	200/381		18.12.75	D.C.Bonsall	Netherthorpe	11. 5.99P
					(Phoenix F/Grp c/s)		
G-BDOL	Piper J3C-65 Cub (L-4J-PI)	13186	F-BCPC	18.12.75	L.R.Balthazor	Lee-on-Solent	28. 9.99P
			45-4446				
	(Frame No.13016 - see comments for G-BCUB; officially has c/n 13370 but has genuine c/n and USAAC plates						
	relating to c/n 13370/ex 45-4630)						
G-BDON	Thunder Ax7-77A HAFB	063		17.12.75	M.J.Smith	York	24. 6.94A
					"Fred"		
G-BDOT	BN-2A mk.III-2 Trislander	1025	ZK-SFF	21. 1.76	Atlantic Bridge Aviation Ltd	Lydd	3.12.98T
			N900TA/N903GD/N3850K/VH-BPB/G-BDOT (Op Sky Trek Airways)				
G-BDOW	Reims Cessna FRA.150M Aerobat	0296		26. 1.76	A.Brinkley (Euroair)	Southend	26. 6.01T
G-BDPA	PA-28-151 Cherokee Warrior			26. 1.76	T.A.Marsh t/a G-BDPA F/Grp		
		28-7615033				Gloucestershire	6.11.00
G-BDPJ*	PA-25-235 Pawnee B	25-3665	PH-VBF	2. 2.76	W.J. & A.E.Taylor RAF West Raynham		
			SE-EPZ		(Crashed Ivychurch, Kent 25.6.80; on rebuild 2.96)		
G-BDPK	Cameron O-56 HAFB	191		4. 2.76	N.H.Ponsford & A.M.Lindsay	Leeds	29.12.88A
					t/a Rango Balloon & Kite Co		
G-BDPV	Boeing 747-136	21213		9. 2.76	British Airways plc	Heathrow	22. 6.99T
					"Blea Water"		
G-BDRD	Reims Cessna FRA.150M Aerobat	0289		9. 2.76	Air Service Training Ltd	Edinburgh	6. 5.00T
G-BDRG	Taylor JT.2 Titch PFA/60-10295			19.12.78	D.R.Gray	(Wilmslow)	
G-BDRJ	DHC.1 Chipmunk 22	C1/0742	WP857	19. 2.76	J.C.Schooling (As "WP857/24")	Elstree	25. 6.99
G-BDRK	Cameron O-65 HAFB	205		12. 2.76	D.L.Smith "Smirk" Eling Hill, Newbury		20. 6.86A
G-BDRL	Stits SA-3A Playboy	P-689	N730GF	12. 2.76	O.C.Bradley	Mullaghmore	17. 6.98P
	(Cont C85)						
G-BDSA	Clutton Fred Srs.II		EI-BFS	23. 2.76	W.D.M.Turtle	(Ballymena)	5. 7.79P
	(VW 1600) LAS.1803 & PFA/29-10141		G-BDSA				
G-BDSB	PA-28-181 Cherokee Archer II		N8221C	23. 2.76	Testfair Ltd	Fairoaks	20. 7.01
		28-7690107					
G-BDSE	Cameron O-77 HAFB	210		27. 2.76	British Airways plc	Worplesdon	31. 3.90A
					"Concorde"		
G-BDSF	Cameron O-56 HAFB	209		1. 3.76	J.H.Greensides	Hull	24. 5.93A
					"Itzuma"		
G-BDSH	PA-28-140 Cherokee Cruiser			1. 3.76	D.Jones	Nottingham	26. 8.99
		28-7625063			t/a The Wright Brothers F/Grp		

Regn	Type	C/n	P/I	Date	Owner/operator	Probable Base	CA Expy
G-BDSK	Cameron O-65 HAFB	166		3. 3.76	Semajan Ltd	Romsey	25. 6.99A
					t/a Southern Balloon Group "Carousel II"		
G-BDSL	Reims Cessna F.150M Commuter	1306		5. 3.76	D.C.Bonsall	Netherthorpe	24. 6.01T
G-BDSM	Slingsby T.31 Motor Cadet III			5. 3.76	N.F.James	Husbands Bosworth	22. 7.98P
G-BDSO*	Cameron O-31 HAFB	207		10. 3.76	Not known "Baby Budget"	Bristol	24. 6.81A
G-BDTB	Evans VP-1 Srs.2 (VW1834)	PFA/7009		15. 3.76	T.F.Crossman	(Loddon, Norwich)	26.11.96P
G-BDTL	Evans VP-1 (VW1600)	PFA/7012		17. 3.76	A.K.Lang (Stoke-sub-Hamdon, Somerset) (Stored 5.98)		5. 9.85P
G-BDTN	BN-2A Mk III-2 Trislander	1026	S7-AAN VQ-SAN/G-BDTN	16. 3.76	Aurigny Air Svs Ltd	Guernsey	10. 6.98T
G-BDTO	BN-2A Mk.III-2 Trislander	1027	G-RBSI G-OTSB/G-BDTO/8P-ASC/G-BDTO/(C-GYOX)/G-BDTO	16. 3.76	Aurigny Air Svs Ltd "Nessie"	Guernsey	31. 3.01T
G-BDTT*	Bede BD-5	3795 & PFA/14-10084		17. 3.76	Martini's Night-Club	Barrow-in-Furness	
G-BDTU	Van Den Bemden Omega III (Gas) Free Balloon (20,000 cu.ft)	VDB-35 & AFB.4		16. 3.76	R.G.Turnbull "Omega III"	Clyro, Hereford	4. 8.99A
G-BDTV	Mooney M.20F Executive	22-1307	N6934V	16. 3.76	S.Redfearn	Netherthorpe	21. 4.00
G-BDTW	Cassutt Racer IIIM (Cont C90)	PFA/34-10102		18. 3.76	R.Mohlenkamp "The Thunder Box"	Damme, Germany	1.11.99P
G-BDTX	Reims Cessna F.150M Commuter	1275		19. 3.76	S.L.Lefley & F.W.Ellis	Water Leisure Park, Skegness	6. 4.00T
G-BDUI	Cameron V-56 HAFB	218		19. 3.76	D.C.Johnson "True Brit"	Farnham	6. 7.91A
G-BDUL	Evans VP-1 (VW1834)	PFA/1557		25. 3.76	C.K.Brown	(Helston)	11. 3.99P
G-BDUM	Reims Cessna F.150M Commuter	1301	F-BXZB	29. 3.76	Techair Aviation Ltd	Norwich	16. 1.97T
G-BDUN	PA-34-200T Seneca II	34-7570163	(EI-BLR) G-BDUN/SE-GIA	29. 3.76	Air Medical Ltd	Oxford	27. 2.01T
G-BDUO	Reims Cessna F.150M Commuter	1304		29. 3.76	C.B.Mellor t/a BM Aviation	(Winchester)	8. 2.01T
G-BDUY	Robin DR.400/140B Major	1120		5. 4.76	J.G.Anderson	Newcastle	20. 1.00
G-BDUZ	Cameron V-56 HAFB	213		30. 3.76	P.J.Bish	Hungerford	13. 5.87A
					t/a Zebedee Balloon Service "Hot Lips"		
G-BDVA	PA-17 Vagabond (Cont C90)	17-206	CN-TVY F-BFFE	23. 4.76	I.M.Callier	Liss	24. 7.99P
G-BDVB	PA-15 Vagabond (Cont C90)	15-229	F-BHHE SL-AAY/F-BETG	23. 4.76	B.P.Gardner Whittles Farm, Mapledurham		5. 6.99P
G-BDVC	PA-17 Vagabond (Cont C90)	17-140	F-BFBL	29. 9.76	A.R.Caveen Sandford Hall, Knockin		13. 8.98P
G-BDVG*	Thunder Ax6-56A HAFB	067		2. 4.76	D.Body "Argonaut"	?	N/E(A)
G-BDVU	Mooney M.20F Executive	22-1380		23. 4.76	D.H.G.Penney	Biggin Hill	22. 7.01
G-BDWA	Socata Rallye 150ST	2695		20. 4.76	J.T.Wilson Bann Foot, Lough Neagh (Stored 6.97)		7. 6.01
G-BDWE	Flaglor Sky Scooter (VW1600)	KF-S-66 & DWE-01 & PFA/1332		12. 4.76	B.A.Schlussler	(Bourne) t/a Flagor Fliers	16. 9.97P
G-BDWH	Socata Rallye 150ST	2697		20. 4.76	M.A.Jones Upper Harford Farm, Bourton-on-the-Water		29. 6.01
G-BDWJ	Replica Plans SE-5A (Cont C90)	PFA/20-10034	"C1904" "F8010"	27. 4.76	C.D.Pidler (Wellington) (As "F8010/Z" in RFC c/s)		18.11.99P
G-BDWL	PA-25-235 Pawnee B	25-3575	PH-IPO N7531Z	4. 5.76	R.Sharman Crowland t/a Peterborough & Spalding Gliding Club		31. 7.00
G-BDWM	Bonsall DB-1 Mustang (Lyc IO-360)	PFA/73-10200		3. 5.76	D.C.Bonsall Netherthorpe (As "FB226/MT-A" in RAF c/s)		15. 6.98P
G-BDWO	Howes Ax6 HAFB	RBH.2		5. 5.76	R.B. & Mrs C.Howes Keysoe, Bedford "Griffin"		
	(Complete and extant 11.88 but never certified)						
G-BDWP	PA-32R-300 Cherokee Lance	32R-7680176	N8784E	7. 5.76	W.M.Brown & B.J.Wood	Coventry	12.10.00
G-BDWV	BN-2A Mk.III-2 Trislander	1035	8P-ASF G-BDWV	11. 5.76	Aurigny Air Svs Ltd	Guernsey	15. 4.99T
G-BDWX	Jodel Wassmer D.120A Paris-Nice	311	F-BNHT	13. 5.76	R.P.Rochester	Bagby	6.10.98P
G-BDWY	PA-28-140 Cherokee E	28-7225378	PH-NSC	14. 5.76	Comed Avn Ltd	Blackpool	27. 2.00
G-BDXA	Boeing 747-236B	21238	N1790B	18. 3.77	British Airways plc "City of Peterborough"	Heathrow	26. 7.99T
G-BDXB	Boeing 747-236B	21239	N8280V	13. 1.77	British Airways plc "City of Liverpool"	Heathrow	15. 6.99T
G-BDXC	Boeing 747-236B	21240		18. 3.77	British Airways plc "City of Manchester"	Heathrow	21. 6.99T
G-BDXD	Boeing 747-236B	21241	N8285V	4. 4.78	British Airways plc (Blue Poole t/s)	Gatwick	11. 4.00T
G-BDXE	Boeing 747-236B	21350		23. 2.78	British Airways plc "City of Glasgow"	Gatwick	4. 4.00T
G-BDXF	Boeing 747-236B	21351		23. 3.78	British Airways plc "City of York"	Gatwick	30. 4.00T
G-BDXG	Boeing 747-236B	21536		16. 6.78	British Airways plc (Blomsterang t/s)	Gatwick	30. 6.00T
G-BDXH	Boeing 747-236B	21635		23. 2.79	British Airways plc "City of Elgin"	Gatwick	2. 5.01T
G-BDXI	Boeing 747-236B	21830		21. 2.80	British Airways plc "City of Cambridge"	Heathrow	13. 3.01T

Regn	Type	C/n	P/I	Date	Owner/operator	Probable Base	CA Expy
G-BDXJ	Boeing 747-236B	21831	N1792B	2. 5.80	British Airways plc "City of Birmingham"	Heathrow	7. 5.01T
G-BDXK	Boeing 747-236B	22303		29. 4.83	British Airways plc (Chelsea Rose t/s)	Gatwick	13. 6.00T
G-BDXL	Boeing 747-236B	22305	N8280V (G-BDXM)	9. 1.84	British Airways plc "City of Winchester"	Gatwick	18. 3.01T
G-BDXM	Boeing 747-236M	23711	N6055X	25. 2.87	British Airways plc "City of Derby"	Heathrow	27. 3.00T
G-BDXN	Boeing 747-236M	23735	N6046P	17. 3.87	British Airways plc "City of Stoke-on-Trent"	Heathrow	12. 4.00T
G-BDXO	Boeing 747-236B	23799	N6055X	22. 4.87	British Airways plc (Paithani t/s)	Heathrow	14. 5.00T
G-BDXP	Boeing 747-236M	24088	N6009F	24. 2.88	British Airways plc "City of Salisbury"	Heathrow	20. 3.01T
G-BDXX	SNCAN NC.858S	110	F-BEZQ	17. 5.76	M.Gaffney & K.Davis	(Waltham Cross)	3. 7.96P
G-BDYD	Rockwell Commander 114	14014	N1914J	21. 5.76	L.A. & A.A.Buckley	Chester	3. 8.00
G-BDYF	Cessna 421C Golden Eagle II	421C-0055	N98468	24. 5.76	Widehawk Aviation t/a Hawkair	Cambridge	24. 6.99T
G-BDYG*	Percival P.56 Provost T.1	PAC/F/056	7696M WV493	25. 5.76	Royal Museum of Scotland/Museum of Flight (As "WV493/29/A-P")	East Fortune	28.11.80P
G-BDYH	Cameron V-56 HAFB	233		24. 5.76	B.J.Godding "Novocastrian"	Didcot	25.11.90A
G-BDYM*	Skysales S·31 HAFB	1		27. 5.76	Not known "Cheeky Devil"	Bristol	N/E(A)
G-BDZA	Scheibe SF-25E Super Falke	4320	(D-KECW)	1. 6.76	Norfolk Gliding Club Ltd	Tibenham	21. 9.01
G-BDZC	Reims Cessna F.150M Commuter	1316		1. 6.76	A.M.Lynn	Norwich	21. 7.99T
G-BDZD	Reims Cessna F.172M Skyhawk II	1478		1. 6.76	Northamptonshire School of Flying Ltd	Sywell	11. 9.00T
G-BDZU	Cessna 421C Golden Eagle II	421C-0094	N98791	14. 6.76	R.Richardson t/a Eagle F/Grp	East Midlands	23. 2.99T
G-BDZX	PA-28-151 Cherokee Warrior	28-7615212	N9559N	14. 6.76	J.Craig	Aldergrove	10.10.99T
G-BDZY*	Phoenix Luton LA-4A Minor	PFA/842		15. 6.76	P.J.Dalby	(Ventnor, IoW)	

(Cancelled as wfu 26.2.99; under construction 11.92 but no Permit issued & not completed)

G-BEAA-BEZZ

Regn	Type	C/n	P/I	Date	Owner/operator	Probable Base	CA Expy
G-BEAB	CEA Jodel DR.1051 Sicile	228	F-BKGH	18. 8.76	R.C.Hibberd	(Swindon)	10.12.99
G-BEAC	PA-28-140 Cherokee	28-21963	4X-AND	4. 6.76	C.E.Stringer	Elstree	18. 5.00T
					t/a Clipwing F/Grp		
G-BEAD*	Westland WG.13 Lynx	WA.00.001	XW835	15. 6.76	Army Air Corps, 9 Regiment RAF Dishforth		
					(Stored 8.93)		
G-BEAG	PA-34-200T Seneca II	34-7670204	N9395K	18. 6.76	Oxford Aviation Services Ltd	Oxford	22.10.00T
G-BEAH	Auster 5 J/2 Arrow	2366	F-BFUV	28. 6.76	W.R. & M.D.Horler	Haverfordwest	13.12.99P
	(Cont C85)		F-BFVV/OO-ABS				
G-BEBC*	Westland WS-55 Whirlwind HAR.10		8463M	25. 6.76	City of Norwich Avn Museum	Norwich	
	(Line No. WAJ/30)	WA/371	XP355		(As "XP355/A")		
G-BEBE	Grumman-American AA-5A Cheetah			28. 6.76	Bills Avn Ltd	Biggin Hill	22.10.99T
		AA5A-0154					
G-BEBG	WSK-PZL SZD-45A Ogar	B-655		29. 6.76	D.W.Coultrip	Hinton-in-the-Hedges	23. 9.99
					t/a The Ogar Syndicate		
G-BEBI	Reims Cessna F.172M Skyhawk II	1461		28. 6.76	R.G.A.Willoughby	Elstree	22.12.99T
					t/a Hatfield F/C		
G-BEBL	McDonnell Douglas DC-10-30	46949	N54643	31. 1.77	British Airways plc	Gatwick	13. 4.01T
					"Forest of Dean"		
G-BEBM	McDonnell Douglas DC-10-30	46921	N54640	23. 2.77	British Airways plc	Gatwick	5. 3.01T
			N8704Q		"Sherwood Forest"		
G-BEBN	Cessna 177B Cardinal	177-01631	4X-CEW	1. 7.76	A.J.Franchi & D.J.French	Earls Colne	6.12.96
			N34031				
G-BEBO	Turner Special TSW.2 PFA/46-10127			30. 6.76	E.Newsham & P.Moffatt	Breighton	19. 3.99P
	(Lyc O-290)				t/a The Turner Special F/Grp		
G-BEBS	Andreasson BA-4B HA/01 & PFA/38-10157			7. 7.76	N.J.W.Reid	Lee-on-Solent	30. 4.99P
	(Cont O-200-A)						
G-BEBT	Andreasson BA-4B HA/02 & PFA/38-10158			7. 7.76	A.Horsfall	Breighton	10. 9.97P
	(Lyc O-235)						
G-BEBU	Rockwell Commander 112A	272	N1272J	8. 7.76	R.Hodgkinson	Cardiff	11.11.00
G-BEBZ	PA-28-151 Cherokee Warrior		N6193J	14. 7.76	Goodwood Road Racing Co Ltd	Goodwood	2. 4.00T
		28-7615328					
G-BECA	Socata Rallye 100ST	2751		14. 7.76	R.J.Gregory & C.Terry		
					t/a Bredon F/Grp Croft Farm, Defford		30. 6.00
G-BECB	Socata Rallye 100ST	2783		14. 7.76	A.J.Trible Henscott Farm, Holsworthy		12. 2.01
G-BECC	Socata Rallye 150ST	2748		14. 7.76	D.T.Price	Cardiff	15. 5.00
G-BECE*	Aerospace Developments	1214/1		14. 7.76	Friends of Cardington	Cardington	1. 4.79P
	AD500 Airship				Airship Station		
					(Damaged Cardington 9.3.79; parts stored for future museum 9.94)		
G-BECF	Scheibe SF-25A Motorfalke	4555	OO-WIZ	14. 7.76	North County Ltd	(Middleton)	1.3.94P*
			(D-KARA)				
G-BECK	Cameron V-56 HAFB	136		27. 7.76	H. & D.J.Farrar	Seacroft, Leeds	29.12.96A
					"Joyride"		
G-BECN	Piper J3C-65 Cub (L-4J-PI)	12776	F-BCPS	27. 7.76	R.C.Partridge & M.Oliver		
			44-80480		Sampsons Hall, Kersey, Suffolk		22. 5.99
					(As "80480/44/E" in US Army c/s)		
G-BECT	CASA I-131E Jungmann	"3974"	E3B-338	3. 8.76	A.Stokes	Shoreham	14. 1.00P
					t/a Shoreham 131 Grp (As "A-57" in Swiss AF c/s)		
G-BECW	CASA I-131E Jungmann	2037	E3B-423	3. 8.76	R.A.Seeley	(London W8)	25. 8.99P
	(Incorporating parts of G-BECY ex E3B-459)				(As "A-10" in Swiss AF c/s)		
G-BECZ	Mudry/CAARP CAP.10B	68	F-BXHK	26. 7.76	Avia Special Ltd	White Waltham	17. 3.01T
G-BEDA	CASA I-131E Jungmann	2099	E3B-504	3. 8.76	M.G.Kates & D.J.Berry t/a DA Grp		2. 2.98P
					Sheffield Park, Haywards Heath		
G-BEDB*	SNCAN 1203 Norecrin II	117	F-BEOB	5. 8.76	J.E.Pierce	Ley Farm, Chirk	11. 6.80PF
					(On rebuild 3.98)		
G-BEDD	SAN Jodel D.117A	915	F-BITY	3. 8.76	P.B.Duhig	Chippenham	29. 6.99P
G-BEDF	Boeing B-17G-105-VE	8693	N17TE	5. 8.76	B-17 Preservation Ltd	Duxford	5. 5.98P
	Flying Fortress		F-BGSR/44-85784		(As "124485/DF-A" in USAAC c/s) "Sally B/Memphis Belle"		
G-BEDG	Rockwell Commander 112A	482	N1219J	5. 8.76	L.E.Blackburn	Newtownards	10. 4.00
G-BEDJ	Piper J3C-65 Cub (L-4J-PI)	12890	F-BDTC	5. 8.76	R.Earl	White Waltham	8.10.96P
	(Frame No.12720)		44-80594		(As "44-805942 in USAAC c/s)		
G-BEDK*	Hiller UH-12E	2300	XS706	5. 8.76	Alpha Aerotech Ltd	Chilbolton	14. 6.85T
					(Cancelled by CAA 6.3.99; pod in open store 1.96)		
G-BEDL	Cessna T337D Turbo Super Skymaster		N86406	12. 8.76	D.T.Colley & T.J.Brammer	Biggin Hill	23. 5.98
		337-01178			(Crashed nr Leatherhead Common 3.10.98)		
G-BEDP	BN-2A mk.III-2 Trislander	1039	ZK-SFG	17. 8.76	Atlantic Bridge Aviation Ltd	Lydd	8.10.99T
			N902TA/N1FY/N401JA/G-BEDP		(Op Sky Trek Airways)		
G-BEDV*	V.668 Varsity T.1	-	WJ945	26. 7.76	Duxford Avn Society	Duxford	15.10.87P
					(As "WJ945/21")		
G-BEEE*	Thunder Ax6-56A HAFB	070		20. 8.76	British Balloon Museum	Newbury	11. 5.84A
					& Library "Avia"		
G-BEEG	BN-2A-26 Islander	550	(C-GYUH)	25. 8.76	North West Parachute Centre Ltd	Cark	30. 3.01T
			G-BEEG				
G-BEEH	Cameron V-56 HAFB	250		24. 8.76	Sade Balloons Ltd	Coulsdon, Surrey	22. 5.99A
					"Tywi"		
G-BEEP	Thunder Ax5-42 HAFB	086		20. 8.76	Mrs B.C.Faithfull Wagenberg, Netherlands		11.5.84A
					"Also Kenneth"		

Regn	Type	C/n	P/I	Date	Owner/operator	Probable Base	CA Expy
G-BEER	Isaacs Fury II (Lyc O-235)	PFA/1588		31. 8.76	N.Davis (Ashford, Kent) (As "K2075" in RAF c/s)		5. 5.99
G-BEEU	PA-28-140 Cherokee F	28-7325247	PH-NSE	9. 9.76	J.Maffia & H.Merkado	Panshanger	28. 2.00
G-BEEV*	PA-28-140 Cherokee F	28-7325229	PH-NSG	29. 9.76	Not known (Damaged Rayne 16.4.91; stored 5.97)	Panshanger	28. 3.93
G-BEEW	Taylor JT.1 Monoplane PFA/55-10189 (VW1600) (Modified to resemble Boeing P-26A Peashooter)			3. 9.76	P.A.Boyden (Godalming) (As "5" in 34th Pursuit Sqdn, US Army c/s) (Damaged early 1989)		
G-BEFA	PA-28-151 Cherokee Warrior	28-7615416	N6978J	8. 9.76	Firmbeam Ltd	Booker	31. 3.00
G-BEFF	PA-28-140 Cherokee F	28-7325228	PH-NSF N33696	27. 9.76	C.Haymes	Tibenham	19. 5.00
G-BEFO	BN-2A mk.III-2 Trislander	1041	5H-AZP G-BEFO G-SARN/F-BYCJ/V2-LMB/VP-LMB/G-BEFO	27. 9.76	Keen Leasing Ltd (Op Woodgate Executive Air Services)	Aldergrove	28.11.99T
G-BEFV*	Evans VP-2 V2-2390, YA-3 & PFA/63-10203 (Cont A65)			5.10.76	Not known Mickleton, Long Marston (Stored incomplete 8.93)		
G-BEGA	Westland-Bell 47G-3Bl (Regd with line No. WAT/227)	WA/705	XW185	19.10.76	Flight 47 Ltd	Fairoaks	23. 7.01
G-BEGG	Scheibe SF-25E Super Falke	4326	(D-KDFB)	15.10.76	R.Culley & A.Collett t/a G-BEGG F/Grp Hall Farm, Turweston		29. 4.00
G-BEHH	PA-32R-300 Cherokee Lance	32R-7680323	N6172J	29.10.76	SMK Engineers Ltd	Sherburn	7. 8.00
G-BEHJ*	Evans VP-1	PFA/1545		26.10.76	C.Bestwick (Stored 1992)	Beeston, Notts	
G-BEHM*	Taylor JT.1 Monoplane (VW1700) (Mod as Wildfire PDH.001; complete 1990 but C of A problems; on rebuild 11.95)	PFA/1420		29.10.76	Not known (Bedfordshire)		
G-BEHS	PA-25-260 Pawnee C	25-5207	OE-AFX N8755L	2.11.76	Southern Sailplanes Ltd (On overhaul 2.95)	Membury	25. 6.93A
G-BEHU	PA-34-200T Seneca II	34-7670265	N6175J	3.11.76	ANT Avn Ltd	Cambridge	21. 2.98T
G-BEHV	Reims Cessna F.172N Skyhawk II	1541		3.11.76	J.Easson (Op Edinburgh Air Centre)	Edinburgh	13. 4.01T
G-BEHX	Evans VP-2 V2-2338 & PFA/7222 (VW1834)			8.11.76	G.S.Adams "Ulster Flyer" (Stored 6.97)	Coalisland	22. 1.90P
G-BEIA	Reims Cessna FRA.150M Aerobat	0317		8.11.76	Rankart Ltd	Oxford	27.10.00T
G-BEIC	Sikorsky S-61N mk.II	61-222	N307Y	28.12.76	Brintel Helicopters Ltd t/a British International Helicopters	Sumburgh	8. 2.00T
G-BEIF	Cameron O-65 HAFB	259		17.11.76	R S Kent "Solitaire" (Balloon Preservation Group 7.98)	Lancing	25. 3.90A
G-BEIG	Reims Cessna F.150M Commuter	1361		18.11.76	D.A.Hardiman	Shobdon	14. 1.02T
G-BEII	PA-25-235 Pawnee D	25-7656059	N54918	16.11.76	Burn Gliding Club Ltd	Burn	7. 4.99
G-BEIL	Socata Rallye 150T	2653	F-BXDL	1.12.76	J.I.Oakes & R.A.Harris t/a The Rallye F/Grp Hill Farm, Nayland		6. 1.00
G-BEIP	PA-28-181 Cherokee Archer II	28-7790158	N6628F	22.11.76	S.W.& J.K.Stevens (Newbury)		16. 8.01
G-BEIS	Evans VP-1 (VW1600)	PFA/7029		25.11.76	P.J.Hunt (Melksham) (Stored Old Sarum 3.91 - status uncertain)		16. 7.90P
G-BEJB	Thunder Ax6-56A HAFB (Flies with second canopy; first one destroyed by fire at Latimer 4.9.77) "Baby J&B"	096		31.12.76	Justerini & Brooks Ltd	Latimer	21. 5.87A
G-BEJD	Avro 748 Srs.1/105	1543	LV-HHE LV-PUF	17.12.76	Emerald Airways Ltd (Reed Avn c/s) "John Case"	Liverpool	29. 3.00T
G-BEJK	Cameron S-31 HAFB	256		1.12.76	N.H.Ponsford & A.Lindsay t/a Rango Balloon & Kite Co "L'Essence" (or "Esso")	Leeds	16. 2.92A
G-BEJL	Sikorsky S-61N mk.II	61-224	EI-BPK G-BEJL/N4606G	30.12.76	Brintel Helicopters Ltd t/a British International Helicopters	Aberdeen	30. 9.98T
G-BEJV	PA-34-200T Seneca II	34-7770062	N7657F	31.12.76	Oxford Aviation Services Ltd	Oxford	8. 6.00T
G-BEKL	Bede BD-4E-150 (Lyc O-320)	151 & BD4E/2	(G-AYKB)	11. 1.77	A.J.Harpley (Hawes, N.Yorks) (On rebuild Bladon-on-Tyne 5.93)		14.10.80PF
G-BEKM	Evans VP-1 (VW 1834)	PFA/7025		12. 1.77	G.J.McDill	Park Farm, Eaton Bray	23. 3.95P
G-BEKN	Reims Cessna FRA.150M Aerobat	0318		12. 1.77	RFC (Bourn) Ltd (Open store 8.97)	Sibson	8.10.89T
G-BEKO	Reims Cessna F.182Q Skylane	0037		12. 1.77	G.J. & F.J.Leese	Sherburn	11. 6.00
G-BEKR	Rand Robinson KR-2 EAA/102591 & PFA/129-11046 (VW1834)			14. 1.77	A.N.Purchase (Status uncertain) (Woodlands Park, Maidenhead)		20. 8.88P
G-BELF	IRMA BN-2A-26 Islander	823	D-IBRA G-BELF	13. 1.77	The Black Knights Parachute Centre Ltd	Cark	12. 3.01
G-BELP	PA-28-151 Cherokee Warrior	28-7715219	N9543N	18. 1.77	R.J.Doughton	Dunkeswell	2. 8.01T
G-BELT	Reims Cessna F.150J (Mainly rebuild of G-AWUV and parts of G-ATND)	0409X		26. 1.77	Yorkshire Light Acft Ltd	Leeds-Bradford	5. 2.01T
G-BELX	Cameron V-56 HAFB	261		31. 1.77	V. & A.M.Dyer "Topsy Taffy"	Launceston	15. 8.93A
G-BEMB	Reims Cessna F.172M Skyhawk II	1487		27. 1.77	Stocklaunch Ltd	Goodwood	6. 4.01
G-BEMM	Slingsby Cadet III (VW1600) (Converted from T.31B)	1247	BGA942 RAFGSA 289/BGA942	27. 1.77	J.Beirne Boleybeg, Ballymore Eustace, Ireland		27.10.99P
G-BEMU	Thunder Ax5-42 HAFB	097		9. 2.77	I.J.Liddiard "Chrysophylax"	Newbury	16. 1.99A
G-BEMW	PA-28-181 Cherokee Archer II	28-7790243	N9566N	9. 2.77	Touch & Go Ltd	White Waltham	24. 5.00

Regn	Type	C/n	P/I	Date	Owner/operator	Probable Base	CA Expy
G-BEMY	Reims Cessna FRA.150M Aerobat	0315		9. 2.77	Euroair Flying Club Ltd	Cranfield	4.11.01T
G-BEND	Cameron V-56 HAFB	260		14. 2.77	P.J.Bish	Hungerford	1. 1.94A
					t/a Dante Balloon Group "Le Billet"		
G-BENF*	Cessna T210L Turbo Centurion II		N732AE	17. 2.77	Not known Cherry Tree Farm, Monewden		24. 5.82
		210-61356	D-EIPY/N732AE		(Crashed Ipswich 29.5.81; wreck in open storage 8.97)		
G-BENJ	Rockwell Commander 112B	522	N1391J	7. 3.77	E.J.Percival	Blackbushe	26. 7.00
G-BENK	Reims Cessna F.172M Skyhawk II	1509		2. 3.77	Graham Churchill Plant Ltd	Turweston	27. 5.00
G-BENL*	PA-25-235 Pawnee D	25-7656038	N54893	1. 3.77	W.J. & A.E.Taylor RAF West Raynham		14.11.85
					(Crashed Sutton Bank 10.7.85; stored 2.96)		
G-BENN	Cameron V-56 HAFB	278		4. 3.77	S.H.Budd "English Rose"	Pewsey	15. 3.87A
G-BEOD*	Cessna 180	32092	OO-SPZ	14. 3.77	I.Addy (Ivychurch, Kent)		6. 9.91
			D-EDAH/SL-AAT/N3294D		(Damaged Errol, Perthshire 29.6.89; stored 3.97)		
G-BEOE	Reims Cessna FRA.150M Aerobat	0322		21. 3.77	W.J.Henderson t/a Air Images	Carlisle	11. 7.00T
G-BEOH	PA-28R-201T Turbo Arrow III		N1905H	11. 3.77	J.J.Evendon	Blackbushe	6. 7.01
		28R-7703038			t/a G-BEOH Grp		
G-BEOI	PA-18-180 Super Cub	18-7709028	N54976	11. 3.77	Southdown Gliding Club Ltd	Parham Park	2.11.01
					(On overhaul 10.97)		
G-BEOK	Reims Cessna F.150M Commuter	1366		14. 3.77	D.C.Bonsall	Netherthorpe	11. 5.00T
G-BEOX*	Lockheed 414 Hudson IIIA	414-6464	VH-AGJ	25. 3.77	RAF Museum	Hendon	
	(A-29A-LO)		VH-SMM/A16-199/FH174/41-36975		(As "A16-199/SF-R")		
G-BEOY	Reims Cessna FRA.150L Aerobat	0150	F-BTFS	30. 3.77	R.W.Denny	Crowfield	14. 5.98T
					(Op Crowfield Flying Club)		
G-BEOZ*	AW.650 Argosy 101	6660	N895U	28. 3.77	East Midlands Aeropark	East Midlands	28. 5.86T
			N6502R/G-1-7		(Elan c/s) "Fat Albert"		
G-BEPB	Pereira Osprey II 88 & PFA/70-10193			29. 3.77	J.J. & A.J.C.Zwetsloot	Bourn	8. 6.98P
	(Lyc IO-320)						
G-BEPC	SNCAN Stampe SV-4C	64	F-BFUM	17.10.77	Dawn Patrol Flight Training Ltd		
			F-BFZM/Fr.Mil			Dunkeswell	24. 3.01T
G-BEPF	SNCAN Stampe SV-4C	424	F-BCVD	30. 3.77	L.J.Rice (On rebuild 1.97)	Chilbolton	
G-BEPH	BN-2A Mk.III-2 Trislander	1052	S7-AAG	4. 4.77	Aurigny Air Svs Ltd	Guernsey	14. 6.98T
			G-BEPH		(Steeple Finance c/s) "Jack"		
G-BEPI	BN-2A Mk.III-2 Trislander	1053		4. 4.77	Aurigny Air Svs Ltd	Guernsey	18.12.99T
					(Hambros Bank c/s)		
G-BEPN*	PA-25-235 Pawnee D	25-7656022	N54877	7. 4.77	Not known	Shobdon	6. 4.79
					(Crashed nr Cirencester 11.2.78; frame in store 3.96)		
G-BEPS	Short SC.5 Belfast C.1	SH.1822	G-52-13	6. 4.77	Heavylift Avn Holdings Ltd	Stansted	31. 8.99T
			XR368		(Op Heavylift Cargo Airlines)		
G-BEPV	Fokker S.11.1 Instructor	6274	PH-ANK	13. 4.77	L.C.MacKnight	Elstree	15. 4.93P
			Dutch Navy 174/Dutch AF E-31		(Frame stored 4.95)		
G-BEPY	Rockwell Commander 112B	524	N1399J	20. 4.77	K.M.Coke t/a G-BEPY Group	Blackbushe	28. 6.01
G-BERA	Socata Rallye 150ST	2821	F-ODEX	13. 4.77	C.S.Randall	Earls Colne	26. 1.00T
G-BERC	Socata Rallye 150ST	2858		13. 4.77	R.Jones & I.Harper	Welshpool	20. 4.98
					t/a The Severn Valley Aero Grp		
G-BERD	Thunder Ax6-56A HAFB	106		25. 4.77	P.M.Gaines	Stockton-on-Tees	15. 5.99A
					"Goldfinger"		
G-BERI	Rockwell Commander 114	14234	N4909W	6. 5.77	K.B.Harper	Blackbushe	12. 5.00
G-BERN	Saffery S.330 HAFB (Model)	4		19. 4.77	B.Martin "Beeze I"	Somersham, Cambs	
G-BERT	Cameron V-56 HAFB	273		19. 4.77	Semajan Ltd	Romsey	15. 5.99A
					t/a Southern Balloon Group "Bert"		
G-BERW	Rockwell Commander 114	14214	N4884W	6. 5.77	Malvern Holdings Ltd	Conington	5. 5.01
G-BERY	Grumman-American AA-1B Trainer	0193	N9693L	27.10.77	R.H.J.Levi	Stapleford	11. 5.01
G-BETD	Robin HR.200/100 Club	20	PH-SRL	28. 4.77	T.Gatland	Booker	21. 6.98
G-BETE	Rollason Beta B.2A	PFA/02-10169		26. 4.77	T.M.Jones	Egginton, Derby	
					(Incorporates parts from PFA/1304; under construction 4.97)		
G-BETF*	Cameron Champion 35SS HAFB	280		17. 5.77	British Balloon Museum	Newbury	6. 4.84A
	(Champion Spark Plug shape)				"Champion"		
G-BETG	Cessna 180K Skywagon	180-52873	N64146	17. 5.77	A.J.Norman	Rendcomb	27. 4.00
					t/a Norman Aeroplane Trust		
G-BETH*	Thunder Ax6-56A HAFB	113		27. 5.77	British Balloon Museum	Newbury	31. 5.78S
G-BETI	Pitts S-1D Special 7-0314 & PFA/09-10156			28. 4.77	P.Metcalfe Morgansfield, Fishburn		10. 6.97P
	(Lyc O-320)						
G-BETL	PA-25-235 Pawnee D	25-7656016	N54874	27. 5.77	Cambridge Gliding Club Ltd		
						Gransden Lodge	15. 9.00
G-BETM	PA-25-235 Pawnee D	25-7656066	N54927	5. 5.77	Yorkshire Gliding Club (Pty) Ltd		
						Sutton Bank	8. 4.01
G-BETO	MS.885 Super Rallye	34	F-BKED	18. 5.77	A.J. & A.Hawley Farley Farm, Romsey		31. 3.01
					t/a G-BETO Group		
G-BETP	Cameron O-65 HAFB	286		3. 5.77	J.R.Rix & Sons Ltd "Rix"	Hull	12. 6.88A
G-BETT	PA-34-200-2 Seneca	34-7250011	EI-BCD	20. 6.77	Andrews Professional Colour Laboratories Ltd		
			PH-AVM/N1978T		(Op London Flight Centre)	Lydd	28. 7.99A
G-BEUA	PA-18-180 Super Cub	18-8212	D-ECSY	21. 6.77	London Gliding Club Pty Ltd	Dunstable	30. 5.00
			N4146Z				
G-BEUD	Robin HR.100/285 Tiara	534	F-BXRC	8. 6.77	E.A. & L.M.C.Payton	Cranfield	18. 7.99
G-BEUI	Piper J3C-65 Cub (L-4H-PI)	12174	F-BFEC	19. 5.77	C.P.L.Jenkins	(Great Yarmouth)	10. 9.99P
			F-OAJF/Fr.AF/44-79878				
	(Frame No.12002 - regd as c/n 10536 ex 45-29245)						

Regn	Type	C/n	P/I	Date	Owner/operator	Probable Base	CA Expy
G-BEUK	Fuji FA.200-160 Aero Subaru	284		24. 5.77	C.B.Mellor t/a BM Avn	Southampton	2.11.00T
					(Damaged Glebe Farm, Stockton, Wilts 8.1.99)		
G-BEUM	Taylor JT.1 Monoplane (VW1700)	PFA/1438		8. 6.77	J.M.Burgess	(Helston)	21. 5.98P
G-BEUN	Cassutt Racer IIIM (Cont C90)	PFA/34-10241		20. 2.78	R.McNulty	Breighton	7. 7.97P
G-BEUP	Robin DR.400/180 Regent	1228		19. 5.77	A.V.Pound & Co Ltd	Biggin Hill	19. 2.01
G-BEUU	PA-18-95 Super Cub (L-18C-PI) 18-1551 (Frame No.should be 18-1523)		F-BOUU ALAT 18-1551/51-15551	27. 6.77	F.Sharples	Sandown	23. 4.99P
G-BEUX	Reims Cessna F.172N Skyhawk II	1596		30. 5.77	Multiflight Ltd	Leeds-Bradford	18.10.00T
G-BEUY	Cameron N-31 HAFB	283		31. 5.77	A.C.Beaumont "Little Red"	Henley-on-Thames	17.10.90A
G-BEVB	Socata Rallye 150ST	2860		2. 6.77	N.R.Haines	Malmesbury	22. 7.01
G-BEVC	Socata Rallye 150ST	2861		2. 6.77	B.W.Walpole		
					Old Hall Farm, St.Nicholas, South Elmham, Harleston		3. 4.00
G-BEVG	PA-34-200T Seneca II	34-7570060	VQ-SAM N32854	31. 5.77	Aranair Ltd	Bournemouth	27. 6.98T
G-BEVI*	Thunder Ax7-77A HAFB	125		30. 5.77	British Balloon Museum & Library "Prime Bang"	Newbury	N/E(A)
G-BEVO	Sportavia Fournier RF5	5107	5N-AIX D-KAAZ	27. 6.77	T.Barlow (Stored 12.97)	Barton	20. 8.96P
G-BEVP*	Evans VP-2 (VW2074)	ISW/7207/1 & PFA/7207		9. 6.77	G.Moscrop & R.C.Crowley	Netherthorpe	22.9.80P*
					(Damaged Truleigh Manor Farm, Edburton 13.6.92; on rebuild 10.95)		
G-BEVS	Taylor JT.1 Monoplane (VW1835)	PFA/1429		8. 6.77	D.Hunter	Kemble	21. 5.99P
G-BEVT	BN-2A Mk.III-2 Trislander	1057		10. 6.77	Aurigny Air Svs Ltd	Guernsey	15.11.00T
					(Islands Insurance c/s) "Polly"		
G-BEVV	BN.2A Mk.111-2 Trislander	1059	6Y-JQK G-BNZD/G-BEVV	10. 6.77	Cormack (A/c Svs) Ltd	Cumbernauld	
G-BEVW	Socata Rallye 150ST	2928		2. 6.77	P.C.Goodwin	RAF Keevil	23. 3.00
G-BEWM	Sikorsky S-61N Mk.II	61-772		14. 9.77	Brintel Helicopters Ltd t/a British International Helicopters	Aberdeen	30.11.00T
G-BEWN	DH(Aust).82A Tiger Moth (DHA rebuild c/n T305)	952	VH-WAL RAAF A17-529	16. 6.77	H.D.Labouchere	Blue Tile Farm, Langham	14. 7.00
G-BEWO	Moravan Zlin Z.326 Trener Master 915		CS-ALU	23.11.77	Nimrod Group Ltd	Gloucestershire	10. 4.00
G-BEWP*	Reims Cessna F.150M	1426		13. 6.77	Perth College	Perth	12. 8.85
					(Crashed Aboyne 4.10.83; instructional airframe 10.97)		
G-BEWR	Reims Cessna F.172N Skyhawk II	1613		13. 6.77	Cheshire Air Training Svs Ltd	Liverpool	7. 4.01T
G-BEWX	PA-28R-201 Cherokee Arrow III	28R-7737070	N5723V	23. 6.77	A.Vickers	North Weald	23. 5.00
G-BEWY	Bell 206B JetRanger	348	G-CULL EI-BXQ/G-BEWY/9Y-TDF	27. 6.77	PLM Dollar Grp Ltd	Inverness/Denham	4. 5.01T
G-BEXK	PA-25-235 Pawnee D	25-7756004	(N82424)	14. 7.77	Eastern Stearman Ltd	East Winch	3. 6.93A
					(Crashed 3/4.10.92; stored for spares 9.97)		
G-BEXN	Grumman-American AA-1C Lynx	AA1C-0045	N6147A	7. 9.77	C.J.Morgan t/a Lynx F/Grp	Elstree	1. 4.00
G-BEXO	PA-23-160 Apache	23-213	OO-APH N1176P	4. 7.77	G.R.Moore & A.K.Hulme	Rayne Hall Farm, Rayne	5.11.96
G-BEXW	PA-28-181 Cherokee Archer II	28-7790521	N38122	11. 7.77	T.R.Kingsley	Norwich	14.10.99
G-BEXX	Cameron V-56 HAFB	274		29. 6.77	K.A.Schlussler "Rupert of Rutland"	Bourne	2. 7.86A
G-BEXZ	Cameron N-56 HAFB	294		7. 7.77	D.C.Eager & G.C.Clark "Valor"	Bracknell/Worcester	13. 4.97A
G-BEYA	Enstrom 280C Shark	1104		15. 8.77	Hovercam Ltd	Plymouth	29. 5.00T
G-BEYB*	Fairey Flycatcher replica (P & W R985)	WA/3		11. 7.77	Fleet Air Arm Museum	RNAS Yeovilton	4. 7.96P
					(As "S1287/5" in 405 Flt FAA c/s)		
G-BEYF	HPR.7 Dart Herald 401	175	FM1022	13. 7.77	Dart Group plc t/a Channel Express	Bournemouth	17. 3.00T
G-BEYL	PA-28-180 Cherokee Archer	28-7405098	PH-SDW	6. 9.77	J. & N.Baker t/a Yankee Lima Group	Compton Abbas	26. 2.98
G-BEYN*	Evans VP-2	V2-3167 & PFA/63-10271		1. 8.77	Not known	East Fortune	
					(Incomplete airframe stored in hangar roof 9.98)		
G-BEYO	PA-28-140 Cherokee Cruiser	28-7725215	N9648N	14. 7.77	W.B.Bateson	Blackpool	12. 5.01
					(Damaged Brittas Bay, Ireland 13.6.97)		
G-BEYT*	PA-28-140 Cherokee	28-20330	D-EBWO N6280W	19. 7.77	B.A.Mills	(Little Eversden)	AC
					(Stored Earls Colne 5.97)		
G-BEYV	Cessna T210M Turbo Centurion II	210-61583	N732KX	19. 7.77	P.J.W. & N.Austen t/a Austen Avn (Damaged at Edinburgh 28.7.98)	Edinburgh	13. 4.01T
G-BEYW	Taylor JT.1 Monoplane RJS.100 & PFA/55-10279 (VW1834)			22. 7.77	R.A.Abrahams "Red Hot"	Barton	11. 3.99P
G-BEYZ	CEA Jodel DR.1050/Ml Sicile Record	588	F-BMGV	22. 7.77	M.L.Balding	Biggin Hill	25. 5.00
G-BEZC	Grumman-American AA-5 Traveler	AA5-0493	F-BUYN (N7193L)	29. 7.77	P.N. & S.E.Field	Elstree	24. 6.01
G-BEZE	Rutan VariEze (Cont O-200-A)	PFA/74-10207		26. 7.77	H.C.MacKinnon (Status uncertain)	(Alton)	2. 6.92P

Regn	Type	C/n	P/I	Date	Owner/operator	Probable Base	CA Expy
G-BEZF	Grumman-American AA-5 Traveler	AA5-0538	F-BVJP	29. 7.77	RAF College Flying Club Ltd	RAF Cranwell	23.10.01T
G-BEZG	Grumman-American AA-5 Traveler		F-BVRJ	29. 7.77	M.D.R.Harling & T.W.Cubbin	Andrewsfield	3. 4.99
G-BEZH	Grumman-American AA-5 Traveler	AA5-0566	F-BVRK N9566L	29. 7.77	L. & S.M.Sims	Fenland	25. 2.01
G-BEZI	Grumman-American AA-5 Traveler	AA5-0567	F-BVRL N9567L	29. 7.77	Heather Matthews t/a The BEZI F/Grp	Cranfield	6. 5.01
G-BEZK	Reims Cessna F.172H	0462	D-EBUD D-ENHC/SLN-07/N20462	17. 8.77	J-A.Kaas-Icleyn t/a Zulu Kilo F/Grp	Earls Colne	22. 5.99
G-BEZL	PA-31-310 Turbo Navajo C	31-7712054	SE-GPA	1. 8.77	London Flt Centre (Stansted) Ltd (Op Love Air)	Biggin Hill	25. 9.98T
G-BEZO	Reims Cessna F.172M Skyhawk II	1392		24. 8.77	Gloucestershire F/Svs Ltd	Gloucestershire	28. 3.01T
G-BEZP	PA-32-300 Cherokee Six	32-7740087	N38572	19. 8.77	Falcon Styles Ltd	White Waltham	22. 1.01
G-BEZR	Reims Cessna F.172M Skyhawk II	1395		24. 8.77	Kirmington Avn Ltd	Sandown	1. 3.01T
G-BEZS*	Reims Cessna FR.172J Rocket	0562	(I-CCAJ)	11. 8.77	Not known	Bourn	22. 9.79
	(Damaged nr Stapleford 15.6.79; front fuselage stored 5.97)						
G-BEZV	Reims Cessna F.172M Skyhawk II	1474	(I-CCAY)	24. 8.77	A.T.Wilson t/a Insch F/Grp	Insch	4. 5.98
G-BEZY	Rutan VariEze (Cont PC60)	1167 & PFA/74-10225		26. 7.77	R.J.Jones	Cranfield	18. 5.96P
G-BEZZ	Jodel D.112 (Built by Passot Avn)	397	F-BHMC	12. 8.77	M.J.Coles t/a G-BEZZ Jodel Grp	Barton	11. 4.99P

G-BFAA-BFZZ

Regn	Type	C/n	P/I	Date	Owner/operator	Probable Base	CA Expy
G-BFAA	Socata GY-80-160 Horizon	78	F-BLVY	20.10.77	Mary Poppins Ltd (Stoke-on-Trent) Status uncertain)		18.11.90
G-BFAB*	Cameron N-56 HAFB	297		15. 8.77	A.Gibson "Phonagram" Stockport (for British Balloon Museum & Library)		N/E(A)
G-BFAF	Aeronca 7BCM Champion (L-16A-AE)	7BCM-11	N797US N2552B/47-797	15. 8.77	D.C.W.Harper Finmere (As "7797" in US Army c/s)		25. 8.99P
G-BFAH	Phoenix Currie Wot (Cont O-200A) (Being built as Replica SE-5A and to be in RFC c/s)	PFA/3017		22. 8.77	R.W.Clarke (Cheadle)		
	(Regd as c/n PFA/58-11376 but mistaken with PFA/101-11376, a Sopwith Pup replica by same owner/builder)						
G-BFAI	Rockwell Commander 114	14304	N4984W	17. 8.77	Aeronautical & Marine Investments Ltd (IoM)		3.10.99
G-BFAK	GEMS MS.892A Rallye Commodore 150	10595	F-BNNJ	9. 8.77	P.G.Wells t/a Draycott Rallye Group Draycott Farm, Chiseldon		19. 4.01
G-BFAO	PA-20-135 Pacer	20-674	ZS-CMH ZS-CAH	10.10.77	Erica A.M.Austin Kemble		14.11.99
G-BFAP	SIAI-Marchetti S.205-20R	4-213	I-ALEN	1. 9.77	A.O'Broin Brook Field Farm, Great Stukeley		22. 5.00
G-BFAS	Evans VP-1 Srs.2 (VW1834)	PFA/7033		15. 8.77	A.I.Sutherland Fearn		10. 3.99
G-BFAW	DHC.1 Chipmunk 22 (Fuselage No. DHB/F/625)	C1/0733	8342M WP848	31. 8.77	R.V.Bowles Husbands Bosworth		7.10.00
G-BFAX	DHC.1 Chipmunk 22 (Fuselage No. DHB/F/364)	C1/0496	8394M WG422	31. 8.77	A.C.Kerr Cumbernauld (As "WG422")		8. 4.99
G-BFBA	SAN Jodel DR.100A Ambassadeur	88	F-BIVU	12. 9.77	W.H.Sherlock Drayton St.Leonard, Oxon		30. 9.99
G-BFBB	PA-23-250 Aztec E	27-7405294	SE-GBI	1. 9.77	Air Training Svs Ltd Booker		16. 6.01T
	(An Aztec wreck was marked "G-BFBB" for film use in Halland Handling Scrapyard, Braydon, Wilts 2.96)						
G-BFBC*	Taylor JT.1 Monoplane (VW1600)	PFA/55-10280		5. 9.77	Not known Linley Hill, Leven (Under construction 2.93)		
G-BFBE	Robin HR.200/100	12	PH-SRK	9. 9.77	A.C.Pearson Denham		28. 2.99
G-BFBF	PA-28-140 Cherokee F	28-7325240	EI-BMG G-BFBF/PH-SRF	9. 9.77	Marnham Investments Ltd Aldergrove (Op Woodgate Executive Air Services)		30. 9.01T
G-BFBM	Saffery S.330 HAFB (Model)	7		1. 9.77	B.Martin "Beeze II" Somersham, Cambs		
G-BFBR	PA-28-161 Cherokee Warrior II	28-7716277	N38845	15. 9.77	Lowery Holdings Ltd Fairoaks		29. 1.01T
G-BFBU	Partenavia P.68B	24	SE-FTM	25. 1.78	Premiair Charter Ltd Southampton		19. 4.00T
G-BFBY	Piper J-3C-65 Cub (L-4H-PI)	10998	F-BDTG 43-29707	29. 9.77	U.Schuhmacher Bolt Head, Salcombe		28. 6.99P
G-BFCT	Cessna TU206F Turbo Stationair II	U206-03202	(LN-TVF) N8341Q	15. 9.77	Cecil Avn Ltd Cambridge		26. 1.01
G-BFCZ	Sopwith Camel F.1 Replica (Clerget 9B)	WA/2		12.10.77	Brooklands Museum Trust Ltd Brooklands (As "B7270")		23. 2.89P
G-BFDC	DHC.1 Chipmunk 22	C1/0525	7989M WG475	15.11.77	N.F.O'Neill Newtownards		6. 2.00
G-BFDE*	Sopwith Tabloid Scout Replica (Cont PC.60)	168 & PFA/67-10186		22. 9.77	RAF Museum Hendon (As "168" in RNAS c/s)		4. 6.83P
G-BFDF	Socata Rallye 235E	12834	F-GAKT	6.10.77	D.J.Lindsay Wood Bournemouth		1. 1.98
G-BFDI	PA-28-181 Cherokee Archer II	28-7790382	N2205Q	5.10.77	Truman Avn Ltd Nottingham		10. 9.01T
G-BFDK	PA-28-161 Warrior II	28-7816010	N40061	23. 9.77	R.D.H.Cole t/a Priory Garage Enstone		8. 4.01T
G-BFDL	Piper J3C Cub (L-4J-PI) (Cont O-200-A) (Frame No.13107)	13277	HB-OIF 45-4537	30.11.77	S.Beresford & G.S.Claybourn Walton Wood (As "454537/04-J" in US Army c/s)		27. 4.99P
G-BFDO	PA-28R-201T Turbo Cherokee Arrow III	28R-7703212	N38396	3.10.77	A.J.Gow Wellesbourne Mountford		30. 6.99
G-BFDZ	Taylor JT.1 Monoplane (VW1600)	PFA/55-10185		5.10.77	G.J.Clare (Bath)		23. 9.99P
G-BFEB	SAN Jodel 150 Mascaret	34	F-BMJR OO-LDY/F-BLDX	14.10.77	S.Russell Wilkieston Farm, Cupar (Damaged Marston Moor 14.4.91; on rebuild 5.98)		19. 4.91P
G-BFEF	Agusta-Bell 47G-3B1	1541	XT132	11.10.77	R.C.Hields Gamston		7. 5.99T
G-BFEH	SAN Jodel D.117A	828	F-BITG	5.10.77	C.V. & S.J.Philpot Kemble		30. 9.94P
G-BFEK	Reims Cessna F.152 II	1442		11.10.77	Gloucestershire F/Svs Ltd Gloucestershire		20. 2.01T
G-BFEO*	Boeing 707-323C	18691	5X-UWM N7557A	14.10.77	Boeing Acft Co/USAF Davis-Monthan AFB, Arizona, USA (Stored for spares use 10.92)		30.12.85T
G-BFER	Bell 212	30835	N18099	7.11.77	Bristow Helicopters Ltd Scatsta		27.11.99T
G-BFEV	PA-25-235 Pawnee D	25-7756060		20.10.77	Trent Valley Aerotowing Club Ltd Kirton-in-Lindsey		18. 4.01
G-BFEW	PA-25-235 Pawnee D	25-7756062		20.10.77	Cornish Gliding & F/C Ltd Perranporth		25. 3.01
G-BFFB*	Evans VP-2	V2-2289 & PFA/63-10159		27.10.77	Not known Park Farm, Eaton Bray (Stored 6.96)		
G-BFFC	Reims Cessna F.152 II	1451		27.10.77	Yorkshire F/Svs Ltd Leeds-Bradford		11. 6.01T
G-BFFE	Reims Cessna F.152 II	1454		27.10.77	J.Easson Edinburgh (Op Edinburgh Air Centre) (Dumped 5.98)		19. 4.98T

Regn	Type	C/n	P/I	Date	Owner/operator	Probable Base	CA Expy
G-BFFJ	Sikorsky S-61N Mk.II	61-777	N6231	17. 1.78	Brintel Helicopters Ltd	Penzance	22. 3.00T
					t/a British International Helicopters "Tresco"		
G-BFFK	Sikorsky S-61N Mk.II	61-778		1. 2.78	Brintel Helicopters Ltd	Aberdeen	11. 3.00T
					t/a British International Helicopters		
G-BFFP	PA-18-180 Super Cub	18-8187	PH-OTC	9.11.77	Booker Gliding Club Ltd	Booker	12. 4.01
	(Frame No. 18-8402)						
G-BFFT	Cameron V-56 HAFB	360		7.11.77	R.I.McKean Kerr & D.C.Boxall	Bristol	23. 7.99A
					t/a The Red Section Balloon Group "Red Leader"		
G-BFFW	Reims Cessna F.152 II	1447		14.11.77	Tayside Avn Ltd	Dundee	28. 5.01T
G-BFFY	Reims Cessna F.150M Commuter	1376		14.11.77	G. & S.A.Jones	Linley Hill, Beverley	3. 3.01T
G-BFFZ	Reims Cessna FR.172K Hawk XPII	0603	F-WZDU	14.11.77	Bravo Avn Ltd	Caernarfon	26. 4.00T
					(Op Air Caernarfon)		
G-BFGD	Reims Cessna F.172N Skyhawk II	1545	F-WZDT	14.11.77	J.T.Armstrong	Denham	6. 9.01T
G-BFGF	Reims Cessna F.177RG Cardinal II	0166		14.11.77	J.E.Searson	Spanhoe	25.11.01
G-BFGG	Reims Cessna FRA.150M Aerobat	0321	F-WZDS	14.11.77	Cornwall Flying Club Ltd	Bodmin	3. 3.01T
G-BFGH	Reims Cessna F.337G Super Skymaster II (Wichita c/n 01754)	0081		14.11.77	T.Perkins	Leeds-Bradford	29. 5.99
G-BFGK	SAN Jodel D.117	644	F-BIBT	27. 6.78	B.F.J.Hope	Stoneacre Farm, Farthing Corner	29. 4.99P
G-BFGL	Reims Cessna FA.152 Aerobat	0339		14.11.77	Yorkshire F/Svs Ltd	Leeds-Bradford	5. 4.01T
G-BFGO	Fuji FA.200-160 Aero Subaru	219	PH-KDB	25.11.77	Butane Buzzard Avn Corporation Ltd	Cranfield	23. 8.92
					(Damaged Rush Green 18.8.93; stored 7.96)		
G-BFGS	Socata MS.893E Rallye 180GT	12571	F-BXYK	31. 8.76	K.M. & H.Bowen	Goldcliff	15. 9.00
			Fr.AF 12571 FSCAZ/"41-AZ"				
G-BFGW	Reims Cessna F.150H	0370	PH-TGO	24.11.77	C.E.Stringer	Humberside	19.10.95T
G-BFGX	Reims Cessna FRA.150M Aerobat	0328	F-BUDX	28.11.77	Air Service Training Ltd	Edinburgh	27. 8.01T
G-BFGZ	Reims Cessna FRA.150M Aerobat	0329		28.11.77	Tollett & Co Ltd	Oxford	10. 3.00T
G-BFHD*	CASA C.352L	146	T2B-255 "721-8"	23.11.77	National Air & Space Museum Dulles Airport, Washington, USA		
					(As "D-ODLH" in Lufthansa c/s)		
G-BFHF*	CASA C.352L	166	T2B-275 "721-15"	23.11.77	Auto und Technik MuseumSinsheim, Germany		
					(As "RJ+NP" in Luftwaffe c/s)		
G-BFHH	DH.82A Tiger Moth	85933	F-BDOH Fr.AF/DF197	25.11.77	P.Harrison & M.J.Gambrell	Swanborough Farm, Lewes	14. 8.00
G-BFHI	Piper J3C-65 Cub (L-4J-PI)	12532	F-BFBT 44-80236	25.11.77	N.Glass & A.Richardson	Bann Foot, Lough Neagh	26. 1.00P
G-BFHP	Champion 7GCAA Citabria	114	HB-UAX	8.12.77	Griffin Marston Ltd	Compton Abbas	4. 9.99T
					(Op Abbas Air)		
G-BFHR	CEA Jodel DR.220 2 + 2	30	F-BOCX	1.12.77	T.W.Greaves	Garton, Hull	3. 6.00
G-BFHT	Reims Cessna F.152 II	1441		7.12.77	Westward Airways (Lands End) Ltd	St.Just	16. 4.01T
G-BFHU	Reims Cessna F.152 II	1461		7.12.77	Deltair Ltd	Chester	30. 8.98T
G-BFHV	Reims Cessna F.152 II	1470		21.12.77	A.S.Bamrah	Blackbushe	27. 8.01T
					t/a Falcon F/Svs (Op European Flyers)		
G-BFHX	Evans VP-1 (VW1600)	PFA/62-10283		2.12.77	A.D.Bohanna & D.I.Trussler	(Swindon)	7. 4.99P
G-BFIB	PA-31 Turbo Navajo	31-684	LN-NPE OY-DVH/LN-RTJ	21.12.77	Richard Hannon Ltd	Thruxton	13. 8.00T
G-BFID	Taylor JT.2 Titch Mk.III (Cont O-200-A)	PFA/60-10311		13.12.77	J.C.Lidgard	North Coates	4. 8.98P
G-BFIE	Reims Cessna FRA.150M Aerobat	0331		12. 1.78	B.J.Parker	Shoreham	13.10.00T
G-BFIG	Reims Cessna FR.172K Hawk XPII	0615		12. 1.78	Tenair Ltd	Barton	1.12.00
G-BFIJ	Grumman-American AA-5A Cheetah	AA5A-0486	N6160A	1. 3.78	T.H.& M.G.Weetman	(West Kilbride)	3.12.00
G-BFIN	Grumman-American AA-5A Cheetah	AA5A-0520	N6145A	22. 3.78	I.W.Lewis	Wellesbourne Mountford	21. 1.02
					t/a G-BFIN F/Grp		
G-BFIP	Wallbro Monoplane replica (McCulloch/Wallis)	WA-1		16.12.77	K.H.Wallis	Shipdham	22. 4.82P
					(No external marks; stored 8.97)		
G-BFIU	Reims Cessna FR.172K Hawk XP	0591	N96098	12. 1.78	B.M.Jobling	Hinton-in-the-Hedges	30. 4.00
G-BFIV	Reims Cessna F.177RG Cardinal II		N96106	12. 1.78	Kingfishair Ltd	Blackbushe	24. 5.99
G-BFIX	Thunder Ax7-77A HAFB	133		9.12.77	R.Owen "Animal Magic"	Wigan	23. 4.95S
G-BFIY	Reims Cessna F.150M	1381	OE-CMT	11. 1.78	Yorkshire Light Acft Ltd	Leeds-Bradford	23. 6.99T
					(Op Yorkshire Aeroplane Club)		
G-BFJJ	Evans VP-1 (VW1800)	PFA/62-10273		30.12.77	Marion J.Collins	Popham	23. 6.96P
G-BFJK	PA-23-250 Aztec F	27-7654137	N62678	16. 1.78	H.G.Keighley	Sherburn	24.11.01
G-BFJR	Reims Cessna F.337G Super Skymaster II (Wichita c/n 01761)	0082	N46297 (N53658)	4. 1.78	Robot (UK) Ltd	East Midlands	11. 2.99
					t/a Mannix Avn		
G-BFJZ	Robin DR.400/140B Major	1290		20. 1.78	Rochester Avn Ltd	Rochester	24. 6.01T
G-BFKB	Reims Cessna F.172N Skyhawk II	1601	PH-AXO	16. 1.78	R.M.Collins	Ludham	19. 2.00T
G-BFKC	Rand Robinson KR-2	KKC.5 & PFA/129-10809		20. 1.78	L.H.S.Stephens & I.S.Hewitt	(Littleover, Derby)	
G-BFKF	Reims Cessna FA.152 Aerobat	0337		26. 1.78	Klingair Ltd	Conington	27. 4.01T
G-BFKG*	Reims Cessna F.152 II	1463		26. 1.78	Not known	Biggin Hill	25.11.90T
					(Damaged Luton 11.11.89; wreck stored 8.97)		
G-BFKH	Reims Cessna F.152 II	1464		26. 1.78	TG Avn Ltd (Op Thanet F/C)	Manston	20. 3.01T
G-BFKL	Cameron N-56 HAFB	369		23. 1.78	Merrythought Ltd	Telford	17. 7.92A

Regn	Type	C/n	P/I	Date	Owner/operator	Probable Base	CA Expy
G-BFKY	PA-34-200-2 Seneca	34-7350318	PH-NAZ N56332	22. 2.78	SLH Construction Ltd	Biggin Hill	24. 9.01T
G-BFLH	PA-34-200T Seneca II	34-7870065	N2126M	16. 2.78	Air Medical Ltd	Oxford	10. 5.00T
G-BFLI	PA-28R-201T Turbo Arrow III	28R-7803134	N2582M	16. 2.78	J.K.Chudzicki	Fairoaks	11. 6.01
G-BFLM*	Cessna 150M Commuter	150-76352	N3017V	15. 6.78	Cornwall F/C Ltd (Crashed nr Bodmin 14.1.97; open store 7.97)	Bodmin	16.11.96T
G-BFLP	Amethyst Ax6-56 HAFB	001		20. 2.78	K.J.Hendry "Amethyst"	Gillingham, Kent	
G-BFLU	Reims Cessna F.152 II	1433		15. 2.78	Bravo Avn Ltd (Op Atlantic Flight Training)	Coventry	8. 5.01T
G-BFLX	Grumman-American AA-5A Cheetah	AA5A-0524	N6147A	14. 3.78	Dynasty Trading Ltd.	(London SE10)	23.11.01T
G-BFLZ	Beechcraft 95-A55 Baron	TC-220	PH-ILE HB-GOV	16. 3.78	K.A.Graham t/a Caterite Food Service	Carlisle	23. 7.01
G-BFME	Cameron V-56 HAFB	371		17. 2.78	A.Mayes & V.Lawton t/a Warwick Balloons "Avon Lad"	Leamington Spa	29. 1.88A
G-BFMF*	Cassutt Racer IIIM (Cont C90)	PFA/34-10147		17. 2.78	Not known (Stored 8.95; cancelled by CAA 27.1.99)	Shaftesbury	24. 5.91P
G-BFMG	PA-28-161 Cherokee Warrior II	28-7716160	N3506Q	11. 5.78	Stardial Ltd	Fairoaks	5. 9.99T
G-BFMH	Cessna 177B Cardinal	177-02034	N34836	18. 4.78	Span Avn Ltd	Newcastle	21. 8.99
G-BFMK	Reims Cessna FA.152 Aerobat	0344		6. 3.78	RAF Halton Aeroplane Club Ltd	RAF Halton	5. 2.99T
G-BFMM	PA-28-181 Archer II	28-7890127	N47735	28. 2.78	K.Hobbs t/a Aldergrove Flight Training Centre	Belfast	26. 8.01T
G-BFMR	PA-20-125 Pacer	20-130	N7025K	20. 2.78	J.Knight	Headcorn	11. 1.00
G-BFMX	Reims Cessna F.172N Skyhawk II	1732		24. 8.78	Broomco (406) Ltd	Farley Farm, Hants	12. 6.00
G-BFMY	Sikorsky S-61N mk.II	61-745	N4040S	14. 3.78	Bristow Helicopters Ltd "Diamond"	Mount Pleasant, Falkland Islands	3. 2.00T
G-BFMZ*	Payne Ax6-62 HAFB	GFP.2		1. 3.78	E.G.Woolnough	Halesworth, Suffolk	
G-BFNG	Wassmer Jodel D.112	1321	F-BNHI	6. 3.78	M.T.Taylor	(Lincoln)	23. 7.99P
G-BFNI	PA-28-161 Warrior II	28-7816215	N9505N	8. 3.78	P.Elliott	Biggin Hill	26. 7.99
G-BFNJ	PA-28-161 Warrior II	28-7816281	N9520N	8. 3.78	Fleetlands Flying Association Ltd	Lee-on-Solent	23. 5.01T
G-BFNK	PA-28-161 Warrior II	28-7816282	N9527N	8. 3.78	Oxford Aviation Services Ltd	Oxford	22.12.99T
G-BFNU*	IRMA BN-2B-21 Islander	877		16. 3.78	Isles of Scilly Skybus Ltd (Fuselage stored 8.96)	St.Just	18. 8.89T
G-BFOD	Reims Cessna F.182Q Skylane II	0068		23. 3.78	G.N.Clarke	Alderney	30. 5.99
G-BFOE	Reims Cessna F.152 II	1475		23. 3.78	Redhill Air Services Ltd	Redhill	19.12.99T
G-BFOF	Reims Cessna F.152 II	1448		9. 3.78	Gloucestershire Flying Services Ltd	Gloucestershire	5. 6.99T
G-BFOG	Cessna 150M	150-76223	N66706	13. 3.78	Griffin Marston Ltd	Compton Abbas	20.11.00T
G-BFOJ	American AA-1 Yankee	AA1-0395	OH-AYB (LN-KAJ)/(N6195L)	4. 4.78	A.J.Morton & N.W.Thomas	Bournemouth	23. 9.99
G-BFOM	Piper PA-31 Turbo Navajo C	31-7512017	EI-DMI G-BFOM/HB-LHH/N59933	17. 3.78	Deer Hill Avn Ltd	(Kingsbridge)	25. 1.01T
G-BFOP	Jodel Wassmer D.120 Paris-Nice	32	F-BHTX	23. 3.78	R.J.Wesley & G.D.Western "Jean"	Sampsons Hall, Kersey	23. 8.99P
G-BFOS	Thunder Ax6-56A HAFB	147		20. 3.78	N.T.Petty "Milton Keynes"	Sudbury, Suffolk	25.11.93A
G-BFOU	Taylor JT.1 Monoplane	PFA/55-10333		17. 3.78	G.Bee	(Stockton-on-Tees)	
G-BFOV	Reims Cessna F.172N Skyhawk II	1675		18. 5.78	D.J.Walker	Shoreham	22. 9.99
G-BFPA	Scheibe SF-25B Falke	46179	D-KAGM	29. 3.78	N.Meiklejohn & J.Steel	Falgunzeon	13. 9.98
G-BFPB	Grumman-American AA-5B Tiger	AA5B-0706		7. 4.78	Aero Stratus Ltd	Guernsey	10. 6.99
G-BFPE*	PA-28-140 Cherokee C	28-26410	OH-PCY	22. 3.78	Not known (Crashed Clacton 9.6.82; wreck stored 4.92)	Framlingham	26. 5.84
G-BFPH	Reims Cessna F.172K	0802	PH-VHN	23. 3.78	M.Pollard t/a Linc-Air F/Grp	Sturgate	13. 6.99
G-BFPL	Fokker D VII Replica (Ranger 6-440-C5)	0033	D-EAWM	11. 8.78	F.Actis (German "Skull & Crossbones" marks)	(Charmey, Switzerland)	11.11.98P
G-BFPM	Reims Cessna F.172M Skyhawk II	1384	PH-MIO	13. 4.78	N.R.Havercroft	Sturgate	19.11.99T
G-BFPO	Rockwell Commander 112B	530	N1412J	10. 5.78	J.G.Hale Ltd	Shoreham	25. 8.00
G-BFPP	Bell 47J-2 Ranger	2851	F-BJAN TR-LKD/F-OCBU	23. 5.78	M.R. Masters	(Southampton)	11.11.99
G-BFPS	PA-25-235 Pawnee D	25-7856013		4. 4.78	Kent Gliding Club Ltd	Challock	19. 1.00
G-BFRA	Rockwell Commander 114	14292	N4972W	28. 3.78	Ischia Investments Ltd	Cascais, Portugal	24.10.00
G-BFRD	Bowers FlyBaby 1A	PFA/16-10300		27. 1.78	R.A.Phillips	(Elgin)	
G-BFRF	Taylor JT.1 Monoplane (VW1500)	PFA/55-10330		7. 4.78	E.R.Bailey	(Hockley, Essex)	
G-BFRI	Sikorsky S-61N Mk.II	61-809		26. 5.78	Bristow Helicopters Ltd "Braeriach"	Unst	14. 6.01T
G-BFRM	Cessna 550 Citation II (Unit No.027)	550-0027	N527CC N3245M	31. 1.78	Marshall of Cambridge Aerospace Ltd	Cambridge	14. 1.02T
G-BFRR	Reims Cessna FRA.150M Aerobat	0326	LN-ALO	19. 4.78	J.R.Duller	Egginton	6. 7.00

Regn	Type	C/n	P/I	Date	Owner/operator	Probable Base	CA Expy
G-BFRS	Reims Cessna F.172N Skyhawk II	1555	LN-ALP	19. 4.78	Poplar Models Ltd		
						Poplar Hall Farm, Elmsett	24. 4.00T
G-BFRV	Reims Cessna FA.152 Aerobat	0345		17. 4.78	Solo Services Ltd	Shoreham	18. 9.99T
G-BFRX*	PA-25-235 Pawnee D	25-7405787	SE-GDZ	23. 5.78	Yorkshire Gliding Club (Pty) Ltd		
				(Damaged Sutton Bank 27.3.94; spares use 1.95) Sutton Bank			28. 2.96
G-BFRY	PA-25-260 Pawnee D	25-7405789	SE-GIB	23. 5.78	Yorkshire Gliding Club (Pty) Ltd		
						Sutton Bank	28. 5.00
G-BFSA	Reims Cessna F.182Q Skylane II	0074	F-WZDG	17. 4.78	Clark Masts Teksam Ltd Zwartberg/Sandown		18. 8.99
G-BFSB	Reims Cessna F.152 II	1506		20. 4.78	M.R.Shelton	Tatenhill	6. 2.00T
					t/a Tatenhill Avn		
G-BFSC	PA-25-235 Pawnee D	25-7656068	N82302	2. 6.78	M.A.Pruden	(Bedford)	17. 6.00A
G-BFSD	PA-25-235 Pawnee D	25-7656084	N82338	2. 6.78	Deeside Gliding Club (Aberdeenshire) Ltd		
						Aboyne	8.11.01
G-BFSR	Reims Cessna F150J	0504	OH-CBN	7. 7.78	Sandra Jayyousi	Bourn	16. 4.01T
G-BFSS	Reims Cessna FR172G Rocket	0167	OH-CDY	7. 7.78	J.R. & S.J.Goddard Grateley, Andover		27. 3.00
					& F.West t/a Minerva Svs		
G-BFSY	PA-28-181 Archer II	28-7890200	N9503N	19. 4.78	A.S.Domone t/a Downland Avn	Goodwood	24. 5.99
G-BFTC	PA-28R-201T Turbo Arrow III	28R-7803197	N3868M	19. 4.78	M.J.Milns	Sherburn	22. 6.00
G-BFTF	Grumman-American AA-5B Tiger	AA5B-0879		7. 9.78	F.C.Burrow Ltd	Sherburn	22. 5.00
G-BFTG	Grumman-American AA-5B Tiger	AA5B-0777		15. 5.78	D.Hepburn & G.R.Montgomery	Perth	29. 8.99
G-BFTH	Reims Cessna F.172N Skyhawk II	1671		3. 5.78	J.Birkett	Wickenby	12. 9.99T
G-BFTT	Cessna 421C Golden Eagle II	421C-0462	N6789C	3. 5.78	P & B Metal Components Ltd	Manston	2. 5.99T
					(Op TG Avn)		
G-BFTX	Reims Cessna F.172N Skyhawk II	1715		2. 5.78	P.Howlett t/a East Kent F/Grp	Manston	28. 3.00
G-BFTZ*	Socata MS.880B Rallye Club	1269	F-BPAX	2. 6.78	The Aeroplane Collection Ltd	Winthorpe	19. 9.81
					(On loan to Newark Air Museum)		
G-BFUB	PA-32RT-300 Lance II	32R-7885052	N9509C	18. 5.78	Jolida Holdings Ltd	Jersey	3. 4.02
G-BFUD	Scheibe SF-25E Super Falke	4313	D-KLDC	19. 5.78	P.A.Lewis	Walney Island	21. 9.01
					t/a The Lakes Libelle Syndicate		
G-BFUF*	PA-30-160 Twin Comanche	30-363	F-OCZF	19. 5.78	Not known	Wilson, Nairobi	
			5R-MCA/N7361Y		(Dismantled & stored 9.92; Kenyan regn not issued)		
G-BFUG	Cameron N-77 HAFB	394		15. 5.78	Cornwall Ballooning Adventures Ltd		
						Newquay	19. 4.99A
G-BFVF	PA-38-112 Tomahawk	38-78A0055	N9691N	1. 6.78	Truman Avn Ltd	Nottingham	26. 6.98T
G-BFVG	PA-28-181 Archer II	28-7890408	N31746	1. 6.78	M.S.Cornah t/a G-BFVG F/Grp	Blackpool	22. 6.99
			N9558N				
G-BFVH	Airco DH.2 Replica	WA/4	"5964"	1. 6.78	M.J.Kirk (Stored/rebuild 1997)	(Barry)	23.7.86P*
	(125 hp Kinner B54)						
G-BFVM*	Westland-Bell 47G-3B1	WA/393	XT234	14. 6.78	Not known (Stored 5.96)	Coventry	20.11.87T
	(Line no. WAP/96)						
G-BFVP	PA-23-250 Aztec F	27-7854096	N63966	6. 7.78	Litton Avn Svs Ltd	Sherburn	14.11.99T
G-BFVS	Grumman-American AA-5B Tiger	0784	N28736	11. 8.78	S.W.Biroth & T.Chapman	Denham	2.10.00
G-BFVU	Cessna 150L Commuter	150-74684	N75189	10. 8.78	Airtime Aviation Ltd	Bournemouth	19. 6.00T
G-BFWB	PA-28-161 Warrior II	28-7816584	N31752	22. 6.78	Mid-Anglia Flying School Ltd	Cambridge	17. 7.99T
G-BFWD	Phoenix Currie Wot	PFA/3009		22. 6.78	F.R.Donaldson	Goodwood	6.10.96P
	(Walter Mikron 3)						
G-BFWE	PA-23-250 Aztec E	27-4583	9M-AQT	13. 7.78	Air Navigation & Trading Co Ltd		
			9V-BDI/N13968			Blackpool	10. 2.00T
G-BFWL	Reims Cessna F.150L	0971	PH-KDC	4.10.78	P.Maher t/a G-BFWL F/Grp	Barton	27. 3.00
G-BFXD	PA-28-161 Warrior II	28-7816583	N31750	10. 7.78	Oxford Aviation Services Ltd	Oxford	23. 5.00T
G-BFXE	PA-28-161 Warrior II	28-7816585	N31802	10. 7.78	Oxford Aviation Services Ltd	Oxford	8. 9.99T
G-BFXF	Andreasson BA.4B	AAB-001 & PFA/38-10351		10. 7.78	A.Brown	(Sherburn-in-Elmet)	
					(Semi-built 3.87)		
G-BFXH*	Reims Cessna F.152 II	1469	(F-BXQJ)	21. 7.78	M.Entwistle	(Warwick)	1. 2.93T
					(Cancelled by CAA 6.3.99; status unknown)		
G-BFXK	PA-28-140 Cherokee F	28-7325387	PH-NSK	1. 8.78	G.S. & Mrs M.T.Pritchard	Southend	16. 4.00
G-BFXL*	Albatros D.Va Replica	0034	D-EGKO	24. 8.78	Fleet Air Arm Museum	RNAS Yeovilton	5.11.91P*
	(Ranger 6-440-C5) (Built by Williams Flugzeugbau)				(As "D5397/17" in German c/s)		
G-BFXM*	Jurca MJ.5 Sirocco	PFA/2205		18. 7.78	R.Bradbury & A.R.Greenfield		
					(Open store incomplete 2.93) Stansted Mountfichet		
G-BFXR	Wassmer Jodel D.112	247	F-BFTM	27. 7.78	P.M.Beresford	Crosland Moor	24.11.97P
					t/a Jodel Group		
G-BFXS	Rockwell Commander 114	14271	N4949W	3. 8.78	Keats Printing Ltd	Denham	30. 7.99
G-BFXW	Gulfstream AA-5B Tiger	AA5B-0940		21. 2.79	Campsol Ltd	Leeds-Bradford	19. 6.00
G-BFXX	Gulfstream AA-5B Tiger	AA5B-0917		3.10.78	M.J.S.Worley	Southampton	11.11.00
G-BFYA	MBB Bo.105DB	S.321	D-HJET	31.10.78	Sterling Helicopters Ltd	Norwich	12. 5.00T
G-BFYB	PA-28-161 Warrior II	28-7816581	N31731	27. 7.78	Oxford Aviation Services Ltd	Oxford	12. 4.00T
G-BFYC	PA-32RT-300 Lance II	32R-7885200	N36645	31. 7.78	A.A.Barnes	Biggin Hill	3. 9.00
					t/a Cyril Silver & Ptnrs		
G-BFYI	Westland-Bell 47G-3B1	WA/326	XT167	24. 1.79	B.Walker & Co (Dursley) Ltd		
	(Line No. WAN/17)					Gloucestershire	1. 6.00
G-BFYK	Cameron V-77 HAFB	433	EI-BAY	16. 8.78	Louise E.Jones	Worcester	31.12.99A
G-BFYL	Evans VP-2	PFA/63-10146		15. 8.78	W.C.Brown	(Camberley)	17.12.98P
	(VW1834)						

Regn	Type	C/n	P/I	Date	Owner/operator	Probable Base	CA Expy
G-BFYM	PA-28-161 Warrior II	28-7816586	N31813	14. 8.78	Oxford Aviation Services Ltd	Oxford	7. 9.99T
G-BFYO*	SPAD XIII replica	0035	D-EOWM	16.11.78	American Air Museum	Duxford	21. 6.82P
	(Lyc AIO-360) (Built by Williams Flugzeugbau)				(As "1/4513" in 3rd Escadrille French AF c/s)		
G-BFYP	Wombat Gyrocopter	AJP.1		7. 7.78	A.J.Philpotts	St.Merryn	
	(Originally regd to unbuilt Bensen B.7 - Wombat built 1995)						
G-BFYU*	Short SC.5 Belfast C.1	SH.1821	G-52-15	13.11.78	Heavylift Avn Holdings Ltd	Southend	10. 4.93T
			XR367		(Heavylift Cargo Airlines) "St.David" (Wfu 27.6.92; stored 3.99)		
G-BFZA	Alpavia Fournier RF3	5	F-BLEL	14. 9.78	T.J.Hartwell & D.R.Wilkinson	(Bedford)	
					(On overhaul nr Thurleigh 3.90)		
G-BFZB	Piper J3C-85 Cub (L-4J-PI)	13019	D-ECEL	21. 9.78	P.F.Ansell & J.Noble t/a Zebedee F/Grp		
	(Frame No.12849)		HB-OSP/44-80723		(On rebuild 9.94)		
						West Chiltington, Pulborough	9. 4.88P
G-BFZD	Reims Cessna FR.182 Skylane RG II	0010		9.10.78	R.B.Lewis t/a R.B.Lewis & Co	Sleap	15. 1.00
G-BFZG	PA-28-161 Warrior II	28-7816582	N31748	18. 9.78	Oxford Aviation Services Ltd	Oxford	8. 2.00T
					(Oxford Air Training School)		
G-BFZH	PA-28R-200 Cherokee Arrow	28R-35307	OY-BDB	25.10.78	W.E.Lowe	Shobdon	25. 9.00
G-BFZM	Rockwell Commander 112TC-A	13191	N4661W	9.10.78	R.J.Lamplough	Filton/North Weald	8. 8.97
G-BFZN	Reims Cessna FA.152 Aerobat	0348		20.10.78	A.S.Bamrah t/a Falcon F/Svs	Biggin Hill	29.11.81T
					(Crashed Narborough, Leics 4.10.80; on rebuild 2.95)		
G-BFZO	Gulfstream AA-5A Cheetah	AA5A-0697		1.11.78	P.Young (Portstewart, Co.Londonderry)		12. 5.00
					t/a Coleraine Landscape Services		
G-BFZT	Reims Cessna FA.152 Aerobat	0356		4. 7.79	Zulu Tango Ltd	Guernsey	6.10.00T
					(Op Guernsey Aero Club)		
G-BFZU	Reims Cessna FA.152 Aerobat	0355		29. 6.79	Redhill Air Services Ltd	Redhill	10. 9.98T
G-BFZV	Reims Cessna F.172M	1093	SE-FZR	2.11.78	R.Thomas	AAC Middle Wallop	7. 3.00T

G-BGAA-BGZZ

Regn	Type	C/n	P/I	Date	Owner/operator	Probable Base	CA Expy
G-BGAA	Cessna 152 II	152-81894	N67529	18. 7.78	PJC (Leasing) Ltd	Stapleford	22. 6.01T
G-BGAB	Reims Cessna F.152 II	1531		13.10.78	TG Avn Ltd (Op Thanet F/C)	Manston	7. 4.00T
G-BGAD	Reims Cessna F.152 II	1532		13.10.78	Keen Leasing (IoM) Ltd	Newtownards	29.10.00T
G-BGAE	Reims Cessna F.152 II	1540		8.11.78	Klingair Ltd	Conington	30. 4.00T
G-BGAF	Reims Cessna FA.152 Aerobat	0349		13.10.78	M.F.Hatt, P.E.Preston, R.W.Harris, A.Jahanfar & D.S.Woolf (Op Southend F/C)	Southend	1. 8.00T
G-BGAG	Reims Cessna F.172N Skyhawk II	1754	"G-KING"	13.10.78	Aerohire Ltd (Op Devon School of Flying)	Dunkeswell	11. 5.01T
G-BGAH*	Clutton Fred Srs.II	PFA/29-10324		15. 2.78	Not known (Under construction 8.97)	Hethersett, Wymondham	
G-BGAJ	Reims Cessna F.182Q Skylane II	0096		13.10.78	Ground Airport Svs Ltd	Guernsey	4. 5.00
G-BGAU*	Rearwin 9000L Sportster	572D	N18548 NC18548	23.10.78	Not known (For rebuild - status uncertain)	(Ventnor,IoW)	
G-BGAX	PA-28-140 Cherokee F	28-7325409	PH-NSH	20.10.78	C.D.Brack	Breighton	17. 7.99
G-BGAZ	Cameron V-77 HAFB (New envelope ?)	439		20.10.78	C.J.Madigan & D.H.McGibbon "Silicon Chip/Robocop"	Bristol	1. 8.97A
G-BGBA	Robin R.2100A Club	133	F-OCBJ	2. 5.78	D.Faulkner	Headcorn	24. 3.00
G-BGBE	SAN Jodel DR.1050 Ambassadeur	260	F-BJYT	29.11.78	J.A. & B.Mawby	(Stevenage)	6. 9.01
G-BGBF	Druine D.31A Turbulent (VW1600)	PFA/1658		24.10.78	S.M.Cryer	(Lincoln)	9. 5.98P
G-BGBG	PA-28-181 Archer II	28-7990012	N39730	2.11.78	Harlow Printing Ltd	Newcastle	27. 4.00
G-BGBI	Reims Cessna F.150L	0688	PH-LUA	28.11.78	A.S.Bamrah t/a Falcon F/Svs	Cardiff	19. 3.01T
G-BGBK*	PA-38-112 Tomahawk	38-78A0433		2.11.78	Not known (Temp unregd 30.12.96)Sandtoft		5. 9.96
G-BGBN	PA-38-112 Tomahawk	38-78A0511		29.11.78	Bonus Avn Ltd	Cranfield	14. 7.00T
G-BGBP	Reims Cessna F.152 II	1546		8.11.78	Stapleford F/C Ltd (Damaged Stapleford 18.8.92; status uncertain)	Stapleford	19. 6.94T
G-BGBR	Reims Cessna F.172N Skyhawk II	1772		8.11.78	A.S.Bamrah t/a Falcon F/Svs (Op European Flyers)	Blackbushe	16. 2.01T
G-BGBU*	Auster AOP.9	B5/10/131	XN435	8.11.78	P.Neilson (On rebuild 1992)	Egham	
G-BGBW	PA-38-112 Tomahawk	38-78A0670		8.11.78	Truman Avn Ltd	Nottingham	19. 6.00T
G-BGBY	PA-38-112 Tomahawk	38-78A0711		8.11.78	Cheshire F/Svs Ltd t/a Ravenair	Manchester	18. 3.00T
G-BGBZ	Rockwell Commander 114	14423	N5878N	9.10.78	R.S.Fenwick	Rochester	7. 5.01
G-BGCG*	Douglas C-47A-85DL Dakota	20002	N5595T	28.11.78	Datran Holdings Ltd Rotary Farm, Hatch		8.8.80PF
	G-BGCG/Sp.AF T3-27/N49V/NC50322/43-15536 (Stored 8.95)						
G-BGCM	Gulfstream AA-5A Cheetah	AA5A-0835		23. 3.79	G. & S.A.Jones	Linley Hill, Beverley	28.10.00T
G-BGCO	PA-44-180 Seminole	44-7995128	N2103D	20.12.78	J.R.Henderson (Op by British Aerospace plc)	Dunsfold	2. 7.00
G-BGCX*	Taylor JT.2 Titch	PFA/3221		23.11.78	G.M.R.Walters (Cancelled as PWFU 27.3.99)	(Kingswinford)	
G-BGCY	Taylor JT.1 Monoplane (VW1600)	PFA/55-10370		23.11.78	M.T.Taylor	(Lincoln)	30. 8.96P
G-BGDA	Boeing 737-236ADV	21790	N1285E	4.12.81	British Airways plc (Martha Masanabo/Ndebele t/s)	Gatwick	3.12.99T
G-BGDE	Boeing 737-236ADV	21794		12. 3.80	British Airways plc (Sterntaler/Bauhaus t/s)	Gatwick	12. 3.01T
G-BGDF	Boeing 737-236ADV	21795		20. 3.80	British Airways plc (Delftblue Daybreak t/s)	Gatwick	20. 3.01T
G-BGDL	Boeing 737-236ADV	21801		9. 6.80	British Airways plc (Mountain of the Birds/Benyhone Tartan t/s)	Gatwick	10. 6.01T
G-BGDO	Boeing 737-236ADV	21803		25. 7.80	British Airways plc (Whale Rider t/s)	Manchester	27. 7.01T
G-BGDR	Boeing 737-236ADV	21805	N1786B	18. 9.80	British Airways plc (Dove/Colum t/s)	Gatwick	7. 9.01T
G-BGDS	Boeing 737-236ADV	21806		18. 9.80	British Airways PLC "Mons Calpe"	Heathrow	28. 9.01T
G-BGDT	Boeing 737-236ADV	21807		4.11.80	British Airways plc (Animals and Trees/Kg-Oocoan-Naka-Hiian-Thee-E t/s)	Manchester	5.11.01T
G-BGEA	Reims Cessna F.150M	1396	OY-BJK	22. 3.79	Agricultural & General Avn Ltd (Op Bournemouth F/C)	Bournemouth	23. 6.00T
G-BGED	Cessna U206F Stationair	U206-02279	LN-BGQ N1911U	12.12.78	Chapman Avn Ltd	Sibson	28. 3.00
G-BGEE	Evans VP-1 (VW1679)	PFA/62-10287		27.11.78	R.Wheeler & B.E.Holmes (Wings only at Priory Farm, Tibenham 8.97)	(Norwich/Ely)	16. 5.95P
G-BGEF*	Wassmer Jodel D.112	1309	F-BMYL	7.12.78	Not known (Damaged North Coates 8.10.95; stored 6.96)	North Coates	12. 9.96P
G-BGEH	Monnett Sonerai II 209 & PFA/15-10254 (VW2340)			1.12.78	P.C.Dowbor	Enstone	16. 8.96P
G-BGEI	Oldfield Baby Lakes (Cont A65)	PFA/10-10016 (Fuselage of PFA/1576 incorporated during construction)		1.12.78	A.R.Robinson	(Macclesfield)	29. 6.99
G-BGEK	PA-38-112 Tomahawk	38-78A0575		13.12.78	Cheshire F/Svs Ltd t/a Ravenair	Manchester	26. 3.00T
G-BGEP	Cameron D-38 Hot-Air Airship	442		6.12.78	Aeronord SAS	Milan, Italy	8. 6.99A
G-BGES*	Phoenix Currie Wot	JR.1 & PFA/58-10291		30.11.78	H.F.Moffatt (Stored 1989)	Woodlow Farm, Bosbury	
G-BGEW	SNCAN NC.854S (Cont A65)	63	F-BFSJ	13.12.78	Tavair Ltd	Emlyn's Field, Rhuallt	11. 5.99P

Regn	Type	C/n	P/I	Date	Owner/operator	Probable Base	CA Expy
G-BGEX*	Brookland Mosquito Mk.2 (VW1800)	JB.1		13.12.78	Not known (Stored 9.97)	Horsford, Norwich	14. 8.81P
G-BGFC	Evans VP-2 V2-1278 & PFA/63-10441 (VW1834)			15.12.78	S.W.C.Hollins	Llandegla	29. 9.93P
G-BGFF	Clutton FRED Srs.II (VW1834)	PFA/29-10261		18.12.78	I.Daniels	Popham	26. 3.99P
G-BGFG	Gulfstream AA-5A Cheetah	AA5A-0687	N6158A	25. 1.79	Plane Talking Ltd	Elstree	22. 5.00T
G-BGFH	Reims Cessna F182Q Skylane II	0105		18. 1.79	R.H.Stradling & J.A.Reid	(Reading)	13. 5.01T
	(Rebuilt with fuselage of G-EMMA 1994/95; original fuselage stored at Blackpool 5.97)						
G-BGFI	Gulfstream AA-5A Cheetah	AA5A-0733	N6142A	5. 3.79	I.J.Hay & A.Nayyar t/a GFI Grp	Biggin Hill	21.10.00
G-BGFJ	Jodel D.9 Bebe (VW1600)	PFA/1324		11.12.78	M.D.Mold	Watchford Farm, Yarcombe	22. 6.99P
G-BGFK	Evans VP-1	PFA/62-10343		20.12.78	I.N.M.Cameron (Stored 10.97) Wathstones Farm, Newby Wiske		
G-BGFT	PA-34-200T Seneca II	34-7870218	N9714C	17. 1.79	Oxford Aviation Services Ltd	Oxford	1. 9.00T
G-BGFX	Reims Cessna F.152 II	1555		28.12.78	A.S.Bamrah t/a Falcon F/Svs (Spares use 2.95)	Biggin Hill	23. 6.91T
G-BGGA	Bellanca 7GCBC Citabria 150S	1104-79		5. 2.79	L.A.King	North Connel	2.11.00
G-BGGB	Bellanca 7GCBC Citabria 150S	1105-79		7. 2.79	G.H.N.Chamberlain	Rattlesden	2.12.01
G-BGGC	Bellanca 7GCBC Citabria 150S	1106-79		5. 2.79	R.P.Ashfield & J.M.Stone Gorwell Farm, Littlebredy, Dorset		18. 9.00
G-BGGD	Bellanca 8GCBC Scout	284-78		5. 2.79	Bristol & Gloucestershire Gliding Club Ltd Nympsfield		22. 6.01
G-BGGE	PA-38-112 Tomahawk	38-79A0161		10. 1.79	Truman Avn Ltd	Nottingham	5. 6.00T
G-BGGF	PA-38-112 Tomahawk	38-79A0162		10. 1.79	Truman Avn Ltd (Stored 10.97) Nottingham		15.10.94T
G-BGGG	PA-38-112 Tomahawk	38-79A0163		10. 1.79	Teesside Flt Centre Ltd	Teesside	13. 5.01T
G-BGGI	PA-38-112 Tomahawk	38-79A0165		10. 1.79	Truman Avn Ltd	Nottingham	12. 2.01T
G-BGGL	PA-38-112 Tomahawk	38-79A0169		10. 1.79	Grunwick Processing Laboratories Ltd (Op Bonus Avn)	Cranfield	5. 6.00T
G-BGGM	PA-38-112 Tomahawk	38-79A0170		10. 1.79	Grunwick Processing Laboratories Ltd (Op Bonus Avn)	Cranfield	12. 6.00T
G-BGGN	PA-38-112 Tomahawk	38-79A0171		10. 1.79	Domeastral Ltd	Elstree	20. 7.00T
G-BGGO	Reims Cessna F.152 II	1569		8. 3.79	East Midlands Flying School Ltd East Midlands		27. 6.00T
G-BGGP	Reims Cessna F.152 II	1580		8. 3.79	East Midlands Flying School Ltd East Midlands		28. 9.00T
G-BGGU	Wallis WA-116/RR	702		28.12.78	K.H.Wallis	Reymerston Hall	
G-BGGV	Wallis WA-120 Srs.2	703		28.12.78	K.H.Wallis (Not built) (Reymerston Hall)		
G-BGGW	Wallis WA-122/RR (Cont O-240-A)	704		28.12.78	K.H.Wallis	Reymerston Hall	24. 4.98P
G-BGHE	Convair L-13A-CO	-	N1132V 47-346	4. 8.80	J.M.Davis (Long-term rebuild)	Wichita, USA	
G-BGHF*	Westland WG.30 Srs.100-60	WA.001.P		4. 1.79	The Helicopter Museum	Weston-super-Mare	1. 8.86S
G-BGHI	Reims Cessna F.152 II	1560		15. 1.79	Taxon Ltd	Shoreham	8. 5.00T
G-BGHM	Robin R.1180T Aiglon	227		19. 2.79	H.Price	Blackpool	23.10.00
G-BGHP	Beechcraft 76 Duchess	ME-190	N60132	16. 1.79	Magenta Ltd	Exeter	22. 4.00T
G-BGHS	Cameron N-31 HAFB	501		15. 1.79	W.R.Teasdale "Blackjack"	Maidenhead	N/E(A)
G-BGHT	Falconar F-12 (Lyc O-290)	PFA/22-10040		17. 1.79	C.R.Coates	Sneaton Thorpe, Whitby	
G-BGHU	North American T-6G-NF Texan	182-729 Fr.AF 115042/51-15042	FAP1707	22. 1.79	C.E.Bellhouse (As "115042/TA-042" in USAF c/s) "Carly"	Headcorn	29. 4.99P
G-BGHV	Cameron V-77 HAFB	483		12. 1.79	E.Davies t/a Adeilad Claddings "Adclad"	Penlan Farm, Llanwrda	5. 7.99A
G-BGHY	Taylor JT.1 Monoplane (VW1600)	PFA/1455		12. 1.79	R.A.Hand "Shy Talk"	RAF Cranwell	5. 6.98P
G-BGHZ	Clutton FRED Srs.II	PFA/29-10445		12. 1.79	A.Smith (Under construction 1991)	(Swansea)	
G-BGIB	Cessna 152 II	152-82161	N68169	3. 7.79	Southern Air Operations Ltd	Shoreham	26. 4.01T
G-BGID	Westland-Bell 47G-3B1 (Line No. WAN/31)	WA/340	XT181	28. 2.79	M.J.Cuttell	Gloucestershire	19.12.98
G-BGIG	PA-38-112 Tomahawk	38-78A0773		23. 1.79	Air Claire Ltd	Manchester	8. 4.01T
G-BGIO	Montgomerie-Bensen B.8MR (Rotax 503)	PFA G/01-1259		11. 1.79	R.M.Savage & F.G.Shepherd t/a Great Orton Group	Carlisle	15. 5.99P
G-BGIP	Colt 56A HAFB	038		2. 2.79	J.G.N.Perfect "The Snake"	Dorking	21. 6.94A
G-BGIU	Reims Cessna F.172H	0620	PH-VIT	26. 2.79	M.Ruggieri & M.Smalley	Top Farm, Tadlow	22. 3.01
G-BGIX	Helio H.295 Super Courier	1467	(G-BGAO) N68861	17.10.79	Caroline M.Lee Fanners Farm, Great Waltham, Essex		23.11.01
G-BGIY	Reims Cessna F.172N Skyhawk II	1824		31. 1.79	S.Kerr t/a Glasgow 172 Grp	Glasgow	21.12.00T
G-BGJE	Boeing 737-236ADV	22026		21. 3.80	British Airways plc (Rendezvous c/s)	Gatwick	21. 3.01T
G-BGJF	Boeing 737-236ADV	22027		17. 4.80	British Airways plc "River Axe"	Gatwick	16. 4.01T
G-BGJH	Boeing 737-236ADV	22029		13. 5.80	British Airways plc "River Lyne"	Gatwick	13. 5.01T
G-BGJU	Cameron V-65 HAFB	499		5. 2.79	Janet A.Folkes "Spoils"	Loughborough	4. 4.93A
G-BGKC	Socata Rallye 110ST	3262		25. 4.79	J.H.Cranmer & T.A.Timms	Bidford	8. 9.99
G-BGKD*	Socata Rallye 110ST	3263		25. 4.79	P.A.Cairns (Damaged Stone Hill, Exeter 27.10.97)	Dunkeswell	23. 7.98T

Regn	Type	C/n	P/I	Date	Owner/operator	Probable Base	CA Expy
G-BGKJ*	MBB Bo.105D	S.128	D-HDDV	20. 4.79	Bond Helicopters Ltd	Bourn	19. 4.88T
	(Ditched nr Mossbank, Shetland Isles 25.4.89; used as demonstration airframe 7.93)						
G-BGKO	Gardan GY-20 Minicab	PFA/1827		14. 2.79	R.B.Webber Hayrish Farm, Okehampton		
					(Stored incomplete 7.97)		
G-BGKS	PA-28-161 Warrior II	28-7916221	N9562N	12. 2.79	Marnham Investments Ltd	Newtownards	20. 3.00T
					(Op Woodgate Executive Air Services)		
G-BGKT	Auster AOP.9	B5/10/137	XN441	28.12.78	E.Wright t/a Auster Nine Group (On rebuild 9.97)		
	(c/n possibly B5/10/139?)				(As "XN441") South Lodge Farm, Widmerpool		
G-BGKU	PA-28R-201 Arrow III	28R-7837237	N31585	8. 3.79	Aerolease Ltd.	(Huntingdon)	12. 1.01T
G-BGKV	PA-28R-201 Cherokee Arrow III	N44985	21. 5.79	R.Haverson & R.G.Watson	Shipdham	2. 3.01
		28R-7737156					
G-BGKY	PA-38-112 Tomahawk	38-78A0737		2. 3.79	Prospect Air Ltd	Manchester	7. 7.00T
					(Op Manchester School of Flying)		
G-BGKZ	Auster J/5F Aiglet Trainer	2776	F-BGKZ	15.12.78	Deborah Hatelie	(Liverpool)	25. 2.95
					(Damaged nr Nayland 30.1.93)		
G-BGLA	PA-38-112 Tomahawk	38-78A0741		9. 3.79	B.H. & P.M.Illston	Norwich	6. 8.00T
					t/a Norwich School of Flying		
G-BGLB*	Bede BD.5B 3796 & PFA/14-10085			2. 3.79	The Science Museum	Wroughton	4. 8.81P*
	(Hirth 230R)						
G-BGLF	Evans VP-1 Srs.2	PFA/62-10388		28. 2.79	R.A.Yates	Sibsey	8. 2.99P
	(VW1834)						
G-BGLG	Cessna 152 II	152-82092	N67909	11. 4.79	A.T. Wright	Leeds-Bradford	1. 7.01T
G-BGLJ	Bell 212	30548	(EC-GHP)	5. 3.79	Bristow Helicopters Ltd	Redhill	10.11.99A
			EC-295/G-BGLJ/9Y-TIJ/G-BGLJ/5N-AJX/G-BGLJ/EP-HBZ/VR-BEJ/N2956W				
G-BGLK*	Monnett Sonerai IIL	PFA/15-10304		24. 2.78	N.M.Smorthit RAF Linton-on-Ouse		31. 8.89P
	(VW1783)				(Cancelled by CAA 6.3.99; stored 10.92)		
G-BGLN	Reims Cessna FA.152 Aerobat	0354		8. 3.79	Bournemouth F/Club Ltd.	Bournemouth	5. 8.00T
G-BGLO	Reims Cessna F.172N Skyhawk II	1900		8. 3.79	A.H.Slaughter	Southend	27.11.00
G-BGLS	Oldfield Super Baby Lakes			11.12.78	J.F.Dowe (Status uncertain)	(Ipswich)	18. 6.88P
	(Lyc O-235)	PFA/10-10237					
G-BGLW	PA-34-200-2 Seneca	34-7250132	OY-BDZ	2. 6.78	London Executive Aviation Ltd Stapleford		28. 8.00T
			SE-FYS				
G-BGLZ	Stits SA-3A Playboy	71-100	N9996	19. 6.79	C.A.Wills	Cambridge	8.11.99P
	(Cont C90)						
G-BGMA	Druine D.31 Turbulent	PFA/48-10438		27.11.78	G.C.Masterton (Not built)	(Guildford)	
G-BGME	SIPA 903	96	G-BCML	1. 1.81	M.Emery & C.A.Suckling	Guildford	17. 6.94P
			"G-BCHU"/F-BGHU		(Stored 1995)		
G-BGMJ	CAB GY-201 Minicab	12	F-BGMJ	19. 6.78	S.L. & A.W.Wakefield,	Sibson	19. 8.99P
					J.F.Hawkins & N.Birchall		
G-BGMN	HS.748 Srs.2A/347	1766	PK-OCH	9. 3.79	Emerald Airways Ltd	Liverpool	19.11.01T
			G-BGMN/9Y-TGH/G-BGMN/9Y-TGH				
G-BGMO	HS.748 Srs.2A/347	1767	ZK-MCB	9. 3.79	Emerald Airways Ltd	Liverpool	22. 4.99T
			G-BGMO/9Y-TGI/V2-LDB/9Y-TGI/(G-BGMO)				
G-BGMP	Reims Cessna F.172G	0240	PH-BNV	26. 3.79	R.W.Collings	Hinton-in-the-Hedges	24. 3.01
G-BGMR	Barritault JB-01 Minicab			12. 3.79	R:A.M.Smith	White Waltham	29. 9.99P
	(Cont C90)	PFA/56-10153			t/a Mike Romeo Flying Group		
G-BGMS	Taylor JT.2 Titch			20.10.78	M.A.J.Spice	(Middlewich, Cheshire)	
		MS.1 & PFA/60-10400					
G-BGMT	Socata Rallye 235E	13126		14. 9.78	C.G.Wheeler	(Newton Aycliffe)	13.12.00
G-BGMU	Westland-Bell 47G-3B1	WA/514	XT807	14. 5.79	V.L.J. & V.English		14. 1.95
	(Line No. WAP/83)					Whittlesey, Peterborough	
G-BGMV	Scheibe SF-25B Falke	4648	D-KEBG	15. 5.79	P.Turner	Halesland	16.11.01
					t/a Mendip Falke F/Grp		
G-BGND	Reims Cessna F.172N Skyhawk II	1576	PH-AYI	3. 3.78	A.J.M.Freeman	Andrewsfield	5. 8.99
			(F-GAQA)				
G-BGNH*	Short SD.3-30 Var.200	SH.3035	N331L	22. 3.79	Newcastle Airport Fire Service		
			G-BGNH			Newcastle	22.9.79F
G-BGNS*	Reims Cessna F.172N Skyhawk II	1901		23.10.79	F & H (Acft) Ltd Tattershall Thorpe		6. 1.89T
					(Damaged Shoreham 16.10.87; wreck stored 10.92)		
G-BGNT	Reims Cessna F.152 II	1644		23.10.79	Klingair Ltd	Conington	1. 3.01T
G-BGNV	Gulfstream GA-7 Cougar	GA7-0078	N790GA	20. 4.79	D.H.Smith	Bagby	25.11.00T
G-BGOD	Colt 77A HAFB	040		4. 4.79	C. & M.D.Steuer	London NW1	18. 6.97A
					"Harvey Wallbanger"		
G-BGOG	PA-28-161 Warrior II	28-7916350	N9639N	8. 6.79	W.D.Moore	Cranfield	8.10.00
G-BGOI	Cameron O-56 HAFB	526		4. 4.79	S.H.Budd "Skymaster"	Pewsey	13. 5.87A
G-BGOL	PA-28R-201T Turbo Arrow III		N36705	11. 4.79	Valley Flying Co Ltd	(Stoke-on-Trent)	14. 5.00
		28R-7803335					
G-BGON	Gulfstream GA-7 Cougar	GA7-0095	N9527Z	24. 4.79	J.P.E.Walsh	Elstree	4. 8.00T
					t/a Walsh Aviation (Op Cabair)		
G-BGOO*	Colt Flame 56SS HAFB	039		27. 4.79	British Balloon Museum	Newbury	N/E(A)
	("Smiling Flame" Shape)				"Mr Gas"		
G-BGOP	Dassault Falcon 20F	406/557	F-WMKF	19. 4.79	Nissan UK Ltd	Heathrow	30. 9.99T
					(Op by Falcon Jet Centre)		
G-BGOR	North American AT-6D-NT	88-14863	FAP1508	28. 3.79	M.L. Sargeant	(Goudhurst)	20. 5.99P
	Harvard III (Reported as c/n 88-14880)	SAAF7504/EX935/41-33908			(As "14863/TA-863" in USAAF c/s)		
G-BGPA	Cessna 182Q Skylane II	182-66538	C-GYBW	11. 7.79	J.J. & J.Walsh	Bodmin	22. 4.01
			(N94935)		t/a Papa Alpha Grp		

Regn	Type	C/n	P/I	Date	Owner/operator	Probable Base	CA Expy
G-BGPB	CCF Harvard 4	CCF4-538	FAP1747	4. 4.79	J.Romain	Duxford	6. 6.90P
	(T-6J-CCF Texan)	WGAF BF+050/WGAF AA+050/53-4619			(Op The Aircraft Restoration Co)		
			(Damaged Little Gransden 15.6.89; on rebuild 11.97) (As "1747" in Portuguese AF c/s)				
G-BGPD	Piper J3C-65 Cub (L-4H-PI)	12040	F-BFQP	18. 4.79	P.D.Whiteman Marsh Hill Farm, Aylesbury		16. 3.99P
			F-BDTP/44-79744		(As "479744/49/M" in 92nd Armoured FA Btn, US 9th Army c/s)		
	(Officially regd as c/n 10478 which is ex 43-29187/OO-ADI/F-BFQP; however G-BGPD has Frame No.11867						
	which is ex 44-79744/F-BDTP; presumably the fuselages were exchanged in France - see G-BCOM)						
G-BGPF*	Thunder Ax6-56Z HAFB	206		13. 7.79	P.J.Bish "Pepsi"	Hungerford	27. 6.82A
G-BGPH	Gulfstream AA-5B Tiger	AA5B-1248	(G-BGRU)	14. 8.79	Shipping & Airlines Ltd	Biggin Hill	30. 9.01T
G-BGPI	Plumb BGP.1 Biplane	PFA/83-10359		26. 6.78	B.G.Plumb	Hinton-in-the-Hedges	2. 6.98P
	(VW1834)						
G-BGPJ	PA-28-161 Warrior II	28-7916288	N9602N	24. 4.79	West Lancs Warrior Co Ltd	Blackpool	24. 6.00
G-BGPK	Gulfstream AA-5B Tiger	AA5B-1258	(G-BGRV)	28. 8.79	Ann Green	Elstree	4. 9.98T
G-BGPL	PA-28-161 Warrior II	28-7916289	N9603N	20. 4.79	TG Avn Ltd (Op Thanet F/C)	Manston	12. 6.00T
G-BGPM	Evans VP-2	PFA/63-10335		17. 4.79	M.G.Reilly	(Basingstoke)	29. 4.86P
	(VW2075)				(Open storage Old Sarum 9.91 - status uncertain)		
G-BGPN	PA-18-150 Super Cub	18-7909044		12. 4.79	Clacton A/C (1988) Ltd	Clacton	7. 3.92T
					(Damaged Nayland 27.1.90; on rebuild 5.93)		
G-BGPU	PA-28-140 Cherokee F	28-7325282	PH-GNT	25. 4.79	Air Navigation & Trading Co Ltd		
						Blackpool	17. 8.00T
G-BGPZ	Morane MS.890A Rallye	10284	F-BLBD	3. 5.79	A.S.Cowan	Popham	28. 1.02
	Commodore 145				t/a Popham F/Grp G-BGPZ		
G-BGRC	PA-28-140 Cherokee B	28-26208	SE-FHF	12. 6.79	Arrow Air Centre Ltd	Shipdham	26.10.97T
G-BGRE	Beechcraft 200 Super King Air	BB-568		8. 5.79	Martin-Baker (Engineering) Ltd	Chalgrove	23.10.99T
G-BGRG	Beechcraft 76 Duchess	ME-233		8. 5.79	Liddell Aircraft Ltd	Bournemouth	30. 1.99T
					(Op Langtry Flying Group)		
G-BGRH	Robin DR.400 2+2	1411		21. 5.79	Rochester Avn Ltd	Rochester	4.11.00T
G-BGRI	CEA Jodel DR.1050 Sicile	540	F-BLZJ	27. 4.79	R.T.Gunn & J.R.Redhead	Sherburn	29. 5.00
G-BGRK	PA-38-112 Tomahawk	38-79A0983		8. 5.79	Goodwood Road Racing Co Ltd	Goodwood	14.12.99T
G-BGRL	PA-38-112 Tomahawk	38-79A0917		25. 4.79	Goodwood Road Racing Co Ltd	Goodwood	3. 5.00T
G-BGRM	PA-38-112 Tomahawk	38-79A1067		1. 8.79	Goodwood Road Racing Co Ltd	Goodwood	8. 5.00T
G-BGRN	PA-38-112 Tomahawk	38-79A0897		25. 4.79	Goodwood Road Racing Co Ltd	Goodwood	12. 2.00T
G-BGRO	Reims Cessna F.172M Skyhawk II	1129	PH-KAB	4. 5.79	Alarmond Ltd	Edinburgh	19.11.00T
					t/a Edinburgh F/C		
G-BGRR	PA-38-112 Tomahawk	38-78A0336	OO-FLT	8. 5.79	Surrey Flying Services Ltd	(London EC1)	7. 9.97T
					(Damaged Woodford 22.8.97)		
G-BGRS	Thunder Ax7-77Z HAFB	203		21. 5.79	P.M.Gaines & P.B.Fountain "Hassall Homes"		
						Stockton/Luton	19. 8.95A
G-BGRT	Steen Skybolt RCT.001 & PFA/64-10171			12. 9.78	J.H.Kimber & O.Meier		
	(Lyc O-360)					Damyns Hall, Upminster	16. 8.99P
G-BGRX	PA-38-112 Tomahawk	38-79A0609		11. 5.79	Bonus Avn Ltd	Cranfield	30.10.00T
G-BGSA	Socata MS.892E Rallye 150GT	12838	F-GAKC	29. 5.79	D.H.Tonkin	Bodmin	4. 6.01
G-BGSB*	Percival P.56 Provost T.1	PAC/F/057		21. 5.79	Military Museum of Oman	Oman	19. 7.82P
		7992M WV494			(As "WV494/04")		
G-BGSG	PA-44-180 Seminole	44-7995004	N36538	21. 5.79	D.J.McSorley	Enniskillen	25. 8.01
G-BGSH	PA-38-112 Tomahawk	38-79A0562		11. 5.79	Scotia Safari Ltd	Carlisle	11. 6.99T
					(Op Carlisle Flt Centre)		
G-BGSI	PA-38-112 Tomahawk	38-79A0564		18. 5.79	Cheshire F/Svs Ltd	Manchester	14. 9.00T
					t/a Ravenair		
G-BGSJ	Piper J3C-65 Cub (L-4A-PI)	8781	F-BGXJ	21. 5.79	A.J.Higgins	(Langport)	20. 9.99P
	(Frame No.8917)		Fr.AF/42-36657				
G-BGST	Thunder Ax7-65 Bolt HAFB	217		14. 5.79	J.L.Bond "Black Fred"	Haywards Heath	23. 3.91A
G-BGSV	Reims Cessna F.172N Skyhawk II	1830		1. 8.79	Southwell Air Svs Ltd Linley Hill, Leven		2.12.00
G-BGSW	Beechcraft F33 Bonanza	CD-1253	OH-BDD	30. 5.79	Marketprior Ltd	Swansea	28. 4.99T
G-BGSX	Reims Cessna F.152 II	1603		29. 5.79	Plane Talking Ltd	Biggin Hill	25. 5.01T
					(Op London Aviation)		
G-BGSY	Gulfstream GA-7 Cougar	GA7-0096		4. 6.79	Plane Talking Ltd	Elstree	17. 7.97
G-BGTC	Auster AOP.9	AUS/168	XP282	12.10.79	P.T.Bolton South Lodge Farm, Widmerpool		9. 6.97P
					(Damaged Widmerpool 2.10.96) (As "XP282")		
G-BGTF	PA-44-180 Seminole	44-7995287	N2131Y	20. 6.79	NG Trustees & Nominees Ltd	Jersey	26. 4.00
G-BGTG	PA-23-250 Aztec F	27-7954061	N2454M	23. 5.79	Keen Leasing (IOM) Ltd	(Castletown)	21.10.00T
G-BGTI	Piper J3C-65 Cub (L-4J-PI)	12940	F-BFFL	17. 5.79	A.P.Broad Brandy Wharf, Waddingham		14. 7.99P
	(Rotax 582) (Frame No.12770)		44-80644				
G-BGTJ	PA-28-180 Cherokee Archer	28-7405083	OY-BIO	3. 7.79	Serendipity Avn Ltd	Gloucestershire	8.12.00
			SE-GAH				
G-BGTP	Robin HR.100/210 Safari	188	(G-BGTN)	25. 6.79	J.C.Parker	Blackbushe	18. 1.99
			F-BVCP				
G-BGTT	Cessna 310R II	310R-1641	N1AN	13. 7.79	Aviation Beauport Ltd	Jersey	5. 2.01T
			(N2635D)				
G-BGTX	SAN Jodel D.117	698	F-BIDI	22. 6.79	C.Adams & D.Wain	Shobdon	4. 8.99P
					t/a The Madley F/Grp		
G-BGUB	PA-32-300 Six	32-7940252	N2387U	29.11.79	A.J.Diplock	Biggin Hill	31. 1.01
G-BGUY	Cameron V-56 HAFB	441		27. 9.78	J.L.Guy "Good Guy"	Skipton	13.10.95A
G-BGVB	CEA DR.315 Petit Prince	308	F-BPOP	20. 7.79	C.P.Jones & J.A.Alliss	Popham	11. 7.99
					t/a Victor Bravo Grp		
G-BGVE	Scintex CP.1310-C3 Super Emeraude		F-BMJE	8. 6.79	R.T.L.Arkell		
		931			t/a Victor Echo Grp "Mon Papillon"		
					Little Battleflats Farm, Ellistown, Coalville		30. 6.99P

Regn	Type	C/n	P/I	Date	Owner/operator	Probable Base	CA Expy
G-BGVH	Beechcraft 76 Duchess	ME-260		8. 6.79	W.J. & J.C.M.Golden t/a Valco Marketing		
						Bowerchalke, Salisbury	22. 6.01
G-BGVK	PA-28-161 Warrior II	28-7816400	PH-WPT	13. 6.79	D.S.Wells	Fenland	17. 5.01
			G-BGVK/N6244C				
G-BGVL*	PA-38-112 Tomahawk	38-78A0263	N9963T	13. 6.79	Shirley A Boyall	(Shipdham)	5. 2.95T
					(Crashed Priory Farm, Tibenham 16.7.93; spares for G-BPHI)		
G-BGVN	PA-28RT-201 Arrow IV	28R-7918168	N2846U	22. 6.79	H.S.Davies	Stapleford	10. 9.00
G-BGVS	Reims Cessna F.172M	0992	PH-HVS	3. 5.79	J.W.Tulloch t/a Kirkwall F/C	Kirkwall	14.12.00T
			(PH-LUK)				
G-BGVT	Cessna R182 Skylane RGII	R182-00244	N3162C	28. 6.79	J.M.Bain t/a Bain Transport	Perth	9.11.00
G-BGVU	PA-28-180 Cherokee D	28-5359	PH-AVU	5. 7.79	P.E.Toleman (Op Ravenair)	Manchester	2. 6.97T
					(Damaged Welshpool 14.1.97)		
G-BGVV	Gulfstream AA-5A Cheetah	AA5A-0750		27. 6.79	A.H.McVicar	Prestwick	1. 4.01T
G-BGVW	Gulfstream AA-5A Cheetah	AA5A-0774		21. 6.79	Plane Talking Ltd	Biggin Hill	14. 8.00T
					(Op Biggin Hill School of Flying)		
G-BGVY	Gulfstream AA-5B Tiger	AA5B-1080	(G-BGVU)	21. 8.79	R.J.C.Neal-Smith	Shoreham	5.10.00
			(F-GBOO)				
G-BGVZ	PA-28-181 Archer II	28-7990528	N2886A	12. 7.79	P.Chandraskaran	Biggin Hill	3. 7.00T
G-BGWC	Robin DR.400/180 Regent	1420		26. 6.79	D.C.Shepherd	Rochester	8. 2.01T
G-BGWH	PA-18-150 Super Cub	18-7605	ST-ABR	18. 6.79	V.D.Speck	Clacton	14. 6.93T
			G-ARSR		(Damaged Clacton 7.7.92; stored 9.97)		
G-BGWJ	Sikorsky S-61N Mk.II	61-819		20. 8.79	British Executive Air Svs Ltd	Aberdeen	12.10.00T
					(Op by Bristow Helicopters) "Monadh Mor"		
G-BGWK	Sikorsky S-61N Mk.II	61-820	N1346C	10. 9.79	British Executive Air Svs Ltd	Aberdeen	28.11.99T
			G-BGWK		(Op by Bristow Helicopters) "Cairngorm"		
G-BGWM	PA-28-181 Archer II	28-7990458	N2817Y	29. 6.79	Thames Valley F/C Ltd	Booker	10. 5.00T
G-BGWN	PA-38-112 Tomahawk	38-79A0918		2. 7.79	Teesside Flight Centre Ltd	Teesside	30.11.98T
G-BGWO	Jodel D.112 (Valladeau built)	227	F-BHGQ	22. 6.79	R.C.Williams t/a G-BGWO Group	Sandtoft	26. 6.98P
G-BGWR	Cessna U206A Super Skywagon	U206-0653	G-DISC	6. 7.79	C.M.J.Parton	Tilstock	20.10.00
			G-BGWR/PH-OTD/N4953F				
G-BGWS	Enstrom 280C Shark	1050		8.11.76	JHS Consultants Ltd	(London W1)	20. 5.99T
G-BGWU	PA-38-112 Tomahawk	38-79A0788		2. 7.79	J.S. & L.M.Markey	Gloucestershire	1.12.00
G-BGWV	Aeronca 7AC Champion	7AC-4082	OO-GRI	23. 8.79	J.A.Webb	(Alton)	10.10.86P
			OO-TWR		t/a RFC F/Grp		
					(Damaged Popham 8.6.86; status uncertain)		
G-BGWW	PA-23-250 Turbo Aztec E	27-4587	OO-ABH	15. 6.79	Kathleen Hobbs	Aldergrove	28. 9.01T
			N13971		t/a Aldergrove Flight Training Centre		
G-BGWY	Thunder Ax6-56Z HAFB	229		23. 8.79	P.J.Eley	Braintree	19. 8.95A
G-BGWZ*	Eclipse Super Eagle	ESE.007		29. 6.79	Fleet Air Arm Museum	Wroughton	
					(Stored 3.96)		
G-BGXA	Piper J3C-65 Cub (L-4H-PI)	10762	F-BGXA	1. 3.78	K.Nicholls	Broadheath, Worcester	16. 8.99P
	(Frame No.10587 - regd with c/n 11170)		Fr.AF/43-29471		(As "329471/F/44" in USAAC c/s)		
G-BGXB	PA-38-112 Tomahawk	38-79A1007		2. 7.79	Signtest Ltd	Cardiff	10. 3.01T
G-BGXC	Socata TB-10 Tobago	35		19.10.79	D.H.Courtley	Guernsey	23. 7.01
G-BGXD	Socata TB-10 Tobago	39		19.10.79	P.N.Atkin, T.M.Sloan,	(Pulborough)	18. 5.01
					R.J.Wright & J.S.Smith		
G-BGXJ	Partenavia P.68B	189		6. 9.79	Cecil Avn Ltd	Cambridge	8. 9.99
G-BGXK	Cessna 310R II	310R-1257	N6070X	7. 8.79	Alarmond Ltd	Edinburgh	1.11.00T
					t/a Edinburgh Flying Club		
G-BGXN	PA-38-112 Tomahawk	38-79A0898		5. 7.79	Panshanger School of Flying Ltd		
					(Damaged 1991; stored for rebuild 3.97)	Manor Farm, Glatton	24. 8.91T
G-BGXO	PA-38-112 Tomahawk	38-79A0982		5. 7.79	Goodwood Road Racing Co Ltd	Goodwood	12. 2.01T
G-BGXP	Westland-Bell 47G-3B1	WA/350	XT191	20. 7.79	A.C. & E.I.Byrne t/a Ace Motor Salvage (Norfolk)		
	(Line no. WAN/41)					Botany Bay, Horsford, Norwich	13. 2.00
G-BGXR	Robin HR.200/100	53	F-BVYH	1.10.79	E.G.Cleobury	Wellesbourne Mountford	27.11.01
G-BGXS	PA-28-236 Dakota	28-7911198	N2836Z	12. 7.79	Bawtry Road Service Station Ltd	Gamston	23. 3.01T
G-BGXT	Socata TB-10 Tobago	40		3.10.79	D.A.H.Morris	Halfpenny Green	18. 8.01
G-BGYG	PA-28-161 Warrior II	28-7916431	N9528N	17. 7.79	Oxford Aviation Services Ltd	Oxford	31. 8.00T
G-BGYH	PA-28-161 Warrior II	28-7916313	N9619N	17. 7.79	Oxford Aviation Services Ltd	Oxford	3. 2.01T
G-BGYN	PA-18-150 Super Cub	18-7709137	N62747	19. 7.79	B.J.Dunford	Long Wood, Morestead	26. 4.01
G-BGYR	HS.125 Srs.F600B	256045	G-5-11	3.12.79	British Aerospace	Warton	30. 9.00
			EC-CQT/G-5-18		(Operations) Ltd		
G-BGYT	Embraer EMB-110P1 Bandeirante	110-234	N104VA	11.10.79	Thonhill Aviation Ltd	(London N1)	12. 1.00T
			G-BGYT/PT-SAA				
G-BGZF	PA-38-112 Tomahawk	38-79A1015		26. 7.79	Aerohire Ltd	Egginton	25. 5.98T
G-BGZJ*	PA-38-112 Tomahawk	38-79A0999		7. 9.79	Midland Aircraft Maintenance Ltd		
					(Damaged Cambridge 5.8.90; stored 9.97)	Halfpenny Green	14. 6.92T
G-BGZK	Westland-Bell 47G-3B1	WA/382	XT223	24. 7.79	Pan Air Ltd	North Weald	29. 5.00
	(Line No.WAP/81)				(As "XT223" in Army Air Corps c/s)		
G-BGZL	Eiri PIK.20E	20218		21. 8.79	F.Casolari	(Castellarano, Italy)	28. 7.01
G-BGZO*	SEEMS MS.880B Rallye Club	378	F-BKZO	24.10.79	Not known	(Shoreham)	9. 4.92
					(Damaged East Meon, Petersfield 3.5.89; stored 12.92)		
G-BGZW	PA-38-112 Tomahawk	38-79A1068		1. 8.79	Cheshire F/Svs Ltd	Manchester	19.11.01T
					t/a Ravenair		
G-BGZY	Jodel Wassmer D.120 Paris-Nice	118	F-BIQU	17. 8.79	M.Hale	(La Trinite Sur Mer, France)	22.11.99P
G-BGZZ	Thunder Ax6-56 Bolt HAFB	220		10. 8.79	Jennifer M.Robinson Milton-under-Wychwood		16. 7.94A
					"Robinson's Cruiser"		

G-BHAA-BHZZ

Regn	Type	C/n	P/I	Date	Owner/operator	Probable Base	CA Expy
G-BHAA	Cessna 152 II	152-81330	N49809	12. 2.79	Herefordshire Aero Club Ltd	Shobdon	14. 5.00T
G-BHAC	Cessna A152 Aerobat	A152-0776	N7595B	12. 2.79	Herefordshire Aero Club Ltd	Shobdon	17. 4.00T
G-BHAD	Cessna A152 Aerobat	A152-0807	N7390L	12. 2.79	Shropshire Aero Club Ltd	Sleap	11. 4.00T
G-BHAF	PA-38-112 Tomahawk	38-79A1092		8. 8.79	Notelevel Ltd Woodford/Manchester (Op Ravenair)		4.10.97T
G-BHAI	Reims Cessna F.152 II	1625	(D-EJAY)	14. 8.79	J.Easson	Netherthorpe	14.10.01T
G-BHAJ	Robin DR.400/160 Major 80	1430		22. 8.79	Rowantask Ltd	Rochester	5. 3.01T
G-BHAL	Rango-Saffery S.200SS HAFB (Model) (Face & pigtails shape)	NHP-2		14. 8.79	Miss A.M.Lindsay Leeds t/a Rango Balloon & Kite Co "Anneky Panky"		
G-BHAM	Thunder Ax6-56 Bolt HAFB	251		28. 1.80	D.M. & K.R.Sandford Knutsford "Levitation"		7. 4.86A
G-BHAR	Westland-Bell 47G-3B1 (Line No.WAN/44)	WA/353	XT194	7. 8.79	E.A.L.Sturmer Wilstone, Tring		10. 6.00
G-BHAT*	Thunder Ax7-77 Bolt HAFB	250		28. 1.80	Not known "Witter"	?	6. 2.83A
G-BHAV	Reims Cessna F.152 II	1633		15. 8.79	T.M. & M.L.Jones Egginton t/a Derby Aero Club		2. 8.98T
G-BHAW	Reims Cessna F.172N Skyhawk II	1858		15. 8.79	E.Alexander	(Braintree)	1. 6.01
G-BHAX	Enstrom F-28C-2-UK	486-2	N5689N	22.10.79	J.L.Ferguson	South Wirral	12. 2.99
G-BHAY	PA-28RT-201 Arrow IV	28R-7918213	N2910N	17. 8.79	Alpha Yankee Ltd	Newcastle	23. 2.01
G-BHBA	Campbell Cricket (Rotax 503)	SMI/1		15. 8.79	S.M.Irwin Armshold Farm, Kingston, Cambs		3. 6.97P
G-BHBE	Westland-Bell 47G-3B1 (Soloy conversion) (Line No.WAP/136)	WA/422	XT510	29.10.79	T.R.Smith (Agricultural Machinery) Ltd	Dereham	21.12.01
G-BHBF	Sikorsky S-76A II Plus	760022	N4247S	9.11.79	Bristow Helicopters Ltd	North Denes	3. 1.01T
G-BHBG	PA-32R-300 Cherokee Lance	32R-7780515	N408RC	18. 9.79	L.T.Halpin	Leicester	4. 6.00T
G-BHBI	Mooney M.20J (201)	24-0842	N4764H	24. 9.79	A.M.McGlone t/a G-BHBI Group Biggin Hill		10. 4.00
G-BHBT	Marquart MA-5 Charger	PFA/68-10190		3. 9.79	R.G. & C.J.Maidment Shoreham (Stored 6.93)		
G-BHBZ	Partenavia P.68B	191		10. 9.79	P.C.Hamer & P.C.W.Landau	Humberside	27. 3.99
G-BHCC	Cessna 172M Skyhawk II	172-66711	(G-BGLY) N80713	26.10.79	Langtry F/Grp Ltd	Bournemouth	16. 6.99T
G-BHCE	SAN Jodel D.117A	381	F-BHME	1.10.79	D.M.Parsons (Highnam, Gloucester) t/a Parwebb Flying Group (Status uncertain)		27. 2.85P
G-BHCM	Reims Cessna F.172H	0468	SE-FBD	25. 9.79	J. Dominic	Denham	24. 4.01
G-BHCP	Reims Cessna F.152 II	1640		31.10.79	D.Copley	Sherburn	12.10.98T
G-BHCT	PA-23-250 Aztec F	27-7954113	G-OLBC G-BHCT/N6925A	18.10.79	A.S.Bamrah Snetterton t/a Falcon F/Svs		3. 6.99T
G-BHCW*	PA-22-150 Tri-Pacer	22-3006	F-BHDT	11. 2.80	Not known (Stored 10.94)	Shoreham	
G-BHCZ	PA-38-112 Tomahawk	38-78A0321	N214MD	26. 9.79	Jennifer E.Abbott	Goodwood	25. 9.00
G-BHDD	V.668 Varsity T.1	-	WL626	18.10.79	G.Vale East Midlands (As "WL626/P") (To East Midlands Aeropark 3.98)		AC
G-BHDE	Socata TB-10 Tobago	58		2. 1.80	A.E.Allsop Antwerp, Belgium (Op ACS Belgium BVBA)		29. 7.01
G-BHDH	McDonnell Douglas DC-10-30	47816		30. 4.80	British Airways plc	Gatwick	29. 4.01T
G-BHDI	McDonnell Douglas DC-10-30	47831		10. 6.80	British Airways plc "Forest of Ae"	Gatwick	20. 7.01T
G-BHDJ	McDonnell Douglas DC-10-30	47840	N19B	30. 7.80	British Airways plc "Glencap Forest"	Gatwick	15.10.01T
G-BHDK*	Boeing TB-29A-45-BN Superfortress	11225	44-61748	27. 9.79	Imperial War Museum Duxford (As "461748/Y" in USAF c/s) "Hawg Wild"		
G-BHDM	Reims Cessna F.152 II	1684		15.10.79	Tayside Avn Ltd	Aberdeen	9. 4.01T
G-BHDP	Reims Cessna F.182Q Skylane	0131		15.10.79	Zone Travel Ltd	Booker	16. 9.99
G-BHDR	Reims Cessna F.152 II	1680		15.10.79	Tayside Avn Ltd	Dundee	2. 7.01T
G-BHDS	Reims Cessna F.152 II	1682		15.10.79	Tayside Avn Ltd	Dundee	27. 6.99T
G-BHDT	Socata TB-10 Tobago	59		29.11.79	D.T.Rasey	Gloucestershire	2.11.98T
G-BHDU	Reims Cessna F.152 II	1681		15.10.79	A.S.Bamrah Biggin Hill t/a Falcon F/Svs		27. 5.01T
G-BHDV	Cameron V-77 HAFB	585		1. 2.80	P.Glydon Barnt Green, Birmingham "Dormouse"		12. 5.99A
G-BHDW	Reims Cessna F.152 II	1652		15.10.79	Tayside Avn Ltd	Dundee	7. 5.01T
G-BHDX	Reims Cessna F.172N Skyhawk II	1889		5.10.79	J.Mitchell Newtownards t/a Skyhawk DX Grp		4. 6.01
G-BHDZ	Reims Cessna F.172N Skyhawk II	1911		3.12.79	Arrow Flying Ltd.	Denham	15. 5.01T
G-BHEC	Reims Cessna F.152 II	1676		3.12.79	Stapleford F/C Ltd	Stapleford	16. 7.01T
G-BHED	Reims Cessna FA.152 Aerobat	0359		3.12.79	TG Avn Ltd (Op Thanet F/C)	Manston	26. 4.01T
G-BHEG	SAN Jodel 150 Mascaret	46	PH-ULS OO-SET	3. 7.80	D.M.Griffiths Dinas Farm, Pwllheli		25. 6.98P
G-BHEH	Cessna 310G	310G-0016	N1720 N8916Z	14. 4.80	F.J.Shevill Bagby (Dismantled & stored 4.97)		9.12.96
G-BHEK	Scintex CP.1315-C3 Super Emeraude	923	F-BJMU	11.10.79	D.B.Winstanley	Barton	14. 9.99P
G-BHEL	SAN Jodel D.117	735	F-BIOA	8.10.79	N.Wright & C.M.Kettlewell Queach Farm, Bury St.Edmunds		17. 7.98P
G-BHEM	Bensen B.8MV EK.14 & PFA G/01-1016 (Rotax 503)			8.10.79	A.J.Maxwell	Great Orton	13. 9.99P
G-BHEN	Reims Cessna FA.152 Aerobat	0363		3. 1.80	Leicestershire A/C Ltd	Leicester	3.12.01T

Regn	Type	C/n	P/I	Date	Owner/operator	Probable Base	CA Expy
G-BHEO	Reims Cessna FR.182 Skylane RG II	0049		3. 1.80	J.G.Hogg	Rochester	6. 6.01
G-BHER	Socata TB-10 Tobago	60	4X-AKK G-BHER	19.10.79	Vale Avn Ltd	Biggin Hill	20. 7.00T
G-BHET	Socata TB-10 Tobago	62		19.10.79	Underwood Kitchens Ltd	Turweston	24. 4.98
G-BHEU	Thunder Ax7-65 Srs.1 HAFB	238		16.10.79	D.G.Such "Polomoche"	Birmingham	24. 2.99A
G-BHEV	PA-28R-200 Cherokee Arrow II	28R-7435159	PH-BOY N41244	23.10.79	P.Hardy t/a 7-Up Group	Netherthorpe	24. 3.00T
G-BHEX	Colt 56A HAFB	056		15.10.79	A.S.Dear, R.B.Green & W.S.Templeton t/a Hale Hot-Air Balloon Group "Superwasp" Fordingbridge		11.11.98A
G-BHEZ	SAN Jodel 150 Mascaret	22	F-BLDO	31. 1.80	A.Shorter t/a Air Yorkshire Group	Sherburn	20. 6.99P
G-BHFC	Reims Cessna F.152 II	1436		7. 4.78	TG Avn Ltd (Op Thanet F/C)	Manston	1. 8.99T
G-BHFE	PA-44-180 Seminole	44-7995324	ADAF 005 G-BHFE/N2383U	22.10.79	Grunwick Ltd (Op Bonus Avn)	Cranfield	9.12.99T
G-BHFF	Dormois Jodel D.112	322	F-BEKJ	19.10.79	P.A.Dowell	Watchford Farm, Yarcombe	28. 3.99P
G-BHFG	SNCAN Stampe SV-4C	45	F-BJDN Fr.Mil	31.10.79	Stormswift Ltd	Kemble	7.10.01T
G-BHFH	PA-34-200T Seneca II	34-7970482	N8075Q	23.10.79	Aerohire Ltd	Halfpenny Green	22. 1.01T
G-BHFI	Reims Cessna F.152 II	1685		22.10.79	R.Bilson & D.Turner t/a BAe Warton F/C	Blackpool	8. 4.01T
G-BHFJ	PA-28RT-201T Turbo Arrow IV	28R-7931298	N8072R	22.10.79	T.L.P.Delaney	White Waltham	6. 8.01
G-BHFK	PA-28-151 Cherokee Warrior	28-7615088	N8325C	12.12.79	Ilkeston Car Sales Ltd Jericho Farm, Lambley		19. 3.01
G-BHFR	Eiri PIK-20E Srs.1	20228	(D-KHJR) G-BHFR	8.11.79	J.T.Morgan "FR"	Husbands Bosworth	5. 8.98
G-BHFS	Robin DR.400/180 Regent	1304		7. 3.78	D.S.Chandler	Shoreham	17.10.99
G-BHGA	PA-31-310 Turbo Navajo	31-7912117	N3539M	12.11.79	Heltor Ltd	Exeter	25. 3.00
G-BHGC	PA-18-150 Super Cub	18-8793	PH-NKH N4447Z	3. 4.79	M.R. & P.A.Dawson	RAF Keevil	4.11.99
G-BHGF	Cameron V-56 HAFB	574		5.11.79	P.Spellward "Biggles"	Bristol	17. 4.99A
G-BHGJ	Jodel Wassmer D.120 Paris-Nice	336	F-BOYB	15. 1.80	Q.M.B.Oswell	RAF Halton	8. 4.99P
G-BHGK	Sikorsky S-76A II Plus	760049	N1545Y	27. 3.80	Bond Helicopters Ltd	Humberside	8. 5.00T
G-BHGO	PA-32-260 Cherokee Six	32-7800007	PH-BGP N9656C	16.11.79	DDCS Ltd (Op Cherokee Six Group)	Newcastle	12. 4.01T
G-BHGP	Socata TB-10 Tobago	100		17. 1.80	Inter Textiles Ltd	Stapleford	11. 3.99
G-BHGX	Colt 56B HAFB	057		22.11.79	M.N.Dixon "Prospect"	Bicester	22. 7.90A
G-BHGY	PA-28R-200-2 Cherokee Arrow II	28R-7435086	PH-NSL N57365	23.11.79	V.Humphries	Nottingham	28. 6.01
G-BHHB	Cameron V-77 HAFB	170		26.11.79	R.M.Powell "Pax"	Stockbridge	3. 9.99T
G-BHHE	CEA Jodel DR.1051/M1 Sicile Record	628	F-BMZC	26. 4.80	P.Bridges	Headcorn	6.12.01
G-BHHG	Reims Cessna F.152 II	1725		4. 3.80	TG Avn Ltd (Op Thanet Flying Club)	Manston	17. 6.01T
G-BHHH	Thunder Ax7-65 Bolt HAFB	245		5.12.79	C.A.Hendley (Essex) Ltd "Christmas"	Loughton	27. 9.87A
G-BHHK	Cameron N-77 HAFB	547		5.12.79	I.S.Bridge "Shadowfax II"	Shrewsbury	7.12.87A
G-BHHN	Cameron V-77 HAFB	549		29.11.79	P.Gooch t/a The Itchen Valley Balloon Group "Valley Crusader" Alresford, Hants		26. 7.99A
G-BHHX	Jodel D.112 (Built Valladeau)	223	F-BFAJ	19. 2.80	P.J.Reed & D.M.Gale	Dunkeswell	29. 6.98P
G-BHHZ	Rotorway Scorpion 133	MSI.1195		12.12.79	L.W. & O.Underwood (Stored 12.94) Stoneacre Farm, Farthing Corner		23. 9.81P
G-BHIB	Reims Cessna F.182Q Skylane II	0134		18.12.79	S.N.Chater & B.Payne	Jersey	3. 4.00
G-BHIC	Reims Cessna F.182Q Skylane II	0135		18.12.79	C.W.Makin	Sherburn	3. 6.99
G-BHIG	Colt 31A Air Chair HAFB	060	SE-... G-BHIG	12.12.79	P.A.Lindstrand Upplands Vasby, Sweden (Op S.Ericsson)		19. 3.98A
G-BHIH	Reims Cessna F.172N Skyhawk II	1945		3. 1.80	M.A.Wilkinson	Sywell	30. 7.01
G-BHII	Cameron V-77 HAFB	548		10.12.79	R.V.Brown "Tosca"	Maidenhead	2. 9.96A
G-BHIJ	Eiri PIK.20E Srs.1	20241		9. 1.80	I.W.Paterson	Portmoak	13. 4.98
G-BHIK	Adam RA.14 Loisirs (Cont A65)	11-bis	F-PHLK	6. 2.80	L.Lewis (Redcar) (Damaged nr Lancaster 17.4.85 - on rebuild)		20. 8.85P
G-BHIN	Reims Cessna F.152 II	1715		28. 1.80	P.Skinner	Egginton	7. 7.98T
G-BHIR	PA-28R-200 Cherokee Arrow	28R-35614	SE-FHP	21. 2.80	Factorcore Ltd (Op Manchester School of Flying)	Woodford	22.10.01T
G-BHIS	Thunder Ax7-65 Bolt HAFB	254		26.11.79	J.R.Wilson t/a The Hedgehoppers Balloon Grp "Yo-Yo"	Didcot	21. 3.96A
G-BHIT	Socata TB-9 Tampico	63		7.12.79	J.E.Iles	Biggin Hill	31. 1.01T
G-BHIY	Reims Cessna F.150K	0627	F-BRXR	18.12.79	G.J.Ball	(Romsey)	8. 4.01
G-BHJA	Cessna A152 Aerobat	A152-0835	N4954A	11. 3.80	Cornwall F/C Ltd (Damaged Bodmin 21.7.90; stored 10.95)	Bodmin	9. 4.92T
G-BHJB	Cessna A152 Aerobat	A152-0856	N4662A	11. 3.80	Sky Pro Ltd	Gamston	21.12.98T
G-BHJF	Socata TB-10 Tobago	83		2. 1.80	P.Crutchfield t/a Flying Fox Group	Blackbushe	16.12.00

Regn	Type	C/n	P/I	Date	Owner/operator	Probable Base	CA Expy
G-BHJI	Mooney M.20J (201)	24-0925	N3753H	11. 2.80	S.F.Lister	Gamston	19.12.98
G-BHJK	Maule M.5-235C Lunar Rocket	7296C	N56359	25. 2.80	S.Sampson	Old Sarum	28. 2.99
G-BHJN	Sportavia Fournier RF4D	4021	F-BORH	3. 1.80	G.E.Reeman & G.R.Beers t/a RF4 F/Grp	Enstone	16. 8.99P
G-BHJO	PA-28-161 Warrior II	28-7816213	OO-FLD N9507N/N6034H	4. 1.80	J.G.Chree, K.J.Utting & A.Sangster t/a The Brackla F/Grp	Inverness	12. 5.01
G-BHJS	Partenavia P.68B	172	I-KLUB	28.12.79	J.J.Watts & D.Fletcher	(Fordingbridge)	27. 5.01T
G-BHJU	Robin DR.400 2+2	1288	D-ECDK	9. 1.80	T.J.Harlow	Frid Farm, Bethersden	29. 5.98
G-BHKA*	Evans VP-1 Srs.2 (VW1834)	PFA/62-10496		4. 1.80	Not known Stoke Orchard, Cheltenham (Open store 7.91)		8.10.90P
G-BHKE	Bensen B.8MS VW.1 & PFA G/01-1009			7. 1.80	C.Baldwin	(Altrincham)	
G-BHKH	Cameron O-65 HAFB	592		7. 1.80	D.G.Body Leighton Buzzard t/a Mid-Bucks Farmers Balloon Grp "Daisy"		11. 8.96A
G-BHKJ	Cessna 421C Golden Eagle III (Robertson STOL conversion) 421C-0848		(N26596)	25. 1.80	Totaljet Ltd	Chester	10. 9.01T
G-BHKN*	Colt 14A Cloudhopper HAFB	068		17. 1.80	British Balloon Museum "Green Ice 2"	Newbury	
G-BHKR*	Colt 14A Cloudhopper HAFB	071		17. 1.80	British Balloon Museum "Green Ice 5"	Newbury	
G-BHKT	Wassmer Jodel D.112	1265	F-BMIQ	10. 1.80	K.A.Stewart & G.Oldfield t/a The Evans F/Grp	Croft-on-Tees	17. 6.99P
G-BHKV*	Gulfstream AA-5A Cheetah	AA5A-0894	N27465	31. 1.80	Not known Biggin Hill (Damaged Deanland 11.6.94; on rebuild 9.94)		24. 4.95T
G-BHLE	Robin DR.400/180 Regent	1466		25. 1.80	L.H.Mayall	Ronaldsway	2. 5.01
G-BHLH	Robin DR.400/180 Regent	1320	F-GBIG	11. 2.80	W.A.Clark	Netherthorpe	28. 6.01
G-BHLJ	Saffery-Rigg S.200 Skyliner HAFB (Model)	IAR/01		23. 1.80	I.A.Rigg "Skyliner"	Manchester	
G-BHLT	DH.82A Tiger Moth (Regd as c/n "911")	84997	ZS-DGA SAAF2272/T6697	9. 6.80	P.J. & A.J.Borsberry (On rebuild 8.90) Kidmore End, Reading		26. 2.90
G-BHLU	Alpavia Fournier RF3	79	F-BMTN	14. 4.80	M.C.Roper Swanton Morley (Op Norwich RF3 Grp)		1. 3.99P
G-BHLW	Cessna 120 (Cont C85)	10210	N73005 NC73005	24. 3.80	L.W.Scattergood "Sky Ranger"	Sherburn	16. 6.95P
G-BHLX	Grumman-American AA-5B Tiger	AA5B-0573	OY-GAR	1. 2.80	Tiger Avn (Jersey) Ltd	Jersey	10. 6.01
G-BHMA	SIPA 903	61	OO-FAE F-BGBK	13. 3.80	H.J.Taggart Ballymoney, Co.Antrim		18. 5.98P
G-BHMG	Reims Cessna FA.152 Aerobat	0368		10. 6.80	R.D.Smith	Popham	12.11.98
G-BHMI	Reims Cessna F.172N Skyhawk II	2036	G-WADE G-BHMI	6. 8.80	GMI Aviation Ltd	Blackpool	4. 3.99T
G-BHMJ	Avenger T.200-2112 HAFB (Model)	002		29. 1.80	R.Light "Lord Anthony I"	Stockport	
G-BHMK	Avenger T.200-2112 HAFB (Model)	003		29. 1.80	P.Kinder "Lord Anthony II"	Stockport	
G-BHMR	Stinson 108-3 Station Wagon	108-4352	F-BABO F-DABO/NC6352M	12. 2.80	D.G.French (Stored 12.95)	Sandown	23.11.90
G-BHMT	Evans VP-1 (VW1834)	PFA/62-10473		18. 2.80	P.E.J.Sturgeon Chestnut Farm, Tipps End		1. 6.99P
G-BHMY	Fokker F-27 Friendship 200	10196	F-GBDK (F-GBRV)/PK-PFS/JA8606/PH-FDL	6. 5.80	Air UK Ltd	Norwich	22. 5.99T
G-BHNA	Reims Cessna F.152 II	1683		12. 2.80	Sheffield A/C Ltd Netherthorpe (Damaged Netherthorpe 17.6.95; stored 5.97)		20.10.95T
G-BHNC	Cameron O-65 HAFB	588		7. 2.80	D. & C.Bareford "Hot N'Cold"	Kidderminster	5. 3.94A
G-BHND	Cameron N-65 HAFB	582		7. 2.80	S.M.Wellband	Frome	24. 6.89A
G-BHNG*	PA-23-250 Aztec E	27-7405432	N54125	13. 5.80	Riverside Metals Ltd (Crashed Shoreham 19.12.81; fuselage stored 3.97) Cradle Hill, Seaford		11. 8.83T
G-BHNK	Jodel Wassmer D.120A Paris-Nice	243	F-BLNK	26. 3.80	D.A.Bates St.Marys, Isles of Scilly t/a G-BHNK F/Grp		16. 2.99P
G-BHNL	Wassmer Jodel D.112	1206	F-BLNL	30. 1.80	J.C.Mansell Watchford Farm, Yarcombe		1. 7.01P
G-BHNO	PA-28-181 Archer II	28-8090211	N81413	7. 2.80	Airfluid Hydraulics & Pneumatics (Wolverhampton) Ltd Halfpenny Green		18. 6.98
G-BHNP	Eiri PIK-20E Srs.1	20253		29. 2.80	D.A.Sutton Sackville Lodge, Riseley (As "NP")		26. 5.99
G-BHNV	Westland-Bell 47G-3B1 (Line No.WAT/222)	WA/700	F-GHNM G-BHNV/XW180	11. 3.80	Leyline Helicopters Ltd	(Billingham)	28. 5.89T
G-BHNX	SAN Jodel D.117	493	F-BHNX	7. 9.78	A.J.Chalkley (On rebuild 4.91)	(Pwllheli)	12. 1.87P
G-BHOA	Robin DR.400/160 Major 80	1478		27. 1.80	M.F.Ferguson	Headcorn	15. 5.99
G-BHOF	Sikorsky S-61N Mk.II	61-824	LN-ONK G-BHOF/LN-ONK/G-BHOF	27. 2.80	Bristow Helicopters Ltd	Aberdeen	9. 7.01T
G-BHOH	Sikorsky S-61N Mk.II	61-827		25. 4.80	Bristow Helicopters Ltd "Ben Avon"	Aberdeen	20. 5.99T
G-BHOJ*	Colt 14A Cloudhopper HAFB	080		27. 2.80	G.Elson "Green Ice 6"	(Spain)	
G-BHOL	CEA Jodel DR.1050 Ambassadeur	35	F-BJQL	6. 2.80	D.G.Hart Inverness t/a Cawdor F/Grp "Nicolette"		28.10.01
G-BHOM	PA-18-95 Super Cub (L-18C-PI) (Frame No.18-1272)	18-1391	OO-PIU OO-HMT/ALAT 51-15391	7. 3.80	C.H.A.Bott Whitehall Farm, Benington		8. 3.99P

Regn	Type	C/n	P/I	Date	Owner/operator	Probable Base	CA Expy
G-BHOO	Livesey-Purves Thunder Ax7-65 HAFB	001		26. 2.80	D.Livesey & J.M.Purves "Scraps"	Crayke, York	
G-BHOR	PA-28-161 Warrior II	28-8016331	N82162	12. 6.80	M.Finta t/a Oscar Romeo F/Grp	Biggin Hill	12. 6.01
G-BHOT	Cameron V-65 HAFB	777		15. 9.81	J.A.Baker t/a The Dante Balloon Group "Le Billet Doux"	Marsh Benham	8. 8.99A
G-BHOZ	Socata TB-9 Tampico	84		11. 3.80	M.Brown		1. 5.99
G-BHPK	Piper J3C-65 Cub (L-4A-PI)	8979	F-BEPK Fr.Mil/42-38410	26. 2.80	P.H.J.Scrase t/a L4 Grp (As "236800/44/A" in USAAF c/s)	Priory Farm, Tibenham	3. 9.99P
	(Frame No.9098; official c/n is 12161/44-79865 which is F-BFYU)						
G-BHPL	CASA I-131E Jungmann	1058	E3B-350	17. 7.80	R.G.Gray (As "E3B-350/97-.." in Spanish AF c/s)	(London N1)	3. 8.99P
G-BHPM	PA-18-95 Super Cub (L-18C-PI)	18-1501	F-BOUR ALAT 51-15501	10. 4.80	P.I.Morgans (Stored 5.95) Furze Hill Farm, Rosemarket, Milford Haven		
	(Frame No.18-1469)						
G-BHPN	Colt 14A Cloudhopper HAFB	081	(SE-) G-BHPN	6. 3.80	Lindstrand Balloons Ltd (Op by S.Ericsson)	Upplands Vasby, Sweden	19. 3.99A
G-BHPS	Jodel Wassmer D.120A Paris-Nice	148	F-BIXI	11. 6.80	T.J. Price	(Aberdare)	27. 4.99P
G-BHPT	Piper J3C-65 Cub	"17792"	F-BSGQ LX-AIH/N70688/NC70688	10. 4.80	J.R.I.Rolfe t/a Rolfe Air Svs	Willington, Beds	12. 5.96P
	(Frame No.17792; the quoted p/i is suspect - possibly c/n 18105 ex NC71076/N71076)						
G-BHPX	Cessna 152 II	152-82994	N46073	26. 3.80	Southern Air Ltd	Shoreham	23. 7.01T
G-BHPY	Cessna 152 II	152-82983	N46009	26. 3.80	A.T.Hooper & T.E.Evans	Wellesbourne Mountford	10. 9.01T
G-BHPZ	Cessna 172N Skyhawk II	172-72017	N6411E	26. 3.80	O'Brien Properties Ltd	Shoreham	12. 9.99T
G-BHRB	Reims Cessna F.152 II	1707		20. 3.80	LAC (Enterprises) Ltd t/a Lancashire Aero Club	Barton	27. 1.02T
G-BHRC	PA-28-161 Warrior II	28-7916430	N9527N	3. 4.80	Sherwood F/Club Ltd (Damaged landing Sandtoft 17.1.99)	Nottingham	5. 1.01T
G-BHRH	Reims Cessna FA.150K Aerobat	0056	PH-ECB D-ECBL/(D-EKKW)	24. 3.80	Merlin F/C Ltd	Hucknall	6. 3.99T
G-BHRI	Saffery S.200 Phoenix HAFB (Model)	20	G-BGHD(1)	12. 3.80	N.J. & H.L.Dunnington "Can-Can"	Bristol	
G-BHRM	Reims Cessna F.152 II	1718	F-GCHR	8. 4.80	Aerohire Ltd	Wellesbourne Mountford	27. 9.02T
G-BHRN	Reims Cessna F.152 II	1728	F-GCHV	8. 4.80	J.Easson	Netherthorpe	25. 2.99T
G-BHRO	Rockwell Commander 112A	364	N1364J	20. 3.80	John Raymond Transport Ltd	Cardiff	17. 8.01
G-BHRP	PA-44-180 Seminole	44-8095021	N81602	1. 4.80	Merlinrun Ltd	Leicester	22.12.00T
G-BHRR	Menavia Piel CP.301A Emeraude	270	F-BISK	28. 3.80	T.W.Offen Lake Farm, Sutton Valence (Status uncertain)		28. 5.87P
G-BHRW	CEA Jodel DR.221 Dauphin	93	F-BPCP	10. 7.80	M.F.Filer & D.H.Williams	Bristol/Lulsgate	4. 3.99
G-BHRY	Colt 56A HAFB	030		2. 4.80	A.S.Davidson "Turkish Delight"	Burton-on-Trent	29. 5.95A
G-BHSA	Cessna 152 II	152-83693	(N4889B)	1. 5.80	D.Copley	Sherburn	11. 4.98T
G-BHSB	Cessna 172N Skyhawk II	172-72977	(N1225F)	25. 6.80	ABK Aviation Svcs Ltd	(Pontefract)	3. 1.02
G-BHSD	Scheibe SF-25E Super Falke	4357	D-KDGG	21. 7.80	Lasham Gliding Society Ltd	Lasham	1. 2.02
G-BHSE	Rockwell Commander 114	14161	N4831W AN-BRL/(N4831W)	15. 5.80	604 Squadron Flying Group Ltd	Booker	7. 5.99
G-BHSL	CASA I-131E Jungmann	1117	E3B-236	18. 6.80	H.I.Taylor (As "05-97") (Damaged Cranfield 6.7.96)	Gloucestershire	19. 7.96P
G-BHSN	Cameron N-56 HAFB	595		10. 4.80	I.Bentley	Bath	9. 5.97A
G-BHSP	Thunder Ax7-77Z HAFB	272		15. 4.80	G.A.Fisher t/a Out-Of-The-Blue "Chicago"	Guildford	23. 2.94A
	(Originally built as D-TRIER c/n 221)						
G-BHSS	Pitts S-1C Special (Lyc O-320)	C.1461M	N1704	19. 9.80	K.Lyons t/a Bottoms Up Syndicate	Chester	23. 6.99P
G-BHSY	CEA Jodel DR.1050 Sicile	546	F-BLZO	6. 5.80	T.R.Allebone	Easton Maudit	3. 9.01
G-BHTA	PA-28-236 Dakota	28-8011102	N8197H	22. 4.80	Dakota Ltd	Jersey	27. 7.96
G-BHTC	CEA Jodel DR.1051/M1 Sicile Record	581	F-BMGR	1. 5.80	G.Clark	Garston Farm, Marshfield	7.10.01
G-BHTD	Cessna T188C AGhusky	T188-03338T	(G-BGTN) N2033J	18. 4.80	ADS (Aerial) Ltd (Status uncertain - probably exported/destroyed)	(Benfleet)	26. 6.83A
G-BHTG	Thunder Ax6-56 Bolt HAFB	273		18. 4.80	F.R. & Mrs S.H.MacDonald "Halcyon"	Newdigate, Surrey	18.12.91A
G-BHTH	North American T-6G-NT Texan	168-176	N2807G 49-3072A	20. 5.80	J.J.Woodhouse (As "2807/V-103" -US Navy/VF-111 Sqdn c/s) (Damaged Bourne Park, nr Andover 13.3.95; on rebuild 8.97)	Shoreham	11. 5.97T
G-BHTR	Bell 206B JetRanger III	3035	N18098	27. 6.80	Galinsky Helicopter Corporation Ltd	(Pudsey)	12. 4.01
G-BHUB*	Douglas C-47A-85DL Dakota	19975	"G-AGIV" Sp.AF T3-29/N51V/N9985F/SE-BBH/43-15509	30. 4.80	Imperial War Museum/American Air Museum (As "315509/W7-S" in USAAF c/s) Duxford		
G-BHUE*	SAN Jodel DR.1050 Ambassadeur	185	F-BERM F-OBRM	21. 4.80	M.J.Harris (Cancelled by CAA 2.3.99; status unknown)	RAF Laarbruch	19.10.92
G-BHUG	Cessna 172N Skyhawk II	172-72985	N1283F	24. 6.80	F.G.Baulch t/a FGT Aircraft Hire	Dunkeswell	14. 9.01T
G-BHUI	Cessna 152 II	152-83144	N46932	27. 5.80	Galair International Ltd	Wellesbourne Mountford	19.11.01T
G-BHUJ	Cessna 172N Skyhawk II	172-71932	N5752E	27. 5.80	Northamptonshire School of Flying Ltd	Sywell	3. 2.99T

Regn	Type	C/n	P/I	Date	Owner/operator	Probable Base	CA Expy
G-BHUM	DH.82A Tiger Moth	85453	VT-DGA	9. 6.80	S.G.Towers	Beckwithshaw, Harrogate	1. 9.99
			VT-DDN/RIAF/SAAF 4622/DE457				
G-BHUO	Evans VP-2 (Cont A65)	PFA/63-10552		12. 5.80	D.A.Wood	Yearby	21.12.94P
G-BHUP*	Reims Cessna F.152 II	1773		2. 5.80	Not known	Stapleford	9.10.89T
					(Damaged nr Barton 17.5.89; stored 10.93)		
G-BHUR	Thunder Ax3 Mini Sky Chariot HAFB	277		9. 5.80	B.F.G.Ribbans "Sheppard"	Lancing	31. 8.90A
					(Op Balloon Preservation Group 10.97)		
G-BHUU	PA-25-260 Pawnee D	25-8056035		28. 5.80	Booker Gliding Club Ltd	Booker	23.10.00A
G-BHVB	PA-28-161 Warrior II	28-8016260	N9638N	16. 5.80	Bobbington Air Training School Ltd	Halfpenny Green	30. 7.01T
G-BHVF	SAN Jodel 150A Mascaret	11	F-BLDF	28.10.80	J.D.Walton	Swanborough Farm, Lewes	20. 4.99P
G-BHVP	Cessna 182Q Skylane II	182-67071	N97374	15.12.80	J.Kettles & C.Stevenson	Perth	22.10.99T
G-BHVR	Cessna 172N Skyhawk II	172-70196	N738SG	27. 5.80	Maxhill Ltd	Elstree	15. 5.00T
G-BHVV	Piper J3C-65 Cub (L-4A-PI)	8953	F-BGXF 42-38384	27. 6.80	P.R.Wright (Stored 8.98)	Aboyne	3. 7.85P
	(Frame No.9048; regd with c/n 10291/43-1430 which was F-BEGF; frames probably exchanged in 1953 rebuild)						
G-BHWA	Reims Cessna F.152 II	1775		28. 3.80	M.Housley & J.H.Mills t/a Lincoln Aviation	Wickenby	2. 6.01T
G-BHWB	Reims Cessna F.152 II	1776	(G-BHWA)	14. 4.80	M.Housley & J.H.Mills t/a Lincoln Aviation	Wickenby	19. 7.01T
G-BHWH	Weedhopper JC-24A (EC-34-PM) (Modified to JC-24C)	0074		23. 4.80	G.A.Clephane "Dream Machine" (As "Bu.126603" in US Navy c/s)	Basingstoke	30.11.86E
G-BHWK	Socata MS.880B Rallye Club	870	F-BONK	27. 8.80	L.L.Gayther	Shobdon	23. 9.01
G-BHWS	Reims Cessna F.152 II	1785	(G-BHHD)	16. 6.80	Alarmond Ltd t/a Edinburgh F/C	Perth	24. 8.95T
	(Damaged Whalsay, Shetland Isles 15.7.94; on rebuild 12.95)						
G-BHWY	PA-28R-200-2 Cherokee Arrow II	28R-7435059	N56904	17. 6.80	P.R.Gould & R.B.Cheek t/a Kilo Foxtrot F/Grp	Sandown	6. 4.99
G-BHWZ	PA-28-181 Archer II	28-7890299	N3379M	8. 4.80	I.R.McCue	Southampton	20. 5.01
G-BHXA	Scottish Avn Bulldog 120/1210	BH120-407	Botswana DF OD1/G-BHXA	9. 6.80	D.A.Williams (Stored 1.97)	Chester	AC
G-BHXB	Scottish Avn Bulldog 120/1210	BH120-408	Botswana DF OD2/G-BHXB	9. 6.80	D.A.Williams (Op Deltair Ltd)	Chester	23. 4.98T
G-BHXD	Jodel Wassmer D.120 Paris-Nice	258	F-BMIA	3. 7.80	P.H.C.Hall	Manor Farm, Inglesham	21. 6.99P
G-BHXK	PA-28-140 Cherokee	28-21106	VR-HGB 9V-BAJ/(9M-AOM)	4. 7.80	J.C.King t/a GXK F/Grp	Southampton	1. 6.00
G-BHXL	Evans VP-2 (VW1834)	PFA/63-10520		17. 6.80	R.S.Wharton	(Cardiff)	
G-BHXN*	Van's RV-3 EAA/105098 & PFA/99-10518			9. 6.80	Not known (Noted 2.99)	Bourn	
G-BHXS	Jodel Wassmer D.120 Paris-Nice	133	F-BIXS	27. 8.80	I.R.Willis	Dundee	19. 7.99P
G-BHXT*	Thunder Ax6-56Z HAFB	281		2. 7.80	Not known "Blue Eagle"	(Wigan)	N/E(A)
G-BHXY	Piper J3C-65 Cub (L-4H-PI) (Frame No.11733)	11905	D-EAXY F-BFQX/44-79609	1. 7.80	F.W.Rogers (As "44-79609"/"PR"-"L4 in USAAC c/s) "Heather"	Bodmin	18. 6.99P
G-BHYA	Cessna R182 Skylane RGII	R182-00532	N1717R	10. 7.80	Card Tech Ltd	Denham	7. 3.99
G-BHYC	Cessna 172RG Cutlass II	172RG-0404	(N4868V)	24. 6.80	IB Aeroplanes Ltd.	(Coleraine, NI)	13. 2.99T
G-BHYD	Cessna R172K Hawk XPII	R172-2734	N736RS	11.12.80	Sylmar Avn & Svs Ltd	Lower Wasing Farm, Aldermaston	16. 9.99
G-BHYE	PA-34-200T Seneca II	34-8070233	N8225U	27. 6.80	Oxford Aviation Services Ltd	Oxford	10. 6.01T
G-BHYF	PA-34-200T Seneca II	34-8070234	N8225V	27. 6.80	Oxford Aviation Services Ltd	Oxford	3.10.01T
G-BHYG	PA-34-200T Seneca II	34-8070235	N8225X	30. 6.80	Oxford Aviation Services Ltd	Oxford	27. 9.01T
G-BHYI	SNCAN Stampe SV-4A	18	F-BAAF Fr.Mil	11. 7.80	P.A.Irwin	White Waltham	21.10.99
G-BHYO	Cameron N-77 HAFB	659		30. 6.80	Adventure Balloon Co Ltd	(London W3)	N/E
G-BHYP	Reims Cessna F.172M Skyhawk II	1108	OY-BFR	30. 6.80	Avior Ltd	Oxford	16. 6.99T
G-BHYR	Reims Cessna F.172M	0922	OY-DZH SE-FZH/(OH-CFQ)	30. 6.80	S.D.Undrill t/a G-BHYR Group	Stapleford	23. 6.99
G-BHYS*	PA-28-181 Archer II	28-8090319	N8218Y	30. 6.80	Not know	Biggin Hill	22. 8.86T
	(Damaged Biggin Hill 7.12.85; wreck in open storage 8.97)						
G-BHYV	Evans VP-1 (VW1600)	LC.2 & PFA/1569		2. 7.80	L.Chiappi	(Blackburn)	
	(Flown 5.89; stored Blackpool 8.90 - status uncertain)						
G-BHYX	Cessna 152 II	152-81832	N67434	4. 7.80	Stapleford F/C Ltd	Stapleford	7. 3.99T
G-BHZE	PA-28-181 Archer II	28-7890291	OO-FLR (OO-HEM)/N3053M	4.11.80	Northfield Garage Ltd (Op Edinburgh F/C)	Edinburgh	18.11.99T
G-BHZF	Evans VP-2 (Cont A65)	PFA/63-10509		9. 7.80	W.J.Evans "Miss Louise" (Damaged nr Swansea 3.7.93)	RAF St.Athan	30. 3.94P
G-BHZH	Reims Cessna F.152 II	1786		25. 7.80	One Zero One Three Ltd (Op Guernsey Flight Training)	Guernsey	21. 9.01T
G-BHZK	Grumman-American AA-5B Tiger	AA5B-0743	N28670	8. 9.80	R.G.Seth-Smith t/a Zulu Kilo Grp	Elstree	23. 5.99
G-BHZO	Gulfstream AA-5A Cheetah	AA5A-0692	N26750	21. 7.80	Scotia Safari Ltd (Op Prestwick Flt Centre)	Prestwick	12.11.01T
G-BHZR	Scottish Avn Bulldog 120/1210	BH120-410	Botswana DF OD4/G-BHZR	23. 7.80	M.A.Elobeid (Stored 8.97)	Henstridge	7.10.80
G-BHZS	Scottish Avn Bulldog 120/1210	BH120-411	Botswana DF OD5/G-BHZS	23. 7.80	D.A.Williams	Chester	8. 2.99T

Regn	Type	C/n	P/I	Date	Owner/operator	Probable Base	CA Expy
G-BHZT	Scottish Avn Bulldog 120/1210			23. 7.80	Jean M.Bax	Old Sarum	29. 1.99T
		BH120-412	Botswana DF OD6/G-BHZT				
G-BHZU	Piper J3C-65 Cub (L-4B-PI)	9775	F-BETO	17. 7.80	J.K.Tomkinson		25. 6.99P
	(Cont O-200-A)		(F-BFKH)/43-914		Brook Farm, Boylestone, Derbyshire		
	(Regd with Frame No.9606 which was fitted to F-BETO in 1961 rebuild replacing c/n 13164 ex 45-4424)						
G-BHZV	Jodel Wassmer D.120A Paris-Nice	278	F-BMON	23. 7.80	K.J.Scott		26. 6.99P
						Stoneacre Farm, Farthing Corner	
G-BHZX	Thunder Ax7-69A HAFB	288		25. 7.80	R.J. & H.M.Beattie	Aylesbury	2. 4.94A
					"After Eight"		

G-BIAA-BIZZ

Regn	Type	C/n	P/I	Date	Owner/operator	Probable Base	CA Expy
G-BIAC	Socata Rallye 235E Gabier	13323		17. 7.80	Aerobatic Displays Ltd & A.E.Kay Oakley		18. 6.99T
G-BIAH	Wassmer Jodel D.112	1218	F-BMAH	20. 8.80	D.Mitchell Muirhouses Farm, Errol		27. 4.99P
G-BIAI	WMB.2 Windtracker HAFB (Model)	008		1. 7.80	I.Chadwick Horsham		
					t/a Unicorn Grp "Amanda I"		
G-BIAK	Socata TB-10 Tobago	150		17. 7.80	Westmead Business Group Ltd Biggin Hill		15. 1.00
G-BIAL	Rango NA.8 Super HAFB (Model)	AL.9		28. 7.80	Anne M.Lindsay Leeds		
					t/a Rango Balloon & Kite Co "Tristophone"		
G-BIAP	PA-16-108 Clipper	16-732	F-BBGM F-OAGS	25. 6.80	P.J.Bish Draycott Farm, Chiseldon		23. 2.01
G-BIAR*	Rigg Skyliner II HAFB (Model)	AKC-59 & IAR/02		9. 7.80	I.A.Rigg Manchester		
G-BIAU*	Sopwith Pup Replica (80hp Le Rhone)	EMK/002		4. 1.83	Fleet Air Arm Museum RNAS Yeovilton (As "N6452" in RNAS c/s)		13. 9.89P
G-BIAX	Taylor JT.2 Titch	GFR-1 & PFA/3228		30. 7.80	J.T.Everest (Fairoaks) (Nearing completion 9.97)		
G-BIAY	Grumman-American AA-5 Traveler	AA5-0423	OY-GAD N7123L	26. 8.80	S.Martin Southend		26. 6.99
G-BIAZ*	Cameron AT-165 (Helium/Hot-Air) Free Balloon	400		7. 2.78	British Balloon Museum Newbury "Zanussi"		31.10.78
			(HAFB part destroyed Trubenbuch, Austria 14.1.80; inner helium cell envelope held)				
G-BIBA	Socata TB-9 Tampico	149		17. 7.80	TB Avn Ltd Denham		14. 7.99
G-BIBB	Mooney M.20C Mark 21	2803	OH-MOD	22. 7.80	P.M.Breton Kemble		2.12.01
G-BIBG	Sikorsky S-76A II Plus	760083		18. 8.80	Bristow Helicopters Ltd Redhill "Loch Seaforth"		9. 5.01T
G-BIBJ	Enstrom 280C-UK-2 Shark	1187		13. 8.80	Kemspray Ltd Coleraine, Co.Londonderry		30.11.01
G-BIBK*	Taylor JT.2 Titch	PFA/3233		12. 8.80	J.G.McTaggart (Cancelled by CAA 17.3.99) North Commonside Farm, Inchinnan, Renfrew		
G-BIBN	Reims Cessna FA150K Aerobat	0078	F-BSHN	29.10.80	G.A.Eaton & C.G.Wilson Shoreham		22.11.01T
G-BIBO	Cameron V-65 HAFB	667		7. 8.80	I.Harris "Diadem" Devizes		30. 6.89A
G-BIBS	Cameron P-20 HAFB	671		14. 8.80	Cameron Balloons Ltd Bristol		
G-BIBT	Gulfstream AA-5B Tiger	AA5B-1047	N4518V	8. 9.80	Vizor Tempered Glass Ltd (Port Talbot)		21. 3.01
G-BIBW	Reims Cessna F.172N Skyhawk II	1756		13.10.78	O. Hill t/a Farley Avn (Winchester)		11. 9.98T
G-BIBX	WMB.2 Windtracker HAFB (Model)	9		18. 8.80	I.A.Rigg "Bumble" Manchester		
G-BICC	Vulture TX3 HAFB (Model)	CC.1		31. 7.80	C.P.Clitheroe (Not built) Altrincham		
G-BICD	Auster 5	735	F-BFXH MT166	20. 8.80	R.T.Parsons Sturgate		1. 7.99P
G-BICE	North American AT-6C-1NT Harvard IIA	88-9755	FAP1545 SAAF 7084/EX302/41-33275	3. 9.80	C.M.L.Edwards Seething (As "41-33275/CE" in US Army c/s)		8. 9.99T
G-BICG	Reims Cessna F.152 II	1796		3. 9.80	A.S.Bamrah Biggin Hill t/a Falcon F/Svs		24. 3.99T
G-BICJ	Monnett Sonerai II	726 & PFA/15-10531		22. 8.80	I.Parr (Berwick-on-Tweed)		20.10.90P
	(VW 1834)				(On rebuild 1997)		
G-BICM	Colt 56A HAFB	095		1. 9.80	W.S.Templeton & R.B.Green Fordingbridge		11.11.98A
					t/a The Avon Advertiser Balloon Club "Ladybird"		
G-BICN	Sequoia Falco F.8L	PU-001-2 & PFA/100-10563		3. 9.80	R.J.Barber (Beccles)		
G-BICP	Robin DR.360 Chevalier	610	F-BSPH	2.10.80	Bravo India F/Grp Ltd Liverpool		13. 5.99
G-BICR	Jodel Wassmer D.120A Paris-Nice	135	F-BIXR	5. 9.80	M.Ashfield White Waltham		23. 5.99P
					t/a Beehive F/Grp		
G-BICS	Robin R.2100A Club	128	F-GBAC	4.12.80	I.Young Sandown		27. 4.00
G-BICT	Evans VP-1	PFA/62-10455		12. 8.80	A.C.Combe & D.L.Tribe Long Marston		20. 2.97P
	(VW1600)				(Damaged nr Evesham 4.8.96)		
G-BICU	Cameron V-56 HAFB	680		9. 9.80	S.D.Bather & D.Scott "Nobby" Melksham		4. 5.98A
G-BICW	PA-28-161 Warrior II	28-7916309	N2091U	8.10.80	D.Gellhorn Blackbushe		3. 2.00
G-BICX	Maule M.5-235C Lunar Rocket	7287C	G-MAUL(1) N56352	2. 2.81	A.T.Jeans & J.F.Clarkson Compton Chamberlayne, Salisbury		19. 7.99
G-BICY	PA-23-160 Apache	23-1640	OO-AOL 5N-ACL/VR-NDF/PH-ACL/N4010P	26. 9.80	A.M.Lynn Sibson (Op Busy Bee)		9. 7.01T
G-BIDD	Evans VP-1	PFA/62-10974		27.10.78	Jane Hodgkinson Dunkirk, Canterbury		29. 9.99P
	(VW1600) (Initially regd with c/n PFA/62-10167 and combined with both projects)						
G-BIDF	Reims Cessna F.172P Skyhawk II	2045	(PH-JPO)	18. 9.80	E.Alexander Redhill		25. 2.00T
G-BIDG	SAN Jodel 150A Mascaret		F-BLDG	11. 9.80	D.R.Gray Barton		26. 6.98P
G-BIDH	Cessna 152 II	152-80546	G-DONA G-BIDH/N25234	12. 9.80	J.A. & R.M.Nichol Carlisle t/a Cumbria A/C		1. 4.99T
G-BIDI	PA-28R-201 Arrow III	28R-7837135	N3759M	11.11.80	Ambrit Ltd Elstree		9. 5.99
G-BIDJ	PA-18A-150 Super Cub (Frame No.18-6089)	18-6007	PH-MAY N7798D	22. 9.80	A.B.Plant (Bristol) Ltd Dunsford, Exeter		15. 7.00
G-BIDK	PA-18-150 Super Cub (L-21A-PI)	"18-6591"	PH-MAI R.Neth AF R-211/51-15679/N7194K	22. 9.80	R.G.Warwick Kilrea, Co.Londonderry t/a Kemspray		19. 8.01
	(This is a composite a/c - PH-MAI was originally c/n 18-6591 (Frame No.18-6714) ex LN-TVB/N9285D but was rebuilt in 1976 using Frame No.18-503 (c/n 18-565) and ex R.Neth AF R-211 as shown)						
G-BIDO	Piel CP.301A Emeraude	327	F-POIO	25. 3.81	A.R.Plumb Hill Farm, Nayland (Stored 9.97)		24. 6.97P
G-BIDU	Cameron V-77 HAFB	660		8. 1.81	E.Eleazor "Margaret" London W1		26. 8.87A
G-BIDV*	Colt 17A Cloudhopper HAFB	789		29. 1.79	British Balloon Museum Newbury & Library "Smirnoff Cloudhopper"		N/E(A)
	(Second canopy - original was Colt 14A c/n 034 which may be held by the Museum)						

Regn	Type	C/n	P/I	Date	Owner/operator	Probable Base	CA Expy
G-BIDW*	Sopwith "1 1/2" Strutter rep (Le Clerget)	WA/5	"9382"	24. 9.80	RAF Museum (As "A8226" in 45 Sqn RFC c/s)	Hendon	29.12.80P*
G-BIDX	Dormois Jodel D.112	876	F-BIQY	19. 9.80	H.N.Nuttall & P.Turton Ash House Farm, Winsford		15.10.99P
G-BIEF	Cameron V-77 HAFB	679		25. 9.80	D.S.Bush "Daedalus"	Hertingfordbury, Herts	6. 3.94A
G-BIEJ	Sikorsky S-76A II Plus	760097		21.10.80	Bristow Helicopters Ltd "Glenlossie"	North Denes	21. 2.01T
G-BIEN	Jodel Wassmer D.120A Paris-Nice	218	F-BKNK	3. 6.81	R.J.Baker "The Lady Savage"	Stapleford	24. 2.99P
G-BIEO	Wassmer Jodel D.112	1296	F-BMOK	19. 3.82	S.C.Solley t/a Clipgate Flyers	Clipgate Farm, Denton	1. 8.99P
G-BIES	Maule M.5-235C Lunar Rocket	7334C	N56394	24. 7.81	W.Procter t/a William Procter Farms	Stowes Farm, Tillingham	26. 3.00
G-BIET	Cameron O-77 HAFB	674		30. 9.80	G.M.Westley "Archimedes"	London SW15	5. 6.91A
G-BIEY	PA-28-151 Cherokee Warrior	28-7715213	PH-KDH OO-HCB	10.11.80	A.S.Bamrah t/a Falcon Flying Services	Southend	1. 1.01T
G-BIFA	Cessna 310R II	310R-1606	N36868	29. 1.81	Booth Plant & Equipment Ltd	Leeds-Bradford	31. 7.00
G-BIFB	PA-28-150 Cherokee C	28-1968	4X-AEC	6.10.80	N.A.Ayub	Biggin Hill	12.12.98T
G-BIFN	Bensen B.8MR KW.1 & PFA G/01-1010			7.10.80	B.Gunn	(North Ferriby)	
G-BIFO	Evans VP-1 PFA/62-10411 (VW1834)			29. 9.80	R.Broadhead	Bagby	6. 7.99P
G-BIFP*	Colt 56C HAFB	097		14.10.80	J.Philp t/a The Serendipity Balloon Grp "Fire Engine"	Liskeard	
G-BIFY	Reims Cessna F.150L	0829	PH-CEZ	9.10.80	B.W.Davis t/a Astra Associates	Elstree	21. 8.99T
G-BIFZ	Partenavia P.68C	229		24. 6.81	Jet Airmotive Ltd	Henstridge	14.10.99T
G-BIGF	Thunder Ax7-77 Bolt HAFB	295		20.10.80	M.D.Steuer & Christine A.Allen "Low Rider"	Monmouth	6. 9.91A
G-BIGJ	Reims Cessna F.172M	0936	PH-SKT	2.12.80	V.D.Speck	Clacton	4. 7.99T
G-BIGK	Taylorcraft BC-12D (Cont A65)	8302	N96002 NC96002	29.10.80	N.P.S.Ramsay	Pauncefoot, Romsey	19. 7.99P
G-BIGL	Cameron O-65 HAFB	690		22.10.80	P.L.Mossman "Biggles"	Bristol	24. 2.97A
G-BIGP	Bensen B.8M PFA G/01-1005 (McCulloch)			14.10.80	R.H.S.Cooper	Cross Houses, Shrewsbury	20.10.97P
G-BIGR	Avenger T.200-2122 HAFB (Model)	004		6.10.80	R.Light	Stockport	
G-BIGT*	Colt 77A HAFB	078		28. 2.80	British Balloon Museum "Big T" (Damaged Belton Hall nr Grantham 23.8.81; stored)	Newbury	20. 2.83A
G-BIGX	Bensen B.8M JRM.2 & PFA G/01-1033			5.11.80	W.C.Turner	Malvern	
G-BIGZ	Scheibe SF-25B Falke	46142	D-KCAI	22.12.80	R.F.Smith & C.R.Sproson t/a G-BIGZ Syndicate	Saltby	22. 7.99
G-BIHD	Robin DR.400/160 Major 80	1510		29.10.80	K.B.Mainstone	Thurrock	13. 5.99
G-BIHE	Reims Cessna FA.152 Aerobat	0373		6.11.80	Walkbury Aviation Ltd (Damaged nr Sheerness 10.3.99)	Sibson	5. 3.99T
G-BIHF	Replica Plans SE.5A (Cont O-200-A) (Plans No. 079275)	PFA/20-10548		27.10.80	K.J.Garrett "Lady Di" (As "F-943" in 92 Sqdn RFC c/s)	White Waltham	15. 6.99P
G-BIHG	PA-28-140 Cherokee	28-24376	OO-JAR N6686J	25.11.80	P.W.Wilson t/a Parham Flying Group	Framlingham	7. 6.99
G-BIHI	Cessna 172M Skyhawk II	172-66854	(G-BIHA) N1125U	18.11.80	L.R.Haunch t/a Fenland Flying School	Fenland	14. 3.99T
G-BIHO	DHC.6 Twin Otter 310	738	A6-ADB G-BIHO	9. 1.81	Isles of Scilly Skybus Ltd	St.Just	18. 4.00T
G-BIHP	Van Den Bemden 1000m3 Gas Free Balloon (C/n quoted as "18" on Belgian C of R; believed rebuilt with 600m3 balloon c/n VDB-47)	VDB-38	OO-VBA	19.12.80	J.J.Harris "Belgica"	London SW6	5. 7.99
G-BIHT	PA-17 Vagabond (Cont A65)	17-41	N138N N8N/N4626H/NC4626H	9. 1.81	G.H.Cork	Orchard Farm, Fradley	16. 6.98P
G-BIHU	Saffery S.200 HAFB (Model)	25		5.11.80	B.L.King	Coulsdon	
G-BIHX	Bensen B.8MR PFA G/01-1003 (Rotax 503)			12.11.80	P.P.Willmott	North Coates	20.10.99P
G-BIIA	Alpavia Fournier RF3	51	F-BMTA	14.11.80	T.M.W.Webster t/a Double M F/Grp (Status uncertain)	(Pershore)	16. 7.87P
G-BIIB	Reims Cessna F.172M Skyhawk II	1110	PH-GRE	18.11.80	Civil Service F/C (Biggin Hill) Ltd	Biggin Hill	24. 4.00T
G-BIID	PA-18-95 Super Cub (L-18C-PI) (Frame No.18-1558)	18-1606	OO-LPA OO-HMK/ALAT 18-1606/51-15606	5. 1.81	D.A.Lacey	Cumbernauld	26. 5.99P
G-BIIE	Reims Cessna F.172P Skyhawk II	2051		31.12.80	Sterling Helicopters Ltd	Norwich	28. 2.99T
G-BIIF*	Sportavia Fournier RF4D	4047	G-BVET F-BOXG	25.11.80	Not known (Stored 8.97)	Biggin Hill	18. 3.93A
G-BIIK	Socata MS.883 Rallye 115	1552	F-BSAP	28.11.80	Chiltern Flyers Ltd Park Farm, Eaton Bray		22.10.01
G-BIIL	Thunder Ax6-56 Bolt HAFB	306		12.11.80	G.W.Reader	Selby	1. 6.84A
G-BIIP	PBN BN-2B-27 Islander	2103	6Y-JQJ 6Y-JKJ/N411JA/G-BIIP	1.12.80	Hebridean Air Services Ltd	Glasgow	AC
G-BIIT	PA-28-161 Warrior II	28-8116052	N82744	1.12.80	Tayside Aviation Ltd	Glenrothes	6. 3.99T
G-BIIV	PA-28-181 Archer II	28-7990028	N20875	19.12.80	Stratton Motor Co (Norfolk) Ltd	Crowfield	10. 9.00T
G-BIIX	Rango NA-12 HAFB (Model) (Regd as c/n NHP-12)	NHP.11		1.12.80	N.H.Ponsford t/a Rango Balloon & Kite Co "Lament for Jok"	Leeds	
G-BIIZ	Great Lakes 2T-1A Sport Trainer	57	N603K NC603K	1. 4.81	C.D.Baird	(Farnham)	4. 2.99P

Regn	Type	C/n	P/I	Date	Owner/operator	Probable Base	CA Expy
G-BIJB	PA-18-150 Super Cub	18-8009001	N23923 (N2573H)	18. 8.80	Essex Gliding Club Ltd	North Weald	31. 3.01
G-BIJD	Bolkow Bo.208C Junior	636	PH-KAE (PH-DYM)/OO-SIS/(D-EGFA)	9.12.80	C.G.Stone	Biggin Hill	29. 7.01
G-BIJE	Piper J3C-65 Cub (L-4A-PI) (Frame No.8504)	8367	F-BIGN Fr.AF/42-15248	5. 5.81	R.L.Hayward & A.G.Scott (On rebuild 4.91)	Cardiff	
G-BIJS	Phoenix Luton LA-4A Minor (VW 1600) PAL/1348 & PFA/835			18. 5.78	I.J.Smith	Brook Farm, Boylestone	14.11.95P
G-BIJU	Menavia Piel CP.301A Emeraude	221	G-BHTX F-BIJU	10. 6.80	A.G.Bailey t/a Eastern Taildraggers F/Grp	Stapleford	20. 4.99P
G-BIJV	Reims Cessna F.152 II	1813		22.12.80	A.S.Bamrah t/a Falcon F/Svs	Biggin Hill	4. 3.99T
G-BIJW	Reims Cessna F.152 II	1820		22.12.80	A.S.Bamrah t/a Falcon F/Svs (Op European Flyers)	Blackbushe	15. 2.99T
G-BIJX	Reims Cessna F.152 II	1829		29.12.80	A.S.Bamrah t/a Falcon F/Svs	Lydd	29. 5.99T
G-BIKA	Boeing 757-236	22172	(N757B)	28. 3.83	British Airways plc (Blue Poole t/s)	Heathrow	28. 3.00T
G-BIKB	Boeing 757-236	22173		25. 1.83	British Airways plc (Chelsea Rose t/s)	Heathrow	26. 1.00T
G-BIKC	Boeing 757-236	22174		31. 1.83	British Airways plc (Emmly Masanabo/Ndebele t/s)	Heathrow	9. 2.00T
G-BIKD	Boeing 757-236	22175		10. 3.83	British Airways plc (Emmly Masanabo/Ndebele t/s)	Heathrow	14. 3.00T
G-BIKE	PA-28R-200 Cherokee Arrow II	28R-7335173	OY-DVT N55047	18. 4.80	R.V.Webb Ltd	Elstree	17. 8.01
G-BIKF	Boeing 757-236	22177	(G-BIKG)	28. 4.83	British Airways plc (Wanula Dreaming t/s)	Heathrow	28. 4.00T
G-BIKG	Boeing 757-236	22178	(G-BIKH)	26. 8.83	British Airways plc "Stirling Castle"	Heathrow	26. 8.00T
G-BIKH	Boeing 757-236	22179	(G-BIKI)	18.10.83	British Airways plc (Golden Khokhloma t/s)	Heathrow	20.10.00T
G-BIKI	Boeing 757-236	22180	(G-BIKJ)	30.11.83	British Airways plc "Tintagel Castle"	Heathrow	1.12.00T
G-BIKJ	Boeing 757-236	22181	(G-BIKK)	9. 1.84	British Airways plc (Waves of the City t/s)	Heathrow	11. 1.01T
G-BIKK	Boeing 757-236	22182	(G-BIKL)	1. 2.84	British Airways plc "Eilean Donan Castle"	Heathrow	1. 2.01T
G-BIKL	Boeing 757-236	22183	(G-BIKM)	29. 2.84	British Airways plc (Mountain of the Birds/Benyhone Tartan t/s)	Heathrow	28. 2.01T
G-BIKM	Boeing 757-236	22184	N8293V (G-BIKN)	21. 3.84	British Airways plc "Glamis Castle"	Heathrow	22. 3.01T
G-BIKN	Boeing 757-236	22186	(G-BIKP)	23. 1.85	British Airways plc "Bodiam Castle"	Heathrow	24. 1.02T
G-BIKO	Boeing 757-236	22187	(G-BIKR)	14. 2.85	British Airways plc "Harlech Castle"	Heathrow	18. 2.02T
G-BIKP	Boeing 757-236	22188	(G-BIKS)	11. 3.85	British Airways plc "Enniskillen Castle"	Heathrow	14. 3.99T
G-BIKR	Boeing 757-236	22189	(G-BIKT)	29. 3.85	British Airways plc "Bamburgh Castle"	Heathrow	2. 4.99T
G-BIKS	Boeing 757-236	22190	(G-BIKU)	31. 5.85	British Airways plc "Corfe Castle"	Heathrow	2. 6.99T
G-BIKT	Boeing 757-236	23398		1.11.85	British Airways plc (Crossing Borders t/s)	Heathrow	3.11.99T
G-BIKU	Boeing 757-236	23399		7.11.85	British Airways plc "Inverary Castle"	Heathrow	7.11.99T
G-BIKV	Boeing 757-236	23400		9.12.85	British Airways plc "Raglan Castle"	Heathrow	11.12.99T
G-BIKW	Boeing 757-236	23492		7. 3.86	British Airways plc (Martha Masanabo/Ndelhone t/s)	Heathrow	9. 3.99T
G-BIKX	Boeing 757-236	23493		14. 3.86	British Airways plc (Delftblue Daybreak t/s)	Heathrow	16. 3.99T
G-BIKY	Boeing 757-236	23533		28. 3.86	British Airways plc (Primavara t/s)	Heathrow	31. 3.99T
G-BIKZ	Boeing 757-236	23532		15. 5.86	British Airways plc "Kenilworth Castle"	Heathrow	15. 5.99T
G-BILA*	Dalotel DM-165L Viking	01	F-PPZE	5. 2.81	Not known (On rebuild 1994)	(Bristol)	14. 9.83P
G-BILB	WMB-2 Windtracker HAFB (Model)	14		22. 1.81	B.L.King	Coulsdon	
G-BILE	Scruggs BL-2B HAFB (Model)	81231		13. 3.81	P.D.Ridout	Botley	
G-BILF	Practavia Sprite 125 PFA/05-10467			17.12.80	G.Harfield	(Derby)	
G-BILG	Scruggs BL-2B HAFB (Model)	81232		13. 3.81	P.D.Ridout	Botley	
G-BILI	Piper J3C-65 Cub (L-4J-PI)	13207	F-BDTB 45-4467	14. 1.81	R.P.Grace & S.C.Wilson t/a G-BILI F/Grp (As "454467/J/44" in US Army c/s)	White Waltham	26. 5.99P
	(Original p/i is unconfirmed; a/c appears to have Frame No.15044 (c/n 15449) but current as N87791)						
G-BILJ	Reims Cessna FA.152 Aerobat	0376		31.12.80	Bournemouth F/Club Ltd	Bournemouth	30. 5.99T
G-BILK	Reims Cessna FA.152 Aerobat	0372		9. 1.81	Exeter F/C Ltd	Exeter	13. 5.99T
G-BILL	PA-25-260 Pawnee D	25-7856028		3. 1.79	W.J. & A.E.Taylor t/a Pawnee Avn	Aboyne	28. 5.00A

Regn	Type	C/n	P/I	Date	Owner/operator	Probable Base	CA Expy
G-BILR	Cessna 152 II	152-84822	N4822P	19. 3.81	Shropshire Aero Club Ltd	Sleap	8. 5.99A
G-BILS	Cessna 152 II	152-84857	N4954P	3. 6.81	Keen Leasing (IOM) Ltd.	(Castletown)	24. 6.99A
G-BILU	Cessna 172RG Cutlass II	172RG-0564	N5540V	29. 1.81	R.M.English & Sons Ltd	Full Sutton	14. 6.00A
G-BILZ	Taylor JT.1 Monoplane	PFA/55-10244		15.12.80	A.Petherbridge	Sibsey	29. 2.91P
	(VW1600) (Regd as c/n PFA/55-10124)				(Damaged Ingoldmells 10.6.90; stored 9.96)		
G-BIMK	Tiger T.200 Srs.1 HAFB (Model)	7/MKB-01		22.12.80	M.K.Baron	Stockport	
G-BIMM	PA-18-150 Super Cub	18-3868	PH-VHO	8. 1.81	Clacton A/C (1988) Ltd	Clacton	6. 8.01T
	(L-21B-PI) (Frame No.18-3881)		R.Neth AF R-178/54-2468				
G-BIMN	Steen Skybolt	PFA/64-10329		31.12.80	G.P.Gregg	Spanhoe Lodge, Northants	21. 6.99P
	(Lyc IO-360)						
G-BIMO	SNCAN Stampe SV-4C	394	F-BADG	5. 3.81	R.A.Robert	Goodwood/Pulborough	9.11.98
	(Gipsy Major II)		Fr.Mil		(As "394" in French AF c/s)		
G-BIMT	Reims Cessna FA.152 Aerobat	0361	N8062L	9. 1.81	Gloucestershire Flying Svs Ltd	Gloucestershire	17. 5.99T
G-BIMU	Sikorsky S-61N Mk II	61-752	N8511Z	9. 1.81	Bristow Helicopters Ltd	Stornoway	23.10.99T
			VH-CRU/N4042S		"Loch Fyne" (HM Coastguard/SAR)		
G-BIMX	Rutan VariEze	PFA/74-10544		6. 1.81	D.G.Crew	Biggin Hill	3. 8.98P
	(Cont O-200-A)						
G-BIMZ	Beechcraft 76 Duchess	ME-169	N6021K	20. 3.81	A.J.Nurse	Gloucestershire	18.11.99
G-BINF	Saffery S.200 Heatwave HAFB (Model)	02		28. 5.81	T.C.B.Lewis	Altrincham	
G-BING	Reims Cessna F.172P Skyhawk II	2084		12. 1.81	Foyle Flyers Ltd	Eglinton	28. 3.99
G-BINL	Scruggs BL-2B HAFB (Model)	81216		5. 2.81	P.D.Ridout	Botley	
G-BINM	Scruggs BL-2B HAFB (Model)	81217		5. 2.81	P.D.Ridout	Botley	
G-BINO	Evans VP-1	PFA/1547		8. 6.78	G.Ravichandran	Chilbolton	
	(Possibly incorporates project PFA/7007)				(Under construction 1.96)		
G-BINR	Unicorn UE-1A HAFB (Model)	81004		20. 1.81	I.Chadwick	Horsham	
					t/a Unicorn Grp "Lady Diana"		
G-BINS	Unicorn UE-2A HAFB (Model)	80002		22.12.80	I.Chadwick	Horsham	
					t/a Unicorn Grp "Caroline"		
G-BINT	Unicorn UE-1A HAFB (Model)	80001		22.12.80	I.Chadwick	Horsham	
					t/a Unicorn Grp "Belinda"		
G-BINU	Saffery S.200 Heatwave HAFB (Model)	TCBL/01		13. 1.81	T.C.B.Lewis	Altrincham	
G-BINX	Scruggs BL-2B HAFB (Model)	81219		5. 2.81	P.D.Ridout	Botley	
G-BINY	Oriental Air-Bag HAFB (Model)	OAB-001		22. 1.81	J.L.Morton	Wokingham	
G-BIOB	Reims Cessna F.172P Skyhawk II	2042		23. 1.81	Aerofilms Ltd	Luton	3. 4.99T
G-BIOC	Reims Cessna F.150L	0848	F-BUEC	3. 2.81	T.J. & M.D.Palmer	Prestwick	9. 6.99T
G-BIOE*	Short SD.3-30 Var.200	SH.3063	N59MM	5. 1.81	Gill Avn Ltd	Newcastle	27. 5.97T
			G-BIOE/VH-KNP/G-BIOE/G-14-3063		(Stored 7.97)		
G-BIOI	SAN Jodel DR.1050/M Excellence	477	F-BLJQ	21. 1.81	H.F.Hambling	Fenland	18. 6.99P
G-BIOJ	Rockwell Commander 112TC-A	13192	N4662W	22. 1.82	A.T.Dalby	Sywell	22.12.99
G-BIOK	Reims Cessna F.152 II	1810		2. 2.81	Tayside Avn Ltd	Glenrothes/Aberdeen	9. 4.99T
G-BIOM	Reims Cessna F.152 II	1815		5. 2.81	A.S.Bamrah	Biggin Hill	18. 4.99T
					t/a Falcon F/Svs		
G-BIOR	Socata MS.880B Rallye Club	1229	OO-SAF	3. 2.81	R.L. & K.P.McLean	Rufforth	8. 5.99
	(Composite rebuild with components from G-AZGJ)				t/a McLean Avn		
G-BIOU	SAN Jodel D.117A	813	F-BIOU	9. 8.78	M.D.Howlett	Ilmer, Bucks	23. 5.99P
					t/a Dubious Grp		
G-BIOW	Slingsby T-67A	1988		26. 2.81	A.B.Slinger	Sherburn	31. 3.00
					t/a Slingsby T67A Grp		
G-BIPA	Grumman-American AA-5B Tiger	AA5B-0200	OY-GAM	24. 3.81	J.Campbell	Walney Island	6. 5.99
G-BIPH	Scruggs BL-2B HAFB (Model)	81224		10. 2.81	C.M.Dewsnap	Camberley	
G-BIPI	Everett Gyroplane	001		30. 4.81	R.Spall	Wolverhampton	29. 4.92P
	(VW1834) (Marks possibly applied to two aircraft stored at Kemble & Ipswich)						
G-BIPN	Alpavia Fournier RF3	35	F-BMDN	26. 2.81	J.C.R.Rogers & I.F.Fairhead	Cranwell	3.10.95P
					(Stored 4.97)		
G-BIPO	Mudry/CAARP CAP.20LS-200	03	F-GAUB	5. 3.81	M.C.Sandford	White Waltham	21. 2.00S
G-BIPS*	Socata Rallye 100ST	3028	F-GBCA	20. 2.81	Not known	Newcastle	27. 9.93T
					(Damaged pre 9.92; stored 5.93))		
G-BIPT	Wassmer Jodel D.112	1254	F-BMIB	11. 3.81	C.R.Davies	Allensmore, Hereford	7. 9.99P
G-BIPV	Gulfstream AA-5B Tiger	AA5B-0981	N28266	10. 3.81	Airtime Aviation Ltd.	Bournemouth	2. 5.99T
G-BIPW	Avenger T200-2112 HAFB (Model)	10		24. 2.81	B.L.King	Coulsdon	
G-BIPY	Montgomerie-Bensen B.8MR			25. 2.81	C.G.Ponsford	(Maldon)	13.10.95P
	(Rotax 532) AJW.01 & PFA G/01-1007						
G-BIPZ*	McCandless M.4 Gyroplane	Mk.4-4		27. 2.81	Not known	Sion Mills, Strabane	
					(Stored 4.96)		
G-BIRB*	Socata MS.880B Rallye 100T	2460	F-BVAQ	30. 3.81	Hawick ATC Squadron	Carlisle	16. 6.90
					(Stored 9.97)		
G-BIRD	Pitts S-1D Special	707-H & PFA/1596		3.11.77	Sandra J.Perkins	Deenethorpe	6. 4.99P
	(Lyc IO-360)				t/a Pitts Artists F/Grp		
G-BIRE	Colt Bottle 56SS HAFB	323		4. 3.81	K.R.Gafney "Satzenbrau"	Bracknell	N/E(A)
	(Satzenbrau Bottle)						
G-BIRH	PA-18-180 Super Cub	18-3853	PH-LET	19. 3.81	Aquila Gliding Club Ltd (Milton Keynes)		16. 4.99
	(L-21B-PI) (Frame No.18-3857)		R Neth AF R-163/54-2453 (As "R-163" in R.Neth AF c/s)				
G-BIRI	CASA I-131E Jungmann	1074	E3B-113	14. 4.81	M.G. & J.R.Jefferies	Little Gransden	20.10.94P
					(Stored 9.96)		

Regn	Type	C/n	P/I	Date	Owner/operator	Probable Base	CA Expy
G-BIRK	Avenger T200-2112 HAFB (Model)	006		10. 3.81	T.A.Smith	Cheadle, Cheshire	
G-BIRL	Avenger T200-2112 HAFB (Model)	008		10. 3.81	R.Light	Stockport	
G-BIRM	Avenger T200-2112 HAFB (Model)	007		10. 3.81	P.Higgins	Hyde	
G-BIRP	Ridout Arena Mk.17 Skyship HAFB (Model)	01		13. 3.81	Annette S.Viel	Botley	
G-BIRS	Cessna 182P Skylane	182-61436	G-BBBS N21131	10. 3.81	Air Nova plc	Liverpool	12. 4.01T
G-BIRT	Robin R.1180TD Aiglon	276		25. 3.81	W.D'A.Hall	White Waltham	10. 9.99
G-BIRW*	Morane-Saulnier MS.505 Criquet	695	OO-FIS F-BDQS	10. 4.81	Royal Museum of Scotland, Museum of Flight (As "F+IS" in Luftwaffe c/s) East Fortune		3. 6.83P
G-BIRY	Cameron V-77 HAFB	715		12. 3.81	P.& H.Mann "Magic Carpet"	Luton	15. 5.99A
G-BIRZ	Zenair CH.250-100 (Lyc O-290-G)	2-454 & PFA/24-10459		10. 3.81	T.N.Fox & I.R.Nash	Popham	4. 8.99P
G-BISG	Clutton FRED Srs.III (VW1600)	RAC 01-224 & PFA/29-10675		13. 3.81	R.A.Coombe (Lymington, Hants) "Fuzz Bee" (Status uncertain)		29.10.86P
G-BISH	Cameron V-65 HAFB	707		16. 3.81	P.J.Bish & C.Hall Hungerford t/a Zebedee Balloon Service "Tsaritsa"		29. 8.99A
G-BISJ	Cessna 340A II	340A-0497	OO-LFK N6328X	10. 4.81	K.J. & J.G.Bill Halfpenny Green t/a Billair		2. 6.99T
G-BISL	Scruggs BL-2B HAFB (Model)	81233		13. 3.81	P.D.Ridout	Botley	
G-BISM	Scruggs BL-2B HAFB (Model)	81234		13. 3.81	P.D.Ridout	Botley	
G-BISS	Scruggs BL-2C HAFB (Model)	81235		13. 3.81	P.D.Ridout	Botley	
G-BIST	Scruggs BL-2C HAFB (Model)	81236		13. 3.81	P.D.Ridout	Botley	
G-BISX	Colt 56A HAFB	324		18. 3.81	Colt G-BISX Ltd Pathhead, Midlothian		18. 8.99
G-BISZ	Sikorsky S-76A II Plus	760155		19. 3.81	Bristow Helicopters Ltd North Denes		23.10.99T
G-BITA	PA-18-150 Super Cub	18-8109037		24. 3.81	D.J.Gilmour North Weald t/a Intrepid Aviation Co		1. 7.99
G-BITE	Socata TB-10 Tobago	193		7. 5.81	M.A.Smith & R.J.Bristow	Fairoaks	22. 9.99
G-BITF	Reims Cessna F.152 II	1822		27. 3.81	Tayside Avn Ltd	Glenrothes	30. 4.00T
G-BITH	Reims Cessna F.152 II	1825		27. 3.81	Tayside Avn Ltd	Dundee	14. 8.00T
G-BITK	Clutton FRED Srs.II (VW1500)	PFA/29-10369		23. 3.81	D.J.Wood	(Dover)	
G-BITM	Reims Cessna F.172P Skyhawk II	2046		13. 4.81	D.G.Crabtree	Liverpool	9. 7.99T
G-BITO	Wassmer Jodel D.112D	1200	F-BIUO	20. 3.81	A.Dunbar	Barton	31. 5.99P
G-BITR	Sikorsky S-76A II Plus	760157	PT-HRW G-BITR	26. 3.81	Bristow Helicopters Ltd North Denes "Glenlassaugh"		21.12.00T
G-BITS	Drayton B-56 HAFB	MJB-01/81		16. 3.81	M.J.Betts "Hedger" Drayton, Norwich t/a Eastern Region, British Balloon & Airship Club		
G-BITW	Short SD.3-30 Var.100	SH.3070	G-EASI (G-BITW)/G-14-3070	26. 3.81	Air Cavrel Ltd (Kingston-upon-Thames)		9. 6.98T
G-BITY	Bell FD.31T Flying Dodo HAFB (Model)	2604		25. 3.81	A.J.Bell	Luton	
G-BIUL*	Cameron 60 Expansion Joint SS HAFB	703		27. 3.81	(To British Balloon Museum & Library 1998) Newbury		
G-BIUM	Reims Cessna F.152 II	1807		3. 4.81	Sheffield A/C Ltd	Netherthorpe	30. 1.00T
G-BIUO*	Rockwell Commander 112A	281	OY-PRH N1281J	30. 3.81	Not known	Bristol/Lulsgate	28.10.84
	(Collided with Cirrus BGA.2138 Longdon 12.5.84; wreck on fire dump 10.98)						
G-BIUP	SNCAN NC.854S	54	(G-AMPE) G-BIUP/F-BFSC	4. 6.81	D.F.Hurn t/a BIUP F/Grp	Popham	6. 6.98P
G-BIUV	HS.748 Srs.2A/266	1701	5W-FAN G-AYYH/G-11-8	11. 5.81	Emerald Airways Ltd Liverpool "City of Liverpool"		16. 6.99T
G-BIUW	PA-28-161 Warrior II	28-8116128	N9506N	14. 4.81	D.R.Staley	Sturgate	27. 6.99
G-BIUY	PA-28-181 Archer II	28-8190133	N8318X	3. 4.81	J.S.Devlin & Z.Islam	(East Grinstead)	27.11.01T
G-BIVA	Robin R.2112	137	F-GBAZ	6. 5.81	P.A. Richardson	Conington	31. 7.99
G-BIVB	Wassmer Jodel D.112	1009	(G-BIVC) F-BMAI	18. 9.81	D.Silsbury	(Ivybridge)	3. 2.99P
G-BIVC	Wassmer Jodel D.112 (Cont A65)	1219	F-BJII	1. 6.81	M.J.Barnby Brickhouse Farm, Frogland Cross		20. 8.96P
G-BIVF	Scintex CP.301C3 Emeraude	594	F-BJVN	4.11.81	R.J.Moore	Bedford	17. 6.92P
G-BIVK	Bensen B.8M (VW1834)	PFA G/01-1008		10. 4.81	J.G.Model "Skyrider"	Redditch	27. 7.98P
G-BIVL*	Bensen B.8M (VW1834)	PFA G/01-1011		10. 4.81	Not known	St.Merryn	29. 4.87P
G-BIVT	Saffery S.80 HAFB (Model)	LFG-001		22. 4.81	L.F.Guyot	London SW19	
G-BIVV	Gulfstream AA-5A Cheetah	AA5A-0857	N26979	26. 5.81	Plane talking Ltd	Elstree	18. 7.99T
G-BIVW	Moravan Zlin Z.326 Trener-Master	932	F-BPNQ	12. 1.82	G.C.Masterton Rushett Farm, Chessington		
	(Imported as wreck from Carcassonne for spares; remains stored 6.96)						
G-BIWA	Stevendon Skyreacher HAFB (Model)	102		8. 6.81	S.D.Barnes	Botley	
G-BIWB	Scruggs RS.5000 HAFB (Model)	81541		8. 6.81	P.D.Ridout	Botley	
G-BIWC	Scruggs RS.5000 HAFB (Model)	81546		26. 6.81	P.D.Ridout "Waterloo"	Botley	
G-BIWD	Scruggs RS.5000 HAFB (Model)	81545		26. 6.81	D.Eaves "Spooky"	Southampton	
G-BIWF	Ridout Warren Windcatcher HAFB WW.013 (Model)			3. 7.81	P.D.Ridout	Botley	
G-BIWG	Ridout Zelenski Mk.2 HAFB (Model) (Regd with c/n 2401)	Z.401		3. 7.81	P.D.Ridout	Botley	
G-BIWH	Cremer Super Fliteliner HAFB (Model)	15.700PC		13. 7.81	L.Griffiths	Morecambe	

Regn	Type	C/n	P/I	Date	Owner/operator	Probable Base	CA Expy
G-BIWJ	Unicorn UE-1A HAFB (Model)	81014		14. 7.81	B.L.King	Coulsdon	
G-BIWK	Cameron V-65 HAFB	719		22. 4.81	I.R.Williams & R.G.Bickerdike "Double Fantasy"	Bedford/Huntingdon	30. 3.99A
G-BIWL	PA-32-301 Saratoga	32-8106056	N83684	23. 4.81	A.R.Ward	Southend	9. 6.99
G-BIWN	Wassmer Jodel D.112	1314	F-BNCN	5. 6.81	C.R.Coates	Sneaton Thorpe, Whitby	26. 4.99P
G-BIWP	Mooney M.20J (201)	24-1094	N9923S	28. 5.81	G.Gore-Browne t/a Whiskey Papa F/Grp	Sherburn	26.11.99
G-BIWR	Mooney M.20F Executive	22-1339	N6972V	1. 6.81	A.C.Brink	Bourn	7.11.99
G-BIWU	Cameron V-65 HAFB	717		15. 5.81	L.P.Hooper "Bumble Bee"	Bristol	3.12.98A
G-BIWW	American AA-5 Traveler	AA5-0263	OY-AYV	2. 6.81	B.M.R. & K.R.Sheppard t/a B & K Avn (Op Sandra's F/Grp) "Kit-Kat"	Deenethorpe	29. 8.99
G-BIWY*	Westland WG-30-100	901		30. 4.81	Westland Helicopters Ltd (Stored 6.91)	Yeovil	30. 3.86T
G-BIXA	Socata TB-9 Tampico	205		7. 5.81	Lord de Saumarez	Shrublands Hall/Crowfield	6. 8.99
G-BIXB	Socata TB-9 Tampico	208		7. 5.81	L.B.W.& F.H.Hancock	(Lyneham)	4. 3.00T
G-BIXH	Reims Cessna F.152 II	1840		30. 4.81	The Cambridge Aero Club Ltd	Cambridge	9. 2.00T
G-BIXI	Cessna 172RG Cutlass II	172RG-0861	N7533B	7. 7.81	J.F.P.Lewis t/a X India Grp	Sandown	10. 6.99
G-BIXL	North American P-51D-20NA Mustang	122-38675	IDF/AF2343 Fv.26116/44-72216	3. 7.81	R.J.Lamplough "Miss L" (As "472216"/"AJ-L" in 354th FG USAAC c/s)	North Weald	28. 5.99P
G-BIXN	Boeing-Stearman A75N1 (PT-17-BW) Kaydet (Cont W670)	75-2248	N51132 41-8689	15. 6.81	R.R.White (Damaged Frensham Pond 21.4.96; stored 10.97)	Swanton Morley	3. 8.96
G-BIXS	Avenger T.200-2112 HAFB (Model)	013		13. 5.81	M.Stuart	Altrincham	
G-BIXV	Bell 212	30870	N16931	27. 5.81	Bristow Helicopters Ltd	Safe Gothia Oil Rig	22. 7.99T
G-BIXW	Colt 56B HAFB	348		18. 5.81	N.A.P.Bates "Spam"	Tunbridge Wells	17. 8.97A
G-BIXX	Pearson Srs.II HAFB (Model)	00327		8. 5.81	D.Pearson	Solihull	
G-BIXZ	Grob G-109	6019	D-KGRO	14. 5.81	D.L.Nind & I.Allum	Booker	13. 5.01
G-BIYI	Cameron V-65 HAFB	722		21. 5.81	P.F.Smart t/a The Sarnia Balloon Group "Penny"	Basingstoke	16. 4.97A
G-BIYJ	PA-18-95 Super Cub (L-18C-PI)	18-1000	MM51-15303/I-EIST/MM51-15303/51-15303	5. 6.81	S.Russell	Wilkieston Farm, Cupar	21. 9.99P
G-BIYK	Isaacs Fury II (Cont C90)	PFA/11-10418		20. 5.81	D.Silsbury	Dunkeswell	19.10.99P
G-BIYO	PA-31-310 Turbo Navajo	31-7912022	PH-ECG N27845	5. 6.81	Executive Jet Leasing Ltd	Ronaldsway/Manchester	14. 8.98T
G-BIYP	PA-20-125 Pacer	20-802	CN-TYP F-DACJ/OO-ADP	25. 5.83	R.J.Whitcombe	Liss, Petersfield	12. 5.99
G-BIYR	PA-18-150 Super Cub (L-21B-PI) (Frame No. 18-3843)	18-3841	(G-BIYB) PH-GER R.Neth AF R-151/5G-96/54-2441	26. 5.81	B.H. & M.J.Fairclough t/a The Delta Foxtrot F/Grp (As "R-151" in R.Neth AF c/s)	Dunkeswell	1. 6.01
G-BIYT	Colt 17A Cloudhopper HAFB	344		13. 7.81	J-M Francois	Salles-Courbatiers, France	2.10.99A
G-BIYU	Fokker S.11-1 Instructor	6206	(PH-HOM) R.Neth AF E-15	13. 5.81	C.Briggs (As "E-15" in R.Neth AF c/s)	Bagby	23. 9.99P
G-BIYW	Wassmer Jodel D.112	1209	F-BLNR	26. 5.81	K.Balaam t/a Pollard/Balaam/Bye F/Grp	Elmsett, Suffolk	14. 7.98P
G-BIYX	PA-28-140 Cherokee Cruiser	28-7625064	OY-BLD	19. 6.81	Comed Aviation Ltd (On rebuild 11.96)	Blackpool	19.12.96T
G-BIYY	PA-18-95 Super Cub (L-18C-PI) (Frame No.18-1914)	18-1979	MM52-2379/I-EIGA/MM52-2379/52-2379	2. 6.81	A.E. & W.J.Taylor	Bunns Bank, Norfolk	13. 6.98T
G-BIZF	Reims Cessna F.172P Skyhawk II	2070		16. 6.81	R.S.Bentley	Bourn	27. 1.01
G-BIZG	Reims Cessna F.152 II	1873		16. 6.81	M.A.Judge t/a Aero Group 78	Netherthorpe	10. 5.00T
G-BIZI	Robin DR.400 2+2	1543		29. 5.81	Rochester Avn Ltd	Rochester	4. 2.00T
G-BIZK	Nord 3202B1	78	N2255E ALAT	22.11.85	A.I.Milne (Luftwaffe c/s)	Little Snoring	23.10.98P
G-BIZM	Nord 3202B	91	N2256K ALAT	22.11.85	Magnificent Obsessions Ltd	Humberside	17. 6.99P
G-BIZN	Slingsby T-67A	1989		16. 6.81	M.B.Smithson & A.Marsland t/a Sport to Business (Damaged Leicester 23.7.97) (Hessle/Holme-on-Spalding Moor)		24. 6.00
G-BIZO	PA-28R-200 Cherokee Arrow II	28R-7535339	OY-DLH	16. 6.81	Bizo Air Ltd	Clutton Hill	14. 1.00T
G-BIZR	Socata TB-9 Tampico	210	G-BSEC G-BIZR	15. 6.81	Rosalind C.Walker	Biggin Hill	28.11.97
G-BIZT*	Bensen B.8M (VW1835)	PFA G/01-1015		10. 6.81	J.Ferguson (Stored 3.93)	Girvan, Ayr	12. 8.88P
G-BIZU	Thunder Ax6-56Z HAFB	358		15. 6.81	M.J.Loades "Greenall Whitley"	Southampton	4. 7.99A
G-BIZV	PA-18-95 Super Cub (L-18C-PI)	18-2001	MM52-2401 I-EIDE/MM52-2401/52-2401	12. 6.81	S.J.Pugh & R.L.Wademan (As "18-2001" in US Army c/s)	Oxenhope	1. 6.99P
G-BIZW	Champion 7GCBC Citabria	0157	D-EGPD	16. 7.81	J.C.Read t/a G.Read & Sons	Hall Farm, Louth	18. 8.01
G-BIZY	Wassmer Jodel D.112	1120	F-BKJL	13. 7.81	W.Tunley t/a Wayland Tunley & Associates	Hinton-in-the-Hedges	20. 5.99P

G-BJAA-BJZZ

Regn	Type	C/n	P/I	Date	Owner/operator	Probable Base	CA Expy
G-BJAE	Lavadoux Starck AS.80 Holiday 04 (Cont A65)		F-PGGA F-WGGA	17. 6.81	D.J. & Mrs S.A.E.Phillips (Damaged Woburn 17.8.91)(Leamington Spa)		8. 8.92P
G-BJAF	Piper J3C-65 Cub (L-4A-PI) 8437 (Frame No.8540)		D-EJAF HB-OAD/42-15318	23. 6.81	P.J.Cottle Craysmarsh Farm, Melksham		3. 3.99P
G-BJAG	PA-28-181 Archer II 28-7990353		PH-LDB (PH-BEG)/(OO-FLM)/N2244W	23. 6.81	J.F.Clark	Fenland	19. 6.99
G-BJAJ	Gulfstream AA-5B Tiger AA5B-1177		N4532V	2. 7.81	A.H.McVicar	Prestwick	20. 6.99T
G-BJAL	CASA I-131E Jungmann 1028 (Spanish AF serial no. conflicts with G-BUCC)		E3B-114	11. 9.78	I.C.Underwood & S.B.J.Chandler Breighton		22. 6.99P
G-BJAN	K & S SA.102.5 Cavalier PFA/1554			20.12.78	J.Powlesland	(Brightlingsea)	
G-BJAO	Montgomerie-Bensen B.8MR (Rotax 582) GLS-01 & PFA G/01-1001 (Regd with c/n GL5-01)			28. 8.81	N.J.Hall (Damaged Kemble 29.12.96)	Kemble	10.12.98P
G-BJAP	DH.82A Tiger Moth 0482 & PFA/157-12897 (Composite rebuild)			15. 6.81	K.Knight (As "K2587" in pre-war 32 Sqn/CFS c/s)	Shobdon	17. 6.99P
G-BJAS	Rango NA-9 HAFB (Model) TL-19			22. 6.81	A.Lindsay	Twickenham	
G-BJAV	Gardan GY-80-160 Horizon 28		OO-AJP F-BLVB	8. 9.81	A.G.Martlew	Henstridge	26. 1.97
G-BJAW	Cameron V-65 HAFB 745			19. 6.81	G.A.McCarthy "Breezin" Shepton Mallet		16. 4.86A
G-BJAY	Piper J3C-65 Cub (L-4H-PI) 12086 (Frame No. 11914)		F-BFBN OO-EAC/44-79790	1.11.78	K.L.Clarke (Horncastle, Lincs)		19. 8.92P
G-BJBK	PA-18-95 Super Cub (L-18C-PI) 18-1431 (Cont O-200-A) (Frame No.18-1370)		F-BOME ALAT/51-15431	21. 8.81	M.S.Bird Pepperbox, Salisbury		28. 4.99P
G-BJBM	Monnett Sonerai I (VW2074) MEA-117 & PFA/15-10022			2. 7.81	G.J.Townshend (Kings Lynn)		9. 1.97P
G-BJBO	CEA Jodel DR.250/160 Capitaine 40		F-BNJG	24. 8.81	R.C.Thornton t/a Wiltshire F/Grp	Oaksey Park	17. 7.00
G-BJBW	PA-28-161 Warrior II 28-8116280		N2913Z	22. 7.81	J.C.Lucas	Popham	21.11.99
G-BJBX	PA-28-161 Warrior II 28-8116269		N8414H	17. 7.81	Haimoss Ltd (Op Old Sarum F/C)	Old Sarum	4. 3.00T
G-BJBZ	Rotorway Exec 133 01-81			17. 7.81	P.J.D.Kerr	(Bridgwater)	
G-BJCA	PA-28-161 Warrior II 28-7916473		N2846D	30. 7.81	QBS Trading Co Ltd (Op Wellesbourne Avn) Wellesbourne Mountford		28.11.99T
G-BJCF	Scintex CP.1310-C3 936 Super Emeraude		F-BMJH	19.11.81	K.M.Hodson & C.G.H.Gurney Manor Farm, Binham		16.12.98P
G-BJCI	PA-18-180 Super Cub 18-6658		N9388D	10. 9.81	The Borders (Milfield) Aero-Tow Club Ltd Galewood Farm, Milfield		1. 6.00
G-BJCW	PA-32R-301 Saratoga SP 32R-8113094		N2866U	6. 8.81	G.R.Patrick & Co Ltd	Fairoaks	5. 5.99
G-BJDE	Reims Cessna F.172M 0984		OO-MSS D-EGBR	25. 8.81	H.P.K.Ferdinand	Elstree	24. 7.00
G-BJDF	Socata MS.880B Rallye 100T 3000		F-GAKP	21. 9.81	W.R.Savin t/a G-BJDF Grp	Willingham	9. 2.00
G-BJDI	Reims Cessna FR.182 Skylane RG 0046		N8062H	7. 8.81	Jones Samuel Ltd t/a JSE Systems	Leicester	3.3.00
G-BJDJ	BAe HS.125 Srs.700B 257142		G-RCDI G-BJDJ/G-5-12	27. 7.81	Falcon Jet Centre Ltd	Fairoaks	6.10.99T
G-BJDK	Ridout European E.157 HAFB (Model) S.2			17. 8.81	E.Osborn t/a Aeroprint Tours Southampton		
G-BJDO	Gulfstream AA-5A Cheetah AA5A-0823		N26936	3. 8.81	J.J.Woodhouse t/a Flying Svs (Fleet)		2. 4.00T
G-BJDT	Socata TB-9 Tampico 227			21. 8.81	C.P.Bignell	Shoreham	25. 3.00T
G-BJDW	Reims Cessna F.172M Skyhawk II 1417		PH-JBE	10. 8.81	J.Rae Poplar Hall Farm, Elmsett (Op Suffolk A/C)		22.12.99T
G-BJEI	PA-18-95 Super Cub 18-1988 (L-18C-PI) (Frame No.18-1938)		MM52-2388 I-EILO/MM52-2388/52-2388	27. 7.81	H.J.Cox Wendover Farm, Sheepwash		8. 8.99P
G-BJEL	SNCAN NC.854S 113		F-BEZT	7. 8.81	N.F. & S.G.Hunter Wolvesnewton, Chepstow		17. 7.98P
G-BJEN	Scruggs RS.5000 HAFB (Model) 81548			5. 8.81	N.J.Richardson	Southampton	
G-BJEV	Aeronca 11AC Chief 11AC-270		N85897 NC85897	12. 8.81	R.F.Willcox (As "E/897" in US Navy c/s) Eastbach Farm, English Bicknor		4.12.99P
G-BJEX	Bolkow Bo.208C Junior 690		F-BRHY D-EEAM	27. 8.81	G.D.H.Crawford (Henley-on-Thames) (Status uncertain)		28. 1.88
G-BJFB	Eaves Dodo Mk.1A HAFB (Model) DD.5			27. 8.81	S.D.Loveridge t/a Aeroprint Photographics	Southampton	
G-BJFC	Ridout European E.8 HAFB (Model) S.1			17. 8.81	P.D.Ridout	Botley	
G-BJFE	PA-18-95 Super Cub 18-2022 (L-18C-PI)		MM52-2422 I-EISU/MM52-2422/52-2422	17. 8.81	P.H.Wilmot-Allistone	Kemble	8.10.98P
G-BJFL	Sikorsky S-76A II Plus 760056		N106BH N1546T/(G-BHRK)	28. 8.81	Bristow Helicopters Ltd "Glen Moray"	Aberdeen	17. 9.99T
G-BJFM	Jodel Wassmer D.120 Paris-Nice 227		F-BLFM	8.10.81	J.V.George & P.A.Smith	Popham	1. 7.99P
G-BJGE*	Thunder Ax3 Sky Chariot HAFB 367			21. 8.81	R.Warner	Cranfield	
G-BJGF	Eaves Dodo Mk.1 HAFB (Model) DD-1			19. 8.81	D. & D.Eaves "Raphus Cacullatus"	Southampton	
G-BJGG	Eaves Dodo Mk.2 HAFB (Model) DD-2			19. 8.81	D. & D.Eaves "Super Dodo"	Southampton	
G-BJGK	Cameron V-77 HAFB 696			3. 9.81	T.J.Orchard, N.J.Glover & S.R.Godfrey "Dollar"	Reading	11. 4.99A
G-BJGL	Cremer Cloud Challenger 15.704 PAC HAFB (Model)			24. 8.81	G.Lowther	Luton	
G-BJGM	Unicorn UE-1A HAFB (Model) 81015			21. 8.81	D.Eaves & P.D.Ridout "Capricorn"	Southampton	

Regn	Type	C/n	P/I	Date	Owner/operator	Probable Base	CA Expy
G-BJGO	Cessna 172N Skyhawk II	172-71985	N6038E	14. 9.81	R.M.Hunt	Gloucestershire	11. 8.00
G-BJGX	Sikorsky S-76A II Plus	760026	N103BH	4. 9.81	Bristow Helicopters Ltd	North Denes	8.10.00T
			N4251S		"Glen Elgin"		
G-BJGY	Reims Cessna F.172P Skyhawk II	2128		13.10.81	Kit Martin (Historic Houses Rescue) Ltd		
						Gunton Hall, Somerton, Norfolk	12. 4.00
G-BJHB	Mooney M.20J (201)	24-1190	N1145G	23.12.81	Zitair F/C Ltd	Booker	25. 3.99T
G-BJHK	EAA Acro-Sport 1	PFA/72-10470		20. 3.80	D.M.Cue	White Waltham	15. 9.96P
	(Lyc IO-360)						
G-BJHP	Osprey Lizzieliner 1C HAFB (Model)			9. 9.81	N.J.Richardson	Southampton	
		AKC.16					
G-BJHT	Thunder Ax7-65 Bolt HAFB	368		27. 8.81	A.H. & L.Symonds "Aura"	Chelmsford	
G-BJHV*	Voisin Scale Replica	MPS-1		1. 9.81	M.P.Sayer	Brooklands	
					(On loan to Brooklands Museum)		
G-BJHW	Osprey Lizzieliner 1C HAFB (Model)			9. 9.81	N.J.Richardson	Southampton	
		AKC.19					
G-BJIA	Allport Aerostatics YUO-1A-1-DA			2. 9.81	D.J.Allport	Bourne, Lincs	
	HAFB (Model)	01					
G-BJIC	Eaves Dodo 1A HAFB (Model)	DD.3		4. 9.81	P.D.Ridout	Botley	
G-BJID	Osprey Lizzieliner 1B HAFB (Model)			4. 9.81	P.D.Ridout	Botley	
		AKC.28					
G-BJIF*	Bensen B.8M	HR-01		7. 9.81	H.Redwin (Damaged 1981/82)	Chiswick	13.7.82P*
	(McCulloch O-90)				(Cancelled as wfu 25.1.99)		
G-BJIG	Slingsby T-67A	1992		16. 9.81	D.Lacy	Redhill	4. 3.01
					t/a G-BJIG Slingsby Syndicate		
G-BJIR	Cessna 550 Citation II	550-0296	N6888C	17. 9.81	Gator Avn Ltd	Jersey	17. 1.00T
	(Unit No.326)				(Op Aviation Beauport Ltd)		
G-BJIV	PA-18-180 Super Cub	18-8262	N5972Z	17. 9.81	Yorkshire Gliding Club (Pty) Ltd		
						Sutton Bank	21. 7.00
G-BJJE	Eaves Dodo Mk.3 HAFB (Model)	DD.7		9. 9.81	D.Eaves	Southampton	
G-BJKF	Socata TB-9 Tampico	240		30. 9.81	P.C.Churcher	Denham	8. 4.01
					t/a Venue Solutions		
G-BJKW	Wills Aera II	A3JKW		1. 3.78	J.K.S.Wills	(London SE3)	
G-BJKX*	Reims Cessna F.152 II	1881		22. 9.81	Not known	Abbeyshrule, Ireland	1. 7.91T
					(Crashed nr Letterkenny 24.9.88; wreck stored 4.96)		
G-BJKY	Reims Cessna F.152 II	1886		22. 9.81	Manx Aero Marine Management Ltd	Blackpool	1.10.01T
					(Op Westair F/Svs)		
G-BJLB	SNCAN NC.854S	58	(OO-MVM)	5.11.81	N.F.Hunter	Wolvesnewton, Chepstow	30. 6.83P
			F-BFSG		(Crashed nr Newport,Gwent 29.7.84; stored 8.90)		
G-BJLC	Monnett Sonerai IIL			18. 9.81	A.R.Ansell "Elsie"	(Andover)	11. 5.98P
	(VW 1835) 942L & PFA/15-10634						
G-BJLF	Unicorn UE-1C HAFB (Model)	81018		21. 9.81	I.Chadwick t/a Unicorn Group	Horsham	
G-BJLG	Unicorn UE-1B HAFB (Model)	81017		21. 9.81	I.Chadwick t/a Unicorn Group	Horsham	
G-BJLH	PA-18-95 Super Cub	18-1541	F-BOUM	26.10.81	Felthorpe Flying Group Ltd	Felthorpe	30. 5.99P
	(L-18C-PI) (Frame No.18-1513)		ALAT 51-15541		(As "K/33" in US Army c/s)		
G-BJLO	PA-31-310 Turbo Navajo	31-815	F-BTQG	23.10.81	RJ Aviation Ltd	Fairoaks	23.12.01
			(F-BTDV)				
G-BJLX	Cremer Cracker HAFB (Model)	15.711 PAC		24. 9.81	P.W.May	Wilmslow	
G-BJLY	Cremer Cracker HAFB (Model)	15.709 PAC		24. 9.81	P.Cannon	Luton	
G-BJMI	Eaves European E.84 HAFB (Model)	S.3		9. 9.81	D.Eaves	Southampton	
G-BJML	Cessna 120	10766	N76349	5.10.81	D.F.Lawlor	Inverness	1. 7.99P
	(Cont C90)		NC76349				
G-BJMO	Taylor JT.1 Monoplane	PFA/55-10612		30. 9.81	R.C.Mark	(Ludlow)	
G-BJMR	Cessna 310R II	310R-1624	N2631Z	16. 7.79	J.M.Robinson	Sherburn	18. 2.01
G-BJMW	Thunder Ax8-105 Srs.2 HAFB	369		14.10.81	G.M.Westley	London SW15	5. 1.89A
G-BJMX	Ridout Jarre JR-3 HAFB (Model)	81601		6.10.81	P.D.Ridout	Botley	
G-BJMZ	Ridout European EA-8A HAFB (Model)	S.5		6.10.81	P.D.Ridout	Botley	
G-BJNA	Ridout Arena Mk.117P HAFB (Model)	202		6.10.81	P.D.Ridout	Botley	
G-BJND	Chown Osprey Mk.1E HAFB (Model)	AKC.53		7.10.81	A.Billington & D.Whitmore	Liverpool	
G-BJNF	Reims Cessna F.152 II	1882		21.10.81	Exeter F/C Ltd	Exeter	28. 1.00T
G-BJNG	Slingsby T-67M	1993		16.10.81	Dolphin Property (Management) Ltd		
						Old Sarum	23. 7.01T
G-BJNH	Chown Osprey Mk.1E HAFB (Model)	AKC.57		8.10.81	D.A.Kirk	Manchester	
G-BJNN	PA-38-112 Tomahawk	38-80A0064		15.10.81	Scotia Safari Ltd	Carlisle	25. 8.00T
G-BJNP	Rango NA-32 HAFB (Model)	NHP-22		1.10.81	N.H.Ponsford	Leeds	
					t/a Rango Balloon & Kite Co		
G-BJNX	Cameron O-65 HAFB	775		21.10.81	B.J.Petteford	Bristol	12. 8.97A
					"Flaming Nuisance"		
G-BJNY	Aeronca 11CC Super Chief	11CC-264	CN-TYZ	28.10.81	P.I. & D.M.Morgans (Stored 4.91)		
			F-OAEE		Furze Hill Farm, Rosemarket, Milford Haven		9. 8.90P
G-BJNZ	PA-23-250 Aztec F	27-7954099	G-FANZ	5.10.81	Bonus Avn Ltd	Cranfield	3. 8.01T
			N6905A				
G-BJOA	PA-28-181 Archer II	28-8290048	N8453H	29.10.81	Channel Islands Aero Services Ltd		
					(Jersey A/C)	Jersey	21. 1.02T
G-BJOB	SAN Jodel D.140C Mousquetaire III		F-BMBD	2.11.81	T.W.M.Beck & M.J.Smith		
		118				Monks Gate, Horsham	20. 6.00

Regn	Type	C/n	P/I	Date	Owner/operator	Probable Base	CA Expy
G-BJOE	Jodel Wassmer D.120A Paris-Nice	177	F-BJIU	12.11.81	J.F.Govan t/a Forth F/Grp	East Fortune	14 6.99P
G-BJOP	PBN BN-2B-26 Islander	2132		29.10.81	Loganair Ltd (Celtic c/s)	Glasgow	3. 9.98T
G-BJOT	SAN Jodel D.117	688	F-BJCO CN-TVH/F-DABU	12.11.81	E.Davies	(Blackpool)	2. 9.99P
G-BJOV	Reims Cessna F.150K	0558	PH-VSD	4. 2.82	J.A.Boyd	(Maidstone)	8. 7.00
G-BJPI	Bede BD-5G 1 & PFA/14-10218 (Hirth 230R)			30.10.81	M.D.McQueen	(Beckenham, Kent)	
G-BJPL	Chown Osprey Mk.4A HAFB (Model) AKC-39			13.10.81	M.Vincent	Jersey	
G-BJPV	Haigh Super Hi-Flyer HAFB (Model) 001			16.10.81	M.J.Haigh	Stockport	
G-BJRA	Chown Osprey Mk.4B HAFB (Model) AKC.87			23.10.81	E.Osborn	Southampton	
G-BJRB	Eaves European E.254 HAFB (Model) S.5			23.10.81	D.Eaves	Southampton	
G-BJRC	Eaves European E.84R HAFB (Model) S.7			23.10.81	D.Eaves	Southampton	
G-BJRD	Eaves European E.84R HAFB (Model) S.8			23.10.81	D.Eaves	Southampton	
G-BJRG	Chown Osprey Mk.4B HAFB (Model) AKC.95			26.10.81	A.de Gruchy	Jersey	
G-BJRH	Rango NA-36/Ax3 HAFB	NHP-23		4.11.81	N.H.Ponsford t/a Rango Balloon & Kite Co	Leeds	
G-BJRP	Cremer Cracker HAFB (Model) 15.712 PAC			29.10.81	M.D.Williams	Dunstable	
G-BJRR	Cremer Cracker HAFB (Model) 15.715 PAC			29.10.81	M.D.Williams	Houghton Regis	
G-BJRV	Cremer Cracker HAFB (Model) 15.713 PAC			29.10.81	M.D.Williams	Dunstable	
G-BJRW	Cessna U206G Stationair 6 II U206-05738		(N5422X)	8. 4.80	A.I.Walgate & Son Ltd Cuxwold Hall, Caistor		23. 5.01
G-BJRZ	Partenavia P.68C	231	G-OAKP G-BJRZ	10.11.81	Ampy Automation Digilog Ltd	Sibson	12. 8.01T
G-BJSA	BN-2A-26 Islander	46	HB-LIC D-IBNB/I-TRAL	15.12.81	Police Avn Svs Ltd (Stored 6.97)	Gloucestershire	25.10.95T
G-BJSC	Chown Osprey Mk.4D HAFB (Model) AKC.84			12.11.81	N.J.Richardson	Southampton	
G-BJSD	Chown Osprey Mk.4D HAFB (Model) AKC.83			12.11.81	N.J.Richardson	Southampton	
G-BJSF	Chown Osprey Mk.4B HAFB (Model) AKC.66			9.11.81	N.J.Richardson	Southampton	
G-BJSG	VS.361 Spitfire LF.IXc 6S/735188 (C/n quoted as 6S/730116 - this is firewall no.)		Indian AF HS543/G-15-11/ML417	29. 1.81	Patina Ltd (Op The Fighter Collection) (As "ML417/2I-T" in 443 (RCAF) Sqdn c/s)	Duxford	21. 4.99P
G-BJSI	Chown Osprey Mk.1E HAFB (Model) AKC.43			9.11.81	N.J.Richardson	Southampton	
G-BJSP	Guido 1A-61 HAFB (Model) GAN01/81-2609			23.11.81	G.A.Newsome	Hull	
G-BJSS	Allport YUO-1B-1-DA Neolithic Invader 01-8101002 Superballoon Srs.2/20 HAFB (Model)			9.11.81	D.J.Allport	Bourne, Lincs	
G-BJST	CCF Harvard 4	CCF4-...	MM53795 SC-66	21.12.81	A.Winter	(Emmelshausen, Germany)	AC
G-BJSU*	Bensen B-8M	PFA G/01-1026		11.11.81	J.D.Newlyn (Stored 3.97)	River, Dover	
G-BJSV	PA-28-161 Warrior II	28-8016229	PH-VZL (OO-HLM)/N35787	25.11.81	Airways Flight Training (Exeter) Ltd	Exeter	9. 9.00T
G-BJSW	Thunder Ax7-65Z HAFB	378		16.11.81	Sandicliffe Garage Ltd "Sandicliffe Ford"	Stapleford, Notts	7. 5.99A
G-BJSX	Unicorn UE-1C HAFB (Model)	82023		10.11.81	N.J.Richardson	Southampton	
G-BJSZ	Piper J3C-65 Cub (L-4H-PI) 12047 (Regd with Frame No.11874)		D-EHID (D-ECAX)/(D-EKAB)/PH-NBP/44-79751	20.11.81	H.Gilbert (Stored 6.95)	Enstone	14. 6.94P
G-BJTB	Cessna A150M Aerobat	A150-0627	(G-BIVN) N9818J	28.10.82	V.D.Speck	Clacton	16. 5.99T
G-BJTF	Skyrider Mk.1 HAFB (Model)	KSR-01		18.11.81	D.A.Kirk	Manchester	
G-BJTN	Chown Osprey Mk.4B HAFB (Model) ASC-112			23.11.81	M.Vincent	Jersey	
G-BJTO	Piper J3C-65 Cub (L-4H-PI) 11527 (Frame No.11352)		F-BEGK OO-AAL/43-30236	1.12.81	K.R.Nunn Fritton Decoy, Great Yarmouth (Stored 1.91)		5. 3.86P
G-BJTP	PA-18-95 Super Cub (L-18C-PI) 18-999		MM51-15302/I-EICO/MM51-15302/51-15302	26.11.81	J.T.Parkins "Sittin'Duck" (As "115302/TP" in VMO-6 Sqn, US Marines c/s)	Bidford	20.10.99P
G-BJTW	Eaves European E.107 HAFB (Model) S.10			23.11.81	C.J.Brealey	Southampton	
G-BJTY	Chown Osprey Mk.4B HAFB (Model) ASC-115			23.11.81	A.E.de Gruchy	Jersey	
G-BJUB	BVS Special 01 HAFB (Model) VS/PW01			25.11.81	P.G.Wild	Beverley	
G-BJUC	Robinson R-22HP	0228		13. 1.82	J.J.Woodhouse	(Fleet)	14. 9.00T
G-BJUD	Robin DR.400/180R Remorqueur 870 (Rebuilt using new fuselage; original scrapped Membury 11.88)		PH-SRM	27.11.81	Lasham Gliding Society Ltd	Lasham	15. 5.00
G-BJUE	Chown Osprey Mk.4B HAFB (Model) ASC-114			23.11.81	M.Vincent	Jersey	
G-BJUI	Chown Osprey Mk.4B HAFB (Model) ASC-116			23.11.81	B.A.de Gruchy	Jersey	
G-BJUR	PA-38-112 Tomahawk	38-79A0915		5. 2.82	Truman Avn Ltd (Op Nottingham School of Flying)	Nottingham	30.10.00T
G-BJUS	PA-38-112 Tomahawk	38-80A0065		10.12.81	Panshanger School of Flying Ltd (Stored 6.96)	High Cross, Ware	24. 4.94T
G-BJUU	Chown Osprey Mk.4B HAFB (Model) ASC-113			23.11.81	M.Vincent	Jersey	
G-BJUV	Cameron V-20 HAFB	792		9.12.81	P.Spellward	Bristol	
G-BJUY	Colt Ax7-77A HAFB	384	EI-BDE	15.12.81	Balloon Sports HB	Partille, Sweden	
	(Special Golf Ball shape; rebuild of Colting Ax7-77A c/n 77A-003) (Op P.Lesser)						
G-BJVB	Cremcorn Ax1-4 HAFB (Model)	82029		11.12.81	P.A.Cremer	Camberley	
G-BJVC	Evans VP-2 PFA/63-10599 (VW1911)			17. 2.82	C.J.Morris (Status uncertain)	(Andover)	19. 6.91P

Regn	Type	C/n	P/I	Date	Owner/operator	Probable Base	CA Expy
G-BJVF	Thunder Ax3 Maxi Sky Chariot HAFB			15.12.81	A.G.R.Calder	California, USA	6.10.91A
	(C/n duplicates G-SPOP)	187					
G-BJVH	Reims Cessna F.182Q Skylane	0106	D-EJMO	21.12.81	R.J.D.Cuming	Bolt Head, Salcombe	27. 5.00
			PH-AXU(2)				
G-BJVJ	Reims Cessna F.152 II	1906		6. 1.82	The Cambridge Aero Club Ltd	Cambridge	17. 3.01T
G-BJVK	Grob G-109	6074		11. 3.82	B.A.Kimberley	(Banbury)	22. 5.92
					(Status uncertain)		
G-BJVM	Cessna 172N Skyhawk II	172-69374	N737FA	14.12.81	I.C.Maclennan	Swanton Morley	15. 7.00T
G-BJVS	Scintex CP.1310-C3	903	F-BJVS	5. 1.79	A.E.Futter	Felthorpe	4. 6.99P
	Super Emeraude				t/a The Aerofel 81 Super Emeraude Group		
G-BJVT	Reims Cessna F.152 II	1904		12. 1.82	The Cambridge Aero Club Ltd	Cambridge	9.10.00T
G-BJVU	Thunder Ax6-56 Bolt HAFB	397		31.12.81	G.V.Beckwith "Cooper"	York	26. 4.91A
G-BJVV	Robin R.1180TD Aiglon	279		5.11.81	Medway F/Grp Ltd	Rochester	1. 5.00
G-BJVX	Sikorsky S-76A II Plus	760100	N108BH	15. 1.82	Bristow Helicopters Ltd	North Denes	23. 3.00T
			N1548G				
G-BJWC*	Saro Skeeter AOP.10	S2/3070	7840M	30.11.82	D.A.George	Sywell	
			XK482		(Sloane Helicopters Ltd) (Stored 5.96)		
G-BJWH	Reims Cessna F.152 II	1919		7. 5.82	Plane Talking Ltd	Biggin Hill	27. 8.00T
G-BJWI	Reims Cessna F.172P Skyhawk II	2172		14. 5.82	Bournemouth F/Club Ltd	Bournemouth	16. 8.01T
G-BJWJ	Cameron V-65 HAFB	802		25. 1.82	R.G.Turnbull & S.G.Farse "Gawain"		
						Glasbury, Hereford	10. 9.97A
G-BJWO	BN-2A-26 Islander	334	4X-AYR	16. 2.82	Peterborough Parachute Centre Ltd Sibson		4. 2.00
			SX-BBX/4X-AYR/G-BAXC				
G-BJWT	Wittman W.10 Tailwind PFA/31-10688			5. 1.82	J.F.Bakewell	Hucknall	26. 5.99P
	(Lyc O-290-G)				t/a Tailwind Group		
G-BJWV	Colt 17A Cloudhopper HAFB	391		22. 1.82	D.T.Meyes "Bryant Homes" Leamington Spa		26. 3.97A
G-BJWW	Reims Cessna F.172P Skyhawk II	2148	(D-EFTV)	1. 2.82	Manx Aero Marine Management Ltd		
					(Op Westair F/Svs)	Blackpool	27. 8.00T
G-BJWX	PA-18-95 Super Cub (L-18C-PI) 18-1985		MM52-2385	23. 2.82	A.White	Redhill	21.10.99P
	(Cont O-200-A)		I-EIME/MM52-2385/52-2385 t/a Acebell JWX Syndicate				
G-BJWY*	Sikorsky S-55 (HRS-2)	55???	A2576	25. 1.82	D.Charles	Carlisle	
	Whirlwind HAR.21		WV198/Bu.130191		(As "WV198/K") (On loan to Solway Avn Society)		
G-BJWZ	PA-18-95 Super Cub (L-18C-PI) 18-1361		OO-HMO	18. 1.82	R.A.G.Lucas	Redhill	23. 9.98P
	(Frame No.18-1262)		ALAT 18-1361/51-15361 t/a G-BJWZ Syndicate				
G-BJXA	Slingsby T-67A	1994		8. 2.82	Comed Avn Ltd	Blackpool	5. 4.01T
G-BJXB	Slingsby T-67A	1995		8. 2.82	A.K.Halvorsen	Barton	5. 8.01
G-BJXK	Sportavia Fournier RF5	5054	D-KINB	3. 2.82	E.Fitzgerald & J.T.Phillips	Usk	3.12.00
					t/a G-BJXK Syndicate		
G-BJXP	Colt 56B HAFB	393		29. 3.82	H.J.Anderson	Oswestry	23. 9.99A
G-BJXR	Auster AOP.9	184	XR267	2. 2.82	A.Southern & R.J.Rudhall	Kemble	23. 6.01
					t/a Cotswold Acft Restoration Grp		
G-BJXX	PA-23-250 Aztec E	27-4692	F-BTCM	7. 4.82	V.Bojovic	Bournemouth	21.10.01
			N14094				
G-BJXZ	Cessna 172N Skyhawk II	172-73039	PH-CAA	24. 3.82	T.M.Jones (Op Derby Aero Club) Egginton		1.11.97T
			N1949F				
G-BJYD	Reims Cessna F.152 II	1915		25. 3.82	Cleveland F/School Ltd	Teesside	8. 9.00T
G-BJYF	Colt 56A HAFB	401		1. 3.82	A.van Wyk	London SE12	9. 8.86A
G-BJYG	PA-28-161 Warrior II	28-8216053	N8458B	4. 3.82	D. & A.M.Lee t/a Lee Air	Liverpool	12. 6.00T
G-BJYK	Jodel Wassmer D.120A Paris-Nice	185	(G-BJWK)	11. 5.82	T.Fox & D.A.Thorpe	Crowland	22. 5.99P
			F-BJPK				
G-BJYN	PA-38-112 Tomahawk	38-79A1076	G-BJTE	12. 3.82	Panshanger School of Flying Ltd		
						High Cross, Ware	6. 3.00T
G-BJZA	Cameron N-65 HAFB	820		4. 3.82	A.D.Pinner "Digby"	Northampton	3. 6.97A
G-BJZB	Evans VP-2	PFA/63-10633		10. 3.82	J.A.Macleod	Stornoway	31. 3.99P
	(VW 1834)						
G-BJZC*	Thunder Ax7-65Z HAFB	416		5. 3.82	K A Kent "Greenpeace Trinity"	Lancing	17. 6.94A
					(Balloon Preservation Group 7.98)		
G-BJZF	DH.82A Tiger Moth	NAS-100		8. 3.82	R.Blasi	White Waltham	1. 4.99P
	(Built by Norfolk Aerial Spraying Ltd from spares)						
G-BJZN	Slingsby T-67A	1997		31. 3.82	A.R.T. Marsland	(York)	19. 7.01
G-BJZR	Colt 42A HAFB	402		18. 3.82	A.F.Selby	Loughborough	21. 7.99A
					t/a Selfish Balloon Grp "Selfish"		
G-BJZX	Grob G-109	6109	(D-KGRO)	3. 9.82	Oxfordshire Sport Flying Ltd	Enstone	4. 9.00
G-BJZY	Bensen B.8MV			18. 3.82	P.C.Dockerill	Market Harborough	
	(VW1700) DNL.21103 & PFA G/01-1012						

G-BKAA-BKZZ

Regn	Type	C/n	P/I	Date	Owner/operator	Probable Base	CA Expy
G-BKAB*	ICA IS-28M2A	23A		19. 3.82	T.Cust	Sandtoft	20. 5.85
	(Crashed Rattlesden 19.5.84; wreck stored 10.97)						
G-BKAE	Jodel Wassmer D.120 Paris-Nice	200	F-BKCE	5. 5.82	M.P.Wakem	Barton	2. 6.98P
G-BKAF	Clutton FRED Srs.II	PFA/29-10337		23. 3.82	J.M.Robinson	(Achill Island, Co.Mayo)	30. 5.97P
	(VW1835)						
G-BKAM	Slingsby T-67M Firefly 160	1999		26. 4.82	A.J.Daley	Wellcross Grange, Slinfold	9. 7.99
G-BKAO	Wassmer Jodel D.112	249	F-BFTO	22. 3.82	R.Broadhead	Bagby	21.12.99P
G-BKAR	PA-38-112 Tomahawk	38-79A1091		16. 4.82	D.A.Williams (Op Deltair)	Chester	8. 7.01T
G-BKAS	PA-38-112 Tomahawk	38-79A1075		16. 4.82	D.A.Williams (Op Deltair)	Chester	25. 5.98T
G-BKAY	Rockwell Commander 114	14411	SE-GSN	28. 9.81	R.S.Morse	Dunkeswell	23. 3.01
					t/a The Rockwell Grp		
G-BKAZ	Cessna 152 II	152-82832	N89705	27. 4.82	A.T.Wright	Leeds-Bradford	19. 4.00A
G-BKBB	Hawker Fury Replica	WA/6	OO-HFU	2. 4.82	R.Landuyt	(Brugge, Belgium)	
	(RR Kestrel 5)		OO-XFU/G-BKBB		(As "K1930" in 43 Sqn c/s)		
	(Damaged Keiheuval, Belgium 1.6.96; on rebuild Rotary Farm, Hatch 9.96)						
G-BKBD	Thunder Ax3 Maxi Sky Chariot HAFB	418		5. 4.82	M.J.Casson	Kendal	
G-BKBF	Socata MS.894A Rallye Minerva 220	11622	F-BSKZ	8. 9.82	J.A.Gibbs	Draycott Farm, Chiseldon	16. 6.99
G-BKBH	HS.125 Srs.600B	256052	5N-DNL	1. 4.82	Beamalong Ltd	Southend/Southampton	Exp
			G-5-698/5N-DNL/5N-NBC/G-5-698/G-BKBH/G-5-698/TR-LAU/G-BKBH/G-BDJE/G-5-11				
G-BKBN	Socata TB-10 Tobago	287		4. 6.82	D.S.& W.A.Newby	(Newquay)	20. 7.01
					t/a David Newby Associates		
G-BKBO	Colt 17A Cloudhopper HAFB	342		1. 9.82	J.Armstrong, M.A.Ashworth	Newquay	23. 3.00A
					& H.Davey "Captain Courageous"		
G-BKBP	Bellanca 7GCBC Scout	465-73	N8693	1. 6.82	M.G. & J.R.Jefferies	Little Gransden	8. 5.95T
					t/a H.G.Jefferies & Son (Damaged Graveley, Herts 23.5.93; stored 9.95)		
G-BKBR*	Cameron Chateau 84SS HAFB	743		11. 5.82	Forbes Europe Inc	Balleroy, Normandy	N/E(A)
	(Special Shape as Forbes "Chateau de Balleroy")				(Stored 6.93)		
G-BKBS*	Bensen B.8MV	PFA G/01-1027		14. 4.82	Not known	(Cornwall)	
G-BKBV	Socata TB-10 Tobago	288	F-BNGO	4. 6.82	R.M.Messenger	Carlisle	14. 4.01
G-BKBW	Socata TB-10 Tobago	289		4. 6.82	P.J.Bramhall & D.F.Woodhouse		
					t/a Merlin Avn	Bristol/Lulsgate	28.12.97
G-BKCB	PA-28R-200 Cherokee Arrow II	28R-7435186	OY-POO	21. 6.82	J.D.Rose	Exeter	8.10.99T
			CS-APD/N41460				
G-BKCC	PA-28-180 Cherokee Archer	28-7405099	OY-BGY	13. 5.82	Archer Aviation Ltd	Gloucestershire	13. 8.01T
G-BKCE	Reims Cessna F.172P Skyhawk II	2135	N9687R	26. 4.82	Far North Flight Training	Wick	15. 5.00T
G-BKCH	Thompson Cassutt Special	PFA/126-10778		21. 4.82	S.C.Thompson	Wellcross Grange, Slinfold	19. 7.99P
	(Cont C90)						
G-BKCI	Brugger MB.2 Colibri	PFA/43-10692		22. 4.82	E.R.Newall "Bugsy"	Breighton	
	(VW1600)						
G-BKCJ	Oldfield Baby Lakes	PFA/10-10714		12. 5.82	S.V.Roberts	Sleap	26. 1.99P
	(Cont O-200-A)						
G-BKCL	PA-30-160 Twin Comanche C	30-1982	G-AXSP	12. 1.81	Yorkair Ltd	Gamston	26. 1.00T
			N8824Y				
G-BKCN	Phoenix Currie Wot	PFA/3018		27. 4.82	N.A.A.Pogmore	Bensons Farm, Laindon	14. 6.99P
	(Cont A65)						
G-BKCR	Socata TB-9 Tampico	297		6. 5.82	A.Whitehouse	(Merriot, Somerset)	3. 8.98T
G-BKCT	Cameron V-77 HAFB	837		10. 5.82	Quality Products General Engineering		
					(Wickwar) Ltd "Quality Products" Bristol		7. 5.93A
G-BKCV	EAA Acro Sport II	430 & PFA/72A-10776		5. 5.82	T.N.Jinks	Charity Farm, Baxterley	19. 8.99P
	(Lyc O-360)						
G-BKCW	Jodel Wassmer D.120A Paris-Nice	285	(G-BKCP)	1. 6.82	A.Greene & G.Kerr	Dundee	21.12.97P
			F-BMYF		t/a The Dundee F/Grp (Damaged Dundee 13.4.97)		
G-BKCX	Mudry/CAARP CAP-10B	149		28. 7.82	Mahon & Associates	Popham	8. 6.01
G-BKCY	PA-38-112 Tomahawk II	38-81A0027	OO-XKU	22. 5.82	Wellesbourne Avn Ltd	Welshpool	7.11.94T
					(Stored 12.97)		
G-BKCZ	Jodel Wassmer D.120A Paris-Nice	207	F-BKCZ	23. 4.82	M.R.Baker (On rebuild 6.92)	Lewes	AC
G-BKDC	Monnett Sonerai IIL	876 & PFA/15-10597		2. 7.82	K.J.Towell	(Guildford)	18. 6.90P
	(VW 1834)				(Damaged Breighton 7.8.90; status uncertain)		
G-BKDH	Robin DR.400/120 Dauphin 80	1582	PH-CAB	25. 5.82	Airbase Aircraft Ltd	Shoreham	6.12.01T
G-BKDI	Robin DR.400/120 Dauphin 80	1583	PH-CAD	25. 5.82	The Cotswold A/C Ltd	Gloucestershire	9.10.00T
G-BKDJ	Robin DR.400/120 Dauphin 80	1584	PH-CAC	25. 5.82	M.D.Joyce & R.R.Wills	Sherburn	28. 4.01
G-BKDK	Thunder Ax7-77Z HAFB	428		21. 6.82	A.J.Byrne "Cider Riser"	Thatcham	17. 9.95A
G-BKDP	Clutton FRED Srs.III	PFA/29-10650		24. 5.82	M.Whittaker	(Wolverhampton)	
G-BKDR	Pitts S-1S Special	PFA/09-10654		14. 6.82	T.J.Reeve	(Bury St. Edmunds)	11. 3.97P
	(Lyc IO-360)						
G-BKDT*	RAF SE.5A replica	278 & PFA/80-10325		26. 5.82	Yorkshire Air Museum	Elvington	
					(As "F943")		
G-BKDX	SAN Jodel DR.1050 Ambassadeur	55	F-BITX	1. 6.82	T.V.Thorp & G.J.Slater	Clench Common	10. 9.99
					t/a DX Group		
G-BKEK	PA-32-300 Cherokee Six	32-7540091	OY-TOP	30. 6.82	P.H.Maynard	Turweston	22. 4.01T
G-BKEP	Reims Cessna F.172M Skyhawk II	1095	OY-BFJ	8. 7.82	R.Green	Cumbernauld	1. 9.01
G-BKER	Replica Plans SE.5A	PFA/20-10641		15. 6.82	N.K.Geddes	Bridge of Weir	9. 7.98P
	(Cont O-200A)				(As "F5447/N")		
G-BKES*	Cameron Bottle 57 SS HAFB	846		25. 6.82	British Balloon Museum	Newbury	N/E(A)
	(Robinsons Barley Water Bottle)				"Robinsons Barley Water" (Stored 1.90)		

Regn	Type	C/n	P/I	Date	Owner/operator	Probable Base	CA Expy
G-BKET	PA-18-95 Super Cub (L-18C-PI)	18-1990	MM52-2390 I-EIBI/MM52-2390/52-2390	17. 6.82	H.M.MacKenzie (Stored 6.98) Inverness		24. 8.96P
G-BKEU	Taylor JT.1 Monoplane (VW 1600)	PFA/55-10553		18. 6.82	R.J.Whybrow & J.M.Springham Knettishall		20. 7.95P
G-BKEV	Reims Cessna F.172M Skyhawk	1443	PH-WLH OO-CNE	8. 7.82	J.W.Finlayson (St. Andrews)		19.11.00T
G-BKEW	Bell 206B JetRanger III	3010	D-HDAD	8. 7.82	N.R.Foster t/a Foster Associates Denham		17. 7.00
G-BKEX	Rich Prototype Glider	1		24. 6.82	D.B.Rich (Callington, Cornwall)		
G-BKEY	Clutton FRED Srs.III (VW1600)	PFA/29-10208		27. 5.82	G.S.Taylor (Bewdley,Worcs)		
G-BKFA	Monnett Sonerai IIL	PFA/15-10524		21. 6.82	R.F.Bridge Bursledon, Southampton		
G-BKFC	Reims Cessna F.152 II	1443	OO-AWB	1. 9.82	Sulby Aerial Surveys Ltd Sibbertoft, Husbands Bosworth		5.10.01T
G-BKFI	Evans VP-1 Srs.2 (VW1834)	PFA/62-10491		24. 6.82	D.Martin Rayne Hall Farm, Rayne t/a Foxtrot India F/Grp		5. 5.99P
G-BKFK	Isaacs Fury II (Lyc O-290-D)	PFA/11-10038		25. 6.82	G.C.Jones (Chelmsford) (Persian AF c/s) "Cia Cia San"		6. 9.95P
G-BKFL	Aerosport Scamp	PFA/117-10814		17. 8.82	J.Sherwood (Barnsley)		
G-BKFM	QAC Quickie 1 (Rotax 503)	PFA/94-10570		28. 6.82	F.Rothera Pent Farm, Postling, Kent		29. 6.98P
G-BKFN	Bell 214ST Super Transport	28109	LZ-CAW G-BKFN/VH-BEE/VH-LHT/G-BKFN	16. 8.82	Bristow Helicopters Ltd Aberdeen "Loch Broome"		24.10.01T
G-BKFP	Bell 214ST Super Transport	28110		16. 8.82	Caledonian Helicopters Ltd Aberdeen (Op Bristow Helicopters) "Loch Roag"		27.10.00T
G-BKFR	Scintex CP.301C Emeraude	519	F-BUUR F-BJFF	30. 6.82	C.R.Beard Grove Moor Farm, Grassthorpe		22. 7.99P
G-BKFW	Percival P.56 Provost T.1	PAC/F/303	XF597	21. 9.82	Sylmar Avn & Svs Ltd (Alan House) (As "XF597/AH" in RAF College c/s) Lower Wasing Farm, Brimpton		8. 4.99P
G-BKFZ	PA-28R-200 Cherokee Arrow II	28R-7635127	OY-BLE	17. 8.82	R.S.Watt Shacklewell Lodge, Empingham t/a Shacklewell F/Grp		28.10.00
G-BKGA	Socata MS.892E Rallye 150GT	13287	F-GBXJ	15. 7.82	J.H.A.Clarke t/a BJJ Avn Wadswick Manor Farm, Corsham		19. 3.00
G-BKGB	Jodel Wassmer D.120 Paris-Nice	267	F-BMOB	21. 6.82	B.A.Ridgway (Pontyclun)		12.11.99P
G-BKGC	Maule M.6-235C Super Rocket	7413C	N56465	23. 7.82	M.C.Woodhouse Oaksey Park		4. 8.00
G-BKGD*	Westland WG.30 Srs.100	002	(G-BKBJ)	15. 7.82	Westland Helicopters Ltd Yeovil (Stored 3.93)		6. 7.93T
G-BKGL	Beechcraft D18S (3TM) (Beech c/n A-764)	CA-164	CF-QPD RCAF 5193/1564	14. 7.82	G.A.Warner Duxford t/a The Acft Restoration Co (Op Classic Wings) (As "1164" in 1942 US Army c/s)		8. 5.99
G-BKGM	Beechcraft 3NM (D18S) (Beech c/n A-853)	CA-203	N5063N G-BKGM CF-SUQ/RCAF 2324	14. 7.82	A.E.Hutton North Weald (Op Harvard Formation Team) (As "HB275" in RAF/SEAC c/s)		21. 5.00
G-BKGR	Cameron O-65 HAFB	864		6. 8.82	K.Kidner & L.E.More Newton Abbot		8. 5.93P
G-BKGT	Socata Rallye 110ST Galopin	3361		23. 7.82	A.G.Morgan Wellesbourne Mountford t/a Long Marston F/Grp		28.10.00
G-BKGW	Reims Cessna F.152 II	1878	N9071N	11. 8.82	Leicestershire A/C Ltd Leicester		18. 6.01T
G-BKHA*	Westland WS-55 Whirlwind HAR.10	WA/109	XJ763	25. 8.82	C.J.Evans Thornicombe (As "XJ763/P" in 103 Sqdn c/s; believed stored)		3. 5.92P
G-BKHD	Oldfield Baby Lakes (Cont O-200-A)	8133-F-802B & PFA/10-10718		25. 8.82	P.J.Tanulak Sleap (Damaged Shrewsbury 22.10.95; on rebuild)		11. 4.96P
G-BKHG	Piper J3C-65 Cub (L-4H-PI)	12062	F-BCPT NC79807/44-79766	13. 9.82	K.G.Wakefield "Puddle Jumper" Brickhouse Farm, Frogland Cross (As "479766/D-63" in HQ 9th Army, USAAC c/s)		18. 3.99P
G-BKHJ	Cessna 182P Skylane II (Reims c/n 0040)	182-64129	PH-CAT D-EATV/N6223F	25. 8.82	Augur Films Ltd Shipdham		7. 8.98
G-BKHR	Luton LA-4A Minor (VW1834)	PFA/51-10228		24. 8.82	C.B.Buscombe & R.Goldsworthy Bodmin		7. 4.99P
G-BKHW	Stoddard-Hamilton Glasair IIRG (Lyc O-320)	357 & PFA/149-11312		27.8.82	G.R.W.Monksfield, D.Callabritto & S.T.Ballard (Woodford Green)		30. 3.99P
G-BKHY	Taylor JT.1 Monoplane (VW 1600)	PFA/1416		8. 9.82	B.C.J.O'Neill Damyns Hall, Upminster		26. 5.99P
G-BKHZ	Reims Cessna F.172P Skyhawk II	2169	D-EJOK	15.10.82	L.R.Leader Clacton		1. 9.01
G-BKIA	Socata TB-10 Tobago	322		25. 8.82	M.F.McGinn Cumbernauld		24. 8.01T
G-BKIB	Socata TB-9 Tampico	323		25. 8.82	G.A.Vickers Chester		22.10.01T
G-BKIC	Cameron V-77 HAFB	859		12. 8.82	C.A.Butter "Passing Wind" Marsh Benham		7. 6.92A
G-BKIE*	Short SD.3-30 Var.100	SH.3005	G-SLUG G-METP/G-METO/G-BKIE/C-GTAS/G-14-3005	15. 9.82	CAA Fire Training Centre Teesside		22. 8.93T
G-BKIF	Fournier RF6B-100	3	F-GADR	8.10.82	G.G.Milton Kimbolton		3. 9.00
G-BKII	Reims Cessna F.172M Skyhawk II	1370	PH-PLO (D-EGIA)	8.10.82	M.S.Knight Goodwood t/a Sealand Aerial Photography		17. 2.01T
G-BKIJ	Reims Cessna F.172M	0920	PH-TGZ	15.10.82	V.D.Speck Clacton/Duxford		2. 9.00T
G-BKIK	Cameron DG-19 Helium Airship	776		23. 8.82	Balloon Preservation Group Farnborough (On loan to Farnborough Air Sciences Trust 7.98)		4. 9.88A
G-BKIN	Alon A-2A Aircoupe	B-253	N5453F	24. 9.82	D.W.Vernon Blackpool		8.10.00
G-BKIR	SAN Jodel D.117	737	F-BIOC	30. 9.82	R.Shaw & D.M.Hardaker (On rebuild 3.96) Birds Edge, Penistone		28. 8.92P
G-BKIS	Socata TB-10 Tobago	329		22. 9.82	I.R.Carver Seething t/a Barber-Cook Carver		9. 6.99

Regn	Type	C/n	P/I	Date	Owner/operator	Probable Base	CA Expy
G-BKIT	Socata TB-9 Tampico	330		22. 9.82	D.N.Garlick, P.D.Foreman & R.M.Pannell	Southend	26. 5.01
G-BKIV*	Colt 21A Cloudhopper HAFB	447		29. 9.82	Not known	?	N/E(A)
G-BKIY	Thunder Ax3 Sky Chariot HAFB	464		7.10.82	Mr Martin "Michaelangelo" (Balloon Preservation Group 7.98)	Lancing	
G-BKIZ	Cameron V-31 Air Chair HAFB	842		1. 2.83	A.P.S.Cox "Camberley"/"Kiss"	Camberley	
G-BKJB	PA-18-135 Super Cub (L-21A-PI) (Frame No.18-522)	18-574	PH-GAI R.Neth AF R-204/51-15657/N1003A	1. 8.83	Haimoss Ltd	Old Sarum	20.12.96T
	(Damaged Kingsmuir House, Anstruther, Fife 4.8.96; stored 1.97)						
G-BKJF	Socata MS.880B Rallye 100T	2300	F-BULF	16.12.82	Journeyman Avn Ltd	Sywell	13. 5.01
G-BKJS	Jodel Wassmer D.120A Paris-Nice	191	F-BJPS	4.10.82	A.J.Bourner	Stoneacre Farm, Farthing Corner	20. 7.99P
G-BKJW	PA-23-250 Aztec E	27-4716	N14153	3.11.78	Alan Williams Entertainments Ltd	Southend	29. 1.98
G-BKKI*	Westland WG.30 Srs.100	003		1.11.82	Westland Helicopters Ltd (Stored 6.91)	Yeovil	28. 6.85P
G-BKKN	Cessna 182R Skylane II	182-67801	N6218N	30.11.82	R.A.Marven t/a Marvagraphic	Coleman Green, Herts	30. 4.01
G-BKKO	Cessna 182R Skylane II	182-67852	N4907H	30.11.82	B & G Jebson Ltd	Crosland Moor	20. 1.99
G-BKKS*	Mercury Dart Srs.1	MA 001		4.11.82	B.A.Mills (Stored 4.95 - construction abandoned)	Great Eversden	
G-BKKZ	Pitts S-1D Special	PFA/09-10525	(G-BIVW)	10.11.82	J.A.Coutts	(Woodbridge)	
G-BKLC	Cameron V-56 HAFB	879		29.11.82	M.A. & J.R.H.Ashworth "Bubbles"	Newquay	6. 5.91A
G-BKLJ*	Westland Scout Srs.1	F.9618	5X-UUX	6. 7.83	R.Dagless (Stored as 5X-UUX 6.93 in poor condition)	East Dereham	
G-BKLO	Reims Cessna F.172M Skyhawk II	1380	PH-BET D-EFMS	22. 3.83	Stapleford F/C Ltd	Stapleford	11. 6.01T
G-BKLP	Reims Cessna F.172N Skyhawk II	1809	PH-BYL	22. 3.83	Euroair Flying Club Ltd	Cranfield	11. 6.01T
G-BKLS*	Aerospatiale SA.341G Gazelle 1	1455	G-TURP G-BKLS/N17MT/N14MT/N49549	11. 1.83	Apollo Helicopters Ltd	Halstead, Essex	2.12.91T
	(Damaged Stanford-le-Hope 9.9.91; on rebuild using fuselage ex N341BB [1421]; orig. fuselage to Redhill 9.93)						
G-BKLZ*	Vinten Wallis WA-116MC (Aka VJ-22 Autogyro)	UMA-01		8.12.82	Wehrtechnische Studiensammlung (As "G-55-2") (On loan to Flugausstellung L & P Junior Museum)	Hermeskeil, Germany	16.12.83P
G-BKMA	Mooney M.20J (201)	24-1316	N1170N	13.12.82	A.C.South t/a Foxtrot Whisky Avn	Cambridge	8. 4.01
G-BKMB	Mooney M.20J (201)	24-1307	N1168P	15.12.82	W.A.Cook, B.Pearson & P.Turnbull	Sherburn	24.11.01
G-BKMD	Short SC.7 Skyvan 3 Var.100	SH.1907	EI-BUB G-BKMD/A40-SK/G-BAHK/G-14-79	20.12.82	R.M.Burnett t/a Army Parachute Association	AAC Netheravon	30. 5.00A
G-BKMG	Handley Page 0/400 Replica (Some components under construction 1993)	TPG-1		8.12.82	M.G.King t/a The Paralyser Grp	(Wroxham, Norwich)	
G-BKMI	VS.359 Spitfire HF.VIIIc	6S/583793	A58-671 MV154	23.12.82	The Aerial Museum (North Weald) Ltd (As "MT928/ZX-M" in 145 Sqn c/s)	North Weald	2. 7.99P
G-BKMK	PA-38-112 Tomahawk	38-80A0081	OO-GME (OO-HKD)	8. 2.83	APB Leasing Ltd	Norwich	12. 2.01T
G-BKMT	PA-32R-301 Saratoga SP	32R-8213013	N8005Z	4. 2.83	P.R. & B.N.Lewis t/a Severn Valley Avn Grp	Welshpool	31. 3.01
G-BKMX	Short SD.3-60 Var.100	SH.3608	G-14-3608	13.12.82	Jersey European Airways (UK) Ltd	Exeter	15. 3.99T
G-BKNA	Cessna 421 Golden Eagle	421-0097	F-BUYB HB-LDZ/N4097L	28. 1.83	Launchapart Ltd (Damaged Penbridge, Hereford 3.8.97)	Barton	13. 8.97
G-BKNB	Cameron V-42 HAFB	887		10. 1.83	D.N.Close	Andover	17. 7.97A
G-BKNI	Gardan GY-80-160D Horizon	249	F-BRJN	28. 1.83	A.Hartigan t/a Blue Horizon F/Grp "Blue Lady"	Bourn	12. 3.99
G-BKNL	Cameron D-96 Hot-Air Airship	805	(I-)	25. 1.83	Sport Promotion SRL	Belbo, Italy	16. 1.97A
	(Rebuilt with new envelope c/n 3192/G-BVHH 1994) G-BKNL/N17830/G-BKNL						
G-BKNO	Monnett Sonerai IIL (VW1834)	792 & PFA/15-10528		11. 3.83	M.D.Hughes	Pauncefoot, Romsey	15. 6.99P
G-BKNP	Cameron V-77 HAFB	874		22.12.82	I.Lilja "Winnie The Pooh"	Kvanum, Sweden	23. 6.99A
G-BKNY*	Bensen B.8M-P-VW	PFA G/01-1030		1. 3.83	D.A.C.MacCormack (Cancelled by CAA 26.2.99; no Permit issued & probably not completed)	Ashford, Kent	
G-BKNZ	Menavia Piel CP.301A Emeraude	296	F-BISZ	21. 1.83	R.N.Crosland & P.R.Teager	Deanland, Hailsham	17.12.98P
G-BKOA	Socata MS.893E Rallye 180GT	12432	F-BOFB F-ODAT/F-BVAT	2. 3.83	N.F.Nowell	(Penzance)	28. 3.99
G-BKOB	Moravan Zlin Z.326 Trener Master	757	F-BKOB	28. 9.81	W.G.V.Hall	Old Sarum	11. 7.99
G-BKOT	Wassmer WA.81 Piranha	813	F-GAIP	17. 2.87	Barbara N.Rolfe	Manor Farm, Glatton	AC
G-BKOU	Hunting P.84 Jet Provost T.3	PAC/W/13901	XN637	17. 2.83	A.Haig-Thomas (As "XN637/03")	North Weald	30. 4.98P
G-BKOW*	Colt 77A HAFB	505		6. 9.84	A D Kent "Lady Di" (Elle c/s) (Balloon Preservation Group 7.98)	Lancing	14. 2.88A
G-BKPA	Hoffmann H-36 Dimona	3522		16. 6.83	A.Mayhew	Rochester	4. 6.99
G-BKPB	Aerosport Scamp (VW1834)	PFA/117-10736		23. 2.83	E.D.Burke	Bidford	28.10.99P
G-BKPC	Cessna A185F AGcarryall	185-03809	N4599E	10. 7.80	The Black Knights Parachute Centre Ltd	Bank End Farm, Cockerham	14. 8.01

Regn	Type	C/n	P/I	Date	Owner/operator	Probable Base	CA Expy
G-BKPD	Viking Dragonfly 302 & PFA/139-10897 (VW1834)			11. 3.83	E.P.Browne & G.J.Sargent (Saffron Walden)		20. 1.00P
G-BKPE	CEA Jodel DR.250/160 Capitaine	35	F-BNJD	18. 3.83	J.S. & J.D.Lewer	Dunkeswell	17.11.01
G-BKPG*	Luscombe P3 Rattler Strike	003		7. 3.83	Not known (Stored 5.95)	Tatenhill	
G-BKPK	Everett Gyroplane (VW 1834)	005		19. 4.83	J.C.McHugh (Stapleford Abbotts) (Stored Sproughton 12.95)		23. 3.93P
G-BKPM	Schempp-Hirth HS.5 Nimbus 2	84	BGA 2025	18. 3.83	J.N.Ellis (See SECTION 3)		
G-BKPN	Cameron N-77 HAFB	923		9. 3.83	R.H.Sanderson "Do It All"	Nuneaton	21. 5.87A
G-BKPS	Grumman-American AA-5B Tiger AA5B-0007		OO-SAS OO-HAO/(OO-WAY)/N1507R	7. 3.83	Scout Centre Ltd	Thruxton	26. 8.00
G-BKPX	Jodel Wassmer D.120A Paris-Nice	240	F-BLNG	19. 1.84	N.H.Martin Skipwith, Selby (Damaged Skipwith, Selby 17.10.96)		12. 2.00P
G-BKPY	SAAB 91B/2 Safir	91321	56321 R.Nor AF "UA-B"	23. 3.83	Newark Air Museum Ltd Winthorpe (As "321" in R.Nor AF c/s)		
G-BKPZ	Pitts S-1T Special PFA/09-10852 (Lyc AEIO-360)			4. 3.83	Mary A.Frost Downland Farm, Redhill		30. 4.99P
G-BKRA	North American T-6G-NH Harvard 188-90		MM53664 RM-9/51-15227	19. 8.83	Transport Command Ltd Shoreham (As "51-15227/10" in US Navy c/s)		25. 6.00T
G-BKRB*	Cessna 172N Skyhawk II	172-72969	EI-BKR G-BHKZ/N1207F	23. 3.83	Not known (Wreck stored 7.95)	Clacton	15. 5.89
G-BKRD*	Cessna 320E Skyknight	320E-0101	D-IACB HB-LDN/N2201Q	24. 3.83	The Fire Service College Moreton-in-Marsh (Crashed Lille, France 5.11.90 & for fire service use 8.98)		30. 9.93
G-BKRF	PA-18-95 Super Cub (L-18C-PI) 18-1525 (Frame No.18-1502)		F-BOUI ALAT/51-15525	7.11.83	K.M.Bishop Croft Farm, Defford		29. 9.98P
G-BKRG*	Beechcraft C-45G-BH AF-222 (Regd as C-45H)		N75WB N9072Z/51-11665	5. 5.83	Aces High Ltd Bruntingthorpe (Spares source for Beechcraft D.18S G-BKRN)		
G-BKRH	Brugger MB.2 Colibri 142 & PFA/43-10150 (VW1835)			15. 3.83	M.R.Benwell Hinton-in-the-Hedges		22. 5.99P
G-BKRI	Cameron V-77 HAFB	909		30. 3.83	D.W.& J.M.Westlake Corlayl, France "Snapdragon II"		24. 6.97A
G-BKRK	SNCAN Stampe SV-4C	57	Fr.Navy	30. 3.83	J.R.Bisset (Stored 8.98) Aboyne t/a Strathgadie Stampe Grp		28. 6.98
G-BKRL*	Chichester-Miles Leopard (Noel Penny 301)	001		21. 3.83	Chichester-Miles Consultants Ltd (Stored 2.97; cancelled as wfu 25.1.99) Cranfield		14.12.91P*
G-BKRN	Beechcraft D.18S CA-75		CF-DTN RCAF A675/RCAF 1500	14. 4.83	A.A.Marshall & P.L.Turland (Ilkeston/Northampton)		26. 6.83PF
G-BKRS	Cameron V-56 HAFB	908		23. 3.83	D.N. & L.J.Close "Bonkers"	Andover	17. 7.97A
G-BKRU	Ensign Crossley Racer PFA/131-10797 (Cont C90)			30. 3.83	M.S.Crossley Redhill (Cancelled by CAA 2.3.99; stored 9.90)		24.1.90P*
G-BKRZ	Dragon 77 HAFB	001		11. 4.83	J.R.Barber "Rupert" Newbury (British Balloon Museum 2.97)		5. 3.94A
G-BKSB	Cessna T310Q II	310Q-0914	VR-CEM G-BKSB/HB-LMO/OE-FYL/(N69680)	22. 4.83	Flightline Ltd	Southend	1. 5.00
G-BKSC	Saro Skeeter AOP.12 S2/7157 (C/n officially S2/7076 but may be component no.)		XN351	23. 5.83	R.A.L.Falconer Ipswich (As "XN351")		8.11.84P
G-BKSD	Colt 56A HAFB	361		11. 4.83	M.J.Casson Kendal "Entwhistle Green"		2. 6.96A
G-BKSE	QAC Quickie 1 PFA/94-10748 (Onan B48M) (Regd with c/n PFA/94-10784)			6. 4.83	M.D.Burns (Glasgow) (Status uncertain)		8. 5.89P
G-BKSP	Schleicher ASK 14	14028	D-KOMO	25. 5.83	J.H.Bryson Bellarena		28. 3.00
G-BKSS	SAN Jodel 150 Mascaret	48	F-BMFC	14. 9.83	D.H.Wilson-Spratt (Peel, IoM) (Status uncertain)		
G-BKST	Rutan VariEze	12718-001		20. 4.83	R.Towle (Hexham)		
G-BKSX	SNCAN Stampe SV-4C	61	F-BBAF Fr.Mil	16. 5.83	C.A.Bailey & J.A.Carr (Stored 8.90) Trenchard Farm, Eggesford		15. 6.89
G-BKTA	PA-18-95 Super Cub 18-3223 (L-18C-PI) (Frame No.18-3246)		OO-HBA OL-L149/53-4823	10. 5.83	M.J.Dyson & M.T.Clark Fradley		19. 5.99P
G-BKTH	Hawker (CCF) Sea Hurricane IB CCF/41H/4013		Z7015	24. 5.83	The Shuttleworth Trust Duxford (As "Z7015/7-L" in 880 Sqdn, RN c/s)		31. 5.99P
G-BKTM	PZL SZD-45A Ogar	B-656		31. 5.83	Repclif Chemical Services Ltd Liverpool		14.10.99
G-BKTR	Cameron V-77 HAFB	951		6. 6.83	C.Wilson "Diddlybopper" Potters Bar		29. 9.99A
G-BKTV	Reims Cessna F.152 II	1450	OY-BJB	8. 8.83	Seawing Flying Club Ltd Southend		24. 6.99T
G-BKTY	Socata TB-10 Tobago	363	F-BNGZ	7. 6.83	B.M. & G.M.McClelland Crosland Moor		22. 4.99
G-BKTZ	Slingsby T-67M Firefly	2004	G-SFTV	26. 8.83	T.D.Reid (Craigavon, NI)		24. 7.99
G-BKUE	Socata TB-9 Tampico	369	F-BNGX	31. 5.83	W.J.Moore Carlisle		15. 7.99
G-BKUJ	Thunder Ax6-56 Srs.1 HAFB	520		17. 6.83	R.J.Bent "Edward Bear" Torquay		28. 9.88A
G-BKUR	Menavia Piel CP.301A Emeraude	280	(G-BKBX) F-BMLX/F-OBLY	19.10.83	R.Wells Peterlee		21. 6.99P
G-BKUS	Bensen B.8M PFA G/01-1045			7. 7.83	A.Charles Newbury		21. 6.88P
G-BKUU	Thunder Ax7-77 Srs.1 HAFB	522		3. 8.83	D.A.Kozuba-Kozubska London WC1 "Tanglefoot"		16. 9.94A
G-BKVA	Socata Rallye 180T Galerien	3274	SE-GFS F-GBXA	30. 6.83	J.M.Airey Saltby t/a Buckminster Gliding Club Syndicate		7. 6.01T
G-BKVB	Socata Rallye 110ST Galopin	3258	OO-PIP	22. 6.83	C.Tilley (Wolverhampton)		16.12.01
G-BKVC	Socata TB-9 Tampico	372	F-BNGQ	4. 7.83	H.P.Aubin-Parvu Biggin Hill		5. 2.99
G-BKVE	Rutan VariEze PFA/74-10236 (Cont O-200-A)		G-EZLT	5. 7.83	Vandgard ACG Ltd & Temporal Songs Ltd (Tunbridge Wells)		3. 9.99P

Regn	Type	C/n	P/I	Date	Owner/operator	Probable Base	CA Expy
G-BKVF	Clutton FRED Srs.III PFA/29-10791			29. 7.83	A.R.Hawes	Stowmarket	
G-BKVG	Scheibe SF-25E Super Falke	4362	(D-KNAE)	25. 8.83	G-BKVG Ltd	North Hill	4. 6.99
G-BKVK	Auster AOP.9	AUS/10/2	WZ662	8. 8.83	J.D.Butcher	AAC Middle Wallop	24. 9.99P
					(Op Military Auster Flt) (As "WZ662" in Army c/s)		
G-BKVL	Robin DR.400/160 Major	1625		26. 7.83	M.R.Shelton	Tatenhill	23.11.98T
					t/a Tatenhill Aviation		
G-BKVM	PA-18-150 Super Cub	18-849	PH-KAZ	26. 8.83	D.G.Caffrey	North Reston, Louth	24. 7.99
	(L-21A-PI) (Frame No.18-824)		R.Neth AF R-214/51-15684		(As "115684" in US Army c/s) "Spirit of Goxhill"		
G-BKVO	Pietenpol Air Camper PFA/47-10799			8. 8.83	B.P.Waites "Emily"		
	(Cont A65)					Spilsted Farm, Sedlescombe	25. 5.99P
G-BKVP	Pitts S-1D Special 002 & PFA/09-10800			19. 8.83	P.J.Leggo	(Linton, Cambs)	27. 8.99P
	(Lyc O-360)						
G-BKVS	Campbell Cricket	G/01-1047		11. 8.83	A.J.Unwin "Yorkie"	Kemble	13. 4.98P
	(VW 1834)						
G-BKVT	PA-23-250 Aztec E	27-7754002	G-HARV N62760	6. 2.84	BKS Surveys Ltd.	Belfast/Exeter	9. 4.00T
G-BKVW	Airtour AH-56 HAFB	AH.003		27. 6.84	L.D. & H.Vaughan "Lunardi"	Tring	
G-BKVX	Airtour AH-56C HAFB	AH.002		27. 6.84	P.Aldridge	Halesworth, Suffolk	
					"Featherspin" or "Liebling"		
G-BKVY	Airtour B-31 HAFB	AH.001		9. 8.83	M.Davies	Callington, Cornwall	17. 6.97A
					"Day Dream"		
G-BKWD	Taylor JT.2 Titch PFA/60-10232			17. 8.83	E.H.Booker	Valley Farm, Winwick	16. 6.99P
	(Cont PC60) (Originally regd as c/n PFA/60-10143; presumed absorbed into both projects)						
G-BKWE	Colt 17A Cloudhopper HAFB	533		1.11.83	Flying Pictures Ltd	Fairoaks	24.11.96A
					"Pooh Bear/DisneyChannel"		
G-BKWG	PZL-104 Wilga 35A	17820687	SP-WAC	10. 8.83	H & C Balfour Paul	Cumbernauld	30. 9.01A
G-BKWR	Cameron V-65 HAFB	970		26. 8.83	K.J.Foster	Coleshill, Birmingham	18. 4.99A
					"White Spirit"		
G-BKWW	Cameron O-77 HAFB	984		13. 9.83	A.M.Marten "Kouros"	Woking	18. 1.89A
G-BKWY	Reims Cessna F.152T	1940		22. 9.83	The Cambridge Aero Club Ltd	Cambridge	23. 6.99T
G-BKXA	Robin R.2100	114	F-GAOS	24.11.83	G.G.Beal t/a G-BKXA Group	Cumbernauld	22.10.99
G-BKXD	Aerospatiale SA.365N Dauphin 2	6088	F-WMHD	7. 9.83	Bond Helicopters Ltd	Blackpool	8.12.01T
G-BKXF	PA-28R-200 Cherokee Arrow II	28R-7335351	OY-DZN N56092	10.11.83	P.L.Brunton	Caernarfon	20. 5.99T
G-BKXG	Cessna T303 Crusader	T303-00195	N9616C	22. 9.83	Wm Ewington & Co Ltd	Woodford	1. 6.01
G-BKXM	Colt 17A Cloudhopper HAFB	531		3.10.83	R.G.Turnbull	Glasbury, Hereford	1. 2.99A
G-BKXN	ICA IS-28M2A	48		24.10.83	T.J.Mills	Shobdon	3. 5.00
G-BKXO	Rutan LongEz PFA/74A-10580			24.10.83	D.F.P.Finan & Cambridge Perfusion Svs Ltd	Teesside	14. 6.99P
	(Cont O-200-A)						
G-BKXP	Auster AOP.6	2830		12.10.83	B.J. & W.J.Ellis		
	(Frame No. TAY841BJ)		Belg AF A-14/VT987		(On rebuild 7.91)	Little Gransden	
G-BKXR	Druine D.31A Turbulent	303	OY-AMW	1.11.83	M.B.Hill	Draycott Farm, Chiseldon	12.11.99P
	(VW1700)						
G-BKXX	Cameron V-65 HAFB	1000	(OO-) G-BKXX	1. 9.83	L.J.H.Decabooter & L.P.Neirynck "Hot Mille"	St.Niklaas/Ostend, Belgium	24. 7.99A
G-BKYA	Boeing 737-236ADV	23159		14. 9.84	British Airways plc	Manchester	27. 9.01T
					"Ariel"		
G-BKYB	Boeing 737-236ADV	23160		27. 9.84	British Airways plc	Birmingham	9.10.01T
					(Blue Poole t/s)		
G-BKYE	Boeing 737-236ADV	23163		1.11.84	British Airways plc	Birmingham	12.11.01T
					(Water Dreaming t/s)		
G-BKYH	Boeing 737-236ADV	23166		13.12.84	British Airways plc	Birmingham	20.12.01T
					"Hotspur"		
G-BKYI	Boeing 737-236ADV	23167		7. 1.85	British Airways plc	Birmingham	16. 1.02T
					"River Waveney"		
G-BKYK	Boeing 737-236ADV	23169		1. 2.85	British Airways plc	Birmingham	11. 2.02T
					"River Foyle"		
G-BKYL	Boeing 737-236ADV	23170		22. 2.85	British Airways plc	Gatwick	3. 3.99T
					"Titania"		
G-BKYM	Boeing 737-236ADV	23171		1. 3.85	British Airways plc	Birmingham	10. 3.99T
					"Moonshine"		
G-BKYN	Boeing 737-236ADV	23172		21. 3.85	British Airways plc	Manchester	31. 3.99T
					"Prince Hal"		
G-BKYO	Boeing 737-236ADV	23225		12. 4.85	British Airways plc	Manchester	18. 4.99T
					"Oberon"		
G-BKYP	Boeing 737-236ADV	23226		24. 4.85	British Airways plc	Manchester	1. 5.99T
					(Waves & Cranes t/s)		
G-BKZB	Cameron V-77 HAFB	995		11.11.83	G.W.G.C. Sudlow	Somerton	30. 4.95A
					"Camelot Clodhopper"		
G-BKZE	Aerospatiale AS.332L Super Puma	2102	F-WKQE	30. 9.83	Brintel Helicopters Ltd	Aberdeen	13. 3.00T
					t/a British International Helicopters		
G-BKZF	Cameron V-56 HAFB	246	F-BXUK	14.11.83	A.D.Brice "Xplorer"	Cowbridge	18. 3.97A
G-BKZG	Aerospatiale AS.332L Super Puma	2106		30. 9.83	Brintel Helicopters Ltd	Aberdeen	26. 1.00T
					t/a British International Helicopters		

Regn	Type	C/n	P/I	Date	Owner/operator	Probable Base	CA Expy
G-BKZH	Aerospatiale AS.332L Super Puma	2107		30. 9.83	Brintel Helicopters Ltd t/a British International Helicopters	Aberdeen	4. 4.00T
G-BKZI	Bell 206A JetRanger (P/i is either 5B-CGC or CGD ntu)	118	(5B-CG?) G-BKZI/N6238N	7.12.83	Dolphin Property (Management) Ltd	Old Sarum	19. 9.01T
G-BKZM	Isaacs Fury II (Cont O-200-A)	PFA/11-10742		27. 9.83	B.Jones (As "K2060") (Stored 8.96)	Haverfordwest	1.10.90P
G-BKZT	Clutton FRED Srs.II (VW1834)	PFA/29-10715		20.10.83	D.C.Mayle & M.V.Pettifer	White Waltham	16.12.99P
G-BKZV	Bede BD-4 (Lyc O-320)	380	ZS-UAB	31. 8.84	G.I.J.Thomson	Little Snoring	4. 8.99P

G-BLAA-BLZZ

Regn	Type	C/n	P/I	Date	Owner/operator	Probable Base	CA Expy
G-BLAA	Sportavia Fournier RF5	5011	D-KIHI	3.10.83	A.D.Wren	Southend	11. 9.99
G-BLAC	Reims Cessna FA.152 Aerobat	0370		25. 3.80	Tilbrook Industries Ltd (Op Osprey F/C) (Stored 7.97)	Cranfield	24. 3.01T
G-BLAD	Thunder Ax7-77 Srs.1 HAFB	485		7.12.83	P.J.Bish "Big Lad" (Stolen from Hungerford 5.8.92)	Hungerford	15.10.92A
G-BLAF	Stolp SA.900 V-Star (Cont O-200-A)	PFA/106-10651		13. 9.83	P.R.Skeels	Tatenhill	13. 9.99P
G-BLAG	Pitts S-1D Special (Lyc AEIO-360)	PFA/09-10195		1.12.83	P.M.Ambrose	Popham	15. 4.99P
G-BLAH	Thunder Ax7-77 Srs.1 HAFB	526		3.10.83	T.M.Donnelly "Blah"	Doncaster	7. 4.96A
G-BLAI	Monnett Sonerai IIL (Regd with c/n PFA/15-10584)	PFA/15-10583		6.12.83	T.Simpson (Noted 9.98)	Breighton	12. 1.99P
G-BLAM	CEA DR.360 Chevalier	345	F-BRCM	6. 2.84	D.J.Durell	Maypole Farm, Chislet	8. 8.99
G-BLAT	SAN Jodel 150 Mascaret	56	F-BNID	30. 1.84	D.J.Dulborough & A.J.Court	Popham	11. 6.99P
G-BLAX	Reims Cessna FA.152 Aerobat	0385		11.10.83	Bournemouth F/Club Ltd	Bournemouth	23. 4.99T
G-BLCA	Bell 206B JetRanger III	3443	N20982	1.12.83	RMH Stainless Ltd (Op Central Helicopters) Orgreave Gorse Farm, Lichfield		27. 3.99T
G-BLCG	Socata TB-10 Tobago	61	G-BHES	17. 3.80	P.Hickey & M.E.Woodroffe t/a Charlie Golf F/Grp	Shoreham	25. 6.01
G-BLCH	Colt 56D HAFB	392		14.11.83	Balloon Flights Club Ltd "Geronimo"	Leicester	
G-BLCI	EAA AcroSport P	P-10A	N6AS	29. 2.84	M.R.Holden "Bluebottle" (Damaged Farthing Corner late 1996) Stoneacre Farm, Farthing Corner		16. 6.97P
G-BLCM	Socata TB-9 Tampico	194	OO-TCT (OO-TBC)	2.12.83	Repclif Chemical Services Ltd (Op Liverpool F/School)	Liverpool	29. 5.99T
G-BLCT	CEA Jodel DR.220 2+2	23	F-BOCQ	22.12.83	C.J.Snell t/a Christopher Robin F/Grp	Shoreham	9. 7.99
G-BLCU	Scheibe SF-25B Falke	4699	D-KECC	30.12.83	C.F.Sellers	Rufforth	7. 6.99
G-BLCV	Hoffmann H-36 Dimona	36113	EI-CJO G-BLCV	21. 3.84	R.L.Braithwaite	(Warton)	4. 6.99
G-BLCW	Evans VP-1 (VW1600)	PFA/62-10835		19.12.83	K.D.Pearce "Le Plank"	Southery	28. 6.96P
G-BLCY	Thunder Ax7-65Z HAFB	487		13. 1.84	C.M.George	Brixton, Plymouth	26. 2.99A
G-BLDB	Taylor JT.1 Monoplane (VW1600)	PFA/55-10506		28.12.83	C.J.Bush	Great Oakley, Harwich	15. 5.99P
G-BLDC*	K & S Jungster 1	PFA/44-10701		29.12.83	A.W.Brown (Cancelled by CAA 6.3.99; no Permit issued)	(Oxenhope)	
G-BLDD	WAG-Aero CUBy AcroTrainer (Lyc O-320)	PFA/108-10653		29.12.83	J.K.Davies	(Chester)	21.12.99P
G-BLDG	PA-25-260 Pawnee C	25-4501	SE-FLB LN-VYM	9. 1.84	Ouse Gliding Club Ltd	Rufforth	16. 6.99
G-BLDK	Robinson R-22	0139	C-GSGU	17. 1.84	Warrenform Ltd	White Waltham	24. 6.99T
G-BLDL*	Cameron Truck 56 SS HAFB	990		10. 1.84	I.Warrington & R.S Kent "Europa" Lancing t/a Balloon Preservation Group Balloon Team		N/E(A)
G-BLDV	PBN BN-2B-26 Islander	2179	D-INEY G-BLDV	13. 1.84	Loganair Ltd Glasgow (Mountain of the Birds/Benyhone Tartan c/s)		10. 7.99T
G-BLEB	Colt 69A HAFB	537		20. 1.84	I.R.M.Jacobs "Gusto"	Reading	N/E(A)
G-BLEJ	PA-28-161 Warrior II	28-7816257	N2194M	8. 2.84	Eglinton F/C Ltd	Eglinton	3. 3.99T
G-BLEL*	Price Ax7-77-245 HAFB	001		23. 1.84	Theresa S.Price "Butterfly"	Edgware	
G-BLEP	Cameron V-65 HAFB	1022		7. 2.84	D.Chapman t/a The Ground Hogs "Manor Marquees"	Maidstone	10. 9.96A
G-BLES	Stolp SA.750 Acroduster Too (Lyc O-360)	197 & PFA/89-10428		8.12.83	T.W.Harris	Little Snoring	11. 3.99P
G-BLET	Thunder Ax7-77 Srs.1 HAFB	539		16. 2.84	Servatruc Ltd "Servatruc"	Nottingham	15. 8.97A
G-BLEW	Reims Cessna F.182Q Skylane II	0039	F-GAQD	21. 6.78	D.J.Cross	Cumbernauld	1. 5.00
G-BLEZ	Aerospatiale SA.365N Dauphin 2	6131		24. 1.84	Bond Helicopters Ltd	Blackpool	27. 8.99T
G-BLFI	PA-28-181 Archer II	28-8490034	N4333Z	22. 2.84	Bonus Avn Ltd	Cranfield	22. 7.00T
G-BLFW	Grumman-American AA-5 Traveler	AA5-0786	OO-GLW	22. 2.84	D.C.A.Milne t/a Grumman Club	Draycott Farm, Chiseldon	13. 6.99
G-BLFY	Cameron V-77 HAFB	1030		16. 3.84	A.N.F.Pertwee "Groupie"	Frinton-on-Sea	5. 4.92A
G-BLFZ	PA-31-310 Turbo Navajo C	31-7912106	PH-RWS N3538W	21. 3.84	London Executive Aviation Ltd Stapleford		10. 7.99T
G-BLGH	Robin DR.300/180R Remorqueur	570	D-EAFL	10. 4.84	Booker Gliding Club Ltd	Booker	15. 2.00
G-BLGO	Bensen B.8MV (VW 1834)	RB-01		18. 6.84	F.Vernon (Stored 8.94)	St.Merryn	15.5.87P*
G-BLGR	Bell 47G-4A	7501	N3236G HC-ASQ/N1186W	2. 5.84	H., J.R. & H.C.Wake & S.P.Broughton & Co Ltd t/a Courteenhall Farms Courteenhall, Northampton		8. 5.99
G-BLGS	Socata Rallye 180T	3206		7. 7.78	Lasham Gliding Society Ltd	Lasham	21. 5.99
G-BLGT	PA-18-95 Super Cub (L-18C-PI) (Frame No.18-1399)	18-1445	D-EAGT D-EOCC/ALAT 51-15445	1. 6.84	T.A.Reed	Watchford Farm, Yarcombe	14. 5.99P
G-BLGV	Bell 206B JetRanger II	982	5B-JSB C-FDYL/CF-DYL	2. 5.84	Partreward Ltd (Op Unique Avn Grp)	Shobdon	29. 5.00T
G-BLGX*	Thunder Ax7-65 HAFB	551		16. 4.84	"The 45"	?	N/E(A)
G-BLHH	CEA DR.315 Petit Prince	324	F-BPRH	3. 7.84	G.G.Milton	Kimbolton	29. 5.00
G-BLHI	Colt 17A Cloudhopper HAFB	506		8. 9.86	Janet A.Folkes "Hopping Mad"	Loughborough	3. 1.96A

Regn	Type	C/n	P/I	Date	Owner/operator	Probable Base	CA Expy
G-BLHJ	Reims Cessna F.172P Skyhawk II	2182		26. 3.84	J.Easson (Op Edinburgh Air Centre)	Edinburgh	2. 5.99T
G-BLHK	Colt 105A HAFB	576		19. 6.84	A.S.Dear, R.B.Green & W.S.Templeton t/a Hale Hot-Air Balloon Grp "Gloworm"	Fordingbridge	12. 7.97A
G-BLHL*	Menavia CP.301A Emeraude	275	F-BLHL F-OBLM	2. 3.78	The Fire Service College (Crashed Slinfold 4.8.81 & for fire service use 8.98)	Moreton-in-Marsh	27. 5.81P
G-BLHM(2)	PA-18-95 Super Cub (L-18C-PI) (Frame No.18-3088)	18-3120	LX-AIM D-EOAB/Belg AF OL-L46/53-4720	23. 7.84	B.N.C.Mogg	Bibberne Farm, Stalbridge	10. 7.99P
G-BLHN	Robin HR.100/285 Tiara	539	F-GABF	20. 2.78	Tarist Ltd	(Llangarron)	15. 5.00
G-BLHR	Gulfstream GA-7 Cougar	GA7-0109	OO-RTI (OO-HRC)/N751G	12. 4.84	T.E.Westley	(Newmarket)	20.11.99T
G-BLHS	Bellanca 7ECA Citabria 115	1342-80	OO-RTQ	12. 4.84	N.J.F.Campbell	Inverness	21. 3.99
G-BLHW	Varga 2150A Kachina	VAC161-80		17. 7.84	W.D.Garlick t/a Kachina Hotel Whiskey Group	Damyns Hall, Upminster	20. 1.00
G-BLID	FFW DH.112 Venom FB.50 (FB.1)	815	J-1605	13. 7.84	P.G.Vallance Ltd (As "J-1605" in Swiss AF c/s)	Charlwood, Surrey	AC
G-BLIE	FFW DH.112 Venom FB.50 (FB.1)	824	J-1614	28. 2.85	Gone Flying Ltd. (As "J-1614" in Swiss AF c/s)	North Weald	AC
G-BLIG	Cameron V-65 HAFB	1045		24. 4.84	W.Davison "Peek-A-Boo II"	Chesterfield	3. 8.91A
G-BLIH	PA-18-135 Super Cub (L-21B-PI) (Frame No.18-3827)	18-3828	(PH-KNG) R Neth AF R-138/54-2428	12.11.84	I.R.F.Hammond	Stubbington	AC
G-BLIK	Wallis WA-116/F/S (Franklin 2A-120)	K-218X		30. 4.84	K.H.Wallis	Reymerston Hall	24. 4.98P
G-BLIO*	Cameron R-42 Gas Free Balloon	1015		17. 4.84	British Balloon Museum & Library	Newbury	17. 5.84P*
G-BLIP*	Cameron N-77 HAFB	1031		17. 4.84	Balloon Preservation Group "Systems 80"	Lancing	26. 3.94A
G-BLIT	Thorp T-18CW (Lyc O-320)	PFA/76-10550		24. 4.84	K.B.Hallam	Fairoaks	16. 6.99P
G-BLIW	Percival P.56 Provost T.53	PAC/F/125	IAC.177	12. 6.85	D.Mould & J.De Uphaugh t/a Provost F/Grp (As "177" in Irish Air Corps c/s)	Shoreham	1. 9.99P
G-BLIX	Saro Skeeter AOP.12	S2/5094	PH-HOF (PH-SRE)/XL809	3. 5.84	K.M.Scholes (As "XL809"in Army c/s)	Wilden	18. 8.99P
G-BLIY	Socata MS.892A Rallye Commodore 150	11639	F-BSCX	9. 5.84	A.J.Brasher & K.R.Haynes Church Farm, North Moreton, Wallingford		14. 5.00
G-BLJD	Glaser-Dirks DG-400	4-85		15. 6.84	M.I.Gee	(London NW3)	17. 6.99
G-BLJF	Cameron O-65 HAFB	1041		14. 5.84	M.D.Mitchell "Fat Lady"	Sevenoaks	19. 5.98A
G-BLJH	Cameron N-77 HAFB	1047		14. 5.84	K A Kent "Daydream" (Balloon Preservation Group 7.98)	Lancing	27. 6.89A
G-BLJM	Beechcraft 95-B55 Baron	TC-1997	SE-GRT	3. 3.78	R.A.Perrot	Guernsey	7. 8.00
G-BLJO	Reims Cessna F.152 II	1627	OY-BNB	21. 6.84	Redhill School of Flying Ltd t/a Redhill F/C	Redhill	17. 8.01T
G-BLKA	FFW DH.112 Venom FB.54 (FB.4) (Regd with c/n 431)	960	(G-VENM) Sw AF J-1790	13. 7.84	De Havilland Aviation Ltd (As "WR410/N" in 6 Sqdn RAF c/s)	Swansea	14. 7.95P
G-BLKJ*	Thunder Ax7-65 HAFB	580		18. 7.84	R S Kent "Up & Coming" (Balloon Preservation Group 7.98)	Lancing	3. 2.96A
G-BLKK	Evans VP-1 (VW1834)	PFA/62-10642		15. 6.84	D.J.Hunter	(Norwich)	5. 8.99P
G-BLKM	CEA Jodel DR.1051 Sicile	519	F-BLRO	26. 6.84	T.C.Humphreys	Goodwood	27. 6.00
G-BLKP	BAe Jetstream 3102	634	(G-BLEX) G-31-634	9. 7.84	British Aerospace (Operations) Ltd	Farnborough/Warton	19. 4.01
G-BLKU*	Colt Flame 56SS HAFB	572		17. 7.84	British Balloon Museum & Library "Mr.Wonderful II"	Newbury	N/E(A)
G-BLKY	Beechcraft 58 Baron	TH-1440		22. 8.84	P.R.Earp	Gloucestershire	4. 3.00
G-BLKZ	Pilatus P.2-05	600-45	U-125 A-125	30. 7.84	R.W.Hinton	Duxford	21.12.99P
G-BLLA	Bensen B.8M (VW1834)	PFA G/01-1055		27. 6.84	K.T.Donaghey	Gerrards Cross	22. 6.98P
G-BLLB	Bensen B.8MR (Rotax 532)	PFA G/01A-1059		4. 9.84	D.H.Moss	Chilbolton	10. 3.99P
G-BLLD	Cameron O-77 HAFB	1060		16. 7.84	G.Birchall	Ormskirk	22. 5.99A
G-BLLH	CEA Jodel DR.220A-B 2+2	131	F-BROM	17. 7.84	P.Chamberlain & D.E.Starkey	White Waltham	18. 6.00
G-BLLM	PA-23-250 Aztec E	27-4619	G-BBNM OY-POR/G-BBNM/N14001	18. 1.84	C & M Thomas t/a Ammanford Trade Sales	Cardiff	21. 8.98
G-BLLN	PA-18-95 Super Cub (L-18C-PI) (Cont O-200A) (Frame No.18-3380)	18-3447	D-ECLN 96+23/PY+901/QZ+011/AC+508/AS+508/54-747	27. 6.84	A.L.Hall-Carpenter	Swanton Morley	21.12.00T
G-BLLO	PA-18-95 Super Cub (L-18C-PI) (Frame No.18-3058)	18-3099	D-EAUB Belg AF OL-L25/53-4699	11. 7.84	D.G. & M.G.Margetts Vaynor Farm, Llanidloes, Powys		12.10.96P
G-BLLP	Slingsby T-67B	2008		19. 7.84	Cleveland Flying School Ltd	Teesside	4.12.00T
G-BLLR	Slingsby T-67B	2011		19. 7.84	R.L.Brinklow	Biggin Hill	12.10.01T
G-BLLS	Slingsby T-67B	2013		19. 7.84	Western Air (Thruxton) Ltd	Thruxton	12.12.99T
G-BLLV	Slingsby T-67C	2015		3. 9.84	R.L.Brinklow	Turweston	10.11.00T
G-BLLW	Colt 56B HAFB	578		11. 9.84	G.Fordyce, R.Wickens & S.A.Sawyer "Angel Clare"	Olney	13.12.98A

Regn	Type	C/n	P/I	Date	Owner/operator	Probable Base	CA Expy
G-BLLZ	Rutan LongEz (Lyc O-235)	PFA/74A-10830		16. 7.84	R.S.Stoddart-Stones	Henstridge	22. 6.94P
G-BLMA	Moravan Zlin Z.526A Trener Master	922	F-BORS	23. 7.84	G.P.Northcott	Redhill	24. 6.01
G-BLMC*	Avro 698 Vulcan B.2A		XM575 R		East Midlands Aeropark (As "XM575")	East Midlands	
G-BLME	Robinson R-22HP	0032	N90261	16. 4.85	Heli Air Ltd	Wellesbourne Mountford	2. 9.99T
G-BLMG	Grob G-109B	6322		27. 9.84	P.R.Holloway t/a Mike Golf Syndicate	Enstone	25.10.99
G-BLMI	PA-18-95 Super Cub (L-18C-PI) (Frame No.18-2086)	18-2066	D-ENWI R	5. 6.84	B.J.Borsberry Kidmore End, Reading Neth AF R-55/52-2466 (Stored 8.90)		31. 5.87P
G-BLMN	Rutan LongEz (Lyc O-235) (Regd as c/n PFA/74A-10648)	PFA/74A-10643		3. 7.84	S.E.Bowers t/a G-BLMN F/Grp	Thruxton	28. 9.99P
G-BLMP	PA-17 Vagabond (Cont A65)	17-193	F-BFMR N4893H	15. 5.84	M.Austin	Lower Upham	29. 6.99P
G-BLMR	PA-18-150 Super Cub (L-18C-PI) (Frame No.18-2070)	18-2057	D-ELGH R	29. 5.84	Bidford Gliding Centre Ltd Bidford Neth AF R-72/52-2457		22. 5.99T
G-BLMT	PA-18-135 Super Cub (Frame No.18-2724)	18-2706	D-ELGH N8558C	12. 9.84	I.S.Runnalls Church Farm, North Moreton, Wallingford		9. 7.99
G-BLMW	Nipper T.66 RA45 Mk.IIIB (Ardem 10)	PFA/25-11020		31. 8.84	S.L.Millar	Crowland	30. 6.99P
G-BLMX	Reims Cessna FR.172H Rocket	0327	PH-RPC	5. 9.84	C.J.W.Littler	Marshland, Wisbech	16.12.99
G-BLMZ	Colt 105A HAFB	404		24. 9.84	Mandy D.Dickinson "Zulu"	Bristol	28. 3.97A
G-BLNJ	PBN BN-2B-26 Islander	2189		3. 9.84	Loganair Ltd (South Africa t/s)	Glasgow	3.12.99T
G-BLNL	PBN BN-2T Islander	2191	PH-RPN G-BLNL	3. 9.84	Britten-Norman Ltd	Bembridge	
G-BLNO	Clutton FRED Srs.III	PFA/29-10559		17.10.84	L.W.Smith	(Sale, Cheshire)	
G-BLNW	PBN BN-2B-26 Islander	2197		3. 9.84	Loganair Ltd Glasgow (Op Scottish Air Ambulance) "Sister Jean Kennedy"		21.12.99T
G-BLOB	Colt 31A Air Chair HAFB	599		11. 9.84	Jacques W.Soukup Enterprises Ltd South Dakota, USA		5. 6.91A
G-BLOL	SNCAN Stampe SV.4A	SS-SV-R1 & 554	G-AXRP	12. 2.85	T Moore (Sandy)		5. 6.76S
	(Originally registered 7.11.69 as SV.4C G-AXRP (554) ex F-BDCZ) t/a Skysport Engineering						
	(Damaged Gransden 19.10.74; restored 9.94 as G-AXRP; stored Rotary Farm, Hatch 7.95)						
G-BLOR	PA-30-160 Twin Comanche	30-59	HB-LAE N7097Y	19. 7.85	R.L.C.Appleton Gloucestershire (On overhaul 10.97)		31. 8.91T
G-BLOS	Cessna 185A Skywagon (Also operates on floats)	185-0359	LN-BDS N4159Y	17. 9.84	Elizabeth Brun	Great Massingham	20. 4.00
G-BLOT	Colt 56B HAFB	424		11. 9.84	H.J.Anderson "Pathfinder"	Oswestry	17. 7.96A
G-BLOU	Rand-Robinson KR-2	PFA/129-11118		4.12.85	D.G.Cole	(Martley, Worcs)	
G-BLOV*	Thunder Ax5-42 Srs.1 HAFB	590		11. 9.84	Not known "Puff The Magic Dragon" (USA)		N/E(A)
	(Cancelled 11.2.91 as sold to USA but noted active as G-BLOV in 9.93)						
G-BLPA	Piper J3C-65 Cub (L-4H-PI) (Frame No.11152)	11327	OO-AJL OO-JOE/43-30036	27. 9.84	C.J.Gray	Turweston	12. 7.99P
G-BLPB	Turner TSW Hot Two Wot (Lyc O-320-A)	PFA/46-10606		19.10.84	I.R.Hannah	Temploux, Belgium	4. 6.98P
G-BLPE	PA-18-95 Super Cub (L-18C-PI) (Cont O-200-A) (Also quoted as 18-3083)	18-3084	D-ECBE Belg Army L-10/53-4684	28. 9.84	A.A.Haig-Thomas	Clacton	5. 5.99P
G-BLPF	Reims Cessna FR.172G Rocket	0187	N4594Q D-EEFL	29. 1.85	W.A.F.Cuninghame	Prestwick	2.11.00
G-BLPG	Auster J/1N Alpha	3395	G-AZIH	21. 5.82	Q.J.Ball Pent Farm, Postling, Kent (As "16693" in RCAF c/s)		25. 3.00
G-BLPH	Reims Cessna FRA.150L Aerobat	0239	EI-BHH PH-ASH	19. 9.84	G.K. & T.G.Solomon Shoreham t/a The New Aerobat Grp		25. 6.00
G-BLPI	Slingsby T-67B	2016		24. 9.84	R.C.McCloud	RAF Laarbruch	21. 7.00T
G-BLPK*	Cameron V-65 HAFB	1069		24. 9.84	A.J. & C.P.Nicholls "Millie" Bristol t/a Bernard Hunter & Bristol Cine Sales (Cancelled by CAA 19.1.99)		9. 8.96A
G-BLPM	Aerospatiale AS.332L Super Puma	2122	LN-ONB	5.10.84	Bristow Helicopters Ltd Aberdeen G-BLPM/G-GQCB/G-BLPM "Balmedie"		18.10.01T
G-BLPP	Cameron V-77 HAFB	432		19. 9.78	L.P.Purfield "Merlin"	Leicester	30. 4.94A
G-BLRA	BAe 146 Srs.100	E-1017	N117TR	3.10.84	British Aerospace (Operations) Ltd Woodford N462AP/CP-2249/N462AP/G-BLRA/G-5-02		15.10.99
G-BLRC	PA-18-135 Super Cub (L-21B-PI) (Frame No.18-3790)	18-3602	OO-DKC PH-DKC/R Neth R-112/54-2402	27.11.84	A.J.McBurnie	Seething	4.12.00
G-BLRD	MBB Bo.209 Monsun 150FV	101	D-EBOA (OE-AHM)	15.10.84	Margaret D.Ward	Kemble	23.11.00
G-BLRF	Slingsby T-67C	2014		30.11.84	Bristow Helicopters Ltd	Redhill	2. 1.00T
G-BLRG	Slingsby T-67B	2020		30.11.84	R.L.Brinklow RAF Wyton (Op Wyton Flying Club)		17. 7.00T
G-BLRH	Rutan LongEz	PFA/74A-11073		7. 2.85	G.L.Thompson	(Kingsbridge, Devon)	
G-BLRJ	CEA Jodel DR.1051 Sicile	502	F-BLRJ	8. 2.78	M.P.Hallam	Jackrells Farm, Horsham	17. 7.00
G-BLRL	Scintex CP-301C1 Emeraude	552	(G-BLNP)	5.11.84	B.C.Davis	Palma/Son Bonet, Mallorca	16. 9.99P
G-BLRM	Glaser-Dirks DG-400	4-107		5. 2.85	D.J.Barke	Tatenhill	14. 4.00
G-BLRN	DH.104 Dove 8 (C.2/2)	04266	N531WB	30.10.84	C.W.Simpson (To Pionier Hangaar Collection) G-BLRN/WB531 (As "WB531" in RAF c/s) Lelystad, Netherlands		13. 3.96
G-BLRW	Cameron Elephant 77SS HAFB	1074		14.12.84	Forbes Europe Inc Balleroy, Normandy "Great Sky Elephant"		4.11.98A

Regn	Type	C/n	P/I	Date	Owner/operator	Probable Base	CA Expy
G-BLSD*	FFW DH.112 Venom FB.54	928	N203DM G-BLSD/J-1758	20. 5.85	R.J.Lamplough North Weald (As "J-1758 in Swiss AF c/s) (Stored 10.97)		
G-BLSF	Gulfstream AA-5A Cheetah	AA5A-0802	G-BGCK	21. 2.83	J.P.E.Walsh Elstree t/a Walsh Avn (Op London School of Flying)		12. 6.00T
G-BLSH*	Cameron V-77	1085		7.12.84	A D Kent "Compass Rose" Lancing (Balloon Preservation Group 7.98)		14. 1.95A
G-BLSK	Colt 77A HAFB	617		29.11.84	R.D.MacKenzie	Gerrards Cross	22. 5.96A
G-BLSM	BAe 125 Srs.700B	NA0346 & 257208	G-5-19 (G-BLMJ)/N710BR	18.10.84	Dravidian Air Svs Ltd	Heathrow	19.11.01
G-BLST	Cessna 421C Golden Eagle III	421C-0623	N88638	29.11.78	Cecil Avn Ltd	Cambridge	9. 7.99T
G-BLSU	Cameron A-210 HAFB	1095		31.12.84	A.C.Elson "Skysales II"	Bristol	7. 6.95T
G-BLSX	Cameron O-105 HAFB	1094		16. 1.85	B.J.Petteford "Flaming Mischief" Bristol (Petteford's Solid Fuels titles)		20. 3.99T
G-BLTA	Colt 77A Coil HAFB	525		8. 6.84	K.A.Schlussler "James Sadler"	Bourne, Lincs	7. 8.91A
G-BLTC	Druine D.31A Turbulent (VW1600)	PFA/48-10964		18.12.84	G.P.Smith & A.W.Burton Little Down Farm, Milson		6. 4.99P
G-BLTF	Robinson R-22 Alpha	0428	N8526A	10. 1.85	S.& J.M.Taylor (Blackburn) t/a Stuart Taylor International		8. 3.01T
G-BLTK	Rockwell Commander 112TC-A	13106	SE-GSD	11.12.84	B.Rogalewski	Denham	26. 5.00
G-BLTM	Robin HR.200/100 Club	96	F-GAEC	21.11.84	B.D.Balcanquall	Barton	19. 6.00
G-BLTN	Thunder Ax7-65 HAFB	621		4. 1.85	J.A.Liddle "Frederica"	Reading	3. 9.88A
G-BLTP	BAe 125 Srs.700B	NA0347 & 257210	G-5-18 (G-BLMK)/N710BQ	18.10.84	Dravidian Air Svs Ltd	Heathrow	15. 1.02
G-BLTR	Sportavia-Putzer Scheibe SF-25B Falke	4823	D-KHEC	23. 1.85	V.Mallon	RAF Bruggen	1. 4.94
G-BLTS	Rutan LongEz	PFA/74A-10741		14. 1.85	R.W.Cutler	(Thorverton, Exeter)	
G-BLTT	Slingsby T-67B	2023		16. 1.85	S.E.Marples	Newcastle	5. 8.00T
G-BLTU	Slingsby T-67B	2024		16. 1.85	W.F.Hall RAF Laarbruch t/a The Neiderrhein Powered F/C		14. 8.00T
G-BLTV	Slingsby T-67B	2025		16. 1.85	R.L.Brinklow	Turweston	2. 7.98T
G-BLTW	Slingsby T-67B	2026		16. 1.85	R.L.Brinklow	Turweston	25. 9.99T
G-BLUE	Colting Ax7-77A HAFB (Regd as Colt 77A c/n 11)	77A-011		2. 5.78	D.P.Busby "Bluebird" Lancing (Balloon Preservation Group 7.98)		20. 9.99A
G-BLUI	Thunder Ax7-65 HAFB	553		22. 2.85	Susan Johnson "Rhubarb & Custard"	Blackpool	12. 4.95A
G-BLUK	Bond Sky Dancer (Mod)	85/1		16. 1.85	J.Owen Spilsted Farm, Sedlescombe (Under construction 8.93 - wings only present 8.94)		
G-BLUL*	CEA Jodel DR.1050/M1 Sicile Record	601	F-BMPJ	7. 3.85	J.Owen Spilsted Farm, Sedlescombe (Cancelled by CAA 2.3.99; last known on overhaul)		24.10.91
G-BLUM	Aerospatiale SA.365N Dauphin 2	6101		21. 1.85	Bond Helicopters Ltd	Liverpool	14. 4.99T
G-BLUN	Aerospatiale SA.365N Dauphin 2	6114	PH-SSS G-BLUN	21. 1.85	Bond Helicopters Ltd	Liverpool	5. 3.99T
G-BLUV	Grob G-109B	6336		1. 2.85	R.J.Buckels & S.K.Durso North Weald t/a The 109 F/Grp		16. 2.00
G-BLUX	Slingsby T-67M Firefly 200	2027	G-7-145 G-BLUX/G-7-113	31. 1.85	R.L.Brinklow Headcorn t/a Richard Brinklow Aviation (Op Tiger Club)		22. 4.99T
G-BLUY*	Colt 69A HAFB	631		7. 3.85	Not known "Bluey"	?	N/E(A)
G-BLUZ	DH.82B Queen Bee	1435 & SAL.150	LF858	9. 4.85	C.I.Knowles & J.Flynn RAF Henlow t/a The Bee Keepers Group (As "LF858")		12. 8.99P
G-BLVA	Airtour AH-31 HAFB	AH.004		12. 2.86	A.van Wyk	London SE12	
G-BLVB	Airtour AH-56 HAFB	AH.005		12. 2.86	T.C.Hinton "Bluejay"	Tunbridge Wells	
G-BLVI	Slingsby T-67M Firefly II	2017	(PH-KIF) G-BLVI	1. 2.85	Hunting Aviation Ltd RAF Barkston Heath (Op Hunting Acft Ltd/JEFTS)		12.12.99T
G-BLVK	Mudry/CAARP CAP-10B	141	JY-GSR	11. 3.85	E.K.Coventry	Childerditch, Brentwood	8. 5.00
G-BLVL	PA-28-161 Warrior II	28-8416109	N43677	11. 2.85	Marair (Jersey) Ltd	Jersey	15. 5.00T
G-BLVN	Cameron N-77 HAFB	1098		4. 2.85	Servo & Electronic Sales Ltd "Connect One"	Lydd	9. 4.96A
G-BLVS	Cessna 150M Commuter	150-76869	EI-BLS N45356	19. 2.85	Tindon Ltd	Little Snoring	30. 7.00T
G-BLVW	Reims Cessna F.172H	0422	D-ENQU	16. 5.85	R & D Holloway Ltd	Stapleford	10. 7.00
G-BLWB	Thunder Ax6-56 Srs 1 HAFB	645		22. 2.85	G.J.Bell "Porky"	Wokingham	10.11.99A
G-BLWD	PA-34-200T Seneca II	34-8070334	ZS-KKV ZS-XAT/N8253E	14. 3.85	Acre 123 Ltd.	(London SW1)	17. 4.99T
G-BLWE	Colt 90A HAFB	648		5. 3.85	Huntair Ltd "Rair Computers"	Aachen, Germany	23. 4.99A
G-BLWF	Robin HR.100/210 Safari	183	F-BUSR	8. 3.85	Starguide Ltd	Stapleford	27. 5.00
G-BLWH	Fournier RF6B-100	7	F-GADF	3. 4.85	R.H.Ashforth Gloucestershire t/a Gloster Aero Grp		11. 8.00
G-BLWM*	Bristol M.1C Replica (110 hp Gnome)	PFA/112-10892	"C4912"	12. 3.85	RAF Museum Hendon (As "C4994" in RFC c/s)		12.8.87P*
G-BLWP	PA-38-112 Tomahawk	38-78A0367	OY-BTW	7. 6.85	A.Dodd	Panshanger	1. 3.01T
G-BLWT	Evans VP-1 Srs.2 (VW1834)	PFA/62-10639		27. 3.85	C.J.Bellworthy	Finmere	2.12.98P
G-BLWV	Reims Cessna F.152 II	1843	EI-BIN	25. 2.85	Redhill Avn Ltd t/a Redhill F/C	Redhill	19. 6.00T
G-BLWW	Aerocar Mini-Imp Model C (Cont O-200-A)	PFA/136-10880		1. 3.85	M.K.Field (Shrewsbury) t/a The Brize Group (Status uncertain)		4. 6.87P

Regn	Type	C/n	P/I	Date	Owner/operator	·Probable Base	CA Expy
G-BLWX*	Cameron N-56 HAFB	1096		15. 2.85	Not known	-	N/E(A)
				(Sold as RP-C1483 9.94 but at Ashton Court, Bristol 8.95 as G-BLWX)			
G-BLWY	Robin R.2160D	176	F-GCUV SE-GXE	15. 4.85	A.Spencer & D.A.Rolfe	Crowfield	23.10.00
G-BLXA	Socata TB-20 Trinidad	284	SE-IMO F-ODOH	11. 4.85	Shropshire A/C Ltd	Sleap	14. 6.00T
G-BLXF	Cameron V-77 HAFB	1144		2. 4.85	P.Lawman "Candytwist III"	Northampton	2. 4.97A
G-BLXG	Colt 21A Cloudhopper HAFB	605		2. 5.85	A.Walker	Richmond, Surrey	6. 5.98A
					"Britannia Park"		
G-BLXH	Alpavia Fournier RF3	39	F-BMDQ	25. 3.85	A.Rawicz-Szczerbo	Eaglescott	16.11.99P
G-BLXI	Scintex CP.1310-C3 Super Emeraude	937	F-BMJI	1. 4.85	R.Howard	Grove Moor Farm, Grasthorpe	10. 4.98P
G-BLXO	SAN Jodel 150 Mascaret	10	F-BLDB	9. 5.85	P.R.Powell	Allensmore, Hereford	10. 6.98P
G-BLXP	PA-28R-200 Cherokee Arrow II	28R-7235200	N5226T	29. 7.85	M.B.Hamlett	Le Plessis-Belleville, France	21. 7.99
G-BLXR	Aerospatiale AS.332L Super Puma	2154		14. 5.85	Bristow Helicopters Ltd	Aberdeen	1. 7.00T
					"Cromarty"		
G-BLXT	RAF SE.5A	-	N4488 USAAS 22-296	2.10.85	V.Lindsay (To USA 1994)		25. 5.94P
	(180hp Wright-Martin Hispano-Suiza)				(As "B4863/G" McCudden's 56 Sqdn in RFC c/s)		
	(Converted from Eberhart SE.5E)						
G-BLXX	PA-23-250 Aztec F	27-7854137	(G-BLVM) G-PIED/N6534A	4. 3.85	A.S.Bamrah t/a Falcon F/Svs	Southend	18. 9.99T
					(Willowair F/C)		
G-BLXY	Cameron V-65 HAFB	1139		9. 4.85	Gone With The Wind Ltd	Seronera, Tanzania	
G-BLYD	Socata TB-20 Trinidad	518		1. 5.85	J.M.White & R.A.Stockdale	Biggin Hill	1. 2.01
					t/a Gourmet Trotters		
G-BLYE	Socata, TB-10 Tobago	521		1. 5.85	G.Hatton	Blackpool	28. 5.01T
G-BLYK	PA-34-220T Seneca III	34-8433083	N4371J	30. 5.85	S.W.Jackson	Gamston	28. 9.00
G-BLYP	Robin R.3000/120	109		15. 5.85	C.J.Freeman t/a Weald Air Svs	Headcorn	5. 5.01T
G-BLYT	Airtour AH-77 HAFB	AH.008		7. 7.87	I.J. & B.A.Taylor "Signal 2"	Corsham	19. 7.99A
G-BLYY	PA-28-181 Archer II	28-7890181	OO-PAV N9792K	17. 5.85	N.J.Skinner t/a G-BLYY Group	Stapleford	18. 9.00
G-BLZA	Scheibe SF-25B Falke	4684	D-KBAJ	22. 5.85	T.A.Lacey	RAF Halton	14. 9.00
					t/a Chiltern Gliding Club		
G-BLZB	Cameron N-65 HAFB	1164		21. 5.85	R S Kent "Pro-Sport"	Lancing	25. 4.90A
					(Balloon Preservation Group 7.98)		
G-BLZE	Reims Cessna F.152 II	1579	G-CSSC PH-AYF(2)	3. 5.85	Redhill Avn Ltd t/a Redhill F/C	Redhill	12. 4.01T
G-BLZF	Thunder Ax7-77 HAFB	660		3. 6.85	H.M.Savage "Hector"	Edinburgh	31. 8.97A
G-BLZH	Reims Cessna F.152 II	1965		21. 6.85	Plane Talking Ltd	Biggin Hill	3. 4.01T
G-BLZM	Rutan LongEz	PFA/74A-10704		10. 6.85	N.J.Rushby t/a Zulu Mike Grp	Shoreham	28. 8.98P
	(Lyc O-235)						
G-BLZN	Bell 206B JetRanger	314	ZS-HMV C-GWDH/N1408W	12. 7.85	L.Smith	Booker	18. 7.00T
					t/a Helicopter Svs (Op Virgin Helicopters)		
					(Damaged Booker 29.6.98)		
G-BLZP	Reims Cessna F.152 II	1959		10. 7.85	East Midlands Flying School Ltd	East Midlands	7.11.00T
G-BLZS	Cameron O-77 HAFB	479		22. 5.85	M.M.Cobbold "Rainbow Brite"	Plymouth	11. 6.97A
					(Henry Africa's Hothouse Restaurant titles)		
G-BLZT	Short SD.3-60 Var.100	SH.3676		18. 6.85	Gill Avn Ltd	Newcastle	29. 8.00T

G-BMAA-BMZZ

Regn	Type	C/n	P/I	Date	Owner/operator	Probable Base	CA Expy
G-BMAD	Cameron V-77 HAFB	1166		10. 6.85	M.A.Stelling "Nautilus"	Bedford	27. 9.99A
G-BMAF*	Cessna 180F	180-51219	G-BDVR	6. 3.81	P.Channon	Rushett Farm, Chessington	6. 8.93T
			ET-ABT/N2119Z		(Cancelled by CAA 2.3.99)		
G-BMAL	Sikorsky S-76A II Plus	760120	F-WZSA	27.11.80	Bond Helicopters Ltd	Humberside	9. 5.01T
			G-BMAL				
G-BMAO	Taylor JT.1 Monoplane	PFA/1411		29. 7.85	V.A.Wordsworth	Hucknall	28. 6.99P
G-BMAR(2)	Short SD.3-60 Var.100	SH.3633	G-BLCR	12. 1.84	BAC Express Airlines Ltd	Gatwick	14. 3.99T
G-BMAV	Aerospatiale AS.350B Ecureuil	1089		1. 6.79	Heli-Trans Ltd.	Belfast	4. 8.00T
G-BMAX	Clutton FRED Srs.II (VW1834)	PFA/29-10322		20.12.78	D.A.Arkley	(Chelmsford)	29. 4.99P
G-BMAY	PA-18-135 Super Cub (L-21B-PI) (Frame No.18-3961)	18-3925	OO-LWB "EI-229" I-EIJZ/MM54-2525/54-2525	3. 7.85	R.W.Davies	Little Robhurst Farm, Woodchurch, Kent	18.10.01
G-BMBB	Reims Cessna F.150L	1136	OO-LWM PH-GAA	2. 8.85	A.H.Glick t/a Dacebow Avn	Leeds-Bradford	2. 8.98T
G-BMBC	PA-31-350 Chieftain	31-7952172	(ZF524) N3519C	9. 7.85	Air Navigation & Trading Co Ltd	Blackpool	12.10.99T
G-BMBE	PA-46-310P Malibu	46-8508063	N6908W	26. 7.85	The Barfax Distributing Co Ltd & Glasdon Grp Ltd	Blackpool	8. 4.01T
G-BMBJ	Schempp-Hirth Janus CM	20/209	(G-BLZL)	9. 9.85	T.M.Holloway t/a RAFGSA	Bicester	19. 3.01
G-BMBS	Colt 105A HAFB	704		18. 7.85	H.G.Davies	Cheltenham	27. 8.91A
G-BMBW	Bensen B.8MR MV-001 & PFA G/01-1064 (Rotax 503)			27. 8.85	M.E.Vahdat	Uxbridge	30. 6.93P
G-BMBZ	Scheibe SF-25E Super Falke	4322	D-KEFQ	17. 7.85	Cornish Gliding & Flying Club Ltd	Perranporth	18. 7.00
G-BMCC	Thunder Ax7-77 HAFB	705		12. 7.85	A.K. & C.M.Russell "Charlie Charlie"	Stafford	9. 3.97A
G-BMCD	Cameron V-65 HAFB	1234		26. 6.85	M.C.Drye "My Second Fantasy"	Winkfield	9. 3.97A
G-BMCG	Grob G-109B	6362	(EAF673)	25. 7.85	Lagerholm Finnimport Ltd	Booker	7. 7.01
G-BMCI	Reims Cessna F.172H	0683	OO-WID	19. 8.85	A.B.Davis (Op Edinburgh Air Centre)	Edinburgh	9. 6.01T
G-BMCK	Cameron O-77 HAFB	1180		9. 7.85	D.L.Smith t/a Smith Smart Partnership "Touchy"	Newbury	20.10.92A
G-BMCN	Reims Cessna F.152 II	1471	D-ELDM	7. 8.85	Lincoln Aero Club Ltd	Sturgate	3.12.00T
G-BMCS	PA-22-135 Tri-Pacer	22-1969	5Y-KMH VP-KMH/ZS-DJI	6. 9.85	Richard Lazenby & Co Ltd & T.A.Hodges	Frinsted, Kent	15. 7.01
G-BMCV	Reims Cessna F.152 II	1963		2.10.85	Leicestershire A/C Ltd	Leicester	19. 3.01T
G-BMCW	Aerospatiale AS.332L Super Puma	2161	F-WYMG	4.10.85	Bristow Helicopters Ltd "Monifieth"	(China)	7.11.99T
G-BMCX	Aerospatiale AS.332L Super Puma	2164		7.10.85	Bristow Helicopters Ltd "Lossiemouth"	Aberdeen	14.11.01T
G-BMDB	Replica Plans SE.5A (Cont O-200-A)	PFA/20-10931		12. 8.85	D.Biggs	Boscombe Down	27. 5.99P
				(Damaged Lymington 2.8.92; stored 9.96)	(As "F235/B" in RFC c/s)		
G-BMDC	PA-32-301 Saratoga	32-8006075	OO-PAC OO-HKK/N8242A	13. 8.85	J.D.M.Tickell t/a MacLaren Avn	Fairoaks	5.10.00T
G-BMDD	Slingsby T-29 Motor Tutor (VW1834)	PFA/42-11070		8. 8.85	A.R.Worters (Status uncertain)	(Dunoon)	7.10.88P
G-BMDE	Pietenpol Air Camper (Cont O-200-A)	PFA/47-10989		12. 8.85	P.B.Childs	Bristol/Lulsgate	12. 8.98P
G-BMDJ	Price Ax7-77S HAFB	TPB.1 & 003		1. 8.85	D.A.Kozuba-Kozubska "Wings of Phoenix"	London WC1	
G-BMDK	PA-34-220T Seneca III	34-8133155	ZS-LOS N84209	16. 9.85	Air Medical Ltd	Oxford	24.11.01T
				(Damaged landing Cardiff-Wales 8.9.98)			
G-BMDO	ARV1 Super 2 K.004 & PFA/152-11127 (Hewland AE75) (Built by Hornet Avn Ltd)			27. 8.85	R.M.Roullier	(Newport, IoW)	12. 6.97P
G-BMDP	Partenavia P.64B Oscar 200	08	HB-EPQ	20. 8.85	T.Gracey	Henstridge	25. 5.01
G-BMDS	Jodel Wassmer D.120 Paris-Nice	281	F-BMOS	12. 8.85	J.V.Thompson	Lumb-in-Rossendale	29. 5.91P
G-BMEA	PA-18-95 Super Cub (L-18C-PI) 18-3204		OL-L07/L130/53-4804	27. 8.85	C.L.Towell	Ranksborough Farm, Langham	5.10.99P
	(Frame No. stated as 18-3206 (c/n 18-3194 ex OL-L20/L120/53-4794); c/n 18-3204 has Frame No.18-3216)						
G-BMEB	Rotorway Scorpion 145	2896	VR-HJB	10.12.85	L.S.Elliott	Coleraine	
G-BMEE	Cameron O-105 HAFB	1189		4. 9.85	A.G.R.Calder	Los Angeles, USA	8.10.89A
G-BMEG	Socata TB-10 Tobago	530		23.10.85	G.H.N. & R.V.Chamberlain t/a Chamberlain Leasing	Great Yeldham, Essex	17.11.01
G-BMEH	Jodel 150 Special Super Mascaret (Lyc O-235) PFA/151-11047			15. 8.85	W.M.Coupar	Muirhouses Farm, Errol	16. 8.99P
			(Rebuild of incomplete SAN Jodel 150 Mascaret c/n 62)				
G-BMET	Taylor JT.1 Monoplane (VW 1600)	PFA/1465		4. 9.85	M.K.A.Blyth	Little Gransden	3. 7.99P
G-BMEU	Isaacs Fury II (90hp Salmson)	PFA/11-10179		11. 9.85	G.R.G.Smith	(Hints Farm, Ludlow)	
G-BMEV	PA-32RT-300T Turbo Lance II	32R-7887056	OO-CHB G-BMEV/ZS-KFK/N36591	30. 4.86	Arrow Avn Ltd	Jersey	14.12.01
G-BMEW*	Lockheed 18-56 (C-60A-LO) 18-2444 Lodestar (Gulfstar conversion)		OH-SIR OH-MAP N283M/N105G/N69898/42-55983	30. 9.85	Forsvarsmuseet Flysamlingn (Norwegian AF Museum) (Stored as OH-SIR 5.94)	Gardermoen, Norway	
G-BMEX	Cessna A150K Aerobat	A150-0169	N8469M	18. 9.85	N.A.M.Brain	Netherthorpe	4. 5.98

Regn	Type	C/n	P/I	Date	Owner/operator	Probable Base	CA Expy
G-BMEZ*	Cameron DP-50 Hot-Air Airship	1130		18. 9.85	British Balloon Museum & Library	Newbury	4. 5.89A
G-BMFD	PA-23-250 Aztec F	27-7954080	G-BGYY N6834A	6. 9.79	N G R Moffat	Carlisle	4.12.00T
G-BMFG	Dornier Do.27A-1	27-1003-342	FAP 3460 AC+955	23. 9.85	R.F.Warner t/a Sigma Services (On rebuild 5.96)	Old Buckenham	
G-BMFI	PZL SZD-45A Ogar	B-657		23. 9.85	S.L.Morrey	Andreas, IoM	1. 4.99
G-BMFL	Rand Robinson KR-2	PFA/129-11050		24. 9.85	E.W.B.Comber & M.F.Leusby	(Huntingdon)	
G-BMFN	QAC Quickie Tri-Q 200 (Cont O-200-A)	EMK-017 & PFA/94A1-11062		27. 9.85	A.H.Hartog	Bournemouth	13.10.99P
G-BMFP	PA-28-161 Warrior II	28-7916243	N3032L	1.11.85	T.J.Froggatt & C.A.Lennard t/a Bravo Mike Fox Papa Grp	Blackbushe	10. 5.01
G-BMFT	HS.748 Srs.2A/266	1714	VP-BFT VR-BFT/G-BMFT/5W-FAO/G11-10	18.10.85	Emerald Airways Ltd	Liverpool	19.8.96T
G-BMFU	Cameron N-90 HAFB	628		1.10.85	J.J.Rudoni	Rugeley, Staffs	24. 6.99T
G-BMFY	Grob G-109B	6401		8.10.85	P.J.Shearer	Kirkwall	11. 6.01
G-BMFZ	Reims Cessna F.152 II	1953		3.12.85	Cornwall F/C Ltd	Bodmin	5. 1.01T
G-BMGB	PA-28R-200 Cherokee Arrow II	28R-7335099	N15864	8.11.85	A.L.Ings t/a Malmesbury Specialist Cars	Kemble	14. 6.01
G-BMGC*	Fairey Swordfish II (Blackburn-built)	-	G-BMGC RCN W5856/RN W5856 (As "W5856/A2A" in 810 Sqn c/s) "City of Leeds"	23.10.85	RN Historic Flight	RNAS Yeovilton	
G-BMGG	Cessna 152 II	152-79592	OO-ADB PH-ADB/D-EHUG/F-GBLM/N757AT t/a Falcon F/Services	10.10.85	A S Bamrah	Biggin Hill	24.10.00T
G-BMGH	PA-31-325 Turbo Navajo C/R	31-7512045	ZS-LEU N8493/A2-CAT	6.12.85	Not known (On rebuild 3.99)	Southend	
G-BMGR t/a BMGR Grp	Grob G-109B	6396		27.11.85	D.S.Hawes & M.Clarke	Lasham	9. 2.01
G-BMGY	Lake LA-4-200 Buccaneer	680	N39RG G-BWKS/G-BDDI/N1087L (Op Ocean Air)	1.11.85	RL Estates Ltd	Bournemouth/Gibraltar	9. 1.98T
G-BMHA	Rutan LongEz	PFA/74A-10973		18.10.85	S.F.Elvins	(Bristol)	
G-BMHC	Cessna U206G Stationair II	U206-03427	N10TB G-BMHC/N8571Q	17.11.76	Clacton A/C (1988) Ltd	Duxford/Clacton	22. 8.97T
G-BMHJ	Thunder Ax7-65 Srs.1 HAFB	743		2. 1.86	M.G.Robinson "Kittylog"	Great Milton, Oxon	19. 5.92A
G-BMHL	Wittman W.8 Tailwind (Cont O-200-A)	PFA/31-10503		28.11.85	T.G.Hoult Octon Grange Farm, Foxholes, Driffield		28. 5.99P
G-BMHS	Reims Cessna F.172M	0964	PH-WAB	7. 4.86	R.A.Hall Rayne Hall Farm, Rayne t/a Tango Xray F/Grp		21. 7.01
G-BMHT	PA-28RT-201T Turbo Arrow IV	28R-8231010	ZS-LCJ N8462Y	18.11.85	Scalpay Ltd t/a Cartel Communications	Birmingham	22. 4.01
G-BMHZ	PA-28RT-201T Turbo Arrow IV	28R-8031001	ZS-KII N8096D	18.11.85	B.L.Tuwie t/a The Arrow Association	Elstree	31. 3.99
G-BMID	Jodel Wassmer D.120 Paris-Nice	259	F-BMID	18. 8.81	P.D.Smoothy	Hinton-in-the-Hedges	27. 4.99P
G-BMIG	Cessna 172N Skyhawk II	172-72376	ZS-KGI (N48630)	13. 5.86	J.R.Nicholls	Sibson	15. 6.01T
G-BMIH	BAe HS.125 Srs.700B	257115	G-5-502 5N-AMX/G-BMIH/HZ-DA3	22. 1.86	Surewings Ltd	Luton	17. 8.99T
G-BMIM	Rutan LongEz (Lyc O-235)	160	OY-CMT OY-8102	12.12.85	R.M.Smith	Biggin Hill	17. 7.99P
G-BMIO	Stoddard-Hamilton Glasair IIRG	PFA/149-11016		25.11.85	J.W.E.de Frayssinet & J.M.Ayres (Under construction 9.93)	Shobdon	
G-BMIP	Wassmer Jodel D.112	1264	F-BMIP	7.12.78	M.T.Kinch Manor Farm, Inglesham t/a The Inglesham F/Grp		17. 9.99P
G-BMIR*	Westland Wasp HAS.1	F.9670	XT788	24. 1.86	Park Avn Supply (Stored as "XT788" 3.93) Little Glovers Farm, Charlwood, Surrey		
G-BMIS	Monnett Sonerai II	755 & PFA/15A-10813	VR-HIS	26. 2.87	B.A.Bower (Status uncertain)	(Andover)	26.10.89P
	(Revmaster R2100DQ)						
G-BMIV	PA-28R-201T Turbo Arrow III	28R-7703154	ZS-JZW N5816V	7. 1.86	Maurice Mason Ltd	Swaffham	21. 4.01
G-BMIW	PA-28-181 Archer II	28-8190093	ZS-KTJ N8301J	6.12.85	Oldbus Ltd	Shoreham	1. 5.01T
G-BMIY	Oldfield Baby Lakes (Cont O-200-A)	PFA/10-10194	G-NOME	3.12.85	J.B.Scott (Stored 6.96)	Blackpool	27. 8.87P
G-BMJA	PA-32R-301 Saratoga SP	32R-8113019	ZS-KTH N8309E	23.12.85	General Airline Ltd t/a European Flyers	Blackbushe	22. 7.99
G-BMJB	Cessna 152 II	152-80030	N757VD	3. 2.86	Bobbington Air Training School Ltd	Halfpenny Green	21. 3.01T
G-BMJC	Cessna 152 II	152-84989	N623AP	3. 2.86	The Cambridge Aero Club Ltd	Cambridge	23. 6.01T
G-BMJD	Cessna 152 II	152-79755	N757HP	21.11.85	Donair F/C Ltd	East Midlands	2. 6.01T
G-BMJG	PA-28R-200 Cherokee Arrow	28R-35046	ZS-TNS ZS-FYC/N9345N	23.12.85	Western Air (Thruxton) Ltd (Damaged on take-off at Thruxton 11.10.98)	Thruxton	4. 2.99T
G-BMJL	Rockwell Commander 114	14006	A2-JRI ZS-JRI/N1906J	8. 1.86	Wardair Ltd.	Blackbushe	12. 6.00T
G-BMJM	Evans VP-1 (VW1834)	PFA/62-10763		21.11.85	M.J.Veary	Sywell	8. 6.98P
G-BMJN	Cameron O-65 HAFB	1212		6.12.85	P.M.Traviss "F'red"	Yarm	15. 5.98A
G-BMJO	PA-34-220T Seneca III	34-8533036	N6919K N9565N	5.12.85	Oxford Aviation Services Ltd	Oxford	14. 4.01

Regn	Type	C/n	P/I	Date	Owner/operator	Probable Base	CA Expy
G-BMJR	Cessna T337H Turbo Super Skymaster II	337-01895	G-NOVA N1259S	10. 7.84	Eastcote Services Ltd	Sturgate	12. 6.99
G-BMJS	Thunder Ax7-77 HAFB	754		3.12.85	S.E.Burton	Northampton	7. 4.96A
G-BMJT	Beechcraft 76 Duchess	ME-376	ZS-KMI N3718W	4.12.85	Mike Osborne Properties Ltd	Ronaldsway	30. 3.01
G-BMJW*	North American AT-6D-NT Harvard III	88-15963	EZ259 SAAF7631/EZ259/42-84182	28.11.85	B.Fenton	Wakefield	
	(Composite with rear fuselage of KF487; fuselage on rebuild 2.96)						
G-BMJX	Wallis WA-116/X Srs.1 (Limbach L-2000)	K/219/X		31.12.85	K.H.Wallis (Stored 8.97) Reymerston Hall		1. 4.89P
G-BMJY	SPP Yakovlev C.18A	-	(France) Egypt AF 627	21. 1.86	R.J.Lamplough (As "07" in Russian AF c/s)	North Weald	19. 1.99P
G-BMJZ	Cameron N-90 HAFB	1219		16.12.85	P.Spellward "Uvistat" t/a Bristol University Hot-Air Ballooning Society	Bristol	31. 3.94A
G-BMKB	PA-18-135 Super Cub (L-21B-PI) (Frame No.18-3818)	18-3817	OO-DKB PH-DKB/(PH-GRP)/R	11.12.85	Cubair Flight Training Ltd Neth AF R-127/54-2417	Redhill	7. 1.00T
G-BMKC	Piper J3C-90 Cub (L-4H-PI) (Frame No.10970)	11145	F-BFBA 43-29854	2. 1.86	R.J.H.Springall (As "329854/R/44" in 533rd BS/381st Bomb Grp, USAAC c/s) "Little Rockette Jnr."	St.Just	22.11.99P
G-BMKD	Beechcraft C90A King Air	LJ-1069	N223CG N67516	30.12.85	A.E.Bristow	Godalming/Fairoaks	25. 3.00
G-BMKF	CEA Jodel DR.221 Dauphin	96	F-BPCS	3. 2.86	L., S.T.Gilbert & L.M.Radcliffe	Enstone	9. 6.00
G-BMKG	PA-38-112 Tomahawk II	38-82A0050	ZS-LGC N91544	3. 2.86	APB Leasing Ltd	Welshpool	24. 8.01T
G-BMKI	Colt 21A Cloudhopper HAFB	753		30.12.85	A.C.Booth	Bristol	11.12.98A
G-BMKJ	Cameron V-77 HAFB	1235		2. 1.86	R.C.Thursby	Barry	14. 5.99A
G-BMKK	PA-28R-200 Cherokee Arrow II	28R-7535265	ZS-JNY N9537N	16. 1.86	Dawcroft Ltd t/a Colony Aviation	(Ulverston)	5. 1.01T
G-BMKP	Cameron V-77 HAFB	724	(G-BMFX)	10. 1.86	R.Bayly "And Baby Makes 10"	Bristol	7. 8.93A
G-BMKR	PA-28-161 Warrior II	28-7916220	G-BGKR N9561N	14. 6.84	D.R.Shrosbee t/a Field F/Grp	Goodwood	19. 6.00
G-BMKV	Thunder Ax7-77 HAFB	772		21. 1.86	A.Hornak & M.J.Nadal	London N1	8.12.93A
G-BMKW	Cameron V-77 HAFB	608		29. 1.86	A.C.Garnett "Aorangi"	Guildford	9. 1.93A
G-BMKX*	Cameron Elephant 77SS HAFB	1196		6. 2.86	A D Kent "Benjamin I" (Balloon Preservation Group 7.98)	Lancing	19. 2.89A
G-BMKY	Cameron O-65 HAFB	1246		4. 3.86	Ann R.Rich "Orion"	Hyde	11. 3.96A
G-BMLB	Jodel Wassmer D.120A Paris-Nice	295	F-BNCI	20. 1.86	W.O.Brown	Seighford	3. 8.99P
G-BMLJ	Cameron N-77 HAFB	1263		7. 3.86	C.J.Dunkley t/a Wendover Trailers "Mr Funshine"	Aylesbury	19. 3.96A
G-BMLK	Grob G-109B	6424		24. 2.86	J.J.Mawson t/a Brams Syndicate	Rufforth	15. 5.01
G-BMLL	Grob G-109B	6420		13. 3.86	P.C.Broome	Denham	24. 7.01
G-BMLM	Beechcraft 95-58 Baron	TH-405	F-GEPV 3D-ADF/ZS-LOZ/G-BMLM/G-BBJF	2. 7.79	Swift Air Ltd	Cranfield	2. 8.01
G-BMLS	PA-28R-201 Cherokee Arrow III	28R-7737167	N47496	11. 2.86	R.M.Shorter	Booker	24. 4.99T
G-BMLT	Pietenpol Air Camper (Cont C90)	PFA/47-10949		28. 1.86	W.E.R.Jenkins	Waits Farm, Belchamp Walter	8.10.99P
G-BMLU	Colt 90A HAFB	786		10. 4.86	L.J.Goldsmith "Firebird"	Biggin Hill	6. 3.97A
G-BMLW	Cameron O-77 HAFB	813		6. 2.86	M.L. & L.P.Willoughby "Stelrad"	Reading	7. 8.95A
G-BMLX	Reims Cessna F.150L	0700	PH-VOV	21. 3.86	C.J.Freeman (Op Weald Air Svs)	Headcorn	14. 8.01T
G-BMLZ	Cessna 421C Golden Eagle II	421C-0223	G-OTAD	17.12.85	Hadagain Investments Ltd		14. 2.89T
G-BMMC	Cessna 310Q	310Q-0041	G-BEVL/N5476G		Swift Air Ltd (To Canada by container 7.97)		14. 2.89T
G-BMMD	Rand Robinson KR-2 (VW1834 ACRO)	PFA/129-10817	YU-BGY N7541Q	11. 2.86	Cooper Clegg Ltd	Gloucestershire	20. 2.99
G-BMMF	Clutton FRED Srs.II (VW1834)	PFA/29-10296		7. 2.86	D.J.Howell	(Kinver, Stourbridge)	14. 6.99P
G-BMMI	Pazmany PL-4A (Cont PC 60)	PFA/17-10149		20. 2.86	J.M.Jones East Pennard, Shepton Mallet "Thankyou Girl"		6. 4.99P
G-BMMJ	Siren PIK-30	720		6. 2.86	M.K.Field	Sleap	2. 9.97P
G-BMMK	Cessna 182P Skylane II (Reims-assembled c/n 0038)	182-64117	OO-AVU N6129F	13. 6.86 24. 3.86	J.R.Greig M.S.Knight t/a Sealand Aerial Photography	Feshiebridge Goodwood	25. 6.01 1. 7.01T
G-BMML	PA-38-112 Tomahawk	38-80A0079	PH-TMG OO-HKD	2. 4.86	Western Air (Thruxton) Ltd	Thruxton	19. 5.01T
G-BMMM	Cessna 152 II	152-84793	N4652P	10. 9.86	A.S.Bamrah t/a Falcon F/Svs	Biggin Hill	20.10.01T
G-BMMP	Grob G-109B	6432		27. 6.86	E.W.Reynolds	Tatenhill	24. 5.99
G-BMMR	Dornier 228-202K	8063	(D-IAOT) D-CAOS	1. 4.86	Suckling Avn (Intl) Ltd t/a Suckling Airways	Cambridge	23. 4.99T
G-BMMU	Thunder Ax7-77 HAFB	719		4. 3.86	Nicola Metcalfe "Pansy"	Didcot	11. 8.97A
G-BMMV	ICA IS-28M2A	57		10. 3.86	F.R.Temple-Brown	Henstridge	5.11.98
G-BMMW	Thunder Ax7-77 HAFB	782		10. 3.86	P.A.George "Ethos" (Sports Council c/s)	Princes Risborough	3. 6.96A
G-BMMX	ICA IS-28M2A	58		14. 4.86	J.Bachelor t/a G-BMMX Syndicate	Kirton-in-Lindsey	29. 9.01
G-BMMY	Thunder Ax7-77 HAFB	716		11. 3.86	S.M.Wade & Sheila E.Hadley "Winco"	Salisbury	2. 6.91A

Regn	Type	C/n	P/I	Date	Owner/operator	Probable Base	CA Expy
G-BMNL	PA-28R-200 Cherokee Arrow II	28R-7535040	N18MW N32280	17. 9.86	Elston Ltd t/a Arrow Flying Group	Elstree	30. 5.99
G-BMNP	PA-38-112 Tomahawk II	38-81A0133	N23352	24. 3.86	APB Leasing Ltd	Welshpool	27. 6.98T
G-BMNT	PA-34-220T Seneca III	34-8133029	N8348T	19. 3.86	Channel Airways Ltd	Guernsey	1.10.01
G-BMNV	SNCAN Stampe SV-4C (Mod) (Lyc IO-360)	108	F-BBNI	14. 3.86	Wessex Avn & Transport Ltd	Chalmington	8. 6.94P
G-BMNX	Colt 56A HAFB	790		14. 4.86	C.N.Marshall "Rosie"	Tonbridge	26. 7.96A
G-BMOE	PA-28R-200 Cherokee Arrow II	28R-7635226	PH-PCB OO-HAS/N9221K	20. 5.86	E.P.C.Rabson	Southampton	14.10.99
G-BMOF	Cessna U206G Stationair II	U206-03658	N7427N	17. 4.86	D.M.Penny Movenis, Co.Londonderry t/a Wild Geese Skydiving Centre		11. 2.00
G-BMOG	Thunder Ax7-77 HAFB	793		2. 4.86	R.M.Boswell Bawburgh, Norwich		28. 8.95A
G-BMOH	Cameron N-77 HAFB	1270		2. 4.86	P.J.Marshall & M.A.Clarke Ruislip "Ellen Gee"		20. 8.91A
G-BMOI	Partenavia P.68B	103	I-EEVA	4. 4.86	Simmette Ltd	Exeter	20. 7.01
G-BMOJ	Cameron V-56 HAFB	1275		4. 4.86	S.R.Bridge	Grantham	27. 7.89A
G-BMOK	ARV1 Super 2	011		14. 4.86	J.C.F.Dalton	(Stevenage)	17. 8.00
G-BMOL*	PA-23-250 Aztec D	27-4394	G-BBSR N6610Y	26. 6.84	Not known (On fire dump 2.96)Bournemouth		26. 7.87T
G-BMOM	ICA IS-28M2A	50		30. 6.86	M.K.Gill Rufforth t/a Brasov F/Grp (Stored 8.96)		12. 7.96
G-BMOO*	Clutton FRED Srs.II (Cont A65)	PFA/29-10770		11. 4.86	N.Purllant (RAF c/s) (Leicester) (Cancelled by CAA 22.2.99; last known on overhaul)		8. 8.91P
G-BMOP	PA-28R-201T Turbo Arrow III	28R-7703194	N38257	18. 4.86	P.Murer	Fairoaks	20. 4.98
G-BMOT	Bensen B.8M (VW 1834)	PFA G/01-1066		17. 4.86	R.S.W.Jones	Tregaron, Dyfed	17. 6.97P
G-BMOV	Cameron O-105 HAFB	1307		11. 4.86	Cheryl Gillott "Up & Down"	Stroud	1. 7.99A
G-BMOX	Hovey Beta Bird	PFA/135-10976		15. 4.86	A.K.Jones	(Stockport)	
G-BMPC	PA-28-181 Archer II	28-7790436	LN-NAT	23. 4.86	C.J. & R.J.Barnes	East Midlands	6. 2.02T
G-BMPD	Cameron V-65 HAFB	1200		4. 6.86	D.E. & J.M.Hartland "Second Dawn"	Matlock	1. 8.99A
G-BMPF*	Optica OA.7 Optica	010		14. 4.86	FLS Aerospace (Light Aircraft) Ltd (Stored 11.95)	Bournemouth	14. 1.93T
G-BMPL	Optica OA.7 Optica	016		14. 4.86	Sunhawk Ltd.	Jersey	2. 8.97T
G-BMPP	Cameron N-77 HAFB	1303		15. 4.86	I.B. & R.J.Lumsden Rickmansworth "Tuppence"		14. 5.93A
G-BMPR	PA-28R-201 Arrow III	28R-7837175	ZS-LMF N417GH	22. 4.86	AH Flight Svs Ltd Moor Farm, Humbleton, Hull		24. 4.99
G-BMPS	Strojnik S-2A	045		18. 4.86	G.J.Green	(Matlock)	
G-BMPY	DH.82A Tiger Moth	"82619"	ZS-CNR SAAF	25. 4.86	S.M.F.Eisenstein Sandford Hall, Knockin		16.11.01
G-BMRA	Boeing 757-236	23710		2. 3.87	British Airways plc (Paithani t/s)	Heathrow	3. 3.00T
G-BMRB	Boeing 757-236	23975		25. 9.87	British Airways plc "Colchester Castle"	Heathrow	29. 9.00T
G-BMRC	Boeing 757-236	24072	(N) G-BMRC	2.12.87	British Airways plc (British Olympic Association t/s)	Heathrow	26. 1.01T
G-BMRD	Boeing 757-236	24073	(N) G-BMRD	2.12.87	British Airways plc (Chelsea Rose t/s)	Heathrow	3. 3.01T
G-BMRE	Boeing 757-236	24074	(N) G-BMRE	2.12.87	British Airways plc (Rendezvous t/s)	Heathrow	28. 3.01T
G-BMRF	Boeing 757-236	24101		13. 5.88	British Airways plc (Water Dreaming t/s)	Heathrow	17. 5.01T
G-BMRG	Boeing 757-236	24102		31. 5.88	British Airways plc (Rendezvous t/s)	Heathrow	2. 6.01T
G-BMRH	Boeing 757-236	24266		21. 2.89	British Airways plc (Nalanji Dreaming t/s)	Heathrow	28. 2.99T
G-BMRI	Boeing 757-236	24267		17. 2.89	British Airways plc (Blomsterang/Flower Field t/s)	Heathrow	23. 2.02T
G-BMRJ	Boeing 757-236	24268		6. 3.89	British Airways plc (Grand Union t/s)	Heathrow	13. 3.99T
G-BMSA	Stinson HW-75 Model 105 (Cont O-200-A)	7040	G-BCUM F-BGQO/NC21189	26. 3.86	M.A.Thomas Barton t/a The Stinson Group "Iron Eagle"		2. 3.99P
G-BMSB	VS.509 Spitfire T.9 (Regd as c/n 6S/R/749433)	CBAF.7722	G-ASOZ IAC158/G-15-171/MJ627	3. 5.78	M.S.Bayliss Coventry (As "MJ627/9G-P" in 441 Sqn c/s) (Damaged Coventry 25.4.98)		12. 3.99P
G-BMSC	Evans VP-2 (VW1834)	V2-482MSC & PFA/63-10785		25. 8.82	J.Holme	(Salisbury)	8.10.99P
G-BMSD	PA-28-181 Cherokee Archer II	28-7690070	EC-CVH N9646N	2. 7.86	General Airline Ltd Blackbushe t/a European Flyers		6. 9.01T
G-BMSE	Valentin Taifun 17E	1082	D-KHVA(17)	20. 5.86	A.J.Nurse	Gloucestershire	1. 4.99
G-BMSF	PA-38-112 Tomahawk	38-78A0524	N4277E	9. 2.79	B.Catlow	Crosland Moor	30. 6.99
G-BMSG*	SAAB 32A Lansen	32028	Fv.32028	22. 7.86	Thamesdown Helicopters Ltd Cranfield (Cancelled by CAA 3.3.99; open storage 7.96 with no Permit or C of A issued)		AC
G-BMSL	Clutton FRED Srs.III (VW1834)	PFA/29-11142		19. 5.86	A.C.Coombe	Long Marston	27. 6.99P

Regn	Type	C/n	P/I	Date	Owner/operator	Probable Base	CA Expy
G-BMST*	Cameron N-31 HAFB	1317		4. 6.86	I M Martin "B&Q" Lancing		N/E(A)
					(Balloon Preservation Group 7.98 for restoration)		
G-BMSU	Cessna 152 II	152-79421	N714TN	29. 8.86	S.Waite t/a G-BMSU Grp	Leeds-Bradford	26. 8.99T
G-BMTA	Cessna 152 II	152-82864	N89776	27. 8.86	Alarmond Ltd	Edinburgh	5.12.98T
					t/a Edinburgh F/C		
G-BMTB	Cessna 152 II	152-80672	N25457	19. 8.86	Sky Leisure Aviation (Charters) Ltd		
						Shoreham	5.11.98T
G-BMTJ	Cessna 152 II	152-85010	N6389P	19. 6.86	Nelson Services Ltd	Shoreham	14. 6.01T
G-BMTL	Reims Cessna F.152 II	1977		11. 9.86	Agricultural & General Avn Ltd		
					(Op Bournemouth F/C)	Bournemouth	1. 5.99T
G-BMTN	Cameron O-77 HAFB	1305		4. 6.86	Industrial Svs (MH) Ltd	Bristol	1. 6.97A
					t/a Flete Rental "Fletie"		
G-BMTO	PA-38-112 Tomahawk II	38-81A0051	N25679	28.11.86	A.S.Bamrah t/a Falcon F/Svs	Cardiff	25. 7.99T
G-BMTP*	PA-38-112 Tomahawk	38-79A0034	N2392B	14. 8.86	Not known	Jersey	26. 4.93T
					(Damaged Alderney 1.9.92; stored 12.96)		
G-BMTR	PA-28-161 Warrior II	28-8116119	N83179	19. 6.86	Aeroshow Ltd	Gloucestershire	23. 9.01T
G-BMTS	Cessna 172N Skyhawk II	172-70606	N739KP	17. 7.86	A.S.Bamrah t/a Falcon F/Svs	Blackbushe	27. 7.01T
					(Op European Flyers)		
G-BMTU	Pitts S-1E Special (Lyc O-360)	PFA/09-10801		4. 6.86	O.R.Howe	Edgehill	9. 9.99P
G-BMTX	Cameron V-77 HAFB	733		19. 6.86	J.A.Langley "Boondoggle"	Stroud	14.11.99A
					(Buses For Bristol titles)		
G-BMUD	Cessna 182P Skylane	182-61786	OY-DVS N78847	6.11.81	Mescal E.Taylor	Netherthorpe	31. 7.00T
G-BMUG	Rutan LongEz (Lyc O-235)	PFA/74A-10987		17. 6.86	P.Richardson & J.Shanley		
						Croft-on-Tees, Darlington	24. 6.99P
G-BMUJ	Colt Drachenfisch SS HAFB	835		3. 6.86	Virgin Airship and Balloon Co Ltd		
					"Drachenfisch"	Telford	27. 7.91A
G-BMUK	Colt UFO SS HAFB	836		3. 6.86	Virgin Airship and Balloon Co Ltd		
					"UFO/Dream Station"	Telford	26. 4.95A
G-BMUL	Colt Kindermond SS HAFB	837		3. 6.86	Virgin Airship and Balloon Co Ltd		
					"Kindermond/Childrens' Moon"	Telford	26. 9.91A
	(G-BMUJ/K/L have futuristic shapes designed by Andre Heller and were flown in various European capital cities in 1986)						
G-BMUN	Cameron Harley 78SS HAFB (Harley Davidson Motorcycle shape)	1188		10. 6.86	Forbes Europe Inc "Harley Davidson"	Balleroy, Normandy	22. 5.99A
G-BMUO	Cessna A152 Aerobat	A152-0788	4X-ALJ N7328L	4. 6.86	A.J.Gomes (Op Sky Leisure Aviation)	Shoreham	15. 8.01T
G-BMUT	PA-34-200T Seneca II	34-7570320	EC-CUH N3935X	23. 1.87	Newcastle Aeroplane Co Ltd	Newcastle	17. 5.99T
G-BMUU	Thunder Ax7-77 HAFB	827		1. 8.86	G.Anorewartha "Fiesta"	Kings Lynn	29.10.98A
G-BMUZ	PA-28-161 Warrior II	28-8016329	EC-DMA N9559N	24. 7.86	Newcastle-upon-Tyne A/C Ltd	Newcastle	7. 1.99T
G-BMVA	Scheibe SF-25B Falke	46223	RAFGGA.512 D-KAEN	28. 7.86	M.L.Jackson	Headcorn	18. 1.02
G-BMVB	Reims Cessna F.152 II	1974		10. 9.86	LAC (Enterprises) Ltd t/a Lancashire Aero Club	Barton	10. 2.00T
G-BMVE	PA-28RT-201 Arrow IV	28R-7918009	N3071K	24. 9.86	ARC Precision Engineering Ltd		
						Bournemouth	28.10.99T
G-BMVG	QAC Quickie Q-1 (Rotax 503)	PFA/94-10749		11. 6.86	P.M.Wright	Coventry	22. 4.98P
G-BMVI	Cameron O-105 HAFB	1326		19. 6.86	M.L.Gabb "Securicor" t/a Heart of England Balloons	Alcester	7. 7.95A
G-BMVJ	Cessna 172N Skyhawk II	172-72232	N9347E	27. 6.86	Green Avn Associates Ltd	Leeds-Bradford	26. 2.99T
G-BMVL	PA-38-112 Tomahawk	38-79A0033	N2391B	5. 9.86	Airways Aero Associations Ltd	Booker	7.12.01T
					(Op British Airways F/C) (Blue Poole t/s)		
G-BMVM	PA-38-112 Tomahawk	38-79A0025	N2359B	5. 9.86	Airways Aero Associations Ltd	Booker	19. 2.01T
					(Op British Airways F/C) (Waves of the City t/s)		
G-BMVO	Cameron N-77 HAFB	1309		23. 6.86	Warners Motors (Leasing) Ltd	Gloucester	3. 5.97A
					"Warners"		
G-BMVS*	Cameron Benihana 70SS HAFB (Also described as Chef's Hat)	1252		27.10.86	Shellrise Ltd "Rocky"	Miami, USA	N/E(A)
G-BMVT	Thunder Ax7-77A HAFB	102	SE-ZYY	15. 7.86	M.L. & L.P.Willoughby "Trygg Hansa"	Reading	
G-BMVU	Monnett Moni (KEF-107)	PFA/142-10948		14. 8.86	I.C.White	Enstone	20. 9.99P
G-BMVW	Cameron O-65 HAFB	1331		27. 6.86	S.P.Richards "Olau Ferries"	Cranbrook	15. 8.91A
G-BMWA	Hughes 269C	14-0271	N8998F	1. 7.86	P.J.Brown	Crawley	5. 9.99T
G-BMWE	ARV1 Super 2	012		1. 7.86	R.J.N.Noble	Goodwood	16. 1.00
G-BMWF	ARV1 Super 2 (Rotax 914 Turbo)	013		1. 7.86	N.R.Beale Deppers Bridge, Leamington Spa		2. 4.90T
					(Under construction 7.96)		
G-BMWJ	ARV1 Super 2 (Norton AE.100R)	017		1.12.86	Mid-West Engines Ltd	Gloucestershire	12.2.96P*
G-BMWM	ARV1 Super 2	020		30. 3.87	P.G.Hayward	(North Walsham)	22. 4.99P
G-BMWN	Cameron Temple 80SS HAFB	1211		9. 7.86	Forbes Europe Inc "Temple"	Balleroy, Normandy	17. 6.96A
G-BMWR	Rockwell Commander 112A	365	N1365J	23. 9.86	M. & J.Edwards	Blackbushe	20. 3.99

Regn	Type	C/n	P/I	Date	Owner/operator	Probable Base	CA Expy
G-BMWU	Cameron N-42 HAFB	1346		22.12.88	R S Kent "Baby Helix"	Lancing	
					(Balloon Preservation Group 7.98)		
G-BMWV	Putzer Elster B	024	D-EEKB	5. 8.86	E.A.J.Hibbard	Hill Farm, Nayland	
			97+14/D-EBGI				
G-BMXA	Cessna 152 II	152-80125	N757ZC	14. 7.86	E.Alexander	Andrewsfield	16. 7.99T
G-BMXB	Cessna 152 II	152-80996	N48840	14. 7.86	H.Daines Electronics Ltd.	(Beccles)	21. 3.93T
G-BMXC	Cessna 152 II	152-80416	N24858	14. 7.86	General Airline Ltd	Blackbushe	7. 1.02T
					t/a European Flyers		
G-BMXD	Fokker F-27 Friendship 500	10417	TF-FLR	6.10.86	BAC Express Airlines Ltd	Gatwick	12.12.01T
			HL-5210/HL-5206/PH-FOR				
G-BMXJ	Reims Cessna F.150L	0853	F-BUBA	18. 7.86	R.Harman t/a Arrow Acft Grp	Tatenhill	25. 3.00
G-BMXL	PA-38-112 Tomahawk	38-80A0018	N25060	4. 9.86	Airways Aero Associations Ltd	Booker	4. 6.99T
					(Op British Airways F/C)		
					(Maintain of the Birds/Benyhone Tartan t/s)		
G-BMXX	Cessna 152 II	152-84953	N5469P	10. 9.86	Aerohire Ltd	Wellesbourne Mountford	16.11.98T
G-BMYA*	Colt 56A HAFB	864		13. 8.86	British Balloon Museum	Newbury	2.12.92A
					& Library "British Gas"		
G-BMYC	Socata TB-10 Tobago	696		1. 9.86	Elizabeth A.Grady	Norwich	30. 4.99
G-BMYD	Beechcraft A36 Bonanza	E-2350		28.11.86	Seabeam Partners Ltd		21. 3.99
						Wellesbourne Mountford	
G-BMYF	Bensen B.8M	PE-01		18. 8.86	G.Callaghan	Richhill, Armagh	
G-BMYG	Reims Cessna FA152 Aerobat	0365	OO-JCA	23.10.86	Club Air Ltd	Aberdeen	24. 3.99T
			(OO-JCC)/PH-AXG		t/a Aberdeen Flying Club		
G-BMYI	Grumman-American AA-5 Traveler		EI-BJF	1. 9.86	W.C. & S.C.Westran	Shoreham	24. 3.99T
		AA5-0568	F-BVRM/N9568L				
G-BMYJ	Cameron V-65 HAFB	726		8. 9.86	A.Lutz "Skylark II"	Westbury	16. 5.99A
G-BMYN	Colt 77A HAFB	873		2. 9.86	W.I.Martyn	Wadebridge	11. 3.99A
					"Spectacles"		
G-BMYP	Fairey Gannet AEW.3	F.9461	8610M	16. 9.86	D.Copley	Sandtoft	29.9.89P*
			XL502		(As "XL502" in 849 Sqdn/"B" Flt RN c/s)		
G-BMYS	Thunder Ax7-77Z HAFB	887		3.11.86	J.E.Weidema t/a Pinkel Balloons		
						Baambrugge, Netherlands	25. 6.97A
G-BMYU	Jodel Wassmer D.120 Paris-Nice	289	F-BMYU	23. 6.78	P.M.Standen & A.J.Roxburgh	Barton	15. 4.99P
G-BMYV	Bensen B.8M	RC-001		23. 9.86	Not known	(London)	
G-BMYW*	Hughes 269C	14-0272	N8999F	22. 9.86	March Helicopters Ltd	Sywell	26. 3.00T
G-BMZA	Air Command 503 Modac	0589		11. 2.87	R.W.Husband	Sheffield	1. 6.99P
	(Rotax 503) (Probably c/n 0389)						
G-BMZB	Cameron N-77 HAFB	1370		30.10.86	D.C.Eager "Dreamland"	Bracknell	30. 4.95A
G-BMZE	Socata TB-9 Tampico	708		5.12.86	R.F.Keene	(Bicester)	14. 6.99T
G-BMZF*	WSK-Mielec LiM 2 (MiG-15bis)	1B01420		18.12.86	Fleet Air Arm Museum	RNAS Yeovilton	
			Polish AF 1420				
G-BMZG	QAC Quickie Q2	PFA/94A-10919		1.10.86	T.D.Edmunds	Haverfordwest	2. 8.99P
	(Revmaster 2100D)						
G-BMZN	Everett Gyroplane 1	008		13.11.86	K.Ashford	Walsall	16. 8.99P
	(VW 1835)						
G-BMZP	Everett Gyroplane 1	010		14.11.86	M.N.Morris-Jones	Kemble	18. 8.98P
	(VW 1835)						
G-BMZS	Everett Gyroplane 1	012		13.11.86	L.W.Cload	St.Merryn	4.11.99P
	(VW 1835)						
G-BMZW	Bensen B.8MR	PFA G/01-1021		16.10.86	P.D.Widdicombe	Huntingdon, York	25. 8.99P
	(Rotax 532)						
G-BMZX	Wolf W-11 Boredom Fighter	PFA/146-11042		31.10.86	A.R.Meakin & S.W.Watkins	Llangarron	26. 5.95P
	(Cont A65) (Represents a Spad replica)				(As "146-11042/7" in 94th Aero Sqdn, AEF France c/s)		
G-BMZZ	Stephens Akro Z	V.57	(HB-)	10.11.86	F.Actis	Charmey, Switzerland	19.10.98P
	(Lyc AE10-360)		G-BMZZ/VH-AUZ				

G-BNAA-BNZZ

Regn	Type	C/n	P/I	Date	Owner/operator	Probable Base	CA Expy
G-BNAD	Rand Robinson KR-2 (VW1834)	PFA/129-11077		10.11.86	P.J.Brookman (Loughborough) (Stored Ottringham, Hull 7.90)		27. 2.90P
G-BNAG	Colt 105A HAFB	906		31.10.86	R.W.Batchelor	Thame	19.12.89A
G-BNAI	Wolf W-11 Boredom Fighter (Cont A65) (Represents a Spad replica)	PFA/146-11083		31.10.86	P.J.D.Gronow Haverfordwest (As "146-11083/5" in 94th Aero Sqdn, AEF France c/s)		12.11.99P
G-BNAJ	Cessna 152 II	152-82527	C-GZWF (N69173)	3.11.86	Galair Ltd (Op Surrey & Kent F/C)	Biggin Hill	15. 3.99T
G-BNAN	Cameron V-65 HAFB	1333		28.10.86	Anne M.Lindsay & N.H.Ponsford Leeds t/a Rango Balloon & Kite Co "Actually"		9.10.94A
G-BNAO	Colt AS-105 Hot Air Airship	897		28.10.86	Heather Flight Ltd (London SE16)		27. 8.90A
G-BNAR	Taylor JT.1 Monoplane (VW1600)	PFA/55-10569		14.11.86	C.J.Smith (Blackfield, Southampton) (Status uncertain)		28.12.90P
G-BNAU	Cameron V-65 HAFB	1395		13.11.86	Cherry L.E.Lewis	Colwyn Bay	19. 2.99A
G-BNAW	Cameron V-65 HAFB	1366		24.10.86	A. & P.A.Walker Richmond, Surrey "Hippo-Thermia" (HMS Recruitment titles)		25. 6.95A
G-BNBL	Thunder Ax7-77 HAFB	910		7. 1.87	E.Stivala Marston Moreteyne, Bedford		21.12.99A
G-BNBP*	Colt Snowflake SS HAFB	913		21.11.86	D.Partridge/Air 2 Air Balloons Ltd (Stored 8.95)	Bristol	
G-BNBR	Cameron N-90 HAFB	1412		2.12.86	Airborne Promotions Ltd "Honda"	Bath	3. 6.94T
G-BNBU*	Bensen B.8MV	PFA G/01-1070		1.12.86	R.Retallick (Newton Abbot) (Cancelled by CAA 6.3.99; no Permit issued)		
G-BNBV	Thunder Ax7-77 HAFB	915		2.12.86	Jennifer M.Robinson "Layla" Milton-under-Wychwood		23. 7.99A
G-BNBW	Thunder Ax7-77 HAFB	914		11.12.86	I.S. & S.W.Watthews Grange-over-Sands "Mutley"		9. 9.99A
G-BNBY	Beechcraft 95-B55A Baron	TC-1347	G-AXXR	14. 2.83	Earthline Aviation Ltd	Thruxton	22.10.01
G-BNBZ	LET L-200D Morava	171329	D-GGDC EI-AOY/(D-GLIN)/EI-AOY/OK-SHB	16.12.86	C.A.Suckling Rushett Farm, Chessington		15. 5.00
G-BNCB	Cameron V-77 HAFB	1401		2.12.86	G.J.Preen Bristol t/a Tyred & Battered Balloon Grp "Cabot Tyres"		12. 5.93A
G-BNCC	Thunder Ax7-77 HAFB	924		11.12.86	Celia J.Burnhope "Charlie"	Leeds	9.10.99A
G-BNCE*	Grumman G.159 Gulfstream I	009	N436M N436/N436M/N43M/N709G		Not known Aberdeen (For Fire Services use 6.98)		9. 4.92T
G-BNCH	Cameron V-77 HAFB	1398		11.12.86	N.F.Mulliner Chatham t/a Royal Engineers Balloon Club "Sapper II"		19. 6.92A
G-BNCJ	Cameron V-77 HAFB	815		16.12.86	I.S.Bridge Shrewsbury "Sunshine Desserts"		8. 5.97A
G-BNCK	Cameron V-77 HAFB	1420		7. 1.87	G.Randall	Bielefeld, Germany	9.11.91A
G-BNCM	Cameron N-77 HAFB	1388		16.12.86	C.A. Stone	Bristol	3. 3.96A
G-BNCN	Glaser-Dirks DG-400	4-198		22. 1.87	M.C.Costin "421"	Husbands Bosworth	25. 3.99
G-BNCO	PA-38-112 Tomahawk	38-79A0472	N2482F	7. 1.87	Diane K.Walker	(Oakham, Leics)	12. 6.97T
G-BNCR	PA-28-161 Warrior II	28-8016111	G-PDMT ZS-LGW/N8103D	10.12.86	Airways Aero Associations Ltd Booker (Op British Airways F/C) (Rendezvous t/s)		2. 5.99T
G-BNCS	Cessna 180	30022	OO-SPA D-ENUX/N2822A	7. 1.87	C.Elwell Transport Ltd	Tatenhill	17. 2.95
G-BNCU	Thunder Ax7-77 HAFB	928		7. 1.87	P.Mann "Skylark"	Luton	27. 8.97A
G-BNCV	Bensen B.8 (VW1835)	LWC-01		8. 1.87	J.M.Benson	St.Merryn	
G-BNCX*	Hawker Hunter T.7	41H/695454	XL621	9. 1.87	Brooklands Museum (As "XL621")	Brooklands	28.3.87P*
G-BNCZ	Rutan LongEz (Lyc O-235)	PFA/74A-10723		8. 1.87	P.A.Ellway "Atlas..T"	Sherburn	4.10.94P
G-BNDG	Wallis WA-201/R Srs.1 (Rotax 532)	K/220/X		22. 1.87	K.H.Wallis Reymerston Hall (Stored 8.97)		3.3.88P*
G-BNDN	Cameron V-77 HAFB	1443		8. 1.87	J.A.Smith	Bristol	22.10.93A
G-BNDO	Cessna 152 II	152-84574	N5387M	11. 2.87	Simair Ltd Andrewsfield (Op Essex School of Flying)		18. 7.99T
G-BNDP	Brugger MB.2 Colibri (VW1834)	PFA/43-10956		8. 1.87	J.P.Kynaston	(Luton)	11.5.93P
G-BNDR	Socata TB-10 Tobago	740		12. 2.87	A.N.Reardon	Blackpool	8. 1.00T
G-BNDT	Brugger MB.2 Colibri (VW 1834)	PFA/43-10981		8. 1.87	S.R.G.Anselm RAF Waddington t/a Colibri F/Grp		23. 8.99P
G-BNDV	Cameron N-77 HAFB	1427		25. 2.87	R.E.Jones Lytham St.Annes "English Lake Hotels"		9. 5.93A
G-BNDW	DH.82A Tiger Moth	3942	N6638	10.12.86	N.D.Welch Shobdon (Components stored Shobdon Acft Maintenance 3.96)		
G-BNDY	Cessna 425 Conquest I	425-0236	N1262T	2. 6.87	Standard Avn Ltd	Newcastle	14.10.99
G-BNED	PA-22-135 Tri Pacer	22-1640	OO-JEF N3385A	26. 1.87	P.Storey Sywell (Stored 1994)		AC
G-BNEE	PA-28R-201 Arrow III	28R-7837084	N630DJ N9518N	28. 1.87	Britannic Management (Avn) Ltd White Waltham		27. 6.99
G-BNEI	PA-34-200T Seneca II	34-7870429	N3058K VQ-LBC/N9646N	12. 6.87	P.J.Morrison	Stapleford	8. 4.00
G-BNEK	PA-38-112 Tomahawk II	38-82A0081	N9096A	28. 1.87	APB Leasing Ltd	Welshpool	28. 5.99T

Regn	Type	C/n	P/I	Date	Owner/operator	Probable Base	CA Expy
G-BNEL	PA-28-161 Warrior II	28-7916314	N2246U	27. 4.87	S.C.Westran	Shoreham	27. 6.99T
G-BNEN	PA-34-200T Seneca II	34-8070262	N8232V	18. 2.87	Warwickshire Aerocentre Ltd	Birmingham	20. 4.99T
G-BNEO	Cameron V-77 HAFB	1408		9. 2.87	J.G.O'Connell "Rowtate"	Braintree	19. 8.95
G-BNES	Cameron V-77 HAFB	1426		19. 2.87	G.Wells	Congleton	7. 1.99A
					t/a Northern Counties Photographers		
G-BNET	Cameron O-84 HAFB	1368		22. 1.87	C.& A.I.Gibson	Stockport	16. 2.99A
G-BNEV	Viking Dragonfly (VW 1834)	PFA/139-10935		28.11.86	N.W.Eyre (Kirkbymoorside) (Nearing completion 6.92)		
G-BNEX	Cameron O-120 HAFB	1414		3. 4.87	The Balloon Club Ltd	Bristol	6. 5.90A
					t/a Bristol Balloons "Sue Sheppard Employment Agency"		
G-BNFG	Cameron O-77 HAFB	1416		5. 3.87	Capital Balloon Club Ltd "Dolores"	London NW1	13. 1.94A
G-BNFI	Cessna 150J	150-69417	N50588	8. 1.87	T.D.Aitken	(Derby)	3. 3.00
G-BNFK	Cameron Egg 89SS HAFB (Faberge Rosebud Egg shape)	1436		20. 2.87	Forbes Europe Inc "Faberge Easter Egg"	Balleroy, Normandy	11. 7.99A
G-BNFM	Colt 21A Cloudhopper HAFB	668		5. 3.87	M.E.Dworski	Vermenton, France	18. 3.96A
G-BNFN	Cameron N-105 HAFB	1442		13. 3.87	P.Glydon	Barnt Green, Birmingham	17. 6.97T
G-BNFO	Cameron V-77 HAFB	816		5. 3.87	D.Newton & M.Sherbourn "Funshine"	Bristol	10. 5.92A
G-BNFP	Cameron O-84 HAFB	1474		29. 4.87	B.F.G.Ribbans "Dragonfly"	Woodbridge	3. 6.99A
G-BNFR	Cessna 152 II	152-82035	N67817	8. 4.87	Eastern Executive Air Charter Ltd (Op Seawing F/C)	Southend	10. 3.00T
G-BNFS	Cessna 152 II	152-83899	N5545B	10. 4.87	C & S Aviation Ltd	Halfpenny Green	9. 7.99T
G-BNFV	Robin DR400/120 Dauphin 80	1767		4. 3.87	J.P.A.Freeman	Headcorn	6. 6.99T
G-BNGE	Auster AOP.6	1925	TW536	18. 3.87	M.Pocock	(Melksham)	29. 4.99P
	(Op by Military Auster Flight as "TW536/TS-V" in 657 AOP Sqn c/s)						
G-BNGJ	Cameron V-77 HAFB	1487		18. 3.87	Latham Timber Centres (Holdings) Ltd "Latham Timber"	High Wycombe	14. 8.93A
G-BNGN	Cameron N-77 HAFB	817		3. 4.87	Catherine B.Leeder "Falcon"	Diss	28. 9.99A
G-BNGO	Thunder Ax7-77 HAFB	971		26. 3.87	J.S.Finlan	Hamilton, New Zealand	14. 3.99A
					t/a The G-BNGO Grp "Thunderbird" (Philips c/s)		
G-BNGP	Colt 77A HAFB	1033		30. 3.87	Cornwall Ballooning Adventures Ltd "Headland Hotel II"	Newquay	1. 8.99A
G-BNGR	PA-38-112 Tomahawk	38-79A0479	N2492F	26. 3.87	Teesside Flight Centre Ltd	Teesside	19. 3.00T
G-BNGS	PA-38-112 Tomahawk	38-78A0701	N2463A	26. 3.87	Frontline Avn Ltd	Carlisle	
					(Damaged in transit to UK 5.87; on rebuild 4.97)		
G-BNGT	PA-28-181 Archer II	28-8590036	N149AV N9559N	29. 4.87	J.H.Berry	Edinburgh	18. 5.99T
					t/a Berry Air (Op Edinburgh F/C)		
G-BNGV	ARV1 Super 2	021		4. 6.87	N.A.Onions	Stapleford	21.11.99
G-BNGW	ARV1 Super 2	022		4. 6.87	Southern Gas Turbines Ltd (Stored 6.94)	Manston	8. 7.90T
G-BNGX	ARV1 Super 2	023		6. 7.87	Southern Gas Turbines Ltd (Stored 2.96)	Goodwood	7. 8.94
G-BNGY	ARV1 Super 2	019	(G-BMWL)	9. 6.87	M.T.Manwaring	RAF Wyton	5. 3.01
G-BNHB	ARV1 Super 2	026		13. 7.87	J.K.Davies	(Chester)	2. 2.01
G-BNHE	ARV1 Super 2	029		14. 8.87	L.J.Joyce	Liverpool	7. 8.99
G-BNHG	PA-38-112 Tomahawk II	38-82A0030	N91435	23. 3.87	D.A.Whitmore	Turweston	14. 5.00T
G-BNHI	Cameron V-77 HAFB	1249		26. 3.87	C.J.Nicholls "Fun-Der-Bird"	Warwick	22. 3.99A
G-BNHJ	Cessna 152 II	152-81249	N49418	4. 6.87	The Pilot Centre Ltd	Denham	11.11.99T
G-BNHK	Cessna 152 II	152-85355	N80161	30. 3.87	General Airline Ltd	Blackbushe	19.12.99T
					t/a European Flyers		
G-BNHL*	Colt Beer Glass 90SS HAFB	1042		24 .3.87	R S Kent "Gatzweiler Alt"	Lancing	4.3.97A
					(Balloon Preservation Group 7.98)		
G-BNHN*	Colt Ariel Bottle SS HAFB	1045		30. 3.87	British Balloon Museum "Ariel "	Newbury	N/E(A)
G-BNHO	Thunder Ax7-77 HAFB	1057		30. 3.87	M.J.Forster "Bloody Mary"	Newcastle	16. 7.97A
G-BNHP	Saffery S.330 HAFB (Model)	9		21. 3.78	N.H.Ponsford	Leeds	
					t/a Rango Balloon & Kite Co "Alpha 2"		
G-BNHT	Alpavia Fournier RF3	80	(D-KITX) G-BNHT/F-BMTO	13. 4.87	D.G.Hey	Little Gransden	15. 7.99P
					t/a G-BNHT Grp		
G-BNID	Cessna 152 II	152-84931	N5378P	24. 4.87	M.J.Ireland	Wellesbourne Mountford	5. 3.00T
G-BNIE	Cameron O-160 HAFB	1450		5. 5.87	D.K.Fish	Bedford	20. 7.95T
G-BNIF	Cameron O-56 HAFB	1464		15. 4.87	D.V.Fowler "Nifty"	Cranbrook, Kent	24. 5.99A
G-BNII	Cameron N-90 HAFB	1497		15. 4.87	S.Saunders	Petworth	14.10.99T
					t/a Topless Balloon Grp		
G-BNIJ	Socata TB-10 Tobago	758		27. 4.87	R.E.Price	(Coalville)	11. 8.01
G-BNIK	Robin HR200/120 Club	43	LX-AIK LX-PAA	15. 4.87	A.W.Eldridge	Leicester	17. 5.00
G-BNIM	PA-38-112 Tomahawk	38-78A0148	N9631T	18. 6.87	S.S.Houston & J.Giltrap	Glasgow	10. 3.00T
G-BNIN	Cameron V-77 HAFB	1079	G-RRSG(1)	15. 4.87	M.K.Grigson	Shoreham	16. 9.99A
					t/a Cloud Nine Balloon Grp "Cloud Nine"		
G-BNIO	Luscombe 8AC Silvaire (Cont A75)	2120	N45593 NC45593	15. 4.87	G.G.Pugh	Stapleford	8. 9.99P
G-BNIP	Luscombe 8A Silvaire (Cont A65)	3547	N77820 NC77820	15. 4.87	D.R.C.Hunter & S.Maric (Stored 6.98)	Cumbernauld	10. 2.93P
G-BNIU	Cameron O-77 HAFB	1499		28. 4.87	M.R.Nanda & Mitchell Air Power Ltd "Mitchell Air Power"	Nottingham	13. 4.96A
					t/a Nottingham Hot-Air Balloon Club		

Regn	Type	C/n	P/I	Date	Owner/operator	Probable Base	CA Expy
G-BNIV	Cessna 152 II	152-84866	N4972P	24. 4.87	Aerohire Ltd (Op Halfpenny Green Flight Centre)	Halfpenny Green	3. 7.00T
G-BNIW	Boeing-Stearman A75N1 (PT-17) Kaydet (P&W R985)	75-1526	N49291 41-7967	22. 4.87	R.C.Goold	East Midlands	26. 3.01
G-BNIZ	Fokker F-27 Friendship 600F	10405	OY-SRA G-BNIZ/9Q-CLQ/PH-FOD	1. 6.87	Dart Group plc t/a Channel Express	Bournemouth	3.11.00T
G-BNJA	WAG-Aero Wag-a-Bond (Cont O-200-A)	PFA/137-10886		3. 4.87	B.E.Maggs	(Bristol)	26. 5.99P
G-BNJB	Cessna 152 II	152-84865	N4970P	27. 4.87	Klingair Ltd	Conington	16. 4.99T
G-BNJC	Cessna 152 II	152-83588	N4705B	27. 4.87	Stapleford F/C Ltd	Stapleford	23. 7.99T
G-BNJD	Cessna 152 II	152-82044	N67833	27. 4.87	Southern Air Ltd	Shoreham	16.10.99T
G-BNJF	PA-32RT-300 Lance II	32R-7885098	N31539	8. 6.78	PFB Aviation Ltd	Birmingham	12.11.99T
G-BNJG	Cameron O-77 HAFB	1502		9. 5.89	A.M.Figiel "Simply Red"	(High Wycombe)	4. 4.97
G-BNJH	Cessna 152 II	152-85401	C-GORA (N93101)	21. 7.87	Alarmond Ltd t/a Edinburgh F/C	Edinburgh	10. 7.00T
G-BNJJ*	Cessna 152 II	152-83625	N4767B	22. 6.87	The Fire Service College	Moreton-in-Marsh	14. 7.90T
				(Damaged Cranfield 18.5.88 & in fire service use 8.98)			
G-BNJK*	BAe HS.748 Srs.2A	1594	C-GEPI HP-432	5. 5.87	Macavia International Ltd	Chateauroux, France	N/E(Exp)
	(Converted to MacAvia 748 Turbine Tanker water-bomber; stored 6.95)						
G-BNJL	Bensen B.8 (VW1835)	PFA G/01-1020		30. 4.87	C.G.Ponsford	(Maldon)	
G-BNJM	PA-28-161 Warrior II	28-8216078	N8015V	27. 5.87	Teesside Flight Centre Ltd	Carlisle	4. 6.90T
				(Damaged Middleton, Cumbria 18.5.89; stored 4.97)			
G-BNJO	QAC Quickie Q2 (Revmaster 2100D)	2217	N17LM	6.10.87	J.D.McKay	Crowfield	14. 5.93P
				(Damaged nr Crowfield 17.1.97; stored Netherthorpe 6.97)			
G-BNJR	PA-28RT-201T Turbo Arrow IV	28R-8031104	N8212U	8. 5.87	Intelligent Micro Software Ltd	Blackbushe	16. 7.99
G-BNJT	PA-28-161 Warrior II	28-8116184	N8360T	11. 6.87	B.J.Newman, B.C.Williams, T.Kermode & M.Jones t/a Chester Flying Group	Chester	21.10.99T
G-BNJU	Cameron Bust 80SS HAFB	1324		13. 5.87	Ballon Team Bonn GmbH & Co. KG "Ludwig von Beethoven"	Meckenheim, Germany	21. 1.00A
G-BNJV*	Cessna 152 II	152-83840	N5333B	13. 5.87	Not known	Biggin Hill	29. 6.93T
				(Crashed Stoneacre Farm, Bredhurst 8.3.92; stored 2.95)			
G-BNJX	Cameron N-90 HAFB	1480		2. 7.87	Mars UK Ltd "Maltesers"	Slough	19. 5.94A
G-BNJZ	Cassutt Racer IIIM (Cont O-200-A)	PFA/34-11228		14. 5.87	A.P.Meredith & Jill R.Burry	Hilden-le-Noble, Hants	21. 6.99P
G-BNKC	Cessna 152 II	152-81036	N48894	26. 5.87	Herefordshire A/C Ltd	Shobdon	6. 8.99T
G-BNKD	Cessna 172N Skyhawk II	172-72329	N4681D	19. 5.87	Bristol Flying Centre Ltd	Bristol/Lulsgate	20. 8.99T
G-BNKE	Cessna 172N Skyhawk II	172-73886	N6534J	20. 5.87	T.Jackson t/a Kilo Echo Flying Group	Manchester	22. 9.99T
G-BNKF	Colt AS-56 Hot-Air Airship	899		20. 5.87	Formtrack Ltd	Tucson, Arizona	14. 9.88A
G-BNKH	PA-38-112 Tomahawk II	38-81A0078	N25874	14. 5.87	Goodwood Road Racing Co Ltd	Goodwood	8. 7.99T
G-BNKI	Cessna 152 II	152-81765	N67337	19. 5.87	RAF Halton Aeroplane Club Ltd	RAF Halton	10. 6.99T
G-BNKP	Cessna 152 II	152-81286	N49460	18. 5.87	Clacton A/C (1988) Ltd	Clacton	19. 8.00T
G-BNKR	Cessna 152 II	152-81284	N49458	18. 5.87	Marnham Investments Ltd (Op Ulster Flying Club)	Newtownards	10. 7.99T
G-BNKS	Cessna 152 II	152-83186	N47202	18. 5.87	Shropshire A/C Ltd	Sleap	9. 5.99T
G-BNKT	Cameron O-77 HAFB	1356		13. 2.87	British Airways plc "Katie II"		13. 5.96A
G-BNKV	Cessna 152 II	152-83079	N46604	18. 5.87	Premi-Air Flying Club Ltd	Shoreham	8. 8.99T
G-BNKX*	Robinson R-22	0149	N9065L	28. 5.87	B.C.Seedle t/a Brian Seedle Helicopters (Stored 12.97)	Blackpool	16. 8.96T
G-BNLA	Boeing 747-436	23908	N60665	30. 6.89	British Airways plc (Chelsea Rose t/s)	Gatwick	29. 6.99T
G-BNLB	Boeing 747-436	23909		31. 7.89	British Airways plc "City of Edinburgh"	Heathrow	31. 7.99T
G-BNLC	Boeing 747-436	23910		21. 7.89	British Airways plc (Dove/Colum t/s)	Gatwick	26. 7.99T
G-BNLD	Boeing 747-436	23911	N6018N	5. 9.89	British Airways plc (Delftblue Daybreak t/s)	Heathrow	5. 9.99T
G-BNLE	Boeing 747-436	24047		14.11.89	British Airways plc "City of Newcastle"	Heathrow	16.11.99T
G-BNLF	Boeing 747-436	24048		23. 2.90	British Airways plc "City of Leeds"	Heathrow	27. 2.00T
G-BNLG	Boeing 747-436	24049		23. 2.90	British Airways plc (Whale Rider t/s)	Heathrow	26. 2.00T
G-BNLH	Boeing 747-436	24050		28. 3.90	British Airways plc (Wings of the City t/s)	Gatwick	29. 3.00T
G-BNLI	Boeing 747-436	24051		19. 4.90	British Airways plc (Mountain of the Birds/Benyhone Tartan t/s)	Heathrow	20. 4.00T
G-BNLJ	Boeing 747-436	24052	N60668	23. 5.90	British Airways plc (Martha Masanabo/Ndebele t/s)	Gatwick	24. 5.00T
G-BNLK	Boeing 747-436	24053	N6009F	25. 5.90	British Airways plc (Water Dreaming t/s)	Heathrow	28. 5.00T
G-BNLL	Boeing 747-436	24054		13. 6.90	British Airways plc (Chelsea Rose t/s)	Heathrow	13. 6.00T

Regn	Type	C/n	P/I	Date	Owner/operator	Probable Base	CA Expy
G-BNLM	Boeing 747-436	24055	N6009F	28. 6.90	British Airways plc (Martha Masanabo/Ndebele t/s)	Gatwick	27. 6.00T
G-BNLN	Boeing 747-436	24056		26. 7.90	British Airways plc (Nalanji Dreaming t/s)	Heathrow	26. 7.00T
G-BNLO	Boeing 747-436	24057		25.10.90	British Airways plc (Emmly Masanabo/Ndebele t/s)	Heathrow	24.10.00T
G-BNLP	Boeing 747-436	24058		17.12.90	British Airways plc "City of Aberdeen"	Gatwick	16.12.00T
G-BNLR	Boeing 747-436	24447	N6005C	15. 1.91	British Airways plc (Rendezvous t/s)	Heathrow	16. 1.01T
G-BNLS	Boeing 747-436	24629		13. 3.91	British Airways plc (Wanula Dreaming t/s)	Heathrow	12. 3.01T
G-BNLT	Boeing 747-436	24630		19. 3.91	British Airways plc (Cockerel of Lowicz/Koguty Lowickie t/s)	Gatwick	18. 3.01T
G-BNLU	Boeing 747-436	25406		28. 1.92	British Airways plc "City of Bangor"	Heathrow	27. 1.02T
G-BNLV	Boeing 747-436	25427		20. 2.92	British Airways plc (Waves of the City t/s)	Gatwick	19. 2.99T
G-BNLW	Boeing 747-436	25432		4. 3.92	British Airways plc "City of Norwich"	Heathrow	4. 3.99T
G-BNLX	Boeing 747-436	25435		1. 4.92	British Airways plc (Waves of the City t/s)	Heathrow	2. 4.99T
G-BNLY	Boeing 747-436	27090	N60659	10. 2.93	British Airways plc "City of Swansea"	Heathrow	9. 2.00T
G-BNLZ	Boeing 747-436	27091		4. 3.93	British Airways plc (Animals and Trees/Kg-Oocoan-Naka-Hiian-Thee-E t/s)	Heathrow	3. 3.00T
G-BNMA	Cameron O-77 HAFB	830		15.12.87	Tracey A.Hains "Finian"	Bristol	13. 3.99A
G-BNMB	PA-28-151 Cherokee Warrior 28-7615369		N6826J	6.10.87	Britannia Airways Ltd	Luton	26. 1.00T
G-BNMC	Cessna .152 II	152-82564	N69218	29. 5.87	Margaret L.Jones (Op Derby A/C)	Egginton	21. 7.00T
G-BNMD	Cessna 152 II	152-83786	N5170B	28. 5.87	T.M.Jones (Op Derby A/C)	Egginton	28. 7.01T
G-BNME	Cessna 152 II	152-84888	N5159P	25. 9.87	Northamptonshire School of Flying Ltd	Sywell	4.12.99
G-BNMF	Cessna 152T	152-85563	N93858	21. 7.87	Aerohire Ltd (Op Midland Flight Centre)	Halfpenny Green	2. 1.00T
G-BNMG	Cameron O-77 HAFB	1500		27. 5.87	J.H.Turner	Bridgnorth	7. 3.97A
G-BNMH	Pietenpol Air Camper	NH-1-001		2. 6.87	N.M.Hitchman	(Stoke Gifford)	
G-BNMI	Colt Black Knight HAFB	1096		1. 6.87	Virgin Airship & Balloon Co.Ltd	Telford	12. 5.99A
G-BNMK	Dornier Do.27A-1	271	OE-DGO 56+04/BD+397/BA+399	14. 8.87	G.Mackie	(Lisburn, NI)	
G-BNML	Rand Robinson KR-2 (VW1834)	PFA/129-11240		23. 6.87	L.G.Horne	(Ashford, Kent)	23. 7.98P
G-BNMO	Cessna R182 Skylane RG II	R182-00956	N738RK	3. 7.87	Surfheath Ltd t/a Safari Aviation Services	Bournemouth	24. 4.00
G-BNMT	Short SD.3-60 Var.100	SH.3723	N160DD G-BNMT/G-14-3723	18. 6.87	Loganair Ltd (Cockerel of Lowicz/Koguty Lowickie t/s)	Glasgow	15.10.99T
G-BNMU	Short SD.3-60 Var.100	SH.3724	N161DD G-BNMU/G-14-3724	18. 6.87	Loganair Ltd (Dove/Colum t/s)	Glasgow	22.11.99T
G-BNMX	Thunder Ax7-77 HAFB	1003		15. 6.87	S.A.D.Beard	Cheltenham	22. 5.99A
G-BNNA	Stolp SA.300 Starduster Too (Lyc O-360)	1462	N8SD	29. 6.87	D.F.Simpson	Standalone Farm, Meppershall	11. 1.99P
G-BNNE	Cameron N-77 HAFB	1413		15. 6.87	Balloon Flights International Ltd	Bath	
G-BNNG*	Cessna T337D Turbo Super Skymaster 337-01096		G-COLD PH-NOS/N86147	23. 6.87	Not known (Damaged Goodwood 1985; on rebuild 3.92)	Farley Farm, Romsey	15. 7.85
G-BNNI	Boeing 727-276	20950	VH-TBK	10.12.86	Swift Airways Ltd (Op Sabre Airways "Lady Patricia")	Gatwick	17. 3.99T
G-BNNK	Boeing 737-4Q8	24069		30.11.88	GB Airways Ltd (Waves of the City t/s)	Gatwick	7.12.01T
G-BNNL	Boeing 737-4Q8	24070		26. 1.89	GB Airways Ltd (Chelsea Rose t/s)	Gatwick	30. 1.02T
G-BNNO	PA-28-161 Warrior II	28-8116099	N8307X	15. 6.87	Lorch Airways (UK) Ltd	Norwich	18. 6.99T
G-BNNR	Cessna 152 II	152-85146	N40SX N40SU/N6121Q	15. 6.87	Sussex F/C Ltd	Shoreham	8.10.99T
G-BNNS	PA-28-161 Warrior II	28-8116061	N8283C	26. 6.87	M.J.Allen & R.Inskip t/a Warrior Aircraft Syndicate	Fowlmere	21. 5.99
G-BNNT	PA-28-151 Cherokee Warrior 28-7615056		N7624C	12. 6.87	S.T.Gilbert & D.J.Kirkwood	Hinton-in-the-Hedges	3. 7.00T
G-BNNU	PA-38-112 Tomahawk II	38-81A0037	N25650	12. 6.87	Edinburgh Flying Club Ltd	Edinburgh	9.10.99T
G-BNNX	PA-28R-201T Turbo Arrow III 28R-7703009		N9005F	14. 7.87	P.J.Lague	Andrewsfield	18.10.97
G-BNNY	PA-28-161 Warrior II	28-8016084	N8092M	1. 9.87	A.S.Bamrah t/a Falcon F/Svs (Op Southern Air)	Shoreham	3.10.99T
G-BNNZ	PA-28-161 Warrior II	28-8016177	N8135Y	24. 7.87	General Airline Ltd t/a European Flyers	Blackbushe	3.10.99T
G-BNOB	Wittman W.8 Tailwind 258/DH1 & PFA/3502 (Cont.PC60)			13. 7.87	M.Robson-Robinson "Imogen"	(Abbots Bromley)	8.12.98P
G-BNOE	PA-28-161 Warrior II	2816013	N9121X N9568N	26. 6.87	Sherburn Aero Club Ltd	Sherburn	9. 2.98T

Regn	Type	C/n	P/I	Date	Owner/operator	Probable Base	CA Expy
G-BNOF	PA-28-161 Warrior II	2816014	N9122B	26. 6.87	British Aerospace Flight Training (UK) Ltd Prestwick		31. 3.01T
G-BNOG	PA-28-161 Warrior II	2816015	N9122D	26. 6.87	British Aerospace Flight Training (UK) Ltd Prestwick		5. 7.01T
G-BNOH	PA-28-161 Warrior II	2816016	N9122L	26. 6.87	Sherburn Aero Club Ltd	Sherburn	25. 1.01T
G-BNOI	PA-28-161 Warrior II	2816017	N9122N	26. 6.87	British Aerospace Flight Training (UK) Ltd Prestwick		17. 5.97T
G-BNOJ	PA-28-161 Warrior II	2816018	N9122R	26. 6.87	W.M.Brown & R.D.Turner t/a British Aerospace (Warton) F/C	Blackpool	26. 6.00T
G-BNOK	PA-28-161 Warrior II	2816019	N9122U	26. 6.87	British Aerospace Flight Training (UK) Ltd Prestwick		19. 5.01T
G-BNOL	PA-28-161 Warrior II	2816023		26. 6.87	British Aerospace Flight Training (UK) Ltd Prestwick		12. 5.01T
G-BNOM	PA-28-161 Warrior II	2816024		26. 6.87	Sherburn Aero Club Ltd	Sherburn	4. 2.01T
G-BNON	PA-28-161 Warrior II	2816025		26. 6.87	British Aerospace Flight Training (UK) Ltd Prestwick		22. 2.01T
G-BNOO	PA-28-161 Warrior II	2816026		26. 6.87	British Aerospace Flight Training (UK) Ltd Prestwick		14. 5.99T
G-BNOP	PA-28-161 Warrior II	2816027		26. 6.87	British Aerospace Flight Training (UK) Ltd Prestwick		25. 6.98T
G-BNOR	PA-28-161 Warrior II	2816028		26. 6.87	British Aerospace Flight Training (UK) Ltd Prestwick		8. 8.99T
G-BNOS	PA-28-161 Warrior II	2816029		26. 6.87	British Aerospace Flight Training (UK) Ltd Prestwick		28. 3.98T
G-BNOT	PA-28-161 Warrior II	2816030		26. 6.87	British Aerospace Flight Training (UK) Ltd Prestwick		24. 6.01T
G-BNOU	PA-28-161 Warrior II	2816031		26. 6.87	British Aerospace Flight Training (UK) Ltd Prestwick		27. 7.98T
G-BNOV	PA-28-161 Warrior II	2816032		26. 6.87	British Aerospace Flight Training (UK) Ltd Prestwick		17. 6.00T
G-BNOW	PA-28-161 Warrior II	2816033		26. 6.87	British Aerospace Flight Training (UK) Ltd Prestwick		1. 5.98T
G-BNOX	Cessna R182 Skylane RG II	R182-01026	N756AW	24. 6.87	B.C.Leahy	Ronaldsway	20. 3.00
G-BNOZ	Cessna 152 II	152-81625	EI-CCP G-BNOZ/N65570	22. 6.87	APB Leasing Ltd	Welshpool	14. 2.99T
G-BNPE	Cameron N-77 HAFB	1519	(G-BNPX)	25. 8.87	Kent Garden Centres Ltd "Kent Garden Centres"	Maidstone	7. 9.95A
G-BNPF	Slingsby T.31M Cadet III (Stark Stamo MS.1400A) 826 & PFA/42-11122 (Contains wings from XE791 which became OO-ZDQ)	XA284		3.11.87	S.Luck, P.Norman & D.R.Winder "Noddy"	Audley End	5. 8.99P
G-BNPH	Hunting-Percival P.66 Pembroke C.1 (Regd with c/n "PAC66/027")	P66/41	WV740	30. 6.87	M.J.Willing (As "WV740" in 60 Sqn RAF c/s)	Jersey	5. 5.99P
G-BNPI	Colt 21A Cloudhopper HAFB	1038		23. 6.87	Virgin Airship & Balloon Co Ltd "Virgin Cloudhopper"	Telford	7. 8.95A
G-BNPL	PA-38-112 Tomahawk	38-79A0524	N2420G	28. 7.87	Modern Air (UK) Ltd	Fowlmere	30. 1.00T
G-BNPM	PA-38-112 Tomahawk	38-79A0374	N2561D	28. 7.87	Papa Mike Avn Ltd (Op Bonus Avn)	Cranfield	10. 5.99T
G-BNPN	PA-28-181 Archer II	28-7890059	N47379	28. 7.87	Z.Mahmood	Elstree	19.12.99T
G-BNPO	PA-28-181 Archer II	28-7890123	N47720	28. 7.87	Bonus Avn Ltd	Cranfield	29. 5.00T
G-BNPU*	Hunting-Percival P.66 Pembroke C.1 (Regd with c/n "K66/089")	P66/87	XL929	30. 6.87	Museum of D-Day Aviation (As "XL929") (Open storage 10.97)	Shoreham	17.5.88P*
G-BNPV	Bowers Fly Baby 1A/1B (Cont C90)	PFA/16-11120		2. 7.87	J.G.Day & R.Gauld-Galliers	Rushett Farm, Chessington	15.10.99P
G-BNPY	Cessna 152 II	152-80249	N24388	30. 6.87	J.C.Birdsall t/a Traffic Management Svs	Gamston	19.11.99T
G-BNPZ	Cessna 152 II	152-85134	N6109Q	30. 6.87	C & S Aviation Ltd	Halfpenny Green	18. 9.99T
G-BNRA	Socata TB-10 Tobago	772		15. 7.87	D.Teece t/a Double D Air Group	Nottingham	8. 5.00
G-BNRG	PA-28-161 Warrior II	28-8116217	N83810	7. 7.87	RAF Brize Norton F/C Ltd RAF Brize Norton		26. 3.00T
G-BNRI	Cessna U206G Stationair II	U206-04024	N756ED	28. 7.87	Target Technology Ltd	Headcorn	10. 4.00
G-BNRK	Cessna 152 II	152-84659	N6297M	29. 7.87	Redhill Avn Ltd t/a Redhill F/C	Redhill	26.11.99T
G-BNRL	Cessna 152 II	152-84250	N5084L	13. 7.87	J.R.Nicholls	Sibson	25. 4.00T
G-BNRP	PA-28-181 Archer II	28-7790528	N984BT	25.11.87	Bonus Aviation Ltd	Cranfield	3. 4.00T
G-BNRR	Cessna 172P Skyhawk II	172-74013	N5213K	13. 7.87	Cornwall Flying Club Ltd	Bodmin	29.11.99
G-BNRX	PA-34-200T Seneca II	34-7970336	N2898A	25.11.87	Truman Aviation Ltd.	Nottingham	9. 2.00
G-BNRY	Cessna 182Q Skylane II	182-65629	N735RR	20. 7.87	Reefly Ltd	Booker	28. 5.00T
G-BNRZ	Robinson R-22 Beta	0670		28. 7.87	R.D.Jordan	Cranfield	24. 8.99
G-BNSG	PA-28R-201 Arrow III	28R-7837205	N9516C	30. 7.87	Armada Avn Ltd	Redhill	9.10.99
G-BNSI	Cessna 152 II	152-84853	N4945P	6. 8.87	Sky Leisure Avn (Charters) Ltd	Shoreham	1.10.99T
G-BNSL	PA-38-112 Tomahawk II	38-81A0086	N25956	21. 7.87	Muriel H.Kleiser (Op Edinburgh F/C)	Edinburgh	23. 1.00T
G-BNSM	Cessna 152 II	152-85342	N68948	23. 7.87	Cornwall F/C Ltd	Bodmin	29. 1.00T
G-BNSN	Cessna 152 II	152-85776	N94738	21. 7.87	M.K.Barnes & G.N.Olson (Op Bristol Flying Centre)	Bristol/Lulsgate	20. 2.00T

Regn	Type	C/n	P/I	Date	Owner/operator	Probable Base	CA Expy
G-BNSO	Slingsby T-67M Firefly II	2021		20. 8.87	Hunting Aviation Ltd RAF Barkston Heath (Op Hunting Acft Ltd/JEFTS)		3. 1.00T
G-BNSP	Slingsby T-67M Firefly II	2044		20. 8.87	Hunting Aviation Ltd RAF Barkston Heath (Op Hunting Acft Ltd/JEFTS)		4. 2.00T
G-BNSR	Slingsby T-67M Firefly II	2047		20. 8.87	Hunting Aviation Ltd RAF Barkston Heath (Op Hunting Acft Ltd/JEFTS)		7. 4.00T
G-BNST	Cessna 172N Skyhawk II	172-73661	N4670J	21. 9.87	B.& R.P.Martin t/a Martin Aviation	Gamston	6. 3.00T
G-BNSU	Cessna 152 II	152-81245	N49410	2.12.87	Channel Avn Ltd	Bourn	21. 8.00T
G-BNSV	Cessna 152 II	152-84531	N5322M	4.12.87	Channel Avn Ltd (Op Rural Flying Corps)	Bourn	12. 7.97T
G-BNSW	Cessna 152 II	152-85621	N94213	1. 9.87	One Zero One Three Ltd (Op Guernsey Flight Training)	Guernsey	7. 4.00T
G-BNSY	PA-28-161 Warrior II	28-8016017	N4512M	18. 8.87	Carill Avn Ltd	Southampton	12. 3.00T
G-BNSZ	PA-28-161 Warrior II	28-8116315	N8433B	20. 8.87	Carill Avn Ltd	Southampton	10.11.99T
G-BNTC	PA-28RT-201T Turbo Arrow IV	28R-8131081	N83428	4.11.87	M.F.Lassan	(Kidderminster)	13. 6.99
G-BNTD	PA-28-161 Cherokee Warrior II	28-7716235	N38490 N9539N	5. 8.87	A.M.Alam & H.S.Patel	Elstree	24.10.99T
G-BNTE	FFA AS.202/18A4 Bravo	224		7. 8.87	British Aerospace Flight Training (UK) Ltd	Prestwick	11. 3.97T
G-BNTF	FFA AS.202/18A4 Bravo	225		7. 8.87	British Aerospace Flight Training (UK) Ltd	Blackpool	24. 8.01T
G-BNTH	FFA AS.202/18A4 Bravo	227		7. 8.87	British Aerospace Flight Training (UK) Ltd	Prestwick	14. 7.97T
G-BNTI	FFA AS.202/18A4 Bravo	228		7. 8.87	British Aerospace Flight Training (UK) Ltd	Prestwick	1. 7.01T
G-BNTJ	FFA AS.202/18A4 Bravo	229		7. 8.87	British Aerospace Flight Training (UK) Ltd	Prestwick	22. 8.97T
G-BNTK	FFA AS.202/18A4 Bravo	230		7. 8.87	British Aerospace Flight Training (UK) Ltd (Status uncertain)	Prestwick	18. 4.91T
G-BNTL	FFA AS.202/18A4 Bravo	231		7. 8.87	British Aerospace Flight Training (UK) Ltd	Prestwick	8. 3.98T
G-BNTM	FFA AS.202/18A4 Bravo	232		7. 8.87	British Aerospace Flight Training (UK) Ltd (Op Anglo American Avtn)	Bournemouth	8. 3.01T
G-BNTN	FFA AS.202/18A4 Bravo	233		7. 8.87	British Aerospace Flight Training (UK) Ltd	Prestwick	1. 5.97T
G-BNTO	FFA AS.202/18A4 Bravo	234		7. 8.87	British Aerospace Flight Training (UK) Ltd	Prestwick	23. 8.96T
G-BNTP	Cessna 172N Skyhawk II	172-72030	N6531E	4. 9.87	Westnet Ltd	Barton	16.12.99T
G-BNTS	PA-28RT-201T Turbo Arrow IV	28R-8131024	N8296R	6. 8.87	Nasaire Ltd	Liverpool	11. 2.00
G-BNTT	Beechcraft 76 Duchess	ME-228	N54SB	8.10.87	L. & J.Donne t/a Donne Enterprise	Perth	6. 4.97T
G-BNTW	Cameron V-77 HAFB	1574		13. 8.87	P.Goss "Cecilia"	Alton	6.11.99A
G-BNTZ	Cameron N-77 HAFB	1518		27. 8.87	P.M.Watkins t/a Balloon Team "Nationwide Anglia"	Chippenham	6. 7.97A
G-BNUC	Cameron O-77 HAFB	1575		18. 8.87	T.J.Bucknall "Bridges Van Hire II"	Chester	
G-BNUI	Rutan VariEze (Cont O-200-A)	PFA/74-10960		12. 8.87	I.T.Kennedy & K.H.McConnell	Aldergrove	1.11.99P
G-BNUL	Cessna 152 II	152-84486	N4852M	2.10.87	Exeter Air Training School Ltd	Exeter	13. 2.00T
G-BNUN	Beechcraft 58PA Baron	TJ-256	N6732Y	19. 8.87	British Midland Airways Ltd	East Midlands	11.10.99T
G-BNUO	Beechcraft 76 Duchess	ME-250	N6635Y	29. 9.87	G.A.F.Tilley (Op Langtry Flying Group)	Bournemouth	19. 4.99T
G-BNUS	Cessna 152 II	152-82166	N68179	26. 8.87	Stapleford F/C Ltd	Stapleford	1. 7.00T
G-BNUT	Cessna 152 II	152-79458	N714VC	26. 8.87	Stapleford F/C Ltd	Stapleford	25. 5.00T
G-BNUV	PA-23-250 Aztec F	27-7854038	N97BB N63894	2.10.87	L.J.Martin	Sandown/Redhill	21.10.99
G-BNUX	Hoffmann H.36 Dimona	36236		26. 8.87	G.Hill t/a Buckminster Dimona Syndicate	Saltby	30. 5.00
G-BNUY	PA-38-112 Tomahawk II	38-81A0093	N26006	10. 9.87	Aerohire Ltd	Cardiff	9. 3.00T
G-BNUZ	Robinson R-22 Beta	0680		28. 8.87	J.C.Reid	Stockton-on-Tees	1. 4.00
G-BNVB	Grumman-American AA-5A Cheetah	AA5A-0758	N26843	28. 8.87	A.M.Glazer	Turweston	23. 2.00
G-BNVD	PA-38-112 Tomahawk	38-79A0055	N2421B	16.11.87	Channel Avn Ltd	Guernsey	10. 4.00T
G-BNVE	PA-28-181 Archer II	28-8490046	N4338D	28. 8.87	S.Parrish t/a Steve Parrish Racing	Fowlmere	30.10.99T
G-BNVT	PA-28R-201T Turbo Cherokee Arrow III	28R-7703157	N5863V	26. 1.88	T.Yeung t/a Victor Tango Grp	Glasgow	6.10.00
G-BNVZ	Beechcraft 95-B55 Baron	TC-2042	N17720	25. 9.87	W.J.Forrest & P.Schon	White Waltham	7. 4.01
G-BNWA	Boeing 767-336ER	24333	N6009F	19. 4.90	British Airways plc (Delftblue Daybreak t/s)	Heathrow	24. 4.00T
G-BNWB	Boeing 767-336ER	24334	N6046P	2. 2.90	British Airways plc (Chelsea Rose t/s)	Heathrow	12. 2.00T
G-BNWC	Boeing 767-336ER	24335		2. 2.90	British Airways plc (Rendezvous t/s)	Heathrow	21. 2.00T

Regn	Type	C/n	P/I	Date	Owner/operator	Probable Base	CA Expy
G-BNWD	Boeing 767-336ER	24336	N6018N	2. 2.90	British Airways plc (Martha Masanabo/Ndebele t/s)	Heathrow	27. 2.00T
G-BNWE	Boeing 767-336ER	24337		23. 2.90	British Airways plc (Chelsea Rose t/s)	Heathrow	17. 3.00T
G-BNWF	Boeing 767-336ER	24338	N1788B	22. 6.90	British Airways plc (Mountain of the Birds/Benyhone Tartan t/s)	Heathrow	22. 6.00T
G-BNWG	Boeing 767-336ER	24339		11. 7.90	British Airways plc (Waves of the City t/s)	Heathrow	12. 7.00T
G-BNWH	Boeing 767-336ER	24340	N6005C	31.10.90	British Airways plc (Waves of the City t/s)	Heathrow	30.10.00T
G-BNWI	Boeing 767-336ER	24341		18.12.90	British Airways plc "City of Madrid"	Gatwick	17.12.00T
G-BNWJ	Boeing 767-336ER	24342		24. 4.91	British Airways plc (Golden Khokhloma t/s)	Heathrow	23. 4.01T
G-BNWK	Boeing 767-336ER	24343		18. 4.91	British Airways plc (Dove/Colum t/s)	Heathrow	17. 4.01T
G-BNWL	Boeing 767-336ER	25203		30. 4.91	British Airways plc "City of Luxembourg"	Heathrow	29. 4.01T
G-BNWM	Boeing 767-336ER	25204		24. 6.91	British Airways plc "City of Toulouse"	Manchester	24. 6.01T
G-BNWN	Boeing 767-336ER	25444		30.10.91	British Airways plc "City of Berlin"	Heathrow	29.10.01T
G-BNWO	Boeing 767-336ER	25442		2. 3.92	British Airways plc "City of Barcelona"	Gatwick	1. 3.99T
G-BNWP	Boeing 767-336ER	25443		9. 3.92	British Airways plc (Rendezvous t/s)	Heathrow	8. 3.99T
G-BNWR	Boeing 767-336ER	25732		20. 3.92	British Airways plc (Chelsea Rose t/s)	Gatwick	19. 3.99T
G-BNWS	Boeing 767-336ER	25826	N6018N	19. 2.93	British Airways plc "City of Oporto"	Heathrow	18. 2.00T
G-BNWT	Boeing 767-336ER	25828		8. 2.93	British Airways plc (Mountain of the Birds/Benyhone Tartan t/s)	Heathrow	7. 2.00T
G-BNWU	Boeing 767-336ER	25829		16. 3.93	British Airways plc (Blomsterang t/s)	Gatwick	15. 3.00T
G-BNWV	Boeing 767-336ER	27140		29. 4.93	British Airways plc (Dove/Colum t/s)	Heathrow	28. 4.00T
G-BNWW	Boeing 767-336ER	25831		3. 2.94	British Airways plc "City of Marseille"	Heathrow	2. 2.00T
G-BNWX	Boeing 767-336ER	25832		1. 3.94	British Airways plc "City of Bilbao"	Heathrow	28. 2.00T
G-BNWY	Boeing 767-336ER	25834	N5005C	22. 4.96	British Airways plc "City of Helsinki"	Heathrow	21. 4.99T
G-BNWZ	Boeing 767-336ER	25733		25. 2.97	British Airways plc	Heathrow	24. 2.00T
G-BNXA	BN-2A Islander	80	V2-LAC VP-LAC/N854JA/G-51-21	17. 9.87	Cormack (A/c Services) Ltd	Cumbernauld	29.12.98T
G-BNXC	Cessna 152 II	152-85429	N93171	24. 9.87	R.A.Page t/a Sir W.G.Armstrong-Whitworth F/Grp	Coventry	30. 1.00T
G-BNXD	Cessna 172N Skyhawk II	172-72692	N6285D	25. 9.87	A.Jahanfar (Op Willowair F/C)	Southend	22. 4.01T
G-BNXE	PA-28-161 Warrior II	28-8116034	N8262D	24. 9.87	M.S.Brown t/a Rugby Autobody Repairs	Coventry	23.12.99
G-BNXI	Robin DR.400/180R Remorqueur	1021	SE-FNI	13.10.87	London Gliding Club Pty Ltd	Dunstable	30.12.99
G-BNXK	Nott/Cameron/Airship Industries ULD/3 Explorer Rozier HAFB 7 & 1110		(G-BLJN)	23. 9.87	J.R.P.Nott	(London NW3)	
	(Hot-air envelope in Twain Harte, California, USA 12.97 - helium inner envelope stored Bristol 1995)						
G-BNXL	Glaser-Dirks DG-400	4-216		2.10.87	J.McLaughlin t/a G-BNXL Grp	Sleap	14. 4.00
G-BNXM	PA-18-95 Super Cub (Cont O-200-A) (L-21B-PI) (Italian Frame rebuild No.0006)	18-4019	MM54-2619 EI-276/I-EIVC/MM54-2619/54-2619	23.11.87	R.Thorp t/a G-BNXM Grp	Gipsy Wood	15. 4.99P
G-BNXR	Cameron O-84 HAFB	1515		23. 9.87	J.A.B. Gray "Bacchus II"	Bowness-on-Windermere	7. 5.99T
G-BNXT	PA-28-161 Cherokee Warrior II	28-7716168	N4047Q	23. 9.87	A.S.Bamrah t/a Falcon F/Svs (Op Euroflyers)	Blackbushe	27.10.99T
G-BNXU	PA-28-161 Warrior II	28-7916129	N2082C	23. 9.87	D.J.G.Carphin & R.E.Woolsey t/a Friendly Warrior Grp	Newtownards	28.12.99
G-BNXV	PA-38-112 Tomahawk	38-79A0826	N2399N	10.12.87	E.Reed t/a The St.George Flying Club	Teesside	5.10.01T
G-BNXX	Socata TB-20 Trinidad	664	N20GZ	15. 9.87	D.M.Carr	Wellesbourne Mountford	12. 5.00
G-BNXZ	Thunder Ax7-77 HAFB	1105		13.10.87	W.S.Templeton, R.B.Green & A.S.Dear t/a Hale Hot-Air Balloon Grp "Dragonfly"	Fordingbridge	21.11.98A
G-BNYB	PA-28-201T Turbo Dakota	28-7921040	N2856A	27. 1.88	A.G.E.Camisa & C.J.Freeman	Elstree	22.10.00T
G-BNYD	Bell 206B JetRanger II	1911	N3254P C-GTWM/N49712	10.10.87	Sterling Helicopters Ltd	Norwich	31.10.99T
G-BNYI	Short SD.3-60 Var.100	SH.3731	N360CC G-BNYI/G-14-3731	12.10.87	Gill Aviation Ltd	Newcastle	10. 5.99T
G-BNYK	PA-38-112 Tomahawk II	38-82A0059	N2376V	23.10.87	APB Leasing Ltd	Welshpool	11. 5.99T

Regn	Type	C/n	P/I	Date	Owner/operator	Probable Base	CA Expy
G-BNYL	Cessna 152 II	152-80671	N25454	6.10.87	APB Leasing Ltd	Barton	24. 9.00T
G-BNYM	Cessna 172N Skyhawk II	172-73854	N6089J	13.11.87	N.B.Lindley	Crosland Moor	20. 1.00
G-BNYN	Cessna 152 II	152-85433	N93185	2.10.87	Redhill Avn Ltd t/a Redhill F/C	Redhill	6. 2.00T
G-BNYO	Beechcraft 76 Duchess	ME-78	N2010P	28.10.87	Sub Marine Services Ltd	(Falmouth)	11.12.01T
G-BNYP	PA-28-181 Archer II	28-8490027	N4330K	19.10.87	R.D.Cooper (Op Sandra's F/Grp)	Cranfield	13. 3.00T
G-BNYS	Boeing 767-204ER	24013	N6009F	22. 2.88	Britannia Airways Ltd	Luton	13. 2.02T
G-BNYV	PA-38-112 Tomahawk	38-78A0073	N9364T	13.11.87	Channel Avn Ltd (Stored 6.97)	Guernsey	4. 3.94T
G-BNYX	Denney Kitfox Mk.1 (Rotax 532)	PFA/172-11285		28.10.87	R.W.Husband Birds Edge, Penistone (Stored 3.96)		14. 3.95P
G-BNYZ	SNCAN Stampe SV-4E (Lyc O-360)	200	F-BFZR Fr Mil	10.12.87	Tapestry Colour Ltd	White Waltham	2.10.00
G-BNZB	PA-28-161 Warrior II	28-7916521	N2900U	18.11.87	A.S.Bamrah t/a Falcon F/Svs	Biggin Hill	24. 1.00T
G-BNZC	DHC.1 Chipmunk 22	C1/0778	7438M/WP905	11.11.87	D.A.Horsley (As "671" in RCAF c/s)	Wombleton	12. 4.00
G-BNZG	PA-28RT-201T Turbo Arrow IV	28R-8031132	N82376	23.11.87	Brightday Ltd	Manchester	15. 2.97
G-BNZJ	Colt 21A Cloudhopper HAFB	1150		27.10.87	N.Charbonnier	Aosta, Italy	31. 8.96A
G-BNZK	Thunder Ax7-77 HAFB	1104		10.11.87	T.D.Marsden "Shropshire Lass"	Grimsby	28. 5.97A
G-BNZL	Rotorway Scorpion 133	2839		2.11.87	J.R.Wraight (Complete but stored 5.95) Stoneacre Farm, Farthing Corner		
G-BNZM	Cessna T210N Turbo Centurion II	210-63640	N4828C	9.11.87	A.J.M.Freeman	Stansted	5. 2.00
G-BNZO	Rotorway Exec 90 (RW152)	3535		9.11.87	M.G.Wiltshire Albany Farm, Hullavington "Bonzo"		24. 6.99P
G-BNZR	Clutton FRED Srs.II (VW 1834)	PFA/29-10727		10.11.87	R.M.Waugh	Newtownards	21. 5.99P
G-BNZV	PA-25-235 Pawnee	25-7405649	C-GSKU N9548P	22. 2.88	Northumbria Gliding Club Ltd	Currock Hill	3. 4.00
G-BNZZ	PA-28-161 Warrior II	28-8216184	N8253Z	17.11.87	Zooom Aviation Ltd	Denham	26. 2.00T

G-BOAA-BOZZ

Regn	Type	C/n	P/I	Date	Owner/operator	Probable Base	CA Expy
G-BOAA	BAC-Aerospatiale Concorde 102	100-006	G-N94AA G-BOAA	3. 4.74	British Airways plc (Union Flag t/s)	Heathrow	24. 2.00T
G-BOAB	BAC-Aerospatiale Concorde 102	100-008	G-N94AB G-BOAB	3. 4.74	British Airways plc (Union Flag t/s)	Heathrow	19. 9.01T
G-BOAC	BAC-Aerospatiale Concorde 102	100-004	G-N81AC G-BOAC	3. 4.74	British Airways plc (Union Flag t/s)	Heathrow	11. 2.01T
G-BOAD	BAC-Aerospatiale Concorde 102	100-010	G-N94AD G-BOAD	9. 5.75	British Airways plc (Union Flag t/s) .	Heathrow	4.11.01T
G-BOAE	BAC-Aerospatiale Concorde 102	100-012	G-N94AE G-BOAE	9. 5.75	British Airways plc (Union Flag t/s)	Heathrow	18. 7.99T
G-BOAF	BAC-Aerospatiale Concorde 102	100-016	G-N94AF G-BFKX	12. 6.80	British Airways plc (Union Flag t/s)	Heathrow	11. 6.01T
G-BOAG	BAC-Aerospatiale Concorde 102	100-014	G-BFKW	9. 2.81	British Airways plc	Heathrow	3. 4.99T
G-BOAH	PA-28-161 Warrior II	28-8416030	N43401	21. 1.88	Keen Leasing (IOM) Ltd. (Castletown)		27. 2.00T
G-BOAI	Cessna 152 II	152-79830	C-GSJH N757LS	8. 1.88	Galair Ltd	Biggin Hill	22. 5.00T
G-BOAK	PA-22-150 Tri-Pacer	22-5101	N7313D	23.11.87	Alison M.Noble Pepperbox, Salisbury (On rebuild to PA-20 configuration 6.93)		
G-BOAL	Cameron V-65 HAFB	1600		5.11.87	A.Lindsay "No Name Balloon" Twickenham		15. 5.97A
G-BOAM	Robinson R-22 Beta	0717		10.12.87	Bristow Helicopters Ltd	Redhill	21.12.99T
G-BOAO	Thunder Ax7-77 HAFB	1162		2.12.87	D.V.Fowler Cranbrook, Kent		16. 6.97A
G-BOAS	Air Command 503 Commander	0388 & PFA G/04-1094		3.12.87	R.Robinson (Leighton Buzzard)		
G-BOAU	Cameron V-77 HAFB	1606		10.12.87	G.T.Barstow Llandrindod Wells "Flying Colours/Duster I"		9.12.96A
G-BOBA	PA-28R-201 Arrow III	28R-7837232	N31249	4. 1.88	RJS Aviation Ltd	Halfpenny Green	26. 3.00T
G-BOBB	Cameron O-120 HAFB	1609		24.11.87	S.E.& V.D.Hurst	Mansfield	28. 3.99A
G-BOBD	Cameron O-160 HAFB	1594		22.12.87	J.Spindler	Kinross	6. 9.95T
G-BOBF*	Brugger MB.2 Colibri	PFA/43-11172	.	10.12.87	R.Bennett Sproughton, Ipswich		
				(Cancelled by CAA 6.3.99; not completed and sold to a new owner in 1997)			
G-BOBH	Airtour AH-77B HAFB	009		2.12.87	J. & K.Francis "Gloworm" Southampton		4. 7.99A
G-BOBJ	PA-38-112 Tomahawk	38-80A0021	N25096 N9656N	4. 1.88	Pearl Technology Ltd	Biggin Hill	8. 5.00T
G-BOBK	PA-38-112 Tomahawk	38-79A0503	N2352G	4. 1.88	Pearl Technology Ltd	Biggin Hill	23. 3.00T
G-BOBL	PA-38-112 Tomahawk II	38-81A0140	N91335	4. 1.88	Aerohire Ltd	Halfpenny Green	18. 8.00T
G-BOBR	Cameron N-77 HAFB	1623		10.12.87	C.Bradley & M.Morris Llanymynech, Powys "Loganair"		29. 4.99A
G-BOBS	QAC Quickie Q2 (Revmaster 2100)	PFA/94A-10840		27. 9.82	M.A.Hales RAF Brize Norton (Wreck stored 4.95)		22.12.92P
G-BOBT	Stolp SA.300 Starduster Too (Lyc O-360)	CJ-01	N690CM	15.12.87	S.C.Lever t/a G-BOBT Group White Waltham		3. 5.98P
G-BOBU	Colt 90A HAFB	900		15.12.87	Prescott Hot Air Balloons Ltd Cheltenham		3.10.99A
G-BOBV	Reims Cessna F.150M Commuter	1415	EI-BCV	14.12.87	Sheffield Aero Club Ltd	Netherthorpe	10. 3.00T
G-BOBY	Monnett Sonerai II (VW2233)	PFA/15-10223		26.10.78	R.G.Hallam Netherthorpe (Damaged nr Barton 31.10.82; stored 9.96)		8.11.82P
G-BOBZ	PA-28-181 Archer II	28-8090257	N81671	21.12.87	Trustcomms Intl Ltd	Goodwood	9. 3.98T
G-BOCB*	HS.125 Srs.1B/522	25106	G-OMCA	14. 9.87	Barry Technical College		
		G-DJMJ/G-AWUF/5N-ALY/G-AWUF/HZ-BIN			Cardiff Airport Industrial Park (Instructional airframe 11.95)		16.10.90T
G-BOCC	PA-38-112 Tomahawk	38-79A0362	N2540D	14.12.87	J.M.Green	Goodwood	14.12.00T
G-BOCF	Colt 77A HAFB	1178		4. 1.88	Lindstrand Balloons Ltd Oswestry (Stored 9.95)		25. 7.94T
G-BOCG	PA-34-200T Seneca II	34-7870359	N36759	30.12.87	Oxford Aviation Services Ltd	Oxford	23.10.00T
G-BOCI	Cessna 140A (Cont C90)	15497	N5366C	17.11.87	J.B.Bonnell "Whitey" (Newbury)		10. 9.99
G-BOCK	Sopwith Triplane Replica 153 & NAW-1 (130 hp Clerget Rotary 9B)			26. 1.88	The Shuttleworth Trust Old Warden (As "N6290" in 8 Sqdn RNAS c/s) "Dixie II"		18. 7.99P
G-BOCL	Slingsby T-67C	2035		5. 1.88	Richard Brinklow Aviation Ltd Gloucestershire		10. 7.00T
G-BOCM	Slingsby T-67C	2036		5. 1.88	Richard Brinklow Aviation Ltd Turweston		27. 4.00T
G-BOCP	PA-34-220T Seneca III	3433089		17.12.87	British Aerospace Flight Training (UK) Ltd Prestwick		6. 5.01T
G-BOCR	PA-34-220T Seneca III	3433111		26. 2.88	British Aerospace Flight Training (UK) Ltd Prestwick		27. 5.01T
G-BOCS	PA-34-220T Seneca III	3433112		26. 2.88	. British Aerospace Flight Training (UK) Ltd Prestwick		24. 9.01T
G-BOCT	PA-34-220T Seneca III	3433113		26. 2.88	British Aerospace Flight Training (UK) Ltd Prestwick		30. 3.98T
G-BOCU	PA-34-220T Seneca III	3433114		26. 2.88	British Aerospace Flight Training (UK) Ltd Prestwick		24. 6.01T
G-BOCV	PA-34-220T Seneca III	3433115		26. 2.88	British Aerospace Flight Training (UK) Ltd Prestwick		9. 1.98T
G-BOCW	PA-34-220T Seneca III	3433120		25. 8.88	British Aerospace Flight Training (UK) Ltd Prestwick		30.11.01T
G-BOCX	PA-34-220T Seneca III	3433121		29. 9.88	British Aerospace Flight Training (UK) Ltd Prestwick		21.11.98T

Regn	Type	C/n	P/I	Date	Owner/operator	Probable Base	CA Expy
G-BOCY	PA-34-220T Seneca III	3433122		29. 9.88	British Aerospace Flight Training (UK) Ltd Prestwick		3.12.01T
G-BODA	PA-28-161 Warrior II	2816037	N9601N	19. 1.88	Oxford Aviation Services Ltd	Oxford	13. 4.00T
G-BODB	PA-28-161 Warrior II	2816042		23. 2.88	Oxford Aviation Services Ltd	Oxford	7. 9.00T
G-BODC	PA-28-161 Warrior II	2816041		23. 2.88	Oxford Aviation Services Ltd	Oxford	7. 4.00T
G-BODD	PA-28-161 Warrior II	2816040		23. 2.88	Oxford Aviation Services Ltd	Oxford	7. 8.00T
G-BODE	PA-28-161 Warrior II	2816039	N9603N	23. 2.88	Oxford Aviation Services Ltd	Oxford	25. 5.00T
G-BODF	PA-28-161 Warrior II	2816038	N9602N	19. 1.88	Oxford Aviation Services Ltd	Oxford	20. 4.00T
G-BODG	Slingsby Cadet III (Conversion of T.31B c/n 706)	PFA/42-11310	WT911	9. 6.88	H.P.Vox (Op East Fortune F/Grp) (Stored incomplete 9.98)	East Fortune	
G-BODH	Slingsby Cadet III (VW1834)	PFA/42-10108	BGA.474	5. 1.88	H.P.Vox "Fochinell" (Op East Fortune F/Grp) (Stored 9.98)	East Fortune	29. 1.99P
	(If p/i is as quoted then conversion from T.8 Tutor c/n MHL/RT.13 ex G-ALNK/BGA.474)						
G-BODI	Stoddard-Hamilton SH-2H Glasair III	3088	(HB-) G-BODI	14. 4.89	C.A.C.Tilney	(Milton Keynes)	18. 6.99P
G-BODM	PA-28-180 Cherokee Challenger	28-7305519	N56016	2. 2.88	R.Emery	Clutton Hill, High Littleton	27. 8.99T
G-BODO	Cessna 152 II	152-82404	N68923	29. 1.88	Annie R.Sarson	Popham	29. 5.00
G-BODP	PA-38-112 Tomahawk II	38-81A0010	N25616	5. 1.88	D.A.Whitmore	Wellesbourne Mountford	1.12.00
G-BODR	PA-28-161 Warrior II	28-8116318	N8436B	5. 1.88	Airways Aero Associations Ltd (Op British Airways F/C) (Waves & Cranes t/s)	Booker	2. 9.00T
G-BODS	PA-38-112 Tomahawk	38-79A0410	N2379F	3. 2.88	Mid-Anglia Flying School Ltd	Cambridge	8. 6.01T
G-BODT	Jodel D.18 173 & PFA/169-11290 (Rotax 912UL)			14. 1.88	L.D.McPhillips t/a Jodel G-BODT Syndicate	Portmoak	6. 5.99P
G-BODU	Scheibe SF.25C-2000 Falke	44434	D-KIAA	19. 1.88	R.G.G.English t/a Monica English Memorial Trust	Rufforth	9. 5.00
G-BODX	Beechcraft 76 Duchess	ME-309	N67094	26. 2.88	R.J.Dajczak	Welshpool	30. 7.00
G-BODY	Cessna 310R II	310R-1503	N4897A	17.12.87	Atlantic Air Transport Ltd	Coventry	23. 2.00T
G-BODZ	Robinson R-22 Beta	0729		8. 1.88	Langley Construction Ltd	Nottingham	21. 4.01
G-BOEC*	PA-38-112 Tomahawk	38-78A0138	N9587T	8. 1.88	Not known (Temp unregd 8.7.97)	Jersey	22. 8.97T
G-BOEE	PA-28-181 Cherokee Archer II	28-7690359	N6168J	20. 1.88	T.B.Parmenter	Lodge Farm, St.Osyth, Clacton	13. 6.00
G-BOEH	Robin DR.340 Major	434	F-BRVN	4. 1.88	G.Bowles Bradleys Lawn, Heathfield t/a Piper Flyers Grp		14. 5.01
G-BOEK	Cameron V-77 HAFB	1658		25. 1.88	A.J.E.Jones "Secret One"	Bristol	7. 8.97A
G-BOEM	Aerotek Pitts S-2A Special (Lyc AEIO-360)	2255	N31525	17. 2.88	Margaret Murphy	(Barnet)	21. 7.01
G-BOEN	Cessna 172M Skyhawk	172-61325	N20482	12. 2.88	H.B.Davies	Elstree	19. 6.00T
G-BOER	PA-28-161 Warrior II	28-8116094	N83030	21. 1.88	M. & W.Fraser-Urquhart	White Waltham	7. 4.00
G-BOET	PA-28RT-201 Arrow IV	28R-8018020	G-IBEC G-BOET/N8116V	28. 1.88	B.C.Chambers	Jersey	4. 8.00
G-BOEW	Robinson R-22 Beta	0750		27. 1.88	Bristow Helicopters Ltd	Redhill	14. 3.00T
G-BOEX	Robinson R-22 Beta	0751		27. 1.88	Bristow Helicopters Ltd	Redhill	12. 2.00T
G-BOEZ	Robinson R-22 Beta	0753		27. 1.88	Bristow Helicopters Ltd	Redhill	9. 3.97T
G-BOFC	Beechcraft 76 Duchess	ME-217	N6628M	28. 1.88	Magenta Ltd	Exeter	18. 2.00T
G-BOFD	Cessna U206G Stationair II	U206-04181	N756LS	27. 1.88	D.M.Penny Movenis, Co.Londonderry (Op Wild Geese Parachute Centre)		24. 6.00
G-BOFE	PA-34-200T Seneca II	34-7870381	N39493	22. 2.88	Alstons Upholstery Ltd	(Colchester)	15. 7.00T
G-BOFF	Cameron N-77 HAFB	1666		26. 1.88	R.C.Corcoran	Bristol	13. 8.98A
G-BOFL	Cessna 152 II	152-84101	N5457H	28. 1.88	Gem Rewinds Ltd	Coventry	23. 2.00T
G-BOFM	Cessna 152 II	152-84730	N6445M	28. 1.88	Gem Rewinds Ltd	Coventry	27. 5.00T
G-BOFO	Ultimate Acft 10 Dash 200 (Lyc HIO-360) 10-200-004 & PFA/180-11319 G-BOFO		(HB-)	15. 2.88	M.Werdmuller (Status uncertain)	(Felton, Bristol)	16. 6.92P
G-BOFW	Cessna A150M Aerobat	A150-0612	N9803J	15. 2.88	Vectair Aviation 1995 Ltd	Goodwood	2. 9.00T
G-BOFX	Cessna A150M Aerobat	A150-0678	N9869J	15. 2.88	K.Hobbs t/a Aldergrove Flight Training Centre	Aldergrove	27.11.00T
G-BOFY	PA-28-140 Cherokee Cruiser	28-7425374	N43521	3. 2.88	BCT Aircraft Leasing Ltd	Bristol/Lulsgate	10.12.00T
G-BOFZ	PA-28-161 Warrior II	28-7816255	N2189M	10. 2.88	R.W.Harris (Op Willowair F/C)	Southend	19. 1.01T
G-BOGC	Cessna 152 II	152-84550	N5346M	8. 2.88	Keen Leasing (IOM) Ltd	(Castletown)	
G-BOGG	Cessna 152 II	152-82960	N45956	15. 2.88	The Royal Artillery A/C Ltd	AAC Middle Wallop	20. 8.00T
G-BOGI	Robin DR.400/180 Regent	1821		15. 2.88	A.L.M.Shepherd	Rochester	13. 5.00T
G-BOGK	ARV Super 2 K.006 & PFA/152-11138 (Hewland AE75)			10. 2.88	D.R.Trouse Cherry Tree Farm, Monewden t/a Suffolk Super Two Grp		21.12.99P
G-BOGM	PA-28RT-201T Turbo Arrow IV	28R-8031077	N8173C	10. 2.88	R.J.Pearce t/a RJP Avn	Halfpenny Green	18. 9.00
G-BOGO	PA-32R-301T Saratoga SP	32R-8029064	N8165W	6. 4.88	G.W.Dimmer	Old Sarum	13. 8.00
G-BOGP	Cameron V-77 HAFB	896		30. 3.88	T.Gunn "Dire Straits"	Crowborough	7. 9.97A
G-BOGR*	Colt 180A HAFB	1183		11. 5.88	British Balloon Museum & Library "Britannia"	Newbury	13. 3.92T
G-BOGT*	Colt 77A HAFB	1212		21. 3.88	R S Kent "British Gas" (Balloon Preservation Group 7.98)	Lancing	2.12.94A
G-BOGV	Air Command 532 Elite 0399 & PFA G/04-1102			10. 3.88	G.M.Hobman	Heworth, York	10. 1.91P
G-BOGW	Air Command 532 Elite AC532-UK001 & 0398			16. 2.88	A.Gault	(Forth, Lanark)	30. 6.89P

Regn	Type	C/n	P/I	Date	Owner/operator	Probable Base	CA Expy
G-BOGY	Cameron V-77 HAFB	1650		15. 2.88	R.A.Preston "Bella"	Bristol	30. 1.99A
G-BOHA	PA-28-161 Warrior II	28-7816352	N3526M	16. 3.88	S.R.V.Clark	Shoreham	16. 6.00T
G-BOHD	Colt 77A HAFB	1214		4. 3.88	D.B.Court "Bluebird"	Ormskirk	12. 4.95A
G-BOHF	Thunder Ax8-84 HAFB	1197		8. 4.88	J.A.Harris	Sturminster Newton	19. 9.94A
G-BOHG	Air Command 532 Elite			10. 3.88	T.E.McDonald	Melrose Farm, Melbourne	4. 6.91P
		0402 & PFA G/04-1122					
G-BOHH	Cessna 172N Skyhawk II	172-73906	N131FR	19. 2.88	T.Scott	Gamston	27. 4.01T
			N7333J				
G-BOHI	Cessna 152 II	152-81241	N49406	29. 2.88	V.D.Speck	Clacton	7. 7.00T
G-BOHJ	Cessna 152 II	152-80558	N25259	29. 2.88	J.M.Hothersall	Beccles	9. 8.98T
G-BOHL	Cameron A-120 HAFB	1701		11. 3.88	T.J.Bucknall	Chester	3. 2.98
					"Son of City of Bath"		
G-BOHM	PA-28-180 Cherokee Challenger		N55000	18. 2.88	M.J.Anthony & B.Keogh		23. 4.00
		28-7305287			Lockmead Farm, South Marston		
G-BOHN*	PA-38-112 Tomahawk II	38-81A0151	N23593	19. 2.88	Not known	Cardiff	19. 6.94T
					(Crashed Cardiff 13.8.93; stored 8.94)		
G-BOHO	PA-28-161 Warrior II	28-8016196	N747RH	25. 2.88	G.J.Craig & D.L.H.Barrel	Cambridge	21. 8.00T
			N9560N		t/a Egressus F/Grp		
G-BOHR	PA-28-151 Cherokee Warrior		C-GNFE	29. 2.88	G.Cockerton	Coventry	13. 4.01
		28-7515245					
G-BOHS	PA-38-112 Tomahawk	38-79A0988	N2418P	26. 2.88	A.S.Bamrah t/a Falcon F/Svs	Biggin Hill	12. 3.01T
G-BOHT	PA-38-112 Tomahawk	38-79A1079	N25304	14. 4.88	E.Reed	Teesside	26. 7.00T
			C-GAYW/N24052		t/a The St.George Flying Club		
G-BOHU	PA-38-112 Tomahawk	38-80A0031	N25093	26. 2.88	Avon A/C Lsg Ltd	Wellesbourne Mountford	1. 5.00T
G-BOHV	Wittman W.8 Tailwind			3. 3.88	R.A.Povall	Teesside	10. 9.99P
	(Cont O-200-A)	621 & PFA/31-11151					
G-BOHW	Van's RV-4	PFA/181-11309		16. 6.88	P.J.Robins	Deenethorpe	20. 8.99P
	(Lyc O-320)						
G-BOHX	PA-44-180 Seminole	44-7995008	N36814	9. 3.88	Airpart Supply Ltd	Oxford	3. 8.00T
G-BOIA	Cessna 180K Skywagon II	180-53121	N2895K	3. 3.88	R.E., P.E.R., J.E.R. & R.J.W.Styles		13.11.00
					t/a Old Warden Flying & Parachute Grp Turweston		
G-BOIB	Wittman W.10 Tailwind	PFA/31-10551		3. 3.88	L.Fairs	Popham	AC
G-BOIC	PA-28R-201T Turbo Arrow III		N2336M	7. 4.88	M.J.Pearson	Stapleford	19. 6.00
		28R-7803123					
G-BOID	Bellanca 7ECA Citabria	1092-75	N8676V	3. 3.88	D.Mallinson	Birds Edge, Penistone	11.12.00
G-BOIG	PA-28-161 Warrior II	28-8516027	N4390B	1. 3.88	D.Vallance-Pell	Gamston	10. 7.00
			N9519N				
G-BOIJ	Thunder Ax7-77 Srs.1 HAFB	964		11. 3.88	R.A.Hughes "Shropshire Lad"	Oswestry	28. 9.96A
G-BOIK	Air Command 503 Commander			8. 3.88	F.G.Shepherd	Alston, Cumbria	22. 1.90P
	(Rotax 503)	0420 & PFA G/04-1087		(Erroneously regd as c/n PFA G/04-1090)			
G-BOIL	Cessna 172N Skyhawk II	172-71301	N23FL	2. 3.88	Upperstack Ltd	Barton	29. 5.00T
			N23ER/(N2494E)				
G-BOIN	Bellanca 7ECA Citabria	1190-77	N4160Y	7. 3.88	LAC (Enterprises) Ltd	Barton	22. 4.01T
					(Op Lancashire Aero Club)		
G-BOIO	Cessna 152 II	152-80260	N24445	7. 3.88	AV Avn Ltd	Carlisle	12. 7.01T
					(Op Cumbria Aero Club)		
G-BOIP	Cessna 152 II	152-83444	N49264	7. 3.88	Stapleford F/C Ltd	Stapleford	26. 5.91T
					(Damaged Uckington 11.1.90; stored 9.93)		
G-BOIR	Cessna 152 II	152-83272	N48041	7. 3.88	Shropshire A/C Ltd	Sleap	13. 6.00T
G-BOIT	Socata TB-10 Tobago	810		10. 3.88	Buckland Newton Hire Ltd	Compton Abbas	27. 8.01T
G-BOIU	Socata TB-10 Tobago	811		10. 3.88	R & B Avn Ltd	Guernsey	20. 4.01
G-BOIV	Cessna 150M Commuter	150-78620	N704HH	30. 3.88	J.B.Green	South Burlingham, Norwich	25.11.00
G-BOIW	Cessna 152 II	152-82845	N89731	6. 4.88	EFG Flying Services Ltd	Biggin Hill	15.10.00T
G-BOIX	Cessna 172N Skyhawk II	172-71206	C-GMMX	9. 3.88	JR Flying Ltd	Bournemouth	27. 1.01T
			N2253E				
G-BOIY	Cessna 172N Skyhawk II	172-67738	N73901	9. 3.88	Aviation Acess Ltd	Leeds-Bradford	1. 7.00T
G-BOIZ	PA-34-200T Seneca II	34-8070014	N81081	25. 2.88	R.W.Tebby t/a S.F.Tebby & Son		29. 6.00T
					(Op Bristol Flying Centre) Bristol/Lulsgate		
G-BOJB	Cameron V-77 HAFB	1615		11. 3.88	K.L.Heron & R.M.Trotter	Bristol	5. 8.99A
G-BOJD	Cameron N-77 HAFB	1653		11. 3.88	L.H.Ellis "Bluebird"	Marlow	20. 5.99
G-BOJF	Air Command 532 Elite	0425		11. 3.88	Not known (Hoofddorp, Netherlands)		4. 6.91P
	(Rotax 532)						
G-BOJH	PA-28R-200 Cherokee Arrow II		N2821T	6. 4.88	Piper-Air (Glasgow) Ltd	Glasgow	22.10.00T
		28R-7235139			(Op Glasgow Flying Club)		
G-BOJI	PA-28RT-201 Arrow IV	28R-7918221	N2919X	31. 3.88	B.A.Mintowt-Czyz & T.A.Stoate Blackbushe		8. 5.00
G-BOJK	PA-34-220T Seneca III	3433020	G-BRUF	11. 3.88	Redhill Avn Ltd t/a Redhill F/C	Redhill	3. 4.00T
			N9113D				
G-BOJL	GEMS MS.885 Super Rallye	122		21. 3.88	J.A.Rees & F.Doncaster	Haverfordwest	
G-BOJM	PA-28-181 Archer II	28-8090244	N8155L	21. 3.88	Fernborough Ltd	Humberside	12. 5.00
G-BOJO*	Colt 120A HAFB	1208		7. 3.88	Not known (Temp unregd 6.8.97) Newcastle		23. 9.97T
G-BOJR	Cessna 172P Skyhawk II	172-75574	N64539	22. 4.88	Exeter F/C Ltd	Exeter	30. 6.00T
G-BOJS	Cessna 172P Skyhawk II	172-74582	N52699	29. 3.88	I.S.H.Paul	Denham	25. 5.00T
G-BOJU	Cameron N-77 HAFB	1718		21. 3.88	M.A.Scholes "GB Transport"	London SE25	7. 9.97A
G-BOJW	PA-28-161 Cherokee Warrior II		N1668H	28. 3.88	S.C.Brown	Enstone	25. 9.00T
		28-7716038					

Regn	Type	C/n	P/I	Date	Owner/operator	Probable Base	CA Expy
G-BOJZ	PA-28-161 Warrior II	28-7916223	N2113J	28. 3.88	Southern Air Ltd	Shoreham	22. 5.00T
G-BOKA	PA-28-201T Turbo Dakota	28-7921076	N2860S	15. 3.88	CBG Avn Ltd	Fairoaks	24. 4.00
G-BOKB	PA-28-161 Warrior II	28-8216077	N8013Y	29. 3.88	Southern Air Ltd	Shoreham	1. 5.00T
G-BOKF	Air Command 532 Elite (Rotax 532)	0404 & PFA G/04-1101		28. 3.88	D.Beevers	Melrose Farm, Melbourne	22. 9.99P
G-BOKH	Whittaker MW.7 (Rotax 532) (Regd as PFA/171-11231)	PFA/171-11281	(G-MTWT)	21. 3.88	I.D.Evans	Thame	1. 7.96P
G-BOKI	Whittaker MW.7 (Rotax 532)	PFA/171-11282	(G-MTWU)	21. 3.88	R.K.Willcox (Damaged Old Sodbury, Bristol 9.4.95)	Chipping Sodbury	28. 7.95P
G-BOKJ	Whittaker MW.7 (Rotax 532)	PFA/171-11283	(G-MTWV)	21. 3.88	M.R.Payne	(Watford)	4. 6.97P
G-BOKK*	PA-28-161 Warrior II	28-8116300	N8427L	6. 4.88	Not known (Damaged Hamgreen nr Redditch 18.5.95; on rebuild 6.96)	Blackpool	7. 6.97T
G-BOKL	PA-28-161 Warrior II	2816044		24. 3.88	British Aerospace Flight Training (UK) Ltd	Prestwick	1.12.91T
G-BOKM	PA-28-161 Warrior II	2816045		24. 3.88	British Aerospace Flight Training (UK) Ltd	Prestwick	12.11.99T
G-BOKN	PA-28-161 Warrior II	2816046		24. 3.88	British Aerospace Flight Training (UK) Ltd	Prestwick	7.11.99T
G-BOKO	PA-28-161 Warrior II	2816049		24. 3.88	British Aerospace Flight Training (UK) Ltd	Prestwick	12.11.99T
G-BOKP	PA-28-161 Warrior II	2816050		24. 3.88	British Aerospace Flight Training (UK) Ltd	Prestwick	18.12.99T
G-BOKR	PA-28-161 Warrior II	2816051		24. 3.88	British Aerospace Flight Training (UK) Ltd	Prestwick	22. 4.01T
G-BOKS	PA-28-161 Warrior II	2816052		24. 3.88	British Aerospace Flight Training (UK) Ltd	Prestwick	18. 1.92T
G-BOKT	PA-28-161 Warrior II	2816053		24. 3.88	British Aerospace Flight Training (UK) Ltd	Prestwick	30. 4.01T
G-BOKU	PA-28-161 Warrior II	2816054		24. 3.88	British Aerospace Flight Training (UK) Ltd	Prestwick	7.11.99T
G-BOKW*	Bolkow Bo.208C Junior	689	G-BITT F-BRHX/D-EEAL	6. 1.88	Not known (Temp unregd 19.7.96)	Croft Farm, Defford	3.11.95P
G-BOKX	PA-28-161 Warrior II	28-7816680	N39709	28. 3.88	C.J.Freeman (Op Weald Air Svs)	Headcorn	22. 8.00T
G-BOKY	Cessna 152 II	152-85298	N67409	6. 4.88	D.F.F.Poore	Bournemouth	8. 3.01T
G-BOLB	Taylorcraft BC-12-65 (Cont A65)	3165	N36211 NC36211	17. 5.88	A.T.E.Pacewicz & R.J.Rhys-Williams "Spirit of California"	Eastbach Farm, English Bicknor	10. 7.98P
G-BOLC	Fournier RF6B-100	1	F-BVKS	28. 3.88	W.H.Hendy	Dunkeswell	27.11.00
G-BOLD	PA-38-112 Tomahawk	38-78A0180	N9740T	8. 7.88	B.R.Pearson & B.F.Fraser-Smith (Stored 10.97)	Eaglescott	21. 1.96T
G-BOLE	PA-38-112 Tomahawk	38-78A0475	N2506E	13. 7.88	M.W.Kibble & E.A.Minard	Eaglescott	27. 5.01
G-BOLF	PA-38-112 Tomahawk	38-79A0375	N583P YV-133E/YV-1696P/N9666N	13. 7.88	Teesside Flight Centre Ltd	Teesside	1. 7.01T
G-BOLG	Bellanca 7KCAB Citabria	517-75	N8706V	25.11.88	B.R.Pearson t/a Aerotug	Eaglescott	24. 5.01
G-BOLI	Cessna 172P Skyhawk II	172-75484	N63794	30. 3.88	A.A.Mackinnon t/a BOLI F/C	Denham	11. 7.00T
G-BOLL	Lake LA-4-200 Skimmer	295	(F-GRMX) G-BOLL/EI-ANR/N1133L	4. 5.88	S.Armstrong	St. Angelo	19. 5.00
G-BOLN	Colt 21A Cloudhopper HAFB	1226		4. 5.88	Virgin Airship & Balloon Co Ltd "Pepsi Cola 1"	Telford	7. 8.95A
G-BOLO	Bell 206B JetRanger II	1522	N59409	2.11.87	Hargreaves Construction Co Ltd (Op Blades Helicopters)	Goodwood	13. 1.00T
G-BOLP	Colt 21A Cloudhopper HAFB	1227		4. 5.88	Virgin Airship & Balloon Co Ltd "Pepsi Cola 2"	Telford	7. 8.95A
G-BOLR	Colt 21A Cloudhopper HAFB	1228		3. 5.88	Virgin Airship & Balloon Co Ltd "Pepsi Cola 3"	Telford	7. 8.95A
G-BOLS	Clutton FRED Srs.II	PFA/29-10676		6. 4.88	I.F.Vaughan "The Ruptured Uck"	(Melton Mowbray)	
G-BOLT	Rockwell Commander 114	14428	N5883N	16.10.78	Betterbox Communications Ltd	Cranfield	30. 7.01
G-BOLU	Robin R.3000/120	106	F-GFAO SE-IMS	14. 4.88	I.W.Goodger t/a Classair	Biggin Hill	6. 7.00T
G-BOLV	Cessna 152 II	152-80492	N24983	8. 4.88	A.S.Bamrah t/a Falcon F/Svs	Biggin Hill	20.12.99T
G-BOLW	Cessna 152 II	152-80589	N25316	9. 6.88	JRB Avn Ltd (Op Seawing F/C)	Southend	30. 8.00T
G-BOLX	Cessna 172N Skyhawk II	172-69099	N734TK	8. 4.88	R.J.Burrough	Headcorn	12.11.00
G-BOLY	Cessna 172N Skyhawk II	172-69004	N734PJ	31. 3.88	D.A.T.Skidmore	Southend	16.10.00T
G-BOLZ	Rand Robinson KR-2 (VW 1834)	PFA/129-10866		6. 4.88	B.Normington	Coventry	24. 7.98P
G-BOMB	Cassutt Racer IIIM (Cont O-200-A)	PFA/34-10386		18.12.78	S.Adams "Blind Panic" (Damaged Weston Park nr Telford 22.6.97)	RAF Weston-on-the-Green	23. 5.98P
G-BOML	Hispano HA-1112-MIL Buchon	151	N170BG Sp AF C4K-107	15. 4.88	Classic Avn Ltd (Op The Old Flying Machine Co) "Red 3"	Duxford	1. 7.99P
	(C/n quoted as 170 originally but may be a corruption of Spanish AF serial)(As W/No "166238" in Luftwaffe c/s)						
G-BOMN	Cessna 150F	150-63089	N6489F	25. 4.89	D.G.Williams	Headcorn	29. 7.00T
G-BOMO	PA-38-112 Tomahawk II	38-81A0161	N91324	8. 4.88	APB Leasing Ltd	Welshpool	13. 7.00T
G-BOMP	PA-28-181 Cherokee Archer II	28-7790249	N8482F	8. 4.88	Skyline School of Flying Ltd & SRC Contractors Ltd	Elstree	27. 8.00T

Regn	Type	C/n	P/I	Date	Owner/operator	Probable Base	CA Expy
G-BOMS	Cessna 172N Skyhawk II	172-69448	N737JG	11. 4.88	Aerohire Ltd Wellesbourne Mountford		2. 7.01
G-BOMT	Cessna 172N Skyhawk II	172-70396	N739AU	12. 7.88	C.E.Derbyshire (Sawbridgeworth)		6. 5.01T
G-BOMU	PA-28-181 Cherokee Archer II	28-7790318	N1631H	8. 4.88	J.Sawyer & P.R.Kinge	Blackbushe	19. 5.00T
					t/a RJ Avn		
G-BOMY	PA-28-161 Warrior II	28-8216049	N8457S	28. 6.88	Carill Avn Ltd	Southampton	7.12.00T
G-BOMZ	PA-38-112 Tomahawk	38-78A0635	N2315A	30. 6.88	D.P.Cloet & R.A.Cook	Booker	25. 4.00T
					t/a BOMZ Avn		
G-BONC	PA-28RT-201 Arrow IV	28R-7918007	C-GXYX	13. 5.88	K.A.Hemming	Fowlmere	7. 7.00T
			N3069K				
G-BOND	Sikorsky S-76A II Plus	760036	N4931Y	31. 1.80	Bond Helicopters Ltd	Aberdeen	5. 3.00T
G-BONE	Pilatus P.2-06	600-62	Sw.AF	8. 7.81	P.S.Watts (As "U-142")	(Dursley)	23. 2.87P
			U-142/U-113		(Stored Hurst Green, Etchingham, E.Sussex 12.95)		
G-BONG	Enstrom F-28A-UK	154	N9604	22. 4.88	M.A.Crook Appleton, Warrington		16. 8.98T
					t/a TR Bitz		
G-BONK	Colt 180A HAFB	1167		14.12.87	Wye Valley Avn Ltd	Ross-on-Wye	2.11.94T
G-BONO	Cessna 172N Skyhawk II	172-70299	C-GSMF	11. 5.88	Mer-Air Aviation Ltd	Fairoaks	23. 9.00T
			N738WS				
G-BONP	CFM Streak Shadow SS-01P & PFA/161A-11344			4. 5.88	T.J.Palmer	(Kilmarnock)	7. 9.99P
	(Rotax 582)						
G-BONR	Cessna 172N Skyhawk II	172-68164	C-GYGK	18. 4.88	D.I.Claik	Biggin Hill	6. 8.00
			(N733BH)				
G-BONS	Cessna 172N Skyhawk II	172-68345	C-GIUF	18. 4.88	M.G.Montgomerie t/a G-BONS Grp Elstree		2. 7.00
G-BONT	Slingsby T-67M Firefly II	2054		3. 5.88	Hunting Aviation Ltd RAF Barkston Heath		7. 9.00T
					(Op Hunting Acft Ltd/JEFTS)		
G-BONU	Slingsby T-67B	2037		3. 5.88	R.L.Brinklow	RAF Wyton	29. 6.00T
					(Op Wyton Flying Club)		
G-BONV	Colt 17A Cloudhopper HAFB	1238		3. 5.88	K A Kent "Bryant Group	Lancing	1. 4.93A
					(Balloon Preservation Group 7.98)		
G-BONW	Cessna 152 II	152-80401	OY-CPL	15. 4.88	Lincoln A/C Ltd	Sturgate	23. 7.00T
			N24825				
G-BONY	Denney Kitfox mk.1 (Rotax 532)	166 & PFA/172-11351		11. 5.88	M.J.Walker	Denham	31. 5.99P
G-BONZ	Beechcraft V35B Bonanza	D-10282	N6661D	6. 4.88	P.M.Coulten Boughton, Norfolk		22. 7.00
G-BOOB	Cameron N-65 HAFB	515		12.11.79	C.V.Legate-Pearce "Cracker" London W2		8. 4.90A
G-BOOC	PA-18-150 Super Cub	18-8279	SE-EPC	29. 4.88	R.R. & S.A.Marriott	Meon	17. 7.00
G-BOOD	Slingsby T.31M Motor Tutor PFA/42-11264			4. 5.88	G.F.M.Garner	Clench Common	17. 6.99P
	(EC-44-2PM) (The wings are ex XE810 c/n 923)						
G-BOOE	Gulfstream GA-7 Cougar	GA7-0093	N718G	7. 6.88	N.Gardner	Southampton	18. 7.00T
G-BOOF	PA-28-181 Archer II	28-7890084	N47510	16. 6.88	General Airline Ltd	Blackbushe	3. 9.00T
					t/a European Flyers		
G-BOOG	PA-28RT-201T Turbo Arrow IV	28R-8331036	N4303K	6. 5.88	Simair Ltd	Andrewsfield	14. 1.02
G-BOOH	Jodel D.112	481	F-BHVK	16. 5.88	M.J.Hayman Watchford Farm, Yarcombe		26. 3.99P
	(Built Ets Valladeau)						
G-BOOI	Cessna 152 II	152-80751	N25590	22. 8.88	Stapleford F/C Ltd	Stapleford	23. 4.01T
G-BOOJ	Air Command 532 Elite II	PB206 & PFA G/04-1098		4. 5.88	Roger Savage (Gyroplanes) Ltd Portmoak		6.12.91P
	(Rotax 532)						
G-BOOL	Cessna 172N Skyhawk II	172-72486	C-GJSY	27. 4.88	Hockstar Ltd (Op Southernair)	Shoreham	16.12.00T
			N5271D				
G-BOOV	Aerospatiale AS.355F2 Twin Squirrel	5374		3. 5.88	Merseyside Police Authority Air Support Grp	Liverpool	2.10.00T
G-BOOW	Aerosport Scamp	PFA/117-10709		10. 5.88	A.P.Daines	Earls Colne	12. 9.95P
	(VW1834)						
G-BOOX	Rutan LongEz	PFA/74A-10844		3. 5.88	I.R.Wilde	Deenethorpe	9. 3.99P
	(Lyc O-235)						
G-BOOZ	Cameron N-77 HAFB	904	(G-BKSJ)	21. 6.83	J.E.F.Kettlety "Bluebell"	Chippenham	
G-BOPA	PA-28-181 Archer II	28-8490024	N43299	28. 4.88	JE Strutt (London) Ltd Andrewsfield		4. 8.00
G-BOPB	Boeing 767-204ER	24239	N6009F	1.11.88	Britannia Airways Ltd	Luton	21. 3.01T
					"Captain Sir Ross Smith"		
G-BOPC	PA-28-161 Warrior II	28-8216006	N2124X	6. 5.88	Channel Avn Ltd	Guernsey	16. 6.00T
G-BOPD	Bede BD-4	632	N632DH	25. 5.88	S.T.Dauncey	Redcar	17. 6.99P
	(Lyc O-320)						
G-BOPG	Cessna 182Q Skylane II	182-66689	N95962	6. 5.88	G.Wimlett	Blackpool	17. 7.00T
G-BOPH	Cessna TR182 Turbo Skylane RG II	R182-01031	N756BJ	11. 5.88	E.A.L.Sturmer	Cranfield	4. 5.00
G-BOPO	FLS OA.7 Optica 301	021	EC-FVM	17. 5.88	Sunhawk Ltd	Jersey	27. 5.96T
			G-BOPO				
G-BOPR	FLS OA.7 Optica 301	023		17. 5.88	Sunhawk Ltd.	Jersey	
G-BOPT	Grob G-115	8046		10. 5.88	LAC (Enterprises) Ltd	Barton	6. 8.00T
					t/a Lancashire Aero Club		
G-BOPU	Grob G-115	8059		10. 5.88	LAC (Enterprises) Ltd	Barton	8. 7.00T
					t/a Lancashire Aero Club		
G-BOPV	PA-34-200T Seneca II	34-8070265	N82323	7. 6.88	G.J.Powell	Biggin Hill	11. 7.00T

Regn	Type	C/n	P/I	Date	Owner/operator	Probable Base	CA Expy
G-BOPW	Cessna A152 Aerobat	A152-0908	N4922A	11. 5.88	Northamptonshire School of Flying Ltd		
					(Damaged Sywell 30.8.95)	Sywell	20. 6.98T
G-BOPX	Cessna A152 Aerobat	A152-0932	N761BK	11. 5.88	Aerohire Ltd	Halfpenny Green	24. 1.98T
					(Op Midland Flight Centre)		
G-BORA*	Colt 77A	1233		19. 5.88	Balloon Preservation Group	Lancing	24. 8.94A
					"Cala Homes"		
G-BORB	Cameron V-77 HAFB	1348		24. 8.88	M.H.Wolff	Liskeard	2. 9.92A
G-BORD	Thunder Ax7-77 HAFB	1164		26. 5.88	D.D.Owen "Marvin"	Wotton-under-Edge	11.12.99A
G-BORE	Colt 77A HAFB	642		24. 5.88	J.D.Medcalf & C.Wilson	Enfield	28. 7.99A
					t/a Little Secret Hot Air Balloon Grp "My Little Secret"		
G-BORF	Colt AS-80 Mk II Hot-Air Airship	1241		22.12.88	Belton Dream Ltd	(Canada)	15. 7.91A
					(Op Sunrise Balloons) (Crashed Brooks, Alberta 9.7.91)		
G-BORG	Campbell Cricket (Rotax 503)	PFA G/03-1085		8. 6.88	N.G.Bailey	Kemble	7. 8.96P
					(Damaged 1996)		
G-BORH	PA-34-200T Seneca II	34-8070352	N8261V	7. 6.88	Aerolease Ltd.	(Huntingdon)	22.11.00T
G-BORI	Cessna 152 II	152-81672	N66936	8. 6.88	Staryear Ltd	Barton	23. 9.00T
G-BORJ	Cessna 152 II	152-82649	N89148	27. 5.88	J.A. & R.M.Nicol	Carlisle	13.11.00T
					t/a Cumbria Aero Club		
G-BORK	PA-28-161 Warrior II	28-8116095	N83036	8. 6.88	A.W.Collett	Turweston	13.11.00T
G-BORL	PA-28-161 Warrior II	28-7816256	N2190M	28. 9.88	Westair F/Svs Ltd	Blackpool	14.12.00T
G-BORM*	HS.748 Srs.2B/217	1670	RP-C1043 V2-LAA/VP-LAA/9Y-TDH	29. 7.88	Exeter Fire Svs	Exeter	
G-BORN	Cameron N-77 HAFB	1777		13. 5.88	I.Chadwick	Partridge Green, W.Sussex	13. 8.99A
					"Ian"		
G-BORO	Cessna 152 II	152-83767 (Damaged Welshpool 26.8.96)	N5130B	27. 5.88	M.R.Shelton	Tatenhill	28. 1.01T
					t/a Tatenhill Aviation		
G-BORS	PA-28-181 Archer II	28-8090156	N8127C	31. 5.88	B.K. & S.C.Ambrose	(Cambridge)	11. 6.00T
					t/a Ambrose Air		
G-BORT	Colt 77A HAFB	1255		7. 6.88	Y.J.Joslyn	Wilhelmshaven, Germany	24. 8.99A
G-BORV	Bell 206B JetRanger II	2202	C-GVTY	8. 6.88	C.A.Rosenberg	Abergavenny	5. 5.99T
G-BORW	Cessna 172P Skyhawk II	172-74301	N51357	23. 8.88	Briter Avn Ltd	Coventry	2. 4.98T
G-BORY	Cessna 150L	150-72292	N6792G	27. 5.88	Harrison Aviation Ltd	Norwich	6. 8.99T
G-BOSB	Thunder Ax7-77 HAFB	1199		7. 6.88	M.Gallagher	Consett	17. 9.99A
	(Regd as c/n 581 but built as c/n 1199)						
G-BOSD	PA-34-200T Seneca II	34-7570085	N33086	7. 6.88	Barnes Olson Aeroleasing Ltd		
					(Op Bristol Flying Centre)	Bristol/Lulsgate	11. 8.01T
G-BOSE	PA-28-181 Archer II	28-8590007	N143AV	17. 5.88	C.Hudson & A.Thomas	(Wokingham)	23. 5.00
G-BOSF	Colt 69A HAFB	1271		23. 6.88	Virgin Airship & Balloon Co Ltd	Telford	28. 1.93A
					"Lloyds Bank"		
G-BOSG	Colt 17A Cloudhopper HAFB	1272		23. 6.88	Virgin Airship & Balloon Co Ltd	Telford	22. 5.89A
					"Lloyds Bank Cloudhopper"		
G-BOSJ	Nord 3400	124	N9048P ALAT "MOO"	26. 5.88	A.I.Milne	Little Snoring	1.11.94P
					(As "124" in Fr.AF c/s)		
					(Damaged Fenland 12.6.94; stored 9.97)		
G-BOSM	CEA Jodel DR.253B Regent	168	F-BSBH	24. 5.88	S.H.Gibson	High Cross, Ware	10.12.01
					t/a Sierra Mike (Ware) Group		
G-BOSO	Cessna A152 Aerobat	A152-0975	N761PD	25. 5.88	Redhill Avn Ltd t/a Redhill F/C	Redhill	20. 8.01T
					(Damaged Fairoaks 4.3.99)		
G-BOSP	PA-28-151 Cherokee Warrior	28-7515307	N1143X N9563N	26. 5.88	A.S.Bamrah	Biggin Hill	17.11.01T
					t/a Falcon Flying Services		
G-BOSR	PA-28-140 Cherokee	28-22092	N7464R	26. 5.88	Clare R.Guggenheim	Bournemouth	3. 6.00T
					t/a Sierra-Romeo Grp		
G-BOSU	PA-28-140 Cherokee Cruiser	28-7325449	N55635	19. 7.88	A. & R.Windley	Tattershall Thorpe	8. 6.01
G-BOSV	Cameron V-77 HAFB	1320		17. 6.88	K.H.Greenaway	Market Harborough	7. 6.97A
					"Joyride II"		
G-BOTB	Cessna 152 II	152-85733	N94571	7. 6.88	Stapleford F/C Ltd	Stapleford	18. 9.00T
G-BOTD	Cameron O-105 HAFB	1611		6. 6.88	P.J.Beglan	Belves, France	10.11.96A
G-BOTE*	Thunder Ax8-90 HAFB	555		14. 6.88	I M Martin "Barge Fox"	Lancing	16. 2.95T
					(Balloon Preservation Group 7.98)		
G-BOTF	PA-28-151 Cherokee Warrior	28-7515436	C-GGIF	8. 6.88	D.S.Woolf	Southend	20. 8.00T
					t/a G-BOTF Grp (Op Southend F/C)		
G-BOTG	Cessna 152 II	152-83035	N46343	9. 6.88	Donington Avn Ltd	East Midlands	20. 8.00T
G-BOTH	Cessna 182Q Skylane II	182-67558	N202PS N114SP/N5172N	9. 6.88	W.J.Forrest t/a G-BOTH Group	Barton	24. 2.01
G-BOTI	PA-28-151 Cherokee Warrior (Convd to Srs.161 status)	28-7515251	C-GNFF	9. 6.88	A.J.Bamrah t/a Falcon F/Svs	Birmingham	29. 8.00T
G-BOTK	Cameron O-105 HAFB	1765		9. 6.88	F.R. & V.L.Higgins	Bath	12. 7.96T
					"Champagne Rides"		
G-BOTL*	Colt 42A SS HAFB	466		23.11.82	British Balloon Museum & Library "Bottle"	Newbury	
G-BOTM	Bell 206B JetRanger III	3881	N31940	9. 6.88	David McLean Homes Ltd	Flint	31. 7.00
G-BOTN	PA-28-161 Warrior II	28-7916261	N2173N	9. 6.88	Premiair Flying Club Ltd	Shoreham	19. 1.01T
G-BOTO	Bellanca 7ECA Citabria	939-73	N57398	9. 6.88	A.K.Hulme	Rayne Hall Farm, Rayne	6.11.97
					t/a G-BOTO Grp		
G-BOTP	Cessna 150J	150-70736	N61017	2. 8.88	M.Colson	(Westbury, Wilts)	29. 3.01
G-BOTT	Rand-Robinson KR-2	PFA/129-11164		16. 6.88	M.D.Ott & M.R.Hutchins	(Dunmow)	
					(Project abandoned)		

Regn	Type	C/n	P/I	Date	Owner/operator	Probable Base	CA Expy
G-BOTU	Piper J3C-75 Cub	19045	N98803 NC98803	8. 7.88	T.L.Giles	Hill Farm, Nayland	28. 6.99P
G-BOTV	PA-32RT-300 Lance II	32R-7885153	N36039	7. 6.88	Robin Lance Avn Associates Ltd Rochester		18.12.97
G-BOTW	Cameron V-77 HAFB	1761		14. 6.88	M.R.Jeynes	(Worcester)	17. 7.99A
G-BOTZ	Bensen B.8MR (Rotax 532)	PFA G/01-1086		17. 6.88	C.Jones	Stonehouse, Ayr	31. 8.99P
G-BOUD	PA-38-112 Tomahawk II	38-82A0017	N91365	26. 7.88	A.J.Wiggins	(Longhope, Glos)	25. 3.01T
G-BOUE	Cessna 172N Skyhawk II	172-73235	N6535F	8. 8.88	Aviation Access Ltd	(Pudsey)	9. 2.01T
G-BOUF	Cessna 172N Skyhawk II	172-71900	N5605E	24. 6.88	M.I. & B.P.Sneap t/a Amber Valley Avn	Ripley, Derby	8. 6.01T
G-BOUJ	Cessna 150M Commuter	150-76373	N3058V	25. 8.88	R.D.Billins	Denham	23.12.99T
G-BOUK	PA-34-200T Seneca II	34-7570124	N33476	31. 8.88	C.J. & R.J.Barnes	East Midlands	9. 6.99T
G-BOUL	PA-34-200T Seneca II	34-7670157	N8936C	28. 6.88	Oxford Aviation Services Ltd	Oxford	5. 4.01T
G-BOUM	PA-34-200T Seneca II	34-7670136	N8401C	3. 8.88	Oxford Aviation Services Ltd	Oxford	5. 8.01T
G-BOUN	Rand-Robinson KR-2 (VW 1834)	PFA/129-10945		23. 6.88	W.J.Allan	Charterhall	27. 7.99P
G-BOUP	PA-28-161 Warrior II	2816059	N9139X	12. 7.88	Oxford Aviation Services Ltd	Oxford	21. 1.00T
G-BOUR	PA-28-161 Warrior II	2816060	N9139Z	12. 7.88	Oxford Aviation Services Ltd	Oxford	14.10.00T
G-BOUS	PA-28RT-201 Arrow IV	28R-7918109	N32WC N9644N	23. 6.88	Air Nova plc	Liverpool	3. 8.00T
G-BOUT	Zenair Colomban MC-12 Cri-Cri	12-0135	N120JN	14. 6.88	C.K.Farley	Southampton	
G-BOUU	Everett Autogyro	015	R		A.Everett (Stored 5.97)	Sproughton, Ipswich	
G-BOUV	Montgomerie-Bensen B.8MR (Rotax 532)	PFA G/01-1092		23. 6.88	A.J.Dickson	Rochdale	28. 7.97P
G-BOUX	Everett Autogyro	016	R		A.Everett (Stored 7.94)	Sproughton, Ipswich	
G-BOUZ	Cessna 150G	150-65606	N2606J	15. 6.88	Atlantic Bridge Avn Ltd (Op Weald Air Svs)	Headcorn	16. 3.00T
G-BOVB	PA-15 Vagabond (Lyc O-145)	15-180	N4396H NC4396H	23. 6.88	M.J.Ebdell & P.Laycock t/a Oscar F/Grp	Shoreham	11. 1.00P
G-BOVG*	Reims Cessna F.172H	0627	OO-ANN D-ELTR	2. 8.88	No.1476 Squadron, ATC (Damaged Southend 1991; instructional airframe 3.99)	Rayleigh, Essex	14. 9.91
G-BOVH	PA-28-161 Warrior II	28-8316091	N4311M	28. 6.88	R.W.Tebby t/a S.F.Tebby & Son (Damaged Bristol/Lulsgate 1.4.94; status uncertain)	(Bristol)	12. 9.94T
G-BOVK	PA-28-161 Warrior II	28-8516061	N69168	7. 9.88	Air Nova plc	Liverpool	14. 5.01T
G-BOVR	Robinson R-22HP	0176	N9069D	28. 6.88	P.J.Homan	Shoreham	19. 8.00T
G-BOVS	Cessna 150M Commuter	150-78663	N704KC	21. 7.88	Griffin Marston Ltd	Compton Abbas	13.11.00T
G-BOVT	Cessna 150M Commuter	150-78032	N8962U	1.12.88	C.J.Hopewell	(Huntingdon)	5. 3.01T
G-BOVU	Stoddard-Hamilton Glasair III (Lyc IO-540)	3090		16. 9.88	B.R.Chaplin	Deenethorpe	15. 1.99P
G-BOVW	Colt 69A HAFB	1286		13. 7.88	V.Hyland "Enderby-Hyland Painting"	Nottingham	6. 4.94A
G-BOVX	Hughes 269C	38-0673	N58170	12. 7.88	Autohaus Ltd	Sywell	16. 7.01T
G-BOVY	Hughes 269C	40-0915	EI-CIL G-BOVY/N1096K	12. 7.88	P.J.Brown	Redhill	15. 5.99T
G-BOWB	Cameron V-77 HAFB	1767		13. 7.88	R.C.Stone "Richard's Rainbow"	Reading	21.12.98A
G-BOWD	Reims Cessna F337G Super Skymaster (Wichita c/n 01791)	0084	N337BC G-BLSB/EI-BET/D-INAI/(N53697)	8. 7.88	Badgehurst Ltd	Southend	4. 4.01T
G-BOWE	PA-34-200T Seneca II	34-7870405	N39668	14. 7.88	Oxford Aviation Services Ltd	Oxford	26.10.01T
G-BOWK	Cameron N-90 HAFB	1764		1. 8.88	S.R.Bridge "Burley Stables"	Grantham	
G-BOWL	Cameron V-77 HAFB	1780		26. 7.88	P.G. & G.R.Hall "Matrix"	Chard	13. 5.99A
G-BOWM	Cameron V-56 HAFB	1781		26. 7.88	C.G.Caldecott & G.Pitt	Newcastle-under-Lyme	17. 5.95A
G-BOWN	PA-12 Super Cruiser (Lyc O-235)	12-1912	N3661N NC3661N	26. 7.88	R.W.Bucknell	Andrewsfield	26. 2.00T
G-BOWO	Cessna R182 Skylane RG II	R182-00146	(G-BOTR) N2301C	20. 7.88	D.P.Bennett	Gamston	15. 3.01
G-BOWP	Jodel Wassmer D.120A Paris-Nice (Cont O-200-A)	319	F-BNZM	26. 7.88	A.R.Gedney, G.Morris & J.M.Palmer	Cowbit, Fenland	16.12.99P
G-BOWU	Cameron O-84 HAFB	1779		1. 8.88	C.F.Pooley & D.C.Ball t/a St.Elmos Fire Syndicate "Elmo"	Gloucester	6. 8.99A
G-BOWV	Cameron V-65 HAFB	1800		24. 8.88	R.A.Harris "Sigmund"	Axminster	13. 5.99A
G-BOWY	PA-28RT-201T Turbo Arrow IV	28R-8131114	N404EL N83648	8. 8.88	A.Davies (Op Redhill Flying Club)	Redhill	27. 7.00T
G-BOWZ	Bensen B.80V (Rotax 532)	PFA G/01-1060		27. 7.88	W.M.Day	Ulverston	31. 7.98P
G-BOXA	PA-28-161 Warrior II	2816075	N9149Q	1.11.88	Channel Islands Aero Services Ltd Jersey t/a Jersey A/C	Jersey	21.12.00T
G-BOXB	PA-28-161 Warrior II	2816064	N9142H	12. 8.88	Channel Islands Aero Services Ltd Jersey t/a Jersey A/C	Jersey	6. 2.00T
G-BOXC	PA-28-161 Warrior II	2816063	N9142D	12. 8.88	Channel Islands Aero Services Ltd Jersey t/a Jersey A/C (Damaged on take-off Jersey 27.1.97)	Jersey	14. 5.00T
G-BOXG	Cameron O-77 HAFB	1792		26. 8.88	R.A.Wicks	Norwich	1. 1.94A
G-BOXH	Pitts S-1S Special (Lyc O-360)	MP4	N8LA	29. 7.88	Diane Medrek	Breighton	2. 1.98T

Regn	Type	C/n	P/I	Date	Owner/operator	Probable Base	CA Expy
G-BOXJ	Piper J3C-90 Cub (L-4H-PI) (Frame No.12021)	12193	OO-ADJ 44-79897	1. 8.88	J.D.Tseliki	Shoreham	20. 3.91P
G-BOXK*	Slingsby T-67C	2063		26. 9.88	Slingsby Avn Ltd (Cancelled as destroyed 14.3.99)	Kirkbymoorside	23. 3.01T
G-BOXR	Gulfstream GA-7 Cougar	GA7-0059	N772GA	19.10.88	Plane Talking Ltd	Elstree	11. 9.00T
G-BOXT	Hughes 269C	104-0367	SE-HMR PH-JOH/D-HBOL	1. 8.88	Goldenfly Ltd	Denham	17. 1.99T
G-BOXU	Grumman-American AA-5B Tiger	AA5B-0026	N1526R	28. 7.88	G.C.Baker t/a Marcher Aviation Group	Welshpool	15. 5.01
G-BOXV	Pitts S-1D Special (Lyc O-360) (Regd with c/n 7-0432)	7-0433	N27822	8. 8.88	G.R.Clark	Sleap	24. 7.98P
G-BOXW	Cassutt Racer IIIM	PFA/34-11317		11. 8.88	D.I.Johnson	(Leigh-on-Sea)	
G-BOXX	Robinson R-22 Beta	0815	N2640D	15. 6.88	Plane Talking Ltd	Redhill	25. 7.00T
G-BOXY	PA-28-181 Archer II	28-7990175	N3073D	29. 7.88	Sheffield A/C Ltd	Netherthorpe	17. 3.01T
G-BOYB	Cessna A152 Aerobat	A152-0928	N761AW	29. 7.88	Northamptonshire School of Flying Ltd	Sywell	14.12.00T
G-BOYC	Robinson R-22 Beta	0837		22. 8.88	M.D.Thorpe t/a Yorkshire Helicopters	Coney Park, Leeds	10. 5.01T
G-BOYF	Sikorsky S-76B	760343		15. 9.88	Darley Stud Management Co Ltd Blackbushe (Op Air Hanson)		24.11.99T
G-BOYH	PA-28-151 Cherokee Warrior (Convd to Srs.161 status)	28-7715290	N8795F	8. 8.88	Superpause Ltd (Op West London A/C)	White Waltham	18. 3.01T
G-BOYI	PA-28-161 Warrior II	28-7816183	N9032K	8. 8.88	S.J.Harris	RAF Woodvale	29.11.97
G-BOYL	Cessna 152 II	152-84379	N6232L	11. 8.88	Aerohire Ltd	Wellesbourne Mountford	26. 2.01T
G-BOYM	Cameron O-84 HAFB	1796		25. 8.88	Frontline Distribution Ltd "Frontline"	Basingstoke	
G-BOYO	Cameron V-20 HAFB	1843		27. 9.88	J.M.Willard	Burgess Hill, W.Sussex	
G-BOYP	Cessna 172N Skyhawk II	172-70349	N738YU	22. 8.88	Guildtons Ltd	North Weald	1. 3.01
G-BOYU	Cessna A150L Aerobat	A150-0497	N8121L	31. 8.88	Upperstack Ltd	Barton	17. 9.00T
G-BOYV	PA-28RT-201T Turbo Arrow III	28R-7703014	N1143H	1. 9.88	Arrow Air Ltd	(Broadway)	14. 1.01
G-BOYX	Robinson R-22 Beta	0862	N90813	25. 8.88	R.Towle (Damaged Teesside 18.7.90)	Hexham	28. 9.91T
G-BOYY	Cameron A-105 HAFB	1786		22. 8.88	Hoyers (UK) Ltd "Hoyer"	Huddersfield	20. 4.97A
G-BOZI	PA-28-161 Warrior II	28-8116120	(G-BOSZ) N8318A	14. 7.88	Klingair Ltd	Conington	25.11.00T
G-BOZK	Aerospatiale AS.332L Super Puma	2179	LN-OMQ G-BOZK/F-GINN	5. 8.88	Brintel Helicopters Ltd t/a British International Helicopters	Aberdeen	8. 7.00T
G-BOZM	PA-38-112 Tomahawk	38-78A0352	N6247A	25. 8.88	A.S.Bamrah t/a Falcon Flying Services	Biggin Hill	17. 6.01T
G-BOZN	Cameron N-77 HAFB	1807		1. 9.88	Calarel Developments Ltd "Calarel Developments"	Chipping Campden	29.10.94A
G-BOZO	Gulfstream AA-5B Tiger	AA5B-1282	N4536Q	12. 8.88	Caslon Ltd	Elstree	27.11.00T
G-BOZP	Beechcraft 76 Duchess	ME-99	N6010Z	26. 8.88	Newcastle-upon-Tyne A/C Ltd	Newcastle	15. 4.01T
G-BOZR	Cessna 152 II	152-84614	N6083M	7. 9.88	Gem Rewinds Ltd	Coventry	18.12.00T
G-BOZS	Pitts S-1C Special (Lyc O-320)	221-H	N10EZ	31. 8.88	R.J. & M.B.Trickey	Perth	5. 5.98P
G-BOZU	Aero Dynamics Sparrow Hawk Mk II	PFA/184-11371		12.12.88	R.V.Phillimore	(Bexhill-on-Sea)	
G-BOZV	Robin DR.340 Major	416	F-BRTS	9. 8.88	A.R.Norman	(London SW10)	27. 8.00
G-BOZW	Bensen B.8MR (Rotax 532)	PFA G/01-1096		1. 9.88	M.E.Wills	Lytchett Matravers	4. 1.99P
G-BOZY	Cameron RTW-120 Airship/HAFB	1770		1. 9.88	L.V.Mastis	Bristol	21. 4.97A
G-BOZZ	Gulfstream AA-5B Tiger	AA5B-1155	N4530N	22. 8.88	A.W.Matthews t/a Solent Tiger Grp	Southampton	14.10.00

G-BPAA-BPZZ

Regn	Type	C/n	P/I	Date	Owner/operator	Probable Base	CA Expy
G-BPAA	Acro Advanced AA-001 & PFA/200-11528 (Acro VW2100)			26. 8.88	Acro Engines & Airframes Ltd	Yearby	7. 6.99P
G-BPAB	Cessna 150M Commuter	150-77244	N63335	21. 9.88	A.N.Wicks & R.Carr-Ellison Wheeler t/a Alpha Bravo Group	(Sudbury)	18. 2.01
G-BPAC	PA-28-161 Cherokee Warrior II	28-7716112	N2567Q	21. 9.88	G.G.Pratt	High Cross	27. 2.01
G-APAD*	PA-34-200T Seneca II	34-7870431	N21208	23.8.88	The Fire Service College	Moreton-in-Marsh	9.4.95T
				(Damaged Bowland, Lancs 15.7.92 & in fire service use 8.98)			
G-BPAE	Cameron V-77 HAFB	1798		1. 9.88	I.J.Jackson	Lytham St.Annes	1. 1.96
G-BPAF	PA-28-161 Cherokee Warrior II	28-7716142	N3199Q	6. 9.88	Red Dragon Aviation Ltd	Cardiff	7. 5.00T
G-BPAH	Colt 69A HAFB	512		2. 6.83	Justerini & Brooks Ltd "Phil"	London SW1	15. 8.88A
G-BPAI	Bell 47G-3B-1 (Mod)	6528	N8588F	9. 9.88	LRC Leisure Ltd (Op Manchester Helicopter Centre)	Barton	29. 3.01
G-BPAJ	DH.82A Tiger Moth (Composite with "real" G-AMNN ?)	83472	G-AOIX T7087	5.11.80	P.A.Jackson	(Huntingdon)	13. 6.00
G-BPAL	DHC.1 Chipmunk 22	C1/0437	G-BCYE WG350	29.10.86	K.F. & P.Tomsett (As "WG350")	(Leatherhead)	9. 6.00
G-BPAO*	Air Command 503 Commander	0424 & PFA G/04-1097		8. 9.88	D.J.Sagar Upton Snodsbury, Worcester (Cancelled as WFU 23.2.99)		8. 8.91P
G-BPAS	Socata TB-20 Trinidad	283	A2-ADR F-GDBO	9.11.88	Syndicate Clerical Services Ltd (Exeter)		1. 3.01T
G-BPAU	PA-28-161 Warrior II	28-7916218	N3063H	3.11.88	Lapwing F/Grp Ltd	Denham	26. 3.01T
G-BPAV	Clutton FRED Srs.II (VW 1600)	PFA/29-10274		21.11.78	P.A.Valentine (Under construction 1990)	(Uxbridge)	
G-BPAW	Cessna 150M Commuter	150-77923	N8348U	5. 9.88	A.Phillips	Watchford Farm, Yarcombe	22. 6.01
G-BPAX	Cessna 150M Commuter	150-77401	N63571	5. 9.88	Barry Avn Ltd	Shoreham	18. 5.01T
G-BPAY	PA-28-181 Archer II	28-8090191	N3568X	12. 9.88	Leicestershire Aero Club Ltd	Leicester	23.12.00T
G-BPBA*	Bensen B.80MR (Rotax 532)	PFA G/01-1036		5. 9.88	M.E.Green	Crewe	17. 9.90P
G-BPBB	Evans VP-2 (Arrow GT500)	PFA/63-11261		2. 9.88	P.J.Manifold	Priory Farm, Tibenham	9. 6.97P
G-BPBG	Cessna 152 II	152-84941	N5418P	16. 9.88	Atlantic Air Transport Ltd	Coventry	18. 6.01T
G-BPBJ	Cessna 152 II	152-83639	N4793B	9. 9.88	W.Shaw & P.G.Haines	(Lincoln)	19. 1.01
G-BPBK	Cessna 152 II	152-83417	N49095	9. 9.88	Burbage Farms Ltd	Claybrooke Lodge Farm, Lutterworth	14. 1.01T
G-BPBM	PA-28-161 Warrior II	28-7916272	N3050N	12. 9.88	Thin Air Aircraft Ltd	Halfpenny Green	14.12.00T
G-BPBO	PA-28RT-201T Turbo Arrow IV	28R-8131195	N8431H	28. 9.88	Music Connections Ltd	Stapleford	11. 5.01
G-BPBP	Brugger MB.2 Colibri mk.II (VW1600)	PFA/43-10246		6. 2.78	D.A.Preston	(Ulverston)	21. 1.99P
G-BPBR	PA-38-112 Tomahawk	38-80A0020	N25082	8. 9.88	Cardiff Wales Flying Club Ltd	Cardiff	30. 6.01T
G-BPBU	Cameron V-77 HAFB	1844		23. 9.88	M.C.Gibbons & J.E.Kite "Sky Maid" t/a G-BPBU Skymaid Balloon (Keep Music Live titles)	Bristol	3. 8.99A
G-BPBV	Cameron V-77 HAFB	1821		21. 9.88	W.E. & L.A.Newman "Sugar Plumb"	Carnforth	
G-BPBW	Cameron O-105 HAFB	1841		14.10.88	R.J.Mansfield "October Gold"	Huddersfield	15. 9.96A
G-BPBY	Cameron V-77 HAFB	1818	(G-BPCS)	9.12.88	Louise Hutley "Brewster's Toy"	Guildford	15. 8.97A
G-BPBZ	Thunder Ax7-77 HAFB	1258		10.10.88	A.W.J.Weston	Ross-on-Wye	13.10.94
G-BPCA	PBN BN-2B-26 Islander	2198	G-BLNX	28. 1.88	Loganair Ltd "Captain David Barclay MBE" (Op Scottish Air Ambulance)	Glasgow	16. 2.99T
G-BPCE*	Stolp SA.300 Starduster Too (Cont O-470-M)	36	N8HM	26. 9.88	Not known (Stored 2.92)	Sabadella, Barcelona	14.2.89PF
G-BPCF	Piper J3C-65 Cub (Cont O-200-A) (Lippert Reed clipped-wing conversion - S/No.SA811SW)	4532	N140DC N28033/NC28033	12. 5.89	A.J.Cooke Neslam Farm, Sempringham Fen		14. 6.99P
G-BPCG	Colt AS-80 Mk.II Hot-Air Airship	1300		14.10.88	N.Charbonnier "Greensport/Napapijri"	Aosta, Italy	22. 9.96A
G-BPCI	Cessna R172K Hawk XP II	R172-2360	N9976V	3. 1.89	H.W.Farnsworth	(Reading)	26. 3.99
G-BPCJ*	Cessna 150J	150-70797	N61096	26. 9.88	Solihull College Engineering Dept Blossomfield Rd, Solihull		3. 8.92T
				(Damaged Compton Abbas 25.1.90; instructional airframe 3.95)			
G-BPCK	PA-28-161 Warrior II	28-8016279	N8529N C-GMEI/(N9519N)	26. 9.88	W.G.Booth	Compton Abbas	10. 8.01T
G-BPCL	Scottish Avn Bulldog Srs.120/128	BH120/393	HKG-6 G-31-19	20. 9.88	Isohigh Ltd t/a 121 Grp (DHL c/s)	Elstree	2. 7.01T
G-BPCM	Rotorway Exec 152 (RW152)	E.3293	N979WP	21. 9.88	R.J.Turner Weavers Loft, Wem t/a Aircare Grp (Stored 7.96)		25.11.91P*
G-BPCR	Mooney M.20K (231)	25-0532	N98433	23. 9.88	T. & R.Harris "Over The Moony"	Biggin Hill	17. 6.01
G-BPCV	Montgomerie-Bensen B-8MR (Rotax 532)	PFA G/01-1088		11.10.88	O.J.Blackbourn	Tremethick Cross, Penzance	25. 7.91P
G-BPCX	PA-28-236 Dakota	28-8211004	N8441S	25.10.88	G.E.J.Spooner	Fenland	11. 6.01T

Regn	Type	C/n	P/I	Date	Owner/operator	Probable Base	CA Expy
G-BPDA	HS.748 Srs.2A/334SCD	1756	G-GLAS 9Y-TFS/G-11-8	7.10.88	Emerald Airways Ltd "John J Goodall"	Liverpool	12.11.99T
G-BPDE	Colt 56A HAFB	1296		26.10.88	J.E.Weidema Baambrugge, Netherlands t/a Pinkel Balloons		25. 6.97A
G-BPDF	Cameron V-77 HAFB	1806		6.10.88	The Ballooning Business Ltd Northampton		9. 1.00T
G-BPDG	Cameron V-77 HAFB	1839		21.10.88	D.F.H.Smith "Pretty Damn Good"	Burnley	4.11.99A
G-BPDJ	Chris Tena Mini Coupe (VW1835)	275	N13877	4.10.88	J.J.Morrissey (Stored 9.98)	Popham	28.10.91P*
G-BPDK*	Sorrell SNS-7 Hyperbipe (Lyc IO-360)	242	N85BL	6.10.88	A.J.Cable (Stored 4.97) (Cancelled by CAA 17.2.99)	Barton	23.6.95P*
G-BPDM	CASA I-131E Jungmann	2058	E3B-369	24.10.88	J.D.Haslam (Northallerton) (As "E3B-369/781-32" in Spanish AF c/s)		22. 6.96P
G-BPDT	PA-28-161 Warrior II	28-8416004	N4317Z	22.12.88	Channel Islands Aero Services Ltd Jersey t/a Jersey Aero Club		21. 8.99T
G-BPDU	PA-28-161 Cherokee Warrior II	28-7716195	N5672V	30. 9.88	Southern Air Ltd	Shoreham	28. 6.99T
G-BPDV	Pitts S-1S Special (Lyc O-360)	27P	N330VE	15. 9.88	J.Vize	Sywell	3. 6.99P
G-BPDY	Westland-Bell 47G-3B1 (Line No.WAN/48)	WA/356	OY-HCO SE-HIF/XT197	10.10.88	M.O.Simpson & A.C.Lindner t/a Howden Helicopters Howden, Humberside		3. 8.01T
G-BPEA	Boeing 757-236ER	24370		31. 3.89	British Airways plc "Castell Cydweli"	Gatwick	5. 6.99T
G-BPEB	Boeing 757-236ER	24371		27. 4.89	British Airways plc	Gatwick	1. 5.99T
G-BPEC	Boeing 757-236ER	24882		6.11.90	British Airways plc "Sir Simon Rattle"	Gatwick	12.11.00T
G-BPED	Boeing 757-236	25059		30. 4.91	British Airways plc (Cockerel of Lowicz/Koguty Lowickie t/s)	Heathrow	29. 4.01T
G-BPEE	Boeing 757-236ER	25060		3. 5.91	British Airways plc "Robert Louis Stevenson"	Gatwick	2. 5.01T
G-BPEF	Boeing 757-236ER	24120	G-BOHC EC-ELA/EC-516/G-BOHC/EC-ELA/EC-202/G-BOHC	18. 5.92	British Airways plc	Gatwick	17. 5.99T
G-BPEI	Boeing 757-236	25806	(G-BMRK)	9. 3.94	British Airways plc "Winchester Castle"	Heathrow	8. 3.00T
G-BPEJ	Boeing 757-236	25807	(G-BMRL)	22. 4.94	British Airways plc "Castell Dinas Bran"	Heathrow	24. 4.00T
G-BPEK	Boeing 757-236	25808	(G-BMRM)	17. 3.95	British Airways plc "Carew Castle"	Heathrow	16. 3.01T
G-BPEL	PA-28-151 Cherokee Warrior	28-7415172	C-FEYM	10.10.88	R.W.Harris & A.Jahanfar (Wreck stored 1.99)	Southend	8. 2.92T
G-BPEM	Cessna 150K	150-71707	N6207G	24.10.88	R.Strong & R.G.Lindsey	Netherthorpe	17. 6.01
G-BPEO	Cessna 152 II	152-83775	N5147B	10.10.88	Seawing Flying Club Ltd Southend & Eastern Executive Air Charter Ltd		1. 7.01T
G-BPER	PA-38-112 Tomahawk II	38-82A0036	N91465	11.10.88	APB Leasing Ltd Welshpool (Damaged Welshpool 30.8.96; stored 9.97)		22. 7.98T
G-BPES	PA-38-112 Tomahawk II	38-81A0064	N25728	2.11.88	Sherwood F/C Ltd	Nottingham	5. 1.01T
G-BPEZ	Colt 77A HAFB	1324		14.10.88	J.E.F.Kettlety & W.J.Honey	Chippenham/Bristol	21. 7.96A
G-BPFB	Colt 77A HAFB	1334		26.10.88	S.Ingram	Oldham	19. 6.95A
G-BPFC	Mooney M.20C Ranger	20-1243	N3606H	21.10.88	D.P.Tinsley	Sleap	22. 2.99
G-BPFD	Jodel D.112	312	F-PHJT	3.11.88	K.Manley Swanborough Farm, Lewes		23.12.99P
G-BPFF	Cameron DP-70 Hot-Air Airship	1831		24.10.88	E.F.H.Wothe Bruhl, Germany		17. 4.94A
G-BPFH	PA-28-161 Warrior II	28-8116201	N83723	3.11.88	Muriel H.Kleiser Edinburgh (Op Edinburgh F/C)		23.11.00T
G-BPFI	PA-28-181 Archer II	28-8090113	N8103G	5. 1.89	F.Teagle	Perranporth	12. 7.01
G-BPFJ*	Cameron Can 90SS HAFB (Budweiser Beer Can Shape)	1834		14.11.88	I M Martin "Budweiser" Lancing (Balloon Preservation Group 7.98)		10.12.93A
G-BPFK	Montgomerie-Bensen B.8MR (Rotax 532) SJB-1 & PFA G/01A-1116			27.10.88	J.W.Birkett (Southampton) (Destroyed Enstone 6.11.94)		9. 6.95P
G-BPFL	Davis DA-2A (Cont O-200-A)	051	N72RJ	27.10.88	B.W.Griffiths Wellesbourne Mountford		26. 1.99P
G-BPFM	Aeronca 7AC Champion	7AC-4751	N1193E NC1193E	13.10.88	Linda A.Borrill	Netherthorpe	6. 2.99P
G-BPFN	Short SD.3-60 Var.100	SH.3747	N747HH N747SA/G-BPFN/G-14-3747	2.11.88	Loganair Ltd. Glasgow (Mountain of the Birds/Benyhone Tartan t/s)		27. 8.99T
G-BPFZ	Cessna 152 II	152-85741	N94594	27.10.88	C.J.Ward Wellesbourne Mountford		3. 8.01T
G-BPGB	Cessna 150J	150-69722	N51042	2.11.88	Magnificent Obsessions Ltd (Grimsby) (Stored 10.92)		1. 3.92T
G-BPGC	Air Command 532 Elite (Rotax 532) 0440 & PFA G/04-1108			11.10.88	E.C.E.Brown Goodworth Clatford, Andover (Stored 5.97)		1. 8.91P
G-BPGD	Cameron V-65 HAFB	2000		9. 9.88	Gone With The Wind Ltd Bristol "Silver Lining"		4.12.99A
G-BPGE	Cessna U206C Super Skywagon	U206-1013	N29017	7.11.88	K.Brady Strathallan t/a The Scottish Parachute Club		14. 5.01
G-BPGF	Thunder Ax7-77 HAFB	1355		22.11.88	M.Schiavo "Dovetail"	Manchester	25. 8.95A
G-BPGH	EAA Acrosport II (Cont IO-346)	422	N12JE	14.11.88	G.M.Bradley	Crowfield	16. 8.99P

Regn	Type	C/n	P/I	Date	Owner/operator	Probable Base	CA Expy
G-BPGJ*	Colt 31A Air Chair HAFB	1333		22.11.88	Airtrack Adventures	Johannesburg, SA	
G-BPGK	Aeronca 7AC Champion	7AC-7187	N4409E	7. 2.89	T.M.Williams	Pencoed Farm, Llanelli	21. 8.91P
	(Cont A65)				(Damaged Llanelli 7.5.91)		
G-BPGM	Cessna 152 II	152-84932	N5380P	14.11.88	J.Easson	Edinburgh	24. 5.98T
G-BPGU	PA-28-181 Archer II	28-8490025	N4330B	26.10.88	G.Underwood	Nottingham	25.11.00
G-BPGV	Robinson R-22 Beta	0887		3.11.88	Polo Avn Ltd	Bristol/Lulsgate	21.11.00T
G-BPGX	Socata TB-9 Tampico Club	884		4.11.88	D.A.Lee	Denham	13. 2.00T
G-BPGY	Cessna 150H	150-67325	N6525S	24. 1.89	Rita A.Watson	Shoreham	16. 9.99T
					(Op Premi-Air Flying Club)		
G-BPGZ	Cessna 150G	150-64912	N3612J	14.11.88	P.G.Gardner	Ely	17. 5.01
G-BPHB	PA-28-161 Warrior II	2816069	N9148G	14.11.88	Channel Islands Aero Services Ltd		
					t/a Jersey Aero Club	Jersey	3. 2.01T
G-BPHD	Cameron N-42 HAFB	1863		21. 2.89	P.J.Marshall & M.A.Clarke	Ruislip	19. 8.95A
					"Ellen Gee II"		
G-BPHE	PA-28-161 Warrior II	28-7916536	N2911D	28.12.88	APB Leasing Ltd	Welshpool	26. 3.01T
G-BPHG	Robin DR.400/180 Regent	1887		29.11.88	K.J. & M.B.White		
					Homefield Farm, Crowhurst, Lingfield		20. 5.01
G-BPHH	Cameron V-77 HAFB	1840		2.12.88	C.D.Aindow "Office Angels"	London SW18	18. 3.96A
G-BPHI	PA-38-112 Tomahawk	38-79A0002	N2535T	22.11.88	D.F.Wright	Gloucestershire	4. 6.01T
G-BPHJ	Cameron V-77 HAFB	1881		23.11.88	C.W.Brown "Twiggy"	Nottingham	9. 1.00A
G-BPHL	PA-28-161 Warrior II	28-7916315	N555PY N2247U	2.12.88	Teesside Flt Centre Ltd	Teesside	2. 7.01T
G-BPHO	Taylorcraft BC-12D	8497	N96197 NC96197	10. 1.89	A.A.Alderdice	(Newry, NI)	10. 7.98P
					"Spirit of Missouri"		
G-BPHP	Taylorcraft BC-12-65	2799	N33948 NC33948	12.12.88	D.C.Stephens	Llangarron	2.11.99P
	(Cont A65)				"Spirit of Mississippi"		
G-BPHR	DH (Aust) 82A Tiger Moth	45	N48DH VH-BLX/A17-48	3. 1.89	N.Parry (As "A17-48" in RAAF c/s)		
					Lotmead Farm, Wanborough, Swindon		11.10.01
G-BPHT	Cessna 152 II	152-82401	N961LP	5.12.88	Bobbington Air Training School Ltd		
						Halfpenny Green	16. 8.01T
G-BPHU	Thunder Ax7-77 HAFB	1365		19.12.88	R.P.Waite	St.Helens	15. 8.99A
G-BPHW	Cessna 140	11035	N76595 NC76595	13. 1.89	M.Day	White Waltham	1. 4.99
	(Cont C85)						
G-BPHX	Cessna 140	12488	N2252N NC2252N	2.12.88	M.McChesney	Enniskillen	23. 5.93
	(Cont C85)				(Stored 2.93)		
G-BPHZ	Morane-Saulnier MS.505 Criquet	53/7	F-BJQC Fr Mil	17. 4.89	G.A.Warner	Duxford	26. 4.99P
					t/a The Acft Restoration Co		
					(As "TA+RC" in I/JG54 Luftwaffe c/s)		
G-BPID	PA-28-161 Warrior II	28-7916325	N2137V	16. 3.89	K.J.Newman	North Coates	19. 5.01
G-BPIE	Bell 206B JetRanger III	2533	N327WM	22.11.88	Frey Avn Ltd (Op Cabair)	Elstree	15. 2.01T
G-BPIF*	Bensen-Parsons Two-Place	UK-01		19.12.88	A.P.Barden	Inverness	28. 3.96P
	(Rotax 532)				(Cancelled by CAA 6.3.99)		
G-BPIH	Rand Robinson KR-2	8023 & PFA/129-11436		19.12.88	J.R.Rowley & T.E.Masters	(Birmingham)	
G-BPII	Denney Kitfox	213 & PFA/172-11496		15.12.88	J.K.Cross	Hurst Green, Lancs	5. 4.94P
	(KFM 112)						
G-BPIJ	Brantly B.2B	465	N2293U	23. 3.89	R.B.Payne	Willand, Cullompton	13. 7.98
G-BPIK	PA-38-112 Tomahawk II	38-82A0028	N3947M ZP-EAP/N91423	2.12.88	R.J.Everett & S.J.Overton	Hill Farm, Nayland	2. 2.95T
G-BPIL	Cessna 310B	35620	N620GS OO-SEF/N5420A	16.11.89	A.L.Brown & R.A.Parsons	Bourn	28. 4.00T
					"Fast Lady"		
G-BPIM	Cameron N-77 HAFB	1896		6. 1.89	Thermalite Ltd	Birmingham	
G-BPIN	Glaser-Dirks DG-400	4-242		14.12.88	M.P.Seth-Smith & J.N.Stevenson	Lasham	10. 4.01
G-BPIO	Reims Cessna F.152 II	1556	PH-VSO PH-AXS	23. 1.89	I.D.McClelland	Biggin Hill	27. 8.01T
G-BPIP	Slingsby T.31 Cadet III PFA/42-10771			14.11.88	J.H.Beard	Bodmin	27. 9.96P
	(VW1600)						
G-BPIR	Scheibe SF-25E Super Falke	4332	N25SF (D-KDFX)	15.12.88	Coventry Gliding Club Ltd		
						Husbands Bosworth	3. 4.01
G-BPIT	Robinson R-22 Beta	0907	N80011	22.12.88	NA Air Ltd	Chester	27. 6.99T
G-BPIU	PA-28-161 Warrior II	28-7916303	N3028T	28.12.88	G.D.Corbin	(Salisbury)	28. 3.01
G-BPIV	Bristol 149 Blenheim IV	-	"Z5722" RCAF 10201	15. 2.89	G.A.Warner	Duxford	4. 6.98P
	(Bolingbroke IVT)				t/a The Aircraft Restoration Co		
					(As "L8841/QY-C" in 254 Sqdn c/s) "Spirit of Britain First"		
G-BPIY	Cessna 152 II	152-84073	N5249H	19.12.88	A.S.Bamrah	Biggin Hill	19.11.97T
					t/a Falcon Flying Services (Damaged Earls Colne 12.8.97)		
G-BPIZ	Gulfstream AA-5B Tiger	AA5B-1154	N4530L	14. 2.89	N.R.F.McNally	Shoreham	30. 7.01
G-BPJA	Beechcraft 58 Baron	TH-1532	N3102A	8.12.88	J.F.Britten	Fairoaks	26. 4.01
G-BPJB	Schweizer Hughes 269C	S.1331	N75065	7.11.88	Elborne Holdings Ltd	Cascais, Portugal	24.10.99
G-BPJD	Socata Rallye 110ST	3253	OY-CAV	22.12.88	D.Carr	Morgansfield, Fishburn	14. 6.01
G-BPJE	Cameron A-105 HAFB	1864		8.11.88	J.S.Eckersley	Henley-on-Thames	28. 6.99A
					"Burley Stables"		
G-BPJG	PA-18-150 Super Cub	18-8350	SE-EZG N4172Z	4. 1.89	M.W.Stein	Oaksey Park	31. 7.01
G-BPJH	PA-18-95 Super Cub	18-1980	MM52-2380 I-EICA/MM52-2380/52-2380	24. 5.83	P.J.Heron	Ballymoney, Co.Antrim	4.10.99P
	(L-18C-PI)						
G-BPJK	Colt 77A HAFB	1362		22.12.88	Saran UK Ltd	Cheltenham	17. 9.97A
G-BPJL	Cessna 152 II	152-81296	N49473	28.12.88	Eastern Executive Air Charter Ltd		
					(Op Seawing F/C)	Southend	27. 5.01T

Regn	Type	C/n	P/I	Date	Owner/operator	Probable Base	CA Expy
G-BPJN	Jodel D.18 254 & PFA/169-11409			19.12.88	W.J.Evans	Rhigos	28.11.96P
	(VW 1834)				(Damaged Pencefen Farm nr Aberystwyth 21.7.96)		
G-BPJO	PA-28-161 Cadet	2841014	N9153Z	15.12.88	Plane Talking Ltd	Denham	20.12.01T
G-BPJP	PA-28-161 Cadet	2841015	N9154K	22.12.88	Oxford Aviation Services Ltd	Oxford	19. 5.01T
G-BPJR	PA-28-161 Cadet	2841024	N9154X	17. 1.89	J.P.E.Walsh t/a Walsh Aviation	Denham	21.12.01T
G-BPJS	PA-28-161 Cadet	2841025	N9154Z	12. 1.89	Oxford Aviation Services Ltd	Oxford	26. 2.01T
G-BPJT*	PA-28-161 Cadet	2841031	N9156X	6. 1.89	The Fire Service College	Moreton-in-Marsh	17. 2.95T
					(Crashed Oxford 12.7.92 & in fire service use 8.98)		
G-BPJU	PA-28-161 Cadet	2841032	N9156Z	11. 1.89	Oxford Aviation Services Ltd	Oxford	22. 2.01T
G-BPJV	Taylorcraft F-21	F-1005	N2004L	12. 1.89	P.Glennon t/a TC F/Grp	Rochester	17. 6.99P
G-BPJW	Cessna A150K Aerobat	A150-0127	C-FAJX CF-AJX/N8427M	4. 1.89	G & S.A.Jones	Linley Hill, Leven	21. 5.00T
G-BPJZ	Cameron O-160 HAFB	1904		4. 1.89	M.L.Gabb	Alcester	3. 7.97T
G-BPKF	Grob G-115	8075		3. 1.89	Radford Bavarian Ltd	Ingestre, Stafford	28.12.00
G-BPKI	EAA Acrosport I PFA/72A-11391			15. 2.89	P.Shaw	(Selby)	3. 9.98P
	(Lyc O-320)						
G-BPKK	Denney Kitfox mk.1 264 & PFA/172-11411			19.12.88	D.Moffat	Blackpool	24. 8.99P
	(Rotax 532)						
G-BPKL	Mooney M.20J (201)	24-1102	N1008K	12. 1.89	London Link Flying Ltd	Stapleford	25. 6.01
G-BPKM	PA-28-161 Warrior II	28-7916341	PH-CKO N2140X/N9630N	6. 1.89	M.J.Greasby	Bicester	20. 6.01T
G-BPKN*	Colt AS-80 Mk.II Hot-Air Airship	1297		11. 1.89	British Balloon Museum	Newbury	14. 3.91A
					(Stored 12.94)		
G-BPKO	Cessna 140	8936	N89891 NC89891	12. 1.89	I.R.March	Booker	18. 5.00
G-BPKR	PA-28-151 Cherokee Warrior	28-7515446	N4341X	13. 3.89	Aeroshow Ltd	Gloucestershire	12. 3.01T
G-BPLF	Cameron V-77 HAFB	1903		16. 1.89	I.R.Warrington & R.A.Macmillan	Stamford	18. 5.99A
					"Star Attraction"		
G-BPLH	CEA Jodel DR.1051 Sicile	401	F-BLAE	27. 2.89	M.N.King	Dunkeswell	24.11.01
G-BPLM	AIA Stampe SV-4C	1004	F-BHET Fr.Mil/F-BDKC	8. 2.89	C.J.Jesson	(Forest Row)	14. 8.91T
					(On rebuild Hedge End 5.95)		
G-BPLV	Cameron V-77 HAFB	1822		23. 1.89	MC VH SA	Brussels, Belgium	14. 6.97A
G-BPLY	Christen Pitts S-2B Special	5149		25. 1.89	M.Mountstephen	Goodwood	13. 5.01
	(Lyc AEIO-540)						
G-BPLZ	Hughes 369HS	91-0342S	N126CM	15. 2.89	Pyramid Precision Engineering Ltd	Halfpenny Green	16.12.00
G-BPMB	Maule M.5-235C Lunar Rocket	7284C	N5635T	13. 8.79	R.A.Fleming	Sherburn	16.12.00
G-BPMC*	Air Command 503 Commander 0403 & PFA G/04-1107			16.12.88	M.A.Cheshire	Exeter	2. 9.91P
					(Cancelled by CAA 8.3.99) (Sold in France ?)		
G-BPME	Cessna 152 II	152-85585	N94021	24. 1.89	Eastern Executive Air Charter Ltd	Southend	26. 7.01T
					(Op Seawing Flying Club)		
G-BPMF	PA-28-151 Cherokee Warrior	28-7515050	C-GOXL	2. 2.89	L. & A.Hill	Walney Island	2. 5.01
G-BPMH	Schempp-Hirth Nimbus 3DM	7/23		20. 3.89	R.Jones "60"	Lasham	20. 4.01
	(Regd as c/n 07)				t/a Southern Sailplanes		
G-BPML	Cessna 172M Skyhawk II	172-67102	N1435U	17.11.89	J.P.Birnie (Op Birnie Air Svs)	Sandown	11. 4.00T
G-BPMM	Champion 7ECA Citabria	7ECA-498	N5132T	22. 3.89	J.Murray	(Ballymoney, Co.Antrim)	25. 2.97P
G-BPMR	PA-28-161 Warrior II	28-8416119	N4373S N9620N	25. 1.89	B.McIntyre	Gloucestershire	2. 6.01T
G-BPMU	Nord 3202B	70	(G-BIZJ) N22546/ALAT "AIX"	26. 1.89	A.I.Milne (Stored 9.97)	Little Snoring	19.10.90P*
G-BPMV	PA-28-161 Warrior II	28-8416127	N4374M N9628N	25. 1.89	Oxford Aviation Services Ltd	Oxford	23. 4.01T
G-BPMW	QAC Quickie Q2 PFA/94A-10790		G-OICI G-OGKN	13. 3.89	C.W.Tattersall	Southampton	17. 8.91T
	(Revmaster R2100DQ)				(Damaged nr Basingstoke 16.2.91)		
G-BPMX	ARV1 Super 2 K.005 & PFA/152-11128			30. 1.89	C.R.James	Ludham	21. 6.99P
	(Hewland AE75)						
G-BPNA	Cessna 150L Commuter	150-73042	N1742Q	10. 2.89	Griffin Marston Ltd	Compton Abbas	2. 3.00T
					(Op Abbas Air)		
G-BPNC	Rotorway Exec 152	3600		3. 2.89	S.J.Hanson	Farleton, Lancaster	30. 5.92P
	(RW152)				(Damaged Quernmore nr Lancaster 16.5.92)		
G-BPND	Boeing 727-2D3	21021	OK-EGK N500AV/G-BPND/PH-AHZ/N500AV/HI-452/JY-ADV	18.12.87	Sabre Airways Ltd "Katie"	Lasham	10. 4.01T
G-BPNF	Robinson R-22 Beta	0967		1. 3.89	Direct Helicopters (Southend) Ltd	Southend	24. 4.01
G-BPNI	Robinson R-22 Beta	0948		6. 2.89	Heliflight (UK) Ltd	Halfpenny Green	8. 2.01T
G-BPNL	QAC Quickie Q2 PFA/94A-11014			6. 2.89	J.Catley	Coventry	16. 1.96P
	(Revmaster 2100D)				(Damaged Swansea 30.4.95; stored Swansea 6.95)		
G-BPNN	Montgomerie-Bensen B.8MR	MV-003		3. 2.89	M.E.Vahdat	(Uxbridge)	
G-BPNO	Moravan Zlin Z.526 Trener Master 930		F-BPNO	18. 2.86	J.A.S.Baldry & S.T.Logan	Little Gransden	11. 9.00
G-BPNT	BAe 146 Srs.300	E-3126		4. 1.89	Flightline Ltd	Bournemouth	31. 5.99T
					(Op Palmair Flightline)		
G-BPNU	Thunder Ax7-77 HAFB	1011		9. 2.89	M.J.Barnes "Firefly"	Ivybridge	1. 8.98T
G-BPNW*	HS.748 Srs.2/217	1584	G-11-4 RP-C1042/V2-LIP/VP-LIP	7. 2.89	British Aerospace plc	Irvine	
					(Stored in Maxi-Haulage Yard 8.94)		
G-BPOA*	Gloster Meteor T.7	-	WF877	16. 3.89	Not known	Kemble	
					(As "WF877") (Stored 6.97)		

Regn	Type	C/n	P/I	Date	Owner/operator	Probable Base	CA Expy
G-BPOB	Tallmantz Sopwith Camel F.1 rep (Warner Scarab 165)	TM-10	N8997	14. 3.89	Bianchi Avn Film Svs Ltd (Op Blue Max Movie Acft Museum) (As "B2458/R" in RFC c/s)	Booker	6. 8.97P
G-BPOL	Pietenpol Air Camper	PFA/47-10941		16. 2.89	G.W.Postance (Burgess Hill, Sussex)		
G-BPOM	PA-28-161 Warrior II	28-8416118	N4373Q N9619N	15. 2.89	APB Leasing Ltd	Norwich	13. 5.01T
G-BPON	PA-34-200T Seneca II	34-7570040	N675ES N32644	13. 2.89	Aeroshow Ltd	Gloucestershire	15. 6.01T
G-BPOO	Montgomerie-Bensen B.8MR	MV-002 & PFA G/01A-1109		3. 2.89	M.E.Vahdat (Not constructed)	(Uxbridge)	
G-BPOR	Bell 206B JetRanger III	3439	N90WM N21153	13. 3.89	P.F.Copeland Ltd (Damaged Newtownards 13.10.95; stored 7.96)	Dublin	20. 5.95T
G-BPOS	Cessna 150M Commuter	150-75905	N66187	21. 2.89	K.J.Goggins	(Stevenage)	10.10.99T
G-BPOT	PA-28-181 Cherokee Archer II	28-7790267	N8807F	7. 2.89	P.Fraser	Cumbernauld	14. 5.01
G-BPOU	Luscombe 8A Silvaire (Cont A65)	4159	N1432K NC1432K	14. 2.89	M.J.Negus & R.Hardley Stoneacre Farm, Farthing Corner		23. 8.99P
G-BPOV	Cameron Magazine 90SS HAFB (Forbes Magazine shape)	1890		10. 3.89	Forbes Europe Inc Balleroy, Normandy "Forbes Capitalist Tool"		31. 5.99A
G-BPOZ	Enstrom F-28A-UK	281	N246Q	6. 3.89	Creswick Engineering Services Ltd Weston Zoyland		9. 5.99T
G-BPPA	Cameron O-65 HAFB	1930		15. 2.89	Rix Petroleum Ltd "Rix Petroleum"		5. 9.99A
G-BPPD	PA-38-112 Tomahawk	38-79A0457	N2456F	15. 2.89	S.Snodgrass & M.A.Wood t/a AS Belting Products	Cardiff	13. 9.01T
G-BPPE	PA-38-112 Tomahawk	38-79A0189	N2445C	15. 2.89	B.H. & P.M.Illston t/a Norwich School of Flying	Norwich	30. 5.98T
G-BPPF	PA-38-112 Tomahawk	38-79A0578	N2329K	15. 2.89	D.J.Bellamy t/a Bristol Strut Flying Group	Bristol/Lulsgate	13. 9.01
G-BPPJ	Cameron A-180 HAFB	1924		2. 3.89	Heather R.Evans	Ross-on-Wye	18. 2.98T
G-BPPK	PA-28-151 Cherokee Warrior	28-7615054	N7592C	10. 3.89	UK Technical Consultants Ltd	(Peterborough)	24. 6.98T
G-BPPL	Enstrom F-28A	251	HB-XER	15. 2.89	M & P Food Products Ltd t/a Coventry Helicopters	Coventry	9. 5.98T
G-BPPM	Beechcraft B200 Super King Air	BB-1044	N7061T C-GJJT/N815CE/(N815CF)/N815CE/N62895	16. 2.89	Gama Avn Ltd (Op Bond Air Svs)	Aberdeen	24. 9.01T
G-BPPO	Luscombe 8A Silvaire (Cont A65)	2541	N3519M N71114/NC71114	15. 2.89	I.K.Ratcliffe	Popham	28. 6.99P
G-BPPP	Cameron V-77 HAFB	1700		29. 2.88	P.F.Smart t/a The Sarnia Balloon Grp "Thruppence"	Basingstoke	28. 6.97A
G-BPPR*	Air Command 532 Elite	0434 & PFA G/04-1105		22. 2.89	T.D.Inch (Cancelled by CAA 10.3.99)	Banstead	14. 5.91T
G-BPPS	Mudry/CAARP CAP.21	9	F-GDTD	3. 5.85	J.E.Davies	Woodford	20. 8.99S
G-BPPU	Air Command 532 Elite	0438 & PFA G/04-1120		22. 2.89	J.Hough	Alresford, Hants	18.10.91P
G-BPPW	Schweizer Hughes 269C (300C)	S.1172	N3624J	22. 2.89	Browns Distribution Services Ltd Ravensdale, Stoke-on-Trent		28. 5.01
G-BPPY	Hughes 269B (300)	20-0448	N9554F	10. 3.89	N.J.Edmonds	Wellesbourne Mountford	29.10.99
G-BPPZ	Taylorcraft BC-12D (Cont C85)	7988	N28286 NC28286	22. 3.89	J.Gordon & M.Hart t/a Zulu Warriors F/Grp	Charterhall	26. 8.99P
G-BPRA	Aeronca 11AC Chief	11AC-1344	N9702E NC9702E	22. 3.89	R.M.C.Hunter	Scotland Farm, Hook	14. 6.99P
G-BPRC	Cameron Elephant 77SS HAFB	1871		21. 2.89	G.V.Beckwith	(Germany)	15. 2.97A
G-BPRD	Pitts S-1C Special (Lyc O-360)	ZZ.1	N10ZZ	21. 2.89	Shiela M.Trickey	Bodmin	26. 2.99P
G-BPRJ	Aerospatiale AS.355F1 Twin Squirrel	5201	N368E	22. 2.89	PLM Dollar Group Ltd	Cumbernauld	14.12.01T
G-BPRL	Aerospatiale AS.355F1 Twin Squirrel	5154	N362E	22. 2.89	Gas & Air Ltd (Op Virgin Helicopters)	Booker	24. 3.00T
G-BPRM	Reims Cessna F.172L	0825	G-AZKG	20. 4.88	D.Rychlik	(Shetland)	19. 4.01
G-BPRN	PA-28-161 Warrior II	28-8116109	N83112	6. 3.89	Air Navigation & Trading Co Ltd	Blackpool	10. 6.01T
G-BPRO	Cessna A150K Aerobat	A150-0221	N221AR VP-LAQ/8P-LAC/N5921J	1. 3.89	Armphase Ltd	Southampton	24. 3.99
G-BPRP	Cessna 150E	150-61269	N3569J	10. 3.89	P.A.Griffin (Op Premi-Air Flying Club)	Shoreham	3. 5.98T
G-BPRR	Rand Robinson KR-2	PFA/129-11105		1. 3.89	R.C.Bowley	(Earls Croome)	
G-BPRS	Air Command 532 Elite	0432		14. 4.89	B.K.Snoxall (Damaged ?)	(Whitchurch, Hants)	
G-BPRX	Aeronca 11AC Chief (Cont A75)	11AC-94	N86288 NC86288	3. 3.89	D.J.Dumolo & C.R.Barnes	Breighton	23. 8.99P
G-BPRY	PA-28-161 Warrior II	28-8416120	N4373Y N9621N	2. 3.89	R.C.White t/a White Wings Avn	East Midlands	4. 6.01T
G-BPSB*	Air Command 532 Elite	0431		10. 3.89	D.K.Duckworth (Cancelled by CAA 3.3.99)	Northampton	
G-BPSH	Cameron V-77 HAFB	1837		21. 2.89	P.G.Hossack "Coconut Ice"	Pewsey	5. 4.97T
G-BPSI	Thunder Ax10-160 HAFB	1420		10. 3.89	Airborne Adventures Ltd "Airborne Adventures"	Skipton	19. 2.96T
G-BPSJ	Thunder Ax6-56 HAFB	1479		13. 3.89	Capricorn Balloons Ltd	Loughborough	22. 4.96A
G-BPSK	Montgomerie-Bensen B.8M	PFA G/01-1100		15. 3.89	G.C.Kerr	Carlisle	25.11.99P

Regn	Type	C/n	P/I	Date	Owner/operator	Probable Base	CA Expy
G-BPSL	Cessna 177 Cardinal	177-01138	N659SR	3. 3.89	N.P.Bendle t/a G-BPSL Group	Dunkeswell	12.11.01
G-BPSO	Cameron N-90 HAFB	1959		10. 3.89	J.Oberprieler	Mauern, Germany	24. 6.99A
G-BPSP	Cameron Ship 90SS HAFB (Columbus "Santa Maria" shape)	1848		10. 3.89	Forbes Europe Inc "Santa Maria"	Balleroy, Normandy	17. 6.94
G-BPSR	Cameron V-77 HAFB	1962		10. 3.89	K.J.A.Maxwell "Norma Jean"	Haywards Heath	23. 3.99T
G-BPSS	Cameron A-120 HAFB	1947		27. 2.89	T.J.Parker t/a Anglian Countryside Balloons	Burnham-on-Crouch	3.11.99T
G-BPSZ	Cameron N-180 HAFB	1911		14. 3.89	A.Bolger "Park Furnishers II"	Salisbury	4. 1.00T
G-BPTA	Stinson 108-2 Station Wagon (Franklin 6A4)	108-3429	N429C NC429C	22. 3.89	M.L.Ryan	Garston Farm, Marshfield	30. 9.01
G-BPTB	Boeing-Stearman A75N1 (PT-17) Kaydet (Lyc R-680)	75-442	N55581 40-1885	22. 3.89	Aero Vintage Ltd (As "FJ992" in RAF c/s)	Andrewsfield	15. 7.99
G-BPTC*	Taylorcraft BC-12D	9388	N94988 NC94988	18. 1.89	Not known (Temp unregd 28.1.97)	(London SW15)	29. 5.96P
G-BPTD	Cameron V-77 HAFB	2001		14. 3.89	J.Lippett "Visions 2001"	South Petherton, Somerset	25. 5.97A
G-BPTE	PA-28-181 Cherokee Archer II	28-7690178	N8553E	9. 3.89	I.Chaplin	Southend	9. 8.01T
G-BPTF	Cessna 152 II	152-81979	N67715	9. 3.89	A.S.Bamrah t/a Falcon Flying Services	Shoreham	12. 8.01T
G-BPTG	Rockwell Commander 112TC	13067	N4577W	31. 3.89	Marita A.Watteau	Shoreham	23. 4.01
G-BPTH	Air Command 532 Elite	01	N532KR	25. 4.89	R.Wheeler (Damaged 1991 - parts only remain 1992) North Green Farm, Reymerston, Norwich		
G-BPTI	Socata TB-20 Trinidad	414	N41BM	21. 4.89	N.Davis	Blackbushe	25. 5.01
G-BPTL	Cessna 172N Skyhawk II	172-68652	N733YJ	22. 3.89	Cleveland Flying School Ltd	Teesside	3.12.01T
G-BPTO	Zenair CH-200-AA (Lyc O-320)	2-563	EI-BKP	22. 3.89	Barbara Philips (Damaged Aldersfield, Worcs 27. 5.91)	Ledbury/Gloucestershire	8. 9.91P
G-BPTP	Robinson R-22	0140	N9056H	17. 3.89	Thorneygrove Ltd	Newcastle	2. 6.01T
G-BPTS	CASA I-131E Jungmann	1....	E3B-153 "781-75"	23. 5.89	Aerobatic Displays Ltd (Op The Old Flying Machine Co) (As "E3B-153/781-75" in Spanish AF c/s)	Duxford	18. 9.99P
G-BPTT	Robin DR400/120 Dauphin 2+2	1906		14. 3.89	The Cotswold A/C Ltd	Gloucestershire	10. 6.01T
G-BPTU	Cessna 152 II	152-82955	N45946	22. 3.89	A.M.Alam	Panshanger	23. 5.99
G-BPTV	Bensen B.8	PFA G/01-1058		30. 3.89	C.Munro	(Colne)	
G-BPTX	Cameron O-120 HAFB	1972		29. 3.89	S.J.Colin & A.S.Pinder t/a Skybus Ballooning	Maidstone	14. 5.97T
G-BPTZ	Robinson R-22 Beta	0958		22. 3.89	J.Lucketti	Barton	16.11.98
G-BPUA	EAA Sport Biplane (Lyc O-235)	SAAC-02	EI-BBF	30. 3.89	V.Millard (Crashed Orchard Farm, Streethay 17.4.93)	(Ipswich)	8. 4.93P
G-BPUB	Cameron V-31 Air Chair HAFB	1114		15. 3.89	M.T.Evans	Bath	3. 6.94A
G-BPUC	QAC Quickie Q.235 (Lyc O-235)	2583	N250CE	22. 3.89	S.R.Harvey	RAF Brize Norton	22.11.96P
G-BPUD*	Ryan PT-22-RY (ST3KR)	1265	N53189 41-15236	22. 3.89	R.I.Warman (As "I-492" in US Army c/s)	Sandown	17. 2.93P
	(Damaged Great Ryburgh, Norfolk 8.11.92; spares use 9.93; cancelled as destroyed 3.3.99)						
G-BPUE	Air Command 532 Elite	0441 & PFA G/04-1136		29. 3.89	A.H.Brent	Brough	11. 9.91P
G-BPUF	Thunder Ax6-56Z HAFB	270	(G-BHRL)	30. 4.80	R.C. & M.A.Trimble "Buf Puf"	Henley-on-Thames	10. 2.90A
G-BPUG	Air Command 532 Elite	0401 & PFA G/04-1157		29. 3.89	T.A.Holmes	Melrose Farm, Melbourne	18. 4.91P
G-BPUI	Air Command 532 Elite	0442 & PFA G/04-1128		31. 3.89	D.C.E.Streeter	Tatenhill	2. 5.91P
G-BPUJ	Cameron N-90 HAFB	1977		17. 4.89	D.Grimshaw	Preston	28.10.98T
G-BPUL	PA-18A-150 Super Cub (L-18C-PI)(Regd with Frame No.18-2517)	18-2017	OO-LUL I-EIRU/EI-87/MM52-2417/52-2417	12. 4.89	C.D.Duthy-James	(Presteigne)	9. 4.99
G-BPUM	Cessna R182 Skylane RG II	R182-00915	N738DZ	2. 5.89	R.C.Chapman	Marley Hall,Ledbury	30. 4.01
G-BPUP	Whittaker MW.7	PFA/171-11473		2. 8.89	J.H.Beard	(Buckfastleigh, Devon)	
G-BPUR	Piper J3L-65 Cub	4708	N30228 NC30228	14. 6.89	H.A.D.Monro	(Hastings)	
G-BPUS	Rans S-9 (Rotax 532)	PFA/196-11487		7. 4.89	T.A.Wright	Langtoft	6. 3.98P
G-BPUU	Cessna 140	13722	N4251N NC4251N	31. 3.89	Sherburn A/Club Ltd	Sherburn-in-Elmet	26.11.99T
G-BPUW	Colt 90A HAFB	1436		12. 4.89	Huntair Ltd	(London SE16)	6. 8.99A
G-BPUX	Cessna 150J Commuter	150-70619	N60851	25. 4.89	BCT A/c Leasing Ltd	(Chesterfield)	13. 2.97
G-BPVA	Cessna 172F Skyhawk	172-52286	N8386U	13. 4.89	South Lancashire Flyers Ltd	Barton	8. 7.00
G-BPVC	Cameron V-77 HAFB	1302		7. 4.89	J.B.R.Elliot	Great Yarmouth	18. 9.97A
G-BPVE	Bleriot XI 1909 replica (Built by R.D.Henry, Texas 1967)	1	N1197	20. 6.89	Bianchi Avn Film Svs Ltd (Blue Max Movie Acft Museum) (As "1197")	Booker	
G-BPVH	Cub J3C-85 Prospector	178C	CF-DRY	7. 4.89	D.E.Cooper-Maguire	Findon, Worthing	4. 4.99P
G-BPVI	PA-32R-301 Saratoga SP	3213021	N91685	24. 4.89	M.T.Coppen	Goodwood	16. 7.01
G-BPVJ	Cessna 152 II	152-82596	N70741	13. 4.89	Multiflight Ltd	Leeds-Bradford	14.10.99T
G-BPVK	Varga 2150A Kachina	VAC85-77	N4626V	4. 5.89	H.W.Hall	Southend	18.10.99P
G-BPVM	Cameron V-77 HAFB	1970		4. 4.89	N.F.Mulliner t/a Royal Engineers Balloon Club "Viscount"	Chatham	6. 9.97A

Regn	Type	C/n	P/I	Date	Owner/operator	Probable Base	CA Expy
G-BPVN	PA-32R-301T Saratoga SP	32R-8029073	N8178W	14. 4.89	Y.Leysen (London SW3)		20. 7.01T
G-BPVO	Cassutt Racer IIIM (Cont O-200-A)	DG.1	N19DD	13. 4.89	R.J.Adams & D.R.Puleston "VooDoo"	Shipdham	22. 9.98P
G-BPVP	Aerotek Pitts S-2B Special	5000	N5302M	13. 4.89	J.A.Harris (Gillingham, Dorset) (Damaged Clacton 19.6.92; on rebuild 5.93)		17. 5.95
G-BPVU	Thunder Ax7-77 HAFB	965		12. 4.89	B.J.Hammond	Chelmsford	18. 9.98T
G-BPVW	CASA I-131E Jungmann	2133	E3B-559	17. 5.89	C. & J.W.Labeij Lelystad, Netherlands		9. 9.97P
G-BPVX	Cassutt Racer IIIM (Cont C90)	99JC	N99JC	17. 4.89	J.H.Milne "Whitey"	Swanton Morley	19. 4.99P
G-BPVY	Cessna 172D Skyhawk	172-50568	N2968U	20. 4.89	Unitek Aviation Ltd	Denham	11. 6.99
G-BPVZ	Luscombe 8E Silvaire (Cont C85)	5565	N2838K NC2838K	9. 5.89	W.E.Gillham & P.Ryman	Croft	31. 5.99P
G-BPWA	PA-28-161 Warrior II	28-7816074	N47450	7. 4.89	Leisure Park Management Ltd	Goodwood	15. 5.01T
G-BPWB	Sikorsky S-61N	61822	EI-BHO G-BPWB/EI-BHO	4. 5.89	Bristow Helicopters Ltd	Aberdeen	10. 7.01T
G-BPWC	Cameron V-77 HAFB	1986		12. 4.89	H.B.Roberts "Hot Flush"	Bristol	14. 5.99T
G-BPWD	Cessna 120 (Cont O-240-E)	10026	N72839 NC72839	14. 4.89	M.B.Horan & M.W.Albery t/a Peregrine F/Grp	Hucknall	23. 6.99P
G-BPWE	PA-28-161 Warrior II	28-8116143	N8330P	2. 5.89	RPR Associates Ltd	Swansea	18. 6.99T
G-BPWG	Cessna 150M Commuter	150-76707	(G-BPTK) N45029	10. 4.89	W.R.Spicer & I.D.Carling Nanbeck Farm, Wilsford, Grantham		26. 7.01T
G-BPWI	Bell 206B JetRanger III	3087	9M-BSR VH-HXZ/ZK-HXX/XC-PFH	14. 4.89	S. & J.M.Taylor	Barton	13. 8.01T
G-BPWK	Sportavia Fournier RF5B Sperber	51036	N56JM (D-KEAR)	17. 4.89	S.L.Reed	Usk	28. 7.99P
G-BPWL	PA-25-235 Pawnee	25-2304	N6690Z G-BPWL/N6690Z	14. 4.89	Marchington Gliding Club Ltd	Tatenhill	19. 6.99
G-BPWM	Cessna 150L	150-72820	N1520Q	17. 4.89	M.E.Creasey	Crowfield	14.10.99
G-BPWN	Cessna 150L Commuter	150-74325	N19308	17. 4.89	International Aerospace Engineering Ltd	Cranfield	13. 6.99T
G-BPWP	Rutan LongEz (Cont O-240)	PFA/74A-11132		17. 4.89	J.F.O'Hara & A.J.Voyle	Denham	1. 4.99P
G-BPWR	Cessna R172K Hawk XPII	R172-2953	N758AZ	21. 4.89	A.M.Skelton	Humberside	9. 8.01
G-BPWS	Cessna 172P Skyhawk II	172-74306	N51387	21. 4.89	Plane Talking Ltd	Redhill	2. 8.01T
G-BPWT	Cameron DG-19 Helium Airship	1772		18. 4.89	Airspace Outdoor Advertising Ltd Southampton		3. 7.90A
G-BPWW	Focke-Wulf Piaggio FWP.149D	087	OO-FDF D-EFDF/(D-EBDF)/90+69/SC+332/AS+496	12. 6.89	J.S.Holborn Standalone Farm, Meppershall t/a G-BPWW Grp		23. 4.01
G-BPWY	Isaacs Fury II	PFA/11-11437		21. 4.89	R.J.Knights (North Weald)		
G-BPXA	PA-28-181 Archer II	28-8390064	N4305T	12. 5.89	D.Howdle & D.L.Heighington t/a Cherokee F/Grp	Netherthorpe	4. 6.01
G-BPXB	Glaser-Dirks DG-400	4-248		2. 5.89	K.M.Fresson & G.C.Westgate	Parham Park	5.10.99
G-BPXE	Enstrom 280C Shark	1089	N379KH C-GMLH/N660H	21. 4.89	A.Healy	Littlehampden, Bucks	4. 1.02
G-BPXF	Cameron V-65 HAFB	2003		21. 4.89	D.Pascall "Gwei-Lo"	Croydon	
G-BPXH	Colt 17A Cloudhopper HAFB	667	OO-BWG	21. 4.89	Sport Promotion SRL	Belbo, Italy	2. 6.99A
G-BPXJ	PA-28RT-201T Turbo Arrow IV	28R-8231023	N8061U	21. 4.89	K.M.Hollamby	Biggin Hill	7. 7.01
G-BPXX	PA-34-200T Seneca II	34-7970069	N923SM N9556N	21. 4.89	Hockstar Ltd	Biggin Hill	29. 6.01T
G-BPXY	Aeronca 11AC Chief	11AC-S-50	N3842E	10. 4.89	J.H.Tetley	Cliffe, Yorks	14. 6.99P
G-BPYI	Cameron O-77 HAFB	1988		9. 5.89	A.J.Clarke t/a Fly By Night Balloon Grp	Godalming	3. 5.99A
G-BPYJ	Wittman W.8 Tailwind (Cont PC60)	PFA/31-11028		12. 5.89	J.Dixon	Bagby	19.10.99P
G-BPYK	Thunder Ax7-77 HAFB	1166		15. 5.89	A.R.Swinnerton "Yorick"	London EC2	29. 5.93
G-BPYL	Hughes 369D	100-0796D	N65AM G-BPYL/HB-XKT	10. 5.89	Morcorp (BVI) Ltd (Jersey)		7. 6.01T
G-BPYN	Piper J3C-65 Cub (L-4H-PI)	11422	F-BFYN HB-OFN/43-30131	14. 3.79	D.W.Stubbs t/a The Aquila Grp	White Waltham	14. 7.99P
G-BPYO	PA-28-181 Archer II	2890114	(SE-KIH)	22. 5.89	Sherburn A/C Ltd	Sherburn	26. 7.01
G-BPYR	PA-31-310 Turbo Navajo	31-7812032	G-ECMA N27493	15. 5.89	Multi Ltd (Op Adam Construction)	Sturgate	13. 8.99T
G-BPYS	Cameron O-77 HAFB	2008		9. 5.89	D.J.Goldsmith "Aqualisa II"	Edenbridge	14.12.99A
G-BPYT	Cameron V-77 HAFB	1984		9. 5.89	M.H.Redman	Sturminster Newton	
G-BPYV	Cameron V-77 HAFB	1992		17. 5.89	M.E.Weston	Cirencester	
G-BPYW	Air Command 532 Elite	PFA G/04-1114		2. 6.89	W.V.Tatters	Keswick	
G-BPYY	Cameron A-180 HAFB	2013		11. 5.89	G.D.Fitzpatrick	Thame	28. 6.96T
G-BPYZ	Thunder Ax7-77 HAFB	1521		11. 5.89	J.E.Astall "Axis" (Stolen Crewkerne, Somerset 23.10.97)	Hinton St.George	7. 7.96A
G-BPZA	Luscombe 8A Silvaire (Cont A65)	4326	N1599K NC1599K	18. 4.89	T.P.W.Hyde Chestnut Farm, Tipps End		13. 5.99P
G-BPZB	Cessna 120 (Cont C90)	8898	N89853 NC89853	25. 5.89	C. & M.A.Grime	Headcorn	26. 4.99P
G-BPZC	Luscombe 8A Silvaire (Cont A65)	4322	N1595K NC1595K	6. 6.89	Not known (Damaged by gales Cranfield 25.1.90; stored 10.96)	Dinton	5. 7.90P
G-BPZD	SNCAN NC.858S	97	F-BEZD	26. 1.79	G.Richards	Headcorn	10. 1.00P

Regn	Type	C/n	P/I	Date	Owner/operator	Probable Base	CA Expy
G-BPZE	Luscombe 8E Silvaire (Cont C85)	3904	N1177K NC1177K	6. 6.89	B.A.Webster t/a WFG Luscombe Associates	Seething	27.10.99P
G-BPZI	Christen Eagle II (Lyc IO-360)	T.0001	N48BB	22. 5.89	S.D.Quigley "Thunder Eagle"	Breighton	9. 9.98P
G-BPZK	Cameron O-120 HAFB	1982		7. 4.89	D.L.Smith "Hot Stuff"	Newbury	12. 5.97T
G-BPZM	PA-28RT-201 Arrow IV	28R-7918238	G-ROYW G-CRTI/SE-ICY	12. 5.89	R.Taylor	Upminster	22. 8.01
G-BPZO	Cameron N-90 HAFB	1998		15. 5.89	Seaward Homes (South) Ltd "Seaward Homes"	Chichester	4. 6.96A
G-BPZP	Robin DR.400/180R Remorqueur	1471	D-EFZP	4. 5.89	Lasham Gliding Society Ltd	Lasham	14. 5.01
G-BPZS	Colt 105A HAFB	1312		25. 5.89	L.V.Mastis West Bloomfield, MI, USA "Chamonix"		29. 6.97A
G-BPZU	Scheibe SF-25C-2000 Falke	44471	D-KIAV	21. 7.89	A.J.Buchanan t/a G-BPZU Grp	Parham Park	12. 8.01
G-BPZX	Cessna 152 II	152-85706	N94530	25. 5.89	J.C.Birdsall t/a Traffic Management Services	Gamston	2.12.01T
	(Destroyed in mid-air collision with RAF Tornado GR.Mk.1 ZA330/B-08 over Mattersey, Notts. 21.1.99)						
G-BPZY	Pitts S-1C Special (Lyc O-320)	RN-1	N1159	15. 5.89	J.S.Mitchell	White Waltham	26. 2.99P
G-BPZZ	Thunder Ax8-105 HAFB	1441		25. 5.89	Capricorn Balloons Ltd	Loughborough	4. 4.99T

Regn	Type	C/n	P/I	Date	Owner/operator	Probable Base	CA Expy
G-BRAA	Pitts S-1C Special (Lyc O-290)	101-GM	N14T	12. 5.89	C.Davidson (Castle Donington) (Stored Blackpool 6.96)		26. 4.91P
G-BRAF	VS.394 Spitfire FR.XVIIIe 6S/663052		Indian AF HS877/SM969	29.12.78	Wizzard Investments Ltd. (As "SM969/D-A" ?)	North Weald	23. 9.93P
G-BRAJ	Cameron V-77 HAFB	1876		25. 5.89	Heather R.Evans	Ross-on-Wye	
G-BRAK	Cessna 172N Skyhawk II	172-73795	C-GBPN (N5438J)	23. 6.88	T.I.Mason	Kemble	15. 1.01T
G-BRAM	Mikoyan MiG-21PF	-	503/ Hungarian AF	22. 5.89	R.Parker t/a Universal Avn Grp (Displayed 2.99) (As "503" in Hungarian AF c/s)	North Weald	
G-BRAP	Thermal Aircraft 104 HAFB	001		11. 5.89	R.A.Patey t/a Thermal Acft (London SE1)		
G-BRAR	Aeronca 7AC Champion	7AC-6564	N2978E NC2978E	14. 6.89	C.D.Ward	Wombleton	20. 8.98P
G-BRAW	Pitts S-1C Special (Lyc O-290)	52544	N24DB	24. 5.89	P.G.Bond & P.B.Hunter	Swanton Morley	31. 8.99P
G-BRAX	Payne Knight Twister 85B (Cont O-200-A)	203	N979	24. 5.89	R.Earl	White Waltham	29. 9.93P
G-BRBA	PA-28-161 Warrior II	28-7916109	N2090B	25. 5.89	Halfpenny Green Flight Centre Ltd	Halfpenny Green	22.11.01T
G-BRBB	PA-28-161 Warrior II	28-8116030	N8260W	28. 6.89	Aeroshow Ltd.	Gloucestershire	13.10.01T
G-BRBC	North American T-6G Texan	182-156 (Reported as c/n 182-155 ex 51-14469)	MM54099 RR-56/51-14470	4. 9.92	A.P.Murphy (Chigwell) (On rebuild Audley End 9.90 - status uncertain)		
G-BRBD	PA-28-151 Cherokee Warrior	28-7415315	N41702	28. 6.89	W.E.Rispin t/a Bravo Delta Group "Shaftesbury Belle"	Compton Abbas	22. 3.02
G-BRBE	PA-28-161 Warrior II	28-7916437	N2815D	13. 6.89	Solo Services Ltd (Op Sussex F/C)	Shoreham	17.12.01T
G-BRBF	Cessna 152 II	152-81993	N67748	8. 6.89	G.Jackson t/a Jacksons Tool & Plant Hire	Carlisle	5. 7.98T
G-BRBG	PA-28-180 Cherokee Archer	28-7505248	N3927X	12. 6.89	Ken MacDonald & Co	Stornoway	19. 8.01
G-BRBH	Cessna 150H Commuter	150-69283	N50410	13. 6.89	Professional Flight Management Ltd & S.J.Reeves	Panshanger	7. 8.01T
G-BRBI	Cessna 172N Skyhawk II	172-69613	N737RJ	7. 7.89	M.D.Harcourt-Brown t/a G-BRBI F/Grp	Popham	3. 9.01
G-BRBJ	Cessna 172M Skyhawk II	172-67492	N73476	26. 5.89	I.R.March	Booker	12. 1.02
G-BRBK	Robin DR.400/180 Regent	1915		31. 5.89	R.Kemp	Thruxton	15.10.01
G-BRBL	Robin DR.400/180 Regent	1920		5. 7.89	C.A.Marren	Upavon	19. 5.01
G-BRBM	Robin DR.400/180 Regent	1921		5. 7.89	R.W.Davies	Little Robhurst Farm, Woodchurch, Kent	24. 1.02
G-BRBN	Pitts S-1S Special (Lyc O-360)	G.3	N81BG	14. 7.89	D.R.Evans	Gloucestershire	14. 6.99P
G-BRBO	Cameron V-77 HAFB	1877		30. 5.89	D.Haynes & I.Jane t/a Cardinal Avn "Patches"	(York)	3. 6.99A
G-BRBP	Cessna 152 II	152-84915	N5324P	14. 6.89	Staverton Flying Svs Ltd Gloucestershire		23. 7.01T
G-BRBS	Bensen B.8M (Rotax 503) PFA G/01-1039			30. 5.89	K.T.MacFarlane	Kilmacolm, Renfrew	
G-BRBT	Trotter Ax3-20 HAFB	RMT-001		13. 6.89	R.M.Trotter	Bristol	
G-BRBU	Colt 17A Cloudhopper HAFB	1506		12. 6.89	Virgin Airship & Balloon Co Ltd "National Theatre"	Telford	29. 5.90A
G-BRBV	Piper J/4A Cub Coupe (Cont A75)	4-1080	N27860 NC27860	13. 6.89	Janette Schonburg & Miriam Yeo	Exeter	18. 4.96P
G-BRBW	PA-28-140 Cherokee Cruiser	28-7425153	N40737	3. 7.89	R.W.Langley t/a Cherokee Cruiser Acft Grp	Shoreham	18.10.01
G-BRBX	PA-28-181 Cherokee Archer II	28-7690185	N8674E	20. 7.89	M.J.Ireland t/a Archer Air	Birmingham	7.12.98T
G-BRBY	Robinson R-22 Beta	1027		15. 6.89	BLS Avn Ltd	Blackbushe	13. 7.01T
G-BRCA	Jodel D.112 (Built Valladeau)	1203	F-BLIU	11. 7.89	R.C.Jordan	Turweston	10.11.99P
G-BRCD	Cessna A152 Aerobat	A152-0796	N7377L	8. 6.89	D.E.Simmons t/a Charlie Delta Group	Shoreham	12. 8.01
G-BRCE	Pitts S-1C Special (Lyc O-290)	1001	N4611G	22. 6.89	R.D.Rogers Hulcote Farm, Salford, Beds (Op Skylark Aerobatic Co)		25.11.97P
G-BRCF	Montgomerie-Bensen B.8MR (Rotax 532) PFA G/01A-1131			12. 6.89	J.S.Walton	Mold	30.10.91P
G-BRCG	Grob G-109	6077	N64BG	15. 6.89	Oxfordshire Sportflying Ltd	Enstone	11.11.01
G-BRCI	Pitts S-1C Special (Lyc O-320)	4668	N351S	6. 7.89	G.L.Carpenter	Sittles Farm, Alrewas	5. 1.01P
G-BRCJ	Cameron H-20 HAFB	2028		13. 6.89	P.de Cock	Waasmunster, Belgium	25. 7.99A
G-BRCM	Cessna 172L Skyhawk	172-59960	N3860Q	19. 6.89	S.G.E.Plessis & D.C.C.Handley Cranfield (Op Osprey F/C)		30. 5.99T
G-BRCO	Cameron H-20 HAFB	2030		19. 6.89	M.Davies "Shell Unleaded"	Callington, Cornwall	17. 6.97A
G-BRCT	Denney Kitfox Mk.2	396		23. 6.89	Wessex Avn & Transport Ltd (Frame stored 4.94)	Chalmington	
G-BRCV	Aeronca 7AC Champion (Cont A65)	7AC-282	N81661 NC81661	19. 9.89	J.M.Gale	Belle Vue, Yarnscombe	8.12.99P

Regn	Type	C/n	P/I	Date	Owner/operator	Probable Base	CA Expy
G-BRCW	Aeronca 11BC Chief (Cont C85)	11AC-366	N85964 NC85964	16.10.89	R.B.McComish	Bow, Totnes	26. 4.99P
G-BRDB	Zenair CH-701 STOL	PFA/187-11412		11. 7.89	D.L.Bowtell	(Ware)	
G-BRDC	Thunder Ax7-77 HAFB	1547		26. 6.89	P.J.Bish & C.Kunert t/a Zebedee Balloon Service "Purple Rising"	Hungerford	5. 5.96A
G-BRDD	Mudry CAP.10B	224		3. 8.88	R.D.Dickson	Coal Aston/Gamston	9. 9.00
G-BRDE	Thunder Ax7-77 HAFB	1538		22. 6.89	C.C.Brash "Veronica"	Maidenhead	24. 7.96A
G-BRDF	PA-28-161 Cherokee Warrior II	28-7716085	N1139Q	26. 6.89	White Waltham Airfield Ltd (Op West London Aero Svs)	White Waltham	27. 3.99T
G-BRDG	PA-28-161 Warrior II	28-7816047	N44934	26. 6.89	White Waltham Airfield Ltd (Op West London Aero Svs)	White Waltham	10.12.01T
G-BRDJ	Luscombe 8A Silvaire (Cont A65)	3411	N71984 NC71984	28. 6.89	J.D.Parker	(Bath)	20. 8.99P
G-BRDM	PA-28-161 Cherokee Warrior II	28-7716004	N8464F	26. 6.89	White Waltham Airfield Ltd (Op West London Aero Svs)	White Waltham	12.11.01T
G-BRDN	Socata MS.880B Rallye Club	1212	OY-DTV	14. 7.89	B.J.D.Peatfield	Redhill	31. 1.99
G-BRDO	Cessna 177B Cardinal II	177-02166	N35030	13. 7.89	P.G.Wood & A.J.Renham t/a Cardinal Grp	Teesside	21.12.01
G-BRDP	Colt Jumbo SS HAFB	1526		3. 7.89	Virgin Airship & Balloon Co Ltd	Florida, USA	3. 8.94A
G-BRDT	Cameron DP-70 Hot-Air Airship	2029		3. 7.89	M.M.Cobbold	Plymouth	11. 8.96A
G-BRDV	VS Spitfire Prototype replica (Jaguar V-12 350hp)	HD36/001 & PFA/130-10796		3. 7.89	Replica Spitfire Ltd (As "K5054" in RAF c/s) (Stored 4.96)	RAF Keevil	18.2.95P*
G-BRDW	PA-24-180 Comanche	24-1733	N6612P	12. 3.90	I.P.Gibson	Southampton	6.12.99
G-BREA	Bensen B.8MR (Rotax 503)	PFA G/01-1006		6. 7.89	T.J.Deane	Kemble	2. 6.99P
G-BREB	Piper J3C-65 Cub	7705	N41094 NC41094	3. 7.89	L.J.A.Cordes	(Northampton)	25. 2.98P
G-BREE	Whittaker MW.7 (Rotax 503)	PFA/171-11497		22. 6.89	G.Hawkins	Newton Peverill	29. 9.98P
G-BREH	Cameron V-65 HAFB	2049		7. 7.89	S.E. & V.D.Hurst "Promise"	Mansfield	28. 3.99A
G-BREL	Cameron O-77 HAFB	386		5. 4.78	R.A.Patey "Gabrielle/Big Six"	London N11	9. 3.93A
G-BREM	Air Command 532 Elite	0614 & PFA G/04-1139		20. 7.89	T.W.Freeman (Stored 7.91)	Fowlmere	25. 3.91P
G-BREP	PA-28RT-201 Arrow IV	28R-7918119	N2230Z	19. 6.90	TDR Aviation Ltd	Enniskillen	22. 1.00
G-BRER	Aeronca 7AC Champion (Cont A65)	7AC-6758	N3157E NC3157E	12. 7.89	B. & S.Meadley	Watchford Farm, Yarcombe	16. 7.99P
G-BREU	Montgomerie-Bensen B.8 (Rotax 582)	PFA G/01A-1137		20. 7.89	M.A.Hayward	(Liskeard)	16. 6.99P
G-BREX	Cameron O-84 HAFB	2019		14. 7.89	Ovolo Ltd	Belfast	2. 8.90A
G-BREY	Taylorcraft BC-12D	7299	N43640 NC43640	14. 7.89	R.J.Pitts t/a BREY Grp	Leicester	25. 3.99P
G-BRFA	PA-31-350 Navajo Chieftain	31-7852154	G-BREW N27729	30. 6.89	Comed Avn Ltd	Blackpool	16. 7.99T
G-BRFB	Rutan LongEz (Lyc O-290)	PFA/74A-10646		14. 7.89	R.A.Gardiner	Cumbernauld	13. 6.99P
G-BRFC	Hunting P.57 Sea Prince T.1	P57/71	WP321	10. 9.80	Aces High Ltd (As "WP321/CU-750" in RN c/s; stored 5.97)	North Weald	9.12.93PF
G-BRFE	Cameron V-77 HAFB	1835		20. 7.89	D.L.C.Nelmes t/a Esmerelda Balloon Syndicate "Esmerelda"	Bristol	3. 8.97A
G-BRFF	Colt 90A HAFB	1548		14. 7.89	M.I. & B.P.Sneap t/a Amber Valley Avn "Zycomm"	Ripley, Derbyshire	17. 7.97A
G-BRFH	Colt 90A HAFB	1543		14. 7.89	Polydron International Ltd "Polydron"	Kemble	14. 3.97A
G-BRFI	Aeronca 7DC Champion (Cont C85)	7AC-4609	N1058E NC1058E	1. 8.89	I.J.Boyd & D.J.McCooke (Damaged 1990; on rebuild 4.96)	Coleraine, Londonderry	19. 2.91P
G-BRFJ	Aeronca 11AC Chief (Cont A65)	11AC-796	N9163E NC9163E	28. 7.89	C.M.G.Ellis	Cowbit, Fenland	24. 6.99P
G-BRFL	PA-38-112 Tomahawk	38-79A0431	N2416F	17. 8.89	Teesside Flight Centre Ltd	Teesside	13. 8.99T
G-BRFM	PA-28-161 Warrior II	28-7916279	N2234P	17.10.89	Air Caernarfon Ltd	Caernarfon	15. 2.01T
G-BRFN	PA-38-112 Tomahawk	38-79A0397	N2326F	23.10.89	Light Aircraft Leasing (UK) Ltd	Norwich	6.11.00T
G-BRFO	Cameron V-77 HAFB	2025		6. 7.89	N.J.Bland t/a Hedgehoppers Balloon Grp "Lurcher"	Oxford	25. 7.99A
G-BRFP	Schweizer Hughes 269C	S.1389		14. 7.89	Heli Hopper Ltd	Yeovil	13. 9.98T
G-BRFR*	Cameron N-105 HAFB	2042		14. 7.89	I M Martin "Rover" (Balloon Preservation Group 7.98)	Lancing	6.12.93A
G-BRFS*	Cameron N-90 HAFB	2041		14. 7.89	Flying Pictures Ltd "Jaguar" (Cancelled as wfu 20.1.99)	Fairoaks	21.11.96A
G-BRFW	Montgomerie-Bensen B.8 Two-Seat (Rotax 582)	PFA G/01-1073		20. 7.89	J.M.Montgomerie	Crosshills, Maybole	7.10.98P
G-BRFX	Pazmany PL-4A (VW1700)	PFA/17-10079		14. 7.89	D.E.Hills	(Ipswich)	
G-BRGD	Cameron O-84 HAFB	2043		20. 7.89	J.R.H. & M.A.Ashworth	Newquay	
G-BRGE	Cameron N-90 HAFB	2047		20. 7.89	Oakfield Farm Products Ltd "Oakfield Farm Products"	Broadway, Worcester	15.12.99A

Regn	Type	C/n	P/I	Date	Owner/operator	Probable Base	CA Expy
G-BRGF	Luscombe 8E Silvaire (Cont C85)	5475	N23FP N944BL/N2748K/NC2748K	20. 7.89	N.Surman t/a Luscombe F/Grp	RAF Henlow	26. 6.99P
G-BRGG	Luscombe 8A Silvaire (Cont A65)	3795	N1068K NC1068K	20. 7.89	M.P. & V.H.Weatherby	Elstree	11. 8.99P
G-BRGI	PA-28-180 Cherokee E	28-5827	N77VG NllVG	24. 7.89	Golf India Avn Ltd	Redhill	16. 2.99
G-BRGN	BAe Jetstream 3102	637	G-BLHC G-31-637	20. 3.87	British Aerospace (Operations) Ltd	Warton	16. 5.01
G-BRGO*	Air Command 532 Elite	0615 & PFA G/04-1149		7. 8.89	D.A.Wood (Cancelled by CAA 10.3.99)	Milton Keynes	13. 2.91P
G-BRGP*	Colt Flying Stork SS HAFB	1409		25. 7.89	Not known "Great Eggspectations" (USA)		N/E(A)
G-BRGT	PA-32-260 Cherokee Six	32-658	N3744W	7.11.89	P.Cowley	East Midlands	28. 6.99
G-BRGW	Barritault JB-01 Minicab (Cont O-200-A)	PFA/1823		13.11.78	R.G.White	Hildon-le-Noble, Hants	18. 6.99P
G-BRGX	Rotorway Exec 152 (RW152D)	3597		3. 8.89	D.W.J.Lee	South Burlingham, Norwich	25. 5.99P
G-BRHA	PA-32RT-300 Lance II	32R-7985076	N2093P	27. 7.89	D.J.Chatterton & P.MacKinnon t/a Lance G-BRHA Grp	Southend	8.11.01
G-BRHB	Boeing-Stearman B75N1 (N2S-3) Kaydet	75-6508	EC-AID N67955/Bu.05334	10. 8.89	D.Calabritto	(Billericay)	AC
G-BRHC	Cameron V-77 HAFB	1842		3. 8.89	Golf Centres Balloons Ltd "Green Dragon"	Gargonza, Italy	30. 8.94T
G-BRHG	Colt 90A HAFB	1568		11. 9.89	Bath University Students Union "Badgerline"	Bath	14. 8.99A
G-BRHL	Montgomerie-Bensen B.8MR (Rotax 503)	PFA G/01A-1123		7. 8.89	A.McCredie	Carlisle	21. 6.99P
G-BRHM	Bensen B.8M	PFA G/01-1144		3. 8.89	H.P.Latham	Stockbridge	
G-BRHN	Robinson R-22 Beta	1093		4. 8.89	Plane Talking Ltd	Elstree	21. 5.01T
G-BRHO	PA-34-200 Seneca	34-7350037	N15222	20. 9.89	D.A.Lewis	Luton	30. 7.01
G-BRHP	Aeronca O-58B Defender (Cont A65)	058B-8533	N58JR N46536/43-1923	2. 8.89	J.G.Townsend (As "3-1923" in US Army c/s)		
	(If US Army serial is correct, type should be L-3C-AE)					Thruxton/Draycott Farm, Chiseldon	4. 1.99P
G-BRHR	PA-38-112 Tomahawk	38-79A0969	N2377P	21. 8.89	Air Nova plc	Liverpool	27. 9.01T
G-BRHT	PA-38-112 Tomahawk	38-79A0199	N2474C	4. 8.89	Air Nova plc	Liverpool	9. 8.01T
G-BRHU	Montgomerie-Bensen B.8MR (Rotax 532)	PFA G/01A-1133		4. 8.89	G.L. & S.R.Moon	Camberley	10. 1.92P
G-BRHW	DH.82A Tiger Moth	85612	7Q-YMY VP-YMY/ZS-DLB/SAAF 4606/DE671	26. 7.89	P.J. & A.J.Borsberry (On rebuild)	Kidmore End, Reading	
G-BRHX	Luscombe 8E Silvaire (Cont C90)	5114	N176M N2387K/NC2387K	8. 8.89	J.Lakin	Eaglescott	19. 3.99P
G-BRHY	Luscombe 8E Silvaire (Cont C85)	5138	N2411K NC2411K	8. 8.89	D.Lofts & A.R.W.Taylor	Sleap	6. 4.99P
G-BRHZ	Stephens Akro Z (Lyc IO-360) (Aka Astro 235)	A-235	N35EJ	20.12.89	T.A.Shears	White Waltham	16. 4.98P
G-BRIA	Cessna 310L	310L-0010	N2210F	4. 8.89	B.J.Tucker & R.C.Pugsley	(Blackwood)	15.10.01T
G-BRIB	Cameron N-77 HAFB	2065		8. 8.89	D.Stitt "American Adventures"	Tunbridge Wells	14. 7.96A
G-BRID*	Cessna U206A Super Skywagon	U206-0574	N4874F	7. 5.87	British Skysports (Used as para-trainer 1.96)	Grindale	20. 5.93
G-BRIF	Boeing 767-204ER	24736	(PH-AHM) G-BRIF	10. 3.90	Britannia Airways Ltd "Lord Horatio Nelson"	Luton	18.11.99T
G-BRIG	Boeing 767-204ER	24757	(PH-AHN) G-BRIG	10. 4.90	Britannia Airways Ltd "Eglantyne Jebb"	Luton	17. 4.00T
G-BRIH	Taylorcraft BC-12D (Cont A75)	7421	N43762 NC43762	24. 8.89	A.D.Duke	(Lichfield)	1. 6.99P
G-BRII	Zenair CH-600 Zodiac	PFA/162-11392		18. 8.89	A.C.Bowdrey	(Hemel Hempstead)	
G-BRIJ	Taylorcraft F-19	F-119	N3863T	23. 8.89	K.E.Ballington	Yeatsall Farm, Abbots Bromley	31. 8.99P
G-BRIK	Nipper T.66S RA45 Srs.3B (VW1834) (Rebuild of G-AVKH c/n 27)	PFA/25-10174		26. 4.77	C.W.R.Piper	Hinton-in-the-Hedges	14. 6.99P
G-BRIL	Piper J/5A Cub Cruiser (Cont A75)	5-572	N35183 NC35183	2. 8.89	P.L.Jobes	Peterlee	13.11.99P
G-BRIM	Cameron O-160 HAFB	1856		10. 8.89	Golf Centres Balloons Ltd	Bridport	11. 8.93T
G-BRIO	Turner Super T-40A (Cont O-200-A) (Regd incorrectly as PFA/104-10736)	PFA/104-10636		7. 8.89	D.McIntyre	Dundee	9. 8.98P
G-BRIR	Cameron V-56 HAFB	2056		17. 8.89	H.G.Davies & C.Dowd "Spirit of Century" (Skyviews Windows c/s)	Cheltenham	6. 9.97A
G-BRIS	Steen Skybolt (Lyc IO-360)	01	N870MC	30. 8.89	P.D.Harrison	Netherthorpe	31. 3.00P
G-BRIV	Socata TB-9 Tampico Club	939		24. 8.89	Gowad Aviation Ltd	(Tadley)	10. 2.00T
G-BRIY	Taylorcraft DF-65 (Cont A65) (Built as TG-6 glider)	6183	N59687 NC59687/42-58678	1. 2.90	J.D.Tseliki (As "42-58678/IY" in L-2A USAAC c/s)	(Brighton)	10. 7.98P
G-BRIZ*	Druine D.31 Turbulent	PFA/48-11513		8. 8.89	M.C.Hunt (Cancelled by CAA 2.3.99; no Permit issued)	(Farnborough)	
G-BRJA	Luscombe 8A Silvaire (Cont A65)	3744	N1017K NC1017K	12. 9.89	A.D.Keen	(Totnes)	14. 1.99P

Regn	Type	C/n	P/I	Date	Owner/operator	Probable Base	CA Expy
G-BRJB	Zenair CH-600 Zodiac	6-1283		2. 8.89	D.Collinson (Incomplete 7.95)	(Durham)	
G-BRJC	Cessna 120 (Cont C85)	12077	N1833N NC1833N	21. 8.89	C.J.Elliott & D.J.Wheeler t/a One Twenty Grp	Nottingham	8. 3.99P
G-BRJK	Luscombe 8A Silvaire (Cont A65)	4205	N1478K NC1478K	21. 8.89	C.J.L.Peat & M.Richardson	Redhill	1. 4.98P
G-BRJL	PA-15 Vagabond (Cont C85)	15-157	N4370H NC4370H	21. 8.89	C.P.Ware & C.R.Leech Garston Farm, Marshfield		25. 6.99P
G-BRJM	Cameron A-210 HAFB	2081		17. 8.89	T.M.Donnelly	Doncaster	11. 8.95T
G-BRJN	Pitts S-1C Special (Lyc O-320)	1-MA	N6A	23. 8.89	W.Chapel	(Halifax)	5. 8.97P
G-BRJR	PA-38-112 Tomahawk	38-79A0144	N2598B	31. 8.89	Chester Avn Ltd	Chester	31. 3.99T
G-BRJT	Cessna 150H	150-68426	N44SS N22649	31. 8.89	J.Eagles	Compton Abbas	2. 8.01T
G-BRJV	PA-28-161 Cadet	2841167	N9185G	24. 8.89	Newcastle upon Tyne A/C Ltd (Damaged at Kirkbride 17.5.98)	Newcastle	4.12.01T
G-BRJW	Bellanca 7GCBC Citabria 150S	1200-80	OO-LPG	7. 4.82	F.A.L.Castleden & A.J.Sillis	Henstridge	4. 8.00
G-BRJX	Rand Robinson KR-2 (Revmaster 2100D)	PFA/129-11386		22. 8.89	D.H.Evans	Cardiff	15. 4.97P
G-BRJY	Rand Robinson KR-2 (Revmaster 2100D)	PFA/129-11308		22. 8.89	R.E.Taylor	Inverness	23. 5.96P
G-BRKA	Luscombe 8F Silvaire (Cont C90)	5084	N2357K NC2357K	13. 3.89	H.Savage-Jones	(Cheltenham)	1. 8.99P
G-BRKC	Auster 5 J/1 Autocrat	2749	F-BFYT	31. 8.89	J.W.Conlon (On rebuild 5.97) High Easter		
G-BRKD	Piaggio P.149D	306	D-EAMS 92+10/AC+457/AS+457	15. 9.89	P.E.H.Scott	(Stockbridge)	5.11.92
G-BRKH	PA-28-236 Dakota	28-7911003	N21444	30. 8.89	P.A.Wright & P.W.Lever	Newcastle	28.12.01
G-BRKL	Cameron H-34 HAFB	2075		29. 8.89	B.J.Newman	Rushden, Northampton	17. 2.99A
G-BRKN	Robinson R-22 Mariner	0578M	N2454M	5. 9.89	P.M.Webber	Koropi Heliport, Greece	9. 6.99
G-BRKO	Oldfield Baby Lakes	1	N8GL	18. 1.90	C.Wren	Stapleford	
G-BRKP*	Colt 31A HAFB	1590		30. 8.89	Bavarian Balloon Co Ltd (Cancelled as PWFU 22.3.99)	(Germany)	
G-BRKR	Cessna 182R Skylane II	182-68468	N9896E	2. 6.89	A.R.D.Brooker Springfield Farm, Ettington		27. 1.02
G-BRKS*	Air Command 532 Elite	GS-01 & PFA G/04-1146		1. 9.89	G.Sandercock (Cancelled by CAA 10.3.99)	Reigate	11. 3.91P
G-BRKW	Cameron V-77 HAFB	2093		1. 9.89	T.J.Parker	Burnham-on-Crouch	3.11.98
G-BRKX	Air Command 532 Elite (Rotax 532)	0619 & PFA G/04-1150		8. 9.89	K.Davis	Alfreton, Derbyshire	10.12.90P
G-BRKY	Viking Dragonfly mk II (VW 2180)	PFA/139-11117		7. 9.89	G.D.Price (Stored 3.97)	Deanland,.Hailsham	8. 6.94P
G-BRLB	Air Command 532 Elite	0622		4. 9.89	F.G.Shepherd	Great Orton	
G-BRLD*	Robinson R-22 Beta	1099		4. 9.89	R.Everett (Damaged Rayleigh 28.3.93; stored 12.95 - pod at Redhill 12.96)	Sproughton, Ipswich	25.10.95
G-BRLF	Campbell Cricket (Rotax 503)	PFA G/03-1077		6. 9.89	D.Wood	Holbeach	22. 5.97P
G-BRLG	PA-28RT-201T Turbo Arrow IV	28R-8431027	N4379P N9600N	12. 9.89	C.G.Westwood	Halfpenny Green	11. 1.02
G-BRLH*	Air Command 532 Elite	0623 & PFA G/04-1148		12. 9.89	Childs Garages (Sherborne) Ltd (Stored 4.96) (Cancelled by CAA 26.1.99)	Henstridge	28.12.90P
G-BRLI	Piper J/5A Cub Cruiser (Lyc O-290)	5-822	N35951 NC35951	23. 8.89	Little Bear Ltd	Exeter	8. 6.99P
G-BRLK*	Air Command 532 Elite	0618 & PFA G/04-1155		7. 9.89	G.L.Hunt (Used for spares 1998; cancelled by CAA 10.3.99)	Ripley, Derbyshire	1. 1.91P
G-BRLL	Cameron A-105 HAFB	2032		7. 9.89	Adventure Flights Ltd "Chris Evan Ltd"	London W7	23.10.99T
G-BRLO	PA-38-112 Tomahawk	38-78A0621	N2397K N9680N	26.10.89	Scotia Safari Ltd	Carlisle	1. 7.99T
G-BRLP	PA-38-112 Tomahawk	38-78A0011	N9301T	4.10.89	D.A.Whitmore	(Aylesbury)	19. 3.01T
G-BRLR	Cessna 150G	150-64822	N4772X	4.10.89	D.C.Maxwell	Morgansfield, Fishburn	17. 5.98
G-BRLS	Thunder Ax7-77 HAFB	1603		29. 9.89	Elizabeth C.Meek	Oswestry	15. 7.99A
G-BRLT	Colt 77A HAFB	1588		12. 9.89	D.Bareford "Pro-Sport"	Kidderminster	3. 5.99A
G-BRLU	Cameron H-24 HAFB	2082		8. 9.89	Not known (Temp unregd 21.5.97)	Bedford	10. 1.97A
G-BRLV	CCF Harvard 4	CCF4-194	N90448 RCAF 20403	14. 9.89	B.C.Abela (Op Bar-Belle Avn) North Weald (As "93542/LTA-542" in 6148th TCS USAF c/s) "Texan Belle"		26. 7.99P
G-BRLX	Cameron N-77 HAFB	2095		13. 9.89	National Power plc "National Power"	Swindon	1. 6.96A
G-BRLY	BAe ATP	2025	TC-THP G-BRLY	22. 9.89	British Regional Airlines Ltd Ronaldsway		29.10.99T
G-BRMA*	Westland WS-51 Dragonfly HR.5	WA/H/50	WG719	15. 6.78	E.D. Ap Rees t/a The Helicopter Museum (As "WG719/705")	Weston-super-Mare	
G-BRMB*	Bristol 192 Belvedere HC.1	13347	7997M XG452	15. 6.78	E.D. Ap Rees t/a The Helicopter Museum (As "XG452")	Weston-super-Mare	
G-BRME	PA-28-181 Cherokee Archer II	28-7790105	OY-BTA	14. 9.89	S.Edgar (Op Woodgate Executive Air Services) (SERE Motors titles)	Aldergrove	3. 4.99T
G-BRMG	VS.384 Seafire F.XVII	FLWA.25488	A2055 SX336	19. 9.89	P.J.Woods (On rebuild 3.96)	Twyford, Bucks	AC
G-BRMI	Cameron V-65 HAFB	2104		14. 9.89	M.Davies "Sapphire"	Callington, Cornwall	17. 6.97A

Regn	Type	C/n	P/I	Date	Owner/operator	Probable Base	CA Expy
G-BRMJ	PA-38-112 Tomahawk	38-79A0784	N2316N	15. 9.89	Aerohire Ltd Wellesbourne Mountford (Op Wellesbourne Avn)		25. 4.96T
G-BRML	PA-38-112 Tomahawk	38-79A1017	N2510P	3.10.89	P.H.Rogers	Manchester	22. 2.99T
G-BRMM	Air Command 532 Elite	0624 & PFA G/04-1159		15. 9.89	R. de Serville	(London SW7)	
G-BRMS	PA-28RT-201 Arrow IV	28R-8118004	N82708	25. 9.89	Fleetbridge Ltd	White Waltham	27. 3.99
G-BRMT	Cameron V-31 Air Chair HAFB	2038		31. 8.89	T.C.Hinton	Tunbridge Wells	
G-BRMU	Cameron V-77 HAFB	2109		19. 9.89	K.J. & G.R Ibbotson	Gloucester	
G-BRMV	Cameron O-77 HAFB	2103		25. 9.89	P.D.Griffiths "Viscount"	Southampton	22. 5.99A
G-BRMW	Whittaker MW.7 (Rotax 532)	PFA/171-11395		25. 9.89	N.Crisp Sittles Farm, Alrewas		8. 7.99P
G-BRNC	Cessna 150M Commuter	150-78833	N704SG	29. 9.89	D.C.Bonsall	Netherthorpe	18. 7.99T
G-BRND	Cessna 152 II	152-83776	N5148B	7.11.89	T.M. & M.L.Jones (Op Derby Aero Club)	Egginton	15. 2.99T
G-BRNE	Cessna 152 II	152-84248	N5082L	4.10.89	Aerohire Ltd	Exeter	21. 2.99T
G-BRNJ	PA-38-112 Tomahawk	38-79A0415	N2395F	22. 9.89	Aerohire Ltd Wellesbourne Mountford		28. 8.99T
G-BRNK	Cessna 152 II	152-80479	N24969	22. 9.89	Sheffield A/C Ltd	Netherthorpe	1. 2.99T
G-BRNM	Chichester-Miles Leopard	002		17.10.89	Chichester-Miles Consultants Ltd	Cranfield	AC
G-BRNN	Cessna 152 II	152-84735	N6452M	22. 9.89	Sheffield A/C Ltd	Netherthorpe	23.12.01T
G-BRNP	Rotorway Exec 152	3578		22. 9.89	C.A.Laycock	Oxenhope	AC
G-BRNT	Robin DR.400/180 Regent	1935		3.10.89	M.J.Cowham	Little Gransden	20.12.01
G-BRNU	Robin DR.400/180 Regent	1937		31.10.89	November Uniform Travel Syndicate Ltd	White Waltham	2. 5.99
G-BRNV	PA-28-181 Cherokee Archer II	28-7790402	N2537Q	7.12.89	B.S.Hobbs	Fairoaks	10. 3.99
G-BRNW	Cameron V-77 HAFB	2138		2.10.89	N.Robertson & G.Smith "Mr Blue Sky"	Truro/Bristol	5. 8.99A
G-BRNX	PA-22-150 Tri-Pacer	22-2945	N2610P	3.10.89	R.S.Tomlinson & B.Yager	Elstree	19.12.99
G-BRNZ	PA-32-300 Cherokee Six B	32-40594	N4229R	7. 2.90	IML Avn Ltd	Cranfield	4. 6.99T
G-BROB	Cameron V-77 HAFB	2073		29. 8.89	R.W.Richardson	Cardiff	20. 3.98A
G-BROE	Cameron N-65 HAFB	2098		5.10.89	R.H.Sanderson "Lancia Dedra"	Nuneaton	3. 8.97A
G-BROF	Air Command 532 Elite	0625 & PFA G/04-1154		5.10.89	M.J.Hoskins (Sold in Spain 1994 ?)	Banbury	
G-BROG	Cameron V-65 HAFB	2121		6. 9.89	R.Kunert "The Dodger"	Wokingham	29. 8.99A
G-BROH	Cameron O-90 HAFB	2120		6.10.89	Patricia A.Wenlock Stretton, Staffs "Linde"		1. 8.99T
G-BROI	CFM Streak Shadow K.115-SA & PFA/161-11586 (Rotax 532)			16.11.89	G.W.Rowbotham	Wymeswold	8. 8.97P
G-BROJ	Colt 31A HAFB	1468		6.10.89	Virgin Airship & Balloon Co Ltd Telford "Fly Virgin"		23. 9.92A
G-BROL	Colt AS-80 Mk.II Hot-Air Airship	1578		6.10.89	G.Gratius Stretten, Germany "Hansa-Dental"		1. 4.99A
G-BROM*	ICA IS-28M2A	04A		5.12.77	Not known Cuatro Vientos, Spain (Open storage/derelict 4.95)		18. 8.87
G-BROO	Luscombe 8F Silvaire 90 (Cont C90)	6154	N75297 HI-20 N1527B/NC1527B	28. 9.89	S.R.Greasley & J.G.Parish t/a Bedwell Hey F/Grp Bedwell Hey Farm, Little Thetford, Ely		6. 7.99P
G-BROP	Van's RV-4 (Lyc O-360)	3	N19AT	25.10.89	K.E.Armstrong Armshold Farm, Kingston, Cambs		15. 7.99P
G-BROR	Piper J3C-65 Cub (L-4H-PI)	10885	F-BHMQ 43-29594	7.12.89	J.H.Bailey & A.P.J.Wiseman Sturgate t/a White Hart F/Grp		16. 6.98P
G-BROX	Robinson R-22 Beta	1127	N8061V	13.10.89	Defence Products Ltd	Blackbushe	9.11.01T
G-BROY	Cameron O-90 HAFB	2173		6. 9.89	T.G.S.Dixon "Oscar"	Bromsgrove	25. 1.99A
G-BROZ	PA-18-150 Super Cub	18-6754	HB-ORC N9572D	20. 9.89	P.G.Kynsey Rushett Farm, Chessington		19.10.98T
G-BRPE	Cessna 120 (Cont C85)	13326	N3068N NC3068N	11.10.89	J.M.Fowler	Nottingham	21. 6.99P
G-BRPF	Cessna 120 (Cont C85)	9902	N72723 NC72723	11.10.89	D.Sharp	Breighton	9. 6.99P
G-BRPG	Cessna 120 (Cont C85)	9882	N72703 NC72703	11.10.89	I.C.Lomax	Ottringham	29. 8.94P
G-BRPH	Cessna 120 (Cont C85)	12137	N1893N NC1893N	11.10.89	J.A.Cook Pent Farm, Postling, Kent		29. 6.99P
G-BRPJ	Cameron N-90 HAFB	2071		11. 9.89	Paul Johnson Consett t/a Cloud Nine Balloon Co "Presto"		10. 3.99T
G-BRPK	PA-28-140 Cherokee Cruiser	28-7325070	N15449	17.11.89	J.P.A.Gomes Cascais, Portugal		17. 6.99
G-BRPL	PA-28-140 Cherokee Cruiser	28-7325160	N15771	13.10.89	Comed Avn Ltd	Blackpool	2. 5.99T
G-BRPM	Nipper T.66 Srs.3B	PFA/25-11038		4. 3.85	T.C.Horner (Under construction 1995)	(Glasgow)	
G-BRPO	Enstrom 280C Shark	1092	N636H	13.10.89	K.Payne Gamlingay & Ampy Automation Digilog Ltd		4. 3.99
G-BRPP*	Brookland Hornet (mod) (VW1776)	DC-1		16.10.89	D.E.Cox (Cancelled by CAA 10.3.99)	St.Merryn	19. 8.93P
G-BRPR	Aeronca L-3C Defender (Cont A65)	058B-8823	N49880 43-1952	17.10.89	C.S.Tolchard Earls Colne (As "31952" in US Army c/s)		14. 9.98P

Regn	Type	C/n	P/I	Date	Owner/operator	Probable Base	CA Expy
G-BRPS	Cessna 177B Cardinal	177-02101	N34935	23.10.89	R.C.Tebbett	(Tenbury Wells)	12. 1.02
G-BRPT	Rans S-10 Sakota	PFA/194-11554		18.10.89	B.G.Morris	Dunkeswell	18. 8.98P
	(Rotax 532)						
G-BRPU	Beechcraft 76 Duchess	ME-140	N6007Z	17.10.89	Air Nova plc	Liverpool	4.10.01T
G-BRPV	Cessna 152 II	152-85228	N6311Q	6.11.89	GEM Rewinds Ltd	Coventry	7. 2.99T
G-BRPX	Taylorcraft BC-12D	6462	N39208	12.12.89	M.J.Brett	Little Gransden	27. 7.98P
	(Cont A65)		NC39208				
G-BRPY	PA-15 Vagabond	15-141	N4356H	23.10.89	Joanne P.Esson	Fareham	18. 5.99P
	(Cont C85)		NC4356H				
G-BRPZ	Luscombe 8A Silvaire	911	N22089	13.12.89	S.L. & J.P.Waring		5. 5.99P
	(Cont A65)		NC22089			Shacklewell Lodge, Empingham	
G-BRRA	VS.361 Spitfire LF.Xc	CBAF.IX.1875		10.10.89	Historic Flying Ltd	Audley End	
	(Regd with c/n CBAF.8185)		R.Belg AF SM-29		(On rebuild 7.97)		
			R.Neth AF H-59/H-119/Fokker B-1/MK912				
G-BRRB	Luscombe 8E Silvaire	2611	N71184	23.10.89	C.G.Ferguson & D.W.Gladwin	RAF Newton	14. 5.99P
	(Cont C85)		NC71184				
G-BRRD	Scheibe SF-25B Falke	4811	D-KBAT	30.10.89	M.N.Martin	Highfield Farm, Empingham	12. 1.01
G-BRRF	Cameron O-77 HAFB	2101		24.10.89	D.G.Body	Leighton Buzzard	14. 3.97T
					t/a Mid-Bucks Farmers Balloon Grp "Daisy Chain"		
G-BRRG	Glaser-Dirks DG-500M	5E7-M5		7.11.89	D.C.Chaplin "492"	Sutton Bank	6.10.00
					t/a Glider Syndicate		
G-BRRJ	PA-28RT-201T Turbo Arrow IV		N4353T	27.11.89	M.Stower	Booker	10. 4.99
		28R-8431021					
G-BRRK	Cessna 182Q Skylane II	182-66160	N759PW	30.10.89	M.G.Mitchell	Great Bentley, Ipswich	7. 5.99
G-BRRL	PA-18-95 Super Cub	18-2050	D-EMKE	17. 9.90	A.J.White	Redhill	
	(L-18C-PI)		R Neth AF R-44/52-2450		t/a Acebell G-BRRL Syndicate		
	(Believed to comprise Frame No.18-1602/G-AYPO [18-1615])				(On rebuild Whitehall Farm,Benington 4.93)		
G-BRRM	PA-28-161 Cadet	2841260	N9194B	25.10.89	R.H.Sellier	Biggin Hill	7.12.01T
G-BRRN	PA-28-161 Warrior II	28-8216043	N84533	30.10.89	Spinseal Ltd	Cranfield	22. 1.02T
G-BRRO	Cameron N-77 HAFB	2142		30.10.89	P.W.Limpus & I.J.Liddiard	Newbury	13. 3.99A
					"Newbury Building Society II"		
G-BRRR	Cameron V-77 HAFB	2070		13.10.89	L.M.Heal & A.P.Wilcox	Chippenham	17. 8.99A
					"Breezy"		
G-BRRS	Pitts S-1S Special	TM-1	N18TM	1.11.89	R.C.Atkinson Ranksborough Farm, Langham		25. 6.93P
	(Lyc O-360)				(Stored 5.95)		
G-BRRU	Colt 90A HAFB	1591		1.11.89	Reach For The Sky Ltd	Guildford	6. 8.99T
G-BRRW	Cameron O-77 HAFB	2125		7.11.89	D.V.Fowler "Mobiloon"	Cranbrook	7. 6.97T
G-BRRY	Robinson R-22 Beta	1193		14.11.89	Bristow Helicopters Ltd	Redhill	11.12.01T
G-BRSA	Cameron N-56 HAFB	2113		8.11.89	C.Wilkinson	Newcastle	17.10.92A
G-BRSC	Rans S-10 Sakota	0589-051		8.11.89	M.A.C.Stephenson	Blackpool	12. 8.97P
	(Rotax 532)						
G-BRSD	Cameron V-77 HAFB	2174		8.11.89	T.J.Porter & J.E.Kelly	Belper, Derby	3. 2.94A
G-BRSE	PA-28-161 Warrior II	28-8016276	N8163R	5.12.89	Startown Ltd	Edinburgh	14.12.98T
					(Op Edinburgh Flying Club)		
G-BRSF*	VS.361 Spitfire HF.IXc		SAAF 5632	22.11.89	J.Peace	Lancing	
		-	RR232		(As "RR232") (Stored 3.96)		
	(Composite including tail/parts from Mk.VIII JF629 ex W.Australia and wings from Mk.XIV						
	ex R.Thai AF U14-6/93/RAF RM873)						
G-BRSG	PA-28-161 Cadet	2841285	N92011	23.11.89	J.Appleton	Denham	4. 1.02T
					t/a Holmes Rentals (Op Cabair)		
G-BRSH	CASA I-131E Jungmann	2156	E3B-540	29.11.89	L.Ness	(Nannestad, Norway)	8. 3.99P
	(Spanish AF serial conflicts with F-AZGG)				(As "781-25" in Spanish AF c/s)		
G-BRSJ	PA-38-112 Tomahawk II	38-81A0044	N25664	29.12.89	APB Leasing Ltd	Welshpool	25. 3.99T
G-BRSK	Boeing-Stearman B75N1	75-1180	N5565N	15.11.89	C.R.Lawrence Priory Farm,	Tibenham	20. 1.97
	(N2S-3) Kaydet (Cont W670)		Bu.3403		t/a Wymondham Engineering (Stored 8.97)		
					(As "1180" in US Navy c/s)		
G-BRSL	Cameron N-56 HAFB	468		21.12.78	S.H.Budd "Boris"	Pewsey	28. 5.87A
G-BRSN	Rand Robinson KR-2	PFA/129-11178		10.11.89	K.W.Darby	(Teignmouth)	
	(VW1834)						
G-BRSO	CFM Streak Shadow			16.11.89	D.J.Smith	Old Sarum	23. 8.99P
	(Rotax 532) K.133-SA & PFA/161A-11601						
G-BRSP	Air Command 532 Elite			13.11.89	G.M. Hobman	(York)	11. 1.92P
	0626 & PFA G/04-1158						
G-BRSW	Luscombe 8AC Silvaire	3249	N71822	15.11.89	P.J.Allitt & M.A.Harris	Fenland	25. 6.99P
	(Cont A75)		NC71822		t/a Bloody Mary Aviation "Bloody Mary"		
G-BRSX	PA-15 Vagabond	15-117	N4334H	27.10.89	C.Milne-Fowler Craysmarsh Farm, Melksham		5. 5.99P
	(Cont A65)		NC4334H				
G-BRSY	Hatz CB-1	6	N2257J	15.11.89	J.P.Barrett	Breighton	10. 7.98P
	(Lyc O-290-D)				t/a G.A.Barrett & Son		
G-BRTA	PA-38-112 Tomahawk	38-79A0047	N2407B	27.11.89	Cardiff-Wales Flying Club Ltd	Cardiff	5. 6.00T
G-BRTD	Cessna 152 II	152-80023	N757UW	11. 1.90	T.G.Phillips, C.Greenland	Popham	9. 7.99
					& J.Page t/a 152 Grp		
G-BRTH	Cameron A-180 HAFB	2016		21.11.89	The Ballooning Business Ltd	Northampton	15. 5.99T
	(Replacement envelope c/n 3199 fitted 1994)				"Burning Ambition II"		
G-BRTI	Robinson R-22 Beta	1130	EI-CDW	23. 2.90	A.J.& P.D.Morgan t/a Morhire	(Usk)	25. 3.00T
			(EI-CFJ)/G-BRTI/N8044U				

Regn	Type	C/n	P/I	Date	Owner/operator	Probable Base	CA Expy
G-BRTJ	Cessna 150F	150-61749	N8149S	22.11.89	Avon Aviation Ltd Bristol/Lulsgate		16. 1.00T
G-BRTK	Boeing-Stearman E75	75-5949	N16716	29.11.89	Eastern Stearman Ltd Swanton Morley		24. 4.93
	(PT-13D) Kaydet (Cont W670)		42-17786/Bu.38728		(As "FJ777" in RCAF c/s)		
G-BRTL	MDH Hughes 369E	0356E	(F-GHLF)	5. 1.90	Crewhall Ltd	Leatherhead	11. 2.99
G-BRTM	PA-28-161 Warrior II	28-8416083	N4334L	12.12.89	Oxford Aviation Services Ltd	Oxford	31. 1.99T
G-BRTN	Beechcraft 58 Baron	TH-1400	N58VF N6763U	29.11.89	Colneway Ltd	Guernsey	28. 1.02
G-BRTP	Cessna 152 II	152-81275	N49448	28.11.89	M.R.Shelton	Tatenhill	6. 3.99T
					t/a Tatenhill Aviation		
G-BRTT	Schweizer Hughes 269C	S.1411		29.11.89	Technical Exponents Ltd	Denham	25. 4.99T
G-BRTV	Cameron O-77 HAFB	2182		1.12.89	Carole Vening	Littlehampton	11. 6.97A
					"Solitaire II"		
G-BRTW	Glaser-Dirks DG-400	4-259		22.12.89	I.J.Carruthers	Great Orton	4. 2.02
G-BRTX	PA-28-151 Cherokee Warrior		N8307C	27.12.89	J.Phelan & D.G.Scott	Aldergrove	9. 4.01T
		28-7615085			t/a Spectrum Flying Group		
G-BRTZ	Slingsby Cadet III	PFA/42-10545		24. 1.90	R.R.Walters	Haamstede, Belgium	14. 3.97P
	(VW1600)						
G-BRUA	Cessna 152 II	152-81212	N49267	11. 1.90	Griffin Marston Ltd	Compton Abbas	18. 8.99T
					(Op Abbas Air)		
G-BRUB	PA-28-161 Warrior II	28-8116177	N8351Y	27.12.89	Flytrek Ltd	Compton Abbas	7.11.99
G-BRUD	PA-28-181 Archer II	28-8390010	N8300S	9. 2.90	Wilkins & Wilkins Special Auctions Ltd		
						RAF Henlow	14. 3.99T
G-BRUE	Cameron V-77 HAFB	2183		15.12.89	B.J.Newman & P.L.Harrison	Kettering	26. 2.99A
					"Bruer"		
G-BRUG	Luscombe 8E Silvaire	4462	N1735K NC1735K	15.12.89	P.A.Cain & N.W.Barratt	Compton Abbas	12. 5.98P
	(Cont C85)						
G-BRUH	Colt 105A HAFB	1650		15.12.89	D.C.Chipping	Evora, Portugal	29. 7.93T
G-BRUI	PA-44-180 Seminole	44-7995150	N2230E G-BRUI/N2230E	15.12.89	M.R.Shelton	Tatenhill	28. 8.99T
					t/a Tatenhill Avn		
G-BRUJ	Boeing-Stearman A75N1	75-4299	N55557	6. 4.90	M.Walker	Liverpool	16. 7.01T
	(PT-17) Kaydet (Cont R670)		42-16136		(As "16136/205" in USN c/s)		
G-BRUM	Cessna A152 Aerobat	A152-0870	N4693A	12. 3.86	Aerohire Ltd	Halfpenny Green	2. 9.01T
G-BRUN	Cessna 120	9294	G-BRDH N72127/NC72127	29. 8.89	O.C.Brun	Great Massingham	12. 2.01P
	(Cont C85)						
G-BRUO	Taylor JT.1 Monoplane	PFA/55-10859		15.12.89	G.Verity	Crosland Moor	4. 8.98P
	(VW1600)						
G-BRUT	Thunder Ax8-90 HAFB	1392		30. 3.89	Moet and Chandon (London) Ltd London SW1		6.12.93A
					"L'Esprit D'Aventure II/Mercier II"		
G-BRUU	EAA Biplane Model P1	1	N41MW N4775G	22.12.89	R.D.Harper	High Ham, Langport	17. 6.98P
	(Lyc O-360)						
G-BRUV	Cameron V-77 HAFB	2100		16. 8.89	T.W. & R.F.Benbrook	Romford	21.10.99A
					"BiGBRUVver"		
G-BRUX	PA-44-180 Seminole	44-7995151	N2245E	8. 3.79	Hambrair Ltd	Tatenhill	27.11.00
G-BRUZ	MFM Raven-Europe FS-57A HAFB	E-066	F-GMFM HB-BKB	1.12.89	R.H.Etherington Rapollano Terme, Italy		15. 4.93A
G-BRVB	Stolp SA.300 Starduster Too	409	N33MH	21.12.89	M.N.Petchey & S.Turner	Andrewsfield	15. 9.98P
	(Lyc O-360)						
G-BRVC	Cameron N-180 HAFB	2180		15.12.89	A.J.Street	Whimple, Exeter	28. 5.99T
G-BRVE	Beechcraft D17S Traveller	6701	N1193V	12. 3.90	D.J.Gilmour	North Weald	16. 7.99
	(UC-43-BH)	NC1193V/Bu.32874/FT475/44-67724/(Bu.23689)			t/a Intrepid Avn Co		
G-BRVF	Colt 77A HAFB	1651		19.12.89	Airborne Adventures Ltd	Skipton	21. 1.92A
G-BRVG	North American SNJ-7C Texan	88-17676	N830X	24. 1.90	D.J.Gilmour	North Weald	15. 8.99
		N4134A/Bu.90678/(42-85895)			t/a Intrepid Avn Co (As "27" in VS-932 Sqn, USN c/s)		
G-BRVH	Smyth Model S Sidewinder	PFA/92-11251		19.12.89	I.S.Bellamy	Netherthorpe	10. 5.99P
	(Lyc O-290)						
G-BRVI	Robinson R-22 Beta	1240		27.12.89	P.M.Whitaker	Ilkley	3. 4.99T
G-BRVJ	Slingsby Cadet III	701 & PFA/42-11382	(BGA3360) WT906	24. 1.90	B.Outhwaite	Breighton	27. 1.95P
	(VW1600) (Modified T.31B)						
G-BRVK	Cameron A-210 HAFB	2144		28.12.89	A.J.Street	Whimple, Exeter	13. 8.97T
G-BRVL	Pitts S-1C Special	559H	N2NW	10. 1.90	M.F.Pocock	RAF Leeming	2.11.99P
	(Lyc IO-320)						
G-BRVN	Thunder Ax7-77 HAFB	1614		28.12.89	D.L.Beckwith	Northampton	2. 7.99A
G-BRVO	Aerospatiale AS.350B Ecureuil	2315		3. 1.90	Malcolm Wilson (Motorsport) Ltd		
						Cockermouth	24. 4.99T
G-BRVR	Barnett Rotorcraft J4B-2	216-2		20. 2.90	M.Richardson	Ilkeston	AC
					t/a Ilkeston Contractors		
G-BRVS	Barnett Rotorcraft J4B-2	210-2		20. 2.90	M.Richardson	Ilkeston	AC
					t/a Ilkeston Contractors (Not constructed)		
G-BRVT	Christen Pitts S-2B Special	5189		6. 4.90	C.J. & M.D.Green	Bournemouth	14. 1.00T
	(Lyc AEIO-540)				(Op SFT Avn) "The Tart"		
G-BRVU	Colt 77A HAFB	1652		4. 1.90	J.K.Woods	Chatham	11. 2.98A
					"Concorde Watches"		
G-BRVV	Colt 56B HAFB	1386		8. 1.90	S.J. & M.P.A.Hollingsworth	Matlock	28. 3.95A
					"Rosie"		
G-BRVY	Thunder Ax8-90 HAFB	1676		9. 1.90	G.E. & J.V.Morris	Cheltenham	21. 3.99A
					"Golden Gem"		
G-BRVZ	SAN Jodel D.117	433	F-BHNR	22.12.89	J.G.Patton South Lodge Farm, Widmerpool		31. 5.99P

Regn	Type	C/n	P/I	Date	Owner/operator	Probable Base	CA Expy
G-BRWA	Aeronca 7AC Champion	7AC-351	N81730 NC81730	20. 3.90	D.D.Smith & J.R.Edwards Siege Cross Farm, Thatcham		16. 8.99P
G-BRWB	North American T-6G Texan	182-213	Fr.Mil 51-14526	28. 3.90	Rentair Ltd (Jersey) (As "526" in USAF c/s)		9. 7.98P
G-BRWC*	Cessna 152 II	152-81918	TF-GMT N67569	19. 1.90	T.Hayselden (Doncaster) Ltd	Sandtoft	15. 5.93T

(Reported as an original Harvard II, s/n 41-32473, rebuilt in 1951)

(Damaged Sandtoft 29.8.90; old fuselage in open store Egginton 3.98; on rebuild using cockpit
and front fuselage of G-BITG 6.96 which became G-ODAC; cancelled as wfu 16.2.99)

Regn	Type	C/n	P/I	Date	Owner/operator	Probable Base	CA Expy
G-BRWD	Robinson R-22 Beta	1231	N8064U	15. 1.90	Matrix Avn Ltd	Fenland	2. 5.99
G-BRWF	Thunder Ax7-77 HAFB	1200		15. 1.90	Deborah J.Greaves	Tenterden, Kent	7. 8.99A
G-BRWH	Cameron N-77 HAFB	2186		15. 1.90	C.P.G.E.Rodrigues	Sint Niklaas, Belgium	24.10.97A
G-BRWO	PA-28-140 Cherokee Cruiser	28-7325548	N55985	11. 1.90	Fergair Ltd	Bournemouth	11. 7.99T
G-BRWP	CFM Streak Shadow	PFA/161A-11596		17. 1.90	M.M.Bain	(Roslin)	18. 6.98
G-BRWR	Aeronca 11AC Chief (Cont A65)	11AC-1319	N9676E	17. 1.90	M.B.Moon & R.M.Lee	Frogland Cross	25. 6.99P
G-BRWT	Scheibe SF-25C-2000 Falke	44480	D-KIAY	11. 1.90	Booker Gliding Club Ltd	Booker	8. 4.99
G-BRWU	Phoenix Luton LA-4A Minor	PAL/1141		18. 1.90	R.B.Webber & P.K.Pike Hayrish Farm, Okehampton		31. 8.99P

(JAP J.99) (Regd as PFA/1141)

(Construction commenced by Russ Hooper; no PFA No. known)

Regn	Type	C/n	P/I	Date	Owner/operator	Probable Base	CA Expy
G-BRWV	Brugger MB.2 Colibri (VW 1834)	PFA/43-11027		18. 1.90	S.J.McCollum	Newtownards	9. 6.98P
G-BRWX	Cessna 172P Skyhawk II	172-74729	N53363	17. 1.90	D.A.Abels	Bristol/Lulsgate	22. 9.99T
G-BRWY	Cameron H-34 HAFB	2214		17. 1.90	E.Krafft	Annweiler, Germany	17. 4.94A
G-BRWZ	Cameron Macaw 90SS HAFB	2206		29. 1.90	Forbes Europe Inc	Balleroy, Normandy	12. 1.99
					"Capitalist Tool"		
G-BRXA	Cameron O-120 HAFB	2217		19. 1.90	Gone With The Wind Ltd & R.J.Mansfield Bowness-on-Windermere/Huddersfield		20. 3.99T
G-BRXB	Thunder Ax7-77 HAFB	1631		18. 1.90	H.Peel	Worcester	24. 4.97A
G-BRXC	PA-28-161 Warrior II	28-8416043	N4339X N9563N	19. 2.90	Oxford Aviation Services Ltd	Oxford	10. 3.99T
G-BRXD	PA-28-181 Archer II	28-8290126	N9690N N8203E	19. 2.90	D.D.Stone	Wellesbourne Mountford	12. 3.00
G-BRXE	Taylorcraft BC-12D (Cont A65)	9459	N95059 NC95059	25. 1.90	Wendy J.Durrad	Eastbach Farm, Coleford	25. 8.99P
G-BRXF	Aeronca 11AC Chief (Cont A65)	11AC-1033	N9396E NC9396E	25. 1.90	A.B.Newman	Andrewsfield	22. 6.99P
G-BRXG	Aeronca 7AC Champion (Cont A65)	7AC-3910	N85178 NC85178	1. 3.90	J.D.Webb t/a X-Ray Golf F/Grp	Hill Farm, Nayland	20. 5.99P
G-BRXH	Cessna 120 (Cont C85)	10462	N76068 NC76068	25. 1.90	J.N.Pittock & A.P.Fox Romney Street Farm, Sevenoaks		7. 2.98P
G-BRXL	Aeronca 11AC Chief (Cont A65)	11AC-1629	N3254E NC3254E	31. 1.90	P.R.A.Hammond	Rush Green	22. 9.99P
					t/a G-BRXL Group "Fat Bullet" (As "42-78044" in US Army L-3F c/s)		
G-BRXN	Montgomerie-Bensen B.8MR (Rotax 532)	PFA G/01-1160		31. 1.90	G.Robertson	Dunblane	18. 6.99P
G-BRXO	PA-34-200T Seneca II	34-7970149	N111ED N9618N	12. 4.90	Aviation Services Ltd	Tenerife North	31. 7.99
G-BRXP	SNCAN Stampe SV-4C (Lyc)	678	N33528 F-BGGU/Fr AF/(F-BDNX)	2. 2.90	P.G.Kavanagh & D.T.Kaberry	(Rossendale)	AC
G-BRXS	Howard Special T-Minus (Lyc O-290) (Modified Taylorcraft BC)	REC-1	N2278C	14. 2.90	A.Shuttleworth	Barton	24. 6.99P
G-BRXU	Aerospatiale AS.332L Super Puma	2092	VH-BHV G-BRXU/HC-BMZ/C-GSLO	6. 3.90	Bristow Helicopters Ltd "Crail"	Scatsta	11. 9.01T
G-BRXV	Robinson R-22 Beta	1246		7. 2.90	J.W.F. & S.M.Tuke t/a Tukair Aircraft Charter	Cranbrook	26. 3.99T
G-BRXW	PA-24-260 Comanche	24-4069	N8621P	16. 2.90	P.A.Jenkins t/a Oak Grp	Coventry	22.12.99
G-BRXY	Pietenpol Air Camper (Cont C90)	PFA/47-11416		7. 2.90	P.S.Ganczakowski	Great Eversden	19. 6.97P
G-BRYA	DHC.7-110 Dash Seven	062		17.11.81	Brymon Airways Ltd (Op Brymon Offshore)	Eindhoven/Aberdeen	19.10.99
G-BRYD	DHC.7-110 Dash Seven	109	C-GEWQ	24.12.87	Brymon Airways Ltd (Op Brymon Offshore)	Eindhoven/Aberdeen	18. 1.00T
G-BRYI	DHC.8-311A Dash Eight	256	C-GEOA	26. 3.91	Brymon Airways Ltd (Chelsea Rose t/s)	Bristol/Lulsgate	27. 3.00T
G-BRYJ	DHC.8-311A Dash Eight	319	C-GEOA	27. 3.92	Brymon Airways Ltd (Grand Union t/s)	Bristol/Lulsgate	2. 4.00T
G-BRYK	DHC.8-311A Dash Eight	284	N431AW C-GETI	2. 4.96	Brymon Airways Ltd	Bristol/Lulsgate	1. 4.99T
G-BRYM	DHC.8-311A Dash Eight	305	N433AW C-GDFT	25. 3.96	Brymon Airways Ltd	Bristol/Lulsgate	24. 3.99T
G-BRYN	Socata TB-20 Trinidad	959		22. 3.89	Anglo American Airmotive Ltd	Bournemouth	28. 3.99
G-BRYO	DHC.8-311A Dash Eight	311	N434AW C-GEVP	26. 4.96	Brymon Airways Ltd	Bristol/Lulsgate	25. 4.99T

Regn	Type	C/n	P/I	Date	Owner/operator	Probable Base	CA Expy
G-BRYP	DHC.8-311A Dash Eight	315	N435AW C-GFCF	22. 4.96	Brymon Airways Ltd	Bristol/Lulsgate	21. 4.99T
G-BRYR	DHC.8-311A Dash Eight	336	N436AW	20. 5.96	Brymon Airways Ltd	Bristol/Lulsgate	19. 5.99T
G-BRYS	DHC.8-311A Dash Eight	296	PH-SDG D-BKIS/C-GFQL	23. 4.97	Brymon Airways Ltd (Waves of the City t/s)	Bristol/Lulsgate	4. 5.00T
G-BRYT	DHC.8-311A Dash Eight	334	D-BKIR C-GFEN	11. 3.97	Brymon Airways Ltd (Colour Down the Side t/s)	Bristol/Lulsgate	25. 3.00T
G-BRYU	DHC.8-311A Dash Eight	458	(9M-PGA) C-GFEN	4. 4.98	Brymon Airways Ltd (Mountain of the Birds/Benyhone Tartan t/s)	Bristol/Lulsgate	3. 4.00T
G-BRYV	DHC.8-311A Dash Eight	462	(9M-PGD) C-GFHZ	10. 4.98	Brymon Airways Ltd (Dove/Colum t/s)	Bristol/Lulsgate	9. 4.00T
G-BRYW	DHC.8-311A Dash Eight	474	(9M-PG.) C-GDIU	26. 5.98	Brymon Airways Ltd (Cockerel of Lowicz/Koguty Lowickie t/s)	Bristol/Lulsgate	25. 5.01T
G-BRYX	DHC-8-311A Dash Eight	508	C-GDOE	25. 9.98	Brymon Airways Ltd.	Plymouth	27. 9.01T
G-BRYY	DHC-8-311A Dash Eight	519	C-FDHD	11.12.98	Brymon Airways Ltd. (Rendezvous t/s)	Plymouth	10.12.01T
G-BRYZ	DHC.8-311A Dash Eight	464	C-FCSG	16.10.98	Brymon Airways Ltd	Plymouth	15.10.01T
G-BRZA	Cameron O-77 HAFB	2231		7. 2.90	L. & R.J.Mold "Breezy"	High Wycombe	7. 1.99A
G-BRZB	Cameron A-105 HAFB	2212		7. 2.90	Cornwall Ballooning Adventures Ltd "Headland Hotel"	Newquay	28. 4.99A
G-BRZC*	Cameron N-90 HAFB	2227		8. 2.90	British Balloon Museum & Library "Unipart II"	Newbury	2.12.92A
G-BRZD	HAPI Cygnet SF-2A (VW2078)	PFA/182-11443		8. 2.90	L.G.Millen	Stoneacre Farm, Farthing Corner	2. 3.99P
G-BRZE	Thunder Ax7-77 HAFB	1633		8. 2.90	G.V.Beckwith & F.Schoeder "Jenlain"	York	31. 8.97A
G-BRZG	Enstrom F-28A	169	N9053	8. 2.90	S.M.Bell	Woodford	7. 4.00
G-BRZI	Cameron N-180 HAFB	2215		8. 2.90	C.E.Wood t/a Eastern Balloon Rides	Witham	25. 2.99T
G-BRZK	Stinson 108-2 Voyager	108-2846	N9846K NC9846K	17. 4.90	P.C.G.Wyld t/a Voyager G-BRZK Syndicate	Booker	15. 8.99
G-BRZL	Pitts S-1D Special (Lyc O-360)	01	N899RN	26. 2.90	R.T.Cardwell (Stored 2.97) Standalone Farm, Meppershall		2. 8.96P
G-BRZO	Jodel D.18	PFA/169-11275		14. 2.90	J.D.Anson	(Liskeard)	
G-BRZP	PA-28-161 Warrior II	28-8616013	N9140Y	17. 4.90	Air Service Training Ltd	Perth	27. 4.99T
G-BRZS	Cessna 172P Skyhawk II	172-75004	N54585	2.10.90	H.Hargreaves & P.F.Hughes t/a G-BHYP F/Grp	Blackpool	20.11.99
G-BRZT	Cameron V-77 HAFB	2241		21. 2.90	Beverley Drawbridge "Hoopla"	Cranbrook, Kent	9.11.96T
G-BRZU	Colt Flying Cheese SS HAFB	1544		26. 2.90	N.Charbonnier "Grana Padano"	Aosta, Italy	25. 9.97A
G-BRZV	Colt Flying Apple SS HAFB	1662		26. 2.90	Thrust Drive Ltd "Bodensee"	(Austria)	14. 9.97A
G-BRZW	Rans S-10 Sakota (Rotax 532) 0789-058 & PFA/194-11932			21. 2.90	D.L.Davies	Emlyns Field, Rhuallt	6. 8.98P
G-BRZX	Pitts S-1S Special (Lyc O-320)	711-H	N272H	22. 2.90	J.H.Milne & T.H.Bishop	Felthorpe	8. 6.94P
G-BRZZ	CFM Streak Shadow (Rotax 532) (C/n duplicates Renegade Spirit G-MWDM)	PFA/161A-11628		22. 2.90	L.P.Townsley t/a Shetland F/Grp	Kirkwall	16. 8.99P

G-BSAA-BSZZ

Regn	Type	C/n	P/I	Date	Owner/operator	Probable Base	CA Expy
G-BSAI	Stoddard-Hamilton Glasair III	3102		31. 1.90	K.J. & P.J.Whitehead		
						Whitchurch Hill, Reading	AC
G-BSAJ	CASA I-131E Jungmann	2209	E3B-209	23. 1.90	P.G.Kynsey	Headcorn	15. 7.99P
G-BSAK	Colt 21A Sky Chariot HAFB	1696		26. 2.90	K.Meehan	Much Wenlock	24. 7.99A
					t/a Northern Flights		
G-BSAR	Air Command 532 Elite	0443		20. 4.89	T.A.Holmes	(Leeds)	
G-BSAS	Cameron V-65 HAFB	2191		27. 2.90	J.R.Barber	Kings Lynn	12. 4.95A
G-BSAV	Thunder Ax7-77 HAFB	1555		26. 2.90	E.A. & H.A.Evans,	Chesterfield	29. 3.99A
					I.G. & C.A.Lloyd "Burnt Savings"		
G-BSAW	PA-28-161 Warrior II	28-8216152	N8203C	27. 2.90	Carill Avn Ltd	Southampton	16. 6.99T
G-BSAX	Piper J3C-65 Cub	18432	N98260	17. 1.91	K.& J.I.Harness	(Louth, Lincs)	
			NC98260				
G-BSAZ	Denney Kitfox mk.2 602 & PFA/172-11664		(G-BRVW)	5. 3.90	A.J.Lloyd, D.M.Garrett & J.T.Lane		
	(Rotax 582)				(Bromyard/Hereford/Brierley Hill)		26. 6.97P
G-BSBA	PA-28-161 Warrior II	28-8016041	N2574U	1. 3.90	R.J.Doughton	Dunkeswell	28. 4.00T
					t/a Doughton Aviation Services		
G-BSBG	CCF Harvard 4	CCF4-483	1753	5. 3.90	A.P.St.John	Liverpool	5. 2.99P
	(T-6J-CCF Texan)		Moz.PLAF		(As "20310/310" in RCAF c/s)		
			FAP 1753/BF+053/AA+053/52-8562				
G-BSBH*	Short SD.3-30	SH.3000		6. 6.74	Belfast Harbour Fire Service		
						Belfast Harbour	13. 4.81S
G-BSBI	Cameron O-77 HAFB	2245		6. 3.90	D.M.Billing	Uckfield	14. 7.96A
G-BSBK	Colt 105A HAFB	1319		6. 3.90	Zebra Ballooning Ltd	Maidstone	12. 6.99T
G-BSBM	Cameron N-77	2229		8. 3.90	R S Kent "Nuclear Electric 1"	Lancing	21.11.96A
					(Balloon Preservation Group 7.98)		
G-BSBN	Thunder Ax7-77 HAFB	1531		6. 3.90	B.Pawson "Venus"	Cambridge	9.12.93A
G-BSBP	Jodel D.18	PFA/169-11613		15. 1.90	R.T.Pratt	(Crickhowell)	
	(Revmaster R2100)						
G-BSBR	Cameron V-77 HAFB	2247		26. 2.90	B.Bromiley "Honey"	Bury	10.10.99A
G-BSBT	Piper J3C-65 Cub	17712	N70694	9. 3.90	I. & L.J.Proudfoot	Booker	22.10.98P
			NC70694				
G-BSBV	Rans S-10 Sakota 1089-064 & PFA/194-11769			9. 3.90	R.G.Cameron	Milson	11. 4.99P
	(Rotax 532)						
G-BSBW	Bell 206B JetRanger III	3664	N43EA	12. 3.90	D.T.Sharpe	Sherburn	20. 6.99T
			9Y-THC				
G-BSBX	Montgomerie-Bensen B.8MR			12. 3.90	B.Ibbott	Hemel Hempstead	26. 5.93P
	(Rotax 503)	PFA G/01A-1135					
G-BSBZ	Cessna 150M Commuter	150-77093	N63086	29. 3.90	D.T.Given t/a DTG Avn	Newtownards	13. 6.99T
G-BSCA	Cameron N-90 HAFB	2237		12. 3.90	P.J.Marshall & M.A.Clarke	Ruislip	29. 1.99A
					"The Graduate"		
G-BSCB	Air Command 532 Elite			16. 3.90	P.H.Smith	Nottingham	18. 9.97P
		0627 & PFA G/04-1172					
G-BSCC	Colt 105A HAFB	1006		15. 3.90	Capricorn Balloons Ltd	Loughborough	5. 4.99T
G-BSCD	Hughes 269C	74-0327	PH-HSH	19. 3.90	The Hughes Helicopter Co Ltd Biggin Hill		29. 5.00T
			SE-HFG		t/a Biggin Hill Helicopters		
G-BSCE	Robinson R-22 Beta	1245		15. 3.90	S.Thompson	(Leamington Spa)	13. 3.99T
G-BSCF	Thunder Ax7-77 HAFB	1537		14. 3.90	V.P.Gardiner	Stoke-on-Trent	8. 9.99A
					"Charlie Farley"		
G-BSCG	Denney Kitfox mk.2	PFA/172-11620		23. 4.90	N.L.Beever	Breighton	28. 9.98P
	(Rotax 582)						
G-BSCH	Denney Kitfox mk.2			16. 3.90	M.P.M.Read	Carlisle	4. 1.99P
	(Rotax 582)	510 & PFA/172-11621					
G-BSCI	Colt 77A HAFB	1683		16. 3.90	J.L. & S.Wrigglesworth "Brody"	Ilminster	1. 8.99A
G-BSCK	Cameron H-24 HAFB	2263		16. 3.90	J.D.Shapland "Monacle"	Wadebridge	11. 6.95A
G-BSCL	Robinson R-22 Beta	1249		28. 3.90	Skyhopper Ltd	Booker	16. 6.99T
G-BSCM	Denney Kitfox mk.2 638 & PFA/172-11745			28. 3.90	S.A.Hewitt	(Stourbridge)	5.10.99P
	(Rotax 582)						
G-BSCN	Socata TB-20 Trinidad	1070	D-EGTC	27. 3.90	B.W.Dye	Biggin Hill	27. 6.99
			G-BSCN				
G-BSCO	Thunder Ax7-77 HAFB	1635		6. 3.90	F.J.Whalley "Bluebell"	Cleish, Kinross	11. 9.99A
G-BSCP	Cessna 152 II	152-83289	N48135	20. 3.90	Moray F/C (1990) Ltd	RAF Kinloss	12. 9.99T
G-BSCR	Cessna 172M Skyhawk II	172-62182	N12693	20. 3.90	London Link Flying Ltd	Stapleford	16. 1.00T
G-BSCS	PA-28-181 Archer II	28-7890064	N47392	3. 4.90	Wingtask Ltd	Seething	30. 5.99T
G-BSCV	PA-28-161 Warrior II	28-7816135	C-GQXW	22. 3.90	S.E.Burton	Earls Colne	26. 9.99
					t/a Southwood F/Grp		
G-BSCW	Taylorcraft BC-65	1798	N24461	22. 3.90	S.Leach	Plymouth	30. 6.99P
			NC24461				
G-BSCX	Thunder Ax8-105 HAFB	1748		21. 3.90	Balloon Flights Club Ltd	Leicester	14. 7.99T
					"Balloon Flights"		
G-BSCY	PA-28-151 Cherokee Warrior 28-7515046		C-GOBE	22. 3.90	A.S.Bamrah t/a Falcon F/Svs	Oxford	1. 8.99T
	(Convd to Srs.161 status)						
G-BSCZ	Cessna 152 II	152-82199	N68226	22. 3.90	Eastern Executive Air Charter Ltd		
						Southend	3. 6.00T
G-BSDA	Taylorcraft BC-12D	7316	N43657	15.11.90	D.G.Edwards	Shoreham	22. 9.99P
	(Cont A75)		NC43657				
G-BSDB	Pitts S-1C Special	01	(N1867)	22. 3.90	S.Adams	Leicester	31. 5.99P
	(Lyc O-320)		N77R				

Regn	Type	C/n	P/I	Date	Owner/operator	Probable Base	CA Expy
G-BSDD	Denney Kitfox mk.2 639 & PFA/172-11797 (Rotax 582)			28. 3.90	J.Windmill	Priory Farm, Tibenham	21. 6.96P
G-BSDG	Robin DR.400/180 Regent	1974		29. 3.90	P.A.Stephens	Manor Farm, Heslerton	30. 6.99
G-BSDH	Robin DR.400/180 Regent	1980		18. 4.90	R.L.Brucciani	Leicester	16. 5.99
G-BSDI	Corben Junior Ace Model E (Cont A75)	3961	N91706	28. 3.90	T.K.Pullen & A.J.Staplehurst	Eaglescott	3.10.98P
G-BSDJ	Piper J/4E Cub Coupe (Cont C85)	4-1456	N35975 NC35975	13. 2.91	B.M.Jackson	(Thame)	16. 4.99P
G-BSDK	Piper J/5A Cub Cruiser (Cont A75)	5-175	N30337 NC30337	28. 3.90	S.Haughton & I.S.Hodge	Field Farm, Great Missenden	1. 4.98P
G-BSDL	Socata TB-10 Tobago	156		7.10.80	P.Middleton & G.Corbin t/a Delta Lima Grp	Sherburn	1. 5.00
G-BSDN	PA-34-200T Seneca II	34-7970335	N2893A	2. 4.90	McCormick Consulting Ltd	Manchester	20. 5.99T
G-BSDO	Cessna 152 II	152-81657	N65894	23. 5.90	J.Vickers	Humberside	17. 9.99T
G-BSDP	Cessna 152 II	152-80268	N24468	11. 6.90	I.S.H.Paul	Denham	10. 7.00T
G-BSDS	Boeing-Stearman E75 (PT-13A) Kaydet (Cont W670)	75-118	N57852 38-470	6. 4.90	E.Hopper (As "118" in US Army c/s)	Bagby	13. 5.00
G-BSDU	Bell 206B JetRanger III	4097	C-FHZV	5. 6.90	Eaglecray Ltd	Cannock	14. 7.99
G-BSDV	Colt 31A HAFB	1722		30. 3.90	Virgin Airship & Balloon Co Ltd "Baby Carrots"	Telford	27. 6.96A
G-BSDW	Cessna 182P Skylane II	182-64688	N9125M	9. 4.90	Delta Whisky Ltd	Little Snoring	4. 7.99
G-BSDX	Cameron V-77 HAFB	2050		30. 3.90	D.K.Fish	Bedford	
	(Canopy fitted to G-SNOW and rebuilt with G-SNOW's original canopy)						
G-BSDZ	Enstrom 280FX	2051	OO-MHV (OO-JMH)/G-ODSC/G-BSDZ	3. 4.90	Avalon Group Ltd	Chester	3. 1.00
G-BSED	PA-22-160 Tri-Pacer (Taildragger conversion)	22-6377	N9404D	7. 6.90	M.Henderson	Dundee	15. 6.00
G-BSEE	Rans S-9 (Rotax 532)	PFA/196-11635		2. 3.90	P.M.Semler	Buttermilk Farm, Easton Maudit	19. 3.99P
G-BSEF	PA-28-180 Cherokee C	28-1846	N7831W	18. 4.90	B.Mills	(Barnsley)	25. 7.99
G-BSEG	Ken Brock KB-2 (Rotax 582) (C/n possibly PFA G/06-1106)	PFA G/01-1106		3. 4.90	S.J.M.Ledingham	Boulmer	5. 6.99P
G-BSEJ	Cessna 150M Commuter	150-76261	N66767	4. 5.90	Halfpenny Green Flight Centre Ltd	Halfpenny Green	12. 9.99T
G-BSEK	Robinson R-22	0027	N45AD N90193	10. 4.90	Heli Air Ltd	Panshanger	28. 4.99T
G-BSEL	Slingsby T-61G Super Falke	1986		31. 3.80	T.Holloway t/a RAFGSA (Op Bannerdown Gliding Club)	RAF Keevil	11. 1.01
G-BSEP	Cessna 172	46555	N6455E	12. 4.90	A.P Wall, R.J.Tyson & R.J Watts	Redhill	19. 8.99
G-BSER	PA-28-160 Cherokee B	28-790	N5665W	19. 4.90	Yorkair Ltd	Sandtoft	15. 8.99T
G-BSES*	Denney Kitfox (Rotax 532)	PFA/172-11587		17. 4.90	M.Albert-Brecht & J.J.M.Donnelly	Aboyne	5. 2.93P
	(Destroyed by fire Aboyne 1992/93; parts only stored 3.94; cancelled by CAA 6.3.99)						
G-BSET	Beagle B.206 Basset CC.1	B.006	XS765	3.12.86	Lawgra (No.386) Ltd t/a International Aerospace Engineering (As "XS765" in RAF Transport Command c/s)	Cranfield	28. 7.98
G-BSEU	PA-28-181 Archer II	28-7890108	N47639	1. 5.90	Euro Avn 91 Ltd	Blackbushe	23. 6.99
G-BSEV	Cameron O-77 HAFB	2271		20. 4.90	The Ballooning Business Ltd	Northampton	
G-BSEX	Cameron A-180 HAFB	2254		18. 4.90	M.L.Gabb t/a Heart of England Balloons	Alcester	3. 7.97T
G-BSEY	Beechcraft A36 Bonanza	E-1873	N1809F	17. 5.90	K.Phillips Ltd	Coventry	6. 8.99
G-BSEZ*	Air Command 532 Elite	0629 & PFA G/04-1165		18. 4.90	D.S.Robinson (Used for spares 1998; cancelled as wfu 29.1.99)	(Swansea)	14. 6.91P
G-BSFA	Aero Designs Pulsar 176 & PFA/202-11754 (Rotax 582)			18. 4.90	S.A.Gill	White Waltham	19. 7.99P
G-BSFB	CASA I-131E Jungmann	2053	E3B-449	27. 4.90	C.G.Dodds t/a G-BSFB Group (As "S5+B06" in Luftwaffe c/s)	(Dunmow)	17. 9.99P
G-BSFD	Piper J3C-65 Cub (Frame No.15443)	16037	N88419 NC88419	25. 5.90	E.G. & N.S.C.English	North Weald	21.12.99P
G-BSFE	PA-38-112 Tomahawk II	38-82A0033	N91452	26. 4.90	Chubbs Aviation Services (UK) Ltd (Op Glasgow F/C)	Glasgow	21.10.99T
G-BSFF	Robin DR.400/180R Remorqueur	1295	D-ELMM	20. 4.90	Lasham Gliding Society Ltd	Lasham	11. 7.99
G-BSFJ	Thunder Ax8-105 HAFB	1762		20. 4.90	C.Gibson, L.Kirby & J.Russon	Stockport	19. 7.99T
G-BSFK	PA-28-161 Warrior II	28-8516062	N6918D	1. 5.90	Oxford Aviation Services Ltd	Oxford	24. 5.99T
G-BSFN	Sud SE.313B Alouette II	1500	XP967	30. 5.90	A.C.Watson	(Barnsley)	2.10.00
G-BSFP	Cessna 152T	152-85548	N93764	9. 5.90	J.R.Nicholls	Sibson	5. 8.99T
G-BSFR	Cessna 152 II	152-82268	N68341	9. 5.90	Galair Ltd	Biggin Hill	10. 7.99T
G-BSFS	Sud SE.313B Alouette II	1582	XR378 F-WIFM	30. 5.90	S.Lee (Possibly ex F-WIEM)	Wilden, Bedford	15. 7.00T
G-BSFU*	Sud SE.313B Alouette II	1645	XR385	30. 5.90	Not known (Stored 7.97)	Coventry	
G-BSFV	Woods Woody Pusher (Cont C85)	201	N16WP	30. 4.90	M.J.Wells "Woody's Pusher"	Draycott Farm, Chiseldon	26. 3.99P
G-BSFW	PA-15 Vagabond (Cont A65)	15-273	N4484H NC4484H	26. 4.90	J.R.Kimberley	Bounds Farm, Ardleigh	2. 9.99P
G-BSFX	Denney Kitfox Mk.2 506 & PFA/172-11723 (Rotax 582)			23. 4.90	T.A.Crone	(Milton Keynes)	3. 8.99P
G-BSFY	Denney Kitfox Mk.2 (Rotax 582)	PFA/172-11632		16. 3.90	A.R.Hawes	Crowfield	9.11.99P
G-BSGB	Gaertner Ax4 Skyranger HAFB	SR.0001		30. 3.90	B.Gaertner	Oxford	

176

Regn	Type	C/n	P/I	Date	Owner/operator	Probable Base	CA Expy
G-BSGC	PA-18-95 Super Cub (L-18C-PI)	18-3227	OO-HBC OL-L53/L-153/53-4827	22. 3.90	G.Churchill (On overhaul 1996)	(Towcester)	
G-BSGD	PA-28-180 Cherokee E	28-5691	N3463R	4. 5.90	R.J.Cleverley	Draycott Farm, Chiseldon	6. 5.00
G-BSGF	Robinson R-22 Beta	1383		1. 5.90	Direct Helicopters (Southend) Ltd	Southend	20. 6.99T
G-BSGG	Denney Kitfox mk.2 (Jabiru 2200A)	PFA/172-11666		1. 5.90	C.G.Richardson	Fulbeck, Lincs	5. 8.98P
G-BSGH	Airtour AH-56B HAFB	014		1. 5.90	G.Luck "Battle of Britain"	Habrough, Lincolnshire	
G-BSGJ	Monnett Sonerai II (VW1835)	300	N34WH	1. 5.90	G.A.Brady	(Burford, Oxon)	6. 9.91P
G-BSGK	PA-34-200T Seneca II	34-7870331	N36450	22. 5.90	R.Hope, M.J.Martin & B.W.Powell t/a GK Aviation	Manston	17.11.99
G-BSGL	PA-28-161 Warrior II	28-8116041	N82690	10. 5.90	Keywest Air Charter Ltd (Op Liverpool F/School) "Liverbird V"	Liverpool	4. 7.99T
G-BSGN	PA-28-151 Cherokee Warrior	28-7615225	N9657K	10. 5.90	J.R.Whetlor & M.Gipps	Denham	13. 6.99T
G-BSGP	Cameron N-65 HAFB	2293		1. 5.90	M.D.Hammond t/a Mid Sussex F/School	Burgess Hill	
G-BSGR*	Boeing-Stearman E75 (PT-17) Kaydet (Reported as c/n 75-6714 ex N66870/Bu.07110)	75-4721	EC-ATY N55050/42-16558	19. 6.90	A.G.Dunkerley (Bury) (On rebuild Brickhouse Farm, Frogland Cross 4.96) (Cancelled by CAA 10.3.97)		
G-BSGS	Rans S-10 Sakota (Rotax 532)	1289-076 & PFA/194-11724		9. 5.90	M.R.Parr (Holmbrook, Cumbria) (Damaged Coventry late 1.93; status uncertain)		4. 3.93P
G-BSGT	Cessna T210N Turbo Centurion II (Reims-assembled with c/n 0020)	210-63361 D-EOGB/N5308A	LX-ATL	21. 5.90	B.J.Sharpe	Booker	17. 3.00
G-BSGV*	Rotorway Exec (RW 152)	3823		8. 5.90	Not known (Stored 5.95)	Elstree	14.7.92P*
G-BSGY	Thunder Ax7-77 HAFB (Envelope ex G-BROA c/n 1535)	1760		18. 7.90	P.B.Kenington "Bugsy"	Winterbourne, Bristol	30. 5.99A
G-BSHA	PA-34-200T Seneca II	34-7670216	N9707K	2. 5.90	JGH Computer Svs Ltd, Maze Computers Ltd	Cardiff	24. 7.99T
G-BSHC	Colt 69A HAFB	1668		8. 5.90	L.V.Mastis	Bristol	12.10.98A
G-BSHD	Colt 69A HAFB	1736		8. 5.90	D.B.Court	Ormskirk	11. 8.99A
G-BSHE	Cessna 152 II	152-81302	N49483	17. 3.89	J.A.Pothecary t/a Air South	Shoreham	28. 1.93
					(Damaged Shoreham 6.11.92; stored for spares 9.93)		
G-BSHH	Luscombe 8E Silvaire (Cont C85)	3981	N1254K NC1254K	11. 5.90	G.M.Wightman	(Leamington Spa)	28.10.99P
G-BSHI	Luscombe 8DF Silvaire Trainer (Cont C90)	1821	N39060 NC39060	11. 5.90	W.H.J.Knowles	Weston Zoyland	8. 9.98P
G-BSHK	Denney Kitfox mk.2 (Rotax 532)	449 & PFA/172-11752		11. 5.90	D.Doyle & C.Aherne	Kilrush, Dublin	24. 6.99P
G-BSHP	PA-28-161 Warrior II	28-8616002	N9107Y	31. 5.90	Keen Leasing (IoM) Ltd	Liverpool	26. 8.99T
G-BSHR	Reims Cessna F.172N Skyhawk II	1616	G-BFGE	23.10.84	A.Simmers Ltd	Aberdeen	22. 5.00
G-BSHS	Colt 105A HAFB	1674	(D-OCAT) G-BSHS	16. 5.90	I.Novosad	Planegg, Germany	11. 8.99A
G-BSHT	Cameron V-77 HAFB	2321		30. 5.90	E.C.Moore "Buckshot II"	Great Missenden	5. 6.99A
G-BSHV	PA-18-135 Super Cub (L-18C-PI)	18-3123	OO-GDG Belgian Army L49/53-4723	5. 7.90	A.Furness t/a Fen Tigers F/Grp	Wilburton	5. 4.01
G-BSHW	Hawker Tempest II (Bristol built)	12177	IAF HA564 MW376	21. 3.91	P.Y.C.Denis (Romans, France) (Stored North Weald 5.96; to be "MW800/HF-V" in 54 Sqn c/s)		
G-BSHX	Enstrom F-28A	155	N9605	16. 5.90	Stephenson Avn Ltd (Stored 4.96)	Goodwood	AC
G-BSHY	EAA Acrosport 1 (Lyc O-290)	PFA/72-10928		17. 4.90	R.J.Hodder	Eastfield Farm, Manby	14. 1.99P
G-BSHZ	Enstrom F-28F	427	N51702	16. 5.90	S.G.Oliphant-Hope	Shoreham	25. 3.00
G-BSIB	PA-28-161 Warrior II	28-8016304	N8182C	13. 6.90	Bobbington Air Training School Ltd (Op Dee Training)	Halfpenny Green	5. 7.99T
G-BSIC	Cameron V-77 HAFB	2322		17. 5.90	C.Wilcock	Rickmansworth	11. 7.91A
G-BSIE	Enstrom 280FX	2052	HA-MIN G-BSIE	17. 5.90	S.G.Oliphant-Hope	(Worthing)	18. 1.00T
G-BSIF	Denney Kitfox mk.2 (Rotax 582)	563 & PFA/172-11889		5. 7.90	J.C.W. & J.Smith	Hungerford	1. 2.00P
G-BSIG	Colt 21A Cloudhopper HAFB	1322		18. 5.90	E.C. & A.J.Moore	Great Missenden	17. 9.98A
G-BSIH	Rutan LongEz	1200-1 & PFA/74A-11492		31. 5.90	W.S.Allen	(Cheltenham)	
G-BSII	PA-34-200T Seneca II	34-8070336	N8253N	16. 5.90	N.H.N.Gardner	Fairoaks	17. 7.99
G-BSIJ	Cameron V-77 HAFB	2164		23. 5.90	A.S.Jones	Wolverhampton	20. 9.99A
G-BSIK	Denney Kitfox Mk.1	51		5. 6.90	G.J.Sargent	(Cambridge)	
G-BSIM	PA-28-181 Archer II	28-8690017	N9092Y	22. 5.90	East Midlands Acft Hire Ltd	East Midlands	10. 8.99T
G-BSIN	Robinson R-22 Beta	1379	N4015H	25. 5.90	P.D.Mardell t/a PDM Aviation	Pulloxhill, Bedford	2. 7.99T
G-BSIO	Cameron Furness House 56SS HAFB	2310		25. 5.90	R.E.Jones "Pinkie"	Lytham St.Annes	2. 9.97A
G-BSIT	Robinson R-22 Beta	0762		9. 3.88	Helicentre Ltd (Damaged Ashcroft, Cheshire 20.4.97)	Blackpool	26. 5.97T
G-BSIU	Colt 90A HAFB	1774		25. 5.90	S.Travaglia	Firenze, Italy	25.11.99A

Regn	Type	C/n	P/I	Date	Owner/operator	Probable Base	CA Expy
G-BSIY	Schleicher ASK14	14005	5Y-AID D-KOIC	4. 6.90	E.V.Goodwin (Huntingdon) t/a Winwick Flying Group		20.10.96
G-BSIZ	PA-28-181 Archer II	28-7990377	N2162Y	25. 5.90	A.M.L.Maxwell	Alderney	20. 6.99
G-BSJB	Bensen B.8	PFA G/01-1080		5. 6.90	J.W.Limbrick	(Bewdley)	
G-BSJU	Cessna 150M Commuter	150-76430	N3230V	14. 6.90	A.C.Williamson (Op Crowfield F/C)	Crowfield	26. 2.01T
G-BSJW	Everett Gyroplane Srs.2 (Rotax 532)	020		6. 6.90	R.Sarwan	(Beccles)	25.10.91P
G-BSJX	PA-28-161 Warrior II	28-8216084	N8036N	30. 5.90	D.A.Shields & L.C.Brekkeflat	Elstree	22. 7.99T
G-BSJZ	Cessna 150J	150-70485	N60661	7. 5.91	BCT Aircraft Lsg Ltd (Chesterfield)		1. 3.00T
G-BSKA	Cessna 150M Commuter	150-76137	N66588	31. 7.90	P.R.Edwards	(Braintree)	13. 3.00T
G-BSKC	PA-38-112 Tomahawk	38-79A0748	OY-PJB N748RM/C-GRQI	27. 7.90	J.Marioni Panshanger (Damaged nr Tewin 2.6.96; stored 9.97)		24. 1.97T
G-BSKD	Cameron V-77 HAFB	2336		4. 6.90	M.J.Gunston "Skulduggery"	Camberley	4. 7.99A
G-BSKE	Cameron O-84 HAFB	1604	ZS-HYD G-BSKE	4. 6.90	B.W.Smith Wisborough Green, W.Sussex t/a The Blunt Arrows Balloon Team		5. 6.99A
G-BSKG	Maule MX-7-180 Star Rocket	11072C		7. 6.90	J.R.Surbey Blockmoor Farm, Barway, Ely		5. 2.00
G-BSKI	Thunder Ax8-90 HAFB	1623		18. 5.90	P.G.Ward Camberley t/a G-BSKI Balloon Grp "Ski Maiden"		22.11.98A
G-BSKK	PA-38-112 Tomahawk	38-79A0671	N2525K	11. 6.90	A.S.Bamrah t/a Falcon F/Svs	Biggin Hill	20.11.99T
G-BSKL	PA-38-112 Tomahawk	38-78A0509	N4252E	11. 6.90	A.S.Bamrah t/a Falcon F/Svs Birmingham (Op Warwickshire Aero Centre)		20.11.99T
G-BSKO	Maule MXT-7-180 Star Rocket	14008C		7. 6.90	M.A.Ashmole	Perth	12. 5.00
G-BSKP	VS.379 Spitfire F.XIVe	6S/663417	RBAF SG-31/RN201	27. 6.90	Historic Flying Ltd Audley End (On rebuild 3.96)		AC
G-BSKS*	Nieuport 28C-1 (Gnome Monosoupape 160hp) (Identity obscure - ex Tallmantz & not ex N4123A)	6531	"N5246" US Navy	27. 6.90	US Army Avn Museum Fort Rucker, Alabama, USA (As "6531/5" in 94th Aero Sqn AEF c/s)		13. 5.93P
G-BSKT	Maule MX-7-180 Star Rocket	11070C		7. 6.90	B.P.Young Dunkeswell t/a Maule F/Grp		11. 1.99
G-BSKU	Cameron O-84 HAFB	2330		8. 6.90	Alfred Bagnall & Sons (West) Ltd "Bagnalls II" Bristol		31. 7.99A
G-BSKW	PA-28-181 Archer II	2890138	N91940	1. 6.90	Shropshire Aero Club Ltd	Sleap	9. 4.00T
G-BSLA	Robin DR.400/180 Regent	1997		22. 6.90	A.B.McCoig Biggin Hill t/a Robin Lima Alpha Group		26. 8.99
G-BSLD	PA-28RT-201 Arrow IV	28R-7918231	N2943D	22. 6.90	E.Gawronek	Barton	20.11.99
G-BSLE	PA-28-161 Warrior II	28-8116028	N8260L	25. 6.90	Oxford Aviation Services Ltd	Oxford	18. 8.99T
G-BSLG	Cameron A-180 HAFB	2332		15. 6.90	B.J.Newman "Spot"	Rushden	7. 4.99T
G-BSLH	CASA I-131E Jungmann	2222	E3B-622	27. 7.90	P.Warden	Brive, France	19. 5.99P
G-BSLI	Cameron V-77 HAFB	2115		15. 6.90	J.D.C. & F.E.Bevan Market Drayton "Blackbird"		5. 6.99T
G-BSLJ*	Denney Kitfox mk.2 364 & PFA/172-11589 (Rotax 532)			15. 6.90	A.F.Reid Comber, NI (Damaged Bundoran Beach, Co.Donegal 28.5.92; stored 6.97; cancelled by CAA 10.3.99)		14. 4.93P
G-BSLK	PA-28-161 Warrior II	28-7916018	N20849	15. 6.90	R.A.Rose	Wellesbourne Mountford	3. 2.00T
G-BSLM	PA-28-160 Cherokee	28-308	N5262W	22. 6.90	C.W.Barker & A.J.Pollinger Old Sarum t/a Old Sarum Cherokee Grp		19. 2.00
G-BSLO	Cameron A-180 HAFB	2162		8. 6.90	Adventure Balloon Co Ltd	London W7	25. 6.99T
G-BSLT	PA-28-161 Warrior II	28-8016303	N81817	19. 6.90	APB Leasing Ltd	Welshpool	18. 1.00T
G-BSLU	PA-28-140 Cherokee	28-24733	OY-PJL OH-PJL/SE-FFA	19. 6.90	D.J.Budden	Shobdon	1. 9.99
G-BSLV	Enstrom 280FX	2054	D-HHAS G-BSLV	26. 6.90	Beaufort Securities Ltd Kings Somborne, Stockbridge		10. 7.00T
G-BSLW	Bellanca 7ECA Citabria	431-66	N9696S	16. 7.90	D.W.Mann Shoreham t/a Shoreham Citabria Group		28. 4.00
G-BSLX	WAR Focke-Wulf 190 Replica	24	N698WW	19. 6.90	E.C.Murgatroyd (Bedford) (As "+4" in Luftwaffe c/s)		
G-BSMB	Cessna U206E Super Skywagon	U206-01659	N9459G C-GUUW/N9459G	25. 6.90	R.M.Burnett AAC Netheravon t/a Army Parachute Assocn		18. 2.00
G-BSMD	SNCAN 1101 Noralpha	139	F-GDPQ F-YEEE/F-YCZK/CAN-11/Fr.Mil	26. 6.90	R.J.Lamplough North Weald (Stored 3.97) (As "+114" in Luftwaffe c/s)		4. 5.96P
G-BSME	Bolkow Bo.208C Junior	596	D-ECGA	25. 6.90	D.J.Hampson	Fenland	11. 2.00
G-BSMF	Avro 652A Anson C.19	-	TX183	5. 9.90	G.M.K.Fraser Friockheim, Arbroath (As "TX183"; on rebuild 12.93)		
G-BSMG	Montgomerie-Bensen B.8M (Rotax 532)	PFA G/01-1170		22. 6.90	A.C.Timperley	Great Orton	16. 7.97P
G-BSMK	Cameron O-84 HAFB	2328		26. 6.90	D.F.Maine & D.M.Newton Redditch t/a G-BSMK Shareholders		16. 8.97A
G-BSML	Schweizer Hughes 269C (300C)	S.1462	PH-HUH N134DM	10.10.90	Triangle Computer Services Ltd Bournemouth		17. 3.00
G-BSMM	Colt 31A Sky Chariot HAFB	1779		27. 6.90	D.V.Fowler	Cranbrook, Kent	16. 6.99A
G-BSMN	CFM Streak Shadow K.137-SA & PFA/161A-11656 (Rotax 582)			26. 6.90	D.K.Daniels	Swansea	26. 4.99P
G-BSMO	Denney Kitfox (Rotax 582)	PFA/172-11773		16. 7.90	R.C.Hanley t/a Kitfox Group	Seething	25. 5.99P
G-BSMS	Cameron V-77 HAFB	2356		26. 6.90	Sade Balloons Ltd "Sadie"	Coulsdon	4. 8.99A

Regn	Type	C/n	P/I	Date	Owner/operator	Probable Base	CA Expy
G-BSMT	Rans S-10 Sakota 1289-077 & PFA/194-11793 (Rotax 532)			29. 6.90	I.M.Ashpole, Wye Valley Aviation Ltd (Ross-on-Wye)		19.10.99P
G-BSMU	Rans S-6 Coyote II 1089-090 & PFA/204-11732		G-MWJE	27. 6.90	J.S.M.Cattle (Newcastle)		23. 8.99P
G-BSMV	PA-17 Vagabond (Cont C85)	17-94	N4696H NC4696H	29. 6.90	A.Cheriton "Sophie"	Wellesbourne Mountford	11. 1.00P
G-BSMX	Bensen B.8MR	PFA G/01-1171		3. 7.90	J.S.E.R.McGregor	(Birmingham)	
G-BSND	Air Command 532 Elite	PFA G/04-1180		16. 7.90	K.Brogden & W.B.Lumb	(Heywood, Manchester)	
G-BSNE	Luscombe 8E Silvaire (Cont C85)	5757	N1130B NC1130B	2.11.90	S.C.Weston t/a Aerolite Luscombe Grp "B's Neez"	Long Marston	2. 7.99P
G-BSNF	Piper J3C-65 Cub (Cont O-200-A) (Frame No.3070) (Lippert Reed conversion)	3070	N23317 NC23317	17. 8.90	D.A.Hammant	Bere Farm, Warnford, Southampton	17. 9.98P
G-BSNG	Cessna 172N Skyhawk II	172-70192	N738SB	19. 7.90	A.J. & P.C.MacDonald (Op Edinburgh F/C)	Edinburgh	11. 9.99T
G-BSNI	Bensen B.8V	PFA G/01-1161		18. 7.90	Not known	(Cumbria)	
G-BSNJ	Cameron N-90 HAFB	2335		6. 7.90	D.P.H.Smith	(France)	6. 4.99A
G-BSNL	Bensen B.8MR (Rotax 532)	PFA G/01-1181		16. 7.90	A.C.Breane	Popham	20. 7.97P
G-BSNN	Rans S-10 Sakota (Rotax 532)	PFA/194-11846		31. 7.90	O. & S.D.Barnard	Packington, Coalville	10. 7.98P
G-BSNP	PA-28R-201T Turbo Arrow III	28R-7703236	N38537	18. 7.90	D.F.K.Singleton	(Teck, Germany)	15.12.99
G-BSNR	BAe 146 Srs.300	E-3165	EC-FGT EC-807/G-6-165/G-BSNR/N886DV/G-BSNR/(N886DV)/G-6-165	13. 7.90	Air UK Ltd	Stansted	20.11.00T
G-BSNS	BAe 146 Srs.300	E-3169	EC-FHU EC-839/G-6-169/G-BSNS/N887DV/G-BSNS/(N887DV)/G-6-169	13. 7.90	Air UK Ltd	Stansted	18.10.00T
G-BSNT	Luscombe 8A Master (Cont A65)	1679	N37018 NC37018	16. 7.90	A.L.Nightingale "Beryl"	(Holyhead)	14. 5.99P
G-BSNU	Colt 105A HAFB	1811		23. 7.90	Sun Life Assurance Society plc "Sun Life"	Bristol	2. 2.97A
G-BSNV	Boeing 737-4Q8	25168		5. 2.92	British Airways (European Operations at Gatwick) Ltd	Gatwick	18. 2.02T
G-BSNW	Boeing 737-4Q8	25169		12. 3.92	British Airways (European Operations at Gatwick) Ltd	Gatwick	19. 3.02T
G-BSNX	PA-28-181 Archer II	28-7990311	N3028S	19. 7.90	G-WATS Aviation Ltd (Op Midland Flight Centre)	Halfpenny Green	16. 8.99T
G-BSNY	Bensen B.8M (Arrow GT500R)	PFA G/01-1176		16. 7.90	H.McCartney	Newtownards, NI	3. 2.99P
G-BSNZ	Cameron O-105 HAFB	2364		16. 7.90	J.M.Stables t/a Aire Valley Balloons	Knaresborough	22. 5.97T
G-BSOE	Luscombe 8A Silvaire	4331	N1604K NC1604K	22. 8.90	S.B.Marsden (Stored dismantled as "N1604K" 8.98)	Sturgate	
G-BSOF	Colt 25A Sky Chariot Mk.II HAFB	1820		27. 7.90	H.C.J.Williams	Bristol	22. 9.92A
G-BSOG	Cessna 172M Skyhawk II	172-63636	N1508V	16. 7.90	B.Chapman & A.R.Budden	Goodwood	12.12.99
G-BSOI	Aerospatiale AS.332L Super Puma	2063	C-GSLE G-BSOI/C-GSLE	21. 9.90	Brintel Helicopters Ltd t/a British International Helicopters	Aberdeen	28. 3.00T
G-BSOJ	Thunder Ax7-77 HAFB	1818	JA- G-BSOJ	31. 7.90	R.J.S.Jones	Stourbridge	20.12.99A
G-BSOK	PA-28-161 Warrior II	28-7816191	N9749K	19. 7.90	Archer Aviation Ltd	Gloucestershire	12. 1.00T
G-BSOM	Glaser-Dirks DG-400	4-126	LN-GMC D-KGDG	12. 7.90	M.J.Watson t/a G-BSOM Grp "403"	Winthorpe	7. 3.00
G-BSON	Green S-25 HAFB	001		7. 6.90	J.J.Green	Newbury	
G-BSOO	Cessna 172F	172-52431	N8531U	19. 7.90	P.W.Lawrence t/a Double Oscar F/Grp	Seething	2.10.99
G-BSOR	CFM Streak Shadow K.131-SA & PFA/161A-11602 (Rotax 532)			23.10.89	J.P.Sorenson	Cranfield	31. 3.99P
G-BSOT	PA-38-112 Tomahawk II	38-81A0053	N25682	23. 7.90	APB Leasing Ltd	Welshpool	25.11.00T
G-BSOU	PA-38-112 Tomahawk II	38-81A0130	N23373	23. 7.90	Chubbs Aviation Services (UK) Ltd (Op Glasgow F/C)	Cumbernauld	10. 9.00T
G-BSOV	PA-38-112 Tomahawk II	38-81A0031	N25637	20. 8.90	A.Dodd (Damaged Panshanger 7.10.95; stored for spares 7.97)	Cranfield	1. 3.98T
G-BSOX	Luscombe 8AE Silvaire (Cont C85)	2318	N45791 NC45791	7. 8.90	D.Gill "Bobby Sox"	Maypole Farm, Chislet	5. 6.99P
G-BSOY	PA-34-220T Seneca III	3433155	OY-CEU	1. 8.90	British Aerospace Flight Training (UK) Ltd	Prestwick	27.11.00T
G-BSOZ	PA-28-161 Warrior II	28-7916080	N30220	14. 8.90	Moray F/C Ltd	RAF Kinloss	19.12.99T
G-BSPA	QAC Quickie Q.2 (Revmaster R2100DQ)	2227	N227T	16. 8.90	G.V.Mckirdy & B.K.Glover (Damaged Winthorpe 17.8.96; for spares ?)	Enstone	13. 5.99P
G-BSPB	Thunder Ax8-84 HAFB	1803		24. 7.90	Nigs Pertwee Ltd	Frinton-on-Sea	19. 7.93T
G-BSPC*	SAN Jodel D.140C Mousquetaire III	150	F-BMFN	2.11.81	(On overhaul 9/97)	Headcorn	31.10.85
G-BSPE	Reims Cessna F.172P Skyhawk II	2073		31.12.80	A.M.J.Clark	(Northallerton)	21. 5.99
G-BSPG	PA-34-200T Seneca II	34-8070168	N8176S	8. 8.90	D.P.Hughes	Elstree	4.11.99
G-BSPI	PA-28-161 Warrior II	28-8116025	N8258V	26. 7.90	Snapfleet Ltd "Funny Mick"	Wellesbourne Mountford	28. 1.00T
G-BSPJ	Bensen B.8	PFA G/01-1061		3. 8.90	C.M.Jones	(Stowmarket)	

Regn	Type	C/n	P/I	Date	Owner/operator	Probable Base	CA Expy
G-BSPK	Cessna 195A	7691	N1079D	14. 8.90	A.G. & D.L.Bompas	Biggin Hill	25. 4.00
G-BSPL	CFM Streak Shadow (Rotax 582)	K.140-SA		26. 7.90	MEL (Avn Oxygen) Ltd	Northrepps	13. 3.99P
G-BSPM	PA-28-161 Warrior II	28-8116046	N82679	27. 7.90	White Waltham Airfield Ltd (Op West London Aero Svs)	White Waltham	13. 8.00T
G-BSPN	PA-28R-201T Turbo Arrow III	28R-7703171	N5965V	31. 7.90	R.G. & W.Allison t/a G-BSPN F/Grp	Sandtoft	21.12.99
G-BSPW	Light Aero Avid Speed Wing (Rotax 582)	PFA/189-11840		17. 7.90	M.J.Sewell	(Windermere)	27. 5.94P
G-BSPX	Neico Lancair 320	521-320-259FB & PFA/191-11865		31. 7.90	C.H.Skelt	(Reigate)	
G-BSPY	BN-2A Islander	156	G-AXYM 5N-AIQ/G-AXYM/G-51-156	1. 6.90	G-WATS Aviation Ltd	Bagby	16. 7.00
G-BSRC	Cessna 150M Commuter	150-77651	N6337K	25. 7.90	Liverpool Flying School Ltd	Liverpool	27. 5.00
G-BSRH	Pitts S-1C Special (Lyc O-360)	LS-2	N4111	7. 8.90	M.R.Janney	(Ashford, Kent)	30. 7.98P
G-BSRI	Neico Lancair 235 (Lyc O-235)	PFA/191-11467		9. 8.90	G.Lewis	Liverpool	14. 6.99P
G-BSRK	ARV1 Super 2 (Hewland AE75)	K.007	ZK-FSQ	8. 8.90	D.M.Blair	(Holywell)	21. 5.99P
G-BSRL	Everett Gyroplane Srs.2	022		8. 8.90	R.F.E.Burley	(Gillingham, Kent)	
G-BSRP	Rotorway Exec (RW152) (Originally quoted c/n 3647)	3824		15. 8.90	R.J.Baker	Bromsgrove	24. 9.92P
G-BSRR	Cessna 182Q Skylane II	182-66915	N96961	25. 7.90	Select Management Svs Ltd	Seething	22. 5.00
G-BSRT	Denney Kitfox mk.2 742 & PFA/172-11873 (Rotax 582)			9. 8.90	A.J.Lloyd	Milson	1. 6.99P
G-BSRX	CFM Streak Shadow K.148-SA & PFA/206-11870 (Rotax 618)			15. 8.90	P.Williams	Netherthorpe	1. 5.98P
G-BSRZ	Air Command 532 Elite Two-Seat PFA G/05-1188			15. 8.90	A.S.G.Crabb	(Beverley)	
G-BSSA	Luscombe 8E Silvaire (Cont C85)	4176	N1449K NC1449K	15. 8.90	Punters Promotions Ltd	White Waltham	26. 3.99P
G-BSSB	Cessna 150L Commuter	150-74147	N19076	15. 8.90	D.T.A.Rees	Haverfordwest	29. 4.00T
G-BSSC	PA-28-161 Warrior II	28-8216176	N81993 N9529N/N8234B	15. 8.90	Oxford Aviation Services Ltd	Oxford	17. 1.00T
G-BSSE	PA-28-140 Cherokee	28-7525192	N33440	22.10.90	Comed Avn Ltd (Damaged Netherthorpe 2.7.97)	Blackpool	30. 4.99T
G-BSSF	Denney Kitfox mk.2 738 & PFA/172-11796 (Rotax 582)			15. 8.90	P.Heckles	(Enfield)	20.10.99P
G-BSSI	Rans S-6 Coyote II (Rotax 582) 0190-112 & PFA/204-11782		(G-MWJA)	17. 8.90	R.W.Skelton	(Craigavon, Co.Armagh)	6.11.99P
G-BSSJ	Clutton FRED Srs.2 (VW 1834)	PFA/29-10753		23. 8.90	R.F.Jopling	Bagby	21. 6.99P
G-BSSK	QAC Quickie Q.200 (Cont O-200-A)	PFA/94A-11354		5. 9.90	D.G.Greatrex	Enstone	23. 9.98P
G-BSSN*	Air Command 532 Elite Two-Seat 0631 (Possibly c/n PFA G/05-1187)			21. 8.90	R.C.Bettany (Cancelled by CAA 10.3.99 - no permit issued)	(Swansea)	
G-BSSO	Cameron O-90 HAFB	2255		23. 7.90	R.R. & J.E.Hatton "Just So"	Warminster	15. 5.99A
G-BSSP	Robin DR.400/180R Remorqueur	2015		24. 9.90	Soaring (Oxford) Ltd (Op Air Cadets Gliding School)	RAF Syerston	8. 1.00
G-BSSR	PA-28-151 Cherokee Warrior	28-7615001	N1190X	29. 8.90	H.M.B.Lundgren	Lydd	19. 2.00
G-BSST*	BAC-Sud Concorde SST	002 & 135208		6. 5.68	The Science Museum	RNAS Yeovilton	31.10.74P*
G-BSSV	CFM Streak Shadow K.129-SA & PFA/206-11657 (Rotax 532)			21. 8.90	R.W.Payne	Langtoft	5. 5.98P
G-BSSW	PA-28-161 Warrior II	28-7816143	N47850	29. 8.90	R.L.Hayward (Op Bristol F/C)	Filton	11. 6.99T
G-BSSX	PA-28-161 Warrior II	2816056	N9141H	11. 9.90	Airways Aero Associations Ltd (Op British Airways F/C) (Martha Masanabo/Ndebele t/s)	Booker	9.11.99T
G-BSTC	Aeronca 11AC Chief (Cont A65)	11AC-1660	N3289E NC3289E	15.10.90	B.Bridgman & N.J.Mortimore Watchford Farm, Yarcombe (Damaged Henstridge 18.4.93; on rebuild 12.95)		26. 6.93P
G-BSTE	Aerospatiale AS.355F2 Twin Squirrel	5453		29. 8.90	Hygrade Foods Ltd	Biggin Hill	1. 8.00
G-BSTH	PA-25-235 Pawnee C	25-5009	N8599L	25. 9.90	Scottish Gliding Union Ltd	Portmoak	17. 3.00
G-BSTI	Piper J3C-85 Cub	19144	N6007H NC6007H	31. 8.90	I.Fraser & G.L.Nunn	Knettishall	28. 3.99P
G-BSTJ	DH.82A Tiger Moth	82309	OO-MEH	6. 9.90	Mavis R.Parker	Sywell	14. 8.99
	OO-GEB/R Neth AF A-13/PH-UFB/A-13/N9192 (As "N9192/RCO-N") (Possibly ex R Neth AF A-23 - c/n 86628 and PG742)						
G-BSTK	Thunder Ax8-90 HAFB	1838		17. 9.90	M.Williams	Wadhurst, E.Sussex	4. 5.95A
G-BSTL	Rand Robinson KR-2	PFA/129-11863		6. 9.90	C.S.Hales	(Walsall)	
G-BSTM	Cessna 172L Skyhawk	172-60143	N4243Q	25. 9.90	A.H.Windle t/a G-BSTM Grp	Cambridge	27. 2.00
G-BSTO	Cessna 152 II	152-82133	N68005	4. 9.90	Plymouth School of Flying Ltd	Plymouth	14.11.99T

Regn	Type	C/n	P/I	Date	Owner/operator	Probable Base	CA Expy
G-BSTP	Cessna 152 II	152-82925	N89953	4. 9.90	Cobham Leasing Ltd	Bournemouth	3.12.99T
G-BSTR	Grumman-American AA-5 Traveler	AA5-0688	OO-ALR OO-HAN/(OO-WAZ)	8.10.90	James Allan (Avn & Engineering) Ltd	Glenrothes	5.12.99
G-BSTS	Schleicher ASW20L	20311	BGA.2618	10. 9.90	T.I.Gardiner (Presumed NTU)	Challock	
G-BSTT	Rans S-6 Coyote II (Rotax 582) 0190-115 & PFA/204-11880			5. 9.90	D.G.Palmer	(Peterhead)	28. 4.99P
G-BSTV	PA-32-300 Cherokee Six	32-40378	N4069R	13. 9.90	B.C.Hudson (Stored 9.94)	Popham	
G-BSTX	Luscombe 8A Silvaire	3301	EI-CDZ G-BSTX/N71874/NC71874	10. 9.90	A.A.Alderdice	Kilkeel, Co.Down	18. 6.99P
G-BSTY	Thunder Ax8-90 HAFB	394		12. 9.90	J.W.Cato	Leicester	15. 6.97A
G-BSTZ	PA-28-140 Cherokee Cruiser	28-7725153	N1674H	10.10.90	Air Navigation & Trading Co Ltd	Blackpool	15.10.99T
G-BSUA	Rans S-6 Coyote II (Rotax 582)	PFA/204-11910		29.10.90	A.J.Todd	Abbey Warren Farm, Bucknall, Lincoln	1.12.99P
G-BSUB	Colt 77A HAFB	1801		30.10.90	R.R.J.Wilson & M.P.Hill	Bristol	20. 3.99A
G-BSUD	Luscombe 8A Master (Cont A65)	1745	N37084 NC37084	14. 9.90	I.G.Harrison	Egginton	26. 6.99P
G-BSUE	Cessna U206G Stationair II	U206-04334	N756TB	6. 9.90	R.A.Robinson	Little Gransden	7.12.00
G-BSUF	PA-32RT-300 Lance II	32R-7885240	N32PL ZP-PJQ/N9641N	17. 9.90	M.J.Parker	Elstree	2. 6.00
G-BSUH*	Cessna 140 (Cont C85)	8092	N89088 NC89088	15.10.90	Not known (Damaged Gowran Grange 6.93; stored 3.98)	Abbeyshrule, Ireland	2. 5.94
G-BSUJ	Brugger MB.2 Colibri	PFA/43-10726		17. 9.90	M.A.Farrelly	(Liverpool)	
G-BSUK	Colt 77A HAFB	1374		21. 9.90	A.J.Moore	Northwood, Middlesex	2. 8.94A
G-BSUM	Scheibe SF.27MB	6303	D-KIBE	31.10.90	M.J.Davies t/a M Syndicate	Winthorpe	
G-BSUO	Scheibe SF-25C-2000 Falke	44501	D-KIOK	6.12.90	British Gliding Association Ltd	Booker	26. 2.00
G-BSUR*	Rotorway Exec 90 (RW 162)	5003		21. 9.90	Coaching For Results Ltd (Stored 6.97 - cancelled by CAA 26.3.99)	Sherburn	1.12.93P
G-BSUT	Rans S-6-ESA Coyote II (Rotax 582) 0990-138 & PFA/204-11897			2.10.90	J.Bell	Barton	4.11.99P
G-BSUU	Colt 180A HAFB	1851		17. 9.90	Heritage Balloons	Bath	26.11.99T
G-BSUV	Cameron O-77 HAFB	2407		26. 9.90	R.Moss	Banchory	15.12.99A
G-BSUW	PA-34-200T Seneca II	34-7870081	N2360M	26. 9.90	TG Avn Ltd (Op Thanet Flying Club)	Manston	5.12.99T
G-BSUX	Carlson Sparrow II (Rotax 532)	PFA/209-11794		5.10.90	J.Stephenson (Stored 4.97)	Bagby	10. 1.00P
G-BSUZ	Denney Kitfox mk.3 (Rotax 582) 745 & PFA/172-11875			10. 9.90	M.J.Clark	(Horsham)	6. 5.99P
G-BSVB	PA-28-181 Archer II	2890098	N9155S	10. 9.90	B.R.Janman & PEPS Intl Ltd	Sywell	30.12.99T
G-BSVE	Binder CP.301S Smaragd	113	HB-SED	27. 9.90	R.E.Perry t/a Smaragd F/Grp	Halesland, Cheddar	3. 4.99P
G-BSVF	PA-28-161 Warrior II	28-8416047	C-GVSJ N9575N	2.10.90	Airways Aero Associations Ltd (Op British Airways F/C) (Wings of the City t/s)	Booker	29.11.99T
G-BSVG	PA-28-161 Warrior II	28-8516013	C-GZAV	2.10.90	Airways Aero Associations Ltd (Op British Airways F/C) (Dove/Colum t/s)	Booker	22.12.99T
G-BSVH	Piper J3C-75 Cub	15360	N87702 NC87702	2.10.90	A.R.Meakin	Eastbach Farm, Coleford	5. 8.99P
G-BSVI	PA-16 Clipper	16-186	N5379H	7.11.90	I.R.Blakemore "Spirit of St.Petersburg"	Old Sarum	30. 6.01
G-BSVJ	Piper J3C-65 Cub	17521	N2MD R N70515/NC70515		V.S.E.Norman	Rendcomb	
G-BSVK	Denney Kitfox mk.2 (Rotax 582)	PFA/172-11731		2.10.90	C.M.Looney	(Leatherhead)	5. 4.94P
G-BSVM	PA-28-161 Warrior II	28-8116173	N8351N	7.11.90	A.S.Bamrah t/a Falcon F/Svs	Biggin Hill	23. 1.00T
G-BSVN	Thorp T-18 (Lyc O-290)	107	N4881	17. 9.90	J.H.Kirkham	Barton	4.10.99P
G-BSVP	PA-23-250 Aztec F	27-7754115	N63787	9. 2.78	Time Electronics Ltd	Biggin Hill	22.11.98
G-BSVR	Schweizer Hughes 269C (300C)	S.1236	OO-JWW D-HLEB	14.11.90	Martinair Ltd	Sherburn	1.12.00
G-BSVS	Robin DR.400/100 Cadet	2017		22.10.90	D.M.Chalmers	Upper Harford	22. 3.00
G-BSVV	PA-38-112 Tomahawk	38-79A0723	N2492L	3.10.90	J.Maffia & H.Merkado	Panshanger	10. 6.00T
G-BSVW	PA-38-112 Tomahawk	38-79A0149	N2606B	9.11.90	EFG Flying Services Ltd	Biggin Hill	27. 7.00T
G-BSVX	PA-38-112 Tomahawk	38-79A0950	N2336P	10. 1.91	D.J.Hockings	Rochester	13. 4.00T
G-BSVY	PA-38-112 Tomahawk	38-79A0038	N2396B	10. 1.91	Cardiff-Wales Flying Club Ltd	Cardiff	23. 7.00T
G-BSVZ	Pietenpol Air Camper (Regd as a Pietenpol/Challis Chaffinch)	1008	N3265	6.11.90	A.F.Cashin (Stored 9.97)	Maypole Farm, Chislet	6.9.93P*
G-BSWB	Rans S-10 Sakota (Rotax 532) 0489-046 & PFA/194-11560			8.10.90	F.A.Hewitt	Garston Farm, Marshfield	5. 3.99P
G-BSWC	Boeing-Stearman E75 (PT-13D) Kaydet (Lyc R-680)	75-5560	N17112 N5021V/42-17397	16.11.90	R.R.White (As "112" in US Army c/s)	Old Sarum	31. 8.00T
G-BSWF	PA-16 Clipper (Lyc O-320)	16-475	N5865H	12.10.90	T.M.Storey	Bolney	30. 8.98
G-BSWG	PA-15 Vagabond (Cont A65)	15-99	N4316H NC4316H	8.10.90	P.E.J.Sturgeon	Priory Farm, Tibenham	31. 8.97P
G-BSWH	Cessna 152 II	152-81365	N49861	15.10.90	Airspeed Avn Ltd	Swansea	25. 1.99T

Regn	Type	C/n	P/I	Date	Owner/operator	Probable Base	CA Expy
G-BSWI	Rans S-10 Sakota (Rotax 532)	PFA/194-11872		16.10.90	J.M.Mooney (Shotts, Lanark) (Damaged Braehead 26.10.93)		11. 6.94P
G-BSWJ	Cameron O-77 HAFB	2433		17.10.90	T.Charlwood "JVC"	Billingshurst	14. 6.99A
G-BSWL	Slingsby T-61F Venture T.2	1974	EI-CCQ G-BSWL/ZA655	15.10.90	K.Richards	(Bridgend)	17. 2.01
G-BSWM	Slingsby T-61F Venture T.2	1965	ZA629	12.10.90	L.J.McKelvie	Bellarena	26. 3.00
G-BSWR	PBN BN-2T Turbine Islander	2245		22.10.90	Police Authority for Northern Ireland	Aldergrove	2. 3.01T
G-BSWV	Cameron N-77 HAFB	2369		22.10.90	Leicester Mercury Ltd "Leicester Mercury"	Leicester	22. 3.99A
G-BSWX	Cameron V-90 HAFB	2401		22.10.90	B.J.Burrows "Beeswax"	Bristol	20. 3.99A
G-BSWY	Cameron N-77 HAFB	2428		12.10.90	M.R.Nanda t/a Nottingham Balloon Club	Nottingham	19. 7.99A
G-BSWZ	Cameron A-180 HAFB	2419	C-FGWZ G-BSWZ	22.10.90	G.C.Ludlow	Hythe	30. 7.97T
G-BSXA	PA-28-161 Warrior II	28-8416121	N4373Z N9622N	11.12.90	A.S.Bamrah t/a Falcon F/Svs	Biggin Hill	31. 7.00T
G-BSXB	PA-28-161 Warrior II	28-8416125	N4374D N9626N	4.12.90	Aeroshow Ltd	Gloucestershire	24. 3.00T
G-BSXC	PA-28-161 Warrior II	28-8416126	N4374F N9627N	4.12.90	L.T.Halpin Clutton Hill Farm, High Littleton		25. 6.00T
G-BSXD	Soko P-2 Kraguj	030	30146 Yugoslav Army	22.10.90	L.C.MacKnight (As "30146" in Yugoslav Army c/s)	Elstree	22. 4.99P
G-BSXI	Mooney M.20E Chapparal	700056	N6766V	31.10.90	L.S. & K.L.Johnson Lodge Farm, Clacton t/a Mooney Grp		4. 5.00
G-BSXM	Cameron V-77 HAFB	2446		5.11.90	C.A.Oxby "Oxby"	Doncaster	27. 7.97A
G-BSXN	Robinson R-22 Beta	1611		14.11.90	J.G.Gray	Berwick-upon-Tweed	23. 1.00
G-BSXP	Air Command 532 Elite	0633 & PFA G/04-1195		5.11.90	B.J.West	(Sevenoaks)	
G-BSXS	PA-28-181 Archer II	28-7990151	N3055C	26.11.90	Pipe-Air Ltd	Shoreham	5. 3.00
G-BSXT	Piper J/5A Cub Cruiser (Cont C85)	5-498	N33409 NC33409	8.11.90	M.G. & K.J.Thompson (Stored 10.97) Belle Vue Farm ,Yarnscombe		12. 5.97P
G-BSXX	Whittaker MW7	PFA/171-11469		16.10.90	H.J.Stanley	(Abingdon)	
G-BSXY	Oldfield Baby Lakes	PFA/10-10094	(G-JENY)	15.10.90	B.Freeman-Jones	(Alford, Aberdeen)	
G-BSYA	Jodel D.18 (VW1834)	PFA/169-11316		7.11.90	S.Harrison	Eshott	5. 2.99P
G-BSYB	Cameron N-120 HAFB	2406		7.11.90	M.Buono	Siena, Italy	6.11.99A
G-BSYC	PA-32R-300 Cherokee Lance	32R-7780159	N7745T N1435H	2. 4.91	T.E. & M.J.Whyton t/a Arrow Avn	Halfpenny Green	4. 4.00
G-BSYD	Cameron A-180 HAFB	2426		18.10.90	A.A.Brown t/a Balloon Company "Discovery"	Guildford	31.10.98T
G-BSYF	Luscombe 8A Silvaire	3455	N72028 NC72028	12.11.90	Atlantic Connexions Ltd (Stored 7.95) t/a Atlantic Avn Manor Farm, Glatton		
G-BSYG	PA-12 Super Cruiser (Lyc O-235)	12-2106	N3228M NC3228M	12.11.90	E.R.Newall t/a Fat Cub Group	Breighton	8. 7.99P
G-BSYH	Luscombe 8A Silvaire (Cont A65)	2842	N71415 NC71415	13.11.90	N.R.Osborne	Insch	31. 8.99P
G-BSYI	Aerospatiale AS.355F1 Twin Squirrel	5197	M-MJI	14.11.90	Lynton Avn Ltd (Op European Helicopters Ltd)	Denham	28.11.99T
G-BSYJ	Cameron N-77 HAFB	2441		13.11.90	Chubb Fire Ltd "Chubb Fire II"	Sunbury-on-Thames	16.12.99A
G-BSYK*	PA-38-112 Tomahawk II	38-81A0143	N23449	30. 1.91	Flychoice Ltd Halfpenny Green (Cancelled by CAA 10.3.99 - no C of A issued)		
G-BSYL*	PA-38-112 Tomahawk II	38-81A0172	N91333	23. 1.91	Flychoice Ltd Halfpenny Green (Stored 9.97; cancelled by CAA 10.3.99 - no C of A issued)		
G-BSYM	PA-38-112 Tomahawk II	38-82A0072	N2507V	30. 1.91	Flychoice Ltd Wellesbourne Mountford (Damaged 27.7.94; open store 5.98)		4. 9.94T
G-BSYO	Piper J3C-90 Cub (L-4B-PI) (Cont O-200-A) (Frame No.12639)	12809	(G-BSMJ) (G-BRHE)/EC-AIY/HB-ODO/44-80513	19. 2.91	C.R.Reynolds & J.D.Fuller Pent Farm, Postling, Kent (Officially regd as c/n 10244 ex 43-1383/F-BFYF which is HB-OVG)		7. 7.99P
G-BSYP	Bensen B.8MR (Rotax 503)	PFA G/01-1186		16.11.90	C.R.Gordon	Carlisle	3. 6.98P
G-BSYU	Robin DR.400/180 Regent	2027		26.11.90	K.J.J.Jarman & P.D.Smoothy	(Brackley)	27. 2.00
G-BSYV	Cessna 150M Commuter	150-78371	N9423U	16.11.90	L.R.Haunch t/a Fenland Flying School	Fenland	28. 2.00T
G-BSYW	Cessna 150M Commuter	150-78446	N9498U	16.11.90	J.A.F.Waller	Barton	25. 3.00
G-BSYY	PA-28-161 Warrior II	2816009	N9100X	26.11.90	Oxford Aviation Services Ltd	Oxford	1. 2.00T
G-BSYZ	PA-28-161 Warrior II	28-8516051	N6908H	22.11.90	Piper Air (Glasgow) Ltd	Glasgow	8. 9.00T
G-BSZB	Stolp SA.300 Starduster Too (Lyc O-360)	545	N5495M	3.12.90	D.T.Gethin	Haverfordwest	7. 1.99P
G-BSZC	Beechcraft C-45H-BH Expeditor AF-258		N9541Z 51-11701	14.12.90	A.A.Hodgson Bryngwyn Bach "Southern Comfort" (As "AF258/51-11701A" in USAF c/s) (Originally built as AT-7 42-2490 c/n 4166; re-manufactured 4.52)		29. 5.00
G-BSZD	Robin DR.400/180 Regent	2029		21.11.90	R.J.Hitchman & P.J.Rowland & Sons (Farmers) Ltd Draycott Farm, Chiseldon		17. 3.00
G-BSZF	CEA Jodel DR.250/160 Capitaine	32	F-BNJB	29.11.90	J.B.Randle	Piltdown, E.Sussex	24. 4.00

Regn	Type	C/n	P/I	Date	Owner/operator	Probable Base	CA Expy
G-BSZG	Stolp SA.100 Starduster (Lyc O-320)	101	N70P	27.11.90	S.W.Watkins & D.F.Chapman Trecorras Farm, Llangarron		21.10.97P
G-BSZH	Thunder Ax7-77 HAFB	1848		27.11.90	K.E.Viney & L.J.Weston "Her Outdoors"	Olney	30.11.99T
G-BSZI	Cessna 152 II	152-85856	N95139	17.12.90	Eglinton F/C Ltd	Eglinton	9. 2.00T
G-BSZJ	PA-28-181 Archer II	28-8190216	N8373Z	6.12.90	R.D.Fuller & M.L.A.Pudney	Earls Colne	3. 5.00
G-BSZL	Colt 77A HAFB	1883		28.11.90	Staedtler Mars GmbH "Staedtler"	Nurnberg, Germany	12.12.97A
G-BSZM	Montgomerie-Bensen B.8MR (Rotax 582)	PFA G/01-1193		30.11.90	J.H.H.Turner	Johnstone, Renfrew	17.12.98P
G-BSZN	Bucker Bu.133D-1 Jungmeister (Siemens Bramo SH14A) (Bitz-built)	2002	N8103 D-ECAY	30.11.90	A.J.Norman t/a Norman Aeroplane Trust	Rendcomb	29. 7.99P
G-BSZO	Cessna 152 II	152-80221	N24334	30.11.90	A.T.Hooper & T.E.Evans (Op RS Pilot Training) Wellesbourne Mountford		19.10.01T
G-BSZS	Robinson R-22 Beta	1235	N8058J	13.12.90	Blade Runner Helicopters Ltd (Kingswinford)		16. 3.00
G-BSZT	PA-28-161 Warrior II	28-8116027	N8260D	31.12.90	Airbase Aircraft Ltd	Shoreham	8. 4.00T
G-BSZU	Cessna 150F	150-63481	N6881F	3.12.90	M.J.Tarrant	Old Sarum	19.12.00T
G-BSZV	Cessna 150F	150-62304	N3504L	3.12.90	Kirmington Avn Ltd	(Bembridge, IOW)	17. 7.00T
G-BSZW	Cessna 152 II	152-81072	N48958	3.12.90	Haimoss Ltd	Old Sarum	6.10.00T
G-BSZY	Cameron A-180 HAFB	2479		3. 1.91	K.H.Benning	Telgte, Germany	2. 1.96A

G-BTAA-BTZZ

Regn	Type	C/n	P/I	Date	Owner/operator	Probable Base	CA Expy
G-BTAB	BAe 125 Srs.800B	258088	G-5-563	12. 7.88	Dean Finance Co Ltd	Heathrow	6. 5.99T
			G-BOOA/(ZK-RHP)/G-5-563		(Op by Aravco)		
G-BTAD	Macair Merlin	PFA/208-11661		6.11.90	A.T. & M.R.Dowie Scotland Farm, Hook		
					(Under construction 5.95)		
G-BTAG	Cameron O-77 HAFB	2454		12.11.90	R.A.Shapland "Tag-Along"	Petworth	21. 9.99A
G-BTAH	Bensen B.8M	PFA G/07-1196		13.12.90	T.B.Johnson	St.Merryn	31. 8.98P
	(Arrow GT500R)						
G-BTAK	EAA Acrosport 2	1-468	N440X	27.12.90	P.G.Harrison "The Duck"	Sywell	2. 3.99P
	(Lyc O-320)						
G-BTAL	Reims Cessna F.152 II	1444		7. 4.78	TG Avn Ltd (Op Thanet F/C)	Manston	14. 3.00T
G-BTAM	PA-28-181 Archer II	2890093	N9153D	10. 1.91	Tri-Star Farms Ltd	Ronaldsway	24. 4.00T
G-BTAN	Thunder Ax7-65Z HAFB	517		4. 5.83	A.S.Newnham	Southampton	4. 7.99A
G-BTAP	PA-38-112 Tomahawk	38-78A0141	N9603T	8. 1.91	Western Air (Thruxton) Ltd	Thruxton	20. 7.00T
G-BTAR	PA-38-112 Tomahawk	38-79A0383	N2584D	13. 2.91	Aerohire Ltd Halfpenny Green		12. 3.00T
					(Damaged Liverpool 19.6.98)		
G-BTAS	PA-38-112 Tomahawk	38-79A0545	F-GTAS	21. 2.91	W.Brooks	Alderney	17. 3.00T
			G-BTAS/N2492G				
G-BTAT*	Denney Kitfox mk.2 689 & PFA/172-11832			6.11.90	O.W.Owen & M.D.Harris	Kemble	15. 4.97P
	(Rotax 582)						
G-BTAU	Thunder Ax7-77 HAFB	1429		13.12.90	Sara L.G.Williams	Bristol	13.12.91A
G-BTAV	Colt 105A HAFB	1858		13.12.90	D.C.Chipping	Evora, Portugal	20.12.93A
G-BTAW	PA-28-161 Warrior II	28-8616031	N9259T	14.12.90	A.J.Wiggins	Gloucestershire	30. 4.00T
					(Op Gloucester & Cheltenham Flying School)		
G-BTAX*	PA-31-350 Navajo Chieftain		N63721	3. 9.87	Meggair Ltd (To Canada by container 7.97)		6.12.91T
		31-7752036					
G-BTAZ	Evans VP-2	PFA/63-11474		13.12.90	G.S.Poulter	(Norwich)	
G-BTBA	Robinson R-22 Beta	1717		18. 3.91	Heliflight (UK) Ltd Halfpenny Green		30. 4.00
G-BTBB	Thunder Ax8-105 Srs.2 HAFB	1871		23.11.90	W.J.Brogan	(London SW6)	3. 3.98T
G-BTBC	PA-28-161 Warrior II	28-7916414	N28755	19.12.90	M.J.L.MacDonald Wellesbourne Mountford		21. 4.00T
					(Op Wellesbourne Avn)		
G-BTBF	Fisher FP.202 Super Koala	(G-MWOZ)	24.12.90	E.A.Taylor	(Southend)	
	SK.067 & PFA/158-11954				(Half completed 1.99)		
G-BTBG	Denney Kitfox	PFA/172-11845		18.12.90	J.Catley	(Bristol)	
G-BTBH	Ryan ST3KR (PT-22-RY)	2063	N854	18. 2.91	A.T.Hooper & C.C.Silk		
	(Kinner R56)		N50993/41-20854		t/a Ryan Group (As "854" in US Army c/s)		
					Bericote Farm, Blackdown, Leamington Spa		17. 1.99P
G-BTBI	WAR P-47 Thunderbolt replica	0054	N47DL	8. 1.91	S.W.Ballantyne	Carlisle	8. 9.98P
	(Cont O-200-A) (Marked as Project No. 52685A)				(As "85" in USAF c/s) "Lil Jug"		
G-BTBJ	Cessna 195B	16046	N4461C	2.10.91	J.Griffin	Kemble	20. 5.00
G-BTBL	Montgomerie-Bensen B.8MR						
	Merlin (Rotax 532) PFA G/01A-1183			21.12.90	R.D.H.Dobree-Carey		
						Blandford Forum/Kemble	2. 9.99P
G-BTBN	Denney Kitfox mk.2 686 & PFA/172-11859			31.12.90	T.M.W.Webster & S.A.Webster		
	(Rotax 582)					Croft Farm, Defford	29. 5.98P
G-BTBP	Cameron N-90 HAFB	2464		21.12.90	Julia B.Turnau Pianella, Italy		1. 6.99A
					t/a Chianti Balloon Club		
G-BTBR	Cameron DP-80 Hot-Air Airship	2344		21.12.90	Cameron Balloons Ltd	Bristol	3.12.97A
					"Cameron Skyship"		
G-BTBS*	Cameron N-180 HAFB	2440		21.12.90	Balloon Preservation Group	Lancing	27. 6.97T
					"The Big Sod"		
G-BTBU	PA-18-150 Super Cub	18-7509010	N9665P	3. 1.91	A.J.White t/a G-BTBU Syndicate	Denham	9. 7.00
G-BTBV	Cessna 140	12727	N2474N	2. 4.91	M.S.Johnson	Enstone	11. 6.00
	(Cont C85)		NC2474N				
G-BTBW	Cessna 120	14220	N2009V	24. 1.91	Melanie J.Willies		
	(Cont C90)		NC2009V			Standalone Farm, Meppershall	13. 7.01
G-BTBX	Piper J3C-65 Cub	6334	N35367	29. 1.91	J.B.Hargrave & D.T.C.Collins RAF Henlow		18. 9.00
			NC35367		t/a Henlow Taildraggers		
G-BTBY	PA-17 Vagabond	17-195	N4894H	4. 1.91	G.J.Smith Clipgate Farm, Denton		1. 5.99P
	(Cont C85)						
G-BTCA	PA-32R-300 Cherokee Lance		N5941V	10. 1.91	P.Taylor t/a Lance Grp Halfpenny Green		26. 5.00
		32R-7780381					
G-BTCB	Air Command 582 Sport			9. 1.91	G.Scurrah	Millom	
	0634 & PFA G/04-1198				(Nearing completion 5.95)		
G-BTCC	Grumman F6F-5K Hellcat	A-11286	(N10CN)	31.12.90	Patina Ltd	Duxford	18. 8.99P
			N100T/FN80142/Bu.80141		(Op The Fighter Collection)		
	(Composite with centre section from F6F-3 Bu.08831 c/n A-218) (As "Bu.40467/19" in VF-6 Sqn US Navy c/s)						
G-BTCD	North American	122-39608	N51JJ	11. 1.91	Patina Ltd	Duxford	28. 4.99P
	P-51D-25NA Mustang		N6340T/RCAF 9568/44-73149		(Op The Fighter Collection) "Candyman"/Moose"		
					(As "463221/G4-S" in 362nd FS/357th FG USAAF c/s)		
G-BTCE	Cessna 152 II	152-81376	N49876	10. 1.91	S.T.Gilbert	Enstone	13. 8.00T
	(Tailwheel conversion)						
G-BTCH	Luscombe 8E Silvaire	6403	N1976B	11. 2.91	J.Grewcock & R.C.Carroll	Popham	9. 9.99P
	(Cont C85)		NC1976B				
G-BTCI	PA-17 Vagabond	17-136	N4839H	11. 1.91	T.R.Whittome	Inverness	5. 7.99P
	(Cont A65)		NC4839H				
G-BTCJ	Luscombe 8AE Silvaire	1869	N41908	16. 1.91	C.C. & J.M.Lovell	Chilbolton	15. 6.99P
	(Cont O-200A)		NC41908				

Regn	Type	C/n	P/I	Date	Owner/operator	Probable Base	CA Expy
G-BTCK	Cameron A-210 HAFB	2451		8. 1.91	M.W.A.Shemilt Henley-on-Thames		8. 5.98T
					t/a H-O-T Air Balloons		
G-BTCM	Cameron N-90 HAFB	1306	(G-BMPW)	8. 5.86	J.D. & K.Griffiths "TCM"	Newark	10.10.00A
G-BTCO	Clutton FRED Srs.II	PFA/29-10558		11. 1.91	I.P.Manley	(Yeovil)	
G-BTCR	Rans S-10 Sakota	PFA/194-11877		11. 1.91	B.J.Hewitt	(Dromore, NI)	11. 5.94P
	(Rotax 532)						
G-BTCS	Colt 90A HAFB	1895		11. 1.91	R.C.Stone	Reading	25.10.98A
					"Rosie Rags" (Variety Club of GB c/s)		
G-BTCT	Aerospatiale AS.332L Super Puma	2129	FAP 1012	14. 1.91	Bristow Helicopters Ltd	Aberdeen	31. 3.01T
					"Anstruther"		
G-BTCW	Cameron A-180 HAFB	2458		17. 1.91	P.Clark t/a Bristol Balloons	Bristol	1. 9.97T
G-BTCZ	Cameron Chateau 84SS HAFB	2246		18. 1.91	Forbes Europe Inc Balleroy, Normandy		19. 6.99
					"Chateau II"		
G-BTDA	Slingsby T-61F Venture T.2	1870	XZ550	17. 4.91	T.Holloway t/a RAFGSA RAF Wattisham		16. 3.00
					(Op Anglia Gliding Club)		
G-BTDC	Denney Kitfox mk.2 405 & PFA/172-11483			11. 1.91	D.Collinson	(Durham)	
G-BTDD	CFM Streak Shadow K.127-SA & PFA/161A-11622			14. 1.91	R.D.Davidson	Perth	1. 9.99P
	(Rotax 582)						
G-BTDE	Cessna C-165 Airmaster	551	N21911 NC21911	18. 1.91	G.S.Moss	Popham	3. 9.00
G-BTDF	Luscombe 8AF Silvaire	2205	N45678 NC45678	17. 4.91	M.Stow Blaydon-on-Tyne		19. 8.93P
	(Cont C90)				(Damaged nr Newcastle 11.4.93; stored 5.93)		
G-BTDH	Hunting-Percival P.56 Provost T.1	N2416R PAC/F/183 7925M/WV666		25. 1.91	J.J.Woodhouse Thruxton		25. 9.98P
					t/a Flying Services (As "WV666/O-D" in 6 FTS c/s)		
G-BTDI	Robinson R-22 Beta	1670		29. 1.91	R.L.Moody	Denham	15. 5.00
G-BTDN	Denney Kitfox mk.2 688 & PFA/172-11826			22. 1.91	S.D.Arnold	(Coventry)	
					t/a Foxy Flyers Grp		
G-BTDP	Grumman TBM-3R Avenger	3381	N3966A Bu.53319	5. 2.91	A.Haig-Thomas North Weald		13. 5.99
					(As "53319/RB-319" in USN c/s)		
G-BTDR	Aero Designs Pulsar	PFA/202-11962		24. 1.91	M.Jordan	Stapleford	12. 6.99P
	(Rotax 582)						
G-BTDS	Colt 77A HAFB	1897		29. 1.91	CP Witter Ltd "Witters II"	Chester	22. 9.96A
G-BTDT	CASA I-131E Jungmann	2131	E3B-505	5. 2.91	T.A.Reed Watchford Farm, Yarcombe		8. 6.94P
					(On rebuild off site 9.98)		
G-BTDV	PA-28-161 Warrior II	28-7816355	N3548M	25. 2.91	R.E.Thorne	Alderney	17. 5.01
G-BTDW	Cessna 152 II	152-79864	N757NC	25. 2.91	J.A.Blenkharn	Carlisle	27. 8.00T
G-BTDX	PA-18-150 Super Cub	18-7809098	N62595	28. 1.91	A.D. Hammond	(Hitchin)	25. 5.00T
					t/a Hammond Aviation		
G-BTDY	PA-18-150 Super Cub	18-8109007	N24570	28. 1.91	Rodger Avn Ltd (Op Medway Flt Training)		23. 7.94T
					(DBF Stoneacre Farm 1993 and used in rebuild of G-HAHA) Stoneacre Farm, Farthing Corner		
G-BTDZ	CASA I-131E Jungmann	2104	E3B-524	5. 2.91	R.J.Pickin & I.M.White	Redhill	29. 5.99P
G-BTEA	Cameron N-105 HAFB	284		31. 5.77	M.W.A.Shemilt Henley-on-Thames		19. 5.96A
					t/a HOT Air Balloons "Big Red"		
G-BTEE	Cameron O-120 HAFB	2499		24. 1.91	W.H. & J.P.Morgan	Swansea	21. 3.99T
					"Y Ddraig Goch/The Red Dragon"		
G-BTEF	Pitts S-1 Special	515H	N88PR	19. 2.91	C.Davidson	Blackpool	28.10.97P
	(Lyc IO-360)				t/a Northwest Aerobatics		
G-BTEI	Everett Campbell Cricket	023		31. 1.91	R.A.Jarvis	Portmoak	21.12.98P
	(Arrow GT500R)				(Damaged nr Great Orton 15.8.95; stored 8.98)		
G-BTEK	Socata TB-20 Trinidad	1240		4. 2.91	D.F.Fagan		13. 8.99
					Vendee Air Park, Talmont, St.Hilaire, France		
G-BTEL	CFM Streak Shadow K.125-SA & PFA/206-11667			31. 1.91	J.E.Eatwell	Boscombe Down	16. 8.99P
	(Rotax 532)						
G-BTES	Cessna 150H	150-68371	N22575	29. 4.91	R.A.Forward	(Crowborough)	20. 8.00
G-BTET	Piper J3C-65 Cub	18296	N98141 NC98141	5. 2.91	R.M.Jones	Blackpool	3. 8.99P
G-BTEU	Aerospatiale SA.365N2 Dauphin 2	6392		11. 2.91	Bond Helicopters Ltd	Humberside	1. 4.01T
G-BTEV	PA-38-112 Tomahawk	38-78A0025	N9315T	13. 2.91	Cardiff Aeronautical Svs Ltd	Cardiff	15. 4.00T
G-BTEW	Cessna 120	10238	CF-ELE	29. 4.91	Kay F.Mason	Little Snoring	21. 6.01
	(Cont C90)						
G-BTEX	PA-28-140 Cherokee	28-23773	CF-XXL N3907X	24. 4.91	McAully F/Grp Ltd	Little Snoring	11. 4.01T
G-BTFA	Denney Kitfox mk.2 566 & PFA/172-11520			13. 2.91	K.R.Peek Church Farm, North Moreton		6.10.94P
	(Rotax 503)				(Damaged North Moreton 18.6.97)		
G-BTFC	Reims Cessna F.152 II	1668		23. 5.79	Tayside Avn Ltd	Aberdeen	8. 1.01T
G-BTFD	Colt AS-105 mk.II Hot-Air Airship	1856		13. 2.91	Media Fantasy Avn UK Ltd	(London SE16)	23. 1.93A
G-BTFE	Parsons Gyroplane Model 1	38		13. 2.91	N.C.White	(Glenlomond)	27.11.98P
	(Rotax 582) (Tandem Trainer)						
G-BTFF	Cessna T310R II	310R-0718	N1363G	25. 2.91	United Sales Equipment Dealers Ltd		29. 5.00
					Sandford Hall, Knockin		
G-BTFG	Boeing-Stearman A75N1	75-3441	N4467N Bu.30010	20. 2.91	D.W.N.Johnson Bunns Bank, Norfolk		19. 6.97
	(N2S-4) Kaydet (Cont W670)				(As "441" in USN c/s)		
G-BTFJ	PA-15 Vagabond	15-159	N4373H NC4373H	13. 2.91	A.V.Norris	(Dorking)	10. 4.98P
	(Lyc O-145)						
G-BTFK	Taylorcraft BC-12D	10540	N599SB N5240M	13. 2.91	D.J.S.McClean	Eglinton	1. 2.99P
	(Cont A65)						

Regn	Type	C/n	P/I	Date	Owner/operator	Probable Base	CA Expy
G-BTFL	Aeronca 11AC Chief	11AC-1727	N3403E NC3403E	18. 2.91	J.G.Vaughan Eastbach Farm, Coleford t/a BTFL Grp		8.11.99P
G-BTFM	Cameron O-105 HAFB	2623		12. 8.91	P.Forster & J.Trehern Edinburgh t/a Edinburgh University Hot-Air Balloon Club		18. 8.99A
G-BTFO	PA-28-161 Warrior II	28-7816580	N31728	12. 3.91	Flyfar Ltd	Blackpool	5. 5.00
G-BTFP	PA-38-112 Tomahawk	38-78A0340	N6201A	17. 4.91	Teesside Flight Centre Ltd	Teesside	6. 8.00T
G-BTFS	Cessna A150M Aerobat	A150-0719	N20331	20. 2.91	K.Ford	Popham	1. 5.00T
G-BTFT	Beechcraft 58 Baron	TH-979	N2036W	14. 3.91	Fastwing Air Charter Ltd	Thruxton	18. 3.01T
G-BTFU	Cameron N-90 HAFB	2391		28. 2.91	J.J.Rudoni & A.C.K.Rawson Stafford t/a Wickers World Hot Air Balloon Co "Maltesers II"		24. 6.99A
G-BTFV	Whittaker MW7 (Rotax 532)	PFA/171-11722		8. 2.91	S.J.Luck Tower Farm, Wollaston		23. 9.99P
G-BTFW	Montgomerie-Bensen B.8MR (Rotax 532)	PFA G/01A-1141		20. 2.91	A.Mansfield	Crowland	24. 6.99P
G-BTFX	Bell 206B JetRanger II	1648	N400MH N90219	20. 2.91	J.Selwyn Smith (Shepley) Ltd Shepley, Huddersfield		28. 3.00T
G-BTFY	Bell 206B JetRanger II	1714	N49590	20. 2.91	M.D.Thorpe (Leeds) t/a Yorkshire Helicopters		31. 8.00T
G-BTGA	Boeing-Stearman A75N1 (PT-17) Kaydet (P+W R985)	75-3132	N65501 41-25625	21. 2.91	J.C.Lister Valley Farm, Winwick		6. 7.01
G-BTGC	PA-38-112 Tomahawk	38-78A0120	N9507T	5. 3.91	Cardiff-Wales Flying Club Ltd	Cardiff	28. 8.00T
G-BTGD	Rand-Robinson KR-2 (VW1915)	PFA/129-11150		22. 2.91	D.W.Mullin "Lucinda Two"	Chester	23. 8.99P
G-BTGG	Rans S-10 Sakota (Rotax 582)	PFA/194-11944		20. 2.91	A.R.Cameron	Oaksey Park	22. 6.96P
G-BTGH	Cessna 152 II	152-81048	N48919	2. 4.91	C & S Aviation Ltd	Halfpenny Green	2. 4.01T
G-BTGI	Rearwin 175 Skyranger (Cont A75)	1517	N32308 NC32308	26. 2.91	A.H.Hunt (Dismantled 5.98) Lower Botrea Farm, Newbridge, Penzance		6. 7.98P
G-BTGJ	Smith DSA-1 Miniplane (Cont C90)	NM.II	N1471	25. 3.91	G.J.Knowles (Hayling Island) (Status uncertain)		20. 5.94P
G-BTGL	Light Aero Avid Speed Wing (Rotax 582)	PFA/189-11885		27. 2.91	A.F.Vizoso	RAF Halton	15. 6.99P
G-BTGM	Aeronca 7AC Champion (Cont A65)	7AC-3665	N84943 NC84943	11. 3.91	J.R.L.White	(Neuilly, France)	11. 2.99P
G-BTGN	Cessna 310R II	310R-1541	N5331C	3. 4.91	Air Service Training Ltd	Edinburgh	27. 1.99T
G-BTGO	PA-28-140 Cherokee D	28-7125613	N1998T	20. 2.91	Rankart Ltd	Oxford	3. 7.00T
G-BTGP	Cessna 150M Commuter	150-78921	N704WA	28. 2.91	Billins Air Svs Ltd (Op City Air)	Cranfield	24. 4.00T
G-BTGR	Cessna 152 II	152-84447	N6581L	28. 2.91	A.J.Gomes (Op Sky Leisure Avn)	Shoreham	25. 7.00T
G-BTGS(2)	Stolp SA.300 Starduster Too (Lyc O-320) EAA/50553 & PFA/35-10076		G-AYMA	30. 9.87	A.E.Bailey (Cranleigh) t/a A.E.Bailey & Partners		28. 5.99P
G-BTGT	CFM Streak Shadow (Rotax 582) K164-SA & PFA/206-11964		(G-MWPY)	1. 3.91	G.Arscott	(Fleet)	27. 4.99P
G-BTGU	PA-34-220T Seneca III	34-8233106	N999PW N8160V	1. 3.91	Carill Avn Ltd	Southampton	30. 5.00T
G-BTGV	PA-34-200T Seneca II	34-7970077	N3004H	26. 3.91	MS 124 Ltd	Shobdon	23. 6.00
G-BTGW	Cessna 152 II	152-79812	N757KY	5. 3.91	Stapleford F/C Ltd	Stapleford	31. 7.00T
G-BTGX	Cessna 152 II	152-84950	N5462P	5. 3.91	Stapleford F/C Ltd	Swansea	20. 8.00T
G-BTGY	PA-28-161 Warrior II	28-8216199	N209FT N9574N	5. 3.91	Stapleford F/C Ltd	Stapleford	23. 6.00T
G-BTGZ	PA-28-181 Archer II	28-7890160	N47956	8. 4.91	Allzones Travel Ltd	Biggin Hill	17. 8.00T
G-BTHA	Cessna 182P	182-63420	N2932P	22. 3.91	T.P.Hall t/a Hotel Alpha Flying Group	Blackpool	5. 8.00
G-BTHD	Yakolev Yak-3U (Conversion of LET Yak C.11)	170101	(France) EAF.533	7. 3.91	Patina Ltd (Duxford) (Op The Fighter Collection) (On rebuild in Russia 1996; for return during 1997)		AC
G-BTHE	Cessna 150L	150-75340	N11348	7. 3.91	S.F.Barnes & W.E.Thorpe Burn t/a Humberside Police F/C		26. 5.00T
G-BTHF	Cameron V-90 HAFB	2543		7. 3.91	N.J. & S.J.Langley	Bristol	27. 4.99T
G-BTHH	CEA Jodel DR.100A Ambassadeur	5	F-BJCH	28. 2.91	H.R.Leefe Bourg-en-Bresse, France		13. 2.99
G-BTHI	Robinson R-22 Beta	1732		26. 3.91	R.Bean t/a R.Bean Commercial Vehicles	Thirsk	19. 6.00
G-BTHJ	Evans VP-2	PFA/63-10901		14. 3.91	C.J.Moseley Bournemouth (Under construction 8.92)		
G-BTHK	Thunder Ax7-77 HAFB	1906		11. 3.91	M.J.Chandler	Cranbrook	29. 9.99A
G-BTHM	Thunder Ax8-105 HAFB	1925		11. 3.91	Anglia Balloon School Ltd Norwich t/a Anglia Balloons		13. 4.96T
G-BTHN	Murphy Renegade 912 384 & PFA/188-12005 (Rotax 912)			12. 3.91	F.A.Purvis Newcastle/Eshott "Spirit of England II"		22. 8.99P
G-BTHP	Thorp T.211	101		13. 6.91	M.J.Newton	Barton	5.10.01T
G-BTHR	Socata TB-10 Tobago	1296		13. 3.91	Computer 100 Ltd	White Waltham	14. 2.99
G-BTHU	Light Aero Avid Flyer PFA/189-11427 (Rotax 532)			14. 3.91	R.C.Bowley (Earls Croome, Worcester) (Damaged at Field Head Farm, Denholme, Bradford 7.6.92; on rebuild 5.95)		
G-BTHV	MBB Bo.105DBS-4	S.855	D-HMBV G-BTHV/D-HFHM	20. 3.91	Bond Helicopters Ltd	Aberdeen	12. 5.00T

Regn	Type	C/n	P/I	Date	Owner/operator	Probable Base	CA Expy
G-BTHW	Beechcraft F33C Bonanza	CJ-130	PH-BNA N23787	18. 3.91	Robin Lance Avn Associates Ltd Rochester		20. 8.00
G-BTHX	Colt 105A HAFB	1939		18. 3.91	R.Ollier	Northwich, Cheshire	19. 3.92A
G-BTHY	Bell 206B JetRanger III	2290	N6606M VH-BIQ/ZK-HBQ/DQ-FEN/ZK-HLU	20. 3.91	Sterling Helicopters Ltd	Norwich	19. 5.00T
G-BTHZ	Cameron V-56 HAFB	486	OO-BBC	20. 3.91	C.N.Marshall	Nairobi, Kenya	
					(Noted as OO-BBC 9.95)		
G-BTIC	PA-22-150 Tri-Pacer	22-6780	N9988D	25. 3.91	T.Richards & G.C.Winters (Colne/Bradford)		24. 6.94
			(N702DE)/N9988D (Damaged Newhouse Farm, Birds Edge, Huddersfield 24.4.93)					
G-BTID	PA-28-161 Warrior II	28-8116036	N82647	25. 6.91	Plymouth School of Flying Ltd	Plymouth	22. 5.00T
G-BTIE	Socata TB-10 Tobago	187		30. 3.81	JGH Computer Services Ltd	Cardiff	7. 9.99T
G-BTIF	Denney Kitfox mk.3			27. 2.91	G.A.Fox	Crowborough	26.10.98P
	(Rotax 582) 684 & PFA/172-11862						
G-BTIG	Montgomerie-Bensen B.8MR			21. 3.91	K.Jarvis	(Sheffield)	4. 1.99P
	(Rotax 532) PFA G/01-1093						
G-BTIH	PA-28-151 Cherokee Warrior		N6158J	20. 3.91	J.S.Edmunds-Jones & M.Stedman Blackbushe		26. 5.00
		28-7615315			t/a MPM Avn		
G-BTII	Gulfstream AA-5B Tiger	AA5B-1256	N4560S	5. 6.91	B.D.Greenwood	Ronaldsway	16. 4.99
G-BTIJ	Luscombe 8E Silvaire	5194	N2467K NC2467K	3. 4.91	S.J.Hornsby	Lee-on-Solent	9. 7.99P
	(Cont C85)						
G-BTIK	Cessna 152 II	152-82993	N46068	26. 3.91	P.R.Edwards & E.Alexander	Andrewsfield	29. 4.99T
G-BTIL*	PA-38-112 Tomahawk	38-80A0004	N24730	26. 3.91	B.R.Pearson	Eaglescott	AC
					(Cancelled by CAA 10.3.99; stored 4.96 - no UK C of A issued)		
G-BTIM	PA-28-161 Cadet	2841159	(SE-KIO) N9185D	24. 8.89	Mid Sussex Timber Co Ltd	Biggin Hill	25.10.01T
G-BTIN	Cessna 150C	150-59905	N7805Z	26. 3.91	Cormack (Acft Svs) Ltd	Cumbernauld	
G-BTIO	SNCAN Stampe SV-4C	303	N73NS F-BCLC	28. 3.91	M.D. & C.F.Garratt	(Bushey, Watford)	23.11.98
G-BTIP	Denney Kitfox mk.3 850 & PFA/172-11973			5. 3.91	P.A.Hardy Wadswick Manor Farm, Corsham		
	(Rotax 582)				(Damaged Wadswick Manor Farm, 31.5.92)		
G-BTIR	Denney Kitfox mk.2 PFA/172-11952			26. 3.91	R.B.Wilson	(Kendal)	9.10.99P
	(Hewland AE75)						
G-BTIS	Aerospatiale AS.355F1 Twin Squirrel		G-TALI	10. 4.91	J.P.E.Walsh	Elstree	9. 6.01T
		5261			t/a Walsh Avn (Op Cabair Helicopters)		
G-BTIU	Socata MS.892A Rallye Commodore 150	10914	F-BPQS	7. 5.91	W.H.Cole Spilsted Farm, Sedlescombe		30. 6.01
G-BTIV	PA-28-161 Warrior II	28-8116044	N82697	10. 5.91	B.R.Pearson t/a Warrior Grp	Eaglescott	3. 7.00T
G-BTIW*	CEA Jodel DR.1050/M1 Sicile Record	618	F-BMPV	28. 6.91	Not known	Crosland Moor	4. 7.94
					(Damaged Westbury-sub-Mendip 1.7.94: stored 9.96)		
G-BTIX	Cameron V-77 HAFB	2087		27. 3.91	D.J.Cook "Sky's The Limit"	Norwich	23. 9.99T
G-BTIZ	Cameron A-105 HAFB	2546		11. 3.91	Wendy A.Board	Penshurst	24. 6.98A
					t/a Gleen Board Promotions		
G-BTJA	Luscombe 8E Silvaire	5037	N2310K NC2310K	4. 4.91	M.W.Rudkin	Woodford	28. 5.99P
	(Cont C85)						
G-BTJB	Luscombe 8E Silvaire	6194	N1567B NC1567B	4. 4.91	M.Loxton Leysdown-on-Sea, Sheppey		15. 5.98P
	(Cont C85)						
	(G-BTJA may be ex NC1567B which suggests the identities of G-BTJA/BTJB were changed on conversion)						
G-BTJC	Luscombe 8F Silvaire	6589	N2162B	4. 4.91	Alison M.Noble	Thruxton	18. 9.99P
	(Lyc O-290)						
G-BTJD	Thunder Ax8-90 Srs.2 HAFB	1865		28. 3.91	S.J.Wardle	Kettering	15. 5.99A
G-BTJF	Thunder Ax10-180 Srs.2 HAFB	1952		28. 3.91	Airborne Adventures Ltd	Skipton	4. 3.99T
					"Yorkshire Lad"		
G-BTJH	Cameron O-77 HAFB	2559		3. 4.91	H.& F.Stringer "Oriel"	Scarborough	13. 9.98T
G-BTJK	PA-38-112 Tomahawk	38-79A0838	N2427N	3. 4.91	Western Air (Thruxton) Ltd	Thruxton	4. 8.00T
G-BTJL	PA-38-112 Tomahawk	38-79A0863	N2477N	3. 4.91	Archer Aviation Ltd	Gloucestershire	23. 7.01T
G-BTJN	Montgomerie-Bensen B.8MR			3. 4.91	A.Hamilton	Larkhall, Lanark	7. 9.99P
	(Rotax 532) PFA G/01-1194						
G-BTJO	Thunder Ax9-140 HAFB	1948		3. 4.91	G.P.Lane	Waltham Abbey	28. 4.92A
G-BTJS	Montgomerie-Bensen B.8MR			8. 4.91	T.C. & P.K.Jackson		6. 9.99P
	(Rotax 532) PFA G/01-1083					Melrose Farm, Melbourne	
G-BTJU	Cameron V-90 HAFB	2554		8. 4.91	C.W.Jones (Floorings) Ltd	Bristol	6. 8.99A
G-BTJX	Rans S-10 Sakota PFA/194-12014			9. 4.91	M.Goacher Linley Hill, Leven		
					(Nearing completion 5.97)		
G-BTKA	Piper J/5A Cub Cruiser	5-954	N38403 NC38403	11. 4.91	Janet M.Lister Valley Farm, Winwick		
					(On rebuild 3.97)		
G-BTKB	Murphy Renegade 912 376 & PFA/188-11876			11. 4.91	G.S.Blundell "Spirit of Kinross" Perth		31. 5.99P
	(Rotax 912)						
G-BTKD	Denney Kitfox mk.4 853 & PFA/172-11941			15. 4.91	J.F.White Walkerburn Farm, Peebles		9. 7.98P
	(Rotax 582) (Denney c/n conflicts with N653CP)				(Op Border Avn Ltd)		
G-BTKG	Light Aero Avid Flyer PFA/189-12037			16. 4.91	M.K.Slaughter	Thruxton	9. 7.99P
	(Rotax 582)				t/a Kilo Golf Group		
G-BTKI	North American T-6G-NF Texan 197-88			17. 4.91	P.S. & S.M.Warner	Bredon, Pershore	
	(C/n also quoted as FO-8002-088)		Fr AF 534592"RA"/53-4592 (On rebuild 3.96)					
G-BTKL	MBB Bo.105DB-4	S.422	D-HDMU Swedish Army/D-HDMU	2. 5.91	Veritair Ltd	Halfpenny Green	2. 3.00T
					(Op by Central Counties Police Air Operations Unit)		
G-BTKP	CFM Streak Shadow PFA/206-12036			24. 4.91	G.D.Martin	(Cambridge)	11. 5.99P
	(Rotax 582)						

Regn	Type	C/n	P/I	Date	Owner/operator	Probable Base	CA Expy
G-BTKS	Rans S-10 Sakota (Rotax 532)	PFA/194-11861		9. 7.91	J.R.I. & S.M.Rolfe, A.J. & M.L.Reed, N.Parkinson, R.Clarke & R.P.Sandford Cranfield (Damaged Insch 19.8.93; stored 7.94)		5. 7.94P
G-BTKT	PA-28-161 Warrior II	28-8216218	N429FT N9606N	9. 5.91	Eastern Executive Air Charter Ltd & E.Alexander t/a General Aero Svs Thurrock (Damaged nr Shoreham 8.8.95; status uncertain)		14. 7.97T
G-BTKV	PA-22-160 Tri-Pacer	22-7157	N3216Z	25. 4.91	R.A.Moore	Newtownards	26. 6.01
G-BTKW	Cameron O-105 HAFB	2566		25. 4.91	P.Spellward	Bristol	13. 6.97A
G-BTKX	PA-28-181 Archer II	28-7890146	N47866	14. 5.91	D.J.Perkins	Tatenhill	30. 4.00
G-BTKZ	Cameron V-77 HAFB	2573		26. 4.91	S.P.Richards "Lancaster Jaguar"	Cranbrook	7. 6.97T
G-BTLA	Sikorsky S-76B	760367		22. 4.91	Falcon of Friendship Ltd	Blackbushe	9. 5.00
G-BTLB	Wassmer WA.52 Europa	42	F-BTLB	17. 4.89	M.D.O'Brien	Shoreham	8. 6.01
G-BTLE	PA-31-350 Navajo Chieftain	31-7405428	D-IBPL N54288	20.10.77	Boal Air Services (UK) Ltd (Loughborough)		10. 9.00
G-BTLG	PA-28R-200 Cherokee Arrow	28R-35811	N5045S	29. 4.91	A.P.Reilly (Crashed Kirkbride 10.2.99)	Blackpool	17. 7.00
G-BTLL*	Pilatus P.3-03	323-5	A-806	18. 4.91	Not known Headcorn (As "A-806" in Swiss AF c/s; stored 9.97)		23. 6.94P
G-BTLM	PA-22-160 Tri-Pacer (Univair tail-wheel conversion)	22-6162	N9025D	16. 5.91	M.D.N. & A.C.Fisher	Leicester	1. 9.00
G-BTLP	Grumman-American AA-1C Lynx	AA1C-0109	N9732U	13. 5.91	Partlease Ltd	Stapleford	22.12.00
G-BTMA	Cessna 172N Skyhawk II	172-73711	N5136J	2. 5.91	East of England F/Grp Ltd	North Weald	7. 8.00T
G-BTMF	Taylorcraft BC-12D	6609	N43990 NC43990	10. 7.91	C.M.Churchill	(Cambridge)	
G-BTMH	Colt 90A HAFB	1963		14. 5.91	European Balloon Corporation Espinette, Belgium		1. 7.99A
G-BTMJ	Maule MX-7-180 Star Rocket	11073C		11. 6.91	C.M.McGill	Biggin Hill	6. 7.01
G-BTMK	Cessna R172K Hawk XPII	R172-2787	N736TZ	10. 6.91	S.P. & A.C.Barker	East Midlands	24.11.00T
G-BTML*	Cameron Rupert Bear 90SS HAFB	2533		16. 5.91	Balloon Preservation Group Lancing "Rupert The Bear" (For restoration 12.98)		31.12.94A
G-BTMN	Thunder Ax9-120	2003		17 .5.91	D J Farrer "Batman"	Leeds	8. 3.99T
G-BTMO	Colt 69A HAFB	2004		20. 5.91	Cameron Balloons Ltd t/a Thunder & Colt	Bristol	
G-BTMP	Everett Campbell Cricket (Rotax 532)	024 & PFA G/03-1226		20. 5.91	P.W.McLaughlin	Kemble	21.10.97P
G-BTMR	Cessna 172M Skyhawk II	172-64985	N64047	20. 5.91	J.A.Nicol t/a Cumbria A/C	Carlisle	29. 5.00T
G-BTMS	Avid Speed Wing	PFA/189-12023	(CS-) G-BTMS	24. 4.91	M.J.Kaye	Mexborough	
G-BTMT	Denney Kitfox mk.1 (Rotax 532)	66		10. 5.91	M.D.Burns t/a Skulk F/Grp North Commonside Farm, Erskine, Renfrew		20.10.99P
G-BTMV	Everett Gyroplane Srs.2	025		21. 5.91	L.Armes	Basildon	
G-BTMW	Zenair CH-701 STOL (Rotax 582)	PFA/187-11808		21. 5.91	L.Lewis (Stored 4.97)	Yearby	9. 4.96P
G-BTMX	Denney Kitfox mk.3 (Rotax 582)	916 & PFA/172-12079		13. 5.91	P.B.Lowry	Deanland	6. 9.99P
G-BTNA	Robinson R-22 Beta	1800	N40820	23. 5.91	Heli Charter Ltd	Manston	24.11.00T
G-BTNB	Robinson R-22 Beta	1802	N23006	30. 5.91	G.Kidger	Netherthorpe	24. 7.00
G-BTNC	Aerospatiale SA.365N2 Dauphin 2	6409		21. 6.91	Bond Helicopters Ltd	Strubby	9.10.01T
G-BTND	PA-38-112 Tomahawk	38-78A0155	N9671T	23. 5.91	R.B.Turner	Gloucestershire	8.12.01T
G-BTNE	PA-28-161 Warrior II	28-8116212	N8379H	22. 7.91	D.Rowe	Wellesbourne Mountford	16. 6.01T
G-BTNL	Thunder AX10-180 HAFB	2006	(OO-ntu) G-BTNL	29. 5.91	M.P.A.Sevrin	Court St.Etienne, Belgium	
G-BTNN	Colt 21A Cloudhopper HAFB	2018		3. 6.91	Cameron Balloons Ltd	Bristol	9. 6.92A
G-BTNO	Aeronca 7AC Champion	7AC-3132	N84441 NC84441	31. 5.91	D.B.Evans & A.McGarrell Netherthorpe t/a November Oscar Grp		4. 8.99P
G-BTNP	Light Aero Avid Commuter (Rotax 582)	PFA/189-11988		31. 5.91	N.Evans Silfield, Wymondham (Damaged Swardeston, Norfolk 25.6.92; stored 8.97)		23.6.92P*
G-BTNR	Denney Kitfox mk.3 (Rotax 582)	921 & PFA/172-12035		31. 5.91	J.W.G.Ellis	Eaglescott	26.11.97P
G-BTNS	WSK PZL-104 Wilga 80	CF.20890883	N71695	22. 7.91	R.W.Husband	Breighton	26.10.00
G-BTNT	PA-28-151 Cherokee Warrior	28-7615401	N6929J	31. 5.91	Britannia Airways Ltd Luton (Op Britannia Airways F/C)		24.11.00T
G-BTNV	PA-28-161 Warrior II	28-7816590	N31878	20. 6.91	D.K.Oakeley & A.M.Dawson	Oxford	6. 7.00
G-BTNW	Rans S-6-ESA Coyote II (Rotax 582)	0391-171 & PFA/204-12077		3. 6.91	A.F.Stafford Melrose Farm, Melbourne		12.11.97P
G-BTOA	Mong Sport MS-2 (Cont C85)	FHC-1	N1067Z	3. 6.91	G.Gilding Priory Farm, Tibenham (Stored 8.97)		28. 9.94P
G-BTOC	Robinson R-22 Beta	1801	N23004	10. 6.91	N.Parkhouse Chelwood Gate, W.Sussex		10. 7.00
G-BTOD	PA-38-112 Tomahawk	38-78A0675	N2421A	7. 6.91	GB Training on Demand Ltd	Gamston	10. 9.00T
G-BTOG	DH.82A Tiger Moth	86500	F-BGCJ Fr.AF/NM192	5. 9.91	P.T.Szluha Audley End (On overhaul 4.94)		
G-BTOI	Cameron N-77 HAFB	2588		20. 6.91	The Nestle Co Ltd "Rowntree/Nestle"	Croydon	29. 6.95A
G-BTOL	Denney Kitfox mk.3 (Rotax 582)	919 & PFA/172-12052		26. 6.91	P.J.Gibbs	(Truro)	6. 4.99P

Regn	Type	C/n	P/I	Date	Owner/operator	Probable Base	CA Expy
G-BTOM*	PA-38-112 Tomahawk	38-78A0763		15. 1.79	Lorch Airways Ltd Norwich		10. 4.94T
					(Crashed Alderney 26.9.92; stored 10.97)		
G-BTON	PA-28-140 Cherokee Cruiser		N43193	15. 7.91	Horizon Flying Club Ltd Earls Colne		2. 7.01T
		28-7425343					
G-BTOO	Pitts S-1C Special	5215-24A	N37H	12. 6.91	G.H.Matthews (On overhaul 5.92) Sandown		
G-BTOP	Cameron V-77 HAFB	2484		14. 6.91	J.J.Winter "Big Top" Cardiff		
G-BTOS	Cessna 140	8353	N89325	7. 6.91	J.L.Kaiser Nancy-Essais, France		1. 7.99
	(Cont C85)		NC89325				
G-BTOT	PA-15 Vagabond	15-60	N4176H	22. 5.91	P.J.Rutter East Farm, Garmondsway		24. 7.99P
	(Lyc O-145)		NC4176H				
G-BTOU	Cameron O-120 HAFB	2606		2. 7.91	C.Monk Bath		27. 1.99T
G-BTOW	Socata Rallye 180T Galerien	3360	F-BNGZ	9.11.82	Cambridge Gliding Club Ltd		
						Gransden Lodge	23. 3.01
G-BTOZ	Thunder Ax9-120 Srs.2 HAFB	2008		28. 6.91	H.G.Davies Cheltenham		11. 5.99T
G-BTPB	Cameron N-105 HAFB	1536		6. 7.87	C.N.Rawnson Stockbridge		21. 9.96A
					t/a Test Valley Balloon Grp "Phone Book"		
G-BTPF	BAe ATP	2013	(N383AE)	2. 9.88	British Airways plc Glasgow		17. 4.99T
					"Strathearn"		
G-BTPG	BAe ATP	2014	(N384AE)	2. 9.88	British Airways plc Glasgow		22. 5.99T
					"Strathfillan"		
G-BTPH	BAe ATP	2015	(N385AE)	2. 9.88	British Airways plc Glasgow		11. 6.99T
					"Strathnaver"		
G-BTPJ	BAe ATP	2016	(N386AE)	2. 9.88	British Airways plc Glasgow		9. 7.99T
					"Strathpeffer"		
G-BTPL	BAe ATP	2042	EC-GLH	10. 6.92	British Aerospace (Operations) Ltd		
			G-BTPL/G-11-042			Woodford	7.11.98T
G-BTPO	BAe ATP	2051	G-5-051	10. 6.92	British Airways plc Glasgow		28. 7.99T
					"Strathclyde"		
G-BTPT	Cameron N-77 HAFB	2575		10. 6.91	Derbyshire Building Society Derby		20.11.99A
G-BTPV*	Colt 90A HAFB	1956		14. 6.91	Virgin Airship & Balloon Co Ltd Telford		1. 8.97A
					"Mondial Assistance" (Cancelled as PWFU 25.3.99)		
G-BTPX	Thunder Ax8-90 HAFB	1873		18. 6.91	E.Cordall Chichester		24. 1.99
G-BTPZ	Isaacs Fury II	PFA/11-11927		1. 7.91	M.A.Farrelly Ormskirk		
					(As "85" in Portuguese AF c/s)		
G-BTRB	Colt Mickey Mouse SS HAFB	1959		4. 7.91	Benedikt Haggeney GmbH "Mickey Mause"		
					Ennigerloh, Germany		28 .5.97A
G-BTRC	Light Aero Avid Speed Wing			2. 7.91	Grangecote Ltd (Brighton)		15. 6.96P
		913 & PFA/189-12076					
G-BTRE	Reims Cessna F.172H	0657	N10657	3. 7.91	M.L.J.Warwick Stapleford		18.10.01T
G-BTRF	Aero Designs Pulsar	PFA/202-12051		4. 7.91	C.Smith Spilsted Farm, Sedlescombe		21. 9.99P
	(Rotax 582)						
G-BTRG	Aeronca 65C Super Chief	C4149	N22466	4. 7.91	H.J.Cox Lukes Farm, Sheepwash		8. 7.98P
	(Cont A65)		NC22466				
G-BTRH	Aeronca 7AC Champion	7AC-2895	N84204	4. 7.91	M.A.N.Newall (Harrogate)		15. 5.99P
	(Cont A65)		NC84204				
G-BTRI	Aeronca 11CC Super Chief	11CC-246	N4540E	4. 7.91	P.A.Wensak Bounds Farm, Ardleigh		30. 6.99P
	(Cont C85)		NC4540E				
G-BTRK	PA-28-161 Warrior II	28-8216206	N297FT	8. 7.91	Stapleford F/C Ltd Stapleford		22.10.00T
			N9594N				
G-BTRL	Cameron N-105 HAFB	2622		5. 7.91	J.Lippett South Petherton, Somerset		29. 4.99A
					"Harrods"		
G-BTRO	Thunder Ax8-90 HAFB	1872		11. 7.91	Capital Balloon Club Ltd London NW1		21. 3.97A
G-BTRP	MDH Hughes 369E (500E)	0475E	N1607D	11. 7.91	P.C.Shann & P.C.Shann Management & Research Ltd		
					Fulford, York		15. 4.01
G-BTRR	Thunder Ax7-77 HAFB	1905		12. 7.91	Sheila M.Roberts Skipton		26. 8.96A
G-BTRS	PA-28-161 Warrior II	28-8116004	N8248V	12. 7.91	I.C.Tyson & G.R.Berry Woodford		16.12.01
					t/a Tyberry Avn		
G-BTRT	PA-28R-200 Cherokee Arrow II		N1189X	24. 7.91	C.E.Yates Barton		9.12.00
		28R-7535270					
G-BTRU	Robin DR.400/180 Regent	2089		12. 7.91	R & M Engineering Ltd Inverness		24.11.00
G-BTRW	Slingsby T-61F Venture T.2	1968	ZA632	5. 7.91	B.Kerby & G.Grainger (Rednal)		1.11.00
G-BTRX*	Cameron V-77 HAFB	1143	VH-HIH	12. 7.91	Not known (Temp unregd 2.5.97) Horsham		16. 4.97A
G-BTRY	PA-28-161 Warrior II	28-8116190	N8363L	18. 7.91	Oxford Aviation Services Ltd Oxford		6.12.01T
G-BTRZ	Jodel D.18 148 & PFA/169-11271			16. 7.91	R.M.Johnson & R.Collin (Falkirk)		18. 8.99P
	(VW1834)						
G-BTSB	Corben Baby Ace D	JC-1	N3599	16. 7.91	D.G.Kelly Shempston Farm, Elgin		11. 2.99P
	(Cont A65)						
G-BTSC	Evans VP-2	PFA/63-10342		20.10.78	G.B.O'Neill (Northampton)		13. 2.96P
	(Arrow GT500)				(On overhaul Chilbolton 6.96)		
G-BTSD	Loehle 5151 Mustang	PFA/213-11867		17. 7.91	R.Fitzpatrick (Newquay)		
G-BTSJ	PA-28-161 Warrior II	28-7816473	N9417C	23. 7.91	Plymouth School of Flying Ltd Plymouth		18.12.00T
G-BTSL	Cameron Glass 70SS HAFB	1627		27. 1.88	M.R.Humphrey & J.R.Clifton Brackley		25. 4.90A
	(Tennent's Lager Glass Shape)				"Tennent's Glass"		
G-BTSM	Cessna 180A	32678	P2-DEQ	9. 7.91	C.Couston t/a Sierra Mike Grp		
			VH-DEQ/VH-DEC/N7781A		Church Farm, North Moreton, Wallingford		2. 5.99
G-BTSN	Cessna 150G	150-65106	N3806J	30. 8.91	N.A.Bilton Priory Farm, Tibenham		12.11.98
G-BTSP	Piper J3C-65 Cub	7647	N41013	30. 8.91	J.A.Walshe & A.Corcoran		
			NC41013		Strandhill, Sligo, Ireland		10. 1.00P

Regn	Type	C/n	P/I	Date	Owner/operator	Probable Base	CA Expy
G-BTSR	Aeronca 11AC Chief (Cont A65)	11AC-785	N9152E NC9152E	30. 8.91	T.J.Goodwin	Ardleigh	17. 3.99P
G-BTST	Bensen B.8M (Mod)	002VS		23. 7.91	V.Scott	Shipdham	
G-BTSU*	Bensen B.8MR	BTG-01		24. 7.91	B.T.Goggin (Cancelled by CAA 22.3.99)	(Swansea)	
G-BTSV	Denney Kitfox mk.3 (Rotax 582)	PFA/172-11920		24. 7.91	D.J.Sharland	Popham	21. 6.99P
G-BTSW	Colt AS-105GD Hot-Air Airship	1999		24. 7.91	Gefa-Flug GmbH (Adler Modemarkt c/s)	Aachen, Germany	24. 3.99A
G-BTSX	Thunder Ax7-77 HAFB	2027		24. 7.91	Christine Moris-Gallimore	Hinton St.George, Somerset	18. 9.94
G-BTSY*	English Electric Lightning F.6 95207		XR724	25. 7.91	B.J.Pover (Stored 4.97) t/a Lightning Association (As "XR724")	Binbrook	
G-BTSZ	Cessna 177A Cardinal	177-01198	N30332	30. 7.91	K.D.Harvey	Cranfield	24.11.99T
G-BTTA	Hawker Iraqi Fury FB.11 37534 & ISS13		VH-HFX N28SF/Iraqi AF 243	25. 7.91	Classic Avn Ltd (Op The Old Flying Machine Co) (As "PR772 in RAF c/s)	Duxford	11. 6.99P
G-BTTB	Cameron V-90 HAFB	2624		22. 7.91	N.F.Mulliner t/a Royal Engineers Balloon Club "Sapper IV"	Chatham	8. 7.99A
G-BTTD	Montgomerie-Bensen B.8MR (Rotax 582)	PFA G/01-1204		31. 7.91	K.B.Gutridge	(London SE5)	20. 7.99P
G-BTTE	Cessna 150L	150-75558	N11602	31. 7.91	Premiair Flying Club Ltd	Shoreham	22. 1.99T
G-BTTK	Thunder Ax8-105 HAFB	2036		9. 8.91	Tempowish Ltd	Frinton-on-Sea	15. 4.98A
G-BTTL	Cameron V-90 HAFB	2649		12. 8.91	A.J.Baird "Hyde Farm Dairy"	Cheltenham	16. 7.96A
G-BTTO	BAe ATP	2033	EC-GJU G-BTTO/G-OEDE/G-BTTO/TC-THV/G-BTTO/S2-ACX/G-11-033	16. 8.91	British Aerospace (Operations) Ltd	Woodford	8.12.97T
G-BTTP	BAe 146 Srs.300	E-3203	G-6-203	20. 8.91	Air UK Ltd	Stansted	11.11.00T
G-BTTR	Aerotek Pitts S-2A Special (Lyc IO-360)	2208	N38MP	16. 8.91	Ebork Ltd	Biggin Hill	22. 3.01
G-BTTS	Colt 77A HAFB	1861		16. 8.91	J.A.Lomas t/a Rutland Balloon Club	Melton Mowbray	7. 7.99A
G-BTTW	Thunder Ax7-77 HAFB	2016		27. 8.91	J.Kenny	Athlone, Co.Roscommon	18. 6.99A
G-BTTY	Denney Kitfox mk.2	PFA/172-11823		29. 7.91	K.J.Fleming	(Liverpool)	
G-BTTZ	Slingsby T-61F Venture T.2	1961	ZA625	30. 7.91	G.J.Bridgewater	(Ulverston)	4. 8.00
G-BTUA	Slingsby T-61F Venture T.2	1985	ZA666	20. 8.91	C.Edmunds t/a Shenington Gliding Club	Edge Hill	29. 5.01
G-BTUB	LET Yakovlev C.11 (Identity of 039 quoted)	172623	(France) Egyptian AF 543	29. 8.91	M.G. & J.R.Jefferies (Soviet AF c/s without serial)	White Waltham	18. 7.99P
G-BTUD*	CFM Image (Rotax 532)	IM-01 & PFA/222-12012	G-MWPV	21. 8.91	D.G.Cook (Cancelled as wfu 5.2.99)	Leiston, Suffolk	21.1.95P*
G-BTUG	Socata Rallye 180T	3208		10. 7.78	Herefordshire Gliding Club Ltd	Shobdon	16. 4.00
G-BTUH	Cameron N-65 HAFB	1452		28. 8.91	B.J.Godding	Didcot	
	(Originally the "attached" balloon to G-WASH c/n 1451)						
G-BTUJ	Thunder Ax9-120 HAFB	2022		30. 8.91	ECM Construction Ltd	Great Missenden	15. 5.99T
G-BTUK	Aerotek Pitts S-2A Special (Lyc AEIO-360)	2260	N5300J	2. 9.91	Wickenby Avn Ltd	Wickenby	9.10.00T
G-BTUL	Aerotek Pitts S-2A Special (Lyc AEIO-360)	2200	N900RS N31467	2. 9.91	J.M.Adams	Nottingham	22.11.00
G-BTUM	Piper J3C-85 Cub (Frame No.19536)	19516	N6335H NC6335H	6. 9.91	C.Johnstone t/a G-BTUM Syndicate "Jingle-Belle"	White Waltham	8. 8.97P
G-BTUR	PA-18-95 Super Cub (L-18C-PI)	18-3205	OO-LVM OL-L08/L-131/53-4805	11. 9.91	P.R.Small t/a L-18 Syndicate	Cumbernauld	21. 5.99
G-BTUS	Whittaker MW7 (Rotax 503)	PFA/171-11999		5. 9.91	J.D.Webb	(Hereford)	9. 6.98P
G-BTUU	Cameron O-120 HAFB	2669		16. 9.91	J.L.Guy	Skipton	29.10.99T
G-BTUV	Aeronca 65TAC Defender	C.1661TA	N36816 NC36816	12. 9.91	J.T.Ingrouille (On rebuild 6.97)	Guernsey	
G-BTUW	PA-28-151 Cherokee Warrior	28-7415066	N54458	12. 9.91	T.S.Kemp	Enstone	25. 6.01T
G-BTUX	Aerospatiale SA.365N2 Dauphin 2	6424		12. 9.91	Bond Helicopters Ltd	Strubby	1. 2.02T
G-BTUZ	American General AG-5B Tiger	10075	N11939	3.10.91	Grocontinental Ltd	Sleap	26. 2.00
G-BTVA	Thunder Ax7-77 HAFB	2009		16. 9.91	A.H.Symonds "Bertie Bassett"	Chelmsford	7. 5.99A
G-BTVB	Everett Gyroplane Srs.3 (Rotax 532)	026		24. 9.91	J.Pumford	Epsom	16.12.99P
G-BTVC	Denney Kitfox mk.2 (Rotax 582)	PFA/172-11784		23. 9.91	P.Mitchell "Zebedee"	Long Marston	18. 1.00P
G-BTVE	Hawker Demon I	-	2292M K8203	18. 9.91	Demon Displays Ltd (As "K8203" in 64 Sqn c/s)	Rotary Farm, Hatch	AC
	(Composite of ex Irish front and K8203 rear)				(On rebuild by Skysport Engineering Ltd 7.96)		
G-BTVF	Rotorway Exec 90	5058		13. 9.91	E.P.Sadler	(Market Drayton)	AC
G-BTVG	Cessna 140 (Cont O-200-A)	12350	N2114N NC2114N	30. 8.91	V.C.Gover	Plockton	15. 4.99
G-BTVH	Colt 77A HAFB	1027	G-ZADT G-ZBCA	24. 9.91	D.N. & L.J.Close	Andover	19. 8.97A
G-BTVR	PA-28-140 Cherokee Cruiser	28-7625012	N4328X	16. 9.91	Full Sutton Flying Centre Ltd	Full Sutton	26. 3.01T
G-BTVU	Robinson R-22 Beta	1937		26. 9.91	B.Enzo	Bologna, Italy	17. 3.00

Regn	Type	C/n	P/I	Date	Owner/operator	Probable Base	CA Expy
G-BTVV	Reims Cessna FA337G Super Skymaster (Wichita c/n 01476)	0058	PH-RPD N1876M	25. 9.91	B.Maddock	Bournemouth	8. 9.99T
G-BTVW	Cessna 152 II	152-79631	N757CK	23. 9.91	A.T.Hooper & T.E.Evans (Op RS Pilot Training) Wellesbourne Mountford		8. 9.99T
G-BTVX	Cessna 152 II	152-83375	N48786	23. 9.91	A.T.Hooper & T.E.Evans (Op RS Pilot Training) Wellesbourne Mountford		30. 6.01T
G-BTWB*	Denney Kitfox mk.3 920 & PFA/172-12278		(G-BTTM)	21. 8.91	J.E.Tootell (Cancelled by CAA 14.3.99)	(Aylesbury)	
G-BTWC	Slingsby T-61F Venture T.2	1975	ZA656	23. 9.91	T.M.Holloway t/a RAFGSA	RAF Upavon	4. 1.02
G-BTWD	Slingsby T-61F Venture T.2	1976	ZA657	23. 9.91	Ouse Gliding Club Ltd t/a York Gliding Centre	Rufforth	26. 9.00
G-BTWE	Slingsby T-61F Venture T.2	1980	ZA661	23. 9.91	T.M.Holloway t/a RAFGSA (Op Four Counties Gliding Club)	RAF Syerston	13. 3.01
G-BTWF	DHC.1 Chipmunk 22	C1/0564	WK549	30. 9.91	J.A. & V.G.Simms (As "WK549") (On rebuild)	Rufforth	
G-BTWI	EAA Acrosport I (Lyc O-290)	230	N10JW	2.10.91	G.K.Brothwood t/a WI Group	Liverpool	26. 1.99P
G-BTWJ	Cameron V-77 HAFB	2670		3.10.91	S.J. & J.A.Bellaby	Nottingham	28. 4.99A
G-BTWL	Wag-Aero CUBy Acro Sport Trainer (Lyc O-235) PFA/108-10893			3.10.91	M.T.Lewis . Eastbach Farm, Coleford		27. 7.99P
G-BTWM	Cameron V-77 HAFB	2163		4.10.91	R.C.Franklin "Aerolus"	Chesham	24. 9.99A
G-BTWN	Maule MXT-7-180 Star Rocket	14025C		7.10.91	C.T.Rolls	Redhill	5. 2.01
G-BTWR	Bell P-63A-7BE Kingcobra	33-397	N52113	7.10.91	Patina Ltd	Duxford	28. 4.99P
	(C/n officially 33-37 but quoted as 296A-5-3) NX52113/42-69097 (B.J.S.Grey t/a The Fighter Collection) (As "269097" in USAAF c/s) "Trust Me"						
G-BTWS*	Thunder Ax7-77 HAFB	1971		9.10.91	Bavarian Balloon Co Ltd (Cancelled as PWFU 22.3.99) (Frinton-on-Sea)		8. 3.96A
G-BTWU	PA-22-135 Tri-Pacer	22-2135	N3320B	10.10.91	Prestige Air (Engineers) Ltd Haverfordwest		
G-BTWV	Cameron O-90 HAFB	2675		10.10.91	C.J.Thomas	Haslemere	15. 5.99A
G-BTWX	Socata TB-9 Tampico	1401		14.10.91	Parkers Properties Ltd	Biggin Hill	30. 7.00T
G-BTWY	Aero Designs Pulsar (Rotax 582)	PFA/202-12040		15.10.91	M.Stevenson	(Salisbury)	19. 5.99P
G-BTWZ	Rans S-10 Sakota	PFA/194-12117		15.10.91	D.G.Hey Little Gransden (Under construction 3.97)		
G-BTXB	Colt 77A HAFB	2072		16.10.91	SGL Ltd t/a Shellgas South West Area "Shellgas"	Bristol	1. 8.99T
G-BTXD	Rans S-6-ESA Coyote II PFA/204-12104 (Rotax 582)			22.10.91	M.Isterling	Insch	3. 6.99P
G-BTXF	Cameron V-90 HAFB	2692		2.10.91	G.Thompson	Ambleside	24. 1.96T
G-BTXH	Colt AS-56 Hot-Air Airship	2078		23.10.91	L.Kiefer March-Flugstetten, Germany		26.11.99A
G-BTXI	Noorduyn AT-16-ND Harvard IIB 14-429		Fv.16105 RCAF FE695/FE695/42-892	25.10.91	Patina Ltd (Op The Fighter Collection) (As "FE695/94")	Duxford	24. 6.99P
G-BTXK	Thunder Ax7-65 HAFB	1910	ZS-HYP G-BTXK	28.10.91	T.M.Dawson	Woodford Green	5.12.96
G-BTXM	Colt 21A Cloudhopper HAFB	2082		29.10.91	Virgin Airship & Balloon Co Ltd Telford "Virgin Megastore Hopper"		22. 8.97A
G-BTXS	Cameron O-120 HAFB	2141		16.10.91	Semajan Ltd t/a Southern Balloon Grp	Romsey	26. 4.99A
G-BTXT	Maule MXT-7-180 Star Rocket	14027C		7.10.91	W.C.Evans	(Bicester)	19.12.00
G-BTXV	Cameron A-210 HAFB	2703		30.10.91	The Ballooning Business Ltd Northampton "Burning Ambition III"		27. 3.99T
G-BTXW	Cameron V-77 HAFB	2717		31.10.91	P.C.Waterhouse Wadhurst, E.Sussex "Scott's Whisky"		29. 8.99A
G-BTXX	Bellanca 8KCAB Decathlon	595-80	OY-CYC SE-IEP/N5063G	1.10.91	Sherwood F/C Ltd	Nottingham	11. 2.01T
G-BTXZ	Zenair CH.250 PFA/113-12170 (Lyc O-290)			24.10.91	I.Parris & P.W.J.Hull Hinton-in-the-Hedges		30.10.99P
G-BTYC	Cessna 150L	150-75767	N66002	4.11.91	Polestar Aviation Ltd	Jersey	5. 3.02T
G-BTYE	Cameron A-180 HAFB	2704		5.11.91	K.J.A.Maxwell & D.S.Messmer "Rolling Rock" Haywards Heath		20. 3.99T
G-BTYF	Thunder Ax10-180 Srs.2 HAFB	2086		7.11.91	P.Glydon Barnt Green, Birmingham		18. 3.99T
G-BTYH	Pottier P.80S PFA/160-11121 (VW1834)			11.11.91	R.Pickett	Tatenhill	18. 8.99P
G-BTYI	PA-28-181 Archer II	28-8190078	N8287T	15.11.91	C.A.Savile (Op Modern Air)	Fowlmere	11. 2.99T
G-BTYK	Cessna 310R II	310R-0138	N200VC N5018J	21.11.91	Revere Aviation Ltd	Jersey	24. 6.00
G-BTYT	Cessna 152 II	152-80455	N24931	25.11.91	M.J.Green	Southend	20. 3.99T
G-BTYW	Cessna 120 (Cont C85)	11725	N77283 NC77283	27.11.91	C.J.Parker Shacklewell Farm, Wittering t/a G-BTYW Group		1.10.01
G-BTYX	Cessna 140 (Cont C90)	11004	N76568 NC76568	27.11.91	A.Coulson & J.R.H.Willis t/a G-BTYX Grp	Rochester	23. 2.98T
G-BTYY	Curtiss Robin C-2 (Cont W-670)	475	N348K NC348K	8.10.91	R.R.L.Windus Truleigh Manor Farm, Edburton		1. 9.97P
G-BTYZ	Colt 210A HAFB	2083		17.10.91	T.M.Donnelly	Doncaster	4. 5.97T
G-BTZA	Beechcraft F33A Bonanza	CE-957	PH-BNT D-EBKX	22.11.91	H.Mendelssohn t/a G-BTZA Grp	Edinburgh	21.12.01

Regn	Type	C/n	P/I	Date	Owner/operator	Probable Base	CA Expy
G-BTZB	Yakovlev Yak-50	801810	DOSAAF 77	27.11.91	J.S.Allison (As "69" in Soviet AF c/s)	RAF Wyton/Duxford	1. 3.99P
G-BTZD	Yakovlev Yak.1 Srs.1 (C/n is identity stamped on engine bearers) (Soviet AF) (Salvaged from lake in N.Russia mid 1991 after forced landing c.1942; stored 3.96)	8188	1342	10.12.91	Historic Acft Collection Ltd	Audley End	AC
G-BTZE	LET Yakovlev C.11	171312	(France) Egypt AF/OK-JIK	11. 2.92	Bianchi Avn Film Svs Ltd (Blue Max Movie Acft Museum 3.96)	Booker	
G-BTZL	Oldfield Baby Lakes (Cont C85)	8506-M-28B	N2288B	12.12.91	J.M.Roach (Stored 3.97)	Little Gransden	16. 6.95P
G-BTZO	Socata TB-20 Trinidad	1409		18.12.91	M.R.Munn	(Leighton Buzzard)	19. 3.01
G-BTZP	Socata TB-9 Tampico Club	1421		18.12.91	Newcastle-upon-Tyne A/C Ltd	Newcastle	14. 6.01T
G-BTZR	Colt 77B HAFB	2087		18.12.91	P.J.Fell "Bullet"	Maidenhead	12. 9.99A
G-BTZS	Colt 77B HAFB	2088		18.12.91	P.T.R.Ollivere	Sutton	8. 3.99A
G-BTZU	Cameron Concept 60 HAFB	2734		20.12.91	A.C.Rackham	Keswick	28. 1.96A
G-BTZV	Cameron V-77 HAFB	2410		20.12.91	A.W.Sumner "Vulcan"	Newark	11. 9.98A
G-BTZX	Piper J3C-65 Cub	18871	N98648 NC98648	27. 2.92	D.A.Woodhams & J.T.Coulthard	Bidford	21.11.99P
G-BTZY	Colt 56A HAFB	2084		17.10.91	T.M.Donnelly	Doncaster	13.10.94A
G-BTZZ	CFM Streak Shadow K.169-SA & PFA/206-12155 (Rotax 582)			23.12.91	D.R.Stennett	Mendlesham	21. 5.99P

Regn	Type	C/n	P/I	Date	Owner/operator	Probable Base	CA Expy
G-BUAA	Corben Baby Ace D (Cont A65)	561	N516DH	19.11.91	J.M.Walsh	Haverfordwest	7.10.98P
G-BUAB	Aeronca 11AC Chief (Cont A65)	11AC-1759	N3458E NC3458E	17. 1.92	J.Reed	Craysmarsh Farm, Melksham	30. 4.99P
G-BUAC	Slingsby Cadet III (VW1200)	PFA/42-12059	(ex)	17. 1.92	D.A.Wilson	Brunton	4.10.94P
	(Original identity unknown, possibly home-built; stored 5.97)						
G-BUAF	Cameron N-77 HAFB (Rebuilt from 5N-ATT)	2746		2. 1.92	S.J.Colin t/a Skybus Ballooning "Ariston"	Maidstone	26. 7.99
G-BUAG	Jodel D.18 (VW1834)	PFA/169-11651		3. 1.92	A.L.Silcox	Bodmin	16. 6.99P
G-BUAI	Everett Gyroplane Srs.3 (Rotax 532)	030		6. 1.92	C.J.Sullivan	Kemble	9.10.97P
G-BUAJ	Cameron N-90 HAFB	2735		7. 1.92	J.R. & S.J.Huggins "Chunnel Plant Hire"	Dover	19. 7.99A
G-BUAM	Cameron V-77 HAFB	2470		10. 1.92	N.Florence "J & E Page Flowers"	London SW11	10. 6.97T
G-BUAN	Cessna 172N Skyhawk II	172-70290	N738WH	23.12.91	R.J.Cawdell	Booker	7. 7.01T
G-BUAO	Luscombe 8A Silvaire (Cont A65)	4089	N1362K NC1362K	15. 1.92	D.Gough	Popham	17. 6.99P
G-BUAR	VS.358 Seafire LF.IIIc (Westland built)	-	PP972/Aeronavale/PP972	21. 1.92	Wizzard Investments Ltd (David Arnold/Flying A Services)	Earls Colne	AC
G-BUAT	Thunder Ax9-120 HAFB	2093		24. 1.92	J.Fenton "Calor"	Preston	14. 3.99T
G-BUAU	Cameron A-180 HAFB	2744		17. 1.92	C.J.Sandell t/a Out of this World Balloons	Sevenoaks	22. 3.96T
G-BUAW	Pitts S-1C Special (Lyc O-320)	1921-77	N29DH	27. 1.92	A.J.Seymour (Damaged Norwich 16.4.95; on rebuild 9.97))	Swanton Morley	26. 4.95P
G-BUAX	Rans S-10 Sakota (Rotax 582)	PFA/194-11848		28. 1.92	S.P.Wakeham	RAF St.Mawgan	12. 7.99P
G-BUAY	Cameron A-210 HAFB	2751		28. 1.92	Virgin Balloon Flights Ltd (London SE16)		3. 5.96T
G-BUBA	PA-18S-150 Super Cub Floatplane	18-7909047	N6BL N83522	17. 1.92	B.Jackson Knepp Castle, West Grinstead (Op Acebell Avn)		22. 5.01T
G-BUBC	QAC Quickie Tri-Q 200 (Cont O-200-A)	PFA/94-11909		3. 2.92	D.J.Clarke	Sturgate	24. 1.00P
G-BUBN	PBN BN-2B-26 Islander	2270		14. 2.92	Isles of Scilly Skybus Ltd	St.Just	18. 2.00T
G-BUBR	Cameron A-250 HAFB	2779		5. 2.92	Balloon Flights Intl Ltd (Op Bath Hot-Air Balloon Club) "BIBS I"	Bath	13.10.99T
G-BUBS	Lindstrand LBL-77B HAFB (Possibly a new envelope cc 9.95?)	144		10.10.94	Beaulah J.Bower "Bubbles Balloon" Middle Wyke Farm, St.Mary Bourne, Andover		8.10.99A
G-BUBT	Stoddard-Hamilton IIS RG Glasair (Lyc IO-320) 2026 & PFA/149-11633			6. 2.92	M.D.Evans	Haverfordwest	5. 5.99P
G-BUBU	PA-34-220T Seneca III	34-8233060	N8043B	9. 7.87	Brinor (Holdings) Ltd Poplar Hall Farm, Elmsett		28. 4.00
G-BUBW	Robinson R-22 Beta	2048		7. 2.92	Forth Helicopter Services Ltd	Edinburgh	16. 4.01T
G-BUBY	Thunder Ax8-105 Srs.2 HAFB	2115		3. 2.92	T.M.Donnelly "Jorvik Viking Centre"	Doncaster	1. 4.97T
G-BUCA	Cessna A150K Aerobat	A150-0220	N5920J	14. 6.89	T.R.Kingsley	Norwich	1. 2.99T
G-BUCB	Cameron H-34 HAFB	2777		11. 2.92	A.S.Jones	Wolverhampton	21.11.96A
G-BUCC	CASA I-131E Jungmann	1109	G-BUEM	11. 9.78	P.L.Gaze (As "BU+CC" in Luftwaffe c/s)	(Pulborough)	11. 6.99P
	(Spanish serial conflicts with G-BJAL)	G-BUCC/E3B-114					
G-BUCG	Schleicher ASW 20L (mod) (Konig SD430)	20396	BGA.3140 I-FEEL	19. 2.92	W.B.Andrews (As "344")	Booker	16. 6.00
G-BUCH	Stinson V-77 (AT-19) Reliant	77-381	N9570H FB531(RN)	21. 2.92	Pullmerit Ltd	White Waltham	12.10.98
G-BUCI	Auster AOP.9	B5/10/150	XP242	10. 2.92	M.Somerton-Rayner AAC Middle Wallop t/a Historic Acft Flight Reserve Collection (As "XP242" in Army Air Corps c/s)		20. 5.99P
G-BUCJ	DHC.2 Beaver AL.1	1442	XP772	23. 3.92	Propshop Ltd & G.Warner t/a British Aerial Museum (As "XP772" in Army c/s)	Duxford	
G-BUCK	CASA I-131E Jungmann Srs.1000	1113	E3B-322	11. 9.78	R.A.Cayless & J.G.Brander White Waltham t/a Jungmann F/Grp (As "BU+CK" in Luftwaffe c/s)		20. 7.99P
G-BUCM	Hawker Sea Fury FB.11	-	VX653	26. 2.92	Patina Ltd Duxford (Op The Fighter Collection) (On rebuild 1.99)		
G-BUCO	Pietenpol Air Camper (Cont C90)	PFA/47-11829		10. 2.92	A.James Siege Cross Farm, Thatcham		25. 6.99P
G-BUCS	Cessna 150F	150-62368	N3568L	25. 8.89	Atlantic Bridge Avn Ltd	Lydd	20.10.99T
G-BUCT	Cessna 150L	150-75326	N11320	14. 6.89	JK Aviation Services Ltd	Lydd	20.10.99T
G-BUDA	Slingsby T-61F Venture T.2	1963	ZA627	18. 2.92	T.M.Holloway t/a RAFGSA	Bicester	11. 9.98
G-BUDB	Slingsby T-61F Venture T.2	1964	ZA628	18. 2.92	T.M.Holloway t/a RAFGSA	Bicester	8. 7.99
G-BUDC	Slingsby T-61F Venture T.2	1971	ZA652	18. 2.92	R.A.Boddy	Rufforth	5. 8.99
G-BUDE	PA-22-135 Tri-Pacer (Tail-wheel conversion)	22-980	N1144C	9. 4.92	B.A.Bower	Hong Kong	
G-BUDF	Rand Robinson KR-2 (HAPI Magnum 75)	PFA/129-11155		26. 2.92	E.C.King	(Calne)	8. 9.98P

Regn	Type	C/n	P/I	Date	Owner/operator	Probable Base	CA Expy
G-BUDI	Aero Designs Pulsar PFA/202-12185 (Rotax 582)			25. 2.92	R.W.L.Oliver	Popham	27. 8.99P
G-BUDK	Thunder Ax7-77 HAFB	2076		2. 3.92	W.Evans	Wrexham	18. 3.99A
G-BUDL	Taylorcraft Auster III (Regd with Frame No.TAY 5810)	458	PH-POL 8A-2 R Neth AF R-17/NX534	5. 3.92 (On rebuild 6.98 and for op by Military Auster Flt as "NX534")	M.Pocock	AAC Middle Wallop	
G-BUDN	Cameron Shoe 90SS HAFB (Converse Allstar Trainers shape)	2761		6. 3.92	L.V.Mastis "Converse Allstar Boot"	Bristol	3. 4.96A
G-BUDO	PZL-110 Koliber 150	03900045	(D-EIVT)	12. 3.92	A.S.Vine	Old Sarum	1. 8.98
G-BUDR	Denney Kitfox Mk.3 (Rotax 582)	1086 & PFA/172-12107		16. 3.92	N.J.P.Mayled	Dunkeswell	17. 8.99P
G-BUDS	Rand Robinson KR-2	PFA/129-10937		31.12.85	D.W.Munday	(Aldershot)	
G-BUDT	Slingsby T-61F Venture T.2	1883	XZ563	30. 3.92	R.V.Andrews t/a G-BUDT Grp	Eaglescott	17. 6.01
G-BUDU	Cameron V-77 HAFB	2447		16. 3.92	T.M.G.Amery Faux Court, Llandeilo, Dyfed		5. 7.99A
G-BUDW	Brugger MB.2 Colibri PFA/43-10644 (VW1600)		G-GODS	19. 3.92	J.M.Hoblyn	Dunkeswell	29. 9.99P
G-BUEA	ATR-42-300	268	F-WWEW	30. 4.92	Cityflyer Express Ltd	Gatwick	29. 4.99T
G-BUEB	ATR-42-300	304	F-WWLE	29. 6.92	Cityflyer Express Ltd	Gatwick	28. 6.99T
G-BUEC	Van's RV-6 (Lyc O-360)	21015 & PFA/181C-11884		17. 3.92	R.D.Harper	High Ham, Langport	23. 7.99P
G-BUED	Slingsby T-61F Venture T.2	1979	ZA660	12. 3.92	D.J.Wood t/a SE Kent Civil Service F/C	Waldershare Park	14. 5.01
G-BUEE	Cameron A-210 HAFB	2803		20. 3.92	The Balloon Club Ltd t/a Bristol Balloons "Wookey Hole Caves"	Bristol	30. 7.99T
G-BUEF	Cessna 152 II	152-80862	N25928	17. 3.92	CBS Aerohire Ltd Wellesbourne Mountford		12.11.98T
G-BUEG	Cessna 152 II	152-80347	N24736	17. 3.92	Plymouth School of Flying Ltd	Plymouth	9.11.01T
G-BUEI	Thunder Ax8-105 HAFB	2172		23. 3.92	Anglia Balloon School Ltd t/a Anglia Balloons	Marlingford, Norwich	14. 3.99A
G-BUEK	Slingsby T-61F Venture T.2	1879	XZ559	30. 3.92	Norfolk Gliding Club Ltd	Tibenham	7. 7.01
G-BUEN	VPM M.14 Scout (Arrow GT1000R)	VPM14-UK101		19. 3.92	W.M.Day	Ulverston	4.12.96P
G-BUEO	Maule MX-7-180 Star Rocket	11082C		24. 3.92	K. & S.C.Knight (Damaged in France 21.8.95)	Shobdon	10. 8.98
G-BUEP	Maule MXT-7-180 Star Rocket	14023C		24. 3.92	G.M.Bunn	Goodwood	1. 5.01
G-BUES	Cameron N-77 HAFB	2828		26. 3.92	R.J.Shortall "Bath in Bloom"	Bath	3. 5.98T
G-BUET*	Colt Flying Drinks Can SS HAFB (Budweiser Can Shape)	2162		30. 3.92	R S Kent "Bud King of Beers" (Balloon Preservation Group 7.98)	Lancing	10.12.93A
G-BUEU*	Colt 21A Cloudhopper HAFB (Budweiser Can Shape)	2163		30. 3.92	R S Kent "Bud King of Beers" (Balloon Preservation Group 7.98)	Lancing	2.12.94A
G-BUEV	Cameron O-77 HAFB	2810	EI-CFW G-BUEV	31. 3.92	R.R.McCormack & R.J.Mercer (Exported 1998)	Belfast	8.7.97Exp
G-BUEX	Schweizer Hughes 269C (300C)	S.1412	G-HFLR	14. 4.92	A.Drewery t/a Fenland Helicopter Centre	Fenland	5. 6.99T
G-BUEZ	Hawker Hunter F.6A (AWA-built)	S4U-3275	8736M XF375	3. 4.92	The Old Flying Machine (Air Museum) Co Ltd (As "XF375/05")	Duxford	
G-BUFA	Cameron R-77 Gas Balloon	2712		19. 3.92	)		10. 6.93A
G-BUFC	Cameron R-77 Gas Balloon	2823		19. 3.92	) Noble Adventures Ltd		23. 6.93A
G-BUFE	Cameron R-77 Gas Balloon	2825		19. 3.92	)	(Netherlands)	21. 6.93A
G-BUFG	Slingsby T-61F Venture T.2	1977	ZA658	3. 4.92	T.W.Eagles	Hinton-in-the-Hedges	27. 7.01
G-BUFH	PA-28-161 Warrior II	28-8416076	N43520	15. 4.92	M.P.Rainford & J.E.Slee t/a The Tiger Leisure Grp	Blackpool	1. 6.01T
G-BUFJ	Cameron V-90 HAFB	2809		7. 4.92	S.P.Richards	Cranbrook	6. 6.98T
G-BUFK	Cassutt Racer IIIM	PFA/34-11069		7. 4.92	D.I.H.Johnstone & W.T.Barnard (Under construction 5.95)	Strathaven	
G-BUFN	Slingsby T-61F Venture T.2	1967	ZA631	8. 4.92	S.C.Foggin Sandhill Farm, Shrivenham t/a BUFN Grp		19. 8.01
G-BUFO	Cameron UFO 70SS HAFB (Flying Saucer shape)	1929		10. 3.89	Virgin Airship & Balloon Co Ltd "UFO"	Telford	26. 4.97A
G-BUFP	Slingsby T-61F Venture T.2	1982	ZA663	8. 4.92	R.A.Winley t/a Venture Grp (As "ZA663")	Currock Hill	28. 4.01
G-BUFR	Slingsby T-61F Venture T.2	1880	XZ560	9. 4.92	R.F.Warren & P.A.Hazell	Upper Broyle Farm, Ringmer	29. 4.01
G-BUFT	Cameron O-120 HAFB	2814		9. 4.92	N.D.Hicks	Alton	24. 9.01T
G-BUFV	Light Aero Avid Speed Wing mk.4 (Rotax 582) PFA/189-12192			15. 4.92	S.C.Ord	Holywell	9. 5.99P
G-BUFX	Cameron N-90 HAFB	2835		22. 4.92	Kerridge Computer Co Ltd "Kerridge II"	Newbury	31. 5.99A
G-BUFY	PA-28-161 Warrior II	28-8016211	N130CT N8TS/N3571K	14. 4.92	Bickertons Aerodromes Ltd	Denham	30. 6.01T
G-BUGB	Stolp SA.750 Acroduster Too PFA/89-11942			22. 4.92	D.Burnham (Nearing completion 9.97)	Andrewsfield	12. 1.99P
G-BUGC	Jurca MJ.5 Sirocco (Regd as PFA/59-2207)	PFA/2207	(G-BWDJ)	14. 4.92	A.Burani Manor Farm, Glatton (Nearing completion 7.95)		
G-BUGD	Cameron V-77 HAFB	2195		23. 4.92	Cameron Balloons Ltd "Bug"	Bristol	25. 7.99A
G-BUGE	Bellanca 7GCAA Citabria	339-77	N4165Y	23. 4.92	P.White	(Fethard, Ireland)	13. 9.01T
G-BUGG	Cessna 150F	150-62479	N8379G	24. 3.92	C.P.J.Taylor & D.M.Forshaw	Panshanger	9. 5.99

Regn	Type	C/n	P/I	Date	Owner/operator	Probable Base	CA Expy
G-BUGH	Rans S-10 Sakota			24. 4.92	D.T.Smith	Bagby	31. 8.99P
	(Rotax 582) 0790-110 & PFA/194-11899						
G-BUGI	Evans VP-2	PFA/7201		16. 4.92	D.G.Gibson	(Braunton)	13. 7.99P
					(Under construction 9.95)		
G-BUGJ	Robin DR.400/180 Regent	2137		28. 4.92	Alfred Graham Ltd	Southend	23. 7.01
G-BUGL	Slingsby T-61F Venture T.2	1966	ZA630	29. 4.92	D.E.Hills & J.Edwards	Tibenham	1. 6.98
					t/a VMG Grp		
G-BUGM	CFM Streak Shadow			29. 4.92	D.Penn-Smith	Sywell	29. 6.99P
	(Rotax 582) K.176-SA & PFA/206-12069				t/a The Shadow Group		
G-BUGN	Colt 210A HAFB	2193		1. 5.92	R.W.Batchelor	Thame	31. 7.99T
G-BUGO	Colt 56B HAFB	2143		18. 5.92	D.W.Allum	Beverley, Hull	2.10.98A
G-BUGP	Cameron V-77 HAFB	2278	OO-BEE	10. 3.92	R.Churcher	Canterbury	26.5.95Exp
					(Exported 1998)		
G-BUGS	Cameron V-77 HAFB	2482		14. 4.92	T J Orchard Booker		19. 6.97T
					t/a A Load of Hot Air "Bugs Bunny"		
G-BUGT	Slingsby T-61F Venture T.2	1871	XZ551	22. 4.92	R.W.Hornsey	(Stanford-le-Hope)	5. 8.99
G-BUGV	Slingsby T-61F Venture T.2	1884	XZ564	28. 4.92	Oxfordshire Sportflying Ltd	Enstone	28. 6.01
G-BUGW	Slingsby T-61F Venture T.2	1962	ZA626	22. 4.92	Rankart Ltd	Hinton-in-the-Hedges	16. 8.01
G-BUGX	Socata MS.880B Rallye Club	2957	OO-FLO	24. 4.92	R.W.H.Watson	Cumbernauld	9. 9.99
G-BUGY	Cameron V-90 HAFB	2800		9. 4.92	I.J.Culley	Hungerford	22. 7.99A
					t/a Dante Balloon Grp "Florance"		
G-BUGZ	Slingsby T-61F Venture T.2	1981	ZA662	22. 4.92	R.W.Spiller	RAF Dishforth	4. 2.99
					t/a Dishforth Flying Group		
G-BUHA	Slingsby T-61F Venture T.2	1970	ZA634	29. 4.92	A.W.Swales (As "ZA634/C")	Rufforth	15. 7.99
G-BUHC	BAe 146 Srs 300	E-3193	G-BTMI	30. 6.92	Air UK Ltd	Stansted	8. 7.01T
			G-6-193				
G-BUHJ	Boeing 737-4Q8	25164		19. 3.93	British Airways (European Operations at Gatwick) Ltd		
						Gatwick	18. 3.00T
G-BUHK	Boeing 737-4Q8	26289		14. 6.93	British Airways (European Operations at Gatwick) Ltd		
						Gatwick	13. 6.00T
G-BUHL	Boeing 737-4S3	25134	9M-MLH	22. 3.93	GB Airways Ltd	Gatwick	6. 4.00T
			N1799B/(G-BSRB)		(Wings of the City t/s)		
G-BUHM	Cameron V-77 HAFB	2481		7. 5.92	L.A.Watts	Pangbourne, Reading	25.11.99A
					"Blue Horizon"		
G-BUHO	Cessna 140	14402	N2173V	1. 5.92	W.B.Bateson	Blackpool	27. 7.01T
	(Cont C90)						
G-BUHP	Ailes De K Flyair 1100	01219935		7. 5.92	R.White	(Henley-on-Thames)	
G-BUHR	Slingsby T-61F Venture T.2	1874	XZ554	8. 5.92	Lleweni Parc Ltd	Lleweni Parc	13.11.98
G-BUHS	Stoddard-Hamilton Glasair I TD	149	C-GYMB	8. 5.92	E.J.Spalding	Dingwall	23. 8.99P
	(Lyc O-360)						
G-BUHU	Cameron N-105 HAFB	2785		13. 5.92	Balloon Preservation Group	Lancing	21.11.96A
					"Land Rover" (For restoration 12.98)		
G-BUHY	Cameron A-210 HAFB	2858		14. 5.92	Adventure Balloon Co Ltd	London W7	24. 8.99T
G-BUHZ	Cessna 120	14950	N3676V	1. 5.92	G.L.Brown	Sibson	
G-BUIB	MBB Bo.105DBS-4	S.138/911	G-BDYZ	21. 5.92	Bond Helicopters Ltd	Inverness	24. 6.01T
			D-HDEF		(Op Scottish Air Ambulance)		
	(Original a/c remanufactured with new pod c/n S.911 in 1992)						
G-BUIC	Denney Kitfox mk.2	PFA/172-11802		1. 5.92	C.R.Northrop & B.M.Chilvers		
						(Huntingdon/Wisbech)	
G-BUIE	Cameron N-90 HAFB	2863		22. 5.92	Flying Pictures Ltd	Fairoaks	14. 7.99A
					"Unipart III"		
G-BUIF	PA-28-161 Warrior II	28-7916406	N28375	29. 5.92	Newcastle upon Tyne A/C Ltd	Newcastle	8. 9.01T
G-BUIG	Campbell Cricket	PFA G/03-1173		27. 5.92	T.A.Holmes	Melrose Farm, Melbourne	9. 6.97P
	(Rotax 532)						
G-BUIH	Slingsby T-61F Venture T.2	1876	XZ556	29. 5.92	Yorkshire Gliding Club (Pty) Ltd		
						Sutton Bank	8. 6.01
G-BUIJ	PA-28-161 Warrior II	28-8116210	N83784	3. 6.92	Ashurst Technologies Ltd	Chilbolton	9. 7.01
G-BUIK	PA-28-161 Warrior II	28-7916469	N2845P	2. 6.92	A.S.Bamrah	Biggin Hill	2. 8.01T
					t/a Falcon Flying Services		
G-BUIL	CFM Streak Shadow K.182-SA & PFA/206-12121			8. 5.92	P.N.Bevan & L.M.Poor	Perth	22. 9.99P
	(Rotax 582)						
G-BUIN	Thunder Ax7-77 HAFB	1882		5. 6.92	J.R.Birkenhead & E.J.Case		
					t/a Free Flight Aerostat Grp (Klea 32 c/s)		
						Runcorn/St.Helens	30. 5.97A
G-BUIP	Denney Kitfox mk.2 710 & PFA/172-11874			8. 6.92	Avcomm Developments Ltd	Enstone	20. 7.99P
	(Rotax 582)						
G-BUIR	Light Aero Avid Speed Wing mk.4			9. 6.92	K.N.Pollard	Sturgate	29. 4.97P
	(Rotax 582)	PFA/189-12213			(Damaged nr Gainsborough 26.1.97; on rebuild 5.97)		
G-BUIU	Cameron V-90 HAFB	2641		11. 6.92	H.Micketeit	Bielefeld, Germany	25. 2.99A
G-BUIW	Robinson R-22 Beta	2049		10. 6.92	J.L. & A.M.Leonard	Thruxton	3. 8.98T
					t/a Findon Air Svs (Crashed nr Amport 9.3.98)		
G-BUIZ	Cameron N-90 HAFB	2850		12. 6.92	Virgin Airship & Balloon Co Ltd	Telford	7. 8.95A
					(Hutchinson Telecom c/s)		
G-BUJA	Slingsby T-61F Venture T.2	1972	ZA653	22. 5.92	T.M.Holloway t/a RAFGSA	RAF Cosford	8. 7.01
					(Op Wrekin Gliding Club)		
G-BUJB	Slingsby T-61F Venture T.2	1978	ZA659	21. 5.92	O.F.Vaughan & D.A.Fall	Shobdon	6. 7.01
					t/a Falke Syndicate		
G-BUJE	Cessna 177B Cardinal	177-01920	N34646	10. 6.92	J.Flux t/a FG93 Grp	Old Sarum	5. 5.01

Regn	Type	C/n	P/I	Date	Owner/operator	Probable Base	CA Expy
G-BUJH	Colt 77B HAFB	2207		23. 6.92	R.P.Cross & R.Stanley	Luton/Harpenden	26. 6.99A
G-BUJI	Slingsby T-61F Venture T.2	1882	XZ562	22. 5.92	R.A.Boddy	Rufforth	1. 6.01
G-BUJJ	Light Aero Avid Speed Wing (Rotax 582)	213	N614JD	20.10.92	A.C.Debrett	Midhurst	21. 6.99P
G-BUJK	Montgomerie-Bensen B.8MR Merlin (Rotax 582)	PFA G/01-1211		25. 6.92	C.Moffat	(Reading)	10. 2.99P
G-BUJL	Aero Designs Pulsar	PFA/202-11892		16. 6.92	J.J.Lynch	(Dunstable)	
G-BUJM	Cessna 120 (Cont C85)	11784	N77343 NC77343	19. 6.92	B.R.Johnstone t/a Cessna 120 F/Grp	(Yeovil)	9.10.99
G-BUJN	Cessna 172N Skyhawk II	172-72713	N6315D	19. 6.92	De Cadenet Engineering Ltd		
	(Damaged Wellesbourne Mountford 18.1.95; on repair 9.97)					Halfpenny Green	30.11.95T
G-BUJO	PA-28-161 Cherokee Warrior II	28-7716077	N1014Q	19. 6.92	Channel Islands Aero Holdings (Jersey) Ltd t/a Jersey Aero Club	Jersey	24. 3.00T
G-BUJP	PA-28-161 Warrior II	28-7916047	N21624	19. 6.92	APB Leasing Ltd	Welshpool	27. 6.99T
G-BUJR	Cameron A-180 HAFB	2821		22. 6.92	W.I.Hooker & C.Parker	Nottingham	31. 7.97T
G-BUJT*	BAe Jetstream 3100	699	N414MX G-31-699	8. 7.92	British Aerospace plc (Stored as N414MX 11.96)	Prestwick	N/E(Exp)
G-BUJU	Cessna 150H	150-67285	N6485S	30. 6.92	P.J.Smith t/a BUJU F/C & Associates	Shoreham	9. 9.01
G-BUJV	Light Aero Avid mk.4 Speed Wing (Rotax 582)	PFA/189-12250		3. 7.92	C.Thomas (Damaged Caernarfon 13.8.93)	(Tamworth)	28. 7.94P
G-BUJW	Thunder Ax8-90 Srs.2 HAFB	2208		6. 7.92	R.T.Fagan	Bath	6. 8.95T
G-BUJX	Slingsby T-61F Venture T.2	1873	XZ553	7. 7.92	J.R.Chichester-Constable	Burton Constable, Hull	6. 3.99
G-BUJY	DH.82A Tiger Moth	"OU/04/1967"	VT-DPE HU-858	1. 7.92	Aero Vintage Ltd St.Leonards-on-Sea (On rebuild 3.94)		
G-BUJZ	Rotorway Exec 90 (RI 162)	5119		9. 7.92	T.W.Aisthorpe & R.J.D.Crick (Damaged Eggesford 23.10.93) Tedburn St.Mary, Exeter		25. 5.94P
G-BUKA	Fairchild SA.227AC Metro III	AC-706B	ZK-NSQ N27185/G-BUKA/N27185	24. 8.88	Atlantic Air Transport Ltd (Atlantic Airways c/s)	Coventry	11. 6.00T
G-BUKB	Rans S-10 Sakota (Rotax 582)	PFA/194-12078		13. 7.92	M.K.Blatch & M.P.Lee	RAF Keevil	16. 6.99P
G-BUKC	Cameron A-180 HAFB	2870		3. 7.92	P.Johnson t/a Cloud Nine Balloon Co	Consett	11. 3.98T
G-BUKE	Boeing-Stearman A75N1 (PT-17) Kaydet	75-2732	(G-BRIP) N53127/41-25243	17. 7.92	R.G.Rance (As "243" in USAAC c/s) "Sharkey's Machine"	Goodwood	27. 8.01T
G-BUKF	Denney Kitfox mk.4 (Rotax 582)	PFA/172A-12247		2. 6.92	A.G.V.McClintock t/a Kilo Foxtrot Group	(Longniddry, NI)	14. 9.99P
G-BUKH	Druine D.31 Turbulent (VW 1600)	PFA/48-11419		14. 8.92	P.M.Newman Stoneacre Farm, Farthing Corner		26. 4.99P
G-BUKI	Thunder Ax7-77 HAFB	2239		8. 7.92	C.Wilkinson t/a Adventures Aloft (Sunderland 92 c/s)	Newcastle	24. 4.97T
G-BUKJ	BAe ATP	2052	EC-GLD G-OEDF/G-BUKJ/TC-THZ/G-BUKJ	5. 8.92	British Aerospace (Operations) Ltd	Woodford	
G-BUKK	Dornier Bucker Bu.133D Jungmeister	27	N44DD HB-MKG/Sw AF U-80	15.11.89	E.J.F.McEntee Kirdford, Billingshurst (As "U-80" in Swiss AF c/s)		7. 7.99P
G-BUKN	PA-15 Vagabond	15-215	N4427H NC4427H	15. 7.92	M.A. & A.M.Watts	(Southampton)	
G-BUKO	Cessna 120 (Cont C85)	13089	N2828N NC2828N	15. 7.92	N.G.Abbott Manor Farm, Bishopstone, Salisbury (Damaged Manor Farm, Bishopstone 28.12.97)		31. 7.98P
G-BUKP	Denney Kitfox mk.2 (Rotax 582)	PFA/172-12301		22. 7.92	T.D.Reid	Newtownards	14.10.98P
G-BUKR	SOCATA MS.880B Rallye 100T	2923	LN-BIY	27. 7.92	G.R.Russell t/a G-BUKR F/Grp	Bridport	20.10.99
G-BUKS	Colt 77B HAFB	2241		6. 7.92	R.& M.Bairstow Middlewich, Cheshire		28. 7.97A
G-BUKT	Luscombe 8E Silvaire (Cont C85)	2197	N45670 NC45670	30. 7.92	M.G.Talbot & J.N.Wilshaw	Sherburn	10. 9.99P
G-BUKU	Luscombe 8E Silvaire (Cont C85)	4720	N1993K NC1993K	30. 7.92	F.G.Miskelly	Thruxton	19. 6.99P
G-BUKV	Colt AS-105 Mk.II Hot-Air Airship	2212	ZS-HYO G-BUKV	3. 8.92	A.Ockelmann t/a Ballon Reisen	Buchholz, Germany	20. 4.99A
G-BUKX	PA-28-161 Warrior II	28-7816674	N231PA	5. 8.92	LNP Ltd	Dunkeswell	28.11.01T
G-BUKY	CCF T-6J Harvard 4	CCF4-464	FAP1766 BF+063/AA+063/52-8543	13. 7.92	R.A.Fleming (As "52-8543/66" in US Navy c/s)	Breighton	4. 4.99P
G-BUKZ	Evans VP-2	PFA/63-10761		5. 8.92	P.R.Farnell (Extant 5.97)	Wombleton	
G-BULB	Thunder Ax7-77 HAFB	1968		3. 7.92	Elinore French Ltd t/a Shiltons of Rothbury	Morpeth	13. 4.97A
G-BULC	Light Aero Avid Flyer mk.4	PFA/189-12202		6. 7.92	C.Nice	(Woking)	
G-BULD	Cameron N-105 HAFB	2136		6. 8.92	S.J.Boxall	Sheffield	14. 2.99T
G-BULE	Price TPB.2 HAFB	004		10. 8.92	A.G.R.Calder	London NW1	
G-BULF	Colt 77A HAFB	2043		10. 8.92	M.V.Farrant "Nursey II" or "Max" ?	Billingshurst	22. 5.99A
G-BULG	Van's RV-4 (Lyc O-320)	JRV4-1	C-FELJ	28. 7.92	R.I.Warman Priory Farm, Tibenham		15.11.98P
G-BULH	Cessna 172N Skyhawk II	172-69869	N738CJ	2. 7.92	Pye Consulting Group Ltd	(Wigan)	18. 7.99T

Regn	Type	C/n	P/I	Date	Owner/operator	Probable Base	CA Expy
G-BULJ	CFM Streak Shadow			10. 8.92	C.C.Brown		
	(Rotax 582) K.191-SA & PFA/206-12199					Papillon Farm, Market Harborough	26. 5.99P
G-BULK	Thunder Ax9-120 Srs.2 HAFB	2237		3. 7.92	S.J.Colin & A.S.Pinder	Maidstone	26. 5.99T
					t/a Skybus Ballooning		
G-BULL	Scottish Avn Bulldog Srs.120/128	HKG-5	20. 9.88		C.D.Weiswall	Elstree	17. 6.98
		BH120/392	G-31-18		(As "HKG-5" in Hong Kong c/s)		
G-BULM	Aero Designs Pulsar PFA/202-12010			11. 8.92	J.Webb	White Waltham	19. 4.99P
	(Rotax 582)						
G-BULN	Colt 210A HAFB	2265		13. 8.92	H.G.Davies	Cheltenham	17. 9.99T
G-BULO	Luscombe 8A Silvaire	4216	N1489K	13. 8.92	A.F.S.Caldecourt	Popham	16. 4.99P
	(Cont A65)		NC1489K				
G-BULR	PA-28-140 Cherokee B	28-25230	HB-OHP	8. 7.92	R & H Wale (General Woodworks) Ltd		
			N7320F		"Margaret Ann"	Little Gransden	15.10.99T
G-BULT	Campbell Cricket PFA G/03-1213			20. 8.92	A.T.Pocklington	(Bishops Stortford)	
G-BULY	Light Aero Avid Flyer PFA/189-12309			12. 8.92	D.R.Piercy	Newton Peverill	6. 7.99P
	(Rotax 582)				"Lady Irene"		
G-BULZ	Denney Kitfox mk.2 PFA/172-11546			31. 7.92	T.G.F.Trenchard	(Blandford Forum)	29. 9.98P
	(Rotax 582)						
G-BUMP	PA-28-181 Cherokee Archer II		PH-MVA	17. 1.79	Marnham Investments Ltd	Ronaldsway	23.10.00T
		28-7790437	OO-HCH/N3105Q		(Op Manx Flyers Aero Club)		
G-BUNB	Slingsby T-61F Venture T.2	1969	ZA633	25. 8.92	T.M.Holloway	RAF Cranwell	14.12.01
					t/a RAFGSA (Op Cranwell Gliding Club)		
G-BUNC	PZL-104 Wilga 35	129444	SP-TWP	2. 9.92	M.Prew t/a Paravia Grp	Framlingham	20. 8.99
G-BUND	PA-28RT-201T Turbo Arrow IV		N8219V	18. 7.88	Jenrick Ltd & A.Somerville	Blackbushe	29. 6.01
		28R-8031107					
G-BUNG	Cameron N-77 HAFB	2905		2. 9.92	A.Kaye	Wellingborough	25. 9.99A
					t/a The Bungle Balloon Group "Bungle"		
G-BUNH	PA-28RT-201T Turbo Arrow IV		N8255H	26. 8.92	Jennifer A.Blenkharn	Carlisle	30.11.01T
		28R-8031166			t/a JB Consultants (Aviation)		
G-BUNI	Cameron Bunny 90SS HAFB	2897		23. 9.92	Virgin Airship & Balloon Co Ltd	Telford	29.10.99A
	(Cadburys Caramel Bunny shape)						
G-BUNJ	K & S SA.102-5 Cavalier PFA/01-10058			10. 9.92	J.A.Smith	Great Massingham	
					(Nearing completion 9.97)		
G-BUNM	Denney Kitfox mk.3 PFA/172-12111			15. 9.92	P.J.Carter	Inverness	19. 5.98P
	(Rotax 582)						
G-BUNO	Neico Lancair 320 PFA/191-12332			11. 9.92	J.Softley	(Newbury)	
G-BUNS	Reims Cessna F150K	0648	F-BSIL	28. 8.92	R.W.H.Cole	Spilsted Farm, Sedlescombe	
					t/a Cole Aviation (Stored 3.97)		
G-BUNV	Thunder Ax7-77 HAFB	1967		23. 9.92	J.A.Lister "Skylark"	Aldershot	11. 8.99A
G-BUNZ	Thunder Ax10-180 Srs.2 HAFB	2271		7. 9.92	T.M.Donnelly	Doncaster	19. 7.97T
G-BUOA	Whittaker MW6S Srs.A Fatboy Flyer			25. 9.92	D.A.Izod	Gerpins Farm, Upminster	1. 6.99P
	(Rotax 582) PFA/164-11959						
G-BUOB	CFM Streak Shadow			29. 9.92	A.M.Simmons	Belle Vue Farm, Yarnscombe	7. 5.99P
	(Rotax 582) K.186-SA & PFA/206-12156						
G-BUOC	Cameron A-210 HAFB	2924		5.10.92	G.N. & K.A.Connolly	Monmouth	2. 4.99T
G-BUOD	Replica Plans SE.5A PFA/20-10474			5.10.92	M.D.Waldron	Braschaat, Belgium	14.12.98P
	(Cont C90)				(As "B595/W" in 56 Sqdn, RFC c/s)		
G-BUOE	Cameron V-90 HAFB	2938		6.10.92	B. & J.Smallwood	Chippenham	2. 4.99A
					t/a Dusters & Co "Duster 2"		
G-BUOF	Druine D.62B Condor PFA/49-11236			6.10.92	R.P.Loxton	(Sherborne)	23. 9.99P
	(Cont O-200-A)						
G-BUOI	PA-20-135 Pacer	20-571	OY-ALS	18. 9.92	R.A.L.Hubbard	Meon	24. 7.99
	(Lyc O-320)		D-EHEN/N7750K		t/a Foley Farm Flying Group		
G-BUOJ	Cessna 172N Skyhawk II	172-71701	N5064E	8.10.92	EFG Flying Services Ltd	Biggin Hill	8. 7.01T
G-BUOK	Rans S-6-116 Coyote II			9.10.92	M.Morris		
	(Rotax 912UL) 0692-314 & PFA/204A-12317					Fieldhead Farm, Denholme, Bradford	30.10.98P
G-BUOL	Denney Kitfox mk.3 PFA/172-12142			12.10.92	J.G.D.Barbour		
	(Rotax 582)					Sheriff Hall, Balgone, Berwick	24. 2.99P
G-BUON	Light Aero Avid Aerobat PFA/189-12160			13.10.92	I.A.J.Lappin	Newtownards	6.10.99P
	(Rotax 582)						
G-BUOO	QAC Quickie Tri-Q 200	01	N10RX	17. 5.93	J.J.Donely & A.D.P.Thompson	Coventry	16. 6.97P
	(Cont O-200-A)				(Damaged Cranfield 4.7.97)		
G-BUOP	Dorrington Skycycle D2 Airship D2-218			15.10.92	G.E.Dorrington (Southampton University)		
G-BUOR	CASA I-131E Jungmann Srs.2000	2134	N89542	21.10.92	M.I.M.Schermer Voest (As "781-26" in Spanish AF c/s)		
			EC-336/E3B-508			Lelystad, Netherlands	13.11.95P
G-BUOS	VS.394 Spitfire FR.XVIIIe 6S/672224		HS687	19.10.92	Historic Flying Ltd	Audley End	AC
	(Regd with c/n 6S/676224)		(IAF)/SM845		(On rebuild 9.96)		
G-BUOW	Aero Designs Pulsar XP PFA/202-12206			22.10.92	T.J.Hartwell & M.J.Riley	(Bedford)	8. 6.95P
	(Rotax 912)				t/a RAE Bedford F/C		
G-BUOX	Cameron V-77 HAFB	2925		23.10.92	R.M.Pursey & C.M.Richardson		
					"High Flyer"	Newbury/Oxford	22. 3.97A
G-BUPA	Rutan LongEz	750	N72SD	22. 9.92	G.J.Banfield	Gloucestershire	12. 8.99P
	(Lyc O-235)						
G-BUPB	Stolp SA.300 Starduster Too RH.100		N8035E	3.11.92	I.D.Trask	Popham	15. 7.99P
	(Lyc IO-360)				t/a Starduster Group		
G-BUPC	Rollason Beta B2 PFA/02-12369			29.10.92	C.A.Rolph	Shoreham	21.10.98P
	(Cont C90)						

Regn	Type	C/n	P/I	Date	Owner/operator	Probable Base	CA Expy
G-BUPF	Bensen B.8MR PFA G/01-1209 (Rotax 532)			5.11.92	P.W.Hewitt-Dean (Wootton Bassett)		11. 5.99P
G-BUPG	Cessna 180J Skywagon	180-52490	N52086	15.10.92	T.P.A.Norman	Rendcomb	13.10.99
G-BUPI	Cameron V-77 HAFB	1778	G-BOUC	28. 7.88	Sally A.Masey "Bristol United Press" (Western Daily Press/Evening Post titles)	Bristol	11. 8.96A
G-BUPJ	Sportavia Fournier RF4D	4119	N7752	10.11.92	M.R.Shelton	Tatenhill	
G-BUPM	VPM M-16 Tandem Trainer VPM16-UK-102 (Arrow GT1000R)			16.10.92	J.G.Erskine	Kemble	12. 5.97P
G-BUPN	PA-46-350P Malibu Mirage	4622086	N91884	18.11.92	W.P.J.Davison (Sutton Coldfield)		4. 2.02
G-BUPO	Moravan Zlin Z.526F Trener Master	1267	YR-OAZ YR-ZAO	23.11.92	P.J.Behr & F.Mendelssohn (Sarreguemines/Strasbourg, France)		31. 1.96
G-BUPP	Cameron V-42 HAFB	2789		21. 7.92	M.W.A.Shemlit	Henley-on-Thames	21.10.95A
G-BUPR	Jodel D.18 PFA/169-11289 (Limbach L2000)			23.11.92	R.W.Burrows Priory Farm, Tibenham		12.11.99P
G-BUPS	ATR-42-300	109	DQ-FEP F-WWEF	16.12.92	Titan Airways Ltd	Stansted	5. 6.99T
G-BUPT	Cameron O-105 HAFB	2960		25.11.92	P.M.Simpson Hemel Hempstead t/a Chiltern Balloons		9. 1.99T
G-BUPU	Thunder Ax7-77 HAFB	2305		25.11.92	R.C.Barkworth & D.G.Maguire (USA) "Puzzle"		8. 6.99A
G-BUPV	Great Lakes 2T-1A Sport Trainer	126	N865K NC865K	26.11.92	R.J.Fray	Sibson	28. 6.99P
G-BUPW	Denney Kitfox mk.3 PFA/172-12281 (Rotax 912)			22.10.92	G.M. Park t/a Kitfox Group (Lochwinnoch)		9. 7.99P
G-BURD	Reims Cessna F.172N Skyhawk II	1677	PH-AXI	26. 4.78	L.M.Bateman & Co Ltd	Leicester	27.10.99
G-BURE	Jodel D.9 Bebe PFA/944			30.11.92	Lucy J.Kingsford	Headcorn	
					(Under construction 12.95)		
G-BURF	Rand Robinson KR-2 PFA/129-11345 (VW1834)			30.11.92	P.J.H.Moorhouse & B.L.Hewart (Stockport)		
G-BURG	Colt 77A HAFB	2042		12. 1.93	S.T.Humphreys "Lily" Great Missenden		28. 3.99A
G-BURH	Cessna 150E	150-61225	EI-AOO G-BURH/EI-AOO/N2125J	2.12.92	C.A.Davis & K.E.Morgan Popham t/a BURH F/Grp		6.11.99
G-BURI	Enstrom F-28C	433	N51743	11.12.92	R.L.Heath Ashford, Kent t/a India Helicopters Group		8. 2.99
G-BURL	Colt 105A HAFB	2297		18.11.92	J.E.Rose	Abingdon	9. 1.99T
G-BURM	English Electric Canberra TT.18	-	WJ680	11.12.92	Mitchell Aircraft Ltd Kemble		18. 8.97P
	(Built by Handley Page)				(Op by Canberra Flight as "WJ680/CT" in 100 Sqdn c/s)		
G-BURN	Cameron O-120 HAFB	2793		18. 2.92	Innovation Ballooning Ltd Bath "Innovations II"		17. 3.99T
G-BURP	Rotorway Exec 90 (RI 162)	5116		8.10.92	N.K.Newman	Sywell	13. 9.96P
G-BURR	Auster AOP.9	-	7851M WZ706	28. 9.92	R.P.D.Folkes AAC Middle Wallop (Op Military Auster Flight as "WZ706")		
G-BURS	Sikorsky S-76A II Plus	760040	(HP-) G-BURS/G-OHTL	4. 5.89	Lynton Avn Ltd Denham (Op European Helicopters Ltd)		13.10.99T
G-BURT	PA-28-161 Cherokee Warrior II	N2459Q 28-7716105		10. 6.81	J.D.F.Fendick	Norwich	2. 6.99
G-BURZ	Hawker Nimrod II	41H-59890	K3661	22.12.91	Historic Acft Collection Ltd (On rebuild 8.95) St.Leonards-on-Sea		AC
G-BUSB	Airbus A320-111 (Originally flown as G-BRSA)	0006	(G-BRAA) F-WWDD	30. 3.88	British Airways plc Heathrow (Cockerel of Lowicz/Koguty Lowickie t/s)		19. 4.01T
G-BUSC	Airbus A320-111	0008	(G-BRAB) F-WWDE	26. 5.88	British Airways plc Heathrow (British Olympic Association t/s)		1. 6.01T
G-BUSD	Airbus A320-111	0011	(G-BRAC) F-WWDF	21. 7.88	British Airways plc Heathrow "Island of Mull"		21. 7.01T
G-BUSE	Airbus A320-111	0017	F-WWDG	1.12.88	British Airways plc Heathrow (Mountain of the Birds/Benyhone Tartan t/s)		30.11.01T
G-BUSF	Airbus A320-111	0018	F-WWDH	26. 5.89	British Airways plc . Heathrow "Isle of Man"		25. 5.99T
G-BUSG	Airbus A320-211	0039	F-WWDM	30. 5.89	British Airways plc Heathrow (Sterntaler/Bauhaus t/s)		30. 5.99T
G-BUSH	Airbus A320-211	0042	F-WWDT	19. 6.89	British Airways plc Heathrow "Isle of Jura"		18. 6.99T
G-BUSI	Airbus A320-211	0103	F-WWDB	23. 3.90	British Airways plc Heathrow (Wings of the City t/s)		21. 3.00T
G-BUSJ	Airbus A320-211	0109	F-WWIC	6. 8.90	British Airways plc Heathrow (Water Dreaming t/s)		5. 8.00T
G-BUSK	Airbus A320-211	0120	F-WWIN	12.10.90	British Airways plc Heathrow (Waves & Cranes t/s)		11.10.00T
G-BUSN	Rotorway Exec 90 (RI 162)	5141		6. 1.93	B.Seymour Castle Eden, Hartlepool		23. 8.99P
G-BUSR	Aero Designs Pulsar PFA/202-12356 (Rotax 582)			15.12.92	S.S.Bateman & R.A.Watts Cheddington		21. 6.98P
G-BUSS	Cameron Bus 90SS HAFB	1685		11. 3.88	L.V.Mastis West Bloomfield, MI, USA "National Express"		31. 1.96A
G-BUST	Neico Lancair IV	LIV-114A		23.10.92	C.C.Butt (Chester)		AC
G-BUSV	Colt 105A HAFB	2324		12. 1.93	M.N.J.Kirby Northwich, Cheshire		26. 1.95
G-BUSW	Rockwell Commander 114	14079	N4749W	18. 1.93	P.A.Nesbitt (Bohemia, NY, USA)		AC

Regn	Type	C/n	P/I	Date	Owner/operator	Probable Base	CA Expy
G-BUSY	Thunder Ax6-56A HAFB	111		20. 6.77	M.E.Hooker "Busy Bodies"	Whitchurch	27. 4.86A
G-BUSZ	Light Aero Avid Speed Wing mk.4			20. 1.93	T.J.Allan	Drayton St.Leonard	21.12.98P
	(Rotax 582)	PFA/189-12280					
G-BUTA	CASA I-131E Jungmann Srs.2000 1101/A		E3B-336	20. 1.93	A.G.Dunkerley	Breighton	1. 2.00P
	(Correct c/n not known)						
G-BUTB	CFM Streak Shadow			20. 1.93	F.A.H.Ashmead	New Milton	16. 2.99P
	(Hirth 2706 R05) K.190 & PFA/206-12243						
G-BUTC	Cyclone Ax3		G-MYHO	11. 1.93	P.R.Berridge	Enniscorthy, Co.Wexford	4.11.98P
	(Rotax 618) B.1122981 & PFA/245-12365						
G-BUTD	Van's RV-6	PFA/181-12152		21. 1.93	N.W.Beadle	Bensons Farm, Laindon	25. 6.99P
	(Lyc O-320)						
G-BUTE	Anderson EA-1 Kingfisher Amphibian		G-BRCK	15. 8.91	T.Crawford	Cumbernauld	15.10.99P
	(Lyc O-235)	PFA/132-10798					
G-BUTF	Aeronca 11AC Chief	11AC-1578	N3231E	21. 1.93	N.J.Mortimore	Watchford Farm, Yarcombe	
			NC3231E		(Stored 1.98)		
G-BUTG	Zenair CH-601HD Zodiac PFA/162-12225			22. 1.93	J.M.Palmer	Willingham	12. 5.99P
	(Cont C90)						
G-BUTH	CEA Jodel DR.220 2+2	6	F-BNVK	10. 2.93	Merlin Flying Club Ltd	Hucknall	29. 5.00
G-BUTJ	Cameron O-77 HAFB	2991		25. 1.93	A.J.A. & P.A.Bubb	Guildford	5. 4.97A
					"Purple Haze"		
G-BUTK	Murphy Rebel	PFA/232-12091		25. 1.93	A.Allen	Aberdeen	3.11.98P
	(Rotax 912-UL)						
G-BUTL	PA-24-250 Comanche	24-2352	G-ARLB	4. 4.84	D.Heater	Blackbushe	28. 7.99
G-BUTM	Rans S-6-116 Coyote II PFA/204A-12414			22. 1.93	W.S.Long	Hermitage	2. 7.99P
	(Rotax 912UL)						
G-BUTN	MBB Bo.105DBS-4	S.34/912	G-AZTI	29. 1.93	Bond Helicopters Ltd	Glasgow Heliport	25. 2.99T
	(Rebuilt with new pod S.912 1993)		EI-BTE/G-AZTI/EC-DRY/G-AZTI/D-HDAN		(Op Scottish Ambulance Service)		
G-BUTP*	Bede BD-5G	008801		5. 2.93	Heather Flight Ltd	(Germany)	
					(Cancelled by CAA 25.3.99)		
G-BUTT	Reims Cessna FA.150K Aerobat	0029	G-AXSJ	18. 8.86	C.R.Guggenheim	Bournemouth	24.10.99T
					(Op Airbourne School of Flying)		
G-BUTX	Bucker 133C Jungmeister	E1-4		3. 2.93	A.J.E.Smith	Breighton	
	(Warner Super Scarab)	Sp AF ES.1-4/35-4					
	(Possibly c/n 1010 or a CASA built I-133L)						
G-BUTY	Brugger MB.2 Colibri	PFA/43-12387		30.11.92	R.M.Lawday	(Milford, Derby)	
G-BUTZ	PA-28-180 Cherokee C	28-3107	G-DARL	23. 4.93	A.J. & J.M.Davis	Cranfield	14. 5.00T
			4R-ARL/4R-ONE/SE-EYD				
G-BUUA	Slingsby T-67M Firefly II	2111		17. 3.93	Hunting Aviation Ltd	RAF Barkston Heath	18. 8.99T
					(Op JEFTS)		
G-BUUB	Slingsby T-67M Firefly II	2112		17. 3.93	Hunting Aviation Ltd	RAF Barkston Heath	2. 8.99T
					(Op JEFTS)		
G-BUUC	Slingsby T-67M Firefly II	2113		17. 3.93	Hunting Aviation Ltd	RAF Barkston Heath	14. 8.99T
					(Op JEFTS)		
G-BUUD	Slingsby T-67M Firefly II	2114		17. 3.93	Hunting Aviation Ltd	RAF Barkston Heath	31. 8.99T
					(Op JEFTS)		
G-BUUE	Slingsby T-67M Firefly II	2115		17. 3.93	Hunting Aviation Ltd	RAF Barkston Heath	29. 9.99T
					(Op JEFTS)		
G-BUUF	Slingsby T-67M Firefly II	2116		17. 3.93	Hunting Aviation Ltd	RAF Barkston Heath	13.10.99T
					(Op JEFTS)		
G-BUUG	Slingsby T-67M Firefly II	2117		17. 3.93	Hunting Aviation Ltd	RAF Barkston Heath	24.10.99T
					(Op JEFTS)		
G-BUUI	Slingsby T-67M Firefly II	2119		17. 3.93	Hunting Aviation Ltd	RAF Barkston Heath	18.11.99T
					(Op JEFTS)		
G-BUUJ	Slingsby T-67M Firefly II	2120		17. 3.93	Hunting Aviation Ltd	RAF Barkston Heath	10.12.99T
					(Op JEFTS)		
G-BUUK	Slingsby T-67M Firefly II	2121		17. 3.93	Hunting Aviation Ltd	RAF Barkston Heath	16. 1.00T
					(Op JEFTS)		
G-BUUL	Slingsby T-67M Firefly II	2122		17. 3.93	Hunting Aviation Ltd	RAF Barkston Heath	16. 1.00T
					(Op JEFTS)		
G-BUUM	PA-28RT-201 Arrow IV	28R-7918090	N2145X	14. 1.93	J.Phelan & J.M.O'Grady	Aldergrove	3. 4.99
					t/a Bluebird F/Grp		
G-BUUN	Lindstrand LBL-105A HAFB	015		9. 2.93	Flying Pictures Ltd	Fairoaks	28. 5.99A
					"British Gas"		
G-BUUO	Cameron N-90 HAFB	2994		9. 2.93	Bryan Brothers Ltd	Bristol	27. 7.99A
G-BUUS	Skyraider Gyrocopter	P.01		9. 2.93	Sycamore Avn Ltd		
	(Arrow GT500)					Healinks Farm, Clitheroe	11.5.95P*
G-BUUT	Interavia 70TA HAFB	04509-92		21. 1.93	Aero Vintage Ltd	Rye	
G-BUUU	Cameron Bottle 77SS HAFB	2980		11. 2.93	United Distillers UK plc	Perth	4. 3.94A
	(Bells Whisky Bottle shape)				"Bells Whisky"		
G-BUUX	PA-28-180 Cherokee D	28-5128	OY-BCW	17. 2.93	M.A.Judge t/a Aero Grp 78	Netherthorpe	9. 3.99T
G-BUVA	PA-22-135 Tri-Pacer	22-1301	N8626C	12. 2.93	R.Howard t/a Oaksey VA Grp	Oaksey Park	14.11.99
G-BUVB	Colt 77A HAFB	2041		22. 2.93	T.L.Regan	Newcastle	23. 3.94A
G-BUVE	Colt 77B HAFB	2376		8. 3.93	M.P. & M.Nicholson	Alverton/Newark	28. 8.99A
G-BUVF	DHC.2 Beaver 1	965		5. 3.93	H.Wade, J.J.van Egmond & P.R.Monk		
	(Regd with US Army "c/n" 1623)		R Neth AF S-9/55-4585 t/a Nostalgic Flying (As "S-9" in R.Neth AF c/s)				
						Lelystad, Netherlands	30. 4.99
G-BUVG	Cameron N-56 HAFB	3012		8. 3.93	Cameron Balloons Ltd	Bristol	20. 4.99A
G-BUVK*	Cameron A-210 HAFB	2996		8. 3.93	Balloon Preservation Group	Lancing	18. 8.97T
					"Burgundy Blaze"		

Regn	Type	C/n	P/I	Date	Owner/operator	Probable Base	CA Expy
G-BUVL	Fisher Super Koala PFA/228-11399 (Jabiru 2200)			3. 3.93	A.D.Malcolm "Spirit of Throwley" Park Farm, Throwley, Faversham		21.10.97P
G-BUVM	CEA Jodel DR.250/160 Capitaine	54	OO-NJR F-BNJR	11. 3.93	G.G.Milton	Kimbolton	AC
G-BUVN	CASA I-131E-2000 Jungmann	2092	EC-333 E3B-487	12. 3.93	W.Van Egmond Hoogeveen, Netherlands (As "BI-005" in R.Neth AF c/s)		14. 8.99P
G-BUVO	Reims Cessna F182P Skylane II	0022	G-WTFA PH-VDH/D-EJCL	10. 3.93	D.W.Wall t/a BUVO Grp	Southend	23. 5.99
G-BUVP	CASA I-131E-2000 Jungmann (Regd with c/n 2155)	2139	EC-338 E3B-539	12. 3.93	M.I.M.Schermer Voest Lelystad, Netherlands		14. 9.98P
G-BUVR	Christen A-1 Husky	1162		12. 3.93	A.E.Poulsom Manor Farm, Tongham		26. 4.99
G-BUVS	Colt 77A HAFB	2381		12. 3.93	Supergas Ltd "Supergas I"	Birmingham	18.11.99A
G-BUVT	Colt 77A HAFB	2382		12. 3.93	Supergas Ltd "Supergas II"	Birmingham	9. 4.94A
G-BUVW	Cameron N-90 HAFB	3020		19. 3.93	Bristol Balloon Fiestas Ltd	Bristol	12. 5.99A
G-BUVX	CFM Streak Shadow PFA/206-12410 (Rotax 582)			22. 3.93	G.K.R.Linney	(Edinburgh)	28. 7.99P
G-BUVZ	Thunder Ax10-180 Srs.2 HAFB	2380		24. 3.93	Lakeside Lodge Balloon Rides (Cambridgeshire) Ltd Huntingdon		13.12.98T
G-BUWA	VS.349 Spitfire F.Vc WASP/20/288		C-FDUY 7555M/5378M/AR614	19. 3.93	Alpine Deer Group Ltd (Wanaka, NZ) (As "AR614/DU-Z" in 312 Sqdn c/s)		AC
G-BUWE	Replica Plans SE.5A PFA/20-11816 (Cont C90)			25. 3.93	P.N.Davis Leicester (As "C9533/M" in RFC c/s)		26. 3.99P
G-BUWF	Cameron N-105 HAFB	3036		26. 3.93	R.E.Jones Lytham St.Annes "British Aerospace II"		17. 9.99T
G-BUWH	Parsons Two-Place Gyroplane (Rotax 532) PFA G/08-1215			1. 4.93	R.V.Brunskill Melrose Farm, Melbourne		22. 8.95P
G-BUWI	Lindstrand LBL-77A HAFB	023		5. 4.93	Capital Balloon Club Ltd London NW1 "Throw Up"		10. 9.99A
G-BUWJ	Pitts S-1C Special (Lyc O-320)	2002	N110R	25. 3.93	P.A.Willmington	(Malmesbury)	23.10.99P
G-BUWK	Rans S-6-116 Coyote II PFA/204A-12448 (Rotax 582)			7. 4.93	R.Warriner Bradleys Lawn, Heathfield		28. 4.98P
G-BUWL	Piper J/4A Cub Coupe	4-1047	N27828 NC27828	8. 4.93	V.F.Kemp	Oaksey Park	
G-BUWM	BAe ATP	2009	CS-TGB G-BUWM/CS-TGB/G-11-9	19. 4.93	British Aerospace (Operations) Ltd (Exported 1998) Woodford		12.6.93Exp
G-BUWP	BAe ATP	2053	G-11-053	30. 3.93	British Airways plc Glasgow "Strathisla"		20. 4.00T
G-BUWR	CFM Streak Shadow K.177-SA & PFA/206-12068 (Rotax 582)			26. 4.93	T.Harvey Grove Farm, Raveningham		2. 4.98P
G-BUWS	Denney Kitfox Mk.2 PFA/172-11831			26. 4.93	J.E.Brewis	(Castletown, IoM)	
G-BUWT	Rand Robinson KR-2 PFA/129-10952			5. 4.93	Cynthia M.Coombe	(Greenford, Middx)	
G-BUWU	Cameron V-77 HAFB	3053		27. 4.93	G.Thompson	Ashford, Kent	1. 6.97A
G-BUWW	Cameron O-105 HAFB	3023		1. 4.93	M.T.Evans	Bath	18. 6.99T
G-BUWY	Cameron V-77 HAFB	2961		27. 4.93	P.A.Sachs	West Byfleet	23. 5.99A
G-BUWZ	Robin HR.200/120B	254		22. 4.93	A.Cox	Boship, Hailsham	27. 1.00
G-BUXA	Colt 210A HAFB	2400		27. 4.93	Balloon School (Intnl) Ltd	Petworth	16. 8.99T
G-BUXB	Sikorsky S-76A	760086	(F-GSJG) G-BUXB/VR-CCZ/N399BB/N39RP	11. 6.93	Air Hanson Ltd	Blackbushe	16. 8.99T
G-BUXC	CFM Streak Shadow PFA/206-12177 (Rotax 582)			20. 4.93	J.P.Mimnagh	(Wirral)	13.12.99P
G-BUXD	Maule MXT-7-160 Star Rocket	17001C	N9231R	4. 5.93	S.Baigent	Jersey	9. 7.99
G-BUXI	Steen Skybolt PFA/64-10755 (Lyc IO-360)			16. 3.93	M.Frankland	Liverpool	5. 8.99P
G-BUXJ	Slingsby T-61F Venture T.2	1878	XZ558	6. 5.93	R.A.P.McLachlan	Redhill	17. 6.99
G-BUXK	Pietenpol Aircamper PFA/47-11901 (Cont C90)			12. 5.93	G.R.G.Smith Shobdon t/a XIX Crawley F/C		14. 7.99P
G-BUXL	Taylor JT.1 Monoplane PFA/55-11819			12. 5.93	M.W.Elliott	(Derby)	
G-BUXM	QAC Quickie Tri-Q (Revmaster 2100D)	2343	N4435Y	23. 2.93	A.J.Ross & D.Ramwell (Stored 10.97)	Tatenhill	10. 8.95P
G-BUXN	Beechcraft C23 Sundowner	M-1752	N9256S	13. 5.93	J.L.Pearce Bournemouth t/a Private Pilots Syndicate		8. 9.99
G-BUXO	Pober P-9 Pixie PFA/105-10647			17. 5.93	J.Mangiapane t/a P-9 F/Grp	(Nottingham)	
G-BUXP	American Aircraft Falcon XPS PFA/250-12439			16. 3.93	J.C. & B.E.Greenslade	(Ilfracombe/Ipswich)	
G-BUXR	Cameron A-250 HAFB	3056		13. 5.93	D.S.King Nottingham t/a Celebration Balloon Flights		15. 6.99T
G-BUXS	MBB Bo.105DBS-4	S.41/913	G-PASA G-BGWP/F-ODMZ/G-BGWP/HB-XFD/N153BB/D-HDAS	19. 5.93	Bond Helicopters Ltd "Irn Bru" Aberdeen		25. 5.99T
	(Rebuilt with new pod S.913 1993 - regn D-HIFA reserved 4.93)						
G-BUXT	Dornier 228-202K	8065	D-CBOL TC-FBM/D-CBOL	24. 5.93	Suckling Avn (International) Ltd Cambridge		26. 5.99T
G-BUXU	Beechcraft D17S (GB-2) Traveler	4823	N9113H Bu 33024	20. 5.93	S.J.Ellis	Bryngwyn Bach	AC

Regn	Type	C/n	P/I	Date	Owner/operator	Probable Base	CA Expy
G-BUXV	PA-22-160 Tri-Pacer (Super Pacer tailwheel conversion)	22-6685	N9769D	20. 5.93	T.McManus & W.Connor Weston, Ireland t/a Bogavia Two		30. 9.00
G-BUXW	Thunder Ax8-90 Srs.2 HAFB	2405		25. 5.93	J.M.Percival	Burton-on-the-Wolds	14. 7.99A
G-BUXX	PA-17 Vagabond (Cont A75)	17-28	N4611H NC4611H	31. 3.93	R.H.Hunt	Old Sarum	15. 4.99P
G-BUXY	PA-25-235 Pawnee	25-2705	C-GZCR N6959Z	18. 3.93	Bath, Wilts & North Dorset Gliding Club Ltd Kingston Deverill		29.12.00
G-BUYB	Aero Designs Pulsar PFA/202-12193 (Rotax 582)			28. 5.93	A.P.Fenn	Shobdon	27. 7.99P
G-BUYC	Cameron Concept 80 HAFB	3095		28. 5.93	P.J.Dorward	Witney	20. 7.94
G-BUYD	Thunder Ax8-90 HAFB	2422		28. 5.93	Anglia Balloon School Ltd t/a Anglia Balloons "Air UK"	Norwich	18. 3.99A
G-BUYE	Aeronca 7AC Champion (Cont A65)	7AC-4327	N85584 NC85584	30. 4.93	R.Mazey	(Bristol)	16.11.96P
G-BUYF	American Aircraft Falcon XP (Rotax 503)	600179	N512AA	13. 5.93	J.C.Greenslade Belle Vue Farm, Huntshaw		2. 2.99P
G-BUYG	Colt Flying Gin Bottle 12 SS HAFB (Gordon's Gin Bottle shape)	2331		28. 5.93	United Distillers plc "Gordon's Gin"	(Spain)	20. 5.96
G-BUYH	Cameron A-210 HAFB	3045		28. 5.93	A.J.Street	Whimple, Exeter	14. 5.98T
G-BUYI	Thunder Ax7-77 HAFB	1266		20. 6.88	Chelmsford Management Ltd "Elevation"	Chelmsford	18. 7.99A
G-BUYJ	Lindstrand LBL-105A HAFB	039		1. 6.93	D.K.Fish	Bedford	8. 5.99T
G-BUYK	Denney Kitfox mk.4 PFA/172A-12214 (Rotax 912UL)			1. 6.93	R.D.L.Mayes	Biggin Hill	30.11.95P
G-BUYL	Rotary Air Force RAF 2000 H2-92-361 (Subaru EJ22)		C-FPFN	2. 6.93	Newtonair Gyroplanes Ltd Newton Abbot/St.Merryn		25. 9.98P
G-BUYM	Thunder Ax8-105 HAFB	2419		3. 6.93	G.M.Houston t/a Scotair Balloons	Lesmahagow, Lanark	7. 2.99T
G-BUYN	Cameron O-84 HAFB	1214	OE-KZG	4. 6.93	J.T.L.Challenger (Challenger Balloons)	(Thailand)	11. 7.94A
G-BUYO	Colt 77A HAFB	2398		4. 6.93	S.F.Burden (Noordwijk, Netherlands)		17. 5.99T
G-BUYR	Mooney M.20C Mark 21	2650	N1369W	7. 6.93	Charmaine R.Weldon	Weston, Ireland	15. 9.00
G-BUYS	Robin DR.400/180 Regent	2197		21. 6.93	F.A.Spear	Nuthampstead	16. 6.99
G-BUYT	Ken Brock KB-2 PFA G/06-1214 (Rotax 582)			7. 6.93	Janet E.Harris	(Ashby-De-La-Zouch)	6. 2.95P
G-BUYU	Bowers Fly Baby 1A PFA/16-12222 (Cont A65)			7. 6.93	J.A.Nugent	Haverfordwest	17. 6.98P
G-BUYY	PA-28-180 Cherokee B	28-1028	C-FXDP CF-XDP/N7214W	18. 3.93	A.J.Hedges & C.E.Yates Bristol/Lulsgate t/a G-BUYY Group		26. 3.99T
G-BUZA	Denney Kitfox mk.3	1178 & PFA/172-12547		10. 6.93	R.Hill	Haverfordwest	6. 9.99P
G-BUZB	Aero Designs Pulsar XP PFA/202-12312 (Rotax 912)			14. 6.93	S.M.Lancashire	Lymmdam	25.11.98P
G-BUZC	Everett Gyroplane Srs.3A	034		14. 7.93	M.P.Lhermette (Faversham) (Damaged 7.94; stored Sproughton 12.95)		
G-BUZD	Aerospatiale AS.332L Super Puma 2069		C-GSLJ N189EH/C-GSLJ/HC-BNB/C-GSLJ/PT-HRN/C-GSLJ	11. 2.93	Brintel Helicopters Ltd Aberdeen t/a British International Helicopters		14.12.99T
G-BUZE	Light Aero Avid Speed Wing PFA/189-12047 (Rotax 582)			16. 6.93	N.L.E. & R.A.Dupee Watchford Farm, Yarcombe		5.11.98P
G-BUZF	Colt 77B HAFB	1993		16. 6.93	I.J.Jackson	Lytham St.Annes	6. 5.99A
G-BUZG	Zenair CH.601HD PFA/162-12457 (Cont O-200-A)			17. 6.93	N.C.White	Portmoak	10. 6.98P
G-BUZH	Star-Lite SL-1	119	N4HC	17. 6.93	I.Burrows	(Dunganon, NI)	2. 8.99P
G-BUZK	Cameron V-77 HAFB	2962		17. 6.93	J.T.Wilkinson	Calne	7. 5.95A
G-BUZL	VPM M-16 Tandem Trainer VPM16-UK-105 (Arrow GT1000R)			18. 6.93	R.M.Savage Carlisle t/a Roger Savage (Photography)		21.11.97P
G-BUZM	Light Aero Avid mk.3 Speed Wing (Rotax 582) PFA/189-12179			30. 4.93	R.McLuckie & O.G.Jones	RAF Mona	21. 6.99P
G-BUZN	Cessna 172H	172-56056	N2856L	24. 6.93	H.Jones	Barton	23. 9.99
G-BUZO	Pietenpol Aircamper PFA/47-12408 (Salmson AD9)			28. 6.93	D.A.Jones	(Maidenhead)	
G-BUZR	Lindstrand LBL-77A HAFB	044		29. 6.93	Lindstrand Balloons Ltd	Oswestry	11. 1.00A
G-BUZS	Colt Flying Pig SS HAFB	2415		2. 7.93	Banco Bilbao Vizcaya	(Spain)	20. 5.96A
G-BUZT	Kolb Twinstar Mk.3 PFA/205-12367			1. 7.93	A.C.Goadby	(Sudbury)	
G-BUZV	Ken Brock KB-2 PFA G/06-1152			1. 7.93	K.Hughes	(Amlwch, Gwynedd)	
G-BUZY	Cameron A-250 HAFB	2936		29. 4.93	P.J.D.Kerr	Bridgwater	15. 1.99T
G-BUZZ	Agusta-Bell 206B JetRanger II	8178	F-GAMS HB-XGI/OE-DXF	13. 4.78	Virgin Helicopters Ltd	Booker	19. 6.99T

G-BVAA-BVZZ

Regn	Type	C/n	P/I	Date	Owner/operator	Probable Base	CA Expy
G-BVAA	Light Aero Avid Speed Wing mk.4 (Rotax 582) PFA/189-12166			10. 6.93	D.T.Searchfield	Popham	28. 7.99P
G-BVAB	Zenair CH.601HDS PFA/162-12475 (Rotax 912UL)			26. 5.93	A.R.Bender	Deanland, Hailsham	19. 5.99P
G-BVAC	Zenair CH.601HD PFA/162-12504 (Rotax 912UL)			1. 6.93	A.G.Cozens	Goodwood	6. 9.98P
G-BVAF	Piper J3C-85 Cub	4645	OO-UBU N28199/NC28199	14. 6.93	N.M.Hitchman	Garston Farm, Marshfield	18. 6.98P
G-BVAG	Lindstrand LBL-90A HAFB	022		7. 7.93	T.Moult, P.Ellis & R.Tillson Nottingham "Gee Tee"		4.10.97A
G-BVAH	Denney Kitfox mk.3 PFA/172-12031 (Rotax 912)			22.10.91	V.A.Hutchinson	Market Bosworth	25. 8.99P
G-BVAI	PZL-110 Koliber 150	03900040	OY-CYJ	7. 7.93	N.J. & R.F.Morgan	Tatenhill	3.11.99
G-BVAJ*	Rotorway Exec 90 (RI 162)	5118		7. 7.93	Rotorbuild Helicopters Ltd (Cancelled by CAA 22.3.99) (Acaster Malbis, York)		AC
G-BVAM	Evans VP-1 PFA/62-12132			7. 7.93	R.F.Selby	(Littlehampton)	
G-BVAN	SOCATA MS.892E Rallye 150GT	12376	F-BVAN	21.11.88	D.R.Stringer	Elstree	26. 4.01
G-BVAO	Colt 25A Sky Chariot HAFB	2024		9. 7.93	Janice M.Frazer Hexham, Northumberland		9. 6.99
G-BVAW	Staaken Z-1 Flitzer PFA/223-12058 (VW1834)			12. 7.93	D.J.Evans & L.R.Williams (As "D692") Brickhouse Farm, Frogland Cross		29. 6.99P
G-BVAX	Colt 77A HAFB	1213		30. 3.88	P.H.Porter "Vax"	Tenbury Wells	5. 8.95A
G-BVAY	Rutan VariEze	RS.8673/345	N5MS	3. 9.93	D.A.Young	(Sunderland)	
G-BVAZ*	Montgomerie-Bensen B.8MR PFA G/01-1190			12. 7.93	R Patrick (Noted 6.98)	Perth	
G-BVBD	Vertical Avn Technologies S-52-3 (Converted Sikorsky S-52) 52014		N4643S Bu.125521	21. 7.93	J.Windmill (Stored 10.95)	Ilkeston	
G-BVBF	PA-28-151 Cherokee Warrior 28-7515206		N31JM N32633	22. 7.93	R.K.Spence	Cardiff	AC
G-BVBG	PA-32R-300 Cherokee Lance 32R-7680151		N19BP	22. 7.93	R.K.Spence	Cardiff	30. 1.00T
G-BVBJ*	Colt Flying Coffee Jar 1 SS HAFB (Maxwell House Jar) 2427			27. 7.93	Balloon Preservation Group Newbury "Maxwell House 1" (On loan to BBM & L 7.98)		21.11.96A
G-BVBK*	Colt Flying Coffee Jar 2 SS HAFB (Maxwell House Jar) 2428			27. 7.93	A D Kent "Maxwell House 2" Lancing (Balloon Preservation Group 7.98)		14. 2.97A
G-BVBL	PA-38-112 Tomahawk II 38-82A0004		N91339	2. 8.93	Aerohire Ltd Wellesbourne Mountford (Op Wellesbourne Avn)		30. 1.00T
G-BVBN	Cameron A-210 HAFB	2904		2. 8.93	M.L. & S.M.Gabb Alcester t/a Heart of England Balloons		10. 3.98T
G-BVBO	Vertical Avn Technologies S-52-3 52046		N9329R Bu.128616	4. 8.93	M.Richardson Ilkeston t/a Ilkeston Contractors (Stored 10.95)		
G-BVBP	Avro 683 Lancaster B.10	-	RCAF KB994 KB994	4. 8.93	Aces High Ltd North Weald (Open storage 5.96)		
G-BVBR	Light Aero Avid Speed Wing (Rotax 582) PFA/189-12085			3. 8.93	H.R.Rowley	Wellesbourne Mountford	14. 6.98P
G-BVBS	Cameron N-77 HAFB	3128		4. 8.93	Marley Building Materials Ltd Birmingham		14.10.99A
G-BVBT	DHC.1 Chipmunk 22 C1/0547 (Fuselage no. DHB/F/432)		WK511	4. 8.93	T.J.Manna (Kennet Avn) Cranfield (As "WK511" in RN c/s)		13.10.97
G-BVBU	Cameron V-77 HAFB	3076	(OO-BYS)	5. 8.93	J.Manclark	Haddington	26. 7.97A
G-BVBV	Light Aero Avid Speed Wing (Rotax 582) PFA/189-12187			4. 8.93	L.W.M.Summers	Sandown	24. 3.99P
G-BVBX*	Cameron N-90M HAFB	3102		10. 8.93	British Balloon Museum Newbury & Library "Mercury"		27. 9.95A
G-BVCA	Cameron N-105 HAFB	3129		11. 8.93	Unipart Group Ltd Cowley t/a Unipart Balloon Club "Unipart 4"		11. 1.99A
G-BVCB	Rans S-10 Sakota PFA/194-11882			11. 8.93	M.D.T.Barley	Top Farm, Tadlow	
G-BVCC	Monnett Sonerai 2LT PFA/15-10547			12. 8.93	J.Eggleston	(Northallerton)	
G-BVCG	Van's RV-6 PFA/181-11783 (Lyc O-320)			17. 8.93	C.A.Simmonds	Leicester	16. 2.99P
G-BVCI	Robinson R-22 Beta	2176		18. 8.93	Boldre Aviation Ltd Bournemouth (Op Bournemouth Helicopters)		30.10.99
G-BVCJ	Agusta A.109A II	7265	G-CLRL G-EJCB	23. 8.93	Castle Air Charters Ltd Trebrown, Liskeard		5. 3.00T
G-BVCL	Rans S-6-116 Coyote II PFA/204A-12551 (Rotax 912UL)			25. 8.93	R.A.Blackbourn & J.K.McFarlane Perth		6. 2.99P
G-BVCM	Cessna 525 Citation Jet 525-0022		N1329N	2. 5.94	Kwik Fit Plc	Edinburgh	22. 5.00
G-BVCN	Colt 56A HAFB	2445		25. 8.93	N.R.Mason	Llandudno	9. 9.94A
G-BVCO	Clutton Fred Srs.2 PFA/29-10947			25. 8.93	I.W.Bremner	(Dornoch, Sutherland)	23. 6.99P
G-BVCP	Piper CP.1 Metisse PFA/253-12512 (VW1835) (Modified Tipsy Nipper)			24. 6.93	C.W.R.Piper	Harpenden	
G-BVCS	Aeronca 7AC Champion 7AC-1346 (Cont A65)		N69BD N82702/NC82702	1. 9.93	P.C.Isbell Cherry Tree Farm, Monewden		5. 8.98P
G-BVCT	Denney Kitfox mk.4-1200 (Rotax 912UL) 1761 & PFA/172A-12456			27. 8.93	A.F.Reid	Comber, NI	19. 4.99P
G-BVCX	Sikorsky S-76A II Plus	760183	N951L N5450M	21. 9.93	Brintel Helicopters Ltd Aberdeen t/a British International Helicopters		1. 2.00T
G-BVCY	Cameron H-24 HAFB	3136		3. 9.93	Bryant Group plc	Solihull	27. 1.99A

Regn	Type	C/n	P/I	Date	Owner/operator	Probable Base	CA Expy
G-BVCZ	Colt 240A HAFB	2480		3. 9.93	Schemedraw Ltd	(USA)	21. 8.96
G-BVDB	Thunder AX7-77 HAFB	2364	G-ORDY	6. 9.93	M.J.Smith & J.Towler	York	17.10.99A
G-BVDC	Van's RV-3	PFA/99-12218		12. 7.93	D.Calabritto	(Billercay)	25. 6.96P
	(Lyc 0-235)						
G-BVDD	Colt 69A HAFB	2170		6. 9.93	R.M.Cambridge & D.Harrison-Morris		
						Oswestry	17. 8.99
G-BVDE	Taylor JT-1 Monoplane	PFA/55-11278		6. 9.93	C.R.J.Norman	(Gravesend)	
G-BVDF	Cameron Doll 105SS HAFB	3112		7. 9.93	Cameron Balloons Ltd	(Germany)	3.11.94A
G-BVDH	PA-28RT-201 Arrow IV	28R-7918030	N2176L	13. 9.93	P.Heffron	Swansea	20.10.99
G-BVDI	Van's RV-4	2058	N55GJ	13. 9.93	J.P.Leigh	(Streethay)	28. 1.99P
	(Lyc 0-320)						
G-BVDJ	Campbell Cricket	PFA G/03-1189		13. 9.93	Shirley Jennings	Crowthorne	26. 4.99P
	(Rotax 582)						
G-BVDM	Cameron Concept 60 HAFB	3141		15. 9.93	M.P.Young	Dover	28. 9.98A
G-BVDN	PA-34-220T Seneca III	34-8133185	G-IGHA	16. 9.93	Convergence Avn. Ltd.	Jersey	19.11.00T
			G-IPUT/N84224D				
G-BVDO	Lindstrand LBL-105A HAFB	055		16. 9.93	J.Burlinson	Aston Clinton	19. 3.99T
G-BVDP	Sequoia F8L Falco	PFA/100-10879		17. 9.93	T.G.Painter	(Felixstowe)	
G-BVDR	Cameron 0-77 HAFB	2452		21. 9.93	T.Duggan	Selby	24. 5.97A
G-BVDS	Lindstrand LBL-69A HAFB	102		23. 9.93	I.Ollerenshaw	Oswestry	27. 6.95A
G-BVDT	CFM Streak Shadow	PFA/206-12462		23. 9.93	H.J.Bennet	Inverness	15. 3.99P
	(Rotax 582)						
G-BVDW	Thunder Ax8-90 HAFB	2507		30. 9.93	J.G.Wilson "Cosmic"	Thirsk	18. 7.99
G-BVDX	Cameron V-90 HAFB	3159	OO-BMY	30. 9.93	R.K.Scott	Yeovil	18. 5.99A
			G-BVDX				
G-BVDY	Cameron Concept 60 HAFB	3167		30. 9.93	K.A. & G.N.Connolly	Monmouth	23. 3.96A
G-BVDZ	Taylorcraft BC-12D	9043	N96743	21. 1.94	P.N.W.England	(Hove)	
			NC96743				
G-BVEA	Nostalgair N.3 Pup		G-MWEA	7. 6.93	N.Lynch	Breighton	26.10.97P
	(Mosler MM-CB35) 01-GB & PFA/212-11837						
G-BVEB	PA-32R-301 Saratoga SP	3213055	N9224X	15. 9.93	Transea Trading Co Ltd	Stapleford	26. 9.99
G-BVEC	ATR-42-300	356	F-WWEW	30. 4.93	Cityflyer Express Ltd	Gatwick	29. 4.00T
G-BVED	ATR-42-300	315	F-WWEN	4.11.93	Cityflyer Express Ltd	Gatwick	3.11.99T
G-BVEF	ATR-42-300	331	F-GKNF	24. 3.94	Cityflyer Express Ltd	Gatwick	23. 3.00T
			F-WWLP				
G-BVEG	Hunting-Percival P.84	PAC/W/13893	XN629	19. 8.93	R.J.Everett	(Ipswich)	28. 5.99P
	Jet Provost T.3A				(As "XN629/49" in RAF c/s)		
G-BVEH	Wassmer Jodel D.112	1294	F-BMOH	29.10.93	M.L.Copland	Breighton	4. 8.98P
G-BVEJ	Cameron V-90 HAFB	3169		5.10.93	J.D.A.Snields & A.R.Craze	Battle	4. 9.99T
G-BVEK*	Cameron Concept 80 HAFB	3133		5.10.93	J.G.Andrews	Pewsey	30. 4.97A
					(Cancelled by CAA 6.3.99)		
G-BVEL*	Evans VP-1 Srs.2	PFA/62-11983		6.10.93	M.J. & S.J.Quinn	(Kilmacolm)	
					(Cancelled by CAA 22.3.99)		
G-BVEN	Cameron Concept 80 HAFB	3164		6.10.93	J.M.Stables	Knaresborough	24. 5.97T
					t/a Aire Valley Balloons		
G-BVEP*	Luscombe 8A Master	1468	N28707	8.10.93	Mid-West Avn Ltd	Oaksey Park	
			NC28707		(Stored 9.98 - cancelled by CAA 22.3.99)		
G-BVER	DHC.2 Beaver 1	1648	G-BTDM	13. 8.91	A.F.Allen	(Leavesden)	23. 4.95T
			XV268		(Status uncertain) (As "XV268" in AAC c/s)		
G-BVES	Cessna 340A II	340A-0077	N1378G	8. 9.93	Firfax Systems Ltd	Gloucestershire	3. 6.99T
G-BVEU	Cameron 0-105 HAFB	3145		12.10.93	H.C.Wright	Kelfield, York	22.11.98T
G-BVEV	PA-34-200 Seneca	34-7250316	N1428T	8.10.93	R.W.Harris, M.F.Hatt	Southend	14. 7.00T
			HB-LLN/D-GHSG/N1428T		& JRB Avn Ltd (Op Southend Flying Club)		
G-BVEW	Lindstrand LBL-150A HAFB	057		14.10.93	P.Trumper	Ashford	2. 9.99T
G-BVEY	Denney Kitfox mk.4/1200	PFA/172A-12527		14.10.93	J.H.H.Turner	Carlisle	12. 5.99P
	(Rotax 582)						
G-BVEZ	Hunting-Percival P.84	PAC/W/9287	XM479	13.10.93	Newcastle Jet Provost Co Ltd	Newcastle	5. 8.98P
	Jet Provost T.3A				(As "XM479/54" in RAF c/s)		
G-BVFA	Rans S-10 Sakota	PFA/194-12298		7. 9.93	D.Parkinson & D.Allam		
	(Rotax 582)					Downland Farm, Redhill	6. 7.99P
G-BVFB	Cameron N-31 HAFB	3175		20.10.93	Bath City Council "Bath Heritage"	Bath	16. 5.99A
G-BVFF	Cameron V-77 HAFB	3161		26.10.93	R.G.Barry	Newbury	7. 4.96A
					"Roy Barry Carpets"		
G-BVFM	Rans S-6-116 Coyote II			2.11.93	P.G.Walton	Morgansfield, Fishburn	26. 6.99P
	(Rotax 912UL) 0793-522 & PFA/204A-12579						
G-BVFN	Pitts S-1E Special	JAS.7	N41JS	1.11.93	N.W.Parkinson	Little Gransden	13. 3.98P
	(Lyc 0-360)						
G-BVFO	Light Aero Avid Speed Wing			9. 9.93	P.Chisman	Enstone	20. 4.99P
	(Rotax 582)	PFA/189-12053					
G-BVFP	Cameron V-90 HAFB	3179		2.11.93	C.Duppa-Miller	Warwick	31.12.99A
G-BVFR	CFM Streak Shadow			3.11.93	R.W.Chatterton		
	(Rotax 582) K.237-SA & PFA/206-12567					Griffins Farm, Temple Bruer	26. 2.99P
G-BVFS	Slingsby T-31M Cadet III	PFA/42-11387	(ex)	3.11.93	V.M.Crabb	High Cross, Ware	
G-BVFT	Maule M.5-235C Lunar Rocket	7183C	N6180M	5.11.93	R.T.Love	Bodmin	1. 4.00
G-BVFU	Cameron Sphere 105SS HAFB	3137		18.11.93	Lascar Investments Ltd		
						Junglinster, Luxembourg	21. 5.99
G-BVFX	Nanchang CJ-6A (Yak-18)	1532008	Chinese AF	9.11.93	Elmair Ltd Wellcross Grange, Slinfold		3. 4.99P
					(As "1532008/08" in Chinese People's Liberation Army c/s)		

Regn	Type	C/n	P/I	Date	Owner/operator	Probable Base	CA Expy
G-BVFZ	Maule M.5-180C Lunar Rocket	8082C	N5664D	21. 2.94	C.N.White		
						Franklyns Field, Chewton Mendip	7. 3.00
G-BVGA	Bell 206B JetRanger III	2922	N54AJ	11.11.93	J.L. & A.M.Leonard	Shoreham	30. 1.00T
			VH-SBC		t/a Findon Air Svs		
G-BVGB	Thunder Ax8-105 Srs.2 HAFB	2408		11.11.93	Flying Pictures Ltd	Fairoaks	24. 1.00A
G-BVGC*	Cessna 411A	411A-0274	EI-BCT	16.11.93	Taylor Acft Svs Ltd	Leicester	
			G-AVEK/N3274R		(Cancelled as WFU 10.2.99)		
G-BVGE	Westland WS-55 Whirlwind HAR.10	8732M	18.11.93	B.H. & E.F.Austen	Oaksey Park	26. 1.99P
		WA/100	XJ729		t/a Austen Associates (As "XJ729" in RAF Rescue c/s)		
G-BVGF	Europa Avn Europa PFA/247-12565			18.11.93	A.Graham & G.G.Beal	Brunton	20.10.99P
	(Rotax 912UL)						
G-BVGG	Lindstrand LBL-69A HAFB	011		30.11.93	Lindstrand Balloons Ltd	Oswestry	11. 1.97A
G-BVGH	Hawker Hunter T.7	HABL.004328	XL573	26.11.93	B.J.Pover	Exeter	28. 7.99P
	(Reported as c/n HABL.003360)				(Op Lightning F/C) (As "XL573")		
G-BVGI	Pereira Osprey 2 PFA/70-10536			29.11.93	A.A.Knight	(Isle of Mull)	8. 2.99P
	(Lyc O-320)						
G-BVGJ	Cameron Concept 80 HAFB	3099		7.12.93	D.T.Watkins "Pizza Express"	Hexham	20. 3.99A
G-BVGO	Denney Kitfox mk.4/1200 PFA/172A-12362			15.11.93	A.Morgan	(Ilkeston)	27. 8.99P
	(Rotax 582)						
G-BVGP	Dornier Bucker Bu.133C Jungmeister		F-AZFQ	3.12.93	J.P.H.A.Delvaux	(Auflance, France)	19. 6.99P
	(Siemens-Bramo SH14A)	42	N15696		(As "U-95" in Swiss AF c/s)		
			HB-MIE/D-EIII/HB-MIE/Sw AF U-95				
G-BVGR	RAF BE.2E	133/A1325 R	Nor AF 37	8.12.93	Aero Vintage Ltd	Rotary Farm, Hatch	
	(RAF 1e)				(On rebuild 8.95)		
G-BVGS	Robinson R-22 Beta	2389	N2363S	9.12.93	Bristol & Wessex Helicopters Ltd		
						Bristol/Lulsgate	16. 1.00T
G-BVGT	Crofton Auster J/1A Special			19.11.93	L.A.Groves	Boarhunt, Stubbington	8. 4.99P
	(Blackburn Cirrus 2) PFA/00-220				t/a Crofton Aeroplane Svs		
	(Rebuild of unregd Auster J/1 Autocrat frame used as an engine test rig)						
G-BVGW	Luscombe 8A Silvaire	4823	N2096K	18.11.93	L.A.Groves	(Stubbington)	
			NC2096K				
G-BVGX	Thunder Ax8-90 Srs.2 HAFB	2490		16.12.93	J.S.Finlan	Hamilton, New Zealand	31. 3.97A
					t/a G-BVGX Grp		
G-BVGY	Luscombe 8E Silvaire	4754	N2027K	18.11.93	Tracey Groves	(Fareham)	
			NC2027K				
G-BVGZ	Fokker DR.1 Triplane rep			20.12.93	The Museum of Army Flying		
	(Lyc AIO-360) VHB-10 & PFA/238-12654				(German AF c/s)	AAC Middle Wallop	21.12.98P
G-BVHC	Grob G-115D-2 Heron	82005	D-EARG	14.12.93	Short Bros plc	Plymouth	9. 3.00T
					(Op for Royal Navy)		
G-BVHD	Grob G-115D-2 Heron	82006	D-EARJ	14.12.93	Short Bros plc	Plymouth	19. 3.00T
					(Op for Royal Navy)		
G-BVHE	Grob G-115D-2 Heron	82008	D-EARQ	14.12.93	Short Bros plc	Plymouth	26. 3.00T
					(Op for Royal Navy)		
G-BVHF	Grob G-115D-2 Heron	82011	D-EARV	14.12.93	Short Bros plc	Plymouth	6. 4.00T
					(Op for Royal Navy)		
G-BVHG	Grob G-115D-2 Heron	82012	D-EARX	14.12.93	Short Bros plc	Plymouth	14. 4.00T
					(Op for Royal Navy)		
G-BVHI	Rans S-10 Sakota PFA/194-12608			20.12.93	P.D.Rowley	Popham	2. 6.99P
	(Rotax 582)						
G-BVHJ	Cameron A-180 HAFB	3155		20.12.93	S.J.Boxall	Sheffield	3. 5.99T
G-BVHK	Cameron V-77 HAFB	3209		23.12.93	Ann R.Rich "Intel Inside"	Hyde	4. 7.99
G-BVHL	Nicollier HN.700 Menestrel II			24.12.93	I.H.R.Walker	(Ashford, Kent)	
	PFA/217-12614						
G-BVHM	PA-38-112 Tomahawk	38-79A0313	G-DCAN	14.11.91	A.J.Gomes (Op Sky Leisure Avn) Shoreham		17. 7.99T
			N9713N				
G-BVHN	Lindstrand LBL-G144 HAFB	076		24.12.93	Lindstrand Balloons Ltd	Oswestry	
G-BVHO	Cameron V-90 HAFB	3158		29.12.93	N.W.B.Bews	Tenbury Wells	7. 1.95
G-BVHP	Colt 42A HAFB	2533		31.12.93	Huntair Ltd	(London SE16)	11. 8.97
G-BVHR	Cameron V-90 HAFB	3174		5. 1.94	G.P.Walton	Bagshot	18. 2.99T
G-BVHS	Murphy Rebel PFA/232-12180			5. 1.94	J.Brown	Breighton	27. 4.99P
	(Lyc O-235)						
G-BVHT	Light Aero Avid mk.4 Speed Wing			28.10.93	R.S.Holt	Long Marston	15. 6.99P
	(Rotax 582) PFA/189-12226						
G-BVHU	Colt Flying Bottle 13 SS HAFB	2499		6. 1.94	Bias International Ltd "Kaiser"		
						Rio De Janeiro, Brazil	19. 2.95A
G-BVHV	Cameron N-105 HAFB	3215		6. 1.94	Flying Pictures Ltd "Rover"	Fairoaks	14.12.98A
G-BVHX	PBN BN-2T-4R Defender 4000	4003		21. 1.94	Britten-Norman Ltd	Bembridge	AC
					(Stored 4.97)		
G-BVHY	PBN BN-2T-4R Defender 4000	4004		21. 1.94	Britten-Norman Ltd	Bembridge	
					(Stored 4.97)		
G-BVIA	Rand Robinson KR-2 PFA/129-11004			14. 1.94	K.Atkinson	(Ulverston)	
G-BVIC	English Electric Canberra B.2/B.6		XH568	25.10.93	Classic Avn Projects Ltd Bruntingthorpe		30. 1.97T
		71105			(As "XH568" in DRA c/s) (Stored 9.97)		
	(C/n relates to nose section only as ex WG788 from 1970 rebuild; XH568 was c/n 71399)						
G-BVID	Lindstrand LBL Lozenge SS HAFB	064		17. 1.94	Respatex International Ltd		
						Chesham, Bucks	29. 4.99A
G-BVIE	PA-18-95 Super Cub (L-18C-PI) 18-1549		G-CLIK	26. 1.94	J.C.Best	(Bishops Stortford)	16. 1.98P
	(Cont O-200-A) (Frame No.18-1521) (G-BLMB)/D-EDRB/ALAT 51-15549/51-15549 t/a C'est La Vie Grp "C'est La Vie"						

Regn	Type	C/n	P/I	Date	Owner/operator	Probable Base	CA Expy
G-BVIF	Montgomerie-Bensen B.8MR (Rotax 582) PFA G/01A-1228			26. 1.94	R.M. & D.Mann (Brodick, Isle of Arran)		21. 8.95P
G-BVIG	Cameron A-250 HAFB	3213		26. 1.94	Balloon Flights Intl Ltd Bath "BIBS II" (Bath Building Society c/s)		31. 8.99T
G-BVIH	PA-28-161 Warrior II	28-7916191	G-GFCE G-BNJP/N2212G	26.10.93	Ocean Developments Ltd	Redhill	23. 1.00T
G-BVIK	Maule MXT-7-180 Star Rocket	14056C		31. 1.94	R.D.Masters	Panshanger	30. 5.00
G-BVIL	Maule MXT-7-180 Star Rocket	14059C		31. 1.94	K. & S.C.Knight	Shobdon	21. 6.00
G-BVIM	Cameron N-77 HAFB	2222		2. 2.94	The Ballooning Business Ltd Northampton "NAPS"		9. 1.00T
G-BVIN	Rans S-6-ESA Coyote II PFA/204-12533 (Rotax 503)			25.10.93	K.J.Vincent	(Bromley)	28. 8.97P
G-BVIO	Colt Flying Drinks Can SS HAFB 2538 (Budweiser Can shape)			4. 2.94	Virgin Balloon & Airship Co Ltd Telford "Budweiser"		21.11.96A
G-BVIR	Lindstrand LBL-69A HAFB	079		2. 2.94	Aerial Promotions Ltd Cannock "Vauxhall"		2. 3.97A
G-BVIS	Brugger MB.2 Colibri PFA/43-10666			2. 2.94	M.J.Sharp RAF Kinloss (Under construction 5.95)		
G-BVIT	Campbell Cricket PFA G/03-1229 (Rotax 582)			4. 2.94	A.N.Nisbet Pitsford, Northampton		24. 7.97P
G-BVIV	Light Aero Avid Speed Wing (Rotax 582) PFA/189-12034			25.10.93	J. & V.Hobday	Barton	27. 1.99P
G-BVIW	PA-18-150 Super Cub	18-8277	SE-EPD	4. 2.94	Rodger Aircraft Ltd	Old Sarum	27. 5.00T
G-BVIX	Lindstrand LBL-180A HAFB	082		8. 2.94	R.T. & H.Revel High Wycombe t/a Humbug Balloon Group		14. 3.99T
G-BVIZ	Europa Avn Europa 52 & PFA/247-12601 (Rotax 912UL)			24. 1.94	T.J.Punter & P.G.Jeffers	Booker	10. 3.99P
G-BVJA	Fokker F.100-650	11489	PH-EZE	22. 4.94	British Midland Airways Ltd East Midlands		24. 4.00T
G-BVJB	Fokker F.100-650	11488	PH-EZD	7. 7.94	British Midland Airways Ltd East Midlands		6. 7.00T
G-BVJC	Fokker F.100-650	11497	PH-EZJ	2.12.94	British Midland Airways Ltd East Midlands		1.12.00T
G-BVJD	Fokker F.100-650	11503	PH-EZO	14.12.94	British Midland Airways Ltd East Midlands		13.12.00T
G-BVJE	Aerospatiale AS.350B1 Ecureuil	1991	SE-HRS	3. 2.94	I.S. & G.Steel Stockholders Ltd (Op PLM Dollar Group Ltd) Cumbernauld		24. 2.00T
G-BVJF	Montgomerie-Bensen B.8MR PFA G/01-1082			18. 2.94	D.M.F.Harvey (Yate, Bristol)		
G-BVJG	Cyclone Ax3/K (Rotax 582) C.3123187 & PFA/245-12663		(G-MYOP)	15. 2.94	T.D.Reid Tandragee, Co.Armagh		14.10.98P
G-BVJH	Aero Designs Pulsar PFA/202-12196 (Rotax 582)			22. 2.94	J.A.C.Tweedie (Wymondham)		26. 4.96P
G-BVJJ	Cameron DP-90 Hot-Air Airship	3216		25. 2.94	Cameron Balloons Ltd Rio De Janeiro, Brazil		
G-BVJK	Glaser-Dirks DG-800A	8-24-A21		30. 3.94	B.A.Eastwell	Ringmer	4. 8.00
G-BVJN	Europa Avn Europa 66 & PFA/247-12666 (Rotax 912UL)			2. 3.94	N.Adam "Better by Redesign"	Bicester	14. 6.99P
G-BVJO	Cameron R-77 Gas Free Balloon	3228		8. 3.94	Bondbaste Ltd Faux Court, St.Etienne, Belgium		25. 5.95A
G-BVJP	ATR-42-300	371	F-WWLN	7. 4.94	Gill Avn Ltd	Newcastle	6. 4.00T
G-BVJS	Colt Piggy Bank SS HAFB	2487		9. 3.94	Iduna-Bausparkasse AG Hamburg, Germany		3. 6.99A
G-BVJT	Reims Cessna F406 Caravan II	0073		2. 2.94	P Madent & M Evans Fairoaks t/a Nor Leasing		29. 3.00
G-BVJU	Evans VP-1 PFA/62-10691			10. 3.94	Barbara A.Schlussler	(Bourne)	
G-BVJX	Marquart MA.5 Charger PFA/68-11239 (Lyc O-360)			12. 1.94	M.L.Martin	Redhill	16. 6.99P
G-BVJZ	PA-28-161 Warrior II	28-7816248	N2088M	22. 3.94	A.R.Fowkes	Denham	16. 4.00T
G-BVKA	Boeing 737-59D	24694	SE-DNA (SE-DLA)	15. 2.94	British Midland Airways Ltd East Midlands		28. 2.00T
G-BVKB	Boeing 737-59D	27268	SE-DNM	24. 3.94	British Midland Airways Ltd East Midlands		11. 4.00T
G-BVKC	Boeing 737-59D	24695	SE-DNB (SE-DLB)	5. 5.94	British Midland Airways Ltd East Midlands		15. 5.00T
G-BVKD	Boeing 737-59D	26421	SE-DNK	25.11.94	British Midland Airways Ltd East Midlands		15.12.00T
G-BVKF	Europa Avn Europa 50 & PFA/247-12638 (Rotax 912UL)			11. 3.94	T.R.Sinclair	(Lamb Holm)	19. 7.99P
G-BVKG	Colt Flying Hot Dog SS HAFB	2571		15. 3.94	Longbreak Ltd Greenwood, MS, USA		24.11.98A
G-BVKH	Thunder Ax-8-90 HAFB	2574		15. 3.94	R.B.Gruzelier	Salisbury	13. 3.99
G-BVKJ	Bensen B.8M PFA G/01-1221 (Arrow GT500R)			17. 3.94	A.G.Foster	Grimsby	27. 8.99P
G-BVKK	Slingsby T-61F Venture T.2	1984	ZA665	22. 2.94	K.E.Ballington	(Burton-on-Trent)	13. 9.01
G-BVKL	Cameron A-180 HAFB	3255		17. 3.94	W.I. & C.Hooker	Nottingham	7.11.99T
G-BVKM	Rutan VariEze (Cont O-200-A)	1933	N7137G	5. 4.94	J.P.G.Lindquist (Kilchberg, Switzerland)		25. 1.00P
G-BVKR	Sikorsky S-76A	760115	RJAF 734	4. 3.94	Bristow Helicopters Ltd	Aberdeen	8.12.00T
G-BVKU	Slingsby T-61F Venture T.2	1877	XZ557	22. 3.94	R.W.Curtis	West Knoyle	4.11.01

Regn	Type	C/n	P/I	Date	Owner/operator	Probable Base	CA Expy
G-BVKV	Cameron N-90 HAFB	3236		24. 3.94	Pringle of Scotland Ltd	Hawick	3. 2.97A
G-BVKW	Lindstrand LBL-240A HAFB	093		25. 3.94	Bridges Van Hire Ltd	Nottingham	11. 8.99T
G-BVKX	Colt 14A Cloudhopper HAFB	2580		28. 3.94	H.C.J.Williams	Bristol	
G-BVKZ	Thunder Ax9-120 HAFB	2547		23. 3.94	D.J.Head	Newbury	31. 3.99T
G-BVLA	NEICO Lancair 320	PFA/191-11751		29. 3.94	A.R.Welstead	(Oxford)	
G-BVLC	Cameron N-42 HAFB	3256		28. 3.94	Cameron Balloons Ltd	Bristol	15. 9.98A
G-BVLD	Campbell Cricket	PFA G/01A-1163		29. 3.94	C.Berry	(Wigston, Leics)	AC
G-BVLE	McCandless M.4	PFA G/10-1232		29. 3.94	H.Walls	Sion Mills, Strabane	
					(Near completion 4.96)		
G-BVLF	CFM Starstreak Shadow SS-D K.250-SSD			4. 3.94	B.R.Johnson	Wokingham	
G-BVLG	Aerospatiale AS.355F1 Twin Squirrel	5011	N57745	31. 3.94	PLM Dollar Group Ltd	Cumbernauld	6. 4.00T
G-BVLH	Europa Avn Europa	PFA/247-12491		30. 3.94	D.Barraclough	(Alnwick)	
G-BVLI	Cameron V-77 HAFB	5568	N9544G	30. 3.94	Janet Lewis-Richardson		
						Waiheke, New Zealand	30. 4.99A
G-BVLK	Rearwin 8125 Cloudster	803	N25403 NC25403	6. 4.94	M.C.Hiscock	Titchfield, Hants	
					(On rebuild 2.96)		
G-BVLL	Lindstrand LBL-210A HAFB	101		9. 3.94	Aerial Promotions Ltd	Cannock	27. 4.99T
G-BVLN	Aero Designs Pulsar XP	PFA/202-12530		6. 4.94	D.A.Campbell	(Leek)	
G-BVLP	PA-38-112 Tomahawk II	38-82A0002	N91355	8. 4.94	D.A.Whitmore	Turweston	29. 4.00T
G-BVLR	Van's RV-4	PFA/181-12306		13. 4.94	S.D.Arnold & S.J.Moodey	(Coventry)	
					t/a RV4 Grp		
G-BVLS	Thunder Ax8-90 Srs.2 HAFB	2577		13. 4.94	J.R.Henderson	Stratford-Upon-Avon	22. 7.99A
G-BVLT	Bellanca 7GCBC Citabria 150S	1103-79	SE-GHV	6. 4.94	M.D.Hinge	Old Sarum	17. 5.97T
G-BVLU	Druine D.31 Turbulent	PFA/1604		18. 4.94	C.D.Bancroft	Milson	
G-BVLV	Europa Avn Europa 39 &	PFA/247-12585		10. 3.94	J.T.Naylor t/a Euro 39 Group	Sywell	9. 4.99P
	(Rotax 912UL)						
G-BVLW	Light Aero Avid Hauler mk.4			24. 3.94	D.M.Johnstone	Shobdon	28. 9.99P
	(Hirth F30)	PFA/189-12577					
G-BVLX	Slingsby T-61F Venture T.2	1973	ZA654	19. 4.94	T.M.Holloway t/a RAFGSA	Bicester	22.10.00
G-BVLZ	Lindstrand LBL-120A HAFB	063		4. 3.94	Balloon Flights Club Ltd		
						Kings Norton, Leicester	21. 3.99T
G-BVMA	Beechcraft 200 Super King Air	BB-797	G-VPLC N84B	22. 7.93	Manhattan Air Ltd	Blackbushe	21.10.99T
G-BVMB	Hawker Hunter T.7A	41H/695347	XL613	26. 4.94	Hunter Avn Ltd	Exeter	28.11.95P*
	(Regd with c/n 41H/695334)				(As "XL613") (Stored 3.96)		
G-BVMC	Robinson R-44 Astro	0060		15. 4.94	E.Wooton	Sywell	9. 7.00T
G-BVMD	Luscombe 8E Silvaire	5265	9Q-CGB KAT-?/VP-YRB/ZS-BWC/NC2538K	15. 4.94	G.M.Scott	(London SW18)	5. 1.00P
G-BVMF	Cameron V-77 HAFB	3195		22. 4.94	P.A.Meecham	Milton-Under-Wychwood	17. 6.99A
G-BVMG	Bensen B.80V	PFA G/01-1056		25. 4.94	D.Moffatt	(Slamannan, Falkirk)	
G-BVMH	Wag-Aero Sport Trainer	PFA/108-12647		28. 4.94	D.M.Jagger	Woodhall Spa	27.10.98P
	(Cont C90)				(As "624/D-39" in US Army c/s)		
G-BVMI	PA-18-150 Super Cub	18-4649	N1136Z D-EIAC/(PH-WDP)/D-EIAC/D-EKAF/N1OF	6. 4.94	T.P. & M.M.Spurge	East Winch	2. 3.01
	(Frame No.18-4613; initially and currently regd with c/n 18-8482 as ex OH-PIN/N4262Z but latterly rebuilt from N1136Z/D-EIAC after crash 15.8.95; original airframe now rebuilt as G-CUBP)						
G-BVMJ	Cameron Eagle 95SS HAFB	3262		28. 4.94	R.D.Sargeant	Maidenhead	17. 9.99A
G-BVML	Lindstrand LBL-210A HAFB	094		29. 4.94	Ballooning Adventures Ltd	Hexham	1. 6.99T
G-BVMM	Robin HR.200/100 Club	41	F-BVMM	18. 8.80	R.H.Ashforth	Gloucestershire	9. 7.01
					(Stored 6.97)		
G-BVMN	Ken Brock KB-2	PFA G/06-1218		29. 4.94	S.McCullagh	(London W3)	17. 6.99P
	(Rotax 582)						
G-BVMR	Cameron V-90 HAFB	3269		28. 3.94	I.R.Comley "Midnight Rainbow"	Gloucester	1. 5.98A
G-BVMU	Aerostar Yakovlev Yak-52	9411809	YR-013	11. 5.94	J.E. & A.Ashby	Little Gransden	1. 7.99P
	(C/n should be 9211809)				(As "09" in DOSAAF c/s)		
G-BVMX	Short SD.3-60 Var.100	SH.3751	G-BPFS G-REGN/G-OCIA/G-BPFS	25.10.93	Aurigny Air Services Ltd	Guernsey	21.11.99T
G-BVMZ	Robin HR.100/210 Safari	198	F-BVMZ	20. 3.85	Chiltern Handbags (London) Ltd		
						Stapleford	16. 7.01
G-BVNA	Aces High Cuby II	G-MYMA		27. 4.94	P.Scott Brickhouse Farm, Frogland Cross		1. 2.99P
	(Rotax 503)	LC2F-931052605 & PFA/257-12584					
G-BVNG	DH.60GIII Moth Major	?	EC-AFK EE1-81/30-81	17. 5.94	J.A.Pothecary	Old Sarum	
					(On rebuild 2.96)		
G-BVNH	Agusta A.109C	7643	G-LAXO	13. 6.94	C.Dawes	Alderney	11. 7.00T
G-BVNI	Taylor JT.2 Titch	PFA/60-11107		20. 5.94	T.V.Adamson	Rufforth	
G-BVNL	Rockwell Commander 114	14118	I-ECCE N4789U	13. 5.94	W.J.Hemmings, R.Lockyer & S.J.Healey	Birmingham	5. 7.00
G-BVNM	Boeing 737-4S3	24163	G-BPKA 9M-MJJ/G-BPKA	31. 3.92	British Airways (European Operations at Gatwick) Ltd (Pause to Remember t/s)	Gatwick	31. 3.99T
G-BVNN	Boeing 737-4S3	24164	G-BPKB 9M-MLA/G-BPKB	18. 3.92	British Airways (European Operations at Gatwick) Ltd	Gatwick	18. 3.02T
G-BVNO	Boeing 737-4S3	24167	G-BPKE 9M-MLB/G-BPKE	18. 3.92	British Airways (European Operations at Gatwick) Ltd (Mountain of the Birds/Benyhone Tartan t/s)	Gatwick	14. 4.99T
G-BVNR	Cameron N-105 HAFB	3288		24. 5.94	Liquigas SpA	Milan, Italy	1. 6.99A
G-BVNS	PA-28-181 Cherokee Archer II	28-7690358	N6163J	13. 4.94	Scottish Airways Flyers (Prestwick) Ltd	Prestwick	11. 8.00T

Regn	Type	C/n	P/I	Date	Owner/operator	Probable Base	CA Expy
G-BVNU	FLS Sprint Club	004		25. 5.94	Sunhawk Ltd	North Weald	17.10.98T
G-BVNY	Rans S-7 Courier (Rotax 582)	PFA/218-11951		24. 5.94	Sport Air UK Ltd	Bagby	5. 1.00P
G-BVOA	PA-28-181 Archer II	28-7990145	N2132C	31. 5.94	M.J. & R.J.Millen t/a Millen Avn Svs	Rochester	30. 7.00T
G-BVOB	Fokker F-27 Friendship 500	10366	PH-FMN PT-LZM/F-BPNA/PH-FMN	5. 7.94	BAC Express Airlines Ltd.	Southend	6.10.00T
G-BVOC	Cameron V-90 HAFB	3291		8. 6.94	Sally A.Masey "Scoop"	Bristol	1. 5.99A
G-BVOD	Montgomerie-Parsons Two-Place Gyroplane	PFA G/08-1238		8. 6.94	J.M.Montgomerie	Maybole, Ayr	
G-BVOG	Cameron RN-9 HAFB	3285		14. 6.94	Cameron Balloons Ltd	Klaus, Austria	12.10.95A
G-BVOH	Campbell Cricket (Rotax 532)	PFA G/03-1220		14. 6.94	G.A.Speich	Beausale, Warwick	16. 1.99P
G-BVOI	Rans S-6-116 Coyote II (Rotax 582)	PFA/204A-12712		14. 6.94	A.P.Bacon	(Wick)	17. 5.99P
G-BVOK	Aerostar Yakovlev Yak-52	9111505	RA-9111505/DOSAAF55	14. 6.94	D.J.Gilmour t/a Intrepid Aviation Co (As "55" in DOSAAF c/s)	North Weald	9.12.99P
G-BVOL*	Douglas C-47B-40DL Dakota 3	9836	ZS-NJE SAAF 6867/FD938/42-23974	14. 6.94	Aviodome "Field Marshall Jan Smuts" (As "KG391/AG" in RAF c/s) (Spares for PH-PBA then as museum exhibit)	Schiphol, Netherlands	19. 9.96
G-BVON	Lindstrand LBL-105A HAFB	001	N532LB G-BVON	16. 6.94	P.A.Lindstrand	Oswestry	15. 4.99
G-BVOO	Lindstrand LBL-105A HAFB	123		16. 6.94	T.G.Church	Blackburn	6.12.99A
G-BVOP	Cameron N-90 HAFB	3317		21. 6.94	Cambury Ltd t/a Mr.Lazenbys	Stockton-on-Tees	20. 3.99T
G-BVOR	CFM Streak Shadow K.238-SA & PFA/206-12695 (Rotax 582)			31. 3.94	J.A.Lord Wickhambrook, Bury St.Edmunds		13. 5.99P
G-BVOS	Europa Avn Europa	PFA/247-12562		11. 4.94	D.Collinson & D.A.Young t/a Durham Europa Grp	(Durham)	6. 1.00P
G-BVOU	HS.748 Srs.2A/270	1721	CS-TAH G-11-6	21. 6.94	Emerald Airways Ltd (Lynx c/s)	Exeter	30. 7.01T
G-BVOV	BAe 748 Srs.2A/372	1777	CS-TAO G-11-4	21. 6.94	Emerald Airways Ltd	Liverpool	11. 5.01T
G-BVOW	Europa Avn Europa 84 & PFA/247-12679 (Rotax 912UL)			27. 6.94	M.W.Cater t/a Europa Syndicate	(Sulby)	25.11.99P
G-BVOX	Taylorcraft F-22	2208	N221UK	20. 5.94	Mousquetaire Ltd (Stored 10.96)	Redhill	AC
G-BVOY	Rotorway Exec 90	5238		17. 6.94	E.Drinkwater	(Warrington)	
G-BVOZ	Colt 56A HAFB	2595		21. 6.94	Balloon School (International) Ltd t/a British School of Ballooning	Petworth	11. 1.99A
G-BVPA	Thunder Ax8-105 Srs.2 HAFB	2600		24. 6.94	J.Fenton t/a Firefly Balloon Promotions	Preston	15. 6.97T
G-BVPD	CASA I-131E Jungmann	2086	F-AZNG E3B-482	12. 7.94	W.R.M.Beesley	Breighton	14. 9.99P
G-BVPH	Bensen-Parsons Two-Place Gyroplane	PFA G/08-1234		30. 6.94	I.A.Leedham	(South Wirral)	
G-BVPI	Evans VP-1 (VW1500)	PFA/1578		7.12.78	C.M.Gibson (Weston-super-Mare) (Damaged Old Sarum 17.4.88; stored 5.89 - status uncertain)		12. 7.88P
G-BVPK	Cameron O-90 HAFB	3313		1. 7.94	D.V.Fowler	Cranbrook	23. 5.98T
G-BVPL	Zenair CH.601HD (Cont O-200-A)	PFA/162-12693		4. 7.94	D.Harker	Yearby	30. 6.99P
G-BVPM	Evans VP-2 Coupe V2-1016 & PFA/7205 (Cont A65)			6.11.78	P.Marigold (Locking, Weston-super-Mare) (Stored 7.95)		31. 5.94P
G-BVPN	Piper J3C-65 Cub	6917	G-TAFY N31073/N38207/N38307/NC38307	6. 7.94	J.Esteban	(Sevilla, Spain)	4. 7.99P
	(Regd as c/n 5298 but has Frame No.7002 which was N38207; probably used in rebuild of N31073 in early 1970s)						
G-BVPP	Folland Gnat T.1	FL.536	8620M XP534	22. 4.94	T.J.Manna t/a Kennet Avn (As "XR993" in Red Arrows c/s)	Cranfield	30.11.99P
G-BVPR	Robinson R-22 Beta	1612	G-KNIT	17. 6.94	E.Bailey	Gloucestershire	4. 2.00T
G-BVPS	Jodel D.112	PFA/917		6. 7.94	P.J.Sharp	(Harpenden)	
G-BVPU	Cameron A-140 HAFB	3296		12. 7.94	Cameron Balloons Ltd	(Canada)	22. 7.97A
G-BVPV	Lindstrand LBL-77B HAFB	119		13. 7.94	A.R.Greensides	Burton Pidsea, Hull	20. 7.99A
G-BVPW	Rans S-6-116 Coyote II PFA/204A-12737 (Rotax 582)			12. 7.94	J.G.Beesley	Halwell, Totnes	2.10.99P
G-BVPX	Lovegrove Tyro Gyro mk.II	PFA G/011-1237		13. 7.94	P.C.Lovegrove	(Didcot)	
G-BVPY	CFM Streak Shadow (Rotax 582)	PFA/206-12375		14. 6.94	R.J.Mitchell	(Tingwall, Shetland)	8.11.99P
G-BVRA	Europa Avn Europa	PFA/247-12635		25. 7.94	E.J.J. & S.W.Pels	(Mold)	
G-BVRD	VPM M-16 Tandem Trainer (Arrow GT1000)	VPM16-UK-108		27. 7.94	Whisky Mike (Avn) Ltd (Damaged Cranfield 12.1.95)	Forfar	
G-BVRE	Van's RV-6A (Lyc O-320)	PFA/181-12677		1. 8.94	T.I.Carlin	(Londonderry)	1.11.99P
G-BVRH	Taylorcraft BL-65	1657	N24322 NC24322	15. 7.94	Ebork Ltd	Walkeridge Farm, Overton	
G-BVRI	Thunder Ax6-56 HAFB	2622		2. 8.94	A.Van Wyk	Caxton, Cambs	14. 4.97A
G-BVRK	Rans S-6-ESA Coyote II	1193-566	G-MYPK	14. 7.94	J.Secular	(Beckenham)	
G-BVRL	Lindstrand LBL-21A HAFB	130		3. 8.94	M.J.Green	Walsall	15. 6.96A
G-BVRM	Cameron A-210 HAFB	3134		4. 8.94	Virgin Balloon Flights Ltd	Muscat, Oman	16.10.98T

Regn	Type	C/n	P/I	Date	Owner/operator	Probable Base	CA Expy
G-BVRN	Fokker F-27 Friendship 500	10427	PH-FPB HL-5211/(HL-5207)/PH-FPB	7. 3.95	Compania Canaria De Transporte Aereo SA Tenerife, Spain		13. 9.98T
G-BVRP	Lindstrand LBL-9A HAFB	108		9. 8.94	Lindstrand Balloons Ltd	(Austria)	1.11.95P
G-BVRR	Lindstrand LBL-77A HAFB	133		9. 8.94	G.C.Elson	(Malaga, Spain)	24. 5.99A
G-BVRS	Beechcraft B90 King Air	LJ-481	G-KJET G-AXFE	29.12.93	The Eight Blew Ltd	(Godalming)	11. 3.99T
G-BVRU	Lindstrand LBL-105A HAFB	131		15. 8.94	Flying Pictures Ltd	Fairoaks	19. 1.00A
G-BVRV	Van's RV-4 (Lyc AEIO-320)	793	N144TH	23. 6.94	A.Troughton Armagh Field, Woodview		17. 9.98P
G-BVRY	Cyclone Ax3K C3013085 & PFA/245-12471 (Rotax 582)			18. 8.94	J.Toone	Popham	2. 3.99P
G-BVRZ	PA-18-95 Super Cub (Regd with Frame No.18-3381)	18-3442	SE-ITP LN-LJG/D-EDCM/96+19/QW+901/QZ+001/AC+507/AS+506/54-752 (Damaged on take off Kilrea 30.7.98)	22.11.94	R.G.Warwick Kilrea, Co.Londonderry		25. 5.01
G-BVSB	Team Minimax 91A PFA/186-12241 (Rotax 503)			1. 7.94	D.G.Palmer	(Peterhead)	22. 6.99P
G-BVSD	Sud SE.3130 Alouette II	1897	V-54 Swiss AF	8. 9.94	M.J.Cuttell Gloucestershire (As "V-54" in Swiss AF c/s)		11. 2.99
G-BVSF	Aero Designs Pulsar PFA/202-12071 (Rotax 582)			1. 7.94	S.N. & R.J.Freestone	Deanland	21. 9.99P
G-BVSJ	PBN BN-2T Turbine Islander	2286		31. 1.95	Britten-Norman Ltd	Bembridge	AC
G-BVSL	PBN BN-2B-26 Islander	2288		31. 1.95	Britten-Norman Ltd	Bembridge	AC
G-BVSM	Rotary Air Force RAF 2000 EW-42 (Subaru EA82)			24. 8.94	K.Quigley	(Dundalk, Co.Louth)	24. 1.97P
G-BVSN	Light Aero Avid Speed Wing (Rotax 582) PFA/189-12088			24. 8.94	D.J. & C.Park	Rush Green	2. 5.99P
G-BVSO	Cameron A-120 HAFB	3339		25. 8.94	Up and Away Ballooning Ltd High Wycombe		7. 8.99T
G-BVSP	Hunting P.84 Jet Provost T.3A PAC/W/6327		XM370	31. 8.94	Shoal Ltd (Frank Heneghan) Norwich (As "XM370")		5. 8.99P
G-BVSR	Colt 210A HAFB	2470		8. 9.94	Eagle Security Ltd	(London EC1)	13.10.96T
G-BVSS	Jodel 150 Mascaret PFA/151-11878			22. 8.94	A.P.Burns	(Formby, Liverpool)	
G-BVST	Jodel 150 Mascaret 130 & PFA/235-12198 (Cont O-200-A)			11. 8.94	A.Shipp	Full Sutton	21. 6.99P
G-BVSW	Cameron C-80 HAFB	3194		5. 9.94	Cameron Balloons Ltd	Beirut, Lebanon	1. 9.95A
G-BVSW	Cameron C-80 HAFB	3210		5. 9.94	Cameron Balloons Ltd	Beirut, Lebanon	1. 9.95A
G-BVSX	Team Minimax 91A PFA/186-12463 (Mosler MM CB-35)			9. 9.94	G.N.Smith	Headcorn	18. 3.98P
G-BVSY	Thunder Ax9-120 HAFB	2631		16. 8.94	G.R.Elson	Malaga, Spain	21. 1.99T
G-BVSZ	Pitts S-1E(S) Special PFA/09-11235 (Lyc AEIO-360)			9. 9.94	R.C.F.Bailey (Swinmore Farm, Ledbury)		11.10.99P
G-BVTA	Tri-R Kis PFA/239-12450			26. 8.94	P.J.Webb	Dunkeswell	
G-BVTC	BAC.145 Jet Provost T.5A EEP/JP/997		XW333	7. 9.94	Global Avn Ltd Binbrook (As "XW333/79")		2. 2.99P
G-BVTD	CFM Streak Shadow K.159-SA & PFA/206-11972 (Rotax 582)			14. 9.94	M.Walton	(Granby, Nottingham)	6. 7.99P
G-BVTE	Fokker F.28-0070	11538	PH-EZX	13. 4.95	British Midland Airways Ltd East Midlands		12. 4.01T
G-BVTF	Fokker F.28-0070	11539	PH-EZZ PH-EZA	24. 5.95	British Midland Airways Ltd East Midlands		23. 5.01T
G-BVTG	Fokker F.28-0070	11551	PH-EZK	1. 9.95	British Midland Airways Ltd East Midlands		31. 8.01T
G-BVTH	Fokker F.28-0070	11577	R		British Midland Airways Ltd East Midlands		
G-BVTJ	ATR-72-202	342	F-WWEV F-GKOI/F-WWLX	7.12.94	Cityflyer Express Ltd Gatwick (Waves & Cranes t/s)		6.12.01T
G-BVTK	ATR-72-202	357	F-WWEW F-GKOJ	21.10.94	Cityflyer Express Ltd Gatwick (Chelsea Rose t/s)		20.10.01T
G-BVTL	Colt 31A Air Chair HAFB	2572		5. 7.94	A.Lindsay	Twickenham	15. 5.97
G-BVTM	Reims Cessna F152 II	1827	G-WACS D-EFGZ	31. 8.94	RAF Halton Aeroplane Club Ltd RAF Halton		25. 8.01T
G-BVTN	Cameron N-90 HAFB	3361		16. 9.94	P.Zulehner Peterskirchen, Austria		25. 9.96A
G-BVTO	PA-28-151 Cherokee Warrior 28-7415253		G-SEWL D-EDOS/N9550N	19. 9.94	A.S.Bamrah Manston t/a Falcon F/Svs (Op SE College of Air Training)		15. 1.01T
G-BVTV	Rotorway Exec 90 (RI 162)	5243		16. 9.94	Southern Helicopters Ltd Street Farm, Takeley, Essex		16. 4.99P
G-BVTW	Aero Designs Pulsar PFA/202-12172			14. 9.94	J.D.Webb	(Hereford)	
G-BVTX	DHC.1 Chipmunk 22A	C1/0705	WP809	2. 8.94	P.B.Cartwright & R.Hannon t/a Airspares UK (As "WP809/78" in RN c/s) Husbands Bosworth		11.11.01
G-BVUA	Cameron O-105 HAFB	3369		27. 9.94	D.C.Eager	Bracknell	20.10.95A
G-BVUC	Colt 56A HAFB	2608	G-639	30. 9.94	Cameron Balloons Ltd Bristol t/a Thunder & Colt		28. 4.99A
G-BVUD	Cameron A-250 HAFB	3370		30. 9.94	) Balloon School· Petworth) (International) Ltd		27. 9.99T
G-BVUE	Cameron C-80 HAFB	3374		30. 9.94	) t/a British School Petworth) of Ballooning		8.10.96T
G-BVUF	Thunder Ax10-180 Srs.2 HAFB (Cameron c/n 3508)	2642		3.10.94	A.J.Nunns	Harare, Zimbabwe	N/E(A)

Regn	Type	C/n	P/I	Date	Owner/operator	Probable Base	CA Expy
G-BVUG	AIA Stampe SV.4C	1045	G-BEUS	3.10.94	William Tomkins Ltd	(Peterborough)	13. 9.99P
	(Regd as Betts TB.1 c/n PFA/265-12770) F-BKFK/F-DAFK/Fr.Mil						
G-BVUH	Thunder Ax6-65B HAFB	243	JA-A0075	3.10.94	N.C.A.Crawley	Great Yarmouth	
G-BVUI	Lindstrand LBL-25A Cloudhopper HAFB	148		5.10.94	Lindstrand Balloons Ltd	Oswestry	12.11.96A
G-BVUJ	Ken Brock KB-2 PFA G/06-1244			10.10.94	R.J.Hutchinson	Kemble	17. 5.99P
	(Rotax 503)						
G-BVUK	Cameron V-77 HAFB	3372		11.10.94	H.G.Griffiths & W.A.Steel	Reading	31. 7.97A
G-BVUM	Rans S-6-116 Coyote II PFA/204A-12685			11.10.94	G.L.Donaldson	Charterhall	11. 5.99P
	(Rotax 582)						
G-BVUN	Van's RV-4 3363UK & PFA/181-12488			11.10.94	I.G. & M.Glenn	Kingston, Cambs	27. 4.99P
	(Lyc O-360)						
G-BVUO	Cameron R-150 Gas Free Balloon	3365		13.10.94	M.Sevrin	Court St.Etienne, Belgium	21.12.95A
G-BVUP	Schleicher ASW24E	24828	D-KEWI	14.10.94	E. & C.F.Specht	Husbands Bosworth	8. 1.98P
G-BVUT	Evans VP-1 Srs.2 PFA/62-12092			24.10.94	P.J.Weston	(Salisbury)	22. 1.01
G-BVUU	Cameron C-80 HAFB	3383		11.10.94	T.M.C.McCoy	Bath	9.10.96T
					(Op Ascent Balloons) "Ascent"		
G-BVUV	Europa Avn Europa PFA/247-12762			23. 9.94	R.J.Mills	(Sheffield)	
G-BVUZ	Cessna 120	11334	Z-YGH	20. 9.94	N.O.Anderson (Trumpington, Cambridge)		
			VP-YGH/VP-NAM/VP-YGH				
G-BVVA	Aerostar Yakovlev Yak-52	877610	LY-ANN	24.10.94	T.W.Freeman	Fowlmere	1. 7.98P
			DOSAAF 52				
	(Has c/n plate 889109 and marked as ex LY-AMV which was based in France 1995)						
G-BVVB	Carlson Sparrow II PFA/209-11809			26. 9.94	L.M.McCullen	North Connel	12.10.99P
	(Rotax 532)						
G-BVVC	Hawker Hunter F.6A	S4/U/3362	8685M	28.10.94	P.Hellier	Exeter	27. 8.99P
	(AWA built)		XF516		(As "XF516/F")		
G-BVVE	Wassmer Jodel D.112	1070	F-BKAJ	28.10.94	G.W.Jarvis	Halfpenny Green	11. 3.98P
G-BVVF	Nanchang CJ-6A (Yak 18)	2232028		10.10.94	R.A.Fleming & A.J.E.Smith	(Leeds)	5. 5.97P
			Chinese PLAF		(As "2028/69" in Chinese Peoples Liberation AF c/s)		
G-BVVG	Nanchang CJ-6A (Yak 18)	2751219		10.10.94	G.Beda	(Paris, France)	AC
			Chinese PLAF		(As "1219/57" in Chinese Peoples Liberation AF c/s)		
G-BVVH	Europa Avn Europa PFA/247-12505			31.10.94	T.G.Hoult	(Driffield)	
G-BVVI	Hawker Audax I	-	2015M	3.11.94	Aero Vintage Ltd St.Leonards-on-Sea		
	(Avro built)		K5600		(On rebuild 8.95)		
G-BVVK	DHC.6-310 Twin Otter	666	LN-BEZ	21.12.94	Loganair Ltd	Glasgow	12. 1.00T
G-BVVL	EAA Acrosport 2 PFA/72A-10887			11.11.94	G.A.Breen	(Algarve, Portugal)	22. 6.99P
	(Lyc O-360)						
G-BVVM	Zenair CH.601HD Zodiac			3.10.94	J.G.Small	Blackpool	9. 5.99P
	(Rotax 912UL)	PFA/162-12539					
G-BVVN	Brugger MB.2 Colibri PFA/43-10979			12.10.94	N.F.Andrews	Emlyns Field, Rhuallt	30. 6.99P
	(VW1834)						
G-BVVP	Europa Avn Europa 88 & PFA/247-12697			20. 9.94	W.Komm	(Munich, Germany)	13.10.99P
	(Rotax 912UL)						
G-BVVR	Stits SA-3A Playboy	P-736	N4620S	14.11.94	A.D.Pearce		
	(Cont A65)				Eastbach Farm, English Bicknor		24. 2.99P
G-BVVS	Van's RV-4 PFA/181-12324			15.11.94	E.C. & N.S.C.English		
	(Lyc O-320)				Blue Tile Farm, Langham		22. 7.98P
G-BVVT	Colt 240A HAFB	2682		17.11.94	R.W.Keron	Dereham	15. 7.99T
G-BVVW	IAV-Bacau Yakovlev Yak-52	844605	RA-01361	16.11.94	J.E.Blackman	(Newton Green)	30. 7.99P
	(C/n plate shows c/n 833519)		DOSAAF15/DOSAAF95				
G-BVVX	Yakovlev Yak-18A	?	307	11.11.94	J.M. & E.M.Wicks (On rebuild 10.96)		
			Russian AF		Boones Farm, High Garrett, Braintree		
G-BVVY	Air Command 532 Elite PFA G/04-1104		G-CORK	22.11.94	T.A.Holmes	(Leeds)	AC
G-BVVZ	Corby CJ-1 Starlet PFA/134-12293			9.11.94	A.E.Morris	Fairoaks	2. 2.99P
	(VW1834)						
G-BVWA	Socata MS.880B Rallye 100T	2747	F-GACD	29.11.94	G.K.Brunwin	Shoreham	14. 4.01
G-BVWB	Thunder Ax8-90 Srs.2 HAFB	3000		2.12.94	S.C.Clayton	Shrewsbury	19. 7.99
G-BVWC	English Electric Canberra B.2(mod)	71399	WK163	2.12.94	Classic Aviation Projects Ltd	Duxford	5. 6.99P
	(C/n relates to nose section originally fitted to XH568)				(As "WK163")		
G-BVWE	Cameron C-80 HAFB	3414		6.12.94	Daicel Polymers Ltd	Milton Keynes	16. 3.98T
G-BVWH	Cameron N-90 Lightbulb SS HAFB	3404		8.12.94	Virgin Airship & Balloon Co Ltd Telford		2. 9.98A
					(Phillips Energy Saving Lightbulbs c/s)		
G-BVWI	Cameron Light Bulb 65SS HAFB	3405		8.12.94	Virgin Airship & Balloon Co Ltd Telford		2. 6.97A
G-BVWK	Air & Space 18-A Gyroplane	18-14	SE-HID	19.12.94	Whisky Mike (Avtn) Ltd		AC
			N6108S			Kinnettles, Forfar	
G-BVWL	Air & Space 18-A Gyroplane	18-63	SE-HIE	19.12.94	Whisky Mike (Avtn) Ltd		AC
			N90588/N6152S			Kinnettles, Forfar	
G-BVWM	Europa Avn Europa PFA/247-12620			14.12.94	A.Aubeelack	(London W5)	
					t/a Europa Syndicate		
G-BVWP	DHC.1 Chipmunk 22	C1/0741	WP856	19.12.94	T.W.M.Beck	Monks Gate, Horsham	26. 4.01
					(As "WP856/904" in RN c/s)		
G-BVWW	Lindstrand LBL-90A HAFB	169		28.12.94	R.B.Naylor	Pulborough	9. 7.97A
G-BVWX	VPM M-16 Tandem Trainer			3. 1.95	M.L.Smith	Chilbolton	14. 6.99P
	(Arrow GT1000R)	VPM16-UK-111					

Regn	Type	C/n	P/I	Date	Owner/operator	Probable Base	CA Expy
G-BVWY	Porterfield CP.65 (Cont A65)	720	N27223 NC27223	23.11.94	B.Morris	Oaksey Park	7. 7.99P
G-BVWZ	PA-32-301 Saratoga	3206055	I-TASP N9184N	3. 1.95	J.W.V.Edmonds	Malaga, Spain	16. 2.01
G-BVXA	Cameron N-105 HAFB	3441		4. 1.95	R.E.Jones	Lytham St.Annes	14. 2.99T
G-BVXB	Cameron V-77 HAFB	3442		4. 1.95	J.A.Lawton "Pat McLean"	Godalming	22. 3.99A
G-BVXC	English Electric Canberra B(I).8	6649	WT333	9. 1.95	Classic Avn Projects Ltd Bruntingthorpe (As "WT333" in DRA c/s)		AC
G-BVXD	Cameron O-84 HAFB	3432		5. 1.95	N.J.Langley "Prudential"	Bristol	2. 2.97A
G-BVXE	Steen Skybolt (Lyc IO-360)	PFA/64-11123	G-LISA	5. 1.95	T.J.Reeve Grange Farm, Boughton		17.11.99P
G-BVXF	Cameron O-120 HAFB	3400		21. 9.94	Gone With The Wind Ltd Carryduff, Co.Down		14. 3.97T
G-BVXG	Lindstrand LBL-90A HAFB	110		5. 1.95	G.C.Elson (Spain) t/a Lindstrand Balloon School		24. 5.99A
G-BVXI	Klemm Kl.35D (Hirth HM504)	1981	D-EFEG SE-BHT/Fv.5052	5. 1.95	J.J.Van Egmond (Nyverdal, Netherlands)		AC
G-BVXJ	CASA Bucker Bu.133 Jungmeister	-	E1-9 11. 1.95 ES1-9/35-9		J.D.Haslam (Northallerton)		
G-BVXK	Aerostar Yakovlev Yak-52	9111306	RA-44508 12. 1.95 DOSAAF 26		E.Gavazzi White Waltham (As "26" in DOSAAF c/s)		16. 4.99P
G-BVXM	Aerospatiale AS.350B Ecureuil	2013	I-AUDI I-CIOC	10. 1.95	The Berkeley Leisure Group Ltd Sparkford		5. 2.99T
G-BVXP	Cameron N-105 HAFB	1311	VH-URU	13. 1.95	P.M.Gaines "El Gas"	Stockton-on-Tees	
G-BVXR	DH.104 Devon C.2	04436	XA880	13. 1.95	M.Whale & M.W.A.Lunn Kemble (As "XA880" in RAE c/s) (Stored 6.97)		
G-BVXS	Taylorcraft BC-12D (Cont A65)	9284	N96984 NC96984	27. 1.95	Janet M.Allison Swanton Morley "Obsession"		5. 2.01P
G-BVXW	Short SC.7 Skyvan 3A-100	SH.1889	LX-DEF 15.11.95 Arg.Coast Guard PA-52/G-14-61		Hunting Avn Ltd Weston-on-the-Green/Oxford		20.11.99T
G-BVYA	Airbus A.320-231	354	F-WQAY 7. 4.95 (N301SA)/F-WWDZ		Caledonian Airways Ltd Gatwick "Loch Katrine"		6. 4.01T
G-BVYB	Airbus A.320-231	357	F-WQAZ 20. 4.95 (N302SA)/F-WWBH		Caledonian Airways Ltd Gatwick "Loch Hourn"		19. 4.01T
G-BVYC	Airbus A.320-231	411	F-WWQB 26. 4.95 (N303SA)/F-WWDX		Caledonian Airways Ltd Gatwick "Loch Tay"		25. 4.01T
G-BVYF	PA-31-350 Navajo Chieftain	31-7952102	F-WQAY 7. 4.95 N3518T	8. 2.95	Warwickshire Aerocentre Ltd Birmingham		23. 1.00T
G-BVYG	Robin DR.300/180R	611	F-BSQB F-BSPI	9. 1.95	London Gliding Club Pty Ltd Dunstable		9. 4.99
G-BVYJ	Cameron Fire Extinguisher 90SS HAFB	3398		2. 2.95	Chubb Fire Ltd Sunbury-on-Thames		16.12.99A
G-BVYK	Team Minimax 91A (Rotax 447)	PFA/186-12598		13. 2.95	S.B.Churchill Eastbach Farm, Coleford		4. 8.98P
G-BVYM	Robin DR.300/180R	656	F-BTBL	9.12.94	London Gliding Club Pty Ltd Dunstable		19. 7.01
G-BVYO	Robin R.2160	288		11. 1.95	The Cotswold Aero Club Ltd Gloucestershire		15. 4.01T
G-BVYP	PA-25-235 Pawnee B	25-3481	N7475D	13. 2.95	Bidford Gliding Centre Ltd Bidford		16. 3.01
G-BVYR	Cameron A-250 HAFB	3411		2. 2.95	Voyager Balloons Ltd	Cambridge	14.10.99T
G-BVYT	QAC Quickie Q-2 (Revmaster R2100D)	2443	N3797S	18. 1.95	I.K.Mitchell (Cullompton) t/a Quickie Club		13. 6.98P
G-BVYU	Cameron A-140 HAFB	3544		17. 2.95	B.J.Petteford "Blue Belle"	Bristol	5. 3.98T
G-BVYX	Light-Aero Avid Speed Wing mk.4 (Rotax 582)	PFA/189-12370		16. 2.95	G.J.Keen	Andrewsfield	29.10.98P
G-BVYY	Pietenpol Aircamper	PFA/47-12559		20. 2.95	J.R.Orchard	(Stourbridge)	28. 6.98
G-BVYZ	Stemme S-10V	14-011	D-KGDD	6. 3.95	L.Gubbay & S.Sagar	Denham	7. 7.01
G-BVZD	Tri-R Kis (CAM.100)	PFA/239-12416		21. 2.95	R.T.Clegg	Netherthorpe	18. 6.99P
G-BVZE	Boeing 737-59D	26422	SE-DNL	7. 3.95	British Midland Airways Ltd East Midlands		22. 3.01T
G-BVZF	Boeing 737-59D	25038	SE-DND (SE-DNC)	3. 4.95	British Midland Airways Ltd East Midlands		2. 5.01T
G-BVZG	Boeing 737-5Q8	25160	SE-DNF	12. 4.95	British Midland Airways Ltd East Midlands		1. 5.01T
G-BVZH	Boeing 737-5Q8	25166	SE-DNG	25. 4.95	British Midland Airways Ltd East Midlands		26. 5.01T
G-BVZI	Boeing 737-5Q8	25167	SE-DNH	15. 5.95	British Midland Airways Ltd East Midlands		11. 6.01T
G-BVZJ	Rand-Robinson KR-2	PFA/129-11049		21. 2.95	J.P.McConnell-Wood Phoenix Farm, Hants (Damaged on landing at Phoenix Farm 15.7.98)		
G-BVZM	Cessna 210M Centurion II	210-61674	OO-CNJ N732PV	28. 2.95	R.W.Bonner-Davies	(London SW11)	25. 3.01
G-BVZN	Cameron C-80 HAFB	3546		28. 2.95	Sally J.Langley Bristol t/a Sky Fly Balloons "Taywood Homes"		27. 4.99A
G-BVZO	Rans S-6-116 Coyote II (Rotax 582) 0494-606 & PFA/204A-12710			1. 3.95	P.Atkinson	Sandtoft	19. 1.01P

Regn	Type	C/n	P/I	Date	Owner/operator	Probable Base	CA Expy
G-BVZR	Zenair CH.601HD (Rotax 912UL)	PFA/162-12417		2. 3.95	J.D.White	Nottingham	11.10.99P
G-BVZT	Lindstrand LBL-90A HAFB	183		9. 3.95	F.W.Farnsworth Ltd t/a Pork Farms Bowyers	Nottingham	1. 6.99A
G-BVZV	Rans S-6-116 Coyote II (Rotax 582)	PFA/204A-12832		16. 2.95	A.G.Cameron & W.G.Dunn	(Winkleigh)	16. 5.99P
G-BVZX	Cameron H-34 HAFB	3564		15. 3.95	Julia B.Turnau t/a Chianti Balloon Club	Siena, Italy	21. 6.96A
G-BVZY	Mooney M.20R Ovation	29-0045		13. 3.95	Ovation Ltd	(Jersey)	9. 4.01
G-BVZZ	DHC.1 Chipmunk 22	C1/0687	WP795	5. 1.95	D.C.Murray t/a Portsmouth Naval Gliding Club (As "WP795/901" in RN c/s)	Lee-on-Solent	2. 6.01

G-BWAA-BWZZ

Regn	Type	C/n	P/I	Date	Owner/operator	Probable Base	CA Expy
G-BWAA	Cameron N-133 HAFB	3471		9. 3.95	Brunel Motor Co Ltd t/a Brunel Ford	Portishead	17. 4.99T
G-BWAB	Jodel D.140 Mousquetaire PFA/251-12469			25. 1.95	W.A.Braim	(Driffield)	
G-BWAC	Waco YKS-7 (Jacobs R-755)	4693	N5ORA N53361/NC50	19. 8.92	D.N.Peters	Little Gransden	29.10.01
G-BWAD	Rotary Air Force RAF 2000 (Subaru EJ22) 147 & PFA G/13-1254			27. 2.95	Newtonair Gyroplanes Ltd	Newton Abbot	26. 1.99P
G-BWAE	Rotary Air Force RAF 2000 (Subaru EA82) PFA G/13-1252			27. 2.95	B.J.Crockett (Damaged Kemble 30.7.96)	Redhill, Hereford	15.11.96P
G-BWAF	Hawker Hunter F.6A S4/U/3393 (Built Armstrong-Whitworth)		8831M XG160	24. 2.95	RV Aviation Ltd (For Royal Jordanian Historic Flight) (Stored as "XG160/U" 9.97)	Bournemouth	
G-BWAG	Cameron O-120 HAFB	3478		3. 2.95	M.F.Glue	Hertford	4. 7.99T
G-BWAH	Montgomerie-Bensen B.8MR PFA G/01-1208			16. 3.95	S.J.O.Tinn	Weymouth	
G-BWAI	CFM Streak Shadow PFA/206-12556 (Rotax 582)			21. 3.95	I.G.Hunt	Headcorn	25.11.99P
G-BWAJ	Cameron V-77 HAFB	3579		22. 3.95	R.S. & S.H.Ham	Axbridge, Somerset	2. 8.97A
G-BWAK	Robinson R-22 Beta	2507	N83311	22. 3.95	Caudwell Communications Ltd	Stoke-on-Trent	17. 6.01
G-BWAN	Cameron N-77 HAFB	3499		24. 3.95	Virgin Airship and Balloon Co Ltd (National Power c/s)	Telford	16. 8.97A
G-BWAO	Cameron C-80 HAFB	3436		24. 3.95	Virgin Airship and Balloon Co Ltd	Telford	20. 7.98T
G-BWAP	Clutton FRED Srs.3 PFA/29-10959			24. 3.95	R.J.Smyth	(York)	27. 8.98P
G-BWAR	Denney Kitfox mk.3 PFA/172-12432 (Rotax 582)			16. 3.95	B.J.Finch	(Cheltenham)	27. 8.98P
G-BWAT	Pietenpol Aircamper PFA/47-11594 (Cont C90)			15. 3.95	D.R.Waters	Leicester	27. 7.99P
G-BWAU	Cameron V-90 HAFB	3569		27. 3.95	K.M. & A.M.F.Hall	London N10	10. 7.99A
G-BWAV	Schweizer Hughes 269C (300C) S.1204		SE-JAY LN-OTS/OY-HDW/N41S	28. 2.95	Oxford Aviation Services Ltd	Oxford	2. 7.01T
G-BWAW	Lindstrand LBL-77A HAFB	207		28. 3.95	D.Bareford	Kidderminster	1. 5.99A
G-BWBA	Cameron V-65 HAFB	3456		27. 2.95	P.G.Dunnington t/a Dante Balloon Grp (British Airways c/s)	Hungerford	10. 5.99A
G-BWBB	Lindstrand LBL-14A HAFB	222		3. 4.95	Oxford Promotions (UK) Ltd	(USA)	
G-BWBC	Cameron N-90AS HAFB	3574		12. 6.95	Radio/Tele FFH GmbH & Co "Zeppelin"	Frankfurt, Germany	3. 4.98A
G-BWBE	Colt Flying Ice Cream Cone SS HAFB 3560			3. 4.95	Benedikt Haggeney GmbH	Ennigerloh, Germany	17. 2.99A
G-BWBF	Colt Flying Ice Cream Cone SS HAFB 3561			3. 4.95	Benedikt Haggeney GmbH	Ennigerloh,Germany	18. 2.99A
G-BWBG	Cvjetkovic CA-65 Skyfly PFA/1566			6. 4.95	T.White & M.C.Fawkes	Charity Farm, Baxterley	
G-BWBH	Thunder Fork Lift Truck 90SS HAFB 3472			6. 4.95	Jungheinrich AG	Hamburg, Germany	17. 2.99A
G-BWBI	Taylorcraft F-22A	2207	N22UK	3. 4.95	P.J.Wallace	Eshott	21. 9.98
G-BWBJ	Colt 21A HAFB	3532		6. 4.95	U.Schneider	Giessen, Germany	22. 2.99A
G-BWBN	Cameron V-90 HAFB	3583		7. 4.95	The Small School at Red House Ltd	Buxton, Norwich	25. 7.97A
G-BWBO	Lindstrand LBL-77A HAFB	157		10. 4.95	R.C.McCarthy "Lost in America"	Galena, Illinois, USA	30. 5.97A
G-BWBS	BAC.145 Jet Provost T.5A EEP/JP/1053		XW431	13. 4.95	N.D.Paterson (As "XW431/A") (Crashed into sea nr Clacton 24.12.98)	North Weald	24. 8.99P
G-BWBT	Lindstrand LBL-90A HAFB	184		3. 4.95	British Telecommunications plc	Newbury	29. 4.97A
G-BWBV	Colt Piggy Bank SS HAFB	3535		19. 4.95	Iduna-Bausparkasse AG	Hamburg, Germany	18. 2.99A
G-BWBY	Schleicher ASH26E	26076		30. 8.95	F.B.Jeynes	Bidford	14.11.01
G-BWBZ	ARV1 Super 2 PFA/152-12802 (Mid-West AE.100R)			10. 3.95	J.N.C.Shields & D.J.Millar	Newtownards	16. 5.99P
G-BWCA	CFM Streak Shadow PFA/206-11985 (Rotax 582)			19. 4.95	R.Thompson	(Redhill)	21. 7.97P
G-BWCC	Van Den Bemden 460m3 (Gas) "022" Free Balloon (C/n may be a corruption of Dutch CofR 622)		PH-BOX	5. 4.95	R.W.Batchelor t/a Piccard Balloon Grp "Prof A.Piccard"	Thame	
G-BWCE	Campbell Cricket PFA G/03-1235			24. 4.95	M.K.Hoban	(Ruislip)	
G-BWCG	Lindstrand LBL-42A HAFB	223		25. 4.95	Oxford Promotions (UK) Ltd	(USA)	10. 1.97A
G-BWCI	Light Aero Avid Hauler mk.4 PFA/189-12299			19. 8.92	M.J. Lowis t/a Avid Group (Damaged nr Fenland 16.5.98)	(Boston)	31. 7.98P
G-BWCK	Everett Gyroplane Srs.3 036 (Rotax 582)			26. 4.95	A.C.S.M.Hart	(Haslemere)	AC
G-BWCL	Lindstrand LBL-180A HAFB	150		27. 4.95	G.McFarland	Towcester	1.10.99T
G-BWCN	Dornier Do.28D-2 Skyservant	4335	5N-AYE D-ILID/9V-BKL/D-ILID	28. 4.95	Wingglider Ltd	Hibaldstow	11. 7.989
G-BWCO	Dornier Do.28D-2 Skyservant	4337	EI-CJU (N5TK)/5N-AOH/D-ILIF	19. 6.95	Wingglider Ltd	Hibaldstow	19. 5.99A

Regn	Type	C/n	P/I	Date	Owner/operator	Probable Base	CA Expy
G-BWCT	Tipsy T.66 Nipper Srs.1	11	"OO-NIC"	27. 4.95	J.S.Hemmings & C.R.Steer		
			PH-MEC/D-EMEC/OO-NIC			(Rye/Bexhill-on-Sea)	
G-BWCV	Europa Avn Europa (NSI EA-81/100)	PFA/247-12591		4. 5.95	M.P.Chetwynd-Talbot	Coxwold, Thirsk	14. 4.98P
					(Damaged Coxwold, Thirsk 31.10.97)		
G-BWCW	Barnett Rotorcraft J4B	PFA G/14-1256		5. 5.95	S.H.Kirkby	Southampton	
G-BWCY	Murphy Rebel (Lyc O-235)	PFA/232-12135		15. 5.95	A.Konieczek	St.Michaels-on-Wyre	26. 7.99P
G-BWCZ	Revolution Helicopters Mini-500 (Rotax 582)	0010		1. 5.95	D.Nieman	(Milton Common, Oxford)	AC
G-BWDA	ATR-72-202	444	F-WWEQ	29. 6.95	Gill Avn Ltd	Newcastle	28. 6.01T
G-BWDB	ATR-72-202	449	F-WWEE	14. 6.95	Gill Avn Ltd "City of Newcastle"	Newcastle	13. 6.01T
G-BWDE	PA-31P Pressurised Navajo	31P-7400193	G-HWKN	12. 5.95	Tomkat Aviation Ltd	Shoreham	18.12.96T
			HB-LIR/D-IAIR/N7304L (Stored 10.97)				
G-BWDF	WSK PZL-104 Wilga 35A	21950955		17. 5.95	Shivair Ltd	White Waltham	30.11.98
G-BWDH	Cameron N-105 HAFB	3549		22. 5.95	Bridges Van Hire Ltd	Awsworth, Nottingham	8. 6.99T
G-BWDM	Lindstrand LBL-120A HAFB	263		26. 5.95	G.D. & L.Fitzpatrick	Thame	N/E(T)
G-BWDO	Sikorsky S-76B	760356	VR-CPN N9HM	2. 6.95	Air Hanson Ltd	Blackbushe	8. 6.99T
G-BWDP	Europa Avn Europa 62 & (Rotax 912UL)	PFA/247-12637		7. 6.95	H.Linke	(Ahrensburg, Germany)	10. 2.99P
G-BWDR	Hunting-Percival P.84 Jet Provost T.3A	PAC/W/6603	XM376	6. 6.95	Global Avn Ltd (As "XM376/27")	Binbrook	7.10.99P
G-BWDS	Hunting P.84 Jet Provost T.Mk.3A (C/n incomplete ?)	'PAC/W/932'	XM424 N77506-ntu?	6. 6.95	J.Sinclair	North Weald	2. 2.99P
G-BWDT	PA-34-220T Seneca II	34-8233045	PH-TWI G-BKHS/N8472H	21. 9.88	A.C.Morgan	Biggin Hill	30. 6.00
G-BWDU	Cameron V-90 HAFB	3143		19. 6.95	C.J.Jenkins & M.Stone t/a Bath & West Security "Stella Tortoise"	Bath	14. 5.99A
G-BWDV	Schweizer Hughes 269C	S.1712	N86G	16. 6.95	Oxford Aviation Services Ltd	Oxford	26. 7.01T
G-BWDX	Europa Avn Europa (Rotax 912UL)	PFA/247-12603		13. 6.95	J.B.Crane	Fenland	22. 5.01P
G-BWDY	Sky 65-24 HAFB	001		13. 6.95	Sky Balloons Ltd	Wrexham	31.10.01T
G-BWDZ	Sky 105-24 HAFB	002		13. 6.95	Skyride Balloons Ltd	Kings Lynn	5.10.01T
G-BWEA	Lindstrand LBL-120A HAFB	252		14. 6.95	S.R.Seager	Aylesbury	20. 7.99T
G-BWEB	BAC.145 Jet Provost T.5A EEP/JP/1044		XW422	19. 6.95	D.W.N.Johnson (Transair Pilot Shop c/s)	North Weald	8.10.99P
G-BWEC	Cassutt-Colson Variant	PFA/34-10444		20.12.78	N.R.Thomson & M.P.J.Hill (On overhaul 5.96)	Sywell	11. 9.91P
G-BWED	Thunder Ax7-77 HAFB	3575		20. 6.95	J.Tod	London WC2	20. 6.96
G-BWEE	Cameron V-42 HAFB	3480		8. 3.95	Aeromantics Ltd	Bristol	
G-BWEF	SNCAN Stampe SV-4C (Gipsy Major 10)	208	G-BOVL	13. 5.93	A.J.White	Redhill	14.12.00
			N20SV/F-BHES/F-BBLC t/a Acebell BWEF Syndicate				
G-BWEG	Europa Avn Europa (Rotax 912UL)	PFA/247-12600		4. 4.95	B.A.Selmes & R.J.Marsh t/a Wessex Europa Grp	Weston Zoyland	23. 4.99P
G-BWEH	HOAC DV-20 Katana	20123		19. 6.95	Diamond Aircraft Industries GmbH (Weiner Neustadt, Austria)		19. 7.01T
G-BWEI	Cessna 172N Skyhawk II	172-67663	N73767	20. 6.95	Atlantic Bridge Aviation Ltd	Lydd	26. 8.01T
G-BWEL	Sky 200-24 HAFB	003		27. 6.95	M.W.A.Shemilt t/a H-O-T Air Balloons	Henley-on-Thames	8. 5.99T
G-BWEM	VS.358 Seafire L.III		IAC.157 RX168	28. 6.95	C.J.Warrilow & S.W.Atkins (On rebuild 6.97)	Norfolk	
G-BWEN	Macair Merlin GT (Jabiru 2200A)	PFA/208A-12859		20. 6.95	B.W.Davies	Hungry Hall Farm, Wyton	7.12.95P*
G-BWEO	Lindstrand LBL-14M HAFB	285		23. 6.95	Lindstrand Balloons Ltd	Oswestry	15.10.98A
G-BWEP	Lindstrand LBL-77M HAFB	286		23. 6.95	Lindstrand Balloons Ltd	Oswestry	9. 3.99A
G-BWER	Lindstrand LBL-14M HAFB	287		23. 6.95	Lindstrand Balloons Ltd	Oswestry	N/E(A)
G-BWEU	Reims Cessna F.152 II	1894	EI-BNC N9097Y	15. 6.95	Sky Pro Ltd	Copse Farm, Bourn	6. 8.01T
G-BWEV	Cessna 152 II	152-83182	EI-BVU N47184	28. 6.95	Haimoss Ltd	Old Sarum	23. 9.01T
G-BWEW	Cameron N-105 HAFB	3637		30. 6.95	Flying Pictures Ltd (Unipart c/s) "Unipart 5"	Fairoaks	17. 1.00A
G-BWEY	Bensen B.8	PFA G/01-1197		3. 7.95	F.G.Shepherd	Alston, Cumbria	
G-BWEZ	Piper J3C-85 Cub	6021	N29050 NC29050	3. 7.95	J.G.McTaggart t/a PJ L4 Group (As "436021" in US Army c/s)	Cumbernauld	15. 7.99P
G-BWFD	HOAC DV-20 Katana	20127		5. 7.95	Diamond Aircraft Industries GmbH (Weiner Neustadt, Austria)		30. 7.01T
G-BWFE	HOAC DV-20 Katana	20129		5. 7.95	Diamond Aircraft Industries GmbH (Weiner Neustadt, Austria)		23. 7.01T
G-BWFG	Robin HR.200/120	293		20. 7.95	Air Caernarfon Ltd	Caernarfon	20. 1.02T
G-BWFH	Europa Avn Europa	PFA/247-12842		14. 7.95	B.L.Wratten	(Uckfield/Crowborough)	5. 3.99T
G-BWFI	HOAC DV-20 Katana	20128		17. 7.95	Diamond Aircraft Industries GmbH (Weiner Neustadt, Austria)		12. 8.01T
G-BWFJ	Evans VP-1 (VW1600)	PFA/62-10349		1. 9.78	P.A.West (Stored Old Sarum 5.94)	(Stroud)	27. 3.93P

Regn	Type	C/n	P/I	Date	Owner/operator	Probable Base	CA Expy
G-BWFK	Lindstrand LBL-77A HAFB	289		17. 7.95	Virgin Airship & Balloon Co Ltd "Orange"	Telford	6. 8.98A
G-BWFM	Yakovlev Yak-50	781208	NX5224R DDR-WQX/DM-WQX	19. 7.95	Classic Avn Ltd (Op The Old Flying Machine Co)	Duxford	27. 7.99P
G-BWFN	HAPI Cygnet SF-2A	PFA/182-11335		19. 7.95	T.Crawford	(Rothesay)	
G-BWFO	Colomban MC-15 Cri-Cri (JPX PUL-212)	PFA/133-11253		19. 7.95	O.G.Jones	(Llanbedr)	
G-BWFP	IAV Yakovlev Yak-52	855503	RA-44501 DOSAAF 43	20. 7.95	M.C.Lee	Liverpool	17.11.99P
	(C/n plate shows c/n 855606 ex DOSAAF 61 (blue) - possibly composite)						
G-BWFR	Hawker Hunter F.58	41H-697398	J-4031	24. 7.95	The Old Flying Machine Air Museum Co Ltd (As "J-4031")	Scampton	3. 8.99P
G-BWFS	Hawker Hunter F.58	41H-697425	J-4058	24. 7.95	The Old Flying Machine Air Museum Co Ltd (As "J-4058")	Scampton	5. 7.99P
G-BWFT	Hawker Hunter T.8M	41H-695332	XL602	24. 7.95	B.R.Pearson t/a T8M Grp (As "XL602")	Exeter	23. 7.99P
G-BWFV	HOAC DV-20 Katana	20132		26. 7.95	HOAC Austria Flugzeugwerk Wiener Neustadt GmbH (Op South Warwickshire F/C)	Wellesbourne Mountford	17. 8.01T
G-BWFX	Europa Avn Europa 38 & PFA/247-12586 (Rotax 912UL)			26. 7.95	A.D.Stewart	Rayne Hall Farm, Rayne	10.11.98P
G-BWFY	Aerospatiale AS.350B1 Ecureuil	1963	N518R	31. 7.95	PLM Dollar Group Ltd	Inverness	21. 7.01T
G-BWFZ	Murphy Rebel	PFA/232-12536	G-SAVS	19. 7.95	I.E.Spencer	(Accrington)	
G-BWGA	Lindstrand LBL-105A HAFB	295		2. 8.95	Virgin Airship & Balloon Co Ltd "Asda"	Telford	24. 3.97A
G-BWGF	BAC.145 Jet Provost T.5A	EEP/JP/989	XW325	10. 8.95	J.W.Cullen t/a Specialscope Jet Provost Group (As "XW325/E")	Woodford	20. 7.99P
G-BWGG	Max Holste MH.1521C1 Broussard	20	F-GGKG F-WGKG/Fr mil	10. 7.95	M.J.Burnett Jnr. & R.B.Maalouf (As "315-SQ" in ALAT c/s)	Aberdeen	29. 7.01
G-BWGH	Europa Avn Europa	PFA/247-12589		23. 8.95	M.H.B.Heathman	(Exeter)	16. 3.99P
G-BWGJ	Chilton DW.1A (Lyc O-145)	PFA/225-12615		11. 8.95	T.J.Harrison (Complete 8.97)	Goodwood	
G-BWGK	Hawker Hunter GA.11	HABL-003032	XE689	15. 8.95	B.J.Pover (As XE689/864/VL")	Exeter	28. 7.99P
G-BWGL	Hawker Hunter T.8C (Regd with c/n 41H-695946)	HABL-003086	XF357	15. 8.95	G.R.Lacey (As "XF357/871/VL")	Bournemouth	5.11.99P
G-BWGM	Hawker Hunter T.8C (Regd with c/n 41H-695940)	HABL-003008	XE665	15. 8.95	B.J.Pover (As "XE665/876/VL")	Exeter	24. 6.98P
G-BWGN	Hawker Hunter T.8C	41H-670689	WT722	15. 8.95	B.J.Pearson t/a T8C Grp (As "WT722/878/VL")	Exeter	3. 9.97P
G-BWGO	Slingsby T-67M-200 Firefly	2048	SE-LBC LN-TFC/G-7-123	15. 8.95	R.Gray	Fairoaks	22.10.98
G-BWGP	Cameron C-80 HAFB	3631		17. 8.95	P.J. & C.M.Gentle "London Camera Exchange"	Bristol	27. 9.99A
G-BWGR	North American TB-25N-NC Mitchell (Regd with c/n 108-30925)	108-34200	NL9494Z 44-30925	18. 8.95	Aces High Ltd (As "151632" in USAF c/s)	North Weald (Stored 10.97)	
G-BWGS	BAC.145 Jet Provost T.5A	EEP/JP/974	XW310	18. 8.95	Katharina K.Gerstorfer (As "XW310/37")	(London SW6)	18. 2.99P
G-BWGT	Hunting-Percival P.84 Jet Provost T.4 (Reported as c/n PAC/W/19992)	PAC/W/21624	8991M XR679	21. 8.95	R.E.Todd (Op The Jet Provost Club)	Sandtoft	19. 5.99P
G-BWGU	Cessna 150F	150-62962	EI-CDU N8862G	18. 8.95	W.Davies (Stored 1.97)	Cardiff	5. 4.01
G-BWGX	Cameron N-42 HAFB	3633		21. 8.95	Newbury Building Society	Newbury	5. 9.96A
G-BWGY	HOAC DV-20 Katana	20134		22. 8.95	HOAC Austria Flugzeugwerk Wiener Neustadt GmbH (Op Plymouth School of Flying)	Plymouth	12.10.01T
G-BWGZ	HOAC DV-20 Katana	20135		22. 8.95	HOAC Austria Flugzeugwerk Wiener Neustadt GmbH (Op Plymouth School of Flying)	Plymouth	12.10.01T
G-BWHA	Hawker Hurricane IIB (Regd with c/n 41H-G3121232)	41H/G5/21232	Z5053 (Soviet AF)/Z5053	23. 8.95	Historic Flying Ltd (On rebuild 8.95 to be as "Z5252/GO-B")	Audley End	
G-BWHB	Cameron O-65 HAFB	2759		24. 8.95	G.Aimo	Mondovi, Italy	1. 6.99A
G-BWHC	Cameron N-77 HAFB	3647		25. 8.95	Travelsphere Ltd	Market Harborough	15. 8.98A
G-BWHD	Lindstrand LBL-31A HAFB	292		29. 8.95	J.C.E.Price t/a Army Air Corps Balloon Club	Portadown	22. 9.97A
G-BWHF	PA-31-325 Navajo C/R	31-7612076	F-GECA D-IBIS/N59862	7. 9.85	Awyr Cymru Cyf	Welshpool	31.10.99T
G-BWHG	Cameron N-65 HAFB	3619		7. 9.95	Coffee Nannini SRL	Siena, Italy	4.10.99A
G-BWHH	PA-18-135 (L-21B-PI) Super Cub (Frame No.18-3789)	18-3605	PH-KNA R.Neth AF R-115/54-2405	9. 8.95	J.W.McLeod (As "44" in US Army c/s)	Felthorpe	31.10.98
G-BWHI	DHC.1 Chipmunk 22A	C1-0637	WK624	8. 9.95	N.E.M.Clare (As "WK624/M")	Duxford	9. 9.01T
G-BWHJ	CFM Starstreak Shadow SA-II (Rotax 618) K.269 & PFA/206-12907			12. 9.95	N.Irwin	(Castle Martyr, Co.Cork)	28. 4.98P
G-BWHK	Rans S-6-116 Coyote II (Rotax 582)	PFA/204A-12908		15. 9.95	N.D.White	Turweston	1.11.99P

Regn	Type	C/n	P/I	Date	Owner/operator	Probable Base	CA Expy
G-BWHM	Sky 140-24 HAFB	006		18. 9.95	Sky Balloons Ltd	Wrexham	13. 5.99T
G-BWHN	Aerospatiale AS.332L Super Puma	2017	C-GSLC	24.10.95	Brintel Helicopters Ltd	Aberdeen	9. 5.00T
			HC-BNC/C-GSLC		t/a British International Helicopters		
G-BWHP	CASA I-131E Jungmann	2109	E3B-513	18. 8.95	J.F.Hopkins Watchford Farm, Yarcombe		16. 7.99P
					(As "S4+A07" in Luftwaffe c/s)		
G-BWHR	Tipsy T.66 Nipper Srs.1 PFA/25-12843		(OO-KAM)	19. 9.95	L.R.Marnef (Koningshooikt, Belgium)		
			OO-69				
	(Composite homebuild of original Fairey built c/n 29 & 71)						
G-BWHS	Rotary Air Force RAF.2000			25. 9.95	V.G.Freke	Kemble	9.11.99P
	(Sabaru EA82) PFA G/13-1253						
G-BWHU	Westland Scout AH.1	F.9517	XR595	27. 9.95	N.J.F.Boston	Plymouth	27. 1.00P
					(As "XR595/M" in Army c/s)		
G-BWHV	Denney Kitfox mk.2	PFA/172-11857		28. 9.95	A.C.Dove (Ashtead, Surrey)		11.12.99P
G-BWHW	Cameron A-180 HAFB	3634		29. 9.95	Societe Bombard SARL Meursanges, France		31.10.99A
G-BWHY	Robinson R-22	0098	N90366	24. 3.87	Helicentre Ltd	Liverpool	18. 4.99T
G-BWIA	Rans S-10 Sakota	PFA/194-12044		15. 9.95	P.A.Beck	Cambridge	1. 4.99P
					(Under construction 3.97)		
G-BWIB	Scottish Avn Bulldog 120/122		G-103	10.10.95	L.Bax	Henstridge	AC
		BH120/227	Ghana AF				
G-BWID	Druine D.31 Turbulent	201	F-PHFR	16.10.95	A.M.Turney (Tring)		20.10.99
G-BWII	Cessna 150G	150-65308	N4008J	22. 9.95	J.D.G.Hicks Beeches Farm, South Scarle		15. 1.99
			(G-BSKB)/N4008J				
G-BWIJ	Europa Avn Europa	PFA/247-12513		19.10.95	R.Lloyd (Tenbury Wells)		
G-BWIK	DH.82A Tiger Moth	86417	7015M	20.10.95	G.H.Fullbrook & B.J.Ellis (On rebuild)		
			NL985		(As "NL985") (Northampton/Slough)		
G-BWIL	Rans S-10 Sakota		G-WIEN	4.10.95	J.C.Longmore	Netherthorpe	29. 5.97P
	(Rotax 582) 1089-065 & PFA/194-11770						
G-BWIO	HOAC DV-20 Katana	20147		24.10.95	HOAC Flugzeugwerk Wiener Neustadt GmbH		
					(Damaged nr Sleap 8.2.97) Woodford		15.11.98T
G-BWIP	Cameron N-90 HAFB	3668		20.10.95	Noble Adventures Ltd	Bristol	27.10.96A
G-BWIR	Dornier 328-100	3023	D-CDXF	20.10.95	Suckling Airways (Norwich) Ltd Cambridge		19.10.99T
			N328DA/D-CDHH		(Op Air UK)		
G-BWIT	QAC Quickie 1	484	N44B2Z	21. 9.95	D.E., M.S. & I.E.Johnson	Coventry	2. 9.97P
	(Rotax 503)				(Damaged nr Coventry 12.10.97)		
G-BWIU	Hawker Hunter F.58	41H-691770	J-4021	26.10.95	Classic Aviation Ltd	Scampton	24. 2.99P
	(Reported as c/n 41H/694926)				(As "XG232" in RAF c/s)		
G-BWIV	Europa Avn Europa			27.10.95	Joan R.Lockwood-Goose	Newton Stewart	9. 9.99P
	(Rotax 912UL) 210 & PFA/247-12871						
G-BWIW	Sky 180-24 HAFB	008		1.11.95	G.D. & L.Fitzpatrick	Thame	30. 6.99T
G-BWIX	Sky 120-24 HAFB	009		31.10.95	J.M.Percival "Mayfly III"	Loughborough	5. 5.99
G-BWIY	Lindstrand LBL-105A HAFB	322		3.11.95	Lindstrand Balloons Ltd	Oswestry	5.11.99A
G-BWIZ	Quickie Tri-Q 200	PFA/94-12330		21. 8.95	B.J.Cain (Stanford-le-Hope)		23. 6.98P
	(Cont O-200-A)						
G-BWJB	Thunder Ax8-105 HAFB	197		15. 6.79	Justerini & Brooks Ltd	London SW1	14. 1.88A
					"Whisky J & B"		
G-BWJC	Cameron N-65 HAFB	3754		3.11.95	Cameron Balloons Ltd	Bristol	19. 7.99
					"Coral Draw"		
G-BWJE	Sky 105-24 HAFB	010		3.11.95	Sky Balloons Ltd	Wrexham	13.11.96A
G-BWJG	Mooney M.20J (201MSE)	24-3319	N1083P	7.11.95	Samic Ltd	Elstree	4. 2.02
G-BWJH	Europa Avn Europa	PFA/247-12643		10.11.95	A.R.D. & J.A.S.T.Hood (London SW6)		26. 9.99P
	(Rotax 912UL)						
G-BWJI	Cameron V-90 HAFB	3727		13.11.95	Calarel Developments Ltd Chipping Camden		16. 8.99A
G-BWJL	Cameron N-120 HAFB	3416		13.11.95	Cameron Balloons Ltd	Bristol	2. 5.99T
G-BWJM	Bristol M.1C Replica	NAW-2		23.11.95	The Shuttleworth Trust	Old Warden	AC
					(As "C4918" in 72 Sqn c/s)		
G-BWJN	Montgomerie-Bensen B.8MR			16.11.95	M.G.Mee	Great Orton	8. 9.99P
	(Rotax 582) PFA G/01-1262						
G-BWJP	Cessna 172C	172-49424	N1824Y	21.11.95	Heron Air Services Ltd (Bournemouth)		
G-BWJR	Sky 120-24 HAFB	007		22.11.95	W.J.Brogan "Filzmooser"		
						Steiermark, Austria	21.12.96
G-BWJT	Yakovlev Yak-50	812003	RA-01385	23.11.95	W.R.M.Beesley	Breighton	11.12.98P
			DOSAAF 50		(As "01385")		
G-BWJW	Westland Scout AH.1	F.9705	XV130	29.11.95	C.L.Holdsworth (Weybridge)		9.11.99P
					(As "XV130/R" in 666 Sqdn c/s)		
G-BWJY	DHC.1 Chipmunk 22	C1/0519	WG469	5.12.95	K.J.Thompson (As "WG469")	Newtownards	14.10.99
G-BWJZ	DHC.1 Chipmunk 22	C1/0653	WK638	23.11.95	J.Zemlik (As "WK638/83")	Breighton	17. 1.02
G-BWKB	Hawker Hunter F.58	41H-697448	J-4081	12.10.95	Classic Aviation Ltd	Duxford	AC
					(As "J-4081") (Stored 9.97)		
G-BWKC	Hawker Hunter F.58	41H-697394	J-4025	12.10.95	RV Avn Ltd	Bournemouth	4. 5.99P
					(Op Royal Jordanian Historic Flight) (As "712/E")		
G-BWKD	Cameron O-120 HAFB	3773		8.12.95	K.E. & L.J.Viney "Rainbow" Olney, Bucks		30.11.99T
G-BWKE	Cameron AS-105GD Hot Air Airship			8.12.95	Gefa-Flug GmbH	Aachen, Germany	14. 3.97A
		3685					
G-BWKF	Cameron N-105 HAFB	3736		8.12.95	R.M.M.Botti	Grosseto, Italy	23. 1.99A
G-BWKG	Europa Avn Europa	PFA/247-12451		28.11.95	T.C.Jackson (Sheffield)		
G-BWKJ	Rans S-7 Courier	PFA/218-12918		14.12.95	J.P.Kovacs	Aboyne	19. 5.99P
	(Rotax 582)						

Regn	Type	C/n	P/I	Date	Owner/operator	Probable Base	CA Expy
G-BWKK	Auster AOP.9 AUS.166 & B5/10/165	XP279		30. 7.79	C.A.Davis & D.R.White (As "XP279" in Army c/s)	Popham	1. 8.96P
G-BWKR	Sky 90-24 HAFB	014		18.12.95	Beverley Drawbridge	Cranbrook	26. 2.97T
G-BWKT	Stephens Akro Lazer	PFA/123-11421		19.12.95	P.D.Begley	Sywell	
G-BWKU	Cameron A-250 HAFB	3730		21.12.95	Balloon School (International) Ltd t/a British School of Ballooning	Petworth	27. 9.99T
G-BWKV	Cameron V-77 HAFB	3780		27.12.95	Poppies (UK) Ltd	Wootton Fitzpaine, Dorset	9. 2.99T
G-BWKW	Thunder Ax8-90 HAFB	3770		28.12.95	Venice Simplon Orient Express Ltd "Road to Mandalay"	Frinton-on-Sea	9. 1.97A
G-BWKX	Cameron A-250 HAFB	3731		2. 1.96	Balloon School (International) Ltd t/a Hot Airlines	Petworth	27. 9.99T
G-BWKZ	Lindstrand LBL-77A HAFB	340		21.12.95	Lambert Smith Hampton Group Ltd	Streatley, Berks	14. 1.00A
G-BWLA	Lindstrand LBL-69A HAFB	339		3. 1.96	Virgin Airship & Balloon Co Ltd	(Telford)	14. 1.97A
G-BWLD	Cameron O-120 HAFB	3774		16. 1.96	D. & P.Pedri & C.Nicolodi	Villalagarina, Italy	22. 1.00A
G-BWLE	Bell 212	31225	N4247M SU-CAA	5. 1.96	Bristow Helicopters Ltd (On rebuild 9.97)	Redhill	AC
G-BWLF	Cessna 404 Titan II	404-0414	G-BNXS HKG-4/(N8799K)	26.10.94	P.Maden & M Evans t/a Nor Leasing	Fairoaks	19. 3.00
G-BWLH	Lindstrand HS-110 Hot Air Airship	331		10. 1.96	J.A.Cooper t/a Ramdon International	Ivybridge	12.12.98A
G-BWLJ	Taylorcraft DCO-65	O-4331	C-GUSA (ex)	16. 1.96	C.Evans	(Ipswich)	
G-BWLL	Murphy Rebel (Lyc O-235)	PFA/232-12499		22. 1.96	F.W.Parker	(Richmond, N.Yorks)	16. 7.99P
G-BWLM	Sky 65-24 HAFB	015		24. 1.96	W.J.Brogan t/a Dachstein Tauern Balloons KG "Innsbruck"	Steiermark, Austria	5. 2.97
G-BWLN	Cameron O-84 HAFB	3737		24. 1.96	Reggiana Riduttori SRL	S.Polo d'Enza, Italy	1. 6.99A
G-BWLO	Bell 206B JetRanger	488	N2290W	22. 1.96	RCR Aviation Ltd	Thruxton	27. 6.99T
G-BWLP	HOAC DV-20 Katana	20141	OE-UDV	6. 2.96	HOAC Austria Wiener Neustadt GmbH (Op Blackbushe School of Flying)	Blackbushe	13. 3.99T
G-BWLR	Max Holste MH.1521C1 Broussard	185	F-GGKJ F-WGKJ/French AF	25. 1.96	Chicory Crops Ltd (As "185" in French AF c/s)	Sywell	4. 2.00
G-BWLS	HOAC DV-20 Katana	20142	OE-UHK	6. 2.96	HOAC Austria Wiener Neustadt GmbH	Leeds-Bradford	13. 3.99T
G-BWLT	HOAC DV-20 Katana	20149		6. 2.96	HOAC Austria Wiener Neustadt GmbH	Gloucestershire	25. 3.99T
G-BWLV	HOAC DV-20 Katana	20151		6. 2.96	HOAC Austria Wiener Neustadt GmbH	Woodford	27. 3.99T
G-BWLW	Light Aero Avid Speed Wing mk.4	PFA/189-12763		26. 1.96	P.C. & Susan A.Creswick	Weston Zoyland	
G-BWLX	Westland Scout AH.1	F.9709	XV134	29.12.95	R.E.Dagless (As "XV134" in AAC c/s)	Yaxham, Dereham	9.11.99P
G-BWLY	Rotorway Exec 90 (RI 162)	5142		11. 1.93	P.W. & I.P.Bewley	Ley Farm, Chirk	18.11.98P
G-BWMA	Colt 105A HAFB	1853		31.10.90	C.C.Duppa-Miller	Warwick	5. 9.97A
G-BWMB	Jodel D.119	77-1492	F-BGMA	17. 2.78	C.Hughes	Finmere	19. 5.99P
	(Original F-BGMA c/n 77 became F-PHQH and was rebuilt as a Larrieu JL.2; this is presumed to be a rebuild using some components of c/n 77 plus newly built c/n 1492)						
G-BWMC	Cessna 182P Skylane II	182-63117	N5462J G-BWMC/OO-RGM	30. 1.96	P.F.N.Burrow & E.N.Skinner t/a Eggesford Eagles F/Grp	Trenchard Farm, Eggesford	3. 7.00
G-BWMD	Enstrom 480	5013		5. 2.96	Southern Air Ltd	Shoreham	24. 6.99T
G-BWMF	Gloster Meteor T.7	G5/356460	7917M WA591	15.12.95	C.C.Rhodes t/a Meteor Flight (Yatesbury) (On rebuild 3.96)	Yatesbury	
G-BWMG	Aerospatiale AS.332L Super Puma	2046	OY-HMG	1. 2.96	Bristow Helicopters Ltd	Aberdeen	24. 6.00T
G-BWMH	Lindstrand LBL-77B HAFB	152		7. 2.96	J.W.Hole	Much Wenlock	2. 4.97A
G-BWMI	PA-28RT-201T Turbo Arrow IV	28R-8031131	F-GCTG N9571N	31. 1.96	C.E.R.Hewitt & D.H.Saunders	Poplar Hall Farm, Elmsett	11. 6.99
G-BWMJ	Nieuport Scout 17/23 replica (Cont A75)	PFA/121-12351		8. 2.96	R.Gauld-Galliers & Lisa J.Day (As "B3459/2" in RFC c/s)	Popham	22. 7.99P
G-BWMK	DH.82A Tiger Moth	84483	T8191	9. 2.96	Schneider Trophy Ltd	Welshpool	AC
G-BWML	Cameron A-275 HAFB	3725		12. 2.96	A.J.Street	Exeter	8. 3.98T
G-BWMN	Rans S-7 Courier (Rotax 912UL)	PFA/218-12446		14. 2.96	T.M.Turnbull	Stoneacre Farm, Farthing Corner	22. 1.98P
G-BWMO	Oldfield Baby Lakes (Cont C85)	JAL.3	G-CIII N11JL	14. 2.96	P.J.Tanulak	Sleap	17. 2.99P
G-BWMS	DH.82A Tiger Moth	82712	OO-EVJ T-29/R4771	14. 2.96	Foundation Early Birds	Lelystad, Netherlands	
G-BWMU	Cameron Monster Truck 105SS HAFB	3607		20. 2.96	Cameron Balloons Ltd "Skycrusher"	(Canada)	4. 5.97A
G-BWMV	Colt AS-105 mk.II Hot Air Airship	3775		22. 2.96	Aereo Grupo Arashi SL	Madrid, Spain	30. 9.98A

Regn	Type	C/n	P/I	Date	Owner/operator	Probable Base	CA Expy
G-BWMX	DHC.1 Chipmunk 22	C1/0481	WG407	19. 2.96	Wendy H.Sanaghan (As "WG407/67")	Spanhoe	2. 4.99
G-BWMY	Cameron Bradford and Bingley 90SS HAFB	3808		23. 2.96	Flying Pictures Ltd	Fairoaks	25. 5.99A
G-BWNB	Cessna 152 II	152-80051	N757WA	23. 8.96	Galair International Ltd	Wellesbourne Mountford	12. 9.99T
G-BWNC	Cessna 152 II	152-84415	N6487L	23. 8.96	Galair International Ltd	Wellesbourne Mountford	21.10.99T
G-BWND	Cessna 152 II	152-85905	N95493	23. 8.96	Galair International Ltd, M.R.Galiffe & G.Davis	Wellesbourne Mountford	12. 9.99T
G-BWNF	PBN BN-2T Turbine Islander	2296		28. 2.96	Britten-Norman Ltd	Bembridge	
G-BWNG	PBN BN-2B-20 Islander	2297		28. 2.96	Britten-Norman Ltd	Bembridge	AC
G-BWNH	Cameron A-375 HAFB	3553		28. 2.96	Noble Adventures Ltd	Bristol	12. 5.97A
G-BWNI	PA-24-180 Comanche	24-136	N5123P	15. 2.96	A.P.Dyer t/a Small World Aviation	(Maldon)	18. 6.99
G-BWNJ	Hughes 269C	86-0528	N42LW N27RD/N7458F	29. 2.96	L.R.Fenwick Long Fosse House, Beelsby, Grimsby		12. 6.99
G-BWNK	DHC.1 Chipmunk 22	C1/0317	WD390	4. 3.96	B.Whitworth (As "WD390")	Netherthorpe	4. 3.00
G-BWNL	Europa Avn Europa	PFA/247-12675		27. 2.96	H.Smith Morgansfield, Fishburn (Damaged Fishburn 14.12.97)		
G-BWNM	PA-28R-180 Cherokee Arrow	28R-30435	N934BD	5. 3.96	D.Houghton	(Pershore)	16. 9.99
G-BWNN	Rand-Robinson KR-2	PFA/129-11342		5. 3.96	C.Clark	(Scunthorpe)	
G-BWNO	Cameron O-90 HAFB	3716		5. 3.96	Action Research	Horsham, W.Sussex	
G-BWNP	Cameron Club-90 SS HAFB (Club Orange Soft Drink Can shape)	1717	EI-BVQ	6. 3.96	C.J.Davies & P.Spellward	Hope Valley	22. 5.99
G-BWNR	PA-38-112 Tomahawk	38-78A0449	N2361E	6. 3.96	APB Leasing Ltd	Welshpool	11. 4.99T
G-BWNS	Cameron O-90 HAFB	3842		6. 3.96	Inland Revenue Corporate Communications "Hector" (Self Assessment Tax c/s)	(London WC2)	24. 4.97T
G-BWNT	DHC.1 Chipmunk 22	C1/0772	WP901	7. 3.96	R.A.Stafford t/a Three Point Avn (As "WP901")	East Midlands	19.12.99T
G-BWNU	PA-38-112 Tomahawk	38-78A0334	N9294T	8. 3.96	Rosemary E.Best t/a G-BWNU Group	Kemble	6. 8.99
G-BWNV	PA-38-112 Tomahawk	38-79A1019	N2538P	8. 3.96	C.P.Ebbs t/a CEA Aircraft Leasing	(Dursley)	
G-BWNX	Thunder Ax10-180 Srs.2 HAFB	2352	G-OWBC	2. 1.96	Airborne Rides Ltd	Longleat	7. 4.99T
G-BWNY	Aeromot AMT-200 Super Ximango	200-055		11. 6.96	H.G.Nicklin	Woodford	20. 5.99
G-BWNZ	Agusta A.109C	7654		3. 4.96	Anglo Beef Processors Ltd	Shrewsbury	3. 4.99T
G-BWOA	Sky 105-24 HAFB	027		13. 3.96	Akhter Group Holdings plc	Harlow	4. 5.99A
G-BWOB	Luscombe 8F Silvaire	6179	N1552B NC1552B	14. 3.96	P.J.Tanulak & H.T.Law	(Shrewsbury)	
G-BWOD	IAV Yakovlev Yak-52	833810	LY-ALY DOSAAF 139	14. 3.96	Insurefast Ltd (As "DOSAAF 139")	Sywell	28. 4.99P
G-BWOE	Yakovlev Yak-3U (Converted from LET Yak C.11)	1701231	(G-BUXZ) NX11SN/(France)/Egyptian AF	14. 3.96	R.G.Hanna (Op The Old Flying Machine Co)	Duxford	AC
G-BWOF	BAC.145 Jet Provost T.5	EEP/JP/955	XW291	18. 3.96	Techair London Ltd	Bournemouth	18. 2.00P
G-BWOH	PA-28-161 Cadet	2841061	D-ENXG N9142S	18. 3.96	Oxford Aviation Services Ltd	Oxford	26. 3.99T
G-BWOI	PA-28-161 Cadet	2841307	D-EJTM N9264N/N9208P	18. 3.96	Oxford Aviation Services Ltd	Oxford	25. 4.99T
G-BWOJ	PA-28-161 Cadet	2841331	D-ESTM N92242/(N123ND)/N92242	18. 3.96	Oxford Aviation Services Ltd	Oxford	26. 3.99T
G-BWOK	Lindstrand LBL-105G HAFB	370		19. 3.96	Lindstrand Balloons Ltd	Oswestry	17. 8.99A
G-BWOL	Hawker Sea Fury FB.11	ES.3617 & 61631	D-CACY G-9-66/WG599	18. 3.96	The Old Flying Machine (Air Museum) Co Ltd (Stored as "D-CACY" 1.99)	Duxford	
G-BWOM	Cessna 550 Citation II	550-0671	N671EA 9M-TAA/(N6761L)	22. 3.96	Ferron Trading Ltd (Op Aviation Beauport Ltd)	Jersey	18. 4.00
G-BWON	Europa Avn Europa (Rotax 912UL)	PFA/247-12720		29. 1.96	G.T.Birks	White Waltham	16. 8.99P
G-BWOR	PA-18-135 Super Cub (L-18C)	18-2547	OO-WIS OO-HMF/ALAT/52-6229	21. 3.96	C.D.Baird	(Farnham)	23. 7.99
G-BWOS	Bell 212	35074	PNC-189 (Colombian Police)/C-FTIP	22. 3.96	Heliwork Services Ltd (Crashed 10.12.94; on rebuild)	Thruxton	
G-BWOT	Hunting P.84 Jet Provost T.3A (Reported as c/n PAC/W/949267)	PAC/W/10138	XN459	25. 3.96	Quasi Mondi Ltd (As "XN459" in all-red Red Pelicans c/s)	North Weald	11.10.99P
G-BWOU	Hawker Hunter F.58A	HABL.003067	J-4105 G-9-315/A2565/XF303	26. 3.96	The Old Flying Machine (Air Museum) Co Ltd (As "105")	Scampton	3. 9.97P
	(Regd with c/n 41H-003067 ex XF306/7776M/G-9-402 which became J-4133:- G-BWOU may be a composite)						
G-BWOV	Enstrom F-28A	222	N690BR G-BWOV/F-BVRG	28. 3.96	B.H.Austen t/a Austen Associates	Thruxton	16.12.99
G-BWOW	Cameron N-105 HAFB	3805		31. 1.96	S.J.Colin & A.S.Pinder t/a Skybus Ballooning	Maidstone	18. 2.99T
G-BWOX	DHC.1 Chipmunk 22	C1/0728	WP844	27. 3.96	J.St Clair-Quentin (As "WP844")	Spanhoe	10. 7.00
G-BWOY	Sky 31-24 HAFB	029		28. 3.96	Virgin Airship & Balloon Co Ltd	(Telford)	5. 4.97A

Regn	Type	C/n	P/I	Date	Owner/operator	Probable Base	CA Expy
G-BWOZ	CFM Streak Shadow SA (Rotax 582) K154SA & PFA/206-12988			1. 4.96	N.P.Harding	(Barnet)	19. 7.99P
G-BWPA	Cameron A-340 HAFB	3714		29. 3.96	A.A.Brown	Guildford	31.10.98T
G-BWPB	Cameron V-77 HAFB	3866		1. 4.96	R.H. & N.K.Calvert t/a The Fair Weather Friends Ballooning Co	Bristol	19. 5.99A
G-BWPC	Cameron V-77 HAFB	3867		1. 4.96	Helen Vaughan "Olive"	Tring	20. 6.99A
G-BWPE	Murphy Renegade Spirit UK PFA/188-12791			2. 4.96	G.Wilson	(Solihull)	
G-BWPF	Sky 120-24 HAFB	028		3. 4.96	Computeraid Services Ltd & H. & R.T.Revel t/a Humbug Balloon Group "Whisper" Farnborough/High Wycombe		18. 5.01T
G-BWPG*	Robin HR.200/120B	299		15. 4.96	Air Alba Ltd	Inverness	7. 7.99T
	(Damaged off Cromarty Gap, Nigg Bay 29.10.97 - fuselage stored Dalcross 6.98)						
G-BWPH	PA-28-181 Cherokee Archer II 28-7790311		N1408H	4. 4.96	J.Maffia	Panshanger	1. 5.99T
G-BWPI	Sky 120-24 HAFB	018		9. 4.96	Sky Balloons Ltd Indio, California, USA "Thunderbird"		12. 8.99
G-BWPJ	Steen Skybolt PFA/64-12854 (Cont IO-346)			9. 4.96	W.R.Penaluna	(Penzance)	1. 2.99P
G-BWPK	PBN BN-2T-4R Defender 4000	4006		24. 4.96	Britten-Norman Ltd	Bembridge	AC
G-BWPL	Airtour AH-56 HAFB	011	G-OAFC	19. 3.96	A.S.Newnham	Southampton	
G-BWPM	PBN BN-2T-4R Defender 4000	4007		24. 4.96	Britten-Norman Ltd	Bembridge	
G-BWPP	Sky 105-24 HAFB	031		9. 4.96	P.F.Smart t/a The Sarnia Balloon Group "Fourpence"	Basingstoke	6. 7.99A
G-BWPR	PBN BN-2T-4S Defender 4000	4010		24. 4.96	Pilatus Britten-Norman Ltd	Bembridge	
G-BWPS	CFM Streak Shadow SA PFA/206-12954 (Rotax 618)			9. 2.96	P.G.A.Sumner Tower Farm, Wollaston, Wellingborough		4. 8.99P
G-BWPT	Cameron N-90 HAFB	3838		5. 3.96	Workplace Technologies Ltd	Huddersfield	1. 5.99A
G-BWPU	PBN BN-2T-4S Defender 4000	4011		24. 4.96	Britten-Norman Ltd	Bembridge	AC
G-BWPV	PBN BN-2T-4S Defender 4000	4012		24. 4.96	Britten-Norman Ltd	Bembridge	AC
G-BWPW	PBN BN-2T-4S Defender 4000	4013		24. 4.96	Britten-Norman Ltd	Bembridge	
G-BWPX	PBN BN-2T-4S Defender 4000	4014		24. 4.96	Britten-Norman Ltd	Bembridge	
G-BWPY	HOAC DV-20 Katana	20158	OE-UDV	10. 6.96	Diamond Aircraft Industries GmbH Weiner Neustadt, Austria		19. 6.99T
G-BWPZ	Cameron N-105 HAFB	3889		19. 4.96	Flying Pictures Ltd "Jaguar"	Fairoaks	19. 3.99A
G-BWRA	Sopwith LC-1T Triplane Replica (Warner Scarab 165) PFA/21-10035		G-PENY	19. 4.96	S.M.Truscott & J.M.Hoblyn (As "N500" in RNAS c/s) Watchford Farm, Yarcombe/RNAS Yeovilton		15.11.99P
G-BWRC	Light Aero Avid Hauler mk.4 (Hirth F30) PFA/189-12979			22. 2.96	B.Williams Chilsfold Farm, Crawley		27. 6.99P
G-BWRM	Colt 105A HAFB	3734		23. 4.96	N.Charbonnier	Aosta, Italy	25. 1.00A
G-BWRO	Europa Avn Europa PFA/247-12849 (Rotax 912UL)			22. 4.96	J.G.M.McDiarmid	(Glasgow)	12.11.99P
G-BWRP	Beechcraft 58 Baron	TH-1737	VR-BVB N3217H	23. 4.96	Astra Aviation Ltd	Guernsey	30. 4.99
G-BWRR	Cessna 182Q Skylane II	182-66660	N95861	29. 3.94	D.O.Halle	(West Bridgford)	13. 7.00T
G-BWRS	SNCAN Stampe SV-4C	437	(N) F-BCVQ	24. 4.96	G.P.J.M.Valvekens	(Diest, Belgium)	
G-BWRT*	Cameron Concept-60 HAFB	3078	EI-BYP	22.10.96	European Balloon Display Co Ltd (Exported 1998) Great Missenden		Exp
G-BWRU	Lindstrand Audi Saloon Car SS HAFB	369		23. 4.96	Flying Pictures Ltd "Audi"	Fairoaks	26. 9.97A
G-BWRV	Lindstrand LBL-90A HAFB	371		23. 4.96	Flying Pictures Ltd "Audi"	Fairoaks	28. 5.99A
G-BWRW	Sky 220-24 HAFB	032		23. 4.96	Sky Trek Ballooning Ltd Longfield, Kent		11. 5.99T
G-BWRY	Cameron N-105 HAFB	3817		24. 4.96	G.Aimo	Mondovi, Italy	1. 6.98a
G-BWRZ	Lindstrand LBL-105A HAFB	383		26. 4.96	Flying Pictures Ltd "Rover"	Fairoaks	13. 4.99A
G-BWSB	Lindstrand LBL-105A HAFB	384		26. 4.96	Flying Pictures Ltd "MG"	Fairoaks	13. 4.99A
G-BWSC	PA-38-112 Tomahawk II	38-81A0125	N23203	29. 4.96	APB Leasing Ltd (Op Norwich Flying Club)	Norwich	23. 6.99T
G-BWSD	Campbell Cricket PFA G/03-1216			3. 5.96	R.F.G.Moyle	(Falmouth)	
G-BWSF	Sky 180-24 HAFB	022		10. 5.96	A.Bolger	Salisbury	9. 7.97T
G-BWSG	BAC.145 Jet Provost T.5 EEP/JP/988		XW324	13. 5.96	Den Air Aviation Ltd North Weald (Op Aviators Flight Center) (As "XW324" in 6FTS c/s)		22. 9.99P
G-BWSH	Hunting P.84 PAC/W/10159 Jet Provost T.3A		XN498	13. 5.96	Global Aviation Ltd	Binbrook	26. 5.99P
G-BWSI	K & S SA.102.5 Cavalier PFA/01-10624 (Lyc O-235)			18. 4.84	B.W.Shaw Wathstow Farm, Newby Wiske		28. 4.99P
G-BWSJ	Denney Kitfox mk.3 PFA/172-12204 (Rotax 582)			15. 5.96	J.M.Miller	Swanton Morley	2.12.99P
G-BWSK	Enstrom 280FX	2016	ZK-HIR JA7724	16. 5.96	M.A. & M.Gradwell	Barton	11. 7.99
G-BWSL	Sky 77-24 HAFB	004		16. 5.96	The Balloon Co Ltd	Cheltenham	6. 4.99A
G-BWSN	Denney Kitfox mk.3 PFA/172-12141 (Rotax 582)			16. 5.96	W.J.Forrest	(Windsor)	27. 8.99P
G-BWSO	Cameron Apple Sainsbury 90SS HAFB	3915		17. 5.96	Flying Pictures Ltd "Sainsbury's Apple"	Fairoaks	5. 8.99A
G-BWSP	Cameron Carrots Sainsbury 80SS HAFB	3914		17. 5.96	Flying Pictures Ltd "Sainsbury's Carrots"	Fairoaks	13. 7.99A

Regn	Type	C/n	P/I	Date	Owner/operator	Probable Base	CA Expy
G-BWSR	Cameron A-210 HAFB	3700		1. 5.96	Gone With The Wind Ltd	Windermere	20. 3.99T
G-BWST	Sky 200-24 HAFB	036		20. 5.96	S.A.Townley t/a Sky High Leisure	Wrexham	6. 8.99T
G-BWSU	Cameron N-105 HAFB	3848		20. 5.96	A.M.Marten "Wonder Bra"	London SW1	23. 9.99A
G-BWSV	IAV-Bacau Yakovlev Yak-52	877601	DOSAAF 43	20. 5.96	P.Traynor	Wellesbourne Mountford	19. 7.99P
G-BWSW*	IAV-Bacau Yakovlev Yak-52	866807	DOSAAF 88	20. 5.96	R.D.Doughton	(Wellington)	
					t/a Doughton Avn Svs (Cancelled as destroyed 26.2.99)		
G-BWSX	PA-28-236 Dakota II	28-7911130	C-FLMJ N2169V	28. 5.96	C. & C.Bowie	Dunkeswell	7. 7.99
G-BWSY	BAe 125 Srs.800B	258201	G-OCCI G-5-699	28. 5.96	British Aerospace Airbus Ltd	Filton	26. 8.00
G-BWSZ	Montgomerie-Bensen B.8MR (Rotax 582)	PFA G/01-1268		14. 5.96	D.Cawkwell	Goole	6. 1.98P
G-BWTA	HOAC DV-20 Katana	20159	OE-UDV	10. 6.96	Diamond Aircraft Industries GmbH	Woodford	19. 6.99T
G-BWTB	Lindstrand LBL-105A HAFB	374		29. 5.96	Servatruc Ltd	Nottingham	15. 6.99A
G-BWTC	Moravan Zlin Z.242L	0697		2. 8.96	Oxford Aviation Services Ltd	Oxford	20. 8.99T
G-BWTD	Moravan Zlin Z.242L	0698		2. 8.96	Oxford Aviation Services Ltd	Oxford	18. 9.99T
G-BWTE	Cameron O-140 HAFB	3885		30. 5.96	R.J. & A.J.Mansfield	Windermere	21. 7.99T
G-BWTF	Lindstrand Bear SS HAFB	375		3. 6.96	Free Enterprise Balloons Ltd "Mr Biddle" East Leroy, MI, USA		27. 8.97A
G-BWTG	DHC.1 Chipmunk 22	C1/0119	WB671	4. 6.96	G.C.Martin (Epse, Netherlands)		4. 8.00
					t/a Chipmunk 4 Ever Foundation (As "WB671")		
G-BWTH	Robinson R-22 Beta	1767	HB-XYD N4052R	5. 6.96	Sloane Helicopters Ltd	Sywell	10. 6.99T
G-BWTJ	Cameron V-77 HAFB	3917		7. 6.96	A.J.Montgomery	Yeovil	25. 7.97A
G-BWTK	Rotary Air Force RAF 2000 GTX-SE (Subaru EJ22)	PFA G/13-1264		7. 6.96	Terrafirma Services Ltd Lamberhurst Farm, Faversham		5. 6.99P
G-BWTL	ATR-72-202	441	F-WWLG	7.12.95	Cityflyer Express Ltd (Cockerel of Lowicz/Koguty Lowickie t/s)	Gatwick	6.12.98T
G-BWTM	ATR-72-202	470	F-WWED	8. 3.96	Cityflyer Express Ltd (Mountain of the Birds/Benyhone Tartan t/s)	Gatwick	7. 3.99T
G-BWTN	Lindstrand LBL-90A HAFB	357		12. 6.96	Clarks Drainage Ltd	Oakham	7. 7.99A
G-BWTO	DHC.1 Chipmunk 22	C1/0852	WP984	5. 6.96	Skycraft Services Ltd (As "WP984/H")	Little Gransden	3. 6.01
G-BWTP	Montgomerie-Parsons Two-Place Gyroplane	PFA G/08-1276		12. 6.96	J.M.Montgomerie	Maybole, Ayr	
G-BWTR	Slingsby T-61F Venture T.2	1881	XZ561	12. 6.96	P.R.Williams	(Brackley)	
G-BWTU	Lindstrand LBL-77A HAFB	376		17. 6.96	Virgin Airship & Balloon Co Ltd "Land Rover"	Telford	2. 9.99A
G-BWTW	Mooney M.20C	20-1188	EI-CHI N6955V	5. 6.96	R.C.Volkers	(London SW1)	22.10.99
G-BWTY*	Air Command 532 Elite Two-Seat	PFA G/05-1274		14. 6.96	A.J.Unwin (WFU 3.6.97)	Kemble	
G-BWUA	Campbell Cricket	PFA G/03-1248		17. 6.96	R.T.Lancaster	Ash, Hants	
G-BWUB	PA-18S-135 Super Cub (L-21C) (Regd with c/n 18-3786)	18-3986	N786CS	13. 6.96	Caledonian Seaplanes Ltd	Cumbernauld	23. 6.99T
		G-BWUB/SX-AHB/EI-263/I-EIUO/MM54-2586/54-2586					
G-BWUD	Lavochkin La-9	828	(Chinese AF)	14. 6.96	Classic Aviation Ltd (Op The Flying Machine Co) (Dismantled 1.99)	Duxford	
G-BWUE	Hispano HA-1112-M1L	223	N9938	14. 6.96	R.A.Fleming	Breighton	
	(C/n 223 was C4K-155; reported as c/n 172) G-AWHK/C4K-102						
G-BWUF	WSK PZL-Mielec Lim-5 (MiG-17)	1C1211	1211 (Polish AF)	14. 6.96	Classic Aviation Ltd (Op The Flying Machine Co; as "1211"in Korean (?) c/s)	Duxford	AC
G-BWUG	Piper J/5C Cub Cruiser (AE-1)	5-1477	ZK-USN N62073/NC62073/Bu.30274	21. 6.96	W.D.Lincoln (On overhaul 8.97)	Henstridge	
G-BWUH	PA-28-181 Archer III	2843048	N9272E	30. 8.96	R.Paston	Birmingham	19. 9.99
G-BWUJ	Rotorway Exec (RW.162F)	6153		2. 7.96	Southern Helicopters Ltd Street Farm, Bishops Stortford		AC
G-BWUK	Sky 160-24 HAFB	043		2. 7.96	Blagdon Balloons Ltd	Bristol	7. 2.99T
G-BWUM	Sky 105-24 HAFB	038		5. 7.96	P.Stern & F.Kirchberger "Wanninger" Regen/Lam, Germany		28. 7.99
G-BWUN	DHC.1 Chipmunk 22	C1/0253	WD310	5. 7.96	T.Henderson (As "WD310") Upper Broyle Farm, Ringmer		5.11.99
G-BWUP	Europa Avn Europa	PFA/247-12703		3. 7.96	T.J.Harrison	Kemble	22.11.99
G-BWUR	Thunder Ax10-210 Srs.2 HAFB	3910		11. 7.96	T.J.Bucknall	Chester	18. 7.99T
G-BWUS	Sky 65-24 HAFB	040		16. 7.96	N.A.P.Bates	Tunbridge Wells	15.12.99A
G-BWUT	DHC.1 Chipmunk 22	C1/0918	WZ879	4. 6.96	Aero Vintage Ltd (As "WZ879/73") Duxford		3.11.99
G-BWUU	Cameron N-90 HAFB	3954		17. 7.96	South Western Electricity plc	Bristol	16. 7.99A
G-BWUV	DHC.1 Chipmunk 22A	C1/0655	WK640	18. 7.96	P.Ray (As "WK640/C")	Bagby	27. 7.01
G-BWUW	BAC.145 Jet Provost T.5A	EEP/JP/1045	XW423	18. 7.96	Lorch Airways (UK) Ltd (As "XW423/14")	Norwich	AC
G-BWUY	Thunder Ax10-180 HAFB	3646		23. 7.96	D.C.Chipping	Evora, Portugal	22. 7.99T
G-BWUZ	Campbell Cricket (Rotax 582)	PFA G/03-1267		24. 6.96	M.A.Concannon	Birmingham	20.11.97P
G-BWVB	Pietenpol Aircamper (Cont O-200-A)	PFA/47-11777		24. 7.96	M.J.Whatley	White Waltham	16.11.99P
G-BWVC	Jodel D.18	PFA/169-11331		29. 7.96	R.W.J. Cripps	(Spondon, Derby)	

Regn	Type	C/n	P/I	Date	Owner/operator	Probable Base	CA Expy
G-BWVE	Bell 206B JetRanger III	3394	G-BOSX N20681	1. 9.88	Bartlett Industrial Holdings Ltd (Op Lanyonair)	Blackbushe	5. 9.00T
G-BWVF	Pietenpol Aircamper	PFA/47-11936		5. 8.96	R.M.Sharphouse	(Thirsk)	
G-BWVG	Robin HR.200/120B	308		16. 7.96	Air Caernarfon Ltd	Caernarfon	15.10.99T
G-BWVH	Robinson R-44 Astro	0072	SX-HDE (D-HBBT)	10. 9.96	Twinlite Developments Ltd	(Dublin)	19. 9.99T
G-BWVI	Stern ST.80 Balade	PFA/166-11190		7. 8.96	P.E.Barker	Great Barford, Bedford	AC
G-BWVK	Cameron Calling Card 110SS HAFB	3947		12. 8.96	Cameron Balloons Ltd	Calgary, Canada	31. 8.99A
G-BWVL	Cessna 150M	150-77229	N50NA N63286	13. 8.96	Dualworld Ltd	Kemble	23.10.99T
G-BWVM	Colt AA-1050 Gas Free Balloon	3806		14. 8.96	D.A.Gleed	Langley, BC, Canada	3. 9.99A
G-BWVN	Whittaker MW.7	PFA/171-11839		19. 8.96	J.W.May	Bicester	
G-BWVP	Sky 160-24 HAFB	044		21. 8.96	Sky Balloons Ltd	Wrexham	N/E(P)
G-BWVR	Aerostar Yakovlev Yak-52	878202	LY-AKQ DOSAAF 134	27. 8.96	Numberprint Ltd. (As "52")	Crosland Moor	16. 1.99P
G-BWVS	Europa Avn Europa	PFA/247-12686		28. 8.96	D.R.Bishop	(Basingstoke)	
G-BWVT	DHA.82A Tiger Moth	1039	N1350 VH-SNZ/A17-604/VH-AIN/A17-604	27. 8.96	R.Jewitt	(Horley)	
G-BWVU	Cameron O-90 HAFB	3204		28. 8.96	J.Atkinson	Dorchester	N/E(A)
G-BWVV	Jodel D.18 (VW 1834)	PFA/169-12699		29. 8.96	P.Cooper	Sherburn	22.11.99P
G-BWVX	Aerostar Yakovlev Yak-52	866811	LY-AOJ DOSAAF	16. 9.96	C.J.M.Van Den Broek & R.V.De Vries	Hoevenen, Netherlands	28.11.99P
G-BWVY	DHC.1 Chipmunk 22A	C1/0766	WP896	3. 9.96	P.W.Portelli (As "WP896/M")	Audley End	AC
G-BWVZ	DHC.1 Chipmunk 22	C1/0614	WK590	16. 7.96	D.Campion (As "WK590/69")	St.Ghislain, Belgium	26. 9.99
G-BWWA	Ultravia Pelican Club GS (Rotax 912UL)	PFA/165-12242		6. 9.96	E.F.Clapham & N.R.Beale	(Bristol/Leamington Spa)	22.12.99P
G-BWWB	Europa Avn Europa (Rotax 912UL)	PFA/247-12670		9. 9.96	M.G.Dolphin "The Wheelbarrow"	RAF Brize Norton	27. 1.98P
G-BWWC	DH.104 Dove 7	04498	XM223	14. 6.96	Cormack (A/c Svcs) Ltd (As "XM223")	Cumbernauld	AC
G-BWWE	Lindstrand LBL-90A HAFB	410		11. 9.96	B.J.Newman	Rushden, Northants	N/E(T)
G-BWWG	Socata Rallye 235E Gabier	13121	EI-BIF HB-EYT/N344RA	23.10.96	J.McEleney	Buncrana, Ireland	3. 4.00
G-BWWH	Yakovlev Yak-50	853010	LY-ABL LY-XNI/DOSAAF	16. 9.96	De Cadenet Motor Racing Ltd (As "853010")	Little Gransden	1. 3.99P
G-BWWI	Aerospatiale AS.332L Super Puma	2040	OY-HMF	11. 9.96	Bristow Helicopters Ltd	Aberdeen	8.11.99T
G-BWWJ	Hughes 269C (300C)	113-0256	G-BMYZ N8996F	25. 2.87	Dave Nieman Toys Ltd	Milton Common, Oxon	28.10.96
G-BWWK	Hawker Nimrod I	41H-43617	S1581	13. 9.96	Historic Aircraft Collection Ltd (Jersey) (On rebuild)		
G-BWWL	Colt Flying Egg SS HAFB	1813	JA-A0513	19. 9.96	L.V.Mastis	(USA)	11.11.97A
G-BWWN	Isaacs Fury II	PFA/11-10957		23. 9.96	D.H.Pattison (As "K8303")	(Swindon)	
G-BWWP	Rans S-6-116 Coyote II (Rotax 582)	PFA/204A-12648		2.10.96	S.A.Beddus	Cherry Tree Farm, Monewden	20. 8.99P
G-BWWS	Rotary Air Force RAF 2000 GTX-SE	PFA G/13-1277		7.10.96	G.R.Williams	(Blackwood, Gwent)	
G-BWWT	Dornier 328-110	3022	D-CDXO VT-VIG/D-CDHG	12.11.96	Suckling Airways (Luton) Ltd	Luton	12.11.99T
G-BWWU	PA-22-150 Tri-Pacer	22-5002	N7139D	9.10.96	Aerocars Ltd	(Hungerford)	AC
G-BWWW	BAe Jetstream 3102	614	G-31-614	18. 7.83	British Aerospace (Operations) Ltd	Warton	23.10.99A
G-BWWX	Yakovlev Yak-50	853003	LY-AOI DOSAAF	11.10.96	J.L.Pfundt	Hilversum, Netherlands	21.11.00P
G-BWWY	Lindstrand LBL-105A HAFB	411		14.10.96	M.J.Smith	Westow, York	29. 4.99T
G-BWWZ	Denney Kitfox mk.3	PFA/172-13054		15.10.96	K.M.Allan	Eshott	
G-BWXA	Slingsby T-67M-260 Firefly	2236		19. 3.96	Hunting Aviation Ltd	RAF Barkston Heath	27. 6.99T
G-BWXB	Slingsby T-67M-260 Firefly	2237		19. 3.96	Hunting Aviation Ltd	RAF Barkston Heath	17. 7.99T
G-BWXC	Slingsby T-67M-260 Firefly	2238		19. 3.96	Hunting Aviation Ltd	RAF Barkston Heath	28. 7.99T
G-BWXD	Slingsby T-67M-260 Firefly	2239		19. 3.96	Hunting Aviation Ltd	RAF Barkston Heath	15. 8.99T
G-BWXE	Slingsby T-67M-260 Firefly	2240		19. 3.96	Hunting Aviation Ltd	RAF Barkston Heath	28. 8.99T
G-BWXF	Slingsby T-67M-260 Firefly	2241		19. 3.96	Hunting Aviation Ltd	RAF Barkston Heath	5. 9.99T
G-BWXG	Slingsby T-67M-260 Firefly	2242		19. 3.96	Hunting Aviation Ltd	RAF Barkston Heath	23. 9.99T
G-BWXH	Slingsby T-67M-260 Firefly	2243		19. 3.96	Hunting Aviation Ltd	RAF Barkston Heath	20.10.99T
G-BWXI	Slingsby T-67M-260 Firefly	2244		19. 3.96	Hunting Aviation Ltd	RAF Barkston Heath	7.10.99T
G-BWXJ	Slingsby T-67M-260 Firefly	2245		19. 3.96	Hunting Aviation Ltd	RAF Barkston Heath	28.10.99T
G-BWXK	Slingsby T-67M-260 Firefly	2246		19. 3.96	Hunting Aviation Ltd	RAF Barkston Heath	5.11.99T
G-BWXL	Slingsby T-67M-260 Firefly	2247		19. 3.96	Hunting Aviation Ltd	RAF Barkston Heath	20.11.99T
G-BWXM	Slingsby T-67M-260 Firefly	2248		19. 3.96	Hunting Aviation Ltd	RAF Barkston Heath	26.11.99T
G-BWXN	Slingsby T-67M-260 Firefly	2249		19. 3.96	Hunting Aviation Ltd	RAF Barkston Heath	4.12.99T
G-BWXO	Slingsby T-67M-260 Firefly	2250		19. 3.96	Hunting Aviation Ltd	RAF Barkston Heath	15.12.99T
G-BWXP	Slingsby T-67M-260 Firefly	2251		19. 3.96	Hunting Aviation Ltd	RAF Barkston Heath	8. 1.00T
G-BWXR	Slingsby T-67M-260 Firefly	2252		19. 3.96	Hunting Aviation Ltd	RAF Barkston Heath	13. 1.00T
G-BWXS	Slingsby T-67M-260 Firefly	2253		19. 3.96	Hunting Aviation Ltd	RAF Barkston Heath	29. 1.00T
G-BWXT	Slingsby T-67M-260 Firefly	2254		19. 3.96	Hunting Aviation Ltd	RAF Barkston Heath	5. 2.00T

Regn	Type	C/n	P/I	Date	Owner/operator	Probable Base	CA Expy
G-BWXU	Slingsby T-67M-260 Firefly	2255		19. 3.96	Hunting Aviation Ltd RAF Barkston Heath		11. 2.00T
G-BWXV	Slingsby T-67M-260 Firefly	2256		19. 3.96	Hunting Aviation Ltd RAF Barkston Heath		20. 2.00T
G-BWXW	Slingsby T-67M-260 Firefly	2257		19. 3.96	Hunting Aviation Ltd RAF Barkston Heath		27. 2.00T
G-BWXX	Slingsby T-67M-260 Firefly	2258		19. 3.96	Hunting Aviation Ltd RAF Barkston Heath		11. 3.00T
G-BWXY	Slingsby T-67M-260 Firefly	2259		19. 3.96	Hunting Aviation Ltd RAF Barkston Heath		13. 3.00T
G-BWXZ	Slingsby T-67M-260 Firefly	2260		19. 3.96	Hunting Aviation Ltd RAF Barkston Heath		26. 3.00T
G-BWYC	Cameron N-90 HAFB	3994		17.10.96	Cameron Balloons Ltd	Bristol	7. 5.99A
G-BWYD	Europa Avn Europa (Rotax 912UL)	PFA/247-12621		28. 8.96	H.J.Bendiksen	Biggin Hill	3. 6.99P
G-BWYE	Cessna 310R II	310R-1654	F-GBPE (N26369)	6. 9.96	Edinburgh Air Centre Ltd	Edinburgh	9.10.99T
G-BWYG	Cessna 310R II	310R-1580	F-GBMY (N1820E)	28.10.96	R.F.Jones t/a Kissair Aviation	(London SE10)	18.11.00T
G-BWYH	Cessna 310R II	310R-1640	F-GBPC N2634Y	28.10.96	Edinburgh Air Centre Ltd	Edinburgh	31. 3.00T
G-BWYI	Denney Kitfox Mk.3 (Rotax 912)	PFA/172-12143		30.10.96	J.Adamson Beeches Farm, South Scarle		31. 3.99P
G-BWYK	Yakovlev Yak-50	812004	RA-01386 DOSAAF 51	9. 8.96	Titan Airways Ltd	North Weald	17.12.99P
G-BWYL	Cameron A-200 HAFB	3996		30. 9.96	J.M.Stables t/a Aire Valley Balloons	Knaresborough	8. 3.99T
G-BWYM	HOAC DV-20 Katana	20067	D-EWAU	27. 1.97	Diamond Aircraft Industries GmbH Gloucestershire		16. 2.00T
G-BWYN	Cameron O-77 HAFB	1162	G-ODER	13.11.96	W.H.Morgan "Hobo"	Swansea	21. 6.97A
G-BWYO	Sequoia Falco F.8L	PFA/100-10920		7.11.96	N.G.Abbott & J.Copeland (Flamstone Park)		1. 4.99P
G-BWYP	Sky 56-24 HAFB	053		8.11.96	S.A.Townley t/a Sky High Leisure	Wrexham	27.10.98A
G-BWYR	Rans S-6-116 Coyote II (Rotax 912-UL)	PFA/204A-13058		8.11.96	Stephen Palmer Ltd	Swinford, Rugby	16. 2.99P
G-BWYS	Cameron O-120 HAFB	3997		30. 9.96	J.M.Stables t/a Aire Valley Balloons	Knaresborough	8. 3.99T
G-BWYU	Sky 120-24 HAFB	052		13.11.96	R.J.Darkin t/a Bramley Park Garages	St.Ives, Hunts	28. 2.99A
G-BWYW	PBN BN-2B-20 Islander	2293		2.12.96	Britten-Norman Ltd (to PK-?)	Bembridge	AC
G-BWYX	PBN BN-2B-20 Islander	2298		2.12.96	Britten-Norman Ltd	Bembridge	AC
G-BWYY	PBN BN-2B-20 Islander	2299		2.12.96	Britten-Norman Ltd	Bembridge	AC
G-BWYZ	PBN BN-2B-20 Islander	2300		2.12.96	Britten-Norman Ltd	Bembridge	AC
G-BWZA	Europa Avn Europa (Rotax 912UL)	PFA/247-12626		1.11.96	M.C.Costin	Sywell	13. 7.99P
G-BWZD	Light Aero Avid Flyer mk.4	PFA/189-12453		29.11.96	B.Moore	(Keady, Armagh)	
G-BWZE	Hunting Percival P.84 Jet Provost T.3A	PAC/W/6605	XM378	29.11.96	Shoal Ltd (As "XM378")	(Douglas, IOM)	24. 3.99P
G-BWZF	PBN BN-2B-20 Islander	2301		12.12.96	Britten-Norman Ltd	Bembridge	AC
G-BWZG	Robin R.2160	311	F-WZZZ	6.11.96	Sherburn Aero Club Ltd Sherburn-in-Elmet		4. 3.00T
G-BWZI	Agusta A.109A II	7269	OH-HAD N109AK	29.11.96	P.W.Harris Pendley Farm, Aldbury, Tring t/a Pendley Farm		3. 2.00T
G-BWZJ	Cameron A-250 HAFB	4021		2.12.96	Balloon School (International) Ltd t/a Balloon Club of Great Britain Petworth		9. 5.99T
G-BWZK	Cameron A-210 HAFB	4020		2.12.96	Balloon School (International) Ltd t/a Balloon Club of Great Britain Petworth		14.10.99T
G-BWZP	Cameron Home Special 105SS HAFB	4051		6.12.96	Flying Pictures Ltd "Barclays Mortgages"	Fairoaks	3. 3.99A
G-BWZT	Europa Avn Europa (Rotax 912-UL)	PFA/247-12727		9.12.96	A.M.Smyth t/a G-BWZT Group	Crowfield	16. 9.99P
G-BWZU	Lindstrand LBL-90B HAFB	418		12.12.96	K.D.Pierce	Cranbrook, Kent	4. 9.99
G-BWZW	Bell 206B Jet Ranger	12	G-CTEK N7812S	26.11.96	Yorkshire Helicopter Centre Ltd	Mexborough	15. 6.98T
G-BWZX	Aerospatiale AS.332L Super Puma	2120	F-WQDX	12.12.96	Bristow Helicopters Ltd	Aberdeen	5. 5.01T
	G-BWZX/F-WQDX/5V-MCD/5V-TAH/LN-OLE						
G-BWZY	Hughes 269A	95-0378	G-FSDT N269CH/N1336D/64-18066	4.12.96	Katharine B.Elliott	Redhill	13. 5.01
G-BWZZ	Hunting Percival P.84 Jet Provost T.3A	PAC/W/9278	XM470	5. 9.96	Jet Aviation (Northwest) Ltd Manchester (As "XM470")		26. 5.99P

G-BXAA-BXZZ

Regn	Type	C/n	P/I	Date	Owner/operator	Probable Base	CA Expy
G-BXAB	PA-28-161 Warrior II	28-8416054	G-BTGK N4344C	7.10.96	Tindon Ltd	Little Snoring	25. 4.00T
G-BXAC	Rotary Air Force RAF 2000 GTX-SE	PFA G/13-1279		21.11.96	D.C.Fairbrass	Kemble	5. 5.99P
G-BXAD	Cameron Thunder Ax11-225 Srs.2 HAFB	4052		18.12.96	C.E.Wood	Witham	25. 2.99T
G-BXAF	Pitts S-1D Special (Lyc O-360)	PFA/09-12258		6.12.96	F.Sharples	Sandown	25.11.99P
G-BXAH	Piel CP.301A Emeraude (Cont C90)	AB.422	D-EBAH	29.10.96	G.E.Valler	(Stafford)	26. 5.99P
G-BXAI	Cameron Colt 120A HAFB	4056		20.12.96	E.F. & R.F.Casswell	Maidstone	11. 1.99T
G-BXAJ	Lindstrand LBL-14A HAFB	425		23.12.96	Oscair Project AB	Taby, Sweden	
G-BXAK	IAV-Bacau Yakovlev Yak-52	811508	LY-ASC DOSAAF	23.12.96	S.L.Flannigan	Compton Abbas	26. 3.99P
G-BXAL	Cameron Bertie Bassett 90SS HAFB	4034		13. 1.97	Trebor Bassett Ltd	Howden, Yorks	13. 7.99A
G-BXAM	Cameron N-90 HAFB	4035		13. 1.97	Trebor Bassett Ltd	Howden, Yorks	9. 3.99A
G-BXAN	Scheibe SF-25C Falke 1700	44299	D-KDGQ	13. 1.97	M.J.Davies & E.R.Boyle t/a C Falke Syndicate	Winthorpe	15.10.00
G-BXAO	Jabiru SK (Jabiru 2200A)	PFA/274-13066		14. 1.97	P.J.Thompson (Damaged Ledicot nr Shobdon 3.5.98)	(Gaerwen)	23. 4.99P
G-BXAP	Cameron Hard Hat 90SS HAFB	4045		16. 1.97	Norwest Holst Ltd & C.S.Perceval	Watford/Great Missenden	15. 5.99A
G-BXAR	BAe 146 RJ100	E-3298	G-6-298	27. 3.97	Cityflyer Express Ltd (Delftblue Daybreak t/s)	Gatwick	29. 3.00T
G-BXAS	BAe 146 RJ100	E-3301	G-6-301	23. 4.97	Cityflyer Express Ltd (Animals and Trees/Kg-Oocoan-Naka-Hiian-Thee-E t/s)	Gatwick	29. 4.00T
G-BXAU	Pitts S-1 Special (Lyc O-320)	GHG.9	N9GG	22. 1.97	D.Dobson	Deenethorpe	29. 4.99P
G-BXAV	Aerostar Yakovlev Yak-52	9111608	RA-01325 DOSAAF 73	24. 1.97	G.M.Sharp (As "DOSAAF 72")	North Weald	18. 2.99P
G-BXAX	Cameron N-77 HAFB	2010		25. 5.89	Flying Pictures Ltd "Citroen"	Fairoaks	21.11.96A
G-BXAY	Bell 206B Jet Ranger III	3946	N85EA N521RC/N3210D	24. 1.97	Mainland Car Deliveries Ltd	Bootle	21. 7.00T
G-BXBA	Cameron A-210 HAFB	4072		10. 1.97	Reach For The Sky Ltd	Guildford	8. 3.99T
G-BXBB	PA-20-150 Pacer	20-959	EC-AOZ N1133C	24. 1.97	M.E.R.Coghlan (On rebuild)	Thornicombe, Dorset	
G-BXBC	Anderson EA-1 Kingfisher Amphibian	PFA/132-11302		28. 1.97	S.Bichan	(Stromness, Orkney)	
G-BXBD	CASA I-131 Jungmann	1052	E3B-317	28. 1.97	B.Childs & B.L.Robinson	(Bristol/Clevedon)	
	(Identity uncertain as another Jungmann "E3B-317" is displayed in Musee de Jean Tinguely, Basel, Switzerland)						
G-BXBG	Cameron A-275 HAFB	4023		28. 1.97	M.L.Gabb	Alcester	16. 2.99T
G-BXBH	Hunting Percival P.84 Jet Provost T.3A	XM365 PAC/W/9241		29. 1.97	G-BXBH Provost Ltd (As "XM365")	(Douglas, IOM)	8. 6.99P
G-BXBI	Hunting Percival P.84 Jet Provost T.3A	XN510 PAC/W/11799		29. 1.97	Global Aviation Ltd	Binbrook	
G-BXBJ	Hunting Percival P.84 Jet Provost T.3A	XN470 PAC/W/10149		29. 1.97	Global Aviation Ltd	Binbrook	
G-BXBK	Mudry/CAARP CAP.10B	17	N170RC French AF "307-SO"	30. 1.97	S.Skipworth	(Newbury)	24. 6.00
G-BXBL	Lindstrand LBL-240A HAFB	317		31. 1.97	J.Fenton t/a Firefly Balloon Promotions	Preston	14. 3.99T
G-BXBM	Cameron O-105 HAFB	3990		31. 1.97	P.Spellward "Buhab's Five" t/a Bristol University Hot Air Ballooning Society	Bristol	13. 3.99A
G-BXBN	Rans S-6-116 Coyote II	PFA/204A-13062		31. 1.97	W.S.Long	Bagby	29. 4.99P
G-BXBO	DH.82A Tiger Moth (DHA rebuild c/n T289)	82360	(D-EAJO) VH-ALC/N9259	3. 2.97	Bavarian Balloon Co Ltd	(Germany)	AC
G-BXBP	Denney Kitfox mk.2	PFA/172-12149		3. 2.97	G.S.Adams	(Dungannon, Co.Tyrone)	
G-BXBR	Cameron A-120 HAFB	1983	SE-ZDY	4. 2.97	M.G.Barlow	Skipton	
G-BXBS	Cameron V-90 HAFB	4096		6. 2.97	D.C.Boxall "Warners"	Bristol	16. 5.99A
G-BXBT	Aerospatiale AS.355F1 Twin Squirrel	5262	G-TMMC G-JLCO	11. 2.97	McAlpine Helicopters Ltd	Oxford	28. 9.01T
G-BXBU	Mudry/CAARP CAP.10B	103	N173RC French AF	11. 2.97	T.J.Caton	Thurrock	24. 6.00
G-BXBV	ATR-42-300	245	TS-LBA (EI-BYQ)/F-WWET	14. 5.97	Gill Aviation Ltd	Newcastle	21. 5.00T
G-BXBW	HOAC DV-20 Katana	20148	D-ESHM	25. 2.97	Diamond Aircraft Industries GmbH (Op Euroflyers)	Blackbushe	31. 3.00T
G-BXBY	Cameron A-105 HAFB	4077		13. 2.97	S.P.Watkins	Bristol	26. 3.99T
G-BXBZ	WSK PZL-104 Wilga 80 (C/n quoted officially as CF21930941)	CF21910941	EC-GDA ZK-PZQ	13. 2.97	RCR Aviation Ltd	Thruxton	25. 6.00
G-BXCA	Hapi Cygnet SF-2A (Rotax 912-UL)	PFA/182-12921		22. 1.97	G.E.Collard	Popham	13. 8.99P

Regn	Type	C/n	P/I	Date	Owner/operator	Probable Base	CA Expy
G-BXCB	Agusta A.109A II	7347	F-GJSH	17. 2.97	Vulture Ventures Ltd	Southampton	28. 4.00T
			G-ISEB/G-IADT/G-HBCA				
G-BXCC	PA-28-201T Turbo Dakota	28-7921068	D-EKBM	19. 2.97	K.L.Cropp	Elmsett	3. 4.00T
			N2855A				
G-BXCD	Team Minimax 91A	PFA/186-12393		18. 2.97	R.Davies	(London NW7)	13.10.99P
G-BXCG	CEA Jodel DR.250/160 Capitaine	60 & PFA/299-13146	D-EHGG	22. 5.97	J.M.Scott t/a G-BXCG Group	Evesham	13. 7.99P
G-BXCH	Europa Avn Europa (Rotax 912UL)	PFA/247-12980		19. 2.97	D.M.Stevens	Haverfordwest	11.10.99P
G-BXCJ	Campbell Cricket	PFA G/03-1177		24. 2.97	R.A.Friend	(Southsea)	17. 2.99P
G-BXCK	Cameron Douglas-Lurpak Butterman 110SS HAFB	4076		25. 2.97	Flying Pictures Ltd "Douglas-Lurpak Butter"	Fairoaks	20. 5.99A
G-BXCL	Montgomerie Bensen B.8MR	PFA G/01-1287		26. 2.97	A.V.Francis	(Dunstable)	24. 8.99P
G-BXCM	Lindstrand LBL-150A HAFB	443		26. 2.97	Blown Away (UK) Ltd	Walsall	29. 4.99T
G-BXCN	Sky 105-24 HAFB	047		27. 2.97	Capricorn Balloons Ltd	Loughborough	16. 3.98T
G-BXCO	Colt 120A HAFB	4086		3. 3.97	G.C.Ludlow	Hythe, Kent	19. 7.99T
G-BXCP	DHC.1 Chipmunk 22	C1/0744	WP859	27. 2.97	S.Conlan	(Kildare, Co.Kildare)	
G-BXCR	DHC.1 Chipmunk 22	C1/0796	WP920	3. 3.97	V.S.E.Norman	Rendcomb	15. 6.01
G-BXCS	Cameron N-90 HAFB	4122		4. 3.97	Flying Pictures Ltd "Lurpak"	Fairoaks	19. 3.99A
G-BXCT	DHC.1 Chipmunk 22	C1/0145	WB697	3. 3.97	Wickenby Aviation Ltd (As "WB697")	Wickenby	19. 5.00T
G-BXCU	Rans S-6-116 Coyote II (Rotax 912UL)	PFA/204A-13105		6. 3.97	M.R.McNeil	Breighton	22. 6.99P
G-BXCV	DHC.1 Chipmunk 22	C1/0807	WP929	3. 3.97	Propshop Ltd (As "WP929/F")	Duxford	6.10.00T
G-BXCW	Denney Kitfox mk.3	PFA/172-12619		6. 3.97	M.J.Blanchard	(Swanage)	
G-BXCX	Robinson R-22 Beta	0885	G-MFHL	17. 1.97	Plane Talking Ltd	Blackbushe	10. 4.01T
G-BXCY	Grumman-American AA-5A Cheetah	AA5A-0646	N26686	31. 1.97	Plane Talking Ltd	Elstree	13. 2.00T
G-BXCZ	Gulfstream AA-5A Cheetah	AA5A-0876	N27152	31. 1.97	Plane Talking Ltd	Elstree	25. 2.00T
G-BXDA	DHC.1 Chipmunk 22	C1/0747	WP860	7. 3.97	S.R.Cleary (As "WP860/6")	Cumbernauld	17. 6.00
G-BXDB	Cessna U206F Stationair	U206-02233	G-BMNZ	18.12.96	Tindon Ltd	Little Snoring	4. 8.01
			F-BVJT/N1519U				
G-BXDC	Montgomerie-Bensen B.8MR	PFA G/01-1219		5. 2.97	D.L.Smerdon	Middlesbrough	
G-BXDD	Rotary Air Force RAF 2000 GTX-SE (Subaru EJ22)	PFA G/13-1284		9. 1.97	R.M.Savage t/a Roger Savage (Photography)	Great Orton	27. 5.01P
G-BXDE	Rotary Air Force RAF 2000 GTX-SE	PFA G/13-1280		14. 1.97	A.McRedie	(Lazonby, Penrith)	
G-BXDF	Beechcraft 95-B55 Baron	TC-2011	SE-IXG	7. 3.97	Malcolm (UK) Ltd	Halfpenny Green	8. 4.00
			OY-ASB				
G-BXDG	DHC.1 Chipmunk 22	C1/0644	WK630	7. 3.97	R.E.Dagless (As "WK630")	Yaxham, Dereham	15. 9.00
G-BXDH	DHC.1 Chipmunk 22	C1/0270	WD331	10. 3.97	Victory Workwear Ltd (As "WD331")	Booker	21. 1.01P
G-BXDI	DHC.1 Chipmunk 22	C1/0312	WD373	10. 3.97	J.R.Gore (As "WD373/12" in RAF c/s)	Perth	10. 8.00
G-BXDL	Hunting Percival P.84 Jet Provost T.3A	8983M PAC/W/9286	XM478	18. 3.97	Jet Provost Promotions Ltd	North Weald	12.11.99P
G-BXDM	DHC.1 Chipmunk 22	C1/0723	WP840	28. 2.97	G.M.Turner (As "WP840/9")	RAF Halton	5. 6.00T
G-BXDN	DHC.1 Chipmunk 22	C1/0618	WK609	18. 3.97	W.D.Lowe & L.A.Edwards (As "WK609")	Booker	2. 9.00
G-BXDO	Rutan Cozy	PFA/159-12032		21. 3.97	C.R.Blackburn	(Kirk Michael, IoM)	
G-BXDP	DHC.1 Chipmunk 22	C1/0659	WK642	27. 2.97	J.S.J.Valentine & J.P.Conlan	(Ballytore/Kildare, Co.Kildare)	9. 7.00
G-BXDR	Lindstrand LBL-77A HAFB	441		25. 3.97	British Telecommunications plc	(Thatcham, Berks)	19. 4.98A
G-BXDT	Robin HR.200/120B	315		25. 3.97	Multiflight Ltd	Leeds-Bradford	5. 6.00T
G-BXDU	Aero Designs Pulsar	PFA/202-11991		25. 3.97	M.P.Board	(London E4)	
G-BXDV	Sky 105-24 HAFB	049		26. 3.97	J.Skinner	Maidstone	2. 7.99T
G-BXDW	Sky 120-24 HAFB	059		26. 3.97	M. & S.M.Sarti	Fowey	14. 7.99T
G-BXDX	Lindstrand LBL-77M HAFB	452		26. 3.97	International Balloons Ltd	(Oswestry)	23. 3.99A
G-BXDY	Europa Avn Europa (Rotax 912UL)	PFA/247-12914		27. 3.97	D.G. & S.Watts "The Rocketeer"	Rochester	23.11.99P
G-BXDZ	Lindstrand LBL-105A HAFB	437		4. 4.97	M.A.Webb	Yarcombe, Honiton	14. 4.99A
G-BXEA	Rotary Air Force RAF 2000 GTX-SE (Subaru EJ22)	PFA G/13-1270		2. 4.97	R.Firth	Netherthorpe	10.12.99P
G-BXEB	Rotary Air Force RAF 2000 GTX-SE (Subaru EJ22)	PFA G/13-1285		2. 4.97	Penny Hydraulics Ltd	Chesterfield	22.12.99P
G-BXEC	DHC.1 Chipmunk 22	C1/0647	WK633	3. 4.97	D.C.Budd t/a Mad F/Grp (As "WK633")	Gamston	27. 4.00
G-BXEE	Enstrom 280C Shark	1117	OH-HAN	9. 4.97	S.T.Raby	Grange Farm, Woodwalton	7. 7.00
			N336AT				
G-BXEF	Europa Avn Europa	PFA/247-12790		7. 4.97	C. & W.P.Busuttil-Reynaud	(Emsworth, Hants)	
G-BXEG	ATR-42-320	329	ZS-NKY	12. 4.95	Cityflyer Express Ltd	Gatwick	11. 4.99T
			F-WQAB/F-GKNE/F-WWLO				

Regn	Type	C/n	P/I	Date	Owner/operator	Probable Base	CA Expy
G-BXEJ	VPM M16 Tandem Trainer (Arrow GT 1000)	D-9302	D-MIFF	8. 4.97	N.H.Collins Alrewas, Derby t/a AES Radionic Surveillance Systems		14. 7.98P
G-BXEL	MDH MD-500N	LN.059	N5207E TC-HIC/N5207E	10. 4.97	Ford Helicopters Ltd Dallas, Texas, USA		
G-BXEM	Campbell Cricket mk.4	PFA G/03-1282		11. 4.97	D.M.Bracken (Port Laoise, Ireland)		3. 3.99P
G-BXEN	Cameron N-105 HAFB	4090		11. 4.97	G.Aimo Mondovi, Italy		2.11.99A
G-BXEP	Lindstrand LBL-14M HAFB	460		14. 4.97	Lindstrand Balloons Ltd Oswestry		2. 4.99A
G-BXER	PA-46-350P Malibu Mirage	4636110		21. 7.97	Sunseeker Sales (UK) Ltd Bournemouth		6. 8.00
G-BXES	Hunting Percival P.66 Pembroke C.1 (Regd with c/n PAC/W/3032)	P66/101	N4234C 9042M/XL954	14. 4.97	Atlantic Air Transport Ltd Coventry		AC
G-BXET	PA-38-112 Tomahawk	38-80A0028	N25089	14. 4.97	APB Leasing Ltd Welshpool		AC
G-BXEX	PA-28-181 Cherokee Archer II	28-7790463	N3562Q	16. 4.97	Tunjet Ltd. Denham		12. 5.00T
G-BXEY	Colt AS-105GD Hot-Air Airship	3936		15. 4.97	D.Mayer Neidenstein, Germany		17. 8.99A
G-BXEZ	Cessna 182P Skylane II (Reims assembled with c/n 0054)	182-64344	OH-CHJ N1479M	16. 4.97	Transport Command Ltd Shoreham		25. 8.00T
G-BXFB	Pitts S-1 Special	9543	N77ZZ	16. 4.97	D.Dobson Deenethorpe		3. 1.00P
G-BXFC	Jodel D.18	PFA/169-11322		17. 4.97	B.S.Godbold (Sandy)		
G-BXFD	Enstrom 280C Shark	1084	N88MD N632H	18. 4.97	A.Smithson Weymouth		24. 7.00
G-BXFE	Mudry/CAARP CAP.10B	135	N175RC French AF	18. 4.97	R.W.H.Cole Spilsted Farm, Sedlescombe t/a Cole Aviation		14. 5.01
G-BXFG	Europa Avn Europa	PFA/247-12500		21. 4.97	A.Rawicz-Szczerbo (Barnstaple)		
G-BXFI	Hawker Hunter T.7	41H-670815	WV372	24. 4.97	Fox-One Ltd Kemble (As "WV372/R" in RAF c/s)		13. 9.99P
G-BXFK	CFM Streak Shadow (Rotax 582)	PFA/206-12329		24. 4.97	D.Adcock Priory Farm, Tibenham		5. 8.98P
G-BXFN	Cameron Colt 77A HAFB	4145		25. 4.97	Cameron Balloons Ltd Bristol		13. 6.99A
G-BXFP	BAC.167 Strikemaster mk.87	PS.71	OJ5 Kenyan AF 602/G-27-192	29. 4.97	C.J.& S.M.Thompson North Weald (As "NZ6361" in RNZAF c/s)		6. 5.99P
G-BXFR	BAC.167 Strikemaster mk.87	PS.73	OJ9 Kenyan AF 604/G-27-194	29. 4.97	Global Aviation Ltd Binbrook		
G-BXFS	BAC.167 Strikemaster mk.87	PS.74	OJ10 Kenyan AF 605/G-27-195	29. 4.97	Gone Flying Ltd North Weald		
G-BXFU	BAC.167 Strikemaster mk.83 (Regd as c/n "805")	PS.158	OJ1 ZG805/Kuwait AF 110/G-27-151	29. 4.97	Global Aviation Ltd Binbrook		6.11.99P
G-BXFV	BAC.167 Strikemaster mk.83 (Regd as c/n "806")	PS.162	OJ7 ZG809/Kuwait AF 114/G-27-155	29. 4.97	Global Aviation Ltd Binbrook		23. 2.99P
G-BXFX	BAC.167 Strikemaster mk.83 (Regd as c/n "809")	PS.167	OJ8 ZG811/Kuwait AF 119/G-27-188	29. 4.97	Global Aviation Ltd Binbrook		23.12.99P
G-BXFY	Cameron Bierkrug 90SS HAFB	4133		29. 4.97	Cameron Balloons Ltd Bristol		25. 5.99A
G-BXFZ	Sky 65-24 HAFB	065		22. 4.97	Aerial Promotions Ltd Cannock		14. 5.99A
G-BXGA	Eurocopter AS.350B2 Ecureuil	2493	OO-RCH OO-XCH/F-WZFX	30. 4.97	PLM Dollar Group Ltd. Inverness		27. 8.00T
G-BXGC	Cameron N-105 HAFB	4137		6. 5.97	R.G.Stevenson Bath "The Royal Crescent Hotel" (Op Ascent Balloons)		2. 6.99T
G-BXGD	Sky 90-24 HAFB	067		6. 5.97	Servo & Electronic Sales Ltd Lydd		2. 6.99A
G-BXGE	Cessna 152 II	152-82700	N89283	8. 5.97	APB Leasing Ltd Welshpool		16. 7.00T
G-BXGG	Europa Avn Europa	PFA/247-12803		29. 4.97	B.W.Faulkner (Godalming)		6. 9.99P
G-BXGH	Diamond DA-20-A1 Katana	10151		20. 5.97	Diamond Aircraft Industries GmbH Norwich		11. 6.00T
G-BXGI	Diamond HK-36TTC Super Dimona	36543	OE-UHK	7. 5.97	T.Miller t/a Enstone Flying Club Enstone		18. 6.00T
G-BXGK	Lindstrand LBL-203M HAFB	468		12. 5.97	Lindstrand Balloons Ltd Oswestry		
G-BXGL	DHC.1 Chipmunk 22	C1/0924	WZ884	12. 5.97	Airways Aero Associations Ltd Booker (Op British Airways Flying Club as "WZ884")		11. 9.00T
G-BXGM	DHC.1 Chipmunk 22	C1/0806	WP928	9. 5.97	M.A.Petrie (As "WP928") (Uckfield)		28.10.00
G-BXGO	DHC.1 Chipmunk 22	C1/0097	WB654	13. 5.97	A.Judd t/a Trees Group Booker (As "WB654")		18. 9.00
G-BXGP	DHC.1 Chipmunk 22	C1/0927	WZ882	12. 5.97	J.Pote Eaglescott t/a Eaglescott Chipmunk Group (As "WZ882/K")		18. 6.01T
G-BXGS	Rotary Air Force RAF 2000 GTX-SE (Subaru EJ22)	PFA G/13-1290		14. 5.97	C.R.Gordon (Cupar)		12. 8.99P
G-BXGT	III Sky Arrow 650T (Rotax 912-UL)	PFA/298-13085		7. 5.97	Sky Arrow (Kits) UK Ltd Old Sarum		29. 6.99P
G-BXGV	Cessna 172R Skyhawk II	172-80240	N9300F	7. 1.98	Grandfort Properties Ltd Elstree		1.12.01T
G-BXGW	Robin HR.200/120B	317		16. 5.97	Multiflight Ltd Leeds-Bradford (Op Multiflight Flying Club)		2.10.00T
G-BXGX	DHC.1 Chipmunk 22	C1/0609	WK586	19. 5.97	Interflight (Air Charter) Ltd Blackbushe		3. 9.00
G-BXGY	Cameron V-65 HAFB	4125		18. 4.97	Gone With The Wind Ltd Hungerford		8. 8.99A
G-BXGZ	Stemme S-10V	14-023	D-KSTE EC-GGD/D-KGDF	18. 8.97	D.B.Smith Aboyne		25. 8.00
G-BXHA	DHC.1 Chipmunk 22	C1/0801	WP925	20. 5.97	A.J.Keeling White Waltham (As "WP925/C" in Army c/s)		16. 9.00
G-BXHD	Beechcraft 76 Duchess	ME-284	OY-ARM N223JC	22. 5.97	Liddell Aircraft Ltd Bournemouth		24. 7.00T
G-BXHE	Lindstrand LBL-105A HAFB	459		23. 5.97	Independent Insurance Co Ltd (London EC3)		25. 3.99T
G-BXHF	DHC.1 Chipmunk 22	C1/0808	WP930	28. 5.97	R.Beresford (Caterham)		28. 1.01

Regn	Type	C/n	P/I	Date	Owner/operator	Probable Base	CA Expy
G-BXHH	Grumman-American AA-5A Cheetah	N9705U	3. 6.97	M.G.Greenslade	Biggin Hill	5. 6.00T
		AA5A-0105			t/a Oaklands Flying		
G-BXHI	Hughes 269C	77-0616	G-GBHH	18. 6.97	Dragon Helicopter Services Ltd	Redhill	13.10.99T
		TF-HRH/TF-HHO/N45CD/N9250F/(N51CC)			t/a Redhill Helicopter Centre		
G-BXHJ	Hapi Cygnet SF-2A	PFA/182-12159		29. 5.97	I.J.Smith	(Uttoxeter)	
G-BXHL	Sky 77-24 HAFB	055		29. 5.97	R.A.Messenger	Melksham	29. 7.99
G-BXHM	Lindstrand LBL-25A	466		30. 5.97	Virgin Balloon & Airship Co Ltd	Telford	22. 7.99A
	Cloudhopper HAFB				"Bud Light"		
G-BXHN	Lindstrand Budweiser Can SS HAFB 465			30. 5.97	Virgin Balloon & Airship Co Ltd	Telford	2. 9.98A
					"Budweiser"		
G-BXHO	Lindstrand Telewest Sphere SS HAFB			30. 5.97	Flying Pictures Ltd	Fairoaks	20. 7.99A
		474			"Telewest"		
G-BXHP	Lindstrand LBL-105A HAFB	458		30. 5.97	Flying Pictures Ltd	Fairoaks	25. 6.99A
					"Britannia"		
G-BXHR	Stemme S-10V	14-030		23. 7.97	J.H.Rutherford	Teesside	12. 8.00
G-BXHT	Bushby-Long Midget Mustang			3. 6.97	P.P.Chapman	(Sevenoaks)	
		PFA/168-13077					
G-BXHU	Campbell Cricket mk.6	PFA G/16-1292		3. 6.97	P.C.Lovegrove	Didcot	
G-BXHY	Europa Avn Europa	PFA/247-12514		6. 6.97	A.L.Thorne & B.Lewis	White Waltham	17. 2.99P
					t/a Jupiter F/Grp		
G-BXHZ	VS 361 Spitfire HF.IX	CBAF.10164	SAAF	9. 6.97	A.G.Dunkerley	(Bury)	
			SM520		(On rebuild in Oxfordshire 6.97)		
G-BXIA	DHC.1 Chipmunk 22	C1/0056	WB615	9. 6.97	W.Askew, G.Bullock	Blackpool	16. 3.01T
					& C.Duckett t/a Dales Aviation (As "WB615/E")		
G-BXIB	Bell 206L-3 Long Ranger	51300	EC-EQQ	9. 6.97	Aeromega Ltd	Stapleford	2. 7.00T
G-BXIC	Cameron A-275 HAFB	4162		9. 6.97	Southern Flight Co Ltd	Winchester	16. 6.99T
G-BXID	IAV-Bacau Yakovlev Yak-52	888802	LY-ALG	10. 6.97	L.F.Clayton	Wellesbourne Mountford	13. 1.00P
			DOSAAF 74		(As "DOSAAF 74")		
G-BXIE	Cameron Colt 77B HAFB	4181		11. 6.97	The Aerial Display Co Ltd	Looe	30. 7.99A
G-BXIF	PA-28-181 Cherokee Archer II		PH-SWM	12. 6.97	Piper Flight Ltd	Kemble	9. 7.00T
		28-7690404	OO-HAY/N6827J				
G-BXIG	Zenair CH-701 STOL	PFA/187-12065		16. 6.97	A.J.Perry	(Cranleigh, Surrey)	
G-BXIH	Sky 200-24 HAFB	076		16. 6.97	G.C.Ludlow	Hythe	19. 7.99T
G-BXII	Europa Avn Europa	PFA/247-12812		30. 4.97	D.A.McFadyean	(Alvechurch, Birmingham)	
G-BXIJ	Europa Avn Europa	PFA/247-12698		16. 6.97	D.G. & E.A.Bligh	Inverness	6. 5.99P
G-BXIM	DHC.1 Chipmunk 22	C1/0548	WK512	13. 5.97	P.R.Joshua & A.B.Ascroft		
					(As "WK512/A")	RAF Brize Norton	1. 7.00
G-BXIO	SAN Jodel DR.1050M Excellance	493	F-BNIO	16. 5.97	D.N.K. & M.A.Symon	Cumbernauld	1. 7.01
G-BXIT	Zebedee V-31 HAFB	Z1/3999		8. 5.97	P.J.Bish	Hungerford	
					t/a Zebedee Balloon Service		
G-BXIV	Agusta A.109A	7135	F-GERU	13. 6.97	Castle Air Charters Ltd		
			HB-XOK/D-HFZF			Trebrown, Liskeard	20.10.01T
G-BXIW	Sky 105-24 HAFB	073		24. 6.97	L.A.Watts	Pangbourne, Reading	26. 6.98
G-BXIX	VPM M-16 Tandem Trainer			13. 6.97	D.Beevers	Pocklington	12. 7.99P
		PFA G/12-1292					
G-BXIY	Blake Bluetit	01	BAPC37	26. 6.97	The Shuttleworth Trust	Old Warden	
	(Gnat 32hp)			(Pre-war composite from Spartans G-AAGN/G-AAJB & Avro 504K; on rebuild 3.96)			
G-BXIZ	Lindstrand LBL-31A HAFB	476		3. 7.97	Hyundai Car (UK) Ltd	High Wycombe	23. 7.99A
G-BXJA	Cessna 402B	402B-0356	N5753M	17. 7.97	Air Ward Ltd	Edinburgh	24. 8.00T
			XA-RFK/N5753M		(Op Edinburgh Air Centre)		
G-BXJB	IAV-Bacau Yakovlev Yak-52	877403	LY-ABR	30. 6.97	D.J.Young & H.Wheldon "15"(Newton Green)		26.11.98P
			DOSAAF 15		t/a Aero Anglia		
G-BXJC	Cameron A-210 HAFB	4191		2. 7.97	Balloon School (International) Ltd		
					t/a British School of Ballooning Petworth		25. 7.99T
G-BXJD	PA-28-180 Cherokee C	28-4215	OY-BBZ	27. 6.97	BCT Aircraft Lsg Ltd	(Chesterfield)	31. 7.00T
G-BXJG	Lindstrand LBL-105B HAFB	478		11. 7.97	C.E.Wood	Witham	20. 7.99T
G-BXJH	Cameron N-42 HAFB	4194		15. 7.97	Flying Pictures Ltd	Fairoaks	26. 7.99A
					"Unipart"		
G-BXJI	Tri-R Kis	PFA/239-12573		2. 7.97	R.M.Wakeford	(Glasgow)	
G-BXJJ	PA-28-161 Cadet	2841200	G-GFCC	26. 6.97	Plane Talking Ltd	Denham	7.12.01T
			N9189N				
G-BXJK	Aerospatiale SA.341G Gazelle 1	1417	F-GEHC	30. 6.97	R.A.Kingston	Sandling, Hythe	11. 8.00
			N341AT/N49536				
G-BXJL	Cameron Real Fruit 90SS HAFB	4172		15. 7.97	Cameron Balloons Ltd	(Canada)	24. 8.99A
G-BXJM	Cessna 152 II	152-82380	OO-HOQ	15. 7.97	E.Alexander	(Braintree)	30. 7.00T
			F-GHOQ/N68797				
G-BXJO	Cameron O-90 HAFB	4190		16. 7.97	W.I. & C.Hooker	Nottingham	6. 7.99T
G-BXJP	Cameron C-80 HAFB	4171		17. 7.97	AR Cobaleno Pasta Fresca SRL		
						Perugia, Italy	18. 7.99A
G-BXJS	Schempp-Hirth Janus CM	35/265	OH-819	7. 7.97	R.A.Hall t/a Janus Syndicate	Enstone	17. 8.00
G-BXJT	Sky 90-24 HAFB	072		18. 7.97	Sky Operations Ltd	Oswestry	24. 7.98A
G-BXJU	Sky 90-24 HAFB	077		18. 7.97	Sky Operations Ltd	Oswestry	24. 7.98A
G-BXJV	Dimona DA-20-A1 Katana	10152		23. 7.97	Tayside Aviation Ltd	Perth	29. 7.00T
G-BXJW	Dimona DA-20-A1 Katana	10211	(OE-)	23. 7.97	Tayside Aviation Ltd	Perth	29. 7.00T
			N811CH				

Regn	Type	C/n	P/I	Date	Owner/operator	Probable Base	CA Expy
G-BXJY	Van's RV-6	PFA/181-12447		23. 7.97	D.J.Sharland	Popham	5. 5.99P
G-BXJZ	Cameron C-60 HAFB	4168		23. 7.97	R.S.Mohr	Chippenham	9. 9.98A
G-BXKC	Airbus A.320-214	730	F-WWBQ	15.12.97	Flying Colours Airlines Ltd	Manchester	14.12.00T
G-BXKD	Airbus A.320-214	735	F-WWBV	17.12.97	Flying Colours Airlines Ltd	Manchester	16.12.00T
G-BXKF	Hawker Hunter T.7 (Regd with c/n 41H-003315)	HABL-003314	8676M XL577	28. 7.97	R.F.Harvey (As "XL577")	Kemble	
G-BXKH	Cameron Colt Sparkasse Box 90SS HAFB	4161		4. 8.97	Westfalisch-Lippischer Sparkassen und Giroverband Münster, Germany		30. 8.99A
G-BXKI	Robinson R-44 Astro	0220	OY-HEK	15. 8.97	A.D.Russell	Bourn	25. 8 00
G-BXKJ	Cameron A-275 HAFB	4215		4. 8.97	The Balloon Club Ltd	Bristol	27. 8.01T
G-BXKK	Cameron Golf Ball 90SS HAFB	4054		4. 8.97	Longbreak Ltd Greenwood, Mi., USA		30. 9.99A
G-BXKL	Bell 206B Jet Ranger III	3006	N5735Y	8.10.97	Swattons Aviation Ltd	Andover	18.11.00T
G-BXKM	Rotary Air Force RAF 2000 GTX-SE	PFA G/13-1291		5. 8.97	J.R.Huggins Lamberhurst Farm, Faversham		20. 5.99P
G-BXKO	Sky 65-24 HAFB	083		11. 8.97	P.J.Beglan Orliac, Belves, France		1. 8.99
G-BXKU	Cameron Colt AS-120 mk.II Hot Air Airship	4165		15. 8.97	D.C.Chipping Evora, Portugal		26.11.99A
G-BXKW	Slingsby T-67M Firefly 200	2061	VR-HZS HKG-13/G-7-129	15. 8.97	W.R.Tandy	Dunstable	23.10.00T
G-BXKX	Auster 5	803	D-EMXA HB-EOK/MS938	19. 8.97	A.L.Jubb	Rochester	19. 4.01
G-BXKY	Cameron DP-90 Hot Air Airship	4198		19. 8.97	Cameron Balloons Ltd "Oceania" (Op Bruno Schwartz) Rio de Janeiro, Brazil		
G-BXLA	Robinson R-22 Beta	1368	SE-HVX N4014G	12. 8.97	Bristow Helicopters Ltd	Redhill	18. 9.00T
G-BXLC	Sky 120-24 HAFB	085		20. 8.97	Sky Balloons Ltd	Wrexham	5.10.99A
G-BXLD	Cameron Colt 120A HAFB	4188		26. 8.97	Cameron Balloons Ltd	Bristol	14. 2.99A
G-BXLF	Lindstrand LBL-90A HAFB	487		3. 9.97	R. & J.Moffatt t/a Variohm Components	Towcester	18.19.99A
G-BXLG	Cameron C-80 HAFB	4250		5. 3.98	D. & L.S.Litchfield	Reading	22. 2.99A
G-BXLI	Bell 206B Jet Ranger III	4041	N206JR G-JODY	8. 9.97	Williams Grand Prix Engineering Ltd	Wantage	28.10.00T
G-BXLJ*	Cessna 172M Skyhawk	172-67065	N1394U	8. 9.97	APB Leasing Ltd	Welshpool	17. 6.01T
	(Crashed into Berwyn Mts, Mid-Wales 12.2.99; cancelled as destroyed 26.2.99)						
G-BXLK	Europa Avn Europa	PFA/247-12613		11. 9.97	R.G.Fairall	Redhill	14. 6.99P
G-BXLM	BAe Jetstream 3108	645	N645JD PH-KJA/G-31-645	16. 9.97	General Electric Capital Equipment Finance AB	Stockholm	
G-BXLN	Sportavia Fournier RF4D	4022	F-BORK	15. 9.97	E.H.Booker	(Peterborough)	
G-BXLO	Hunting Percival P.84 Jet Provost T.4	PAC/W/19986	9032M XR673	14. 8.97	HCR Aviation Ltd	(Hastings)	AC
G-BXLP	Sky 90-24 HAFB	084		18. 9.97	Sky Balloons Ltd	Wrexham	23.11.98A
G-BXLR	PZL-110 Koliber 160A (Regd with c/n 04970077)	04980077	SP-WGF(2)	10. 6.98	PZL Intnl Avn Marketing & Sales plc	(London EC2)	23. 9.01T
G-BXLS	PZL-110 Koliber 160A (Regd with c/n 04970078)	04980078	SP-WGG	23. 6.98	PZL Intnl Avn Marketing & Sales plc	(London EC2)	15. 9.01T
G-BXLT	Socata TB-200 Tobago XL	1457	F-GRBB EC-FNX/EC-234/F-GLFP	28. 4.97	R.M.Shears	Blackbushe	29. 4.00
G-BXLV	Enstrom F-28F	733	1711 Thai Government/KASET	11. 9.97	Dixon Development Corporation Ltd (IoM)		16. 2.01T
G-BXLW	Enstrom F-28F	734	1712 Thai Government/KASET	11. 9.97	Dixon Development Corporation Ltd (IoM)		
G-BXLX	Enstrom F-28F	735	1713 Thai Government/KASET	11. 9.97	Dixon Development Corporation Ltd (IoM)		
G-BXLY	PA-28-151 Cherokee Warrior	28-7715220	G-WATZ N7641F	19. 9.97	Air Nova plc	Liverpool	16. 7.01T
G-BXLZ	Europa Avn Europa	PFA/247-12815		24. 6.97	A.R.Round	(Guernsey)	22. 4.99P
G-BXMA	Beechcraft 200 Super King Air	BB-726	N622JA N522JA/N222JD	31. 7.97	Manhattan Air Ltd	Blackbushe	7. 8.00T
G-BXMF	Cassutt Racer IIIM	PFA/34-13003		19. 9.97	J.F.Bakewell	(Hucknall)	
G-BXMG	Rotary Air Force RAF 2000 GTX	H2-92-3-59	PH-TEN	18. 8.97	B.D.Jones	Solihull	
G-BXMH	Beechcraft 76 Duchess	ME-168	F-GDMO N6021Y	19. 9.97	R.Clarke	Halfpenny Green	22. 1.01T
G-BXML	Mooney M.20A	1594	OY-AIZ	26. 9.97	A.L.Hall-Carpenter	Shipdham	25. 1.02
G-BXMM	Cameron A-180 HAFB	4252		28.10.97	Flying Pictures Ltd "Unipart"	Fairoaks	18.10.99A
G-BXMN	DH.82A Tiger Moth	86243	N82RD N8353/ZS-IGJ/CR-AGL/FAP/NL772 (As "NL772")	2.10.97	Linda V.Handley	Blackpool	26.11.01
G-BXMR	Robinson R-22 Beta	1932	N923FM N2306E	9.10.97	Sloane Helicopters Ltd	Sywell	21.10.00T
G-BXMP	Bell 206L-4 Long Ranger (mod.)	52062	N58968 G-OCOP/N58968	9.10.97	Textron Ltd	Fairoaks	3. 9.00
G-BXMU	WSK PZL-104 Wilga 80	20890880	EC-GMH ZK-PZP/SP-FWP	9.10.97	RCR Aviation Ltd	Thruxton	AC
G-BXMV	Scheibe SF-25C Falke 1700	44223	D-KDFV	7. 8.97	J.B.Marett t/a Falcon F/Grp	(Swindon)	6.11.00
G-BXMW	Cameron A-275 HAFB	4247		19. 2.98	Balloon Flights International Ltd Bath		1. 2.99T
G-BXMX	Phoenix Currie Wot	PFA/58-13055		23. 9.97	M.J.Hayman	(Totnes)	
G-BXMY	Hughes 269C	74-0328	N9599F	20.10.97	G.R.Lloyd	Swansea	7.12.00T

Regn	Type	C/n	P/I	Date	Owner/operator	Probable Base	CA Expy
G-BXMZ	Diamond DA-20-A1 Katana	10236		4.12.97	Tayside Aviation Ltd	Dundee	6. 1.01T
G-BXNA	Light Aero Avid Flyer	118	N5531J	10.10.97	Isobel Brooks	(Cublington)	
G-BXNC	Europa Avn Europa	PFA/247-12970		13.10.97	J.K.Cantwell	(Ashton-under-Lyne)	
					"The Magic Leprechaun"		
G-BXND	Cameron Thomas The Tank Engine 110SS HAFB	4254		2. 2.98	Flying Pictures Ltd	Fairoaks	29. 1.99A
G-BXNF	Fokker F.100-650	11316	TU-TIV	15.10.97	Airline Facilities Pty. Ltd		
			PH-RRG/G-FIOO/PH-EZW		(Eagle Farm, Qld, Australia)		14. 2.92T
G-BXNG	Beechcraft 58 Baron	TH-874	N18747	13.10.97	Bonanza Flying Club Ltd	Booker	23.10.00
G-BXNH	PA-28-161 Warrior II	28-7816314	N2828M	22.10.97	CC Management Associates Ltd	Redhill	30.11.00T
G-BXNL	Cameron A-120 HAFB	4241		3. 3.98	R.G.Griffin t/a Newbury Balloons & Land		
					Securities Properties Ltd	Newbury	25. 3.99T
G-BXNM	Cameron A-210 HAFB	4245		12.12.97	N.D.Hicks t/a Horizon Ballooning	Alton	10.12.99T
G-BXNN	DHC.1 Chipmunk 22	C1/0849	WP983	4. 8.97	J.N.Robinson	(Frensham)	18. 6.01
					(As "WP983 in RAF c/s)		
G-BXNO	Yakovlev Yak-50	822305	LY-ASD	13.10.97	N.J.Radford	Denham	12.11.99P
			DOSAAF 82				
G-BXNS	Bell 206B Jet Ranger III	2385	N16822	3.11.97	Sterling Helicopters Ltd	Norwich	3.12.00T
G-BXNT	Bell 206B Jet Ranger III	2398	N94CA	11.11.97	Sterling Helicopters Ltd	Norwich	3.12.00T
			N123AL				
G-BXNU	Jabiru SK	PFA/274-13218		31.10.97	J.Smith	(Downham Market)	24. 6.99P
G-BXNV	Cameron Colt AS-105 GD Hot-Air Airship	4231		19. 2.98	The Sleeping Society	Edegem, Belgium	2. 4.99A
G-BXNX	Lindstrand LBL-210A HAFB	318		3.11.97	Jane H.Cuthbert	Sevenoaks	11.11.98T
					t/a Spirit of Adventure		
G-BXNZ	Hawker Hunter F.58	41H-697433	J-4066	7.11.97	Classic Aviation Ltd	Kemble	AC
	(Regd with c/n 41H-28364)						
G-BXOA	Robinson R-22 Beta	1614	N41132	10.11.97	MG Group Ltd	Sywell	4. 1.01
			JA7832				
G-BXOB	Europa Avn Europa	PFA/247-12892		6.11.97	S.J.Willett	(Maidstone)	
G-BXOC	Evans VP-2	PFA/63-10305		29. 9.97	H.J. & E.M.Cox	(Bideford)	
G-BXOF	Diamond DA-20-A1 Katana	10256		4.12.97	Tayside Aviation Ltd	Dundee	6. 1.01T
G-BXOI	Cessna 172R Skyhawk II	172-80145	N9990F	17.11.97	Wycombe Air Centre Ltd	Booker	2. 2.01T
					(Damaged Guernsey 26.11.98)		
G-BXOJ	PA-28-161 Warrior III	2842010	N9265G	15.12.97	Bournemouth F/Club Ltd	Bournemouth	15.12.00T
G-BXOL	Boeing 757-23A	24528	SE-DSM	26.11.97	Britannia Airways Ltd	Luton	5. 2.01T
			OO-ILI				
G-BXOM	Isaacs Spitfire	PFA/27-12768		25.11.97	J.H.Betton	(Ammanford)	
G-BXON	Auster AOP.9	AUS/10/60	WZ729	1.12.97	C.J. & D.J.Baker	Carr Farm, Newark	
G-BXOO	Grumman-American AA-5A Cheetah	AA5A-0674	N26721	10.12.97	Blackbushe School of Flying Ltd	Blackbushe	15.12.00T
G-BXOR	Robin HR.200/120B	321		1.12.97	Multiflight Ltd	Leeds-Bradford	19. 2.01T
G-BXOS	Cameron A-200 HAFB	4286		19. 2.98	Airbourne Balloon Mangmnt Ltd	Longleat	13. 3.99T
G-BXOT	Cameron C-70 HAFB	4200		21.10.97	Gone With The Wind Ltd	Bristol	28.10.99A
					(Op Dante Balloon Group)		
G-BXOU	CEA Jodel DR.360 Chevalier	312	F-BPOU	6.10.97	S.H. & J.A.Williams	Blackpool	15.12.00
G-BXOV	Cameron Colt 105A HAFB	4227		12.12.97	The Aerial Display Co Ltd	Looe	30.12.99A
G-BXOW	Cameron Colt 105A HAFB	4228		9. 1.98	The Aerial Display Co Ltd	Looe	11. 1.00A
G-BXOX	Grumman American AA-5A Cheetah	AA5A-0694	F-GBDS	27. 2.98	Plane Talking Ltd	Elstree	2. 3.01T
G-BXOY	QAC Quickie Q.200	PFA/94-12183		17.11.97	C.C.Clapham	(Chelmsford)	
G-BXOZ	PA-28-181 Cherokee Archer II	28-7790173	N6927F	14.10.97	Spritetone Ltd	(London W12)	8. 1.01T
G-BXPB	Diamond DA-20-A1 Katana	10257		4.12.97	Tayside Aviation Ltd	Glenrothes	8. 1.01T
G-BXPC	Diamond DA-20-A1 Katana	10258		4.12.97	Tayside Aviation Ltd	Glenrothes	8. 1.01T
G-BXPD	Diamond DA-20-A1 Katana	10259		4.12.97	Tayside Aviation Ltd	Dundee	5. 3.01T
G-BXPE	Diamond DA-20-A1 Katana	10263		4.12.97	Tayside Aviation Ltd	Dundee	5. 3.01T
G-BXPF	Venture Thorp T.211	105	N6524Y	8.12.97	AM Aerospace Ltd	Fradley	29. 3.01T
G-BXPH	Sky 220-24 HAFB	096		4.12.97	J.Nolte	Aachen, Germany	3.12.98
G-BXPI	Van's RV-4	PFA/181-12426		2. 1.98	Cavendish Aviation Ltd	(Bakewell)	20. 8.99P
G-BXPK	Cameron A-250 HAFB	4226		2. 2.98	Broadland Balloons Ltd	Norwich	6. 8.99T
G-BXPL	PA-28-140 Cherokee	28-24560	N7224J	10.11.97	M.Jones	RAF Brize Norton	3. 2.99T
G-BXPM	Beechcraft 58 Baron	TH-1677	N207ZM	10.10.97	Foyle Flyers Ltd	Eglinton	5.11.00
G-BXPO	Venture Thorp T.211	104	N6524Q	10.12.97	DM Aerospace Ltd	Fradley	29. 3.01T
G-BXPP	Sky 90-24 HAFB	092		17.12.97	Adam Associates Ltd	Thatcham, Berks	21.12.98A
G-BXPR	Cameron Colt Can 110SS HAFB	4218		2. 2.98	FRB Fleishwarenfabrik Rostock-Bramow	Rostock, Germany	22. 2.99A
G-BXPS	PA-23-250 Aztec C	27-3498	G-AYLY	10.12.90	Wendy A.Moore	Redhill	16.10.97T
			N6258Y				
G-BXPT	Ultramagic H-77 HADB	77-140		22.12.97	G.D.O.Bartram	Ordino, Andorra	AC
G-BXPV	PA-34-220T Seneca IV	3448035	A7-FCH	24.12.97	Flight Safety International (UK) Ltd		
			N9198X			Dundee	13. 1.01T
G-BXPW	PA-34-220T Seneca IV	3448034	A7-FCG	9. 2.98	Flight Safety International (UK) Ltd		
			N9171R			Dundee	12. 2.01T
G-BXPX	Agusta A.109A II	7390	(N) G-BXPX/I-DVRE	12.12.97	Castle Air Charters Ltd	Trebrown, Liskeard	
G-BXPY	Robinson R-44 Astro	0154	OY-HFV	22.12.97	O.Desmet & B.Mornie	Maarkedal, Belgium	23.12.00
G-BXPZ	DHC.8-311A Dash Eight	422	N377DC OE-LTE/C-GLOT	6. 3.98	Brymon Airways Ltd	Bristol/Lulsgate	15. 3.01T

Regn	Type	C/n	P/I	Date	Owner/operator	Probable Base	CA Expy
G-BXRA	Mudry/CAARP CAP.10B	03	FrAF 03 F-TFVR	12.12.97	P.A.Soper	(Ipswich)	17. 8.01
G-BXRB	Mudry/CAARP CAP.10B	100	FrAF 100	12.12.97	T.T.Duhig	(London WC1)	5. 7.01
G-BXRC	Mudry/CAARP CAP.10B	134	FrAF 134	12.12.97	I.F.Scott t/a Group Alpha	Sibson	AC
G-BXRD	Enstrom 280FX	2012	PH-JVM N213M	22.12.97	G.Firbank Eastwood End Farm, Macclesfield		28. 1.01
G-BXRE	Fokker F.28 Mk.4000	11187	N102EW 9G-ADA/PH-EXW	5. 1.98	Aero Engine Support Ltd	(London W6)	
G-BXRF	Scintex CP.1310-C3 Super Emeraude	935	OO-NSF F-BMJG	9. 1.98	D.T.Gethin	(Swansea)	AC
G-BXRG	PA-28-181 Archer II	28-7990036	PH-LEC N21173	29. 1.98	Alderney Flying Training Ltd	Guernsey	1. 3.01T
G-BXRH	Cessna 185A Skywagon	185-0413	HB-CRX N1613Z	10.12.97	R.E.M.Holmes	(IoM)	4. 6.01
G-BXRI	Cessna T303 Crusader	T303-00133	HB-LNI (N5143C)	27. 1.98	I.F.Vaughan	Guernsey	4. 3.01
G-BXRK	Robinson R-22 Beta	1341	N341MB	20. 1.98	Sloane Helicopters Ltd	Sywell	5. 2.01T
G-BXRM	Cameron A-210 HAFB	4237		23. 4.98	W. & C.Hooker	(Nottingham)	19. 4.99T
G-BXRN	Reims Cessna F.152 II	1440	G-RICH OO-FTC	27. 1.98	A.T.Hooper & T.E.Evans Wellesbourne Mountford		21. 9.01T
G-BXRO	Cessna U.206G Stationair II	U206-04217	OH-ULK N756NE	9. 2.98	M.Penny	(Coleraine, NI)	24. 3.01
G-BXRP	Schweizer Hughes 269C	S.1334	OH-HSP	27. 1.98	B.Wronski	Gloucestershire	18. 3.01
G-BXRR	Westland Scout AH.1	F.9740	XW612	28. 1.98	R.P.Coplestone	(Marlborough)	7. 2.00P
G-BXRS	Westland Scout AH.1	F.9741	XW613	28. 1.98	R.P.Coplestone	(Marlborough)	AC
G-BXRT	Robin DR.400/180	2382		23. 2.98	Mistral Aviation Ltd	Goodwood	2. 4.01
G-BXRV	Van's RV-4	PFA/181-12482		12. 1.98	B.J.Oke	(Wotton-under-Edge)	
G-BXRX	Airbus A.320-231	314	EC-GLT R N314RX/LZ-ABD/F-WWDO		Airworld Aviation Ltd	Manchester	
G-BXRY	Bell 206B JetRanger	208	N4054G	19. 3.98	R & M International Ltd	Dereham	27. 5.01T
G-BXRZ	Rans S-6-116 Coyote II	PFA/204A-13195		3. 2.98	C.M.White	(Dunblane)	
G-BXSA	Cameron PM-80 HAFB (Coca Cola bottle)	4297		11. 3.98	Flying Pictures Ltd	(Dubai)	11. 3.99A
G-BXSB	Cameron PM-80 HAFB (Coca Cola bottle)	4298		11. 3.98	Flying Pictures Ltd	(Dubai)	7.12.99A
G-BXSC	Cameron C-80 HAFB	4251		12.12.97	S.J.Coates	Barton-le-Clay, Bedford	31.10.99A
G-BXSD	Cessna 172R Skyhawk II	172-80310	N431ES	12. 3.98	K.J.Freeman & J.A.Barlow t/a Sierra DeltaGroup	(Launceston)	26. 3.01
G-BXSE	Cessna 172R Skyhawk II	172-80352	N9321F	19. 5.98	Dingle Star Ltd	Elstree	26. 5.01
G-BXSF	Cessna 172R Skyhawk II	172-80419	N9967F	15. 5.98	Oxford Aviation Services Ltd	Oxford	28. 5.01T
G-BXSG	Robinson R-22 Beta	2789		3. 2.98	R.M.Goodenough	Wotton-under-Edge	26. 2.01T
G-BXSH	Glaser-Dirks DG-800B	8-121-B50		5. 2.98	D.S.MaKay	(Brackley)	4. 6.01
G-BXSI	Jabiru SK	PFA/274-13204		5. 2.98	V.R.Leggott	Willingham	5. 5.99P
G-BXSJ	Cameron C-80 HAFB	4330		24. 3.98	Balloon School (International) Ltd t/a British School of Ballooning Petworth		24. 3.99T
G-BXSK	Beechcraft 76 Duchess	ME-192	EI-CMX N60450	12. 2.98	Building and Commercial Ltd	Gloucestershire	11. 3.01T
G-BXSL	Westland Scout AH.1	F.9762	XW799	17. 2.98	R.P.Coplestone	(Marlborough)	26. 7.99P
G-BXSM	Cessna 172R Skyhawk II	172-80320	N432ES	10. 3.98	East Midlands Flying School Ltd	East Midlands	19. 3.01T
G-BXSN	Sikorsky S-61N	61721	EI-BLY C-GPOH/VH-IMQ/VH-PTF/N611EH	17. 2.98	Bristow Helicopters Ltd	Aberdeen	AC
G-BXSO	Lindstrand LBL-105A HAFB	114	HB-BBJ	18. 2.98	Lindstrand Balloons Ltd	Oswestry	24. 3.99A
G-BXSP	Grob G-109B	6335	D-KNEA	25. 3.98	I.M.Donnelly	Aboyne	7. 4.01
G-BXSR	Reims Cessna F.172N	2003	PH-SPY D-EITH	6. 2.98	J.A.Havers	Elstree	21. 4.01
G-BXST	PA-25-235 Pawnee C	25-4952	PH-BAT N8532L	9. 2.98	P.Channon	Lands End	AC
G-BXSU	Team Minimax 91A	PFA/186-12357	G-MYGL	20. 2.98	C.D.Brack	(York)	28. 9.99P
G-BXSW	Cameron Mountie 120SS HAFB	4299		20. 2.98	Cameron Balloons Ltd	(Canada)	1. 6.99A
G-BXSX	Cameron V-77 HAFB	4329		6. 4.98	D.R.Medcalf	(Bromsgrove)	7. 4.99A
G-BXSY	Robinson R-22 Beta	2778		27. 1.98	N.M.G.Pearson	Bristol	5. 2.01T
G-BXTA	Airbus A.320-214	764	F-WWDF	29. 4.98	Flying Colours Airlines Ltd	Manchester	29. 4.01T
G-BXTB	Cessna 152 II	152-82516	OH-CMS N69151	25. 2.98	Haimoss Ltd	Old Sarum	1. 4.01T
G-BXTC	Taylor JT.1 Monoplane	PFA/55-13142		25. 2.98	R.Holden-Rushworth	(Devizes)	
G-BXTD	Europa Avn Europa	PFA/247-12772		26. 2.98	P.R.Anderson	(Southwell)	
G-BXTE	Cameron A-275 HAFB	4028		30. 3.98	Adventure Balloon Co Ltd	Hook	1. 4.01T
G-BXTF	Cameron N-105 HAFB	4304		2. 4.98	Flying Pictures Ltd	Fairoaks	1. 4.99A
G-BXTG	Cameron N-42 HAFB "Sainsbury"	4305		2. 4.98	Flying Pictures Ltd	Fairoaks	24. 3.99A
G-BXTH	Westland Gazelle HT.3	WA.1120	XW866	13. 3.98	Flightline Ltd (As "E" in RAF c/s)	Southend	AC
G-BXTI	Pitts S-1S Special	NP-1	ZS-VZX	9. 3.98	A.B.Treherne-Pollock	(London SW4)	30. 6.99P
G-BXTJ	Cameron N-77 HAFB	4332		6. 4.98	Chubb Fire Ltd	(Sunbury-on-Thames)	16.12.99A

Regn	Type	C/n	P/I	Date	Owner/operator	Probable Base	CA Expy
G-BXTK	Dornier Do.28D-2	4080	D-IDBB German AF 58+05	15. 5.98	R.Ebke (Porta Westfalica, Germany)		
G-BXTL	Schweizer Hughes 269C-1	0075		13. 3.98	Oxford Aviation Services Ltd	Oxford	2. 4.01T
G-BXTM	Schweizer Hughes 269C-1	0076		13. 3.98	Oxford Aviation Services Ltd (Damaged Oxford 4.1.99)	Oxford	2. 4.01T
G-BXTN	ATR-72-202	483	F-WWEV	24.10.97	Cityflyer Express Ltd (Whale Rider t/s)	Gatwick	23.10.00T
G-BXTO	Hindustan HAL-26 Pushpak	PK-128	9V-BAI VT-DWM	12. 2.98	A.A.Marshall	(Ilkeston)	
G-BXTP	Diamond DA-20-A1 Katana	10306	N636DA	10. 3.98	Solent Flight Aircraft Ltd	Southampton	23. 4.01T
G-BXTR	Diamond DA-20-A1 Katana	10307	N607DA	10. 3.98	Solent Flight Aircraft Ltd	Southampton	23. 4.01T
G-BXTS	Diamond DA-20-A1 Katana	10308	N638DA	10. 3.98	Solent Flight Aircraft Ltd	Southampton	23. 4.01T
G-BXTT	Grumman-American AA-5B Cheetah	AA5B-0749	F-GBDH	27. 2.98	Plane Talking Ltd	Elstree	2. 3.01
G-BXTU	Robinson R-22 Beta	2790		3. 3.98	TDR Aviation Ltd	(Craigavon, NI)	7. 4.01T
G-BXTV	Bug	BUG.2		12. 3.98	B.R.Cope	(Bewdley)	
G-BXTW	PA-28-181 Archer III	2843137	N41279	26. 2.98	J.N.Davison t/a Davison Plant Hire	(Wolverhampton)	25. 5.01
G-BXTX	PA-28-161 Warrior II	28-8516008	PH-LEH N130AV/N43682	11. 3.98	Plane Talking Ltd	Elstree	2. 4.01T
G-BXTY	PA-28-161 Cadet	2841179	PH-LED	11. 3.98	Plane Talking Ltd	Elstree	7. 6.01T
G-BXTZ	PA-28-161 Cadet	2841181	PH-LEE	11. 3.98	Plane Talking Ltd	Elstree	12. 3.01T
G-BXUA	Campbell Cricket Mk.5	PFA G/03-1272		12. 3.98	P.C.Lovegrove	(Didcot)	
G-BXUB	Lindstrand Syrup Bottle SS HAFB	508		30. 4.98	Free Enterprise Balloons Ltd	(London SE16)	5. 5.99A
G-BXUC	Robinson R-22 Beta	0908	OY-HFB	17. 3.98	C.W.B.Wrightson	Yarm	29. 3.01T
G-BXUE	Sky 240-24 HAFB	098		30. 4.98	G.M.Houston t/a Scotair Balloons	Lesmahagow	22. 4.99T
G-BXUF	Agusta-Bell 206B JetRanger II	8633	EC-DUS OE-DXE	12. 5.98	SJ Contracting Services Ltd	Oxford	7. 7.01T
G-BXUG	Lindstrand Baby Bel SS HAFB	512		14. 5.98	Virgin Airship & Balloon Co Ltd	Telford	2. 7.99A
G-BXUH	Lindstrand LBL-31A HAFB	513		2. 6.98	Virgin Airship & Balloon Co Ltd	Telford	7. 6.99A
G-BXUI	Glaser-Dirks DG-800B	8-105-B39	BGA.4382 D-KKLC	12. 5.98	J.Le Coyte	(Swindon)	25. 5.01P
G-BXUK	Robinson R-44 Astro	0093	D-HIFF	19. 6.95	Adrian Raymond Ltd Gurney Slade, Bath		19. 6.01T
G-BXUL	Vought (Goodyear) FG-1D Corsair (Officially regd as c/n P32823) (P/i of Bu.88439 quoted)	3205	N55JP "NZ5611"/NZ5648/Bu.88391	25. 3.98	The Old Flying Machine (Air Museum) Co Ltd Duxford (As "NZ5648/648" in RNZAF c/s)		2. 7.99P
G-BXUM	Europa Avn Europa	PFA/247-12611		19. 3.98	D.Bosomworth	(Camberley)	
G-BXUO	Lindstrand LBL-105A HAFB	520		27. 3.98	Lindstrand Balloons Ltd	Oswestry	2. 4.99A
G-BXUP	Schweizer Hughes 269C	S.1317	SE-HTB	30. 3.98	D.R.Kenyon t/a Aviation Bureau	Biggin Hill	6. 4.01T
G-BXUS	Sky 65-24 HAFB	111		6. 4.98	Sky Balloons Ltd	(Wrexham)	16. 4.99A
G-BXUT	PA-34-200 Seneca	34-7250315	N1427T HB-LMK/N1427T	11. 5.98	H.Merkado & D.Webber	Panshanger	25. 5.01T
G-BXUU	Cameron V-65 HAFB	4362		23. 4.98	D.I.Gray-Fisk	(Slough)	26. 4.99A
G-BXUV	PA-31-50 Navajo Chieftain	31-7552075	PH-OTH N59979	14. 4.98	KLM Aerocarto BV (Arnem, Netherlands)		26. 4.99T
G-BXUW	Cameron Colt 90A HAFB	4317		23. 4.98	Zycomm Electronics Ltd	(Derby)	19. 4.99A
G-BXUX	Fountain MF Cherry BX-2	PFA/179-12571		14. 4.98	M.F.Fountain	(Dover)	
G-BXUY	Cessna 310Q	310Q-0231	N137SA D-IHMT/N7731Q	16. 4.98	D.A.De Horne Rowntree	(London NW3)	23. 4.01
G-BXUZ	Cessna 152 II	152-82810	N89638	14. 4.98	Stapleford Flying Club Ltd	Stapleford	AC
G-BXVA	Socata TB-200 Tobago XL	1325	F-GJXL F-WJXL	15. 4.98	AMC Ltd	(Thornton-Cleveleys)	18. 5.01
G-BXVB	Cessna 152 II	152-82584	N69250	15. 4.98	PJC (Leasing) Ltd	Stapleford	14. 9.01T
G-BXVC	PA-28RT-201T Turbo Arrow IV	28R-7931113	D-ELIV N2152V	20. 4.98	J.S.Develin & I.Zahurul (East Grinstead) (Damaged nr Rye 22.8.98)		28. 6.01T
G-BXVD	CFM Streak Shadow SA	PFA/206-13304		1. 4.98	CFM Aircraft Ltd	Leiston	
G-BXVE	Lindstrand LBL-330A HAFB	492		6. 5.98	Adventure Balloon Co Ltd	London W7	23. 6.99T
G-BXVF	Thunder Ax11-250 Srs.2 HAFB	4371		22. 5.98	T.J.Parker Burnham-on-Crouch t/a Anglian Countryside Balloons		5. 6.99T
G-BXVG	Sky 77-24 HAFB	99		28. 5.98	M.Wolf	Wallingford	26. 4.99
G-BXVH	Sky 25-16 HAFB	120		23. 4.98	Flying Pictures Ltd	Fairoaks	
G-BXVI	VS 361 Spitfire LF.XVIe	CBAF.IX.4644 "RF114"/RW386	6944M	27.12.84	Wizzard Investments Ltd North Weald (On rebuild 4.89)		AC
G-BXVJ	Cameron O-120 HAFB	2201	PH-VVJ G-IMAX	12. 3.98	Gone with the Wind Ltd Clonskeagh, Co.Dublin		22. 3.99T
G-BXVK	Robin HR.200/120B	326		1. 7.98	Mistral Aviation Ltd	Guildford	23. 6.01T
G-BXVL	Sky 180-24 HAFB	113		16. 6.98	S.Stanley t/a Purple Balloons	Sudbury	11. 6.99T
G-BXVM	Van's RV-6A	PFA/181-13103		26. 2.98	J.G.Small	(Southport)	
G-BXVN	Sky 105-24 HAFB	115		17. 9.98	L.V.D. Avyle, Wachtebetie, Belgium t/a Skydance		
G-BXVO	Van's RV-6A	PFA/181-12575		28. 4.98	P.J.Hynes & M.E.Holden	(Shrewsbury)	
G-BXVP	Sky 31-24 HAFB	056		28. 4.98	Sky Balloons Ltd	Wrexham	4. 5.99A

Regn	Type	C/n	P/I	Date	Owner/operator	Probable Base	CA Expy
G-BXVR	Sky 90-24 HAFB	061		20. 7.98	P.Hegarty	Magherafelt, NI	25. 6.99
G-BXVS	Brugger Colibri MB.2	PFA/43-11948		5. 5.98	G.T.Snoddon	(Belfast)	
G-BXVT	Cameron O-77 HAFB	1444	PH-MKB	30. 7.98	R.P.Wade	Wigan	
G-BXVU	PA-28-161 Warrior II	28-7816063	N47372	5. 5.98	Atlantic Bridge Aviation Ltd	Lydd	7. 7.01T
G-BXVV	Cameron V-90 HAFB	4369		5. 5.98	Floating Sensations Ltd	Thatcham	8. 6.99A
G-BXVW	Colt Piggy Bank SS HAFB	4366		2. 7.98	G.Binder	Sonnerbuhl, Germany	
G-BXVX	Rutan Cozy	PFA/159-12680		6. 5.98	G.E.Murray	(Swansea)	
G-BXVY	Cessna 152	152-79808	N757KU	11. 5.98	Stapleford Flying Club Ltd	Stapleford	9.11.01T
G-BXVZ	WSK-PZL Mielec TS-11 Iskra	3H-1625	SP-DOF Polish AF?/SP-DOF	27. 3.98	J.Ziubrzynski	Shoreham	
G-BXWA	Beechcraft 76 Duchess	ME-232	OY-CYM (SE-IUY)/D-GBTD	8. 4.98	Liddel Aircraft Ltd (Op Langtry F/Grp)	Bournemouth	23. 6.01T
G-BXWB	Pierre Robin HR.100/200B Royale	08	HB-EMT	29. 4.98	W.A.Brunwin	Bristol/Lulsgate	24. 6.01T
G-BXWC	Cessna 152	152-83640	N4794B	11. 5.98	PJC (Leasing) Ltd	Stapleford	8. 7.01T
G-BXWD	Agusta A.109A-II	7266	N565RJ I-URIA/D-HEMZ/N109BD	14. 5.98	Castle Air Charters Ltd	Trebrown, Liskeard	AC
G-BXWE	Fokker F.100-650	11327	PH-CFE F-GJAO/PH-CFE/PH-EZL/(G-FIOX)/PH-EZL	6. 7.98	British Midland Airways Ltd	East Midlands	30. 8.01T
G-BXWF	Fokker F.100-650	11328	PH-CFF F-GKLX/PH-CFF/PH-EZM/(G-FIOY)/PH-EZM	13. 7.98	British Midland Airways Ltd	East Midlands	31. 8.01T
G-BXWG	Sky 120-24 HAFB	114		28. 5.98	Airbourne Adventures Ltd	Skipton	25. 5.99T
G-BXWH	Denney Kitfox 4-1200 Sportster	PFA/172A-12343		4. 3.98	R.Horton	(Harrogate)	
G-BXWI	Cameron N-120 HAFB	4395		12. 6.98	Flying Pictures Ltd	Fairoaks	8. 6.99A
G-BXWJ	Robinson R-22 Beta	1685	N4060W	19. 5.98	M.Horrell	(Huntingdon)	4. 6.01T
G-BXWK	Rans S-6-ESA Coyote II	PFA/204-13317		19. 5.98	Sport Air UK Ltd	Felixkirk	
G-BXWL	Sky 90-24 HAFB	117		20. 7.98	I.S.Bridge t/a The Shropshire Hills Balloon Company	Shrewsbury	29. 6.99A
G-BXWO	PA-28-181 Archer II	28-8190311	D-ENHA(2) N8431C	22. 5.98	J.S.Develin & Z.Islam	(East Grinstead)	30. 6.01T
G-BXWR	CFM Streak Shadow	PFA/206-13205	G-MZMI	22. 5.98	M.A.Hayward	Bodmin	7. 1.00P
G-BXWS	Scheibe SF-25E Super Falke	4304	F-CHCG D-KEYB	26. 5.98	M.M.Martin	Leicester	
G-BXWT	Van's RV-6	PFA/181-12639		19. 7.96	R.C.Owen	(Haywards Heath)	
G-BXWU	Sprint 160	003	G-70-503	5. 6.98	Sunhawk Ltd	North Weald	
G-BXWV	Sprint 160	005	G-70-505	5. 6.98	Sunhawk Ltd	North Weald	
G-BXWX	Sky 25-16 HAFB	082		29. 5.98	Sky Balloons Ltd	Wrexham	
G-BXWY	Cameron A-105 HAFB	4410		12. 6.98	Richard Nash Cars Ltd	Norwich	15. 6.99A
G-BXWZ	Cameron A-210 HAFB	4083		9. 6.98	G.C.Ludlow t/a Kent & Canterbury Ballooning	(Canterbury)	8. 6.99T
G-BXXA	ATR-72-202	301	F-WQGJ F-OHAG/F-WWLY	27. 4.98	Gill Aviation Ltd (Op Euroscot Express)	Bournemouth	15. 6.01T
G-BXXC	Scheibe SF-25C Falke 1700	44151	D-KEFA(2)	3. 6.98	K.E.Ballington	(Burton-on-Trent)	AC
G-BXXD	Cessna 172R Skyhawk	172-80068	N9739F	15. 6.98	R.MacAire t/a Denston Hall Estate	(Newmarket)	30. 6.01T
G-BXXE	Rand KR-2	PFA/129-10927		8. 6.98	N.Rawlinson	(Leek)	
G-BXXF	Cameron A-210 HAFB	4300		2. 4.98	Gone With The Wind Ltd	(Bristol)	7. 4.99T
G-BXXG	Cameron N-105 HAFB	3662		19. 6.98	Allen Owen Ltd	Wotton-under-Edge	24. 6.99A
G-BXXH	Hatz CB-1	PFA/143-12445		9. 6.98	R.D.Shingler	(Shrewsbury)	
G-BXXI	Grob G-109B	6400	F-CAQR F-WAQR	9. 6.98	Richard Collings Ltd	(Daventry)	13. 7.01
G-BXXJ	Colt Flying Yacht SS HAFB	1797	JA-A015	10. 6.98	L.V.Mastis (Exported 1998)	Bristol	
G-BXXK	Reims Cessna F.172N	1806	D-EOPP	15. 6.98	E.Alexander	(Braintree)	29. 7.01T
G-BXXL	Cameron N-105 HAFB	4408		16. 7.98	Flying Pictures Ltd	Fairoaks	7. 7.99A
G-BXXN	Robinson R-22 Beta	0720	N720HH	16. 6.98	Sloane Helicopters Ltd	Sywell	2. 7.01T
G-BXXO	Lindstrand LBL-90B HAFB	534		6. 7.98	Lindstrand Balloons Ltd	Oswestry	15. 7.99A
G-BXXP	Sky 77-24 HAFB	124		20. 7.98	L.van den Avyle	Wachebetie, Belgium	15. 7.99A
G-BXXR	AV-8 Gyroplane	PFA G/15-1263		29. 6.98	P.C.Lovegrove	Didcot	
G-BXXS	Sky 105-24 HAFB	116		30. 7.98	Flying Pictures Ltd	Fairoaks	27. 7.99A
G-BXXT	Beechcraft 76 Duchess	ME-212	(N212BE) F-GBOZ	17. 7.98	Solent Flight Aircraft Ltd	Southampton	21. 7.01T
G-BXXU	Colt 31A HAFB	4427		21. 8.98	Sade Balloons Ltd	Coulsdon	3. 8.99
G-BXXV	Eurocopter EC-135T-1	0049		2. 7.98	Multiflight Ltd	Leeds-Bradford	6. 8.01
G-BXXY	PA-34-220T Seneca III	34-8333061	PH-TLN N4295X	3. 7.98	Air Medical Ltd	Oxford	15. 7.01T
G-BXXZ	CFM Starstreak Shadow SA-II	PFA/206-13171		19. 5.98	A.V. & B.T.Orchard	(Cemaes Bay)	6.10.01T
G-BXYC	Schweizer 269C	S.1716	D-HFDZ	8. 7.98	L.Williamson & A.Hamilton	(Rotherham)	6. 8.01T
G-BXYD	Eurocopter EC-120B	1006		7. 7.98	John Finlay (Concrete Pipes) Ltd	(Dungannon, NI)	13.12.01
G-BXYE	Scintex CP.301-C1 Emeraude	559	F-BTEO F-PTEO/F-WTEO/F-BJFV	8. 7.98	D.T.Gethin	Swansea	
G-BXYF	Colt AS-105 GD Airship	4433		7. 8.98	D.Stuber	Aachen, Germany	24. 8.99A
G-BXYG	Cessna 310D	310-39089	HB-LSF F-GEJT/3A-MCA/F-BBOT/F-OBOT/(N6789T)	14. 8.98	Equitus SARL	(Bailleul, France)	7.12.01T
G-BXYH	Cameron N-105 HAFB	4441		7. 8.98	Virgin Airship & Balloon Co Ltd	Telford	23. 7.99A

Regn	Type	C/n	P/I	Date	Owner/operator	Probable Base	CA Expy
G-BXYI	Cameron H-34 HAFB	4442		7. 8.98	Virgin Airship & Balloon Co.Ltd	Telford	23. 7.99A
G-BXYJ	SAN Jodel DR.1050 Ambassadeur	143	F-BJNA	28. 7.98	R.Manning	Netherthorpe	21.10.01
G-BXYK	Robinson R-22 Beta	1579	N4037B	27. 7.98	R.C.Hields t/a Hields Aviation	(Leeds)	19. 8.01T
G-BXYL	Cameron A-275 HAFB	4450		22. 7.98	The Balloon Club Ltd t/a Bristol Balloons	Bristol	22. 7.99T
G-BXYM	PA-28-235 Cherokee B	28-10858	SE-FAM	18. 8.98	E.Francis	Compton Abbas	22.12.01T
G-BXYN	Van's RV-6	PFA/181-13265		29. 7.98	J.A.Tooley	(Thatcham)	
G-BXYO	PA-28RT-201 Arrow IV	28R-8018046	PH-SDD N8164M	18. 8.98	Oxford Aviation Services Ltd	Oxford	1.12.01T
G-BXYP	PA-28RT-201 Arrow IV	28R-8018050	PH-SBO N8168H	18. 8.98	Oxford Aviation Services Ltd	Oxford	1.12.01T
G-BXYR	PA-28RT-201 Arrow IV	28R-8018101	PH-SDA N8251B	3. 8.98	Oxford Aviation Services Ltd	Oxford	11.11.01T
G-BXYS	PA-28RT-201 Arrow IV	28R-7918145	PH-SBS N29561	3. 8.98	Oxford Aviation Services Ltd	Oxford	8.10.01T
G-BXYT	PA-28RT-201 Arrow IV	28R-7918198	PH-SBN (PH-SBM)/OO-HLA/N2878W	3. 8.98	Oxford Aviation Services Ltd	Oxford	9. 9.01T
G-BXYU	Reims Cessna F.152 II	1804	OH-CKD SE-IFY	31. 7.98	Exeter Flying Club Ltd	Exeter	24. 8.01T
G-BXYV	ATR 72-202	322	B-22708 F-WWEQ	12.10.98	Gill Aviation Ltd.	Newcastle	15.10.01T
G-BXYX	Van's RV-6 (Built by M.T.Hathaway)	22293	N2399C	31. 7.98	D.Coles	(Hampton, Middx)	18.10.99P
G-BXYY	Reims Cessna FR.172E	0016	OY-AHO F-WLIP	20. 4.98	Haimoss Ltd	Old Sarum	19. 5.01T
G-BXZA	PA-38-112 Tomahawk	38-79A0864	N2480N	6. 8.98	D.A.Whitmore	Booker	1. 9.01T
G-BXZB	Nanchang CJ-6A	2632019	Chinese	18. 9.98	Elmair Ltd.	Slinfold	AC
G-BXZC							
G-BXZD	Westland Gazelle HT.2	WA/1174	XW895	25. 8.98	K.W.Brigden t/a KB Aviation Services	(Truro)	AC
G-BXZE	Westland Gazelle HT.3	WA/1228	XW910	25. 8.98	K.W.Brigden t/a KB Aviation Services	(Truro)	AC
G-BXZF	Lindstrand LBL-90A HAFB	575		8. 1.99	L.Van Den Avyle	(Cascais, Portugal)	7. 1.00A
G-BXZG	Cameron A-210 HAFB	4424		21. 8.98	Societe Bombard SARL	Beaume, France	13. 8.99A
G-BXZH	Cameron A-210 HAFB	4423		21. 8.98	Societe Bombard SARL	Beaume, France	13. 8.99A
G-BXZI	Lindstrand LBL-90A HAFB	543		14. 8.98	S.Stanley t/a Purple Balloons	Sudbury	13. 8.99A
G-BXZJ	Sky 70-16 HAFB	131		14. 8.98	Sky Balloons Ltd	Wrexham	5.10.99
G-BXZK	Boeing MDH MD-900 Explorer	900-00057	N9238T	27. 8.98	Dorset Police Air Support Unit	Dorchester	1. 2.02T
G-BXZM	Cessna 182S	182-80310	N2683L	8.10.98	Oxford Aviation Services Ltd	Oxford	8.10.01T
G-BXZN	CH1 ATI	00002	N8186E	25. 8.98	Intora-Firebird PLC	Southend	

(This small helicopter exhibited at Farnborough 1998 and marketed as "Intora Firebird" probably began life as a Liteco Helicopter Systems ATLAS (Advanced Technology Light Airborne System). The original design was known as the Rotorcraft RH-1 Pinwheel)

Regn	Type	C/n	P/I	Date	Owner/operator	Probable Base	CA Expy
G-BXZO	Pietenpol Air Camper	PFA/47-12818		10. 7.98	P.J.Cooke	(Uckfield)	
G-BXZS	Sikorsky S-76A (mod)	760287	N190AL N190AE/N153AE/N7265A	14. 9.98	Bristow Helicopters Ltd.	Redhill	AC
G-BXZT	MS.880B Rallye Club	1733	OO-EDG D-EBDG/F-BSVL	2.9.98	K.P. Snipe	(Swindon)	8.12.01
G-BXZU	Bantam B22 S	98-015	ZK-JJL	21. 9.98	M.R.M. Welch	(Lewes)	26. 9.99P
G-BXZV	CFM Streak Shadow SA	PFA/206-13357		18. 9.98	CFM Aircraft Ltd.	Leiston	
G-BXZW	Fokker F.27-050	20154	OY-MMV PH-EXO	18. 9.98	QIP Aviation III Ltd (Stored at Norwich)	(Georgetown, Cayman Islands)	
G-BXZX	Bell 206B Jet Ranger III	2288	N27EA N286CA/N93AT/N16873	28. 8.98	R & M Engineering Ltd	Dereham	15.10.01T
G-BXZY	CFM Streak Shadow Srs.DD	296-DD		21. 9.98	CFM Aircraft Ltd	Leiston	16.12.99P
G-BXZZ	Sky 160-24 HAFB	109		14. 7.98	S.J.Colin & A.S.Pinder t/a Skybus Ballooning	Maidstone	24. 6.99T

G-BYAA-BYZZ

Regn	Type	C/n	P/I	Date	Owner/operator	Probable Base	CA Expy
G-BYAA	Boeing 767-204ER	25058	PH-AHM G-BYAA/N60659	23. 4.91	Britannia Airways Ltd	Luton	13.11.99T
G-BYAB	Boeing 767-204ER	25139	(PH-AHN) G-BYAB	11. 6.91	Britannia Airways Ltd	Luton	26. 3.99T
G-BYAD	Boeing 757-204ER	26963		6. 5.92	Britannia Airways Ltd	Luton	22. 2.02T
G-BYAE	Boeing 757-204ER	26964		12. 5.92	Britannia Airways Ltd	Luton	26. 4.01T
G-BYAF	Boeing 757-204ER	26266		13. 1.93	Britannia Airways Ltd	Luton	19. 1.00T
G-BYAG	Boeing 757-204ER	26965		22. 1.93	Britannia Airways Ltd	Luton	22. 2.01T
G-BYAH	Boeing 757-204ER	26966		5. 2.93	Britannia Airways Ltd	Luton	10. 2.00T
G-BYAI	Boeing 757-204	26967		1. 3.93	Britannia Airways Ltd	Luton	4. 3.00T
G-BYAJ	Boeing 757-204	25623		4. 3.93	Britannia Airways Ltd	Luton	23. 1.02T
G-BYAK	Boeing 757-204	26267		6. 4.93	Britannia Airways Ltd	Luton	13. 4.00T
G-BYAL	Boeing 757-204	25626		13. 5.93	Britannia Airways Ltd	Luton	18. 5.00T
G-BYAM	Boeing 757-2T7	23895	G-DRJC	15. 3.93	Britannia Airways Ltd	Luton	14. 1.00T
G-BYAN	Boeing 757-204	27219		26. 1.94	Britannia Airways Ltd	Luton	14. 2.01T
G-BYAO	Boeing 757-204	27235		3. 2.94	Britannia Airways Ltd	Luton	2. 2.00T
G-BYAP	Boeing 757-204	27236		15. 2.94	Britannia Airways Ltd	Luton	14. 2.00T
G-BYAR	Boeing 757-204	27237		1. 3.94	Britannia Airways Ltd	Luton	28. 2.00T
G-BYAS	Boeing 757-204	27238		9. 3.94	Britannia Airways Ltd	Luton	31. 1.02T
G-BYAT	Boeing 757-204	27208		21. 3.94	Britannia Airways Ltd	Luton	24. 3.01T
G-BYAU	Boeing 757-204	27220		18. 5.94	Britannia Airways Ltd	Luton	17. 5.00T
G-BYAV	Taylor JT.1 Monoplane	PFA/055-11010		27. 8.98	C.D.Pidler	Dunkeswell	
G-BYAW	Boeing 757-204	27234		3. 4.95	Britannia Airways Ltd "Eric Morecambe OBE"	Luton	2. 4.01T
G-BYAX	Boeing 757-204	28834		24. 2.99	Britannia Airways Ltd	Luton	
G-BYAZ	CFM Streak Shadow	PFA/206-12656		1. 9.98	A.G.Wright	(Camberley)	22.11.99P
G-BYBA	Agusta-Bell 206B JetRanger III	8596	G-BHXV G-OWJM/G-BHXV	31. 3.98	R.Forests Ltd	(Banbury)	8. 8.99T
G-BYBC	Agusta-Bell 206B JetRanger II	8567	G-BTWW EI-BJV/G-BTWW	31. 3.98	RCR Aviation Ltd	Thruxton	5. 6.00T
G-BYBD	Reims Cessna F.172H	0487	G-OBHX G-AWMU	6. 7.98	J.M.Cubley	(Atherstone)	29. 7.99T
G-BYBE	Wassmer Jodel D.120A Paris-Nice	269	OO-FDP	24. 7.98	R.J.Page	(Haywards Heath)	27. 1.02
G-BYBF	Robin R.2160i	329		1.10.98	Mistral Aviation Ltd	(Guildford)	AC
G-BYBI	Bell 206B Jet Ranger III	3668	ZS-RGP N5757M	19.10.98	R & M Engineering Ltd	Dereham	AC
G-BYBJ	Hybred 44XLR	MR156/135		22. 1.99	M Gardner	Rochester	
G-BYBK	Murphy Rebel	260R	N95LD	19. 8.98	D.Webb	Worcester	8.11.99P
G-BYBL	Gardan GY-80 Horizon 160D	127	F-BMUY	25. 9.98	P.T.Harmsworth	Exeter	AC
G-BYBM	Jabiru SK	274-13377		18. 9.98	M.Rudd	Dorchester	
G-BYBN	Cameron N-77 HAFB	3082		30. 9.98	M.G.& R.D.Howard	Bristol	
G-BYBO	Hybred 44XLR Eclipser	155134		14. 9.98	R.Skene	Dartford	
G-BYBP	Cessna A185F	185-03804	OO-DCD F-GDCD/F-ODIA/N4593E	15.10.98	J.M.Thorpe	Llangarron	AC
G-BYBR	Rans S-6-116 Coyote II	PFA/204A-13081		10. 7.98	J.B.Robinson	(Preston)	
G-BYBS	Sky 80-16 HAFB	136		27.10.98	G.W.G.C. Sudlow	Somerton	18.10.99
G-BYBT	Fokker F27-050	20153	OY-MMU PH-EXO	13.10.98	QIP Aviation IV Ltd	Norwich	
G-BYBU	Renegade Spirit UK	PFA/188-13229		12.10.98	K.R.Anderson	(Shrewsbury)	
G-BYBV	Rapier	1183-1198-7-W986		20.10.98	M.W.Robson	York	
G-BYBW	Team Minimax	PFA/186-12120		19.10.98	N.E.Johnson	Kettering	
G-BYBX	Slingsby T67M-260	2261		21.10.98	Slingsby Aviation Ltd	York	
G-BYBY	Thorp T-18C Tiger	492	N77KK	17. 7.98	L.J.Joyce	Liverpool	
G-BYBZ	Jabiru SK	PFA/274-13290		7. 9.98	A.W.Harris	(Birmingham)	
G-BYCA	PA-28-140 Cherokee D	28-7125223	PH-VRZ N11C	24. 9.98	Pilotime Ltd t/a GT Aviation	Bournemouth	16.11.01
G-BYCB	Sky 21-16 HAFB	142		28.10.98	Sky Balloons Ltd.	Wrexham	
G-BYCC	Jabiru SK	PFA/274-13225		24. 7.98	A.R.Silvester	(Milton Keynes)	2. 9.99P
G-BYCD	Cessna 140 (modified)	13744	N4273N NC4273N	28. 9.98	G.P.James	(London E1)	AC
G-BYCE	Robinson R-44 Astro	0520		12.10.98	Heli Air Ltd	Wellesbourne Mountford	15.10.01T
G-BYCF	Robinson R-22 Beta	2866		12.10.98	Stableauto Ltd t/a Lisair	Liverpool	19.10.01T
G-BYCG*	Agusta-Bell 47G-3B1	1513	EC-EGO	12.10.98	Nash Group Ltd	(Warwick)	
			Spanish AF 751-12/HE7B-22/Z7B-22 (Cancelled by CAA 9.2.99)				
G-BYCH*	Agusta-Bell 47G-4A	2519	EC-BMB	12.10.98	Nash Group Ltd	(Warwick)	
			Italian AF MM80504 (Cancelled by CAA 9.2.99)				
G-BYCI*	Agusta-Bell 47G-4A	2530	EC-BSC	12.10.98	Nash Group Ltd (Cancelled by CAA 9.2.99)	(Warwick)	
G-BYCJ	Shadow Series DD	PFA/161-13258		14.10.98	J.W.E.Pearson	St Albans	
G-BYCL	X'Air 582	BMAA/HB/088		15.10.98	Camelford & Wessex Light Aeroplane Co Ltd	(Camelford)	
G-BYCM	Rans S6-ES Coyote II	PFA/204-13315		15. 9.98	E.W.McMullan	(Ballyclare, NI)	
G-BYCN	Rans S6-ES Coyote I	PFA/204-13314		15. 9.98	J.K.Dunseath & R.L.Dunseath		
G-BYCO	Rans S6-ES Coyote II	PFA/204-13318		17. 9.98	T.J.Croskery	(Coleraine, NI)	
G-BYCP	Beechcraft B200 Super King Air	BB-966	F-GDCS	15.10.98	Comex Services Ltd	Ronaldsway	17.11.01
G-BYCS	CEA Jodel DR.1051 Sicile	201	F-BJUJ	28.10.98	R.A.Bragger	(Ringwood) (Lisburn, NI)	AC

Regn	Type	C/n	P/I	Date	Owner/operator	Probable Base	CA Expy
G-BYCT	Aero L-29A Delfin	395142	ES-YLH	29.10.98	Fast Jets Ltd	(Canterbury)	AC
			Estonian AF/Soviet AF				
G-BYCU	Robinson R-22 Beta	1094	G-OCGJ	3.11.98	Sloane Helicopters Ltd	Sywell	15. 9.01T
G-BYCV	Murphy Maverick	PFA/259-12925		24. 9.98	P.C.Vallence	Arclid, Sandbach	1. 1.00P
G-BYCW	Mainair Blade 912	1185-1198-7-W988		5.11.98	P.Hacking	Ince Blundell	
G-BYCX	Westland Wasp HAS.Mk.1	"W1A-B-Z3"	ZK-HOX	9.11.98	B.H.Austen	(Swindon)	AC
			NZ390?		t/a Austen Associates		
G-BYCY	III Sky Arrow 650T	PFA/298-13332		10.11.98	A.S.Sprigings	(Bury St. Edmunds)	
G-BYCZ	Jabiru SK	PFA/274-13388		16.10.98	Business Operational Services Ltd		
						Carlisle	
G-BYDA	Mc Donnell Douglas DC-10-30	46990	OY-CNO	25. 3.99	Airtours Intnl Airways Ltd	Manchester	
			XA-SYE/F-GGMZ/C-GFHX/9V-SDA				
G-BYDB	Grob G-115B	8025	VH-JVL	26 3.99	A F Jones	(Stafford)	
			D-EFCG				
G-BYDD	Mooney M.20J	24-0847	D-EIWM	19.10.98	Pilotime Ltd t/a GT Aviation	(Weymouth)	AC
G-BYDE	VS.361 Spitfire IX	-	Sov AF	11.11.98	A.H.Soper	(Romford)	
			PT879				
G-BYDF	Sikorsky S-76A	760364	JA6615	9. 1.98	Brecqhou Development Ltd	Guernsey	8. 7.01T
G-BYDG	Beechcraft C24R Sierra	MC-627	OY-AZL	9.11.98	Liddell Aircraft Ltd.	Bournemouth	AC
G-BYDH	Airbus A.300B4-203	210	F-OHPO	14. 1.99	TNT Express Worldwide (UK) Ltd		
			F-WHPK/SX-BAZ/N213PA/F-WZMK				
G-BYDI	Cameron A-210 HAFB	4495		4. 2.99	N.J.Appleton t/a First Flight	Bristol	12. 1.00T
G-BYDJ	Colt 120A HAFB	3527		17.11.99	Cameron Balloons Ltd	Bristol	23.11.99A
G-BYDK	Stampe SV-4C	55	F-BCXY	20.11.98	Bianchi Aviation Film Services Ltd		
	(P/I quoted officially as F-BCXV which was c/n 298)					Booker	
G-BYDL	Hawker Hurricane IIB	-	Sov AF	17.11.98	R.A.Roberts	(Billingshurst)	
			Z5207				
G-BYDM	Cyclone Pegasus Quantum 15-912	7488		18.11.98	B.J.Fallows	(Ammanford)	15.11.99P
G-BYDP	Fokker F.28-100 (F.100-650)	11321	F-WQJA	18. 2.99	Gill Aviation Ltd	Newcastle	
			N132ML/SE-DUA/PH-RRC/G-FIOS/PH-EZA				
G-BYDR	North American B-25D-30NC	100-20644	N88972	22. 3.99	Patina Ltd	Duxford	
	Mitchell II		CF-OGQ		(B J S Grey/The Fighter Collection)		
	(C/n 100-23644 reported)		RCAF KL161/43-3318	(As "KL161/VO-B" in 98 Sqdn RAF c/s) "Grumpy"			
G-BYDS	Messerschmitt Bf109E-3	1342	Luft'ffe	24.11.98	Alpine Deer Group Ltd	Duxford	
					(On rebuild in UK)		
G-BYDT	Cameron N-90 HAFB	4499		28. 1.99	Virgin Airship & Balloon Co Ltd	Telford	28. 1.00A
G-BYDU	Cameron Cart SS HAFB	4500		28. 1.99	Virgin Airship & Balloon Co Ltd	Telford	28. 1.00A
G-BYDV	Van's RV-6	PFA/181-13264		3.12.98	G.L.Carpenter	Birmingham	
G-BYDW	Rotary Air Force RAF 2000 GTX-SE	PFA G/13-1302		4.12.98	M.T.Byrne	(London E5)	
G-BYDY	Beech 58 Baron	TH-1852	C-GBWF	10.11.98	J.F.Britten	Fairoaks	19.11.01
G-BYDX	American General AG-5B Tiger	10051	N374SA	25. 3.99	A.J.Watson t/a Bibit Group	Southampton	
			G-AYDX/F-GKBH/N1191Y				
G-BYDZ	Cyclone Pegasus Quantum 15-912	7493		22.12.98	W.McCormack	(West Calder)	16.12.99
G-BYEA	Cessna 172P	172-75464	PH-ILL	7.10.98	Plane Talking Ltd	Elstree	19.10.01T
			N63661				
G-BYEB	Cessna 172P	172-74634	PH-ILM	7.10.98	Plane Talking Ltd	Elstree	18.10.01T
			N52917				
G-BYEC	Glaser-Dirks DG-800B	8-102-B36	D-KSDG	13.11.98	R.L.Mclean	Rufforth	23.11.01
G-BYED	BAC Jet Provost T.MK.5A	EEP/JP/966	N166A	23.11.98	R.E.Todd	Sandtoft	AC
			XW303				
G-BYEE	Mooney M.20K (231)	25-0282	N231JZ	20. 7.88	R.J.Baker & W.Woods	Coventry	26. 3.01
					t/a Double Echo Flying Group		
G-BYEF	Lockheed L.188CF Electra	2086	EI-CHX	14.12.98	Dart Group plc	Bournemouth	
			SE-IVR/N853U/PH-LLC	(Op Channel Express)			
G-BYEG	Cessna 182S Skylane	182-80404	N23697	3. 3.99	High Flying Aviation Ltd	Jersey	
G-BYEH	CEA DR.250/160 Capitaine	15	OO-SOL	6.10.98	E.J.Horsfall	Blackpool	AC
			F-BMZL				
G-BYEJ	Scheibe SF-28A Tandem Falke	5713	OE-9070	18.12.98	Total Support Inc (UK) Ltd	(Barnstaple)	AC
			(D-KDAM)				
G-BYEK	Stoddard-Hamilton Glastar	PFA/295-13087		14. 9.98	G.M.New	(York)	
G-BYEL	Van's RV-6	PFA/181-12560		7. 1.99	D.T.Smith	(Stockton-on-Tees)	
G-BYEM	Cessna R182 Skylane RG II	R182-00822	N494	8. 1.99	Swiftair Ltd	Elstree	AC
			D-ELVI/N737FT				
G-BYEN	Cessna 172P	172-74163	PH-ILU	6.10.98	Plane Talking Ltd.	Elstree	12.11.01T
			N97003				
G-BYEO	Zenair CH.601HDS	PFA/162-13345		11. 1.99	M.J.Diggins	(High Wycombe)	
					t/a Cloudbase F/Grp		
G-BYEP	Lindstrand LBL 90B HAFB	560		20.11.98	D.G Macguire	Pulborough	2.12.99A
G-BYER	Cameron C-80 HAFB	4513		19.11.98	Cameron Balloons Ltd	Bristol	7. 1.00A
G-BYES	Cessna 172P	172-74514	PH-ILN	7.10.98	Plane Talking Ltd	Elstree	15.10.01T
			N172TP/N52424				
G-BYET	Cessna 172P	172-75122	PH-ILP	7.10.98	Plane Talking Ltd	Elstree	15.10.01T
			N55158				
G-BYEU	Pegasus Quantum 15	7495		28. 1.99	T.C.Brown	Shifnal	
G-BYEW	Cyclone Pegasus Quantum 15	7499		15. 1.99	D McCormack	(West Calder)	13. 1.00P
G-BYEX	Sky 120-24 HAFB	135		21. 1.99	Ballongflyg Upp and Ner AB		11. 1.00A
						Stockholm, Sweden	

Regn	Type	C/n	P/I	Date	Owner/operator	Probable Base	CA Expy
G-BYEY	Lindstrand LBL-21 Silver Dream	577		15. 1.99	Oscair Project Ltd	Taby, Sweden	11. 1.00A
G-BYEZ	Dyn'Aero MCR-01	PFA 301-13185		25.11.98	J.P.Davies	(Lyndhurst)	
G-BYFA	Reims Cessna F.152 II	1968	G-WACA	19.11.98	A.J.Gomes	Biggin Hill	5. 5.96
G-BYFB	Cameron N-105 HAFB	4532		15. 1.99	Cameron Balloons Ltd	Bristol	
G-BYFC	Jabiru SK	PFA/274-13344		5. 2.99	A.C.N.Freeman	(High Wycombe)	
G-BYFD	Grob G-115A	8110	EI-CCN	15. 1.99	R Jones	Membury	
			G-BSGE		t/a Southern Sailplanes		
G-BYFF	Pegasus Quantum 15-912	7500		1. 2.99	D.Young t/a Kemble Flying Club	Kemble	31. 1.00P
G-BYFG	Europa Avn Europa XS	PFA/247-13407		22. 1.99	P R Brodie	(Guildford)	
G-BYFH	Bede BD-5B	665		22. 1.99	G M J Monaghan	(Bury St Edmunds)	AC
G-BYFI	CFM Starstreak Shadow SA	PFA/206-13300		11. 2.99	D.G.Cook	Leiston	
G-BYFJ	Cameron N-105 HAFB	4545		4. 3.99	Flying Pictures Ltd	Fairoaks	
G-BYFK	Cameron Printer-105 SS HAFB	4522		4. 3.99	Flying Pictures Ltd	Fairoaks	
G-BYFL	Diamond HK 36 TTS	36623		5. 2.99	C.N.J.Squibb	RNAS Culdrose	
					t/a Seahawk Gliding Club		
G-BYFM	Jodel DR.1050-MI Sicile Record	PFA/304-13237		26. 2.99	P.M.Standen & A.J.Roxburgh	(Bolton)	
G-BYFN	Thruster T600N	9029-T600N-030		8. 2.99	Thruster Air Services Ltd	Wantage	
G-BYFS	Airbus A.320-231	230	A40-MA	27. 3.99	Airtours Intl Airways Ltd	Manchester	
			N230RX/SX-BSJ/N230RX/F-WWOI				
G-BYFT	Pietenpol Aircamper	PFA/47-13057		22.12.98	M W Elliott	(Tamworth)	
G-BYFU	Lindstrand LBL-105B HAFB	594		9. 3.99	Balloons Lindstrand France	Curcay Sur Dive, France	
G-BYFV	Team Minimax 91	PFA/186-13431		5. 2.99	W.E.Gillham	(County Durham)	
G-BYFW	Cameron Rugby-90 SS HAFB	4533		4. 3.99	Cameron Balloons Ltd	Bristol	
G-BYFX	Colt 77A HAFB	4547		4. 3.99	Flying Pictures Ltd	Fairoaks	
G-BYFY	Avions Mudry CAP.10B	263	F-GKKD	9. 3.99	R.W.H.Cole Spilsted Farm, Sedlescombe		
					t/a Cole Aviation		
G-BYGA	Boeing 747-436	28855		15.12.98	British Airways plc	Heathrow	13.12.01T
					(Chelsea Rose t/s)		
G-BYGB	Boeing 747-436	28856		17. 1.99	British Airways plc	Heathrow	16. 1.02T
					(Dove/Colum t/s)		
G-BYGC	Boeing 747-436	25823		19. 1.99	British Airways plc	Heathrow	18. 1.02T
					(Chelsea Rose t/s)		
G-BYGD	Boeing 747-436	28857		26. 1.99	British Airways plc	Heathrow	25. 1.02T
					(Rendezvous t/s)		
G-BYGE	Boeing 747-436	28858		5. 2.99	British Airways plc	Heathrow	AC
					(Rendezvous t/s)		
G-BYGF	Boeing 747-436	25824		17. 2.99	British Airways plc	Heathrow	
					(Chelsea Rose t/s)		
G-BYGG	Boeing 747-436	28859		R	British Airways plc	Heathrow	
					(Rendezvous t/s) (For dely 5.99)		
G-BYHA	ATR-42-320	190	HS-TRK	15.12.98	Cabot 396 Ltd	(Hassocks)	AC
			F-WWEF				
G-BYHB	ATR-42-320	206	HS-TRL	15.12.98	Cabot 396 Ltd	(Hassocks)	AC
			F-WWEU				
G-BYHC	Cameron Z-90 HAFB	4555		16. 3.99	N.Appleton, R.Waycott	Bristol	
					t/a The Balloon Co & Darlows Ltd		
G-BYHD	Robinson R-22 Beta	1455	N900AB	22. 3.99	A S Owen	(Motherwell)	
G-BYHE	Robinson R-22 Beta	2023	N82128	14. 1.99	L Smith t/a Helicopter Services	Booker	AC
			LV-VAB				
G-BYHI	PA-28-161 Warrior II	28-8116084	SE-IDP	4. 1.99	Phoenix House Developments Ltd (Reading)		AC
					t/a Aviation 2000		
G-BYHL	DHC-1 Chipmunk 22	C1/0361	WG308	15. 3.99	W.F., M.R.& I.D.Higgins	Gamston	
	(Fuselage No.DHBF260 quoted as c/n)						
G-BYHM	BAe 125-800B	258233	VP-BTM	12. 2.99	Corporate Aircraft Leasing Ltd	Jersey	
			VR-BTM/(VR-BQH)/F-WQCD/D-CAVW/G-5-770				
G-BYHO	Mainair Blade 912	1197-0599-7-W1000		16. 3.99	P.J.Morton	(High Peak)	
G-BYHS	Mainair Blade 912	1187-0299-7-W990		11. 3.99	D.A.Bolton	(Rochdale)	
G-BYHV	X'Air	BMAA/HB/090		25. 3.99	B J Bowditch	Bristol	
G-BYHW	Cameron A-160	2848	D-OWEH	25. 3.99	R H Etherington	Siena, Italy	
G-BYHY	Cameron V-77	4493		22. 3.99	P Spellward	Bristol	
G-BYIA	Jabiru SK	PFA/274-13436		10. 2.99	M.F.Cottam	(Lincoln)	
G-BYIB	Rans S6-ES	PFA/204-13387		26. 3.99	G A Clayton	(Chesterfield)	
G-BYIF	Jabiru XL	PFA/274A-13364		26. 3.99	D Cassidy	(Canterbury)	
G-BYIG	Murphy Renegade Spirit	PFA/188-12519		26. 2.99	J.Hatswell	(Menton, France)	
G-BYII	Team Minimax	PFA/186-11820		22. 1.99	J S R Moodie	(Rogart)	
G-BYIJ	CASA I-131E Jungmann	2110	E3B-514	16. 7.90	K.B.Palmer	Headcorn	28. 4.98P
G-BYIK	Europa Avn Europa	PFA/247-12771		2. 2.99	P.M.Davis	(Abingdon)	
G-BYIM	Jabiru UL	PFA/274A-13397		22.12.98	W J Dale	(Nottingham)	
G-BYIN	RAF 2000	PFA G/13-1305		19. 1.99	J.R.Legge	(Rossendale)	
G-BYIP	Aerotek Pitts S-2A	2244	N109WA	23. 2.99	Hampshire Aeroplane Co. Ltd	St.Just	
			TC-ECN				
G-BYIR	Aerotek Pitts S-1S Special	1-0063	N103WA	23. 2.99	Hampshire Aeroplane Co. Ltd	St.Just	
			TC-ECP				
G-BYIS	Pegasus Quantum 15-912	7508		25. 2.99	Light Flight Ltd	(Newark)	
G-BYIT	Robin DR400/500	0010		27. 1.99	P.R.Liddle	(Maidstone)	

Regn	Type	C/n	P/I	Date	Owner/operator	Probable Base	CA Expy
G-BYIY	Lindstrand LBL-105B	601		26. 3.99	Lindstrand Balloons Ltd	Oswestry	
G-BYIZ	Pegasus Quantum 15-912	7504		8. 2.99	J.D.Gray	Ryton	
G-BYJO	Rans S6-ES Coyoye II	PFA/204-13338		4. 3.99	G.Ferguson	(Kings Lynn)	
G-BYJP	Aerotek Pitts S-1S Special	1-0064	N105WA TC-ECR	16. 3.99	T.Riddle t/a Eaglescott Pitts Grp	(Rickmansworth)	
G-BYJS	Socata TB-20 Trinidad	1875	F-OIGE	15. 1.99	J K Sharkey	(London NW5)	25. 1.02
G-BYKE	Rans S6-ESA	PFA/204-13327		22. 1.99	C.Townsend	(Malmesbury)	
G-BYKK	Robinson R-44 Astro	0572		4. 3.99	Heliflight (UK) Ltd	(Stourbridge)	
G-BYKZ	Sky 140-24 HAFB	147		25. 2.99	D.J.Head	Newbury	
G-BYLL	Sequoia Falco F.8L (Lyc O-320)	PFA/100-10843		6.12.85	N.J.Langrick	Breighton	4. 3.99P
G-BYLS	Bede BD-4 (Lyc O-320)	PFA/37-11288		13.12.90	G.H.Bayliss	Shobdon	14. 6.99P
G-BYLY	Cameron V-77 HAFB	3375	G-ULIA(2)	16.7.97	R.Bayly	Bristol	7. 8.99A
G-BYNA	Reims Cessna F.172H	0626	OO-VDW PH-VDW/(G-AWTH)/F-WLIT	15. 1.99	R E Knapton	(Aylesbury)	AC
G-BYNG	Cessna T303 Crusader	T303-00306	G-PTWB N6312V	3.11.88	J.M.E.Byng	Elstree	10. 3.00
G-BYPM	Europa Avn Europa XS	PFA/247-13418		16.12.98	P.Mileham	(Saffron Walden)	
G-BYRE	Rans S-10 Sakota	PFA/194-11729		23. 7.91	R.J. & M.B.Trickey	(Ellon, Aberdeen)	
G-BYSE	Agusta-Bell 206B JetRanger II	8553	G-BFND	3.11.81	Bewise Ltd (Op PLM Dollar Group)	Inverness/Coventry	11. 7.99T
G-BYSL	Cameron O-56 HAFB	1269		10. 4.86	S.M.M.Askey	Tring	22. 8.96A
G-BYTE	Robinson R-22 Beta	1250		18. 4.90	Manhattan Associates (UK) Ltd	(Neath)	31. 5.99T
G-BYXU	PA-28-161 Cherokee Warrior II	28-7716097	EI-BXU G-BNUP/N2282Q	8. 1.99	W T King	Brittas Bay	27. 8.90

G-BZAA-BZZZ

Regn	Type	C/n	P/I	Date	Owner/operator	Probable Base	CA Expy
G-BZAT	BAe 146 RJ100	E-3320	G-6-320	18.11.97	Cityflyer Express Ltd (Waves of the City t/s)	Gatwick	8. 1.00T
G-BZAU	BAe 146 RJ100	E-3328		25. 4.98	Cityflyer Express Ltd (Dove/Colum t/s)	Gatwick	11. 6.01T
G-BZAV	BAe 146 RJ100	E-3331		19. 5.98	Cityflyer Express Ltd (Chelsea Rose t/s)	Gatwick	23. 7.01T
G-BZBH	Thunder Ax7-65 Bolt HAFB	173		28.11.78	R.B. & G.Craik "Serendipity II"	Northampton	8. 5.99A
G-BZGC	Aerospatiale AS.355F1 Twin Squirrel	5077	G-CCAO G-SETA/G-NEAS/G-CMMM/G-BNBJ/C-GLKH	26. 3.99	McAlpine Helicopters Ltd	Oxford	21.11.99T
G-BZGH	Reims Cessna F.172H Skyhawk II	1789	EI-BGH	1.12.98	D.Behan t/a Golf Hotel Group	(Dublin)	AC
G-BZHA	Boeing 767-336ER	29230	N60668	22. 5.98	British Airways plc (Wings of the City t/s)	Heathrow	21. 5.01T
G-BZHB	Boeing 767-336ER	29231		30. 5.98	British Airways plc (Delftblue Daybreak t/s)	Heathrow	29. 5.01T
G-BZHC	Boeing 767-336ER	29232		29. 6.98	British Airways plc (Waves & Cranes t/s)	Heathrow	28. 6.01T
G-BZKK	Cameron V-56 HAFB	396		2. 8.78	P.J.Green & C.Bosley t/a Gemini Balloon Group "Gemini II"	Newbury	13. 8.96A
G-BZZD	Reims Cessna F.172M Skyhawk II	1436	G-BDPF	14. 4.98	S.& C.Barry	Shoreham	28. 7.99T

G-CAAA-CZZZ

Regn	Type	C/n	P/I	Date	Owner/operator	Probable Base	CA Expy
G-CAHA	PA-34-200T Seneca II	34-7770010	N23PL SE-GPY/(D-IICC)/SE-GPY	7. 7.98	R.Marshall	Sandtoft	31. 7.01
G-CAIN	CFM Shadow Srs.CD (Rotax 503)	062	G-MTKU	26. 1.99	A.J.Cain	(Corby)	13. 5.99P
G-CALL	PA-23-250 Aztec F	27-7754061	N62826	21.12.77	Woodgate Avn (IOM) Ltd	Aldergrove/Ronaldsway	29. 5.01T
G-CAMB	Aerospatiale AS.355F2 Twin Squirrel	5416	N813LP	17.12.96	Cambridge & Essex Air Support Consortium	Huntingdon	16. 4.00T
G-CAMM	Hawker Cygnet replica (Mosler MM-CB35)	PFA/77-10245	(G-ERDB)	30. 5.91	D.M.Cashmore (On loan to The Shuttleworth Collection)	Old Warden	17. 7.99P
G-CAMP	Cameron N-105	4546		24. 3.99	R D Parry t/a Hong Kong Balloon & Airship Club	Hong Kong	
G-CAMR	BFC Challenger II	PFA/177-12569		26. 3.99	P R A Walker	Ringwood	
G-CAPI	Mudry/CAARP CAP.10B	76	G-BEXR	16. 3.99	I.Valentine	(Dungannon)	28. 7.00
G-CAPX	Avions Mudry CAP.10B	280		21. 9.98	R.W.H.Cole Spilsted Farm, Sedlescombe t/a Cole Aviation		21.12.01T
G-CBAC	Short SD.3-60 Var.200	SH.3675	B-3608 G-BLYH/G-14-3675	20.10.95	BAC Leasing Ltd (Stored Baiyun, Guangzhou, China 2.97)	Exeter	19.11.95F
G-CBAL	PA-28-161 Warrior II	28-8116087	LN-MAD N83007	25. 3.94	Britannia Airways Ltd	Redhill	13. 4.00T
G-CBCL	Stoddard-Hamilton Glastar PFA/295-13089			5. 9.97	C.F.M.Norman	(Somerton)	
G-CBIL	Cessna 182K Skylane	182-57804	(G-BFZZ) D-ENGO/N26040	9.10.78	G.H.Parsons	East Midlands	2. 9.99
G-CBKT	Cameron O-77 HAFB	1754		7. 6.88	Caledonian Airways Ltd "Caledonian"	Gatwick	22. 6.99A
G-CBOR	Reims Cessna F172N Skyhawk II	1656	PH-BOR PH-AXG(1)	28. 5.87	Pauline Seville	Barton	8. 5.00T
G-CCAR	Cameron N-77 HAFB	464		5.12.78	D.P.Turner "Mitsubishi Cars"	Bath	23. 7.99A
	(Rebuilt 8.1980 after write off Newton Abbot 13.7.80 using new envelope c/n 670; c 1989 with c/n 2108 and in 1992 with c/n 2658 !)						
G-CCAT	Gulfstream AA-5A Cheetah	AA5A-0893	G-OAJH G-KILT/G-BJFA/N27169	16. 1.92	Plane Talking Ltd	Elstree	30.10.99T
G-CCAU	Eurocopter EC-135T-1	0040	G-79-01	30. 6.98	West Mercia Constabulary	(Hindlip)	21. 7.01T
G-CCCC	Cessna 172H	172-55822	SE-ELU N2622L	9. 2.79	K.E.Wilson	Bourn	16.10.01
G-CCCP	IAV Bacau Yakovlev Yak-52	899404	LY-AKV DOSAAF16 (Yellow)	30.11.93	R.J.N.Howarth	North Weald	27. 1.99P
G-CCIX*	VS.361 Spitfire LF.IXe (C/n is firewall no.)	CBAF.IX.558	IDF/AF2046/Czech AF/TE517 (Stored pending rebuild 3.96)	9. 4.85	K.Weeks	Booker	16.10.01
G-CCLY	Bell 206B JetRanger III	3594	G-TILT G-BRJO/N2295Z	26. 4.95	Ciceley Ltd	Samlesbury Helipad	17.10.98
G-CCOA	Scottish Avn Bulldog 120/122 BH120-375		G-111 Ghana AF/G-BCUU	4. 9.96	Cranfield University	Cranfield	23. 2.00T
G-CCOL	Gulfstream AA-5A Cheetah	AA5A-0772	G-BIVU N26859	24. 4.92	Lowlog Ltd (Op Cabair)	Elstree	24. 6.99T
G-CCOZ	Monnett Sonerai II 0197 & PFA/15-10107 (VW1900)			31. 5.78	P.R.Cozens	Hinton-in-the-Hedges	21. 6.98P
G-CCSC	Cameron N-77 HAFB	4282		16. 1.98	C.J.Royden "Coherent"	Stroud	7. 1.99A
G-CCUB	Piper J3C-65 Cub	2362A	N33528 NC33528	2. 4.81	Cormack (Acft Svs) Ltd (On rebuild 8.94)	Carlisle	
G-CCVV*	VS.379 Spitfire FR.XIVe	6S/649186	IAF"42" MV262	18. 5.88	K.Weeks (On rebuild 3.96)	Booker	
G-CDAV	PA-34-220T Seneca V	3449033	N9284Q	27.11.97	Saratoga Air Club SRL	(Navarra, Spain)	26.11.00T
G-CDBS	MBB Bo.105DBS-4 (See also G-BCXO)	S.738	D-HDRZ VH-MBK/N970MB/D-HDRZ	29. 9.89	Bond Helicopters Ltd (Op Cornwall Ambulance Service)	St.Mawgan	7.11.01T
G-CDET	Culver LCA Cadet (Cont O-200-A)	129	N29261 NC29261	10.11.86	H.B.Fox (As "29261" in USAAF c/s)	Booker	31. 7.99P
G-CDGA	Taylor JT.1 Monoplane 6020/1 & PFA/55-10382			28.12.78	R.M.Larimore	(Spondon, Derby)	
G-CDON	PA-28-161 Warrior II	28-8216185	N8254D	24. 5.88	East Midlands Flying School Ltd	East Midlands	30. 6.00T
G-CDRU	CASA I-131E Jungmann	2321	EC-DRU E3B-530	19. 1.90	P.Cunniff "Yen a Bon"	White Waltham	30. 6.99P
G-CEAA	Airbus A.300B2-1C	062	F-WQGQ F-BUAI	2. 7.98	European Aviation Ltd (Open store 1.99)	Bournemouth	AC
G-CEAB	Airbus A.300B2-1C	027	F-WQGS F-BUAH/F-WLGC/F-WLGB (Open store 1.99)	. 1.98R	European Aviation Ltd	Bournemouth	
G-CEAL	Short SD.3-60 Var.100	SH.3761	N161CN N161SB/G-BPXO	11. 9.95	BAC Express Airlines Ltd		12. 1.00T
G-CEAS*	HPR.7 Dart Herald 214	186	G-BEBB PP-SDH	31. 1.86	Dart Group plc t/a Channel Express (Stored 7.97)	Bournemouth	4. 6.99T
G-CEGA	PA-34-200T Seneca II	34-8070367	N8272B	20.11.80	Oxford Aviation Services Ltd	Oxford	
G-CEGR	Beechcraft 200 Super King Air BB-351		N68CP N351FW/N6666C/N6666K	23. 7.97	Caga Aviation Ltd	Goodwood	18. 8.00T

Regn	Type	C/n	P/I	Date	Owner/operator	Probable Base	CA Expy
G-CEJA	Cameron V-77 HAFB	2469	G-BTOF	17. 6.91	L. & C.Gray	Farnborough	3. 5.99A
G-CERT	Mooney M.20K (252TSE)	25-1134		5.10.87	S.T.Newington	Conington	5. 2.00
G-CEXA	Fokker F-27 Friendship 500RF	10503	N703A	19. 1.96	Dart Group plc	Bournemouth	24.3.02TC
			PH-EXK		t/a Channel Express		
G-CEXB	Fokker F-27 Friendship 500RF	10550	N743A	15.11.95	Dart Group plc	Coventry/Bournemouth	30.1.99TC
			PH-EXF		t/a Channel Express (Parcel Force titles)		
G-CEXC	Airbus A.300B4-103F	124	N407U	18. 7.97	Dart Group plc	Stansted	17. 7.00T
			N407UA/N220EA/F-GBNO		t/a Channel Express		
G-CEXD	Fokker F-27 Friendship 600	10351	PH-KFE	18. 2.97	Dart Group plc	Bournemouth	18.2.00TC
			HB-AAX/PH-FLX				
G-CEXE	Fokker F-27 Friendship 500	10654	SU-GAF	2. 4.97	Dart Group plc	Bournemouth	14.5.00TC
			PH-EXJ		t/a Channel Express		
G-CEXF	Fokker F-27 Friendship 500	10660	SU-GAE	2. 4.97	Dart Group plc	Bournemouth	30.6.00TC
			PH-EXC		t/a Channel Express		
G-CEXH	Airbus A.300B4-203F	117	D-ASAZ	30. 3.98	Dart Group plc	Liege	1. 4.00T
			N14966/N966C/F-OGTB/9V-STA/F-WZER t/a Channel Express				
G-CEXI	Airbus A.300B4-203 (mod)	121	D-ASAA	3. 9.98	Dart Group plc (Op TNT)	Liege	3. 9.01T
			N15967/N967C/F-OGTC/9V-STB/F-WZEK				
G-CEXP*	HPR.7 Dart Herald 209	195	I-ZERC	29.10.87	BAA plc	Gatwick	7.11.96T
			G-BFRJ/4X-AHO		(On display on Terminal Building 8.98)		
G-CEXS	Lockheed L.188CF Electra	1091	N5539	14. 4.92	Dart Group plc	Bournemouth	15. 4.99T
			N171PS/N971HA/N171PS t/a Channel Express				
G-CFBI	Colt 56A HAFB	570		11. 7.84	G.A.Fisher	Guildford	24. 7.91A
					t/a Out-of-the-Blue "Air O"		
G-CFLY*	Cessna 172F	172-52635	PH-SNO	25. 8.78	Not known (Stored 6.96)	Blackpool	13. 7.95
			N8731U				
G-CFME	Socata TB.10 Tobago	1795	F-GNHU	15. 4.98	Charles Funke Associates Ltd (Godalming)		4. 5.01T
G-CGHM	PA-28-140 Cruiser	28-7425143	PH-NSM	25. 4.79	C.M.Jones	Shoreham	8.10.00
G-CGOD	Cameron N-77 HAFB	2647		5. 9.91	G.P.Lane	Waltham Abbey	13. 6.96A
					"Neptune"		
G-CGON	Beechcraft F33C Bonanza	CJ-145	G-CCON	13. 7.98	Aces High Ltd	North Weald	19. 5.00
			PH-BNM				
G-CHAA	Cameron O-90 HAFB	2471		24.10.91	P.Farmer	Wadhurst	4. 6.99T
G-CHAM	Cameron Pot 90SS HAFB	2912		29. 9.92	B.J.Reeves & C.Walker	Brighouse	6. 8.99A
	(Chambourcy Pot shape)				t/a High Exposure Balloons		
G-CHAP	Robinson R-44 Astro	0326		9. 4.97	Monitron International Ltd		
						Halfpenny Green	30. 4.00T
G-CHAR	Grob G-109B	6435		21. 5.86	T.Holloway t/a RAFGSA	RAF Bicester	26. 6.99
G-CHAS	PA-28-181 Archer II	28-8090325	N82228	18. 3.91	C.H.Elliott	Stapleford	7. 5.00
G-CHAV	Europa Avn Europa	PFA/247-12769		28.12.94	M.B.Stoner t/a Chavenage F/Grp (Tetbury)		
G-CHAZ	Rans S-6-ESA Coyote II	1291-250		7.10.93	C.H.Middleton	(Borrowash, Derby)	
G-CHCA	Aerospatiale AS.332L-1	2007	F-WQDZ	13. 1.98	Brintel Helicopters Ltd	Aberdeen	26. 4.01T
	Super Puma		C-GSEM		t/a British International Helicopters		
			HC-B../C-GSEM/HC-BPE/C-GSEM/HK-3197X/C-GSEM/N332CH/OE-GXB				
G-CHCB	Aerospatiale AS.332L-1	2015	F-....	29. 6.98	Brintel Helicopters Ltd	Aberdeen	21. 2.01T
	Super Puma		C-GQYX		t/a British International Helicopters		
			HC-BRH/C-GQYX/HC-BOZ/C-GQYX/P2-PHY/C-GQYX/N5789M				
G-CHCC	Aerospatiale AS.332L-1	2087	N25AN	27. 8.98	Brintel Helicopters Ltd	Aberdeen	AC
	Super Puma		N77GY/N58023		t/a British International Helicopters		
G-CHCD	Sikorsky S-76A II Plus	760101	G-CBJB	16. 1.98	Brintel Helicopters Ltd	Aberdeen	18. 2.01T
			N288SP/C-GIMN/YV-326C t/a British International Helicopters				
G-CHEB	Europa Avn Europa	PFA/247-12967		16. 9.96	C.H.P.Bell	Wombleton	16. 6.98P
	(NSI EA-81/100)						
G-CHEM	PA-34-200T Seneca II	34-8170032	N8292Y	26. 8.87	London Executive Avn Ltd	London City	28. 1.00T
G-CHES	BN-2A-26 Islander	2011	G-PASY	19. 4.94	The Cheshire Constabulary	Chester	2. 6.00T
			G-BPCB/G-BEXA/G-MALI/(ZB503)/G-DIVE/G-BEXA				
G-CHET	Europa Avn Europa	PFA/247-13277		12. 2.98	H.P.Chetwynd-Talbot	(York)	
G-CHGL	Bell 206B JetRanger II	1669	G-BPNG	29. 4.98	Helisport Ltd	Kintore, Inverurie	3. 3.00T
			G-ORTC/G-BPNG/N20EA/C-GHVB				
G-CHIK	Reims Cessna F.152 II	1628	G-BHAZ	19.10.81	Stapleford F/C Ltd	Stapleford	3.11.00T
			(D-EHLE)				
G-CHIP	PA-28-181 Archer II	28-8290095	N81337	22. 2.82	C.M.Hough	Fairoaks	21. 4.00
G-CHIS	Robinson R-22 Beta	1740		5. 4.91	I.R.Chisholm	Costock, Loughborough	30. 7.00T
					t/a Bradmore Helicopter Leasing		
G-CHKL	Cameron Kookaburra 120SS HAFB	3733		8.11.95	Eagle Ltd	Canowindra, Australia	19. 3.97A
G-CHLT	Stemme S-10	10-30	D-KGCD	3. 7.91	F.C.Y.Cheung	Quasada, Alicante, Spain	24.11.00
					(Op B.J.Willson)		
G-CHMP	Bellanca 7ACA Champ	62-72	N68556	21.12.92	I.J.Langley (Llanllawddog, Carmarthen)		
					(Stored Bidford 10.92)		
G-CHNL	Fokker F-27 Friendship 600	10508	OY-SRZ	20. 3.95	Dart Group plc	Bournemouth	18. 5.01T
			N61AU/OB-R-1042/PH-EXA t/a Channel Express				
G-CHNX	Lockheed L.188AF Electra	1068	EI-CHO	1.11.94	Channel Express (Air Svs) Ltd		
			(G-CHNX)/N5535			Bournemouth	31.10.01
G-CHOK	Cameron V-77 HAFB	1752		25. 5.88	Amanda J.Moore	Great Missenden	21. 3.99T
					"S'il Vous Plais"		
G-CHOP	Westland-Bell 47G-3B1	WA/380	XT221	19.12.78	Image Computer Systems Ltd	Wimborne	28. 8.99T
	(Line No.WAN/79)						
G-CHPY	DHC.1 Chipmunk 22	C1/0093	WB652	7. 3.97	JGH Computer Services Ltd	(Cardiff)	15.10.01T
G-CHSU	Eurocopter EC.135 T1	0079		4. 2.99	McAlpine Helicopters Ltd	Oxford	

Regn	Type	C/n	P/I	Date	Owner/operator	Probable Base	CA Expy
G-CHTA	Grumman-American AA-5A Cheetah	AA5A-0631	G-BFRC	3. 3.86	Quickspin Ltd (Op Biggin Hill School of Flying)	Biggin Hill	12. 1.00T
G-CHTT*	Varga 2150A Kachina	VAC162-80		7. 9.84	H.W.Hall	Southend	6. 9.87
					(Damaged nr Hatherleigh, Devon 27.4.86; spares for G-BPVK 3.99)		
G-CHUB	Colt Cylinder Two N-51 HAFB (Fire Extinguisher shape)	1720		11. 4.90	Chubb Fire Ltd "Chubb Fire Extinguisher" (British Balloon Museum 2.97)	Newbury	19.12.95A
G-CHUG	Europa Avn Europa	PFA/247-12960		29. 7.96	C.M.Washington	(Stoke-on-Trent)	
G-CHUK	Cameron O-77 HAFB	2773		6. 3.92	L.C.Taylor	Burton-on-Trent	5. 4.93A
G-CHYL	Robinson R-22 Beta	1197		28.11.89	Caroline M.Gough-Cooper	Ringwood	10. 1.02
G-CIAO	III Sky Arrow 1450L	PFA/298-13095		23. 7.97	J.Hosier	Draycott Farm, Chiseldon	10. 1.02
G-CIAS	PBN BN-2B-21 Islander	2162	HC-BNS G-BKJM	1. 5.91	Channel Island Air Search Ltd	Guernsey	20. 4.99
G-CICI	Cameron R-15 Gas/HAFB	673	(N) G-CICI/(G-BIHP)	11.11.80	Ballooning Endeavours Ltd	Bristol	5.6.91P*
G-CIFR	PA-28-181 Cherokee Archer II	28-7790208	PH-MIT OO-HBB/N7654F	18. 6.97	Aeroshow Ltd	Gloucestershire	9. 7.00T
G-CIGY	Westland-Bell 47G-3B1	WA/350	G-BGXP XT191	26.10.98	R.A. Perrot	Guernsey	13. 2.00
G-CIPI	AJEP Wittman W.8 Tailwind (Cont O-200-A)	AJEP/2 & PFA/1363	G-AYDU	22. 7.87	N.R.Hurley (Roquefort Les Pins, France)		15. 6.99P
G-CITA	Bellanca 7KCAB Citabria	543-75	N14091 G-CITA/N53785/SE-KUI/N53785	2. 2.96	J.R.K.Pardoe	Hove	21. 3.99T
G-CITI	Cessna 501 Citation	501-0084	VP-CDM VR-CDM/G-CITI/(N11JC)/(N463CJ)/N3160M	21. 9.87	Euro Executive Jet Ltd	Southampton	8. 9.99T
G-CITY	PA-31-350 Navajo Chieftain	31-7852136	N27741	12. 9.78	Woodgate Avn (IOM) Ltd	Ronaldsway/Aldergrove	5.11.00T
G-CITZ	Bell 206B Jet Ranger II	1997	G-BRTB N9936K	19. 2.99	Euro Executive Jet Ltd	Southampton	4. 6.99T
G-CIVA	Boeing 747-436	27092		19. 3.93	British Airways plc (Op British Asia Airways) "City of St.Davids"/"Dinas Tyddewi"	Heathrow	18. 3.00T
G-CIVB	Boeing 747-436	25811	(G-BNLY)	15. 2.94	British Airways plc "City of Lichfield"	Heathrow	14. 2.01T
G-CIVC	Boeing 747-436	25812	(G-BNLZ)	26. 2.94	British Airways plc (Delftblue Daybreak t/s)	Heathrow	25. 2.00T
G-CIVD	Boeing 747-436	27349		14.12.94	British Airways plc (Waves of the City t/s)	Gatwick	13.12.00T
G-CIVE	Boeing 747-436	27350		20.12.94	British Airways plc (Op British Asia Airways) "City of Sunderland"	Heathrow	19.12.00T
G-CIVF	Boeing 747-436	25434	(G-BNLY)	29. 3.95	British Airways plc "City of St.Albans"	Gatwick	28. 3.01T
G-CIVG	Boeing 747-436	25813	N6009F	20. 4.95	British Airways plc "City of Wells"	Heathrow	18. 4.01T
G-CIVH	Boeing 747-436	25809		23. 4.96	British Airways plc "City of Hereford"	Gatwick	22. 4.99T
G-CIVI	Boeing 747-436	25814		2. 5.96	British Airways plc "City of Gloucester"	Gatwick	1. 5.99T
G-CIVJ	Boeing 747-436	25817		11. 2.97	British Airways plc	Heathrow	10. 2.00T
G-CIVK	Boeing 747-436	25818		28. 2.97	British Airways plc (Op British Asia Airways)	Heathrow	27. 2.00T
G-CIVL	Boeing 747-436	27478		28. 3.97	British Airways plc	Heathrow	27. 3.00T
G-CIVM	Boeing 747-436	28700		5. 6.97	British Airways plc (Waves & Cranes t/s)	Heathrow	4. 6.00T
G-CIVN	Boeing 747-436	28848		29. 9.97	British Airways plc (Delftblue Daybreak t/s)	Heathrow	28. 9.00T
G-CIVO	Boeing 747-436	28849	N6046P	5.12.97	British Airways plc (Mountain of the Birds/Benthone Tartan t/s)	Heathrow	4.12.00T
G-CIVP	Boeing 747-436	25850		17. 2.98	British Airways plc (Dove/Colum t/s)	Heathrow	16. 2.01T
G-CIVR	Boeing 747-436	25820		2. 3.98	British Airways plc (Waves & Cranes t/s)	Gatwick	1. 3.01T
G-CIVS	Boeing 747-436	28851		13. 3.98	British Airways plc (Whale Rider t/s)	Heathrow	12. 3.01T
G-CIVT	Boeing 747-436	25821	(G-CIVN)	20. 3.98	British Airways plc (Delftblue Daybreak t/s)	Heathrow	19. 3.01T
G-CIVU	Boeing 747-436	25810	(G-CIVO)	24. 4.98	British Airways plc (Wings of the City t/s)	Heathrow	23. 4.01T
G-CIVV	Boeing 747-436	25819	N6009F (G-CIVP)	23. 5.98	British Airways plc (Rendezvous t/s)	Heathrow	21. 5.01T
G-CIVW	Boeing 747-436	25822	(G-CIVR)	15. 5.98	British Airways plc (Mountain of the Birds/Benyhone Tartan t/s)	Heathrow	14. 5.01T
G-CIVX	Boeing 747-436	28852		3. 9.98	British Airways plc (Waves & Cranes t/s)	Heathrow	2. 9.01T
G-CIVY	Boeing 747-436	28853		29. 9.98	British Airways plc (Whale Rider t/s)	Heathrow	28. 9.01T
G-CIVZ	Boeing 747-436	28854		31.10.98	British Airways PLC (Mountain of the Birds/Benyhone Tartan t/s)	Heathrow	30.10.01T
G-CJBC	PA-28-180 Cherokee D	28-5470	OY-BDE	28.11.80	J.B.Cave	Halfpenny Green	16. 7.99

Regn	Type	C/n	P/I	Date	Owner/operator	Probable Base	CA Expy
G-CJCI	Pilatus P.2-06	600-63	U-143	30. 7.84	J.Briscoe & P.G.Bond t/a Pilatus P2 F/Grp (As "CC+43"" in Luftwaffe c/s in Arado Ar.96B guise)	Norwich	27. 9.99P
G-CJIM*	Taylor JT.1 Monoplane	PFA/1419		28.12.78	J.Crawford (Under construction 7.95 - cancelled by CAA 24.3.99)	Farnborough	
G-CJUD	Denney Kitfox mk.3 847 & PFA/172-11939 (Rotax 582)			17. 1.91	M.D.Hamwee "Dougal"	(London SW4)	25.11.99P
G-CKCK	Enstrom 280FX Shark	2071	OO-PVL	5. 5.95	Farmax Ltd	(Maidstone)	14. 5.98T
G-CKEN*	Wombat Autogyro	CJ-002		1. 6.90	K.H.Durran (Not constructed)(Dorchester)		
G-CLAC	PA-28-161 Warrior II	28-8116241	N8369U	18. 5.87	PBD Techtronics Ltd	Blackbushe	3.11.99
G-CLAG	Lindstrand LBL-90A HAFB	582		26. 1.99	Cargolifter AG	Wiesbaden, Germany	
G-CLAS	Short SD.3-60 Var.200	SH.3635	EI-BEK G-BLED/G-14-3635	7.93	BAC Express Airlines Ltd (Op Jersey European Airways Ltd)	Exeter	20. 7.99T
G-CLEA	PA-28-161 Warrior II	28-7916081	N30296	28. 8.80	R.J.Harrison & A.R.Carpenter Oaksey Park		30.11.01
G-CLEM	Bolkow Bo.208A-2 Junior	561	G-ASWE D-EFHE	22. 9.81	J.J.Donely & A.D.P.Thompson t/a Bolkow Group	Coventry	8.12.99P
G-CLIC	Cameron A-105 HAFB (New envelope c/n 3395 4.95)	2557		18. 4.91	R.S.Mohr "Clic Trust"	Corsham	14. 5.01A
G-CLIP	Eurocopter AS.355N Twin Squirrel	5580		25.11.94	Quantel Ltd	Thruxton	11. 4.98T
G-CLKE	Robinson R-44 Astro	0185	G-HREH D-HREH	22. 9.98	J.Clarke t/a Clarke Business	(Burnley)	10. 9.00T
G-CLOE	Sky 90-24 HAFB	019		11. 3.96	C.J.Sandell "Headfirst"	Sevenoaks	1. 4.99T
G-CLOS	PA-34-200T Seneca II	34-7870361	HB-LKE N36783	17. 6.86	P.S.Kirby	Coventry	12. 9.01T
G-CLRK	Sky 77-24 HAFB	101		3. 3.98	William Clark & Son (Parkgate) Ltd	Dumfries	2.12.99A
G-CLUB	Reims Cessna FRA.150N Aerobat	0347	OO-AWZ F-WZAZ/(F-WZDZ)	10. 2.83	D.C.C.Handley	Cranfield	1. 5.99T
G-CLUE	PA-34-200T Seneca II	34-7970502	N8089Z	15. 9.92	Bristol Office Machines Ltd	Bristol/Lulsgate	25. 1.02T
G-CLUX	Reims Cessna F.172N Skyhawk II	1996	PH-AYG(3)	1. 5.80	J.G.Jackman & K.M.Drewitt t/a J & K Avn	Chester	20. 8.01T
G-CMGC	PA-25-235 Pawnee D	25-7756042	G-BFEX N82525	19.11.91	Midland Gliding Club Ltd	Long Mynd	19. 4.01
G-CNDY	Robinson R-22 Beta	2677	G-BXEW	15. 5.97	Testgate Ltd	Dunsfold	27. 5.00T
G-COAI	Cranfield A.1	001	G-BCIT	1. 6.98	Cranfield University	Cranfield	
G-COCO	Reims Cessna F.172M Skyhawk II	1373	PH-SMO OO-ADI	27.10.80	P.C.Sheard & R.C.Larder	North Reston, Louth	15. 2.99
G-CODE	Bell 206B Jet Ranger III	3850	N222DM N84TC	27. 8.96	Datel Direct Ltd	Stone	19. 9.99
G-COEZ	Airbus A.320-231	179	OY-CNH F-WWIS	10. 2.97	Airtours International Airways Ltd	Manchester	11. 2.00T
G-COIN	Bell 206B JetRanger II	897	EI-AWA	11. 3.85	C.Sarno	Luton	22. 6.00
G-COLA	Beechcraft F33C Bonanza	CJ-137	G-BUAZ PH-BNH	31. 3.92	J.A.Kelman & Cola Aviation Ltd	Spilsted Farm, Sedlescombe	3. 4.98
G-COLB	Boeing 737-3Q8	26283	N373TA	28. 5.98	Color Air AS (Op by Air Foyle Charter Airlines Ltd)	Oslo-Gardermoen, Norway	6. 8.01T
G-COLC	Boeing 737-3Q8	26286	N374TA	26. 5.98	Color Air AS (Op by Air Foyle Charter Airlines Ltd)	Oslo-Gardermoen, Norway	30.7.01T
G-COLE	Boeing 737-3Q8	24962	PP-VOX	13.11.98	Color Air A/S	Oslo-Gardermoen, Norway	20.11.01T
G-COLL	Enstrom 280C-UK-2 Shark	1223		17. 8.81	SG Avn Svs Ltd	Olney	11. 1.01
G-COLR*	Colt 69A HAFB	780		8. 4.86	K.A Kent "Colourtech" (Balloon Preservation Group 7.98)	Lancing	N/E(A)
G-COMB	PA-30-160 Twin Comanche B	30-1362	G-AVBL N8236Y	14. 9.84	J.T.Bateson	Weston, Ireland	28.10.01
G-COMP	Cameron N-90 HAFB	1564		24. 9.87	Computacenter Ltd "Computacenter"	London SE1	20. 5.97A
G-CONB	Robin DR.400/180 Regent	2176	G-BUPX	14. 4.93	C.C. & C.Blakey t/a Winchcombe Farm (Stored 3.97)	Redhill	24. 2.02
G-CONC	Cameron N-90 HAFB	2139		13.11.89	British Airways plc "Concorde"	Heathrow	30.10.93T
G-CONI*	Lockheed 749A-79 Constellation	2553	N7777G	12. 5.82	The Science Museum	Wroughton	
	(N173X)/N7777G/TI-1045P/PH-LDT/PH-TET (As "N7777G" in TWA c/s)						
G-CONL	Socata TB.10	173	F-GCOR	22.12.98	J Macgilvray	(Oban)	
G-COOP	Cameron N-31 HAFB	382		2. 3.78	D P Bushby "Co-op" (Balloon Preservation Group 7.98)	Lancing	13. 5.87A
G-COOT	Taylor Coot A	EE-1A		16. 9.81	P.M.Napp	(Newcastle)	
G-COPS	Piper J3C-65 Cub (L-4H-PI)	11911	F-BFYC Fr.AF/44-79615	17. 7.79	R.W.Sproat & C.E.Simpson	Lennox Plunton, Borgue	29. 6.99P
	(Regd as c/n 36-817 which is a USAAC Contract No.; Frame No.11739)						
G-COPT	Aerospatiale AS.350B Ecureuil	2168	9M-FSA 9V-BOR	25. 2.98	Owenlars Ltd	(Odiham)	6. 5.01T
G-CORC	Bell 206B JetRanger II	1129	G-CJHI G-BBFB/N18094	18.12.89	Air Corcoran Ltd	Redhill	27.10.00
G-CORD	Slingsby Nipper T.66 RA.45 Srs.3 (Rebuild from S.105/1565) S.129/1676		G-AVTB	21. 3.88	B.A.Wright & K.E.Wilson	Little Gransden	1.11.99P
G-CORP	BAe ATP	2037	G-BTNK N860AW/G-BTNK/G-11-037	2. 3.98	British Aerospace (Operations) Ltd	Warton	28. 3.01T

Regn	Type	C/n	P/I	Date	Owner/operator	Probable Base	CA Expy
G-CORT	Agusta-Bell 206B Jet Ranger III	8739		21. 6.96	Helicopter Training & Hire Ltd		
						Aldergrove	30. 7.99T
G-COSY	Lindstrand LBL-56A HAFB	017		18. 2.93	D.D.Owen	Wotton-under-Edge	10.12.99A
G-COTT	Cameron Flying Cottage 60SS HAFB	687	"G-HOUS"	13. 2.81	M.R.Nanda	Nottingham	15. 6.98A
					t/a Nottingham Hot-Air Balloon Club "Cottage"		
G-COUP	Ercoupe 415C	1903	N99280	27. 5.93	S.M.Gerrard "Jenny Lin"	Goodwood	17. 7.99
	(Cont C75)		NC99280				
G-COWS	ARV Super 2	K.009 & PFA/152-11182	(G-BONB)	27. 5.88	T.C.Harrold	Felthorpe	10. 3.99P
	(Hewland AE75)						
G-COZI	Rutan Cozy III	PFA/159-12162		19. 7.93	D.G.Machin	Biggin Hill	14. 1.99P
	(Lyc O-320)						
G-CPCD	CEA Jodel DR.221 Dauphin	81	F-BPCD	11.12.90	P.G.Bumpus & R.Thwaites		
						Spilsted Farm, Sedlescombe	9. 6.01
G-CPCH	PA-28-151 Cherokee Warrior		G-BRGJ	11.11.93	Cardiff Wales Flying Club Ltd	Cardiff	14. 1.00T
		28-7715131	(G-BPGP)/N5425F				
G-CPEL	Boeing 757-236	24398	N602DF	24. 8.92	British Airways plc	Heathrow	26.10.99T
			EC-EOL		(Animals and Trees/Kg-Oocoan-Naka-Hiian-Thee-E t/s)		
			EC-597/G-BRJE/EC-EOL/EC-278/G-BRJE				
G-CPEM	Boeing 757-236	28665		28. 3.97	British Airways plc	Heathrow	27. 3.00T
					(Blue Poole t/s)		
G-CPEN	Boeing 757-236	28666		23. 4.97	British Airways plc	Heathrow	22. 4.00T
G-CPEO	Boeing 757-236	28667		11. 7.97	British Airways plc	Heathrow	10. 7.00T
					(Whale Rider t/s)		
G-CPEP	Boeing 757-2Y0	25268	C-GTSU	16. 4.97	British Airways plc	Heathrow	9. 7.00T
			EI-CLP/N400KL/XA-TAE		(Dove/Colum t/s)		
G-CPER	Boeing 757-236	29113		29.12.97	British Airways plc	Gatwick	28.12.00T
					(Wings of the City t/s)		
G-CPES	Boeing 757-236	29114		17. 3.98	British Airways plc	Heathrow	16. 3.01T
					(Wings of the City t/s)		
G-CPET	Boeing 757-236	29115		12. 5.98	British Airways plc	Heathrow	11. 5.01T
					(Sterntaler/Bauhaus t/s)		
G-CPEU	Boeing 757-236			R	British Airways plc	Heathrow	
					(For delvy 4.99)		
G-CPEV	Boeing 757-236			R	British Airways plc	Heathrow	
					(For delvy 6.99)		
G-CPFC	Reims Cessna F.152 II	1430		1.12.77	A.S.Bamrah t/a Falcon F/Svs	Southend	25. 6.01T
					(Op Willowair Flying Club)		
G-CPMK	DHC.1 Chipmunk 22	C1/0866	WZ847	28. 6.96	Towerdrive Ltd	Bradley, Ashbourne	19. 9.97
					(As "WZ847")		
G-CPMS	Socata TB.20 Trinidad	1607	F-GNHA	7. 4.98	Charlotte Park Management Services Ltd		
						(Chichester)	7. 4.01T
G-CPOL	Aerospatiale AS.355F1 Twin Squirrel		N5775T	30.11.95	Thames Valley Police Authority	Luton	30. 1.02T
		5007	C-GJJB/N5775T		(Op Chiltern Air Support Unit)		
G-CPTM	PA-28-151 Cherokee Warrior		G-BTOE	9. 7.91	T.J.Mackay & C.M.Pollett	Manchester	4. 9.00T
		28-7715012	N4264F				
G-CPTS	Agusta-Bell 206B JetRanger II	8556		1. 6.78	A.R.B.Aspinall	Skipton	6. 5.00
G-CRAK	Cameron N-77 HAFB	2291		7. 6.90	Mobile Windscreens Ltd	Bristol	14. 7.97A
					"Mobile Windscreens"		
G-CRAY	Robinson R-22 Beta	0919		12. 1.89	W.H.Grimshaw	Barton	7. 4.98
G-CRES	Denney Kitfox mk.2	PFA/172-11574		7. 6.90	K.M.James	High Barn Farm, Houghton	3. 8.99P
	(Rotax 912)						
G-CRIC	Colomban MC.15 Cri-Cri	PFA/133-10915		22. 7.83	R.S.Stoddart-Stones	(Caterham)	5. 5.99P
	(JPX PUL.212)						
G-CRIL	Rockwell Commander 112B	521	N1388J	22. 6.79	J.W.Reynolds	Cardiff	21.10.00
					t/a Rockwell Avn Grp		
G-CRIS	Taylor JT.1 Monoplane	PFA/55-10318		5. 6.79	C.R.Steer	(Bexhill-on-Sea)	
G-CRML	Cessna 414A Chancellor III	414A-1209	N1246D	18. 6.92	Anglo International Holdings Ltd		
						Ronaldsway/Blackpool	8.10.98
G-CROL	Maule MXT-7-180 Star Rocket	14032C	N9232F	24.11.93	D.C.,C.& K.Croll Heron Hall, Brentwood	17. 2.00
					(Damaged Brentwood 3.5.97)		
G-CROY	Europa Avn Europa	PFA/247-12896		7. 2.97	A.Croy	(Kirkwall)	
G-CRPH	Airbus A.320-231	424	F-WQBB	10. 4.95	Airtours International Airways Ltd		
			F-WWIV			Manchester	14. 4.99T
G-CRPS	Bell 206B Jet Ranger II	1967	A6-BCC	22. 9.97	Helisport Ltd	Biggin Hill	
G-CRUM	Westland Scout AH.1	F.9712	XV137	17. 3.98	Crummock Development Ltd	(Bonnyrigg)	14. 4.01T
	(Pod No.F8-6151)						
G-CRUS	Cessna T303 Crusader	T303-00313	N6498V	27. 2.90	B.A.Groves	Shoreham	18. 4.99T
G-CRUZ	Cessna T303 Crusader	T303-00004	N9336T	7.12.90	Bank Farm Ltd Bank Farm, Benwick, Cambs	5. 3.00
G-CSBM	Reims Cessna F.150M	1359	PH-AYC	24. 5.78	Motorglider Centre Ltd		
						Hinton-in-the-Hedges	14.11.00T
G-CSCS	Reims Cessna F.172N Skyhawk II	1707	PH-MEM	28.11.86	Cheryl Sullivan	Stapleford	21. 5.99T
			(PH-WEB)/N9899A				
G-CSDJ	Jabiru UL	PFA/274A-13337		23. 3.99	D W Johnston	Northwich	
G-CSFC	Cessna 150L Commuter	150-75360	(G-BFLX)	21. 3.78	J.L. & L.J.Eden	(Sutton Coldfield)	6. 3.02
			N11370				
G-CSFT*	PA-23-250 Aztec D	27-4521	G-AYKU	20. 9.84	Aces High Ltd (Stored 5.97)	North Weald	3.12.94T
			N13885				
G-CSNA	Cessna 421C Golden Eagle III		(D-IOSS)	11. 6.79	Claessens International Ltd	Blackbushe	18. 8.99T
		421C-0677	N26522				

Regn	Type	C/n	P/I	Date	Owner/operator	Probable Base	CA Expy
G-CSPJ	Hughes 369HS	55-0745S	G-BXJF N99KS/N9KS	24. 7.97	Helisport Ltd	Biggin Hill	3. 9.00T
G-CSWL	Bell 206L-1 Long Ranger	45565	G-SIRI G-CSWL/F-GDAD	6. 5.97	Capital Helicopter Group Ltd	Biggin Hill	5. 6.00T
G-CTCL	Socata TB-10 Tobago	1107	G-BSIV	16. 7.90	Merryfield Leasing Ltd	Jersey	30. 9.99
G-CTEL	Cameron N-90 HAFB	3933		27. 8.96	Cabletel Surrey & Hampshire Ltd	Farnborough	24. 8.99A
G-CTGR	Cameron N-77 HAFB	1775	G-CCDI	28. 8.97	T.G.Read	Knutsford	8. 4.97T
G-CTIX	VS.509 Spitfire Tr.IX (Major rebuild from parts pre 1994)		N462JC G-CTIX/IDFAF 2067/0607/MM4100/PT462	9. 4.85	A.A.Hodgson	Duxford	25. 8.99P
G-CTKL	Noorduyn Harvard IIB (C/n quoted as "76-80")	07-30	(G-BKWZ) MM54137/RCAF3064	22.11.83	A.P.Williams (As "5413769" in US Navy c/s)	(Ware)	7. 2.00P
G-CTOY	Denney Kitfox mk.3 1176 & PFA/172-12150 (Rotax 582)			14.10.91	B.McNeilly	Newtownards	10. 5.93P
G-CTPW	Bell 206B JetRanger 4	4374	(N9145B)	30.11.95	C.T.Wheatley	Newtown, Powys	19. 2.99T
G-CTWW	PA-34-200T Seneca II	34-7970191	G-ROYZ G-GALE/N3052X	21. 7.93	Seneca Consortium Ltd	Welshpool	16. 8.99
G-CUBB	PA-18-180 Super Cub (L-18C-PI) (Frame No.18-3009)	18-3111	PH-WAM	5.12.78	Bidford Gliding Centre Ltd Belgian AF OL-L37/53-4711 (Damaged Bidford 2.5.95)	Bidford	18. 4.01
G-CUBI*	PA-18-135 Super Cub (Mod.) (L-18C-PI) PH-VCV/R.Neth R-83/Belgian AF L-107/53-4781 (Official c/n is 18-559 which relates to PH-GAV prior to a 1970 rebuild when it incorporated Frame No.18-3170 from PH-VCV; cancelled by CAA 29.1.99)	18-3181	PH-GAV	26. 2.79	Teresa Watson	Clacton	4.11.94
G-CUBJ	PA-18-150 Super Cub (L-18C-PI) (Frame No.18-2035) (Regd with c/n 18-5395 following 1974 rebuild of PH-NLF which acquired data plate from, and took up, the identity of PH-MBF - note G-SUPA carries this c/n)	18-2036	PH-MBF PH-NLF R.Neth AF R-43/8A-43/52-2436	15.12.82	J.G.Waller (As "56-5395/CDG" in French Army c/s)	Shotteswell	10. 8.00
G-CUBP	PA-18-150 Super Cub (Frame No.18-8725; regd with c/n 18-8823 which is the "official" identity of N1136Z/D-EIAC but which was rebuilt 1984/85 with Frame No.18-4613 from D-EKAF. This latter frame was fitted to G-BVMI following an accident on 15.8.95; the repaired frame of G-BVMI has become G-CUBP)	18-8482	G-BVMI OH-PIN/N4262Z	8. 8.96	P.Grenet	Oaksey Park	18. 8.99
G-CUBY	Piper J3C-65 Cub (Rebuilt with new fuselage 1996/97)	16317	G-BTZW N88689/NC88689	2. 3.95	Claudine A.Bloom (F/f 19.2.98)	Shoreham	18. 8.99P
G-CUCU	Colt 180A HAFB	3869		22. 4.96	G.M.N. & S.Spencer "Commercial Union"	Watford	31. 3.99T
G-CUPN	PA-46-350P Malibu Mirage	4636144		11. 2.98	K.Fletcher t/a Airpark	Coventry	23. 4.01
G-CURE*	Colt 77A HAFB (Standard shape plus Alka Seltzer tablet blisters)	1424		3. 7.89	T Gunn "Alka Seltzer 3" (Balloon Preservation Group 7.98)	Lancing	21.11.96A
G-CURR	Cessna 172R Skyhawk II	172-80143	G-BXOH N9989F	27. 5.98	JS Aviation Ltd	Luton	2. 3.01T
G-CUTY	Europa Avn Europa PFA/247-12910			20. 8.96	D.J. & M.Watson	(Selby)	
G-CVBF	Cameron A-210 HAFB	3588		2. 6.95	Virgin Balloon Flights Ltd	Bath	26. 9.99T
G-CVIL	Piper J3C-65 Cub (L-4H-PI)	12005	OO-VIL OO-VVV/44-79709	23. 8.96	H.A.D.Munro	(Hastings)	
G-CVIX	DH.110 Sea Vixen D.3 (Regd as FAW.2 with c/n 10132)	10125	XP924	26. 2.96	De Havilland Aviation Ltd (As "XP924")	Swansea	AC
G-CVPM	VPM M-16 Tandem Trainer VPM16-UK-110			26. 3.98	C.S.Teuber (Hannover, Germany)		AC
G-CVYD	Airbus A.320-231	0393	B-HYO VR-HYO/F-WWIR	24. 2.98	Caledonian Airways Ltd	Gatwick	16. 3.01T
G-CVYE	Airbus A.320-231	0394	B-HYP VR-HYP/F-WWBB	23. 3.98	Caledonian Airways Ltd	Gatwick	6. 4.01T
G-CVYG	Airbus A.320-231	0443	B-HYT VR-HYT/F-WWBV	10.11.98	Caledonian Airways Ltd.	Gatwick	30.11.01T
G-CWAG	Sequoia Falco F.8L PFA/100-10895			11. 5.92	B.B.Wagner	Glasgow	29. 6.99P
G-CWBM	Phoenix Currie Wot PFA/3020 (Cont C85)		G-BTVP	28. 3.94	B.V.Mayo Maypole Farm, Chislet		8. 9.98P
G-CWCW	Cameron R-900 HAFB	4386		9.11.98	Around The World Balloon Ltd Glastonbury (Cable & Wireless c/s) (Ditched into Pacific Ocean nr Omaezaki, Japan 7.3.99)		
G-CWIZ	Aerospatiale AS.350B Ecureuil	1847	CS-HDF G-DJEM/G-ZBAC/G-SEBI/G-BMCU	18.10.95	Kensington Aviation Ltd (Blairgowrie)		23. 5.99T
G-CWOT	Phoenix Currie Wot PFA/3019 (Walter Mikron II)			31. 1.78	J.P.Conlan "Jonah" (Kildare, Ireland)		15.12.99P
G-CXCX	Cameron N-90 HAFB (Replacement envelope c/n 3332)	1242		14. 3.86	Cathay Pacific Airways (London) Ltd "Cathay Pacific IV" (London SW1)		26. 2.99A
G-CYGI	Hapi Cygnet SF-2A PFA/182-12084			17.12.93	B.Brown (Melton Mowbray)		
G-CYLS	Cessna T303 Crusader	T303-00005	N20736 G-BKXI/N303CC/(N9355T)	20.12.90	Gledhill Water Storage Ltd	Blackpool	16. 3.00
G-CYMA	Gulfstream GA-7 Cougar	GA7-0083	G-BKOM N794GA	15. 8.83	Cyma Petroleum Ltd	Elstree	4. 6.01
G-CZAR	Cessna 560 Citation V	560-0046	(N26656)	29.11.89	Chauffair (CI) Ltd	Farnborough	6. 3.99T
G-CZCZ	Mudry/CAARP CAP.10B	54	OE-AYY F-WZCG/HB-SAK/F-BUDT	28. 7.94	P.R.Moorhead & M.F.R.B.Collett Garston Farm, Marshfield		1. 8.00

G-DAAA-DZZZ

Regn	Type	C/n	P/I	Date	Owner/operator	Probable Base	CA Expy
G-DAAH	PA-28RT-201T Turbo Arrow IV	N3026U	27. 4.79	R.Peplow	Halfpenny Green	21. 5.00
		28R-7931104					
G-DAAM	Robinson R-22 Beta	2043		3. 6.92	Grampian Helicopter Charter Ltd		
						Kintore, Inverurie	2. 7.01T
G-DACA	Percival P.57 Sea Prince T.1	P57/12	WF118	6. 5.80	P.G.Vallance Ltd	Charlwood, Surrey	17. 7.81P
					(Stored 6.97)		
G-DACC	Cessna 401B	401B-0112	N77GR	1. 9.86	Niglon Ltd	Coventry	9. 9.01
			N4488A/G-AYOU/N79720				
G-DACF	Cessna 152 II	152-81724	G-BURY	13. 6.97	T.M. & M.L.Jones	Egginton	10. 7.00T
			N67285		t/a Derby Aero Club		
G-DACS	Short SD.3-30 Var.100	SH.3089	C-GLAL	6. 7.98	Air Cavrel Ltd (Kingston-upon-Thames)		
G-DADS	Hughes 369HS	22-0369S	N888SS	11. 6.90	Executive Avn Svs Ltd	Gloucestershire	26. 7.99
			N9101F				
G-DAFY	Beechcraft 58 Baron	TH-1591	N5684C	6.10.93	P.R.Earp	Gloucestershire	10.11.01
G-DAIR	Luscombe 8A Master	1474	G-BURK	3.10.97	D.F.Soul	Emberton	19.10.99P
	(Cont A65)		N28713/NC28713				
G-DAJB	Boeing 757-2T7ER	23770		26. 2.87	Monarch Airlines Ltd	Luton	13. 5.99T
G-DAJC	Boeing 767-31KER	27206		15. 4.94	Airtours International Airways Ltd		
						Manchester	14. 4.00T
G-DAKK	Douglas C-47A-35DL Dakota 4	9798	(G-OFON)	26. 7.94	Meridian Aircraft Ltd (Op South Coast Airways)		
			F-GEOM/Fr Navy 36/OK-WZB/OK-WDU/42-23936			Bournemouth	23. 4.99T
G-DAMY	Europa Avn Europa			21.10.94	M.J.Ashby-Arnold	(Knaresborough)	20.11.98P
	(Rotax 912UL) 105 & PFA/247-12781						
G-DAND	Socata TB-10 Tobago	72		5.12.79	Whitemoor Engineering Co Ltd	Coventry	21. 6.010
G-DANS	Aerospatiale AS.355F2	5480	G-BTNM	28. 4.93	Frewton Ltd	Oxford/Jersey	14. 6.99T
	Twin Squirrel						
G-DANT	Rockwell Commander 114	14298	N4978W	9. 7.96	D.P.Tierney	Biggin Hill	17. 7.99T
G-DANZ	Eurocopter AS.355N Twin Squirrel 5658			14. 9.98	McAlpine Helicopters Ltd	Oxford	AC
G-DAPH	Cessna 180K Skywagon II	180-53016	N2620K	29. 1.92	M.R.L.Astor	East Hatley, Tadlow	19.11.98
G-DARA	PA-34-220T Seneca III	34-8333060	PH-TCT	8.11.88	Sys (Scaffolding Contractors) Ltd		
			N83JR/N4297J/N9632N			Gamston	25. 2.01
G-DASH	Rockwell Commander 112A	237	G-BDAJ	31. 3.87	Josef D.J.Jons & Co Ltd	Woodford	26. 3.00
			N1237J				
G-DASI	Short SD.3-60 Var.100	SH.3606	G-14-3606	14. 2.83	Gill Avn Ltd	Newcastle	21. 3.99T
			G-BKKW				
G-DASU	Cameron V-77 HAFB	2300		6. 4.90	D. & L.S.Litchfield "Borne Free" Reading		11. 8.97A
G-DAVE	Jodel D.112 (Valladeau)	667	F-BICH	16. 8.78	D.A.Porter Griffins Farm, Temple Bruer		2. 2.99P
G-DAVO	Gulfstream AA-5B Tiger	AA5B-1226	G-GAGA	5. 1.96	Kadala Aviation Ltd	Elstree	19. 1.01T
			G-BGPG/(G-BGRW)				
G-DAVT	Schleicher ASH26E	26090		24. 4.96	D.A.Triplett	Sleap	15. 4.99
G-DAYI	Europa Avn Europa	PFA/247-13027		19. 8.96	A.F.Day	(West Wickham)	
G-DAYS	Europa Avn Europa	PFA/247-12810		9. 5.95	D.J.Bowie	(Ellesmere)	21. 7.99P
	(Rotax 912UL)						
G-DBAL*	HS.125 Srs.3B	25117	G-BSAA	20. 7.84	Southampton Airport Fire Services		
			5N-AKT/5N-AET			Southampton	16. 6.92
G-DBHH	Agusta-Bell 206B JetRanger	8111	G-AWVO	24. 5.96	UK Helicopter Charter Ltd	(Chatham)	22. 6.01
			VH-BHI/PK-HCA/G-AWVO/9Y-TDN/PK-HBG/G-AWVO				
G-DBMW	Bell 206B Jet Ranger 4	4401		8. 3.96	Lind Ltd	Attlebridge, Norwich	2. 6.99T
G-DBYE	Mooney M.20M	27-0098	N91462	24. 3.98	Axe & Status Ltd	Cranfield	23. 3.01
G-DCAV	PA-32R-301 Saratoga IIHP	3246075	N92864	8. 5.97	Airsys Communications Technology Ltd		
						Southampton	7. 5.00
G-DCCH	MBB Bo.105DBS/4	S-770	D-HDYF	19. 9.86	Bond Helicopters Ltd	Aberdeen	10.12.01T
G-DCDB	Bell 407	53137	N7238A	R.97			
G-DCEA	PA-34-200T Seneca II	34-8070079	N3567D	13. 2.91	M.J.Greasby	Booker	14. 5.00T
G-DCIO	McDonnell Douglas DC-10-30	48277		27. 1.81	British Airways plc	Gatwick	14. 4.01T
					"Epping Forest"		
G-DCKK	Reims Cessna F.172N Skyhawk II	1589	PH-GRT	19. 5.80	M.Manston	Panshanger	24. 4.01
			PH-AXA				
G-DCPA	MBB BK-117C-1C	7511	D-HECU	16.12.97	Devon & Cornwall Constabulary		
			D-HXXL/G-LFBA/D-HECU/D-HMBF			Middlemoor, Exeter	16. 6.99T
G-DCXL	SAN Jodel D.140C Mousquetaire III	101	F-BKSM	27. 5.88	C.F.Mugford	Little Gransden	22.12.99
					t/a X-Ray Lima Grp		
G-DDAY	PA-28R-201T Turbo Arrow III		G-BPDO	24.11.88	K.E.Hogg t/a G-DDAY Grp	Tatenhill	15. 4.01
		28R-7703112	N34960				
G-DDMV	North American T-6G-NF Texan 168-313		N3240N	30. 4.90	E.A.Morgan	Sywell/Gloucestershire	13.11.99
			Haitian AF 3209/49-3209		(As "493209" in Calif ANG c/s)		
G-DDSC	Europa Avn Europa XS	PFA/247-13291		14. 4.98	G.Holland	(Bath)	
G-DEAN	Solar Wings Pegasus XL-Q		G-MVJV	30.11.98	D.C.P.Cardey & G.D.Tannahill	Hereford	4. 9.99P
	(Rotax 462) SW-TE-0117 & SW-WQ-0123						
G-DEBA	BAe 146 Srs.200	E-2028	N171US	1. 5.96	Debonair Airways Ltd	Luton	30. 4.99T
			N351PS		"Sir Anthony"		
G-DEBC	BAe 146 Srs.200	E-2024	N166US	23. 5.96	Debonair Airways Ltd	Luton	22. 5.99T
			N348PS		"Team Spirit"		
G-DEBD	BAe 146 Srs.200	E-2034	N174US	23. 5.96	Debonair Airways Ltd	Luton	18. 6.99T
			N354PS		"Lady M"		

Regn	Type	C/n	P/I	Date	Owner/operator	Probable Base	CA Expy
G-DEBE	BAe 146 Srs.200	E-2022	N163US N346PS	5. 8.96	Debonair Airways Ltd "Bird of Paradise"	Luton	6. 8.99T
G-DEBF	BAe 146 Srs.200	E-2023	N165US N347PS	25. 9.96	Debonair Airways Ltd	Luton	26. 9.99T
G-DEBG	BAe 146 Srs.200	E-2040	N178US N357PS	1. 4.97	Debonair Airways Ltd "Jumbolino"	Luton	31. 3.00T
G-DEBH	BAe 146 Srs.200	E-2045	N185US N362PS	27. 8.97	Debonair Airways Ltd "Prosperity"	Luton	27. 8.00T
G-DEBJ	BAe 146 Srs.100	E-1004	VH-NJA	6. 8.98	Debonair Airways Ltd	Luton	10. 8.01T
			PK-MTA/G-OJET/G-5-537/(N346SS)/G-BRJS/G-5-04/ZD695/G-OBAF/(G-SSCH)/(G-BIAG)				
G-DEBK	BAe 146 Srs.200	E-2012	C-FHAV N601AW	19. 2.99	Debonair Airways Ltd	Luton	
G-DEBL	BAe 146 Srs.200	E-2014	C-FHAX N602AW	2.12.98	Debonair Airways Ltd	Luton	AC
G-DEBM	BAe 146 Srs.200	E-2016	C-FHAZ	8. 1.99	Debonair Airways Ltd	Luton	AC
G-DEBN	BAe 146 Srs.100	E-1015	EC-GEP	15.12.98	Debonair Airways Ltd	Luton	22.12.01T
			EC-971/N568BA/XA-RST/N461AP/G-5-01				
G-DEER	Robinson R-22 Beta	2827		17. 7.98	M.Taylor	(Godalming)	28.12.01T
G-DEJL	Robinson R-22 Beta	2001		31. 3.92	G.& B.Dobson Ltd	(Louth)	18. 5.01T
G-DELF	Aero L-29A Delfin	194555	ES-YLM Soviet AF 12 (red)	28. 8.97	P.A.Greenhalgh & B.R.Green	Manston	23. 4.99P
G-DELT	Robinson R-22 Beta	0898		11.11.88	Virgin Helicopters Ltd	Booker	15. 4.99T
G-DEMH	Reims Cessna F.172M Skyhawk II (Modified)	1137	G-BFLO PH-DMF/(EI-AYO)	18.11.91	M.Hammond	Crowfield/Hardwick	11. 6.01
G-DENA	Reims Cessna F.150G	0204	G-AVEO EI-BOI/G-AVEO	14.12.95	D.G.Kipling t/a Aviators Flight Center	Southend	20. 1.02T
G-DENB	Reims Cessna F.150G	0136	G-ATZZ	14.12.95	D.G.Kipling t/a Aviators Flight Center	Southend	11.12.98T
G-DENC	Reims Cessna F.150G	0107	G-AVAP	14.12.95	D.G.Kipling t/a Aviators Flight Center	Southend	18. 7.99T
G-DEND	Reims Cessna F.150M	1201	G-WAFC G-BDFI/(OH-CGD)	6. 6.97	Den Air Aviation Ltd t/a Aviators Flight Center	Southend	3. 8.01T
G-DENE	PA-28-140 Cherokee	28-21710	G-ATOS	5. 2.98	Den Air Aviation Ltd t/a Aviators Flight Center	Southend	2. 4.99T
G-DENH	PA-28-161 Warrior II	28-8216202	G-BTNH N253FT/N9577N	14. 4.97	Den Air Aviation Ltd t/a Aviators Flight Center	Norwich	1. 3.01T
G-DENI	PA-32-300 Cherokee Six	32-7340006	G-BAIA	7.12.95	A.Bendkowski	Rochester	14. 3.01T
G-DENK	PA-28-181 Archer II	28-8290108	G-BXRJ HB-PGO	5. 2.98	Den Air Aviation Ltd t/a Aviators Flight Center (Swiss Cross on fin)	Southend	10. 2.01T
G-DENN	Bell 206B Jet Ranger 4	4409	N75486	10. 6.96	Abbey Flight Ltd	Fairoaks	3. 7.99
G-DENR	Reims Cessna F.172N Skyhawk II	1839	G-BGNR	30. 4.97	Den Air Aviation Ltd t/a Aviators Flight Center	Southend	22.10.00T
G-DENS	Binder CP.301S Smaragd	121	D-ENSA	20.11.85	J.S.Hemmings t/a Rother F/Grp	Rye	3. 9.99P
G-DENT	Cameron N-145 HAFB	4135		8. 4.97	Deproco UK Ltd	Dorking	6. 7.99A
G-DENZ	PA-44-180 Seminole	44-7995327	G-INDE G-BHNM/N8077X	3. 7.97	Den Air Aviation Ltd t/a Aviators Flight Center	Southend	22. 2.99T
G-DERB	Robinson R-22 Beta	1005	G-BPYH	28. 6.95	P.N. & J.E.Thornton t/a Derbyshire Helicopters	Matlock	25. 6.01T
G-DERV	Cameron Truck 56SS HAFB	1719		21. 3.88	J.M.Percival "Shell UK Truck"	Loughborough	15.12.88A
G-DESI	Aero Designs Pulsar XP PFA/202-12147			14.11.91	D.F.Gaughan	(Minehead)	
G-DESS	Mooney M.20J (201)	24-1272	N11598	20.10.87	W.E.Newnes	Birmingham	14. 1.00
G-DEST	Mooney M.20J	24-3429		6.11.98	Flemming Frandsen Aircraft Sales Ltd	Biggin Hill	12. 1.02
G-DESY	Cessna A152 Aerobat	A152-0805	G-BNJE N7386L	20.10.97	General Airline Ltd	(Reading)	23. 3.00T
G-DEVN*	DH.104 Devon C.2/2	04269	WB533	26.10.84	Air Classic GmbH (As "WB533") Frankfurt Rhein-Main, Germany		4. 2.85P*
G-DEVS	PA-28-180 Cherokee	28-830	G-BGVJ D-ENPI/N7066W	5. 3.85	B.J.Hoptroff & J.M.Whiteley t/a 180 Grp	Blackbushe	9. 1.02
G-DEXP	ARV1 Super 2 003 & PFA/152-11154 (Hewland AE75)			24. 4.85	W.G.McKinnon	Perth	15. 4.99P
G-DEXY	Beechcraft E90 King Air	LW-136	N750DC N30CW/N84GA/N328TB/TR-LTT	6. 4.89	Specsavers Avn Ltd	Guernsey	18. 1.00
G-DEZC	BAe HS.125 Srs.700B	257070	G-BWCR G-5-604/HB-VGG/G-5-604/HB-VGG	28. 5.96	Frewton Ltd	Jersey	17. 7.99
G-DFLY	PA-38-112 Tomahawk	38-79A0450		15. 2.79	Western Air Training Ltd	Thruxton	4.12.00T
G-DGDG	Glaser-Dirks DG-400-17	4-27		25. 3.83	M.Clarke t/a DG-400 F/Grp	Lasham	2. 5.01
G-DGIV	Glaser Dirks DG-800B	8-145-B69		27.11.98	W.R. McNair	(Holywood, NI)	23.11.01
G-DGWW	Rand Robinson KR-2 PFA/129-11044 (Hapi Magnum 75)			7. 3.91	W.Wilson	Liverpool	23. 6.99P
G-DHAV	DH.115 Vampire T.11 (T.55)	15682	U-1234 XH308	13.10.95	Jacquelyn Jones (De Havilland Aviation Ltd) (As "U-1234" in Swiss AF c/s)	Swansea	27. 8.99P
	(Regd with nacelle no. DHP.48913) (Reported as FFW built with c/n 994)						
G-DHCB	DHC.2 Beaver 1 Floatplane	1450	G-BTDL XP779	20. 6.91	Seaflite Ltd	Loughearnhead	16. 9.97T
G-DHCC	DHC.1 Chipmunk 22	C1/0393	WG321	28. 5.97	Eureka Aviation NV	Wevelgem, Belgium	3. 9.00

Regn	Type	C/n	P/I	Date	Owner/operator	Probable Base	CA Expy
G-DHCI	DHC.1 Chipmunk 22	C1/0884	G-BBSE WZ858	12. 7.89	Felthorpe F/Grp Ltd	Felthorpe	14. 8.00
G-DHDV	DH.104 Dove 8	04205	VP981	26.10.98	Air Atlantique Ltd	Coventry	AC
G-DHGS	Robinson R-22 Beta	2592		19. 4.96	Driver Hire Group Services Ltd	Leeds-Bradford	12. 5.99T
G-DHLB	Cameron N-90 HAFB	3261		20. 4.94	DHL International (UK) Ltd	Hounslow	28.10.96A
G-DHLI	Colt World 90SS HAFB	2603		2. 6.94	Virgin Airship & Balloon Co Ltd	Telford	17.12.98A
G-DHLZ	Colt 31A Air Chair HAFB	2604		2. 6.94	Virgin Airship & Balloon Co Ltd	Telford	23. 7.99A
G-DHSS	FFW DH.112 Venom FB.50 (FB.1)	836	J-1626	26. 3.99	D J L Wood	Bournemouth	
G-DHTM	DH.82A Tiger Moth	PFA/157-11095		6. 1.86	E.G.Waite-Roberts	(Basingstoke)	
					(On rebuild from original unidentified components)		
G-DHTT	FFW DH.112 Venom FB.50 (FB.1)	821	(G-BMOC) J-1611	17.10.96	D.J.Lindsay Wood (Source Classic Jet Flight) (As "WR421" in all-red c/s)	Bournemouth	17. 7.99P
G-DHUU	FFW DH.112 Venom FB.50 (FB.1)	749	(G-BMOD) J-1539	26. 2.96	D.J.Lindsay Wood (Source Classic Jet Flight) (As "WR410" in 6 Sqdn RAF c/s)	Bournemouth	17. 7.99P
G-DHVV	DH.115 Vampire T.55 (Also quoted as c/n 974)	55092	U-1214	5. 9.91	Lindsay Wood Promotions Ltd (Op Source Classic Jet Flight) (As "WZ589" in 54 Sqdn RAF c/s)	Bournemouth	17. 7.99P
G-DHWW	FFW DH.115 Vampire T.55	979	U-1219	5. 9.91	Lindsay Wood Promotions Ltd (Op Source Classic Jet Flight) (As "XG775/VL" in RN c/s)	Bournemouth	27. 1.00P
G-DHXX	FFW DH.100 Vampire FB.6	682	J-1173	5. 9.91	Lindsay Wood Promotions Ltd (Op Source Classic Jet Flight) (As "VT871" in 54 Sqdn RAF c/s)	Bournemouth	27. 1.00P
G-DHYY	DH.115 Vampire T.11	15112	WZ553	17. 3.95	Lindsay Wood Promotions Ltd (As "WZ553/40") (Stored 3.96)	Bruntingthorpe	
G-DHZZ	FFW DH.115 Vampire T.55	990	U-1230	5. 9.91	Lindsay Wood Promotions Ltd Bournemouth (Op Source Classic Jet Flight) (As "WZ589" in 56 Sqdn RAF c/s)		24.11.98P
G-DIAL	Cameron N-90 HAFB	1851		7.11.88	A.J.Street "London"	Exeter	29. 5.99T
G-DIAT	PA-28-140 Cherokee Cruiser	28-7425322	G-BCGK N9594N	19. 7.89	The RAF Benevolent Fund Enterprises Ltd (Op Disabled Flyers Grp/Bristol & Wessex Aeroplane Club)	Bristol/Lulsgate	2. 9.00T
G-DICE	Enstrom F-28F	787	D-HANA	8.11.96	Dice Aviation Services Ltd	Goodwood	5.12.99
G-DICK	Thunder Ax6-56Z HAFB	159		6. 7.78	R.D.Sargeant "Dandag"	(Switzerland)	13. 9.00A
G-DIET	Lindstrand Drinks Can SS HAFB (Diet Pepsi Can)	220		1. 5.95	Pepsi Cola Overseas Ltd	Des Moines, IA, USA	19. 4.99A
G-DIGI	PA-32-300 Cherokee Six	32-7940224	D-EIES N2947M	13.10.98	D.Stokes t/a Security UN Ltd Grp	(London E4)	19.11.01T
G-DIKY	Murphy Rebel	PFA/232-13182		13. 2.98	R.J.P.Herivel	(Alderney)	
G-DIMB	Boeing 767-31KER	28865		28. 4.97	Airtours International Airways Ltd	Manchester	2. 7.01T
G-DIME	Rockwell Commander 114	14123	N49829	9. 3.88	H.B.Richardson	(Chippenham)	28. 9.97
G-DINA	Gulfstream AA-5B Tiger	AA5B-1218	N4555Y	27. 2.81	J.Gosling & N.R.J.Mifflin t/a Portway Aviation	Shobdon	13. 4.99T
G-DING	Colt 77A HAFB	1862		28. 6.91	G.J.Bell "Dingbat"	Wokingham	10.11.99A
G-DINO	Cyclone Pegasus Quantum 15 (Rotax 582)	7225	G-MGMT	15.12.98	G.D.Hall	(March)	23. 7.99P
G-DINT	Bristol 156 Beaufighter IF	STAN B1 184604 3858M	X7688	17. 6.91	T.E.Moore (On rebuild from various ex Australian components 8.95)	Rotary Farm, Hatch	
G-DIPI	Cameron Tub 80SS HAFB	1745		6. 5.88	D.K.Fish "KP Choc Dips Tub"	Bedford	11. 7.98A
G-DIPS	Taylor JT.1 Monoplane (VW1500)	PFA/55-10320		19.12.78	B.J.Halls (Project stored 1990)	(Boston)	
G-DIRE	Robinson R-22 Beta	1663		29. 1.91	Heli Air Ltd	Wellesbourne Mountford	19. 3.00T
G-DIRK	Glaser-Dirks DG-400	4-124	D-KEKT	18. 9.86	C.J.Lowrie	(Horsham)	29. 1.02
G-DISK	PA-24-250 Comanche	24-1197	G-APZG EI-AKW	9. 8.89	A.Johnston	Guernsey	29. 5.00
G-DISO	SAN Jodel 150 Mascaret	24	9Q-CPK OO-APK/F-BLDT	16.12.86	P.F.Craven & J.H.Shearer	Cumbernauld	30. 5.99P
G-DIVA	Cessna R172K Hawk XPII	3071	N758FX	10. 2.86	SPD Ltd	Old Sarum	20. 8.01T
G-DIWY	PA-32-300 Cherokee Six	32-40731	OY-DLW D-EHMW/N8931N	26.11.91	Industrial Foam Systems Ltd	East Winch	19. 5.01
G-DIXY	PA-28-181 Archer III	2843195	N41284	10.12.98	S.Dixon-Smith t/a Lyons Aviation	(Haverhill)	
G-DIZO	Jodel Wassmer D.120A Paris-Nice	326	G-EMKM F-BOBG	30. 5.91	D. & E.Aldersea	Breighton	22. 9.99P
G-DIZY	PA-28R-201T Turbo Arrow III	28R-7703401	N47570	13.10.88	T.D.Melen t/a Medway Arrow Grp	Rochester	9.12.00
G-DIZZ	Hughes 369HE	89-0105E	N9029F	19. 2.97	H.J.Pelham	Cleeves Farm, Salisbury	22. 4.00T
G-DJAE	Cessna 500 Citation (Unit No.339)	500-0339	G-JEAN N300EC/N707US/G-JEAN/(N5339J)	3.11.98	Source Ltd.	Bournemouth	27. 3.99T
G-DJAR	Airbus A.320-231	164	OY-CNE (D-ACSL)/OY-CNE/F-WWIE	18. 3.97	Airtours International Airways Ltd	Manchester	17. 3.00T
G-DJCR	Varga 2150A Kachina	VAC 155-80	EI-CFK G-BLWG/OO-HTD/N8360J	11. 4.96	D.J.C.Robertson	Perth	30. 4.99
G-DJEA	Cessna 421C Golden Eagle II	421C-0654	TC-AAA N37379/(N24BS)/N37379	16. 4.98	Source Ltd	Bournemouth	11.10.01T
G-DJHB	Beechcraft A23-19 Musketeer Sport III	MB-200	G-AZZE LN-TVH	6. 8.82	W.B.Murray t/a Nayland Aiglet Grp	Hill Farm, Nayland	19. 7.98
G-DJIM*	DHCA.1	DHCA.1		28.12.78	J.Crawford (Cancelled by CAA 24.3.99)	(Oxford)	

Regn	Type	C/n	P/I	Date	Owner/operator	Probable Base	CA Expy
G-DJJA	PA-28-181 Archer II	28-8490014	N4326D	14. 9.87	B.Cheese & S.M.Price t/a Choice Acft (Op Modern Air)	Fowlmere	18.12.99T
G-DJLW	HS.125 Srs.3B/RA	25140	G-AVVB G-5-17/(G-5-16)	19. 1.89	Osprey Aviation Ltd	Southampton	14. 6.99T
G-DJNH	Denney Kitfox mk.3 772 & PFA/172-11896 (Rotax 582)			20. 9.90	D.J.N.Hall	Downwood, Dorset	20. 7.98P
G-DKDP	Grob G-109	6100	(G-BMBD) D-KAMS	9. 7.85	D.W. & J.E.Page	Tibenham	12. 8.00
G-DKGF	Viking Dragonfly mk.1 PFA/139-10898 (VW1834)			16.10.86	P.C.Dowbor (Stored 10.97)	Enstone	
G-DLCB	Europa Avn Europa 46 & PFA/247-12652 (Rotax 912UL)			16.11.95	D.J.Lockett & C.R.C.Bowen	Inverness	14. 6.99P
G-DLDL	Robinson R-22 Beta	1971		2. 1.92	A.J.Wagstaff (Damaged Cambridge 28.11.98)	Sywell	5. 2.01
G-DLFN	Aero L-29 Delfin	294872	ES-YLE Estonian AF/Soviet AF	28. 5.98	T.W.Freeman & N.Gooderham	North Weald	AC
G-DLOM	Socata TB-20 Trinidad	1102	N2823Y	13.12.90	J.N.A.Adderley	Rochester	30. 9.00
G-DLTR	PA-28-180 Cherokee E	28-5803	G-AYAV	15. 3.96	D.A.Williams (Op Deltair)	Chester	20. 6.99T
G-DMAC	Pearce Jabiru UL	PFA/274-13321		15.10.98	B.McFadden	(Cottingham)	
G-DMCA	McDonnell Douglas DC-10-30	48266	N3016Z	12. 3.96	Monarch Airlines Ltd	Luton	11. 3.99T
G-DMCD	Robinson R-22 Beta	1201	G-OOLI G-DMCD	14.11.89	R.W.Pomphrett	Thruxton	10.12.01T
G-DMCS	PA-28R-200 Cherokee Arrow II 28R-7635284		G-CPAC PH-SMW/OO-HAU/N75220	29. 5.84	Command Performance Ltd	Goodwood	20.11.00T
G-DMWW	CFM Shadow Srs.DD	304-DD		12.10.98	CFM Aircraft Ltd	Leiston	
G-DNCN	Agusta-Bell 206A Jet Ranger	8185	9H-AAJ Libyan Arab Rep.AF 8185/5A-BAM	21.11.97	Heli-Tele Ltd	Newbury	20.11.00T
G-DNCS	PA-28R-201T Turbo Arrow III 28R-7803024		N47841	3. 1.89	BC Arrow Ltd.	Barton	6. 4.01
G-DNLB	MBB Bo.105DBS-4 (Rebuilt with new pod S.850 1992)	S.60/850	G-BUDP G-BTBD VH-LCS/VH-HRM/G-BCDH/EC-DUO/G-BCDH/D-HDBK	10. 4.92	Bond Helicopters Ltd (Op for Northern Lighthouse Board)	Oban/Aberdeen	23. 4.98T
G-DNVT	Gulfstream G.1159C Gulfstream IV	1078	(G-BPJM) N17589	29. 9.89	Shell Acft Ltd	Heathrow	28. 9.00T
G-DOBN	Cessna 402B II	402B-1243	N24PL N4604G	25. 4.96	Edinburgh Air Centre Ltd	Edinburgh	27. 6.00T
G-DOCA	Boeing 737-436	25267		21.10.91	British Airways plc "River Ballindery"	Heathrow	20.10.01T
G-DOCB	Boeing 737-436	25304		16.10.91	British Airways plc (Wings of the City t/s)	Heathrow	16.10.01T
G-DOCC	Boeing 737-436	25305		24.10.91	British Airways plc (Blomsterang t/s)	Heathrow	24.10.01T
G-DOCD	Boeing 737-436	25349		6.11.91	British Airways plc (Animals & Trees t/s)	Heathrow	6.11.01T
G-DOCE	Boeing 737-436	25350		20.11.91	British Airways plc (Blomsterang t/s)	Heathrow	19.11.01T
G-DOCF	Boeing 737-436	25407		9.12.91	British Airways plc (Cockerel of Lowicz/Koguty Lowickie t/s)	Heathrow	9.12.01T
G-DOCG	Boeing 737-436	25408		16.12.91	British Airways plc (Chelsea Rose t/s)	Heathrow	15.12.01T
G-DOCH	Boeing 737-436	25428		19.12.91	British Airways plc (Grand Union t/s)	Heathrow	18.12.01T
G-DOCI	Boeing 737-436	25839		8. 1.92	British Airways plc "River Carron"	Heathrow	7. 1.02T
G-DOCJ	Boeing 737-436	25840		15. 1.92	British Airways plc "River Glass"	Heathrow	14. 1.02T
G-DOCK	Boeing 737-436	25841		25. 2.92	British Airways plc "River Lochay"	Manchester	24. 2.02T
G-DOCL	Boeing 737-436	25842		2. 3.92	British Airways plc (Martha Masanabo/Ndebele t/s)	Gatwick	1. 3.02T
G-DOCM	Boeing 737-436	25843		19. 3.92	British Airways plc (Rendezvous t/s)	Heathrow	18. 3.02T
G-DOCN	Boeing 737-436	25848		21.10.92	British Airways plc "River Ottery"	Gatwick	20.10.99T
G-DOCO	Boeing 737-436	25849		26.10.92	British Airways plc "River Parett"	Heathrow	25.10.99T
G-DOCP	Boeing 737-436	25850		2.11.92	British Airways plc "River Swift"	Gatwick	1.11.99T
G-DOCR	Boeing 737-436	25851		6.11.92	British Airways plc "River Tavy"	Gatwick	5.11.99T
G-DOCS	Boeing 737-436	25852		1.12.92	British Airways plc "River Teifi"	Gatwick	30.11.99T
G-DOCT	Boeing 737-436	25853		22.12.92	British Airways plc (Crossing Borders t/s)	Heathrow	23.12.99T
G-DOCU	Boeing 737-436	25854		18. 1.93	British Airways plc (Martha Masanabo/Ndebele t/s variant)	Heathrow	19. 1.00T
G-DOCV	Boeing 737-436	25855		25. 1.93	British Airways plc (Mountain of the Birds/Benyhone Tartan t/s)	Heathrow	24. 1.00T

Regn	Type	C/n	P/I	Date	Owner/operator	Probable Base	CA Expy
G-DOCW	Boeing 737-436	25856		2. 2.93	British Airways plc (Rendezvous t/s)	Heathrow	3. 2.00T
G-DOCX	Boeing 737-436	25857		29. 3.93	British Airways plc (Dove/Colum t/s)	Heathrow	28. 3.00T
G-DOCY	Boeing 737-436	25844	OO-LTQ G-BVBY/TC-ALS/G-BVBY/(G-DOCY) "River Weaver"	17.10.96	British Airways plc	Heathrow	17.10.99T
G-DOCZ	Boeing 737-436	25858	EC-FXJ EC-657/G-BVBZ/(G-DOCZ)	12.12.94	British Airways plc	Gatwick	11. 1.01T
G-DODB	Robinson R-22 Beta	0911	N8005R	3. 5.96	Exmoor Helicopters Ltd Withiel Farm, Minehead		9. 7.99T
G-DODD	Reims Cessna F.172P Skyhawk II	2175		5.10.82	K.Watts	Denham	4.10.98
G-DODI	PA-46-350P Malibu Mirage	4636019		26.10.95	CAVOK SRL	(Milan)	24.11.00
G-DODR	Robinson R-22 Beta	1325	N80721	5. 6.96	Exmoor Helicopters Ltd Withiel Farm, Minehead		25. 7.99T
G-DOEA	Gulfstream AA-5A Cheetah	AA5A-0895	G-RJMI N27170	30. 4.96	Plane Talking Ltd (Op Cabair Aerospace Education Sevice) (Duke of Edinburgh Award & British Aerospace c/s)	Elstree	28. 7.00T
G-DOFY	Bell 206B JetRanger III	3637	N2283F	26. 8.87	Cinnamond Ltd (Op Cabair Helicopters)	Elstree	3.10.99T
G-DOGZ	Horizon 1	PFA/241-13129		10. 8.98	J.E.D.Rogerson	(Ferryhill)	
G-DOLY	Cessna T303 Crusader	T303-00107	N303MK G-BJZK/(N3645C)	20. 7.94	R.M.Jones	Blackpool	12. 8.00
G-DONG	Sky 105-24 HAFB	011	G-BWKP	5. 2.97	G.J.Bell	Wokingham	10. 9.99A
G-DONI	Gulfstream AA-5B Tiger	AA5B-1029	G-BLLT OO-RTG/(OO-HRS)	20. 7.95	D.M.McLean	Wellesbourne Mountford	1.10.00
G-DONS	PA-28RT-201T Turbo Arrow IV	28R-8131077	N8336L	22. 4.88	D.J.Murphy t/a Arrow One Grp	Blackbushe	29. 9.00
G-DONZ	Europa Avn Europa	PFA/247-12545		1. 6.94	D.J.Smith & D.McNicholl (Muir of Ord/Tain, Ross-shire)		
G-DOOZ	Aerospatiale AS.355F2 Twin Squirrel	5367	G-BNSX	13. 5.88	Lynton Avn Ltd (Op European Helicopters Ltd)	Denham	1. 4.00T
G-DORB	Bell 206B JetRanger III	3955	SE-HTI TC-HBN	15. 8.90	Dorbcrest Homes Ltd Wrightington, Wigan		28.11.99
G-DORN	EKW C-3605	332	HB-RBJ SwissAF C-552	15. 5.98	R.G.Gray	(London E1)	AC
G-DOVE	Cessna 182Q Skylane II	182-66724	N96446	26. 6.80	Carel Investments Ltd	Bournemouth	21. 7.01
G-DOWN	Colt 31A Air Chair HAFB	1570		3. 8.89	M.Williams "Up & Down" Wadhurst, Sussex		18. 8.95A
G-DPST	Phillips ST-2 Speedtwin	PFA/207-12674		10. 5.96	S.E.Phillips Upper Cae Garw Farm, Trelleck, Monmouth		
G-DPUK	Mooney M.20K (231)	25-0631	G-BNZS N1154A	2. 4.98	K.A.Horne	(Bourne End)	26. 3.00
G-DRAC	Cameron Dracula Skull SS HAFB	2655		14.11.91	Shiplake Investments Ltd	(Guernsey)	10. 1.93A
G-DRAG	Cessna 152 II (Tailwheel conversion)	152-83188	G-REME G-DRAG/G-BRNF/N47217 (Op Old Sarum F/C)	27. 4.90	L.A.Maynard & M.E.Scouller	Old Sarum	11. 7.99T
G-DRAI	Robinson R-22 Beta	0918	N8008V	2. 2.89	L.L.F.Smith (Op Virgin Helicopters)	Booker	6. 5.01T
G-DRAM	Reims Cessna FR.172F Rocket (Floatplane)	0102	OH-CNS	18. 9.98	A.F.Allen t/a Off-Water Group	(Lochearnhead)	AC
G-DRAR	MDH Hughes 369E (500E)	0486E	N101LH N1608Z	15. 9.95	Readmans Ltd	Leeds-Bradford	9.10.01T
G-DRAW	Colt 77A HAFB	1830		31. 8.90	The Readers Digest Association Ltd London W1		9. 9.91A
G-DRAY	Taylor JT-1 Monoplane	PFA/1452		13. 7.78	L.J.Dray	Sidmouth	
G-DRBG	Cessna 172M Skyhawk	172-65263	G-MUIL N64486	18. 1.95	J.W.Halfpenny	(Landbeach, Cambridge)	13. 5.01T
G-DREX	Cameron Saturn 110SS HAFB	4217		28.10.97	LRC Products Ltd	Broxbourne, Herts	3.11.99A
G-DRGN	Cameron N-105 HAFB	2024		13. 6.91	W.I.Hooker & C.Parker	Nottingham	7. 7.99T
G-DRGS	Cessna 182S	18280375	N2389X	17.11.98	Walter Scott and Partners Ltd	Edinburgh	14.12.01
G-DRHL	Eurocopter AS.350B2 Ecureuil	3032		12. 1.98	David Reed Homes Ltd	Cambridge	29. 4.01
G-DRMM	Europa Avn Europa	PFA/247-13201		27. 7.98	M.W.Mason	(Nantwich)	
G-DRNT	Sikorsky S-76A II Plus	760201	N93WW N3WQ/N3WL/N3121G	5. 4.90	Bristow Helicopters Ltd	Redhill	1. 5.99T
			(Static "G-DRNT" in use Petak Offshore Industry Training Centre, Norwich 10.97)				
G-DROP	Cessna U206C Super Skywagon	U206-1230	G-UKNO G-BAMN/4X-ALL/N71943	7. 8.87	Peterborough Parachute Centre Ltd Sibson		1.10.00
G-DRSV	Robin DR.315X Petit Prince (Regd with c/n PFA/210-11765 following major rebuild)	624	F-ZWRS	6. 7.90	R.S.Voice	Rushett Farm, Chessington	14. 9.99P
G-DRUM	Thruster TST Mk.1 (Rotax 503)	8068-TST-081	G-MVBR	12. 1.99	C.C.Mercer	Saltash	31. 1.00P
G-DRYI	Cameron N-77 HAFB	2046		7. 8.89	J.Barbour & Sons Ltd "Barbour"	Marsh Benham	4. 6.94A
G-DRYS	Cameron N-90 HAFB	3377		1.12.95	J.Barbour & Sons Ltd	Marsh Benham	7. 7.99A
G-DRZF	CEA DR.360 Chevalier	451	F-BRZF	4. 9.91	Mavis R.Parker	Sywell	28.11.00
G-DSGC	PA-25-260 Pawnee C	25-4890	OY-BDA	3. 5.95	Devon & Somerset Gliding Club Ltd North Hill		14. 8.01
G-DSID	PA-34-220T Seneca	3447001		21. 7.95	R.Howton	Biggin Hill	3. 8.01
G-DTCP	PA-32R-300 Cherokee Lance	32R-7780255	G-TEEM N2604Q	26. 1.93	Campbell Avn Ltd	Denham	23.36.01

Regn	Type	C/n	P/I	Date	Owner/operator	Probable Base	CA Expy
G-DTOO*	PA-38-112 Tomahawk	38-79A0312		15. 2.79	Not known	Panshanger	29. 7.94T
					(Damaged Seething 9.7.94; stored 9.97)		
G-DUCK*	Grumman G.44 Widgeon	1218	N3103Q	15.11.88	Musee Historique de L'Hydraviation		
			N58337/42-38217/NC28679		(On rebuild 10.93)	Biscarosse, France	
G-DUDS	CASA I-131E Jungmann	2108	D-EHDS	27. 6.90	D.H.Pattison	Draycott Farm, Chiseldon	11. 6.01T
			E3B-512				
G-DUDZ	Robin DR.400/180	2367	G-BXNK	3.12.97	D.H.Pattison	Draycott Farm, Chiseldon	22.12.00
G-DUET	Wood Duet	D.001		19.12.78	C.Wood	(Aston Clinton)	
	(May be a modified Brugger Colibri c/n PFA/43-10468)						
G-DUNC	Cessna 182S Skylane	182-80195	N9305F	27. 5.98	D.C.Bain	(Leighton Buzzard)	11. 6.01T
G-DUNG	Sky 65-24 HAFB	125		20. 7.98	G.J.Bell	Wokingham	15. 6.99A
G-DUNN	Zenair CH.200 AD-1 & PFA/24-10450			5.10.78	A.Dunn t/a Chevalier F/Grp	(Lancing)	
	(Lyc O-320)				(Under construction 1988)		
G-DURO	Europa Avn Europa	PFA/247-12554		15.11.93	R.Swinden	(Witney)	
G-DURX	Colt 77A HAFB	1522		25. 5.89	V.Trimble	Henley-on-Thames	22. 3.99A
					"Featherlite/Durex" (You're Safer With Durex titles)		
G-DUSK	DH.115 Vampire T.Mk.11	15596	XE856	1. 2.99	R.M.A.Robinson & R.Horsfield	(Hornsea)	
G-DUST	Stolp SA.300 Starduster Too	JP-2	N233JP	28. 4.88	J.V.George	Popham	22. 5.90P
					(Damaged in collision with G-AKTM Badminton 16.7.89)		
G-DUVL	Reims Cessna F.172N Skyhawk II	1723	G-BFMU(1)	16. 8.78	A.J.Simpson	Sibson	11. 1.01
G-DVBF	Lindstrand LBL-210A HAFB	188		6. 3.95	Virgin Balloon Flights Ltd (London SE16)		16. 7.99T
G-DVON	DH.104 Devon C.2/2 (Dove 8)	04201	(G-BLPD)	26.10.84	C.L.Thatcher	Little Staughton	29. 5.96
			VP955		t/a The 955 Preservation Group		
					(As "VP955") (Stored 4.97)		
G-DWIA	Chilton DW.1A	PFA/225-12256		25. 1.93	D.Elliott	(Horsham)	
G-DWIB	Chilton DW.1B	PFA/225-12374		22.12.93	J.Jennings	(Bedford)	
G-DWPH	UltraMagic M-77 HAFB	77/109		17. 3.95	Jennifer M.Robinson	Chipping Norton	23. 7.99
					t/a UltraMagic UK "Miguel"		
G-DYAK	LET Yakovlev C-11	170103	G-BWFU	27.10.98	M.Rusche	(Hannover, Germany)	
			OK-...		(Being rebuilt at Little Gransden 11.96)		
G-DYNE	Cessna 414 Chancellor	414-0070	N8170Q	4. 8.87	Commair Avn Ltd	Nottingham	3. 9.99
					t/a Commodore Intl		
G-DYNG	Colt 105A HAFB	1721	G-HSHS	9. 2.98	G.J.Bell	Wokingham	17. 2.99A
G-DYOU*	PA-38-112 Tomahawk	38-78A0436		19.10.78	Not known	Booker	3. 3.94T
					(Damaged Booker 23.7.92; stored 6.97)		

G-EAAA-EZZZ - See Page 5 for 1919/1928 G-E allocations

Regn	Type	C/n	P/I	Date	Owner/operator	Probable Base	CA Expy
G-EAGA(2)	Sopwith Dove Replica (Le Rhone 80hp)	3004/1	(G-BLOO)	22.11.89	A.Wood (On loan to The Shuttleworth Collection)	Old Warden	14. 8.98P
G-EAGL(2)	Cessna 421C Golden Eagle III	421C-0713	(N2656G)	8. 8.79	Moseley Group (PSV) Ltd & Clowes (Estates) Ltd	East Midlands	20. 7.99
G-EBJI(2)	Hawker Cygnet replica	PFA/77-10240		9. 8.77	C.J.Essex (Under construction 12.96)	(Coventry)	
G-EBZN(2)	DH.60X Moth (Cirrus I)	608	VP-NAA VP-YAA/ZS-AAP/G-UAAP	28.10.88	Jane Hodgkinson (On rebuild from some original components)	(Gravesend)	
G-ECAS	Boeing 737-36N	28554		16.12.96	British Midland Airways Ltd	East Midlands	19.12.99T
G-ECAV	Beechcraft 200 Super King Air	BB-561	N36GA N963JC	17. 4.86	GEC-Marconi Avionics Ltd	Rochester	4. 6.00
G-ECBH	Reims Cessna F.150K	0577	D-ECBH	16. 5.85	J.P.Hosford	Henstridge	21. 8.97T
G-ECDX	DH.71 Tiger Moth replica (Gipsy I)	SP.7		1.11.94	M.D.Souch & N.Parkhouse (Nearing completion 8.97)	Hill Farm, Durley	
G-ECGC	Reims Cessna F.172N Skyhawk II	1850		10.10.79	Euroair Flying Club Ltd	Cranfield	29. 6.01T
G-ECGO	Bolkow Bo.208C Junior	599	D-ECGO	24. 8.89	A Flight Aviation Ltd	(Clydebank)	20. 3.00
G-ECHO	Enstrom 280C-UK-2 Shark	1017	G-BDIB	28. 5.82	A.L.Pattinson t/a ALP Electrical (Maidenhead)	Booker	7. 6.00
G-ECJM	PA-28R-201T Turbo Arrow III	28R-7803178	G-FESL G-BNRN/N321EC/N3561M	25. 9.90	Regishire Ltd	Southampton	1. 3.01
G-ECKE	Avro 504K replica (Warner Scarab SS-50) (Built AJD Engineering Ltd)	0014		6.10.93	N.Wright & C.M.Kettlewell (As "D8781" in RFC c/s)	Bury St.Edmunds	23. 7.99P
G-ECOS	Aerospatiale AS.355F1 Twin Squirrel	5300	G-DOLR G-BPVB/OH-HAJ/D-HEHN	24. 9.92	Multiflight Ltd (Op Northern Helicopters (Leeds) Ltd)	Leeds-Bradford	2.10.00T
G-ECOX	Grega GN.1 Air Camper	WLAW.1 & PFA/47-10356		5.12.78	H.C.Cox Brickhouse Farm, Frogland Cross (Under construction 12.93)		
G-EDEN	Socata TB-10 Tobago	66		8. 1.80	N.G.Pistol, J.R.Priest, G.W.Bevan & A.K.Hilton	Elstree	17. 4.99
G-EDFS	Pietenpol Aircamper	PFA/47-13206		24. 3.98	D.F.Slaughter	(Redhill)	
G-EDGE	Jodel 150 Mascaret (Cont O-200-A)	111 & PFA/151-11223		14. 9.88	A.D.Edge	(Derby)	
G-EDGI	Piper PA-28-161 Warrior	28-7916565	D-EBGI N2941R	19. 1.99	A.P.Dyer t/a Small World Aviation	North Weald	AC
G-EDMC	Pegasus Quantum 15-912	7513		11. 3.99	E.McCallum	(Gateshead)	
G-EDNA	PA-38-112 Tomahawk	38-78A0364	OY-BRG	4. 9.84	D.J.Clucas	Woodford	21.10.99T
G-EDRY	Cessna T303 Crusader	T303-00280	N4817V	9. 3.87	Pat Eddery Ltd	Turweston	3. 4.99
G-EDVL	PA-28R-200 Cherokee Arrow II	28R-7235245	G-BXIN D-EDVL/N1243T	30. 6.97	J.S.Develin & Z.Islam	Redhill	30. 7.00
G-EEAC	PA-31 Turbo Navajo	31-761	G-SKKA G-FOAL/G-RMAE/G-BAEG/N7239L	5. 5.94	London Flight Centre (Stansted) Ltd (Op Love Air)	Biggin Hill	27. 6.99T
G-EEGL	Christen Eagle II (Lyc AEIO-360)	AES/01/0353	5Y-EGL	14.12.90	A.J.Wilson	Deenethorpe	2. 6.99P
G-EELS	Cessna 208B Caravan I	208B-0619		3. 3.97	Glass Eels Ltd	Gloucestershire	20. 8.00T
G-EEMV	Hawker Sea Fury FB.Mk.11	41H-636335	N588 VH-BOU/WH588 (RAN)/WH588	10.12.97	P.J.Morgan "Baby Gorilla" (As "WH588/NW-114" in RAN c/s)	Sywell	5. 4.99P
G-EENA	PA-32R-301 Saratoga SP	32R-8013011	C-GBBU	3.10.97	Gamit Ltd	Andrewsfield	16.10.00
G-EENI	Europa Avn Europa	PFA/247-12831		28. 7.98	M.P.Grimshaw	(London W5)	
G-EENY	Gulfstream GA-7 Cougar	GA7-0094	N721G	21. 6.79	J.P.E.Walsh t/a Walsh Aviation (Op Cabair)	Cranfield	20. 7.00T
G-EESA	Europa Avn Europa (NSI EA-81/100)	PFA/247-12535	G-HIIL	9. 4.96	C.B.Stirling	Damyns Hall	27. 1.99P
G-EESE*	Cessna U206G Stationair	U206-03883	OO-DMA N7344C	28. 2.85	Not known Movenis, Co.Londonderry (Crashed Magilligan, Co.Londonderry 31.12.88; wreck stored 6.97)		1. 4.91
G-EEUP	SNCAN Stampe SV-4C	451	F-BCXQ	1. 9.78	A.M.Wajih	Redhill	18. 8.99
G-EEZE	Rutan LongEz (Originally regd to VariEze c/n 1567, possibly a new kit)	11 & PFA/74-10308		13.12.77	A.J.Nurse	(Bristol)	
G-EFRY	Light Aero Avid Aerobat (Rotax 582)	PFA/189-12096		22. 3.93	F.E.Telling	(Esher)	25.11.99P
G-EFSM	Slingsby T-67M Firefly 260	2072	G-BPLK	16. 7.92	Slingsby Avn Ltd	Kirkbymoorside	29. 4.99T
G-EFTE	Bolkow Bo.207	218	D-EFTE	4. 1.90	L.J. & A.A.Rice	Bishopstrow Farm, Warminster	7. 5.99
G-EGAL	Christen Eagle II (Lyc AEIO-360)	0042-86	SE-XMU	11. 3.96	P.N.Davis	Coventry	22. 9.99P
G-EGEE	Cessna 310Q	310Q-0040	G-AZVY SE-FKV/N7540Q	14.11.83	A.Dervan	Fairoaks	30. 6.00
G-EGEL	Christen Eagle II (Lyc AEIO-360)	S.308		4. 2.91	R.Kirchhofer, P.Miny & U.Fritz	(Steinen, Germany)	26. 7.99P
G-EGGS	Robin DR.400/180 Regent	1443		15.11.79	R.Foot	Henstridge	16. 7.01
G-EGHB	Ercoupe 415D (Cont O-200-A)	1876	N3414G N99253/NC99253	1. 9.95	J.H.Spanton	Maypole Farm, Chislet	13. 7.01
G-EGHH	Hawker Hunter F.58	41H-697450	J-4083	4. 7.95	Jet Heritage Charitable Foundation Ltd (As "J-4083")	Bournemouth	27. 1.01T
G-EGHR	Socata TB-20 Trinidad	795	F-GGIQ	19.12.97	B.M.Prescott	Goodwood	
G-EGJA	Socata TB-20 Trinidad	1101	N2807D	13.12.90	D.A.Williamson	Alderney	6. 1.00

Regn	Type	C/n	P/I	Date	Owner/operator	Probable Base	CA Expy
G-EGLD	PA-28-161 Cadet	2841283	N92007	23.11.89	J.Appleton t/a Holmes Rentals (Op Denham School of Flying)	Denham	6. 1.02T
G-EGLE	Christen Eagle II (Lyc AEIO-360) (Built by Airmore Avn)	F.0053		30. 3.81	R.L.Mitcham, P.J.Meaton, S.R.Flack & I.Dinermann	Booker	3. 8.99P
G-EGLT	Cessna 310R II	310R-1874	G-BHTV N1EU/(N3206M)	9. 9.93	Tilling Associates Ltd (Op Eagle Airways)	Guernsey	21.12.01T
G-EGNR	PA-38-112 Tomahawk	38-79A0233	OY-VIG SE-KNI/N2570C	6.10.97	Chester Aero Services Ltd	Chester	9.10.00T
G-EGTR	PA-28-161 Cadet	2841281	G-BRSI N92001	25. 4.98	Plane Talking Ltd	Elstree	17.12.02T
G-EGUL	Christen Eagle II (Lyc AEIO-360)	Argence 0001	G-FRYS N66EA	19. 1.93	I.S.Smith t/a G-EGUL Flying Group	Coventry	18. 3.99P
G-EGUY	Sky 220-24 HAFB	103		24. 4.98	J.L.Guy t/a Black Sheep Balloons	(Skipton)	8. 4.99T
G-EHBJ	CASA I-131E Jungmann 2000	2150	E3B-550	19. 7.90	E.P.Howard Priory Farm, Tibenham		26. 5.99P
G-EHIL	EH Industries EH-101 (Airframe No.PP3)	50003		9. 7.87	Westland Helicopters Ltd (To MoD as ZH647 1993)		
G-EHMJ	Beechcraft S35 Bonanza	D-7879	D-EHMJ	12. 1.99	A.L.Burton & A.J.Daley	(Worksop)	AC
G-EHMM	Robin DR.400/180R Remorqueur	867	D-EHMM	10.12.84	Booker Gliding Club Ltd	Booker	1. 4.00
G-EHUP	Aerospatiale SA.341G Gazelle 1	1407	F-GIJR N869GT/N869/N49523	3.10.97	MW Helicopters Ltd	(Ware)	2.12.00
G-EIBM	Robinson R-22 Beta	1993	G-BUCL	25. 3.94	Abbey Management Ltd t/a Abbey Quantity Surveyors	Dundee	5. 3.01T
G-EIIR	Cameron N-77 HAFB	358		16.11.77	D.V.Howard "Silver Jubilee"	Bath	14. 5.93A
G-EIKY	Europa Avn Europa (Rotax 912UL)	PFA/247-12634		27. 9.94	J.D.Milbank	Insch	19. 8.99P
G-EIWT	Reims Cessna FR.182 Skylane RG	0052	D-EIWT OO-BLI	28. 1.86	P.P.D.Howard-Johnston (Op Edinburgh Air Centre)	Edinburgh	1. 4.01
G-EJGO	Zlin Z.226 Trener 6HE Spezial	199	D-EJGO OK-MHB	7. 8.85	S.Gibbins t/a Golf Oscar Flying Group	Rochester	15. 4.01
G-EJMG	Reims Cessna F.150H	0301	D-EJMG	27. 4.98	T.A.White t/a Bagby Aviation	Bagby	26.10.01T
G-EJOC	Aerospatiale AS.350B Ecureuil	1465	G-GEDS G-HMAN/G-SKIM/G-BIVP	21.12.94	Elmsdale (UK) Ltd	Fairoaks	8. 7.99T
G-EKKL	PA-28-161 Warrior 11	28-8416087	D-EKKL N43588	24. 3.99	B W Davis t/a Astra Associates	(St.Albans)	
G-EKOS	Reims Cessna FR.182 Skylane RG	0017	D-EKOS	15. 7.98	S.Charlton	(York)	9. 9.01
G-ELBC	PA-34-200 Seneca	34-7350021	G-BANS N15110	4. 4.91	Stapleford F/C Ltd (Op for LBC Radio -"London Lookout")	Stapleford	23.12.00T
G-ELEN	Robin DR.400/180	2363		16. 9.97	N.R. & E.Foster	Biggin Hill	10.11.00
G-ELFI	Robinson R-22 Beta	1126	N80513	2.10.89	A.L.Ramsden	Shobdon	11.11.01T
G-ELIZ	Denney Kitfox mk.2 717 & PFA/172-11835 (Rotax 582)			19. 7.90	A.J.Ellis t/a Tiger Helicopters Sandown (Damaged Brightstone, IoW 10.5.93)		5.11.93P
G-ELKA	Christen Eagle II (Lyc AEIO-360)	0001	N121DJ	18.10.94	D.Aitken & Skydance Aviation Ltd (Aberdeen/Dundee)		29. 4.99P
G-ELKS	Avid Speed Wing MK.4	PFA/189-13109		6. 1.98	H.S.Elkins	(Gloucester)	9. 7.99P
G-ELLA	PA-32R-301 Saratoga IIHP	3246050	N92279Q G-ELLA	13. 8.96	C.C.W.Hart	(London W11)	21.10.99T
G-ELLE	Cameron N-90 HAFB	4498		11. 1.99	S.A.Lacey t/a L.E.Electrical	Norwich	15.12.99A
G-ELLI	Bell 206B Jet Ranger III	4231	D-HMOF	24. 6.97	RA Fleming Ltd Brandon Hall, Leeds		3. 7.00T
G-ELMH	North American AT-6D-NT Harvard III	88-16336 EZ341/42-84555	FAP1662	22. 7.92	M.Hammond "Fools Rush-In" Hardwick (As "42-84555/EP-H" in USAAC c/s to commemorate 100th BG B-17G)		26. 5.99P
G-EMAK	PA-28R-201 Cherokee Arrow III	28R-7737082	D-EMAK N38180	30. 8.85	D. & G.Rathbone (Stored 12.97)	Barton	18. 9.94
G-EMAX	PA-31-350 Navajo Chieftain	31-7952029	N276CT SE-KKP/54202	8.12.98	AM & T Aviation Ltd Bristol/Lulsgate Swedish Navy/SE-KKP/LN-PAI		15.12.01T
G-EMAZ	PA-28-181 Archer II	28-8290088	N8073W	26. 4.90	E.J.Stanley	Blackpool	17.10.99T
G-EMBA	Embraer EMB-145EU	145-016	PT-SYM	17. 7.97	British Regional Airlines Ltd (Dove/Colum t/s) East Midlands		14. 8.00T
G-EMBB	Embraer EMB-145EU	145-021	PT-SYR	27. 8.97	British Regional Airlines Ltd (Sterntaler/Bauhaus t/s) East Midlands		1. 9.00T
G-EMBC	Embraer EMB-145EU	145-024	PT-SYU	1.10.97	British Regional Airlines Ltd (Cockerel of Lowicz/Koguty Lowickie t/s) East Midlands		8.10.00T
G-EMBD	Embraer EMB-145EU	145-039		7. 1.98	British Regional Airlines Ltd (Animals and Trees/Kg-Oocoan-Naka-Hiian-Thee-E t/s) East Midlands		11. 1.01T
G-EMBE	Embraer EMB-145EU	145-042		3. 2.98	British Regional Airlines Ltd (Waves of the City t/s) East Midlands		2. 2.01T
G-EMBF	Embraer RJ-145EU	145-088		10.11.98	British Regional Airlines Ltd Ronaldsway (Grand Union t/s)		9.11.01T
G-EMBG	Embraer RJ-145EU	145-094		18.11.98	British Regional Airlines Ltd Ronaldsway (Water Dreaming t/s)		17.11.01T
G-EMBH	Embraer RJ-145EU	145-107		20. 1.99	British Regional Airlines Ltd Birmingham (Blomsterang t/s)		19. 1.02T
G-EMBI	Embraer RJ-145EU	145-...		R.99	British Regional Airlines Ltd Birmingham (Youm-al-Suq t/s)		
G-EMBJ	Embraer RJ-145EU	145-...		R	British Regional Airlines Ltd Birmingham (For delvy 5.99)		

Regn	Type	C/n	P/I	Date	Owner/operator	Probable Base	CA Expy
G-EMBJ	Embraer RJ-145EU	145-...		R	British Regional Airlines Ltd Birmingham (For delvy 5.99)		
G-EMBK	Embraer RJ-145EU	145-...		R	British Regional Airlines Ltd Birmingham (For delvy 8.99)		
G-EMBL	Embraer RJ-145EU	145-...		R	British Regional Airlines Ltd Birmingham (For delvy 9.99)		
G-EMBM	Embraer RJ-145EU	145-...		R	British Regional Airlines Ltd Birmingham (For delvy 11.99)		
G-EMBN	Embraer RJ-145EU	145-...		R	British Regional Airlines Ltd Birmingham (For delvy 1.00)		
G-EMBO	Embraer RJ-145EU	145-...		R	British Regional Airlines Ltd Birmingham (For delvy 3.00)		
G-EMER	PA-34-200 Seneca	34-7350002	N3081T	29. 7.91	Haimoss Ltd & R.P.Thomas (Op Old Sarum F/C)	Old Sarum	26. 1.01T
G-EMIN	Europa Avn Europa (Rotax 912UL)	PFA/247-12673		1. 3.94	G.M.Clarke t/a Gemini Grp	Perth	3. 6.99P
G-EMJA	CASA I-131E-2000 Jungmann 013 & PFA/242-12340 (Composite from Spanish spares imported in 1991)		(Sp.AF)	2. 9.94	P.J.Brand (As "D-EMJA" in pre-war German c/s)	Audley End	3. 2.99P
G-EMMS	PA-38-112 Tomahawk	38-78A0526	OO-TKT N4414E	14. 9.79	Cheshire F/Svs Ltd t/a Ravenair	Blackpool	22. 9.00T
G-EMMY	Rutan VariEze 577 & PFA/74-10222 (Lyc O-235)			21. 8.78	M.J.Tooze	Biggin Hill	9. 2.99P
G-EMNI	Phillips ST.1 Speedtwin Mk.2 006 & PFA/207-12880			25. 5.95	A.J.Clarry	(Pewsey, Wilts)	
G-EMRD	BAe 748 Srs.2B/378	1797	G-HDBD G-11-747/CS-TAR/G-11-1/D-AHSF/G-11-2	11.10.96	Emerald Airways Ltd	Liverpool	16.10.99T
G-EMSI	Europa Avn Europa	PFA/247-12817		24. 1.95	P.W.L.Thomas	(York)	
G-EMSY	DH.82A Tiger Moth	83666	G-ASPZ D-EDUM/T7356	27. 6.91	B.E.Micklewright (On rebuild 3.98 with parts from OO-MOT)	Chilbolton	28.10.65
G-ENCE	Partenavia P.68B	141	G-OROY G-BFSU	1. 6.84	Bettany Aircraft Holdings Ltd	Jersey	2. 9.00
G-ENIE	Nipper T.66 Srs.IIIB (VW1800)	PFA/25-10214		17. 3.78	E.J.Clarke	Seighford	24. 8.99P
G-ENII	Reims Cessna F.172M Skyhawk II	1352	PH-WAG (D-EDQM)	18. 1.79	J.Howley	Fenland	10.10.99T
G-ENNY	Cameron V-77 HAFB	1399		1.12.86	B.G.Jones "Crocks of Frome"	Devizes	16. 5.99A
G-ENOA	Reims Cessna F.172F	0138	G-ASZW	2. 9.81	M.K.Acors	Thurrock	1. 4.00
G-ENRI	Lindstrand LBL-105A HAFB	294		4. 8.95	P.G.Hall (Henry Numatic Vacuum Cleaners c/s)	Chard	13. 5.96T
G-ENRY	Cameron N-105 HAFB	2096		26. 9.89	P.G. & G.R.Hall "Henry"	Chard	7. 7.94T
G-ENSI	Beechcraft F33A Bonanza	CE-699	D-ENSI	17. 3.78	J.M.Eskes	Booker	19. 5.99
G-ENTT	Reims Cessna F152 II	1750	G-BHHI (PH-CBA)	9.11.93	Southern Flight Training Ltd	Bournemouth	28. 3.99T
G-ENTW	Reims Cessna F152 II	1479	G-BFLK	21. 1.93	Southern Flight Training Ltd	Bournemouth	21. 7.99T
G-ENUS	Cameron N-90 HAFB	1914		18. 1.89	Wye Valley Avn Ltd "Guinness"	Ross-on-Wye	30. 6.99T
G-EOFS	Europa Avn Europa	PFA/247-13033		22. 7.98	G.T.Leedham	(Swadlincote)	
G-EOHL	Cessna 182L Skylane	182-59279	D-EOHL N70505	4. 3.99	G.B.Dale & M.C.Terris	(Armagh, NI)	
G-EOMA	Airbus A.330-243	265	F-WWKU	R	Monarch Airlines Ltd (For dlvy 4.99)	Luton	
G-EORG	PA-38-112 Tomahawk (Rebuilt with new fuselage; old one stored 2.95)	38-78A0427		18. 9.78	Airways Aero Associations Ltd (Op British Airways F/C) (Whale Rider t/a)	Booker	14. 7.00T
G-EPAR	Robinson R-22 Beta	2781		26. 2.98	J.W.Ramsbottom t/a Jepar Rotorcraft	(Preston)	26. 2.00T
G-EPDI	Cameron N-77 HAFB	370		25. 1.78	R.Moss "Pegasus"	Banchory	29. 6.91A
G-EPED	PA-31-350 Chieftain	31-8252040	G-BMCJ N121CF/N41060	22. 3.95	Pedley Furniture International Ltd	Duxford	21.12.98T
G-EPFR	Airbus A.320-231	0437	F-FTDF G-BVJV/N437RX/G-BVJV/C-FWDQ/G-BVJV/N437RX/F-WWDM	18.11.97	Airtours International Airways Ltd	Manchester	28. 4.01T
G-EPJM	PA-28-181 Archer III	2843166	N41268	10. 9.98	E.J.Moorey	(Brockenhurst)	15. 9.01
G-EPOL	Aerospatiale AS.355F1 Twin Squirrel	5302	G-SASU G-BSSM/G-BMTC/G-BKUK	13. 1.98	Cambridge and Essex Air Support Unit	Boreham	24.10.99T
G-EPOX	Aero Designs Pulsar XP	PFA/202-12355		27. 4.94	K.F.Farey	(Bourne End)	
G-EPTR	PA-28R-200 Cherokee Arrow II	28R-7235090	D-EPTR OH-PTR/(SE-KVF)/N4558T	26. 5.98	T.I.Moore	Aberdeen	26. 6.01
G-ERBL	Robinson R-22 Beta	2711		26. 6.97	G.V.Maloney	Biggin Hill	27. 7.00T
G-ERCO	Ercoupe 415D (Cont C85)	3210	N2585H NC2585H	7. 4.93	A.R. & M.V.Tapp	Maypole Farm, Chislet	15. 8.99
G-ERDS	DH.82A Tiger Moth	85028	ZS-BCU SAAF 2267/T6741	27. 7.94	W.A.Gerdes	Lee-on-Solent	21. 6.01
G-ERIC	Rockwell Commander 112TC	13010	SE-GSA	26. 9.78	Atomchoice Ltd	Cranfield	15. 4.00
G-ERIK	Cameron N-77 HAFB	1753		18. 5.88	T.M.Donnelly "Norsewind"	Doncaster	8. 2.96A
G-ERIS	Hughes 369D (500D) (Mod to 500E standard)	11-0871D	G-PJMD G-BMJV/N1110S	1. 3.96	R.J.Howard	Leeds	12. 8.01T
G-ERIX	Boeing-Stearman E75 (PT-13D) Kaydet (P+W R985)	75-5093	N5055V 42-16930	9. 3.88	P.P.Stanitzeck (As "985" in US Navy c/s)	(Munchen, Germany)	3.12.00

Regn	Type	C/n	P/I	Date	Owner/operator	Probable Base	CA Expy
G-ERMO	ARV Super 2	018	G-BMWK	7. 1.87	P.R.Booth	(Ripon)	2. 1.94
G-ERMS	Thunder AS-33 Hot Air Airship	A.1		28.11.78	B.R. & M.Boyle	Newbury	
	(Now regd as Ax3 Sky Chariot)				"Microbe" (On loan to British Balloon Museum 12.93)		
G-ERNI	PA-28-181 Archer II	28-8090146	G-OSSY N81215	9.10.91	D.C. & M.A.Greenaway	Biggin Hill	15. 2.01
G-EROS	Cameron H-34 HAFB	2296		6. 4.90	Evening Standard Co Ltd "Eros" London W8		
G-ERRY	Grumman-American AA-5B Tiger	AA5B-0725	G-BFMJ	20. 3.84	M.D.Savage & A.F.K.Horne t/a Gemini Aviation	Shobdon	10. 5.99
G-ESFT	PA-28-161 Warrior II	28-7916060	G-ENNA N22065	16. 5.97	SFT Europe Ltd	Bournemouth	21. 4.00T
G-ESKU	PA-23-250 Aztec C	27-3823	G-AWIY N6599Y	11. 4.96	A.J.Keen	Aldergrove	16. 7.98
G-ESKY	PA-23-250 Aztec D	27-4172	G-BBNN N6832Y	24.11.95	A.Watson (Op Premi-Air Flying Club)	Shoreham	18. 4.00T
G-ESSX	PA-28-161 Warrior II	28-8016261	G-BHYY N9639N	30. 7.82	S.Harcourt t/a Courtenay Enterprises	Compton Abbas	16. 1.97T
G-ESTA	Cessna 550 Citation II (Unit No.143)	550-0217	G-GAUL N550TJ/(N27TG)/N29TC/N2631N	24. 6.98	Executive Aviation Services Ltd	Gloucestershire	17. 8.99T
G-ESTE	Gulfstream AA-5A Cheetah	AA5A-0780	G-GHNC N26877	28. 4.87	Plane Talking Ltd	Elstree	8.12.01T
G-ESUS	Rotorway Exec 162F	6169		7.10.96	J.Tickner	(Kings Lynn)	
G-ETBY	PA-32-260 Cherokee Six (Rebuild using spare Frame No.32-858S)	32-211	G-AWCY N3365W	13. 7.89	S.R.Nash & K.Richards-Green t/a G-ETBY Group	Enstone	25. 1.99T
G-ETDA	PA-28-161 Warrior II	28-8116256	N84051	9. 3.88	T.Griffiths	Oaksey Park	26. 3.00
G-ETDC	Cessna 172P Skyhawk II	172-74690	N53133	4. 5.88	Osprey Air Svs Ltd	Exeter	22. 6.00T
G-ETFT	Colt Financial Times SS HAFB	1792	G-BSGZ	11. 1.91	Financial Times Ltd "Financial Times II"	London SE19	11. 1.99A
G-ETIN	Robinson R-22 Beta	0853	N9081D	7. 9.88	Forestdale Hotels Ltd	Burley	24. 9.00T
G-EUOA to G-EUOZ	Airbus A.320				)) Reservations for British Airways plc)		
G-EUPA	Airbus A.319	1082	R		British Airways plc (Chelsea Rose t/s) (For delvy 9.99)	Heathrow	
G-EUPB	Airbus A.319	1115	R		British Airways plc	Heathrow	
G-EUPC	Airbus A.319	1116	R		British Airways plc	Heathrow	
G-EUPD to G-EUPZ	Airbus A.319				)) Reservations for British Airways plc)		
G-EURA	Agusta-Bell 47J-2 Ranger	2061	G-ASNV	21. 7.83	L.Goddard	Thornicombe, Dorset	23.10.00
G-EVAN*	Taylor JT.2 Titch	PFA/3231		14.12.78	E.Evans	(Stanford-le-Hope)	
					(Construction suspended- cancelled by PWFU 24.3.99)		
G-EVER	Robinson R-22 Beta	1109		25. 8.89	Bucks Joinery (Mfg) Ltd	Aston Clinton	6.11.98T
G-EVES	Dassault Falcon 900B	165	F-WWFD	13.11.97	Northern Executive Aviation Ltd (Op for David Crossland/Airtours) Jersey/Manchester		12.11.00T
G-EVET	Cameron Concept 80 HAFB	3703		30.10.95	K.J.Foster	Coleshill, Birmingham	18. 4.99A
G-EVNT	Lindstrand LBL-180A HAFB	071		13.12.93	Redmalt Ltd (Op Bailey Balloons)	Bristol	2. 4.99T
G-EWAN	Protech PT-2C Sassy	PFA/249-12425		23. 6.93	C.G.Shaw	(Littlehampton)	AC
G-EWFN	Socata TB-20 Trinidad	1009	G-BRTY	22. 1.90	Trinidair Ltd	Bristol/Lulsgate	21. 4.99T
G-EWIZ	Pitts S-2SE Special (Lyc AEIO-540)	S.18	VH-EHQ	12.11.82	S.J.Carver & D.Howdle	Netherthorpe	17.10.99P
G-EWUD*	Reims Cessna F.172F	0137	(G-ESSO) G-EWUD/G-ATBK	26. 5.87	Not known (Damaged in Dee Estuary nr West Kirby 14.8.92; stored 2.93)	Wickenby	12.12.93
G-EXEA	Extra EA.300/L	082		9. 3.99	Brandish Holdings Ltd	(Jersey)	
G-EXEC	PA-34-200 Seneca	34-7450072	(G-EXXC) OY-BGU	11. 5.78	Sky Air Travel Ltd	Stapleford	15.12.99T
G-EXEX	Cessna 404 Titan II	404-0037	SE-GZF (N5418G)	3. 5.79	Atlantic Air Transport Ltd (Op for Dept of Transport)Inverness/Coventry		29. 7.00A
G-EXIT	Socata MS.893E Rallye 180GT	12979	F-GARX	22. 9.78	K.J.Reynolds Middle Stoke, Isle of Grain t/a Medway Microlights		12. 2.01
G-EXPL	American Champion 7GCBC Citabria	1220-96		9. 5.96	J.J.Young	Church Farm, Shipmeadow	18.11.99
G-EXPR	Colt 90A HAFB	1064		17. 8.87	D.P.Hopkins t/a Lakeside Lodge Golf Centre	Pidley, Huntingdon	13.12.98A
G-EXTR	Extra EA.260 (Lyc AEIO-540)	004	D-EDID	10. 8.92	Diana M.Britten (Morse titles)	Fairoaks	29. 4.99P
G-EYAS	Denney Kitfox mk.2 (Rotax 582)	PFA/172-11858		3. 3.93	E.J.Young	(Sheffield)	1. 9.94P
G-EYCO	Robin DR.400/180 Regent	1949		12. 3.90	L.M.Gould	Jersey	14. 4.99
G-EYES	Cessna 402C II	402C-0008	SE-IRU G-BLCE/N4648N	16. 7.90	Atlantic Air Promotions Ltd (Op for National Rivers Authority)	Coventry	15. 8.99T
G-EYET	Robinson R-44 Astro	0052	G-JPAD	30.11.98	Eye-T Aviation Ltd	(Shipley)	29. 4.00
G-EYNL	MBB Bo.105DBS-5	S.382	LN-OTJ D-HDLR/EC-DSO/D-HDLR	19. 8.96	Humberside Police Helicopter Support Unit Normandy Barracks, Leconfield		4.12.99T
G-EYRE	Bell 206L-1 Long Ranger II	45229	G-STVI N60MA/N5091K	12.11.90	Hideroute Ltd	Stapleford	30. 6.00T

Regn	Type	C/n	P/I	Date	Owner/operator	Probable Base	CA Expy
G-EZOS	Rutan VariEze (Cont O-200-A)	002 & PFA/74-10221		10. 7.78	O.Smith	Croft-on-Tees, Darlington	18.10.99P
G-EZYA	Boeing 737-3Y0	23498	G-MONG C-GPWG/G-MONG/C-GPWG/G-MONG	30. 5.96	easyJet Airline Co Ltd	Luton	5. 6.99T
G-EZYB	Boeing 737-3M8	24020	N797BB I-TEAA/OO-LTA/(OO-BTA)	17.10.96	easyJet Airline Co Ltd	Luton	20.10.99T
G-EZYC	Boeing 737-3Y0	24462	G-BWJA EC-FJR/EC-897/G-TEAA/EI-BZQ/(N116WA)/EI-BZQ/EC-ENS/EC-244/N5573K	28. 5.97	easyJet Airline Co Ltd	Luton	4. 4.99T
G-EZYD	Boeing 737-3M8	24022	N798BB I-TEAE/OO-LTC/(OO-BTC)	5. 2.97	easyJet Airline Co Ltd	Luton	10. 2.00T
G-EZYE	Boeing 737-3Q8	24068	SE-DTA G-OCHA/G-BNNJ	4. 6.97	easyJet Airline Co Ltd	Luton	13. 7.00T
G-EZYF	Boeing 737-375	23708	D-AGEX (G-EZYC)/4L-AAA/PT-TEC/(C-GZPW)	3.11.97	easyJet Airline Co Ltd	Luton	9.11.00T
G-EZYG	Boeing 737-33V	29331	N1768B	19. 8.98	easyJet Airline Co Ltd	Luton	18. 8.01T
G-EZYH	Boeing 737-33V	29332		17. 9.98	easyJet Airline Co Ltd	Luton	17. 9.01T
G-EZYI	Boeing 737-33V	29333		24.11.98	easyJet Airline Co Ltd	Luton	22.11.01T
G-EZYJ	Boeing 737-33V	29334		18.12.98	easyJet Airline Co Ltd	Luton	17.12.01T
G-EZYK	Boeing 737-33V	29335		31. 1.99	easyJet Airline Co.Ltd	Luton	AC
G-EZYL	Boeing 737-33V	29336		12. 3.99	easyJet Airline Co Ltd	Luton	
G-EZYM	Boeing 737-33V	29337		R	easyJet Airline Co Ltd (For dlvy 5.99)	Luton	
G-EZYN	Boeing 737-33V	29338		R	easyJet Airline Co Ltd (For dlvy 7.99)	Luton	
G-EZYO	Boeing 737-33V	29339		R	easyJet Airline Co Ltd (For dlvy 8.99)	Luton	
G-EZYP	Boeing 737-33V	29340		R	easyJet Airline Co Ltd (For dlvy 9.99)	Luton	
G-EZYR	Boeing 737-33V	29341		R	easyJet Airline Co Ltd (For dlvy 10.99)	Luton	
G-EZYS	Boeing 737-33V	29352		R	easyJet Airline Co Ltd (For dlvy 12.99)	Luton	

G-FAAA-FZZZ

Regn	Type	C/n	P/I	Date	Owner/operator	Probable Base	CA Expy
G-FABB	Cameron V-77 HAFB	822	LX-FAB	13.12.89	P.Trumper	Ashford, Kent	7. 9.99T
G-FABI	Robinson R-44 Astro	0325		25. 4.97	P.Caswell	Blackpool	24. 4.00T
G-FABM	Beechcraft 95B55A Baron	TC-2259	G-JOND	22. 2.91	F.B.Miles	Gloucestershire	17. 8.01
			G-BMVC/N66456				
G-FABS	Thunder Ax9-120 Srs.2 HAFB	2399		8. 6.93	Not known	Felixstowe/Woodbridge	10. 5.96T
					(Temp unregd 29.5.96)		
G-FAGN	Robinson R-22 Beta	0615	(N2566W)	28.11.86	C.R.Weldon	Dublin	25. 5.01
G-FALC	Aeromere F.8L Falco 3	224	G-AROT	19. 2.81	P.W.Hunter	Old Sarum	28. 6.98
G-FAME	CFM Starstreak Shadow SA-II			23. 5.96	T.J.Palmer	(Kilmarnock)	
	(Jabiru 2200) K.273SA & PFA/206-12973						
G-FAMH	Zenair ZH.701 Stol PFA/187-13301			26. 6.98	A.M.Harrhy	(Ventnor)	
G-FAMY	Maule M.5-180C	8089C	N5668B	24. 1.91	R.J. & K.C.Grimstead	Petworth	2. 7.00
G-FANC	Temco Fairchild 24R-46	R46-347	N77647	16.10.89	A.T.Fines	Felthorpe	26. 5.00
			NC77647				
G-FANL	Cessna R172K Hawk XPII	R172-2873	N736XQ	7. 6.79	J.A.Rees	Haverfordwest	24. 6.00T
G-FANN*	HS.125 Srs.600B	256019	HZ-AAI	13. 2.89	Not known	Dunsfold	
	(Also quoted as ex HZ-AA1)		G-BARR		(On fire dump 6.96 - "HZ-AAI")		
G-FARM	Socata Rallye 235E	12832	F-GARF	10.10.78	Bristol Cars Ltd	White Waltham	26.10.00
G-FARO	Star-Lite SL-1 PFA/175-11359			19. 6.89	M.K.Faro	(Wimborne)	16. 4.98P
	(Rotax 447)						
G-FARR	SAN Jodel 150 Mascaret	58	F-BNIN	21. 7.81	G.H.Farr Dairy House Farm, Nantwich		19. 5.99P
G-FATB	Commander 114B	14624	N6037Y	3. 7.96	J.W.F.McIllwraith	Shoreham	28. 7.99
G-FAYE	Reims Cessna F.150M	1252	PH-VSK	24. 1.80	Cheshire Air Training Svs Ltd	Liverpool	21. 6.01T
G-FBHH	Hughes 369HS	33-0461S	N2186K	1. 8.96	G.R. Lloyd	Pembrey	9. 9.99T
			PK-AVH/PK-PDO		t/a Dragon Helicopters		
G-FBIX	DH.100 Vampire FB.9	22100	7705M	24. 7.91	D.G.Jones	(Bridgend)	
			WL505		(As "WL505") (On rebuild 2.96)		
G-FBMW	Cameron N-90 HAFB	3019		23. 4.93	K-J.Schwer Erbach-Donaurieden, Germany		4. 3.97A
G-FBPI	ANEC IV Missel Thrush PFA/312-13417			19. 1.99	R.Trickett.	(Kings Lynn)	
G-FBRN	PA-28-181 Archer II	28-8290166	D-ERBN	3. 8.98	Herefordshire Aero Club Ltd	Shobdon	26. 8.01T
			N82628				
G-FBWH	PA-28R-180 Cherokee Arrow	28R-30368	SE-FCV	23. 8.78	F.T.Short	Fenland	24. 1.01
G-FCAL	Cessna 441 Conquest II	441-0293	C-FMHD	19. 3.96	Cobham Leasing Ltd	Bournemouth	17.10.00T
			N88723		(Op FR Aviation)		
G-FCLA	Boeing 757-28A	27621	N1789B	26. 2.97	Flying Colours Airlines Ltd	Manchester	25. 2.00T
G-FCLB	Boeing 757-28A	28164	N751NA	25. 3.97	Flying Colours Airlines Ltd	Manchester	8. 5.00T
			G-FCLB				
G-FCLC	Boeing 757-28A	28166		9. 5.97	Flying Colours Airlines Ltd	Manchester	8. 5.00T
G-FCLD	Boeing 757-25F	28718		25. 4.97	Flying Colours Airlines Ltd	Manchester	24. 4.00T
G-FCLE	Boeing 757-28A	28171		24. 5.98	Flying Colours Airlines Ltd	Manchester	23. 5.01T
G-FCLF	Boeing 757-28A	28835		24. 3.99	Flying Colours Airlines Ltd	Manchester	AC
G-FCLG	Boeing 757-28A	24367	N701LF	18.12.98	Flying Colours Airlines Ltd	Manchester	
			EI-CLM/N381LF/N240LA/C-GTSK/C-GNXI/G-GAWB				
G-FCLH	Boeing 757-28A	26274	N751LF	17. 2.99	Flying Colours Airlines Ltd	Manchester	
			EI-CLU/N161LF				
G-FCLI	Boeing 757-28A	26725	N651LF	17. 3.99	Flying Colours Airlines Ltd	Manchester	
G-FCSP	Robin DR.400/180 Regent	2022		24.10.90	F.C.Smith	Biggin Hill	23. 1.00
					t/a FCS Photochemicals		
G-FDAV	Westland SA.341G Gazelle 1	WA/1108	G-RIFA	17. 5.93	Federal Avn Ltd	Denham	15.12.98
			G-ORGE/G-BBHU				
G-FEBE	Cessna 340A II	340A-0345	N405LS	12. 7.88	C.Dugard Ltd & E.C.Dugard	Shoreham	11. 4.01
			(N37320)				
G-FEFE	Scheibe SF-25B Falke	46126	EI-BVZ	11. 4.94	R.Bagley	Aston Down	22. 9.99
			D-KADB		t/a Aston Down Falke Syndicate		
G-FELL	Europa Avn Europa PFA/247-13208			17. 3.98	J.A.Fell	(Peterborough)	
G-FELT	Cameron N-77 HAFB	1174		19. 7.85	Allan Industries Ltd	Chinnor	14. 3.99A
					"Fuzzy Felt"		
G-FEZZ	Agusta Bell 206B Jet Ranger II	8317	SU-YAD	16. 9.98	L.Smith t/a Helicopter Services	Booker	23. 9.01T
			YU-HAT				
G-FFAB	Cameron N-105 HAFB	4067		20. 2.97	The Andrew Brownsword Collection	Bath	5. 5.99A
G-FFEN	Reims Cessna F.150M	1204	PH-VGL	25. 8.78	Suffolk Aero Club Ltd		26. 3.00T
						Poplar Hall Farm, Elmsett	
G-FFOR	Cessna 310R II	310R-1889	G-BMGF	31. 3.87	ILS Air Ltd	Bristol/Lulsgate	14. 5.01T
			ZS-KU/N3276M				
G-FFOX	Hawker Hunter T.7B	41H-670792	WV318	10. 1.96	Delta Engineering Avn Ltd	Kemble	14. 5.99P
	(Composite, possibly including components of WV322)				(As "WV318" in all-black c/s)		
G-FFRA	Dassault Falcon 20DC	132	N902FR	28. 5.92	Cobham Leasing Ltd	Bournemouth	20.10.99A
			(N23FR)/(N149FE)/N2FE/N560L/N4348F/F-WMKG				
G-FFRI	Aerospatiale AS.355F1 Twin Squirrel		G-GLOW	15. 4.93	C.B. & C.M.Smith	Fairoaks	5. 5.00T
		5120	G-PAPA/G-CNET/G-MCAH t/a Ford Farm Racing (Op Alan Mann Helicopters)				
G-FFTI	Socata TB-20 Trinidad	1065		23. 2.90	Romsure Ltd	Cambridge	21. 5.99T
G-FFWD	Cessna 310R II	310R-0579	G-TVKE	20. 2.90	Keef & Co Ltd	Booker	16. 2.00
			G-EURO/N87468				
G-FGID	Vought (Goodyear) FG-1D Corsair	3111	N8297	1.11.91	Patina Ltd	Duxford	10. 8.99P
			N9154Z/Bu.88297		(B J S Grey/The Fighter Collection)		
					(As "KD345/130" in 1850 Sqn RN c/s)		
G-FHAS	Scheibe SF-25E Super Falke	4359	(D-KOOG)	14. 5.81	Burn Gliding Club Ltd	Burn	28.10.99

Regn	Type	C/n	P/I	Date	Owner/operator	Probable Base	CA Expy
G-FIAT	PA-28-140 Cherokee F	28-7425162	G-BBYW N9622N	19. 7.89	The RAF Benevolent Fund Enterprises Ltd (Op Disabled Flyers Grp) Hinton-in-the-Hedges		10. 6.99T
G-FIBS	Aerospatiale AS.350BA Ecureuil	2074	JA9732	14. 6.94	Irvine Avn Ltd	Denham	8. 8.00T
G-FIFE	Reims Cessna FA.152 Aerobat	0351	G-BFYN	15. 2.95	Tayside Aviation Ltd	Glenrothes	23.12.99T
G-FIFI	Socata TB-20 Trinidad	688	G-BMWS	16. 1.87	OLM Avn Ltd	Denham	1. 7.99
G-FIGA	Cessna 152 II	152-84644	N6243M	3. 6.87	Aerohire Ltd Halfpenny Green (Op Midland Flight Centre)		22. 8.99T
G-FIGB	Cessna 152 II	152-85925	N95561	16.11.87	Aerohire Ltd	Wellesbourne Mountford	12. 2.00T
G-FIJR	Lockheed L.188PF Electra	1138	(EI-HCF) G-FIJR/C-FIJR/CF-IJR/N134US	12. 9.91	Atlantic Air Transport Ltd	Coventry	12. 9.01T
G-FIJV	Lockheed L.188C Electra	1129	EI-HCE G-FIJV/C-FIJV/CF-IJV/N7143C	29. 8.91	Atlantic Air Transport Ltd	Coventry	27. 9.01T
G-FILE	PA-34-200T Seneca II	34-8070108	N8140Z	23. 7.87	Barnes Olson Aeroleasing Ltd	Bristol/Lulsgate	14.11.99T
G-FILL	PA-31-310 Navajo C	31-7912069	OO-EJM N3521C	28. 6.96	P.V.Naylor-Leyland	Deenethorpe	8. 8.99
G-FILO	Robin DR.400/180 Regent	2063		16. 4.91	Baron G.van der Elst Gosselies, Belgium		4. 9.00
G-FINA	Reims Cessna F150L	0826	G-BIFT PH-CEW	12.10.93	D.Norris	Finmere	8. 5.99T
G-FINS	Agusta-Bell 206B JetRanger II	8507	G-FSCL D-HASE/SE-HGI/OY-HCR/SE-HGI/HB-XFI t/a Whyles International	3.12.87	Leverton Farms Ltd & D.Whyles	Lincoln	19. 8.00
G-FIRS	Robinson R-22 Beta	2807		15. 4.98	M. & S.Chantler	(Crewe)	
G-FISH	Cessna 310R II	310R-1845	N2740Y	8. 5.81	R.W.F & R.B.Warner t/a Warner Group (Damaged Little Ness nr Shrewsbury 11.11.95; stored 7.97)	Edinburgh	14. 5.96
G-FISK	Pazmany PL-4A (VW1834)	PFA/17-10129		14.12.88	K.S.Woodard (Stored 9.97) Little Snoring		11. 4.96P
G-FIST*	Fieseler Fi 156C-3 Storch (Argus AS.10C)	156-5802	D-EDEC I-FAGG/MM12822	23.11.83	Italian Air Force Museum Vigna De Valle (As "MM12822" in Italian AF c/s)		6. 3.96P
G-FITZ	Cessna 335	335-0044	G-RIND N2710L	20. 4.95	White Knuckle Airways Ltd Leeds-Bradford		20. 1.02
G-FIZU	Lockheed L.188CF Electra	2014	EI-CHY G-FIZU/SE-IZU/(N857ST)/N857U/Ph-LLG	6. 4.93	Atlantic Air Transport	Coventry	3. 1.02T
G-FIZZ	PA-28-161 Warrior II	28-7816301	N2721M	1.12.78	Arrow Air Centre Ltd	Shipdham	30. 4.00T
G-FJCE	Thruster T600T	9120-T600T-032		25.11.98	Thruster Air Services Ltd	Wantage	
G-FJET	Cessna 550 Citation II	550-0419	G-DCFR G-WYLX/VH-JVS/G-JETD/N1217N	7. 7.97	London Executive Avn Ltd	London City	27.12.99T
G-FJMS	Partenavia P.68B	113	G-SVHA OY-AJH	7. 9.92	F.J.M.Sanders (Op Bonus Avn)	Cranfield	13. 6.99T
G-FKNH	PA-15 Vagabond (Cont C85)	15-291	CF-KNH N4517H/NC4517H	19. 3.97	M.J.Mothershaw	Woodford	15. 5.00
G-FLAG	Colt 77A HAFB	2000		20. 9.90	B.A.Williams	Maidstone	10. 6.97T
G-FLAK	Beechcraft E55 Baron	TE-1128	N4771M	26. 9.89	Thunder Avn Ltd (De Haan, Belgium) "Red Baron"		6. 3.99T
G-FLAV	PA-28-161 Warrior II	28-8016283	N8171X	7. 4.94	S.W.Parker t/a The Crew F/Grp Nottingham		17. 5.00
G-FLCA	Fleet 80 Canuck	068	CS-ACQ CF-DQP	18. 7.90	E.C.Taylor (On rebuild 3.96)	(Warwick)	
G-FLCT	Hallam Fleche	PFA/309-13389		21.10.98	R G Hallam	(Macclesfield)	
G-FLEW	Lindstrand LBL-90A HAFB	586		21. 1.99	Lindstrand Balloons Ltd	Oswestry	21. 8.00A
G-FLII	Grumman-American GA-7 Cougar	GA7-0003	G-GRAC C-GRAC/(N1367R)/N730GA (Op as Capital Radio's "Flying Eye")	18.12.91	Plane Talking Ltd	Elstree	23.10.01T
G-FLIK	Pitts S-1S Special (Lyc O-320)	PFA/09-10513		7. 1.81	R.P.Millinship	Leicester	22. 5.99P
G-FLIP	Reims Cessna FA152 Aerobat	0375	G-BOES G-FLIP	29.12.80	J.R.Nicholls	Sibson	8. 5.00T
G-FLIT	Rotorway Exec 162F	6324		22.12.98	R.F.Rhodes.	(Maldon)	AC
G-FLIZ	Staaken Z-21 Flitzer 006 & PFA/223-13115			24. 3.97	G.P.Gregg (As "D-694")	(Oakham)	
G-FLOA	Cameron O-120 HAFB	4006		4.10.96	Floating Sensations Ltd Thatcham, Berks		5.11.99T
G-FLOR	Europa Avn Europa	PFA/247-12793		11.11.98	A.F.C.Van Eldik	(Hythe)	
G-FLOX	Europa Avn Europa	PFA/247-12732		28. 6.95	P.S.Buchan t/a DPT Grp	(Horsham)	25.11.99P
G-FLPI	Rockwell Commander 112A	205	SE-FLP (N1205J)	16. 3.79	L.Freeman & Son Ltd	Newcastle	13. 3.00
G-FLSI	FLS Sprint 160	001		20. 8.93	Sunhawk Ltd	North Weald	AC
G-FLTA	BAe 146 Srs.200	E-2048	N189US N365PS	25. 2.98	Flightline Ltd	Southend	26. 2.01T
G-FLTI	Beechcraft F90 King Air	LA-59	N7P	16. 3.90	Flightline Ltd	Southend/Guernsey	19. 7.99
G-FLTY	Embraer EMB-110P1 Bandeirante	110-215	G-ZUSS G-REGA/N711NH/PT-GMH	28. 8.92	Not known	Southend	21. 4.98T
G-FLTZ	Beechcraft 58 Baron	TH-1154	G-PSVS N5824T/YV-266P	21. 9.93	Stesco Ltd (Flightline Ltd)	Southend/Guernsey	11. 5.01
G-FLUF	Lindstrand Bunny SS HAFB	002		7. 4.93	Lindstrand Balloons Ltd (Oswestry) (Not built)		
G-FLVU	Cessna 501 Citation I (C/n 501-580 reported)	501-0178	N83ND	11. 6.98	Neonopal Ltd	Liverpool	23. 6.01T
G-FLYA	Mooney M.20J (201SE)	24-3124		8. 6.89	BRF Aviation Ltd	Full Sutton	3.12.01
G-FLYE	Cameron A-210 HAFB	4216		12.12.97	Bakers World Travel Ltd	Langford, Somerset	4.12.99T
G-FLYI*	PA-34-200 Seneca	34-7250144	G-BHVO SE-FYY	1. 9.81	Routair Ltd (Damaged Elstree 21.11.91; on rebuild 3.99)	Southend	12. 5.92T

Regn	Type	C/n	P/I	Date	Owner/operator	Probable Base	CA Expy
G-FLYP	Beagle B.206 Srs 2	B.058	N4OCJ N97JH/G-AVHO/VQ-LAY/G-AVHO	24. 2.67	Key Publishing Ltd. (Stamford)		AC
G-FLYS	Robinson R-44 Astro	0347		5. 6.97	N.Ferris t/a Brilliant PR	Cookham, Maidenhead	12. 6.00
G-FLYT	Europa Avn Europa 57 & PFA/247-12653 (NSI EA-81/100)			15. 5.95	D.W.Adams	Kings Langley	24. 3.99P
G-FLYZ	Robinson R-44 Astro	0490		7. 7.98	P., M. & K.I.Smith (Newport Pagnell) t/a Rotaflite Helicopter Sales		18.10.01T
G-FMAM	PA-28-151 Cherokee Warrior	28-7415056	G-BBXV N9603N	7. 6.90	B.Barr	Seething	23.10.99
G-FMSG	Reims Cessna FA.150K Aerobat	0081	G-POTS G-AYUY	4. 1.95	G.Owen	Humberside	15.10.00T
G-FNLD	Cessna 172N Skyhawk II	172-70596	(G-BOUG) N739KD	3. 8.88	D.Wright & R.C.Laming t/a Papa Hotel F/Grp	Fenland	11. 1.01
G-FNLY	Reims Cessna F.172M	0910	G-WACX G-BAEX	20. 3.89	P.M.Hopkinson	(Truro)	25. 7.00T
G-FODI	Robinson R-44 Astro	0513		21. 9.98	Sanna Industries Ltd	(Birmingham)	
G-FOGG	Cameron N-90 HAFB	1365		21.11.86	J.P.E.Money-Kyrle "Phileas Fogg"	Chippenham	15.10.01T
G-FOKW	Focke-Wulf Fw190A-5	0151227	"A"(white) DG+HO (Luftwaffe)	6. 3.96	Wizzard Investments Ltd Earls Colne (David Arnold/Flying A Services) (Crashed nr Leningrad 19.7.43; on rebuild 9.96)		
G-FOLD	Light Aero Avid Speed Wing PFA/189-12041 (Rotax 582)			30.10.92	R.H.Green	(Lyndhurst)	20. 2.99P
G-FOLI	Robinson R-22 Beta	2813		25. 4.98	K.Duckworth	(Northampton)	17. 5.01
G-FOLY	Aerotek Pitts S-2A Special (Lyc AEIO-360)	2213	N31477	26. 7.89	A.A.Laing	Dundee	21.12.98
G-FOPP	Neico Lancair 320	PFA/191-12319		14. 8.92	Airsport (UK) Ltd	Abbots Langley	
G-FORC	SNCAN Stampe SV-4C	665	(G-BLTJ) F-BDNJ	6. 6.85	I.A.Marsh	(Borehamwood)	23. 4.00
G-FORD	SNCAN Stampe SV-4C (Gipsy Major 10)	129	F-BBNS	7. 2.78	P.H.Meeson Oaklands Farm, East Tytherley, Wilts (Damaged East Tytherley, nr Romsey 16.7.96)		31. 7.98
G-FORZ	Pitts S-1S Special	PFA 009-13393		3.11.98	N.W. Parkinson	(Bedford)	
G-FOTO	PA-E23-250 Aztec F	27-7654089	G-BJDH G-BDXV/N62614	27. 2.79	Aerofilms Ltd	(Borehamwood)	13. 3.00A
G-FOWL	Colt 90A HAFB	1198		11. 3.88	N.A.Fishlock t/a G-FOWL Ballooning Group "Chicken"	Cheltenham	10. 7.99A
G-FOWS	Cameron N-105 HAFB	3995		11.12.96	Fowlers of Bristol Ltd	Bristol	7. 1.00T
G-FOXA	PA-28-161 Cadet	2841240	N9192B	17.11.89	Leicestershire A/C Ltd	Leicester	7. 3.99T
G-FOXC	Denney Kitfox mk.3 773 & PFA/172-11900 (Rotax 582)			8. 1.91	I.H.Clarke	Portmoak	10. 9.99P
G-FOXD	Denney Kitfox (Rotax 582)	PFA/172-11618		22.11.89	M.Hanley	Deenethorpe	24. 7.99P
G-FOXE	Denney Kitfox mk.2 740 & PFA/172-11994 (Rotax 582)			1. 8.90	K.M.Pinkard "Foxe Lady" (Chester) (Damaged Stewartby Lake, Beds 3. 7.94)		31. 5.95P
G-FOXG	Denney Kitfox mk.2 452 & PFA/172-11886 (Rotax 532)			15. 8.90	S.M.Jackson t/a Kitfox Grp Romney Street Farm, Sevenoaks		6. 5.99P
G-FOXI	Denney Kitfox mk.2 (Rotax 532)	PFA/172-11508		21. 9.89	B.Johns Combrook, Stratford-on-Avon		16. 8.99P
G-FOXM	Bell 206B JetRanger II	1514	G-STAK G-BNIS N35HF/N135VG	5. 2.93	R.P.Maydon t/a Milton Keynes City Air (Op by CSE Helicopters for Fox FM Radio)	Oxford	22.12.97T
G-FOXS	Denney Kitfox mk.2 465 & PFA/172-11571 (Rotax 582)			15. 8.90	S.P.Watkins & C.C.Rea	Sheepcote	25. 8.99P
G-FOXX	Denney Kitfox	PFA/172-11509		1.11.89	R.O.F.Harper	(Lymm)	
G-FOXZ	Denney Kitfox	PFA/172-11834		4.12.90	S.C.Goozee	(Wimborne)	19.10.98
G-FPLA	Beechcraft B200 Super King Air	BB-944	N31WL HB-GHZ/HL5260/N1824V	3.12.97	FR Aviation Ltd	Bournemouth	9. 3.01T
G-FPLB	Beechcraft B200 Super King Air	BB-1048	N739MG N223MD/9Y-TGY	3.12.97	FR Aviation Ltd	Bournemouth	11. 1.01T
G-FPLC	Cessna 441 Conquest II	441-0207	G-FRAX G-BMTZ/N27280	14. 1.98	FR Aviation Ltd	Bournemouth	29. 3.00T
G-FRAD	Dassault Falcon 20E	304/511	G-BCYF F-WRQP	26.11.86	Cobham Leasing Ltd (Op FR Aviation)	Bournemouth	2. 9.00A
G-FRAE	Dassault Falcon 20E	280/503	N910FR I-EDIS/F-WPXK	23. 9.87	Cobham Leasing Ltd (Op FR Aviation)	Bournemouth	19. 1.00A
G-FRAF	Dassault Falcon 20E	295/500	N911FR I-EDIM/F-WRQQ	1. 9.87	Cobham Leasing Ltd (Op FR Aviation)	Bournemouth	18.10.99A
G-FRAG	PA-32-300 Six	32-7940284	N3566L	21. 1.80	A.M.Sierant t/a G-FRAG Grp	Sherburn	21. 5.01
G-FRAH	Dassault Falcon 20DC	223	G-60-01 N900FR/(N904FR)/N22FE/N4407F/F-WPUX (Op FR Aviation)	31. 5.90	Cobham Leasing Ltd	Teesside	7.10.99A
G-FRAI	Dassault Falcon 20E	270	N901FR N37FE/N4435F/F-WPUZ (Op FR Aviation)	17.10.90	Cobham Leasing Ltd	Teesside	18. 4.99A
G-FRAJ	Dassault Falcon 20DC	20	N903FR (N25FR)/N5FE/(N146FE)/N5FE/N367GA/N367/N842F/F-WMKJ (Op FR Aviation)	30. 4.91	Cobham Leasing Ltd	Bournemouth	12.12.99A
G-FRAK	Dassault Falcon 20DC	213	N905FR N32FE/N4390F/F-WJMM (Op FR Aviation)	9.10.91	Cobham Leasing Ltd	Bournemouth	9. 4.99A

Regn	Type	C/n	P/I	Date	Owner/operator	Probable Base	CA Expy
G-FRAL	Dassault Falcon 20DC	151	N904FR	17. 3.93	Cobham Leasing Ltd	Teesside	22.12.99A
	(N24FR)/N3FE/(N148FE)/N3FE/N810PA/N810F/N4360F/F-WMKI (Op FR Aviation)						
G-FRAM	Dassault Falcon 20DC	224	N907FR	13. 5.93	Cobham Leasing Ltd	Bournemouth	26. 5.99A
			N23FE/N4408F/F-WPUY (Op FR Aviation)				
G-FRAN	Piper J3C-90 Cub (L-4J-PI)	12617	G-BIXY	14. 7.86	I.Dole	Rayne Hall Farm, Rayne	19. 4.99P
	(Frame No.12447)		F-BDTZ/44-80321		t/a Essex L-4 Grp (As "480321/44/H" in USAAC c/s)		
G-FRAO	Dassault Falcon 20DC	214	N906FR	23.10.92	Cobham Leasing Ltd	Bournemouth	28. 1.00A
			N33FE/N4400F/F-WNGO (Op FR Aviation)				
G-FRAP	Dassault Falcon 20DC	207	N908FR	12. 7.93	Cobham Leasing Ltd	Bournemouth	19.10.99A
			N27FE/N4395F/F-WMKF (Op FR Aviation)				
G-FRAR	Dassault Falcon 20DC	209	N909FR	2.12.93	Cobham Leasing Ltd	Bournemouth	15. 2.00A
			N28FE/N4396F/F-WLCX (Op FR Aviation)				
G-FRAS	Dassault Falcon 20C	82/418	CAF 117501	31. 7.90	Cobham Leasing Ltd	Bournemouth	1.12.99A
			20501/F-WJMM		(Op FR Aviation)		
G-FRAT	Dassault Falcon 20C	87/424	CAF 117502	31. 7.90	Cobham Leasing Ltd	Teesside	21. 2.00A
			20502/F-WJMJ		(Op FR Aviation)		
G-FRAU	Dassault Falcon 20C	97/422	CAF 117504	31. 7.90	Cobham Leasing Ltd	Teesside	15.12.99A
			20504/F-WJMJ		(Op FR Aviation)		
G-FRAW	Dassault Falcon 20C	114/420	CAF 117507	31. 7.90	Cobham Leasing Ltd	Bournemouth	9. 4.99A
			20507/F-WJMM		(Op FR Aviation)		
G-FRAY	Cassutt Racer IIIM (Mod)	PFA/34-11211		24.10.90	C.I.Fray	(Macclesfield)	
G-FRAZ	Cessna 441 Conquest II	441-0035	SE-GYC	14. 9.87	Cobham Leasing Ltd	Bournemouth	24. 9.99A
			(N36965)		(Op FR Aviation)		
G-FRBA	Dassault Falcon 20C	178/459	OH-FFA	16. 7.96	FR Finances Ltd	Bournemouth	AC
			F-WPXF		(Op FR Aviation)		
G-FRBY	Beechcraft E55 Baron	TE-868	N78PS	23. 9.94	FR Finances Ltd	Bournemouth	16.11.00A
			N77PS		(Op FR Aviation)		
G-FRCE	Folland Gnat T.1	FL.598	8604M	28.11.89	Butane Buzzard Avn Corpn Ltd	Cranfield	17. 4.95P
			XS104		(Op Kennet Avn) (Stored 3.96)		
G-FRED*	Clutton Fred Srs.II	PFA/29-10339		18. 5.78	Not known	Priory Farm, Tibenham	
					(Incomplete and stored 4.96)		
G-FRGN	PA-28-236 Dakota	2811046	N9244N	8. 2.96	Fregon Aviation Ltd	Enstone	5. 3.99T
G-FRJB*	Britten SA-1 Sheriff	0001		18. 5.81	East Midlands Aeropark	East Midlands	
	(Not completed)						
G-FRST	PA-44-180T Turbo Seminole	44-8207020	N8236B	5.11.82	WAM (GB) Ltd	Blackpool/Newtownards	28. 5.01
			N9615N				
G-FRYI	Beechcraft 200 Super King Air	BB-210	G-OAVX	15. 3.96	London Executive Aviation Ltd	Stapleford	26. 3.98T
			G-IBCA/G-BMCA/N5657N				
G-FSFT	PA-44-180 Seminole	44-7995190	EI-CCO	12.10.98	Magenta Ltd	Oxford	12.10.01T
			N2135G				
G-FSII*	Gregory Free Spirit mk.II	004		26. 2.91	M.J.Gregory & R.P.Hallam		AC
					(Cancelled by CAA 27.3.99) (Huntingdon/Aldershot)		
G-FTAX	Cessna 421C Golden Eagle II	421C-0308	N8363G	23. 8.84	C.R.Venner	Cambridge	4. 5.99T
			G-BFFM/N8363G		t/a CRV Leasing (Op Hawkair)		
G-FTFT*	Colt Financial Times 90SS HAFB	1163		14. 1.88	Financial Times Ltd	Newbury	5. 6.95A
					"Financial Times" (To British Balloon Museum 2.97)		
G-FTIL	Robin DR.400/180 Regent	1825		10. 3.88	G.M.Pearce	Niederrhein, Netherlands	25. 9.00T
					t/a Niederrhein Powered F/C		
G-FTIM	Robin DR.400/100 Cadet	1829		6. 5.88	Bird Investment Properties Ltd	Kemble	28. 4.01
G-FTIN	Robin DR.400/100 Cadet	1830		6. 5.88	G.D.Clark & M.J.D.Theobald	Blackpool	17. 8.00
					t/a YP F/Grp		
G-FTUO	Van's RV-4	926	C-FTUQ	23.12.97	Euroclip 2000 Ltd	(Banbury)	5. 3.99P
G-FTWO	Aerospatiale AS.355F2 Twin Squirrel	5347	G-OJOR	27. 1.87	McAlpine Helicopters Ltd	Oxford	18. 2.99T
			G-FTWO/G-BMUS				
G-FUEL	Robin DR.400/180 Regent	1537		15. 5.81	R.Darch	East Chinnock, Yeovil	27. 5.00
G-FUGA	Fouga CM-170R Magister	045	G-BSCT	12. 4.90	Dutch Historic Jet Association BV		1. 7.99P
			Fr.AF 45		(Hilversum, Netherlands)		
G-FUJI*	Fuji FA.200-180 Aero Subaru	156	D-EMMI	14. 9.79	F & H (Acft) Ltd	Tattershall Thorpe	29. 6.92
					(Damaged Newton, Powys 5. 5.92; stored 7.95)		
G-FULL	PA-28R-200 Cherokee Arrow II	28R-7435248	G-HWAY	26.11.84	M.Pugh	Stapleford	25.11.99
			G-JULI/(G-BKDC)/OY-POV/N43128				
G-FUND	Thunder Ax7-65Z HAFB	376		3.11.81	Soft Sell Ltd "Paddy Wagon"	Wallingford	6.12.92A
G-FUNK	Yakovlev Yak-50	852908	RA-852908	27. 3.98	D.J.Gilmour	North Weald	21. 5.99P
					t/a Intrepid Avn Co		
G-FUNN	Plumb BGP-1 Biplane	PFA/83-12744		16.10.95	J.D.Anson	(Liskeard)	
G-FUSI	Robinson R-22 Beta	2506	N83306	16. 3.95	F.M.Usher-Smith	Saffron Walden	5. 5.01
G-FUZY	Cameron N-77 HAFB	1751		6. 5.88	Allan Industries Ltd	Chinnor	5.11.96A
					"Fuzzy Felt II"		
G-FUZZ	PA-18-95 Super Cub (L-18C-PI)	18-1016	(OO-HMY)	11. 9.80	G.W.Cline	(Gipsy Wood)	8. 4.99P
	(Frame No. 18-1086)		ALAT-FMBIT/51-15319				
G-FVBF	Lindstrand LBL-210A HAFB	311		6.12.95	Virgin Balloon Flights Ltd	(London SE16)	17.22.99T
					"Red November"		
G-FWPW	PA-28-236 Dakota	2811018	N9145L	10.10.88	P.A. & F.C.Winters	Oxford	22.10.00
G-FWRP	Cessna 421C Golden Eagle III	421C-0418	N3919C	9.12.82	Adavia Ltd	Sturgate	5. 9.99T
					(Op Eastern Air Executive)		

Regn	Type	C/n	P/I	Date	Owner/operator	Probable Base	CA Expy
G-FXII	VS.366 Spitfire F.XII 6S/197707		EN224	4.12.89	P.R.Arnold (Newport Pagnell)		
					t/a Peter R.Arnold Collection		
					(On rebuild from components 3.96)		
G-FXIV*	VS.379 Spitfire FR.XIV		T44	11. 4.80	Luftfahrtmuseum Laatzen-Hannover		
	HS... (Indian AF)/MV370 (As "MV370/EB-Q" in 41 Sqdn c/s) Laatzen-Hannover, Germany						
G-FYAN	Williams Westwind HAFB (Model)	MDW-1		6. 1.82	M.D.Williams	Dunstable	
G-FYAO	Williams Westwind HAFB (Model)	MDW-001		6. 1.82	M.D.Williams	Dunstable	
G-FYAU	Williams Westwind Two HAFB (Model)	MDW-002		6. 1.82	M.D.Williams	Dunstable	
G-FYAV	Osprey Mk.4E2 HAFB (Model)	ASC-247		12. 1.82	C.D.Egan & C.Stiles	Hounslow	
G-FYBD	Osprey Mk.1E HAFB (Model)	ASC-136		20. 1.82	M.Vincent	Jersey	
G-FYBE	Osprey Mk.4D HAFB (Model)	ASC-128		20. 1.82	M.Vincent	Jersey	
G-FYBF	Osprey Mk.5 HAFB (Model)	ASC-218		20. 1.82	M.Vincent	Jersey	
G-FYBG	Osprey Mk.4G2 HAFB (Model)	ASC-204		20. 1.82	M.Vincent	Jersey	
G-FYBH	Osprey Mk.4G HAFB (Model)	ASC-214		20. 1.82	M.Vincent	Jersey	
G-FYBI	Osprey Mk.4H HAFB (Model)	ASC-234		20. 1.82	M.Vincent	Jersey	
G-FYBP	European E.84PW HAFB (Model)	S.20		29. 1.82	D.Eaves	Southampton	
G-FYBR	Osprey Mk.4G2 HAFB (Model)	ASC-203		29. 1.82	A.J.Pugh	Lakenheath	
G-FYCL	Osprey Mk.4G HAFB (Model)	ASC-213		9. 2.82	P.J.Rogers	Banbury	
G-FYCV	Osprey Mk.4D HAFB (Model)	ASK-276		19. 2.82	M.Thomson	London SW11	
G-FYCZ	Osprey Mk.4D2 HAFB (Model)	ASC-244		24. 2.82	P.Middleton	Colchester	
G-FYDC	European EDH.1 HAFB (Model)	S.24		17. 3.82	D.Eaves & H.W.Goddard	Southampton	
G-FYDF	Osprey Mk.4D HAFB (Model)	ASK-278		22. 3.82	K.A.Jones	Thornton Heath	
G-FYDI	Williams Westwind Two HAFB (Model)	MDW-005		29. 3.82	M.D.Williams	Dunstable	
G-FYDN	European 8C HAFB (Model)	DD34/S.22		5. 4.82	P.D.Ridout	Botley	
G-FYDO	Osprey Mk.4D HAFB (Model)	ASK-262		15. 4.82	N.L.Scallan	Hayes	
G-FYDP	Williams Westwind Three HAFB (Model)	MDW-006		29. 3.82	M.D.Williams	Dunstable	
G-FYDS	Osprey Mk.4D HAFB (Model)	ASK-261		15. 4.82	M.E.Scallan	Hayes	
G-FYDW	Osprey Mk.4B HAFB (Model)	ASK-282		27. 4.82	R.A.Balfre	Hayes	
G-FYEB	Rango Rega Srs.II (Gas Airship) (Model)	NHP-31		18. 5.82	N.H.Ponsford	Leeds	
					t/a Rango Balloon & Kite Co "Maegaera"		
G-FYEJ	Rango NA-24 (Gas FB) (Model) (Half-scale Chartres Balloon replica)	NHP-30		27. 5.82	N.H.Ponsford	Leeds	
					t/a Rango Balloon & Kite Co		
G-FYEK	Unicorn UE-1C HAFB (Model)	82024		2. 7.82	D. & D.Eaves	Southampton	
G-FYEL	European E.84Z HAFB (Model)	S.25		24. 6.82	D.Eaves	Southampton	
G-FYEM	Rango NA-8 HAFB (Model)	RGS-32		2. 8.82	R.G.Strathdee	Aylesbury	
G-FYEO	Scallan Eagle Mk.1A HAFB (Model)	001		20. 7.82	M.E.Scallan	Hayes	
G-FYEV	Osprey Mk.1C HAFB (Model)	ASK-294		10. 8.82	M.E.Scallan	Hayes	
G-FYEZ	Scallan Firefly Mk.1 HAFB (Model)	MNS-748		22. 9.82	M.E. & N.L.Scallan	Hayes	
G-FYFA	European E.84LD HAFB (Model)	S.26		12.10.82	D.Goddard & D.Eaves	Southampton	
G-FYFG	European E.84DE HAFB (Model)	S.28		26.11.82	D.Eaves	Southampton	
G-FYFH	European E.84DS HAFB (Model)	S.30		26.11.82	D.Eaves	Southampton	
G-FYFI	European E.84PS HAFB (Model)	S.29		1.12.82	M.A.Stelling	Barton-le-Clay	
G-FYFJ	Williams Westwind Two HAFB (Model)	MDW-010		14.12.82	M.D.Williams	Dunstable	
G-FYFN	Osprey Saturn 2 DC3 HAFB (Model)	ATC-250/MJS-11		17. 2.83	J.Woods & M.Woods	Bracknell	
G-FYFT	Rango NA-32BC HAFB (Model)	NHP-37		12. 3.84	N.H.Ponsford & A.M.Lindsay	Leeds	
					t/a Rango Kite & Balloon Co "Bear Chair"		
G-FYFW	Rango NA-55 (Radio Controlled Balloon) (Model)	NHP-40		8.10.84	N.H.Ponsford & A.M.Lindsay	Leeds	
					t/a Rango Kite & Balloon Co "Vaughan Williams"		
G-FYFY	Rango NA-55RC HAFB (Model)	AL-43		28. 2.85	A.M.Lindsay "Fifi"	Leeds	
G-FYGA	Rango NA-50RC HAFB (Model)	NHP-47		7. 1.86	N.H.Ponsford & A.M.Lindsay	Leeds	
					t/a Rango Kite & Balloon Co "Tallis"		
G-FYGB	Rango NA-105RC (Gas Airship) (Model)	NHP-45		7. 1.86	N.H.Ponsford & A.M.Lindsay	Leeds	
					t/a Rango Kite & Balloon Co		
G-FYGF	Busby Buz-B20 HAFB (Model)	DSD-001		8. 7.87	D.P. & D.S.Busby	Southampton	
G-FYGI	Rango NA-55RC HAFB (Model)	NHP-54		26. 6.90	D.K.Fish	Bedford	
G-FYGJ	Airspeed-300 HAFB (Model)	001		8.10.91	N.Wells	Tunbridge Wells	
G-FYGK	Rango NA-42 POC HAFB (Model)	NHP-55		31.10.91	N.H.Ponsford & A.M.Lindsay	Leeds	
					t/a Rango Kite & Balloon Co		
G-FYGM	Saffery/Smith Princess HAFB (Model)	551		24.11.97	A. & N.Smith	Goole	
G-FZZA	Aeronautiche F22-A	018		13. 8.98	APB Leasing Ltd	Welshpool	15.10.10T
	(Manufactured General Avia Construzioni Aeronautiche SRL)						
G-FZZI	Cameron H-34 HAFB	2105		30.10.89	L.V.Mastis	Bristol	30. 7.96A
					"Andrews" ??		
G-FZZY*	Colt 69A HAFB	779		19. 2.86	T Gunn "Alka-Seltzer 2"	Lancing	16. 2.90A
					(Balloon Preservation Group 7.98)		

G-GAAA-GZZZ

Regn	Type	C/n	P/I	Date	Owner/operator	Probable Base	CA Expy
G-GABD	Gulfstream GA-7 Cougar	GA7-0043	D-GABD	13. 4.82	Scotia Safari Ltd	Prestwick	25. 9.99T
G-GACA	Hunting Percival P.57 Sea Prince T.1	P57/58	WP308	2. 9.80	P.G.Vallance Ltd Charlwood, Surrey (Stored 6.97 - coded CU/572")		4.11.80P*
G-GAII	Hawker Hunter GA.11 (Officially regd with c/n 41H-004038)	HABL-003028	XE685	7.12.94	B.J.Pover (As "XE685/861/VL" in RN c/s)	Exeter	24. 6.98P
G-GAIW	Cameron A-140 HAFB	4131		21. 5.97	Cameron Balloons Ltd (Re-regd C-GAIW 1998)	Bristol	31. 8.99A
G-GAJB	Gulfstream AA-5B Tiger	AA5B-1179	G-BHZN N37519	6. 4.87	G.A.J.Bowles	Elstree	7. 1.02T
G-GALA	PA-28-180 Cherokee E	28-5794	G-AYAP	31. 7.89	E.Alexander (Op Alouette F/C)	Biggin Hill	19.10.98T
G-GAME	Cessna T303 Crusader	T303-00098	(F-GDFN) N2693C	25. 2.83	M.C.Choksey	(Leamington Spa)	14. 6.01
G-GANE	Sequoia F.8L Falco 906 & PFA/100-11100 (Lyc IO-320)			25. 9.85	S.J.Gane	Kemble	26. 7.99P
G-GANJ	Fournier RF6B-100	38	F-GANJ	16. 8.84	Soaring Equipment Ltd (Stored 5.95) Shacklewell Lodge, Empingham		31. 7.94
G-GASC	Hughes 369HS (500)	110-0270S	G-WELD G-FRO/OO-KAR	11. 7.85	Crewhall Ltd	Effingham	21. 6.99
G-GASP	PA-28-181 Cherokee Archer II	28-7790013	N4328F	15.10.90	D.J.Turner t/a G-GASP F/Grp	Fairoaks	21.11.99
G-GASS	Thunder Ax7-77 HAFB	1746		19. 4.90	M.W.Axon London E9 t/a Servowarm Balloon Syndicate "Travel Gas III"		13. 5.99A
G-GAWA	Cessna 140 (Cont C85)	9619	G-BRSM N72454/NC72454	17. 9.91	E.C.Murgatroyd	(Bedford)	30. 5.99T
G-GAZA	Aerospatiale SA.341G Gazelle 1	1187	G-RALE G-SFT/N87712	19. 6.92	The Auster Aircraft Co Ltd (Melton Mowbray)		23. 7.01
G-GAZI	Aerospatiale SA.341G Gazelle 1	1136	G-BKLU N32PA/N341VH/N90957	29. 6.90	Stratton Motor Co (Norfolk) Ltd & UCC Intl Grp Ltd (Op Cheqair) Long Stratton		28. 6.00T
G-GAZZ	Aerospatiale SA.341G Gazelle 1	1271	F-GFHD YV-242CP/HB-XGA/F-WMHC	14. 3.90	Stratton Motor Co (Norfolk) Ltd & UCC Intl Grp Ltd (Op Cheqair) Long Stratton		13. 6.99T
G-GBAO	Robin R.1180TD Aiglon (Rebuild of R.1180 prototype F-WVKU c/n 01)	277	F-GBAO	9. 9.81	J.Kay-Movat	Cherbour/Jersey	13. 9.01
G-GBHI	Socata TB-10 Tobago	19	F-GBHI	12.11.97	N.J.Webb	(Arlesey, Beds)	27.11.00
G-GBLP	Reims Cessna F.172M Skyhawk II	1042	G-GWEN G-GBLP/N14496	9.11.84	Edinburgh Air Centre Ltd	Edinburgh	9. 7.00T
G-GBLR	Reims Cessna F.150L	1109	N961L (D-EDJE)	30. 4.85	G.Matthews Sywell t/a Blue Max F/Grp (Damaged Sywell 15.1.96; stored 5.96)		24. 1.96T
G-GBSL	Beechcraft 76 Duchess	ME-265	G-BGVG	27. 3.81	M.H.Cundey	Redhill	2. 5.99
G-GBTA	Boeing 737-436	25859	G-BVHA (G-GBTA)	7. 2.94	British Airways plc (Youm-al-Suq t/s)	Manchester	31.10.99T
G-GBTB	Boeing 737-436	25860	OO-LTS G-BVHB/OO-LTS/G-BVHB/(G-GBTB)	23.10.96	British Airways plc	Heathrow	28.10.99T
G-GBUE	Robin DR.400/120A Petit Prince	1354	G-BPXD F-GBUE	11. 5.89	R.F.Jopling t/a G-GBUE Grp	Bagby	2. 6.01
G-GBXS	Europa Avn Europa XS	0005	"G-2000" G-GBXS	1. 4.98	Europa Aircraft Co Ltd	Wombleton	28. 6.99
G-GCAT	PA-28-140 Cherokee B	28-26032	G-BFRH OH-PCA	22.10.81	H.Skelton t/a Group CAT	Humberside	18. 8.99
G-GCCL	Beechcraft 76 Duchess	ME-322	(G-BNRF) N6714U	5. 8.87	A.J. & S.B.Duckworth	Tatenhill	15. 8.99
G-GCJL	BAe Jetstream 4100	41001		5. 2.91	British Aerospace (Operations) Ltd Prestwick		29. 4.95S
G-GCKI	Mooney M.20K (231)	25-0401	N4062H	15. 8.80	A.L.Burton & A.J.Daley	Netherthorpe	6. 8.01
G-GCNZ	Cessna 150M Commuter	150-75933	C-GCNZ	8.11.88	Firecrest Avn Ltd	Elstree	17. 6.01T
G-GCUB	PA-18-150 Super Cub	18-7922	SE-GCO Swedish Army 51249	11. 2.99	N.J.Morgan	(Ashbourne)	
G-GDAM	PA-18-135 Super Cub (L-21B-PI) (Frame No.18-3648)	18-3535	PH-PVW (PH-DKE)/R-107/54-2335	30. 6.81	A.D.Martin (Stored 1996)	Reading	11. 8.91
G-GDAY	Robinson R-22 Beta	0676		10. 8.87	C.J.H. & P.A.J.Richardson Bremridge Farm, Shillingford, Devon		10.12.99
G-GDER	Robin R.1180TD	280	F-GDER	15. 5.97	Berkshire Aviation Services Ltd Fairoaks		15. 5.00
G-GDEZ	BAe 125 Srs.1000B	259026	N9026 G-5-743/ZS-ACT/ZS-CCT/G-5-743	30.10.95	Frewton Ltd	Jersey	9.11.98
G-GDGR	Socata TB-20 Trinidad	378	F-GDGR	23. 7.97	R.D.Hill	Enstone	3. 8.00T
G-GDOG	PA-28R-200 Cherokee Arrow II	28R-7635227	G-BDXW N9235K	17. 4.89	R.K.& S.Perry	Blackbushe	30. 6.99
G-GDXK	Cameron A-140 HAFB	4467		22. 9.98	Cameron Balloons Ltd	Bristol	22. 9.99A
G-GEAR	Reims Cessna FR.182 Skylane RG	0004		21. 6.78	Wycombe Air Centre Ltd	Booker	11. 6.00T
G-GEDI	Dassault Falcon 2000	49	VP-BEF F-WWMD	23. 7.98	Victoria Aviation Ltd	(Guernsey)	22. 7.99
G-GEEE	Hughes 369HS	45-0738S	G-BDOY	2. 3.90	B.P.Stein	Denham	7. 9.01
G-GEEP	Robin R.1180TD Aiglon	266		9. 4.80	Organic Concentrates Ltd	Booker	7. 8.01
G-GEES	Cameron N-77 HAFB	357		8.11.77	N.A.Carr "Gee-Gees"	Leicester	18. 5.99A

Regn	Type	C/n	P/I	Date	Owner/operator	Probable Base	CA Expy
G-GEEZ	Cameron N-77 HAFB	1159		3. 5.85	Charnwood Forest Turf Accountants Ltd "Tic Tac"	Leicester	7. 4.96A
G-GEHP	PA-28RT-201 Arrow IV	28R-8218014	F-GEHP N82023	24. 4.98	Aeroshow Ltd	Gloucestershire	2. 7.01T
G-GEMS	Thunder Ax8-90 Srs.2 HAFB	2287	G-BUNP	6.11.92	Alexanders The Jewellers Ltd	Farnham	17. 1.00T
G-GENN	Gulfstream GA-7 Cougar	GA7-0114	G-BNAB G-BGYP	2.12.94	Chalrey Ltd (Op Cabair)	Elstree	15. 1.01T
G-GEOF	Pereira Osprey 2	PFA/70-10384		7. 9.78	G.Crossley	(Blackpool)	
G-GEUP	Cameron N-77 HAFB	880		8.12.82	D.P. & B.O.Turner "Gee-Up"	Bath	19. 7.96A
G-GFAB	Cameron N-105 HAFB	2048		4. 8.89	The Andrew Brownsword Collection Ltd	Bath	8..8.97a
G-GFCA	PA-28-161 Cadet	2841100	N9174X	24. 4.89	A.M.Norman & A.N.Cox	Rendcomb	4.10.01
G-GFCB	PA-28-161 Cadet	2841101	N9175F	24. 4.89	AM & TAviation Ltd	Bristol/Lulsgate	11. 7.01T
G-GFCD	PA-34-220T Seneca III	34-8133073	G-KIDS N83745	31. 5.90	Stonehurst Avn Ltd	Coventry	13.10.99T
G-GFCF	PA-28-161 Cadet	2841259	G-RHBH N9193Z	28. 6.90	Aerohire Ltd .	Halfpenny Green	27. 1.02T
G-GFEY	PA-34-200T Seneca II	34-7870343	D-GFEY D-IFEY/N36599	13. 5.98	Topa Panama Inc	Guernsey	28. 5.01
G-GFKY	Zenair CH.250 (Lyc O-235)	34	C-GFKY	23. 4.93	B.F.Hill	Hinton-in-the Hedges	6. 6.99P
G-GFLY	Reims Cessna F.150L	0822	PH-CES	28. 8.80	Lorch Airways (UK) Ltd	Norwich	1.12.02T
G-GGGG	Thunder Ax7-77 HAFB	162		2. 8.78	T.A.Gilmour t/a Flying G Grp "Flying G"	Stockbridge	17. 8.99A
G-GGLE	PA-22-108 Colt	22-8914	N5234Z	13. 5.93	J.Ivory	(Edinburgh)	1. 7.99T
	(Taildragger conversion incorporating parts from G-AROM c/n 22-8805)						
G-GGOW	Colt 77A HAFB	1542		19. 6.89	G.Everett "Charles Rennie Mackintosh"	Dartford	1.10.99A
G-GGTT	Agusta-Bell 47G-4A	2538	F-GGTT I-ANDO	21. 8.97	Thorneygrove Ltd	Newcastle	16. 2.01
G-GHCL	Bell 206B JetRanger II	925	G-SHVV N72GM/N83106	8. 7.92	Grampian Helicopters Charter Ltd	Kintore, Inverurie	3. 6.99T
G-GHIA	Cameron N-120 HAFB	2442		13.11.90	J.A.Marshall	Billingshurst	13. 2.97T
G-GHIN	Thunder Ax7-77 HAFB	1802		16. 7.90	N.T.Parry "Pegasus"	Binfield	17. 8.99A
G-GHRW	PA-28RT-201 Arrow IV	28R-7918140	G-ONAB G-BHAK/N29555	8.12.83	Bonus Aviation Ltd	Cranfield	22.12.00T
G-GHSI	PA-44-180T Turbo Seminole	44-8107026	SX-ATA N8278Z	2.12.94	M.G.Roberts (Damaged late 1994; on rebuild 8.95)	Bournemouth	1.12.97
G-GHZJ	Socata TB-9 Tampico	941	F-GHZJ	4. 3.98	M.Haller	Shipdham	30. 4.01
G-GHZM	Robinson R-22 Beta	0884	G-FENI	1. 8.95	County Garage (Cheltenham) Ltd	Gloucestershire	5.10.98T
G-GIGI	Socata MS.893A Rallye Commodore 180	11637	G-AYVX F-BSFJ	28. 9.81	D.J.Moore	(Vanhill Farm)	13. 4.00
G-GILT	Cessna 421C Golden Eagle III	421C-0515	G-BMZC N555WV/N555WW/N885WW/N885EC/N88541	3. 7.97	Air Nova plc	Liverpool	25. 9.00T
G-GINZ	Hughes 269C	129-0869	F-GINZ SE-HMX/PH-HAN/C-GFKF/N1091N	31.10.97	Heliplus Ltd	Biggin Hill	28. 5.01T
G-GIRO	Schweizer Hughes 269C	S.1328	N41S	16. 9.88	D.E.McDowell	Wantage	8.10.01
G-GIRY	American General AG-5B Tiger	10146	F-GIRY	5. 2.99	M.J.Sparshatt-Worley	Southampton	AC
G-GJCD	Robinson R-22 Beta	0966		2. 2.89	J.C.Lane	Green Crize, Hereford	21. 5.01T
G-GJET	Gates Learjet 35A	35A-365	G-CJET G-SEBE/G-ZIPS/(N4564S)/G-ZONE	9. 3.95	DPS Aviation Ltd	Fairoaks/Heathrow	10. 2.00T
G-GJKK	Mooney M.20K (252TSE)	25-1227	F-GJKK	26.11.93	C.J.Davey & S.C.Shaw	Biggin Hill	11. 3.00
G-GKAT	Enstrom 280C Shark	1200	F-GKAT N5694Y	26. 8.97	Thorneygrove Ltd	Newcastle	29. 1.01
G-GKFC	Tiger Cub RL5A LW Sherwood Ranger	PFA/237-12947	G-MYZI	24.11.98	K.F.Crumplin	(Wells)	
G-GLAD	Gloster Gladiator II	-	"N2276" N5903	5. 1.95	Patina Ltd (Op The Fighter Collection) (On rebuild 1.99 unmarked)	Duxford	
G-GLAW	Cameron N-90 HAFB	1808		10.10.88	George Law Plant Ltd "Law Civil Engineers"	Kidderminster	17. 8.99A
G-GLBL	Lindstrand AM.32000 HAFB	444		3.10.96	Lindstrand Balloons Ltd	Oswestry	
G-GLED	Cessna 150M Commuter	150-76673	C-GLED	6. 1.89	Firecrest Avn Ltd	Elstree	22.10.01T
G-GLTT	PA-31-350 Chieftain	31-8452004	N27JV N606SM	19. 9.97	J.A.Robson	Gloucestershire	16. 3.01T
G-GLUE	Cameron N-65 HAFB	390		17. 3.81	L.J.M.Muir & G.D.Hallett	East Molesey	17. 7.90A
					"Tacky Jack"/"Jack of Hearts" (Mobile Windscreens titles)		
G-GLUG	PA-31-350 Chieftain	31-8052077	N2287J G-BLOE/G-NITE/N3559A	1. 9.94	Champagne-Air Ltd	Newcastle	31.10.99T
G-GMAX	SNCAN Stampe SV-4C	141	G-BXNW F-BBPB	19. 6.87	Glidegold Ltd (Damaged in crash Booker 3.6.91; on rebuild 5.96)	Booker	29. 8.93T
G-GMPA	Aerospatiale AS.355F2 Twin Squirrel	5409	G-BPOI	26. 9.89	Greater Manchester Police Authority	Barton	9.11.01T
G-GMSI	Socata TB-9 Tampico	145		18. 9.80	M.L.Rhodes	Halfpenny Green	28. 5.00T
G-GNAT	Folland Gnat T.1	FL.595	8638M XS101	14. 4.82	Brutus Holdings Ltd (As "XS101" in Red Arrows c/s)	Cranfield	8. 8.99P

Regn	Type	C/n	P/I	Date	Owner/operator	Probable Base	CA Expy
G-GNSY*	HPR.7 Dart Herald 209	197	I-ZERD	30. 6.87	Channel Express Grp plc	Bournemouth	1. 8.99T
			G-BFRK/4X-AHN		(Broken up 1998 ?)		
G-GNTA	Saab-Scania SF.340A	340A-049	HB-AHK	5. 4.91	Business Air Ltd	Aberdeen	11. 4.99T
			SE-E49				
G-GNTB	Saab-Scania SF.340A	340A-082	HB-AHL	30. 9.91	Business Air Ltd	Aberdeen	10.10.99T
			SE-E82				
G-GNTC	Saab-Fairchild SF.340A	340A-020	HB-AHE	25. 9.92	Business Air Ltd	Aberdeen	24. 9.99T
			SE-E20				
G-GNTD	Saab-Scania SF.340A	340A-100	SE-ISK	30.12.92	Business Air Ltd	Aberdeen	3. 1.00T
			SE-E01				
G-GNTE	Saab-Scania SF.340A	340A-133	SE-ISM	22. 1.93	Business Air Ltd	Aberdeen	21. 1.01T
			SE-F33		(Mountain of the Birds/Benyhone Tartan t/s)		
G-GNTF	Saab-Scania SF.340A	340A-113	HB-AHO	27.10.94	Business Air Ltd	Aberdeen	27.10.99T
			SE-F13				
G-GNTG	Saab-Scania SF.340A	340A-126	HB-AHR	18.11.94	Business Air Ltd	Aberdeen	18.11.99T
			SE-F26				
G-GNTH	Saab-Scania SF.340B	340B-169	N588MA	23. 1.97	Business Air Ltd	Aberdeen	4. 2.00T
			SE-F69				
G-GNTI	Saab-Scania SF.340B	340B-172	N589MA	30. 1.97	Business Air Ltd	Aberdeen	5. 2.00T
			SE-F72				
G-GNTJ	Saab-Scania SF.340B	340B-192	N591MA	26. 2.97	Business Air Ltd	Aberdeen	4. 3.99T
			SE-F92				
G-GNTZ	BAe 146 Srs.200	E-2036	HB-IXB	26.11.94	British Regional Airlines Ltd	Manchester	25.11.00T
			N175US/N355PS		(Mountain of the Birds/Benyhone Tartan t/s)		
G-GOBT	Colt 77A HAFB	1815		13. 2.91	British Telecommunications plc	Thatcham	26. 6.97A
					"Sky Piper"		
G-GOCC	Gulfstream AA-5A Cheetah	AA5A-0811	G-BPIX	2. 9.92	Lowlog Ltd (Op Cabair)	Elstree	17. 3.01T
			N26916				
G-GOCX	Cameron N-90 HAFB	2619		7. 8.91	R.D.Parry	Hong Kong, PRC	9. 1.00A
G-GOGW	Cameron N-90 HAFB	3304		31. 8.94	Great Western Trains Co Ltd	Swindon	10. 5.99A
G-GOKT	McDonnell Douglas DC-10-30	47838	RP-C2114	1. 5.96	Caledonian Airways Ltd	Gatwick	2. 5.99T
			(RP-C2004)		"Loch Roag"		
G-GOLF	Socata TB-10 Tobago	250		21.12.81	E.H. & A.C.Scammell, G.J.Powell & B.Bain		
						Biggin Hill	2. 5.00
G-GONE	FFW DH.112 Venom FB.50 (FB.1)	752	J-1542	17. 9.84	Not known	Bournemouth	7.11.95P
G-GOOD	Socata TB-20 Trinidad	1657	F-GNHJ	4.11.94	Skyforce Charters Ltd	Goodwood	25.11.00T
G-GORE	CFM Streak Shadow	.		12. 4.90	M.S.Clinton	(Farnborough)	11. 5.99P
	(Rotax 532) K.138-SA & PFA/206-11646		(PFA c/n duplicates Minimax G-MWFD)				
G-GOSS	CEA Jodel DR.221 Dauphin	125	F-BPRA	4.12.80	M.J.Milner	Bidford	12. 5.00
					t/a Avon Flying Group		
G-GOTC	Gulfstream GA-7 Cougar	GA7-0074	G-BMDY	25. 6.97	Plane Talking Ltd	Elstree	9. 1.99T
			OO-LCR/OO-HRA				
G-GOTO	PA-32R-301T Saratoga II TC	3257026	N92965	8. 1.98	J.A.Varndell	Blackbushe	7. 1.01
G-GOZO	Cessna R182 Skylane RG II	R182-01883	G-BJZO	9. 1.85	Transmatic Fyllan Ltd	Little Staughton	11. 2.01
			(G-BJYE)/N5521T				
G-GPMW	PA-28R-201T Turbo Arrow IV		N3576V	3. 7.89	M.Worrall, J.Riley & I.R.Court	Coventry	23. 7.01T
		28R-8031041					
G-GPST	Phillips ST.1 Speedtwin			21. 6.90	Susan E.Phillips	Old Sarum	16. 7.99P
	(Cont O-200-A) 1 & PFA/207-11645		(PFA c/n conflicts with Kolb Twinstar G-MWWM)				
G-GRAM	PA-31-350 Navajo Chieftain		G-BRHF	14. 3.91	BAC Leasing Ltd	Plymouth	5. 2.98T
		31-7305006	N7679L		(Op Air South West)		
G-GRAY	Cessna 172N Skyhawk II	172-72375	N4859D	3.12.79	Truman Avn Ltd	Nottingham	13. 2.95T
					(Damaged in Firth of Forth, nr Mussleburgh 2.4.93; stored 4.97)		
G-GREN	Cessna T310R II	310R-1282	N426CB	24. 7.90	D.Hughes	Sherburn	1. 1.00
			N6015X				
G-GRID	Aerospatiale AS.355F1 Twin Squirrel	5012	TG-BOS	28. 3.89	National Grid Co plc	Oxford	18. 6.01T
G-GRIF	Rockwell Commander 112TC-A	13258	G-BHXC	2.10.81	N.G.W.Cragg & E.T.N.Sutherland		
			N1005C		t/a Nicholas Aviation	(Rotherham)	26. 3.01
G-GRIN	Van's RV-6	PFA/181-12409		8. 1.98	A.Phillips	(Fareham)	
G-GRIP	Colt Bibendum 110SS HAFB	4224		5. 1.98	The Aerial Display Co Ltd	Looe	19.11.99
G-GROL	Maule MXT-7-180 Star Rocket	14091C		16. 6.98	D.C., C.& C.Croll	Southend	16. 6.01
G-GRRC	PA-28-161 Warrior II	2816076	G-BXJX	9. 3.98	Goodwood Road Racing Co Ltd	Goodwood	8.10.00T
			HB-POM/D-EJTB/N9149X				
G-GRRR	Scotish Avn Bulldog 120/122	BH120/229	G-BXGU	15. 5.97	L Bax	(Salisbury)	
			Ghana AF G-105				
G-GSEB	Dassault Falcon 900	161	VP-CTT	14. 4.98	Walkfine Ltd/Mere Golf & Country Club		
			F-GSAA/F-WWFF			Manchester	14. 4.01T
G-GSFC	Robinson R-22 Beta	0569	N2425J	3. 7.86	Weller Helicopters Ltd	Redhill	4.10.98T
G-GSFT	PA-44-180 Seminole	44-7995202	EI-BYZ	12.10.98	Magenta Ltd.	Oxford	28.10.01T
			N2193K				
G-GTAX	PA-31-350 Navajo Chieftain		G-OIAS	11. 3.88	Hadagain Investments Ltd		4. 4.98T
		31-7405442	OY-CBF/D-IGSA/N54322		(To Canada by Container 7.97)		
G-GTHM	PA-38-112 Tomahawk II	38-81A0171	C-GTHM	17.11.86	G.Fleck	Prestwick	19.10.01T
G-GTPL	Mooney M.20K (231)	25-0301	G-BHOS	15. 7.80	W.R.Emberton		
			N231LQ			Cuidad Quesada, Alicante, Spain	27. 6.01

Regn	Type	C/n	P/I	Date	Owner/operator	Probable Base	CA Expy
G-GUAY	Enstrom 480	5036		1.12.98	Testactual Ltd t/a Heliway Avn (Fareham)		31.12.01
G-GUCK	Beechcraft C23 Sundowner 180	M-2221	G-BPYG N6638R	9. 4.92	D.J.McWilliams t/a G-GUCK Grp	Sandtoft	9. 1.01
G-GUFO	Cameron Saucer 80SS HAFB	1641	C-GUFO G-BOUB	10. 6.98	L.V.Mastis	Bristol	23. 6.89A
G-GUGI	Eurocopter EC.135T 1	0065		9.10.98	McAlpine Helicopters Ltd	Oxford	AC
G-GULF	Lindstrand LBL-105A HAFB	320		3.11.95	Virgin Balloon Flights Ltd Muscat, Oman		9. 3.99A
G-GULL	SMAN Petrel Amphibian PFA/269-12833 (Rotax 912UL)		29-DX/ F-JBS/G-GULL	6. 3.95	Amphibians UK Ltd Dunkeswell/Salcombe		9.10.95P*
G-GUNS	Cameron V-77 HAFB	2221		9. 5.90	Royal School of Artillery Hot Air Balloon Club "Guns"	Larkhill	28. 8.97A
G-GURL*	Cameron A-210 HAFB	2387		3. 9.90	R S Kent "Hot Airlines" (Balloon Preservation Group)	Lancing	29. 8.96T
G-GUSS	PA-28-151 Cherokee Warrior	28-7415497	G-BJRY N43453	16. 8.95	A.M.B.Dudley (Op Flywatch UK Ltd)	Southend	6. 6.00T
G-GUST	Agusta-Bell 206B Jet Ranger	8192	G-CBHH F-GALU/G-AYBE	30. 8.96	Arena Aviation Ltd	Redhill	25. 4.99T
G-GUYS	PA-34-200T Seneca II	34-7870283	G-BMWT N31984	14. 7.87	G.B.Faulkner	Gamston	29. 3.99
G-GVBF	Lindstrand LBL-180A HAFB	250	PH-VBF G-GVBF	19. 5.95	Virgin Balloon Flights Ltd (London SE16)		15. 1.99T
G-GVIP	Agusta A.109E Power	11024		1. 7.98	Sloane Helicopters Ltd	Sywell	26. 8.01T
G-GWIZ	Colt Clown SS HAFB	1369	(G-BPWU)	25. 4.89	Oxford Promotions (UK) Ltd Kentucky, USA		13. 4.99A
G-GWYN	Reims Cessna F.172M Skyhawk II	1217	PH-TWN	5. 3.81	C.Bosher & D.J.Bruford t/a Gwyn Avn	Exeter	18. 4.99
G-GYAV	Cessna 172N Skyhawk II	172-71362	C-GYAV	26. 8.87	Southport & Merseyside A/C (1979) Ltd	Liverpool	8. 3.00T
G-GYBO	Gardan GY-80-180 Horizon	228	OY-DTN	4. 8.98	M.J.Strother	(Leeds)	AC
G-GYMM	PA-28R-200 Cherokee Arrow	28R-7135049	G-AYWW	22. 2.90	J.B.A.Ainsworth t/a Gymm Group	Leicester	5. 2.01
G-GYRO	Campbell Cricket PFA G/03-1046 (Rotax 532)			26. 2.82	J.W.Pavitt	St.Merryn	26. 4.99
G-GZDO	Cessna 172N Skyhawk II	172-71826	C-GZDO (N5299E)	11.10.88	G.Cambridge & G.W.J.Hall t/a Cambridge Hall Avn (Op Firecrest Avn)	Elstree	31. 3.01T

G-HAAA-HZZZ

Regn	Type	C/n	P/I	Date	Owner/operator	Probable Base	CA Expy
G-HACK	PA-18-150 Super Cub	18-7168	SE-CSA	20.11.97	S.J.Harris	North Weald	2.12.00
G-HADA	Enstrom 480	5017		17. 9.96	W.B.Steele	Whitchurch, Shropshire	24. 9.99
G-HAEC	Commonwealth CAC-18	CACM-192-1517	VR-HIU	1. 5.85	R.W.Davies "Big Beautiful Doll") Duxford		30. 5.99P
	Mustang 22		(RP-C651)/PI-C651		(Op The Old Flying Machine Ltd)		
			VH-FCB/A68-192		(As "472218/WZ-I" in 78th FG USAAF c/s)		
	(Composite rebuilt 1974-76 using major components from Philippine AF P-51D 44-72917)						
G-HAIG	Rutan LongEz 1983-L & PFA/74A-11149			20. 5.86	R.Casey & D.W.Parfrey	Coventry	7. 7.99P
	(Lyc O-235)						
G-HAJJ	Glaser-Dirks DG-400	4-225		15. 2.88	P.W.Endean	Perranporth	21. 4.00
G-HALC	PA-28R-200 Cherokee Arrow II		N91253	26.11.90	Halcyon Avn Ltd	Barton	28. 5.00
		28R-7335042	C-FFQO/CF-FQO				
G-HALE	Robinson R-44 Astro	0492		6. 8.98	Barhale Surveying Ltd	Elstree	19. 8.01T
G-HALJ	Cessna 140	8336	N89308	30. 4.96	H.A.Lloyd-Jennings	Old Sarum	16. 6.99
	(Cont C85)		NC89308				
G-HALL	PA-22-160 Tri-Pacer	22-7423	G-ARAH	8.11.79	F.P.Hall	Maypole Farm, Chislet	29. 6.00
G-HALO	Elisport CH-7 Angel	A.031	I-2858	12.11.93	Taylor Woolhouse Ltd	Gloucestershire	30.7.94P*
					(Stored 6.97)		
G-HALP	Socata TB-10 Tobago	192	G-BITD	19. 8.81	Delia H.Halpern	Elstree	30. 5.97
G-HAMA	Beechcraft 200 Super King Air	BB-30	N244JB	16.11.84	Gama Avn Ltd	Heathrow/Fairoaks	19.11.99T
			N211JB/N3090C/N3030C/N200CA				
G-HAMI	Fuji FA.200-180 Aero Subaru		G-OISF	31. 1.92	S.A.R.Rose & K.G.Cameron	Biggin Hill	31. 3.02
		FA200-188	G-BAPT				
G-HAMP	Bellanca 7ACA Champ	30-72	N9173L	8. 8.88	K.Macdonald	(Clapham, Bedford)	13. 9.99P
G-HAND	Cameron Startac 105SS HAFB	3895		19. 8.96	Redmalt Ltd	Witham, Essex	19. 2.99A
G-HANS	Robin DR.400 2 + 2	1384		2. 3.79	Rochester Avn Ltd	Rochester	20. 6.00T
G-HAPR	Bristol 171 Sycamore HC.14	13387	8010M	15. 6.78	E.D. Ap Rees	Weston-super-Mare	
			XG547		t/a The Helicopter Museum	(As "XG547/T-S" in CFS c/s)	
G-HAPY	DHC.1 Chipmunk 22	C1/0697	WP803	3. 7.96	G-HAPY Ltd (as WP803)	Booker	29. 8.99
G-HARE	Cameron N-77 HAFB	1467		12. 3.87	C.E. & J.Falkingham	Stevenage	4. 7.99A
G-HARF	Gulfstream Aerospace Gulfstream IV		N1761J	9.10.91	Fayair (Jersey) Co Ltd	Stansted/Jersey	20.12.99T
		1117			(Op Harrods)		
G-HARH	Sikorsky S-76B	760391	N7600U	30. 9.91	Air Harrods Ltd	Stansted	17. 1.02T
G-HARO	Aerospatiale AS.355F2 Twin Squirrel		G-DAFT	21. 8.96	Air Harrods Ltd	Denham	17. 1.00T
		5364	G-BNNN				
G-HART	Cessna 152 II	152-79734	(G-BPBF)	2. 2.89	Atlantic Air Transport Ltd	Coventry	25. 6.01T
	(Tailwheel conversion)		N757GS				
G-HARY	Alon A-2 Aircoupe	A.188	G-ATWP	15. 3.93	M.C.Clark	Newcastle	22. 4.01
G-HASI	Cessna 421B Golden Eagle	421B-0654	G-BTDK	17. 2.98	C.C.Butt	Chester	5. 3.99T
			OY-BFA/N1558G				
G-HATZ	Hatz CB-1	17	N54623	11. 5.89	S.P.Rollason	Charity Farm, Baxterley	16. 8.99P
	(Lyc O-320)						
G-HAUL*	Westland WG.30-300	020	G-17-22	3. 7.86	The Helicopter Museum	Weston-super-Mare	27.10.86P
G-HAZE	Thunder Ax8-90 HAFB	989		3. 8.88	T.G.Church	Blackburn	23. 6.97T
G-HBBC	DH.104 Dove 8	04211	G-ALFM	24. 1.96	BBC Air Ltd	Compton Abbas	25. 6.01
			VP961/G-ALFM/VP961				
G-HBMW	Robinson R-22	0170	G-BOFA	7. 7.94	J.Anderson	Edinburgh	26. 9.00T
			N9068D				
G-HBUG	Cameron N-90 HAFB	1991	G-BRCN	21. 6.89	R.T. & H.Revel "Humbug"	High Wycombe	18. 5.99T
G-HCFR	BAe 125 Srs.800B	258240	HB-VLT	23. 7.98	Chauffair (CI) Ltd	Farnborough	26. 7.99T
			G-SHEA/G-BUWC/G-5-772				
G-HCSL	PA-34-220T Seneca III	34-8133237	N84375	9. 5.91	Dawcroft Ltd	(Ulverston)	31. 8.00T
					t/a Colony Aviation		
G-HDEW	PA-32R-301 Saratoga SP	3213026	G-BRGZ	4.12.89	Lord Howard de Walden	Oxford	11. 3.01
			N91787				
G-HDIX	Enstrom 280FX	2076	N506DH	19. 2.98	J.Poupard	(Kings Lynn)	12. 3.01T
			D-HDIX				
G-HDPP	Eurocopter EC-135T-1	0055	G-HDDP	3. 7.98	McAlpine Helicopters Ltd	Oxford	
G-HEAD	Colt 56SS Flying Head HAFB	304	SE-ZHE	18. 8.81	E.K.Nyberg	Stockholm, Sweden	24. 4.97A
	(Compac Computerised Head shape)		G-HEAD		(Exported 1998)		
G-HEBE	Bell 206B Jet Ranger III	3745	CS-HDN	5. 2.97	Heli-Hire Ltd	Didcot	9. 3.00T
			N3179A				
G-HELE	Bell 206B Jet Ranger III	3789	G-OJFR	21. 2.91	MGGR (UK) Ltd	White Waltham	12. 5.00T
			N18095				
G-HELI*	Saro Skeeter AOP.12	S2/5110		15. 6.78	Luftwaffen Museum	Uetersen, Hamburg	
	(Composite of cabin/7870M/XM556 & boom/7979M/XM529)				(Delivered 1995) (In German Army c/s)		
G-HELN	PA-18-95 Super Cub	18-3365	G-BKDG	10. 1.86	J.J.Anziani	Booker	9. 3.99P
	(L-21B-PI) (Frame No.18-3400)		MM52-2392/EI-69/EI-141/I-EIWB/MM53-7765/53-7765				
	(Regd as c/n 18-1992 but frame exchanged in Italian AF service; c/n 18-3365 was officially regd as N9837Q)						
G-HELP*	Colt 17A Cloudhopper HAFB	902		16. 2.87	Virgin Airship & Balloon Co Ltd	Telford	7. 8.95A
					"Mondial Cloudhopper" (Cancelled as PWFU 27.3.99)		
G-HELV	FFW DH.115 Vampire T.55	975	U-1215	17. 9.91	Hunter Wing Ltd	Bournemouth	4. 5.99P
					(As "215" in RAF c/s)		
G-HEMS	Aerospatiale SA.365N Dauphin 2	6009	F-WYMJ	22. 8.88	Virgin Executive Aviation Ltd		
			G-HEMS/N365AM/N365AH		(Op for London Hospitals Emergency Medical Service)		
					The Royal London Hospital, Whitechapel/Denham		21.12.99T

Regn	Type	C/n	P/I	Date	Owner/operator	Probable Base	CA Expy
G-HENS*	Cameron N-65 HAFB	740		8. 7.81	Balloon Preservation Group "Free Range" (Noted 12.98)	Lancing	N/E(A)
G-HENY	Cameron V-77 HAFB	2486		9. 1.91	R.S.D'Alton "Henny"	Newbury	1. 8.99A
G-HERA	Robinson R-22 Beta	1426		26. 6.90	G.R.Day (Damaged Blackpool 24.2.99)	(Boston)	21. 8.99T
G-HERB	PA-28R-201 Arrow III	28R-7837118	ZS-LAG N3504M	5. 6.86	Appleton Aviation Ltd	(York)	14.10.01
G-HERO	PA-32RT-300 Lance II	32R-7885086	G-BOGN N33LV/N30573	26. 4.88	Air Alize Communication	Stapleford	9. 7.97
G-HERS	Jodel D.18 255 & PFA/169-11410		R		Angela Usherwood	Ammanford	
G-HEWI	Piper J3C-90 Cub (L-4J-PI) (Frame No.12396)	12566	G-BLEN D-EBEN/HB-OFZ/44-80270	20. 7.84	R.Preston t/a Denham Grasshopper F/Grp	Denham	3.10.99
G-HEYY	Cameron Bear 72SS HAFB (Hofmeister Lager Bear)	1244		21. 1.86	L.V.Mastis "George"	Bristol	31.11.98A
G-HFBM	Curtiss Robin C-2 (Cont W-670)	352	LV-FBM NC9279	24. 4.90	D.M.Forshaw	Panshanger	17. 3.99P
G-HFCA	Cessna A150L Aerobat (Texas Tailwheel conversion)	A150-0381	N6081J	30. 8.91	Horizon F/C Ltd	Earls Colne	3. 9.01T
G-HFCB	Reims Cessna F.150L	0798	G-AZVR	10. 2.87	Horizon F/C Ltd	Earls Colne	11. 2.00T
G-HFCI	Reims Cessna F.150L	0823	PH-CET	11. 9.80	Horizon F/C Ltd	Earls Colne	27. 1.02T
G-HFCL	Reims Cessna F.152 II	1663	G-BGLR	11.10.88	Horizon F/C Ltd	Earls Colne	23. 4.00T
G-HFCT	Reims Cessna F.152 II	1861		27. 1.81	Stapleford F/C Ltd	Stapleford	21. 5.99T
G-HFIX	VS.361 Spitfire HF.IXe	CBAF.7243	G-BLAS	22. 8.89	D.W.Pennell	Gloucestershire	17. 6.99P
	(C/n quoted also as CBAF.78883) IDF/AF 2066/06-06/MM4094/MJ730 (As "MJ730/GZ-?" in 32 Sqn c/s)						
G-HFLA	Schweizer Hughes 269C (300C)	S.1428		8.12.89	Sterling Helicopters Ltd	Norwich	4. 2.02T
G-HFTG	PA-23-250 Aztec E	27-7405378	G-BSOB G-BCJR/N54040	30. 4.87	Widehawk Avn Ltd t/a Hawkair	Cambridge	2. 4.99T
G-HGAS	Cameron N-77 HAFB	1969		4. 5.89	N.J.Tovey	Bristol	13. 5.97A
G-HGPI	Socata TB-20 Trinidad	851		4. 8.88	M.J.Jackson	Bournemouth	21.12.00
G-HIAH*	Revolution Helicopters Mini-500	0052		4. 3.96	H.I.A.Hopkinson (Cancelled by CAA 10.3.99; no Permit issued)	(Huddersfield)	
G-HIBM	Cameron N-145 HAFB	3197		8. 2.94	L.& R.J.Mold t/a Dragonfly Balloons	High Wycombe	28. 5.99T
G-HIEL	Robinson R-22 Beta	1120		28. 9.89	R.C.Hields t/a Hields Avn	Sherburn	16.11.98
G-HIHI	PA-32R-301 Saratoga SP (Regd with c/n 32R-13012)	3213012		11. 5.88	Godolphin Management Co Ltd	(Newmarket)	11. 3.01
G-HIII	Extra EA.300	057	D-ETYD	10. 1.95	Firebird Aerobatics Ltd (Rover c/s)	Denham	29. 1.01T
G-HILO	Commander 114	14224	N4894W	6. 2.98	F.H.Parkes	(Chelmsford)	7. 4.01
G-HILS	Reims Cessna F.172H	0522	G-AWCH	20.12.88	B.F.W.Lowdon t/a Lowdon Avn Grp	Blackbushe	12. 1.01
G-HILT	Socata TB-10 Tobago	298	(G-BMYB) EI-BOF/G-HILT	13. 5.82	Insight Marketing & Communications Ltd	Woodford	7. 5.99T
G-HIND	Maule MT-7-235 Star Rocket	18037C		26. 3.98	R.G.Humphries	(Hook)	29. 4.01T
G-HIPE	Sorrell SNS-7 Hyperbipe (Lyc IO-360)	209	N18RS	6. 4.93	T.A.S.Rayner	Glenrothes	30. 4.99P
G-HIPO	Robinson R-22 Beta	1719	G-BTGB	11. 9.92	Fleet Street Travel Ltd	(Chertsey)	19. 5.00T
G-HIRE	Gulfstream GA-7 Cougar	GA7-0091	G-BGSZ N704G	10.12.81	London Aerial Tours Ltd	Rochester	28. 5.00T
G-HISS	Aerotek Pitts S-2A Special (Lyc AEIO-360)	2137	G-BLVU SE-GTX	17. 3.92	L.V.Adams & J.Maffia "Always Dangerous" (Stored 11.97)	Panshanger	24. 8.98T
G-HIVA	Cessna 337A Super Skymaster	337-0429	G-BAES SE-CWW/N5329S	28. 3.88	G.J.Banfield	Gloucestershire	9. 7.00
G-HIVE	Reims Cessna F.150M	1186	G-BCXT	19. 4.85	M.P.Lynn	Sibson	30. 4.01
G-HJSS	AIA Stampe SV-4C	1101	G-AZNF F-BGJM/Fr mil	7. 9.92	H.J.Smith	Shoreham	24. 5.99
G-HKIT	BAC One Eleven 521FH	BAC.196	VP-BEC VR-BEC/LV-JNT/G-16-10	17. 6.97	European Aviation Ltd (Austral c/s) (Stored 11.98)	Bournemouth	
G-HLAA	Airbus A.300B4-203	047	EI-TLN G-HLAA/N740SC/F-BVGJ/F-WUAX	6.10.97	Heavylift Cargo Airlines Ltd	Stansted	7. 7.01T
G-HLAB	Airbus A.300B4-203F	045	N743SC F-BVGI/F-WNDA	20. 2.98	Heavylift Cargo Airlines Ltd	Stansted	26. 2.01T
G-HLAC	Airbus A.300B4-203	074	N829SC F-BVGL	23.11.98	Heavylift Cargo Airlines Ltd	Stansted	3.12.01T
G-HLCF	CFM Starstreak Shadow SA-II (Rotax 618)	PFA/206-12796		10. 5.96	S.M.E.Solomon	North Weald	4.12.98P
G-HLEN	Aerospatiale AS.350B Ecureuil	1836	G-LOLY JA9897/N5805T/HP-.../N5805T	22. 4.93	N.Edmonds	Okehampton	15. 2.01T
G-HLFT	Short SC.5 Belfast C.1 (Modified to Mk.2)	SH.1819	XR365	11. 9.81	Heavylift Avn Holdings Ltd t/a Heavylift Cargo Airlines "St.George"	Stansted	20. 6.99T
G-HLIX*	Cameron Helix Oilcan 61SS HAFB	1192		20. 9.85	R S Kent "Helix Oil Can" (Balloon Preservation Group 7.98 for restoration)	Lancing	25. 4.90A
G-HMBJ	Commander 114B	14636	N6036F	30. 6.97	B.A.Groves	Shoreham	24. 7.00
G-HMED	PA-28-161 Warrior III	2842020	LX-III	21. 7.97	H.Faizal	Denham	31. 7.00
G-HMES	PA-28-161 Warrior II	28-8216070	OY-CSN N8471N	21. 4.89	Cleveland Flying School Ltd (Op Teesside A/C)	Teesside	20. 8.01T
G-HMJB	PA-34-220T Seneca III	34-8133040	N8356R	12. 7.89	Overview Europe Ltd	Gamston	1. 9.02

Regn	Type	C/n	P/I	Date	Owner/operator	Probable Base	CA Expy
G-HMPH	Bell 206B JetRanger II	1232	G-BBUY N18090	20. 6.88	Mightycraft Ltd	White Waltham	31. 3.02T
G-HMPT	Agusta-Bell 206B JetRanger II	8168	D-HARO	7.11.91	Kensington Avn Ltd	Blairgowrie	26. 1.01T
G-HNRY	Cessna 650 Citation VI	650-0219	N219CC	23.10.92	Quantel Ltd	Farnborough	12. 1.00
G-HNTR*	Hawker Hunter T.7	HABL-003311	8834M XL572	7. 7.89	Yorkshire Air Museum (As "XL572/83")	Elvington	
G-HOBO	Denney Kitfox Mk.4 PFA/172A-12140 (Rotax 582)			10. 9.92	W.M.Hodgkins & C.A.Boswell "Navy Baby"	Chalgrove	6. 5.99P
G-HOCK	PA-28-180 Cherokee D	28-4395	G-AVSH	15. 5.86	Arabact Ltd	Goodwood	12. 8.01T
G-HOFC	Europa Avn Europa 119 & PFA/247-12736 (Rotax 912UL)			25. 9.95	J.W.Lang Hilton of Carslogie, Fife		26. 6.99P
G-HOFM	Cameron N-56 HAFB	1245		21. 1.86	L.V.Mastis	Bristol	30.11.98A
G-HOGS	Cameron Pig 90SS HAFB	4121		7. 4.97	Flying Pictures Ltd "Britannia Piggy Bank"	Fairoaks	1. 7.99A
G-HOHO	Colt Santa Claus SS HAFB	1671		21.12.89	Oxford Promotions (UK) Ltd	Kentucky, USA	14. 4.99A
G-HOLY	Socata ST-10 Diplomate	108	F-BSCZ	31. 1.90	M.K.Barsham	Booker	31. 3.99
G-HOME	Colt 77A HAFB	032		26. 2.79	Anglia Balloon School Ltd "Tardis" (To British Balloon Museum & Library)	Newbury	27. 5.86A
G-HONG	Slingsby T-67M Firefly 200	2060	VR-HZR HKG-12/G-7-128	24. 3.94	Hunting Avn Ltd RAF Barkston Heath (Op JEFTS)		26. 6.00T
G-HONK	Cameron O-105 HAFB	1813		30. 9.88	T.F.W.Dixon & Son Ltd "Dixons"	Bromsgrove	14. 9.97A
G-HONY	Lilliput Type 1 Srs.A HAFB	L-01		31. 7.98	A.E. & D.E.Thomas	Honiton	
G-HOOV	Cameron N-56 HAFB	388		2. 3.78	Heather R.Evans "Hoover"	Ross-on-Wye	26. 5.89A
G-HOPE	Beechcraft F33A Bonanza	CE-805	N2024Z	27. 2.79	Bournemouth Avn Ltd	Bournemouth	12. 3.01
G-HOPI	Cameron N-42 HAFB	2724		5.12.91	Ballonverbung Hamburg GmbH	Kiel, Germany	29. 4.97A
G-HOPS	Thunder Ax8-90 Srs.1 HAFB	1220		11. 3.88	A.C. & B.Munn	Hastings	20. 5.96T
G-HOPY	Van's RV-6A PFA/181-12742			4.12.95	R.C.Hopkinson	Booker	28. 1.99P
G-HORN	Cameron V-77 HAFB	570		29.11.79	S.Herd	Mold	11.12.98A
G-HOST	Cameron N-77 HAFB	434		4. 9.78	D.Grimshaw "Suzanna"	Preston	18. 5.93A
G-HOTI	Colt 77A HAFB	750		13. 7.87	R.Ollier Northwich, Cheshire "Horace Hot One"		30. 9.90A
G-HOTT	Cameron O-120 HAFB	2581		30. 4.91	D.L.Smith "Floating Sensations"	Newbury	17. 5.97T
G-HOTZ	Colt 77B HAFB	2218		16. 6.92	C.J. & S.M.Davies Castleton, Sheffield		10. 9.99A
G-HOUS	Colt 31A Air Chair HAFB	099		7.10.80	Anglia Balloon School Ltd "K9" t/a Anglia Balloons (Barratts c/s) (To British Balloon Museum & Library)	Newbury	3. 5.90A
G-HOWE	Thunder Ax7-77 HAFB	1340		10. 4.89	M.F.Howe "Howie/Howzat"	Beverley	15. 8.95A
G-HPAA	PBN BN-2B-20 Islander	2244	G-BSWP	14. 8.91	Hampshire Police Authority Air Support Unit	Lee-on-Solent (Jersey)	22.12.99T
G-HPSE	Commander 114B	14638	N6038V	26. 8.97	Al Nisr Ltd		16. 9.00A
G-HPUX	Hawker Hunter T.Mk.7	41H-693455	8807M XL587	12. 3.99	Classic Aviation Ltd	Duxford	
G-HRHE	Robinson R-22 Beta	1950	G-BTWP	24. 1.97	R.H.Everett Upton Lovell, Warminster/Thruxton		11.12.00
G-HRHI	Beagle B.206 Basset Srs.1	B.014	XS770	6. 7.89	Lawgra (No.386) Ltd Cranfield t/a International Aerospace Engineering (As "XS770" in Queens Flight c/s)		15. 4.00
G-HRHS	Robinson R-44 Astro	0323		15. 4.97	Sloane Helicopters Ltd	Sywell	16. 4.00
G-HRIO	Robin HR.100/210 Safari	149	F-BTZR	22. 1.87	D.Peters Hurstbourne Tarrant, Hants (Stored 1.97)		17.12.01
G-HRLK	Saab 91D/2 Safir	91376	G-BRZY PH-RLK	6. 3.90	Sylmar Avn & Svs Ltd Lower Wasing Farm, Brimpton		12. 5.01
G-HRLM	Brugger MB.2 Colibri PFA/43-10118 (VW1834)			28.12.78	S.J.Perkins & D.Dobson "Titch"	Deenethorpe	21.10.99P
G-HRNT	Cessna 182S Skylane	18-280395	N2369H	29.1.99	Dingle Star Ltd	(London NW10)	AC
G-HROI	Rockwell Commander 112A	326	N1326J	19. 6.89	Intereuropean Aviation Ltd	Jersey	28. 4.01
G-HRON	DH.114 Heron 2B	14102	XR442 G-AORH	4. 4.91	M.E.R.Coghlan Gloucestershire (Unmarked 6.98)		AC
G-HRVD	CCF Harvard 4 (T-6J-CCF Texan)	CCF4-548	G-BSBC Moz PLAF PLAF/FAP	8.12.92	M.Slater 1741/BF+055/AA+055/53-4629 (On rebuild 12.95) 1780/AA+614/53-4622)	Coventry	
	(Possibly a composite with rear fuselage of Moz PLAF/FAP 1780/AA+614/53-4622)						
G-HRZN	Colt 77A HAFB	536		14.12.83	A.J.Spindler "Tequila Sunrise"	Kinross	4. 5.88A
G-HSDW	Bell 206B JetRanger II	1789	ZS-HFC	16.12.85	Winfield Shoe Co & Stott Demolition Ltd	Rossendale	2. 2.02
G-HSOO	Hughes 369HE	109-0208E	G-BFYJ F-BRSY	3.11.93	Edwards Aviation Ltd	Wilmslow	27. 9.99T
G-HSTH	Lindstrand HS-110 Hot-Air Airship	546		20. 8.98	Ballonsport Helmet Seitz Kisslegg, Germany		14. 1.00A
G-HTAX	PA-31-350 Navajo Chieftain	31-7405435	N54305	7. 6.88	Hadagain Investments Ltd		AC
G-HTPS	Aerospatiale SA.341G Gazelle 1	1301	G-BRNI YU-HBI	16.11.89	J.Malcolm	Wolverhampton	24. 7.00
G-HTVI	Cameron N-90 HAFB	1375	G-PRIT	29.10.96	HTV Group plc	Cardiff	6.10.97T
G-HUBB	Partenavia P.68B	194	OY-BJH SE-GXL	27. 5.83	G-HUBB Ltd	Denham	29. 7.01
G-HUCH	Cameron Carrots 80SS HAFB	2258	G-BYPS	13. 3.91	L.V.Mastis "Magic Carrots"	Bristol	29.10.98A

Regn	Type	C/n	P/I	Date	Owner/operator	Probable Base	CA Expy
G-HUEY	Bell UH-1H-BF Iroquois .	13560	AE-413 (Arg.Army)/73-22077	23. 7.85	Butane Buzzard Avn Corporation Ltd Luton (Op Kennet Avn)		5.10.98P
G-HUFF	Cessna 182P Skylane II (Reims-assembled with c/n 0033)	182-64076	PH-CAS N6059F	31.10.78	A.E.G.Cousins (Op Seawing F/C)	Southend	8. 5.00T
G-HUGG	Gates Learjet 35A	35A-432	VR-CAD N330BC/N4445Y/F-GDCN	9. 4.96	1427 Ltd (A & D Crosland/Airtours plc) Manchester/Jersey		11. 4.00T
G-HUGO	Colt 260A HAFB	2559		20. 1.94	P.G.Hall t/a Adventure Ballooning Chard		13. 5.99T
G-HULL	Reims Cessna F.150M	1255	PH-TGR	19. 1.79	A.D.McLeod	Linley Hill, Leven	21. 4.01T
G-HUMF	Robinson R-22 Beta	0534	N23743	18. 2.86	Plane Talking Ltd (Op Cabair)	Elstree	25. 6.01
G-HUNI	Bellanca 7GCBC Scout	541-73	OO-IME D-EIME	21.10.96	T.I.M.Paul	Denham	16.12.99T
G-HUNK	Lindstrand LBL 77A HAFB	551		9. 9.98	Lindstrand Balloons Ltd	Oswestry	30. 9.99A
G-HUNY	Reims Cessna F.150G	0157	G-AVGL	27. 6.83	M.P.Lynn (Damaged in storms Denham 16.10.87; stored 11.94)	Sibson	18. 4.88T
G-HURI	Hawker (CCF) Hurricane XIIA (IIB) (Composite - probably includes parts from c/n 44019/RCAF 5424, RCAF 5625 and RCAF 5547)	72036	RCAF 5711	9. 6.83	Patina Ltd (B J S Grey) Duxford (Op The Fighter Collection) (As "Z3781/XR-T" in 71 Sqn RAF c/s)		6. 5.99P
G-HURN	Robinson R-22 Beta	1441		18. 7.90	Coventry Helicopter Centre Ltd Coventry		5. 9.99T
G-HURR	Hawker (CCF) Hurricane XII (IIB)	52024	RCAF 5589	30. 7.90	R.A.Fleming (As "LK-A")	Breighton	30. 7.98P
G-HURY	Hawker Hurricane IV (RAF p/i unlikely as KZ321 was written off 23.5.43; frame off-site - unmarked wings only 1.99)	-	(Israel) Yugoslav AF/KZ321	31. 3.89	Patina Ltd (B J S Grey/The Fighter Collection)	Duxford	AC
G-HUTT	Denney Kitfox mk.2 (Rotax 582)	509 & PFA/172-11634		24. 1.90	D.Watt Conington/Yaxley, Peterborough		30. 7.98P
G-HVAN	Tiger Cub RL5A LW Sherwood Ranger	PFA/237-13074		10.12.98	H.T.H.Van Neck	(Wirral)	
G-HVBF	Lindstrand LBL-210A HAFB	372		23. 5.96	Virgin Balloon Flights Ltd (London SE16)		29. 4.99T
G-HVDM	VS.361 Spitfire LF.IXc	CBAF.IX.1732 R.Neth AF	8633M 3W-17/H-25/MK732	18. 1.91	H.Wade & P.R.Monk t/a Nostalgic Flying & J.J.Van Egmond (Op Dutch Spitfire Flt) Biggin Hill/Lelystad, Netherlands (As "MK732/OU-U" in 485 Sqn c/s) "Baby Bea V"		19. 9.98P
G-HVIP	Hawker Hunter T.68	HABL-003215 G-9-415/Fv.34080/G-9-56	J-4208	7. 7.95	Golden Europe Jet De Luxe Club Ltd (Op Dr.Karl Theurer)	Bournemouth	10. 4.99P
G-HVRD	PA-31-350 Navajo Chieftain	31-7305052	G-BEZU SE-GDP	11. 6.87	London Flt Centre (Stansted) Ltd t/a Love Air	Biggin Hill	13.11.97T
G-HVRS	Robinson R-22 Beta	1225		22.12.89	M.D.Thorpe t/a Yorkshire Helicopters (Damaged at RAF Church Fenton 19.7.98)	Coney Park, Leeds	29.10.99T
G-HWKR	Colt 90A HAFB	1610		4.12.89	P.A.Henderson Stratford-Upon-Avon "Hawker Siddeley"		18. 4.99T
G-HYHY	PA-46-350P Malibu Mirage	4636131		13. 8.97	Longslow Dairy Ltd	(Market Drayton)	21. 1.01
G-HYLT	PA-32R-301 Saratoga SP	32R-8213001	N84588	23. 4.86	H.Young Transport Ltd	Southampton	31. 1.02
G-HYST	Enstrom 280FX Shark	2082		9. 7.98	Ocean Shields Ltd	(Newton Abbot)	16. 8.01

G-IAAA-IZZZ

Regn	Type	C/n	P/I	Date	Owner/operator	Probable Base	CA Expy
G-IAFT	Cessna 152 II	152-85123	EI-BVW N60939	20. 6.95	Marnham Investments Ltd Aldergrove (Op Woodgate Executive Air Services)		22. 7.01T
G-IAMP	Cameron H-34 HAFB	2541		11. 3.91	Virgin Airship & Balloon Co Ltd Telford "National Power"		14. 6.97A
G-IANG	Bell 206L Long Ranger	45132	SE-HSV PH-HMH/N16845	22. 1.98	Lothian Helicopters Ltd East Fortune		29.1.01T
G-IANJ	Reims Cessna F.150K	0548	G-AXVW	19. 5.98	B.Murelli	Thurrock	31. 7.01T
G-IASL	Beechcraft 60 Duke	P-21	G-SING D-IDTA/SE-EXT	18. 4.97	Applied Sweepers Ltd	Dundee	13. 4.01
G-IBBC	Cameron Sphere 105SS HAFB	4082		2. 4.97	Virgin Airship & Balloon Co Ltd Telford		14. 5.99A
G-IBBO	PA-28-181 Archer II	28-7790107	D-EPCA N5389F	17.12.98	M.Gibbon	Elstree	6. 1.02
G-IBBS	Europa Avn Europa	PFA/247-12745		8. 9.94	R.H.Gibbs	Popham	14. 4.99P
G-IBED	Robinson R-22 Alpha	0500	G-BMHN N50022	7. 9.93	B.C.Seedle t/a Brian Seedle Helicopters	Blackpool	30. 9.94
G-IBET	Cameron Can 70SS HAFB	1625		25. 1.88	M.R.Humphrey & J.R.Clifton "Carling Black Label"	Brackley	15. 8.97A
G-IBFC	BFC Challenger II	PFA/177B-13369		9.11.98	K.N.Dickinson (Lytham St. Annes)		
G-IBFW	PA-28R-201 Arrow III	28R-7837235	N31534	22. 1.79	A.W.Collett	Turweston	25. 8.00T
G-IBRO	Reims Cessna F.152 II	1957	EI-BRO	11.10.95	Leicestershire Aero Club Ltd Leicester		19. 2.99T
G-ICAB	Robinson R-44 Astro	0086		28.11.94	JR Clark Ltd Culverthorpe, Grantham		14.12.00
G-ICAS	Aviat Pitts S-2B Special	5344	N511P	19. 6.97	J.C.Smith	Sherburn	10. 7.00T
G-ICCL	Robinson R-22 Beta	1608	G-ORZZ	25.11.93	G.Kidger	Netherthorpe	6. 2.00T
G-ICES	Thunder Ax6-56 SP.1 HAFB (Ice Cream special shape)	283		3. 7.80	British Balloon Museum & Library Ltd	Newbury	3. 6.94A
G-ICEY	Lindstrand LBL-77A HAFB	043		11. 8.93	Iceland Frozen Foods plc Deeside		19. 9.96A
G-ICFR	BAe 125 Srs.800B	258050	N9LR G-5-503/I-OSLO/G-5-503/G-BUCR/HZ-OFC/G-5-503	23.11.94	Chauffair (CI) Ltd Heathrow/Farnborough		1.12.99T
G-ICKY	Lindstrand LBL-77A HAFB	029		19. 5.93	R.R., M.J. & B.Green Kenilworth/Walsall		18. 5.99A
G-ICOI	Lindstrand LBL-105A HAFB	564		3.11.98	Virgin Airship and Balloon Co Ltd Telford		12.11.99A
G-ICOM	Reims Cessna F172M Skyhawk II	1212	G-BFXI PH-ABA/D-EEVC	25. 4.94	T.J. & P.S.Nicholson Maypole Farm, Chislet		23. 6.00
G-ICOZ	Lindstrand LBL-105A HAFB	565		3.11.98	Virgin Airship and Balloon Co Ltd Telford		12.11.99A
G-ICSG	Aerospatiale AS.355F1 Twin Squirrel	5104	G-PAMI G-BUSA	6. 4.93	MW Helicopters Ltd	Ware	2. 5.00T
G-IDAY	Skyfox CA-25N Gazelle (Rotax 912)	CA25N-028	VH-RCR	29. 4.96	The Anglo-Pacific Aircraft Co (UK) Ltd & G.Horne	Glenrothes	23. 5.99T
G-IDDI	Cameron N-77 HAFB	2383		21. 8.90	Allen & Harris Ltd Newbury "Allen & Harris II"		
G-IDDY	DHC.1 Chipmunk (Modified) (Lyc O-540) HA/MM/4-81, NB.130 & C1/0359 WG306		G-BBMS	26. 9.79	W.Senior "Mighty Munk"	Breighton	19. 2.99P
G-IDEA	Gulfstream AA-5A Cheetah	AA5A-0871	G-BGNO	7. 2.84	Lowlog Ltd (Op Cabair)	Elstree	16. 3.01T
G-IDUP	Enstrom 280C Shark	1163	G-BRZF N5687D	11. 5.92	Antique Buildings Ltd Hunterswood Farm, Dunsfold		31. 5.01
G-IDWR	Hughes 369HS	69-0101S	G-AXEJ	26. 5.81	Ainderfield Ltd Tadcaster t/a Copley Electrical Contractors		25.12.00
G-IEJH	SAN Jodel 150A Mascaret	02	G-BPAM F-BLDA/F-WLDA	28. 2.95	E.J.Horsfall	Blackpool	26. 3.99P
G-IEYE	Robin DR.400/180 Regent	2123		29. 1.92	E.Hopper	Sherburn	28. 6.01
G-IFAB	Reims Cessna F.182Q Skylane	0127	OO-ELM (OO-HNU)	6. 1.98	Chatham Glyn Fabrics Ltd Thurrock/Southend		25. 5.01
G-IFFR	PA-32-300 Cherokee Six	32-7340123	G-BWVO OO-JPC/N55520	1. 4.97	D.J.D. & G.D.Ritchie & J.C.Gilbert (Letchworth/Meppershall)		20. 3.00
G-IFIT	PA-31-350 Navajo Chieftain	31-8052078	G-NABI G-MARG/N3580C	31.12.85	Dart Group plc Bournemouth (Op Channel Express)		31.10.99T
G-IFLI	Gulfstream AA-5A Cheetah	AA5A-0831	N26948	7. 7.82	ABC Avn Ltd	Biggin Hill	17. 7.00T
G-IFLP	PA-34-200T Seneca II	34-8070029	N81WS N81149	4. 1.88	AD Aviation Ltd	Barton	19. 6.00T
G-IFTC	HS.125 Srs F3B/RA	25171	G-OPOL G-BXPU/(N171AV)/G-BXPU/G-AXPU/G-IBIS/G-AXPU/HB-VBT/G-5-19	21. 7.94	Albion Aviation Management Ltd Gatwick		28. 7.01T
G-IFTE	BAe HS.125 Srs.700B	257037	G-BFVI G-5-18	16. 5.96	Albion Aviation Management Ltd Gatwick		17. 8.99T
G-IFTS	Robinson R-44 Astro	0366		16. 9.97	Dawcroft Ltd Ulverston t/a Colony Aviation		24. 9.00T
G-IGEL	Cameron N-90 HAFB	2726		7. 4.92	Computacenter Ltd London SE1 "Computacenter II"		12. 5.97A
G-IGGL	Socata TB-10 Tobago	146	G-BYDC F-GCOL	26. 3.99	M & J S Perkin	(Wokingham)	2.12.01
G-IGHH	Enstrom 480	5034		1.12.98	G.H.Harding	(Whitchurch)	17.12.01T
G-IGLA	Colt 240A HAFB	2228		3. 7.92	M.L. & S.M.Gabb Alcester t/a Heart of England Balloons (Barclaycard c/s)		31. 3.97T
G-IGLE	Cameron V-90 HAFB	2609		11. 6.91	A.A.Laing	Aberdeen	7. 5.99A
G-IGOA	Boeing 737-3Y0	24678	EI-BZK	16. 7.98	GO Fly Ltd	Stansted	19. 7.01T
G-IGOB	Boeing 737-3..	2....		. .98R	GO Fly Ltd	Stansted	
G-IGOC	Boeing 737-3Y0	24546	EI-BZH	1. 5.98	GO Fly Ltd	Stansted	7. 5.01T
G-IGOD	Boeing 737-3..	2....		. .98R	GO Fly Ltd	Stansted	

Regn	Type	C/n	P/I	Date	Owner/operator	Probable Base	CA Expy
G-IGOE	Boeing 737-3Y0	24547	EI-BZI	19. 5.98	GO Fly Ltd	Stansted	20. 5.01T
G-IGOF	Boeing 737-3Q8	24698	PK-GWF	2. 4.98	GO Fly Ltd	Stansted	3. 6.01T
G-IGOG	Boeing 737-3Y0	23927	F-GLLE	3. 9.98	GO Fly Ltd	Stansted	3. 9.01T
			PT-TEK				
G-IGOH	Boeing 737-3Y0	23926	F-GLLD	6.11.98	GO Fly Ltd	Stansted	12.12.01T
			PT-TEJ				
G-IGOI	Boeing 737-33A	24092	G-OBMD	30.12.98	GO Fly Ltd	Stansted	13. 2.99T
G-IGOJ	Boeing 737-36N	28872	N1795B	11.11.98	GO Fly Ltd	Stansted	20.11.01T
G-IGOK	Boeing 737-3..	28574	R		GO Fly Ltd	Stansted	
G-IGOL	Boeing 737-3..	28596	R		GO Fly Ltd	Stansted	
G-IGOM	Boeing 737-3..	28599	R		GO Fly Ltd	Stansted	
G-IGOP	Boeing 737-3..	28602	R		GO Fly Ltd	Stansted	
G-IGOR	Boeing 737-3..	28606	R		GO Fly Ltd	Stansted	
G-IHSB	Robinson R-22 Beta	0982		16. 3.89	M.Walker	Kington, Hereford	1. 2.01T
G-IIAC	Aeronca 11AC Chief	11AC-169	(G-BTPY)	2. 7.91	P.K.Sheppard & R.Elliott	Compton Abbas	4.10.98P
	(Cont A65)		N86359/NC86359				
G-IIAN	Aero Designs Pulsar	PFA/202-12123		10. 9.91	I.G.Harrison	(Derby)	
G-IIFR	Robinson R-22 Beta	2841		2. 9.98	Sloane Helicopters Ltd	Sywell	1.10.01T
G-IIIG	Boeing-Stearman A75N1	75-4354	G-BSDR	25. 3.91	Aerosuperbatics Ltd "Annie"		
	(PT-17) Kaydet (Cont W670)		N61827/42-16191		(Crunchie c/s) (To Flight Incentives NV 9.97)		
						Antwerp, Belgium	11. 5.00T
G-IIIH	BAC One Eleven 518FG	BAC.200	VP-BED	17. 6.97	European Aviation Ltd	Bournemouth	
			VR-BED/LV-MEX/(G-AXMF)/PT-TYV/G-AXMF				
G-IIII	Pitts S-2B Special	5010	N5330G	6. 1.89	B.K.Lecomber (Microlease c/s)	Denham	20. 6.01T
	(Lyc AEIO-540)						
G-IIIR	Pitts S-1S Special	604	N27M	21. 1.93	R.O.Rogers Hulcote Farm, Salford, Bucks	15. 9.99P
	(Lyc IO-360)						
G-IIIT	Aerotek Pitts S-2A Special	2222	N7YT	16. 1.89	Aerobatic Displays Ltd	Shoreham	13. 8.01A
	(Lyc AEIO-360)				(Toyota c/s)		
G-IIIV	Pitts Super Stinker 11-260	PFA/273-13005		4. 2.97	A.N.R.Houghton		
						Ranksborough Farm, Langham	
G-IIIX	Pitts S-1S Special	AJT	G-LBAT	22. 5.89	P.Shaw	Breighton	16. 7.98P
	(Lyc O-360)		G-UCCI/G-BIYN/N455T				
G-IIPM	Aerospatiale AS.350B Ecureuil	1790	G-GWIL	18.12.96	CSR Ltd	Chester	10.10.99
G-IIRB	Bell 206B JetRanger III	3958	N903CA	22.11.89	Robard Consultants Ltd		
					Reem Hill Farm, Weeton, Preston	6. 6.99
G-IIRG	Stoddard-Hamilton Glasair IIS RG			29. 6.93	D.S.Watson	Fairoaks	26. 3.99P
	(Lyc IO-360)	PFA/149-11937					
G-IITI	Extra EA.300	018	D-EFRR	12. 5.92	Aerobatic Displays Ltd	Booker	13. 8.01A
					(Nigel Lamb) (Lexus c/s)		
G-IIXX	Montgomerie-Parsons Two Place			13.10.93	J.M.Montgomerie	(Mayboole)	14. 6.94*
	(Rotax 912)	PFA G/08-1225			(Unmarked 2.98)		
G-IIZI	Extra EA.300	037	JY-RNB	12.12.96	P.J.Pengilly & S.G.Jones		
			D-ETXA		t/a 11-21 Flying Group (Fleet/Hungerford)	11. 2.01T
G-IJAC	Light Aero Avid mk.4	PFA/189-12095		31.12.92	I.J.A.Charlton	(Petworth)	
	Speed Wing						
G-IJCB	Sikorsky S-76C (Modified)	760464		16.12.96	JC Bamford Excavators Ltd		
						Rocester, Uttoxeter	25. 3.00
G-IJMC	VPM M-16 Tandem Trainer		G-POSA	10. 6.98	I.J.McTear	(Whitehaven)	AC
		VPM16-UK-106	G-BVJM				
G-IJOE	PA-28RT-201T Turbo Arrow IV		N8265X	14. 8.90	R.P.Wilson	Gamston	22. 5.99
		28R-8031178	N9599N				
G-IJYS	BAe Jetstream 3102	715	G-BTZT	5.10.92	Air Kilroe Ltd	Manchester	18.11.00T
			N416MX/G-31-715		"Flying Scotsman"		
G-IKAP	Cessna T303 Crusader	T303-00182	N63SA	4. 3.99	T.M.Beresford	Cambridge	
			D-IKAP/N9518C				
G-IKBP	PA-28-161 Warrior II	28-8216132	N81762	16. 7.90	K.B.Page	Shoreham	26. 7.99
G-IKIS	Cessna 210M Centurion II	210-61754	N732TD	15. 5.78	A.C.Davison	(Tzaneen, South Africa)	25.12.01
	(Reims-assembled with c/n 0002)						
G-IKPS	PA-31-310 Navajo C	31-7912098	D-IKPS	9. 8.96	Channel Aviation Ltd	Biggin Hill	24. 9.00T
			(N444BK)/D-IKPS/N3539G				
G-ILEA	PA-31-310 Navajo C	31-7812117	D-ILEA	7. 7.97	Guernsey Colour Laboratories Ltd		
			N27775			Guernsey	13. 7.00
G-ILEE	Colt 56A Duo Chariot HAFB	2624		29. 7.94	G.I.Lindsay	Pulborough	28. 2.97A
G-ILES	Cameron O-90 HAFB	2360		29. 6.90	G.N.Lantos	Craven Arms	
					(Not build 1998)		
G-ILGW	Cessna 404 Titan II	404-0690	D-ILGW	21. 1.98	Edinburgh Air Charter Ltd	Edinburgh	1. 2.01T
			N404MW/N25DC/N616R/(N6763Y)				
G-ILLE	Boeing-Stearman E75	75-5028	N68979	7. 3.90	J.Griffin	Compton Abbas	6. 6.99T
	(PT-13D) Kaydet (Cont W670)		42-16865/Bu.60906		(As "379" in USAAC c/s)		
G-ILLY	PA-28-181 Archer II	28-7690193	SE-GND	21. 2.80	A.G. & K.M.Spiers Ltd		
						Hinton-in-the-Hedges	19.12.93
G-ILSE	Corby CJ-1 Starlet	PFA/134-10818		9. 1.84	S.Stride	Halfpenny Green	
	(VW1835)				(Nearing completion 9.97)		
G-ILTS	PA-32-300 Six	32-7940217	G-CVOK	28. 3.90	P.G.Teasdale	Boonhill, Fadmoor	6.10.01T
			OE-DOH/N2941C				
G-ILYS	Robinson R-22 Beta	1142		5.10.89	R.S.Jones t/a BJ Avn	Welshpool	24.11.01T

Regn	Type	C/n	P/I	Date	Owner/operator	Probable Base	CA Expy
G-IMAG	Colt 77A HAFB	1718		9. 3.90	Flying Pictures Ltd "Agfa"	Fairoaks	19. 1.00A
	(Second envelope c/n 2254; c/n 1718 dbf 6.92)						
G-IMAN	Colt 31A Sky Chariot HAFB	2605		23. 6.94	Benedikt Haggeney GmbH		
						Ennigerloh, Germany	17. 2.99A
G-IMAX	Cameron O-120	2201	PH-VVJ	?. 5.98	Not known	????	
G-IMBY	Pietenpol Air Camper	PFA/47-12402		22.12.93	P.F.Bockh	(Horsham)	
G-IMLI	Cessna 310Q	310Q-0491	G-AZYK N4182Q	3. 4.86	M.V.Rijkse & N.M.R.Richards	Oxford	30. 4.00T
G-IMOK	Hoffmann HK-36R Super Dimona	36317	I-NELI OE-9352	31. 7.97	A.L.Garfield	(London N12)	3. 8.00
G-IMPX	Rockwell Commander 112B	512	N1304J	25.10.90	T.L. & S.Hull	Aberdeen	10. 4.00
G-IMPY	Light Aero Avid Flyer C PFA/189-11439			10. 4.89	T.R.C.Griffin	Haverfordwest	3. 8.99P
	(Rotax 532)						
G-INAV	Aviation Composites Europa	AC.001		23. 2.87	I.Shaw	(York)	AC
G-INCA	Glaser-Dirks DG-400	4-199		22. 1.87	H.W.Ober "CA"	Rufforth	29. 3.99
G-INCH	Montgomerie-Bensen B.8MR		G-BRES	20. 8.91	I.H.C.Branson	Great Orton	17. 8.95P
	(Rotax 532)	PFA G/01A-1117					
G-INDC	Cessna T303 Crusader	T303-00122	G-BKFH N4766C	28. 6.83	Godolphin Management Co Ltd	(Newmarket)	19. 5.01
G-INDY	Robinson R-44 Astro	0071		11. 7.94	Reynard Racing Cars Ltd	Sywell	19.10.00
G-INGA	Thunder Ax8-84 HAFB	2149		16. 6.92	M.L.J.Ritchie	Weybridge	14. 9.94A
G-INGE	Thruster T600N	9039-T600N-033		23. 2.99	Thruster Air Services Ltd	(Wantage)	
G-INGR	Reims Cessna F.150J	0492	G-AWXU	1. 8.96	KJC Bradmar Communications Ltd	Southend	11. 7.99T
					(Op Willowair Flying Club)		
G-INNI	Wassmer Jodel D.112	540	F-BHPU	30. 8.94	R.G.Andrews	Damyns Hall, Upminster	28. 7.99P
G-INNY	Replica Plans SE.5A	PFA/20-10439		18.12.78	K.S.Matcham	Goodwood	14. 5.98P
	(Cont C90)				(As "F5459/Y" in RFC c/s)		
G-INOW	ARV Monnett Moni 223 & PFA/142-10953			30. 3.84	W.C.Brown (Stored 8.97)	Fairoaks	20. 8.88P
	(KFM 107)						
G-INSR	Cameron N-90 HAFB	4320		23. 4.98	M.J.Betts & The Smith & Pinching Grp Ltd		
						(Norwich)	20. 4.99
G-INVU	Agusta-Bell 206B JetRanger II	8530	G-XXII G-GGCC/G-BEHG	1. 3.95	Burman Aviation Ltd	Cranfield	28. 3.00T
G-IOCO	Beechcraft 58 Baron	TH-1783		6. 6.96	Sea & Air Charter Ltd	Blackbushe	20. 6.99
G-IOCS	Short SD.3-30 Var.100	SH.3057	G-BIFH N488NS/LV-OJH/G-BIFH	25. 7.96	Air Tabernacle Ltd (Op Willow Air) (Overseas Courier Service c/s)	Southend	10.10.98T
					(Open store 3.99)		
G-IOIO	Bell 206B Jet Ranger III	4359	N47EA	11. 4.96	Lynton Air Ltd	Denham	13. 5.99T
G-IOOI	Robin DR.400/160 Major 80	1700		31. 5.85	N.B.Mason & S.J.O'Rourke	Rendcomb	11.11.01
G-IOPT	Cessna 182P Skylane	182-61731	N182EE D-ECVM/N21585	9. 6.98	Swift Air Ltd	Elstree	7. 7.01
G-IOSI	CEA Jodel DR.1050 Sicile	526	F-BLRS	6.10.80	G.A.Saxby	Bidford	25. 6.99
					t/a Sicile Flying Group		
G-IPSI(2)	Grob G-109B	6425	G-BMLO	29. 5.86	G-IPSI Ltd	Woodford	20.11.99
G-IPSY	Rutan VariEze 1512 & PFA/74-10284		(G-IPSI)	19. 6.78	R.A.Fairclough	Biggin Hill	30. 6.98P
	(Cont PC60)						
G-IPUP	Beagle B.121 Pup 2	B121-036	HB-NAC G-35-036	17. 7.95	M.Sowerby	Elstree	15.10.01T
G-IRAF	Rotary Air Force RAF 2000 GTX-SE			17. 6.96	J.P.Wood	Kemble	30. 3.99P
	(Subaru EJ22)	PFA G/13-1278					
G-IRAN	Cessna 152 II	152-83907	OH-CKM C-GBJY/(N6150B)	19. 8.97	E.Alexander	Andrewsfield	
G-IRIS	Gulfstream AA-5B Tiger	AA5B-1184	G-BIXU N4533N	14.12.87	A.H.McVicar	Carlisle	22. 4.00T
					(Op Carlisle Flight Centre)		
G-IRLY	Colt 90A HAFB	1620		28.12.89	S.A.Burnett & L.P.Purfield	Leicester	6. 8.94A
					"Air Canada Cargo II"		
G-IROY	Rotorway Exec 152	3525		24. 2.98	R.R.Orr	(Dromore, NI)	
	(RW-152)						
G-IRPC	Cessna 182Q Skylane II	182-66039	G-BSKM N559CT/N759JV	15. 5.91	C.A.Morris t/a Barmoor Avn	Top Farm, Royston	19. 7.99T
G-ISCA	PA-28RT-201 Arrow IV	28R-8118012	N8288Y N9608N	12. 2.91	D.J. & P.Pay	Exeter	15. 4.00
G-ISDB	PA-28-161 Cherokee Warrior II		G-BWET SX-ALX/D-EFFQ/N9612N	19. 2.96	Action Air Services Ltd	White Waltham	22. 3.01T
		28-7716074					
G-ISDN	Boeing-Stearman A75N1	75-1263	N4197X XB-WOV/Bu.3486	6. 2.95	D.R.L.Jones (As "14" in US Army c/s)	Kemble	8.10.98
	(N2S-3) Kaydet						
G-ISEH	Cessna 182R Skylane II	182-67843	G-BIWS N6601N	9.11.90	Hadsley Ltd	Guernsey	8. 5.00
G-ISFC	PA-31-310 Turbo Navajo B	31-7300970	G-BNEF N7574L	23. 3.94	SFC (Air Taxis) Ltd	Stapleford	21. 9.99T
G-ISIS	DH.82A Tiger Moth	86251	G-AODR NL779	20.12.83	D.R. & M.Wood	Tunbridge Wells	29. 3.62
					(Crashed Nympsfield 18.9.61; on rebuild)		
G-ISKY	Bell 206B JetRanger III	3654	G-PSCI G-BOKD/N3171A	5. 4.95	Kwik-Fit (GB) Ltd	Edinburgh	13. 4.00T
G-ISLA	BN-2A-26 Islander	206	PH-PAR G-BNEA/SE-FTA/G-51-206	7. 5.97	Hoe Leasing Ltd	Cranfield	12. 6.00T

Regn	Type	C/n	P/I	Date	Owner/operator	Probable Base	CA Expy
G-ISPL	Robinson R-22 Mariner	1771M	SE-JAL	3. 2.99	Selectpile Ltd	(Warminster)	AC
G-ISTT	Thunder Ax8-84 HAFB	1787		12. 6.90	RAF Halton Hot Air Balloon Club		
					"RAF Halton"	RAF Halton	17. 9.98A
G-ITII	Aerotek Pitts S-2A Special	2223	I-VLAT	5. 7.95	Aerobatic Displays Ltd	Booker	13. 8.01A
	(Lyc AEIO-360)						
G-ITON	Maule MX-7-235 Star Rocket	10050C	N5670R	11. 9.96	J.R.S.Heaton Hawksbridge Farm, Oxenhope		3.11.99
G-IVAC	Airtour AH-77B HAFB	012		28.11.89	T.D.Gibbs	Billingshurst	18. 8.97A
G-IVAN	Shaw Twin-Eze 39 & PFA/74-10502			11. 9.78	A.M.Aldridge	(North Walsham)	5.10.90P*
	(2/Norton NR642)				"Mistress" (Stored Ostend 9.96)		
G-IVAR	Yakovlev Yak-50	791504	D-EIVI	24. 2.89	R.A.L.Hubbard & S.Whitcombe (West Meon)		18. 6.99P
			(N5219K)/DDR-WQT/DM-WQT t/a Foley Farm Flying Group				
G-IVEL	Sportavia Fournier RF4D	4029	G-AVNY	29. 6.95	V.S.E.Norman	Rendcomb	14. 4.01A
					(St.Ivel/Utterly Butterly c/s)		
G-IVET	Europa Avn Europa PFA/247-12511			23. 5.97	K.J.Fraser	(Abingdon)	
G-IVIV	Robinson R-44 Astro	0016	(N803EH)	2. 8.93	Rahtol Ltd	Sywell	10. 3.99
G-IVOR	Aeronca 11AC Chief	11AC-1035	EI-BKB	18. 6.82	P.R.White & C.P.Matthews	Bodmin	10. 3.99P
			G-IVOR/EI-BKB/N9397E t/a South Western Aeronca Grp				
G-IWON	Cameron V-90 HAFB	2504	G-BTCV	17. 2.92	D.P.P.Jenkinson "Twenty One"	Tring	25. 7.99A
G-IXCC	VS.361 Spitfire LF.IXe	-	(Fokker)	18. 5.88	Personal Plane Svs Ltd	Booker	9.12.93P
			PL344 (Blue Max Movie Acft Museum as "PL344/Y2-B" in 442 Sqn RAF c/s)				
G-IYAK	SPP Yakovlev Yak.C11	171103	OK-JIM	12. 1.94	E.K.Coventry	Earls Colne	AC
			(Ex Jean Salis, France and Egyptian AF)				
G-IZIT	Rans S-6-116 Coyote II PFA/204A-12965			7. 3.96	C.Wren	(Hockley)	5. 5.99P
	(Rotax 912UL)				(Damaged at Southend 6.9.98)		

G-JAAA-JZZZ

Regn	Type	C/n	P/I	Date	Owner/operator	Probable Base	CA Expy
G-JACK	Cessna 421C Golden Eagle III	421C-1411	N421GQ N125RS/N12028	29. 4.97	JCT 600 Ltd (Jack Tordoff)Leeds-Bradford		28. 4.01
G-JACS	PA-28-181 Archer III	2843078	N9278J	15. 4.97	Vector Air Ltd	Fowlmere	1. 5.00T
G-JAHL	Bell 206B Jet Ranger III	3565	N666ST	2. 1.98	D.T.Gittins & J.A.Ruck t/a Jet Air Helicopters	(Ludlow)	22. 2.01T
G-JAKE	DHC.1 Chipmunk 22	C1/0584	G-BBMY WK565	21. 1.80	K.Ritter	(Bangor)	11.12.01
G-JAKI	Mooney M.20R Ovation	29-0030		7. 2.95	A.Pound	(Leighton Buzzard)	31. 3.01
G-JALC	Boeing 757-225	22194	N504EA	6. 3.95	Airtours International Airways Ltd Manchester		22. 4.01T
G-JAMP	PA-28-151 Cherokee Warrior	28-7515026	G-BRJU N44762	3. 4.95	ANP Ltd White Waltham (Op West London Aero Club)		19. 5.01T
G-JANA	PA-28-181 Archer II	28-7990483	N2838X	12. 2.87	C.Dashfield t/a Croaker Avn	Stapleford	21. 5.99
G-JANB	Colt Flying Bottle SS HAFB (J & B Whisky Bottle shape)	1643		16. 2.90	Justerini & Brooks Ltd London SW1 "Whisky Too"		30. 9.96A
G-JANI	Robinson R-44 Astro	0110	D-HIMM	21. 7.95	Heli Air Ltd Wellesbourne Mountford		10.12.01T
G-JANK	PA-E23-250 Aztec C	27-2754	EI-BOO G-ATCY/N5640Y	24. 4.95	Liverpool Flying School Ltd	Liverpool	3. 3.99T
G-JANN	PA-34-220T Seneca III	3433133	N9154W	23. 6.89	MBC Aviation Ltd	Headcorn	5. 8.01T
G-JANO	PA-28RT-201T Arrow IV	28R-7918091	SE-IZR N2146X	14. 5.98	Abertawe Aviation Ltd	Swansea	17. 6.01T
G-JANS	Reims Cessna FR.172J Rocket	0414	PH-GJO D-EGJO	11. 8.78	I.G.Aizlewood	Rush Green	6. 9.01
G-JANT	PA-28-181 Archer II (Originally built as c/n 28-8290117/N81992/YV-2234P; not delivered and re-manufactured as 8390075)	28-8390075	N4297J	23. 2.87	Janair Avn Ltd	Denham	10. 3.99T
G-JARA	Robinson R-22 Beta	1837		11. 6.91	J.A.R.Allwright	Clacton-on-Sea	18. 7.00
G-JASE	PA-28-161 Warrior II	28-8216056	N8461R	13. 2.91	Mid-Anglia Flying School Ltd	Cambridge	2. 7.01T
G-JAVO	PA-28-161 Warrior II	28-8016130	G-BSXW N8119S	17. 9.97	I.N.T.Thornhill	Wellesbourne Mountford	11. 6.00T
G-JAWZ	Pitts S-1S Special (Lyc AEIO-360)	PFA/09-12846		6.11.95	A.R.Harding	(Ipswich)	12. 6.98P
G-JAYI	Auster 5 J/1 Autocrat	2030	OY-ALU D-EGYK/OO-ABF	5. 2.93	Bravo Avn Ltd (Air Atlantique)	Coventry	25. 4.99
G-JAZZ	Gulfstream AA-5A Cheetah	AA5A-0819	N26932	30. 3.82	R.W.Taylor t/a Jazz Club	Southend	26. 6.99
G-JBAC	Embraer EMB-110P1 Bandeirante	110-249	G-BGYV N105VA/G-BGYV/PT-SAP	20.10.94	BAC Leasing Ltd (Op Skydrift)	Newcastle	26.11.99T
G-JBDB	Agusta-Bell 206B Jet Ranger	8238	G-OOPS G-BNRD/Oman AF 602	11. 4.96	Brad Helicopters Ltd	Denham	28.11.99T
G-JBDH	Robin DR.400/180 Regent	1901		17. 3.89	P.R.Liddle	Rochester	23. 5.01
G-JBJB	Colt 69A HAFB	1274		26. 7.88	Justerini & Brooks Ltd London SW1 "J & B Jeremy"		15. 5.99A
G-JBPR	Wittman W.10 Tailwind	PFA/31-11490		25. 5.89	P.A.Rose & J.P.Broadhurst	Walney Island	
G-JBWI	Robinson R-22 Beta	1040		19. 6.89	J.B.Wagstaff Costock, Loughborough t/a N.J.Wagstaff Leasing (Op East Midlands Helicopters)		19. 7.01T
G-JCAS	PA-28-181 Archer II	28-8690036	N9093N (N170AV)/N9648N	12. 6.89	Charlie Alpha Ltd	Jersey	19. 6.01T
G-JCBI	Dassault Falcon 2000	27	F-WWMM	13.11.96	JC Bamford Excavators Ltd	East Midlands	17.11.00
G-JCFR	Cessna 550 Citation II (Unit No.315)	550-0282	G-JETC N68644	14. 7.95	Chauffair Ltd	Farnborough	28. 2.99T
G-JCKT	Stemme S-10VT	11-004		8. 4.98	J.C.Taylor	(Castletown/IoM)	
G-JCUB	PA-18-135 Super Cub (L-21B-PI)(Frame No. 18-3630)	18-3531	PH-VCH R.Neth AF R-103/54-2331	21. 1.82	Piper Cub Consortium (Jersey) Ltd Jersey		16. 6.99
G-JCMW	Rand KR-2	PFA/129-11064		3. 2.99	M.Wildish & J.Cook	(Gainsborough)	
G-JDEE	Socata TB-20 Trinidad	333	G-BKLA F-BNGX	1. 5.84	P.A.Bennett t/a JDEE Grp	Edinburgh	3. 5.99
G-JDEL	Jodel 150 Mascaret	112 & PFA/151-11276	G-JDLI	19. 9.95	K.F. & R.Richardson	(Solihull)	
G-JDIX	Mooney M.20B Mark 21	1866	G-ARTB	28.11.85	ADH Ltd	Tibenham	16. 1.00
G-JDTI	Cessna 421C Golden Eagle III	421C-1226	N42E	11. 8.87	MCP Aviation (Charter) Ltd (Op Hawkair)	Cambridge	23.12.99T
G-JEAD	Fokker F-27 Friendship 500	10627	VH-EWU PH-EXL	14.11.90	Jersey European Airways Ltd (Op BAC Express)	Jersey	21.11.99T
G-JEAE	Fokker F-27 Friendship 500	10633	VH-EWV PH-FSO	2. 1.91	Jersey European Airways Ltd Bournemouth (Op Channel Express)		15. 1.00T
G-JEAF	Fokker F-27 Friendship 500	10637	OY-SRD G-JEAF/VH-EWW/PH-EXE	2. 1.91	Jersey European Airways (UK) Ltd	Exeter	16. 9.99T
G-JEAG	Fokker F-27 Friendship 500	10639	D-ADAP G-JEA/VH-EWX/PH-EXG	14.11.90	Jersey European Airways Ltd	Jersey	3.10.01T
G-JEAH	Fokker F-27 Friendship 500	10669	VH-EWY PH-EXL	21. 1.91	Jersey European Airways Ltd	Jersey	14. 2.02T
G-JEAI	Fokker F-27 Friendship 500	10672	VH-EWZ PH-EXS	18.12.90	Jersey European Airways Ltd	Jersey	16.12.99T
G-JEAJ	BAe 146 Srs.200	E-2099	G-OLCA G-5-099	20. 9.93	Jersey European Airways (UK) Ltd Exeter "Pride of Guernsey"		17. 7.99T
G-JEAK	BAe 146 Srs.200	E-2103	G-OLCB G-5-103	18. 3.93	Jersey European Airways (UK) Ltd Exeter "Pride of Birmingham"		20. 6.99T

Regn	Type	C/n	P/I	Date	Owner/operator	Probable Base	CA Expy
G-JEAM	BAe 146 Srs.300	E-3128	G-BTJT HS-TBK/G-11-128	24. 5.93	British Regional Airlines Ltd Manchester (Mountain of the Birds/Benyhone Tartan t/s)		23. 5.00T
G-JEAO	BAe 146 Srs.100	E-1010	G-UKPC C-GNVX/N802RW/G-5-512/PT-LEP/G-BKXZ/PT-LEP	19. 9.94	Jersey European Airways (UK) Ltd (Op Air France Express)	Heathrow	29. 4.99T
G-JEAP	Fokker F-27 Friendship 500	10459	9Q-CBI OY-APF/9Q-CBI/PH-RUA/VH-EWR/F-BYAH/OY-APF/PH-EXD	13. 4.95	Jersey European Airways Ltd Bournemouth (Op Channel Express)		15. 6.01T
G-JEAR	BAe 146 Srs.200	E-2018	G-HWPB G-6-018/G-BSRU/G-OSKI/N603AW (Air France c/s)	14.11.95	Jersey European Airways (UK) Ltd Exeter		7. 4.01T
G-JEAS	BAe 146 Srs.200	E-2020	G-OLHB G-BSRV/G-OSUN/C-FEXN/N604AW (Air France c/s)	13. 2.96	Jersey European Airways (UK) Ltd Exeter		13. 7.00T
G-JEAT	BAe 146 Srs.100	E-1071	N171TR J8-VBB/G-BVUY/B-2706/G-5-071	11.10.96	Jersey European Airways (UK) Ltd (Op Air France Express)	Heathrow	23.10.99T
G-JEAU	BAe 146 Srs.100	E-1035	N135TR J8-VBC/G-BVUW/B-584L/B-2704/G-5-035	30.12.96	Jersey European Airways (UK) Ltd Exeter		24. 1.00T
G-JEAV	BAe 146 Srs.200	E-2064	N764BA CC-CEN/N414XV/G-5-064/N404XV	17. 6.97	Jersey European Airways (UK) Ltd Exeter		19. 6.00T
G-JEAW	BAe 146 Srs.200	E-2059	(N759BA) CC-CEJ/N401XV/G-5-059/N401XV/G-5-059	21. 7.97	Jersey European Airways (UK) Ltd Exeter		21. 8.00T
G-JEAX	BAe 146 Srs.200	E-2136	N136JV C-FHAP/N136TR/N882DV/(N719TA)/N882DV/G-5-136	16. 2.98	Jersey European Airways (UK) Ltd Exeter		19. 2.01T
G-JEBA	BAe 146 Srs.300	E-3181	HS-TBL G-6-181/G-BSYR/G-6-181	16. 6.98	Jersey European Airways (UK) Ltd Exeter		27. 2.01T
G-JEBB	BAe 146 Srs.300	E-3185	HS-TBK G-6-185	26. 6.98	Jersey European Airways (UK) Ltd Exeter		1.11.01T
G-JEBC	BAe 146 Srs.300	E-3189	HS-TBO G-6-189	4. 6.98	Jersey European Airways (UK) Ltd Exeter		1. 7.01T
G-JEBD	BAe 146 Srs.300	E-3191	HS-TBJ G-6-191	14. 7.98	Jersey European Airways (UK) Ltd Exeter		17. 9.01T
G-JEBE	BAe 146 Srs.300	E-3206	HS-TBM G-6-206	28. 5.98	Jersey European Airways (UK) Ltd Exeter		25. 6.01T
G-JEDH	Robin DR.400/180	2343		3. 2.97	J.B.Hoolahan	Lasham	14. 5.00
G-JEET	Reims Cessna FA.152 Aerobat	0369	G-BHMF	10.12.87	A.S.Bamrah t/a Falcon F/Svs (Op Willowair Flying Club)	Southend	18.10.01T
G-JEFF	PA-38-112 Tomahawk	38-79A0763		8. 3.79	R.J.Alford (Op Channel Avn) (Stored 6.97)	Guernsey	15.10.95T
G-JEFS	PA-28R-201T Turbo Arrow III	28R-7703365	G-BFDG N47381	14. 4.97	Barneyline Ltd	White Waltham	23. 7.01
G-JEKP	Agusta-Bell 206B Jet Ranger III	8598	D-HMSF G-ESAL/G-BHXW	13. 2.97	K.Payne	Maxey, Peterborough	1. 4.00
G-JENA	Mooney M.20J (201)	24-1304	N1168D	5. 7.82	P.Leverkuehn t/a Mooney Partnership (To Mr.Allgeier) Antwerp-Deurne, Belgium		12.11.00
G-JENI	Cessna R182 Skylane RG II	R182-00267	N3284C	17. 9.87	R.A.Bentley	Stapleford	23. 4.00
G-JENN	Gulfstream AA-5B Tiger	AA5B-1187	N4533T	7.12.81	Plane Talking Ltd (Op Cabair)	Elstree	21. 2.00T
G-JERS	Robinson R-22 Beta	1610		21.12.90	Preveda Ltd	(Wotton-under-Edge)	30. 4.00T
G-JESS	PA-28R-201T Turbo Arrow III	28R-7803334	G-REIS N36689	18. 9.95	N.E. & M.A.Bedggood	White Waltham	11. 5.00
G-JETA	Cessna 550 Citation II (Unit No.101)	550-0094	(N26630)	3. 9.79	IDS Acft Ltd (Op Dynamic Air)	Bournemouth	17. 5.99T
G-JETG	Gates Lear Jet 35A	35A-324	G-JETN G-JJSG	5. 3.98	Gama Aviation Ltd	Fairoaks	28. 7.98T
G-JETH	Armstrong-Whitworth AW.6385 Sea Hawk FGA.6 (Composite with WM983/A2511)		"XE364" XE489	10. 8.83	P.G.Vallance Ltd	Charlwood, Surrey	
G-JETI	BAe 125 Srs.800B	258056	G-5-509	9. 7.86	Ford Motor Co Ltd	Stansted	19.10.99T
G-JETJ	Cessna 550 Citation II (Unit No.171)	550-0154	G-EJET G-DJBE/(N8887N)	9. 2.93	Widehawk Aviation Ltd	Cambridge	15. 8.99T
G-JETM	Gloster Meteor T.7	-	VZ638	10. 8.83	P.G.Vallance Ltd (As "VZ638/HF" in RN/FRU c/s)	Charlwood, Surrey	
G-JETP	Hunting P.84 Jet Provost T.52A (T.4) (Possibly ex 105 not 107)	PAC/W/17635	Sing AF 355 S.Yemen AF 107 G-27-92 or 94/XP666	13.12.83	Shadow Valley Investments Ltd (S.Constantinides)	Paphos, Cyprus	10.12.93P
G-JETU	Aerospatiale AS.355F2 Twin Squirrel	5450	VR-CET JA6623	18. 4.96	Helimand Ltd.	(London SE1)	22. 5.99T
G-JETX	Bell 206B JetRanger III	3208	N3898L	9. 2.88	Heli Charter Ltd	Rochester	3. 3.00T
G-JETZ	MDH Hughes 369E (500E)	0450E	VR-HJI	26. 3.97	John Matchett Ltd	Oxford	5. 6.00
G-JFWI	Reims Cessna F.172N Skyhawk II	1622	PH-DPA PH-AXY	1. 9.80	Staryear Ltd	Barton	16.12.99T
G-JGMN	CASA I-131E Jungmann (Carries c/n plate 2104 in rear cockpit)	2011	E3B-407	17. 4.91	P.D.Scandrett	Rendcomb	4. 1.99P
G-JHAS	Schweizer Hughes 269C (300C)	S.1493		14. 9.90	Barton & Co (Farmers) Ltd Hall Farm, Saundby, Retford		9. 1.00
G-JHEW	Robinson R-22 Beta	0672	N23677	20. 7.87	Burbage Farms Ltd	Hinckley	21.10.99
G-JIII	Stolp SA.300 Starduster Too (Lyc IO-360)	2-3-12	N9043	27. 5.93	J.G.McTaggart t/a VTIO Company	Cumbernauld	1.2.97P
G-JILL	Rockwell Alpine Commander 112TC-A	13304	(OO-HPB) G-JILL/N8070R/HB-NCW	25. 7.80	Westcroft American Motorhomes Ltd	Halfpenny Green	6. 1.02

Regn	Type	C/n	P/I	Date	Owner/operator	Probable Base	CA Expy
G-JIMB	Beagle B.121 Pup 1	B121-033	G-AWWF G-35-033	7. 4.94	K.D.H.Gray & P.G.Fowler	Enstone	21. 9.01T
G-JIMW	Agusta-Bell 206B JetRanger II	8440	G-UNIK G-TPPH/G-BCYP	4. 1.96	R.J.Watt (To Van Cauwelaert) St.Pieters Leeuw, Belgium		4. 4.01T
G-JJAN	PA-28-181 Archer II	2890007	N9105Z	28. 3.88	Redhill Aviation Ltd Redhill t/a Redhill F/C		1. 5.00T
G-JLCA	PA-34-200T Seneca II	34-7870428	G-BOKE N21030	3. 9.97	C.A.S.Atha (Saltburn-by-the-Sea)		29.10.00T
G-JLEE	Agusta-Bell 206B JetRanger III	8588	G-JOKE G-CSKY/G-TALY	10. 2.88	Lee Avn Ltd	Denham	25. 6.00
G-JLHS	Beechcraft A36 Bonanza	E-2571	N8046U	30.11.90	I.G.Meredith	Lydd	16. 1.00
G-JLMW	Cameron V-77 HAFB	1768		23. 6.88	J.L.M.Watkins	Ivybridge	26. 2.99T
G-JLRW	Beechcraft 76 Duchess	ME-165	N60206	4.11.87	Moorfield Developments Ltd	Elstree	6. 1.00
G-JMAC	BAe Jetstream 4100	41004	G-JAMD G-JXLI	12. 6.92	British Aerospace (Operations) Ltd (Stored 7.97)	Prestwick	6.10.97A
G-JMDI	Schweizer Hughes 269C (300C)	S.1398	G-FLAT	24. 9.91	J.J.Potter	Morley, Leeds	2.12.01
G-JMTS	Robin DR.400/180 Regent	2045		29.11.90	J.R.Whiting	Exeter	7. 5.00
G-JMTT	PA-28R-201T Turbo Arrow III	28R-7803190	G-BMHM N3735M	8. 7.86	C.E.Passmore	Southend	14. 3.99
G-JNEE	Cameron R-420 Gas Balloon	4232		21.10.97	Bondbaste Ltd "J Renee" ? Chicago, USA (Damaged Rockford, Illinois, USA 31.12.97 on RTW attempt)		
G-JNNB	Colt 90A HAFB	2063		20.12.91	Justerini & Brooks Ltd "J&B" London SW1		15. 5.99A
G-JOCK	Beechcraft A36 Bonanza	E-2782	G-OVVB N82469	26. 3.97	Minster Enterprises Ltd	Oxford	29. 9.99
G-JODL	SAN Jodel DR.1050/M Excellence	99	F-BJJC	28. 4.86	P.A.Marsh Old Sarum 26.11.99 (Damaged on landing Wharf Farm, Market Bosworth 10.10.98)		
G-JOEY	BN-2A Mk.III-2 Trislander	1016	G-BDGG C-GSAA/G-BDGG	27.11.81	Aurigny Air Svs Ltd "Joey"	Guernsey	26. 8.01T
G-JOIN	Cameron V-65 HAFB	1257		8. 5.86	Derbyshire Building Society "Derbyshire Building Society"	Derby	31. 7.93A
G-JOJO	Cameron A-210 HAFB	2674		20. 9.91	Joanna Barber Ledbury 10. 3.99T t/a Worcester Balloons		
G-JOLY	Cessna 120 (Cont C85)	13872	OO-ACE	3. 9.81	B.V.Meade Garston Farm, Marshfield		16. 6.99P
G-JONB	Robinson R-22 Beta	2593		29. 4.96	J.Bignall Mistletoe Farm, Pinner/Denham		15. 5.99
G-JONE	Cessna 172M Skyhawk II	172-64490	N9724V	2.12.80	A.Pierce	Stapleford	13. 5.00
G-JONH	Robinson R-22 Beta	2170		3. 6.93	Scotia Helicopters Ltd	Cumbernauld	12. 6.99T
G-JONI	Reims Cessna FA.152 Aerobat	0346	G-BFTU	6. 7.84	Euroair Flying Club Ltd	Cranfield	15. 5.00T
G-JONO	Colt 77A HAFB	1086		22. 6.87	The Sandcliffe Motor Group Ltd "Sandcliffe Ford" Stapleford, Notts		17. 9.95A
G-JONY	Cyclone AX2000 HKS	7503		12. 3.99	A.Parker	(Bingley)	
G-JONZ	Cessna 172P Skyhawk II	172-76233	N97835	28. 9.89	Truman Aviation Ltd	Nottingham	20. 5.99T
G-JOON	Cessna 182D	182-53067	(N) G-JOON/OO-ACD/N99967T	9. 6.81	G.Jackson	Sibson	15. 7.01T
G-JOST	Europa Avn Europa	PFA/247-12916		17. 6.98	J.A.Austin	(Bangor)	
G-JOYS	Beechcraft 58 Baron	TH-1556	N1556U	4. 8.94	Dunmhor Transport Ltd	Cumbernauld	21.10.00
G-JOYT	PA-28-181 Archer II	28-7990132	G-BOVO N2239B	13. 2.90	John K.Cathcart Ltd	St. Angelo	30. 3.00T
G-JOYZ	PA-28-181 Archer III	2843018	N9262R	19. 1.96	S.W. & Joy E.Taylor	Biggin Hill	23. 1.02
G-JPOT	PA-32R-301 Saratoga SP	32R-8113065	G-BIYM N8385X	1. 8.94	S.W.Turley	Wickenby	9. 6.99T
G-JPRO	BAC.145 Jet Provost T.5A EEP/JP/1055		XW433	10. 8.95	Ruddington Avn Ltd (As "XW433/63")	Nottingham	2. 2.99P
G-JPTV	BAC.145 Jet Provost T.5A EEP/JP/1005		XW355	2. 5.96	M P Grimshaw	(London W5)	26. 1.00P
G-JPVA	BAC.145 Jet Provost T.5A EEP/JP/953		G-BVXT XW289	22. 2.95	T.J.Manna Cranfield 10. 5.99P t/a Kennet Avn (As "XW289/73" in 1FTS c/s)		
G-JRBH	Robinson R-22 Beta	2852		11. 8.98	B.C.Hunter Edinburgh 7. 9.01T & C.S.N.Eaton Trustees of Bernard Hunter		
G-JRSL	Agusta A.109E	11036		9.11.98	Sloane Helicopters Ltd	Sywell	22.12.01T
G-JSAT	PBN BN-2T Turbine Islander	2277	G-BVFK	5. 2.98	J.H.Horne (BFPO 16, Germany) 5. 3.01A t/a Rhine Army Parachute Association		
G-JSCL*	Rans S-10 Sakota 1289-075 & PFA/194-11781 (Rotax 532)			12. 4.90	Not known Emlyns Field, Rhuallt 16. 5.92P (Damaged Emlyns Field, Rhuallt 16.7.91; stored 9.96)		
G-JSJX	Airbus A.321-213	0808	(EC-) D-AVZP	3. 4.98	Air World Aviation Ltd	Manchester	27. 4.01T
G-JSON	Cameron N-105 HAFB	2933		21. 5.92	Up & Away Ballooning Ltd High Wycombe 1. 7.97T "Jason"		
G-JSPC	PBN BN-2T Turbine Islander	2264	G-BUBG	21.12.94	J.H.Horne Sennelager, Germany 16. 1.00A t/a Rhine Army Parachute Association		
G-JSSD*	HP.137 Jetstream 3001	227	N510F N510E/N12227/G-AXJZ	14. 6.79	Museum of Flight	East Fortune	9.10.90S
G-JTCA	PA-23-250 Aztec E	27-7305112	G-BBCU N40297	29.12.80	J.D.Tighe Norwich 2. 9.00T t/a Eastern Air Executive		
G-JTPC	Aeromot AMT-200 Super Ximango	200-067		28. 5.97	J.T.Potter & P.G.Cowling Dishforth 11. 6.00 t/a G-JTPC Falcon 3 Group		

Regn	Type	C/n	P/I	Date	Owner/operator	Probable Base	CA Expy
G-JTWO	Piper J/2 Cub	1754	G-BPZR	23.10.89	A.T.Hooper & C.C.Silk		
	(Cont A65) (f/f 12.8.37)		N19554/NC19554		Bericote Farm, Blackdown, Leamington Spa		17. 8.99P
G-JTYE	Aeronca 7BM Champion	7AC-4185	N85445	26. 9.91	G.D.Horn	Old Sarum	17. 6.99P
	(Cont C85) (Modified from 7AS standard)		NC85445		(Damaged Longwood Farm, Southampton 2.8.98)		
G-JUDE	Robin DR.400/180 Regent	1869		14.10.88	R.G.Carrell	Goodwood	7.12.00
G-JUDI	North American AT-6D-NT	88-14722	FAP 1502	17.11.78	A.A.Hodgson	Bryngwyn Bach	3. 2.99P
	Harvard III		SAAF7439/EX915/41-33888		(As "FX301/FD-NQ")		
	(Regd with c/n "EX915-326165")						
G-JUDY	Grumman-American AA-5A Cheetah		(G-BFWM)	31. 8.78	Plane Talking Ltd	Biggin Hill	18.11.99T
		AA5A-0620	N26480				
G-JUIN	Cessna T303 Crusader	T303-00014	OO-PEN	29. 2.88	M.J.Newman	Denham	8. 5.00
			N9401T				
G-JULS	Stemme S-10V	14-028	D-KGDC	12. 6.97	J.P.C.Fuchs	(Rochdale)	18. 6.00
G-JULU	Cameron V-90 HAFB	3611		7. 7.95	Datacentre Ltd	Bristol	2. 8.97A
G-JULZ	Europa Avn Europa	PFA/247-13045		8.10.96	M.Parkin	(Doncaster)	
G-JUNG	CASA I-131E Jungmann	1121	E3B-143	23.11.88	K.H.Wilson	White Waltham	10. 3.99P
					(As "E3B-143" in Spanish AF c/s)		
G-JURE	Socata TB-10 Tobago	597	N106U	6.11.92	P.M.Ireland South Lodge Farm, Widmerpool		14. 1.01
G-JURG	Rockwell Commander 114A GT	14516	N4752W	19. 9.79	R.D., S.R. & N.Spencer	Fenland	6. 4.01
	(Laid-down as c/n 14449)				t/a Blue Line Trailers (To P J Taylor)		
G-JVBF	Lindstrand LBL-210A HAFB	265		5. 6.95	Virgin Balloon Flights Ltd (London SE16)		21. 3.99T
G-JVMD	Cessna 172N Skyhawk II	172-67794	G-BNTV	7. 2.92	P.W.Speller	Biggin Hill	19.11.99T
			N75539		t/a Brandon Avn (Op King Air F/C)		
G-JWBB	CEA Jodel DR.1050 Sicile	534	G-LAKI	17. 8.92	B.F.Baldock Maypole Farm, Chislet		30. 6.99
			F-BLZD				
G-JWBI	Agusta-Bell 206B Jet Ranger II	8435	G-RODS	3. 4.96	J.W.Bonser (Walsall) Ltd	Walsall	6. 3.99T
			G-NOEL/G-BCWN				
G-JWDG	Grumman-American AA-5A Cheetah		G-OCML	9.10.91	Lowlog Ltd	Blackbushe	20.11.00T
		AA5A-0662	G-JAVA/N26705				
G-JWDS	Reims Cessna F.150G	0216	G-AVNB	15.12.88	C.R. & S.A.Hardiman	Shobdon	29. 9.94T
G-JWFT	Robinson R-22 Beta	0989		16. 3.89	J.W.F & S.M.Tuke	Headcorn	6. 5.01T
					t/a Tukair Acft Charter		
G-JWIV	CEA Jodel DR.1051 Sicile	431	F-BLMD	6. 9.78	C.M.Fitton	(Stoke Fleming)	22.10.95
					(Damaged Hobbynoor Cross, Coldridge, Devon 23.9.95)		
G-JWLS	Bell 206B JetRanger	1114	G-BSXE	8. 1.99	W.Lowry t/a J.W.L.Services	(Bromley)	29.12.99T
			N40EA/C-GMVM/N83150				

G-KAAA-KZZZ

Regn	Type	C/n	P/I	Date	Owner/operator	Probable Base	CA Expy
G-KADY	Rutan LongEz	PFA/74A-11094		3. 9.85	M.W.Caddy	(Mansfield)	
G-KAFC*	Cessna 152 II	152-84394	N6443L	24. 8.81	Not known	Biggin Hill	15. 4.90T
					(Damaged Biggin Hill 16.10.87; spares use 12.95)		
G-KAFE	Cameron N-65 HAFB	1505		18. 5.87	M.Sarti	Fowey	31. 5.99A
G-KAIR	PA-28-181 Archer II	28-7990176	N3075D	28.12.78	Belfast Flying Club Ltd	Belfast	3. 9.00
G-KAMM	Hawker CCF Hurricane XIIA	CCF/R32007	BW881	23. 2.95	Alpine Deer Group Ltd	Wananka, NZ	
G-KAMP	PA-18-135 Super Cub (L-18C)	18-3451	D-EDPM	9. 5.97	P.R.Edwards & E.Alexander	Andrewsfield	30. 7.00T
			96+27/NL+104/AC+502/AS+501/54-751				
G-KAOM	Scheibe SF.25C Falke	4417	D-KAOM	3. 2.98	K.J.Sleigh, M.A.Robinson & K.Nicholson	(Bury St.Edmunds)	AC
G-KAPW	Percival P.56 Provost T.1	PAC/F/311	XF603	22. 9.97	T.J.Manna	Cranfield	17. 3.99P
					(Op Kennet Aviation) (As "XF603/H")		
G-KARA	Brugger MB.2 Colibri	PFA/43-10980	G-BMUI	1. 6.95	Cara L.Reddish	Netherthorpe	14. 6.99P
		(VW1834)					
G-KARI	Fuji FA.200-160 Aero Subaru	236	G-BBRE	19.12.84	I.Mansfield & F.M.Fiore	Old Sarum	2. 4.00
G-KART	PA-28-161 Warrior II	28-8016088	N8097B	10. 7.91	Newcastle-upon-Tyne A/C Ltd	Newcastle	12.11.00T
G-KARY	Fuji FA.200-180AO Aero Subaru	285	G-BEYP	28. 3.89	M.J.Nairn & J.Davis	Old Buckenham	11. 6.01
					t/a Kary-On Flying Group		
G-KATA	HOAC DV-20 Katana	20021	OE-UDV	4. 2.94	Total Support Inc (UK) Ltd	Dunkeswell	12. 1.00
G-KATE*	Westland WG.30 Srs.100	010		7. 7.83	Westland Helicopters Ltd	Yeovil	16. 9.88T
					(Dumped 10.93)		
G-KATI	Rans S-7 Courier	PFA/218-12917		5. 3.96	S.M. & K.E.Hall	Netherthorpe	7.12.99P
		(Rotax 582)					
G-KATS	PA-28-140 Cherokee Cruiser	28-7325022	G-BIRC OY-BGE	26. 8.83	A.G.Knight t/a Airlaunch	Old Buckenham	7.11.99T
G-KATT	Cessna 152 II	152-85661	G-BMTK N94387	10. 6.93	Aerohire Ltd	Oxford	27. 6.99T
G-KAUR	Colt 315A HAFB	2536		1. 3.94	Balloon School (International) Ltd		
					t/a Balloon Safaris	Petworth	7. 4.98T
G-KAWA	Denney Kitfox mk.2	PFA/172-11822		11. 3.91	T.W.Maton	Enstone	5. 7.95P
		(Rotax 582)			(Damaged Wavendon, Bucks 30. 6.95)		
G-KAXF	Hawker (AWA) Hunter F.6A	S4/U/3361	8830M XF515	20.12.95	T.J.Manna	Cranfield	13. 8.99P
					t/a Kennet Avn (As "XF515/C") (Stored 7.96)		
G-KAXL	Westland Scout AH.1	F.9715	XV140	16.11.95	T.J.Manna	Cranfield	8. 7.99P
		(Regd with c/n F8-7976)			t/a Kennet Avn (As "XV140")		
G-KBAC	Short SD.3-60 Var.100	SH.3758	VH-MJH G-BPXL	2. 1.98	BAC Leasing Ltd	Newcastle	21. 1.00T
					(Op Gill Airways)		
G-KBKB	Thunder Ax8-90 Srs.2 HAFB	2089		30.10.91	G.Boulden "KB Cars"	Aldershot	8. 9.99A
G-KBOT	Hughes 369HM (500M)	52-0214M	G-RAMM EI-AVN/N9037F	30. 7.98	K.H.Bott	(Wigan)	19. 9.99
G-KBPI	PA-28-161 Warrior II	28-7816468	G-BFSZ N9556N	21. 5.81	Goodwood Road Racing Co Ltd	Goodwood	1. 9.99T
G-KCIG	Sportavia Fournier RF5B Sperber	51005	D-KCIG	19. 6.80	J.R.Bisset	Aboyne	18.12.98P
					t/a Deeside Fournier Group		
G-KDET	PA-28-161 Cadet	2841158	(SE-KIR) N91842	8. 8.89	Rapidspin Ltd	Biggin Hill	22.11.99T
					(Op Biggin Hill School of Flying)		
G-KDEY	Scheibe SF-25E Super Falke	4325	D-KDEY	8. 1.99	J.French	Aston Down	
					t/a Falke Syndicate		
G-KDFF	Scheibe SF-25E Super Falke	4330	D-KDFF	25. 4.83	K. & S.C.A.Dudley	Sandtoft	25. 6.01
G-KDIX	Jodel D.9	PFA/54-10293		23.11.78	D.J.Wells	Fenland	20. 4.99P
		(VW1600)					
G-KDLN	LET Zlin Z.37A-2 Cmelak	19-05	OK-DLN	14. 8.95	J.Richards	Dunkeswell	20.12.98
G-KEAB*	Beechcraft 65-B80 Queen Air	LD-344	G-BSSL	3. 8.88	Northbrook College	Shoreham	27. 9.87T
			G-BFEP/F-BRNR/OO-VDE		(Instructional airframe 8.97)		
G-KEAC	Beechcraft 65-A80 Queen Air	LD-176	G-REXY	3. 8.88	E.A.Prentice	Little Gransden	18. 9.89T
			G-AVN/D-ILBO		t/a G-KEAC F/Grp (Stored 11.96)		
G-KEEN	Stolp SA.300 Starduster Too	800	PH-HAB	19. 7.78	H.Sharp t/a Sharp Aerobatics	Eglinton	6. 4.99P
		(Lyc IO-540)		(PH-PET)/G-KEEN/N800RE			
G-KEES	PA-28-180 Cherokee Archer	28-7505025	OO-AJV OO-HAC/N32102	29. 5.97	C.N.Ellerbrook	(Wymondham)	27. 8.00
G-KELL	Van's RV-6	PFA/181-12845		16. 5.95	J.D.Kelsall	Netherthorpe	14. 6.99P
G-KEMC	Grob G-109	6024	D-KEMC	19.10.84	D.L.H.Person, G.H.N.Chamberlain & R.S.Kiddy		
					t/a Eye-Fly	Rattlesden	25. 2.00
G-KEMI	PA-28-181 Archer III	28-43180	N41493	28.10.98	R.B. Kempster	Panshanger	
G-KENB	Air Command 503 Commander	PFA G/04-1153		7.11.89	K.Brogden	Heywood, Lancs	24.9.93P*
G-KENI	Rotorway Exec 152	3599		14. 3.89	A.J.Wheatley	Ley Farm, Chirk	6. 1.95P
		(RW 152)			(Stored 8.93)		
G-KENM	Luscombe 8EF Silvaire	2908	N21NK N71481/NC71481	9. 1.91	M.G.Waters	Compton Abbas	29. 9.99P
G-KENN*	Robinson R-22 Beta	0715		10.12.87	The Hangar Nightclub	Stamford, Lincs	1. 1.97T
					(Damaged Sandtoft 31.10.94; rebuilt to static condition)		
G-KERY	PA-28-180 Cherokee C	28-3049	G-ATWO N9021J	5.10.83	Seawing F/C Ltd & E.Alexander	Southend	13. 4.01T
					t/a General Aero Svs		
G-KEST	Steen Skybolt	1	G-BNKG	11. 6.91	B.Tempest	Leicester	16.10.99P
		(Lyc IO-360)	G-RATS/G-RHFI/N443AT		t/a G-KEST Syndicate		

Regn	Type	C/n	P/I	Date	Owner/operator	Probable Base	CA Expy
G-KEVB	PA-28-181 Archer III	2843098	N9289E	29. 8.97	Palmair Ltd	(London NW11)	3. 9.00
G-KEVN	Robinson R-22 Beta	0781	G-BONX	5. 6.91	Burman Aviation Ltd	Cranfield	22. 4.00T
G-KEYS	PA-23-250 Aztec F	27-7854052	N63909	6.10.78	T.M.Tuke & W.T.McCarter	Eglinton	4. 6.00T
G-KEYY	Cameron N-77 HAFB	1748	G-BORZ	14. 6.88	B.N.Trowbridge	Derby	29. 8.99A
G-KFAN	Scheibe SF-25B Falke	46301	D-KFAN	14. 5.96	R.G & J.A.Boyes	Eaglescott	29. 5.99
G-KFOX	Denney Kitfox mk.2 298 & PFA/172-11447 (Rotax 582)			11.10.88	I.R.Lawrence	Eaglescott	16.12.99P
G-KFRA	PA-32-300 Six	32-7840182	G-BGII N20879	9. 9.97	M.Drake & W.Rankin Weston, Ireland t/a West India Flying Group		10.11.00
G-KFZI	Williams KFZ-1 Tigerfalck PFA/153-11054 (Cont C90) (Originally laid-down as Kestrel Sport c/n PFA/1530)			2. 2.89	L.R.Williams	(Aberdare)	
G-KGMT	Aerospatiale AS.355F1 Twin Squirrel		G-PASE N57818	7. 8.98	Police Aviation Services Ltd	Rochester	18. 7.99T
G-KHOM	Aeromot AMT-200 Super Ximango 200-091			5. 5.98	O.C.Masters & K.M.Haslett	Rufforth	4. 5.01
G-KHRE	Socata Rallye 150SV Garnement	2931	F-GAYR	25. 3.82	J.L.Clarke Kilrea, Co.Londonderry		19.10.00
G-KIMB	Robin DR.300/140 Major	470	F-BPXX F-WPXX	23. 3.90	R.M.Kimbell	Sywell	8. 5.00
G-KINE	Gulfstream AA-5A Cheetah	AA5A-0896	N27173	20. 7.82	J.P.E.Walsh Elstree t/a Walsh Avn (Op London School of Flying)		24. 7.00T
G-KIRK	Piper J3C-65 Cub (Frame No.12490)	10536	F-BBQC F-OAJF/Fr AF/43-29245	28. 2.79	M.J.Kirk Barry, S.Glamorgan		15. 9.99P
G-KISS	Rand Robinson KR.2 (VW1835)	PFA/129-10899		2. 8.83	E.A.Rooney	(Whitstable)	
G-KITE	PA-28-181 Archer II	28-8490053	N4338X	12. 4.88	L.G.Kennedy	Liverpool	13. 4.98T
G-KITF	Denney Kitfox mk.1 (Rotax 532)	156	N156BH	10. 5.89	R.Burgun	Melbourne, Derby	16. 1.98P
G-KITI	Pitts S-2E Special (Lyc IO-360)	002	N36BM	21. 6.90	B.R.Cornes "Super Turkey II" RAF Lyneham		15. 4.99P
G-KITS	Europa Avn Europa Tri-gear (Midwest AE100R) 003 & PFA/247-12844			13. 6.94	Europa Avn Ltd	Wombleton	3.12.99P
G-KITT	Curtiss TP-40M Kittyhawk 27490 (Officially c/n quoted as "31423") (C/n 31423 was P-40N 43-23484/RCAF 877/N1009N(1) & was scrapped in 1965. The identity was adopted by RCAF 840)		F-AZPJ N1009N/N1233N/RCAF 840/43-5802	4. 3.98	Patina Ltd Duxford (Op The Fighter Collection) (As "49/Bengal Tiger" in US Army c/s)		28. 6.99P
G-KITY	Denney Kitfox mk.2 456 & PFA/172-11565			18. 8.89	T.Ringshaw t/a Kitfox KFM Grp	(Nottingham)	13.12.99P
G-KIWI	Cessna 404 Titan Courier II 404-0644		G-BHNI LN-LGM/SE-IFV/G-BHNI/(N5302J)	25. 1.90	Aviation Beauport Ltd	Jersey	5. 2.00T
G-KKDL	Socata TB-20 Trinidad	1096	G-BSHU	3.12.90	Egerton Hospital Equipment Ltd Biggin Hill		14. 8.99
G-KKES	Socata TB-20 Trinidad	1316	G-BTLH	2. 3.92	Polestar Holdings Ltd		15. 4.01T
G-KLEE	Bell 206B JetRanger III	3370	G-SIZL G-BOSW/N2063T	11.10.95	L.D.Taylor-Ryan White Waltham t/a Taylor-Ryan Avn		1. 4.01T
G-KLIK	Air Command 532 Elite PFA G/04-1113 (Arrow GT500)			21. 4.89	R.M.Savage Penrith t/a Roger Savage (Photography)		6. 8.99P
G-KNAP	PA-28-161 Warrior II	28-8116129	G-BIUX N9507N	15. 2.90	Newland Aeroleasing Ltd	Humberside	28. 4.99T
G-KNOB	Lindstrand LBL-180A HAFB	065		20.12.93	Wye Valley Avn Ltd	Ross-on-Wye	18. 2.99T
G-KNOW	PA-32-300 Six	32-7840111	N9694C	21. 9.88	Hi Fly Ltd	(London W1)	15. 3.01
G-KODA	Cameron O-77 HAFB	1448		26. 3.87	N.J.Milton "Kodasnap"	Bristol	
G-KOKL	Hoffmann H-36 Dimona	36276	D-KOKL	4. 3.98	R.Smith & R.Stembrowicz	(York)	30. 3.01
G-KOLB	Kolb Twinstar mk.3A (Rotax 912UL)	PFA/205-12228		30. 6.93	T.R.Sinclair	Insch	4. 8.99P
G-KOLI	PZL-110 Koliber 150 (Licence-built Socata Rallye)	03900038		23. 7.90	D.Sadler	Insch	17.10.99
G-KONG	Slingsby T-67M Firefly 200	2041	VR-HZP HKG-10/G-7-119	24. 3.94	Hunting Avn Ltd RAF Barkston Heath		3. 8.00T
G-KOOL*	DH.104 Devon C.2/2	04220	VP967	12. 1.82	East Surrey College Gatton Point, Redhill (Instructional airframe 4.93)		
G-KORN	Cameron Berentzen Bottle 70SS HAFB	1655		10. 5.88	R.S.Kent, I M Martin & I Chadwick "Berentzen" Lancing t/a Balloon Preservation Flying Group		4. 7.99A
G-KOTA	PA-28-236 Dakota	28-8011044	N8130R	23.12.88	D.J.Fravigar t/a JF Packaging Church Farm, Croft, Skegness		18. 2.01
G-KPAO	Robinson R-44 Astro	0382	G-SSSS	19.11.98	Avonline Group Ltd Bristol/Lulsgate		20.11.00T
G-KRAY	Robinson R-22HP	0266	EI-CEF G-BOBO/N712BH/N100GV/N90763	25. 5.95	Direct Helicopters (Southend) Ltd Southend		11. 6.01T
G-KRES	Stoddard-Hamilton Glasair IIS RG PFA/149-12984			12. 6.96	G.Kresfelder	(London SW11)	
G-KRII	Rand-Robinson KR-2	PFA/129-10934		4. 8.89	M.R.Cleveley	(Halesworth, Suffolk)	
G-KRIS	Maule M.5-235C Lunar Rocket	7357C	N56420	21. 4.81	Maggie Penny Movenis, Co.Londonderry		26. 3.99
G-KSIR	Stoddard-Hamilton Glasair IIS RG (Lyc IO-360) 2151 & PFA/149-12137			15. 4.94	The Hon R.Cayzer	Oxford	6. 8.98P
G-KSVB	PA-24-260 Comanche B	24-4657	G-ENIU G-AVJU/N9199P	8.11.91	Janice R.Pettit	Stapleford	28. 5.01
G-KTEE	Cameron V-77 HAFB	2177		28.12.89	D.C. & N.P.Bull "Katie"	Aylesbury	9. 5.99A
G-KTKT	Sky 260-24 HAFB	110		19. 5.98	T.M.Donnelly	Doncaster	

Regn	Type	C/n	P/I	Date	Owner/operator	Probable Base	CA Expy
G-KUTU	QAC Quickie Q.2 (Limbach L2000)	PFA/94A-10758		8. 3.82	J.Parkinson & R.Nash (Damaged Cranfield 18.5.85; stored 6.97)	Booker	29. 4.86P
G-KVBF	Cameron A-340HL HAFB	4313		6. 4.98	Virgin Balloon Flights Ltd	London SE16	7. 4.99T
G-KWAX	Cessna 182E Skylane	182-53808	N9902 YV-T-PTS/N2808Y	18. 5.78	J.E. & V.T.Brewis	Ronaldsway	7. 4.00
G-KYAK	SPP Yakovlev YAK C-11	171101	F-AZQI G-KYAK/F-AZHQ/G-KYAK/Israeli DFAF/Egyptian AF 590/Czech AF	21.12.78	M.Gainza	(London SW3)	
G-KWIK	Partenavia P.68B	152		27. 9.78	ACD Cidra NV	Wevelgem, Belgium	3. 6.00T
G-KWIP	Europa Avn Europa 27 & (Rotax 912UL)	PFA/247-12557		26. 9.95	D.Elliott	Ashbourne	30. 6.99P
G-KWKI	QAC Quickie Q.200 (Cont O-200-A)	PFA/94-12158		22.10.91	B.M.Jackson	Enstone	17. 9.99P
G-KWLI	Cessna 421C Golden Eagle II	421C-0168	G-DARR G-BNEZ/N87386	13.11.98	Golden Eagle Haulage Ltd	(York)	12.11.99

G-LAAA-LZZZ

Regn	Type	C/n	P/I	Date	Owner/operator	Probable Base	CA Expy
G-LABS	Europa Avn Europa PFA/247-12595			1. 3.94	C.T.H.Pattinson	(Bicester)	
G-LACA	PA-28-161 Warrior II	28-7816036	N44883	22. 6.90	LAC (Enterprises) Ltd	Barton	9. 1.99T
					t/a Lancashire A/C		
G-LACB	PA-28-161 Warrior II	28-8216035	N8450A	12. 6.90	LAC (Enterprises) Ltd	Barton	5. 7.99T
					t/a Lancashire A/C		
G-LACD	PA-28-181 Archer III	28-43157	G-BYBG	11.11.98	A.W.Brown	Barton	28. 9.01T
			N47BK		t/a Cavok Aviation		
G-LACE	Europa Avn Europa PFA/247-12962			15. 4.96	J.H.Phillingham	(Wallingford)	
G-LACR	Denney Kitfox PFA/172-11945			4.12.90	C.M.Rose	(Edinburgh)	
G-LADE	PA-32-300 Six	32-7940030	N3008L	21.11.80	Telefax 2000 Ltd "Harry O"	White Waltham	19. 2.99
G-LADI	PA-30-160 Twin Comanche	30-334	G-ASOO	8. 4.94	E.C.Clark	Biggin Hill	5. 5.00T
G-LADS	Rockwell Commander 114	14314	N4994W	6.12.90	D.F.Soul	Emberton, Olney	5. 1.00
			(N114XT)/N4994W				
G-LAGR	Cameron N-90 HAFB	1628		25. 1.88	J.R.Clifton	Brackley	9. 9.99A
G-LAIN	Robinson R-22 Beta	1992		7. 2.92	Quay Contracts Ltd	(Portsmouth)	23. 4.01T
G-LAIR	Stoddard-Hamilton Glasair IIS	2106		12. 9.91	D.L.Swallow	(Norwich)	
G-LAKE	Lake LA-250 Renegade	70	(EI-PJM)	12. 7.88	Stanford Ltd (Op P.J.McGoldrick)		
			G-LAKE/N8415B			Lough Derg Marina, Killaloe	31. 8.01
G-LAMA	Aerospatiale SA.315B Lama	2348	SE-HET	17. 3.98	PLM Dollar Group Ltd	Cumbernauld	19. 3.01T
G-LAMM	Europa Avn Europa PFA/247-12941			20.11.95	S.A.Lamb	(Paddock Wood)	
G-LAMS	Reims Cessna F.152 II	1431	N54558	23. 6.88	Rentair Ltd	Earls Colne	2.10.00T
					(Op Essex Flying School)		
G-LANC*	Avro 683 Lancaster B.X	-		31. 1.85	Imperial War Museum	Duxford	
			RCAF KB889		(As "KB889/NA-I" in 428 Sqn c/s)		
G-LAND	Robinson R-22 Beta	0639		28. 4.87	Helicopter Training & Hire Ltd		
						Aldergrove	29. 3.02T
G-LANE	Reims Cessna F.172N Skyhawk II	1853		27. 6.79	G.C.Bantin	Sproatley	26. 5.00
G-LAPN	Light Aero Avid Aerobat PFA/189-12146			4. 3.93	R.M. & A.P.Shorter	White Waltham	26.10.98P
	(Rotax 582)						
G-LARA	Robin DR.400/180 Regent	2050		14. 2.91	K.D. & C.A.Brackwell	Goodwood	23. 4.00
G-LARE	PA-39 Twin Comanche C/R	39-16	N8861Y	20. 2.91	Glareways (Neasden) Ltd	Biggin Hill	12. 6.00
G-LARK	Helton Lark 95	9517	N5017J	3.12.85	J.Fox	Booker	26. 3.99P
G-LASR	Stoddard-Hamilton Glasair II	2106		8. 1.90	G.Lewis	(Wirral)	
G-LASS	Rutan VariEze PFA/74-10209			20. 9.78	S.Roberts	Enstone	16. 8.99P
	(Cont O-200-A)						
G-LAST	Cessna 340 II	340-0305	G-UNDY	2. 9.96	Last Engineering Ltd	Cambridge	30. 4.00
			G-BBNR/N69452				
G-LATK	Robinson R-44 Astro	0064	G-BVMK	18. 7.94	Holly Aviation Ltd	Cambridge	27. 8.00
G-LAVE	Cessna 172R Skyhawk	172-80663	G-BYEV	10. 3.99	Wycombe Air Centre Ltd	Booker	
			N2377J/N41297				
G-LAXY	Everett Gyroplane Srs.3			17. 2.94	G.D.Western	(Ipswich)	
	035 & PFA G/03-1233						
G-LAZA	Lazer Z.200 PFA/123-12682			15. 6.95	M.Hammond	Hardwick	27. 8.99P
	(Lyc AEIO-360)						
G-LAZR	Cameron O-77 HAFB	2240		6. 3.90	Laser Civil Engineering Ltd	Pershore	10. 6.97A
					"Laser Engineering"		
G-LAZY	Lindstrand LBL Armchair SS HAFB	129		18. 9.94	The Air Chair Co Ltd "The Chair"		
						Westville, Indiana, USA	16. 4.99A
G-LAZZ	Stoddard-Hamilton Glastar			31.10.96	A.P.Hinchcliffe	(Bristol)	
	PFA/295-13059						
G-LBCS	Colt 31A HAFB	1891		10. 1.91	Virgin Airship & Balloon Co Ltd	Telford	13. 1.96A
					"Lloyds Bank I"		
G-LBLI	Lindstrand LBL-69A HAFB	010		4.11.92	N.M.Gabriel	Kimberley, Notts	22.10.99A
G-LBMM	PA-28-161 Warrior II	28-7816440	N6940C	28.11.89	Flexi-Soft Ltd	Wellesborne Mountford	27. 3.99
G-LBNK	Cameron N-105 HAFB	3559		20. 3.95	Virgin Airship & Balloon Co Ltd	Telford	25. 3.99A
					"Lloyds Bank"		
G-LBRC	PA-28RT-201 Arrow IV	28R-7918051	N2245P	20. 7.88	D.J.V.Morgan	Halfpenny Green	3.12.00
G-LCGL	Comper CLA.7 Swift replica PFA/103-11089			1.7.92	J.M.Greenland		
	(Pobjoy Niagara 1A)					Blackacre Farm, Holt, Wilts	15.11.99P
G-LCIO*	Colt 240A HAFB	1381		23. 1.89	British Balloon Museum	Newbury	
					(Stored 12.94)		
G-LCON	Eurocopter AS.355N Twin Squirrel	5572		28. 6.94	Lancashire Constabulary	Warton	19.10.00T
					(Op Lancashire Air Support Unit)		
G-LCRC	Boeing 757-23A	24636	G-IEAB	27.10.93	Airtours International Airways Ltd		
						Manchester	9. 5.99T
G-LDYS	Thunder Ax6-56Z HAFB	347		18. 5.81	P.Glydon & M.J.Myddelton "Gladys"		
	(Regd as Colt 56A)					Birmingham/Keynsham	3. 6.97A
G-LEAF	Reims Cessna F.406 Caravan II	0018	EI-CKY	7. 3.96	Atlantic Air Transport Ltd	Coventry	20. 5.00T
			PH-ALN/OO-TIW/F-WZDX				
G-LEAM	PA-28-236 Dakota	28-8011061	G-BHLS	1. 7.80	C.S.Doherty	Gamston	8. 7.01
			N35650				
G-LEAP	PBN BN-2T Turbine Islander	2183	G-BLND	19. 8.87	R.M.Burnett	AAC Netheravon	17. 4.00A
					t/a Army Parachute Association		
G-LEAR	Gates Learjet 35A	35A-265	G-ZEST	20. 8.79	Northern Executive Avn Ltd	Manchester	10. 1.00T
			N1462B				
G-LEAU	Cameron N-31 HAFB	761		5. 8.81	P.L.Mossman "Perrier"	Bristol	24. 2.97A

Regn	Type	C/n	P/I	Date	Owner/operator	Probable Base	CA Expy
G-LECA	Aerospatiale AS.355F1 Twin Squirrel	5043	G-BNBK C-GBKH	6. 2.87	South Western Electricity plc	Bristol/Lulsgate	2. 5.99T
G-LEDA	Robinson R22 Beta	1938	G-IFOX	12.11.98	E.D.Obeng t/a Pentacle	Denham	13.11.00T
G-LEDN	Short SD.3-30 Var.100	SH.3064	5N-AOX G-BIOF/G-14-3064/EI-BNM/G-BIOF/N280VY/N4270A/G-BIOF	12. 1.89	Streamline Avn (SW) Ltd	Luton	5.4.99TC
G-LEED	Denney Kitfox Mk.2 450 & PFA/172-11577 (Rotax 582)			24. 4.91	G.T.Leedham	Netherseal	25. 6.99P
G-LEEM*	PA-28R-200 Cherokee Arrow II	28R-7435289	G-BJXW OY-CB/SE-GID/OO-HJN/N43700	28. 5.85	Not known	Aldergrove	30. 6.91
					(Damaged nr Newtownards 14.5.91; wreck stored 1.93)		
G-LEES	Glaser-Dirks DG-400	4-238		4.10.88	C.A.Marren t/a G-LEES Grp "800"	RAF Upavon	25. 1.01
G-LEEZ	Bell 206L-1 LongRanger II	45761	G-BPCT D-HDBB/N3175G	22. 1.92	Pennine Helicopters Ltd	Oldham	13.11.00T
G-LEGG	Reims Cessna F.182Q Skylane II	0145	G-GOOS	26. 6.96	P.J.Clegg	Barton	11.11.99
G-LEGO	Cameron O-77 HAFB	1975		14. 4.89	C.H.Pearce Construction plc "Jigsaw II"	Bristol	10. 8.96A
G-LEGS	Short SD.3-60 Var.100	SH.3637	G-BLEF	7. 3.84	Loganair Ltd	Glasgow	8. 3.99T
G-LEIC	Reims Cessna FA.152 Aerobat	0416		16. 9.86	Leicestershire Aero Club Ltd	Leicester	24. 4.99T
G-LEMJ	Hughes 269C	14-0272	G-BMYW N8999F	27. 8.98	L.J.J.Leeman (Buggen Hout, Belgium)		26. 3.00T
G-LEND	Cameron N-77 HAFB	2012		25. 5.89	Southern Flight Co Ltd "Southern Finance Co"/"Glenda"	Southampton	12. 9.96T
G-LENI	Aerospatiale AS.355F1 Twin Squirrel	5311	G-ZFDB G-BLEV	9. 8.95	Grid Aviation Ltd	Denham	21. 4.00T
G-LENN	Cameron V-56 HAFB	1833		29. 9.88	M.D.H.Jenkins	Edinburgh	6. 5.91A
G-LENS*	Thunder Ax7-77Z HAFB	168		3.11.78	Not known (Noted 2.97)	-	N/E(A)
G-LEOS	Robin DR.400/120 Dauphin 2+2	1884		29.11.88	P.G.Newens	Fairoaks	7. 4.01
G-LEPF	Fairchild F.24R-46A Argus III	952	HB-EPF N1041/HB714/43-14988	31. 7.87	J.M.Greenland Blackacre Farm, Holt, Wilts		25.11.99
G-LESJ	Denney Kitfox mk.3 PFA/172-12001 (Rotax 582)			4.10.94	J.H.Mawson t/a G-LESJ Flying Group	Kirkbride	2. 3.99P
G-LEVI	Aeronca 7AC Champion	7AC-4001	N85266 NC85266	17. 4.90	Jean P.A.Pumphrey t/a G-LEVI Grp	White Waltham	9. 7.99P
G-LEXI	Cameron N-77 HAFB	438		26.10.78	D.I.Shuffleton t/a Sedgemoor 500 Balloon Group	Saxmundham	7. 3.93A
G-LEZE	Rutan LongEz PFA/74A-10702 (Cont O-200-A)			31. 3.82	K.G.M.Loyal, A.J.Draper, J.R.J.Giesler & C.McGeachy	Fairoaks	7. 7.98P
G-LEZJ	Denney Kitfox 4-1200 Speedster (Rotax 912UL) PFA/172B-12529			7. 3.96	C.E.Brookes	Egginton	9. 5.99P
G-LEZZ	Stoddard-Hamilton Glastar PFA/295-13241		G-BYCR	4.11.98	L.A.James	(Nuneaton)	
G-LFIX	VS.509 Spitfire Trainer 9 CBAF.8463 (C/n is firewall plate no.)		IAC162 G-15-175/ML407	1. 2.80	Carolyn S.Grace "Nicholson Leslie"	Duxford	8. 5.99P
	(As "ML407/OU-V" (stbd)" in 485 Sqn c/s & "ML407/"NL-D" (port) in 341 Sqn c/s)						
G-LFSA	PA-38-112 Tomahawk	38-78A0430	G-BSFC	22.10.90	Liverpool Flying School Ltd	Liverpool	15. 1.00T
G-LFSB	PA-38-112 Tomahawk	38-78A0072	G-BLYC D-ELID	20.10.94	Liverpool Flying School Ltd	Liverpool	7.10.00T
G-LFSC	PA-28-140 Cherokee Cruiser	28-7425005	G-BGTR OY-BGO	4. 9.95	Liverpool Flying School Ltd "Liverbird I"	Liverpool	27.10.01T
G-LFSD	PA-38-112 Tomahawk II	38-82A0046	G-BNPT N91522	21.10.96	Liverpool Flying School Ltd	Liverpool	22.12.99T
G-LFSE	PA-28R-200 Cherokee Arrow II	28R-7335157	G-BAXT	9. 6.97	Liverpool Flying School Ltd	Liverpool	3. 4.92T
G-LFSI	PA-28-140 Cherokee C	28-26850	G-AYKV	14. 7.89	J.Vickers	Humberside	15.11.01T
G-LFVB	VS.349 Spitfire LF.VB	CBAF.2403 5377M/EP120	8070M	9. 5.94	Patina Ltd (Op The Fighter Collection) "City of Winnipeg" (As "EP120/AE-A" in 402 Sqn c/s)	Duxford	10. 7.99P
G-LGRM	Bell 206B JetRanger II	1376	G-OBRU G-GOBP/G-BOUY/N1PE/XC-GUW	7. 1.99	Aeromega Ltd	Stapleford	3.12.00T
G-LIBB	Cameron V-77 HAFB	2463		21. 6.91	R.R.McCormick & R.J.Mercer	Belfast	9. 5.99A
G-LIBS	Hughes 369HS (500C)	43-0469S	N9147F	20. 8.85	A.Harvey & R.White Whimple, Exeter		14. 5.01T
G-LICK	Cessna 172N Skyhawk II	172-70631	G-BNTR N739LQ	19. 4.88	A.H.Glick t/a Dacebow Avn Leeds-Bradford		1.11.99
G-LIDA	Hoffman HK.36R Super Dimona	36355		15. 4.92	W.D.Inglis	Thruxton	23. 7.98
G-LIDE	PA-31-350 Navajo Chieftain	31-7852156	N27800	26.10.78	Keen Leasing Ltd (Op Woodgate Executive Air Services)	Aldergrove	11.10.00T
G-LIDR	Hoffmann H-36 Dimona	36208	G-BMSK	1. 4.96	J.MacGilvray	North Connel	16. 9.01
G-LIDS	Robinson R-22 Beta	2808		21. 4.98	A.Wall t/a Direct	(Morecambe)	7. 5.01
G-LIFE	Thunder Ax6-56Z HAFB	135		11. 1.78	D.F.Maine "Golden Delicious"	Redditch	31. 7.99A
G-LILY	Bell 206B JetRanger III	4107	G-NTBI C-FIJD	14. 3.95	T.S.Brown	Goodwood	11. 4.99T
G-LIMA	Rockwell Commander 114	14415	N5870N	17.10.78	Tricolore Aeroclub Ltd Biggin Hill		1. 7.01T
G-LINC	Hughes 369HS	43-0467S	C-FDUZ CF-DUZ	14. 5.87	Sleekform Ltd (Sowerby Bridge)		21.11.99T
G-LINE	Eurocopter AS.355N Twin Squirrel	5566		22. 3.94	National Grid Co plc	Oxford	12. 5.00T

Regn	Type	C/n	P/I	Date	Owner/operator	Probable Base	CA Expy
G-LIOA*	Lockheed 10A Electra	1037	N5171N	6. 5.83	The Science Museum	Wroughton	
			NC243/NC14959		(As "NC5171N")		
G-LION	PA-18-135 Super Cub	18-3857	PH-KLB	29. 9.80	C.Moore	Turweston	10. 6.99
	(L-21B-PI) (Frame No.18-3841)		(PH-DKG)		(As "R-167" in R.Neth AF c/s) "Grin 'n Bare It"		
			R.Neth AF R-167/54-2457				
G-LIOT	Cameron O-77 HAFB	2378		7. 8.90	D.Eliot	Aberdeen	21. 8.99A
G-LIPE	Robinson R-22 Beta	1882	G-BTXJ	23. 1.92	F.C.Owen	Burnley	4. 2.01T
G-LISE	Robin DR.500/200i President	0001		27. 7.98	J.Marks	Goodwood	24. 8.01
G-LITE	Rockwell Commander 112A	291	OY-RPP	13. 6.80	J.E.Dixon	Norwich	21. 8.00
G-LITZ	Pitts S-1E Special PFA/09-11131			3. 3.92	Jennifer A.Hughes "Glitz"	Leicester	15.10.99P
	(Lyc IO-360)						
G-LIVA	Enstrom 480	5010	N900SA	27. 8.98	P.D.Bundy	(Stafford)	
			G-PBTT/JA6169				
G-LIVH	Piper J3C-65 Cub (L-4H-PI)	11529	OO-JAN	31. 3.94	M.D.Cowburn	Barton	1. 5.00
	(Frame No.11354)		OO-AAT/OO-PAX/43-30238		(As "330238/A-24" in US Army c/s)		
G-LIZA	Cessna 340A II	340A-1021	G-BMDM	15. 2.90	J.H.Fry & J.C.Merkens	Perth	9.11.98
			ZS-KRH/N4620N				
G-LIZI	PA-28-160 Cherokee	28-52	G-ARRP	26. 1.89	R.J.Walker & J.R.Lawson	Cranwell	19. 6.99
G-LIZY*	Westland Lysander III "504/39"		RCAF 1558	20. 6.86	Imperial War Museum	Duxford	
	(C/n also quoted as "Y1351")		V9300		(As "V9673/MA-J" in 161 Sqn c/s)		
G-LIZZ	PA-E23-250 Aztec E	27-7405268	G-BBWM	26. 7.93	T.D.Nathan, M.J.Barge & G.Walker		
			N40532			Fairoaks	28. 1.00
G-LJCC	Murphy Rebel PFA/232-13355			8. 7.98	J.H.A. Clarke	(Chippenham)	
G-LJET	Gates Learjet 35A	35A-643	(N35NK)	2.12.88	Gama Aviation Ltd	Heathrow	23. 5.01T
			G-LJET/N39418				
G-LLTT	PA-32R-301 Saratoga IIHP	3246060	N9283P	31. 1.97	M.J.Start	Guernsey	30. 1.00
G-LLYD	Cameron N-31 HAFB	3558		20. 3.95	Virgin Airship & Balloon Co Ltd	Telford	17. 7.97A
G-LNYS	Reims Cessna F177RG Cardinal	0120	G-BDCM	30.11.92	J.W.Clarke	Egginton	19.12.99
			OY-BIP				
G-LOAF	Schempp-Hirth Janus CM	36/269	OH-830	10. 3.93	G.W.Kirton	Saltby	19. 8.99
					(Damaged nr Sheffield 14.10.96)		
G-LOAG*	Cameron N-77 HAFB	359		10.11.77	British Balloon Museum	Newbury	6. 4.84A
					"Famous Grouse" (Stored 12.94)		
G-LOAN	Cameron N-77 HAFB	1434		9. 1.87	P.Lawman	Northampton	16. 1.99A
					"Newbury Building Society"		
G-LOAT	Rutan Cozy PFA/159-13213			28. 5.98	P.S. & N.G.Pritchard	(Usk)	
G-LOBO	Cameron O-120 HAFB	3389		3. 1.95	C.A.Butter t/a Solo Aerostatics	Newbury	1. 8.99A
G-LOCH	Piper J3C-90 Cub (L-4J-PI)	12687	HB-OCH	10.12.84	J.M.Greenland		
	(Frame No.12517)		44-80391			Blackacre Farm, Holt, Wilts	5.11.98P
G-LOFA*	Lockheed L.188CF Electra	2002	N359Q	10. 2.94	Atlantic Air Transport Ltd	Coventry	9. 2.00T
			F-OGST/N359AC/TI-LRM/N359AC/HC-AVX/N359AC/VH-ECA		("Pandalink" c/s)		
					(Wfu Coventry for spares 7.98)		
G-LOFB	Lockheed L.188CF Electra	1131	N667F	28. 6.94	Atlantic Air Transport Ltd	Coventry	28. 6.00T
			N133AJ/CF-IJW/N131US				
G-LOFC	Lockheed L.188CF Electra	1100	N665F	15. 6.95	Atlantic Air Transport Ltd	Coventry	15. 6.01T
			N289AC/N6123A				
G-LOFD	Lockheed L-188CF Electra	1143	LN-FOG	12. 6.97	Atlantic Air Transport Ltd	Coventry	15.6.00TC
			LN-MOD/N9745C/(CF-IJC)/N9745C				
G-LOFE	Lockheed L-188CF Electra	1144	EI-CET	5. 1.99	Atlantic Air Transport Ltd	Coventry	AC
			(G-FIGF)/N668Q/N688F/N24AF/N138US				
G-LOFM	Maule MX-7-180A Star Rocket	20027C	N31110	19. 7.95	Atlantic Air Transport Ltd	Coventry	10. 9.01T
G-LOFT	Cessna 500 Citation I	500-0331	LN-NAT	12. 1.95	Atlantic Air Transport Ltd		
	(Unit No.331)		EC-FUM		(Op Atlantic Executive Avn)	Jersey/Coventry	25. 3.00T
			EC-500/LN-NAT/N40AC/N96RE/N86RE/N331CC/(N5331J)				
G-LOGO	MDH Hughes 369E (500E)	0454E	G-BWLC	4.10.96	R.M.Briggs	Brough	27. 2.99T
			HB-XIJ/SE-JAM				
G-LOLL	Cameron V-77 HAFB	2964		4.12.92	C.N.Rawnson	Stockbridge	3. 5.99A
					t/a Test Valley Balloon Group		
G-LOOP	Pitts S-1C Special	850	5Y-AOX	11. 5.78	M.Persaud	White Waltham	19. 5.99P
	(Lyc O-320)				t/a G-LOOP F/Grp		
G-LOOK*	Reims Cessna 172M Skyhawk	1234	PH-MIG	4. 5.79	Not known	Fenland	
					(Damaged Laarbruch 11.8.85; mainplanes stored 8.98)		
G-LOOT*	Embraer EMB-110P1 Bandeirante		G-BNOC	17. 1.91	Not known (Open store 3.99)	Southend	5.10.90T
		110-223	PT-GMP				
G-LORA	Cameron A-250 HAFB	3828		22. 1.96	Global Ballooning Ltd	Uckfield	20. 3.99T
G-LORC	PA-28-161 Cadet	2841339	D-ESTC	12. 1.99	Tindon Ltd	Fakenham	AC
			N9184W/(SE-KMP)/(N620FT)				
G-LORD	PA-34-200T Seneca II	34-7970347	N2908W	6. 5.88	Aerohire Ltd	Manchester	23. 4.00T
G-LORI*	HS.125 Srs.403B	25246	G-AYOJ	19. 7.83	Not known	Lagos, Nigeria	26. 8.84
			9Q-COH/G-AYOJ/(G-5-16)		(Open storage 3.95)		
G-LORN	Avions Mudry CAP.10B	282		4. 3.99	AWE Aeronautics Ltd	Jersey	
G-LORR	PA-28-181 Archer III	2843037		19. 4.96	B.Galt	Edinburgh	14. 5.99
G-LORT	Light Aero Avid mk.4 Speed Wing			12. 2.92	G.E.Laucht	Long Marston	31. 5.99P
	(Rotax 582) 1124 & PFA/189-12219						
G-LORY	Thunder Ax4-31Z HAFB	171		28.11.78	A.J.Moore "Glory"	Northwood, Middx	
G-LOSM	Armstrong-Whitworth Meteor NF.11		WM167	8. 6.84	Hunter Wing Ltd	Bournemouth	6. 5.99P
		S4/U/2342			(Op Jet Heritage Ltd) (As "WM167/M" in 141 Sqdn c/s)		

Regn	Type	C/n	P/I	Date	Owner/operator	Probable Base	CA Expy
G-LOSS	Cameron N-77 HAFB	1369		23. 9.86	D.K.Fish "Crown" (Crown Paints titles)	Bedford	10. 1.97A
G-LOST	Denney Kitfox mk.3 Floatplane (Rotax 618)	PFA/172-12055		10. 8.95	P.N.& S.E.Akass	Beauly, Inverness	2. 6.99P
G-LOTI	Bleriot Type XI rep (ABC Scorpion II)	PFA/88-10410		21.12.78	Brooklands Museum Trust Ltd	Brooklands	19.7.82P*
G-LOTO	BN-2A-26 Islander	530	G-BDWG (N90255)/(C-GYUF)/G-BDWG	27. 7.95	Scottish Parachute Club (Islander) Ltd	Strathallan	2. 8.00A
G-LOUN	Eurocopter AS.355N Twin Squirrel	5627		24. 1.97	Loune Ltd	Oxford	12. 6.00T
G-LOVA	BAe Jetstream 3102	640	G-OAKA 28. 5.98 G-BUFM/G-LAKH/G-BUFM/N410MX/G-31-640 t/a Love Air			London Flight Centre (Stansted) Ltd	Stansted	15. 7.99T
G-LOWA	Colt 77A HAFB	1451		14. 4.89	K.D.Peirce	Cranbrook	7. 6.97A
G-LOWS	Sky 77-24 HAFB	025		19. 3.96	A.J.Byrne & D.J.Bellinger "Dawn Treader"	Thatcham	1. 8.98
G-LOYA	Reims Cessna FR.172J Rocket	0352	G-BLVT PH-EDI/D-EEDI	4. 8.89	T.R.Scorer	Boones Farm, High Garrett, Braintree	31. 5.00
G-LOYD	Aerospatiale SA.341G Gazelle Srs.1 1289 (Rebuilt 1990 using major components of N6957 c/n 1060)		G-SFTC N47298	19. 6.85	Apollo Manufacturing (Derby) Ltd	Ripley, Derbys	13. 3.00
G-LPGI	Cameron A-210 HAFB	4196		13. 8.97	A.Derbyshire	Stretton	29.10.99T
G-LSFI	Gulfstream AA-5A Cheetah	AA5A-0770	G-BGSK	13. 2.84	T.G.Dughan	Linley Hill, Leven	12. 6.00
G-LSHI	Colt 77A HAFB	1264		20. 7.88	Lambert Smith Hampton Group Ltd "Lambert Smith Hampton" Streatley, Berks		12. 7.95A
G-LSKW	Cessna 182P Skylane	182-61095	OO-PWW N7455Q	11. 1.99	B.F.E.Segers & B.Blommarr	(Ekeren, Belgium)	
G-LSMI	Reims Cessna F.152 II	1710		1. 2.80	A.S.Bamrah t/a Falcon F/Svs (Op European Flyers)	Blackbushe	20. 3.99T
G-LSTR	Stoddard-Hamilton Glastar	PFA/295-13093		20. 4.98	R.Y.Kendal	(Newcastle)	
G-LTFB	PA-28-140 Cherokee	28-23343	G-AVLU	28. 2.97	London Transport F/C Ltd	Fairoaks	2. 4.01T
G-LTFC	PA-28-140 Cherokee B	28-26259	G-AXTI	8. 6.94	London Transport F/C Ltd	Fairoaks	1. 9.00T
G-LTRF	Sportavia Fournier RF7	7001	G-EHAP (G-BGVC)/D-EHAP/F-WPXV	10.12.97	L.J.Trute	Belle Vue Farm, Huntshaw, Devon	16. 4.98P
G-LTSB	Cameron LTSB-90 HAFB	4483		15. 1.99	Virgin Airship & Balloon Co Ltd	Telford	12. 1.00
G-LUBE	Cameron N-77 HAFB	1127		25. 2.85	A.C.Rawson "Lubey Loo"	Stafford	6. 8.99A
G-LUCK	Reims Cessna F.150M	1238	PH-LEO D-EHRA	13.12.79	Taylor Aviation Ltd	Rochester	5. 3.01T
G-LUED	Aero Designs Pulsar (Rotax 582)	PFA/202-12122		9. 3.92	J.C.Anderson	Sturgate	4. 2.99P
G-LUFF	Rotorway Exec 90	6191		24. 4.97	D.C.Luffingham	Dymock, Glos	
G-LUFT	Putzer Elster C	011	G-BOPY D-EDEZ	31. 3.92	Bath Stone Co Ltd (Stored as "D-EDEZ" 9.96)	North Coates	
G-LUKE	Rutan LongEz (Lyc O-235)	PFA/74A-10978		4. 7.84	S.G.Busby	Booker	7. 4.99P
G-LUKY	Robinson R-44 Astro	0357		10. 7.97	English Braids Ltd	Gloucestershire	7. 8.00
G-LULU	Grob G-109	6137		6. 9.82	A.P.Bowden	Enstone	15. 5.01
G-LUNA	PA-32RT-300T Turbo Lance II	32R-7987108	N2246Q	19. 3.79	R.J.H.Creese	Fenland	16. 3.00T
G-LUSC	Luscombe 8E Silvaire	3975	D-EFYR LN-PAT/(NC1248K)	1.11.84	M.Fowler (On rebuild 9.97)	Bruntingthorpe	
G-LUSI	Temco Luscombe 8F Silvaire (Cont C85)	6770	N838B	3.10.89	J.P.Hunt & D.M.Robinson	Hurstbourne Tarrant, Hants	20. 5.99P
G-LUST	Luscombe 8E Silvaire (Cont C85)	6492	N2065B NC2065B	9.11.89	M.Griffiths	Gloucestershire	9. 7.98P
G-LUXE	BAe 146 Srs.300	E-3001	G-5-300 G-SSSH/(G-BIAD)	9. 4.87	British Aerospace (Operations) Ltd	Woodford	8. 5.98S
G-LYDA	Hoffmann H-36 Dimona	3515	OE-9213	5. 4.94	M.A.Holmes & M.J.Philpott t/a G-LYDA Flying Group	Booker	18. 9.00
G-LYDD*	PA-31 Turbo Navajo	31-537	G-BBDU N6796L	8. 5.89	Not known (Damaged Lydd 17.7.91; fuselage stored 6.96)	Blackpool	12. 5.89T
G-LYND	PA-25-235 Pawnee (Rebuild of G-BSFZ c/n 25-2246 with new frame)	25-6309	SE-IXU G-BSFZ/G-ASFZ/N6672Z	8. 9.93	Lleweni Parc Ltd	Lleweni Parc	18. 9.99
G-LYNE	North American P-51D-20NA Mustang	122-31887	IDF/AF 41 N22B/44-72028	5.12.95	E.N.Robinson & M.C.B.Anderson Darlington t/a P-51D Restoration Grp (On rebuild 12.95)		
G-LYNK	CFM Shadow Srs.DD	303-DD		12.10.98	G.Linskey	(Douglas, IOM)	AC
G-LYNX*	Westland WG.13 Lynx 800	WA/102	(ZA500) G-LYNX	6.11.78	Westland Helicopters Ltd (As "ZB500" in Army c/s) (To The Helicopter Museum 8.98)	Weston-super-Mare	13.12.83PF
G-LYON	McDonnell Douglas DC-10-30	47818	N537MD S2-ADB/N115WA/N519MD/PP-VMS/9V-SDG	11. 3.98	Caledonian Airways Ltd	Gatwick	17. 3.01T
G-LYTE	Thunder Ax7-77 HAFB	1113		29. 9.87	G.M.Bulmer "Crispen"	Hereford	19. 5.91A

G-MAAA-MAZZ

Regn	Type	C/n	P/I	Date	Owner/operator	Probable Base	CA Expy
G-MAAC	Advanced Airship Corpn ANR-1	01		16. 1.89	Advanced Airship Corpn Ltd (Sold incomplete 12.93)	Oswestry	
G-MAAH	BAC One-Eleven 488GH	BAC.259	PK-TAL	26. 6.95	Aravco Ltd (Exported 1998)	Farnborough	
			G-BWES/PK-TAL/G-BWES/5N-UDE/LX-MAM/HZ-MAM				
G-MABE	Reims Cessna F.150L Commuter	1119	G-BLJP N962L	20. 6.97	Herefordshire Aero Club Ltd	Shobdon	
G-MACH	SIAI-Marchetti SF.260	1-14	F-BUVY	29.10.80	Cheyne Motors Ltd	Old Sarum	3. 9.99
			OO-AHR/OO-HAZ/(OO-RAB)				
G-MACK	PA-28R-200 Cherokee Arrow II	28R-7635449	N5213F	18. 8.78	Haimoss Ltd	Old Sarum	8.12.01T
G-MAFA	Reims Cessna F.406 Caravan II	0036	G-DFLT F-WZDZ	2. 6.98	Directflight Ltd	Prestwick	6. 6.01T
G-MAFB	Reims Cessna F.406 Caravan II	0080	F-WWSR	27. 5.98	Directflight Ltd	Prestwick	28. 9.01T
G-MAFE	Dornier 228-202K	8009	G-OALF	21.12.92	FR Aviation Ltd	Bournemouth	4.11.99T
			G-MLDO/PH-SDO/D-IDON				
					(Op on behalf of Ministry of Agriculture, Fisheries & Food)		
G-MAFF	PBN BN-2T Turbine Islander	2119	G-BJED	20. 4.82	Cobham Leasing Ltd	Teesside/Bournemouth	25. 9.99T
					(Op on behalf of Ministry of Agriculture, Fisheries & Food)		
G-MAFI	Dornier 228-200	8115	D-CAAE	16. 2.87	Cobham Leasing Ltd	Bournemouth	15. 7.99T
					(Op on behalf of Ministry of Agriculture, Fisheries & Food)		
G-MAGC	Cameron Grand Illusion SS HAFB	4000		19. 1.95	L.V.Mastis	Bristol	30. 5.99A
G-MAGG	Pitts S-1SE Special (Lyc O-360)	PFA/09-10873		17. 3.83	C.A.Boardman	Little Gransden	1. 4.98P
G-MAIK	PA-34-220T Seneca IV	3448078	N73BS	17.11.97	Mydon Enterprises Ltd	(Greece)	26.11.00
G-MAIR	PA-34-200T Seneca II	34-7970140	N3029R	15. 2.89	Barnes Olson Aeroleasing Ltd		
					(Op Bristol Flying Centre)	Bristol/Lulsgate	9. 4.01T
G-MAJA	BAe Jetstream 4100	41032	G-4-032	22. 4.94	British Regional Airlines Ltd	Ronaldsway	24. 5.99T
G-MAJB	BAe Jetstream 4100	41018	G-BVKT N140MA/G-4-018	1. 6.94	British Regional Airlines Ltd	Ronaldsway	8. 6.00T
G-MAJC	BAe Jetstream 4100	41005	G-LOGJ	12. 9.94	British Regional Airlines Ltd	Ronaldsway	20.12.00T
G-MAJD	BAe Jetstream 4100	41006	G-WAWR	27. 3.95	British Regional Airlines Ltd	Ronaldsway	2. 3.01T
G-MAJE	BAe Jetstream 4100	41007	G-LOGK	12. 9.94	British Regional Airlines Ltd	Ronaldsway	24. 2.00T
G-MAJF	BAe Jetstream 4100	41008	G-WAWL	6. 2.95	British Regional Airlines Ltd	Ronaldsway	18. 3.99T
G-MAJG	BAe Jetstream 4100	41009	G-LOGL	16. 8.94	British Regional Airlines Ltd	Ronaldsway	30. 3.99T
G-MAJH	BAe Jetstream 4100	41010	G-WAYR	4. 4.95	British Regional Airlines Ltd "Viscount Tonypandy"	Ronaldsway	13. 4.00T
G-MAJI	BAe Jetstream 4100	41011	G-WAND	20. 3.95	British Regional Airlines Ltd	Ronaldsway	27. 4.01T
G-MAJJ	BAe Jetstream 4100	41024	G-WAFT G-4-024	27. 2.95	British Regional Airlines Ltd	Ronaldsway	28.10.99T
G-MAJK	BAe Jetstream 4100	41070	G-4-070	27. 7.95	British Regional Airlines Ltd (Wings of the City t/s)	Ronaldsway	2. 9.00T
G-MAJL	BAe Jetstream 4100	41087	G-4-087	1. 4.96	British Regional Airlines Ltd	Ronaldsway	16. 5.00T
G-MAJM	BAe Jetstream 4100	41096	G-4-096	23. 9.96	British Regional Airlines Ltd	Ronaldsway	29.10.99T
G-MAJR	DHC.1 Chipmunk 22	C1/0699	WP805	25. 9.96	C.Adams t/a Chipmunk Shareholders	(Gosport)	
G-MAJS	Airbus A.300B4-605R	604	F-WWAX	26. 4.91	Monarch Airlines Ltd	Luton	25. 4.99T
G-MALA	PA-28-181 Archer II	28-8190055	G-BIIU N82748	6. 3.81	D.C. & M.E.Dowell t/a M & D Avn	Kemble	16. 4.99T
G-MALC	Grumman-American AA-5 Traveler	AA5-0664	G-BCPM N6170A	19.11.79	B.P.Hogan	Sywell	22. 5.00
G-MALS	Mooney M.20K (231)	25-0573	N1061T	16. 8.84	J.Houlberg t/a G-MALS Grp	Blackbushe	25. 4.99
G-MALT	Colt Flying Hop SS HAFB	1447		14. 4.89	P.J.Stapley "Hoppie"	Redcar	11. 9.97A
G-MAMC	Rotorway Exec 90 (RI 162)	5057		24. 5.94	J.R.Carmichael (Damaged Cumbernauld 22.9.98)	Cumbernauld	
G-MAMO	Cameron V-77 HAFB	1616		17.11.87	The Marble Mosaic Co Ltd "Osprey"	Portishead	17. 4.99A
G-MANA	BAe ATP	2056	G-LOGH G-11-056	21. 2.94	British Regional Airlines Ltd	Ronaldsway	21. 3.98T
G-MANB	BAe ATP	2055	G-LOGG G-JATP/G-11-055	14. 9.94	British Regional Airlines Ltd	Ronaldsway	26. 9.99T
G-MANC	BAe ATP	2054	G-LOGF G-11-054	7.11.94	British Regional Airlines Ltd	Ronaldsway	20.10.00T
G-MAND	PA-28-161 Warrior II	28-8116284	G-BRKT N8082Z	8. 3.93	Halfpenny Green Flight Centre Ltd	Halfpenny Green	3.12.01T
G-MANE	BAe ATP	2045	G-LOGB G-11-045	7. 6.94	British Regional Airlines Ltd	Ronaldsway	26. 2.99T
G-MANF	BAe ATP	2040	G-LOGA	19. 9.94	British Regional Airlines Ltd	Ronaldsway	5.11.99T
G-MANG	BAe ATP	2018	G-LOGD G-OLCD	22. 8.94	British Regional Airlines Ltd (Damaged on landing Manchester 18.3.98)	Ronaldsway	28. 9.99T
G-MANH	BAe ATP	2017	G-LOGC G-OLCC	16.11.94	British Regional Airlines Ltd	Ronaldsway	14. 8.99T
G-MANI	Cameron V-90 HAFB	3038		8. 3.93	M.P.G.Papworth	Ilkley	30. 8.01T
G-MANJ	BAe ATP	2004	G-LOGE G-BMYL	6. 9.94	British Regional Airlines Ltd	Ronaldsway	14. 4.01T

Regn	Type	C/n	P/I	Date	Owner/operator	Probable Base	CA Expy
G-MANL	BAe ATP	2003	G-ERIN	3.10.94	British Regional Airlines Ltd		
			G-BMYK		(Op British Midland Airways Ltd)	East Midlands	25. 5.99T
G-MANM	BAe ATP	2005	G-OATP	17.10.94	British Regional Airlines Ltd		
			G-BZWW/(N375AE)/G-BZWW "Elaine Griffiths"			Ronaldsway	20. 3.99T
G-MANN	Aerospatiale SA.341G Gazelle 1	1295	G-BKLW	14. 4.86	First City Air plc	Thruxton	11. 7.01T
			N4DQ/N4QQ/N444JJ/N47316/F-WKQH				
G-MANO	BAe ATP	2006	OK-TFN	28.11.94	Manx Airlines Ltd	Ronaldsway	18. 1.02T
			G-MANO/G-UIET/G-11-5/(N376AE) (Rendezvous t/s)				
G-MANP	BAe ATP	2023	OK-VFO	28.10.94	Manx Airlines Ltd	Ronaldsway	25.10.00T
			G-MANP/G-PEEL				
G-MANS	BAe 146 Srs.200	E-2088	G-CHSR	5. 5.94	Manx Airlines Ltd	Ronaldsway	25. 4.00T
			G-5-088				
G-MANT*	Cessna 210L Centurion II	210-60970	G-MAXY	22. 5.85	Not known	Great Yarmouth	2.10.94
			N550SV				
			(Damaged nr Kidlington 16.2.92; displayed Sea-front Crazy Golf course 8.97)				
G-MANU	BAe ATP	2008	G-BUUP	20. 8.97	British Regional Airlines Ltd Ronaldsway		24. 3.00T
			CS-TGA/G-11-8/(N378AE)				
G-MANW	Tri-R Kis	PFA/239-12628		12. 9.96	M.T.Manwaring	(Barking)	
G-MANX	Clutton FRED Srs.II PW.2 &	PFA/29-10327		31. 5.78	S.Styles	(Birmingham)	17. 8.82P
	(Ardem 4C02)						
			(Crashed nr Ronaldsway 30.10.81; on rebuild Wellesbourne Mountford 7.90)				
G-MAPR	Beechcraft A36 Bonanza	E-2713	N55916	17. 9.92	Openair Ltd	Blackbushe	2. 9.01
G-MAPS	Sky Flying Map SS HAFB	105		20. 7.98	Virgin Airship & Balloon Co Ltd	Telford	2. 7.99
G-MARA	Airbus A.321-231	983	D-AVZ.	R	Monarch Airlines Ltd	Luton	
					(For dlvy 3.99)		
G-MARE	Schweizer Hughes 269C	S-1320		12. 8.88	The Earl of Caledon		
						Caledon Castle, Co.Tyrone	9.10.00
G-MARY*	Cassutt Racer	2		14. 3.80	Not known Standalone Farm, Meppershall		
					(Under construction 4.91 but see G-TRUC)		
G-MASC	SAN Jodel 150A Mascaret	37	F-BLDZ	1. 2.91	K.F. & R.Richardson		
						Wellesbourne Mountford	12. 5.99P
G-MASF	PA-28-181 Cherokee Archer II		OY-EPT	24. 6.97	Mid-Anglia Flying School Ltd	Cambridge	21. 7.00T
		28-7790191	LN-NAP				
G-MASH	Westland-Bell 47G-4A	WA/725	G-AXKU	3.11.89	Defence Products Ltd	Redhill	4. 2.99
			G-17-10		(US Army c/s)		
G-MASS	Cessna 152 II	152-81605	G-BSHN	6. 3.95	MK Aero Support Ltd	Denham	23. 7.99T
			N65541				
G-MASX	Masquito M.80	03		19. 6.98	Masquito Aircraft NV (Roosdaal, Belgium)		
G-MASY	Masquito M.80	02		19. 6.98	Masquito Aircraft NV (Roosdaal, Belgium)		
G-MASZ	Masquito M.58	01		29. 4.97	Masquito Aircraft NV (Roosdaal, Belgium)		
G-MATE	Moravan Zlin Z.50LX	0068		26.10.90	D.T.Kaberry	Barton	21. 4.01
G-MATT	Robin R.2160	97	G-BKRC	7. 5.85	D.J.Nicholson	East Midlands	15.10.99
			F-BZAC/F-WZAC				
G-MATZ	PA-28-140 Cherokee Cruiser		G-BASI	11.12.90	R.B.Walker	Coventry	13.10.00T
		28-7325200			t/a Midland Air Training School		
G-MAUD	BAe ATP	2002	(G-MANK)	14.12.93	British Regional Airlines Ltd		
			G-MAUD/G-BMYM		(Blue Poole t/s)	East Midlands	13. 6.01T
G-MAUK	Colt 77A HAFB	901		16. 2.87	B.Meeson "Mondial Assistance"	Walsall	4. 6.92A
G-MAVI	Robinson R-22 Beta	0960		7. 2.89	R.M.Weyman	Coventry	26. 4.01T
G-MAWL	Maule M.4-210C Rocket	1065C	D-EEAO	29. 5.81	D.Wallace	Aboyne	3. 4.00
			N2011U				
G-MAXI	PA-34-200T Seneca II	34-7670150	N8658C	11. 2.81	Draycott Seneca Syndicate Ltd		
						(London SW6)	8. 4.00
G-MAYA	Aero L-29 Delfin	394912	ES-YLO	16. 6.98	B.R.Green & P.A.Greenhalgh	Lydd	25.10.99
			Estonian AF 64/Soviet AF 64 (red) t/a Fast Jets Group				
G-MAYO	PA-28-161 Warrior II	28-7716278	G-BFBG	20. 2.81	M.P.Catto	Fairoaks	17. 3.01T
			N38846		t/a Jermyk Engineering		

G-MBAA-MBZZ

Regn	Type	C/n	P/I	Date	Owner/operator	Probable Base	CA Expy
G-MBAA	Hiway Skytrike Mk.II/Excalibur	01		23. 4.81	M.J.Aubrey	Kington, Hereford	
G-MBAB	Hovey WD-II Whing Ding II			26. 5.81	M.J.Aubrey	Kington, Hereford	1. 2.98P
	(Konig SC430) MA-59 & PFA/116-10706						
G-MBAD	Weedhopper JC-24A	0382		3. 6.81	M.Stott	Prudhoe	
G-MBAL	Ultrasports Tripacer/Hiway Demon HD.51			29. 6.81	I.M.Munster	Nottingham	24.10.91E
	(EC-25-PS)						
G-MBAP*	Rotec Rally 2B	PL-1		16. 7.81	P.D.Lucas (Stored 1.91)	Needham	
G-MBAR	Wheeler Scout	389W		8. 7.81	L.Chiappi	Blackburn	
G-MBAW	Pterodactyl Ptraveler	017		14. 7.81	J.C.K.Scardifield	Lymington	31. 8.86E
G-MBBB	Wheeler Scout II	0388W		3. 8.81	A.J. & B.Chalkley	Pwllheli	
G-MBBM	Eipper Quicksilver MX	10960		11. 9.81	J.Brown	Markfield, Leics	
G-MBBY	Ultrasports Tripacer/Flexiform Solo			22. 9.81	R.A.Martin	Rotherham	9. 2.94P
	Sealander (EC-34-PM)	JEH-1					
G-MBBZ*	Volmer VJ-24W (Yamaha KT100)	7		23. 9.81	Not known (Stored 10.97)	Old Sarum	23. 9.93E
G-MBCI	Hiway Skytrike II/Solar Wings Typhoon			30. 9.81	P.A.Kilburn	Urmston, Manchester	3. 9.93P
	T481-119P						
G-MBCJ	Mainair Tri-Flyer/Solar Wings Typhoon S			30. 9.81	R.A.Smith	Doncaster	30. 4.86E
	JRN-1						
G-MBCK	Eipper Quicksilver MX	GWR-10962		30. 9.81	P.Rowbotham	Loughborough	N/E
	(Rotax 377)						
G-MBCL	Hiway Skytrike 160/Solar Wings Typhoon			30. 9.81	P.J.Callis	Kibworth, Leicester	N/E
	2332 & T1181-07 (C/n probably T1181-307)						
G-MBCU	American Aerolights Eagle Amphibian 3181			5.10.81	J.L.May	Portsmouth	22. 4.98P
	(Rotax 377)						
G-MBCX	Hornet 250/Airwave Nimrod 165			12.10.81	M.Maylor	Louth	31.12.87E
	H090 & 0090 LJH						
G-MBDD*	Hiway Skytrike/Demon 175	MM17D		14.10.81	Not known	Newbury	9. 7.98P
	(EC-34-PM) (Regd as MM175D & reported as Mainair Tri-Flyer) (Temp unregd 6.10.97)						
G-MBDE	Sharp & Sons Tartan/Flexiform Solo Striker			15.10.81	A.R.Cantrill	Kirkmichael, IoM	3. 9.96P
	(EC-34-PM)	FS-1					
	(Regd as Ultrasports Tripacer)						
G-MBDG	Eurowing Goldwing	E.20		19.10.81	B.Fussell	Llanelli	14.12.94P
	(Konig SC430)						
G-MBDI*	Flexiform Sealander	KB-1		2.11.81	K.Bryan Sutton-in-Ashfield, Notts		
					(Cancelled by CAA 17.2.99)		
G-MBDJ	Mainair Tri-Flyer/Flexiform Sealander			19.10.81	J.W.F.Hargrave	High Wycombe	10. 2.92E
	(EC-25-PS)	LHP-1					
G-MBDL*	Striplin (AES) Lone Ranger	109		21.10.81	North East Acft Museum	Usworth	
					(Stored in poor condition 4.96)		
G-MBDM	Southdown Sigma	SST/001		26.10.81	A.R.Prentice	Dartford	N/E
	(EC-25-PS)						
G-MBEP*	American Aerolights Eagle 215B	2877		9.11.81	Caernarfon Air Museum	Caernarfon	N/E
	(Cuyuna 215)						
G-MBEI	MEA Mistral Trainer	MEA.103		10.11.81	B.H.Stephens	Southampton	27. 9.98P
	(EC-44-PM)						
G-MBEU	Chargus T.250/Hiway Demon	T.250/06		10.11.81	R.C.Smith	Clacton	31. 5.86E
G-MBEV	Chargus Titan 38	LUFC-01		11.11.81	N.Hooper		
	(EC-44-PM)					Lower Mountpleasent Farm, Wiblington	6. 2.94E
G-MBFK	Hiway Skytrike/Demon 175	LR17D		16.11.81	D.W.Stamp	Kidderminster	N/E
	(EC-25-PS)						
G-MBFO	Eipper Quicksilver MX	MLD-01		17.11.81	J.C.Larkin	Maryport, Cumbria	20. 8.93P
	(Cuyuna 430R)						
G-MBFU*	Ultrasports Tripacer/Hiway Demon THJP-01			23.11.81	Not known	Lyndhurst	16.10.95P
	(EC-25-PS)				(Temp unregd 30.1.96)		
G-MBFZ	MSS Eurowing Goldwing	MSS-01		25.11.81	P.C.Piggott	Lutterworth	5. 9.99P
	(EC-34-PM)						
G-MBGA	Mainair Tri-Flyer/Flexiform Solo Sealander			25.11.81	C.Murphy Ince Blundell, Liverpool		14. 9.97P
	(EC-34-PM)	001					
G-MBGB*	American Aerolights Eagle	JCM-01		25.11.81	J.C.Miles	Blackburn	
					(Cancelled as WFU 2.3.99)		
G-MBGF	Twamley Trike/Birdman Cherokee RWT-01			26.11.81	T.B.Woolley	Leicester	
G-MBGP	Hiway Skytrike/Solar Wings Typhoon			1.12.81	W.Niblett	Frome	9. 1.99P
	(EC-34-PM)	T481-141L					
G-MBGS	Rotec Rally 2B	PCB-1		2.12.81	P.C.Bell	Yalding, Kent	
G-MBGW*	Hiway Skytrike/Super Scorpion			3.12.81	Not known (Stored 10.95)	Davidstow Moor	26. 9.91E
	GWRC-1 & 23						
G-MBGX	Southdown Lightning DS	RBDB-1		7.12.81	T.Knight	Newton Abbot	7. 3.92E
	(EC-44-PM)						
G-MBHE	American Aerolights Eagle	4210		18.12.81	R.J.Osborne	Long Marston	12.10.96P
	(Cuyuna 430R)						
G-MBHJ*	Hornet 250/Skyhook Cutlass B	GH-1		30.12.81	Not known (Stored 12.97)		
					Guy Lane Farm, Waverton, Chester		
G-MBHK	Mainair Tri-Flyer 250/Flexiform Solo Striker			30.12.81	K.T.Vinning	Stratford-on-Avon	11. 8.98P
	(EC-34-PM) EB-1 & 036-241181						
G-MBHZ	Pterodactyl Ptraveler	TD-01		6. 1.82	J.C.K.Scardifield	Lymington	28. 2.86E

Regn	Type	C/n	P/I	Date	Owner/operator	Probable Base	CA Expy
G-MBIA	Hiway Skytrike/Flexiform Sealander (EC-34-PM)	6172349/336		6. 1.82	I.P.Cook	Oldham	N/E
G-MBIO	American Aerolights Eagle 215B (Zenoah G25B1)	E.4007-Z		12. 1.82	B.J.C.Hill	Bridgnorth	N/E
G-MBIT	Hiway Skytrike/Demon (EC-25-PS)	2501		18. 1.82	Kverneland (UK) Ltd	Yarm, Cleveland	N/E
G-MBIY	Ultrasports Tripacer/Lightning Phase II	330		19. 1.82	D.Hamilton-Brown	Crawley	18. 4.99P
G-MBIZ	Mainair Tri-Flyer/Hiway Vulcan	039-251181 & SD9V		20. 1.82	E.F.Clapham, W.B.S.Dobi, S.P.Slade & D.M.A.Templeman	Bristol	
G-MBJA	Eurowing Goldwing (EC-34-PM)	EW-34		20. 1.82	R.McBlain	Maybole, Ayr	29. 8.96P
G-MBJD	American Aerolights Eagle 215B (Zenoah G25B1)	4169		21. 1.82	R.W.F.Boarder	Tring	N/E
G-MBJF	Hiway Skytrike Mk.II/Vulcan 80-00099 (C/n is engine no) (EC-25-PS)			22. 1.82	C.H.Bestwick	Nottingham	31. 1.87E
G-MBJG	Chargus T.250/Airwave Nimrod UP (EC-25-PS)	CMT165045		25. 1.82	D.H.George	Sandown	8. 9.98P
G-MBJK	American Aerolights Eagle	2742		16. 1.82	B.W.Olley	Ely	
G-MBJL	Hornet/Airwave Nimrod (EC-25-PS)	JSRM-01		26. 1.82	A.G.Lowe	Dyce	20.10.96P
G-MBJM	Striplin Lone Ranger	LR-81-00138		26. 1.82	C.K.Brown	Loughborough	
G-MBJN	American Aerolights Eagle 215B MEC-01 (EC-25-PS)			26. 1.82	Mary M.Wallace	Jurby, IoM	29. 6.97P
G-MBJO*	Birdman Cherokee mk.I	CHL-5100680		28. 1.82	C.A.James & T.T.Parr (Cancelled by CAA 15.3.99)	Bristol	
G-MBJS*	Hiway Skytrike/Solar Wings Typhoon S2 (EC-34-PM)	26X7 & T383-731L		28. 1.82	Not known (Rebuild with Trike from G-MWXE)	Mill Farm, Hughley	
G-MBKB*	Pterodactyl Ptraveler	47		3. 2.82	Not known (Stored 8.92)	Longacre Farm, Sandy	
G-MBKC*	Southdown Lightning Phase I 250	DAI-01		3. 2.82	R.I.Deakin (Cancelled by CAA 23.3.99)	Rugby	
G-MBKW*	MEA Pterodactyl Ptraveler (EC-34-PM)	PT-105		10. 2.82	M.L.Smith (Cancelled by CAA 14.5.98)	Sudbury	N/E
G-MBKY	American Aerolights Eagle 215B	ZFE-15288 (C/n is probably engine no.)		12. 2.82	M.J.Aubrey	Kington, Hereford	
G-MBKZ	Hiway Skytrike/Super Scorpion (EC-25-PS)	EC25P8-04 (C/n is corruption of engine type)		12. 2.82	S.I.Harding	Camberley	
G-MBLM	Hiway Skytrike 250/Southdown Sigma	25R7		18. 2.82	D.E.Peace	Leeds	
G-MBLN	MEA Pterodactyl Ptraveler 430D (EC-34-PM)	HCM-01		19. 2.82	F.D.C.Luddington	Bledsoe, Bedford	2. 4.94P
G-MBLO*	Mainair Tri-Flyer/Flexiform Sealander 160	10676		22. 2.82	M.W.Olliver (Cancelled by CAA 10.2.99)	Ringwood	
G-MBLU	Ultrasports Tripacer/Southdown Lightning L195 (EC-25-PS)	L195/191		26. 2.82	C.R.Franklin	Barnstaple	N/E
G-MBMG	Rotec Rally 2B	RJP-01		3. 3.82	J.R.Pyper	Craigavon, Co.Armagh	
G-MBMT	Mainair Tri-Flyer/Southdown Lightning 195 (EC-25-PS)	TRY-01		8. 3.82	D.Hamilton-Brown	Crawley	N/E
G-MBNH*	Southern Aerosports Scorpion	4		23. 3.82	Not known (Stored 7.92)	Branscombe	
G-MBNK	American Aerolights Eagle	E.2398MJ		17. 3.82	R.Moss	Manchester	
G-MBNT	American Aerolights Eagle (EC-25-PS)	MDO-01		24. 3.82	M.P.Harper (Stored 9.95)	Priory Farm, Tibenham	10. 4.95P
G-MBNV	Sheffield Trident	816		24. 3.82	F.Elmore	Sheffield	
G-MBNY	Steer Terror/Manta Pfledge II MJS.II			24. 3.82	M.J.Steer	East Molesey	
G-MBOD*	American Aerolights Eagle	3082		26. 3.82	M.A.Ford, A.F.Little & D.Young (Cancelled by CAA 27.1.98)	Maidenhead/Kemble	
G-MBOF	Pakes Jackdaw	LGP-01		26. 3.82	L.G.Pakes	Ryde, IoW	
G-MBOH	MEA Mistral Trainer (EC-44-PM)	008		29. 3.82	N.A.Bell	Fordingbridge	N/E
G-MBOK	Brooks Pulsar/Solar Wings Typhoon S4 (Sachs Dolmar 153)	153/042/6		1. 4.82	P.Huddleston	Marlborough	9. 5.93E
G-MBON	Eurowing Goldwing	EW-33 & SWA-02		1. 4.82	A.H.Dunlop	Devizes	30. 6.86E
G-MBOU*	Wheeler Scout Mk III/3/R (Regd as c/n 43ZR3)	432R/3		2. 4.82	J.S.Millard (Cancelled as WFU 10.3.99)	Newport, Gwent	
G-MBPG	Mainair Tri-Flyer/Solar Wings Typhoon (EC-25-PS)	189-1983 & T381-105		13. 4.82	S.D.Thorpe	Walsall	30. 4.95P
G-MBPJ	Centrair Moto-Delta G.11	001		14. 5.82	J.B.Jackson	Chester	
G-MBPM	Eurowing Goldwing (EC-34-PM)	EW-21		14. 4.82	A.Gibson t/a Gartmore F/Grp	Wishaw, Strathclyde	21. 8.98P
G-MBPU	Hiway Skytrike/Demon (EC-25-PS)	DSS-01		21. 4.82	B.Curtis	Harlow	4.12.94P
G-MBPW*	Weedhopper JC-24	1306		8. 2.82	D.H.Whisker (Cancelled by CAA 24.3.99)	Sheriff Hutton, York	
G-MBPX	Eurowing Goldwing SP (Konig SC430)	EW-42		21. 4.82	A.R.Channon	Sawston, Cambridge	6.11.96P
G-MBPY	Ultrasports Tripacer 330/Wasp Gryphon (EC-34-PM)	RKP-01		21. 4.82	J.L.Thomas	Bristol	24.10.98P

Regn	Type	C/n	P/I	Date	Owner/operator	Probable Base	CA Expy
G-MBPZ*	Mainair Tri-Flyer 250/Flexiform Striker			23. 8.82	C.R.Harris	Bensons Farm, Laindon	N/E
		CRH-01 & 047-241281			(Stored 3.94)		
G-MBRB	Electraflyer Eagle Mk.I	E.2229		9.12.81	R.C.Bott	Tywyn	
G-MBRD	American Aerolights Eagle 215B	E.2635		20. 4.82	R.J.Osborne	Tiverton	31. 8.85E
G-MBRE	Wheeler Scout	73962		21. 4.82	C.A.Foster	Leicester	
G-MBRH	Ultraflight Mirage Mk.II	RALH-01		20. 4.82	R.W.F.Boarder	Oakley	13. 6.99P
	(Rotax 447)						
G-MBRS	American Aerolights Eagle 215B	RWC.1		23. 4.82	W.J.Phillips (Stored 6.90)	Haverfordwest	31. 8.85E
G-MBSF*	Ultraflight Mirage Mk.II	234		19. 4.82	A.J.Horne	Saffron Walden	
					(Cancelled as wfu 16.2.99)		
G-MBSG*	Ultraflight Mirage Mk.II	235		19. 4.82	P.E.Owen	Dorchester	
					(Cancelled by CAA 12.2.99)		
G-MBST	Mainair Gemini/Southdown Sprint			10. 4.84	G.J.Bowen	Llanelli	9. 4.97P
	(EC-44-PM)	141-29383	(Trike from G-MJXA ?)				
G-MBSX	Ultraflight Mirage II	240		14. 6.82	P.J.Careless & P.Samal	Sandy	20. 9.98P
	(Cuyuna 428)						
G-MBTC	Weedhopper JC-24B	ANM-01		11. 5.82	C.A.Reed (Stored 8.97)	Long Marston	
G-MBTE	Hiway Skytrike/Demon H050			26. 4.82	K.A.Armstrong	Brough	1. 5.95P
	(Hiro 125) (Regd with former Hornet Trike c/n)				(Damaged mid 1994)		
G-MBTF	Mainair Gemini/Southdown Sprint			26. 4.82	J.R.Pyper	Craigavon, Co.Armagh	11.10.98P
	(EC-44-PM)	168-30683					
G-MBTG	Mainair Gemini/Southdown Sprint			26. 4.82	D.M.Pearson	Wallingford	15.10.94P
	(EC-44-PM)	064-19482 & P.431					
G-MBTH	Whittaker MW-4	001	(G-MBPB)	6. 4.82	L.Greenfield & M.Whittaker (Stored 8.97)		
	(EC-34-PM)				t/a The MW4 F/Gtp	Otherton, Cannock	1.12.91E
G-MBTJ	Ultrasports Tripacer/Solar Wings Typhoon			2. 4.82	H.A.Comber	Poole	13. 9.93P
	(EC-25-PS)	CSRS-01					
G-MBTS*	Hovey WD-II Whing-Ding	PFA 8484/7		4. 2.82	T.G.Solomon	Shoreham	
	(C/n is probably owner's PFA membership no)				(Stored in North hangar 10.96)		
G-MBTW	Aerodyne Vector 600	1188		10. 5.82	W.I.Fuller	Cambridge	N/E
G-MBTY*	American Aerolights Eagle	3207		11. 5.82	P.Raymond (Stored 2.96)	Camberley	
G-MBUA	Hiway Demon	RJN-01		30. 4.82	R.J.Nicholson	Lightwater	
G-MBUE*	MBA Tiger Cub 440	MBA-001		29. 4.82	Newark Air Museum	Winthorpe	
	(EC-44-PM)				"The Dormouse Zeitgeist"		
G-MBUK*	Mainair Tri-Flyer/Solar Wings Tyhpoon			30. 4.82	M.J.Curley	London W3	20. 7.95P
	(EC-34-PM)	063-31382 & T582-473			(Cancelled by CAA 26.6.98).		
G-MBUZ	Wheeler (Skycraft) Scout II	0366		4. 5.82	A.B.Cameroon	Auchinleck, Ayr	
					t/a The Affleck Aero Wing F/Grp		
G-MBVS	Hiway Skytrike 250/Super Scorpion 25T3			14. 5.82	M.A.Brown	Hinckley	
G-MBVV	Hiway Skytrike Mk II/Demon 175	IS-01		14. 5.82	G.Hayton	Skipton	27. 1.95P
	(EC-34-PM)						
G-MBVW	Skyhook TR2/Cutlass	TR2/23		14. 5.82	M.Jobling	Harrogate	28. 5.87E
G-MBWE*	American Aerolights Eagle	2937		18. 5.82	A.M.Blackmun	Melton Constable	
					(Cancelled by CAA 24.3.99)		
G-MBWF	Mainair Tri-Flyer/Flexiform Solo Striker			19. 5.82	J.B.Brierley	Tarn Farm, Cockerham	29. 6.95P
	(EC-34-PM)	GAA-01 & 682-01					
G-MBWG	Huntair Pathfinder 1 (EC-34-PM)	006		19. 5.82	R.D.Groves	Magherafelt, Co.Londonderry	14. 7.99P
G-MBWH	Jordan Duet 1	D82001		20. 5.82	Designability Ltd (To Jordan Avn Ltd)		
						St.Leonards-on-Sea	
G-MBWI*	Lafayette Hi-Nuski mk.1	30680		8. 6.82	N.H.Ponsford (Stored 3.96)	Leeds	
G-MBWY*	American Aerolights Eagle	CCCW-1		24. 5.82	J.P.Donovan	Milton Keynes	
					(Cancelled by CAA 15.3.99)		
G-MBXJ*	Hiway Skytrike 250/Demon 175	DM17D		25. 5.82	S.Ward	East Kilbride	
					(Cancelled by CAA 24.3.99)		
G-MBXX	Ultraflight Mirage II	111		21. 1.82	E.J.Girling (Stored St.Just 5.94)		
						Plymouth	N/E
G-MBYD	American Aerolights Eagle 215B	3510		3. 6.82	J.A.Hambleton	Market Drayton	30. 1.92E
	(EC-25-PS)						
G-MBYI	Ultraflight Lazair IIIE	A464/001		4. 6.82	M.Sumner	Market Drayton	5. 3.99P
	(Rotax 185) (Previously quoted c/n A522)						
G-MBYK	Huntair Pathfinder 1	012		4. 6.82	R.C.Barnett	Billericay	17. 6.97P
	(EC-44-2PM)						
G-MBYL	Huntair Pathfinder 1	009		4. 6.82	J.Morton t/a Crazy Capers	Mullaghmore	23. 7.98P
	(EC-44-PM)						
G-MBYM	Eipper Quicksilver MX	JW-01		4. 6.82	M.P.Harper & L.L.Perry		
	(Cuyuna 430R)					Priory Farm, Tibenham	21. 9.96P
G-MBYO*	American Aerolights Eagle	4467		8. 6.82	B.J.& M.G.Ferguson	Crawley	
					(Cancelled by CAA 24.3.99)		
G-MBYR*	American Aerolights Eagle	3310		25. 6.82	G.Walker	Burnley	
					(Cancelled by CAA 24.3.99)		
G-MBYT*	Ultraflight Mirage Mk.II	98		14. 6.82	Not known	Letterkenny, Ireland	26. 9.93E
	(Kawasaki TA440)				(Stored 8.95)		
G-MBYX*	American Aerolights Eagle	E 2904		9. 6.82	N.P.Austen	Liskeard	
					(Cancelled by CAA 24.3.99)		
G-MBZA*	Ultrasports Tripacer/Hiway Demon 175			10. 6.82	Not known	Chandlers Ford	8. 1.95P
	(EC-25-PS)	MAR-01 & 100873	(Regd as Mainair Tri-Flyer 330) (Temp unregd 29.6.95)				

Regn	Type	C/n	P/I	Date	Owner/operator	Probable Base	CA Expy
G-MBZH	Eurowing Goldwing (EC-34-PM)	EW-50		14. 6.82	J.Spavins	Long Acre Farm, Sandy	31. 3.99P
G-MBZJ	Southdown Puma (Lightning) (EC-34-PM)	L170-415		14. 6.82	A.K.Webster	Wallingford	1. 8.98P
G-MBZK	Ultrasports Tripacer 250 /Solar Wings Typhoon	AAL-01		14. 6.82	J A Crofts	Carmarthen	
G-MBZN	Southdown Puma (Lightning DS) (EC-44-PM)	80-00131 & DJC-01		14. 6.82	A.Brown	Ely	N/E
G-MBZO	Mainair Tri-Flyer/Flexiform Medium Striker (EC-34-PM)	GRH-01 & 021-101081		15. 6.82	A.N.Burrows	Kirk Michael, IOM	15. 4.98P

G-MCAA-MCZZ

Regn	Type	C/n	P/I	Date	Owner/operator	Probable Base	CA Expy
G-MCAR	PA-32-300 Cherokee Six D	32-7140008	G-LADA G-AYWK/N8616N	11.11.83	B.M.Jordan	Leicester	1. 7.99
G-MCEA	Boeing 757-225	22200	N510EA	6. 2.95	Airtours International Airways Ltd	Manchester	23. 3.01T
G-MCJL	Pegasus Quantum 15-912	7497		16. 3.99	M.C.J.Ludlow	(Ashford)	
G-MCMS	Aero Designs Pulsar (Rotax 582)	PFA/202-11982		3. 2.93	M.C.Manning	Spanhoe Lodge	19. 5.99P
G-MCOX	Fuji FA.200-180AO Aero Subaru	296	(G-BIMS)	29.12.81	West Surrey Engineering Ltd	Fairoaks	30. 4.00
G-MCPI	Bell 206B JetRanger III	3191	G-ONTB N3896C	4. 4.90	D.A.C.Pipe	Westbury-sub-Mendip	9. 3.00T

G-MDAA-MDZZ

Regn	Type	C/n	P/I	Date	Owner/operator	Probable Base	CA Expy
G-MDAC	PA-28-181 Archer II	28-8290154	N8242T	6.11.87	B.R.McKay t/a Alpha Charlie Flying Club	Jersey/Compton Abbas	17. 4.00
G-MDBD	Airbus A.330-243	266	F-WW..	R	Airtours International Airways Ltd	Manchester	
G-MDEW	Lindstrand LBL Drinks Can SS HAFB (Mountain Dew Can Shape)	099		4. 3.94	Pepsi Cola Overseas Ltd "Mountain Dew Supercan"	Des Moines, IA, USA	7. 3.97A
G-MDKD	Robinson R-22 Beta	1247		18. 4.90	B.C.Seedle t/a Brian Seedle Helicopters	Blackpool	3. 5.99

G-MEAA-MEZZ

Regn	Type	C/n	P/I	Date	Owner/operator	Probable Base	CA Expy
G-MEAH	PA-28R-200 Cherokee Arrow II	28R-7435104	G-BSNM N46PR/G-BSNM/N46PR/N54439	14. 6.91	Stapleford F/C Ltd (Damaged at Stapleford 17.8.98)	Stapleford	26. 3.00T
G-MEDA	Airbus A.320-231	480	N480RX F-WWDU	12.10.94	British Mediterranean Airways Ltd (Whale Rider t/s)	Heathrow	11.10.00T
G-MEDB	Airbus A.320-231	376	3B-RGY F-OHMB/(XA-SGB)/F-WWIK	19. 3.97	British Mediterranean Airways Ltd (Rendezvous t/s)	Heathrow	7. 4.00T
G-MEDD	Airbus A.320-231	386	3B-RGZ F-OHMC/(XA-SGC)/F-WWBI	19. 3.97	British Mediterranean Airways Ltd (Crossing Borders t/s)	Heathrow	1. 4.00T
G-MEGA	PA-28R-201T Turbo Arrow III	28R-7803303	N999JG	13. 2.86	Multi Ltd	Breighton	14. 6.01T
G-MELD	Gulfstream AA-5A Cheetah	AA5A-0863	G-BHCB	18. 2.85	A.S.Bamrah t/a Falcon Flying Svs	Biggin Hill	15. 1.01T
G-MELT	Reims Cessna F.172H	0580	G-AWTI	23. 9.83	Vectair Avn Ltd	Goodwood	27. 2.00T
G-MELV	Socata Rallye 235E Gabier	13328	G-BIND	21. 5.86	Wallis & Son Ltd	Little Staughton	24.10.99
G-MEME	PA-28R-201 Arrow III	2837051	N9219N	17. 8.90	Henry J.Clare Ltd	Bodmin	4. 9.99
G-MEOW	CFM Streak Shadow (Rotax 582)	PFA/206-12025		23. 4.93	S.D.Hicks	Draycott Farm, Chiseldon	11. 1.98P
G-MERC	Colt 56A HAFB	842		11. 6.86	A.F. & C.D.Selby	Loughborough	5. 4.99A
G-MERE	Lindstrand LBL-77A HAFB	092		7. 4.94	G.T.Restell	Folkestone	9. 5.96A
G-MERF	Grob G-115A	8091	EI-CAB	24. 7.95	W.Murphy	White Waltham	24. 3.99
G-MERI	PA-28-181 Archer II	28-8090267	N8175J	17. 7.80	Scotia Safari Ltd (Op Carlisle Flt Centre)	Carlisle	12. 3.99T

Regn	Type	C/n	P/I	Date	Owner/operator	Probable Base	CA Expy
G-MERL	PA-28RT-201 Arrow IV	28R-7918036	N2116N	27. 6.86	M.Giles	Cardiff	20. 7.01
G-METE	Gloster Meteor F.8	G5/361641	VZ467	5.11.91	Sark International Airways Ltd	Kemble	AC
					(A.Gjertsen/Classic Jets Aircraft) "Winston"		
					(As "VZ467/A" in 601 Sqn)		
G-MEUP	Cameron A-120 HAFB	2117		5.10.89	Innovation Ballooning Ltd	Bath	13. 5.99A
G-MEYO	Enstrom 280FX	2059	SX-HCN	13. 1.95	L.G.King	Shoreham	16. 3.01

G-MFAA-MFZZ

Regn	Type	C/n	P/I	Date	Owner/operator	Probable Base	CA Expy
G-MFHI	Europa Avn Europa	PFA/247-12841		14.11.97	M.F.Howe	(Beverley)	3.11.99P
G-MFHT	Robinson R-22 Beta	2601	N8334H	20. 6.96	MFH Helicopters Ltd	(London W1)	19. 6.99T
G-MFLI	Cameron V-90 HAFB	2650		14. 8.91	J.M.Percival "Mayfly"	Loughborough	3. 9.99A
G-MFMF	Bell 206B JetRanger III	3569	G-BJNJ	4. 6.84	South Western Electricity plc		
						Bristol/Lulsgate	4.11.00T
G-MFMM	Scheibe SF-25C Falke	4412	(G-MBMM)	20. 4.82	J.A.Rees	Haverfordwest	2. 8.99
			D-KAEU				

G-MGAA-MGZZ

Regn	Type	C/n	P/I	Date	Owner/operator	Probable Base	CA Expy
G-MGAA	BFC Quad City Challenger II			18. 8.97	G.A.Archer & J.W.E.Pearson		
	(Rotax 582) CH2-..97-1568 & PFA/177A-13124				Plaistows Field, Hemel Hampstead		22.12.99P
G-MGAG	Aviasud Mistral 870545 & BMAA/HB/009			20. 6.89	M.Raj	Wolverhampton	27. 6.99P
	(Rotax 532)						
G-MGCA	Pearce Jabiru UL	PFA/274-13228		8. 5.98	Cloudbase Aviation Services Ltd	Redhill	
G-MGCB	Cyclone Pegasus XL-Q			16.10.96	C.W.Barnes & M.G.Gomez		
	(Rotax 462)	SW-TE-0344 & 7267	(Trike ex G-MWUT)			Knapthorpe Lodge, Caunton	29.10.98P
G-MGCK	Whittaker MW-6 Merlin	PFA/164-11262		30. 3.93	M.H.Arrowsmith	Lincoln	
G-MGDB	CFM Shadow Srs.DD	300-DD		19.12.97	D.V.Brunt	St. Albans	
G-MGDL	Cyclone Pegasus Quantum 15	7400		17. 2.98	G.D.Lusk	Wellingborough	15. 2.99P
G-MGDM	Cyclone Pegasus Quantum 15	7406		19. 3.98	R.Jeffes	London SW13	17. 3.99P
	(Rotax 912)						
G-MGEC	Rans S-6-ESD Coyote II XL			13.10.97	E. & M.Carter	Thirsk	28. 1.00P
		PFA/204-13209					
G-MGEF	Cyclone Pegasus Quantum 15	7261		18. 9.96	G.D.Castell	Sandy	17.11.99P
	(Rotax 912)						
G-MGFK	Cyclone Pegasus Quantum 15	7396		2. 2.98	F.A.A.Kay	Chorleywood	10. 2.99P
	(Rotax 912)						
G-MGFO	Cyclone Pegasus Quantum 15	7410		24. 3.98	A.Gulliver	Harrogate	19. 3.99P
	(Rotax 912)						
G-MGGG	Cyclone Pegasus Quantum 15	7377		3.11.97	R.A.Beauchamp	Shenstone	2.11.98P
	Super Sport (Rotax 912)						
G-MGGT	CFM Streak Shadow Srs.M			3. 6.94	R.K.& J.Hyatt	Newquay	23.11.99P
	(Rotax 618)	K.252 & PFA/206-12723					
G-MGGV	Cyclone Pegasus Quantum 15	7484		12.10.98	R.W.Krake	Andover	12.11.99P
	(Rotax 912)						
G-MGMC	Cyclone Pegasus Quantum 15	7430		28. 4.98	M.Clare	Gayton, Northampton	23. 4.99P
	(Rotax 912)						
G-MGMT	Cyclone Pegasus Quantum 15	7225		28. 5.96	N.Pugh	Stonea	23. 7.98P
	(Rotax 582)						
G-MGND	Rans S-6-ESD Coyote II XL			27. 6.97	N.N.Ducker	Ashbourne,Derbyshire	14. 9.99P
	(Rotax 503)	PFA/204-13152					
G-MGOD	Medway Raven X	MRB110/106		6. 7.93	P.C.Collins	Bath	20. 3.99P
	(Rotax 447)						
G-MGOM	Medway Hybrid 44XLR	MR125/103		22.11.91	T.Bradfield	Kenley	24. 9.99P
	(Rotax 503) (Reported as being a Medway Raven)						
G-MGOO	Murphy Renegade Spirit UK			14.11.89	A.R.Max	White Waltham	12.11.99P
	(Rotax 582) & PFA/188-11580						
G-MGPD	Solar Wings Pegasus XL-R	6905		9. 1.95	P.C.Davis	Weston Zoyland	22. 2.99P
	(Rotax 462)						
G-MGPH	CFM Streak Shadow SA-M	PFA/206-13166	G-RSPH	27.11.97	CFM Aircraft Ltd	Leiston	7. 8.98P
	(Rotax 582)						
G-MGRH	Quad City Challenger II	CH2-1189-0482		20. 2.90	R.A. & B.M.Roberts		
	(Hirth 2705.R06)				Griffins Farm, Temple Bruer		2. 2.99P
G-MGRW	Cyclone AX3/S	BMAA/HB/024		8.11.93	R.J.White	Ongar	10. 2.99P
	(Rotax 503) (Originally regd with c/n C.3093155/S)						
G-MGTG	Cyclone Pegasus Quantum 15	7369		19.12.97	R.B.Milton	(London E2)	6.11.99P
	(Rotax 912)						

Regn	Type	C/n	P/I	Date	Owner/operator	Probable Base	CA Expy
G-MGTR	Hunt Wing/Experience	BMAA/HB/067		24. 7.97	A.C.Ryall	Cardiff	
G-MGTW	CFM Shadow Srs.DD	287-DD		23. 1.98	G.T.Webster	Helensburgh	8. 3.99P
G-MGUN	Cyclone AX2000 (Rotax 582/48)	7284		18.12.96	D.J.Clark	Sywell	19. 3.99P
G-MGUX	Hunt Wing/Experience	BMAA/HB/064		24. 7.97	B.D.Attwell	Caerphilly	
G-MGUY	CFM Shadow Srs.CD (Rotax 447)	078		23.11.87	F.J.Luckhurst & R.G.M.Proost t/a The Shadow Flt Centre	Old Sarum	16. 8.91P
G-MGWH	Thruster T300 (Rotax 582)	9013-T300-507		8.12.92	W.Corps & A.Bass	Eastbourne	8.10.99P

G-MHAA-MHZZ

Regn	Type	C/n	P/I	Date	Owner/operator	Probable Base	CA Expy
G-MHCA	Enstrom F-28C	348	G-SHWW G-SMUJ/G-BHTF	10. 5.90	A.G.Forshaw	Barton	12. 3.99
G-MHCB	Enstrom 280C Shark	1031	N892PT	11.10.95	J.W.Beswick (Op Manchester Helicopter Centre)	(Bury)	15. 2.99T
G-MHCD	Enstrom 280C-UK Shark	1112	G-SHGG N627H	12. 7.96	Checksent Ltd (Op Manchester Helicopter Centre)	Barton	24. 8.01T
G-MHCE	Enstrom F-28A	150	G-BBHD	22. 8.96	K.Bickley (Op Manchester Helicopter Centre)	Barton	3. 4.99T
G-MHCF	Enstrom 280C-UK Shark	1149	G-GSML G-BNNV/SE-HIY	19. 9.96	K., H.K. & D.Collier t/a HKC Helicopter Services (Op Manchester Helicopter Centre)	Barton	3. 6.01T
G-MHCG	Enstrom 280C-UK Shark	1155	G-HAYN G-BPOX/N51776	7. 3.97	D & E Motor Factors Ltd (Op Manchester Helicopter Centre)	Barton	27. 1.00T
G-MHCH	Enstrom 280C Shark	1043	N557H	19. 5.97	J.& S.Lewis Ltd	Barton	29. 7.00T
G-MHCI	Enstrom 280C Shark	1152	N100WZ	20. 5.97	B & B Helicopters Ltd	Barton	27. 7.00T
G-MHCJ	Enstrom F-28C-UK	453	G-CTRN	30. 3.98	Euro Marine Group Ltd	Southampton	21. 5.01T
G-MHCK	Enstrom 280FX	2006	G-BXXB ZK-HHN/JA7702	5. 6.98	N., C. & N.C. Bailey t/a Manchester Helicopter Centre	Barton	23. 6.01T
G-MHCL	Enstrom 280C Shark	1144	N51740	30. 6.98	N., C. & N.C.Bailey t/a Manchester Helicopter Helicopter Centre	Barton	24.11.01T

G-MIAA-MIZZ

Regn	Type	C/n	P/I	Date	Owner/operator	Probable Base	CA Expy
G-MICH	Robinson R-22 Beta	0647	G-BNKY	3. 9.87	A.L.Ramsden t/a Tiger Helicopters	Shobdon	4.10.99T
G-MICK	Reims Cessna F.172N Skyhawk II	1592	PH-JRA PH-AXB	9. 1.80	A.W.Moate t/a G-MICK Flying Group	Blackpool	7. 8.01
G-MICY	Everett Gyroplane Srs.1 (VW1835)	018	(G-BOVF)	26. 2.90	D.M.Hughes	St.Merryn	2. 5.92P
G-MICZ	PA-46-310P Malibu	46-8508096	N2494X	3. 7.95	Michell Instruments Ltd	Fowlmere	25. 8.01T
G-MIDA	Airbus A.321-231	806	D-AVZQ	31. 3.98	British Midland Airways Ltd	East Midlands	30. 3.01T
G-MIDC	Airbus A.321-231	835	D-AVZZ	12. 6.98	British Midland Airways Ltd	East Midlands	11. 6.01T
G-MIDD	PA-28-140 Cherokee Cruiser	28-7325444	G-BBDD N55687	20. 1.97	R.B.Walker t/a Midland Air Training School	Coventry	25. 5.01T
G-MIDE	Airbus A.321-231	864	D-AVZB	14. 8.98	British Midland Airways Ltd	East Midlands	13. 8.01T
G-MIDF	Airbus A.321-231	810	D-AVZS	24. 4.98	British Midland Airways Ltd	East Midlands	23. 4.01T
G-MIDG	Bushby-Long MM-1 Midget Mustang (Lyc O-320)	385	N11DE	14. 3.90	C.E.Bellhouse	Headcorn	2. 9.99P
G-MIDH	Airbus A.321-231	968	D-AVXZ	22. 3.99	British Midland Airways Ltd	East Midlands	
G-MIDI	Airbus A.321-231	974	D-AVZA	26. 3.99	British Midland Airways Ltd	East Midlands	
G-MIDJ	Airbus A.321-231		R		British Midland Airways Ltd (For dlvy 1999)	East Midlands	
G-MIDK	Airbus A.320-232		R		British Midland Airways Ltd (For dlvy 1999)	East Midlands	
G-MIDL	Airbus A.321-231		R		British Midland Airways Ltd (For dlvy 1999)	East Midlands	
G-MIDM	Airbus A.320-232		R		British Midland Airways Ltd (For dlvy 1999)	East Midlands	

Regn	Type	C/n	P/I	Date	Owner/operator	Probable Base	CA Expy
G-MIDN	Airbus A.321-231		R		British Midland Airways Ltd (For dlvy 2000)	East Midlands	
G-MIDO	Airbus A.321-231		R		British Midland Airways Ltd (For dlvy 2000)	East Midlands	
G-MIDP	Airbus A.320-232		R		British Midland Airways Ltd (For dlvy 2000)	East Midlands	
G-MIDR	Airbus A.320-232		R		British Midland Airways Ltd (For dlvy 2000)	East Midlands	
G-MIDS	Airbus A.320-232		R		British Midland Airways Ltd (For dlvy 2000)	East Midlands	
G-MIDT	Airbus A.321-231		R		British Midland Airways Ltd (For dlvy 2000)	East Midlands	
G-MIDU	Airbus A.321-231		R		British Midland Airways Ltd (For dlvy 2001)	East Midlands	
G-MIDV	Airbus A.320-232		R		British Midland Airways Ltd (For dlvy 2001)	East Midlands	
G-MIDW	Airbus A.320-232		R		British Midland Airways Ltd (For dlvy 2001)	East Midlands	
G-MIDX	Airbus A.320-232		R		British Midland Airways Ltd (For dlvy 2001)	East Midlands	
G-MIDY	Airbus A.320-232		R		British Midland Airways Ltd (For dlvy 2002)	East Midlands	
G-MIDZ	Airbus A.320-232	934	F-WWII	19. 1.99	British Midland Airways Ltd	East Midlands	
G-MIFF	Robin DR.400/180 Regent	2076		31. 5.91	G.E.Snushall	Leicester	6. 8.00
G-MIII	Extra EA.300/L (Lyc AEIO-540)	013	D-EXFI	5. 9.95	Firebird Aerobatics Ltd (Microlease c/s)	Denham	21. 9.01T
G-MIKE	Brookland Hornet (VW1830)	MG.1		15. 5.78	M.H.J.Goldring	St.Merryn	25. 9.92P
G-MIKI	Rans S-6-ESA Coyote II (Rotax 912UL)	PFA/204-13094		28. 2.97	S.P.Slade	Kemble	16. 6.99P
G-MILA	Reims Cessna F.172N Skyhawk II	1686	D-EGHC(2) PH-AYJ	9. 6.98	P.J.Miller	(Sudbury)	29. 7.01A
G-MILE	Cameron N-77 HAFB	2411		26. 9.90	Miles Air Ltd "Miles Architectural"	Bristol	20. 7.99A
G-MILI	Bell 206B JetRanger III	2275	C-GGAR 5H-MPV	5.10.94	C.Kiley t/a CK's Supermarket	Swansea	15. 9.01
G-MILY	Grumman American AA-5A Cheetah	AA5A-0672	G-BFXY	2. 9.96	Plane Talking Ltd	Elstree	7.10.99T
G-MIMA	BAe 146 Srs.200	E-2079	G-CNMF G-5-079	3. 3.93	Manx Airlines Ltd (Three Legs of Man t/s)	Ronaldsway	25.11.99T
G-MIME	Europa Avn Europa	PFA/247-12850		26. 9.97	N.W.Charles	(Devizes)	
G-MIND	Cessna 404 Titan II	404-0004	G-SKKC G-OHUB/SE-GMX/(N3932C)	27. 4.93	Atlantic Air Transport Ltd	Coventry	13. 2.00T
G-MINI	Phoenix Currie Wot	PFA/58-10294		4. 8.78	D.Collinson	(Durham)	
G-MINS	Nicollier HN.700 Menestrel II	PFA/217-12354		23.10.92	R.Fenion	Kirkbride	AC
G-MINT	Pitts S-1S Special (Lyc AEIO-360)	PFA/09-10292		7. 2.83	T.G.Sanderson	Leicester	22.11.99P
G-MINX	Bell 47G-4A (Mod)	7604	N6242N G-FOOR/N6242N	16. 3.90	R.F.Warner	Elstree	22. 5.93T
G-MIOO	Miles M.100 Student 2	100/1008	G-APLK G-MIOO/G-APLK/XS941/G-APLK/G-35-4	26.10.84	Aces High Ltd	Woodley	6. 5.86P
	(Damaged Duxford 24.8.85; to Museum of Berkshire Aviation Trust 4.97 and stored for rebuild)						
G-MISH	Cessna 182R Skylane II	182-67888	G-RFAB G-BIXT/N6397H	16. 6.95	M.Konstantinovic	Stapleford	1. 4.00
G-MISS	Taylor JT.2 Titch	PFA/3234		18.12.78	Pamela L.Brenen	(Abingdon)	
G-MITS	Cameron N-77 HAFB	1115		20. 2.85	The Colt Car Co Ltd "Mitsubishi Motors"	Cirencester	25. 7.99T
	(Rebuilt with new envelope c/n 3217 1994)						
G-MITZ	Cameron N-77 HAFB	1638		17. 3.88	The Colt Car Co Ltd "Mitsubishi Motors II"	Cirencester	10. 8.90A
G-MIWS	Cessna 310R II	310R-1585	G-ODNP N19TP/N2DD/N1836E	1. 2.96	R.W.F. & R.B.Warner t/a Bob Warner Aviation	Hawarden	22. 8.99

G-MJAA-MJZZ

Regn	Type	C/n	P/I	Date	Owner/operator	Probable Base	CA Expy
G-MJAE	American Aerolights Eagle (C/n is probably the engine no.)	1021		12. 7.82	T.B.Woolley	Leicester	
G-MJAF*	Southdown Puma (Lightning DS) (EC-44-PM)	BHA-01		17. 6.82	S.I.Robertson (Cancelled by CAA 16.4.98)	Glasgow	20. 9.93E
G-MJAJ	Eurowing Goldwing (EC-44-PM)	EW-36		18. 6.82	J.S.R.Moodie	Rogart, Sutherland	18. 4.99P
G-MJAL	Wheeler Scout Mk.III/3/R (EC-25-PS)	0433 R/3		18. 6.82	G.W.Wickington	Hamble	
G-MJAM	Eipper Quicksilver MX (Cuyuna 430)	JCL-01		18. 6.82	J.C.Larkin	Maryport, Cumbria	20. 8.93P
G-MJAN	Hiway Skytrike/Flexiform Hilander (Valmet)	RPFD-01 & 21U9		21. 6.82	G.M.Sutcliffe	Stockport	4. 3.92E
G-MJAP	Hiway Skytrike/Vulcan 160	21W3		22. 6.82	A.L.Flude	Baldock	N/E
G-MJAV	Hiway Skytrike/Demon 175 (EC-25-PS)	817003		23. 6.82	J.N.J.Roberts (Stored 7.96)	Long Acre Farm, Sandy	N/E
G-MJAY	Eurowing Goldwing (EC-34-PM)	EW-58		23. 6.82	M.Anthony	Alfreton	N/E
G-MJAZ	Aerodyne Vector 610 (Konig SC430)	1251	PH-1J1 G-MJAZ	23. 6.82	B.Fussell (Stored 1.97)	Swansea	23. 9.93E
G-MJBI	Eipper Quicksilver MX (Cuyuna 430R)	3075		24. 6.82	E.J.H.Blackbourn	Louth	1. 3.94P
G-MJBL	American Aerolights Eagle	2892		25. 6.82	B.W.Olley	Ely	
G-MJBN*	American Aerolights Rainbow Eagle	3132		28. 6.82	Not known (Open store 7.95)	Manor Farm, Glatton	
G-MJBS	UAS Storm Buggy	JL814S		29. 6.82	G.I.Sargeant	Bridgwater	
G-MJBT*	Eipper Quicksilver MX II (Cuyuna 430R)	DJ/NBII & 3662		30. 6.82	Not known (Stored 8.95)	Letterkenny, Ireland	N/E
G-MJBV	American Aerolights Eagle 215B (EC-25-PS)	RSP-001		1. 7.82	B.H.Stephens	Southampton	11. 8.96P
G-MJBX*	Pterodactyl Ptraveler	BJE-01		1. 7.82	R.E.Hawkes (Cancelled by CAA 24.3.99)	Wellingborough	
G-MJBZ	Huntair Pathfinder 1 (EC-34-PM)	PK-17		2. 7.82	J.C.Rose	Eastbach Farm, English Bicknor	28.12.93P
G-MJCE	Southdown Panther Sprint X (EC-44-PM)	RGC-01		5. 7.82	L.I.Bateup & N.D.Dykes	Olney/Bedford	1.12.99P
G-MJCL	Eipper Quicksilver MX II (Cuyuna 430R)	RFW-01		5. 7.82	K.J.Bunn	East Kirkby	21. 1.95P
G-MJCN	Southern Flyer Mk.1 (EC-44-PM)	005		5. 7.82	C.W.Merriam	Billingshurst	11. 6.99P
G-MJCU	Tarjani/Solar Wings Typhoon (EC-25-PS)	SCG-01		7. 7.82	J.K.Ewing	Old Sarum	1. 9.94P
G-MJCW	Hiway Skytrike/Super Scorpion	MGS-01		7. 7.82	M.G.Sheppard	Bournemouth	
G-MJCX	American Aerolights Eagle 215B (Chrysler 820)	2759		7. 7.82	J.Channer	Nottingham	11. 8.94P
G-MJDA	Hornet Executive 330/Skyhook Sabre C	H340		12. 7.82	J.Hainsworth	Pudsey	28. 2.87E
G-MJDE	Huntair Pathfinder 1 (EC-34-PM)	020		9. 7.82	P.Rayson	Swadlincote	17.10.99P
G-MJDH	Huntair Pathfinder 1 (EC-34-PM)	015		9. 7.82	T.Mahmood	Insch	8. 6.99P
G-MJDJ	Hiway Skytrike/Demon	VW17D		9. 7.82	A.J.Cowan	Billingham	
G-MJDP	Eurowing Goldwing (EC-34-PM)	GW-001		12. 7.82	J.R.Ledbrook & F.C.James	Camberley	15.11.92P
G-MJDR	Hiway Skytrike/Demon	PJB-01		14. 7.82	D.R.Redmile	Leicester	
G-MJDU	Eipper Quicksilver MXII (Rotax 503)	14002		15. 7.82	J.Brown	Markfield, Leics	N/E
G-MJDW	Eipper Quicksilver MXII (Cuyuna 430)	RI-01		15. 7.82	T.Scarborough	Boston	7. 7.98P
G-MJEB	Southdown Puma Sprint (Rotax 447)	1231/0041		18. 4.85	R.J.Shelswell	Warwick	2. 5.96P
G-MJEE	Mainair Tri-Flyer 250/Solar Wings Typhoon (EC-25-PS)	038-251181		20. 7.82	M.F.Eddington	Wincanton	6.11.99P
G-MJEG	Eurowing Goldwing (EC-34-PM)	GJS-01		20. 7.82	G.J.Stamper	Penrith	N/E
G-MJEH	Rotec Rally 2B	018T		20. 7.82	E.L.G.Brocklehurst	Manningtree	
G-MJEO	American Aerolights Eagle 215B (Zenoah G25B1)	4562		26. 7.82	A.M.Shaw	Stoke-on-Trent	25. 6.93E
G-MJER	Ultrasports Tripacer/Flexiform Solo Striker (Rotax 447)	DSD-01		23. 7.82	D.S.Simpson	Radwell, Letchworth	21.11.98P
G-MJEY	Mainair Tri-Flyer/Southdown Lightning DS (EC-44-PM)	PMC-01		27. 7.82	M.McKenzie	Insch	7. 6.96P
G-MJFB	Ultrasports Tripacer/Flexiform Solo Striker (EC-34-PM)	AJK-01		27. 7.82	B.Tetley	Cowes	21. 3.99P
G-MJFH*	Eipper Quicksilver MX (Cuyuna 430R)	3077		28. 7.82	C.T.Lamb (Stored 1.94)	Road End Farm, Great Casterton	N/E
G-MJFK	Mainair Tri-Flyer/Flexiform Dual Sealander	JH-01		28. 7.82	J.J.Woollen	Huby, York	N/E

Regn	Type	C/n	P/I	Date	Owner/operator	Probable Base	CA Expy
G-MJFM	Huntair Pathfinder 1 (EC-34-PM)	ML-01		2. 9.82	R.Gillespie & S.P.Girr	Mullaghmore	23. 7.99P
G-MJFP	American Aerolights Eagle 215B (Cuyuna 215R)	5010		2. 8.82	R.C.Colbeck	Henley-on-Thames	N/E
G-MJFX	Skyhook TR1/Sabre	TR1/38		2. 8.82	M.R.Dean	Hebden Bridge	28. 2.87E
G-MJGO	Barnes Avon/Wasp Gryphon (EC-34-PM)	2510		5. 8.82	B.R.Barnes	Bristol	31.12.87E
G-MJHB*	AES Sky Ranger	SR.100		9. 8.82	Not known (Fuselage stored 3.97)	Enstone	
G-MJHC	Ultrasports Tripacer 330/Southdown Lightning Mk II	82-00044		9. 8.82	E.J.Allen	Cambridge	N/E
G-MJHM	Ultrasports Tripacer/Hiway Demon 175 (Regd with c/n ME-170)	ME17D		11. 8.82	D.B.Markham	Lincoln	
G-MJHR	GS Trike/Southdown Lightning DS	GNS-01		12. 8.82	B.R.Barnes	Bristol	
G-MJHU	Eipper Quicksilver MX (Cuyuna 430R)	10692		13. 8.82	P.J.Hawcock, J.W.Lupton & R.F.Hinton (Stored 9.96) Hougham, Lincs		N/E
G-MJHV	Hiway Skytrike 250/Demon	AG-17		13. 8.82	A.G.Griffiths	Avenchurch, Birmingham	
G-MJHX	Eipper Quicksilver MXII (Rotax 503)	1033		13. 8.82	P.D.Lucas Needham, Harleston (Stored 9.97)		14. 5.95P
G-MJHZ	Ultrasports Tripacer/Southdown L170/267 Lightning 170 (Puma DS) (EC-34-PM)			13. 8.82	M.J.Luton	Farnborough	8.11.98P
G-MJIA	Ultrasports Tripacer/Flexiform Solo Striker (Rotax 377)	SE-007		13. 8.82	D.G.Ellis	Tamworth	20. 9.96P
G-MJIB*	Hornet 250/Skyhook Sabre	H.350		13. 8.82	S.H.Williams St Yon, France (Cancelled by CAA 25.3.99)		
G-MJIC	Ultrasports Tripacer/Flexiform Solo Striker (EC-34-PM)	82-00043		13. 8.82	J.Curran	Newry, Co.Down	15.10.94P
G-MJIF	Mainair Tri-Flyer/Flexiform Striker (EC-34-PL) "E-1 EC25PS-04" (C/n was original engine type)			16. 8.82	R.J.Payne	Newmarket	31.10.91E
G-MJIO*	American Aerolights Eagle	2625		18. 8.82	R.Apps & J.Marshall Tetbury (Cancelled by PWFU 25.3.99)		
G-MJIR	Eipper Quicksilver MXII (Rotax 503)	1392		18. 8.82	H.Feeney (Stored 8.96)	Long Marston	26. 1.95P
G-MJIY	Flexiform Striker/Solar Wings Panther 002CSRS (Originally regd as Ultrasports Tripacer/Flexiform Striker) t/a McClelland Aviation			23. 8.82	M.I.McClelland	Old Sarum	28. 2.86E
G-MJIZ	Ultrasports Tripacer/Southdown Lightning JS-189			23. 8.82	Jacqueline J.Crudington	Hockley, Essex	
G-MJJA	Huntair Pathfinder 1	031		23. 8.82	R.D.Bateman & J.M.Watkins	Fareham	N/E
G-MJJB	Eipper Quicksilver MX (Cuyuna 430R)	3526		23. 8.82	S.A.P.Rowberry	Wallingford	22. 7.98P
G-MJJF	Ultrasports Tripacer/Solar Wings Medium Typhoon (EC-34-PM) JGS-01 & 116-108			25. 8.82	G.Ravichandran	London N13	21. 6.96P
G-MJJK	Eipper Quicksilver MXII (Rotax 503)	3397		25. 8.82	M.J.O'Malley	Northolt	8. 7.96P
G-MJJO	Mainair Tri-Flyer/Flexiform Dual Striker (EC-44-PS) JDH-01 (Mainair c/n probably 073-31582)			26. 8.82	T.R.Marsh	Frome	5.11.96P
G-MJKB	Striplin Sky Ranger (Also quoted as c/n SRI-6-I)	ST 161		2. 9.82	A.P.Booth	Newbury	
G-MJKF	Hiway Demon	WGR-01		2. 9.82	S.D.Hill	Henley-on-Thames	
G-MJKH	Eipper Quicksilver MXII (Rotax 503)	1020		28. 1.83	D.O'Neill (Stored 1.98)	Long Marston	23. 8.96P
G-MJKO	Farnell Trike/Goldmarque Gyr 188 (EC-25-PS)	90030P		7. 9.82	M.J.Barry	Bridgwater	18.11.91E
G-MJKX	Skyrider Airsports Phantom (EC-48)	PH.82005		14. 9.82	W.E.Willets	Bewdley	1. 8.98P
G-MJLK*	Dragonfly 250-II	D.105		10. 9.82	Not known Breighton (Stored completely dismantled 6.96)		
G-MJLY*	American Aerolights Eagle	AMR-01		30. 9.82	A.M.Read Plymouth (Cancelled by CAA 15.3.99)		
G-MJMA	Hiway Skytrike/Demon (EC-25-PS)	JCC-01		22. 9.82	R.V.Parks & S.C.Hewett Faversham/Herne Bay		N/E
G-MJMD	Hiway Skytrike/Demon 175 (EC-34-PM)	OE17D		27. 9.82	T.A.N.Brierley Baxby Manor, Husthwaite		1. 8.97P
G-MJMI*	Skyhook Sabre	260A-138824		27. 9.82	Not known Longacre Farm, Sandy (Stored 8.92)		
G-MJMN	Mainair Tri-Flyer/Flexiform Striker (EC-34-PM) 087-04882			29. 9.82	E.D.Locke (Stored 12.97)	Barton	24. 6.97P
G-MJMR	Mainair Tri-Flyer 250/Solar Wings Typhoon DR-01 & 048-5182			30. 9.82	J.C.S.Jones (Stored 12.97)	Rhuallt	
G-MJMS	Hiway Skytrike/Demon 175	EEW-01		30. 9.82	D.E.Peace	Rawdon, Leeds	
G-MJMT	Hiway Skytrike/Demon 175 (EC-25-PS)	RL17D		30. 9.82	K.H.Roberts	Eshott	9.10.93P
G-MJMU	Hiway Skytrike 250/Demon 817003 (C/n duplicates that of both PH-1B2 & G-MJOI)			1.10.82	P.Hunt	Bishop Auckland	
G-MJMX	Mainair Tri-Flyer/Flexiform Dual Striker (EC-44-PM) 179-5883 & RM-01			4.10.82	N.Cockburn	Swanley, Kent	18. 6.97P
G-MJNH*	Skyhook Cutlass	260A 156824		13.10.82	M.E.James Telford (Cancelled by CAA 25.3.99)		

Regn	Type	C/n	P/I	Date	Owner/operator	Probable Base	CA Expy
G-MJNK	Hiway Skytrike/Demon 175 (EC-34-PM)	EA17D		14.10.82	E.W.Barker	Baxby Manor, Husthwaite	28.10.96P
G-MJNM	American Aerolights Double Eagle 430B (Cuyuna 430R)	702		25.11.82	B.H.Stephens	Southampton	19. 9.93P
G-MJNO	American Aerolights Double Eagle Amphibian (Rotax 447)	703		24.11.82	R.S.Martin	Gosport	3. 3.93P
G-MJNS	Swallow AeroPlane Swallow B (Cuyuna 430R)	782039-2		9. 7.86	F.J.Marton (Stored 7.93)	Dunkeswell	9. 2.93E
G-MJNT	Hiway Skytrike/Demon 175 (EC-25-PS)	R017D		18.10.82	F.Tyreman	Whitby	N/E
G-MJNU	Skyhook TR1/Cutlass	TR1/17		19.10.82	R.W.Taylor	Sheffield	
G-MJNV*	Eipper Quicksilver MX	10537		19.10.82	W.Toulmin (Cancelled as destroyed 25.3.99)	Peterborough	
G-MJNY	Skyhook TR1/Sabre	TR1/35		3.11.82	P.Ratcliffe	Sheffield	
G-MJOC	Huntair Pathfinder (EC-34-PM)	048		25.10.82	A.J.Glynn	Southend	31. 7.99P
G-MJOD	Rotec Rally 2B	AK-01		28.10.82	E.L.G.Brocklehurst & A.S.L.Root	Manningtree	
G-MJOE	Eurowing Goldwing (Rotax 377)	EW-55		29.10.82	R.J.Osborne	Tiverton	N/E
G-MJOU	Hiway Skytrike II/Demon 175 (EC-34-PM) (Probably shares trike with G-MMBS)	HP-01		8.11.82	R.J.Thompson (Stored 9.96)	Milson	31. 5.86E
G-MJPA	Rotec Rally 2B	AT-01		5. 1.83	R.Boyd	Armagh	
G-MJPB*	Manuel Ladybird	WLM-14		9.11.82	Estate of W.L.Manuel (On loan to Brooklands Museum)	Brooklands	
G-MJPC*	American Aerolights Double Eagle 430B	PHH-01		9.11.82	D.M.Jackson (Stored 9.96; cancelled as WFU 17.2.99)	Hougham, Lincs	
G-MJPE	Hiway Skytrike/Demon 175 (EC-34-PM) (Reported as Mainair Tri-Flyer)	OG17D		10.11.82	E.G.Astin	Whitby	7. 8.96P
G-MJPO	Eurowing Goldwing	018		16.12.82	M.E.Merryman	Dronfield	
G-MJPP	Hiway Skytrike/Solar Wings Typhoon (Hiro 125)	KLM-01		28.11.82	A.B.Greenbank	Bradford	16. 9.97P
G-MJPU	Ultrasports/Solar Wings Panther XL (EC-44-PM)	KND-01 & T1283-948X	(Regd with wing later fitted to G-MMHZ)	8. 2.83	M.B.Saunders	Poole	2.12.93P
G-MJPV	Eipper Quicksilver MX (Cuyuna 430R)	JBW-01		30.11.82	F.W.Ellis	Skegness	1. 2.95P
G-MJRL	Eurowing Goldwing (Rotax 377)	EW-79 & SWA-5K		30.12.82	V.J.Morris	Truro	15. 6.99P
G-MJRO	Eurowing Goldwing (Rotax 447)	EW-77 & SWA-04		31.12.82	H.P.Welch	Taunton	22. 9.99P
G-MJRP	Mainair Tri-Flyer/Hiway Demon 175 (EC-34-PM)	118-161282 & OF17D		4. 1.83	W.H.Newton	Wombleton	9.11.97P
G-MJRR	Reece SkyRanger Srs.1	JR-3		26. 4.82	J.R.Reece	Formby	
G-MJRS	Eurowing Goldwing (Rotax 377)	EW-80 & SWA-6K		5. 1.83	S.J.Spavins (Damaged mid 1996)	St.Albans	30. 3.97P
G-MJRT	Southdown Puma (Lightning DS) (EC-44-PM)	TJF-01		5. 1.83	B.D.Ronaghan	Northampton	16. 7.97P
G-MJRU	MBA Tiger Cub 440	SO.86		6. 1.83	D.J.Short	Nailsea, Bristol	31. 1.86E
G-MJRV	Eurowing Goldwing EW-69 & BMAA/HB/084			7. 1.83	N.W.Beadle (W/O on second flight)	Billericay	
G-MJSE	Skyrider Airsports Phantom (EC-44-PL)	SF-101		24. 1.83	C.J.Meadows	Franklyns Field, Chewton Mendip	21. 1.00P
G-MJSF	Skyrider Airsports Phantom	SF-105	SE-G-MJSF	24. 1.83	B.J.Towers	Pershore	
G-MJSL	Dragon 200 (Rotax 503)	0018		24. 2.83	G.Kingston & N.J.Warner	Long Marston	22. 9.99P
G-MJSO	Hiway Skytrike II/Demon 175 (Hiro 22)	SA17D		1. 2.83	D.C.Read	Ledbury	N/E
G-MJSP	Romain MBA Super Tiger Cub Special 440 (Nosewheel conversion)	SO.54		7. 2.83	A P Chapman	Grimsby	31. 1.86E
G-MJST	MEA Pterodactyl Ptraveler (EC-34-PM)	GCS-01		2.12.81	C.H.J.Goodwin	Bedford	7. 5.99P
G-MJSU*	MBA Tiger Cub 440 (Regd with c/n SO.175)	SO.75/1		2. 2.83	Not known (Stored 9.97)	Swanton Morley	31. 1.86E
G-MJSV*	MBA Tiger Cub 440	SO.87/2		2. 2.83	Not known (Stored 5.95)	RAF Kinloss	31. 1.86E
G-MJSY	Eurowing Goldwing (Rotax 377)	EW-63		8. 2.83	A.J.Rex	Wrexham	N/E
G-MJSZ	Harker DH Wasp (Rotax 447)	HA.5		10. 2.83	J.J.Hill	Middlesbrough	28. 7.98P
G-MJTD	Gardner T-M Scout (Thomas-Morse S4 Scout 2/3rd scale replica; as "41386" in US Army Signal Corps c/s) (Possibly c/n PFA/111-10664)	83/001		14. 2.83	D.Gardner	Rugby	AC
G-MJTE	Skyrider Airsports Phantom (EC-44-PM)	SF-106		15. 2.83	C.J.Tomlin	Desborough	1. 7.98P
G-MJTM	Aerostructure Pipistrelle P2B (KFM-107ER)	019 & SAL/P2B/002		21. 2.83	K.S.Matcham	Soberton, Southampton	18. 9.99P
G-MJTO	Jordan Duet Srs.1 (Rotax 503)	D 101		19. 7.83	M.E.Bates	Chesterfield	6. 3.94E

Regn	Type	C/n	P/I	Date	Owner/operator	Probable Base	CA Expy
G-MJTP	Mainair Tri-Flyer/Flexiform Dual Sealander		25. 2.83		P.Milton	Bedford	16. 6.98P
	(EC-44-PM)	AJDH-01 & 139-7383 (Possibly Dual Striker)					
G-MJTR	Southdown Puma DS Mk.1	H362		9. 3.83	D.W.Palmer	Bexhill-on-Sea	15. 7.96P
	(EC-44-PM)						
G-MJTX	Skyrider Airsports Phantom	SF-110		1. 3.83	G.C.Thomas	Long Marston	22. 4.96P
	(EC-44-PM)						
G-MJTZ	Skyrider Airsports Phantom	MBS-01		29. 4.83	B.J.Towers	Pershore	N/E
	(EC-44-PM) (Eng No.82-00119)						
G-MJUC	MBA Tiger Cub 440			7. 3.83	J.A.Harker	Southampton	20. 1.92E
	(EC-44-PM)	RRH-01 & PFA/140-10908			(Stored Kirkbride 5.96)		
G-MJUE	Southdown Puma	82-00435 & P.109		8. 3.83	J.Rae	Largs	N/E
	(Southdown Wildcat II Trike with Lightning II wing)						
G-MJUF*	MBA Super Tiger Cub 400	MCT-01		8. 3.83	Not known	Full Sutton	
					(Stored 6.96)		
G-MJUJ	Eipper Quicksilver MXII	1025		10. 3.83	J.F.A.Cooke	Llanbedr	27. 6.92E
	(Rotax 503)						
G-MJUM	Hiway Skytrike/Flexiform Striker			28. 3.83	M.J.W.Holding	Stafford	N/E
	(EC-25-PS)	82-00493 (C/n is Engine No.)					
G-MJUO*	Eipper Quicksilver MXII	1043		22. 3.83	Not known	Strathaven	
	(Cuyana 430R)				(Noted 8.98)		
G-MJUR	Skyrider Airsports Phantom	SF-108		5. 4.83	A.L.Lewis	Milson	20. 9.98P
	(EC-44-PM)						
G-MJUT	Eurowing Goldwing	DLE-01		23. 3.83	D.L.Eite	Newark	
G-MJUU	Eurowing Goldwing	EW-70		28. 3.83	E.F.Clapham	Oldbury-on-Severn	3. 5.97P
	(EC-344-PM)						
G-MJUV	Huntair Pathfinder mk.1	045		18. 5.83	S.J.Overton	(Colchester)	31. 3.99P
	(EC-44-PM)						
G-MJUW	MBA Tiger Cub 440	SO.69		29. 3.83	D.G.Palmer	Mintlaw	3. 5.99P
	(EC-44-PM)						
G-MJUX	Skyrider Airsports Phantom	RFF-01		29. 2.84	C.A.Crick	Desborough	6. 8.97P
	(EC-44-PM)						
G-MJUY*	Eurowing Goldwing	EW-82		6. 4.83	Not known	Hougham, Lincs	N/E
					(Stored complete 9.96)		
G-MJUZ	Dragon 150	015		30. 3.83	G.S.Richardson	North Coates	28. 2.87E
	(Robin EC-57)				(Stored 9.96)		
G-MJVE	Medway Hybred 44XL/Solar Wings Typhoon XLII			19. 4.83	T.A.Clark	Manningtree	16. 8.97P
	(EC-44-PM)	4483/1					
G-MJVF	CFM Shadow Srs.CD	002		12. 4.83	J.A.Cook	Thorpeness	16.12.99P
	(Rotax 503)						
G-MJVN	Southdown Puma/Flexiform Striker			18. 4.83	R.McGookin	West Kilbride	5.10.93P
	(EC-44-PM)	82-00030-PR1			(WFU and engine to G-MJRP)		
G-MJVP	Eipper Quicksilver MXII	1149		19. 4.83	G.J.Ward	Dorchester	10. 7.96P
G-MJVT	Eipper Quicksilver MX	10961		20. 4.83	L.Swift	Skegness	4. 5.94P
	(Cuyuna 430R)						
G-MJVU	Eipper Quicksilver MXII	1118		3. 4.84	F.J.Griffith	Denbigh	11. 6.99P
	(Rotax 503)						
G-MJVX	Skyrider Airsports Phantom			27. 4.83	J.R.Harris	Bewdley, Worcs	13. 4.99P
	(EC-44-PM)	JAG-01 & SF-102					
G-MJVY	Dragon 150	D.150/013		4. 5.83	J.C.Craddock	Freshwater, IoW	25. 7.99P
	(Rotax 503)						
G-MJWB	Eurowing Goldwing	EW-59		24. 5.83	F.C.Claydon	Newmarket	25. 8.93P
	(Rotax 447)						
G-MJWF	MBA Tiger Cub 440	BRH-001		4. 5.83	B.R.Hunter	Glasgow	
G-MJWG	MBA Tiger Cub 440			4. 5.83	W.K.Evans	Llanelli	18.10.98P
	(EC-44-PM) DHC-001, PFA/140-10961 & BMAA/HB/001						
G-MJWH*	Chargus Vortex 120		R		Midland Air Museum	Coventry	
	(Regn reserved in 1983 for a Chargus T.250 plus engine for F.Embleton, fitted to a 1974 Vortex hang glider; this was abandoned and only the wing is on display)						
G-MJWI*	Twamley Trike/Flexiform Striker			8. 7.83	M.P.Challis	Northampton	
		RWT-01			(Cancelled by CAA 27.3.99)		
G-MJWJ	MBA Tiger Cub 440	013/191		9. 5.83	G.Whitaker	Pontypridd	18. 3.96P
	(EC-44-PM)						
G-MJWK	Huntair Pathfinder 1	JWK-01		1.10.82	R.J.F.Coates	Kemble	23. 5.99P
	(Rotax 447)						
G-MJWN	Hornet/Flexiform Solo Striker			10. 5.83	G.de Clara	Stoke-on-Trent	26. 7.91E
	(EC-34-PM)	H430					
G-MJWS*	Eurowing Goldwing	EW-22		16. 5.83	Not known (Stored 4.94)	Newtownards	N/E
G-MJWW	MBA Super Tiger Cub 440	MU-001		11. 5.83	R.J.Tobin	Sudbrook, Lincoln	23. 5.98P
	(EC-44-PM) (Possibly c/n PFA/140-10904)						
G-MJWZ	Ultrasports/Solar Wings Panther XL-S			9. 9.85	C.P.Hughes	Rhuallt	27.10.98P
	(EC-44-2PM)	T583-781XL					
G-MJXD	MBA Tiger Cub 440	011/061		16. 5.83	W.L.Rogers	Totnes	
G-MJXE	Mainair Tri-Flyer/Hiway Demon 175			17. 5.83	H.Sykes	Manchester	21. 3.95P
	(EC-34-PM)	102-131082 & HS-001					
G-MJXJ*	MBA Tiger Cub 440	SO.100		20. 5.83	P.J.Wright	Whitstable	
					(Cancelled as WFU 6.3.99)		
G-MJXS	Huntair Pathfinder II	134		25. 5.83	A.E.Sawyer	Melrose Farm, Melbourne	
					(Stored 6.96)		

Regn	Type	C/n	P/I	Date	Owner/operator	Probable Base	CA Expy
G-MJXX	Lancashire Micro-Trike/Flexiform Dual Striker (EC-44-2PM)	AAL-01		16. 6.83	H.A.Ward (Possibly now a Mainair Tri-Flyer)	Popham	24. 2.92E
G-MJXY	Hiway Skytrike/Demon 175 (EC-34-PM)	KQ17D		31. 5.83	P.A.Ord	Redcar	17.11.98P
G-MJYC	Ultrasports/Solar Wings Panther XL (EC-44-PM)	JM-01		1.10.85	R.J.Humphries	Southampton	21. 4.98P
G-MJYF	Mainair Gemini/Flash 305-585-3 & W45 (EC-44-PM)			18. 4.85	W.D.Crooks	Richhill, Armagh	5. 5.97P
G-MJYP	Mainair Gemini/Flexiform Dual Striker (EC-44-PM)	167-13683		7. 6.83	R.Taylor & M.V.Rainford	Ormskirk	20.12.98P
G-MJYV	Mainair/Flexiform Rapier 1 + 1 (EC-34-PM)	175-19783		23.11.83	L.H.Phillips	Solihull	17.10.99P
G-MJYW	Lancashire Micro-Trike Dual 330/Wasp Gryphon III	2/330PM/PGK/6.83/K		28. 6.83	P.D.Lawrence	Munlochy, Ross-shire	
G-MJYX	Mainair Tri-Flyer/Hiway Demon (EC-33-PM)	108-251182		9. 6.83	I.Dzialowski	Grimsby	27. 6.94P
G-MJYY	Hiway Skytrike/Demon 175 (EC-34-PM)	ZD17D		9. 6.83	N.Smith	Brunton	N/E
G-MJZC	MBA Tiger Cub 440 (EC-44-PM)	SO.169		14. 6.83	R.D.Slegg	Haywards Heath	17. 1.94P
G-MJZD	Mainair Gemini/Flash (EC-44-PM)	311-585-3 & W50		18. 4.85	A.R.Gaivoto	Popham	15. 8.98P
G-MJZH	Mainair Tri-Flyer/Southdown Lightning 195 (EC-25-PS)	BFC-01 & 002-781 (Trike unit from G-MBCC)		27. 6.83	A.G.Thelwall	Bedford	N/E
G-MJZK(2)	Southdown Puma Sprint (EC-44-PM)	1111/0081		3. 3.86	R.J.Osborne	Tiverton	18.10.91P*
G-MJZL	Eipper Quicksilver MXII (Rotax 503)	EEW-01		15. 6.83	A.P.Kenning	Boston	7. 7.98P
G-MJZO	Lancashire Micro-Trike/Flexiform Solo Striker (EC-34-PM)	1/330PM/LM/683/2		24. 6.83	B.P.Barker	Ley Farm, Chirk	5. 4.96P
G-MJZU	Mainair Tri-Flyer/Flexiform Dual Striker (EC-44-PM)	JDR-02		21. 6.83	P.D.Mickleburgh	Fleckney, Leicester	3. 6.99P
G-MJZX*	Maxair Hummer TX	TX/16		21. 6.83	R.J.Folwell (Cancelled by CAA 27.3.99)	Bristol	

G-MKAA-MKZZ

Regn	Type	C/n	P/I	Date	Owner/operator	Probable Base	CA Expy
G-MKAK	Colt 77A HAFB	2039		15. 8.91	Virgin Airship & Balloon Co Ltd	Telford	13. 6.97A
G-MKAS	PA-28-140 Cherokee Cruiser	28-7425338	G-BKVR OY-BGV	30. 4.98	MK Aero Support Ltd	Andrewsfield	8. 7.01T
G-MKIV*	Bristol 149 Bolingbroke IVT	-	(G-BLHM) RCAF 10038	26. 3.82	G.A.Warner (As "V6028/GB-D" in 105 Sqdn c/s) (Damaged Denham 21.6.87; stored 3.96 for spares)	Duxford	28. 5.88P
G-MKIX	VS.361 Spitfire IXe CBAF.IX.2200 (Firewall no. CBAF.8563)		N238V OO-ARE Belg.AF SM-36/Fokker B-8/R.Neth AF H-60/H-103/NH238	12.12.83	D.W.Arnold t/a Warbirds of GB (As "NH238") (Stored 1996) (Bournemouth)		22. 5.93P
G-MKPU	Europa Avn Europa	PFA/247-12569	G-DZEL	22.12.97	M.K.Papworth (Upwood, Cambs)		
G-MKVB	VS.349 Spitfire LF.Vb CBAF.2461		5718M BM597	2. 5.89	Historic Acft Collection Ltd (As "BM597/JH-C" in 317 Sqdn c/s)	Duxford	17. 3.99P
G-MKVI	FFW DH.100 Vampire FB.6	676	J-1167	2. 6.92	T.C.Topen (To De Havilland Aviation Ltd) (As "WL505" in 614 Sqn c/s) (Stored 3.97)	Swansea	14. 9.95P
G-MKXI	VS.365 Spitfire PR.XI (Packard Merlin 266)	6S/504719	R Neth AF PL965	13.11.89	R.A.Fleming & A.J.E.Smith (Op Real Aeroplane Co) (As "PL965/R" in 16 Sqn RAF c/s) (Damaged nr Ashford, Kent 2.8.98)	Breighton	11. 6.99P

G-MLAA-MLZZ

Regn	Type	C/n	P/I	Date	Owner/operator	Probable Base	CA Expy
G-MLAS*	Cessna 182E	182-53826	OO-HPE D-EGPE/N2826Y	2. 5.79	Not known (Crashed 14.12.80; cabin used as para-trainer 5.94)	St.Merryn	2.10.82
G-MLFF	PA-23-250 Aztec E	27-7305194	G-WEBB G-BJBU/N40476	31. 1.90	Channel Islands Aero Services Ltd Jersey t/a Jersey Aero Club		19.11.99T
G-MLTI	Dassault Falcon 900B	164	F-WWFC	13. 6.97	Multiflight Ltd	Leeds-Bradford	12. 6.99T
G-MLWI	Thunder Ax7-77 HAFB	1000		3. 9.86	M.L. & L.P.Willoughby "Mr Blue Sky"	Reading	7. 8.95A

G-MMAA-MMZZ

Regn	Type	C/n	P/I	Date	Owner/operator	Probable Base	CA Expy
G-MMAC	Dragon Srs.200 (EC-44-PM)	003	OY-... G-MMAC	14. 7.82	J.F.Ashton & J.Kirwan	Ince Blundell	N/E
G-MMAE	Dragon Srs 200 (EC-44-PM)	005		7. 9.82	B.P.Walmbley	Davidstow Moor	29. 7.96P
G-MMAG	MBA Tiger Cub 440 (EC-44-PM)	SO.47		22. 6.83	M.J.Aubrey	Kington, Hereford	14. 9.93P
G-MMAI	Dragon Srs.150	0032		1. 7.83	G.S.Richardson	North Coates	13. 7.97P
G-MMAJ	Mainair Gemini/Southdown Sprint X (EC-44-PM) MLS.01 & 193-14983			12.10.83	D.M.Pearson Chiltern Park, Wallingford		19. 3.98P
G-MMAK	MBA Tiger Cub 440	SO.155		20. 9.83	G.E.Heritage	Corley, Coventry	
G-MMAL	Mainair Tri-Flyer/Flexiform Dual Striker (EC-44-PM) DHM-01			20. 9.83	Tina E.Simpson (On rebuild 10.97)	Bewdley, Worcs	1. 4.94P
G-MMAM	MBA Tiger Cub 440 (EC-44-PM)	SO.197		23. 9.83	M.G.Reilly	Old Sarum	14. 6.96P
G-MMAN	Mainair Tri-Flyer 330/Flexiform Solo Striker 192-6983			27. 9.83	K.F.Gittins	Billingham	8.12.98P
G-MMAO	Southdown Puma Sprint X (EC-44-PM)	HS.549		28.12.83	P.A.Kershaw (Stored 8.97)	Tarn Farm, Cockerham	14. 3.99P
G-MMAP	Maxair Hummer TX (Zenoah G25B1)	250TX-17		29. 9.83	L.Gerrard	Groby, Leicester	5. 9.93E
G-MMAR	Southdown Puma Sprint MS 195-11083-2 (Mainair Gemini) (EC-44-PM)			23. 9.83	A.R. & J.Fawkes	Newbury	17. 9.98P
G-MMAW	Mainair/Flexiform Rapier 1+1 (Solo Striker) (EC-34-PM) 131-10283			18. 7.83	G.B.Hutchison	Bury St.Edmunds	29. 7.96P
G-MMAX	Hiway Skytrike/Flexiform Dual Striker 0011			5. 8.93	D A Hopewell & M T Wells	Newcastle	N/E
G-MMAZ	Southdown Puma Sprint X (EC-44-PM)	MAPB-01		5. 8.83	A.R.Smith	Chelmsford	22. 7.96P
G-MMBJ	Hiway Skytrike/Solar Wings Medium Typhoon (EC-34-PM) RFB-01			5. 7.83	W.Wells	Belvedere, Kent	11. 6.96P
G-MMBL	Southdown Puma DS (EC-44-PM)	80-00083		4. 7.83	B.J.Farrell	Preston, Lancs	7. 3.92E
G-MMBN	Eurowing Goldwing (Rotax 447)	EW-89		28. 6.83	W.G.Reynolds (Stored 8.93)	Overstrand, Cromer	27. 8.92E
G-MMBS	Hiway Skytrike/Flexiform Striker (EC-34-PM) JTRC-01 (Possibly shares trike with G-MJOU)			6. 7.83	R.J.Thompson (Stored 9.96)	Milson	5. 3.94E
G-MMBT	MBA Tiger Cub 440 SO.131 & TA.01 (Probably either c/n PFA/140-10924 or 10990)			19. 7.83	F.F.Chamberlain (Stored 1.91)	Ipswich	31. 1.86E
G-MMBU	Eipper Quicksilver MXII (Rotax 503)	CAL-222		8. 7.83	G.Lockwood	Bridlington	11. 5.99P
G-MMBV	Huntair Pathfinder (EC-34-PM)	044		8. 7.83	P.J.Bishop	Tarn Farm, Cockerham	17. 5.97P
G-MMBY	Ultrasports/Solar Wings Panther XL (EC-44-PM) T483-759XL			20. 7.83	R.M.Sheppard & P.Huddleston	Wantage/Marlborough	29. 7.99P
G-MMBZ	Solar Wings Typhoon P T981-5217 (EC-34-PM) (C/n probably T981-217)			20. 7.83	T.J.Birkbeck	Rufforth	28. 4.96P
G-MMCB*	Huntair Pathfinder II	136		13. 7.83	The Science Museum (On display 7.92)	Wroughton	
G-MMCG	Eipper Quicksilver MX I (Cuyuna 430R)	10990		14. 7.83	D.Pick	Boston	7. 7.98P
G-MMCI	Southdown Puma Sprint X (EC-44-PM) DMP-01 & P.421			28. 9.83	R.J.Webb	Long Marston	3. 6.99P
G-MMCJ	Flexiform Dual Striker	JJ-165		13. 2.87	L.G.Martindale	Liverpool	N/E
G-MMCM	Mainair Tri-Flyer/Southdown Puma Sprint (EC-44-PM) CM-2			28. 6.83	J.McAvoy	Bishopton, Renfrew	17. 7.98P
G-MMCV	Hiway Skytrike II/Solar Wings Typhoon (EC-34-PM) T583-783			27. 7.83	G.Addison	Kinross	8. 6.97P
G-MMCW	Southdown Puma Sprint 572 & 1121/0124			16. 9.83	J.Brandrick Cwmdwyfran Farm, Carmarthen		6. 8.97P
G-MMCX	MBA Super Tiger Cub 440	MU.002		8. 8.83	D.Harkin	Johnstone, Renfrew	
G-MMCZ	Mainair Tri-Flyer/Flexiform Dual Striker (EC-44-PM) TE-01 (Mainair Trike c/n 180-...)			10. 8.83	T.D.Adamson	Morgansfield, Fishburn	12.12.99P
G-MMDF	Southdown Wild Cat Mk.II/Lightning Phase II (EC-34-PM) 007			24. 8.83	J.C.Haigh	Tonbridge	27. 1.99P
G-MMDK	Mainair Tri-Flyer/Flexiform Striker (EC-34-PM) 181-16883			7. 9.83	P.E.Blyth	Rotherham	30. 5.99P
G-MMDN	Mainair Tri-Flyer/Flexiform Dual Striker RPO.12			30. 9.83	M.G.Griffiths	Monmouth	N/E
	(Initially had Hornet Invader trike and still regd with Hornet c/n)						
G-MMDP	Mainair Gemini/Southdown Sprint X (EC-44-PM) 183-22883			20. 9.83	J.D.Bridgewater & C.H.Prince	Kirkmichael, IoM	25. 1.95P
	(C/n duplicates G-MMPD; probably fitted with new Gemini trike)						
G-MMDR	Huntair Pathfinder II	137		30. 8.83	C.Dolling	Swindon	
G-MMDS	Ultrasports/Solar Wings Panther XL-S (EC-34-PM) KND-02			13. 7.84	C.C.Exton	London E15	10. 1.94P

Regn	Type	C/n P/I	Date	Owner/operator	Probable Base	CA Expy
G-MMDT*	Mainair Tri-Flyer/Flexiform Striker (EC-44-PM) 178-20583		1. 9.83	Not known (Stored 8.95)	Long Marston	N/E
G-MMDU*	MBA Tiger Cub 440 SO.49 (EC-44-PM)		5. 9.83	Not known (Stored dismantled 3.98)	Chirk	N/E
G-MMDX	Lloyd Trident/Solar Wings Typhoon EJL-01		7. 9.83	E.J.Lloyd (Status uncertain)	Caterham, Surrey	
G-MMDY	Southdown Puma Sprint X S.064 (EC-44-PM)		7. 9.83	C.Duffin	Portlaoise, Co.Laois	N/E
G-MMEF	Hiway Skytrike/Super Scorpion SM160B 10664		13. 9.83	R.H.Evans	Bury St.Edmunds	
G-MMEG*	Eipper Quicksilver MX DJND-02		14. 9.83	Not known (Stored 1994)	Rayne Hall Farm, Rayne	N/E
G-MMEI	Hiway Skytrike/Demon 3644C (EC-34-PM)		21. 9.83	W.H.Shakeshaft	Chelmsford	30.11.94P
G-MMEJ	Mainair Tri-Flyer/Flexiform Striker (EC-34-PM) 215-41183 & FF/LAI/83/JDR/03		15. 9.83	R.B.Tweedie	Stoke-on-Trent	9.11.97P
G-MMEO	Ultrasports Tripacer/Southdown Lightning Phase II 135		21. 9.83	G.C.Rogers	Dartford	4. 1.95P
G-MMES*	Southdown Puma Sprint SS.582 (EC-44-PM)		21.12.83	S.E.Balley t/a Balleys Forecourt Sves (Cancelled by CAA 27.3.99)	Newbury	11. 8.98P
G-MMEY	MBA Tiger Cub 440 SO.206 (EC-44-PM)		21.10.83	G.Norton	Lincoln	26. 5.95P
G-MMFC*	Mainair Gemini/Flexiform Dual Striker (EC-44-PM) KR235-484-2 & FF/LAI/83/JDR/11		20. 9.83	L.R.Orriss (Cancelled by CAA 25.8.98)	Rotherham	29.12.94P
G-MMFD	Mainair Tri-Flyer/Flexiform Dual Striker (EC-44-PM) 210-31083-2 & FF/LAI/83/JDR/12		20. 9.83	M.E. & W.L.Chapman	Oldham	6.12.93P
G-MMFE	Mainair Tri-Flyer/Flexiform Striker (EC-44-PM) FF/LAI/83/JDR/13		20. 9.83	W.Camm	Barnsley	16. 6.94P
G-MMFG	Lancashire Micro-Trike/Flexiform Dual Striker (EC-44-PM) FF/LAI/83/JDR/15		20. 9.83	M.G.Dean & M.J.Hadland	Tarn Farm, Cockerham	18. 3.93E
G-MMFK	Mainair Tri-Flyer/Flexiform Dual Striker (Rotax 447) 234-284-2 & FF/LAI/83/JDR/19		20. 9.83	M.J.Robbins	Tunbridge Wells	19. 7.96P
G-MMFL	Ultrasports Tripacer/Flexiform Solo Sealander (EC-34-PM) JGM-01		25.10.83	T.C.Bradley	Gloucester	N/E
G-MMFN	MBA Tiger Cub 440 (EC-44-PM) SO.113		31.10.83	J.S.Skipp	Bromyard, Hereford	30.11.95P
G-MMFS	MBA Tiger Cub 440 (EC-44-PM) SO.64		1.11.83	P.J.Taylor	Stafford	11.12.98P
G-MMFT	MBA Tiger Cub 440 (EC-34-PM) SO.56		2.11.83	E.N.Simmons	Wyberton	23. 1.95P
G-MMFV	Mainair Tri-Flyer/Flexiform Dual Striker (EC-44-PM) 212-271083		8.12.83	R.A.Walton	Basingstoke	26. 4.97P
G-MMFZ	Striplin Sky Ranger HAW-01		18.11.83	H.A.Ward	Winchester	
G-MMGF	MBA Tiger Cub 440 SO.124		18.11.83	A.P.Chapman	Grimsby	12. 5.93P
G-MMGL	MBA Tiger Cub 440 SO.148 & BMAA/HB/050 (EC-44-PM)		23.11.83	H.E.Dunning (Stored Rufforth 8.95)	Knaresborough	
G-MMGP	Southdown Puma Sprint X RGC-01 (EC-44-PM)		24.11.83	J.Garcia	Kilmarnock	5. 2.92E
G-MMGS	Ultrasports/Solar Wings Panther XL (EC-44-PM) T1283-939XL		28.12.83	D.W.Bock	Saltash	12. 8.98P
G-MMGT	Hunt Avon Skytrike/Hunt Wing JAH-7 (Rotax 462) (Also reported as Solar Wings Typhoon wing)		28.11.83	J.A.Hunt	Hereford	17. 4.99P
G-MMGU	SMD Gazelle/Flexiform Sealander (EC-44-PM) 30-4883		1.12.83	A.D.Cranfield	Wincanton	19. 9.93E
G-MMGV	Microknight Whittaker MW-5 Sorcerer Srs.A 001		2.12.83	G.N.Haffey & M.W.J.Whittaker	Chatham/Doncaster	6. 5.89P
G-MMHE*	Mainair Gemini/Southdown Sprint MS (EC-44-PM) 229-184-2		8.12.83	L.Fekete & J.Sharp (Cancelled by CAA 30.10.98)	Rhuallt	27. 5.98P
G-MMHF	Southdown Puma Sprint EBDA-01 (EC-44-PM)		8.12.83	B.R.Claughton	Whitstable	2.10.99P
G-MMHK	Hiway Skytrike/Super Scorpion KSC.83 (EC-25-PS)		19.12.83	C.N.Bradley	Darlington	N/E
G-MMHL	Hiway Skytrike/Super Scorpion KSC.84		19.12.83	E.J.Blyth	Pickering	N/E
G-MMHN	MBA Tiger Cub 440 SO.136		19.12.83	M.J.Aubrey	Kington, Hereford	
G-MMHP	Hiway Hiro Skytrike/Demon 175 PCC-01 & OL17D (Regd with c/n OL175)		19.12.83	P.A.Bedford	Tewkesbury	N/E
G-MMHR	Mainair Gemini/Southdown Sprint (EC-44-PM) 213-271083-2 & P.427		29.12.83	C.A.Eagles	Basingstoke	2. 9.90P
G-MMHS	SMD Gazelle/Flexiform Dual Striker 104-11283		21.12.83	C.J.Meadows	Shepton Mallet	
G-MMHY	Hornet Invader 440/Flexiform Dual Striker RPO.17		21.12.83	W.Finlay	Leeds	
G-MMHZ	Ultrasports/Solar Wings Panther XL-S (EC-44-PM) TP2-0001 & T1283-948XL (Wing ex G-MJPU)		3. 1.84	S.J.Pain	Hulcote Farm, Nottingham	26. 9.98P
G-MMIE	MBA Tiger Cub 440 G7-7		3. 1.84	B.W.Olliver	Telford	31. 1.86E
G-MMIH	MBA Tiger Cub 440 SO.130 (EC-44-PM)		25. 4.84	R.A.Davis	Gloucester	19. 8.93P
G-MMII	Southdown Puma Sprint P.500 (EC-44-PM)		26. 1.84	P.J.Daulton	Billingshurst	24. 6.96P
G-MMIJ	Ultrasports Tripacer/Airwave Nimrod 165 (EC-34-PM) ZX-00165		1.11.83	R.J.Wheeler	Haverfordwest	9.12.96P

Regn	Type	C/n	P/I	Date	Owner/operator	Probable Base	CA Expy
G-MMIL	Eipper Quicksilver MXII (Rotax 503) (C/n duplicates G-MMNA)	1046		6. 1.84	C.K.Brown	Loughborough	24. 3.94P
G-MMIM	MBA Tiger Cub 440 (EC-44-PM)	SO.28 & BMAA/HB/060		11. 1.84	T.J.Bidwell	Newtown, Powys	19.12.97P
G-MMIO*	Huntair Pathfinder II	159		16. 1.84	Not known (Stored 6.96)	Melrose Farm, Melbourne	
G-MMIR	Mainair Gemini/Southdown Sprint (EC-44-PM) 051-20182 (Regd with original Trike c/n ex G-MBKX then G-MJDO; now rebuilt with Trike 314-585-3 ex G-MMZK; wing ex G-MMTI)			25. 1.84	J.P.Wilson (Stored 1.98)	Long Marston	15. 8.97P
G-MMIV*	Mainair Gemini/Southdown Sprint (EC-44-PM) 231-184-2			3. 2.84	W.Anderson (Cancelled by CAA 21.1.98)	Linlithgow	30. 4.98P
G-MMIW	Southdown Puma Sprint (EC-44-PM)	590		9. 2.84	F.H.Cook	Whitchurch	1. 8.98P
G-MMIX	MBA Tiger Cub 440 (EC-44-PM)	MBCB-01		14. 2.84	J.S.Morgan	Long Marston	N/E
G-MMJB*	American Aerolights Eagle	JB-01		21. 3.83	Not known	Long Marston	31. 8.85E
G-MMJD	Southdown Puma Sprint (EC-44-PM)	SP/1001		28. 6.83	A.C.Snowling	Dereham	1. 6.99P
G-MMJF	Ultrasports/Solar Wings Panther Dual XL-S (EC-44-PM) T284-988XL			27. 2.84	D.J. & M.E.Walcroft	Great Missenden	20. 4.99P
G-MMJG	Mainair Tri-Flyer/Flexiform Dual Striker (EC-44-PM) 185-1983			31. 9.83	A.D.Stewart	Dollar, Clackmannan	1. 7.99P
G-MMJM	Southdown Puma Sprint (EC-44-PM) PD.500 & 1111/0001			27. 2.84	R.J.Sanger	Wickford	31. 5.97P
G-MMJS*	MBA Tiger Cub 440	WAM.1		8. 1.87	J.M.Robinson (Stored 1.93)	Bann Foot, Lough Neagh	
G-MMJT	Mainair Gemini/Southdown Sprint X (EC-44-PM) JBT-01			20.12.83	W.F.Murray	Swinford, Rugby	6. 7.99P
G-MMJV	MBA Tiger Cub 440 (EC-44-PM) SO.195 & PFA/140-10902			5. 3.84	D.G.Palmer	Mintlaw, Peterhead	9. 5.93P
G-MMJX	Teman Mono-Fly (Rotax 377)	01		6. 3.84	M.Ingleton	Sheerness	27. 5.99P
G-MMKA	Ultrasports/Solar Wings Panther Dual XL (EC-44-PM) T284-986XL			8. 3.84	R.S.Wood	Wallacestone, Falkirk	30. 4.86E
G-MMKD	Southdown Puma Sprint (EC-44-PM)	P.514		27. 2.84	G.G.Stokes	Stourport-on-Severn	11. 6.95P
G-MMKE	Birdman WT-11 Chinook	01817		2. 4.84	D.M.Jackson	Belper	31.12.87E
G-MMKG	Medway Hybred 44XL/Solar Wings Typhoon XL2 (EC-44-PM) 22284/7			9. 3.84	G.P.Lane (Reported with wing marked G-MNYX 8.96)	Bristol	18. 7.97P
G-MMKH	Medway Hybred 44XL/Solar Wings Typhoon XL (EC-44-PM) 22284/8			9. 3.84	K.W.E.Brunnenkant	Lincoln	1.10.97P
G-MMKL	Mainair Gemini/Flash 238-384-2 & W11 (EC-44-PM)			12. 3.84	D.W.Cox	Coventry	29. 9.93P
G-MMKM	Mainair Gemini/Flexiform Dual Striker (EC-44-PM) 221-184-2 (Regd/stamped with c/n 221-0184-0002)			12. 3.84	N.J.Raeside & M.Grundmann Baxby Manor, Husthwaite		11. 6.99P
G-MMKP	MBA Tiger Cub 440	SO.203		13. 3.84	J.W.Beaty	Kettering	
G-MMKR	Mainair Tri-Flyer/Southdown Lightning DS (EC-44-PM) 209-171083			14. 3.84	C.R.Madden	Great Orton	2. 6.96P
G-MMKU	Mainair Gemini/Southdown Sprint MS (EC-44-PM) 232-284-2 & P.519			19. 3.84	T.J.Ford & R.D.McManus	Stone	2.10.94P
G-MMKV	Southdown Puma Sprint (EC-44-PM)	P.521		24. 4.84	A.Turnbull	Clitheroe	24. 2.99P
G-MMKX*	Skyrider Airsports Phantom 330 PH-107R (EC-34-PL-02)			18. 3.85	D.B.White (Cancelled by CAA 15.3.99)	Little Gransden	11.12.98P
G-MMLB	MBA Super Tiger Cub 440	SO.57		19. 3.84	A.Newton	Hull	
G-MMLE	Eurowing Goldwing SP	EW-81		21. 3.84	D.Lamberty	Linlithgow	
G-MMLF	MBA Tiger Cub 440 (EC-44-PM)	SO.115		23. 3.84	W.M.Wilson	Doncaster	31.12.91E
G-MMLH	Hiway Skytrike Mk.II 330/Demon PMH-01 & DJL-01			28. 3.84	P.M.Hendry & D.J.Lukey	Folkestone	
G-MMLM	MBA Tiger Cub 440	SO.172		26. 3.84	J.Scholefield	Glasgow	N/E
G-MMLP	Mainair Gemini/Southdown Sprint (EC-44-PM) 242-484-2			3. 4.84	S.F.K.Blakeman	Eaglescott	24. 7.99P
G-MMLV	Southdown Puma 330 (Lightning) (EC-34-PL) P3-84-4-164 (C/n quoted as P3-84-164)			29.11.84	C.L.Newcombe	Ashford, Kent	31. 5.97P
G-MMLX	Ultrasports/Solar Wings Panther XL-S (EC-44-PM) T584-1063XL			3. 7.84	M.J.Curnow	Marazon	7. 8.99P
G-MMMB	Mainair Tri-Flyer/Southdown Sprint (EC-44-PM) CR-01/170 & 170-16583 (Trike unit ex G-MJYU)			5. 4.84	K.Birkett	Southampton	18. 8.99P
G-MMMD	Mainair Gemini/Southdown Sprint (EC-44-PM) 224-184-2 & P.504			30.12.83	R.J.Newsham	Clench Common	14. 8.97P
G-MMMG	Eipper Quicksilver MXL (Rotax 377)	1383		5. 6.84	J.J.James	Spilsby, Lincs	29. 6.99P
G-MMMH	Hadland Willow/Flexiform Striker (BMW R80/7) MJH 383			9.12.83	M.J.Hadland	Wigan	11. 4.98P
G-MMMI	Ultrasports Tripacer/Southdown Lightning DS Phase II (EC-34-PM) SW-01			30. 3.84	S.Moore Lower Mountpleasant Farm, Wimblington		8. 7.96P

298

Regn	Type	C/n	P/I	Date	Owner/operator	Probable Base	CA Expy
G-MMML	Dragon Srs.150 (EC-44-PM)	D150/002	OY-... G-MMML	28. 6.83	R.G.Huntley	Bradford-on-Avon	6. 9.98P
G-MMMN	Ultrasports/Solar Wings Panther Dual XL-S (EC-44-2PM)	PXL 843-150		4. 4.84	C.Downton	Newton Abbot	5.12.99P
G-MMMR	Ultrasports Tripacer/Flexiform Striker (EC-34-PM)	MAR-01		14. 3.84	H.A.Lloyd-Jennings	London SW6	10.11.98P
G-MMMW	Hornet Invader/Flexiform Dual Striker (EC-44-2PM)	KMS-01 & RPO.18		29. 3.84	A.Worthington	Chorley	19.11.97P
G-MMNA*	Eipper Quicksilver MXII (C/n duplicates G-MMIL)	1046		30. 3.84	K.R.Daly St.Marys, Isles of Scilly (Cancelled by CAA 28.1.99)		2.11.93P
G-MMNB	Eipper Quicksilver MX (Cuyuna 430R)	4286		30. 3.84	J.T.Lindop	Long Marston	12.10.97P
G-MMNC	Eipper Quicksilver MX (Cuyuna 430R)	4276		30. 3.84	K.R.Daly St.Marys, Isles of Scilly		31. 5.96P
G-MMND	Eipper Quicksilver MXII Q2 (Rotax 503)	1038		30. 3.84	G.B.Burby Tarn Farm, Cockerham (Status uncertain)		13.11.94P
G-MMNH	Dragon Srs.150 (EC-44-PM)	D150/42		27. 7.83	T.J.Barlow	Dromore	30. 3.93E
G-MMNM	Hornet 330/Skyhook Sabre	H310		9. 4.84	T.Pearson	Huddersfield	
G-MMNN	Sherry Buzzard	1		6. 4.84	E.W.Sherry	Stoke-on-Trent	
G-MMNS	Mitchell Super Wing U-2	PFA/114-10690		11. 4.84	C.Baldwin & J.C.Lister Valley Farm, Winwick		
G-MMNT	Flexiform Solo Striker (Rotax 277)	SSL-1		16. 4.84	C.R.Thorne	Lyndhurst, Hants	N/E
G-MMNW	Mainair Tri-Flyer/Hiway Demon 175 (EC-34-PM)	TJ-01		2. 8.84	T.Cottrell	Douglas, IoM	29. 6.97P
G-MMNX	Ultrasports/Solar Wings Panther XL	PXL 844-153		8. 5.84	B.Montsern	Lenham Heath, Maidstone	AC
G-MMOB	Mainair Gemini/Southdown Sprint (EC-44-PM)	244-584-2		11. 5.84	D.Woolcock	Preston	3. 9.99P
G-MMOF	MBA Tiger Cub 440 (EC-44-PM)	SO.76		14. 6.83	D.Gee	Barnsley	30.11.92E
G-MMOH	Solar Wings Pegasus XL-R	SW-TB-1450 & T484-1054XL		4. 5.84	T.H.Scott	Rayne Hall Farm, Rayne	
	(New Trike fitted replacing one formerly on G-MBTT)						
G-MMOK	Ultrasports/Solar Wings Panther XL-S (EC-44-PM)	T584-1066XL		9. 5.84	R.F. & A.J.Foster	Woodbridge	6. 5.99P
G-MMOW	Mainair Gemini/Flash (EC-44-PM)	246-684-3		21. 5.84	J.Wakelin	Boscastle	20. 4.99P
G-MMPG	Southdown Puma Sprint (EC-34-PM) (Tripacer/Lightning II)	NEA-01		8. 6.84	W.Parsons	Royston	14. 2.98P
G-MMPH	Southdown Puma Sprint (EC-44-PM)	P.545		20. 6.84	J.E.Mills	Shifnal	5.11.98P
G-MMPL	Lancashire Micro-Trike 440/Flexiform Dual Striker PDL-02 & 2/330PM/PGK/683/K (EC-44-PM)			5.12.83	P.D.Lawrence	Munlochy, Ross-shire	28. 8.99P
G-MMPO	Mainair Gemini/Flash (EC-44-PM)	325-785-3 & W65		18. 4.85	H.B.Baker	Chilbolton	3. 6.99P
G-MMPR*	Dragon Srs.150	0011		18. 4.83	Not known	Letterkenny, Ireland	28. 2.87E
G-MMPT	SMD Gazelle/Flexiform Dual Striker	ECP-01		5. 6.84	A.K.Buttle	Sherborne	N/E
G-MMPU	Ultrasports Tripacer/Solar Wings Typhoon S4 (EC-34-PM)	RJH-01		5. 6.84	J.T.Halford	Holt, Norfolk	22. 5.96P
G-MMPZ	Teman Mono-Fly (Rotax 447)	JWH-01		2. 7.84	R.V.Brunskill	Wallsend	6.11.99P
G-MMRH	Hiway Skytrike/Demon	JSM-01 & 25Rl		20. 6.84	J.S.McCaig	North Berwick	
G-MMRJ*	Ultrasports/Solar Wings Panther XL-S (EC-44-PM)	PXL846-167 & T684-1098XL		21. 6.84	Not known (Stored 5.93)	Hatherton, Cannock	18. 4.90P
G-MMRK	Ultrasports/Solar Wings Panther XL-S (EC-44-PM)	PXL846-175 & T684-1107XL		9. 7.84	L.S.Broom	London W12	28. 9.95P
G-MMRL	Ultrasports/Solar Wings Panther XL-S (EC-44-PM)	PXL846-174 & T684-1102XL		17. 7.84	A.B.Cameron	Preston	7. 1.00P
G-MMRN	Southdown Puma Sprint (EC-44-PM)	P.544		16. 7.84	T.F.R.Calladine	Selston, Nottingham	2. 2.99P
G-MMRO	Mainair Gemini/Southdown Sprint (EC-44-PM)	258-784-2 & P.557		17.10.84	M.A.Sims (Stored 8.97)	Old Sarum	7. 4.96P
G-MMRP	Mainair Gemini/Southdown Sprint (EC-44-PM)	259-884-2 & P.561		7. 2.85	J.C.S.Jones	Rhuallt	24. 2.99P
G-MMRT	Southdown Raven X 2232/0175 (Rotax 447) (Originally regd to Puma Sprint (EC-44-PM) c/n T.513 & P.532; amended 8.1986 but possibly reverted in 1987)			11. 7.84	V.A.Brierley (Damaged mid.1996)	Dover	11. 8.99P
G-MMRW	Mainair Gemini 440/Flexiform Dual Striker LAI/DS/25 & 216-71283-2			5. 1.84	M.D.Hinge	Salisbury	N/E
G-MMRY	Chargus T.250/Hiway Vulcan	EDG-01		17. 7.84	D.L.Edwards, I.R.Davis & R.J.Grantham Weston-super-Mare/Bath		
G-MMRZ	Ultrasports/Solar Wings Panther XL-S (EC-44-PM)	PXL847-168 & T684-1099XL		16. 7.84	A.L.Lyall	East Fortune	13. 6.98P
G-MMSA	Ultrasports/Solar Wings Panther XL-S (EC-44-2PM) PXL847-189 & T184-1142XL (C/n probably T784-1142XL)			9. 8.84	A.Draper, G.Jones & D.A.Breeze Newtown, Powys		27. 5.98P

Regn	Type	C/n	P/I	Date	Owner/operator	Probable Base	CA Expy
G-MMSE	Eipper Quicksilver MX	10021		23. 7.84	P.Rowbotham	Loughborough	31.10.85E
G-MMSG	Ultrasports/Solar Wings Panther XL-S			6. 9.85	R.W.McKee	Deeside	12.11.98
	(EC-44-2PM)	T884-1165XL		(Regd with c/n 8841/65XC; c/n duplicates G-MMTT)			
G-MMSH	Ultrasports/Solar Wings Panther XL-S			28. 5.85	I.J.Drake	Billericay	7. 5.90P
	(EC-44-PM)	PXL984-192 & T884-1163XL					
G-MMSO	Mainair Gemini/Southdown Sprint			14. 1.86	K.A.Maughan	Sandtoft	26. 7.99P
	(EC-44-PM)	255-784-2 & P.539					
G-MMSP	Mainair Gemini/Flash	265-984-2		17. 8.84	R.I.Henderson	Lanark	24. 1.99P
	(EC-44-PM)						
G-MMSS*	Ultrasports Tri-pacer/Southdown Lightning			27. 3.84	G.Norn	East Kirkby	7. 7.98P
	(EC-34-PM)	SRS/HJ2426			(Cancelled by CAA 11.12.98)		
G-MMST	Southdown Puma Sprint	1221/0003		7. 1.85	A.G.Cooper	Chesterfield	14. 9.97P
	(EC-44-PM)						
G-MMSV	Southdown Puma Sprint	1221/0004		21. 5.86	J.Ridgewell	Long Marston	25. 5.92P
	(EC-44-PM)						
G-MMSW	MBA Tiger Cub 440	SO.68		8. 8.84	D.R.Hemmings	Ringwood	
G-MMSZ	Medway Half Pint/Aerial Arts 130SX			27. 3.85	Lancaster Partners (Holdings) Ltd		
	(JPL PUL425)	2/21385				Ash Croft Farm, Winsford	N/E
G-MMTA	Ultrasports/Solar Wings Panther XL-S			25.10.84	R.E.Goodwin	Olney	29. 1.99P
	(EC-44-PM)	PXL884-194 & T884-1164XL					
G-MMTB*	Mainair Gemini/Southdown Sprint			R	Not known	Lagos, Algarve, Portugal	
G-MMTC	Solar Wings Pegasus XL-R	T684-1101XL		28. 9.84	P.J.Sheehy	Warsash, Southampton	22. 3.99P
	(Rotax 447)						
G-MMTD	Mainair Tri-Flyer/Hiway Demon 175			16. 8.84	W.E.Teare	Ramsey, IoM	1. 9.99P
	(EC-34-PM)	EIA-01					
G-MMTG	Mainair Gemini/Southdown Sprint			21. 8.84	H.A.Rose	Durham	13. 8.94P
	(EC-44-PM)	267-984-2 & P.577					
G-MMTH	Southdown Puma Sprint	P.538		4. 9.84	R.G.Tomlinson	Yeovil	8.12.92P
	(EC-44-PM)						
G-MMTI	Southdown Puma Sprint	1221/0005		13. 9.84	P.A.C.Bailey	Tonbridge	29. 4.99P
	(EC-44-PM) (C/n duplicates ZS-VLZ) (See G-MMIR - possibly fitted with new wing)						
G-MMTJ	Southdown Puma Sprint	1221/0006		17. 1.85	R.A.Redmond & A.J.Murray		
	(EC-44-PM)					Celbridge/Dublin	25. 9.98P
G-MMTK	Medway Hybred 44XL/Solar Wings Typhoon			30. 8.84	J.F.Nicholls	Rochester	9.10.95P
	(EC-44-PM)	12784/9					
G-MMTL	Mainair Gemini/Southdown Sprint			3.10.84	T.W.Faragher	Jurby, IoM	6. 7.99P
	(EC-44-PM)	268-1084-2 & P.576					
G-MMTM	Mainair Gemini/Southdown Sprint			12. 7.85	D.H.George	Sandown	25. 3.90P*
	(EC-44-PM)	141-29383 & P.575		(Initially regd with Trike 269-1084-27)			
G-MMTO	Mainair Tri-Flyer/Southdown Sprint			6. 9.84	R.W.Kelly	New Ross, Co.Wexford	7. 8.98P
	(EC-44-PM)	236-384-2 & P.498					
G-MMTR	Ultrasports/Solar Wings Pegasus XL-R			27. 9.84	P.Sarfas	Billericay	20. 9.99P
	(Rotax 447)	KND-03					
G-MMTS	Ultrasports/Solar Wings Panther XL			18. 9.84	A.S.Wason	Wootton Bassett	1.10.97P
	(EC-44-PM)	T784-1157XL					
G-MMTT	Ultrasports/Solar Wings Panther XL-S			12.12.84	C.T.H.Tenison	Abergavenny	7.11.97P
	(EC-44-PM)	T684-1165XL		(C/n possibly T884-1165XL but duplicates G-MMSG)			
G-MMTV	American Aerolights Eagle 215B Seaplane			25. 5.84	P.J.Scott	Seaview, IoW	21.11.96P
	(EC-25-PS)	SGP-1					
G-MMTX	Mainair Gemini/Southdown Sprint			25. 3.85	J.Burke	Popham	17. 5.98P
	(EC-44-PM)	275-1284-2 & P.590					
G-MMTY	Fisher FP202U	2140		28. 9.84	B.E.Maggs Brickhouse Farm, Frogland Cross		
					(Stored 4.96)		
G-MMTZ	Eurowing Goldwing	EW-60 & SWA-7		28. 9.84	R.B.D.Baker	Torquay	11. 7.99P
	(Rotax 447)						
G-MMUA	Southdown Puma Sprint	1221/0007		21.12.84	C.R.Gale	Kirk Michael, IoM	12. 9.98P
	(EC-44-PM)						
G-MMUE	Mainair Gemini/Flash			16.10.84	B.P.Hately	Ashton-in-Makerfield	29. 3.97P
	(EC-44-PM)	273-1284-2 & W10					
G-MMUG*	Mainair Tri-Flyer 250/Solar Wings Typhoon S4			6. 9.82	Not known	Tonbridge	26. 5.97P
	(EC-34-PM)	032-221181 & T884-1178S		(Wing confirmed as ex G-MJKY: temp unregd 21.10.96)			
G-MMUH	Mainair Tri-Flyer/Southdown Sprint			8.11.84	J.P.Nicklin	Hayling Island	22. 7.99P
	(EC-44-PM)	270-1084-2 & P.579					
G-MMUJ*	Southdown Puma Sprint/Cougar 1121/0009			6.12.84	C.C.Muir	Bristol	18. 7.97P
	(EC-44-PM)				(Cancelled as WFU 6.3.99)		
G-MMUK	Ultrasports Tripacer II/Solar Wings			15.10.84	W.G.F.Ditcham	Newbury	18. 9.99P
	Typhoon S4 (Rotax 447) BRK-01 & T782-532						
G-MMUM	MBA Tiger Cub 440	SO.019		8. 3.83	Coulson Flying Services Ltd	Skegness	
G-MMUN	Ultrasports/Solar Wings Panther Dual XL			23.10.84	P.J.Kirwan	Geashill, Ireland	
		T1084-1231XL					
G-MMUO	Mainair Gemini/Flash 272-1084-2 & W08			29.10.84	B.D.Bastin & D.R.Howells	Long Marston	30. 1.99P
	(EC-44-PM)						
G-MMUR	Hiway Skytrike 250/Solar Wings Storm			28.12.84	R.J.Ripley	Oakley, Bedford	
		SL.180180					
G-MMUS	Mainair Gemini/Flash 284-185-3 & W24			29. 1.85	R.L.Feechan	St.Michaels-on-Wyre	1. 3.97P
	(EC-44-PM)						
G-MMUT	Mainair Gemini/Flash 262-884-2 & W04			5.10.84	L.R.Orriss	Rotherham	5. 7.99P
	(EC-44-PM) (Restored 29.6.98 with c/n 235-484-2-W04)						

Regn	Type	C/n P/I	Date	Owner/operator	Probable Base	CA Expy
G-MMUV	Southdown Puma Sprint (EC-44-PM)	1121/0010	7.11.84	D.C.Read	Ledbury	2.11.89P*
G-MMUW	Mainair Gemini/Flash 260-784-2 & W13 (EC-44-PM)		17. 1.85	J.C.K.Scardifield	Lymington	23. 3.87P
G-MMUX	Mainair Gemini/Southdown Sprint (EC-44-PM)	285-185-3 & P.587	28.12.84	D.Uff	Hatfield	7. 7.95P
G-MMVA	Southdown Puma Sprint (EC-44-PM)	1121/0011 & P.588	7.11.84	C.H.Tomkins	Kettering	26. 3.92P
G-MMVC	Ultrasports/Solar Wings Panther XL-S (EC-44-PM)	T684-1106XL	13.11.84	E.R.Holton	Lichfield	18.1.90P*
G-MMVG*	MBA Tiger Cub 440	SO.139	14.11.84	C.W.Grant (Cancelled by CAA 15.3.99)	Salisbury	
G-MMVH	Southdown Raven X (Mosler MM-CB)	2122/0015	10. 1.85	G.W. & K.M.Carwardine	Isle of Grain	16.11.99P
G-MMVI	Southdown Puma Sprint (EC-44-PM)	1121/0012	28.11.84	G.R.Williams	Haverfordwest	2.11.97P
G-MMVO	Southdown Puma Sprint (Rotax 447)	1232/0017	20. 3.85	N.F.Thomas	Newton Abbot	7.10.98P
G-MMVP	Mainair Gemini/Flash 276-1284-2 & W12 (EC-44-PM)		17.12.84	S.C.McGowan	Rufforth	16.10.99P
G-MMVS	Skyhook Pixie/Zeus (Solo 210) TR1/52		28. 2.85	B.W.Olley	Ely	18.11.91E
G-MMVX	Southdown Puma Sprint 41183 & P.452 (EC-44-PM) (Possibly Mainair Gemini Trike)		29.11.83	R.J.Wheeler	Haverfordwest	10. 9.99P
G-MMVZ	Southdown Puma Sprint (EC-44-PM)	1121/0016	15. 1.85	J.Channer	Selston, Nottingham	1. 8.99P
G-MMWA	Mainair Gemini/Flash 271-1184-1 & W07 (EC-44-PM)		22.11.84	D.Muir	Lancaster	12. 4.99P
G-MMWB*	Huntair Pathfinder II	LWB.3	28. 6.84	Bryant Aircraft Ltd (Cancelled by CAA 27.3.99)	Bishop Auckland	
G-MMWC	Eipper Quicksilver MXII (Rotax 503)	1041	22.10.84	G.N.Harris	Billingshurst	14. 1.97P
G-MMWG	Mainair Tri-Flyer/Flexiform Solo Striker (Rotax 377) FF/LAI/83/JDR/11		17.12.84	C.R.Green	Redruth	26. 6.99P
G-MMWH	Southdown Puma Sprint (EC-44-PM)	P.548	21. 6.84	S.Giles	Oxford	21. 5.93P
G-MMWI	Southdown Puma (Lightning 190) CAC-01 (EC-34-PM)		3. 1.85	A.W.Cove	Wellingborough	5. 9.93E
G-MMWJ	Pterodactyl Ptraveler (EC-34-PM)	WFX-33	5. 3.85	G.A.Harman	Sandy	9.11.97P
G-MMWL	Eurowing Goldwing (Rotax 447)	SWA-09 & EW-91	9. 4.85	P.J.Brookman	Lymeswold	14. 4.99P
G-MMWN	Mainair Tri-Flyer/Flexiform Striker 1283.NH (Rotax 377) (Possibly Ultrasports Tripacer)		21.11.84	D.H.George	Sandown	30. 3.97P
G-MMWO	Ultrasports/Solar Wings Panther XL-S (EC-44-PM)	T1184-1281XL	22. 1.85	M.J.Chance	Rainham	8.12.93P
G-MMWS	Ultrasports Tripacer/Flexiform Solo Striker (Rotax 377)	983.SH	21.11.84	P.H.Risdale	Woolaston	28.11.99P
G-MMWT	CFM Shadow Srs C (Rotax 503)	B.009	27. 3.85	H.R.Block	Terrington, Kings Lynn	3. 6.98P
G-MMWX	Southdown Puma Sprint (EC-44-PM)	1121/0047	10. 4.85	S.J.Ball	Swadlincote	24.11.99P
G-MMWZ	Southdown Puma Sprint (EC-44-PM)	1121/0030	19. 2.85	D.C.Olson	Cambridge	12.11.98P
G-MMXC	Mainair Gemini/Flash 279-1284-2 & W17 (EC-44-PM) (Trike reported as c/n 292 9.96 - see G-MMXL)		28.12.84	M.P.Birks	St.Michaels-on-Wyre	9. 6.94P
G-MMXD	Mainair Gemini/Flash 282-185-3 & W20 (Rotax 447)		28.12.84	D.Lund	Preston	7.10.99P
G-MMXG	Mainair Gemini/Flash 288-485-1 & W32 (EC-44-PM)		17. 1.85	S.D.Hill	Henley-on-Thames	26. 5.94P
G-MMXH	Mainair Gemini/Flash 210-121283-2 & W25 (EC-44-PM)		4. 2.85	I.C.Willetts	Barton Turf, Norwich	28. 8.95P
G-MMXJ	Mainair Gemini/Flash 289-185-3 & W22 (Rotax 447)		17. 1.85	R.Meredith-Hardy	Radwell, Letchworth	6. 8.96P
G-MMXK	Mainair Gemini/Flash 274-485-2 & W35 (EC-44-PM)		17. 1.85	G.K.Thornton	High Barn Farm, Houghton	11. 6.99P
G-MMXL	Mainair Gemini/Flash 292-385-3 & W36 (EC-44-PM)		17. 1.85	J.M.Marshall	Urmston	16. 5.97P
G-MMXN	Southdown Puma Sprint (EC-44-PM)	1121/0021	24. 1.85	A.D.Ramsay & G.Hawes	Great Glen, Leicester	28.12.98P
G-MMXO	Southdown Puma Sprint (EC-44-PM)	1121/0018	23. 1.85	D.J.Tasker	Swinford, Rugby	6. 7.99P
G-MMXP	Southdown Puma Sprint (EC-44-PM)	1121/0014	19. 7.85	I.J.Knott	RAF Marham	21. 4.93P
G-MMXT	Mainair Gemini/Flash 302-485-3 & W41 (EC-44-PM)		29. 1.85	L.R.Orriss	Rotherham	24.11.97P
G-MMXU	Mainair Gemini/Flash 254-784-2 & W21 (EC-44-PM)		29. 1.85	T.J.Franklin	Graveley	18. 2.95P

Regn	Type	C/n	P/I	Date	Owner/operator	Probable Base	CA Expy
G-MMXV	Mainair Gemini/Flash 298-385-3 & W37 (EC-44-PM)			29. 1.85	A.E.Ciantar	Bury St.Edmunds	12. 3.99P
G-MMXW	Mainair Gemini/Southdown Sprint (EC-44-PM) 286-185-3 & P.597			23. 1.85	A.Hodgson	Milton Keynes	3. 5.97P
G-MMYA	Solar Wings Pegasus XL-P/Se (Rotax 447) XL-P Proto & T784-1151XL			30. 1.85	M.Harris	Clench Common	14. 9.99P
G-MMYF	Southdown Puma Sprint (EC-44-PM)	1121/0026		28. 3.85	B.R.Underwood & D.Thorpe	Swinford, Rugby	12. 5.99P
G-MMYI	Southdown Puma Sprint (EC-44-PM)	1121/0036		6. 3.85	D.J.Brixton t/a Shropshire Tow Group	Bishops Castle	20. 9.99P
G-MMYJ	Southdown Puma Sprint (EC-44-PM)	1121/0031		18 .2.85	R.K.Seddon	High Barn Farm, Houghton	3. 5.97P
G-MMYL	Cyclone 70/Aerial Arts 130SX (Rotax 277)	CH.01		8. 3.85	J.T.Halford	Holt, Norfolk	26. 7.99P
G-MMYN	Ultrasports/Solar Wings Panther XL-R (Rotax 447) T784-1158XL			27. 2.85	C.G.Johns Pound Green, Buttonoak, Kidderminster		13. 4.97P
G-MMYO	Southdown Puma Sprint (EC-44-PM)	1121/0037		11. 4.85	M.Mills	Otherton, Cannock	10. 4.98P
G-MMYR	Eipper Quicksilver MXII (Rotax 503)	3345		27. 2.85	M.Reed	Newhouse Farm, Loughborough	3. 7.99P
G-MMYT	Southdown Puma Sprint (EC-44-PM)	1121/0046		15. 4.85	J.K.Divall	Chichester	25. 3.94P
G-MMYU	Southdown Puma Sprint (Rotax 447)	1231/0045		11. 6.85	S.J.Firth	Crieff	30. 7.99P
G-MMYV	Mainair Tri-Flyer/Flexiform Striker (Rotax 277)	JW-2		22. 3.85	S.B.Herbert	Presteigne	20.12.95P
G-MMYY	Southdown Puma Sprint (Rotax 447)	1231/0042		18. 7.85	D.G.Emery & M.R.Smith Dudley/Warley, W.Midlands		17. 6.98P
G-MMYZ	Southdown Puma Sprint (Rotax 447)	1231/0034		28. 2.85	M.Bodill West Bridgeford (Damaged in gales Roddidge 1.98)		19. 2.99P
G-MMZA	Mainair Gemini/Flash 266-984-3 & W60 (EC-44-PM) (Wing c/n may be W06)			4. 3.85	G.T.Johnston	Craigavon, Co.Armagh	3. 5.99P
G-MMZB	Mainair Gemini/Flash 319-685-3 & W58 (EC-44-PM)			4. 3.85	M.A.Nolan	Great Orton	23. 5.99P
G-MMZD	Mainair Gemini/Flash 309-585-3 & W49 (EC-44-PM)			4. 3.85	J.C.Ettridge	Kendal	4. 9.97P
G-MMZE	Mainair Gemini/Flash 300-485-3 & W39 (EC-44-PM)			4. 3.85	I.P.Stubbins	Scunthorpe	13. 9.97P
G-MMZF	Mainair Gemini/Flash 299-485-3 & W38 (EC-44-PM)			4. 3.85	A.R.Rhodes	Great Orton	17. 6.99P
G-MMZG	Ultrasports/Solar Wings Panther XL-S (EC-44-PM) SW-WA-1022			12. 8.85	P.A.Jones	North Coates	30. 1.99P
G-MMZI	Medway Half Pint Srs.1/Aerial Arts 130SX (JPX PUL425) 57			6. 3.85	J.Messenger	Workington	28. 3.93E
G-MMZJ	Mainair Gemini/Flash 312-585-3 & W51 (EC-44-PM)			18. 3.85	M.Moulai	Scunthorpe	15. 8.98P
G-MMZK	Mainair Gemini/Flash 326-785-3 & W53 (EC-44-PM) (Trike ex G-MMEZ; originally regd with trike c/n 314-585-3; to G-MMIR)			18. 3.85	G.Jones & B.Lee	Warrington	3.11.99P
G-MMZM	Mainair Gemini/Flash 304-585-3 & W44 (EC-44-PM)			18. 3.85	K.W.Roberts	Barnsley	12. 5.99P
G-MMZN	Mainair Gemini/Flash 283-185-3 & W23 (EC-44-PM)			18. 3.85	W.K.Dalus	Nottingham	28. 9.93P
G-MMZP	Ultrasports/Solar Wings Panther XL (EC-44-PM) HP-01			14. 3.85	B.Richardson	Sunderland	12. 1.94P
G-MMZR	Southdown Puma Sprint (EC-44-PM)	1121/0039		4. 7.85	J.E.Hicks t/a Intl Animal Rescue	Dunkeswell	6.12.93P
G-MMZU*	Southdown Lightning/Puma	006		12. 4.85	E.Clark (Cancelled by CAA 17.2.99)	Oakham	
G-MMZV	Mainair Gemini/Flash 313-585-3 & W52 (Rotax 447)			18. 4.85	P.R.M.Spengler	Bracknell	17. 5.99P
G-MMZW	Southdown Puma Sprint (EC-44-PM)	1121/0043		28. 3.85	M.G.Ashbee	Cranbrook	30. 9.98P
G-MMZX	Southdown Puma Sprint (Rotax 447)	1231/0051		17. 4.85	J.V.Rozentals	Sutton-in-Ashfield	10. 4.95P
G-MMZZ	Maxair Hummer	0010		8. 4.82	P.J.Brookman	Loughborough	

G-MNAA-MNZZ

Regn	Type	C/n	P/I	Date	Owner/operator	Probable Base	CA Expy
G-MNAE	Mainair Gemini/Flash 343-885-3 & W77 (EC-44-PM)			18. 4.85	G.C.Luddington	Bletsoe	19. 8.97P
G-MNAF*	Ultrasports/Solar Wings Pegasus XL-S (EC-44-PM) SW-WA-1001			24. 4.85	C.W.Payne (Cancelled by CAA 21.1.99)	Worcester	7. 8.98P
G-MNAH	Ultrasports/Solar Wings Panther XL-S (EC-44-PM) SW-WA-1002			24. 4.85	J.H.Button & G.A.Harman	Sandy	18. 9.99P
G-MNAI	Ultrasports/Solar Wings Panther XL-S (EC-44-PM) SW-WA-1003			15. 5.85	R.G.Cameron	Dundee	23. 6.98P
G-MNAJ	Ultrasports/Solar Wings Panther XL-S (EC-44-PM) SW-TA-1004 & SW-WA-1004			17. 5.85	C.Lonsdale	Morgansfield, Fishburn	22. 1.00P
G-MNAK	Ultrasports/Solar Wings Panther XL-S (EC-44-PM) SW-WA-1005			15. 5.85	R.J.Porter	Insch	2. 5.99P
G-MNAM	Ultrasports/Solar Wings Panther XL-S (EC-44-2PM) SW-WA-1006			17. 5.85	T.M.Gilsenan & G.E.C.Burgess	Dunstable	13.10.95P
G-MNAN	Solar Wings Pegasus XL-R (Rotax 447) SW-TB-0001 & SW-WA-1007			2. 7.85	J.W.F.Hargreave	High Wycombe	30. 4.95P
G-MNAO	Solar Wings Pegasus XL-R (Rotax 447) SW-TB-0002 & SW-WA-1008			2. 6.85	R.H.Cooke	Southampton	15. 8.99P
G-MNAR	Solar Wings Pegasus XL-R SW-WA-1011 (Rotax 447)			6. 8.85	C.R.Wasmuth	London Colney	13. 2.99P
G-MNAU	Solar Wings Pegasus XL-R SW-WA-1013 (Rotax 447)			30. 9.85	R.J.Ridgway	High Wycombe	25. 9.93P
G-MNAV	Southdown Puma Sprint 1121/0033 (EC-44-PM)			28. 2.85	A.W.Smith	Peel, IoM	22. 8.99P
G-MNAW	Solar Wings Pegasus XL-R (Rotax 447) SW-TB-1010 & SW-WA-1014			16. 8.85	D.J.Harber	Henley-on-Thames	10.11.99P
	(Trike c/n believed correct but reported on LN-YCO with Flash wing W686)						
G-MNAX	Solar Wings Pegasus XL-R SW-WA-1015 (Rotax 447)			16. 8.85	B.J.Phillips	Newbury	21. 7.96P
G-MNAY	Solar Wings Pegasus XL-R (Rotax 447) SW-TB-1015 & SW-WA-1016			6. 8.85	S.J.Honeybourne	Lowdham	11. 9.99P
G-MNAZ	Solar Wings Pegasus XL-R (Rotax 447) SW-TB-1016 & SW-WA-1017			6. 8.85	R.W.Houldsworth	Rochford	18. 4.99P
G-MNBA	Solar Wings Pegasus XL-R (Rotax 447) SW-TB-1024 & SW-WA-1018			6. 9.85	K.D.Baldwin "Tigerfish"	Long Acre Farm, Sandy	14. 5.99P
G-MNBB	Solar Wings Pegasus XL-R (Rotax 447) SW-TB-1020 & SW-WA-1019			20. 9.85	M.Sims	Brynmawr, Gwent	26. 5.95P
G-MNBC	Solar Wings Pegasus XL-R (Rotax 447) SW-TB-1026 & SW-WA-1020			11.10.85	W.M.Rowley	Slough	21. 2.97P
G-MNBD	Mainair Gemini/Flash 341-585-3 & W42 (EC-44-PM)			6. 1.86	G.B.Mitchell	Nottingham	21.10.96
G-MNBE	Southdown Puma Sprint 1121/0050 (EC-44-PM)			17. 5.85	A.Wherrett	Bristol	5. 7.98P
G-MNBF	Mainair Gemini/Flash 306-585-3 & W46 (EC-44-PM)			2. 5.85	H.G.Denton	Newhouse Farm, Loughborough	5. 5.99P
G-MNBG	Mainair Gemini/Flash 347-585-3 & W66 (Rotax 447)			9. 5.85	J.W. & C.Richardson	New Ellerby, Hull	20. 7.98P
G-MNBH	Southdown Puma Sprint 1231/0056 (Rotax 447)			20. 5.85	D.W.B.Crang	RAF Wyton	1.10.97P
G-MNBI	Ultrasports/Solar Wings Panther XL-S (EC-44-PM) PXL884-178 & T884-1161XL		(C/n duplicates G-MMVF)	3. 5.85	G.R.Cox	Northampton	29. 4.97P
G-MNBL	American Aerolights Eagle 215B (Cuyuna 215R) BA-1001			9. 1.84	T.S.Mangat	Long Marston	20. 9.97P
G-MNBM	Southdown Puma Sprint 1231/0058 (EC-44-PM)			25. 6.85	A.F.Hicks	Shelmore Valley Farm, Stafford	23. 6.97P
G-MNBN	Mainair Gemini/Flash 303-485-3 & W43 (EC-44-PM)			11. 6.85	S.Allison & D.Kelly	Long Marston	5. 7.98P
G-MNBP	Mainair Gemini/Flash 338-885-3 & W75 (EC-44-PM)			15. 5.85	A.L.Alexandrou	Camberley	18.12.93P
G-MNBR	Mainair Gemini/Flash 345-985-3 & W79 (Rotax 447)			15. 5.85	N.A.P.Gregory (Stored 1.98)	Long Marston	5. 2.94P
G-MNBS	Mainair Gemini/Flash 308-585-3 & W48 (EC-44-PM)			15. 5.85	P.A.Comins	Nottingham	20. 6.94P
G-MNBT	Mainair Gemini/Flash 322-685-3 & W62 (EC-44-PM)			15. 5.85	C.J.R.Hardman	St.Michaels-on-Wyre	4.11.99P
G-MNBU	Mainair Gemini/Flash 337-885-3 & W74 (Rotax 447)			15. 5.85	A.S.Dalby	Thirsk	23. 7.96P
G-MNBV	Mainair Gemini/Flash 333-685-3 & W70 (Rotax 447)			15. 5.85	P.Lowham	Caledon, Co.Tyrone	25.10.98P
G-MNBW	Mainair Gemini/Flash 332-685-3 & W69 (Rotax 447)			15. 5.85	G.A.Brown & N.S.Brotherton	Weston Zoyland	8. 1.00P
G-MNCA	Hunt Avon/Hiway Demon 175 DA-01			28. 5.85	C.Kett	Bridgwater	26. 3.94E
G-MNCF	Mainair Gemini/Flash 321-685-3 & W61 (Rotax 447)			3. 6.85	T.C.Edwards	Ware	10.11.95P
G-MNCG	Mainair Gemini/Flash 320-685-3 & W59 (Rotax 447)			3. 6.85	G.Hartley	Kendal	5. 5.97P

Regn	Type	C/n	P/I	Date	Owner/operator	Probable Base	CA Expy
G-MNCI	Southdown Puma Sprint (Rotax 447)	1231/0059		7. 6.85	R.M.Wait	Stourbridge	12.11.99P
G-MNCJ	Mainair Gemini/Flash 351-785-3 & W83 (Rotax 447)			3. 6.85	R.S.McLeister	Accrington	16.11.93P
G-MNCK	Southdown Puma Sprint (Rotax 447)	1231/0055		11. 7.85	R.A.Beauchamp (Damaged in gales Roddidge 1.98)	Alrewas	3. 1.98P
G-MNCL	Southdown Puma Sprint (EC-44-PM)	1121/0060		3. 6.85	S.A.P.Rowberry	Wallingford	20. 7.98P
G-MNCM	CFM Shadow Srs C (Rotax 503)	006		31. 5.85	K.W.Allan Drummiard Farm, Bonnybank		30. 8.98P
G-MNCO	Eipper Quicksilver MX II	1045		3. 6.85	S.Lawton	Colne	
G-MNCP	Southdown Puma Sprint (Rotax 447)	1231/0071		24. 6.85	R.A.Willetts & W.Atkinson	Long Marston	8.11.98P
G-MNCS	Skyrider Airsports Phantom (EC-44-PM)	PH.00098		2. 1.86	C.G.Johns	Bewdley, Worcs	24. 5.99P
G-MNCU	Medway Hybred/Solar Wings Typhoon 44XL (EC-44-PM)	26485/10		13. 6.85	A.P.Norman	Swinford, Rugby	10. 6.99P
G-MNCV	Medway Hybred/Solar Wings Typhoon 44XL (EC-44-PM)	26485/11 (Reported as Pegasus XL-R Wing SW-WA-1030 1997)		13. 6.85	P.D.Mickleburgh	Swinford, Rugby	6. 9.99P
G-MNDC	Mainair Gemini/Flash 336-885-3 & W73 (Rotax 447)			12. 6.85	C.G.Jarvis	Southampton	10. 3.98P
G-MNDD	Mainair Scorcher 358-885-1 & W85 (Rotax 447)			12. 6.85	W.J.Heap	Ince Blundell, Liverpool	23. 6.98P
G-MNDE	Medway Half Pint/Aerial Arts 130SX (JPL PUL425) 3/8685 (Wing ex G-MNBZ)			19. 6.85	N.J.Dea	Birmingham	27. 3.99P
G-MNDF	Mainair Gemini/Flash 327-785-3 & W67 (Rotax 447)			25. 6.85	S.K.Starling	Hethersett	13. 5.99P
G-MNDG	Southdown Puma Sprint (EC-44-PM)	1121/0057		18. 7.85	C.Kiernan	Mostrim, Ireland	14. 6.99P
G-MNDM	Mainair Gemini/Flash 324-785-3 & W64 (Rotax 447)			11. 7.85	A.N.McDonough	Arclid Green, Sandbach	7. 4.98P
G-MNDO	Solar Wings Pegasus/Flash SW-WF-0001 (Rotax 447)			2. 7.85	D.Buchanan	Southsea	16. 8.98P
G-MNDP	Southdown Puma Sprint (EC-44-PM)	1121/0063		28. 6.85	S.C.Davidson	Haverfordwest	26. 4.93P
G-MNDU	Midland Ultralights Sirocco 377GB (Rotax 377) MU-011			22. 7.85	D.Dugdale	Bruntingthorpe	19.11.98P
G-MNDV	Midland Ultralights Sirocco 377GB (Rotax 377) MU-012			1. 4.86	L.J.Dutch (Stored Tarn Farm, Cockerham 5.93)	Wigan	13. 7.92P
G-MNDW	Midland Ultralights Sirocco 377GB (Rotax 377) MU-014			30. 7.85	G.C.Reid	Olney	26. 9.98P
G-MNDZ	Southdown Puma Sprint (EC-44-PM)	1121/0062		28. 6.85	Wendy A.Guest	Bridgnorth	29. 4.99P
G-MNEF	Mainair Gemini/Flash 344-885-3 & W78 (Rotax 447)			8. 7.85	J.P.Faver	East Fortune	19.12.99P
G-MNEG	Mainair Gemini/Flash 360-885-3 & W92 (Rotax 447)			8. 7.85	T.K.Duffy	Ballyclare, Co.Antrim	18.10.99P
G-MNEH	Mainair Gemini/Flash 361-885-3 & W90 (Rotax 503)			8. 7.85	I.Rawson	St.Michaels-on-Wyre	5. 7.99P
G-MNEI	Medway Hybred/Solar Wings Typhoon 44XL (EC-44-PM) 8785/12 & SW-WA-1035			9. 7.85	L.G.Thompson (Stored 8.96) Long Marston		26. 7.93P
G-MNEK	Medway Half Pint/Aerial Arts 130SX (JPX PUL425) 4/8785			12. 7.85	M.I.Dougall	Maidstone	25. 9.94P
G-MNEL	Medway Half Pint/Aerial Arts 130SX (JPX PUL425) 5/8785			12. 7.85	K.J.Hitch	Westerham	26. 9.94P
G-MNEM	Solar Wings Pegasus XL-R (Rotax 447) SW-TB-1007 & SW-WA-1034			16. 7.85	M.D.Foster	Hastings	31. 7.93P
G-MNER	CFM Shadow Srs.CD (Rotax 462)	008		15. 7.85	F.C.Claydon Wickham Brook, Newmarket		27. 2.99P
G-MNET	Mainair Gemini/Flash 349-885-3 & W81 (EC-44-PM)			23. 7.85	S.W.Barker	Scarborough	5. 7.99P
G-MNEV	Mainair Gemini/Flash 362-1085-3 & W108 (Rotax 447)			23. 7.85	A.A.White	St.Michaels-on-Wyre	28. 8.97P
G-MNEY	Mainair Gemini/Flash 365-1085-3 & W94 (Rotax 447)			23. 7.85	A.G.Phillips	East Fortune	4. 7.99P
G-MNFA	Mainair Tri-Flyer/Solar Wings Typhoon (EC-34-PM) DRJ-01 & GWW-01			29.12.83	R.S.Lee Pontesbury, Shrewsbury (Trike ex G-MJFA)		10.10.92P
G-MNFB	Southdown Puma Sprint (Rotax 447)	1231/0077		22. 7.85	C.Lawrence	Tiverton	26. 7.98P
G-MNFE	Mainair Gemini/Flash 350-885-3 & W82 (EC-44-PM)			29. 7.85	D.R.Kennedy	East Fortune	18.11.95P
G-MNFF	Mainair Gemini/Flash 371-1185-3 & W110 (Rotax 447)			29. 7.85	R.P.Cook & C.H.Spencer Manor Farm, Inskip		8. 6.94P
G-MNFG	Southdown Puma Sprint (Rotax 447)	1231/0078		31. 7.85	A.C.Hing	Leighton Buzzard	29. 4.99P
G-MNFH	Mainair Gemini/Flash 364-1085-3 & W93 (Rotax 447)			6. 8.85	P.A.Martindale (Stored 9.97) Great Orton		30. 6.95P

Regn	Type	C/n P/I	Date	Owner/operator	Probable Base	CA Expy
G-MNFJ	Mainair Gemini/Flash 346-985-3 & W80 (Rotax 447)		20. 9.85	S.C.Marshall	Market Harborough	21. 3.90P
G-MNFK	Mainair Gemini/Flash 2 359-885-3 & W91 (Rotax 462)		12. 8.85	S.L.Larter-Whitcher & A.L.Carroll Hertford/Harlow		6. 5.93P
G-MNFL	AMF Microflight Chevvron CH.002 (Konig SD570)		19. 8.85	P.W.Wright	Fradley, Lichfield	13.12.99P
G-MNFM	Mainair Gemini/Flash 366-1085-3 & W98 (Rotax 447)		10.10.85	P.M.Fidell	Wombleton	6. 8.99P
G-MNFN	Mainair Gemini/Flash 367-1085-3 & W99 (Rotax 447)		6.11.85	J.R.Martin	Bedale	30. 4.94P
G-MNFP	Mainair Gemini/Flash 368-1085-3 & W100 (Rotax 447)		23.10.85	S.Farnsworth & P.Howarth	Clitheroe	3. 6.98P
G-MNFR*	Mainair Tri-Flyer/Solar Wings Medium Typhoon T981-272		15. 8.85	R.L.Arscott (Cancelled by CAA 23.6.98)	Taunton	
G-MNFW	Medway Hybred 44XL 10885/13 (EC-44-PM)		15. 8.85	A.T.Palmer	Plymouth	15. 8.99P
G-MNFX	Southdown Puma Sprint 1231/0079 (Rotax 447)		14. 8.85	A.M.Shaw	Stoke-on-Trent	26. 7.99P
G-MNFZ	Southdown Puma Sprint (Rotax 447) T.597 & 1231/0080		22. 8.85	M.J.Devane	Killarney, Ireland	22. 7.99P
G-MNGB	Mainair Gemini/Flash (EC-44-PM) 218-81183-2 & W01		14.12.83	S.L.Rowlands	Wirral	19. 4.98P
G-MNGD	Ultrasports Tripacer/Solar Wings Medium Typhoon (EC-34-PM) 012 & T681-171		13. 8.85	F.H.Cook	Whitchurch	4. 5.97P
G-MNGF	Solar Wings Pegasus/Flash (Rotax 447) W-TB-1022 & SW-WF-0003		21. 8.85	D.R.Stapleton	Tarn Farm, Cockerham	14. 8.98P
G-MNGG	Solar Wings Pegasus XL-R T784-1159XL (Rotax 447)		21. 8.85	T.Peckham	Faversham	28. 6.98P
G-MNGH	Skyhook TR1 Pixie/Zeus TR1/61		24. 9.85	A.R.Smith	Chelmsford	
G-MNGK	Mainair Gemini/Flash 374-1085-3 & W112 (Rotax 447)		5. 9.85	A.R.White	Popham	15. 8.98P
G-MNGL	Mainair Gemini/Flash 376-1085-3 & W114 (Rotax 447)		5. 9.85	G.Cusden	Davidstow Moor	21. 3.99P
G-MNGM	Mainair Gemini/Flash 394-1285-3 & W109 (Rotax 447)		5. 9.85	J.E.Caffull & D.R.Beale	Long Marston	10. 6.99P
G-MNGN	Mainair Gemini/Flash 378-1185-3 & W115 (Rotax 447)		5. 9.85	T.B.Margetts	Poole	17. 6.99P
G-MNGR	Southdown Puma Sprint 1231/0086 (Rotax 447)		18. 9.85	A.K.Webster	Wallingford	29. 8.93P
G-MNGS	Southdown Puma (Lightning 195) (EC-34-PM) GJS-02 (Tripacer trike unit from G-MJRF)		8. 5.84	C.R.Mortlock & B.P.Cooke	Newmarket	N/E
G-MNGT	Mainair Gemini/Flash 372-1085-3 & W106 (Rotax 447) (Reported 4.96 as Huntwing 462LC)		30. 9.85	M.R.Lycett	Arclid Green, Sandbach	14. 2.99P
G-MNGU	Mainair Gemini/Flash 373-1085-3 & W111 (Rotax 503)		30. 9.85	J.K.Bathurst	London E4	21. 3.99P
G-MNGW	Mainair Gemini/Flash 386-1185-3 & W121 (Rotax 447)		30. 9.85	D.G.Baker	Petersfield	25.10.98P
G-MNGX	Southdown Puma Sprint 1231/0088		26. 9.85	R.J.Morris	Ely	26. 9.99P
G-MNGZ	Mainair Gemini/Flash 385-1085-3 & W120 (Rotax 447)		10.10.85	G.T.Snoddon	Newtownards	4. 9.97P
G-MNHB	Solar Wings Pegasus XL-R/Se SW-WA-1045 (Rotax 447)		1.11.85	A.F.J.Freiherr-Knigge Pattensen, Germany		28. 7.98P
G-MNHC	Solar Wings Pegasus XL-R (Rotax 447) SW-TB-1032 & SW-WA-1046		31.10.85	P.Mathews	Shobdon	27. 5.99P
G-MNHD	Solar Wings Pegasus XL-R (Rotax 447) SW-TB-1033 & SW-WA-1047		5.11.85	P.D.Stiles	Ashley Down, Bristol	1. 6.99P
G-MNHE	Solar Wings Pegasus XL-R (Rotax 447) SW-TB-1036 & SW-WA-1048		11.12.85	J.R.Austin	Truro	3. 7.99P
G-MNHF	Solar Wings Pegasus XL-R (Rotax 447) SW-TB-1037 & SW-WA-1049		29.11.85	J.Cox	Hereford	22. 6.88P
G-MNHH	Solar Wings Pegasus XL-S SW-WA-1051 (EC-44-PM)		22. 1.86	F.J.Williams	Shefford, Beds	7. 8.99P
G-MNHI	Solar Wings Pegasus XL-R (Rotax 447) SW-TB-1042 & SW-WA-1052		8. 1.86	I.D.R.Hyde	Enstone	13. 7.95P
G-MNHJ	Solar Wings Pegasus XL-R SW-WA-1053 (Rotax 447)		11. 3.86	S.J.Woodd	Oxford	26. 6.93P
G-MNHK	Solar Wings Pegasus XL-R SW-WA-1054 (Rotax 462)		9. 7.86	R.D.Proctor	Stamford, Lincs	13. 6.92P
G-MNHL	Solar Wings Pegasus XL-R SW-WA-1055 (Rotax 447)		9. 7.86	Deborah A.R.Palmer	Bexleyheath	14. 5.98P
G-MNHM	Solar Wings Pegasus XL-R (Rotax 447) SW-TB-1078 & SW-WA-1056		11. 7.86	J.Ellis	Baxby Manor, Husthwaite	3. 6.98P
G-MNHN	Solar Wings Pegasus XL-R SW-WA-1057 (Rotax 447)		11. 8.86	N.J.Howarth	Kettering	16. 6.99P
G-MNHP	Solar Wings Pegasus XL-R SW-WA-1059 (Rotax 447)		11. 8.86	P.N.Bailey & D.M.Smith (Damaged nr Bristol 18.11.95)	Swindon	28. 9.96P
G-MNHR	Solar Wings Pegasus XL-R (Rotax 447) SW-TB-1081 & SW-WA-1060		7. 8.86	B.D.Jackson	Wincanton	6.11.99P

Regn	Type	C/n	P/I	Date	Owner/operator	Probable Base	CA Expy
G-MNHS	Solar Wings Pegasus XL-R (Rotax 447) SW-TB-1082 & SW-WA-1061			21. 8.86	T.J.Gayton-Polley	Billingshurst	7. 9.99P
G-MNHT	Solar Wings Pegasus XL-R SW-WA-1062 (Rotax 447)			4. 8.86	J.W.Coventry	Plymouth	4. 9.98P
G-MNHU	Solar Wings Pegasus XL-R SW-WA-1063 (Rotax 447)			4. 8.86	B.A.Wright & D.Lyon	Dunkeswell	16. 1.99P
G-MNHV	Solar Wings Pegasus XL-R (Rotax 447) SW-TB-1095 & SW-WA-1064			18. 8.86	E.Jenkins	Crymych, Dyfed	31. 7.99P
G-MNHZ	Mainair Gemini/Flash 310-585-3 & W118 (EC-44-PM)			15.10.85	M.Salvini & S.P.Rouse Baxby Manor, Husthwaite		28. 5.99P
G-MNIA	Mainair Gemini/Flash 370-1185-3 & W105 (Rotax 447)			10.10.85	A.E.Dix	Bromsgrove	10. 4.89P
G-MNID	Mainair Gemini/Flash 369-1185-3 & W104 (Rotax 447)			7. 2.86	P.Fowler (Stolen from Rufforth 10/11.97; Engine No.3706877)	Rufforth	24. 3.98P
G-MNIE	Mainair Gemini/Flash 388-1185-3 & W123 (Rotax 447)			21.11.85	A.D.Partington	Long Marston	1.11.98P
G-MNIF	Mainair Gemini/Flash 403-286-4 & W147 (Rotax 462)			7. 1.86	D.Yarr	Stockport	18. 6.99P
G-MNIG	Mainair Gemini/Flash 391-1285-3 & W139 (Rotax 447)			9. 1.86	I.S.Everett	Astwood	18. 5.99P
G-MNIH	Mainair Gemini/Flash 379-1185-3 & W116 (Rotax 447)			10.12.85	A.R.Richardson	Barnsley	10. 8.99P
G-MNII	Mainair Gemini/Flash 390-1285-3 & W128 (Rotax 447)			6.11.85	R.F.Finnis (Trike reported at St.Michaels-on-Wyre 9.96)	Guildford	6. 9.91P
G-MNIK*	Solar Wings Pegasus Photon SW-TP-0002 & SW-WP-0002			29.10.85	Not known (Stored for possible rebuild 4.96)	Clench Common	
G-MNIL	Southdown Puma Sprint 1231/0094 (Rotax 447)			4.11.85	I.K.Hogg	Kirkbride	20. 7.99P
G-MNIM	Maxair Hummer PJB-01			29.10.85	K.Wood	Leicester	
G-MNIP	Mainair Gemini/Flash 393-1285-3 & W134 (Rotax 447)			6.11.85	G.S.Bulpitt	Chilbolton	12. 6.97P
G-MNIS	CFM Shadow Srs.C (Rotax 447) 014			11.11.85	R.W.Payne	Peterborough	25. 4.92P
G-MNIT	Aerial Arts Alpha Mk.II/130SX (Rotax 227) 130SX-176			27. 2.86	M.J.Edmett	London N3	15. 8.99P
G-MNIU	Solar Wings Pegasus Photon (Rotax 185) SW-WP-0003			27.11.85	K.Roberts (Damaged & stored 3.90)	Tarn Farm, Cockerham	N/E
G-MNIW	Mainair Tri-Flyer/Airwave Nimrod 165 (EC-25-PS) 050/19181	EI-BOB		29.11.85	J.A.McIntosh & R.W.Mitchell	Perth	13. 5.98P
G-MNIX	Mainair Gemini/Flash 395-1285-3 & W136 (Rotax 447)			29.11.85	S.Farnworth	Kempston, Bedford	11. 7.98P
G-MNIZ	Mainair Gemini/Flash 392-1285-3 & W130 (Rotax 447)			26. 2.86	B.Fletcher	St.Michaels-on-Wyre	20. 3.99P
G-MNJB	Southdown Raven X 2232/0098 (Rotax 447)			10.12.85	G.Elwes	Longacre Farm, Sandy	7. 2.99P
G-MNJC	MBA Tiger Cub 440 SO.215			8. 6.84	J.G.Carpenter	Romsey	N/E
G-MNJD	Mainair Gemini/Southdown Puma Sprint MS (EC-44-PM) 243-10484-2 & P.537			2. 4.84	M.E.Smith	Verwood	8. 8.99P
G-MNJF	Dragon Srs.150 (EC-44-PM) 0068	(OY)9-17		2. 1.86	B.W.Langley	Bradford-on-Avon	21. 7.98P
G-MNJG	Mainair Gemini/Southdown Puma Sprint MS (EC-44-PM) SA.2030 & 251-684-2 & P.593			29. 9.83	P.Batchelor	Crawley	31. 8.97P
G-MNJH	Solar Wings Pegasus/Flash (Rotax 447) SW-TB-1023 & SW-WF-0004			22.10.85	C.P.Course Church Farm, Wellingsborough		19. 5.99P
G-MNJJ	Solar Wings Pegasus/Flash (Rotax 447) SW-TB-1029 & SW-WF-0006			22.10.85	P.A.Shelley	Sutton Meadows, Ely	26.11.96P
G-MNJK	Solar Wings Pegasus/Flash (Rotax 447) SW-TB-1027 & SW-WF-0007			21.10.85	A.Jones	Ley Farm, Chirk	3. 8.94P
G-MNJL	Solar Wings Pegasus/Flash SW-WF-0008 (Rotax 447)			21.10.85	S.D.Thomas	Bilston, W.Midlands	11.11.94P
G-MNJN	Solar Wings Pegasus/Flash SW-WF-0010 (Rotax 447)			19.11.85	D.Thorn	St. Austell	17. 7.99P
G-MNJO	Solar Wings Pegasus/Flash (Rotax 447) SW-TB-1035 & SW-WF-0011			19.11.85	S.Clarke	Long Marston	5. 7.98P
G-MNJP*	Solar Wings Pegasus/Flash (Rotax 447) SW-TB-1040 & SW-WF-0012 (Mainair wing c/n W127-1185-1)			30.12.85	K.J.Ball (Stored 10.97; cancelled as WFU 31.7.98)	Mill Farm, Hughley	2. 5.93P
G-MNJR	Solar Wings Pegasus/Flash SW-WF-0013 (Rotax 447)			30.12.85	T.A.Heathcote	Burwash, East Sussex	15. 9.99P
G-MNJS	Southdown Puma Sprint 1231/0085 (Rotax 447)			18. 9.85	W.E.Pepper	Royston	12. 7.94P
G-MNJT	Southdown Raven X 2232/0087 (Rotax 447)			20. 9.85	R.C.Hinkins	RAF Wyton	5. 3.99P
G-MNJU	Mainair Gemini/Flash 384-1185-3 & W119 (Rotax 447)			20. 9.85	E.J.Wells	Lower Wanborough, Swindon	18. 6.99P
G-MNJV	Medway Half Pint/Aerial Arts 130SX 8/19985		(Regd as c/n 9/19985)	10.10.85	D.J.Lewis	Cheltenham	20. 8.92E
G-MNJW	Mitchell Wing B-10 JDW-01			26. 1.84	J.D.Webb	Hereford	

Regn	Type	C/n	P/I	Date	Owner/operator	Probable Base	CA Expy
G-MNJX	Medway Hybred 44XL (EC-44-PM)	15885/14		9.12.85	H.A.Stewart	Sittingbourne	23. 7.98P
G-MNKB	Solar Wings Pegasus/Photon (Solo 210)	SW-WP-0005		14. 1.86	M.E.Gilbert	Dunfermline	27. 4.99P
G-MNKC	Solar Wings Pegasus/Photon (Solo 210)	SW-TP-0006 & SW-WP-0006		14. 1.86	A.C.Carter	Rufforth	31. 8.97P
G-MNKD	Solar Wings Pegasus/Photon (Solo 210)	SW-WP-0007		14. 1.86	F.Walton	Bishop Auckland	28. 8.92P
G-MNKE	Solar Wings Pegasus/Photon (Solo 210)	SW-WP-0008		14. 1.86	M.J.Olsen	Middlesbrough	13. 5.99P
G-MNKG	Solar Wings Pegasus/Photon (Solo 210)	SW-TP-0010 & SW-WP-0010		28. 1.86	T.W.Thompson (Trike stored 9.97) Eshott		11. 6.95P
G-MNKH	Solar Wings Pegasus/Photon (Solo 210)	SW-TP-0011 & SW-WP-0011		28. 1.86	L.M.Ball	Maidenhead	25. 8.93P
G-MNKI	Solar Wings Pegasus/Photon (Solo 210)	SW-WP-0012	(EI-) G-MNKI	28. 1.86	T.Shivner	Salthill, Galway	1. 8.98P
G-MNKK	Solar Wings Pegasus/Photon (EC-44-PM)	SW-WP-0014		28. 1.86	M.E.Gilbert	Dunfermline	7. 5.95P
G-MNKL	Mainair Gemini/Flash (Rotax 447)	397-1285-3 & W143		6. 1.86	R.Thorpe	Pontefract	21. 5.94P
G-MNKM	MBA Tiger Cub 440 (EC-44-PM)	SO.213		30.12.85	M.S.Wood	Batley	23. 9.97P
G-MNKN*	Wheeler (Skycraft) Scout Mk.III/3/R	410		6. 1.86	E.A.Diamond (Cancelled as WFU 19.2.99)	Barrow-in-Furness	
G-MNKO	Solar Wings Pegasus XL-Q (Rotax 447)	SW-TB-1158 & SW-WX-0001		2. 1.86	G.Sharp	Eshott	18. 8.99P
G-MNKP	Solar Wings Pegasus/Flash (Rotax 447)	SW-TB-1043 & SW-WF-0014		9. 1.86	C.Hasell	Longacre Farm, Sandy	24.10.99P
G-MNKR	Solar Wings Pegasus/Flash (Rotax 447)	SW-TB-1045 & SW-WF-0015		14. 1.86	M.A. & P.A.Hornsby	Sutton Meadows, Ely	16. 6.95P
G-MNKS	Solar Wings Pegasus/Flash (Rotax 447)	SW-TB-1044 & SW-WF-0016		9. 1.86	W.J.Walker	Drummiard Farm, Bonnybank	10. 4.99P
G-MNKU	Southdown Puma Sprint (Rotax 447)	1231/0100		29. 1.86	S.P.O'Hannrachain	Naas, Co.Kildare	21.10.98P
G-MNKV	Solar Wings Pegasus/Flash (Rotax 447)	SW-TB-1047 & SW-WF-0017		15. 1.86	R.A Banks t/a G-MNKV Group	Dunkeswell	4. 4.99P
G-MNKW	Solar Wings Pegasus/Flash (Rotax 447)	SW-WF-0018		28. 1.86	S.Rumens	Etchingham, E.Sussex	11. 3.96P
G-MNKX	Solar Wings Pegasus/Flash (Rotax 447)	SW-WF-0019		28. 2.86	P.Samal	Sandy	5.12.99P
G-MNKZ	Southdown Raven X (Rotax 447)	2232/0102		4. 2.86	G.B.Gratton	Andover	27.12.97P
G-MNLB	Southdown Raven X (Rotax 447)	2232/0117		11. 4.86	D.A.Chamberlain	Long Marston	7. 6.98P
G-MNLE	Southdown Raven X (Rotax 447)	2232/0128		30. 4.86	I.D. & P.G.Cresswell	Rochester	6.10.98P
G-MNLH	Romain Cobra Biplane (Midwest AE50R)	001		23. 1.86	J.W.E.Romain	Welwyn	5.11.98P
G-MNLI	Mainair Gemini/Flash 2 (Rotax 503)	407-286-4 & W152		28. 1.86	C.E. & P.M.Fessi	Coventry/Bolton	6. 6.99P
G-MNLK	Southdown Raven X (Rotax 447)	2232/0108		4. 2.86	M.J.Robbins	Tunbridge Wells	27. 7.98P
G-MNLL	Southdown Raven X (Rotax 447)	2232/0109		4. 2.86	S.Barrass	Doncaster	15. 8.93P
G-MNLM	Southdown Raven X (Rotax 447)	2232/0110		6. 2.86	A.P.White	Exmouth	9. 6.93P
G-MNLN	Southdown Raven X (Rotax 447)	2232/0111		6. 2.86	R.Locke	Newark	13.12.99P
G-MNLO	Southdown Raven X (Rotax 447)	2232/0112		6. 2.86	D.Kiddy (Damaged Upottery nr Honiton 6.4.86)	Torquay	1. 6.87P
G-MNLT	Southdown Raven X (Rotax 447)	2232/0115		6. 2.86	J.L.Stachini	Borehamwood	5. 3.98P
G-MNLU	Southdown Raven X (Rotax 447)	2232/0116		6. 2.86	D.J.Ainsworth	Preston	25. 6.99P
G-MNLV	Southdown Raven X (Rotax 447)	2232/0118		6. 2.86	J.Murphy	London EC1	16. 7.90P
G-MNLW	Medway Half Pint/Aerial Arts 130SX (JPX PUL 425)	10/31186		10. 2.86	M.I.Dougall	Maidstone	15. 9.93E
G-MNLX	Mainair Gemini/Flash 2 (Rotax 462)	413-386-4 & W165		6. 2.86	K.J.Jarmin	Rushden	21. 4.98P
G-MNLY	Mainair Gemini/Flash (Rotax 503)	406-386-4 & W151		14. 2.86	J.L.Finney	Ince Blundell, Liverpool	5. 4.99P
G-MNLZ	Southdown Raven X (Rotax 447)	2232/0123		6. 2.86	E.L.Jenkins	Bexleyheath	27. 5.99P
G-MNMC	Mainair Gemini/Southdown Puma Sprint MS (EC-44-PM)	222-284-2 & P524		20. 3.84	J.J.Milliken	Winchester	20. 9.96P
G-MNMD	Southdown Raven X (Rotax 447) (Originally regd with c/n 2232/0121)	2000/0121		10. 2.86	P.G.Overall	Crawley	10.11.99P

Regn	Type	C/n P/I	Date	Owner/operator	Probable Base	CA Expy
G-MNME	Hiway Skytrike/Demon WTP-01 & 3535009 (Rotax 377)		12. 2.86	J.C.P.Greene	Hereford	10. 6.93E
G-MNMG	Mainair Gemini/Flash 2 419-386-4 & W177 (Rotax 447)		11. 2.86	N.A.M.Beyer-Kay	Southport	20. 8.94P
G-MNMH	Mainair Gemini/Flash 2 417-486-4 & W168 (Rotax 462)		11. 2.86	A.B.Legge	Windermere	4.10.98P
G-MNMI	Mainair Gemini/Flash 2 317-685-3 & W178 (EC-44-PM) (Trike ex G-MMZL)		11. 2.86	S.D.Titman	RAF Wyton	8. 8.99P
G-MNMJ	Mainair Gemini/Flash 2 387-1185-3 & W122 (Rotax 447)		11. 2.86	P.J.Burrow	Crediton	18. 9.99P
G-MNMK	Solar Wings Pegasus XL-R SW-WA-1038 (Rotax 447)		19. 8.85	G.P.Wayne	Okehampton	4.10.98P
G-MNML	Southdown Puma Sprint 1111/0065 (EC-44-PM)		4. 8.83	R.C.Carr	Launceston	14. 7.97P
G-MNMM	Aerotech MW-5(K) Sorcerer 5K-0001-02 (Rotax 447) (Regd with c/n SK-0001-01)		11. 2.86	G.R.Horner	York	17. 8.99P
G-MNMN	Medway Hybred 44XLR 8286/16 (Rotax 447)		7. 3.86	D.S Blofeld	Orpington	16.12.99P
G-MNMO	Mainair Gemini/Flash 2 398-186-4 & W141 (Rotax 447)		27. 2.86	P.D.Hawkesworth & G.Wigglesworth Guy Lane Farm, Waverton		28. 5.99P
G-MNMS*	Wheeler Scout 0010		25. 5.84	M.I.Smith (Cancelled by CAA 27.3.99)	Alton	
G-MNMU	Southdown Raven X 2232/0127 (EC-44-PM)		17. 2.86	M.J.Curley	London Colney	7. 5.99P
G-MNMV	Mainair Gemini/Flash 375-1085-3 & W113 (Rotax 447)		3. 3.86	D.Shackleton	Wakefield	6. 1.99P
G-MNMW	Whittaker MW-6-1-1 Merlin PFA/164-11144 (Rotax 582)		16. 4.86	E.F.Clapham Oldbury-on-Severn t/a G-MNMW Flying Group		27. 7.99P
G-MNMY	Cyclone 70/Aerial Arts 110SX CH-02 (Rotax 277)		6. 3.86	N.R.Beale	Leamington Spa	29. 9.96P
G-MNNA	Southdown Raven X 2232/0129 (Rotax 447)		4. 3.86	D. & G.D.Palfrey	Tiverton	20. 7.88P
G-MNNB	Southdown Raven 2122/0130 (EC-44-PM)		4. 3.86	J.K.Ewing	Poole	15. 8.99P
G-MNNC	Southdown Raven X 2232/0131 (Rotax 447)		4. 3.86	S.A.Sacker	Grantham	29.10.98P
G-MNND	Solar Wings Pegasus/Flash 2 SW-WF-0100 (Rotax 447)		27. 2.86	M.J.Matthews	Crewe	2. 7.94P
G-MNNE	Mainair Gemini/Flash 2 410-386-4 & W154 (Rotax 462)		27. 2.86	R.N.Watts	Wirral	1. 7.93P
G-MNNF	Mainair Gemini/Flash 2 402-286-4 & W148 (Rotax 447)		28. 2.86	W.J.Gunn (Stored 1.98)	Long Marston	8. 4.97P
G-MNNG	Squires Lightfly/Solar Wings Photon (Rotax 277) SW-WP-0019		25. 2.86	C.C.Bilham	Huntingdon	30. 1.99P
G-MNNI	Mainair Gemini/Flash 2 427-486-4 & W170 (Rotax 503) (Wing also quoted as c/n W173)		28. 2.86	J.C.Miller	East Fortune	2. 6.98P
G-MNNJ*	Mainair Gemini/Flash 2 405-286-4 & W150 (Rotax 503)		28. 2.86	G.D.Tannahill Broadmeadow Farm, Hereford (Cancelled as destroyed 17.8.98)		12. 4.98P
G-MNNK	Mainair Gemini/Flash 2 428-486-4 & W185 (Rotax 503) (Trike stolen from Fradley 1.1.93)		28. 2.86	M.P.Shea	Newcastle, Staffs	8. 4.93P
G-MNNL	Mainair Gemini/Flash 2 429-486-4 & W186 (Rotax 503)		28. 2.86	D.Wilson & A.Bielawski	Nottingham	15. 5.99P
G-MNNM	Mainair Scorcher Solo 424-486-1 & W182 (Rotax 447)		20. 3.86	D.A.Whiteside	Ulverston	8. 9.91P
G-MNNN	Southdown Raven X 2232/0132 (Rotax 447)		4. 3.86	F.Byford & S.Hooker	Dover	21. 8.90P
G-MNNO	Southdown Raven X 2232/0133 (Rotax 447)		26. 3.86	M.J.Robbins	Tunbridge Wells	9. 5.96P
G-MNNP	Mainair Gemini/Flash 2 409-386-4 & W155 (Rotax 462)		5. 3.86	K.J.Regan	Billericay	28. 8.94P
G-MNNR	Mainair Gemini/Flash 2 430-586-4 & W188 (Rotax 503) (Wing originally quoted as c/n W157)		6. 3.86	W.A.B.Hill	Davidstow Moor	8. 4.99P
G-MNNS	Eurowing Goldwing EW-74		8. 4.86	D.Johnstone & R.J.Wood	Dunbar	
G-MNNU	Mainair Gemini/Flash 2 408-386-4 & W153 (Rotax 447) (See G-MTBK)		19. 3.86	M.Hurn	Graveley	13. 7.97P
G-MNNV	Mainair Gemini/Flash 2 431-586-4 & W187 (Rotax 503)		10. 3.86	R.P.Wilkinson	Bath	24. 1.89P
G-MNNY	Solar Wings Pegasus/Flash (Rotax 447) SW-TB-1059 & SW-WF-0023		14. 3.86	K.B.Stokes	Davidstow Moor	30. 8.98P
G-MNNZ	Solar Wings Pegasus/Flash 2 (Rotax 447) SW-TB-1060 & SW-WF-0101		24. 4.86	R.D.A.Henderson	Exeter	1. 4.98P
G-MNPA	Solar Wings Pegasus/Flash 2 SW-WF-0102 (Rotax 462)		18. 4.86	J.M.MacDonald Mill Farm, Hughley, Much Wenlock		30. 5.98P
G-MNPB	Solar Wings Pegasus/Flash 2 SW-WF-0103 (Rotax 447)		18. 4.86	M.R.Truran	Old Sarum	29. 5.95P
G-MNPC	Mainair Gemini/Flash 2 423-586-4 & W181 (Rotax 462)		17. 3.86	M.J.Holmes	Northampton	13. 4.98P

Regn	Type	C/n P/I	Date	Owner/operator	Probable Base	CA Expy
G-MNPG	Mainair Gemini/Flash 2 437-686-4 & W204 (Rotax 447)		20. 3.86	P.Kirton	Cumbernauld	14. 6.99P
G-MNPI	Southdown Pipistrelle 2C SAL-P2C-003 (JPX PUL505)		17. 3.86	R.Riley (Damaged 1994)	Ashford, Kent	25. 7.94P
G-MNPV	Mainair Scorcher Solo 432-586-1 & W189 (Rotax 447)		24. 3.86	F.Colman	Eshott	17. 5.98P
G-MNPX	Mainair Gemini/Flash 2 412-486-4 & W164 (Rotax 447)		24. 3.86	B.R.Ginger	Colchester	9.11.99P
G-MNPY	Mainair Scorcher Solo 452-886-1 & W229 (Rotax 447)		25. 3.86	R.N.O.Kingsbury	Tunbridge Wells	15. 6.99P
G-MNPZ	Mainair Scorcher Solo 449-886-1 & W226 (Rotax 503/3-blade prop test a/c)		25. 3.86	S.Stevens	North Shields	4. 9.93P
G-MNRD	Ultraflight Lazair IIIE (Rotax 185) 81		17. 6.83	J.K.Evans	Northampton	15. 9.99P
G-MNRE	Mainair Scorcher Solo 453-886-1 & W230 (Rotax 447)		25. 3.86	G.R.Hill	Staines	30. 7.97P
G-MNRF	Mainair Scorcher Solo 461-986-1 & W238 (Rotax 447)		25. 3.86	Flylight Airsports Ltd	Sywell	19. 5.99P
G-MNRG	Mainair Scorcher Solo 462-986-1 & W239 (Rotax 447)		25. 3.86	C.Murphy	Ince Blundell, Liverpool	8.12.97P
G-MNRI	Hornet Dual Trainer/Raven (Rotax 462) HRWA 0051 & 2000/0119		26. 3.86 (Replacement Trike HRWA-0082 now fitted)	D.A.Robinson	Sandtoft	1. 7.99P
G-MNRJ	Hornet Dual Trainer/Raven (Rotax 447) HRWA 0052 & 2000/0120		26. 3.86	S.R., S.M. & R.W.Morris	Coventry	10.11.90P
G-MNRK	Hornet Dual Trainer/Raven (Rotax 447) HRWA 0053 & 2000/0183		26. 3.86	R.K.Beynon	Aberdeen	30. 7.95P
G-MNRL	Hornet Dual Trainer/Raven (Rotax 462) HRWA 0054 & 2000/0184		26. 3.86	A.G.Ward	Royston	30. 1.00P
G-MNRM	Hornet Dual Trainer/Raven (Rotax 447) HRWA 0055 & 2000/0214		26. 3.86	R.I.Cannan	Ramsey, IoM	26.12.99P
G-MNRP	Southdown Raven X 2232/0135 (Rotax 447)		7. 4.86	C.Moore	Egremont	5. 7.95P
G-MNRS	Southdown Raven X 2232/0137 (Rotax 447)		7. 4.86	A.J.Denhart	Crawley	8. 6.99P
G-MNRT	Midland Ultralights Sirocco 377GB (Rotax 377) MU-016		1. 4.86	R.F.Hinton	Mansfield	7. 8.99P
G-MNRW	Mainair Gemini/Flash 2 411-486-4 & W156 (Rotax 462)		7. 4.86	L.A.Maynard	Old Sarum	1. 8.99P
G-MNRX	Mainair Gemini/Flash 2 434-686-4 & W220 (Rotax 503)		8. 4.86	S.Foster	St.Michaels-on-Wyre	8. 5.99P
G-MNRY	Mainair Gemini/Flash 2 418-486-4 & W169 (Rotax 462)		7. 4.86	T.K.Duffy	Insch	8. 8.99P
G-MNRZ	Mainair Scorcher Solo 426-586-1 & W184 (Rotax 447)		4. 4.86	J.N.Wrigley	Ley Farm, Chirk	17. 5.94P
G-MNSA	Mainair Gemini/Flash 2 442-786-4 & W219 (Rotax 503)		18. 4.86	R.E.Morris	Kidwelly, Dyfed	10.10.96P
G-MNSB	Southdown Puma Sprint 539 & 1121/0066 (EC-44-PM)		15. 6.83	A.C.Cale	Ledbury	9.10.96P
G-MNSD	Ultrasports Tripacer/Solar Wings Typhoon S4 (Hunting HS.260A) T182-341L		23. 4.86	N.D.Dykes	Marston Moreteyne, Bedford	N/E
G-MNSE	Mainair Gemini/Flash 2 444-886-4 & W224 (Rotax 503)		4. 4.86	H.T.H. van Neck	Wirral	1. 4.98P
G-MNSH	Solar Wings Pegasus Flash 2 SW-WF-0104 (Rotax 447)		14. 4.86	M.J.Aubrey	Kington, Hereford	22. 7.98P
G-MNSI	Mainair Gemini/Flash 2 445-786-4 & W213 (Rotax 462)		9. 4.86	S.Wheeldon	Manchester	3. 6.98P
G-MNSJ	Mainair Gemini/Flash 2 443-886-4 & W223 (Rotax 503)		11. 4.86	A.Simon	Dingwall	4.10.99P
G-MNSL	Southdown Raven X 2232/0145 (Rotax 447)		17. 4.86	P.B.Robinson	Ely	8. 7.99P
G-MNSN	Solar Wings Pegasus Flash 2 (Rotax 447) SW-TB-1066 & SW-WF-0105		25. 4.86	F.R. & V.L.Higgins	Leigh-upon-Mendip, Bath	19. 4.97P
G-MNSR	Mainair Gemini/Flash 2 399-486-4 & W144 (Rotax 503)		17. 4.86	A.M.Bell	Rufforth	2. 5.99P
G-MNSS	American Aerolights Eagle 215B 4131 (Zenoah G25Bl)		24. 4.86	G.P.Jones	Caernarfon	N/E
G-MNSV	CFM Shadow Srs.B (Rotax 447) 012		24. 4.86	P.J.W.Rowell	Southport	20.11.99P
G-MNSW	Southdown Raven X 2232/0147 (Rotax 447)		23. 4.86	A.H.Gray	Tonbridge	22. 7.93P
G-MNSX	Southdown Raven X 2232/0148 (Rotax 447)		30. 4.86	S.F.Chave	Honiton	11. 9.98P
G-MNSY	Southdown Raven X 2232/0149 (Rotax 447)		30. 4.86	J.B.Carter	Hatherton, Cannock	7. 7.99P
G-MNTC	Southdown Raven X 2232/0150 (Rotax 447)		30. 4.86	J.R.Brabbs	Brandon	12.10.92P
G-MNTD	Aerial Arts Chaser/110SX 110SX/255 (C/n duplicates G-MTSF)		24. 4.86	B.Richardson	Sunderland	
G-MNTE	Southdown Raven X 2232/0151 (Rotax 447)		30. 4.86	D.Kiddy	Torquay	

Regn	Type	C/n	P/I	Date	Owner/operator	Probable Base	CA Expy
G-MNTF	Southdown Raven X	2232/0152		30. 4.86	M.D.Phillips	Mayfield, E.Sussex	24. 7.94P
G-MNTG	Southdown Raven X (Rotax 447)	2232/0153		30. 4.86	D.Thorpe (Stored 5.97)	Dunkeswell	24. 7.96P
G-MNTI	Mainair Gemini/Flash 2 447-886-4 & W231 (Rotax 503)			8. 5.86	R.T.Strathie	Melrose, Roxburgh	7. 8.99P
G-MNTK	CFM Shadow Srs.CD (Rotax 503)	024		8. 5.86	T.A.R.Davies	Brixham	4. 8.99P
G-MNTM	Southdown Raven X (Rotax 447)	2232/0154		19. 5.86	D.M.Garland	Atherstone	24. 7.98P
G-MNTN	Southdown Raven X (Rotax 447)	2232/0155		2. 6.86	J.Hall	Wolverhampton	31.12.97P
G-MNTO	Southdown Raven X (Rotax 447)	2232/0156		5. 6.86	D.J.Poole	Longacre Farm, Sandy	9. 7.98P
G-MNTP	CFM Shadow Srs.B (Rotax 447)	K.022		19. 5.86	P.K.Hope-Lang	Milton Keynes	5. 2.00P
G-MNTS	Mainair Gemini/Flash 2 450-886-4 & W227 (Rotax 462)			3. 4.86	K.J.Cole	Highnam, Glos	2. 5.96P
G-MNTT	Medway Half Pint/Aerial Arts 130SX 12/1486			7. 4.86	Lancaster Partners (Holdings) Ltd Ashcroft Farm, Winsford		N/E
G-MNTU	Mainair Gemini/Flash 2 460-886-4 & W233 (Rotax 503)			9. 7.86	T.J.Barley	Sawbridgeworth	8. 6.99P
G-MNTV	Mainair Gemini/Flash 2 455-886-4 & W241 (Rotax 462)			9. 7.86	P.Dunstan	Redruth	10.10.99P
G-MNTW	Mainair Gemini/Flash 2 456-886-5 & W242 (Rotax 462)			11. 9.86	C.L.Bowen	Liverpool	4. 6.99P
G-MNTX	Mainair Gemini/Flash 2 415-486-4 & W166 (Rotax 503)			20. 5.86	S.Isherwood	St.Michaels-on-Wyre	29. 6.99P
G-MNTY	Southdown Raven X (Rotax 447)	2232/0157		29. 5.86	B.J.Holloway	Bicester	6. 3.99P
G-MNTZ	Mainair Gemini/Flash 2 457-886-4 & W243 (Rotax 503)			3. 6.86	M.Harris	Brierley Hill	20. 3.99P
G-MNUA	Mainair Gemini/Flash 2 458-886-4 & W235 (Rotax 462)			29. 5.86	J.McCullough	Castlewellan, Co.Down	14. 2.99P
G-MNUB	Mainair Gemini/Flash 2 459-986-4 & W236 (Rotax 462)			3. 6.86	M.J.Hammond	South Ockendon, Essex	11. 8.97P
G-MNUD	Solar Wings Pegasus Flash 2 (Rotax 462) SW-TE-0003 & SW-WF-0110			10. 6.86	P.G.H.Milbank	Over, Cambridge	3. 8.99P
G-MNUE	Solar Wings Pegasus Flash 2 SW-WF-0108 (Rotax 462)			10. 6.86	P.M.Rogers	Rochdale	5. 6.99P
G-MNUF	Mainair Gemini/Flash 2 472-786-4 & W252 (Rotax 503)			13. 6.86	C.Hannaby (Stored 12.97)	Guy Lane Farm, Waverton	4. 2.96P
G-MNUG	Mainair Gemini/Flash 2 465-986-4 & W245 (Rotax 462)			13. 6.86	M.L.Harris	Sittles Farm, Alrewas	1. 2.99P
G-MNUH	Southdown Raven X (Rotax 447)	2232/0158		17. 6.86	A.L.Flude	Newnham	3. 5.97P
G-MNUI	Mainair Tri-Flyer/Skyhook Cutlass (EC-44-PM)	MH-01		21. 5.86	M.Holling	Goole	28. 2.87E
G-MNUJ*	Solar Wings Pegasus Photon SW-TP-0018 & SW-WP-0018			11. 6.86	W.G.Farr (Stored 9.97; cancelled by CAA 27.3.99)	Eshott	
G-MNUM	Mainair Gemini/Southdown Puma Sprint MS (EC-44-PM) 226-184-2 & P.508			12. 3.84	J.A.Sims	Farnham	31. 1.99P
G-MNUO	Mainair Gemini/Flash 2 421-586-4 & W179 (Rotax 462)			9. 7.86	C.L.G.Innocent	Worthing	8. 5.99P
G-MNUR	Mainair Gemini/Flash 2 470-986-4 & W250 (Rotax 503)			14. 8.86	J.C.Greves	Cobham	30. 3.90P
G-MNUT	Southdown Raven X (Rotax 447)	2232/0160		10. 6.86	Irene A.De Groot (Stored 7.95) Lower Mountpleasant Farm, Wimblington		15. 7.93P
G-MNUU	Southdown Raven X (Rotax 447)	2232/0162		26. 6.86	P.N.Jackson	Launceston	7. 8.99P
G-MNUW	Southdown Raven X (Rotax 447)	2232/0163		17. 6.86	B.A.McDonald	Sutton Meadows, Ely	19.12.96P
G-MNUX	Solar Wings Pegasus XL-R SW-WA-1076 (Rotax 447)			24. 6.86	N.Smith	Hebburn	29. 9.99P
G-MNUY	Mainair Gemini/Flash 2 422-586-4 & W180 (Rotax 503)			23. 6.86	R.M.Cornwell	Kemble	20. 6.99P
G-MNVB	Solar Wings Pegasus XL-R (Rotax 447) SW-TB-1073 & SW-WA-1077			7. 7.86	M.J.Melvin	Spalding	2. 1.99P
G-MNVC	Solar Wings Pegasus XL-R (Rotax 447) SW-TB-1074 & SW-WA-1078			7. 7.86	M.N.C.Ward	Shobdon	2. 3.98P
G-MNVE	Solar Wings Pegasus XL-R SW-WA-1079 (Rotax 447)			19. 6.86	M.P.Aris	Welwyn	19. 6.99P
G-MNVF*	Solar Wings Pegasus Flash 2 SW-WF-0112 (Rotax 447)			26. 6.86	A.Rooker (Damaged mid 1996; cancelled as WFU 17.6.98)	Cambridge	23. 6.97P
G-MNVG	Solar Wings Pegasus Flash 2 SW-WF-0109 (Rotax 447)			11. 6.86	D.J.Ward	Low Farm, South Walsham	7. 6.99P
G-MNVH	Solar Wings Pegasus Flash 2 (Rotax 462) SW-TE-0001 & SW-WF-0122			23. 6.86	J.A.Clarke & C.Hall	London N22/E8	9. 4.97P
G-MNVI	CFM Shadow Srs.C (Rotax 503)	026		17. 6.86	D.R.C.Pugh	Caersws, Powys	13. 9.99P

Regn	Type	C/n	P/I	Date	Owner/operator	Probable Base	CA Expy
G-MNVJ	CFM Shadow Srs.CD	028		17. 6.86	V.C.Readhead	Saxmundham	23. 9.99P
	(Rotax 447) (Originally regd as Srs.BD)						
G-MNVK	CFM Shadow Srs.CD	029		17. 6.86	K.C.Lye	Melksham	16. 8.99P
	(Rotax 503)						
G-MNVN	Southdown Raven (EC-34-PM)	2132/0165		27. 6.86	N.Cowlen & D.J.Francis	Spalding	26. 4.97P
G-MNVO	Hovey Whing-Ding II	CW-01		14. 8.86	C.Wilson	Basildon	
G-MNVP	Southdown Raven X	2232/0166		23. 6.86	M.J.Carnell	Belper	15. 9.97P
	(Rotax 447)				(Damaged late 1996)		
G-MNVR	Mainair Gemini/Flash 2	471-986-4 & W251		27. 6.86	S.Farrow Botany Bay, Horford, Norwich		13.11.99P
	(Rotax 503)				"Loopy"		
G-MNVS	Mainair Gemini/Flash 2	476-986-4 & W257		9. 7.86	J.D.Potts	Telford	29. 1.98P
	(Rotax 503)						
G-MNVT	Mainair Gemini/Flash 2	477-786-4 & W258		27. 6.86	A.C.Barker t/a ACB Hydraulics	Cheadle	28. 7.87P
	(Rotax 503)				(Stored Hinton-in-the-Hedges 4.90)		
G-MNVU	Mainair Gemini/Flash 2	468-986-4 & W248		26. 6.86	W.R.Marsh		
	(Rotax 503)				Newhouse Farm, Hardwicke, Hereford		28. 6.99P
G-MNVV	Mainair Gemini/Flash 2	467-986-4 & W247		26. 6.86	R.P.Hothersall	Clitheroe	30. 3.99P
	(Rotax 503)						
G-MNVW	Mainair Gemini/Flash 2	466-986-4 & W246		26. 6.86	J.C.Munro-Hunt	Milson	20. 9.98P
	(Rotax 503)						
G-MNVY*	Solar Wings Pegasus Photon	SW-WP-0020		27. 6.86	Not known Hughley, Much Wenlock		N/E
					(On rebuild 3.97)		
G-MNVZ	Solar Wings Pegasus Photon	SW-WP-0021		27. 6.86	J.J.Russ	Eshott	27. 6.94P
	(Solo 210)						
G-MNWA	Southdown Raven X	2232/0167		26. 6.86	J.B.Mayes	Newmarket	14. 5.99P
	(Rotax 447)						
G-MNWB	Thruster TST	086-118-UK-001		25. 6.86	Heather E.Hewitt		
	(Rotax 503)				Clontilew Farm, Portadown, Co.Armagh		3. 1.95P
G-MNWC*	Mainair Gemini/Flash 2	416-486-4 & W167		27. 6.86	Not known	Kilmarnock	8. 6.98P
	(Rotax 503)				(Temp unregd 20.10.97)		
G-MNWD	Mainair Gemini/Flash 2	474-986-4 & W254		27. 6.86	M.B.Rutherford	Swinford, Rugby	28.12.99P
	(Rotax 462)						
G-MNWG	Southdown Raven X	2232/0170		4. 8.86	A.J.McShane & M.J.Reeve	Sywell	5. 1.99P
	(Rotax 447)						
G-MNWI	Mainair Gemini/Flash 2	478-986-4 & W264		9. 7.86	I.B.Rushbrooke Arclid Green, Sandbach		3.11.99P
	(Rotax 503)						
G-MNWK	CFM Shadow Srs.C (Rotax 503)	030		9. 7.86	J.E.Hunt	Welling, Kent	19. 8.98P
G-MNWL	Arbiter Svs Trike/Aerial Arts 130SX	130SX/333		23. 7.86	Arbiter Svs Ltd	Newport Pagnell	
G-MNWO	Mainair Gemini/Flash 2	490-1086-4 & W287		15. 7.86	G.Neal & Y.G.G.Lewis	Ruislip	8. 8.98P
	(Rotax 503)						
G-MNWP	Solar Wings Pegasus/Flash 2			4. 8.86	A.G. & C.Smith	Swanton Morley	24. 8.99P
	(Rotax 447) SW-TB-1083 & SW-WF-0113						
G-MNWR	Medway Hybred 44XLR	23686/17		4. 8.86	P.Collins	Grays	23. 7.96P
	(Rotax 447)						
G-MNWU	Solar Wings Pegasus/Flash 2LC			4. 8.86	F.J.E.Brownshill & W.Parkin	Oakley	18. 4.99P
	(Rotax 462) SW-TE-0006 & SW-WF-0111						
G-MNWV	Solar Wings Pegasus/Flash 2			4. 8.86	M.N.Tope & D.J.Brenchley	Davidstow Moor	11. 3.96P
	(Rotax 447) SW-TB-1090 & SW-WF-0121						
G-MNWW	Solar Wings Pegasus XL-R/Se			8.10.86	N.P.Chitty	Ginge, Wantage	13. 3.99P
	(Rotax 462) SW-TE-0008 & SW-WA-1085				t/a Chiltern Flyers Aero Tow Grp		
G-MNWX	Solar Wings Pegasus XL-R			4. 8.86	J.A.Crofts & G.M.Birkett	Haverfordwest	5. 5.96P
	(Rotax 447) SW-TB-1093 & SW-WA-1086						
G-MNWY	CFM Shadow Srs.CD K.021 & PFA/161-11130			28. 7.86	R.Savage Ballynahinch, Co.Down		1. 8.98P
	(Rotax 503)				t/a Air Photographic Ireland		
G-MNWZ	Mainair Gemini/Flash 2	436-686-4 & W203		19. 8.86	W.T.Hume	Newmilns, Ayr	16. 6.98P
	(Rotax 503)						
G-MNXA	Southdown Raven X	2232/0180		5. 8.86	P.Johnson	Kettering	27. 7.99P
	(Rotax 447)						
G-MNXB	Mainair Tri-Flyer/Solar Wings Photon			29. 7.86	J.F.Phillips Drummiard Farm, Bonnybank		16. 6.98P
	(EC-34-PM) SW-WP-0022						
G-MNXC	Aerial Arts Chaser/110SX	110SX/335		4. 8.86	J.E.Sweetingham	Basildon	27. 4.95P
	(Rotax 377)						
G-MNXD	Southdown Raven	2132/0173		13. 8.86	P.Jephcott	Solihull	25.10.98P
	(EC-44-PM)						
G-MNXE	Southdown Raven X	2232/0202		7. 8.86	A.E.Silvey	Wilburton, Ely	24. 7.98P
	(Rotax 447)						
G-MNXF	Southdown Raven	2132/0176		2. 9.86	D.E.Gwenin	Tring	13. 5.99P
	(EC-44-PM)						
G-MNXG	Southdown Raven X	2232/0181		3. 9.86	M.A. & E.M.Williams	Tonbridge	9. 4.96P
	(Rotax 447)						
G-MNXI	Southdown Raven X	2232/0179		19. 8.86	A.M.Yates	Wisbech	13. 7.96P
	(Rotax 447)						
G-MNXN	Medway Hybred 44XLR	28786/18		3. 9.86	E.C.D.Williams & J.Dinwoodey		
	(Rotax 447)				(Stored 7.97) Tarn Farm, Cockerham		16. 5.95P
G-MNXO	Medway Hybred 44XLR	29786/19		3. 9.86	D.L.Turner	Chatham	6. 7.99P
	(Rotax 447)						

Regn	Type	C/n P/I	Date	Owner/operator	Probable Base	CA Expy
G-MNXP	Solar Wings Pegasus Flash 2 (Rotax 447) SW-TB-1094 & SW-WF-0117		16. 9.86	D.Harrison	Bewdley	6. 8.96P
G-MNXR	Mainair Gemini/Flash 2 479-986-4 & W265 (Rotax 462)		19. 8.86	N.T.Wainwright	Bromyard	14. 6.97P
G-MNXS	Mainair Gemini/Flash 2 480-986-4 & W267 (Rotax 462)		8. 9.86	F.T.Rawlings	Hereford	16. 3.89P
G-MNXT	Mainair Gemini/Flash 2 481-986-4 & W268 (Rotax 503)		19. 8.86	B.K.Robinson	Shobdon	27. 3.96P
G-MNXU	Mainair Gemini/Flash 2 482-1086-4 & W272 (Rotax 503)		18. 8.86	J.M.Hucker	Abertillery	10. 3.98P
G-MNXX	CFM Shadow Srs.CD (Rotax 447) K.027		13. 8.86	P.G.Gale "Shadowfax"	Old Sarum	13. 5.99P
G-MNXZ	Whittaker MW-5 Sorcerer PFA/163-11156 (EC-34-PM)		13. 8.86	P.J.Cheyney	Newhouse Farm, Loughborough	29. 5.99P
G-MNYA	Solar Wings Pegasus Flash 2 (Rotax 447) SW-TB-1098 & SW-WF-0119		3. 9.86	D.J.Gardner	Wellingborough	3.10.99P
G-MNYB	Solar Wings Pegasus XL-R (Rotax 447) SW-TB-1096 & SW-WA-1089		8. 9.86	P.J.Conaghy	Drogheda, Co.Louth, Ireland	27. 6.99P
G-MNYC	Solar Wings Pegasus XL-R (Rotax 447) SW-TB-1097 & SW-WA-1090		3. 9.86	F.C.Handy	Hatherton, Cannock	31.10.98P
G-MNYD	Aerial Arts Chaser/110SX 110SX/320 (Rotax 377)		19. 8.86	B.Richardson	Sunderland	24. 6.99P
G-MNYE	Aerial Arts Chaser/110SX 110SX/321		19. 8.86	D.A.Breeze	Welshpool	18.11.99P
G-MNYF	Aerial Arts Chaser/110SX 110SX/322 (Rotax 377)		19. 8.86	B.Richardson	Sunderland	24. 6.99P
G-MNYG	Southdown Raven (EC-44-PM) 2122/0172		19. 8.86	K.Clifford	Stanmore	20. 6.99P
G-MNYI	Southdown Raven X 2232/0211 (Rotax 447)		3. 9.86	N.P.Lloyd	Wrexham	17. 8.99P
G-MNYJ	Mainair Gemini/Flash 2 485-1086-4 & W275 (Rotax 462)		8. 9.86	S.J.Bristow	Malvern	17. 6.99P
G-MNYK	Mainair Gemini/Flash 2 494-1086-4 & W296 (Rotax 503)		11. 9.86	D.E.Williams	Coleford, Glos	4.10.95P
G-MNYL	Southdown Raven X 2232/0195 (Rotax 447)		2. 9.86	A.D.F.Clifford	Broadmeadow Farm, Hereford	9. 6.99P
G-MNYM	Southdown Raven X 2232/0196 (Rotax 447)		2. 9.86	R.W.Scarr	Dunkeswell	13. 8.99P
G-MNYP	Southdown Raven X 2232/0207 (Rotax 447)		3. 9.86	A.G.Davies	Bristol	11. 8.99P
G-MNYS	Southdown Raven X 2232/0208 (Rotax 447)		8. 9.86	S.Connolly	Braintree	9. 1.99P
G-MNYT	Solar Wings Pegasus XL-R (Rotax 447) SW-TB-1099 & SW-WA-1091		11. 9.86	V.Gadhia (Damaged mid 1997; stored 1.98)	Roddidge, Fradley	8. 3.98P
G-MNYU	Solar Wings Pegasus XL-R/Se (Rotax 447) SW-TB-1100 & SW-WA-1092		16. 9.86	S.R.Wiggins	Rhuallt	1. 5.99P
G-MNYV	Solar Wings Pegasus XL-R/Se (Rotax 447) SW-TB-1101 & SW-WA-1093		11. 9.86	P.Devlin	Hungerford	30.11.99P
G-MNYW	Solar Wings Pegasus XL-R SW-WA-1094 (Rotax 447)		11. 9.86	M.P.Waldock	Selsdon, Surrey	7. 8.98P
G-MNYX	Solar Wings Pegasus XL-R/LC (Rotax 462) SW-TE-0009 & SW-WA-1095		19. 9.86	P.Mayes & J.P.Widdowson (See G-MMKG)	Bridgnorth	13. 5.98P
G-MNYZ	Solar Wings Pegasus Flash 2 SW-WF-0114 (Rotax 462)		11. 9.86	A.C.Bartolozzi	Ely	14. 6.99P
G-MNZA	Solar Wings Pegasus Flash 2 (Rotax 462) SW-TB-1103 & SW-WF-0120 (Mainair Alpha c/n W127-1185-1)		3.10.86	J.M.MacDonald	Mill Farm, Hughley, Much Wenlock	24. 8.90P
G-MNZB	Mainair Gemini/Flash 2 483-1086-4 & W273 (Rotax 503)		8. 9.86	A.G.Carter	Oxton, Nottingham	2. 3.98P
G-MNZC	Mainair Gemini/Flash 2 484-1086-4 & W274 (Rotax 503)		16. 9.86	C.J.Whittaker	Ledbury	19. 1.89P
G-MNZD	Mainair Gemini/Flash 2 493-1086-4 & W295 (Rotax 503)		8. 9.86	N.D.Carter (Stored 9.96)	Little Gransden	4. 4.96P
G-MNZE	Mainair Gemini/Flash 2 495-1086-4 & W297 (Rotax 503) (Wing regd as W279 - see G-MTEK)		8. 9.86	A.Shand	Insch	6. 4.99P
G-MNZF	Mainair Gemini/Flash 2 496-1186-4 & W291 (Rotax 503)		8. 9.86	B.J.Marshall	Swinford, Rugby	14. 3.98P
G-MNZI*	Prone Power Mk.2/Solar Wings Typhoon PP-01		22. 9.86	R.J.Folwell (Cancelled by CAA 27.3.99)	Bristol	
G-MNZJ	CFM Shadow Srs.BD 033 (Rotax 447)		19. 9.86	T.E.P.Eves & A.Rothery	Baxby Manor, Husthwaite	26.11.99P
G-MNZK	Solar Wings Pegasus XL-R/Se SW-WA-1096 (Rotax 447)		24. 9.86	J.G.Campbell & P.J.Perkins	Barnsley	23. 7.99P
G-MNZL	Solar Wings Pegasus XL-R (Rotax 447) SW-TB-1106 & SW-WA-1097		1.10.86	M.A.Concannon (Stored 6.96)	Long Marston	27. 9.95P
G-MNZO	Solar Wings Pegasus Flash 2 (Rotax 462) SW-TE-0012 & SW-WF-0125		30. 9.86	K.B.Woods & D.Johnson	Newnham	14. 2.99P
G-MNZP	CFM Shadow Srs.BD (Rotax 447) K.039 & PFA/161-11206		19. 9.86	J.G.Wakeford	Bexhill-on-Sea	18. 5.99P
G-MNZR	CFM Shadow Srs.BD 040 (Rotax 447)		19. 9.86	J.S.Wilson	Swanton Morley	7. 9.99P

Regn	Type	C/n	P/I	Date	Owner/operator	Probable Base	CA Expy
G-MNZS	Aerial Arts Alpha/130SX (Rotax 277)	130SX/376		23. 9.86	S.B.Walters	Sidcup	1. 8.99P
G-MNZU	Eurowing Goldwing (EC-34-PM)	EW-88		24. 9.86	H.B.Baker	Salisbury	15. 7.99P
G-MNZW*	Southdown Raven X (Rotax 447)	2232/0220		17.10.86	C.A.James (Cancelled by CAA 15.3.99)	Filton	5. 7.98P
G-MNZY	Mainair Tri-Flyer 330/Airwave Nimrod	078-14682		17.10.86	P.W.Fieldman	Petersfield, Hants	N/E
G-MNZZ	CFM Shadow Srs.CD (Rotax 503)	036		19. 9.86	P.J.Lynch	Farnborough	18. 9.99P

G-MOAA-MOZZ

Regn	Type	C/n	P/I	Date	Owner/operator	Probable Base	CA Expy
G-MOAC	Beechcraft F33A Bonanza	CE-1349	N1563N	25. 5.89	R.L.Camrass	La Rochelle, France	30. 5.01
G-MOAK	Schempp-Hirth Nimbus 3DM	19/46		23. 5.91	P.W.Lever "929"		28. 5.01
						Carr Hill Farm, Corbridge	
G-MOBI	Aerospatiale AS.355F1 Twin Squirrel	5260	G-MUFF	11.11.93	M.J.O'Brien	Redhill	3. 4.00T
			G-CORR		t/a Castle Aviation (Op Gemini Redhill Ltd)		
G-MOFB	Cameron O-120 HAFB	4275		13. 1.98	D.M.Moffat	Alveston, Bristol	
G-MOFF	Cameron O-77 HAFB	2040		27. 7.89	D.M.Moffat "Moff"	Alveston, Bristol	19.12.99A
G-MOFZ	Cameron O-90 HAFB	3350		7. 9.94	D.M.Moffat	Alveston, Bristol	15. 9.96A
G-MOGI	Grumman-American AA-5A Cheetah	AA5A-0630	G-BFMU	1. 5.86	TL Avn Ltd	Jersey	24.10.99
G-MOGY	Robinson R-22 Beta	0899		23.11.88	Heli Air Ltd	Wellesbourne Mountford	8. 6.01
G-MOHS	PA-31-350 Chieftain	31-8152115	G-BWOC N40898	29. 4.96	Sky Air Travel Ltd	Stapleford	17. 9.99T
G-MOKE	Cameron V-77 HAFB	3686		4.10.95	D.D.Owen	(Luxembourg)	3. 1.00A
G-MOLE	Taylor JT.2 Titch (Cont O-200-A)	PFA/60-10725		20. 1.87	S.R.Mowle (Under construction 10.90)	(Kenley)	
G-MOLI	Cameron A-250 HAFB	3429		26. 1.95	J.J.Rudoni	Rugeley	12. 2.99T
G-MOLL	PA-32-301T Turbo Saratoga	32-8024040	N82535	25. 3.91	M.S.Bennett	Netherthorpe	12. 5.00
G-MOLY	PA-23-160 Apache	23-1686	EI-BAW G-APFV/EI-ALK	7. 6.79	R.R. & M.T.Thorogood	Gloucestershire	28. 2.99
G-MONB	Boeing 757-2T7ER	22780		7. 3.83	Monarch Airlines Ltd	Luton	1. 2.00T
G-MOND	Boeing 757-2T7	22960	D-ABNZ G-MOND	28. 4.83	Monarch Airlines Ltd	Luton	13. 5.99T
G-MONE	Boeing 757-2T7ER	23293		27. 2.85	Monarch Airlines Ltd (Renaissance Cruise c/s)	Luton	25. 2.00T
G-MONI	Monnett Moni (KFM.107)	PFA/142-10925		12. 1.84	B.S.Carpenter	RAF Brize Norton	23.11.98P
G-MONJ	Boeing 757-2T7ER	24104		26. 2.88	Monarch Airlines Ltd	Luton	23. 1.00T
G-MONK	Boeing 757-2T7ER	24105		26. 2.88	Monarch Airlines Ltd	Luton	31. 5.99T
G-MONR	Airbus A.300B4-605R	540	VH-YMJ G-MONR/F-WWAT	15. 3.90	Monarch Airlines Ltd	Luton	2. 4.99T
G-MONS	Airbus A.300B4-605R	556	VH-YMK G-MONS/F-WWAY	17. 4.90	Monarch Airlines Ltd	Luton	23. 3.00T
G-MONW	Airbus A.320-212	391	F-WWDO	24. 2.93	Monarch Airlines Ltd	Luton	7. 3.00T
G-MONX	Airbus A.320-212	392	F-WWDR	19. 3.93	Monarch Airlines Ltd	Luton	17. 3.00T
G-MONY	Airbus A.320-212	279	C-GVNY G-MONY/C-GVNY/G-MONY/C-FLSF/F-WWDU	11. 1.93	Monarch Airlines Ltd	Luton	1. 4.99T
G-MOON	Mooney M.20K (252TSE)	25-1143	N252BT	22. 6.88	Moira A.Eccles	Binton, Stratford-upon-Avon	14. 8.00
G-MOOR	Socata TB-10 Tobago	82	G-MILK	23. 7.91	J.R.Smith & WG & R Communications Ltd	Sandtoft	21.10.01
G-MOOS	Hunting-Percival P.56 Provost T.1	PAC/F/335	G-BGKA 8041M/XF690	5. 4.91	T.J.Manna t/a Kennet Avn (As "XF690" in RAF c/s)	Cranfield	17. 6.99P
G-MOSI*	DH.98 Mosquito TT.35	-	N9797 G-ASKA/RS709	10.11.81	USAF Museum (As "NS519/P" in USAAF c/s) Wright Patterson AFB, Dayton, Ohio, USA		17.12.84P*
G-MOSS	Beechcraft D55 Baron	TE-548	G-AWAD	12. 6.95	A.W.Moss & Son (Civil & Railway Engineering) Ltd	Coal Aston/Gamston	17. 3.00
G-MOSY	Cameron O-84 HAFB	2315	EI-CAO	17. 4.96	P.L.Mossman	Bristol	
G-MOTA	Bell 206B Jet Ranger III	4494	N81521	20.10.98	J W Sandle	(Kings Lynn)	28.10.01T
G-MOTH	DH.82A Tiger Moth (Rebuilt to DH.82 standard)	85340	7035M DE306	31. 1.78	M.C.Russell (As "K2567")	Top Farm, Tadlow	4. 6.01
G-MOTI	Robin DR.400/500	0006		23.11.98	O.Graham-Flatebo & The Lord Saville of Newdigate t/a The Tango India F/Grp	Biggin Hill	2. 2.02
G-MOTO	PA-24-180 Comanche	24-3239	G-EDHE N51867/G-ASFH/EI-AMM	24. 3.87	L.T. & S.Evans	Sandown	21. 7.99
G-MOTT	Light Aero Avid Speed Wing (Rotax 582)	PFA/189-11738		29. 5.92	J.B.Ott	Cambridge	26. 2.99P
G-MOUL	Maule M.6-235C Super Rocket	7518C		1. 5.90	M.Klinge	(Troon, Ayrshire)	10. 4.00
G-MOUR	Folland Gnat T.1	FL.596	8624M XS102	16. 5.90	D.J.Gilmour t/a Intrepid Avn Co (As "XR991" in Yellowjacks c/s)	North Weald	28. 4.99P
G-MOVE	PA-60-601P Aerostar 61P-0593-7963263		OO-PKB G-MOVE/(N8144J)	5. 1.79	A. Kazaz & A1 Hydraulics Ltd	Leicester	26. 6.99
G-MOVI	PA-32R-301 Saratoga SP	32R-8313029	G-MARI N8248H	6. 2.89	G-BOON Ltd	(Stevenage)	24. 5.00T
G-MOZZ	Mudry CAP.10B	256		30.10.90	M.B.Smith & N.Skipworth	Booker	2. 5.00

G-MPAA-MPZZ

Regn	Type	C/n	P/I	Date	Owner/operator	Probable Base	CA Expy
G-MPBH	Reims Cessna FA.152 Aerobat	0374	G-FLIC G-BILV	8.12.88	S.Gwilliam & C.Hopwood t/a Metropolitan Police F/C	Biggin Hill	1. 8.99T
G-MPBI	Cessna 310R II	310R-0584	F-GEBB HB-LMD/N87473	21. 7.97	M.P.Bolshaw & Co Ltd	Elstree	7. 8.00
G-MPCD	Airbus A.320-212	379	C-FTDU G-MPCD(x4)/F-WWDY	14. 3.94	Monarch Airlines Ltd	Luton	30. 4.01T
G-MPWH	Rotorway Exec	3579		22. 6.90	Thistle Aviation Ltd (Stored 5.94)	Henley-on-Thames	AC
G-MPWI	Robin HR.100/210	163	F-GBTY F-ODFA/F-BUPD	3. 3.80	Propwash Investments Ltd	Swansea	6. 3.99
G-MPWT	PA-34-220T Seneca III (Originally built as c/n 34-8233163)	34-8333068	N4294X N9539N/N8218K	26. 9.88	Neric Ltd (Op Modern Air)	Guernsey/Fowlmere	19. 5.01T

G-MRAA-MRZZ

Regn	Type	C/n	P/I	Date	Owner/operator	Probable Base	CA Expy
G-MRAJ	MDH Hughes 369E (500E)	0010E	N51946	19. 3.98	A.Jardine	Dundee	5. 5.01T
G-MRED	Elmwood CA-05 Christavia mk.1	PFA/185-12935		2. 8.96	E.Hewett	(Fareham)	
G-MRKT	Lindstrand LBL-90A HAFB	037		7. 6.93	Marketplace Public Relations (London) Ltd "Kaytee"	Crowthorne, Berks	31. 3.99A
G-MRMR	PA-31-350 Chieftain	31-7952092	OH-PRE G-WROX/G-BNZI/N3517T	21. 8.97	I.D. & P.J.Margetson-Rushmore t/a MRMR Flight Services	Stapleford	2. 2.99T
G-MROC	Pegasus Quantum 15-912	7498		22. 1.99	M.Convine	(Wellingborough)	21. 1.00P
G-MRPP	PA-34-220T Seneca III	34-8233134	N8202P	8. 5.90	Dagless Ltd	Conington	6. 8.99
G-MRSN	Robinson R-22 Beta	1654		21. 1.91	Leeds Lighting Ltd	(Leeds)	7. 4.00T
G-MRST	PA-28RT-201 Arrow IV	28R-7918068	9H-AAU 5B-CEC/N3019U	27.11.86	C.P.Scamp	Gloucestershire	13. 3.01
G-MRTN	Socata TB-10 Tobago	62	G-BHET	9. 7.98	Underwood Kitchens Ltd	(Aylesbury)	30. 4.01
G-MRTY	Cameron N-77 HAFB	1008		24. 4.84	P.G. & R.A.Vale "Marty"	Kidderminster	19. 5.96A

G-MSAA-MSZZ

Regn	Type	C/n	P/I	Date	Owner/operator	Probable Base	CA Expy
G-MSAL	Morane-Saulnier MS.733 Alcyon	143	F-BLXV Fr.Mil	16. 6.93	North Weald Flying Svs Ltd (As "143" in Aeronavale c/s)	North Weald	
G-MSDJ	Aerospatiale AS.350B1 Ecureuil	2174	G-BPOH	28. 3.89	Denis Ferranti Hoverknights Ltd	Llanfairfechan	3. 5.01
G-MSFC	PA-38-112 Tomahawk II	38-81A0067	N25735	11. 5.90	Sherwood F/C Ltd	Nottingham	18. 7.99T
G-MSFT	PA-28-161 Warrior II	28-8416093	G-MUMS N118AV	2. 4.97	M.J.Love (Op SFT Aviation)	Bournemouth	1. 5.00T
G-MSKA	Boeing 737-5L9	24859	OY-MAC (OY-MMZ)	18.10.96	Maersk Air Ltd (Blue Poole t/s)	Birmingham	17.10.99T
G-MSKB	Boeing 737-5L9	24928	OY-MAD (OY-MMO)	12.11.96	Maersk Air Ltd (Dove/Colum t/s)	Birmingham	11.11.99T
G-MSKC	Boeing 737-5L9	25066	OY-MAE	3.12.96	Maersk Air Ltd (Waves of the City t/s)	Birmingham	2.12.99T
G-MSKD	Boeing 737-5L9	24778	HL7230 OY-MAA/(OY-MMW)	14. 1.98	Maersk Air Ltd (Whale Rider t/s)	Birmingham	21. 1.02T
G-MSKE	Boeing 737-5L9	28084	OY-APB	4. 1.99	Maersk Air Ltd (Delftblue Daybreak t/s)	Birmingham	28. 1.02T
G-MSKJ	BAe Jetstream 4100	41034	N434JX G-BWIH/VH-SMH/G-4-034	4. 7.96	Maersk Air Ltd (Martha Masanabo/Ndebele t/s)	Birmingham	29. 8.00T
G-MSKK	Canadair RJ100 Regional Jet (CL.600-2B19)	7226	C-GCBS C-FMKZ	25. 5.98	Maersk Air Ltd (Wings of the City t/s)	Birmingham	23. 5.01T
G-MSKL	Canadair RJ100 Regional Jet (CL.600-2B19)	7247		1. 7.98	Maersk Air Ltd (Martha Masanabo/Ndebele t/s)	Birmingham	30. 6.01T
G-MSKM	Canadair RJ100 Regional Jet (CL.600-2B19)	7248		28. 7.98	Maersk Air Ltd (Sterntaler/Bauhaus t/s)	Birmingham	29. 7.01T
G-MSKN	Canadair RJ100 Regional Jet (CL.600-2B19)	7283		14. 1.99	Maersk Air Ltd (Chelsea Rose t/s)	Birmingham	18. 1.02T
G-MSKO	Canadair RJ100 Regional Jet (CL.600-2B19)	7299		R	Maersk Air Ltd (Crossing Borders t/s) (For dlvy 4.99)	Birmingham	
G-MSOO	Revolution Helicopters Mini-500	0016		16.10.95	R.H.Ryan	(Sunderland)	
G-MSMS	Eurocopter AS.350B2 Ecureuil	3119		21. 8.98	Fairview Securities (Investments) Ltd	(London SW3)	11. 1.02T
G-MSTC	Gulfstream AA-5A Cheetah	AA5A-0833	G-BIJT N26950	30. 1.95	Mid-Sussex Timber Co Ltd	Biggin Hill	4. 2.02T
G-MSTG	North American P-51D-25-NT Mustang	124-48271	NZ2427 45-11518	2. 9.97	M.Hammond	(Eye)	

G-MTAA-MTZZ

Regn	Type	C/n P/I	Date	Owner/operator	Probable Base	CA Expy
G-MTAA	Solar Wings Pegasus XL-R (Rotax 447) SW-TB-1108 & SW-WA-1102		15.10.86	R.Scott	London Colney	7. 2.99P
G-MTAB	Mainair Gemini/Flash 2 (Rotax 503) 492-1086-4 & W290		8.10.86	S.Moreton (Stored 1.98)	Long Marston	31. 3.97P
G-MTAC	Mainair Gemini/Flash 2 (Rotax 503) 486-1086-4 & W278		15.10.86	A.Jackson	St.Michaels-on-Wyre	17. 6.99P
G-MTAE	Mainair Gemini/Flash 2 (Rotax 503) 500-1186-4 & W302		15.10.86	S.W.Tallamy	Davidstow Moor	27.12.99P
G-MTAF	Mainair Gemini/Flash 2 (Rotax 503) 499-1186-4 & W301		5.10.86	P.A.Long	Altrincham	30.10.98P
G-MTAG	Mainair Gemini/Flash 2 (Rotax 503) 487-1086-4 & W281		15.10.86	B.Read	Wallasey	21.10.98P
G-MTAH	Mainair Gemini/Flash 2 (Rotax 503) 488-1086-4 & W282		16.10.86	T.G.Elmhirst	St.Michaels-on-Wyre	18. 8.99P
G-MTAI	Solar Wings Pegasus XL-R (Rotax 447) SW-TB-1109 & SW-WA-1103		14.10.86	J.Becskehazy	Oxton, Notts	4. 5.96P
G-MTAJ	Solar Wings Pegasus XL-R SW-WA-1104 (Rotax 447)		16.10.86	G.A. & S.D.Batchelor	Launceston	27.12.98P
G-MTAL	Solar Wings Pegasus Photon SW-WP-0023 (Solo 210)		15.10.86	R.P.Wilkinson	Bath	29.10.95P
G-MTAO	Solar Wings Pegasus XL-R (Rotax 447) SW-TB-1107 & SW-WA-1107		21.10.86	S.P.Disney & R.Jones	Swinford, Rugby	17. 5.99P
G-MTAP	Southdown Raven X 2232/0225 (Rotax 447)		15.10.86	D.B.McCalvey	Hailsham	13. 6.98P
G-MTAS	Whittaker MW-5C Sorcerer PFA/163-11166 (Norton Rotary 50hp)		14.10.86	E.A. & R.E.Henman	Old Sarum	21.4.93P*
G-MTAT	Solar Wings Pegasus XL-R (Rotax 447) SW-TB-1113 & SW-WA-1108		28.10.86	J.Ryan	Enniscorthy, Co.Wexford	17. 7.98P
G-MTAV	Solar Wings Pegasus XL-R (Rotax 447) SW-TB-1115 & SW-WA-1110		21.10.86	Susan Fairweather & Carolyn L.Harris (Stored 9.96) Nottingham/Warrington		14. 2.99P 21.10.95P
G-MTAW	Solar Wings Pegasus XL-R SW-WA-1111 (Rotax 447)		21.10.86	J.P.Stannard	Weston Zoyland	1.10.96P
G-MTAX	Solar Wings Pegasus XL-R (Rotax 447) SW-TB-1117 & SW-WA-1112		27.10.86	R.C.Young	Kingsthorpe, Northampton	7. 8.98P
G-MTAY	Solar Wings Pegasus XL-R (Rotax 447) SW-TB-1118 & SW-WA-1113		27.10.86	S.A.McLatchie	Enstone	3. 9.98P
G-MTAZ	Solar Wings Pegasus XL-R (Rotax 447) SW-TB-1119 & SW-WA-1114		28.10.86	H.W.Banham Lower Mountpleasant Farm, Wimblington		2.10.99P
G-MTBA	Solar Wings Pegasus XL-R SW-WA-1115 (Rotax 447)		27.10.86	R.J.W.Franklin & M.C.Buffery (Stored 5.97) Redlands, Swindon		24. 6.93P
G-MTBB	Southdown Raven X 2232/0226 (Rotax 447)		16.10.86	A.Miller	Woking	2. 6.92P
G-MTBC	Mainair Gemini/Flash 2 (Rotax 503) 501-1186-4 & W303		16.10.86	Not known (Trike stored 5.96)	Popham	11. 5.92P
G-MTBD	Mainair Gemini/Flash 2 (Rotax 503) 498-1186-4 & W299 (Wing regd as W229)		16.10.86	J.Williams	Oxton, Notts	20.12.96P
G-MTBE	CFM Shadow Srs.CD K.035 (Rotax 462HP)		16.10.86	S.K.Brown	Farnborough	10. 5.99P
G-MTBG	Mainair Gemini/Flash 2 (Rotax 503) 506-1286-4 & W309		27.10.86	N.Spencer-Brayn	Winchester	23. 6.90P
G-MTBH	Mainair Gemini/Flash 2 (Rotax 462) 524-187-5 & W327		28.10.86	D.E.Williams	Coleford	30. 5.99P
G-MTBI	Mainair Gemini/Flash 2 (Rotax 462) 508-1286-4 & W311		27.10.86	A.Ormson	Eshott	29. 9.99P
G-MTBJ	Mainair Gemini/Flash 2 (Rotax 503) 509-1286-4 & W312		27.10.86	R.M. & P.J.Perry Otherton, Cannock (Op Staffordshire Aero Club)		18. 5.99P
G-MTBK	Southdown Raven X 2232/0230 (Rotax 447) (Wing reported as from G-MNNU)		28.10.86	R.J.Grimwood Plaistows Field, Hemel Hampstead		29. 9.99P
G-MTBL	Solar Wings Pegasus XL-R (Rotax 447) SW-TB-1121 & SW-WA-1117		6.11.86	R.N.Whiting Lower Mountpleasant Farm, Wimblington		18. 1.00P
G-MTBN	Southdown Raven X 2232/0227 (Rotax 447)		28.10.86	A.J. & S.E.Crosby-Jones	Hailsham	11. 7.98P
G-MTBO	Southdown Raven X 2232/0233 (Rotax 447)		28.10.86	D.C.Britton	Bristol	11. 8.99P
G-MTBP	Aerotech MW-5B Sorcerer SR102-R440B-02 (Rotax 447)		28.10.86	R.Thompson (Stored 5.96)	Shobdon	21. 9.94P
G-MTBR	Aerotech MW-5B Sorcerer SR102-R440B-03 (EC-44-PM)		20. 1.87	J.H.Cooling	Crowland	26.10.99P
G-MTBS	Aerotech MW-5B Sorcerer SR102-R440B-04 (EC-44-PM)		27.10.86	J.M.Benton	Wetheroak	28. 3.99P
G-MTBT*	Aerotech MW-5B Sorcerer (EC-44-PM) SR102-R440B-05 & BMAA/HB/027 (Wings possibly from G-MWGI)		10. 4.87	N.W.Finn-Kelcey Weston Underwood, Olney (Stored 7.96)		19. 5.92P
G-MTBW*	Mainair Gemini/Flash 2 (Rotax 503) 520-187-5 & W322		6.11.86	J.Sharman Otherton, Cannock (Crashed Old Airfield, Aldridge 15.4.97 & cancelled by CAA 23.2.98)		21. 9.97P

Regn	Type	C/n P/I	Date	Owner/operator	Probable Base	CA Expy
G-MTBX	Mainair Gemini/Flash 2 (Rotax 447)	510-1286-4 & W313	6.11.86	J.E.Orbell	Spean Bridge, Inverness	21. 3.99P
G-MTBY	Mainair Gemini/Flash 2 (Rotax 447)	507-1286-4 & W310	6.11.86	R.P.Wilkinson	Bath	5. 4.97P
G-MTBZ	Southdown Raven X (Rotax 447)	2232/0232	10.11.86	S.Haywood	Stoke-on-Trent	19. 7.99P
G-MTCA	CFM Shadow Srs.C (Rotax 447)	K.011	6.11.86	J.R.L.Murray (Damaged mid 1997)	Edinburgh	18. 1.98P
G-MTCC	Mainair Gemini/Flash 2 (Rotax 503)	497-1186-4 & W298	13.11.86	J.Madhvani	Barnet	21.10.96P
G-MTCD*	Southdown Raven X	2232/0236	21.11.86	R.Green (Cancelled as wfu 6.4.98)	Lincoln	10. 7.96P
G-MTCE	Mainair Gemini/Flash 2 (Rotax 462)	511-1286-4 & W314	2.12.86	R.S.Acreman	Hatherton, Cannock	23. 5.99P
G-MTCG	Solar Wings Pegasus XL-R/Se (Rotax 447)	SW-TB-1125 & SW-WA-1123	16.12.86	R.W. & M.W.Allan (Stored 9.97)	Eshott	11. 2.95P
G-MTCH	Solar Wings Pegasus XL-R (Rotax 447)	SW-TB-1126 & SW-WA-1124	28.11.86	R.E.H.Harris	Davidstow Moor	29.11.95P
G-MTCK	Solar Wings Pegasus Flash 2 (Rotax 447)	SW-WF-0127	11.12.86	A.R.R.Williams	St.Andrews, Bristol	11. 8.99P
G-MTCM	Southdown Raven X (Rotax 447)	2232/0239	11.12.86	J.C & A.M.Rose	Oakley	2. 7.97P
G-MTCO	Solar Wings Pegasus XL-R (Rotax 447)	SW-TB-1129 & SW-WA-1127	7. 1.87	A.J.Nesom	Husthwaite	31. 5.99P
G-MTCP	Aerial Arts Chaser/110SX (Rotax 377)	110SX/476	16.12.86	B.Richardson	Sunderland	24. 6.99P
G-MTCR	Solar Wings Pegasus XL-R (Rotax 447)	SW-WA-1128	16.12.86	S.Walker	South Milford, Leeds	3. 6.99P
G-MTCT	CFM Shadow Srs.CD (Rotax 503)	042	16.12.86	F.W.McCann	Johnstone	20. 6.99P
G-MTCU	Mainair Gemini/Flash 2A (Rotax 503)	451-1286-4 & W228	5. 1.87	B.E.Hiscock	Alrewas	17. 6.98P
G-MTCW	Mainair Gemini/Flash 2 (Rotax 462)	502-1186-4 & W304	5. 1.87	R.A.Watering	Bourne, Lincs	6. 5.98P
G-MTCX	Solar Wings Pegasus XL-R (Rotax 447)	SW-TB-1131 & SW-WA-1129	9. 1.87	A.L.Davies	Rhuallt	30. 6.99P
G-MTDA	Hornet Dual Trainer/Southdown Raven (Rotax 462)	HRWA 0060 & 2000/0245	5. 1.87	B.D.Atkinson & I.R.Buckle	Oxford	2. 9.96P
G-MTDB*	Owen Pola Mk.1	POLA/X001/001	19.12.86	P.E.Owen (Cancelled by CAA 16.2.99)	Dorchester	
G-MTDC*	Owen Pola Mk.1	POLA/X001/002	19.12.86	P.E.Owen (Cancelled by CAA 16.2.99)	Dorchester	
G-MTDD	Aerial Arts Chaser/110SX (Rotax 377) (Originally regd as c/n 110SX/437)	110SX/137	26. 1.87	B.Richardson	Sunderland	24. 6.99P
G-MTDE	Aerial Arts Chaser/110SX (Rotax 377)	110SX/438	5. 1.87	M.M.Bowyer	Southampton	27.12.98P
G-MTDF	Mainair Gemini/Flash 2 (Rotax 503)	515-287-5 & W319	5. 1.87	A.R.Haydock	St.Michaels-on-Wyre	4. 4.99P
G-MTDG	Solar Wings Pegasus XL-R/Se (Rotax 447)	SW-WA-1130	20. 1.87	E.W.Laidlaw (Stored 9.97)	Great Orton	27. 8.96P
G-MTDH	Solar Wings Pegasus XL-R (Rotax 447)	SW-TB-1133 & SW-WA-1131	22. 1.87	M.Shiner	Birmingham	8. 4.99P
G-MTDI	Solar Wings Pegasus XL-R/Se (Rotax 447)	SW-TB-1134 & SW-WA-1132	22. 1.87	W.Wood (Stored 9.97)	Eshott	13. 5.91P
G-MTDJ	Medway Hybred 44XL (Rotax 447)	1587/23	20. 1.87	J.A.Slocombe & C.D.Gates	Gillingham	4. 4.96P
G-MTDK	Aerotech MW-5B Sorcerer (EC-44-PM)	SR102-R440B-06	22. 1.87	R.H.Borland	Nunthorpe, Cleveland	13. 3.99P
G-MTDN	Ultraflight Lazair IIIE (Rotax 185)	A465/002	22. 1.87	B.H.Ashman	Buttermilk Hall Farm, Blisworth	27. 6.97P
G-MTDO	Eipper Quicksilver MXII (Rotax 503)	1124	27. 2.87	D.L.Ham	Long Marston	N/E
G-MTDP	Solar Wings Pegasus XL-R (Rotax 447)	SW-TB-1136 & SW-WA-1134	22. 1.87	M.J.Powell	Shobdon	29. 5.99P
G-MTDR	Mainair Gemini/Flash 2 (Rotax 503)	516-287-5 & W276	26. 1.87	J.W. & C.Richardson	Baxby Manor, Husthwaite	28. 6.99P
G-MTDS	Solar Wings Pegasus Photon (Solo 210)	SW-WP-0024	29. 1.87	M.J.Wooldridge (Stored 5.97)	Clench Common	27. 4.97P
G-MTDT	Solar Wings Pegasus XL-R (Rotax 447)	SW-TB-1137 & SW-WA-1135	2. 2.87	K.H.A.Negal	London SW7	14. 2.99P
G-MTDU	CFM Shadow Srs.CD (Rotax 503)	K.037	26. 1.87	M.Jones	Leicester	23. 8.99P
G-MTDV	Solar Wings Pegasus XL-R (Rotax 447)	SW-WA-1136	3. 2.87	S.J.Adcock	Broxbourne	28. 8.94P
G-MTDW	Mainair Gemini/Flash 2 (Rotax 503)	517-387-5 & W212	2. 2.87	S.R.Leeper	Priory Farm, Tibenham	21.11.98P
G-MTDX	CFM Shadow Srs.CD (Rotax 503)	K.043	10. 2.87	L.Fekete	Ellesmere Port	21. 5.99P
G-MTDY	Mainair Gemini/Flash 2 (Rotax 462)	513-187-5 & W317	11. 2.87	S.Penoyre	Windlesham	22. 9.99P

Regn	Type	C/n	P/I	Date	Owner/operator	Probable Base	CA Expy
G-MTEB	Solar Wings Pegasus XL-R SW-WA-1139 (Rotax 447)			9. 2.87	F.Watt (Stored 8.98)	Insch	18.10.98P
G-MTEC	Solar Wings Pegasus XL-R SW-TB-1142 & SW-WA-1140 (Rotax 447)			9. 2.87	R.W.Glover (Stored 6.97)	Kemble	11. 6.94P
G-MTED	Solar Wings Pegasus XL-R SW-WA-1141 (Rotax 447)			9. 2.87	D.Marsh	Charminster, Bournemouth	27. 5.95P
G-MTEE	Solar Wings Pegasus XL-R (Rotax 447) SW-TB-1144 & SW-WA-1142 (C/n plate incorrectly shows SW-WA-1144 & SW-WA-1142) (New wing ? - see G-MTLG)			13. 2.87	S.M.Dewson	Shenstone Hall Farm, Shenstone	4. 8.99P
G-MTEH	Mainair Gemini/Flash 2 521-387-5 & W262 (Rotax 503)			13. 2.87	M.P.Challis	Northampton	24. 7.97P
G-MTEJ	Mainair Gemini/Flash 2 522-387-5 & W277 (Rotax 462)			18. 2.87	D.E.Bassett	St.Michaels-on-Wyre	5. 4.99P
G-MTEK	Mainair Gemini/Flash 2 523-387-5 & W279 (Rotax 503)			3. 3.87	M.O'Hearne & G.M.Wrigley	Rufforth	3.10.94P
G-MTEN	Mainair Gemini/Flash 2 527-487-5 & W285 (Rotax 503)			25. 2.87	B.Bennison	Brough	10. 9.99P
G-MTEO*	Midlands Ultralight Sirocco 377GB (Rotax 377) MU-019			27. 2.87	Not known (Stored 8.96)	Manston	6. 3.93P
G-MTER	Solar Wings Pegasus XL-R/Se (Rotax 447) SW-TB-1146 & SW-WA-1144			19. 2.87	K.A.Wright	Grimsby	31. 1.99P
G-MTES	Solar Wings Pegasus XL-R (Rotax 447) SW-TB-1147 & SW-WA-1145			19. 2.87	K.A.Lyons	Tregavethan, Truro	8. 5.99P
G-MTET	Solar Wings Pegasus XL-R SW-WA-1146 (Rotax 447)			19. 2.87	P.A.S.Talbot	Camborne	5.10.98P
G-MTEU	Solar Wings Pegasus XL-R/Se SW-WA-1147 (Rotax 447)			19. 2.87	B.Harris	Northwich	5. 1.00P
G-MTEV*	Solar Wings Pegasus XL-R SW-WA-1148 (Rotax 447)			19. 2.87	N.P.D.Lambert (Cancelled as destroyed 27.7.98)	London SW11	1. 5.97P
G-MTEW	Solar Wings Pegasus XL-R/Se (Rotax 447) SW-TB-1151 & SW-WA-1149			19. 2.87	R.W. & P.J.Holley	Shifnal	30.11.99P
G-MTEX	Solar Wings Pegasus XL-R (Rotax 447) SW-TB-1152 & SW-WA-1150			19. 2.87	R.J.H. & A-M.Hayward	Hereford	11. 8.99P
G-MTEY	Mainair Gemini/Flash 2 518-387-5 & W217 (Rotax 503)			20. 2.87	A.Wells	Baxby Manor, Husthwaite	4. 6.98P
G-MTFA	Solar Wings Pegasus XL-R (Rotax 462) SW-TE-0014 & SW-WA-1156			24. 2.87	D.Baillie	Great Orton	14. 3.94P
G-MTFB	Solar Wings Pegasus XL-R SW-WA-1157 (Rotax 462)			24. 2.87	I.D.Stokes	Camelford	10. 4.98P
G-MTFC	Medway Hybred 44XLR 22087/24 (Rotax 447)			23. 3.87	J.K.Masters	Chigwell	25. 7.97P
G-MTFE	Solar Wings Pegasus XL-R (Rotax 447) SW-TB-1157 & SW-WA-1155			6. 3.87	R.H.L.Cope-Lewis	Bath	1. 8.98P
G-MTFF	Mainair Gemini/Flash 2 528-487-5 & W286 (Rotax 503)			12. 3.87	T.N.Taylor	Sidcup	19. 4.96P
G-MTFG	AMF Chevvron 2-32C CH.004 (Konig SD570)			9. 3.87	R.Gardner	Stratford-on-Avon	24. 7.99P
G-MTFH	Aerotech MW-5B Sorcerer SR102-R440B-07 (EC-44-PM)			5. 3.87	M.Wade	Dublin	27. 5.97P
G-MTFI	Mainair Gemini/Flash 2 531-487-5 & W289 (Rotax 503)			12. 3.87	T.L.Purves	Carrickfergus, NI	25. 2.99P
G-MTFJ	Mainair Gemini/Flash 2 532-487-5 & W320 (Rotax 503)			12. 3.87	G.Souch & M.D.Peacock	Leatherhead/Guildford	6. 5.97P
G-MTFK*	Moult Trike/Flexiform Striker DIM-01			23. 3.87	The Norfolk & Suffolk Avn Museum Flixton (Stored 7.97)		
G-MTFL	Ultraflight Lazair IIIE A466/003 (Rotax 185)			12. 3.87	P.J.Turrell	Halesowen	26. 9.89P
G-MTFM	Solar Wings Pegasus XL-R SW-WA-1158 (Rotax 462)			13. 3.87	P.R.G.Morley	Sutton Meadows, Ely	20. 6.99P
G-MTFN	Whittaker MW-5 Sorcerer PFA/163-11207			13. 3.87	A.Donowho & K.A.Stewart	Newcastle	
G-MTFO	Solar Wings Pegasus XL-R/Se (Rotax 447) SW-TB-1159 & SW-WA-1159			18. 3.87	D.S.Parker & R.J.Hodgson	Great Orton	14. 3.98P
G-MTFP	Solar Wings Pegasus XL-R (Rotax 447) SW-TB-1160 & SW-WA-1160			18. 3.87	Swansea Avn Ltd	Swansea	29. 6.99P
G-MTFR	Solar Wings Pegasus XL-R (Rotax 447) SW-TB-1161 & SW-WA-1161			18. 3.87	S.Ballantyne	Blanefield, Glasgow	19. 9.99P
G-MTFT	Solar Wings Pegasus XL-R SW-WA-1163 (Rotax 447)			18. 3.87	A.T.Smith	Hughley, Much Wenlock	21. 5.99P
G-MTFU	CFM Shadow Srs.BD (Rotax 447) K.034			18. 3.87	G.R.Eastwood	Full Sutton	6. 8.99P
G-MTFX	Mainair Gemini/Flash 2 534-487-5 & W321 (Rotax 503)			26. 3.87	R.J.Green (Damaged nr Sandtoft 28.7.96)	Pontefract	1. 1.97P
G-MTFZ	CFM Shadow Srs.CD (Rotax 503) 053			24. 3.87	R.P.Stonor	Long Marston	22. 3.99P
G-MTGA	Mainair Gemini/Flash 2 535-587-5 & W293 (Rotax 503)			26. 3.87	B.E.Warburton	Barton	14. 9.99P
G-MTGB	Thruster TST Mk.1 837-TST-011 (Rotax 503)			10. 4.87	G.Arthur	Cheltenham	9.10.94P

Regn	Type	C/n P/I	Date	Owner/operator	Probable Base	CA Expy
G-MTGC	Thruster TST Mk.1 (Rotax 503)	837-TST-012	10. 4.87	B.Foster & P.Smith	London E13	14. 2.99P
G-MTGD	Thruster TST Mk.1 (Rotax 503)	837-TST-013	10. 4.87	W.J.Lister	Glasgow	30. 4.99P
G-MTGE	Thruster TST Mk.1 (Rotax 503)	837-TST-014	10. 4.87	G.W.R.Swift	Hartfield	17.10.99P
G-MTGF	Thruster TST Mk.1 (Rotax 503)	837-TST-015	10. 4.87	B.Swindon	Chesham	30. 7.99P
G-MTGH	Mainair Gemini/Flash 2 (Rotax 462)	536-587-5 & W294	31. 3.87	J.R.Gillies	Waltham Cross	12. 6.99P
G-MTGJ	Solar Wings Pegasus XL-R (Rotax 447)	SW-TB-1165 & SW-WA-1165	1. 4.87	M.S.Taylor	Gillingham	9. 7.98P
G-MTGK	Solar Wings Pegasus XL-R (Rotax 447)	SW-WA-1166	1. 4.87	I.A.Smith	Canterbury	1. 8.91P
G-MTGL	Solar Wings Pegasus XL-R (Rotax 447)	SW-WA-1167	1. 4.87	R.D.Thomasson	London Colney	7. 2.99P
G-MTGM	Solar Wings Pegasus XL-R (Rotax 447)	SW-WA-1168	1. 4.87	A.W.Rawlings & J.Smith	Cannock	18. 7.97P
G-MTGN	CFM Shadow Srs.BD (Rotax 447)	K.041	31. 3.87	N.G.Price	Bricket Wood, Radlett	24. 8.98P
G-MTGO	Mainair Gemini/Flash 2 (Rotax 462)	550-587-5 & W336	10. 4.87	A.W.Fish	Eshott	13. 3.99P
G-MTGP	Thruster TST Mk.1 (Rotax 503)	847-TST-016	10. 4.87	A.E.Sellers & J.H.Cooling Lower Mountpleasant Farm, Wimblington		19.12.99P
G-MTGR	Thruster TST Mk.1 (Rotax 503)	847-TST-017	10. 4.87	M.R.Grunwell	Brentwood	26. 7.90P
G-MTGS	Thruster TST Mk.1 (Rotax 503)	847-TST-018	10. 4.87	G.J.Chadwick	Huddersfield t/a G-MTGS F/Grp	3. 5.99P
G-MTGT	Thruster TST Mk.1 (Rotax 503)	847-TST-019	10. 4.87	R.T.Manderson	Glasgow	15.11.99P
G-MTGU	Thruster TST Mk.1 (Rotax 503)	847-TST-020	10. 4.87	B.J.Robe	Park Farm, Carlisle	20. 6.99P
G-MTGV	CFM Shadow Srs.CD (Rotax 503)	052	8. 4.87	V.R.Riley	Manchester	7. 5.98P
G-MTGW	CFM Shadow Srs.CD	054 I-G-MTGW	8. 4.87	D.Cioffi	Brighton	25. 5.99P
G-MTGX	Hornet Dual Trainer/Southdown Raven (Rotax 462)	HRWA 0061 & 2000/0270	13. 4.87	S.J.M.Morling	Taunton	11. 4.97P
G-MTHB	Aerotech MW-5B Sorcerer SR102-R440B-08 (EC-44-PM)		10. 4.87	J.C.P.Thornber	Peterborough	22. 4.97P
G-MTHC	Raven X (Rotax 447)	2232/0257	15. 4.87	P.Beauchamp & S.R.Dunton	Hinckley	9. 5.99P
G-MTHD	Ultrasports Tripacer/Hiway Demon 195	JMS-01	13. 4.87	J.D.Frost	Beeston, Notts	
G-MTHG	Solar Wings Pegasus XL-R (Rotax 447)	SW-WA-1171	13. 4.87	S.T.Felton	Stockport	19. 2.99P
G-MTHH	Solar Wings Pegasus XL-R (Rotax 447)	SW-WA-1172	13. 4.87	J.Palmer	Winkleigh	28.12.98P
G-MTHI	Solar Wings Pegasus XL-R (Rotax 447)	SW-TB-1172 & SW-WA-1173	13. 4.87	J.R.Bowman	Oxford	9. 2.98P
G-MTHJ	Solar Wings Pegasus XL-R (Rotax 447)	SW-TB-1173 & SW-WA-1174	13. 4.87	S.A.Watson	Longacre Farm, Sandy	31. 3.99P
G-MTHN	Solar Wings Pegasus XL-R (Rotax 447)	SW-WA-1178	13. 4.87	G.E.Murphy	Cardigan	30. 6.99P
G-MTHO	Solar Wings Pegasus XL-R (Rotax 447)	SW-WA-1179	13. 4.87	R.C.Hinds	Newnham, Gloucester	17. 8.96P
G-MTHS	CFM Shadow Srs.CD (Rotax 503)	059	22. 4.87	A.J.McMenmamin	Oakley	17. 5.97P
G-MTHT	CFM Shadow Srs.CD (Rotax 447)	058	22. 4.87	B.J.Topham	Long Marston	13.10.99P
G-MTHU	Hornet Dual Trainer/Raven (Rotax 462)	HRWA 0062 & 2000/0269	30. 4.87	J.Barlow	Castletown, IoM	4. 9.93P
G-MTHV	CFM Shadow Srs.BD (Rotax 447)	K.049	7. 5.87	J.W.Taylor	Ross-on-Wye	24. 7.99P
G-MTHW	Mainair Gemini/Flash 2 (Rotax 462)	540-587-5 & W325	14. 5.87	M.D.Kirby	Billericay	30. 3.99P
G-MTHY	Mainair Gemini/Flash 2A (Rotax 503)	543-687-5 & W331	14. 5.87	M.Stevenson	Ringwood	27. 6.94P
G-MTHZ	Mainair Gemini/Flash 2A (Rotax 503)	541-587-5 & W329	14. 5.87	B.Berry	Manchester	11. 8.98P
G-MTIA	Mainair Gemini/Flash 2A (Rotax 503)	544-687-5 & W332	14. 5.87	A.R.Hawkins	Farnham	27. 7.99P
G-MTIB	Mainair Gemini/Flash 2A (Rotax 503)	545-687-5 & W333	14. 5.87	P.Millership	St.Michaels-on-Wyre	1.11.99P
G-MTIC	Mainair Gemini/Flash 2A (Rotax 462)	546-587-5 & W334	14. 5.87	B.J.Magill	Bishops Stortford	5. 8.95P
G-MTID	Raven X (Rotax 447)	2232/0276	18. 5.87	R.G.Featherby	Kings Lynn	23. 2.99P
G-MTIE	Solar Wings Pegasus XL-R (Rotax 462)	SW-WA-1183	18. 5.87	A.H.Paterson & I.M.Vass	Wick	24. 6.96P
G-MTIH	Solar Wings Pegasus XL-R (Rotax 447)	SW-WA-1186	18. 5.87	R.J.Humphries	Southampton	21. 4.98P

Regn	Type	C/n	P/I	Date	Owner/operator	Probable Base	CA Expy
G-MTII	Solar Wings Pegasus XL-R SW-WA-1187 (Rotax 447)			18. 5.87	H.Greef & G.Sharp (Damaged mid 1995)	Eshott	22.10.95P
G-MTIJ	Solar Wings Pegasus XL-R/Se (Rotax 447) SW-TB-1185 & SW-WA-1188			18. 5.87	M.J.F.Gilbody	Urmston, Manchester	1. 4.98P
G-MTIK	Raven X (Rotax 447)	2232/0272		19. 5.87	J.M.Barber	Peterborough	5. 1.99P
G-MTIL	Mainair Gemini/Flash 2A 549-687-5 & W338 (Rotax 462)			21. 5.87	S.Lunney	Ince Blundell, Liverpool	21. 8.98P
G-MTIM	Mainair Gemini/Flash 2A 553-687-5 & W341 (Rotax 503)			21. 5.87	W.M.Swan	East Fortune	17. 4.99P
G-MTIN	Mainair Gemini/Flash 2A 547-687-5 & W335 (Rotax 503)			1. 6.87	D.M.Newton	Forfar	23. 5.99P
G-MTIO	Solar Wings Pegasus XL-R SW-WA-1190 (Rotax 447)			26. 5.87	M.A.Coe	Kettering	10. 6.99P
G-MTIP	Solar Wings Pegasus XL-R (Rotax 447) SW-TB-1188 & SW-WA-1191			26. 5.87	W.B.Cooper	Sutton Meadows, Ely	3.12.99P
G-MTIR	Solar Wings Pegasus XL-R/Se SW-WA-1192 (Rotax 447) (Original wing apparently fitted to G-MTZI in Portugal ?)			26. 5.87	S.J.Spearey	Bristol	19. 4.98P
G-MTIS	Solar Wings Pegasus XL-R SW-WA-1193 (Rotax 447)			26. 5.87	N.P.Power	Eastbourne	25. 8.99P
G-MTIU	Solar Wings Pegasus XL-R (Rotax 447) SW-TB-1191 & SW-WA-1194			26. 5.87	D.Burdett	Chatteris	30. 6.99P
G-MTIV	Solar Wings Pegasus XL-R (Rotax 447) SW-TB-1192 & SW-WA-1195			26. 5.87	P.J.Culverhouse t/a Syndicate IV	Sittles Farm, Alrewas	25.10.99P
G-MTIW	Solar Wings Pegasus XL-R (Rotax 447) SW-TB-1193 & SW-WA-1196			26. 5.87	R.N.Whittall	Tunbridge Wells	15.12.97P
G-MTIX	Solar Wings Pegasus XL-R SW-WA-1197 (Rotax 447)			26. 5.87	S.Pickering	Sutton Meadows, Ely	27. 9.98P
G-MTIY	Solar Wings Pegasus XL-R SW-WA-1198 (Rotax 447)			26. 5.87	R.W.Surmon	Somerton	27. 9.99P
G-MTIZ	Solar Wings Pegasus XL-R (Rotax 447) SW-TB-1196 & SW-WA-1199			26. 5.87	S.L.Blount	St.Ives, Huntingdon	29. 9.99P
G-MTJA	Mainair Gemini/Flash 2A 551-687-5 & W339 (Rotax 503)			15. 6.87	S.A.Robinson	Roddidge, Fradley	11. 8.99P
G-MTJB	Mainair Gemini/Flash 2A 554-687-5 & W343 (Rotax 462)			2. 6.87	K.Worthingon	Chorley	20. 9.99P
G-MTJC	Mainair Gemini/Flash 2A 555-687-5 & W344 (Rotax 503)			1. 6.87	A.J.Calvert	Oxton, Notts	29. 7.98P
G-MTJD	Mainair Gemini/Flash 2A 552-687-5 & W340 (Rotax 462)			5. 6.87	M.Bond	Bristol	21.11.99P
G-MTJE	Mainair Gemini/Flash 2A 556-687-5 & W345 (Rotax 503)			24. 6.87	C.J.Dyke	Redlands, Swindon	30. 5.99P
G-MTJF*	Mainair Gemini/Flash 2A 557-687-5 & W346 (Rotax 503)			15. 6.87	Not known (Stored 7.96)	Bruntingthorpe	13. 4.91P
G-MTJG	Medway Hybred 44XLR (Rotax 447)	22587/25		16. 6.87	Margaret A.Trodden	Tupton, Chesterfield	24. 2.99P
G-MTJH	Solar Wings Pegasus/Flash (Rotax 447) SW-TB-1050 & W342-687-3 (Trike previously fitted to G-MMUF)			17. 6.87	C.L.Parker	Ampthill	7. 7.99P
G-MTJI	Raven X (Rotax 447)	2232/0260		23. 6.87	E.J.MacPherson	Desborough	12.10.92P
G-MTJK	Mainair Gemini/Flash 2A 559-787-5 & W348 (Rotax 503)			17. 6.87	R.C.White	Aldermaston	1. 9.98P
G-MTJL	Mainair Gemini/Flash 2A 548-687-5 & W337 (Rotax 503)			17. 6.87	D.J.Tuplin & B.G.M.Chapman	Grimsby/Louth	15. 7.99P
G-MTJM	Mainair Gemini/Flash 2A 560-787-5 & W349 (Rotax 462)			24. 6.87	M.E.Jeffreys	Uxbridge	2. 2.97P
G-MTJN	Midland Ultralights Sirocco 377GB (Rotax 377)	MU-020		23. 6.87	R.Harris	Hailsham	19. 3.94P
G-MTJP	Medway Hybred 44XLR (Rotax 447)	25687/27		6. 7.87	P.S.Hunt t/a G-MTJP Group	Plaistows Field, Hemel Hempstead	15. 5.99P
G-MTJR	Solar Wings Pegasus XL-R SW-WA-1209 (Rotax 462)			15. 7.87	Ultralight Training Ltd (Damaged late 1997)	Coventry	14.12.99P
G-MTJS	Solar Wings Pegasus XL-Q (Rotax 462) SW-TE-0022 & SW-WX-0013			6. 7.87	A.R.Watt	Insch	9. 5.99P
G-MTJT	Mainair Gemini/Flash 2A 558-787-5 & W347 (Rotax 462)			16. 7.87	D.T.A.Rees	Haverfordwest	22.12.99P
G-MTJV	Mainair Gemini/Flash 2A 562-787-5 & W351 (Rotax 503)			16. 7.87	N.Charles & J.Richards	Swinford, Rugby	1. 7.98P
G-MTJW	Mainair Gemini/Flash 2A 563-787-5 & W352 (Rotax 503)			16. 7.87	J.F.Ashton	Liverpool	4.10.95P
G-MTJX	Hornet Dual Trainer/Southdown Raven (Rotax 462) HRWA 0063 & 2000/0279			5. 8.87	J.P.Kirwan	Liverpool	31. 5.99P
G-MTJY	Mainair Gemini/Flash 2A 564-887-5 & W353 (Rotax 503)			15. 7.87	D.L.Silver (Damaged mid 1994; stored 9.95)	Swinford, Rugby	9.10.94P
G-MTJZ	Mainair Gemini/Flash 2A 561-787-5 & W350 (Rotax 503)			16. 7.87	G.A.Murphy	Ballincollig, Ireland	17. 5.99P
G-MTKA	Thruster TST Mk.1 (Rotax 503)	867-TST-021		21. 7.87	C.W.Payne	Worcester	9. 7.98P

Regn	Type	C/n	P/I	Date	Owner/operator	Probable Base	CA Expy
G-MTKB	Thruster TST Mk.1 (Rotax 503)	867-TST-022		21. 7.87	M.Hanna	Rathfriland, Co.Down	1. 2.99P
G-MTKD	Thruster TST Mk.1	867-TST-024		21. 7.87	M.J.R.Corney (Damaged mid 1996)	Denbigh	14.10.99P
G-MTKE	Thruster TST Mk.1 (Rotax 503)	867-TST-025		21. 7.87	W.Wells & D.F.Hughes Belvedere/London SE9		3. 5.99P
G-MTKG	Solar Wings Pegasus XL-R/Se (Rotax 447) SW-TB-1199 & SW-WA-1201			13. 7.87	W.J.Hodgins	Buckingham	13. 5.99P
G-MTKH	Solar Wings Pegasus XL-R (Rotax 447) SW-TB-1200 & SW-WA-1202			13. 7.87	N.Harford	Horley	14. 5.99P
G-MTKI	Solar Wings Pegasus XL-R (Rotax 447) SW-TB-1201 & SW-WA-1203 (Reported as c/n SW-TB-1204)			13. 7.87	I.D.A.Spanton	Malvern	7. 9.99P
G-MTKJ	Solar Wings Pegasus XL-R/Se (Rotax 447) SW-TB-1202 & SW-WA-1204			13. 7.87	P.E.Hudson	Warrington	2.12.99P
G-MTKM	Gardner T-M Scout S2	87/003		12. 8.87	D.Gardner (As "38674" in USAS c/s)	Rugby	
G-MTKN	Mainair Gemini/Flash 2A (Rotax 503) 566-887-5 & W355			15. 7.87	A.J.Taylor	Preston	9. 6.99P
G-MTKO	Mainair Gemini/Flash 2A (Rotax 503) 567-787-5 & W356			13. 7.87	M.Leavesley	Sittles Farm, Alrewas	30.10.97P
G-MTKP	Solar Wings Pegasus XL-R SW-WA-1207 (Rotax 462)			13. 7.87	J.Chapman (Damaged mid 1995)	Tarn Farm, Cockerham	1. 5.96P
G-MTKR	CFM Shadow Srs.CD (Rotax 503)	067	9H-ABL G-MTKR	20. 7.87	Cloudbase Avn Svs Ltd	Redhill	19. 5.99P
G-MTKV	Mainair Gemini/Flash 2A (Rotax 503) 565-887-5 & W354			26. 8.87	L.A.Davidson	Scunthorpe	9. 3.99P
G-MTKW	Mainair Gemini/Flash 2A (Rotax 503) 569-887-5 & W358			13. 7.87	R.T.Henry	Newtownards	3. 3.99P
G-MTKX	Mainair Gemini/Flash 2A (Rotax 503) 568-887-5 & W357			13. 7.87	A.S.Leach	Warrington	7. 2.99P
G-MTKZ	Mainair Gemini/Flash 2A 571-887-5 & W360 (Rotax 503)			31. 7.87	A.H.F.Wilks	Carnbo, Kinross	21. 6.99P
G-MTLB	Mainair Gemini/Flash 2A 573-887-5 & W362 (Rotax 503)			31. 7.87	D.N.Bacon	Hucknall	29. 8.99P
G-MTLC	Mainair Gemini/Flash 2A 574-887-5 & W363 (Rotax 503)			31. 7.87	R.J.Alston	Cromer	15. 7.99P
G-MTLD	Mainair Gemini/Flash 2A 575-887-5 & W364 (Rotax 503)			31. 7.87	I.A.Forrest	East Fortune	28. 3.99P
G-MTLG	Solar Wings Pegasus XL-R (Rotax 447) SW-TB-1207 & SW-WA-1211 (Fitted with wing ex G-MTEE; thus is SW-WA-1142)			31. 7.87	D.Young t/a Kemble Flying Club	Kemble	19.10.96P
G-MTLH	Solar Wings Pegasus XL-R (Rotax 447) SW-TB-1208 & SW-WA-1212 (Trike stored 4.96)			31. 7.87	B.S.Waite	Clench Common	18. 5.95P
G-MTLI	Solar Wings Pegasus XL-R SW-WA-1213 (Rotax 447)			31. 7.87	M.McKay	Robertsbridge	6. 6.97P
G-MTLJ	Solar Wings Pegasus XL-R/Se (Rotax 447) SW-TB-1210 & SW-WA-1214			31. 7.87	R.E.Pratt	Sandtoft	27. 7.99P
G-MTLL	Mainair Gemini/Flash 2A 578-987-5 & W367 (Rotax 503)			14. 8.87	M.F.Shaw & M.J.Bird t/a Wrekin Communications (Stored 3.93)	Long Marston	4. 1.93P
G-MTLM	Thruster TST Mk.1 (Rotax 503)	887-TST-027		5. 8.87	E.F.Howells t/a Chloe's F/Grp "Chloe"	Manor Farm, Croughton	19. 5.99P
G-MTLN	Thruster TST Mk.1 (Rotax 503)	887-TST-028		5. 8.87	L.A.Maynard	Old Sarum	23. 8.98P
G-MTLO	Thruster TST Mk.1 (Rotax 503)	887-TST-029		5. 8.87	A.Emmanuel	Haverfordwest	5. 8.96P
G-MTLR	Thruster TST Mk.1 (Rotax 503)	887-TST-031		5. 8.87	J.C.Miller	Strathaven	7.12.98P
G-MTLT	Solar Wings Pegasus XL-R SW-WA-1216 (Rotax 447)			12. 8.87	S.P.MacDonald	Stamford, Lincs	11. 2.99P
G-MTLU	Solar Wings Pegasus XL-R/Se (Rotax 447) SW-TB-1213 & SW-WA-1217			12. 8.87	B.Richardson	Eshott	12. 9.99P
G-MTLV	Solar Wings Pegasus XL-R (Rotax 447) SW-TB-1214 & SW-WA-1218			12. 8.87	D.E.Watson	Long Marston	27. 9.90P
G-MTLW	Solar Wings Pegasus XL-R (Rotax 447) SW-TB-1215 & SW-WA-1219			12. 8.87	S.R.Sutch t/a Pegasus Flt Training	Sutton Meadows, Ely	30. 8.98P
G-MTLX	Medway Hybred 44XLR (Rotax 447)	20687/26		14. 8.87	D.A.Coupland	RAF Wyton	29. 1.00P
G-MTLY	Solar Wings Pegasus XL-R SW-WA-1220 (Rotax 462)			12. 8.87	I.Johnston	Bolton	5. 7.92P
G-MTLZ	Whittaker MW-5 Sorcerer PFA/163-11241 (Rotax 377)			13. 8.87	M.J.Davenport	Weymouth	1. 8.97P
G-MTMA	Mainair Gemini/Flash 2A 579-987-5 & W368 (Rotax 503)			14. 8.87	D.Bussell	St.Michaels-on-Wyre	31. 5.99P
G-MTMB*	Mainair Gemini/Flash 2A 580-987-5 & W369 (Rotax 503)			14. 8.87	C.Lavender (Cancelled by CAA 1.12.98)	Kendal	1. 6.97P
G-MTMC	Mainair Gemini/Flash 2A 581-987-5 & W370 (Rotax 503)			14. 8.87	A.R.Johnson	Brenzett, Kent	22. 4.98P

Regn	Type	C/n	P/I	Date	Owner/operator	Probable Base	CA Expy
G-MTMD	Whittaker MW-6 Merlin PFA/164-11225 (Rotax 503)			12. 8.87	G.C.Steele	Otherton, Cannock	1.10.97P
G-MTME	Solar Wings Pegasus XL-R SW-WA-1221 (Rotax 447)			18. 8.87	M.T.Finch	Sutton Meadows, Ely	27. 8.99P
G-MTMF	Solar Wings Pegasus XL-R SW-WA-1222 (Rotax 447)			18. 8.87	J.T.W.Smith	Mallaig, Inverness	30. 5.99P
G-MTMG	Solar Wings Pegasus XL-R SW-WA-1223 (Rotax 447)			18. 8.87	C.W. & P.E.F.Suckling	Rushden	18. 8.99P
G-MTMH	Solar Wings Pegasus XL-R SW-WA-1224 (Rotax 447)			18. 8.87	P.J.McQuie & C.N.Jones	Longacre Farm, Sandy	21. 6.94P
G-MTMI	Solar Wings Pegasus XL-R/Se (Rotax 447) SW-TB-1220 & SW-WA-1225			18. 8.87	J.S.Hogg	Eshott	26. 9.97P
G-MTMJ*	Maxair Hummer MJM-01			18. 8.87	A.Cuthbertson (Cancelled as WFU 10.3.99)	Port Talbot	
G-MTMK	Raven X (Rotax 447) 2000/0289			2. 9.87	D.W.Thomas	Dartford	27. 7.97P
G-MTML	Mainair Gemini/Flash 2A 582-1087-5 & W371 (Rotax 462)			27. 8.87	J.F.Ashton	Liverpool	14. 5.99P
G-MTMO	Raven X (Rotax 447) 2232/0278 (G-MTKL)			11. 9.87	H.Tuvey	South Ockendon	22. 5.97P
G-MTMP	Hornet Dual Trainer/Raven (Rotax 462) HRWA 0064 & 2000/0288			28. 8.87	P.G.Owen	Baxby Manor, Husthwaite	6. 8.99P
G-MTMR	Hornet Dual Trainer/Raven (Rotax 462) HRWA 0065 & 2000/0297			28. 8.87	D.J.Smith	Hucknall	10. 5.99P
G-MTMT	Mainair Gemini/Flash 2A 583-1087-5 & W372 (Rotax 462)			3. 9.87	I.Howes	Penrith	31. 3.99P
G-MTMV	Mainair Gemini/Flash 2A 585-1087-5 & W374 (Rotax 503)			3. 9.87	A.J.Cropper	St.Michaels-on-Wyre	8. 4.99P
G-MTMW	Mainair Gemini/Flash 2A 587-1087-5 & W376 (Rotax 503)			9. 9.87	A.J.Howard & L.Jensen-Robertson t/a G-MTMW Grp Ince Blundell, Liverpool		24. 9.99P
G-MTMX	CFM Shadow Srs.CD (Rotax 503) 070			4. 9.87	I.M.Cross	Enstone	25. 8.99P
G-MTMY	CFM Shadow Srs.CD (Rotax 503) 071			4. 9.87	R.F.Learney t/a G-MTMY Syndicate Redhill		6. 1.00P
G-MTMZ	CFM Shadow Srs.BD (Rotax 447) 074			4. 9.87	C.A.Keens	Blackbushe/Woking	29.10.97P
G-MTNB	Raven X (Rotax 447) 2232/0305			9. 9.87	R.Coar	High Barn Farm, Houghton	15. 9.97P
G-MTNC	Mainair Gemini/Flash 2A 588-1087-5 & W377 (Rotax 503)			15. 9.87	B.Collier	Wolverhampton	15. 4.00P
G-MTNE	Medway Hybred 44XLR 7987/32 (Rotax 447) (Presumed fitted with new trike as original was transferred to G-MVDC in 1988)			12.10.87	A.D.Chapman	Orpington	8. 9.99P
G-MTNF	Medway Hybred 44XLR 1987/31 (Rotax 447)			12.10.87	P.A.Bedford	Tewkesbury	21.11.98P
G-MTNG	Mainair Gemini/Flash 2A 590-1087-5 & W379 (Rotax 503)			21. 9.87	G.M.Yule	Shobdon	2. 6.98P
G-MTNH	Mainair Gemini/Flash 2A 589-1087-5 & W378 (Rotax 462)			17. 9.87	J.R.Smart	Churchdown, Gloucester	29. 5.99P
G-MTNI	Mainair Gemini/Flash 2A 595-1187-5 & W384 (Rotax 503)			18. 9.87	A.R.Mikolajczyk	Knapthorpe Lodge, Caunton, Notts	24. 8.99P
G-MTNJ	Mainair Gemini/Flash 2A 593-1187-5 & W382 (Rotax 462)			17. 9.87	R.H.Hunt	Old Sarum	17.12.99P
G-MTNK	Weedhopper JC-24B (EC-34-PM) 1936			28. 9.87	K.J.Tomlinson	Derby	N/E
G-MTNL	Mainair Gemini/Flash 2A 591-1187-5 & W380 (Rotax 503)			21. 9.87	A.K.Munro	Stoke-on-Trent	29. 8.99P
G-MTNM	Mainair Gemini/Flash 2A 592-1187-5 & W381 (Rotax 503)			22. 9.87	C.J.Janson	Shobdon	28. 6.98P
G-MTNO	Solar Wings Pegasus XL-Q (Rotax 447) SW-TB-1252 & SW-WQ-0001			23. 9.87	A.F.Batchelor	Rayne Hall Farm, Rayne	2. 5.99P
G-MTNP	Solar Wings Pegasus XL-Q (Rotax 447) SW-TB-1253 & SW-WQ-0002			23. 9.87	G.G.Roberts	Rayne Hall Farm, Rayne	15. 6.99P
G-MTNR	Thruster TST Mk.1 897-TST-032 (Rotax 503)			1.10.87	R.B.M.Etherington	Totnes	17. 6.99P
G-MTNS	Thruster TST Mk.1 897-TST-033 (Rotax 503)			1.10.87	S.J.Wilkinson	Tarn Farm, Cockerham	12.11.99P
G-MTNT	Thruster TST Mk.1 897-TST-034 (Rotax 503)			1.10.87	G.Bennett	Caister-on-Sea	19.12.99P
G-MTNU	Thruster TST Mk.1 897-TST-035 (Rotax 503)			1.10.87	A.Deer	Surbiton	8. 7.99P
G-MTNV	Thruster TST Mk.1 897-TST-036 (Rotax 503)			1.10.87	J.B.Russell	Larne, Co.Antrim	11.10.88P
G-MTNW	Thruster TST Mk.1 897-TST-037 (Rotax 503)			1.10.87	S.D. & M.D.Barnard	Coalville, Leicester	17. 8.97P
G-MTNX	Mainair Gemini/Flash 2A 606-1187-5 & W393 (Rotax 503)			29. 9.87	C.Evans (Damaged late 1997)	Grimsby	9. 5.99P
G-MTNY	Mainair Gemini/Flash 2A 594-1187-5 & W383 (Rotax 503)			2.10.87	R.A.McClure & A.J.Wallace	Taunton/Weymouth	11. 7.99P
G-MTOA	Solar Wings Pegasus XL-R (Rotax 447) SW-TB-1226 & SW-WA-1226			15. 9.87	R.A.Bird	East Hunsbury, Northampton	17. 8.99P
G-MTOB	Solar Wings Pegasus XL-R (Rotax 447) SW-TB-1222 & SW-WA-1227			15. 9.87	P.S.Lemm	Hatherton, Cannock	1.10.97P
G-MTOC	Solar Wings Pegasus XL-R (Rotax 447) SW-TB-1223 & SW-WA-1228			15. 9.87	S.B.Perez	Monteleger, France	26. 5.96P

Regn	Type	C/n P/I	Date	Owner/operator	Probable Base	CA Expy
G-MTOD	Solar Wings Pegasus XL-R SW-WA-1229 (Rotax 447)		15. 9.87	G.J.Crago	Liskeard	17. 7.99P
G-MTOE	Solar Wings Pegasus XL-R SW-WA-1230 (Rotax 447)		15. 9.87	A.J.Sims	Salisbury	13. 3.99P
G-MTOF	Solar Wings Pegasus XL-R/Se (Rotax 447) SW-TB-1226 & SW-WA-1231		15. 9.87	A.B.Potts	Eshott	26. 4.99P
G-MTOG	Solar Wings Pegasus XL-R SW-WA-1232 (Rotax 447)		15. 9.87	C.R.M.Bannerman	Balfron, Glasgow	17. 4.99P
G-MTOH	Solar Wings Pegasus XL-R (Rotax 447) SW-TB-1228 & SW-WA-1233		15. 9.87	H.Cook	Pontypool	18. 7.98P
G-MTOI	Solar Wings Pegasus XL-R (Rotax 447) SW-TB-1229 & SW-WA-1234		15. 9.87	S.C.Key	Sutton Meadows, Ely	14. 6.99P
G-MTOJ	Solar Wings Pegasus XL-R/Se SW-WA-1235 (Rotax 447)		15. 9.87	P.G.Lloyd	Old Sarum	20. 9.99P
G-MTOK	Solar Wings Pegasus XL-R SW-WA-1236 (Rotax 447)		2.10.87	W.S.Davis	Oxton, Nottingham	13. 2.99P
G-MTOL	Solar Wings Pegasus XL-R SW-WA-1237 (Rotax 447)		2.10.87	R.D.Bertram	Gillingham	4.12.98P
G-MTOM	Solar Wings Pegasus XL-R/Se (Rotax 447) SW-TB-1233 & SW-WA-1238		2.10.87	A.R.Walker	Sandtoft	23. 4.99P
G-MTON	Solar Wings Pegasus XL-R (Rotax 447) SW-TB-1234 & SW-WA-1239		2.10.87	D.J.Cook	Northwich, Cheshire	19. 3.99P
G-MTOO	Solar Wings Pegasus XL-R (Rotax 447) SW-TB-1235 & SW-WA-1240		2.10.87	G.W.Bulmer	Bristol	5. 6.99P
G-MTOP	Solar Wings Pegasus XL-R/Se SW-WA-1241 (Rotax 447)		2.10.87	P.D.Larkin	Bourne End	2.10.99P
G-MTOR	Solar Wings Pegasus XL-R (Rotax 447) SW-TB-1237 & SW-WA-1242		9.10.87	M.A.Pantling	Weston Zoyland	15. 7.98P
G-MTOS	Solar Wings Pegasus XL-R (Rotax 447) SW-TB-1238 & SW-WA-1243		9.10.87	R.A.Young	Ginge, Wantage	29. 8.99P
G-MTOT	Solar Wings Pegasus XL-R SW-WA-1244 (Rotax 447)		9.10.87	G.J.Howley	Coleford	10.11.99P
G-MTOU	Solar Wings Pegasus XL-R/Se (Rotax 447) SW-TB-1240 & SW-WA-1245		9.10.87	I.E.Wallace	Eshott	18.12.99P
G-MTOW	Solar Wings Pegasus XL-R SW-WA-1247 (Rotax 447)		19.10.87	G.A.Hagger	Bristol	28. 4.94P
G-MTOX	Solar Wings Pegasus XL-R (Rotax 447) SW-TB-1243 & SW-WA-1248		19.10.87	I.Fernihough	Ashbourne	19.11.99P
G-MTOY*	Solar Wings Pegasus XL-R SW-WA-1249 (Rotax 447)		19.10.87	D.Halstead (Damaged mid 1997; cancelled by CAA 27.10.98)	London N4	14.12.97P
G-MTOZ	Solar Wings Pegasus XL-R (Rotax 447) SW-TB-1245 & SW-WA-1250		19.10.87	P.J.McCool	Enstone	12. 2.99P
G-MTPA	Mainair Gemini/Flash 2A 598-1187-5 & W394		13.10.87	K.R.Bircher	Longhope, Glos	19. 6.99P
G-MTPB	Mainair Gemini/Flash 2A 599-1187-5 & W387 (Rotax 503)		15.10.87	N.Sutcliffe	Northenden, Manchester	26.10.98P
G-MTPE	Solar Wings Pegasus XL-R (Rotax 447) SW-TB-1258 & SW-WA-1260		21.10.87	J.Bassett	Kemble	13. 9.98P
G-MTPF	Solar Wings Pegasus XL-R (Rotax 447) SW-TB-1259 & SW-WA-1261		21.10.87	P.J.C.Martins	Kingsbridge	27. 8.98P
G-MTPG	Solar Wings Pegasus XL-R SW-WA-1262 (Rotax 447)		21.10.87	W.H.Morrow	Dunkeswell	27. 6.99P
G-MTPH	Solar Wings Pegasus XL-R (Rotax 447) SW-TB-1261 & SW-WA-1263		30.10.87	L.M.Sams	Long Marston	29. 3.98P
G-MTPI	Solar Wings Pegasus XL-R/Se (Rotax 447) SW-TB-1262 & SW-WA-1264		30.10.87	R.J.Bullock	Long Marston	1. 2.98P
G-MTPJ	Solar Wings Pegasus XL-R (Rotax 447) SW-TB-1263 & SW-WA-1265		30.10.87	D.A.Whittaker	Roddige, Fradley	31. 7.99P
G-MTPK	Solar Wings Pegasus XL-R SW-WA-1266 (Rotax 447)		30.10.87	S.H.James	Peterborough	17.10.99P
G-MTPL	Solar Wings Pegasus XL-R (Rotax 447) SW-TB-1265 & SW-WA-1267		30.10.87	I.R.F.King	Tunbridge Wells	2. 9.98P
G-MTPM	Solar Wings Pegasus XL-R (Rotax 447) SW-TB-1266 & SW-WA-1268		30.10.87	I.J.Butler	Sittles Farm, Alrewas	29. 5.99P
G-MTPN*	Solar Wings Pegasus XL-R (Rotax 447) SW-TB-1267 & SW-WQ-0004		21.10.87	C.G.Johns (Cancelled by CAA 2.12.98)	Kidderminster	13. 4.94P
G-MTPO	Solar Wings Pegasus XL-Q (Rotax 462) SW-TE-0032 & SW-WQ-0005		21.10.87	P.Devlin	Hungerford	3. 8.98P
G-MTPP	Solar Wings Pegasus XL-R SW-WA-1259 (Rotax 447)		21.10.87	D.G.Salmon	Ashford, Kent	31.10.98P
G-MTPR	Solar Wings Pegasus XL-R SW-WA-1257 (Rotax 447)		21.10.87	M.Castle & S.Fairclough	Shrewsbury	16. 6.96P
G-MTPS	Solar Wings Pegasus XL-Q SW-WX-0011 (Rotax 462)		23.10.87	M.Collinson	Ely	18. 4.98P
G-MTPT	Thruster TST Mk.1 8107-TST-038 (Rotax 503)		23.10.87	J.T.Kendrick	Popham	3.11.96P

Regn	Type	C/n	P/I	Date	Owner/operator	Probable Base	CA Expy
G-MTPU	Thruster TST Mk.1 (Rotax 503)	8107-TST-039		23.10.87	M.R.Jones "Poppy"	Compton Abbas	1. 8.99P
G-MTPV	Thruster TST Mk.1 (Rotax 503)	8107-TST-040		23.10.87	E.Bentley	Stockton-on-Tees	23. 5.99P
G-MTPW	Thruster TST Mk.1 (Rotax 503)	8107-TST-041		23.10.87	C.J.E.Nagle	Chipping Sodbury	20. 8.99P
G-MTPX	Thruster TST Mk.1 (Rotax 503)	8107-TST-042		23.10.87	T.Snook	Long Marston	2. 5.93P
G-MTPY	Thruster TST Mk.1 (Rotax 503)	8107-TST-043		23.10.87	A.N.Wicks	Sudbury	17. 7.99P
G-MTRA	Mainair Gemini/Flash 2A (Rotax 503)	605-1187-5 & W395		28.10.87	E.N.Alms	Guy Lane Farm, Waverton	2. 2.98P
G-MTRB	Mainair Gemini/Flash 2A (Rotax 503)	600-1187-5 & W388		27.10.87	N.Braude	Ely	8. 6.98P
G-MTRC	Midland Ultralights Sirocco 377GB (Rotax 377)		MU-021	2.11.87	D.Thorpe	Grantham	11. 8.98P
G-MTRE	Whittaker MW-6 Merlin (Rotax 532)	PFA/164-11168		27.10.87	M.J.Batchelor	Wickwar	19. 7.99P
G-MTRF	Mainair Gemini/Flash 2A (Rotax 503)	601-1187-5 & W389		30.10.87	J.McGaughran	Long Marston	28. 5.99P
G-MTRJ	AMF Chevvron 2-32C (Konig SD570)	CH.006		30.10.87	R.J.Wells	Chorley	27. 7.99P
G-MTRK	Hornet Dual Trainer/Raven (Rotax 462)	HRWA 0067 & 2000/0324		4.11.87	P.M.Gilfoyle	Leeds	8. 5.94P
G-MTRL	Hornet Dual Trainer/Raven (Rotax 462)	HRWA 0068 & 2000/0326		4.11.87	J.McAlpine	Largs	31. 7.99P
G-MTRM	Solar Wings Pegasus XL-R (Rotax 462)	SW-TE-0030 & SW-WA-1276		10.11.87	D.B.Jones	Longacre Farm, Sandy	5. 6.99P
G-MTRN	Solar Wings Pegasus XL-R (Rotax 447)	SW-WA-1269		2.12.87	P.Vallis	Alfreton	3. 8.99P
G-MTRO	Solar Wings Pegasus XL-R/Se (Rotax 447)	SW-TB-1271 & SW-WA-1270		2.12.87	H.Lloyd-Hughes	Rhuallt	5. 9.99P
G-MTRR	Solar Wings Pegasus XL-R (Rotax 447)	SW-WA-1272		3.12.87	A.Docherty	Cleveland	26. 7.99P
G-MTRS	Solar Wings Pegasus XL-R (Rotax 447)	SW-WA-1273		2.12.87	J.J.R.Tickle	Llanerchymedd, Gwynedd	10. 6.99P
G-MTRT	Raven X (Rotax 447)	2232/0325		12.11.87	D.Hines	Fordhall Villa Farm, Ternhill	5. 8.95P
G-MTRU	Solar Wings Pegasus XL-Q (Rotax 447)	SW-WQ-0009		10.11.87	A.Barnish	Waterlooville	31.10.98P
G-MTRV	Solar Wings Pegasus XL-Q (Rotax 477)	SW-TB-1276 & SW-WX-0010		10.11.87	D.A.Poole	Swindon	18. 6.98P
G-MTRW	Raven X (Rotax 447)			12.11.87	S-A Wensley & T P Hale	Weston-super-Mare	31. 7.99P
G-MTRX	Whittaker MW-5 Sorcerer (Rotax 447)	PFA/163-11202		11.11.87	W.Turner (Stored 8.96)	Otherton, Cannock	13. 2.95P
G-MTRY	Noble Hardman Snowbird Mk.IV (Rotax 532)	SB-005		24.11.87	D.J.Gage & G.Simpson	Kilmarnock/Cumnock	4. 7.90P
G-MTRZ	Mainair Gemini/Flash 2A (Rotax 503)	611-1287-5 & W400		17.11.87	S.J.Doyle	Ince Blundell, Liverpool	12. 5.99P
G-MTSB	Mainair Gemini/Flash 2A (Rotax 503)	608-1187-5 & W397		16.11.87	P.Carter, D.Gabbott & B.F.Stephenson Liverpool		22. 3.99P
G-MTSC	Mainair Gemini/Flash 2A (Rotax 503)	618-188-5 & W407		17.11.87	D.Gabbott	Preston	27. 7.99P
G-MTSD	Raven X (Rotax 447)	2232/0312		24.11.87	D.Turner	Manor Farm, Croughton	20. 7.98P
G-MTSG	CFM Shadow Srs.CD (Rotax 503)	079		24.11.87	C.A.Purvis	St Albans	20. 2.99P
G-MTSH	Thruster TST Mk.1 (Rotax 503)	8117-TST-044		3.12.87	J.I.V.Hill	Newtownards	13. 4.99P
G-MTSI	Thruster TST Mk.1 (Rotax 503)	8117-TST-045		3.12.87	P.P.Trangmar	Hailsham	21. 4.99P
G-MTSJ	Thruster TST Mk.1 (Rotax 503)	8117-TST-046		3.12.87	L.J.Forinton	Gainsborough	8. 4.99P
G-MTSK	Thruster TST Mk.1 (Rotax 503)	8117-TST-047		3.12.87	J.S.Pyke	Westfield Farm, Hailsham	10. 5.99P
G-MTSL	Thruster TST Mk.1 (Rotax 503)	8117-TST-048		3.12.87	J.W.H.Giles & T.A.Porter Newton Abbot/Okehampton		27. 3.96P
G-MTSM	Thruster TST Mk.1 (Rotax 503)	8117-TST-049		3.12.87	Environment Agency, Thames Region Ginge, Wantage		9. 2.00P
G-MTSN	Solar Wings Pegasus XL-R (Rotax 447)	SW-TB-1278 & SW-WA-1280	(Reported	14.12.87	G.P.Lane as trike c/n SW-TB-1272)	Pucklechurch	9. 1.00P
G-MTSO	Solar Wings Pegasus XL-R/Se (Rotax 447)	SW-WA-1281		14.12.87	I.E.Evans	Chesterfield	4. 5.97P
G-MTSP	Solar Wings Pegasus XL-R (Rotax 447)	SW-WA-1282		14.12.87	R.J.Nelson	Swinford, Rugby	14. 9.99P
G-MTSR	Solar Wings Pegasus XL-R (Rotax 447)	SW-TB-1281 & SW-WA-1283		14.12.87	J.Norman	Watford	7. 8.99P
G-MTSS	Solar Wings Pegasus XL-R (Rotax 462)	SW-WA-1284		14.12.87	T.M.Evans	Haywards Heath	23.11.99P

Regn	Type	C/n	P/I	Date	Owner/operator	Probable Base	CA Expy
G-MTST(2)	Thruster TST Mk.1	8128-TST-111		12.12.88	D.J.Flower Baxby Manor, Husthwaite t/a Husthwaite Thruster Grp		21. 5.99P
G-MTSU	Solar Wings Pegasus XL-R SW-WA-1285 (Rotax 447)			4. 1.88	J.McAldney Ballymena, Co.Antrim		20. 3.99P
G-MTSV	Solar Wings Pegasus XL-R SW-WA-1286 (Rotax 447)			4. 1.88	R.J.Bowden	Dunkeswell	18. 8.99P
G-MTSX	Solar Wings Pegasus XL-R (Rotax 447) SW-TB-1282 & SW-WA-1288			4. 1.88	M.R.L.Smith	Lichfield	5. 4.99P
G-MTSY	Solar Wings Pegasus XL-R/Se (Rotax 447) SW-TB-1283 & SW-WA-1289			14. 1.88	N.F.Waldron	Swinford, Rugby	24. 5.99P
G-MTSZ	Solar Wings Pegasus XL-R/Se (Rotax 447) SW-TB-1284 & SW-WA-1290			14. 1.88	J.R.Appleton	Colne	17. 2.99P
G-MTTA	Solar Wings Pegasus XL-R (Rotax 462) SW-TE-0035 & SW-WA-1291			14. 1.88	D.Verdon Morgansfield, Fishburn		28. 2.99P
G-MTTB	Solar Wings Pegasus XL-R SW-WA-1292 (Rotax 447)			14. 1.88	P.M.Golden	Reading	20.10.99P
G-MTTD	Solar Wings Pegasus XL-Q (Rotax 447) SW-TB-1286 & SW-WQ-0011			15. 1.88	R.S.Noremberg	Clacton-on-Sea	12. 4.99P
G-MTTE	Solar Wings Pegasus XL-Q (Rotax 447) SW-TB-1287 & SW-WQ-0012			15. 1.88	C.R.W.Masterton	Clench Common	25. 2.99P
G-MTTF	Whittaker MW-6 Merlin PFA/164-11273 (Rotax 532)			14.12.87	P.Cotton	Long Marston	29. 3.95P
G-MTTH	CFM Shadow Srs.BD (Rotax 447) K.061			15.12.87	C.S.Smith	Shenstone	15. 5.99P
G-MTTI	Mainair Gemini/Flash 2A 620-188-5 & W409 (Rotax 503)			14.12.87	S.M.Savage	Guildford	19. 7.96P
G-MTTK	Southdown Puma (Lightning DS) (EC-44-PM)	DO-8477		15.12.87	D.E.Oakley	West Bromwich	22. 8.93E
G-MTTM	Mainair Gemini/Flash 2A 609-1287-5 & W398 (Rotax 503)			5. 1.88	Valerie C.Ruck	Lydney, Glos	6. 4.97P
G-MTTN	Skyrider Airsports Phantom PH.00100			22. 1.88	H.R.Duggins	Matlock	N/E
G-MTTP	Mainair Gemini/Flash 2A 612-188-5 & W401 (Rotax 462)			18. 1.88	M.J.Rawlins Oxton, Nottingham		11. 8.98P
G-MTTR	Mainair Gemini/Flash 2A 614-188-5 & W403 (Rotax 462)			27. 1.88	A.Westoby	Hucknall	12. 7.99P
G-MTTS	Mainair Gemini/Flash 2A 621-188-5 & W410 (Rotax 503)			4. 1.88	J.B.Bailey	Shrewsbury	23. 4.91P
G-MTTU	Solar Wings Pegasus XL-R (Rotax 447) SW-TB-1332 & SW-WA-1294			25. 2.88	N.L.Walsh & A.T.Farmer Shifnal		9. 7.99P
G-MTTW	Mainair Gemini/Flash 2A 622-188-5 & W411 (Rotax 462)			15. 1.88	M.W.Holmes	Ilkeston	29. 6.99P
G-MTTX	Solar Wings Pegasus XL-Q (Rotax 447) SW-TB-1293 & SW-WQ-0013			15. 2.88	P.G.Moss Baxby Manor, Husthwaite		30. 4.99P
G-MTTZ	Solar Wings Pegasus XL-Q SW-WQ-0015 (Rotax 462)			21. 1.88	J.Haskett	Kings Lynn	7. 8.99P
G-MTUA	Solar Wings Pegasus XL-R/Se (Rotax 447) SW-TB-1294 & SW-WA-1295			15. 1.88	A.J.Varga	Redcar	14. 6.99P
G-MTUB	Thruster TST Mk.1 8018-TST-050 (Rotax 503)			15. 1.88	G.Millar Dungannon, Co.Tyrone		17. 3.99P
G-MTUC	Thruster TST Mk.1 8018-TST-051 (Rotax 503)			15. 1.88	E.J.Girling	Plymouth	10. 8.99P
G-MTUD	Thruster TST Mk.1 8018-TST-052 (Rotax 503)			15. 1.88	J.D.Smith Husthwaite t/a Baxby Airsports Club		5.10.00P
G-MTUE	Thruster TST Mk.1 8018-TST-053 (Rotax 503)			15. 1.88	J.P.McVitty Armagh Field, Woodview		11. 6.94P
G-MTUF	Thruster TST Mk.1 8018-TST-054 (Rotax 503)			15. 1.88	P.Stark	Strathaven	22. 9.99P
G-MTUG	Thruster TST Mk.1 8018-TST-055 (Rotax 503)			15. 1.88	T.L.Davis	Popham	28. 5.94P
G-MTUI	Solar Wings Pegasus XL-R/Se SW-WA-1296 (Rotax 447)			21. 1.88	N.J.Garrett	Enstone	28. 1.99P
G-MTUJ	Solar Wings Pegasus XL-R SW-WA-1297 (Rotax 447)			21. 1.88	R.W.Pincombe Chumleigh, Devon		31. 5.94P
G-MTUK	Solar Wings Pegasus XL-R SW-WA-1298 (Rotax 447)			21. 1.88	D.L.Pickover Nelson, Lancs		28. 3.99P
G-MTUL	Solar Wings Pegasus XL-R/Se (Rotax 447) SW-TB-1299 & SW-WA-1299			21. 1.88	A.G.Curtis	Wellingborough	11. 2.99P
G-MTUN	Solar Wings Pegasus XL-Q (Rotax 447) SW-TB-1301 & SW-WQ-0016 (Fitted with Wing from G-MVUK ?)			20. 1.88	J.P.Feeney & C.G.Notarantonio (Stored 1.98) Long Marston		6. 9.95P
G-MTUP	Solar Wings Pegasus XL-Q (Rotax 447) SW-TB-1303 & SW-WA-0018			20. 1.88	S.J.Allen Blisworth, Northampton		25. 1.99P
G-MTUR	Solar Wings Pegasus XL-Q (Rotax 447) SW-TB-1304 & SW-WQ-0019			20. 1.88	G.Ball	Tewkesbury	28. 8.99P
G-MTUS	Solar Wings Pegasus XL-Q (Rotax 447) SW-TB-1305 & SW-WQ-0020			20. 1.88	I.Haddow	Campbeltown	6. 8.98P

Regn	Type	C/n	P/I	Date	Owner/operator	Probable Base	CA Expy
G-MTUT	Solar Wings Pegasus XL-Q			21. 1.88	L.F.Tanner & D.D.Lock		
	(Rotax 462) SW-TE-0040 & SW-WQ-0021					Sutton Meadows, Ely	26. 4.99P
G-MTUU	Mainair Gemini/Flash 2A 623-288-5 & W412			10. 2.88	M.Harris	Eshott	26. 3.97P
	(Rotax 503)						
G-MTUV	Mainair Gemini/Flash 2A 624-288-5 & W413			28. 1.88	R.J.Griffiths	Rush Green	2. 4.99P
	(Rotax 462)						
G-MTUX	Medway Hybred 44XLR	241287/33		2. 2.88	P.A.R.Wilson	Husthwaite	29. 8.99P
	(Rotax 503)						
G-MTUY	Solar Wings Pegasus XL-Q			28. 1.88	H.C.Lowther	Penrith	18. 3.99P
	(Rotax 462) SW-TE-0041 & SW-WQ-0022						
G-MTVB	Solar Wings Pegasus XL-R			28. 1.88	N.A.Martin, D.M.Roberts & T.Quantril		
	(Rotax 447) SW-TB-1307 & SW-WA-1302					Clench Common	29. 9.97P
G-MTVC	Solar Wings Pegasus XL-R			28. 1.88	M.R.Nurse	Milton Keynes	6. 7.97P
	(Rotax 447) SW-TB-1308 & SW-WA-1303						
G-MTVG	Mainair Gemini/Flash 2A 628-388-6 & W417			12. 2.88	D.A.Whitworth	Swanton Morley	10. 3.99P
	(Rotax 503)						
G-MTVH	Mainair Gemini/Flash 2A 626-288-6 & W415			17. 2.88	N.S.Payne	Broadmeadow Farm, Hereford	12.12.99P
	(Rotax 503)						
G-MTVI	Mainair Gemini/Flash 2A 629-388-6 & W416			12. 2.88	R.A.McDowell	Slough	10. 5.92P
	(Rotax 503)						
G-MTVJ	Mainair Gemini/Flash 2A 627-388-6 & W418			12. 2.88	I.D.Remizo-Clarke	Accrington	3. 6.99P
	(Rotax 503)						
G-MTVK	Solar Wings Pegasus XL-R SW-WA-1306			15. 2.88	C.J.Finnigan	(BFPO 140)	17. 3.98P
	(Rotax 447)						
G-MTVL	Solar Wings Pegasus XL-R/Se SW-WA-1307			15. 2.88	J.K.Pattison	Weston Zoyland	2. 8.97P
	(Rotax 447)						
G-MTVM	Solar Wings Pegasus XL-R SW-WA-1308			15. 2.88	S.I.French	Ventnor, IoW	22. 5.99P
	(Rotax 447)						
G-MTVN	Solar Wings Pegasus XL-R SW-WA-1309			15. 2.88	A.I.Crighton		
	(Rotax 447)					Lower Mountpleasant Farm, Wimblington	4. 4.98P
G-MTVO	Solar Wings Pegasus XL-R			15. 2.88	A.L.Brown	Long Marston	9. 1.00P
	(Rotax 447) SW-TB-1315 & SW-WA-1310						
G-MTVP	Thruster TST Mk.1	8028-TST-056		10. 2.88	J.M.Evans	Abingdon	4.12.98P
	(C/n plate marked incorrectly as 8208-TST-056)						
G-MTVR	Thruster TST Mk.1	8028-TST-057		10. 2.88	A.J.Wood	Baxby Manor, Husthwaite	27. 5.99P
	(Rotax 503)						
G-MTVS	Thruster TST Mk.1	8028-TST-058		10. 2.88	W.J.Burrell	Banbridge, Co.Down	22. 9.99P
	(Rotax 503)						
G-MTVT	Thruster TST Mk.1	8028-TST-059		10. 2.88	J.R.Lukey	Popham	14. 5.99P
	(Rotax 503)						
G-MTVV	Thruster TST Mk.1	8028-TST-061		10. 2.88	R.S.O'Carroll	Craigavon, Co.Armagh	2. 8.99P
	(Rotax 503)						
G-MTVX	Solar Wings Pegasus XL-Q			3. 3.88	J.G.Spinks	Swinford, Rugby	10. 8.99P
	(Rotax 462HP) SW-TE-0042 & SW-WQ-0025						
G-MTVZ	Powerchute Raider (Rotax 447)	80104		3. 3.88	A.Cronin	Loughborough	23. 1.97P
G-MTWA	Solar Wings Pegasus XL-R SW-WA-1311			25. 2.88	J.C.Corrall	Chatteris	14.11.99P
	(Rotax 447)						
G-MTWB	Solar Wings Pegasus XL-R			25. 2.88	M.W.A.Shemilt	Henley-on-Thames	13.11.98P
	(Rotax 447) SW-TB-1342 & SW-WA-1312						
G-MTWC	Solar Wings Pegasus XL-R			25. 2.88	L.C.Wellington-Graham & J.P.Clements		
	(Rotax 447) SW-TB-1321 & SW-WA-1313					Baxby Manor, Husthwaite	6. 4.99P
G-MTWD	Solar Wings Pegasus XL-R			25. 2.88	J.A.Valentine	Sutton Meadows, Ely	30. 4.99P
	(Rotax 447) SW-TB-1320 & SW-WA-1314						
G-MTWE	Solar Wings Pegasus XL-R SW-WA-1315			25. 2.88	A.Thomas	London NW10	22. 9.90P
	(Rotax 447)						
G-MTWF	Mainair Gemini/Flash 2A 630-388-6 & W419			25. 2.88	W.Porter	Nottingham	18. 8.99P
	(Rotax 503)						
G-MTWG	Mainair Gemini/Flash 2A 631-288-6 & W420			25. 2.88	J.R.Mosey	Liverpool	13. 6.99P
	(Rotax 503)						
G-MTWH	CFM Shadow Srs.CD (Rotax 503) K.064			25. 2.88	V.A.Hutchinson	Nuneaton	23. 8.99P
	(Rotax 503)						
G-MTWK	CFM Shadow Srs.CD (Rotax 503) 073			25. 2.88	R.C.Fendick	Westbury-sub-Mendip	25. 9.98P
	(Rotax 503)						
G-MTWL	CFM Shadow Srs.BD (Rotax 447) 076			25. 2.88	M.J.Gray	Manor Farm, Croughton	15. 4.99P
G-MTWM	CFM Shadow Srs.CD (Rotax 503) 080			25. 2.88	U.A.Schliessler & R.J.Kelly		
	(Rotax 503)					"Kiwa" Plaistows Field, Hemel Hampstead	9.10.99P
G-MTWN	CFM Shadow Srs.CD (Rotax 503) 081			25. 2.88	P.W.Heywood	Davidstow Moor	17. 6.99P
	(Rotax 503)						
G-MTWP	CFM Shadow Srs.BD (Rotax 447) K.069			29. 2.88	L.J.Chapman	Alresford, Hants	7.9.88P*
					(See G-MZBN)		
G-MTWR	Mainair Gemini/Flash 2A 632-388-6 & W421			3. 3.88	J.B.Hodson	Arclid Green, Sandbach	8. 4.99P
	(Rotax 503)						
G-MTWS	Mainair Gemini/Flash 2A 633-388-6 & W422			3. 3.88	A.R.Walker	Doncaster	5. 7.99P
	(Rotax 503)						
G-MTWX	Mainair Gemini/Flash 2A 634-488-6 & W423			11. 3.88	G.A.Barrett	St.Michaels-on-Wyre	5. 6.99P
	(Rotax 503)						
G-MTWY	Thruster TST Mk.1	8038-TST-062		15. 3.88	M.F.Eddington	Wincanton	10. 2.99P
	(Rotax 503)						

Regn	Type	C/n	P/I	Date	Owner/operator	Probable Base	CA Expy
G-MTWZ	Thruster TST Mk.1 (Rotax 503)	8038-TST-063		15. 3.88	A.Makepeace	Guildford	17. 2.99P
G-MTXA	Thruster TST Mk.1 (Rotax 503)	8038-TST-064		15. 3.88	S.Whittaker	Sandtoft	21. 4.99P
G-MTXB	Thruster TST Mk.1 (Rotax 503)	8038-TST-065		15. 3.88	J.J.Hill	Middlesbrough	25. 8.99P
G-MTXC	Thruster TST Mk.1 (Rotax 503)	8038-TST-066		15. 3.88	Joan A.Huntley	Bradford-on-Avon	13. 6.99P
G-MTXD	Thruster TST Mk.1 (Rotax 503)	8038-TST-067		15. 3.88	B.E.Holloway	Harrogate	3. 2.99P
G-MTXE	Hornet Dual Trainer/Raven (Rotax 462)	HRWA 0070 & 2000/0332		11. 3.88	F.J.Marton t/a Charter Systems	Long Marston	27. 5.98P
G-MTXH	Solar Wings Pegasus XL-Q (Rotax 447)	SW-WQ-0030		11. 3.88	J.Rhodes	Pontefract	21. 7.97P
G-MTXI	Solar Wings Pegasus XL-Q (Rotax 447)	SW-TB-1329 & SW-WQ-0031		11. 3.88	R.Lewis-Evans	Poole	5.10.98P
G-MTXJ	Solar Wings Pegasus XL-Q (Rotax 447)	SW-TB-1330 & SW-WQ-0032		11. 3.88	J.Fuller	Enstone	24. 5.99P
G-MTXK	Solar Wings Pegasus XL-Q (Rotax 447)	SW-WQ-0033		11. 3.88	M.J.McManamon	East Fortune	2. 5.99P
G-MTXL	Noble Hardman Snowbird Mk.IV (Rotax 532)	SB-006		4. 5.88	R.M.Davies & P.I.Hodgson	Amersham/Ilford	16. 5.99P
G-MTXM	Mainair Gemini/Flash 2A (Rotax 503)	636-488-6 & W425		10. 5.88	E.M.Escalante	Borehamwood	29. 1.00P
G-MTXO	Whittaker MW-6 Merlin (Rotax 503)	PFA/164-11326		11. 3.88	S.J.Whyatt	Brighton	4. 8.98P
G-MTXP	Mainair Gemini/Flash 2A (Rotax 503)	637-488-6 & W426		23. 3.88	N.Fielding	St.Michaels-on-Wyre	26. 6.99P
G-MTXR	CFM Shadow Srs.CD (Rotax 503)	K.038		23. 3.88	A.L.R.Middleton	Redhill	1. 8.99P
G-MTXS	Mainair Gemini/Flash 2A (Rotax 503)	638-488-6 & W427		23. 3.88	F.Sempebwa	Roddige, Fradley	17.10.99P
G-MTXY	Hornet Dual Trainer/Raven (Rotax 462)	HRWA 0073 & 2000/0354		30. 3.88	J.McAvoy	Bishopton	17. 8.99P
G-MTXZ	Mainair Gemini/Flash 2A (Rotax 503)	641-588-6 & W430		10. 5.88	S.S.Raines	Market Drayton	4. 9.99P
G-MTYA	Solar Wings Pegasus XL-Q (Rotax 462HP)	SW-TE-0047 & SW-WQ-0037		29. 3.88	I.Clarkson	Long Marston	22. 9.99P
G-MTYC	Solar Wings Pegasus XL-Q (Rotax 462)	SW-WQ-0039		30. 3.88	C.I.D.H.Garrison	Huntingdon	13. 9.99P
G-MTYD	Solar Wings Pegasus XL-Q (Rotax 462)	SW-TE-0050 & SW-WQ-0040		29. 3.88	Fiona E.Treveil	Liphook	16. 9.99P
G-MTYE	Solar Wings Pegasus XL-Q (Rotax 462)	SW-WQ-0041		29. 3.88	K.L.Chorley & A.Cook	Enstone	24. 2.99P
G-MTYF	Solar Wings Pegasus XL-Q (Rotax 462)	SW-WQ-0042		29. 3.88	J.Hyde	Spalding	19. 9.99P
G-MTYH	Solar Wings Pegasus XL-Q (Rotax 462)	SW-TE-0054 & SW-WQ-0044		30. 3.88	J.F.R.Rendell	Cheltenham	25.11.95P
G-MTYI	Solar Wings Pegasus XL-Q (Rotax 462)	SW-WQ-0045		30. 3.88	R.H.Stokes	Warboys	24. 5.99P
G-MTYL	Solar Wings Pegasus XL-Q (Rotax 462)	SW-TE-0058 & SW-WQ-0048 & c/n 6412		30. 3.88	G.T.Hanson	Sywell	30. 7.99P
G-MTYM	Solar Wings Pegasus XL-Q (Rotax 462)	SW-WQ-0049		30. 3.88	Margaret E.Merrison	Chard	20. 6.98P
G-MTYN	Solar Wings Pegasus XL-Q (Rotax 462)	SW-TE-0060 & SW-WQ-0050		30. 3.88	R.P.A.Turner & E.H.Jenkins (Stored 6.97) Broadmeadow Farm, Hereford		18.10.93P
G-MTYP	Solar Wings Pegasus XL-Q (Rotax 462)	SW-WQ-0052		30. 3.88	W.G.Dent (Stored 9.97)	Eshott	14. 7.99P
G-MTYR	Solar Wings Pegasus XL-Q (Rotax 462)	SW-WQ-0053		30. 3.88	C.J.Hill (Stored 6.97)	Broadmeadow Farm, Hereford	30. 4.99P
G-MTYS	Solar Wings Pegasus XL-Q (Rotax 462)	SW-TE-0064 & SW-WQ-0054		30. 3.88	R.G.Wall	Caerleon	13. 8.99P
G-MTYT	Solar Wings Pegasus XL-Q (Rotax 462HP)	SW-TE-0065 & SW-WQ-0055		30. 3.88	M.G.Walsh	Rufforth	30. 8.97P
G-MTYU	Solar Wings Pegasus XL-Q (Rotax 462HP)	SW-WQ-0056		30. 3.88	N.I.Garland & M.Powell	Taunton	10. 3.99P
G-MTYV	Raven X (Rotax 447)	2232/0341		8. 4.88	R.E.J.Pattenden	Maidstone	26. 2.00P
G-MTYW	Raven X (Rotax 447)	2232/0344		8. 4.88	R.Solomans	Tunbridge Wells	10. 6.99P
G-MTYX	Raven X (Rotax 447)	2232/0345		8. 4.88	J.C.Hawkins	Selsey	15. 8.99P
G-MTYY	Solar Wings Pegasus XL-R (Rotax 447)	SW-WA-1326		6. 5.88	G.J.Slater	Marlborough	13. 1.00P
G-MTZA	Thruster TST Mk.1 (Rotax 503)	8048-TST-068		13. 4.88	M.G.Davidson	Craigavon, Co.Armagh	24.11.98P
G-MTZB	Thruster TST Mk.1 (Rotax 503)	8048-TST-069		13. 4.88	S.J.O.Tinn	Weymouth	22.11.97P
G-MTZC	Thruster TST Mk.1 (Rotax 503)	8048-TST-070		13. 4.88	R.Morton	Newtownabbey, NI	25. 1.99P

Regn	Type	C/n	P/I	Date	Owner/operator	Probable Base	CA Expy
G-MTZD	Thruster TST Mk.1 (Rotax 503)	8048-TST-071		13. 4.88	M.Medlock & A.Stephenson	Popham	8.10.99P
G-MTZE	Thruster TST Mk.1 (Rotax 503)	8048-TST-072		13. 4.88	N.A.Reed	Rufforth	13. 2.99P
G-MTZF	Thruster TST Mk.1 (Rotax 503)	8048-TST-073		13. 4.88	D.Large t/a Zulu Fox Grp	Long Marston	25. 8.97P
G-MTZG	Mainair Gemini/Flash 2A (Rotax 503)	642-588-6 & W431		10. 5.88	T.G.Greenhill	Leicester	22. 5.99P
G-MTZH	Mainair Gemini/Flash 2A (Rotax 462)	643-588-6 & W433		9. 6.88	D.C.Hughes	St.Michaels-on-Wyre	20. 3.99P
G-MTZI	Solar Wings Pegasus XL-R (Rotax 447) (Fitted with wing ex G-MTIR)	SW-WA-1327		6. 5.88	E.A.S.Freitas	Lagos, Algarve	2. 6.94P
G-MTZJ	Solar Wings Pegasus XL-R (Rotax 447) SW-TB-1335 & SW-WA-1328			6. 5.88	P.J.Burns	Kemble	19.12.99P
G-MTZK	Solar Wings Pegasus XL-R (Rotax 447) SW-TB-1336 & SW-WA-1329			6. 5.88	Sara J.Singlehurst Long Acre Farm, Sandy		19.10.98P
G-MTZL	Mainair Gemini/Flash 2A (Rotax 503)	645-588-6 & W435		10. 5.88	N.S.Brayn	Popham	18. 9.99P
G-MTZM	Mainair Gemini/Flash 2A (Rotax 503)	646-588-6 & W436		3. 5.88	K.L.Smith	Leicester	4. 2.99P
G-MTZO	Mainair Gemini/Flash 2A (Rotax 462)	649-688-6 & W439		6. 5.88	R.C.Hinds	Newnham, Glos	7. 6.99P
G-MTZP	Solar Wings Pegasus XL-Q (Rotax 447)	SW-WQ-0059		6. 5.88	Island Micro Aviation Ltd	Ventnor, IoW	30. 5.99P
G-MTZR	Solar Wings Pegasus XL-Q (Rotax 447) SW-TB-1338 & SW-WQ-0060			6. 5.88	P.J.Hatchett	Rhuallt	19. 8.98P
G-MTZS	Solar Wings Pegasus XL-Q (Rotax 447)	SW-WQ-0061		6. 5.88	P.A.Darling	Wilmslow	15. 7.93P
G-MTZT	Solar Wings Pegasus XL-Q (Rotax 447)	SW-WQ-0062		6. 5.88	M.Y.Brown	Eshott	14. 7.99P
G-MTZV	Mainair Gemini/Flash 2A (Rotax 503)	650-688-6 & W440		6. 5.88	G.J.Donnellon	Barton	21. 3.99P
G-MTZW	Mainair Gemini/Flash 2A (Rotax 503)	651-688-6 & W441		25. 5.88	L.McIntyre	Ince Blundell, Liverpool	4.10.98P
G-MTZX	Mainair Gemini/Flash 2A (Rotax 503)	652-688-6 & W442		23. 6.88	J.G.Stancombe	Rufforth	27.12.98P
G-MTZY	Mainair Gemini/Flash 2A (Rotax 503)	653-688-6 & W443		24. 5.88	P.K.Dale	Bagby	1. 8.99P
G-MTZZ	Mainair Gemini/Flash 2A (Rotax 503)	654-688-6 & W444		14. 6.88	P.J.Litchfield	Tarn Farm, Cockerham	1. 8.99P

G-MUAA-MUZZ

Regn	Type	C/n	P/I	Date	Owner/operator	Probable Base	CA Expy
G-MUFY	Robinson R-22 Beta	1248	D-HICH	13.12.96	Rotormurf Ltd	Wirral	AC
G-MUIR	Cameron V-65 HAFB	2037		23. 6.89	Lindsay J.M.Muir "Muriel"	East Molesey	25. 3.99A
G-MULL	McDonnell Douglas DC-10-30	47888	YA-LAS	21. 3.85	British Airways plc "New Forest"	Gatwick	20. 5.01T
G-MUNI	Mooney M.20J (201SE)	24-3118		12. 5.89	M.W.Fane	Fairoaks	25. 8.01
G-MURI	Gates Lear Jet 35A	35A-646	N712JB	19. 2.98	G-MURI Ltd	Edinburgh	18. 2.00T
	N717JB/N646EA/XA-UMA/N3812G (Op Northern Executive Aviation)						
G-MURY	Robinson R-44 Astro	0201		19. 7.95	Simlot Ltd (Op Jennifer Murray)	Denham	27. 7.01T
G-MUSO	Rutan LongEz (Lyc O-235)	PFA/74A-10590		11. 6.83	M.Moran	North Weald	14. 6.99P
G-MUST*	Commonwealth CA.18 Mustang 22	1524	VH-BOZ A68-199	20.12.79	Fighter World Museum RAAF Williamtown, NSW, Australia		
G-MUTE	Colt 31A Air Chair HAFB	2099		2.12.91	Redmalt Ltd "Motorola"	Witham, Essex	11.11.99A
G-MUVG	Cessna 421C Golden Eagle III	421C-1064	N421DD	13. 1.97	Air Montgomery Ltd	Leeds-Bradford	7. 2.00T
G-MUZO	Europa Avn Europa	PFA/247-12623		11. 1.94	J.T.Grant	(Norwich)	

G-MVAA-MVZZ

Regn	Type	C/n	P/I	Date	Owner/operator	Probable Base	CA Expy
G-MVAA	Mainair Gemini/Flash 2A (Rotax 503) 655-688-6 & W445			8. 6.88	T.D.Holder	Worksop	24. 2.99P
G-MVAB	Mainair Gemini/Flash 2A (Rotax 503) 656-688-6 & W446			10. 5.88	W.Anderson	Linlithgow	19.11.99P
G-MVAC	CFM Shadow Srs.CD (Rotax 503) K.077			12. 5.88	A.C.MacDonald	Insch	22. 3.99P
G-MVAD	Mainair Gemini/Flash 2A (Rotax 503) 657-688-6 & W447			10. 5.88	N.G.Woodall	Warrington	9. 8.99P
G-MVAF	Southdown Puma Sprint (EC-44-2PM)	P.455	G-MBAF	24. 6.87	J.F.Horn	Yelverton	19. 3.99P
G-MVAG	Thruster TST Mk.1 (Rotax 503)	8058-TST-074		18. 5.88	N.S.Brown	High Barn Farm, Houghton	9. 8.99P
G-MVAH	Thruster TST Mk.1 (Rotax 503)	8058-TST-075		18. 5.88	M.W.H.Henton "Times Four"	Popham	27. 6.99P
G-MVAI	Thruster TST Mk.1 (Rotax 503)	8058-TST-076		18. 5.88	G.D.Bailey	Popham	18. 8.99P
G-MVAJ	Thruster TST Mk.1 (Rotax 503)	8058-TST-077		18. 5.88	B.W.Savory	Long Marston	28. 4.99P
G-MVAK	Thruster TST Mk.1 (Rotax 503)	8058-TST-078		18. 5.88	A.J.Dunlop & S.J.Pettitt	Long Acre Farm, Sandy	29. 1.00P
G-MVAL	Thruster TST Mk.1 (Rotax 503)	8058-TST-079		18. 5.88	G.C.Brooke	Colchester	7. 8.96P
G-MVAM	CFM Shadow Srs.CD (Rotax 503) 082			18. 5.88	K.E.Wedl	St.Michaels-on-Wyre	9. 7.99P
G-MVAN	CFM Shadow Srs.CD K.048 & PFA/161-11219 (Rotax 503)			18. 5.88	I.Brewster	Nuthampstead	16.10.99P
G-MVAO	Mainair Gemini/Flash 2A 658-688-6 & W448 (Rotax 503)			24. 5.88	S.W.Grainger	Wirral	30. 6.99P
G-MVAP	Mainair Gemini/Flash 2A 659-688-6 & W449 (Rotax 503)			24. 5.88	R.J.Miller	Long Marston	21. 9.99P
G-MVAR	Solar Wings Pegasus XL-R SW-WA-1331 (Rotax 447)			24. 5.88	K.H.Creeo	Langar	31.10.99P
G-MVAS	Solar Wings Pegasus XL-R SW-WA-1332 (Rotax 447)			24. 5.88	J.F.P.Marreiros	Lagos, Algarve	14. 4.99P
G-MVAT	Solar Wings Pegasus XL-R SW-WA-1333 (Rotax 447)			24. 5.88	S.Ward	Strathaven	28. 8.99P
G-MVAU	Solar Wings Pegasus XL-R (Rotax 447) SW-TB-1346 & SW-WA-1334			24. 5.88	B.S.Miley & J.H.M.Perry	Eshott	1. 7.98P
G-MVAV	Solar Wings Pegasus XL-R (Rotax 447) SW-TB-1347 & SW-WA-1335			24. 5.88	P.L.Alsop	Sutton Meadows, Ely	11. 8.99P
G-MVAW	Solar Wings Pegasus XL-Q (Rotax 447) SW-TB-1348 & SW-WQ-0064			24. 5.88	L.R.Fox	Aylesbury	1. 8.99P
G-MVAX	Solar Wings Pegasus XL-Q (Rotax 447) SW-TB-1349 & SW-WQ-0065			24. 5.88	G.R.Ward	Cowbridge	9. 6.99P
G-MVAY	Solar Wings Pegasus XL-Q SW-WQ-0066			24. 5.88	V.O.Morris	Swansea	16. 4.97P
G-MVBB	CFM Shadow Srs.BD (Rotax 447) K.051			24. 5.88	R.Garrod	Mendlesham	8.10.00P
G-MVBC	Mainair Tri-Flyer/Aerial Arts 130SX 130SX-616			24. 5.88	D.Beer	Ilfracombe	
G-MVBD	Mainair Gemini/Flash 2A 660-688-6 & W450 (Rotax 462)			8. 6.88	P.A.Morris	St.Michaels-on-Wyre	15.12.99P
G-MVBE	Mainair Scorcher 661-688-6 & W451 (Rotax 503)			28. 7.88	B.L.Cook	Bradford	28. 8.99P
G-MVBF	Mainair Gemini/Flash 2A 662-688-6 & W452 (Rotax 462)			14. 6.88	K.Laud	Swadlincote	3. 8.99P
G-MVBG	Mainair Gemini/Flash 2A 663-688-6 & W453 (Rotax 503)			25. 5.88	A.Dennison	Hughley, Much Wenlock	6.12.99P
G-MVBH	Mainair Gemini/Flash 2A 664-688-6 & W454 (Rotax 503)			25. 5.88	S.H.Harrison	Manor Farm, Inskip	10. 7.98P
G-MVBI	Mainair Gemini/Flash 2A 665-788-6 & W455 (Rotax 503)			7. 6.88	E.R.Wilson	Barrow-in-Furness	6. 9.92P
G-MVBJ	Solar Wings Pegasus XL-R SW-WA-1338 (Rotax 462)			7. 6.88	J.Fleming	Grantown-on-Spey	14. 4.98P
G-MVBK	Mainair Gemini/Flash 2A 666-788-6 & W456 (Rotax 462)			7. 6.88	C.S.Bowen & M.D.Carruthers	Manor Farm, Inskip	8.12.99P
G-MVBL	Mainair Gemini/Flash 2A 669-788-6 & W459 (Rotax 503)			7. 6.88	P.M.Wright	High Barn Farm, Houghton	27. 9.99P
G-MVBM	Mainair Gemini/Flash 2A 667-788-6 & W457 (Rotax 503)			7. 6.88	I.R.Thomas	Buntingford	15. 3.99P
G-MVBN	Mainair Gemini/Flash 2A 668-788-6 & W458 (Rotax 503)			8. 6.88	M.Frankcom	Darwen	2. 6.99P
G-MVBO	Mainair Gemini/Flash 2A 671-788-6 & W461 (Rotax 503)			8. 6.88	R.Brasher	Rugeley	27. 7.99P
G-MVBP	Thruster TST Mk.1 (Rotax 503)	8068-TST-080		14. 6.88	K.J.Crompton	Bangor, Co.Down	8. 3.99P
G-MVBR*	Thruster TST Mk.1 (Rotax 503)	8068-TST-081		14. 6.88	A. Stanford (Cancelled by CAA 5.11.98)	Dunkeswell	24. 9.99P

Regn	Type	C/n	P/I	Date	Owner/operator	Probable Base	CA Expy
G-MVBS	Thruster TST Mk.1 8068-TST-082 (Rotax 503) (Regd as c/n 8060-TST-082)			14. 6.88	P.G.Lowrie	Tarn Farm, Cockerham	22.11.96P
G-MVBT	Thruster TST Mk.1 8068-TST-083 (BMW R100)			14. 6.88	E.L.Everitt	Ley Farm, Chirk	12.11.99P
G-MVBU	Thruster TST Mk.1 8068-TST-084 (Rotax 503)			14. 6.88	J.H.M.Weir (Stored 9.97)	Great Orton	26. 5.93P
G-MVBY	Solar Wings Pegasus XL-R SW-WA-1344 (Rotax 447)			17. 6.88	D.C.de La Haye	Newton Abbot	26. 8.99P
G-MVBZ	Solar Wings Pegasus XL-R (Rotax 447) SW-TB-1358 & SW-WA-1345			17. 6.88	A.G.Butler	Shenstone Hall Farm, Shenstone	24. 7.99P
G-MVCA	Solar Wings Pegasus XL-R SW-WA-1346 (Rotax 447)			17. 6.88	R.Walker	Sutton Meadows, Ely	7. 3.99P
G-MVCB	Solar Wings Pegasus XL-R (Rotax 447) SW-TB-1360 & SW-WA-1347			17. 6.88	G.T.Clipstone	Ipswich	16. 7.97P
G-MVCC	CFM Shadow Srs.CD (Rotax 503) K.045			17. 6.88	K.D.Mitchell	Hassocks	1. 4.99P
G-MVCD	Medway Hybred 44XLR MR001/34 (Rotax 447) (Marked as Raven)			14. 6.88	A.Cochrane	Houghton Conquest	15. 6.99P
G-MVCE	Mainair Gemini/Flash 2A 672-788-6 & W462 (Rotax 503)			23. 6.88	J.D.Berry	Ince Blundell, Liverpool	5. 4.99P
G-MVCF	Mainair Gemini/Flash 2A 673-788-6 & W463 (Rotax 462)			14. 7.88	J.L.Hamer	Hartpury, Glos	19. 7.99P
G-MVCI	Noble Hardman Snowbird Mk.IV SB-011 (Rotax 532)			11.10.88	W.L.Chapman	Tarn Farm, Cockerham	13. 4.95P
G-MVCJ	Noble Hardman Snowbird Mk.IV SB-012 (Rotax 532)			11.10.88	D.A. & A.H.Hopewell "The Strumpet"	Newcastle, Staffs	31. 3.99P
G-MVCK	Cosmos Trike/La Mouette Profil 19 SDA-01			19. 7.88	S.D.Alsop	Bath	
G-MVCL	Solar Wings Pegasus XL-Q SW-WQ-0075 (Rotax 462HP)			27. 6.88	T.E.Robinson	Insch	22. 5.99P
G-MVCM	Solar Wings Pegasus XL-Q (Rotax 462) SW-TE-0070 & SW-WQ-0076			27. 6.88	J.C.Ferris	Sandtoft	3. 4.99P
G-MVCN	Solar Wings Pegasus XL-Q SW-WQ-0077 (Rotax 462)			27. 6.88	S.R.S.Evans	Chelmsford	5. 1.99P
G-MVCO	Solar Wings Pegasus XL-Q (Rotax 462) SW-TE-0072 & SW-WQ-0078			27. 6.88	C.F.Grainger	Fiskerton, Nottingham	8. 8.91P
G-MVCP	Solar Wings Pegasus XL-Q (Rotax 462) SW-TE-0073 & SW-WQ-0079			27. 6.88	D.Blunt & G.Handyside	Deenethorpe	9.10.96P
G-MVCR	Solar Wings Pegasus XL-Q SW-WQ-0080 (Rotax 462)			27. 6.88	G.D.Isaacs	London Colney	1. 8.99P
G-MVCS	Solar Wings Pegasus XL-Q (Rotax 462) SW-TE-0075 & SW-WQ-0081			27. 6.88	J.J.Sparrow	Sywell	15. 4.99P
G-MVCT	Solar Wings Pegasus XL-Q (Rotax 462) SW-TE-0076 & SW-WQ-0082			27. 6.88	G.J.Lampitt	Pound Green, Buttonoak, Kidderminster	19. 9.99P
G-MVCV	Solar Wings Pegasus XL-Q SW-WQ-0084 (Rotax 462)			27. 6.88	D.J.Taylor & G.G.Ansell	Long Acre Farm, Sandy	29. 3.99P
G-MVCW	CFM Shadow Srs.BD (Rotax 447) 084			28. 6.88	T.Green	Full Sutton	26. 5.99P
G-MVCY	Mainair Gemini/Flash 2A 674-788-6 & W464 (Rotax 503)			14. 7.88	A.M.Smith	Stafford	6. 9.99P
G-MVDA	Mainair Gemini/Flash 2A 676-788-6 & W466 (Rotax 447)			13. 7.88	C.Tweedley	Great Orton	3. 7.99P
G-MVDB	Medway Hybred 44XLR MR005/36 (Rotax 447)			28. 7.88	G.P.Barnes & J.W.Davies	Sawbridgeworth	19.10.99P
G-MVDC	Medway Hybred 44XL MR009/37 (Rotax 447) (Fitted with trike from G-MTNE)			13. 7.88	K.B.Kealy	RAF Wyton	7. 4.98P
G-MVDD	Thruster TST Mk.1 8078-TST-086 (Rotax 503)			12. 7.88	D.J.Love	Witton, Norwich	9.11.99P
G-MVDE	Thruster TST Mk.1 8078-TST-087 (Rotax 503)			12. 7.88	R.H.Davis	Severn Beach, Bristol	20. 8.99P
G-MVDF	Thruster TST Mk.1 8078-TST-088 (Rotax 503)			12. 7.88	J.Walsh & A.R.Sunley	Rayne Hall Farm, Rayne	3.11.99P
G-MVDG	Thruster TST Mk.1 8078-TST-089 (Rotax 503)			12. 7.88	D.G., P.M. & A.B.Smith	Popham	26. 7.99P
G-MVDH	Thruster TST Mk.1 8078-TST-090 (Rotax 503)			12. 7.88	M.L.Roberts	St.Austell	30. 6.99P
G-MVDJ	Medway Hybred 44XLR MR010/38 (Rotax 447)			20. 7.88	W.D.Hutchings	Nottingham	1. 4.99P
G-MVDK	Aerial Arts Chaser S CH.702 (Rotax 377)			5. 8.88	S.Adams	Scraptoft, Leicester	29.11.99P
G-MVDL	Aerial Arts Chaser S CH.701 (Rotax 377)			11. 8.88	J.M.Hucker	Abertillery, Gwent	9. 5.99P
G-MVDN	Aerial Arts Chaser S CH.704 (Rotax 377)			11. 8.88	Oban Divers Ltd	North Connel	11. 2.94P
G-MVDP	Aerial Arts Chaser S CH.706 (Rotax 447)			11. 8.88	M.A.Concannon	Long Marston	13. 9.96P
G-MVDR	Aerial Arts Chaser S CH.708 (Rotax 377)			11. 8.88	J.J.Smith t/a Avon Chasers Group	Long Marston	1. 8.99P
G-MVDT	Mainair Gemini/Flash 2A 670-788-6 & W460 (Rotax 503)			20. 7.88	D.C.Stephens	Coleford, Glos	26. 8.97P

Regn	Type	C/n	P/I	Date	Owner/operator	Probable Base	CA Expy
G-MVDU	Solar Wings Pegasus XL-R SW-WA-1348 (Rotax 447)			13. 7.88	I.K. & B.A.Marshall	Weston Zoyland	12. 2.99P
G-MVDV	Solar Wings Pegasus XL-R SW-WA-1349 (Rotax 447)			13. 7.88	D.A.Preston	Ulverston	24. 8.97P
G-MVDW	Solar Wings Pegasus XL-R SW-WA-1350 (Rotax 447)			13. 7.88	R.P.Brown	Longacre Farm, Sandy	20. 7.97P
G-MVDX	Solar Wings Pegasus XL-R SW-WA-1351 (Rotax 447)			13. 7.88	C.Kett	Weston Zoyland	8. 8.98P
G-MVDY	Solar Wings Pegasus XL-R SW-WA-1352 (Rotax 447)			13. 7.88	C.G.Murphy	Biggin Hill	1. 6.92P
G-MVDZ	Solar Wings Pegasus XL-R SW-WA-1353 (Rotax 447)			12. 7.88	A.K.Pickering	Robertsbridge	17. 5.99P
G-MVEA	Solar Wings Pegasus XL-R (Rotax 447) SW-TB-1367 & SW-WA-1354			20. 7.88	A.J.Jackson	Rufforth	7.12.97P
G-MVEC	Solar Wings Pegasus XL-R (Rotax 447) SW-TB-1369 & SW-WA-1356			20. 7.88	J.A.Jarvis	Bodmin	28. 1.00P
G-MVED	Solar Wings Pegasus XL-R/Se (Rotax 447) SW-TB-1370 & SW-WA-1357			20. 7.88	P.A.Sleightholme	Helmsley	1. 4.99P
G-MVEE	Medway Hybred 44XLR MR004/35 (Rotax 447)			22. 7.88	D.S.L.Evans	Gravesend	18. 4.99P
G-MVEF	Solar Wings Pegasus XL-R SW-WA-1358 (Rotax 462)			19. 7.88	N.J.Stoner	Wombleton	15.11.93P
G-MVEG	Solar Wings Pegasus XL-R (Rotax 462) SW-TE-0080 & SW-WA-1359			19. 7.88	A.W.Leadley	Strabane, NI	15. 5.99P
G-MVEH	Mainair Gemini/Flash 2A 677-788-6 & W468 (Rotax 503)			26. 8.88	D.L.Morris	Dawlish	15. 7.99P
G-MVEI	CFM Shadow Srs.CD (Rotax 503) 085			26. 7.88	T.J.McKean	Castle Douglas	23. 4.99P
G-MVEJ	Mainair Gemini/Flash 2A 678-888-6 & W469 (Rotax 462)			27. 7.88	M.Thornburn & S.Mair	Moffat/Lockerbie	22.11.99P
G-MVEK	Mainair Gemini/Flash 2A 679-888-6 & W470 (Rotax 503)			27. 7.88	J.R.Spinks	Ludlow	20. 9.99P
G-MVEL	Mainair Gemini/Flash 2A 680-888-6 & W471 (Rotax 503)			27. 7.88	M.R.Starling	Overstrand	3.11.99P
G-MVEN	CFM Shadow Srs.CD (Rotax 503) K.047			26. 7.88	J.P.Davis	Thorney Island	6.11.99P
G-MVEO	Mainair Gemini/Flash 2A 682-888-6 & W472 (Rotax 503)			28. 7.88	E.J.Robson	Gorebridge	30. 1.00P
G-MVER	Mainair Gemini/Flash 2A 684-888-6 & W474 (Rotax 503)			28. 7.88	J.R.Davis	Cheltenham	26. 7.99P
G-MVES	Mainair Gemini/Flash 2A 685-888-6 & W475 (Rotax 503)			5. 8.88	R.H.Ferguson & F.W.McLean	East Fortune	13. 3.99P
G-MVET	Mainair Gemini/Flash 2A 686-888-6 & W476 (Rotax 503)			19. 8.88	T.Bailey	Otherton, Cannock	3. 2.99P
G-MVEV	Mainair Gemini/Flash 2A 687-888-6 & W477 (Rotax 503)			5. 8.88	S.M.Ellwood & P.Chapman	Crosland Moor	16.10.98P
G-MVEW	Mainair Gemini/Flash 2A 688-988-6 & W478 (Rotax 503)			16. 9.88	N.A.Dye	Swanton Morley	27. 7.98P
G-MVEX	Solar Wings Pegasus XL-Q SW-WQ-0088 (Rotax 462)			5. 8.88	R.Morelli	Malahide, Ireland	21. 3.99P
G-MVEZ	Solar Wings Pegasus XL-Q (Rotax 462) SW-TE-0084 & SW-WQ-0090			9. 8.88	P.W.Millar	Newnham	13. 6.99P
G-MVFA	Solar Wings Pegasus XL-Q (Rotax 462HP) SW-TE-0085 & SW-WQ-0091			9. 8.88	G.Frogley & P.J.Garrett	Swinford, Rugby	30. 5.99P
G-MVFB	Solar Wings Pegasus XL-Q (Rotax 462) SW-TE-0086 & SW-WQ-0092			9. 8.88	M.O.Bloy	Chatteris	14. 4.99P
G-MVFC	Solar Wings Pegasus XL-Q SW-WQ-0093 (Rotax 462)			9. 8.88	D.R.Joint	Bournemouth	25. 6.95P
G-MVFD	Solar Wings Pegasus XL-Q (Rotax 462) SW-TE-0088 & SW-WQ-0094			9. 8.88	C.D.Humphries	Long Marston	21. 5.99P
G-MVFE	Solar Wings Pegasus XL-Q SW-WQ-0095 (Rotax 462)			9. 8.88	S.J.Weeks	Weston Zoyland	11. 4.98P
G-MVFF	Solar Wings Pegasus XL-Q (Rotax 462) SW-TE-0090 & SW-WQ-0096			9. 8.88	A.Makepeace	Guildford	22.11.99P
G-MVFG	Solar Wings Pegasus XL-Q (Rotax 462) SW-TE-0091 & SW-WQ-0097			9. 8.88	R.F.Cooper	Oakley	5.10.99P
G-MVFH	CFM Shadow Srs.CD 086 (Rotax 447)			9. 8.88	G.R.Read	Mendlesham	8. 1.00P
G-MVFJ	Thruster TST Mk.1 8088-TST-092 (Rotax 503)			11. 8.88	B.E.Renehan t/a Kestrel F/Grp	Popham	4.12.99P
G-MVFK	Thruster TST Mk.1 8088-TST-093 (Rotax 503)			11. 8.88	E.J.Rossouw	Wetherby	21. 6.98P
G-MVFL	Thruster TST Mk.1 8088-TST-094			11. 8.88	G.Hawkins	Bere Regis	14. 3.99P
G-MVFM	Thruster TST Mk.1 8088-TST-095			11. 8.88	W.J.H.Orr	Blandford Forum	20. 6.99P
G-MVFN	Thruster TST Mk.1 8088-TST-096			11. 8.88	B.Wood	Letchworth	22. 7.98P
G-MVFO	Thruster TST Mk.1 8088-TST-097			11. 8.88	A.L.Higgins & D.H.King t/a G-MVFO Grp	Newport Pagnell	17.10.99P

Regn	Type	C/n	P/I	Date	Owner/operator	Probable Base	CA Expy
G-MVFP	Solar Wings Pegasus XL-R (Rotax 447) SW-TB-1371 & SW-WA-1365			9. 8.88	M.F.Tobin	North Coates	27. 7.97P
G-MVFR	Solar Wings Pegasus XL-R (Rotax 447) SW-TB-1372 & SW-WA-1366			9. 8.88	P.Newton	Macclesfield	21.11.99P
G-MVFS	Solar Wings Pegasus XL-R/Se (Rotax 447) SW-TB-1373 & SW-WA-1367			9. 8.88	S.Derwin	Rufforth	3. 5.99P
G-MVFT	Solar Wings Pegasus XL-R SW-WA-1368 (Rotax 447)			9. 8.88	J.E.Halsall	Ashby-de-la-Zouche	24.10.99P
G-MVFV	Solar Wings Pegasus XL-R SW-WA-1370 (Rotax 447)			9. 8.88	R.J.A.Warren & K.Sullivan Peterborough/Corby		12. 2.99P
G-MVFW	Solar Wings Pegasus XL-R SW-WA-1371 (Rotax 447)			9. 8.88	S.F.Chaplin	Whitland, Dyfed	29. 9.98P
G-MVFX	Solar Wings Pegasus XL-R SW-WA-1372 (Rotax 447)			9. 8.88	S.J.Park	Sywell	30. 6.96P
G-MVFY	Solar Wings Pegasus XL-R SW-WA-1373 (Rotax 447)			9. 8.88	D.A.Linsey-Bloom	Long Ashton, Bristol	8. 1.00P
G-MVFZ	Solar Wings Pegasus XL-R (Rotax 447) SW-TB-1380 & SW-WA-1374			9. 8.88	R.K.Johnson	Popham	8. 5.99P
G-MVGA	Aerial Arts Chaser S CH.707 (Rotax 508)			11. 8.88	I.F.Bastin	Liskeard	29. 7.99P
G-MVGB	Medway Hybred 44XLR MRO11/39 (Rotax 447)			1. 9.88	R.Graham	Gravesend	25. 6.99P
G-MVGC	AMF Chevvron 2-32C (Konig SD570) 010			2. 9.88	A.E.Dobson Broadmeadow Farm, Hereford		6. 8.99P
G-MVGD	AMF Chevvron 2-32 (Konig SD570) 011			5. 9.88	Calvert Holdings Ltd Park Farm, Eaton Bray		1. 6.98P
G-MVGE	AMF Chevvron 2-32C (Konig SD570) 012			26. 9.88	J.Lawley	Blandford Forum	19. 1.99P
G-MVGF	Aerial Arts Chaser S CH.720 (Rotax 377)			2. 9.88	R.Nicklin	Otherton, Cannock "The Dingbat"	15. 9.99P
G-MVGG	Aerial Arts Chaser S CH.721 (Rotax 377)			2. 9.88	M.I.Hubbard	Horley	14. 4.99P
G-MVGH	Aerial Arts Chaser S CH.722 (Rotax 447)			2. 9.88	R.W.Cooper	Douglas, IoM	4.10.99P
G-MVGI	Aerial Arts Chaser S CH.723 (Rotax 462)			1. 9.88	J.Bagnall	Congleton	13. 7.97P
G-MVGJ	Aerial Arts Chaser S CH.724 (Rotax 377)			2. 9.88	P.J.McNamee	Rickmansworth	8.12.89P
G-MVGK	Aerial Arts Chaser S CH.726 (Rotax 462)			2. 9.88	P.S.Flynn (Stored 5.97)	Sandtoft	1. 9.99P
G-MVGL	Medway Hybred 44XLR MRO12/40 (Rotax 447)			1. 9.88	S.Tensch	Chelmsford	1. 6.98P
G-MVGM	Mainair Gemini/Flash 2A 691-988-6 & W481 (Rotax 503)			25. 8.88	A.R.Pitcher	Cranbrook, Kent	27. 8.99P
G-MVGN	Solar Wings Pegasus XL-R/Se (Rotax 447) SW-TB-1381 & SW-WA-1377			23. 8.88	W.Timbrell	Martock	11. 2.99P
G-MVGO	Solar Wings Pegasus XL-R (Rotax 447) SW-TB-1382 & SW-WA-1378			23. 8.88	J.B.Peacock Lower Mountpleasant Farm, Wimblington		14. 3.99P
G-MVGP	Solar Wings Pegasus XL-R SW-WA-1379 (Rotax 447)		(EC-) G-MVGP	23. 8.88	J.P.Cox	Kettering	8. 6.98P
G-MVGR	Solar Wings Pegasus XL-R/Se SW-WA-1380 (Rotax 447)			23. 8.88	G.R.Leport	Barnet, Herts	30.12.91P
G-MVGS	Solar Wings Pegasus XL-R (Rotax 447) SW-TB-1385 & SW-WA-1381			23. 8.88	N.P.Greenslade	Churchdown, Glos	31. 5.96P
G-MVGT	Solar Wings Pegasus XL-Q (Rotax 462) SW-TE-0092 & SW-WQ-0099			23. 8.88	R.Saunders	Portland	25. 9.98P
G-MVGU	Solar Wings Pegasus XL-Q SW-WQ-0100 (Rotax 462)			23. 8.88	T.D.Turner	Clench Common	11. 6.99P
G-MVGV	Solar Wings Pegasus XL-Q (Rotax 462) SW-TE-0094 & SW-WQ-0101			23. 8.88	J.L.Richards	Waltham Cross	7. 3.99P
G-MVGW	Solar Wings Pegasus XL-Q SW-WQ-0102 (Rotax 462)			23. 8.88	M.J.L.de Carvalho & V.V.P.Pedro t/a G-MVGW Grp Lagos, Algarve, Portugal		8. 2.92P
G-MVGY	Medway Hybred 44XLR MRO15/41 (Rotax 447)			31. 8.88	G.S.Cridland	Alton	1. 6.98P
G-MVGZ	Ultraflight Lazair IIIE A.338 (Rotax 185)		(ex?)	21.10.88	M.F.Briggs	Yateley	24. 9.98P
G-MVHA	Aerial Arts Chaser S-1000 CH.729 (Mosler MM-CB)			24. 8.88	R.Meredith-Hardy Radwell Lodge, Baldock		9. 7.97P
G-MVHB	Powerchute Raider (Rotax 447) 80105			26. 8.88	A.E.Askew	Melton Mowbray	18. 4.95P
G-MVHC	Powerchute Raider (Rotax 447) 80106			26. 8.88	D.J.Whysall	Ripley, Derby	17.10.99P
G-MVHD	CFM Shadow Srs.CD (Rotax 503) 088			8. 9.88	Susan R Groves Plaistows Field, Hemel Hempstead		1. 4.99P
G-MVHE	Mainair Gemini/Flash 2A 692-988-6 & W482 (Rotax 503)			4.10.88	P.G.Richards	East Fortune	2. 9.99P
G-MVHF	Mainair Gemini/Flash 2A 693-988-6 & W483 (Rotax 503)			4.10.88	P.N.Walker & J.Laurie St.Michaels-on-Wyre		7. 5.99P
G-MVHG	Mainair Gemini/Flash 2A 694-988-6 & W484 (Rotax 503)			14.10.88	M.J.W.Brouse	Hethersett	15. 799P
G-MVHH	Mainair Gemini/Flash 2A 607-1187-5 & W485 (Rotax 503) (Originally Trike No.695 replaced by No.607 ex G-MTSA 1995)			24.10.88	G.Addison	Kinross	29. 5.99P

Regn	Type	C/n	P/I	Date	Owner/operator	Probable Base	CA Expy
G-MVHI	Thruster TST Mk.1 (Rotax 503)	8098-TST-100		26. 9.88	P.D.Gill	Popham	16. 9.99P
G-MVHJ	Thruster TST Mk.1 (Rotax 503)	8098-TST-101		26. 9.88	A.P.Harvey & R.L.Barker	Basildon/Billericay	19. 3.99P
G-MVHK	Thruster TST Mk.1 (Rotax 503)	8098-TST-102		27. 9.88	A.L.Rowland	Davidstow Moor	30. 6.99P
G-MVHL	Thruster TST Mk.1 (Rotax 532)	8098-TST-103		27. 9.88	D.Sweeney & G.R.Thomas	Redlands, Swindon	22. 1.00P
G-MVHM	Whittaker MW-5 Sorcerer (Rotax 447)	PFA/163-11314		8. 9.88	E.M.Morris	Bexhill	4. 2.93P
G-MVHN	Aerial Arts Chaser S (Rotax 377)	CH.728		9. 9.88	M.Stoney	Chigwell	11. 8.99P
G-MVHO	Solar Wings Pegasus XL-Q (Rotax 462HP)	SW-WQ-0104		23. 9.88	S.J.Barkworth	Rufforth	21. 3.99P
G-MVHP	Solar Wings Pegasus XL-Q (Rotax 462)	SW-WQ-0105		23. 9.88	J.B.Gasson	Lower Mountpleasant Farm, Wimblington	28. 6.98P
G-MVHR	Solar Wings Pegasus XL-Q (Rotax 462)	SW-TE-0099 & SW-WQ-0106		23. 9.88	J.M.Hucker	Full Sutton	26. 5.98P
G-MVHS	Solar Wings Pegasus XL-Q (Rotax 462)	SW-WQ-0107		23. 9.88	S.Sebastian	Long Acre Farm, Sandy	19. 3.99P
G-MVHT	Solar Wings Pegasus XL-Q (Rotax 462)	SW-WQ-0108		23. 9.88	A.M.Gould	Bristol	2.10.99P
G-MVHU	Solar Wings Pegasus XL-Q (Rotax 462HP)	SW-TE-0182 & SW-WQ-0109		23. 9.88	A.McDermid	Addlestone, Surrey	11. 7.99P
G-MVHV	Solar Wings Pegasus XL-Q (Rotax 462)	SW-WQ-0110		23. 9.88	K.J.Tomlinson	Mackworth, Derby	1. 3.93P
G-MVHW	Solar Wings Pegasus XL-Q (Rotax 462)	SW-TE-0101 & SW-WQ-0111		23. 9.88	P.E.Vincent	Tamworth	31. 8.99P
G-MVHX	Solar Wings Pegasus XL-Q (Rotax 462HP)	SW-TE-0105 & SW-WQ-0112		23. 9.88	D.F.Randall	Plaistows Field, Hemel Hempstead	27. 3.99P
G-MVHY	Solar Wings Pegasus XL-Q (Rotax 462HP)	SW-TE-0106 & SW-WQ-0113		23. 9.88	R.P.Paine	Mansfield	2. 5.99P
G-MVHZ	Hornet Dual Trainer/Raven (Rotax 462)	HRWA 0076 & MHR-101		26. 9.88	B.G.Colvin	Kings Lynn	10.11.99P
G-MVIA	Solar Wings Pegasus XL-R (Rotax 462)	SW-WA-1375		4.10.88	K.P.Taylor	Benington	16. 2.99P
G-MVIB	Mainair Gemini/Flash 2A (Rotax 503)	700-1088-4 & W490		14.10.88	LSA Systems Ltd	Arclid, Sandbach	30. 4.98P
G-MVIC	Mainair Gemini/Flash 2A (Rotax 503)	699-1188-4 & W489		4.10.88	G.Tomlinson	Eshott	16. 3.99P
G-MVIE	Aerial Arts Chaser S (Rotax 377)	CH.732		14.10.88	T.M.Stiles	Heathfield	6. 6.97P
G-MVIF	Medway Hybred 44XLR (Rotax 447)	MR020/43		4.10.88	J.R.Harrison	Bolsover	14. 8.98P
G-MVIG	CFM Shadow Srs.B (Rotax 447)	K.044		5.10.88	M.P.& P.A.G.Harper (Damaged 1993: stored 8.93)	Priory Farm, Tibenham	20. 1.94P
G-MVIH	Mainair Gemini/Flash 2A (Rotax 503)	697-1088-6 & W487		14.10.88	M.D.Bainbridge	Honiton	7. 4.99P
G-MVIL	Noble Hardman Snowbird Mk.IV (Rotax 532)	SB-014		6. 2.89	G.R.Graham	Carlisle	5.10.99P
G-MVIM	Noble Hardman Snowbird Mk.IV (Rotax 532)	SB-015		6. 2.89	R.H.Whitaker (Stored 6.96)	Wombleton	28. 6.91P
G-MVIN	Noble Hardman Snowbird Mk.IV (Rotax 532)	SB-016		6. 2.89	G. & A.J.Rollin	Willerby, Hull	28. 5.94P
G-MVIO	Noble Hardman Snowbird Mk.IV	SB-017		12. 4.89	D.H.S.Williams	Ely	7. 4.99P
G-MVIP	AMF Chevvron 2-32 (Konig SD570)	008		11. 5.88	C.D.Marsh t/a Chilbolton Chevvron Grp	Chilbolton	21. 2.00P
G-MVIR	Thruster TST Mk.1 (Rotax 503) (C/n plate marked as 8118-TST-104)	8108-TST-104		21.10.88	E.R.Butterfield	Kingsclere, Hannington	18. 6.99P
G-MVIS	Thruster TST Mk.1 (Rotax 503)	8108-TST-105		21.10.88	J.D.Taylor t/a Taylor Project Svs (Damaged mid 1995)	Warrington	21.10.95P
G-MVIU	Thruster TST Mk.1 (Rotax 503)	8108-TST-107		21.10.88	G.J.Chater	Popham	9.11.98P
G-MVIV	Thruster TST Mk.1 (Rotax 503)	8108-TST-108		21.10.88	P.J.Sears	Ivybridge	19. 6.99P
G-MVIW*	Thruster TST Mk.1 (Rotax 532)	8108-TST-109		21.10.88	M.P.Walsh & L.W.Stevens (Cancelled by CAA 23.3.99)	Deenethorpe	7.11.98P
G-MVIX	Mainair Gemini/Flash 2A (Rotax 503)	702-1088-6 & W492		14.10.88	T.D.Grieve (Damaged mid 1996)	Hamilton	18. 4.97P
G-MVIY	Mainair Gemini/Flash 2A (Rotax 503)	701-1088-6 & W491		14.10.88	D.H.Brown	Ince Blundell, Liverpool	8. 5.99P
G-MVIZ	Mainair Gemini/Flash 2A (Rotax 503)	703-1088-6 & W493		14.10.88	W.E.Richards & P.Lockey	Redlands, Swindon	8. 5.99P
G-MVJA	Mainair Gemini/Flash 2A (Rotax 503)	696-988-6 & W486		5.12.88	J.R.Harrison	Wisbech	1. 8.99P
G-MVJB	Mainair Gemini/Flash 2A (Rotax 503)	704-1088-6 & W494		24.10.88	M.R.Starling	Northrepps	29. 7.97P

Regn	Type	C/n	P/I	Date	Owner/operator	Probable Base	CA Expy
G-MVJC	Mainair Gemini/Flash 2A 705-1088-6 & W495 (Rotax 503)			24.10.88	B.Temple	Swanton Morley	8. 7.99P
G-MVJD	Solar Wings Pegasus XL-R (Rotax 462) SW-TE-0109 & SW-WA-1386			24.10.88	D.M.Wood	Enstone	15. 6.98P
G-MVJE	Mainair Gemini/Flash 2A 706-1188-6 & W496 (Rotax 503)			21.10.88	S.J.Whistance	Bromyard	30. 4.95P
G-MVJF	Aerial Arts Chaser S (Rotax 377)	CH.743		21.11.88	G.P.Jones	Stoke-on-Trent	17.10.99P
G-MVJG	Aerial Arts Chaser S (Rotax 377)	CH.749		22.11.88	J.T.Houghton	Andreas, IoM	24. 5.99P
G-MVJH	Aerial Arts Chaser S (Rotax 377)	CH.751		14.11.88	P.N.Crowther-Wilton	Enstone	7. 5.99P
G-MVJI	Aerial Arts Chaser S (Rotax 377)	CH.752		17.11.88	J.P.Kynaston	Luton	13. 4.98P
G-MVJJ	Aerial Arts Chaser S (Rotax 508)	CH.753		14.11.88	W.A.Emmerson	Newcastle	25. 4.99P
G-MVJK	Aerial Arts Chaser S (Rotax 377)	CH.754		14.11.88	T.L.Travis	Stafford	28. 5.98P
G-MVJL	Mainair Gemini/Flash 2A 698-1188-6 & W488 (Rotax 503)			21.10.88	A.R.Trace & V.C.Cowles	Sittles Farm, Alrewas	20. 5.99P
G-MVJM	Microflight Spectrum (Rotax 503) 007			21.10.88	Corbett Farms Ltd	Shobdon	27. 8.96P
G-MVJN	Solar Wings Pegasus XL-Q (Rotax 462) SW-TE-0110 & SW-WQ-0116			26.10.88	J.W.Wall (Stored 6.96)	Enstone	18. 2.96P
G-MVJO	Solar Wings Pegasus XL-Q (Rotax 462)	SW-WQ-0117		26.10.88	J.R.Pearce	Andover	20. 4.99P
G-MVJP	Solar Wings Pegasus XL-Q (Rotax 462)	SW-WQ-0118		26.10.88	W.G.Colyer	Paddock Wood	28. 2.99P
G-MVJR	Solar Wings Pegasus XL-Q (Rotax 462)	SW-WQ-0119		26.10.88	A.D.Woodroffe	Henley-on-Thames	30. 8.97P
G-MVJS	Solar Wings Pegasus XL-Q (Rotax 462)	SW-WQ-0120		26.10.88	S.D.Morley	Rayne Hall Farm, Rayne	13.12.98P
G-MVJT	Solar Wings Pegasus XL-Q (Rotax 462HP) SW-TE-0115 & SW-WQ-0121			26.10.88	R.D.McKellar & M.Howland t/a Juliet Tango Group	Ginge, Wantage	10. 8.98P
G-MVJU	Solar Wings Pegasus XL-Q (Rotax 462) SW-TE-0116 & SW-WQ-0122			26.10.88	G.B.Hutchison	Sandtoft	16. 7.99P
G-MVJV	Solar Wings Pegasus XL-Q (Rotax 462) SW-TE-0117 & SW-WQ-0123			26.10.88	D.C.P.Cardey & G.D.Tannahill	Hereford	12. 4.98P
G-MVJW	Solar Wings Pegasus XL-Q (Rotax 462) SE-TE-0118 & SW-WQ-0124			26.10.88	R.Dainty & D.W.Stamp	Pound Green, Buttonoak, Kidderminster	31. 7.99P
G-MVJX*	Solar Wings Pegasus XL-Q	SW-WQ-0125		26.10.88	Not known (Wing stored 9.97)	Long Marston	
G-MVKB	Medway Hybred 44XLR (Rotax 447)	MR023/45		11.11.88	J.Newby	Sandtoft	15. 6.99P
G-MVKC	Mainair Gemini/Flash 2A 709-1188-6 & W499 (Rotax 503)			16.11.88	J.E.Gattrell	Sittles Farm, Alrewas	14. 4.99P
G-MVKE	Solar Wings Pegasus XL-R (Rotax 447)	SW-WA-1391		14.11.88	M.R.Allan (Stored 6.96)	Wombleton	27. 3.93P
G-MVKF	Solar Wings Pegasus XL-R (Rotax 447)	SW-WA-1392		14.11.88	M.Convine	Woolaston	22. 7.99P
G-MVKG	Solar Wings Pegasus XL-R (Rotax 447) SW-TB-1390 & SW-WA-1393			14.11.88	N.D.Meer	Alrewas	24.10.99P
G-MVKH	Solar Wings Pegasus XL-R (Rotax 447) SW-TB-1391 & SW-WA-1394			14.11.88	K.M.Elson	Roddige, Fradley	29.10.99P
G-MVKJ	Solar Wings Pegasus XL-R (Rotax 447) SW-TB-1393 & SW-WA-1396			14.11.88	G.V.Warner	Finmere	13. 4.99P
G-MVKK	Solar Wings Pegasus XL-R (Rotax 462)	SW-WA-1397		14.11.88	P.G.Sayers	London Colney	22. 3.99P
G-MVKL	Solar Wings Pegasus XL-R (Rotax 462)	SW-WA-1398		14.11.88	J.T.Powell-Tuck	Pontypool	6. 6.99P
G-MVKM	Solar Wings Pegasus XL-R (Rotax 462) SW-TE-0136 & SW-WA-1399			14.11.88	D.T.Evans	Broadmeadow Farm, Hereford	19. 5.99P
G-MVKN	Solar Wings Pegasus XL-Q (Rotax 462) SW-TE-0120 & SW-WQ-0126			14.11.88	T.A.Colman	London NW8	13. 1.99P
G-MVKO	Solar Wings Pegasus XL-Q (Rotax 462HP) SW-TE-0121 & SW-WQ-0127			14.11.88	B.J.Lyford	Swanage	19. 6.99P
G-MVKP	Solar Wings Pegasus XL-Q (Rotax 462) SW-TE-0122 & SW-WQ-0128			14.11.88	J.Urwin	Eshott	16. 8.99P
G-MVKS	Solar Wings Pegasus XL-Q (Rotax 462) SW-TE-0124 & SW-WQ-0130			14.11.88	K.S.Wright (Stored 8.95)	Long Marston	13. 5.94P
G-MVKT	Solar Wings Pegasus XL-Q (Rotax 462)	SW-WQ-0131		14.11.88	M.J.Bell	Enstone	19.10.99P
G-MVKU	Solar Wings Pegasus XL-Q (Rotax 462) SW-TE-0126 & SW-WQ-0132			14.11.88	J.R.F.Shepherd	Wooton	2. 7.99P
G-MVKV	Solar Wings Pegasus XL-Q (Rotax 462)	SW-WQ-0152		14.11.88	J.Howard	Enstone	4. 6.99P
G-MVKW	Solar Wings Pegasus XL-Q (Rotax 462)	SW-WQ-0134		14.11.88	A.T.Scott	London SW17	11. 5.99P

Regn	Type	C/n	P/I	Date	Owner/operator	Probable Base	CA Expy
G-MVKX	Solar Wings Pegasus XL-Q (Rotax 462)	SW-TE-0129 & SW-WQ-0135		14.11.88	G.R.Soper	Popham	21. 3.99P
G-MVKY	Aerial Arts Chaser S (Rotax 377)	CH.755		5.12.88	R.W.Whitehead	Swinford, Rugby	12.12.98P
G-MVKZ	Aerial Arts Chaser S (Rotax 377)	CH.756		5.12.88	N.D.Meer	Tamworth	11. 9.99P
G-MVLA	Aerial Arts Chaser S (Rotax 377)	CH.762		12.12.88	T.M.Toothill Franklyns Field, Chewton Mendip		30. 7.99P
G-MVLB	Aerial Arts Chaser S (Rotax 377)	CH.763		5.12.88	C.R.Read	Didcot	13. 9.97P
G-MVLC	Aerial Arts Chaser S (Rotax 377)	CH.764		22.11.88	B.R.Barnes	Bristol	5. 4.99P
G-MVLD	Aerial Arts Chaser S (Rotax 377)	CH.765		22.11.88	G.F.Atkinson	Rufforth	26. 2.99P
G-MVLE	Aerial Arts Chaser S (Rotax 377)	CH.766		5.12.88	R.G.Hooker	Cramlington	29. 8.99P
G-MVLF	Aerial Arts Chaser S (Rotax 377)	CH.767		11. 1.89	J.R.Moore	Baxby Manor, Husthwaite	25. 6.98P
G-MVLG	Aerial Arts Chaser S (Rotax 377)	CH.768		14.11.88	S.Bradie	Great Orton	25.11.96P
G-MVLH	Aerial Arts Chaser S (Rotax 377)	CH.769		22.11.88	A.W.Cove	Wellingborough	13.11.97P
G-MVLJ	CFM Shadow Srs.CD (Rotax 503)	092		11.11.88	B.Gallacher	East Kilbride	2.12.99P
G-MVLL	Mainair Gemini/Flash 2A (Rotax 503)	708-1188-6 & W498		23.11.88	J.W.Peake	Stafford	29. 9.99P
G-MVLM*	Solar Wings Pegasus Bandit SW-WX-0015			23.11.88	Not known (Trike stored for rebuild 4.96)	Clench Common	
G-MVLP	CFM Shadow Srs.B (Rotax 447)	095		22.11.88	D.Bridgland & D.T.Moran	Reading	24. 5.94P
G-MVLR	Mainair Gemini/Flash 2A (Rotax 503)	713-1288-6 & W503		30.11.88	S.R.Winter	Broxbourne, Herts	18.11.99P
G-MVLS	Aerial Arts Chaser S (Rotax 377)	CH.773		21. 2.89	E.W.P.Van Zeller	Ashford, Kent	30. 1.00P
G-MVLT	Aerial Arts Chaser S (Rotax 377)	CH.774		5.12.88	B.D.Searle	Portsmouth	22. 3.99P
G-MVLU	Aerial Arts Chaser S	CH.775		5.12.88	M.J.Aubrey	Kington, Hereford	11.2.89P*
G-MVLW	Aerial Arts Chaser S (Rotax 377)	CH.778		28.12.88	T.W.Harrold	Redditch	5. 9.99P
G-MVLX	Solar Wings Pegasus XL-Q (Rotax 462)	SW-TE-0133 & SW-WQ-0114		30.11.88	D.O'Keeffe	London N3	27. 5.99P
G-MVLY	Solar Wings Pegasus XL-Q (Rotax 462)	SW-WQ-0142		5.12.88	I.Glover	Nottingham	23. 6.96P
G-MVMA	Solar Wings Pegasus XL-Q (Rotax 462)	SW-TE-0139 & SW-WQ-0144		5.12.88	B.D.Clapp	Weston Zoyland	26. 4.99P
G-MVMB	Solar Wings Pegasus XL-Q (Rotax 462)	SW-WQ-0145		5.12.88	J.C.Sear	Chelmsford	23. 6.93P
G-MVMC	Solar Wings Pegasus XL-Q (Rotax 462HP) SW-TE-0141 & SW-WQ-0146			5.12.88	P.G.Becker	Washingborough, Lincoln	4. 4.99P
G-MVMD	Powerchute Raider (Rotax 447)	80924		15.12.88	A K Webster	Wallingford	13. 7.90P
G-MVME	Thruster TST Mk.1 (Rotax 503)	8128-TST-110		12.12.88	N.A.Bell & G.W.Hockey	Fordingbridge	16. 7.95P
G-MVMG	Thruster TST Mk.1 (Rotax 503)	8128-TST-112		12.12.88	A.S.G.Henry (Damaged mid 1996)	Banbridge, Co.Down	31. 8.97P
G-MVMI	Thruster TST Mk.1 (Rotax 503)	8128-TST-114		12.12.88	J.Norton	Thorney, Newark	9.10.99P
G-MVMK	Medway Hybred 44XLR (Rotax 447)	MR022/46		12.12.88	D.J.Lewis	Damyns Hall, Upminster	5. 2.94P
G-MVML	Aerial Arts Chaser S (Rotax 377)	CH.781		28.12.88	F.D.C.Luddington	Bledsoe, Bedford	16.11.97P
G-MVMM	Aerial Arts Chaser S (Rotax 377)	CH.797		21. 2.89	S.C.Reeve	Slipperlow Farm, Belper	9. 1.00P
G-MVMN	Mainair Gemini/Flash 2A (Rotax 503)	714-1288-6 & W506		18. 1.89	C.D.C.Ashdown	Fairlie, Ayrshire	4. 4.99P
G-MVMO	Mainair Gemini/Flash 2A (Rotax 503)	715-1288-6 & W507		12.12.88	N.Redmond	Sandtoft	20. 9.99P
G-MVMR	Mainair Gemini/Flash 2A (Rotax 503)	717-1288-6 & W509		9. 1.89	P.W.Ramage	Manor Farm, Inskip	20. 9.96P
G-MVMT	Mainair Gemini/Flash 2A (Rotax 503)	718-189-6 & W510		22.12.88	R.F.Sanders Hatherton, Cannock t/a Independent Financial Advisory Service		25. 9.98P
G-MVMU	Mainair Gemini/Flash 2A (Rotax 503)	719-189-6 & W511		22.12.88	M.J.A.New & A.Clift "Icarus" Mill Farm, Hughley, Much Wenlock		12. 5.98P
G-MVMV	Mainair Gemini/Flash 2A (Rotax 503)	720-189-6 & W512		22.12.88	D.Shuttleworth	Otherton, Cannock	27. 5.99P
G-MVMW	Mainair Gemini/Flash 2A (Rotax 503)	710-1188-6 & W500		11.11.88	K.Downes & B.Nock	Wolverhampton	26. 7.99P
G-MVMX	Mainair Gemini/Flash 2A (Rotax 462) (Trike stamped incorrectly as W512)	721-189-6 & W513		23.12.88	A.L.Bentham	Telford	24. 1.98P

Regn	Type	C/n	P/I	Date	Owner/operator	Probable Base	CA Expy
G-MVMY	Mainair Gemini/Flash 2A 722-189-6 & W514 (Rotax 503)			22.12.88	D.J.Higham	Stafford	15. 5.99P
G-MVMZ	Mainair Gemini/Flash 2A 723-189-6 & W515 (Rotax 503)			22.12.88	A.L.Neenan	Otherton, Cannock	29.10.99P
G-MVNA	Powerchute Raider (Rotax 447)	81230		12. 7.89	C.N.Bond	RAF Manston	24. 5.93P
G-MVNB	Powerchute Raider (Rotax 447)	81231		12. 7.89	E.Nicell	Londonderry	23. 3.97P
G-MVNC	Powerchute Raider (Rotax 447)	81232		12. 7.89	W.R.Hanley	Edinburgh	3. 6.99P
G-MVNE	Powerchute Raider (Rotax 447)	90219		12. 7.89	R.Crawley	Hitchin	26.11.93P
G-MVNI	Powerchute Raider (Rotax 447)	90625		12. 7.89	N.J.Staib	Kemble	7. 8.98P
G-MVNK	Powerchute Raider (Rotax 447)	90623		12. 7.89	J.Cunliffe	Stoke-on-Trent	16. 7.95P
G-MVNL	Powerchute Raider (Rotax 447)	90624		12. 7.89	G.R.P.Clarke	Burton-on-Trent	3. 6.93P
G-MVNM	Mainair Gemini/Flash 2A 725-189-6 & W517 (Rotax 503)			6. 1.89	M.Castle & T.Hartwig	Shrewsbury	14. 5.98P
G-MVNN	Aerotech MW-5(K) Sorcerer (Rotax 447) 5K-0003-02 & BMAA/HB/022			28. 3.90	K.N.Dando	Shobdon	12.11.98P
G-MVNO	Aerotech MW-5(K) Sorcerer 5K-0004-02 (Rotax 447)			4. 5.89	R.L.Wadley	London SW19	10. 2.99P
G-MVNP	Aerotech MW-5(K) Sorcerer 5K-0005-02 (Rotax 447)			13. 7.89	R.A.Davis	Leamington Spa	24. 9.96P
G-MVNR	Aerotech MW-5(K) Sorcerer 5K-0006-02 (Rotax 447)			4. 5.89	S.N.F.Warnell	Staines	11. 6.99P
G-MVNS	Aerotech MW-5(K) Sorcerer 5K-0007-02 (Rotax 447)			19. 7.89	R.D.Chiles Shenstone Hall Farm, Shenstone		15. 7.99P
G-MVNT	Aerotech MW-5(K) Sorcerer 5K-0008-02 (Rotax 447)			28. 3.90	P.E.Blyth	Wombleton	23. 4.99P
G-MVNU	Aerotech MW-5(K) Sorcerer 5K-0009-02 (Rotax 447)			4. 5.89	J.C.Rose	Oakley	25. 4.99P
G-MVNW	Mainair Gemini/Flash 2A 726-189-6 & W518 (Rotax 503)			25. 1.89	A.Weatherall	Preston	4. 4.99P
G-MVNX	Mainair Gemini/Flash 2A 727-289-6 & W519 (Rotax 503)			10. 1.89	I.Sidebotham	Barton	16. 9.99P
G-MVNY	Mainair Gemini/Flash 2A 724-189-6 & W516 (Rotax 462)			11. 1.89	M.K.Buckland	Daventry	7. 5.99P
G-MVNZ	Mainair Gemini/Flash 2A 728-289-6 & W520 (Rotax 503)			11. 1.89	B.Crouch	Oxton, Notts	3. 6.99P
G-MVOA	Aerial Arts Chaser S (Rotax 462) CH.780 (Reported as Aerial Arts Alligator)			16. 1.89	A.B.Potts	Eshott	30.10.99P
G-MVOB	Mainair Gemini/Flash 2A 729-289-6 & W521 (Rotax 503)			16. 1.89	B.J.Bader	Taunton	16. 2.99P
G-MVOD	Aerial Arts Chaser/110SX 110SX/653 (Rotax 377)			16. 1.89	M.A.Hodgson	Northallerton	13. 8.98P
G-MVOE	Solar Wings Pegasus XL-R SW-WA-1401 (Rotax 462)			23. 1.89	P.Ray	London N18	29. 6.94P
G-MVOF	Mainair Gemini/Flash 2A 730-289-6 & W522 (Rotax 503)			31. 1.89	C.Pearce	Swanton Morley	24. 8.99P
G-MVOH	CFM Shadow Srs.CD (Rotax 447) K.090			23. 1.89	D.I.Farmer	Paignton	23. 8.99P
G-MVOI	Noble Hardman Snowbird Mk.IV SB-018 (Rotax 532)			6. 2.89	K.W. & C.A.Warn	Newbury/Uxbridge	2. 7.98P
G-MVOJ	Noble Hardman Snowbird Mk.IV SB-019 (Rotax 532)			26. 7.89	T.D.Thwaites t/a The HFC Group	Penrith	28. 3.99P
G-MVOL	Noble Hardman Snowbird Mk.IV SB-021 (Rotax 532)			29. 8.89	E.J.Lewis t/a Swansea Snowbird Fliers	Swansea	8. 5.99P
G-MVON	Mainair Gemini/Flash 2A 731-289-6 & W523 (Rotax 503)			30. 1.89	J.V.Bailey	Leigh, Lancs	15. 8.98P
G-MVOO	AMF Chevvron 2-32C (Konig SD570) 014			10. 1.89	I.R.F.Hammond	Fareham	1. 8.98P
G-MVOP	Aerial Arts Chaser S CH.787 (Rotax 377)			21. 2.89	D.Thorpe	Grantham	28.10.96P
G-MVOR	Mainair Gemini/Flash 2A (Rotax 462) 732-289-6 & W524		(EC-) G-MVOR	6. 2.89	P.T. & R.M.Jenkins	Dunkeswell	17. 8.99P
G-MVOS	Southdown Puma/Raven PJB-02 (EC-44-PM)			6. 2.89	B.Kirkland	Tarn Farm, Cockerham	22. 8.97P
G-MVOT	Thruster TST Mk.1 8029-TST-116 (Rotax 503)			17. 2.89	H.W.Vasey	Davidstow Moor	18. 7.99P
G-MVOU	Thruster TST Mk.1 8029-TST-117 (Rotax 503)			17. 2.89	A.T.Murray	Great Orton	28. 5.98P
G-MVOV	Thruster TST Mk.1 8029-TST-118 (Rotax 503)			17. 2.89	J.N.W.Moss t/a G-MVOV Grp	Templecombe	27. 4.99P
G-MVOW	Thruster TST Mk.1 8029-TST-119 (Rotax 503)			17. 2.89	J.Short & B.J.Merret Ilfracombe/Barnstaple		3.10.98P
G-MVOX	Thruster TST Mk.1 8029-TST-120 (Rotax 503)			17. 2.89	J.E.Davies	Haverfordwest	19. 2.99P
G-MVOY	Thruster TST Mk.1 8029-TST-121 (Rotax 503)			17. 2.89	G.R.Breaden (Damaged mid 1996)	Blackpool	25. 6.97P
G-MVPA	Mainair Gemini/Flash 2A 735-289-7 & W527 (Rotax 503)			29. 3.89	J.E.Milburn	Eshott	30. 8.95P
G-MVPB	Mainair Gemini/Flash 2A 736-389-7 & W528 (Rotax 503)			29. 3.89	J.R.Moore	Darlington	9. 5.99P

Regn	Type	C/n P/I	Date	Owner/operator	Probable Base	CA Expy
G-MVPC	Mainair Gemini/Flash 2A 737-389-7 & W529 (Rotax 503) (Has c/n stamp 740-389-7-W532 - see G-MVPI)		7. 2.89	G.D.Scott	Ince Blundell, Liverpool	26. 5.98P
G-MVPD*	Mainair Gemini/Flash 2A 738-389-7 & W530 (Rotax 503)		7. 2.89	P.Jackson (Cancelled by CAA 14.12.98)	Baxby Manor, Husthwaite	30. 8.97P
G-MVPE	Mainair Gemini/Flash 2A 739-389-7 & W531 (Rotax 503)		7. 2.89	E.A.Wrathall & H.N.Houghton	St.Michaels-on-Wyre	10. 2.00P
G-MVPF	Medway Hybred 44XLR	MR036/52	27. 2.89	M.Sandereson	Purley	14. 8.98P
	(Rotax 447)					
G-MVPG	Medway Hybred 44XLR	MR026/53	15. 2.89	M.A.Jones	Wigan	30.12.98P
	(Rotax 447)					
G-MVPH	Whittaker MW-6S Fatboy Flyer (Rotax 503)	PFA/164-11404	7. 2.89	P.L.Corder & A.Rowson	Emlyns Field, Rhuallt	23. 8.99P
G-MVPI	Mainair Gemini/Flash 2A 740-389-7 & W532 (Rotax 503) (See G-MVPC)		9. 2.89	C.R. & P.Squibbs	Franklyns Field, Chewton Mendip	7. 4.99P
G-MVPJ	Rans S-5 Coyote 88-083 & PFA/193-11470 (Rotax 447)		15. 2.89	D.Harker	Middlesbrough	2. 8.99P
G-MVPK	CFM Shadow Srs.BD (Rotax 447) K.091		15. 2.89	G.Dalton	Davidstow Moor	25. 4.99P
G-MVPL	Medway Hybred 44XLR MR034/50		1. 3.89	J.N.J.Roberts	Long Acre Farm, Sandy	30. 4.98P
G-MVPM	Whittaker MW-6 Merlin PFA/164-11272 (Rotax 503)		21. 2.89	P.R.A. & S.Elliston	Gaerwen, Gwynedd	6. 7.98P
G-MVPN	Whittaker MW-6 Merlin PFA/164-11280 (Rotax 503)		21. 2.89	A.M.Field	Glastonbury	18. 5.93P
G-MVPO	Mainair Gemini/Flash 2A 741-389-7 & W533 (Rotax 503)		3. 3.89	A.H. & C.I.King	Rye	9. 8.99P
G-MVPR	Solar Wings Pegasus XL-Q (Rotax 462) SW-TE-0149 & SW-WQ-0163		14. 3.89	R.S.Swift	Milton Keynes	25. 5.99P
G-MVPS	Solar Wings Pegasus XL-Q SW-WQ-0140 (Rotax 462HP)		14. 3.89	B.R.Chamberlain	London Colney	22. 3.99P
G-MVPU	Solar Wings Pegasus XL-Q (Rotax 462) SW-TE-0150 & SW-WQ-0164		29. 3.89	C.W.Lark	Long Marston	7. 8.99P
G-MVPW	Solar Wings Pegasus XL-R SW-WA-1411 (Rotax 462)		28. 3.89	C.A.Mitchell	Newport, Gwent	24.10.98P
G-MVPX	Solar Wings Pegasus XL-Q SW-WQ-0158 (Rotax 462)		28. 3.89	M.M.P.Evans	Romford	16. 3.99P
G-MVPY	Solar Wings Pegasus XL-Q SW-WQ-0188 (Rotax 462)		28. 3.89	G.H.Dawson	Swavesey, Cambridge	6. 6.99P
G-MVPZ*	Rans S-4 Coyote 88-084 & PFA/193-11494 (Rotax 447) (Damaged Rushmead Farm, South Wraxall, Wilts 17.8.97 & cancelled by CAA 2.3.98)		31. 3.89	G.A.Hagger & D.Murray	Charmy Down, Bath	11. 8.98P
G-MVRA	Mainair Gemini/Flash 2A 743-489-7 & W535 (Rotax 503)		10. 4.89	A.J.Lowe-Jones	Dukinfield	4. 7.99P
G-MVRB	Mainair Gemini/Flash 2A 747-489-7 & W539 (Rotax 503)		29. 3.89	M.J.Burns & P.A.McGivern	Castlewellan	17. 4.99P
G-MVRC	Mainair Gemini/Flash 2A 748-489-7 & W540 (Rotax 503)		29. 3.89	M.O'Connell	Rufforth	7.11.98P
G-MVRD	Mainair Gemini/Flash 2A 749-489-7 & W541 (Rotax 503)		9. 5.89	J.A. & S.E.Robinson	Kendal	24. 7.99P
G-MVRE	CFM Shadow Srs.CD (Rotax 503) K.087		10. 4.89	G.F.Hartfield & D.A.Chamberlain	Hemel Hempstead	22. 5.99P
G-MVRF	Rotec Rally 2B	AIE-01	28. 4.89	A.I.Edwards	Stafford	
G-MVRG	Aerial Arts Chaser S (Rotax 337)	CH.798	14. 4.89	J.P.Kynaston	Luton	31. 8.99P
G-MVRH	Solar Wings Pegasus XL-Q (Rotax 462) SW-TE-0160 & SW-WQ-0177		10. 4.89	K.Farr	Swinford, Rugby	4. 8.99P
G-MVRI	Solar Wings Pegasus XL-Q (Rotax 462) SW-TE-0145 & SW-WQ-0159		10. 4.89	J.E.Morrison & J.D.Fisher	Long Acre Farm, Sandy	19. 9.99P
G-MVRJ	Solar Wings Pegasus XL-Q SW-WQ-0154 (Rotax 462HP)		10. 4.89	D.J.Cook	Eaglescott	18. 8.99P
G-MVRL	Aerial Arts Chaser S (Rotax 447)	CH.801	18. 4.89	G.P.Hodgson	Bolton	30. 4.99P
G-MVRM	Mainair Gemini/Flash 2A 752-489-7 & W545 (Rotax 462)		12. 4.89	G.A.McKay	East Fortune	19. 6.99P
G-MVRN	Rans S-4 Coyote 88-085 & PFA/193-11503 (Rotax 447)		10. 4.89	C.Briggs	Brafferton, York	23. 1.93P
G-MVRO	CFM Shadow Srs.BD (Rotax 447) K.105		3. 4.89	J.R.Fairweather t/a G-MVRO F/Grp	Hougham, Lincs	28.11.99P
G-MVRP	CFM Shadow Srs.CD (Rotax 503) 097		7. 4.89	D.R.G.Whitelaw	Oban	27. 7.99P
G-MVRR	CFM Shadow Srs.CD (Rotax 503) 098		7. 4.89	S.P.Christian & M.Mears	Hougham, Lincs	17. 4.99P
G-MVRT	CFM Shadow Srs.BD (Rotax 447) 104		7. 4.89	S.C.Cornock	Birmingham	13. 7.99P
G-MVRU	Solar Wings Pegasus XL-Q (Rotax 462) SW-TE-0166 & SW-WQ-0183		12. 4.89	P.J.Edwards	Newmarket	9.10.99P
G-MVRV	Powerchute Kestrel (Rotax 503) 90210		28. 4.89	G.M.Fletcher	Chesterfield	3. 2.97P
G-MVRW	Solar Wings Pegasus XL-Q (Rotax 462) SW-TE-0161 & SW-WQ-0178		12. 4.89	W.H.Mills	Lampeter	9. 4.99P
G-MVRX	Solar Wings Pegasus XL-Q SW-WQ-0165 (Rotax 462HP)		12. 4.89	M.Everest	Hailsham	22. 5.99P
G-MVRY	Medway Hybred 44XLR	MR049/56	12. 4.89	K.Dodman	Cambridge	4. 3.99P
	(Rotax 447)					

Regn	Type	C/n	P/I	Date	Owner/operator	Probable Base	CA Expy
G-MVRZ	Medway Hybred 44XLR (Rotax 503)	MR043/57		9. 5.89	I.Oswald	London SE9	2.10.99P
G-MVSB	Solar Wings Pegasus XL-Q (Rotax 462) SW-TE-0184 & SW-WQ-0193			18. 4.89	M.J.Olsen	Middlesbrough	8.10.99P
G-MVSD	Solar Wings Pegasus XL-Q (Rotax 462) SW-TE-0186 & SW-WQ-0195			18. 4.89	J.A.Flock	Kemble	14. 5.99P
G-MVSE	Solar Wings Pegasus XL-Q (Rotax 462) SW-TE-0187 & SW-WQ-0196			18. 4.89	T.R.Grief	Middlesborough	4. 8.99P
G-MVSG	Aerial Arts Chaser S (Rotax 377)	CH.804		24. 4.89	M.Roberts	Melksham	16. 8.99P
G-MVSI	Medway Hybred 44XLR (Rotax 447)	MR040/58		18. 4.89	L.Marson (Stored 1.98)	Long Marston	23. 7.95P
G-MVSJ	Aviasud Mistral (Rotax 532)	072 & BMAA/HB/013		18. 4.89	A.J.Record	Selby	25. 9.99P
G-MVSK	Aerial Arts Chaser S (Rotax 377)	CH.806		27. 4.89	D.E.Morgan	Deenethorpe	8. 1.00P
G-MVSL	Aerial Arts Chaser S (Rotax 377)	CH.807		15. 5.89	J.M.Hucker	Abertillery	29. 8.98P
G-MVSM	Midland Ultralights Sirocco 377GB (Rotax 377)	MU-023		21. 4.89	J.A.Hambleton	Market Drayton	12.10.99P
G-MVSN	Mainair Gemini/Flash 2A 754-589-7 & W547 (Rotax 503)			28. 4.89	P.Shore	South Normanton, Derby	30. 1.99P
G-MVSO	Mainair Gemini/Flash 2A 755-589-7 & W548 (Rotax 503)			27. 4.89	A.T.Cossey	Great Yarmouth	16. 3.99P
G-MVSP	Mainair Gemini/Flash 2A 756-589-7 & W549 (Rotax 503)			27. 4.89	D.R.Buchanan	Pulborough	25. 5.98P
G-MVSR	Medway Hybred 44XLR (Rotax 447)	MR038/59		15. 5.89	G.Tate	Great Orton	25.10.98P
G-MVST	Mainair Gemini/Flash 2A 750-589-7 & W543 (Rotax 462)			12. 6.89	G.B.Mountain	Rufforth	19. 4.99P
G-MVSU	Microflight Spectrum (Rotax 503) 008			4. 5.89	R.Nicklin	Wolverhampton	28. 1.99P
G-MVSV	Mainair Gemini/Flash 2A 757-589-7 & W550 (Rotax 503)			11. 5.89	P.Shelton	St.Michaels-on-Wyre	2. 7.99P
G-MVSW	Solar Wings Pegasus XL-Q (Rotax 462HP) SW-TE-0189 & SW-WQ-0198			17. 5.89	W.A.Holland	Kidderminster	15.11.99P
G-MVSX	Solar Wings Pegasus XL-Q SW-WQ-0199 (Rotax 462)			11. 5.89	A.R.Law	Plymouth	22. 5.99P
G-MVSY	Solar Wings Pegasus XL-Q SW-WQ-0200 (Rotax 462)			11. 5.89	P.L.Cummings & R.J. Turner	Eaglescott	25. 3.99P
G-MVSZ	Solar Wings Pegasus XL-Q SW-WQ-0201 (Rotax 462HP)			11. 5.89	R.Gulliver	Eshott	7. 8.99P
G-MVTA	Solar Wings Pegasus XL-Q SW-WQ-0202 (Rotax 462)			11. 5.89	S.Vestuti	Kidwelly, Dyfed	20. 9.99P
G-MVTC	Mainair Gemini/Flash 2A 759-689-7 & W552 (Rotax 503)			30. 5.89	B.D.Bowen	Pontypool	14. 5.99P
G-MVTD	Whittaker MW-6 Merlin PFA/164-11367 (Rotax 503)			11. 5.89	G.J.Green	Matlock	28. 4.97P
G-MVTE	Whittaker MW-6 Merlin PFA/164-11372 (Rotax 503)			17. 5.89	P.D.Burnett	Gravesend	11. 7.96P
G-MVTF	Aerial Arts Chaser S (Rotax 377)	CH.808		30. 5.89	J.Collyer	St.Leonards-on-Sea	15. 7.92P
G-MVTG	Solar Wings Pegasus XL-Q SW-WQ-0204 (Rotax 462)			25. 5.89	D.L.Hadley	Canterbury	15.11.99P
G-MVTI	Solar Wings Pegasus XL-Q SW-WQ-0206 (Rotax 462)			25. 5.89	D.H.Leech	Saffron Walden	30. 8.99P
G-MVTJ	Solar Wings Pegasus XL-Q (Rotax 462) SW-TE-0197 & SW-WQ-0207			25. 5.89	P.D.Rowe	Taunton	15.11.97P
G-MVTK	Solar Wings Pegasus XL-Q (Rotax 462) SW-TE-0198 & SW-WQ-0208			25. 5.89	S.Davis & S.E.Strangeway	Hungerford/Reading	22.10.99P
G-MVTL	Aerial Arts Chaser S (Rotax 337)	CH.809		13. 6.89	R.J.Grainger	Northampton	20. 3.98P
G-MVTM	Aerial Arts Chaser S (Rotax 447)	CH.810		13. 6.89	C.C.W.Mates	Billericay	8. 8.99P
G-MVUA	Mainair Gemini/Flash 2A 760-689-7 & W553 (Rotax 462)			14. 6.89	P.Alexander & S.Hewitt	St Helens/Wigan	10. 9.98P
G-MVUB	Thruster T.300 (Rotax 532)	089-T300-373		13. 6.89	A.R.Hughes	Yatesbury, Wilts	12.10.97P
G-MVUC	Medway Hybred 44XLR (Rotax 447)	MR046/60		13. 6.89	B.Pounder	Longacre Farm, Sandy	29. 8.95P
G-MVUD	Medway Hybred 44XLR (Rotax 503)	MR037/55		19. 6.89	B.H.Morton	Great Orton	6. 7.99P
G-MVUF	Solar Wings Pegasus XL-Q (Rotax 462) SW-TE-0203 & SW-WQ-0213			13. 6.89	T.Read	Old Sarum	21. 4.99P
G-MVUG	Solar Wings Pegasus XL-Q (Rotax 462) SW-TE-0204 & SW-WQ-0214			13. 6.89	P.Nicholls	Alton	15. 7.99P
G-MVUH	Solar Wings Pegasus XL-Q (Rotax 462) SW-TE-0205 & SW-WQ-0215			13. 6.89	A.Davis	Macclesfield	17. 8.99P

Regn	Type	C/n	P/I	Date	Owner/operator	Probable Base	CA Expy
G-MVUI	Solar Wings Pegasus XL-Q			13. 6.89	J.K.Edgecombe	Coalville	6. 7.99P
	(Rotax 462) SW-TE-0206 & SW-WQ-0216 (Wing incorrectly marked as c/n SW-TE-0216)						
G-MVUJ	Solar Wings Pegasus XL-Q SW-WQ-0217			13. 6.89	I.R.Buckle	Littlemore, Oxon	26. 3.99P
	(Rotax 462)						
G-MVUL	Solar Wings Pegasus XL-Q SW-WQ-0219			13. 6.89	M.Morris t/a G-MVUL Grp	Swansea	24. 5.99P
	(Rotax 462HP)						
G-MVUM	Solar Wings Pegasus XL-Q SW-WQ-0220			13. 6.89	I.M.Munster	Fiskerton, Nottingham	5.11.95P
	(Rotax 462)						
G-MVUN	Solar Wings Pegasus XL-Q SW-WQ-0221			13. 6.89	J.A.Crofts	Carmarthen	19. 5.95P
	(Rotax 462)						
G-MVUO	AMF Chevvron 2-32C (Konig SD570) 015			14. 6.89	D.Beevers	Pocklington	6. 7.99P
G-MVUP	Aviasud Mistral		83-CQ	10. 8.89	D.G.Salt	Ashbourne, Derbyshire	1. 8.99P
	(Rotax 532) 1087-48 & BMAA/HB/003						
G-MVUR	Hornet RS-ZA HRWA-0050 & ZA107			3. 7.89	N.J.Frost	Gloucester	20. 5.96P
	(Rotax 532) (Originally regd as c/n HRWA-0076; HRWA-0050 was G-MVLK)						
G-MVUS	Aerial Arts Chaser S CH.813			3. 7.89	H.Poyzer	Eshott	7. 6.99P
	(Rotax 377)						
G-MVUT	Aerial Arts Chaser S CH.814			4. 7.89	L.L.Perry	Diss	18. 4.99P
	(Rotax 377)						
G-MVUU	Hornet R-ZA HRWB-0061 & ZA110			13. 7.89	M.J.Allen	St.Helens	17. 8.92P
	(Rotax 462)						
G-MVVF	Medway Hybred 44XLR MR054/61			11. 7.89	S.F.Carey	Strood, Kent	2. 8.96P
	(Rotax 447)						
G-MVVG	Medway Hybred 44XLR MR045/62			12. 7.89	C.Smith	Hastings	24. 6.94P
	(Rotax 447)					t/a Avialite Southeast	
G-MVVH	Medway Hybred 44XLR MR047/63			11. 7.89	C.R.Thorne & I.G.Reason		
	(Rotax 447)					Lyndhurst/Salisbury	5. 4.98P
G-MVVI	Medway Hybred 44XLR MR050/64			12. 7.89	C.J.Newell	Leigh, Surrey	5. 6.99P
	(Rotax 447)						
G-MVVJ*	Medway Hybred 44XLR MR056/65			12. 7.89	S.D.Bowie	Beckenham	5. 5.98P
	(Rotax 447)					(Cancelled by CAA 30.9.98)	
G-MVVK	Solar Wings Pegasus XL-R			11. 7.89	A.Williams	Yate, Bristol	15. 5.99P
	(Rotax 447) SW-TB-1414 & SW-WA-1423					(Damaged Belluton Farm, Pensford 6.7.97)	
G-MVVM	Solar Wings Pegasus XL-R			12. 7.89	N.B.Mehew	Oxton, Nottingham	28. 8.99P
	(Rotax 447) SW-TB-1416 & SW-WA-1425						
G-MVVN	Solar Wings Pegasus XL-Q			11. 7.89	J.R.Francis	Long Marston	12.12.99P
	(Rotax 462) SW-TE-0214 & SW-WQ-0226						
G-MVVO	Solar Wings Pegasus XL-Q			11. 7.89	R.B.Milton	London E2	12. 4.98P
	(Rotax 462) SW-TE-0215 & SW-WQ-0227						
G-MVVP	Solar Wings Pegasus XL-Q			11. 7.89	B.J.Fallows	Ammanford	19. 3.98P
	(Rotax 462) SW-TE-0216 & SW-WQ-0228					(Damaged late 1997)	
G-MVVR	Medway Hybred 44XLR MR058/66			20. 7.89	J.McMillan & A.A.Ellman	Purley	9. 9.96P
	(Rotax 503)						
G-MVVT	CFM Shadow Srs.CD			26. 7.89	J.N.Fugl	Uckfield	21. 2.99P
	(Rotax 503) K.101 & PFA/161-11569						
G-MVVU	Aerial Arts Chaser S CH.816			19. 7.89	S.Jackson	Eshott	13. 1.99P
	(Rotax 377)						
G-MVVV	AMF Chevvron 2-32C (Konig SD570) 016		PH-1W9	11. 5.89	P.R.Turton	Ferndown	20.12.99P
			G-MVVV				
G-MVVW	Aerial Arts Chaser S CH.817			26. 7.89	J.B.Allan	Stanford-le-Hope	30. 4.99P
	(Rotax 508)						
G-MVVZ	Powerchute Raider (Rotax 447) 90628			25. 7.89	P.R.Sale	Tamworth	19.12.99P
G-MVWB	Powerchute Raider (Rotax 447) 90630			25. 7.89	R.Featherstone	Salisbury	12. 9.95P
G-MVWD	Powerchute Raider (Rotax 447) 90732		9H-ACH	25. 7.89	H.Rota	St.Andrew, Malta	20. 4.96P
			G-MVWD				
G-MVWF	Powerchute Raider (Rotax 447) 90734			25. 7.89	J.Doyle	Castlebar, Co.Mayo	12. 4.93P
G-MVWH	Powerchute Raider (Rotax 447) 90736			25. 7.89	S.Penn	Bridport	15. 6.99P
G-MVWI	Powerchute Raider (Rotax 447) 90737			25. 7.89	C.Charlton	Shrewsbury	16. 8.96P
G-MVWN	Thruster T300 089-T300-374			26. 7.89	T.B.Reakes t/a Whisky November Group		
	(Rotax 503)					Franklyns Field, Chewton Mendip	13. 3.99P
G-MVWP	Thruster T300 089-T300-376			26. 7.89	D.R.G.Whitelaw & C.D.Taylor		
	(Rotax 503)					t/a Connel F/C	North Connel	2.11.94P
G-MVWR	Thruster T300 089-T300-377			26. 7.89	A.Allan	Muir of Ord	11. 7.99P
	(Rotax 503)						
G-MVWS	Thruster T300 089-T300-378			26. 7.89	R.J.Humphries	Southampton	15. 8.95P
	(Rotax 503)						
G-MVWU*	Medway Hybred 44XLR MR057/68			24. 7.89	T.L.Purves	Carrickfergus	7. 7.98P
	(Rotax 447)					(Cancelled as destroyed 16.9.98)	
G-MVWV	Medway Hybred 44XLR MR060/69 & BMAA/HB/005			24. 7.89	K.Smith	Rainham	17. 1.99P
	(Rotax 447)						
G-MVWW	Aviasud Mistral 532 0389-81			25. 7.89	P.S.Balmer & B.H.D.Minto		
	(Rotax 532)					Tarn Farm, Cockerham	16. 9.99P
G-MVWX	Microflight Spectrum (Rotax 503) 009			24. 7.89	G.S.Taylor	Otherton, Cannock	3.12.99P
						t/a Spectrum Otherton Syndicate	
G-MVWZ	Aviasud Mistral BMAA/HB/008			2. 8.89	B.R.Underwood & P.Bennett		
	(Rotax 532) (Originally regd with c/n 1288-70)					Swinford, Rugby	10. 5.99P
G-MVXA	Whittaker MW-6 Merlin PFA/164-11337			17. 8.89	I.Brewster	Little Gransden	21. 4.99P
	(EC-44-PM)						

Regn	Type	C/n P/I	Date	Owner/operator	Probable Base	CA Expy
G-MVXB	Mainair Gemini/Flash 2A 762-789-7 & W555 (Rotax 462)		3. 8.89	J.M.Davidson	Tewkesbury	19. 6.99P
G-MVXC	Mainair Gemini/Flash 2A 763-889-7 & W556 (Rotax 503)		4. 8.89	D.Wood	Arclid Green, Sandbach	6.12.99P
G-MVXD	Medway Hybred 44XLR MR061/70 (Rotax 447)		3. 8.89	J.J.Littler	Chichester	3. 5.99P
G-MVXE	Medway Hybred 44XLR MR063/71 (Rotax 447)		23. 8.89	A.M.Brittle	Sittles Farm, Alrewas	8. 7.98P
G-MVXF*	Weedhopper JC-31A RAS-01		28. 7.89	R.A.Sammons (Cancelled by CAA 27.3.99)	Looe	
G-MVXG	Aerial Arts Chaser S CH.820 (Rotax 377)		5. 9.89	R.J.Cook	Glasgow	18. 7.97P
G-MVXH	Microflight Spectrum (Rotax 503) 010		2. 8.89	Medway Microlights Ltd	Rochester	29. 1.98P
G-MVXI	Medway Hybred 44XLR MR064/72 (Rotax 447)		9. 8.89	G.R.Roach	Maidstone	10. 9.98P
G-MVXJ	Medway Hybred 44XLR MR065/73 (Rotax 447)		25. 8.89	P.J.Wilks	Edenbridge	26. 9.90P
G-MVXL	Thruster TST Mk.1 8089-TST-122 (Rotax 503)		18. 8.89	K.B.Stokes	Davidstow Moor	28. 8.99P
G-MVXM	Medway Hybred 44XLR MR055/75 (Rotax 503) (Reported as Medway Raven)		17. 8.89	T.Thomson	Hereford	2. 8.97P
G-MVXN	Aviasud Mistral 65 & BMAA/HB/002 (Rotax 532)		18. 8.89	G.A.Davidson	Nelson	25. 8.99P
G-MVXP	Aerial Arts Chaser S CH.822 (Rotax 377)		17. 8.89	E.J.MacPherson	Desborough	29. 5.95P
G-MVXR	Mainair Gemini/Flash 2A 764-889-7 & W557 (Rotax 462)		22. 8.89	J.D.Bayne	East Fortune	25. 6.99P
G-MVXS	Mainair Gemini/Flash 2A 766-889-7 & W559 (Rotax 503)		22. 8.89	J.W.Wood	Tarn Farm, Cockerham	14. 3.98P
G-MVXU*	Aviasud Mistral 93 & BMAA/HB/006		29. 8.89	S.J.Fretwell (Stored 8.95; cancelled by CAA 23.4.98)	Rufforth	
G-MVXV	Aviasud Mistral 92 & BMAA/HB/004 (Rotax 532)		22. 8.89	P.H.Ronfell	Tarn Farm, Cockerham	11.12.98P
G-MVXW	Rans S-4 Coyote 89-098 & PFA/193-11545 (Rotax 447)		22. 8.89	G.Lombardi & R.A.Rawes	Wyton/Bristol	29. 6.99P
G-MVXX	AMF Chevvron 2-32 (Konig SD570) 018		27. 7.89	C.Dews & H.T.Boal	Ely/Bottisham	20. 5.99P
G-MVXZ	Team MiniMax 91 PFA/186-11429 (Arrow GT250R)		4. 9.89	P.Harvey	Dursley, Glos	26. 4.93P
G-MVYB	Solar Wings Pegasus XL-Q (Rotax 462) SW-TE-0223 & SW-WQ-0238		8. 9.89	C.J.Williams	Wisbech	7. 7.97P
G-MVYC	Solar Wings Pegasus XL-Q SW-WQ-0239 (Rotax 462HP)		8. 9.89	I.W.Barlow	Ilkeston	31. 3.99P
G-MVYD	Solar Wings Pegasus XL-Q (Rotax 462) SW-TE-0225 & SW-WQ-0240		8. 9.89	M.Beake	Long Marston	7. 5.99P
G-MVYE	Thruster TST Mk.1 8089-TST-123 (Rotax 503)		13. 9.89	S.J.Spavins	St.Albans	4. 7.96P
G-MVYG	Hornet R-ZA HRWB-0067 & ZA119 (Rotax 462)		22. 9.89	H.Knox	Larbert, Stirling	20. 4.96P
G-MVYH	Hornet R-ZA HRWB-0072 & ZA125 (Rotax 462)		22. 9.89	H.Greef (Damaged early 1997)	Eshott	13. 1.98P
G-MVYI	Hornet R-ZA HRWB-0074 & ZA122 (Rotax 462) (A trike unit with c/n HRWB-0074 amended to HRWB-0081 was noted @ Popham 4.96)		22. 9.89	N.J.Warner	Redditch	21. 9.95P
G-MVYJ	Hornet R-ZA HRWB-0075 & ZA111 (Rotax 462) (Trike unit shows deleted c/n HRWB-0070)		22. 9.89	R.Williamson	Great Orton	26. 3.98P
G-MVYK	Hornet R-ZA HRWB-0076 & ZA117 (Rotax 462)		22. 9.89	P.Asbridge	Rhuallt	22. 7.99P
G-MVYL*	Hornet R-ZA HRWB-0077 & ZA115 (Rotax 462)		22. 9.89	R.Hogarch	Maasmechelen, Belgium	3. 6.91P
G-MVYM	Hornet R-ZA HRWB-0078 & ZA130 (Rotax 462)		22. 9.89	D.M.Smith	Old Sarum	21. 2.95P
G-MVYN	Hornet R-ZA HRWB-0079 & ZA136 (Rotax 462)		22. 9.89	W.M.Studley	Weston Zoyland	15. 3.99P
G-MVYO	Hornet R-ZA HRWB-0080 & ZA134 (Rotax 462)		22. 9.89	R.W.Swain & C.K.Ford	Barnet	15. 6.97P
G-MVYP	Medway Hybred 44XLR MR071/77 (Rotax 447)		19. 9.89	P.D.Burnett	Gravesend	25. 5.98P
G-MVYR	Medway Hybred 44XLR MR068/76 (Rotax 447)		19. 9.89	A.MacDonald	Chorley	28. 8.97P
G-MVYS	Mainair Gemini/Flash 2A 770-989-7 & W563 (Rotax 503)		19. 9.89	J.E.Walewdowski	Crosland Moor	9. 7.99P
G-MVYT	Noble Hardman Snowbird Mk.IV SB-022 (Rotax 532)		26. 9.89	D.T.A.Rees	Haverfordwest	22.12.99P
G-MVYU	Noble Hardman Snowbird Mk.IV SB-023 (Rotax 532)		7.11.89	P.J.McEvoy t/a Phoenix Avn	Romford	26. 6.99P
G-MVYV	Noble Hardman Snowbird Mk.IV SB-024 (Rotax 532)		21. 8.90	D.W.Hayden t/a G-MVYV Group	Swansea	13. 3.99P
G-MVYW	Noble Hardman Snowbird Mk.IV SB-025 (Rotax 532)		22.10.90	T.J.Harrison	Dalton-in-Furness	9. 5.99P

Regn	Type	C/n	P/I	Date	Owner/operator	Probable Base	CA Expy
G-MVYX	Noble Hardman Snowbird Mk.IV (Rotax 532)	SB-026		25.11.91	R.McBlain	Kilkerran	22. 4.99P
G-MVYY	Aerial Arts Chaser S (Rotax 508)	CH.824		26. 9.89	J.M.Spatcher	Guildford	31. 7.98P
G-MVYZ	CFM Shadow Srs.BD (Rotax 447)	121		25. 9.89	Erindale Products Ltd	Langar	17. 7.99P
G-MVZA	Thruster T300 (Rotax 503)	089-T300-379		26. 9.89	C.C.Belcher	Popham	10. 1.99P
G-MVZB	Thruster T300 (Rotax 503)	089-T300-380		26. 9.89	J.F.Kenyon	Holsworthy	24. 6.99P
G-MVZC	Thruster T300 (Rotax 532)	089-T300-381		26. 9.89	R.A.Knight	Popham	18. 7.99P
G-MVZD	Thruster T300 (Rotax 532)	089-T300-382		26. 9.89	T.Pearce t/a G-MVZD Syndicate	Twickenham	5.11.99P
G-MVZE	Thruster T300 (Rotax 532)	089-T300-383		26. 9.89	R.A.Kehoe, R.Nunn & J.H.Smith	Andrewsfield	20. 9.98P
G-MVZG	Thruster T300 (Rotax 532)	089-T300-385		26. 9.89	M.L.Smith (Stored 5.97)	Popham	1. 7.95P
G-MVZI	Thruster T300 (Rotax 503)	089-T300-387		26. 9.89	R.R.R.Whittern	Trowbridge	14. 6.99P
G-MVZJ	Solar Wings Pegasus XL-Q (Rotax 462)	SW-WQ-0241		26. 8.89	M.Price	Shobdon	4. 8.99P
G-MVZK	Quad City Challenger II UK (BMW R.100)	PFA/177-11498		28. 9.89	M.J.Downes	Pool Quay, Breidden	7. 9.97P
G-MVZL	Solar Wings Pegasus XL-Q (Rotax 462)	SW-TE-0227 & SW-WQ-0242		4.10.89	G.J.Pearce	Horsham	22. 3.99P
G-MVZM	Aerial Arts Chaser S (Rotax 377)	CH.825		2.11.89	P.S.Herbert	Godalming	18. 9.99P
G-MVZO	Medway Hybred 44XLR (Rotax 503)	MR072/78		25.10.89	P.Smith	Hinton-in-the-Hedges	24. 9.97P
G-MVZP	Murphy Renegade Spirit UK (Rotax 582)	256 & PFA/188-11630		17.10.89	Full Sutton Flying Centre Ltd	Full Sutton	7. 8.95P
G-MVZR	Avidsud Mistral (Rotax 532)	90 & BMAA/HB/011		9.10.89	D.M.Whitham	Crosland Moor	22. 5.99P
G-MVZS	Mainair Gemini/Flash 2A (Rotax 503)	771-1089-7 & W564		17.10.89	M.Brooke	Rufforth	22. 5.99P
G-MVZT	Solar Wings Pegasus XL-Q (Rotax 462HP)	SW-TE-0228 & SW-WQ-0243		6.10.89	C.J.Meadows	Shepton Mallet	25. 5.99P
G-MVZU	Solar Wings Pegasus XL-Q (Rotax 462)	SW-TE-0229 & SW-WQ-0244		6.10.89	R.D.Proctor	RAF Wittering	8. 6.99P
G-MVZV	Solar Wings Pegasus XL-Q (Rotax 462HP)	SW-TE-0230 & SW-WQ-0245		6.10.89	S.R.Bowsher	Bristol	9. 5.99P
G-MVZW	Hornet R-ZA (Rotax 462)	HRWB-0063 & ZA142		27.10.89	R.W.Swain	Popham	3. 8.97P
G-MVZX	Murphy Renegade Spirit UK (Rotax 582)	PFA/188-11590		18.10.89	G.Holmes	Pickering	30.11.99P
G-MVZY	Aerial Arts Chaser S (Rotax 377)	CH.827		2.11.89	N.W.O'Brien (Damaged mid 1995)	Leicester	7. 4.96P
G-MVZZ	AMF Chevvron 2-32 (Konig SD570)	019		27. 7.89	Lancaster Partners (Holdings) Ltd (B.Lockyear) Ashcroft Farm, Winsford		19. 4.98P

G-MWAA-MWZZ

Regn	Type	C/n	P/I	Date	Owner/operator	Probable Base	CA Expy
G-MWAB	Mainair Gemini/Flash 2A (Rotax 503)	772-1089-7 & W565		24.10.89	C.G.Deeley	Lichfield	12. 4.99P
G-MWAC	Solar Wings Pegasus XL-Q (Rotax 462)	SW-TE-0236 & SW-WQ-0260		25.10.89	P.A.Tabberer	Rhuallt	3. 6.99P
G-MWAD	Solar Wings Pegasus XL-Q (Rotax 462)	SW-WQ-0261		25.10.89	N.Wannop	Sutton Meadows, Ely	20. 1.00P
G-MWAE	CFM Shadow Srs.CD (Rotax 503)	130		24.10.89	D.J.Adams	North Coates	11. 4.99P
G-MWAF	Solar Wings Pegasus XL-R (Rotax 447)	SW-TB-1422 & SW-WA-1441		30.10.89	B.B.Boniface	Knutsford	16. 6.98P
G-MWAG	Solar Wings Pegasus XL-R (Rotax 447)	SW-WA-1442		30.10.89	D.Foster	Leek	12.12.99P
G-MWAH	Hornet RS-ZA (Rotax 532)	HRWB-0052 & ZA137		1.11.89	W.M.Rowley	Slough	1. 8.99P
G-MWAI	Solar Wings Pegasus XL-R (Rotax 462)	SW-WA-1443		1.11.89	T.G.Hunt	Rochester	25. 3.99P
G-MWAJ	Murphy Renegade Spirit UK (BMW R.100)	PFA/188-11438		1.11.89	M.W.Hanley	Truro	25. 2.99P
G-MWAL	Solar Wings Pegasus XL-Q (Rotax 462)	SW-TE-0240 & SW-WQ-0263		2.11.89	A.W.Hill	Bluntisham	29. 8.98P
G-MWAM	Thruster T300 (Rotax 532)	089-T300-388		14.11.89	S.R.Monkcom	Long Marston	30. 9.99P
G-MWAN	Thruster T300 (Rotax 532)	089-T300-389		14.11.89	A.R.Tomlinson	Swanton Morley	13. 9.99P
G-MWAP	Thruster T300 (Rotax 503)	089-T300-391		14.11.89	S.F.Chave & A.G.Spurway	Honiton/Chard	2. 6.99P
G-MWAR	Thruster T300 (Rotax 532)	089-T300-392		14.11.89	T.J.Bax	Dorchester	18. 5.99P
G-MWAS	Thruster T300 (Rotax 532)	089-T300-393		14.11.89	A.W.Vaughan (Damaged mid 1994)	Crieff	2. 6.95P
G-MWAT	Solar Wings Pegasus XL-Q (Rotax 462)	SW-WQ-0265		13.11.89	S.C.Beale	Bristol	4. 4.99P
G-MWAU	Mainair Gemini/Flash 2A (Rotax 582)	773-1189-7 & W566		7.12.89	L.Roberts	Ammanford	5. 5.99P
G-MWAV	Solar Wings Pegasus XL-R (Rotax 447)	SW-WA-1444		13.11.89	A.Caie	Stoke D'Abernon	25. 7.99P
G-MWAW	Whittaker MW-6 Merlin (Rotax 503)	PFA/164-11460		10.11.89	D.J.Flanagan	Hyde	15. 4.99P
G-MWBH	Hornet RS-ZA (Rotax 532)	HRWB-0071 & ZA120		14.11.89	A.F.Neale & C.P.Anderton Tarn Farm, Cockerham		20. 5.98P
G-MWBI	Medway Hybred 44XLR (Rotax 503)	MR073/79		21.11.89	A.J.Wilkinson	Wolverhampton	13. 4.99P
G-MWBJ	Medway Puma Sprint (Rotax 447)	MS003/1		21.11.89	C.C.Strong	Buaes	22.11.98P
G-MWBK	Solar Wings Pegasus XL-Q (Rotax 462)	SW-TE-0248 & SW-WQ-0271		16.11.89	D.G.Benson	Clench Common	4.10.98P
G-MWBL	Solar Wings Pegasus XL-R/Se (Rotax 447)	SW-TB-1424 & SW-WA-1446		16.11.89	C.J.Arthur	Eshott	25. 4.99P
G-MWBM	Hornet R-ZA (Rotax 462)	HRWB-0082 & ZA141		29.11.89	K.D.Shadforth	RAF Dishforth	2. 5.94P
G-MWBN	Hornet R-ZA (Rotax 522) (Trike regd as HRWB-0081 but frame restamped as 0103; wing originally ZA143)	HRWB-0103 & ZA155		21.11.89	J.Batchelor	Benfleet	22. 8.97P
G-MWBO	Rans S-4 Coyote (Rotax 447)	89-097 & PFA/193-11583		29.11.89	D.S.Coutts t/a G-MWBO Group	Linlithgow	26. 4.99P
G-MWBP	Hornet R-ZA (Rotax 462)	HRWB-0083 & ZA144		29.11.89	J.Rossall (Damaged mid 1995)	Poulton-le-Fylde	28. 3.99P
G-MWBR	Hornet RS-ZA (Rotax 462)	HRWB-0084 & ZA145		29.11.89	J.W.Coventry	Davidstow Moor	22. 9.95P
G-MWBS	Hornet R-ZA (Rotax 462)	HRWB-0085 & ZA146		29.11.89	P.D.Jaques	Sandtoft	23. 4.98P
G-MWBU	Hornet R-ZA (Rotax 462)	HRWB-0087 & ZA148		29.11.89	K.C.Wigley	Belper	26.11.96P
G-MWBW	Hornet R-ZA (Rotax 462)	HRWB-0089 & ZA150		29.11.89	P.R.A.Walker	Ringwood	15. 5.99P
G-MWBX	Hornet R-ZA (Rotax 462)	HRWB-0090 & ZA151		29.11.89	J.Johnson	Bootle	22.10.92P
G-MWBY	Hornet R-ZA (Rotax 462)	HRWB-0091 & ZA152		29.11.89	R.M.Hardy	Preston	23. 6.97P
G-MWBZ	Hornet R-ZA (Rotax 462) (Trike unit originally marked as HRWB-0096; then HRWB-0104 - both overstamped)	HRWB-0092 & ZA153		29.11.89	T.M.Gilsenan & G.E.C.Burgess	Stock	15. 6.99P
G-MWCA	Hornet R-ZA (Rotax 462)	HRWB-0093 & ZA154		29.11.89	M.J.Knight	Fareham	3. 4.97P
G-MWCB	Solar Wings Pegasus XL-Q (Rotax 462)	SW-WQ-0273		1.12.89	I.P.Joyce	Long Acre Farm, Sandy	25. 5.99P
G-MWCC	Solar Wings Pegasus XL-R/Se (Rotax 447)	SW-TB-1387 & SW-WA-1447		1.12.89	J.W.Glendenning	Eshott	7. 8.99P
G-MWCE	Mainair Gemini/Flash 2A (Rotax 503)	775-1289-7 & W568		19.12.89	B.A.Tooze	Shobdon	30. 4.98P

Regn	Type	C/n	P/I	Date	Owner/operator	Probable Base	CA Expy
G-MWCF	Solar Wings Pegasus XL-Q SW-WQ-0276 (Rotax 462)			13.12.89	D.V.Lawrence	Stourbridge	14. 8.99P
G-MWCG	Microflight Spectrum (Rotax 503)	011		15.12.89	P.J.Collicutt	Long Marston	23. 8.99P
G-MWCH	Rans S-6-ESD Coyote II (Rotax 503) 0989-067 & PFA/204-11632 (PFA c/n duplicates Kitfox G-BSFY)			15.12.89	W.Lucy & J.Burns	Eshott	10. 8.99P
G-MWCI	Powerchute Kestrel (Rotax 503)	91245		3. 1.90	E.G.Bray	Clacton	31.10.98P
G-MWCJ	Powerchute Kestrel (Rotax 503)	91246		3. 1.90	B.A.Dowland	Peterborough	16.10.97P
G-MWCK	Powerchute Kestrel (Rotax 503)	91247		3. 1.90	M.A.Avossa	Leicester	7.12.97P
G-MWCL	Powerchute Kestrel (Rotax 503)	91248		3. 1.90	G.F.Smith	Milton Keynes	5. 4.99P
G-MWCN	Powerchute Kestrel (Rotax 503)	91250		3. 1.90	H.J.Goddard	Fleet	2.12.99P
G-MWCO	Powerchute Kestrel (Rotax 503)	91251		3. 1.90	T.F.Bakker	Fairford	17. 5.93P
G-MWCP	Powerchute Kestrel (Rotax 503)	91252		3. 1.90	J.L.Thomas	Bridlington	23.10.99P
G-MWCR	Southdown Puma Sprint (EC-44-PM) P.516 & 1121/0070			24. 2.84	S.F.Chave	Honiton	31. 1.99P
G-MWCS	Powerchute Kestrel (Rotax 503)	91253		3. 1.90	B.J.L.Clark t/a Fly High (KSPT)	Maidstone	25.10.98P
G-MWCU	Solar Wings Pegasus XL-R SW-WA-1449 (Rotax 447)			27.12.89	D.A.Bannister	Langtoft, Peterborough	3. 9.99P
G-MWCV	Solar Wings Pegasus XL-Q (Rotax 462HP) SW-TE-0256 & SW-WQ-0278			27.12.89	J.B.Hobbs	Bedford	20. 5.99P
G-MWCW	Mainair Gemini/Flash 2A (Rotax 462) 776-0190-7 & W569			29.12.89	B.C.Jones	St.Michaels-on-Wyre	28. 4.99P
G-MWCX	Medway Hybred 44XLR (Rotax 503)	MR076/80		8. 1.90	P.A.Harris	Petersfield	31. 3.96P
G-MWCY	Medway Hybred 44XLR (Rotax 503)	MR077/81		15. 1.90	J.K.Masters	Chigwell	14. 5.99P
G-MWCZ	Medway Hybred 44XLR (Rotax 503)	MR078/82		10. 1.90	B.W.Bland	London W2	20. 8.97P
G-MWDB	CFM Shadow Srs.CD (Rotax 503)	100		3. 7.89	M.D.Meade	St. Albans	23. 7.99P
G-MWDC	Solar Wings Pegasus XL-R/Se (Rotax 462) SW-TE-0255 & SW-WA-1450			5. 1.90	A.N.Edwards	Great Orton	20. 3.99P
G-MWDD	Solar Wings Pegasus XL-Q SW-WQ-0280 (Rotax 462)			15. 1.90	T.P.Toth	Enstone	28. 8.99P
G-MWDE	Hornet RS-ZA HRWB-0094 & ZA126 (Rotax 532)			10. 1.90	H.G.Reid	Roddige, Fradley	13. 6.98P
G-MWDF*	Hornet RS-ZA HRWB-0095 & ZA155 (Rotax 532)			10. 1.90	Not known (Stored 4.96)	Clench Common	31. 5.92P
G-MWDI	Hornet RS-ZA HRWB-0098 & ZA158 (Rotax 532)			10. 1.90	R.J.Perrin	Tarn Farm, Cockerham	2. 8.99P
G-MWDJ	Mainair Gemini/Flash 2A 777-0190-7 & W570 (Rotax 503)			17. 1.90	M.Gardiner	St.Michaels-on-Wyre	10. 2.99P
G-MWDK	Solar Wings Pegasus XL-Q SW-WQ-0281 (Rotax 462)			17. 1.90	T.Wicks	Devizes	14.10.99P
G-MWDL	Solar Wings Pegasus XL-Q (Rotax 462) SW-TE-0260 & SW-WQ-0282			17. 1.90	J.N.Whelan	Stock	30. 6.99P
G-MWDM	Murphy Renegade Spirit UK (Rotax 582) 319 & PFA/188A-11628 (PFA c/n duplicates Streak Shadow G-BRZZ)			18. 1.90	M.A. & S.J.Wood "Iouna"	RAF Laarbruch	6. 3.99P
G-MWDN	CFM Shadow Srs.CD (Rotax 503)	K.102		17. 1.90	D.J.Abbott	St.Albans	1. 8.98P
G-MWDP	Thruster TST Mk.1 (Rotax 503)	8129-TST-124		30. 1.90	J.Walker	Ballymena	5. 5.95P
G-MWDS	Thruster T300 (Rotax 532)	089-T300-395		30. 1.90	C.M.White	East Fortune	8.11.99P
G-MWDZ	Eipper Quicksilver MXL Sport II (Rotax 503)	022		29. 1.90	R.G.Cook	Newport Pagnell	30. 3.97P
G-MWEE*	Solar Wings Pegasus XL-Q SW-WQ-0147 (Rotax 462)			12.12.88	Not known (Temp unregd 17.11.97)	Sidcup	25. 8.97P
G-MWEF	Solar Wings Pegasus XL-Q (Rotax 462HP) SE-TE-0261 & SW-WQ-0283			30. 1.90	N.R.Williams (Stored 9.97)	Long Marston	21. 7.99P
G-MWEG	Solar Wings Pegasus XL-Q SW-WQ-0284 (Rotax 462)			30. 1.90	R.H.Marshall	Defford	3. 3.95P
G-MWEH	Solar Wings Pegasus XL-Q SW-WQ-0286 (Rotax 462HP)			7. 2.90	B.M.Weinrabe	Borehamwood	8. 8.99P
G-MWEK	Whittaker MW-5 Sorcerer (Rotax 447) PFA/163-11284			20. 2.90	J.T.Francis	Crowthorne, Berks	15.10.99P
G-MWEL	Mainair Gemini/Flash 2A (Rotax 503) 780-0290-7 & W573			13. 2.90	B.L.Benson	Malpas, Cheshire	15. 3.99P
G-MWEN	CFM Shadow Srs.CD (Rotax 503)	K.113		20. 2.90	K.G.D.MacRae	Drummiard Farm, Bonnybank	8. 8.99P
G-MWEO	Whittaker MW-5 Sorcerer (EC-34-PM) PFA/163-11263			21. 2.90	H.A.Evans	Movenis, Co.Londonderry	14. 7.99P
G-MWEP	Rans S-4 Coyote (Rotax 447) 89-096 & PFA/193-11616			21. 2.90	A.P.Walsh	Ludham	12. 8.97P
G-MWER	Solar Wings Pegasus XL-Q (Rotax 462) SW-TE-0265 & SW-WQ-0287			1. 3.90	S.V.Stojanovic	Swansea	14. 4.99P
G-MWES	Rans S-4 Coyote (Rotax 447) 89-099 & PFA/193-11737			1. 2.90	R.W.Sage & I.Fleming	Priory Farm, Tibenham	28. 6.99P
G-MWEU	Hornet RS-ZA HRWB-0100 & ZA160 (Rotax 532)			21. 2.90	Tracy A.Simpson	Graveley	11.11.99P

Regn	Type	C/n	P/I	Date	Owner/operator	Probable Base	CA Expy
G-MWEV	Hornet RS-ZA			21. 2.90	I.D.McCaig Tarn Farm, Cockerham		13. 6.95P
	(Rotax 532) HRWB-0101 & ZA161				(Stolen 4.1995 - Engine No.3799219)		
G-MWEZ	CFM Shadow Srs.CD (Rotax 503) 136			22. 2.90	K.G.Diamond & J.Ball Redhill		10. 7.99P
					t/a WEZ Group Assets		
G-MWFA	Solar Wings Pegasus XL-R SW-WA-1454			27. 2.90	A.W.Edwards	Davidstow Moor	10. 9.97P
	(Rotax 447)						
G-MWFB	CFM Shadow Srs.CD (Rotax 503) K.119			1. 3.90	D.P.Cripps	Sandown	30. 4.99P
G-MWFC	Team Minimax 294 & PFA/186-11648		G-BTXC	1. 3.90	A.E.Sellers & J.H.Cooling	Fenland	3. 4.99P
	(Rotax 447)		G-MWFC				
G-MWFD	Team Minimax 293 & PFA/186-11646			1. 3.90	M.A.Bolshaw Tarn Farm, Cockerham		19. 1.99P
	(Rotax 447) (PFA c/n duplicates Shadow G-GORE)						
G-MWFF	Rans S-4 Coyote 89-106			10. 1.90	F.Colman	East Boldon	
G-MWFG	Powerchute Kestrel (Rotax 503) 00358			20. 3.90	J.O.Jones	Llandeilo	13. 5.98P
G-MWFI	Powerchute Kestrel (Rotax 503) 00360			20. 3.90	S. & G.Millar Dungannon, Co.Tyrone		27.11.99P
G-MWFL	Powerchute Kestrel (Rotax 503) 00363			20. 3.90	J.G.Bolitho	Penzance	17. 8.97P
G-MWFN	Powerchute Kestrel (Rotax 503) 00365			20. 3.90	I.R.Henson	Nottingham	15. 7.93P
G-MWFO*	Solar Wings Pegasus XL-R SW-WA-1455			8. 3.90	Not known (Temp unregd 17.4.97)		
	(Rotax 462)				Lower Mountpleasant Farm, Wimblington		14. 5.97P
G-MWFP	Solar Wings Pegasus XL-R			12. 3.90	G.G.Thorpe	Weston Zoyland	12. 8.95P
	(Rotax 447) SW-TB-1406 & SW-WA-1456						
G-MWFS	Solar Wings Pegasus XL-Q			14. 3.90	A.T.Smith Tarn Farm, Cocherham		3. 6.99P
	(Rotax 462) SW-TE-0267 & SW-WQ-0289						
G-MWFT	MBA Tiger Cub 440 (EC-44-PM) WFT-02			24.11.83	J.R.Ravenhill	Kemble	3. 3.99P
G-MWFU	Quad City Challenger II UK			16. 3.90	M.E.Chamberlain High Barn Farm, Houghton		8. 1.99P
	(Rotax 503) PFA/177-11654						
G-MWFV	Quad City Challenger II UK			16. 3.90	W.D.Gordon	Dumfries	16. 7.98P
	(Rotax 503) PFA/177-11655						
G-MWFW	Rans S-4 Coyote PFA/193-11662			16. 3.90	C.C.B.Soden	Dunkeswell	14. 9.99P
	(Rotax 447)						
G-MWFX	Quad City Challenger II UK			20. 3.90	I.M.Walton	Coventry	5. 6.92P
	CH2-1189-UK-0485 & PFA/177-11706						
G-MWFY	Quad City Challenger II UK			20. 3.90	P.J.Ladd Craysmarsh Farm, Melksham		28. 4.98P
	PFA/177-11668						
G-MWFZ	Quad City Challenger II UK			20. 3.90	A.Slade	Enfield	
	CH2-0190-UK-0506 & PFA/177-11707						
G-MWGA	Rans S-5 Coyote			20. 3.90	D.B.Casley-Smith	East Kirkby	11. 2.99P
	(Rotax 447) 89-092 & PFA/193-11810						
G-MWGC	Medway Hybred 44XLR MR087/85			26. 3.90	I.Nicholls	Gravesend	7. 8.99P
	(Rotax 503)						
G-MWGD	Medway Hybred 44XLR MR088/86			26. 3.90	P.A.Harris	Harlow	3.12.94P
	(Rotax 503)				(Fitted with new wing after original stolen 12.1994)		
G-MWGE*	Medway Hybred 44XLR MR089/87			26. 3.90	A.R.Silvester Horseheath, Haverhill		1. 8.96P
	(Rotax 503)				(Damaged Popham 29.2.96; cancelled by CAA 10.9.98)		
G-MWGF	Murphy Renegade Spirit UK			21. 3.90	J.A.Cuthbertson	Malton	19. 6.98P
	(Rotax 582) 220 & PFA/188-11771						
G-MWGG	Mainair Gemini/Flash 2A 785-0390-7 & W578			26. 3.90	J.R.Phillips	Gosport	26.12.99P
	(Rotax 462)						
G-MWGI	Aerotech MW-5B Sorcerer 5K-0012-02			28. 3.90	B.Barrass	Stamford	3. 9.91P
	(Rotax 447)						
G-MWGJ	Aerotech MW-5(K) Sorcerer 5K-0014-02			6. 9.90	J.Hollis	Redhill	18. 3.99P
	(Rotax 447)						
G-MWGK	Aerotech MW-5(K) Sorcerer 5K-0015-02	(G-MWLV)		19. 9.90	R.M.Thomas	Wombleton	26.11.99P
	(Rotax 447)						
G-MWGL	Solar Wings Pegasus XL-Q SW-WQ-0293			28. 3.90	J.Walker	Corby	3. 6.99P
	(Rotax 462)						
G-MWGM	Solar Wings Pegasus XL-Q W-WQ-0294			28. 3.90	P.J. & L.S.Kirkpatrick	Cambridge	19. 3.99P
	(Rotax 462)						
G-MWGN	Rans S-4 Coyote			26. 3.90	R.H.S.Cattle		
	(Rotax 447) 89-113 & PFA/193-11709				Plaistows Field, Hemel Hempstead		17. 8.98P
G-MWGO	Aerial Arts 110SX/Chaser 110SX/566			28. 3.90	B.Nicolson	Middlesbrough	28. 4.97P
	(Rotax 377)						
G-MWGR	Solar Wings Pegasus XL-Q			6. 4.90	M.D.Hurtubise	Long Marston	19. 6.99P
	(Rotax 462) SW-TE-0272 & SW-WQ-0296						
G-MWGT	Powerchute Kestrel (Rotax 503) 00367			26. 4.90	G.McAleer	Carrickfergus	11. 5.98P
G-MWGU	Powerchute Kestrel (Rotax 503) 00368	(9H-)		26. 4.90	M.Pandolfino	Luqa, Malta	19. 7.91P
		G-MWGU					
G-MWGV	Powerchute Kestrel (Rotax 503) 00369			26. 4.90	E.G.Bray	Clacton	20. 1.00P
G-MWGW	Powerchute Kestrel (Rotax 503) 00370			26. 4.90	S.P.Tomlinson	Leominster	13. 7.97P
G-MWGY	Powerchute Kestrel (Rotax 503) 00372			26. 4.90	C.N.Bond	RAF Manston	12. 8.94P
G-MWGZ	Powerchute Kestrel (Rotax 503) 00373			26. 4.90	L.J.Lynch	Ventnor, IoW	27. 5.97P
G-MWHC	Solar Wings Pegasus XL-Q (Rotax 462)			24. 4.90	P.J.Lowery	Leighton Buzzard	14. 5.99P
	SW-TE-0274 & SW-WQ-0304						
G-MWHD	Microflight Spectrum (Rotax 503) 012			18. 4.90	P.B.& M.A.Howson	Sheffield	18. 7.99P
G-MWHE*	Microflight Spectrum (Rotax 503) 014			18. 4.90	P.J.Taylor Otherton, Cannock		3. 9.97P
					(Cancelled by CAA 11.12.98)		
G-MWHF	Solar Wings Pegasus XL-Q (Rotax 462)			24. 4.90	N.J.Troke & S.Cox Swinford, Rugby		17. 6.99P
	SW-TE-0275 & SW-WQ-0305						
G-MWHG	Solar Wings Pegasus XL-Q			24. 4.90	I.A.Lumley	Great Orton	9. 9.99P
	(Rotax 462) SW-TE-0276 & SW-WQ-0306						

Regn	Type	C/n P/I	Date	Owner/operator	Probable Base	CA Expy
G-MWHH	Team Minimax 326 & PFA/186-11814 (Rotax 447)		23. 4.90	B.F.Crick	Desborough	30. 6.99P
G-MWHI	Mainair Gemini/Flash 784-0390-5 & W577 (Rotax 503)		26. 4.90	I.Vardy & M.A.Noakes	Sandtoft	14. 4.97P
G-MWHJ	Solar Wings Pegasus XL-Q (Rotax 462) SW-TE-0277 & SW-WQ-0307		27. 4.90	A.J.Bacon Botany Bay, Horsford, Norwich		7. 3.98P
G-MWHL	Solar Wings Pegasus XL-Q SW-WQ-0308 (Rotax 462)		1. 5.90	T.G.Jackson	London SW11	13. 5.99P
G-MWHM	Whittaker MW-6S Fatboy Flyer (Rotax 532) PFA/164-11463		18. 5.90	D.W. & M.L.Squire	St.Austell	18.12.99P
G-MWHO	Mainair Gemini/Flash 2A 778-0190-5 & W571 (Rotax 503)		10. 5.90	B.Epps	Arclid Green, Sandbach	28. 1.00P
G-MWHP	Rans S-6-ESD Coyote II (Rotax 532) 1089-093 & PFA/204-11768		8. 5.90	J.F.Bickerstaffe High Barn Farm, Houghton		13. 5.99P
G-MWHR	Mainair Gemini/Flash 2A 787-0590-7 & W580 (Rotax 503)		16. 5.90	P.Jones & B.Brazier	Darwen	16.10.99P
G-MWHS	AMF Chevvron 2-32C (Konig SD570) 021		18. 5.90	Airshare Flying Clubs Ltd	Abington	26. 2.98P
G-MWHT	Solar Wings Pegasus Quasar TC (Rotax 503) SW-TQ-0005 & SW-WQQ-0314		15. 5.90	E.H.Gatehouse & D.M.Walters Pound Green, Buttonoak, Kidderminster		1. 8.98P
G-MWHU	Solar Wings Pegasus Quasar SW-WQQ-0315 (Rotax 503)		15. 5.90	A.F.Frost & S.J.Park	Sywell	16. 9.99P
G-MWHV	Solar Wings Pegasus Quasar SW-WQQ-0316 (Rotax 503)		15. 5.90	I.M.J. & A.J.Mitchell Otherton, Cannock		3. 2.99P
G-MWHW	Solar Wings Pegasus XL-Q SW-WQ-0317 (Rotax 462)		15. 5.90	P.Brown	Newcastle	20. 7.99P
G-MWHX	Solar Wings Pegasus XL-Q (Rotax 462) SW-TE-0280 & SW-WQ-0318		15. 5.90	N.P.Kelly	Navan, Co.Meath	15. 7.99P
G-MWHY	Mainair Gemini/Flash 2A 788-0590-7 & W581 (Rotax 462)		16. 5.90	G.C.Wright (Damaged mid 1997)	Dunkeswell	28.11.97P
G-MWHZ*	Trion J.1 J-001 & BMAA/HB/018		18. 5.90	J.Wibberley	Needham, Harlesdon	
	(Damaged Needham, Norfolk 1990; stored 9.97; cancelled by CAA 9.7.98)					
G-MWIA	Mainair Gemini/Flash 2A 789-0690-7 & W582 (Rotax 503)		21. 5.90	M.Raj	Otherton, Cannock	29. 5.98P
G-MWIB	Aviasud Mistral 094 & BMAA/HB/010 (Rotax 532)		16. 5.90	N.W.Finn-Kelcey Weston Underwood, Olney "Weston Belle"		14. 6.99P
G-MWIC	Whittaker MW-5C Sorcerer PFA/163-11224 (Rotax 447)		20. 2.90	M.A.C.Stephenson "Freyja"	Torquay	23. 8.99P
G-MWID	Solar Wings Pegasus XL-Q (Rotax 462) SW-TE-0281 & SW-WQ-0324		30. 5.90	A.J.Pike Lower Mountpleasant Farm, Wimblington		16. 7.96P
G-MWIE	Solar Wings Pegasus XL-Q (Rotax 462) SW-TE-0282 & SW-WQ-0325		30. 5.90	J.S.Palmer	Wolverhampton	17. 6.99P
G-MWIF	Rans S-6-ESD Coyote II (Rotax 503) 1089-095 & PFA/204-11749		30. 5.90	S.P.Slade & R.Thorpe	Wickwar	16. 2.99P
G-MWIG	Mainair Gemini/Flash 2A 790-0690-7 & W583 (Rotax 462)		4. 6.90	J.Cresswell	Roddige	15. 2.99P
G-MWIH	Mainair Gemini/Flash 2A 791-0690-5 & W584 (Rotax 503)		4. 6.90	G.Collins & L.J.Hill	Rufforth	6. 9.99P
G-MWIK	Medway Hybred 44XLR MR094/89 (Rotax 503)		7. 6.90	J.L.Gowens	Maidstone	27. 8.99P
G-MWIL	Medway Hybred 44XLR MR096/90 (Rotax 447)		8. 6.90	J.W.Savage	St Albans	13. 9.95P
G-MWIM	Solar Wings Pegasus Quasar TC (Rotax 503) SW-TQ-0008 & SW-WQQ-0326		11. 6.90	P.J.Bates & T.S.Smith	Long Marston	6. 8.99P
G-MWIN	Mainair Gemini/Flash 2A 793-0690-7 & W586 (Rotax 462)		12. 6.90	C.D.Lingard	Eshott	13.12.99P
G-MWIO	Rans S-4 Coyote 90-117 & PFA/193-11774 (Rotax 447)		11. 6.90	R.E.Harris	Leicester	27. 1.99P
G-MWIP	Whittaker MW-6 Merlin PFA/164-11360 (Rotax 582)		7. 6.90	D.Beer & B.J.Merrett	Ilfracombe	25. 1.99P
G-MWIR	Solar Wings Pegasus XL-Q (Rotax 462HP) SW-TE-0283 & SW-WQ-0330		8. 6.90	C.E.Dagless	Dereham	13. 8.98P
G-MWIS	Solar Wings Pegasus XL-Q SW-WQ-0331 (Rotax 462HP)		8. 6.90	M.Mazure	Edgware	19. 4.99P
G-MWIT	Solar Wings Pegasus XL-Q (Rotax 462) SW-TE-0285 & SW-WQ-0332		8. 6.90	G.F.Ryland	Oxton, Nottingham	6. 9.99P
G-MWIU	Solar Wings Pegasus Quasar TC (Rotax 503) SW-TQ-0010 & SW-WQQ-0333		8. 6.90	M.E.Howard	Aston Clinton	7. 3.99P
G-MWIV	Mainair Gemini/Flash 792-0690-5 & W585 (Rotax 503)		15. 6.90	A.M.Hemmings	Scunthorpe	22. 9.99P
G-MWIW	Solar Wings Pegasus Quasar (Rotax 503) SW-TQ-0011 & SW-WQQ-0334		18. 6.90	T.Yates	Alfreton	2.10.99P
G-MWIX	Solar Wings Pegasus Quasar TC (Rotax 503) SW-TQ-0012 & SW-WQQ-0335		18. 6.90	T.D.Neal	Shobdon	10.12.99P
G-MWIY	Solar Wings Pegasus Quasar (Rotax 503) SW-TQ-0014 & SW-WQQ-0336		22. 6.90	D.J.Payne	Enstone	26. 1.99P
G-MWIZ	CFM Shadow Srs.CD (Rotax 462) 096		22.11.88	I.E.Bloys	Ely	10. 9.99P
G-MWJD	Solar Wings Pegasus Quasar (Rotax 503) SW-TQ-0016 & SW-WQQ-0339		22. 6.90	A.J.Blackwell	Long Marston	30. 9.99P

Regn	Type	C/n	P/I	Date	Owner/operator	Probable Base	CA Expy
G-MWJF	CFM Shadow Srs.BD (Rotax 447) K.123			26. 6.90	P.J.Kelly	Tarn Farm, Cockerham	15. 7.99P
	(Damaged mid 1996; wings stored 8.97)						
G-MWJG	Solar Wings Pegasus XL-R			26. 6.90	M.J.Piggott	Little Gransden	14. 6.99P
	(Rotax 447) SW-TB-1415 & SW-WA-1472						
G-MWJH	Solar Wings Pegasus Quasar SW-WQQ-0340			29. 6.90	A.W.Reed	Broadmeadow Farm, Hereford	29. 4.98P
	(Rotax 503)						
G-MWJI	Solar Wings Pegasus Quasar SW-WQQ-0341			29. 6.90	R.J.Howell	Bristol	12. 8.97P
	(Rotax 503)						
G-MWJJ	Solar Wings Pegasus Quasar			29. 6.90	E.Daleki	Drayton St.Leonard	11. 9.99P
	(Rotax 503) SW-TQ-0019 & SW-WQQ-0342						
G-MWJK	Solar Wings Pegasus Quasar SW-WQQ-0343			29. 6.90	N.P.Chitty	Didcot	16. 9.99P
	(Rotax 503)						
G-MWJL	AMF Chevvron 2-32 (Konig SD570) 023			16. 7.90	M.Nooshabadi	Co.Meath, Ireland	2. 6.99P
G-MWJM	AMF Chevvron 2-32C (Konig SD570) 024			31. 7.90	Airshare Flying Clubs Ltd	Abington	17. 9.98P
G-MWJN	Solar Wings Pegasus XL-Q			29. 6.90	R.J.Williamson		
	(Rotax 462) SW-TE-0288 & SW-WQ-0344				Lower Mountpleasant Farm, Wimblington		1. 7.97P
G-MWJO	Solar Wings Pegasus XL-Q			29. 6.90	C.Serra	Wareham, Dorset	11.10.99P
	(Rotax 462HP) SW-TE-0289 & SW-WQ-0345						
G-MWJP	Medway Hybred 44XLR MR097/91			29. 6.90	D.W.Beach	Stock	14. 5.99P
	(Rotax 503)						
G-MWJR	Medway Hybred 44XLR MR098/92			28. 6.90	J.Stokes	Tilbury	7. 7.96P
	(Rotax 503)						
G-MWJS	Solar Wings Pegasus Quasar TC SW-WQQ-0349			6. 7.90	C.R.Ashley	Sittles Farm, Alrewas	27. 6.99P
	(Rotax 503)						
G-MWJT	Solar Wings Pegasus Quasar TC			16. 7.90	K.V.Rands-Allen		
	(Rotax 503) SW-TQ-0022 & SW-WQQ-0350				Nether Heyford, Northampton		22. 1.00P
G-MWJU	Solar Wings Pegasus Quasar			6. 7.90	S.Baker	Alrewas	21.12.98P
	(Rotax 503) SW-TQ-0023 & SW-WQQ-0351						
G-MWJV	Solar Wings Pegasus Quasar			6. 7.90	J.S.Seddon-Harvey		
	(Rotax 503) SW-TQ-0024 & SW-WQQ-0352				Broadmeadow Farm, Hereford		4. 5.99P
G-MWJW	Whittaker MW-5 Sorcerer			11. 5.90	S.Badby	Banbury	10. 8.98P
	(EC-44-PM) JDW-02 & PFA/163-11186						
G-MWJX	Medway Puma Sprint			17. 7.90	A.Tristram		
	(Rotax 447) MS009/3				Pound Green, Buttonoak, Kidderminster		14. 9.99P
G-MWJY	Mainair Gemini/Flash 2A			16. 7.90	R.E.Parker	Harlow	11. 5.97P
	(Rotax 503) 797-0790-7 & W590						
G-MWJZ	CFM Shadow Srs.CD (Rotax 503) K.132			19. 7.90	D.Mahajan	West Wickham, Kent	23. 7.99P
G-MWKA	Murphy Renegade Spirit UK PFA/188-11864			26. 7.90	C.E.Neill t/a Downlands F/Grp	Deanland	1. 4.99P
	(Rotax 582) (Incorporates project PFA/188-11690)				"Spirit of Lewes"		
G-MWKE	Hornet RS-ZA HRWB-0108 & ZA167			30. 7.90	D.R.Stapleton	Blackpool	22.10.99P
	(Rotax 532) (Trike c/n overstamped on HRWB-0107)						
G-MWKF*	Hornet R-ZA HRWB-0109 & ZA168			30. 7.90	Not known	Clench Common	9.3.91P*
	(Rotax 532) (Trike unit originally stamped as HRWB-0099)				(Trike stored 5.97)		
G-MWKO	Solar Wings Pegasus XL-Q SW-WQ-0357			31. 7.90	R.G.Hearsey	Rye	16.10.99P
	(Rotax 462)						
G-MWKP	Solar Wings Pegasus XL-Q			31. 7.90	P.G.Ford	Sutton Meadows, Ely	19. 5.99P
	(Rotax 462HP) SW-TE-0291 & SW-WQ-0358						
G-MWKW	Microflight Spectrum (Rotax 503) 015			3. 8.90	P.B. & M.Robinson	Sutton Meadows, Ely	19.12.98P
G-MWKX	Microflight Spectrum (Rotax 503) 016			3. 8.90	C.R.Ions	Eshott	27. 7.98P
G-MWKY	Solar Wings Pegasus XL-Q			3. 8.90	C.R.Wright	Roddige, Fradley	17. 3.99P
	(Rotax 462HP) SW-TE-0292 & SW-WQ-0362						
G-MWKZ	Solar Wings Pegasus XL-Q			3. 8.90	P.L.Cummings	Long Marston	16.12.99P
	(Rotax 462HP) SW-TE-0293 & SW-WQ-0363						
G-MWLA	Rans S-4 Coyote 89-114 & PFA/193-11787			3. 8.90	B.R.Hunter	Cumbernauld	19. 5.99P
	(Rotax 447)						
G-MWLB	Medway Hybred 44XLR MR104/93			15. 8.90	M.W.Harmer	Welwyn Garden City	21. 9.99P
	(Rotax 503)						
G-MWLC*	Medway Hybred 44XLR MR086/94			15. 8.90	G.J.Slater		20.2.91P*
	(Rebuilt as G-MWRM 1991; cancelled by CAA 3.12.98)						
G-MWLD	CFM Shadow Srs.CD (Rotax 503) 106			9. 5.89	T.J. & M.D.Palmer	Kilmarnock	20.10.99P
G-MWLE	Solar Wings Pegasus XL-R			9. 8.90	D.Stevenson	London Colney	26. 2.99P
	(Rotax 447) SW-TB-1425 & SW-WA-1474						
G-MWLF	Solar Wings Pegasus XL-R SW-WA-1475			9. 8.90	G.Rainey	Weston Zoyland	31. 3.96P
	(Rotax 447)						
G-MWLG	Solar Wings Pegasus XL-R			9. 8.90	D.P.Green	Weston Zoyland	2. 6.99P
	(Rotax 447) SW-TB-1427 & SW-WA-1476						
G-MWLH	Solar Wings Pegasus Quasar			9. 8.90	R.A.Duncan	Drummiard Farm, Bonnybank	15. 6.99P
	(Rotax 503) SW-WQQ-0364						
G-MWLI	Solar Wings Pegasus XL-Q	G-65-8		9. 8.90	I.A.MacAdam	Bedford	31. 7.96P
	(Rotax 447) SW-TQ-0031 & SW-WQQ-0365	G-MWLI			(Damaged mid 1996)		
G-MWLJ	Solar Wings Pegasus Quasar			9. 8.90	C.G.Rouse	Chandlers Ford	18. 9.99P
	(Rotax 503) SW-WQQ-0366						
G-MWLK	Solar Wings Pegasus Quasar TC			9. 8.90	R.P.Wilkinson	Charmy Down, Bath	19. 4.99P
	(Rotax 503) SW-TQ-0033 & SW-WQQ-0367						
G-MWLL	Solar Wings Pegasus XL-Q			16. 8.90	Hereford Airsports Ltd (Stored 9.96)		
	(Rotax 462) SW-TE-0287 & SW-WQ-0338				Newhouse Farm, Hardwicke, Hereford		28. 8.99P
G-MWLM	Solar Wings Pegasus XL-Q SW-WQ-0322			17. 8.90	R.J.Hawkins	Kettering	28.11.99P
	(Rotax 462)						

Regn	Type	C/n P/I	Date	Owner/operator	Probable Base	CA Expy
G-MWLN	Whittaker MW-6S Fatboy Flyer (Rotax 503) PFA/164-11844		16. 8.90	S.J.Field "Red Lips"	Bridgwater	5. 6.92P
G-MWLO	Whittaker MW-6 Merlin PFA/164-11373 (Rotax 503)		21. 8.90	S.P.Ganecki & L.Prew	Hatherton, Cannock	2.11.98P
G-MWLP	Mainair Gemini/Flash (Rotax 503) 801-0990-5 & W594		24. 8.90	J.S.Potts	Kilmarnock	24. 8.98P
G-MWLS	Medway Hybred 44XLR MR081/95 (Rotax 503)		29. 8.90	J.Rochead	Oban	29. 5.99P
G-MWLT	Mainair Gemini/Flash 2A (Rotax 503) 804-0990-7 & W597		31. 8.90	K.Roberts & J.E.Mann	Caernarfon/Wigan	15. 8.98P
G-MWLU	Solar Wings Pegasus XL-R/Se (Rotax 462) SW-TE-0304 & SW-WA-1478		6. 9.90	T.P.G.Ward (Stored 9.97)	Great Orton	14.10.91P
G-MWLW	Team Minimax PFA/186-11717 (Rotax 377)		14. 9.90	S.Hobday (Damaged Deanland 4.6.93)	Salisbury	11. 6.93P
G-MWLX	Mainair Gemini/Flash 2A 805-0990-7 & W598 (Rotax 503)		5.10.90	G.Good & E.J.Robson	East Fortune	27. 1.00P
G-MWLY	Rans S-4 Coyote PFA/193-11691 (Rotax 447)		20. 9.90	A.Bulling	Fraserburgh	20. 7.95P
G-MWLZ	Rans S-4 Coyote 90-116 & PFA/193-11887 (Rotax 447)		8.10.90	I.W.Critchley	Stafford	24. 2.99P
G-MWMA	Powerchute Kestrel (Rotax 503) 00398		7.11.90	G.Webb	Selby	24.11.96P
G-MWMB	Powerchute Kestrel (Rotax 503) 00399		7.11.90	D.J.Whysall	Ripley, Derby	17.10.99P
G-MWMC	Powerchute Kestrel (Rotax 503) 00400		7.11.90	K.James	Kemble	19. 7.98P
G-MWMD	Powerchute Kestrel 00401		7.11.90	D.J.Jackson	Melton Constable	20.11.91P
G-MWMG	Powerchute Kestrel (Rotax 503) 00404		7.11.90	M.D.Walton	Tregaron	26.10.99P
G-MWMH	Powerchute Kestrel (Rotax 503) 00405		7.11.90	J.D.Smith & A.C.Turnbull	Ferryhill	17.10.99P
G-MWMI	Solar Wings Pegasus Quasar (Rotax 503) SW-TQ-0043 & SW-WQQ-0383		21. 9.90	P.Richardson	Newark	30. 3.99P
G-MWMJ	Solar Wings Pegasus Quasar (Rotax 503) SW-TQ-0044 & SW-WQQ-0384		21. 9.90	D.Webb	Kemble	13. 2.99P
G-MWMK	Solar Wings Pegasus Quasar SW-WQQ-0385 (Rotax 503)		21. 9.90	R.J.Donkin	Devizes	23. 2.99P
G-MWML	Solar Wings Pegasus Quasar SW-TQ-0046 & SW-WQQ-0386		21. 9.90	A.Rokker	Cambridge	31. 7.99P
G-MWMM	Mainair Gemini/Flash 2A 800-0890-7 & W593 (Rotax 462)		24. 8.90	R.H.Church	Croft Farm, Defford	12. 4.99P
G-MWMN	Solar Wings Pegasus XL-Q (Rotax 462HP) SW-TE-0297 & SW-WQ-0387		2.10.90	N.A.Rathbone & P.A.Arnold	Swinford, Rugby	9. 1.00P
G-MWMO	Solar Wings Pegasus XL-Q (Rotax 462) SW-TE-0298 & SW-WQ-0388		2.10.90	B.J.Kitson	Great Stukeley	21. 5.99P
G-MWMP	Solar Wings Pegasus XL-Q SW-WQ-0389 (Rotax 462HP)		2.10.90	J.A.Way	Ramsgate	22. 7.99P
G-MWMR	Solar Wings Pegasus XL-R SW-WA-1483 (Rotax 462)		2.10.90	J.A.Crofts	Meidrim, Carmarthen	14.12.98P
G-MWMS	Mainair Gemini/Flash 807-1090-5 & W600 (Rotax 503)		3.10.90	C.K.Richardson	East Fortune	18.12.99P
G-MWMT	Mainair Gemini/Flash 2A 808-1090-7 & W601 (Rotax 503)		3.10.90	B.Berrington & D.Foxley	Crosby, Liverpool	13. 4.99P
G-MWMU	CFM Shadow Srs.CD (Rotax 503) 150		2.10.90	D.Reeve	Lower Mountpleasant Farm, Wimblington	30.10.96P
G-MWMV	Solar Wings Pegasus XL-R (Rotax 462) SW-TE-0307 & SW-WA-1484		5.10.90	G.M.Stevens	Sutton Meadows, Ely	26. 5.99P
G-MWMW	Murphy Renegade Spirit UK (Rotax 532) 254 & PFA/188-11544		21. 8.89	H.Feeney "Spirit of Cornwall"	Long Marston	15.12.99P
G-MWMX	Mainair Gemini/Flash 2A 810-1090-7 & W603 (Rotax 462)		17.10.90	G.T.Snoddon	Dundonald, Belfast	19.11.99P
G-MWMY	Mainair Gemini/Flash 2A 809-1090-7 & W602 (Rotax 462)		17.10.90	C.W.Lowe	Grove Farm, Raveningham	5. 5.97P
G-MWMZ	Solar Wings Pegasus XL-Q SW-WQ-0393 (Rotax 462)		8.10.90	P.C.Ockwell	Swindon	6. 8.99P
G-MWNA	Solar Wings Pegasus XL-Q SW-WQ-0394 (Rotax 462)		8.10.90	J.M.Kirtley	Eshott	14. 9.99P
G-MWNB	Solar Wings Pegasus XL-Q (Rotax 462) SW-TE-0303 & SW-WQ-0395		8.10.90	P.F.J.Rogers	London SW17	26. 4.99P
G-MWNC	Solar Wings Pegasus XL-Q SW-WQ-0396 (Rotax 462HP)		8.10.90	G.Evans	Chatteris	28. 3.99P
G-MWND	Tiger Cub RL5A Sherwood Ranger (Rotax 532) 001 & PFA/237-12229		9.10.90	Tiger Cub Developments Ltd	Doncaster	1. 5.96P
G-MWNE	Mainair Gemini/Flash 2A 803-1090-7 & W596 (Rotax 503)		17.10.90	T.C.Edwards	Ware	21. 3.99P
G-MWNF	Murphy Renegade Spirit UK PFA/188-11853 (Rotax 582)		15.10.90	D.J.White	Matlock	31. 8.99P
G-MWNG	Solar Wings Pegasus XL-Q (Rotax 462HP) SW-TE-0305 & SW-WQ-0399		17.10.90	M.A.McClelland t/a McClelland Aviation	Old Sarum	21. 6.99P
G-MWNK	Solar Wings Pegasus Quasar TC (Rotax 503) SW-WQQ-0403		1.11.90	G.S.Lyon	RAF Wyton	1. 8.99P
G-MWNL	Solar Wings Pegasus Quasar (Rotax 503) SW-TQ-0055 & SW-WQQ-0404		1.11.90	Creation Company Films Ltd	Popham	9. 8.98P

Regn	Type	C/n	P/I	Date	Owner/operator	Probable Base	CA Expy
G-MWNO	AMF Chevvron 2-32 (Konig SD570)	025		12.11.90	I.K.Hogg	Kirkbride	30. 4.99P
G-MWNP	AMF Chevvron 2-32C (Konig SD570)	026		31.10.90	D.G.Titterton & D.A.Norwood "Gwenric-J"	Ashcroft Farm, Winsford	13. 7.99P
G-MWNR	Murphy Renegade Spirit UK PFA/188-11926 (Rotax 582)			12.11.90	J.J.Lancaster t/a RJR F/Grp	Cublington	11. 7.99P
G-MWNS	Mainair Gemini/Flash 2A 811-1190-7 & W604 (Rotax 503)			6.11.90	S.Woolmington	Colchester	12. 6.99P
G-MWNT	Mainair Gemini/Flash 2A 812-1190-7 & W605 (Rotax 582)			6.11.90	P. & V.C.Reynolds	East Fortune	4. 6.99P
G-MWNU	Mainair Gemini/Flash 2A 813-1190-5 & W606 (Rotax 503)			6.11.90	C.C.Muir	Bristol	27. 3.99P
G-MWNV	Powerchute Kestrel	00406		12.11.90	K.N.Byrne	Isle of Colonsay	13. 3.92P
G-MWNX	Powerchute Kestrel (Rotax 503)	00408		12.11.90	J.H.Greenroyd	Hebden Bridge	1. 8.99P
G-MWNY	Powerchute Kestrel (Rotax 503)	00409		12.11.90	P.T.T.Williams	Farnham	18. 6.97P
G-MWNZ	Powerchute Kestrel	00410		12.11.90	M.J.Boase	Leeds	10. 2.93P
G-MWOC	Powerchute Kestrel	00413		12.11.90	G.Lorking (Damaged late 1994)	Sunnyhill, Derby	24. 4.95P
G-MWOD	Powerchute Kestrel (Rotax 503)	00414		12.11.90	T.Morgan	Kidderminster	29. 4.98P
G-MWOE	Powerchute Kestrel	00415		12.11.90	E.G.Woolnough & P.K.Reason	Halesworth	20. 1.00P
G-MWOF*	Microflight Spectrum (Rotax 503)	018		13.11.90	Not known (Temp unregd 4.6.96; on rebuild 6.97)	Shobdon	29. 5.96P
G-MWOH	Solar Wings Pegasus XL-R/Se SW-WA-1485 (Rotax 447)			28.11.90	J.Walter	Great Orton	27. 3.99P
G-MWOI	Solar Wings Pegasus XL-R (Rotax 447) SW-TB-1430 & SW-WA-1486			29.11.90	P.Maller	Cheltenham	6. 5.99P
G-MWOJ	Mainair Gemini/Flash 2A 814-1290-7 & W608 (Rotax 503)			6.12.90	J.K.Nicol	Southport	8. 8.99P
G-MWOK	Mainair Gemini/Flash 2A 815-1290-7 & W609 (Rotax 462)			6.12.90	J.C.Miller	East Fortune	5. 7.99P
G-MWOL	Mainair Gemini/Flash 2A (Rotax 503) 816-1290-7 & W610			6.12.90	I.V.Watters	Swansea	31. 1.94P
G-MWOM	Solar Wings Pegasus Quasar TC (Rotax 503) SW-WQQ-0412			1. 3.91	T.J.Williams	Tuam, Co.Galway	17. 4.95P
G-MWON	CFM Shadow Srs.CD (Rotax 503) K.128			18.12.90	C.J.Ball	Cheltenham	14. 7.99P
G-MWOO	Murphy Renegade Spirit UK (Rotax 582) 318 & PFA/188-11811			14. 9.90	R.C.Wood	Chatteris	12. 7.99P
G-MWOP	Solar Wings Pegasus Quasar TC (Rotax 503) SW-TQC-0059 & SW-WQQ-0410			31.12.90	A.Baynes	Sywell	2.10.99P
G-MWOR	Solar Wings Pegasus XL-Q SW-WQ-0411 (Rotax 462)			21.12.90	I.D.Chantler	Long Acre Farm, Sandy	29. 7.98P
G-MWOV	Whittaker MW-6 Merlin PFA/164-11301 (Rotax 503)			9. 1.91	S.J.Field	Bridgwater	24.10.95P
G-MWOW	CFM Shadow Srs.B (Rotax 447)	007	83-AG	16. 9.85	Global Avn Projects Ltd (Stored Davidstow Moor 10.95)	Torrington	2. 7.91P
G-MWOX	Solar Wings Pegasus XL-Q SW-WQ-0413 (Rotax 462)			7. 1.91	G.Milo	Popham	16. 6.99P
G-MWOY	Solar Wings Pegasus XL-Q (Rotax 462HP) SW-TE-0310 & SW-WQ-0414			7. 1.91	G.S.Beeby	Sutton Meadows, Ely	17. 4.99P
G-MWPA	Mainair Gemini/Flash 2A (Rotax 462) 817-0191-7 & W611			9. 1.91	T.Beckham	Newcastle	20. 4.99P
G-MWPB	Mainair Gemini/Flash 2A (Rotax 503) 823-0191-7 & W617			3. 1.91	J.Fenton	St.Michaels-on-Wyre	4. 6.99P
G-MWPC	Mainair Gemini/Flash 2A (Rotax 503) 826-0191-7 & W620			3. 1.91	I.Shaw	Arclid Green, Sandbach	25. 5.99P
G-MWPD	Mainair Gemini/Flash 2A (Rotax 503) 824-0191-7 & W618			9. 1.91	G.A.McKay	Linlithgow	25. 5.96P
G-MWPE	Solar Wings Pegasus XL-Q (Rotax 462HP) SW-TE-0096 & SW-WQ-0416		(Trike ex G-MVGX)	9. 1.91	E.C.R.Hudson	Upper Stow, Weedon	19. 4.99P
G-MWPF	Mainair Gemini/Flash 2A (Rotax 503) 825-0191-7 & W619			11. 1.91	S.R.Simms	Roddige, Fradley	2. 7.99P
G-MWPG	Microflight Spectrum (Rotax 503)	019		9. 1.91	P.F.Craggs	Eshott	11. 7.98P
G-MWPH	Microflight Spectrum (Rotax 503)	020		9. 1.91	S.B.Mance & K.R.Wootton	Wombleton	8. 6.99P
G-MWPI	Microflight Spectrum TI (Rotax 503)	021		9. 1.91	B.W.Peacock (Damaged early 1997)	Peterborough	28. 2.98P
G-MWPJ	Solar Wings Pegasus XL-Q (Rotax 462) SW-TE-0312 & SW-WQ-0418			17. 1.91	D.A. & M.J.Slater	Carshalton, Surrey	30. 4.99P
G-MWPK	Solar Wings Pegasus XL-Q (Rotax 462) SW-TE-0313 & SW-WQ-0419			17. 1.91	G.D.Peplow	Pound Green, Buttonoak, Kidderminster	5. 9.97P
G-MWPN	CFM Shadow Srs.CD (Rotax 503) K.147			22. 1.91	W.R.H.Thomas	Swansea	11. 6.99P
G-MWPO	Mainair Gemini/Flash 2A (Rotax 503) 827-0191-7 & W621			29. 1.91	J.H.Brooks	Oxton, Nottingham	20. 5.98P
G-MWPP	CFM Streak Shadow Srs.M (Rotax 582) K.166-SA & PFA/206-11992		G-BTEM	14. 2.91	W.C.Yates	Ireston	13. 4.98P
G-MWPR	Whittaker MW-6 Merlin PFA/164-11260			16.10.90	P.J.S.Ritchie	Worthing	
G-MWPS	Murphy Renegade Spirit UK (Rotax 582) PFA/188-11931			18. 2.91	A.R.Broughton-Tompkins (As "0347"in pseudo US Navy c/s)	Elstead	1. 7.98P

Regn	Type	C/n	P/I	Date	Owner/operator	Probable Base	CA Expy
G-MWPT	Hunt Avon/Hunt Wing (EC-44-PM) JAH-8 & BMAA/HB/015		EI-CKF G-MWPT	18. 2.91	G.A.Murphy Ballincollig, Cork (Destroyed in accident ?)		10. 5.97P
G-MWPU	Solar Wings Pegasus Quasar TC (Rotax 503) SW-WQQ-0426			20. 2.91	N.J.Holt	Street	13. 4.99P
G-MWPW	AMF Chevvron 2-32C (Konig SD570) 027			26.11.90	E.L.T.Westman	Teangue, Isle of Skye	22.11.99P
G-MWPX	Solar Wings Pegasus XL-R SW-WA-1488			27. 2.91	R.S.Amor	Bristol	9. 5.99P
G-MWPZ	Murphy Renegade Spirit UK PFA/188-11631			18. 3.91	J.Ievers	Pains Castle	24. 2.99P
G-MWRA	Mainair Gemini/Flash 2A 818-0191-7 & W612 (Rotax 503)			5. 2.91	A.W.Austin	Treddington, Cheltenham	30. 6.99P
G-MWRB	Mainair Gemini/Flash 2A 819-0191-7 & W613 (Rotax 503)			5. 2.91	A.S.Harvey	RAF Wyton	25. 4.99P
G-MWRC	Mainair Gemini/Flash 2A 820-0191-7 & W614 (Rotax 503)			5. 2.91	D.R.Talbot	Chilton Park, Wallingford	7. 7.99P
G-MWRD	Mainair Gemini/Flash 2A 821-0191-7 & W615 (Motavia engine)			5. 2.91	D.M.Law	Redlands, Swindon	14.11.96P
G-MWRE	Mainair Gemini/Flash 2A 822-0191-7 & W616 (Rotax 503)			5. 2.91	A.J.Baldwin	Oxton, Nottingham	29. 6.99P
G-MWRF	Mainair Gemini/Flash 2A 829-0191-7 & W623 (Rotax 503)			4. 2.91	R.D.Ballard	Bexhill	12. 5.99P
G-MWRG	Mainair Gemini/Flash 2A 830-0191-7 & W624 (Rotax 503)			5. 2.91	B.R.Lamming	Seaton, Hull	28. 2.99P
G-MWRH	Mainair Gemini/Flash 2A 831-0191-7 & W625 (Rotax 503)			5. 2.91	K.Hodgson	Doncaster	26. 5.99P
G-MWRI	Mainair Gemini/Flash 2A 828-0191-7 & W622 (Rotax 462)			1. 3.91	R.N.Scarr	Marlborough	12.12.99P
G-MWRJ	Mainair Gemini/Flash 2A 832-0291-7 & W626 (Rotax 462)			28. 2.91	J.S.Walton	Mold	10. 9.99
G-MWRK	Rans S-6 Coyote II (Rotax 503) 0191-154 & PFA/204-11930			13. 2.91	R.H.Bambury	Breighton	10. 5.99P
G-MWRL	CFM Shadow Srs.CD (Rotax 503) K.152			13. 2.91	D.G.Brennan "Shadow Hawk" Old Sarum		24. 5.99P
G-MWRM	Medway Hybred 44XLR MR086/94/91/S (Rotax 503)		G-MWLC	26. 2.91	J.P.Bennett	RAF Wyton	5. 6.99P
G-MWRN	Solar Wings Pegasus XL-R (Rotax 462) SW-TE-0316 & SW-WA-1489			5. 3.91	D.T.MacKenzie	Downhill, Glasgow	5.12.99P
G-MWRO	Solar Wings Pegasus XL-R SW-WA-1490 (Rotax 462)			5. 3.91	I.D.Stokes	Camelford	8. 6.99P
G-MWRP	Solar Wings Pegasus XL-R SW-WA-1491			1. 3.91	M.Russell	Bristol	22. 5.99P
G-MWRR	Mainair Gemini/Flash 2A 834-0391-7 & W628 (Rotax 503)			7. 3.91	D.J.Tootell, G.Evans & R.Hughes Sandbach		14. 3.99P
G-MWRS	Ultravia Super Pelican E001-201			9. 5.84	T.B.Woolley	Narborough, Leics	9. 9.87P*
G-MWRT	Solar Wings Pegasus XL-R (Rotax 447) SW-TB-1431 & SW-WA-1492			15. 3.91	G.L.Gunnell	Luton	17. 5.99P
G-MWRU	Solar Wings Pegasus XL-R SW-WA-1493 (Rotax 447)			15. 3.91	J.McIver	West Kilbride	25. 8.96P
G-MWRV	Solar Wings Pegasus XL-R (Rotax 447) SW-TB-1433 & SW-WA-1494			15. 3.91	M.S.Adams	Roddige, Fradley	10.10.99P
G-MWRW	Solar Wings Pegasus XL-Q (Rotax 462) SW-TE-0320 & SW-WQ-0431			25. 3.91	E.Lewis Franklyn's Field, Chewton Mendip		25. 5.99P
G-MWRX	Solar Wings Pegasus XL-Q SW-WQ-0432 (Rotax 462)			25. 3.91	M.A.E.Harris	Swansea	6. 4.96P
G-MWRY	CFM Shadow Srs.CD (Rotax 503) K.162			26. 3.91	A.W.Hodder Belle Vue Farm, Yarnscombe		6.10.99P
G-MWRZ	AMF Chevvron 2-32C (Konig SD570) 028			10. 4.91	M.J.Barrett	Davidstow Moor	3. 7.99P
G-MWSA	Team Minimax (Rotax 377) PFA/186-11855			8. 4.91	A.N.Baumber Overseal, Burton-on-Trent "The Flying Cobbler"		8. 6.99P
G-MWSB	Mainair Gemini/Flash 2A 837-0591-7 & W631 (Rotax 582)			30. 4.91	T.Slevin	Mansfield	13. 7.97P
G-MWSC	Rans S-6-ESD Coyote II PFA/204-12019 (Rotax 503)			13. 5.91	B.E.Francis	Newton Peverill	30. 6.96P
G-MWSD	Solar Wings Pegasus XL-Q (Rotax 462) SW-TE-0319 & SW-WQ-0430			6. 3.91	J.D.Buchanan	Willingham	18. 7.99P
G-MWSE	Solar Wings Pegasus XL-R (Rotax 462) SW-TE-0323 & SW-WA-1496			10. 4.91	Ultra Light Training Ltd	Coventry	15. 8.98P
G-MWSF	Solar Wings Pegasus XL-R (Rotax 462) SW-TE-0324 & SW-WA-1497			10. 4.91	V.A.M.Bourne Long Newnton, Malmesbury		3. 9.98P
G-MWSG	Solar Wings Pegasus XL-R (Rotax 462) SW-TE-0325 & SW-WA-1498			10. 4.91	J.Eddon	Pickering	19. 9.99P
G-MWSH	Solar Wings Pegasus Quasar TC (Rotax 503) SW-TQC-0064 & SW-WQQ-0435			30. 4.91	T.W.Newton	Tarn Farm, Cockerham	30. 8.98P
G-MWSI	Solar Wings Pegasus Quasar TC (Rotax 503) SW-TQC-0065 & SW-WQQ-0436			23. 5.91	B.J.Kelly & P.J.Prescott	Daventry	21. 7.99P
G-MWSJ	Solar Wings Pegasus XL-Q SW-WQ-0437 (Rotax 462)			12. 4.91	R.A.Barrett Lower Mountpleasant Farm, Wimblington		29. 5.99P
G-MWSK	Solar Wings Pegasus XL-Q SW-WQ-0438 (Rotax 462)			12. 4.91	J.Doogan t/a Scottglass	Galashiels	5. 9.98P
G-MWSL	Mainair Gemini/Flash 2A 835-0491-7 & W629 (Rotax 503)			16. 4.91	C.W.Frost	Rufforth	11. 6.98P

Regn	Type	C/n	P/I	Date	Owner/operator	Probable Base	CA Expy
G-MWSM	Mainair Gemini/Flash 2A 836-0491-7 & W630 (Rotax 503)			16. 4.91	R.M.Wall & P.A.Garside St.Michaels-on-Wyre		23. 8.99P
G-MWSO	Solar Wings Pegasus XL-R (Rotax 462) SW-TE-0329 & SW-WA-1503			25. 4.91	M.A.Clayton	New Romney	28.11.98P
G-MWSP	Solar Wings Pegasus XL-R (Rotax 462) SW-TE-0330 & SW-WA-1504			25. 4.91	F.Pickering Knapthorpe Lodge, Caunton, Notts		9.10.99P
G-MWSR	Solar Wings Pegasus XL-R (Rotax 462) SW-TE-0331 & SW-WA-1505			25. 4.91	M.E.T.Taylor	Newport	7. 8.99P
G-MWSS	Medway Hybred 44XLR (Rotax 503)	MR117/97		7. 5.91	F.S.Ogden West Hoathly, Haywards Heath		15. 9.98P
G-MWST	Medway Hybred 44XLR (Rotax 503)	MR118/98		8. 5.91	A.Ferguson (Damaged mid 1997)	Insch	7. 8.98P
G-MWSU	Medway Hybred 44XLR (Rotax 503)	MR119/99		1. 5.92	G.R.Craig	Insch	24. 7.98P
G-MWSW	Whittaker MW-6 Merlin PFA/164-11328			15. 2.91	S.N.F.Warnell	Staines	
G-MWSX	Aerotech MW-5 Sorcerer PFA/163-11549 (Rotax 447)			3. 5.91	A.T.Armstrong	Yelverton	20. 1.99P
G-MWSY	Aerotech MW-5 Sorcerer PFA/163-11218 (Rotax 447)			3. 5.91	J.E.Holloway	Saltash	24.11.97P
G-MWSZ	CFM Shadow Srs.CD (Rotax 503) K.158			4. 4.91	P.G.Bibbey	Old Sarum	24. 9.99P
G-MWTA	Solar Wings Pegasus XL-Q SW-WQ-0444 (Rotax 462)			8. 5.91	T.W.Phipps Craysmarsh Farm, Melksham		10. 7.99P
G-MWTB	Solar Wings Pegasus XL-Q (Rotax 462) SW-TE-0333 & SW-WQ-0445			8. 5.91	I.A.Baker	Kettering	14. 8.98P
G-MWTC	Solar Wings Pegasus XL-Q SW-WQ-0446 (Rotax 462)			8. 5.91	P.Nicholson	London SE18	2. 7.99P
G-MWTD	Microflight Spectrum (Rotax 503) 022			13. 5.91	J.V.Harris Faringdon, Oxon t/a Group Delta		23.10.99P
G-MWTE	Microflight Spectrum (Rotax 503) 023			13. 5.91	R.H.Braithwaite RAF Halton t/a RAF Microlight Flying Association		28. 1.00P
G-MWTF	Mainair Gemini/Southdown Sprint 249-684-2 (EC-44-PM)			30. 7.84	G.D.C.Buyers	Popham	19. 7.95P
G-MWTG	Mainair Gemini/Flash 2A 838-0591-7 & W632 (Rotax 582)			16. 5.91	D.G.Emery & M.R.Smith	Dudley	10. 6.98P
G-MWTH	Mainair Gemini/Flash 2A 839-0591-7 & W633 (Rotax 503)			21. 5.91	T.Coughlan	Cumbernauld	9. 6.95P
G-MWTI	Solar Wings Pegasus XL-Q SW-WQ-0274 (Rotax 462HP)			23. 5.91	A.Crozier	East Fortune	15. 5.99P
G-MWTJ	CFM Shadow Srs.CD (Rotax 503) K.167			16. 5.91	H.F.Blakeman	Crewe	15. 8.99P
G-MWTK	Solar Wings Pegasus XL-R/Se (Rotax 462) SW-TE-0335 & SW-WA-1507			28. 5.91	R.T.Meeson Jacksdale, Nottingham		7. 4.99P
G-MWTL	Solar Wings Pegasus XL-R (Rotax 462) SW-TE-0336 & SW-WA-1508			28. 5.91	B.Lindsay Chipping Sodbury		25.10.98P
G-MWTM	Solar Wings Pegasus XL-R SW-WA-1509 (Rotax 462)			28. 5.91	I.R.F.King	Tunbridge Wells	4. 5.97P
G-MWTN	CFM Shadow Srs.CD (Rotax 503) K.153			23. 5.91	M.J.Broom	Long Marston	28. 7.99P
G-MWTO	Mainair Gemini/Flash 2A 840-0591-7 & W634 (Rotax 503)			28. 5.91	J.Greenhalgh St.Michaels-on-Wyre		13. 6.98P
G-MWTP	CFM Shadow Srs.CD (Rotax 503) K.107			23. 5.91	D.A.Crosbie	Sudbury	14. 7.99P
G-MWTR	Mainair Gemini/Flash 2A 842-0591-7 & W636 (Rotax 503)			31. 5.91	A.A.Howland	Battle	1.10.98P
G-MWTS	Whittaker MW-6S Fatboy Flyer PFA/164-12015 (Rotax 582)			31. 5.91	P.G.Evans & K.N.Lovett	Alford	17. 4.97P
G-MWTT	Rans S-6-ESD Coyote II (Rotax 503) 20391-175 & PFA/204-12016			30. 4.91	L.E.Duffin "Warrior 2"	Insch	21.10.99P
G-MWTU	Solar Wings Pegasus XL-R SW-WA-1501 (Rotax 447)			21. 6.91	J.D.Doran Mullingar, Co.Westmeath		25. 9.99P
G-MWTY	Mainair Gemini/Flash 2A 843-0691-7 & W637 (Rotax 503)			12. 6.91	K.B.Pownall	Stoke-on-Trent	19. 4.98P
G-MWTZ	Mainair Gemini/Flash 2A 844-0691-7 & W638 (Rotax 503)			12. 6.91	C.W.R.Felce	Riseley, Bedford	23. 6.98P
G-MWUA	CFM Shadow Srs.CD (Rotax 503) K.161			10. 6.91	Cloudbase Avtn Svs Ltd	Crawley	2. 6.99P
G-MWUB	Solar Wings Pegasus XL-R SW-WA-1510 (Rotax 462)			12. 6.91	J.A.Horn	Peterlee	29. 4.99P
G-MWUC	Solar Wings Pegasus XL-R SW-WA-1511 (Rotax 462)			12. 6.91	J.R.Hall Bibberne Farm, Stalbridge		6. 7.98P
G-MWUD	Solar Wings Pegasus XL-R SW-WA-1512 (Rotax 462)			12. 6.91	N.A.Martin	Marlborough	6.12.99P
G-MWUE	Solar Wings Pegasus XL-R SW-WA-1513 (Rotax 447)		EI-CGL G-MWUE	13. 6.91	R.M.Balfe Drogheda, Co.Louth		11. 4.99P
G-MWUF	Solar Wings Pegasus XL-R (Rotax 447) SW-TB-1439 & SW-WA-1514			13. 6.91	J.G.Jackson	Woodley	13. 2.99P
G-MWUG	Solar Wings Pegasus XL-R (Rotax 447) SW-TB-1440 & SW-WA-1515			14. 6.91	G.C.Weighell	Enstone	18. 7.99P
G-MWUH	Murphy Renegade Spirit UK 343 (Built in Canada/Saudi Arabia)			12. 6.91	Choicesource Ltd (Stored 4.97) Inverness		2.10.95P
G-MWUI	AMF Chevvron 2-32C (Konig SD570) 029			2. 7.91	B.McFadden Linley Hill, Leven t/a Microflight Avn		28. 2.99P

Regn	Type	C/n	P/I	Date	Owner/operator	Probable Base	CA Expy
G-MWUJ	Medway Hybred 44XLR (Rotax 503)	MR122/101		27. 6.91	P.C.Cowling	Sleaford	25. 1.98P
G-MWUK	Rans S-6-ESD Coyote II (Rotax 503)	PFA/204-12090		1. 7.91	G.K.Hoult	Long Marston	5.10.99P
G-MWUL	Rans S-6-ESD Coyote II (Rotax 503) 0391-172 & PFA/204-12054			10. 6.91	D.M.Gale	Franklyns Field, Chewton Mendip	16. 8.99P
G-MWUN	Rans S-6-ESD Coyote II PFA/204-12075 (Rotax 503) (Rebuilt with new airframe after w/o 13.10.94) t/a Coyote Flying Group			10. 6.91	M.L.Robinson	Kirkbride	14. 7.99P
G-MWUO	Solar Wings Pegasus XL-Q (Rotax 462) SW-TE-0296 & SW-WQ-0379			26. 6.91	A.P.Slade	High Wycombe	20. 7.99P
G-MWUP	Solar Wings Pegasus XL-R (Rotax 462) SW-WA-1517			21. 6.91	R.G.Mulford	Gillingham	13.12.98P
G-MWUR	Solar Wings Pegasus XL-R (Rotax 462) SW-TE-0342 & SW-WA-1518			21. 6.91	A.W.Buchan & C.D.Creasey t/a Nottingham Aerotow Club Knapthorpe Lodge, Causton, Notts		19. 8.98P
G-MWUS	Solar Wings Pegasus XL-R (Rotax 462) SW-TE-0343 & SW-WA-1519			21. 6.91	H.R.Loxton	Weston Zoyland	12.10.98P
G-MWUU	Solar Wings Pegasus XL-R (Rotax 462) SW-TE-0346 & SW-WA-1521			28. 6.91	B.R.Underwood & P.E.Hadley	Swinford, Rugby	13. 6.99P
G-MWUV	Solar Wings Pegasus XL-R (Rotax 462) SW-TE-0347 & SW-WA-1522			28. 6.91	L.Birkett t/a Blast Clean	Great Orton	15. 5.99P
G-MWUW*	Solar Wings Pegasus XL-R (Rotax 462) SW-TE-0348 & SW-WA-1523			28. 6.91	Ultraflight Microlights Ltd (Cancelled by CAA 16.2.98)	Alrewas	29. 1.98P
G-MWUX	Solar Wings Pegasus XL-Q (Rotax 462HP)	SW-WQ-0454		28. 6.91	B.D.Attwell	Caerphilly	13. 9.98P
G-MWUY	Solar Wings Pegasus XL-Q (Rotax 462) SW-TE-0345 & SW-WQ-0455			28. 6.91	F. & E.Gallagher	Glasgow	17. 5.99P
G-MWUZ	Solar Wings Pegasus XL-Q (Rotax 462) SW-TE-0350 & SW-WQ-0456			28. 6.91	N.K.Allen	Ongar	13. 9.98P
G-MWVA	Solar Wings Pegasus XL-Q (Rotax 462) SW-TE-0351 & SW-WQ-0457			28. 6.91	G.T.Collar	Eshott	28.10.99P
G-MWVE	Solar Wings Pegasus XL-R (Rotax 447) SW-TB-1441 & SW-WA-1524			18. 7.91	W.A.Keel-Stocker	Long Marston	13. 4.99P
G-MWVF	Solar Wings Pegasus XL-R/Se (Rotax 447) SW-TB-1442 & SW-WA-1525			18. 7.91	M.Tomlinson	Hatherton, Cannock	9. 4.99P
G-MWVG	CFM Shadow Srs.CD (Rotax 503)	151		5. 8.91	Shadow Flight Centre Ltd	Old Sarum	16.10.99P
G-MWVH	CFM Shadow Srs.CD (Rotax 503)	181		5. 8.91	D.J.Cross	Inverness	4. 5.99P
G-MWVI*	Whittaker MW-6 Merlin	PFA/164-11432		1. 9.89	B.H. & P.M.Gilmore Whitminster, Glos (Cancelled by CAA 3.3.99)		
G-MWVK	Mainair Mercury (Rotax 503)	849-0891-5 & W643		13. 8.91	J.Northage	Ilkley	10. 7.99P
G-MWVL	Rans S-6 ESD Coyote II (Rotax 503) 0892-341 & PFA/204-12118			13. 8.91 (Originally built with frame c/n 0491-186)	G.G.Hunt	Melksham	28. 5.99P
G-MWVM	Solar Wings Pegasus Quasar IIIC (Rotax 503) SW-TQ-0031 & SW-WX-0020		G-65-8	2. 9.91	S.B.Wilkes t/a G-MWVM Group	Roddige, Fradley	29. 8.99P
G-MWVN	Mainair Gemini/Flash 2A (Rotax 503) 850-0891-7 & W644			19. 8.91	J.McCafferty	Enstone	20.11.99P
G-MWVO	Mainair Gemini/Flash 2A (Rotax 582) 852-0891-7 & W646			27. 8.91	B. & J.D.Caudwell	Stafford	9. 1.97P
G-MWVP	Murphy Renegade Spirit UK (Rotax 582) PFA/188-11735			22. 8.91	T.B.Woolley "Spirit of Lancashire" (Damaged Redlands, Swindon 3.7.93)	Leicester	29. 4.94P
G-MWVR	Mainair Gemini/Flash 2A (Rotax 503) 855-0991-7 & W650			30. 8.91	A.M.Dalgetty	Perth	8. 4.99P
G-MWVS	Mainair Gemini/Flash 2A 856-0991-7 & W651			30. 8.91	S.J.Yates & R.L.Ashton	Cannock	13.12.99P
G-MWVT	Mainair Gemini/Flash 2A (Rotax 503) 860-1091-7 & W655			2. 9.91	J.Barlow & C.Osiejuk	Oxton, Nottingham	8.11.99P
G-MWVU	Medway Hybred 44XLR (Rotax 503)	MR123/102		18. 9.91	Medway Microlights Ltd	Rochester	19. 9.99P
G-MWVW	Mainair Gemini/Flash 2A (Rotax 503) 853-0891-7 & W647			9. 9.91	W.O'Brien	Arclid Green, Sandbach	12. 7.99P
G-MWVY	Mainair Gemini/Flash 2A (Rotax 503) 854-0991-7 & W649			4. 9.91	J.D.Hinton	Tunbridge Wells	3. 5.99P
G-MWVZ	Mainair Gemini/Flash 2A (Rotax 503) 863-1091-7 & W658			4. 9.91	K.T.Leach	Skelmersdale	14. 3.99P
G-MWWA	Solar Wings Pegasus Quasar IIIC (Rotax 503) SW-TQC-0073 & SW-WQT-0467			17. 9.91	C.Long	Pontypool	6.10.99P
G-MWWB	Mainair Gemini/Flash 2A (Rotax 503) 864-1091-7 & W659			18. 9.91	D.K.Royle	Guy Lane Farm, Waverton	30. 8.99P
G-MWWC	Mainair Gemini/Flash 2A (Rotax 582) 868-1191-7 & W663			23. 9.91	A. & D.Margereson	Chesterfield	15. 4.98P
G-MWWD	Murphy Renegade Spirit UK (Rotax 582) 344 & PFA/188-11719			23. 9.91	S.Hill t/a Doctor & The Medics "Winning Spirit"	Long Marston	29. 7.99P
G-MWWE	Team Minimax (Rotax 447) PFA/186-11925			1.10.91	J.Entwistle	Tarn Farm, Cockerham	23. 7.97P
G-MWWG	Solar Wings Pegasus XL-Q	SW-WQ-0468 (Rotax 462HP)		3.10.91	A.W.Guerri	York	3. 7.99P
G-MWWH	Solar Wings Pegasus XL-Q (Rotax 462) SW-TE-0356 & SW-WQ-0469			3.10.91	M.R.Dunnett	Ludham	10. 7.99P
G-MWWI	Mainair Gemini/Flash 2A (Rotax 503) 870-1291-7 & W665			11.10.91	N.R.Osborne	Huddersfield	29. 9.99P

Regn	Type	C/n	P/I	Date	Owner/operator	Probable Base	CA Expy
G-MWWJ	Mainair Gemini/Flash 2A (Rotax 503)	865-1191-7 & W660		22.10.91	J.Garcia	Kilmarnock	17. 8.98P
G-MWWK	Mainair Gemini/Flash 2A (Rotax 582)	866-1191-7 & W661		22.10.91	B.N.Thresher	Dunkeswell	21. 3.99P
G-MWWL	Rans S-6-ESD Coyote II (Rotax 503)	PFA/204-11849	(G-BTXD)	17.10.91	D.W.Lloyd	St.Neots	13. 5.99P
G-MWWM	Kolb Twinstar mk.2 (Rotax 503) (C/n duplicates G-GPST)	PFA/205-11645	(G-BTXC)	17.10.91	D.Jordan	RAF Brize Norton	26. 5.99P
G-MWWN	Mainair Gemini/Flash 2A (Rotax 503)	872-1291-7 & W667		22.10.91	J.Nowill	Dunkeswell	16. 9.99P
G-MWWO	Solar Wings Pegasus XL-R/Se (Rotax 447)	SW-TB-1443 & SW-WA-1528		22.10.91	J.M.Cooper (Stored 9.97)	Great Orton	7. 7.96P
G-MWWP	Rans S-4 Coyote (Rotax 447)	PFA/193-12073		21.10.91	R.McKinlay	Galston, Ayr	16. 2.99P
G-MWWR	Microflight Spectrum (Rotax 503)	024		23.10.91	C.S.Warr & B.Fukes	Market Rasen	14. 2.99P
G-MWWS	Thruster T300 (Rotax 532)	089-T300-370	EI-BYW	4.11.91	S.P.McCaffrey (Stored 3.97)	Ginge, Wantage	7. 7.95P
G-MWWT	Thruster Super T300 (Rotax 582)	9012-ST300-503		25.10.91	Tempest Avn Ltd	Wantage	1. 9.93P
G-MWWV	Solar Wings Pegasus XL-Q (Rotax 462HP)	SW-WQ-0470		30.10.91	R.W.Livingstone	Enniskillen	30.10.99P
G-MWWX	Microflight Spectrum (Rotax 503)	025		25.10.91	D.Moorhead	Eshott	7. 3.99P
G-MWWZ	Cyclone Chaser S (Rotax 447)	CH.829		29.10.91	G.F.Clews	Roddige, Fradley	17. 6.99P
G-MWXA	Mainair Gemini/Flash 2A (Rotax 503)	873-0192-7 & W668		30.10.91	G.Sipson	Aldermans Green, Coventry	15. 8.97P
G-MWXB	Mainair Gemini/Flash 2A (Rotax 503)	869-1191-7 & W664		6.11.91	D.A.Smith	Rufforth	14. 7.99P
G-MWXC	Mainair Gemini/Flash 2A (Rotax 503)	874-0192-7 & W669		6.11.91	G.Dufton-Kelly	Wirral	4. 8.99P
G-MWXD	Mainair Gemini/Flash 2A (Rotax 462)	876-0192-7 & W671		6.11.91	D.H.Wood	Heysham	20. 3.99P
G-MWXF	Mainair Mercury (Rotax 503)	867-1191-5 & W662		12.11.91	T.R.Southall	Halesowen	14. 6.99P
G-MWXG	Solar Wings Pegasus Quasar IITC (Rotax 503)	SW-TQC-0074 & SW-WQT-0471		7.11.91	C.A.Thomas	Chatteris	27. 4.99P
G-MWXH	Solar Wings Pegasus Quasar IITC (Rotax 503)	SW-TQC-0075 & SW-WQT-0472		7.11.91	G.A.Horrocks	Long Marston	20. 7.98P
G-MWXI	Solar Wings Pegasus Quasar IITC (Rotax 503)	SW-WQT-0473		7.11.91	F.Tibone	Abingdon	1. 4.94P
G-MWXJ	Mainair Mercury (Rotax 503)	861-1091-5 & W656		15.11.91	P.L.Parker	Baxby Manor, Husthwaite	31. 1.99P
G-MWXK	Mainair Mercury (Rotax 503)	862-1191-5 & W657		15.11.91	M.P.Wilkinson	Sandtoft	18. 7.96P
G-MWXL	Mainair Gemini/Flash 2A (Rotax 582)	859-1091-7 & W654		12.12.91	C.D.Joyner	Bognor Regis	17. 5.99P
G-MWXN	Mainair Gemini/Flash 2A (Rotax 582)	878-0192-7 & W673		20.11.91	S.C.Reeve	Oxton, Notts	28. 3.99P
G-MWXO	Mainair Gemini/Flash 2A (Rotax 582)	880-0192-7 & W675		25.11.91	R.Pass	Roddige, Fradley	7.11.99P
G-MWXP	Solar Wings Pegasus XL-Q (Rotax 462)	SW-TE-0359 & SW-WQ-0475		26.11.91	A.P.Attfield	Sutton Meadows, Ely	18. 8.99P
G-MWXR	Solar Wings Pegasus XL-Q (Rotax 462)	SW-WQ-0476		26.11.91	G.W.Craig	Insch	21. 3.99P
G-MWXS	Mainair Gemini/Flash 2A (Rotax 503)	883-0292-7 & W678		4.12.91	P.Hall	Clay Cross	18. 7.96P
G-MWXU	Mainair Gemini/Flash 2A (Rotax 582)	882-0192-7 & W677		9.12.91	C.M.Mackinnon	East Fortune	11. 6.99P
G-MWXV	Mainair Gemini/Flash 2A (Rotax 582)	879-1291-7 & W674		9.12.91	Launch Link Systems Ltd (Stored 4.97) Oxton, Nottingham		11.12.93P
G-MWXW	Cyclone Chaser S (Rotax 377)	CH.830		9.12.91	K.C.Dodd	Roddige, Fradley	22. 4.99P
G-MWXX	Cyclone Chaser S (Rotax 447)	CH.831	(G-MWEB) (G-MWCD)	9.12.91	R.J.Moore	Folkestone	3. 6.99P
G-MWXY	Cyclone Chaser S (Rotax 447)	CH.832	(G-MWEC)	19.12.91	G.Doughty	East Fortune	1. 9.98P
G-MWXZ	Cyclone Chaser S (Rotax 508)	CH.836		31.12.91	M.J.A.New	Hughley, Much Wenlock	19. 4.99P
G-MWYA	Mainair Gemini/Flash 2A (Rotax 462)	886-0292-7 & W681		3. 1.92	R.F.Hunt	St.Michaels-on-Wyre	7. 6.93P
G-MWYB	Solar Wings Pegasus XL-Q (Rotax 462)	SW-TE-0364 & SW-WQ-0485		15. 1.92	P.A.West	Old Sarum	3. 4.99
G-MWYC	Solar Wings Pegasus XL-Q (Rotax 462)	SW-TE-0365 & SW-WQ-0486		15. 1.92	A.R.Hood	Knapthorpe Lodge, Caunton, Notts	20. 6.99P
G-MWYD	CFM Shadow Srs.C (Rotax 503)	K.179		8. 1.92	J.Anderson	Plaistows Field, Hemel Hampstead	28. 5.99P
G-MWYE	Rans S-6-ESD Coyote II (Rotax 503)	0591-189 & PFA/204-12223		10. 1.92	D.K.Seath	RAF Benson	1. 6.99P
G-MWYG	Mainair Gemini/Flash 2A (Rotax 582)	884-0292-7 & W679		15. 1.92	M.S.McCrudden	Holywood, NI	11. 6.99P
G-MWYH	Mainair Gemini/Flash 2A (Rotax 503)	887-0292-7 & W682		15. 1.92	D.C.Jackson	Nottingham	9. 5.99P

Regn	Type	C/n	P/I	Date	Owner/operator	Probable Base	CA Expy
G-MWYI	Solar Wings Pegasus Quasar IITC (Rotax 503) SW-TQC-0083 & SW-WQT-0488			30. 1.92	T.S.Chadfield	Graveley	1. 4.98P
G-MWYJ	Solar Wings Pegasus Quasar IITC (Rotax 503) SW-TQC-0084 & SW-WQT-0489			24. 1.92	R.E.Quine	Jurby, IoM	1. 2.99P
G-MWYL	Mainair Gemini/Flash 2A (Rotax 503) 877-0192-7 & W672			17. 1.92	A.Gannon	East Fortune	16. 5.99P
G-MWYM	Cyclone Chaser S 1000 CH.838 (Mosler MM-CB35)			21. 1.92	K.H.A.Negal	London SW7	27.11.99P
G-MWYN	Rans S-6-ESD Coyote II (Rotax 503) 0491-185 & PFA/204-12168			22. 1.92	W.R.Tull	Milton-under-Wychwood	29. 9.98P
G-MWYS	CGS Hawk I Arrow (Rotax 447) H-T-470-R447 & BMAA/HB/020			17. 2.93	D.W.Hermiston-Hooper t/a Civilair	Ryde, IoW	
G-MWYT	Mainair Gemini/Flash 2A (Rotax 503) 881-0392-7 & W676			3. 2.92	M.A.Hodgson	Northallerton	17. 9.99P
G-MWYU	Solar Wings Pegasus XL-Q SW-WQ-0491 (Rotax 462)			30. 1.92	Hannah L.Rogers	Hailsham, E.Sussex	17.11.99P
G-MWYV	Mainair Gemini/Flash 2A (Rotax 582) 896-0392-7 & W691			3. 2.92	J.N.Whitworth	Chesterfield	31.10.97P
G-MWYY	Solar Wings Pegasus XL-Q (Rotax 462) SW-TE-0365 & SW-WQ-0492			17. 2.92	R.D.Allard Elm Tree Park, Marlborough (Stored 8.97)		15. 3.99P
G-MWYZ	Solar Wings Pegasus XL-Q SW-WQ-0474 (Rotax 462HP)			20.11.91	P.V.Stevens	Oakley	2. 4.99P
G-MWZA	Mainair Mercury 888-0292-5 & W683 (Rotax 503)			7. 2.92	A.J.Malham	Rufforth	7. 2.00P
G-MWZB	AMF Chevvron 2-32C (Konig SD570) 033			10. 2.92	A.J.Pickup	Didcot	1. 8.98P
G-MWZC	Mainair Gemini/Flash 2A (Rotax 503) 899-0492-7 & W694			7. 2.92	R.W.Taylor	St.Michaels-on-Wyre	22. 9.99P
G-MWZD	Solar Wings Pegasus Quasar IITC (Rotax 503) SW-TQC-0086 & SW-WQT-0494			2. 3.92	B.Hamilton	Long Marston	1. 4.99P
G-MWZE	Solar Wings Pegasus Quasar IITC (Rotax 503) SW-TQC-0087 & SW-WQT-0495			17. 2.92	J.Nicholson	Great Orton	18. 7.99P
G-MWZF	Solar Wings Pegasus Quasar IITC (Rotax 582/40) SW-TQD-0108 & SW-WQT-0496 (Trike c/n duplicates G-MYEK)			17. 2.92	R.G.T.Corney	Clench Common	29. 6.99P
G-MWZG	Mainair Gemini/Flash 2A (Rotax 582) 889-0392-7 & W684			7. 2.92	P.L.Braniff	Belfast	24. 5.99P
G-MWZH	Solar Wings Pegasus XL-R SW-WA-1532 (Rotax 462)			17. 2.92	P.A.Ord	Redcar	29.12.97P
G-MWZI	Solar Wings Pegasus XL-R (Rotax 462) SW-TE-0367 & SW-WA-1533			17. 2.92	S.A.Oerton	Roddige, Fradley	11. 4.99P
G-MWZJ	Solar Wings Pegasus XL-R/Se (Rotax 462) SW-TE-0368 & SW-WA-1534			17. 2.92	P.Kitchen	Eshott	12. 6.99P
G-MWZL	Mainair Gemini/Flash 2A (Rotax 582) 900-0492-7 & W695			17. 2.92	G.Kerr	East Fortune	24. 6.99P
G-MWZM	Team Minimax 91 PFA/186-12211 (Mosler MM-CB40)		G-BUDD G-MWZM	18. 2.92	C.Leighton-Thomas "My Buddy"	Bath	19. 8.97P
G-MWZN	Mainair Gemini/Flash 2A (Rotax 582) 902-0492-7 & W697			25. 2.92	J.G.Boxall	Inverurie	17.11.97P
G-MWZO	Solar Wings Pegasus Quasar IITC (Rotax 503) SW-WQT-0498			26. 2.92	R.Oseland	Shifnal	29. 3.99P
G-MWZP	Solar Wings Pegasus Quasar IITC (Rotax 503) SW-TQC-0090 & SW-WQT-0499			26. 2.92	C.D.Hogbourne	Longacre Farm, Sandy	17. 8.99P
G-MWZR	Solar Wings Pegasus Quasar IITC (Rotax 503) SW-WQT-0500			26. 2.92	J.A.Robinson	Kendal	7. 7.99P
G-MWZS	Solar Wings Pegasus Quasar IITC (Rotax 503) SW-WQT-0501		EI-CIP G-MWZS	26. 2.92	B.H.A.Van Duykeren Grange Bannow, Co.Wexford		4. 7.99P
G-MWZT	Solar Wings Pegasus XL-R (Rotax 462) SW-TE-0370 & SW-WA-1535			26. 2.92	S.Kilpin	Sutton Meadows, Ely	5. 8.99P
G-MWZU	Solar Wings Pegasus XL-R SW-WA-1536 (Rotax 462)			26. 2.92	D.W.Palmer	Bexhill	11. 2.99P
G-MWZV	Solar Wings Pegasus XL-R SW-WA-1537 (Rotax 462)			26. 2.92	D.J.Newby	Clench Common	8. 8.99P
G-MWZW	Solar Wings Pegasus XL-R (Rotax 462) SW-TE-0373 & SW-WA-1538			26. 2.92	W.D.Fanshawe	Salisbury	16. 6.99P
G-MWZX	Solar Wings Pegasus XL-R (Rotax 462) SW-TE-0374 & SW-WA-1539			26. 2.92	N.M.S.Waters	Arundel	12. 8.99P
G-MWZY	Solar Wings Pegasus XL-R (Rotax 462) SW-TE-0375 & SW-WA-1540			26. 2.92	T.J.Birkbeck & P.G.Moss Rufforth t/a Vale of York Hang Gliding Club		30. 1.99P
G-MWZZ	Solar Wings Pegasus XL-R (Rotax 462) SW-TE-0376 & SW-WA-1541			26. 2.92	M.P.Shea	Hixon	9. 7.99P

G-MXAA-MXZZ

Regn	Type	C/n	P/I	Date	Owner/operator	Probable Base	CA Expy
G-MXVI	VS.361 Spitfire LF.XVIe CBAF.IX.4394	6850M TE184		17. 2.89	De Cadenet Motor Racing Ltd North Weald (As "TE184")		28.11.98P

G-MYAA-MYZZ

Regn	Type	C/n	P/I	Date	Owner/operator	Probable Base	CA Expy
G-MYAA	CFM Shadow Srs.CD (Rotax 503)	K.139		11. 4.90	R.Riley	Ashford, Kent	18. 4.99P
G-MYAB	Solar Wings Pegasus XL-R/Se (Rotax 462) SW-TE-0377 & SW-WA-1542			26. 2.92	A.N.F.Stewart (Stored 1.98)	Long Marston	20. 3.97P
G-MYAC	Solar Wings Pegasus XL-Q (Rotax 462) SW-TE-0378 & SW-WQ-0502			26. 2.92	M.A.Garner	Thetford	29. 8.99P
G-MYAD	Solar Wings Pegasus XL-Q (Rotax 462HP) SW-TE-0379 & SW-WQ-0503			26. 2.92	P.Byrne	Hacketstown, Ireland	19. 6.99P
G-MYAE	Solar Wings Pegasus XL-Q (Rotax 462) SW-TE-0380 & SW-WQ-0504			26. 2.92	R.J.Waller	Redlands, Swindon	9. 1.99P
G-MYAF	Solar Wings Pegasus XL-Q (Rotax 462) SW-WQ-0505			26. 2.92	K.N.Rigley	Newark	3. 6.99P
G-MYAG	Quad City Challenger II (Rotax 503) PFA/177-12167			25. 2.92	J.W.G.Andrews	Welwyn	20. 8.97P
G-MYAH	Whittaker MW-5 Sorcerer (Rotax 447) PFA/163-11233			2. 3.92	W.G.Tait	Exmouth	22.10.98P
G-MYAI	Mainair Mercury (Rotax 503) 892-0392-5 & W687			11. 3.92	J.M.Hodgson	Baxby Manor, Husthwaite	28. 4.99P
G-MYAJ	Rans S-6-ESD Coyote II (Rotax 503) PFA/204-12227			3. 3.92	S.R.Green	Bristol	19. 5.99P
G-MYAK	Solar Wings Pegasus Quasar IITC (Rotax 503)	SW-WQT-0506	D-G-MYAK	5. 3.92	R.S.McMaster	Sywell	1. 9.99P
G-MYAL	Rotec Rally 2B	DJC-01		5. 3.92	D.J.Cooper	Kings Lynn	
G-MYAM	Murphy Renegade Spirit UK (Rotax 582) PFA/188-11907			6. 3.92	A.F.Reid	Newtownards, NI	14. 7.98P
G-MYAN	Aerotech MW-5(K) Sorcerer 5K-0017-02 (Rotax 447) (Full Lotus floats)		(G-MWNI)	24. 3.92	J.Hollings	Melbourne, Derby	9.10.99P
G-MYAO	Mainair Gemini/Flash 2A (Rotax 503) 894-0392-7 & W689			11. 3.92	P.Millar	Cumbernauld	1. 8.98P
G-MYAP	Thruster T300 (Rotax 582) 9022-T300-501			12. 3.92	R.E.Williams & W.Fletcher (Damaged late 1994)	Swansea	28.11.95P
G-MYAR	Thruster T300 (Rotax 503) 9022-T300-502			12. 3.92	R.J.Ripley	Woolaston	25. 9.99P
G-MYAS	Mainair Gemini/Flash 2A (Rotax 503) 895-0392-7 & W690			11. 3.92	A.N.Duncanson	Redlands, Swindon	8. 5.99P
G-MYAT	Team Minimax PFA/186-12017 (Rotax 447)			6. 3.92	M.A.Perry	Rayleigh, Essex	29. 9.99P
G-MYAU	Mainair Gemini/Flash 2A (Rotax 462) 890-0392-7 & W685			25. 3.92	P.P.Allen	Ely	15. 7.99P
G-MYAV	Mainair Mercury 893-0392-5 & W688 (Rotax 503)			23. 3.92	J.Lynch	Baxby Manor, Husthwaite	20. 5.99P
G-MYAW	Team Minimax 91 PFA/186-12164 (Rotax 447)			11. 3.92	J.L.Hamer	Hartpury, Glos	1. 4.99P
G-MYAY	Microflight Spectrum (Rotax 503)	027		13. 3.92	S.A.Clarehugh	Eshott	21.12.99P
G-MYAZ	Murphy Renegade Spirit UK (Rotax 582) PFA/188-12027			16. 3.92	R.Smith	Kilkerran	18. 6.99P
G-MYBA	Rans S-6-ESD Coyote II PFA/204-12210 (Rotax 503)			12. 3.92	M.R.Cann t/a Climsland Climber Society	Dunkeswell	30.11.99P
G-MYBB	Maxair Drifter MD.001 & BMAA/HB/014			10. 4.92	M.Ingleton	Sheerness	12.6.92P*
G-MYBC	CFM Shadow Srs.CD BMAA/HB/047 (Rotax 503) (Originally regd with c/ns K.195 & PFA/206-12221 - PFA c/n indicates a Streak Shadow incorrectly)			18. 3.92	M.E.Gilbert	Drummiard Farm, Bonnybank	24. 5.99P
G-MYBD	Solar Wings Pegasus Quasar IITC (Rotax 503) SW-WQT-0511			26. 3.92	A.M.Brumpton	Horncastle, Lincs	27. 5.99P
G-MYBE	Solar Wings Pegasus Quasar IITC (Rotax 503) SW-WQT-0512			26. 3.92	R.H.Thomson & C.Lamb	Rye	17. 9.99P
G-MYBF	Solar Wings Pegasus XL-Q (Rotax 462) SW-TE-0384 & SW-WQ-0513			26. 3.92	M.R.Williamson	Sutton Meadows, Ely	17. 2.99P
G-MYBG	Solar Wings Pegasus XL-Q (Rotax 462) SW-TE-0385 & SW-WQ-0514			26. 3.92	I.R.Russell & P.A.Henretty	Swinford, Rugby	8. 5.99P
G-MYBH	Eipper Quicksilver GT500	0173		25. 3.92	D.Smith	Goole	
G-MYBI	Rans S-6-ESD Coyote II (Rotax 503) PFA/204-12186			26. 3.92	J.C.O'Donnell	Shotteswell	14. 9.99P
G-MYBJ	Mainair Gemini/Flash 2A (Rotax 462) 908-0593-7 & W706			2. 4.92	C.Nicholson	Sandtoft	31. 7.99P
G-MYBL	CFM Shadow Srs.CD K.194 (Rotax 503)			2. 4.92	R.Garrod & S.M.Hart	Stowmarket/Ipswich	8. 1.00P
G-MYBM	Team Minimax 91 PFA/186-12212 (Mosler MM-CB35)			3. 4.92	M.K.Dring	East Kirkby	22.10.99P
G-MYBN	Hiway Skytrike mkII/Demon 175 BRL-01			14. 4.92	B.R.Lamming	Seaton, Hull	
G-MYBO	Solar Wings Pegasus XL-R SW-WA-1545 (Rotax 447)			16. 4.92	K.Sene	Chesham	27. 1.00P
G-MYBP	Solar Wings Pegasus XL-R/Se (Rotax 447) SW-TB-1446 & SW-WA-1546			16. 4.92	N. & J.M.Hodgkinson	Great Orton	27. 6.99P

Regn	Type	C/n	P/I	Date	Owner/operator	Probable Base	CA Expy
G-MYBR	Solar Wings Pegasus XL-Q (Rotax 462) SW-TE-0386 & SW-WQ-0517			16. 4.92	M.J.Larbey & G.T.Hunt	Watford	16. 6.99P
G-MYBS	Solar Wings Pegasus XL-Q (Rotax 462) SW-WQ-0518			16. 4.92	J.L.Parker	Maidstone	17. 7.99P
G-MYBT	Solar Wings Pegasus Quasar IIITC (Rotax 503) SW-WQT-0519			16. 4.92	I.D.Rutherford	High Wycombe	13. 8.99P
G-MYBU	Cyclone Chaser S (Rotax 447)	CH.837		28. 4.92	R.L.Arscott	Taunton	21. 1.00P
G-MYBV	Solar Wings Pegasus XL-Q (Rotax 462) SW-TE-0393 & SW-WQ-0522			5. 5.92	G.M.Balaam	Long Acre Farm, Sandy	1.10.99P
G-MYBW	Solar Wings Pegasus XL-Q SW-WQ-0523 (Rotax 462)			5. 5.92	B.J.Palfreyman	Newthorpe, Notts	15. 7.99P
G-MYBX	Solar Wings Pegasus XL-Q SW-WQ-0524 (Rotax 462)		(F-) G-MYBX	5. 5.92	P.A.Mowbray	Newark	28.11.92P*
G-MYBY	Solar Wings Pegasus XL-Q (Rotax 462) SW-TE-0396 & SW-WQ-0525			5. 5.92	P.R.Brooker	Smarden, Kent	12. 8.99P
G-MYBZ	Solar Wings Pegasus XL-Q (Rotax 462) SW-TE-0397 & SW-WQ-0526			5. 5.92	J.M.Todd	Long Marston	27. 9.97P
G-MYCA	Whittaker MW-6 Merlin PFA/164-11821 (Rotax 532)			14. 5.92	R.B.Skinner	Beaworthy, Devon	2. 4.99P
G-MYCB	Cyclone Chaser S (Rotax 447)	CH.839		18. 5.92	E.B.Jones	Crickhowell	15. 8.99P
G-MYCE	Solar Wings Pegasus Quasar IIITC (Rotax 503) SW-TQC-0098 & SW-WQT-0527			14. 5.92	J.G.Robinson	Scarborough	20. 6.99P
G-MYCF	Solar Wings Pegasus Quasar IIITC (Rotax 503) SW-TQC-0099 & SW-WQT-0528			14. 5.92	I.J.Bratt	Telford	26. 5.99P
G-MYCJ	Mainair Mercury 906-0592-5 & W704 (Rotax 503) (Wing c/n unconfirmed & duplicates G-MYAX)			19. 5.92	C.G.Rodger	East Fortune	17.11.99P
G-MYCK	Mainair Gemini/Flash 2A 909-0592-7 & W707 (Rotax 462)			19. 5.92	D.N.Powell	Ince Blundell, Liverpool	11. 6.99P
G-MYCL	Mainair Mercury 910-0592-5 & W708 (Rotax 503)			19. 5.92	Palladium Leisure Ltd	Fenland	10. 6.97P
G-MYCM	CFM Shadow Srs.CD	196		20. 5.92	T.Jones	Redhill	20. 5.99P
G-MYCN	Mainair Mercury 901-0492-5 & W696 (Rotax 503)			22. 5.92	C.S.Robinson	Newtownards	23. 2.99P
G-MYCO	Murphy Renegade Spirit UK PFA/188-12020 (Rotax 582)			28. 5.92	V.A. & C.V.Brierley	Dover	8. 3.98P
G-MYCP	Whittaker MW-6 Merlin PFA/164-11505 (Rotax 532)			2. 6.92	M. & S.E.L.Grocott	Otherton, Cannock	24.11.98P
G-MYCR	Mainair Gemini/Flash 2A 875-0192-7 & W670 (Rotax 503)			10. 6.92	L.M.S.Collier	Urmston, Manchester	9. 7.97P
G-MYCS	Mainair Gemini/Flash 2A 911-0592-7 & W710 (Rotax 503)			12. 6.92	G.Penson Baxby Manor, Husthwaite t/a Husthwaite Alpha Grp		23. 7.99P
G-MYCT	Team Minimax 91 PFA/186-12163 (Rotax 447)			30. 3.92	S.R.Roberts	Stowmarket	2.11.99P
G-MYCU	Whittaker MW-6 Merlin PFA/164-11627 (Rotax 532) (PFA c/n duplicates Streak Shadow G-ORAF)			9. 6.92	R.D.Thomasson	Romford	24. 8.99P
G-MYCV	Mainair Mercury 913-0792-5 & W712 (Rotax 503)			12. 6.92	D.P.Creedy	Crewe	11. 7.99P
G-MYCW	Powerchute Kestrel (Rotax 503)	00420		15. 6.92	C.D.Treffers	Basildon	1. 7.93P
G-MYCX	Powerchute Kestrel (Rotax 503)	00421		15. 6.92	D.Pedlow	Oswestry	24. 7.99P
G-MYCY	Powerchute Kestrel (Rotax 503)	00422		15. 6.92	D.S.Baber	Amersham	16. 8.99P
G-MYCZ	Powerchute Kestrel (Rotax 503)	00423		15. 6.92	A.F.Hardy	Newtownards	10.10.95P
G-MYDA	Powerchute Kestrel (Rotax 503)	00424		15. 6.92	K.J.Greatrix	Sleaford	17.11.99P
G-MYDB	Powerchute Kestrel (Rotax 503)	00425		15. 6.92	Coppard Plant Hire Ltd	Crowborough	28.10.93P
G-MYDC	Mainair Mercury 916-0792-5 & W715 (Rotax 503)			23. 6.92	D.J.Boylan & D.Gordon	Rufforth	9. 9.99P
G-MYDE	CFM Shadow Srs.CD (Rotax 503)	K.187		24. 6.92	T.W.Seymour	Tilehurst	11. 1.99P
G-MYDF	Team Minimax 91 PFA/186-12129 (Rotax 447)			24. 6.92	A.R.Mikolajczyk	Mansfield	7. 9.99P
G-MYDI	Solar Wings Pegasus XL-R SW-WA-1557 (Rotax 462HP)			26. 6.92	W.Greenwood(Stored 8.98) Swanborough t/a Southern Hang Gliding Aerotow Group		24. 4.99P
G-MYDJ	Solar Wings Pegasus XL-R SW-WA-1558 (Rotax 462)			1. 7.92	A.M.Webb Swanton Morley t/a Norfolk Aero Tow		7. 5.99P
G-MYDK	Rans S-6-ESD Coyote II (Rotax 503) 0392-276 & PFA/204-12239			21. 4.92	E.Gordon t/a G-MYDK Grp	Eshott	20. 4.99P
G-MYDL	Aerotech MW-5(K) Sorcerer PFA/163-12106			26. 6.92	S.J.Field	Bridgwater	
G-MYDM	Whittaker MW-6S Fatboy Flyer (Rotax 582) PFA/164-12105			26. 6.92	A.L. & A.R.Roberts	Lincoln	29. 1.99P

Regn	Type	C/n P/I	Date	Owner/operator	Probable Base	CA Expy
G-MYDN	Quad City Challenger II UK (Rotax 462) CH2-1091-UK-0736 & PFA/177-12245		30. 6.92	T.C. & R.Hooks	Newtownards	9. 7.99P
G-MYDO	Rans S-5 Coyote (Rotax 447) 89-110 & PFA/193-12274		6. 7.92	B.J.Benton	Long Marston	19. 8.98P
G-MYDP	Kolb Twinstar Mk.3 PFA/205-12231 (Rotax 503)		15. 7.92	M.H.Rollins & J.W.Harrison	Solihull	14. 4.99P
G-MYDR	Thruster T300 9072-T300-505 (Rotax 582)		21. 7.92	H.G.Soper	Lewes	19. 7.99P
G-MYDS	Quad City Challenger II UK (Rotax 503) CH2-1289-UK-0500 & PFA/177-11716		6. 3.90	A.C.Ryall	Swansea	26. 6.99P
G-MYDT	Thruster T300 9072-T300-506 (Rotax 582)		21. 7.92	A.W.Brandsom Ford Hill Farm, Ternhill		10. 1.96P
G-MYDU	Thruster T300 9072-T300-504 (Rotax 582)		21. 7.92	Euroflight Microlight Club Ltd Dromore, Co.Down		18. 4.99P
G-MYDV	Mainair Gemini/Flash 2A 917-0892-7 & W716 (Rotax 462)		29. 7.92	A.Gibson	St.Michaels-on-Wyre	27. 8.99P
G-MYDW	Whittaker MW-6 Merlin PFA/164-12184 (Rotax 503)		27. 7.92	W.R.G.West	Taunton	26. 4.96P
G-MYDX	Rans S-6-ESD Coyote II PFA/204-12238 (Rotax 503)		27. 7.92	R.J.Goodburn "The Ruptured Duck"	Spanhoe	27. 4.99P
G-MYDZ	Mignet HM-1000 Balerit 66 (Rotax 582)		3. 8.92	Fleaplanes UK Ltd	Rush Green	12.12.99P
G-MYEA	Solar Wings Pegasus XL-Q (Rotax 462HP) SW-TE-0404 & SW-WQ-0537		28. 7.92	A.M.Taylor	Long Marston	18. 9.99P
G-MYEC	Solar Wings Pegasus XL-Q (Rotax 462HP) SW-TE-0406 & SW-WQ-0539		28. 7.92	D.Young t/a Pegasus Flight Training	Kemble	7. 5.99P
G-MYED	Solar Wings Pegasus XL-R (Rotax 462HP) SW-TE-0405 & SW-WA-1559		28. 7.92	I.A.Clark (Trike may be SW-TE-0403)	Grimsby	13. 3.99P
G-MYEE*	Thruster TST mk.1 087-TST-206 (Rotax 503) (Imported 12.90 - ex ZK-FRW ?)		11. 8.92	A.P.Gornall (Cancelled as destroyed 16.10.98)	Popham	1.12.98P
G-MYEF*	Whittaker MW-6 Merlin PFA/164-11327		28. 5.92	S.Meadowcroft (Cancelled by CAA 6.3.99)	Manchester	
G-MYEG	Solar Wings Pegasus XL-R (Rotax 447) SW-TB-1447 & SW-WA-1560		4. 8.92	D.G.Matthews	London Colney	1.10.98P
G-MYEH	Solar Wings Pegasus XL-R SW-WA-1561 (Rotax 447)		4. 8.92	J.Hardy	Kettering	25.10.98P
G-MYEI	Cyclone Chaser S CH.841 (Rotax 447)		18. 8.92	T.Cottrell	Douglas, IOM	18. 4.99P
G-MYEJ	Cyclone Chaser S CH.842 (Rotax 447)		18. 8.92	D.A.Cochrane	Newnham	27. 9.98P
G-MYEK	Solar Wings Pegasus Quasar IITC (Rotax 582/40) SW-TQD-0108 & SW-WQT-0540		7. 8.92	B.A.McWilliams (See G-MWZF)	Droitwich	17. 8.95P
G-MYEM	Solar Wings Pegasus Quasar IITC (Rotax 582/40) SW-TQD-0101 & SW-WQT-0542		7. 8.92	D.J.Moore	Oakington, Cambs	31. 7.99P
G-MYEN	Solar Wings Pegasus Quasar IITC (Rotax 582/40) SW-TQD-0105 & SW-WQT-0543		7. 8.92	P.R.Jeffcoat & D.Johnson	Upton Snodsbury	24. 1.00P
G-MYEO	Solar Wings Pegasus Quasar IITC (Rotax 582/40) SW-TQD-0106 & SW-WQT-0544		7. 8.92	Avelec Ltd	Enstone	20. 7.99P
G-MYEP	CFM Shadow Srs.CD K.205 (Rotax 503)		13. 8.92	R.Powers	Walsall	15. 4.99P
G-MYER	Cyclone AX2000 B.1052901 & CA.001 G-69-3 (Rotax 582/48) 59-GD		19. 8.92	W.J.Whyte	Insch	24. 6.99P
G-MYES	Rans S-6-ESD Coyote II (Rotax 503) 0392-283 & PFA/204-12254		3. 7.92	W.R.Gilgrist t/a Dairy House Flyers	Tarporley	3. 1.00P
G-MYET	Whittaker MW-6 Merlin PFA/164-12318 (Rotax 503)		19. 8.92	M.B.Haine	Christchurch	3. 8.98P
G-MYEU	Mainair Gemini/Flash 2A 918-0892-7 & W718 (Rotax 503)		1. 9.92	G.J.Webster & G.J.Williams	Telford	6. 5.99P
G-MYEV	Whittaker MW-6 Merlin PFA/164-11250		25. 8.92	M.M.Ruck	Pontyclun	
G-MYEX	Powerchute Kestrel 00426 (Rotax 503)		28. 8.92	R.S.McFadyen	Tamworth	5.11.99P
G-MYFA	Powerchute Kestrel 00429 (Rotax 503)		28. 8.95	D.A.Gardner	Balfron, Glasgow	23. 3.98P
G-MYFE	Rans S-6-ESD Coyote II PFA/204-12232 (Rotax 503)		1. 9.92	K.A.Mitchell	Henley-in-Arden	22. 9.99P
G-MYFG	Hunt Avon Skytrike/Hunt Wing 92040006 & BMAA/HB/017		4. 9.92	S.F.Carey (Cancelled by CAA 16.7.98)	London SE19	
G-MYFH	Quad City Challenger II UK (Rotax 503) CH2-0292-0798 & PFA/177-12282		9. 9.92	R.J. & C.J.Lines	Sandtoft	26. 2.99P
G-MYFI	Cyclone AX3 C.3093159 & CA.002 (Rotax 503)		9. 9.92	C.M.Bulmer & P.M.Voznick Hitchin/London N1		5.12.99P
G-MYFJ	Solar Wings Pegasus Quasar IITC SW-WQT-0552 (Rotax 582/40)		11. 9.92	J.Mannion	Kettlethorpe, Lincoln	20.3.93P*
G-MYFK	Solar Wings Pegasus Quasar IITC (Rotax 582/40) SW-TQD-0113 & SW-WQT-0553		11. 9.92	P.Corke	Long Acre Farm, Sandy	9. 6.99P
G-MYFL	Solar Wings Pegasus Quasar IITC (Rotax 582/40) SW-TQD-0103 & SW-WQT-0541/A		11. 9.92	G.P.Austin Mill Farm, Hughley, Much Wenlock		30. 5.99P

(Originally regd as c/n SW-WQT-0554; replacement wing fitted to trike G-MYEL after wing stolen 1.1.93)

Regn	Type	C/n P/I	Date	Owner/operator	Probable Base	CA Expy
G-MYFM	Murphy Renegade Spirit UK (Rotax 582)	PFA/188-12249	9. 9.92	A.C.Cale	Long Marston	3.11.99P
G-MYFN	Rans S-5 Coyote (Rotax 447)	89-112 & PFA/193-12273	16. 9.92	D.J.Minary	Rufforth	25. 2.99P
G-MYFO	Cyclone Chaser S (Rotax 377)	CH.843	22. 9.92	A.P.Skipper	Wollaston	3. 5.99P
G-MYFP	Mainair Gemini/Flash 2A (Rotax 503)	920-0992-7 & W719	2.10.92	G.T.Corfield	Otherton, Cannock	9.11.99P
G-MYFR	Mainair Gemini/Flash 2A (Rotax 503)	921-0992-7 & W720	30. 9.92	M.A.Pugh	London N10	10. 7.97P
G-MYFS	Solar Wings Pegasus XL-R (Rotax 447)	SW-TB-1453 & SW-WA-1564	30. 9.92	A.Godber (Damaged mid 1995; stored 4.96)	Alrewas	2. 7.95P
G-MYFT	Mainair Scorcher (Rotax 503)	922-0992-3 & W234	30. 9.92	M.P.Law	Rochdale	10. 8.99P
G-MYFU	Mainair Gemini/Flash 2A (Rotax 462)	924-1092-7 & W722	7.10.92	S.Meadowcroft	Barton	8. 5.99P
G-MYFV	Cyclone AX3 (Rotax 503)	C.2083050	6.10.92	P.J. Barton	Sandy	24.11.99P
G-MYFW	Cyclone AX3 (Rotax 503)	C.2083051	13.10.92	T.W.Stewart & D.L.Frankland t/a G-MYFW F/Grp	Eshott	29. 7.99P
G-MYFX	Solar Wings Pegasus XL-Q (Rotax 462)	SW-WQ-0378 (ex)	25. 6.93	M.M.Danek	Clench Common	19. 7.98P
G-MYFY	Cyclone AX3 (Rotax 503)	C.2083047	1.10.92	P.Rielly & F.J.Lloyd	Tarn Farm, Cockerham	15.11.99P
G-MYFZ	Cyclone AX3 (Rotax 503)	C.2083048	20.10.92	M.L.Smith t/a Buzzard Flying Group	Popham	25.11.99P
G-MYGD	Cyclone AX3 (Rotax 503)	C.2083049	21.10.92	D.Young t/a Kemble Flying Club (Stored 6.97)	Kemble	3.12.99P
G-MYGE	Whittaker MW-6 Merlin (Rotax 532)	PFA/164-11650	20.10.92	M.D. & S.M.North	Manor Farm, Croughton	24. 6.97P
G-MYGF	Team Minimax 91 (Rotax 447)	PFA/186-12175	22.10.92	R.D.Barnard	Stockport	9. 4.98P
G-MYGG*	Mainair Mercury (Rotax 503)	927-1192-7 & W724	18.11.92	Not known (Crashed nr Sandtoft 31.8.95: wreck stored 5.97)	Sandtoft	17.11.95P
G-MYGH	Rans S-6-ESD Coyote II (Rotax 503)	0692-318 & PFA/204-12335	30.10.92	J.A.Moss	Needham, Harleston	19. 8.97P
G-MYGI	Cyclone Chaser S (Rotax 447)	CH.844	2.11.92	A.D.Stanyer	Sywell	26. 7.99P
G-MYGJ	Mainair Mercury (Rotax 503)	923-0992-7 & W721	5.10.92	N.E.Parkinson	Arclid Green, Sandbach	22.10.99P
G-MYGK	Cyclone Chaser S (Rotax 508)	CH.846	3.11.92	P.C.Collins	Bath	14.11.95P
G-MYGM	Quad City Challenger II UK (Rotax 503) PFA/177-12261 & CH2-0391-UK-0662		6.11.92	R.Holt	Mill Farm, Hughley, Much Wenlock	29. 7.99P
G-MYGN	AMF Super Chevvron 2-32C (Konig SD.570)	034	29.12.92	Finish Design Ltd t/a Air-Share	Tarn Farm, Cockerham	1. 8.98P
G-MYGO	CFM Shadow Srs.CD (Rotax 503)	K.114	28. 7.92	R.C.S.Mason	Wootton, Bedford	22.10.98P
G-MYGP	Rans S-6-ESD Coyote II (Rotax 503)	0992-349 & PFA/204-12368	10.11.92	J.H.Kempton	Salcombe	16. 4.98P
G-MYGR	Rans S-6-ESD Coyote II (Rotax 503)	PFA/204-12378	16.11.92	D.Wallace	Plymouth	14. 2.99P
G-MYGT	Solar Wings Pegasus XL-R (Rotax 462)	SW-WA-1569	13.11.92	J.J.Hoer t/a Condors Aerotow Syndicate	Dunkeswell	18. 2.99P
G-MYGU	Solar Wings Pegasus XL-R (Rotax 462)	SW-TE-0414 & SW-WA-1570	13.11.92	W.H.J.Knowles	Weston Zoyland	11. 8.99P
G-MYGV	Solar Wings Pegasus XL-R (Rotax 462HP)	SW-TE-0415 & SW-WA-1571	13.11.92	D.J.Brixton t/a Shropshire Tow Grp	Bishops Castle, Shropshire	7. 5.99P
G-MYGZ	Mainair Gemini/Flash 2A (Rotax 582)	928-1192-7 & W726	18.11.92	J.G.Lloyd	Harlow	20.11.99P
G-MYHF	Mainair Gemini/Flash 2A (Rotax 503)	929-1092-7 & W727	25.11.92	J.R.Gibson	St.Michaels-on-Wyre	17. 6.99P
G-MYHG	Cyclone AX3 (Rotax 503)	C.2103070	27.11.92	I.McDiarmid t/a G-MYHG F/Grp	Strathaven	10. 6.99P
G-MYHH	Cyclone AX3 (Rotax 503)	C.2103069 & CA.006	30.11.92	M.L.Smith	Popham	29. 3.99P
G-MYHI	Rans S-6-ESD Coyote II (Rotax 503)	PFA/204-12279	8.12.92	L.N.Anderson	Weston Zoyland	30. 6.99P
G-MYHJ	Cyclone AX3 (Rotax 503) C.2103073 (Reported as c/n C.3093157 - see G-MYME)		11.12.92	P.E.Clarke	Long Marston	7. 2.99P
G-MYHK	Rans S-6-ESD Coyote II (Rotax 503)	0692-311 & PFA/204-12349	3.12.92	K.Joynson & M.A.Dunn	Sandtoft	27. 4.99P
G-MYHL	Mainair Gemini/Flash 2A (Rotax 503)	932-0193-7 & W730	21.12.92	P.J.Morton	New Mills	3. 2.99P
G-MYHM	Cyclone AX3 (Rotax 503)	C.2103068 & CA.007	18.12.92	A.J.Bergman	Popham	17. 7.99P
G-MYHN	Mainair Gemini/Flash 2A (Rotax 582)	933-0193-7 & W731	29.12.92	D.M.Waddle	Pontefract	18. 5.99P
G-MYHP	Rans S-6-ESD Coyote II (Rotax 503)	0892-313 & PFA/204-12406	8. 1.93	J.M.Swash "Grass Stripper"	Sittles Farm, Alrewas	25. 6.99P
G-MYHR	Cyclone AX3 (Rotax 503)	C.2103071	15. 1.93	Aerolite Flight Parks Ltd t/a Aerolite	Long Marston	14. 3.99P

Regn	Type	C/n	P/I	Date	Owner/operator	Probable Base	CA Expy
G-MYHS	Powerchute Kestrel (Rotax 503)	00433		26. 1.93	R.Kent	Newark	6. 4.99P
G-MYHX	Mainair Gemini/Flash 2A (Rotax 582)	930-1292-7 & W728		2.12.92	M.J.Allan	Lasswade, Midlothian	22.12.99P
G-MYIA	Quad City Challenger II UK (Rotax 503)		PFA/177-12400	21. 1.93	I.J.Arkieson	Hawarden	26. 3.97P
G-MYIE	Whittaker MW-6S Fatboy Flyer (Rotax 532)		PFA/164-11800	26. 1.93	P.A.Mercer	St.Michaels-on-Wyre	20. 5.99P
G-MYIF	CFM Shadow Srs CD (Rotax 503)	217		2. 2.93	A.W.Shellis & S.D.Taylor, Otherton, Cannock		15. 4.99P
G-MYIG*	Murphy Renegade Spirit		PFA/118-11725	2. 2.93	J R Peters	Birmingham	
	(Cancelled as temporarily wfu 26.7.94: not completed and will now emerge as G-TBMW)						
G-MYIH	Mainair Gemini/Flash 2A 937-0293-7 & W734 (Rotax 582)			9. 3.93	C.A.Murray t/a G-MYIH F/Grp	Loughton, Essex	27. 5.99P
G-MYII	Team Minimax 91 (Mosler CB40)		PFA/186-12119	10.11.92	K.R.H.Wingate	Hallwell, Totnes	23. 3.99P
G-MYIJ	Cyclone AX3 (Rotax 503)	C.2103072		8. 2.93	G.A.Breen	Lagos, Algarve	15. 4.99P
G-MYIK	Kolb Twinstar mk.3		PFA/205-12220	13. 1.93	J.Latimer	Altrincham	21. 5.99P
G-MYIL	Cyclone Chaser S (Rotax 508)	CH.849		3. 3.93	R.A.Rawes "Fricky"	Bradley Stoke, Bristol	23. 1.00P
G-MYIM	Solar Wings Pegasus Quasar IITC (Rotax 582/40)	SW-WQT-0579	(EI-) G-MYIM	22. 2.93	D.Forde	Co. Galway, Ireland	3. 6.97P
G-MYIN	Solar Wings Pegasus SW-TQD-0123 & SW-WQT-0580 Quasar IITC (Rotax 582/40)			22. 2.93	M.P.Hadden	Long Marston	17. 7.98P
G-MYIO	Solar Wings Pegasus SW-TQD-0124 & SW-WQT-0581 Quasar IITC (Rotax 582/40)			22. 2.93	K.W.Brock	London SW19	11. 6.97P
G-MYIP	CFM Shadow Srs.CD (Rotax 503)	K.198		16. 3.93	S.S.M.Allardice	Old Sarum	18.11.99P
G-MYIR	Rans S-6-ESD Coyote II (Rotax 503)	0892-344	& PFA/204-12458	17. 3.93	I.R.Westrope	Haverhill, Suffolk	19. 8.99P
G-MYIS	Rans S-6-ESD Coyote II PFA/204-12382 (Rotax 503)			31.12.92	A.J.Wyatt	Haverfordwest	26. 5.99P
G-MYIT	Cyclone Chaser S (Rotax 508)	CH.850		19. 3.93	R.Barringer	Ravensthorpe, Northampton	28. 3.99P
G-MYIU	Cyclone AX3 (Rotax 503)	C.3013084		22. 3.93	S.Armstrong	Enniskillen	10. 3.99P
G-MYIV	Mainair Gemini/Flash 2A 938-0393-7 & W735 (Rotax 582)			30. 3.93	P.S.Nicholls	Finmere	5. 4.99P
G-MYIX	Quad City Challenger II UK (Rotax 503) CH2-0191-UK-0615 & PFA/177-12260			5. 1.93	A.Studley	Crewkerne	20. 7.99P
G-MYIY	Mainair Gemini/Flash 2A 942-0493-7 & W737 (Rotax 503)			1. 4.93	J.H.Bradbury	Sandbach	10. 5.99P
G-MYIZ	Team Minimax 91 (Rotax 447)		PFA/186-12347	31. 3.93	S.E.Richardson	Escrick, York	26. 4.99P
G-MYJB	Mainair Gemini/Flash 2A 943-0593-7 & W738 (Rotax 503)			7. 4.93	D.J.A.Sim & J.A.Parry-Sim	Spalding	6.11.99P
G-MYJC	Mainair Gemini/Flash 2A 944-0593-7 & W739 (Rotax 462)			7. 4.93	J.E.Cunliffe	Rufforth	14. 4.99P
G-MYJD	Rans S-6-ESD Coyote II (Rotax 503) 0792-324 & PFA/204-12360			23. 4.93	D.M.Newbould	Macclesfield	8. 9.99P
G-MYJE	CFM Shadow Srs.CD (Rotax 503)	185		26. 9.91	A.K.Paterson	Sleaford	26. 4.97P
G-MYJF	Thruster T.300 (Rotax 582)	9013-T300-509		14. 4.93	B.McConville	Craigavon, NI	11. 9.99P
G-MYJG	Thruster T.300 (Rotax 582)	9043-T300-510		14. 4.93	J.E.L.Goodall	Broadway	17. 3.99P
G-MYJH	Thruster T.300 (Rotax 582)	9013-T300-508		14. 4.93	B.O. & B.C.McCartan	Banbridge, Co.Down	13.12.99P
G-MYJJ	Solar Wings Pegasus Quasar IITC (Rotax 582/40) SW-TQD-0131 & SW-WQT-0591			27. 4.93	J.H.Sparks	Franklyns Field, Chewton Mendip	13. 9.98P
G-MYJK	Solar Wings Pegasus Quasar IITC SW-WQT-0592 (Rotax 582/40)			27. 4.93	P.Kneeshaw	Alford	9. 5.99P
G-MYJL	Rans S-6-ESD Coyote II PFA/204-12476 (Rotax 503)			28. 4.93	R.J.Giddings & C.R.Marriott	Sutton Meadows, Ely	27. 6.99P
G-MYJM	Mainair Gemini/Flash 2A 945-0593-7 & W740 (Rotax 582)			29. 4.93	A.J.Boyd	Bangor, NI	25. 9.99P
G-MYJN	Mainair Mercury 946-0593-7 & W741 (Rotax 503)			29. 4.93	J.Howarth	Mansfield	24. 5.95P
G-MYJO	Cyclone Chaser S (Rotax 508)	CH.851		30. 4.93	J.F.Phillips	Liskeard	24. 7.99P
G-MYJP	Murphy Renegade Spirit UK (Rotax 582)	357	& PFA/188-12045	3. 4.91	J.W.E.Pearson "Cloud Dancer/The Spirit of Luck"	Burstom, St.Albans	27.10.99P
G-MYJR	Mainair Mercury 947-0593-7 & W742 (Rotax 503)			12. 5.93	T.C.F.Heaney	Epping	27. 1.99P
G-MYJS	Solar Wings Pegasus Quasar IITC 6581 (Rotax 582/40)			19. 5.93	P.J.Barton	Long Acre Farm, Sandy	7. 7.96P
G-MYJT	Solar Wings Pegasus Quasar IITC 6582 (Rotax 582/40)			19. 5.93	G.Stadler	Eshott	12. 9.99P
G-MYJU	Solar Wings Pegasus Quasar IITC 6573 (Rotax 582)			19. 5.93	P.G.Penhaligan	Hemel Hempstead	30. 5.99P
G-MYJW	Cyclone Chaser S (Rotax 508)	CH.856		19. 5.93	P.M.Coppola (Stored 8.96)	East Fortune	10. 9.94P

Regn	Type	C/n	P/I	Date	Owner/operator	Probable Base	CA Expy
G-MYJX	Whittaker MW-8 001 & PFA/243-12345 (Rotax 508)			24. 5.93	M.W.J.Whittaker	Doncaster	3.12.95P*
G-MYJY	Rans S-6-ESD Coyote II (Rotax 503) 0692-317 & PFA/204-12346			24. 5.93	F.N.Pearson	Baxby Manor, Husthwaite	23. 8.99P
G-MYJZ	Whittaker MW-5D Sorcerer (Rotax 447) PFA/163-12385			22. 4.93	P.A.Aston	Newton Abbot	2.12.99P
G-MYKA	Cyclone AX3 C.3013086 (Rotax 503)			25. 5.93	J.Thomas	Sandy	3. 1.00P
G-MYKB	Kolb Twinstar mk.3 PFA/205-12398 (Rotax 582)			31. 3.93	D.Young	Coleford	27. 8.99P
G-MYKC	Mainair Gemini/Flash 2A 948-0593-7 & W743 (Rotax 582)			26. 5.93	J.Summersgill	Warrington	22.12.99P
G-MYKD	Cyclone Chaser S CH.857 (Rotax 447)			26. 5.93	J.V.Clewer	Ashford, Kent	9. 8.98P
G-MYKE	CFM Shadow Srs.BD K.031 (Rotax 447)			14. 1.88	M.Hughes Emlyn's Field, Rhuallt t/a MKH Engineering		26.10.96P
G-MYKF	Cyclone AX3 C.3013083 (Rotax 503)			8. 6.93	P.Jones	Tarn Farm, Cockerham	10. 7.99P
G-MYKG	Mainair Gemini/Flash 2A 950-0693-7 & W745 (Rotax 582)			21. 6.93	P.G.Angus	High Barn Farm, Houghton	27. 9.99P
G-MYKH	Mainair Gemini/Flash 2A 951-0693-7 & W746 (Rotax 582)			21. 6.93	K.G. & G.F.Atkinson Rufforth t/a F.Atkinson & Sons		4. 9.99P
G-MYKI	Mainair Mercury 953-0693-7 & W748 (Rotax 503)			21. 6.93	B.J.Webster	Ormskirk	4.10.98P
G-MYKJ	Team Minimax PFA/186-12215 (Rotax 508)			10. 6.93	P.I.Frost	Guilsborough, Northampton	3. 9.99P
G-MYKL	Medway Raven X MRB116/104 (Rotax 447)			6. 7.93	S.Hutchinson	RAF Wyton	6. 9.99P
G-MYKN	Rans S-6-ESD Coyote II PFA/204-12361 (Rotax 503)			23. 6.93	S.E. & L.Hartles "Captain Airfix" Lower Mountpleasant Farm, Chatteris		9.11.99P
G-MYKO	Whittaker MW-6S Fatboy Flyer (Hirth 2706) PFA/164-11919			25. 6.93	J.Glover	Bristol	23. 6.99P
G-MYKP	Solar Wings Pegasus Quasar IITC 6627 (Rotax 582/40)			7. 7.93	J.Mayer	Stoke-on-Trent	29. 8.98P
G-MYKR	Solar Wings Pegasus Quasar IITC 6635 (Rotax 582/40)			7. 7.93	C.Stallard	Jersey	8. 7.99P
G-MYKS	Solar Wings Pegasus Quasar IITC 6636 (Rotax 582/40)			7. 7.93	P.W.Sandwith	Pinner	14. 5.99P
G-MYKT	Cyclone AX3 (Rotax 503) C.3013082			5. 7.93	A.Cooke-Sanderson t/a G-MYKT Grp	Popham	8. 7.99P
G-MYKU	Medway Raven X MRB117/107 (Rotax 447)			9. 7.93	M.Woodmansey	Davidstow Moor	18. 6.99P
G-MYKV	Mainair Gemini/Flash 2A 954-0793-7 & W749 (Rotax 503)			13. 7.93	J.White & P.Gulliver	Telford	2. 2.99P
G-MYKW	Mainair Mercury 960-0893-7 & W755 (Rotax 503)			9. 7.93	N.O.Marsh	Rufforth	1. 3.99P
G-MYKX*	Mainair Mercury 961-0893-7 & W756 (Rotax 503)			3. 9.93	L.R.Bain (Cancelled by CAA 27.3.99)	Perth	30.10.99P
G-MYKY	Mainair Mercury 962-0893-7 & W757 (Rotax 503)			6. 8.93	R.P.Jewitt	York	14.12.99P
G-MYKZ	Team Minimax 91 PFA/186-11841	G-BVAV		26. 7.93	W.W.Vinton	Cinderford	14. 7.98P
	(Rotax 503)						
G-MYLA	Rans S-6-ESD Coyote II PFA/204-12543 (Rotax 503)			30. 7.93	W.A.Stevens	Colchester	18. 5.99P
G-MYLB	Team Minimax 91 PFA/186-12419 (Rotax 532)			2. 8.93	S.Stockill	Buckingham	5. 8.98P
G-MYLC	Solar Wings Pegasus Quantum 15 6634 (Rotax 503)			9. 8.93	T.E.Pedley	Earlswood	12. 6.98P
G-MYLD	Rans S-6-ESD Coyote II PFA/204-12394 (Rotax 503)			1. 3.93	F.Overall	Priory Farm	25. 6.99P
G-MYLE	Solar Wings Pegasus Quantum 15 6609 (Rotax 503)			9. 8.93	Susan E.Powell	Enstone	19.12.99P
G-MYLF	Rans S-6-ESD Coyote II (Rotax 503) 0493-483 & PFA/204-12544			4. 8.93	G.R. & J.A.Pritchard "Low Flyer" Newhouse Farm, Hardwicke, Hereford		16.11.99P
G-MYLG	Mainair Gemini/Flash 2A 959-0893-7 & W754 (Rotax 503)			6. 8.93	B.A.Coombe	Weybridge	2.12.98P
G-MYLH	Solar Wings Pegasus Quantum 15 6632 (Rotax 503)			27. 8.93	T.D'Amico	Northampton	26. 7.98P
G-MYLI	Solar Wings Pegasus Quantum 15 6645 (Rotax 503)			11. 8.93	E.Jenkins & S.Walters t/a Metropolitan Police SE Area Microlight Acft Club		9. 5.99P
G-MYLJ	Cyclone Chaser S (Rotax 447) CH.858			24. 8.93	B.W.Atkinson	North Coates	30. 1.99P
G-MYLK	Solar Wings Pegasus Quantum 15 6602 (Rotax 503)			27. 8.93	C.L.Minter t/a G-MYLK Group	Northampton	7. 9.99P
G-MYLL	Solar Wings Pegasus Quantum 15 6650 (Rotax 462HP)			31. 8.93	N.Demmar	Warminster	21. 3.99P
G-MYLM	Solar Wings Pegasus Quantum 15 6651 (Rotax 582/40)		(EC-) G-MYLM	31. 8.93	P.A.Banks	Milton Keynes	29. 7.99P

Regn	Type	C/n	P/I	Date	Owner/operator	Probable Base	CA Expy
G-MYLN	Kolb Twinstar mk.3 PFA/205-12430 (Rotax 582)			3. 9.93	C.D.Hatcher	Peterborough	14. 6.99P
G-MYLO	Rans S-6-ESD Coyote II PFA/204-12334 (Rotax 503)			9. 9.93	M.J.W.Holding & A.W.Brandsom	Stafford/Stone	25. 6.99P
G-MYLP	Kolb Twinstar mk.3 PFA/205-12391 (Rotax 582)		(G-BVCR)	9. 9.93	R.Thompson	Bristol	27. 5.99P
G-MYLR	Mainair Gemini/Flash 2A 964-0993-7 & W759 (Rotax 582)			17. 9.93	S.A.Owen	East Fortune	24. 3.99P
G-MYLS	Mainair Mercury 966-0993-7 & W761 (Rotax 503)			5.10.93	D.Burnell-Higgs	Shobdon	6.11.96P
G-MYLT	Mainair Blade 967-1093-7 & W762 (Rotax 582)			23. 9.93	A.R.Walsh	Preston	27. 5.99P
G-MYLV	CFM Shadow Srs.CD (Rotax 503) 220			24. 9.93	G.Gilhead & R.G.M.Proost t/a Aviation for Paraplegics & Tetraplegics Trust	Old Sarum	20.12.99P
G-MYLW	Rans S-6-ESD Coyote II (Rotax 503) 1292-401 & PFA/204-12560			4. 8.93	M.J.Phillips	Priory Farm, Tibenham	8.12.97P
G-MYLX	Medway Raven X (Rotax 447)MRB113/109			6.10.93	T.M.Knight	Luton	13.12.98P
G-MYLY	Medway Raven X (Rotax 447)MRB001/108			23. 9.93	C.R.Smith	Stanford-le-Hope	3.10.94P
G-MYLZ	Solar Wings Pegasus Quantum 15 6672 (Rotax 462)			6.10.93	J.L.Pollard & K.M.Walter Knapthorpe Lodge, Caunton, Notts		21.11.99P
G-MYMB	Solar Wings Pegasus Quantum 15 6674 (Rotax 582/40)			6.10.93	C.A.Green "Firebird"	Winterborne Earls	6. 2.99P
G-MYMC	Solar Wings Pegasus Quantum 15 6675 (Rotax 582/40)			6.10.93	D.W.Johnston & C.D.Slater	Northwich/Canterbury	20.12.97P
G-MYMD	Solar Wings Pegasus Quantum 15 6655 (Rotax 503)			8.10.93	P.Simpson	Potters Bar	4.12.99P
G-MYME	Cyclone AX3 (Rotax 503) C.3093157			13.10.93	M.L.Smith (See G-MYHJ)	Popham	16.11.99P
G-MYMF	Cyclone AX3 (Rotax 503) C.3093158			18.10.93	M.McClelland t/a McClelland Aviation	Old Sarum	5.11.99P
G-MYMG	Team Minimax 91 PFA/186-12336			18.10.93	D.Bannister	West Kilbride	
G-MYMH	Rans S-6-ESD Coyote II (Rotax 503) 0793-520 & PFA/204-12576			20.10.93	E.O.Otun	Maidenhead	22. 3.99P
G-MYMI	Kolb Twinstar mk.3 PFA/205-12537 (Rotax 582)			21.10.93	R.P.T.Harris	High Wycombe	21. 7.99P
G-MYMJ	Medway Raven X (Rotax 447)MRB004/110			28.10.93	N.Brigginshaw	Fenland	24. 1.99P
G-MYMK	Mainair Gemini/Flash 2A 968-1193-7 & W763 (Rotax 582)			29.10.93	A.Britton	Rickmansworth	27.11.99P
G-MYML	Mainair Mercury 969-1193-7 & W765 (Rotax 503)			29.10.93	D.J.Dalley	Weymouth	21.10.98P
G-MYMM	Air Creation Fun 18S GT bis 93/001 (Rotax 503)			30. 9.93	A.B.Greenbank High Barn Farm, Houghton		23.10.98P
G-MYMN	Whittaker MW-6 Merlin PFA/164-12124 (Rotax 582)			29.10.93	K.J.Cole	Highnam, Gloucester	17. 5.99P
G-MYMO	Mainair Gemini/Flash 2A 955-0793-7 & W750 (Rotax 503)			24. 6.93	R.C.Colclough Ince Blundell, Liverpool		13. 8.99P
G-MYMP	Rans S-6-ESD Coyote II (Rotax 503) 1291-250 & PFA/204-12436		(G-CHAZ)	5.11.93	G.P.Jones	Stoke-on-Trent	4.11.99P
G-MYMR	Rans S-6-ESD Coyote II PFA/204-12580 (Rotax 503)			17.11.93	J.Neilands	Ballybofey, Co.Donegal	11.10.99P
G-MYMS	Rans S-6-ESD Coyote II (Rotax 503) 0893-526 & PFA/204-12581			17.11.93	M.R.Johnson & P.G.Briscoe	Warwick	23. 8.99P
G-MYMT	Mainair Mercury 970-1193-7 & W766 (Rotax 503)			19.11.93	W. & C.A.Bradshaw	St.Michaels-on-Wyre	7.12.99P
G-MYMV	Mainair Gemini/Flash 2A 971-1193-7 & W767 (Rotax 503)			26.11.93	W.A.Edwards Guy Lane Farm, Waverton		14. 2.99P
G-MYMW	Cyclone AX3 (Rotax 503) C.3093156			23.11.93	L.J.Perring	Oakley	2.12.99P
G-MYMX	Solar Wings Pegasus Quantum 15 6705 (Rotax 582/40)			1.12.93	J.E.McGee	Hexham	24.11.98P
G-MYMY	Cyclone Chaser S (Rotax 508) CH.860			7. 9.93	R.A.Keene	Over, Gloucester	7. 4.99P
G-MYMZ	Cyclone AX3 (Rotax 503) C.3093154			7.12.93	L.G.Dobinson	Otherton, Cannock	15. 4.99P
G-MYNA	CFM Shadow Srs.C (Rotax 447) K.023			10. 2.88	P.J.Walker	Lincoln	4. 7.99P
G-MYNB	Solar Wings Pegasus Quantum 15 6719 (Rotax 582/40)			14.12.93	S.B.C.Wall	Melton Mowbray	23. 4.99P
G-MYNC	Mainair Mercury 973-1293-7 & W769 (Rotax 503)			17.12.93	A.Brotheridge	Redlands, Swindon	12. 8.98P
G-MYND	Mainair Gemini/Flash 2A 841-0591-7 & W635 (Rotax 503)			28. 5.91	G.C.Baird	Ludlow	4.12.98P
G-MYNE	Rans S-6-ESD Coyote II PFA/204-12497 (Rotax 503)			25. 6.93	J.N.W.Moss	Templecombe	20. 6.99P
G-MYNF	Mainair Mercury 974-1293-7 & W770 (Rotax 503)			17. 1.94	E.D.Locke	Barton	24. 1.00P
G-MYNH	Rans S-6-ESD Coyote II (Rotax 462) 0493-487 & PFA/204-12616			30.12.93	E.F. & V.M.Clapham	Oldbury-on-Severn	9. 5.99P

Regn	Type	C/n	P/I	Date	Owner/operator	Probable Base	CA Expy
G-MYNI	Team Minimax 91 (Mosler MM-CB35)	PFA/186-12314		22. 2.93	J.J.Penney	Neath	17.11.99P
G-MYNJ	Mainair Mercury (Rotax 503)	972-1293-7 & W768		14. 1.94	B.Roberts	York	13. 4.99P
G-MYNK	Solar Wings Pegasus Quantum 15 (Rotax 582/40)	6614		17.11.93	D.L.Goode	Enstone	17. 4.99P
G-MYNL	Solar Wings Pegasus Quantum 15 (Rotax 582/40)	6648		17.11.93	B.S.Smy	Poringland, Norwich	18. 9.99P
G-MYNM*	Solar Wings Pegasus Quantum 15	6723		17.11.93	Not known (Stored 2.97)	Al Rafaah, UAE	
G-MYNN	Solar Wings Pegasus Quantum 15 (Rotax 582/40)	6679		17.11.93	P.H.E.Woodliffe-Thomas	Thame	19.11.99P
G-MYNO	Solar Wings Pegasus Quantum 15 (Rotax 582/40)	6724		10. 1.94	S.J.Baker	Sutton Meadows, Ely	22. 3.99P
G-MYNP	Solar Wings Pegasus Quantum 15 (Rotax 582/40)	6688		17.11.93	R.H.Braithwaite t/a RAF Microlight Flying Association	RAF Cottesmore	12.12.99P
G-MYNR	Solar Wings Pegasus Quantum 15 (Rotax 582/40)	6692		17.11.93	D.Pick	Boston	30. 3.99P
G-MYNS	Solar Wings Pegasus Quantum 15 (Rotax 582/40)	6694		17.11.93	T.R.Marsh	Frome	13. 2.99P
G-MYNT	Solar Wings Pegasus Quantum 15 (Rotax 582/40)	6693		17.11.93	P.A.Vernon	Devizes	27. 3.97P
G-MYNU	Solar Wings Pegasus Quasar IITC	6695		5. 1.94	R.Sfredda	Luxembourg	
G-MYNV	Solar Wings Pegasus Quantum 15 (Rotax 582/40)	6725		10. 1.94	S.C.Jackson	York	28. 5.99P
G-MYNW	Cyclone Chaser S (Rotax 447)	CH.855		6. 1.94	M.T.G.Pope	Dubai, UAE	30. 1.95P
G-MYNX	CFM Streak Shadow SA-M (Rotax 618)	K.193-SA-M & PFA/206-12268		15. 6.92	T.J. & M.D.Palmer	Cumbernauld	7. 5.99P
G-MYNY	Kolb Twinstar mk.3 (Rotax 582)	PFA/205-12478		22.11.93	B.Alexander	Swinford, Rugby	25. 8.98P
G-MYNZ	Solar Wings Pegasus Quantum 15 (Rotax 582/40)	6709		18. 1.94	N.S.Lynall	Walsall	11. 3.97P
G-MYOA	Rans S-6-ESD Coyote II (Rotax 503)	PFA/204-12578		23.11.93	M.Leavesley	Lichfield	4. 1.00P
G-MYOB	Mainair Mercury (Rotax 503)	976-1293-7 & W772		8.12.93	J.C. & B.E.Barnes	Wisbech	19. 9.99P
G-MYOE	Solar Wings Pegasus Quantum 15	6668		31. 1.94	J.P.Foret	Aron, France	
G-MYOF	Mainair Mercury (Rotax 503)	975-1293-7 & W771		3.12.93	B.S.Ogden	Barton	2. 2.99P
G-MYOG	Kolb Twinstar mk.3 (Hirth 2706)	PFA/205-12449		19. 1.94	A.P. de Legh	Redhill	23. 3.99P
G-MYOH	CFM Shadow Srs.CD (Rotax 503)	K.201		27. 1.94	S.C.Smith	Popham	22. 3.99P
G-MYOI	Rans S-6-ESD Coyote II (Rotax 503)	PFA/204-12503		3. 2.94	J.Meijerink	Willingham	7. 8.99P
G-MYOL	Air Creation Fun 18S GT bis (Rotax 447)	94/001		7. 2.94	I.R.Scott & K.J.O'Grady	Lichfield	11.10.97P
G-MYOM	Mainair Gemini/Flash 2A (Rotax 582)	981-0294-7 & W777		14. 2.94	A.L.Walmsley	Rufforth	27. 3.99P
G-MYON	CFM Shadow Srs.CD (Rotax 503)	240		12. 1.94	P.M.McNair-Wilson	Old Sarum	28. 2.99P
G-MYOO	Kolb Twinstar mk.3M (Rotax 582)	PFA/205-12200		11. 5.92	P.D.Coppin	Colemore Common	15.10.99P
G-MYOR	Kolb Twinstar mk.3 (Rotax 582)	PFA/205-12602		16. 2.94	J.J.Littler	Chichester	24. 8.99P
G-MYOS	CFM Shadow Srs.CD (Rotax 503)	246		18. 2.94	E.J. & C.A.Bowles	Melksham	7. 5.99P
G-MYOT	Rans S-6-ESD Coyote II (Rotax 503)	PFA/204-12668		21. 2.94	R.T.Mosforth	Netherthorpe	6. 4.99P
G-MYOU	Solar Wings Pegasus Quantum 15 (Rotax 582/40)	6726		?. 3.94	D.W.General Wood Machinists Ltd	London Colney	17. 6.99P
G-MYOV	Mainair Mercury (Rotax 503)	979-0294-7 & W775		1. 3.94	P.Brownrigg	Chester	12. 6.99P
G-MYOW	Mainair Gemini/Flash 2A (Rotax 503)	983-0294-7 & W779		16. 3.94	P.W.F.Coleman	Adversane, Billingshurst	19. 9.99P
G-MYOX	Mainair Mercury (Rotax 503)	984-0294-7 & W780		23. 2.94	A.D.Dudding	Sandtoft	20. 4.99P
G-MYOY	Cyclone AX3 (Rotax 503)	C.3123191		23. 2.94	D.O.Herbert t/a Cyclone F/Grp	Shobdon	4. 5.99P
G-MYOZ	BFC Quad City Challenger II UK (Rotax 503)	CH2-1093-1045 & PFA/177A-12640		24. 2.94	T.J.Wickham	Bordon, Hants	21. 9.99P
G-MYPA	Rans S-6-ESD Coyote II (Rotax 503)	0893-527 & PFA/204-12678		24. 2.94	L.J.Dutch	Tarn Farm, Cockerham	18. 1.99P
G-MYPC	Kolb Twinstar mk.3 (Rotax 582)	PFA/205-12437		2. 3.94	J.E.Twigge	Newcastle-under-Lyme	31. 5.99P
G-MYPD	Mainair Mercury (Rotax 462)	982-0294-7 & W778		11. 3.94	A.Bennion	Northwich	14. 7.99P
G-MYPE	Mainair Gemini/Flash 2A (Rotax 582)	985-0394-7 & W781		11. 3.94	J.D.Capewell	East Fortune	21. 3.99P
G-MYPF	Solar Wings Pegasus Quasar IITC	SW-WQT-0564		5. 4.94	Articles de Vol Libre	Luxembourg	
G-MYPG	Solar Wings Pegasus XL-Q (Rotax 462)	SW-WQ-0176		29. 3.89	P.Gibbs	Rickmansworth	26. 5.99P

Regn	Type	C/n	P/I	Date	Owner/operator	Probable Base	CA Expy
G-MYPH	Solar Wings Pegasus Quantum 15 6764 (Rotax 582/40)			?. 3.94	P.M.J.White	Pickering	7. 5.99P
G-MYPI	Solar Wings Pegasus Quantum 15 6767 (Rotax 582/40)			?. 3.94	E.M.Woods	Lydney, Glos	8. 5.99P
G-MYPJ	Rans S-6-ESD Coyote II (Rotax 503) 1293-569 & PFA/204-12692			18. 3.94	A.W.Fish (Damaged by fire RAF Boulmer 11.1.98)	Eshott	8. 5.99P
G-MYPL	CFM Shadow Srs.CD K.213 & BMAA/HB/080 (Rotax 503)			14. 2.94	G.I.Madden	Milton Keynes	25. 8.99P
G-MYPM	Cyclone AX3 (Rotax 503) C.3123188			23. 3.94	Microflight Ireland Ltd	Portrush, Co.Antrim	10. 4.99P
G-MYPN	Solar Wings Pegasus Quantum 15 6727 (Rotax 582/40)			12. 4.94	D.R.Jarvis	Melton Mowbray	14. 6.99P
G-MYPO	Hunt Wing/Experience (Rotax 503) 9409011, BMAA/HB/019 & BMAA/HB/026			28. 3.94	W.I.McMillan	Northwich	11.12.99P
G-MYPP	Whittaker MW-6S Fatboy Flyer PFA/164-12413			11. 4.94	D.S.L.Evans	Gravesend	
G-MYPR	Cyclone AX3 (Rotax 503) C.3123190			13. 4.94	N.E.Ashton Ince Blundell, Liverpool		3. 6.99P
G-MYPS	Whittaker MW-6 Merlin PFA/164-11585			19. 4.94	I.S.Bishop	Bicester	
G-MYPT	CFM Shadow Srs.CD (Rotax 503) K.212			22. 4.94	M.G. & S.A.Collins	Oldbury-on-Severn	23. 6.99P
G-MYPU	Airwave Microchute UQ/Motor 27 (Rotax 503) 023, PSP.101746 & BMAA/HB/023			22. 4.94	S.E.Jones	Cardiff	20. 6.96P
G-MYPV	Mainair Mercury 986-0394-7 & W782 (Rotax 582)			18. 3.94	L.T.Neve	Nazeing	21. 5.99P
G-MYPW	Mainair Gemini/Flash 2A 991-0494-7 & W787 (Rotax 582)			3. 5.94	N.A.Porter	Hoddesdon	18. 5.99P
G-MYPX	Solar Wings Pegasus Quantum 15 6785 (Rotax 582/40)			28. 4.94	P.J.Callis & M.Aylett	Kibworth/Loughborough	21.11.99P
G-MYPY	Solar Wings Pegasus Quantum 15 6786 (Rotax 582/40)			12. 5.94	J.Hood	Eshott	25. 7.99P
G-MYPZ	BFC Quad City Challenger II UK (Hirth 2706) CH2-1093-UK-1046 & PFA/177A-12689 (Regd incorrectly as CH2-0194-UK-1046)			2. 3.94	E.G.Astin t/a BFC	Whitby	
G-MYRA	Kolb Twinstar mk.3 PFA/205-12434 (Rotax 503)			29. 3.94	S.J.Fox & A.P.Pickford	Popham	16. 4.99P
G-MYRB	Whittaker MW-5 Sorcerer PFA/163-11543			14. 4.94	P.J.Careless	Sandy	
G-MYRC	Mainair Blade 988-0594-7 & W784 (Rotax 462)			1. 6.94	A.T.Hayward	Broseley	11. 8.99P
G-MYRD	Mainair Blade 989-0594-7 & W785 (Rotax 582)			20. 5.94	W.G.Minns	Burwash, East Sussex	11. 8.99P
G-MYRE	Cyclone Chaser S (Rotax 377) CH.863			10. 5.94	M.P.Dodgson	Wallsend	24. 7.99P
G-MYRF	Solar Wings Pegasus Quantum 15 6795 (Rotax 462HP)			13. 5.94	J.D.Gray	Eshott	22. 8.99P
G-MYRG	Team Minimax PFA/186-11891			17. 5.94	D.G.Burrows	Presteigne	
G-MYRH	BFC Quad City Challenger II UK (Rotax 582) CH2-1093-1044 & PFA/177A-12690			10. 3.94	R.T.Hall	Thorney Island	11. 2.99P
G-MYRI	Medway Hybred 44XLR MR180/841 (Rotax 503)			23. 5.94	P.R.Garrett	Rainham, Kent	12. 4.99P
G-MYRJ	BFC Quad City Challenger II UK (Hirth 2706.R05) CH2-1093-1042 & PFA/177A-12658			28. 3.94	H.F.Breakwell & P.Woodcock	Sittles Farm, Alrewas	20. 7.99P
G-MYRK	Murphy Renegade Spirit UK (Rotax 582) 215 & PFA/188-11425			3.10.89	M.A.J.Queiroz & J.R.Francis Long Marston "Spirit of Yorkshire"		16. 7.99P
G-MYRL	Team Minimax 91 PFA/186-11967 (Rotax 447)			17. 5.94	D.J.Flanagan	Glossop	23. 8.99P
G-MYRM	Solar Wings Pegasus Quantum 15 6800 (Rotax 582/40)			26. 5.94	R.C.Budden	Old Sarum	28. 1.00P
G-MYRN	Solar Wings Pegasus Quantum 15 6801 (Rotax 582/40)			26. 5.94	P.C.Kind	Swinford, Rugby	21.11.99P
G-MYRO	Cyclone AX3 (Rotax 503) C.4043211			6. 6.94	R.I.Simpson & R.Tarplee	Broadstairs	26. 7.98P
G-MYRP	Letov LK-2M Sluka PFA/263-12725 & 0209 (Rotax 447)			6. 6.94	J.W.Hiestand	Dereham	11. 5.99P
G-MYRR	Letov LK-2M Sluka (Rotax 447) 0205 (Regd with c/n 05)			10. 6.94	G.W.L.Howarth	Aylesbury	19. 5.99P
G-MYRS	Solar Wings Pegasus Quantum 15 6803 (Rotax 582/40)			13. 6.94	R.M.Summers	Insch	6. 5.99P
G-MYRT	Solar Wings Pegasus Quantum 15 6732 (Rotax 582/40)			1. 3.94	M.C.Taylor	Coleford	22. 3.99P
G-MYRU	Cyclone AX3 (Rotax 503) C.4043210			7. 6.94	L.W. & C.Scarlett	Eshott	17. 9.99P
G-MYRV	Cyclone AX3 (Rotax 503) C.4043209			8. 6.94	T.E. & A.T.Owen	Holyhead	4. 7.99P
G-MYRW	Mainair Mercury 999-0694-7 & W795 (Rotax 503)			17. 6.94	G.C.Hobson	St.Michaels-on-Wyre	16. 6.99P
G-MYRX	Mainair Gemini/Flash 2A 995-0694-7 & W792 (Rotax 462)			22. 6.94	L.J.Latter	London N19	23. 8.95P
G-MYRY	Solar Wings Pegasus Quantum 15 6813 (Rotax 582/40)			15. 6.94	P.G.Jackson & D.Roberts	Shobdon	25. 8.99P
G-MYRZ	Solar Wings Pegasus Quantum 15 6812 (Rotax 582/40)			15. 6.94	C.Judd	Ely	27. 6.99P
G-MYSA	Cyclone Chaser S (Rotax 508) CH.864			15. 6.94	D.W.M.Hamer	Banbury	3. 9.99P

Regn	Type	C/n	P/I	Date	Owner/operator	Probable Base	CA Expy
G-MYSB	Solar Wings Pegasus Quantum 15 6809 (Rotax 582/40)			22. 6.94	D.Margereson	Chesterfield	10. 8.99P
G-MYSC	Solar Wings Pegasus Quantum 15 6811 (Rotax 582/40)			22. 6.94	O.W.Achurch	Weedon	13. 2.99P
G-MYSD	BFC Quad City Challenger II CH2-1093-1043 & PFA/177A-12688			23. 6.94	C.E.Bell	Oakham	
G-MYSG	Mainair Mercury 993-0694-7 & W790 (Rotax 503)			12. 7.94	B.M.Jones	Shifnal	30. 4.99P
G-MYSH	Mainair Blade 994-0694-7 & W791 (Rotax 582)			12. 7.94	J.Lamont		13. 9.95P
G-MYSI	HM.14/93 PFA/255-12700			18. 7.94	A.R.D.Seaman	Dagenham	
G-MYSJ	Mainair Gemini/Flash 2A 1001-0894-7 & W797 (Rotax 503)			2. 8.94	L.Cottle	Baxby Manor, Husthwaite	9. 8.99P
G-MYSK	Team Minimax 91 PFA/186-12203 (Rotax 447)			25. 7.94	A.D.Bolshaw	Wolverhampton	11.10.99P
G-MYSL	Aviasud Mistral 66 & BMAA/HB/007 (Rotax 532)		83-DE	27. 2.92	P.C.Piggott & M.E.Hughes	Lutterworth	5. 7.99P
G-MYSM	CFM Shadow Srs.CD K.243 & BMAA/HB/049 (Rotax 503)			22. 3.94	L.W.Stevens	Grantham	14. 9.99P
G-MYSN	Whittaker MW-6S Fatboy Flyer PFA/164-12285 (Rotax 532)			27. 7.94	T.A.Dockrell	Weston-super-Mare	11.10.99P
G-MYSO	Cyclone AX3 (Rotax 503) C.4043215			1. 8.94	M.L.Smith	Popham	22. 2.98P
G-MYSP	Rans S-6-ESD Coyote II (Rotax 503) 0392-284 & PFA/204-12265			26. 5.92	G.C.Holmes	Sittle Farm, Alrewas	17.12.98P
G-MYSR	Solar Wings Pegasus Quantum 15 6837 (Rotax 582)			?. 8.94	D.O.Crane	Lutterworth	13. 6.99P
G-MYST	Aviasud Mistral 0489-83, GB.01 & BMAA/HB/012 (Rotax 532)			11. 7.89	T.E.Taylor	Otherton, Cannock	5. 8.98P
G-MYSU	Rans S-6-ESD Coyote II PFA/204-12753 (Rotax 503)			5. 8.94	C.C.Wright	Laurencekirk	6.11.98P
G-MYSV	Aerial Arts Chaser S CH.812 (Rotax 377)		(ex)	24. 8.94	M.O'Hearne	Tadcaster	13. 3.99P
G-MYSW	Solar Wings Pegasus Quantum 15 6834 (Rotax 582)			13. 7.94	A.R.Lloyd	Kettering	21. 8.99P
G-MYSX	Solar Wings Pegasus Quantum 15 6832 (Rotax 503)			13. 7.94	J.L.Treves	London Colney	27. 6.99P
G-MYSY	Solar Wings Pegasus Quantum 15 6864 (Rotax 582)			15. 8.94	C.Lamb	Rye	2.10.99P
G-MYSZ	Mainair Mercury 1006-0894-7 & W802 (Rotax 503) (C/n confirmed but see G-MYYY)			2. 9.94	N.Cox	Leominster	18. 9.99P
G-MYTA	Team Minimax 91 PFA/186-12461 (Rotax 447)			20. 5.94	R.E.Gray	Oxted, Surrey	4. 6.99P
G-MYTB	Mainair Mercury 1004-0894-7 & W800 (Rotax 582)			19. 8.94	P.J.Higgins	Fenland	4.12.98P
G-MYTC	Solar Wings Pegasus XL-Q SW-WQ-0246		(ex)	28. 9.94	M.J.Edmett	London N3	
G-MYTD	Mainair Blade 1002-0894-7 & W798 (Rotax 582)			18. 8.94	D.M.Dunphy	Barton	29. 4.98P
G-MYTE	Rans S-6-ESD Coyote II PFA/204-12718 (Rotax 503)			22. 7.94	D.Cassidy	Stoneacre Farm, Farthing Corner	9.11.99P
G-MYTG	Mainair Blade 1008-0994-7 & W804 (Rotax 582)			16. 9.94	P.Lenk	Barton	1. 2.00P
G-MYTH	CFM Shadow Srs.CD 089 (Rotax 503)			7.11.88	J.E.Neil Sheriff Hall, Balgone, Berwick		23. 6.99P
G-MYTI	Solar Wings Pegasus Quantum 15 6874 (Rotax 582/40)			6.10.94	J.Madhvani	Plaistows Field, Hemel Hampstead	21. 2.99P
G-MYTJ	Solar Wings Pegasus Quantum 15 6877 (Rotax 582/40)			29. 9.94	T.J.Cale	Defford	12. 4.99P
G-MYTK	Mainair Mercury 1009-1094-7 & W805 (Rotax 503)			29. 9.94	D.A.Holroyd	London W14	19.10.99P
G-MYTL	Mainair Blade 1010-1094-7 & W807 (Rotax 582)			4.10.94	S.Ostrowski	Davidstow Moor	5. 4.99P
G-MYTM	Cyclone AX3 (Rotax 503) C.3123189			13. 4.94	T.S.Mangat	Long Marston	22. 7.99P
G-MYTN	Solar Wings Pegasus Quantum 15 6878 (Rotax 503)			30. 9.94	R.Redman	Grantham	17. 1.99P
G-MYTO	Quad City Challenger II UK (Hirth 2705.R06) PFA/177-12583			22. 7.94	K.B.Tolley & D.M.Cottingham	Axminster/Sidmouth	20. 2.00P
G-MYTP	CGS Arrow Flight Hawk II 215 (Rotax 503) H-CGS-489-P & PFA/266-12801			6.10.94	R.J.Turner	Otherton, Cannock	8. 5.97P
G-MYTR	Solar Wings Pegasus Quasar IIIC 6880 (Rotax 582/40)			11.10.94	I.Jones	Dunkeswell	31. 1.00P
G-MYTS*	Hunt Wing/Avon 92009014 & BMAA/MB/032 (Rotax 447)			12.10.94	C.Jenkins (Cancelled by CAA 30.9.98)	Ballina, Co.Mayo	12.1.96P*
G-MYTT	Quad City Challenger II PFA/177-12761 (Rotax 503)			11.10.94	R.J.Shave t/a Challenger G-MYTT	Bristol	19.10.99P
G-MYTU	Mainair Blade 1011-1094-7 & W808 (Rotax 582)			21.10.94	R.M.A.Woodward	Stony Stratford	19.10.99P

Regn	Type	C/n	P/I	Date	Owner/operator	Probable Base	CA Expy
G-MYTV	Hunt Wing/Avon 92040010 & BMAA/HB/029 (Rotax 503)			13.10.94	P.J.Sutton	Bristol	3. 7.99P
G-MYTW	Mainair Blade 1012-1194-7 & W809 (Rotax 582)			4.11.94	J.Parker	Fenland	27.11.97P
G-MYTX	Mainair Mercury 1003-0894-7 & W799 (Rotax 503)			23. 9.94	S.G.A.Heward	Rufforth	28. 9.98P
G-MYTY	CFM Streak Shadow Srs.M PFA/206-12607 (Rotax 912UL) (Possibly c/n K.242)			11. 7.94	Skydrive Ltd	Leamington Spa	31. 8.99P
G-MYTZ	Air Creation Fun 18S GT bis 94/003 (Rotax 503)			7.11.94	J.K.Evans	Husbands Bosworth	22. 1.99P
G-MYUA	Air Creation Fun 18S GT bis 94/002 (Rotax 503)			8.11.94	D.Mahajan	West Wickham	31. 7.99P
G-MYUB	Mainair Mercury 1014-1194-7 & W812 (Rotax 503)			14.12.94	T.A. & C.M.Ross	Arclid Green, Sandbach	22. 9.99P
G-MYUC	Mainair Blade 1015-1294-7 & W813 (Rotax 462)			16.11.94	A.D.Clayton	St.Michaels-on-Wyre	4.11.98P
G-MYUD	Mainair Mercury 1016-1294-7 & W814 (Rotax 582)			24.11.94	S.A.Noble	Audley End	13. 2.99P
G-MYUE	Mainair Mercury 1017-1294-7 & W815 (Rotax 582)			22.11.94	R.J.Speight	Amersham	10. 3.99P
G-MYUF	Murphy Renegade Spirit PFA/188-12795			16.11.94	C.J.Dale	Beverley	13. 9.99P
G-MYUG	Hunt Wing/Avon BMAA/HB/038 & 9409034			21.11.94	C.W.Green	High Wycombe	AC
G-MYUH	Solar Wings Pegasus XL-Q 6810 (Rotax 462)			28.11.94	K.S.Daniels	London Colney	28. 8.99P
G-MYUI	Cyclone AX3 C.4043213 (Rotax 503) (Frame stamped with c/n 0102822; possibly rebuilt)			13.12.94	R. & M.Bailey Plaistows Field, Hemel Hempstead		13. 3.99P
G-MYUJ	Meridian Ultralights Maverick (Rotax 503) 402 & PFA/259-12750			30.12.94	K.Anderson "69"	Stafford	12.12.97P
G-MYUK	Mainair Mercury 1020-0195-7 & W818 (Rotax 462)			12.12.94	S.Lear	London N15	28.11.97P
G-MYUL	Quad City Challenger II UK (Rotax 503) PFA/177-12687			10. 1.95	A.G.Easson	Dunfermline	4. 4.99P
G-MYUM	Mainair Blade 1018-1294-7 & W816 (Rotax 582)			24.11.94	M.E.Keefe & G.P.Hodgson St.Michaels-on-Wyre		10. 1.00P
G-MYUN	Mainair Blade 1019-0195-7 & W817 (Rotax 582)			5.12.94	P.Harper	Thornton Cleveleys	17. 1.00P
G-MYUO	Cyclone Pegasus Quantum 15 6911 (Rotax 582)			23. 1.95	D.J.Harris (Damaged late 1997)	St.Albans	18. 4.99P
G-MYUP	Letov LK-2M Sluka (Rotax 447) 829409x24, PFA/263-12785 & UK.2			20.12.94	R.D.Proctor	RAF Wyton	27.11.99P
G-MYUR	Hunt Wing/Avon BMAA/HB/034 (Rotax 582)			24. 1.95	S.D.Pain	Rayne	17. 9.99P
G-MYUS	CFM Shadow Srs.CD (Rotax 503) 257			26. 1.95	G.Gilhead & R.G.M.Proost Old Sarum t/a Aviation for Paraplegics and Tetraplegics Trust		15. 7.99P
G-MYUT*	Hunt Wing/Experience 9409039 & BMAA/HB/042			26. 1.95	R.A.Kehoe (Cancelled by CAA 23.6.98)	Chelmsford	
G-MYUU	Cyclone Pegasus Quantum 15 6917 (Rotax 462)			30. 1.95	Lynette J.Ryals	Enstone	23. 3.99P
G-MYUV	Cyclone Pegasus Quantum 15 6918 (Rotax 582)			6. 2.95	D.Baillie	Great Orton	27. 6.99P
G-MYUW	Mainair Mercury 1024-0295-7 & W822 (Rotax 503)			7. 2.95	G.Suckling	Saffron Walden	11. 7.99P
G-MYUY	Airwave Microchute UQ/Reggae Motor 30 (Rotax 503) PSP.104006			9. 2.95	S.E.Jones	Cardiff	19.10.95P*
G-MYUZ	Rans S-6-ESD Coyote II (Rotax 503) 1293-568 & PFA/204-12741			5. 1.95	D.K.Ross & B.Davies	Lichfield	16. 4.99P
G-MYVA	Kolb Twinstar mk.3 PFA/205-12756 (Rotax 582)			13. 2.95	S.P.Read	Henstridge	14. 6.99P
G-MYVB	Mainair Blade 1021-0195-7 & W819 (Rotax 582)			15.12.94	P.C.Watson	Arclid Green, Sandbach	22. 3.99P
G-MYVC	Cyclone Pegasus Quantum 15 6904 (Rotax 582)			13. 2.95	G.Lace	Liverpool	17. 5.99P
G-MYVE	Mainair Blade 1027-0295-7 & W825 (Rotax 582)			8. 2.95	C.W.Laskey Risca, Newport t/a Blue Blade Syndicate G-MYVE		28. 2.99P
G-MYVG	Letov LK-2M Sluka (Rotax 447) PFA/263-12786 & 829409x26			15. 2.95	M.Tormey	Co.Meath, Ireland	8. 2.99P
G-MYVH	Mainair Blade 1028-0295-7 & W826 (Rotax 582)			21. 2.95	D.Sugden	Liversedge	27. 3.99P
G-MYVI	Air Creation Fun 18S GT bis 94/004 (Rotax 503)			17. 2.95	P.Osborne Northampton t/a Northampton Aerotow Club		7. 5.98P
G-MYVJ	Cyclone Pegasus Quantum 15 6974 (Rotax 582/40)			24. 2.95	G.R.Hall	Canterbury	28. 4.99P
G-MYVK	Cyclone Pegasus Quantum 15 6970 (Rotax 582/40)			27. 2.95	J.P.Metcalfe	Ashford, Kent	9. 4.99P
G-MYVL	Mainair Mercury 1030-0395-7 & W828 (Rotax 462)			1. 3.95	T.Pollard	Cambourne, Cornwall	7. 7.99P

Regn	Type	C/n	P/I	Date	Owner/operator	Probable Base	CA Expy
G-MYVM	Cyclone Pegasus Quantum 15 (Rotax 582/40)	6893		9. 3.95	A.F.A.Marreiros	Lisboa, Portugal	23. 6.99P
G-MYVN	Cyclone AX3 (Rotax 503)	C.4043212		16. 3.95	F.Watt	Insch	6. 6.99P
G-MYVO	Mainair Blade 1013-1194-7 & W811 (Rotax 582)			8.11.94	K.R.Anderson	Shrewsbury	9. 1.99P
G-MYVP	Rans S-6-ESD Coyote II PFA/204-12828 (Rotax 503)			27. 3.95	R.H.Tait	Eshott	29.11.99P
G-MYVR	Cyclone Pegasus Quantum 15 (Rotax 582)	6980		21. 3.95	M.P.Wimsey	Louth	26. 4.99P
G-MYVS	Mainair Mercury 1037-0495-7 & W835 (Rotax 462)			12. 4.95	P.S.Flynn	Sandtoft	25. 4.99P
G-MYVT	Letov LK-2M Sluka PFA/263-12835 & 829409x25 (Rotax 447)			17. 3.95	J.Hannibal	Kidderminster	9.11.99P
G-MYVU*	Medway Budget Raven (Rotax 447)	MRB126/108		3. 4.95	Not known (Temp unregd 25.10.95)	Chislehurst, Kent	9. 4.96P
G-MYVV	Medway Hybred 44XLR (Rotax 503)	MR127/109		3. 4.95	A.I.Dawson	Chesterfield	24. 2.99P
G-MYVW	Medway Raven X (Rotax 447)	MRB128/110		15. 5.95	J.C.Woolgrove	Beckenham	5. 6.97P
G-MYVX	Medway Hybred 44XLR (Rotax 503)	MR129/111		3. 4.95	S.J.Martin	Belvedere, Kent	9. 7.99P
G-MYVY	Mainair Blade 1033-0495-7 & W831 (Rotax 582)			29. 3.95	N.Purdy	Sutton-in-Ashfield	30. 6.99P
G-MYVZ	Mainair Blade 1034-0495-7 & W832 (Rotax 582)			31. 3.95	M.Morris	Preston	6. 4.99P
G-MYWA	Mainair Mercury 1035-0495-7 & W833 (Rotax 503)			30. 3.95	D.James	Neath	5. 5.99P
G-MYWB*	Edel Corniche/Scorpion 004 & BMAA/HB/071			31. 3.95	P.F.Funnell (Cancelled by CAA 7.8.98)	Cranbrook, Kent	
G-MYWC	Hunt Wing/Avon 9409038 & BMAA/HB/043 (Rotax 503)			3. 4.95	F.J.C.Binks	Saffron Walden	29. 7.99P
G-MYWD	Thruster T.600N (Rotax 503)	9035-T600-511	(G-MYOJ)	18. 4.95	G.J.Slater	Marlborough	16. 3.99P
G-MYWE	Thruster T.600T (Rotax 503)	9035-T600-512	(G-MYOK)	18. 4.95	P.J.Reed	Temple Cloud, Bristol	9. 1.00P
G-MYWF	CFM Shadow Srs.CD (Rotax 503) K.248 & BMAA/HB/068			18. 4.95	M.A.Newman	Saxmundham	8. 1.99P
G-MYWG	Cyclone Pegasus Quantum 15 (Rotax 582/40)	6998		20. 4.95	N.S.McNaughton	Auchincruive, Ayr	20. 8.99P
G-MYWH	Hunt Wing/Experience 9409025 & BMAA/HB/037			20.12.94	G.N.Hatchett	Gloucester	
G-MYWI	Cyclone Pegasus Quantum 15 (Rotax 582)	7006		1. 5.95	W.H.McMinn	Craigavon	6. 6.99P
G-MYWJ	Cyclone Pegasus Quantum 15 (Rotax 582)	6919		24. 1.95	W.C.Jones	Long Acre Farm, Sandy	22. 2.99P
G-MYWK	Cyclone Pegasus Quantum 15 (Rotax 582/40)	7011		1. 5.95	Euroflight Microlight Club Ltd Dromore, Co.Down		20. 5.99P
G-MYWL	Cyclone Pegasus Quantum 15 (Rotax 582)	6995		2. 5.95	J.S.Hamilton	Edenbridge, Kent	19. 3.99P
G-MYWM	CFM Shadow Srs.CD K.227 & BMAA/HB/056 (Rotax 503)			9. 5.95	R.E.Peirse	Kingston, Royston	23. 7.99P
G-MYWN	Cyclone Chaser S (Rotax 508)	CH.865		9. 5.95	J.E.Borrill	Fort William	22. 8.99P
G-MYWO	Cyclone Pegasus Quantum 15 (Rotax 582)	6932		9. 5.95	B.D.Avery	Chippenham	4. 9.99P
G-MYWP	Kolb Twinstar mk.3 PFA/205-12561 (Rotax 582)			7. 3.95	B.J.M.Albiston	Long Marston	27. 9.99P
G-MYWR	Cyclone Pegasus Quantum 15 (Rotax 582/40)	7002		10. 5.95	T.A.Chambers	Long Marston	11. 8.99P
G-MYWS	Cyclone Chaser S 6946 & CH.866 (Rotax 447)			17. 5.95	M.H.Broadbent	Bexhill-on-Sea	4. 8.99P
G-MYWT	Cyclone Pegasus Quantum 15 (Rotax 582/40)	6997		19. 5.95	H.Hall	Willenhall	5. 7.99P
G-MYWU	Cyclone Pegasus Quantum 15 (Rotax 582)	7024		25. 5.95	J.R.Buttle	Dunkeswell	24. 7.99P
G-MYWV	Rans S-4C Coyote (Rotax 447) 093-212 & PFA/193-12826			30. 5.95	A.H.Trapp	Bewdley, Worcs	19. 6.99P
G-MYWW	Cyclone Pegasus Quantum 15 (Rotax 503)	7021		30. 5.95	K.J.Gay	Bangor, Co.Down	1. 7.99P
G-MYWX	Cyclone Pegasus Quantum 15 (Rotax 582)	7019		6. 6.95	D.J.Revell	Chatteris	13. 7.99P
G-MYWY	Cyclone Pegasus Quantum 15 (Rotax 582)	6982		20. 3.95	D.Young	Kemble	10. 8.99P
G-MYWZ	Thruster TST mk.1 (Rotax 503)	8128-TST-115	G-MVMJ	22. 2.93	D.L.Hendry	Appin, Argyll	24. 5.99P
G-MYXA	Team Minimax 91 PFA/186-12266 (Rotax 447)			13. 6.95	G.M.Johnson	Huntingdon	14. 4.99P
G-MYXB	Rans S-6-ESD Coyote II PFA/204-12787 (Rotax 503)			20. 6.95	A.Aldridge	Kings Lynn	30.10.98P

Regn	Type	C/n P/I	Date	Owner/operator	Probable Base	CA Expy
G-MYXC	BFC Quad City Challenger II UK CH2-0294-UK-1099		16. 5.95	K.N.Dickinson	High Barn Farm, Houghton	
G-MYXD	Cyclone Pegasus Quasar IITC (Rotax 582)	7029	21. 6.95	C.Lee	Long Acre Farm, Sandy	30. 8.99P
G-MYXE	Cyclone Pegasus Quantum 15 (Rotax 582)	7061	23. 6.95	D.Little	Crawley	7. 9.98P
G-MYXF	Air Creation Fun 18S GT bis (Rotax 503)	94/005	23. 6.95	T.A.Morgan	Popham	11.10.99P
G-MYXG	Rans S-6-ESD Coyote II PFA/204-12879 (Rotax 503)		29. 6.95	G.H.Lee	High Barn Farm, Houghton	21.12.98P
G-MYXH	Cyclone AX3 (Rotax 503)	7028	3. 7.95	E.G.White	Wantage	10. 9.98P
G-MYXI	Cook Aries 1	BMAA/HB/048	4. 7.95	H.Cook	Newport, Gwent	
G-MYXJ	Mainair Blade 1048-0795-7 & W846 (Rotax 582)		17. 7.95	V.G. & D.Concannon	Oxton, Nottingham	19. 8.98P
G-MYXK	BFC Quad City Challenger II (Rotax 503) CH2-1194-1254 & PFA/177A-12877		11. 7.95	V.Vaughan & N.O'Brien Mullinahone, Co.Tipperary		30. 6.99P
G-MYXL	Mignet HM-1000 Balerit (Rotax 582)	112	11. 7.95	R.W.Hollamby	Bardown, Wadhurst	17. 7.99P
G-MYXM	Mainair Blade 1047-0795-7 & W845 (Rotax 582)		19. 7.95	T.F.J.Roach	Mansfield	7. 8.99P
G-MYXN	Mainair Blade 1046-0795-7 & W844 (Rotax 582)		27. 7.95	M.R.Sands	Peterlee	19. 7.99P
G-MYXO	Letov LK-2M Sluka (Rotax 447) 8295s001 & PFA/263-12873		27. 7.95	K.H.A.Negal	London SW7	24.11.98P
G-MYXP	Rans S-6-ESD Coyote II PFA/204-12886 (Rotax 503)		31. 7.95	K.J.Lywood	Bradford-on-Avon	2. 9.99P
G-MYXR	Murphy Renegade Spirit UK PFA/188-12755		2. 8.95	S.Hooker	Ashford, Kent	
G-MYXS	Kolb Twinstar mk.3 PFA/205-12528 (Rotax 582)		4. 5.94	R.Coar High Barn Farm, Houghton (On rebuild 8.97)		11. 7.97P
G-MYXT	Cyclone Pegasus Quantum 15 (Rotax 582)	7073	4. 8.95	D.M.Mackenzie	Beauly, Inverness	26. 9.99P
G-MYXU	Thruster T.300 (Rotax 582)	9024-T300-513	16. 8.95	D.W.Wilson	Collone, Co.Armagh	18.12.99P
G-MYXV	Quad City Challenger II UK (Rotax 503) CH2-1194-UK-1243		19. 7.95	A.Hipkin	Bewdley, Worcs	18. 6.99P
G-MYXW	Cyclone Pegasus Quantum 15 (Rotax 582)	7090	24. 8.95	M.A.Pantling	Gillingham	4.12.99P
G-MYXX	Cyclone Pegasus Quantum 15 (Rotax 582)	7081	25. 8.95	J.H.Arnold	Milverton, Taunton	13. 8.99P
G-MYXY	CFM Shadow Srs.CD K.245 & BMAA/HB/059 (Rotax 503)		29. 8.95	N.H.Townsend	Old Sarum	21. 7.99P
G-MYXZ	Cyclone Pegasus Quantum 15 (Rotax 582)	7023	21. 6.95	K.L.Baldwin	Clench Common	24. 8.99P
G-MYYA	Mainair Blade 1052-0995-7 & W850 (Rotax 462)		1. 9.95	J.N.Hanson	St.Michaels-on-Wyre	17. 9.99P
G-MYYB	Cyclone Pegasus Quantum 15 (Rotax 582)	7079	4. 9.95	A.L.Johnson	Long Acre Farm, Sandy	17.10.99P
G-MYYC	Cyclone Pegasus Quantum 15 (Rotax 582)	7094	12. 9.95	B.Kirkland	Tarn Farm, Cockerham	26. 2.99P
G-MYYD	Cyclone Chaser S (Rotax 447)	CH.7099	15. 9.95	D.Kingslake	Long Acre Farm, Sandy	7.11.99P
G-MYYE	Hunt Wing/Hunt Avon BMAA/HB/041 (EC-44-PM)		21. 9.95	P.J.Dickinson	Stoke-on-Trent	
G-MYYF	Quad City Challenger II UK PFA/177-12811 (Rotax 503)		27. 9.95	G.Ferries	Insch	11.11.99P
G-MYYG	Mainair Blade 1054-0995-7 & W852 (Rotax 462)		4.10.95	P.McCormick	Shobdon	23.10.99P
G-MYYH	Mainair Blade 1056-1095-7 & W854 (Rotax 582)		3.10.95	B.Hunter	Bridlington	11. 2.99P
G-MYYI	Cyclone Pegasus Quantum 15 (Rotax 582)	7101	23. 9.95	S.Etches	Sheffield	23. 7.99P
G-MYYJ	Hunt Wing/Hunt Avon BMAA/HB/033 (Rotax 503)		29. 9.95	M.J.Slater (Stored 5.97)	Clench Common	
G-MYYK	Cyclone Pegasus Quantum 15 (Rotax 582)	7100	2.10.95	L.Scarse	Melksham	12. 4.99P
G-MYYL	Cyclone AX3 (Rotax 503)	7110	4.10.95	P.M.Dewhurst & K.Meredith-Jones	Sywell	9.11.99P
G-MYYM	Trekking Microchute/Motor 27 TH10124M		17.10.95	S.E.Jones Cardiff t/a Motor Gliders Group		
G-MYYN	Cyclone Pegasus Quantum 15 (Rotax 582)	7022	3.10.95	Kwik, Kwek Kwak SA	Marbella, Spain	2.10.96P
G-MYYO	Medway Raven X (Rotax 447)	MRB134/114	5.10.95	W.E.Richards	Redlands, Swindon	8. 5.99P
G-MYYP	AMF Chevvron 2-32C (Konig SD570) 036		31.10.95	G.A.Pentelow	Rothwell Lodge, Kettering	5.11.99P
G-MYYR	Team Minimax 91 PFA/186-12724 (Rotax 447)		31.10.95	P.Palmer Crosland Moor (Damaged at Cranfield 5.7.98)		22. 6.99P

Regn	Type	C/n	P/I	Date	Owner/operator	Probable Base	CA Expy
G-MYYS	Team Minimax	PFA/186-11989		7.11.95	J.R.Hopkinson	Chesterfield	
G-MYYT	Hunt Wing/Experience	BMAA/HB/065		14.11.95	E.Finnamore	Tullamore, Co.Offauy	
G-MYYU	Mainair Mercury 1062-1295-7 & W862 (Rotax 503)			17.11.95	G.V.Willder	Arclid Green, Sandbach	26. 3.99P
G-MYYV	Rans S-6-ESD Coyote IIXL (Rotax 503) 0896-1026XL & PFA/204-12943			17.11.95	B.W.Drake	Long Marston	16. 7.99P
G-MYYW	Mainair Blade 1051-0895-7 & W849 (Rotax 582)			8. 8.95	J.E.L.Woodward	Oxton, Nottingham	18. 8.99P
G-MYYX	Cyclone Pegasus Quantum 15 (Rotax 582)	7126		17.11.95	K.M.MacRae	East Fortune	3. 4.99P
G-MYYY	Mainair Blade 1031-0495-7 & W829 (Rotax 582) (Incorrectly stamped with wing c/n W802 - see G-MYSZ)			15. 3.95	D.A.Lane	Barton	30. 3.99P
G-MYYZ	Medway Raven X (Rotax 447)	MRB135/116		10. 1.96	S.G.Beeson	Stoke-on-Trent	8. 9.99P
G-MYZA	Whitaker MW-6 Merlin	PFA/164-11396		17. 7.95	D.C.Davies	Lover Farm	9. 3.99P
G-MYZB	Cyclone Pegasus Quantum 15 (Rotax 582)	7124		22.11.95	A.D.Griffin	Long Marston	14.12.98P
G-MYZC	Cyclone AX3 (Rotax 503)	7125		5.12.95	Alison M.Lowrie	Liverpool	14. 2.98P
G-MYZE	Team Minimax 91 (Global GMT-35)	PFA/186-12570		28. 9.95	A.W.Austin	Cheltenham	2. 6.98P
G-MYZF	Cyclone AX3 (Rotax 503)	7133		11.12.95	R.L.H.Alexander	Holywood, NI	7. 3.99P
G-MYZG	Cyclone AX3 (Rotax 503)	7137		11. 1.96	R.A.Johns	Weston Zoyland	9. 1.00P
G-MYZH	Chargus Titan 38	JPA-1		16. 1.96	P.A.James	Crawley	
G-MYZI	Tiger Cub RL5A-LW Sherwood Ranger	PFA/237-12947		17. 1.96	K.F.Crumplin	Wells	
G-MYZJ	Cyclone Pegasus Quantum 15 (Rotax 582)	7150		24. 1.96	G.G.Rowley	Great Orton	12. 4.99P
G-MYZK	Cyclone Pegasus Quantum 15 (Rotax 582/40)	7157		5. 2.96	T.D.Grieve	Hamilton	11. 7.99P
G-MYZL	Cyclone Pegasus Quantum 15 (Rotax 582/40)	7158		5. 2.96	Flight Aid Ltd	Ilminster	20. 7.99P
G-MYZM	Cyclone Pegasus Quantum 15 (Rotax 582/40)	7159		5. 2.96	D.Hope	Uckfield	28. 3.99P
G-MYZN	Whittaker MW-6S-LW Fatboy Flyer (Rotax 582)	PFA/164-12431		31. 1.96	M.K.Shaw	Leighton Buzzard	18. 6.99P
G-MYZO	Medway Raven X (Rotax 447)	MRB136/115		12. 2.96	E.M.Middleton	Hereford	3. 5.99P
G-MYZP	CFM Shadow Srs.DD (Rotax 582)	249 & PFA/161-12914		7. 2.96	R.M.Davies & P.I.Hodgson	Amersham	13. 7.99P
G-MYZR	Rans S-6-ESD Coyote II XL (Rotax 503)	PFA/204-12958		9. 2.96	S.E.J.McLaughlin	Sutton Meadows, Ely	9. 4.99P
G-MYZS	Airwave Rave/Vega 1 001 & BMAA/HB/054			16. 2.96	Paratrike Ltd	Colchester	
G-MYZT	Airwave Rave/Vega 2	002		16. 2.96	Paratrike Ltd	Colchester	
G-MYZU	Airwave Rave/Scorpion	005		16. 2.96	Paratrike Ltd	Colchester	
G-MYZV	Rans S-6-ESD Coyote II XL (Rotax 503)	PFA/204-12946		26. 2.96	D.R.Godby & C.J.Cullen Yelverton/Ilminster		26. 6.99P
G-MYZW	Cyclone Chaser S (Rotax 508)	7165		27. 2.96	P.Harris	Cannock	22. 4.99P
G-MYZX	Cyclone Chaser S (Rotax 508)	7172		28. 2.96	A.J.Blake	Buxton	1. 4.97P
G-MYZY	Cyclone Pegasus Quantum 15 (Rotax 582)	7156		8. 2.96	D.Young t/a Kemble Flying Club	Kemble	17. 4.99P

G-MZAA-MZZZ

Regn	Type	C/n	P/I	Date	Owner/operator	Probable Base	CA Expy
G-MZAA	Mainair Blade 1059-1195-7 & W857 (Rotax 462)			24.10.95	J.C.Kitchen	London SE15	6. 1.00P
G-MZAB	Mainair Blade 1043-0695-7 & W841 (Rotax 582)			26. 5.95	S.M.Holroyd	Wakefield	9. 6.99P
G-MZAC	BFC Quad City Challenger II CH2-0294-1100 & PFA/177A-12716			21. 7.95	M.N.Calhaem	Fradswell, Stafford	20. 4.99P
G-MZAD	Mainair Blade 1061-1295-7 & W861 (Rotax 912)			29.11.95	T.Kidd (Stored 4.97)	Oxton, Notts	
G-MZAE	Mainair Blade 1063-1295-7 & W863 (Rotax 582)			4.12.95	A.C.Rowlands	Dalscote, Nether Heyford	21. 3.99P
G-MZAF	Mainair Blade 1045-0795-7 & W843 (Rotax 582)			1.12.95	G.C.Brown	Barton	18. 4.99P
G-MZAG	Mainair Blade 1042-0695-7 & W840 (Rotax 582)			26. 5.95	P.D.Gurney	Blackpool	30.12.99P
G-MZAH	Rans S-6-ESD Coyote II (Rotax 503) 0393-470 & PFA/204-12553			3. 9.93	D.G.Matthews	Chipping Norton	15. 6.98P
G-MZAI	Mainair Blade 1065-0196-7 & W867 (Rotax 912UL)			4.12.95	P. & M.Boultby	Oxton, Notts	4. 3.98P
G-MZAJ	Mainair Blade 1067-0196-7 & W869 (Rotax 582)			20.12.95	K.W.Palmer	Benfleet	5. 2.00P
G-MZAK	Mainair Mercury 1070-0296-7 & W872 (Rotax 503)			15. 1.96	S.J.Joseph	Cheshunt	5. 2.99P
G-MZAL	Mainair Blade 1076-0396-7 & W878			21. 2.96	T.Dunn	Nottingham	31. 3.99P
G-MZAM	Mainair Blade 1044-0695-7 & W842 (Rotax 582)			31. 5.95	B.K.Robinson	Droitwich	11. 8.99P
G-MZAN	Cyclone Pegasus Quantum 15 7188 (Rotax 582/40)			7. 3.96	S.Payne t/a Zanco Syndicate	Dunkeswell	30. 4.99P
G-MZAO	Mainair Blade 1069-0296-7 & W871 (Rotax 912UL)			15. 3.96	P.A.B. & B.A.Morgan	Sandy	7. 4.99P
G-MZAP	Mainair Blade 1036-0495-7 & W834 (Rotax 582)			31. 3.95	J.G.Lloyd	Harlow	28. 2.99P
G-MZAR	Mainair Blade 1072-0296-7 & W874 (Rotax 582)			13. 2.96	S.M.Hillyer-Jones	Shobdon	24. 2.99P
G-MZAS	Mainair Blade 1049-0895-7 & W847 (Rotax 582)			15. 8.95	T.Carter	Shobdon	25. 8.99P
G-MZAT	Mainair Blade 1060-1195-7 & W860 (Rotax 582)			29.11.95	P.Carmassi	Southport	6.12.98P
G-MZAU	Mainair Blade 1064-0196-7 & W864 (Rotax 582)			29.11.95	I.Caslin & I.Simpson	Carlisle	28. 4.99P
G-MZAV	Mainair Blade 1078-0396-7 & W881 (Rotax 582)			11. 3.96	D.L.Pollitt	St.Michaels-on-Wyre	8. 5.99P
G-MZAW	Cyclone Pegasus Quantum 15 7160 (Rotax 503)			14. 2.96	M.J.Mawle	Kemble	13. 3.99P
G-MZAX	Cyclone Pegasus Quantum 15 7152			11. 3.96	Kwik Kwek Kwak SA	Marbella, Spain	
G-MZAY	Mainair Blade 1077-0396-7 & W880 (Rotax 462)			15. 3.96	M.D.Harris	Earls Barton, Northampton	13. 3.99P
G-MZAZ	Mainair Blade 1040-0595-7 & W838 (Rotax 462)			26. 5.95	P.J.Kay	Barton	30. 6.99P
G-MZBA	Mainair Blade 1068-0296-7 & W870 (Rotax 912UL)			15. 3.96	M.K.Mitchell	Hertford	27. 3.98P
G-MZBB	Cyclone Pegasus Quantum 15 7139 (Rotax 582/40)			13. 3.96	P.D.Willan	Rhuallt	27. 4.99P
G-MZBC	Cyclone Pegasus Quantum 15 7077 (Rotax 582)			15. 8.95	B.M.Quinn	Barlow, Sheffield	30. 3.99P
G-MZBD	Rans S-6-ESD Coyote II XL (Rotax 503) 0795-850XL & PFA/204-12957			15. 3.96	S.J.Marshall	Lichfield	9. 2.99P
G-MZBE	CFM Streak Shadow SA-M PFA/206-12905 (Rotax 618)			18. 3.96	N.J.Bushell	Southampton	3. 9.99P
G-MZBF	Letov LK-2M Sluka (Rotax 447) PFA/263-12881			18. 3.96	C.R.Stockdale	Movenis, Co.Londonderry	25. 1.00P
G-MZBG	Whittaker MW-6S Fatboy Flyer (Rotax 503) PFA/164-12891			20. 3.96	A.W.Hodder	RAF Cranwell	22. 5.99P
G-MZBH	Rans S-6-ESD Coyote II PFA/204-12244 (Rotax 503)			21. 3.96	D.Sutherland	Breighton	22. 4.99P
G-MZBI	Cyclone Pegasus Quantum 15 7189 (Rotax 582/40)			21. 3.96	C.A.Campbell	Kirkhill, Inverness	9. 5.99P
G-MZBK	Letov LK-2M Sluka 8295s 002 & PFA/263-12872			26. 3.96	R.Painter	Bridgnorth	
G-MZBL	Mainair Blade (Rotax 582) 1080-0496-7 & W883			11. 4.96	C.Jackson	Ince Blundell, Liverpool	13. 6.99P
G-MZBM	Cyclone Pegasus Quantum 15 7196 (Rotax 582/40)			12. 4.96	Flight Aid Ltd	Ilminster	10.10.98P
G-MZBN	CFM Shadow Srs.CD 069 & BMAA/HB/073 (Rotax 503) (Manufacturer's c/n duplicates G-MTWP - was that aircraft rebuilt ?)			22. 4.96	Cloudbase Aviation Services Ltd	Redhill	19. 6.99P
G-MZBO	Cyclone Pegasus Quantum 15 7218 (Rotax 582)			3. 5.96	B.H.Ashman	Sywell	17. 6.98P

Regn	Type	C/n	P/I	Date	Owner/operator	Probable Base	CA Expy
G-MZBP	Airwave Microchute UQ/Motor BMAA/HB/028 and/or BMAA/HB/075	27		29. 3.96	V.G.Pearson	Guildford	
G-MZBR	Southdown Raven	2232/0082		24. 5.96	D.M.Lane	Stourbridge	
G-MZBS	CFM Shadow Srs.D (Rotax 582/47)	PFA/161-13008		14. 5.96	P.B.Merritt	Newbury	17. 6.99P
G-MZBT	Cyclone Pegasus Quantum 15 (Rotax 912)	7224		22. 5.96	T.M.Clark	Guildford	20. 7.99P
G-MZBU	Rans S-6-ESD Coyote II XL (Rotax 503)	PFA/204-12992		30. 5.96	J.B.Marshall	Scarborough	3.10.99P
G-MZBV	Rans S-6-ESD Coyote II XL (Rotax 503) 0396-950XL & PFA/204-13009			30. 5.96	P.A.Gilford	Penrith	29. 7.98P
G-MZBW	Quad City Challenger II UK (Rotax 582)	PFA/177-12971		19. 2.96	R.T.L.Chaloner	Grisborough, Cleveland	29. 7.99P
G-MZBX	Whittaker MW-6S-LW Fatboy Flyer	PFA/164-12563		16. 5.96	S.Rose & P.Tearall	Ilford/Camberley	18.10.99P
G-MZBY	Cyclone Pegasus Quantum 15 (Rotax 582) (C/n 7224 reported - see G-MZBT)	7227		30. 5.96	D.M.Holmam	Northwich	24. 9.99P
G-MZBZ	Quad City Challenger II UK	PFA/177-12928		11. 3.96	J.Flisher	Honiton	
G-MZCA	Rans S-6-ESD Coyote II XL (Rotax 503) 0396-953XL & PFA/204-12997			31. 5.96	S.J.Everett, K.Kettles & F.Williams Stratford-on-Avon		26. 6.99P
G-MZCB	Cyclone Chaser S (Rotax 447)	7220		4. 6.96	A.R.Turk	Rickmansworth	1. 8.99P
G-MZCC	Mainair Blade (Rotax 912UL)	1086-0696-7 & W889		7. 6.96	D.E.McGauley	Ince Blundell, Liverpool	18. 7.99P
G-MZCD	Mainair Blade (Rotax 582)	1087-0696-7 & W890		10. 6.96	J.R.Caylow	Nottingham	30. 9.99P
G-MZCE	Mainair Blade (Rotax 462)	1088-0696-7 & W891		17. 6.96	P.Hayes	Ince Blundell, Liverpool	15.12.99P
G-MZCF	Mainair Blade (Rotax 462)	1089-0696-7 & W892		30. 8.96	J.White	Ince Blundell, Liverpool	29. 8.97P
G-MZCG	Mainair Blade (Rotax 462)	1090-0696-7 & W893		17. 6.96	M.J.Wilson	Childwall, Liverpool	17.10.99P
G-MZCH	Whittaker MW-6S Fatboy Flyer	PFA/164-12131		7. 6.96	E.J.Blake	Totnes	
G-MZCI	Cyclone Pegasus Quantum 15 (Rotax 503)	7231		10. 6.96	P.H.Risdale	Wollaston	13. 7.99P
G-MZCJ	Cyclone Pegasus Quantum 15 (Rotax 582/40)	7233		14. 6.96	A.W.Hay	Insch	19. 7.99P
G-MZCK	AMF Chevvron 2-32C (Konig SD570)	038		11. 7.96	Finish Design Ltd	Cambridge	9. 7.97P
G-MZCL	Ultrasports Tripacer/Moyes Mega II	JAJ-01		21. 6.96	J.A.Jones	Winchester	
G-MZCM	Cyclone Pegasus Quantum 15 (Rotax 582)	7219		3. 5.96	A.J.Harper	Croughton	5. 6.98P
G-MZCN	Mainair Blade (Rotax 582)	1079-0396-7 & W882		27. 6.96	P.C.Nelstrop	Barton	30. 6.99P
G-MZCO	Mainair Mercury (Rotax 462)	1091-0796-7 & W894		26. 6.96	P.A.Bott	Northwich	14. 8.99P
G-MZCP	Solar Wings Pegasus XL-Q (Rotax 462) SW-TE-0434 & SW-WQ-0576			11. 2.93	C.A.Palmer	Clench Common	22. 5.99P
G-MZCR	Cyclone Pegasus Quantum 15 (Rotax 503)	7234		28. 6.96	J.E.P.Stubberfield	Kenley	20. 4.99P
G-MZCS	Team Minimax 91	PFA/186-12646		20.12.95	C.E.Cox	Leominster	7. 5.99P
G-MZCT	CFM Shadow Srs.CD (Rotax 503)	277		11. 7.96	W.G.Gill Plaistows Field, Hemel Hampstead		16. 9.97P
G-MZCU	Mainair Blade (Rotax 462)	1082-0496-7 & W885		1. 5.96	B.L.Cook	Sandtoft	5. 7.99P
G-MZCV	Cyclone Pegasus Quantum 15 (Rotax 503)	7235		11. 7.96	B.S.Toole	Rhuallt	8. 8.98P
G-MZCX	Hunt Wing/Avon Skytrike BMAA/HB/072 (Rotax 503) (Originally regd with c/n 9510055)			17. 7.96	R.Harrison	High Barn Farm, Houghton	10. 2.99P
G-MZCY	Cyclone Pegasus Quantum 15 (Rotax 582)	7236		19. 7.96	B.G.Simons	Craysmarsh Farm, Melksham	26. 7.99P
G-MZCZ	Hunt Wing/Experience BMAA/HB/039 (Originally regd with c/n 9409024)			24. 7.96	C.Kiernan	Mostrim, Co.Longford	
G-MZDA	Rans S-6-ESD Coyote II XL (Rotax 503)	PFA/204-13019		29. 7.96	J.Dent & W.C.Lombard Thirsk/Northallerton		5. 9.99P
G-MZDB*	Cyclone Pegasus Quantum 15 (Rotax 912)	7237		31. 7.96	Not known (Temp unregd 15.11.96)	Marlborough	26. 7.97P
G-MZDC	Cyclone Pegasus Quantum 15 (Rotax 582)	7246		2. 8.96	M.T.Jones	Witney	7.11.99P
G-MZDD	Cyclone Pegasus Quantum 15 (Rotax 503)	7114	G-69-23	11. 7.96	L.A.Hosegood	Swindon	16. 1.98P
G-MZDE	Cyclone Pegasus Quantum 15 (Rotax 582)	7238		12. 7.96	D.J.Taylor	St.Neots	26. 1.00P

Regn	Type	C/n	P/I	Date	Owner/operator	Probable Base	CA Expy
G-MZDF	Mainair Blade (Rotax 462)	1093-0896-7 & W896		15. 8.96	R.Ratcliffe	Arclid Green, Sandbach	11. 4.99P
G-MZDG	Rans S-6-ESD Coyote II XL (Rotax 503)	PFA/204-13030		7. 8.96	R. & J.A.Rhodes	Eshott	7. 4.99P
G-MZDH	Cyclone Pegasus Quantum 15 (Rotax 912)	7248		12. 8.96	R.Germany Knapthorpe Lodge, Caunton t/a Germany Transport		8. 9.98P
G-MZDI	Whittaker MW-6S Fatboy Flyer Srs.A (Rotax 503)	PFA/164-11929	G-BUNN	15. 8.96	G.T.Harris	East Grinstead	10.11.99P
G-MZDJ	Medway Raven X (Rotax 447)	MRB138/119		19. 8.96	R.Bryan & S.Digby	Bristol	2. 9.98P
G-MZDK	Mainair Blade (Rotax 582) (C/n reported as 1084-0696-7)	1084-0596-7 & W887		9. 5.96	K.J.Miles	St.Michaels-on-Wyre	29. 5.99P
G-MZDL	Whittaker MW-6S Fatboy Flyer	PFA/164-12412		19. 8.96	C.D. & S.J.Wills	Andover	
G-MZDM	Rans S-6-ESD Coyote II XL (Rotax 503)	0396-954XL & PFA/204-13022		2. 9.96	M.E.Nicholas	Stafford	25. 8.99P
G-MZDN	Cyclone Pegasus Quantum 15 (Rotax 582)	7255		5. 9.96	A.Cox	Winks Farm, Hailsham	16. 3.99P
G-MZDO	Cyclone AX3 (Rotax 503)	7252		11. 9.96	I.P.Noonan	Weston Zoyland	17. 4.99P
G-MZDP	AMF Chevvron 2-32C (Konig SD570)	020		3. 4.90	A.S.Nicol & A.S.Gunn Billericay t/a G-MZDP Group (Damaged mid 1995)		16. 3.96P
G-MZDR	Rans S-6-ESD Coyote II XL (Rotax 503)	PFA/204-13012		8. 8.96	R.Pyper & P.McGill Newtownards/Holywood		4.11.99P
G-MZDS	Cyclone AX3 (Rotax 503)	7253		16. 9.96	A.B.Askew	Kettering	3.10.98P
G-MZDT	Mainair Blade (Rotax 582)	1096-0996-7 & W899		19. 9.96	G.Sipson	Otherton, Cannock	14. 8.98P
G-MZDU	Cyclone Pegasus Quantum 15 (Rotax 912)	7260		19. 9.96	G.A.Breen	Lagos, Portugal	26.10.98P
G-MZDV	Cyclone Pegasus Quantum 15 (Rotax 582)	7199		9. 4.96	P.M.Wilkinson	Great Orton	19. 5.99P
G-MZDW	Trekking Microchute UQ/Motor 27	BMAA/HB/078		23. 9.96	C.Kiernan	Mostrim, Co.Longford	
G-MZDX	Letov LK-2M Sluka	PFA/263-12882		30. 9.96	R.P.Stonor	London W3	8. 2.99P
G-MZDY	Cyclone Pegasus Quantum 15 (Rotax 462HP)	7263		2.10.96	E.R.Bone	Newmarket	21.10.99P
G-MZDZ	Hunt Avon/Wing 9501042 & BMAA/HB/045			23.10.96	E.W.Laidlaw	Langholm, Dumfries	
G-MZEA	BFC Quad City Challenger II CH2-0294-1101 & PFA/177A-12728			22. 4.96	G.S.Cridland	Thorney Island	8. 2.99P
G-MZEB	Mainair Blade (Rotax 462)	1074-0396-7 & W876		22. 7.96	G.R.Barker	Epping	21. 7.99P
G-MZEC	Cyclone Pegasus Quantum 15 (Rotax 582/40)	7278		24.10.96	A.B.Godber Bradley Ashbourne, Derby		10.11.99P
G-MZED	Mainair Blade (Rotax 582)	1092-0796-7 & W895		3. 7.96	P.Lavender	Barton	31. 7.99P
G-MZEE	Cyclone Pegasus Quantum 15 (Rotax 582)	7245		9. 8.96	D.R.Willson	Oakham	28. 8.99P
G-MZEF*	Mainair Blade (Rotax 462)	1094-0896-7 & W897		12. 8.96	D.A.Bolton Rochdale (Cancelled as destroyed 19.2.99)		23. 9.99P
G-MZEG	Mainair Blade (Rotax 582)	1095-0896-7 & W898		8. 8.96	J.Jasinczuk Otherton, Cannock		5. 9.99P
G-MZEH	Cyclone Pegasus Quantum 15 (Rotax 582/40)	7259		19. 9.96	P.S.Hall	Sywell	16.10.99P
G-MZEI	Whittaker MW-5D Sorcerer (Rotax 447)	PFA/163-12011		28.10.96	W.G.Reynolds	Cromer	23. 7.98P
G-MZEJ	Mainair Blade (Rotax 462)	1097-0996-7 & W900		8.10.96	D.Jones	Liverpool	13. 8.99P
G-MZEK	Mainair Mercury (Rotax 462)	1098-1096-7 & W901		14.10.96	G.Crane	Stoke-on-Trent	4.11.99P
G-MZEL	Cyclone AX3 (Rotax 503)	7250		30.10.96	T.I.Bull	Tarn Farm, Cockerham	18. 3.99P
G-MZEM	Cyclone Pegasus Quantum 15 (Rotax 912)	7277		8.11.96	C.A.W.Godfrey	London W4	6. 1.00P
G-MZEN	Rans S-6-ESD Coyote II (Rotax 503)	PFA/204-12823		9. 7.96	P.Bottomley Damyns Hill, Upminster		18. 2.99P
G-MZEO	Rans S-6-ESD Coyote II XL (Rotax 503)	PFA/204-13046		19.11.96	J.R.Dobson Cramlington t/a G-MZEO Group		25. 2.99P
G-MZEP	Mainair Rapier (Rotax 503)	1103-1296-7 & W906		13.12.96	A.J. & M.S.Haworth Arclid Green, Sandbach		10. 3.99P
G-MZER	Cyclone AX2000 (Rotax 582/48)	7251		4.12.96	B.H.Stephens Old Sarum t/a Sarum AX2000 Group		16. 3.99P
G-MZES	Letov LK-2M Sluka (Rotax 447)	8296K10 & PFA/263-13064		5.12.96	C.Parkinson	Sandtoft	14. 6.99P
G-MZET	Cyclone Pegasus Quantum 15 (Rotax 503)	7288		9.12.96	D.L.Walker Medernach, Netherlands		17. 2.99P
G-MZEU	Rans S-6-ESD Coyote II XL (Rotax 503)	PFA/204-13023		23.12.96	P.W.Cole & J.E.Holloway Hereford/Saltash		23. 6.98P
G-MZEV	Mainair Rapier (Rotax 503)	1101-1296-7 & W904		7. 1.97	I.D.Woolley	Barton	30. 3.99P

Regn	Type	C/n	P/I	Date	Owner/operator	Probable Base	CA Expy
G-MZEW	Mainair Blade 1105-0197-7 & W908 (Rotax 462)			13. 1.97	M.Rhodes	Arclid Green, Sandbach	5. 2.99P
G-MZEX	Cyclone Pegasus Quantum 15 7292 (Rotax 582/40)			19.11.96	J.W.Barr	Long Marston	30. 1.00P
G-MZEY	Micro Aviation B.22S Bantam 96-002 (Rotax 582)		ZK-TII	7. 1.97	C.A.Bagshaw Pound Green, Kidderminster t/a Pound Green Syndicate		9. 1.99P
G-MZEZ	Cyclone Pegasus Quantum 15 7285 (Rotax 912)			8.11.96	E.Daleki	Oakley	17. 2.99P
G-MZFA	Cyclone AX2000 7301 (Rotax 582/48)			17.12.96	P.J.Howard	Ennis, Co.Clare	16. 1.00P
G-MZFB	Mainair Blade 1108-0197-7 & W911 (Rotax 462)			7. 1.97	R.J.Allarton	Newark	3. 6.99P
G-MZFC	Letov LK-2M Sluka PFA/263-13063 (Rotax 447)			7. 1.97	J.van der Broek	Tewksbury	24. 6.99P
G-MZFD	Mainair Rapier 1109-0197-7 & W912 (Rotax 462)			24. 1.97	R.Gill	Knapthorpe Lodge, Caunton	17. 3.99P
G-MZFE	Hunt Avon/Wing 9507049 & BMAA/HB/061 (Rotax 503)			16. 1.97	G.J.Latham	Sittles Farm, Alrewas	10. 6.99P
G-MZFF	Hunt Avon/Wing 960458 & BMAA/HB/074			22. 1.97	B.J.Adamson	Stockport	
G-MZFG	Cyclone Pegasus Quantum 15 7305 (Rotax 582/40)			21. 1.97	P.Smith	Ulverston	17. 3.99P
G-MZFH	AMF Chevvron 2-32C (Konig SD570) 039			27. 3.97	Finish Design Ltd Tarn Farm, Cockerham t/a Air-Share		21. 4.98P
G-MZFI	Lorimer Iolaire (BMW) BMAA/HB/035			30. 1.97	H.Lorimer	Mauchline, Ayr	
G-MZFK	Whittaker MW-6 Merlin PFA/164-11626 (Rotax 532)			10. 2.97	K.Worthington	Chorley	19.11.99P
G-MZFL	Rans S-6-ESD Coyote II XL (Rotax 503) 0696-999XL & PFA/204-13041			12. 2.97	D.L.Robson & U.Y.S.O'Reilly	Eshott	19. 8.99P
G-MZFM	Cyclone Pegasus Quantum 15 7310 (Rotax 582/40)			21. 2.97	T.Holford	Cannock	9. 3.99P
G-MZFN	Rans S-6-ESD Coyote II PFA/204-12977 (Rotax 503)			26. 2.97	C.J. & W.R.Wallbank	Ley Farm, Chirk	14. 9.99P
G-MZFO	Thruster T.600N 9037-T600N-001 (Rotax 503)			4. 3.97	Mainair Sports Ltd	Barton	8. 4.99P
G-MZFP	Thruster T.600T 9047-T600T-002 (Rotax 503)			4. 3.97	A.R.Emerson	Priory Farm, Tibenham	12. 5.99P
G-MZFR	Thruster T.600N 9047-T600N-003 (Rotax 503)			4. 3.97	H.Larmour Stourbridge t/a Blue Bird Syndicate		18. 5.99P
G-MZFS	Mainair Blade 1110-0297-7 & W913 (Rotax 582) (Regd with Trike c/n 1010-0297-7)			8. 1.97	S.P.Stone & F.A.Stephens Baxby Manor, Husthwaite		11. 3.99P
G-MZFT	Cyclone Pegasus Quantum 15 7264 (Rotax 912)			2.10.96	J.F.Woodham	Oakley	8.10.99P
G-MZFU	Thruster T.600N 9047-T600N-004 (Rotax 503)			4. 3.97	Thruster Air Services Ltd	Ginge, Wantage	17. 9.99P
G-MZFV	Cyclone Pegasus Quantum 15 7324 (Rotax 912)			13. 3.97	G.J.Slater	Marlborough	22. 4.99P
G-MZFW	Mainair Rapier 1111-0297-7 & W914 (Rotax 462)			17. 1.97	C.S.M.Hallam	Rochdale	23. 4.99P
G-MZFX	Cyclone AX2000 7322 (Rotax 582/48)			14. 3.97	Flylight Airsports Ltd	Sywell	30. 4.99P
G-MZFY	Rans S-6-ESD Coyote II XL (Rotax 503) PFA/204-13043			17. 3.97	L.G.Tserkezos	Reigate	27. 5.99P
G-MZFZ	Mainair Blade 1119-0497-7 & W922 (Rotax 582/2V)			2. 4.97	S.M.Park Rufforth t/a Phoenix Flying Group		21. 5.99P
G-MZGA	Cyclone AX2000 7303 (Rotax 582/48)			17.12.96	Microflight Ireland Ltd	Mullaghmore	18. 5.99P
G-MZGB	Cyclone AX2000 7302 (Rotax 582/48)			28. 1.97	P.Hegarty Magherafelt, Co.Londonderry		10.11.99P
G-MZGC	Cyclone AX2000 7304 (Rotax 582/2V)			20.12.96	Carol E.Walls	Mullaghmore	23. 1.99P
G-MZGD	Rans S-5 Coyote PFA/193-13096			1. 4.97	A.G.Headford	Barton	
G-MZGE	Medway Hybred 44XLR MR143/125 (Rotax 503)			8. 4.97	Eclectic Computer Software Ltd	Westerham	27. 5.99P
G-MZGF	Letov LK-2M Sluka PFA/263-13073 (Rotax 447)			8. 4.97	G.Lombardi	RAF Wyton	16. 9.99P
G-MZGG	Cyclone Pegasus Quantum 15 7327 (Rotax 503)			10. 4.97	A.J.Ridell	Graveley	16. 5.99P
G-MZGH	Hunt Avon/Hunt Wing BMAA/HB/070			20.12.96	G.C.Horner	Tyldesley, Manchester	
G-MZGI	Mainair Blade 1117-0397-7 & W920 (Rotax 912UL)			11. 4.97	N.E.King	Bolton	7. 5.99P
G-MZGJ	Kolb Twinstar Mk.3 PFA/205-12421			16. 4.97	P.Coppock	Kemble	12. 8.99P
G-MZGK	Cyclone Pegasus Quantum 15 7331 (Rotax 582/40)			30. 4.97	G.C.Weighell	Chipping Norton	14. 5.99P
G-MZGL	Mainair Rapier 1104-0197-7 & W907 (Rotax 503)			18.12.96	L.R.Fox	Aylesbury	6. 3.98P
G-MZGM	Cyclone AX2000 7334 (Rotax 582/48)			1. 5.97	W.G.Dunn	Winkleigh, Devon	3. 7.99P

Regn	Type	C/n	P/I	Date	Owner/operator	Probable Base	CA Expy
G-MZGN	Cyclone Pegasus Quantum 15 (Rotax 503)	7332		2. 5.97	R.J.Townsend	Welwyn Garden City	16. 6.99P
G-MZGO	Cyclone Pegasus Quantum 15 (Rotax 582/40)	7320		20. 3.97	S.F.G.Allen	Knapthorpe Lodge, Caunton	16. 5.99P
G-MZGP	Cyclone AX2000 (Rotax 582/48)	7333		7. 5.97	M.W.Taylor	Insch	10. 6.99P
G-MZGR	Team Minimax	PFA/186-12323		8. 5.97	K.G.Seeley	Reading	
G-MZGS	CFM Shadow Srs.DD	PFA/161-13050		8. 5.97	M.J.McCrystal	Dingwall	10. 8.99P
G-MZGT	RH7B Tiger Light (Five eights scale Tiger Moth)	PFA/230-13013		10. 3.97	J.B.McNab	Coventry	
G-MZGU	Arrowflight Hawk II (UK) (Rotax 503)	PFA/266-13075		8. 5.97	Arrowflight Aviation Ltd	Cowes, IoW	27. 7.99P
G-MZGV	Cyclone Pegasus Quantum 15 (Rotax 582/40)	7339		12. 6.97	J.I.Greenshields	Taunton	22. 6.99P
G-MZGW	Mainair Blade (Rotax 462)	1112-0297-7 & W915		19. 2.97	R.Almond	Bury St.Edmunds	3. 5.99P
G-MZGX	Thruster T.600N (Rotax 503)	9057-T600N-005		28. 4.97	R.L.Barton	Arclid Green, Sandbach	17. 6.99P
G-MZGY	Thruster T.600N (Rotax 503)	9057-T600N-006		28. 4.97	Financial Planning (Wells) Ltd	Wells	12. 8.98P
G-MZGZ	Thruster T.600N (Rotax 503)	9057-T600N-007		28. 4.97	A.Stanford	Newton Abbot	29. 9.99P
G-MZHA	Thruster T.600T (Rotax 503)	9057-T600T-008		28. 4.97	R.V.Buxton	Feshiebridge	29. 7.99P
G-MZHB	Mainair Blade (Rotax 462)	1114-0297-7 & W917		19. 2.97	R.J.Butler	Guy Lane Farm, Waverton	22. 3.99P
G-MZHC	Thruster T.600T	9067-T600T-009		13. 5.97	Thruster Air Services Ltd	Wantage	16. 3.99P
G-MZHD	Thruster T.600T	9067-T600T-010		13. 5.97	B.E.Foster	Tain, Ross-shire	4. 1.99P
G-MZHE	Thruster T.600N (Rotax 503)	9067-T600N-011		13. 5.97	K.R.Jenkins	Honiton	5. 1.00P
G-MZHF	Thruster T.600N (Rotax 503)	9067-T600N-012		13. 5.97	Thruster Air Services Ltd	Wantage	AC
G-MZHG	Whittaker MW-6T	PFA/164-11420		16. 6.97	M.G.Speers	Douglas, IoM	21. 9.99P
G-MZHI	Cyclone Pegasus Quantum 15 (Rotax 582/40)	7337		27. 5.97	V.Causey t/a Quantum HI Group	Chesterfield	3. 7.99P
G-MZHJ	Mainair Rapier (Rotax 462)	1123-0697-7 & W926		17. 6.97	T.D.Guest	Shifnal	22. 6.99P
G-MZHK	Cyclone Pegasus Quantum Super Sport 15 (Rotax 582/40)	7352		24. 6.97	B.J.Partridge	Cambridge	20. 7.99P
G-MZHL	Mainair Rapier (Rotax 503)	1126-0797-7 & W929		30. 6.97	A.N.W.Fletcher	Bodmin	19. 7.99P
G-MZHM	Team Himax 1700R (Rotax 447)	PFA/272-12912		8. 1.97	M.H.McKeown	Enniskillen	2. 4.99P
G-MZHN	Cyclone Pegasus Quantum 15 (Rotax 462HP)	7351		27. 6.97	T.G.Jones	Rhuallt	10. 8.99P
G-MZHO	Quad City Challenger II	PFA/177-12936		15. 7.97	J.Pavelin	Southend	5. 5.99P
G-MZHP	Cyclone Pegasus Quantum 15 (Rotax 582/40)	7353		15. 7.97	A.S.Findley	Cardington	20. 8.99P
G-MZHR	Cyclone AX2000 (Rotax 582)	7307		7. 3.97	Opus Software Ltd	Swayfield	22. 4.99P
G-MZHS	Thruster T.600T	9077-T600T-013		4. 7.97	D.Mahajan	West Wickham	9.10.99P
G-MZHT	Whittaker MW-6 Merlin (Rotax 503)	PFA/164-11244		12. 6.97	P.J.Mogg	Bibberne Farm, Stalbridge	22.10.99P
G-MZHU	Thruster T.600T	9077-T600T-019		4. 7.97	M.S.Shelton	London SE13	26. 4.99P
G-MZHV	Thruster T.600T	9077-T600T-018		4. 7.97	K.M.Jones	Leicester	29. 7.99P
G-MZHW	Thruster T.600N	9077-T600N-017		4. 7.97	K.N.Hopewell	Queniborough	26. 4.99P
G-MZHX	Thruster T.600N	9077-T600N-016		4. 7.97	Thruster Air Services Ltd	Wantage	
G-MZHY	Thruster T.600N	9077-T600N-015		4. 7.97	J.R.North t/a West Lancashire Microlight School	Liverpool	17. 2.99P
G-MZHZ	Thruster T.600N	9077-T600N-014		4. 7.97	G.E.Hillyer-Jones	Kington	17. 9.99P
G-MZIA	Team Himax 1700R	PFA/272-13020		25. 4.97	I.J.Arkieson	Meols, Wirral	
G-MZIB	Cyclone Pegasus Quantum 15 (Rotax 582/40)	7354		15. 7.97	K.W.A.Ballinger	Wokingham	2. 9.99P
G-MZIC	Cyclone Pegasus Quantum 15 (Rotax 503)	7348		24. 6.97	Helen M.Squire & C.F.Two t/a Swansea Airsports Services	Swansea	20. 7.99P
G-MZID	Whittaker MW-6 Merlin	PFA/164-11383		15. 7.97	M.G.A.Wood	Tadcaster	
G-MZIE	Cyclone Pegasus Quantum 15 (Rotax 582/40)	7359		6. 8.97	Flylight Airsports Ltd	Sywell	25. 8.99P
G-MZIF	Cyclone Pegasus Quantum 15 (Rotax 503)	7355		16. 7.97	P.Simpson	Weston Favell, Northampton	20. 8.99P
G-MZIH	Mainair Blade (Rotax 462)	1128-0797-7 & W931		16. 7.97	E.Scarisbrick	Preston	5. 8.99P
G-MZII	Team Minimax 88 (Rotax 377)	PFA/186-11842		19. 3.97	G.F.M.Garner	Clench Common	15. 9.99P
G-MZIJ	Cyclone Pegasus Quantum 15 (Rotax 582/40)	7362		14. 8.97	B.Errington-Weddle	North Shields	31. 8.99P

Regn	Type	C/n	P/I	Date	Owner/operator	Probable Base	CA Expy
G-MZIK	Cyclone Pegasus Quantum 15 (Rotax 582/40)	7368		8. 9.97	D.Kiddy & P.Davies	Torquay/Totnes	7. 9.99P
G-MZIL	Mainair Rapier 1132-0897-7 & W935 (Rotax 462)			1. 9.97	G.R.Stockdale	Sherburn	8. 9.99P
G-MZIM	Mainair Rapier 1124-0697-7 & W927 (Rotax 462)			9. 6.97	M.J.McKegney	Batley	9. 7.99P
G-MZIN	Whittaker MW-6 Merlin PFA/164-12820			9. 9.97	R.F.Bayford Newnham, St.Neots (Crashed Newnham 28.3.99)		20.10.99P
G-MZIP	Murphy Renegade Spirit UK (Rotax 532) 216 & PFA/188-11426			4. 7.89	C.I.Bates	Evesham	1.11.99P
G-MZIR	Mainair Blade 1134-0997-7 & W937 (Rotax 582)			18. 9.97	I.Callaghan t/a Moorland Flying Club	Davidstowe	28. 9.99P
G-MZIS	Mainair Blade 1115-0397-7 & W918 (Rotax 462)			17. 2.97	G.C.Long	Kettering	23. 3.99P
G-MZIT	Mainair Blade 1129-0897-7 & W932 (Rotax 912UL)			16. 7.97	K.M.Jones	Tring	24. 7.99P
G-MZIU	Cyclone Pegasus Quantum 15 (Rotax 582/40)	7371		15.10.97	S.F.Winter	Calne	2.10.99P
G-MZIV	Cyclone AX2000 (Rotax 582/48)	7372		21.10.97	C.J.Tomlin	Kettering	16.10.99P
G-MZIW	Mainair Blade 1127-0797-7 & W930 (Rotax 582)			16. 7.97	N.Creeney	St.Michaels-on-Wyre	11. 9.99P
G-MZIX	Mignet HM-1000 Balerit	130		23. 9.97	P.E.H.Scott	Stockbridge	27. 1.99P
G-MZIY	Rans S-6-ESD Coyote II XL (Rotax 503) 1096-1050XL & PFA/204-13184			29. 9.97	P.A.Bell	Barton	16.10.99P
G-MZIZ	Murphy Renegade Spirit UK (Rotax 582) 257 & PFA/188-11701		G-MWGP	21.10.92	J.G.McMinn	Movenis, Co.Londonderry	5.11.99P
G-MZJA	Mainair Blade 1135-0997-7 & W938 (Rotax 582)			30. 9.97	R.Cookson	Wirral	1.11.99P
G-MZJB	Aviasud Mistral	047	(ex ?)	30. 9.97	D.M.Whitham	Crosland Moor	
G-MZJC	Micro Aviation B.22S Bantam 97-011 (Rotax 582)		ZK-JIK	14.10.97	A.S.Moore	Stafford	1.12.99P
G-MZJD	Mainair Blade 1130-0897-7 & W933 (Rotax 503)			7. 8.97	R.J.Davey	Sleaford	18. 8.99P
G-MZJE	Mainair Rapier 1136-1097-7 & W939 (Rotax 503)			17.10.97	J.E.Davies	Southport	23.11.99P
G-MZJF	Cyclone AX2000 (Rotax 582/48)	7378		2.12.97	J.A.R.Hartley	Long Marston	1.12.99P
G-MZJG	Cyclone Pegasus Quantum 15 (Rotax 462)	7335		2. 5.97	J.Gamlen	Oakley	28. 5.99P
G-MZJH	Cyclone Pegasus Quantum 15 (Rotax 503)	7350		25. 6.97	J.Hardy	Kettering	17. 7.99P
G-MZJI	Rans S-6-ESD Coyote II XL (Rotax 503) 1096-1046XL & PFA/204-13221			3.11.97	A.T.Morgan	Bishops Stortford	18.12.99P
G-MZJJ	Meridian Ultralights Maverick PFA/259-13016			5.11.97	M.F.Cottam	Welton, Lincoln	1.10.99P
G-MZJK	Mainair Blade 1100-1196-7 & W903 (Rotax 582)			19.11.96	A.H.Kershaw	Bury	12.10.98P
G-MZJL	Cyclone AX2000 (Rotax 503)	7363		11. 8.97	A.J.Longbottom	Smeathorpe, Honiton	18. 9.99P
G-MZJM	Rans S-6-ESD Coyote II XL PFA/204-13215			19.11.97	R.J.Hopkins	Popham	26. 3.99P
G-MZJN	Cyclone Pegasus Quantum 15 (Rotax 582/40)	7376		11.11.97	J.Nelson	Belper	16.11.99P
G-MZJO	Cyclone Pegasus Quantum 15 (Rotax 582/40)	7338		17. 6.97	D.C.Lennard	Richmond, Surrey	1. 7.98P
G-MZJP	Whittaker MW-6S Fatboy Flyer PFA/164-13049			21.10.97	D.J.Burton & C.A.J.Funnell	Brighton	
G-MZJR	Cyclone AX2000	7385		11.11.97	Cyclone Airsports Ltd t/a Pegasus Aviation	Marlborough	18. 5.99P
G-MZJS	Meridian Ultralights Maverick PFA/259-13017			12.12.97	R.D.Barnard	Stockport	5.10.99P
G-MZJT	Cyclone Pegasus Quantum 15 (Rotax 912)	7399		23.12.97	C.M.Theakstone	Northampton	23.12.99P
G-MZJU	Cyclone Pegasus Quantum 15	7382		23.12.97	L.M.King	Telford	18. 2.99P
G-MZJV	Mainair Blade 1141-0198-7 & W944 (Rotax 912)			7. 1.98	M.A.Roberts	West Malling	3. 2.99P
G-MZJW	Cyclone Pegasus Quantum 15	7390		27. 1.98	I.D.Stokes	Camelford	27. 1.99P
G-MZJX	Mainair Blade 1139-0198-7 & W942			9. 1.98	D.J.Clark	West Malling	10. 2.99P
G-MZJY	Cyclone Pegasus Quantum 15 7394 (Rotax 912)			23.12.97	C.K.Jones	Northampton	23.12.99P
G-MZJZ	Mainair Blade 1121-0597-7 & W924 (Rotax 912UL)			23. 6.97	P.Crosby	Ince Blundell, Liverpool	22. 6.99P
G-MZKA	Cyclone Pegasus Quantum 15 (Rotax 912)	7380		1.12.97	A.S.R.McSherry	West Kilbride	26.11.99P
G-MZKB	Kolb Twinstar Mk.3 PFA/205-13160 (Rotax 582)			18. 7.97	K.R.Blades	Louth	19.11.98P

Regn	Type	C/n	P/I	Date	Owner/operator	Probable Base	CA Expy
G-MZKC	Cyclone AX2000	7398		22. 1.98	A.G. & G.L.Higgins	Bitteswell	21. 1.99P
G-MZKD	Cyclone Pegasus Quantum 15	7404		19. 3.98	S.J.E.Smith	Newcastle	17. 3.99P
G-MZKE	Rans S-6-ESD Coyote II XL			19. 1.98	I.Findlay	Wallsend	8. 3.99P
	PFA/204-13248						
G-MZKF	Cyclone Pegasus Quantum 15	7407		21. 1.98	G.J.Slater	Marlborough	16. 2.99P
G-MZKG	Mainair Blade	1145-0198-7 & W948		23. 1.98	P.Olsson	Ulverston	10. 2.99P
G-MZKH	CFM Shadow Srs.DD	292-DD		23. 1.98	K.D.Mitchell	Shoreham	8. 3.99P
G-MZKI	Mainair Rapier	1147-0298-7 & W950		12. 2.98	C.A.Benjamin	Prestwich	18. 5.99P
G-MZKJ	Mainair Blade	1039-0595-7 & W837		19. 5.95	L.G.M.Maddick	Barton	14. 6.98P
	(Rotax 582)						
G-MZKK	Mainair Blade	1140-0198-7 & W943		12. 2.98	D.L.Handley	Canterbury	23. 2.99P
	(Rotax 912)						
G-MZKL	Cyclone Pegasus Quantum 15	7360		18. 8.97	S.Pearce & K.J.Fish	Woodhall Spa	31. 8.98P
	(Rotax 582/40)						
G-MZKM	Mainair Blade	1133-0897-7 & W936		15. 8.97	C.Bodill	Nottingham	18. 8.98P
	(Rotax 912UL)						
G-MZKN	Mainair Rapier	1138-1297-7 & W941		12.12.97	G.Craig	Dundonald, Belfast	23. 1.00P
G-MZKO	Mainair Blade	1131-0897-7 & W934		5. 8.97	A.M.Durose	Nottingham	16. 9.99P
	(Rotax 503)						
G-MZKP	Thruster T.600N	9038-T600N-020		27. 1.98	Thruster Air Services Ltd	Wantage	
G-MZKR	Thruster T.600N	9038-T600N-021		27. 1.98	Thruster Air Services Ltd	Wantage	AC
G-MZKS	Thruster T.600N	9038-T600N-022		27. 1.98	Thruster Air Services Ltd	Wantage	
G-MZKT	Thruster T.600T	9038-T600T-023		27. 1.98	M.J.O'Connor	Carshalton	7. 7.99P
G-MZKU	Thruster T.600T	9038-T600T-024		27. 1.98	A.S.Day	RAF Wyton	1.10.99P
G-MZKV	Mainair Blade	1144-0198-7 & W947		28. 1.98	M.P.J.Moore	Stoke-on-Trent	18. 3.99P
	(Rotax 912)						
G-MZKW	Quad City Challenger II	PFA/177-12518		22. 3.94	K.W.Warn	Newbury	26. 9.99P
	(Hirth 2705 R06)						
G-MZKX	Cyclone Pegasus Quantum 15	7395		15. 1.98	T.J.Hector	Royston	14. 1.00P
G-MZKY	Cyclone Pegasus Quantum 15	7403		16. 1.98	G.N.S.Farrant	Wallingford	28. 1.00P
G-MZKZ	Mainair Blade	1137-0298-7 & W940		18. 2.98	R.P.Wolstenholme	Warrington	26. 2.99P
G-MZLA	Cyclone Pegasus Quantum 15	7415		27. 2.98	D.A.Morgan	Plymouth	26. 2.99P
G-MZLB	Hunt Wing/Experience	BMAA/HB/058		25. 2.98	M.Ffrench	New Ross, Ireland	
G-MZLC	Mainair Blade	1146-0298-7 & W949		26. 2.98	J.R.North	Barton	6. 4.99P
	(Rotax 912)						
G-MZLD	Cyclone Pegasus Quantum 15	7416		24. 3.98	E.Clarke	Accrington	15. 3.99P
	(Rotax 912)						
G-MZLE	Meridian Ultralights Maverick		G-BXSZ	27. 2.98	A.A.Plumridge	Yevlverton	
	PFA/259-12955						
G-MZLF	Cyclone Pegasus Quantum 15	7417		30. 3.98	J.H.Tope	Newton Abbot	31. 3.99P
G-MZLG	Rans S-6-ESD Coyote II XL	PFA/204-13192		3. 3.98	R.H.J.Jenkins	Liverpool	20. 5.99P
G-MZLH	Cyclone Pegasus Quantum 15	7426		1. 4.98	R.J.Philpotts	Stourbridge	31. 3.99P
G-MZLI	Mignet HM-1000 Balerit	133		5. 3.98	D.S.Tye	Oban	22. 3.99P
G-MZLJ	Cyclone Pegasus Quantum 15	7421		20. 3.98	M.H.Colin & A.C.Jones	Otherton	19. 3.99P
G-MZLK	Hunt Avon Skytrike/Solar Wings Typhoon			9. 3.98	J.A.Jones	Winchester	28.12.99P
	T285-1471						
G-MZLL	Rans S-6-ESD Coyote II	PFA/204-13067		23. 9.97	J.A.Willats & G.W.Champion	Crawley	2. 8.99P
G-MZLM	Cyclone Pegasus AX2000	7425		22. 4.98	P.Bennett	Hinckley	20. 4.99P
G-MZLN	Cyclone Pegasus Quantum 15	7431		14. 4.98	S.H.James	Corby	19. 4.99P
G-MZLO	CFM Shadow Srs.D	K.298-D		1. 4.98	CFM Aircraft Ltd	Leiston	24.10.99P
G-MZLP	CFM Shadow Srs.D	K.299-D		1. 4.98	CFM Aircraft Ltd	Leiston	AC
G-MZLR	Cyclone Pegasus XL-Q	7441		28. 5.98	T.I.Courtney	Jacksdale	31. 5.99P
G-MZLS	Cyclone Pegasus AX2000	7428		6. 7.98	G.Forster	Market Rasen	5. 7.99P
G-MZLT	Cyclone Pegasus Quantum 15	7438		24. 4.98	C.S.Bourne	Stone	22. 4.99P
	(Rotax 912)						
G-MZLU	Cyclone Pegasus AX2000	7439		28. 7.98	M.L.Smith	Verwood	20. 7.99P
G-MZLV	Cyclone Pegasus Quantum 15	7437		29. 4.98	C.J.Finnigan	(BFPO 140)	7. 5.99P
G-MZLW	Cyclone Pegasus Quantam 15	7440		28. 4.98	G.Clipston	Kettering	27. 4.99P
G-MZLX	Micro Aviation B.22S Bantam	97-013	ZK-JIV	9.12.97	R.Smith	Bedford	14.12.98P
	(Rotax 582)						
G-MZLY	Letov LK-2M Sluka	PFA/263-13065		20. 4.98	B.G.M.Chapman	Louth	28. 7.99P
G-MZLZ	Mainair Blade	1154-0498-7 & W957		21. 4.98	S.Blackmore	Basingstoke	21. 4.99P
	(Rotax 912)						
G-MZMA	Solar Wings Pegasus Quasar IIITC	6611		1. 9.93	C.M.Addison		11.11.99P
	(Rotax 582/40)					Knapthorpe Lodge, Caunton, Notts	
G-MZMB	Mainair Blade	1149-0398-7 & W952		5. 3.98	G.Faulkner	Rugeley	29. 3.99P
G-MZMC	Cyclone Pegasus Quantum 15	7206		10. 5.96	J.J.Baker	Kettering	29. 5.98P
	(Rotax 912)						
G-MZMD	Mainair Blade	1148-0398-7 & W951		5. 3.98	T.Gate	Clitheroe	18. 3.99P
	(Rotax 912)						
G-MZME	Medway Hybred 44XLR Eclipser	151/129E		28. 4.98	T.Bowles	Liverpool	17. 9.99P
G-MZMF	Cyclone Pegasus Quantum 15 (HKS)	7387		30. 4.98	J.W.Teesdale	Sheriff Hutton	2. 9.99P
G-MZMG	Cyclone Pegasus Quantum 15	7446		27. 5.98	P.Baker	Bath	27. 5.99P
G-MZMH	Cyclone Pegasus Quantum 15	7402		27. 1.98	M.Hurtubise	Leamington Spa	27. 1.99P
	(Rotax 912)						
G-MZMI	CFM Streak Shadow	PFA/206-13205		30. 4.98	M.A.Hayward	Liskeard	
G-MZMJ	Mainair Blade	1155-0598-7 & W958		8. 5.98	S.Miles	Sutton-in-Ashfield	18. 5.99P
	(Rotax 912)						

Regn	Type	C/n	P/I	Date	Owner/operator	Probable Base	CA Expy
G-MZMK	AMF Chevvron 2-32C	040		19. 5.98	K.D.Calvert	Milton Keynes	3. 6.99P
G-MZML	Mainair Blade 1158-0698-7 & W961 (Rotax 912)			19. 5.98	D.McCormack	Livingstone	11. 6.99P
G-MZMM	Mainair Blade 1162-0698-7 & W965 (Rotax 912)			19. 5.98	J.F.Shaw	York	12. 7.99P
G-MZMN	Cyclone Pegasus Quantum 15 7445 (Rotax 912)			21. 5.98	W.H.J.Knowles	Tiverton	20. 5.99P
G-MZMO	Team Minimax 91 PFA/186-12951			20. 5.98	I.M.Ross	Banchory	
G-MZMP	Mainair Blade 1160-0698-7 & W963			20. 5.98	F.C.Tomlin	Linlithgow	21. 6.99P
G-MZMR	Rans S-6-ESA Coyote II PFA/204-13315			21. 5.98	E.W.McMullan	Ballyclare	
G-MZMS	Rans S-6-ES Coyote II PFA/204-13294			26. 5.98	J.G.Dungey	Norwich	21.10.99P
G-MZMT	Cyclone Pegasus Quantum 15 7449			18. 6.98	C.I.D.H.Garrison	Huntingdon	16. 6.99P
G-MZMU	Rans S-6-ESD Coyote II PFA/204-13242			5. 6.98	S.Cox	Hinckley	28. 9.99P
G-MZMV	Mainair Blade 1152-0496-7 & W955			30. 3.98	R.Nicklin	Wolverhampton	11. 5.99P
G-MZMW	Mignet HM-1000 Balerit 125 (Rotax 582)			2.10.96	M.E.Whapham	Burwash, East Sussex	6.11.99P
G-MZMX	Cyclone AX2000 7451			8. 9.98	R.H.Braithwaite t/a RAF Microlight Flying Association	RAF Cottesmore	6. 9.99P
G-MZMY	Mainair Blade 1153-0498-7 & W956			16. 3.98	C.J.Millership	Stoke-on-Trent	10. 5.99P
G-MZMZ	Mainair Blade 1081-0496-7 & W884 (Rotax 582)			22. 4.96	M.K.O'Donnell	Rainham, Essex	17. 5.99P
G-MZNA	Quad City Challenger II UK (Rotax 503) CH2-0894-UK-1193		EI-CLE	19. 3.98	R.S.O'Carroll	Craigavon, NI	11.10.99P
G-MZNB	Cyclone Pegasus Quantum 15 7456 (Rotax 912)			17. 7.98	W.D.Fanshawe	Old Sarum	12. 7.99P
G-MZNC	Mainair Blade 1161-0698-7 & W964 (Rotax 912)			22. 6.98	A.Costello	Manchester	22. 6.99P
G-MZND	Mainair Rapier 1170-0898-7 & W973			24. 6.98	S.D.Hutchinson	Preston	12. 7.99P
G-MZNE	Whittaker MW-6-2 Fatboy Flyer PFA/164-13120			26. 6.98	V.E.Booth	Twekesbury	
G-MZNF	Tiger Cub RL5A-LW Sherwood Ranger PFA/237-12964			29. 6.98	B.J.Chester-Master	Hereford	
G-MZNG	Cyclone Pegasus Quantum 15 7457 (Rotax 912)			11. 8.98	A.W.Buchan	Newark	13. 8.99P
G-MZNH	CFM Shadow Srs.DD K.297-DD			30. 6.98	CFM Aircraft Ltd	Leiston	6. 7.99P
G-MZNI	Mainair Blade 1163-0698-7 & W966 (Rotax 912)			3. 7.98	D.Armstrong	Ruislip	9. 8.99P
G-MZNJ	Mainair Blade 1168-0798-7 & W971			6. 7.98	G.E.Cole	Chepstow	10. 8.99P
G-MZNK	Mainair Blade 1164-0798-7 & W967			6. 7.98	R.P.Taylor	Folkestone	11.11.99P
G-MZNL	Mainair Blade 1165-0798-7 & W968 (Rotax 912)			6. 7.98	D.S.Taylor	Maidstone	11.11.99P
G-MZNM	Team Minimax 91 PFA/186-12304			10. 7.98	N.P.Thomson	North Berwick	
G-MZNN	Team Minimax 91 PFA/186-13125			10. 7.98	D.M.Dronsfield	Thornton-Cleveleys	
G-MZNO	Mainair Blade 1167-0798-7 & W970			9. 6.98	R.C.Colclough	Stoke-on-Trent	3. 8.99P
G-MZNP	Cyclone Pegasus Quantum 15 Super Sport (HKS) 7466 (Rotax 912)			22. 7.98	O.W.Achurch	Northampton	4.11.99P
G-MZNR	Cyclone Pegasus Quantum 15 7465			17. 8.98	E.S.Wills	Paignton	17. 8.99P
G-MZNS	Cyclone Pegasus Quantum 15 7473 (Rotax 912)			31. 7.98	Cyclone Airsports t/a Pegasus Aviation	Marlborough	13. 9.99P
G-MZNT	Cyclone Pegasus Quantum 15 7470 (Rotax 912)			25. 9.98	M.P.Lewis	Market Harborough	22. 9.99P
G-MZNU	Mainair Rapier 174-0898-7 & W977			5. 8.98	D.M.Hepworth	West Linton	2. 9.99P
G-MZNV	Rans S-6-ESD Coyote II PFA/204-12884			7. 8.98	D.E.Rubery & A.P.Thomas	Reading	2. 9.99P
G-MZNW	Thruster T.600N HKS 9098-T600N-025			10. 8.98	Thruster Air Services Ltd	Wantage	
G-MZNX	Thruster T.600N 9098-T600N-026			10. 8.98	D.Clarke t/a David Clarke Microlight Aircraft	Swanton Morley	14. 9.99P
G-MZNY	Thruster T.600N 9098-T600N-027			10. 8.98	Thruster Air Services Ltd	Wantage	AC
G-MZNZ	Letov LK-2M Sluka PFA/263-13274			21. 4.98	K.T.Vinning	Stratford-Upon-Avon	
G-MZOA	Thruster T.600T 9108-T600T-028			10. 8.98	Thruster Air Services Ltd	Wantage	
G-MZOB	Thruster T.600T 9098-T600T-029			10. 8.98	Thruster Air Services Ltd	Wantage	
G-MZOC	Mainair Blade 1172-0898-7 & W975 (Rotax 912)			10. 8.98	G.M.Prowling	Sowerby Bridge	1. 9.99P
G-MZOD	Cyclone Pegasus Quantum 15 7435 (Rotax 912)			28. 4.98	J.W.Mann	Witney	26. 4.99P
G-MZOE	Cyccone AX2000 7472			17. 9.98	York Microlight Centre Ltd	York	16. 9.99P
G-MZOF	Mainair Blade 1122-0697-7 & W925 (Rotax 462)			5. 6.97	A.P.S.John, T.D.Holland-Martin & P.J.Bossom t/a Overbury Farms	Tewkesbury	28. 7.99P
G-MZOG	Cyclone Pegasus Quantum 15 7471 (Rotax 912)			12.10.98	T.S.Sayers	Bristol	13.10.99P
G-MZOH	Whittaker MW-5D Sorcerer PFA/163-13060			14. 8.98	D.M.Precious	Camelford	
G-MZOI	Letov LK-2M Sluka PFA/263-13238			17. 8.98	K.P.Taylor	Welwyn Garden City	
G-MZOJ	Pegasus Quantum 15 7478			9.11.98	A.C.Lane	(Luton)	15.11.99P
G-MZOK	Whittaker MW-6 Merlin PFA/164-11568			24. 8.97	T.A.Willcox	Bristol	
G-MZOM	CFM Shadow Srs.DD 302-DD			8. 9.98	CFM Aircraft Ltd	Leiston	21. 9.99P

Regn	Type	C/n	P/I	Date	Owner/operator	Probable Base	CA Expy
G-MZON	Mainair Rapier	1180-1098-7-W983		11. 9.98	K.A.Armstrong	Brough	22. 9.99P
G-MZOP	Mainair Blade (Rotax 912)	1178-0998-7-W981		11. 9.98	P.Barrow	Macclesfield	15.10.99P
G-MZOR	Mainair Blade (Rotax 912)	1173-0898-7-W976		21. 9.98	Mainair Microlight School Ltd	Rochdale	21. 9.99P
G-MZOS	Pegasus Quantum 15 (Rotax 912)	7458		6.10.98	J.P.Appleby	Leicester	11.10.99P
G-MZOT	Letov LK-2M Sluka	PFA/263-13346		21. 9.98	J.R.Walter	Hollybush, Ayr	
G-MZOV	Pegasus Quantum 15	7512		9. 3.99	J.C.Tunstall	(Banbury)	
G-MZOW	Pegasus Quantum 15-912	7502		9. 3.99	G.R.Craig	(Insch)	
G-MZOX	Letov LK-2M Sluka	PFA/263-13415		15. 2.99	C.M.James	(Canterbury)	
G-MZOZ	Rans S-6-ESD Coyote II XL	PFA/204-13168		20. 5.98	D.C. & S.G.Emmons	Reading	13. 8.99P
G-MZPB	Mignet HM-1000 Balerit (Rotax 582)	124		4.10.96	P.M.Baker	Billingshurst	20.11.99P
G-MZPD	Solar Wings Pegasus Quantum 15 (Rotax 582)	7013		9. 5.95	P.M.Dewhurst	Sywell	31. 5.99P
G-MZPH	Mainair Blade	1177-0998-7-W980		26. 8.98	P.M.Hopewell	Loughborough	11.10.99P
G-MZPJ	Team Minimax 91 (Rotax 503)	PFA/186-12277		23.11.92	P.R.Jenson	Sittles Farm, Alrewas	14.10.98P
G-MZPW	Solar Wings Pegasus Quasar IITC (Rotax 582)	6892		26.10.94	P.R.Wilkinson	Newark	14. 2.99P
G-MZRC	Pegasus Quantum 15	7482		25.11.98	R.J.Cook	(Glasgow)	15.11.99P
G-MZRH	Cyclone Pegasus Quantum 15 (Rotax 582/40)	7269		11.10.96	A.J.Boulton	Roddige, Fradley	21.11.99P
G-MZRM	Cyclone Pegasus Quantum 15 (Rotax 912)	7455		10. 7.98	M.R.Mosley	Retford	9. 7.99P
G-MZRS	CFM Shadow Srs.CD (Rotax 503)	141		4. 4.90	M.R.Lovegrove	Worcester	8. 8.98P
G-MZSC	Cyclone Pegasus Quantum 15 (Rotax 503)	7370		3.10.97	R.J.Greaves	Hockliffe	6.10.99P
G-MZSD	Mainair Blade (Rotax 912)	1179-0998-7 & W978		21. 8.98	D.Sampson	Edinburgh	21. 9.99P
G-MZSM	Mainair Blade (Rotax 582)	1000-0794-7 & W796		15. 7.94	P.R.Anderson	Oxton, Nottingham	23. 8.99P
G-MZTA	Mignet HM-1000 Balerit (Rotax 582)	120		14. 5.96	A.Fusco t/a Sky Light Group	Burwash	5. 5.99P
G-MZTS	Aerial Arts Chaser S (Rotax 377)	CH703	G-MVDM	19. 3.96	D.G.Ellis	Tamworth	11. 8.98P
G-MZUB	Rans S-6-ESD Coyote II XL	PFA/204-13244		30. 4.98	B.O.Dowsett	Biggleswade	30. 7.99P
G-MZZT	Kolb Twinstar Mk.3	PFA/205-12596		1. 5.98	P.I.Morgans	Milford Haven	
G-MZZY	Mainair Blade (Rotax 912UL)	1050-0895-7 & W848		13.11.95	A.Mucznik	Oxton, Nottingham	28. 2.99P
G-MZZZ	Whittaker MW-6S Fatboy Flyer (Rotax 532)	PFA/164-11908		21.12.90	P.M.N.Richardson	Haywards Heath	

G-NAAA-NZZZ

Regn	Type	C/n	P/I	Date	Owner/operator	Probable Base	CA Expy
G-NAAB	MBB Bo.105DBS/4	S.416	D-HDMO D-HSTP/D-HDMO	23. 3.99	Bond Helicopters Ltd	Aberdeen	
G-NAAS	Aerospatiale AS.355F1 Twin Squirrel 5203		G-BPRG G-NWPA/G-NAAS/G-BPRG/N370E	23. 3.90	Northumbria Ambulance Service NHS Trust	Blyth Heliport	18. 4.99T
G-NAAT*	Folland Gnat T.1	FL.507	XM697	27.11.89	Hunter Wing Ltd	Bournemouth	
					(As "XM697") (Open storage 1.97)		
G-NACA	Norman NAC-2 Freelance 180	2001		23.11.87	NDN Aircraft Ltd	Bembridge	
					(Stored 11.97)		
G-NACI	Norman NAC-1 Freelance 180	NAC.001	G-AXFB	20. 6.84	L.J.Martin	Bembridge	7. 4.94P
					(Stored 10.95)		
G-NACL*	Norman NAC-6 Firemaster 65	6001	G-BNEG	23. 4.87	EPA Acft Co Ltd	Sandown	5.12.90P*
	(Note - fitted with rudder/marks of G-NACM 2.96)				(Stored 8.97- cancelled by CAA 22.3.99)		
G-NACO*	Norman NAC-6 Firemaster 65	6004		2.12.87	EPA Acft Co Ltd	Bournemouth	27. 8.92A
					(Stored 8.97 - cancelled by CAA 22.3.99)		
G-NACP*	Norman NAC-6 Fieldmaster 34	6005		2.12.87	EPA Acft Co Ltd	Bournemouth	6. 9.93A
					(Stored 3.97 - cancelled by CAA 22.3.99)		
G-NADS	Team Minimax 91	PFA/186-12995		8. 2.99	P.M.Spencer	(Thornton-Cleveleys)	
G-NANA	VPM M-16 Tandem Trainer PFA G/112-1249 (Arrow GT1000R)			29.11.94	J.W.P.Lewis	Haverfordwest	27. 8.99P
G-NARO	Cassutt Racer	M.14372	G-BTXR	14. 4.98	D.A.Wirdnam	Oxford	12. 5.99P
	(Cont O-200-A) (Aka Musso Racer Original) N68PM						
G-NASA	Lockheed T-33A-5-LO	580-6350	G-TJET	3. 6.91	De Havilland Aviation Ltd	Swansea	7. 5.87P
			RDAF DT-566/51-8566 (As "91007" in USAF c/s)				
G-NASH	Grumman-American AA-5A Cheetah AA5A-0617		(G-BFWL) N26477	13. 9.78	J.J.Woodhouse t/a Flying Services	Blackbushe	14.10.99T
G-NATT	Rockwell Commander 114A	14538	N5921N	14. 1.80	Northgleam Ltd	Woodford	3. 9.01T
G-NATX	Cameron O-65 HAFB	1681		3. 3.88	A.G.E.Faulkner	Willenhall, W.Midlands	5. 5.91T
					"National Express Rapide"		
G-NATY	Folland Gnat T.1	FL.548	8642M XR537	19. 6.90	F.C.Hackett-Jones	Bournemouth	
					(Displayed by Jet Heritage Ltd 1.99 as "XR537")		
G-NAVO	PA-31-325 Navajo C/R	31-8212031	G-BMPV N4109V	6. 7.90	Air Care (South West) Ltd	Plymouth	24. 7.99T
G-NAVY*	DH.104 Sea Devon C.20 (Dove 6) 04406		XJ348 G-AMXX	6. 1.82	Flugausstellung L & P Junior Museum		
					(As "XJ348" in Royal Navy c/s)		
						Hermeskeil, Germany	23. 1.87
G-NBDD	Robin DR.400/180 Regent	1103	F-BXVN	26. 9.88	J.N.Binks	Sherburn	28.12.00
G-NCFC	PA-38-112 Tomahawk	38-81A0107	N737V G-BNOA/N23272	14. 1.99	Light A/c Leasing (UK) Ltd	(London EC1)	
G-NCFR	BAe HS.125 Srs.700B	257054	G-BVJY RA-02802/G-BVJY/C6-BET	28. 4.97	Chauffair (CI) Ltd	Farnborough	5. 2.99T
G-NCUB	Piper J3C-65 Cub (L-4H-PI)	11599	G-BGXV F-BFQT/OO-GAB/43-30308 t/a G-NCUB Flying Group	6. 7.84	N.Thomson	Grove Farm, Raveningham	1. 8.98P
G-NDGC	Grob G-109	6150		7. 4.83	M.Newton "Babs"	Lydd	17. 5.99
G-NDNI	Norman NDN-1 Firecracker	001		30. 3.77	N.W.G.Marsh (Stored 7.97)	Coventry	AC
G-NDOL	Europa Avn Europa 44 & PFA/247-12594 (Subaru EA81)			30.11.93	S.Longstaff	(Sheffield)	4.11.98P
G-NDRW	Colt AS-80 mk.II Hot-Air Airship 2085			2.12.91	Huntair Ltd "NDR"	(Germany)	21. 1.99A
G-NEAL	PA-32-260 Cherokee Six	32-1048	G-BFPY N5588J	7.11.83	V.Walker t/a VSD Group	(Kingswinford)	30. 7.00
G-NEAT	Europa Avn Europa 65 & PFA/247-12642 (Rotax 912UL)			28. 6.94	M.Burton	Nympsfield	25. 5.99P
G-NEEL	Rotorway Exec 90 (RW 162)	5002		7. 8.90	M.B.Sims	(Whitby)	17. 6.98P
G-NEGS	Thunder Ax7-77 HAFB	1059		18. 3.87	M.Rowlands	Ashton-in-Makerfield	26. 8.96A
					"Hot-Shot"		
G-NEIL	Thunder Ax3 Maxi Sky Chariot HAFB	379		2.12.81	N.A.Robertson	Combe Hay Manor, Bath	2. 7.90A
					"Neil"		
G-NEPB	Cameron N-77 HAFB	1264		7. 3.86	The Post Office (Royal Mail North East)		
					"Royal Mail"	Leeds	5. 3.97A
G-NERC	PA-31-350 Navajo Chieftain 31-7405402		G-BBXX N66869	26. 4.94	Natural Environment Research Council (Op Air Atlantique)	Coventry	21. 5.99T
G-NESI	Van's RV-6	PFA/181-13381		24.11.98	G.Ness	(Wakefield)	
G-NESU	PBN BN-2B-20 Islander	2260	G-BTVN	30. 5.95	Northumbria Police Authority	Newcastle	20. 2.00T
					(Op North East Air Support Unit)		
G-NESV	Eurocopter EC.135 T1	0067		4. 2.99	McAlpine Helicopters Ltd	Oxford	
G-NETY	PA-18-150 Super Cub	1809108	N4159K	8. 9.95	N.B.Mason	Rendcomb	19. 1.02
G-NEUF	Bell 206L-1 Long Ranger II	45547	G-BVVV D-HUGO/OE-KXT/C-GLMM	20.11.98	Yendle Roberts Ltd	(Henley-on-Thames)	6. 9.98
G-NEVS	Aero Designs Pulsar XP PFA/202-12283			12.11.93	N.Warrener	(Stockport)	
G-NEWR	PA-31-350 Navajo Chieftain 31-7952129		N35251	23. 8.79	Eastern Air Executive Ltd	Sturgate	8. 1.00T
G-NEWS	Bell 206B JetRanger III	2547	N18098	29.11.78	Abington Aviation Ltd	(Abington)	3. 4.00

Regn	Type	C/n	P/I	Date	Owner/operator	Probable Base	CA Expy
G-NEWT	Beechcraft 35 Bonanza (Modified to C35 engine status)	D-1168	G-APVW EI-BIL/G-APVW/N9866F/4X-ACL/ IDF/AF 0604/ZS-BTE	28. 2.90	J.A.West	RAF Newton	9. 8.97
G-NEWZ	Bell 206B Jet Ranger III	4475	C-GBVZ	28. 1.98	Peter Press Ltd	Southampton	2. 4.01T
G-NEXT	Aerospatiale AS.355F1 Twin Squirrel	5115	G-WDKR G-NEXT/I-NEXT/G-NEXT/G-OMAV	21.10.87	RCR Aviation Ltd	Thruxton	3. 8.00T
G-NFLC	HP.137 Jetstream 1	222	G-AXUI G-8-9	12.12.95	Cranfield University (National Flying Laboratory Centre)	Cranfield	3. 6.00T
G-NGRM	Spezio DAL-1 Tuholer (Lyc O-290-G)	134	N6RM	14. 8.90	S.H.Crook	Damyns Hall, Upminster	1. 2.99P
G-NHRH	PA-28-140 Cherokee	28-22807	OY-BIC SE-EZP	19. 5.82	J.E.Parkinson	Newcastle	24. 4.01
G-NHVH	Maule M.5-235C Lunar Rocket	7276C	N5634N	4. 7.80	Commercial Go-Karts Ltd	Exeter	5. 2.99
G-NICH	Robinson R-22 Beta	0937		4. 1.89	Virgin Helicopters Ltd	Booker	5. 4.01T
G-NICK*	PA-18-95 Super Cub (L-18C-PI) (Frame No.18-2085)	18-2065	PH-CWA R.Neth AF R-79/8A-79/52-2465 "Jose" (On rebuild 2.96)	17.10.79	I.Woolacott	Headcorn	26. 6.85P
G-NIGE	Luscombe 8E Silvaire (Cont C85)	3525	G-BSHG N72098/NC72098	6. 6.90	Gardan Party Ltd	Popham	19. 9.99P
G-NIGL	Europa Avn Europa	PFA/247-12775		6. 7.95	N.M.Graham	(Southampton)	
G-NIGS	Thunder Ax7-65 HAFB	1663		30. 1.90	A.N.F.Pertwee "Bang Sai"	Frinton-on-Sea	19. 6.97A
G-NIKE	PA-28-181 Archer II	28-8390086	N4315N	7. 4.89	Key Properties Ltd	White Waltham	8. 8.01T
G-NINA	PA-28-161 Cherokee Warrior II	28-7716162	G-BEUC N3507Q	29. 7.88	P.A.Layzell	(Attleborough)	28.10.00
G-NINE	Murphy Renegade 912 (Rotax 912)	448 & PFA/188-12191		16. 6.93	R.F.Bond	Garston Farm, Marshfield	29. 5.98P
G-NIOS	PA-32R-301 Saratoga SP	32R-8513004	N4381Z N105DX/N4381Z	28. 9.90	L.A.Dingemans & D.J.Everett t/a Plant Aviaton	Stapleford	16. 4.99
G-NIPA	Slingsby Nipper T.66 RA.45 Srs.3 (Acro/VW1834)	S.120/1627	G-AWDD	7. 6.96	R.J.O.Walker	(Lincoln)	3.11.93P
G-NIPY	Hughes 369HS	124-0676S	OH-HMD SE-JAK/N65BL/N9232F	26.11.97	Arena Aviation Ltd	Redhill	8.12.00T
G-NISR	Rockwell Turbo Commander 690A	11243	HB-GFS	10. 7.85	Ziad Isma'il Bilbeisi	Fairoaks	28. 4.99
G-NITA	PA-28-180 Cherokee C (Used spare frame no. 28-3807S)	28-2909	G-AVVG	16. 1.84	T.Clifford	(Dunstable)	17.11.97T
G-NIUK	McDonnell Douglas DC-10-30	46932	9Q-CLT	27. 8.85	British Airways plc	Gatwick	29. 9.99T
G-NJAG	Cessna 207 Skywagon	207-00093	D-EMDN (N91152)	2. 8.78	G.H.Nolan	Biggin Hill	17. 6.00T
G-NJSH	Robinson R-22 Beta	0780		19. 4.88	T.F.Hawes	Sywell	19. 6.00
G-NLEE	Cessna 182Q Skylane II	182-65934	G-TLTD N759EL	1.12.93	J.S.Lee	Booker	15. 8.99
G-NMHS	Eurocopter AS.355N Twin Squirrel	5502	G-DPPS F-WYMM	26. 3.98	North Midlands Helicopter Support Unit Derbyshire HQ		29. 3.01T
G-NNAC	PA-18-135 Super Cub (L-21B-PI) (Frame No. 18-3820)	18-3820	PH-PSW R.Neth AF R-130/54-2420	19. 5.81	P.A.Wilde t/a PAW F/Svs	Bagby	14. 8.00T
G-NOBI	Spezio HES-1 Tuholer Sport (Cont C125)	162	N1603	28.11.90	A.D.Pearce	(Lydney)	26. 4.98P
G-NOCK	Reims Cessna FR182 Skylane RGII	0036	G-BGTK (D-EHZB)	18. 1.94	R.D.Masters	Top Farm, Tadlow	17.11.00
G-NODE	Gulfstream AA-5B Tiger	AA5B-1182	N4533L	22. 5.81	Abraxas Avn Ltd	Elstree	3. 7.99T
G-NODY	American General AG-5B Tiger	10076	N1194C	3.10.91	Curd & Green Ltd (Op Cabair)	Elstree	8.12.01T
G-NOIR	Bell 222	47031	G-OJLC G-OSEB/G-BNDA/A40-CG	9. 8.91	Arlington Securities plc	Blackbushe	31. 5.99T
G-NONI	Grumman-American AA-5 Traveler	AA5-0383	G-BBDA (EI-AYL)/G-BBDA	1. 8.88	P.T.Harmsworth t/a November India F/Grp	Exeter	26. 4.01
G-NOOR	Commander 114B	14656		6. 2.98	As-Al Ltd	Guernsey	19. 5.01
G-NORD	SNCAC NC.854	7	F-BFIS	20.10.78	W.J.McCollum (On rebuild) (Magherafelt, Co.Londonderry)		27. 5.82P
G-NOSE	Cessna 402B	402B-0823	N98AR G-MPCU/SE-IRL/OO-TAT/(OO-SEL)/N3946C	23. 4.96	Atlantic Air Transport Ltd	Coventry	11. 5.00T
G-NOTE	PA-28-181 Archer III	2843082	D-ESPI N9282N	19. 9.97	General Aeroplane Trading Co Ltd	Elstree	18. 9.00T
G-NOTT	Nott ULD/2 HAFB	06		11. 6.86	J.R.P.Nott	London NW3	
G-NOTY	Westland Scout AH.1	F.9630	XT624	5.11.97	R.P.Coplestone	Ogborne	26. 1.99P
G-NOVO	Colt AS-56 Hot-Air Airship	1067		20. 5.87	Astec Group plc	Cheltenham	22. 4.97A
G-NPKJ	Van's RV-6	PFA/181-13138		12. 2.98	K.Jones	(Sheffield)	
G-NPNP	Cameron N-105 HAFB	2959	G-BURX	18. 1.93	Virgin Airship & Balloon Co Ltd "National Power II"	Telford	18. 8.98T
G-NPWR*	Cameron RX-100 HAFB	2849		13. 7.92	R S Kent "Nuclear Electric 2" (Balloon Preservation Group 7.98)	Lancing	21.11.96A
G-NRDC*	Norman NDN-6 Fieldmaster	004		8. 6.81	Not known (Stored 8.97)	Sandown	17.10.87P
G-NROY	PA-32RT-300 Lance II	32R-7985070	G-LYNN G-BGNY/N30242	26.11.93	R.L.West t/a Roy West Cars, J.E.Dixon & W.Wells	Norwich	6. 1.02
G-NSHR	Robinson R-22 Beta	2809		8. 5.98	Gnashair Ltd	(St.Helens)	14. 5.02T
G-NSTG	Reims Cessna F.150F (Wichita c/n 63499) (Tail-wheel conversion)	0058	G-ATNI	16. 8.89	N.S.Travers-Griffin "Iris"	Blackpool	23. 8.01
G-NTEE	Robinson R-44 Astro	0024		14.12.93	Central Aviation (Helicopters) Ltd	Nottingham	3. 2.00T

Regn	Type	C/n	P/I	Date	Owner/operator	Probable Base	CA Expy
G-NUTS*	Cameron Mr Peanut 35SS HAFB	711		18. 2.81	British Balloon Museum & Library Newbury "Mr Peanut II"		1. 4.84A
G-NUTY	Aerospatiale AS.350B Ecureuil	1490	G-BXKT F-GXRT/N333FH/N5797V	20. 7.98	Arena Aviation Ltd	(Crawley)	10. 9.00T
G-NVBF	Lindstrand LBL-210A HAFB	249		19. 5.95	Virgin Balloon Flights Ltd (London SE16)		14. 3.99T
G-NVSA	DHC-8-311 Dash Eight	451	C-GDNG	20.11.98	Brymon Airways Ltd	Plymouth	20.11.01T
G-NVSB	DHC-8-311 Dash Eight	517	C-GHRI	14. 1.99	Brymon Airways Ltd	Plymouth	13. 1.02T
G-NVSC	DHC-8-311 Dash Eight	519	C-FDHO	R	Brymon Airways Ltd (For dlvy 1999)	Plymouth	
G-NWAC	PA-31-310 Turbo Navajo	31-7612040	G-BDUJ N59814	18. 2.94	North West Air Charters Ltd	Liverpool	15. 7.99
G-NWPI	Aerospatiale AS.355F2 Twin Squirrel	5348	F-GMAO	9. 2.94	North Wales Police Authority Kimmel Army Camp, Bodelwyddan, Clwyd		28. 3.00T
G-NWPS	Eurocopter EC.135T 1	0063		15.10.98	McAlpine Helicopters Ltd	Oxford	AC
G-NYTE	Reims Cessna F.337G Super Skymaster (Wichita c/n 01465)	0056	G-BATH N10631	12. 5.86	Photoair Ltd	Little Staughton	9. 6.00T
G-NZGL	Cameron O-105 HAFB	1361		3. 9.86	P.G.Vale "Nazgul"	Kidderminster	23. 4.97A
G-NZSS	Boeing-Stearman E75 (N2S-5) Kaydet (Lyc R-680)	75-8611	N4325 Bu.43517/42-109578	31. 1.89	Ace Aviation Ltd (As "343251/27" in USAAC c/s)	Swanton Morley	6. 1.02T

G-OAAA-OZZZ

Regn	Type	C/n	P/I	Date	Owner/operator	Probable Base	CA Expy
G-OAAA	PA-28-161 Warrior II	2816107	N9142N	8. 9.93	Halfpenny Green Flight Centre Ltd	Halfpenny Green	12. 9.99T
G-OAAC	Airtour AH-77B HAFB	010		13. 9.88	Army Air Corps, Historic A/c Board of Management "Go AAC"	AAC Middle Wallop	2. 5.96A
G-OAAL	PA-38-112 Tomahawk	38-78A0623	N4471E	25.10.88	Red Dragon Aviation Ltd	Cardiff	15.12.00T
G-OABA	Boeing 737-33A	24097	VT-JAD G-BUSM/PP-SNZ/(PP-SNX)	15. 5.98	AB Airlines Ltd	Stansted	4. 6.01T
G-OABB	SAN Jodel D150 Mascaret	01	F-BJST F-WJST	21. 1.97	A.B.Bailey	Popham	12. 3.00
G-OABC	Colt 69A HAFB	1159		17.11.87	P.A.C.Stuart-Kregor	Newbury	20. 3.99A
G-OABL	Boeing 737-33A	24096	VT-JAC G-BUSL/PP-SNW	6. 5.98	AB Airlines Ltd	Stansted	11. 6.01T
G-OABO	Enstrom F-28A	097		10. 7.98	ABO Ltd	(Pulborough)	2. 6.01T
G-OABR	American General AG-5B Tiger	10124	C-GZLA N256ER	15. 4.98	Abraxas Aviation Ltd	Elstree	23. 4.01
G-OACE	Valentin Taifun 17E	1017		22. 1.87	J.E.Dallison	Enstone	26. 2.99
G-OACG	PA-34-200T Seneca II	34-7870177	G-BUNR EI-CFI/N9245C	10. 3.94	ACG Building Contractors Ltd	Goodwood	9.11.01T
G-OACI	Socata MS.893E Rallye 180GT	13086	G-DOOR EI-BHD/F-GBCF	5. 5.98	R.A.Wakefield & A.M.Quayle	Alderney	6. 4.01
G-OACP	OGMA DHC.1 Chipmunk 20 (Lyc O-360)	OGMA.35	(CS-DAO) FAP 1345	20. 8.96	Aeroclub de Portugal	(Lisbon)	19.12.99
G-OADY	Beechcraft 76 Duchess	ME-56	N5022M	27.10.86	Multiflight Ltd	Leeds-Bradford	31. 1.02T
G-OAER	Lindstrand LBL-105A HAFB	359		4. 3.96	T.M.Donnelly "Aero"	Doncaster	21. 5.99T
G-OAFC*	Airtour AH-56	011		15. 6.89	P J Donnellan (Balloon Preservation Group 12.98)	Lancing	
G-OAFT	Cessna 152 II	152-85177	G-BNKM N6161Q	19. 4.88	Bobbington Air Training School Ltd	Halfpenny Green	3.11.99T
G-OAHC	Beechcraft F33C Bonanza	CJ-133	G-BTTF PH-BND	2. 9.91	V.D.Speck	Clacton	18. 5.01
G-OAJB	Cyclone AX2000 (Rotax 582/48)	7281	G-MZFJ	16. 2.99	A.J.Blackwell	(Banbury)	8. 4.98P
G-OAJS	PA-39 Twin Comanche C/R	39-15	G-BCIO N49JA/N57RG/G-BCIO/N8860Y	9. 3.94	Go-AJs Ltd	Sherburn	16. 3.01
G-OAKI	BAe Jetstream 3102	718	N417MX G-31-718	5. 5.92	Air Kilroe Ltd	Manchester	25. 6.01T
G-OAKJ	BAe Jetstream 3202	795	G-BOTJ G-OAKJ/G-BOTJ/G-31-795	20. 7.89	Air Kilroe Ltd	Manchester	31. 8.99T
G-OALD	Socata TB-20 Trinidad	490	N54TB F-GBLL	17. 3.88	D.A.Grief t/a Gold Avn	Biggin Hill	24. 5.00
G-OAMG	Bell 206B JetRanger III	2901	G-COAL	25. 2.86	Alan Mann Helicopters Ltd	Fairoaks	18. 5.01T
G-OAML	Cameron AML-105 HAFB	3881		4.12.96	Cheqair Ltd	Long Stratton	13. 2.99A
G-OAMP	Reims Cessna F177RG Cardinal (Wichita c/n 00098)	0006	G-AYPF	30.11.93	K.Payne	Spanhoe	6. 7.00
G-OAMS	Boeing 737-37Q	28548		9.12.97	British Regional Airlines Ltd (Rendezvous t/s)	Manchester	9.10.01T
G-OAMT	PA-31-350 Navajo Chieftain	31-7752105	G-BXKS N350RC/EC-EBN/N27230	23. 1.98	AM & T Solutions Ltd	Bristol/Lulsgate	18.11.00T
G-OAMY	Cessna 152 II	152-84639	N6214M	5. 8.85	Red Dragon Aviation Ltd	Cardiff	12.11.00T
G-OANC	PA-28-161 Warrior II	28-7716206	G-BFAD N5850V	29. 4.87	Millwood Ltd	Humberside	15.12.99T
G-OANI	PA-28-161 Warrior II	28-8416091	N43570	8. 1.91	J.F.Mitchell (Damaged Upton Farm, Dover 16.6.96; wreck at Oxford 9.96)	(Burgess Hill)	8. 9.97
G-OANN	Zenair CH.601HDS	PFA/162-12932		2. 2.96	P.Noden	(Stoke-on-Trent)	
G-OAPB	Colt Bottle 14 SS HAFB	4406		9.11.98	Airborne Images Ltd	Singapore	24.11.99A
G-OAPE	Cessna T303 Crusader	T303-00245	N303MF D-INKA/N9960C/M303HW/N9960C	3. 2.99	C.I.Travel (Holdings) Ltd & C.Twiston-Davies	Jersey	AC
G-OAPR	Brantly B-2B	446	(G-BPST) N2280U	21. 4.89	E.D.Ap Rees t/a Helicopter Intl Magazine	Weston-super-Mare	26. 6.01
G-OAPW	Glaser-Dirks DG-400	4-268		17. 4.90	D.T.S.Walsh "434"	(Hitchin)	10. 6.99
G-OARA	PA-28R-201 Arrow	28-37002	N802ND N9622N	28.10.98	Plane Talking Ltd	Elstree	19.11.01T
G-OARG	Cameron C-80 HAFB	3379		20.10.94	G. & R.Madelin	Farnham/London SW15	5.12.99A
G-OART	PA-23-250 Aztec D	27-4293	G-AXKD N6936Y	26.11.93	Levenmere Ltd (Op Skydrift)	Little Snoring	15. 3.00T
G-OARV	ARV-1 Super 2 (Hewland AE75)	001 & PFA/152-11060		18. 6.84	N.R.Beale (Rebuilt with Kit No.008 1986; stored Sproughton 1.91)	(Leamington Spa)	12.10.87P
G-OASH	Robinson R-22 Beta	0761	N2627Z	13. 6.88	J.C.Lane (Op Heliflight)	Halfpenny Green	18. 6.00T
G-OASP	Aerospatiale AS.355F2 Twin Squirrel	5479	F-GJAJ F-WYMH	3. 8.95	Avon & Somerset Constabulary & Gloucestershire Constabulary	Filton	9. 9.01T
G-OATD*	Short SD.3-30 Var.100	SH.3096	N332SB G-BKSV/G-14-3096	23. 2.89	Wingspares Ltd (Damaged Belfast Harbour 27.11.89; fuselage in open store 12.94)	Shoreham	
G-OATS	PA-38-112 Tomahawk	38-78A0007	N9659N	14. 3.78	Truman Avn Ltd	Nottingham	28. 8.00T
G-OATV	Cameron V-77 HAFB	2149		14. 2.90	W.G.Andrews	Plymouth	23.10.93A

Regn	Type	C/n	P/I	Date	Owner/operator	Probable Base	CA Expy
G-OAUS	Sikorsky S-76A	760219	(G-BKGU) N3122M	11. 8.82	Darley Stud Management Co Ltd Blackbushe (Op by Air Hanson)		2.10.99T
G-OAWS	Cameron Colt 77A HAFB	4340		23. 4.98	Auto Windscreens Ltd (Chesterfield)		26. 4.99A
G-OBAL	Mooney M.20J (201LM)	24-1601	N56569	27.11.86	Britannia Airways Ltd (Op Britannia F/C)	Luton	24. 3.99T
G-OBAN	SAN Jodel D.140B Mousquetaire II 80		G-ATSU F-BKSA	20. 2.92	S.R.Cameron	North Connel	3. 3.91
G-OBAT*	Reims Cessna F.152 II	1771	G-OENT G-OBAT/(D-EMIN)	25. 7.80	M.Entwistle	Coventry	10. 1.93T
	(Damaged Sladbury's Farm, Holland-on-Sea 11.12.92; cancelled by CAA 8.3.99)						
G-OBAY	Bell 206B JetRanger	276	G-BVWR	27. 7.98	Helixair Ltd (Chorley)		2. 3.00T
G-OBBC	Colt 90A HAFB	1358		11. 5.89	R.A. & M.A.Riley "Beeb" (BBC in the Midlands c/s)	Bromsgrove	31.10.98A
G-OBDA	Diamond DA-20-A1 Katana	10260		2. 7.98	Diamond Aircraft Industries GmbH	Gloucestershire	31. 7.01T
G-OBEN	Cessna 152 II	152-81856	G-NALI G-BHVM/N67477	16. 8.93	Airbase Aircraft Ltd	Shoreham	26. 3.00T
G-OBEV	Europa Avn Europa	PFA/247-12813		3. 2.98	M.B.Hill & N.I.Wingfield (Dursley)		
G-OBEY	PA-23-250 Aztec C	27-2569	G-BAAJ SE-EIU	11. 5.79	Creaton Acft Svs Ltd	Halfpenny Green	4. 8.86T
G-OBFC	PA-28-161 Warrior II	2816118	N9252X	15. 7.96	Bournemouth F/Club Ltd	Bournemouth	AC
G-OBFS	PA-28-161 Warrior III	2842039	N41274	4.12.98	Bournemouth F/Club Ltd	Bournemouth	3.12.01T
G-OBHD	Short SD.3-60 Var.100	SH.3714	G-BNDK G-OBHD/G-BNDK	20. 1.87	Jersey European Airways Ltd	Exeter	5. 3.98T
G-OBIB	Colt 120A HAFB	4229		9. 1.98	The Aerial Display Co Ltd	Looe	16.11.99A
G-OBIG	Aerospatiale AS.355F1 Twin Squirrel	5157	G-SVJM G-BOPS/I-MOST	28. 8.96	Plane Talking Ltd (Op Cabair Helicopters)	Elstree	22. 5.00T
G-OBIL	Robinson R-22 Beta	0792		10. 5.88	C.A.Rosenberg	Abergavenny	3. 7.00T
G-OBIO	Robinson R-22 Beta	1402	N7724M	29. 6.98	A.E.Churchill (Huntingdon)		2. 7.01
G-OBJH	Colt 77A HAFB	2569		11. 3.94	UK Petroleum Products Ltd t/a Eurogas & Corralgas	Alcester	7. 6.97
G-OBLC	Beechcraft 76 Duchess	ME-249	N6635R	3. 6.87	Pridenote Ltd (Knaresborough)		9.10.99T
G-OBLK	Short SD.3-60 Var.100	SH.3712	G-BNDI G-OBLK/G-BNDI	20. 1.87	Jersey European Airways Ltd	Exeter	11. 2.99T
G-OBLN	DH.115 Vampire T.11 (Regd with Nacelle No.DHP.48700)	15664	XE956	14. 9.95	De Havilland Aviation Ltd (As "XE956") (On rebuild 2.96)	Bridgend	
G-OBMF	Boeing 737-4Y0	23868		14.10.88	British Midland Airways Ltd	East Midlands	11.11.01T
G-OBMG	Boeing 737-4Y0	23870	N1791B	31. 3.89	British Midland Airways Ltd	East Midlands	14. 4.99T
G-OBMH	Boeing 737-33A	24460		19. 3.90	British Midland Airways Ltd	East Midlands	21. 3.99T
G-OBMJ	Boeing 737-33A	24461		22. 3.90	British Midland Airways Ltd	East Midlands	27. 3.99T
G-OBMM	Boeing 737-4Y0	25177		4.12.91	British Midland Airways Ltd	East Midlands	6. 4.99T
G-OBMO	Boeing 737-4Q8	26280		13. 3.92	British Midland Airways Ltd	East Midlands	29. 4.99T
G-OBMP	Boeing 737-3Q8	24963		8. 1.92	British Midland Airways Ltd	East Midlands	19. 3.99T
G-OBMR	Boeing 737-5Y0	25185	XA-RJS	7. 5.96	British Midland Airways Ltd	East Midlands	4. 6.99T
G-OBMS	Reims Cessna F.172N Skyhawk II	1584	OO-BWA (OO-HWA)/D-EBYX	16. 4.84	D.Beverley & W.F.van Schoten	Sherburn	23. 5.99
G-OBMW	Grumman-American AA-5 Traveler	AA5-0805	G-BDFV	4. 7.79	Fretcourt Ltd	Sherburn	25. 2.00
G-OBMX	Boeing 737-59D	25065	SE-DNE (SE-DND)	23. 9.93	British Midland Airways Ltd	East Midlands	22. 9.99T
G-OBMZ	Boeing 737-53A	24754	SE-DNC	22. 9.93	British Midland Airways Ltd	East Midlands	20. 9.99T
G-OBNF	Cessna 310K	310K-0109	F-BNFI N7009L	20. 7.94	P.H.Johnson t/a Fadmoor F/Grp	Boonhill, Fadmoor	20. 5.00T
G-OBPL	Embraer EMB-110P2 Bandeirante	110-199	PH-FVB G-OEAB/G-BKWB/G-CHEV/(PT-GLR)	27.11.98	Comed Aviation Ltd	Blackpool	6.12.99T
G-OBRY	Cameron N-180 HAFB	3010		1. 3.93	Bryant Group plc	Solihull	6. 4.99T
G-OBTS	Cameron C-80 HAFB	3589		18. 4.95	Bedford Tyre Service (Chichester) Ltd	Chichester	27. 7.99A
G-OBUD*	Colt 69A HAFB	698		26. 6.85	British Balloon Museum & Library Newbury "Budweiser"		1. 2.90A
G-OBUS*	PA-28-181 Archer II	28-7990242	G-BMTT N3002K	4. 8.86	Northbrook College	Shoreham	14. 8.89T
	(Crashed Goodwood 18. 4.89; instructional airframe 8.97)						
G-OBUY	Colt 69A HAFB	2031		7. 8.91	Virgin Airship & Balloon Co Ltd Telford "Virgin Megastore"		28. 6.99A

Regn	Type	C/n	P/I	Date	Owner/operator	Probable Base	CA Expy
G-OBWA	BAC One-Eleven 518FG	BAC.232	G-BDAT G-AYOR	1.12.92	British World Airlines Ltd (Iberia Regional Air Nostrum titles)	Southend	12. 4.00T
G-OBWB	BAC One-Eleven 518FG	BAC.202	G-BDAS G-AXMH	8.12.92	British World Airlines Ltd	Southend	18. 4.99T
G-OBWC	BAC One-Eleven 520FN	BAC.230	G-BEKA 4X-BAR/G-16-22/G-BEKA/PP-SDR	8.12.92	British World Airlines Ltd	Southend	11.10.98T
G-OBWD	BAC One-Eleven 518FG	BAC.203	G-BDAE G-AXMI	14. 1.93	British World Airlines Ltd	Southend	14. 4.99T
G-OBWE	BAC One-Eleven 531FS	BAC.242	G-BJYM TI-LRI/TI-1095C	7. 4.93	British World Airlines Ltd	Southend	26. 5.99T
G-OBWL	BAe ATP	2057	G-11-057	26. 9.97	British World Airlines Ltd	Southend	25. 9.00T
G-OBWM	BAe ATP	2058	G-11-058	22.12.97	British World Airlines Ltd	Southend	21.12.00T
G-OBWN	BAe ATP	2059	G-BVEO G-11-059	22.12.98	British World Airlines Ltd	Southend	AC
G-OBWO	BAe ATP	2060	(EI-COS) G-11-060	6. 6.98	British World Airlines Ltd	Southend	15. 6.01T
G-OBYA	Boeing 767-304ER	28039	D-AGYA G-OBYA	15. 5.96	Britannia Airways Ltd	Luton	11. 6.01T
G-OBYB	Boeing 767-304ER	28040		17. 5.96	Britannia Airways Ltd	Luton	16. 5.99T
G-OBYD	Boeing 767-304ER	28042		4. 3.97	Britannia Airways Ltd	Luton	3. 3.00T
G-OBYG	Boeing 767-304ER	29137		13. 1.99	Britannia Airways Ltd	Luton	12. 1.02T
G-OBYT	Agusta-Bell 206A JetRanger	8237	G-BNRC Oman AF 601	30. 1.95	Sloane Helicopters Ltd	Sywell	12. 7.00T
G-OCAA	HS.125 Srs.700B	257091	G-BHLF	22. 4.92	Magec Avn Ltd (Op for CAA)	Luton	28. 4.99T
G-OCAD	Sequoia Falco F8L (Lyc IO-320)	PFA/100-12114		8. 6.92	C.W.Garrard t/a Falco F/Grp (Damaged Tatenhill 10.8.97)	Leicester	12. 3.99P
G-OCAM	Gulfstream AA-5A Cheetah	AA5A-0741	G-BLHO OO-RTJ/OO-HRN	24. 3.94	Plane Talking Ltd (Op Cabair)	Elstree	4.10.00T
G-OCAR	Colt 77A HAFB	1099		6. 8.87	I.Purvis t/a Ridgeway Balloon Grp "Toyota"	Oxford	5. 8.95A
G-OCAT	Eiri PIK.20E	20226	(D-KGAT) G-OCAT	19.11.79	D.Bonucci	(Croxley Green)	13. 5.01
G-OCAW	Lindstrand Bananas SS HAFB	388		22. 5.96	Flying Pictures Ltd	Fairoaks	1. 8.97A
G-OCBB	Bell 206B JetRanger II	969	G-BASE N18093	16.11.90	Helispeed Ltd	Wellesbourne Mountford	30.10.00T
G-OCCA	PA-32R-301 Saratoga SP	32R-8113030	G-BRIX N8319S	12. 5.89	R.L. & J.D.Walls t/a Waterfresh	Redhill	30. 6.99
G-OCDB	Cessna 550 Citation II	550-0601	G-ELOT (N1303M)	20. 8.92	Paycourt Ltd (Op Eurojet)	Birmingham	28. 2.99T
G-OCDS	Aviamilano F.8L Falco Srs.II	114	G-VEGL OO-MEN/I-VEGL	6. 9.85	C.O.P.Barth	Hartenholm, Germany	6. 8.99
G-OCEA	Short SD.3-60 Var.100	SH.3762	N162CN N162SB/G-BRMX	26.10.95	BAC Express Airlines Ltd	(Horley)	26. 3.99T
G-OCFR	Gates Learjet 35A	35A-614	G-VIPS G-SOVN/HB-VJC/G-PJET/N3815G	15. 6.92	Chauffair (CI) Ltd	Heathrow/Farnborough	12. 4.99T
G-OCJK	Schweizer Hughes 269C (300C)	S.1294	N69A	10.12.87	P.Crawley	Shipley	27. 5.00
G-OCJS	Cameron V-90 HAFB	2805		24. 4.92	C.J.Sandell	Sevenoaks	19. 3.99T
G-OCJW	Cessna 182R Skylane II	182-68316	G-SJGM N357WC	18. 4.97	C.J.Ward	Wellesbourne Mountford	9. 7.00
G-OCME*	BN-2A Mk.III-1 Trislander	262	G-AYWI G-51-262	14. 5.86	Eccles Demolition Ltd Tenax Road, Trafford Park (Damaged Hale, Cheshire 9.2.87; stored in scrapyard 1.93)		29. 5.87
G-OCND*	Cameron O-77 HAFB	1020		6. 2.84	K A Kent "CND Airborne" (Balloon Preservation Group 7.98)	Lancing	N/E(A)
G-OCPC	Reims Cessna FA.152 Aerobat	0343		20. 1.78	Westward Airways (Lands End) Ltd	St.Just	22. 7.99T
G-OCPF	PA-32-300 Cherokee Six	32-7640082	G-BOCH N9292K	22. 9.97	Syndicate Clerical Services Ltd	(Exeter)	8. 9.00
G-OCPS	Colt 120A HAFB	2047		27. 5.92	CPS Fuels Ltd "CPS Gas"	Norwich	12. 6.97T
G-OCRI	Colomban MC-15 Cri-Cri	524 & PFA/133-12288		24. 6.92	M.J.J.Dunning	(Coventry)	
G-OCSB	Cessna 525 Citation Jet	525-0177	N1280A (RP-C717)/N1280A/N5163C	28. 1.98	Kestrel Aviation Ltd	Guernsey	
G-OCSI	Embraer EMB-110P2 Bandeirante	110-270	G-BHJZ PT-SBH	29.12.94	Air Tabernacle Ltd (Op Willow Air) (Overseas Courier Service c/s)	Bembridge	3. 7.98T
G-OCST	Agusta-Bell 206B JetRanger III	8694	N39AH VR-CDG/G-BMKM	14.12.94	G.J.Plumstead t/a Fieldgrove Trading (Op Polo Avn)	Bristol/Lulsgate	7. 1.01T
G-OCTA	BN-2A Mk.III-2 Trislander	1008	VR-CAA DQ-FCF/G-BCXW	14. 7.87	Aurigny Air Svs Ltd (ITEX c/s)	Guernsey	17. 7.00T
G-OCTI	PA-32-260 Cherokee Six	32-288	G-BGZX 9XR-MP/5Y-ADH/N3427W	26. 7.88	J.K.Sharkey	Denham	23. 4.01
G-OCTU	PA-28-161 Cadet	2841280	N91997	16.11.89	J.P.E.Walsh t/a Walsh Aviation (Op Denham School of Flying)	Denham	13.12.01T
G-OCUB	Piper J3C-90 Cub (L-4J-PI) (Frame No.13078)	13248	OO-JOZ PH-NKC/PH-UCH/45-4508	21. 4.81	C.A.Foss & P.A.Brook t/a Florence F/Grp "Florence"	Shoreham	23. 6.98P

(Official c/n of 13215 is 45-4475/PH-UCW and was rebuilt as PH-UCH)

Regn	Type	C/n	P/I	Date	Owner/operator	Probable Base	CA Expy
G-ODAC	Reims Cessna F.152 II	1824	G-BITG	19.12.96	T.M. & M.L.Jones (Op Derby Aero Club)	Egginton	22. 7.01T
G-ODAD	Colt 77A HAFB	2001		20. 2.91	K.Meehan "Odyssey"	Much Wenlock	28. 8.99A
G-ODAM	Gulfstream AA-5A Cheetah	AA5A-0818	G-FOUX N8488H	16.11.88	Stop & Go Ltd (Op London Avn)	Biggin Hill	21. 3.99T
G-ODBN	Lindstrand Flowers SS HAFB	389		22. 5.96	Flying Pictures Ltd "Sainsbury's Flowers"	Fairoaks	25. 6.99A
G-ODCS	Robinson R-22 Beta	2828		19. 5.98	DCS Helicopters Ltd	(Broadway)	1. 6.01T
G-ODDY	Lindstrand LBL-105A HAFB	042		15. 7.93	P.& T.Huckle	Oakwood	8. 8.99A
G-ODEB	Cameron A-250 HAFB	4328		23. 4.98	A.Derbyshire	(Stafford)	7. 4.99T
G-ODEL	Falconar F-11-3 (Cont O-200-A)	PFA/32-10219		14. 8.78	G.F.Brummell (Damaged Little Gransden 4.9.88; on rebuild)	(Bedford)	17. 7.89P
G-ODEN	PA-28-161 Cadet	2841282	N92004	22.11.89	J.Appleton t/a Holmes Rentals (Op Denham School of Flying)	Denham	18.12.01T
G-ODHL	Cameron N-77 HAFB	1538		22. 2.88	DHL Intl (UK) Ltd "DHL"	Hong Kong	17. 6.94A
G-ODIG	Bell 206B JetRanger II	2142	G-NEEP N777FW/N3CR	11. 6.93	Vallely Engineering Ltd	(Leeds)	30.10.98T
G-ODIN	Mudry CAARP CAP-10B	192	F-GDTH	16.12.93	T.W.Harris	(Hunstanton)	1. 5.00
G-ODIY	Colt 69A HAFB	1786		12. 6.90	P.Glydon	Barnt Green, Birmingham	18. 3.99A
G-ODJG	Europa Avn Europa	PFA/247-12889		3. 5.96	D.J.Goldsmith	(Edenbridge)	
G-ODJH	Mooney M.20C Ranger	690083	G-BMLH N9293V	19. 1.93	R.M.Schweitzer	(Amsterdam, Netherlands)	6. 2.99
G-ODLY	Cessna 310J	310J-0077	G-TUBY G-ASZZ/N3077L	21. 3.88	R.J.Huband	Gloucestershire	3. 6.00
G-ODMC	Aerospatiale AS.350B1 Ecureuil	2200	G-BPVF	17.10.89	D.M.Coombs t/a DM Leasing Co	Denham	25.10.01T
G-ODOC	Robinson R-44 Astro	0372		27. 8.97	Gas & Air Ltd	Thaxted, Essex	21. 9.00T
G-ODOG	PA-28R-200 Cherokee Arrow II	28R-7235197	EI-BPB	2. 8.96	Advanced Investments Ltd	Sibson	22.10.99
G-ODOT	Robinson R-22 Beta	2779	G-BAAR/N11C	23. 1.98	Farm Aviation Ltd	Booker	17. 2.01T
G-ODSK	Boeing 737-37Q	28537		23. 7.97	British Midland Airways Ltd	East Midlands	27. 7.00T
G-ODTI	Europa Avn Europa 004 & PFA/247-13010 (Rotax 912UL)			26. 2.96	Europa Aviation Ltd	Wombleton	19. 6.98P
G-ODTW	Europa Avn Europa	PFA/247-12890		7. 9.95	D.T.Walters	(Longfield, Kent)	
G-ODUS	Boeing 737-36Q	28659	D-ADBX	17. 3.98	British Regional Airlines Ltd (Waves & Cranes t/s)	Manchester	15. 4.01T
G-ODVB	CFM Shadow Srs.DD	300-DD	G-MGDB	3.11.98	D.V. Brunt Plaistows Field,	St.Albans	8. 3.99P
G-OEAC	Mooney M.20J (201)	24-1636	N57656	16. 6.88	N.R.Capon	Fowlmere	1. 7.00
G-OEAT	Robinson R-22 Beta	0650	G-RACH	8. 1.98	C.Y.O.Seeds Ltd	(Didcot)	21. 1.02T
G-OECH	Gulfstream AA-5A Cheetah	AA5A-0836	G-BKBE (G-BJVN)/N26952	24. 1.89	Plane Talking Ltd (Op London School of Flying)	Elstree	1. 5.00T
G-OEDB	PA-38-112 Tomahawk	38-79A0167	G-BGGJ N9694N	9. 5.89	Air Delta Bravo Ltd (Op Bonus Avn)	Cranfield	21. 5.00T
G-OEDP	Cameron N-77 HAFB	2189		28.12.89	M.J.Betts "Eastern Counties Press"	Norwich	16. 5.99A
G-OEGG	Cameron Egg 65SS HAFB (Cadbury's Creme Egg shape)	2140		4.12.89	Virgin Airship & Balloon Co Ltd "Cadburys Creme Egg"	Telford	4. 1.97A
G-OEGL	Christen Eagle II	001	N46JH	12. 1.98	D.I.Cooke & J.Penfold	Swanborough Farm	31. 3.99P
G-OEJA	Cessna 500 Citation	500-0264	G-BWFL F-GLJA/N205FM/N5264J	2. 8.96	Eurojet Aviation Ltd	Birmingham	20. 7.99T
G-OERR	Lindstrand LBL-60A HAFB	469		30. 6.97	Lindstrand Balloons Ltd	Oswestry	9. 1.00
G-OERS	Cessna 172N Skyhawk II	172-68856	G-SSRS N734HA	24. 5.94	E.R.Stevens	Leicester	29.10.99T
G-OERX	Cameron O-65 HAFB	4004		23. 1.96	R.Roehsler	Vienna, Austria	27. 2.97A
G-OEWA	DH.104 Dove 8	04528	G-DDCD G-ARUM	10. 6.98	D.C.Hunter	East Midlands	
G-OEYE	Rans S-10 Sakota (Rotax 582)	PFA/194-11955		25. 4.91	P.Thompson "Dancing Doll"	Crosland Moor	19. 5.99P
G-OEZY	Europa Avn Europa 42 & PFA/247-12590 (Rotax 912UL)			8. 8.95	A.W.Wakefield	Sibson	26. 6.98P
G-OFAS	Robinson R-22 Beta	0559		17. 6.86	J.L.Leonard t/a Findon Air Svs (Fast Helicopters)	Thruxton	3. 4.99T
G-OFBJ	Thunder Ax7-77A HAFB	2050		2. 9.91	N.D.Hicks "Blue Horizon"	Alton	25. 9.99A
G-OFCM	Reims Cessna F.172L	0839	G-AZUN (OO-FCB)	21.10.81	FCM Avn Ltd	Guernsey	31. 3.00
G-OFER	PA-18-150 Super Cub	18-7709058	N83509	29.12.89	Mary S.W.Meagher	Edgehill	2. 3.00
G-OFFA	Pietenpol Aircamper	PFA/047-13181		3.11.98	D.J. Street t/a Offa Group	(Chinnor)	
G-OFHJ	Cessna 441 Conquest II	441-0294	G-HSON (N88724)	3.10.86	Tilling Associates Ltd (Op Eagle Airways Ltd)	Guernsey	9. 6.99T
G-OFHL	Aerospatiale AS.350B Ecureuil	1805	EI-BPM G-BLSP	25. 6.93	Ford Helicopters Ltd	Brentwood	15. 7.99T
G-OFIL	Robinson R-44	0555		15. 1.99	P.& J.Twigg	(Gloucester)	2. 2.02T
G-OFIT	Socata TB-10 Tobago	938	G-BRIU	11. 9.89	G.S.M.Brain	White Waltham/Alderney	19. 1.02T
G-OFIZ*	Cameron Can 80SS HAFB	2106		30.10.89	British Balloon Museum & Library Newbury "Andrews Can"		2.12.91A
G-OFJC	Eiri Pik-20E	20291	OH-641	19. 3.93	M.J.Aldridge	Tibenham	3. 6.99
G-OFJS	Robinson R-22 Beta	0699	G-BNXJ	28. 5.91	Burman Aviation Ltd	Cranfield/Newcastle	4.11.99

Regn	Type	C/n	P/I	Date	Owner/operator	Probable Base	CA Expy
G-OFLG	Socata TB-10 Tobago	11	G-JMWT F-GBHF	11.12.91	R.Noble Ltd	(Teddington)	2. 8.01T
G-OFLI	Colt 105A HAFB	991		20. 1.87	Virgin Airship & Balloon Co Ltd Telford "Virgin Atlantic"		22.11.90A
G-OFLT	Embraer EMB-110P1 Bandeirante	110-211	G-MOBL (G-BGCS)/PT-GMD	11.12.90	Flightline Ltd	Southend	1. 1.99T
G-OFLY	Cessna 210M Centurion II	210-61600	(D-EBYM) N732LQ	13.10.79	A.P.Mothew	Southend	7. 5.01
G-OFMB	Rand Robinson KR-2	7808	N5337X	29. 4.97	F.M. & S.I.Burden	(Bracknell)	
G-OFOA	BAe 146 Srs.100	E-1006	G-BKMN EI-COF/SE-DRH/G-BKMN/G-ODAN	3. 3.98	Formula One Adminstration Ltd	(London SW7)	30. 6.99
G-OFOR	Thunder Ax3 Maxi Sky Chariot HAFB	596		5.10.84	T.J.Ellenreider, G.D.Bartram & P.Spellward "Go For It"	Bristol	17. 4.97A
G-OFOX	Denney Kitfox	PFA/172-11523		1.11.89	P.R.Skeels	Barton	
G-OFRA	Boeing 737-36Q	29327		5. 5.98	British Regional Airlines Ltd Manchester (Sterntaler/Bauhaus t/s)		17. 5.01T
G-OFRB	Everett Gyroplane Srs.2 (Rotax 503)	006	(G-BLSR)	7. 8.85	R.M.Savage t/a Roger Savage (Photography) "Little Patty"	Kemble	17. 6.92P
G-OFRT	Lockheed L.188CF Electra	1075	N347HA N423MA/N23AF/N64405/SE-FGC/N5537 t/a Channel Express	29.10.91	Dart Group plc	Bournemouth	28.10.01T
G-OFRY	Cessna 152 II	152-81420	G-BPHS N49971	8. 2.93	Devon School of Flying Ltd	Dunkeswell	23. 8.01T
G-OFTI	PA-28-140 Cherokee Cruiser	28-7325201	G-BRKU N15926	11. 6.90	E.Alexander	(Braintree)	4. 6.99T
G-OGAN	Europa Avn Europa	PFA/247-12734		28. 7.94	M.A.Jackson t/a G-OGAN Grp	(Ingham, Lincoln)	
G-OGAR	PZL SZD-45A Ogar	B-601	SP-0004	29. 1.90	N.C.Grayson	Boscombe Down	9. 6.00
G-OGAS*	Westland WG.30 Srs.100	008	G-17-1 G-OGAS/G-BKNW	23. 3.83	Westland Helicopters Ltd (Open storage 9.97)	Yeovil	19. 5.88T
G-OGAV	Lindstrand LBL-240A HAFB	074		4. 2.94	C.J.Sandell t/a Out of this World Balloons	Sevenoaks	18. 3.99T
G-OGAZ	Aerospatiale SA.341G Gazelle 1	1274	G-OCJR G-BRGS/F-GEQA/N341SG/(N341P)N341SG/N47295 t/a Killochries Fold	12. 1.94	I.M.& S.M. Graham	(Kilmalcolm)	7. 3.00T
G-OGBA	Boeing 737-4S3	25596	G-OBMK	4. 4.97	GB Airways Ltd (Waves & Cranes t/s)	Gatwick	7. 5.99T
G-OGBB	Boeing 737-34S	29108		27. 1.98	GB Airways Ltd (Dove/Colum t/s)	Gatwick	26. 1.01T
G-OGBC	Boeing 737-34S	29109	N1787B	26. 2.98	GB Airways Ltd (Cockerel of Lowicz/Koguty Lowickie t/s)	Gatwick	25. 2.01T
G-OGBD	Boeing 737-3L9	27833	OY-MAR D-ADBJ/OY-MAR	16. 3.98	GB Airways Ltd (Martha Masanabo/Ndebele t/s)	Gatwick	12. 3.01T
G-OGBE	Boeing 737-3L9	27834	OY-MAS	24.11.98	GB Airways Ltd	Gatwick	17.12.01T
G-OGCA	PA-28-161 Warrior II	28-8016262	N8154L	16. 8.90	Aerohire Ltd (Op Midland Flight Centre)	Halfpenny Green	4. 7.99T
G-OGEE	Christen Pitts S-2B Special (Lyc AEIO-540)	5200	OH-SKY	1. 6.95	Management Consultancy Svcs Inc Ltd & GB-European Ltd	(Ipswich)	28. 6.01
G-OGEM	PA-28-181 Archer II	28-8190226	N83816	10. 3.88	GEM Rewinds Ltd	Coventry	8. 5.00T
G-OGET	PA-39-160 Twin Comanche C/R	39-87	G-AYXY N8930Y	14. 3.83	P.G.Kitchingman	White Waltham	21.12.01
G-OGGS	Thunder Ax8-84 HAFB	1595		1. 9.89	G.Gamble & Sons (Quorn) Ltd "Gamblis Quorn"	Loughborough	10. 2.95T
G-OGHH	Enstrom 480	5015		14. 2.96	G.H.Harding	Whitchurch	12. 3.02T
G-OGHL	Aerospatiale AS.355F1 Twin Squirrel	5164	N5796S	18. 4.97	Grampian Helicopter Charter Ltd	Kintore, Inverurie	27. 5.00T
G-OGIL*	Short SD.3-30 Var.100	SH.3068	G-BITV G-14-3068	23. 1.89	North East Aircraft Museum (Damaged Newcastle 1.7.92)	Usworth	21. 4.93T
G-OGJS	Rutan Puffer Cozy (Lyc 0-360)	PFA/159-11169		27. 1.89	G.J.Stamper	Carlisle	14. 9.98P
G-OGOA	Aerospatiale AS.350B Ecureuil	1745	G-PLMD G-NIAL	16. 1.90	Lomas Helicopters Ltd	Lake Heliport, Abbotsham	23. 5.99T
G-OGOB	Schweizer Hughes 269C (300C)	S.1315	G-GLEE G-BRUW/N86G	2.10.90	Kingfisher Helicopters Ltd	Exeter	3. 3.97T
G-OGOG	Robinson R-22 Beta	1475	G-TILL	2. 7.97	D.Thomas Lake Heliport, Abbotsham t/a Lake Services		9.10.99T
G-OGOS	Everett Gyroplane (VW1834)	004	7Q-YES G-OGOS	30. 7.84	R.Abercrombie	Rainham, Essex	12. 9.90P
			(Damaged St.Merryn 1.10.89 & possibly rebuilt; stored Sproughton 12.95)				
G-OGRK	Aerospatiale AS.355F1 Twin Squirrel	5185	(G-MOBZ) N107KF/N5799R	26. 3.99	Kelwaiver Ltd	Ipswich	12. 2.00T
G-OGTS	Air Command 532 Elite (Rotax 532)	0432 & PFA G/104-1125		19.12.88	GTS Engineering (Coventry) Ltd Coventry t/a GTS Cars		1.10.90P
G-OHAJ	Boeing 737-36Q	29141		2. 6.98	British Regional Airlines Ltd Manchester (Delftblue Daybreak t/s)		15. 6.01T
G-OHAL	Pietenpol Aircamper	PFA/47-12840		25.11.96	H.C.Danby	(Sudbury)	
G-OHCP	Aerospatiale AS.355F1 Twin Squirrel	5249	G-BTVS G-STVE/G-TOFF/G-BKJX	14. 3.94	Cabair Helicopters Ltd	Elstree	10. 2.01T

Regn	Type	C/n	P/I	Date	Owner/operator	Probable Base	CA Expy
G-OHDC	Colt Film Cassette SS HAFB (Agfa Film shape)	2633		8. 8.94	Flying Pictures Ltd "Agfa"	Fairoaks	26. 8.99A
G-OHEA*	HS.125 Srs 3B/RA	25144	G-AVRG G-5-12	25.11.86	Cranfield University (Fire Service use)	Cranfield	7. 8.92T
G-OHHI	Bell 206L-1 Long Ranger	45552	G-BWYJ D-HOBD/D-HGAD	30. 4.98	Hancocks Holdings Ltd	(Loughborough)	25. 2.00T
G-OHLL	Robinson R-22 Beta	1087	G-CHAL	2.12.97	Plane Talking Ltd	Elstree	26. 4.01T
G-OHMS	Aerospatiale AS.355F1 Twin Squirrel	5194	N367E	15. 6.90	South Western Electricity plc	Bristol/Lulsgate	23. 6.99T
G-OHNA	Mainair Blade 912	1189-0199-7-W992		6.11.98	P.A. Lee	(Harlow)	
G-OHSA	Cameron N-77 HAFB	4269		2. 2.98	D.N. & L.J.Close	Andover	1. 2.99A
G-OIBM	Rockwell Commander 114	14295	G-BLVZ SX-AJO/N4957W	14.10.88	I.Rosewell	Blackbushe	4. 7.00
G-OIBO	PA-28-180 Cherokee C	28-3794	G-AVAZ	21. 1.87	Britannia Airways Ltd	Luton	24. 3.00T
G-OICE	Cessna 525 Citation Jet	G525-0028	N1330S	5.10.93	Iceland Frozen Foods plc	Chester	17.10.99
G-OICO	Lindstrand LBL-42A HAFB	566		3.11.98	Virgin Airship and Balloon Co Ltd	Telford	11.11.99A
G-OICV	Robinson R-22 Beta	0991	G-BPWH	11. 2.93	C.J.Sharples	London SW3	18. 3.01
G-OIDW	Reims Cessna F.150G	0188	N70163 D-EGTI	24. 4.90	I.D.Wakeling	Franklyns Field, Chewton Mendip	5. 8.99
G-OIEA	PA-31P Pressurised Navajo	31P-7300141	G-BBTW N7660L	13. 7.89	Skyrock Avn Ltd "Anastasia"	Cardiff	19.10.96
G-OIFM	Cameron Dude 90SS HAFB (Radio One FM DJ's head/headphones)	2841		18. 6.92	L.N.Mastis "Cool Dude"	West Bloomfield, MI, USA	29. 5.99A
G-OILA	ATR-72-212	472	F-WWEJ	28. 3.96	British World Airlines Ltd "Shetland Lady"	Aberdeen	27. 3.99T
G-OILB	ATR-72-212	473	F-WWEG	30. 5.96	British World Airlines Ltd "Grampian Lady"	Aberdeen	29. 5.99T
G-OILX*	Aerospatiale AS.355F1 Twin Squirrel	5327	G-RMGN G-BMCY	27. 1.93	Firstearl Ltd (To Ministry of Defence 25.2.99)	Oxford	27. 2.99T
G-OIMC	Cessna 152 II	152-85506	N93521	15. 5.87	East Midlands Flying School Ltd	East Midlands	28. 6.99T
G-OINK	Piper J3C-65 Cub (L-4J-PI) (Frame No.12443)	12613	G-BILD G-KERK/F-BBQD/44-80317	22. 3.83	A.R.Harding	Newton Green, Sudbury	19. 7.99P
G-OIOZ	Thunder AX9-120 S2 HAFB	4434		17.11.98	The Flying Doctors Hot Air Balloon Co Ltd	Salisbury	2.11.99T
G-OISK	Cameron N-90 HAFB	3747		23. 1.96	S.A.Simington & J.D.Rigden	Norwich	26. 2.97A
G-OISO	Reims Cessna FRA.150L Aerobat (Modified to FA.150 standard)	0213	G-BBJW	3. 4.90	Valerie J.Wilce t/a Les Oiseaux	Poplar Hall Farm, Elmsett	13. 8.99T
G-OITN	Aerospatiale AS.355F1 Twin Squirrel	5088	N400HH N5788B	3.10.89	Independent Television News Ltd (Op by Lynton Avn Ltd)	Denham	13.12.01T
G-OITV	Enstrom 280C Shark	1038	G-HRVY G-DUGY/G-BEEL	9. 4.96	M.A.Crook & A.Wright	Barton	19. 9.99T
G-OJAB	Pearce Jabiru SK (Jabiru 2200)	PFA/274-13031		19. 9.96	ST Aviation Ltd	Southery, Downham Market	14. 4.99P
G-OJAC	Mooney M.20J (201)	24-1490	N5767E	20. 8.90	Hornet Engineering Ltd	Biggin Hill	22. 1.00T
G-OJAE	Hughes 269C	90-0966	N1101W	12. 2.90	J.A. & C.M.Wilson	Slaithwaite, Huddersfield	17. 9.99
G-OJAV	BN-2A Mk.III-2 Trislander	1024	G-BDOS (4X-CCI)/G-BDOS	6. 6.90	Air Tabernacle Ltd (Op Sky Trek)	Lydd	24.11.99T
G-OJBW	Lindstrand J & B Bottle SS HAFB	436		26. 8.97	Justerini & Brooks Ltd	(London SW1)	15. 5.99A
G-OJCB	Agusta-Bell 206B JetRanger II	8554		7. 4.78	Yorkshire Helicopter Centre Ltd	Swinton	7. 5.99T
G-OJCM*	Rotorway Exec 90 (RI 162)	5117		4. 8.92	Not known (Damaged Whitchurch, Shropshire 25.9.95; stored 3.96)	Chester	28. 6.96P
G-OJCW	PA-32RT-300 Lance II	32R-7985062	N3016K	9. 1.80	P.G.Dobson t/a CW Grp	Blackbushe	19. 5.01T
G-OJDA	EAA Acrosport 2	PFA/72-11067		1. 4.98	D.B.Almey	Spalding	
G-OJDC	Thunder Ax7-77 HAFB	875		9. 1.89	Julia Crosby	Brighton	29. 7.99A
G-OJEG	Airbus A.321-231	1015	D-AVZ.	R	Monarch Airlines Ltd (For dlvy 4.99)	Luton	
G-OJEN	Cameron V-77 HAFB	3302		26. 5.94	Jensport Ltd	Bedale	18. 7.96A
G-OJGT	Maule M.5-235C Lunar Rocket	7285C	LN-AEL (LN-BEK)/N5635V	30. 6.98	J.G.Townsend	(Swindon)	23. 7.01
G-OJHB	Colt Flying Ice Cream Cone SS HAFB	2591		23. 6.94	Benedikt Haggeney GmbH	Ennigerloh, Germany	29. 5.97A
G-OJHL	Europa Avn Europa	PFA/247-13039		12. 5.97	J.H.Lace	(Kilmarnock)	
G-OJIL	PA-31-350 Navajo Chieftain	31-7625175	OY-BTP	28. 5.97	Redhill Aviation Ltd (Op Redhill Charters)	Redhill	7.12.00T
G-OJIM	PA-28R-201T Turbo Arrow III	28R-7703200	N38299	4. 8.86	R.C.Wood	(Portsmouth)	13.12.01
G-OJJB	Mooney M.20K (252TSE)	25-1161		12. 8.88	Fly Over Ltd	(London SW1)	17. 5.99
G-OJJF	Druine D.31 Turbulent (VW1300)	378 & 31	OO-30	6. 1.97	J.J.Ferguson	(Bideford)	
G-OJMR	Airbus A.300B4-605R	605	F-WWAY	3. 5.91	Monarch Airlines Ltd	Luton	2. 5.99T
G-OJNB	Lindstrand LBL-21A HAFB	085		14. 2.94	Justerini & Brooks Ltd	London SW1	30. 9.96A
G-OJON	Taylor JT.2 Titch III (Cont C90)	PFA/3208		6.10.78	J.H.Fell	Great Massingham	15. 5.99
G-OJPB	HS.125 Srs.F600B	25258	VP-CJP VR-CJP/G-BFAN/G-AZHS	25. 9.97	Widehawk Aviation Ltd	Cambridge	9. 4.99T

Regn	Type	C/n	P/I	Date	Owner/operator	Probable Base	CA Expy
G-OJRH	Robinson R-44 Astro	0321		11. 4.97	Holgate Construction Ltd		
						Emley Moor, Huddersfield	10. 4.00
G-OJSW	Boeing 737-8Q8	28218		11.12.98	Sabre Airways Ltd	Gatwick	AC
G-OJSY	Short SD.3-60 Var.100	SH.3603	N368MQ	26. 3.86	BAC Leasing Ltd	Exeter	22. 4.99T
			G-BKKT				
G-OJTA	Stemme S-10V	14-018	D-KGDA	18. 9.95	O.J.Truelove	(Wadebridge)	15.10.98
					t/a OJT Associates		
G-OJTW	Boeing 737-36N	28558	(G-JTWF)	26. 4.97	British Midland Airways Ltd		
						East Midlands	1. 5.00T
G-OJVA	Van's RV-6	PFA/181-12292		6. 9.96	J.A.Village	(Sheffield)	
G-OJVH	Reims Cessna F.150H	0356	G-AWJZ	27. 3.81	Yorkshire Light Acft Ltd	Leeds-Bradford	17. 5.01T
G-OJVI	Robinson R-22 Beta	0818	(G-OJVJ)	13. 7.88	Sloane Helicopters Ltd	Sywell	21. 5.00T
G-OJWE	Cameron A-210 HAFB	4081		20. 2.97	John Weatherill Electronics Ltd		
					(Damaged North Ferriby, Hull 20.7.97) Pocklington		27. 4.98T
G-OJWS	PA-28-161 Warrior II	28-7816415	N6377C	13. 7.88	L.E.Guernieri	Denham	10. 7.00
G-OKAG	PA-28R-180 Cherokee Arrow	28R-30075	N3764T	15. 4.88	N.F. & B.R.Green	Stapleford	3. 4.00T
G-OKAY	Pitts S-1E Special	12358	N35WH	27. 5.80	J.S.Mortimer & R.J.Allan	Barton	26. 3.99P
	(Lyc IO-360)						
G-OKBT	Colt 25A Sky Chariot mk.II HAFB	2301		10.11.92	British Telecommunications plc	Thatcham	24. 9.99A
					"Skypiper II"		
G-OKCC	Cameron N-90 HAFB	1741		6. 5.88	D.J.Head	Newbury	3. 4.97A
G-OKDN	Boeing 737-8Q8	28226		27. 7.98	Sabre Airways Ltd	Gatwick	26. 7.01T
G-OKED	Cessna 150L	150-74250	N19223	29. 1.93	Haimoss Ltd	Old Sarum	14.11.99T
					(Op Old Sarum Flying Club)		
G-OKEN	PA-28R-201T Turbo Arrow III		N47518	20.10.87	W.B.Bateson	Blackpool	25. 2.00T
		28R-7703390					
G-OKES	Robinson R-44 Astro	0053		16. 3.94	Direct Helicopters (Southend) Ltd		
						Southend	11. 5.00T
G-OKEV	Europa Avn Europa	PFA/247-13091		11. 6.97	K.A.Pilcher	(Wolverhampton)	
G-OKEY	Robinson R-22 Beta	2004		14. 1.92	Key Properties Ltd	Denham	12. 6.01
G-OKIS	Tri-R Kis	PFA/239-12248		15. 6.92	B.W.Davies	Fenland	31. 3.99P
	(CAM.100)				t/a Junipa Sales (Avn) Ltd (Stored 8.98)		
G-OKMA	Tri-R Kis	PFA/239-12808		22.11.95	K.Miller	(Coventry)	
G-OKPW	Tri-R Kis	PFA/239-12359		17. 8.93	K.P.Wordsworth	Shoreham	12. 2.98P
	(Cont O-200-A)						
G-OKYA	Cameron V-77 HAFB	1259		4. 3.87	D.J.B.Woodd	BFPO.17, Germany	
	(Replacement envelope c/n 3331)				t/a Army Balloon Club "Fly Army II"		
G-OKYM	PA-28-140 Cherokee	28-23303	G-AVLS	10. 5.88	D.Hotham	North Coates	8. 7.00
			N11C				
G-OLAH	Short SD.3-60 Var.100	SH.3604	G-BPCO	14. 8.91	Gill Avn Ltd	Newcastle	27.12.01T
			G-RMSS/G-BKKU				
G-OLAU	Robinson R-22 Beta	1119		5. 9.89	Thistle Aviation Ltd	Booker	15. 2.99
G-OLAW	Lindstrand LBL-25A Cloudhopper HAFB			9.12.94	George Law Plant Ltd	Kidderminster	24. 4.97A
	170				"Law Hopper"		
G-OLBL	Lindstrand LBL-90A HAFB	419		24. 2.97	Lindstrand Balloons Ltd	Oswestry	16. 2.99A
G-OLDB	PA-31-350 Chieftain	31-8152014	OY-SKY	29. 5.97	Shed Three Ltd	Biggin Hill	24. 7.00T
			G-DIXI/N40717		(Op Gold Air International)		
G-OLDD	BAe 125-800B	258106	PK-RGM	11. 3.99	Gold Air International Ltd.	Cambridge	
			PK-WSJ/G-5-580				
G-OLDN	Bell 206L LongRanger	45077	G-TBCA	2.10.84	Gulfstream Air Svs (UK) Ltd	Thruxton	29. 5.00T
			G-BFAL/N64689/A6-BCL				
G-OLDV	Colt 90A HAFB	2592		5. 5.94	Virgin Airship & Balloon Co Ltd	Telford	10.11.98A
					"LDV"		
G-OLDZ	Beechcraft 200 Super King Air	BB-828	G-MCEO	28. 6.96	Shed One Ltd	Biggin Hill	21. 5.99T
		(N828AB)/G-SWFT/G-SIBE/G-MCEO/G-BILY (Op Gold Air International)					
G-OLEE	Reims Cessna F.152 II	1797		11. 9.80	Aerohire Ltd	Wellesbourne Mountford	30. 5.99T
					(Op South Warwickshire F/School)		
G-OLEO	Thunder Ax10-210 Srs.2 HAFB	3974		9. 1.97	P.J.Waller	Norwich	14. 3.98T
G-OLFC	PA-38-112 Tomahawk	38-79A0995	G-BGZG	6.12.85	M.W.Glencross	Luton	21. 5.01T
G-OLFT	Rockwell Commander 114	14274	G-WJMN	28. 3.85	B.C.Richens & B.N.Woodward	Redhill	25. 1.99
			N4954W				
G-OLGA	CFM Starstreak Shadow SA.II			15.10.97	N.F.Smith	Halstead	20. 4.99P
		PFA/206-13164					
G-OLIN*	PA-30-160 Twin Comanche B	30-1716	OY-DLC	22.12.81	Not known	(Henstridge)	3. 3.88T
			G-AWMB/N8569Y		(Crashed Stapleford 16.8.87; stored 1992)		
G-OLIZ	Robinson R-22 Beta	0779		29. 9.88	L.T.Alderman	Baldock, Herts	5. 8.01T
					t/a Randall Photographic		
G-OLJT	Mainair Gemini/Flash 2A		G-MTKY	16. 9.98	L.J.Taylor	Darlington	21.12.99P
	(Rotax 503)	570-887-5 & W359					
G-OLLE	Cameron O-84 HAFB	1520		15. 4.87	N.A.Robertson	Combe Hay Manor, Bath	5. 8.99A
					"Golly IV"		
G-OLLI	Cameron O-31 HAFB	196		11. 5.76	N.A.Robertson	Combe Hay Manor, Bath	17. 7.97A
	(Special Shape - Golly)				"Golly III"		
G-OLLY	PA-31-350 Navajo Chieftain		G-BCES	27. 1.76	Barnes Olson Aeroleasing Ltd		
		31-7405418	N66916		(Op Bristol Flying Centre)	Bristol/Lulsgate	6. 5.01T
G-OLMA	Partenavia P.68B	159	G-BGBT	15. 4.85	C.M.Evans	Plymouth	15. 5.99T
G-OLOW	Robinson R-44 Astro	0100		3.10.94	Rotaspot Ltd	Sywell	17.11.00

Regn	Type	C/n	P/I	Date	Owner/operator	Probable Base	CA Expy
G-OLPG	Colt 77A HAFB	2568		11. 3.94	UK Petroleum Products Ltd t/a Eurogas & Corralgas	Leeds	16. 5.99
G-OLRT	Robinson R-22 Beta	1378	N4014R	21. 5.90	A.J. & P.D.Morgan t/a Morhire	Usk	15. 7.99T
G-OLSC*	Cessna 182A	34078	G-ATNU EI-ANC/N6078B	19. 8.87	Not known	St.Merryn	3. 7.93
			(Crashed Knettishall 6.6.93; for film use as "G-ATCX" - fuselage stored 4.94)				
G-OLSF	PA-28-161 Cadet	2841284	G-OTYJ G-OLSF/N9200B	23.11.89	Plane Talking Ltd	Elstree	22. 1.99T
G-OLVR	Clutton FRED Srs.II (Cont A65)	PFA/29-10321		17.11.78	C.P.Whitwell	Spalding	12. 8.97P
G-OLYD	Beechcraft 58 Baron	TH-1427	N7255H ZS-LYC/N7255H	12. 9.97	I.G.Lloyd	Nottingham	13.10.00
G-OLYN	Sky 260-24 HAFB	088		24. 4.98	C.J.Sandell	Sevenoaks	22. 4.99
G-OMAC	Reims Cessna FR.172E Rocket	0022	PH-HAI (PH-KRC)/D-EDDC	3. 7.84	R.J.Knibbs t/a RK Consultants	Maypole Farm, Chislet	5.11.01
G-OMAF	Dornier 228-200	8112	D-CAAD	16. 2.87	Cobham Leasing Ltd	Bournemouth	22. 6.99T
			(Op for Ministry of Agriculture & Fisheries/Fisheries Patrol)				
G-OMAP	Rockwell Commander 685	12036	F-GIRX F-OCGX/F-ZBBU/N6525V	4.11.94	Cooper Aerial Surveys Ltd (Exported 1998)	Sandtoft	27.2.98Exp
G-OMAR	PA-34-220T Seneca III	34-8233142	N82033	17. 6.88	Redhill Aviation Ltd t/a Redhill F/C	Redhill	19.10.00T
G-OMAT	PA-28-140 Cherokee D	28-7125139	G-JIMY G-AYUG	27. 8.87	R.B.Walker t/a Midland Air Training School	Coventry	3.11.00T
G-OMAX	Brantly B.2B	473	G-AVJN	7. 8.87	P.D.Benmax	Costock, Leics	9.12.99
G-OMDD	Cameron Thunder AX8-90 S2 HAFB	4345		2. 4.98	M.D.Dickinson	(Bristol)	
G-OMDG	Hoffmann H-36 Dimona	3510	OE-9215	19.11.98	P.Turner t/a Mendip Dimona Group	Halesland	7.12.01
G-OMDH	MDH Hughes 369E (500E)	0293E		14.11.88	Stiltgate Ltd	Booker	28. 4.01T
G-OMDR	Agusta-Bell 206B JetRanger III	8610	G-HRAY G-VANG/G-BIZA	8.12.97	Aeromega Ltd	Stapleford	15.12.00T
G-OMEC	Agusta-Bell 206B JetRanger III	8716	G-OBLD	16. 1.90	Kallas Ltd	(Monaco)	21.10.01
G-OMEL	Robinson R-44 Astro	0073	G-BVPB	30. 9.96	Nedair Ltd	Blackpool	2.11.00
G-OMGD	BAe HS.125 Srs.700B	257184	9K-AGA YI-AKG/9K-AGA/G-5-12	28.12.94	Magec Avn Ltd	Luton	21. 2.99T
G-OMGE	BAe 125 Srs.800B	258197	G-5-696 G-BTMG	1. 7.91	Marconda Services Ltd	Luton	22. 5.99T
G-OMGG	BAe 125 Srs.800B	258058	N125JW G-5-637/N125JW/VH-NMR/ZK-EUI/(ZK-EUR)/G-5-510	21.11.94	Magec Avn Ltd	Luton	23.11.99T
G-OMHC	PA-28RT-201 Arrow IV	28R-7918105	N3072Y	10. 2.81	M.R.Shelton t/a Tatenhill Avn	Tatenhill	2. 5.99T
G-OMHI	Mills MH-1	MH.001		8.10.97	J.P.Mills	(Stockport)	
G-OMIA	Socata MS.893A Rallye Commodore 180	12074	D-ENME F-BUGE/(D-ENMH)	21. 7.98	P.W.Portelli	(London SW10)	23.10.01
G-OMIG	WSK SBLim-2A (MiG 15UTI)	622047	6247 (Polish AF)	10.11.92	Classic Avn Ltd (Op by The Old Flying Machine Co)	Duxford	18. 5.99P
			(Built by Aero Vodochody as S.103/MiG 15bis; later rebuilt in Poland) (As "6247"in Soviet AF c/s)				
G-OMIK	Europa Avn Europa	PFA/247-12991		12. 1.98	M.J.Clews	(Maidenhead)	
G-OMJB	Bell 206B JetRanger II	2051	N315JP N712WG/N712WC/N9989K	20. 4.89	Coventry Helicopter Centre Ltd	Coventry	7. 6.01T
G-OMJT	Rutan LongEz 968 & PFA/74A-10703 (Lyc O-235)			14.10.92	M.J.Timmons	Prestwick	31. 7.99P
G-OMKF	Aero Designs Pulsar (Rotax 582)	PFA/202-11866		15. 1.91	M.K.Faro	Old Sarum	16. 4.99P
G-OMMG	Robinson R-22 Beta	1041	G-BPYX	25. 2.94	BLS Avn Ltd	Blackbushe	27. 1.01T
G-OMMM	Colt 90A HAFB	2328		20. 1.93	3M Health Care Ltd	Loughborough	11. 4.99A
G-OMNH	Beechcraft 200 Super King Air	BB-108	N108BM RP-C1979/TR-LWC	19. 8.98	Maynard & Harris Holdings Ltd	(Beccles)	20. 8.99T
G-OMNI	PA-28R-200 Cherokee Arrow II	28R-7335130	G-BAWA	3. 1.84	Excel Automation Ltd	Gloucestershire	8. 6.00
G-OMOG	Gulfstream AA-5A Cheetah	AA5A-0793	G-BHWR N26892	4. 3.88	J.R. & S.Nutter t/a Solent Flight Leasing	Southampton	18. 2.99T
G-OMPS*	PA-28-161 Warrior II	28-8016050	G-BOHP N8079Z	14. 2.89	Not known Montpellier/Frejorques, France		29. 3.94T
			(Crashed Tours 20.8.92; wreck in open store 5.97)				
G-OMRB	Cameron V-77 HAFB	2184		29. 8.90	M.R.Bayne "Harlequin"	Dunnington, Yorks	3. 9.99A
G-OMRG	Hoffmann H-36 Dimona	36132	G-BLHG	15.11.88	M.R.Grimwood	Gloucestershire	7. 2.00
G-OMSG	Robinson R-22 Beta	2738		8.10.97	Aviation Corporation plc	Cheltenham	23.10.00T
G-OMUC	Boeing 737-36Q	29405		29. 6.98	British Regional Airlines Ltd (Dove/Colum t/s)	Manchester	16. 7.01T
G-OMUM	Rockwell Commander 114	14067	PH-JJJ (PH-MMM)/N4737W	24. 1.97	Armadafleet Ltd	Blackbushe	3. 3.00
G-OMWE	Zenair CH.601HD (Mid-West AE.100R)	PFA/162-12740	G-BVXU	21. 3.97	Mid-West Engines Ltd	Gloucestershire	13. 7.98P
G-OMXS	Lindstrand LBL-105A HAFB	172		7.12.94	Virgin Airship & Balloon Co Ltd "Mazda"	Telford	1. 4.97A
G-ONAF	Naval Acft Factory N3N-3 (Wright Whirlwind R.760)	-	N45192 Bu.4406	31. 1.89	R.P.W.Steele & J.D.Hutchinson	Sandown	24. 7.99
G-ONAV	PA-31-310 Turbo Navajo C	31-7812004	G-IGAR D-IGAR/N27378	29. 1.93	Panther Avn Ltd	Elstree	28. 3.98T
G-ONCB	Lindstrand LBL-31A HAFB	393		4. 6.96	Flying Pictures Ltd	Fairoaks	6. 9.99A

Regn	Type	C/n	P/I	Date	Owner/operator	Probable Base	CA Expy
G-ONCL	Colt 77A HAFB	1637		4. 4.90	D.R.Pearce	Slimbridge	23. 6.98A
G-ONEB	Westland Scout AH.1	F.9761	G-BXOE XW798	21. 1.98	N.E.Bailey Ogbourne Maizey, Marlborough		29. 3.99P
G-ONET	PA-28-180 Cherokee E	28-5802	G-AYAU	3. 6.98	J.Blackburn & J.J.Feeney	Elstree	10. 7.99T
G-ONFL	Meridian Ultralights Maverick (Rotax 503) 402 & PFA/259-12750		G-MYUJ	27.11 98	K.Anderson "69"	Stafford	12.12.98P
G-ONGC	Robin DR.400/180R Remorquer	1385	EI-CKA SE-GHM	11.11.98	Norfolk Gliding Club Ltd	Tibbenham	3.12.01
G-ONHH	Forney F-1A Aircoupe	5725	G-ARHA N3030G	13.12.89	Bob Crowe A/c Sales Ltd	Cranfield	5. 3.01P
G-ONIX	Cameron C-80 HAFB	4411		12. 8.98	Hillwalk Ltd	Pewsey	22. 7.99A
G-ONKA	Aeronca K (Lyc O-145)	K283	N19780 NC19780	21.10.91	N.J.R.Minchin "Aggnes"	Sandown	15. 5.99P
G-ONOW	Bell 206A JetRanger	605	G-AYMX	8. 8.88	J.Lucketti	Fenland	27. 4.00T
G-ONPA(2)	PA-31-350 Navajo Chieftain	31-7952110	N89PA N35225	6. 5.98	Anglo American Airmotive Ltd	Bournemouth	15.10.01T
G-ONTV	Agusta-Bell 206B JetRanger III	8733	D-HUNT TC-HKJ/(D-HSAV)/I-GPFP/I-PIEF	1. 4.98	Castle Air Charters Ltd	Trebrown, Liskeard	7. 4.01T
G-ONUN	Van's RV-6A	PFA/181-12976		20. 2.96	R.E.Nunn	(Herne Bay)	
G-ONYX	Bell 206B Jet Ranger III	4160	G-BXPN N18EA/D-HOBA/(D-HOBE)	22. 1.98	D.C. & A.J.Burgoyne t/a Burgoyne Group	(Hereford)	10. 3.01T
G-ONZO	Cameron O-77 HAFB	1089		13.11.84	K.Temple "Gonzo"	Diss	19. 7.99A
G-OOAA	Airbus A.320-231	291	F-WWBZ	11. 4.92	Air 2000 Ltd	Manchester	14. 4.99T
G-OOAB	Airbus A.320-231	292	F-WWDN	24. 4.92	Air 2000 Ltd	Manchester	23. 4.99T
G-OOAC	Airbus A.320-231	327	F-WWDQ	15. 9.92	Air 2000 Ltd	Manchester	14. 9.99T
G-OOAD	Airbus A.320-231	336	F-WWIG	24. 9.92	Air 2000 Ltd	Manchester	23. 9.99T
G-OOAE	Airbus A.321-112	852	(G-UNIF) D-AVZG	14. 7.98	Air 2000 Ltd	Manchester	13. 7.00T
G-OOAF	Airbus A.321-211	677	G-UNID G-UKLO/D-AVZO	4.12.98	Air 2000 Ltd	Manchester	
G-OOAH	Airbus A.321-211	781	G-UNIE D-AVZK	4. 1.99	Air 2000 Ltd	Manchester	2. 3.01T
G-OOAN	Boeing 767-39HER	26256	G-UKLH	26. 1.99	Air 2000 Ltd	Manchester	
G-OOAO	Boeing 767-39HER	26257	G-UKLI	11. 1.99	Air 2000 Ltd	Manchester	14. 4.00T
G-OODE	SNCAN Stampe SV-4C (Gipsy Major 10)	500	G-AZNN F-BDGI	9. 5.77	Chocks Away Ltd	Goodwood	28. 4.99T
G-OODI	Pitts S-1D Special (Lyc IO-360)	KH.1	G-BBBU	23.12.80	M.J.Walden	Cheddington	30. 4.99P
G-OODW	PA-28-181 Archer II	28-8490031	N4332C	14. 7.87	Goodwood Road Racing Co Ltd	Goodwood	3.11.99T
G-OOER	Lindstrand LBL-25A Cloudhopper HAFB 125			15. 8.94	Airborne Adventures Ltd	Skipton	18.10.95A
G-OOGA	Gulfstream GA-7 Cougar	GA7-0111	SE-IEA N758G	3. 2.86	Plane Talking Ltd (Op Denham School of Flying)	Denham	25.11.01T
	(Althouh YV-1334P is registered with c/n 0111 G-OOGA is confirmed correct)						
G-OOGI	Gulfstream GA-7 Cougar	GA7-0077	G-PLAS G-BGHL/N789GA	16. 1.95	Plane Talking Ltd	Biggin Hill	10. 8.00T
G-OOGO	Grumman-American GA-7 Cougar	GA7-0049	N762GA	12.11.97	Leonard F.Jollye (Brookmans Park) Ltd	Elstree	2.12.00T
G-OOGS	Gulfstream American GA-7 Cougar	GA7-0105	G-BGJW N737G	19. 6.98	Bournemouth Flying Club Ltd	Bournemouth	
G-OOJB	Cessna 421C Golden Eagle III	421C-1006	G-BKSO N6333X	13. 3.91	Melman Investments Ltd	Guernsey	21. 5.99
G-OOJC	Bensen B.8MR	PFA G/101-1303		4.12.98	J.R.Cooper	(Swansea)	
G-OOLE	Cessna 172M Skyhawk II	172-66712	G-BOSI N80714	25. 8.89	P.S.Eccersley	Humberside	15. 1.01
G-OONE	Mooney M.20J (205)	24-3039		31. 7.87	J.H.Donald & K.B.Moore	Cumbernauld	8. 4.00
G-OONI	Thunder Ax7-77 HAFB	1534		9. 3.90	Fivedata Ltd "Bridesnightie"	Todmorden, Lancs	4. 8.96A
G-OONY	PA-28-161 Warrior II	28-8316015	N83071	26. 7.89	D.A.Field & P.B.Jenkins	Compton Abbas	24. 9.99T
G-OOOA	Boeing 757-28AER	23767	C-FOOA G-OOOA/C-FOOA/G-OOOA/C-FOOA/G-OOOA	6. 3.87	Air 2000 Ltd	Manchester	6. 4.01T
G-OOOB	Boeing 757-28AER	23822	C-FOOB G-OOOB (x9)	19. 2.87	Air 2000 Ltd	Manchester	28. 4.01T
G-OOOC*	Boeing 757-28AER	24017	C-FXOC G-OOOC (x6)	19. 1.88	Air 2000 Ltd (Leased Air 3000 C-FXOC 12.98)	Manchester	10. 4.00T
G-OOOD*	Boeing 757-28AER	24235	C-FXOD G-OOOD/C-FXOD/G-OOOD (Leased Air 3000 C-FXOD 12.98)	25. 2.88	Air 2000 Ltd	Manchester	6. 5.99T
G-OOOG	Boeing 757-23AER	24292	C-FOOG G-OOOG (x5)	29. 3.89	Air 2000 Ltd	Manchester	29.10.01T
G-OOOI	Boeing 757-23AER	24289	N510SK EC-EMV/EC-247	19.10.89	Air 2000 Ltd	Manchester	19.10.99T
G-OOOJ	Boeing 757-23AER	24290	N510FP EC-EMU/EC-248	19.10.89	Air 2000 Ltd	Manchester	1.11.99T
G-OOOO	Mooney M.20J (205)	24-3046	N205EE	25. 1.88	Pergola Ltd	Weston, Ireland	7. 7.00
G-OOOS	Boeing 757-236ER	24397	G-BRJD EC-ESC/EC-349/G-BRJD	14. 5.91	Air 2000 Ltd	Manchester	18.10.99T
G-OOOU	Boeing 757-2Y0ER	25240		30. 8.91	Air 2000 Ltd	Manchester	24.10.99T

Regn	Type	C/n	P/I	Date	Owner/operator	Probable Base	CA Expy
G-OOOV	Boeing 757-225	22211	N521EA	12. 2.92	Air 2000 Ltd	Manchester	17. 2.00T
G-OOOW	Boeing 757-225	22611	N522EA	20. 1.92	Air 2000 Ltd	Manchester	20. 1.00T
G-OOOX	Boeing 757-2Y0	26158		24. 2.93	Air 2000 Ltd	Manchester	22. 3.00T
G-OOOY	Boeing 757-28A	28203		21. 5.98	Air 2000 Ltd	Manchester	20. 5.01T
G-OOSE	Rutan VariEze	1536 & PFA/74-10326		7.12.78	J.A.Towers	Yearby	
					(Under construction 8.91)		
G-OOSY	DH.82A Tiger Moth	85831	F-BGFI	6. 9.94	M.Goosey	Eccleshall, Stafford	
	(Composite rebuild)		Fr AF/DE971		(On rebuild 9.94)		
G-OOTC	PA-28R-201T Turbo Arrow III		G-CLIV	18. 1.94	H.Daines Electronics Ltd	(Beccles)	14. 5.00
		28R-7703086	N3011Q				
G-OOUT	Colt Flying Shuttlecock SS HAFB 1938			16. 5.91	Shiplake Investments Ltd	(Switzerland)	26.11.98A
					"Shuttlecock"		
G-OOXP	Aero Designs Pulsar XP PFA/202-11915			25.10.90	T.D.Baker	Corby	18. 4.96P
	(Rotax 912)						
G-OPAG	PA-34-200 Seneca	34-7250348	N506DM	16.10.90	A.H.Lavender	Biggin Hill	10. 4.00
			G-BNGB/F-BTQT/(F-BTMT)				
G-OPAL	Robinson R-22 Beta	0535	N23750	11. 2.86	Pebblestar Ltd	Hareford	13. 4.01T
G-OPAM	Reims Cessna F.152 II	1536	G-BFZS	5. 9.86	PJC (Leasing) Ltd	Egginton	17. 6.00T
	(Texas Tail-wheel conversion)				"Little Red Rooster" (Op Derby Aero Club)		
G-OPAT	Beechcraft 76 Duchess	ME-304	G-BHAO	6.12.82	R.D.J.Axford	White Waltham	30. 1.00
G-OPAZ	Pazmany PL-2	PFA/69-10673		20. 3.98	K.Morris	(Salisbury)	
G-OPDM	Enstrom 280FX Shark	2021	N8627Q	7. 1.98	Lancroft Air Ltd	(Oswestry)	15. 1.01T
			PH-GBL/N650PG				
G-OPDS	Denney Kitfox mk.4	PFA/172A-12259		8. 1.93	P.D.Sparling	Popham	27. 6.99P
	(Rotax 582)						
G-OPEP	PA-28RT-201T Turbo Arrow IV		OY-PEP	3.12.97	A.J.Keen	(Castletown, IOM)	12. 1.01T
		28R-7931070	N2217Q				
G-OPFI	Vickers Viscount 802	170	G-BLNB	1. 3.94	British World Airlines Ltd	Southend	13. 8.00T
			G-AOHV				
G-OPFT	Cessna 172R Skyhawk II	172-80316	N9491F	11. 3.98	Rankart Ltd	(Brackley)	19. 3.00T
G-OPFW	HS.748 Srs.2A/266	1714	G-BMFT	1. 7.98	Emerald Airways Ltd	Liverpool	16. 2.01T
			VP-BFT/VR-BFT/G-BMFT/5W-FAO/G11-10				
G-OPHT	Schleicher ASH 26E	26105		6. 2.97	Scheibler Filters Ltd "T1"	Gamston	11. 3.00
G-OPIC	Reims Cessna FRA.150L Aerobat	0234	G-BGNZ	20. 6.95	S.J.Burke	Bodmin	10.12.99T
			PH-GAB/D-EIQE		t/a Peak Aviation Photography		
G-OPIK	Eiri PIK-20E Srs.1	20233	PH-651	27. 1.82	A.J.McWilliam	Newtownards	1.10.97
G-OPIT	CFM Streak Shadow			22.11.89	W.M.Kilner High Barn Farm, Roach Bridge		17. 6.97P
	(Rotax 532) K.126-SA & PFA/161A-11624						
G-OPJC	Cessna 152 II	152-82280	N68354	7. 6.88	PJC (Leasing) Ltd	RAF Henlow	9.10.00T
G-OPJD	PA-28RT-201T Turbo Arrow IV		N8097V	2.10.89	F.T.Ahmed, J.G.McVey & K.G.Ward		
		28R-8231028				Liverpool	15.12.01T
G-OPJH	Rollason Druine D.62B Condor RAE/619		G-AVDW	15. 4.97	P.J.Hall	Old Sarum	9.12.01
G-OPJK	Europa Avn Europa 17 & PFA/247-12487			29. 4.93	P.J.Kember Laddingford, Paddock Wood		1.12.98P
	(Rotax 912UL)				"The First of the Many"		
G-OPLB	Cessna 340A II	340-0486	G-FCHJ	11. 7.95	Ridgewood Ltd	Jersey	13. 5.00
			G-BJLS/(N6315X)				
G-OPLC	DH.104 Dove 8	04212	G-BLRB	10. 1.91	W.G.T.Pritchard & I.D'Arcy-Bean		
			VP962		(Op Mayfair Dove)	Redhill/Biggin Hill	30. 3.99T
G-OPME	PA-23-250 Aztec D	27-4099	G-ODIR	31. 3.94	Oxspeed Ltd	Southampton	26. 9.01T
			G-AZGB/N878SH/N10F				
G-OPMT	Lindstrand LBL-105A HAFB	052		30. 9.93	Pace Micro Technology Ltd "Pace" Shipley		31. 7.99A
G-OPNH	Stoddard-Hamilton Glasair IIRG		G-CINY	14.10.98	P N Haigh	(Huddersfield)	
		PFA/149-13011					
G-OPNI	Bell 206B Jet Ranger	83	G-BXAA	24. 4.96	P & I Data Services Ltd	Denham	30. 5.99
			F-GKYR/HB-XOR/G-BHMV/VH-SJJ/VH-FVR (Crashed in Lyme Bay, Dorset 5.4.99)				
G-OPPL	Gulfstream AA-5A Cheetah	AA5A-0867	G-BGNN	11.10.85	J.P.E.Walsh	Elstree	8. 8.00T
					t/a Walsh Avn (Op Cabair)		
G-OPPS	Mudry CAP.231	11	F-GGYN	12. 3.90	Bianchi Avn Film Svs Ltd	Booker	20. 7.00
			F-WZCI/G-OPPS		(Proteus Petrol c/s)		
G-OPRA	PA-31 Turbo Navajo	31-109	G-VICK	26. 2.92	Comed Aviation Ltd	Blackpool	9. 9.98T
			G-AWED/N9076Y				
G-OPSF	PA-38-112 Tomahawk	38-79A0998	EI-BLT	13.10.82	Panshanger School of Flying Ltd		
			G-BGZI			High Cross, Ware	17. 8.00T
G-OPSL	PA-32R-301 Saratoga SP	32R-8013085	G-IMPW	4. 1.99	Photonic Science Ltd	(Robertsbridge)	15. 1.00
			N8186A				
G-OPST	Cessna 182R Skylane II	182-67932	N9317H	16. 6.88	Lota Ltd	Shoreham	9. 7.00
G-OPTS	Robinson R-22 Beta	2712		16. 7.97	ZB Ltd	(Stockport)	17. 7.00T
G-OPUB	Slingsby T-67M Firefly 160	2002	G-DLTA	18.10.96	P.M.Barker	Bagby	3. 2.01T
			G-SFTX				
G-OPUP	Beagle B.121 Pup 2	B121-062	G-AXEU	31.10.84	A.Brinkley Standalone Farm, Meppershall		4. 2.01
			(5N-AJC)		t/a Brinkley Light Aircraft Services		
G-OPUS	Pearce Jabiru SK	PFA/274-13343		16. 7.98	Opus Software Ltd	(Grantham)	16. 2.99P
G-OPWH	Dassault Falcon 900B	151	F-WWFK	31.10.95	P.B.W.Hamlyn & Lynton Corporate Jet Ltd		
					t/a Aviation Partnership	Oxford	31.10.01T
G-OPWK	Grumman-American AA-5A Cheetah		G-OAEL	26. 5.92	A.H.McVicar	Prestwick	23. 8.98T
		AA5A-0663	N26706				

Regn	Type	C/n	P/I	Date	Owner/operator	Probable Base	CA Expy
G-OPWS	Mooney M.20K (231)	25-0663	N1162W	12. 4.91	A.R.Mills	Fowlmere	10. 7.00
G-OPYE	Cessna 172S Skyhawk	172S-8059	N653SP	19. 2.99	Pye Consulting Group Ltd	(Wigan)	
G-ORAF	CFM Streak Shadow K.134-SA & PFA/161A-11627			18. 5.90	A.P.Hunn	(Norwich)	1.10.90P
	(Rotax 532) (PFA c/n duplicates MW6 G-MYCU)						
G-ORAR	PA-28-181 Archer II	2890224	N9255G	6. 6.95	P.N. & S.M.Thornton	Goodwood	26. 6.01T
G-ORCL	Cessna 421C Golden Eagle III	421C-1223	N27089	8. 5.87	T.& G.Engineering Co Ltd	Fairoaks	25. 8.00
G-ORDN*	PA-28R-200 Cherokee Arrow II	28R-7235294	G-BAJT	21. 7.89	Not known	Stapleford	9. 4.99
					(Damaged Stapleford 27.5.96; open store 5.97)		
G-ORDO	PA-30-160 Twin Comanche B	30-1648	N8485Y	19. 4.91	C.A.Ringrose	Biggin Hill	28. 4.00
G-ORED	PBN BN-2T Turbine Islander	2142	G-BJYW	10. 1.85	Red Devils Aviation Ltd	AAC Netheravon	25. 9.00A
G-OREV	Revolution Helicopters Mini 500 0112			8. 8.96	R.H.Everett	Thruxton	AC
G-ORFC	Jurca MJ.5 Sirocco	PFA/2210		16. 5.85	D.J.Phillips	Lasham	6. 5.99P
	(Lyc O-290)						
G-ORFH	ATR-42-300	346	F-WWEI	29.12.93	Gill Avn Ltd	Newcastle	28.12.99T
					(Op Air France Express)		
G-ORHE	Cessna 500 Citation	500-0220	(N619EA)	25. 3.96	R.H.Everett	Thruxton	22. 5.00T
	(Unit No.220)		G-OBEL/G-BOGA/N932HA/N93WD/N5220J				
G-ORIG	Glaser-Dirks DG-800A	8-39-A29		5. 4.94	I.Godfrey "386"	Lasham	17.11.00
G-ORIX	ARV K1 Super 2 034 & PFA/152-12424		G-BUXH	16. 9.93	Burel Air Ltd	(Cheltenham)	1. 4.99P
	(Norton AE.100R)		(G-BNVK)				
G-ORJB	Cessna 500 Citation	500-0364	G-OKSP	2. 7.92	L'Equipe Air Ltd	Gamston	20.10.01T
	(Unit No.392)		N40DA/N20WP/(N221JB)/N221AC/HB-VFF/N36892				
G-ORJW	Laverda F.8L Falco Srs.4	403	(PH-)	2. 8.93	W.R.M.Sutton	Seppe, Netherlands	1. 9.01
			G-ORJW/D-ELDV/D-ELDY				
G-ORMA	AS.355F1 Twin Squirrel	5192	G-SITE	9.11.98	Autopilot Ltd	Elstree	7. 6.01T
			G-BPHC/N365E				
G-ORMB	Robinson R-22 Beta	1607		14.12.90	R.M.Bailey	Cumbernauld	24. 2.00T
G-ORMG	Cessna 172R Skyhawk II	172-80344	N9518F	25. 9.98	J.R.T.Royle	Audley End	30. 9.01
G-OROB	Robinson R-22 Beta	0965	G-TBFC	11. 6.90	R.Culf	Redhill	25. 6.95T
			N80287		t/a Corniche Helicopters (Spares use 9.97)		
G-OROD	PA-18-150 Super Cub	18-7856	SE-CRD	27. 6.89	R.J.O.Walker Griffins Farm, Temple Bruer		10.12.98
G-ORON	Colt 77A HAFB	1149		8. 3.88	J.Charley	Wymeswold	29. 9.99A
					t/a Orion Hot Air Balloon Group		
G-OROZ	Aerospatiale AS.350B2 Ecureuil	2617		26. 2.92	Tyrone Fabrication Ltd		
						Dungannon, Co.Tyrone	30. 4.01
G-ORPR	Cameron O-77 HAFB	2341		26. 6.90	T.Strauss & A.Sheehan	(London SW1)	8. 8.99A
					"Batman"		
G-ORSP	Beechcraft A36 Bonanza	E-2723	N56037	26.10.92	Select Plant Hire Co Ltd	North Weald	7. 1.02
G-ORTM	Glaser-Dirks DG-400	4-209		6. 3.87	D.P.Holdcroft	(Brackley)	29. 4.00
G-ORTW	Lindstrand AM.25000 HAFB	304		15. 8.95	Lindstrand Balloons Ltd	Oswestry	9. 4.96E
G-ORVB	McCulloch J.2	039	(G-BLGI)	2. 8.89	R.V.Bowles (On overhaul 7.91)	Coventry	AC
			(G-BKKL)/Bahrain Public Security BPS-3/N4329G				
G-ORVR	Partenavia P.68B	115	G-BFBD	2.10.95	Cheshire F/Svs Ltd	Manchester	13. 3.99T
					t/a Ravenair		
G-OSAL	Cessna 421C Golden Eagle II	421C-0218	OY-BEC	13. 7.83	M.D.Thorpe	Leeds-Bradford	13. 1.99T
			SE-GZI/N5471G		t/a Yorkshire Helicopters		
G-OSCA	Cessna 500 Citation	500-0270	G-SWET	31. 1.96	Oscar Aviation Ltd	(Romsey)	25. 4.99T
	(Unit No.270)		N4238X/N68CB/N72BC/N712N/N712J/N5270J				
G-OSCC	PA-32-300 Cherokee Six	32-7540020	G-BGFD	27.11.84	BG & G Airlines Ltd	Jersey	27. 6.99
			D-EOSH/N32186				
G-OSCH	Cessna 421C Golden Eagle III	421C-0706	G-SALI	13. 9.95	Sureflight Avn Ltd	(Birmingham)	8.11.99
			N26552				
G-OSCO	Team Minimax	PFA/186-12878		24.12.96	P.J.Schofield	(Sproston, Crewe)	
G-OSDI	Beechcraft 58 Baron	TH-1111	G-BHFY	27. 7.84	D.Darling	Wellesbourne Mountford	2. 4.98
G-OSEA	PBN BN-2B-26 Islander	2175	G-BKOL	27. 8.85	W.T.Johnson & Sons (Huddersfield) Ltd		
						Crosland Moor	23. 3.01
G-OSEE	Robinson R-22 Beta	0917		11. 1.89	J.P.Dennison	Stockport	20.11.98
G-OSFC	Reims Cessna F.152 II	1872	G-BIVJ	31. 1.86	Stapleford F/C Ltd	Stapleford	12. 6.00T
G-OSGB	PA-31-350 Navajo Chieftain 31-7952155		G-YSKY	25.01.99	Gold Air International Ltd	Cambridge	1. 5.99T
			N3529D				
G-OSHL	Robinson R-22 Beta	1000		19. 4.89	Sloane Helicopters Ltd	Sywell	27. 8.01T
G-OSII	Cessna 172N Skyhawk II	172-67768	G-BIVY	17.10.95	K.J.Abrams	(Great Dunmow)	17. 1.99T
			N73973				
G-OSIP	Robinson R-22 Beta	2916		9. 2.99	Heli Air Ltd	Wellesbourne Mountford	
G-OSIS	Pitts S-1S Special	PFA/09-12043		19. 9.94	M.C.Boddington & I.M.Castle	Sywell	
G-OSIX	PA-32-260 Cherokee Six	32-499	G-AZMO	5. 8.86	A.E.Whittie	Blackpool	18.12.98T
			SE-EYN				
G-OSKP	Enstrom 480	5002	F-GSOT	6. 6.94	Astral Communications (Wakefield) Ltd		
			G-OSKP/N480EN		t/a Astral Helicopters	Tadcaster	25. 3.00
G-OSKY	Cessna 172M Skyhawk II	172-67389	A6-KCB	27. 2.79	Skyhawk Leasing Ltd		
			N73343			Wellesbourne Mountford	8. 7.00T
G-OSLO	Schweizer Hughes 269C	S.1360	N7507L	15. 3.89	AH Helicopter Services Ltd	Newton Abbot	3. 3.01T
G-OSMD	Bell 206B JetRanger II	2034	G-LTEK	12. 2.99	Stuart Aviation Ltd	White Waltham	7. 5.01T
			G-BMIB/ZS-HGH				
G-OSMR	Lake LA-4-200 Buccaneer	650	EI-BNB	13. 3.96	J.P.Billingham	Gloucestershire	25. 7.99
			N1057L				

Regn	Type	C/n	P/I	Date	Owner/operator	Probable Base	CA Expy
G-OSMS	Robinson R-22 Beta	1528	G-BXYW	22. 2.99	Speed Services plc (St.Ives, Hunts)		22. 9.01T
			HA-MIU/N528SH				
G-OSMT	Europa Avn Europa	PFA/247-12705		15. 6.94	S.M.Thomas (Stockton-on-Tees)		
G-OSND	Reims Cessna FRA.150M Aerobat	0272	G-BDOU	16.10.84	Wilkins & Wilkins Special Auctions Ltd		
						RAF Henlow	30. 1.00T
G-OSNI	PA-23-250 Aztec C	27-3852	G-AWER	2. 7.98	Marham Investments Ltd (Castletown, IoM)		17. 5.01T
			N6556Y				
G-OSOE	HS.748 Srs.2A/275	1697	G-AYYG	17.11.97	Emerald Airways Ltd	Liverpool	10.11.99T
			ZK-MCF/C-GRCU/ZK-MCF/G-AYYG/(x3)/G-11-9 (Securicor Omega Express c/s)				
G-OSOO	MDH Hughes 369E (500E)	0298E		10. 5.89	Tyrone Fabrication Ltd		
						Dungannon, Co.Tyrone	25. 5.01T
G-OSOW	PA-28-140 Cherokee	28-23780	G-AVWH	13. 6.94	Go-Hog Flying Ltd	Bournemouth	3. 8.00T
					(Op Airbourne School of Flying)		
G-OSPS	PA-18-95 Super Cub (L-18C-PI)		OO-SPS	9. 7.92	J.W.Macleod	Felthorpe	28. 3.99
	(Frame No.18-1527)	18-1555	G-AWRH/OO-HMI/ALAT 51-15555				
G-OSST	Colt 77A HAFB	737		28.10.85	British Airways plc	Heathrow	10.10.96A
					"Concorde II"		
G-OSTC	Gulfstream AA-5A Cheetah	AA5A-0848	N26967	22. 4.91	5th Generation Designs Ltd	Goodwood	29. 9.00T
G-OSTU	Gulfstream AA-5A Cheetah	AA5A-0807	G-BGCL	18. 4.95	Airhouse Corporation Ltd	Elstree	3. 7.00T
G-OSTY	Reims Cessna F.150G	0129	G-AVCU	21. 3.97	C.R Guggenheim	Bournemouth	10.10.99T
					(Op Airbourne School of Flying)		
G-OSUP	Lindstrand LBL-90A HAFB	098		17. 3.94	T.J.Orchard	Booker	19. 4.97T
					t/a British Airways Balloon Club "Goes Up"		
G-OSUS	Mooney M.20K (231)	25-0429	OY-SUS	7.11.94	J.B. & M.O.King	Goodwood	25.11.00
			(N3597H)				
G-OSVO	Cameron Hopper Servo 30SS HAFB	3077		30. 4.93	Servo & Electronic Sales Ltd	Lydd	26. 6.97A
					"Twocon"		
G-OSVY	Sky 31-24 HAFB	104		28. 5.98	Virgin Airship & Balloon Co Ltd	Telford	28. 5.99A
G-OTAC	Robinson R-22 Beta	2737		8.10.97	Aviation Corporation plc	Cheltenham	23.10.00T
G-OTAF	Aero L-39ZO Albatros	232337	N40VC	9. 2.95	C.P.B.Horsley	Duxford	25. 4.99P
			N159JC/(N4321X)/Chad AF/Libyan Arab AF 2337				
G-OTAL	ARV1 Super 2	024	G-BNGZ	10. 9.87	N.R.Beale	Shotteswell	1. 3.99P
	(Rotax 912)						
G-OTAM	Cessna 172M Skyhawk II	172-64098	N29060	13. 2.89	Tecair Aviation Ltd	Norwich	28.10.01T
G-OTAN	PA-18-135 Super Cub (L-21B-PI)		OO-TAN	28.10.96	S.D.Turner	Andrewsfield	13. 4.00
	(Frame No.18-3850)	18-3845	(OO-DPD)/R.Neth AF R-155/54-2445				
G-OTBY	PA-32-300 Six	32-7940219	N2932G	14. 2.91	GOTBY Ltd	Jersey	29. 3.00
G-OTCH	CFM Streak Shadow	K.207 & PFA/206-12401		28.10.93	H.E.Gotch	Redhill	9. 6.99P
	(Rotax 582)						
G-OTDB	MDHC Hughes 369E	0210E	G-BXUR	7. 4.98	Helisport Ltd	Biggin Hill	9. 7.01T
			HA-MSC				
G-OTED	Robinson R-22HP	0209	G-BMYR	17. 1.96	Andrews Heli-Lease Ltd	Denham	8. 2.99T
			ZS-HLG				
G-OTEL	Thunder Ax8-90 HAFB	1790		13. 6.90	D.N.Belton	Chard	3.12.92A
G-OTFT	PA-38-112 Tomahawk	38-78A0311	G-BNKW	14. 3.97	N.Papadroushotis	Luton	9. 4.00T
			N9274T				
G-OTHE	Enstrom 280C-UK Shark	1226	G-OPJT	22. 9.87	GTS Engineering (Coventry) Ltd	Coventry	27. 6.99
			G-BKCO				
G-OTHL	Robinson R-22 Beta	0738	G-DSGN	28.11.94	Thurston Helicopters (Engineering) Ltd		
						Redhill	2. 3.00T
G-OTIM	Bensen B.8MV	PFA G/101-1084		5. 6.90	T.J.Deane	Tilehurst, Reading)	
G-OTNT	Cameron Cider Bottle 120SS HAFB	3067		9. 7.93	A.J.Round	Wantage	24. 8.95A
G-OTOE	Aeronca 7AC Champion	7AC-4621	G-BRWW	2. 4.90	J.M.Gale Coombe Farm, Spreyton, Crediton		10. 5.95P
			N1070E/NC1070E		(Damaged Coombe Farm 31. 5.95)		
G-OTOO	Stolp SA.300 Starduster Too			26. 8.98	I.M.Castle (Market Harborough)		
		PFA/035-13352					
G-OTOY	Robinson R-22 Beta	0888	G-BPEW	5. 9.97	Tickstop Ltd Kimpton Park, Hitchin		4. 9.00T
G-OTRG	Cessna TR182 Turbo-Skylane RG II		(N736SU)	14. 3.79	M.J. & A.M.Bonnick t/a Thermodata Components		
		R182-00766				Little Shelford, Cambridge	22.10.01
G-OTRV	Van's RV-6	PFA/181-13302		27. 5.98	W.R.C.Williams-Wynne	(Tywyn)	
G-OTSP	Aerospatiale AS.355F1 Twin Squirrel		G-XPOL	31. 3.98	Aeromega Ltd	Boreham, Essex	23. 2.00T
		5177	G-BPRF/N363E		(Op Essex Police Air Support Unit)		
G-OTTI	Cameron OTTI 34SS HAFB	3490		23. 3.95	Ballonverbung Hamburg GmbH Kiel, Germany		17. 7.99A
G-OTTO	Cameron Katalog 82SS HAFB	2843		15. 6.92	Ballonverbung Hamburg GmbH Kiel, Germany		14. 7.99A
					"Otto Versand Katalog"		
G-OTUG	PA-18-150 Super Cub	18-5352	(G-BKNM)	17. 2.83	M.C.Woodhouse & B.F.Walker		
	(Frame No.18-5424)		PH-MBA/ALAT 18-5352			Oaksey Park/Nympsfield	16. 7.01
G-OTUP	Lindstrand LBL-180A HAFB	111		28. 3.94	Airborne Adventures Ltd	Skipton	19. 2.96T
G-OTVS*	Britten-Norman BN-2T Turbine Islander		G-BPBN	14. 2.83	Headcorn Parachute Club Ltd	Headcorn	18. 5.90
		419	G-BCMY		(Damaged Headcorn 11.3.89; open store 3.96)		
G-OTWO	Rutan Defiant	114		24. 6.87	A.J.Baggarley (Littlehampton)		21.8.88P*
	(Lyc O-320)				(Stored Lydd 11.97)		
G-OURO	Europa Avn Europa 16 & PFA/247-12522			13.12.93	J.R.Malpass	(Dronfield)	16.12.99P
	(NSI EA-81/100) (Tricyle u/c)						
G-OUVI	Cameron O-105 HAFB	1766		4. 5.89	P.Spellward "Uvistat II"	Bristol	31. 3.94A
					t/a Bristol University Hot Air Ballooning Society		
G-OUZO	Airbus A.320-231	449	EI-VIR	8.11.95	Virgin Atlantic Airways Ltd	Gatwick	7.11.01T
			N449RX/SX-BSV/N449RX/F-WWIG "Spirit of Melina"				

Regn	Type	C/n	P/I	Date	Owner/operator	Probable Base	CA Expy
G-OVAA	Colt Jumbo SS HAFB	1426		11. 5.89	Virgin Airship & Balloon Co Ltd	Telford	21. 9.96A
	(Conventional HAFB with nose/wings/tail of Virgin 747)				"Virgin Jumbo II"		
G-OVAX	Colt AS-80 Mk II Hot-Air Airship			3. 7.89	Vax Appliances Ltd	Droitwich	3. 8.92A
		1501			"Vax Airship"		
G-OVBF	Cameron A-250 HAFB	3494		1. 3.95	Virgin Balloon Flights Ltd	Northampton	4.11.99T
					"Virgin Oscar"		
G-OVBJ	Bell 206B Jet Ranger III	2734	G-BXDS	19. 2.98	Aeromega Helicopters (Engineering) Ltd		
			OY-HDK/N661PS			Stapleford	9. 7.00T
G-OVET	Cameron O-56 HAFB	3939		25. 6.96	E.J.A.Macholc	Saltburn-by-the-Sea	1. 5.99A
G-OVFM	Cessna 120	14720	N2119V	29. 4.88	G.Stevenson t/a Commair Grp	Nottingham	12. 7.99P
	(Cont O-200-A)		NC2119V				
G-OVFR	Reims Cessna F.172N Skyhawk II	1892		23. 5.79	Western Air (Thruxton) Ltd	Thruxton	13. 5.01T
G-OVID	Light Aero Avid Flyer	NMFC.11760	N879UP	31. 5.91	J.M.Walsh & D.F.Chamberlain		
	(Rotax 532)				(Stored 1.97)	Haverfordwest	30. 9.99P
G-OVMC	Reims Cessna F.152 II	1667		29. 5.79	J.A.Lyons	Gloucestershire	16. 8.01T
					t/a Staverton Flying School		
G-OVNR	Robinson R-22 Beta	1634		24.12.90	S.Lancaster & L.Clarke	Breighton	14. 5.00T
					t/a Rally Repaints		
G-OWAC	Reims Cessna F.152 II	1678	G-BHEB	25. 2.80	Barnes Olson Aeroleasing Ltd		
			(OO-HNW)		(Op Bristol Flying Centre) Bristol/Lulsgate		30. 4.01T
G-OWAK	Reims Cessna F.152 II	1677	G-BHEA	25. 2.80	A.S.Bamrah t/a Falcon F/Svs	Blackbushe	23.11.01T
					(Op European Flyers)		
G-OWAL	PA-34-220T Seneca III	3448030	D-GAPN	7. 7.98	Parkers Properties Ltd	(London EC4)	1. 9.01
			N9163K				
G-OWAR	PA-28-161 Warrior II	28-8616054	TF-OBO	18. 2.88	Bickertons Aerodromes Ltd	Denham	27. 3.00T
			N9521N		(Op Denham School of Flying)		
G-OWAZ	Pitts S-1C Special	43JM	G-BRPI	22.11.94	P.E.S.Latham "Tiny Dancer"	RAF Shawbury	13.12.99P
	(Lyc O-320)		N199M				
G-OWCG	Bell 222	47041	G-VERT	12. 8.94	Phoenix Helicopter Charters Ltd		
			G-JLBZ/G-BNDB/A40-CH			(Douglas, IOM)	9. 3.99T
G-OWDB	HS.125 Srs.700B	257040	G-BYFO	18. 2.99	Bizair Ltd.	Jersey	
			HB-VMD/VP-BPE/VR-BPE/N47TJ/EC-ETI/EC-375/G-OWEB/HZ-RC1				
G-OWEL	Colt 105A HAFB	1773		18. 5.90	S.R.Seager	Aylesbury	16. 3.98T
G-OWEN	K & S Jungster 1	PFA/44-10124		13.11.78	R.C.Owen	Danehill	
	(Cont C90)						
G-OWET	Thurston TSC-1A2 Teal	037	C-FNOR	28. 9.94	D.Nieman	Turweston	9. 4.98
			(N1342W)				
G-OWGC	Slingsby T-61F Venture T.2	1875	XZ555	14. 8.91	Wolds Gliding Club Ltd	Pocklington	1.11.00
G-OWIN	IRMA BN-2A-8 Islander	653	EI-AWM	22. 3.83	North London Parachute Centre Ltd		
			G-AYXE			Chatteris	1. 6.00A
G-OWIZ	Luscombe 8A Silvaire	3071	N71644	18.10.89	R.J.Pearson	(Cere-La-Ronde, France)	2. 8.99P
	(Cont A65)		NC71644				
G-OWLC	PA-31 Turbo Navajo	31-679	G-AYFZ	13. 6.91	Top Nosh Ltd	Jersey	1. 8.00
			N6771L				
G-OWOW	Cessna 152 II	152-83199	G-BMSZ	10. 5.95	A.S.Bamrah	Blackbushe	5.11.01T
			N47254		t/a Falcon F/Svs (Op European Flyers)		
G-OWWW	Europa Avn Europa	PFA/247-12683		9. 6.94	W.R.C. & J.F.Williams-Wynne		
						(Tywyn, Gwynedd)	
G-OWYN	Aviamilano F.14 Nibbio	208	HB-EVZ	2. 2.87	J.R.Wynn	Willingham	18. 8.99P
			I-SERE				
G-OXBY	Cameron N-90 HAFB	1993	PH-DUM	9. 6.94	C.A.Oxby "The Zit"	Doncaster	
G-OXKB	Cameron Jaguar XK8 Sports Car 110SS			9. 7.96	Flying Pictures Ltd	Fairoaks	8. 8.99T
	HAFB	3941			"Jaguar XK8"		
G-OXLI*	BAe Jetstream 4100	41003		5. 2.91	FR Aviation Ltd	Bournemouth	
					(For use in Hong Kong GFS static trials)		
G-OXTC	PA-23-250 Aztec D	27-4344	G-AZOD	31. 5.89	A.S.Bamrah	Biggin Hill	15. 6.98T
			N697RC/N6976Y		t/a Falcon F/Svs		
G-OXVI	VS.361 Spitfire LF.XVIe	CBAF.IX.4262	7246M	22. 8.89	Silver Victory BVBA (As "TD248/D" in 41 Sqn c/s)		
			TD248		(Karel Bos)	Antwerp-Deurne, Belgium	30. 7.99P
G-OYAK	SPP Yakovlev C.11	171205	EAF 705	25. 2.88	A.H.Soper	Earls Colne	5 1.00P
	(C/n quoted as 1701139 and/or 690120)		OK-KIH		(As "27" in Soviet AF c/s)		
G-OYES	Mainair Blade 912	1186-1198-7-W989		12.11.98	M.Irving	(Ware)	
G-OZAP	Hughes 369HS	33-0461S	G-FBHH	19. 2.99	G.R.Lloyd	Swansea	9. 9.99T
			N2186K/PK-AVH/PK-PDO				
G-OZAR	Enstrom 480	5007	G-BWFF	31. 7.95	Lancroft Air Ltd	(Oswestry)	5. 8.01T
G-OZBA	Airbus A.320-212	422	F-WWIP	25. 3.94	Monarch Airlines Ltd	Luton	24. 3.00T
G-OZBC	Airbus A.321-231	633	D-ASSE	24. 4.97	Monarch Airlines Ltd	Luton	23. 4.00T
			D-AVZJ/F-WWIJ				
G-OZEE	Light Aero Avid Speed Wing mk.4			18. 4.94	S.C.Goozee	Newton Peverill	4. 9.99P
	(Rotax 582)	PFA/189-12308					
G-OZLN	Moravan Zlin Z.242L	0651	OK-XNA	2.10.92	G.G.L.Thomas	Swansea	28. 3.99
			(SE-KMM)				
G-OZOI	Cessna R182 Skylane RGII	R182-01950	G-ROBK	31. 5.85	J.R. & F.L.Gibson Fleming t/a Ranston Farms		
						Ranston, Blandford Forum	28. 6.01
G-OZRH	BAe 146 Srs.200	E-2047	N188US	29. 1.96	Flightline Ltd	Stansted	1. 2.02T
			N364PS		(Op Alpine Flightline)		
G-OZZI	Pearce Jabiru SK	PFA/274-13176		15. 8.97	A.H.Godfrey & E.J.Stradling		
						(Weston-Super-Mare)	22. 6.99P

G-PAAA-PZZZ

Regn	Type	C/n	P/I	Date	Owner/operator	Probable Base	CA Expy
G-PACE	Robin R.1180T Aiglon	218		16.10.78	Millicron Instruments Ltd	Cranfield	14.10.00
G-PACL	Robinson R-22 Beta	1893	N2314S	17.12.91	R.Wharam	(Rotherham)	3. 2.01T
G-PADI	Cameron V-77 HAFB	1809		18. 8.88	R.F.Penney	Watford	3. 9.94A
G-PADS	Commander 114B	14637	N60987	15. 1.98	J.D'Arcy Mounter	Guernsey	27. 1.01T
G-PAGS	Aerospatiale SA.341G Gazelle 1	1155	G-OAFY	11. 3.96	P.A.G.Seers	North Weald	7.11.99T
			G-SFTH/G-BLAP/N62406				
G-PAIZ	PA-12 Super Cruiser	12-2018	N3215M	11. 4.94	B.R.Pearson	Eaglescott	11. 6.00T
G-PALL	PA-46-350P Malibu Mirage	4636091	G-RMST	4. 3.99	Pressurised A/c Leasing Ltd	(Sutton)	1. 4.00
G-PALS	Enstrom 280C-UK-2 Shark	1191	N5688M	17. 7.80	G.Firbank		
					Eastwood End Farm, Adlington, Macclesfield		22. 8.99
G-PAMS	Ted Smith Aerostar 601P	61P-0275-060	G-GAIR	27. 7.89	Oxspeed Ltd	Southampton	7.12.01
			N90488				
G-PAPS	PA-32R-301T Turbo Saratoga SP	32R-8529005	F-GELX	8. 7.97	Pump & Plant Services Ltd		
			N4385D			Halfpenny Green	23. 7.00
G-PAPU	Beechcraft 58PA Baron	TJ-74	G-NIPU	6. 7.89	Jetmore Ltd	Bristol/Lulsgate	10.12.00T
			N1PU/N313A/N1PU/N1PT/N1899L				
G-PARI	Cessna 172RG Cutlass II	172RG-0010	N4685R	19.11.79	Applied Signs Ltd	Tatenhill	22.11.98
G-PARR*	Colt Bottle 90SS HAFB	1953		15. 3.91	British Balloon Museum & Library	Newbury	29. 9.94A
	(Old Parr Whisky bottle shape)				"Old Parr"		
G-PASB*	MBB Bo.105D	S.135	VH-LSA	2. 3.89	The Helicopter Museum	Weston-super-Mare	
	(Original pod from 1994 rebuild; see G-WMAA)		G-BDMC/D-HDEC	(On rebuild 3.96)			
G-PASC	MBB Bo.105DBS/4	S.421	G-BNPS	27.10.89	Police Aviation Services Ltd		
			N4929M/D-HDMT		(Op Lincolnshire Ambulance Service)		
						RAF Waddington	9. 9.99T
G-PASD	MBB Bo.105DBS/4	S.656	G-BNRS	27.10.89	Police Aviation Services Ltd		26. 6.00T
			N14ES/N4572Q/D-HDTZ			Gloucestershire	
G-PASF	Aerospatiale AS.355F1 Twin Squirrel	5033	G-SCHU	7. 3.91	Police Aviation Services Ltd	Newcastle	16.12.01T
			N915EPFA	G/1N5777H	(Op Northumbria Police Air Support Unit)		
G-PASG	MBB Bo.105DBS/4	S.819	G-MHSL	7.12.92	Police Aviation Services Ltd		
			D-HFCC			Gloucestershire	1. 4.99T
G-PASH	Aerospatiale AS.355F1 Twin Squirrel	5040	F-GHLI	17. 5.96	Police Aviation Services Ltd		
			LX-HUPFA	G/1F-GHLI/N356E		Gloucestershire	24. 3.01T
G-PASS	Boeing MDH MD.900 Explorer	900-00056	N9234P	12.10.98	Police Aviation Services Ltd		
	(MD.902 configuration)					Gloucestershire	AC
G-PASU	PBN BN-2T Turbine Islander	2144	5T-BSA	27. 5.93	Police Aviation Services Ltd		
			G-BJYY			Gloucestershire	10. 7.00T
G-PASV	PBN BN-2B-21 Islander	2157	G-BKJH	26. 2.92	Police Aviation Services Ltd	Teesside	18. 7.00T
			HC-BNR/G-BKJH				
G-PASX	MBB Bo.105DBS/4	S.814	D-HDZX	20.12.89	Police Aviation Services Ltd	Shoreham	10. 1.02T
					(Op Sussex Police Helicopter Unit)		
G-PATF	Europa Avtn Europa	PFA/247-12757		5. 1.99	E P Farrell	(Beaconsfield)	
G-PATG	Cameron O-90 HAFB	3856		13. 3.96	P.A. & A.J.A.Bubb	Guildford	16. 5.99A
					"Purple Rain"		
G-PATN	Socata TB-10 Tobago	307	G-LUAR	25. 3.97	A.T.Paton	Blackbushe	23.11.00
G-PATP	Lindstrand LBL-77A HAFB	471		8. 7.97	P.Pruchnickyj	Weston Turville, Bucks	3. 7.99
G-PATS	Europa Avn Europa	PFA/247-12888		19. 7.95	D.J.G.Kesterton	(Milton Keynes)	
G-PATZ	Europa Avn Europa	PFA/247-12625		2. 6.98	H.P.H.Griffin	(Uxbridge)	
G-PAVL	Robin R.3000/120	170		22.11.96	Newcharter (UK) Ltd	Elstree	6. 2.00T
G-PAWL	PA-28-140 Cherokee	28-24456	G-AWEU	8. 9.82	C.M.Howells (Stored 12.97)	Barton	13. 5.01
G-PAWS	Gulfstream AA-5A Cheetah	AA5A-0806	N2623Q	8. 2.82	Plane Talking Ltd	Elstree	11. 5.01T
G-PAXX	PA-20-135 Pacer	20-1107	(G-ARCE)	20. 5.83	D.W. & M.R.Grace	Truro	1. 6.01
			F-BLLA/CN-TDJ/F-DADR				
G-PAZY	Pazmany PL-4A	PFA/17-10378	G-BLAJ	20.11.89	C.R.Nash	(Fordingbridge)	3.10.95P
	(Cont A65)						
G-PBBT	Cameron N-56 HAFB	1535		23. 6.87	E.C.Moore "Little Book"	Great Missenden	21. 9.96A
G-PBEL	CFM Shadow Srs.DD	305-DD		27.10.98	CFM Aircraft Ltd	Leiston	
G-PBES	Robinson R-22 Beta	1491	G-EXOR	17. 3.95	B.C.Seedle	Blackpool	17.10.99T
			G-CMCM		t/a Brian Seedle Helicopters		
G-PBUS	Pearce Jabiru SK	PFA/274-13269		18. 8.98	G.R.Pybus	Durham	
G-PBYY	Enstrom 280FX	2077	G-BXKV	15. 8.97	Southern Air Ltd	Shoreham	28. 8.00
			D-HHML				
G-PCAF	Pietenpol Aircamper	PFA/47-12433		1. 6.94	C.C. & F.M.Barley	(Farnborough)	16. 7.01
G-PCDP	Moravan Zlin Z.526F Trener Master	1163	SP-CDP	24.10.94	R.A.Mills t/a Zlin Group	Fairoaks	25. 1.01
G-PCOM	PA-30-160 Twin Comanche B	30-1053	HB-LDD	15.10.97	H. & P.Robinson	(Cheltenham)	21. 5.01
			N7957Y				
G-PCUB*	PA-18-135 Super Cub	18-3874	(PH-KER)	16. 2.81	M.J.Wilson	Turweston	28. 3.98
	(L-21B-PI) (Frame No.18-3893)		R.Neth AF R-184/54-2474	(Op Florence F/Grp)	(Cancelled by CAA 10.3.99)		
	(Regd incorrectly as c/n 18-3674)						
G-PDGG	Aeromere F.8L Falco Srs.3	208	OO-TOS	6. 1.98	P.D.G.Grist	(Stamford)	7. 5.01
			I-BLIZ				
G-PDHJ	Cessna T182R Turbo Skylane II	T182-68092	N6888H	3. 1.85	P.G.Vallance Ltd	Charlwood/Redhill	5.11.00
G-PDMH	Cessna 340A II	340A-0461	N6282N	20. 4.98	D.R.C.Knight	(Thame)	22. 4.01
			G-RITA/N6282N				
G-PDOC	PA-44-180 Seminole	44-7995090	G-PVAF	17.12.85	T.White t/a Medicare	Newcastle	5. 5.01T
			N2242A				

Regn	Type	C/n	P/I	Date	Owner/operator	Probable Base	CA Expy
G-PDOG	Cessna L-19E Bird Dog (Regd as Cessna 305C)	24550	F-GKGP ALAT	25. 9.98	N.D.Needham	(Sleaford)	AC
G-PDSI	Cessna 172N Skyhawk II	172-70420	N739BU	4. 1.88	P.A.Hosey & A Clements t/a DA F/Grp	Lasham	2. 2.01T
G-PDWI	Revolution Helicopters Mini-500	0248		14. 2.97	P.Waterhouse	(Stockport)	
G-PEAK	Agusta-Bell 206B JetRanger II	8242	G-BLJE SE-HBW	7. 3.94	J.D.Downes t/a Peak Air Charter	Costock, Loughborough	9. 2.00T
G-PEAL	Aerotek Pitts S-2A Special (Lyc AEIO-360)	2048	N81LF N48KA	11. 5.88	Plymouth Executive Avn Ltd (Damaged nr Kidderminster 28.6.91; stored 9.97)	Plymouth	21. 2.92T
G-PEAT	Cessna 421B Golden Eagle	421B-0432	G-BBIJ N41073	5. 4.84	Golden Airways Ltd	Cambridge	12. 8.01T
G-PEGG	Colt 90A HAFB	1550		28. 6.89	Ballon Vole Association	Fontaine Les Dijon, France	19. 5.99A
G-PEGI	PA-34-200T Seneca II	34-7970339	N2907A	27.11.89	Tayflite Ltd	Dundee/Manchester	20. 7.01T
G-PEKT	Socata TB-20 Trinidad	532	N24AS	28. 7.89	A.J.Dales	(Hull)	11. 1.99
G-PENN	Gulfstream AA-5B Tiger	AA5B-0996	(I-TIGR) N3756L	4. 7.80	L.F.Banks	Denham	30. 9.01T
G-PERR*	Cameron Bottle 60SS HAFB	699		28. 1.81	British Balloon Museum "Perrier" (Stored 9.93)	Newbury	3. 6.84A
G-PERZ	Bell 206B Jet Ranger III	4411	N6272T	7. 1.97	D.J.Gilmour t/a Intrepid Avn Co	North Weald	27. 2.00T
G-PEST	Hawker Tempest II (Bristol-built) (Regd with c/n "1181")	12202	HA604 (RIAF)/MW401	9.10.89	Tempest Two Ltd (On rebuild 11.96)	Sandtoft	AC
G-PETR	PA-28-140 Cherokee Cruiser	28-7425320	G-BCJL	23. 9.85	Marnham Investments Ltd	(Castletown, IOM)	22. 1.00
G-PFAA	EAA Model P2 Biplane PEB/03 & PFA/1338 (Cont PC90)			19. 9.78	E.W.B.Comber	Willingham	1. 5.99P
G-PFAD*	Wittman W.8 Tailwind (Cont PC60)	PFA/31-10259		19. 9.78	Not known (Stored 8.93)	Priory Farm, Tibenham	21. 4.87P
G-PFAF	Clutton FRED Srs.II	PFA/29-10310		30.10.78	M.S.Perkins	(Hinckley)	
G-PFAG	Evans VP-1 (VW1600)	PFA/7022		13.11.78	J.A.Hatch	Netherthorpe	30. 6.89P
G-PFAH	Evans VP-1 (VW1834)	PFA/7004		23.11.78	J.A.Scott	Chestnut Farm, Tipps End	1. 6.98P
G-PFAL	Clutton FRED Srs.II (VW1600)	PFA/29-10243		7.12.78	J.M.Robinson (Stored 4.96)	Bann Foot, Lough Neagh	27. 7.88P
G-PFAO	Evans VP-1	PFA/7008		12.12.78	P.W.Price	(Cheadle)	
G-PFAP	Phoenix Currie Wot (Cont O-200-A) (Built as an SE-5A replica)	PFA/58-10315		12.12.78	J.H.Seed (As "C1904" in RFC c/s)	Black Spring Farm, Castle Bytham	17.12.96P
G-PFAR	Isaacs Fury II (Cont O-200-A)	PFA/11-10220		18.12.78	K.M.Potts (As "K2059" in 25 Sqdn RAF c/s)	Dunkeswell	26. 1.99P
G-PFAT	Monnett Sonerai II (VW1834)	PFA/15-10312		26.10.78	H.B.Carter (Stored Newcastle 5.93)	(St.Clement, Jersey)	24.10.92P
G-PFAW	Evans VP-1 (VW1834)	PFA/62-10183		18.12.78	R.F.Shingler	Forest Farm, Welshpool	9. 9.99P
G-PFAY	EAA Biplane	PFA/1525		18.12.78	A.K.Lang & A.L.Young (Project abandoned 5.98)	(Stoke-sub-Hamdon)	
G-PFBT	Vickers Viscount 806	265	G-AOYP	22. 3.94	Heli-Lift Ltd (Parcelforce c/s)	Rand, South Africa	19. 5.99T
G-PFML	Robinson R-44 Astro	0082		9. 9.94	Helicopter Training & Hire Ltd	Belfast	9.10.00T
G-PGAC	Dyn'Aero MCR-01	PFA/301-13186		27. 1.99	G.A.Coatesworth	(Cambridge)	
G-PHAA	Reims Cessna F.150M Commuter	1159	G-BCPE	19. 6.97	PHA Aviation Ltd	Elstree	17. 3.01T
G-PHEL	Robinson R-22 Beta	1669	G-RUMP N2405T	15. 8.96	Focal Point Communications Ltd	Denham	30. 4.00
G-PHIL	Brookland Hornet (VW1600)	17		7. 7.78	A.J.Philpotts (Stored 5.90)	St.Merryn	11. 8.89P
G-PHON	Cameron Phone SS HAFB (Motorola Microtac Mobile Phone)	2505	G-BTEY	13.12.91	Redmalt Ltd "Motorola Microtac"	Witham, Essex	14. 7.97A
G-PHOT	Thunder & Colt Film Cassette SS HAFB	4507		3. 2.99	Flying Pictures Ltd	Fairoaks	
G-PHSI	Colt 90A HAFB	2181		12. 5.92	P.H.Strickland & Simpson (Piccadilly) Ltd "Daks"	Bedford/London W1	8. 7.99A
G-PHTG	Socata TB-10 Tobago	1008		15.11.89	A.R.Murray	Shoreham	13.10.99
G-PHYL	Denney Kitfox Mk.4	PFA/172A-12189		14. 9.98	J.Dunn	(Basingstoke)	
G-PIAF	Thunder Ax7-65 HAFB	1885		19.11.90	L.Battersey "No Regrets/La Vie en Rose"	Newbury	24. 3.94A
G-PICT	Colt 180A HAFB	1723		22. 3.90	J.L.Guy	Skipton	29. 6.99T
G-PIDS	Boeing 757-225	22195	N505EA	9. 1.95	Airtours International Airways Ltd	Manchester	23. 2.01T
G-PIEL	Menavia Piel CP.301A Emeraude	218	G-BARY F-BIJR	17.11.88	P.R.Thorne	Cublington	17. 2.99P
G-PIES*	Thunder Ax7-77Z HAFB	263		13. 2.80	Not known	(Nottingham)	N/E(A)
G-PIET	Pietenpol Air Camper	PFA/47-12267		1. 4.93	N.D.Marshall	(Hemel Hempstead)	
G-PIGG	Lindstrand Flying Pig SS HAFB	473		18. 8.97	Iris Heidenreich	Remscheid, Germany	31.10.99A
G-PIGS	Socata Rallye 150ST	2696	G-BDWB	13. 6.88	D.Hodgson t/a Boonhill F/Grp	Wombleton	24. 4.00
G-PIGY	Short SC.7 Skyvan 3A-100	SH.1943	LX-JUL 5T-MAM/(G-14-111)	21.12.95	Hunting Avn Ltd	Oxford/Weston-on-the-Green	28. 1.00T

Regn	Type	C/n	P/I	Date	Owner/operator	Probable Base	CA Expy
G-PIIX	Cessna P210N Pressurised P210-00130 Centurion II		G-KATH (N4898P)	12. 6.95	D.E.Glass	Edinburgh	8.11.98
G-PIKE	Robinson R-22 Mariner	1718M		18. 3.91	Sloane Helicopters Ltd	Sywell	23.11.00T
G-PIKK	PA-28-140 Cherokee	28-22932	G-AVLA N11C/(N9509W)	19. 8.88	L.P. & I.Keegan	Dundee	4. 3.01
G-PILE	Rotorway Exec 90 (RI 162)	5143		27. 7.93	J.B.Russell	Magheramorne, Co.Antrim	5.11.98P
G-PILL	Light-Aero Avid Flyer mk.4	PFA/189-12333		12. 8.97	D.R.Meston	(Poole)	
G-PINE	Thunder Ax8-90 HAFB	1546		30. 5.89	J.A.Pine	London W4	15. 8.92A
G-PING	Gulfstream AA-5A Cheetah	AA5A-0878	G-OCWC G-WULL/N27153	6.12.95	Plane Talking Ltd (Op London School of Flying)	Elstree	4. 6.00T
G-PINT	Cameron Barrel 60 SS HAFB (Wells Brewery Beer Barrel shape)	794		4. 1.82	D.K.Fish "Charles Wells"	Bedford	13. 2.98A
G-PINX	Lindstrand Pink Panther SS HAFB	032		23. 4.93	L.V.Mastis	(USA)	30. 5.99A
G-PIPA	PA-28-181 Archer III	2890215		14.12.94	N.J. & P.D.Fuller	Cambridge	10. 3.01
G-PIPR	PA-18-95 Super Cub (Frame No.18-832)	18-826	G-BCDC 4X-ANQ/IDF/AF/4X-ADE	11.10.96	R.G.Trute	(Braunton)	15. 7.01T
G-PIPS	Van's RV-4	PFA/181-11836		3. 8.90	C.J.Marsh	(Reading)	
G-PIPY	Cameron Scottish Piper 105SS HAFB	3815		30. 1.96	Cameron Balloons Ltd Almondsbury, Glos (To Muir Moffat) "The Scotsman"		19. 2.99A
G-PITS	Pitts S-2AE Special (Lyc IO-360)	PFA/09-11001		4. 7.85	T.McManus & D.F.van Lonkhuyzen t/a The Eitlean Grp	Weston, Ireland	24. 6.99P
G-PITZ	Pitts S-2A Special (Lyc AEIO-360)	100ER	N183ER	2.10.87	A.K.Halvorsen	Barton	1.10.98P
G-PIXS	Cessna 336 Skymaster	336-0130	N86648	9. 9.88	Atlantic Bridge Avn Ltd (Stored 11.97)	Lydd	29. 1.95T
G-PJMT	Lancair 320	PFA/191-12348		8. 5.98	M.T.Holland	(Torquay)	7. 2.01P
G-PJRT*	BAe Jetstream 4100	41002		5. 2.91	British Aerospace (Operations) Ltd (Stored 7.97 - cancelled as PWFU 27.3.99)	Prestwick	1. 5.94S
G-PJTM	Reims Cessna FR.172K Hawk II	0611	EI-CHJ G-BFIF	13.10.98	P J McNamara t/a Jane Air	(Milford Haven)	12.10.01T
G-PKPK	Schweizer Hughes 269C (300C)	S.1454	EI-CAR N69A	3. 8.93	Carla Sidney-Woollett	(London SW3)	13. 8.99T
G-PLAC	PA-31-350 Chieftain	31-8052038	G-OLDA G-BNDS/N131PP/N3550N	23.12.98	Vale Aviation Ltd	(London SW1)	7.10.00T
G-PLAN	Reims Cessna F.150L Commuter	1066	PH-SPR	11. 8.78	D.A.Johnson t/a G-PLAN F/Grp	Barton	11.11.99
G-PLAY	Robin R.2112	170	F-ODIT	1. 8.79	D.R.Austin	High Cross, Ware	20.12.97
G-PLEE	Cessna 182Q Skylane II	182-66570	N95538	4.12.87	Sunderland Parachute Centre Ltd Peterlee t/a Peterlee Parachute Centre		11. 3.00
G-PLGI	BAe HS.125 Srs.700B	257034	N510HS N7007X/(XA-....)/N7007X/G-BFXT/G-5-14	26. 7.95	Polygram Record Operations Ltd	Heathrow	11. 9.99T
G-PLIV	Pazmany PL-4 (Cont A65)	PFA/17-10155		19.12.78	B.P.North	(Aylesbury)	
G-PLMB	Aerospatiale AS.350B Ecureuil	1207	G-BMMB C-GBEW/(N36033)	26. 3.86	PLM Dollar Group Ltd	Inverness	15. 2.01T
G-PLMC	Aerospatiale AS.350B Ecureuil	1731	G-BKUM	23. 8.88	PLM Dollar Group Ltd	Cumbernauld	3.11.01T
G-PLMH	Eurocopter AS.350B2 Ecureuil	2156	F-WQDJ G-PLMH/HB-XTE/F-WQPK/HB-XTE	9. 1.95	PLM Dollar Group Ltd	Inverness	25. 2.01T
G-PLMI	Aerospatiale SA.365C1 Dauphin 2	5001	F-GFYH F-WZAE	19. 6.95	PLM Dollar Group Ltd	Inverness	8. 7.98T
G-PLOW	Hughes 269B	67-0317	G-AVUM	13. 9.83	Sulby Aerial Surveys Ltd (Cockpit section only stored Bruntingthorpe 8.97)	Sywell	29.11.92
G-PLPC	Schweizer Hughes 269C (300C)	S.1558	G-JMAT	14. 4.97	Power Lines, Piper & Cables Ltd	Carluke, Lanark	3. 6.01
G-PLUG*	Colt 105A HAFB	1958		17. 4.91	British Balloon Museum & Library Newbury		14. 8.95T
G-PLUS	PA-34-200T Seneca II	34-8070111	N81406	25. 3.80	C.G.Strasser t/a Skycabs	Jersey	9. 5.01
G-PLXI	BAe ATP (Development a/c with PW 127D engines)	2001	G-MATP (G-OATP)	26. 8.94	British Aerospace (Aircraft) Ltd (Stored 10.97)	Woodford	2.12.92P
G-PMAM	Cameron V-65 HAFB	1155		29. 5.85	P.A.Meecham "Tempus Fugit"	Milton-under-Wychwood	23. 7.99A
G-PMNF	VS.361 Spitfire HF.IX CBAF.10372		SAAF TA805	29. 4.96	P.R.Monk (On rebuild 1995)	(Maidstone)	
G-PNEU	Colt Bibendum 110SS HAFB	4223		5. 1.98	The Aerial Display Co Ltd	Looe	22.11.99A
G-PNUT*	Cameron Mr.Peanut 35SS HAFB	643	N400AB G-PNUT	4. 2.80	British Balloon Museum & Library Newbury "Mr.Peanut" (Stored)		
G-POAH	Sikorsky S-76B	760399		30. 3.92	The Peninsula & Oriental Steam Navigation Co Ltd (Op P&O Avn Ltd)	Stansted	17. 5.01T
G-POLT	Robinson R-44 Astro	0370		24. 9.97	Lyntonworth Ltd	Solihull	24. 9.00T
G-POLY	Cameron N-77 HAFB	428		13. 7.78	D.M.Barnes, N.F.Biggs, J.L.Hinton, M.A.C.Life & D.J.Thornley t/a The Empty Wallets Balloon Grp "Polywallets"	Bristol	25. 7.88A
G-POND	Oldfield Baby Lakes (Cont A80)	01	N87ED	2.10.90	H.Hillenbrand Rothenburg-Tauber, Germany		16.12.99P
G-POOH	Piper J3C-65 Cub (Frame No.7015)	6932	F-BEGY NC38324	17.10.79	P. & H.Robinson Upper Harford Farm, Bourton-on-the-Water		8. 4.01

Regn	Type	C/n	P/I	Date	Owner/operator	Probable Base	CA Expy
G-POOL	ARV1 Super 2	025	G-BNHA	28. 8.87	P.A.Dawson (Stored 6.97)	Kemble	9. 9.90T
G-POOP	Dyn'Aero MCR-01	PFA/301-13190		5.11.97	P.Bondar	(Moulton, Newmarket)	
G-POPA	Beechcraft A36 Bonanza	E-2177	N7007F	20. 5.92	R.G.Jones	Southend	28. 1.02
			N7204R				
G-POPE	Eiri PIK.20E Srs.1	20257		5. 3.80	C.J.Hadley "PE"	Membury/Bidford	6. 6.01
G-POPI	Socata TB-10 Tobago	315	G-BKEN	20. 4.90	I.S.Hacon & C.J.Earle	Seething	27. 3.01
			(G-BKEL)				
G-POPP*	Colt 105A HAFB	1776		1. 3.91	Flying Pictures Ltd	Fairoaks	21.11.96A
					"Champagne Mercier" (Cancelled as WFU 5.02.99)		
G-POPS	PA-34-220T Seneca III	34-8133150	N8407H	11. 6.90	Alpine Ltd	Jersey	20. 6.99
G-POPW	Cessna 182S Skylane	182-80204	N9451F	10. 7.98	Billy Blue Ltd	(Olney)	15. 7.01
G-PORK	Grumman-American AA-5B Tiger		EI-BMT	28. 2.84	J.W. & B.A.Flint	Southampton	27. 5.99T
		AA5B-0625					
G-PORT	Bell 206B JetRanger III	2784	N37AH	23. 8.89	Image Computer Systems Ltd	Thruxton	15. 8.01T
			N39TV/N397TV/N2774R	(Op Fast Helicopters)			
G-POSH	Colt 56A HAFB	822	G-BMPT	10. 6.86	B.K.Rippon	Didcot	24. 7.99A
G-POTT	Robinson R-44 Astro	0383		21.11.97	W.W.Potter International (1991) Ltd		
						Sowerby Bridge	27.11.00T
G-POWL	Cessna 182R Skylane II	182-67813	N9070G	11.11.82	Hillhouse Estates Ltd		
			D-EOMF/N6265N			Bowldown Farm, Tetbury	27. 4.01
G-POWR	Agusta A.109E Power	11014	G-BXUD	20. 7.98	Powersene Ltd	(London W1)	16. 6.01T
G-PPAH	Enstrom 480	5032		9. 3.98	Cumbrian Seafoods Ltd	(Maryport)	8. 4.01
G-PPLH	Robinson R-22 Beta	1007		11. 5.89	Status Investments Ltd	(Sheffield)	22. 4.99T
G-PPPP	Denney Kitfox mk.3 771 & PFA/172-11830			9. 1.91	S.P.Woodhouse & S.A.Tuff		
	(Rotax 582)					Goosedale Farm, Market Bosworth	31. 5.99P
G-PRAG	Brugger MB.2 Colibri	PFA/43-10362		29.11.78	D.Frankland t/a Colibri F/Grp	RAF Mona	31. 7.99P
	(VW1835)						
G-PRET	Robinson R-44 Astro	0381		8.10.97	J.Metcalfe t/a Air Charter	(London SW1)	15.10.00T
G-PRIM	PA-38-112 Tomahawk	38-78A0669	N2398A	28. 1.87	Braddock Ltd	White Waltham	25.12.01T
G-PRNT	Cameron V-90 HAFB	2819		23. 3.92	E.K.Gray	Droitwich	30.10.98A
G-PROD	Eurocopter AS.350B2 Ecureuil	2825		7. 2.95	Prodrive Ltd	Banbury	29. 3.01T
G-PROM	Aerospatiale AS.350B Ecureuil	1486	G-MAGY	11.10.96	JPM Ltd	Horsham	23.10.99T
			G-BIYC				
G-PROP	Gulfstream AA-5A Cheetah	AA5A-0845	G-BHKU	16. 2.84	Fortune Technology Ltd	Biggin Hill	28. 5.01T
			(OO-HTF)		(Op Biggin Hill School of Flying)		
G-PROV	Hunting P.84	PAC/W/23905		13.12.83	Bushfire Investments Ltd	North Weald	11.12.99P
	Jet Provost T.52A (T.4)		Sing.AF 352/S.Yemen AF 104/G-27-7/XS228 (R.McCathy)				
G-PRSI	Cyclone Pegasus Quantum 15-912	7492		17.12.98	P.R.Stevens	(New Milton)	16.12.99P
G-PRTT	Cameron N-31 HAFB	1374		6.11.86	J.M.Albury "Baby Pritt"	Cirencester	14.11.99A
G-PRXI	VS.365 Spitfire PR.XI 6S/583723		PL983	6. 6.83	Wizzard Investments Ltd	North Weald	22. 5.93P
	(C/n quoted as 6S/501431)		G-15-109/N74138/PL983 (As "PL983" in 4 Sqdn, 2 TAF c/s)				
G-PSFT	PA-28-161 Warrior II	28-8416021	N4328P	1. 8.96	SFT Europe Ltd	Bournemouth	6.11.00T
			N4328P				
G-PSIC	North American P-51C-10 Mustang		N51PR	16. 4.98	Patina Ltd	Chino, USA	AC
		103-26778	43-25147		(Op by The Fighter Collection) "Princess Elizabeth"		
	(Composite from major components P-51D	IDF/AF 13)	(As "2106449/HO-W" in 487th FS/362nd FS USAAF c/s)				
G-PSON	Colt Cylinder One SS HAFB	1780	PH-SON	14. 3.95	M.E.White	Dublin	7. 8.99A
	(Panasonic Battery Shape)						
G-PSST	Hawker Hunter F.58A	HABL-003115	J-4104	12. 2.97	Heritage Aviation Developments Ltd		
			G-9-317/A2568/XF947 (As "J-4104")			Kemble	22.10.99P
G-PTAG	Europa Avt Europa	PFA/247-13121		14.12.98	R.C.Harrison	(Market Raisen)	
G-PTRE	Socata TB-20 Trinidad	762	G-BNKU	14. 6.88	Trantshore Ltd	Rochester	21. 4.01
G-PTWO	Pilatus P.2-05	600-30	U-110	26. 2.81	Rentair Ltd	(Jersey)	12. 8.94P
			A-110		(As "U-110" in Swiss AF c/s)		
G-PTYE	Europa Avn Europa 1 & PFA/247-12496			22. 1.96	J.Tye "Harriet"	Ashbourne	24. 2.01P
	(Rotax 912UL)						
G-PUBS*	Colt Beer Glass 56SS HAFB	037		7. 6.79	Not known "Beer Glass"	?	
G-PUDL	PA-18-150 Super Cub	18-7292	SE-CSE	24. 2.98	R.A.Roberts	(Billingshurst)	24. 2.01
G-PUDS	Europa Avn Europa	PFA/247-12999		9.10.97	I.Milner	(Appleby-in-Westmorland)	
G-PUFF	Thunder Ax7-77 Bolt HAFB	165		17.11.78	C.A.Gould	Ipswich	20. 8.99A
					t/a Intervarsity Balloon Club "Puffin II"		
G-PUFN	Cessna 340A II	340A-0114	N532KG	4.12.96	The Puffin Club Ltd	Leicester	3.12.99T
			N532KC/N5477J				
G-PULL*	PA-18-150 Super Cub	18-5356	PH-MBB	17. 2.83	R.A.Yates	Sibsey	2. 4.89A
	(Frame No.18-5429)		ALAT 18-5356		(Crashed Eaglescott 13.6.86; stored 8.90)		
G-PUMA	Aerospatiale AS.332L Super Puma	2038	F-WMHB	31. 1.83	Bond Helicopters Ltd	Aberdeen	12. 4.00T
G-PUMB	Aerospatiale AS.332L Super Puma	2075		31. 1.83	Bond Helicopters Ltd	Aberdeen	15. 5.00T
G-PUMD	Aerospatiale AS.332L Super Puma	2077	F-WXFD	31. 1.83	Bond Helicopters Ltd	Aberdeen	23. 8.99T
G-PUME	Aerospatiale AS.332L Super Puma	2091		3. 8.83	Bond Helicopters Ltd	Aberdeen	6. 9.00T
G-PUMG(2)	Aerospatiale AS.332L Super Puma	2018	F-ODOS	3. 8.83	Bond Helicopters Ltd	Aberdeen	14. 5.99T
G-PUMH	Aerospatiale AS.332L Super Puma	2101		3. 8.83	Bond Helicopters Ltd	Aberdeen	22. 5.01T
G-PUMI	Aerospatiale AS.332L Super Puma	2170		27. 1.86	Bond Helicopters Ltd	Aberdeen	21. 5.99T
G-PUMM	Eurocopter AS.332L-2 Super Puma	2477		29. 7.98	Bond Helicopters Ltd	Aberdeen	21. 9.99T
G-PUMO	Eurocopter AS.332L-2 Super Puma	2467		30. 9.98	Bond Helicopters Ltd	Aberdeen	25.10.99T
G-PUNK	Thunder Ax8-105 HAFB	1719		28. 3.90	D.J.Farrar	Leeds	15. 5.99T
G-PUPP	Beagle B.121 Pup 2	B121-174	G-BASD	23.11.93	P.A.Teichman	Elstree	16. 4.99
			(SE-FOG)/G-BASD				

Regn	Type	C/n	P/I	Date	Owner/operator	Probable Base	CA Expy
G-PURR	Gulfstream AA-5A Cheetah	AA5A-0794	G-BJDN N26893	22. 2.82	N.Bass t/a Nabco Retail Display	Elstree	29. 8.99T
G-PURS	Rotorway Exec 152 (RW152)	3827		19. 1.90	J.E.Houseman	Clitheroe	5. 6.96P
G-PUSH	Rutan LongEz	PFA/74A-10740		11. 7.83	E.G.Peterson	(Nottingham)	
G-PUSI	Cessna T303 Crusader	T303-00273	N3479V	26. 7.88	Walter Swinburn Ltd	Oxford	18. 5.00T
G-PUSS	Cameron N-77 HAFB	1577		6.10.87	The Balloon Club Ltd t/a Bristol Balloons "Dick Whittington"	Bristol	20. 3.99A
G-PUTT	Cameron Golfball 76SS HAFB	2060	LX-KIK	8. 8.95	D.P.Hopkins t/a Lakeside Lodge Golf Centre	Pidley, Huntingdon	
G-PVBF	Lindstrand LBL-260S HAFB	504		7. 4.98	Virgin Balloon Flights Ltd (London SE16)		27. 4.99T
G-PVCU	Cameron N-77 HAFB	4376		22. 5.98	R.G.March	Market Harborough	4. 6.99A
G-PVET	DHC.1 Chipmunk 22	C1/0017	WB565	23. 5.97	Connect Properties Ltd (As "WB565")	(Abingdon)	9. 9.00T
G-PYLN	Cameron Pylon 80SS HAFB (Electricity Pylon shape)	2958	G-BUSO	18. 1.93	Virgin Airship and Balloon Co Ltd	Telford	25. 4.97A
G-PYOB	Aerospatiale SA.341G Gazelle 1	1145	G-IYOB G-WELA/G-SFTD/G-RIFC/G-SFTD/N641HM/N341BB/F-WKQH	8. 8.95	Henry Starnes (Holdings) Ltd (Maidstone)		23. 7.00
G-PYRO	Cameron N-65 HAFB	567		8. 1.80	A.C.Booth "Pyromania"	Bristol	4. 8.99A
G-PZAZ	PA-31-350 Navajo Chieftain	31-7405214	G-VTAX (G-UTAX)/N54266	18. 1.95	Air Medical Ltd	Oxford	22. 5.00T
G-PZIZ	PA-31-350 Navajo Chieftain	31-7405429	G-CAFZ G-BPPT/N54297	30.10.98	Air Medical Ltd	Oxford	10.10.98T

G-RAAA-RZZZ

Regn	Type	C/n	P/I	Date	Owner/operator	Probable Base	CA Expy
G-RACA*	Hunting-Percival P57/49		WM735	2. 9.80	Not known Long Marston		4.11.80P*
	P.57 Sea Prince T.1				(Open storage 8.96 - for removal to Carlisle)		
G-RACO	PA-28R-200 Cherokee Arrow II		N1498X	12. 9.91	Graco Grp Ltd	Barton	2. 2.01
		28R-7535300					
G-RADA	Soko P-2 Kraguj	024	30140	25. 9.96	Steerworld Ltd	Fairoaks	22. 6.98P
			(Yugoslav AF)				
G-RADI	PA-28-181 Archer II	28-8690002	N2582X	6. 5.98	G.S. & D.V.Foster	(Ashtead)	21. 5.01
			N9608N				
G-RAEM	Rutan LongEz 557 & PFA/74A-10638			15. 3.82	G.F.H.Singleton t/a Easy Grp	(Matlock)	18. 6.93P
	(Lyc O-235)						
G-RAES	Boeing 777-236ER	27491	(G-ZZZN)	10. 6.97	British Airways plc	Heathrow	9. 6.00T
					(Delftblue Daybreak t/s)		
G-RAFA	Grob G-115A	8081	D-EGVV	2. 3.89	RAF College F/C Ltd	RAF Cranwell	31. 3.01T
G-RAFB	Grob G-115A	8079	D-EGVV	2. 3.89	RAF College F/C Ltd	RAF Cranwell	22. 3.01T
G-RAFC	Robin R.2112 Alpha	192		19. 5.80	J.E.Churchill	(Huntingdon)	25. 6.01
					t/a RAF Charlie Group		
G-RAFE	Thunder Ax7-77 Bolt HAFB	176		18.12.78	L.P.Hooper	Bristol	9. 8.99A
					t/a Giraffe Balloon Syndicate		
G-RAFF	Gates Learjet 35A	35A-504	N8568B	12. 6.84	Graff Avn Ltd	Coventry	26. 6.00T
			N10871		(Op Aerocharter (Midlands) Ltd)		
G-RAFG	Slingsby T-67C	2076		2.11.89	Arrow Flying Ltd	(Alton)	30. 1.99T
G-RAFI	Hunting-Percival PAC/W/17641		8458M	18.12.92	G.R.Lacey	(Epsom)	AC
	P.84 Jet Provost T.4		XP672		(As "8458M/7") (On rebuild 10.96)		
G-RAFT	Rutan LongEz PFA/74A-10734			9. 8.82	H.C.Mackinnon	Tatenhill	19. 7.96P
	(Cont O-240-A)				"A Craft of Graft" (Stored 10.97)		
G-RAFW	Mooney M.20E Super 21	805	G-ATHW	14.11.84	Vinola (Knitwear) Manufacturing Co Ltd		14. 7.01
			N5881Q			Leicester	
G-RAGG	Maule M.5-235C Lunar Rocket	7260C	N5632M	8. 9.95	P.Ragg	(Austria)	12.10.01
G-RAGS	Pietenpol Aircamper PFA/47-11551			8. 6.94	R.F.Billington	(Kenilworth)	
G-RAID	Douglas AD-4NA Skyraider	7722	F-AZED	7. 6.93	Patina Ltd	Duxford	25. 8.99P
	(SFERMA c/n 42)		TR-K../Fr AF	42/Bu.126922 (Op B J S Grey/The Fighter Collection)			
					(As "126922/AK/402" in VA-176 Sqn USN c/s)		
G-RAIL	Colt 105A HAFB	1434		31. 3.89	Ballooning World Ltd	London NW1	31.10.96T
					"Railfreight"		
G-RAIN	Maule M.5-235C Lunar Rocket	7262C	N5632J	26. 7.79	D.S.McKay & J.A.Rayment		22. 9.01
						Hinton-in-the-Hedges	
G-RAIX	CCF T-6J Texan (Harvard 4) CCF4...		G-BIWX	16. 2.98	D.R.G.Baillie (As "FT239")	(Helensburgh)	8. 3.99P
	(Possibly c/n CCF4-409 ex 51-17227)		MM53846/RM-22/51-17...				
G-RALD	Robinson R-22HP	0218	G-CHIL	25. 1.96	Heli Air Ltd		8. 2.99T
			(G-BMXI)/N9074K			Wellesbourne Mountford/Denham	
G-RAMI	Bell 206B JetRanger III	2955	N1080N	18.10.90	M.D.Thorpe	Coney Park, Leeds	10. 2.00T
					t/a Yorkshire Helicopters		
G-RAMP	Piper J3C-65 Cub	6658	N35941	5. 7.90	J.Whittall	(Bristol)	18. 2.99P
			NC35941				
G-RAMS	PA-32R-301 Saratoga SP	32R-8013134	N8271Z	17.10.80	Air Tobago Ltd	Gamston	14. 6.99
G-RAMY	Bell 206B JetRanger	1401	N59554	22. 9.95	Eastman Aviation Ltd	Lincoln	15.10.99T
G-RANA	Cameron Cheese 82SS HAFB	1996	I-IORE	4.10.95	Consorzio Per La Tutela del Formaggio		21. 5.97A
			G-BSFM			Milan, Italy	
G-RAND	Rand Robinson KR-2	RLW-01		19.10.78	R.L.Wharmby	(Milton Keynes)	
G-RANG	Cameron A-340 HAFB	4024		3.10.96	Champagne Balloon Flights Ltd	Alton	4. 5.99T
G-RANS	Rans S-10 Sakota PFA/194-11537			17. 8.89	J.D.Weller	Egginton	20. 7.97P
	(Rotax 532)						
G-RANZ	Rans S-10 Sakota PFA/194-11536			2.11.89	B.A.Phillips (Open store 9.97)	Popham	12. 5.97P
	(Rotax 532)						
G-RAPA	PBN BN-2T-4R Defender 4000	2115 & 4001	N360WT	11. 5.82	Britten-Norman Ltd	Bembridge	31. 7.91T
			G-RAPA/G-51-2115/G-BJBH		(Stored 4.97)		
G-RAPH	Cameron O-77 HAFB	1673		21. 3.88	P.B.D.Bird	Winscombe, Somerset	26. 3.99A
					"Blagdon Water Gardens"		
G-RAPP	Cameron H-34 HAFB	2380		16. 8.90	Cameron Balloons Ltd	St.Louis, USA	25. 6.99A
G-RARB	Cessna 172N Skyhawk II	172-72334	G-BOII	4. 6.96	Richlyn Aviation Ltd	Biggin Hill	10. 4.00T
			N4702D				
G-RARE	Thunder Ax5-42 SS HAFB	266		20. 2.80	Justerini & Brooks Ltd	London SW1	14. 8.88A
	(J & B Rare Whisky Bottle shape)				"J & B Hamish"		
G-RASC*	Evans VP-2 V2-1178 & PFA/63-10422			14.12.78	Not known (Stored 4.97)	Yearby	29. 5.94P
	(Cont C90)						
G-RATE	Gulfstream AA-5A Cheetah	AA5A-0781	G-BIFF	11. 6.84	J.Appleton	Blackbushe	13.11.01T
			(G-BIBR)/N26879		t/a Holmes Rentals		
G-RATZ	Europa Avn Europa PFA/247-12582			16. 6.95	W.Goldsmith	(Boldon Colliery)	23. 8.99P
	(Rotax 912UL)						
G-RAVE	Southdown Raven X	2232/0219	G-MNZV	22.12.98	M.J.Robbins	Tunbridge Wells	15.12.95P
	(Rotax 447)						
G-RAVL	HP.137 Jetstream 200	208	G-AWVK	2.12.86	Cranfield University	Cranfield	26. 2.94A
			N1035S/G-AWVK				
G-RAYA	Denney Kitfox mk.4 PFA/172A-12403			14.12.92	A.K.Ray	(Stone)	
G-RAYE	PA-32-260 Cherokee Six	32-460	G-ATTY	30. 5.96	F.J.Wadia	Edinburgh	8. 8.00

Regn	Type	C/n	P/I	Date	Owner/operator	Probable Base	CA Expy
G-RAYS	Zenair CH.250 RED.001 & PFA/24-10460 (Lyc O-235)			26.10.78	Acro Engines & Airframes Ltd	Yearby	
G-RBBB	Europa Avn Europa (Rotax 912UL)	PFA/247-12664		6. 5.94	W.M.Goodburn & I.H.MacLeod	Portmoak	7. 5.99P
G-RBOS*	Colt AS-105 Hot-Air Airship	390		9. 2.82	The Science Museum	Wroughton	6. 3.87A
G-RBOW	Thunder Ax7-65 HAFB	1439		24. 4.89	A.C.Hall "Rain-Beau-Lune"	Melton Mowbray	10. 8.99A
G-RCED	Rockwell Commander 114	14241	VR-CED N4917W	19. 6.92	Echo Delta Ltd	Guernsey	13. 5.01
G-RCEJ	BAe 125 Srs.800B	258021	VR-CEJ G-GEIL/G-5-15	15. 6.95	Aravco Ltd	Farnborough	14. 6.99T
G-RCHA	PA-28-181 Archer IV	2843094	N9269S	30. 7.97	Plane Talking Ltd	Cranfield	6. 8.00T
G-RCMC	Murphy Renegade 912 (Rotax 912)	485 & PFA/188-12483		1. 2.93	R.C.M.Collisson	Turweston	29. 6.99P
G-RCMF	Cameron V-77 HAFB	1618		23.11.87	Mouldform Ltd "Mouldform I"/"Mayfly"	Loughborough	19. 8.97A
G-RCML	Sky 77-24 HAFB	148		9. 3.99	R.C.M.Sarl	Luxembourg	
G-RDCI	Rockwell Commander 112A	345	G-BFWG ZS-JRX/N1345J	15. 5.85	J.G.Hinley	Coventry	5. 2.01
G-RDVE	Airbus A.320-231	163	OY-CND F-WWDU	26. 2.97	Airtours International Airways Ltd	Manchester	2. 3.00T
G-READ	Colt 77A HAFB	1158	EI-BYI G-READ	16.11.87	J.Keena (Flying as EI-BYI 9.98)	Athlone, Co.Westmeath	2. 5.97A
G-REAH	PA-32R-301 Saratoga SP	32R-8413017	G-CELL (G-BLRI)/N4361D	15. 8.94	M.Q.Tolbod & S.J.Rogers	(Reading)	5. 8.00
G-REAP	Pitts S-1S Special (Lyc O-360)	PFA/09-11557		7. 2.90	R.Dixon "The Grim Reaper"	Netherthorpe	22. 9.99P
G-REAS	Van's RV-6A (Lyc O-320)	PFA/181-12188		16. 8.94	E.J.D.Proctor	(Bewdley)	23. 5.99P
G-REAT	Grumman-American GA-7 Cougar	GA7-0033	N29699	6.10.78	Goodtechnique Ltd	Leeds-Bradford	18. 7.00T
G-REBK	Beechcraft B200 Super King Air	BB-1202	D-IHAP N44VM/N7207M	22. 5.97	Planstable Enterprises Ltd (Op Reebok)	Biggin Hill	17. 6.01T
G-REBL	Hughes 269B	67-0318	N9493F	25. 7.89	GTS Engineering (Coventry) Ltd (Stored 3.97)	Gamlingay	9.10.95
G-RECK	PA-28-140 Cherokee B	28-25656	G-AXJW N11C	17. 3.88	R.J.Grantham & D.Boatswain Clutton Hill Farm, High Littleton		29. 7.01
G-REDB	Cessna 310Q	310Q-0811	G-BBIC N69600	17. 6.93	Leisure Park Management Ltd	Goodwood	22. 3.01T
G-REDD	Cessna 310R II	310R-1833	G-BMGT ZS-KSY/(N2738X)	2.10.96	G.Wightman	(Kendal)	17.12.01T
G-REDX	Experimental Avn Berkut	PFA/252-12481		27. 1.95	G.V.Waters	(Attleborough)	
G-REEC	Sequoia F.8L Falco (Lyc IO-320)	654	LN-LCA	2. 7.96	J.D.Tseliki	Kittyhawk Farm	17. 8.98P
G-REEK	Grumman-American AA-5A Cheetah	AA5A-0429		12. 9.77	J.& A.Pearson	Dundee	10. 2.01
G-REEM	Aerospatiale AS.355F1 Twin Squirrel	5175	G-EMAN G-WEKR/G-CHLA/N818RL/C-FLXH/N818RL/N818R/N5798U	9. 3.98	Heliking Ltd	Redhill	9.10.00T
G-REEN	Cessna 340	340-0063	G-AZYR N5893M	2. 2.84	E. & M.Green	Guernsey	28. 7.99
G-REES	SAN Jodel D.140C Mousquetaire III	156	F-BMFR	23. 4.80	W.H.Greenwood	Swanborough Farm, Lewes	21.10.99
G-REFI*	Enstrom 280C-UK Shark	1090	N638H	2. 5.89	Not known (Destroyed Dublin 22. 9.95; stored for rebuild 1.97)	Coventry	15.10.95
G-REID	Rotorway Scorpion 133	1147	G-BGAW	7.12.81	G.F.Burridge & S.B.Evans	Bedford	18.3.91P
G-RENE	Murphy Renegade 912 (Rotax 912)	PFA/188-12030		6.11.91	J.A.Cuthbertson	Full Sutton	3. 9.98P
G-RENO	Socata TB-10 Tobago	249		10.12.81	Lamond Ltd	Birmingham	21. 5.98T
G-RENT	Robinson R-22 Beta	0758	N2635M	17. 3.88	Rentatruck (Self Drive) Ltd (Op Helicopter Training & Hire) (Damaged Newtownards 30.9.92)	Newtownards	12. 6.94T
G-REPM	PA-38-112 Tomahawk	38-79A0354	N2528D	8. 1.87	Nultree Ltd (Stored 6.96)	Chilbolton	9.10.95T
G-REST	Beechcraft P35 Bonanza	D-7171	G-ASFJ	14.12.82	C.R.E.S.Taylor	Biggin Hill	15. 8.99
G-RETA	CASA I-131E Jungmann 2000	2197	E3B-305	24. 3.80	N.S.C.& G.English	Dereham	11.11.99P
G-REXS	PA-28-181 Archer II	28-8090102	N8093Y	14. 1.80	M.R.Shelton t/a Tatenhill Aviation	Tatenhill	18. 6.01T
G-REZE	Rutan VariEze (Cont O-200-A)	PFA/74-11086		28. 9.89	S.D.Brown & S.P.Evans (Destroyed Bembridge 19.11.95)	Biggin Hill	29. 8.96P
G-RFIL	Thunder Colt 77A HAFB	1496		16. 4.98	G.Davis	(Reading)	1. 4.99T
G-RFIO	Aeromot AMT-200 Super Ximango (Licence-built Fourner RF10)	200-048		6. 3.95	G.McLean & R.P.Beck	Rufforth	30. 6.01
G-RFSB	Sportavia Fournier RF5B Sperber	51045	N55HC	2.12.88	S.W.Brown	Sibson	1. 4.01
G-RGEN	Cessna T337D Turbo Super Skymaster	T337-1062	G-EDOT G-BJIY/9Q-CPF/PH-JWL/N86056	24. 5.96	R.J.Willies Honeydon Farm, Colmworth, Bedford		19. 9.99
G-RGUS*	Fairchild 24R-46A Argus III (UC-61K-FA)	1145	(PH-) G-RGUS/ZS-UJZ/ZS-BAY/KK527/44-83184	16. 9.86	Fenlands Ltd (As "44-83184/7" in USAAC c/s; on rebuild 8.98)	Sturgate	15. 5.93
G-RHCB	Schweizer 269C-1	0036	N201WL	20. 3.98	Oxford Aviation Services Ltd	Oxford	

Regn	Type	C/n	P/I	Date	Owner/operator	Probable Base	CA Expy
G-RHHT	PA-32RT-300 Lance II	32R-7885190	N36476	3. 7.78	R.W. & M.Struth	Southend	18.12.99T
G-RHYS	Rotorway Exec 90 (RI 162)	5140		8.11.93	A.K.Voase & K.Matthews	(Hornsea)	6.12.99P
G-RIAN	Agusta-Bell 206A JetRanger	8056	G-SOOR G-FMAL/G-RIAN/G-BHSG/PH-FSW	16. 9.87	Thorneygrove Ltd	Newcastle	14.10.99T
G-RIAT	Robinson R-22 Beta	2684		27. 5.97	Heli Air Ltd	Wellesbourne Mountford/Denham	2. 6.00T
G-RIBS	Diamond DA.20-A1 Katana	10143	G-BWWM	7. 7.97	J.T.H.McAlpine t/a West London Models	Oxford	6. 8.99
G-RICC	Aerospatiale AS.350B2 Ecureuil	2559	G-BTXA	30.10.91	Specialist Helicopters Ltd	Inverness	8. 2.01
G-RICE	Robinson R-22 Beta	2509	N93MK	14. 3.97	Rivermead Aviation Ltd	(Reading)	3. 4.00T
G-RICK	Beechcraft 95-B55 Baron	TC-1472	G-BAAG	23. 5.84	James Jack (Invergordon) Ltd (Damaged Stornoway 8.12.98)	Inverness	16. 6.99T
G-RICS	Europa Avn Europa	PFA/247-12747		19. 3.96	R.G.Allen t/a The Flying Property Doctor	(Epsom)	27. 5.99P
G-RIDE	Stephens Akro (Lyc AIO-360)	111	N81AC N55NM	10. 8.78	R.Mitchell t/a Mitchell Avn (PSA c/s) (Stored 3.95)	RAF Cosford	13. 8.92P
G-RIFB	Hughes 269C	116-0562	N7428F	17. 5.90	R.F.Rhodes & J.C.McHugh	Maldon/Stapleford	16.10.99
G-RIFN	Mudry CAP.10B	276		6. 6.96	S.A.W.Becker	Goodwood	30. 6.99
G-RIGB	Thunder Ax7-77 HAFB	1201		16. 3.88	Antrum & Andrews Ltd t/a Duck Lane Productions "Rigby"	London W1	15. 2.96A
G-RIGH	PA-32R-301 Saratoga	32R-3246123	N41272	23.12.98	G M R & I H L Graham (Bishops Stortford) t/a Rentair		22.12.01
G-RIGS	PA-60-601P Aerostar	61P-0621-7963281	N8220J	18. 5.79	Tecno Engineering 2C SRL	Rome/Ciampiano, Italy	2.12.01
G-RILY*	Monnett Sonerai IIL (VW1834)	PFA/15-10353		20.12.78	Not known (Stored 4.95)	Hill Farm, Nayland	5.10.89P
G-RIMM	Westland Wasp HAS.Mk.1	F9605	NZ3908 XT435	11. 3.99	M.P.Grimshaw	(London W5)	
G-RINO	Thunder Ax7-77 HAFB	975		24. 6.87	D.J.Head "Cerous"	Newbury	5. 3.94T
G-RINS	Rans S6-ESD Coyote II	PFA/204-13361		15. 3.99	D.Watt	(Kirkby Stephen)	
G-RINT	CFM Streak Shadow (Rotax 582) K199-SA & PFA/206-12251			7.12.93	D. & J.S.Grint	Shoreham	3.11.99P
G-RIPS	Cameron Action Man/Parachutist 110SS HAFB	4092		29. 4.97	Virgin Airship & Balloon Co Ltd "Action Man"	Telford	24. 6.98A
G-RISE	Cameron V-90 HAFB	2395		21. 9.90	D.L.Smith "Rise N' Shine"	Newbury	21.11.98T
G-RIST	Cessna 310R II	310R-1294	G-DATS (N6128X)	28. 4.81	Pilotime Ltd t/a GT Aviation	Bournemouth	22. 6.01
G-RIVT	Van's RV-6 (Lyc O-320)	PFA/181-12743		31. 7.95	N.Reddish	Netherthorpe	28. 5.99P
G-RIZE	Cameron O-90 HAFB	3163		13.12.93	S.F.Burden	Noordwijk, Netherlands	17. 5.99A
G-RIZI	Cameron N-90 HAFB	3080		12. 5.93	R.Wiles	Wadhurst	18. 9.95A
G-RIZZ	PA-28-161 Warrior II	28-7816494	D-EMFW N9563N	11. 2.99	Northamptonshire School of Flying Ltd	Sywell	
G-RJAH	Boeing-Stearman D75N1 (PT-27BW) Kaydet (Cont W670)	75-4041	N75957 RCAF FJ991/42-15852 (As "44" in US Army c/s)	6. 4.90	R.J.Horne	Rendcomb	16. 7.99
G-RJCP	Commander 114B	14606	N6001M	3. 7.96	J.C.Hall	Guernsey	28. 7.99
G-RJGR	Boeing 757-225	22197	N701MG N507EA	22.11.94	Airtours International Airways Ltd	Manchester	1. 2.01T
G-RJMS	PA-28R-201 Arrow III	28R-7837059	N6223H	19. 1.88	M.G.Hill	Crosland Moor	20. 4.00
G-RJWW	Maule M.5-235C Lunar Rocket	7250C	G-BRWG N5632H	6.10.87	PAW F/Svs Ltd	Sandtoft	25. 9.00T
G-RLFI	Reims Cessna FA.152 Aerobat	0340	G-DFTS	17. 1.90	Tayside Avn Ltd	Aberdeen/Dundee	18.11.01T
G-RLMC	Cessna 421C Golden Eagle II	421C-0118	PH-SBI D-IMAZ/I-CCNN/N3849C	9. 3.88	R.D.Lygo	Fairoaks	17. 1.07
G-RMAC	Europa Avn Europa	PFA/247-12717		3. 7.97	P.J.Lawless	(Bath)	
G-RMAN	Aero Designs Pulsar	PFA/202-13071		6. 6.97	M.B.Redman	(Wilton, Salisbury)	
G-RMCT	Short SD.3-60 Var.100	SH.3656	EI-BPD G-BLPU/G-14-3656	27.11.92	Gill Avn Ltd	Newcastle	21.12.99T
G-RMIT	Van's RV-4	PFA/181-12207		4. 9.96	J.P.Kloos (f/f 1.3.99)	Shoreham	
G-RMUG	Cameron Nescafe Mug 90SS HAFB	3450		3. 5.95	Nestle UK Ltd "Nescafe"	Croydon	14. 6.99A
G-RNAS*	DH.104 Sea Devon C.20 (Dove 6)	04473	XK896	16.11.82	Not known (As "XK896" in RN c/s) (Stored 12.95)	North Coates	3. 7.84
G-RNBW	Bell 206B Jet Ranger II	2270	F-GQFH F-WQFH/HB-XUF/F-GFBP/N900JJ/N16UC	9. 1.98	Rainbow Helicopters Ltd	Exeter	22. 2.01T
G-RNEE	Cameron R-420 HAFB	4426		15. 9.98	Bondbaste Ltd	Bristol	
G-RNIE	Cameron Ball 70SS HAFB	2333		3. 8.90	Virgin Airship & Balloon Co Ltd "Schwarzenegger"	Telford	16. 5.97A
G-RNLD	Agusta A.109C	7633	I-ANAG	21. 6.96	Irvine Aviation Ltd	Elstree	25. 7.99
G-RNLI	VS.236 Walrus 1	S2/5591	W2718	13.12.90	R.E.Melton (As "W2718/AA5Y" in 751 Sqn RN c/s; on rebuild 6.95)	Great Yarmouth	
G-RNRM	Cessna A185F Skywagon	A185-02541	N1826R	20. 1.87	A T Usher t/a Royal Navy & Royal Marines Sport Parachute Association	Dunkeswell	2. 4.99
G-ROAM	Schempp-Hirth Nimbus 4DM	22/32		24. 9.96	B.A.Eastwell	Lasham	29. 4.00
G-ROAR	Cessna 401	401-0166	G-BZFL G-AWSF/N4066Q	8. 3.82	Special Scope Ltd	Woodford	3. 7.99
G-ROBD	Europa Avn Europa	PFA/247-12671		23. 2.94	R.D.Davies	(Cowbridge)	

Regn	Type	C/n	P/I	Date	Owner/operator	Probable Base	CA Expy
G-ROBN	Robin R.1180T Aiglon	220		16. 8.78	Jane E.Beaumont	Popham	13. 8.00T
G-ROBT	Hawker Hurricane I		P2902	19. 9.94	R.A.Roberts	Moat Farm, Milden	
	(Gloster built) (On rebuild by Hawker Restorations Ltd from remains salvaged in 1988 from wreck site						
	at Dunkirk Beach; to be "P2902/DX-X")						
G-ROBY	Colt 17A Cloudhopper HAFB	483		7. 2.83	Virgin Airship & Balloon Co Ltd "Continental Cloudhopper"	Telford	26. 9.92A
G-ROCH	Cessna T303 Crusader	T303-00129	N4962C	29. 3.90	R.S.Bentley	Cambridge	22. 4.99
G-ROCK	Thunder Ax7-77 HAFB	781		25. 2.86	M.A.Green "Rocky"	Rednal	3. 5.97A
G-ROCR	Schweizer Hughes 269C	S.1336	N219MS	14. 6.90	Oxford Aviation Services Ltd	Oxford	28. 1.00T
G-RODD	Cessna 310R II	310R-0544	G-TEDD	2.10.89	RJ Herbert Engineering Ltd		
			G-MADI/N87396/G-MADI/N87396			Marshland, Wisbech	10. 6.99
G-RODI	Isaacs Fury (Lyc O-290)	PFA/11-10130		22.12.78	M.R.Baker	Westfield Farm, Hailsham, E.Sussex	17. 8.95P
					(As "K3731" in 43 Sqdn c/s; stored 3.97)		
G-ROGG	Robinson R-22 Beta	1487		31. 8.90	Burman Aviation Ltd	Cranfield	9. 9.99T
G-ROGY	Cameron Concept 60 HAFB	3055		11. 5.93	A.A.Laing "Cameron Voyager"	Aberdeen	3. 5.97A
G-ROIN	Aerospatiale AS.350BA Ecureuil	2344	F-GMAR N516AJ	5. 6.98	C.C.Blake	(Hythe)	
G-ROLA	PA-34-200T Seneca II	34-7670066	N4537X G-ROLA/N4537X	4.12.85	Deer Hill Aviation Ltd	(Kingsbridge)	25.10.01T
G-ROLF	PA-32R-301 Saratoga SP	32R-8113018	N83052	7. 1.81	P.F.Larkins	High Cross, Ware	14. 2.99
G-ROLL	Aerotek Pitts S-2A Special (Lyc AEIO-360)	2175	N31444	20. 2.80	N.Lamb t/a Aerial & Aerobatic Svs (Marlboro' c/s)	Booker	13. 8.01A
G-ROLO	Robinson R-22 Beta	1226		24. 1.90	Plane Talking Ltd (Op Cabair Helicopters)	Elstree	22.12.01T
G-ROMA	Hughes 369HS	13-0442S	G-ROPI G-ROMA/G-ONPP/OY-HCP/D-HGER	16. 1.84	Helicopters (Northern) Ltd	Sywell	27.10.95T
			(Damaged early 1993; to March Helicopters for spares; pod in store 6.96)				
G-ROMS	Lindstrand LBL-105G HAFB	401		13. 9.96	International Balloons Ltd	Oswestry	24. 8.99A
G-ROMW	Cyclone AX2000	7486		4. 2.99	Financial Planning (Wells) Ltd	Wells	
G-RONA	Europa Avn Europa (Rotax 912UL)	PFA/247-12588		17. 1.95	C.M.Noakes	Tatenhill	9. 4.98P
G-RONG	PA-28R-200 Cherokee Arrow II	28R-7335148	N16451	14. 6.90	E.Tang	(London W1)	22. 8.99
G-RONI	Cameron V-77 HAFB	2349		27. 7.90	R.E.Simpson t/a Elbow Beach Balloon Club "Roni"	Great Missenden	15. 5.99A
G-RONN	Robinson R-44 Astro	0267	N770SC G-RONN/D-HIRR	8. 1.98	R Hallam & S E Watts	Leicester	15. 2.01
G-RONS	Robin DR.400/180 Regent	2088		17. 7.91	R. & K.Baker	Newcastle	10. 8.00
G-RONW	Clutton FRED Srs.II (VW1834)	PFA/29-10121		18.12.78	K.Atkinson	Haverfordwest	9. 3.99P
G-ROOK	Reims Cessna F.172P Skyhawk II	2081	PH-TGY G-ROOK	12. 1.81	Rolim Ltd	(Sonehaven)	30.10.99
G-ROOV	Europa Avn Europa XS	PFA/247-13204		16. 7.98	D.K.Richardson	(Malvern)	
G-ROPA	Europa Avn Europa	PFA/247-12396		27.11.92	R.G.Gray	(London N1)	
G-RORI	Folland Gnat T.1	FL.549	8621M XR538	18.10.93	Bushfire Investments Ltd	North Weald	10.12.99P
G-RORO	Cessna 337B Super Skymaster	337-0554	G-AVIX N5454S	8. 1.80	H.D.Hezlett	(Douglas, IOM)	15. 7.00
G-RORY	Focke-Wulf Piaggio FWP.149D (Piaggio c/n 338)	014	G-TOWN D-EFFY/90+06/BB+394	2. 8.88	Bushfire Investments Ltd	Denham	19. 4.99
G-ROSE	Evans VP-1	PFA/7031		22. 1.79	A.P.M.Long	(Leighton Buzzard)	
G-ROSI	Thunder Ax7-77 HAFB	1284		29. 6.88	J.E.Rose "Rosi"	Abingdon	21. 9.96A
G-ROSS	Practavia Pilot Sprite 132 & PFA/05-10404			28. 2.80	A.D.Janaway	(Wellington)	
G-ROTI	Luscombe 8A (Cont A65)	2117	N45590 NC45590	18. 4.89	R.Ludgate & A.L.Chapman	Old Hay,Paddock Wood	9.10.97P
G-ROTR	Brantly B.2B	403	N2192U	9.12.91	D.N.Yardley t/a GP Svs	Old Sarum	26. 3.98
G-ROTS	CFM Streak Shadow	K.120-SA & PFA/161A-11603		21.12.89	P.White	Caernarfon	26. 6.98P
G-ROUP	Reims Cessna F.172M Skyhawk II	1451	G-BDPH	23. 5.84	Stapleford F/C Ltd	Blackbushe	23. 4.00T
G-ROUS	PA-34-200T Seneca II	34-7870187	N9412C	26. 4.78	Oxford Aviation Services Ltd	Oxford	8.12.99T
G-ROUT	Robinson R-22 Beta	1241	N8068U	23. 1.90	Ramsgill Aviation Ltd	(Bingley)	25. 9.00T
G-ROVE	PA-18-135 Super Cub (L-21B-PI) (Frame No.18-3853)	18-3846	PH-VLO (PH-DKF)/R-156/54-2446	6. 5.82	Caledonian Seaplanes Ltd	Carlisle	21. 7.98T
G-ROWE	Reims Cessna F.182P Skylane II	0007	OO-CNG	18.12.95	D.Rowe	Liverpool	29. 1.99
G-ROWL	Grumman-American AA-5B Tiger	AA5B-0595	(N28410)	26.10.77	Plane Talking Ltd	Elstree	9. 5.01T
G-ROWN	Beechcraft 200 Super King Air	BB-684	G-BHLC N27L/N8511L/G-BHLC	13.10.87	Valentia Air Ltd.	Oxford	27. 3.01T
G-ROWS	PA-28-151 Warrior	28-7715296	N8949F	15. 9.78	Mustarrow Ltd	Woodford	2. 3.00
G-ROZI	Robinson R-44 Astro	0252		26. 3.96	Vitapage Ltd	(Tring)	21. 4.99T
G-ROZY	Cameron R-36 Gas Free Balloon	1141		20. 5.85	Jacques W.Soukup Enterprises Ltd	Beaulieu Court, Wilts	N/E(A)
					(Stored uncomplete 1.94)		
G-RPEZ	Rutan LongEz	PFA/74A-10746		3. 4.84	B.A.Fairston & D.Richardson	Booker	
G-RRGN	VS.390 Spitfire PR.XIX	6S/594677	G-MXIX PS853	23.12.96	Rolls-Royce plc (As "PS853/C" in 2nd TAF/PRU c/s)	Filton	28. 8.99P
G-RRSG(2)	Thunder Ax7-77 HAFB	874		24. 9.86	M.T.Stevens "Silver Ghost"	Solihull	1. 8.97A

Regn	Type	C/n	P/I	Date	Owner/operator	Probable Base	CA Expy
G-RSCJ	Cessna 525 Citation Jet	525-0298		15. 1.99	SMD Investments Ltd	Guernsey	AC
G-RSFT	PA-28-161 Warrior II	28-8616038	G-WARI N9276Y	15.12.95	SFT Europe Ltd	Bournemouth	22. 2.01T
G-RSKR	PA-28-161 Warrior II	28-7916181	G-BOJY N3030G	27. 4.95	Southern Air Ltd, P.M.Forte, R.Sherwin-Smith, R.Stammers & R.W.Broad	Shoreham	25. 5.00T
G-RSSF	Denney Kitfox mk.2 (Rotax 582)	PFA/172-12125		9.10.92	R.W.Somerville	Comber, NI	15. 5.97P
G-RSVP	Robinson R-22 Beta	2788		5. 2.98	Pearce Enterprise Ltd	(Tonbridge)	8. 3.01T
G-RSWO	Cessna 172R Skyhawk II	172-80206	N9401F	25. 2.98	Eye-T Aviation Ltd	(Shipley)	2. 3.01T
G-RSWW	Robinson R-22 Beta	1775	N40815	16. 5.91	R.S.Weston-Woods Brands Hatch, Dartford t/a Woodstock Enterprises		21. 5.00T
G-RTBI	Thunder Ax6-56 HAFB	2584		19. 4.94	P.J.Waller	Norwich	25. 5.95A
G-RTWI	Cameron R-550 HAFB	4384		3. 6.98	Spirit of Peace Ltd	(Chippenham)	
G-RTWW	Robinson R-44 Astro	0438		20. 3.98	R.Woods t/a Rotorvation	(Longfield)	30. 4.01T
G-RUBB	Gulfstream AA-5B Tiger	AA5B-0928	(G-BKVI) OO-NAS/(OO-HRC)	20. 9.83	D.E.Gee	Blackbushe	23.11.01
G-RUBI	Thunder Ax7-77 HAFB	1051		27. 2.87	G.Warren t/a Warren & Johnson "Rubicon Computer Systems"	Norwich	20.11.93A
G-RUBY	PA-28RT-201T Turbo Arrow IV	28R-8331037	G-BROU N4306K	5. 1.90	R.Harman t/a Arrow Acft Grp	Tatenhill	14. 2.99
G-RUDD	Cameron V-65 HAFB	844		19. 5.82	N.A.Apsey "Smilie" (Kodak c/s)	High Wycombe	18. 3.96A
G-RUDI	QAC Quickie Q.2 (Revmaster 2100D)	PFA/94A-11209		3. 9.91	R.Brandenberger	(Wilmslow)	
G-RUGS	Campbell Cricket Mk.4	PFA G/103-1307		11. 2.99	J.L.G.Mclane	(York)	
G-RUIA	Reims Cessna F.172N Skyhawk II	1856	PH-AXA(3)	4.10.79	Knockin Flying Club Ltd	Sleap	13. 7.01
G-RUMM	Grumman F8F-2P Bearcat	D.1088	NX700HL NX700H/N1YY/N4995V/Bu.121714	20. 3.98	Patina Ltd (Op The Fighter Collection) (As "21714/201B" in USN c/s)	Duxford	29. 6.99P
G-RUMN	Grumman-American AA-1A Trainer	AA1A-0086	N87599 D-EAFB/(N9386L)	30. 5.80	D.W.Reast	Nottingham	17. 3.00
G-RUMT	Grumman F7F-3P Tigercat	C.167	N7235C BuA.80425	6. 4.98	Patina Ltd (Op The Fighter Collection) (As "80425 4-WT" in US Marines c/s)	Duxford	21.10.98P
G-RUMW	Grumman FM-2 Wildcat	5765	N4845V BuA.86711	15. 4.98	Patina Ltd (Op The Fighter Collection) (As "F" in FAA c/s)	Duxford	28. 6.99P
G-RUNG	SAAB-Scania SF.340A	340A-086	F-GGBV SE-E86	3. 6.97	Business Air Ltd	Aberdeen	5. 6.99T
G-RUNT	Cassutt Racer IIIM 161149 & PFA/34-10860 (Lyc O-235)			12. 4.83	Coulson Flying Services Ltd	(Croft, Skegness)	24. 8.96P
G-RUSO	Robinson R-22 Beta	1387		25. 5.90	R.M.Barnes-Gorell	Thruxton	25. 7.99T
G-RUSS*	Cessna 172N Skyhawk 100	172-68563	N733UR	30. 6.80	Not known (Wings stored 6.95)	Southend	19. 9.86T
G-RVAN	Van's RV-6	PFA/181-12657		25. 4.97	J.R.Heaps & D.Broom	Panshanger	31. 3.99P
G-RVAW	Van's RV-6	PFA/181-13234		24.11.97	A.A.Wordsworth	(Sutton-in-Ashfield)	
G-RVCL	Van's RV-6	PFA/181A-13439		18. 2.99	C.T.Lamb	(Stamford)	
G-RVDJ	Van's RV-6	PFA/181-12938		8. 2.99	J.D.Jewitt	(Selby)	
G-RVEE	Van's RV-6	PFA/181-12262		16. 2.93	J.C.A.Wheeler	(Banchory)	22.11.99P
G-RVET	Van's RV-6	PFA/181-12852		9. 3.98	D.R.Coleman	(Bexley)	
G-RVGA	Van's RV-6A	PFA/181-13079		11. 5.98	D.P.Dawson	(Hitchin)	20. 8.99P
G-RVIA	Van's RV-6A	PFA/181-12289		13. 8.97	A.J.Rose	(Aboyne)	13. 9.99P
G-RVIN	Van's RV-6	PFA/181-13236		28.11.97	N.Reddish	(Mansfield)	29. 7.99P
G-RVIT	Van's RV-6 (Lyc O-360)	PFA/181-12422		1. 5.95	P.J.Shotbolt	(Great Casterton, Lincs)	23. 4.98P
G-RVIV	Van's RV-4	PFA/181-12366		31.12.97	G.S.Scott	Burgess Hill, W.Sussex	
G-RVMJ	Van's RV-4	PFA/181-13433		16. 2.99	M.J.de Ruiter	(Craigavon, NI)	
G-RVRA	PA-28-140 Cherokee Cruiser	28-7625038	G-OWVA N4459X	14. 1.97	Cheshire Flying Services Ltd t/a Ravenair	Manchester	12. 3.00T
G-RVRB	PA-34-200T Seneca II	34-7970440	G-BTAJ N22MJ/N45113	24. 2.97	Cheshire Flying Services Ltd t/a Ravenair	Manchester	2. 6.01T
G-RVRC	PA-23-250 Aztec E	27-7405336	G-BNPD N101VH/N40591	14.10.97	Cheshire Flying Services Ltd t/a Ravenair	Manchester	22.12.00T
G-RVRD	PA-23-250 Aztec E	27-4634	G-BRAV G-BBCM/N14021	16. 3.98	Cheshire Flying Services Ltd t/a Ravenair	Manchester	22. 7.99T
G-RVRF	PA-38-112 Tomahawk	38-78A0714	G-BGEL	21.11.97	Cheshire Flying Services Ltd t/a Ravenair	Manchester	7. 5.00T
G-RVRG	PA-38-112 Tomahawk	38-79A1092	G-BHAF	3. 8.98	Cheshire Flying Services Ltd t/a Ravenair	Manchester	AC
G-RVRV	Van's RV-4	PFA/181-13024		29. 9.98	P Jenkins	(Nairn)	
G-RVSX	Van's RV-6	PFA/181-13090		18. 9.97	R.L. & V.A.West	(Worthing)	
G-RVVI	Van's RV-6	PFA/181-12418		26. 1.93	J.E.Alsford & J.N.Parr	(Peterborough)	
G-RWHC	Cameron A-180 HAFB	2700		16. 4.92	J.J.Rudoni & A.C.K.Rawson t/a Wickers World Hot Air Balloon Co	Stafford	22. 4.99T
G-RWIN	Rearwin 175 Skyranger (Cont A75)	1522	N32391 NC32391	12. 9.90	G.Kay	Yew Tree Farm, Lymm Dam	15. 6.98P
G-RWSS	Denney Kitfox mk.2 (Rotax 582)	PFA/172-12008		16. 4.91	R.W.Somerville (Damaged Comber 18.8.92)	Comber, Newtownards	14. 6.93P
G-RWWW	Westland WS-55 Whirlwind HCC.12	WA/418	8727M XR486	21. 6.90	Whirlwind Helicopters Ltd (As "XR486" in Queens Flight c/s) (Stored 9.97)	Redhill	25. 8.96P
G-RXUK	Lindstrand LBL-105A HAFB	232		29. 3.95	P.A.Hames	Reading	14.12.98A

G-SAAA-SZZZ

Regn	Type	C/n	P/I	Date	Owner/operator	Probable Base	CA Expy
G-SAAB	Rockwell Commander 112TC	13002	G-BEFS N1502J	5.12.79	R.L.Thomas t/a SAAB Grp	Bournemouth	28. 6.00
G-SAAM	Cessna T182R Turbo Skylane II	182-68200	G-TAGL G-SAAM/N2399E	23. 5.84	H.C.Danby & M.D.Harvey	Earls Colne	15.11.01
G-SABA	PA-28R-201T Turbo Arrow III	28R-7703268	G-BFEN N38745	22. 8.79	R.J.Howard	(Leeds)	6. 4.98
G-SABR	North American F-86A-5NA Sabre (Regd with c/n 151-083)	151-43547	N178 N68388/48-178	6.11.91	Golden Apple Operations Ltd (Op by The Old Flying Machine Co) (As "8178/FU-178" in 4th Fighter Wing USAF c/s)	Duxford	1. 6.99P
G-SACB	Reims Cessna F.152 II	1501	G-BFRB	7. 3.84	Sky Pro Ltd	Barton	16. 2.00T
G-SACD	Reims Cessna F.172H	0385	G-AVCD	13. 6.83	Northbrook College of Design & Technology (Op Sky Leisure Aviation)	Shoreham	27. 7.00T
G-SACF*	Cessna 152 II	152-83175	G-BHSZ N47125	21. 3.85	T M & A L Jones (Derby A/C) (Damaged Egginton 21.3.97 - fuselage noted 3.98)	Egginton	8. 6.95T
G-SACI	PA-28-161 Warrior II	28-8216123	N81535	26. 7.89	PJC (Leasing) Ltd	Stapleford	12. 4.99T
G-SACK	Robin R.2160	316		2. 5.97	Sherburn Aero Club Ltd	Sherburn	14. 5.00T
G-SACO	PA-28-161 Warrior II	28-8416085	N4358Z	1. 6.89	D.C. & M.Brooks t/a The Barn Gallery	Oxford	23. 7.01
G-SACR	PA-28-161 Cadet	2841046	N91618	6. 2.89	Sherburn A/C Ltd	Sherburn	19. 2.01T
G-SACS	PA-28-161 Cadet	2841047	N91619	6. 2.89	Sherburn A/C Ltd	Sherburn	19. 2.01T
G-SACT	PA-28-161 Cadet	2841048	N9162D	6. 2.89	Sherburn A/C Ltd	Sherburn	19. 2.01T
G-SACU	PA-28-161 Cadet	2841049	N9162X	6. 2.89	Sherburn A/C Ltd (Damaged on landing Sherburn 29.6.96)	Sherburn	19. 2.98T
G-SACZ	PA-28-161 Warrior II	28-7916258	N2098N	26. 7.89	Cee-Zed Aviation Ltd	Jersey	28. 3.99
G-SADE	Reims Cessna F.150L	0752	G-AZJW	28. 5.91	N.E.Sams (Op Billins Air Services)	Cranfield	21. 9.97T
G-SAEW	Aerospatiale AS.355F2 Twin Squirrel	5435	N244BB N244BH	20.12.96	Veritair Ltd (Op South & East Wales ASU)	Cardiff Heliport	30. 1.00T
G-SAFE	Cameron N-77 HAFB	511		14. 2.79	P.J.Waller "The High Flyer"	Norwich	21. 4.91A
G-SAFR	Saab 91D Safir	91-382	PH-RLR	10.10.95	B.Johansson	Bruntingthorpe	AC
G-SAGA	Grob G-109B	6364	OE-9254	28. 6.90	G-GROB Ltd	Booker	16. 7.99
G-SAGE	Luscombe 8A Silvaire (Cont A65)	2581	G-AKTL N71154/NC71154	15. 8.90	R.J.P.Herivel	Alderney	12. 7.99P
G-SAHI	FLS Sprint 160 (Lyc O-235) (Design originally known as Trago Mills SAH-1)	001		21.10.80	Sunhawk Ltd	North Weald	30. 4.94P
G-SAIL*	Boeing 707-323C	18690	(N7556A) N7556A	29. 9.78	Boeing Acft Co/USAF David-Monthan AFB, Arizona, USA (Stored for spares use 10.92)		8.12.86T
G-SAIR	Cessna 421C Golden Eagle III	421C-0471	G-OBCA N6812C	1. 4.86	Air Support Avn Svs Ltd	Aberdeen	21. 4.00
G-SAIX	Cameron N-77 HAFB	626	N386CB	14. 1.99	C.Walther, B.Sevenich, B. & S.Harren	Aachen, Germany	
G-SALA	PA-32-300 Six	32-7940106	(G-BHEJ) N2184Z	17.10.79	Stonebold Ltd	Elstree	16. 3.01
G-SALL	Reims Cessna F.150L	0682	PH-LTY D-ECPH	19. 1.79	D.& P.A.Hailey	(Tadley)	7. 8.00T
G-SAMG	Grob G-109B	6278		16. 5.84	T.Holloway t/a RAFGSA	RAF Bicester	31. 5.99
G-SAMI	Cameron N-90 Sainsbury Strawberry SS HAFB	3907	G-BWSE	21. 8.96	Flying Pictures Ltd	Fairoaks	30.11.99A
G-SAMM	Cessna 340A II (RAM-conversion)	340A-0742	N37TJ N2671A	7. 3.88	M.R.Cross	Exeter	24. 6.00
G-SAMY	Europa Avn Europa	PFA/247-12901		17. 8.95	K.R.Tallent	(Chertsey)	
G-SAMZ	Cessna 150D	150-60536	G-ASSO N4536U	19. 4.84	N.E.Sams	Cranfield	14. 9.01T
G-SAND	Schweizer Hughes 269C (300C)	S.1399		17. 8.89	Aerocroft Ltd	Oxford	5.11.01T
G-SANS	Robinson R-22 Beta	2012	G-BUHX	31.10.97	J.E. & M.J.Morris t/a The Type Marketing Co	Cheltenham	6. 7.01T
G-SARA	PA-28-181 Archer II	28-7990039	N21270	6. 4.81	R.P.Lewis (Op Airbase Flying Club)	Shoreham	16. 4.01T
G-SARH	PA-28-161 Warrior II	28-8216173	N8232Q	18. 2.91	Sussex F/C Ltd	Shoreham	6. 2.01T
G-SARK	BAC.167 Strikemaster 84	EEP/JP/1931	N2146S Sing.AF 311 G-27-140	13. 1.95	Sark International Airways Ltd (A.Gjertsen Classic Jets Aircraft) Biggin Hill (Stored 8.97)		AC
G-SARO	Saro Skeeter AOP.12	S2/5097	XL812	17. 7.78	Major F.F.Chamberlain (As "XL812")	Old Buckenham	19. 9.99P
G-SASK	PA-31P Pressurised Navajo	31P-39	G-BFAM SE-GLV/OH-PNF	30.10.97	Middle East Business Club Ltd (Guernsey)		30. 8.91T
G-SATL	Cameron Sphere 105SS HAFB	2696		5.12.91	Ballonverbung Hamburg GmbH Kiel, Germany		29. 4.97A
G-SAUF	Colt 90A HAFB (New envelope c/n 2492 1990/1)	1497		25. 5.89	K.H.Medau	Baden, Germany	8. 7.99A
G-SAXO	Cameron N-105 HAFB	3864		1. 4.96	Flying Pictures Ltd (Citroen Saxo titles)	Fairoaks	25. 5.99A
G-SBAE	Reims Cessna F.172P Skyhawk	2200	D-EOCD(3)	3. 6.98	British Aerospace (Operations) Ltd	Warton	16. 7.01T
G-SBAS	Beechcraft B200 Super King Air	BB-1007	SE-IVZ N777GA/G-BJJV	16.11.90	Bond Helicopters Ltd	Aberdeen	20.12.00T

Regn	Type	C/n	P/I	Date	Owner/operator	Probable Base	CA Expy
G-SBLT	Steen Skybolt	MH-01		14. 4.92	M.A.McCallum & H.Lees		
						(London N22/Surbiton)	
G-SBMO	Robin R.2160I	116	EI-BMO	12. 2.99	D.Henderson, U.Simpson & M.Mannion		
			SE-GSZ			Weston	
G-SBUS	PADC BN-2A-26 Islander	3013	G-BMMH	31.10.86	Isles of Scilly Skybus Ltd	St.Just	17. 4.00T
			RP-C578				
G-SBUT	Robinson R-22 Beta	2739	G-BXUT	18. 5.98	Princepro Ltd	(Alfreton)	6.10.00T
G-SCAH	Cameron V-77 HAFB	788		18. 1.82	D.P.Busby "Orpheus"	Lancing	24. 7.87A
					(Balloon Preservation Group 7.98)		
G-SCAN	Vinten Wallis WA-116 Srs.100	001		5. 7.82	K.H.Wallis (Stored 8.97) Reymerston Hall		10. 7.91P
G-SCAT	Reims Cessna F.150F	0054	G-ATRN	15. 9.86	Hunt & Partners Ltd	(Newbury)	26. 3.99T
	(Taildragger conversion) (Wichita c/n 63455) (G-ATMN)						
G-SCFO	Cameron O-77 HAFB	1131		3. 5.85	M.K.Grigson "Southern Counties" Lancing		24. 5.95A
					(Balloon Preservation Group 7.98)		
G-SCLX	FLS Aerospace Sprint 160	002	G-PLYM	14. 7.94	Sunhawk Ltd	North Weald	3. 7.00T
G-SCOX	Enstrom F-28F	771	N330SA	3. 9.98	S.Cox	(Barnsley)	14. 9.01
			G-BXXW/JA7823				
G-SCPL	PA-28-140 Cherokee Cruiser		G-BPVL	4. 5.89	Aeroshow Ltd	Gloucestershire	5. 8.01T
		28-7725160	N1785H				
G-SCRU	Cameron A-250 HAFB	3935	G-BWWO	30. 9.96	Societe Bombard SARL Meursanges, France		3.10.99A
G-SCTA	Westland Scout AH.1	F.9701	XV126	18.12.95	B.H.& E.F.Austen	(Cricklade)	5.12.97P
					t/a Austen Associates (As "XV126/X" in AAC c/s)		
G-SCTT*	HPR.7 Dart Herald 210	173	F-BLOY	30. 8.88	Channel Express Group plc	Bournemouth	27. 7.99T
			F-OCLY/HB-AAK/G-ASPJ (Stored 8.97)				
G-SCUB	PA-18-135 Super Cub	18-3847	PH-GAX	13.12.78	N.D. & Mrs.C.L.Needham t/a N.D.Needham (Farms)		
	(L-21B-PI) (Frame No.18-3849)		R.Neth AF R-157/54-2447		Old Manor Farm, Anwick		15. 8.00
					(As "54-2447" in US Army c/s)		
G-SCUD	Montgomerie-Bensen B.8MR PFA G/101-1294			18. 8.97	D.Taylor	Belper	
G-SCUL	Rutan Cozy	PFA/159-13212		28. 5.98	K.R.W.Scull	(Usk)	
G-SDEV	DH.104 Sea Devon C.20 (Dove 6) 04472		XK895	29. 3.90	Wyndham Press Group plc	Shoreham	17. 9.99
					(As "XK895/CU19" in 771 Sqn RN c/s)		
G-SDLW	Cameron O-105 HAFB	2460		11. 3.91	P.J.Smart	Bath	15. 5.99A
G-SEAB	Republic RC-3 Seabee	413	N6210K	6. 5.88	Barbara A.Farries	Nottingham	AC
			NC6210K				
G-SEAI	Cessna U206G Stationair II Seaplane		N756FQ	20. 3.92	Aerofloat Ltd	Cumbernauld	8. 6.98T
		U206-04059					
G-SEAT	Colt 42A HAFB	817		28. 5.86	Virgin Airship & Balloon Co Ltd Telford		28. 7.88A
					"Virgin Atlantic"		
G-SEED	Piper J3C-90 Cub (L-4H-PI)	11098	EI-BAP	28. 1.80	J.H.Seed		
	(Frame No.10932)		F-BFBZ/44-80203/43-29807		Black Spring Farm, Castle Bytham, Grantham		4. 8.97P
	(Official identity is c/n 12499/44-80203 and probably rebuilt 1945)						
G-SEEK	Cessna T210N Turbo-Centurion II		N9721Y	14.10.83	A.Hopper	(Little Shelford, Cambs)	24. 1.99
		210-64579					
G-SEGA	Cameron Sonic 90SS HAFB	2896		16. 9.92	Virgin Airship & Balloon Co Ltd Telford		24. 4.97A
	(Sonic The Hedgehog shape)				"Sonic The Hedgehog"		
G-SEGO	Robinson R-22 Beta	0871	N9081N	12.10.88	Burman Aviation Ltd	Cranfield	13.11.00T
G-SEJW	PA-28-161 Warrior II	28-7816469	N9557N	19. 4.78	Keen Leasing Ltd	Aldergrove	19. 4.00T
G-SELL	Robin DR.400/180 Regent	1153	D-EEMT	7. 3.85	A.Burbidge	Tatenhill	14. 6.00
					t/a G-SELL Regent Group		
G-SELY	Agusta-Bell 206B Jet Ranger III 8740			26. 7.96	Petrochem Aviation Services Ltd		
						(Wimbledon)	3. 9.99T
G-SEMI	PA-44-180 Seminole	44-7995052	G-DENW	23. 2.99	T.Hiscox	Halfpenny Green	20. 4.98T
			N21439				
G-SENA	Rutan LongEz	1325	F-PZSQ	11.11.96	G.Bennett	(Great Yarmouth)	
			F-WZSQ				
G-SEND	Colt 90A HAFB	2100		2.12.91	Redmalt Ltd	Witham, Essex	4. 6.99T
					"Motorola III"		
G-SENX	PA-34-200T Seneca II	34-7870356	G-DARE	15. 5.95	Senair Charter Ltd	Southend	30. 5.01T
			G-WOTS/G-SEVL/N36742				
G-SEPA	Eurocopter AS.355N Twin Squirrel		G-METD	25. 7.96	The Metropolitan Police		
		5525	G-BUJF/F-WYMF		Fairoaks/Lippitts Hill, Loughton		4. 8.99T
G-SEPB	Eurocopter AS.355N Twin Squirrel		G-BVSE	1. 2.95	The Metropolitan Police		
		5574			Fairoaks/Lippitts Hill, Loughton		1. 3.98T
G-SEPC	Eurocopter AS.355N Twin Squirrel		G-BWGV	29.11.95	The Metropolitan Police		
		5596			Fairoaks/Lippitts Hill, Loughton		20. 3.99T
G-SEPT	Cameron N-105 HAFB	1880		22.11.88	P.Gooch "Septodont"	Alresford	23. 6.99A
G-SERA	Enstrom F-28A-UK	103	G-BAHU	14. 3.91	W.R.Pitcher	Leatherhead	12. 3.00
			EI-BDF/G-BAHU		t/a Regal Rabbits		
G-SERL	Socata TB-10 Tobago	109	G-LANA	28. 5.92	R.J. & G.J.Searle	Rochester	26. 3.00
			EI-BIH				
G-SEUK	Cameron TV 80SS HAFB	3810		12. 4.96	Flying Pictures Ltd "Samsung"	Fairoaks	11. 3.99A
	(Samsung Computer Shape)						
G-SEVA	Replica Plans SE.5A	PFA/20-10955		19. 6.85	I.D.Gregory	Boscombe Down	20.12.99P
	(Cont C90)				(As "F-141/G" in 141 Sqn RFC c/s)		
G-SEVE	Cessna 172N Skyhawk II	172-69970	N738GR	10. 1.90	MK Aero Support Ltd	Andrewsfield	28. 1.01T
G-SEXI	Cessna 172M Skyhawk II	172-63806	N1964V	21. 4.92	General Airline Ltd	Blackbushe	13. 8.01T
					t/a European Flyers		

Regn	Type	C/n	P/I	Date	Owner/operator	Probable Base	CA Expy
G-SEXY	American AA-1 Yankee AA1-0442 (Regd as c/n 0042 incorrectly)		G-AYLM	30. 6.81	I.C.Kenyon Liverpool (Liverpool Flying School c/s) (Damaged Burscough, Lancs 11.2.94; stored 1.97)		17. 3.95
G-SFBH	Boeing 737-46N	28723		28. 5.97	British Midland Airways Ltd East Midlands		5. 6.00T
G-SFHR	PA-23-250 Aztec F	27-8054041	G-BHSO N2527Z	24. 6.82	Comed Avn Ltd Blackpool		22.11.01T
G-SFOX	Rotorway Exec 90 (RW5055)	5059	G-BUAH	11.10.93	Magpie Computer Svs Ltd (Stored Chester 7.97) Crabtree Farm, Crowborough		12. 9.96P
G-SFPA	Reims Cessna F406 Caravan II	0064		11.11.91	Secretary of State for Scotland - Dept of Agriculture & Fisheries (Op Fisheries Protection Agency) Prestwick		12. 3.00T
G-SFPB	Reims Cessna F406 Caravan II	0065		11.11.91	Secretary of State for Scotland - Dept of Agriculture & Fisheries (Op Fisheries Protection Agency) Prestwick		26. 4.00T
G-SFRY	Thunder Ax7-77 HAFB	1667		23. 1.90	K.J.Baxter & P.Szczepanski Birmingham		12. 8.95A
G-SFTA*	Westland SA.341G Gazelle 1	1039	"G-BAGJ" G-SFTA/HB-XIL/G-BAGJ/(XW858)	10. 9.82	North East Acft Museum Usworth		24. 2.86
			(Crashed nr Alston, Cumbria 7.3.84; rebuilt to static condition in Army c/s)				
G-SFTZ	Slingsby T-67M Firefly 160	2000		7. 2.83	Airborne Services Ltd (Manchester)		24. 1.02T
G-SGAS	Colt 77A HAFB	2073		31.10.91	SGL Ltd Barton t/a Shellgas South West Area "Shell Gas"		17. 7.99A
G-SGSE	PA-28-181 Archer II	28-7890332	G-BOJX N3774M	2.12.96	Mountune Racing Ltd Andrewsfield		4. 9.00
G-SHAA	Enstrom 280-UK Shark	1011	N280Q	8. 7.88	Ribble Aviation Ltd Barton		17.11.01T
G-SHAH	Reims Cessna F.152 II	1839	OH-IHA SE-IHA	7. 2.97	E.Alexander Andrewsfield		24. 4.00T
G-SHAW	PA-30-160 Twin Comanche B	30-1221	LN-BWS	21. 3.78	E.R.Meredith & M.D.Faiers Gloucestershire		6. 4.00
G-SHCB	Schweizer Hughes 269C-1	0038	N41S	28. 6.96	Oxford Aviation Services Ltd Oxford		8. 9.99T
G-SHCC	Bell 206B JetRanger II	1172	N280C	14.11.88	Yorkshire Helicopter Centre Ltd Swinton		30. 4.01T
G-SHEC	BAe 125 Srs 1000B	259037	G-SCCC G-5-771	19.12.95	Shell Aircraft Ltd Heathrow		2. 4.98T
G-SHED	PA-28-181 Archer II	28-7890068	G-BRAU N47411	12. 6.89	P.T.Crouch & R.M.Gingell Gloucestershire		14. 8.01
G-SHIM	CFM Streak Shadow (Rotax 582) K.228-SA & PFA/206-12501			19. 5.93	E.G.Shimmin Hadley		13. 9.99P
G-SHIP*	PA-23-250 Aztec F	27-7654015	N62490	18. 1.77	Not known Hockley Heath, Solihull (Crashed Keystone 4.12.83; displayed in "paint-ball" Woodland 11.92)		1. 7.85T
G-SHIV	Gulfstream GA-7 Cougar	GA7-0092	N713G	22.11.84	S.J.Westley Cranfield t/a Westley Avn Svs		18. 1.98T
G-SHNN	Enstrom 280C Shark	1119	N51685	22. 5.89	C.J.Roberts Northwich, Cheshire t/a CJ Svs		28. 4.98
G-SHOE*	Cessna 421C Golden Eagle II 421C-0123		G-BHGD D-IASC/OE-FLR/N3862C	15. 1.81	Not known Southampton (Damaged Deauville, France 8.11.85; fuselage on fire dump 9.96)		1. 5.86T
G-SHOG	Colomban MC-15 Cri-Cri (JPX PUL-212)	001	G-PFAB F-PYPU	3.10.96	V.S.E.Norman Rendcomb (Mitsubishi Shogun c/s) (A second static G-SHOG exists)		20.12.99P
G-SHOT	Cameron V-77 HAFB	972		14.12.83	E.C.Moore "Buckshot" Great Missenden		20. 5.97A
G-SHOW*	Morane-Saulnier MS.733 Alcyon	125	F-BMQJ Fr.AF 125/MZ	1.10.80	Not known ?? (Stored Bruntingthorpe until roaded out 8.96)		24. 5.83P
G-SHPP	Hughes 269A (TH-55A)	36-0481	N80559 64-18169	24. 7.89	R.P.Bateman White Waltham		25. 4.99
G-SHRL	Jodel D.18	PFA/169-12217		18. 9.92	M.W.Kilvert & G.Trevor (Newtown, Powys)		
G-SHSH	Europa Avn Europa	PFA/247-12722		7. 4.98	D.G.Hillam (Birkenhead)		
G-SHSP	Cessna 172S	172S-8079	N9552Q	25. 3.99	Oxford Aviation Services Ltd Oxford		
G-SHSS	Enstrom 280C-UK Shark	1060	N6892X G-SHSS/EI-CHG/G-SHSS/G-BENO	11.10.89	R.J.Patten St. Angelo t/a St. Angelo Helicopters		11.11.00T
G-SHUG	PA-28R-201T Turbo Arrow III 28R-7703048		N1026Q	17. 5.88	Nicola E.Rennie Booker		10. 7.00T
G-SHUU	Enstrom 280C-UK-2 Shark	1221	G-OMCP G-KENY/G-BJFG/N8617N	16.10.89	D.Ellis Wigan		23. 6.01
G-SIAL	Hawker Hunter F.58	41H-697457	J-4090	2.10.95	Classic Aviation Ltd Scampton (As "J-4090")		27. 9.99P
G-SIGN	PA-39 Twin Comanche C/R	39-8	OY-TOO N8853Y	9. 2.78	D.Buttle (Wokingham)		10.12.99
G-SIIB	Aviat Pitts S-2B Special (Lyc AEIO-540)	5218	G-BUVY N6073U	24. 3.93	G.Ferriman Papplewick, Nottingham		30. 4.99
G-SIII	Extra EA.300	058	D-ETYE	10. 1.95	Firebird Aerobatics Ltd Denham (MG F c/s)		22. 1.01T
G-SILS	Pietenpol Air Camper	PFA/47-13331		29. 6.98	D.Silsbury Ivybridge		
G-SIMI	Cameron A-315 HAFB	3391		10. 3.95	Balloon School (International) Ltd t/a Balloon Safaris Petworth		7. 4.99T
G-SIMN	Robinson R-22 Beta	2769		10.12.97	Simlot Ltd (Jersey)		22.12.00T
G-SION	PA-38-112 Tomahawk II	38-81A0146	N23661	30. 1.91	F.N.Dunstan Gloucestershire t/a Naiad Air Svs (Op Avon Flying School)		28.12.00
G-SIPA	SIPA 903	63	G-BGBM F-BGBM	31. 5.83	G.K.Brothwood & P.R.Tonks Liverpool t/a Mersey SIPA Group		14. 2.89P

Regn	Type	C/n	P/I	Date	Owner/operator	Probable Base	CA Expy
G-SIRR	North American P-51D-25NA Mustang	122-39798	N51RR (N151MC)/TNI-AU F-3../44-73339	3. 2.97	D.J.Gilmour t/a Intrepid Aviation Co (As "474008/VF-R" in 4th FG/1336th FS USAAF c/s)	North Weald	8. 5.99P
	(A/c adopted identity of c/n 122-40548/44-74008/RCAF 9274/N8676E/N76AF/(N151MC) during 1982-84 rebuild)						
G-SIVA	MDC Hughes 369E (500E)	0372E	G-TBIX	21. 1.94	Southern Air Ltd	Shoreham	13. 3.99T
G-SIXC	Douglas DC-6A/B	45550	N93459 N90645/B-1006/XW-PFZ/B-1006	20. 3.87	Atlantic Air Transport Ltd	Coventry	4. 4.99T
G-SIXD	PA-32-300 Cherokee Six D	32-7140007	HB-OMH N8615N	25. 3.98	G-SIXD Ltd	(Basildon)	28. 7.01
G-SIXX	Colt 77A HAFB	1327		21.10.88	P.B.D.Bird & R.J.Maud	Bristol	12. 1.99A
G-SIXY	Van's RV-6	PFA/181-13368		9. 3.99	C.J.Hall & C.R.P.Hamlett	(Cambridge)	
G-SIZE	Lindstrand LBL-310A HAFB	028		9. 6.93	Adventure Balloon Co Ltd	London W7	25. 3.99T
G-SJAB	PA-39-160 Twin Comanche C/R	39-85	(N) G-AYWZ/N8928Y	14. 9.81	J.L.Way t/a Smith & Way	Blackpool	24. 4.01
G-SJMC	Boeing 767-31KER	27205	N6038E	16. 3.94	Airtours International Airways Ltd	Manchester	15. 3.00T
G-SKAN	Reims Cessna F.172M Skyhawk II	1120	G-BFKT F-BVBJ	8. 7.85	Bustard Flying Club Ltd	Boscombe Down	1. 4.00T
G-SKIE	Steen Skybolt	AACA/357	ZK-DEN	29. 8.97	S.Gray Rushett Farm, Chessington		
G-SKIL	Cameron N-77 HAFB	2264		19. 3.90	Sky Trek Ballooning Ltd Longfield, Kent "Skillball"		20. 7.99T
G-SKIS	Tri-R Kis	PFA/239-12630		3. 2.94	S.D.Barnard	(Coalville)	
G-SKYC	Slingsby T-67M Firefly	2009	G-BLDP	13. 6.97	T.W.Cassells	Sherburn	12. 9.99T
G-SKYD	Christen Pitts S-2B Special (Lyc AEIO-540)	5057	N5331N	15.10.92	S.D.Harris t/a G-SKYD Syndicate	Redhill	6. 3.99
G-SKYE	Cessna TU206G Turbo Stationair 6 II	U206-04568	(G-DROP) N9783M	1. 8.79	P.M.Hall Weston-on-the-Green t/a RAF Sport Parachute Association		5. 4.01
G-SKYG	III Sky Arrow 650 TC	C008		15.12.98	G.F.Smith	(Milton Keynes)	13. 1.02
G-SKYH*	Cessna 172N Skyhawk 100	172-68098	A6-GRM N76034	20. 2.79	Not known Abbeyshrule, Ireland (Crashed Connaught, Ireland 21.7.91; stored 4.96)		9. 8.91T
G-SKYI	Air Command 532 Elite (Rotax 532)	0430		1. 9.88	P.J.Troy-Davies	Royston	29. 5.91P
G-SKYL	Cessna 182S Skylane	182-80176	N4104D	19. 6.98	Skylane Aviation Ltd	Sherburn-in-Elmet	24. 6.01
G-SKYR	Cameron A-180 HAFB	2826		31. 3.92	PSH Skypower Ltd Pewsey, Wilts "Candy Floss"		18. 5.99T
G-SKYT	III Sky Arrow 650TC (Rotax 912)	C.004		6. 9.96	I.R.Malby	Thruxton	26. 2.00T
G-SKYY	Cameron A-250 HAFB	3402		9. 3.95	PSH Skypower Ltd Pewsey, Wilts "City of Southampton"		1. 4.01T
G-SKYZ	PA-34-200T Seneca II	34-7870260	N31712	20. 1.95	Park Aeroleasing Ltd	Humberside	15. 3.01T
G-SLAC	Cameron N-77 HAFB	2295		7. 6.90	The Scottish Life Assurance Co "Scottish Life"	Manchester	20. 4.97A
G-SLCE	Cameron C-80 HAFB	4022		24. 2.97	SLC Europe Ltd	Bristol	21.11.98A
G-SLEA	Mudry/CAARP CAP.10B	124		19.12.80	P.D.Southerington	Cranwell North	13. 4.00
G-SLII	Cameron O-90 HAFB	2388		20. 9.90	R.B. & A.M.Harris "Mad Dash"	Huntingdon	12. 5.98A
G-SLNE	Agusta A.109A II	7393	G-EEVS G-OTSL	23. 7.96	Sloane Helicopters Ltd	Sywell	3. 7.00T
G-SLYN	PA-28-161 Warrior II	28-8116204	N161WA N8373K	12. 4.89	G.E.Layton	Dunkeswell	25. 5.01
G-SMAF	Sikorsky S-76A	760149	N130TL N5425U	6. 9.88	Air Harrods Ltd	Stansted	3.10.98T
G-SMAN	Airbus A.330-243	261	F-WWKR	26. 3.99	Monarch Airlines Ltd	Luton	
G-SMDB	Boeing 737-36N	28557		15. 3.97	British Midland Airways Ltd	East Midlands	20. 3.00T
G-SMDH	Europa Avtn Europa XS	PFA/247-13367		8.10.98	S.W.Pitt	(Petersfield)	
G-SMIG	Cameron O-65 HAFB	922		6. 6.83	G.Green & R.W.Taaffe Kowloon, Hong Kong t/a The Hong Kong Balloon & Airship Club "San Miguel Brewery"		28. 7.87A
G-SMIT*	Messerschmitt Bf.109G-6/U-2	163824		10.12.79	Australian War Memorial Luftwaffe 163824 Mitchell, Canberra, ACT, Australia (Displayed in Treloar Warfare Technology Centre 1996)		
G-SMJJ	Cessna 414A Chancellor II	414A-0425	N2694H	24. 3.81	Gull Air Ltd	Guernsey	30. 5.00
G-SMTC	Colt Flying Hut SS HAFB	1828		7. 1.91	Shiplake Investments Ltd	(Switzerland)	23. 9.93A
G-SMTH	PA-28-140 Cherokee C	28-26916	G-AYJS	28. 9.90	D.M.Banner	Barton	14. 1.02
G-SNAK	Lindstrand LBL-105A HAFB	404		23. 9.96	Ballooning Adventures Ltd	Hexham	N/E(T)
G-SNAP	Cameron V-77 HAFB	1217		29.11.85	C.J.S.Limon "Snapshot"	Great Missenden	26. 6.97A
G-SNAX	Colt 69A HAFB	1680		6. 3.90	United Biscuits (UK) Ltd "Phileas Fogg II"	Consett	16. 7.97A
G-SNAZ	Enstrom F-28F	761	G-BRCP	31.10.94	Thornhill Aviation Ltd	Shoreham	5. 1.02T
G-SNDY	Piper J3C-65 Cub	3751	N25797 NC25797	1. 3.90	R.R.K.Mayall (Stored 4.94)	Carlisle	
G-SNEV	CFM Streak Shadow SA (Rotax 582)	PFA/206-13042		17. 9.96	N.G.Smart	(Feltham)	26. 1.99P
G-SNOW	Cameron V-77 HAFB	541	(G-BGWA)	21. 6.79	M.J.Ball	Clitheroe	3. 4.99A
	(Fitted with replacement envelope 1989 - c/n 2050 which was the original G-BSDX)						
G-SOAR	Eiri PIK-20E	20214		21. 6.79	F.W.Fay "AR"	Bidford	3. 6.99

Regn	Type	C/n	P/I	Date	Owner/operator	Probable Base	CA Expy
G-SOEI	HS.748 Srs.2A/242	1689	ZK-DES	25. 2.98	Emerald Airways Ltd	Liverpool	17. 4.01T
G-SOFA	Cameron N-65 HAFB	968		30. 8.83	M.J.Axtell	Todmorden	10. 6.90A
G-SOFT	Thunder Ax7-77 HAFB	1339		5.12.88	A.J.Bowen	Edinburgh	11. 9.99A
					"Enterprise Software"		
G-SOLA	Star-Lite SL-1 203TG & PFA/175-11311			9. 6.88	J.P.Lethaby	(Lynton, Devon)	31. 3.93P
	(Rotax 447)				"A Star Is Born" (Stored 6.93)		
G-SOLD	Robinson R-22 Alpha	0471	N8559X	16. 5.85	J.F.H.James	(Chipping-Norton)	12. 6.00
G-SOLH	Bell 47G-5	2639	G-AZMB	5. 3.97	Sol Helicopters Ltd	Elstree	13. 2.00T
			CF-NJW				
G-SOLO	Anvil-Pitts S-2S Special	AA/1/1980		30. 5.80	Landitfast Ltd	Denham	6. 4.96P
	(Lyc AEIO-540)						
G-SONA	Socata TB-10 Tobago	151	G-BIBI	24.10.80	The Real Aeroplane Co Ltd	Breighton	26. 6.93
G-SONY	Aero Commander 200D	358	G-BGPS	24.11.88	General Airline Ltd	Blackbushe	27. 7.01
			5Y-AFT/N2985T		t/a European Flyers		
G-SOOC	Hughes 369HS (500C)	111-0354S	G-BRRX	6.10.93	Repetek Ltd	Dungannon, Co.Tyrone	14.10.99
			N9083F				
G-SOOE	Hughes 369E (500E)	0227E		27. 4.87	R.W.Nash	Gravesend	24. 5.99
G-SOOK	Sukhoi SU-26M	04-01	RA-0401	23. 3.95	V.Rahmani "30"	(London SW6)	25. 6.99P
			DOSAAF30				
G-SOOM	Glaser-Dirks DG-500M	5E42-M20		14. 5.92	R.L.McLean & J.Ellis	Rufforth	2. 6.01
					t/a Glaser-Dirks UK "112"		
G-SOOS	Colt 21A Cloudhopper HAFB	1263		7. 6.88	P.J.Stapley	Redcar	25. 3.95A
G-SOOT	PA-28-180 Cherokee C	28-4033	G-AVNM	19. 8.88	Thornton Browne Group plc	Earls Colne	26. 8.01T
			N11C				
G-SOPP	Enstrom 280FX	2024	G-OSAB	23.10.97	F.P. & M.Sopp & L.A.Moore		18. 5.01
			N86259		Jefferies Farm, Billingshurst		
G-SORT	Cameron N-90 HAFB	2878		13. 7.92	A.Brown "Streamline"	Bristol	8. 8.98A
G-SOUL	Cessna 310R II	310R-0140	N5020J	27. 6.88	Atlantic Air Transport Ltd	Coventry	10. 6.01T
G-SOUP	Cameron C-80 HAFB	3387		24.10.94	M.G.Barlow (Not built)	(Skipton)	
G-SPAM	Light Aero Avid Aerobat	829 & PFA/189-12074		9. 5.91	R.W.Fair	(Chester)	23. 8.99P
	(Rotax 582)						
G-SPEE	Robinson R-22 Beta	0939	G-BPJC	20. 7.94	Speed Helicopters Ltd	Redhill	28. 9.00T
G-SPEL	Sky 220-24 HAFB	045		26. 7.96	T.G.Church	Blackburn	5.12.99T
					t/a Pendle Balloon Co		
G-SPEY	Agusta-Bell 206B JetRanger III	8608	G-BIGO	1. 4.81	Castle Air Charters Ltd		
						Trebrown, Liskeard	24. 4.99T
G-SPFX	Rutan Cozy	PFA/159-13113		30. 4.97	B.D.Tutty	(Gillingham, Kent)	
G-SPIN	Aerotek Pitts S-2A Special	2110	N5CQ	13. 3.80	R.P.Grace & P.L.Goldberg	White Waltham	28. 3.99
	(Lyc AEIO-360)						
G-SPIT	VS.379 Spitfire FR.XIVe 6S/649205		(G-BGHB)	2. 3.79	Patina Ltd (Op The Fighter Collection)		
			Indian AF T-20/MV293		(As "MV293/OI-C"" in 2 Sqn c/s) Duxford		6. 5.99P
G-SPOG	San Jodel DR.1050 Ambassadeur	155	G-AXVS	25. 9.95	A.C.Frost	(Ware)	13. 6.77S
			F-BJNL		(Damaged Stonacre Farm, Bredhurst 17.2.91: on rebuild 1995)		
G-SPOL	MBB Bo.105DBS-4	S-392	VR-BGV	23. 3.90	Bond Helicopters Ltd	Glasgow Heliport	5. 6.99T
			D-HDLH		(Op Strathclyde Police Air Support Unit)		
G-SPUR	Cessna 550 Citation II	550-0714	N593EM	27.10.98	Amsail Ltd	(Brentwood)	15.11.99T
			N12035				
G-SPYI	Bell 206B Jet Ranger III	3689	G-BVRC	9. 5.96	A.J.Sinclair	Ringwood	24. 6.99T
			G-BSJC/N3175S				
G-SROE	Westland Scout AH.1	F.9508	XP907	26.10.95	Bolenda Engineering Ltd	Ipswich	5.10.99P
					(As "XP907")		
G-SRVO	Cameron N-90 HAFB	3551		10. 4.95	Servo & Electronic Sales Ltd	Lydd	23. 6.99A
					"Connect One"		
G-SSCL	MDC Hughes 369E (500E)	0491E	N684F	25. 4.98	Shaun Stevens Contractors Ltd		
						(Maidstone)	
G-SSFC	PA-34-200 Seneca	34-7450016	G-BBXG	28. 4.94	SFC (Air Taxis) Ltd	Stapleford	26. 3.01T
			N56647				
G-SSFT	PA-28-161 Warrior II	28-8016069	G-BHIL	16. 7.86	SFT Europe Ltd	Bournemouth	15. 3.98T
			N80821				
G-SSGS	Europa Avn Europa	082		25. 1.94	G. & S.G.Schwetz	Old Sarum	13. 7.98P
	(Rotax 912UL)				t/a SGS Partnership "Fledermaus"		
G-SSIX	Rans S-6-116 Coyote II PFA/204A-12749			5. 9.94	J.V.Squires	(Didcot)	10.12.98P
	(Rotax 582)				(Damaged Parc Coed Machen Farm nr Cardiff 4.6.98)		
G-SSKY	PBN BN-2B-26 Islander	2247	G-BSWT	11. 5.92	Isles of Scilly Skybus Ltd	St.Just	29. 4.00T
G-SSSC	Sikorsky S-76C	760408		26.10.93	Bond Helicopters Ltd	Aberdeen	13. 1.01T
G-SSSD	Sikorsky S-76C	760415		26.10.93	Bond Helicopters Ltd	Aberdeen	22.12.99T
G-SSSE	Sikorsky S-76C	760417		23.11.93	Bond Helicopters Ltd	Aberdeen	2. 2.00T
G-SSTI	Cameron N-105 HAFB	3238		30. 3.94	British Airways plc	Heathrow	26. 6.99T
G-SSWT	Short SD.3-30 Var.100	SH3095		9. 5.96	Freshleave Ltd	Exeter	18. 6.99T
			G-BNYA/G-BKSU/G-14-3095 (Damaged Luton 13.2.99)				
G-SSWU	Short SD.3-30 Var.100	SH3076	C-FYXF	24. 2.99	Streamline Aviation (SW) Ltd	Exeter	
			G-BIYH/N183AP/N338MV/G-BIYH/G-14-3076				
G-SSWV	Sportavia Fournier RF5B Sperber		N55WV	31. 5.90	E.C.Neighbour & J.A.Melville	Camphill	3. 8.99P
		51032			t/a Skylark F/Grp		
G-STAT	Cessna U206F Stationair II		A6-MAM	20. 2.79	Wingglider Ltd	Hibaldstow	11. 9.98
		U206-03485	N8732Q				
G-STAV	Cameron O-84 HAFB	2913		29. 9.92	F.Horsfall	Moreton-in-Marsh	20. 4.97A

Regn	Type	C/n	P/I	Date	Owner/operator	Probable Base	CA Expy
G-STEF	Hughes 369HS	114-0673S	G-BKTK OY-HCL/OO-JGR	7.11.84	Source Ltd	Bournemouth	29.11.98
G-STEM	Stemme S-10V	14-027		2. 7.97	Warwickshire Aerocentre Ltd	Birmingham	15. 7.00
G-STEN	Stemme S-10	10-32	D-KGCH	9. 1.92	W.A.H.Kahn "4"	Lasham	19. 3.01
G-STEP	Schweizer Hughes 269C	S.1494		1.10.90	Geraint Hill Car Sales Ltd	Aberdare	29.10.00
G-STER	Bell 206B JetRanger III	4116	OO-EGA	23. 3.94	P.J.Brown t/a P.J.Brown Civil Engineer & Haulage Contractors	(Crawley)	24. 3.00T
G-STEV	CEA Jodel DR.221 Dauphin	61	F-BOZD	9. 3.82	S.W.Talbot	Long Marston	24.10.98
G-STMP	SNCAN Stampe SV-4A	241	F-BCKB	11. 3.83	A.C.Thorne (On overhaul Ivybridge 5.93)	(Yelverton)	
G-STNO	Socata TB-20 Trinidad	1815	F-OHUY	15. 7.97	Eclipse (UK) Ltd	Bristol/Lulsgate	17. 7.00
G-STOW	Cameron Wine Box-90 SS HAFB	4420		2.10.98	I.Martin & D.Groombridge t/a Flying Enterprises Partnership	Bristol	
G-STOX	Bell 206B JetRanger II	1513	G-BNIR N59615	27. 4.89	Burman Aviation Ltd	Cranfield	7. 6.99T
G-STOY	Robinson R-22 Beta	0700		10.11.87	Burman Aviation Ltd	Cranfield	29.11.99T
G-STPI	Cameron A-250 HAFB	4102		26. 2.97	A.D.Pinner (Central Auto Supplies c/s)	Northampton	3. 5.99T
G-STRK	CFM Streak Shadow (Rotax 582) K.143-SA & PFA/161-11762			4. 4.90	E.J.Hadley	(Arch, Switzerland)	27. 7.99P
G-STRM	Cameron N-90 HAFB	3568		3. 7.95	Royal Mail Streamline	(Oxford)	8. 8.97T
G-STUA	Aerotek Pitts S-2A Special (Lyc AEIO-360)	2164	N13GT	6. 3.91	Rollquick Ltd	Stapleford	21. 3.00T
G-STUB	Christen Pitts S-2B Special (Lyc AEIO-540)	5163	N260Y	5. 5.94	R.N.Goode & T.L.P.Delaney	White Waltham	19. 6.00
G-STVN*	HPR.7 Dart Herald 210	188	F-BOIZ F-OCLZ/HB-AAL	30. 8.88	Dart Group plc t/a Channel Express	Bournemouth	24.10.99T
G-STWO	ARV1 Super 2 002 & PFA/152-11048 (Hewland AE75)			24. 4.85	G.E.Morris	Gloucestershire	18. 6.99P
G-STYL	Pitts S-1S Special (Lyc-O-320)	GJSN-1P	N665JG	26. 1.88	D.B.Almey	(Spalding)	6. 6.94P
G-SUEE	Airbus A.320-231	363	G-IEAG F-WWBX	23. 9.93	Airtours International Airways Ltd	Manchester	18. 3.00T
G-SUEZ	Agusta-Bell 206B Jet Ranger II	8319	SU-YAE YU-HAZ	16. 9.98	Capital Helicopter Group Ltd	Biggin Hill	AC
G-SUIT	Cessna 210N Centurion II	210-64576	N9698Y	17.11.92	Edinburgh Air Centre Ltd	Edinburgh	28.11.98T
G-SUKI	PA-38-112 Tomahawk	38-79A0260	G-BPNV N2313D	22. 5.91	Western Air (Thruxton) Ltd	Thruxton	8. 5.99T
G-SULL*	PA-32R-301 Saratoga SP	32R-8113002	N82818	19. 6.86	The Fire Service College (Crashed Crowfield 1.2.95 & in fire service use 8.98)	Moreton-in-Marsh	27. 7.95T
G-SULY	Monnett Moni	PFA/142-11208		15. 7.87	M.J.Sullivan	(London W13)	
G-SUMT	Robinson R-22 Beta	2147	G-BUKD N23381	24. 9.92	Frankham Brothers Ltd	Leicester	1.12.01
G-SUPA	PA-18-150 Super Cub (Frame No.18-5512)	18-5395	PH-BAJ PH-MBF/ALAT 18-5395	13.12.78	J.M. Roach t/a Supa Group	Welshpool	5. 8.98
G-SURG	PA-30-160 Twin Comanche B	30-1424	G-VIST G-AVHZ/N8287Y	18. 6.90	A.R.Taylor	Turweston	20. 1.02T
G-SURV	PBN BN-2T-4S Defender 4000	4005	G-BVHZ	14. 4.94	Britten-Norman Ltd	Bembridge	26. 6.99
G-SUSI	Cameron V-77 HAFB	1133		22. 7.85	H.S.Dryden "Susi"	London EC2	25. 7.99A
G-SUSY	North American P-51D-25NA Mustang	122-39232	N12066 FAN GN120/44-72773	23. 7.87	P.J.Morgan "Susy" (As "472773/AJ-C" in 354th FG USAF c/s)	Sywell	10. 5.99P
G-SUTN	III Sky Arrow 650TC	C007		27. 8.98	G.C.Sutton	(London W1)	18.10.01
G-SUZI	Beechcraft 95-B55 Baron	TC-1574	G-BAXR	11. 3.84	Bebecar (UK) Ltd	Elstree	7. 7.01
G-SUZN	PA-28-161 Warrior II	28-8016187	N3573C N9540N	16. 1.91	E.Reed t/a The St.George F/C	Teesside	17. 3.00T
G-SUZY	Taylor JT.1 Monoplane (VW1600)	PFA/55-10395		1.12.78	D.I.Law	Dunkeswell	4. 8.98P
G-SVBF	Cameron A-180 HAFB	3587		2. 6.95	Virgin Balloon Flights Ltd	(London SE16)	17. 3.99T
G-SUNY	Robinson R-44 Astro	0540		8.12.98	Delice De France plc	Southall	13. 2.01T
G-SVEA	PA-28-161 Warrior II	28-7916082	N30299	16.12.98	A.Hastings & E.Lowery t/a Avion Aviation	Birmingham	15.12.01T
G-SVIP	Cessna 421B Golden Eagle II	421B-0820	G-BNYJ N4686Q/D-IMVB/N1590G	12. 3.97	Stephenson Marine Co Ltd	Southampton	28.11.00T
G-SVIV	SNCAN Stampe SV-4C (Gipsy Major)	475	N65214 F-BDBL	7. 8.90	A.J.Clarry & S.F.Bancroft	Thruxton	12. 6.99
G-SWEB	Cameron N-90 HAFB	2413		1.10.90	South Western Electricity plc "SWEB"	Bristol	22. 3.96T
G-SWEL	Hughes 369HS	61-0328S	G-RBUT C-FTXZ/CF-TXZ	18. 7.96	I.C. & L.E.Stilwell	Leamington Spa	13. 3.00
G-SWIF	VS.552 Swift F.7	VA.9597	XF114	1. 6.90	Heritage Aviation Developments Ltd	Scampton	AC
G-SWIM	Aerocar Super Coot	PFA/18-11486		21. 8.90	R.J.Hopkins	(Exmouth)	
G-SWIS*	FFW DH.100 Vampire FB.6	658	J-1149	21. 5.91	Hunter Wing Ltd (As "J-1149" in Swiss AF c/s) (Stored 9.97)	Bournemouth	

Regn	Type	C/n	P/I	Date	Owner/operator	Probable Base	CA Expy
G-SWJW	Airbus A.300B4-203	302	OH-LAB F-WZMY	19. 5.98	OY Air Scandic International Aviation AB Manchester		18. 5.01T
G-SWOT	Phoenix Currie Super Wot (Cont O-200-A)	PFA/3011		10. 9.80	R.T.Bennett (Cotgrave) (As "C3011/S" in SE.5A guise)		15.11.99P
G-SWPR	Cameron N-56 HAFB	829		16. 3.82	A.Brown "Post Code"	Bristol	5. 7.95A
G-SWSH	Revolution Helicopters Mini-500	0049		10.10.95	Aerial Enterprises Ltd (London SW19)		
G-SWUN	Pitts S-1M Special (Lyc O-320)	338-H	G-BSXH N14RM	18. 4.95	T.G.Lloyd (Stored 3.97)	Little Gransden	5. 6.92P
G-SYCO	Europa Avn Europa (NSI EA-81/118)	PFA/247-12540		27.11.95	J.T.Fillingham	Kemble	28. 5.99P
G-SYFW	WAR Focke-Wulf 190 Replica (Cont O-200-A)	269 & PFA/81-10584		28. 2.83	M.R.Parr Les Padins Farm, St.Saviour, Guernsey (As "WNo.7334/2+1" in Luftwaffe c/s) (Stored 1.98)		29. 6.87P
G-SYPA	Aerospatiale AS.355F2 Twin Squirrel	5193	LV-WHC F-WYMS/G-BPRE/N366E	25. 9.96	South Yorkshire Police Authority Sheffield City		2. 4.00T

G-TAAA-TZZZ

Regn	Type	C/n	P/I	Date	Owner/operator	Probable Base	CA Expy
G-TABS	Embraer EMB.110P1 Bandeirante		G-PBAC	18. 8.98	Thornhill Aviation Ltd	Plymouth	21.10.99T
		110-212	F-GCLA/F-OGME/F-GCLA/PT-GME				
G-TACE*	HS 125 Srs.403B	25223	G-AYIZ	23. 1.81	British Aerospace plc	Dunsfold	16. 7.86F
			F-BSSL/PJ-SLB/G-AYIZ/G-5-15 (Open store 10.95)				
G-TACK	Grob G-109B	6279		30. 5.84	A.P.Mayne	Exeter	18. 4.99
G-TAFF	CASA I-131E Jungmann	1129	G-BFNE	7. 9.84	A.Horsfall	Breighton	11. 5.99P
			E3B-148				
G-TAFI	Dornier Bucker Bu133C Jungmeister 24		N2210	27. 1.93	R.J.Lamplough	North Weald	30. 7.97P
			HB-MIF/SwAF U-77				
G-TAGS	PA-28-161 Warrior II	28-8416026	N4329D	6. 5.88	Oxford Aviation Services Ltd	Oxford	3. 8.00T
G-TAIL	Cessna 150J	150-70152	N60220	21. 4.89	D.G.Kipling	Blackpool	15. 1.98T
					t/a Aviators Flight Center		
G-TAIR	PA-34-200T Seneca II	34-7970055	N3059H	17.11.87	D.I.G. & J.de Souza	Bournemouth	3. 3.00T
					t/a Branksome Dene Garage		
G-TAMY	Cessna 421B Golden Eagle	421B-0512	SE-FNS	14.11.77	Malcolm Enamellers (Midlands) Ltd		
			N2BH/N69865			Halfpenny Green	2. 6.00
G-TAND	Robinson R-44 Astro	0478		12. 6.98	Southwest Helicharter Ltd		
						Gloucestershire	2. 7.01T
G-TANI	Gulfstream GA-7 Cougar	GA7-0107	G-VJAI	18. 5.95	S.Spier	Denham	1. 2.02T
			G-OCAB/G-BICF/N8500H/N29707 (Op Denham School of Flying)				
G-TANK	Cameron N-90 HAFB	3625		20. 6.95	Hoyers (UK) Ltd	Huddersfield	21. 3.99A
G-TANS	SOCATA TB-20 Trinidad	1870	F-GRBX	25. 9.98	K.& G.Threfall	(Wolverhampton)	24. 9.01
					t/a Tettenhall Leisure		
G-TAPE	PA-23-250 Aztec D	27-4054	G-AWVW	7.10.83	D.J.Hare (Op Merlix Air)	Fairoaks	11. 2.00T
			OY-RPF/G-AWVW/N6799Y				
G-TARN	Pietenpol Air Camper	PFA/47-13349		3. 8.98	P.J.Heilbron	(Guildford)	
G-TART	PA-28-236 Dakota	28-7911261	N2945C	18.12.90	Caroline A.Herbert	Bournemouth	18. 6.00
G-TARV	ARV.1 Super 2	PFA/152-12627		1. 6.94	M.F.Filer	(Bristol)	
G-TASH	Cessna 172N (modified)	172-70531	PH-KOS	4.11.98	A. Ashpitel	Popham	30.11.01T
			N739GL				
G-TASK	Cessna 404 Titan II	404-0829	PH-MPC	10. 3.93	Bravo Avn Ltd	Coventry	8. 7.00T
			SE-IHL/N6806Q		(Op Air Atlantique)		
G-TATT	Gardan GY-20 Minicab	PFA/56-10347		30.11.78	L.Tattersall	(Blackburn)	
G-TAXI	PA-23-250 Aztec E	27-7305085	N40270	6. 4.78	M.L.D.Levi & S.Waite	Barton	22. 9.01T
					t/a SWL Leasing (Stored 8.97)		
G-TAYI	Grob G.115	8008	(D-ENFT)	12. 9.90	K.P.Widdowson	(Doncaster)	10. 7.00
			G-TAYI/G-DODO/D-ENFT				
G-TAYS	Reims Cessna F.152 II	1697	G-LFCA	28.10.91	Tayside Avn Ltd	Aberdeen/Dundee	28. 5.01T
G-TBAG	Murphy Renegade 912	PFA/188-11912		11.12.90	M.R.Tetley	Newton-on-Rawcliffe, Yorks	12.10.99P
	(Rotax 912)						
G-TBGL	Agusta A.109A II	7412	G-VJCB	6. 1.99	Thomas Bolton Group Ltd (Stoke-on-Trent)		8.12.00T
			G-BOUA				
G-TBIC	BAe 146 Srs.200	E-2025	N167US	15. 1.97	Flightline Ltd	Dublin	16. 1.00T
			N349PS		(Aer Lingus Commuter c/s)		
G-TBIO	Socata TB-10 Tobago	340	F-BNGZ	10. 2.83	Rutland Ltd	Guernsey	14.12.98
G-TBMW	Murphy Renegade Spirit	PFA/118-11725	(G-MYIG)	20.10.98	S J Spavins (See G-MYIG)	(St Albans)	
G-TBRD	Canadair CL-30 (T-33AN)	T33-261	N33VC	18.12.96	Golden Apple Operations Ltd.	Duxford	AC
	Silver Star mk.3		G-JETT/G-OAHB		(Op The Old Flying Machine Co)		
			CF-IHB/CAF 133261/RCAF 21261 (As "54-21261" in USAF c/s)				
G-TBXX	Socata TB-20 Trinidad	276		16. 3.82	D.A.Phillips & C.S.Swaine	Headcorn	21. 5.00
G-TBZI	Socata TB-21 Trinidad TC	871	N21HR	25. 7.96	W.R.M.Beesley	Blackbushe	22. 9.99
G-TBZO	Socata TB-20 Trinidad	444		8. 8.84	D.L.Clarke & M.J.M.Hopper	Shoreham	24. 4.00
G-TCAN	Colt 69A HAFB	1996		19. 7.91	H.C.J.Williams "Toucan"	Bristol	7. 4.97A
G-TCAP	BAe 125 Srs 800B	258115	G-5-599	24. 4.96	British Aerospace plc	Warton	28. 8.00
			R. Saudi AF 104/G-5-665/RSAF 104/G-BPGR/G-5-599				
G-TCDI	HS.125 Srs.F400B	25248	N792A	10.10.96	Aravco Ltd	Farnborough	19.12.99T
			G-5-707/G-SHOP/G-BTUF/G-5-707/D-CFCF				
G-TCMP	Robinson R-22 Beta	0890		3.11.88	Thornhill Aviation Ltd	Shoreham	19. 2.01T
G-TCOM	PA-30-160 Twin Comanche B	30-1967	N555JC	29. 1.96	C.A.C.Burrough	Jersey	9. 4.99
			N8810Y				
G-TCSL*	Rockwell Commander 112A	322	N506CA	17. 9.92	The Works Night Club	(Corby)	26. 3.99
					(Damaged Spanhoe 5.12.94)		
G-TCTC	PA-28RT-201T Turbo Arrow IV	2831001	N9130B	1.12.89	S.C.Tysoe t/a STMS	Leicester	26. 3.99
	(Originally built as N9524N c/n 28R-8631006)						
G-TCUB	Piper J3C-65 Cub (NE-2)	13970	N9039Q	31. 7.87	C.Kirk	Wyberton	13. 4.01
	(Frame No.13805)		N67666/NC67666/Bu.29684/45-55204				
G-TDFS	IMCO Callair A.9	1200	G-AVZA	8.10.86	Dollarhigh Ltd	Sturgate	11.12.00A
			SE-EUA/N26D		t/a TD Flight Svs		
G-TDTW	CCF Hawker Hurricane	-	RCAF 5450	R	Hawker Restorations Ltd		
					(Composite rebuild 6.96) Moat Farm, Milden		
G-TEAL	Thurston TSC-1A1 Teal	15	C-GDQD	8.12.92	K.Heeley	Crosland Moor	AC
			(Damaged Crosland Moor 3.93; wings only stored 9.96 - fuselage on rebuild off-site)				
G-TECC	Aeronca 7AC Champion	7AC-5269	N1704E	26. 6.91	T.E.C.Cushing	Little Snoring	12.10.99P
			NC1704E				
G-TECH	Rockwell Commander 114	14074	G-BEDH	8. 8.85	P.A.Reed	Elstree	7. 8.00
			N4744W				

Regn	Type	C/n	P/I	Date	Owner/operator	Probable Base	CA Expy
G-TECK	Cameron V-77 HAFB	625		21. 3.86	G.M.N.Spencer "Spring Fever" Watford		18. 3.99A
G-TEDF	Cameron N-90 HAFB	2634		8. 8.91	Fort Vale Engineering Ltd	Nelson	10. 7.99A
G-TEDS	Socata TB-10 Tobago	57	G-BHCO	29. 3.83	E.W.Lyon	Halfpenny Green	14.11.98
G-TEDY	Evans VP-1 (VW1834)	PFA/62-10383	G-BHGN	4.10.90	N.K.Marston "The Plank"	(Harrow)	1. 7.97P
G-TEDZ	Nipper T.66 Srs.3B (Fairey c/n 30)	PFA/25-11051		27. 2.96	C.J.D.Edwards	(Wickford)	
G-TEEZ	Cameron N-90 HAFB	4005		27.11.96	Fresh Air Ltd	London NW2	29. 1.99T
G-TEFC	PA-28-140 Cherokee F	28-7325088	OY-PRC N15530	18. 6.80	A.R.Knight	Andrewsfield	1. 2.99
G-TEHL	CFM Streak Shadow Srs.M (Rotax 503)	185	G-MYJE	20.11.98	A.K. Paterson	Sleaford	26. 4.97P
G-TELY	Agusta A.109A II	7326	N1HQ N200SH	10. 3.89	Castle Air Charters Ltd Trebrown, Liskeard		23. 7.99T
G-TEMP	PA-28-180 Cherokee E	28-5806	G-AYBK	15. 5.89	M.J.Groome t/a Bev Piper Grp	Andrewsfield	8. 7.01T
G-TEMT	Hawker Tempest II	420	HA586 (RIAF)/MW763	9.10.89	Tempest Two Ltd Sandtoft (To be "MW763/HF-A" in 183 Sqn c/s) (On rebuild 11.96)		
G-TENT	Auster J/1N Alpha	2058	G-AKJU TW513	1. 2.90	R.C.Callaway-Lewis	Oaksey Park	21. 7.86
G-TERN	Europa Avn Europa	PFA/247-12780		18. 7.97	J.E.G.Lundesjo	(Taplow, Berks)	11. 8.99P
G-TERY	PA-28-181 Archer II	28-7990078	G-BOXZ N22402	13. 1.89	T.Barlow	Barton	26. 6.98T
G-TEST	PA-34-200 Seneca	34-7450116	OO-RPW G-BLCD/PH-PLZ/N41409	28. 7.89	Stapleford F/C Ltd	Stapleford	23.12.01T
G-TEWS	PA-28-140 Cherokee B	28-25128	G-KEAN G-AWTM	23. 5.88	M.J.Tew t/a G-TEWS Flying Group	Liverpool	1. 7.01T
G-TFCI	Reims Cessna FA.152 Aerobat	0358		25.10.79	Tayside Avn Ltd	Dundee	11. 6.01T
G-TFOX	Denney Kitfox mk.2 (Rotax 582)	PFA/172-11817		3. 6.91	F.A.Bakir	(Sale)	12.12.99P
G-TFRB	Air Command 532 Elite Sport	0628 & PFA G/104-1167		26. 4.90	F.R.Blennerhassett Wingate, Hartlepool		6. 8.98P
G-TFUN	Valentin Taifun 17E	1011	D-KIHP	28.12.83	G.F.Wynn & D.H.Evans t/a North West Taifun Grp	Blackpool	7. 7.00
G-TGAS	Cameron O-160 HAFB	1315		12. 8.87	P.J.Bish t/a Zebedee Balloon Service	Hungerford	13.12.96T
G-TGER	Gulfstream AA-5B Tiger	AA5B-0952	G-BFZP	20. 2.86	Plane Talking Ltd	Biggin Hill	26. 3.00T
G-TGRS	Robinson R-22 Beta	1069	G-DELL N80466	5.11.97	A.L.Ramsden t/a Tiger Helicopters	Shobdon	21. 9.01T
G-THCL	Cessna 550 Citation II	550-0563	N1298P	15.10.87	Tower House Consultants Ltd	Southampton	7. 1.99
G-THEA	Boeing-Stearman E75 (N2S-5) Kaydet (Lyc R-680)	75-5736A	N1733B USN Bu.38122	18. 3.81	L.M.Walton Duxford (As "33" in Navy c/s)		28. 5.99

(Converted by Eastern Stearman at Swanton Morley 1997/98: the plate shows c/n 75-5736 which corresponds to
N2PP ex 42-17573 but also records BuA No.38122 [c/n 75-7744] ex N5714N. This is now confirmed as ex
N1733B. The a/c has a non-standard c/n 75-5736A. The original airframe c/n 75-5736 was built as a
USN N2S-5 in 1943 and sold in 5.47. It was stored for some time before becoming N1733B. After many years
crop-dusting it was rebuilt by N.Norigan at Fresno, California in 1974 during which parts from N2S-4
c/n 75-7743/BuA38122 (and possibly from 75-7744/N5714N) were incorporated. The two aircraft which
emerged post-1974 rebuild were thus:-
(i) c/n 75-5736 - N244E,later N2PP, and (ii) c/n 75-5736A - N1733B
The plate on G-THEA is an amalgam of the c/n 75-5736 and the original identity of c/n 75-7743.
It was sold to Chris Ryan in 5.97 after five years of inactivity and arrived at Swanton Morley for
rebuild in 7.97. Marks EI-RYR were reserved in 3.98 but it was still present 4.99)

Regn	Type	C/n	P/I	Date	Owner/operator	Probable Base	CA Expy
G-THEL	Robinson R-44 Astro	0159	G-OCCB G-STMM	2. 9.98	Thurston Helicopters (Engineering) Ltd Redhill		3. 5.01T
G-THEO	Team Minimax 91	PFA/186-13099		9. 2.99	T.Willford	Blandford Forum	
G-THLS	MBB Bo.105DBS-4 (Rebuilt with new pod c/n S.859 1992)	S.80/859	G-BCXO D-HDCE	20. 2.92	Bond Helicopters Ltd RAF St.Mawgan (Op by Trinity House Lighthouse Service)		27. 2.01T
G-THOM	Thunder Ax6-56 HAFB	366		14. 7.81	T.H.Wilson "Macavity"	Diss	29. 8.99A
G-THOS	Thunder Ax7-77 HAFB	769		20. 2.86	C.E.A.Breton	Bristol	17. 4.91A
G-THOT	Pearce Jabiru SK	PFA/274-13159		16. 9.97	N.V.Cook	(Cranleigh)	
G-THSL	PA-28R-201 Arrow III	28R-7837278	N36396	11. 9.78	D.M.Markscheffel	Southend	28. 4.00
G-THZL	Socata TB-20 Trinidad	534	F-GJDR N65TB	9. 5.96	Ewan Ltd	Gloucestershire	22. 7.99T
G-TICL	Airbus A.320-231	169	OY-CNG F-WWIH	10.12.96	Airtours International Airways Ltd Manchester		11.12.99T
G-TIDS	SAN Jodel 150 Mascaret	44	OO-GAN	15. 4.86	J.B.Dovey	Crowfield	16.11.98P
G-TIGA	DH.82A Tiger Moth	83547	G-AOEG T7120	5. 6.85	D.E.Leatherland	Nottingham	20. 8.01T
G-TIGB	Aerospatiale AS.332L Super Puma	2023	G-BJXC F-WTNM	31. 3.82	Bristow Helicopters Ltd "City of Aberdeen"	Aberdeen	27. 4.01T
G-TIGC	Aerospatiale AS.332L Super Puma	2024	G-BJYI F-WTNJ	14. 4.82	Bristow Helicopters Ltd "Royal Burgh of Montrose"	Aberdeen	17. 5.99T
G-TIGE	Aerospatiale AS.332L Super Puma	2028	G-BJYJ F-WTNM	15. 4.82	Bristow Helicopters Ltd "City of Dundee"	Aberdeen	7. 6.01T
G-TIGF	Aerospatiale AS.332L Super Puma	2030	F-WKQJ	15. 4.82	Bristow Helicopters Ltd "Peterhead"	Aberdeen	27. 6.00T
G-TIGG	Aerospatiale AS.332L Super Puma	2032	F-WXFT	15. 4.82	Bristow Helicopters Ltd "Macduff"	Aberdeen	1. 8.01T

Regn	Type	C/n	P/I	Date	Owner/operator	Probable Base	CA Expy
G-TIGH*	Aerospatiale AS.332L Super Puma	2034	F-WXFL	15. 4.82	Bristow Helicopters Ltd	Aberdeen	24. 8.92T
	(Damaged 100m NE of Shetland Isles 14.3.92; used as Escape trainer 12.95)						
G-TIGI	Aerospatiale AS.332L Super Puma	2036	F-WTNP	15. 4.82	Bristow Helicopters Ltd "Fraserburgh"	Aberdeen	5. 9.99T
G-TIGJ	Aerospatiale AS.332L Super Puma	2042	VH-BHT G-TIGJ	15.4.82	Bristow Helicopters Ltd	Aberdeen	29. 6.99T
G-TIGL	Aerospatiale AS.332L Super Puma	2050		15. 4.82	Bristow Helicopters Ltd "Portsoy"	Aberdeen	9.12.99T
G-TIGM	Aerospatiale AS.332L Super Puma	2045		15. 4.82	Bristow Helicopters Ltd "Banff"	Aberdeen	1. 8.00T
G-TIGO	Aerospatiale AS.332L Super Puma	2061	F-WMHH	18. 2.83	Bristow Helicopters Ltd "Royal Burgh of Arbroath"	Scatsta	30. 3.00T
G-TIGP	Aerospatiale AS.332L Super Puma	2064		11. 3.83	Bristow Helicopters Ltd "Carnoustie"	(China)	8. 5.00T
G-TIGR	Aerospatiale AS.332L Super Puma	2071	F-WTNW	11. 3.83	Bristow Helicopters Ltd "Stonehaven"	(Vietnam)	19. 5.99T
G-TIGS	Aerospatiale AS.332L Super Puma	2086		6. 5.83	Bristow Helicopters Ltd "Findochty"	Aberdeen	27. 6.99T
G-TIGT	Aerospatiale AS.332L Super Puma	2078		6. 5.83	Bristow Helicopters Ltd "Portknockie"	Aberdeen	2. 5.01T
G-TIGU	Aerospatiale AS.332L Super Puma	2096		12. 1.84	Bristow Helicopters Ltd "Branderburgh"	Scatsta	27. 4.00T
G-TIGV	Aerospatiale AS.332L Super Puma	2099	LN-ONC G-TIGV/LN-ONC/G-TIGV/LN-OPF/G-TIGV	12. 1.84	Bristow Helicopters Ltd.	Aberdeen	25. 6.01T
G-TIGZ	Aerospatiale AS.332L Super Puma	2115	C-GQKK G-TIGZ	8. 8.84	Brintel Helicopters Ltd t/a British International Helicopters	Aberdeen	14.10.00T
G-TIII	Aerotek Pitts S-2A Special (Lyc AEIO-360)	2196	G-BGSE N947	27. 2.89	D.G.Cowden	Uckfield	14. 7.01T
G-TILE	Robinson R-22 Beta	1100		4. 8.89	M.J.Webb & C.R.Woodwiss	Coventry	2.11.98T
G-TILI	Bell 206B Jet Ranger II	2061	F-GHFN N7037A/XC-BOQ	8. 3.96	C.I.Threlfall t/a CIM Helicopters Ream Hill Farm, Weeton, Preston		2. 4.99
G-TIMB	Rutan VariEze (Cont O-200-A)	PFA/74-10795	G-BKXJ	11. 6.85	T.M.Bailey "Kitty"	Shoreham	14. 6.99P
G-TIME	PA-61P Aerostar 601P	61P-0541-230	(N8058J)	21. 7.78	Business Aircraft Rental Service Ltd Jonkoping, Sweden		7. 3.00
G-TIMJ	Rand Robinson KR-2 (VW1834)	PFA/129-11112		25.11.85	N.Seaton	Bidford	
G-TIMK	PA-28-181 Archer II	28-8090214	OO-TRT PH-EAS/OO-HLN/N8142H	25. 8.81	T.Baker	Halfpenny Green	12. 2.00
G-TIMM	Folland Gnat T.1	FL.519	8618M XP504	19. 2.92	T.J.Manna t/a Kennet Avn (As "XM693")	Cranfield	17. 2.99P
G-TIMP	Aeronca 7BCM Champion (Cont C85)	7AC-3392	N84681 NC84681	14. 8.92	T.E.Phillips "Nancy" Hill Farm, Nayland		5.11.98P
G-TIMS	Falconar F-12A	PFA/22-12134		1.10.91	T.Sheridan	Wellingborough	
G-TIMW*	PA-28-140 Cherokee C	28-26404	G-AXSH	22. 3.85	Taylor Acft Svs Ltd (Crashed nr Netherthorpe 25.3.90; stored 3.91)	Sywell	15. 5.91T
G-TINA	Socata TB-10 Tobago	67		30.10.79	A.Lister	Shipdham	13. 8.01
G-TING	Cameron O-120 HAFB	4007		4.10.96	Floating Sensations Ltd Thatcham, Berks		5.11.99T
G-TINS	Cameron N-90 HAFB	1626		27. 1.88	J.R.Clifton	Brackley	15. 8.99A
G-TINY	Moravan Zlin Z.526F Trener Master	1257	OK-CMD G-TINY/YR-ZAD	4.94	Air V8 Ltd	North Weald	17. 8.98
G-TIPS	Tipsy Nipper T.66 Srs.5 (Rebuild of Fairey c/n 50)	PFA/25-12696	OO-VAL 9Q-CYJ/9O-CYJ/(OO-CYJ)/(OO-CCD)	27. 3.95	R.F.L.Cuypers	Keiheuvel, Belgium	10. 5.99P
G-TJAY	PA-22-135 Tri-Pacer	22-730	N730TJ N2353A	11. 5.93	D.D.Saint	Garston Farm, Marshfield	15. 7.99
G-TJHI	Cessna 500 Citation I (Unit No.363)	500-0354	G-CCCL N51GA/G-BEIZ/(N5363J)	17. 1.92	Trustair Ltd	Blackpool	21. 7.01T
G-TJPM	BAe 146 Srs.300QT	E-3150	SE-DIM G-BRGK	4. 7.94	TNT Express Worldwide (UK) Ltd Stansted (Skypak International Couriers c/s)		3. 7.00T
G-TKGR	Lindstrand Racing Car SS HAFB	380		28. 8.96	Brown & Williamson Tobacco Corporation (Export) Ltd "Team Green" Louisville, KY, USA		20. 8.99A
G-TKIS	Tri-R Kis 029 & PFA/239-12358 (Lyc O-290) (Tailwheel variant)			23.12.93	J.L.Bone	Biggin Hill	15.12.99P
G-TKPZ	Cessna 310R II	310R-1225	G-BRAH N1909G	19. 3.90	Ace Avn Consultancy Enterprises Ltd & Edinburgh Air Charter Ltd Humberside/Edinburgh		1. 4.99T
G-TLDK	PA-22-150 Tri-Pacer	22-4726	N6072D	27. 1.97	A.M.Thomson	(King's Lynn)	
G-TLME	Robinson R-44 Astro	0062		13. 4.94	TJB Associates Ltd	Blackpool	22. 7.00T
G-TMCC	Cameron N-90 HAFB	4327		30. 3.98	Prudential Assurance Co Ltd "The Mall"	Bristol	7. 4.99A
G-TMDP	Airbus A.320-231	168	OY-CNF (D-ADSL)/OY-CNF/F-WWIF	19.11.96	Airtours International Airways Ltd Manchester		19.11.99T
G-TMKI	Percival P.56 Provost T.1	PAC/F/268	WW453	1. 7.92	T.J.Manna t/a Kennet Avn Cranfield (As "WW453/W-S" in RAF c/s) (Stored 7.96)		
G-TNTA	BAe 146 Srs.200QT	E-2056	G-5-056 (G-OTNT)/N146QT/(N146FT)/G-5-056	9. 4.87	TNT Express Worldwide (UK) Ltd	Luton	12. 4.99T
G-TNTB	BAe 146 Srs.200QT	E-2067	G-5-067 (N145AC)/(G-BNFG)	3. 3.87	TNT Express Worldwide (UK) Ltd	Luton	17. 9.99T

Regn	Type	C/n	P/I	Date	Owner/operator	Probable Base	CA Expy
G-TNTE	BAe 146 Srs.300QT	E-3153	G-BRPW	8. 6.90	TNT Express Worldwide (UK) Ltd	Luton	5. 6.99T
G-TNTG	BAe 146 Srs.300QT	E-3182	G-BSUY	21.10.91	TNT European Airlines Ltd	Luton	1.10.99T
G-TNTK	BAe 146 Srs.300QT	E-3186	G-BSXL G-6-186	30. 1.92	TNT European Airlines Ltd	Luton	10.10.01T
G-TNTL	BAe 146 Srs.300QT	E-3168	RP-C479 G-TNTL/G-BSGI/(RP-C479)/G-BSGI/G-6-168	7. 2.92	TNT European Airlines Ltd	Luton	27.10.00T
G-TNTM	BAe 146 Srs.300QT	E-3166	RP-C480 G-TNTM/G-BSLZ/G-6-166	28. 2.92	TNT European Airlines Ltd	Luton	27.10.00T
G-TNTN	Thunder Ax6-56 HAFB	1991		25. 4.91	D.P. & A.Dickinson	Oswestry	29. 4.92A
G-TNTR	BAe 146 Srs.300QT	E-3151	SE-DIT G-BRGM	4. 7.94	TNT Express Worldwide (UK) Ltd (XP Parcel System c/s)	Luton	3. 7.00T
G-TOAD	SAN Jodel D.140 Mousquetaire	27	F-BIZG	27. 9.88	J.H.Stevens	Headcorn	25.10.98
G-TOAK	Socata TB-20 Trinidad	468	N83AV	5.12.89	R.Chown	Teesside	12. 6.99
G-TOBA	Socata TB-10 Tobago	625	N600N	4. 4.91	E.J.Downing	Compton Abbas	31. 7.00
G-TOBE*	PA-28R-200 Cherokee Arrow II	28R-7435148	G-BNRO N40979	25.11.87	Not known (Damaged nr Cranbrook, Kent 6.3.92; stored 8.96)	Headcorn	6. 3.94
G-TOBI	Reims Cessna F.172K	0792	G-AYVB	5. 1.84	G.Hall	Compton Abbas	8. 8.98
G-TOBY*	Cessna 172B	47852	G-ARCM N6952X	8. 4.81	Northbrook College (Damaged Sandown 15.10.83; instructional airframe 10.96)	Shoreham	28. 4.85
G-TODD	ICA IS-28M2A	59		18. 4.86	C.I.Roberts & C.D.King	Shobdon	7. 9.01
G-TODE	Ruschmeyer R90-230RG	016	D-EEAX	20. 6.94	Tode Ltd	Denham	8.10.00
G-TOFT	Colt 90A HAFB	1693		8. 3.90	C.S.Perceval "Bumble"	Great Missenden	15. 5.99A
G-TOGA*	PA-32-301 Saratoga	32-8006028	G-BIEG N81852	15.11.82	Not known (Damaged Belmont, Lancs 29. 8.93; status unknown)	Blackpool	1. 2.95
G-TOMA	Curtis P-40C	194	N80FR Soviet AF/41-13390	30.11.98	Patina Ltd (Op The Fighter Collection)	Duxford	AC
G-TOMG	Hunting P.84 Jet Provost T.4	PAC/W/19987	9030M XR674	31. 8.94	Kingspride Associates Ltd (As "XW428" in Sword's Aerobatic Team c/s)	Lydd	26.11.99P
G-TOMS	PA-38-112 Tomahawk	38-79A0453		22. 1.79	R.J.Alford (Op Channel Avn)	Guernsey	5. 8.00T
G-TOOL	Thunder Ax8-105 HAFB	1670		29. 3.90	W.J.Honey "Trademaster"	Bristol	16. 5.99A
G-TOPC	Aerospatiale AS.355F1 Twin Squirrel	5313	I-LGOG 3A-MCS/D-HOSY/OE-BXV/D-HOSY	29. 7.97	Virgin Helicopters Ltd	Booker	6.11.00T
G-TOPS	Aerospatiale AS.355F1 Twin Squirrel	5151	G-BPRH N360E/N5794F	7. 5.91	Sterling Helicopters Ltd	Norwich	7.12.01T
G-TORE	Hunting-Percival P.84 Jet Provost T.3A (See comments under G-BVBE)	PAC/W/9212	XM405	14. 6.91	Butane Buzzard Avn Corpn Ltd (Op Kennet Avn) (As "XM405") (Stored 7.96)	Cranfield	5. 5.95P
G-TOSH	Robinson R-22 Beta	0933	N2629S LV-RBD/N8012T	14. 3.97	Heli Air Ltd	Denham/Wellesbourne Mountford	20. 3.00T
G-TOTO	Reims Cessna F.177RG Cardinal	0049	G-OADE G-AZKH	29. 8.89	C.R. & J.Cox	Hayrish Farm, Okehampton	14. 8.97
G-TOUR	Robin R.2112	187		9.10.79	Mardenair Ltd	Goodwood	12. 3.01T
G-TOWS	PA-25-260 Pawnee C (Mod 4 blade Hoffman propellor)	25-4853	PH-VBT D-EAVI/N4370Y	17. 7.91	Lasham Gliding Society Ltd	Lasham	23.12.00
G-TOYS	Enstrom 280C-UK-2 Shark	1218	G-BISE	17. 6.82	Stephenson Avn Ltd (Stored 4.96)	Goodwood	26. 2.94T
G-TOYZ	Bell 206B Jet Ranger III	3949	G-RGER N75EA/JA9452/N32018	21.11.96	P.B.Ellis	Blackpool	29. 9.00T
G-TPSL	Cessna 182S	182-80398	N23700	11.12.98	A.N.Purslow	(Hook)	17.12.01T
G-TPTS	Robinson R-44 Astro	0457		24. 4.98	Superstore Ltd	(Runcorn)	6. 5.01
G-TPTT	Airbus A.320-212	348	F-GLGE F-WWBT	29. 2.96	Airtours International Airways Ltd	Manchester	28. 2.02T
G-TRAN	Beechcraft 76 Duchess	ME-408	G-NIFR N1808A	15. 3.93	O.J.Hutcheon	Guernsey	17. 9.01
G-TRAV	Cameron A-210 HAFB	3181		6.12.93	N.J.Appleton t/a First Flight "Bakers Dolphin"	Bristol	12.11.98T
G-TREC	Cessna 421C Golden Eagle III	421C-0838	G-TLOL (N2659K)	2. 7.96	C.P.Lockyer	Coventry	18 2.99
G-TRED	Cameron Colt Bibendum 110SS HAFB	4222		12.12.97	The Aerial Display Co Ltd	Looe	23. 9.99A
G-TREE	Bell 206B JetRanger III	2826	N2779U	15. 6.87	LGH Avn Ltd (Op Alan Mann Helicopters)	Fairoaks	3.11.99T
G-TREK	Jodel D.18 (Limbach L.2000)	182 & PFA/169-11265		1. 5.92	R.H.Mole	Leicester	27. 7.99P
G-TREN	Boeing 737-4S3	24796	G-BRKG	3. 4.91	GB Airways Ltd (Blue Poole t/s)	Gatwick	11. 7.99T
G-TRIB	Lindstrand HS-110 Hot-Air Airship	174		23. 1.95	J.Addison	(USA)	17. 8.99A
G-TRIC	DHC.1 Chipmunk 22A	C1/0080	G-AOSZ WB635	18.12.89	D.M.Barnett (As "18013" in RCAF c/s)	North Weald	7. 9.00
G-TRIM	Monnett Moni	00258T & PFA/142-11012		16. 2.84	J.E.Bennell	(High Wycombe)	
G-TRIN	Socata TB-20 Trinidad	1131		25. 6.90	Isnet Ltd	Cambridge	7. 1.00
G-TRIO	Cessna 172M Skyhawk II	172-66271	G-BNXY N9621H	30. 7.91	C.M.B.Reid	Biggin Hill	30.12.99T
G-TRIP	PA-32R-301 Saratoga SP	32R-8013132	G-HOSK PH-WET/OO-HKN/N8261X	10.12.85	K.L.Burnett	(North Ferriby)	26. 6.00
G-TRIX	VS.509 Spitfire Trainer IX	CBAF.9590	(G-BHGH) IAC161/G-15-174/PV202	2. 7.80	R.A.Roberts (As "PV202/5R-Q" in 33 Sqdn c/s)	Goodwood	28. 4.99P

Regn	Type	C/n	P/I	Date	Owner/operator	Probable Base	CA Expy
G-TROP	Cessna T310R II	T310R-1381	N4250C	31.12.86	Southern Aircharter Ltd	Shoreham	10. 4.99T
G-TRUC	Cassutt Speed One (Possibly a re-registration of G-MARY)	PFA/34-11400		20. 6.89	J.A.H.Chadwick	(London NW8)	
G-TRUE	MDH Hughes 369E	0490E	N6TK ZK-HFP	12. 9.94	B.M.Christie t/a Horizon Helicopter Hire	Goodwood	28.10.00T
G-TRUK	Stoddard-Hamilton Glasair IIRG (Lyc O-320) 575R & PFA/149-11015			23. 7.84	M.P.Jackson	Fairoaks	26. 4.99P
G-TRUX	Colt 77A HAFB	1860		13.11.90	Highway Truck Rental Ltd	Gateshead	2.12.99A
G-TSAM	BAe 125 Srs.800B	258028	G-5-12	31. 1.85	British Aerospace (Operations) Ltd	Warton	13. 6.00
G-TSAR	Beechcraft 58 Baron	TH-1698	N81287	9. 2.94	Thornfield Enterprises Ltd	Guernsey	24. 3.00
G-TSFT	PA-28-161 Warrior II	28-8216117	G-BLDJ N9632N	5. 4.89	SFT Europe Ltd	Bournemouth	7. 2.99T
G-TSGJ	PA-28-181 Archer II	28-8090109	N8097W	12. 9.88	A.Dove & A.D.S.Peat t/a Golf Juliet F/C	Teesside	23.11.00
G-TSIX	North American AT-6C-1NT Harvard IIA	88-9725	FAP1535 SAAF7183/EX289/41-33262 (As "111836/JZ/6" in USN c/s)	19. 3.79	J.Zemlik	Spanhoe	29. 1.00P
G-TSKY	Beagle B.121 Pup Srs.2	B121-010	OE-CFM HB-NAA/G-AWDY/HB-NAA/G-AWDY	6. 4.98	R.G.Hayes	(Pinner)	7. 5.01T
G-TSMI	Rockwell Commander 114	14249	OO-TSM	8. 6.93	J.J.J.C.Herbaux	St.Ghislain, Belgium	5. 9.99
G-TTAM	Taylor JT.2 Titch (VW1600)	PFA/3229		14.12.78	C.H.Morris	(Polegate, E.Sussex)	
G-TTDD	Zenair CH.701 STOL	PFA/187-13106		1. 9.97	B.E.Trinder & D.B.Dainton	(Rushden/Huntingdon)	9. 2.00T
G-TTHC	Robinson R-22 Beta	1196		21.12.89	P.N.Briggs t/a North West Auto Engineering	Bristol/Lulsgate	23. 5.99T
G-TTIM	Cassutt Racer IIIM	PFA/34-13116		10. 7.98	J.D.Llewellyn	(Coalville)	
G-TTMC	Airbus A.300B4-203	299	OH-LAA (LX-LGP)/F-WZMX	25. 4.98	OY Air Scandic International Aviation	Manchester	29. 4.01T
G-TTOY	CFM Streak Shadow SA (Rotax 618)	PFA/206-12805		15. 4.96	S.Marriott	Old Sarum	13. 7.99P
G-TTWO*	Colt 56A HAFB	087		14. 5.80	R S Kent "Tea 4 Two" (Balloon Preservation Group 7.98)	Lancing	1. 9.87A
G-TUDR	Cameron V-77 HAFB	1135		20. 5.85	Jacques W.Soukup Enterprises Ltd "Tudor Rose/HVIIIR"	Chippenham	21. 3.99A
G-TUGG	PA-18-180 (Mod) Super Cub (Frame No.18-8497)	18-8274	PH-MAH N5451Y	10. 1.83	Ulster Gliding Club Ltd	Bellarena	30. 3.01
G-TUGY	Robin DR.400/180 Regent	2052	D-EPAR	27. 4.98	J.M.Airey	Saltby	19. 5.01T
G-TUKE	Robin DR.400/160 Major 80	1542		2. 6.81	J.W.F. & S.M.Tuke t/a Tukair Acft Charter	Headcorn	3. 3.99T
G-TUNE	Robinson R-22 Beta	0818	N60661 G-OJVI/(G-OJVJ)	12. 1.99	Ecurie Ecosse (Scotland) Ltd (Pitlochry)		21. 5.00
G-TURF	Reims Cessna F.406 Caravan II	0020	PH-FWF (EI-CND)/PH-FWF/F-WZDS (Air Atlantic c/s)	17.10.96	Atlantic Air Transport Ltd	Coventry	21.11.00T
G-TURK	Cameron Sultan 80SS HAFB	1711		12. 4.88	Forbes Europe Inc "Suliman"	Balleroy, Normandy	25. 9.99A
G-TURN	Steen Skybolt 003 & PFA/64-11349 (Lyc IO-360)			14. 7.88	M.L.Sargeant	Goudhurst	27.10.98P
G-TUSK	Bell 206B Jet Ranger 4	4406	G-BWZH N53114	13. 1.97	Zeuros Ltd	(Hook)	23. 2.00T
G-TVBF	Lindstrand LBL-310A HAFB	439		2. 4.97	Virgin Balloon Flights Ltd (London SE16)		13. 4.98T
G-TVII	Hawker Hunter T.7	41H-693834	XX467 RJAF 836/RSAF 70-617/G-9-214/XL605	8.12.97	G.R.Montgomery	Perth	
G-TVIJ	CCF Harvard 4 (T-6J-CCF Texan)	CCF4-442 Moz PLAF 1730/FAP 1730/AA+652/52-8521	G-BSBE	10.12.93	R.W.Davies (As "28521/TA-521" in USAF c/s) Little Robhurst Farm, Woodchurch		6. 4.99P
G-TVPA	Aerospatiale AS.355F1 Twin Squirrel	5181	G-BPRI N364E	18. 5.93	Thames Valley Police Authority (Op Chiltern Air Support Unit)	Oxford	3. 8.99T
G-TVSI	Campbell Cricket (Rotax 503)	CA/340	G-AYHH	8. 4.82	C.Smith	Kemble	16. 4.98P
G-TVTV	Cameron TV 90SS HAFB	2357		14. 9.90	J.Krebs	Erfstadt, Germany	2. 6.99A
G-TWEL	PA-28-181 Archer II	28-8090290	N81963	12. 6.80	International Aerospace Engineering Ltd	Cranfield	16.11.98T
G-TWEY	Colt 69A HAFB	700		24. 7.85	N.Bland	Didcot	9. 1.99A
G-TWIG	Reims Cessna F.406 Caravan II	0014	PH-FWD F-WZDS	21.10.98	Highland Airways Ltd	Inverness	22.10.01T
G-TWIN	PA-44-180 Seminole	44-7995072	N30267	6.11.78	Bonus Avn Ltd	Cranfield	25. 3.00T
G-TWIZ	Rockwell Commander 114	14375	SE-GSP N5808N	9. 5.90	B.C.Cox & K.E.Kirkland	Biggin Hill	21. 6.99
G-TWTD	CCF Hawker Sea Hurricane X	CCF/41H/8020	(Russia) AE977	6. 5.94	Hawker Restorations Ltd Moat Farm, Milden		
G-TXSE	Rotary Air Force RAF 2000 GTX-SE (Subaru EJ22)	PFA G/113-1271		1. 3.96	Software Development International Ltd Long Acre Farm, West Clandon		1. 1.98P
G-TYGA	Gulfstream AA-5B Tiger	AA5B-1161	G-BHNZ (D-EGDS)/N4547L	22. 2.82	G.J.Wilmshurst	Biggin Hill	25. 1.01T
G-TYNE	Socata TB-20 Trindad	1523	F-GRBM F-WWRW/CS-AZH/F-OHDE	6.11.97	D.T.Watkins	Newcastle	19.11.00
G-TYRE	Reims Cessna F.172M Skyhawk II	1222	OY-BIA	16. 2.79	J.A.Lyons t/a Staverton Flying School	Gloucestershire	2. 9.00T

G-UAAA-UZZZ

Regn	Type	C/n	P/I	Date	Owner/operator	Probable Base	CA Expy
G-UAPA	Robin DR.400/140B Major	2213	F-GMXC	11. 1.95	Aeromarine Ltd Owslebury, Southampton		10. 6.01
G-UAPO	Ruschmeyer R90-230RG	019	D-EECT	2. 3.95	S.J.Green	Lagoa, Portugal	21. 6.01
G-UCCC	Cameron Sign 90SS HAFB	3918		5. 7.96	Flying Pictures Ltd	Fairoaks	6. 9.99A
					"Unipart Car Care Centres"		
G-UDAY	Robinson R-22 Beta	1101		4. 8.89	Cambridge Helicopters Ltd	Cambridge	29.10.98T
G-UEST	Bell 206B JetRanger II	1484	G-RYOB	8. 9.89	E.& S.Vandyk	(Newbury)	20. 1.00T
			G-BLWU/ZS-PAW				
G-UESY	Robinson R-22 Beta	2801		13. 3.98	EW Guess (Holdings) Ltd	(Stamford)	2. 4.01
G-UFLY	Reims Cessna F.150H	0264	G-AVVY	29. 9.89	Westair F/Svs Ltd	Blackpool	11. 3.99T
G-UIDA	Star-Lite SL-1 211 & PFA/175-11440		G-BRKK	23. 9.91	I.J.Widger		
	(Rotax 447)				(Rancho Palos Verdes, California)		31.10.94P
G-UIDE	Jodel Wassmer D.120 Paris-Nice	262	F-BMIY	27. 5.80	S.T.Gilbert	(Burnham, Slough)	16. 6.89P
					(Damaged Aldbury, Bucks 10.9.88)		
G-UILD	Grob G-109B	6419		28. 1.86	Runnymede Consultants Ltd	Blackbushe	22. 3.01
G-UILE	Neico Lancair 320	PFA/191-12538		17. 1.94	R.J.Martin	(Alresford, Hants)	
G-UINN	Stolp SA.300 Starduster Too	16. 3.98	EI-CDQ	16. 3.98	J.D.H.Gordon	(Galashiels)	21. 5.99P
	(Lyc O-360)	HB.1980-1	C-GTLJ				
G-UJAB	Jabiru UL	PFA/274A-13373		27. 1.99	C.A.Thomas	(Huntingdon)	
G-UKAC	BAe 146 Srs.300	E-3142	G-5-142	25.10.89	Air UK Ltd	Stansted	19.11.01T
G-UKAG	BAe 146 Srs.300	E-3162	G-6-162	28.11.90	Air UK Ltd	Stansted	11.12.01T
G-UKFA	Fokker F.28-0100	11246	N602RP	1. 7.92	Air UK Ltd	Norwich	12.10.99T
			C-FICY/PH-EZB				
G-UKFB	Fokker F.28-0100	11247	N602TR	1. 7.92	Air UK Ltd	Norwich	12. 8.99T
			C-FICW/PH-EZC				
G-UKFC	Fokker F.28-0100	11263	N602DG	1. 7.92	Air UK Ltd	Norwich	27. 7.99T
			C-FICL/PH-EZF				
G-UKFD	Fokker F.28-0100	11259	C-FICP	22. 7.92	Air UK Ltd	Norwich	9.11.99T
			PH-EZJ				
G-UKFE	Fokker F.28-0100	11260	C-FICQ	22. 7.92	Air UK Ltd	Norwich	30.11.99T
			PH-EZK				
G-UKFF	Fokker F.28-0100	11274	PH-ZCK	9.11.93	Air UK Ltd	Norwich	8.11.00T
			(G-FIOB)/PH-ZCK/PH-EZB/(PH-KLK)				
G-UKFG	Fokker F.28-0100	11275	PH-ZCL	19.11.93	Air UK Ltd	Norwich	18.11.00T
			(G-FIOC)/PH-ZCL/PH-EZV/(PH-KLL)				
G-UKFH	Fokker F.28-0100	11277	PH-ZCM	29. 9.93	Air UK Ltd	Norwich	28. 9.00T
			(G-FIOD)/PH-ZCM/PH-EZW/(PH-KLN)				
G-UKFI	Fokker F.28-0100	11279	PH-ZCN	12.10.93	Air UK Ltd	Norwich	11.10.00T
			(G-FIOE)/PH-ZCN/PH-EZX/(PH-KLO)				
G-UKFJ	Fokker F.28-0100	11248	PH-GIOV	30. 1.96	Air UK Ltd	Norwich	22. 2.99T
			C-FICB/PH-INC/PH-EZD				
G-UKFK	Fokker F.28-0100	11249	F-GIOX	19. 2.96	Air UK Ltd	Norwich	1. 4.99T
			C-FICO/PH-INA/PH-EZE				
G-UKFL	Fokker F.28-0100	11268	PH-KLC	14. 8.97	Air UK Ltd	Norwich	18. 8.00T
			F-GIDT/F-OGDI/F-GIDT/F-OGQI/PH-KLC				
G-UKFM	Fokker F.28-0100	11269	PH-KLD	27.10.98	Air UK Ltd.	Stansted	25.11.01T
			F-GIDQ/PH-KLD				
G-UKFN	Fokker F.28-0100	11270	PH-KLE	16. 6.97	Air UK Ltd	Norwich	21. 7.00T
			F-GIDP/PH-KLE				
G-UKFO	Fokker F.28-0100	11271	PH-KLG	20.10.97	Air UK Ltd	Norwich	20.10.00T
			F-GIDO/PH-KLG				
G-UKFP	Fokker F.28-0100	11272	PH-KLH	27.10.98	Air UK Ltd.	Stansted	28.10.01T
			F-GIDN/F-OGQA/F-GIDN/F-OGQA/PH-KLH				
G-UKFR	Fokker F.28-0100	11273	PH-KLI	21. 3.97	Air UK Ltd	Norwich	26. 3.00T
			F-GIDM/F-OGQB/PH-KLI				
G-UKHP	BAe 146 Srs.300	E-3123	G-5-123	26.10.88	Air UK Ltd	Stansted	26. 2.99T
G-UKID	BAe 146 Srs.300	E-3157	G-6-157	28. 2.90	Air UK Ltd	Stansted	6. 3.99T
G-UKLH	Boeing 767-39HER	26256		1. 4.93	Leisure International Airways Ltd		
					"Caribbean Star"	Stansted	4. 4.00T
G-UKLL	Airbus A.320-212	189	C-GRYY	17. 4.96	Leisure International Airways Ltd		
			G-BWCP/N483GX/F-WWDC			Stansted	29. 4.99T
G-UKRB	Colt 105A HAFB	1769		10.12.90	Virgin Airship & Balloon Co Ltd	Telford	16. 5.97A
					"Lloyds Bank II"		
G-UKRC	BAe 146 Srs.300	E-3158	G-BSMR	14. 2.91	Air UK Ltd	Stansted	24. 2.99T
			G-6-158				
G-UKSC	BAe 146 Srs.300	E-3125	G-5-125	26.10.88	Air UK Ltd "City of Innsbruck"	Stansted	9. 3.99T
G-UKTA	Fokker F.27-050	20246	PH-KXF	22. 2.95	Air UK Ltd "City of Norwich"	Norwich	21. 2.01T
G-UKTB	Fokker F.27-050	20247	PH-KXG	21. 3.95	Air UK Ltd "City of Aberdeen"	Norwich	21. 3.01T
G-UKTC	Fokker F.27-050	20249	PH-KXH	25. 1.95	Air UK Ltd "City of Bradford"	Norwich	25. 1.01T
G-UKTD	Fokker F.27-050	20256	PH-KXT	20. 1.95	Air UK Ltd "City of Leeds"	Norwich	19. 1.01T
G-UKTE	Fokker F.27-050	20270	PH-LXJ	14. 2.95	Air UK Ltd "City of Hull"	Norwich	14. 2.01T
G-UKTF	Fokker F.27-050	20271	PH-LXK	31. 1.95	Air UK Ltd "City of York"	Norwich	31. 1.01T
G-UKTG	Fokker F.27-050	20276	PH-LXP	28. 2.95	Air UK Ltd "City of Durham"	Norwich	28. 2.01T
G-UKTH	Fokker F.27-050	20277	PH-LXR	28. 3.95	Air UK Ltd "City of Amsterdam"	Norwich	28. 3.01T
G-UKTI	Fokker F.27-050	20279	PH-LXT	17. 3.95	Air UK Ltd "City of Stavanger"	Norwich	16. 3.01T
G-UKTJ	ATR-72-202	509		19.12.97	Air UK Ltd	Norwich	18.12.00T
G-UKTK	ATR-72-202	519	F-WWLQ	30. 1.98	Air UK Ltd	Norwich	29. 1.00T

Regn	Type	C/n	P/I	Date	Owner/operator	Probable Base	CA Expy
G-UKTL	ATR-72-202	523	F-WWLD	10. 3.98	Air UK Ltd (Damaged at Norwich 14.5.98)	Stansted	9. 3.01T
G-UKTM	ATR-72-202	508	F-WWLU	23. 4.98	Air UK Ltd	Stansted	22. 4.01T
G-UKTN	ATR-72-202	496	F-WWLT	4. 6.98	Air UK Ltd	Stansted	3. 6.01T
G-UKUK	Head Ax8-105 HAFB	248	N8303U	1. 9.97	P.A.George	Princes Risborough	27.10.98A
G-ULAB	Robinson R-22 Beta	2444	N8311Z	18. 8.94	I.R.Chisholm Costock, Loughborough t/a Bradmore Helicopter Leasing		10. 9.00T
G-ULAS	DHC.1 Chipmunk 22	C1/0554	WK517	14. 6.96	Search & Management Services Ltd Booker (As "WK517")		30. 7.99
G-ULLS	Lindstrand LBL-90A HAFB	434		18. 2.97	Tanswell of Towcester Ltd	Towcester	21.12.99A
G-ULPS	Everett Gyroplane Srs.1 (VW1835)	007	G-BMNY	13. 7.93	The Aziz Corporation Ltd	Winchester	13. 6.99P
G-ULTR	Cameron A-105 HAFB	4100		24. 2.97	P.Glydon	Birmingham	12. 5.99T
G-UMBO	Colt Jumbo SS HAFB (Special shape with nose/tail/wings of Virgin 747) (Built as c/n 816 but amended) (Replacement envelope c/n 1645 fitted 1990)	747		2. 4.86	Virgin Airship & Balloon Co Ltd Telford "Virgin Jumbo"		21. 5.96A
G-UMMI	PA-31-310 Turbo Navajo	31-7912060	G-BGSO N3519F	11. 8.92	Alpine Food Machinery Ltd	Humberside	26. 7.99T
G-UNGE	Lindstrand LBL-90A HAFB	122	G-BVPJ	6.12.96	M.T.Stevens t/a Silver Ghost Balloon Club	Solihull	10.12.97A
G-UNIA	Airbus A.330-2..		F-WW..	R	Leisure International Airways Ltd (For dely 2.00)	Manchester	
G-UNIB	Airbus A.330-2..		F-WW..	R	Leisure International Airways Ltd (For dely 2.00)	Manchester	
G-UNIG	Airbus A.321-211		D-AVZ.	R	Leisure International Airways Ltd	Manchester	
G-UNIH	Airbus A.321-211		D-AVZ.	R	Leisure International Airways Ltd	Manchester	
G-UNII	Airbus A.3			R	Leisure International Airways Ltd	Manchester	
G-UNIJ	Airbus A.3			R	Leisure International Airways Ltd	Manchester	
G-UNIP	Cameron Oil Container SS HAFB (Unipart Sureflow Oil Can)	2532		15. 3.91	Balloon Preservation Group "Unipart Oil" (For restoration 12.98)	Lancing	7.11.96A
G-UNIT	Partenavia P.68B	23	G-BCNT	21.10.93	Phlight Avn Ltd	Coventry	16.12.01T
G-UNNY	BAC 167 Strikemaster mk.87 (Regd with c/n "601")	PS.70	G-AYHR OJ4/Kenya 601/G-27-141/G-AYHR/G-27-191	19. 3.98	Gone Flying Ltd	(Woking)	24. 4.99P
G-UNRL	Lindstrand RR-21 HAFB	260		25. 5.95	Virgin Airship & Balloon Co Ltd Telford "Virgin Cola"		23. 7.99A
G-UNYT	Robinson R-22 Beta	0985	G-BWZV G-LIAN	17.11.97	Cambridge Helicopters Ltd	Cambridge	13.11.00T
G-UPHL	Cameron Concept 80 HAFB	3002		23. 2.93	Uphill Motor Co Ltd Langford, Somerset		22. 9.00T
G-UPMW	Robinson R-22 Beta	1982		31.12.91	Burman Aviation Ltd Newcastle/Cranfield		5. 2.01T
G-UPPP	Colt 77A HAFB	852		4. 8.86	M.Williams "Nugget"	Wadhurst	25. 3.95A
G-UPPY	Cameron DP-80 Hot-Air Airship	2274		29. 3.90	Jacques W.Soukup Enterprises Ltd "Jacques Soukup" Beaulieu Court, Wilts/Great Missenden		11. 7.94A
G-UPUP	Cameron V-77 HAFB	1828		21. 7.89	S.R.Burden Noordwijk, Netherlands "Fantasia"		17. 5.99T
G-UROP	Beechcraft B55 Baron	TC-2452	N64311	17. 9.90	Pooler International Ltd	Sleap	27. 2.00
G-URRR	Air Command 582 Sport 0630 & PFA G/104-1200			13. 6.90	L.Armes	(Basildon)	
G-URUH	Robinson R-44 Astro	0354		3. 7.97	Heli Air Ltd Wellesbourne Mountford		10. 8.00T
G-USAM	Cameron Uncle Sam SS HAFB (Uncle Sam head shape)	1120		20. 5.85	Jacques W.Soukup Enterprises Ltd	S.Dakota, USA	31. 5.97A
G-USFT	PA-23-250 Aztec F	27-7654174	G-BEGV N62720	8. 5.97	SFT Europe Ltd	Bournemouth	4. 9.00T
G-USGB	Colt 105A HAFB	1130		26. 8.87	Virgin Airship & Balloon Co Ltd Telford "Virgin Replica"		22.11.92A
G-USIL	Thunder Ax7-77 HAFB	1587		22. 8.89	Window on the World Ltd London SE1 "Mantis"		27. 5.99A
G-USMC	Cameron Chestie 90SS HAFB (US Marine Corps Bulldog shape)	1251		24. 4.86	Jacques W.Soukup Enterprises Ltd	S.Dakota, USA	31. 5.97A
G-USSR	Cameron Doll 90SS HAFB (Russian Doll shape)	2273		29. 3.90	Jacques W.Soukup Enterprises Ltd (USA) "Matrioshka"		30. 5.97A
G-USSY	PA-28-181 Archer II	28-8290011	N8439R	7.11.88	Western Air (Thruxton) Ltd	Thruxton	1. 2.01T
G-USTA	Agusta A.109A	7170	G-MEAN G-BRYL/G-ROPE/G-OAMH	3.12.96	Markoss Aviation Ltd	Biggin Hill	21. 4.00T
G-USTB	Agusta A.109A	7163	D-HEEG (D-HEEF)/VR-CKN/HB-XKM	9. 6.97	Newton Aviation Ltd.	(Chigwell)	26. 6.00T
G-USTE	Robinson R-44 Astro	0315		11. 3.97	Westleigh Developments Ltd	Whetstone, Leics	6. 4.00
G-USTV*	Messerschmitt Bf.109G-2/Trop (Built by Erla)	10639	8478M RN228/Luftwaffe	26.10.90	RAF Museum Hendon (As "6" in Luftwaffe III/JG77 c/s)		30. 5.98P
	(Damaged Duxford 12.10.97: to be rebuilt to static display standard for eventual display at the RAF Museum)						
G-USTY	Clutton FRED Srs.III PFA/29-10390 (VW1834)			11.10.78	R.T.Mosforth t/a GUSTY Grp (Sheffield)		9. 6.97P

Regn	Type	C/n	P/I	Date	Owner/operator	Probable Base	CA Expy
G-USUK*	Colt 2500A HAFB	1100		1. 6.87	Virgin Atlantic Airways Ltd "Virgin Atlantic Flyer" (Gondola displayed 1.99 - remainder stored)	Duxford	19. 8.87P
G-UTSI	Rand-Robinson KR-2	KBG-01		2.10.89	K.B.Gutridge	Biggin Hill	
G-UTSY	PA-28R-201 Cherokee Arrow III 28R-7737052		N3346Q	29. 8.86	Arrow Aviation Ltd	Southend	20.12.98
G-UTZY	Aerospatiale SA.341G Gazelle 1	1307	G-BKLV N341SC	21.12.87	Goldcalm Ltd	(London SW1)	4. 3.01T
G-UVIP	Cessna 421C Golden Eagle III	421C-0603	G-BSKH N88600	23.11.98	Capital Trading Aviation Ltd	Exeter	2.11.01T
G-UZEL	Aerospatiale SA.341G Gazelle 1	1413	G-BRNH YU-HBO	21.11.89	S.E.Hobbs (UK) Ltd	Biggin Hill	30. 4.00
G-UZLE	Colt 77A HAFB	2021		1. 8.91	Flying Pictures Ltd "John Courage"	Fairoaks	28. 5.99A

G-VAAA-VZZZ

Regn	Type	C/n	P/I	Date	Owner/operator	Probable Base	CA Expy
G-VAEL	Airbus A.340-311	015	F-WWJG	15.12.93	Virgin Atlantic Airways Ltd "Maiden Toulouse"	Gatwick	14.12.99T
G-VAGA	PA-15 Vagabond (Lyc O-145)	15-248	N4458H NC4458H	14.11.80	L.W. & O.Usherwood (Maidstone) (Damaged Beauship, Horsebridge 15.5.98)		29. 8.98P
G-VAIR	Airbus A.340-313	164	F-WWJA	21. 4.97	Virgin Atlantic Airways Ltd	Gatwick	20. 4.00T
G-VAJT	Socata MS.894E Rallye 220GT	12195	EI-BAB (S9-NAF)/EI-BAB/(G-BLPN)/EI-BAB(Manorcunningham, Co.Donegal)	25. 7.89	W.M.Patterson		29. 9.01
G-VALS	Pietenpol Aircamper	PFA/47-13157		30. 7.97	I.G.& V.A.Price	(Liphook)	
G-VANS	Van's RV-4 (Lyc O-320)	355	N16TS	7. 9.92	T.R.Grief	Bagby	22.12.98P
G-VANZ	Van's RV-6A	PFA/181-12531		15. 7.93	S.J.Baxter	(Macclesfield)	
G-VARG	Varga 2150A Kachina	VAC 157-80	OO-RTY N80716	14. 5.84	K.Fletcher	Coventry	19. 6.99
G-VASA	PA-34-200 Seneca	34-7350080	G-BNNB N15625	29. 3.96	V.Babic	Bournemouth	15.12.99T
G-VAST	Boeing 747-41R	28757		17. 6.97	Virgin Atlantic Airways Ltd "Ladybird"	Heathrow	16. 6.00T
G-VAUN	Cessna 340 II	340-0538	D-IOWS N5148J	25.11.77	K.L.Burnett	Humberside	16.11.01
G-VBAC	Short SD.3-60 Var.100	SH.3736	VH-MJU G-BOEJ/G-14-3736	15. 9.97	BAC Leasing Ltd (Op Jersey European Airways)	Exeter	15. 9.99T
G-VBEE	Boeing 747-219B		ZK... R		Virgin Atlantic Airways Ltd		
G-VBIG	Boeing 747-4Q8	26255		10. 6.96	Virgin Atlantic Airways Ltd "Tinker Belle"	Gatwick	9. 6.99T
G-VBUS	Airbus A.340-311	013	F-WWJE	26.11.93	Virgin Atlantic Airways Ltd "Lady in Red"	Gatwick	25.11.00T
G-VCAT	Boeing 747-267B	22872	B-HIE VR-HIE	16.10.98	Virgin Atlantic Airways Ltd	Heathrow	20.10.01T
G-VCED	Airbus A.320-231	193	OY-CNI F-WWIX	21. 1.97	Airtours International Airways Ltd	Manchester	30. 1.00T
G-VCIO	EAA Acrosport 2	PFA/72-12388		9.10.97	R.F.Bond	(Corsham, Wilts)	
G-VCJH	Robinson R-22 Beta	1569		26.10.90	Great Northern Helicopters Ltd	Sywell	13. 1.00T
G-VCML	Beechcraft 58 Baron	TH-1346	N2289R	31.10.97	St.Angelo Aviation Ltd	(London EC3)	27.11.00T
G-VCSI*	Rotorway Exec	3660		25.10.90	Not known (Stored 5.94)	Ley Farm, Chirk	
G-VDIR	Cessna T310R II	310R-0211	N5091J	31. 1.91	Thornhill Aviation Ltd (Op Airbase)	Shoreham	2.11.00T
G-VEGA*	Slingsby T.65 Vega				See BGA.2729		
G-VELA	SIAI-Marchetti S.205-22R (Confirmed as S.208A Waco Vela)	4-149	N949W	30.10.89	K.R.Allen t/a G-VELA Partnership	(Chesterfield)	29. 4.99
G-VELD	Airbus A.340-313X	214	F-WWJY	16. 3.98	Virgin Atlantic Airways Ltd "African Queen"	Gatwick	15. 3.01T
G-VENI	FFW DH.112 Venom FB.50 (FB.1)	733	J-1523	8. 6.84	Lindsay Wood Promotions Ltd (Op Source Classic Jet Flight) (As "WE402")	Bournemouth	29. 6.98P
G-VERA	Garden GY-201 Minicab	PFA/56-12236		7. 6.94	D.K.Shipton	(Peterborough)	
G-VETA	Hawker Hunter T.7	41H-693751	G-BVWN XL600	2. 7.96	Jet Heritage Ltd	Bournemouth	16. 4.98P
G-VETS	Enstrom 280C-UK Shark	1015	G-FSDC G-BKTG/OY-HBP	11. 9.95	C.Upton	Barton	17. 4.99
G-VEZE	Rutan Varieze	PFA/74-10285		2. 9.77	S.D.Brown, S.Evans & M.Roper (West Wickham/Haywards Heath)		
G-VFAB	Boeing 747-4Q8	24958		28. 4.94	Virgin Atlantic Airways Ltd "Lady Penelope"	Gatwick	27. 4.00T
G-VFAR	Airbus A.340-313X	225	(G-VPOW) F-WWJZ	12. 6.98	Virgin Atlantic Airways Ltd "Diana"	Gatwick	
G-VFLY	Airbus A.340-311	058	F-WWJE	24.10.94	Virgin Atlantic Airways Ltd "Dragon Lady"	Gatwick	23.10.00T
G-VFSI	Robinson R-22 Beta	1785	N4081L	19.12.96	Survey & Construction (Roofing) Ltd	Redhill	18.12.99T
G-VGIN	Boeing 747-243B	19732	N747BL B-2440/N358AS/I-DEMU "Scarlet Lady"	30. 1.86	Virgin Atlantic Airways Ltd	Gatwick	1.10.99T
G-VHOL	Airbus A.340-311	002	F-WWAS	30. 5.97	Virgin Atlantic Airways Ltd "Jetstreamer"	Gatwick	29. 5.00T
G-VHOT	Boeing 747-4Q8	26326		12.10.94	Virgin Atlantic Airways Ltd "Tubular Belle"	Gatwick	11.10.00T
G-VIBA	Cameron DP-80 Hot Air Airship	1729		28. 5.91	Jacques W.Soukup Enterprises Ltd Beaulieu Court, Wilts/Great Missenden		3. 2.99A
G-VICC	PA-28-161 Warrior II	28-7916317	G-JFHL N2249U	3. 3.92	A.W.Collett	Bicester	4. 8.01T
G-VICE	MDH Hughes 369E (500E)	0365E	D-HLIS	16. 5.95	Controlled Demolition Group Ltd	Barton	21. 8.01
G-VICI	FFW DH.112 Venom FB.50	783	HB-RVB (G-BMOB)/J-1573	6. 2.95	Lindsay Wood Promotions Ltd (Op Source Classic Jet Flight) (As "J-1573" in Swiss AF c/s)	Bournemouth	24.11.99P
G-VICM	Beechcraft F33C Bonanza	CJ-136	PH-BNG	3. 7.91	Velocity Engineering Ltd	(Watford)	18. 3.01
G-VICS	Commander 114B	14655	N655V	3. 2.98	Millennium Aviation Ltd	Guernsey	
G-VIEW	Vinten Wallis WA-116L Srs.100 (Limbach L2000)	002		5. 7.82	K.H.Wallis (Stored 8.97)	Reymerston Hall	6.10.85P*

Regn	Type	C/n	P/I	Date	Owner/operator	Probable Base	CA Expy
G-VIIA	Boeing 777-236ER	27483	N5022E (G-ZZZF)	3. 7.97	British Airways plc (Waves of the City t/s)	Gatwick	2. 7.00T
G-VIIB	Boeing 777-236ER	27484	N5023Q (G-ZZZG)	23. 5.97	British Airways plc "Cities of Dallas/Forth Worth"	Heathrow	22. 5.00T
G-VIIC	Boeing 777-236ER	27485	N5013R (G-ZZZH)	6. 2.97	British Airways plc (Reported as ex N5016R)	Heathrow	5. 2.00T
G-VIID	Boeing 777-236ER	27486	(G-ZZZI)	18. 2.97	British Airways plc	Heathrow	17. 2.00T
G-VIIE	Boeing 777-236ER	27487	(G-ZZZJ)	27. 2.97	British Airways plc	Heathrow	26. 2.00T
G-VIIF	Boeing 777-236ER	27488	(G-ZZZK)	19. 3.97	British Airways plc	Heathrow	18. 3.00T
G-VIIG	Boeing 777-236ER	27489	(G-ZZZL)	9. 4.97	British Airways plc	Heathrow	8. 4.00T
G-VIIH	Boeing 777-236ER	27490	(G-ZZZM)	7. 5.97	British Airways plc	Heathrow	6. 5.00T
G-VIIJ	Boeing 777-236ER	27492	(G-ZZZP)	29.12.97	British Airways plc (Mountain of the Birds/Benyhone Tartan t/s)	Gatwick	28.12.00T
G-VIIK	Boeing 777-236ER	28840		3. 2.98	British Airways plc (Animals and Trees t/s)	Gatwick	2. 2.00T
G-VIIL	Boeing 777-236ER	27493		13. 3.98	British Airways plc (Wings of the City t/s)	Heathrow	12. 3.01T
G-VIIM	Boeing 777-236ER	28841		26. 3.98	British Airways plc (Waves & Cranes t/s)	Heathrow	25. 3.01T
G-VIIN	Boeing 777-236ER	29319		21. 8.98	British Airways plc (Whale Rider t/s)	Heathrow	20. 8.01T
G-VIIO	Boeing 777-236	29320		26. 1.99	British Airways plc	Heathrow	25.01.02T
G-VIIP	Boeing 777-236	29321		9. 2.99	British Airways plc	Heathrow	
G-VIIR	Boeing 777-236ER	29322	R		British Airways plc (Mountain of the Birds/Benyhone Tartan t/s)	Heathrow	
G-VIIS	Boeing 777-236ER	29323	R		British Airways plc (Chelsea Rose t/s) (For dlvy 4.99)	Heathrow	
G-VIIT	Boeing 777-236ER		R		British Airways plc (For dlvy 5.99)	Heathrow	
G-VIIU	Boeing 777-236ER		R		British Airways plc (For dlvy 5.99)	Heathrow	
G-VIIV	Boeing 777-236ER		R		British Airways plc (For dlvy 6.99)	Heathrow	
G-VIIW	Boeing 777-236ER		R		British Airways plc (For dlvy 6.99)	Heathrow	
G-VIIX	Boeing 777-236ER		R		British Airways plc (For dlvy 8.99)	Heathrow	
G-VIIY	Boeing 777-236ER		R		British Airways plc (For dlvy 9.99)	Heathrow	
G-VIKE	Bellanca 17-30A Super Viking 300A	79-30911	N302CB	8. 7.80	W.G.Prout	(Fareham)	27. 6.99
G-VIKY	Cameron A-120 HAFB	3068		27. 4.93	D.W.Pennell	Broadway	27. 5.97A
G-VILL	Carmichael Lazer Z.200 (Lyc AEIO-360)	10	G-BOYZ	10. 6.96	M.G.Jefferies (Global Village titles)	Little Gransden	13. 7.99P
G-VINO	Sky 90-24 HAFB	102		25. 2.98	Fivedata Ltd	Todmorden	19. 2.99A
G-VIPI	BAe 125 Srs.800B	258222	G-5-745	27. 7.92	Yeates of Leicester Ltd	Southampton	16. 9.99T
G-VIPP	PA-31-350 Navajo Chieftain	31-7952244	G-OGRV G-BMPX/N3543D	6. 8.93	Capital Trading Aviation Ltd	Filton/Chester	16. 8.99T
G-VIPY	PA-31-350 Navajo Chieftain	31-7852143	EI-JTC G-POLO/N27750	10.10.97	Capital Trading Aviation Ltd	Filton	9.10.99T
G-VIRG	Boeing 747-287B	21189	N354AS LV-LZD/N1791B	14. 6.84	Virgin Atlantic Airways Ltd "Maiden Voyager"	Gatwick	1. 8.99T
G-VITE	Robin R.1180T Aiglon	219		16.10.78	D.C.Perrett & D.T.Scrutton t/a G-VITE F/Grp	Stapleford	20. 4.00
G-VIVA	Thunder Ax7-65 Bolt HAFB	190		28.11.78	R.J.Mitchener	Andover	18. 3.99A
G-VIVI	Taylor JT.2 Titch	PFA/60-12405		4.11.96	D.G.Tucker	Hill Farm, Nayland	
G-VIVM	BAC P.84 Jet Provost T.5	PAC/W/23907	G-BVWF XS230	25. 3.96	Flight Test Associates Ltd	Woodford	3. 6.99P
G-VIXN	HS.110 Sea Vixen FAW.2 (TT)	10145	8828M XS587	5. 8.85	P.G.Vallance Ltd (As "XS587/252/V" in RN c/s)	Charlwood, Surrey	AC
G-VIZZ	Sportavia RS.180 Sportsman	6018	D-EFBK	25.10.79	M.J.Revill t/a Exeter Fournier Grp	Exeter	20. 7.01
G-VJAB	Pearce Jabiru UL	PFA/274-13322		25. 6.98	ST Aviation Ltd	Downham Market	
G-VJET	Avro 698 Vulcan B.2		XL426	7. 7.87	R.J.Clarkson t/a The Vulcan Restoration Trust (As "XL426")	Southend	
G-VJFK	Boeing 747-238B	20842	VH-EBH	4. 2.91	Virgin Atlantic Airways Ltd "Boston Belle"	Gatwick	3. 3.00T
G-VJIM	Colt Jumbo 77SS HAFB	1298	(G-BPJI)	7. 8.89	L.V.Mastis "Jumbo Jim" (Virgin Atlantic titles)	W Bloomfield, Mi., USA	29. 5.99A
G-VLAD	Yakovlev Yak-50	791502	D-EIVR N51980/DDR-WQR/DM-WQR	14.11.88	M.B.Smith (Vladivar Vodka c/s)	(Stokenchurch)	6. 8.99P
G-VLAX	Boeing 747-238B	20921	VH-EBI	1. 5.91	Virgin Atlantic Airways Ltd "California Girl"	Gatwick	26. 5.99T
G-VLCN	Avro 698 Vulcan B.2		XH558	6. 2.95	C.Walton Ltd (As "XH558")	Bruntingthorpe	AC
G-VMAX	Mooney M.20K	25-0504	ZS-KYP N9716G	12. 2.86	Glidegold Ltd	Booker	20.12.98T
G-VMDE(2)	Cessna P210N Pressurised Centurion II	P210-00088	(N4717P)	20. 7.78	Royton Express Deliveries (Welwyn) Ltd	North Weald	26. 4.00

Regn	Type	C/n	P/I	Date	Owner/operator	Probable Base	CA Expy
G-VMIA	Boeing 747-123	20108	EI-CAI VH-EEI/G-HIHO/(LX-NCV)/N14939/N9669	23. 3.90	Virgin Atlantic Airways Ltd "Spirit of Sir Freddie"	Gatwick	7. 5.99T
G-VMJM	Socata TB-10 Tobago	1361	G-BTOK	21. 4.92	J.H.Michaels	Denham	20. 4.01
G-VMPR	DH.115 Vampire T.11	15621	8196M XE920	13. 3.95	J.N.Kerr & J.Jones (As "XE920/D")	Swansea	8. 1.99P
G-VMSL	Robinson R-22 Beta	0483	G-KILY N8561M	5. 2.98	L.L.F.Smith	Booker	18.12.00T
G-VNOM	FFW DH.112 Venom FB.50	842	J-1632	13. 7.84	De Havilland Aviation Ltd (As "J-1632")	(Bridgend)	AC
G-VOAR	PA-28-181 Archer III	2843011	N9256Q	3.11.95	Jeff Brown Ltd	(Weston-super-Mare)	15.12.01
G-VODA	Cameron N-77 HAFB (New envelope 12.97)	2208		8. 2.90	Vodafone Group plc "Vodafone"	Newbury	7. 6.96A
G-VOID	PA-28RT-201 Arrow IV	28R-8118049	ZS-KTM N83232	17. 8.87	Newbus Avn Ltd	Shoreham	3.12.99
G-VOLH	Airbus A.321-211	823	(EC-) D-AVZX	15. 5.98	OY Air Scandic International Aviation AB	Manchester	14. 5.01T
G-VOLT	Cameron N-77 HAFB	2157		8.11.89	National Power plc "National Power"	Swindon	25. 4.97A
G-VOTE	Ultramagic M-77 HAFB	77-164		10. 3.99	Window on the World Ltd	(London SE1)	
G-VPII	Evans VP-2 (Cont A65)	PFA/63-10262	(G-EDIF)	4.10.88	V.D.J.Hitchings Rayne Hall Farm, Rayne (Wings stored 2.92)		
G-VPSJ	Europa Avn Europa	PFA/247-12520		29. 7.93	J.D.Bean	(Oxford)	
G-VPUF	Boeing 747-219B		ZK...	R	Virgin Atlantic Airways Ltd		
G-VROE	Avro 652A Anson T.21	3634	G-BFIR 7881M/WD413	3. 3.98	Air Atlantique Ltd (As "WD413" in RAF Transport Command c/s)	Coventry	4. 6.99P
G-VRST	PA-46-350P Malibu Mirage	4636189		7.12.98	Winchfield Development Ltd	Biggin Hill	AC
G-VRUM	Boeing 747-267B	23048	B-HIF VR-HIF/N6066U	2.11.98	Virgin Atlantic Airways Ltd	Heathrow	1.11.01T
G-VRVI	Cameron O-90 HAFB	2522		27. 2.91	Cooling Svs Ltd "Daikin"	Portishead	4. 9.99A
G-VSBC	Beechcraft B200 Super King Air	BB-1290	N3185C JA8859/N3185C	17. 6.93	Vickers Shipbuilding & Engineering Ltd	Walney Island	21. 6.00
G-VSEA	Airbus A.340-311	003	F-WWDA	7. 7.97	Virgin Atlantic Airways Ltd	Gatwick	6. 7.00T
G-VSFT	PA-23-250 Aztec F	27-7754144	G-TOMK G-BFEC/N63823	23. 4.96	SFT Europe Ltd	Bournemouth	4. 5.01T
G-VSKY	Airbus A.340-311	016	F-WWJH	21. 1.94	Virgin Atlantic Airways Ltd "China Girl"	Gatwick	20. 1.00T
G-VSSS	Boeing 747-219B		ZK...	R	Virgin Atlantic Airways Ltd	Gatwick	
G-VSUN	Airbus A.340-313	114	F-WWJI (F-GLZJ)	30. 4.96	Virgin Atlantic Airways Ltd "Rainbow Lady"	Gatwick	29. 4.99T
G-VTEN*	Vinten-Wallis WA.117 Venom UMA-01 & 003 (Cont O-200-B)			22. 4.85	K.H.Wallis (Unmarked frame stored 8.97)	Reymerston Hall	3.12.85P*
G-VTII	DH.115 Vampire T.11 (Fuselage No.DHP40273)	15127	WZ507	9. 1.80	De Havilland Aviation Ltd (As "WZ507")	Swansea	13. 8.95P
G-VTOL*	Hawker Siddeley Harrier T.52	B3/41H/735795	ZA250 G-VTOL	27. 7.70	British Aerospace plc (On loan to Brooklands Museum 10.96)	Brooklands	2.11.86S
G-VTOP	Boeing 747-4Q8	28194		28. 1.97	Virgin Atlantic Airways Ltd "Virginia Plain"	Gatwick	17. 3.00T
G-VULC	Avro 698 Vulcan B.2A		N655AV G-VULC/XM655	27. 2.84	Radarmoor Ltd Wellesbourne Mountford (As "XM655")		
G-VVBF	Colt 315A HAFB	4058		3. 3.97	Virgin Balloon Flights Ltd (London SE16)		3. 5.99T
G-VVBK	PA-34-200T Seneca II	34-7570303	G-BSBS G-BDRI/SE-GLG	26. 1.89	Magyar Construction Co Ltd(Douglas, IOM)		30.10.01
G-VVIP	Cessna 421C Golden Eagle III	421C-0699	G-BMWB N2655L	7. 7.92	Capital Trading Avn Ltd	Filton	30. 4.98T
G-VXLG	Boeing 747-41R	29406		30. 9.98	Virgin Atlantic Airways Ltd	Heathrow	20. 9.01T
G-VYGR	Colt 120A HAFB	2479		24. 9.93	A.van Wyk	Caxton	27.10.95T
G-VZZZ	Boeing 747-219B		ZK...	R	Virgin Atlantic Airways Ltd		

G-WAAA-WZZZ

Regn	Type	C/n	P/I	Date	Owner/operator	Probable Base	CA Expy
G-WAAC	Cameron N-56 HAFB	492		14. 2.79	N.P.Hemsley Crawley		26. 6.97A
					t/a Whacko Balloon Group "Whacko"		
G-WACB	Reims Cessna F.152 II	1972		16. 9.86	Wycombe Air Centre Ltd	Booker	24. 2.99T
G-WACE	Reims Cessna F.152 II	1978		16. 9.86	Wycombe Air Centre Ltd	Booker	23. 4.99T
G-WACF	Cessna 152 II	152-84852	N628GH	20. 1.87	Wycombe Air Centre Ltd	Booker	24.11.00T
			(LV-PMB)/N628GH				
G-WACG	Cessna 152 II	152-85536	ZS-KXY	4.11.86	Wycombe Air Centre Ltd	Booker	3. 4.01T
			(N93699)				
G-WACH	Reims Cessna FA.152 Aerobat	0425		18. 6.87	Wycombe Air Centre Ltd	Booker	4. 8.99T
G-WACI	Beechcraft 76 Duchess	ME-289	N6703Y	26. 7.88	Wycombe Air Centre Ltd	Booker	14.11.00T
G-WACJ	Beechcraft 76 Duchess	ME-278	N6700Y	3. 1.89	Wycombe Air Centre Ltd	Booker	6. 5.99T
G-WACL	Reims Cessna F.172N Skyhawk II	1912	G-BHGG	19. 6.89	Wycombe Air Centre Ltd	Booker	20. 4.01T
G-WACO	Waco UPF-7	5400	N29903	28. 1.87	R.G.Vincent Gloucestershire		13. 5.90
			NC29903		t/a RGV (Acft Svs) & Co		
					(Damaged Liverpool 15.4.89; on rebuild 4.97)		
G-WACP	PA-28-180 Cherokee Archer	28-7405007	G-BBPP	5. 4.89	Wycombe Air Centre Ltd	Booker	9. 7.01T
			N9559N				
G-WACR	PA-28-180 Archer	28-7505090	G-BCZF	18.12.86	Wycombe Air Centre Ltd	Booker	9. 7.00T
			N9517N				
G-WACT	Reims Cessna F.152 II	1908	G-BKFT	24. 6.86	Wycombe Air Centre Ltd	Booker	5.10.00T
G-WACU	Reims Cessna FA.152 Aerobat	0380	G-BJZU	10. 7.86	Wycombe Air Centre Ltd	Booker	9. 6.00T
G-WACW	Cessna 172P Skyhawk II	172-74057	N5307K	16. 5.88	Wycombe Air Centre Ltd	Booker	16. 6.00T
G-WACY	Reims Cessna F.172P Skyhawk II	2217	F-GDOZ	3.10.86	Wycombe Air Centre Ltd	Booker	14. 1.02T
G-WACZ	Reims Cessna F.172M Skyhawk II	1311	G-BCUK	19. 5.86	Professional Air Training Ltd		15. 4.99T
						Bournemouth	
G-WADS	Robinson R-22 Beta	1224	G-NICO	25. 4.96	Pyramid Precision Eng Ltd (Telford)		3. 3.99
G-WAIR	PA-32-301 Saratoga	32-8506010	N2607X	14. 1.91	P.H.Burtwhistle (Thorne, Doncaster)		13. 5.00
			N9577N		t/a Thorne Aviation		
G-WAIT	Cameron V-77 HAFB	2390		20.11.90	C.P.Brown	Ely	24. 9.99A
G-WALS	Cessna A152 Aerobat	A152-0843	N4614A	27. 9.88	Redhill Aviation Ltd	Redhill	5. 2.01T
					t/a Redhill F/C		
G-WARA	PA-28-161 Warrior III	2842021	N9289N	3. 9.97	London School of Flying Ltd	Elstree	14. 9.00T
G-WARB	PA-28-161 Warrior III	2842034	N41286	4. 9.98	London School of Flying Ltd	Elstree	7. 9.01T
G-WARC	PA-28-161 Warrior III	2842035	N41244	11. 9.98	London School of Flying Ltd	Elstree	13. 9.00T
G-WARD	Taylor JT.1 Monoplane WB.VI & PFA/1407			1.12.80	R.P.J.Hunter	Redhill	24.11.98P
	(VW1834)						
G-WARE	PA-28-161 Warrior II	28-8416080	N4357L	21. 7.89	W.B.Ware Bristol/Lulsgate		17.11.01
G-WARK	Schweizer Hughes 269C (300C)	S.1354		13.11.89	J.M. & E.M.Wicks Boones Farm, Braintree		15. 4.99T
G-WARO	PA-28-161 Warrior III	2842015	N92946	24.10.97	London School of Flying Ltd	Elstree	23.10.00T
G-WARP	Cessna 182F	182-54633	G-ASHB	6. 6.95	R.M.Burnett	Netheravon	14. 7.01
			N3233U		t/a Army Parachute Association		
G-WARR	PA-28-161 Warrior II	28-7916321	N3074U	15. 9.88	T.J. & G.M.Laundy	RAF Halton	1. 1.01T
					(Op RAF Halton Aeroplane Club)		
G-WARS	PA-28-161 Warrior III	2842022	N9281X	7.11.97	London School of Flying Ltd	Elstree	6.11.00T
G-WARU	PA-28-161 Warrior III	2842023	N92880	6.11.97	Solent Flight A/c Ltd	Southampton	6.11.00T
G-WARV	PA-28-161 Warrior III	2842036	N41247	9.10.98	London Aviation Ltd	Biggin Hill	13.10.01T
G-WARW	PA-28-161 Warrior III	2842037	N41254	17.11.98	London School of Flying Ltd.	Elstree	19.11.01T
G-WARX	PA-28-161 Warrior III	2842038	N41260	15.12.98	London Aviation Ltd	Biggin Hill	AC
G-WARY	PA-28-161 Warrior III	2842024	N9287X	13.11.97	London School of Flying Ltd	Elstree	18.11.00T
G-WARZ	PA-28-161 Warrior III	2842025	N92944	26.11.97	London School of Flying Ltd	Elstree	27.11.00T
G-WASH	Cameron N-850 HAFB	1451		3. 3.87	Noble Adventures Ltd	Bristol	18. 8.87P
G-WASP	Brantly B-2B	445	G-ASXE	7. 2.77	N.J.R.Minchin Hill Top Farm, Godalming		21. 5.99
G-WATS	PA-34-220T Seneca III	34-8333058	G-BOVJ	3. 2.89	Oxford Aviation Services Ltd	Oxford	26. 5.01T
			N8202J				
G-WATT	Cameron Cooling Tower SS HAFB	2158		8.11.89	National Power plc	Swindon	22. 8.96A
					"Enterprise"		
G-WAVE(2)	Grob G-109B	6381		1. 8.85	M.L.Murdoch Park Farm, Eaton Bray		21. 2.01
G-WAZZ	Pitts S-1S Special	7-0332	G-BRRP	17. 6.94	D.T.Knight	White Waltham	14. 6.99P
	(Lyc O-360)		N3TD				
G-WBAT	Wombat Gyrocopter	CJ-001	G-BSID	31. 5.90	C.D.Julian	St.Merryn	4. 3.97*
	(Rotax 532)						
G-WBMG	Cameron N Ele 90SS HAFB	3086	G-BUYV	5. 7.93	M.Severin Court St.Etienne, Belgium		25. 7.99A
G-WBPR	BAe 125 Srs.800B	258085	G-5-551	29. 9.87	Granada Group plc	Luton	13.11.99
G-WBTS	Falconar F-11W-200 PFA/32-10070		G-BDPL	22.10.90	W.C.Brown	Fleet	21. 7.87P
	(Cont O-200-A)				(Damaged Hook 16.10.87; on rebuild 1996)		
G-WCAT*	Colt Flying Mitt SS HAFB	1744		30. 5.90	R S Kent & I M Martin "Washcat" Lancing		N/E(A)
					(Balloon Preservation Group 7.98)		
G-WCEI	Socata MS.894E Rallye 220GT	12141	G-BAOC	28. 5.85	R.A.L.Lucas	Walney Island	12. 7.01
G-WDEB	Thunder Ax7-77 HAFB	1606		26. 9.89	W. de Bock "Landplan"	Peterborough	23. 6.97A
G-WDEV	Westland SA.341G Gazelle 1	WA/1098	G-IZEL	30. 9.98	Wickford Development Co Ltd (Chelmsford)		21.11.99T
			G-BBHW				
G-WEAC	BN-2A mk.III-2 Trislander	1042	5H-AZD	16.12.94	Keen Leasing Ltd	Aldergrove	12.12.99T
	G-BEFP/(4X-CCL)/G-BEFP/N30WA/JA6401/G-BEFP (Op Woodgate Executive Air Services)						

Regn	Type	C/n	P/I	Date	Owner/operator	Probable Base	CA Expy
G-WELI	Cameron N-77 HAFB	1078		26. 9.84	M.A.Shannon "Wellie"	Southampton	7. 7.99A
G-WELL	Beechcraft E90 King Air	LW-198	N202CC (N7PB)/N202CC	18. 7.85	Colt Transport Ltd	Goodwood	5. 6.00T
G-WELS	Cameron N-65 HAFB	1297		7. 4.86	K.J.Vickery "Talisman"	Billingshurst	26. 6.92A
G-WEND	PA-28RT-201 Arrow IV	28R-8118026	PH-SYL N8296L	8.11.82	C.P.Edgar t/a G-WEND Group	Prestwick	14. 2.99
G-WERY	Socata TB-20 Trinidad	305		2. 4.82	G.L.Appleyard & M.T.Jenkins t/a WERY F/Grp	Sherburn	3. 4.00
G-WEST	Agusta A.109A	7213		21. 1.81	Westland Helicopters Ltd	Yeovil	28. 3.99
G-WESX	CFM Streak Shadow (Rotax 582) K.116-SA & PFA/161A-11561			2. 2.90	D.J.Sagar	Croft Farm, Defford	14. 8.98P
G-WETI	Cameron N-31 HAFB	449		27.11.78	C.A.Butter & J.J.T.Cooke "Puddleduck"	Marsh Benham	5. 7.88A
G-WFEP	ATR-42-300	149	N4210G F-WWEV	9. 2.98	Gill Airways Ltd	Newcastle	26. 2.01T
G-WFFW	PA-28-161 Warrior II	28-8116161	N8342A	26.10.93	N.F.Duke	Bournemouth	27.11.99
G-WFOX	Robinson R-22 Beta	2826		2. 6.98	Heli-Air Ltd Wellesbourne Mountford		25. 6.01T
G-WGAL	Bell 206B JetRanger III	3165	G-OICS N678TM	22. 3.93	Watkiss Group Avn Ltd	Keysoe	19. 3.01
G-WGCL	Rockwell Commander 685	12043	CS-AQO N57028	7.11.95	Cooper Aerial Surveys Ltd	Sandtoft	20. 5.99A
G-WGCS	PA-18-95 Super Cub (L-18C-PI) (Frame No.18-1500)	18-1528	(G-BLSV) ALAT F-MBCH/51-15528	21.12.84	S.C.Thompson	Newells Farm, Bolney	25. 6.98P
G-WGHB	Canadair (CL-30) T-33AN Silver Star mk.3	T33-640	CF-EHB CAF 133640/RCAF 21640	9. 5.74	R.H.& G.C. Cooper	Sandtoft	13. 6.77P
G-WGSC	Pilatus PC-6/B2-H4 Turbo-Porter	848	OE-ECS	2. 1.90	D.M.Penny Movenis, Co.Londonderry (Op Wild Geese Parachute Centre)		23. 3.01
G-WHAT	Colt 77A HAFB	1911		15. 3.91	M.A.Scholes "Chad"	London SE25	2. 8.98A
G-WHAZ	Agusta-Bell 206A Jet Ranger	8112	OH-HRE G-WHAZ/OH-HRE	26. 6.97	Claygate Distribution Ltd Paynetts Farm, Goudhurst, Kent		28. 7.00
G-WHDP	Cessna 182S	182-80178	N178TC	12. 5.98	Heatherford Ltd	(London N6)	14. 5.01T
G-WHEE	Pegasus Quantum 15-912	7510		26. 3.99	N & R Harwood	Littlehampton	
G-WHIM	Colt 77A HAFB	1476		10. 4.89	D.L.Morgan	Ilford	15. 6.96A
G-WHOG	CFM Streak Shadow (Rotax 618) K.253-SA & PFA/206-12776			21. 9.94	B.R.Cannell "Wart Hog"	Old Sarum	27. 7.99P
G-WHST	Eurocopter AS.350B2 Ecureuil	2915	G-BWYA	9. 8.96	Hawkrise Ltd	Sutton Coldfield	26. 9.99T
G-WIBB	Jodel D.18 (Subaru EA81)	PFA/169-11640		18. 6.96	J.& D.Wibberley	Priory Farm, Tibenham	6. 3.99P
G-WIBS	CASA I-131E Srs 2000	2005	E3B-401	25. 3.99	C Willoughby	(Ashford)	
G-WILD	Aerotek Pitts S-1T Special (AEIO-360)	1017	ZS-LMM	6.12.85	J.D.Haslam (Microlease c/s)	Breighton	1. 5.01
G-WILG	WSK PZL-104 Wilga 35	62153	G-AZYJ	15. 4.97	Taylor Aircraft Services Ltd "The Startled Fart !"	Sywell	29. 9.00
G-WILS	PA-28RT-201T Turbo Arrow IV	28R-8431005	PH-DPD N4330W	16. 1.96	W.S.Stanley & V.F.A.Dimock	Gloucestershire	7. 2.99T
G-WILY	Rutan LongEz 1200 & PFA/74A-10724 (Lyc O-320)			8. 6.83	W.S.Allen & B.Wronski "Time Flies"	Gloucestershire	26. 1.99P
G-WIMP	Colt 56A HAFB	755		13. 2.86	T.& B.Chamberlain	York	17. 8.97A
G-WINE	Thunder AX7-77Z HAFB	472		25.11.82	S.M.Miles (Balloon Preservation Group 12.98)	Lancing	17. 6.97A
G-WINK	Grumman-American AA-5B Tiger	AA5B-0327	N74658	14.12.90	B.S.Cooke	Elstree	22. 3.00
G-WINS	PA-32-300 Cherokee Six	32-7640065	N8476C	24. 4.91	Cheyenne Ltd	Jersey	26. 2.00
G-WIRE	Aerospatiale AS.355F1 Twin Squirrel	5312	G-CEGB G-BLJL	22. 1.90	National Grid Co plc	Oxford	12. 6.00T
G-WIRL	Robinson R-22 Beta	0671		27. 7.87	C.A.Rosenberg	Shobdon	9. 8.99T
G-WISH	Lindstrand Cake SS HAFB (Birthday Cake shape)	006		14.12.92	Oxford Promotions (UK) Ltd Kentucky, USA		13. 4.99A
G-WISP	Robinson R-44 Astro	0566		16. 3.99	Heli-Air Ltd Wellesbourne Mountford		
G-WIXI	Avions Mudry CAP.10B	279		27. 1.98	J.M. & E.M.Wicks	(Braintree)	26. 7.01
G-WIZA	Robinson R-22 Beta	0861	G-PERL N90815	16.11.94	Burman Avn Ltd (Op Burman Helicopters)	Cranfield	12. 1.01T
G-WIZB	Grob G.115A	8104	EI-CAD	2. 9.98	A.G.Wisbey	Sywell	22.10.01T
G-WIZD	Lindstrand LBL-180A HAFB	066		12.11.93	T.H.Wilson	Diss	28. 9.99
G-WIZO	PA-34-220T Seneca III	34-8133171	N8413U	16.12.86	Bignell Surgical Instruments Ltd	Shoreham	5. 2.01T
G-WIZR	Robinson R-22 Beta	2799		9. 3.98	J.D.Forbes-Nixon & N.H.Taylor t/a Clifton Helicopter Hire Bristol/Lulsgate		25. 3.01T
G-WIZY	Robinson R-22 Beta	0566	G-BMWX N24196	26. 8.97	Central Aviation (Helicopters) Ltd	Nottingham	5. 6.00T
G-WIZZ	Agusta-Bell 206B JetRanger II	8540		7.12.77	Cavenhurst Ltd	Newark	3.10.99T
G-WJAN	Boeing 757-21K	28674		18. 3.97	Airtours International Airways Ltd	Manchester	19. 3.00T
G-WKRD	Eurocopter AS.350B2 Ecureuil	2668	G-BUJG G-HEAR/G-BUJG	16. 3.99	Wickford Development Co	(Chelmsford)	22. 9.01
G-WLAC	PA-18-150 Super Cub	18-8899	G-HAHA G-BSWE/N9194P	2. 6.98	J.S.R.Pearson (Rebuilt 1994/95 using major parts from G-BTDY)	White Waltham	14. 6.01T

Regn	Type	C/n	P/I	Date	Owner/operator	Probable Base	CA Expy
G-WLGA	WSK PZL-104 Wilga 80	CF21910932	EC-FYY F-GMLR	8.11.96	A.J.Renham	Morgansfield, Fishburn	2. 3.00
G-WLLY	Bell 206B JetRanger	405	G-OBHH G-WLLY/G-RODY/G-ROGR/G-AXMM/N1469W	24. 3.93	Blue Five Aviation Ltd	Redhill	11. 7.99T
G-WMAA	MBB Bo.105DBS-4 (Rebuilt using new airframe S.914 1994)	S.135/914	VH-LSA/G-BDMC/D-HDEC (Op West Midlands Air Ambulance)	8. 9.94	Bond Helicopters Ltd	RAF Cosford	29. 9.00T
G-WMPA	Aerospatiale AS.355F2 Twin Squirrel	5401		7. 2.89	West Midlands Police Authority	Birmingham	10. 5.01T
G-WMTM	Gulfstream AA-5B Tiger	AA5B-1035	N4517V	8. 1.91	Susan A.Westhorp	(Godalming)	10. 8.99T
G-WNGS	Cameron N-105 HAFB	4385		15. 7.98	Redmalt Ltd	Witham	7. 7.99A
G-WOLF	PA-28-140 Cruiser	28-7425439	OY-TOD	20. 3.80	Werewolf Aviation Ltd	Elstree	4. 2.02
G-WOOD	Beechcraft 95-B55A Baron	TC-1283	SE-GRC G-AYID/SE-EXK	17. 9.79	T.D.Broadhurst t/a Baron Avn	Tilstock	10.12.02
G-WOOF	Enstrom 480	5027		3. 3.98	Westover Park Ltd	Guernsey	6. 4.01
G-WOOL	Colt 77A HAFB	2044		23. 2.93	T.G.Pembrey, N.P.Helmsley & C.L.Pembrey t/a Whacko Balloon Group	Steyning	9. 9.99
G-WOTG	PBN BN-2T Turbine Islander	2139	(ZF444) G-WOTG/G-BJYT	10.11.83	P.M.Hall t/a RAF Sport Parachute Association	Weston-on-the-Green	30. 1.00
G-WOZA	PA-32RT-300 Lance II	32R-7885144	G-BYBB N31957	23. 5.91	O.C.Kruppa	(Kiel, Germany)	24. 6.99
G-WPAS	Boeing MD-900 Explorer	900-00053		1. 7.98	Police Aviation Services Ltd	Devizes	28.10.01T
G-WREN	Aerotek Pitts S-2A Special (Lyc AEIO-360)	2229	N947	28. 1.81	Northamptonshire School of Flying Ltd	Sywell	24. 3.99T
G-WRFM	Enstrom 280C-UK Shark	1202	G-CTSI G-BKIO/(G-BKHN)/SE-HLB t/a Skywalker Enterprises	21. 4.89	A.J.MacFarlane	Goodwood	19. 5.01
G-WRIT	Colt 77A HAFB	1328		15. 9.88	G.Pusey "Legal Eagle"	Seville, France	31. 5.97A
G-WSEC	Enstrom F-28C	398	G-BONF N51661	19.12.88	M.J.Easey	Town Farm, Hoxne, Eye	10.12.01
G-WSFT	PA-23-250 Aztec F	27-7754059	G-BTHS N62824	18. 6.86	SFT Europe Ltd	Bournemouth	15. 6.01T
G-WSKY	Enstrom 280C-UK-2 Shark	1037	G-BEEK	25. 7.83	M.I.Edwards	Brandon, Suffolk	23. 4.00
G-WUFF	Europa Avtn Europa	PFA/247-12942		19. 1.99	M.A.Barker.	(Doncaster)	
G-WULF	WAR Focke-Wulf 190 204 & PFA/81-10328 (Cont O-200-A)			24. 2.78	S.N.Lester (As "8+-" in Luftwaffe c/s)	Popham	22. 6.99P
G-WURL	Robinson R-22 Beta	2740	G-BXMS	13.10.97	Heli Air Ltd	Wellesbourne Mountford	15.10.00T
G-WVBF	Lindstrand LBL-210A HAFB	312		6.12.95	Virgin Balloon Flights Ltd (London SE16)		25. 9.99T
G-WWAL	PA-28R-180 Cherokee Arrow	28R-30461	G-AZSH N4612J	23.10.98	C.& G.Clarke	Goodwood	1. 7.99T
G-WWAS	PA-34-220T Seneca III	34-8133222	G-BPPB N83270	2. 3.95	D.Intzevidis	Athens, Greece	10. 9.01
G-WWIZ	Beechcraft 58 Baron	TH-429	G-GAMA G-BBSD	18.10.96	Chase Aviation Ltd	Bournemouth	6. 6.99T
G-WWWG	Europa Avn Europa 40 & PFA/247-12597 (NSI EA-81/118)			31. 7.95	Chloe F.Williams-Wynne Talybont, Gwynedd		10.11.98P
G-WYAT	CFM Streak Shadow SA	PFA/206-12993		9. 6.97	M.G.Whyatt	(High Peak, Derbyshire)	5. 5.99P
G-WYCH	Cameron Witch 90SS HAFB (Witch on broomstick plus cat!)	1330		30. 9.86	Jacques W.Soukup Enterprises Ltd "Hilda"	(USA)	22. 6.95A
G-WYMP	Reims Cessna F.150J	0521	G-BAGW SE-FKM	26. 2.82	R.Hall	Full Sutton	18. 8.99T
G-WYMR	Robinson R-44 Astro	0439		15. 4.98	Heli Air Ltd	Wellesbourne Mountford	30. 4.01T
G-WYNN	Rand Robinson KR-2 PFA/129-11141 (Originally regd as c/n PFA/129-11093; probably composite of both projects)			28. 8.85	W.Thomas	(Wrexham)	
G-WYNS	Aero Designs Pulsar XP PFA/202-11976 (Rotax 912)			22. 2.91	S.L.Bauza	(Palma de Mallorca)	27. 4.98P
G-WYNT	Cameron N-56 HAFB	1038		3. 4.84	Jacques W.Soukup Enterprises Ltd "Gwyntoedd Dros Cymru/Winds over Wales"	St.Croix, Virgin Islands	21. 3.98A
G-WYPA	MBB Bo.105DBS/4	S.815	D-HDZY	27.10.89	West Yorkshire Police Authority	Carr Gate, Wakefield	19.12.98T
G-WYZZ*	Air Command 532 Elite 0429 & PFA G/104-1103		G-BPAK	22. 1.90	C.H.Gem (Cancelled by CAA 22.3.99)	(London SW9)	27. 3.90P
G-WZOL	Tiger Cub RL5B LWS Sherwood Ranger PFA/237-12887		G-MZOL	20. 1.99	G.W.F.Webb	(Cambridge)	
G-WZZZ	Colt AS-42 Hot Air Airship 459 (Rebuilt 1984/85 using new AS-56 envelope c/n 607)			10.12.82	Lindstrand Balloons Ltd "Kit Kat"	Oswestry	17. 9.98A

G-XAAA-XZZZ

Regn	Type	C/n	P/I	Date	Owner/operator	Probable Base	CA Expy
G-XALP	Schweizer Hughes 269C (300C)	S.1314		27. 6.88	Teknowledge Ltd	(Lincoln)	13. 8.00T
G-XANT	Cameron N-105 HAFB	3003		4. 3.93	Flying Pictures Ltd "Citroen Xantia"	Fairoaks	21.11.96A
G-XARV	ARV1 Super 2	010	G-OPIG G-BMSJ	8.11.95	N.R.Beale	Shotteswell	1.10.99P
G-XBHX	Boeing 737-36N	28572		21. 5.98	British Regional Airlines Ltd	Manchester	4. 6.01T
G-XCEL	Aerospatiale AS.355F1 Twin Squirrel	5324	G-HBAC G-HJET/F-GEOX/F-WYMC/OY-HDL	16. 5.95	Tri-Ventures Group Ltd	Denham	23. 1.00T
G-XCUB	PA-18-150 Super Cub	18-8109036		1. 5.81	M.C.Barraclough	Selborne, Alton	26. 4.01
G-XENA	PA-28-161 Warrior II	28-7716158	N3486Q	29. 6.98	Tradecliff Ltd	Stockbridge	AC
G-XIIX	Robinson R-22 Beta	0736		8. 2.88	Helitech (Luton) Ltd	Luton	21. 3.97T
G-XITD*	Cessna 310G	310G-0048	G-ASYV HB-LBY/N8948Z	15.10.87	Not known Arbury College, Cambridge (Crashed Leavesden 14.7.88; instructional airframe 1.92)		14. 9.86
G-XLTG	Cessna 182S Skylane	182-80234	N9571L	17. 7.98	GX Aviation Ltd	(London W5)	30. 7.01
G-XLXL	Robin DR.400/160 Knight	813	G-BAUD	3. 1.92	R.Bailes-Brown & D.O.Hallett t/a 40-40 Aero Group	Gamston	5. 5.00
G-XMAN	Boeing 737-36N	28573		18. 6.98	British Regional Airlines Ltd (Golden Khokhlava t/s)	Manchester	7. 7.01T
G-XPBI	Letov LK-2M Sluka	PFA/263-13341		4.12.98	P.Bishop	(Melton Constable)	
G-XPTS	Robinson R-44 Astro	0433		11. 3.98	Heliair Ltd	Wellesbourne Mountford	4. 6.01T
G-XPXP	Aero Designs Pulsar XP (Rotax 912)	218 & PFA/202-11958		30. 3.92	B.J.Edwards	Belle Vue Farm, Huntshaw	22. 5.99P
G-XRAY	Rand Robinson KR-2	PFA/129-11227		30. 4.87	R.S.Smith	(Inverurie)	
G-XRMC	BAe 125 Srs.800B	258180	G-5-675	3. 7.90	RMC Group Svs Ltd	Farnborough	11.12.99
G-XSDJ	Europa Avtn Europa XS	PFA/247-13378		3. 2.99	D.N.Joyce	(Berkeley)	
G-XSFT	PA-23-250 Aztec F	27-7754103	G-CPPC G-BGBH/N63773	18. 6.86	SFT Europe Ltd	Bournemouth	1. 6.00T
G-XSKY	Cameron N-77 HAFB	2508		26. 3.91	T.D.Gibbs	Billingshurst	13. 2.99
G-XTEC	Robinson R-22 Beta	1478	G-BYCK N101EJ	23.10.98	XTEC Software plc	(Milton Keynes)	11.11.01T
G-XTOR	BN-2A Mk.III-2 Trislander (New fuselage from c/n 1065/N3266G (NTU) fitted 2.96)	359	G-BAXD	1. 4.96	Aurigny Air Services Ltd	Guernsey	5. 7.00T
G-XTRA	Extra EA.230 (Lyc AEIO-360)	012A	D-EDLF	21. 1.87	AJD Engineering Ltd Moat Farm, Milden (Sunday/Daily Express c/s)		14. 7.98P
G-XTRS	Extra EA.300/L	047	D-EXJH	8.10.98	D.J.& L.F.Daly	Inverness	23. 9.01
G-XVIE	VS.361 Spitfire LF.XVIe	CBAF.IX.3807 8073M 7281M/7257M/TB252		3. 7.92	Historic Flying Ltd (As "TB252/GW-H") (Stored 7.97)	Audley End	
G-XWWF	Lindstrand LBL-56A HAFB	595		25. 2.99	D.D.Maimone	Guildford	
G-XXEA	Sikorsky S-76C	760492		21.12.98	T.C.Elworthy, Director of Royal Travel (Op Queen's Flight)	Blackbushe	4. 1.00T
G-XXIV	Agusta-Bell 206B JetRanger III	8717		27. 4.89	Hampton Printing (Bristol) Ltd	Bristol	28. 6.01T
G-XXVI	Sukhoi SU-26M	0410	CCCP-0401	2. 4.93	A.N.Onn & T.R.G.Barnby	Headcorn	25. 6.99P

G-YAAA-YZZZ

Regn	Type	C/n	P/I	Date	Owner/operator	Probable Base	CA Expy
G-YAKA	Yakovlev Yak-50	822303	LY-ANJ DOSAAF 80	10.11.94	J.Griffin	Compton Abbas	23. 1.99P
G-YAKI	Aerostar Yakovlev Yak-52	866904	LY-ANM DOSAAF 100	20. 9.94	Yak One Ltd (As "100" in DOSAAF c/s)	Popham	5. 1.00P
G-YAKM	Yakovlev Yak-55M	920506	RA-01333 R DOSAAF 40		Mrs B.Abela "40"	White Waltham	
G-YAKS	Aerostar Yakovlev Yak-52	9311708		16.12.93	Two Bees Associates Ltd "2"	North Weald	15. 4.99P
G-YAKX	Aerostar Yakovlev Yak-52	9111307	RA-9111307/DOSAAF 27	13. 3.96	The X Fliers Ltd (As "27" in DOSAAF c/s)	(Farnham)	25. 5.99P
G-YAKY	Aerostar Yakovlev Yak-52	844109	LY-AKX DOSAAF 24	26. 2.96	T.K.Butcher & I.A.Reid t/a Kilo Yankee Group (As "52" in DOSAAF c/s)	Duxford/Clacton	3. 9.99P
G-YANK	PA-28-181 Archer II	28-8090163	N81314	19. 3.93	Janet A.Millar-Craig t/a G-YANK F/Grp	Tatenhill	2. 5.99
G-YAWW	PA-28RT-201T Turbo Arrow IV	28R-8031024	N2929Y	15.11.90	Barton Avn Ltd	Barton	1. 5.00
G-YBAA	Reims Cessna FR.172J Rocket	0579	5Y-BAA	15.11.84	H.Norman	Bourn	26.10.00
G-YCUB	PA-18-150 Super Cub	1809077	N4993X N4157T	23. 8.96	F.W.Rogers Garage (Saltash) Ltd	(Saltash)	14. 1.00
G-YEAR	Revolution Helicopters Mini-500 0050 (Rotax 582)			6.10.95	D.J.Waddington	(Preston)	AC
G-YELL	Murphy Rebel	PFA/232-12381		1. 5.95	A.D.Keen	(Totnes)	
G-YEOM	PA-31-350 Chieftain	31-8352022	N41108	3. 1.89	Foster Yeoman Ltd	Bristol/Lulsgate	16. 3.99
G-YEWS*	Rotorway Exec 152	DGP-1 & 3850		22. 6.89	D.G.Pollard	Yews Hotel, Great Glen, Leicester	17. 6.93P
		(Stored 8.95 - cancelled by CAA 22.3.99)					
G-YFLY	VPM M-16 Tandem Trainer VPM16-UK114 (Arrow GT1000R)		G-BWGI	14.10.96	A.J.Unwin	Kemble	11. 6.99P
G-YIII	Reims Cessna F.150L	0827	PH-CEX	5. 6.80	Sherburn Aero Club Ltd	Sherburn-in-Elmet	21. 8.00T
G-YJBM	Airbus A.320-231	362	G-IEAF F-WWIN	28. 9.93	Airtours International Airways Ltd	Manchester	26. 1.00T
G-YJET	Montgomerie-Bensen B.8MR (Rotax 582)	PFA G/101-1072	G-BMUH	25. 9.96	A.Shuttleworth	Barton	16. 2.99P
G-YKEN	Robinson R-22 Beta	2875		22.10.98	S M & Y J Kenmore	(London NW1)	5. 1.01
G-YKSZ	Aerostar Yakovlev Yak-52	9311709		16.12.93	J.N. & C.J.Carter (As "01" in Soviet AF c/s)	Old Buckenham	15. 4.99P
G-YLYB	Cameron N-105 HAFB	4482		15. 1.99	Virgin Airship & Balloon Co Ltd	Telford	7. 1.00
G-YMBO	Robinson R-22 Mariner	2054M	OY-HFR	21. 8.95	Coax Connectors Ltd	Sywell	10. 9.00T
G-YMMA to G-YMMP	)) Boeing 777)				British Airways plc (For delvy 2000/2002)		
G-YMYM	Lindstrand Ice Cream Cone SS HAFB 007			7. 7.93	Lindstrand Balloons Ltd	USA	1. 3.97A
G-YNOT	Rollason Druine D.62B Condor	RAE/649	G-AYFH	10.11.83	A.Littlefair	Lymington	9. 9.97P
G-YOGI	Robin DR.400/140B Major	1090	G-BDME	1.10.86	R.M. & A.M.Gosling Stones Farm, Wickham St.Pauls, Essex		19. 4.01
G-YORK	Reims Cessna F.172M Skyhawk II	1354	PH-LUY F-WLIT	14.12.78	B.Berry	Weston, Ireland	6. 7.00
G-YOYO	Pitts S-1E Special (Lyc O-360)	PFA/09-10885	G-OTSW G-BLHE	22. 5.96	J.D.L.Richardson	Exeter	21. 7.99P
G-YPSY	Andreasson BA.4B (Cont O-200-A)	PFA/38-10352		7. 6.78	C.W.N.Huke & A.N.M.Cox (Damaged Bagby 31. 8.93)	(Colchester)	16. 9.99P
G-YRAT*	VPM M-16 Tandem Trainer VPM16-UK104 (Arrow GT1000R)			16.11.92	A.J.Unwin (Damaged nr Kemble 23. 2.96; stored 6.97)	Kemble	31. 8.96P
G-YRIL	Luscombe 8E Silvaire (Cont O-200-A)	5945	N1318B NC1318B	3. 2.92	C.Potter	North Weald	4.10.99P
G-YROI*	Air Command 532 Elite (Rotax 532)	0002	N532CG	3. 9.87	W.B.Lumb Melrose Farm, Melbourne (Cancelled by CAA 22.3.99)		17.12.90P
G-YROS	Montgomerie-Bensen B.8M (HAPI 60-6M)	PFA G/101-1004		29. 1.81	N.B.Gray	Worsley, Manchester	6. 6.97P
G-YROY	Montgomerie-Bensen B.8MR (Rotax 532)	PFA G/101A-1145		12. 9.89	R.D.Armishaw	Insch	13. 1.99P
G-YSFT	PA-23-250 Aztec F	27-7754038	G-BEJT N62805	1.12.87	SFT Europe Ltd	Bournemouth	19. 4.00T
G-YSTT	PA-32R-301 Saratoga IIHP	3246056	N848T	4. 8.97	A.W.Kendrick	Halfpenny Green	5. 8.00
G-YTWO	Reims Cessna F.172M Skyhawk II	1396	PH-CIA	8. 6.79	Sherburn Aero Club Ltd (Damaged Cromer 12.10.97)	Sherburn	29.11.97T
G-YUGO*	HS.125 Srs.1B/R-522	25094	G-ATWH HZ-BO1/G-ATWH	25. 8.88	British Aerospace plc (Open store 9.97)	Dunsfold	19. 4.91
G-YULL	PA-28-180 Cherokee E	28-5603	G-BEAJ 9H-AAC/N2390R	30. 3.79	Fortescue Investments & Consulting Ltd Gloucestershire/Guernsey		18. 9.00
G-YUMM	Cameron N-90 HAFB	2723		12.12.91	Wunderbar Ltd "Boulevard"	York	6.11.99A
G-YUPI	Cameron N-90 HAFB	1602		12. 1.88	ASTP SRL	Rixensart, Belgium	22.11.98A
G-YURO*	Europa Avn Europa 001 & PFA/220-11981 (Rotax 912UL)			6. 4.92	Yorkshire Air Museum (To Museum 1996)	Elvington	9. 6.95P
G-YVBF	Lindstrand LBL-317S HAFB	505		2. 4.98	Virgin Balloon Flights Ltd (London SE16)		18. 3.99T
G-YVET	Cameron V-90 HAFB	3182		11.10.93	K.J.Foster	Coleshill, Birmingham	23. 4.96A

G-ZAAA-ZZZZ

Regn	Type	C/n	P/I	Date	Owner/operator	Probable Base	CA Expy
G-ZABC	Sky 90-24 HAFB	062		10. 4.97	Rishtons (Chichester) Ltd	Chichester	17. 5.99A
G-ZACH	Robin DR.400/100 Cadet	1831	G-FTIO	20.10.92	A.P.Wellings	Sandown	22. 7.01
G-ZAIR	Zenair CH.601HD	PFA/162-12194		21. 2.92	C.B.Shaw	Cambridge	22. 6.99P
	(Rotax 912UL)						
G-ZAPD	Short SD.3-60 Var.100	SH.3741	G-OLGW	6. 8.92	Titan Airways Ltd	Stansted	4. 8.98T
			G-BOFK/G-14-3741				
G-ZAPI	Cessna 500-1 Citation	500-0404	G-BHTT	13. 9.94	Titan Airways Ltd	Stansted	29. 8.99T
	(Unit No.560)		N2614H				
G-ZAPJ	ATR-42-312	113	EI-CIQ	17. 5.96	Titan Airways Ltd	Stansted	19. 5.99T
			DQ-FEQ/F-WWEJ				
G-ZAPK	BAe 146 Srs.200QC	E-2148	G-BTIA	25. 4.96	Titan Airways Ltd	Stansted	17. 4.00T
			ZS-NCB/G-BTIA/G-6-148/G-PRIN				
G-ZAPL	BAe 146 Srs.200	E-2030	G-WLCY	9. 5.97	Titan Airways Ltd	Stansted	25. 3.99T
			N172US/N352PS		(Planet c/s)		
G-ZAPY	Robinson R-22 Beta	0788	G-INGB	8. 7.98	Heli Air Ltd	Wellesbourne Mountford	6. 8.01T
G-ZARI	Grumman-American AA-5B Tiger		G-BHVY	7. 3.86	S.J.Richardson	(Leatherhead)	5. 5.98
		AA5B-0845	N28835				
G-ZARV	ARV1 Super 2	PFA/152-13035		26. 2.97	P.R.Snowden	Cambridge	23. 2.01
G-ZAZA	PA-18-95 Super Cub	18-2041	D-ENAS	1. 5.84	Airborne Taxi Svs Ltd	Wantage	11. 4.99P
	(L-18C-PI)		R.Neth AF R-66/52-2441		(Adrian Swire)		
G-ZBRA	Thunder Ax10-160 HAFB	1530		4. 4.91	Zebra Ballooning Ltd "Zebra"	Maidstone	2. 2.96T
G-ZEBO	Thunder Ax8-105 Srs.2 HAFB	2197		22. 5.92	Redmalt Ltd "Gazebo"	Witham, Essex	10. 8.99T
G-ZEBR	Colt 210A HAFB	2272		10. 9.92	Zebra Ballooning Ltd	Maidstone	16. 2.99T
					"Zebra II"		
G-ZEIN	Slingsby T-67M-260 Firefly	2234		19. 7.95	RV Aviation Ltd	Blackbushe	29.10.98T
G-ZENO	Gates Learjet 35A	35A-429	G-GAYL	16. 5.96	Northern Executive Aviation Ltd		
			G-ZING			Manchester	19. 3.00T
G-ZEPI	Colt GA-42 Gas Airship	878	G-ISPY	9. 4.92	Lindstrand Balloons Ltd	Oswestry	12. 5.93A
			(G-BPRB)				
G-ZEPY	Colt GA-42 Gas Airship	1299	G-BSCU	6. 2.92	Keelex 195 Ltd	Telford	8. 8.97A
G-ZERO	Grumman-American AA-5B Tiger		OO-PEC	3. 9.80	D.M.Ashford	Southampton	24. 1.99T
		AA5B-0051			t/a G-ZERO Syndicate		
G-ZIGI	Robin DR.400/180 Regent	2107		19.11.91	R.J.Dix	Callington	5. 3.01
G-ZIPA	Rockwell Commander 114A	14505	G-BHRA	3. 9.98	M.F.Luke	(Farnham)	26. 1.01
	(Originally laid down as c/n 14436)		N5891N				
G-ZIPI	Robin DR.400/180 Regent	1557		22. 2.82	H.U. & D.C.Stahlberg	Rochester	11. 5.01
G-ZIPY	Wittman W.8 Tailwind	PFA/31-11339		29. 5.91	M.J.Butler	Ranksborough Farm, Langham	30. 1.99P
	(Lyc O-235)						
G-ZLIN	Moravan Zlin Z.326 Trener Master	916	G-BBCR	30. 6.81	N.J.Arthur	Finmere	6.10.01
	(Modified to Z.526 standard)		OH-TZF				
	(C/n confirmed but duplicates I-ETRM)						
G-ZLOJ	Beechcraft A36 Bonanza	E-1677	ZS-LOJ	11. 9.98	C.J.Parker	(Stamford)	12.11.01
			N6748J				
G-ZLYN	Moravan Zlin Z.526F Trener Master		OK-CMC	4. 8.95	Air V8 Ltd	North Weald	17. 8.98
		1255	YR-ZAB				
G-ZONK	Robinson R-44 Astro	0179	G-EDIE	16. 7.97	Zonk Aviation Ltd	Booker	25. 6.01T
G-ZOOI	Lindstrand LBL-105A HAFB	390		22. 5.96	Flying Pictures Ltd	Fairoaks	
G-ZOOL	Reims Cessna FA152 Aerobat	0357	G-BGXZ	11.11.94	A.S.Bamrah	Blackbushe	17. 2.01T
					t/a Falcon F/Svs (Op European Flyers)		
G-ZORO	Europa Avn Europa	PFA/247-12672		20. 6.95	N.T.Read	(Gillingham, Kent)	
G-ZSFT	PA-23-250 Aztec F	27-7954063	G-SALT	5. 4.89	SFT Europe Ltd	Bournemouth	8. 3.01T
			G-BGTH/N2551M				
G-ZTED	Europa Avn Europa	PFA/247-12492		30. 4.96	J.J.Kennedy & E.W.Gladstone	(Edinburgh)	
G-ZULU	PA-28-161 Warrior II	28-8316043	N4292X	25. 2.88	R.W.Tebby	Bristol/Lulsgate	19. 6.00T
					t/a S.F.Tebby & Son (Op Bristol Flying Centre)		
G-ZUMY	Task Silhouette	25		30.12.93	P.M.Wells	(Aylesbury)	
G-ZVBF	Cameron A-400 HAFB	4280		21. 1.98	Virgin Balloon Flights Ltd	London SE16	28. 1.99T
G-ZZIP	Mooney M.20J (205)	24-3167	N1086N	14. 6.91	D.A.H.Dixon	Bournemouth	27. 6.01
G-ZZZA	Boeing 777-236	27105	N77779	20. 5.96	British Airways plc	Heathrow	19. 5.99T
					"Sir Frank Whittle"		
G-ZZZB	Boeing 777-236	27106	N77771	28. 3.97	British Airways plc	Heathrow	27. 3.00T
					"Sir William Branker"		
G-ZZZC	Boeing 777-236	27107	N5014K	11.11.95	British Airways plc	Heathrow	10.11.01T
					(Rendezvous t/s)		
G-ZZZD	Boeing 777-236	27108		28.12.95	British Airways plc	Heathrow	27.12.01T
					"Wilbur Wright/Orville Wright"		
G-ZZZE	Boeing 777-236	27109		12. 1.96	British Airways plc	Heathrow	11. 1.02T
					"Sir Arthur Whitten Brown/Sir John Alcock"		

SECTION 2 - IRELAND REGISTER

The Register is compiled by Paul Cunniffe from the official records of the Irish Aviation Authority, Dublin and is current to 12.3.99. Paul is the Editor/Publisher of "Irish Air Letter" and we extend our thanks for his contribution. No official C of A data is available but Paul has annotated which aircraft have been seen active (A) or extant (E) during 1998 and this is recorded below. Details relating to other preserved or non-currently registered Irish civil aircraft are shown and are marked with an asterisk. Thanks to Wal Gandy for additional information in this area.

Regn	Type	C/n	P/I	Date	Owner/operator	Probable Base	Remarks
EI-AUY*	Morane MS.502 Criquet	338	F-BCDG Fr Mil	30.10.70	Not known (As "CF+HF" 1.99)	Duxford	E1.99
EI-ABI(2)	DH.84 Dragon 2	6105	EI-AFK G-AECZ/AV982/G-AECZ	12. 8.85	Aer Lingus plc "Iolar"	Dublin	A10.98
EI-ADV	PA-12 Super Cruiser (Lyc O-235)	12-3459	NC4031H	11. 5.48	R.E.Levis	Weston	
EI-AFE	Piper J3C-90 Cub	16687	OO-COR D-ELAB/N9954F/EI-AFE/NC79076	11. 3.49	J.Conlon (On rebuild 4.96)	Kildare	
EI-AFF	BA L.25C Swallow II (Pobjoy Cataract II)	406	G-ADMF	18. 5.49	J.Molloy, J.J.Sullivan & B.Donoghue (Damaged Coonagh 24.10.61; on rebuild 4.96)	Ashbourne	
EI-AGD	Taylorcraft Plus D	108	G-AFUB HL534/G-AFUB	26. 5.53	B. & K.O'Sullivan (On rebuild 4.96)	Abbeyshrule	
EI-AGJ	Auster 5 J/1 Autocrat	2208	G-AIPZ	3.11.53	T.G.Rafter Ballyboughal, Co.Dublin (On rebuild 6.96)		
EI-AHI	DH.82A Tiger Moth	85347	G-APRA DE313	17. 9.93	High Fidelity Flyers Harriston Nurney, Monasterevin		
EI-AKM	Piper J3C-65 Cub	15810	N88194 NC88194	17.11.58	Setanta F/Grp (Stored)	Kilmoon	
EI-ALH	Taylorcraft Plus D	106	G-AHLJ HH987/G-AFTZ	5. 5.60	N.Reilly	Ballyjamesduff	
EI-ALP	Avro 643 Cadet (Genet Major)	848	G-ADIE	12. 9.60	J.C.O'Loughlin (Engine seizure 12.6.77; awaiting spares & stored 12.98)	Weston	
EI-ALU*	Avro 631 Cadet	657	G-ACIH	14. 3.61	Not known Newcastle, Dublin (Stored 4.96)		
EI-AMF*	Taylorcraft Plus D	157	G-ARRK G-AHUM/LB286	26. 4.62	G.Lynch (On rebuild 5.96)	Abbeyshrule	
EI-AMK	Auster 5 J/1 Autocrat	1838	G-AGTV	19. 9.62	Irish Aero Club Newcastle,nr Dublin (Wfu after engine failure 5.79; sold 4.95; stored 4.96)		
EI-AMY	Auster J/1N Alpha	2634	G-AJUW	9. 4.63	T.Lennon Maynooth, Co.Kildare (For rebuild 4.92)		
EI-ANA*	Taylorcraft Plus D	206	G-AHCG LB347	29. 8.63	N.Reilly Ballyjamesduff, Co.Cavan (Stored 4.92)		
EI-AND	Cessna 175A	56444	G-APYA N6944E	29. 8.63	M. & A.Cooke (Crashed in Irish Sea nr Formby Point, Lancs 30.10.94)		
EI-ANN*	DH.82A Tiger Moth	83161	G-ANEE T5418	6.10.64	Not known Abbeyshrule (Damaged Culmullen 18.10.64; stored 5.96)		
EI-ANT	Champion 7ECA Citabria	7ECA-38		13. 1.65	Talbury Ltd "The Colonel"	Trim	A8.98
EI-ANY	PA-18-95 Super Cub	18-7152	G-AREU N3096Z	18.11.64	The Bogavia Grp	Weston	A8.98
EI-AOB	PA-28-140 Cherokee	28-20667		28. 4.65	J.Surdival, L.Moran, J.Kilcoyne Knock & J.Cowell		A8.98
EI-AOK	Reims Cessna F.172G	0208		14. 3.66	D.Bruton	Abbeyshrule	E8.98
EI-AOP*	DH.82A Tiger Moth	84320	G-AIBN T7967	24. 9.65	Not known (Stored 5.96)	Abbeyshrule	
EI-AOS	Cessna 310B	35578	G-ARIG EI-AOS/G-ARIG/N5378A	1.11.65	Joyce Avn Ltd (Wfu and to scrapyard)	Kildimo	
EI-APF	Reims Cessna F.150G	0112		6. 3.66	Sligo Aero Club Ltd	Strandhill	A8.98
EI-APS	Schleicher ASK 14 (See EI-114 - SECTION 5)	14008	G-AWVV D-KOBB	24.11.69	SLG Group	Gowran Grange	
EI-ARH	Slingsby T.56 SE5 Replica (Lyc O-235)	1590	G-AVOT	22. 6.67	L.Garrison (Reported at Flabob, California 5.86)		
EI-ARM	Slingsby T.56 SE5 Replica (Lyc O-235) (Regd with c/n 1595, ex G-AVOY)	1594	G-AVOX	22. 6.67	L.Garrison (Powerscourt) (Probably sold in USA)		
EI-ARW	SAN Jodel DR.1050 Ambassadeur	118	F-BJJH	14. 8.67	P.Walsh & P.Ryan Abbeyshrule (Damaged nr Carnmore 28.7.86; stored 4.96)		
EI-ASR	McCandless M.4 Gyroplane (VW)	M.4/5	G-AXHZ	29. 9.69	G.J.J.Fasenfeld Sion Mills, Strabane (Sold to R.McGregor; stored 4.96)		
EI-AST	Reims Cessna F.150H	0273		30. 1.68	P.McKenna	Galway	E8.98
EI-ASU*	Beagle A.61 Terrier 2	B.633	G-ASRG WE599	10. 1.68	Not known (On rebuild 4.96)	Trim	
EI-ATJ	Beagle B.121 Pup 2	B121-029	G-35-029	10. 2.69	L.O'Leary	Waterford	E8.98
EI-ATK	PA-28-140 Cherokee	28-24120	G-AVUP	18.10.68	Mayo F/Club (Damaged Connaught 14.2.87; stored - spares use 4.96)	Abbeyshrule	
EI-ATL	Aeronca 7AC Champion	7AC-4674	N1119E	22. 9.69	Kildare F/Club (Damaged Weston 26.11.75; status uncertain)	Abbeyshrule	

Regn	Type	C/n	P/I	Date	Owner/operator	Probable Base	Remarks
EI-ATP*	Phoenix Luton LA-4A Minor	PAL/1124	G-ASCY	29. 8.69	Not known Miami International		
					(Displayed in Concourse E 10.94)		
EI-ATS	Socata MS.880B Rallye Club	1582		20. 4.70	ATS Group (Stored 4.96)	Abbeyshrule	
EI-AUC	Reims Cessna FA150K Aerobat	0040		10. 4.70	Garda Aviation Club Ltd	Weston	A5.98
EI-AUE	Socata MS.880B Rallye Club	1359	G-AXHU	1. 4.70	Kilkenny F/Club Ltd	Kilkenny	A9.98
EI-AUG	Socata MS.894A Rallye Minerva 220	11080		17. 6.70	K.O'Leary	Rathcoole	
EI-AUJ	Socata MS.880B Rallye Club	1370	G-AXHF	12. 6.70	Ormond F/C Ltd	Abbeyshrule	E8.98
			F-BNGV		(Stored 3.98)		
EI-AUM	Auster 5 J/1 Autocrat	2612	G-AJRN	11. 9.70	T.G.Rafter Ballyboughal, Co.Dublin		
					(On rebuild 6.96)		
EI-AUO	Reims Cessna FA.150K Aerobat	0074		2. 3.70	Kerry Aero Club Ltd	Farranfore	A7.98
EI-AUP*	Socata MS.880B Rallye Club	1143	G-AVVK	30. 9.70	Not known		
					(Damaged Coonagh 1.9.83; stored - spares use 4.96)		
EI-AUS	Auster J/5F Aiglet Trainer	2779	G-AMRL	17.11.70	T.Stevens & T.Lennon	Powerscourt	
					(On rebuild 4.95)		
EI-AUT	Forney F-1A Aircoupe	5731	G-ARXS	21.12.70	Joyce Avn Ltd Bann Foot, Lough Neagh, NI		
			D-EBSA/N3037G		(To N.Glass & A.Richardson) (Stored 4.96)		
EI-AUY	Morane-Saulnier MS.502	338	F-BCDG	30.11.70	Historic Acft Preservation Group Duxford		
	(Argus AS.10)		Fr.Mil (to Imperial War Museum as "CF+HF"; in Luftwaffe c/s)					
EI-AVB	Aeronca 7AC Champion	7AC-1790	7P-AXK	14. 6.71	T.Brett	Galway	
	(Cont A65)		ZS-AXK		(Reserved as N151JC 11.97)		
EI-AVC	Reims Cessna F.337F Super Skymaster	N4757	26. 8.71	Christy Keane (Saggart) Ltd	Abbeyshrule	E8.98
	(Wichita c/n 01355)	0032					
EI-AVM	Reims Cessna F.150L	0745		3. 3.72	J.Cowell	Castlebar	
EI-AWD	PA-22-160 Tri-Pacer	22-6411	G-APXV	17. 1.73	J.P.Montcalm Carrigtwohil, Co.Cork		
			N9437D		(Blown over in gales Cork 12.81; stored 1989)		
EI-AWE	Reims Cessna F.150L	0877		22. 2.73	Third Flight Group	Abbeyshrule	E8.98
					(Stored 3.98)		
EI-AWH	Cessna 210J Centurion	210-59067	G-AZCC	19. 1.73	Rathcoole F/C Ltd	Rathcoole	
			(EI-AWH)/G-AZCC/5N-AIE/N1734C/(N6167F)				
EI-AWP	DH.82A Tiger Moth	85931	F-BGCL	4. 7.72	Anne.P.Bruton	Abbeyshrule	
	(Regd with c/n 19577)		Fr.AF/DF195				
EI-AWR	Malmo MFI-9 Junior	010	LN-HAG	12. 6.73	M.Bevan & P.Byrne	Powerscourt	
			(SE-EBW)				
EI-AWU	Socata MS.880B Rallye Club	880	G-AVIM	12. 1.74	Longford Avn Ltd	Abbeyshrule	
					(Status uncertain)		E8.98
EI-AYA	Socata MS.880B Rallye Club	2256	G-BAON	27. 7.73	Limerick F/C (Coonagh) Ltd	Coonagh	
EI-AYB	Gardan GY-80-180 Horizon	156	F-BNQP	5.10.73	J.B.Smith	Abbeyshrule	
EI-AYD	Grumman-American AA-5 Traveler	0380	G-BAZE	9. 7.73	P.Howick, H.Martini & V.O'Rourke		
			N5480L			Powerscourt	
EI-AYF	Reims Cessna FRA.150L Aerobat	0218		26. 3.74	K.A.O'Connor	Weston	A8.98
EI-AYI	Morane MS.880B Rallye Club	189	F-OBXE	21.11.73	J.McNamara	Trim	
EI-AYK	Reims Cessna F.172M Skyhawk II	1092		25. 3.74	D.Gallagher	Trim	
EI-AYL	Beagle A.109 Airedale	B.507	G-ARRO	12. 3.74	J.Ronan	Abbeyshrule	
			(EI-AVP)/G-ARRO		(Stored for rebuild 4.96)		
EI-AYN	IRMA BN-2A-8 Islander	704	G-BBFJ	26. 3.74	Galway Avn Svs Ltd	Connemara	
					(Op Aer Arann) "Inis-Mor"		
EI-AYO*	Douglas DC-3A-197	1911	N655GP	5. 3.76	The Science Museum	Wroughton	
			N65556/N255JB/N8695E/N333H/NC16071				
EI-AYR	Schleicher ASK 16	16022		5. 4.74	Kilkenny Airport Ltd		
	(See EI-119 - SECTION 3)					Boleybeg, Ballymore Eustace	A8.98
EI-AYS	PA-22-108 Colt	22-8448	G-ARKT	28. 6.74	M.F.Skelly (Stored 3.98)	Abbeyshrule	
EI-AYT	Socata MS.894A Rallye Minerva 220	11065	G-AXIU	6. 8.74	K.A.O'Connor	Abbeyshrule	
					(Damaged en route Weston/Coonagh 12.11.89; stored 4.96)		
EI-AYV	SEEMS MS.892A Rallye Commodore 150	10482	F-BLSP	27. 8.74	P.Murtagh	Strandhill	
EI-AYY	Evans VP-1 MD-01 & SAAC-03			18. 8.75	M.Donohue	Newcastle, Co.Wicklow	A10.98
	(VW1500)						
EI-BAF*	Thunder Ax6-56 HAFB	027	G-BCFU	31. 7.74	W.G.Woollett "Dew"	Newbury	
		(CA expired 31.7.86: to British Balloon Museum 3.95: cancelled 3.9.98)					
EI-BAG*	Cessna 172A	172-47571	G-ARAV	7. 8.74	Not known Portadown, Belfast		
			N9771T		(On rebuild 4.96)		
EI-BAJ	SNCAN Stampe SV-4C	171	F-BBPN	17.10.74	Dublin Tiger Group	Trim	E8.98
EI-BAL*	Beagle A.109 Airedale	B.515	G-ARZS	17.10.74	S.Bruton (Stored 4.96)	Abbeyshrule	
EI-BAO	Reims Cessna F.172G	0278	G-ATNH	11. 2.75	D.Bruton	Abbeyshrule	A8.98
EI-BAR	Thunder Ax8-105 HAFB	014	G-BCAM	26. 2.75	J.Burke & V.Hourihane		
					"Rockwell" Cahir, Co.Tipperary		
EI-BAS	Reims Cessna F.172M Skyhawk II	1262		2. 5.75	Falcon Avn Ltd	Waterford	A8.98
EI-BAT	Reims Cessna F.150M	1196		2. 5.75	K.A.O'Connor	Weston	E5.98
EI-BAV	PA-22-108 Colt	22-8347	G-ARKO	30. 4.75	J.Davy (Stored 4.96)	Thurles	A8.98
EI-BAY*	Cameron O-84 HAFB	16	G-AYJZ	28. 5.75	British Balloon Museum & Library Newbury		
	(Original canopy replaced by c/n 433)				"Godolphin"		
EI-BBC	PA-28-180 Cherokee B	28-1049	G-ASEJ	18. 6.75	Piper Aero Club Ltd	Strandhill	A8.98
EI-BBD	Evans VP-1 VP-1-No.2 & SAAC-02			13. 8.76	The Volksplane Group	Celbridge	
	(VW1600)				(On rebuild 8.81)		

Regn	Type	C/n	P/I	Date	Owner/operator	Probable Base	Remarks
EI-BBE	Champion 7FC Tri-Traveler	7FC-393	G-APZW	7. 9.75	P.Forde & D.Connaire	Newtown Abbey	
	(Tail wheel conversion to 7EC Traveler status)						
EI-BBG	Socata Rallye 100ST	2592		27.10.75	Weston Ltd	Weston	
					(Stored 5.98 with c/n only)		
EI-BBI	Socata Rallye 150ST	2663		13.10.75	Kilkenny Airport Ltd	Kilkenny	A11.98
EI-BBJ	Socata MS.880B Rallye 100S	2361	F-BUVX	7.11.75	Weston Ltd	Weston	A5.98
EI-BBK	Beagle A.109 Airedale	B.509	G-ARXB	18.11.75	H.F.Igoe	Abbeyshrule	
			(EI-ATE)/G-ARXB		(Stored for rebuild 4.96)		
EI-BBM	Cameron O-65 HAFB	195		14. 1.76	The Dublin Ballooning Club Ltd	Dublin	
	(Now uses original canopy from EI-BGT)				"Scath-Na-Greine"		
EI-BBN*	Reims Cessna F.150M	1281		27. 2.76	Sligo North West A/C Ltd		
					(Cancelled as destroyed 23.6.98) Strandhill, Sligo		
EI-BBO	Socata MS.893E Rallye 180GT	12522	F-BVNM	8. 3.76	G.P.Moorhead		
					Moorhead Garage, Hacketstown		
EI-BBV	Piper J3C-65 Cub (L-4J-PI)	13058	D-ELWY	14. 6.76	F.Cronin (Stored 5.97)	Weston	
	(Frame No.12888)		F-BEGB/44-80762				
EI-BCE	BN-2A-26 Islander	519	G-BDUV	14. 9.76	Galway Avn Svs Ltd	Connemara	A4.98
					(Op Aer Arann) "Inis-Meain"		
EI-BCF	Bensen B-8M Gyrocopter	47491	N....	24. 8.76	P.Flanagan	Kilrush,Co. Clare	
	(McC.O-100) (C/n quoted as 47941)						
EI-BCH	GEMS MS.892A Rallye Commodore 150	10561	G-ATIW	17. 9.76	B Foley	Waterford	A8.98
EI-BCJ	Aeromere F.8L Falco 3	204	G-ATAK	19. 1.77	D.Kelly (On rebuild 6.97)	Abbeyshrule	
			D-ENYB				
EI-BCK	Reims Cessna F.172N Skyhawk II	1543		22.11.76	H.Caulfield	Weston	A5.98
EI-BCL	Cessna 182P Skylane II	182-64300	N1366M	22.11.76	L.Burke	Newcastle, Dublin	
	(Reims assembled with c/n 0045)						
EI-BCM	Piper J3C-65 Cub (L-4H-PI)	11983	F-BNAV	26.11.76	Kilmoon F/Grp	Trim	
			N9857F/44-79687				
EI-BCN	Piper J3C-65 Cub (L-4H-PI)	12335	F-BFQE	26.11.76	Snowflake F/Grp	Trim	
			OO-PIE/44-80039				
EI-BCO	Piper J3C-65 Cub	"1"	F-BBIV	26.11.76	J.Molloy	Kilmoon	
					(Not yet converted and stored)		
EI-BCP	Rollason Druine D.62B Condor	RAE/618	G-AVCZ	27. 1.77	A.Delaney	Dolla	
EI-BCS	Socata MS.880B Rallye 100T	2550	F-BVZV	4. 2.77	Organic Fruit & Vegetables of Ireland Ltd		A8.98
						Waterford	
EI-BCU	Socata MS.880B Rallye 100T	2595	F-BXTH	10. 2.77	Weston Ltd (Dismantled 12.98)	Weston	
EI-BCW	Socata MS.880B Rallye Club	1783	G-AYKE	18. 4.77	Kilkenny F/C (Stored 6.97)	Abbeyshrule	
EI-BDH	Socata MS.880B Rallye Club	1270	G-AWOB	18. 7.77	Munster Wings Ltd	Abbeyshrule	
					(Status uncertain - probably scrapped)		
EI-BDK	Socata MS.880B Rallye 100T	2561	F-BXMZ	10. 8.77	Limerick F/C (Coonagh) Ltd	Coonagh	E8.98
EI-BDL	Evans VP-2 V2-2101 & PFA/7213 & SAAC-04			7. 9.77	P.Buggle	Kilrush	
	(VW)						
EI-BDM	PA-23-250 Aztec D	27-4166	G-AXIV	10.10.77	G.A.Costello	Waterford	
			N6826Y		t/a Executive Air Svs		
					(To SE Avn Enthusiasts' Museum; stored 4.96)		
EI-BDP*	Cessna 182P Skylane	182-60867	G-AZLC	14.11.77	O.Bruton	Abbeyshrule	
			N9327G (Damaged 1988 & airframe stored: cancelled 27.11.98 as WFU)				
EI-BDR	PA-28-180 Cherokee C	28-3980	G-BAAO	8.12.77	Cherokee Grp	Farranfore	E11.98
			LN-AEL/(SE-FAG)				
EI-BEA	Socata Rallye 100ST	3007		28. 2.78	Weston Ltd (Stored 12.98)	Weston	
EI-BEN	Piper J3C-65 Cub (L-4J-PI)	12546	G-BCUC	28. 4.78	J.J.O'Sullivan	Weston	A8.98
	(Frame No.12376)		F-BFMN/44-80250				
EI-BEO	Cessna 310Q II	310Q-0233	D-ICEG	13. 4.78	C.Keane	Carrickfin	
			N7733Q		(Stored 1995; status uncertain 1997)		
EI-BEP	Socata MS.892A Rallye Commodore 150	11947	F-BTJT	14. 4.78	H.Lynch & J.O'Leary	Abbeyshrule	
					(Stored 4.96)		
EI-BFB*	Socata Rallye 100ST	3044		12. 6.78	Weston Ltd	Weston	
					(Crashed nr Weston 18.10.87; wreck stored 2.95)		
EI-BFE	Reims Cessna F.150G	0158	G-AVGM	3. 8.78	Joyce Avn Ltd	Waterford	E8.98
					(Stored dismantled 1.99)		
EI-BFF	Beechcraft A23-24 Musketeer Super III	MA-352	G-AXCJ	20. 8.78	P.Furlong	Waterford	A8.98
EI-BFI	Socata Rallye 100ST	2618	F-BXDK	10. 8.78	J.O'Neill	Abbeyshrule	
					(Crashed 14.12.85; stored 4.96)		
EI-BFM	Socata MS.893E Rallye 180GT	12958	F-GARN	12.10.78	Limerick Flying Group (Coonagh) Ltd	Coonagh	
EI-BFO	Piper J3C-90 Cub (L-4J-PI)	12701	F-BFQJ	11. 9.78	D.Gordon	Weston	
	(Frame No.12531 - regd as c/n 8911)		N79856/NC79856/44-80405				
EI-BFP	Socata Rallye 100ST	2942	F-GARR	6.10.78	Weston Ltd	Weston	A5.98
EI-BFR	Socata Rallye 100ST	2429	F-OCVK	9.11.78	J.Power	Waterford	A8.98
EI-BFV	Socata MS.880B Rallye 100T	2415	F-BVAH	2. 2.79	Ormond Flying Club Ltd (Stored 8.93)		
EI-BGA	Socata Rallye 100ST	2549	G-BCXC	23.11.78	J.J.Frew	Mullaghmore, NI	
			F-OCZQ				
EI-BGB	Socata MS.880B Rallye Club	1913	G-AZKB	22. 1.79	Limerick F/C (Coonagh) Ltd	Abbeyshrule	
					(Stored 3.98)		
EI-BGC	Socata MS.880B Rallye Club	1265	F-BRDC	22.12.78	P.Moran	Roscommon	
EI-BGD	Socata MS.880B Rallye Club	2287	F-BUJI	18.12.78	N.Kavanagh (Stored 3.98)	Abbeyshrule	
			(D-EKHD)				

Regn	Type	C/n	P/I	Date	Owner/operator	Probable Base	Remarks
EI-BGF	PA-28R-180 Cherokee Arrow	28R-30121	SE-FAS	30. 1.79	Arrow Group	??	
	(Crashed into Mynydd Prescelly nr Haverfordwest, Dyfed 6.10.83)						
EI-BGG	Socata MS.892E Rallye 150GT	12824	F-GAFS	30. 1.79	O.Bruton	Abbeyshrule	E8.98
EI-BGJ	Reims Cessna F.152 II	1664		14. 5.79	Sligo Aero Club Ltd	Strandhill	A6.98
EI-BGS	Socata MS.893E Rallye 180GT	12675	F-BXTY	25. 4.79	M.Farrelly	Abbeyshrule	
	(Damaged Claive, Co.Kildare 3.91; wreck stored 4.96)						
EI-BGT	Colt 77A HAFB	041		14. 5.79	K.Haugh "Ryan Air"	Dublin	
	(Has new envelope c/n 1092 - original to EI-BBM)						
EI-BGU	Socata MS.880B Rallye Club	875	F-BONM	9. 5.79	M.F.Neary (Wreck stored 6.95)		
						Abbeyshrule	
EI-BHB	Socata MS.887 Rallye 125	2162	F-BUCH	7. 6.79	Hotel Bravo F/C Ltd (Stored 4.96)		
						Abbeyshrule	
EI-BHC	Reims Cessna F.177RG Cardinal	0010	G-AYTG	11. 7.79	B.J.Palfrey & ptnrs	Dublin	A3.98
	(Wichita c/n 00117)						
EI-BHF	Socata MS.892A Rallye Commodore 150	10742	F-BPBP	10. 7.79	B.Mullen	Strandhill	
EI-BHI	Bell 206B JetRanger II	906	G-BAKX	14. 8.79	J.Mansfield	Rathcoole	
EI-BHK	Socata MS.880B Rallye Club	1307	F-BRJE	20. 8.79	D.Bruton	Gowran Grange	
					(Op Dublin Gliding Club)		
EI-BHL	Beechcraft E90 King Air	LW-321	N60253	7. 9.79	Stewart Singlam Fabrics Ltd	Roborough	A8.98
EI-BHM	Reims Cessna F.337E Super Skymaster	0004	OO-PDC OO-PDG	1.11.79	City of Dublin VEC	Bolton St, Dublin	
	(Wichita c/n 01217)				(Dublin College of Technology)		
					(Instructional airframe 5.92)		
EI-BHN	Socata MS.893A Rallye Commodore 180	11422	F-BRRO	11.10.79	T.Garvan (On overhaul 6.96)	Hacketstown	
EI-BHP	Socata MS.893A Rallye Commodore 180	11459	F-BSAA	12.10.79	Spanish Point F/C		
						Spanish Point, Co.Clare	
EI-BHT	Beechcraft 77 Skipper	WA-77		17.10.79	Waterford A/C Ltd	Waterford	A8.98
EI-BHV	Champion 7EC Traveler	7EC-739	G-AVDU N9837Y	30.10.79	M.McDowell	Dolla	
					(To Condor Grp) (On rebuild 5.92)		
EI-BHW	Reims Cessna F.150F	0013	G-ATMK	22.11.79	R.Sharpe	Weston	
	(Wichita c/n 62671)						
EI-BHY	Socata Rallye 150ST	2929	F-GARL	19.11.79	Liberty Flying Group	Cork	A8.98
EI-BIB	Reims Cessna F.152 II	1724		30.11.79	Galway F/C Ltd	Galway	A1.98
EI-BIC	Reims Cessna F.172N Skyhawk II	1965	(OO-HNZ)	15. 2.80	Oriel F/Grp Ltd	Abbeyshrule	
					(Damaged on landing Castlebar 13.4.95: stored 3.98)		
EI-BID	PA-18-95 Super Cub (L-18C-PI)	18-1524	D-EAES ALAT1-15524	30.11.79	S.Coghlan & P.Ryan	Galway	A8.98
	(Possibly c/n 18-1571 ex 51-15571)						
EI-BIG	Moravan Zlin 526 Trener Master	1086	D-EBUP OO-BUT	7.12.79	P.von Lonkhuyzen	Rushett Farm, Chessington	
					(Damaged on landing 9.91; stored 10.97)		
EI-BIJ	Agusta-Bell 206B JetRanger II	8432	G-BCVZ	29. 1.80	Medavia Properties Ltd	Dublin Heliport	A10.98
					(Op by Celtic Helicopters Ltd)		
EI-BIK	PA-18-180 Super Cub	18-7909088	N82276	1. 2.80	Dublin Gliding Club Ltd	Gowran Grange	
EI-BIM	Morane MS.880B Rallye Club	305	F-BKYJ	28. 3.80	D.Millar (Stored 6.97)	Abbeyshrule	
EI-BIO	Piper J3C-65 Cub (L-4J-PI)	12657	F-BGXP OO-GAE/44-80361	27. 5.80	Monasterevin F/Grp	Harristown Nurney, Monasterevin	
EI-BIR	Reims Cessna F.172M Skyhawk II	1225	F-BVXI	24. 3.80	B.Harrison, K.Brereton, P.Rogers & F.Maher	Clonbullogue	A8.98
EI-BIS	Robin R.1180TD Aiglon	268		14. 5.80	The Robin Aiglon Group	Abbeyshrule	A8.98
EI-BIT	Socata MS.887 Rallye 125	2169	F-BULQ	18. 3.80	Spanish Point F/C		
						Spanish Point, Co.Clare	
EI-BIU	Robin R.2112A Alpha	175		14. 5.80	Wicklow F/Grp	Weston	E8.98
EI-BIV	Bellanca 8KCAB Super Decathlon	464-79	N5032Q	3. 6.80	Aerocrats F/Grp Ltd	Weston	A8.98
EI-BIW	Socata MS.880B Rallye Club	1144	F-BPGB	19. 5.80	E.J.Barr	Buncrana, Co.Donegal	
EI-BJB	Aeronca 7DC Champion	7AC-925	G-BKKM	16. 4.80	L.Maddock		
	(Cont C85)		EI-BJB/N82296/NC82296 Killamaster, Castledermot, Co.Kildare					
EI-BJC	Aeronca 7AC Champion	7AC-4927	N1366E NC1366E	2. 4.80	E.Griffin	Blackwater, Co.Limerick	
EI-BJI	Reims Cessna FR.172E Rocket	0040	G-BAAS	23. 5.80	Irish Parachute Club Ltd	Dublin	
			SE-FBW/OY-DKN (Crashed Edenderry 9.82; probably scrapped pre 1990)					
EI-BJJ	Aeronca 15AC Sedan	15AC-226	(G-BHXP) EI-BJJ/N1214H	6. 6.80	O.Bruton (Stored 3.98)	Abbeyshrule	
EI-BJK	Socata Rallye 110ST	3226	F-GBKY	8. 7.80	Jordan Larkin F/Grp	Weston	A5.98
EI-BJM	Cessna A152 Aerobat	A152-0936	N761CC	18. 9.80	Leinster A/C Ltd	Dublin	A9.98
EI-BJO	Cessna R172K Hawk XP II	R172-3340	N758TD	6. 8.80	P.Hogan & G.Ryder	Galway	
EI-BJS	Gulfstream AA-5B Tiger	AA5B-0979	G-BFZR	3. 9.80	P.Morrissey	Newcastle, Dublin	A9.98
EI-BJT	PA-38-112 Tomahawk	38-78A0818	N9650N N9650N	16.10.80	S.Corrigan & W.Lennon	Abbeyshrule	
EI-BJW*	DH.104 Dove 6	04485	G-ASNG	7.11.80	Waterford Airport Fire Service	Waterford	
			HB-LFF/G-ASNG/HB-LFF/G-ASNG/PH-IOM (As "G-ASNG")					
EI-BKC	Aeronca 15AC Sedan	15AC-467	N1394H	5.11.80	J.Lynch	Birr	
EI-BKE*	Morane MS.885 Super Rallye	278	F-BKUN	9. 2.81	Not known	Abbeyshrule	
			F-WKUN (Crashed Ballyclumack, Wexford 5.4.81; wreck stored 4.96)					

Regn	Type	C/n	P/I	Date	Owner/operator	Probable Base	Remarks
EI-BKF	Reims Cessna F.172H	0476	G-AVUX	4.12.80	E.McEllin	Castlebar	
EI-BKK	Taylor JT.1 Monoplane (VW1500)	PFA/1421	G-AYYC	2. 2.81	Waterford A/C (Stored dismantled 1.99)	Waterford	E8.98
EI-BKN	Socata Rallye 100ST	3035	F-GBCK	18. 2.81	Weston Ltd	Weston	A5.98
EI-BKS	Eipper Quicksilver (Yamaha KT100SD)	IMA-001		15. 4.81	Irish Microlight Acft Ltd	Shannon	
EI-BKT	Agusta-Bell 206B JetRanger III	8562	D-HAFD HB-XIC	6. 4.81	Irish Helicopters Ltd	Dublin	A11.98
EI-BKU	Socata MS.892A Rallye Commodore 150	10990	F-BRLG	21. 5.81	Limerick F/C (Coonagh) Ltd (Stored 3.98)	Abbeyshrule	
EI-BLB	SNCAN Stampe SV-4C	323	F-BCTE	27. 7.81	J.E.Hutchinson & R.A.Stafford (Crashed Drumsna, Carrick-on-Shannon 1.6.97)	Abbeyshrule	
EI-BLD	MBB Bo.105DB	S.381	D-HDLQ	21. 7.81	Irish Helicopters Ltd	Dublin	
EI-BLE	Eipper Quicksilver (Yamaha KT100SP)	IMA-003		20. 8.81	R.P.St.George-Smith	Kilkenny	
EI-BLN	Eipper Quicksilver MX (Cuyana 340)	MX.01		26. 8.81	O.J.Conway & B.Daffy	Ennis, Co.Clare	
EI-BLU	Evans VP-1 (VW)	SAAC-05		13.10.81	S.Pallister	Kilkenny	
EI-BLW*	PA-23-250 Aztec C	27-3173	G-BBAV PH-KNV/LN-NPD/SE-EPW	16.11.81	Not known (Stored on Industrial Estate 8.97)	Shannon	
EI-BMA	Socata MS.880B Rallye Club	1965	F-BTJR	26. 1.82	W.Rankin & M.Kelleher	Abbeyshrule	
EI-BMB	Socata MS.880B Rallye 100T	2505	F-BJCO F-BVLB	5. 1.82	Glyde Court Developments Ltd	Weston	A5.98
EI-BMF	Laverda F.8L Super Falco Srs.IV	416	G-AWSU	28. 1.82	M.Slazenger & H.McCann	Powerscourt	
EI-BMH	Socata MS.880B Rallye Club	1277	(G-BIDS) F-BSTJ	19. 2.82	N.S.Bracken	Donegal	
EI-BMI	Socata TB-9 Tampico	203	F-GCOV	12. 5.82	Ashford F/Grp	Weston	
EI-BMJ	Socata MS.880B Rallye 100T	2594	F-BXTG	10. 3.82	Weston Ltd	Weston	E5.98
EI-BMM	Reims Cessna F.152 II	1899		10. 3.82	P.Redmond	Weston	
EI-BMN	Reims Cessna F.152 II	1912		10. 3.82	BMN Group	Abbeyshrule	E8.98
EI-BMU	Monnett Sonerai IIL (VW2100)	01224		19. 5.82	A.Fenton	Ballyshannon, Donegal	
EI-BMV	American Avn AA-5 Traveler	AA5-0200	G-BAEJ	28. 7.82	E.Tierney & K.A.Harold (Damaged Brittas Bay 3.93; stored 6.97)	Abbeyshrule	
EI-BMW	Maddock Skytrike/Hiway Vulcan LM-100 (Fuji-Robin)			1. 6.82	L.Maddock	Carlow	
EI-BNA	McDonnell-Douglas DC-8-63CF	45989	LX-ACV (CX-BOU/TF-ACV/LX-ACV/N779FT	15. 4.83	Aer Turas Teoranta "City of Dublin" (Op by Saudia)	Dublin	
EI-BNF	Eurowing Goldwing (Fuji Robin)	-		22. 9.82	A.Morelli	Malahide	
EI-BNH	Hiway Skytrike (EC-25-PS)	AS.09		18.10.82	M.Martin	Tullamore	
EI-BNJ	Evans VP-2 (VW2000)	-		24. 1.83	G.A.Cashman	Weston	
EI-BNK	Cessna U206F Stationair	U206-01706	G-HILL PH-ADN/D-EEXY/N9506G	23.12.82	Irish Parachute Club Ltd	Clonbulloge	A10.98
EI-BNL	Rand Robinson KR-2 (VW2000)	-		13. 1.83	K.Hayes	Birr	
EI-BNP	Rotorway Exec 145	-		1. 3.83	R.L.Renfroe Letterkenny (Not completed 1989)		
EI-BNR*	American Avn AA-5 Traveler	AA5-0203	N9992Q CS-AHM	12. 4.83	Victor Mike F/Grp Ltd (Crashed 21.2.88; stored 4.96 - spares use)	Abbeyshrule	
EI-BNT	Cvjetkovic CA-65	-		23. 3.83	B.Tobin & P.G.Ryan (Tallaght, Co.Dublin)		
EI-BNU	Socata MS.880B Rallye Club	1204	F-BPQV	7. 4.83	P.A.Doyle	Coonagh	
EI-BOA	Pterodactyl	-		3. 5.83	A.Murphy	Athenry, Co.Galway	
EI-BOE	Socata TB-10 Tobago	301	F-GDBL	12. 9.83	P.Byron, K.Lawford, L.Naye, E.Murtagh, G.Haughey, M.Verling & J.Byron	Weston	A5.98
EI-BOH	Eipper Quicksilver (Yamaha 970cc)	-		8. 9.83	J.Leech	Waterford	
EI-BOP*	Socata MS.892A Rallye Commodore 150	11748	G-BKGS F-BSXS	13. 3.84	Not known (Crashed Coonagh 29.3.86; stored 3/98 - spares use)	Abbeyshrule	
EI-BOR	Bell 222A	47021	LN-OSB	24. 2.84	Westair Avn Ltd (Op for GPA Grp plc)	Shannon	A11.98
EI-BOV	Rand Robinson KR-2 (VW1835)	SAAC-11		7. 5.84	G.O'Hara & G.Callan (Damaged Carnmore 3.91; stored 3.91)	Abbeyshrule	
EI-BOX	Duet (Rotax 503)	-		12.10.84	Dr.K.Riccius (Newcastle, Co.Wicklow)		
EI-BPE	Viking Dragonfly (VW1835)	SAAC-16		15.10.84	G.G.Bracken	Castlebar	
EI-BPJ	Cessna 182A Skylane	34949	G-BAGA N4849D	4.12.84	Falcon Parachute Club Ltd (Damaged pre 7.95; fuselage stored 3.98)	Abbeyshrule	
EI-BPL	Reims Cessna F.172K	0758	G-AYSG	28. 3.85	Phoenix Flying Ltd	Shannon	E8.98
EI-BPN	Flexiform Striker (Fuji Robin)	-		12. 3.85	P.H.Collins	Dunlaoghaire, Co.Dublin	
EI-BPO	Southdown Puma (EC-44-PM) (C/n quoted also as ENo.82-00108)	1923		12. 3.85	A.Channing	Coolock, Co.Dublin	

Regn	Type	C/n	P/I	Date	Owner/operator	Probable Base	Remarks
EI-BPP	Eipper Quicksilver MX (Cuyana 430)	3207		12. 3.85	J.A.Smith (Stored 8.93)	Abbeyshrule	
EI-BPT	Skyhook Sabre (Solo 210)	-		26. 3.85	T.McGrath	Glounthane, Co.Cork	
EI-BPU	Hiway Demon (EC-25-PS)	-		26. 3.85	A.Channing	Coolock, Co.Dublin	
EI-BRH	Mainair Gemini/Flash (EC-44-PM)	316-585-3		15. 5.85	J.Deeney	Carrigaline, Co.Cork	
EI-BRK	Flexiform Trike (Fuji Robin)	LM.102		17. 6.85	L.Maddock	Carlow	
EI-BRS	Cessna P172D	P172-57173	G-WPUI G-AXPI/9M-AMR/N11B/(N8573X)	2. 9.85	D. & M.Hillary	Weston	A5.98
EI-BRT*	Flexwing M17727 (EC-44-PM)	990059		5.11.85	Not known (Stored 8.97)	Millicent Field, Clane	
EI-BRU	Evans VP-1 V-12-84-CQ & SAAC-18 (VW1600)			5.11.85	Home Bru F/Grp	Weston	
EI-BRV	Hiway Skytrike/Demon (EC-25-PS)	-		5.11.85	M.Garvey & C.Tully	Kells	
EI-BRW	Hovey Delta Bird (VW 1300)	-		5.11.85	A & E Aerosport	Curraglass, Co.Cork	
EI-BRX	Reims Cessna FRA.150L Aerobat	0160	G-BACM	9. 1.86	Trim F/C Ltd	Trim	
EI-BSB	Wassmer Jodel D.112	1067	G-AWIG F-BKAA	23. 6.87	J.M.Finnan & M.O'Reilly	Kilrush	
EI-BSC	Reims Cessna F.172N Skyhawk II	1651	G-NIUS	10.12.85	S.Phelan	Weston	E8.98
EI-BSD	Enstrom F-28A	153	G-BBHE	10. 2.86	Clarke Avn Ltd	Waterford	A8.98
EI-BSF*	Avro 748 Srs.1/105	1544	EC-DTP G-BEKD/LV-HHF/LV-PUM	28. 5.86	Ryanair Ltd "Spirit of Tipperary" (Cabin crew trainer 11.95)	Dublin	
EI-BSG	Bensen B-80 Gyrocopter (McC.4318)	-		30. 1.86	J.Todd (Stored 3.90)	Riverstick, Co.Cork	
EI-BSK	Socata TB-9 Tampico	618		9. 4.86	Weston Ltd	Weston	A5.98
EI-BSL	PA-34-220T Seneca III	34-8233041	N8468X	27. 6.86	E.L.Symmons	Weston	A10.98
EI-BSN	Cameron O-65 HAFB	1278		14. 4.86	W.G.Woollett "Erin-Go-Bragh"	Birr	
EI-BSO	PA-28-140 Cherokee B	28-25449	C-GOBL N8241W	16. 4.86	H.M.Hanley	Na Minna	A8.98
EI-BSU	Champion 7KCAB Citabria	124	N1621G	15. 6.87	S. & S.Donohue	Proudstown	
EI-BSV	Socata TB-20 Trinidad	579	G-BMIX	15. 8.86	J.Condron	Abbeyshrule	E8.98
EI-BSW	Solar Wings Pegasus XL-R SW-TB-1124&SW-WA-1122 (Rotax 447)			22. 6.87	E.Fitzgerald	Waterford	
EI-BSX	Piper J3C-65 Cub (Frame No.8999)	8912	G-ICUB F-BEGT/NC79805/45-4515/42-36788	25. 3.86	J. & T.O'Dwyer	Gowran Grange	
	(Official c/n 13255 is incorrect as a/c probably rebuilt c.1945)						
EI-BTX	McDonnell Douglas MD-82	49660	(N59842)	23. 3.88	Air Tara Ltd (Op by Aeromexico)	Mexico City, Mexico	
EI-BTY	McDonnell Douglas MD-82	49667	N12844	6. 5.88	Air Tara Ltd (Op by Aeromexico)	Mexico City, Mexico	
EI-BUA	Cessna 172M Skyhawk II	172-65451	N5458H	8. 8.86	Skyhawks F/C Ltd	Weston	A6.98
EI-BUC	Jodel D.9 Bebe (VW 1500)	PFA/929	G-BASY	20. 1.87	D.Lyons	Thurles	
EI-BUF	Cessna 210N Centurion II	210-63070	G-MCDS G-BHNB/N6496N	18.12.86	210 Group	Abbeyshrule	A9.98
EI-BUG	Socata ST-10 Diplomate	125	G-STIO OH-SAB	4. 2.87	J.Cooke	Weston	A8.98
EI-BUH	Lake LA-4-200 Buccaneer	543	G-PARK G-BBGK/N39779	27. 5.87	T.Henderson	Lough Derg Marina, Killaloe	A8.98
EI-BUJ	Socata MS.892A Rallye Commodore 150	10737	G-FOAM G-AVPL	27. 2.87	T.Cunniffe (Damaged pre 1992; stored 3.98)	Abbeyshrule	
EI-BUL	Whittaker MW.5 Sorcerer (Citroen 602cc)	1		4. 3.87	J.Culleton	Mountmellick, Co.Laois	
EI-BUN	Beechcraft 76 Duchess	ME-371	(EI-BUO) N37001	26. 6.87	L.O'Connor, M.Mellett & K.O'Driscoll	Weston	A8.98
EI-BUO	Aero Composites Sea Hawker (Lyc O-320) (Now regd as Glass S.005E)	80		25. 8.87	C.Donaldson & C.Lavery (Damaged Strangford Lough 9/91; stored 6.97)	Newtownards	
EI-BUR	PA-38-112 Tomahawk	38-79A0363	G-BNDE N2541D	10. 7.87	Westair Avn Ltd	Shannon	A5.98
EI-BUS	PA-38-112 Tomahawk	38-79A0186	G-BNDF N2439C	10. 7.87	Westair Avn Ltd	Shannon	A11.98
EI-BUT	GEMS MS.893A Rallye Commodore 180	10559	SE-IMV	30. 7.87	T.Keating (Galerien c/s)	Weston	A9.98
EI-BUW	Noble-Hardman Snowbird IIIA SB-F001 (Rotax 532)		77-DS (French)	8. 9.87	TIFC & IS Ltd (Damaged Dromiskin, Co.Louth 1.6.92)	Dundalk	
EI-BUX	Agusta A.109A	7147	N790SC (N466MP)/N790SC/N72521	10. 6.88	Orring Ltd	Rathcoole	
EI-BVB	Whittaker MW.6 Merlin (Rotax)	1		14. 9.87	R.England	Mallow	
EI-BVF	Reims Cessna F.172N Skyhawk II	1777	G-BGHJ	30.10.87	First Phantom Grp Ltd	Dublin	A8.98
EI-BVJ(2)	AMF Chevvron 2-32 (Konig SD570)	009		16. 2.88	S.J.Dunne	Bolybeg, Ballymore Eustace	

Regn	Type	C/n	P/I	Date	Owner/operator	Probable Base	Remarks
EI-BVK	PA-38-112 Tomahawk	38-79A0966	OO-FLG OO-HLG/N9705N	2. 3.88	Pegasus F/Grp Ltd	Weston	A5.98
EI-BVT	Evans VP-2 V2-2129/PFA/7221/SAAC-20 (VW 1834)		G-BEIE	29. 4.88	P.Morrison	Cobh, Co.Cork	
EI-BVY	Heintz Zenith CH.200AA-RW (Lyc O-320)	2-582		7. 6.88	J.Matthews, M.Skelly & T.Coleman	Abbeyshrule	A11.98
EI-BWD	McDonnell Douglas DC-9-83 (MD-83)	49575	9Y-THT EI-BWD/EC-EFJ/EC-102	13. 4.88	Airplanes IAL Ltd Kansas City, USA (Op by Trans World Airlines)		
EI-BWH	Partenavia P.68C	212	G-BHJP	11.12.87	K.Buckley	Cork	A10.98
EI-BWJ*	BAC One-Eleven 201AC	BAC.009	N102EX (N29967)/G-ASJE	30. 8.88	Air Tara Ltd Orlando, Florida, USA (Stored 4.95)		
EI-BXA	Boeing 737-448	24474		28. 6.89	Aer Lingus plc "St.Conleth/Connlaodh"	Dublin	
EI-BXB	Boeing 737-448	24521		27.10.89	Aer Lingus plc "St.Gall/Gall"	Dublin	
EI-BXC	Boeing 737-448	24773		26. 4.90	Aer Lingus plc "St.Brendan/Brendan"	Dublin	
EI-BXD	Boeing 737-448	24866		1. 6.90	Aer Lingus plc "St.Colman/Colman"	Dublin	
EI-BXI	Boeing 737-448	25052		29. 4.91	Aer Lingus plc "St.Finnian/Finnian"	Dublin	
EI-BXK	Boeing 737-448	25736		14. 4.92	Aer Lingus plc "St.Caimin/Caimin" (Leased to Ryan International Winter 1998/99)	Dublin	
EI-BXL	Polaris F1B OK350 Microlight (Rotax 503)	M.561628		27. 6.91	M.McKeon	Lough Gowna, Co.Cavan	
EI-BXO	Fouga (Valmet) CM-170 Magister (C/n not confirmed)	213	N18FM FM-28	21.11.88	G.W.Connolly Saggart, Co.Dublin (Sold to Garage at Swords, Dublin; stored 4.96)		
EI-BXT	Rollason Druine D.62B Condor RAE/626		G-AVZE	24. 8.88	J.Sweeney	Letterkenny	
EI-BXX	Agusta-Bell 206B JetRanger III	8560	G-JMVB G-OIML	15.11.88	Westair Avn Ltd	Shannon	A10.98
EI-BYA	Thruster TST Mk.1	8504	G-MNDA	1. 2.89	E.Fagan	Ballyheelan, Co.Cavan	
EI-BYE	PA-31-350 Navajo Chieftain	31-7305118	G-BFDA SE-GDR	29. 5.89	Ireland Airways (Holdings) Ltd Weston (For Westair Cargo, Shannon 2.98)		A5.98
EI-BYF	Cessna 150M Commuter	150-76654	N3924V	20.11.89	Twentieth Air Training Grp Ltd	Dublin	
EI-BYG	Socata TB-9 Tampico Club	928		23. 8.89	Weston Ltd	Weston	A10.98
EI-BYJ	Bell 206B JetRanger II	1897	N49725	23. 6.89	Celtic Helicopters Ltd	Dublin Heliport	
EI-BYL	Heintz Zenith CH-250 MS/FAS 2866 (Lyc O-320) (C/n quoted as c/n A2-866)		(EI-BYD)	14. 6.89	M.Guckian	Strandhill, Sligo	
EI-BYR	Bell 206L-3 Long Ranger III	51284	(EI-LMG) EI-BYR/D-HBAD	15. 8.89	Donloe Management Services Ltd	Dublin	
EI-BYX	Champion 7GCAA Citabria	7GCAA-40	N546DS	4. 4.90	P.J.Gallagher	Coonagh	
EI-BYY	Piper J3C-85 Cub (Frame No.12322)	12494	EC-AQZ HB-OSG/44-80198	12. 4.90	V.Murphy	Thurles	
	(Regd with c/n 22288 and officially ex G-AKTJ/N3595K/NC3595K)						
EI-BZE	Boeing 737-3Y0	24464		2. 8.89	Air Tara Ltd (Op Philippine Airlines)	Manila	
EI-BZF	Boeing 737-3Y0	24465		7. 8.89	Pergola Ltd (Op Philippine Airlines)	Manila	
EI-BZJ	Boeing 737-3Y0	24677		29. 3.90	Pergola Ltd (Op Philippine Airlines)	Manila	
EI-BZL	Boeing 737-3Y0	24680		4.10.90	GECAS Technical Services Ltd (Op Philippine Airlines)	Manila	
EI-BZM	Boeing 737-3Y0	24681		15.10.90	GECAS Technical Services Ltd (Op Philippine Airlines)	Manila	
EI-BZN	Boeing 737-3Y0	24770		30.10.90	Airplanes Finance Ltd (Op Philippine Airlines)	Manila	
EI-CAA*	Reims Cessna FR.172J Rocket	0486	G-BHTW 5Y-ATO	17. 8.89	O.Bruton Abbeysrule (Damaged 1993/94: airframe stored: canc 27.11.98 as WFU)		
EI-CAC	Grob G-115A	8092		22.10.89	Exchequer Leasing Ltd	Weston	A10.98
EI-CAE	Grob G-115A	8105		5. 4.90	D.Kehoe	Waterford	A8.98
EI-CAN	Aerotech MW.5(K) Sorcerer (Rotax 447)	5K-0011-02	(G-MWGH)	15. 6.90	V.Vaughan	Abbeyshrule	
EI-CAP	Cessna R182 Skylane RGII	R182-00056	G-BMUF N7342W	27. 4.90	M.J.Hanlon	Weston	A11.98
EI-CAQ	Allocated to Aer Lingus 2.3.91 for ACARS testing using "c/n" 1.666.						
EI-CAU	AMF Chevvron 2-32 (Konig SD32)	022		14.11.90	J.Farrant	Rathcoole, Co.Cork	
EI-CAW	Bell 206B JetRanger	780	N2947W	11. 7.90	Celtic Helicopters (Maintenance Svs) Ltd	Dublin Heliport	
EI-CAX	Cessna P210N Pressurized Centurion II	P210-00215	(EI-CAS) G-OPMB/N4553K	9. 7.90	J.J.Dunne	Weston	
EI-CAY	Mooney M.20C Ranger	690074	N9272V	14.11.90	Ranger Flights Ltd	Dublin	
EI-CAZ*	Fairchild-Hiller FH-227D	519	SE-KBR C-FNAK/CF-NAK/(N701U)/N2735R	23. 9.91	Norwich Airport Fire Service	Norwich	
EI-CBF	ATR 42-300	176	(N426TE) F-WWEG	23. 2.90	Air Tara Ltd (Op Air Sicilia)	Palermo	

Regn	Type	C/n	P/I	Date	Owner/operator	Probable Base	Remarks
EI-CBJ	DHC-8-102 Dash Eight	215	C-GFCF	25. 5.90	Aerfi Jetprop Ltd (Leased to US Air)	(USA)	
EI-CBK	ATR 42-312	199	F-WWEM	25. 7.90	GPA-ATR Ltd (Leased to Italair Ltd)	(Italy)	
EI-CBO	McDonnell Douglas DC-9-83 (MD-83)	49442	HB-IUL SE-DRU/TC-TRU/EI-CBO/EC-ECO/N6203D	6.11.90	Airplanes IAL Ltd (Op Nouvelair Tunisie)	Tunis-Monastir	
EI-CBR	McDonnell Douglas DC-9-83 (MD-83)	49939		3.12.90	Airplanes 111 Ltd (Op Avianca)	Bogota	
EI-CBS	McDonnell Douglas DC-9-83 (MD-83)	49942		10.12.90	GECAS Technical Services Ltd (Op Avianca) "Ciudad De Cucuta"	Bogota	
EI-CBY	McDonnell Douglas DC-9-83 (MD-83)	49944		30. 7.91	GECAS Technical Services Ltd (Op Avianca) "Ciudad De Barranquilla"	Bogota	
EI-CBZ	McDonnell Douglas DC-9-83 (MD-83)	49945		13. 8.91	GECAS Technical Services Ltd (Op Avianca) "Ciudad Santiago De Cali"	Bogota	
EI-CCA	Beechcraft 19A Musketeer Sport	MB-411	G-AWTR N2758B	18. 7.90	P.F.McCoole	Coonagh	A8.98
EI-CCB	PA-44-180 Seminole	44-7995179	N2093K	6. 9.90	S.Bruton (Stored 3.98)	Abbeyshrule	
EI-CCC	McDonnell Douglas DC-9-83 (MD-83)	49946		27. 9.91	Airplanes 111 Ltd (Op Avianca) "Ciudad De Pereira"	Bogota	
EI-CCD	Grob G-115A	8108	D-EIUD or D-EIWD ?	15. 8.90	MOD Avn Ltd	Weston	A8.98
EI-CCE(2)	McDonnell Douglas DC-9-83 (MD-83)	49947		19. 9.91	GECAS Technical Services Ltd (Op Avianca)	Bogota	
EI-CCF	Aeronca 11AC Chief (Cont A65)	11AC-S-40	N3826E NC3826E	10. 1.91	O.Bruton	Abbeyshrule	
EI-CCH	Piper J3C-65 Cub	7278	N38801 NC38801	24. 1.91	M.Slattery	Trim	
EI-CCJ	Cessna 152 II	152-80174	N24251	9.10.90	M.P.Cahill (Op Irish A/C) (Stored 2.95)	Dublin	
EI-CCK	Cessna 152 II	152-79610	N757BM	9.10.90	M.P.Cahill (Damaged in heavy landing pre 1995)	Newcastle, Dublin	
EI-CCL	Cessna 152 II	152-80382	N24791	9.10.90	M.P.Cahill (Damaged Bray Head, Co.Wicklow 4.5.93; status uncertain)	Dublin	
EI-CCM	Cessna 152 II	152-82320	N68679	9.10.90	M.P.Cahill	Newcastle, Dublin	
EI-CCV	Cessna R172K Hawk XPII	R172-3039	N758EP	2. 3.91	Kerry A/C Ltd	Farranfore	
EI-CCY	Grumman-American AA-1B Trainer	AA1B-0617	G-BDYC	19. 3.91	N.F. & C.Whisler (Crashed Galway/Carnmore 5.11.94; wreck stored 4.96)	Galway	
EI-CDA	Boeing 737-548	24878	EI-BXE	26. 6.91	Aer Lingus plc "St.Columba/Colum"	Dublin	
EI-CDB	Boeing 737-548	24919	EI-BXF	27. 5.91	Aer Lingus plc "St.Albert/Ailbhe"	Dublin	
EI-CDC	Boeing 737-548	24968	EI-BXG	19. 6.91	Aer Lingus plc "St.Munchin/Maincin"	Dublin	
EI-CDD	Boeing 737-548	24989	EI-BXH	3. 7.91	Aer Lingus plc "St.Macartan/Mac Carthain"	Dublin	
EI-CDE	Boeing 737-548	25115	PT-SLM EI-CDE/(EI-BXJ)	21. 5.91	Aer Lingus plc "St.Jarlath/Larfhlaith"	Dublin	
EI-CDF	Boeing 737-548	25737		23. 3.92	Aer Lingus plc "St.Cronan/Cronan"	Dublin	
EI-CDG	Boeing 737-548	25738		7. 4.92	Aer Lingus plc "St.Moling/Molling"	Dublin	
EI-CDH	Boeing 737-548	25739		14. 4.92	Aer Lingus plc "St.Ronan/Ronan"	Dublin	
EI-CDP	Cessna 182L	182-58955	G-FALL OY-AHS/N4230S	20. 5.91	Irish Parachute Club Ltd	Clonbulloge	
EI-CDS	Boeing 737-548	26287		2. 2.93	Aer Lingus plc "St.Malachy/Maolmhaodhog"	Dublin	
EI-CDV	Cessna 150G	150-66677	N2777S	17. 7.91	K.A.O'Connor	Weston	E5.98
EI-CDX	Cessna 210K Centurion	210-59329	G-AYGN N9429M	14. 8.91	Falcon Avn Ltd (Taunton Cider titles)	Waterford	A8.98
EI-CDY	McDonnell Douglas DC-9-83 (MD-83)	49948		27. 9.91	GECAS Technical Services Ltd (Op Avianca)	Bogota	
EI-CEG	Socata MS.893E Rallye 180GT	13083	SE-GTS	31.10.91	M.Farrelly	Powerscourt	
EI-CEK	McDonnell Douglas DC-9-83 (MD-83)	49631	EC-FMY EC-113/EI-CEK/EC-EPM/EC-261 (Op Eurofly)	13.12.91	Airplanes IAL Finance Ltd	Turin, Italy	
EI-CEN	Thruster T.300 (Rotax 582)	9012-T300-500		2. 3.92	P.J.Murphy	Macroom, Co.Cork	
EI-CEP	McDonnell Douglas DC-9-83 (MD-83)	53122		14. 4.92	GECAS Technical Services Ltd (Op Avianca)	Bogota	
EI-CEQ	McDonnell Douglas DC-9-83 (MD-83)	53123		14. 4.92	GECAS Technical Services Ltd (Op Avianca) "Ciudad De Leticia"	Bogota	
EI-CER	McDonnell Douglas DC-9-83 (MD-83)	53125	N9017P	20. 5.92	Airplanes 111 Ltd (Op Avianca)	Bogota	
EI-CES	Taylorcraft BC-65	2231	G-BTEG N27590/NC27590	25. 3.92	N.O'Brien	Kilkenny	

Regn	Type	C/n	P/I	Date	Owner/operator	Probable Base	Remarks
EI-CEX	Lake LA-4-200 Buccaneer	1115	N8VG N3VC/N8544Z	18. 5.92	Derg Developments Ltd Lough Derg Marina, Killaloe		A6.98
EI-CEY	Boeing 757-2Y0	26152		10. 8.92	Pergola Ltd (Op Avianca)	Bogota	
EI-CEZ	Boeing 757-2Y0	26154		18. 9.92	Airplanes Holdings Ltd Bogota (Op Avianca)		
EI-CFE	Robinson R-22 Beta	1709	G-BTHG	15. 5.91	Toriamos Ltd	Weston	E8.98
EI-CFF	PA-12 Super Cruiser (Lyc O-235)	12-3928	N78544 NC78544	23. 5.91	J.O'Dwyer & J.Molloy	Gowran Grange	
EI-CFG	Rousseau Piel CP.301B Emeraude	112	G-ARIW F-BIRQ	1. 6.91	Southlink Ltd (Stored 1.99)	Waterford	
EI-CFH	PA-12 Super Cruiser (Lyc O-320)	12-3110	(EI-CCE) N4214M/NC4214M	1. 6.91	G.Treacy	Shinrone, Co.Offaly	
EI-CFM	Cessna 172P Skyhawk II	172-74656	N53000	19. 5.92	Hibernian Flying Club (Damaged in gales Cork 24.12.97)	Cork	
EI-CFN	Cessna 172P Skyhawk II	172-74113	N5446K JA4172/N5446K	10. 5.92	B.Fitzmaurice & G.O'Connell	Weston	A5.98
EI-CFO	Piper J3C-65 Cub	11947	OO-RAZ OO-RAF/44-79651	13. 5.92	J.Mathews & Ptnrs (USAAF c/s)	Trim	E8.98
EI-CFP	Cessna 172P Skyhawk II	172-74428	N52178	15. 7.91	K A O'Connor	Weston	A7.98
EI-CFV	Socata MS.880B Rallye Club	1850	G-OLFS G-AYYZ	13. 5.92	Kilkenny F/C "Liverbird"	Kilkenny	A9.98
EI-CFX	Robinson R-22 Beta	0793	G-OSPI	16. 6.92	Glenwood Transport Ltd	Weston	
EI-CFY	Cessna 172N Skyhawk II	172-68902	N734JZ	18. 6.92	K.A.O'Connor	Weston	A8.98
EI-CFZ	McDonnell Douglas DC-9-83 (MD-83)	53120	N6206F	29. 7.92	Airplanes 111 Ltd (Op Avianca)	Bogota	
EI-CGB	Team Minimax	36		20. 8.92	M.Garvey	Abbeyshrule	
	(Previously thought to be a Medway Hybred (Rotax 227); possibly the second use of marks ?)						
EI-CGC	Stinson 108-3 Station Wagon	108-5243	OO-IAC OO-JAC/N3B	17. 7.92	Anne P.Bruton	Abbeyshrule	
EI-CGD	Cessna 172M Skyhawk II	172-62309	OO-BMT N12846	30. 7.92	W.Phelan & M.Casey	Weston	A10.98
EI-CGE	Hiway Demon (C/n is engine type)	EC-25PS-04		19. 8.92	Not known (Temp unregd 11.2.97)	Kilpedder	
EI-CGF	Luton LA-5 Major	PFA/1208	G-BENH	31. 7.92	F.Doyle & J.Duggan (Newlands, Co.Wexford)		A10.98
EI-CGG	Ercoupe 415C (Cont C75)	3147	N2522H NC2522H	10. 9.92	Irish Ercoupe Grp	Weston	A5.98
EI-CGH	Cessna 210N Centurion II	210-63524	N6374A	16.11.92	J.J.Spollen	Abbeyshrule	A11.98
EI-CGI	McDonnell Douglas DC-9-83 (MD-83)	49624	EC-279 EC-EKM/EC-178	19.10.92	Airplanes IAL Ltd (Op Nouvelaire)	Monastir, Tunisia	
EI-CGJ	Solar Wings Pegasus XL-R (Rotax 447)	SW-WA-1506	G-MWTV	5. 4.93	P.Hearty	Portarlington	
EI-CGM	Solar Wings Pegasus XL-R (Rotax 447)	SW-WA-1502	G-MWVC	14.11.92	Microflight Ltd	Ballyfore	
EI-CGN	Solar Wings Pegasus XL-R (Rotax 447)	SW-WA-1529	G-MWXM	14.11.92	V.Power	Donamore, New Ross	
EI-CGO	McDonnell Douglas DC-8-63AF	45924	N353AS (N791AL)/SE-DBH/OY-SBM/HS-TGZ/SE-DBH	25. 4.89	Aer Turas Teo	Dublin	
EI-CGP	PA-28-140 Cherokee C	28-26928	G-MLUA G-AYJT	25.11.92	A.Barlow (Op Euroair Training)	Waterford	A8.98
EI-CGQ	Aerospatiale AS.350B Ecureuil	2076	G-BUPK JA9740	21. 1.93	Caulstown Air Ltd	Dublin Heliport	A9.98
EI-CGT	Cessna 152 II	152-82331	G-BPBL N16SU/N68715	10.12.92	J.J.Dunne	Stamullen	
EI-CGV	Piper J/5A Cub Cruiser	5-624	G-BPKT N35372/NC35372	11.12.92	J5 Grp	Trim	E8.98
EI-CGX	Cessna 340	340-0106	(EI-CHH) N51388/G-BALM/N4553L	27. 3.93	Meckfield Construction Co Ltd Dublin (Crashed nr Knock 19.8.94; stored Galway 1.95)		
EI-CHF	PA-44-180 Seminole	44-7995112	G-BGJB N3046B	22. 2.93	A.Barlow (Op Euroair Training)	Waterford	A8.98
EI-CHK	Piper J3C-65 Cub	23019	C-FHNS CF-HNS/N1492N/NC1492N	10. 3.93	N.Higgins	Longwood, Co.Meath	
EI-CHM	Cessna 150M Commuter	150-79288	G-BSZX N714MU	2. 3.93	K.A.O'Connor	Weston	
EI-CHN	Socata MS.880B Rallye Club	901	G-AVIO	22. 2.93	Limerick Flying Club (Coonagh) Ltd Coonagh		A8.98
EI-CHP	DHC-8-103 Dash Eight	258	VH-FNQ C-GFRP	7. 4.93	Airplanes Jetprop Finance Ltd (Op US Air Express) Harrisburg, PA, USA		
EI-CHR	CFM Shadow Srs.BD (Rotax 447)	063	G-MTKT	20. 5.93	J.Smith	Laytown, Co.Meath	
EI-CHS	Cessna 172M Skyhawk II	172-66742	G-BREZ N80775	26. 4.93	Kerry Aero Club Ltd	Farranfore	A11.98
EI-CHT	Solar Wings Pegasus XL-R (Rotax 447) (Possibly c/n SW-TB-1449)	1449		16. 4.93	G.W.Maher	Loughlinstown, Co.Dublin	
EI-CHV	Agusta A.109A II	7149	VR-BMM HB-XTJ/D-HASV	10. 6.93	Celtic Helicopters Ltd	Dublin Heliport	A6.98
EI-CIA	Socata MS.880B Rallye Club	1218	G-MONA G-AWJK	26. 4.93	M.Maher	Thurles	

Regn	Type	C/n	P/I	Date	Owner/operator	Probable Base	Remarks
EI-CIF	PA-28-180 Cherokee C	28-2853	G-AVVV	12. 6.93	AA Flying Group	Weston	A10.98
			N8880J	(Rebuilt 1967 using spare frame c/n 28-3808S - dism 12.98 ?)			
EI-CIG	PA-18-150 Super Cub (Frame No.18-7360)	18-7203	G-BGWF ST-AFJ/ST-ABN	12. 6.93 (Derelict fuselage by 12.98 ?)	K.A.O'Connor	Weston	A6.98
EI-CIH	Ercoupe 415CD (Cont C85)	4834	OO-AIA (PH-NDO)/N94723/NC94723	25. 6.93	J.T.Haycock	Weston	A5.98
EI-CIJ	Cessna 340	340-0304	G-BBVE N69451	2. 7.93 (Damaged Dublin 28.12.97; under repair)	Airlink Airways Ltd	Sligo	A1.99
EI-CIK	Mooney M.20C Mark 21	2620	G-BFXC 9H-ABD/G-BFXC/OH-MOA/N1349W	2. 7.93	A & P Avn Ltd	Galway	A8.98
EI-CIM	Light Aero Avid mk.IV (Rotax 582)	1125D		17. 8.93	P.Swan	Weston	A10.98
EI-CIN	Cessna 150K	150-71728	G-BSXG N6228G	6. 9.93	F.McGovern	Brittas Bay	
EI-CIO	Bell 206L-3 Long Ranger III	51436	JA6075 N6546Q	24.10.93	Sean Quinn Properties Ltd	Ballyconnel	A10.98
EI-CIR	Cessna 551 Citation II (Built as Cessna 550 c/n 550-0128)	551-0174	N60AR EI-CIR/F-WLEF/9A-BPU/RC-BPU/YU-BPU/N220LA/N536M/N2631V	29.11.93	Air Group Finance Ltd	Dinard, France	
EI-CIV	PA-28-140 Cherokee Cruiser	28-7725232	G-BEXY N9639N	20.11.93 (Damaged in gales Cork 24.12.97)	G.Cashman & E.Callanan	Abbeyshrule	A11.98
EI-CIW	McDonnell Douglas DC-9-83 (MD-83)	49785	HL-7271	30.12.93	Carotene Ltd (Op Meridiana)	Olbia, Italy	
EI-CIZ	Steen Skybolt (Lyc IO-360)	001	G-BSAO N303BC	12.12.93	J.Keane	Coonagh	A8.98
EI-CJA	Boeing 767-35HER	26387	S7-AAQ (I-AEJD)	22.12.93	Hikone Ltd (Op Air Europe Italy)	Malpensa, Italy	
EI-CJB	Boeing 767-35HER	26388	S7-AAV (I-AEJE)	23.12.93	Hikone Ltd (Op Air Europe Italy)	Malpensa, Italy	
EI-CJC	Boeing 737-204ADV	22640	G-BJCV CS-TMA/G-BJCV/C-GCAU/G-BJCV/C-GXCP/G-BJCV	25. 1.94	Ryanair Ltd	Dublin	
EI-CJD	Boeing 737-204ADV	22966	G-BKHE (G-BKGU)	18. 2.94	Ryanair Ltd (Eirecell c/s)	Dublin	
EI-CJE	Boeing 737-204ADV	22639	G-BJCU EC-DVE/G-BJCU	10. 3.94	Ryanair Ltd (Jaguar c/s)	Dublin	
EI-CJF	Boeing 737-204ADV	22967	G-BTZF G-BKHF/(G-BKGV)	24. 3.94	Ryanair Ltd	Dublin	
EI-CJG	Boeing 737-204ADV	22058	G-BGYK PP-SRW/G-BGYK/(G-BGRV)	25. 3.94	Ryanair Ltd	Dublin	
EI-CJH	Boeing 737-204ADV	22057	G-BGYJ (G-BGRU)/N8278V	30. 3.94	Ryanair Ltd	Dublin	
EI-CJI	Boeing 737-2E7	22875	G-BMDF (PK-RI.)/G-BMDF/4X-BAB/N4570B	8. 7.94	Ryanair Ltd	Dublin	
EI-CJK	Airbus A.300B4-103	020	F-BUAR D-AMAY/(F-WLGB)	13. 1.94	Airplanes Holdings Ltd (Op TransAer)	Dublin	
EI-CJR	SNCAN Stampe SV-4A	318	G-BKBK OO-CLR/F-BCLR	28. 2.94	C.Scully & P.Ryan	Galway	A8.98
EI-CJS	Jodel Wassmer D.120A Paris-Nice	339	F-BOYF	28. 2.94	L.Maddock	Killamaster	A8.98
EI-CJT	Slingsby Cadet III (VW 1835)	830 & PCW-001	G-BPCW XA288	25. 2.94	J.Tarrant	Rathcoole	
EI-CJV	Moskito 2 (Rotax 582)	004	D-MBGM	12. 3.94	Peril, Kingston, Hanly & Fitzgerald	Coonagh	
EI-CJZ	Whittaker MW-6S Fatboy Flyer (Rotax 503)	PFA/164-11493	G-MWTW	24. 3.94	M.McCarthy	Watergrasshill, Co.Cork	
EI-CKD	Boeing 767-3Y0ER	26205	N6046P	13. 9.94	GECAS Technical Services Ltd (Op Aeroflot)	Moscow, Russia	
EI-CKE	Boeing 767-3Y0ER	26208	N6009F	15. 9.94	GECAS Technical Services Ltd (Op Aeroflot)	Moscow, Russia	
EI-CKG	Hunt Avon (Rotax 447)	92009013		2. 7.94	B.Kenny	Clara,Co. Offaly	
EI-CKH	PA-18-95 Super Cub	18-7248	G-APZK	3. 6.94	G.Brady & C.Keenan	Weston	
EI-CKI	Thruster TST mk.1 (Rotax 503)	8078-TST-091	G-MVDI	3. 6.94	S.Pallister	Brannockstown	
EI-CKJ	Cameron N-77 HAFB	3305		6. 7.94	F.Meldon "Goodfellas"	Blackrock, Co.Dublin	
EI-CKM	McDonnell Douglas DC-9-83 (MD-83)	49792	TC-INC EI-CKM/(D-ALLW)/EI-CKM/XA-RPH/EC-FFF/EC-733/XA-RPH	10. 8.94	Airplanes Finance Ltd	(Shannon)	
EI-CKN	Whittaker MW-6S Fatboy Flyer (Rotax 462)	BCA.8942		29. 7.94	B.Audoire	Dunnmaggin, Co.Kilkenny	
EI-CKP	Boeing 737-2K2ADV	22296	PH-TVS PP-SRV/PH-TVS/LV-RBH/PH-TVS/LV-RAO/PH-TVS/EC-DVN/PH-TVS	7.10.94	Ryanair Ltd	Dublin	
EI-CKQ	Boeing 737-2K2ADV	22906	PH-TVU G-BPLA/PH-TVU/C-FCAV/PH-TVU	20. 2.95	Ryanair Ltd	Dublin	
EI-CKR	Boeing 737-2K2ADV	22025	PH-TVR C-FICP/PH-TVR/(D-AJAA)/PH-TVR	4. 5.95	Ryanair Ltd	Dublin	
EI-CKS	Boeing 737-2T5ADV	22023	PH-TVX OE-ILE/PH-TVX/G-BGTW	1. 6.95	Ryanair Ltd	Dublin	

Regn	Type	C/n	P/I	Date	Owner/operator	Probable Base	Remarks
EI-CKT	Mainair Gemini/Flash 307-585-3 & W47 (EC-44-PM)		G-MNCB	27. 9.94	C.Burke	Bartlemy	
EI-CKU	Solar Wings Pegasus XL-R (Rotax 447)	SW-TB-1434 & SW-WA-1500	G-MWVB	14.10.94	M.O'Regan	Edenderry	
EI-CKX	Wassmer Jodel D.112	1166	G-ASIS F-BKNR	7.12.94	J.Greene	Killamaster, Castle Dermott	
EI-CKZ	Jodel D.18 (VW1834)	229		5. 4.95	J.O'Brien	Glen of Imall	
EI-CLA	HOAC DV-20 Katana	20106		24. 3.95	Weston Ltd	Weston	E8.98
EI-CLB	ATR-72-212	423	F-WWEB	23. 2.95	Tarquin Ltd (Op Avianova/Alitalia) "Lago di Bracciano"	Rome-Fiumicino	
EI-CLC	ATR-72-212	428	F-WWEF	24. 2.95	Tarquin Ltd (Op Avianova/Alitalia) "Fiume Simeto"	Rome-Fiumicino	
EI-CLD	ATR-72-212	432	F-WWEL	3. 3.95	Tarquin Ltd (Op Avianova/Alitalia)	Rome-Fiumicino	
EI-CLF	Fairchild-Hiller FH-227E	505	SE-KBP C-FNAI/CF-NAI/PP-BUK/N7802M	12. 7.95	Ireland Airways Holdings Ltd (For Westair Cargo, Shannon 2.98)	Dublin	
EI-CLG	BAe 146 Srs.300	E-3131	G-BRAB HS-TBL/G-BRAB/G-11-131	7. 6.95	Aer Lingus Commuter Ltd "St.Finbarr/Fionbarr"	Dublin	
EI-CLH	BAe 146 Srs.300	E-3146	G-BOJJ I-ATSC/G-BOJJ/G-6-146	2. 6.95	Aer Lingus Commuter Ltd "St.Aoife/Aoife"	Dublin	
EI-CLI	BAe 146 Srs.300	E-3159	G-BVSA I-ATSD/G-6-159/G-5-159	19. 4.95	Aer Lingus Commuter Ltd "St.Eithne/Eithne"	Dublin	
EI-CLJ	BAe 146 Srs.300	E-3155	G-BTNU (G-BSLS)/G-6-155	1. 3.96	Aer Lingus Commuter Ltd "St.Senan/Seanan"	Dublin	
EI-CLL	Whittaker MW-6S Fatboy Flyer (Rotax 503)	1069		2. 4.95	M.McCarthy	Watergrasshill, Co.Cork	
EI-CLN	Boeing 737-2C9	21443	RA-73000 LX-LGH/N8277V	17. 5.95	Airlease (103) Ltd (Op Transaero)	Moscow, Russia	
EI-CLO	Boeing 737-2C9	21444	RA-73001 LX-LGI	16. 5.95	Airlease (103) Ltd) (Op Transaero)	Moscow, Russia	
EI-CLQ	Reims Cessna F.172N Skyhawk II	1653	G-BFLV	26. 5.95	K.Dardis & ptnrs	Abbeyshrule	A8.98
EI-CLS	Boeing 767-325ER	26262	(N808AM) N171LF	28. 7.95	ILFC Ireland Ltd (Op Air Europe Italy)	Malpensa, Italy	
EI-CLT	Bell 206B JetRanger	1727	N90158	17. 7.95	Mistwood Ltd	Cloghran Heliport	A10.98
EI-CLW	Boeing 737-3Y0	25187	XA-SAB	10. 6.95	Airplanes Finance Ltd (Op Air One)	Pescara, Italy	
EI-CLY	BAe 146 Srs.300	E-3149	G-BTZN N146PZ/ZP-CCY/N146PZ/G-BTZN/HS-TBN/G-11-149	16. 4.97	Aer Lingus Commuter Ltd "St.Eugene/Eoghan"	Dublin	
EI-CLZ	Boeing 737-3Y0	25179	XA-RJR N3521N	27. 7.95	Airplanes Finance Ltd (Op Air One)	Pescara, Italy	
EI-CMB	PA-28-140 Cherokee Cruiser	28-7725094	G-BELR N9541N	5. 9.95	Kestrel F/Grp Ltd	Dublin	A9.98
EI-CMF	CFM Streak Shadow (Rotax 582)	K.260	G-MTFY	13. 9.95	O.Williams	Galway	
EI-CMI	Robinson R-22 Beta	1129	G-BRRZ N8050N	30.11.95	Santail Ltd	Weston	A10.98
EI-CMJ	ATR-72-210	467	F-WWLU	21.12.95	Tarquin Ltd (Op Avianova) "Fiume Volturno"	Milan-Linate	
EI-CMK	Eurowing Goldwing ST (EC-PM-34)	76		22.12.95	M.Garrigan	Clondara, Longford	
EI-CML	Cessna 150M	150-76786	G-BNSS N45207	5. 1.96	K.A.O'Connor	Weston	A5.98
EI-CMM	McDonnell Douglas DC-9-83 (MD-83)	49937	G-COES N30010	1. 2.96	Irish Aerospace Ltd (Op Eurofly)	Turin, Italy	
EI-CMN	PA-12 Super Cruiser (Lyc O-235)	12-1617	N2363M NC2363M	26. 1.96	D.Graham & Ptnrs	Birr	E8.98
EI-CMR	Rutan LongEz (Lyc O-235)	1716		2. 5.96	F. & C.O'Caoimh	Waterford	A8.98
EI-CMS	BAe 146 Srs.200A	E-2044	N184US N361PS	24. 4.96	Cityjet Ltd	Dublin	
EI-CMT	PA-34-200T Seneca II	34-7870088	G-BNER N2590M	23. 4.96	Atlantic Air Ltd	Cork	A10.98
EI-CMU	Mainair Mercury 1071-0296-7 & W873 (Rotax 462)			3. 5.96	J.Deeney	Carrigaline, Co.Cork	
EI-CMV	Cessna 150L	150-72747	G-MSES N1447Q	17. 5.96	Santail Ltd	Weston	A11.98
EI-CMW	Rotorway Exec (RW162D)	3550		13. 5.96	B.McNamee	Dunboyne, Co.Meath	
EI-CMY	BAe 146 Srs.200A	E-2039	N177US N365PS	19. 6.96	Cityjet Ltd	Dublin	
EI-CMZ	McDonnell Douglas DC-9-83 (MD-83)	49390	9Y-THN	20. 7.96	Airplanes Finance Ltd (Op Eurofly)	Turin, Italy	

Regn	Type	C/n	P/I	Date	Owner/operator	Probable Base	Remarks
EI-CNA	Letov LK-2M Sluka (Rotax 447)	8295S005		28. 6.96	G.Doody	Portlaoise, Co.Laois	A8.98
EI-CNB	BAe 146 Srs.200A	E-2046	(EI-CMZ) N187US/N363PS	3. 8.96	Cityjet Ltd (Op Malmo Aviation)	Dublin	
EI-CNC	Team Minimax 1600 (Rotax 447)	514		10. 9.96	A.M.S.Allen	Trim	
EI-CNG	Air & Space 18-A Gyroplane	18-75	G-BALB N6170S	10. 9.96	P.Joyce	Newmarket-on-Fergus, Co.Clare	
EI-CNI	BAe 146 RJ85	E-2299	G-6-299	26.11.96	Peregrine Aviation Leasing Co Ltd (Op Azzurra Air) "Lombardia"	Bergamo, Italy	
EI-CNJ	BAe 146 RJ85	E-2300	G-6-300	2.12.96	Peregrine Aviation Leasing Co Ltd (Op Azzurra Air)	Bergamo, Italy	
EI-CNK	BAe 146 RJ85	E-2306	G-6-306	8. 5.97	Peregrine Aviation Leasing Co Ltd (Op Azzurra Air) "Lazio"	Bergamo, Italy	
EI-CNL	Sikorsky S-61N Mk.II	61746	G-BDDA ZS-RBU/G-BDDA/N91201/G-BDDA	19.12.96	Bond Helicopters (Ireland) Ltd (Op Irish Marine Emergency Service)	Shannon	A12.98
EI-CNM	PA-31-350 Navajo Chieftain	31-7305107	N1201H G-BBNT/N74958	16.12.96	M.Goss	Dublin	A10.98
EI-CNN	Lockheed L.1011-385-1 Tristar	1024	VR-HHV G-BAAA	30. 1.97	Aer Turas Teoranta (Op Iberia)	Madrid, Spain	
EI-CNO	McDonnell Douglas DC-9-83 (MD-83)	49672	EC-FTU EC-487/EC-EJQ/EC-150	19. 2.97	Airplanes Finance Ltd (Op Nouvelair Tunisie)	Monastir, Tunisia	
EI-CNP	Boeing 737-266ADV	21192	TF-ABG N192GP/4R-ULO/SU-AYI	12. 3.97	Airplanes Finance Ltd (Op Aerolineas Argentinas)	Buenos Aires	
EI-CNQ	BAe 146 Srs.200	E-2031	G-OWLD N173US/N353PS	2. 7.97	Cityjet Ltd (Op Business City Express) (Air France c/s)	Dublin	
EI-CNR	McDonnell Douglas DC-9-83 (MD-83)	53199	SE-DLU N13627	10. 4.97	GECAS Technical Serices Ltd (Op Eurofly)	Turin, Italy	
EI-CNS	Boeing 767-3Q8ER	27600	N6005C	16. 4.97	ILFC (Ireland) Ltd (Op Air Europe Italy)	Malpensa, Italy	
EI-CNT	Boeing 737-230ADV	22115	D-ABFC	5.12.96	Ryanair Ltd (News of the World/The Sun c/s)	Dublin	
EI-CNU	Cyclone Pegasus Quantum 15 (Rotax 912)	7326		10. 4.97	M.Ffrench	Donamore, New Ross	A10.98
EI-CNV	Boeing 737-230ADV	22128	D-ABFX (D-ABFW)	26. 3.97	Ryanair Ltd	Dublin	
EI-CNW	Boeing 737-230ADV	22133	D-ABHC (B-)/D-ABHC/(D-ABHB)	31. 5.97	Ryanair Ltd	Dublin	
EI-CNX	Boeing 737-230ADV	22127	D-ABFW N5573K/(D-ABFU)	4. 7.97	Ryanair Ltd (Tipperary Crystal titles)	Dublin	
EI-CNY	Boeing 737-230ADV	22113	D-ABFB N5573K	10.10.97	Ryanair Ltd (Kilkenny Irish Beer c/s)	Dublin	
EI-CNZ	Boeing 737-230ADV	22126	D-ABFU (D-ABFT)	5.11.97	Ryanair Ltd	Dublin	
EI-COA	Boeing 737-230ADV	22637	CS-TES D-ABHX	16.12.97	Ryanair Ltd	Dublin	
EI-COB	Boeing 737-230ADV	22114	D-ABFR	16. 1.98	Ryanair Ltd	Dublin	
EI-COD	ATR-42-312	052	N4203G F-WWEG	24. 7.97	Duntington Ltd (Op Italair)	(Italy)	
EI-COE	Europa Avn Europa (Jabiru 2200)	286		29. 5.97	F.Flynn	(Urlanmore, Co.Clare)	
EI-COG	Gyroscopic Gyroplane	G.120		11. 3.98	R.C.Fidler & D.Bracken	Letterkenny	A8.98
	(Imported from Australia during 1996 and flown without marks in 8.97; the design is a 2-seat side by side open cockpit gyro and the quoted c/n G.120 may be the type designation)						
EI-COH	Boeing 737-430	27001	D-ABKB (VT-S)/D-ABKB	6. 6.97	Flightlease (Ireland) Ltd (Op Air One)	Fiumicino, Italy	
EI-COI	Boeing 737-430	27002	D-ABKC	13.11.97	Challey Ltd (Op Air One)	Pescara, Italy	
EI-COJ	Boeing 737-430	27005	D-ABKK (D-ABKF)	13.11.97	Challey Ltd (Op Air One)	Pescara, Italy	
EI-COK	Boeing 737-430	27003	D-ABKD	23. 2.98	Flightlease (Ireland) Ltd (Op Air One)	Fiumicino, Italy	
EI-COL	Lockheed L.1011-385-1 Tristar	1036	(N660AT) N31014	1. 5.98	Aer Turas Teoranta "Charlie Too" (Open store 3.99)	Southend	
EI-COM	Whittaker MW-6S Fatboy Flyer (Rotax 582)	1		10.10.97	M. Watson	Clonbullogue	
EI-CON	Boeing 737-2T5	22396	PK-RIW EI-CON/PK-RIW/VT-EWF/A40-BM/C-GVRE/(EI-B)/G-BHVH	21. 7.97	Ryanair Ltd	Dublin	
EI-COO	Carlson Sparrow II (Rotax 532)	302		13. 8.97	D.Logue	Weston	
EI-COP	Reims Cessna F.150L Commuter	1058	G-BCBY PH-TGI/(G-BCBY)	26. 6.97	A.Nee	Weston	
EI-COQ	BAe 146 RJ70	E-1254	9H-ACM (9H-ABW)/G-BVRJ/G-6-254	17.10.97	Peregrine Aviation Leasing Co Ltd	Bergamo, Italy	
EI-COS	BAe ATP	2060	G-11-060 R		Ireland Airways Ltd	Dublin	
EI-COT	Reims Cessna F.172N Skyhawk II	1884	D-EIEF	24.11.97	Kawasaki Distributors (Ireland) Ltd	Newcastle	A10.98

Regn	Type	C/n	P/I	Date	Owner/operator	Probable Base	Remarks
EI-COV	BAe 125 Srs.700B	257178	N621S	28. 5.98	Wilton Bridge Ltd	Dublin	
			N700CJ/G-5-747/VH-LMP/G-5-570/G-BMYX/G-5-530/4W-ACM/G-5-14				
EI-COX	Boeing 737-230ADV	22123	D-ABFP	9. 1.98	Ryanair Ltd	Dublin	
EI-COY	Piper J-3C-65 Cub	22519	N3319N	5.11.97	P.McWade	Abbeyshrule	A8.98
			NC3319N				
EI-COZ	Piper PA-28-140C Cherokee	28-26796	G-AYMZ	5.11.97	Euroaer Flight Training School Ltd		A8.98
			N11C			Waterford	
EI-CPB	McDonnell Douglas DC-9-83 (MD-83)	49940	TC-IND	27.11.97	Irish Aerospace Ltd (Op Eurofly)	Milan, Italy	
			G-TTPT/N30016				
EI-CPC	Airbus A.321-211	815	D-AVZT	8. 5.98	ILFC (Op Aer Lingus) "St.Fergus/Feargus"	Dublin	
EI-CPD	Airbus A.321-211	841	D-AVZA	19. 6.98	ILFC (Op Aer Lingus) "St.Davnet/Damhnat"	Dublin	
EI-CPE	Airbus A.321-211	926	D-AVZQ	11.12.98	ILFC (Op Aer Lingus) "St.Enda"	Dublin	
EI-CPF	Airbus A.321-211	991	D-AV..	R	Aer Lingus (For dely 3.99)	Dublin	
EI-CPG	Airbus A.321-211	1013		R	Aer Lingus (For dely 5.99)	Dublin	
EI-CPH	Airbus A.321-211	1094		R	Aer Lingus (For dely late 1999)	Dublin	
EI-CPI	Rutan LongEz (Lyc O-235)	17		18.12.97	D.J.Ryan	Waterford	
EI-CPJ	BAe 146-RJ70	E-1258	9H-ACN	27. 3.98	Peregrine Aviation Leasing Co Ltd (Op Azzura Air) "Puglia"	Bergamo, Italy	
			(9H-ABX)/G-6-258				
EI-CPK	BAe 146-RJ70	E-1260	9H-ACO	27. 3.98	Peregrine Aviation Leasing Co Ltd (Op Azzura Air)	Bergamo, Italy	
			(9H-ABY)/G-6-261				
EI-CPL	BAe 146-RJ70	E-1267	9H-ACP	31. 3.98	Peregrine Aviation Leasing Co Ltd (Op Azzura Air)	Bergamo, Italy	
			(9H-ABZ)/G-6-267				
EI-CPM	SAAB 2000	028	SE-KCF	18. 3.98	Cityjet Ltd	Dublin	
			F-GMVR/(V7-9509)/SE-028				
EI-CPN	Auster J/4	2073	G-AIJR	1. 4.98	E.Fagan	Killykeen, Co.Cavan	
EI-CPO	Robinson R-22B2 Beta	2775	G-BXUJ	23. 9.98	Santail Ltd	Weston	
EI-CPP	Piper J-3C-65 Cub (Rebuilt Glasthule, Dublin 1994/1998)	12052	G-BIGH	23. 3.98	E.Fitzgerald	Newcastle	
			F-BFQV/OO-GAS/OO-GAZ/44-79756				
EI-CPQ	SAAB 2000	013	F-GTSA	9. 4.98	DB Export Leasing GmbH (Op Cityjet Ltd)	Dublin	
			D-ADSA/SE-013				
EI-CPR	Short SD.3-60 Var.200	SH.3713	G-OBOH	1. 2.99	Comhfhorbairt (Gaillimh) Teo (Op Aer Arann)	Dublin	
			G-BNDJ/G-14-3713				
EI-CPS	Beechcraft 58 Baron	TH-862	G-BEUL	21. 5.98	F.Doherty	Donegal	
EI-CPT	ATR-42-312	191	C-GIQS	12. 6.98	GPA-ATR Ltd (Leased to Italair Spa) ??		
			(ZS-NYP)/C-GIQS/F-WWEA				
EI-CPU	Boeing 737-430	27004	D-ABKF	15. 5.98	Flightlease (Ireland) Ltd (Op Air One Italy)	Pescara, Italy	
			(D-ABKK)/(D-ABKE)				
EI-CPV	Boeing 767-36E	25132	N132KR	4. 6.98	ILFC Ireland Ltd (Leased to Air Europe Italy)	Milan, Italy	
			HL7268				
EI-CPW	SAAB 2000	016	F-GTSC	12. 6.98	DB Export Leasing GmbH (Cityjet Ltd)	Dublin	
			D-ADSC/SE-016				
EI-CPX	III Sky Arrow 650T	K.122 & SAAC 67		24. 6.98	N.Irwin	Cork	
EI-CPY	BAe 146 Srs.100	E-1003	N246SS	13. 7.98	CityJet Ltd	Dublin	
			(N631AW)/N246SS/G-5-14/G-SCHH/G-5-14/G-SCHH/(G-BIAF)				
(EI-CPZ)	Boeing 737-86N	28575	N1786B	.98R	GECAS (Jet Airways) Marks NTU - became VT-JNB 8.98.		
(EI-CRA)	Boeing 737-86N	28578	N1786B	.98R	GECAS (Jet Airways) Marks NTU - became VT-JNA 8.98		
EI-CRB	Lindstrand LBL-90A HAFB	550		23. 9.98	J.& C.Concannon	Tuam	
EI-CRC	Boeing 737-46B	24124	EC-GNC	3.11.98	Aer Lingus Ltd (CIT Leasing Corp)		
			SU-SAB/EC-GHF/EC-309/SU-SAA/EC-FYG/EC-655/N689MA/G-BOPK (Leased to Ryan International)			Cleveland, USA	
EI-CRD	Boeing 767-31BER	26259	B-2565	29.10.98	ILFC Ireland Ltd (EuroFly Italy)	Italy	
EI-CRE	McDonnell Douglas DC-9-83 (MD-83)	49854	D-ALLL	11.12.98	Crane Aircraft Ltd (Believed leased to Meridiana)	Olbia, Sardinia	
EI-CRF	Boeing 767-31B	25170	B-2566	4.12.98	ILFC Ireland Ltd (Leased to Eurofly & op for Alitalia)	Rome	
EI-CRG	Robin DR.400-180R	2021	D-EHEC	11.12.98	D & B Lodge	Waterford	
EI-CRH	McDonnell Douglas DC-9-83 (MD-83)	49935	HB-IKM	10. 2.99	Airplanes 111 Ltd (Leased to Meridiana)	Olbia, Sicily	
			G-DCAC/N3004C				
EI-CRJ	McDonnell Douglas DC-9-83 (MD-83)	53013	D-ALLP	27. 1.99	C A Aviation Ltd (Leased to Meridiana)	Olbia, Sicily	
EI-CRK	Airbus A.330-301	070	(EI-NYC)	18.11.94	Aer Lingus Ltd "St Brigid"	Dublin	
			F-WWKV				
EI-CRL	Boeing 767-343ER	30008		R	GECAS (Leased to Alitalia)	Rome	
EI-CRN	Boeing 737-228	23008	F-GBYI	18. 2.99	Rancemont Ltd (Op Air Sicilia)	Sicily	
EI-CRV	Hoffman H.36 Dimona	3674	OE-9319	R	Not known	Waterford	
			HB-2081				

Regn	Type	C/n	P/I	Date	Owner/operator	Probable Base	Remarks
EI-CSA	Boeing 737-8AS	29916	N5537L	R	Ryanair Ltd	Dublin	
			N1786B		(For dlvy 3.99)		
EI-CSB	Boeing 737-8AS			R	Ryanair Ltd	Dublin	
EI-CSC	Boeing 737-8AS			R	Ryanair Ltd	Dublin	
EI-CSD	Boeing 737-8AS			R	Ryanair Ltd	Dublin	
EI-CSE	Boeing 737-8AS			R	Ryanair Ltd	Dublin	
EI-CSF	Boeing 737-8AS			R	Ryanair Ltd	Dublin	
EI-CSG	Boeing 737-8AS			R	Ryanair Ltd	Dublin	
EI-CSH	Boeing 737-8AS			R	Ryanair Ltd	Dublin	
EI-CSI	Boeing 737-8AS			R	Ryanair Ltd	Dublin	
EI-CSK	BAe 146 Srs.200A	E-2062	N810AS	3. 4.98	Jet Acceptance Corp	Dublin	
			N880DV/G-5-062/N406XV/(G-BNDR)/G-5-062 "St.Ciara/Ciara"				
					(Op Aer Lingus Commuter)		
EI-CSL	BAe 146 Srs.200A	E-2074	N812AS	8. 5.98	Jet Acceptance Corp "St.Cormac"	Dublin	
			N881DV/G-5-074/G-BNND/HS-TBQ/G-BNND/N146SB/N192US/N368PS/(G-BNND)/G-5-074				
					(Op Aer Lingus Commuter)		
EI-CSM	Boeing 737-8AS			R	Ryanair Ltd	Dublin	
EI-CTM	BAe 146 Srs.300	E-3129	G-JEAL	R	Aer Lingus Ltd	Dublin	
			G-BTXN/HS-TBM/G-5-129 (For dlvy 3.9) 9(Op Aer Lingus Commuter)				
EI-CUB	Piper J3C-65 Cub	16010	G-BPPV	17. 7.91	J.Connelly & Ptnrs	Galway	
			N88392/NC88392				
EI-DLA	McDonnell Douglas DC-10-30	46958	N883LA	22. 6.94	GECAS Technical Servives Ltd		
		EI-DLA/RP-C2003/(RP-C2000)/(PH-DTM)			(Op Continental Airlines)	Houston, USA	
EI-DUB	Airbus A.330-301	055	F-WWKP	6. 5.94	Aer Lingus plc	Dublin	
					"St.Patrick/Padraig"		
EI-DWN	Cessna 421C Golden Eagle III		N422GC	5. 4.96	Dawn Meats (Waterford) Ltd	Waterford	A10.98
		421C-0641	N307SP/ZS-KEP/N88582				
EI-EAA	Airbus A.300B4-203F	150	F-WQGT	2. 4.98	Air Contractors (Ireland) Ltd (DHL c/s)		
			SU-BCC/F-WZMD		Pyramid Leasing Inc Dublin/East Midlands		
EI-EAB	Airbus A.300B4-203F	199	F-WQFO	R	Air Contractors (Ireland) Ltd (DHL c/s)		
			SU-BDF/(SU-BCD)/F-WZMF		Pyramid Leasing Inc Dublin/East Midlands		
EI-EAC	Airbus A.300B4-203F	250	N10970	20.11.98	Air Contractors (Ireland) Ltd	Dublin	
			N970C/F-WZMU		(Household Commercial Services)		
EI-EAD	Airbus A.300B4-203F	289	(N922C)	R	Air Contractors (Ireland) Ltd	Dublin	
			N13972/N972C/F-WZMM (Household Commercial Services)				
EI-EAT	Airbus A.300B4-203F	116	F-WQFR	16.12.97	Air Contractors (Ireland) Ltd (DHL c/s)		
			D-ASAY/SU-BCB/F-WZES		Pyramid Leasing Inc Dublin/East Midlands		
EI-ECA	Agusta A.109A II	7387	N109RP	28. 2.97	Backdrive Ltd	Drogheda	A12.98
			JA9662		(Op Ace Helicopters Ltd)		
EI-EDR	PA-28R-200 Cherokee Arrow II		G-BCGD	19.11.87	Victor Mike F/C Ltd	Dublin	A11.98
		28R-7435265	N9628N				
EI-EEC	PA-23-250 Aztec E	27-7554045	G-SATO	6. 2.92	Westair Avn Ltd	Shannon	A9.98
			G-BCXP/N54257				
EI-EIO	PA-34-200T Seneca II	34-7670274	N6257J	1.10.91	K.A.O'Connor	Weston	A12.98
EI-ETC	Aeronca 15AC Sedan	15AC-429	G-CETC	9.10.93	H.Moreau	Ballyboy, Co.Meath	
			EI-ETC				
EI-EXP	Short SD.3-30 Var.100	SH.3092	G-BKMU	23. 7.92	Ireland Airways Holdings Ltd	Dublin	
		SE-IYO/G-BKMU/G-14-3092/EI-BEH/EI-BEG/G-14-3092 (For Westair Cargo, Shannon 2.98)					
EI-FKA	Fokker 50	20118	PH-LMA	18. 1.89	Aer Lingus Commuter plc	Dublin	
			PH-EXB		"St.Fintan/Fionntan"		
EI-FKB	Fokker 50	20119	PH-LMB	17. 2.89	Aer Lingus Commuter plc	Dublin	
			PH-EXC		"St.Fergal/Fearghal"		
EI-FKC	Fokker 50	20177	PH-EXC	23. 2.90	Aer Lingus Commuter plc	Dublin	
					"St.Fidelma/Fedeilme"		
EI-FKD	Fokker 50	20181	PH-EXG	12. 4.90	Aer Lingus Commuter plc	Dublin	
					"St.Flannan/Flannan"		
EI-FKE	Fokker 50	20208	PH-EXA	28. 1.91	Aer Lingus Commuter plc	Dublin	
					"St.Pappin/Paipan"		
EI-FKF	Fokker 50	20209	PH-EXE	8. 2.91	Aer Lingus Commuter plc	Dublin	
					"St.Ultan/Ultan"		
EI-FLY	Socata TB-9 Tampico	186	G-BIRA	13.10.93	Hotel Bravo F/C Ltd "Goldangel"	Weston	
					(Crashed Weston 3.1.99 & w/o)		
EI-GER	Maule MX7-180A Star Rocket	20006C		7. 1.94	P.J.Lanigan Ryan	Trim	A8.98
EI-GFC	Socata TB-9 Tampico	141	G-BIAA	9.10.93	B.McGrath, J.Ryan & D.O'Neill	Waterford	A8.98
EI-GHL	Bell 206B Jet Ranger III	3379	N16Q	4. 2.97	Marwing Trading Ltd (Op ICC Bank)		A9.98
			N2069A			Dromahane, Mallow,Co.Cork	
EI-GSM	Cessna 182S	182-80188	N9541Q	17. 6.98	Westpoint F/Grp Ltd	Dublin	A11.98
EI-GWY	Cessna 172R Skyhawk	172-80162	N9497F	31.12.97	Galway Flying Club Ltd	Galway	A10.98
EI-HAM	Light-Aero Avid Flyer	1072-90		18.11.96	H.Goulding	Bray, Co.Wicklow	
	(Rotax 582)						
EI-HCA	Boeing 727-225F	20382	N8839E	15. 4.94	Air Contractors (Ireland) Ltd "Eagle/Iolar"		
					(TTC Hunt 11 Leasing Corp) Dublin/East Midlands		
EI-HCB	Boeing 727-223F	19492	N6817	2. 9.95	Air Contractors (Ireland) Ltd		
			EI-HCB/N6817 (TTC Hunt 11 Leasing Corp) Dublin/East Midlands				
EI-HCC	Boeing 727-223F	19480	N6805	26. 9.95	Air Contractors (Ireland) Ltd		
					(TTC Hunt 11 Leasing Corp) Dublin/East Midlands		

Regn	Type	C/n	P/I	Date	Owner/operator	Probable Base	Remarks
EI-HCD	Boeing 727-223F	20185	N6832	8.11.95	Air Contractors (Ireland) Ltd		
					(TTC Hunt 11 Leasing Corp) Dublin/East Midlands		
EI-HCF	Lockheed L.188PF Electra	1138	G-FIJR	R	Hunting Cargo Airlines (Ireland) Ltd		
			C-FIJR/CF-IJR/N134US			Dublin/East Midlands	
EI-HCI	Boeing 727-223F	20183	N6830	23. 5.95	Air Contractors (Ireland) Ltd		
					(TTC Hunt 11 Leasing Corp) Dublin/East Midlands		
EI-HCS	Grob G-109B	6414	G-BMHR	18. 8.95	H.Sydner	Boleybeg, Ballymore Castle	A3.98
EI-HER	Bell 206B JetRanger III	3408	G-HIER	1. 7.94	SELC Ireland Ltd & Ptnrs		
			G-BRFD/N2069N			Belmullet, Co.Mayo	A11.98
EI-IRV	Aerospatiale AS.350B Ecureuil	1713	D-HENY	7.10.96	Santail Ltd (Op Eddie Irvine)	Weston	A6.98
EI-JAK	Pearce Jabiru UL	0144 & SAAC 68		9. 7.98	S.Walshe	Waterford	A8.98
EI-JBC	Agusta A.109A	7126	F-GATN	24. 7.97	Medeva Properties Ltd	Dublin	A11.98
EI-JFK	Airbus A.330-301	086	F-GMDE	11. 7.95	Aer Lingus plc "St.Colmcille"	Dublin	
EI-JWM	Robinson R-22 Beta	1386	G-BSLB	21.11.92	C.Shiel	Weston	A5.98
EI-LAX	Airbus A.330-202	269	F-WWKV	R	Air Lingus plc		
					(For delvy 5.99)		
EI-LCH	Boeing 727-281F	20466	N903PG	6. 2.95	Air Contractors (Ireland) Ltd "Sylvia"		
			N527MD/HL7355/JA8332 (TTC Hunt 11 Leasing Corp) Dublin/East Midlands					
EI-LIT	MBB Bo.105S	S.434	A6-DBH	20. 2.96	Irish Helicopters Ltd	Cork	A12.98
			Dubai 105/D-HDMH				
EI-LRS	Schweizer Hughes 269C	S.1701	N41S	6. 3.95	Lynch Roofing Systems Ltd	Galway	
EI-MAC	Robinson R-22 Beta	1433	G-OHHL	18. 4.97	McAuliffe Trucking Ltd		
						Castleisland, Co.Kerry	
EI-MAT	Pearce Jabiru UL	0129 & SAAC 66		9. 7.98	M.Tormey	Abbeyshrule	A9.98
EI-MES	Sikorsky S-61N	61776	G-BXAE	27. 3.97	Bond Helicopters (Ireland) Ltd	Shannon	A8.98
			LN-OQO		(Op Irish Marine Emergency Service)		
EI-MIP	Aerospatiale SA.365N Dauphin 2	6119	G-BLEY	20. 3.96	Bond Helicopters (Ireland) Ltd	Cork	A9.98
			F-WTNM				
(EI-MLA)	Fokker F-27 Friendship 600	10304	HZ-KA8	R	NTU		
			VH-FNO/PH-FIY				
EI-ONE	Bell 206B JetRanger	1761	EI-CJM	30. 5.96	E.M.Corcoran	Dublin Heliport	A6.98
			N281C/N49582				
EI-ORD	Airbus A.330-301	059	(EI-USA)	6. 6.97	Aer Lingus plc "St.Ide"	Dublin	
			F-GMDD				
EI-PMI	Agusta-Bell 206B JetRanger III	8614	EI-BLG	19. 9.96	Ping Golf Equipment Ltd	Dublin	A8.98
			G-BIGS				
EI-POD	Cessna 177B Cardinal	177B-02729	N1444C	3. 8.95	Trim Flying Club Ltd	Trim	A11.98
EI-RYR	Boeing Stearman	75-5736A	G-THEA	.99R	Ryanair	Swanton Morley	
			N1733B		"Spirit of Tipperary" (See SECTION 1 for full history)		
EI-SAR	Sikorsky S-61N	61-143	G-AYOM	26. 6.98	Bond Helicopters (Ireland) Ltd	Shannon	A12.98
		(Mitsubishi c/n M61-001)	N4585/JA9506/N94565		(Op Irish Marine Emergency Service)		
EI-SHN	Airbus A.330-301	054	F-WWKJ	27. 4.94	Aer Lingus plc	Dublin	
					"St.Flannan/Flannan"		
EI-STR	Bell 430	53282	N44504	R	Westair Aviation	Shannon	
					(Delivered 27.10.98)		
EI-SXT	Canadair CL.600 Challenger 3R	5159	C-FTNN	25. 4.95	S Ireland Ltd	Zurich	A11.98
			C-GLWR				
EI-TAR	Bell 222A	47029	N121NN	10. 9.98	Westair Ltd	Jersey	
			N121NC/N120NC		(Leased to Confucious Ltd)		
EI-TCK	Cessna 421A	421A-0038	G-AXAW	5.11.91	Dr.T.C.Killeen	Weston	
			N2238Q				
EI-TKI	Robinson R-22 Beta	1195	G-OBIP	22. 8.91	J.McDaid	Weston	A6.98
EI-TLB	Airbus A.300B4-103	012	F-GIJU	2. 4.96	Airplanes Holdings Ltd	Dublin	
			G-BMNC/D-AMAX/F-WLGC (Op TransAer)				
EI-TLE	Airbus A.320-231	429	D-AORX	25. 9.93	TransAer International Airlines Ltd		
			N429RX/F-WWIZ		"Caitlin Shlgigh"	Newark, USA	
					(Leased Transmeridian Winter 1998/99)		
EI-TLF	Airbus A.320-231	476	F-WWBR	10. 6.94	TransAer International Airlines Ltd		
						St.Petersburg, Russia	
					(Leased Transmeridian Winter 1998/99)		
EI-TLG	Airbus A.320-231	428	C-GMPG	20. 5.94	TransAer International Airlines Ltd	???	
			EI-TLG/C-GMPG/EI-TLG/(D-ANDY)/N391LF/F-WWIL				
					(Op Novair Airlines)		
EI-TLH	Airbus A.320-231	247	G-OALA	22.12.94	TransAer International Airlines Ltd		
			EI-TLH/N247RX/F-WWDK (Leased Cubana 11.98-5.01)			(Cuba)	
EI-TLI	Airbus A.320-231	405	N141LF	26. 5.95	TransAer International Airlines Ltd		
			HC-BTV/N441LF/F-WWDK			Philadelphia, USA	
					(Leased Transmeridian Winter 1998/99)		
EI-TLJ	Airbus A.320-231	257	N257RX	29. 9.95	TransAer International Airlines Ltd		
			LZ-ABA/F-WWBI		(Leased Cubana 11.98)	(Cuba)	
EI-TLK	Airbus A.300B4-203	161	N226GE	12. 3.97	GECAS Technical Services Ltd	Dublin	
			TC-JUV/N226EA/F-GBNU (Op TransAer)				
EI-TLL	Airbus A.300B4-203	158	N225GE	20. 6.97	GECAS Technical Services Ltd		
			TC-JUY/N225EA/F-GBNT			Karachi, Pakistan	
					(Leased PIA 11.98-4.99)		
EI-TLM	Airbus A.300B4-203	046	RP-C8882	18. 9.97	TransAer International Airlines Ltd		
			SX-BEB/F-WZER/F-WZEK/F-WLGB			Dublin	

Regn	Type	C/n	P/I	Date	Owner/operator	Probable Base	Remarks
EI-TLO	Airbus A.320-232	758	F-WWDC	9. 1.98	TransAer International Airlines Ltd (Op Novair Airlines)	Dublin	
EI-TLP	Airbus A.320-232	760	F-WWDD	20. 1.98	TransAer International Airlines Ltd (Leased Aeropostal 11.98)	Dublin	
EI-TLQ	Airbus A.300B4-203	131	6Y-JMK G-BIMB/F-WZEL	2. 4.98	Airplanes Finance Ltd (TransAer International Airlines)		
EI-TLR	Airbus A.320-231	414	B-HYR VR-HYR/F-WWIU	16. 6.98	TransAer International Airlines Ltd	Dublin	
EI-TLS	Airbus A.320-231	430	(N430CR) B-HYS/VR-HYS/F-WWBH	19. 8.98	TransAer International Airlines Ltd (Leased Transmeridian Winter 1998/99)	Philadephia, USA	
EI-TVA	Boeing 737-43Q	28489	B-18671	21.11.98	Aldebaran FSE-One Corp Op Virgin Express (Ireland) Ltd	Shannon	
EI-TVB	Boeing 737-43Q	28493	B-18676	9.12.98	Virgin Express (Ireland) Ltd	Shannon	
EI-TVC to EI-TVM	Reserved for Virgin Express (Ireland) Ltd 1999						
EI-TVN	Boeing 737-36N	28586	N1768B	19. 1.99	Virgin Express (Ireland) Ltd	Shannon	
EI-TVO to EI-TVZ	Reserved for Virgin Express (Ireland) Ltd 1999						
EI-TWO	Type unknown			12.12.96R	P.A.Wynne		
EI-UFO	PA-22-150 Tri-Pacer (Tail-wheel conversion)	22-4942	G-BRZR N7045D	12. 2.94	W.Treacy	Trim	
EI-VIP	Hughes 269C	21-1024	G-BOTS EI-VIP/G-BOTS/N13048/(N229SC)/N1105Z	27. 3.95	Cloughran Helicopter Club Ltd	Weston	
EI-WAC	PA-23-250 Aztec E	27-4683	G-AZBK N14077	26. 5.95	Westair Avn Ltd	Shannon	A8.98
EI-WAV	Bell 430	49028	N4213V	24.12.97	Westair Avn Ltd	Shannon	A12.98
EI-WCC	Robinson R-22 Beta	1044	G-OLUM	30.10.93	Westair Avn Ltd	Shannon	
EI-WDC	HS.125 Srs.3B	25132	G-OCBA EI-WDC/G-OCBA/G-MRFB/G-AZVS/OY-DKP	2. 7.94	Westair Avn Ltd	Shannon	A12.98
EI-WGV	Gulfstream G.1159 Gulfstream V	505	N505GV	21.11.97	Westair Avn Ltd	Shannon	A12.98
EI-WHE	Beechcraft B200 Super King Air	BB-1569	VP-CHE N20505	7. 5.98	Westair Avn Ltd	Shannon	
EI-XMA	Robinson R-22 Beta	0681	G-BNVC	20.10.87	Westair Avn Ltd (Xtravision c/s) (Op for RTE 2 as "Eye in the Sky")	Dublin	
EI-XMC	Robinson R-22 Beta	1655		17. 5.91	McAuliffe Photographic Laboratories Ltd (Crashed Dingle Harbour, Co.Kerry 31.5.92; wreck to store)	Dublin	

Registrations awaited:

Regn	Type	C/n	P/I	Date	Owner/operator	Probable Base	Remarks
EI-...	Bensen B8MV	PFA G/01-1044	G-BKZJ	.99	(Cancelled by CAA 22.12.98)		
EI-EA.	Airbus A.300B4-203F	152	N221EA F-GBNP	R	Air Contractors (Ireland) Ltd		
EI-EA.	Airbus A.300B4-203F	259	N885PA TC-ALG/OB-1634/(AP-BFG)/SE-DSG/N72990/(N990C)/N232EA/F-GBNZ	R	Air Contractors (Ireland) Ltd		

SECTION 3A - THE BRITISH GLIDING ASSOCIATION REGISTER

The BGA Register shows the "three-letter" registration (or "trigraph") system sometimes marked on the tails of gliders and the corresponding BGA number, or Certificate of Airworthiness reference, as issued by the BGA. This is usually found below the tailplane in small characters. The identities marked + are gliders known to be wearing their three-letter trigraphs. BGA Competition Numbers etc are also shown where these are known to be carried. More details of these are contained in SECTIONS 3F & 3G. The official BGA list is extended by including non-current gliders and those with recently lapsed Certificates of Airworthiness (CA) for which no cancellation details are known but may survive. These are identified by "*" in the CA expiry column.

Many thanks, once again, to Phil Butler and Wal Gandy for updating the BGA register and to Tony Morris for his further notes. Special thanks are given to the British Gliding Assocation's Secretary, Barry Rolfe, for his valued assistance. We are grateful to Richard Causey for additional observations. The information is current to 1.2.99.

Regn	BGA No.	Type	C/n	P/I	Regn	Owner/operator	Probable Base	CA Expy
AAA-AZZ								
-	162	Manuel Willow Wren	-		9.34	M.L.Beach "The Willow Wren" (Extant 7.97) Dunstable		*
AAA	231	Abbott-Baynes Scud II (b. Slingsby)	215B	G-ALOT BGA.231	8.35	M.L.Beach (On display 3.96) Brooklands		9.95*
(AAF)	236	Slingsby T.6 Kite 1	27A	G-ALUD BGA.236/(BGA.222)	11.35	(Stored pending rebuild 12.95) Dunstable		*
AAX	251	Slingsby T.6 Kite 1	227A	(ex RAF) BGA.251	3.36	R.Boyd Chipping		5.99
ABG	260	Schleicher Rhonsperber	32-16		5.36	F.K.Russell t/a Rhonsperber Syndicate Dunstable		7.99
(ABN)	266	Slingsby T.1 Falcon 1 Waterglider	237A		5.36	Windermere Steamboat Museum (On display 5.95) Windermere		*
ABZ	277	Grunau Baby 2 (b. F.Coleman)	?	RAFGSA.270 BGA.277/G-ALKU/BGA.277	8.36	J.L.Smoker & Ptnrs Weston-on-the-Green		7.95*
ACF	283	Abbott-Baynes Scud III	2	G-ALJR BGA.283	12.36	L.P.Woodage "Scud III" Dunstable		9.98
ACH	285	Slingsby T.6 Kite 1	247A	G-ALNH BGA.285	12.36	E.B.Scott AAC Middle Wallop (On loan to The Museum of Army Flying) (As "G285/E" in 1 GTS RAF c/s) (On display 5.94)		5.99*
ADJ	310	Slingsby T.6 Kite 1 (Rebuilt 1982 with components from BGA.327 c/n 285A)	258B		2.37	A.M.Maufe Tibenham		8.99
AEM	337	Schleicher Rhonbussard	620	G-ALME BGA.337	4.38	C.Wills & S.White Booker		3.96
AGE	378	Slingsby T.12 Gull I	312A	G-ALPJ BGA.378	9.38	T.Smallwood & Ptnrs Booker		5.97
AGW	394	Slingsby T.6 Kite 1 (Rebuild of BGA.317 c/n 277A)	331A		3.39	J.S.Allison RAF Halton		6.98
AHC	400	Slingsby T.6 Kite 1 (Wings from Special T.6 c/n 355A)	336A	VD165 BGA.400	5.39	R.Hadlow & Ptnrs Brooklands (As "F" in 1 GTS RAF c/s) (On display 11.93)		4.97
AHU	416	Scott Viking 1	114	G-ALRD BGA.416	6.39	L.Glover (As "G-ALRD") Husbands Bosworth		5.99
AHW	418	Slingsby T.13 Petrel 1	348A	G-ALNP BGA.418	.39	R.I.Davidson Husbands Bosworth		5.97
AJW +	442	Slingsby T.8 Tutor	MHL/RC/8	G-ALMX BGA.442	8.46	M.Hodgson Dunstable		8.98
(AKC)	448	DFS 108-68 Weihe (Damaged Thun, Switzerland 20.7.79)	000348	G-ALJW BGA.448/LO+WQ	6.47	D.Philips Solihull (On rebuild 1994)		*
AKD	449	DFS/70 Olympia-Meise	227	LF+VO	7.47	L.S.Phillips (Stored)Perranporth		5.85*
AKW	466	Slingsby T.8 Tutor	MHL/RT/7		11.46	D.Kitchen Tibenham		7.96
(ALA)	470	Short Nimbus	S.1312		.47	Ulster Folk & Transport Museum (Stored 6.97) Holywood, Belfast		8.75*
ALR	485	Slingsby T.8 Tutor	513	G-ALPE BGA.485	11.46	M.H.Birch Booker		6.97
ALW	490	Hutter H-17A (Built D.Campbell)	-	G-ALRK BGA.490	8.48	G.Saw & N.I.Newton Booker (Also wears "G-ALRK")		4.99
(ALX)	491	Hawkridge Dagling	08471		2.47	N.H.Ponsford (Stored 1.98) (Breighton)		*
(ALZ)	493	Hawkridge Nacelle Dagling	10471		7.47	P. & D.Underwood (On rebuild 12.95) Eaton Bray (Also allotted BAPC.81)		*
AMK +	503	EoN AP.5 Olympia 2	EoN/O/003	G-ALJP BGA.503	5.47	D.T.Staff Booker		5.95*
AMP	507	EoN AP.5 Olympia 2	EoN/O/008	G-ALJO BGA.507	6.47	M.Briggs Cranfield		6.95*
AMR +	509	EoN AP.5 Olympia 2	EoN/O/011	G-ALLA BGA.509	5.47	B.Perkins Rhigos		10.97
AMT +	511	EoN AP.5 Olympia 2	EoN/O/005	G-ALLM BGA.511	5.47	E.W.Burgess Lyveden		7.97

Regn	BGA No.	Type	C/n	P/I	Regn	Owner/operator	Probable Base	CA Expy
AMW +	514	EoN AP.5 Olympia 2	EoN/O/015	G-ALKM BGA.514	6.47	M R.Fox	Pocklington	10.99
ANW +	538	EoN AP.5 Olympia 2B	EoN/O/040	G-ALNE BGA.538	7.47	D.C.Phillips	Snitterfield	1.99
APC +	544	EoN AP.5 Olympia 2	EoN/O/046	G-ALMJ BGA.544	9.47	J.Graham & Ptnrs	Seighford	5.98
APV	561	EoN AP.5 Olympia 2B	EoN/O/032	G-ALKN BGA.561	6.47	A.Kepley t/a Fenland & West Norfolk Aviation Museum (Stored 8.97) Crowland		8.78*
APZ	565	Slingsby T.25 Gull 4	505	G-ALPB (BGA.565)	.	E.A.Arthur	Tibenham	8.99
AQE	570	Slingsby T.21B	538	G-ALNJ BGA.570		Not known (Stored pending rebuild 10.97) Camphill		*
(AQG)	572	Slingsby T.21B Sedbergh TX.1	539	8884M VX275/BGA.572	.	RAF Museum (Stored 5.93) RAF Cardington		*
AQH	573	Slingsby T.21B	540	G-ALJU BGA.573	.	(To Zimbabwe)		9.90*
AQN	578	Hawkridge Grunau Baby 2B	G.3348	G-ALSO BGA.578	.48	R G Hood	Lasham	7.99
(AQQ)	580	EoN AP.7 Primary	EoN/P/003	G-ALPS BGA.580	.	Imperial War Museum (Stored)	Duxford	*
AQY	588	EoN AP.7 Primary	EoN/P/011		.	N.H.Ponsford (Stored 1.98) (Breighton)		*
(AQZ)	589	EoN AP.7 Primary	EoN/P/012	G-ALMN BGA.589	.	Not known (Farnborough) (Stored 1992)		4.51*
ARK +	599	Slingsby T.30A Prefect	548	PH-1 BGA.599/G-ALLF/BGA.599 (As "G-ALLF")	.	K.M.Fresson	Parham Park	7.99
ARM +	601	Slingsby T.21B	543	G-ALKX BGA.601	8.48	Surrey Hills GC	Kenley	5.99
ART +	606	EoN AP.5 Olympia 2	EoN/O/078	RAFGSA.266 BGA.703/G-ALLB/BGA.606	5.48	G3 Syndicate (To N606BG 6.97)		6.97
ASB	614	Slingsby T.21B	549	RNGSA G-ALLT/BGA.614	9.48	J.L.Rolls & Ptnrs "T42"	Talgarth	6.99
ASC	615	Grunau Baby 2B (Built by Hawkridge)	G-4848	G-ALMM BGA.615	2.49	C.D.Stainer & Ptnrs (Stored 8.95 - but possibly sold in Germany) Rufforth		8.94*
ASN	625	Slingsby T.30B Prefect	567	G-ALPC BGA.625	1.49	Culdrose GC "T30"	Culdrose	5.96
(ASR)	628	EoN AP.8 Baby	EoN/B/004	G-ALRU BGA.628	3.49	Not known Aston Down (Crashed Bardney 28.5.71; stored 9.98)		*
AST	629	EoN AP.8 Baby (Currently regd as G-ALRH)	EoN/B/005	G-ALRH BGA.629	3.49	EoN Baby Syndicate "Liver Bird" (As "G-ALRH") (Extant 9.97) Chipping		9.96
ATH	643	Slingsby T.15 Gull III	364A	TJ711	11.49	M.L.Beach (On display 3.96) Brooklands		9.94*
ATL	646	Slingsby T.21B	536	G-ALKS	6.50	G.Markham (Stored 3.97)	Enstone	7.96
ATR	651	Slingsby T.13 Petrel 1	361A	EI-101 IGA.101/IAC.101/BGA.651/G-ALPP	7.50	G.Saw	Booker	7.98
ATV	655	Zlin 24 Krajanek	101	G-ALMP OK-8592	4.50	M.H.Birch (As "OK-8592")	Booker	4.99
AUD	663	Slingsby T.26 Kite 2B	727		1.52	R.S.Hooper "663"	Dunstable	5.99
AUG	666	Slingsby T.21B	643		6.51	Cambridge University GC Gransden Lodge		6.99
AUJ	668	Slingsby T.21B (Built by Aero & Engineering)	639		6.51	Not known (Stored 7.97) Rufforth (Damaged Feshiebridge 16.7.85)		6.86*
AUP	673	Slingsby T.21B	636		7.51	Portsmouth Naval GC (RNGSA.N21) Lee-on-Solent		3.99
AUU +	678	EoN AP.5 Olympia	EoN/O/076		4.52	J.M.Lee	Parham Park	7.99
AUW	680	Avia 40P	117		8.52	F.Ragot	Booker	7.98
AVA	684	Abbott-Baynes Scud III	3		1.53	E.A.Hull	Dunstable	6.99
AVB +	685	Slingsby T.34 Sky	644	G-644	2.53	R.Moyse	Lasham	3.99
AVC +	686	Slingsby T.34 Sky	670		3.53	P.J.Teagle "Kinder Scout II" Sutton Bank		8.99
AVD +	687	Eon AP.5 Olympia 2	EoN/O/092		3.53	A.C.Jarvis	Parham Park	7.98
AVF +	689	Slingsby T.26 Kite 2A	728	RAFGSA.294 BGA.689	4.53	P.M.Warren "Percy"	Tatenhill	8.99
AVL	694	Slingsby T.34 Sky	671	G-671	5.53	M.P.Wakem	Long Mynd	6.99
AVQ	698	Slingsby T.34 Sky	645	G-645	8.53	Miss A.G.Veitch & B.Middleton "Gertie" "G" Easterton		6.99
AVT	701	Slingsby T.30B Prefect	857	AGA... BGA.701	1.53	Booker GC	Booker	4.99
AWD	711	Slingsby T.21B	950		9.54	D.B.Brown t/a T.21 Syndicate Chipping		6.99
AWU +	726	EoN AP.5 Olympia 2	EoN/O/082		5.55	M J Riley	Cranfield	3.99
AWX +	729	Slingsby T.41 Skylark 2	946		1.56	R.Burtenshaw & Ptnrs	Cranfield	7.99
AWZ +	731	Slingsby T.7 Cadet	SSK/FF/169	RA847	1.57	R.Moyse	Lasham	5.99

Regn	BGA No.	Type	C/n	P/I	Regn	Owner/operator	Probable Base	CA Expy
AXB +	733	Slingsby T.41 Skylark 2	926		2.55	A.L.Shaw	Lyveden	3.99
AXD +	735	Slingsby T.43 Skylark 3	1014		.55	F.G.T.Birlison	Aston Down	3.99
AXE +	736	Slingsby T.43 Skylark 3	1029		3.57	R.J.Hopkins & Ptnrs	Snitterfield	5.98
AXJ	740	Slingsby T.42A Eagle 2	994		.55	P.C.Horn t/a The Eagle Syndicate	Parham Park	3.99
AXL	742	Slingsby T.43 Skylark 3	1030		6.56	M.Chalmers & Ptnrs	Kingston Deverill	2.99
AXP +	745	Slingsby T.41 Skylark 2	949		4.55	M.Sanderson	Milfield	3.99
AXR	747	Slingsby T.41 Skylark 2	945		.56	Lincolnshire GC	Strubby	5.98
AXU +	750	Slingsby T.41 Skylark 2	944		3.55	M.A.Langhurst	Halesland	6.95*
AYD +	759	Slingsby T.41 Skylark 2	1048		.56	J.R.Dickson	Currock Hill	5.99
AYF +	761	Slingsby T.43 Skylark 3B	1058		9.56	A.Jenkins	Enstone	9.98
AYH +	763	Slingsby T.43 Skylark 3B	1066		.56	A.Griffiths	Crowland	7.97
AYY	778	Slingsby T.41 Skylark 2C	1073		.56	H.Johnson "33"	Long Mynd	6.96
AZA +	780	Slingsby T.42 Eagle 3	1085	RNGSA 2-08 BGA.780		J.M.Crewe	Weston on the Green	6.99
AZC	782	Slingsby T.21B	1096		5.57	C.Stachulla	(Augsberg)	8.99
AZF	785	Slingsby T.30B Prefect	1100		.56	L.J.Smith t/a The Prefect Syndicate	Culdrose	3.96*
AZK	789	Slingsby T.8 Tutor	-	VM650	6.57	Not known (Stored 5.93)	Croft, Skegness	7.90*
AZP	793	Slingsby T.41 Skylark 2	999		1.57	G.Dixon & Ptnr "136"	Currock Hill	8.97
AZQ	794	Slingsby T.8 Tutor	-	VM687	.57	J.M.Brookes (As "VM687")	Strubby	10.98
AZR +	795	EoN AP.5 Olympia 2	EoN/O/101		7.58	S.Mooring	Dunstable	7.95*
AZT	797	EoN AP.5 Olympia 2	EoN/O/063	ZS-GCM	3.57	J.Starling	Camphill	8.99
AZY +	802	Slingsby T.41 Skylark 2 (mod)	963		4.57	A.J.Jackson	Burn	6.97

Regn	BGA No.	Type	C/n	P/I	Regn	Owner/operator	Probable Base	CA Expy

BAA-BZZ

Regn	BGA No.	Type	C/n	P/I	Regn	Owner/operator	Probable Base	CA Expy
BAA	804	Slingsby T.8 Tutor	931	XE761 VM589	5.57	A.Chadwick	Rufforth	3.97

(A Cadet TX.1 purporting to be "BGA.804 ex VM589" is stored by Midland Air Museum, Coventry 12.97; this came from Perranporth in 1968)

Regn	BGA No.	Type	C/n	P/I	Regn	Owner/operator	Probable Base	CA Expy
BAC	806	Slingsby T.43 Skylark 3B	1101	RNGSA CU19 BGA.806	6.58	M.Stokeld	Carlton Moor	5.97
BAH +	810	Slingsby T.41 Skylark 2	1104		7.58	B.Jackson	Cranfield	9.97
BAM +	814	Slingsby T.41 Skylark 2	1108		1.58	B.Thwaites	Wormingford	4.99
BAN	815	Slingsby T.30B Prefect	1120		1.58	J.S.Allison	Halton	11.98
BAV +	822	Slingsby T.41 Skylark 2B	1113		2.58	T.Cushion	Kingston Deverill	7.97
BAW +	823	Slingsby T.43 Skylark 3B	1126		2.58	D.Heslop	North Weald	5.99
BAY +	825	Slingsby T.42B Eagle 3	1116		3.58	M.Lodge	Cranwell	5.99
BAZ +	826	Slingsby T.41 Skylark 2	1112		3.58	W.Fuller	Currock Hill	5.99
BBA +	827	Slingsby T.41 Skylark 2	1128		3.58	M.Bosher	Winthorpe	5.99
BBB +	828	Slingsby T.42B Eagle 3	1118		4.58	I.K.Mitchell	North Hill	7.99
(BBG)	833	Slingsby T.8 Tutor	-	VW535	9.57	Not known (On rebuild 12.95) Dunstable		*
BBH +	834	EoN Olympia 2	EoN/O/041	BGA.539	8.57	J.W.Bonham	Cranfield	6.99
BBQ +	841	Slingsby T.42B Eagle 3	1115		5.58	Eagle Syndicate	Milfield	6.99
BBT +	844	Slingsby T.43 Skylark 3B	1134	RAFGSA.234 BGA.844	.58	J.P.Gilbert	Wormingford	4.99
BBU +	845	Slingsby T.41 Skylark 2B	1135		.58	J.A.Timpany	Lleweni Parc	11.97
(BCB)	852	Slingsby T.8 Tutor	-	TS291	7.58	Royal Museum of Scotland - Museum of Flight (As "TS291") (On display 3.96)	East Fortune	*
BCF	856	Slingsby T.21B (Built Leighton Park School)	1		10.58	P.Underwood (Stored 12.95)	Eaton Bray	*
BCH +	858	Slingsby T.8 Tutor	SSK/FF/489	VM547	9.58	N.James	Lyveden	5.99
BCK	860	EoN AP.5 Olympia 2B	EoN/O/081		4.59	C.D.Street	Lasham	7.99
BCL +	861	Slingsby T.43 Skylark 3B	1139		9.58	R.Aylett	Bidford	5.96
BCP +	864	Slingsby T.43 Skylark 3B	1140		11.58	M Cummings	Milfield	2.99
BCS	867	Slingsby T.43 Skylark 3B	1144		12.58	M.Wright & Ptnrs "549"	Wormingford	4.99
BCU	869	Slingsby T.21B	1148		1.59	Not known "2" (Stored)	North Connel	*
BCV +	870	Slingsby T.43 Skylark 3B	1195		4.59	W R Davis "155"	Parham Park	2.99
BCW +	871	Slingsby T.43 Skylark 3B	1147		3.59	I.Tittensor	Bidford	10.97
BCX +	872	Slingsby T.41 Skylark 2B	1197		4.59	G W Haworth	Tibenham	9.98
BCY +	873	Slingsby T.45 Swallow	1198		4.59	D.C Urwin "T45"	Talgarth	6.99
BDA	875	Slingsby T.21B	1205	AGA.7 BGA.875	6.59	W Grobkinsey (Stored 8.98)	Edgehill	5.99
BDF +	880	Slingsby T.42B Eagle 3	1213		9.59	D.C.Phillips	Long Mynd	4.99
BDM +	886	Slingsby T.21B	1216		11.59	D.G.Cooper	Wormingford	7.98
BDR +	890	Slingsby T.45 Swallow	1243		6.60	Channel GC	Waldershare Park	7.98
BDW	895	Slingsby T.8 Tutor TX.2	-	VM637	4.59	R.Patrick & Ptnrs (On rebuild 1.96) (Probably to be as "VM637")	Winthorpe	6.93*
BDX +	896	Slingsby T.41 Skylark 2 (Built C Hurst)	CH.095/1		6.59	H D Maddams	Wormingford	7.99
BEA +	899	Slingsby T.41 Skylark 2	1194		7.59	M.L.Ryan	Hullavington	8.98
BED	902	Slingsby T.12 Gull I	-	VW912(?)	5.59	Royal Museum of Scotland - Museum of Flight	East Fortune	*
BEF +	904	Slingsby T.8 Tutor (Frame No SSK/FF 934)	-	(ex RAF)	10.59	D.Chaplin (Tutor Syndicate)	Sutton Bank	5.96
BEL +	909	EoN AP.5 Olympia 2B	EoN/O/126		12.59	J.G.Gilbert & Ptnrs	Wormingford	2.99
BEM +	910	Slingsby T.45 Swallow	1221		2.60	I.D.Smith	Kingston Deverill	8.97
BER +	914	Slingsby T.43 Skylark 3B	1225		3.60	K.V.Payne	Bryngwyn Bach	2.99
BET	916	Slingsby T.43 Skylark 3B	1227		3.60	A.C.Robertson & Ptnrs "600"	Feshiebridge	5.98
BEX +	920	Slingsby T.43 Skylark 3F	1229		4.60	P.J.Mortimer	Rivar Hill	7.99
BEY	921	Slingsby T.45 Swallow	1230		4.60	R.C.Martin	Lasham	5.99
BEZ +	922	Slingsby T.43 Skylark 3F	1232		4.60	J.Shaw & Ptnrs	Perranporth	7.99
BFB	924	Slingsby T.45 Swallow	1235		5.60	D.Jones & Ptnrs	North Weald	8.99
BFC +	925	Slingsby T.43 Skylark 3F	1239		5.60	Strathclyde GC	Strathaven	8.99
BFD	926	Slingsby T.21B	1240	RAFGSA BGA.926	5.60	B.Jaessing	(Hamburg)	7.96*
BFE +	927	Slingsby T.43 Skylark 3F	1244		6.60	Essex Skylark Gliding Syndicate	North Weald	10.98
BFG	929	Slingsby T.43 Skylark 3F	1245		7.60	T.J.Wilkinson "161"	Sackville Lodge, Riseley	6.99
BFL +	933	Slingsby T.41 Skylark 2B	1220		5.60	D G Coats	Milfield	8.99
BFP	936	Schleicher Ka7 Rhonadler	702/60		5.60	Dartmoor GC (Damaged Brent Tor 15.11.95)	Brent Tor	4.96*

Regn	BGA No.	Type	C/n	P/I	Regn	Owner/operator	Probable Base	CA Expy
BFY +	945	Slingsby T.21B	1251	RAFGGA.515 RAFGSA.286/BGA.945	9.60	D.M.Hayes & Ptnrs	Sutton Bank	10.99
BGB	948	Slingsby T.21B (Robin EC-33)	1274	RAFGSA.282 BGA.948	11.60	Shenington GC (Stored 8.98)	Edgehill	12.97
BGD +	950	Slingsby T.43 Skylark 3F	1276		11.60	Essex University GC	Wormingford	8.99
BGG	953	Slingsby T.21B	1294		12.60	West Wales Gliding Trust	Templeton	3.98
BGH +	954	Slingsby T.43 Skylark 3F	1295		12.60	Glyndwr Soaring Club	Lleweni Parc	2.99
BGL +	957	Slingsby T.43 Skylark 3F	1296		3.61	C.Willey & Ptnrs	Eaglescott	4.99
BGP +	960	Slingsby T.21B	1297	RAFGSA.283 BGA.960	1.61	P.A.Dawson	Keevil	6.99
BGR +	962	EoN AP.5 Olympia 2B	EoN/O/124		6.60	M.H.Gagg	Cosford	1.00
BGT	964	DFS/30 Kranich II (Built AB Flygplan)	087	SE-STF Fv.8226	.60	C.Wills	Booker	4.96*
BGX	968	EoN AP.5 Olympia 2	EoN/O/123	(BGA.892)	8.60	C.Kominski	Eaglescott	7.97*
BGY +	969	Slingsby T.21B	558	SE-SHM	8.60	P.J.Wilby	Wormingford	8.98
BHC +	973	EoN AP.5 Olympia 2B	EoN/O/138		1.61	M Pedwell	Bidford	7.99
BHQ	985	Slingsby T.43 Skylark 3F	1304		4.61	R.Furness "760"	Cranfield	5.96
BHT +	988	Slingsby T.43 Skylark 3F	1306		4.61	K.Chichester & Ptnrs	Camphill	6.99
BHV +	990	Slingsby T.45 Swallow	1308	NEJSGSA.4 BGA.990	4.61	S.Thom	Lyveden	1.99
BJB +	996	Slingsby T.43 Skylark 3F (Built Jones, Pentelow & Saint)	SSK/JPS/1		4.61	R.A.Mills	Turweston	9.99
BJC +	997	EoN AP.5 Olympia 2B	EoN/O/135		4.61	A.Vidion & Ptnrs	Lyveden	6.99
BJD +	998	PZL SZD-9 bis Bocian 1D	P-391		5.61	D.L.Martlew (Bocian Syndicate)	Lasham	12.99
BJF +	1000	Slingsby T.21B	1309		6.61	Dukeries GC	Gamston	5.98
BJK	1004	Slingsby T.43 Skylark 3F	1311		7.61	F.J.Wiseman & Ptnrs	Wormingford	5.97*
BJP +	1008	Slingsby T.45 Swallow	1316		9.61	S R Grant	Stow Maries	8.99
BJQ +	1009	Slingsby T.49A Capstan	1314		.	L.Glover & Ptnrs	Husbands Bosworth	10.99
BJV	1014	Slingsby T.21B	556	SE-SHK	1.62	Royal Museum of Scotland - Museum of Flight	East Fortune	*
BJW	1015	Slingsby T.43 Skylark 3G	1321		3.62	J.B.Strzebrakowski "198"	Crowland	4.99
BJY +	1017	Slingsby T.45 Swallow	1324		3.62	C.Devine	Portmoak	9.99
BJZ	1018	Slingsby T.45 Swallow	1325		3.62	J.P.Marshall	North Connel	11.96*
BKA +	1019	Slingsby T.50 Skylark 4	1326	EI-117 BGA.1019	6.62	W.A.Horne	Camphill	5.99
BKC +	1021	DFS 108-68 Weihe (AB Flygindustri-built)	231	SE-SNE Fv.8312	4.61	B.Briggs	Cranwell	9.96*
BKE +	1023	Slingsby T.43 Skylark 3F (Built C Ross)	1715/CR/1		7.61	G.Smith	Kingston Deverill	4.99
BKJ +	1027	Schleicher Ka6CR	565/59	9G-AAR	7.61	P.M.Hogan	Sandhill Farm, Shrivenham	5.99
BKK	1028	EoN AP.5 Olympia 2	EoN/O/139	RNGSA.CU11 BGA.1028	7.61	J.Bradley	Thruxton	7.99
BKL +	1029	EoN AP.5 Olympia 2B	EoN/O/134		6.61	J.S.Orr	Lasham	5.99
BKN +	1031	Schleicher Ka7 Rhonadler	1091/61		9.61	East Sussex GC "B"	Ringmer	4.99
BKP +	1032	Slingsby T.45 Swallow	1203		10.61	E.Traynor	(Currock Hill)	10.96*
BKS +	1035	EoN AP.5 Olympia 2B	EoN/O/144		11.61	N W Woodward	Booker	3.99
BKU +	1037	EoN AP.5 Olympia 2B	EoN/O/153		1.62	D. & C.MacKay	Aboyne	4.99
BKW +	1039	Schleicher Ka6 Rhonsegler	295	OH-RSA	10.62	I.D.Macro	Rattlesden	4.99
BKX +	1040	EoN AP.5 Olympia 2B	EoN/O/148		3.62	E.T.Samways & Ptnrs	Old Sarum	6.99
BLA	1043	Slingsby T.50 Skylark 4	1331		5.62	I.A.Masterton "327"	Portmoak	6.96*
BLE +	1047	Slingsby T.50 Skylark 4	1335	RNGSA 1-228 BGA.1047	6.62	S.Frank "228"	Easterton	5.99
BLH +	1050	Slingsby T.50 Skylark 4	1338	RAFGSA BGA.1050	7.62	M.D.Cohler	Rufforth	4.99
BLJ +	1051	EoN AP.6 Olympia 419X	EoN/4/009		3.62	G.Balshaw & Ptnrs "Big Bird"	Lleweni Parc	10.96*
BLK	1052	EoN AP.6 Olympia 419X	EoN/4/007	G-APSX	4.62	C.J.Abbott & Ptnrs "Wild Goose" "67"	Long Mynd	5.99
BLL +	1053	Slingsby T.34 Sky	821	PH-203	4.62	M.Wilson	Burn	8.99
BLN +	1055	EoN AP.5 Olympia 2B	EoN/O/152		5.62	M.R.Derwent	Cranwell	2.98
BLP +	1056	EoN AP.5 Olympia 2B	EoN/O/149		3.62	D.Birtwhistle & Ptnrs (Stored 9.97)	Chipping	5.95*
BLQ +	1057	EoN AP.5 Olympia 2 Special	EoN/O/042	RAFGSA 145 BGA.540	7.62	R.C Patrick & Ptnrs	Winthorpe	5.99
BLS +	1059	EoN AP.5 Olympia 2B (EoN rebuild of BGA.897 c/n EoN/O/128)	EoN/O/151		7.62	D.J.Wilson	Seighford	11.97
BLU	1061	Slingsby T.45 Swallow	1340		7.62	Not known (Stored 1.98)	Burn	7.94*
BLW +	1063	Slingsby T.50 Skylark 4	1342		8.62	A.J.Preston	Dunstable	5.99
BLZ	1066	Slingsby T.50 Skylark 4	1346		11.62	R.M Lambert	Easterton	5.99
BML	1077	Slingsby T.45 Swallow	1328		6.62	Dartmoor GS	Burnford Common	7.97*

Regn	BGA No.	Type	C/n	P/I	Regn	Owner/operator	Probable Base	CA Expy
BMQ +	1081	Slingsby T.21B	1351		11.62	I H Davies	Seighford	7.99
BMU	1085	Slingsby T.21B (T) (Rotax 503)	1355	9G-ABD BGA.1085	12.62	D.Woolerton & Ptnrs "Spruce Goose"	East Kirkby	9.97
BMW +	1087	Slingsby T.50 Skylark 4	1357		12.62	M.J.R.Lindsay	Tibenham	6.98
BMX	1088	Slingsby T.50 Skylark 4	1358	RAFGSA.308 BGA.1088	1.63	C.B.Hogarth (789 Syndcate)	Nympsfield	4.99
BMY	1089	Slingsby T.50 Skylark 4	1361		1.63	J.Page "163"	Sutton Bank	4.98
BNA	1091	Shenstone Harbinger Mk.2	1		12.62	A.C.Wood	Camphill	7.97*
BNC	1093	DFS 108-68 Weihe (AB Kockums Flygindustri-built)	1	SE-SHU	3.63	K.S.Green	Lasham	8.99
BND +	1094	Schleicher Ka6CR	1157		3.63	E.G.Harris	Tibenham	6.99
BNE +	1095	Slingsby T.50 Skylark 4 (Reported as c/n 137<u>5</u>; 1343 was N707TN 7.98 & ex C-FOUA/CF-AUO)	1343		4.63	M.Rossiter & Ptnrs	Usk	5.99
BNH +	1098	Schleicher Ka6CR	6115		3.63	Bath, Wilts & N.Dorset GC	Kingston Deverill	3.99
BNK	1100	Slingsby T.50 Skylark 4	1362		2.63	E.D.Weekes & Ptnrs	Weston-on-the-Green	5.99
BNM	1102	Slingsby T.50 Skylark 4 (Reported as "BMN")	1367		3.63	D.Hertzburg	North Weald	5.99
BNN +	1103	Slingsby T.50 Skylark 4	1366		3.63	J R Robinson	Pocklington	12.98
BNP +	1104	Slingsby T.50 Skylark 4	1368		3.63	A.R.Worters "653"	Milfield	5.98
BNQ +	1105	Slingsby T.50 Skylark 4	1369		3.63	R Pye	Chipping	3.99
BNR +	1106	Slingsby T.49B Capstan	1370		8.63	A.R.Bushnell	Crowland	5.99
BNS	1107	Slingsby T.45 Swallow	1373	XS652 BGA.1107	3.63	York GC Swallow Syndicate (As "XS652")	Rufforth	4.99
BNU	1109	Slingsby T.45 Swallow	1377		5.63	K.D.Bagshaw	Lasham	5.97*
BPA +	1115	Slingsby T.50 Skylark 4	1383		5.63	D.Penney	Lasham	12.99
BPB	1116	Slingsby T.50 Skylark 4	1384	RNGSA BGA.1116	6.63	A.J.Hall "255"	Lasham	6.99
BPC +	1117	Slingsby T.50 Skylark 4	1389		7.63	J.L.Grayer & Ptnr	Ringmer	9.98
BPD	1118	Slingsby T.49B Capstan	1390		7.63	Culdrose GC (RNGSA.N55)	Culdrose	2.99
BPE +	1119	Slingsby T.50 Skylark 4	1391		6.63	D.H.Scales	Currock Hill	4.99
BPG	1121	Slingsby T.50 Skylark 4	1393		7.63	R.M.Neill & Ptnrs "741"	Long Mynd	11.99
BPJ	1123	Slingsby T.50 Skylark 4	1360		4.63	M.Cooper "809" (Damaged Challock 26.3.97)	Challock	3.98*
BPK +	1124	Slingsby T.50 Skylark 4	1381		6.63	D.Crowhurst	Crowland	5.98
BPL +	1125	EoN AP.5 Olympia 2B	EoN/O/136	G-APXC	6.63	D.Harris & Ptnrs	Camphill	5.97*
BPN	1127	Oberlerchner Standard Austria	003	OE-0496	6.63	R.K.Avery & Ptnrs "571"	Eaglescott	7.98
BPS +	1131	Slingsby T.49B Capstan	1399		9.63	Capstan Gliding Group	Aboyne	12.98
BPT	1132	Slingsby T.49B Capstan	1400		10.63	J.E.Neville	Laurencekirk	2.95*
BPU	1133	Slingsby T.49B Capstan	1402		11.63	I.T.Godfrey t/a Capstan Syndicate	Dunstable	3.98
BPV	1134	Slingsby T.49B Capstan	1404		12.63	C R Partinton "N31"	Currock Hill	7.99
BPW +	1135	Slingsby T.49B Capstan	1408		1.64	Ulster GC	Bellarena	5.99
BPX	1136	Slingsby T.45 Swallow	1397	XS859 BGA.1136	1.64	F.Pape & Ptnrs "859"	Rufforth	7.98
BPZ +	1138	Slingsby T.50 Skylark 4	1406		3.64	A.Pattermore & Ptnrs	Old Sarum	6.99
BQE	1143	Slingsby T.7 Cadet	-	RAFGSA.273 RA905	8.63	P.A.Dawson	Aston Down	7.97*
BQF	1144	Slingsby T.21B	1168	XN189	10.63	Connel GC "1"	North Connel	7.99
BQJ	1147	DFS/30 Kranich II (Schleicher-built)	821	RAFGSA.215 D-11-0442(?)	11.63	M.C.Russell (As "D-11-3224") (Stored 3.96)	Bishops Stortford	*
BQK +	1148	Schleicher Ka7 Rhonadler	7120		12.63	R.B Armitage (Damaged Waldershare Park 21.8.95)	Waldershare Park	6.96*
BQL	1149	Schleicher Ka6CR	725/60	D-7117	12.63	C.Boyd & Ptnrs	Eaglescott	6.98
BQM +	1150	EoN AP.10 460 Srs.1B	EoN/S/002	RAFGSA.276	12.63	A.Duncan	Portmoak	12.98
BQQ	1153	EoN AP.5 Olympia 2B (Rebuilt 1993 using wings from BGA.678)	EoN/O/121	RAFGSA.244	2.64	I.D.Smith "Dopey"	Nympsfield	7.99
BQS +	1155	EoN AP.10 460 Srs.1	EoN/S/008		3.64	P.Williams	Snitterfield	4.97*
BQT +	1156	EoN AP.10 460 Srs.1	EoN/S/007	BGA.2666 AGA.6/BGA.1156	1.64	J.H.May	Seighford	4.97*
BQU	1157	Schleicher Ka7 Rhonadler	7141	RNGSA AR66 BGA.1157	4.64	Portsmouth Naval GC (RNGSA.N27)	Lee-on-Solent	4.99
BQZ +	1162	Slingsby T.50 Skylark 4	1416		4.64	G.Colledge	Edgehill	6.99
BRA +	1163	Slingsby T.49B Capstan	1417		4.64	K.R.Brown	Nympsfield	5.99
BRB	1164	Slingsby T.51 Dart 15	1423	RAFGSA.334 BGA.1164	4.64	M.Sansom "T51"	Gallows Hill	2.99
BRC +	1165	Slingsby T.45 Swallow 1	1407		5.64	J.R.Smalley	Kirton-in-Lindsey	4.99
BRD +	1166	Slingsby T.51 Dart 15	1425	RAFGSA.335 BGA.1166	5.64	V.Day	Lyveden	6.99
BRE +	1167	Slingsby T.45 Swallow 2	1415		5.64	A.Swannock & Ptnrs	Gamston	6.99
BRG	1169	Slingsby T.45 Swallow	1410		5.64	A.W.F.Edwards	Gransden Lodge	2.98
BRL	1173	EoN AP.5 Olympia 2B	EoN/O/132		5.64	A.Cutts & Ptnrs	Ridgewell	3.99

Regn	BGA No.	Type	C/n	P/I	Regn	Owner/operator	Probable Base	CA Expy
BRM +	1174	Schleicher Ka7 Rhonadler	776/60	D-4635	5.64	D.S.Driver	Currock Hill	1.99
BRQ +	1177	EoN AP.10 460 Srs.1C	EoN/S/003	G-ARFU	6.64	J.Steel & Ptnrs	Falgunzeon	8.96*
BRT	1180	Slingsby T.51 Dart 15	1430		6.64	H.E.Birch & Ptnrs	Dishforth	4.99
BRU +	1181	Slingsby T.51 Dart 15	1429		6.64	M.Charlton	Currock Hill	2.99
BRW +	1183	Slingsby T.49B Capstan	1413		6.64	A.West & Ptnrs	Lasham	11.99
BRY +	1185	Slingsby T.51 Dart 15	1434		7.64	S.Wilkinson & Ptnrs Kirton-in-Lindsey		4.98
BSA +	1187	Slingsby T.51 Dart 15	1405		7.64	N G Oultram	Camphill	6.99
BSC	1189	Slingsby T.50 Skylark 4	1422		8.64	A.Etchells "H23"	Bidford	10.99
BSE +	1191	Slingsby T.49B Capstan	1414		9.64	D.A Bullock	Seighford	1.99
BSG	1193	Slingsby T.50 Skylark 4	1436		9.64	North Wales GC	Bryngwyn Bach	4.99
BSH +	1194	Slingsby T.50 Skylark 4	1444		11.64	M Mathieson	Wormingford	7.99
BSK +	1196	Slingsby T.49B Capstan	1418		10.64	Kermit Syndicate	Pocklington	6.98
BSL +	1197	Slingsby T.51 Dart 17	1445		10.64	C.J.Owles	Tibenham	7.98
BSM	1198	Slingsby T.51 Dart 15	1439		10.64	M.Robertson "597"	Strathaven	9.97*
BSQ	1201	EoN AP.10 460 Srs.1	EoN/S/014		5.64	K.G.Ashford "463" Husbands Bosworth		7.99
BSR +	1202	Slingsby T.50 Skylark 4	1443		12.64	D.Johnstone	Rattlesden	9.98
BSS +	1203	Slingsby T.49B Capstan	1449		12.64	J.F.Rogers "T49"	Booker	8.99
BST	1204	Slingsby T.49 Capstan	1451		1.65	P H Pickett	Husbands Bosworth	7.99
BSV +	1206	Slingsby T.51 Dart 15	1454		7.65	G.G.Butler	Snitterfield	2.97*
BSW +	1207	Slingsby T.51 Dart 17R	1459		2.65	M.R.C.Bean & Ptnrs "310"Tibenham		2.99
BSX +	1208	Slingsby T.45 Swallow	1461	OO-ZWC F-OTAN-C5/BGA.1208	4.65	P.Brownlow & Ptnrs Sackville Lodge, Riseley		7.98
BSY +	1209	Slingsby T.50 Skylark 4	1448		4.65	G B Dennis	Nympsfield	2.99
BSZ +	1210	Slingsby T.50 Skylark 4	1460		4.65	B.Ling	Lleweni Parc	2.99
BTA +	1211	Slingsby T.45 Swallow	1473		6.65	M.Morley	Odiham	8.99
BTD +	1214	DFS/49 Grunau Baby 2C	?	(ex RAFGSA)	8.64	Bidford Gliding Centre	Bidford	5.97*
BTG +	1217	EoN AP.10 460 Srs.1	EoN/S/024		2.65	A.W Hearney	Strubby	9.99
BTH	1218	Slingsby T.21B	JHB/2		3.65	M.Lake (As "WB981")	Aston Down	4.99
		(Built by J.Hulme: restored 1995 with wings from BGA.3238/WB981)						
BTJ +	1219	Schleicher Ka6CR	6367		3.65	M S Lomas	Kingston Deverill	5.99
BTK	1220	Slingsby T.50 Skylark 4	1364	SE-SZW	3.65	J.A.Lewis & Syndicate "368"	Lasham	7.96*
BTM	1222	Schleicher Ka6CR	6174		3.65	P.Maller "211"	Aston Down	4.99
BTN +	1223	EoN AP.10 460 Srs.1	EoN/S/022	AGA.15 BGA.1223	4.65	S.C.Thompson	Parham Park	8.99
BTQ +	1225	EoN AP.10 460 Srs.1	EoN/S/029		4.65	P.Etherington & Ptnrs Husbands Bosworth		2.97*
BTV	1230	DFS/68 Weihe	0-00358	RAFGGA	5.65	Not known	Cranwell	5.93*
BUC +	1237	Slingsby T.49B Capstan	1472		6.65	Lakes GC	Walney Island	2.97
BUE +	1239	Slingsby T.50 Skylark 4	1468		7.65	D.Holt & I.H.Davies	Seighford	4.99
BUF	1240	Slingsby T.51 Dart 17R	1469		7.65	C.H.Brown & Ptnrs "366" Chipping		3.99
BUG +	1241	EoN AP.10 460 Srs.1	EoN/S/028		5.65	A.Rowson & Ptnrs	Long Mynd	3.97*
BUH	1242	Eon AP.10 460 Srs.1	EoN/S/021	G-ASMP	.65	A.E.Lawrence		
			(Damaged Gransden Lodge 29. 6.95) Sackville Lodge, Riseley						5.96*
BUK	1244	EoN AP.10 460 Srs.1	EoN/S/027		5.65	M.Hodgson	Booker	6.97*
BUL +	1245	Slingsby T.51 Dart 17R	1470		7.65	A.Parrish & Ptnr Husbands Bosworth		6.99
BUP +	1247	Slingsby T.51 Dart 17R	1478		9.65	D.S.Carter "837"	Enstone	6.99
BUR +	1249	Slingsby T.49B Capstan	1482		11.65	Bidford Gliding Centre	Bidford	7.99
BUT +	1251	Slingsby T.43 Skylark 3F	VRT.1		7.65	I.Bannister t/a Sky Syndicate		
		(Built by V.R.Tull & Ptnrs)					Chipping	5.99
BUV	1253	EoN AP.10 460 Srs.1	EoN/S/030		7.65	S.H.Gibson	Dunstable	9.98
BUW	1254	Slingsby T.21B	?	RAFGSA.242	8.65	J.N.Wardle	Lasham	6.99
BUZ +	1257	Schleicher Ka6CR	6418		8.65	R.Leacroft	Lyveden	9.99
BVB +	1259	Schleicher Ka7 Rhonadler	7230		9.65	York Gliding Centre	Rufforth	4.99
		(Mod to ASK 13 standard)						
BVC	1260	Slingsby T.51 Dart 17R	1479		3.66	R.M.Hitchin & Ptnrs Kingston Deverill		3.99
BVE +	1262	Slingsby T.51 Dart 17R	1483		11.65	P.Leach & Ptnr "61" Sandhill Farm, Shrivenham		6.99
BVF +	1263	Slingsby T.45 Swallow	1481		11.65	Pershore F/C	Bidford	2.95*
		(Stored 6.98)						
BVH +	1265	Slingsby T.51 Dart 17R	1485		12.65	D.J.Simpson	Halesland	6.99
BVJ +	1266	Slingsby T.51 Dart 17R	1486		1.66	R.& M.Weaver	Usk	12.99
BVL +	1268	Slingsby T.51 Dart 15	1487		1.66	D.Stabler & Ptnrs "404" Tibenham		6.98
BVM +	1269	Slingsby T.51 Dart 17R	1492		1.66	N.H.Ponsford "150" (Stored 1.99) (Breighton)		5.89*
BVN +	1270	EoN AP.10 460 Srs.1	EoN/S/023		3.65	F J Clarke & Ptnrs	North Hill	9.98
BVR +	1273	Schleicher Ka6CR	6441		10.65	R.C Cannon & Ptnrs	Lasham	3.98
BVS +	1274	PZL SZD-9 bis Bocian 1D	F-831		.	Aquila GC Hinton-in-the-Hedges		8.96*
BVW	1278	EoN AP.6 Olympia 403	EoN/4/001	RAFGSA.306 G-APEW	8.65	J.B. & K.D.Dumville	Camphill	7.99
BVX +	1279	Schleicher Ka6CR	6439		10.65	C.G.Stoves	Burn	6.99
BVY +	1280	LET L-13 Blanik	173121		10.65	Strathclyde GC	Strathaven	7.98

Regn	BGA No.	Type	C/n	P/I	Regn	Owner/operator	Probable Base	CA Expy
BVZ +	1281	Schleicher Ka6CR	6446		10.65	J.C.Taggart	Bellarena	3.99
BWB	1283	EoN AP.10 460 Srs.1	EoN/S/036		12.65	S Metcalfe "B96"	Tibenham	6.99
BWC	1284	Schleicher Ka6CR	6449		12.65	M.E.Hazlewood "424"	Lasham	4.98
BWE +	1286	EoN AP.10 460 Srs.2	EoN/S/035		12.65	C.Hughes	Nympsfield	8.99
BWG	1288	EoN AP.10 465 Srs.2	EoN/S/038		12.65	K.S.Green & Ptnr "465"	Lasham	4.97*
BWJ	1290	Slingsby T.51 Dart 17R	1495		2.66	D.Godfrey & Ptnrs "377"	Edgehill	7.96*
BWK	1291	Slingsby T.45 Swallow	1493		2.66	K.Hubbard & Ptnrs	North Hill	6.98
BWM	1293	Slingsby T.51 Dart 17R	1500		4.66	P.L. & L.E.Poole "182"	Lasham	8.96*
BWP	1295	Slingsby T.51 Dart 17R	1501		3.66	D Champion "861"	Parham Park	3.98
BWQ +	1296	Slingsby T.51 Dart 15	1505		3.66	C.Uncles	Halesland	6.99
BWR	1297	DFS 108-68 Weihe	224	G-ASCV	3.66	P.Molloy & Ptnrs	Ridgewell	9.96*
		(Built by AB Flygindustri, Sweden 1943)		SE-STN/Fv.8306		(As "Fv.8306" in 4 Sqdn Swedish AF c/s)		
						(De-registered 26.8.98 - sold to Germany)		
BWS	1298	Slingsby T.51 Dart 17R	1502		4.66	R.D.Broom & E.A.Chalk "517"		
							Cranfield	6.99
BWT	1299	Slingsby T.51 Dart 15R	1508		4.66	R.Parker "163" (Stored)	Dishforth	8.96*
BWU +	1300	EoN AP.10 460 Srs.1	EoN/S/034		1.66	G.Booth	Ridgewell	7.99
BWX +	1303	EoN AP.5 Olympia 2B	101		2.66	P.Kent	Seighford	5.99
		(Built from spares)						
BXC +	1308	EoN AP.10 460 Srs.1	EoN/S/006		4.66	D.D.Copeland "781"	Dunstable	4.96*
BXE +	1310	Slingsby T.51 Dart 15R	1509		5.66	M.P.Holburn	Currock Hill	5.97*
BXG	1312	Slingsby T.51 Dart 17R	1512		5.66	B.W.Compton "686"	Usk	4.99
BXH +	1313	Slingsby T.51 Dart 17R	1516		6.66	B.Crow	Usk	12.98
BXK	1315	Slingsby T.21B	1510		6.66	Not known	Rufforth	*
						(Damaged Falgunzeon 18.5.80; stored 10.93)		
BXL	1316	Slingsby T.51 Dart 17R	1517		6.66	W.R.Longstaff & Ptnr "121"		
							Feshiebridge	5.98
BXM	1317	Slingsby T.51 Dart 17R	1521		7.66	C.A.P.Ellis "9"	Ridgewell	7.98
BXP +	1319	Slingsby T.45 Swallow 2	1522		7.66	Carlton Moor GC	Carlton Moor	4.99
BXR	1321	LET L-13 Blanik	173301	G-ATPX	5.66	Not known	Cranfield	12.92*
						(Stored 7.98)		
BXT +	1323	Schleicher Ka6CR	6492		4.66	J.& A.Briggs	Tibenham	3.99
BXV	1325	LET L-13 Blanik	173304	G-ATRA	5.66	Blanik Syndicate		
						(As "G-ATRA")	Husbands Bosworth	4.99
BXW +	1326	LET L-13 Blanik	173305	G-ATRB	6.66	K A Hale	Bidford	5.99
BXY +	1328	EoN AP.10 460 Srs.1	EoN/S/042		6.66	G.K.Stanford	Brent Tor	7.98
BYA +	1330	Slingsby T.51 Dart 17R	1518		7.66	J.A.Thomson & D.Archer	Easterton	1.00
BYB +	1331	Slingsby T.45 Swallow	1525		7.66	Surrey Hills GC "352"	Kenley	7.97*
BYC +	1332	Slingsby T.51 Dart 17R	1526		8.66	G.Woodman		
							Sandhill Farm, Shrivenham	3.99
BYE +	1334	EoN AP.10 463 Srs.1	EoN/S/044		9.66	C.Bushell	Long Mynd	4.97*
BYG	1336	Slingsby T.51 Dart 17R	1535	RAFGSA	11.66	W.T.Emery "225"	Rufforth	6.99
				BGA.1336				
BYJ	1338	Slingsby T.45 Swallow	1568		2.67	D.I.Johnstone t/a Swallow Soaring		
						Group	Strathaven	11.96*
BYK +	1339	Slingsby T.45 Swallow	1566		1.67	K.Summers	Lasham	2.97*
BYL +	1340	Schleicher Ka6CR	6517		7.66	J.P.Bedingfield	Lleweni Parc	9.99
BYM +	1341	Schleicher Ka6CR	6518	RAFGSA.381	7.66	C J Bailey	Rattlesden	4.98
				BGA.1341				
BYU	1348	Schleicher Ka6CR	6525	XW640	9.66	M.K.Collingham Syndicate "350"		
				BGA.1348			Dunstable	8.99
BYX	1351	Schleicher Ka6E	4055		12.66	J.Dent & D.B.Andrews	Chipping	2.99
BZA +	1354	Slingsby T.21B	1162	RAFGSA.318	11.66	A Hill	Wattisham	10.99
				XN183				
BZB +	1355	EoN AP.10 460 Srs.1	EoN/S/047		10.66	D.C.Ratcliffe Syndicate		
							Parham Park	5.99
BZC +	1356	Slingsby T.51 Dart 17R	1563		2.67	A.N.Ely	Strubby	5.99
BZF	1359	Slingsby T.51 Dart 17R	1570		3.67	P.C.Gill & Ptnrs "311"	Ridgewell	9.99
BZG	1360	Slingsby T.49B Capstan	1581		4.67	Culdrose GC (RNGSA.N54)	Culdrose	5.99
BZH	1361	Slingsby T.51 Dart 17R	1580		4.67	C.Long "406"	Bidford	7.97*
BZJ	1362	Slingsby T.51 Dart 17R	1567		4.67	D.M.Steed "Anastasia" "362"		
							Enstone	8.98
BZL +	1364	Slingsby T.45 Swallow	1596		7.67	Cairngorm Swallow Syndicate		
							Feshiebridge	7.98
BZM	1365	Slingsby T.45 Swallow	1597		7.67	F.Webster	Arbroath	5.97*
BZP	1367	PZL SZD-24-4A Foka 4	W-301		1.67	I.K.Mitchell "F4"	Halesland	3.97*
BZQ	1368	Schleicher Ka6CR	6551		2.67	A.Holland "453"	North Hill	8.99
BZR	1369	EoN AP.10 460 Srs.1	EoN/S/049		2.67	M.P.Dale & T Pond "471"		
							Sutton Bank	6.99
BZS +	1370	EoN AP.10 460 Srs.1	EoN/S/052		2.67	R.Hutchinson	Carlton Moor	4.97*
BZV +	1373	EoN AP.10 460 Srs.1	EoN/S/046		2.67	I.Smith	Lasham	6.99
BZW +	1374	EoN AP.10 460 Srs.1	EoN/S/053		3.67	J.Bradley & Ptnrs "Z11"		
							Lleweni Parc	4.97*
BZX +	1375	Schleicher Ka6CR	6571		3.67	Leeds University GC	Rufforth	7.98
BZY	1376	Slingsby T.31B	SSK/FF1817	BGA.1175	3.67	A.L.Higgins t/a The Blue Brick		
		(BGA.1175 rebuilt)				Syndicate	Cranfield	5.98
BZZ	1377	PZL SZD-24-4A Foka 4	W-308		3.67	M.Hudson & Ptnrs "77"	Booker	4.99

Regn	BGA No.	Type	C/n	P/I	Regn	Owner/operator	Probable Base	CA Expy

CAA-CZZ

Regn	BGA No.	Type	C/n	P/I	Regn	Owner/operator	Probable Base	CA Expy
CAB +	1379	EoN AP.10 460 Srs.1	EoN/S/033	RAFGSA.344	3.67	P.Green & Ptnr	Pershore	10.98
CAC	1380	Schleicher Ka6E	4054		3.67	L.I.Rigby "994"	Crowland	2.99
CAE	1381	Schleicher Ka6E	4076		4.67	P.P.Brightman & G D A.Green "5"	Dunstable	5.99
CAF	1382	EoN AP.5 Olympia 2B	EoN/O/131	RAFGSA.254	4.67	G.D.Griffiths	Brent Tor	1.99
CAG	1383	Schleicher Ka6E	4080		4.67	Peterborough & Spalding GC "715"	Crowland	2.99
CAK	1386	EoN AP.5 Olympia 2B	EoN/O/122	RAFGSA.246	3.67	P.Hatfield t/a Olympia 2B Syndicate "117"	Rufforth	4.99
CAN +	1389	EoN AP.10 460 Srs.1	EoN/S/050		3.67	R.Russon	Snitterfield	2.97*
CAQ	1391	Schempp-Hirth SHK	37		3.67	M.A.Thorne "812"	Old Sarum	4.99
CAR	1392	Schempp-Hirth SHK-1	40		4.67	P.Gentil & M.Gresty "422"	Aston Down	7.98
CAS	1393	Schleicher Ka6E	4029	RAFGSA.372	5.67	R.F.Tindall "372"	Gransden Lodge	1.95*
CAT +	1394	EoN AP.10 460 Srs.1	EoN/S/051		5.67	A.Jackson & Ptnrs	Sackville Lodge, Riseley	4.97*
CAV +	1396	Schleicher ASK13	13015		5.67	M.Cuming (Stored Kemble 7.97)	Edgehill	6.97*
CAW	1397	LET L-13 Blanik	173202	RAFGSA.357 G-ASZK	5.67	Not known "357" (Stored - spares use 6.96)	Enstone	2.83*
CAX +	1398	Slingsby T.45 Swallow	1598		7.67	R.B Armitage	Waldershare Park	3.99
CAZ	1400	Slingsby T.51 Dart 17WR	1611		7.68	J.M.Young & Ptnrs "702"	Easterton	5.98
CBA	1401	Slingsby T.51 Dart 17WR	1612		7.68	D.Bennett & P.H.Pickett "679"	Snitterfield	1.99
CBK	1410	Grunau Baby III (Built by Sfg. Schaffin)	-	RAFGSA.378 D-4676	9.68	N.H.Ponsford (Op Real Aeroplane Club) (Stored 1.98)	Breighton	4.83*
CBM	1412	Schleicher Ka6CR	6607		7.67	I.R.Starfield "343"	Nympsfield	11.99
CBN +	1413	PZL SZD-30 Pirat	W-320		5.67	B.C.Cooper	Burn	2.99
CBP +	1414	PZL SZD-24C Foka	W-198	OY-BXR	7.67	G.Sutton	Sutton Bank	7.98
CBR +	1416	Aeromere M.100S	044		7.67	K.George & Ptnrs	Wormingford	4.97*
CBS	1417	EoN AP.5 Olympia 2B	EoN/O/143	RAFGSA.291	7.67	G.Moden & Ptnrs (Stored 6.95)	Edgehill	9.94*
		(C/n unlikely as EoN/O/143 was BGA.1034 and sold to Zambia; possibly kit-built)						
CBU	1419	Schempp-Hirth SHK-1	53	D-8441	10.67	M.Dodd "905"	Shobdon	12.99
CBV	1420	EoN AP.10 460 Srs.1	EoN/S/055		6.67	J.Sharples & Ptnr "362"	Burn	10.96*
CBW +	1421	Schleicher ASK13	13034		8.67	Stratford-upon-Avon GC	Snitterfield	1.99
CBY	1423	Schleicher Ka6CR	960	RAFGSA.322 D-3222	10.67	L.C.Bradley "475"	Talgarth	6.99
CCA +	1425	Schleicher Ka6E	4126		10.67	R.K.Forrest	Nympsfield	2.99
CCB +	1426	Schempp-Hirth SHK-1	52		7.67	R.M.Johnson	Milfield	6.99
CCD	1428	Schleicher Ka6E	4127		12.67	M.J.Birch & Ptnr "373"	Dunstable	4.99
CCE +	1429	Schleicher ASK13	13047		12.67	Oxford GC	Weston-on-the-Green	1.99
CCF +	1430	Schleicher ASK13	13042		12.67	Norfolk GC	Tibenham	1.99
CCG +	1431	Schleicher Ka6E	4125		12.67	G.A.Fudge	Kenley	3.99
CCJ	1433	Schleicher Ka6CR	6145	RAFGSA.323	10.67	P.Green "878"	Weston-on-the-Green	4.99
CCL	1435	Schleicher Ka6E	4129		3.68	S.J.Hill "47"	Sutton Bank	2.99
CCM +	1436	Schleicher ASK13	13053		2.68	Burn GC	Burn	2.99
CCN +	1437	PZL SZD-9 bis Bocian 1E	P-431		3.68	Surrey Hills GC	Kenley	4.99
CCP +	1438	Schleicher ASK13	13052		2.68	DRA GC "L99"	Odiham	2.99
CCR +	1440	Schleicher Ka6E	4149		2.68	A E Burgess	Enstone	9.99
CCS +	1441	Slingsby T.41 Skylark 2	1008	PH-230	3.68	S.L.Benn	Cranfield	10.97*
CCT +	1442	Schleicher ASK13	13057		3.68	Stratford-upon-Avon GC	Snitterfield	1.99
CCU	1443	Schleicher Ka6E	4122		3.68	D.C.Findlay	Keevil	3.99
CCV	1444	Schleicher Ka6E	4160		3.68	C.J.Nicholas	Ridgewell	6.99
CCW +	1445	Schleicher ASK13	13051		3.68	J E.Hart & Ptnrs	Sutton Bank	2.99
CCX +	1446	Schleicher ASK13	13054		3.68	Trent Valley GC	Kirton-in-Lindsey	3.99
CCY +	1447	Schleicher ASK13	13050		3.68	D.Woolf & Ptnrs	Long Mynd	5.99
CCZ +	1448	Schleicher ASK13	13070		3.68	Trent Valley GC	Kirton-in-Lindsey	2.99
CDA +	1449	Schleicher Ka6E	4136		3.68	F.Bick & Ptnrs	Aboyne	3.99
CDB +	1450	Schleicher Ka6E	4137		3.68	K.L.Holburn	Currock Hill	5.99
CDC +	1451	Schleicher K8B	8743		3.68	Enstone Eagle GC	Enstone	3.99
CDD	1452	Schleicher Ka6E	4165		3.68	D.T.Staff	Booker	3.99
CDF	1454	Schleicher Ka6E	4162		3.68	J.Reid & Ptnrs "683"	Upavon	4.97*
CDG +	1455	FFA Diamant 18	35		3.68	J.A.Luck	Cranfield	7.99
CDH	1456	Schempp-Hirth HS.2 Cirrus	10		4.68	D.T.Owen "619"	Odiham	2.98
CDJ +	1457	Schleicher ASK13	13077		4.68	Southdown GC	Parham Park	4.99
CDK +	1458	Schleicher K8B	8747		5.68	Burn GC (Damaged Burn 24.5.97: wreck noted 1.99)	Burn	1.99
CDR +	1464	Scheibe Bergfalke III	5625		8.68	N.M Neil	Hinton-in-the-Hedges	9.98
CDV +	1468	Schleicher Ka6E	4159		5.68	Not known (Wreck stored 7.97)	Cranfield	4.87*
CDW +	1469	FFA Diamant 18	033		8.68	J.McIver	Falgunzeon	12.99

Regn	BGA No.	Type	C/n	P/I	Regn	Owner/operator	Probable Base	CA Expy
CDX	1470	PZL SZD-30 Pirat	W-392		5.68	S.Cynalski "303"	Rufforth	5.99
CDZ +	1472	Schleicher Ka6E	4177		5.68	J R Minnis	North Weald	8.99
CEA +	1473	Schempp-Hirth HS.2 Cirrus	21	XZ405 BGA.1473/D-8437	8.68	M.Whitton	Long Mynd	3.99
CEB +	1474	PZL SZD-9 bis Bocian 1E	P-433		5.68	Bath, Wilts & N.Dorset GC	Kingston Deverill	6.99
CEC	1475	Schempp-Hirth HS.2 Cirrus	22		7.68	C.R.Ellis "782"	Long Mynd	12.99
CED	1476	Schleicher Ka6E	4196		6.68	H.G.Williams & Ptnrs "18"	Snitterfield	2.99
CEG	1479	Schleicher Ka6E	4203		6.68	J.C.Boley	Halesland	3.96*
CEH +	1480	Wassmer WA.22 Super Javelot	68	F-OTAN-C6 F-CCLU	7.68	E.Hill & Ptnrs	Camphill	9.98
CEJ +	1481	Schleicher ASK13	13102		8.68	Devon & Somerset GC	North Hill	3.99
CEK	1482	Slingsby T.21B (T) (Robin EC34PM s/n 82-00676)	1151	RAFGSA.369	7.68	D.Woolerton	East Kirkby	11.99
CEL	1483	Schleicher Ka6E	4174		8.68	Essex & Suffolk GC "JD"	Wormingford	7.98
CEM +	1484	Schleicher Ka6E	4212		8.68	V D Long	Tibenham	7.99
CEN +	1485	PZL SZD-30 Pirat	W-393	SP-2520	7.68	A.Bogan	Kirton-in-Lindsey	2.99
CEQ	1487	Schleicher Ka6E	4230		8.68	C.L.Lagden & Ptnrs "458"	Ridgewell	8.99
CEV	1492	Scheibe Bergfalke II	184	???	8.68	A.Lewis (Stored 10.96)Jurby, IoM		12.93*
CEW +	1493	Schleicher Ka6E	4209		8.68	J.W.Richardson "177"	Dunstable	4.99
CEX +	1494	Schleicher ASK13	13108		9.68	Newcastle & Teesside GC	Carlton Moor	10.99
CEY +	1495	Schleicher Ka6E	4222		8.68	S.N.Longland & Ptnrs	Gransden Lodge	3.99
CFA +	1497	Schleicher ASK13	13113		10.68	Booker GC	Booker	3.99
CFB	1498	Schleicher ASK13	13110		10.68	Not known (Wreck)	Burn	*
CFC +	1499	Schleicher Ka7 Rhonadler	470	RAFGSA.387 F-OTAN-C1	11.68	J H Mare	Edgehill	9.99
CFD	1500	LET L-13 Blanik	173214	G-ATCG	10.68	M D White "B1"	Burn	12.98
CFF +	1502	Schleicher K8B	8765		10.68	Norfolk GC	Tibenham	4.99
CFG +	1503	Schleicher ASK13	13115		10.68	Staffordshire GC	Seighford	3.99
CFK +	1506	Schempp-Hirth HS.2 Cirrus	38		11.68	C.V Webb & Ptnrs	Sleap	11.99
CFL +	1507	Schleicher Ka6E	4215		10.68	Bath, Wilts & N.Dorset GC	Kingston Deverill	6.98
CFM +	1508	Schleicher ASK13	13121		12.68	Vale of White Horse GC	Sandhill Farm, Shrivenham	3.99
CFS +	1513	Glasflugel H.201 Standard Libelle	83		4.70	J.L.H.Pegman "271"	Currock Hill	5.99
CFT	1514	Slingsby T.59A Kestrel 17	1729		3.73	J.A.Kane "62"	Carlton Moor	5.99
CFX +	1518	Glasflugel H.201 Standard Libelle	274		2.72	A.R Head & Ptnrs	Gransden Lodge	4.99
CFY +	1519	Glasflugel H.201 Standard Libelle	270		3.72	C.W.Stevens "862"	Camphill	3.99
CGB +	1522	Schleicher Ka6E	4247		12.68	M.S Colebrook & Ptnrs	Bembridge	4.99
CGD	1524	Schleicher Ka6E	4202		1.69	I F Smith "418"	Lasham	3.99
CGE	1525	Schleicher Ka6E	4246		1.69	R.J.Brown	Bellarena	4.99
CGH	1528	Schleicher K8B	8772		2.69	Surrey & Hants GC "153"	Lasham	3.99
CGJ +	1529	Schleicher K8B	8773		2.69	Nene Valley GC	Upwood	3.99
CGK	1530	Schleicher Ka6E	4261		3.69	J.A.F.Barnes & Ptnrs "124"	Wormingford	8.99
CGM +	1532	FFA Diamant 18	053		5.69	M.C.Ogglesby	Hinton-in-the Hedges	3.99
CGN	1533	Schleicher Ka6E	4173		3.69	K.R Brown & Ptnr "309"	Nympsfield	9.99
CGQ +	1535	Schleicher ASK13	13153		4.69	Oxford GC	Weston-on-the-Green	3.99
CGR	1536	Schleicher ASK13	13142		3.69	Bristol & Glos GC "913" (Damaged nr Nympsfield 2.6.96)	Nympsfield	12.96*
CGS +	1537	FFA Diamant 18	055		7.69	C.J.Wimbury	Ringmer	2.99
CGT	1538	Schempp-Hirth SHK-1	38	D-1966	4.69	G.Jones & B.W.Svenson "449"	Pocklington	2.98
CGU +	1539	EoN AP.5 Olympia 2B	EoN/O/115	RAFGSA.228	4.69	M.Skinner & Ptnrs	Pocklington	8.97*
CGV +	1540	PIK-16C Vasama	48		4.69	D.J.Osborne & Ptnrs	Currock Hill	7.99
CGX +	1542	Bolkow Phoebus C	869		4.69	W.N.Smith & Ptnrs	Sackville Lodge, Riseley	5.99
CGY	1543	Schempp-Hirth HS.2 Cirrus	51		4.69	R.Munday & Ptnrs "337"	Eaglescott	5.98
CGZ +	1544	Schempp-Hirth SHK	39		5.69	M.C.Ridger	Saltby	12.98
CHB	1546	Schleicher Ka6E	4235		5.69	D.J.Jones "577"	Weston-on-the-Green	4.99
CHC	1547	Bolkow Phoebus C	858		5.69	D.Garner Syndicate	Rhigos	5.99
CHE +	1549	Slingsby T.41 Skylark 2 (Built by Doncaster Sailplane Svs)	DSS.002		6.69	M.S.Howey	Burn	3.99
CHF +	1550	PZL SZD-9 bis Bocian 1E	P-432		5.69	T.J.Wilkinson (Damaged Sackville Lodge 27. 8.95)	Sackville Lodge, Riseley	8.96*
CHG	1551	PZL SZD-30 Pirat	B-294		6.69	Culdrose GC (RNGSA.N52)	Culdrose	3.99
CHJ	1553	Bolkow Phoebus 17C	879		6.69	D.C.Austin	Sutton Bank	3.98
CHK	1554	EoN AP.5 Olympia 2B	?	RAFGSA	6.69	Oly Gliding Syndicate	Halesland	4.99

Regn	BGA No.	Type	C/n	P/I	Regn	Owner/operator	Probable Base	CA Expy
CHL +	1555	PZL SZD-30 Pirat	B-295		6.69	W.Sage & Syndicate	Rufforth	3.99
CHQ	1559	Slingsby T.31B	1186	XN247	6.69	N.H.Ponsford (Stored 1.98) Wigan		7.82*
CHT	1562	Schleicher ASW15	15013		8.69	J.N.Kelly & Ptnrs "846"	Lasham	5.99
CHU +	1563	Schleicher K8B	8794		8.69	H B Chambers (Highland GC Syndicate)		
							Easterton	2.99
CHW +	1565	Schleicher ASK13	13187		8.69	Dorset GC	Gallows Hill	4.99
CHY +	1567	Slingsby T.45 Swallow	RG.103		9.69	J.L.H.Pegman & Ptnrs		
		(Built from kit by R.Greenslade)					Currock Hill	7.98
CHZ	1568	Schleicher Ka6E	4153	N6916	9.69	M.Uphill "357"	Usk	5.99
CJB	1570	Bolkow Phoebus C	919		12.69	T.J.Wilkinson "764"		
						Sackville Lodge, Riseley		5.99
CJC	1571	Ginn-Lesniak Kestrel	1		10.69	P.G.Fairness & K Burns		
							Strathaven	9.99
CJD	1572	Schleicher ASK13	13182		10.69	Shenington GC "S14"	Edgehill	1.00
CJF	1574	Schleicher K8B	8803		11.69	Surrey & Hants GC "474"	Lasham	2.99
CJG +	1575	Wassmer WA.21 Javelot II	38	F-OTAN-C4	1.70	R S Hanslip	Burn	5.99
				F-CCEZ				
CJJ +	1577	Bolkow Phoebus C	913		1.70	P Maddocks	Falgunzeon	8.99
CJK +	1578	Schempp-Hirth SHK	35	RAFGSA.25	2.70	R.H.Short	Lyveden	8.99
CJL	1579	Schempp-Hirth SHK-1	42	OO-ZLG	2.70	M.F.Brook "222"	Camphill	3.99
CJM +	1580	Schleicher K8B	8814		3.70	Surrey & Hants GC	Lasham	3.99
CJN	1581	Schempp-Hirth SHK-1	55		3.70	G.Kench	Dunstable	8.98
CJP +	1582	Schleicher ASW15	15041		3.70	C.Pain	Cranfield	9.98
CJR	1584	Schempp-Hirth HS.2 Cirrus	87		3.70	J.H.Stanley "83"	Lasham	4.99
CJY +	1591	Schleicher Ka6CR	555	(RAFGSA)	4.70	Bristol & Glos GC	Nympsfield	11.98
CJZ +	1592	Schempp-Hirth SHK	03	D-9349	3.70	T.J Frazier & Ptnrs	Pocklington	10.99
CKC +	1595	Bolkow Phoebus C	936	(BGA.1590)	4.70	S.J.Bennett	Bidford	9.98
CKD +	1596	PZL SZD-30 Pirat	B-327		4.70	P.H.Turner	Gamston	4.98
CKF	1598	Glasflugel H.201 Standard Libelle	101		4.70	S.M.Turner "961"	Crowland	7.99
		(BGA.3371 wears owner's initials "CKF")						
CKJ	1601	Slingsby T.30B Prefect	740	PH-197	4.71	Not known (Stored at Crosshill)		4.90*
CKL +	1603	Schleicher Ka6E	4336		4.70	I.Lowes & Ptnrs	Milfield	7.99
CKN +	1605	PZL SZD-9 bis Bocian 1E	P-496		5.70	Strubby GC "Enola Gay"	Strubby	2.99
CKP +	1606	Schleicher ASW15	15058		7.70	M.G.Shaw & Ptnrs	Portmoak	9.99
CKR +	1608	Schleicher ASK13	13247		7.70	Essex GC	North Weald	10.98
CKU +	1611	Schleicher ASK13	13243		8.70	Glyndwr Soaring Club		
							Lleweni Parc	6.98
CKV +	1612	Schleicher ASK13	13253		8.70	D C Hardwick	Challock	6.99
CKW +	1613	Schleicher K8B	8836		9.70	D.R Crompton	Bidford	6.98
CKY	1615	Glasflugel H.201 Standard Libelle	139		8.70	P G Mullis "743"	Snitterfield	2.99
CKZ	1616	Schempp-Hirth HS.4 Standard Cirrus	52	RAFGSA	8.70	M.E.Kingston "724"	Dunstable	5.99
				BGA.1616				
CLA +	1617	Schempp-Hirth HS.4 Standard Cirrus	63		11.70	J.A.Wight & D.Dye	Nympsfield	12.99
CLF +	1622	Schleicher Ka7 Rhonadler	931	D-5062	1.71	P.Morgan & Ptnrs	Tibenham	8.99
CLG +	1623	Schempp-Hirth SHK-1	36	RAFGSA.27	1.71	J.E.Kenny	Bembridge	5.99
CLH	1624	Schempp-Hirth HS.4 Standard Cirrus	77			P.C.Bray & Ptnrs "252"Nympsfield		2.99
CLJ	1625	EoN AP.7 Primary	EoN/P/035	WP267	2.71	Not known	Bicester	2.72*
						(On rebuild 8.98)		
CLK +	1626	Schleicher Ka7 Rhonadler (Mod)	607	D-5714	2.71	Cornish GC	Perranporth	5.99
CLM +	1628	Glasflugel H.201 Standard Libelle	178		2.71	J.N.Cochrane "535"	Lasham	2.99
CLN +	1629	Glasflugel H.201 Standard Libelle	175		4.71	J.N.Wardle "142"	Lasham	5.99
CLP +	1630	Glasflugel H.201B Standard Libelle	176		2.71	G.D.Sutherland "948"	Booker	3.99
CLQ +	1631	Schempp-Hirth HS.2 Cirrus	99		1.71	K.Bastenfield	Brent Tor	3.99
CLR +	1632	Glasflugel H.201B Standard Libelle	173		4.71	D G.Shepherd "284"	Aboyne	4.99
CLT +	1634	Schleicher Ka7 Rhonadler (Mod)	251	D-5529	4.71	R.Spencer t/a The Syndicate		
							Rhigos	10.99
CLV +	1636	Glasflugel H.201 Standard Libelle	180		3.71	G.B.Monslow	Bidford	4.99
CLW +	1637	Glasflugel H.201 Standard Libelle	174		3.71	N.A.Dean & Ptnrs "937"		
							Kirton-in-Lindsey	8.99
CLX +	1638	Schleicher K8B	8851		3.71	Midland GC	Long Mynd	12.99
CLY	1639	Hirth Go.III Minimoa	378	PH-390	3.72	Not known (On rebuild 12.95)		
				D-5076			Dunstable	1.79*
CLZ	1640	Schleicher Ka6E	4056	AGA.2	4.71	H.N.Craven "799"	Pocklington	6.98
CMF +	1646	PZL SZD-32A Foka 5	W-534		7.71	D J Linford	Lasham	4.99
CMG +	1647	Schleicher Ka7 Rhonadler	462	D-8116	7.71	D.MacMillan "Fledermaus"	Lasham	2.99
CMH	1648	Glasflugel H.201B Standard Libelle	224		7.71	D.N Greig "165"	North Hill	3.99
CMK +	1650	Schleicher ASK13	13305		8.71	South Wales GC	Usk	12.99
CML +	1651	Schleicher K8B	8862		8.71	Vectis GC	Bembridge	3.99
CMN +	1653	Schleicher K8B	8870		8.71	Bristol & Glos GC	Nympsfield	2.99
CMQ	1655	Glasflugel H.201 Standard Libelle	233		8.71	P.Winter & Ptnrs "986"	Ridgewell	5.99
CMR +	1656	Glasflugel H.201 Standard Libelle	225		8.71	J.A.Dandie & Ptnrs	Portmoak	8.99
CMS	1657	Glasflugel H.201 Standard Libelle	234		8.71	D.Manser & Ptnrs "602"	Challock	4.99
CMV	1660	Glasflugel H.201 Standard Libelle	235		8.71	S.E.Evans & Ptnrs "184"	Enstone	4.99
CMW +	1661	Glasflugel H.201B Standard Libelle	242		9.71	A M Dalton	Dunstable	2.99
CMX	1662	Glasflugel H.201 Standard Libelle	232		9.71	W D Johnson "226"	Burn	4.99
(CMY)	1663	Grunau Baby IIIC (Built LSV Fussen)	1	RAFGSA.373	1.72	Not known (Stored for rebuild 7.95)		
				D-1090			Manor Farm, Glatton	*

Regn	BGA No.	Type	C/n	P/I	Regn	Owner/operator	Probable Base	CA Expy
CMZ +	1664	Schleicher Ka7 Rhonadler (Mod)	323	D-5589	6.72	Cornish GC	Perranporth	3.99
CND	1668	PZL SZD-9 bis Bocian 1E	P-428	RAFGSA.392	1.72	Angus GC "628"	Drumshade	2.99
CNE	1669	Glasflugel H.201 Standard Libelle	266		1.72	N.Buchan "525"	Portmoak	9.99
CNF	1670	Glasflugel H.201B Standard Libelle	271		1.72	A.S.McWhirter & Ptnrs "709"	Pocklington	5.99
CNG	1671	Glasflugel H.201 Standard Libelle	265		2.72	C.F.Smith & Ptnr "622"	Nympsfield	11.99
CNH	1672	Glasflugel H.201 Standard Libelle	269		2.72	R.M.Grant "442" (or "142"?)	Lasham	6.98
CNJ +	1673	Glasflugel H.201 Standard Libelle	272		2.72	R.E.Gretton	Crowland	7.99
CNK +	1674	PZL SZD-30 Pirat	B-459		3.72	H.Forshaw & Ptnrs	Rufforth	6.99
CNM +	1676	PZL SZD-9 bis Bocian 1E	P-551		2.72	M.Williamson & Ptnrs	Crowland	5.99
CNN +	1677	Schempp-Hirth HS.4 Standard Cirrus	173		2.72	R.W.Asplin	Camphill	4.99
CNP +	1678	Glasflugel H.201 Standard Libelle	264		3.72	S. & J.McKenzie	Camphill	7.99
CNV	1683	Slingsby T.59F Kestrel 19	1790		6.72	P.H.Fanshawe & E.A.Smith "229"	Snitterfield	1.99
CNW	1684	Slingsby T.59F Kestrel 19	1791		7.72	A.R.Jones "625"	Camphill	2.99
CNX	1685	Slingsby T.59F Kestrel 20	1792		7.72	D.Starer "818"	Dunstable	1.99
CNY	1686	Glasflugel H.201 Standard Libelle	322		9.72	S.B.Marshall & Ptnrs "151"	Portmoak	8.99
CPA	1688	Glasflugel H.201B Standard Libelle	328		9.72	A.T.Hirst & S.Pugh "466" Booker		3.99
CPB	1689	Slingsby T.59D Kestrel 19	1796		10.72	P.Turner & Ptnrs "985"	North Hill	6.99
CPC +	1690	PZL SZD-32A Foka 5	W-546		3.72	J.Davidson	Enstone	5.99
CPD	1691	Schleicher ASW17	17026		3.74	E.F.Allsop "292"	Long Mynd	3.99
CPE +	1692	EoN AP.5 Olympia 2B	EoN/O/120	RAFGSA.233	3.72	Not known	Edgehill	8.95*
						(W/O Arbroath 10. 9.94; stored 5.97)		
CPF	1693	Glasflugel H.201 Standard Libelle	267		3.72	J.M.Norman & P.Elvidge "T15"	Pocklington	3.99
CPG +	1694	Schleicher Ka7 Rhonadler	7036	D-4029	4.72	Queens University GC	Bellarena	8.99
CPJ +	1696	Schleicher Ka6E	4059	OO-ZDA	4.72	J.Herd & Ptnrs "521" Pocklington		3.99
CPM +	1699	Glasflugel H.201 Standard Libelle	179		4.72	D.J.Gilder	Aston Down	3.99
CPU	1706	Schempp-Hirth HS.4 Standard Cirrus	194		4.72	J P J.Ketelaar "761" Feshiebridge		11.99
CPV +	1707	PZL SZD-30 Pirat	B-470		3.72	D.Hale & Ptnrs	Bidford	2.98
CPX +	1709	PZL SZD-30 Pirat	B-460		4.72	J.Murphy "552"	Usk	5.99
CQC	1714	PZL SZD-30 Pirat	B-472		4.72	P.R.Tavener & Ptnrs "601"	Tibenham	7.99
CQD +	1715	Schleicher K8B	419/58	D-5625	4.72	Burn GC	Burn	6.99
CQG +	1718	EoN AP.5 Olympia 2B	EoN/O/044	RAFGSA.206 BGA.542	4.72	L.McKenzie	Sutton Bank	2.99
CQJ	1720	Slingsby T.59A Kestrel 17	1727		5.72	A.Shelton "17K"	Portmoak	6.99
CQL	1722	Schempp-Hirth HS.5 Nimbus 2	11		5.72	M N Erlund "339"	East Kirkby	4.99
CQM	1723	Slingsby T.59F Kestrel 19	1765		5.72	J.A.Knowles "234"	Odiham	4.99
CQN +	1724	Schempp-Hirth HS.4 Standard Cirrus	204G		5.72	M.G.Sankey & Ptnrs	Lasham	3.99
CQP	1725	Schempp-Hirth HS.5 Nimbus 2	4		4.72	D.Caunt & Ptnrs "918"	Booker	2.99
CQQ	1726	Schempp-Hirth HS.5 Nimbus 2	5		4.72	G.L.Barrett "139"	Bidford	8.99
CQR	1727	Schempp-Hirth HS.4 Standard Cirrus	220G		5.72	G.W.Burge & R.N.Kill "703"	Sandhill Farm, Shrivenham	8.98
CQT +	1729	Schleicher Ka7 Rhonadler (mod)	603	D-5712	6.72	Shenington GC (Stored Kemble 7.97)	Edgehill	7.96*
CQW	1732	PZL SZD-36A Cobra 15	W-572		6.72	C.R.H.Partington "342"	Carlton Moor	6.99
CQX	1733	PZL SZD-30 Pirat	B-483		6.72	The "B" Syndicate "789"	Lleweni Parc	5.99
CQY	1734	Schempp-Hirth HS.4 Standard Cirrus	214		6.72	S.R.Blackmore "D49"	Edgehill	1.99
CRA +	1736	Schleicher Ka7 Rhonadler	7009	???	7.72	Welland GC	Lyveden	4.99
CRB	1737	Glasflugel H.201 Standard Libelle	243		6.72	A.I.Mawer "241"	Winthorpe	5.99
CRD	1739	PZL SZD-36A Cobra 15	W-578		7.72	J.Durman	Pocklington	6.94*
CRF	1741	Birmingham Guild BG-135	001		2.72	C D Stevens "351"	Lee-on-Solent	5.99
CRH	1743	Schempp-Hirth HS.4 Standard Cirrus	233G		8.72	E MacDonald "650"	Portmoak	2.99
CRK	1745	Slingsby T.8 Tutor	930	XE760 VM539	7.72	I.D.Smith (On rebuild 9.97)	Nympsfield	8.82*
CRL +	1746	Schleicher ASK13	13013	???	8.72	Midland GC	Long Mynd	3.99
CRM	1747	Grunau Baby III	1	RAFGSA.361 D-8061	7.72	R.Wasey & Ptnrs "Grumpy" (On display 3.97)	Sandown	11.96*
CRN	1748	Schempp-Hirth HS.4 Standard Cirrus	234G		8.72	M.G.Woollard "566"	Aston Down	3.99
CRQ +	1750	Glasflugel H.201B Standard Libelle	326		7.72	K.Counsell & Ptnrs	Usk	4.99
CRS	1752	Glasflugel H.201B Standard Libelle	325		8.72	J.E.F.Porter & Ptnrs "707" Booker		7.99
CRT +	1753	Schleicher ASK13	13396		8.72	Bowland Forest GC	Chipping	2.99
CRV +	1755	Glasflugel H.201B Standard Libelle	329		8.72	P.Arthur & Ptnr	Perranporth	5.99
CRW	1756	Glasflugel H.201 Standard Libelle	324		9.72	M.Buick "417"	Nympsfield	5.98
CRZ	1759	Slingsby T.8 Tutor	-	RAFGSA.178	10.72	Not known (Stored 9.96) Chipping		*
CSA	1760	Slingsby T.59F Kestrel 19	1797		11.72	P.L Poole "182"	Parham Park	4.99
CSB +	1761	Slingsby T.59F Kestrel 19	1798		11.72	N.D.Paveley	Pocklington	6.99
CSD	1763	Slingsby T.59D Kestrel 19	1800		12.72	M.J.Silver "53"	Pocklington	6.99
CSF	1765	Slingsby T.59F Kestrel 19	1802		1.73	G.R.Glazebrook "347"	Dunstable	1.99

Regn	BGA No.	Type	C/n	P/I	Regn	Owner/operator	Probable Base	CA Expy
CSG	1766	Slingsby T.59D Kestrel 19	1804		3.73	A.Swann & D.Williams "217"		
							Lasham	6.99
CSJ +	1768	Glasflugel H.201B Standard Libelle	372		1.73	B.Searle	Enstone	7.99
CSK	1769	Slingsby T.59D Kestrel 20	1806		3.73	H.A. & J.E.Torode "387"(Belgium)		4.99
CSL	1770	Slingsby T.8 Tutor	928	XE758 VF181	10.72	W.D.Baars	(Netherlands)	1.99
CSN	1772	Pilatus B4 PC-11	021		12.72	M.Hine "527"	North Hill	9.99
CSP +	1773	Pilatus B4 PC-11	027		3.73	V.Howells	Chipping	3.99
CSR	1775	Glasflugel H.201 Standard Libelle	368		1.73	W.G.Miller & Ptnrs "808"		
							North Connel	6.99
CSV	1779	PZL SZD-30 Pirat	B-515		12.72	P.Udell & Ptnrs	Gamston	8.98
CSW +	1780	Pilatus B4 PC-11	022		12.72	I.H.Keyser	Waldershare Park	2.99
CTA +	1784	EoN AP.5 Olympia 2B	EoN/O/146	RAFGSA.285	12.72	A.Roberts	Wormingford	6.98
CTB	1785	Schempp-Hirth HS.4 Standard Cirrus	264G		1.73	M.J.Gibbons & Ptnrs "579"		
							Weston-on-the-Green	4.99
CTE	1788	Schleicher ASW17	17012		1.73	D.Edwards & S.Blackmore "40"		
							Lasham	2.99
CTF	1789	Schleicher Ka4 Rhonlerche	01	D-3574	1.73	M.Goodman	Winthorpe	9.98
CTJ +	1792	Slingsby T.59D Kestrel 19	1810		3.73	H.B.Walrond & Ptnrs	Rattlesden	2.99
CTL +	1794	Slingsby T.59D Kestrel 19	1812		3.73	P.Codd "116"	Wormingford	4.99
CTM	1795	Slingsby T.59D Kestrel 19	1813		3.73	A S Raffan "401"	Crowland	3.99
CTN +	1796	Slingsby T.59D Kestrel 19	1814		4.73	J.T Goodall	Sutton Bank	2.99
CTP	1797	Slingsby T.59D Kestrel 19	1815		4.73	D.C.Austin "49"	Sutton Bank	6.99
CTQ	1798	Slingsby T.59D Kestrel 20	1816		4.73	K.A.Moules "924"	Bicester	4.99
CTR	1799	Slingsby T.59D Kestrel 19	1817		5.73	D.J.Marpole "402"		
							Kingston Deverill	2.99
CTS +	1800	EoN AP.5 Olympia 2B	EoN/O/157	RNGSA	1.73	P.J.Thornbury	Kingston Deverill	4.99
CTT	1801	Schempp-Hirth HS.4 Standard Cirrus	277G		1.73	S.M.L.Young "873"	Nympsfield	2.99
CTU	1802	Glasflugel H.201 Standard Libelle	371		2.73	J.R.Humpherson "501"	Camphill	6.99
CTV	1803	PZL SZD-30 Pirat	B-528		2.73	B.Fantham	Rhigos	5.99
CTW	1804	PZL SZD-9 bis Bocian 1E	P-598		2.73	Mendip GC "1"	Halesland	8.99
CTX +	1805	PZL SZD-30 Pirat	B-527		2.73	M.W Fisher	Parham Park	7.99
CTZ +	1807	Schleicher K8B	8035/B5	D-KOCU	4.73	Scottish Gliding Union Ltd		
							Portmoak	4.99
CUB +	1809	Pilatus B4 PC-11	047		3.73	P.Noonan & D.Wardell	Enstone	6.99
CUC +	1810	Pilatus B4 PC-11	003	HB-1102	5.73	H.M.Pantin & Ptnrs	Dishforth	3.98
CUD	1811	Yorkshire Sailplanes YS-53 Sovereign 02			7.72	D R Bricknell "158"	Saltby	3.99
		(Built from Slingsby T.53B XV951 c/n 1574 w/o 11.4.72)						
CUF	1813	Yorkshire Sailplanes YS-55 Consort	04		11.73	C.G.Taylor & Ptnrs "331"		
							Sutton Bank	7.98
CUJ	1816	Glasflugel H.201B Standard Libelle	370		2.73	T.G.B.Hobbis & Ptnrs "706"Lasham		3.99
CUK	1817	Glasflugel H.201 Standard Libelle	367		3.73	G.R.Brown "380"	Dunstable	3.99
CUL	1818	Schempp-Hirth HS.4 Standard Cirrus	265G		4.73	L.G.Watts "550/10"		
							Husbands Bosworth	7.98
CUM +	1819	PZL SZD-30 Pirat	B-534		2.73	T.J.Mottershead	Pocklington	1.00
CUQ	1821	Pilatus B4 PC-11	040		2.73	A.E.Hayes & Ptnrs "633"		
							Aston Down	11.99
CUS	1822	Schempp-Hirth HS.2 Cirrus VTC	126Y		3.73	G.F.Wearing "842"	Chipping	5.99
CUT	1823	Pilatus B4 PC-11	041		3.73	N.R.Cawte (On repair 1997)		
							Gamston	10.95*
CUZ +	1829	LET L-13 Blanik	025409		4.73	East Sussex GC	Ringmer	11.98
CVA +	1830	LET L-13 Blanik	025418		3.73	D.Wiseman	Andreas, IoM	4.99
CVB +	1831	LET L-13 Blanik	025419		3.73	Farnborough GC		
							Sackville Lodge, Riseley	5.99
CVC +	1832	PZL SZD-30 Pirat	B-535		3.73	J.P.Batty	Dunstable	5.99
CVE	1834	Schempp-Hirth HS.2 Cirrus VTC	127Y		3.73	I.M.Stenning "BZ Gransden Lodge		3.99
CVF +	1835	Schempp-Hirth HS.2 Cirrus VTC	128Y		3.73	I.Hamilton	Chipping	5.99
CVG	1836	Pilatus B4 PC-11	045		3.73	I H Keyser "656"		
							Waldershare Park	4.99
CVH +	1837	Schempp-Hirth SHK	34	N6524A	3.73	A.K.Mitchell	Parham Park	4.98
CVJ +	1838	Breguet Br.905S Fauvette	37	F-CCJH	6.73	M.P Maughan	Burn	5.99
CVK	1839	Pilatus B4 PC-11	048		3.73	T.M.Perkins "92"	Dunstable	6.99
CVL	1840	Glasflugel H.201B Standard Libelle	369		2.73	T.R.Graham "253"		
							Kirton-in-Lindsey	3.99
CVM	1841	Pilatus B4 PC-11 (powered)	036		3.73	J.A.Mace	Old Sarum	3.99P
CVN	1842	PZL SZD-36A Cobra 15	W-608		3.73	N.Bickham "818"	Dunkeswell	9.96*
CVP +	1843	PZL SZD-9 bis Bocian 1E	P-597		3.73	Deeside GC	Aboyne	11.99
CVQ	1844	Glasflugel H.201 Standard Libelle	374		3.73	C.J.Taunton & Ptnrs "428"		
							Dunstable	4.99
CVR +	1845	PZL SZD-30 Pirat	B-538		3.73	L.J.Bevan	Weston-on-the-Green	12.97
CVS +	1846	PZL SZD-36A Cobra 15	W-610		3.73	E.W.Room	Pocklington	6.99
CVT	1847	PZL SZD-36A Cobra 15	W-609		3.73	J.Amor	Ridgewell	1.95*
CVV +	1849	Pilatus B4 PC-11	028		3.73	F.R.Wolff & Ptnrs	Brent Tor	12.99
CVW	1850	Slingsby T.59D Kestrel 19/22	1818		5.73	P.Hogarth "423"	Aston Down	4.99
CVX	1851	Slingsby T.59D Kestrel 19	1823		7.73	Not known "3"	Aston Down	*
						(Crashed on launch Portmoak 6.9.80: wreck stored 6.98)		
CVY	1852	Slingsby T.59D Kestrel 19	1821		7.73	J.Ainsworth "355"	Sleap	6.98*
						(Damaged Upavon 15.6.97)		

Regn	BGA No.	Type	C/n	P/I	Regn	Owner/operator	Probable Base	CA Expy
CVZ	1853	Slingsby T.59D Kestrel 19	1824		8.73	T.R.F.Gaunt & Ptnrs "269" Kingston Deverill		3.99
CWA	1854	Slingsby T.59D Kestrel 19	1825		9.73	D.K.Gardiner & Ptnrs "363" Portmoak		7.99
CWB +	1855	Slingsby T.59D Kestrel 19	1833		1.74	K.Fairness	Milfield	3.99
CWD +	1857	Slingsby T.59D Kestrel 19	1835		1.74	A.Kennedy & J.R.Dransfield "998" Aboyne		2.99
CWE	1858	Glasflugel H.201 Standard Libelle	482		1.74	T.W.S.Stoker "468"	Rufforth	4.99
CWF +	1859	Slingsby T.59D Kestrel 19	1838		2.74	P.Nicholson	Thame	3.99
CWG	1860	Glasflugel H.201 Standard Libelle	391		4.73	K.H.Gregory "322"	Camphill	7.99
CWH +	1861	Schleicher ASK13	13424		4.73	York Gliding Centre	Rufforth	7.99
CWJ +	1862	Schleicher Ka7 Rhonadler	630	D-6057 D-5723	4.73	Wolds GC	Pocklington	5.99
CWL +	1864	Schempp-Hirth HS.2 Cirrus VTC	125Y		4.73	J.Richardson	Chipping	1.98*
CWN +	1866	Glasflugel H.201B Standard Libelle	386		4.73	R.B.Petrie	Portmoak	2.99
CWR	1869	Schempp-Hirth HS.2 Cirrus VTC	133Y		4.73	S.T.Bonser "917"	Dunstable	4.99
CWS	1870	Schempp-Hirth HS.2 Cirrus VTC	129Y		4.73	R.W.Cassels & Ptnrs	Ridgewell	5.99
CWT	1871	Glasflugel H.201B Standard Libelle	384		4.73	R.J.Peck "978"	Camphill	3.98
CWV	1873	Schleicher Rhonlerche II	123	D-8226	4.73	11th Bristol (Headley Park) Scout Troop "Z" (Stored 8.98) Aston Down		5.94*
CWX	1875	Glasflugel H.201 Standard Libelle	36	RAFGSA.132	4.73	C.A.Weyman & Ptnrs "832" Gallows Hill		3.99
CWY	1876	Glasflugel H.201 Standard Libelle	387		4.73	J Dixon "146"	Drumshade	1.99
CWZ +	1877	Glasflugel H.201 Standard Libelle	392		4.73	Derby & Lancs GC	Camphill	8.99
CXH +	1885	PZL SZD-36A Cobra 15	W-619		6.73	C D Street "544"	Lasham	9.99
CXJ	1886	PZL SZD-36A Cobra 15	W-618		6.73	S R Bruce "791"	Portmoak	7.99
CXK +	1887	Glasflugel H.201 Standard Libelle	383		6.73	C.A Turner	Tatenhill	11.99
CXL +	1888	PZL SZD-30 Pirat	B-548		6.73	R.T.Page & Ptnrs	Wormingford	9.98
CXM	1889	Slingsby T.59D Kestrel 19	1820		7.73	R.P.Beck & Ptnrs "532"	Dishforth	4.99
CXN	1890	Yorkshire Sailplanes YS-55 Consort	05		12.73	A.A.Priestley & Ptnrs "508" Sutton Bank		5.99
CXP	1891	Yorkshire Sailplanes YS-55 Consort	07	BGA.1892	5.76	A.D.Coles	North Hill	10.96*
CXV +	1897	Yorkshire Sailplanes YS-53 Sovereign	03		7.74	C.Wright	Chipping	4.99
CXW +	1898	Yorkshire Sailplanes YS-53 Sovereign	1654		3.74	The Tin Bird Syndicate Aboyne (Wreck stored 5.94)		7.93*
CYA	1902	Pilatus B4 PC-11	072		7.73	E.J.Bromwell & Ptnrs "503" North Hill		4.99
CYC +	1904	Pilatus B4 PC-11	029	N47247	7.73	B.Gent & Ptnrs Ringmer (As "N47247")		4.99
CYD +	1905	PZL SZD-30 Pirat	B-559		7.73	I.Johnstone	Portmoak	4.98
CYG +	1908	Glasflugel H.201 Standard Libelle	441		8.73	M.J Guard	Husbands Bosworth	2.99
CYH +	1909	Slingsby T.41 Skylark 2	995	AGA.4 BGA.801	8.73	B.J.Griffin	Kirton-in-Lindsey	8.99
CYJ +	1910	DFS/49 Grunau Baby 2B (Built 1943 by Petera)	031000	D-6021	8.73	C.Bird (Stored 12.95)	Dunstable	1.90*
CYK	1911	Pilatus B4 PC-11	078		8.73	A.M.Walker t/a Pilatus Soaring Syndicate "248"	Strathaven	4.99
CYM	1913	Schempp-Hirth HS.4 Standard Cirrus	48	RAFGSA D-0578	9.73	L.J.Hartfield "299"	Lasham	3.99
CYN	1914	Slingsby T.59D Kestrel 19 (Built D Jones & T Pentelow)	JP.054		10.74	S.Cooke & Ptnrs "N4" Gransden Lodge		11.99
CYP	1915	Schempp-Hirth HS.4 Standard Cirrus	369		9.73	O.Stuart-Menteth "982" Cranfield		2.99
CYQ	1916	Schempp-Hirth HS.4 Standard Cirrus	364		9.73	D.A.Smith & P.Dunthorne "477" Nympsfield		2.99
CYR +	1917	LET L-13 Blanik	025610		10.73	Not known	Cranfield	12.90*
		(Damaged nr Bidford 8.7.90; rebuilt using fuselage of BGA.2958 c/n 025817; stored 7.97)						
CYT +	1919	Schempp-Hirth HS.4 Standard Cirrus	357G		9.73	R.Francis	Lleweni Parc	7.99
CYZ +	1925	Schleicher K8B	8882	RAFGSA	9.74	Oxford GC	Weston-on-the-Green	3.99
CZD +	1929	Pilatus B4 PC-11	081		12.73	S.R.Evans	Aston Down	6.99
CZE +	1930	PZL SZD-30 Pirat	S-0114		12.73	L E Ingram	Snitterfield	4.99
CZG +	1932	PZL SZD-30 Pirat	S-0116		12.73	I.Lang	Snitterfield	4.98
CZJ +	1934	PZL SZD-30 Pirat	S-0115		12.73	C.L Groves & Ptnrs Husbands Bosworth		5.99
CZL	1936	Glasflugel H.201 Standard Libelle	483		1.74	L P Woodage "504"	Dunstable	1.00
CZM +	1937	Munchen Mu-13D-III	10/52	D-1488	9.74	H.Chapple	Bicester	7.98
CZN +	1938	Schleicher ASW15B	15329		3.74	P.Tuppen & Ptnrs	Bembridge	4.99
CZQ +	1940	Slingsby T.59D Kestrel 19	1840		4.74	J.P.Walker & Ptnrs Husbands Bosworth		5.99
CZR +	1941	Slingsby T.59D Kestrel 19	1842		4.74	R.P.Brisbourne	Rufforth	11.99
CZS +	1942	Slingsby T.59D Kestrel 22	1844		5.74	P.Glennie	Portmoak	3.97*
CZT	1943	Slingsby T.59D Kestrel 19	1848		5.74	G.W.Camp "A3"	Enstone	3.99
CZU	1944	Slingsby T.59D Kestrel 19	1849		6.74	L.Merrett & P.F.Croote	Halesland	5.99
CZV	1945	Slingsby T.59D Kestrel 19	1850		7.74	V.F.G.Tull "415"	Dunstable	7.99
CZW +	1946	Slingsby T.59D Kestrel 20	1846		10.76	C.D Berry "667"	Cranfield	5.99
CZZ	1949	Slingsby T.59D Kestrel 19	1739		6.74	R.M.Grant "900"	Lasham	11.96*

Regn	BGA No.	Type	C/n	P/I	Regn	Owner/operator	Probable Base	CA Expy

DAA-DZZ

Regn	BGA No.	Type	C/n	P/I	Regn	Owner/operator	Probable Base	CA Expy
DAA +	1950	PZL SZD-9 bis Bocian 1E	P-639		3.74	Highland GC	Easterton	3.99
DAC	1952	PZL SZD-36A Cobra 15	W-656		3.74	C.D.Peacock	Husbands Bosworth	9.95*
DAJ	1958	Schempp-Hirth HS.5 Nimbus 2	50		3.74	J.D.Jones "14"	Nympsfield	4.99
DAL +	1960	EoN AP.6 Olympia 419	EoN/4/010	RAFGSA.301	4.74	D.M.Judd & Ptnrs	Snitterfield	9.99
DAM	1961	ICA IS-29D	27		4.74	W.T.Barnard "675"	Strathaven	9.97*
DAN	1962	PZL SZD-30 Pirat	S-0145		3.74	W.Pottinger & Ptnrs "526"	Ridgewell	3.99
DAP +	1963	PZL SZD-30 Pirat	S-0147		4.74	N.Crawford	Currock Hill	4.99
DAQ +	1964	PZL SZD-36A Cobra 15	W-657		4.74	C.Bigwood & Ptnrs	Lyveden	7.97*
DAR +	1965	Slingsby T.21B	?	RAFGSA.404	6.74	Nene Valley GC	Upwood	6.99
DAS +	1966	Schempp-Hirth HS.4 Standard Cirrus	378	(BGA.1925)	4.74	A.Hobson & Ptnrs	Burn	4.99
DAT +	1967	PZL SZD-30 Pirat	S-0149		4.74	The Borders GC	Milfield	4.99
DAU +	1968	PZL SZD-30 Pirat	S-0150		4.74	J.Sentance	Winthorpe	8.99
DAV	1969	PZL SZD-38A Jantar-1	B-608		4.74	R.M.Roberts "240"	Brent Tor	8.99
DAW +	1970	Schleicher Ka6CR	951	RAFGSA D-2025	6.74	R.Lapsley & B.Irwin	Bellarena	3.99
DBA	1974	EoN AP.5 Olympia 2B	EoN/O/156	RNGSA.208	6.74	W.R.Williams "207"	Halton	1.98
DBB +	1975	Slingsby T.51 Dart 17R (Built by Greenfly Avn)	DG/51/01		2.76	S.C.Fear	Crowland	3.99
DBC +	1976	Pilatus B4 PC-11	135		6.74	J.H.France & Ptnrs "851"	Shobdon	12.99
DBD +	1977	PZL SZD-30 Pirat	S-0202		6.74	E W Burgess	Cranfield	3.99
DBF +	1979	Schleicher Ka7 Rhonadler	179	RAFGSA RAFGSA.552/D-5473	6.74	Welland GC	Lyveden	1.99
DBG +	1980	ICA IS-29D	31		6.74	N.D Hughes	Lasham	5.99
DBJ +	1982	Slingsby T.59D Kestrel 19	1856	BGA.1892 BGA.1982	10.74	P L Sanderson "691"	Syerston	3.99
DBK	1983	Slingsby T.59D Kestrel 19	1861		12.74	R.E.Perry & C.Crabb "523"	North Hill	10.98
DBN	1986	Slingsby T.59D Kestrel 19	1857		3.75	A.C.Wright "617"	Sutton Bank	12.99
DBP	1987	Glasflugel H.205 Club Libelle	51		4.75	N.A.White "551"	Rattlesden	8.99
DBQ	1988	Slingsby T.59D Kestrel 19	1863		4.75	P.Ramsden "101"	Rufforth	5.99
DBR	1989	Slingsby T.59D Kestrel 19	1858		4.75	J.G.Bell "95"	Parham Park	5.99
DBS +	1990	Slingsby T.59D Kestrel 19	1864		4.75	J.W.Rice	Kirton-in-Lindsey	4.99
DBT +	1991	Schempp-Hirth Standard Austria S	35	F-CCPQ	7.74	F.J.Tucker "11"	Parham Park	7.99
DBV +	1993	PZL SZD-30 Pirat	S-0227		8.74	M.H.Bryan & Ptnrs	Usk	11.99
DBW +	1994	PZL SZD-9 bis Bocian 1E	P-641		8.74	Sackville GC	Sackville Lodge, Riseley	4.99
DBX +	1995	PZL SZD-9 bis Bocian 1E	P-642		8.74	Miss A.G.Veitch t/a Highland Bocian Syndicate	Easterton	10.99
DCA +	1998	PZL SZD-36A Cobra 15	W-686		9.74	M.J.North	Husbands Bosworth	9.98
DCC	2000	Glasflugel H.201B Standard Libelle	585		11.74	J.Warbey & M.Hutchinson "324"	Shobdon	2.99
DCE +	2002	Slingsby T.41 Skylark 2	1003	RAFGGA.540 PH-225	11.74	C.P.Race	Winthorpe	6.99
DCF	2003	Schleicher Ka6CR	6520	RAFGSA.356	11.74	R.Spencer "356"	Burn	7.95*
DCG	2004	Schleicher Ka2B	2	D-7064	12.74	Not known (Stored)	Falgunzeon	*
DCH +	2005	PZL SZD-30 Pirat	S-0315		11.74	Aquila GC	Hinton-in-the-Hedges	8.96*
DCJ	2006	PZL SZD-30 Pirat	S-0316		11.74	N.Jones (Crashed nr North Hill 29.3.97)	North Hill	3.98*
DCL	2008	LET L-13 Blanik	026154		12.74	Enstone Eagles GC (Wreck stored 6.96)	Enstone	8.92*
DCN	2010	Slingsby T.21B	?	RAFGGA.501	1.75	A.R.Worters	North Connel	7.95*
DCR +	2013	PZL SZD-9 bis Bocian 1E	P-670		1.75	Mendip GC (Crashed Halesland 13.6.96)	Halesland	10.96*
DCS +	2014	Slingsby T.45 Swallow	1538	RAFGGA.544	4.74	H.Dale & Ptnrs	Sutton Bank	6.99
DCW +	2018	Schleicher Ka6CR	1076	D-5228	2.75	Trent Valley GC	Kirton-in-Lindsey	7.99
DCY +	2020	Swales SD.3-15V (Rebuild of incomplete Yorkshire Sailplanes YS-55 Consort c/n 09)	01		2.75	J.C.Gibson & Ptnrs	Chipping	5.97*
DCZ +	2021	King-Elliott-Street Osprey (Believed to be converted Slingsby T.51 Dart but c/n conflicts BGA.1245)	1470		10.75	G.R.Burkert	Lasham	10.98P
DDA +	2022	Schempp-Hirth HS.4 Standard Cirrus	532G		2.75	M.J.Woodhead	Parham Park	3.99
DDB +	2023	Schleicher ASK13	13493		2.75	Norfolk GC	Tibenham	3.99
DDC	2024	Slingsby T.21B	1157	RAFGSA.313	3.75	J.Shaw & Ptnrs	Perranporth	5.99
DDD	2025	Schempp-Hirth HS.5 Nimbus 2	84	G-BKPM BGA.2025	3.75	D.D.Copeland "695"	Dunstable	2.99
DDE +	2026	PZL SZD-38A Jantar-1	B-641		4.75	B.Jones	Bidford	3.98
DDJ +	2030	ICA IS-29D	37		3.75	P.Andrews	Lyveden	7.98*
DDK	2031	PZL SZD-30 Pirat	S-0408		4.75	Portsmouth Naval GC (RNGSA N13)	Lee-on-Solent	9.99
DDL +	2032	Schleicher K8B	218/61	D-5156	4.75	Ouse GC	Rufforth	5.99
DDM	2033	Schempp-Hirth HS.2 Cirrus VTC	164Y		3.75	C.K.Davis & Ptnrs "959"	Gransden Lodge	2.99

Regn	BGA No.	Type	C/n	P/I	Regn	Owner/operator	Probable Base	CA Expy
DDN +	2034	PZL SZD-9 bis Bocian 1E	P-429	RAFGSA.393	3.75	Bath, Wilts & N.Dorset GC Kingston Deverill		5.99
DDR	2037	Schempp-Hirth HS.4 Standard Cirrus 531G			3.75	B.A.Pocock & Ptnrs "680" Kingston Deverill		2.99
DDS	2038	Schleicher ASW15	15009	D-0256	4.75	C.Skeate & Ptnrs "647"	Lasham	3.99
DDV	2041	PZL SZD-38A Jantar-1	B-664		4.75	G.V.McKirdy "536"	Edgehill	5.98*
DDW +	2042	PZL SZD-30 Pirat	S-0433		4.75	M.Dixon & Ptnrs	Parham Park	3.99
DDY +	2044	Schleicher Ka6CR	678	D-8841	4.75	Marchington GC	Tatenhill	2.99
DEB +	2047	Slingsby T.59D Kestrel 19	1866		10.75	T.Moss "169" Weston-on-the-Green		9.98
DEG +	2051	ICA IS-28B2	48		.	P. & H.Whitehead	Sutton Bank	5.99
DEN	2057	ICA IS-29D	41		4.75	S Struthers "586"	Feshiebridge	10.99
DEP +	2058	Schleicher Ka6CR	6452	AGA... BGA.2058/RAFGSA.350	4.75	C.Lawrence	Husbands Bosworth	3.99
DEQ	2059	Glasflugel H.205 Club Libelle	97		4.75	J.A.Holland & Ptnrs "716" Kingston Deverill		8.98
DEV +	2064	Schleicher Ka6CR	6453	RAFGSA.354	5.75	P.J.Groves & Ptnrs	Long Mynd	5.99
DEX +	2066	LET L-13 Blanik	026348	RAFGSA.R4 BGA.2066	6.75	N.Kelly	Talgarth	11.99
DEY +	2067	LET L-13 Blanik	026352	RAFGSA.R12 BGA.2067	6.75	Bath, Wilts & N.Dorset GC Kingston Deverill		7.99
DEZ	2068	ICA IS-29D	43		6.75	R.J.Everett "977" Sproughton (Damaged Lewknor 7.3.90: stored 12.95)		4.91*
DFC	2071	Schempp-Hirth HS.4 Standard Cirrus 592G			7.75	R.J.Marriott & A.Weatherhead "128" Cranfield		3.99
DFE +	2073	Molino PIK-20	20052		7.75	M.Roff-Jarrett	Parham Park	3.99
DFJ	2077	Schleicher Rhonbussard	?	D-5700 RAFGSA	9.75	R.Abrahams & Syndicate	Dunstable	10.98
DFK +	2078	Molino PIK-20	20039	OH-500	9.75	M.J Fairclough	North Hill	2.99
DFL +	2079	PZL SZD-38A Jantar-1	B-682		9.75	R.J.Sharman ("245" under wing) Kenley		7.99
DFN	2081	Glaser-Dirks DG-100	30		9.75	D.J.Clarke "899"	Wormingford	7.99
DFP +	2082	Aeromere M.100S	029	I-LSUO	9.75	D. & J.Lee	Pocklington	6.98
DFR	2084	Grob G.102 Astir CS	1038		10.75	T.A.Polak "906"	Lasham	3.99
DFU	2087	PZL SZD-38A Jantar-1	B-685		10.75	J.E.New & Ptnrs "30"	Lasham	3.96*
DFV	2088	PZL SZD-38A Jantar-1	B-684		10.75	R.R.Rodwell "164"	Bellarena	5.98
DFW +	2089	PZL SZD-30 Pirat	S-0545		10.75	M.J.Appleby	Strubby	1.99
DFX	2090	PZL SZD-41A Jantar Standard	B-691		10.75	J.C.Tait & Ptnrs "767"	Easterton	12.98
DFY +	2091	Schempp-Hirth HS.4 Standard Cirrus 396		AGA...	11.75	G.Lambert Sth Kensington, London (The Science Museum Flight Gallery 12.97)		1.93*
DFZ	2092	Molino PIK-20	20080		11.75	M.J.Leach & J.P.Ashcroft "774" Sandhill Farm, Shrivenham		8.99
DGA +	2093	Schleicher K8B	8587	RAFGSA BGA.1926/D-....	11.75	Welland GC	Lyveden	1.99
DGB +	2094	LET L-13 Blanik	026459		11.75	Black Mountains GC Bidford (Damaged Bidford 21.10.95; stored 5.98)		2.96*
		(Rebuilt with fuselage from BGA.2061 pre 1995)						
DGE +	2097	Schempp-Hirth HS.4 Standard Cirrus 75 606			12.75	T.E.Snoddy	Bellarena	8.99
DGG +	2099	Schleicher Ka6E	4061	RAFGSA.263	12.75	N.Holmes & Ptnrs	Long Mynd	7.98
DGH +	2100	PZL SZD-30 Pirat	B-533	RNGSA BGA.2100	12.75	D.Hilton & Ptnr	Pocklington	7.97*
DGK +	2102	Schleicher Ka6CR	6287	D-3224	12.75	IBM GC "Betty Blue"	Lasham	5.99
DGP +	2106	LET L-13 Blanik	026560		4.76	J.M.Purves "631"	Rufforth	6.99
DGT	2110	Schleicher Ka2B	181	D-5469	5.76	Not known (Stored)	Falgunzeon	*
DGV	2112	Breguet Br.905S Fauvette	2	HB-632	5.76	T.Cust & Ptnrs	Burn	6.97*
DGX	2114	Schempp-Hirth HS.4 Standard Cirrus 75 619		AGA.3 BGA.2114	5.76	G.R.Seaman & Ptnrs "610"	Lasham	5.99
DGY	2115	Schempp-Hirth HS.5 Nimbus 2	105		5.76	J.H.Taylor "195"	Nympsfield	1.99
DHA +	2117	Schleicher K8B	1055	D-8848 D-5148	5.76	Booker GC	Booker	1.99
		(C/n conflicts with D-8616)						
DHB +	2118	PZL SZD-30 Pirat	S-0643		5.76	J.Winsworth	Tibenham	6.98
DHC	2119	PZL SZD-41A Jantar Standard	B-710	(BGA.2109)	5.76	M.C.Burlock "811"	Aston Down	8.99
DHG +	2123	Schleicher Ka6CR	1131	D-5170	5.76	Angus GC	Drumshade	8.99
DHH	2124	Molino PIK-20B	20124		5.76	R.A.Holroyd "116"	Pocklington	5.99
DHJ +	2125	Glaser-Dirks DG-100	48		1.76	H.D.Armitage	Shobdon	3.99
DHK	2126	Glaser-Dirks DG-100	50		1.76	R.Dell & B.J.Griffin "A30" Kirton-in-Lindsey		3.99
DHL +	2127	Glaser-Dirks DG-100	52		1.76	K.Adam	Aboyne	7.99
DHM +	2128	Schleicher Ka6E	4124	RAFGSA.26	1.76	J.G.Heard	Seighford	2.99
DHN	2129	Molino PIK-20B	20082		1.76	G J Bass "824"	Challock	4.99
DHP	2130	Slingsby T.45 Swallow	45176		1.76	Dumfries & Galloway GC Falgunzeon		10.89*
		(C/n is type/year)						
		(Components ex BGA.1041 c/n 1329: w/o 3.4.64 with parts from BGA.1032; on rebuild 5.95)						
DHR +	2132	Slingsby T.53B	1718		2.76	E.MacDonald	Portmoak	6.95*
DHT +	2134	Schleicher Ka6E	4065	???	2.76	I.G Lumley & Ptnrs Bryngwyn Bach		11.98
DHV +	2136	Molino PIK-20B	20111		3.76	J.D. & G.J.Walker	Booker	5.99

Regn	BGA No.	Type	C/n	P/I	Regn	Owner/operator	Probable Base	CA Expy
DHW	2137	Schempp-Hirth HS.5 Nimbus 2	106		3.76	A.J.Bauld "951"	Portmoak	2.99
DHY +	2139	Schleicher Ka7 Rhonadler	1137	RAFGSA.266 D-5162	4.76	G.Whittaker	Chipping	5.99
DHZ +	2140	PZL SZD-30 Pirat	S-0641		4.76	Peterborough & Spalding GC Crowland		3.99
DJA +	2141	PZL SZD-30 Pirat	S-0642		4.76	Northumbria GC	Milfield	9.99
DJB	2142	Schleicher K8B	8879	AGA.17 BGA.2142/RAFGSA.397	4.77	Portsmouth Naval GC (RNGSA.N11) Lee-on-Solent		2.99
DJD	2144	Grob G.102 Astir CS	1226		6.76	P.Gascoigne & Ptnrs Kingston Deverill		2.99
DJE +	2145	Schleicher Ka6CR	6412	D-3682	6.76	M.Burton	Shobdon	5.98
DJG	2147	Schleicher Ka2B Rhonschwalbe	231	D-6179	6.76	J.Harmer "K2"	Lasham	5.99
DJJ +	2149	Schleicher ASK18	18029		6.76	Mendip GC	Halesland	3.99
DJK +	2150	Schleicher ASK18	18030		6.76	Booker GC	Booker	5.99
DJL +	2151	PZL SZD-41A Jantar Standard	B-714		6.76	A.M.Cooper	Bryngwyn Bach	3.99
DJM +	2152	PZL SZD-41A Jantar Standard	B-715		6.76	T.E.Betts	Tatenhill	7.99
DJN	2153	Molino PIK-20B	20140C		7.76	S.L.Cambourne "407"	Lasham	4.99
DJP +	2154	Schleicher K8B	8588	RAFGSA	7.76	Sackville GC Sackville Lodge, Riseley		5.99
DJQ	2155	Grob G.102 Astir CS	1258		7.76	H.Evans & D.J.Jeffries "214" Usk		5.98
DJR	2156	Schleicher Ka6CR	680	D-8423	7.76	J.A.Walker	Thruxton	11.96*
DJS	2157	Schempp-Hirth SHK-1	51	SE-TNF OY-MFX/HB-898	7.76	S.J.Collins	Nympsfield	5.98
DJT +	2158	Schleicher Ka7 Rhonadler (Mod) (See BGA.4271 which is marked "DJT")	?	RAFGSA	7.76	Enstone Eagles GC	Enstone	7.99
DJW	2161	Manuel Condor	1		7.76	C.V. & R.C.Inwood	Booker	5.98
DJX +	2162	Grob G.102 Astir CS	1259		7.76	D.Cruickshank & Ptnrs "614" Aboyne		2.99
DJZ	2164	Eiri PIK-20B	20144		7.76	D.S.Puttock "989"	Halesland	8.99
DKB +	2166	Schempp-Hirth Standard Austria S	32	F-CCPR	8.76	J R Parr	Burn	11.99
DKC +	2167	Schleicher K8B	8261	D-1431	8.76	Yorkshire GC	Sutton Bank	12.99
DKD	2168	Glasflugel H.206 Hornet	67	(BGA.2165)	8.76	I.M.Evans "759"	Usk	8.98
DKE +	2169	Schleicher ASK13	13548		8.76	South Wales GC	Usk	1.99
DKG +	2171	Schleicher Ka6CR	6233	D-4327	8.76	C.Nunn & Ptnrs	Wormingford	4.99
DKH	2172	LET L-13 Blanik	026644		8.76	H.E.Birch "769"	Rufforth	4.99
DKK	2174	Schempp-Hirth SHK-1	32	HB-864	8.76	C.Buzzard & D.J.Deacon "884" Husbands Bosworth		5.95*
DKL	2175	Schempp-Hirth HS.5 Nimbus 2	086	D-2111	9.76	G.J.Croll "444"	Snitterfield	3.99
DKM +	2176	Glasflugel H.206 Hornet	49	D-7816	9.76	M.Lee	Rattlesden	4.99
DKN +	2177	Schleicher Ka6CR	6456	D-9358	3.77	D.Lees & Ptnrs	Wormingford	4.98
DKQ +	2179	Glaser-Dirks DG-100G	91G11		9.76	G.Peters	North Hill	2.99
DKR	2180	Grob G.102 Astir CS	1327		9.76	G.D.Crawford "360" Weston-on-the-Green		4.99
DKS	2181	Grob G.102 Astir CS	1330		12.76	C.K.Lewis "788"	Lasham	5.98
DKT	2182	Eiri PIK-20B	20155		9.76	G.Barnham "185"	Rufforth	2.99
DKU +	2183	Grob G.102 Astir CS	1326		11.76	G.Jennings	Lasham	3.99
DKV	2184	Grob G.102 Astir CS	1328		9.76	T.J.Ireson "391" Sandhill Farm, Shrivenham		7.99
DKW +	2185	Grob G.102 Astir CS	1329		9.76	D.H.Smith	Edgehill	1.99
DKX	2186	Grob G.102 Astir CS	1331		9.76	L.R. & J.M.Bennett "353"	Booker	3.99
DKY +	2187	Schleicher Ka7 Rhonadler	7187	RAFGSA.342	9.76	Defford Aero Club	Pershore	4.98
DKZ +	2188	Glasflugel H.205 Club Libelle	111	RAFGSA.774	11.76	P.Jackson & C.Parsons	Bidford	5.99
DLA +	2189	Pilatus B4 PC-11	149	RAFGSA	9.76	A.Hodges	Camphill	2.99
DLB +	2190	Schleicher ASK18	18040		9.76	Vale of White Horse GC Sandhill Farm, Shrivenham		8.99
DLC	2191	Schleicher ASK13	13549		10.76	Lasham Gliding Society "C" Lasham		12.99
DLD +	2192	Schleicher K8B	8766	RAFGSA.383	10.76	Shalbourne SG	Rivar Hill	5.99
DLE +	2193	Schleicher Ka6E	4074	AGA.8 RAFGSA	10.76	W.P.Grundy	Talgarth	8.96*
DLG	2195	Schempp-Hirth HS.4 Standard Cirrus	579	AGA.2	10.76	S.Naylor "596"	Burn	9.99
DLH	2196	Grob G.102 Astir CS77	1646		2.77	B.Bamber & R.Smith "378"	Lasham	4.99
DLJ +	2197	Molino PIK-20B	20157		12.76	M.S Parks	Milfield	6.99
DLM	2200	Grob G.102 Astir CS	1260	(BGA.2163)	11.76	Highland GC "266"	Easterton	3.99
DLP +	2202	Schleicher Ka6CR	6519	RAFGSA.355	11.76	J.R Crosse	Crowland	5.99
DLR +	2204	Scheibe L-Spatz 55	647	BGA.2654	11.76	Dumfries & District GC		
		(Quoted as ex D-3659 but unconfirmed)		BGA.2204/D-5638		Falgunzeon		8.99
DLS +	2205	Schleicher K8B	8650	D-5718	11.76	Devon & Somerset GC	North Hill	6.98
DLT	2206	ICA IS-28B2	32		12.76	A.Woodrow "485"	Tibenham	5.99
DLU	2207	ICA IS-28B2	33	RAFGSA.R92 EI-141/BGA.2207	12.76	Crusaders GC "R92" Kingsfield, Dhekelia		11.99
DLW +	2209	PZL SZD-30 Pirat	B-467	PH-433	12.76	G.Bryce & Ptnrs	North Connel	4.96*
DLX +	2210	Slingsby T.45 Swallow	1494	RAFGGA.539	12.76	M.Sanderson	Milfield	5.95*
DLY +	2211	Eiri PIK-20D	20509		1.77	D.C Adlam & Ptnrs	Dunstable	3.99
DLZ	2212	Swales SW.3-15T	03		12.76	R.Harris "456"	Thruxton	4.98

Regn	BGA No.	Type	C/n	P/I	Regn	Owner/operator	Probable Base	CA Expy
DMB	2214	Schleicher K8B	8209	D-4331	1.77	DRA GC "Kate" "831" Odiham		7.99
DMD	2216	Glaser-Dirks DG-100	75		12.76	B.T.Payne & A.Jenkins "251"		1.99
							Weston-on-the-Green	
DMF +	2218	Schleicher Ka7 Rhonadler	7073	D-4313	1.77	Staffordshire GC Seighford		7.99
DMG +	2219	Schleicher K8B	8763	RAFGSA.382	1.77	Dorset GC Gallows Hill		5.99
DMH +	2220	Grob G.102 Astir CS	1511		1.77	Oxford GC Weston-on-the-Green		4.99
DMJ	2221	Schleicher K8B	8077	PH-290	2.77	Not known (Stored) Strathaven		*
DMK	2222	Schempp-Hirth SHK	25	D-5401	2.77	T.Barnes "593" Aston Down		
DML +	2223	Schleicher Ka7 Rhonadler	929	D-6194 D-5005	2.77	Newark & Notts GC Winthorpe		3.98
DMM	2224	Schempp-Hirth HS.5 Nimbus 2	125		2.77	T.E.Linee "338" Gallows Hill		2.99
DMN +	2225	Glasflugel H.303 Mosquito	20		2.77	A.Crowden Booker		3.99
DMP	2226	Grob G.102 Astir CS	1239	ZS-GKF	2.77	D.G.Nisbet "233" Dunstable		3.99
DMQ +	2227	Schleicher Ka6E	4062	RAFGSA.254	2.77	A.R.Bushnell & Ptnr Crowland		5.99
DMR +	2228	Grob G.102 Astir CS	1435		2.77	L.Beale & Ptnrs "511"		
							Parham Park	3.99
DMS	2229	Glasflugel H.201B Standard Libelle	385	RNGSA	3.77	M.D.White & Ptnrs "259" Burn		4.99
DMU	2231	Eiri PIK-20D	20524		3.77	A.C.Wanford & Ptnrs "392"		
		(C/n confirmed although duplicates C-GOPN)					Gransden Lodge	2.99
DMV +	2232	Eiri PIK-20D	20526		3.77	F.S.Parkhill "333" Crowland		9.99
DMX +	2234	Schleicher ASK13	13567		3.77	Kent GC Challock		12.99
		(Incorrectly marked as BGA.2294)						
DMY	2235	Eiri PIK-20D	20532		3.77	G.A.Piper "371" Parham Park		6.99
DNA +	2237	DFS/49 Grunau Baby 2B	?	RAFGSA.377 D-1821	2.77	H.Chapple Bicester		5.99
DNB	2238	DFS/49 Grunau Baby 2B	2	RAFGSA.380 D-8039	2.77	P.Underwood Eaton Bray		*
		(Flg.u.Arbeitsg.Hall built)				(On rebuild 12.95; to be in Luftwaffe c/s)		
DNC	2239	Grob G.102 Astir CS	1428		3.77	A.J.Carpenter "Natural High" "588"		
							Edgehill	6.99
DND +	2240	Pilatus B4 PC-11AF	136		3.77	R J Happs Lasham		11.99
DNE +	2241	Grob G.102 Astir CS77	1631		3.77	S P Woolcock Cranfield		4.99
DNF +	2242	PZL SZD-9 bis Bocian 1D	P-354	HB-657	4.77	M.G.Shaw Portmoak		3.99
DNG	2243	Schempp-Hirth HS.5 Nimbus 2	126		4.77	A.O.Harkins & A Brown "265"		
							Gallows Hill	2.99
DNJ +	2245	Schleicher ASK18	18042		4.77	Derby & Lancs GC Camphill		4.99
DNK	2246	Grob G.102 Astir CS	1434		4.77	A. & H.Page "745" Wormington		4.99
DNL +	2247	Glasflugel H.201 Standard Libelle	382	RAFGSA.742	4.77	P.R.Bergson Thame		5.99
DNQ	2251	Rolladen-Schneider LS-3	3035		1.77	M.Cooper "307" Challock		2.99
DNT +	2254	PZL SZD-30 Pirat	S-0712		4.77	M.Davidson & Ptnrs Drumshade		3.99
DNU +	2255	PZL SZD-42-1 Jantar 2	B-783		4.77	C.Rowland & Ptnrs "U2" Booker		5.99
DNV +	2256	Schleicher ASK13	13568		4.77	Buckminster GC Saltby		6.96*
DNW +	2257	Schleicher Ka6CR	829	???	5.77	F G Broom Rhigos		12.99
DNX +	2258	Schleicher Ka6CR	6094Si	D-5107	5.77	W.R.Schofield Burn		9.99
DNZ +	2260	Schleicher K8B	8095	???	5.77	North Wales GC Bryngwyn Bach		6.99
DPA +	2261	Schleicher ASK18	18044		5.77	Norfolk GC Tibenham		4.99
DPD +	2264	LET L-13 Blanik	026860		5.77	J.L.Whiting Bidford		3.96*
DPG +	2267	Munchen Mu-13D III	005	D-1327	5.77	G.J.Moore Dunstable		1.00
DPH	2268	Schempp-Hirth HS.7 Mini Nimbus	009		5.77	J.W.Murdoch "287" Strathaven		4.99
DPJ +	2269	Grob G.102 Astir CS77	1641		6.77	J.Liddiard & Ptnrs Lasham		3.99
DPK +	2270	Glasflugel H.303 Mosquito	27		6.77	G.Lawley Tatenhill		7.98
DPL	2271	Eiri PIK-20D	20549		6.77	D.W.Standen "437" Dunstable		6.99
DPP +	2274	Schleicher Ka2B Rhonschwalbe	105	D-1880	6.77	A.L.Roseberry & Ptnrs Aston Down		9.96*
DPQ	2275	Grob G.102 Astir CS77	1632		6.77	D.Patrick Falgunzeon		6.99
DPR	2276	Scheibe L-Spatz	05	D-1265	6.77	V.W.Jennings Parham Park		4.99
						t/a Shoreham Soaring Group		
						(As "D-1265") "Sparrowfahrt"		
DPT	2278	Scheibe L-Spatz 55	01	???	7.77	B.V.Smith Rufforth		7.98
DPU	2279	EoN AP.5 Olympia 2B	EoN/0/142	RAFGSA.274	7.77	C.H.Thompson Crowland		7.99
DPX +	2282	Schleicher ASW19	19126		7.77	G.L.Boaler & Ptnrs "440"		
							Nympsfield	3.99
DPY	2283	Grob G.102 Astir CS77	1652		8.77	D.S.Burton "375" Lasham		2.98
DPZ +	2284	Slingsby T.34A Sky	822	HB-561	8.77	N.McLaughlin Saltby		8.98
DQA +	2285	Schleicher ASK13	13582		8.77	Essex & Suffolk GC Wormington		3.99
DQB	2286	Grob G.102 Astir CS77	1653		8.77	G.R.Davey "848"Kirton-in-Lindsey		4.99
DQC	2287	Schleicher Ka6CR	6373Si	D-5725	8.77	R.J.Whitaker & I.F.Smith "572"		
							Lasham	3.98
DQD +	2288	Slingsby T.8 Tutor	-		8.77	K.Nurcombe Husbands Bosworth		6.99
		(Built from parts by F.Breeze)						
DQE	2289	Grob G.102 Astir CS77	1636		8.77	Heron GC "480" (RNGSA.N34)		
							RNAS Yeovilton	5.99
DQF	2290	Schleicher Ka6CR	6417	D-5827	9.77	P.James Saltby		2.99
DQG	2291	Grob G.102 Astir CS77	1649		9.77	Miss A.G.Veitch "770" Easterton		4.99
DQH	2292	Schmetz Condor IV	V2	D-8538	7.78	M.H.Birch Lasham		1.00
						(As "D-8538")		
DQJ +	2293	Schleicher Ka6CR	228	D-5467	9.77	Lakes GC Walney Island		3.99
DQK	2294	Schleicher Ka6E	4341	D-0541	9.77	S.Y.Duxbury & R.S.Hawley "542"		
		(See BGA.2234)					Camphill	5.99

Regn	BGA No.	Type	C/n	P/I	Regn	Owner/operator	Probable Base	CA Expy
DQL +	2295	Schleicher Ka8	509	D-5675	9.77	Aquila GC	Hinton-in-the-Hedges	2.99
DQM	2296	Pilatus B4 PC-11	138	RAFGSA	9.77	A.R.Dearden "196"	Ringmer	9.99
DQP +	2298	Schleicher K8B	1181	???	10.77	Coventry GC	Husbands Bosworth	6.99
DQR	2300	Grob G.102 Astir CS77	1667		10.77	N.R.Warren & Ptnrs "556"	Kingston Deverill	4.99
DQS +	2301	Schleicher Ka6CR	1065	D-5144	10.77	L.Hill	North Hill	3.99
DQU +	2303	Eiri PIK-20D	20579		10.77	A.Duncan	Portmoak	3.99
DQX +	2306	Schleicher Ka7 Rhonadler (Mod)	743	D-9127	11.77	Scottish Gliding Union Ltd	Portmoak	5.99
DQY	2307	Schleicher K8B	647	D-4375	11.77	Mendip GC	Halesland	8.99
DRA	2309	Schleicher Ka6CR	1118	D-9041	11.77	P Davis "904"	Bidford	8.99
DRB	2310	Glaser-Dirks DG-100	31	PH-532	11.77	J.D.Peck "86"	Bicester	3.99
DRD +	2312	Schleicher Ka6CR	6377Si	D-9080	11.77	Essex & Suffolk GC	Wormingford	3.99
DRE +	2313	Schleicher Ka6CR	6197	D-8558	11.77	J.H.Jowett	North Hill	3.99
DRF +	2314	Schleicher Ka6CR	943	D-8600	11.77	Devon & Somerset GC	North Hill	4.98*
		(Damaged North Hill 14.7.97)						
DRG +	2315	Schleicher Ka6CR	6157	D-4090	11.77	W.E.Smith t/a Summer Wine Syndicate	Gallows Hill	5.99
DRJ	2317	Schleicher ASK13	13583		11.77	Lasham Gliding Society "D"	Lasham	12.99
DRK +	2318	Grob G.102 Astir CS77	1686		12.77	Cambridge University GC	Gransden Lodge	4.99
DRL +	2319	Scheibe SF-26 Standard	5040	D-7073	12.77	T McKinley	Kirton-in-Lindsey	6.99
DRM +	2320	Schleicher Ka7 Rhonadler	7017	D-4666	12.77	L.Cross & Syndicate	Dunstable	2.99
DRN	2321	Glasflugel H.303 Mosquito	082		12.77	A.Roberts "821"	North Hill	3.99
DRP +	2322	Pilatus B4 PC-11	080	RAFGSA BGA.1927	12.77	H.J.Stone & Ptnrs	Weston-on-the-Green	4.99
DRQ	2323	Grob G.103 Twin Astir	3027		12.77	V.C.Carr & Ptnrs "258"	Sleap	5.99
DRR +	2324	Schleicher Ka2B Rhonschwalbe	49	D-8108	12.77	Dumfries & District GC	Falgunzeon	4.99
DRS +	2325	PZL SZD-9 bis Bocian 1E	P-783		12.77	Mendip GC	Halesland	5.99
DRT	2326	Eiri PIK-20D	20587		1.78	P F Fowler "688"	Sleap	4.99
DRU	2327	Grob G.102 Astir CS77	1685		1.78	A.R.Wilkinson "334"	Wormingford	3.99
DRV +	2328	Schleicher K8B	8026	D-6169	1.78	Buckminster GC	Saltby	12.98
DRW	2329	Grob G.102 Astir CS	1081	D-3311	1.78	J.C.Bittle "798"	Lasham	6.99
DRY	2331	Schleicher Ka6BR	370	D-5553	1.78	A.May	Crowland	7.99
DRZ +	2332	Schleicher K8B	668	D-4622 D-KANB/D-4622	1.78	East Sussex GC	Ringmer	6.99
DSA	2333	Slingsby T.30 Prefect	575	WE985	1.78	R.J.Sharman	Crowland	5.99
DSB +	2334	Schleicher Ka6E	4300	D-0263	1.78	M.H.Yates	Ridgewell	6.98
DSE	2337	Schempp-Hirth HS.7 Mini Nimbus	36		2.78	G.Binnie "227"	Portmoak	1.97*
DSF +	2338	Schleicher K8B	8220	D-7114	2.78	Edinburgh University GC "Snoopy"	Portmoak	10.99
DSG	2339	Schleicher Ka6CR	6393	D-5696	2.78	R.P Maddocks	Booker	6.98
DSH	2340	Grob G.102 Astir CS77	1696		2.78	R.B.Petrie "648"	Portmoak	1.99
DSJ +	2341	Grob G.103 Twin Astir	3050		2.78	L.J Kaye	Shobdon	3.99
DSL	2343	Grob G.103 Twin Astir	3041		3.78	J.G.Hampson "447"	Enstone	4.99
DSM	2344	Fauvel AV.22S	3	F-CCGM	4.78	I.Dunkley	Camphill	8.95*
DSN	2345	Grob G.102 Astir CS77	1698		3.78	J J M Riach "893"	Drumslade	5.99
DSP	2346	Schempp-Hirth HS.7 Mini Nimbus	33		3.78	R.I.Hey & Ptnrs "270"	Nympsfield	3.99
DSR +	2348	Schleicher Ka6CR	970	D-5040	3.78	Cornish GC	Perranporth	5.98
DST	2350	Schleicher ASW20L	20059		3.78	J.E.Gatfield "972"	Husbands Bosworth	12.98
DSU +	2351	Grob G.102 Astir CS77	1663		3.78	Bowland Forest GC	Chipping	3.99
DSV	2352	Pilatus B4 PC-11	134	RAFGSA.718 RAFGSA.518	3.78	Staffordshire GC "718"	Seighford	11.95*
DSW	2353	Schempp-Hirth HS.7 Mini Nimbus	37	RNGSA.N33	3.78	P.I.Fenner & Ptnrs "533"	Lasham	11.99
DSX	2354	Schleicher ASW19	19188		4.78	T.R.Dews "877"	Kingston Deverill	4.99
DSY +	2355	Schleicher Ka6CR	561	D-5702	4.78	G.Harris	Rufforth	5.99
DTA	2357	Glaser-Dirks DG-200	2-27		4.78	R P Hardcastle "699"	Tatenhill	3.99
DTC	2359	Schempp-Hirth HS.6 Janus B	63	RAFGSA.R9 RAFGSA 16/BGA.2359	4.78	Dukeries GC	Gamston	5.99
DTD +	2360	Schleicher ASW19	19187		4.78	R.K.Warren	Tatenhill	3.98
DTE +	2361	Schleicher ASW19	19185		4.78	M.H Langton	Gransden Lodge	3.98
DTG	2363	Schempp-Hirth SHK-1	012	D-2034	4.78	M.A.T.Jones & F.A.W.Elliott	Rattlesden	8.98
DTK	2366	Glasflugel H.303 Mosquito B	109		4.78	P.France "760"	Usk	4.99
DTM +	2368	Glaser-Dirks DG-200	2-34		4.78	Miss J.Walker & Ptnrs	Lasham	2.99
DTN +	2369	Schleicher K8B	117/58	???	5.78	P.J.Gibbs & Syndicate	Edgehill	10.99
DTP	2370	Schleicher ASW20	20078		5.78	T.S.Hills & Ptnrs "915"	Lasham	12.98
DTQ +	2371	Schleicher ASW20	20054		5.78	D.H.Garrard	Cranfield	4.99
DTR +	2372	EoN AP.6 Olympia 401	EoN/4/005	NEJSGSA.7 RAFGSA.252/G-APSI	5.78	B D Clarke	Ringmer	3.99
DTS	2373	CARMAM M.100S Mesange	031	F-CCST	5.78	C.Holmes	Bryngwyn Bach	1.98
DTU +	2375	Schempp-Hirth HS.5 Nimbus 2B	167		5.78	C.J.Short	Lasham	3.99
DTV	2376	Glasflugel H.303 Mosquito B	110		5.78	A.J.Watson "704"	Lasham	3.97*
DTW +	2377	PZL SZD-30 Pirat	S-0711		5.78	C Kaminskui	North Hill	8.99

Regn	BGA No.	Type	C/n	P/I	Regn	Owner/operator	Probable Base	CA Expy
DTX	2378	Glasflugel H.303 Mosquito B	111		5.78	K.D.Hook "320"	Portmoak	1.99
DTY	2379	Glasflugel H.303 Mosquito B	112		5.78	R.Ward "766"	Gransden Lodge	4.99
DTZ	2380	Slingsby T.30 Prefect	573	WE983	5.78	C.Hughes "S30"	Nympsfield	12.99
DUB	2382	Glasflugel H.303 Mosquito B	113		5.78	A.G.Reid & Ptnrs "911"	Kenley	3.99
DUC	2383	CARMAM M.100S Mesange	012	F-CCSA	6.78	Not known (Stored 5.94)		
							Carlton Moor	5.88*
DUF +	2386	Schleicher K8B	8296A	D-5294	6.78	Essex GC	Ridgewell	4.99
DUH +	2388	Scheibe L-Spatz 55	760	???	6.78	R J Aylesbury	Crowland	6.99
DUK +	2390	Schleicher K8B	752	D-4048	6.78	Bristol & Glos GC	Nympsfield	11.99
DUL	2391	Grob G.102 Astir CS77	1720		6.78	K.J.Screen "642"	Long Mynd	3.99
DUQ +	2394	Glaser-Dirks DG-200	2-43		7.78	D.M.Cottingham	North Hill	3.99
DUR +	2395	Schleicher Ka6CR	6273	OY-DLX	7.78	Rattlesden GC	Rattlesden	2.99
DUS	2396	Schleicher Ka6E	4263	OY-XCB	7.78	M.Toon & C.S.Crocker "638"		
				HB-948			Tibenham	5.99
DUT	2397	Schleicher ASW20	20089		7.78	T.J.Murphy "T34"	Portmoak	4.99
DUU	2398	Grob G.103 Twin Astir	3156		8.78	A.F.Coombes & Ptnrs "21"	Lasham	2.98*
DUW	2400	DFS 108/49 Grunau Baby 2B	-	VN148	12.77	C.Tonks	(North Wales)	*
		(Also BAPC.33)		LN+ST		(On rebuild 1995)		
DUX	2401	Grob G.102 Club Astir	2140		7.78	B.T.Spreckley "885"		
							Le Blanc, France	5.99
DUY	2402	Glaser-Dirks DG-100	24	PH-525	7.78	A.C.Saxton & Ptnrs "652"		
							Carlton Moor	7.99
DVB +	2405	Schleicher ASK13	13596		8.78	Essex & Suffolk GC	Wormingford	3.99
		(Components, incl c/n plate, donated to BGA.3493; possible discarded parts from crash Dunstable 5.6.82)						
DVC +	2406	Schleicher ASK13	13597		8.78	Southdown GC	Parham Park	2.99
DVD +	2407	LET L-13 Blanik	027021		8.78	Vectis GC	Bembridge	2.99
DVE	2408	Schleicher Ka6E	4226	RAFGSA.379	8.78	M.J.Leach & S.Foggin "879"		
							Sandhill Farm, Shrivenham	2.97*
DVG +	2410	Schleicher Ka6CR	003	D-1916	8.78	R.F.Warren	Ringmer	9.99
		(Built by Holzmann-Drespack)						
DVH	2411	Schleicher Ka6E	4117	RAFGSA	8.78	P.Burridge & I.Foster "615"		
							Perranporth	1.96*
DVJ +	2412	Eiri PIK-20D	20638		8.78	M.C.Hayes "869"	Bidford	2.99
DVK	2413	PZL SZD-48 Jantar Standard 2	W-868		8.78	R.F.Gray & Ptnrs "732"		
							Gransden Lodge	4.99
DVL	2414	Schleicher ASW19	19222		9.78	P.T Healy & Ptnrs "X96"	Lasham	2.99
DVM +	2415	Glasflugel H.205 Club Libelle	52	RAFGGA.581	9.78	M.J.Gooch	Rattlesden	3.99
DVN +	2416	Eiri PIK-20D	20641		9.78	N Taylor	Husbands Bosworth	3.99
DVP	2417	Schleicher ASW19	19220		9.78	E.F.Davies "971"	Booker	4.99
DVQ +	2418	Schleicher K8B	8134	D-0288	9.78	Staffordshire GC	Seighford	6.99
				D-KICE/D-5235				
DVR	2419	Scheibe L-Spatz 55	663	D-1565	9.78	J.Young	Lyveden	6.96*
DVS	2420	Schempp-Hirth HS.4 Standard Cirrus	380	RAFGSA.824	9.78	D.Hands & Ptnr "VS"	Parham Park	2.99
		(C/n duplicates VH-GGC)						
DVV	2423	Schleicher ASW20L	20100		9.78	Mrs A.F.Coppen "810"	Lasham	2.99
DVW	2424	Schleicher ASW20	20099		9.78	Not known "590"	Aston Down	2.85*
		(Damaged in collision with BGA.2618 Lasham 17.8.84; wreck stored 6.98)						
DVX	2425	Schleicher ASK13	13598		9.78	Shenington GC "S13"	Edgehill	12.99
DVY	2426	Schempp-Hirth HS.2 Cirrus	52	OO-ZIR	10.78	J.Patchett & syndicate "272"		
							Nympsfield	7.99
DVZ	2427	Glasflugel H.303 Mosquito B	133		10.78	B.H.Shaw "Z25" Husbands Bosworth		4.99
DWB	2429	Glasflugel H.303 Mosquito B	135		10.78	C.G.Salt & Ptnrs "733"	Lasham	3.99
		(Marked as BGA.2924)						
DWC +	2430	Schleicher Ka6E	4111	AGA.11	10.78	J Osment	Nympsfield	7.99
DWE +	2432	Schleicher Ka7 Rhonadler	7132	D-5427	10.78	UWE GC	Nympsfield	4.99
DWF +	2433	DFS/49 Grunau Baby 2B	-	AGA.16	11.78	L.P.Woodage	Dunstable	4.99
		(Built RNAY Fleetlands)		RNGSA 1-13/VW743				
DWG +	2434	Schleicher K8B	165/60	D-5750	11.78	Newark & Notts GC	Winthorpe	3.99
DWH +	2435	Schleicher K8B	1	D-8614	11.78	Essex GC	Ridgewell	9.96*
		(Built by Gebr. Huber)		D-8331				
DWJ	2436	Glaser-Dirks DG-200	2-59		11.78	D Evans "191"	Chipping	3.99
DWL	2438	Glasflugel H.303 Mosquito B	141		12.78	A.Stanford & Ptnrs "755"		
							Husbands Bosworth	9.99
DWN	2440	Schleicher Ka7 Rhonadler	7101	D-5360	12.78	L.R.Merritt	Edgehill	11.98
DWP +	2441	Glasflugel H.303 Mosquito B	136		12.78	Mosquito Syndicate	Bicester	6.99
DWQ +	2442	Grob G.102 Astir CS77	1758		12.78	F.Prime	Gransden Lodge	2.99
DWR	2443	Glasflugel H.303 Mosquito B	134	(BGA.2428)	1.79	C.D.Lovell "P9"	Lasham	2.99
DWS	2444	Eiri PIK-20D	20652		1.79	R. & B.Madelin "728"	Lasham	8.98
DWT	2445	Slingsby T.65A Vega	1898		1.79	A.P.Grimley "886"		
							Husbands Bosworth	8.99
DWU +	2446	Grob G.102 Astir CS	1201	D-7269	1.79	G.V.McKirdy	Parham Park	5.98
DWW +	2448	Slingsby T.65A Vega	1896		1.79	E.Fitzgerald	Usk	5.99
DWZ +	2451	Schleicher ASW19	19243		2.79	J.A.Stirk & Ptnrs	Burn	4.99
DXA	2452	Glasflugel H.303 Mosquito B	137		2.79	S H Gibson "483"	Dunstable	4.99

Regn	BGA No.	Type	C/n	P/I	Regn	Owner/operator	Probable Base	CA Expy
DXB	2453	Schleicher ASW20	20142		.	J.Timpany & Ptnrs "81"	Nympsfield	2.99
DXD	2455	Slingsby T.65A Vega	1901		2.79	T.C.Harrington & Ptnrs "132"	Bicester	4.99
DXE +	2456	Slingsby T.65A Vega	1902		2.79	L.M.Astle Husbands Bosworth		7.99
DXF	2457	Slingsby T.65A Vega	1903		2.79	P.Kitchen "815"	Talgarth	9.99
DXG +	2458	Slingsby T.65A Vega 17L	1906		2.79	M.H.Pope	Bidford	7.99
DXH +	2459	Schleicher Ka6E	4198	RAFGSA.489 D-4093	2.79	B.Hughes	Bicester	2.99
DXJ +	2460	Grob G.102 Astir CS77	1762		3.79	R.Maskell & Ptnrs Gransden Lodge		4.99
DXK	2461	Centrair ASW20F	20108		3.79	A.Townsend "160"	Booker	5.99
DXL +	2462	Schempp-Hirth HS.4 Standard Cirrus 203G		AGA.1	3.79	P. & A.Gelsthorpe	Lasham	2.99
DXM +	2463	Schleicher Ka7 Rhonadler (Mod.)	626	RAFGGA.551 D-5707	3.79	Vale of Neath GC	Rhigos	8.97*
DXN	2464	Glaser-Dirks DG-200	2-63		3.79	J.A.Johnston "267"	Gransden Lodge	2.99
DXP +	2465	Schleicher K8B	8646A	D-8537	3.79	Stratford-upon-Avon GC	Snitterfield	2.99
DXQ	2466	Schempp-Hirth HS.7 Mini Nimbus C (Build No.MN97)	96		3.79	T.Lamb & P.Hawkins "147"	Weston-on-the-Green	4.99
DXR	2467	Slingsby T.65A Vega	1905		3.79	D.R.Sutton	Sutton Bank	8.94*
DXT	2469	Schempp-Hirth HS.7 Mini Nimbus C	97		3.79	J.M.Beattie "286"	Booker	12.99
DXU +	2470	Slingsby T.59J Kestrel 22	1867	G-BDWZ	3.79	P.J.Bisgood & Ptnrs	Cranfield	3.99
DXV +	2471	Schleicher ASK13	13602		3.79	Cambridge University GC	Gransden Lodge	2.99
DXW	2472	Glasflugel H.303 Mosquito B	142		3.79	P.Newark & Ptnrs "354"	Burn	1.99
DXX	2473	Schleicher ASW19B	19245		3.79	P.F.Whitehead "580"	Bicester	1.00
DXY	2474	Muller Moswey III	?	HB-474	3.79	G.M.Bacon & Ptnrs Gransden Lodge (As "HB-474")		9.99
DYB	2477	Schleicher Ka7 Rhonadler (Reported as "DYN")	167/59	D-5775	3.79	Surrey Hills GC "6"	Kenley	4.99
DYC +	2478	Schleicher Ka6CR	6390	D-1545	3.79	F.J.Smith	Burn	3.99
DYE	2479	Schleicher ASW20L	20143		3.79	T.A.Sage "828"	Dunstable	1.00
DYF	2480	Grob G.102 Astir CS77	1805		3.79	York Gliding Centre "850"	Rufforth	4.99
DYG	2481	Slingsby T.59H Kestrel 22	1868	G-BDZG	3.79	R.E.Gretton & R.L.Darby "592"	Crowland	7.99
DYH +	2482	Glaser-Dirks DG-200	2-75		4.79	A.Urwin	Milfield	5.96*
DYJ +	2483	Schleicher Ka6CR	6583	D-5838	4.79	R.M.Morris	Dunstable	6.99
DYL +	2485	CARMAM JP/15-36A Aiglon	37		4.79	M.P.Edwards	Crowland	3.99
DYN +	2486	Schleicher Ka6CR (See BGA.2477)	6129Si	D-8458	4.79	C.N.Harder	Lasham	9.98
DYP	2487	Schleicher Ka6BR	191	OO-ZXL D-5482	4.79	D.Ling "BR" (Crashed Ridgewell 31.5.97)	Ridgewell	3.98*
DYQ +	2488	Schleicher Ka6CR	6178	D-5328	4.79	Dorset GC	Gallows Hill	8.99
DYR +	2489	Schleicher Ka7 Rhonadler (Mod.)	766	D-5220	4.79	Avon Soaring Centre	Bidford	8.99
DYT	2490	Eiri PIK-20D	20657		4.79	P.J.Hampshire "537" Parham Park (Damaged nr Parham 12.4.97)		3.98*
DYU	2491	Schempp-Hirth HS.5 Nimbus 2C	181		4.79	A.Pickles "531"	Lasham	7.99
DYX	2494	Schleicher ASW20	20135		4.79	R.Cousins "102"	Challock	4.99
DYZ	2495	Schempp-Hirth HS.5 Nimbus 2C	180		4.79	N.A.Britton "943"	Bidford	3.99
DZA	2496	Slingsby T.65A Vega 17L (Mod)	1907		4.79	M.P.Garrod	Lasham	2.99
DZB +	2497	Slingsby T.65A Vega	1908		4.79	G.W.M.Neill & Ptnrs	Drumshade	7.99
DZC +	2498	Scheibe L-Spatz 55	642	RAFGGA D-5629	4.79	G.A.Ford	Nympsfield	10.98
DZD	2499	Schleicher ASW19B	19268		4.79	D.E.Townsend "573" Lleweni Parc		5.99
DZF	2501	Schempp-Hirth HS.4 Standard Cirrus 421G		RAFGSA.27	4.79	L.S.Hood "152"	Bicester	4.99
DZG	2502	Schleicher ASW19B	19267		4.79	S.P.Wareham "909"	Gallows Hill	2.99
DZJ	2504	Grob G.102 Club Astir	2230		5.79	J. & R.Acreman "576"	North Hill	4.99
DZK	2505	Schempp-Hirth HS.5 Nimbus 2C (Fuselage No.195)	198		5.79	R Hudson "957"	Sutton Bank	2.99
DZM +	2507	Slingsby T.65A Vega	1909		5.79	L.P.Taylor	Long Mynd	5.99
DZN	2508	Slingsby T.65A Vega 17L	1910		5.79	L.E.N.Tanner "990"	Aboyne	6.99
DZP +	2509	Slingsby T.65A Vega	1911		5.79	M.T.Crews	Currock Hill	6.99
DZR +	2511	ICA IS-28B2	87		5.79	Lakes GC	Walney Island	3.99
DZS	2512	PZL SZD-8bis-0 Jaskolka	183	HB-583	5.79	N.A Clark	Parham Park	7.99
DZT	2513	Eiri PIK-20D	20661		5.79	A.C.Garside "106"	Challock	3.99
DZU +	2514	Grob G.102 Astir CS	1076	D-3308	6.79	M.L.Jenkins & I.N.Lingham Booker		1.99
DZV	2515	Scheibe SF-27A Zugvogel V	6065	D-5839	6.79	A.P.Montague "839"	Nympsfield	4.99
DZW +	2516	Schleicher Ka6CR	6628	D-1045	6.79	A.Head Husbands Bosworth		2.99
DZY	2518	Schleicher ASW19B	19275		6.79	M.C.Fairman & T.Marlow "757"	Dunstable	12.98

Regn	BGA No.	Type	C/n	P/I	Regn	Owner/operator	Probable Base	CA Expy

EAA-EZZ

Regn	BGA No.	Type	C/n	P/I	Regn	Owner/operator	Probable Base	CA Expy
EAC	2522	Grob G.102 Astir CS77	1803		6.79	B.T.Pratt "367" Husbands Bosworth		4.99
EAD +	2523	Slingsby T.65A Vega	1912		6.79	P.R.Norrison	Pocklington	4.99
EAE	2524	Schleicher ASW20L	20224		6.79	L.Clayton "107"	Challock	2.99
EAF +	2525	Grob G.102 Astir CS77	1830		6.79	G.J.Wilkins	Booker	5.98
EAG +	2526	Slingsby T.65A Vega	1913		6.79	D.R.Moore	Gransden Lodge	4.99
EAH +	2527	Schleicher Ka6E	4085	D-7542 D-7142	6.79	M.Lodge	Lasham	7.99
EAJ	2528	Schempp-Hirth HS.5 Nimbus 2	7	D-0699	6.79	M.Randle "79"	Aston Down	4.99
EAK	2529	Glasflugel H.303 Mosquito B	155		6.79	A.R.L.Parker & Ptnrs "594" Aston Down		2.99
EAL	2530	Schleicher Rhonlerche II	3051/BR	PH-331	7.79	Newcastle & Teesside GC (Stored 5.94) Carlton Moor		9.91*
EAM +	2531	Schempp-Hirth HS.5 Nimbus 2B	93	D-2787	7.79	P.G.Myers & Syndicate Chipping		4.99
EAR +	2535	Eiri PIK-20D	?		7.79	W.Munns	Syerston	12.99
EAT	2537	Eiri PIK-20D	20664		7.79	P.T.Reading & Ptnrs "786" Lasham		3.99
EAU +	2538	Schleicher Ka7 Rhonadler (Mod.)	7092	PH-304	7.79	Welland GC	Upwood	12.98
EAV	2539	Schempp-Hirth HS.7 Mini Nimbus C	136		7.79	W.Cook & K.Porter	Lasham	8.99
EAW +	2540	Grob G.102 Astir CS77	1831		7.79	W.Severn "342"	Tatenhill	7.99
EAZ +	2543	Schleicher K8B	8138	D-5256 D-KANO/D-5256	7.79	Shalbourne Soaring Group (Crashed Rivar Hill 25.7.97) Rivar Hill		6.98*
EBA +	2544	Slingsby T.65A Vega 17L	1914		7.79	S.M.Smith	Gransden Lodge	3.99
EBB	2545	Grob G.102 Speed Astir IIB	4040		7.79	M.Malcolm & A.F.Grinter "881" Pocklington		5.99
EBC	2546	Slingsby T.30B Prefect	583	RAFGSA."33" WE993	7.79	K.R.Reeves	Syerston	7.98
		(Rebuilt with components ex BGA.808 & BGA.1618?)						
EBD +	2547	Scheibe Bergfalke IV	5822	D-1005	7.79	Burn GC	Burn	4.98
EBE +	2548	Issoire E78 Silene	07		8.79	B.A.Burgess Husbands Bosworth		9.99
EBF +	2549	Schempp-Hirth HS.7 Mini Nimbus C	138		8.79	P.H.Waite & Ptnrs Sandhill Farm, Shrivenham		3.99
EBJ	2552	Schleicher ASW19B	19282		8.79	D.P.Taylor "h11"	Sutton Bank	11.98
EBK	2553	Schempp-Hirth HS.7 Mini Nimbus C	139	AGA.2 BGA.2553	8.79	J.B.Burgoyne "552"	Lyveden	4.99
EBL +	2554	Schleicher ASK13	13610		8.79	Bristol & Glos GC	Nympsfield	10.99
EBM	2555	Grob G.102 Astir CS77	1843		8.79	S.R.Domoney "807"	Ringmer	6.99
EBN +	2556	Centrair ASW20F	20118		8.79	K.W.Blake & Ptnrs "37"	Camphill	6.99
EBP +	2557	Allgaier Geier I	3/4	D-9025	8.79	G.A.Steel & Co	RAF Marham	6.97*
EBR +	2559	Glaser-Dirks DG-200/17	2-89/1706	D-6893	9.79	J.W.Davidson	Aboyne	6.99
EBS +	2560	Scheibe Zugvogel IIIA	1054	LX-CAF D-8363	9.79	I.D.McLeod "Schwarzhornfalke" Challock		3.99
EBX	2565	Schleicher ASW20	20058	D-7973	9.79	J P Davies "644" Gransden Lodge		2.99
EBZ +	2567	Schleicher ASK13	13614		9.79	Booker GC	Booker	1.99
ECA	2568	Wright Falcon	1		9.79	P.W.Wright	Saltby	8.98
ECC +	2570	Schleicher Ka6CR	60/01	D-5080	9.79	N.Lyons & Ptnrs	Burn	3.99
ECF +	2573	Schleicher Ka6CR	856	D-5808	10.79	D.Goldup	Aston Down	6.99
ECG +	2574	Schempp-Hirth SHK	19	D-5359 D-1329	10.79	M.F.Hardy	Upavon	2.99
ECH +	2575	Glasflugel H.303 Mosquito B	173		10.79	A.Walker & Ptnrs	Rattlesden	5.99
ECJ +	2576	Slingsby T.65A Vega	1916		10.79	J.E.B.Hart & Ptnrs	Sutton Bank	4.99
ECK +	2577	Slingsby T.65A Vega	1917		10.79	L.Gibson	Milfield	4.97*
ECL +	2578	Slingsby T.65A Vega 17L	1918		10.79	B.H.Bryce-Smith	Gransden Lodge	3.99
ECM +	2579	Slingsby T.65A Vega	1919		10.79	F.L.Wilson	Aston Down	9.99
ECN	2580	Slingsby T.65A Vega 17L	1920		10.79	C.Claxton Syndicate "645" Booker		3.99
ECP +	2581	Rolladen-Schneider LS-3-17	3426		10.79	M.Collins	Parham Park	1.99
ECQ +	2582	Grob G.102 Astir CS77	1837		10.79	M I Orry	Tibenham	6.99
ECS	2584	Glasflugel H.303 Mosquito B	166		10.79	R.C.Adams & P.Robinson "955" Wormingford		3.99
ECT	2585	Glasflugel H.604	2	I-FEVG D-0279	10.79	F.K.Russell "604"	Dunstable	3.99
ECW +	2588	Schleicher ASK21	21008		11.79	Norfolk GC	Tibenham	10.99
ECX	2589	Schleicher ASW20L	20315		6.80	R.M.Lambert "600"	Feshiebridge	4.99
ECY +	2590	Glasflugel H.201B Standard Libelle	530	RAFGGA.557	11.79	G.Kelly & E.Fry	Bidford	5.99
ECZ +	2591	Schleicher ASK21	21009		4.80	Booker GC	Booker	3.99
EDA +	2592	Slingsby T.65A Vega 17L (Mod)	1888	G-BFYW	11.79	A.R.Worters "647"	Strathaven	5.98
EDB +	2593	CARMAM JP-15-36AR Aiglon	40		11.79	P.J.Martin & Ptnrs	Crowland	3.99
EDC +	2594	Schleicher Ka7 Rhonadler	244	D-8527	12.79	J.C.Shipley ("8527" under wing) Camphill		3.98
EDD	2595	Schleicher ASW17	17043	D-6865	12.79	S.Mulholland & Ptnrs "69" Syerston		5.99
EDE	2596	Centrair ASW20F	20128		1.80	G.M.Cumner "750"	Aston Down	12.98
EDF	2597	Schempp-Hirth HS.7 Mini Nimbus C	149		1.80	C.W.Boutcher "530"	Snitterfield	4.99
EDG +	2598	Schleicher Ka6CR	6512	RAFGSA	1.80	S.J.Wood	Cranwell	4.99
EDH +	2599	Glasflugel H.303 Mosquito B	184		1.80	D.G.Cooper	Tibenham	7.99
EDJ +	2600	Glasflugel H.303 Mosquito B	185		1.80	A.J.Leigh & Ptnrs	Camphill	5.99
EDK	2601	Schleicher Ka7	791	D-1633	1.80	York Gliding Centre	Rufforth	1.00

Regn	BGA No.	Type	C/n	P/I	Regn	Owner/operator	Probable Base	CA Expy
EDL	2602	Focke-Wulf Weihe 50	4	D-0893 HB-555	1.80	F.K.Russell	Dunstable	10.96*
EDM +	2603	Glaser-Dirks DG-200	2-98		1.80	A.H.St Pierre	Sutton Bank	3.99
EDN	2604	Glaser-Dirks DG-100G Elan	E12G6		1.80	A.P.Scott & Ptnrs "820"	Currock Hill	6.99
EDP	2605	Glaser-Dirks DG-100G Elan	E19G7		1.80	J.F.Beach & Ptnrs "448"	Nympsfield	2.98
EDS +	2608	Scheibe SF-26 Standard (Probably ex RAFGGA.548)	5038	RAFGGA.??? D-8454	1.80	I.Davidson	Long Mynd	3.96*
EDU +	2610	Schleicher ASK13	13613		1.80	Kent GC	Challock	2.99
EDV	2611	Slingsby T.65A Vega 17L	1893	G-BGCU	2.80	D.J.Gilder "541"	Aston Down	2.99
EDW +	2612	Schleicher ASK21	21010		5.80	London GC	Dunstable	7.99
EDX +	2613	Slingsby T.65D Vega	1928		5.80	M.W.Cater	Husbands Bosworth	4.99
EDY +	2614	Slingsby T.65D Vega	1929		5.80	C.J.Steadman	Husbands Bosworth	4.99
EDZ +	2615	Slingsby T.65C Sport Vega	1931		5.80	R.C.Copley	Chipping	10.99
EEA +	2616	Slingsby T.65C Sport Vega	1932		5.80	Peterborough & Spalding GC	Crowland	2.99
EEC +	2618	Schleicher ASW20L	20311	(G-BSTS) BGA.2618	3.80	D.Cushway	Challock	3.99
EEE +	2620	Schleicher ASW20L	20312		3.80	T.E.MacFadyen	Aston Down	4.99
EEF +	2621	Rolladen-Schneider LS-3-17	3441		3.80	G.Nicholas	Rivar Hill	6.99
EEG +	2622	Slingsby T.65C Sport Vega	1922	EI-129 BGA.2622	3.80	S.Hopkins	Rufforth	9.99
EEH +	2623	Schleicher ASW19	19042	RAFGGA	2.80	K.Kiely "166"	Dishforth	4.99
EEJ +	2624	Schleicher ASW20L	20314		9.80	R.R.Stoward	Dunstable	2.99
EEK	2625	Schempp-Hirth HS.5 Nimbus 2C	201		2.80	R.E.Cross "141"	Lasham	4.99
EEM +	2627	Schleicher K8B	8688AB	D-0254	2.80	South Wales GC	Usk	4.99
EEN +	2628	Schempp-Hirth HS.4 Standard Cirrus	75 621	(BGA.2609) RAFGSA 87	2.80	J.Hanlon	Weston-on-the-Green	3.99
EEP +	2629	Wassmer WA.26P Squale	36	F-CDSX	3.80	R.H.Parker	Bidford	2.99
EEQ +	2630	Grob G.102 Standard Astir II	5015S	RNGSA.N12	3.80	S.W.Bradford	Dunstable	2.99
EER	2631	Schempp-Hirth HS.7 Mini Nimbus	150		3.80	W.T.Lewis	Perranporth	4.99
EES	2632	Rolladen-Schneider LS-3-17	3248		3.80	R.Illidge & Ptnrs "50"	Camphill	10.99
EEU +	2634	Issoire E78 Silene	08		3.80	M.B.Jefferyes & Ptnrs "456"	Ridgewell	8.98
EEV +	2635	Centrair ASW20FL	20145		3.80	J.P.Lyell & Ptnr "129"	Lasham	3.99
EEW +	2636	Schleicher Ka6CR	6188	RAFGGA D-6151	3.80	P.E.Lowden	Winthorpe	9.99
EEX +	2637	Rolladen-Schneider LS-3-17	3442		3.80	W A.Dalimer & Ptnr	Aston Down	5.99
EEZ +	2639	Rolladen-Schneider LS-3A	3458		3.80	P.Holland "157"	Sutton Bank	12.99
EFA +	2640	Schleicher ASW20L	20326		4.80	P.J.Warner "470"	Dunstable	1.99
EFB +	2641	Schempp-Hirth HS.5 Nimbus 2C	216		4.80	N.Revell & Ptnrs	Gamston	6.99
EFC +	2642	Siebert Sie-3	3018	D-0811	4.80	M.S.A.Skinner	Tatenhill	6.99
EFD +	2643	Schleicher Ka7 Rhonadler	7007	PH-277	7.80	Surrey Hills GC	Kenley	1.99
EFE	2644	Centrair ASW20F	20139		5.80	J.A.Quartermaine & Ptnrs "586"	Sutton Bank	1.99
EFF	2645	Schempp-Hirth HS.5 Nimbus 2C	208		4.80	E.R.Duffin & D.L.Jobbins "737"	Rhigos	3.98
EFG +	2646	Schleicher K8B	?	RAFGGA	4.80	Rattlesden GC	Rattlesden	2.98
EFH	2647	Schleicher ASW20	20308		4.80	M B Judkins "939"	Lasham	1.99
EFJ	2648	Centrair ASW20F	20127		4.80	D.Ball	(Surrey)	6.97*
EFK	2649	Centrair ASW20FL	20140		5.80	B.Kerby "543"	Long Mynd	4.99
EFL	2650	Centrair ASW20FL	20133		5.80	D.J.Connolly "297"	Kingston Deverill	4.99
EFM +	2651	Schleicher Ka6E	4103	RAFGSA	6.80	G.S.Foster	Parham Park	7.99
EFN +	2652	Scheibe L-Spatz 55	635	D-1617	5.80	E F Weaver	Halton	7.99
EFP	2653	Schleicher K8B	E.01	D-8859	5.80	Not known (Stored 3.95)	Portmoak	7.88*
EFR +	2655	Scheibe L-Spatz	320	RAFGGA	4.80	H. & A.Purser	Cranfield	9.98
EFS	2656	Rolladen-Schneider LS-3	3022	HB-1356	5.80	G.I Boswell "636"	Dunstable	6.99
EFT	2657	Schempp-Hirth HS.5 Nimbus 2B	26	HB-1160	4.80	N.L.Jennings "145"	Lleweni Parc	2.99
EFV	2659	Schleicher ASW20	20041		6.80	A.R McKillen	Bellarena	9.99
EFW +	2660	Slingsby T.65C Sport Vega	1938		7.80	Dukeries GC	Gamston	5.99
EFX	2661	LET L-13 Blanik	026460	AGA.21 RAFGSA.R7/BGA.2095	.80	Enstone Eagles GC	Edgehill	11.94*
		(Crashed Enstone 25.6.94; parts to BGA.3666; wreck stored 6.95)						
EFZ +	2663	Rolladen-Schneider LS-3A	3273		5.80	D.H.Gardner & J.Higgins	Aston Down	2.99
EGD	2667	Schleicher ASW17	17028	D-2343	6.80	W.J.Dean "D3"	Booker	7.98
EGE +	2668	Rolladen-Schneider LS-3A	3465		6.80	D.Barker	Nympsfield	1.99
EGF +	2669	Slingsby T.65C Sport Vega	1936		6.80	B.Snook	Old Sarum	1.99
EGG +	2670	Slingsby T.65C Sport Vega	1939		6.80	J.Milson "JH"	Usk	5.99
EGH +	2671	Slingsby T.65C Sport Vega	1943		6.80	M.J Davies & Ptnrs	Winthorpe	5.99
EGJ	2672	Slingsby T.65C Sport Vega	1944		6.80	K.J.Towell & Ptnrs "672"	Lasham	5.99
EGK	2673	Schempp-Hirth HS.4 Standard Cirrus	542G	RAFGSA.569 RAFGSA.R2	6.80	I.M.Deans & Ptnrs "569"	Lasham	2.99

Regn	BGA No.	Type	C/n	P/I	Regn	Owner/operator	Probable Base	CA Expy
EGL +	2674	Schleicher Ka6CR	6330	D-6037	6.80	G.B.Dennis t/a Mendip K6 Syndicate (Damaged North Hill 9.7.97)	Halesland	11.97*
EGN +	2676	Grob G.103 Twin II	3542		7.80	Enstone Eagles GC	Enstone	7.99
EGP	2677	Schleicher ASW20L	20336		7.80	A.W.Gillett & Ptnrs "172"	Nympsfield	3.99
EGR +	2679	Breguet Br.905SA Fauvette	18	F-CCGT	7.80	P.Parker	Tibenham	7.99
EGS	2680	Schempp-Hirth HS.5 Nimbus 2CS	192	D-2111	7.80	P.G.Myers "2"	Chipping	5.99
EGT	2681	Slingsby T.65D Vega	1933		7.80	D.M.Badley & Ptnrs	Sleap	2.99
EGU +	2682	Slingsby T.65A Vega	1921		7.80	K.W.Balcombe & Ptnrs	Parham Park	4.99
EGW	2684	Schempp-Hirth HS.7 Mini Nimbus B (Mod to Mini Nimbus C?)	78	HB-1447	8.80	I F Barnes "844"	Ridgewell	5.99
EGX +	2685	Slingsby T.65C Sport Vega	1937	RAFGSA.R23 BGA.2685	8.80	M.D.Organ	Weston-on-the-Green	2.99
EGZ +	2687	Schleicher ASK21	21030		8.80	Marchington GC	Tatenhill	2.99
EHA	2688	Schleicher K8B	136/59	D-5084	8.80	Not known (Stored marked as D-5084 1.97)	Fairwood Common	*
EHC	2690	Eichelsdorfer SB-5B	5017	D-9310	8.80	R.I.Davidson	Husbands Bosworth	6.99
EHD	2691	Schleicher ASW20L	20386		10.80	E.A.Arthur & Ptnr "891"	Tibenham	1.00
EHE	2692	Slingsby T.30B Prefect	582	WE992	10.80	A.P.Stacey t/a A.T.C.Syndicate (As "WE992")	Keevil	3.98
EHF	2693	Caudron C.801	320/4	F-CBTE	5.89	Dutch Aircastle Society	Loosdrecht, Netherlands	4.99
EHG	2694	Slingsby T.65C Sport Vega	1940		10.80	M.J.Vicery & Ptnrs "453"	Lasham	1.99
EHH	2695	Schempp-Hirth Ventus A	07		10.80	P.G.Sheard & A.Stone "V7"	Lasham	2.99
EHK	2697	Rolladen-Schneider LS-4	4068		10.80	S.J.C.Parker "490"	Nympsfield	12.99
EHL	2698	Rolladen-Schneider LS-4	4024		10.80	C.J.Evans "138"	Booker	4.99
EHM +	2699	Schleicher Ka6E	4118	RAFGSA.318	11.80	D.J.Pengally	Kingston Deverill	7.99
EHN +	2700	Slingsby T.65C Sport Vega	1942	G-BILH BGA.2700	11.80	G.D.Hayter	Challock	2.99
EHP +	2701	Schempp-Hirth HS.5 Nimbus 2C	234		11.80	L.Kirkham	Seighford	2.99
EHQ	2702	Schleicher ASK21	21035		11.80	University of Surrey GC "431"	Lasham	4.98
EHS +	2704	ICA IS-28B2	89		12.80	B.Crowhurst	Crowland	9.99
EHT	2705	Schempp-Hirth HS.5 Nimbus 2C	235		12.80	S.R.Ell "E11"	Camphill	11.99
EHU	2706	Glasflugel H.304	209		12.80	F. & J.M.Townsend "849"	Camphill	12.99
EHV	2707	Schleicher ASW20L	20385		12.80	G.S.Neumann & Ptnrs "481"	Booker	1.98
EHW +	2708	ICA IS-28B2	86		12.80	M Sanderson	Milfield	11.99
EHX +	2709	DFS/49 Grunau Baby 2B	134	D-1128	12.80	J.A.Knowles "1128"	Odiham	3.98
EHY +	2710	Slingsby T.65D Vega	1941		1.81	R.Spear	Ringmer	11.99
EHZ	2711	Schleicher ASW20L	20388		12.80	D.Hoolahan "413"	Challock	4.99
EJA +	2712	ICA IS-28B2	88		1.81	DRA GC	Odiham	5.98
EJB +	2713	Slingsby T.65C Sport Vega	1945		1.81	I.G.Walker & Ptnrs	Camphill	4.99
EJC +	2714	Slingsby T.65C Sport Vega	1946		2.81	A M.Raper & Ptnrs	Rattlesden	3.99
EJD	2715	Slingsby T.65D Vega 17L	1930		6.81	A.J.French "261" (Damaged Dunstable 28.3.97)	Booker	5.97*
EJE +	2716	Slingsby T.65C Sport Vega	1947		2.81	DRA GC	Odiham	5.99
EJF +	2717	Schleicher K8B	8966	D-2328	1.81	Cambridge University GC	Gransden Lodge	11.99
EJG +	2718	Schleicher K8B	01	D-5679	1.81	Kent GC	Challock	2.99
EJH +	2719	Eichelsdorfer SB-5E	5041A	D-5430 D-0087	1.81	H.J.McEvaddy	Husbands Bosworth	6.99
EJJ	2720	Slingsby T.21B	?	RAFGSA.120	2.81	N.P.Marriott	Parham Park	5.99
EJK	2721	Centrair ASW20FLP	20172		2.81	A.M.Blackburn "76"	Camphill	4.99
EJL +	2722	Centrair ASW20FL	20183		2.81	T.T.Caswell	Parham Park	3.99
EJP +	2725	Slingsby T.21B	1131	RAFGSA.238 BGA.846	2.81	Upward Bound Trust	Thame	6.96*
EJQ	2726	Centrair ASW20FL	20184		2.81	G.Falcke & Ptnrs	Gransden Lodge	11.99
EJR	2727	Schleicher ASW19B	19334		2.81	Bristol & Glos GC "193"	Nympsfield	3.99
EJS	2728	Slingsby T.65C Sport Vega	1948		2.81	A.D.McLeman "319"	Portmoak	7.99
EJT	2729	Slingsby T.65A Vega	1889	G-VEGA (G-BFZN)	2.81	R A Rice "890" (As "G-VEGA")	Long Mynd	5.99
EJW +	2732	Issoire D77 Iris	04		4.81	T.Hurley	Husbands Bosworth	2.95*
EJY +	2734	PZL SZD-9 bis Bocian 1D	P-351	D-1587	3.81	The Borders GC	Milfield	5.98
EKA +	2736	Glaser-Dirks DG-200/17	2-128/1730		3.81	M J Lindsey	Tibenham	4.99
EKB	2737	Schempp-Hirth HS.6 Janus C	129		3.81	D.A.Head "710"	Bicester	2.99
EKC +	2738	Schleicher Ka6E	4079	OO-ZDV OE-0813	4.81	S L Benn	Cranwell	4.99
EKD +	2739	Schleicher ASK13	13539	OH-494	4.81	Devon & Somerset GC	North Hill	12.98
EKE	2740	Schleicher ASW20L	20387		4.81	J K Williams "20L"	Ringmer	2.99
EKF +	2741	Grob G.102 Club Astir III	5519C		4.81	Bristol & Glos GC	Nympsfield	2.99
EKG +	2742	Schleicher ASK21 (See AGA.8)			4.81			
EKH	2743	Schempp-Hirth Ventus B	32		4.81	R Bottomley "714"	Lasham	4.99
EKJ	2744	Schempp-Hirth Ventus B	36		4.81	I.J.Metcalfe "186"	Nympsfield	4.99

Regn	BGA No.	Type	C/n	P/I	Regn	Owner/operator	Probable Base	CA Expy
EKK +	2745	PZL SZD-48 Jantar Standard 2	W-853		4.81	G V McKirdy	Nympsfield	9.99
EKP +	2749	Glaser-Dirks DG-100G Elan	E71G46		5.81	P.A Green	Lasham	3.99
EKR	2751	Schempp-Hirth HS.5 Nimbus 2C	195	D-4904	5.81	J.W.Evans "117"	Bidford	3.99
EKS +	2752	Scheibe SF-27A Zugvogel V	6096	D-8166	5.81	A.B.Pemberton	Parham Park	2.99
EKU	2754	Schleicher ASW20L	20384		5.81	A.R.Levi & Ptnrs "408"	Rufforth	1.00
EKV +	2755	Rolladen-Schneider LS-4	4102		5.81	M.Ray	Lasham	2.99
EKW	2756	Schempp-Hirth HS.5 Nimbus 2B	111	D-7245	5.81	R.S.Jobar "430"	Lasham	5.99
EKX +	2757	Schleicher Ka6E	4027	D-1221	6.81	A.Coatsworth (As "D-1221")	Gallows Hill	8.99
EKY +	2758	Slingsby T.65C Sport Vega	1949		6.81	Essex & Suffolk GC	Wormingford	5.99
ELA +	2760	Schleicher ASW19B	19346		6.81	A.G.Stark	Aboyne	4.99
ELC +	2762	Slingsby T.45 Swallow	1474	AGA. RAFGSA.346	7.81	J.Povall	Dishforth	3.99
ELD +	2763	Slingsby T.65C Sport Vega	1950		8.81	D.J Clark & Ptnrs	Challock	2.99
ELE	2764	Schleicher ASK21	21065		7.81	Midland GC "797"	Long Mynd	3.99
ELG +	2766	Schempp-Hirth Ventus B	46		8.81	H.Forshaw "931"	Burn	4.99
ELH +	2767	Slingsby T.21B (Possibly c/n 627 ex WB966)	?	RAFGSA.314 (RAF)	7.81	Not known (Stored 3.97)	Enstone	7.91*
ELJ +	2768	Breguet Br.905SA Fauvette	21	F-CCGU	8.81	E.A.Hull	Dunstable	11.99
ELK	2769	Slingsby T.9 King Kite Replica	-		8.83	D.G.Jones	Husbands Bosworth	5.99
ELL	2770	Vogt Lo-100 Zwergreiher	25	HB-591	7.81	I.E.Tunstall "LO1"	Syerston	8.99
ELN +	2772	Grob G.102 Astir CS Jeans	2024	???	8.81	J.M.Hughes	Dunstable	3.99
ELQ +	2774	Slingsby T.65D Vega	1934		8.81	J.Bell	Milfield	8.99
ELR	2775	Schempp-Hirth Ventus B	45		8.81	I.D.Smith "188"	Nympsfield	2.99
ELS +	2776	EoN AP.10 460 Srs.1	EoN/S/020	RAFGGA.530	8.81	D.G.Shepherd	Easterton	5.97*
ELT +	2777	Rolladen-Schneider LS-4	4186		9.81	N.Pringle & J.Woods	Lasham	1.99
ELU	2778	Schleicher ASW20L	20462		9.81	D.W.Lilburn "696"	Aston Down	3.99
ELV +	2779	Scheibe Zugvogel IIIB	1088	F-CCPX	9.81	C.R.W.Hill	Crowland	7.99
ELX +	2781	Schleicher Ka7 Rhonadler	928	D-4023	9.81	Rattlesden GC	Rattlesden	6.99
ELY +	2782	Schleicher Ka6CR	6485Si	D-5172	9.81	P.F Richardson & Ptnrs	Bellarena	3.99
ELZ	2783	Schleicher ASW20L	20310		10.81	D.A.Fogden "719"	Booker	3.99
EMB	2785	Rolladen-Schneider LS-4	4185		10.81	L S Hood "352"	Winthorpe	1.99
EME	2788	Glaser-Dirks DG-202/17C	2-176CL18		11.81	F.Boyce "515"Weston-on-the-Green		3.99
EMF	2789	Rolladen-Schneider LS-4	4187		11.81	E.R.Smith & Ptnrs "452"	Thruxton	3.99
EMG +	2790	Rolladen-Schneider LS-4	4242		5.82	R C Bowsfield	Nympsfield	2.99
EMH +	2791	Schleicher ASK18 (Officially regd with c/n 18096)	18009	D-6872	11.81	Staffordshire GC (W/O in mid-air collision Seighford 2.5.98)	Seighford	1.99*
EMJ +	2792	Slingsby T.65C Sport Vega	1951		1.82	Staffordshire GC	Seighford	4.99
EMK +	2793	Slingsby T.45 Swallow	1514	RAFGGA.545	12.81	A.Povey & Ptnrs	Syerston	5.99
EML	2794	Slingsby T.65A Vega	1892	G-BGCB	12.81	P.W.Williams "218"	North Hill	1.99
EMN +	2796	Slingsby T.65D Vega	1935		1.82	C.D.Sword & Ptnrs	Currock Hill	7.99
EMP +	2797	Slingsby T.65C Sport Vega	1952		2.82	D.R Freehold	Kenley	7.99
EMR +	2799	Slingsby T.65C Sport Vega	1954		2.82	P.Greenway & Ptnrs	Shobdon	7.99
EMS	2800	Slingsby T.65A Vega 17L	1890	G-BGBV	2.82	M.P.Day "T65" (As "G-BGBV")	Kenley	8.99
EMT	2801	Rolladen-Schneider LS-4	4243		12.81	D.B.Eastell "55"	Challock	1.99
EMU	2802	Glaser-Dirks DG-202/17	2-162/1753		1.82	P.B.Gray & Ptnrs "606"	Camphill	3.99
EMV +	2803	Schleicher Ka7 Rhonadler	?	AGA.13	1.82	Shalbourne Soaring Group	Rivar Hill	6.99
EMW	2804	Grunau Baby III	?	D-1373	7.89	M.T.A.Sands "17"	(France)	9.99
EMY	2806	Rolladen-Schneider LS-4	4189		1.82	N.V.Parry "264"	Nympsfield	3.99
EMZ +	2807	Slingsby T.65A Vega	1891	G-BGCA	2.82	F.S.Smith	Portmoak	4.99
ENA	2808	Rolladen-Schneider LS-4	4191		2.82	J.D.Collins & Ptnr "288"	Bidford	5.99
ENC +	2810	Schleicher Ka7 Rhonadler (Mod to ASK13 status)	384	D-8111	2.82	I.H.Keyser (Over-stressed in spin Bidford 29.7.96; stored 8.97)	Bidford	9.96*
ENE	2812	Rolladen-Schneider LS-4	4271		3.82	D.M.Abbey "281"	Husbands Bosworth	3.99
ENG +	2814	Focke-Wulf Kranich III	79	D-5420	3.82	P.Davie & Ptnrs	Dunstable	8.98
ENJ	2816	Schempp-Hirth Ventus B	62		3.82	S.J.Boyden "771"	Lasham	6.99
ENK +	2817	Schleicher ASK21	21106		4.82	H Jakeman	Aston Down	3.99
ENN	2820	Schempp-Hirth Nimbus 3	9		4.83	R.Kalin & Ptnrs "345"	Gransden Lodge	11.99
ENP +	2821	Schempp-Hirth Nimbus 3	10		11.82	L.Bleaken "626"	Aston Down	4.99
ENT	2825	Glasflugel H.304	210		5.82	P.D.Light "902"	Dunstable	4.98
ENU	2826	Glaser-Dirks DG-100G Elan	E108G78		5.82	F.D.Platt "435"	Camphill	3.99
ENV +	2827	Schleicher ASW20L	20554		5.82	R.Hone "181"	Booker	5.99
ENW +	2828	Schleicher ASW20L	20567		5.82	A.Hunter	Pocklington	3.99
ENY +	2830	Schleicher ASK13	13606	RAFGSA.R17	6.82	Aquila GC	Hinton-in-the-Hedges	2.99
ENZ	2831	Schleicher ASW19B	19366		6.82	O.Pugh	Booker	8.97*
EPD +	2835	Schleicher ASK21	21119		8.82	B.Purslow & Ptnrs	Chipping	4.99
EPE +	2836	Schleicher ASW19B	19335	RAFGSA.R18 BGA.2836	6.82	J.Horner	Pocklington	3.99
EPF	2837	Centrair ASW20FLP	20515		7.82	D.J.Howse "323"	Gransden Lodge	2.99
EPG	2838	CARMAM M.100S Mesange	3	F-CCPB	7.82	P.Shanahan	Templeton	2.95*
EPJ +	2840	Nord 2000 (Olympia)	10399/69	F-CACX	8.82	B.V.Smith	Dishforth	5.99

Regn	BGA No.	Type	C/n	P/I	Regn	Owner/operator	Probable Base	CA Expy
EPK	2841	Centrair 101A Pegase	101-012		10.82	742 Syndicate "742"	Bicester	4.99
EPM +	2843	Scheibe SFH-34 Delphin	5115		8.82	Angus GC	Drumshade	3.98
EPN	2844	Breguet Br.905SA Fauvette	11	F-CCIO	8.82	P.F.Woodcock	Camphill	7.95*
EPP	2845	Schleicher ASK13	1609		1.83	Black Mountains GC "T10"	Talgarth	4.99
		(C/n is spare fuselage no) (Rebuild of PH-368 c/n 13064)						
EPR	2847	Hutter H-17	-	(Kenya) PH-269	9.82	D.Shrimpton	Halesland	6.97
EPS	2848	Schleicher ASW20L	20245	RAFGSA.87	7.85	D.Richardson "765"	Booker	4.98
EPT +	2849	Schleicher K8B	?	RAFGGA.504	9.82	Trent Valley GC	Kirton-in-Lindsey	10.99
EPU +	2850	Glaser-Dirks DG-100G Elan	E116G85	(BGA.2833)	10.82	J.E.Rogers "647"	Booker	3.99
EPV +	2851	Schleicher Ka7 Rhonadler	7148	D-5468	10.82	Newark & Notts GC	Winthorpe	2.99
EPW +	2852	Schleicher Ka6CR	6537	(Kenya)	10.82	J.Kitchen	Strubby	2.99
EPX	2853	Schempp-Hirth Ventus B/16.6	107		10.82	W.T.Craig "906"	Saltby	4.99
EPZ	2855	Scheibe Bergfalke II/55	370	D-4012	1.83	G.W.Sturgess	Thruxton	8.96*
EQA	2856	Rolladen-Schneider LS-4	4259		10.82	M.R.Fountain "275"	Booker	2.99
EQB +	2857	PZL SZD-30 Pirat	S-0648	D-2702	10.82	R.Firman	Booker	8.99
EQD +	2859	Grob G.102 Astir CS77	1614	PH-570	11.82	D.S.Fenton & Ptnrs	Rhigos	7.99
EQE +	2860	Schleicher ASK13	13627		12.82	Essex GC	Ridgewell	8.98
EQF +	2861	Schleicher ASK13	13626		3.85	Essex GC	Ridgewell	8.99
EQG	2862	Schleicher ASW19B	19265	PH-665	12.82	C.M.Whittington & Ptnrs "239"	Challock	4.99
EQJ	2864	Centrair ASW20FL	20512		1.83	N.S.Roberts "968"	Lasham	10.98
EQK +	2865	Centrair 101A Pegase	101-054		2.83	F.G.Irving & Ptnrs	Lasham	3.99
EQL	2866	Avialsa (Rocheteau) CRA-60 Fauconnet	F-CDNR 03K		1.86	J.James	Saltby	5.99
EQM +	2867	CARMAM M.100S Mesange	81	F-CDKQ	3.83	R.Boyd	Nympsfield	8.99
EQN	2868	Schempp-Hirth Nimbus 3	31		3.83	A.D.Purnell "340"	Lasham	2.99
EQQ	2870	Schleicher Ka6CR	6541	AGA.24 BGA.1353	4.83	G.H.Costin & Ptnrs "451"	Challock	3.99
EQR +	2871	Schleicher ASK21	21157		3.83	London GC	Dunstable	10.99
EQU +	2874	Pilatus B4 PC-11	201	PH-535	4.83	W.Green & Ptnrs	Chipping	4.99
EQX +	2877	CARMAM M.200 Foehn	54	F-CDKR	4.83	C.A.McLay & Ptnrs	Chipping	4.99
EQY	2878	BAC.VII rep	01		9.91	M.H.Maufe	Brooklands	5.96P*
		(Rebuild of BAC Drone using wings of G-AEJR and new fuselage)						
EQZ +	2879	Schleicher K8B	8113A	D-8763	4.83	Cambridge University GC	Gransden Lodge	11.98
ERA	2880	Centrair ASW20FL	20526		4.83	C.C.Pike "283"	Booker	3.99
ERB +	2881	Slingsby T.50 Skylark 4 Special	001		4.83	B.V.Smith	Dishforth	8.99
		(Built by C.Almack)						
ERH +	2887	Schleicher ASK21	21147	ZD647 BGA.2887	4.83	Burn GC	Burn	3.99
ERU +	2898	Schempp-Hirth Nimbus 3	13	RAFGSA.R26 D-6330	5.83	L.Urbani	Rieti, Italy	7.99
ERV	2899	Rolladen-Schneider LS-4	4257		5.83	R E Francis "854"	Nympsfield	10.99
ERW	2900	Slingsby T.21B	1130	RAFGSA.237 BGA.842	5.83	High Moor GC "The Spruce Goose"	Hafotty Bennett	6.99
ERX	2901	Centrair 101A Pegase	101-058		6.83	V.Sinclair & Ptnrs "180"	Lasham	1.99
ERY +	2902	Slingsby T.59D Kestrel 22	1839	EI-125 D-9253	6.83	R.J.Hart & Ptnr "983"	Crowland	3.99
ERZ	2903	Oberlerchner Mg19a Steinadler	015	OE-0324	6.83	C.Wills (As "OE-0324")	Booker	6.99
ESA +	2904	PZL SZD-9 bis Bocian 1E	P-750		6.83	Coventry GC	Husbands Bosworth	8.99
ESB +	2905	Schleicher ASK21	21176		6.83	A.L.Garfield	Dunstable	2.99
ESC	2906	Rolladen-Schneider LS-4	4261		6.83	J.M.Staley "379"	Bicester	4.99
ESD	2907	Centrair 101A Pegase	101-065		6.83	R.I.Cowderoy "640"	Lasham	3.97*
ESE	2908	Rolladen-Schneider LS-4	4260		6.83	P.C.Fritche "LS4"	Parham Park	1.99
ESH	2911	Centrair 101A Pegase	101-069		7.83	D.M.Byass "118"	Booker	12.99
ESJ +	2912	Schleicher K8B	8730	D-5010	7.83	Bowland Forest GC	Chipping	5.99
ESK	2913	Schleicher Ka2B	697	RAFGSA.594 D-5947	7.83	W.R.Williams	Odiham	5.99
ESM	2915	Breguet Br.905SA Fauvette	30	F-CCJA	8.83	A C Jarvis	Parham Park	7.99
ESP +	2917	PZL SZD-48-3 Jantar Standard 3	B-1294		4.84	J.Durman	Pocklington	3.99
ESQ	2918	Glaser-Dirks DG-300 Elan	3E10		4.84	G.Huggins "231"	Sandhill Farm, Shrivenham	3.99
ESU +	2922	Schleicher ASK21	21180	RAFGSA.R40 BGA.2922	9.83	Southdown GC	Parham Park	5.99
		(Composite with RAFGSA.R28 c/n 21154)						
ESV	2923	LET L-13 Blanik	173328	EI-110 G-ATWW	5.84	Herefordshire GC	Shobdon	4.98
ESW	2924	Centrair 101A Pegase	101-068		3.84	A.F.Thomas "590"	Usk	2.99
ESX	2925	Schleicher K8B	.	(ex)	9.83	Wolds GC	Pocklington	12.96*
ESY +	2926	Rolladen-Schneider LS-4	4334		2.84	L.Hill & Ptnrs	North Hill	2.99
ETA	2928	Schleicher ASK21	21181		11.83	R W Collings	Husbands Bosworth	4.99
ETB +	2929	Schleicher Ka6E	4365	HB-1021	11.83	A.J.Padgett "A6"	Tibenham	9.97*
ETE	2932	Fauvel AV.36C	214	RAFGSA.R53 D-5353/D-8259	8.87	J.F.Beringer "The Budgie"	Wormingford	6.98

Regn	BGA No.	Type	C/n	P/I	Regn	Owner/operator	Probable Base	CA Expy
ETG +	2934	Rolladen-Schneider LS-4	4349		12.83	M.W.Rebbeck & Ptnrs	Rattlesden	4.99
ETH +	2935	Schleicher K8B	120	D-5755	4.84	North Wales GC	Bryngwyn Bach	4.99
ETJ	2936	Centrair 101A Pegase	101A-0110		10.84	K.J.Bye "223"	Wormingford	1.00
ETK	2937	PZL SZD-48 Jantar Standard 2	W-876	OY-XJO	2.84	J.A.Cowie "215"	Portmoak	6.99
ETL	2938	Jansson BJ-1B Duster	01		1.85P	I.Beckett	North Hill	3.96*
		(Built by I.Beckett)						
ETM	2939	Centrair 101 Pegase	101-111		5.84	Booker GC "312"	Booker	5.99
ETN	2940	CARMAM M.100S Mesange	23	F-CCSL	2.84	T.E.Betts	Seighford	8.96*
ETP	2941	Slingsby T.21B	610	WB943	7.84	P.Hepworth t/a Ouse T.21 Syndicate		
						"943" (As "WB943")	Rufforth	3.99
ETQ +	2942	Centrair 101A Pegase	101A-0123		5.84	A R Jennings	Gransden Lodge	2.98
ETR	2943	Schleicher Ka7 Rhonadler	3	D-8339	1.84	Shenington GC "2"	Edgehill	3.99
ETS +	2944	Schleicher ASK13	13635AB		3.84	Upward Bound Trust	Thame	7.99
ETU +	2946	Schleicher Ka7 Rhonadler	?	RAFGSA R.8	4.84	R.Cullum	Strubby	6.99
ETV +	2947	Rolladen-Schneider LS-4	4314	(BGA.2919)	3.84	T.A.Meaker	Kirton-in-Lindsey	2.99
ETY	2950	Rolladen-Schneider LS-4	4368		4.84	R.Harris "249"	Booker	2.99
ETZ	2951	Schleicher ASW20CL	20730		3.84	R.R.Page "20"	Lasham	2.99
EUC +	2954	Schleicher ASK13	13104	AGA.12	4.84	Bristol & Glos GC	Nympsfield	12.99
EUD	2955	Schleicher ASW20C	20734		6.84	D.J.Tagg "56"	Lasham	3.99
EUE +	2956	Scheibe SF-27A Zugvogel V	6106	D-5342	5.84	Newark & Notts GC	Winthorpe	2.99
EUF +	2957	PZL SZD-50-3 Puchacz	B-1090		5.84	D.B.Meeks t/a Bidford Gliding Centre		
							Bidford	3.99
EUG +	2958	LET L-13 Blanik	025817	RAFGSA.R56	5.84	Avon Soaring Centre	Bidford	5.93*
				RAFGSA.426/BGA.1953		(Wreck stored 8.94)		
		(Composite rebuild - fuselage/tail: BGA.1917 [025610], port [025817] & starboard wings (BGA.2028 [026257])						
EUH	2959	Rolladen-Schneider LS-4	4382		4.84	W.P.Winterton "446"	Parham Park	2.99
EUJ +	2960	Schempp-Hirth Ventus B/16.6	162		4.84	T.Paterson & Ptnrs	Portmoak	11.99
EUK +	2961	Centrair ASW20FL	20530		5.84	J.L.Caton "992"	Lasham	4.99
EUM +	2963	Scheibe SF-26A Standard	5039	RAFGSA	5.84	Vale of Neath GC	Rhigos	7.97*
EUN	2964	Slingsby T.21B	588	RAFGSA.R92	4.84	Booker GC	Booker	6.99
				RAFGSA.212/WB925				
EUQ +	2966	Schleicher Ka7 Rhonadler	863	D-4639	5.84	Kent GC	Challock	4.99
EUS	2968	Schempp-Hirth Ventus B/16.6	192		5.84	J.C.Bastin "443"	Rivar Hill	4.99
EUT +	2969	Schleicher Rhonlerche	?	RAFGSA	5.84	G.De"Orfe & Ptnrs Gransden Lodge		11.99
EUV +	2971	PZL SZD-42-2 Jantar 2B	B-934		5.84	G.V.McKirdy	Edgehill	5.98
EUX +	2973	Schleicher ASK18	18005	D-3988	5.84	Southdown GC	Parham Park	11.99
EUY	2974	Schleicher ASW20BL	20645		6.84	D.G.Roberts & Ptnrs "88"		
							Aston Down	4.99
EUZ	2975	Slingsby T.21B	620	WB959	6.84	Dartmoor Gliding Association		
						(Stored 6.94)	Burnford Common	9.93*
EVA +	2976	Slingsby T.31B	683	WT873	9.84	T.Bull	Parham Park	6.99
EVB +	2977	Schleicher Ka7 Rhonadler	7004	D-5109	6.84	R.Armitage t/a Channel GC		
							Waldershare Park	12.99
EVC +	2978	CARMAM M.200 Foehn	55	F-CDKT	6.84	W.Young & Ptnrs	Pocklington	7.98
EVD	2979	Rolladen-Schneider LS-3	3024	N63LS	8.84	C.R.Appleyard "382"	Lasham	2.99
				D-7914				
EVE	2980	Centrair 101A Pegase	101A-0141		6.84	B.M.Chaplin "491"	Lasham	3.99
EVF	2981	Schempp-Hirth Nimbus 3T	15/76	D-KHIJ	3.85	R.A.Foot & Ptnrs "90"	Lasham	4.99
EVG +	2982	Schleicher Ka7 Rhonadler (Mod.)	396	D-0018	7.84	Derby & Lancs GC	Camphill	8.99
EVH +	2983	Schleicher Ka10	10008	HB-791	5.86	J.W Bolt	Brent Tor	5.99
EVJ	2984	Schleicher ASK13	13637AB		7.84	Lasham Gliding Society "H"		
							Lasham	11.99
EVK +	2985	Grob G.102 Astir CS	1397	PH-546	12.86	D.R.Taylor	Tibenham	6.99
EVL	2986	Grob G.102 Astir CS77	1638	PH-575	8.84	Southdown Aero Service "SA1"		
							Lasham	4.98
EVM	2987	Centrair 101A Pegase	101A-0157		8.84	Culdrose GC (RNGSA.N51)		
							RNAS Culdrose	3.99
EVP	2989	Schleicher ASK13	13638AB		8.84	Lasham Gliding Society "K"		
							Lasham	11.98
EVQ	2990	Centrair 101A Pegase	101A-0149		8.84	R.J.Dann & Ptnr "682"		
							Rivar Hill	5.99
EVR +	2991	LET L-13 Blanik	172604	G-ASVS	8.84	D.Latimer	Hinton-in-the-Hedges	6.99
				OK-3840				
EVS +	2992	PZL SZD-50-3 Puchacz	B-1091		9.84	Connel GC	North Connel	8.99
EVT +	2993	Scheibe Bergfalke IV	5807	D-0730	9.84	Shalbourne Soaring Society		
							Rivar Hill	5.99
EVU	2994	Raab Doppelraab	515	RAFGSA.666	R	Not known	Bicester	*
		(Built Wolf Hirth 1952)		D-5223		(Frame stored 9.94)		
EVV +	2995	Schleicher ASK23	23004		10.84	Midland GC	Long Mynd	12.98
EVW +	2996	Schleicher ASK23	23006		1.85	London GC	Dunstable	12.99
EVX +	2997	Schleicher ASK23	23007		1.85	London GC	Dunstable	11.99
EVY +	2998	Schleicher ASK23	23008		1.85	London GC	Dunstable	10.99
EWP +	3013	Grob G.103A Twin II Acro	33892-K-130	ZE523	11.84	Cambridge University GC		
				BGA.3013			Gransden Lodge	2.99
EWR	3015	Grob G.103A Twin II Acro	33894-K-132	RAFGSA.R70	11.84	Anglia GC	Wattisham	12.99
				ZE525/BGA.3015				
EZE +	3076	Grob G.103A Twin II Acro	33981-K-214	ZE634	5.85	Oxford GC	Weston-on-the-Green	4.99
				BGA.3076				

Regn	BGA No.	Type	C/n	P/I	Regn	Owner/operator	Probable Base	CA Expy

FAA-FZZ

Regn	BGA No.	Type	C/n	P/I	Regn	Owner/operator	Probable Base	CA Expy
FAF	3101	Schleicher ASW20	20214	RAFGSA.271 RAFGSA.R27	10.84	M.S.Armstrong "271" Gallows Hill		4.99
FAJ	3103	Glaser-Dirks DG-300 Elan	3E50		10.84	B A Brown "790"	Lyveden	3.99
FAK +	3104	Avialsa A.60 Fauconnet	104K	F-CDFG	5.85	I.Gumbrell Kingston Deverill		7.98
FAM	3106	Schempp-Hirth Nimbus 3	79		3.85	I.M.Stromberg "115"	Camphill	12.99
FAN	3107	Centrair 101A Pegase	101A-0161		10.84	M Heslop "202"	Parham Park	11.99
FAP	3108	Monnett Monerai	123		5.86P	D.B Rich	Eaglescott	5.99
FAQ	3109	Rolladen-Schneider LS-4	4465		3.85	C.J.Alldis "646"	Bryngwyn Bach	10.99
FAR +	3110	Glasflugel H.205 Club Libelle	58	HB-1262	6.85	G.A.Gair	Kenley	3.99
FAT +	3112	Schleicher ASK13	13528	PH-456	1.85	Dorset GC Gallows Hill		1.00
FAV +	3114	ICA IS-32A	05		12.84	Black Mountains GC	Talgarth	3.99
FAW +	3115	Schempp-Hirth Ventus B/16.6	26	D-6768	2.85	P.Stafford-Allen "333" Crowland		2.99
FAZ +	3118	Schleicher K8B	8558	D-1043	3.85	Southdown GC "Katie" Parham Park		12.98
FBA	3119	Schleicher ASW20BL	20665		1.85	R.W.Prestwich "178"	Sleap	12.99
FBB	3120	Schempp-Hirth HS.4 Standard Cirrus	327G	RAFGGA "312"	1.85	M.Andrewartha "822"	Bidford	1.00
FBC +	3121	Schleicher ASW15B	15356	OH-439	5.85	J.M.Dougans "439"	Dunstable	4.99
FBD +	3122	Schleicher ASW15B	15407	OH-445	5.85	R.Pettifer & C.A.McLay Chipping		4.99
FBE	3123	Rolladen-Schneider LS-6	6028	D-9384	7.85	T.J.Wills "1"	Booker	7.99
FBF	3124	Glaser-Dirks DG-300 Elan	3E9	BGA.2952	1.85	A.L.Garfield "175"	Dunstable	3.99
FBG	3125	PZL SZD-50-3 Puchacz	B-1081		2.85	Not known	Rivar Hill	3.90*
						(Wrecked in gales Booker 25.1.90; stored 5.94)		
FBH	3126	Glaser-Dirks DG-100G Elan	E156G123		4.85	IBM (S.Hants) GC "177"	Lasham	5.99
FBJ +	3127	Schleicher K8B	8221	D-6340	2.85	Bidford GC	Bidford	5.99
FBL	3129	Schleicher Ka2B Rhonschwalbe	373	HB-606	2.85	J.D.Melling Hall Caine, IoM		5.96*
FBM	3130	Schempp-Hirth Nimbus 3/24.5	73		2.85	T.P.Docherty "727"	Portmoak	7.95*
FBN +	3131	Glasflugel H.303 Mosquito B	167	D-6364	5.85	D.R Andrews & Ptnrs	Sleap	2.99
FBQ	3133	Schleicher ASW20BL	20669		4.85	D.W.Gosden "464"	Usk	3.99
FBR	3134	Grob G.102 Astir CS77	1701	SE-TSV	2.88	G.Smith & Ptnrs "773"		8.98
							Pocklington	
FBT	3136	Schempp-Hirth Ventus BT	218/35		3.85	S.M.Young "488"	Talgarth	4.99
FBV +	3138	Schleicher ASK21	21223		5.85	London GC	Dunstable	3.99
FBW	3139	Glaser-Dirks DG-101G Elan	E174G140		4.85	Surrey & Hants GC "395"	Lasham	3.99
FBY	3141	Schempp-Hirth Discus B	20		4.85	D Latimer "780"	Dunstable	3.99
FBZ	3142	Schleicher Ka6CR	6016	D-4667 D-KIMN/D-4667	5.85	R.Martin & Ptnrs (As "D-4667")	Booker	9.98
FCB +	3144	Centrair 101 Pegase	101-0178	F-CGEA	4.85	N.Stratton	Portmoak	2.99
FCC	3145	Slingsby T.31B	1182	XN243	5.85	D.A.Head & Ptnrs (As "XN243")	Bicester	7.97*
FCD	3146	Centrair 101A Pegase B	101A-0207		5.85	G.K.Drury "841"	Challock	4.99
FCF	3148	Slingsby T.21B	MHL.017	WB990	5.85	N.Worrell "993"	Lasham	5.99
FCG	3149	Slingsby T.31B	681	WT871	5.85	J.Desmond (As "WT871")	RAF Marham	1.99
FCH +	3150	CARMAM M.100S Mesange	72	F-CDKD	5.85	P A Pickering	Upwood	4.99
FCJ	3151	Grob G.102 Astir CS	1231	D-4205	5.85	M.Levitt & G.Fellows "571"		1.99
							Aston Down	
FCK	3152	Schempp-Hirth Ventus B/16.6	241		5.85	L.J.Scott "671" Bryngwyn Bach		3.99
FCL +	3153	Schleicher K8B	8045E	D-5225	5.85	M.Jackson	Challock	4.98
FCM	3154	Glaser-Dirks DG-300 Elan	3E94		5.85	R.B.Coote "411"	Parham Park	12.99
FCN	3155	Schempp-Hirth HS.4 Standard Cirrus	131	D-0191	6.85	P.Burniss & Syndicate "920"		12.99
							Nympsfield	
FCP	3156	Rolladen-Schneider LS-6	6030		7.85	E.W.Johnston "721"	Aston Down	2.99
FCQ +	3157	Schleicher K8B	1	RAFGGA... D-8322 or D-0322?	4.85	M.W.Meagher	Edgehill	3.98
		(Build Bayer)						
FCR	3158	Schleicher Ka6E	4223	OH-375 OH-REC	6.85	J.L.Caton & Ptnrs "113"		2.99
							Parham Park	
FCS	3159	Schempp-Hirth HS.5 Nimbus 2C	233/81	D-5993	7.85	R.W.Hawkins "N2"	Parham Park	12.99
FCT +	3160	Slingsby T.21B	611	WB944	12.86	Upward Bound Trust	Thame	7.99
FCV +	3162	Schleicher ASW20	20076	RAFGSA.R24	6.85	M.J.Davis & Ptnrs	RAF Cosford	4.99
FCW	3163	Schleicher ASK13	13642AB		6.85	Lasham Gliding Society "L"		11.99
							Lasham	
FCX +	3164	Schleicher ASK23	23011		7.85	Midland GC Long Mynd (Damaged Long Mynd 26.7.97)		1.98*
FCY +	3165	Schleicher ASW15	15122	D-0748	6.85	M.Evershed & Ptnrs	Dunstable	2.98
FCZ	3166	Slingsby T.1 Falcon 1 rep (Built Southdown Aero Svs)	-		7.85	D.D.Knight & J.Harber RAF Halton		N/E(P)
FDA	3167	Schleicher ASW15	15050	D-0511	7.85	N W Woodward "7D"	Booker	4.99
FDB +	3168	ICA IS-30	07		9.85	Black Mountains GC	Talgarth	5.98
FDC +	3169	CARMAM JP-15/34 Kit Club	TAH.50/60		3.87	T.A.Hollins	Rufforth	5.99
FDD	3170	Schleicher K8B	8972	AGA.5	7.85	L.D.Young "348"	Rivar Hill	3.99
FDE	3171	Schempp-Hirth Ventus BT	256/53		8.85	P.L.Roberts "510"	Tatenhill	3.99
FDF +	3172	Grob G.102 Astir CS	1321	D-7338	9.85	P.Andrews	Aston Down	4.99
FDG +	3173	ICA IS-29D2 Club	02		8.85	D.C.Wales		6.99
							Sackville Lodge, Riseley	
FDL	3177	Schleicher Ka8	Liz.105/58	D-4650	9.85	G.Millar & Ptnrs	Cranfield	11.95*

Regn	BGA No.	Type	C/n	P/I	Regn	Owner/operator	Probable Base	CA Expy
FDP	3180	ICA IS-30	08		5.86	Staffordshire GC "996" Seighford		6.99
FDQ +	3181	Slingsby T.31B	710	WT915	9.85	J.F.J.M.Forster "Chris Wills"		7.99
							Maastricht, Netherlands	
FDR +	3182	Schleicher Ka6CR	6119	D-8456	11.85	P.Hill & R.Grayling		12.99
							Burnford Common	
FDT	3184	Schleicher ASW22	22025	D-7709	10.85	D.P.Taylor "W22"	Sutton Bank	4.99
						(As "BGA.4195" 8.98)		
FDU	3185	Schempp-Hirth Discus B	87		6.86	P.M.Shelton "D1"	Tatenhill	3.99
FDV +	3186	LET L-13 Blanik	173333	D-5826	4.86	T.Wiltshire	East Kirkby	7.98
				D-KOEB/D-5826		(Carries "D-5826" under wing)		
FDW +	3187	Glaser-Dirks DG-300 Elan	3E143		1.86	N Kelly	Enstone	2.99
FDX +	3188	PZL SZD-48-1 Jantar Standard 2	B-1251	(BGA.2916)	11.85	L.Mathews & Ptnrs	Ringmer	9.99
FEA +	3191	Grob G.103 Twin Astir	3151	RAFGSA.R83	12.85	G.M.Brightman	Edgehill	4.99
				RAFGSA "833"				
FEB	3192	Grob G.102 Club Astir III	5643C		11.85	Surrey & Hants GC "398"	Lasham	4.99
FEE +	3195	Slingsby T.21B	MHL.016	WB989	1.86	K.Schickling		
							Aschaffenburg, Germany	5.99
FEF +	3196	Grob G.102 Astir CS	1164	OY-XGC	2.86	Oxford University GC	Bicester	3.99
FEG	3197	Schempp-Hirth Ventus B/16.6	279		2.86	K.Moorhouse & Ptnr "120"		
							Rivar Hill	3.99
FEH	3198	Centrair 101A Pegase Club	101A-0268		5.86	Booker GC "318"	Booker	2.99
		(Rebuilt with new fuselage c/n 01304 and original fuselage rebuilt as BGA.3560)						
FEJ	3199	Schempp-Hirth Discus B	76		2.86	D.Geddes "538"	Lasham	2.99
FEL +	3201	Schleicher Ka7 Rhonadler	7231	RAFGGA...	9.86	Burn GC	Burn	11.99
		(See BGA.3231)		D-???				
FEN +	3203	PZL SZD-50-3 Puchacz	B-1326		3.86	Northumbria GC	Currock Hill	6.99
FEP	3204	Schempp-Hirth Ventus BT	284/69		4.86	R.J.Nicholls "209"		
							Husbands Bosworth	11.99
FEQ	3205	Schleicher ASK13	13650AB		4.86	Lasham Gliding Society "M"		
							Lasham	12.99
FER	3206	Schempp-Hirth Discus B	75		3.86	D.R.Campbell & Ptnr "370" Booker		4.99
FES	3207	Schempp-Hirth Discus B	88		4.86	N.G.Storer "564"	Lasham	2.99
FEU	3209	Schleicher ASW22	22030	D-8888	4.86	A.J.French & P.Harvey "89"		
						(Damaged nr Mitcheldean 24.5.97) Dunstable		11.98
FEV	3210	Glasflugel H.301B Libelle	100	ZS-GFZ	5.86	T.J.Wills	(New Zealand)	9.99
FEX +	3212	Grob G.102 Astir CS77	1660	D-7492	4.86	D.Hartley	Upwood	4.99
FEZ	3214	EoN AP.7 Primary	EoN/P/013	BGA.590??	9.86	G.J.Moore	Brooklands	5.99
		(Reported as ex R13 (c/n EoN/P/037 ex RAFGSA R.13/RAFGSA 113/WP929)						
FFA +	3215	Schleicher ASK13	13651AB		5.86	Staffordshire GC	Seighford	4.99
FFC +	3217	Centrair 101A Pegase	101A-0255		5.86	C.A Hitchin	Kingston Deverill	6.99
FFG	3221	Slingsby T.21B	559	WB920	6.86	J.H.Wisselink (As "WB920")		
							Roosendaal, Netherlands	4.99
FFH +	3222	Schleicher ASW20	20037	D-7947	4.87	J.Hayes "H4"	Dishforth	6.99
FFJ	3223	Grob G.103A Twin II Acro	34075-K-305		6.86	Derby & Lancs GC "623"	Camphill	11.99
FFK	3224	Schempp-Hirth Nimbus 3	87		4.87	Dr.Brennig-James "7"	Booker	6.99
		(BGA.4149 wears "FFK")						
FFL	3225	Slingsby T.21B	MHL.020	WB993	6.87	J.van Os		
							Hilversum, Netherlands	5.99
FFM	3226	Grob G.102 Club Astir IIIb	5609CB	PH-730	7.86	Imperial College GC "296" Lasham		3.99
FFN +	3227	ICA IS-29D	21	D-9223	8.86	A.Sutton & Ptnrs "987"		
							Snitterfield	5.99
FFP	3228	Schleicher ASW19B	19317	RAFGSA.R19	6.86	K A Ford "93"	Lasham	3.99
FFQ +	3229	Slingsby T.31B	913	XE800	8.86	I.F.Smith	Booker	3.99
FFS +	3231	Centrair 101A Pegase	101A-0265		6.86	W Murray	Gransden Lodge	3.99
		(Marked as BGA.3201)						
FFT +	3232	Schempp-Hirth Discus B	110		6.86	R.Maskell & Ptnrs	Ridgewell	3.99
FFU +	3233	Glaser-Dirks DG-100G Elan	E200G166		1.87	S.Robinson	Chipping	2.99
FFV +	3234	PZL SZD-51-1 Junior	B-1616	F-WGJA	8.86	Herefordshire GC	Shobdon	7.99
FFX	3235	Schempp-Hirth Discus B	109		7.86	C.Bainbridge "871"	Wormingford	3.99
FFY +	3237	PZL SZD-51-1 Junior	W-938		11.86	Cornish GC	Perranporth	4.99
FFZ	3238	Slingsby T.21B	MHL.008	WB981	8.86	M.Lake (As "WB981")	Aston Down	6.95*
						(Wfu and wings to BGA.1218 1995; fuselage stored 8.98)		
FGA	3239	Slingsby T.31B	708	WT913	10.86	J.M.Brookes & Ptnrs	Rufforth	7.96*
FGB +	3240	Slingsby T.21B	654	WJ306	8.86	Oxford GC	Weston-on-the-Green	7.99
FGC	3241	Slingsby T.31B	713	WT918	8.86	U.Seegers	(Germany)	4.96*
FGF	3244	Schempp-Hirth Nimbus 3T	25/91		8.86	D.S.Innes "110"	Lasham	3.99
FGG	3245	Slingsby T.21B	665	WG498	9.86	G.A.Ford & Ptnrs	Aston Down	9.98
						(As "WG498")		
FGJ	3247	Schleicher Ka6CR	6634	D-1041	9.86	A.Clark	Booker	7.95*
FGK +	3248	Grob G.102 Astir CS	1323	RAFGSA.R61	9.86	E.Bertoya	Thruxton	4.99
				RAFGSA.316				
FGM +	3250	Slingsby T.21B	1160	XN156	7.87	R.B.Petrie	Strathaven	7.99
		(Mod with 330cc engine)						
FGP +	3252	Schleicher ASW19	19121	C-GJXG	11.86	C.Sullivan	Gransden Lodge	3.99
FGR	3254	Schleicher ASK13	13655AB		10.86	Portsmouth Naval GC (RNGSA.N29)		
		(Jubi-built)					Lee-on-Solent	4.99

Regn	BGA No.	Type	C/n	P/I	Regn	Owner/operator	Probable Base	CA Expy
FGS	3255	Slingsby T.21B	1161	XN157	10.86	D.W.Cole & Ptnrs	Long Mynd	7.95*
		(Fuselage No.SSK/FF/1745)				(As "XN157")		
FGT +	3256	Glaser-Dirks DG-300 Elan	3E217		3.87	B.J Edwards	Booker	1.00
FGU	3257	Schempp-Hirth HS.4 Standard Cirrus	147	D-0193	4.87	M.Wild & Ptnrs "806"	Kenley	2.99
FGV +	3258	Schleicher Ka7 Rhonadler	?	OO-Z..	12.86	Nene Valley GC	Upwood	1.99
		(Hybrid using ex Belgian Ka7 fuselage & wings from Ka2 BGA.2662)						
FGW	3259	Centrair 101A Pegase	101A-0275		6.87	L.P.Smith "701"	Nympsfield	4.99
FGY	3261	Schleicher ASW22	22027	D-3527	1.87	M.Bird "527"	Dunstable	4.99
FGZ +	3262	Schleicher Ka7 Rhonadler	7238	D-5376	1.87	Dartmoor GC "D2"	Brent Tor	10.99
FHB	3264	Slingsby T.21B(T)	MHL.018	WB991	2.87	G.Traves	East Kirkby	3.99
		(Robin EC-34PM s/n 82-00391))						
FHC	3265	Slingsby T.21B	MHL.013	WB986	6.87	G.Traves	East Kirkby	7.97
FHD	3266	Schleicher ASW20BL	20694	RAFGGA...	3.87	K.J.Hartley "196"	Bicester	4.99
FHE	3267	Scheibe L-Spatz III	817	LX-CLM	3.87	C.W.Matten & Ptnrs	Culdrose	3.98
FHF +	3268	PZL SZD-51-1 Junior	W-952		3.87	Black Mountains GC	Talgarth	2.99
FHG	3269	Schempp-Hirth HS.7 Mini Nimbus C	140	(BGA.3213) ZS-GNI	3.87	R.W.Weaver "187"	Usk	1.99
FHJ	3271	Centrair 101A Pegase	101A-0278		5.87	Booker GC "987"	Booker	5.99
FHK +	3272	Slingsby T.31B	695	WT900	4.87	N.Scully & Ptnrs "Tweety"	Dunstable	5.99
FHL	3273	Rolladen-Schneider LS-4	4633		4.87	I.P.Hicks "136"	Cranfield	12.98
FHM	3274	Schleicher ASK13	13662AB		6.87	Lasham Gliding Society "P"	Lasham	12.98
FHN +	3275	Schleicher K8B	?	RAFGSA.R85 RAFGSA.385/RAFGSA.360	6.87	Buckminster GC	Saltby	1.00
FHQ	3277	Hols-der-Teufel Replica	-		6.87	M.L.Beach (On display 3.96)	Brooklands	N/E(P)
		(Built M.L.Beach)						
FHR	3278	Schempp-Hirth Discus B	152		6.87	P.Tratt & Syndicate "Q5"	Parham Park	1.99
FHS	3279	Schempp-Hirth Ventus CT	326/82		6.87	R.Andrews "154"	Long Mynd	1.99
FHT +	3280	Grob G.102 Astir CS	1234	D-4208	6.87	M.A Taylor	Rattlesden	2.99
FHU +	3281	Schleicher Ka7 Rhonadler	629	RAFGSA.R15 RAFGGA/D-5722	6.87	Dartmoor GC	Brent Tor	5.99
		(Mod to ASK13 standard)						
FHV +	3282	PZL SZD-48-1 Jantar Standard 2	B-1036	D-4516	6.87	R.A.Williams & Ptnrs	Long Mynd	4.99
FHW +	3283	Grob G.102 Astir CS	1087	D-6987	6.87	P.W.Roberts "698"	Lasham	4.99
FHY +	3285	Scheibe SF-27A Zugvogel V	6045	D-1868	7.87	J.M.Pursey "H5"	North Hill	7.99
						(As "D-1868")		
FHZ +	3286	Schleicher Ka6CR	949	D-4661	8.87	D.Farmilo & Ptnr	Husbands Bosworth	4.99
FJA +	3287	Slingsby T.21B	1152	XN148	7.87	East Sussex GC	Ringmer	7.99
FJB +	3288	Slingsby T.21B	MHL.002	WB975	7.87	Angus GC	Drumshade	3.99
FJD +	3290	Slingsby T.21B	MHL.007	WB980	8.87	R.H.Short & Ptnrs	Lyveden	6.99
FJE	3291	Schleicher ASW20BL	20953		7.87	B.Pridal "744"	Booker	12.97
FJF	3292	Slingsby T.21B	586	WB923	9.87	R.L.Hill	Snitterfield	8.99
		(Frame No. SSK/FF 1085)						
FJH +	3294	Grob G.102 Astir CS77	1763	AGA.7	8.87	Shalborne Soaring Society "330"	Rivar Hill	2.99
FJJ	3295	Schempp-Hirth Ventus BT	344.93		8.87	R.T.Cole & Ptnrs "134"	Lasham	3.99
FJK +	3296	Centrair 101A Pegase	101-070		4.88	J.R.Martindale	Walney Island	11.99
FJM	3298	Rolladen-Schneider LS-4A	4665	D-1431	12.87	G.C.Beardsley & Ptnr "143"	Dunstable	2.99
FJN	3299	Slingsby T.31B	698	WT903	2.88	R.R.Beazer	Camphill	9.99
FJQ +	3301	Schempp-Hirth Ventus CT	104/365		3.88	B.Rood	Hinton-in-the-Hedges	9.98
FJR	3302	Glaser-Dirks DG-300 Club Elan	3E270C2		2.88	G Smith "950"	(France)	3.99
FJS	3303	Glaser-Dirks DG-300 Club Elan	3E271C3		5.88	Yorkshire GC "257"	Sutton Bank	1.00
FJT	3304	Centrair 101A Pegase	101A-0284		2.88	D.M.Smith & A.Marlow "997"	Booker	5.99
FJU	3305	Schleicher K8B	976	OH-240 OH-RTC	11.87	Northumbria GC	Currock Hill	5.99
		(Marked as "FJT")						
FJV	3306	Schleicher ASW15	15109	D-0710	11.87	G.N.Turner & Ptnr "713"	Sandhill Farm, Shrivenham	3.99
FJX	3308	Glaser-Dirks DG-300 Elan	3E261		2.88	D.S Jones "728"	North Hill	7.99
FJZ +	3310	Schempp-Hirth SHK	14	D-9330	4.88	R H.Hanna & A. & R.Willis	Bellarena	8.99
FKA +	3311	Schleicher Ka6CR	6239	D-7037 D-5435	2.88	S.T.Dry & B.Davies	Kingston Deverill	3.99
FKB +	3312	Glaser-Dirks DG-600	6-08		10.88	J.A.Watt	Dunstable	4.99
FKE	3315	Schleicher ASW15	15146	D-0794	3.88	D.G.Lloyd & Syndicate "G2"	Bidford	2.99
FKG	3317	Rolladen-Schneider LS-4A	4673		5.88	R.Lynch "125"	Kingston Deverill	3.99
FKH +	3318	Schleicher Ka6CR	6343	EI-109 IGA.106	3.88	Ulster GC	Bellarena	6.99
FKJ +	3319	Schleicher K8B	8032	OH-264 OH-RTE	4.88	Aquila GC	Hinton-in-the-Hedges	6.99
FKK	3320	Schempp-Hirth Discus B	219		3.88	D.J.Eade "406"	Lasham	2.99

Regn	BGA No.	Type	C/n	P/I	Regn	Owner/operator	Probable Base	CA Expy
FKL	3321	Schleicher ASW20BL	20954		3.88	J.M.Ley & J.Rollason "152" Ridgewell		12.98
FKM	3322	Schempp-Hirth Discus B	212		3.88	Surrey & Hants GC "399"	Lasham	2.99
FKN	3323	Schleicher ASH25	25042	(BGA.3491) BGA.3323	7.88	M Bird "13"	Dunstable	11.99
FKP	3324	Slingsby T.21B	632	WB971	2.88	M.Powell (As "WB971")	Booker	4.99
FKQ +	3325	Scheibe SFH-34 Delphin	5119	D-1412	4.88	Bristol & Glos GC	Nympsfield	4.99
FKT +	3328	Schleicher K8B	8382	D-5366	4.88	Herefordshire GC	Shobdon	6.99
FKU	3329	Schleicher Ka6CR (Wears "FKY")	822	D-0025	4.88	Mrs C.Roberts	Camphill	5.99
FKV +	3330	CARMAM M.100S Mesange	60	F-CDDV	5.88	G.G Hunt	Bidford	7.97*
FKW +	3331	Schleicher Ka7 Rhonadler	7145	OH-302 OH-KKJ	4.88	Welland GC	Lyveden	6.99
FKX +	3332	Schleicher Ka6CR	6433	D-4316	4.88	D.Bartel & Ptnrs	Lasham	3.99
FKY ·	3333	(See BGA.3329)						
FLC	3337	Glaser-Dirks DG-300 Elan	3E310		9.88	A.R.Milne "808"	Gallows Hill	3.99
FLE	3339	Schempp-Hirth Discus B	207		5.88	R.A.Sandford "414"	Rivar Hill	2.99
FLF	3340	Rolladen-Schneider LS-4A	4694		3.88	D.E.Lamb "Z4"	Booker	2.99
FLG	3341	Schleicher ASH25E (Turbo)	25044		6.88	D.S.McKay "A25"	Enstone	5.99
FLH +	3342	Schleicher K8B (Built by KK Lehtovaara O/Y)	22	OH-361 OH-RTW	5.88	Aquila GC Hinton-in-the-Hedges		6.99
FLK +	3344	Schleicher Ka7 Rhonadler	985	D-5047	1.89	Dukeries GC	Gamston	1.99
FLL +	3345	PZL SZD-9 bis Bocian 1D (C/n probably "877")	F-877	OH-336 OH-KBP	7.88	R.G.Wardell-Yerburgh Kingston Deverill		1.99
FLN	3347	Schleicher ASW24	24011		6.88	D.M.Byass & Ptnrs "161" Dunstable		4.99
FLP	3348	Schleicher K8B (Built by KK Lehtovaara O/Y)	07	OH-316 OH-RTP	5.88	Bath, Wilts & North Dorset GC (Marked as "FLN" 7.98) Kingston Deverill		2.99
FLQ	3349	Schleicher K8B	8195A	D-8887	8.88	Surrey & Hants GC "887"	Lasham	8.97*
FLS +	3351	Schleicher Ka6CR	6180	D-4001	11.88	P.B.Arms	Halton	3.99
FLT +	3352	Glasflugel H.201B Standard Libelle	41	D-0211	12.88	C.Glover	Husbands Bosworth	7.99
FLU	3353	Glasflugel H.201B Standard Libelle	52	D-0298	6.88	C.D.Duthy-James "DJ2"	Talgarth	6.97*
FLV +	3354	LET L-13 Blanik	173312	D-1335	7.88	North Devon GC "Jenny" "3354" Eaglescott		5.96*
FLW +	3355	Schempp-Hirth HS.4 Standard Cirrus	75 656	F-CEMT	7.88	J.R.Taylor "127"	Perranporth	12.99
FLX +	3356	Glaser-Dirks DG-300 Club Elan	3E304C19		10.88	R.Walker	Rufforth	3.99
FLY	3357	Schleicher ASW24	24012		7.88	I.J.Lewis "983"	North Weald	3.98
FLZ +	3358	Scheibe SF-27A Zugvogel V	6061	D-5378	7.88	R Russon	Long Mynd	1.99
FMA*	3359	Slingsby T.38 Grasshopper	793	WZ797	8.88	Not known (On rebuild 8.98)	Edgehill	8.89
FMC	3361	Rolladen-Schneider LS-6B	6184		7.88	B.L.Cooper "68"	Booker	12.99
FMD +	3362	Schleicher Ka7 Rhonadler	343	D-2877 HB-603	7.88	Not known Aston Down (Damaged Ringmer 6.5.92: stored 8.98)		12.92*
FME +	3363	Schleicher ASW15	15164	D-0825	8.88	A.P.Crowley & Ptnrs "927" Carlton Moor		4.99
FMG	3365	Schempp-Hirth Discus B	242		8.88	D.R.Zarb "969"	Nympsfield	2.99
FMH	3366	Schleicher ASK13	13673AB		8.88	Lasham Gliding Society "B" Lasham		1.99
FMK +	3368	Centrair 101 Pegase	101-0293		1.90	A.Bailey	Bidford	5.99
FML +	3369	Schleicher ASW15B	15294	F-CEGR	11.89	A.D.Duke & Ptnrs	Nympsfield	2.99
FMM +	3370	Schleicher Ka6CR	6328	D-1260	10.88	K.E Hebdon	Gamston	7.99
FMN	3371	Schempp-Hirth Ventus CT	123/397		9.88	S C.Kovac "CKF"	Lasham	1.99
FMP	3372	Schleicher ASW24	24023		1.89	A.Hegner "357"	Booker	2.99
FMQ	3373	Schempp-Hirth Discus B	243		10.88	A.L Harris "158"	Nympsfield	3.99
FMR +	3374	Neukom Standard Elfe S-2	05	HB-801	11.88	M.Powell & Ptnrs	Camphill	4.99
FMS	3375	Schleicher ASW15	15061	N111SP	11.88	A.J.Pettit "519"	Lasham	12.99
FMT +	3376	Schempp-Hirth HS.4 Standard Cirrus	249	N2HM	10.89	W.Schmidt	Chipping	3.99
FMU +	3377	Schempp-Hirth HS.4 Standard Cirrus	236	N3LB	7.90	S.A Manktelow	Aston Down	4.99
FMX +	3380	Schleicher ASW24	24014		3.90	D.T.Reilly	North Hill	3.99
FMY	3381	Rolladen-Schneider LS-7	7004	D-1256	12.88	D.F.Holmes "371"	Camphill	5.99
FMZ +	3382	Schleicher Ka7 Rhonadler	7018	D-6035	11.88	Nene Valley GC "2	Upwood	4.99
FNA +	3383	Schleicher K8B	8499	D-5670	11.88	Bowland Forest GC	Chipping	1.99
FNC	3385	Slingsby T.21B	SSK/FF1091	WB9..	11.88	Mrs A.Hartley	(Germany)	4.99
FND +	3386	Schleicher Ka6E	4069	PH-366	11.88	J.M.Smith	North Hill	5.99
FNE +	3387	PZL SZD-38A Jantar-1	B-612	HB-1215	12.88	D.A Salmon & Ptnrs	Camphill	5.99
FNF	3388	Schleicher ASW22B	22053		12.88	T.J.Parker "461"	Dunstable	2.99
FNG	3389	Schleicher ASW24	24015		5.89	G.C.Metcalfe "104"	Lasham	2.99
FNH	3390	Schleicher ASW19	19174	D-7969	2.89	Mrs V.P.Hayley & Ptnrs "A19" Ridgewell		1.00
FNK +	3392	Slingsby T.65A Vega	1897	N9023H	12.88	A.P.Brown	Kenley	4.99
FNL	3393	Schempp-Hirth Discus B	253		11.88	P.A.Holland "705" Kirton-in-Lindsey		4.99
FNM +	3394	Centrair 101B Pegase	101B-0289	F-CGSE	3.89	D.I.Watson	Dunstable	4.99
FNN	3395	Schempp-Hirth Ventus CT	130/407		12.88	C.J.Clarke "109"	Aston Down	11.99
FNP +	3396	Schleicher Ka6CR	567	D-4657	1.89	Notts University GC	Syerston	5.99
FNQ	3397	Schempp-Hirth Discus B	259		12.88	Deeside ASW20 Group "282"	Aboyne	5.99
FNR	3398	Schempp-Hirth Discus B	255		3.89	R.Lemin "130"	Nympsfield	3.99

Regn	BGA No.	Type	C/n	P/I	Regn	Owner/operator	Probable Base	CA Expy
FNS +	3399	Glaser-Dirks DG-300 Club Elan	3E314C23		4.89	R.Arkle	Aboyne	4.99
FNT +	3400	Glaser-Dirks DG-600	6-12		12.88	D.M.Hayes "674"	Rufforth	3.99
FNU +	3401	Rolladen-Schneider LS-4A	4732	D-1376	4.89	R J Simpson "190"	Nympsfield	2.99
FNW +	3403	Schleicher Ka6CR	598	HB-634	3.89	Cotswold GC	Aston Down	1.99
FNX +	3404	Wassmer WA.30 Bijave	84	F-CCTJ	1.89	The Borders GC	Milfield	5.99
FPB +	3408	Schleicher ASW15B	15243	D-2068	12.88	R C Tatlow	Winthorpe	5.99
FPD	3410	Rolladen-Schneider LS-7	7033	D-5178	1.89	P.H.Rackham "973"	Dunstable	12.99
FPE	3411	Schempp-Hirth Ventus CT	131/408		1.89	P.Whitt & N.Francis "238"	Shobdon	3.99
FPF +	3412	Scheibe L-Spatz 55	2720	RAFGGA...	2.89	M.P.Dunlop	Usk	6.99
FPH +	3414	Centrair ASW 20F	20132	F-CFFX	1.89	R.Gibson & Ptnrs	Bidford	4.99
FPJ +	3415	Schleicher ASW19	19001	D-1909	1.89	F.W.Pinkerton "459"	Lyveden	3.98
FPK +	3416	Glaser-Dirks DG-300 Elan	3E6	D-1233	1.89	G.C.Keall & Ptnrs "Y1"	Husbands Bosworth	5.99
FPL	3417	Schempp-Hirth Ventus C	409		1.89	R.V Barrett "242"	Nympsfield	1.99
FPM +	3418	PZL SZD-51-1 Junior	B-1788		3.89	Kent GC	Challock	12.99
FPN	3419	Schleicher ASW20	20376	RAFGGA... D-8780	3.89	E C Wright "545"	Syerston	4.99
FPP	3420	Schemmp-Hirth HS.5 Nimbus 2B	142	D-6779 D-2111	3.89	R.Jones "N2"	Walney Island	2.99
FPQ +	3421	Schleicher Ka7 Rhonadler	EB180/61	D-5184	2.89	East Sussex GC	Ringmer	6.99
FPT	3424	Schleicher ASW20	20007	D-7574	2.89	L.Hornsey & Ptnrs "574"	Halton	1.99
FPU +	3425	Schleicher Ka2B Rhonschwalbe (Built by Segelfluggruppe Zwingen)	-	HB-698	2.89	T.J.Wilkinson	Sackville Lodge, Riseley	3.99
FPV +	3426	Schleicher Ka6E	4123	N29JG G-AWTP	3.89	J.E.Stewart	Bembridge	5.99
FPW	3427	Glaser-Dirks DG-600	6-17		4.89	W.S.Stephen "39"	Aboyne	1.99
FPX +	3428	Schleicher ASK13	13325	F-CDYR	6.89	Booker GC	Booker	5.99
FQB +	3432	Schleicher ASW15B	15340	D-2345	8.89	P.Usborne	Dunstable	9.99
FQC	3433	Glaser-Dirks DG-202/17c	2-178CL19	HB-1645	3.89	A.T.MacDonald "201"	Ridgewell	4.99
FQD +	3434	Schleicher K8B	8289	D-1908	3.89	Kent GC	Challock	12.99
FQE +	3435	Schleicher K8	3	D-6329	4.89	Cotswold GC	Aston Down	7.99
FQF +	3436	Scheibe SF-27A Zugvogel V	6025	D-0009	2.89	S.Maddox	Winthorpe	9.99
FQG	3437	Rolladen-Schneider LS-7	7050	D-1712	6.89	R.W.Spiller "952"	Sutton Bank	6.99
FQH	3438	Rolladen-Schneider LS-7	7029	D-1316	4.89	P.J.Lazenby "98"	Rufforth	6.99
FQK +	3440	Grob G.103C Twin III Acro	34123		8.89	K.Nicholson	Challock	3.99
FQL	3441	Schleicher Ka6CR	6235	HB-772	3.89	C. & N.Worrell "772"	Lasham	12.99
FQM +	3442	Scheibe SF-27A Zugvogel V	6098	D-9421	2.89	R.F.Carver (As "D-9421")	Winthorpe	6.99
FQN	3443	Schempp-Hirth Ventus B/16.6	141	D-8772 D-KHIB	3.89	R.Parsons & Ptnrs "479"	Challock	12.98
		(Composite rebuild of D-8772 - ex Ventus BT D-KHIB (10/141) - w/o 27.5.85 & possibly HB-1626 (91) as FQN holds build plate "V91")						
FQQ	3445	Glaser-Dirks DG-600	6-11		3.89	M.B.Jefferyes & Ptnr "656"	Ridgewell	5.99
FQR +	3446	Schleicher K8B	8537	PH-349	3.89	Dorset GC "B"	Gallows Hill	3.99
FQT	3448	PZL SZD-48-3 Jantar Standard 3	B-1891	(BGA.3409)	3.90	T H Greenwood "484"	Sandhill Farm, Shrivenham	3.99
FQU +	3449	Schleicher Ka7 Rhonadler	1139	D-8614 HB-709	3.89	J.E.Harber	Halton	3.99
FQV	3450	CARMAM JP-15/36AR Aiglon	28	F-CETX	3.89	K.H.Withey "P"	Perranporth	4.98
FQX +	3452	Schleicher K8B	8037	D-5205	4.89	Burn GC	Burn	1.96*
FQY	3453	Schempp-Hirth Discus B	274		4.89	R.D.Payne "781"	Nympsfield	2.99
FQZ	3454	Rolladen-Schneider LS-1F	391	F-CEKH	6.89	G.P.Hibberd "L57"	Sleap	4.99
FRA	3455	Rolladen-Schneider LS-6B	6151	D-8081	4.89	P.J.Haseler "32"	Enstone	4.99
FRB	3456	Schempp-Hirth Ventus C	404		3.89	P.McLean "758"	Crowland	5.99
FRC	3457	Schempp-Hirth HS.5 Nimbus 2B	151	D-4980	5.89	C.F.Whitbread "988"	Challock	4.99
FRD	3458	Centrair 101A Pegase (Reported as wearing "FRG" 6.95 & 7.96)	101A-0311		4.89	A.Kangars "JPB"	Husbands Bosworth	12.99
FRE +	3459	Schleicher Ka6E	4349	F-CDTL	4.89	D.J.Stewart	Parham Park	6.99
FRF +	3460	Schleicher Ka7 Rhonadler	450/58	D-5653	4.89	P.Roberts & Co	Dunstable	5.99
FRG	3461	Siebert Sie-3 (See BGA.3458)	3009	D-0739	4.89	I.R.Taylor & Co	Tatenhill	4.96*
FRH	3462	Schleicher ASW20CL	20740	D-9229	4.89	J.N.Wilton & Ptnr "634"	Husbands Bosworth	4.99
FRJ	3463	Schempp-Hirth HS.4 Standard Cirrus	103	HB-1041	4.89	P.D.Oswald & Ptnrs "48"	Portmoak	4.99
FRK +	3464	Schleicher ASW15B	15214	D-0941	3.89	A.D.Smith	Booker	11.99
FRL	3465	Grob G.102 Astir CS	1373	D-7402	4.89	South Wales GC "609"	Usk	3.99
FRM +	3466	Scheibe SF-27A Zugvogel V	6040	D-3644	4.89	Burn GC	Burn	5.98
FRP	3468	Schempp-Hirth Nimbus 3/24.5	43	N697L D-2518	7.89	T.R.Gardner & J.Mardon "995"	Aston Down	10.95*
FRQ	3469	Slingsby T.45 Swallow	1420	XT653	4.89	D.Shrimpton	Halesland	6.98
FRR	3470	Centrair 101A Pegase	101A-0034	(BGA.3451) F-CFQA	4.89	P.A.Lewis "495" "Scoundrel"	Walney Island	5.99
FRS	3471	Scheibe Zugvogel IIIB	1097	D-2171 HB-749	4.89	R.J.Dann & N.Kent	Rivar Hill	10.97*

Regn	BGA No.	Type	C/n	P/I	Regn	Owner/operator	Probable Base	CA Expy
FRT	3472	Schempp-Hirth Ventus CT	137/421		4.89	C.G.Corbett "170"	Dunstable	3.99
		(Reported identity of D-4349 was Type Certificate 04.349)						
FRV +	3474	Centrair 101A Pegase	101A-0325		10.89	N.J.Robinson	Gransden Lodge	2.99
FRW	3475	Schleicher ASW20L	20202	D-5981	5.89	K.Challinor & Syndicate "268"		
							Booker	5.99
FRX +	3476	Centrair 101A Pegase	101A-0315		5.89	BBC Gliding Grp	Booker	3.99
FRZ	3478	Schempp-Hirth HS.4 Standard Cirrus	348G	HB-1194	5.89	M.Kent "H6"	Lasham	3.99
				D-2172				
FSA	3479	Grob G.102 Astir CS	1277	D-7371	4.89	J.Claxton "498"	Dunstable	5.99
FSC*	3481	Slingsby T.38 Grasshopper	751	WZ755	4.90	Not known	Gallows Hill	4.91
						(Stored 5.98)		
FSD	3482	Schleicher ASK13	13367	D-0863	5.89	Portsmouth Naval GC (RNGSA.N28)		
							Lee-on-Solent	4.99
FSE	3483	Schleicher Ka6CR	6021	D-1946	8.89	G.W.Lobb "964"	North Hill	4.99
FSF +	3484	Schleicher Ka2	120	D-1688	6.89	B.T.Spreckley	Le Blanc, France	10.99
FSH +	3486	Grob G.102 Astir CS Jeans	2090	D-7532	5.89	Buckminster GC	Saltby	11.99
FSJ	3487	Slingsby T.31B	703	WT908	5.89	R.J.Abraham	Dunstable	1.99
						(As "WT908")		
FSL	3489	Schempp-Hirth HS.7 Mini Nimbus	52	HB-1413	6.89	S.C.Waddell "F11"	Booker	2.99
FSQ +	3493	Schleicher ASK13	"13596"		6.89	London GC	Dunstable	1.99
		(Composite containing c/n plate from BGA.2405)						
FSR +	3494	Glaser-Dirks DG-300 Elan	3E343		8.89	E.J.Dent	Nympsfield	11.99
FSS +	3495	Schleicher Ka6E	4019	D-5260	8.89	K.J.Hill & Ptnrs	Lasham	3.99
FST +	3496	Schleicher ASH25E	25073	(BGA.3530)	10.89	K.H.Lloyd & Ptnrs	Aston Down	2.99
				(BGA.3496)				
FSU	3497	Scheibe Zugvogel IIIA	1060	D-9055	6.89	P.W.Williams	Brent Tor	1.99
FSV	3498	Slingsby T.38 Grasshopper	800	WZ819	6.89	P.D.Mann (As "WZ819") RAF Halton		9.97
FSX	3500	Glaser-Dirks DG-300 Elan	3E344		7.89	C.Hyett "405"	Lasham	2.99
FSY	3501	Schleicher ASH25	25064	D-1578	7.89	B.T.Spreckley "162"		
							Le Blanc, France	10.99
FSZ +	3502	Grob G.102 Astir CS77	1841	D-2908	7.89	D.Gardiner & Ptnr	Aston Down	2.99
FTA +	3503	Schleicher K8B	8702	D-0048	7.89	Lincolnshire GC	Strubby	3.97*
FTB +	3504	Schleicher Ka6CR	019	D-8900	7.89	P.J.Blair	Bidford	3.99
		(Bitz-built)						
FTC	3505	PZL SZD-51-1 Junior	B-1860		7.89	Culdrose GC (RNGSA.N56)		
							RNAS Culdrose	3.99
FTD	3506	Schleicher ASW15B	15191	D-0872	8.89	L.G.Callow "205"	Dunstable	8.98
FTF	3508	Schleicher Ka6CR	6294	D-6081	8.89	A.Sparrow	Parham Park	3.99
FTG +	3509	Schleicher Ka7 Rhonadler	535	D-8321	10.89	Angus GC	Drumshade	3.99
FTH +	3510	PZL SZD-50-3 Puchacz	B-1881		8.89	Buckminster GC	Saltby	2.99
FTJ	3511	PZL SZD-48 Jantar Standard 2	W-889	HB-1472	8.89	G.J.Burton & Ptnrs "FTI" Enstone		3.99
FTK	3512	Grob G.102 Astir CS Jeans	2059	OE-5152	10.89	R.Lapsley "518"	Bellarena	4.99
FTL	3513	Schleicher ASW20CL	20751	D-3564	9.89	J.S.Shaw "127"	Dunstable	4.99
FTM	3514	Schleicher K8B	513	D-5708	8.89	West Wales GC	Usk	5.99
FTN	3515	Schleicher K8B	996	D-8539	3.89	Vale of White Horse GC "853"		
				D-KAEL/D-8539		Sandhill Farm, Shrivenham		12.98
FTP	3516	Schleicher ASW20CL	20733	D-3640	1.90	A J Mainwaring "332"	Dunstable	4.99
FTQ +	3517	Centrair ASW20FL	20123	F-CFFR	8.89	C.Wilby	Camphill	11.99
FTR +	3518	Grob G.102 Astir CS77	1606	D-4807	10.89	Lakes GC	Walney Island	2.99
FTS +	3519	Glaser-Dirks DG-300 Club Elan	3E349C38		10.89	Southdown GC	Parham Park	12.99
FTT	3520	Slingsby T.21B	589	WB926	9.89	R.Acreman	Gallows Hill	6.99
						(As "WB926")		
FTU +	3521	Schleicher Ka7 Rhonadler	302	HB-599	9.89	Dartmoor GS "Fondue" Brent Tor		6.99
FTV +	3522	Rolladen-Schneider LS-7	7073		10.89	D.Hilton & S.White "944" Booker		3.99
FTW	3523	Schempp-Hirth Discus B	292		10.89	N.H.Wall & Ptnrs "230"		
							Nympsfield	2.99
		(Rebuilt with new fuselage after accident 21.6.91; original fuselage rebuilt as BGA.3879)						
FTY	3525	Rolladen-Schneider LS-7	7075		10.89	A.M.Burgess "753"	Drumshade	4.99
FUB	3528	Schleicher Ka6CR	6007	D-8573	11.89	D.E.Hooper	Eaglescott	7.99
FUD +	3529	PZL SZD-9 bis Bocian 1E	P-689	SP-2807	11.89	Mendip GC	Halesland	8.99
FUF +	3531	Scheibe SF-27A Zugvogel V	6089	D-6068	9.89	East Sussex GC	Ringmer	4.99
FUG	3532	Schleicher ASH25	25074	(BGA.3526)	10.89	J.P.Gorringe & D.S.Hill "BB"		
							Lasham	2.99
FUH	3533	Schempp-Hirth Ventus C	438		10.89	M.A.Gale & Ptnrs "192"		
							Gallows Hill	4.99
FUJ +	3534	Glaser-Dirks DG-300 Elan	3E353		12.89	J.Cook & Ptnrs	Strathaven	2.99
FUL	3535	Schemmp-Hirth Discus B	293		3.90	N.D.Tillett "803"	Dunstable	2.99
FUM +	3536	Schleicher Ka6CR	808	D-6289	3.90	A.C.Marvin	Rufforth	5.99
FUN	3537	Schleicher ASW20CL	20813	D-3432	4.91	W.H.Parker "432"	Dunstable	2.99
FUP	3538	Schempp-Hirth Discus B	291		10.89	Surrey & Hants GC "397"	Lasham	1.99
FUQ +	3539	Scheibe SF-27A Zugvogel V	6090	D-5196	3.90	G.Elliott & Ptnrs	Ringmer	1.00
FUR	3540	Schempp-Hirth Ventus CT	145/446		3.90	D.S.Towson "256"	Shobdon	4.99
FUS +	3541	PZL SZD-51-1 Junior	B-1912		11.89	Scottish Gliding Union Ltd		
							Portmoak	5.99
FUT	3542	Glaser-Dirks DG-300 Club Elan	3E350C39		3.90	M.J.Barnett & Ptnr "612"		
							Rivar Hill	5.99
FUU +	3543	Glaser-Dirks DG-300 Club Elan	3E360C45		3.90	A.R.MacGregor Kingston Deverill		3.99

Regn	BGA No.	Type	C/n	P/I	Regn	Owner/operator	Probable Base	CA Expy
FUV	3544	Rolladen-Schneider LS-7	7068		11.89	B.C.Morris "194"	Booker	1.00
FUW	3545	Slingsby T.31B Cadet TX.3	920	XE807	11.89	D.Shrimpton (As "XE807")	Halesland	6.98
FUY +	3546	PZL SZD-50-3 Puchacz	B-1983		11.89	M.G.Ashton	Eaglescott	3.99
FVA	3548	Schleicher K8B	1051	D-5117	4.90	Portsmouth Naval GC (RNGSA.N15) Lee-on-Solent		3.99
FVB +	3549	Schempp-Hirth Ventus CT	144/445		1.90	M.J.Sesemann "228"	Challock	12.98
FVC +	3550	Schleicher ASK13 (Jubi-built)	13682AB		12.89	Devon & Somerset GC	North Hill	2.99
FVD +	3551	Scheibe Bergfalke IV	5806	D-0729	12.89	North Wales GC	Bryngwyn Bach	4.99
FVE	3552	Rolladen-Schneider LS-4	4190	RAFGSA"232" RAFGSA R30/D-4542	1.90	R.J.Rebbeck "232"	Edgehill	2.99
FVF +	3553	Schempp-Hirth HS.5 Nimbus 2C	202	D-2880	3.90	J C Mitchell & J.Wood	Chipping	3.99
FVG +	3554	Glaser-Dirks DG-600	6-41		12.89	F.L.Cox "660"	Winthorpe	4.99
FVH +	3555	Rolladen-Schneider LS-7	7067	(BGA.3527)	12.89	B.R.Forrest & A.Hallum "246" Booker		3.99
FVL +	3558	Scheibe Zugvogel IIIB	1082	D-5224	12.89	F.Hunt	Kirton-in-Lindsey	7.99
FVM	3559	Centrair 101A Pegase	101A-0345		3.90	S.H.North "369"	Yeovilton	4.99
FVN +	3560	Centrair 101A Pegase	101A-0268/2		1.90	G.G.Butter	Snitterfield	1.99
		(Rebuild of BGA.3198 and carries c/n 10100268)						
FVP +	3561	Centrair 101A Pegase	101A-0350		4.90	J.R.Parry & Ptnr	Long Mynd	4.99
FVQ +	3562	Rolladen-Schneider LS-7	7079		1.90	R.C.Willis-Fleming	Brent Tor	11.99
FVS +	3564	Schempp-Hirth HS.4 Standard Cirrus	359G	D-2168	3.90	P.A Clark	Lasham	3.99
FVT	3565	Schempp-Hirth HS.5 Nimbus 2	18	N795	5.90	I.Dunkley "760"	Camphill	7.98
FVU +	3566	Schleicher ASK13	13062	D-1348	4.90	Edinburgh University GC	Portmoak	11.99
FVV +	3567	Centrair 101A Pegase	101A-0353		4.90	Cambridge University GC Gransden Lodge		2.99
FVW +	3568	Schempp-Hirth Ventus BT	252/51	D-KORN	1.90	I.Champness	Lasham	4.99
FVY +	3570	Scheibe Zugvogel IIIA	1046	D-8323	2.90	S.Ottner & Ptnrs	Rivar Hill	5.99
FVZ	3571	Schleicher Ka6E	4007	D-4104	2.90	R.P.Filipkiewicz "PS"	Booker	4.99
FWA +	3572	Schleicher Ka6CR	6227	D-1062	3.90	N.M.Hill	Weston-on-the-Green	8.99
FWB +	3573	Schleicher ASK13	13224	HB-989	4.90	Cotswold GC	Aston Down	11.99
FWC	3574	Grob G.103C Twin III Acro	34154		4.90	Lasham Gliding Society Ltd "45" Lasham		3.99
FWD +	3575	Schempp-Hirth Ventus CT	148/468		5.90	R.S.Maxwell-Fendt "888"	Lasham	3.99
FWE +	3576	PZL SZD-50-3 Puchacz	B-1984	(BGA.3547)	2.90	Deeside GC	Aboyne	2.99
FWF	3577	Rolladen-Schneider LS-7	7097		2.90	P.A & D.King "618"	Long Mynd	11.99
FWG +	3578	Centrair 101A Pegase	101A-0252	PH-793	2.90	Devon & Somerset GC	North Hill	2.99
FWH +	3579	Scheibe SF-27A Zugvogel V	6024	D-4733	2.90	R.Sampson	Husbands Bosworth	4.99
FWJ +	3580	Rolladen-Schneider LS-7WL	7078		3.90	J.P.Popika "S3"	Gransden Lodge	2.99
FWK	3581	Schempp-Hirth Nimbus 3DT	32		3.90	J.D.J.Glossop "A29" Gransden Lodge		2.99
FWL +	3582	Schleicher K8B	106/58	D-7151	2.90	Dukeries GC (As "-7151" underwing) Gamston		6.99
FWM +	3583	Glaser-Dirks DG-300 Club Elan	3E373C50		6.90	G.J.T.Underwood	Challock	3.99
FWN +	3584	Schleicher ASK13	13285	HB-1023	4.90	Booker GC	Booker	3.99
FWP	3585	Schleicher ASW19B	19262	D-5980	4.90	K.Harris & Ptnrs "980"	Dunstable	3.99
FWQ +	3586	Schleicher ASK21	21460		5.90	Midland GC	Long Mynd	12.99
FWR	3587	Glasflugel H.303 Mosquito	34	N77RL	3.90	S.J.Ferguson "277"	Aston Down	8.99
FWS	3588	Schleicher ASW20C	20765	D-6623	2.90	G.W.Lynch "662"	North Weald	5.99
FWT +	3589	PZL SZD-50-3 Puchacz	B-1988		3.90	Coventry GC	Husbands Bosworth	2.99
FWU	3590	Rolladen-Schneider LS-7	7080		3.90	G.E.Thomas "768" Husbands Bosworth		2.99
FWW +	3592	Schleicher ASH25E	25093		6.90	A.T.Farmer	Weston-on-the-Green	3.99
FWX +	3593	Centrair 101A Pegase	101A-033	F-CFRZ	3.90	R A Adam "B38"	Husbands Bosworth	5.99
FWY +	3594	Centrair 101A Pegase	101A-071	F-CFXE	3.90	C.Leeseman & Ptnrs	Lasham	7.99
FWZ +	3595	Schleicher ASW19B	19342	D-2603	4.90	C.Fowler	Camphill	1.99
FXA	3596	Grob G.102 Speed Astir IIB	4083	D-2671	4.90	A.D.Duke "567"	Nympsfield	9.99
FXB	3597	Schleicher K8B	8193/A	D-5597	3.90	R.J.Morris	Brent Tor	5.99
FXC +	3598	Schleicher Ka6E	4268	D-0150	8.90	B.L.Anson	Halton	4.99
FXD	3599	Centrair 101A Pegase	101A-0346	(BGA.3563)	3.90	Coventry GC "285" Husbands Bosworth		10.99
FXE	3600	Rolladen-Schneider LS-7	7090		3.90	J.C.Kingerlee "35" Weston-on-the-Green		4.99
FXF +	3601	Slingsby T.50 Skylark 4	1455	HB-812	5.90	S.White	Booker	5.99
FXG +	3602	Schempp-Hirth HS.2 Cirrus	23	N1216	8.90	S.Veness	Enstone	2.99
FXH +	3603	Schleicher Ka7 Rhonadler	353	D-4040	4.90	Vale of Neath GC	Rhigos	8.99
FXJ	3604	Schleicher ASW24	24086		5.90	A.K.Laylee "247"	Booker	1.99
FXL	3606	Schleicher ASH25	25088		4.90	C.R.Simpson & Ptnrs "108" Husbands Bosworth		2.99
FXM	3607	Schempp-Hirth Discus BT	16/301	D-KHIA	4.90	R.J.H.Fack "173"	Shobdon	11.99
FXN +	3608	CARMAM M.200 Foehn	4	OO-ZNI (OO-ZXS)/F-CCXS	4.90	I.Gutzell & Ptnrs	Pocklington	9.99
FXP +	3609	LET L-23 Super Blanik	907609		7.90	R.O.Windley t/a The Blanik Syndicate Sutton Bank		6.99

Regn	BGA No.	Type	C/n	P/I	Regn	Owner/operator	Probable Base	CA Expy
FXQ	3610	Schempp-Hirth Nimbus 3DT (See BGA.3658)	31		4.90	G.O.Wynne & Ptnrs "954"	Lasham	3.99
FXR	3611	LAK-12 Lietuva	6162		9.90	S R Blackmore "L12"	Enstone	5.99
FXS +	3612	Schleicher Ka6E	4228	D-0073	5.90	R.Woodhouse & B.Wade	Tibenham	6.98
FXU +	3614	Schleicher Ka6E	4071	OH-343 OH-RSY	6.90	M E Mann Syndicate	Lasham	3.99
FXW +	3616	Schleicher K8B	8651	D-7203 D-KOLA/D-7203	5.90	South Wales GC	Usk	2.99
FXX +	3617	Scheibe L-Spatz 55	756	D-3598	8.91	P.Brown	Ridgewell	6.99
FXY	3618	Schleicher ASW15B	15348	F-CEJL	5.90	V W Jennings "723"	Dunstable	9.98
FYA	3620	PZL SZD-50-3 Puchacz	B-2022		5.90	Cairngorm GC	Feshiebridge	3.99
FYB	3621	Rolladen-Schneider LS-7	7102		5.90	J.T.Hitchcock "779"	Sandhill Farm, Shrivenham	2.99
FYC	3622	Schempp-Hirth Ventus B	83	N90DM F-CEDR/F-WEDR	5.90	D.B.Meeks "A10"	Sutton Bank	9.99
FYD	3623	Schleicher ASH25	25095		5.90	K.M.H.Wilson "942"	Challock	4.99
FYE	3624	Scheibe Zugvogel IIIB	1067	OY-MHX SE-TCE/OY-EFX/D-1814	5.90	R.J.Hawley "94"	Brent Tor	12.98
FYF +	3625	Schleicher ASK21	21470		8.90	London GC	Dunstable	5.99
FYG +	3626	Glasflugel H.205 Club Libelle	22	OH-545	5.90	I.H Shattock	Usk	8.99
FYH	3627	Rolladen-Schneider LS-4A	4804		7.90	G.W.Craig "224"	Weston-on-the-Green	6.99
FYJ +	3628	Schempp-Hirth HS.4 Standard Cirrus 581G		D-8931	7.90	J.Smith	Pocklington	4.99
FYK	3629	Rolladen-Schneider LS-7	7108		6.90	T J Murphy "34"	Portmoak	3.99
FYL +	3630	PZL SZD-50-3 Puchacz	B-1990		6.90	Deeside GC	Aboyne	4.99
FYM	3631	Schempp-Hirth Discus BT	31/328		6.90	J.A.Denne "326"	Enstone	3.99
FYN	3632	Schempp-Hirth Discus B	179	N75J	7.90	K J Seigh "J3"	Rattlesden	5.99
FYP +	3633	LET L-23 Super Blanik	907620		8.90	Marchington GC	Tatenhill	1.99
FYR +	3635	LET L-23 Super Blanik	917816		7.92	North Wales GC	Bryngwyn Bach	3.99
FYS +	3636	LET L-23 Super Blanik	938011		4.93	P.Clifford	Bicester	4.97*
FYU	3638	Glaser-Dirks DG-100 Elan	E111	OY-XMR SE-TYO	6.90	J.L Brigbee "M5"	North Hill	6.99
FYV +	3639	Schleicher ASK21	21468		7.90	Yorkshire GC	Sutton Bank	1.99
FYW	3640	Rolladen-Schneider LS-7	7111		6.90	J.D.Williams "27"	Saltby	1.00
FYX	3641	Schempp-Hirth Discus BT	32/333		7.90	M.P.Brockington "208"	Talgarth	6.99
FYY	3642	Schleicher ASK13	13685AB		7.90	Lasham Gliding Society "S"	Lasham	2.99
FYZ	3643	Schleicher ASH25	25097		7.90	M.G.Thick "171"	Sutton Bank	12.99
FZA +	3644	PZL SZD-51-1 Junior	B-1913		7.90	Booker GC	Booker	3.99
FZB	3645	Glasflugel H.201B Standard Libelle	112	OH-388 OH-GLA	7.90	C.Thomas & J.E.Herring "669"	Lasham	5.99
FZC	3646	Schempp-Hirth SHK-1	58	OH-357 OH-SHA	8.91	J.F Mills	Talgarth	6.99
FZF +	3649	PZL SZD-51-1 Junior	B-1861		7.90	Devon & Somerset GC	North Hill	3.99
FZG +	3650	PZL SZD-9 bis Bocian 1D	F-859	SP-2450	9.90	The Borders GC	Milfield	3.99
FZH	3651	Schempp-Hirth Ventus C	455		7.90	P.C.Naegeli "520"	Rivar Hill	3.99
FZK +	3653	Schempp-Hirth HS.4 Standard Cirrus	81	HB-967	7.90	J.L.Rodgers & Syndicate	Aston Down	8.99
FZL	3654	Schleicher ASW20CL	20764	D-5937	8.90	R.M.Housden "Z6"	Aston Down	9.99
FZM	3655	Scheibe SF-27A Zugvogel V	6103	D-1772	8.90	D.Thorpe t/a Safety First SG	Camphill	3.99
FZN +	3656	Schleicher ASK13	13045	D-5759	8.90	Black Mountains GC "K13"	Talgarth	7.99
FZP	3657	PZL SZD-51-1 Junior	B-1926		8.90	Portsmouth Naval GC (RNGSA.N16)	Lee-on-Solent	4.99
FZQ	3658	PZL SZD-50-3 Puchacz (Marked as "FXQ")	B-2024	(BGA.3637)	8.90	Coventry GC	Husbands Bosworth	12.98
FZR +	3659	Schleicher Ka6CR	6136	D-8459	12.90	P.S.Huggins	North Hill	11.99
FZS	3660	LET L-13 Blanik (Rebuild with parts from BGA.2661)	025609	NEJSGSA.8	8.90	B.J.Shackell & A.Pattemore "L13"	Gallows Hill	4.99
FZU	3662	Slingsby T.38 Grasshopper	761	WZ765	8.91	H.Chapple (As "WZ765") (To Luftwaffen Museum, Berlin 1996)		12.96*
FZV	3663	Rolladen-Schneider LS-7	7116		12.90	R Roddy "280"	Booker	4.99
FZW +	3664	Glaser-Dirks DG-300 Club Elan	3E378C53		8.90	Mr & Mrs S.Barter	Ringmer	11.98
FZX +	3665	PZL SZD-51-1 Junior	B-1925		9.90	Nene Valley GC	Upwood	4.99
FZY +	3666	LET L-33 Solo	940206		3.94	A.W.Cox	Bicester	3.95*
FZZ +	3667	LET L-33 Solo	940220		4.95	D.A Wiseman	Jurby, IoM	4.99

(Probably composite with wings from WZ765 and spare fuselage c/n SSK/FF2069)

Regn	BGA No.	Type	C/n	P/I	Regn	Owner/operator	Probable Base	CA Expy

GAA-GZZ

Regn	BGA No.	Type	C/n	P/I	Regn	Owner/operator	Probable Base	CA Expy
GAB +	3669	LAK-12 Lietuva	6170		1.91	M.Wilshere	Halton	6.99
GAC +	3670	Schleicher Ka6CR	6301	(BGA.3647) D-5572	11.90	York Gliding Centre	Rufforth	2.99
GAD	3671	Rolladen-Schneider LS-3	3032	HB-1363	11.90	M.J.Towler "L5"	Bidford	3.99
GAF	3673	Schleicher ASK21	21152	ZD652 BGA.2892	11.90	Lasham Gliding Society "778"	Lasham	2.99
GAG +	3674	Schleicher ASK21	21143	ZD645 BGA.2885	1.91	Stratford-upon-Avon GC	Snitterfield	3.99
GAH +	3675	Schempp-Hirth HS.4 Standard Cirrus	572	HB-1240	12.90	M.G.Harris	Nympsfield	11.99
GAJ +	3676	Glaser-Dirks DG-300 Club Elan	3E385C56		12.90	M.R Wooley & Ptnrs	Long Mynd	2.99
GAK	3677	LET L-13 Blanik	174522	2-84 (Lithuania)	7.97	North Wales GC	Bryngwyn Bach	8.99
GAL +	3678	Schempp-Hirth HS.4 Standard Cirrus	335	HB-1150	4.91	D.Reynolds & S.Cooke	Aston Down	4.99
GAM +	3679	Schleicher ASK21	21144	ZD646 BGA.2886	11.90	Oxford University GC	Bicester	1.99
GAN +	3680	Glasflugel H.301 Libelle	8	D-4111	12.90	T.J.Harrison & T.Smallwood	Long Mynd	4.99
GAP +	3681	Schempp-Hirth Ventus BT	14/150	OH-774 N416DP	4.91	J.R.Greenwell	Currock Hill	7.99
GAQ	3682	Schleicher Ka7 Rhonadler	3	PH-788 D-5550	4.91	York Gliding Centre "K7"	Rufforth	7.99
GAR	3683	Rolladen-Schneider LS-6C	6205		11.90	A.J.Burton "148"	Shobdon	2.99
GAS +	3684	Schempp-Hirth Ventus CT	157/509		5.91	M W Edwards	Kingston Deverill	5.99
GAT +	3685	Grob G.102 Astir CS	1130	D-4176	11.90	P.J.Bramley	Lasham	2.99
GAU	3686	Glasflugel H.201B Standard Libelle	498	F-CELA	6.93	D.R.Pickett "725"	Crowland	2.99
GAV +	3687	Scheibe SF-27A Zugvogel V	6073	D-5287	11.90	W.Waite	Lleweni Parc	8.99
GAW +	3688	Schleicher Ka6CR	61/08	D-6320	12.90	C.Davison	Winthorpe	3.99
GAX	3689	PZL SZD-55-1	551190008		12.90	A.V.Nunn "302"	Booker	4.99
GBA +	3692	Schleicher ASK13	13417	D-2114	12.90	Burn GC	Burn	3.99
GBB +	3693	Schleicher ASK21	21073	D-3239	12.90	B.T.Spreckley	Le Blanc, France	3.99
GBD +	3695	PZL SZD-50-3 Puchacz	B-2028		4.91	Northumbria GC	Currock Hill	4.99
GBE +	3696	Schleicher Ka6CR (Pe)	6133A	D-4085	12.90	J.Swannock	Gamston	5.99
GBF +	3697	Schleicher ASK21	21142	ZD644 BGA.2883	2.91	BBC Gliding Group	Booker	3.99
GBG	3698	Rolladen-Schneider LS-6C	6214		12.90	M.J.Jordy "676"	Enstone	3.99
GBJ +	3700	Grob G.102 Astir CS	1107	D-4167	1.91	R.S.Stuart	Rhigos	5.98
GBK +	3701	Grob G.102 Astir CS	1461	D-7451	1.91	G R.Jenkins & Ptnrs "Mountain Man"	Lasham	2.99
GBL	3702	Rolladen-Schneider LS-7	7119		11.90	P.B.Walker "720"	Nympsfield	2.99
GBM +	3703	Scheibe SF-27A Zugvogel V	6060	RAFGGA D-5409	1.91	F.C.Sloggett t/a BFMT Syndicate	North Hill	4.99
GBN	3704	Schleicher ASK21	21141	ZD643 BGA.2884	.91	L.W.Evans "843"/"MD"	Wormingford	2.98
GBP +	3705	Schleicher ASK21	21150	ZD650 BGA.2890	.91	London GC	Dunstable	11.99
GBQ	3706	Rolladen-Schneider LS-6	6082	D-3725	.91	A. & P.R.Pentecost "630"	Kingston Deverill	11.99
GBR	3707	Rolladen-Schneider LS-6C	6196	D-3482	11.90	S.Hurd "218"	Dunstable	2.99
GBS	3708	Glaser-Dirks DG-300 Club Elan	3E389C58		.91	Yorkshire GC "206"	Sutton Bank	2.99
GBT	3709	Rolladen-Schneider LS-4A	4355	N220BB N97SL	4.91	S.A.Adlard "690"	Long Mynd	4.95*
GBU	3710	Centrair 101A Pegase	101A-0394		4.91	S.I.Ross "922"	Parham Park	3.99
GBV	3711	Schleicher ASK21	21149	ZD649 BGA.2889	4.91	Wolds GC "649"	Pocklington	2.99
GBX	3713	Schleicher ASW22	22029	D-4325	2.91	M.C.Russell & Ptnrs "290"	Gransden Lodge	5.99
GBY	3714	Rolladen-Schneider LS-7	7121		1.91	G.W.Kirton & Ptnrs "901"	Saltby	2.99
GBZ +	3715	Glaser-Dirks DG-500 Elan Trainer	5E34T10		8.91	Marchington GC	Tatenhill	4.99
GCA +	3716	Schleicher ASW19B	19281	D-3179	3.91	Deeside GC	Aboyne	3.99
GCB	3717	LAK-12 Lietuva	647		3.91	B.Middleton "637"	Dunstable	6.99
GCC +	3718	PZL SZD-51-1 Junior	B-1928		3.91	Coventry GC	Husbands Bosworth	1.99
GCD	3719	Schempp-Hirth HS.4 Standard Cirrus	476	PH-507	2.91	D.B.Brown "507"	Chipping	9.99
GCE	3720	Schleicher ASH25	25105		2.91	C.L.Withall "8"	Dunstable	3.99
GCF +	3721	Schleicher ASK23	23010	AGA.9	2.91	Marchington GC	Tatenhill	3.99
GCG	3722	Schleicher K8B	8186	D-5227	2.91	Shenington GC "S81"	Edgehill	8.99
GCH	3723	Schleicher ASW15B	15212	PH-438 D-0950	4.91	M.D.Woodman-Smith & Ptnr "438"	Dunstable	4.99
GCJ +	3724	LAK-12 Lietuva	626		3.91	P.Crowhurst	Crowland	5.99
		(New wings with reconditioned 1982-built fuselage)						
GCK +	3725	PZL SZD-50-3 Puchacz	B-2025	(G-BTJV) BGA.3725	3.91	Kent GC	Challock	3.99
GCL +	3726	Grob G.102 Astir CS	1194	D-7311	3.91	D.Draper	Rivar Hill	2.99

Regn	BGA No.	Type	C/n	P/I	Regn	Owner/operator	Probable Base	CA Expy
GCM	3727	Rolladen-Schneider LS-6C	6216		3.91	Gliding Expedition Ltd "Z29" Lasham		3.99
GCN	3728	Centrair 101A Pegase	101A-0035	(BGA.3694)	3.91	B.T.Spreckley "B35"		
				F-CFQB (Damaged Nympsfield 18.6.95) Le Blanc, France				3.96*
GCP +	3729	Schleicher Ka6CR	6416	D-6369	5.91	D.Clarke	Burn	5.99
GCQ	3730	Schempp-Hirth HS.2 Cirrus VTC	135Y	D-2945	4.91	P.Jones & Ptnrs "845"	Lasham	5.99
GCR	3731	Schleicher ASW15B	15447	D-6887	3.91	C.J.Anson & Ptnrs "748"	Dunstable	2.99
GCS	3732	Glasflugel H.205 Club Libelle	159	F-CEQL	7.91	N.Stainton "H12"	Bidford	9.99
GCT	3733	Schempp-Hirth Discus B	360		3.91	M.F.Evans "540"	Lasham	2.99
		(Not ex RAFGSA.R6 as reported)						
GCU +	3734	PZL SZD-50-3 Puchacz	B-2023	(BGA.3619)	3.91	Buckminster GC	Saltby	3.99
GCX +	3736	Schleicher ASW15	15034	D-0420	5.91	A.S.Edlin	Husbands Bosworth	5.99
GCY	3737	Centrair 101A Pegase	101A-0392		4.91	London GC "908"	Dunstable	11.99
GCZ	3738	Rolladen-Schneider LS-7WL	7130		3.91	S.G.Olender & Ptnr "244" (Spain)		3.99
GDA	3739	Rolladen-Schneider LS-3-17M	3448	RAFGGA.546	5.91	D.J.Moore "546/545"	Aston Down	5.99
GDB +	3740	Schleicher K8B	8152	HB-738	3.91	Welland GC	Lyveden	2.99
GDC +	3741	Slingsby T.38 Grasshopper	FF.1795		5.91	F.K.Russell & Ptnrs	Dunstable	5.97*
		(Built from spare frame - also carries c/n SSK/RF.3107)						
GDD +	3742	Bolkow Phoebus 17C	836	D-0060	4.91	I.D.McLeod	Challock	3.99
						(As "D-0060")		
GDE +	3743	Schleicher Ka6CR	6570Si	D-5306	4.91	D.N.Jones	Kingston Deverill	3.98
GDF +	3744	Schleicher Ka6BR	389	D-8544	4.91	W.M.Ulyett	Burn	5.99
GDJ	3747	Rolladen-Schneider LS-4A	4832		4.91	A Clark "450"	Aboyne	3.99
GDK +	3748	Schleicher K8B	8240	D-5381	4.91	East Sussex GC	Ringmer	4.99
				D-KANU/D-5381				
GDM	3750	Glasflugel H.201B Standard Libelle	597	D-6666	4.91	K.Fear & Syndicate "668" Crowland		3.99
GDN	3751	Rolladen-Schneider LS-3-17M	3291	D-6932	4.91	S.J Peppler "294"		
		(Marked as "GDS")				Sandhill Farm, Shrivenham		5.99
GDP +	3752	Schleicher ASW19B	19285	D-3160	5.91	W.M.Leutfeld "ED"	Cranfield	4.99
GDQ +	3753	Grob G.102 Astir CS	1145	D-7229	5.91	J.T.Harrison	Camphill	4.99
GDR +	3754	Schempp-Hirth Discus CS	016CS		5.91	R.H.Wright	Husbands Bosworth	6.99
		(Orlican-built)						
GDS +	3755	Schleicher ASW15B	15205	D-0902	6.91	G.D.E.Edwards	Dunstable	8.99
		(See BGA.3751)						
GDT	3756	Schleicher ASW24	24120		5.91	D.Bower "T54"	Rufforth	3.99
GDU	3757	Schleicher ASW24	24118		6.91	G.J.Mosore "801"	Dunstable	2.99
GDV +	3758	Schleicher Ka6E	4099	OO-ZWQ	6.91	P.Potter	Snitterfield	4.99
				I-NEST/OE-0807				
GDW +	3759	Scheibe SF-27A Zugvogel V	6116	D-1997	5.91	V Grayson	Challock	5.99
GDX	3760	Schempp-Hirth Discus CS	023CS		7.91	The Soaring Centre "896" Husbands Bosworth		4.99
GDY +	3761	Schleicher ASW15B	15220	D-0947	5.91	J Archer	Bidford	12.99
GDZ	3762	Schleicher ASW24	24116		5.91	I.C.Lees "524"	Pocklington	3.99
GEA +	3763	Schleicher Ka6CR	849	(BGA.3605)	6.91	M Wood	Rufforth	5.99
				D-5801				
GEB +	3764	Grob G.102 Astir CS77	1628	PH-576	6.91	J.O.Lavery	Bellarena	6.99
GEE	3767	Glasflugel H.201B Standard Libelle	94	D-0928	6.91	V.Geraghty "928"	Gamston	4.99
GEF +	3768	Schleicher Ka6CR	6459	D-1068	5.91	J.B Christie	Nympsfield	7.98
GEG +	3769	Schleicher K8B	689	HB-639	4.91	Newark & Notts GC	Winthorpe	2.99
GEH	3770	Schleicher ASW15B	15276	D-2124	7.91	K.G.Vincent & Ptnrs "219" Challock		4.99
GEL	3772	PZL SZD-50-3 Puchacz	B-2030		5.91	Portsmouth Naval GC (RNGSA.N23) Lee-on-Solent		12.98
GEM +	3773	Schleicher Ka6CR	6249	D-8486	6.91	D.Arkley	Rivar Hill	6.98
GEN +	3774	Slingsby T.21B	1154	RAFGGA.550	5.92	A.Harris	RAF Bruggen	5.99
				XN150				
GEP +	3775	Schempp-Hirth HS.4 Standard Cirrus	205G	D-0917	6.91	D.Walker	Gamston	3.99

Regn	BGA No.	Type	C/n	P/I	Regn	Owner/operator	Probable Base	CA Expy

HAA-HZZ

Regn	BGA No.	Type	C/n	P/I	Regn	Owner/operator	Probable Base	CA Expy
HAA	3777	Glasflugel H.201B Standard Libelle	356	HB-1090	6.91	T.Mormin & Ptnrs "99"	Gransden Lodge	2.99
HAB +	3778	Schleicher Ka6CR	6596	D-1596	1.92	M Greenwood	Rhigos	6.99
HAC +	3779	PZL SZD-50-3 Puchacz	B-2035		6.91	Peterborough & Spalding GC	Crowland	5.99
HAD	3780	Glasflugel H.201 Standard Libelle	3	D-8914	7.91	G.S Roe & Ptnrs "429"	Lasham	2.99
HAE +	3781	Glasflugel H.205 Club Libelle	75	D-8687	7.91	J.C Leonard	Bembridge	4.99
HAF	3782	PZL SZD-50-3 Puchacz	B-2031		7.91	Culdrose GC (RNGSA.N53)	RNAS Culdrose	3.99
HAG +	3783	Schleicher Ka7 Rhonadler	834	D-5795	5.92	Glyndwr SG	Lleweni Parc	10.98
HAJ	3785	Schempp-Hirth Ventus C	517		7.91	Surrey & Hants GC "391"	Lasham	3.99
HAK	3786	Slingsby T.31B	844	XA302	8.91	W.Walker (As "XA302")	Syerston	5.96*
HAL +	3787	Schleicher ASK13	13690AB		9.91	Cotswold GC	Aston Down	12.99
HAN	3789	Schempp-Hirth HS.4 Standard Cirrus	130	D-0326	8.91	M.Hastings & Syndicate "278"	Weston-on-the-Green	5.99
HAP +	3790	Schleicher Ka6E	4335	HB-985	8.91	C.Delahunt	Long Mynd	8.99
HAQ +	3791	Rolladen-Schneider LS-6B	6150	D-8079	9.91	A R Hughes "114"	Gransden Lodge	2.99
HAR +	3792	Schleicher K8B	8151	D-8453	9.91	T. & R.M.Roberts	Brent Tor	7.97*
HAS +	3793	PZL SZD-50-3 Puchacz	B-2043		8.91	The Soaring Club	Husbands Bosworth	1.99
HAT +	3794	Glaser-Dirks DG-200/17	2-93/1709	D-6843	8.91	D.Simon	Carlton Moor	6.99
HAU +	3795	Grob G.102 Astir CS Jeans	2043	D-3887	9.91	Yorkshire GC	Sutton Bank	3.99
HAV +	3796	Glasflugel H.201B Standard Libelle	40	HB-950	8.91	P.W.Andrews	Husbands Bosworth	1.99
HAX +	3798	Schempp-Hirth HS.4 Standard Cirrus	02	ZS-GHZ ZS-TIM/ZS-GGR/D-0302	10.91	A J Pettit	Rivar Hill	1.00
HAY	3799	Rolladen-Schneider LS-7	7154		10.91	N.Leaton & Ptnrs	Challock	7.96*
HAZ	3800	Schleicher ASH25	25130	(G-BTYJ)	11.91	A.P.Moulang "666"	Challock	2.99
HBA	3801	Rolladen-Schneider LS-7	7156	D-6041	10.91	P.O'Donald "729"	Gransden Lodge	11.99
HBB	3802	Schleicher ASW24	24132		9.91	S.D.Steinberg "S1"	Gransden Lodge	11.99
HBC	3803	Rolladen-Schneider LS-6C	6209	D-....	9.91	J.Burry "301"	Lasham	3.99
HBD +	3804	Glaser-Dirks DG-200	2-12	HB-1384	10.91	L.Marshall & Ptnrs	Rattlesden	3.99
HBE +	3805	Glaser-Dirks DG-300 Elan	3E237	SE-UFB	5.92	A.W.Cox & Ptnrs "356"	Enstone	6.99
HBF +	3806	Schempp-Hirth HS.5 Nimbus 2C	191	D-3369	10.91	T.Cauldwell	Sackville Lodge, Riseley	5.98
HBG	3807	Schleicher ASW24	24133		12.91	Imperial College GC "96"	Lasham	2.99
HBH	3808	Grob G.103C Twin III	36006		10.91	Imperial College GC "496"	Lasham	2.99
HBJ	3809	Rolladen-Schneider LS-6C-18	6230		9.91	D.Hill "949"	Edgehill	3.99
HBK +	3810	Grob G.103 Twin Astir	3254-T-31	RAFGGA... D-2389	9.91	R.W.Idle	Burn	7.98
HBL +	3811	Grob G.102 Astir CS77	1626	RAFGSA R78 RAFGSA.778	10.91	S.Glazzard	Bidford	5.99
HBM +	3812	Grob G.102 Astir CS77	1633	RAFGSA R65 RAFGSA.R66/RAFGSA.546	12.91	M.Wood	Syerston	4.99
HBP	3814	Glaser-Dirks DG-500/22 Elan	5E36S8		10.91	A.Leigh "522"	Camphill	7.99
HBQ +	3815	Schleicher Ka6CR	6611	D-5616	11.91	H Porter	Snitterfield	5.99
HBR	3816	Schempp-Hirth Nimbus 4T	3/6	(BGA.3784)	7.92	P S Hawkins "PM"	Keiheuvel, Belgium	5.99
HBS	3817	PZL SZD-41A Jantar Standard	B-852	D-4160	12.91	A.Henderson	Milfield	7.99
HBT +	3819	Grob G.102 Club Astir	2235	PH-675	2.92	G.M.Hall	Winthorpe	3.99
HBU	3820	Centrair ASW20F	20527	F-CFSI	11.91	R.Palmer & R.Mann "605"	Bidford	1.99
HBV	3821	Schempp-Hirth HS.5 Nimbus 2B	143	D-7850	11.91	C.J.Teagle "827"	Sutton Bank	2.99
HBW	3822	Glaser-Dirks DG-300 Club Elan	3E405C64		12.91	P.C.Cannon "829"	Lasham	4.99
HBX +	3823	Slingsby T.45 Swallow	1386	8801M XS650	5.93	C.D.Street & Ptnrs	Lasham	6.99
HBY	3824	Rolladen-Schneider LS-7	7148		11.91	R.C.Bridges "664"	Husbands Bosworth	4.99
HBZ +	3825	Slingsby T.15 Gull III Replica	-		6.92	P.R.Philpot	Chipping	6.99
HCA +	3826	Grob G.103 Twin Astir	3289	D-0094 OO-ZOH/D-3063	12.91	M.Wright "P5"	Rattlesden	3.98
HCB	3827	Schempp-Hirth Nimbus 3DT	47		12.91	R.B.Witter "754"	Lleweni Parc	5.99
HCC +	3829	PZL SZD-50-3 Puchacz	B-2048		1.92	Heron GC	RNAS Yeovilton	12.99
HCD +	3830	PZL SZD-50-3 Puchacz	B-2049		1.92	Coventry GC	Husbands Bosworth	4.99
HCE	3831	Schleicher ASW19B	19305	D-6527	1.92	N.J.Morgan "346"	Dunstable	12.98
HCF +	3832	PZL SZD-50-3 Puchacz	B-2047		1.92	Shalbourne Soaring Society	Rivar Hill	3.99
HCG	3833	Maupin Woodstock One (Built R.Harvey)	-		10.92	R.Harvey	Swanton Morley	10.99
HCH	3834	Centrair ASW20FP	20178	F-CEUL	3.92	M.P.Eastburn "355"	Saltby	4.99
HCJ +	3835	Grob G.103 Twin II	3709	D-2611	1.92	Peterborough & Spalding GC	Crowland	6.99
HCK	3836	Slingsby T.21B	623	RAFGGA5.. WB962	1.92	V.Mallon (As "WB962")	Laarbruch, Germany	8.99

Regn	BGA No.	Type	C/n	P/I	Regn	Owner/operator	Probable Base	CA Expy
HCL	3837	Schempp-Hirth Discus B	136	D-4682	3.92	P.E. & R.J.Baker "144"		
							Gransden Lodge	2.99
HCM +	3838	Schleicher Ka7 Rhonadler	498	D-5669	3.92	M.Barnard	Dunstable	8.99
HCN +	3839	CARMAM M.200 Foehn	24	F-CDDR	12.92	J S Shaw	Perranporth	7.99
HCP +	3840	Avialsa A.60 Fauconnet	123K	F-CDLA	3.93	B.H.George	Edgehill	7.95*
HCQ +	3841	Glasflugel H.201B Standard Libelle	197	HB-999	1.92	E.K.Harris	Dunstable	2.99
HCR	3842	PZL SZD-51-1 Junior	B-2003		4.92	Surrey & Hants GC "394"	Lasham	3.99
HCS +	3843	Grob G.102 Astir CS77	1727	RAFGSA.R84 RAFGSA.884	2.92	Buckminster GC	Saltby	4.97*
HCU +	3845	Glaser-Dirks DG-300 Club Elan	3E407C66		2.92	M.S Smith & Ptnrs	Aston Down	5.99
HCV +	3846	Schleicher ASW19B	19084	D-4486	5.93	Miss W.J.Palmer	Dunstable	4.99
HCW +	3847	PZL SZD-51-1 Junior (Marked as "HCN")	B-2002	(BGA.3844)	2.92	Deeside GC	Aboyne	4.99
HCX +	3848	Schleicher ASK21	21541		5.92	Devon & Somerset GC	North Hill	6.99
HCY +	3849	Glaser-Dirks DG-300 Club Elan	3E413C67		5.94	M.A.Thorne	Old Sarum	5.99
HCZ +	3850	Schleicher K8B	8114A	D-4675	2.92	Surrey Hills GC	Kenley	8.99
HDA +	3851	Pilatus B4 PC-11AF	017	D-0964	3.92	R.C.Mummery	Lasham	7.99
HDB +	3852	PZL SZD-51-1 Junior	B-1997		3.92	Stratford-upon-Avon GC		
							Snitterfield	1.99
HDC +	3853	Schleicher ASK13	13308	D-0750	3.93	Bowland Forest GC	Chipping	1.99
HDD	3854	Centrair 101B Pegase	101B-0425		4.92	R.C.Bell "591"	Booker	2.99
HDE +	3855	Pilatus B4 PC-11AF	223	VH-XOZ VH-WQP	4.92	A.J.Hamilton	Aston Down	7.99
HDF	3856	Schempp-Hirth Discus B	404		2.92	T.M.Lipscombe "910"	Lasham	12.98
HDG	3857	Schempp-Hirth HS.6 Janus C	144	D-3666	2.92	D.Aknai & Ptnrs "197"	Bicester	3.99
HDH	3858	Glaser-Dirks DG-202-15 (See BGA.3862)	2-197	???	5.92	R.J.Pirie "991"	Parham Park	5.99
HDJ +	3859	Schleicher ASW20CL	20828	D-8442	3.92	M.Challans & Ptnrs	Booker	1.99
HDL	3861	Schleicher ASW20	20082	D-1617 OH-495	4.92	S.Thackray "137"	Booker	3.99
HDM	3862	PZL SZD-12A Mucha 100A	448	SP-1987	4.92	T.J.Wilkinson (As "HDH")		
							Sackville Lodge, Riseley	5.99
HDN +	3863	Schleicher K8B	2	D-8017	3.92	Upward Bound Trust	Thame	9.98
HDP +	3864	PZL SZD-50-3 Puchacz	B-2050		3.92	Heron GC (RNGSA.N36)		
							RNAS Yeovilton	6.99
HDR	3866	Glaser-Dirks DG-300 Elan	3E95	RAFGSA R30	3.92	C.J.Cornish "467"	Booker	4.99
HDT	3868	Schempp-Hirth Discus BT	76/405		3.92	J.D.J.Glossop & Ptnrs "291"		
							Gransden Lodge	2.99
HDU +	3869	PZL SZD-51-1 Junior	B-1996		3.92	Cambridge University GC		
							Gransden Lodge	2.99
HDV	3870	Schleicher ASW19B	19345	D-2876	4.92	R.J.Hinley "882"	Camphill	4.98
HDW +	3871	Centrair 101A Pegase	101A-0179	F-CGEE	3.92	T.Head	Husbands Bosworth	6.99
HDX +	3872	Rolladen-Schneider LS-7	7161		3.92	P.W.Rodwell "A2"	Crowland	1.99
HDY	3873	Schleicher K8B	8277	D-4094	3.92	M.A Everett	Crowland	2.99
HDZ	3874	Schempp-Hirth Discus CS	078CS		7.92	J.P.Wright & G.Bennett "W1"		
							Challock	4.99
HEA +	3875	Slingsby T.38 Grasshopper (Identity unknown - not ex WZ822)	SSK/FF529	(RAF)	7.92	R.L.McLean	Rufforth	7.99
HEB +	3876	Schleicher Ka6CR	6289	HB-773	5.92	J.W Watt	North Hill	3.99
HEC	3877	PZL SZD-55-1	551191019		5.92	G.P Davis "308"	Aston Down	3.99
HED	3878	Schempp-Hirth Ventus A	17	D-2524	4.92	M.R.Dawson "840"	Hullavington	3.99
HEE	3879	Schempp-Hirth Discus B (Rebuild of BGA.3523 after accident 21.6.91 but see BGA.4047)	292		4.92	Booker GC "316"	Booker	5.99
HEF +	3880	Glaser-Dirks DG-500 Elan Trainer	5E53T20		5.92	Yorkshire GC	Sutton Bank	3.99
HEG +	3881	LAK-12 Lietuva	6206		6.92	R.Kmita & Ptnrs		
							Kirton-in-Lindsey	5.99
HEH	3882	Rolladen-Schneider LS-7WL	7163	D-6078	6.92	R.J.Welford "795" Gransden Lodge		3.99
HEJ	3883	Schleicher ASW15B	15441	D-6871	5.92	P.D.Candler "687"	Dunstable	4.99
HEK +	3884	PZL SZD-51-1 Junior	B-2009	BGA.3893 (BGA.3884)	5.92	Cambridge University GC		
							Gransden Lodge	1.99
HEL	3885	Rolladen-Schneider LS-4	4027	D-6431	5.92	G.C.Alison "A9"	Dunstable	1.98
HEM	3886	Schempp-Hirth Discus CS	073CS		5.92	J.H.Nunnerley "473"	Enstone	2.99
HEN	3887	Schempp-Hirth Discus B	422		6.92	A.R.Verity & Ptnrs "735"		
							Challock	7.99
HEP +	3888	PZL SZD-50-3 Puchacz	B-2057		5.92	Peterborough & Spalding GC		
							Crowland	11.99
HEQ	3889	Schleicher ASW20L	20410	D-6747	6.92	M.Chant "611"	Brent Tor	2.99
HER +	3890	Schleicher ASW19	19240	F-CERR	4.93	B.T.Spreckley Le Blanc, France		10.99
HES	3891	Centrair 101A Pegase	101A-039	F-CFQF	3.93	B.T.Spreckley "B39"		
							Le Blanc, France	3.99
HET	3892	Rolladen-Schneider LS-6C	6263		6.92	M P Brooks "335"	Lasham	2.99
HEV +	3894	Schempp-Hirth HS.2 Cirrus	41	OO-ZXY (OO-ZOZ)/D-0104	5.92	D.A Clempson	Portmoak	3.99
HEW	3895	Rolladen-Schneider LS-6C	6250		4.92	R.M.Underhill "486"	Bicester	1.99

Regn	BGA No.	Type	C/n	P/I	Regn	Owner/operator	Probable Base	CA Expy
HEY	3897	Hutter H-17A	02		6.92	J.M.Lee	Parham Park	9.98
		(Built by J.M.Lee - possibly the same specimen as BGA.3661 ?)						
HEZ +	3898	Rolladen-Schneider LS-6C	6264		7.92	J.E.Cruttenden "607"	Lasham	3.99
HFA	3899	Schempp-Hirth Ventus B/16.6	251	RAFGSA.R24	6.92	D.R.Stewart "425"	Winthorpe	6.95*
HFB +	3900	Schleicher Ka6CR	6344Si	D-5825	7.92	S.Tomlinson	Templeton	12.99
HFC	3901	Slingsby T.21B	587	WB924	7.92	M.G Stringer	Dunstable	7.99
						(As "WB924")		
HFD	3902	Grob G.102 Astir CS Jeans	2229	D-5912	6.92	East Sussex GC "289"	Ringmer	8.97*
						(Damaged Kitson Field 15.6.97)		
HFE	3903	Slingsby T.21B	1166	XN187	6.92	A.J.Oultram	Seighford	5.99
						(As "XN187")		
HFF	3904	Schempp-Hirth Standard Cirrus	539	D-8916	2.93	M.S.Morrisroe "870"	Upwood	1.99
HFG	3905	Slingsby T.21B	1165	XN186	6.92	A.S.Raffan	RAF Marham	7.98
HFH +	3906	PZL SZD-50-3 Puchacz	B-2059		8.92	Trent Valley GC		4.99
							Kirton-in-Lindsey	
HFJ +	3907	PZL SZD-42-1 Jantar 2A	B-792	RAFGGA... OO-ZDE	4.92	P.Stein	RAF Bruggen	4.99
HFL	3909	Schleicher ASH25	25147		7.92	T.W.Slater "925/SSC"	Portmoak	1.99
HFM	3910	Rolladen-Schneider LS-6C	6266		7.92	F.J.Shepherd "747"	Booker	6.99
HFN	3911	Wassmer WA-26P Squale	18	F-CDQP	6.92	C.Duthy-James	Talgarth	8.96*
HFP	3912	CARMAM M.100S Mesange	87K	F-CDPQ	6.92	D.Patrick & Ptnr	Falgunzeon	9.96*
HFQ	3913	Rolladen-Schneider LS-6C	6260	(BGA.3908)	6.92	R A Brown "126"	Gamston	3.99
HFU +	3917	PZL SZD-9 bis Bocian 1D	P-334	SP-2038	6.94	T.Wiltshire	(Spilsby)	8.96*
HFV	3918	Schempp-Hirth Ventus B 16.6	204	D-5235	10.92	A.Cliffe "F2"	Camphill	12.98
HFW +	3919	Schleicher K8B	8108	HB-705	9.92	Oxford GC Weston-on-the-Green		2.99
HFX	3920	Schempp-Hirth Nimbus 4T	12		7.92	R.Jones "82"	Lasham	3.99
HFY	3921	Schempp-Hirth Ventus CT	168/554	(BGA.3916) (BGA.3867)	7.92	M.Day & D.J.Ellis "940"	Lasham	4.99
HFZ	3922	Abbott-Baynes Scud I Replica	001		R	M.L.Beach	Brooklands	-
						(On display 3.96)		
HGA +	3923	Wassmer WA-26P Squale	43	F-CDUH	3.93	E.C.Murgatroyd		
							Sackville Lodge, Riseley	5.99
HGB	3924	Grob G.102 Astir CS	1356	D-7386	11.92	P.J.Hollamby & Ptnrs "509"		
		(Rebuild with wings & components from RAFGGA.507)					Lee-on-Solent	2.99
HGC +	3925	Schleicher Ka7 Rhonadler	540	D-5689	3.94	T.J.Ireson Kingston Deverill		8.98
HGF +	3928	Schleicher ASW15B	15264	D-2128	8.92	I.Thompson	Camphill	2.98
HGG +	3929	Schempp-Hirth HS.4 Standard Cirrus	362	HB-1172	12.92	W.R.Hibberd	Seighford	11.99
HGH +	3930	Schleicher ASW19B	19351	D-1199	8.92	A.Wood	Brent Tor	4.99
HGJ	3931	CARMAM M.200 Foehn	33	F-CDHG	9.92	M.Skinner	Tatenhill	11.95*
HGK +	3932	Schempp-Hirth Discus BT	96/435		10.92	C.T.Skeate	Parham Park	11.98
HGL	3933	Schempp-Hirth Discus B	431		7.92	P.J.Ward "183"	Aston Down	11.98
HGM +	3934	Scheibe SF-27A Zugvogel V	6017	D-9351	9.92	S.Algeo	Lyveden	5.99
HGN	3935	Schempp-Hirth Ventus CT	172/562		9.92	Diamond Sailplanes Ltd "740"		
							North Hill	8.99
HGP +	3936	Rolladen-Schneider LS-6C	6270		11.92	E.C.Neighbour	Camphill	8.99
HGQ +	3937	LAK-12 Lietuva	6208		.94	R.A.M.Lovegrove "637"	Dunstable	5.99
HGR +	3938	LAK-12 Lietuva	6186		3.93	R.G Stevens Husbands Bosworth		5.99
HGS	3939	Schempp-Hirth Discus B	439		11.92	J.C.Bailey "730"	Challock	11.99
HGT +	3940	FFA Diamant 16.5	40	HB-929	4.94	R.W.Collins	Burn	3.99
HGU +	3941	Avionautica Rio M.100S	048	HB-1038 I-RIKI	6.93	R.D.Colman	Old Sarum	5.98
HGV +	3942	Glaser-Dirks DG-500/22 Elan	5E70S11		2.93	B.H.Bryce-Smith Gransden Lodge		3.99
HGW +	3943	Centrair ASW20F	20102	F-CFFB	1.93	A.M.Smith Husbands Bosworth		2.99
HGX +	3944	LAK-12 Lietuva	6201		5.93	K.Pickering "783" Parham Park		12.98
HGY	3945	PZL SZD-24C Foka (Mod.)	W-180	SP-2385	12.92	Peterborough & Spalding GC		
							Crowland	5.99
HGZ	3946	Schempp-Hirth Discus BT	95/434		12.92	R.F.Aldous & Ptnrs "502"	Booker	3.99
HHA +	3947	PZL SZD-50-3 Puchacz	B-2058		2.93	Derby & Lancs GC	Camphill	5.99
HHC +	3949	PZL SZD-50-3 Puchacz	B-2080		4.93	Derby & Lancs GC	Camphill	2.99
HHD +	3950	PZL SZD-51-1 Junior	B-2010		3.93	Derby & Lancs GC	Camphill	2.99
HHE +	3951	PZL SZD-51-1 Junior	B-2008		6.93	Derby & Lancs GC	Camphill	4.99
HHG	3953	Slingsby T.31B	705	WT910	1.93	P.Wickwar & Ptnr	Challock	5.97*
						(As "WT910")		
HHH	3954	Rolladen-Schneider LS-6C	6289		12.92	I.M.Hargrove "963"	Booker	2.99
HHJ +	3955	Glaser-Dirks DG-500/22 Elan	5E71S12		2.93	British Gliding Association "97"		
							Bicester	11.99
HHK	3956	Schleicher ASW19B	19384	ZD661 BGA.2897	3.93	A.J.Peters Syndicate "838"		
							Lasham	3.99
HHL +	3957	Schleicher Ka7 Rhonadler	446	OY-XCK D-5619	7.93	Lincolnshire GC "Buttercup"	Strubby	12.98
HHM +	3958	LAK-12 Lietuva	6195		8.93	R.Parayre	(France)	5.99
HHN	3959	Schempp-Hirth Ventus B/16.6	205	RAFGSA.R27	2.93	N.A.C.Norman "979"	Aboyne	2.99
		(Build No. V-204)						
HHP	3960	Schempp-Hirth Discus B	399	SE-UKL	2.93	L.B.Walker "KL"	Nympsfield	1.99
HHQ	3961	Schempp-Hirth Discus BT	106/453		2.93	J.P.Galloway "977"	Portmoak	1.00

Regn	BGA No.	Type	C/n	P/I	Regn	Owner/operator	Probable Base	CA Expy
HHR	3962	PZL SZD-55-1	551191020		4.93	R.T.Starling "100"	Nympsfield	2.99
HHS	3963	Schleicher ASW20	20008	SE-TTU	3.93	D.P.Holdcroft "746"	Crowland	2.99
HHT	3964	Rolladen-Schneider LS-6C	6292		7.93	R.C.Bromwich "855"		2.99
							Kingston Deverill	2.99
HHU	3965	Rolladen-Schneider LS-6C	6296		2.93	P.R.Redshaw "23"	Walney Island	3.99
HHW	3967	LAK-12 Lietuva	6212		3.93	A.J.Dibdin "237"	Dunstable	2.99
HHX	3968	Wassmer WA-26P Squale	14	F-CDQJ	2.93	M.H.Gagg	Long Mynd	2.99
HHY +	3969	Glasflugel H.201B Standard Libelle	119	SE-TIU	3.93	R.Tietma & M.Ainsworth		
							Husbands Bosworth	1.99
HJA +	3971	VFW-Fokker FK-3	0008	D-0409	8.93	M.A Johnson & Ptnrs		
							Sackville Lodge, Riseley	1.99
HJC	3973	Rolladen-Schneider LS-6C	6290		3.93	F.J Davis & I.C.Woodhouse "25"		
							Enstone	1.00
HJD +	3974	Schleicher Ka6E	4141	D-....	2.94	D.Weitzel	Edgehill	2.99
				OH-505/SE-TFM				
HJE	3975	Schleicher K8B	8259	(BGA.3926)	4.93	S.J.Crabb "505"	Edgehill	7.98
				RAFGGA.505 (&/or RAFGGA.981?)				
HJF	3976	Rolladen-Schneider LS-6C	6291		4.93	J.L.Bridge "245"	Gransden Lodge	12.99
HJH +	3978	Schempp-Hirth Discus BT	65/391	(N32086)	4.93	P.J.Goulthorpe "Z1"	Crowland	12.98
				BGA.3978/N224WT				
HJJ	3979	Slingsby T.38 Grasshopper	797	WZ816	R	J.Wilkins		
HJK	3980	Schleicher Ka7 Rhonadler	795	RAFGSA.R5	6.93	Leeds University GC	Rufforth	9.96*
				D-5791				
HJL	3981	Schempp-Hirth Discus BT	105/451		5.93	A.R.MacGregor "306"		
							Kingston Deverill	1.00
HJM +	3982	Hutter H.28-III Replica	ED.02		5.93	E.R.Duffin	Rhigos	6.99
		(Built E.R.Duffin)						
HJN +	3983	Grob Standard Cirrus	440G	HB-1206	6.93	D.F Marlow	Aston Down	5.99
HJP	3984	Rolladen-Schneider LS-6C	6303		5.93	T.Stuart "621"	Nympsfield	2.99
HJR	3986	Glasflugel H.201B Standard Libelle	102	SE-TIO	5.95	B Magnani "89"	Wormingford	4.99
HJT	3988	Centrair ASW20F	20115	F-CFFL	6.93	C.I Roberts & Ptnrs "X16"		
							Snitterfield	5.99
HJU +	3989	Schempp-Hirth Standard Cirrus	134	EC-DNE	7.93	A M Cooper	Usk	7.99
				D-0327				
HJV +	3990	Grob G.102 Astir CS	1007	D-7000	6.93	Cotswold GC	Aston Down	11.99
HJX	3991	Rolladen-Schneider LS-6C	6271		5.93	R.S.Hatwell & M.Haynes "203"		
							Swanton Morley	1.00
HJY +	3992	Schempp-Hirth Standard Cirrus	459	HB-1207	6.93	W.W Turnbull & Ptnrs		
							Currock Hill	7.99
HJZ	3993	Schleicher ASW15B	15190	OH-408	5.94	R.R.Beezer "865"	Camphill	5.98
HKA	3994	Schempp-Hirth Discus CS	120CS		5.93	Coventry GC "135"		
							Husbands Bosworth	2.99
HKB +	3995	Grob G.102 Astir CS77	1658	D-7491	10.93	K.J.McPhee	Kingston Deverill	2.99
HKC +	3996	Grob Standard Cirrus	520G	D-3268	8.93	L.White	Dunstable	5.99
HKD	3997	Grob Standard Cirrus	576G	F-CEMF	7.93	T.G.Whiting "C34"	Edgehill	5.99
HKF +	3999	CARMAM JP-15/36AR Aiglon	23	F-CETU	7.93	K. & C.Vincent	Bidford	9.99
HKJ	4002	Penrose Pegasus 2	001		7.93	J.M.Lee	Parham Park	9.98
		(Built J.M.Lee)						
HKK +	4003	Schleicher K8B	8886	D-0866	1.94	Highland GC	Easterton	3.99
HKL	4004	Schempp-Hirth Discus BT	120/476		2.94	D.P.Knibbs "919"	Seighford	3.99
HKM +	4005	Grob G.102 Astir CS Jeans	2108	D-7636	3.94	P Foulger	Ridgewell	1.99
HKN +	4006	Centrair 101C Pegase	101-902	N101CR	7.93	J.A.Sutton	Currock Hill	2.99
				F-WFXB				
HKP +	4007	Schleicher ASK23B	23100	D-2935	8.93	N.R.Cawte	Winthorpe	3.99
				HB-1935				
HKQ	4008	Schempp-Hirth Nimbus 3DT	63		8.93	R.I.Hey & Syndicate "970"		
							Nympsfield	11.99
HKR +	4009	Jastreb Standard Cirrus G/81	276	OH-663	10.93	J.Evans	Lyveden	5.99
HKS	4010	Jastreb Standard Cirrus G/81	361	SE-TZS	11.93	E.W.Richards	Booker	3.99
HKT +	4011	Schleicher ASW19	19168	D-7958	10.93	A.Birkenshaw & Ptnr	Burn	9.99
		(C/n duplicates OE-5174 but is believed correct)						
HKU	4012	Grob Standard Cirrus	513G	F-CEMA	12.93	T.J Wheeler & Ptnr "C29"	Lyveden	3.99
HKV +	4013	Scheibe Zugvogel IIIA	1034	D-8294	10.93	Dartmoor GC	Brent Tor	6.99
HKW +	4014	Marco J-5	009	G-BSBO	6.94	G.K Owen	Usk	6.99
		(Built D.Austin - regd with c/n 001)						
HKX +	4015	Rolladen-Schneider LS-4B	4933		12.93	D.J Hughes	Long Mynd	12.99
HKY	4016	Schempp-Hirth Discus B	461		10.93	J.G Arnold "JA"	Thruxton	2.99
HKZ	4017	CARMAM JP-15/36AR Aiglon	31	F-CFGA	9.93	R.Borthwick "P31"	Milfield	6.99
HLB	4019	Rolladen-Schneider LS-4	4935		4.94	A.W.Edwards "365"	Gransden Lodge	5.99
HLC +	4020	Pilatus B4 PC-11	177	SE-UFX	3.94	C.J Pollard	Wormingford	2.99
				OH-455				
HLD	4021	Schempp-Hirth Discus BT	122/479		10.93	C.M.Robinson & Ptnrs "462"	Kenley	10.95*
						(Damaged Parham 7.5.95)		
HLG +	4024	Schleicher ASK21	21596		3.95	London GC	Dunstable	3.98
HLH +	4025	Schleicher K8B	8637	RAFGGA.569	2.94	R.Das	Usk	5.99
		(See BGA.4162)		D-5691				

Regn	BGA No.	Type	C/n	P/I	Regn	Owner/operator	Probable Base	CA Expy
HLK +	4027	Glasflugel H.301 Libelle	85	SE-TFS	4.95	B.Amos	Booker	2.99
HLM	4029	Schleicher ASW19B	19269	OH-538	2.94	R.A.Colbeck "819"	Booker	3.99
HLN	4030	Schempp-Hirth Discus CS	143CS		1.94	Portsmouth Naval GC "805"		
							Lee-on-Solent	3.99
HLP +	4031	Schleicher ASK21	21597		3.94	Yorkshire GC	Sutton Bank	2.99
HLQ	4032	Schempp-Hirth Discus B	490		12.93	J.F.Goudie "381"	Portmoak	1.99
HLS	4034	Schempp-Hirth Discus B	114	RAFGSA.R11	1.94	C.L.Withall "V8"	Dunstable	1.99
HLT	4035	LAK-12 Lietuva	6190		2.94	Baltic Sailplanes Ltd	Rufforth	2.95*
						(Damaged Rufforth 16.7.94; stored 7.97)		
HLU +	4036	Scheibe SF-27A Zugvogel V	6101	SE-TGP	2.94	G.M.Brightman	Dunstable	2.99
HLV +	4037	Schleicher K8B	8760	SE-UIM D-5005	2.94	M.Cuming "UIM"	Edgehill	1.97*
HLW +	4038	Schleicher ASW19B	19325	D-8799	4.94	F.J.Hayden	Gransden Lodge	2.99
HLX +	4039	Schleicher ASH25	25124	D-3988	2.94	P.Pozerskis "260"		
							Husbands Bosworth	3.99
HLY +	4040	Schempp-Hirth Discus CS (Not ex RAFGSA.561)	161CS		6.94	F.G.Birlison "561"	Aston Down	11.99
HLZ	4041	Schleicher ASW20BL	20951	D-8188	3.94	T Vines "359"	Dunstable	4.99
HMA +	4042	PZL SZD-51-1 Junior	B-2132		3.94	Coventry GC	Husbands Bosworth	3.99
HMB	4043	Glaser-Dirks DG-300 Elan	3E105	D-4676	3.94	J.S.Weston "445"	Bellarena	2.99
HMG +	4044	ICA IS-28B2	353	HA-....	4.94	G.L.Nunn	Tibenham	4.99
HMH	4045	Schleicher K8B (Officially regd as c/n 2330)	5	D-5735	4.94	Shenington GC "S82"	Edgehill	10.99
HMK	4046	Rolladen-Schneider LS-6-18W	6324		3.94	A.E.Kay "941"	Booker	12.99
HML	4047	Schempp-Hirth Discus CS (Composite with wings from BGA.3879)	114CS	OO-ZTU	3.94	M.E.Hahnefeld "38"	Parham Park	3.99
HMM	4048	Glasflugel H.304B	322	SE-UGZ D-1005	3.94	I.P.Freestone "D19"		
							Husbands Bosworth	4.99
HMP	4050	Schempp-Hirth Discus B	497		3.94	E.R.Lysakowski "71"	Booker	3.99
HMQ	4051	Schempp-Hirth Discus CS	099CS	D-7160	3.94	S.A.Hindley "364"	Edgehill	4.99
HMR	4052	Wassmer WA.30 Bijave	140	F-CCZV	4.94	Bidford GC (As "-CCZV")	Bidford	4.95*
						(Stored 9.97)		
HMS +	4053	Glaser-Dirks DG-100	40	D-2579	4.94	B.Walton-Knight	Tatenhill	5.99
HMT	4054	Glasflugel H.303 Mosquito B	153	F-CEDY	3.94	B.T.Spreckley "380"		
							Le Blanc, France	4.99
HMU +	4055	CARMAM JP-15/36AR Aiglon	22	F-CETT	5.94	J.R.Holmes	Kingston Deverill	3.99
HMV	4056	Schleicher ASK13	13177	D-0268	5.94	Portsmouth Naval GC (RNGSA.N26)		
							Lee-on-Solent	6.99
HMW +	4057	Scheibe SF-27A Zugvogel V	AB.6111	D-0289	5.94	Surrey Hills GC	Kenley	8.98
HMX +	4058	Rolladen-Scheider LS.4B	4230	OO-ZNN F-CEIO	5.94	D.Robson "V19"	Currock Hill	5.99
HMY +	4059	Schempp-Hirth HS.4 Standard Cirrus	121	HB-1034	4.94	C.P.Woodcock & B.J.Thomas		
							Weston-on-the-Green	3.99
HMZ	4060	Federov Me-7 Mechta	M.004		4.94	R.Ellis t/a Kenilworth Intl "469"		
							Long Mynd	2.96*
HNA +	4061	Glaser-Dirks DG-500/20 Elan	5E128W3		7.94	P.Boneham	Winthorpe	12.98
					(Major components from crash Camphill 12.6.96 stored Rufforth 7.97)			
HNB	4062	Schempp-Hirth HS.6 Janus C	215	D-4149	4.94	C.M.Fox "563"	Lleweni Parc	3.99
HNC +	4063	Schleicher ASW19B	19297	OH-515	4.94	J.B.Clarke	Lleweni Parc	2.99
HND +	4064	Scheibe Zugvogel IIIA	1044	HB-735 D-9119	5.94	A J.Sadler	Lyveden	4.99
HNE	4065	Schempp-Hirth HS.5 Nimbus 2B	91	D-2786	5.94	S.Noad & Ptnrs "708"	Challock	5.99
HNF	4066	Schempp-Hirth Duo Discus	11		5.94	Booker GC "315"	Booker	5.99
HNG +	4067	Schleicher K8B	132/59	D-8378	4.94	Bidford GC "8378"	Bidford	5.99
HNH	4068	Schempp-Hirth HS.5 Nimbus 2C	187	D-2830	3.94	A.P.Hatton "599"	Winthorpe	1.99
HNJ +	4069	Schleicher Ka7 Rhonadler	7031	D-1667 RAFGGA.../D-6233	5.94	N.J.Orchard-Armitage "861"		
							Waldershare Park	1.99
HNK +	4070	PZL SZD-51-1 Junior	B-1496	SP-3299 (SP-3290)	5.94	Booker GC	Booker	2.99
HNM	4072	Jastreb Standard Cirrus G/81	360	SE-TZT	7.94	V.L.Brown & Ptnr "167"		
							Snitterfield	3.99
HNN +	4073	Schempp-Hirth Duo Discus	21		9.94	D.Smith	Aboyne	2.99
HNS	4077	Slingsby T.21B	1164	8942M XN185	6.94	B.Walker (As "XN185")	Syerston	8.99
HNT	4078	Schleicher ASW15	15167	F-CEAQ	6.94	A.P.Moulang "105"	Challock	4.99
HNU	4079	Schempp-Hirth Nimbus 4DT	3/5	D-KHIA	5.94	D.E.Findon "48"	Bidford	2.99
HNV	4080	Rolladen-Schneider LS-4B	4960		12.94	P.W.Armstrong "692"		
							Kirton-in-Lindsey	1.99
HNW	4081	Schempp-Hirth Duo Discus	25		11.94	B.A.Bateson & Ptnr "2UP"		
							Parham Park	1.99
HNX	4082	Rolladen-Schneider LS-4B	4937		7.94	C.S.Crocker "585"	Long Mynd	3.99
HNY +	4083	Centrair 101A Pegase	101A-020	F-CFRP	10.95	M.Breen	Booker	10.98
HNZ	4084	Centrair 101A Pegase	101A-032	F-CFRY	7.94	R.H.Partington "RY"		
							Kirton-in-Lindsey	12.98
HPA	4085	Issoire E78 Silene	4	F-CFEA	R	T.M.Perkins	Dunstable	-
HPB	4086	Hutter H.28 II Replica	-		8.94	D.G.Jones	Husbands Bosworth	8.95P*

Regn	BGA No.	Type	C/n	P/I	Regn	Owner/operator	Probable Base	CA Expy
HPC +	4087	Schleicher ASW20CL	20787	D-3424	7.94	D.R.Sutton	Pocklington	6.99
HPD +	4088	Rolladen-Schneider LS-6C-18	6331	D-1054	10.94	S.G.Sampson "717"	Lasham	3.99
HPE +	4089	Schleicher ASK13	13510	D-3992	10.94	Nottingham University GC	Syerston	10.99
HPF	4090	PZL SZD-9 bis Bocian 1E (Wears "HPH")	P-740	OH-508	8.94	Bath, Wilts & North Dorset GC	Kingston Deverill	10.99
HPG +	4091	Maupin Woodstock (Built J.M.Stockwell)	551	VR-HKI	8.94	J.M.Stockwell	Perranporth	8.99
HPH +	4092	Schempp-Hirth Discus CS (See BGA.4090)	174CS		9.94	M.E.Newland-Smith	Ridgewell	9.99
HPJ +	4093	Edgley EA.9 Optimist	EA9/001		5.94	Edgley Aeronautics Ltd	Lasham	4.99
HPK	4094	Bibby G.1	1		R	K.Bibby		
HPL	4095	Rolladen-Schneider LS-4B	4959	(BGA.4071)	7.94	P.G.Mellor "655"	Booker	4.99
HPM +	4096	Grob G.102 Astir CS	1072	D-3304	11.94	S.McQuillan	Lasham	12.99
HPP	4098	Slingsby T.38 Grasshopper	863	XA230	2.95	S.Butler	Gransden Lodge	7.99
HPQ +	4099	Schleicher Ka6CR	6200	D-1933	10.94	E.A.Hull	Dunstable	11.99
HPR +	4100	Schempp-Hirth Discus B	532		2.95	A.S.Decloux	Dunstable	10.98
HPS +	4101	Federov Me-7 Mechta	M.005		5.95	R.Ellis t/a Kenilworth Intl "469"	Long Mynd	6.98
HPT +	4102	Federov Me-7 Mechta	M.006		3.96	A E.Griffiths	Long Mynd	11.99
HPU	4103	Glaser-Dirks DG-800S	8-38S9	(BGA.4074)	11.94	R.J.Middleton "848"	Portmoak	12.98
HPV +	4104	Schleicher ASK21	21608		10.94	Scottish Gliding Union Ltd	Portmoak	10.99
HPW +	4105	Schleicher ASK21	21609		11.94	Scottish Gliding Union Ltd	Portmoak	1.00
HPX	4106	Schempp-Hirth Discus CS	177CS		4.95	P.C.Witmore & M.Whitehead "693"	Gransden Lodge	2.99
HPY	4107	ASC Spirit	EUR.001		5.95	Repclif Avn Ltd	Crewe	6.98
HPZ	4108	ASC Falcon	EUR.002		1.96	Repclif Avn Ltd	Crewe	11.97
HQA	4109	Rolladen-Schneider LS-8	8001	D-6353	10.94	M.D.Wells	Edgehill	8.96P*
HQB	4110	Slingsby T.21B	602	WB935	10.94	C.J.Anson	(Germany)	8.99
		(Officially regd with c/n 1099 which is a corruption of fuselage no.SSK/FF/1099)						
HQC +	4111	Scheibe Bergfalke II/55	322	D-9004	12.94	S.H.Gibson	Bidford	5.99
HQD	4112	Schleicher ASW20	20288	SE-ULA OH-548	11.94	D.G.Brain & Ptnrs "A20"	Dunstable	3.99
HQE	4113	Schempp-Hirth Duo Discus	29		2.95	D.K.McCarthy "620"	Lasham	1.99
HQF +	4114	CARMAM M.100S Mesange	26	F-CCSO	11.94	R.E.Stokes	Rhigos	4.99
HQG +	4115	LAK-12 Lietuva	6222		4.95	M.Boyle & Ptnrs	Rufforth	5.99
HQH +	4116	Schleicher Ka4 Rhonlerche II	3072/Br	(BGA.4097) HB-877	5.95	D.Fulchiron	(France)	7.99
HQJ	4117	Schempp-Hirth Discus B	336	D-1762	2.95	D.G.Lingafidelter "762"	Dunstable	2.99
HQK	4118	Schleicher ASW20CL	20854	D-3366	1.95	S.D.Minson "S2"	Halesland	1.99
HQL	4119	Rolladen-Schneider LS-6C-18W	6352	D-0794	3.95	B.A.Fairston & A.Stotter "LS6"	Husbands Bosworth	3.99
HQM +	4120	Schempp-Hirth Discus B	44	RAFGSA.R10	1.95	Cambridge University GC	Gransden Lodge	5.99
HQN	4121	Schempp-Hirth HS.5 Nimbus 2B	139	D-6494	1.95	D.Peters "D-64"	Burn	1.99
HQR	4123	Schempp-Hirth Discus B	531		4.95	British Gliding Association "19"	Lasham	3.99
HQS +	4124	Grob G.103 Twin Astir	3155	OO-ZEG	2.95	Essex & Suffolk GC	Wormingford	2.99
HQT	4125	Grob G.102 Astir CS77	1678	RAFGGA.561	2.95	D.F.Barley "A77"	Kenley	2.99
HQU +	4126	PZL SZD-9 Bocian 1D	F-848	SP-2439	7.97	T.Wiltshere	(Spilsby)	7.98
HQV +	4127	PZL SZD-51-1 Junior	B-2139		3.95	Coventry GC	Husbands Bosworth	11.98
HQW	4128	Schempp-Hirth Discus B	538		3.95	J.E.May "329"	Nympsfield	3.99
HQX +	4129	Schleicher ASW15B	15326	D-2315	3.95	R.Emms	Crowland	3.99
HQY	4130	Schempp-Hirth HS.7 Mini Nimbus C	"328"	D-....	3.95	D.S.Hill "487"	Lasham	3.99
HQZ	4131	Rolladen-Schneider LS-6C-18W	6353	D-1486	3.95	R.E.Jones "U2"	Lasham	3.99
HRA	4132	Grob G.102 Astir CS	1109	D-4169	4.95	Portsmouth Naval GC (RNGSA.N19)	Lee-on-Solent	5.98
HRB +	4133	LAK-12 Lietuva	6223		3.95	J.E.Neville	Portmoak	12.99
HRC	4134	Glaser-Dirks DG-500-20 Elan Trainer	5E136W5		3.95	N.J.Allcoat "390"	Portmoak	4.99
HRD	4135	Slingsby T.21B	634	WB973	3.95	U.Seegers	(Germany)	3.99
HRE +	4136	Schleicher Ka6CR	572	D-9326	4.96	R.J.Playle "932"	Dunstable	3.99
HRF +	4137	Schleicher Ka6E	4272	OO-ZJR D-0165	5.95	R.J.Rebbeck	Dunstable	7.99
HRG +	4138	PZL SZD-51-1 Junior	B-2013		4.95	Scottish Gliding Union Ltd	Portmoak	5.99
HRJ +	4139	Schleicher K8B	8093Ei	D-5048	4.95	M.Barnard "504"	Turweston	4.99
HRK +	4140	Centrair 101A Pegase	101A-048	F-CFQJ	5.95	I.P Bramley	Dunstable	2.99
HRL +	4141	Schempp-Hirth HS.4 Standard Cirrus	525	D-3099	4.95	M.Harbour	Camphill	2.99
HRN +	4143	Schleicher ASK18	18026	HB-1308	4.95	Stratford-upon-Avon GC	Snitterfield	3.99
HRP +	4144	PZL SZD-51-1 Junior	B-1805	SP-3440	5.95	Wolds GC	Pocklington	3.99

Regn	BGA No.	Type	C/n	P/I	Regn	Owner/operator	Probable Base	CA Expy
HRQ	4145	Schempp-Hirth HS.7 Mini Nimbus C	123	(BGA.4122) SE-TVB	4.95	T.C Wright & Ptnrs "169" Seighford		4.99
HRR	4146	Schleicher ASK21	21033	D-7083	2.95	Lakes GC "D70"	Walney Island	2.99
HRS	4147	Schempp-Hirth Discus CS	100CS	D-5100	4.95	M.E.Hughes "B33" Husbands Bosworth		3.99
HRT +	4148	Schleicher K8B	8390A	D-5599	3.96	Heron GC (RNGSA.N..) RNAS Yeovilton		3.99
HRU	4149	Centrair ASW20F	20114	F-CFFK	7.95	European Soaring Club "FFK" Le Blanc, France		5.99
HRV +	4150	PZL SZD-55-1	551195076		11.95	R.W.Southworth	Warsaw, Poland	2.99
HRW	4151	Schempp-Hirth Duo Discus	43		6.95	A.J.Davis "802"	Nympsfield	12.99
HRX	4152	Schempp-Hirth Discus A	545		5.95	P.G.Sheard "P5"	Dunstable	1.99
HRY	4153	Rolladen-Schneider LS-6C-18W	6362		6.95	F.K.Russell "L8"	Dunstable	3.99
HSA	4155	Rolladen-Schneider LS-6C-18W	6361		8.95	D.A.Benton "A1"	Long Mynd	4.99
HSB +	4156	Glaser-Dirks DG-300 Elan	3E461		7.95	J S.Foster	Parham Park	3.99
HSC	4157	PZL SZD-50-3 Puchacz	B-2079		8.95	British Gliding Association "99" Bicester		2.99
HSD	4158	Schempp-Hirth Discus B (Rebuild of BGA.3406 c/n 258 w/o 26.8.94)	258/1	(BGA.4142)	6.95	C.E.Collingham & J.R.Reed "D15" Dunstable		3.99
HSE +	4159	Grob G.102 Astir CS77	1635	RAFGSA.R68 RAFGSA.548	9.95	J.Hull & Ptnr	Keevil	11.98
HSG +	4161	Scheibe SF-27A Zugvogel V	1705/E	D-7827 OE-0827	7.95	Welland GC "7827"	Lyveden	7.99
HSH	4162	Scheibe Zugvogel IIIB (Marked "HLH" 7.96)	7/1041	D-6558	7.95	J.E.Harman "Brigitta"	Lasham	7.97*
HSJ +	4163	Schempp-Hirth Discus B	546		6.95	K.L.Rowley "D54"	Pocklington	4.99
HSK	4164	Schleicher ASW20CL	20827	D-3499	7.95	T.M.World "933"	Lasham	4.99
HSL	4165	Schempp-Hirth Ventus 2C (Incomplete airframe assembled by Southern Sailplanes)	1/2	(BGA.4154)	7.95	S.G.Jones "410"	Membury	2.99
HSM +	4166	Schleicher ASK13	13145	D-0168	7.95	Stratford-upon-Avon GC Snitterfield		1.99
HSN +	4167	Schleicher Ka6CR	6218	OO-ZZF D-8546	7.95	M.Brennan	Enstone	9.98
HSP	4168	Schempp-Hirth HS.6 Janus C	112	RAFGSA.R1 BGA.2723/D-7013	R	D.H.Garrard "385" Gransden Lodge		-
HSQ	4169	Schempp-Hirth Discus B	99	D-2943	8.95	Midland GC "493"	Long Mynd	1.99
HSR	4170	LAK-12 Lietuva	6178		8.95	J.F.Morris & Ptnr "313" Gransden Lodge		7.99
HSS	4171	Schleicher Ka7 Rhonadler (Mod)	7015	RAFGSA.R29 D-5241	8.95	M.Cuming	Edgehill	8.96*
HSU	4173	Schleicher ASK18	18025	AGA.16	R	R.C.Martin "A17"		
HSV +	4174	Schempp-Hirth HS.4 Standard Cirrus	195	D-0785	3.96	H.Gunther-Heinen	Edgehill	6.99
HSW	4175	Schempp-Hirth Duo Discus	48		8.95	C.R.Simpson "895" Husbands Bosworth		7.99
HSX +	4176	Scheibe SF-27A Zugvogel V	6031	SE-TDT	9.95	J A Horne	Wormingford	3.99
HSY	4177	Pilatus B4 PC-11	050	SE-UFF OH-431	9.95	A.L.Dennis "A15"	Walney Island	9.99
HSZ	4178	Rolladen-Schneider LS-8	8030		9.95	European Soaring Club "197" Le Blanc, France		12.99
HTA +	4179	Centrair C-201B1 Marianne	201-014	F-CGMM	10.95	E.Crooks	Kirton-in-Lindsey	10.98
HTB +	4180	Schempp-Hirth HS.6 Janus A	007	D-3114	7.95	P.J.Gibbs & Ptnrs "TE"	Edgehill	9.99
HTC +	4181	Schleicher ASW15B	15188	OE-0930	10.95	N.A.Page	Camphill	12.97
HTD	4182	Grob G.102 Astir CS	1012	D-6508	1.96	G.V McKirdy "VMC" (As "D-6508")	Edgehill	5.98
HTE +	4183	Grob G.102 Astir CS77	1716	RAFGSA.R82 RAFGSA.882	11.95	J.R.Whittington	Challock	5.99
HTF +	4184	LAK-12 Lietuva	6180		5.96	D.Stidwell	Tatenhill	4.99
HTG +	4185	Grob G.102 Astir CS	1510	RAFGSA.R59 RAFGSA.R69/RAFGSA.519	10.95	Trent Valley GC	Kirton-in-Lindsey	1.99
HTH	4186	Schempp-Hirth Janus CT	185/2	N137DB D-KHIE	10.95	S.A.Adlard "C4" Long Mynd (Cambridge Aero Instruments Research Aircraft)		4.99
HTJ +	4187	Schleicher ASK13	13125	D-6048	12.95	Ulster GC	Bellarena	3.99
HTL	4189	Rolladen-Schneider LS-8-18	8038	D-3156	10.95	A. & L.Wells "LS"	Bidford	12.99
HTM	4190	Rolladen-Schneider LS-8-18	8036		10.95	T.J.Scott "Z8"	Booker	4.99
HTN	4191	Schleicher ASW22	22013	ZS-GLN	4.96	S.Bates "S22"	Edgehill	3.99
HTP	4192	Rolladen-Schneider LS-8	8039	D-3175	11.95	R.A.Browne "L58"	Crowland	12.99
HTQ	4193	Rolladen-Schneider LS-8-18	8037	D-2993	11.95	P.G. & S.J.Crabb "C64" Sandhill Farm, Shrivenham		10.99
HTR +	4194	Grob G.102 Astir CS	1190	D-7307	11.95	I.Wright	Kingston Deverill	2.99
HTS	4195	Rolladen-Schneider LS-8-18 (See BGA.3184)	8040		11.95	R.A.Cheetham "E1"	Dunstable	12.99
HTT +	4196	Schleicher ASW20CL	20627	D-2410	11.95	G.D Clack	Lasham	2.99
HTU +	4197	Schempp-Hirth HS.2 Cirrus	88	D-0478	12.95	S.Kochanowski	Lasham	2.99
HTV +	4198	Schleicher ASK21	21624	D-8355	3.96	Cambridge University GC Gransden Lodge		2.99

Regn	BGA No.	Type	C/n	P/I	Regn	Owner/operator	Probable Base	CA Expy
HTW +	4199	Pottier JP15-34 Kit Club	50-39	F-CFGF	12.95	R.P Halton	Bidford	2.98
HTX	4200	Schleicher ASW20	20239	D-3180	3.96	C.B.Starkey "900"	Lasham	2.99
HTY +	4201	LET L-13 Blanik	026318	LY-GDT DOSAAF	4.96	North Devon GC	Brent Tor	4.99
HTZ	4202	Bolkow Phoebus 17C	908	OO-ZDJ BGA.1573	12.95	A.de Tourtoulon "833" Wormingford		12.98
HUA +	4203	Schleicher ASW19	19091	D-3840	12.95	M.T Davenport	Lasham	3.99
HUB +	4204	PZL SZD-48-3 Jantar Standard	B-1527	DOSAAF	3.96	S.G.Back	Crowland	3.99
HUC +	4205	Schempp-Hirth Janus CE	170	(BGA.4188) D-3189	2.96	C.W.Price	Wormingford	12.99
HUD +	4206	Schleicher ASK13	13018	D-9203	2.96	London GC	Dunstable	8.99
HUE	4207	Schleicher ASW27	27022		10.96	E.H.Downham "N5"	Dunstable	2.99
HUF +	4208	Schleicher ASK13	13109	OO-ZWE	3.96	London GC	Dunstable	8.99
HUG +	4209	Rolladen-Schneider LS-8-18	8047	D-3472	3.96	A.O'Regan (to ZS-GUY 9.98 - same owner)	Sutton Bank	6.98
HUH	4210	Schempp-Hirth HS.6 Janus A	15	D-3116	5.96	B.A.Fairston "D31" Husbands Bosworth		4.99
HUJ +	4211	Centrair ASW20F	20170	F-CFLY	3.96	S.Lee	Rattlesden	3.99
HUK +	4212	Schleicher Ka6CR	6385	SE-TCN	4.96	T.J Donovan & Ptnr	Lyveden	4.99
HUL +	4213	Schempp-Hirth HS.2 Cirrus	V3	HB-900	2.96	I.Ashton & Ptnrs "624"	Chipping	5.99
HUM +	4214	Rolladen-Schneider LS-6C	6267	OO-ZXS D-4350	3.96	A.Hall "241"	Lasham	12.99
HUN +	4215	Grob G.102 Astir CS Jeans	2089	D-7531	2.96	D P.Manchett	Lleweni Parc	11.99
HUP +	4216	Schempp-Hirth Ventus 2CT	4/11		2.96	C G Corbett "170"	Tibenham	11.97
HUQ +	4217	Federov Me-7 Mechta	007		6.96	J S Fielden	Brent Tor	8.99
HUR +	4218	Schempp-Hirth HS.2 Cirrus	12	HB-927	4.96	D G Slocombe	Burn	4.99
HUS +	4219	Scheibe SF-27A Zugvogel V	6010	D-1035	8.97	C J Palmer	Booker	8.99
HUT +	4220	Centrair ASW20F	20187	F-CEUQ	4.96	G.A MacFadyen	Nympsfield	11.99
HUU +	4221	Schleicher ASK13	13527AB	D-7506 D-8945	4.96	Upward Bound Trust	Thame	7.99
HUV	4222	Rolladen-Schneider LS-8A-18	8056	D-3823	4.96	C.P.Jeffery "197" Gransden Lodge		3.99
HUW	4223	Rolladen-Schneider LS-8A	8058		3.96	B.T.Spreckley "S8" Le Blanc, France		10.99
HUX	4224	Schempp-Hirth Ventus 2C	7/12		3.96	E.R.Lysakowski "58"	Lasham	3.99
HUY +	4225	Schempp-Hirth Ventus CT	84/372	D-KILZ	4.96	M A Challans "880"	Lasham	12.99
HUZ	4226	Schempp-Hirth Discus BT	158/559		3.96	J.Lynchenhaun "200" Lleweni Parc		2.99
HVA +	4227	PZL SZD-59 Acro	B-2169		5.96	C.Williams	Lasham	12.99
HVB	4228	Slingsby T.31B	850	(BGA.3249) XA308	4.96	M.Hoogenbosch Maastrict, Netherlands		5.99
HVC	4229	Slingsby T.38 Grasshopper	766	WZ770	R	J.Forster (Netherlands)		
HVD	4230	PZL SZD-55-1	551193052		4.96	Anglo-Polish Sailplanes Ltd "304" Booker		4.99
HVE	4231	Schempp-Hirth Ventus 2CT	8/19	D-KHIA	3.96	Glyndwr Soaring Club "W54" Lleweni Parc		4.99
HVF	4232	Rolladen-Schneider LS-8-18	8059	D-1683	4.96	M.D.Wells "321"	Bidford	4.99
HVG	4233	Schleicher ASK21	21062	D-2606	4.96	Rattlesden GC "RP1"	Rattlesden	4.99
HVH +	4234	Pilatus B4 PC-11	067	D-2156	5.96	C.Cain	Lasham	5.98
HVJ	4235	Scheibe SF-27A Zugvogel V	6012	OE-0762	6.96	C.Bleaden "962" Kirton-in-Lindsey		7.98
HVK +	4236	Grob G.102 Astir CS	1161	D-4182	4.96	F.R.Panter	Tibenham	4.99
HVL +	4237	Rolladen-Schneider LS-8-18	8060		4.96	D.W Allison "LS8"	RAF Wyton	2.99
HVM	4238	Glaser-Dirks DG-300 Elan	3E177	D-4314	5.96	Surrey & Hants GC "393"	Lasham	2.99
HVP	4240	Schleicher ASW20	20374	D-1961 BGA.4076/EC-DLN	5.96	E.J.Smallbone "930"	Lasham	3.99
HVQ +	4241	Schleicher ASK13	13251	D-0605	4.96	R.R Brown	Edgehill	4.99
HVR +	4242	Schempp-Hirth Discus B	560		5.96	Yorkshire Gliding Club (Pty) Ltd Sutton Bank		4.99
HVT	4244	Schempp-Hirth Ventus 2B	37		5.96	P.R.Jones "210"	Booker	3.99
HVU	4245	Rolladen-Schneider LS-8A	8066		4.96	S.J.Crabb "C65" Sandhill Farm, Shrivenham		9.99
HVV +	4246	Rolladen-Schneider LS-4B	41009		1.97	A.Bardgett	Currock Hill	1.00
HVW +	4247	Schleicher ASK13	13431	D-2140	6.96	Rattlesden GC	Rattlesden	6.99
HVX +	4248	Centrair ASW20F	20528	F-CFSJ	6.96	A.S Goldsmith	Camphill	6.99
HVY	4249	Schempp-Hirth Ventus 2C	9/21		5.96	R.Ashurst "584"	Lasham	1.99
HVZ	4250	Schempp-Hirth HS.4 Standard Cirrus	567G	HB-1269	6.96	M. & J.Miles Hinton-in-the-Hedges		6.99
HWA	4251	Schempp-Hirth Ventus 2C	8/20		6.96	C.Garton "31"	Lasham	11.99
HWB	4252	Schempp-Hirth Duo Discus	84		5.96	Lasham Gliding Society "775" "Duo-Tubbies"	Lasham	3.99
HWC	4253	Glasflugel H.201B Standard Libelle	310	HB-1076	7.96	J.C.Rogers "L18"	Winthorpe	3.99
HWD +	4254	Schempp-Hirth HS.4 Standard Cirrus	97	HB-987	6.96	M.A.Edmonds Sandhill Farm, Shrivenham		1.99
HWE +	4255	Schleicher K8B	1151	HB-700	5.96	J.P.Brady	Brent Tor	2.99
HWF +	4256	Jastreb Standard Cirrus G/81	281	SE-TZC	6.96	G.Earle "ZC"	Booker	6.99
HWG +	4257	Glasflugel H.201B Standard Libelle	259	HB-1051	6.96	M.R Fox	Pocklington	6.99
HWH	4258	Schempp-Hirth Ventus CT	182/599	RAFGGA.506	7.96	H.R.Browning "712"	Lasham	10.99

Regn	BGA No.	Type	C/n	P/I	Regn	Owner/operator	Probable Base	CA Expy
HWK	4260	Grob G.104 Speed Astir IIB	4070	OO-ZVQ LX-CRT	7.96	P.Gilbert	Tours, France	7.97*
HWL	4261	Rolladen-Schneider LS-8A	8076		6.96	M.Coffee "84"	Bidford	3.99
HWM	4262	Rolladen-Schneider LS-8A	8079		7.96	B.C.Marsh "847"	Bidford	3.99
HWN	4263	Schempp-Hirth Nimbus 3T	8/60	D-KHIF	7.96	H.N.Lenz "598"	Lasham	7.99
HWP +	4264	Glaser-Dirks DG-100G Elan	E24G13	D-3772	7.96	C.A.Sheldon	Pocklington	7.99
HWQ +	4265	Scheibe L-Spatz 55	607	D-6195	7.96	A.Gruber	Usk	3.99
HWR	4266	Rolladen-Schneider LS-3A	3098	D-3902	7.96	G.L.Askew & Ptnr "M1"	Seighford	7.97
HWS	4267	Rolladen-Schneider LS-8A	8080		2.97	E.A.Coles "75"	Dunstable	2.98
HWT	4268	Schleicher K8B	8780	HB-958	7.96	Shenington GC "S83"	Edgehill	5.99
HWV	4270	Schempp-Hirth Discus B	561		8.96	N.J Passmore "526"	Parham Park	5.99
		(Rebuild of fuselage of AGA.4 c/n 206 with new wings c/n 561)						
HWW	4271	Grob G.103 Twin II Acro	3658-K-27	OE-5285	8.96	T.Gage "DJT"	Lasham	2.99
HWX	4272	PZL SZD-59 Acro	B-2170		9.96	Anglo-Polish Sailplanes Ltd	Booker	7.99
HWY	4273	Jastreb Standard Cirrus VTC G/81	359	LN-GAL	9.96	S.R.Kronfield "168"	Booker	9.97
HWZ +	4274	Schleicher ASW19B	19316	HB-1524	9.96	D.Housky	Winthorpe	3.99
HXA +	4275	Scheibe Zugvogel IIIB	1107	D-2005	3.97	B W Millar	Portmoak	3.99
HXB +	4276	Grob G.102 Astir CS77	1819	D-6755	9.96	K.S.Wells	Crowland	9.99
HXC	4278	Rolladen-Schneider LS-8A	8094		2.97	S.M.Smith "M8"	Gransden Lodge	2.99
HXD +	4279	Schleicher ASW27	27030		3.97	M.Jerman	Wormingford	2.99
HXE	4280	Schleicher ASW19B	19053	D-6699	9.96	M.Lloyd-Owen "Y4"	Lasham	10.99
HXH	4283	Schempp-Hirth Discus B	573	(BGA.4375) (BGA.4283)	6.97	Deeside GC	Aboyne	6.99
		(Originally NTU then re-allotted as BGA.4375 and finally reverted to BGA.4283)						
HXJ +	4284	Schleicher ASK13	13216	D-0417	11.96	Cotswold GC	Aston Down	11.99
HXL	4286	Letov LF-107 Lunak	039	OK-0927	11.96	G.Saw (As "OK-0927")	Booker	12.99
HXM +	4287	Grob G.102 Astir CS	1272	D-7367	11.96	D.P.Compston	Bicester	1.99
HXN	4288	Rolladen-Schneider LS-8A	8095		1.97	J.L Birch "57"	Dunstable	2.99
HXP	4289	Schleicher ASK13	13023	D-3656	11.96	Vale of White Horse GC "856" Sandhill Farm, Shrivenham		1.99
HXQ	4290	Schleicher ASH25B	25187	OH-874	11.96	R.A Cheetham "156"	Rufforth	11.99
HXR	4291	Schempp-Hirth Ventus CT	88/333	D-KESH	2.97	W.A'Court "560"	Lasham	3.99
HXS	4292	Schempp-Hirth Ventus 2CT	10/41		11.96	I.R.Cook "V11"	Thruxton	2.99
HXT	4293	Rolladen-Schneider LS-4A	4325	ZS-GNV	3.97	B.T.Spreckley "LS4" Le Blanc, France		3.99
HXU +	4294	Schleicher ASW19B	19359	SE-TXN	4.97	G A Chalmers	Drumshade	4.99
HXV +	4295	Schleicher ASK13	13080	D-5462	12.96	Aquila GC Hinton-in-the-Hedges		12.99
HXW	4296	Rolladen-Schneider LS-8A	8097		3.97	W.Aspland "325"	Dunstable	3.99
HXX +	4297	Schempp-Hirth HS.4 Standard Cirrus 154G	154G	D-0363	1.97	E J Winning	Templeton	2.99
		(Built by Grob)						
HXY +	4298	Grob G.102 Astir Jeans	1781	D-7689	12.96	I.Worten	Bidford	3.99
HXZ	4299	Rolladen-Schneider LS-4	4249	SE-TXF	3.97	I.P.Freestone "S5"	Lyveden	4.99
HYA	4300	Rolladen-Schneider LS-6	"634B"		2.97	R.H.Dixon "DD"	Parham Park	3.99
HYB	4301	Schempp-Hirth Discus B	140	D-4684	4.97	T.P.Browning "T5"	Lasham	1.99
HYC +	4302	Eichelsdorfer SB-5E Sperber	5042	D-2009	3.97	H.Hughson (As "D-2009")	RAF Bruggen	5.99
		(Akaflieg Braunschweig built)		BGA.3447/RAFGGGA/D-2009				
HYD +	4303	Schleicher ASW24	24039	OE-5460	2.97	P J.Metcalfe	Lasham	4.99
HYE +	4304	Glaser-Dirks DG-505 Elan Orion	5E167X22		12.96	Bristol & Glos GC "913" 	Nympsfield	12.98
HYF	4305	Rolladen-Schneider LS-8-18	8106		3.97	K.M.Barker "KM"	Nympsfield	3.99
HYH +	4307	Rolladen-Schneider LS-3-17	3186	D-6650	1.97	J.Lamb	Bellarena	4.99
HYJ +	4308	Schleicher ASK21	21066	D-2724	1.97	Highland GC	Easterton	2.99
HYK +	4309	Centrair ASW20FLP	20176	F-CEUN	9.97	J.C.Riddell	Rufforth	10.99
HYL	4310	Schempp-Hirth Ventus 2A	44		5.97	A J Stone "K4"	Booker	1.99
HYM	4311	DWLKK PW-5 Smyk	100		1.97	T.Joint "PW5"	Lasham	12.98
		(C/n is probably 17.06.020)						
HYN	4312	Schleicher K8B	8310A	D-1018	11.97	G.Brook	Crowland	11.98
HYP +	4313	PZL SZD-50-3 Puchacz	B-2082		2.97	Rattlesden GC	Rattlesden	4.99
HYQ	4314	Grob G.102 Astir CS	1332	AGA.6	R			
HYR	4315	Schleicher ASW27	27013	D-8733	3.97	A.R.Hutchings "432"	Dunstable	3.99
HYS	4316	Schleicher ASK21	21519	RAFGGA.514	R	AGA "A14"	Wattisham	4.99
HYT	4317	Schleicher ASK21	21568	RAFGGA.515	R	To AGA.20		
HYU	4318	Schempp-Hirth Discus CS	192CS	RAFGGA.561	R	"A61"	Wattisham	
HYV	4319	Schleicher K8B	558	RAFGGA.558	R			
HYW +	4320	Schleicher K8B	8163A	D-5316 D-3202	3.97	Lincs GC	Strubby	4.99
HYX	4321	Schleicher K8B	686	D-5742		M.O.Breen	Bicester	1.99
HYY	4322	Schempp-Hirth Nimbus 3DT	21	RAFGSA.R26 D-KAFA/D-5847	3.97	N.J.Wright "A26"	Bidford	4.99
HYZ	4323	Rolladen-Schneider LS-8-18	8104		4.97	P J Coward "L88"	Crowland	1.00
HZA	4324	Schempp-Hirth Nimbus 3/24.5	94	SE-UFO	4.97	C.J.Short "376"	Lasham	4.99
HZB	4325	DWLKK PW-5 Smyk	17.06.021		2.97	J.D.Scott "JS1"	Gransden Lodge	2.99
HZC	4326	Grob G.102 Astir CS	1092	D-6991	3.97	G.S.Roe "216"	Lasham	1.00
HZD +	4327	Schleicher ASW15B	15327	D-2191	3.97	G.E.Gillard	Winthorpe	3.98
HZE	4328	Schempp-Hirth Discus CS	121CS	D-6946	3.97	A.D.Irving "T3"	Kenley	3.98

Regn	BGA No.	Type	C/n	P/I	Regn	Owner/operator	Probable Base	CA Expy
HZF	4329	Centrair 101A Pegase	101A-0262	PH-796	5.97	B.R.George "G7"	Gransden Lodge	3.99
HZG	4330	Rolladen-Schneider LS-8-18	8118		3.97	N.G.Hackett "X7"	Husbands Bosworth	4.99
HZH +	4331	Schleicher Ka6CR	6461	HB-836	5.97	M.E.de Torre	Gamston	6.99
HZJ +	4332	Schempp-Hirth HS.4 Standard Cirrus	23	HB-981	3.97	A.B.Stokes	Enstone	1.00
HZK +	4333	Not allotted						
HZL +	4334	Schempp-Hirth HS.4 Standard Cirrus	304	D-2060	4.97	P.Cousan	Dunstable	1.99
HZM +	4335	Rolladen-Schneider LS-4A	4762	D-1394	4.97	P G Dowse "U1"	Edgehill	3.99
HZN	4336	Schleicher Ka2B Rhonschwalbe	195	D-6173	3.97	D.E.Lamb (As "D-6173")	Booker	3.99
HZP	4337	Rolladen-Schneider LS-8A	8117		3.97	S.J.Redman "56"	Gransden Lodge	5.99
HZQ	4338	Schleicher ASW27	27018	D-4499	3.97	M.D.Rogers "K5"	Dunstable	1.99
HZR +	4339	Schleicher ASK21	21079	D-4491	5.97	A.Roseberry	Aston Down	5.99
HZS	4340	Schempp-Hirth Ventus 2A	43		3.97	A.E.Kay "K1"	Weston-on-the-Green	3.99
HZT	4341	Centrair ASW20F	20150	F-CFLL	8.97	T.J.Banks "X50"	Ringmer	8.99
HZU	4342	Schempp-Hirth HS.4 Standard Cirrus	366	HB-1258 N71KW	4.97	D.R.Piercy "B11"	Winthorpe	11.99
HZV	4343	Schempp-Hirth HS.4 Standard Cirrus	305	HB-1457 D-2061	4.97	P.Cox "P61"	Enstone	3.99
HZW	4344	Schempp-Hirth Nimbus 3T	22/88	D-KILO	6.97	J.Ellis "112"	Sutton Bank	3.99
HZX	4345	Schleicher K8B	8257	D-8476	4.97	G.E.W.Woodward "476"	Upwood	4.99
HZY	4346	Rolladen-Schneider LS-4A	4479	D-3458	4.97	N.P.Wedi "EN"	Booker	2.99
HZZ	4347	Schleicher ASW20L	20273	N727AM	4.97	P.E.Rice "LD"	Wormingford	4.99

Regn	BGA No.	Type	C/n	Previous identity	Regn	Owner/operator	Probable Base	CA Expy

JAA-JZZ

Regn	BGA No.	Type	C/n	Previous identity	Regn	Owner/operator	Probable Base	CA Expy
JAA +	4348	Schempp-Hirth HS.6 Janus B	163	D-3147	4.97	A.A.Baker	Lasham	4.99
JAB +	4349	Glaser-Dirks DG-300 Elan	3E320	OY-XTC	4.97	P.B.Jones	Lasham	4.99
JAC	4350	Schempp-Hirth Duo Discus	128		5.97	British Gliding Association "98" Bicester		3.99
JAD +	4351	Schleicher ASK21	21659		10.97	Borders GC	Milfield	3.99
JAE	4352	Glaser-Dirks DG-200/17C	2-62	HB-1443	4.97	S.A.White "N8" Hinton-in-the-Hedges		3.99
JAF	4353	Schempp-Hirth Ventus 2B	33	(BGA.4306)	4.97	M.J.Young "V57" Gransden Lodge		2.99
JAG +	4354	Schleicher ASW20L	20136	HB-1474	7.97	654 Syndicate "654" Currock Hill		7.99
JAH	4355	Schempp-Hirth Discus B	572		5.97	K.Neave "921"	Nympsfield	5.99
JAJ	4356	Glaser-Dirks DG-202/17	2-150/1744	D-4154	5.97	T.R Dews "916" Kingston Deverill		3.99
JAK	4357	Schleicher Ka6E	4301	F-CDRJ	R			
JAL +	4358	Schleicher Ka6E	4360	F-CDTX	6.97	N.Gilkes	Lasham	6.98
JAM	4359	Schleicher ASW15B	15353	D-2360	5.97	T.J.Beckwith "777" Sackville Lodge, Riseley		1.99
JAN +	4360	Schempp-Hirth Discus B	575		10.97	Wolds GC	Pocklington	10.99
JAP	4361	Slingsby T.38 Grasshopper	779	WZ783	R			
JAQ +	4362	Schempp-Hirth Discus B	190	D-0960	6.97	P.D.Duffin "823"	Wormingford	1.99
JAR	4363	Schempp-Hirth Discus BT	83/417	D-KHEI	5.97	C.J.Partridge "P3"	Lasham	4.99
JAS	4364	Glasflugel H.201 Standard Libelle	109	SE-TIS	5.97	M.D.Wells "7Q"	Enstone	5.98
JAT +	4365	Schleicher K8B	8150	D-4390	6.97	Wolds GC	Pocklington	5.99
JAU	4366	Slingsby T.21B	585	WB922	5.97	J.Priddle (As "WB922") Kingston Deverill		6.99
JAV +	4367	Schleicher ASK21	21662		11.97	Wolds GC	Pocklington	11.99
JAW	4368	Glaser-Dirks DG-200/17	2-180/1759	D-5618	6.97	J.Walker "M4"	Lasham	1.99
JAX +	4369	Schleicher ASK21	21665		1.98	Wolds GC	Pocklington	1.99
JAY	4370	Schleicher ASW20	20034	D-7941	6.97	D.A.Smith "123" Kingston Deverill		6.99
JAZ +	4371	Grob G.102 Astir Jeans	2073	D-7586	8.97	Bath, Wilts & Dorset GC Kingston Deverill		8.99
JBA +	4372	Slingsby T.38 Grasshopper (Assembled from components; p/i is starboard wing only)	1262	XP463	6.98	J A Northern & Pntr	Challock	6.99
JBB	4373	Rolladen-Schneider LS-8	8003	D-8023	8.97	R F Thirkell "B3"	Lasham	11.99
JBC	4374	Schempp-Hirth Ventus 2CT	15/61		6.97	B.A.Bateson "2B"	Ringmer	5.99
JBD	4375	See BGA.4283						
JBE	4376	ISF Mistral C	MC.020/79	OY-XLX PH-667	7.97	H.H.Crowther "LX"	Aston Down	6.99
JBF	4377	Glasfugel H.201 Standard Libelle	246	F-CDPV	7.97	L Coles	Booker	5.99
JBG	4378	Schempp-Hirth Ventus B	135	OE-5315	7.97	W.R.Longstaff "U9"	Easterton	5.99
JBH	4379	Eiri PIK-20D	20621	OH-529	7.97	537 Syndicate "537"	Parham Park	5.99
JBJ	4380	Jastreb Standard Cirrus G/81	280	SE-TZD	7.97	T.Rendell "G81"	Lasham	3.99
JBK	4381	Schleicher ASW19B	19204	D-4099 PH-602	11.97	R.E.Robertson "L3"	Booker	12.99
JBM	4383	Schleicher ASK21	21089	D-6391	7.97	Staffs GC "S21"	Seighford	7.99
JBN	4384	Schempp-Hirth Discus B	94	D-7175	R			
JBP	4385	Rolladen-Schneider LS-6-18W	6378		7.97	I.C.Baker "B21"	Nympsfield	7.99
JBQ	4386	Rolladen-Schneider LS-8-18	8148		9.97	L.Hill "LH7"	North Hill	9.99
JBR	4387	Schempp-Hirth Discus B	90	F-CGGD F-WGGD	8.97	A.A.Baker "AB"	Odiham	9.99
JBS +	4388	LAK-12 Lietuva	6115	???	8.97	I.G.Smith & Ptnrs	Ringmer	8.98
JBT +	4389	Schleicher ASW19	19075	D-4477	8.97	Aquila GC Hinton-in-the-Hedges		1.99
JBU	4390	Rolladen-Schneider LS-6-18W	6350	D-0462	9.97	J.Gorringe "HL"	Lasham	9.98
JBV	4391	Monnett Monerai (Built J.Foxson/B.Nibett)	-		7.97	B.Nibett	Keevil	7.98
JBW	4392	Schempp-Hirth Discus BT	34/337	D-KBJR	8.97	N.C.Pringle "710"	Lasham	8.99
JBX +	4393	Rolladen-Schneider LS-4A	4293	D-9111	4.98	P Lee & Pntr	Aston Down	4.99
JBY +	4394	LAK-12 Lietuva	6185		8.97	Baltic Sailplanes Ltd Husbands Bosworth		8.99
JBZ +	4395	Grob G.102 Astir CS	1492	D-4794	8.97	M.J.Fogarty	Booker	8.99
JCA +	4396	Schleicher ASW15B	15202	(BGA.4049) OH-410	9.97	R.H. & A.Moss	Nympsfield	9.99
JCB +	4397	Rolladen-Schneider LS-6C-18WL	6234	D-6116	4.98	K Nicholson	Dunstable	10.98
JCD	4399	Schleicher ASW24	24101	D-6091	10.97	M.D.Evershed "H5"	Crowland	10.98
JCE	4400	Schempp-Hirth Ventus BT	46/240	D-KFMS	9.97	A.G.Reid "911"	Kenley	9.99
JCF +	4401	Grob G.102 Astir CS77	1705	PH-1012 D-7634	9.97	Northumbria GC	Currock Hill	9.99
JCG +	4402	DWLKK PW-5 Smyk	17.09.003		9.97	V.H.Spencer	Dunstable	11.99
JCH +	4403	MDM-1 Fox	218		.97	C.Cain	Lasham	7.99
JCJ	4404	Grob Standard Cirrus	434G	SE-TNC	5.98	M R Garwood "C7"	Crowland	5.99
JCK	4405	Schempp-Hirth Discus BT	92/430	D-KIDE	10.97	D.Coppin "DC"	Lasham	10.99
JCL	4406	Rolladen-Schneider LS-8-18	8147		10.97	T.W.Slater "T2"	Aboyne	10.99
JCM	4407	Schleicher ASW24	27064		12.97	M.Clayton "W27"	Bidford	12.98
JCN +	4408	Schempp-Hirth HS.4 Standard Cirrus	646	D-7247	10.97	P.W.Reavell	Camphill	10.99
JCP +	4409	Rolladen-Schneider LS-8-18	8146		10.97	A.J.Emck "36"	Lasham	11.99
JCQ	4410	Schleicher ASW19B	19086	PH-562	12.97	A.J.Preston "W19"	Dunstable	12.99

Regn	BGA No.	Type	C/n	P/I	Regn	Owner/operator	Probable Base	CA Expy
JCR +	4411	Grob G.102 Astir CS	1181	OE-5188	10.97	B Harrison	Kingston Deverill	11.99
JCS	4412	Slingsby T.31B	693	BGA.3284 WT898	10.97	M.Steiner (As "WT898")	(Germany)	10.98
JCT	4413	Schempp-Hirth Nimbus 4T	7/21	D-KKKL	10.97	D S Innes "176"	Lasham	11.99
JCU	4414	Schempp-Hirth HS.4 Standard Cirrus	75 688	D-6604	10.97	N.Swinton "616"	Halton	11.99
JCV	4415	Schleicher ASH25E	25069	D-KAIM	11.97	B.R.George "IM"	Gransden Lodge	11.98
JCW +	4416	Grob G.102 Astir CS77	1612	PH-573	10.97	C.R.Phipps	Bryngwyn Bach	10.98
JCX +	4417	Schempp-Hirth Discus BT	"D432"		10.97	J.E.Bowman	Bidford	11.99
JCY	4418	Rolladen-Schneider LS-8-18	8171		12.97	M.C.Foreman "F3"	Lasham	12.99
JCZ +	4419	Schleicher Ka6CR	6108	D-7152	11.97	V.Phillips	Kingston Deverill	11.98
JDA	4420	Schempp-Hirth Nimbus 3/24.5	8	D-1788	11.97	G.R.Ross "GR"	Lasham	11.98
JDB	4421	Slingsby T.38 Grasshopper	809	WZ828	11.97	H.Chapple (As "WZ828")	Bicester	12.99
JDC	4422	Schleicher ASW27	27010	D-6209	12.97	P.J.Henderson "A27"	Challock	11.99
JDD +	4423	Glaser-Dirks DG-200/17C	2-171/CL17	PH-717	12.97	J.Richardson	Chipping	1.00
JDE	4424	Rolladen-Schneider LS-8-18	8151		5.98	I M Evans "EZ"	Shobdon	4.99
JDF	4425	Schleicher ASH25E	25150	D-KPAS	11.97	J.Bell & Ptnrs "907"	Lasham	11.99
JDG	4426	Rolladen-Schneider LS-6B	6145	D-5675	2.98	A Jelden "KW"	Booker	2.99
JDH	4427	Rolladen-Schneider LS-6C-18W	6287	D-9128	2.98	K H Dietrich "2F"	(Germany)	2.99
JDJ	4428	Rolladen-Schneider LS-3	3010	D-7729	11.97	J.C.Burdett	Chipping	11.99
JDK	4429	Rolladen-Schneider LS-8-18	8153		3.98	K Nicholson "SK1"	Verbier, Switzerland	3.99
JDL	4430	Schempp-Hirth Discus BT	165/5..		4.98	S Robinson "SR"	Chipping	4.99
JDM	4431	Schleicher ASW15B	15280	F-CEGL	1.98	D C Blyth	Tibenham	1.99
JDN +	4432	Glaser-Dirks DG-505	5E180X31		3.98	Devon & Somerset GC	North Hill	3.99
JDP +	4433	Glaser-Dirks DG-200/17	2-136/1734	D-0152	12.97	J.J.Benton	Camphill	12.98
JDQ +	4434	Schleicher ASW19	19106	D-3862	R	Not known	Lasham	
JDR	4435	Schleicher ASW15A	15053	D-6910	2.98	L Whitaker	Booker	2.99
JDS +	4436	Schempp-Hirth HS.4 Standard Cirrus	75 638	D-4057 OY-XCZ	3.98	Burn GC	Burn	3.99
JDT	4437	Rolladen-Schneider LS-8	8172		1.98	R.J.Rebbeck "232"	Dunstable	12.99
JDU +	4438	LET L-13 Blanik	026303	D-8919	12.97	Herefordshire GC	Shobdon	12.99
JDV +	4439	Glaser-Dirks DG-303	3E481A24		3.98	I N Busby	Booker	2.99
JDW +	4440	DWLKK PW-5 Smyk	17.09.018		12.97	G.Pledger	Currock Hill	12.99
JDX +	4441	Wassmer WA-28F Espadon	101	F-CDZU	12.97	K.Ballington	Tatenhill	12.98
JDY	4442	Rolladen-Schneider LS-8	8173		2.98	J Gorringe "P2"	Booker	2.99
JDZ	4443	Schempp-Hirth Nimbus 4T	18	D-KOLF	1.98	T P Browning "111"	Lasham	1.99
JEA +	4444	Rolladen-Schneider LS-8	8158		3.98	R I Davidson "D4"	Husbands Bosworth	3.99
JEB +	4445	Schleicher ASW24	24172	D-9344	2.98	M.A.& J.Taylor	Rattlesden	2.99
JEC +	4446	PZL SZD-50-3 Puchacz	B-2197		4.98	Cambridge University GC	Gransden Lodge	4.99
JED	4447	Schleicher ASW15B	15427	D-3976	1.98	P.R.Williams	Lyveden	1.99
JEE	4448	Schleicher ASW20L	20073	(BGA.4456) D-7666	2.98	C.J.Bailey	Wormingford	2.99
JEF	4449	Schempp-Hirth Ventus CT	126/400	D-KFWH	1.98	M.R.Emmett "M2"	Booker	1.99
JEG	4450	Rolladen-Schneider LS-8-18	8150		1.98	H.Luxton "685"	Booker	1.99
JEH	4451	Glasflugel H.303 Mosquito B	172	OY-XKE	2.98	M.J.Stephens "KE"	Booker	2.99
JEJ	4452	Rolladen-Schneider LS-7WL	7074	OE-5477	3.98	I.Mountain "F1"	Dunstable	3.99
JEK	4453	Grob G.102 Astir CS	1374	(BGA.4398) D-7403	R			
JEL	4454	Schleicher ASW24	24044	PH-866	2.98	M.Dawson"W2"	Keevil	2.99
JEM	4455	Schempp-Hirth Duo Discus	146	-	3.98	H.Kindell "570"	Lasham	3.99
JEN	4456	Schleicher ASW20L	20073			See BGA.4448		
JEP	4457	Rolladen-Schneider LS-4B	41021		R			
JEQ	4458	Schempp-Hirth Nimbus 3D	1	OO-ZOZ	2.98	M.Pocock "OZ"	Rivar Hill	2.99
JER	4459	Schempp-Hirth Std. Cirrus	654	D-6475 OO-ZBM	4.98	J.Hoskins "JH"	Thruxton	4.99
JES	4460	Schleicher ASW19	19119	SE-TTV	3.98	M.Dale "V4"	Sutton Bank	3.99
JET +	4461	Schempp-Hirth Ventus CT	161	RAFGSA.R38	2.98	B.Bryce-Smith	Gransden Lodge	2.99
JEU +	4462	Glasflugel H201 Std. Libelle	55	SE-TIC	4.98	S.Crabb	Cork (Ireland)	4.99
JEV	4463	Schempp-Hirth Std. Cirrus B	650	OE-5072	2.98	M.White	Camphill	2.99
JEW	4464	Schleicher Ka6CR	6493	D-4116	2.98	J.McLaughlin "D42"	Sleap	2.99
JEX	4465	Schempp-Hirth Ventus 2A	64		3.98	D.Watt "DW"	Bicester	3.99
JEY	4466	Schempp-Hirth Std Cirrus	456G	D-3255	3.98	R.Lockett"T7"	North Weald	3.99
JEZ	4467	Glaser-Dirks DG-100	3	PH-792 D-3721	3.98	G.Dale "274"	Lasham	3.99
JFA +	4468	Schempp-Hirth Std. Cirrus	225	D-0974	4.98	M.Sheahan,	Lasham	4.99
JFB	4469	Rolladen-Schneider LS-8-18	8152		3.98	I.Freestone "S6"	Lyveden	3.99
JFC	4470	Schempp-Hirth Discus CS	054	RAFGSA.R55	3.98	RAFGSA Fenland GC "R55"	Marham	3.99
JFD	4471	Grob G.102 Astir CS	1429	RAFGSA.742 D-7425	3.98	RAFGSA Centre "742"	Bicester	3.99
JFE	4472	Schempp-Hirth Janus C	299	RAFGSA.R16	3.98	RAFGSA Centre "R16"	Bicester	3.99
JFF	4473	Schempp-Hirth Duo Discus	131	RAFGSA.R26	3.98	RAFGSA Centre "26"	Bicester	3.99
JFG	4474	Schempp-Hirth Discus b	254	RAFGSA.R15	3.98	RAFGSA Centre "R15"	Bicester	3.99
JFH	4475	Schempp-Hirth Duo Discus	118	RAFGSA R1	3.98	RAFGSA Centre "R1"	Bicester	3.99

Regn	BGA No.	Type	C/n	P/I	Regn	Owner/operator	Probable Base	CA Expy
JFJ +	4476	Schleicher ASW20CL	20830	D-8307 F-CGCS	4.98	W.R.Mills	Usk	4.99
JFK +	4477	Schleicher ASW20L	20201	D-5979	4.98	S.Housden	Aston Down	4.99
JFL	4478	Rolladen-Schneider LS-8	8178	-	3.98	G.Smith "42"	Dunstable	3.99
JFM	4479	Schleicher ASK13	13222	D-0396	3.98	Newark & Notts GC	Winthorpe	3.99
JFN	4480	Schleicher ASH25E	25060	D-KCOH	6.98	R.Baker "OH"	Cranfield	6.99
JFP	4481	Schempp-Hirth Ventus A	19	PH-707	3.98	S.Harris "HB"	(London)	3.99
JFQ	4482	Schempp-Hirth Nimbus 4DT	9/40	-	5.98	J.Delafield "66"	Bicester	5.99
JFR	4483	Schempp-Hirth Ventus cT	170	RAFGSA.R24	12.97	Not known (sold)	??	12.98
JFS	4484	Schempp-Hirth Ventus cT	147	RAFGSA.R28	7.98	RAFGSA "528"	??	7.99
JFT +	4485	Schleicher K8B	8451	D-1883	3.98	Surrey Hills GC	Kenley	3.99
JFU +	4486	Schleicher ASW19	19038	D-4531	3.98	East Sussex GC	Ringmer	3.99
JFV	4487	Schleicher ASK21	21675	-	6.98	Scottish GU "WA1"	Portmoak	6.99
JFW +	4488	LAK-12 Lietuva	6192		4.98	A.Hatfield	Crowland	4.99
JFX	4489	Rolladen-Schneider LS-8A	8174		3.98	D.Campbell "370"	Booker	3.99
JFY	4490	Federov Me-7b	8		10.98	D.Adams	Booker	10.99
JFZ	4491	Federov Me-7b	9		10.98	M.Powell-Brett	Long Mynd	10.99
JGA	4492	Federov Me-7b	10	-	10.98	M.Wilkinson	Challock	10.99
JGB	4493	Schleicher K8B	AB.02	D-8868	5.98	Cambridge UGC "CU" Gransden Lodge		5.99
JGC	4494	Rolladen-Schneider LS-6A	6031	D-6699 PH-763	4.98	Gliding Expeditions Ltd "CC" Les Ages		3.99
JGD +	4495	Schleicher K8B	8214A-SH	D-??..	4.98	S.Pacey Kingston Deverill		4.99
JGE	4496	Schleicher ASK21	21068	RAFGSA.R21	2.98	N.Wall "R21"	Long Mynd	2.99
JGF +	4497	Neukom Elfe S4D	416	- ? -	5.98	C.Inwood	Lasham	5.99
JGG +	4498	Schleicher ASW15B	15332	D-2325	4.98	L.Groves	Ringmer	4.99
JGH +	4499	Schempp-Hirth Nimbus 2c	188	D-2834	4.98	D.Prosolek	Gamston	4.99
JGJ +	4500	Schleicher ASK21	21039	RAFGSA.R22	4.98	Midland GC	Long Mynd	4.99
JGK	4501	Molino Pik-20D	20571	OO-ZDL D-6707	4.98	R.Cassidy "ZDL"	Milfield	4.99
JGL	4502	Schempp-Hirth Discus CS	148	RAFGSA.R27	4.98	Chilterns GC "27"	Halton	4.99
JGM	4503	Schempp-Hirth Discus CS	36	RAFGSA.R53	4.98	Chilterns GC "R53"	Halton	4.99
JGN	4504	Schempp-Hirth Std. Cirrus	554	D-8674	4.98	F.Wilson	Pocklington	4.99
JGP	4505	Schempp-Hirth Ventus 2cT	3	N200EE	4.98	C.Morris "E8"	Bidford	7.98
JGQ +	4506	LET L-13 Blanik	026224	- ? -	6.98	Joint Aviation Services	Lasham	5.99
JGR	4507	Schempp-Hirth Discus bT	10/275	D-KGPS D-5461	5.98	J.Horne "BT"	Wormingford	5.99
JGS	4508	Rolladen-Schneider LS-8-18	8180	-	5.98	G Stingmore "X1"	Winthorpe	5.99
JGT +	4509	Scheibe SF27A	6021	D-1126	4.98	Surrey Hills GC	Kenley	4.99
JGU +	4510	Schempp-Hirth Mini Nimbus	69	HB-1427	5.98	P.Etheringham Husbands Bosworth		5.99
JGV	4511	Schempp-Hirth Duo Discus	173	D-4020	R			
JGW +	4512	Schleicher ASK13	13146	D-0169	5.98	Newark & Notts GC.	Winthorpe	5.99
JGX +	4513	Schleicher K8B	753	D-1878	5.98	J.Fisher	Andreas	5.99
JGY	4514	Schempp-Hirth Std. Cirrus	333	SE-TMU	5.98	P.Chapman "C3" Husbands Bosworth		5.99
JGZ	4515	Glasflugel H-201 Std Libelle	193	D-0697	5.98	J.Edwards	Pocklington	5.99
JHA	4516	Schempp-Hirth Std. Cirrus	645	D-4240	5.98	J.Lee	Pocklington	5.99
JHB +	4517	Scheibe L-Spatz 55	552	D-1618	8.98	A.Gruber	Rhigos	8.99
JHC +	4518	Schleicher ASW19B	19304	OO-ZBN	8.98	W.R.Mills	Usk	8.99
JHD	4519	Schleicher Ka6E	4307	OY-XGS D-0272	5.98	P.Francon-Smith "Y1" &"OY-XGS" Crowland		5.99
JHE	4520	Grob G.102 Astir CS Jeans	2189	CS-PBI BGA3977/D-7764	5.98	AC de Portugal	Lisbon	5.99
JHF	4521	Schempp-Hirth Nimbus 4T	30/44	-	5.98	G.Kerstens "VW"	Enstone	5.99
JHG	4522	Grob G.102 Astir CS	1084	D-6984	5.98	J.Pack "BIT"	The Park	5.99
JHH +	4523	Schempp-Hirth Std. Cirrus	349G	D-3006	5.98	R.L.Fox	Rufforth	5.99
JHJ	4524	Glasflugel H-201 Std. Libelle	495	HB-1187	R			
JHK +	4525	Schleicher K8B	558	AGA21 BGA4319/RAFGSA.558	8.98	AGA Kestrel GC "A55"	Odiham	8.99
JHL +	4526	Schleicher Ka6E	4073	SE-TFB	6.98	V.Long & Ptnr	Tibenham	6.99
JHM +	4527	Schempp-Hirth Discus b	373	???	6.98	J.May	Camphill	6.99
JHN +	4528	Grob G.102 Astir Jeans CS	2110	D-7638	5.98	Derby & Lancs GC	Camphill	5.99
JHP +	4529	Valentin Mistral C	MC048-82	D-4948	6.98	K.Sleigh	Rattlesden	5.99
JHQ	4530	Schleicher ASK18	18021	RAFGSA.R43 RAFGSA.713/RAFGSA.113	9.98	RAFGSA Centre "R43"	Bicester	9.99
JHR	4531	Centrair Alliance SNC-34c	34026	-	6.98	Nevyn International "A34" Bicester		6.99
JHS	4532	Schleicher ASW19B	19047	D-6716	R			
JHT	4533	Schempp-Hirth Discus 2A	2	- ? -	5.98	W.Murray "D2"	Membury	5.99
JHU	4534	Rolladen-Schneider LS-8-18	8197		7.98	S.Thompson "OP8"	Parham Park	7.99
JHV	4535	Schempp-Hirth Discus b	265	RAFGGA547 RAFGGA500	5.98	RAFGSA Phoenix GC "547"	RAF Bruggen	5.99
JHW +	4536	Glaser-Dirks DG-200	2-19	HB-1400	6.98	A.Thornhill	Burn	6.99
JHX	4537	Bolkow Phoebus C	930	OO-ZYN F-CDON	6.98	M.Dunlop	Usk	6.99
JHY	4538	Rolladen-Schneider LS-8a-18	8181	-	7.98	L.E.N.Tanner "LT"	Aboyne	7.99
JHZ	4539	Schleicher ASW20	20313	D-6532	6.98	S.Hughes "G41"	Camphill	6.99

Regn		BGA No.	Type	C/n	P/I	Regn	Owner/operator	Probable Base	CA Expy
JJA		4540	Schempp-Hirth Cirrus	13	D-8114	7.98	P.Tolson "A71"	Saltby	7.99
JJB		4541	Rolladen-Schneider LS-4	4542	D-2397	6.98	M.Tomlinson "TF"	Rhigos	6.99
JJC	+	4542	Schleicher ASK13	13661		7.98	East Sussex GC	Ringmer	7.99
JJD		4543	Schempp-Hirth Discus bT	5/262	D-KIHS	7.98	D.Wilson "SUF" & "K11"	Burn	7.99
JJE		4544	Schempp-Hirth Discus b	379	OE-5530	7.98	N.Braithwaite "JO1"	Long Mynd	7.99
JJF		4545	Schleicher ASW27	27086	-	6.98	G.Read "G1"	Booker	6.99
JJG	+	4546	Schempp-Hirth Nimbus 4T	3	D-KIXL	7.98	P.G.Sheard "V1"	Dunstable	7.99
JJH		4547	Glaser-Dirks DG-800S	8-137S30	R				
JJJ		4548	Schempp-Hirth Std. Cirrus	284	D-2946	7.98	R.Stevens	Bidford	6.99
JJK		4549	Rolladen-Schneider LS-8	8199		8.98	K.Payne "K8" Husbands Bosworth		8.99
JJL		4550	Schleicher ASW19B	19302	D-4227	R			
JJM		4551	Schempp-Hirth Std Cirrus	403G	D-2933	7.98	B.Dakin Husbands Bosworth		7.99
JJN	+	4552	Slingsby T.38	2067	XP490	7.98	Swanton Morley Collection	Swanton Morley	7.99
JJP		4553	Schempp-Hirth Duo Discus	180	-	7.98	R.Fack "494"	Long Mynd	7.99
JJQ	+	4554	PZL SZD-51-1 Junior	B-2191		9.98	Norfolk GC	Tibenham	9.99
JJR		4555	Schleicher ASK21	21054	RAFGSA.R73 RAFGGA.513	8.98	RAFGSA Centre "R73"	Bicester	8.99
JJS		4556	Slingsby T.38	"3254"		R			
JJT		4557	Schleicher ASW27	27070	D-6209	8.98	P.Wells "Z1"	Booker	8.99
JJU		4558	Rolladen-Schneider LS-8a	8200		8.98	P.Harvey "H2"	Cranfield	8.99
JJV	+	4559	Schleicher Ka6CR	1001	D-1719	8.98	L.Simpson	Long Mynd	8.99
JJW		4560	Schleicher ASK13	13281	D-0051	R			
JJX	+	4561	Schleicher ASW15B	15323	D-2321	9.98	T.Davis	Portmoak	9.99
JJY	+	4562	Schempp-Hirth Ventus bT	273/61	PH-981 D-KMIH	9.98	A.J.Leigh	Camphill	9.99
JJZ		4563	Schempp-Hirth Discus bT	156/556	OO-ZQX	9.98	B.Walker "BW"	Aston Down	9.98
JKA	+	4564	Schleicher ASK21	21059	D-8835	10.98	E Sussex GC	Ringmer	10.99
JKB	+	4565	DWLKK PW-5	"1710.08"		9.98	J.Gibson	Chipping	9.99
JKC	+	4566	MDM-1 Fox	224	SP-P632	9.98	G.Westgate & Ptnr	Ringmer	9.99
JKD		4567	Rolladen-Schneider LS-8-18	8215		10.98	R.Large "P1"	Lyveden	10.99
JKE		4568	DWLKK PW-5	17.11.025		10.98	Burn GC	Burn	10.99
JKF	+	4569	Glaser-Dirks DG-200	2-35	D-6069	10.98	L.Rayment	Sutton Bank	10.99
JKG		4570	Schleicher ASK18	18021	RAFGSA.R43	9.98	RAFGSA Centre "R43"	Bicester	9.99
JKH		4571	Schempp-Hirth Ventus cT	174	RAFGSA.R30	10.98	RAFGSA Centre "R30"	Bicester	10.99
JKJ		4572	Schleicher ASK21	21679	(RAFGSA.R21)	10.98	RAFGSA Centre "R21"	Bicester	10.99
JKK		4573	Schleicher ASK21	21182	AGA.11	10.98	AGA Kestrel GC "A7"	Odiham	10.99
JKL		4574	Rolladen-Schneider LS-8	8218		R	R.Welford		
JKM		4575	Glaser-Dirks DG-202-17M	2-148/1746	D-4155	10.98	A.Brown "Z10"	Strathaven	10.99
JKN		4576	Rolladen-Schneider LS-8-18	8214		10.98	D.Booth "790"	Crowland	10.99
JKP		4577	Rolladen-Schneider LS-4B	41000	PH-1089	12.98	M Hope "PH1"	Booker	12.99
JKQ		4578	Schleicher ASK21	21098	RAFGSA.R20	R	RAFGSA Bannerdown GC	RAF Keevil	
JKR		4579	Schempp-Hirth Discus B	151	RAFGSA.R12	R	RAFGSA Bannerdown GC	RAF Keevil	
JKS		4580	Schleicher ASW19B	19362	D-1273	11.98	P Tavener "S19"	Tibenham	11.99
JKT		4581	Schleicher ASK13	13615	RAFGSA.R7	R	RAFGSA Clevelands GC	RAF Dishforth	
JKU		4582	Schleicher ASK18	18022	RAFGSA.R33	R	RAFGSA Clevelands GC	RAF Dishforth	
JKV		4583	Grob G103 Twin II Astir	34042-K-273	RAFGSA.R52	R	RAFGSA Clevelands GC	RAF Dishforth	
JKW		4584	Grob G.102 Astir CS 77	1666	RAFGSA.R60	R	RAFGSA Clevelands GC	RAF Dishforth	
JKX		4585	Schempp-Hirth Discus B	247	RAFGSA.R17	R	RAFGSA Clevelands GC	RAF Dishforth	
JKY		4586	Schempp-Hirth Ventus cT	181	RAFGSA.R24	11.98	RAFGSA Clevelands GC "R24"	RAF Dishforth	11.99
JKZ		4587	Schleicher ASK21	21123	RAFGSA.R25	12.98	RAFGSA Centre "R25"	Bicester	12.99
JLA	+	4588	Schempp-Hirth Ventus 2cT	26/94	PH-1129	11.98	C.Neighbour	Camphill	11.99
JLB		4589	Schempp-Hirth Ventus 2A	74		11.98	R.Knight "70"	Milfield	11.99
JLC		4590	Schempp-Hirth Discus CS	193CS	RAFGSA.R10	11.98	RAFGSA Centre "R10"	Bicester	11.99
JLD		4591	Grob G.103 Twin II Astir	3531	SE-UHH OH-662	R	T Joint	Lasham	
JLE		4592	Schleicher ASK13	13245	RAFGSA.R90 NEJSGSA.1	10.98	RAFGSA Crusaders GC Kingsfield, Dhekelia		10.99
JLF	+	4593	Schleicher ASK13	13150	AGA.14	12.98	Wyvern GC	Upavon	12.99
JLG		4594	PZL SZD-51-1 Junior	B.1933	AGA.5	R	Wyvern GC	Upavon	
JLH		4595	Rolladen-Schneider LS-4	4256	AGA.1	R	Wyvern GC	Upavon	
JLJ		4596	Rolladen-Schneider LS-4B	4997	AGA.2	12.98	Wyvern GC "A8"	Upavon	12.99
JLK		4597	Rolladen-Schneider LS-7	7112	AGA.3	R	Wyvern GC	Upavon	
JLL		4598	Schleicher ASK13	13144	HB-952	11.98	Portsmouth Naval GC "N25" Lee-on-Solent		11.99
JLM		4599	Schempp-Hirth HS.6 Janus C	210	RAFGSA.R2	R	Cranwell GC	Cranwell	
JLN		4600	Rolladen-Schneider LS-8-18	8169	RAFGSA.R4	R	Cranwell GC	Cranwell	
JLP		4601	Schempp-Hirth Discus CS	034CS	RAFGSA.R39	R	Cranwell GC	Cranwell	
JLQ		4602	Schleicher ASK13	13608	RAFGSA.R40 RAFGSA.R4	R	Cranwell GC	Cranwell	
JLR		4603	Grob G.102 Astir CS	1509	RAFGSA.R57	R	Cranwell GC	Cranwell	
JLS		4604	Schleicher K8B	8950	RAFGSA.R75	R	Cranwell GC	Cranwell	
JLT		4605	Schleicher Ka6E	4115	D-6082	11.98	M.Thompson Husbands Bosworth		11.99
JLU		4606	Schempp-Hirth Ventus cT	37		R	J.Mitchell		

Regn	BGA No.	Type	C/n	P/I	Regn	Owner/operator	Probable Base	CA Expy
JLV	4607	Schleicher Ka6E	4192	OY-XEU D-4424	R	M.Neal		
JLW	4608	Schempp-Hirth Discus CS	033CS	RAFGSA.R87	12.98	RAFGSA Centre "87"	Bicester	12.99
JLX +	4609	Grob Std. Cirrus	279G	OO-ZGL D-1985	11.98	M.Fisher	?	11.99
JLY	4610	Schleicher ASW27 27111			R	P.C.Piggott		
JLZ	4611	Grob G.103 Twin Astir II	3633-K-15	D-7912	12.98	T.Dews "21" Kingston Deverill		12.99
JMA	4612	Schleicher ASK18	18038	RAFGSA.R36	R	Four Counties GC	Syerston	
JMB	4613	Rolladen-Schneider LS-8	8130	RAFGSA.R5	R	Four Counties GC	Syerston	
JMC +	4614	Schleicher ASK21	21681	(RAFGSA.R22)	12.98	RAFGSA "R22"	Bicester	12.99
JMD	4615	Schempp-Hirth Discus b	241	RAFGSA.R23	R	RAFGSA		
JME	4616	Schleicher Ka7	5	D-8867	R	T.Joint Lasham		
JMF	4617	Rolladen-Schneider LS-8-18	8232		R	P.Onn		
JMG	4618	PZL SZD-51-1 Junior	B.2192		R	Kent GC	Challock	
JMH +	4619	Schempp-Hirth Std. Cirrus	571	HB-1263	12.98	M.Fryer	Rufforth	12.99
JMJ	4620	Schleicher ASK13	13616	RAFGSA.R46	R	Fenland GC	Marham	
JMK	4621	Schleicher ASK18	18023	RAFGSA.R49	R	Fenland GC	Marham	
JML	4622	Grob G.102 Astir CS 77	1718	RAFGSA.R63	R	Fenland GC	Marham	
JMM	4623	Schempp-Hirth Discus b	254	RAFGSA.R15	12.98	P.Crabb "R15"	Crowland	12.99
JMN +	4624	Schempp-Hirth Nimbus 2B	38	HB-1159	12.98	M.Holroyd	Pocklington	12.99
JMO	4625	Rolladen-Schneider LS-8-18	8225		12.98	J Langrick "781" Husbands Bosworth		12.99
JMP	4626	Schleicher ASK13	13446	D-2984	R	East Sussex GC	Ringmer	
JMQ	4627	Schleicher ASW20L	20499	F-CADB	R			
JMR	4628	Rolladen-Schneider LS8	8198		12.98	D.Williams	?	12.99
JMS	4629	Schleicher ASK21	21212	RAFGGA.521	11.98	Phoenix GC	RAF Bruggen	11.99
JMT	4630	Rolladen-Schneider LS-8-18	8223		R	J.Burry		
JMU	4631	Rolladen-Schneider LS-8	"15308"		R	R.Payne		
JMV	4632	Schempp-Hirth HS.5 Nimbus 2C	179	D-6738	R			
JMW	4633	Schleicher ASK13	13688AB	RAFGGA.567	?	RRAFGSA		

SECTION 3B - RAF GLIDING & SOARING ASSOCIATION REGISTER

RAFGSA numbers have often been re-issued. The "R" prefix to the serial is not always carried. The BGA recognises those marked without the prefix in the normal Competition Number sequence. Those marked * are recognised by the BGA as having the "R" prefix. In 1998 it was decided that the separate RAFGSA series would be discontinued and that BGA Numbers be used in future. The notes indicate that the process is well underway.

RAFGSA No.	Type	c/n	Previous identity	Operator	Probable base	Notes
R1	Schempp-Hirth Duo Discus	118		RAFGSA Centre	Bicester	To BGA.4475
R2 *	Schempp-Hirth HS.6 Janus C	210		Cranwell GC	Cranwell	
R3	Schleicher ASK13	13599		RAFGSA Centre	Bicester	To BGA.4599
R4	Rolladen-Schneider LS-8-18	8169		Cranwell GC	Cranwell	
R5	Rolladen-Schneider LS-8-18	8130		Four Counties GC	Syerston	To BGA.4600
R6 *	Schempp-Hirth Discus B	175		Wrekin GC	Cosford	To BGA.4613
R7 *	Schleicher ASK13	13615		Clevelands GC	Dishforth	To BGA.4581
R8	Grob G.102 Astir CS	1379	OY-XGE	RAFGSA Centre	Bicester	
R9	Schempp-Hirth HS.6 Janus B	63	RAFGSA.16 BGA.2359			To BGA.2359
R9	Grob G.102 Astir CS	1123	RAFGSA R97 BGA.3216/D-6977	Four Counties GC	Syerston	To BGA.3216
R10 *	Schempp-Hirth Discus CS	193CS		RAFGSA Centre	Bicester	To BGA.4590
R12 *	Schempp-Hirth Discus B	151		Bannerdown GC	Keevil	To BGA.4579
R15 *	Schempp-Hirth Discus B	254		RAFGSA Centre	Bicester	To (BGA.4474), BGA.4623
R16	Schempp-Hirth Janus CE	21/299		RAFGSA Centre "16"	Bicester	To BGA.4472
R17 *	Schempp-Hirth Discus B	247		Clevelands GC	Dishforth	To BGA.4585
R18	Grob G.102 Astir	1487	RAFGGA.540 D-4791	Two Rivers GC	Laarbruch	
R19	Grob G.102 Astir	1429	RAFGGA.742 D-7425	Phoenix GC	Bruggen	
R20	Schleicher ASK21	21098		Bannerdown GC	Keevil	To BGA.4578
R21	Schleicher ASK21	21068		(Sold during 1998)		To BGA.4496
R21	Schleicher ASK21	21679		RAFGSA Centre	Bicester	To BGA.4572
R22	Schleicher ASK21	21039		(Sold during 1998)		To BGA.4500
R22	Schleicher ASK21	21681		RAFGSA Centre	Bicester	To BGA.4614
R23 *	Schempp-Hirth Discus B	241		RAFGSA Centre	Bicester	To BGA.4615
R24	Schempp-Hirth Ventus cT	170/560		(Sold during 1998)		To BGA.4483
R24	Schempp-Hirth Ventus cT	181/597	RAFGGA.557	Clevelands GC	Dishforth "24"	To BGA.4586
R25	Schleicher ASK21	21123		RAFGSA Centre	Bicester	To BGA.4587
R26	Schempp-Hirth Duo Discus	131		RAFGSA Centre	Bicester "26"	To BGA.4473
R27	Schempp-Hirth Discus CS	148CS		Chilterns GC	Halton	To BGA.4502
R28 *	Schempp-Hirth Ventus CT	147/456		Cranwell GC	Cranwell	To BGA.4484
R30	Schempp-Hirth Ventus CT	174/566		RAFGSA Centre	Bicester	To BGA.4571
R31	Schleicher ASK13	13609	BGA.2533	Fulmar GC	Kinloss	
R32	Schleicher ASK18	18002	RAFGSA.213 D-3978	Fulmar GC	Kinloss	
R33	Schleicher ASK18	18022	RAFGSA.223	Clevelands GC	Dishforth	To BGA.4582
R34	Schleicher ASK13	13542	F-CERF	Chilterns GC	Halton "34"	
R35	Schleicher ASK21	21148	ZD648	Cranwell GC	Cranwell	To BGA.2888
R36	Schleicher ASK18	18038	RAFGSA.236	Four Counties GC	Syerston	To BGA.4612
R37	Schleicher ASK13	13099	RAFGSA.378	Wrekin GC	Cosford	
R38	Schempp-Hirth Ventus CT	161/521		(Sold during 1988)		To BGA.4461
R39	Schempp-Hirth Discus CS	034CS		Cranwell GC	Cranwell	To BGA.4601
R40	Schleicher ASK13	13608	RAFGSA.R4	Cranwell GC	Cranwell	To BGA.4602
R41	Schleicher ASK13	13375	RAFGSA.241?	Chilterns GC Halton		
R42	Schleicher K8B	8854	RAFGSA.323	Anglia GC Wattisham		
R43	Schleicher ASK18	18021	RAFGSA.713 RAFGSA.113	RAFGSA Centre	Bicester	To BGA.4570
R44	Schleicher K8B	8923	RAFGSA.538 RAFGSA.R38/BGA.2931	Bannerdown GC	Keevil	
R45	Schleicher K8B	8916	RAFGSA.245	Chilterns GC	Halton	
R46	Schleicher ASK13	13616	RAFGSA.R16	Fenlands GC	Marham	To BGA.4620
R47	Schleicher K8B	8795	BGA.1564	Chilterns GC	Halton	
R48	Schleicher ASK18	18036	RAFGSA.448	RAFGSA Centre	Bicester	
	(Composite rebuild 1986/89 of crashed c/n 18036 plus another unknown)					
R49	Schleicher ASK18	18023	RAFGSA.318	Fenlands GC	Marham	To BGA.4621
R50	Grob G.103A Twin II Acro	33964-K-197		Fulmar GC	Kinloss	
R51	Schleicher ASK13	13656		Anglia GC	Wattisham	
	(C/n conflicts with JA2389; but is confirmed correct)					
R52	Grob G.103A Twin II Acro	34042-K-273		Clevelands GC	Dishforth	To BGA.4583
R53	Schempp-Hirth Discus CS	036CS		Chilterns GC	Halton	To BGA.4503
R55	Schempp-Hirth Discus CS	054CS		Fenlands GC	Marham	To BGA.4470
R57	Grob G.102 Astir CS	1509	RAFGSA.507	Cranwell GC	Cranwell	To BGA.4603

RAFGSA No.	Type	c/n	Previous identity	Operator	Probable Base	Notes
R58	Grob G.103A Twin II Acro		BGA.2873	Four Counties GC	Syerston	
		3787-K-65				
R60	Grob G.102 Astir CS77	1666	RAFGSA.560	Clevelands GC	Dishforth	To BGA.4584
R61	Schempp-Hirth Discus CS	192CS	RAFGSA.561			To BGA.4318
R63	Grob G.102 Astir CS77	1718	RAFGSA.883	Fenland GC	Marham	To BGA.4622
R67	Grob G.102 Astir CS77	1634	RAFGSA.547	Anglia GC	Wattisham	
R69	Rolladen-Schneider LS-6-18W		RAFGSA.553	Phoenix GC	Bruggen	
		6345	RAFGSA.R69/D-8037			
R70	Grob G.103A Twin II Acro		ZE525	Anglia GC	Wattisham	To BGA.3015
		33894-K-132	BGA.3015			
R71	Grob G.103A Twin II Acro		ZE612	Fenlands GC	Marham	
		33961-K-194	BGA.3064			
R73	Schleicher ASK21	21054	RAFGGA.513	RAFGSA Centre	Bicester	To BGA.4555
R75	Schleicher K8B	8950	RAFGSA.285	Cranwell GC	Cranwell	To BGA.4604
R77	Grob G.102 Astir CS	1133	D-4177	Wrekin GC	Cosford	
R80	Schleicher ASK13	13127	BGA.1509	Bannerdown GC	Keevil	
R83	Schleicher ASK13	13035	BGA.1427	Four Counties GC	Syerston	
R86	Scleicher ASK13	13312	RAFGSA.386	Fulmar GC	Kinloss	
R87 *	Schempp-Hirth Discus CS	033CS		RAFGSA Centre "87"	Bicester	To BGA.4608
R88	Schleicher ASK13	13312	RAFGSA.186	Wrekin GC	Cosford	
R90	Schleicher ASK13	13245	NEJSGSA.1	Crusaders GC	Kingsfield, Dhekelia	To BGA.4592
R91	Schleicher K8B	590	NEJSGSA	Crusaders GC	Kingsfield, Dhekelia	
			BGA.2619/D-5703			
R92	Slingsby T.21B	666	NEJSGSA.4	Crusaders GC	Kingsfield, Dhekelia	
			WG499			
R93	ICA-Brasov IS-28B	33	EI-141	Crusaders GC	Kingsfield, Dhekelia	To BGA.2207
			BGA.2207			
R95	Schleicher K8B	8778	RAFGSA.395	Wrekin GC	Cosford	
	(Composite with RAFGSA.R96 c/n 8806 ex RAFGSA.396; c/n officially quoted as 8878, but this is D-0848)					
R97	Grob G.102 Astir CS	1123	BGA.3216	Bannerdown GC	Keevil	
			D-6977		(Became R9)	
R98	Schleicher K8B	8880	RAFGSA.398	Fenlands GC	Marham	
R99	Slingsby T.45 Swallow	1387	NEJSGSA.3	Crusaders GC	Kingsfield, Dhekelia	
			XS651			

SECTION 3C - RAF GERMANY GLIDING ASSOCIATION REGISTER

The RAF Germany Gliding Association was disbanded and its constituent clubs incorporated into the RAFGSA at the end of March 1997. The majority of its fleet has now been identified by RAFGSA "R-numbers" and are included in the RAFGSA list above, with the exception of those shown below. Note that the former British Forces Germany Gliding Centre at Achmer (which has itself been disbanded) was jointly funded by the British Army, so that a number of the Centre's aircraft have joined Army GA clubs or retain Army identities with RAFGSA clubs. In 1998 it was decided that the separate service series would be discontinued and that BGA Numbers be used in future. The notes indicate that the process is well underway.

RAFGGA No.	Type	C/n	Previous identity	Operator	Probable Base	Notes
RAFGGA.312	Glaser-Dirks DG-300 Elan	?		Two Rivers GC	Laarbruch	Fate not known
RAFGGA.501	Schempp-Hirth Discus CS	075CS		Two Rivers GC	Laarbruch	Fate not known
	(RAFGGA No. conflicts with DCN/BGA.2010)					
RAFGGA.502	Scheibe L-Spatz 55	-		A.Taylor	RAF West Raynham	
	(Identity unconfirmed: ex RAF Bruggen)			(Stored 11.93)		
RAFGGA.509	Schleicher ASK13	13653		Phoenix GC	Bruggen	
RAFGGA.513	Schleicher ASK21	21054			Bicester	(Noted 7.98)
RAFGGA.514	Schleicher ASK21	21519				To BGA.4316
RAFGGA.515	Schleicher ASK21	21568				To BGA.4317
RAFGGA.521	Schleicher ASK21	21212		Phoenix GC	Bruggen	To BGA.4629
RAFGGA.540	Grob G.102 Astir CS	1487	D-4791	Two Rivers GC	Laarbruch	To RAFGSA.R18
RAFGGA.547 *	Schempp-Hirth Discus B	265	RAFGGA.500	Phoenix GC	Bruggen	To BGA.4535
RAFGGA.556	Grob G.103A Twin II Acro	?		Two Rivers GC	Laarbruch	
	(Type possibly a G.103 Twin Astir)					
RAFGGA.562	Schleicher K8B	?		Two Rivers GC	Laarbruch	Fate not known
RAFGGA.563	Schleicher ASK18	18027		Phoenix GC	Bruggen	
RAFGGA.567	Schleicher ASK13	13688AB		Two Rivers GC	Laarbruch	To BGA.4633
RAFGGA.591	Schleicher Ka.4 Rhonlerche II	D-0359		Museum of Flight/Royal Museum of Scotland		
		209	F-C...	(On display 3.96) East Fortune		

SECTION 3D - RN GLIDING & SOARING ASSOCIATION REGISTER

Until recently the RNGSA operated on a different basis to the RAFGSA & AGA in that their gliders came with the aegis of the BGA and held current certificates. The other service organisations are now adopting this procedure. In 1998 it was decided that the separate RNGSA series would be discontinued and that BGA Numbers be used in future. The notes indicate that the process is well underway.

There are three clubs in the RNGSA as follows:

1.   Portsmouth Naval Gliding Club, Lee-on-Solent

RNGSA.N11	Schleicher K8B	BGA.2142
N13	SZD-30 Pirat	BGA.2031
.N15	Schleicher K8B	BGA.3548
.N16	SZD-51-1 Junior	BGA.3657
.N19	Grob G.102 Astir CS	BGA.4132
.N21	Slingsby T.21B	BGA. 673
.N23	SZD-50-3 Puchacz	BGA.3772
.N25	Schleicher ASK-13	BGA.4598
.N26	Schleicher ASK13	BGA.4056
.N27	Schleicher Ka7 Rhonadler	BGA.1157
.N28	Schleicher ASK13	BGA.3482
.N29	Schleicher ASK13	BGA.3254
.N..	Schempp-Hirth Discus CS	BGA.4030 "805"

2.   Heron Gliding Club, RNAS Yeovilton

RNGSA.N31	Slingsby T.49B Capstan	BGA.1134	
.N34	Grob G.102 Astir CS77	BGA.2289	"480"
.N36	SZD-50-3 Puchacz	BGA.3864	"HDP"
.N..	Schleicher K8B	BGA.4148	

3.   Culdrose Gliding Club, RNAS Culdrose/Predannack

RNGSA.N51	Centrair 101A Pegase	BGA.2987	"70"
.N52	SZD-30 Pirat	BGA.1551	
.N53	SZD-50-3 Puchacz	BGA.3782	
.N54	Slingsby T.49B Capstan	BGA.1360	
.N55	Slingsby T.49B Capstan	BGA.1118	
.N56	SZD-51-1 Junior	BGA.3505	

SECTION 3E - ARMY GLIDING ASSOCIATION REGISTER

Although the AGA HQ is at Middle Wallop gliders are based at either Odiham or Upavon. The "A" tail codes which are sometimes carried do not always relate to the AGA number. In 1998 it was decided that the separate AGA series would be discontinued and that BGA Numbers be used in future. The notes indicate that the process is well underway.

AGA No.	Type	c/n	Previous identity	Operator	Probable Base	Notes
AGA. 1	Rolladen-Schneider LS-4	4256		Wyvern GC "412"	Upavon	To BGA.4595
AGA. 2	Rolladen-Schneider LS-4B	4997		Wyvern GC "A8"	Upavon	To BGA.4596
AGA. 3	Rolladen-Schneider LS-7	7112		Wyvern GC "12"	Upavon	To BGA.4597
AGA. 4	Schempp-Hirth Discus B	206		Wyvern GC "388"	Upavon	@
AGA. 5	SZD-51-1 Junior	B-1933	(BGA.3699)	Wyvern GC "A6"	Upavon	To BGA.4594
AGA. 6	Grob G.102 Astir CS	1332		Sold		To BGA.4314
AGA. 8	Schleicher ASK21	21067	BGA.2742	Wyvern GC "EKG"	Upavon	To BGA.2742
AGA.11	Schleicher ASK21	21182		Kestrel GC "A7"	Odiham	To BGA.4573
AGA.14	Schleicher ASK13	13150		Wyvern GC "A2"	Upavon	
AGA.15	Schleicher ASK13	13591	BGA.2385	Kestrel GC "A1"	Odiham	
AGA.18	Schleicher ASK23	23005		Kestrel GC "A5"	Odiham	
AGA.20	Schleicher ASK-21	21568	RAFGGA.515 BGA.4317	"A16"		To BGA.4317
AGA.21	Schleicher K-8B	558	RAFGGA.558	"A55"		To BGA.4525

@ AGA.4 was badly damaged after spinning-in nr Reading 14.5.95 and was rebuilt with new fuselage. The remains of AGA.4 were rebuilt with wings from Discus B c/n 561 as BGA.4270.

SECTION 3F - BGA COMPETITION NUMBERS

BGA Competition Numbers are issued to members/pilots and not to individual gliders. They change frequently. There is no formal list of Competition Numbers and little control over other gliders wearing similar or past numbers, or other (tail) codes - see SECTION 3G. The listing below is a composite based on BGA information and sightings. Competition Numbers marked with an * indicate where gliders have been noted with the numbers shown and that these have been alloted to persons other than the Competition Number owners. In some cases because joint (syndicate) ownership is common this means that the Competition Number belongs to a member of a syndicate other than the one whose name appears as owner in the BGA's records (!) The members name/glider type is shown where the glider concerned is not identified.

No.	Entry	No.	Entry	No.	Entry	No.	Entry	No.	Entry
1	1144*	56	4337	114	3791*	171	3643	227	(A.T.Farmer)
1	1804*	57	(J.M.Young)	115	3106	172	(G.D.Morris)	227	2337*
1	3123	57	4288*	116	1794	172	--	228	1047*
2	869*	58	4224*	116	2124	173	3607	228	--
2	2680	59	(B.T.Spreckley)	117	1386*	174	(C.B.Hogarth)	228	3549
2	2943*	60	G-BPMH*	117	2751	175	3124	229	1683
2	3382*	60	(S.H.Marriott)	118	2911	176	4413	230	3523
3	(J.D.Bally)	61	1262	119	(E.W.Richards)	177	(I.D.Wheway)	231	2918
3	1851*	62	1514	120	3197	177	1493*	232	3552*
4	G-STEN	63	(S.G.Olender)	121	1316	177	3126*	232	4437
5	1381	64	(C.P.Jeffery)	123	4370	178	3119	233	(J.A.Stephens)
6	(G.H.Herringshaw)	65	(A.K.Lincoln)	124	1530	179	--	233	2226*
6	2477*	66	4482	125	(S.R.Grzeskowiak)	180	(A.Jacobs)	234	1723
7	3224	67	1052	125	3317*	180	2901*	235	(D.Briggs)
8	3720	68	3361	126	3913	181	2827	236	3717
9	1317	69	(E.C.Wright)	127	3355	182	1293*	237	3967
10	1818	69	2595*	128	2071	182	1760	238	3411
11	(P.Potgeiter)	71	4050*	129	2635	183	3933	239	2862
11	1991	72	(S.Sturland)	130	3398	184	1660	240	1969
12	AGA.3	73	4092	131	(W.J.Dean)	185	2182*	241	1737*
13	3323	74	2224	132	2455	186	2744	241	4214
14	1958	75	4267	134	(A.D.W.Mattin)	187	3263	242	3417
15	(G.D.Ackroyd)	76	2721	134	3295*	188	2775	243	(J.A.McCoshim)
16	4472	77	1377	135	3994	189	2371	244	3738
17	2804	78	2345	136	793*	190	3401	245	2079*
18	1475	79	2528	136	3273	191	2436	245	3976
19	4123	80	3141	137	(S.J.Parsonage)	192	3533	246	3555
20	(J.S.Langberg)	81	(J.R.Upton)	137	3861*	193	2727	247	3604
20	2951*	81	2453*	138	2698	194	3544	248	1911
21	4611	82	3920	139	1726	195	2115	249	2950*
22	(T.S.Zealley)	83	1584*	140	(R.D.Payne)	196	2296*	250	4016
23	3965	83	3680	141	2625	196	3266	251	2216
24	RAFGSA.R24	84	4261	142	1629	197	(P.M.Jessop)	252	1624
25	3973	85	(D.J.Robertson)	143	3298	197	4178*	253	1840
26	RAFGSA R26	86	2310	144	3837	197	4222*	254	(D.A.Smith)
27	4502	87	RAFGSA.R87	145	2657	198	1015	255	1116
28	(D.S.McKay)	88	2974	146	1876	199	(J.P.C.Fuchs)	256	3540
29	(J.D.J.Glossop)	89	(J.A.K.Millar)	147	2466	200	4226	257	3303
30	2087	89	3209*	148	3683	201	(C.J.Lowrie)	258	(B.D.Bate)
31	4251	90	2981	150	1269*	201	3433*	258	2323*
32	3455	91	(R.K.Hendra)	151	1686	202	3107	259	2229
33	778	92	1839	152	2501	203	3991	260	4039
34	2397*	93	(K.A.Ford)	152	3321*	204	(M.A.Taylor)	261	2715
34	3629	93	3228*	153	1528	205	3506*	262	(D.Allison/LS.8)
35	3600	94	(S.A.White LS.7)	154	3279	206	3708	263	3777*
36	4409	94	3624*	155	(W.R.Davis)	207	1974	263	(R.N.Turner)
37	(S.P.Robertshaw)	95	1989	156	(J.M.Airey)	208	3641	264	2806
37	2556*	96	3807	157	2639	209	3204	265	(A.Brown)
38	(N.P.Marriott)	97	3955	158	1811*	210	4244	265	2243*
38	4047*	98	2692*	158	2869*	211	(G.A.Childs)	266	2200
39	3427	99	4157*	158	3373	211	1222*	267	2464
40	(B.Fitchett)	100	3962	159	(I.Johnston)	212	2155*	268	(G.K.Payne)
40	1788*	101	1988	160	2461	213	(K.S.Matcham)	268	3475*
41	(R.Rutherford)	102	2494	161	(J.A.McCoshim)	214	(N.S.Jones)	269	1853
42	4478	103	(C.J.Mayhew)	161	929*	215	(M.H.Jones & Ptnrs)	270	2346
43	(R.M.Grant)	104	3389	162	(B.H.Owen)	215	2937*	271	1513*
44	(T.B.Sargeant)	105	4078	162	3501*	216	(K.G.Laws)	271	3101
45	3574	106	2513	163	(C.R.Dearman)	216	4326*	272	2426
46	2458	107	(G.O.Avis)	163	1089*	217	2960*	273	(J.H.Fox)
47	(M.T. Stanley)	107	2524*	163	1299*	218	2794*	274	4467
47	1435*	108	3606	164	2088	218	3707	275	2856
48	3463*	109	3395	165	(D.N.Greig)	219	(C.J.Ireland)	276	(C.D.Lovell)
48	4079	110	3244*	165	1648*	219	3770*	277	3587
49	1797	111	(T.A.Joint)	166	(K.Kiely)	221	(P.J.Stratten)	278	3789
50	2632	111	G-BPIN*	167	3972*	222	1579	280	(M.Strathern)
51	(P.S.Hawkins)	112	4344	167	4072	223	2936	280	3663*
52	(Army GA)	112	G-SOOM*	168	4273	224	3627	281	2812
53	1763	113	(R.F.Whittaker)	169	(C.Buzzard)	225	1336	282	(K J Kingsland)
54	(R.Jones)	113	3158*	170	3472*	226	1662	282	3397*
55	2801	114	(A.R.Hughes)	170	4216			283	(D.J.Maynard)
								283	2880*

284	1632	357	1568*	430	2756	505	(R.W.Harding)	573	2499*
285	3599	357	3372*	431	2702	505	3975*	574	3424
286	2469	358	(J.Sleigh-Ives)	432	(A.R.Hutchins)	506	RAFGSA.506	575	(P.P.Brightman)
287	2268	359	4041	433	(W.P.Grundy)	507	(B.van Woereden)	576	2504
288	2808	360	2180	434	4428	507	3719*	577	(D.L.Jones)
289	3902	361	(J.F.Beringer)	434	G-OAPW*	508	1890	577	1546*
290	3713	362	1362	435	2826	509	(D.E.Kearns)	579	1785
291	3868	362	1420*	436	(C.P.Long)	509	3924*	580	2473
292	(A.S.Edlin)	363	1854	437	(W.A.Coates)	510	3171	581	(P.S.Worth)
293	(D.E.Lamb)	364	4051	437	2271*	511	(J.C.Ennis)	584	4249
294	(S.C.Foggin)	365	4019	438	3723	511	2228*	585	4082
294	3751*	366	1240	439	3121	512	(A.K.Mitchell)	586	2644
295	(R.M.Hitchin)	367	2522	440	2282*	513	(D.B.Almey)	588	2239
296	3226	368	1220*	442	(M.D'Otreppe)	514	(I.P.Freestone)	590	2924
297	2650	369	3559	442	1672*	515	2788	591	3854
298	(M.B.Hill)	370	3206	443	2968	517	1298	592	2481
299	1913	371	2235*	444	2175	517	2123*	593	(M.Hajukewicz)
300	(A.D.Evans)	371	3381	445	4043	518	(T.Busby)	593	2222*
301	3803	372	1393	446	2959	518	3512*	594	2529
302	3689	373	1428	447	(S.E.Evans)	519	(A.F.Brind)	595	(J.W.Bennett)
303	(S.G.Olender)	374	(A.D.Hyslop)	447	2343*	519	3375*	596	2195
303	1470*	375	2283	448	2605	520	3651	597	1198
304	4230	376	4324	449	1538	521	1696*	598	4263*
306	3981	377	(F.B.Jeynes)	450	3747*	522	3814	599	4068
307	2251	377	1290*	450	(A.Clark)	523	1983*	600	(A.C.Robertson)
308	3877	378	2196	451	(D.N.Griffiths)	524	3762	600	25898
309	(G.F.Fisher)	379	2906	451	2870*	525	(J.Fisher)	601	(J.D.Spencer)
309	1533*	380	(P.J.Kite)	452	2789	525	1669*	601	1714*
310	(S.Sheard)	380	1817*	453	1368*	526	(N.Crawshaw)	602	1657
310	1207*	380	4054*	453	2694	526	1962*	604	2585
311	1359	381	4032	454	(B.H.Owen)	526	4270*	605	3820
312	2939	382	2979*	454	--	527	(P.Shrosbree)	606	2802
313	4170	385	4168	456	2212*	527	1772*	607	3898
314	(Booker GC)	386	G-ORIG	456	2634	527	3261*	608	(D.S.Taylor)
315	4066	387	1769*	457	(G.B.Hibberd)	528	4484	609	3465
316	3879	388	AGA.4	458	1487	529	(J.A.Tanner)	610	2114
318	3198	389	(D.Peters)	459	3415	530	(A.A.A.Maitland)	611	(R.S.Johns)
319	2728	390	4134	460	(N Wales GC)	530	2597*	611	3889*
320	2378	391	2184*	461	3388	531	2491	612	3542
320	2788*	391	3785	462	4021	532	1889	614	2162
321	4232	392	2231	463	1201*	533	2353	615	2411*
322	1860	393	4238	464	3133	535	1628	616	4414
323	2837	394	3842	465	1288	536	(M.D.White)	617	1986
324	2000	395	3139	466	1688	536	2041*	618	3577
325	(P.F.Bryce)	396	(Surrey & Hants GC)	467	(R.Starmer)	537	2490*	619	(A.A.Jenkins)
325	4296*	397	3538	467	3866*	537	4379	619	1436*
326	3631	398	3192	468	1858	538	3199	619	1456*
327	1043	399	3322	469	4060	540	3733	620	4113
328	(J.T.Phillips)	400	(R.L.McLean)	469	4101*	541	2611	621	3984
329	4128	401	1795	470	2640	542	2294	622	1671
330	3294	402	1799	471	1369	543	(D.C.Phillips)	623	3223
331	1813	403	(J.A.Ayers)	472	(C.J.Davies)	543	2649*	624	4213
332	3516	403	G-BSOM*	474	1574	544	1885*	625	(S.R.Watson)
333	3115	404	1268	475	1423*	544	G-BVOT	625	1684*
334	2327	405	3500	475	3886	545	(C.V.J.Heames)	626	2821
335	(M.P.Brooks)	406	1361*	476	4345	545	3419*	628	(D.Williams)
335	3892*	406	3320	477	1916	545	3739*	628	1668*
336	(A.B.Adams)	407	2153	478	(P.McLean)	546	3739*	629	(B.A.Jones)
337	1543*	408	2754	479	3443	547	4535	630	3706
338	(S.M.Turner)	410	4165	480	2289*	549	867	633	(R.J.Large)
339	1722	411	3154	481	2707	550	1818	633	1821*
340	2868	412	AGA.1	483	(K.S.Whiteley)	551	1987	634	3462
341	(C.J.Cornish)	413	2711	483	2452*	552	1709*	636	(R.A.Holroyd)
342	1732	414	3339	484	3448	552	2553	636	2656
342	2540*	415	1945	485	2206*	553	(Phoenix GC)	637	(J.Dalrymple-Smith)
343	1412	416	(H.T.Morris)	486	3895	555	(R.S.Maxwell-Fendt)	637	3917*
345	2820	417	1756	487	4130	556	2300	638	2396
346	(G.G.Pursey)	418	(J.C.M.Docherty)	488	3136	557	(RAFGSA)	639	2497*
346	1562*	418	1524*	490	2697	558	(M.J.Friend)	640	2907
346	3831*	419	(M.L.Boxall)	491	2980	560	4291	642	(W.J.Tolley)
347	1765	420	(G.E.McAndrew)	492	(A.W.White)	562	2057	644	2565
348	3170	421	G-BNCN	492	G-BRRG*	563	4062	645	(D.G.Tanner)
350	1348	422	1392	493	4169*	564	3207	645	2580*
351	1741	423	1850	494	4553	565	4040	646	3109
352	(L.S.Hood)	424	(K.M.Davis)	495	3470	566	1748	647	2038*
352	1331*	424	1284*	496	3808	567	3596	647	2592
353	2186	425	3899*	498	3479	568	2301*	647	2850*
354	2472	425	3714	499	(D.P.Taylor)	569	2673	648	2340
355	1852*	426	(J.E.Evason)	500	(J.S.Halford)	570	4455	649	3711*
355	3834	427	(G.B.Brown)	501	(A.B.Dickinson)	571	1127*	650	1743
356	2003*	428	--	501	1802*	571	3151	652	(M.A.Fellis)
356	3805	428	1844	502	3946	572	(I.F.Smith)	652	2402*
357	(M.P.Brooks)	429	(C.M.Elsden)	503	1902	572	2287*	653	1104
357	1397*	429	3780*	504	1936	573	(J.M.Anderson)	654	(R.Strange)

655 4095	734 (F.G.Bradney)	810 2423*	896 3760	971 2417
656 1836*	735 3887	811 (M.C.Burlock)	898 (I.W.Paterson)	972 2350
656 3445	737 2645	811 2119*	899 2081*	973 (P.H.Rackham)
658 ZD658 "YX"	739 1088	812 1391	900 1949*	973 3410*
659 ZD659 "YY"	740 3935	814 1476	900 4200	974 ZD974 "SY"
660 (R.G.Tomlinson)	741 1121	815 2457	901 (C.D.Stainer)	975 ZD975 "SZ"
660 3554*	742 2841*	818 1685	902 3714*	976 (P.L.Bisgood)
662 (P.C.Gill)	742 (E.K.Stephenson)	818 1842*	902 2825	977 2068*
662 3588*	742 4471*	819 4029	903 (R.A.Johnson)	977 3961
663 663*	743 1615	820 (S.M.Hall)	904 (T.T.Caswell)	978 1871
664 (R.A.Johnson)	744 3291	820 2604*	904 2309*	979 3959
664 3824	745 2246	821 2321	905 1419	980 (A.G.Kefford)
665 (J.B.Dalton)	746 3963	822 3120	906 2084*	980 3585*
666 3800	747 3910	823 2129*	906 2853	982 1915
667 (T.J.Scott)	748 (J.Hodgkinson)	823 4362	907 4425	983 2902
668 3750	748 3731*	824 2129	908 3737	983 3357*
669 3645	750 2596	825 (Essex & Suffolk GC)	909 2502	985 (S.E.Crozier)
670 (D.J.Hill/Ventus)	753 3525	826 (P.F.Croote)	910 3856	986 1655
671 3152	754 3827	827 3821	911 2382	987 3227*
672 2672	755 2438*	828 2479	911 4400	987 3271*
673 (D.W.Lilburn)	757 2518	829 3822	912 (F.B.Reilly)	988 3457
674 3400	758 (J.Nash)	830 916	913 1536	989 2164
675 1961	758 3456*	831 2214*	913 4304*	990 2508
676 3698	759 2168	832 1875	914 (J.Archer)	991 3858
677 (K.Fairness)	760 985*	833 4202	915 2370	992 2961
678 (H.M.Pantin)	760 2366	837 1247	916 (P.I.Fenner)	993 3148
679 1401	760 3565*	838 3956	916 4356*	994 1380
680 2037	761 1706	839 2515	917 (A.I.Galbraith)	995 3468
681 (M.P.Weaver)	762 4117	840 (S.J.Ayres)	917 1869*	996 3180
682 2990	764 (J.F.Morris)	840 3878*	918 1725	997 3304
683 1454	764 1570*	841 3146	919 4004	998 (A.J.Clarke)
684 (S.C.Fear)	765 2848	842 1822	920 (K.Neave)	998 1857*
685 4450	766 2379	843 3704	920 3155*	
686 (S.J.Jenkins)	767 2090	844 2684*	921 4355	
686 1312*	768 3590	845 3730*	922 3710	
687 3883	769 (M.Tolson)	846 1562	924 1798	
688 (L.Dent)	769 2172*	847 4262	925 (G.Douglas)	
688 2326*	770 2291	848 2286*	925 3909*	
690 3709	771 (C.E.Wick)	848 4103	927 (T.J.Stanlry)	
691 1982	771 2816*	849 2706	927 3363*	
692 4080	772 3441	850 2480	928 (G.Metcalfe)	
693 4106	773 3134	851 1976	928 3767*	
695 2025	774 2092	853 3515	929 G-MOAK	
696 (E.R.Walker)	775 4252	854 2899	930 4240	
696 2778*	776 (N.J.Leaton)	855 3964	931 (R.J.Fox)	
698 3283	777 (C.Paylor)	856 (Vale of White	931 2766*	
699 2357*	777 4359*	Horse GC)	932 4136*	
700 (S.J.McNeil)	778 3673	857 (M.Uphill)	933 4164	
701 3259	779 3621	858 1689*	935 (G.W.Lynch)	
702 1400	780 (D.Latimer)	858 (D.Heslop)	937 (J.Williams)	
703 1727	781 (D.J.Langrick)	859 1136*	937 1637*	
704 2376	781 1308*	861 1295	939 2647	
705 3393	781 3453*	861 4069*	940 3921	
706 1816	781 4625	862 1519	941 (R.J.Smith)	
707 (G.J.Lyons)	782 (B.R.Bartlett)	864 (J.C.Rogers)	941 4046*	
707 1752*	783 3944	865 3993*	942 (C.C.Lyttelton)	
708 (R.G.Green)	784 (P.M.Shelton)	866 (H.S.Franks)	942 3623*	
708 4065*	785 (P.Studer)	867 (F.G.Wilson)	943 2495	
709 1670	786 2537	868 (D.F.Teasdel)	943 2941*	
710 2737*	787 (C.J.Bailey)	869 2412	944 3522	
710 4392	788 2181	870 3904	948 1630	
711 (M.Chant)	789 (S.J.Wright)	871 3236	949 (G.J.Lyons)	
711 3578*	789 1088*	873 (S.J.Chalmers)	949 3809*	
712 4258	789 1733*	873 1801*	950 3302	
713 3306	790 3103*	875 (R.B.Christy)	951 (D.Hatton)	
714 2743	790 4576	876 (See Note)	951 2137*	
715 1383	791 1886	877 2354*	952 (D.W.Smith)	
716 2059	795 3882*	877 (R.Grundy)	952 3437*	
717 4088	797 2764	878 1433	954 (J.W.Hoskins)	
718 2352*	798 (P.A.Brooks)	879 2408	954 3610*	
719 2783	798 2329*	880 4225	955 2584	
720 3702	799 1640*	881 2545	957 2505	
721 3156	800 G-LEES	882 3870	959 2033	
723 3618	801 3757	883 G-ORTM	960 3611	
724 1616	802 4151	884 2174	961 1598	
725 3686	803 3535	885 2401*	962 4235	
727 3130	804 2785*	886 2445	963 3954	
728 (D.S.Jones)	805 4030	887 3349	964 3483*	
728 2444*	806 3257	888 3575	966 (G.Martin)	
728 3308*	807 (D.O.Sephton)	890 2729	968 (R.Grey)	
729 3801	807 2555*	891 2691	968 2864*	
730 3939	808 1775*	893 2345	969 3365	
732 2413	809 1123*	895 (D.A.Asquith)	970 (P.Harper-Little)	
733 2429	810 (G.J.Hinder)	895 4175*	970 4008*	

SECTION 3G - ALPHA/NUMERIC TAILCODES

Code	Ref	Code	Ref	Code	Ref	Code	Ref	Code	Ref
2B	4374	CKF	3371*	H5	4399*	N27	1157	S5	4299
2F	4427	C1	(J.B.Christey)	H6	3478	N31	1134	S6	4469
2UP	(R.A.Walker)	C3	(P.A.Chapman)	H11	(J.D.Hill)	N52	1551	S7	2943
2UP	4081*	C4	4186	H11	2552*	N54	1360	S8	4223
7D	3167*	C7	4404	H12	3732	OP8	(S.C.Thompson)	S13	2425
7H	4377	C8	(C.Bradley)	H17	490	OZ	4458	S14	1572
7Q	4364*	C29	(C.R.Greengrass)	H20	(J.L.Whiting)	PH1	4577	S19	4580
17K	1720	C29	4012*	H23	1189	PM	3816	S21	4383
20L	2740	C34	3997	IM	(E.J.Rogers)	PN	(P.C.Naegli)	S22	4191
B	1031*	C64	4193	IM	4415*	PS	3571	S30	2380
B	3366	C65	4245*	JA	4016	PW5	4311	S32	(M.P.Wakem)
B	3446*	CB	(J.P.Ben-David)	JD	1483	P1	(R.J.Large)	S70	(S.Edwards)
C	2191	CC	(B.T.Spreckley)	JH	4459	P2	(P.O.Paterson)	S82	4045
D	2317	CL	(C.L.Lyttleton)	J01	(N.Braithwaite)	P2	4442*	S83	4268
E	285*	CU	(Camb Univ GC)	JPB	3458*	P3	4363*	TE	4180
F	400*	CW	(C.C.Watt)	JS1	4325	P4	(P.Onn)	TJ	4443*
G	698*	CZ	(D.H.Conway)	J2	(D.Chalmers-	P5	(G.Bird)	T1	G-OPHT
H	2984	DC	(D.Coppin)		Brown)	P5	3826*	T2	(T.W.Slater)
K	2989	DC	4405	J3	3632	P5	4152*	T3	4328
L	3163	DD	4300	J4	(P.G.Sheard)	P9	2443	T5	4301
M	3205	DJT	4271*	KE	4451	P31	4017	T7	4466*
P	3274	DJ2	3353*	KL	(D.J.Knowles)	P61	4343	T10	2845
P	3450*	DV8	(P.E.Thelwall)	KL	3960*	Q5	3278	T15	1693
S	3642	DW	4465	KM	4305	RP1	4233	T21	948
Z	1873	DY	4054*	KR	(S.G.Back)	RW	(J.E.C.White)	T27	(P.C.Jarvis)
AB	4387	D1	3185	KW	(A.Jelden)	RY	4084	T30	625
A1	4155	D2	(I.D.Smith)	KW	4426	R1	4475	T34	2397*
A1	AGA.15*	D3	2667	K1	4340	R2	)	T34	(E.T.Murphy)
A2	AGA.14*	D4	(D.J.Westwood)	K2	2147	R3	)	T42	(S.Rogers)
A2	3872	D4	4444*	K4	4310	R4	) RAFGSA	T42	614
A3	1943*	D7	4262	K5	4338	R5	) Centre	T45	873
A5	AGA.18	D15	4158	K7	3682*	R6	)	T49	1203
A6	2929*	D19	4048	K8	(K.W.Payne)	R8	)	T51	1164
A6	AGA.5	D31	4210	K11	(D.Wilson)	R9	)	T54	3756
A7	AGA.11	D41	(J.McLaughlan)	K13	3656	R10)		T65	2800
A8	AGA.2	D42	4464	K21	(N.Wall)	R12)		UIM	4037*
A9	3885	D49	1734	LD	4347	R15	4474	U1	4335
A10	3622	D64	4121	LE5	(L.Clark)	R16	4472*	U2	2255*
A14	4316	D70	4146	LH7	4386	R17)	RAFGSA	U2	4131
A15	4177	ED	3752*	LS	4189	R18)	Centre	U9	4378
A16	4317	EN	4346	LS4	2908	R19)		VB	4334
A17	4173	ET	(P.N.Tolson)	LS4	4293*	R21	4496	VMC	4182*
A19	3390	EU	(J.Lee)	LS6	4119	R22	4500*	VS	2420*
A20	(P.Stammell)	EW	(K.R.Walton)	LS8	4237	R23	RAFGSA Centre	V1	4546
A20	4112*	EZ	4424	LT	4358	R24	4483*	V2	(S.G.Jones)
A25	(G.W.Lynch)	E1	4195	LX	4376	R25	RAFGSA Centre	V2T	(P.A.Hearne)
A25	3341*	E2	(R.A.Cheetham)	L1	(R.M.Davies)	R26	4473*	V3	(P.G.Sheard)
A26	4322	E8	4505	L3	4381	R27	4502*	V4	4460
A27	4422	E11	2705	L4	(A.J.Limb)	R28		V7	2695*
A29	3581*	E60	(I.Dunkley)	L5	3671	R30		V7	(J.A.White)
A30	2126	FFK	4149*	L8	4153	R38		V8	4034
A34	4531	FK	(B.T.Spreckley)	L01	2770	R39	RAFGSA Centre	V11	4292
A55	AGA.21	FTI	3511*	L12	3611	R43	4530*	V19	4058
A61	4318	F1	(A.J.Clarke)	L13	3660	R53	4503	V57	4353
A71	(P.N.Tolson)	F1	4452*	L17	(A.Pozerskis)	R55	4470	W1	3874
A77	4125	F2	(D.P.Francis)	L18	4253	R57)		WA1	(Scottish Gliding
A98	3438	F2	3918*	L57	3454	R60)	RAFGSA		Union)
AV8	(M.Wright)	F3	4418	L58	4192	R67)	Centre	W2	4454
BB	3532	F4	1367	L77	(A.A.Darlington)	R69)		W8	(R.J.Welford)
BR	2487*	F11	3489	L88	(P J Howard)	R70	3015	W19	4410
BT	(J.A.Horne)	F15	(I.Mountain)	L99	1438*	R73)		W22	3184
BW	4563	GR	4420	MD	3704*	R77)	RAFGSA	W27	4407
BZ	1834	G1	(G.F.Reid)	M1	4266*	R90)	Centre	W54	4231
B1	1500*	G2	3315	M2	4449	R92	2207*	XY	(See Notes)
B1	(M.Griffiths)	G3	(I.D.Smith)	M3	1035*	R97	RAFGSA Centre	X1	4508
B2	4385	G7	4329	M4	4368	SA1	2986	X7	4330
B2	(I.C.Baker)	G41	4539	M5	3638*	SA2	(Southdown AS)	X16	(A.S.Edlin)
B3	(R.F.Thirkell)	G46	698	M8	4278	SB8	(J.E.Bowman)	X16	3988*
B3	4373*	G81	4380	N2	3159	SK1	4429	X32	(A.J.O'Regan)
B4	(N.A.Scully)	HB	(The Soaring	N2	3420*	SR	4430*	X50	4341
B9	3986		Centre)	N4	1914	SSC	3909*	X70	(R.S.Lee)
B11	4342	HCN	3847*	N5	4207	SY	ZD974	X96	(M.B.Delaney)
B21	3357	HF5	(H.Smith)	N6	(S.Edlin)	SZ	ZD975	X96	2414*
B33	4147	HH5	(D.L.Jobbins)	N8	4352	S1	(S.J.Harland)	Y1	3416
B35	3728*	HL	4390	N11	2142	S1	3802*	Y4	4280
B38	3593	H2	(P.J.Harvey)	N13	2031	S2	4118	ZC	4256
B39	3891	H4	3222	N21	(K.W.Morton)	S3	3580	Z1	3727*
B96	1283	H5	3285	N25	4598	S4	4293	Z1	3978*

```
Z1    4557
Z2    (P.M.Wells)
Z3    (P.M.Wells)
Z4    3340
Z5    (E.W.Johnston)
Z6    (A J.Preston)
Z6    3654*
Z7    3640
Z8    4190
Z9    (A.Hegner)
Z10   (G.A.Marshall)
Z11   1374
Z12   (I.N.Lingham)
Z25   2427
Z29   (M.H.Hardwick)
```

NOTE: Codes "SY" to "ZZ" are allocated to the Air Cadets Central Gliding School.

There remain a few gliders which wear their foreign identities without the nationality mark, namely:

CCZV	4052	7151	3582
1128	2709	7827	4161
1545	2478	8527	2594
3354	3354		

Some imported, or ex British civil, gliders still carry their previous marks. Known examples include:-

G-ALLF	599	TS291	852
G-ALRD	416	VM637	895
G-ALRH	629	VM687	794
G-ALRK	490	WB920	3221
G-APWL	1172	WB922	4366
G-ATRA	1325	WB924	3901
G-BGBV	2800	WB926	3520
D-0060	3742	WB943	2941
D-1221	2757	WB962	3836
D-1868	3285	WB971	3324
D-2009	4302	WB975	3288
D-4667	3142	WB981	1218
D-5084	2688	WE992	2692
D-5826	3186	WG498	3245
D-6173	4336	WT871	3149
D-6508	4182	WT898	4412
D-8006	(See Note)	WT903	3299
D-8538	2292	WT908	3487
D-9421	3442	WT910	3953
D-3-340	(See Note)	WZ819	3498
D-11-3224	1147	WZ828	4421
G285	285	XA302	3786
HB-474	2474	XE807	3545
N47247	1904	XN157	3255
OE-0324	2903	XN185	4077
OK-0927	4286	XN187	3903
OK-8592	655	XN243	3145
Fv.8306	1297	XP463	4372
		XS652	1107

NOTES:

D-8006, a Grunau Baby II, coded "XY", was seen dismantled 4.87 & 9.88 at Bidford, the VAC Rally, Lasham 8.94 & Membury 10.94. The BGA number, if allocated, is not known.

"D-3-340", a Grunau Baby was on display at Kent Battle of Britain Museum, Hawkinge 3.96. No identity is known.

BGA.876 Slingsby T.34A Sky 1 c/n 672 ex XA876/G-672; damaged Lasham 1983 & was on rebuild Lasham 8.94 & 5.95.

FDM An unidentified glider reported at Weston-on-the-Green 8.97.

SECTION 3H - IRISH GLIDING ASSOCIATION REGISTER

The system is similar to the British Glider Association with the register maintained by the Irish Gliding Association. The IGA listing has been updated from Air-Britain sources but the C of A status is at 31 January 1997.

Regn	Type	C/n	P/I		Owner/operator	Probable Base	CA Expy
IGA.6*	Slingsby T.8 Tutor	-	IAC.6 VM657	.56	Eyre Square Shopping Centre	Galway City	
EI-100	SZD-12A Mucha 100A	494	OY-XAN	.95	J.Finnan & M.O'Reilly	Gowran Grange	1. 7.97
EI-102	Slingsby T.26 Kite 2	?	IGA.102 IAC.102/BGA...	.54	Dublin GC (Stored 1.97)	Gowran Grange	--
EI-105	Schleicher Ka7 Rhonadler	775	IGA.7	.60	Dublin GC	Gowran Grange	14. 6.97
EI-108	Schleicher K8B (Logbook shows c/n 8468)	8486		.65	Dublin GC "08"	Gowran Grange	13. 4.97
EI-111	Schleicher Ka6CR	6565		.67	(Private) "11"	Gowran Grange	30. 3.97
EI-112	Schleicher ASK13	13131		.69	Dublin GC	Gowran Grange	9. 3.97
EI-113	Schleicher ASK13	13189		.69	Clonmel GC	Kilkenny	17. 7.97
EI-114	Schleicher ASK14	14008	EI-APS G-AWVV/D-KOBB	.69	SLG Grp (Not Used; see EI-APS)	Gowran Grange	
EI-115	EoN AP.5 Olympia 2B	EoN/O/155	BGA.1097		Dublin GC (On rebuild 4.96)	Gowran Grange	
EI-118	EoN AP.8 Baby	EoN/B/001	BGA.608 RAFGSA.217/BGA.608/G-ALLU/BGA.608	.73	B.Douglas (Stored 6.95)	Gowran Grange	
EI-119	Schleicher ASK16	16022	EI-AYR	.	(Not used)		
EI-120	LET L-13 Blanik	175205	RAFGSA BGA.1730	.75	Private Syndiate	Gowran Grange	
EI-121	Pilatus B4 PC11AF	199		.77	Clonmel GC (Stored 6.95)	Kilkenny	
EI-124	Grob G.102 Astir Standard CS 77	1761	D-....	.80	Nutgrove Shopping Centre Churchtown, Dublin		
EI-127	Schleicher Ka6CR	662	PH-259	.	(Current 1993)		
EI-128	Schleicher Ka6CR	6649	???	.	Dublin GC (On rebuild 4.96)	Gowran Grange	
EI-130	Scheibe L-Spatz	200	BGA.2199 D-4707	.	J.J.Sullivan "White Cloud"	Gowran Grange	
EI-132	Schleicher ASW17	17031	D-2365	.	(Private) "TK"	Gowran Grange	17. 6.97
EI-133	Schleicher K8B	8557	D-8517 D-9367	.91	Dublin GC "33"	Gowran Grange	14. 6.97
EI-134	Schleicher ASW15B	15249	D-1087	.91	(Private) "34"	Gowran Grange	7. 5.97
EI-135	Slingsby T.38 Grasshopper	758	WZ762	.91	(Syndicate) (Wings from WZ756 or WZ768; stored as "WZ762" 4.96)	Gowran Grange	
EI-136	Schleicher ASK18	18007	BGA.2945 D-6868	.91	Dublin GC	Gowran Grange	30. 7.97
EI-137	Rolladen-Schneider LS3-17	3308	D-3521	.92	(Private)	Gowran Grange	1. 3.97
EI-138	Schempp-Hirth Discus CS	089CS		.92	B.Ramseyer "BR"	Gowran Grange	
EI-139	Slingsby T.31B	902	BGA.3485 G-BOKG/XE789	.93	P.Bedford Syndicate	Gowran Grange	2. 8.97
EI-140	SZD-12A Mucha 100A	491	HB-647	.93	D.Mongey	Gowran Grange	
EI-142	Scheibe SF-27A Zugvogel V	6049	(EI-144) D-1444	.94	Not known	Gowran Grange	19. 7.97
EI-143	Schleicher ASK13	13112	BGA.1501	.94	Dublin GC	Gowran Grange	
EI-144	Scheibe SF-27A Zugvogel V	6049	(EI-142) D-1444	.94R	(NTU - to EI-142)		
EI-145	Glaser-Dirks DG-200	2-88	PH-930 D-7610	.95		Gowran Grange	17. 2.97
EI-146	Scheibe SF-27 Zugvogel IIIB	1085	D-4096	.96	N Short & T Daly "TK"	Gowran Grange	17. 5.97
EI-147	Glaser-Dirks DG-200	2-22	D-6780	.97		Gowran Grange	

SECTION 4A BRITISH AIRCRAFT PRESERVATION COUNCIL REGISTER

We continue to update the register of the British Aircraft Preservation Council (BAPC), devised in 1967 to give an identity to the numerous anonymous aircraft held by various public and private collections. The scope has been extended to identify static and taxiable reproductions, film extras and "plastic" display pieces. All Museum exhibits are on display. As usual our thanks to Ken Ellis, the official keeper of the Register, for most of the information presented hereunder with the latest updates taken from Ken's excellent 1998 edition of "Wrecks & Relics No.16".

BAPC No.	Identity carried	Type	C/n	P/I	Owner	Probable Base
1					See G-ARSG in SECTION 1	
2					See G-ASPP in SECTION 1	
3					See G-AANG in SECTION 1	
4					See G-AANH in SECTION 1	
5					See G-AANI in SECTION 1	
6	14	Roe Triplane Type IV rep (JAP 9hp)			The Aeroplane Collection Ltd (On loan to Manchester Museum of Science & Industry) "Bullseye Avroplane"	Manchester
7		Southampton University Manpowered Aircraft ("Sumpac")			Southampton Hall of Aviation	Southampton
8		Dixon Ornithopter			The Shuttleworth Collection (Stored 1.90)	Old Warden
9		Bleriot XI Monoplane rep (Humber) (Conv to 1911 Humber Bleriot Monoplane; assembled from some original parts Old Warden 1959)			The Midland Air Museum	Coventry
10		Hafner R.II Revoplane (Salmson 45hp)			Mrs E.Hafner (On loan to Museum of Army Flying)	AAC Middle Wallop
11					See G-EBNV in SECTION 1	
12		Mignet HM.14 Pou-Du-Ciel (Scott A2S)			The Aeroplane Collection (On loan to Manchester Museum of Science & Industry)	Manchester
13	BAPC 13	Mignet HM.14 Pou-Du-Ciel (Douglas 600cc)			Brimpex Metal Treatments Ltd (Under restoration 3.96)	(Sheffield)
14		Addyman Standard Training Glider			A.Lindsay & N.H.Ponsford (Stored 3.98)	(Selby)
15		Addyman Standard Training Glider (Yorkshire Aeroplanes rebuild)	YA2		N.H.Ponsford (Stored 3.98)	Wigan
16		Addyman Ultralight			A.Lindsay & N.H.Ponsford (Stored incomplete 3.98)	(Selby)
17		Woodhams Sprite (Project active 1960/65 but not completed)			BB Aviation (Stored 3.98)	Canterbury
18		Killick Gyroplane			A.Lindsay & N.H.Ponsford (Stored by The Aeroplane Collection Ltd 3.98)	(Selby)
19	B4	Bristol F2B Fighter (Rebuilt to static condition by Skysport Engineering 6.89 with parts from J8264)			Musee Royal De L'Armee (As "66" in Belgian AF c/s)	Brussels, Belgium
20		Lee Richards Annular Biplane rep ("Those Magnificent Men in Their Flying Machines"film)			Newark Air Museum (Stored 3.98)	Winthorpe
21		Thruxton Jackaroo (Used as spares in rebuild of G-APAL; status unknown)			M.J.Brett	??
22	"G-AEOF"	Mignet HM.14 Pou-Du-Ciel (Scott A2S) (Fictitious registration adopted in 1964; loaned to Aviodome and stored 1992)	WM.1		R.R.Mitchell	Schiphol, Netherlands
23		Allocation cancelled - originally used by half scale SE.5 rep at Newark Air Museum				
24		Allocation cancelled - originally used by 2/3 scale Currie Wot rep at Newark Air Museum				
25		Nyborg TGN.III Sailplane			Paul Williams (On rebuild 1.92)	Warwick
26		Auster AOP.6 - fuselage frame only since scrapped Swansea				
27		Mignet HM.14 Pou-Du-Ciel			M J Abbey (Under construction 1988)	
28		Wright Flyer rep			Leeds Corn Exchange	Leeds
29	"G-ADRY"	Mignet HM.14 Pou-Du-Ciel (Anzani "V") (Built by P.D.Roberts, Swansea 1960/78)			Brooklands Museum	Brooklands
30		DFS Grunau Baby			Destroyed by fire Swansea 1969	
31		Slingsby T.7 Tutor			Status unknown - believed scrapped Swansea	
32		Crossley Tom Thumb (Not completed Banbury 1937)			Midland Air Museum (Stored 4.96)	Coventry
33		DFS 10849 Grunau Baby IIB	VN148 LN+ST		Russavia Collection (On rebuild as BGA.2400 1978; status unknown)	Bishops Stortford
34		DFS 10849 Grunau Baby IIB	030892	RAFGSA.281 RAFGGA GK.4/LZ+AR	D.Elsdon	Hazlemere, Bucks
		(On rebuild as BGA.2362; status unknown but possibly used for spares)				
35		EoN AP.7 Primary	EoN/P/063		Not known (ex Russavia Collection) (On rebuild as BGA.2493 8.89)	Pocklington
36		Fieseler Fi 103 V1 model ("Operation Crossbow" film)			Kent Battle of Britain Museum (On loan from Shuttleworth Trust)	Hawkinge
37					See G-BXIY in SECTION 1	
38	A1742	Bristol Scout D rep (80 hp Gnome)			K Williams & M Thorn (For restoration 11.97)	Solihull

BAPC No.	Identity carried	Type	C/n	P/I	Owner	Probable Base
39		Addyman Zephyr sailplane			A Lindsay & N.Ponsford (Parts held for eventual rebuild 3.98)	(Selby)
40		Bristol Boxkite rep (Gnome) ("Those Magnificent Men in Their Flying Machines"film)	BM.7281		Bristol City Museum & Art Gallery Clifton, Bristol	
41		RAF BE.2C rep		6232	Yorkshire Air Museum (Stored 3.98)	Elvington
42	H1968	Avro 504K rep			Yorkshire Air Museum (Stored 3.98)	Elvington
43		Mignet HM.14 Pou-Du-Ciel (Scott A2S)			Newark Air Museum (Stored 3.96)	Winthorpe
44	L6906	Miles M.14A Magister			See G-AKKY in SECTION 1	
45		Pilcher Hawk glider rep (Built by AWA apprentices 1957/58)			Lord Braye/Percy Pilcher Museum Stanford Hall, Rugby	
46		Mignet HM.14 Pou-Du-Ciel			Not known Tump Farm, Coleford, Glos (Probably scrapped; status uncertain)	
47	BAPC 47	Watkins CHW Monoplane (Watkins 40hp)			National Museum of Wales	Cardiff
48		Pilcher Hawk glider rep (Built by No.2175 Sqdn ATC, Glasgow 1966)			Museum of Transport (Stored 3.96) Kelvin Hall, Glasgow	
49		Pilcher Hawk glider (1896 original) (Rebuilt after fatal crash Stanford Hall, Leics 30.9.1899)			National Museum of Scotland - Museum of Flight East Fortune	
50		Roe Triplane Type I (JAP 9hp) (1909 original)			The Science Museum	South Kensington, London
51		Vickers FB.27 Vimy IV (RR Eagle VIII 360hp)	13		The Science Museum	South Kensington, London
52		Lilienthal Glider Type XI (1895 original)			The Science Museum (Stored 6.94)	South Kensington, London
53		Wright Flyer rep			The Science Museum	South Kensington, London
54		JAP/Harding Monoplane (JAP Anzani 45hp) (Modified Bleriot XI built by J.A.Prestwich & Co 1910)			The Science Museum	South Kensington, London
55		Levasseur-Antoinette Developed Type VII Monoplane (1910 original) (Antoinette V8 50hp)			The Science Museum	South Kensington, London
56		Fokker E.III (Oberusal 100hp) (Captured in Somme 1916; reported as ex XG4 of RFC)	210/16		The Science Museum (Skeletal airframe)	South Kensington, London
57		Pilcher Hawk glider rep (Built by Martin & Miller, Edinburgh 1930)			The Science Museum (Stored 6.94)	Wroughton
58	15-1585	Yokosuka MXY7 Ohka model 11			The Science Museum (Loaned to Fleet Air Arm Museum)	RNAS Yeovilton
59	D3419	Sopwith F1 Camel rep		"F1921"	Cosford Aerospace Museum (Stored 3.96)	RAF Cosford
60		Murray M.1 Helicopter (JAPJ99 36hp)			The Aeroplane Collection Weston-super-Mare (On loan to The Helicopter Museum) (Stored 3.96)	
61		Stewart Ornithopter			Lincolnshire Aviation Heritage Centre "Bellbird II" (Stored 12.96) Tumby Woodside, Lincs	
62	304	Cody Type V Bi-plane (Austro-Daimler 120hp) (1912 original)			The Science Museum	South Kensington, London
63	P3208	Hawker Hurricane model ("Battle of Britain" film)		"L1592"	Hawkinge Aeronautical Trust (Kent Battle of Britain Museum) (As "SD-T"in 501 Sqdn c/s)	Hawkinge
64	P3059	Hawker Hurricane model ("Battle of Britain" film)			Hawkinge Aeronautical Trust (Kent Battle of Britain Museum) (As "SD-N" in 501 Sqdn c/s)	Hawkinge
65	N3289	Supermarine Spitfire model ("Battle of Britain" film)			Hawkinge Aeronautical Trust (Kent Battle of Britain Museum) (As "DW-K" in 610 Sqdn c/s)	Hawkinge
66		Messerschmitt Bf109 (Hispano HA.1112) model ("Battle of Britain" film)	1480		Hawkinge Aeronautical Trust (Kent Battle of Britain Museum) (As "6")	Hawkinge
67	14	Messerschmitt Bf109 (Hispano HA.1112) model (Battle of Britain" film)			Hawkinge Aeronautical Trust (Kent Battle of Britain Museum) (As "14"; JG52 c/s) (Probably previously as "KM+JI")	Hawkinge
68	H3426	Hawker Hurricane model ("Battle of Britain" film)			Not known (Status uncertain; stored 12.94)	(Coventry)
69	N3313	Supermarine Spitfire rep ("Battle of Britain" film)		"MH314" "N3313"	Hawkinge Aeronautical Trust (Kent Battle of Britain Museum) (As "KL-B" in 54 Sqn c/s)	Hawkinge
70	TJ398	Auster AOP.5	TAY/33153	"GALES"	Acft Preservation Society of Scotland/ Museum of Flight	East Fortune
71	P8140	Supermarine Spitfire model ("Battle of Britain" film)		"P9390" "N3317"	Norfolk & Suffolk Avn Museum "Nuflier" (As "ZP-" in 74 Sqn c/s)	Flixton

BAPC No.	Identity carried	Type	C/n	P/I	Owner	Probable Base
72	V7767	Hawker Hurricane model		"KIT 3"	Gloucestershire Aviation Collection (Stored pending rebuild 2.98)	Gloucestershire
73		Hawker Hurricane rep			Not known	(Bishops Stortford)
					(Displayed at "Queens Head" Public House; status unconfirmed)	
74		Messerschmitt Bf109 (Hispano HA.1112) rep ("Battle of Britain" film)	6357		Hawkinge Aeronautical Trust (Kent Battle of Britain Museum) (As "6")	Hawkinge
75	"G-AEFG"	Mignet HM.14 Pou-Du-Ciel			A Lindsay & N H Ponsford (Under restoration 3.98)	(Selby)
76	"G-AFFI"	Mignet HM.14 Pou-Du-Ciel (Scott) (Modern reproduction)			Yorkshire Air Museum	Elvington
77	"G-ADRG"	Mignet HM.14 Pou-Du-Ciel (Citroen 425cc) (Modern reproduction)			Stondon Transport Museum & Garden Centre	Lower Stondon
78					See G-AENP in SECTION 1	
79	ZI-4	Fiat G.46-4b	71	FHE MM53211	T P Luscombe/British Air Reserve (Not constructed)	
80	KJ351	Airspeed AS.58 Horsa II (Composite from LH208, TL659, 8569M & others)			Museum of Army Flying	AAC Middle Wallop
81		RFD (Hawkridge) Dagling	10471	BGA.493	Russavia Collection (On rebuild)	Hemel Hempstead
82		Hawker Afghan Hind (RR Kestrel)	41H/81899		RAF Museum (R.Afghan AF c/s)	Hendon
83	8476M	Kawasaki Ki 1001b			Cosford Aerospace Museum	RAF Cosford
84		Mitsubishi Ki 46III (Dinah) (Allotted 8484M)	5439	(ATAIU/SEA)	Cosford Aerospace Museum (ex Jap Army AF/81st Sentai)	RAF Cosford
85	W2	Weir W2 (Weir Dryad II 50hp)			Museum of Flight/Royal Museum of Scotland	East Fortune
86		DH.82A Tiger Moth			Yorkshire Acft Preservation Society (Status unknown)	(Acaster Malbis)
87	"G-EASQ"	Bristol 30/46 Babe III rep (Construction commenced in 1970s by W.Sneesby)	1		Bristol Aero Collection	Kemble
88	102/17	Fokker DR.1 5/8th rep (Modified Lawrence Parasol airframe)			Fleet Air Arm Museum	RNAS Yeovilton
89		Cayley Glider rep			Manchester Museum of Science & Industry	Manchester
90		Colditz Cock rep (BBC "The Colditz Story" film)			Lincolnshire Avn Heritage Centre	East Kirkby
91		Fieseler Fi 103R-IV (Believed a genuine piloted version)			Lashenden Air Warfare Museum	Headcorn
92		Fieseler Fi 103 (V1)			RAF Museum	Hendon
93		Fieseler Fi 103 (V1)			Imperial War Museum	Duxford
94	8583M	Fieseler Fi 103 (V1) (P/I unconfirmed)		418947	Cosford Aerospace Museum	Cosford
95		Gizmer Autogyro			F.Fewsdale (Status unknown)	(Darlington)
96		Brown Helicopter			North East A/c Museum (Stored 3.98)	Sunderland
97	"G-AFUG"	Luton LA.4 Minor (JAP J99)			North East A/c Museum (Under restoration by K Fern 3.98)	(Stoke-on-Trent)
98	997	Yokosuka MXY7 Ohka model 11		8485M	Manchester Museum of Science & Industry	Manchester
99	8486M	Yokosuka MXY7 Ohka model 11			Cosford Aerospace Museum	RAF Cosford
100		Clarke TWK Chanute biplane glider			The Science Museum (Loaned to RAF Museum)	Hendon
101		Mignet HM.14 Pou-Du-Ciel			Newark Air Museum (Fuselage stored 3.98)	Winthorpe
102		Mignet HM.14 Pou-Du-Ciel			Not constructed - parts to BAPC.75	
103		Hulton Hang-glider (Built by E.A.S.Hulton, London 1969)			Personal Plane Services Ltd ("Blue Max" Movie A/c Museum 3.96)	Booker
104					See G-AVXV in SECTION 1	
105		Bleriot XI (Anzani "V" 25hp)	54		Arango Collection Los Angeles, California, USA	
		(Composite from original components including c/n 54; built by L.D.Goldsmith in 1976 @ RAF Colerne)				
106	164	Bleriot XI (Anzani 40hp) (1910 original) (Allotted 9209M)			Royal Aeronautical Society (On loan to RAF Museum) (Stored 10.95)	RAF Cardington
107	433	Bleriot XXVII (1911 original) (Allotted 9202M)			Royal Aeronautical Society (On loan to RAF Museum)	Hendon
108		Fairey Swordfish IV (Identity not confirmed)		HS503	Cosford Aerospace Museum (Stored 3.96)	RAF Cosford
109		Slingsby T.7 Cadet (Modified) (Allotted 8599M)	28	BGA.679	RAF Museum (Presumed stored; status unconfirmed)	(RAF Henlow)
110	5125/18	Fokker D.VII rep			Leisure Sport Ltd (JG1 c/s) (Sold 10.87)	(Thorpe Park, Surrey)
111	N5492	Sopwith Triplane rep			Fleet Air Arm Museum ("B" Flt/10 Sqdn RNAS c/s)	RNAS Yeovilton

BAPC No.	Identity carried	Type	C/n	P/I	Owner	Probable Base
112	5964	De Havilland DH.2 rep			Museum of Army Flying	AAC Middle Wallop
113	B4863	RAF SE.5A rep			Leisure Sport Ltd (Thorpe Park, Surrey) (As "G" in 56 Sqdn c/s) (Sold 10.87)	
114	"G-EBED"	Vickers 60 Viking IV rep ("The Land Time Forgot" film)		"R4"	Brooklands Museum	Brooklands
115		Mignet HM.14 Pou-Du-Ciel (Douglas 500cc)			I Hancock (On loan to Norfolk & Suffolk Avtn Museum)	Flixton
116		Santos-Dumont Demoiselle XX rep (JAP J99)			Flambards Triple Theme Park (Helston) (Sold 1993)	
117	1701	RAF BE.2C rep (Gipsy Major for taxying) (Built by Ackland & Shaw for "Wings" BBC TV 1976) (Two similar a/c were built but only one has appeared on the BAPC register)			Friends of Biggin Hill (Stored 3.96)	Orpington
118	C19/15	Albatros D.V static rep			North Weald A/c Restoration Flt	North Weald
119		Bensen B.7 Gyroglider			North East A/c Museum	Sunderland
120		See G-AEJZ in SECTION 1				
121		See G-AEKR in SECTION 1				
122	1881	Avro 504 rep (Ford 1300 for taxying) (Built by PPS Booker for "Wings" BBC TV in 1976)			Not known (Status unknown)	???
123	P641	Vickers FB.5 Gunbus rep (Built IES Projects Ltd 1975 for "Shout at the Devil" film)	1186/2	ZS-UHN	A.Topen (Small components only remain & stored 3.90)	Cranfield
124		Lilienthal Glider Type XI rep (Display reproduction of BAPC.52)			The Science Museum	South Kensington, London
126		Rollason-Druine D.31 Turbulent (Static airframe)			Midland Air Museum (Stored 4.96)	Coventry
127		Halton MPA			C.Roper Filching Manor, Wannock (On loan to the Foulkes-Halbard Collection) "Jupiter"	
128		Watkinson CG-4 rotorcraft			The Helicopter Museum	Weston-super-Mare
129		Blackburn " 1911 Monoplane rep (Built for TV series "The Flambards")			Flambards Triple Theme Park (Helston) "Mercury" (Sold 1993)	
130		Blackburn 1911 Monoplane rep (Built for TV series "The Flambards")			Yorkshire Air Museum	Elvington
131		Pilcher Hawk glider rep (Built by C.Paton for film 1972)			C.Paton (London E) (Status unknown; probably stored)	
132		Bleriot XI (Anzani 25hp) (L.D.Goldsmith 1976 rebuild from original components; rebuilt again by EMK in 1982 & initially allotted G-BLXI; reported as sold to unidentified Musee de l'Automobile, France in 1986; possibly the same a/c as BAPC.189)	EMK010 & PFA/8810864		Not known	
133	425/17	Fokker DR.1 model			Kent Battle of Britain Museum	Hawkinge
134		Pitts S.2A		"G-RKSF"	Toyota (Northampton) See "G-CARS" in SECTION 4	
135	C4912	Bristol M.1C Monoplane rep			Leisure Sport Ltd (Thorpe Park, Surrey) (150 Sqdn c/s) (Sold 10.87)	
136	19	Deperdussin 1913 floatplane rep			Planes of Fame Air Museum Chino, California, USA	
137	8151	Sopwith Baby floatplane rep (Built FEM Displays Ltd 1978)			Leisure Sport Ltd (Thorpe Park, Surrey) (RNAS c/s) (Sold 10.87)	
138	2292	Hansa Brandenberg W.29 rep (Ford 1300 for taxying)			Not known (Thorpe Park, Surrey) (Status unknown; sold prior to 10.87)	
139	DR1/17	Fokker DR.1 Triplane rep			Leisure Sport Ltd (Jasta II c/s) (Sold 10.87)	
140	3	Curtiss 42A R3C2 rep			Planes of Fame Air Museum Chino, California, USA (US Army c/s)	
141	5	Macchi M.39 rep (Gipsy Queen for taxying)			Fighter Jets & Air Racing Museum Chino, California, USA	
142	F5459	RAF SE.5A rep			Not known (Switzerland) (As "Y") (Sold 1.5.93)	
143		Paxton MPA			R.A.Paxton (Gloucestershire) (Status unknown; presumed stored)	
144		Weybridge MPA (Previously "Dumbo" rebuilt)			Not known "Mercury" (Cranwell) (Status unknown)	
145		Oliver MPA			Not known (Warton) (Status unconfirmed, possibly scrapped)	
146		Pedal Aeronauts MPA			Not known "Toucan" ??? (Status uncertain: centre section/power train only departed London Colney 1995)	
147	LHS-1	Bensen B7 Gyroglider			Norfolk & Suffolk Aviation Museum	Flixton
148	K7271	Hawker Fury II rep			High Ercall Aviation Museum (1 Sqdn c/s) (Stored 10.98)	High Ercall
149		Short S.27 rep			Fleet Air Arm Museum (Stored 4.98)	RNAS Yeovilton
150	XX725	BAC/Sepecat Jaguar GR.1 model		"XX718" "XX732"	RAF Exhibition, Production & Transportation Unit (As "GU" in 54 Sqdn c/s) (RAF St.Athan) (Extant 9.96)	
151	XZ226	BAC/Sepecat Jaguar GR.1A model		"XX824"	RAF Exhibition, Production & Transportation Unit (As "A" in 41 Sqdn c/s) (RAF St.Athan) (Extant 7.96)	

BAPC No.	Identity carried	Type	C/n	P/I	Owner	Probable Base
152	XX226	BAe Hawk T.1A model		"XX262" "XX162"	RAF Exhibition, Production & Transportation Unit (As "74 in 74 Sqdn c/s) (Extant 9.96)	(RAF St.Athan)
153		Westland WG33 (Engineering mock-up)			The Helicopter Museum (Stored 2.98)	Weston-super-Mare
154		Druine D.31 Turbulent (Unfinished)	PFA/1654		Lincolnshire Aviation Society (Stored for sale 3.96)	East Kirkby
155	ZA446	Panavia Tornado GR.1 model		"ZA446" "ZA600/ZA322"	RAF Exhibition, Production & Transportation Unit (As "AJ-P")	(RAF St.Athan)
156	S1595	Supermarine S.6B rep			Museum of Flying	Santa Monica, California, USA
157	237123	WACO CG-4A Hadrian (Fuselage frame section only & tail pieces ex 456476) (Stored 3.98)			Yorkshire Air Museum	Elvington
158		Fieseler Fi 103 (V1)			Defence Explosives Ordnance Disposal School	Lodge Hill Camp, Chattenden
159		Yokosuka MXY7 Ohka model 11			Defence Explosives Ordnance Disposal School	Lodge Hill Camp, Chattenden
160		Chargus 18/50 Hang-Glider			National Museum of Scotland-Museum of Flight	East Fortune
161		Stewart MP Ornithopter			?? Stewart "Coppelia" (Stored 1991)	(Lincolnshire)
162		Goodhart MPA			The Science Museum "Newbury Manflier" (Parts only stored 9.93)	Wroughton
163	B415	Hafner AFEE 10/42 Rotabuggy rep			Wessex Aviation Society (On loan to Museum of Army Flying)	AAC Middle Wallop
164	N546	Wight Quadruplane Type 1 rep			Southampton Hall of Aviation	Southampton
165	E2466	Bristol F.2B Fighter (RR Falcon rep)			RAF Museum (22 Sqdn c/s)	Hendon
166	D7889	Bristol F.2B Fighter	G-AANM		Aero Vintage (AV) (Under restoration 8.95)	St.Leonards-on-Sea
167		RAF SE.5A rep			TDL Replicas Ltd (Stored 12.97)	Lowestoft
168	"G-AAAH"	DH.60G Moth rep	8058		Gatwick Hilton Hotel "Jason"	Gatwick
169	XX110	BAC/Sepecat Jaguar GR.1 (Engine systems static demonstration airframe)			No.1 School of Technical Training (Extant 11.93)	RAF Halton
170		Pilcher Hawk glider rep ("Kings Royal" BBC film; built 1983 by A.Gourlay)			Not known (Stored 3.93)	Strathallan
171	XX297	BAe Hawk T.1 model		"XX262"	RAF Exhibition, Production & Transportation Unit	(RAF St.Athan)
172		Chargus Midas Super E Hang-Glider			The Science Museum	Wroughton
173		Birdman Grasshopper Hang-Gglider (Power assisted)			The Science Museum	Wroughton
174		Bensen B.7 Gyro-glider			The Science Museum	Wroughton
175		Volmer VJ-23 Swing-wing (9 hp McCulloch)			Manchester Museum of Science & Industry	Manchester
176	A4850	RAF SE.5A scale rep (Currie Wot basic airframe built by Slingsby for "The Blue Max" film)			Macclesfield Historial Avn Society	Barton
177	"G-AACA"	Avro 504K rep (Clerget 130hp)		"G1381"	Brooklands Museum (Brooklands School of Flying c/s)	Brooklands
178		Avro 504K rep		"E373"	By-gone Times Antique Warehouse Eccleston, Lancs (German marks)	
179	A7317	Sopwith Pup rep ("Wings" film)			Epping Forest Council (On loan to Midland Air Museum 4.96)	Coventry
180		McCurdy Silver Dart rep			Reynolds Pioneer Museum (Delivered 4.94)	Wetaskiwin, Alberta, Canada
181	687	RAF BE.2b (Renault V8) (Restoration from original components)			RAF Museum	Hendon
182		Wood Ornithopter			Manchester Museum of Science & Industry (Stored 3.96)	Manchester
183		Zurowski ZP.1 (850 cc Panhard)			Newark Air Museum (Polish AF c/s)	Winthorpe
184	EN398	Supermarine Spitfire IX model (Built 1985 by Specialised Mouldings Ltd)			R.J.Lamplough (As "WO-A")	North Weald
185	243809	WACO CG-4A Hadrian (Restoration from original unidentified components)			Museum of Army Flying	AAC Middle Wallop
186	LF789	DH.82B Queen Bee (Correct identity ?)	K3584		De Havilland Aircraft Museum (As "R2-K")	Salisbury Hall, London Colney
187		Roe Type I Biplane rep (ABC 24hp) (Built by M.L.Beach)			Brooklands Museum	Brooklands
188		McBroom Cobra 88 Hang-Glider			The Science Museum	Wroughton
189		Bleriot XI rep (Anzani) (Some original parts ex Goldsmith Trust)			Not known (Status uncertain; see BAPC.132) (Sold at Christies 31.10.86, probably to France)	
190	K5054	Supermarine Spitfire prototype rep			P.Smith (Stored 8.95) (On loan to Macclesfield Historical Avn Society)	Barton

BAPC No.	Identity carried	Type	C/n	P/I	Owner	Probable Base
191	ZD472	BAe Harrier GR.7 model			RAF Exhibition, Production & Transportation Unit (As Code "01") (Extant 5.96)	(RAF St.Athan)
192		Weedhopper JC24			N.Dykes	Bacup, Lancs
193		Hovey WDII Whing Ding			N.Dykes	Bacup, Lancs
194		Santos Dumont Type 20 Demoiselle rep (ABC Scorpion 30hp) ("Those Magnificent Men in Their Flying Machines" film)	PPS/DEM/1	24 bis	RAF Museum (On loan to Brooklands Museum)	Brooklands
195		Birdman Sports Moonraker 77 Hang-Glider (Built c.1977)			National Museum of Scotland-Museum of Flight	East Fortune
196		Southdown Sailwings Sigma 2m Hang-Glider (Built c.1980)			National Museum of Scotland-Museum of Flight	East Fortune
197		Scotkites Cirrus III Hang-Glider (Built 1977)			National Museum of Scotland-Museum of Flight	East Fortune
198		Fieseler Fi 103 (V1)	477663		Imperial War Museum	South Lambeth, London
199		Fieseler Fi 103 (V1)	442795		The Science Museum	South Kensington, London
200		Bensen B.7 Gyroglider (Composite of three airframes)			Not known (Stored 11.93)	(Leeds)
201	BAPC 201	Mignet HM.14 Pou-Du-Ciel			Caernarfon Air World	Caernarfon
202	MAV467	Vickers Supermarine Spitfire V model ("A Piece of Cake" film)			Maes Artro Village (As "RO")	Llanbedr
203	"G-AFIN"	Chrislea LC.1 Airguard rep			Ponsford Collection (Stored 3.98)	Wigan
204		McBroom Hang-Glider			The Aeroplane Collection (On loan to Newark Air Museum) (Stored 3.98)	Winthorpe
205	BE421	Hawker Hurricane IIc model			RAF Museum (As "XP-G" in 174 Sqn c/s)	Hendon
206	MH486	Vickers Supermarine Spitfire IX model			RAF Museum (As"FF-A" in 132 Sqn c/s)	Hendon
207	"K.158"	Austin Whippet rep		"G-EAGS"	K.Fern t/a Vintage & Rotary Wing Collection (To North East A/c Museum)	Sunderland
208	D276	RAF SE.5A rep (Built AJD Engineering)			Prince's Mead Shopping Precinct	Farnborough, Hants
209	MJ751	Vickers Supermarine Spitfire LF.IXC model ("Piece of Cake" film)			Museum of D-Day Aviation (As "DU-V" in 321 Sqn c/s)	Shoreham
210	C4451	Avro 504J rep (Gnome Monosoupape 100hp) (Built AJD Engineering)			Southampton Hall of Aviation	Southampton
211	"G-ADVU"	Mignet HM.14 Pou-Du-Ciel (Built by Ken Fern/Vintage & Rotary Wing Collection 1993; in North East A/c Museum 4.98)			I.Burns t/a Burns Garage	Sunderland
212		Bensen B.6 Gyrocopter			The Helicopter Museum (Stored 2.98)	Weston-super-Mare
213		Cranfield Vertigo MP Helicopter			The Helicopter Museum (Stored 2.98)	Weston-super-Mare
214	K5054	Supermarine Spitfire prototype model			The Spitfire Society (On loan to Tangmere Military Avtn Museum)	Tangmere
215		Airwave Hang Glider prototype			Southampton Hall of Aviation	Southampton
216	"G-ACSS"	DH.88 Comet model (Taxying)			G.Gayward Home Park, Kings Langley t/a Trout Lake Air Force	
217	K9926	Vickers Supermarine Spitfire I rep			RAF Inspectorate of Recruiting (As "JH-C" in 317 Sqn c/s)	RAF Bentley Priory
218	P3386	Hawker Hurricane IIc model			RAF Inspectorate of Recruiting (As "FT-I"in 43 Sqn c/s)	RAF Bentley Priory
219	L1710	Hawker Hurricane I model			RAF Memorial Chapel (As "AL-D" in 79 Sqn c/s)	Biggin Hill
220	N3194	Vickers Supermarine Spitfire I model			RAF Memorial Chapel (As "GR-Z" in 92 Sqn c/s)	Biggin Hill
221	MH777	Vickers Supermarine Spitfire LF.IX model			RAF Museum (As "RF-N" in 303 Sqn c/s)	RAF Northolt
222	BR600	Vickers Supermarine Spitfire IX model			RAF Museum (As "SH-V" in 64 Sqn c/s)	RAF Uxbridge
223	V7467	Hawker Hurricane I model			RAF Museum (As "LE-D"in 242 Sqn c/s)	RAF Coltishall
224	BR600	Vickers Supermarine Spitfire V model (Built by TDL Replicas)			Stakis Ambassador Hotel (As "JP-A" in 64 Sqn c/s)	Norwich Airport
225	P8448	Vickers Supermarine Spitfire IX model			RAF Museum (As "UM-D" in 52 Sqn c/s)	RAF Cranwell
226	EN343	Vickers Supermarine Spitfire XI model			RAF Museum (PRU c/s)	RAF Benson
227	L1070	Vickers Supermarine Spitfire IA model			RAF Museum (As "XT-A" in 603 Sqn c/s)	Edinburgh
228		Olympus Hang Glider			North East A/c Museum (Stored 3.98)	Sunderland
229	MJ832	Vickers Supermarine Spitfire IX model		"L1096"	RAF Museum "City of Oshawa" (As "DN-Y" in 416 Sqn c/s)	RAF Digby
230	AA908	Vickers Supermarine Spitfire rep (Built by TDL Replicas 1993)		"AA908"	Eden Camp Modern History Theme Museum (As "GE-P" in 152 Sqn c/s)	Old Malton, N.Yorks

-

BAPC No.	Identity carried	Type	C/n	P/I	Owner	Probable Base
231	"G-ADRX"	Mignet HM.14 Pou-Du-Ciel (Probably built Ulverston 1936 with Anzani engine; on rebuild at HM Prison, Haverigg, Millom 3.94 with modern DAF engine, from original remains acquired from Torver, Cumbria)			South Copeland Avn Group	Haverigg, Millom
232		Airspeed AS.58 Horsa I/II (Composite airframe from unidentified components)			De Havilland Heritage Museum	Salisbury Hall, London Colney
233		Broburn Wanderlust Sailplane (Built 1946)			Museum of Berkshire Avn	Woodley
234	GBH-7	Vickers FB.5 Gunbus rep (Built 1985 for "Gunbus" film)			Macclesfield Historical Avn Society (Stored 3.98)	Barton
235		Fieseler Fi 103 V1 model (Built by TDL Replicas 1993)			Eden Camp Modern History Theme Museum	Old Malton, N.Yorks
236	P2793	Hawker Hurricane model (Built by TDL Replica 7.93)			Eden Camp Modern History Theme Museum (As "SD-M" in 501 Sqn c/s)	Old Malton, N.Yorks
237		Fieseler Fi 103 (V1)			RAF Museum (Stored 11.93)	RAF Cardington
238		Waxflatter Ornithopter rep ("Young Sherlock Holmes" film & built by PPS)			Personal Plane Services Ltd ("Blue Max" Movie Acft Museum 7.96)	Booker
239		Fokker D.VIII 5/8 Scale rep			Norfolk & Suffolk Avtn Museum	Flixton
240		Messerschmitt Bf.109G model (Built by D.Thorton 1994)			Yorkshire Air Museum	Elvington
241	L1679	Hawker Hurricane I model (Built by Aerofab 1994)			Tangmere Military Aviation Museum (As "JX-G" in 1 Sqn c/s)	Tangmere
242	BL924	Vickers Supermarine Spitfire VB rep (Built by TDL Reps 1994)			Tangmere Military Aviation Museum (As "AZ-G" in 234 Sqn c/s)	Tangmere
243	"G-ADYV"	Mignet HM.14 Pou-Du-Ciel (Scott A2S) (Modern reproduction built 1995 by Bill Francis; stored 8.95)			P.Ward	Malvern Wells
244		Solar Wings Typhoon Hang-Glider (Wing only) (Built 1981)			National Museum of Scotland - Museum of Flight	East Fortune
245		Electraflyer Floater Hang-Glider (Wing only) (Built 1979)			National Museum of Scotland - Museum of Flight	East Fortune
246		Hiway Cloudbase Hang-Glider (Built 1978)			National Museum of Scotland - Museum of Flight	East Fortune
247		Albatros ASG.21 Hang-Glider (Built 1977)			National Museum of Scotland - Museum of Flight	East Fortune
248		McBroom Hang-Glider (Built 1974)			Museum of Berkshire Aviation	Woodley
249	K5673	Hawker Fury I model			Brooklands Museum (As "A" Flt in 1 Sqn c/s)	Brooklands
250	F5475	RAF SE.5A rep			Brooklands Museum "1st Battalion Honourable Artillery Company" (As "A" in 41 Sqn c/s)	Brooklands
251		Hiway Spectrum Hang-Glider (Built 1980)			Manchester Museum of Science & Industry (Stored 3.98)	Manchester
252		Flexiform Wing Hang-Glider (Built 1982)			Manchester Museum of Science & Industry (Stored 3.98)	Manchester
253	"G-ADZW"	Mignet HM.14 Pou-Du-Ciel (Modern reproduction built in 1990s)			H.Shore (On loan to The Island Aeroplane Co Collection)	Sandown
254	R6690	Supermarine Spitfire 1 model			No.609 (West Riding) Squadron Association (On loan to Yorkshire Air Museum) (As "PR-A" in 609 Sqn c/s)	Elvington
255	463209	NA P-51D Mustang model		"88"	American Air Museum (As "WZ-S" in 78th FS c/s)	Duxford
256		Santos Dumont Type 20 Demoiselle rep (Built by J Aubot 1996/97)			Brookland Museum	Brooklands
257	"G-ACSS"	DH.88 model			Galleria Leisure Experience "Grosvenor House"	Hatfield
258		Adams Balloon (14,000 cu.ft) (Built by GQ Parachutes)			British Balloon Museum & Library	Newbury

SECTION 4B - IRISH AVIATION HISTORICAL COUNCIL REGISTER

The IAHC Register came into existence with similar objectives to the BAPC.   There has been little fresh information this year.

IAPC No.	Identity carried	Type	C/n	P/I	Owner	Probable Base
1		Mignet HM.14 Pou-Du-Ciel			South East Avtn Enthusiasts Group "Patrick" (Stored 4.96)	New Ross, Wexford
2		Aldritt Monoplane			Foulkes-Halbard Collection (Under restoration 4.98)	Filching Manor, Wannock
3		Mignet HM.14 Pou-Du-Ciel (1937 original but unflown)			M.Donohoe (On rebuild 4.96)	Delgany, Co.Wicklow
4		Hawker Hector		IAAC.	D.McCarthy (Believed components on rebuild in Florida, USA)	??
5		Not known				
6		Ferguson Monoplane rep (Built by Capt J.Kelly Rogers 1974; original engine)			Ulster Folk & Transport Museum (On loan from Irish Avn Museum)	Holywood, Belfast
7		Sligo Concept			G.O'Hara (Stored incomplete 8.91)	Sligo
8		O'Hara Autogyro			G.O'Hara (Stored unflown 8.91)	Sligo
9		Ferguson Monoplane rep (Built by L.Hannah 1980)			Ulster Folk & Transport Museum (Stored 4.98)	Holywood, Belfast

SECTION 5 - NON-UK AIRCRAFT LOCATED IN UK

Many thanks to Mike Cain, Paul Hewins, Bernard Martin & Steve Sowter for considerable input and, of course, "Wrecks & Relics No.16".

Regn	Type	C/n	P/I	Owner/(operator)	Probable Base
A40-AB	Vickers VC-10-1103	820	G-ASIX	Brooklands Museum	Brooklands
A6-HHH	Gulfstream G.1159C Gulfstream IV	1011	(A6-DLF) N17581	Govt of Dubai (Noted 9.98)	Farnborough
03 (red)	Mil Mi-24D Hind D	3532461715415		Hawarden Air Services (Stored 4.98)	Chester
04 (red)	Mikoyan MiG-23ML Hind D	024003607		Hawarden Air Services (Noted 11.97)	Chester
05 (blue)	Yakovlev Yak-50	832507	YL-CBH DOSAAF 05	Hawarden Air Services (Noted 11.97)	Chester
05 (red)	Yakovlev Yak-50	832507	YL-YAK	Hawarden Air Services (Noted 11.95)	Chester
06 (yellow)	Mil Mi-24D Hind D	3532464505029		Hawarden Air Services (Stored11.97)	Chester
09 (green)	Yakovlev Yak-52	811202	YL-CBI DOSAAF 09	Hawarden Air Services (Noted 11.96)	Chester
20 (black)	Yakovlev Yak-52	790404	YL-CBJ DOSAAF 20	Hawarden Air Services (Noted 11.97)	Chester
20	Lavochkin La-11	-		The Fighter Collection (Still awaiting rebuild 2.99)	Duxford
23 (red)	Mikoyan MiG-27D	83712515040		Hawarden Air Services (Stored 6.97)	Chester
35 (red)	Sukhoi SU-17M-3 Fitter H	25102		Hawarden Air Services (Stored 4.98)	Chester
	(Reported as SU-22M-3; and possibly 25103)				
50 (red)	Mikoyan MiG-23ML	023003508		Hawarden Air Services (Stored 4.98)	Chester
53 (Soviet AF)	Curtiss P-40B Tomahawk	2380	41-13390	The Fighter Collection (On rebuild in Chino 3.96)	Duxford
54 (red)	Sukhoi SU-17 Fitter C	69004		Hawarden Air Services (Stored 4.98)	Chester
71 (red)	Mikoyan MiG-27D	61912507006		Hawarden Air Services (Stored 4.98)	Chester
-	Mil Mi-24RKR Hind	3532424810853		Hawarden Air Services (Stored 4.98)	Chester
30151	Soko Kraguj		30151 Yugoslav AF	Not known (Noted 12.98)	Bournemouth
Z5207 (Sov AF)	Hawker Hurricane 2B	-		R.A.Roberts	Billingshurst
				(Ex N.Russia - on rebuild by Historic Flying Ltd 7.94)	
RK858 (Sov AF)	V-S Spitfire F.IX	CBAF.9746		The Fighter Collection	Duxford
				(Imported 9.92; wreck recovered from Russia; stored 3.96)	
CF-BXO	V-S.304 Stranraer	RCAF 920 CV-209		RAF Museum (As "920/QN-" in RCAF c/s)	Hendon
CF-EQS	Boeing-Stearman A75N1 (PT-17-BW) Kaydet	41-8169 75-1728		IWM Collection/American Air Museum (As "42-17786/25" in USAAF c/s)	Duxford
CF-KCG	Grumman TBM-3E Avenger AS.3	2066	RCN326 Bu.69327	IWM Collection (As "46214/3-X 69327" in USN c/s)	Duxford
C-FDFC	Bristol 170 Freighter 31M	13218	G-BISU ZK-EPH/NZ5912/ZK-BVI/NZ5912/G-18-194	British Airways Employees	Enstone
				(Damaged Enstone 18.7.96; wreck in open store 4.97)	
C-FJNU	Cessna 182P Skylane II	182-62147	CF-JNU N58573	Not known (Noted 12.98)	Blackbushe
C-FQIP	Lake LA-4			Not known (Noted 3.99)	Elstree
C-GYZI	Cameron N-77			Balloon Preservation Group "Aeolus" (Held 12.98)	Lancing
RCAF 9893	Bristol 149 Bolingbroke IVT	-		IWM Collection (Stored 3.96)	Duxford
RCAF 9940	Bristol 149 Bolingbroke IVT	-		Museum of Flight/Royal Museum of Scotland (Stored 3.96)	East Fortune
CN-TTO	DH.89A Dragon Rapide 4	6940	(F-DAFS) G-AKRP/RL958	R.Ford t/a Fordaire (On rebuild 6.97)	Sywell
CS-AQW	Reims Cessna F.172N Skyhawk II	1914	(G-BOJJ) CS-AQW	C.Wagner/Cormack (A/c Svs) Ltd (Stored 6.98)	Cumbernauld
CS-DAP	OGMA DHC.1 Chipmunk T.20	OGMA-50	FAP 1360	(R.Farrer) (On overhaul Spanhoe 3.96; sold 1997)	(Bedfordshire)
CS-DAQ	OGMA DHC.1 Chipmunk T.20	OGMA-57	FAP 1367	(R.Farrer) (On overhaul Spanhoe 3.96; sold 1997)	(Bedfordshire)
FAP 1366	OGMA DHC.1 Chipmunk T.20	OGMA-58		(R.Farrer) (On overhaul Spanhoe 3.96; sold 1997)	(Bedfordshire)
FAP 1513	North American AT-6D-NT Harvard III	88-14555	SAAF 7426 EX884/41-33857	Air Engineering Services (On rebuild 4.95) (As "FT323/GN")	Swansea
D-CATA	Hawker Sea Fury T.20	ES.8503	D-FATA G-9-30/VZ345	Fleet Air Arm Museum (Stored 9.95) (As "VZ345" in RN c/s)	Brough
	(Damaged Boscombe Down 17.4.85)				
D-EASB	Cessna 177RG Cardinal	177RG-0776	N1603H	C.Hardiman (Wreck stored 9.96)	Shobdon
D-EAZO	Bucker Bu.131 Jungmann	52	HB-UTK SwAF A-41	J.Koch (On rebuild 2.97)	Sandown
D-EFTH	Cessna 195B	16087	N195MB N2102C	J.Koch (Noted 2.97)	Sandown
D-FABE	CCF T-6J Harvard 4	CCF4-499	AA+624 52-8578	J.Koch (Noted 2.97) (As "78" in USN c/s)	Sandown

Regn	Type	C/n	P/I	Owner/(operator)	Probable Base
D-FEHD	Hispano HA-1112-M1L	213	C4K-40?	H.Dittes	Duxford
	(Mod to Messerschmitt Bf.109G-10			(On loan to The Old Flying Machine Co 7.95)	
	- complete with ex Czech WNo.151591 parts)			(As "-+2" in G II Luftwaffe c/s)	
D-FOFM	Antonov AN-2T	12802	LSK-802	J.Koch (Noted 2.97)	Sandown
				(As "12802" in East German AF c/s)	
D-HMQV	Bolkow Bo.102 Helitrainer	6216		The Helicopter Museum	Weston-super-Mare
	(Development aircraft)				
D-HOAY	Kamov Ka.26	7001309	DDR-SPY	The Helicopter Museum	Weston-super-Mare
			DM-SPY		
D-IFSB	DH.104 Dove 6	04379	D-CFSB	De Havilland Aircraft Museum	
			G-AMXR/N4280V		Salisbury Hall,London Colney
D-NFBU	Hang-glider			(Noted 1.99)	Edburton
D-OPHA	Fire Balloons 3000 HAFB	057	D-TALCID	R S Kent t/a Balloon Preservation Group	
				"Talcid" (Stored 7.98)	Lancing
D-PAMGAS	Cameron N-90 HAFB	1288		A Kirk t/a Balloon Preservation Group	
				"Pamgas" (Stored 7.98)	Lancing
V7+1H	Aero Focke-Wulf Fw.189A-1 Uhu	0112100		J.Pearce (For rebuild ex Russia 2.92)	Lancing
				(To Czech Republic for rebuild 1995)	
+4	Messerschmitt Bf.109E WerkeNr 1190			Imperial War Museum (Static rebuild 2.99)Duxford	
3579	Messerschmitt Bf.109E-4	3579		D.Price (Op Santa Monica Museum of Flying)	
					Colchester
	(Imported ex Murmansk late 1992; coded 14 (white) ex I/LG2, or 4/JG51) (On rebuild by C.Charleston 6.95)				
8347	Messerschmitt Bf.109F-4 (Erla b.) 8347			D.Price (Op Santa Monica Museum of Flying)	
	(Wreck found Lubjan, 75 ml SE St.Petersburg; coded 10 (Yellow) ex II/JG54; also reported as WNo.8147)				
	(On rebuild Colchester or spares by C.Charleston 12.94)				
10132	Messerschmitt Bf.109F-4	10132		Aero Vintage Ltd (St.Leonards-on-Sea)	
	(Recovered ex Russia 1995; shot down nr Murmansk 12.8.42) (On rebuild Moat Farm, Milden 8.95)				
D2-TOU	Boeing 707-351C	18964	5Y-BFB	Central Training Establishment	Manston
			5A-DJS/TF-VLP/N88TF/VR-HGQ/(VR-HGR)/N363US (Fire Training use 4.96)		
EC-AOY	Aero-Difusion Jodel D.1190-S	E.56		G.Janney (On rebuild 9.97)	Dunkirk, Canterbury
	Compostela				
B2I-103	CASA 2.111B (Heinkel He.111)	17		The Old Flying Machine Co (Noted 2.99)	Duxford
C4E-88 (Sp.AF)	Messerschmitt Bf.109E	-	Sp AF 6-88	R.Lamplough	Denford Manor, Hungerford
				(Poor condition - stored 12.93)	
ES1-16	CASA I-133L Jungmeister	?		J.Sykes (On rebuild 3.94)	Stretton
EL-AJT	Boeing 707-344BA	18891	(N7000Y)	Omega Air (Spares use 2.97)	Manston
			3B-NAE/VP-WKW/ZS-SAD/LX-LGR/ZS-SAD/ZS-DYL		
EL-AKJ	Boeing 707-321C	19375		Omega Air (Open store 3.99)	Southend
			(PP-BRR)/EL-AKJ/9Q-CSW/5N-TAS/N864BX/OB-R-1243/HK-2473/HK-2473X/N473RN/N473PA		
EL-WXA	Bristol 175 Britannia 253F	13508	9Q-CJH	Britannia Aircraft Preservation Trust	Kemble
			CU-T120/G-BDUP/XM496 (Stored 6.98) (As "XM496" in RAF c/s)		
ES-YLK	Aero L-29A Delfin	194521	Est.AF	Not known (Noted 8.97)	Enniskillen
			Soviet AF		
ES-YLO	Aero L-29A Delfin	294912	Est.AF 64	Not known (Noted 11.97)	Lydd
			Soviet AF 64(red) (Reported as G-MAYA reserved)		
F-AZJD	Dewoitine D.27-SA	SA-290 & 322	F-AZBF	The Old Flying Machine Co	Duxford
	(P & W R985)		(F-AZBC)/HB-RAC/U-290 (Noted 2.99)		
F-AZFV	NA T-28B Trojan	174-545	Fr AF 142	Not known	Duxford
			51-7692	(As "51-7692 Fennec No.142" 1.99)	
F-BBQE	Morane-Saulnier MS.315	7603/345		J.Koch (On rebuild 2.97)	Sandown
	(Reported as ex F-BCNL)				
F-BBSO	Auster 5	1792	G-AMJM	C.J.Baker (On rebuild 9.96)	Carr Farm, Newark
			TW452		
F-BDRS	Boeing B-17G-95DL Flying Fortress		N68269	IWM Collection/American Air Museum	Duxford
		32736	NL68269/44-83735 "Mary Alice"		
			(As "231983/IY-G" in 401st BG/615th BS USAAF c/s)		
F-BFUT	Auster J/1N Alpha	3357		T.Cox (On rebuild)	Bristol
				See G-AJEI	
F-BGEQ	DH.82A Tiger Moth	86305	Fr.AF	Brooklands Museum	Rushett Farm, Chessington
			NL846	(On rebuild 11.93)	
F-BGNR	Vickers Viscount 708	35	(OY-AFO)	Not known	Rotary Farm, Hatch
			(OY-AFN)/F-BGNR (Stored 2.99)		
F-BGNX	DH.106 Comet 1XB			See G-AOJT	
F-BMCY	Potez 840	02	N840HP	Shetland Fire Service	Sumburgh
			F-BJSU/F-WJSU (Damaged Sumburgh 29.3.81; extant 12.95)		
F-BMKC	Sportavia Fornier RF4D	4006		(Spares use 2.95)	Biggin Hill
F-BTGV	Aero Spacelines 377SGT Super Guppy	201	N211AS	British Aviation Heritage Collection	
		001	(Airbus Skylink c/s) (Stored 9.97)		Bruntingthorpe
F-BTRP	Sud SA.321F Super Frelon	01	F-WMHC	The Helicopter Museum	Weston-super-Mare
	(Converted from SA.321 c/n 116)		F-BTRP/F-WKQC/F-OCZV/F-RAFR/F-OCMF/F-BMHC/F-WMHC		
			(As "F-OCMF" in Olympic Airways c/s)		
F-BVGB	Airbus A.300B2-1C	06	F-WVGB	Channel Express Air Services Ltd	Bournemouth
				(Spares use 4.98)	
F-BVGC	Airbus A.300B2-1C	07	F-WVGC	Channel Express Air Services Ltd	Bournemouth
				(Spares use 4.98)	
F-GALL	Beechcraft 58P Baron	TJ-83		T.Hayselden (Doncaster) Ltd	Sandtoft
				(Noted 2.96)	

Regn	Type	C/n	P/I	Owner/(operator)	Probable Base
F-GDPA	Cessna 172RG Cutlass	172RG-1091	N9945B	Not known (Wreck stored 12.96)	Shobdon
F-GFLD	Beechcraft C90 King Air	LJ-741	HB-GGW	RFS Aircraft Engineering	Southend
			I-AZIO	(French reg cancelled 4.96 "as sold") (On rebuild 1.99)	
F-GFNO	Robin ATL	16	F-WFNO	Not known (Noted 12.97)	Kemble
F-GFOR	Robin ATL	42		Not known (Noted 12.97)	Gloucestershire
F-GGKR	Max Holste 1521M Broussard	316	F-WGKR	Not known	Duxford
			Fr Mil	(As "316/315-SN" 1.99)	
F-GHOB	Chaize CS.2200-F12 HAFB	30		M.Hammond "Hobicat"	Lindfield, W.Sussex
				(Active 6.97)	
F-GHRI	Colt AS-261 Hot-Air Airship	1380	F-WGGM	British Balloon Museum & Library	Newbury
			G-BPLD	(Stored 1997)	
F-GOBF	SF.260	BF8431		Not known (Noted 3.99)	Elstree
F-HMFI	Farman F.40	6799		RAF Museum (On rebuild 10.95)	RAF Cardington
	(On rebuild to F.141 status ?)				
F-OCMF				See F-BTRP	
F-PYOY	Heintz Zenith 100	52		B.Featherstone (Noted 1.99)	Southend
F-PYVA	Colomban MC-15 Cri-Cri	371		(Stored Guernsey 8.96 - current status uncertain)	
F-PYYV	Rutan LongEz	1046		Not known (Noted 9.97)	
					Poplar Hall Farm, Elmsett
F-WGTX	Heli Atlas			Interflora Firebird plc	Southend
F-WGTY	Heli Atlas			Interflora Firebird plc	Southend
50-BH	Fisher Super Koala Cub 202	-		K.Riches t/a MUL Intl	Guernsey
				(Stored off airfield 1.92: thought still present 1.95)	
114700 (Fr.AF)	North American T-6G-NH Texan	182-387	51-14700	Aces High Ltd	North Weald
				(Wreck stored 3.96 - in Jap AF c/s "2-134")	
HA-MEP	WSK-PZL Antonov AN-2R	1G190-25		V.S.E.Norman t/a Aerosuperbatics	Rendcomb
				(Utterly Butterly/St.Ivel c/s) (Noted 8.98)	
HA-MKA	WSK-PZL Antonov AN-2			Not known (Noted 12.98)	White Waltham
HA-MKE	WSK-PZL Antonov AN-2R	1G158-34	UR-07714	Air Foyle (Noted 12.98)	White Waltham
			CCCP-07714		
HA-MKF	WSK-PZL Antonov AN-2TP	1G233-43	OM-248	Transair Pilot Shop (Noted 12.98)	White Waltham
			OM-UIN/OK-UIN		
HB-IVR	Canadair CL-604 Challenger	5318	HB-IKQ	Sintec SA	Luton
			(TC-DHE)/C-FYYH/C-GLXO		
HB-NAV	Beagle B.121 Pup 2	B121-155	G-AZCM	447 ATC Sqdn	Henley-on-Thames
				(Fuselage only stored 12.94)	
C-558 (Sw.AF)	EKW C-3605	338		Not known (Stored 3.97)	Little Gransden
J-1626	DH Venom			Not known (Noted 10.98)	
HZ-DG1	Boeing 727-51	19124	N604NA	Dallah Avco (Noted 12.97)	Stansted
			(N5604)/N478US		
HZ-KAA	Grumman Gulfstream IV	1294	(HZ-MAL)	Mawarid Ltd	Farnborough
			N416GA		
HZ-SAK1	Boeing 707-351B	18586	VR-BOR	Al Wisar Trading (Stored 2.97)	Manston
			VR-BMV/G-BSZA/EL-SKD/N351SR/N651TF/VR-CAO/VR-HGO/N353US		
HZ-SJP3	Canadair CL-604 Challenger	5346	N604JP	Jouannou & Parskevaides	Farnborough/Riyadh
I-4818	Groppino Microlight	?		(Noted 6.97)	Gloucestershire
MM53432	N.A. AT-6D-NT Harvard	88-16086	42-84305	D.Baker (Coded "RM-11")	Swansea
	(Plates marked "88-3160" and "AF33-038-2117")			(On rebuild 1.99)	
MM54-2372	PA-18-95 Super Cub	18-3572	I-EIXM	Not known (Open store 7.95)	Kesgrave, Ipswich
			54-2372	(Coded "EI-184")	
JY-RJU	DH.104 Dove 7	04540	RJAF 121	Not known (Noted 12.97)	
					Gloucestershire/Blackbushe
LN-AMY	North American AT-6D Harvard	88-16849	(LN-LCS)	The Old Flying Machine Co	Duxford
			(LN-LCN)/N10595/42-85068 (SEAC/RAF c/s 1.99)		
LN-BNM	Noorduyn AT-16-ND Harvard IIB	14-639	R.Dan AF	RAF Museum (As "FE905" in RAF/RCAF c/s)	Hendon
			31-329/FE905/42-12392		
LV-RIE	Nord 1002 Pingouin	-		R.J.Lamplough (Stored 3.97)	North Weald
LY-ABQ	Yakovlev Yak-52	866915	DOSAAF 111	A.Hyatt "15" (Noted 7.98)	Leicester
LY-ABW	Antonov AN-2	1G195-26	DOSAAF	Not known (Noted 6.98)	Kemble
			CCCP-68121		
LY-ABZ	Yakovlev Yak-52	?		(Noted 7.98)	Panshanger
LY-AFA	Yakovlev Yak-52	822608	DOSAAF 110	"110" (Noted 12.97)	Barton
LY-AFB	Yakovlev Yak-52	822610	DOSAAF 112	Termikas Co "112" (Noted 10.97)	Little Gransden
LY-AFH	Yakovlev Yak-52	9612001		(Noted 10.97)	Halfpenny Green
LY-AFV	Yakovlev Yak-52	899915		A Fraser (Noted 7.98)	Oxford
LY-AFX	Yakovlev Yak-52	899413		D Hawkins (Noted 7.98)	
					Bagber Farm, Milbourne St.Andrew, Dorset
LY-AKW	Yakovlev Yak-52	855601	DOSAAF 56	A.Harris "56" (Noted 1.99)	Swanton Morley
LY-ALJ	Yakovlev Yak-52	8910115	DOSAAF 132	D.Hawkins	
				(Damaged Bagber Farm, Milbourne St Andrew 23.7.97)	
LY-ALN	Yakovlev Yak-52	800708	DOSAAF	D.Lewendon "52" (Noted 7.98)	(Alcester)
	(Regd as c/n 800910 but wears c/n plate from 800708 - see LY-AMP below)				
LY-ALO	Yakovlev Yak-52	844815	DOSAAF 135	Sky Associates (UK) Ltd	Old Buckenham
				(Noted 7.97)	
LY-ALS	Yakovlev Yak-52	855509	DOSAAF 69	M.Jefferies "69"	Little Gransden
			DOSAAF 49	"Once a Knight" (Noted 3.98)	
LY-ALT	Yakovlev Yak-52	822704	DOSAAF 121	Titan Airways Ltd (Noted 6.97)	Stansted

Regn	Type	C/n	P/I	Owner/(operator)	Probable Base
LY-ALU	Yakovlev Yak-52	9011107	DOSAAF 124	S.Goodridge (Noted 7.98)	Exeter
LY-AMI	Yakovlev Yak-18T	22202034143	DOSAAF	M Webb (Noted 12.98)	White Waltham
LY-AMJ	Yakovlev Yak-18T	22202047812	DOSAAF	Not known (Noted 2.99)	Earls Colne
LY-AMP	Yakovlev Yak-52	800708	DOSAAF 52	B Brown "52" (Noted 7.98)	Breighton
	(Wears c/n plate 856103 but offically registered as 800708 - see LY-ALN below)				
LY-AMS	Yakovlev Yak-52	844306	DOSAAF 51(red)	Willowair F/C (Noted 3.99)	Southend
LY-AMU	Yakovlev Yak-52	833901	DOSAAF 42(red)	G.Sharp "42" (Noted 5.98)	North Weald
LY-ANI	Yakovlev Yak-52	9411812	DOSAAF	Not known (Noted 4.95)	Little Gransden
LY-AOB	Yakovlev Yak-52	9211517	DOSAAF	M.Schwarz (Noted 6.97)	Enstone
LY-AOC	Yakovlev Yak-52	811308	DOSAAF 30(?)	T Boxhall (Noted 3.99)	Headcorn
LY-AOK	Yakovlev Yak-52	877404	DOSAAF 16	I.Vaughan (Noted 7.98)	Nottingham
LY-AOO	Yakovlev Yak-18T	22202040425		Not known (Noted 8.98)	Sturgate
LY-AOT	Yakovlev Yak-50	?		Not known (Noted 12.98)	White Waltham
LY-AOX	Yakovlev Yak-52	833708	DOSAAF 122	Not known (Noted 8.97)	Biggin Hill
	(Previously reported as c/n 877604 - correct position unconfirmed)				
LY-AOZ	Yakovlev YAK-52	?		Not known (Noted 11.97)	Biggin Hill
LY-ASA	Antonov AN-2	1G139-49	UR-70290 CCCP-70290	Not known (Noted 12.97)	Turweston
LY-FKD	Yakovlev YAK-12			Not known (Noted 2.99)	Oaksey Park
N1FD	Socata TB-200	1614		Not known (Noted 9.98)	Fairoaks
N2CL	PA-28RT-201T Turbo Arrow IV	28R-8131054	N8333S	Speedbird Air Inc (Noted 3.99)	Elstree
N2FU	Gates Lear Jet 31	31-027	N30LJ N91201	Motor Racing Development Corp (Noted 8.97)	Biggin Hill
N2MD	Piper J3C-65 Cub	17521	N70515 NC70515	V.S.E.Norman Not known (Noted 7.97) (G-BSVJ reserved)	Rendcomb
N3CX	Sikorsky S-76B		N762TC	Not known (Noted 9.98)	
N3TQ	Cessna 310Q	310Q-0752	N1534T	Not known (Noted 12.98)	Blackbushe
N5NN	Cessna 421C Golden Eagle III	421C-0446	G-BRIT N6713C	Mistair Inc (Noted 9.97) (Old Britannia Airways c/s)	Elstree
N6FL	Latulip LM-3X	LM-3X-1001		J.Parkins (Stored 9.95 - USAAF c/s)	Bidford
	(Aeronca 7AC scale rep) (Rotax 377)				
N6NE	Lockheed Jetstar 731	5006/40	(VR-CCC) N6NE/N222Y/N731JS/N227K/N12R/N9280R	Aerospace Finance Leasing Inc (Damaged Southampton 27.11.92; dumped 2.98)	Southampton
N8PY	Beechcraft 200 Super King Air	BB-487	VH-PIL N198SC/PT-OYR/N40QN/VH-NIC/N40QN/N40ON/N243KA	Manxtrust/Euroair Inc (Noted 4.98)	Chester/Ronaldsway
N9AY	Cessna 421C Golden Eagle III	421C-0844	G-NSGI N421EL/XA-RAE/N421EB/(N21MW)/N421EB/N2659Z	D & J Avtn (Noted 6.98)	Elstree
(N10LC)	Leopoldoff L-6	129	F-BGIT F-WGIT	I.M.Callier	(Hungerford)
	(On rebuild 9.96 - registration cancelled 1.95 & re-used on Bell OH-58A in 5.97)				
N12FU	Gates Lear Jet 60	60-027	N4230S XA-ICA/N4027S	B.Ecclestone/Motor Racing Development Corporation (Noted 8.97)	Biggin Hill
N12NM	Cessna 501 Citation I/SP (Unit No.660)	501-0257	OE-FLY N500NW/(N992NW)/N2631V	Pektron Aviation Inc/L'Equipe Air (Noted 9.97)	Gamston
N15FH	Cessna 340A II	340A-0722	G-CMAC G-JIMS/G-PETE/N2667N	F.R.Foran & D.Hanley (Noted 9.98)	Liverpool
N18E	Boeing 247D	1722	NC18E NC18/NC13340	The Science Museum	Wroughton
N18V	Beechcraft UC-43-BH Traveler	6869	NC18 Bu 32898/FT507/44-67761	R.J.Lamplough ("As "DR628") (Noted 5.97)	Newbury/North Weald
N19F	Cessna 337A Super Skymaster (Robertson STOL conversion)	337A-0289	N6289F	Not known (Stored 8.97)	Shoreham
N20RJ	Beechcraft H35 Bonanza	D-5193	N7945D	Not known (Noted 7.97)	Shobdon
N23PL	PA-34-200T Seneca II	34-7770010	SE-GPY (D-IICC)/SE-GPY	Not known (Noted 12.97)	Elstree
N25PJ	Cessna 340A II	340A-0912	HB-LNM LN-TEA/N27026	Not known (Noted 6.97)	Guernsey
N26ET	Aerospatiale AS.355F2 Twin Squirrel	5454	PT-HXV N84CC	Multiflight Aviation Inc (Noted 10.97)	Leeds-Bradford
N27BG	Cessna 340	0656		B Gregory (Noted 7.98)	Cardiff
N27MW	Beechcraft B58 Baron	TH995		Not known (Noted 2.98)	Fairoaks
N31NB	PA-31-310 Navajo B	31-7401239	G-OSFT G-MDAS/5N-AEP/G-BJCZ/N61427	N.Brown (Noted 2.99)	Deenethorpe
N31RB	Grumman-American AA-5B Tiger	AA5B-0156		Forest Aviation Ltd (Noted 6.97)	Guernsey
N33EW	Mitsubishi MU-2B-60	1519S.A.	N331W N33TW/N434MA	King Aviation (Noted 3.99)	Southend
N34FA	SOCATA TB-20	866		Not known (Noted 3.99)	Elstree
N36NB	Beechcraft A36 Bonanza	E-2274	F-GKTZ N7249H	Air Bickerton Inc	Biggin Hill
N36SF	Hawker Iraqi Fury FB.11	37539	Iraqi AF 315	J.Bradshaw (Noted 6.97) (As "361" in composite RAN/RCN/RN/Dutch c/s)	Kemble
N36VU	Beechcraft A36 Bonanza	E-2429	G-BWAY N3113F	T.Henshall (Noted 5.97)	Crosland Moor/Ronaldsway
N37WC	Cessna 401	401-0183	N917WS N4083Q	R.H.Durston/Durston Air Service (Noted 5.98)	Liverpool
N40BJ	Dornier Bucker Bu.133 Jungmeister	4	G-AYFO HB-MIO/U-57	K.Weeks (On rebuild by PPS 3.96 as G-AYFO)	Booker

Regn	Type	C/n	P/I	Owner/(operator)	Probable Base
N40D	Stolp SA-100 Starduster 1	4258549		Not known (Noted 9.96)	Biggin Hill
N45AW	PA-28RT-201T Turbo Arrow IV	28R-8431003	N43230	Powersway Aviation (Noted 1.99)	White Waltham
N45CD	PA-28-161 Warrior II	28-7916467	PH-AND	Not known (Noted 4.98)	Old Sarum
			N2841J		
N45JB	Dassault Falcon 100	203	XA-TBL	Barron International Holdings	London/Gibraltar
			N100CT/VR-CLA/N267FJ/F-WZGJ		
N46EA	Percival P.66 Pembroke C.1	P66/83	8452M	P.G.Vallance Ltd	Charlwood, Surrey
	(Regd with c/n K66-046)		XK885	(Stored 6.97)	
N47BK	PA-32RT-301T Turbo Saratoga		N41283	B Kreiskey (Noted 1.99)	Blackbushe
N47DD	Republic P-47D-40RA Thunderbolt		Peru AF 119	Imperial War Museum/American Air Museum Duxford	
	(Composite rebuild)	399-55731	FAP 545/45-49192 (As "226413/ZU-N" in 56th FG USAAF c/s 1.99)		
N47DD	Republic P-47D/N (P-47M) Thunderbolt	-		B.J.S.Grey t/a The Fighter Collection	Duxford
				(As "226671/MX-X" in 78th FG/82nd FS, USAAF c/s)	
				"No Guts - No Glory" (Noted 1.99)	
	(Composite re-build from wreck of original N47DD plus new P-47N fuselage identified unknown)				
N47DG	Republic P-47G Thunderbolt	21962	N42354	Flying A Services (Noted 1996)	Earls Colne
			42-25068		
N47FK	Douglas C-47A Dakota III	9700	EC-FNS	MLP Avn (Stored 2.99)	North Weald
		EC-187/N2669A/C-FEEX/CF-EEX/N308FN/N3PG/N3W/N7V/NC49538/42-23838			
N47FL	Douglas C-47A Dakota III	13087	EC-FIN	MLP Avn	North Weald
	EC-659/N7164E/C-GCTE/C-GXAV/(N92A)/C-GXAV/CAF 12952/RCAF 968/42-93202				
				(Damaged Elstree 17.7.96; stored 2.99 for spares)	
NL51EA	NA P-51D-20NA Mustang	122-31233	N6345T	The Old Flying Machine Co	Duxford
			9554 RCAF "Double Trouble Too" (As "44-63507") (For dlvy 1999)		
N52NW	Grumman G1159 Gulfstream II	52	N211MT	Global Trading Ltd	Bristol/Lulsgate
			N711MT/(N52TJ)/(N52NE)/N5SJ/N38KM/N69SF/C-FFNM/CF-FNM		
N55BN	Beechcraft 95-B55 Baron	TC-1572	G-KCAS	C.Butler (Noted 8.98)	Denham
			G-KCEA/N2840W		
N55EN	Beechcraft 95-E55 Baron			Not known (Noted 3.99)	Elstree
N56ME	Cessna 340A/RAM II	340A-0316	EI-BYH	K.Hawes (Noted 9.97)	Elstree
			N4146G		
N60FM	Boeing 727-27	19535	N7294	Aimes Co (Stored 6.97)	Lasham
N60NB	Mitsubishi Mu-2b Marquise		5Y-VIZ	Dogfox Aviation (Noted 1.99)	Southend/Guernsey
N60VB	Ted Smith Aerostar 600A	60-0182-080		Not known (Noted 7.98)	Compton Abbas
N61HB	PA-31 Turbo Navajo B Panther			Holding & Barnes Ltd (Noted 2.99)	Thurrock
N61SL	Antonov An-2			Not known (Noted 12.98)	White Waltham
N65TD	IAI 1125A Astra-SPX	093		Helios Ltd/Vitol SA	Luton
N66SW	Cessna 340	340-0011	N5035Q	Cabledraw Inc (Noted 9.98)	Elstree
N70AA	Beechcraft 70 Queen Air	LB-35	G-KEAA	Glidair Inc (Op Airwing Services)	Southend
			G-REXP/G-AYPC (Noted 3.99)		
N70VB	Ted Smith Aerostar 600A	60-0446-150	C-GVHQ	(Not known) (Noted 7.98)	Compton Abbas
			N9805Q		
N70XX	Mitsubishi MU.300 Diamond 1	A052SA	I-FRAB	Lovair Inc (Noted 10.96)	Luton
			HB-VHT/N352DM		
NX71MY	Vickers Vimy Replica	01		Greenco (UK) Ltd/K.Snell	Kemble
				(Noted 6.97) (As "G-EAOU")	
N71VE	North American Rockwell	11043	N71VT	Cooper Aerial Surveys Ltd	Sandtoft
	Turbo Commander 690		N2VQ/N2VA	(Noted 2.98)	
N72FG	Mooney M.20M TLS	27-0118		Not known (Noted 3.98)	Jersey
N74DC	Pitts S-2A Special	2228	I-ALAT	D.Cockburn (Noted 3.99)	Elstree
N75	Hanriot HD.1	75	G-AFDX	RAF Museum	Hendon
			OO-APJ/H-1/75 (As "HD-75" in Belgian AF c/s)		
N75TL	Boeing-Stearman A75N1 (N2S-4) Kaydet		N5148N	Not known (As "669" in US Army c/s) (Noted 9.97)	
		75-3616	Bu.37869		Headcorn/Goudhurst, Kent
N79AP	Beechcraft 58P Baron	TJ-206	VH-ORP	R & B Services Ltd (Noted 3.99)	Southend
			ZK-TML/N6648Z		
N79EL	Beechcraft 400A Beechjet	RK-214		Edra Lauren Leasing/DFS Furniture	East Midlands
N80BA	Pitts S-2A Special	648-4		T.Stronge (Noted 6.97)	Newtownards
N80CP	PA-31T-620 Cheyenne II	31T-7920040	N23185	Not known (Noted 7.98)	Thruxton/Blackbushe
N80RF	Beechcraft 60 Duke	P-17	(G-BMSO)	MLP Avn/E.Lundquist (Noted 5.98)	Elstree
			I-DUKA/F-BRAX/HB-GDO		
N86Y	Beechcraft 200 Super King Air	BB-302	N300BW	York International Corporation	Oxford
			N600CP	(Noted 4.97)	
N88PL	PA-46-310P Malibu	46-8508099		D.Clark Grove Fields/Wellesbourne Mountford	
				(Noted 7.98)	
N93GS	Grumman G-21A Goose (P & W R-985)	B-76	C-FBAE	T.Friedrich "Caribbean Clipper"	Elstree
			CF-BAE/CF-FEM/RCAF 392/Bu.37823 (Noted 7.97)		
N97RJ	PA-31 Turbo Navajo	31-7300956	G-SKKB	JRB Aviation Ltd (Noted 2.99)	Earls Colne
			G-BBDS/N7565L		
N99ET	Socata TB-10 Tobago	226	G-BJDG	E.A.Terris (Noted 7.96)	Oxford
			F-BNGR		
N109TW	Agusta A.109C	7650	D-HCKM	Tom Walkinshaw Racing (Noted 7.98)	Oxford
N112JS	Cessna 550 Citation II	550-0032	N905EM	Hamlin Jet Ltd/Flamingo 500 Inc	Luton
	(Unit No.032)		N50US/N66ES/N55BP/N810SG/N810SC/N3251M (Noted 10.97)		
N112WG	Westland WG-30-100	012		The Helicopter Museum	Weston-super-Mare
				(Stored 8.98)	
N113WG	Westland WG-30-100	013		Not known (Dumped 7.98)	Yeovil

Regn	Type	C/n	P/I	Owner/(operator)	Probable Base
N114WG	Westland WG-30-100	014	G-EFIS G-17-18	The Helicopter Museum (Noted 8.98)	Weston-super-Mare
N115WG	Westland WG-30-100	015		Not known (Dumped 7.98)	Yeovil
N116WG	Westland WG-30-100	016	(G-BLLG)	The Helicopter Museum (Stored 8.98)	Weston-super-Mare
N118WG	Westland WG-30-100	018		The Helicopter Museum (Stored 8.98)	Weston-super-Mare
N125GP	Gates Learjet 31A	31A-162	N162LJ N525GP	Damon Hill	Dublin
N125XX	BAe HS.125 Srs.700A	NA0254 & 257075	N124AR N125TR/N125AM/(G-BHKF)/G-5-13 (Noted 5.97)	Connex Aviation/Ambrion Aviation	Luton
N126NH	Bell 412HP	36067	OE-XLL D-HHJJ/N7078L (Noted 9.96)	Bell Helicopter Textron Ltd	Redhill
N133H	Agusta A.109C	7609	N1NQ	Graff Aviation Ltd (Noted 9.98)	Fairoaks
N139DB	PA-23-250 Aztec E	27-4611	G-AYUL N13992 (Damaged in gales Shoreham 26.1.99)	Not known (Noted 1.99)	White Waltham
N139DP	Bell P-39Q-5BE Airacobra	?	(New Guinea) 42-19993	The Fighter Collection (As "219993" in USAAC c/s) "Brooklyn Bum 2nd" (On rebuild in USA for dely)	Duxford
N139XX	Gates Learjet 31A	60-139	N233FX	Corporate Jets Ltd	Prestwick
N142TW	Beech 58	TH-1841		(Noted 1.99)	Fairoaks
N145DF	Cessna 501 I/SP	501-0055		Ambrion Aviation	Luton
N146GA	Cessna 425 Conquest I	425-0074	HB-LPU N6845Y	Davis Aircraft Operations Inc (Noted 9.97)	Edinburgh
N150JC	Beechcraft A35 Bonanza	D.2084	N8674A	M.Hornblower (Damaged Wick 18.6.83; on rebuild 3.98)	Hurstbourne Tarrant, Hants
N159M	Dasssult Falcon 50EX	276	F-WWHB	Motorola inc	Farnborough
N172AM	Cessna 172M			Not known (Noted 3.99)	Seething
N177CE	Cessna 177RG Cardinal	177RG-1308	N52914	Not known (Noted 11.98)	Farnborough
N179PT	Vought F4U-5N Corsair	-	N171NP N179PT N4903M/FAH 604/N...../Bu.122179	Wizzard Investments/David Arnold (Op Flying A Services) (Noted 10.97)	Earls Colne
N181WW	Beagle B.206 Srs.1	B.018	G-BCJF N181WW/G-BCJF/XS773	Not known (Open Store 2.99)	Biggin Hill
N190RM	Beechcraft E90 King Air	LW-1	N64RJ N64RA/N934K	R & M Aviation Inc (Noted 11.97)	Norwich
N196B	North American F-86A Sabre	151-43611	48-242	American Air Museum (As "80242/FU-242" in USAF c/s 1.99)	Duxford
N201XJ	Mooney M.20J	240494		Not known (Noted 10.98)	
N206NT	Bell 206B JetRanger III	4216		Bell Helicopter Textron (Noted 6.96)	Redhill
N210MP	Cessna T210N Turbo Centurion II	T210-63193	(G-BPGO) N210MP	Welback Estates Ltd (Noted 12.98)	Compton Abbas
N220TW	Piaggio P.180 Avanti	1018	LZ-VPA	Tom Walkinshaw Racing/Marbrite Inc (Noted 4.97)	Oxford
N228CX	Socata TBM-700	84		B.Holmes (Noted 1.99)	Southend/Cannes
N250MC	PA-23-250 Aztec E	27-7305142	EI-BXP G-BSFL/PH-NOA/9M-AUS/PH-NOA/N40378	Oilsearch (US) Inc (Noted 6.97)	Gloucestershire
N250TP	Beechcraft A36 Bonanza (Allison 250-B17)	E-2408	N416HC N600TT/N3107K (Willie Carson) (Noted 3.98)	Minster Enterprises Inc	Oxford
N252BH	Mooney M.20K (252TSE)	25-1137		L.Marks (Noted 6.98)	Bournemouth
N252JP	Hughes 369E	0346E		Not known (Noted 6.97)	Banchory
N252RM	Mooney M.20K (252TSE)	25-1061		Not known (Noted 4.96)	Denham
N252JS	Grumman Gulfstream V	525	N594GA	Smurfitt Group	Dublin
N260KH	SIAI-Marchetti SF-260D	739	I-SMAD	Cheyne Motors Ltd (Noted 3.98)	Old Sarum
N260QB	Aerotek Pitts S-2S Special	3002		D.Baker (Noted 12.95)	Exeter
N273TB	Beech Baron			Not known (Noted 6.98)	Welshpool
N281Q	Enstrom F.28A	266		Stephenson Avn Ltd (Wreck stored 2.96)	Goodwood
N295SS	PA-46 Malibu	46-36174		(Noted 1.99)	Fairoaks
N310QQ	Cessna 310			(Noted 3.99)	Elstree
N311QQ	Cessna 560 Citation V	560-0167	N211DG (167WE)/N20CN/(N68873)	Woodlands Ltd	Manchester
NL314BG	North American P-51D-20NA Mustang	-	C-GZQX	Flying A Services/David Arnold (Noted 1996)	Earls Colne
	(Regd with c/n 122-39599 ex C-FBAU/44-73140 which crashed/dbf 7.7.84; possibly a composite rebuild)				
N321DH	Pilatus PC.XII	116	HB-FQJ	Not known (Noted 3.97)	Farnborough
N331SJ	Gates Lear Jet 31A	31A-113	N31LJ	Sterling Jet (Noted 8.97)	Prestwick
N340AS	Cessna 340A II	340A-0989	LX-GIA 5B-CHN/G-PJAY/N98DA/N3967C	S.Fawcett (Noted 7.98)	Guernsey
N340SC	Cessna 340			Not known (Noted 2.99)	North Weald
N340YP	Cessna 340A II	340A-0990	VR-CHR G-OCAN/D-ICIC/(N3970C)	Not known (Noted 2.98)	Biggin Hill/Guernsey
N347GS	Gates Lear Jet 60	60-026	N60LJ N700GS/N60LJ/N4026Z	Heron 550 Inc (Noted 4.97)	Farnborough
N352AE	Dassault Falcon	172	N352AF N/177FJ/F-WFFD	Fayair Inc	Stansted/White Plains, New York
N360Q	Lockheed L.188CF Electra	1112	N360WS N360Q/N8LG/PT-DZK/N777DP/N129US	Air Atlantique Ltd (Noted 7.97)	Coventry
N367M	Raytheon Hawker 800XP	258367	N3236E	Dudmaston Ltd/Bruno de Mico	Luton/Milan

Regn	Type	C/n	P/I	Owner/(operator)	Probable Base
N370SA	PA-23-250F Aztec		G-BKVN	R K Pugh (Noted 3.99)	Guernsey/Shoreham
N388CA	Commander 114B	14588		Not known (Noted 5.98)	White Waltham
N402R	Cessna 402B II	402B-1364	G-BTVY	Not known (Noted 1.97)	Cardiff
			N402R/N888EE/(N4609A)		
N407FD	Siai-Marchetti SF-260D	772		M.Clarke	Newcastle
				(As "MC-04" in French AF c/s; noted 7.98)	
N413JB	Cameron O-84			D P Busby "Midnight Aurora"	Lancing
				(Balloon Preservation Group 7.98)	
N414FZ	Cessna 414	414-0175	G-AZFZ	Not known (Noted 2.99)	Jersey
			N8245Q		
N417CL	Canadair CL-601-3A Challenger	5107	C-GLWZ	Electronic Data Systems Corp	Farnborough
N425TV	Cessna 425 Conquest I	425-0176	ZS-LDR	Not known (Noted 3.98)	Aberdeen
			N6873T		
N459LJ	Gates Learjet 45	45-009	N984GC	Stealth Aviation	Jersey
N473BS	PA-28RT-201T Turbo Arrow IV	28R-8631003	G-BNYY	B.Strickland (Noted 3.99)	Southend
			N25WA/N77860/G-BNYY/N9129X/N9517N		
N500LN	Howard 500	500-113	N381RD	D.Baker (Noted 12.95)	Exeter
	(Conversion of Lockheed PV-1 Ventura c/n 5560) N206G/N200G/N539N/SAAF 6417/FP579/Bu.34670				
N501CF	Cessna 501 Citation I/SP	501-0128	N900MM	Inductoheat Corporation Inc	Birmingham
	(Unit No.522)		N522CC/(N26504) (Noted 3.97)		
N501D	Cessna 501 Citation I/SP	501-0298	VR-CMS	Cirrus Aviation Inc (Noted 6.98)	Guernsey
	(Unit No.511)		N65M/OE-FIW/I-GERA/(PH-JOB)/N26498		
N502TC	PA-30-160 Twin Comanche	30-881	G-BMSX	Not known (Noted 8.98)	Blackbushe
			N502TC/N7802Y		
N510PS	Cessna 310N	310N-0054	G-AWTA	Heliscott Ltd	Walton Wood, Pontefract
			EI-ATB/N4154Q (Noted 11.97)		
N519MC	PA-28-140 Cherokee Cruiser	28-7325519	G-BBID	Not known (Noted 3.99)	Elstree
N560MM	Cessna 560 Citation V	560-0235	N129PJ	Sagesoft Ltd	Newcastle/Luton
			N52RG/N22RG/N1288D		
N606LG	American Blimp A60			Not known (Noted 1.99)	Halfpenny Green
N624TC	Cessna T303 Crusader	303-00130	EC-DRR	Not known (Dumped 12.98)	Prestwick
			N4971C		
N636N	Cessna 501 Citation I/SP	501-0069	N501EF	Pelmont Avn (Noted 9.96)	Southampton
	(Unit No.441)		N2906A		
N650J	Cessna 650 Citation			Not known (Noted 12.98)	Farnborough
N666GA	Gulfstream AA-5B Tiger	AA5B-1136		Mr.Fasano (Noted 8.97)	Enniskillen
N666LP	PA-46 Malibu	46-36130		Not known (Noted 1.99)	Guernsey
N700JJ	Socata TBM-700	2	F-GLBA	JCT Aviation Ltd (Noted 1.98)	Fairoaks
N703JS	Dassault Falcon 10	157	N64AM	Medusa International	Farnborough
			N157EA/F-GFBG/N80GP/N101EF/(N900AR)/N222FJ/F-WZGF		
N707KS	Boeing 707-321B	20025	N728Q	Kalair Corporation (Noted 5.97)	Stansted
			N886PA		
N707TJ	Boeing-Stearman A75N1 (N2S-1) Kaydet		N9PK	V.S.E.Norman t/a Aerosuperatics Ltd	Rendcomb
	(Mod to Super Stearman -	75-950	N50057	(Crunchie c/s) "Honey" (Noted 7.97)	
	450 hp P & W R-985)		Bu.3173		
N709EL	Beechcraft 400A Beechjet	RK-52	(N709EW)	Edra Lauren Leasing/DFS Furniture	East Midlands
			N709JB	(Noted 9.97)	
N709PC	Boeing 707-323B	20175	N8436	Omega Air (Stored 9.96)	Shannon
N735CX	Cessna 182Q Skylane II	182-65329		B.Holmes (Noted 5.98)	Barnard Farm, Thurrock
	(Mod to Advanced Lift 260 STOL)				
N735XQ	Cessna 182	182-65570		Not known (Noted 1.99)	Bournemouth
N747SY	Mitsubishi MU-2B-60 Maquise	1556.SA	N277JR	Smith Young Partnership (Noted 1.97)	Liverpool
			N277JR/N482MA		
N766AM	Aerospatiale AS.355N Twin Sqirrel	5601		Beacon Energy (Aviation) Ltd	Beacon Farm, Leics
N768WM	Boeing-Stearman B75N-1 Kaydet (N2S-3)	75-7394	G-ROAN	V.S.E.Norman (On overhaul 7.97)	Rendcomb
			N4685N/Bu.07790		
N772H	Cessna T337GP Turbo Pressurised Super		N1ZG	R.M.English & Co (Noted 7.97)	Full Sutton
	Skymaster II (Conv to Riley Rocket) P337-0265				
N773DC	Beechcraft 58 Baron	TH-755	G-BDWK	DC Energy Ltd (Noted 5.97)	Gamston
			(G-BEET)		
N797HG	PA-46-310P Malibu	46-8408064	N43644	(Noted 9.97)	Guernsey
N800H	Grumman F8F-2 Bearcat	D.1126	N2YY	BJS Grey t/a The Fighter Collection	Duxford
			N7827C/Bu.121752 (As "106/A" in USN c/s) (Noted 11.97)		
N800LA	Cessna 550 Citation II	550-0295	N483G	Hamlin Jet	Luton
			N68876		
N809SW	PA-31T Cheyenne II	31T-8020080	(F-ODMM)	Volkl Inc/Demolition Services Ltd (Noted 3.98)	Leeds-Bradford
N816RL	Beechcraft E90 King Air	LW-187	N66BP	L'Equipe Air Ltd/Gamston Aviation (Noted 12.97)	Gamston
			N816EP/N900MH/N2187L		
N829CB	Cessna 550 Citation Bravo	550-0829	N5096S	JJB Sports (Noted 1.99)	Blackpool
N836TP	Beechcraft A36TP Bonanza	E-2124	N6770M	Velcourt East plc (Noted 7.98)	Anwick
N840LE	Gulfstream 690C Commander 840	11709	N690BA	O.Henriksen (Noted 6.97)	Guernsey
			ZS-KZM/N5961K		
N841WS	Cessna 550 Citation Bravo	550-0849	N5086W	Walter Scott & Ptnrs	Edinburgh
N904RE	Rotec Rally III	25513		Not known (Stored 8.95)	Bantry
N909RM	Mooney M.20J (201)	24-0636		I.M.Johnson (Noted 1.99)	Southend

Regn	Type	C/n	P/I	Owner/(operator)	Probable Base
N909WJ	Grumman FM-2 Wildcat (Regd as ex.Bu.16203)	2020	Bu.46867	Wizzard Investments/D.Arnold (Op Flying A Services) (Noted 10.97)	Duxford
N951SF	Beechcraft 56TC Baron	TG-83	N23PB	Not known (Noted 3.99)	Elstree
N961EL	Beechcraft 60 Duke	P-154	N961LL N7187D	Roughaire Inc (Stored 7.97)	Newcastle
N966SW	Cessna 560 Citation V Ultra	560-0284	N5108G	Terry Coleman Ltd	Manchester
N991RV	Dassault Falcon 10	24	N301JJ F-GBTI/N1924V/N116FJ/F-WJML	Eddie Irvine	Dublin
N995MH	Cessna 195	7168		Not known (Noted 7.98)	Compton Abbas
N997JB	Partenavia P.68C-TC	288-20-TC	F-GROG HB-LSB/F-GEQD/N60CH/YV-2318P	Not known (Noted 8.97)	Fairoaks
N999DF	Cessna 441 Conquest II	441-0185	N999DB N441CM/(N2724R)	Semitool Europe Inc (Noted 6.96)	Cambridge
N999MH	Cessna 195			Not known (Noted 7.98)	Compton Abbas
N999PJ	Morane-Saulnier MS.760 Paris 2	089	F-BJLY	R.J.Lamplough (Noted 5.97)	North Weald
N1012W	Beechcraft 58 Baron	TH-305		Not known (Stored 7.97) (Reserved as N273TR 6.97)	Welshpool
N1024L	Beechcraft 60 Duke	P-78	C-FOPH CF-OPH/N1024L/CF-OPH	R.Ogden (Noted 8.97)	Barton
N1069S	Beechcraft B200 Super King Air	BB-1549		JJB Sports (Noted 9.98)	Leeds-Bradford
N1134K	Luscombe 8AE Silvaire (Cont C85)	3861	NC1134K	M.Masters (Noted 10.97) (Damaged Turweston 28.8.96)	Lower Upham
N1158V	Cessna 310J	0172		Not known (Noted 9.98 in poor condition)	Popham
N1172X	PA-34-200T Seneca II	34-7570228		Not known (Noted 11.97)	Lydd
N1207V	Bell 430	49017		Not known (Noted 10.98)	Fairoaks
N1234T	Beechcraft C33A Bonanza	CE-141		Not known (Noted 6.97)	Fairoaks
N1325M	Boeing-Stearman E75 (N2S-5) Kaydet	75-8484	Bu.43390	R.W.Sage t/a Blackbarn Avn (Stored 10.97)	Priory Farm, Tibenham
NC1328	Fairchild 24KS	3310		R.W.Sage t/a Blackbarn Avn (Stored 9.97)	Priory Farm, Tibenham
N1344	Ryan PT-22-RY Recruit	2086	41-20878	Mrs.H.Mitchell t/a PT Flt (Noted 3.95)	RAF Cosford
N1350J	Rockwell Commander 112B	516		G.Richards (Noted 3.97)	Cardiff
N1351H	PA-32-300 Cherokee Six	32-7740034		Not known (Noted 10.97) "Gabriel"	Shoreham
N1407J	Rockwell Commander 112A	407		Not known (Noted 12.98)	Blackbushe
N1565B	Beechcraft 400 Beechjet	RJ-65		A.Ogden & Sons plc (Noted 12.97)	Leeds-Bradford
N1745M	Cessna 182P Skylane II	182-64424		Not known (Noted 1.97)	Cardiff
N1778X	Cessna 210L Centurion	210-60798		Not known (Noted 8.98)	Jersey
N2000M	Cessna 560 Citation V	560-0146	(N6877Q)	Siebe Inc (Noted 12.98)	Farnborough
N2099L	Beechcraft Baron			Not known (Noted 6.98)	Blackbushe
N2121T	Gulfstream AA-5B Tiger	AA5B-1031		J.Siebols (Noted 3.99)	Southend
N2138J	English Electric Canberra TT.18 (Built Avro)	TT.18 R3/EA3/6640	WK126	Biggles Air Inc (Loaned to Gloucestershire Avn Collection 4.96) (As "WK126/843")	Gloucestershire
N2273Q	PA-28-181 Cherokee Archer II	28-7790389		Not known (Noted 7.98)	Panshanger
N2495Q	PA-34-200T Seneca II	34-7770188		Not known (Noted 6.97)	Alderney
NC2612	Stinson Junior SR	8754		A.L.Young (Stored 4.96)	Henstridge
N2652P	PA-22-150 Tri-Pacer	22-2992		Anne Lait "Jeff Jeff" (Noted 5.98)	Weston
N2657N	Cessna 421C Golden Eagle	421C-0811	G-TELL N2657N	Not known (Noted 1.98)	
N2668Z	Cessna 340A II	340A-0731		Not known (Noted 6.97)	Luton
N2675Y	Cessna 340	340-0760		Not known (Noted 9.98)	Fairoaks
N2706X	Cessna 335	335-0018		Not known (Noted 3.99)	Elstree
N2923N	PA-32-300 Cherokee Six	32-7940207		G.Semler (Noted 12.98)	Buttermilk Hall Farm, Blisworth
N2929W	PA-28-151 Cherokee Warrior	28-7415457	OO-GPE N9619N	R.Lobell (Noted 3.99)	Elstree
N2967N	PA-32-300 Six	32-7940242		(Noted 2.98)	Guernsey/Bournemouth
N2989Q	Cessna 421			(Noted 10.98)	Farnborough
N3023W	Beechcraft V35B Bonanza	D-9517		(Noted 11.97)	Guernsey
N3036A	PA-34-200T Seneca II	34-7970003		Biggles Avn (Noted 11.98)	Birmingham
N3044B	PA-34-200T Seneca II	34-7970012		(Noted 5.97)	East Winch
N3188H	Ercoupe 415C	3813	NC3188H	(Damaged on landing c 7.92; stored for spares 9.97)	Maypole Farm, Chislet
N3839H	Ted Smith Aerostar			(Noted 9.98)	Elstree
N3922B	Boeing-Stearman E75 (PT-17) Kaydet (Cont W670)	75-5805	42-17642	Eastern Stearman Ltd (Noted 7.97)	Swanton Morley
N3995W	PA-32-260 Cherokee Six	32-963		(Noted 5.98)	Blackbushe
N4050S	Sikorsky YUH-60A Blackhawk	70-005		Westland Helicopters Ltd (Apprentice Training/Installation Trials 3.93)	Yeovil
N4081J	Cessna 150G	150-65381		G.Sargeant/J.Winder (Noted 7.97)	Hundon
N4085E	PA-18-150 Super Cub	18-7809059		Not known (Noted 6.97)	Top Farm, Tadlow
N4173T	Cessna 320D Skyknight	320D-0073		J.Irwin (Noted 2.97)	Cranfield
N4232Y	Cessna F150G	0098	D-EBYW	Not known (Noted 3.98)	Stapleford
N4306Z	PA-28-161 Warrior II	28-8316073		USAF F/C (Noted 9.98)	RAF Lakenheath
N4337K	Cessna 150K	150-71583	G-BTSA N6083G	Not known (Noted 9.98)	Watchford Farm, Yarcombe

Regn	Type	C/n	P/I	Owner/(operator)	Probable Base
N4565L	Douglas DC-3-201A (Regn N3TV reserved but NTU)	2108	LV-GYP LV-PCV/N129H/N512/N51D/N80C/NC21744	390th BG Memorial Air Museum	Framlingham
				(Damaged in gales 10.87 & 25.1.90; on rebuild 8.97)	
N4596N	Boeing-Stearman E75 (PT-13D) Kaydet (Lyc R680-7)	42-17782 75-5945		N.Mason & D.Gilmour t/a Intrepid Avn Co (Noted 5.97) (US Mail c/s)	North Weald
N4647J	PA-28R-180 Cherokee Arrow	28R-30541		R.Breckell (Noted 7.97)	Barton
N4698W	Rockwell Commander 112TC-A	13274		W.Haynes (Noted 2.99)	Gamston
N4806E	Douglas A-26B-45DL Invader	27451	44-34172	A-26 Europe Inc (R & R Cadman) (3rd BW c/s) (Stored 3.95) "Kunsan Killer"	Manston
N4893K	Cessna 185A	1850240		Not known (Noted 8.98)	Hinton-in-the Hedges
N5025J	Hiller UH-12B	726	G-AVAJ Thai AF 116	C.R.James t/a Flight "C" Helicopters (Stored 4.93)	Whitehall Farm, Benington
N5052P	PA-24-180 Comanche	24-56	G-ATFS N5052P	T.A.G.Randell (Stored 2.97)	Nuthampstead
N5057V	Boeing-Stearman PT-13D Kaydet	75-5598	42-17435	V.S.E.Norman (Crunchie c/s) "Charlie Brown" (Noted 7.97)	Rendcomb
N5092P	PA-24-180 Comanche	24-101		(Rear fuselage stored 9.96)	Little Staughton
N5115C	Robinson R-22 Beta	1564	G-NABS	Burman Aviation Ltd	Cranfield
	(W/off 30.6.91 Cumbernauld as G-NABS, US reg canx 10.96; wreck stored 2.97)				
NC5171N	Lockheed 10A Electra			See G-LIOA	
N5237V	Boeing B-17G-95DL Flying Fortress	32509	(N6466D) N5237V/Bu.77233/44-83868	RAF Museum (As "483868/N" in 94th BG USAAF c/s)	Hendon
N5240H	PA-16 Clipper	16-44	NC5240H	D.Hillier (Noted 7.98) Bagber Farm, Milbourne St.Andrews, Dorset	
N5345N	Boeing-Stearman PT-13D Kaydet	75-5718	42-17555	Eastern Stearman Ltd (On rebuild 6.96 - for Holland)	Swanton Morley
N5419	Bristol Scout D Replica (Built by Leo Opdycke 1983)	-		Bristol Aero Collection (As "N5419" in RFC c/s)	Kemble
N5428C	Cessna 170A	19462		P.Norman (Noted 7.98)	Audley End
N5632R	Maule MX7-180 Star Rocket	7344R		D.Group (Noted 8.98)	Stowes Farm, Tillingham
N5644L	American AA-1 Yankee	AA1-0044		S.Matterface (Noted 10.97)	Biggin Hill
N5668H	Maule MX7-180 Star Rocket	11028C		Not known (Noted 9.97)	Headcorn
N5718H	PA-16 Clipper	16-323		Paul Penn-Sayers (Stored 6.95)	Scaynes Hill, Haywards Heath
N5820T	Westland WG-30	004	G-BKFD G-17-28	The Helicopter Museum (Stored 8.98)	Weston-super-Mare
N5824H	PA-38-112 Tomahawk II	38-81A0118	D-EFFX	Lakenheath F/C (Noted 3.98)	RAF Lakenheath
N5832M	Aero Dynamics Sparrowhawk	8411-2		Not known (Noted 6.96)	Swanton Morley
N5834N	Rockwell Commander 114	14383		Not known (Noted 10.98) (Damaged River Severn 23.10.98)	Cardiff
N5840T	Westland WG-30	006	G-BKFF G-17-30	The Helicopter Museum (Stored 8.98)	Weston-super-Mare
N5880T	Westland WG-30	009		The Helicopter Museum (Stored 8.98)	Weston-super-Mare
N6010Y	Commander 114B	14589		Not known (Noted 8.97)	Biggin Hill
N6039X	Commander 114B	14639		G.Bishop (Noted 7.98)	White Waltham
N6107Y	Commander 114B	14627		Not known (Noted 11.97)	Guernsey
N6182G	Cessna 172N Skyhawk II	172-73576		Not known (Noted 5.97)	North Weald
N6191K	Republic RC-3 Seabee	382	NC6191K	D.T.Smollett (Noted 5.96)	Bratton Clovelly, Okehampton
N6251S	Beechcraft T-34A Mentor	G-101	N34AB 53-3340	D.Arnold (Noted 9.97)	North Weald
N6268	Travel Air Model 2000	707	NC6268	Bianchi Avn Film Svs Ltd (As "Fokker D.VII 626/8" in Ernst Udet c/s) (Blue Max Movie Acft Museum 7.96)	Booker
N6339U	PA-28-236 Cherokee Dakota	28-8011089	OO-JFD F-GCMV/OO-HLM/N8152S	Thistle Aviation Inc	
N6526D	North American P-51D-25NA Mustang	RCAF 9289 122-39874	44-73415	RAF Museum (As "413573/B6-V" in 361st FS/357th FG USAAF c/s)	Hendon
	(Composite - mainly based on ex AURI airframe)				
N6601Y	PA-23-250 Aztec C	27-3905		Not known (Noted 7.97)	Guernsey
N6632L	Beechcraft C23 Musketeer	M-2188		Not known (Noted 11.98)	White Waltham
N6699D	Piasecki HUP-3 Retriever	51	RCN 622 USN/51-16622	The Helicopter Museum (Noted 8.98) (As "622" in RCN c/s)	Weston-super-Mare
N6834L	Cessna T310R II	310R-2137		P.Basch/Tropair Engineering Ltd (Noted 1.97)	Leeds-Bradford
N6907E	Cessna 175			(Noted 3.99)	Elstree
N7027E	Hawker Tempest V	-	EJ693	K.Weeks (On rebuild by Aerofab 10.95)	Andover
N7070A	Cessna S550 Citation SII	S550-0068	N4049 N404G/N1272Z	Omega Air Inc (Noted 10.98)	Dublin
N7133J	Mooney M.20C Mark 21	3116	G-BJAK OO-CAB/OO-VLB/N5814Q	Not known (Noted 4.96)	Belle Vue Farm, Huntshaw
N7148R	Beechcraft B55 Baron	TC-2028	N2198L C-GWFD/N2198L/D-IGRW/N2198L	Not known (Noted 3.98)	Fairoaks/Guernsey
N7263S	Cessna 150H	150-67963		Not known (Noted 9.96)	Elstree
N7348P	PA-24-250 Comanche	24-2526		J.Bown (Noted 3.99)	Netherthorpe
N7374A	Cessna A150M Aerobat 135 (Tailwheel conversion)	A150-0726		J.Thomas "Turnin' Tricks" (Noted 7.98)	Watchford Farm, Branscombe

Regn	Type	C/n	P/I	Owner/(operator)	Probable Base
N7614C	North American B-25J/PBJ-1J Mitchell	44-31171		Imperial War Museum/American Air Museum Duxford	
		108-37246		(As "31171" in US Marines c/s 1.99)	
N7777G	Lockheed L.749A-79 Constellation			See G-CONI	
N7813M	PA-28-180 Cherokee D	28-5227	G-AZYF	Not known (Noted 5.98)	Leicester
			5Y-AJK/N7813N		
N7832P	PA-24-250 Comanche	24-3052		Not known (Noted 6.97)	Elstree/Guernsey
N7997E	Cessna 150	17797		Flt C Helicopters	Bramford, Ipswich
				(Stored 9.92)	
N8153E	PA-28RT-201T Turbo Arrow IV	28R-8131185		Not known (Noted 12.97)	Caernarfon
N8162G	Boeing-Stearman PT-17 Kaydet	75-323	YS-177P	Eastern Stearman Ltd	Swanton Morley
			N52061/40-1766 (Noted 9.96) (As "28" in US Army c/s)		
N8258F	Beech 36			Not known (Noted 3.99)	Elstree
N8360Y	PA-28-181 Archer II	28-8190195		Not known (Noted 9.97)	Booker
N8471Y	PA-28-236 Dakota	28-8211019		Not known (Noted 1.99)	Panshanger
N8618G	Cessna 340A/RAM	340A-0708		Dogfox Aviation (Noted 1.99)	Southend/Dublin
N8728A	Aero Dynamics Sparrow Hawk II	87005-26		F.Beckett/Highland Aero Dynamics Ltd	
	(Rotax 532)	(Status uncertain but believed unmarked specimen stored 10.95)			Swanton Morley
N8754J	Christen A-1 Husky	1160	(ex)	A.Febrache (Noted 7.98)	Guernsey
N8862V	Bellanca 17-31ATC Turbo Viking	31022		M Hales (Noted 7.98)	Little Staughton
N9050T	Douglas C-47A-10DK Dakota 3	12472	5N-ATA	J.Woodhouse/Dakota's American Bistro	Fleet
			PH-MAG	(Parts displayed in restaurant 3.96)	
			G-AGYX/KG437/42-92648		
N9059H	Reims Cessna F.172N Skyhawk II	1815	OY-CBZ	A.Nutbrown (Noted 7.98)	Jersey
			D-EOSS		
N9089Z	North American TB-25J-25NC Mitchell		"HD368"	Aces High Ltd	North Weald
		108-34136	N9089Z	(As "44-30861" in USAAF c/s) "Bedsheet Bomber"	
			44-30861	(G-BKXW reserved 1983 but NTU; stored 10.97)	
N9115Z	North American TB-25N-20NC Mitchell		44-29366	RAF Museum	Hendon
		108-32641		(As "34037" in USAAF c/s; allotted 8838M)	
N9122N	PA-46-310P Malibu	46-8097		Not known (Noted 12.97)	Booker
N9143C	Rockwell Commander 685	12040	G-BWEK	Cooper Aerial Surveys Ltd Sandtoft	
			CS-APB/N9132N (Stored 10.97)		
N9146N	Cessna 401B/RAM conv.	401B-0010		Not known (Noted 5.98)	Weston
N9303W	PA-28-235 Cherokee B	28-10981		R.K.Spence (Noted 1.97)	Cardiff
N9381P	PA-24-260 Comanche C	24-4882		Not known (Noted 6.97)	Guernsey
N9469P	PA-24-260 Comanche C	24-4979		Not known (Noted 12.98)	Guernsey
N9606H	Fairchild M.62A-4 Cornell (PT-26-FA)	FH768		Rebel Air Museum (On rebuild 3.96)	Earls Colne
	(Quoted p/i thought unlikely)	T43-4361	42-14361	(C/n T43-3642?)	
N9694Q	Cessna 172M	172-65778		Not known (Noted 9.97)	Elstree
N9727G	Cessna 180	180-52227	G-FESC	B Richardson (Noted 7.98)	Slinfold Farm
N9987Q	Westland WS-51 Dragonfly HR.5	WA/H/56	7703M	Flambards Village Theme Park	Helston
			WG725	(As "WG754/912/CU")	
N11824	Cessna 150L	150-75652		Not known (On rebuild 8.97)	Framlingham
N12426	SNCAN Stampe SV-4C	677	F-BGGT	D.Kaberry	
	(Lyc VO-360)		Fr AF (Damaged Middleton Sands, Heysham 16.7.94; status uncertain)		
N14113	North American T-28B Trojan	174-398		FA Haiti 1236 Radial Revelations Ltd (USN c/s)	Duxford
			N14113/FrAF 119/51-7545 (As "51-7545 Fennec No.119" 1.99)		
N14234	HP.137 Jetstream	234	N102SC	British Aerospace plc	East Fortune
	(Conv to Jetstream 31 mobile display unit)	N1BE/(N200SE)/G-BBBV/G-8-12 (On loan to Museum of Flight 3.96)			
NC14485	Rearwin 7000 Sportster	403		Not known (Stored 8.94)	Thruxton
NC16676	Fairchild 24C-8F	3101		R.W.Sage	Priory Farm ,Tibenham
				t/a Blackbarn Avn (Stored 9.97)	
NC18028	Beechcraft D17S	147	NC18028	P.H.McConnell (Noted 6.98)	Popham
N21381	PA-34-200 Seneca	34-7350274	F-BUTM	Not known (Noted 5.97)	Dunkeswell
			F-ETAL		
N23659	Beechcraft 58 Baron	TH-893		P.R.Earp (Noted 6.97)	Guernsey
N23840	Beechcraft C24R Sierra 200	MC-556		A.Hall (Noted 3.97)	Liverpool
N27495	PA-31-310 Navajo	31-7812041		Not known (Noted 6.97)	Biggin Hill/Guernsey
N27597	PA-31-350 Navajo	31-7852073		Matair (Noted 3.99)	Southend
N27850	PA-31-350 Navajo Panther	31-7912024		Not known (Noted 7.97)	Elstree
N32625	PA-34-200T Seneca II	34-7570039	G-PALM	Not known	Sleap/Alderney
			SE-LAN/N32625 (Damaged 19.1.98 Guernsey)		
N33528	SNCAN Stampe SV-4C			See G-BRXP	
N33600	Cessna L-19A-CE Bird Dog	22303	51-11989	Museum of Army Flying	AAC Middle Wallop
				(As "111989" in US Army c/s)	
N33870	Fairchild M62A (PT-19-FA)	T40-237	G-BTNY	R.Lamplough	North Weald
	Cornell		N33870/US Army (As "02538" in US Army c/s) (Noted 6.98)		
NC33884	Aeronca 65CA	CA.14101		N.A.Evans (Noted 7.98)Watchford Farm, Branscombe	
N36362	Cessna 180	180-31691		W Burgess (Noted 7.98)	Sibson
N38273	PA-28R-201 Cherokee Arrow III			L.Slater (Noted 12.98)	Blackbushe
		28R-7737086			
N38940	Boeing-Stearman A75N1 (PT-17) Kaydet	75-1822	(G-BSNK)	R.W.Sage	Priory Farm, Tibenham
	(Cont R670)		N38940/N55300/41-8263 t/a Blackbarn Avn		
				(As "18263/822" in US Army c/s) (Noted 8.97)	
N41098	Cessna 421B Golden Eagle	421B-0448		Not known (Noted 7.98)	Biggin Hill
N43069	PA-28-161 Warrior II	28-8316075		D.Wards (Noted 1.99)	RAF Lakenheath
N43230	PA-28RT Turbo Arrow			Not known (Noted 10.98)	White Waltham

Regn	Type	C/n	P/I	Owner/(operator)	Probable Base
N46294	1990 Steen Skybolt	SB-1990		Not known (Noted 3.98)	Maypole Farm, Chislet
N47914	PA-32-300 Six	32-7840018		Not known (Noted 5.97)	Alderney
N49272	Fairchild M.62/PT-23-HO Cornell	HO-437	42-.....	R.E.Mitchell	RAF Cosford
	(Cont W670) (Marked as being ex US Army 43-437)			t/a PT Flt (As "23" in USAAC c/s) (Noted 6.96)	
N50029	Cessna 172	28807	LX-AIB	E.Byrd (Noted 2.99)	Cardiff
			N6707A		
N50755	Boeing-Stearman D75N1 (PT-27)	75-4020	RCAF FJ970	Eastern Stearman Ltd	Swanton Morley
	Kaydet (Rebuilt with new fuselage 1993, original fuselage frame stored Carleton Rode, Norfolk 8.93; now marked as A75N1 "211672" (sic); noted 4.94)				
N53091	Boeing-Stearman A75N1 (PT-17)	75-2795	41-25306	Eastern Stearman Ltd	Swanton Morley
	Kaydet			(On rebuild 10.97)	
N54211	PA-23	23-7664006	G-ITTU	Not known (Noted 1998)	Elstree
N54922	Boeing-Stearman A75N1 (N2S-4)	75-3491	Bu.30054	V.S.E.Norman	Rendcomb
	Kaydet			(Crunchie c/s) "Sweetie" (Noted 7.98)	
N56421	Ryan PT-22-RY Recruit	1539	41-15510	R.E.Mitchell t/a PT Flt	RAF Cosford
				(As "855" in US Army c/s) (Noted 6.96)	
N56643	Maule M.5-180C	8086C		Not known (Noted 6.97)	Langar
N58566	Vultee BT-15-VN Valiant	10670	42-41882	R.E.Mitchell t/a PT Flt	RAF Cosford
				(US Army c/s) (Noted 6.96)	
N60526	Beechcraft E55 Baron	TE-1159		Not known (Noted 3.99)	Elstree
N61422	PA-31-310 Turbo Navajo B Panther			Swiftair Inc (Noted 3.99)	Elstree
		31-7401236			
N62842	Boeing-Stearman PT-17 Kaydet	?		R.W.Sage	Priory Farm, Tibenham
	(Registration not confirmed - if so then ex RCAF FJ801 [75-3851] t/a Blackbarn Avn (Stored 10.97)				
N63590	Boeing-Stearman N2S-3 Kaydet	75-7143	Bu.07539	R.W.Sage	Priory Farm, Tibenham
				t/a Blackbarn Avn (Stored 10.97)	
N65200	Boeing-Stearman D75N1 Kaydet	75-3817	FJ767	Eastern Stearman Ltd	Swanton Morley
				(On rebuild 10.95)	
N66630	Schweizer TG-3A	63	42-52983	Imperial War Museum	Duxford
	(P/i assumed but unconfirmed)			(As "252983" in USAAC c/s 1.99)	
N68200	Boeing-Stearman PT-17 Kaydet	75-7415	Bu.07811	Eastern Stearman Ltd	Swanton Morley
				(For spares use 10.95)	
N68427	Boeing-Stearman A75N1 (N2S-4)	75-5008	Bu.55771	R.W.Sage	Priory Farm, Tibenham
	Kaydet			t/a Blackbarn Avn (Stored 10.97)	
N70727	DHC.1 Chipmunk 22	C1/0783	9M-ANN	L.A.Groves	Stubbington
			FM1026/WP909	t/a Crofton Aeroplane Svs (For spares or rebuild)	
N73410	Boeing-Stearman B75N1 (N2S-3)	75-7761	Bu.38140	R.W.Sage	Priory Farm, Tibenham
	Kaydet			t/a Blackbarn Avn (Stored 10.97)	
N76402	Cessna 140	10828	NC76402	C.Murgatroyd	Standalone Farm, Meppershall
				(Noted in damaged state 1.99)	
N79863	Grumman F6F-5K Hellcat	A-11008	Bu.79863	Flying A Services (Noted 5.98)	North Weald
N80302	PA-34-220T Seneca III	34-8233055		Ambrian Avtn (Noted 6.98)	Elstree
N82507	PA-28RT-201 Arrow IV	28R-8018100		(Damaged Earls Colne 7.3.93; stored 6.96)	Stapleford
N83196	PA-28RT-201T Turbo Arrow IV	28R-8118045		Not known (Noted 11.97)	Cardiff
N90005	Gulfstream G.1159C Gulfstream IV	1103	N433GA	GECC/Siebe plc (Noted 3.98)	Heathrow
N91342	PA-38-112 Tomahawk II	38-82A0009		Falcon Flying Services (Noted 1.99)	Biggin Hill
N91384	Rockwell Commander 690A	11118	SE-FLN	Coopers Aerial Surveys Ltd	Sandtoft
				(Noted 8.97)	
N91457	PA-38-112 Tomahawk II	38-82A0034		Falcon Flying Services (Noted 1.99)	Biggin Hill
N96240	Beechcraft D18S (3TM)	CA-159	G-AYAH	Visionair Intl Avn	Rochester
			N6123/RCAF 1559	"Snapdragon" (Stored 11.97)	
N97121	Embraer EMB-110P1 Bandeirante	110-334	PT-SDK	Guernsey Fire Services (Extant 6.97)	Guernsey
N99153	North American T-28C Trojan	252-52		Norfolk & Suffolk Avn Museum	Flixton
			Zaire AF FG-289/Congo AF FA-289/Bu.146289 (As "146289/2W")		
				(Crashed Limoges, France 14.12.77; fuselage only)	
OE-FBC	LET L-200D Morava	171120	OK-RFW	M.Emery (Spares use)	Hertford
				(Status uncertain - reported reverted to OK-RFW 10.74)	
OK-JIY	Yakovlev C.11	-	(Egypt AF)	Personal Plane Svs Ltd	(High Wycombe)
	(Probably c/n 172673; stored 3.96 for rebuild)				
OO-ARK	Cameron O-84			R S Kent "Princess Alex"	Lancing
				(Balloon Preservation Group 7.98)	
OO-BDO	Cameron N-56			I M Martin "Profo"	Lancing
				(Balloon Preservation Group 7.98)	
OO-DOL	Beechcraft C35 Bonanza	D-3346	OO-JAN	Not known	Hurstbourne Tarrant, Hants
				(Stored 3.98)	
OO-FAN	Beechcraft 56TC Baron	TG-10	G-AZOJ	Not known (Stored 10.97)	Shoreham
			N5443U		
OO-JAT	Cameron Zero 25 Airship			Balloon Preservation Group	Farnborough
				(On loan to Farnbrough Air Sciences Trust 7.98)	
OO-JPJ	PA-34-200 Seneca	34-7350335	OO-GPC	Routair	(Southend)
			N56464		
			(Cabin section removed by 3.99; fuselage West Hanningfield for scrap 12.98)		
OO-MHB	PA-28-236 Dakota	28-8011143	G-BMHB		Blackpool
			D6-PAD/N81321/N9593N (Damaged Southend 20.10.90; stored 6.96)		

Regn	Type	C/n	P/I	Owner/(operator)	Probable Base
OO-VPC	Cessna 182P Skylane II (Reims-assembled c/n 0019)	182-63928	D-EHTW	Not known	Romsey
OY-ANZ	Maule M.5-210C Strata Rocket	6027C	N9859E	(Damaged Maasbree, Holland 26.7.94; wreck in store 1.96)	
			D-EMKK	Not known	East Winch
OY-JRR	DHC.2 Turbo Beaver III	1632/TB-18	N15B	(Damaged in gales 11/12.4.82; on rebuild 9.97)	
			N911CC	Ipswich Parachute Centre	Elmsett/Windrush
P4-FDH	Boeing 707-351B	18586	C-FUKK/CF-UKK	(Noted 6.96)	
			HZ-SAK1	Not known (Noted 3.99)	Southend
PH-NLK	PA-23-160 Apache	23-1694	VR-BOR/VR-BMV/G-BSZA/EL-SKD/N351SR/N651TF/VR-CAO/VROHGO/N353US		
			OY-DCG	Not known	Burgh-le-Marsh, Skegness
			SE-CKW	(Wreck stored 10.93)	
B-163 (R Neth AF)	Noorduyn AT-16 Harvard IIB	14-664	FE930	G.King (On rebuild to SNJ standard 6.95)	
			42-12417	Thameside Avn Museum, Coalhouse Fort, East Tilbury	
56 (Red)	Yakovlev Yak-52	811504	DOSAAF	Not known (Noted 5.95)	Chester
-00153	Yakovlev Yak-18T	22202047817		Not known (Noted 1997)	Haverfordwest
RA-01277	Sukhoi SU-29	80-02		Not known (Noted 8.96)	White Waltham
RA-01333	Yakovlev Yak-55M (G-YAKM reserved)	920506	DOSAAF 40	Mrs B.Abela "40" (Noted 8.98)	White Waltham
RA-01370	Yakovlev Yak-18T	?		F.M.Govern (Noted 2.98)	Oxford
RA-01378	Yakovlev Yak-52	833004	DOSAAF 14	T.Evans	Wellesbourne Mountford
	(Composite with c/n 833805/DOSAAF 134 which is now N54GT) (Open storage - unflyable 5.98)				
RA-01480	Sukhoi SU-31	02-04		L.Perry (Noted 5.98)	White Waltham
RA-01493	Yakovlev Yak-52			D Featherby (Noted 7.98)	White Waltham
RA-01496(2)	Sukhoi SU-29	78-03	RA-7803	R.Goode (Noted 12.95)	White Waltham
RA-01606	Suhkoi SU-29	81-02		Not known (Noted 3.98)	Goodwood
RA-01607	Sukhoi SU-29	77-02	RA-7702	S Jones (Noted 7.98)	White Waltham
RA-01608	Sukhoi SU-31	01-04	RA-0104	R.Goode "03" (Noted 11.97)	White Waltham
RA-01609	Sukhoi SU-29	75-03	RA-7503	Not known (Noted 3.98)	White Waltham
RA-01610	Sukhoi SU-29	78-02	RA-7802	P.Williams (Noted 7.98)	White Waltham
RA-02050	Yakovlev Yak-52	855907	DOSAAF 107	"Tatjana" "107" (Noted 5.98)	Old Sarum
RA-02135	Aeropract A-21M Solo	01		Not known (Noted 3.97)	Newcastle, Co.Wicklow
RA-02209	Yakovlev Yak-52	9111311	DOSAAF 31	P.Scandrett "31" (Noted 7.98)	Rendcomb
RA-02293	Yakovlev Yak-52	9011013	DOSAAF 115	A.Tyler (Noted 7.97)	Halfpenny Green
RA-02622	Yakovlev Yak-52	9612001		Not known (Noted 9.98)	White Waltham
RA-22521	Yakovlev Yak-52	9211612	DOSAAF 04	D.Squires "04" (Noted 9.97)	Wellesbourne Mountford
RA-44463	Yakovlev Yak-52	888912	DOSAAF	Not known (Noted 5.97)	White Waltham
RA-44464	Yakovlev Yak-52	9111415	DOSAAF 50	Not known "50" (Noted 12.98)	White Waltham
RA-44465	Yakovlev Yak-55			Barbelle Aviation (Noted 9.97)	White Waltham
RA-44467	Technoavia Yak-18T	15-33	CCCP-44467	(Noted 7.96)	Little Gransden
RA-44470	Technoavia Yak-18T	18-33		B.Austen (Noted 9.98)	RAF Brize Norton
RA-44480	Technoavia Yak-18T	08-34	CCCP-44480	R.Goode (Noted 12.98)	White Waltham
RA-44483	Technoavia Yak-18T	10-34	DOSAAF 221	R.Goode (Noted 11.95)	White Waltham
RA-44485	Technoavia SM-92 Finist	03		M.A.Crymble (Noted 5.98)	RAF Cranwell
RA-44488	Technoavia SM-93			Not known (Noted 3.98)	White Waltham
RA-44510	Yakovlev Yak-55			T Shears (Noted 10.98)	White Waltham
RA-44514	Yakovlev Yak-52			Not known (Noted 3.98)	Manston
RA-44515	Yakovlev Yak-52	9111515		M.Stebbing "65" (Noted 7.98)	Poplar Hall Farm, Elmsett
RA-44516	Yakovlev Yak-52	9111506		Not known "56" (Noted 12.98)	White Waltham
RA-44517	Sukhoi SU-29			Not known "18" (Noted 1.98)	White Waltham
RA-44518	Yakovlev Yak-52			M Revill (Noted 7.98)	Exeter
RA-44527	Yakovlev Yak-18T			Not known (Noted 12.98)	White Waltham
RA-76401	Ilyushin IL-76TD	1023412399	CCCP-76401	Heavylift Cargo Airlines Ltd/Volga-Dnepr (Noted 4.97)	Stansted
RA-76758	Ilyushin IL-76TD	0073474203	CCCP-76758	Heavylift Cargo Airlines Ltd/Volga-Dnepr (Noted 2.97)	Stansted
RA-82042	Antonov AN-124-100 Ruslan	9773054055093	CCCP-82042	Heavylift Cargo Airlines Ltd/Volga-Dnepr (Noted 7.98)	Stansted
RA-82043	Antonov AN-124-100 Ruslan	9773054155101	CCCP-82043	Heavylift Cargo Airlines Ltd/Volga-Dnepr (Noted 9.97)	Stansted
RA-82044	Antonov AN-124-100 Ruslan	9773054155109	CCCP-82044	Heavylift Cargo Airlines Ltd/Volga-Dnepr (Noted 5.97)	Stansted
RA-82045	Antonov AN-124-100 Ruslan	9773052255113	CCCP-82045	Heavylift Cargo Airlines Ltd/Volga-Dnepr (Noted 8.97)	Stansted
RA-82046	Antonov AN-124-100 Ruslan	9773052255117	CCCP-82067	Heavylift Cargo Airlines Ltd/Volga-Dnepr (Noted 8.97)	Stansted
RA-82047	Antonov AN-124-100 Ruslan	9773053259121	CCCP-82068	Heavylift Cargo Airlines Ltd/Volga-Dnepr (Noted 5.98)	Stansted
SE-AZB	Avro 671 Cierva C.30A Autogiro	R3/CA.954	K4232	RAF Museum (As "K4232")	Hendon
SE-BNN	Saab 91A Safir	91130	OY-DBT	L.de Jonge	Luxters Farm, Hambledon
			OO-MUG/OO-HUG/PH-UEB/SE-BNN	(Stored 10.97)	
SE-GVH	PA-38-112 Tomahawk	38-78A0053			Little Staughton
	(Open storage unmarked 4.97 & used in rebuild of G-CGFC as G-BLNN 1990/1)				
SE-LBR	Yakovlev YAK-50			Not known (Noted 9.98)	Biggin Hill
SP-CHD	PZL-101A Gawron	74134		J.Koch	Sandown
SP-FBO	Antonov AN-2T	1G108-55	PLW-0855	Not known (Noted 8.97)	Priory Farm, Tibenham

Regn	Type	C/n	P/I	Owner/(operator)	Probable Base
SP-FKD	Yakovlev Yak-12M			M Jefferies (Noted 7.98)	Little Gransden
SP-SAY	Mil Mi-2	529538125		The Helicopter Museum (Noted 8.98)	Weston-super-Mare
008 (Polish AF)	WSK SBLim 2A (MiG 15)	1A09-008		G.P.Hinckley (Stored 8.96)	Channons Hall, Tibenham
ST-AHZ	PA-31-310 Turbo Navajo	31-473	G-AXMR	Not known	Elstree
			N6558L	(Fire practice; burnt-out fuselage remains 11.97)	
TF-ABP	Lockheed L.1011-385-100 Tristar	1045	VR-HOG	British Aviation Heritage Collection	
			N323EA		Bruntingthorpe
				(Istanbul Airlines c/s) (Stored 9.97)	
UR-67199	LET L-410UVP Turbolet	790305	CCCP-67199	Not known (Noted 4.97)	Langar
UR-67477	LET L-410UVP Turbolet	841302	CCCP-67477	(Universal Avia c/s) (Noted 8.97)	Sibson
UR-67519	LET L-410UVP Turbolet	851423	CCCP-67519	East West Aviation Ltd (Noted 9.95)	Wymeswold
UR-78755	Ilyushin IL-76MD	0083484531	CCCP-78755	Air Foyle UK	Luton
				(Op for Oil Spill Response Ltd) (Noted 12.96)	
VH-ALB	Supermarine 228 Seagull V	-	A2-4	RAF Museum (As "A2-4")	Hendon
VH-ASM	Avro 652A Anson I	72960	W2068	RAF Museum (As "W2068/68" in RAF c/s)	Hendon
VH-BRC	Short S.24 Sandringham IV	SH.55C	N158C	The Science Museum	Southampton
			VP-LVE	(On loan to Southampton Hall of Aviation)	
			N158C/VH-BRC/ZK-AMH/JM715 (Ansett c/s) "Beachcomber"		
VH-FHJ	Cessna 560 Citation V Ultra	560-0278	N2HJ	Eagle Airways/F.Hackett-Jones	Guernsey
			N5103J	"Cuillon of True Flight" (Noted 6.97)	
VH-SNB	DH.84A Dragon	2002	VH-ASK	Museum of Flight/Royal Museum of Scotland	
			A34-13		East Fortune
VH-UQB	DH.80A Puss Moth	2051	(G-ABDW)	Museum of Flight/Royal Museum of Scotland	
			VH-UQB/G-ABDW		East Fortune
VH-UTH	GAL Monospar ST-12	ST12/36		Newark Air Museum	Winthorpe
				(On rebuild by Cotswold Acft Restoration Grp, Innsworth 7.95)	
VH-UUP	Short S.16 Scion 1			See G-ACUX	
VH-WGL	Short Skyvan			Not known (Noted 10.98)	Fairoaks
VH-YOT	Skyfox Gazelle CA25N (Rotax 912)	CA25N030		Not known (Noted 8.97)	Dunkirk, Canterbury
VP-BBK	Beechcraft B200 Super King Air	BB-1519	VR-BBK	Videovision Ltd (Noted 11.98)	Guernsey
			N10827		
VP-BBN	PA-23-250 Aztec E	27-7305224	VR-BBN	M.J.L.Batt/Inter City Air Ltd	Booker
			(VR-BDM)/G-BCBG/N40494 (Noted 9.97)		
VP-BCC	Canadair CL.601 Challenger 3R	5162	VR-BCC	Consolidated Contractors (UK) Ltd	
			C-FTNE/C-GLXF (Noted 6.97)		Athens/Farnborough
VP-BCI	Canadair CL.601 Challenger 3R	5193	VR-BCI	Consolidated Contractors (UK) Ltd	
			N604D/C-GLYK (Noted 5.97)		Athens/Farnborough
VP-BDR	Cessna 425 Conquest I	425-0199	VR-BDR	M.J.L.Batt/Inter City Air Ltd	Booker
			G-BLGM/(N1223A) (Noted 9.97)		
VP-BHJ	Dassault Falcon 900B	138	VR-BHJ	F.Hackett-Jones/Eagle Airways Ltd	Guernsey
				(Noted 6.97)	
VP-BIE	Canadair CL.601 Challenger 1A	3016	N601CL	Inflite Executive Charter (Noted 8.98)	Stansted
			N1107Z/N4562Q/C-GLWV		
VP-BIS	Grumman Gulfstream IV	1150	N151G	ISPAST Group Ltd	Luton
			V8-SRI/V8-009/V8-ALI/N433GA		
VP-BJV	Grumman Gulfstream II			Not known (Noted 3.98)	Heathrow
VP-BKC	Boeing 727-1H2	20533	VR-BKC	USAL Inc (Noted 6.98)	Stansted/Heathrow
			HZ-122/N228G/N320HG		
VP-BKK	HS.125 Srs.400A/731	25238	VR-BKK	Air 125 Ltd/Business Real Estates	Southampton
			N808V/N125GC/G-TOPF/G-AYER/9K-ACR/G-AYER (Noted 3.97)		
VP-BKQ	Bell 430	49008	N62833	Jud Investments Co Ltd (Noted 5.97)	Fairoaks
VP-BKY	HS.125 Srs.F3A	25150	VR-BKY	Corporate Jet Svs Inc/Bay Investments Ltd	
			N511BX/G-AWMS/G-5-13 (Noted 12.97)		Filton/Gloucestershire
VP-BLA	Canadair CL.601 Challenger 1A	3013	VR-BLA	Granaway Ltd/Sun International Hotels	
			N601TG/C-GLXD (Noted 4.97)		Farnborough
VP-BLK	Gulfstream 690C Commander 840	11672	VR-BLK	Control Techniques (Bermuda) Ltd	Welshpool
			OE-FIT/D-IKOM/(N5924K) (Noted 12.98)		
VP-BLS	Pilatus PC-XII	176	N176BS	B.L.Schroeder (Noted 12.98)	Fairoaks
			VP-BLS/HB-FSL		
VP-BMZ	Gulfstream 690D Commander 900	15033	VR-BMZ	Aviatica Trading Co Ltd/Marlborough Fine Art Ltd	
			G-MFAL/N49GA/(N5925N) (Noted 8.98)		Fairoaks
VP-BNJ	Dassault Falcon 900B	120	VR-BNJ	Triair (Bermuda) Ltd/Silver Sand Ltd	Southampton
			F-WWFN	(Noted 6.97)	
VP-BNM	Cessna 425 Conquest I	425-0027	VR-BNM	Rig Design Services Ltd (Noted 10.96)	Fairoaks
			N181AA/HI-598SP/N97DA/(N711EF)/N97DA/N67720		
VP-BNU	Robin DR400/180 Regent	2047	VR-BNU	N.French (Noted 10.97)	Biggin Hill
			G-BTDU		
VP-BNZ	Gulfstream G.1159A Gulfstream III	452	VR-BNZ	Dennis Vanguard (International) Ltd	Coventry
			N633P/N27R/N331GA (Noted 11.97)		
VP-BOO	McDonnell Douglas MD-87	49778	VR-BOO	Interlocutary Ltd/Ford Motor Co Ltd	Stansted
			N806ML	(Noted 5.98)	
VP-BOP	McDonnell Douglas MD-87	49725	VR-BOP	Interlocutary Ltd/Ford Motor Co Ltd	Stansted
			N802ML	(Noted 5.98)	

Regn	Type	C/n	P/I	Owner/(operator)	Probable Base
VP-BPS	Consolidated 28-5ACF (PBY-5A) Catalina	1997	VR-BPS G-BLSC C-FMIR/N608FF/CF-MIR/N10023/Bu.46633	PS (Bermuda) Ltd/Planesailing Air Displays (Crashed Southampton Water 7.98)	Hamble
VP-BPW	Dassault Falcon 900B	135	VR-BPW F-WWFJ	N.Somers/Tower House Consultants Ltd (Noted 12.97)	Jersey/Southampton
VP-BQK	Agusta A.109A II	7410	VR-BKQ	Patriot Aviation (Bermuda) Ltd (Noted 8.97)	Sywell
VP-BSA	Dassault Falcon 50			Shell Aircraft Ltd (Noted 1998)	Heathrow
VP-BSL	Dassault Falcon 50			Shell Aircraft Ltd (Noted 1998)	Heathrow
VP-BSI	BAe 125 Srs.800B	258073	VR-BSI N802MM/G-5-532/G-BVBH/D-CFVW/G-5-532 (Noted 11.97)	Group 4 Securities Ltd	Gloucestershire
VP-BUS	Gulfstream G.1159C Gulfstream IV	1127	VR-BUS VR-BLR/N427GA (Noted 12.98)	AEC International Ltd/BP Flight Operations Ltd	Farnborough
VP-BZZ	Cessna 525 CitationJet	525-0235	N5246Z	Fegotila Ltd	Gloucestershire
VP-CAM	Canadair CL-601-3A Challenger	5090	N400KC N818TH/N818LS/N404CB/N601CB/C-GLXF	Qamar Ltd	(Jersey)
VP-CAS	BAe 125 Srs.800A	258167	VR-CAS N125AS/G-5-662/N125AS/G-5-662 (Noted 5.97)	Cavalier Air Corpn/A.Senna	Southampton
VP-CAT	Cessna 501 Citation 1/SP (Unit No.637)	501-0232	VR-CAT VR-CHF/N35TL/N853KB/N2616C/(N2616G) (Noted 11.97)	Kestrel Avn/Aviation Jet	Elstree
VP-CBE	Cessna 550 Citation II (Unit No.119)	550-0108	N4EK (N65SA)/N4EK/N4TL/(N2665P)	Eurojet Ltd (Noted 12.97)	Birmingham
VP-CBM	Cessna 550 Citation II	550-0729	VR-CBM N1210V	Bernard Matthews plc (Noted 7.97)	Norwich
VP-CBQ	Boeing 727-212	21460	VR-CBQ HZ-DA5/9V-SGF (Noted 12.97)	Precision Air/FR Aviation Group	Bournemouth
VP-CBW	Gulfstream G.1159C Gulfstream IV	1096	VR-CDW N17589	Rolls-Royce plc (Noted 8.98)	Farnborough
VP-CBX	Grumman Gulfstream V	511	N511GA	Not known	Farnborough
VP-CCK	Agusta A.109A II	7357	VR-CCK N109JD/N90GA	Tarmac plc (Noted 3.98)	Wolverhampton/Sywell
VP-CCT	Beechcraft C90-1 King Air	LJ-1028	VR-CCT G-BKFY/N6420H (Noted 6.97)	Corgi Investments Ltd (Op Corgi Toys)	Oxford
VP-CCV	Cessna 560 Citation V	560-0320	VR-CCV (N28ET)/N46WB/N5262B (Noted 2.99)	Pace Electronics	Leeds-Bradford
VP-CDC	McDonnell Douglas MD500N (520N)	LN050	VR-CDC N52210/HP-1170P/N102TA/C-GQJK/N102TA/(N74996)	Weetabix Ltd (Noted 8.97)	Sywell/Drayton, Leics
VP-CDW	Cessna 650 CitationJet	650-7034	N4360S XA-SWM/N1264E	Grosvenor Estates/Duke of Westminster	Chester
VP-CEZ	Dassault Falcon 50	138	VR-CEZ N138NW/I-CAFB/N941CC/N75G/F-WPXD	IIR Avn (Noted 6.97)	Biggin Hill
VP-CFG	Cessna 501 Citation I/SP (Unit No.577)	501-0176	VR-CFG (VR-CIA)/N49LC/N44LC/N6779L (Noted 7.98)	Alpha Golf Aviation Ltd	Oxford
VP-CHC	Sikorsky S-76C	760377	G-BXGR I-PRLT/N62375/JA6692 (Noted 9.97)	Williams Grand Prix Engineering Ltd	Oxford
VP-CHE	Beechcraft B200 Super King Air	BB-1569	N20505	Not known (Noted 7.97)	Gamston
VP-CHJ	Agusta A.109C	7634	VR-CHJ VR-CEC/3A-MSG	Eagle Airways (Noted 6.97)	Guernsey
VP-CIC	Canadair CL.601 Challenger 3A	5011	VR-CIC N602UK/N611MH/JA8283/N603CC/C-GLXD (Noted 8.98)	TGC Avn Ltd/Fakhar Ltd	Stansted
VP-CIS	Cessna 525 CitationJet	525-0252	N740JV (N5223P) (Noted 3.99)	Lambert Lakes Ltd/Flightline Ltd	Southend
VP-CIZ	Agusta A.109C	7662	VR-CIZ HB-XYY (Noted 11.97)	Williams Grand Prix Engineering Ltd	Oxford
VP-CJB	Cessna 501 Citation I/SP (Unit No.564)	501-0155	VR-CJB N800DW/N110TP/N110TV/(N108CT)/N2617B	Brown Pestell Ltd (Noted 11.97)	Biggin Hill
VP-CJR	Cessna 550 Citation II (Unit No.388)	550-0354	VR-CJR N121C/N121CG (Noted 7.97)	Broome & Wellington (Avn) Ltd/Air Kilroe	Manchester
VP-CLA	Agusta A.109A II	7411	VR-CLA G-BOLA/VR-CMP/VR-CLA/G-BOLA (Noted 9.97)	Laura Ashley Holdings Ltd	Fairoaks
VP-CLL	Cessna 421C Golden Eagle III	421C-0663	VR-CLL G-RILL/G-BGZM/N3839G	Channel Avn Ltd (Noted 7.98)	Guernsey
VP-CMA	Beechcraft B200 Super King Air	BB-1564	N205JT	International Motors Ltd/Rangemile Ltd (Noted 8.97)	Coventry
VP-CMF	Gulfstream G.1159C Gulfstream IV	1062	VR-CMF N688H/N462GA/N17583 (Noted 10.97)	Aravco Ltd/Sheikh Mohammed Fakhry	Heathrow
VP-CMM	Boeing 727-30	18368	VR-CMM N841MM/N728JE/N72700/N92342/D-ABIM	MME Farms Maintenance (Noted 11.97)	Stansted
VP-CMO	Cessna 500 Citation (Unit No.070)	500-0070	VR-CMO YV-707CP/N600MT/N500TD/N570CC	Tunstall Group (Noted 9.97)	Leeds-Bradford
VP-CNM	Cessna 550 Ciation Bravo	550-0857	N51246	Nigel Mansell	Exeter
VP-CNP	Grumman Gulfstream III	496	N843HS (N99SU)/N99SC/N89AB/N89AE/N21NY/N310SL/N327GA	Fitzwilton plc	Dublin
VP-COM	Cessna 500 Citation (Unit No.318)	500-0318	VR-COM N9448/N518CC/N5318J (Noted 8.97)	Rapid 3864 Ltd (C.McGill)	Biggin Hill
VP-CPO	Canadair CL.601 Challenger 3R	5165	VR-CPO C-FTOH/C-GLXO	P & O Containers Ltd (Noted 8.98)	Stansted

Regn	Type	C/n	P/I	Owner/(operator)	Probable Base
VP-CPR	Cessna 421C Golden Eagle III	421C-0837	VR-CPR N2659F	Fifty North (Chris Ryecroft) (Noted 11.97)	Leeds-Bradford/Guernsey
VP-CPT	BAe 125 Srs.1000B	259004	G-LRBJ G-5-779	Reno Investments Inc (Noted 1.99)	Biggin Hill
VP-CRB	Gates Learjet 60	60-125	N60LR	Lisane Ltd	Jersey
VP-CRY	Grumman Gulfstream IV	1176	N176G V8-008/N468GA	Avia Carriers	Luton/Moscow
VP-CSC	Cessna 560 Citation V Ultra	560-0439	(N39LX) N50612	Stadium City Ltd (Noted 10.97)	Humberside
VP-CSN	Cessna 560 Citation V Ultra	560-0401	N401CV	Scottish & Newcastle Breweries Ltd (Noted 10.97)	Edinburgh
VP-CSP	Cessna 500 Citation (Unit No.165)	500-0165	VR-CSP G-PNNY/N19MQ/N19M	SP Metal Ltd (Noted 11.98)	Biggin Hill
VP-CTF	Cessan 550 Citation II	550-0716	VP-CTE (N800KC)/N4VR/N1205A	Not known	Jersey/Chester
VP-CWM	Cessna 550 Citation II	550-0667	VR-CWM N668EA/EC-FDL/EC-621 (Noted 7.97)	Forbane Investment Ltd	Jersey
VP-CYM	Gulfstream G.1159C Gulfstream IV	1090	VR-CYM N466GA	Jet Fly Avn Ltd (Noted 11.97)	Heathrow
VP-FAZ	DHC.6-310 Twin Otter	748	C-GEOA (FAP-2029)/C-GEOA (Noted 5.98)	British Antarctic Survey	Oxford
VP-FBB	DHC.6-310 Twin Otter	783	C-GDKL	British Antarctic Survey (Noted 3.97)	Oxford
VP-FBC	DHC.6-310 Twin Otter	787	C-GDIU	British Antarctic Survey (Noted 3.97)	Oxford
VP-FBL	DHC.6-310 Twin Otter	839	C-GDCZ	British Antarctic Survey (Noted 7.98)	Oxford
VP-KJL	Miles M.38 Messenger 4A	-	G-ALAR RH371	Miles Acft Collection (For rebuild off-site 3.96)	Woodley
VP-YKF	DH.104 Dove 6	04292	3D-AAI VQ-ZJC/G-AMDD	South East Avn Enthusiasts Grp New Ross, Ireland (Damaged 9.8.82; stored 3.97) (As "IAC 176")	
VR-BEA	BAC One-Eleven 524FF	BAC.195	RP-C1185 D-AMUR/G-AXSY/D-AMUR	European Aviation Ltd (Stored 7.97)	Bournemouth
VR-BEB	BAC One-Eleven 527FK	BAC.226	RP-C1181 PI-C1181	European Aviation Ltd (Stored 1.99)	Bournemouth
VR-BEP	Westland WS-55 Whirlwind 3	WA.83	G-BAMH XG588	East Midlands Aeropark (As "XG588 in SAR c/s) "Cormorant"	East Midlands
VR-BET	Westland WS-55 Whirlwind 3			See G-ANJV	
VR-BEU	Westland WS-55 Whirlwind 3	WA.493	G-ATKV EP-HAN/G-ATKV	The Helicopter Museum (Stored for spares 8.98)	Weston-super-Mare
VR-BMB	HS.125 Srs.400B	25240	VR-BKN I-GJBO/G-AYLI/G-5-11	Speedflight Ltd (Stored 8.98)	Stansted
VT-DOU	DH.82A Tiger Moth	"OU/05/68"	HU-483	J.Pearce (Stored 1995)	(Findon, Worthing)
VT-DOX	DH.82A Tiger Moth	"OU/02/66"	HU-492	J.Pearce (Stored 1995 ?)	(Findon, Worthing)
VT-DOY	DH.82A Tiger Moth	"OU/03/66"	HU-498	J.Pearce (Stored 1995)	(Findon, Worthing)
VT-DOZ	DH.82A Tiger Moth	"OU/07/68"	HU-504	J.Pearce (Stored 1995)	(Findon, Worthing)
VT-DPA	DH.82A Tiger Moth	"OU/10/69"	HU-511	J.Pearce (Stored 1995)	(Findon, Worthing)
VT-DPB	DH.82A Tiger Moth	"OU/08/69"	HU-708	J.Pearce (Stored 1995 ?)	(Findon, Worthing)
VT-DPC	DH.82A Tiger Moth	-	"HU-187"	J.Pearce (Stored 1995 ?)	(Findon, Worthing)
VT-DPH	DH.82A Tiger Moth	"OU/09/69"	HU-887	J.Pearce (Stored 1955 ?)	(Findon, Worthing)
HA557 (RIAF)	Hawker Tempest II (Reported as HA577)	12205	MW404	C.P.B.Horsley (On rebuild by Osprey Aviation 9.96)	Dunsfold
XT-BBE	Boeing 727-14	18990	N21UC N2741A/(N975PS)/D-AHLP/N975PS	Not known (Stored 6.97)	Lasham
YL-LEU	WSK-PZL Antonov AN-2R	1G165-45	CCCP-19731 SP-ZFP/CCCP-19731 (Noted 11.97 as CCCP-19731)	Hawarden Air Services	Chester
YL-LEV	WSK-PZL Antonov AN-2R	1G148-32	CCCP-07268	Hawarden Air Services (Noted 4.98 as CCCP-07268)	Chester
YL-LEW	WSK-PZL Antonov AN-2R	1G182-28	CCCP-56471	Hawarden Air Services (Noted 4.98 as CCCP-56471)	Chester
YL-LEX	WSK-PZL Antonov AN-2R	1G187-58	CCCP-54949	Hawarden Air Services (Noted 4.98 as CCCP-54949)	Chester
YL-LEY	WSK-PZL Antonov AN-2R	1G173-11	CCCP-40784	Hawarden Air Services (Noted 4.98 as CCCP-40784)	Chester
YL-LEZ	WSK-PZL Antonov AN-2R	1G165-47	CCCP-19733	Hawarden Air Services (Noted 4.98 as CCCP-19733)	Chester
YL-LFA	WSK-PZL Antonov AN-2R	1G172-20	CCCP-40748	Hawarden Air Services (Noted 4.98 as CCCP-40748)	Chester
YL-LFB	WSK-PZL Antonov AN-2R	1G173-12	CCCP-40785	Hawarden Air Services (Noted 4.98 as CCCP-40785)	Chester
YL-LFC	WSK-PZL Antonov AN-2R	1G206-44	CCCP-17939	Hawarden Air Services (Noted 4.98 as CCCP-17939)	Chester
YL-LFD	WSK-PZL Antonov AN-2R	1G172-21	CCCP-40749	Hawarden Air Services (Noted 4.98 as CCCP-40749)	Chester
YL-LHN	Mil Mi-2	524006025	CCCP-20320	Hawarden Air Services (Noted 4.98 as CCCP-20320)	Chester
YL-LHO	Mil Mi-2	535025126	CCCP-20619	Hawarden Air Services (Noted 3.96)	Chester
YL-MIG	Aviatika MAI-890 Baby MIG	037		Hawarden Air Services (Stored 7.97)	Chester

Regn	Type	C/n	P/I	Owner/(operator)	Probable Base
YL-	Aviatika MAI-890 Baby MIG	034		Hawarden Air Services (Noted 10.93)	Cumbernauld
YL-	Aviatika MAI-890 Baby MIG	038		Hawarden Air Services (Stored 5.95)	Chester
YL-	Aviatika MAI-890 Baby MIG	039		Hawarden Air Services (Noted 10.93)	Cumbernauld
YL-	Aviatika MAI-890 Baby MIG	042		R.J.Everett (Noted 7.94)	Sproughton
YL-	Aviatika MAI-890 Baby MIG	043		Hawarden Air Services (Noted 10.93)	Cumbernauld
YL-	Aviatika MAI-890 Baby MIG	069		Pilatus Britten-Norman Ltd	Bembridge
				(As G-51-890-69) (Noted 5.96)	
YN-CCN	Boeing 707-123B	18054	5B-DAO	Omega Air (Stored 5.97)	Shannon
			G-BGCT/N7526A		
YU-DMN	UTVA-66	-	JRV51182	Not known(Noted 11.97)	Biggin Hill
				(As "51182" in Serbia AF c/s)	
YU-HCE	Bell 212	5173		Not known (For rebuild 12.98)	Redhill
YU-HEH	Aerospatiale Gazelle	011	12619	Not known (Noted 5.98)	
	(SOKO built)				
YU-HEI	Aerospatiale Gazelle		126..	Not known (Noted 5.98)	
	(SOKO built)				
YU-HEK	Aerospatiale Gazelle	012	12620	Not known (Noted 5.98)	
	(SOKO built)				
ZK-RMH	Curtiss P-40E-1-CU Kittyhawk	19669	NZ3009	The Old Flying Machine Co	Duxford
			ET482/41-25158 (For delvy 1999) (As "NZ3009")		
ZS-RSI	Lockheed L.100-30 Hercules	4600	F-GIMV	Hunting Cargo Airlines/Safair	East Midlands
			ZS-RSI/TN-.../F-GDAQ/F-WDAQ/ZS-RSI/C-FNWY/ZS-RSI (Noted 2.97)		
ZS-VFW	SNCAN Stampe SV-4C	186	G-AXCZ	Not known (Stored 10.95)	Bristol/Lulsgate
			F-BCFG		
4K-AZ3	Boeing 707-341C	19321	N107BV	Not known (Open store 3.99)	Southend
			PP-VJS/(FAB2405)/PP-VJS		
Israel	Hawker Hurricane IV	-	KZ191	R.J.Lamplough (For rebuild 3.96)	North Weald
5B-DBE	Boeing 727-30	18371	9M-SAS	Aimes Co (Noted 9.98)	Luton
			V8-BG2/V8-BG1/V8-UHM/N727CH/VS-UHM/VR-UHM/VR-BHP/N727CH/D-ABIQ		
5N-ABJ	Boeing 707-3F9C	20474		Not known	Shannon
				(Stored 5.97; being broken up 1.98)	
5N-ABW	Westland Widgeon 2			See G-AOZE	
5N-ANO	Boeing 707-3F9C	21428		Not known (Dumped 5.98)	Dublin
5N-AOK	BAC One-Eleven 320L-AZ	BAC.113	G-BKAW	Fire Training College	Chorley
			G-AVBY	(Noted 9.98)	
5N-ATU	Beechcraft A90 King Air	LJ-136	F-BFRE	Not known (On fire dump 1.97)	Gamston
			HB-GDF		
5N-AVC	PA-31-350 Navajo Chieftain	31-7305122	NAF 1003	Shoreham Airport Fire Service	Shoreham
			N74970	(Open store 10.96)	
5N-BAB	BAC One Eleven 414EG	BAC.127	EI-BWT	Not known (Open store 1.99)	Bournemouth
			N174FE/G-AZED/(N174FE)/G-AZED/(G-AZDG)/D-ANDY/G-16-3		
5N-HTC	BAC One-Eleven 208AL	BAC.049	EI-ANE	(Hold-Trade Air c/s) (Open store 3.99)	Southend
5N-MXX	Boeing 707-323C	18940	N1088V	Not known (Open store 3.99)	Southend
			PP-VLP/N7561A		
5X-UUW	Westland Scout Srs.1	F9617	G-17-1	R.Dagless (Stored 6.93)	East Dereham
5Y-SIL	Cameron A-140 HAFB	138	F-BTVO	British Balloon Museum	Newbury
			F-WTVO/G-AZUW "Cumulo Nimbus" (Stored)		
9G-LCA	Canadair Cl-44-0			First International A/wys (Noted 3.99)	Southend
9G-SGF	Boeing 707-321C		9G-EBK	Heavylift Cargo Airlines (Noted 11.98)	Southend
			9G-ESI/5N-AWO/TF-IUE/HL7427/N462PA		
9M-ANN	DHC.1 Chipmunk			See N70727 above	
9Q-CBW	Boeing 707-329C	20200	9Q-CBS	Not known (Open store 3.99)	Southend
			OO-SJO		
G-102 Ghana	Scottish Avn Bulldog 120/122	BH120-226		Not knownn	Hurstbourne Tarrant, Hants
				(Stored 3.98)	
G-108 Ghana	Scottish Avn Bulldog 120/122	BH120-372	G-BCUP	Not known	Hurstbourne Tarrant, Hants
				(Stored 3.98)	

SECTION 6 - AIRCRAFT WHICH FAILED TO MAKE SECTION 1 IN 1998

These are the UK Registrations added and removed since the last edition.

Regn	Type	C/n	P/I	Date	Owner/operator	Cancellation Details
G-BXRJ	PA-28-181 Archer II	28-8290108	HB-PGO	16. 1.98	T.A. Holding	To G-DENK 5. 2.98
G-BXRU	Airbus A.300B4-2C	31	N63661	3. 2.98	SARL Ham LOC & EURL GP LOC	To F-OHLE 27. 5.98
			HL7238/F-WZEQ/F-WUAY/F-WLGC			
G-BXRW	Airbus A.320-231	308	EC-GNB	30. 3.98	Airworld Aviation Ltd	To EC-GUR 30. 3.98
			N308RX/LZ-ABC/F-WWDL			
G-BXSS	AS.365N3 Dauphin 3	6537		20. 2.98	McAlpine Helicopters Ltd	To JA60TH 1. 9.98
G-BXSZ	Murphy Maverick	PFA/259-12955		24. 2.98	A.A. Plumridge	To G-MZLE 27. 5.98
G-BXUD	Agusta A.109E	11014		5. 5.98	Sloane Helicopters Ltd	To G-POWR 20. 7.98
G-BXUJ	Robinson R-22 Beta	2775		27. 3.98	Heli Air Ltd	To EI-CPO 7. 9.98
G-BXUN	Robinson R-44 Astro	0435		31. 3.98	Heli Air Ltd	To CS-HEH 15. 4.98
G-BXUR	MDH Hughes 369E	0204E	HA-MSC	2. 4.98	Helisport Ltd	To G-OTDB 7. 4.98
G-BXWM	BAe Jetstream 4124	41102	G-4-102	22. 5.98	British Aerospace (Ops) Ltd t/a British Aerospace Regional Aircraft	To B-HRS 22. 2.99
G-BXWN	BAe Jetstream 4124	41104	G-4-104	22. 5.98	British Aerospace (Ops) Ltd t/a British Aerospace Regional Aircraft	To B-HRT 22. 2.99
G-BXWP	PA-32-300 Cherokee Six	32-7340088	N8143D OE-DRR/N16452	26. 5.98	J.M.Wellfair	To C- 6.98
G-BXWW	Robinson R-22 Beta	0847	EI-CCT G-STOI	2. 6.98	Heli-Air Ltd	To N82222 22. 7.98
G-BXXB	Enstrom 280FX	2006	ZK-HHN JA7702	1. 6.98	S.G.Oliphant-Hope	To G-MHCK 5. 6.98
G-BXXM	Robinson R-44 Astro	0448		16. 6.98	Heli-Air Ltd	To CS- 20 .8.98
G-BXXW	Enstrom F-28F	771	JA7823	2. 7.98	S.G.Oliphant-Hope	To N330SA 23. 7.98
G-BXYA	CSS-13 (Licence built Polikarpov PO-2)	0365	SP-ACP PLW-...	3. 7.98	Personal Plane Services Ltd	To N 13.11.98
G-BXYW	Robinson R-22 Beta	1528	HA-MIU N528SH	4. 8.98	Quasar Communications Ltd	To G-OSMS 22. 2.99
G-BXZL	Bell 47G-5	7801	ZS-HDT Z-WNR/Z-WKC/VP-WKC/ZS-HDT/(ZS-HST)/N8544F	18. 8.98	Helitechnique Ltd	To N7801R 18. 1.99
G-BXZP	Pilatus P3-05	462-11	HB-RCM Swiss AF A-824	25. 8.98	I.Michalke	To HB- 19. 1.99
G-BXZR	Cameron R-650 HAFB	4380		10. 9.98	Cameron Balloons Ltd	To HB-BRA 26.10.98
G-BYBG	PA-28-181 Archer III	28-43157	N47BK	21. 9.98	Anglo American Airmotive Ltd	To G-LACD 13.11.98
G-BYCG	Agusta-Bell 47G-3B1	1513	EC-EGO Spanish AF 751-12/HE7B-22/Z7B-22	12.10.98	Nash Group Ltd	Canc by CAA 9. 2.99
G-BYCH	Agusta-Bell 47G-4A	2519	EC-BMB Italian AF MM80504	12.10.98	Nash Group Ltd	Canc by CAA 9. 2.99
G-BYCI	Agusta-Bell 47G-4A	2530	EC-BSC	12.10.98	Nash Group Ltd	Canc by CAA 9. 2.99
G-BYCK	Robinson R-22 Beta	1478	N101EJ	20.10.98	Sloane Helicopters Ltd	To G-XTEC 23.10.98
G-BYCR	Stoddard-Hamilton Glastar	PFA/295-13241		28.10.98	L.A.James	To G-LEZZ 4.11.98
G-BYDC	Socata TB-10 Tobago	146	F-GCOL	11.11.98	Air Touring Ltd	To G-IGGL 26. 3.99
G-BYEV	Cessna 172R Skyhawk	172-80663	N2377J	9. 2.99	Wycombe Air Centre	To G-LAVE 10 .3.99
G-BYFO	HS.125 Srs.700B	257040	HB-VMD VP-BPE/VR-BPE/N47TJ/EC-ETI/EC-375/G-OWEB/HZ-RC1	11. 2.99	Bizair Ltd	To G-OWDB 18. 2.99
G-BYFZ	Cessna TU.206G Turbo Stationair II	U206-05128	EC-ESG N4855U	8. 3.99	Bob Crowe Aircraft Sales Ltd	To N 9. 3.99
G-ETHY	Cessna 208 Caravan	208-0293		19.10.98	N.Moore	To N1295M 10.11.98
G-HDDP	Eurocopter EC.135 T 1	0055		29. 6.98	McAlpine Helicopters Ltd	To G-HDPP 3. 7.98
G-IOIT	Lockheed L1011-385-1 Tristar 100	1145	G-CEAP SE-DPM/G-BEAL	6. 5.98	Classic Airways Ltd	Canc by CAA 1.10.98
G-MZMI	CFM Streak Shadow	PFA/206-13205		30. 4.98	M.A.Hayward	To G-BXWR 22. 5.98
G-MZOL	RL5B LWS Sherwood Ranger	PFA/237-12887		26. 8.98	G.W.F.Webb	To G-WZOL 20. 1.99
G-OABE	Boeing 737-4Y0	24545	EC-ETB EC-401/C-FVND	29. 4.98	AB Airlines Ltd	To PP- 2.11.98
G-OABF	Boeing 737-4Y0	24688	EC-FZT EC-738/9M-MJI/(G-OOAB)	19. 6.98	AB Airlines Ltd	To EC-GYK 14.10.98
G-OBYE	Boeing 767-304	28979		26. 2.98	Britannia Airways Ltd	To D-AGYE 30.10.98
G-OBYF	Boeing 767-304	28208		8. 6.98	Britannia Airways Ltd	To D-AGYF 9. 6.98
G-OBYH	Boeing 767-304ER	28883		4. 2.99	Britannia Airways Ltd	To D- 22. 3.99
G-OMAK	Airbus A.319-132	913	D-AVYL	7. 1.99	Alkharafi Aviation 2000 Ltd	To F-WWIF 26. 1.99
G-PBTT	Enstrom 480	5010	JA6169	30. 6.98	P.D.Bundy	To N900SA 23. 7.98
G-RITZ	Cessna 182S Skylane	182-80029	N9872F	12. 2.98	S.J.G.Mole	To N 22.3.99
G-SIRI	Bell 206L-1 Long Ranger	45565	G-CSWL F-GDAD	5. 5.98	Heli-Flight Ltd	To G-CSWL 20. 5.98
G-SIVB	MDH MD 600N	RN023	N9223Y (N958SD)	24. 4.98	C.J.Siva-Jothy	To N511VB 2.10.98
G-SPRT	Cameron R-450 HAFB	4350		23. 4.98	Bondbaste Ltd	Destroyed 6.10.98
G-UNID	Airbus A.321-211	677	G-UKLO D-AVZO	15. 1.98	Leisure Intnl Airways Ltd	To G-OOAF 4.12.98
G-UNIE	Airbus A.321-211	781	D-AZVK	3. 3.98	Leisure Intnl Airways Ltd	To G-OOAH 4. 1.99

SECTION 7 - PART 1 - ALPHABETICAL TYPE INDEX - UNITED KINGDOM

ACES HIGH CUBY: G-BVNA

ACRO ADVANCED: G-BPAA

ADAM RA.14 LOISIRS: G-BHIK

ADVANCED AIRSHIP CORPN ANR-1: G-MAAC

AERIAL ARTS:
110/130SX (wing) (ALPHA/AVENGER) (combi): G-MMSZ MYL MZI NDE NEK NEL NIT NJV NLW NMY NTT NWL NZS VBC

CHASER (including CYCLONE): G-MNTD NXC NYD NYE NYF TCP TDD TDE MVDK VDL VDN VDP VDR VGA VGF VGG VGH VGI VGJ VGK VHA VHN
VIE VJF VJG VJH VJI VJJ VJK VKY VKZ VLA VLB VLC VLD VLE VLF VLG VLH VLS VLT VLU VLW VML VMM VOA VOD VOP VRG VRL VSG VSK
VSL VTF VTL VTM VUS VUT VVU VVW VXG VXP VYY VZM VZY WGO WWZ WXW WXX WXY WXZ WYM YBU YCB YEI YEJ YFO YGI YGK YIL YIT YJO
YJW YKD YLJ YMY YNW YSA YSV YWN YWS YYD YZW YZX ZCB ZTS

AERO (CZECH) - see CZL/LET
L-29 DELFIN: G-BYCT DELF LFN MAYA

L-39 ALBATROS: G-BWTT OTAF

AERO COMMANDER - see ROCKWELL
200: G-SONY

500S SHRIKE (ROCKWELL production): G-BDAL

560: G-ARDK

680/685/690/900 (including ROCKWELL/GULFSTREAM production): G-AWOE NISR OMAP WGCL

AERO COMPOSITES SEA HAWKER: EI-BUO

AERO DESIGNS PULSAR: G-BSFA TDR TRF TWY UDI UJL ULM UOW USR UYB UZB VJH VLN VSF VTW XDU DESI EPOX IIAN LUED MCMS NEVS
OMKF OXP RMAN WYNS XPXP

AERO-DIFUSION - see JODEL

AERO DYNAMICS SPARROWHAWK: G-BOZU

AEROCAR MINI IMP: G-BLWW

SOOPER COOT (including TAYLOR): G-COOT SWIM

AERODYNE VECTOR - see RAVEN

AEROMERE - see AVIAMILANO

AEROMOT AMT-200 SUPER XIMANGO (FOURNIER RF10): G-BWNY JTPC KHOM RFIO

AERONCA
C-3/100: G-ADRR DYS EFT ESB ETG EVS EXD

K: G-ONKA

7 CHAMPION series - see CHAMPION

11AC CHIEF/11CC SUPER CHIEF: G-AKTK KUO KVN BJEV JNY PRA PRX PXY RCW RFJ RWR RXF RXL STC TFL TRI TSR UAB UTF IIAC VOR

15AC SEDAN: G-AREX

A65TAC/O-58B/L-3 DEFENDER (including 65C SUPER CHIEF): G-BRHP RPR TRG TUV

AERONAUTICHE F22: G-FZZA

AEROSPACE DEVELOPMENTS AD.500: G-BECE

AEROSPATIALE - see ATR, SOCATA & SUD AVN
AS.332 SUPER PUMA: G-BKZE KZG KZH LPM LXR MCW MCX OZK RXU SOI TCT UZD WHN WMG WWI WZX
CHCA HCB HCC PUMA UMB UMD UME UMG UMH UMI UMM UMO TIGB IGC IGE IGF IGG IGH IGI IGJ IGL IGM IGO IGP IGR IGS IGT IGU
IGV IGZ

AS.350B ECUREUIL (including EUROCOPTER production): G-BMAV GRVO VJE VXM WFY XGA XNE XNJ XNY XOG XOK XPG XPJ
COPT WIZ DRHL EJOC FIBS HLEN IIPM MSDJ SKM ODMC FHL GOA ROZ NUTY PLMB LMC LMH ROD RICC OIN WHST RKD

AS.355 TWIN SQUIRREL (including EUROCOPTER production): G-BOOV PRJ PRL STE SYI TIS VLG XBT ZGC
CAMB CAO LIP POL DANS ANZ OOZ ECOS MAN POL FFRI TWO GMPA RID HARO ICSG JETU KGMT LCON ECA ENI INE OUN MOBI
NAAS EXT MHS WPI OASP BIG GHL GRK HCP HMS ILX ITN ROM RMA TSP PASF ASH REEM SAEW ASU EPA EPB EPC YPA TOPC OPS VPA
WIRE MPA XCEL

AEROSPORT
 SCAMP: G-BKFL KPB OOW

 WOODY PUSHER: G-AWWP YVP BSFV

AEROSTAR - see TED SMITH

AEROSTRUCTURE PIPISTRELLE (including SOUTHDOWN): G-MJTM NPI

AEROTEC/AEROTEK - see PITTS

AEROTECH - see WHITTAKER

AES SKY RANGER: G-MJHB

AESL - see VICTA

AGUSTA A.109 - see BELL: G-BVCJ VNH WNZ WZI XCB XIV XWD XPX GVIP JRSL POWR RNLD SLNE TBGL ELY USTA STB WEST

AILES DE K FLYAIR: G-BUHP

AIR COMMAND 503 COMMANDER/532 ELITE: G-BMZA OAS OGV OGW OHG OIK OJF OKF OOJ PAO PGC PMC PPR PPU PRS PSB PTH PUE PUG PUI
 PYW REM RGO RKS RKX RLB RLK RMM ROF RSP SAR SCB SND SRZ SSN SXP TCB VVY WTY KENB LIK OGTS SKYI TFRB URRR WYZZ YROI

AIR CREATION FUN 18 GT: G-MYMM YOL YTZ YUA YVI YXF

AIR & SPACE 18A: G-BVWK VWL

AIRBUS INDUSTRIE
 A.300B: G-BYDH CEAA EAB EXC EXH EXI HLAA LAB LAC MAJS ONR ONS OJMR SWJW TTMC

 A.319: G-EUPA UPB UPC

 A.320/A.321: G-BUSB USC USD USE USF USG USH USI USJ USK VJW VYA VYB VYC XKA XKC XKD XRX XTA YFS
 COEZ RPH VYD VYE VYG DJAR EPFR EUOA/UOZ JSJX MEDA EDB EDD IDA IDC IDE IDF IDH IDI IDJ IDK IDL IDM IDN IDO IDP IDR IDS
 IDT IDU IDV IDW IDX IDY IDZ ONW ONX ONY PCD OOAA OAB OAC OAD OAE OAF OAH MAK UZO ZBA RDVE SUEE TICL MDP PTT UKLJ KLL
 KLO NIE NIF NIG NIH VCED OLH YJBM

 A.330: G-EOMA MDBD SMAN UNIA NIB

 A.340: G-VAEL ELD AIR BUS FAR FLY HOL SKY SEA SUN

AIRMARK TSR.3 - see CASSUTT: G-AWIV

AIRSPEED
 AS.40 OXFORD: G-AHTW ITB ITF

 AS.57 AMBASSADOR: G-ALZO

AIRSPEED: G-FYGJ

AIRTOUR
 AH-31: G-BKVY

 AH-56: G-BKVW KVX LVA LVB SGH WPL OAFC

 AH-77: G-BLYT OBH IVAC OAAC

AIRWAVE
 MERLIN (wing): G-MMIJ

 MICROCHUTE (including TREKKING): G-MYPU YUY YYM ZBP ZDW

 NIMROD (wing): G-MBCX BJG BJL NIW NZY

 RAVE: G-MYZS YZT YZU

ALLPORT: G-BJIA JSS

AMERICAN AEROLIGHTS EAGLE/DOUBLE EAGLE (including ELECTRAFLYER): G-MBCU BEP BGB BHE BIO BJD BJK BJN BKY BNK BNT BOD BRB
 BRD BRS BTY BWE BWY BYD BYO BYR BYX JAE JBL JBN JBV JCX JEO JFP JIO JLY JNM JNO MJB MTV NBL NSS

AMERICAN AVN - see GRUMMAN-AMERICAN

AMETHYST Ax6-56: G-BFLP

AMF CHEVVRON: G-MNFL TFG TRJ VGC VGD VGE VIP VOO VUO VVV VXX VZZ WHS WJL WJM WNO WNP WPW WRZ WUI WZB MYGN YYP ZCK ZDP
 ZFH

ANDERSON EA-1 KINGFISHER AMPHIBIAN: G-BUTE XBC

ANDREASSON BA.4B (CROSBY): G-AWPZ YFV BEBS EBT FXF YPSY

ANEC
  II: G-EBJO

  IV MISSEL THRUSH: G-FBPI

ARKLE KITTIWAKE - see MITCHELL

ARBITER SVS TRIKE: G-MNWL

ARMSTRONG-WHITWORTH METEOR - see GLOSTER
  SEAHAWK: G-JETH

  AW.650 ARGOSY: G-APRL BEOZ

ARROW ACTIVE: G-ABVE

ARROWFLIGHT - see CGS

ARV1 SUPER 2: G-BMDO MOK MWE MWF MWJ MWM NGV NGW NGX NGY NHB NHD NHE NVI OGK PMX SRK WBZ COWS DEXP ERMO OARV RIX
  TAL POOL STWO TARV XARV ZARV

ATR
  ATR 42: G-BUEA UEB UPS VEC VED VEF VJP XBV XEG XEH YHA YHB ORFH WFEP ZAPJ

  ATR 72: G-BVTJ VTK WDA WDB WTL WTM XTN XXA XYV OILA ILB UKTJ KTK KTL KTM KTN

AUSTER - see TAYLORCRAFT & BEAGLE
  III: G-AHLI HLK REI BUDL

  4/5/5D (including ALPHA 5 variant): G-AGLK IKE JGJ JHJ JVT JXC JXV JXY KOW KPI KSY KSZ KWS KWT KXP LBJ LBK LFA LNV LXZ
  LYB LYG MVD NFU NHR NHS NHU NHW NHX NIE NIJ NIS NLU NRP OCP OCR OCU OFJ OVW PAF PAH PBE PBW PRF PTU BDFX ICD XKX

  6A/AOP.6/TUGMASTER: G-ARDX RGB RGI RHM RIH RRX RXU RYD SEF SIP SNB SOC STI BKXP NGE

  AOP.9/11 (including BEAGLE E.3 variant): G-ASCC VHT VXY XRR XWA YUA ZBU BDFH GBU GKT GTC JXR KVK UCI URR WKK XON

  D.4: G-ARLG

  D.5 - see BEAGLE-AUSTER

  D.6: G-ARCS RDJ

  J/1 AUTOCRAT & J/1N ALPHA (including KINGSLAND/CROFTON SPECIAL variants): G-AGTO GTT GVN GXN GXU GXV GYD GYH GYK GYT
  HAL HAM HAP HAT HAU HAV HCK HCL HHH HHP HHT HHU HSO HSP HSS HST IBH IBM IBR IBW IBX IBY IFZ IGD IGF IGP IGR IGT IGU IJI
  IJZ IPV IRC IZU IZY JAE JAJ JAS JDW JEB JEE JEH JEI JEM JIH JIS JIT JIU JIW JPZ JRB JRC JRE JUD JUE JUL JYB MTM PIK PJZ
  PKM PKN PTR PUK RRL RUY SEE XUJ BLPG RKC VGT JAYI TENT

  J/1B AIGLET: G-AMKU RBM

  J/1U WORKMASTER: G-AGVG PMH PSR

  J/2 ARROW: G-AJAM WLX BEAH

  J/4: G-AIJK IJM IJS IJT IPR

  J/5B AUTOCAR (including J/5G, J/5P, J/5V variants): G-AOBV OFM OHZ OIY PUW RKG RLY RNB RUG SFK XMN

  J/5F AIGLET TRAINER (including J/5K, J/5L variants): G-AMMS MRF MTA MUI MUJ MYD MZI MZT MZU NWX OFS PVG BGKZ

  J/5Q ALPINE (including J/5R variant): G-ANXC OGV OZL PCB

AVENGER (Roger Light): G-BHMJ HMK IGR IPW IRK IRL IRM IXS

AVIA FL.3: G-AGFT

AVIAMILANO (including AEROMERE, LAVERDA & SEQUOIA homebuilts)
  F.8L FALCO: G-BICN VDP WYO YLL CWAG FALC GANE KYNG OCAD CDS RJW PDGG REEC

  F.14 NIBBIO: G-OWYN

AVIASUD MISTRAL: G-MGAG VSJ VUP VWW VWZ VXN VXV VZR WIB YSL YST ZJB

AVIONS LOBET GANAGOBIE: G-BAMG

AVIONS MUDRY - see CAARP

AVRO
  TRIPLANE: see ROE

  504K/L: G-EASD EBJE ECKE BAA DEV ECKE

  534 BABY: G-EACQ

  594 AVIAN: G-EBOV EBZM G-ACGT

621 TUTOR: G-AHSA

652A ANSON/NINETEEN: G-AGPG GWE HKX MDA PHV VVO WRS WSA YWA BFIR SMF VROE

683 LANCASTER: G-ASXX BVBP LANC

685 YORK: G-AGNV NTK

694 LINCOLN: G-APRJ

698 VULCAN: G-BLMC VJET VLCN VULC

748 (including HSA & BAe production): G-ARAY RMX TMI TMJ VXI VXJ YIM BEJD GMN GMO IUV NJK ORM PDA PNW VOU VOV EMRD OJEM PFW SOE SOEI

AVRO (CANADA) CF-100 CANUCK: G-BCYK

BA:
EAGLE 2: G-AFAX

SWALLOW 2 - see BRITISH KLEMM & KLEMM: G-ADPS EVZ FCL FGC FGD FGE FHC

BAC
DRONE (including KRONFELD): G-ADPJ EDB

PETREL - see PROCTOR

BAC ONE-ELEVEN - see HUNTING: G-ASYD VMH VMI VMJ VMK VML VMM VMN VMO VMP VMR VMS VMT VMU VMV VMW VMX VMY VMZ WYV XLL YOP ZMF BEJM HKIT IIIH MAAH OBWA BWB BWC BWD BWE

BAC-SUD/AEROSPATIALE CONCORDE: G-AXDN BBDG OAA OAB OAC OAD OAE OAF OAG SST

BAe - see HAWKER SIDDELEY (HSA)
JETSTREAM (to Srs.30/31) (including HANDLEY-PAGE & SCOTTISH AVTN): G-ATXJ BBYM KUY LKP RGN UJT WWW XLM CBEA IJYS JSSD NFLC OAKI AKJ LOVA OBWN BWO RAVL

JETSTREAM 41: G-BWUI GCJL JMAC MAJA AJB AJC AJD AJE AJF AJG AJH AJI AJJ AJK AJL AJM SKJ OXLI PJRT

ATP (including JETSTREAM 61): G-BRLY TPF TPG TPH TPJ TPL TPO TTO UKJ UWM UWP CORP MANA MANB MANC MANE MANF MANG MANH MANJ MANL MANM MANO MANP MANU MAUD OBWL OBWM OEDJ PLXI WISS

BAe 146 (all variants): G-BKMN LRA PNT SNR SNS TTP UHC XAR XAS ZAT ZAU ZAV
DEBA EBC EBD EBE EBF EBG EBH EBJ EBK EBL EBM EBN FLTA GNTZ JEAJ EAK EAM EAO EAR EAS EAT EAU EAV EAW EAX EBA EBB EBC EBD EBE LUXE MANS IMA OFOA ZRH TBIC JPM NTA NTB NTE NTG NTK NTL NTM NTR UKAC KAG KHP KID KRC KSC ZAPK APL

BARNES AVON (Trike): G-MJGO

BARNETT ROTORCRAFT J4B: G-BRVR RVS WCW

BARRITAULT - see GARDAN

BAT FK-23 BANTAM: G-EACN

BEAGLE - see AUSTER

BEAGLE-AUSTER
A.61 TERRIER: G-ARLO RLP RLR RNO RSL RTM RUI SAJ SAK SAN SAX SBU SCD SDK SDL SEG SKJ SMZ SOI SOM SUI SYG SYN SZE SZX TBU TDN THU VCS VYK YDW YDX

A.109 AIREDALE: G-ARNP ROJ RXC RXD RYZ SAI SBH SBY SRK SWB TCC VKP WGA

B.121 PUP: G-AVDF VLM VLN VZN VZP WKM WKO WVC WWE WYJ WYO XCX XDU XDV XDW XEV XHO XIA XIE XIF XJH XJI XJJ XJO XMW XMX XNL XNM XNN XNP XNR XNS XOJ XOZ XPA XPB XPC XPM XPN XSC XSD XTZ XUA ZCK ZCL ZCN ZCP ZCT ZCU ZCV ZCY ZCZ ZDA ZDG ZEU ZEV ZEW ZEY ZFA ZGF ZSW BAKW ASP DCO IPUP JIMB OPUP PUPP TSKY

B.125 BULLDOG - see SCOTTISH AVN

B.206: G-ARRM SWJ TZO BSET HRHI FLYP

D.5 HUSKY: G-ASNC TCD TMH VOD VSR WSW XBF

E.3 - see AUSTER AOP.9/11

BEDE
BD.4: G-BEKL KZV OPD BYLS

BD.5: G-BCOX DTT GLB JPI UTP YFB

BEECHCRAFT
17 TRAVELER (including UC-43 variant): G-BRVE UXU

18 (including 3NM, 3TM, C-45 variants): G-ASUG BKGL KGM KRN SZC

23 MUSKETEER/SUNDOWNER: G-ASBB SJO SWP TBI WFZ WTS WTV YYU BAHO ARH ARI ASN BSB BTX BTY UXN DJHB GUCK

24R SIERRA: G-BBSC BVJ BXU YDG

33 DEBONAIR (including 33 BONANZA variant): G-BGSW THW TZA CGON OLA ENSI HOPE MOAC OAHC VICM

35 BONANZA ("V" tail version - see 33 & 36 variants): G-APTY RKJ RZN SJL TSR BBTS ONZ
EHMJ NEWT REST

36 BONANZA: G-BMYD SEY JLHS OCK MAPR ORSP POPA ZLOJ

T-34 MENTOR: N6251S

55/56/58 BARON: G-ASDO SOH WAH WAJ YKA YPD ZDK ZXA BFLZ LJM LKY MLM NBY NUN NVZ PJA RTN TFT WRP XDF XNG XPM YDY
DAFY FABM LAK LTZ RBY IOCO JOYS MOSS OLYD SDI PAPU RICK SUZI TSAR UROP VCML WOOD WIZ

60 DUKE: G-IASL

65/70/80 QUEEN AIR: G-ASDA VDR VDS WKX KEAB EAC TUBS WJPN

76 DUCHESS: G-BGHP GRG GVH HGM IMZ MJT NTT NUO NYO ODX OFC OZP RPU XHD XMH XSK XWA XXT
GBSL CCL JLRW OADY BLC PAT TRAN WACI ACJ

77 SKIPPER: EI-BHT

90 KING AIR: G-BMKD VRS DEXY FLTI WELL

95 TRAVEL AIR: G-ASMF SYJ TRC

200/350 SUPER KING AIR: G-BGRE PPM VMA XMA YCK YCP CEGR ECAV FPLA PLB RYI HAMA KMCD OLDZ MNH REBK OWN SBAS VSBC WRCF

BELL
P-63 KINGCOBRA: G-BTWR

BELL HELICOPTERS (including AGUSTA & WESTLAND (47D/G) & AGUSTA (47H/J) production
47D/G: G-ARXH SOL XKN XKO XKS XKW XKX XKY YOE BAXS BRI BVP EGA FEF FVM FYI GID GMU GZK HAR HBE HNV LGR PAI PDY
CHOP IGY GGTT MASH INX SOLH

47H/J: G-ATFV ZYB BFPP EURA

206 JET RANGER (including AGUSTA production): G-AVII VSZ WMK YMW BAKS AML ARP AUN BCA BNG BOR EWY HTR KEW KZI LCA LGV
LZN NYD OLO ORV OTM PIE POR PWI SBW SDU TFX TFY THY UZZ VGA WLO WVE WZW XAY XDS XKL XLI XNS XNT XPN XRY XUF XZX YBA YBC
YBI YSE
CCLY HGL ITZ ODE OIN ORC ORT PTS RPS TPW DBMW ENN NCN OFY ORB ELLI FEZZ INS OXM GHCL UST HEBE ELE MPH MPT SDW IIRB NVU
OIO SKY JAHL BDB EKP ETX IMW LEE WBI WLS KLEE LGRM ILY MCPI FMF ILI OTA NEWS EWZ OAMG BEY BYT CBB CST DIG DIL JCB MDR
MEC MJB NOW NTV NYX OTA PNI SMD VBJ PEAK ORT RAMI AMY IAN NBW SMA SELY HCC PEY PYI TER TOX UEZ TILI OYZ REE UEST WFRD
GAL HAZ IZZ LLY XXIV

206L LONG RANGER: G-BXIB XMP CSWL EYRE IANG LEEZ NEUF OHHI LDN

212: G-BFER GLJ IXV WLE WOS

214ST SUPER TRANSPORT: G-BKFN KFP

222: G-NOIR OWCG

UH-1H IROQUOIS: G-HUEY

BELLANCA
17-30 SUPER VIKING: G-VIKE

CITABRIA - see CHAMPION

BENES-MRAZ M.1 SOKOL: G-AIXN BWRG

BENSEN (including CAMPBELL-BENSEN & MONTGOMERIE-BENSEN variants)
B.7/B.8 GYROCOPTER: G-APSY PUD RTJ SCT SME SNY SWN SYP TLP TOZ WAS WDW WLM WPY XBG XCI ZAZ BCGB DJF GIO HEM HKE IFN IGP
IGX IHX IPY IVK IVL IZT JAO JSU JZY KBS KNY KUS LGO LLA LLB MBW MOT MYF MYV MZW NBU NCV NJL OTZ OUV OWZ OZW PBA PCV PFK
PIF PNN POO PSK PTV RBS RCF REA REU RFW RHL RHM RHU RXN SBX SJB SMG SMX SNI SNL SNY SPJ SZM TAH TBL TFW TIG TJN TJS TST
TSU TTD UJK UPF VAZ VIF VJF VKJ VMG WAH WEY WJN WSZ XCL XDC HAGS INCH OOJC TIM SCUD YJET ROS ROY

BETTS TB.1 - see STAMPE

BFC - see QUAD-CITY

BINDER CP.301S SMARAGD - see PIEL

BIRDMAN
CHEROKEE (Wing): G-MBJO

WT-11 CHINOOK: G-MMKE

BLACKBURN
B.2: G-ACBH DFV EBJ

MONOPLANE: G-AANI

BLAKE BLUETIT: G-BXIY

BLERIOT XI: G-AANG BPVE WRH LOTI

BOEING
B-17G FLYING FORTRESS: G-BEDF

B-29 SUPERFORTRESS: G-BHDK

707: G-APFG PFJ BFEO SAIL

727: G-BNNI PND

737: G-BGDA GDB GDE GDL GDO GDP GDR GDS GDT GDU GJE GJF GJH KYA KYB KYE KYH KYI KYK KYL KYM KYN KYO KYP NNK NNL SNV SNW
UHJ UHK UHL VKA VKB VKC VKD VNM VNN VNO VZE VZF VZG VZH VZI
COLB OLC OLE DOCA OCB OCC OCD OCE OCF OCG OCH OCI OCJ OCK OCL OCM OCN OCO OCP OCR OCS OCT OCU OCV OCW OCX OCY OCZ
GBTA BTB ECAS ZYA ZYB ZYC ZYD ZYE ZYF ZYG ZYH ZYI ZYJ ZYK ZYL IGOA GOB GOC GOD GOE GOF GOG GOH GOI GOJ GOK GOL GOM GOP
GOR MONG ONV SKA SKB SKC SKD SKE OABA ABL AMS BMD BMF BMG BMH BMJ BMM BMO BMP BMR BMX BMZ DSK DUS FRA GBA GBB GBC GBD
GBE HAJ JSW JTW KDN MUC SFBH MDB TREN XBHX MAN

747: G-AWNC WNE WNF WNH WNM WNN WNO WNP BBPU DPV DXA DXB DXC DXD DXE DXF DXG DXH DXI DXJ DXK DXL DXM DXN DXO DXP NLA
NLB NLC NLD NLE NLF NLG NLH NLI NLJ NLK NLL NLM NLN NLO NLP NLR NLS NLT NLU NLV NLW NLX NLY NLZ YGA YGB YGC YGD YGE YGF
YGG CIVA IVB IVC IVD IVE IVF IVG IVH IVI IVJ IVK IVL IVM IVN IVO IVP IVN IVO IVP IVR IVS IVT IVU IVV IVW IVX IVY IVZ
VAST BIG CAT FAB GIN HOT IRG JFK LAX MIA RUM TOP XLG

757: G-BIKA IKB IKC IKD IKF IKG IKH IKI IKJ IKK IKL IKM IKN IKO IKP IKR IKS IKT IKU IKV IKW IKX IKY IKZ MRA MRB MRC MRD
MRE MRF MRG MRH MRI MRJ PEA PEB PEC PED PEE PEF PEI PEJ PEK PET XOL YAD YAE YAF YAG YAH YAI YAJ YAK YAL YAM YAN YAO YAP
YAR YAS YAT YAU YAW YAX CPEL PEM PEN PEO PEP PER PES PET DAJB FCLA CLB CLC CLD CLE CLF CLG CLH CLI JALC LCRC MCEA MONB
OND ONE ONJ ONK OOOA OOB OOG OOI OOJ OOS OOU OOV OOW OOX OOY PIDS RJGR WJAN

767: G-BNWA NWB NWC NWD NWE NWF NWG NWH NWI NWJ NWK NWL NWM NWN NWO NWP NWR NWS NWT NWU NWV NWW NWX NWY NWZ NYS OPB RIF
RIG YAA YAB ZHA ZHB ZHC DAJC IMB OBYA BYB BYC BYD BYG BYH OAN OAO SJMC UKLI

777: G-RAES VIIA IIB IIC IID IIE IIF IIG IIH IIJ IIK IIL IIM IIN IIO IIP IIR IIS IIT YMMA/YMMP ZZZA ZZB ZZC ZZD ZZE

BOEING-STEARMAN 75 KAYDET (including N2S/N3N/PT-13/PT-17 variants): G-AROY WLO ZLE BAVO IXN NIW PTB RHB RSK RTK RUJ SDS
SGR SWC TFG TGA UKE ERIX IIIG LLE SDN NZSS ONAF RJAH

BOLKOW
Bo.207: G-EFTE

Bo.208 JUNIOR (including MALMO): G-ASFR SZD TDO TRI TSI TSX TTR TUI TVX TZA TXZ VKR VLD VZI BIJD OKW SME CLEM ECGO

(MBB) Bo.209 MONSUN: G-AYPE ZBB ZDD ZOA ZOB ZRA ZTA ZVA ZVB BLRD

BOND SKY DANCER: G-BLUK

BONSALL DB-1 MUSTANG: G-BDWM

BOWERS FLY BABY: G-AFRD NPV UYU

BRADSHAW HAB-76: G-AXXP

BRANDLII BX-2 CHERRY: G-BXUX

BRANTLY
B.2: G-ASHD SXD TFG VIP WDU WIO XSR BPIJ OAPR MAX ROTR WASP

305: G-ASXF

BREMNER - see MITCHELL WING

BRIGHTON Ax7-65: G-AVTL

BRISTOL
BOXKITE: G-ASPP

BABE: G-EASQ

SCOUT D: N5419

F.2B FIGHTER: G-AANM CAA EPH

M.1C REPLICA: G-BLWM WJM

105 BULLDOG: G-ABBB

149 BOLINGBROKE (BLENHEIM): G-BPIV MKIV

156 BEAUFIGHTER: G-DINT

171 SYCAMORE: G-ALSX HAPR

175 BRITANNIA: G-ANCF OVF OVT

192 BELVEDERE: G-BRMB

BRITISH KLEMM L.25 SWALLOW - see BA & KLEMM: G-ACXE

BRITTEN SHERIFF: G-FRJB

BRITTEN-NORMAN
 BN.1F: G-ALZE

 BN.2A/B/T ISLANDER/DEFENDER (including IRMA & PILATUS production): G-AWNT XHE XUB XZK YGK YRU YYW BCEN EEG ELF FNU IIP
 JOP JSA JWO LDV LNJ LNL LNW NXA PCA SPY SWR UBN VFK VHX VHY VSJ VSL WNF WNG WPK WPM WPR WPU WPV WPW WPX WYW WYX WYY WYZ
 WZF CHES CIAS HPAA ISLA JSAT SPC LEAP OTO MAFF NESU ORED SEA TVS WIN PASU ASV RAPA SBUS SKY URV WOTG

 BN.2A/III TRISLANDER: G-AZLJ BBYO CCU DOT DTN DTO DWV EDP EFO EPH EPI EVT EVV JOEY OCME CTA JAV WEAC XTOR

BROCHET
 MB.50 PIPISTRELLE: G-AVKB BADV

 MB.84: G-AYVT

BROOKLAND
 HORNET: G-BRPP MIKE PHIL

 MOSQUITO: G-AWIF BGEX

BROOKLANDS - see OPTICA

BROOKS PULSAR: G-MBOK

BRUGGER MB.2/MB.3 COLIBRI: G-BKCI KRH NDP NDT OBF PBP RWV SUJ UDW UTY VIS VVN XVS HRLM KARA PRAG

BUCKER Bu.131 JUNGMANN (CASA 1.131): G-BECT ECW EDA HPL HSL IRI JAL PDM PTS PVW RSH SAJ SFB SLH TDT TDZ UCC UCK UOR UTA
 UVN UVP VPD WHP XBD YIJ CDRU DUDS EHBJ MJA JGMN UNG RETA TAFF WIBS

 Bu.133 JUNGMEISTER (including CASA & DORNIER): G-AEZX XMT YSJ BSZN UKK UTX VGP VXJ TAFI

 Bu.181 BESTMANN (ZLIN Z.381): G-AMYA

BUG: G-BXTV

BUSBY: G-FYGF

BUSHBY-LONG MIDGET MUSTANG - see LOEHLE: G-AWIR BDGA XHT MIDG

BVS: G-BJUB

CAARP - see PIEL
 CAP.10: G-BECZ KCX LVK RDD XBK XBU XFE XRA XRB XRC YFY CAPI APX ZCZ LORN MOZZ ODIN RIFN SLEA WIXI

 CAP.20/21: G-BIPO PPS

 CAP.231 (MUDRY production): G-OPPS

CAB MINICAB/SUPERCAB - see GARDAN

CALLAIR A.9: G-TDFS

CAMBRIDGE HABA: G-BBGZ

CAMERON - see CAMERON-COLT & CAMERON-THUNDER
 Airship (Gas) variants:
 DG-19: G-BKIK PWT
 D-38: G-BGEP
 DP-50: G-BMEZ
 DP-70: G-BPFF RDT
 DP-80: G-BTBR UPPY VIBA
 DP-90: G-BVJJ XKY
 D-96: G-BAMK KNL

 Balloon (Gas) variants:
 R-15: G-CICI
 R-36: G-ROZY
 R-42: G-BLIO
 R-77: G-BUFA UFC UFE VJO
 R-150: G-BVUO
 R-420: G-JNEE RNEE
 R-550: G-RTWI
 R-900: G-CWCW

 Balloon (Hot Air) variants:
 RW-9: G-BVOG

 H-20/P-20/V-20: G-BIBS JUV OYO PRU RCJ RCO

H-24: G-BRLU SCK VCY

N-31/O-31/S-31/V-31: G-BAGI DSO EJK EUY GHS KIZ MST PUB RMT VFB COOP LEAU LYD PRTT WETI

H-34: G-BRKL RWY UCB VZX XYI EROS FZZI IAMP RAPP

N-42/O-42/V-42: G-AZER BCDL ISH KNB MWU PHD UPP VLC WEE WGX XJH XTG HOPI

N-56/O/56/V-56: G-AZKK BADU BYU CAP COJ CXZ DPK DSF DUI DUZ DYH ECK EEH ELX END ENN ERT EXX EXZ FAB FFT FKL FME GLX GOI GUY HGF HSN ICU KLC KRS KZF LWX MOJ NIF OWM RIR RSA RSL THZ UVG YSL ZKK HOFM OOV LENN OVET PBBT SWPR WAAC YNT

N-65/O-65/V-65: G-AZIP ZUP ZUV ZXB BAOW BGR BYR CFC CFN CRI DFG DGP DRK DSK EIF ETP GJU HKH HNC HND HOT HOU IBO IGL IWK IWU IYI JAW JNX JWJ JZA KGR KWR KXX LEP LJF LXY LZB MCD MJN MKY MPD MVW MYJ NAN NAU NAW OAL OOB OWV PGD PPA PXF REH RMI ROE ROG SAS SGP TUH WBA WHB WHG WJC XGY XUU GLUE HENS JOIN KAFE MUIR NATX OERX PMAM YRO RUDD SMIG OFA WELS

CONCEPT C-60/70/80/PM-80: G-BTZU UYC VDM VDY VEK VEN VGJ VSV VSW VUE VUU VWE VZN WAO WGP WRT XJP XJZ XLG XOT XSC XSA XSB XSJ YER EVET OARG BTS NIX ROGY SLCE OUP UPHL

N-77/O-77/V-77: G-BAXF BOC BYL CNP CRE CZO DAC DBI DNZ DSE FUG FYK GAZ GHV HDV HHB HHK HHN HII HYO IDU IEF IET IRY JGK KCT KIC KNP KPN KRI KTR KWW KZB LFY LIP LJH LLD LPP LSH LVN LXF LZS MAD MCK MKJ MKP MKW MLJ MLW MOH MPP MTN MTX MVO MZB NCB NCH NCJ NCK NCM NDN NDV NEO NES NFG NFO NGJ NGN NHI NIN NIU NJG NKT NMA NMG NNE NPE NTW NTZ NUC OAU OBR OEK OFF OGP OJB OJD OJU OOZ ORB ORN OSV OTW OWB OWL OXG OZN PAE PBU PBV PBY PDF PDG PHH PHJ PIM PLF PLV PPP PSH PSR PTD PVC PVM PWC PYI PYS PYT PYV RAJ RBO REL RFE RFO RHC RIB RKW RLX RMU RMV RNW ROB RRF RRO RRR RRW RSD RTV RUE RUV RWH RZA RZT SBI SBM SBR SDX SEV SGY SHO SHT SIC SIJ SKD SLI SMS SUV SWJ SWV SWY SXM SYJ TAG TIX TJH TKZ TOI TOP TPT TRX TWJ TWM TXW TZV UAF UAM UDU UES UEV UGD UGP UGS UHM UNG UOX UPI UTJ UWU UWY UZK VBS VBU VDR VFF VHK VIM VLI VMF VUK VXB WAJ WAN WHC WKV WPB WPC WTJ WYN XAX XSX XTJ XVT YBN YHY YLY
CBKT CAR CSC EJA GOD HOK HUK RAK TGR DASU RYI EIIR NNY PDI RIK FABB ELT UZY GEES EEZ EUP UNS HARE ENY GAS ORN OST IDDI JLMW KEYY ODA TEE LAZR EGO END EXI IDD IOT OAG OAN OLL OSS UBE MAMO ILE ITS ITZ OFF OKE RTY NEPB OATH CND DHL EDP HSA JEN KYA MRB NZO RPR PADI OLY USS VCU RAPH CMF ONI SAFE AIX CAH CFO HOT KIL LAC NOW USI TECK UDR UPUP VODA OLT WAIT ELI XSKY

O-84: G-AYAJ YVA ZBH ZNT ZRN ZSP BAGY AKO ALD AST BLL CEZ NET NFP NXR OWU OYM REX RGD SKE SKU SMK UYN VXD WLN KEYB MOSY OLLE STAV

LTSB-90/N-90/O-90/V-90/Z-90: G-BMFU MJZ NBR NII NJX OWK PSO PUJ PZO RGE ROH ROY RPJ RZC SCA SNJ SSO SWX TBP TCM TFU THF TJU TTB TTL TWV TXF UAJ UFJ UFX UGY UIE UIU UIZ UOE UUO UVW VBX VDX VEJ VFP VHO VHR VKV VMR VOC VOP VPK VTN WAU WBC WBN WDU WIP WJI WNO WNS WPT WUU WVU WYC XAM XBS XCS XJO XVV YDT YHC
CHAA OMP ONC TEL XCX DHLB IAL RYS ELLE NUS FBNW OGG GLAW OCX OGW HBUG TVI IGEL GLE LES NSR WON JULU LAGR TSB MANI FLI OFZ OCJS ISK JBM XBY PATG KCC RNT RISE IZE IZI SLII ORT RVO TRM WEB TANK EDF EEL INS MCC VRVI YUMM UPI VET

RX-100: G-NPWR

A-105/N-105/O-105/AML-105: G-BAVU LSX MEE MOV MVI NFN OTD OTK OYY PBW PJE RFR RLL RZB SNZ TEA TFM TIZ TKW TPB TRL UHU ULD UPT UWF UWW VCA VEU VHV VNR VUA VXA VXP WDH WEW WKF WOW WPZ WRY WSU XBM XBR XBY XEN XGC XTF XWY XXG XXL XYG YFB YFJ
CAMP LIC DRGN ENRY FOWS GFAB HONK JSON LBNK NPNP ZGL OAML UVI SAXO DLW EPT STI ULTR WNGS XANT YLYB

A-120/O-120/RTW-120: G-BNEX OBB OHL OZY PSS PTX PZK RXA SYB TEE TKN TOU TUU TXS UDV UFT URN VSO VXF WAG WJL WKD WLD WYS XNL XVJ XWI FLOA GHIA HOTT LOBO MEUP OFB TING VIKY

N-133: G-BWAA

A-140/O-140: G-BVPU VYU WTE GAIW DXK

N-145: G-DENT HIBM

A-160/N-160/O-160: G-BNIE OBD PCN PJZ PLE RIM YHW TGAS

AT-165: G-BIAZ

A-180/N-180: G-BPPJ PSZ PYY RTH RVC RZI SEX SLG SLO SWD SWZ SYD SZY TBS TCW TYE UAU UJR UKC VHJ VKL WBR WHW XMM OBRY RWHC SKYR VBF

A-200: G-BWYL XOS

A-210: G-BLSU RJM RVK TCK TXV UAY UEE UHY UOC UVK UYH VBN VRM WSR WZK XBA XJC XNM XRM XWZ XXF XZG XZH YDI CVBF FLYE JOJO LPGI OJWE TRAV

A-250: G-BUBR UXE UXR UZY VIG VUD VYR WKU WKX WZJ XPK LORA MOLI ODEB VBF SCRU KYY TPI

A-275: G-BWML XIC XKJ XMW XTE XYL

A-315: G-SIMI

A-340: G-BWPA KVBF YBF RANG

A-375: G-BWNH

A-400: G-ZVBF

N-1250: G-WASH

SPECIAL SHAPES:

ACTION MAN PARACHUTIST	- G-RIPS	MOBILE PHONE	- G-PHON
APPLE	- G-BWSO	MONSTER TRUCK	- G-BWMU
BALL	- G-RNIE	MOUNTIE	- G-BXSW
BEER BARREL	- G-PINT	MR.PEANUT	- G-NUTS PNUT
BEER CAN	- G-IBET	MUG	- G-RMUG
BEETHOVEN BUST	- G-BNJU	N ELE	- G-WBMG
BELLS WHISKY BOTTLE	- G-BUUU	OIL CAN	- G-UNIP
BENIHANA	- G-BMVS	OTTI	- G-OTTI
BERENTZEN BOTTLE	- G-KERN ORN	PERRIER BOTTLE	- G-PERR
BERTIE BASSETT	- G-BXAL	PIG	- G-HOGS
BIERKRUG	- G-BXFY	POT	- G-CHAM
BRADFORD AND BINGLEY	- G-BWMY	PRINTER	- G-BYFK
BUDWEISER CAN	- G-BPFJ	REAL FRUIT	- G-BXJL
BULB	- G-BVWI	ROBINSON'S BARLEY WATER	- G-BKES
BUS	- G-BUSS	RUGBY	- G-BYFW
CADBURY'S CARAMEL BUNNY	- G-BUNI	RUPERT BEAR	- G-BTML
CADBURY'S CREME EGG	- G-OEGG	RUSSIAN DOLL	- G-USSR
CALLING CARD	- G-BWVK	SAMSUNG COMPUTER	- G-SEUK
CAN	- G-OFIZ	SANTA MARIA SHIP	- G-BPSP
CARROTS	- G-BWSP HUCH	SATURN	- G-DREX
CART	- G-BYDU	SAUCER	- G-GUFO
CHAMPION SPARK PLUG	- G-BETF	SCOTTISH PIPER	- G-PIPY
CHATEAU DE BALLEROY	- G-BKBR TCZ	SIGN	- G-UCCC
CHEESE	- G-RANA	SONIC THE HEDGEHOG	- G-SEGA
CHESTIE	- G-USMC	SPHERE	- G-BVFU IBBC SATL
CIDER BOTTLE	- G-OTNT	STARTAC	- G-HAND
CLUB	- G-BWNP	STRAWBERRY	- G-SAMI
COOLING TOWER	- G-WATT	SULTAN	- G-TURK
COTTAGE	- G-COTT	TEMPLE	- G-BMWN
DOLL	- G-BVDF	TENNENT'S LAGER GLASS	- G-BTSL
DOUGLAS- LURPAK BUTTERMAN	- G-BXCK	THOMAS	- G-BXND
DRACULA SKULL	- G-DRAC	TRAINER'S SHOE	- G-BUDN
DUDE	- G-OIFM	TRUCK	- G-BLDL DERV
EAGLE	- G-BVMJ	TV	- G-TVTV
ELEPHANT	- G-BLRW MKX PRC	UFO	- G-BUFO
EXPANSION JOINT	- G-BIUL	UNCLE SAM	- G-USAM
FABERGE EGG	- G-BNFK	WINE BOX	- G-STOW
FIRE EXTINGUISHER	- G-BVYJ	WITCH	- G-WYCH
FORBES' MAGAZINE	- G-BPOV		
FURNESS BUILDING	- G-BSIO		
GOLFBALL	- G-BXKK PUTT		
GOLLY	- G-OLLI		
GRAND ILLUSION	- G-MAGC		
HARD HAT	- G-BXAP		
HARLEY DAVIDSON MOTOCYCLE	- G-BMUN		
HELIX OIL CAN	- G-HLIX		
HOFMEISTER LAGER BEAR	- G-HEYY		
HOME SPECIAL	- G-BWZP		
HOPPER SERVO	- G-OSVO		
JAGUAR XK8 SPORTS CAR	- G-OXKB		
KATALOG	- G-OTTO		
KOOKABURRA	- G-CHKL		
KP CHOC DIPS TUB	- G-DIPI		
LIGHTBULB	- G-BVWH		
MACAW	- G-BRWZ		
MICKEY MOUSE	- G-MOUS		

CAMPBELL
COUGAR: G-BAPS

CRICKET (including BENSEN & EVERETT): G-AXPZ XRC XVL XVM YCC YHI YPZ YRA YRC BHBA KVS ORG RLF TEI TMP UIG ULT VDJ
VIT VLD VOH WCE WSD WUA WUZ XCJ XEM XHU XUA GYRO RUGS TVSI

CANADAIR CL.600/601 CHALLENGER: G-MSKK SKL SKM SKN

CARLSON SPARROW: G-BSUX VVB

CASA - see BUCKER (1.131 JUNGMANN), HEINKEL (2.111) & JUNKERS (C.352L)

CASSUTT RACER (including MUSSO/SPECIAL variants): G-AXDZ BDTW EUN KCH NJZ OMB OXW PVO PVX UFK WEC XMF FRAY MARY NARO
RUNT TTIM RUC

CAUDRON
G.III: G-AETA

C.270 LUCIOLE: G-BDFM

CCF HARVARD - see NORTH AMERICAN

CENTRAIR MOTO-DELTA: G-MBPJ

CENTRE EST (CEA) - see JODEL

CESSNA (including REIMS [F.prefix] production)
C.165 AIRMASTER: G-BTDE

120/140 variants: G-AHRO JJS JJT KTS KUR KVM LOD LTO NGK BHLW JML OCI PHW PHX PKO PUU PWD PZB RJC RPE RPF RPG RPH RUN
RXH SUH TBV TBW TEW TOS TVG TYW TYX UHO UHZ UJM UKO VUZ YCD GAWA HALJ JOLY OVFM

150: G-APXY PZR RAU RFI RFO RSB RTY SMS SMU SMW SST SUE SYP SZB SZU TEF THV THZ TIE TKF TMC TML TMM TMY TNE TNL TOE TOF
TRK TRL TRM TUF TYM TYN TZY VAR VCU VEM VEN VER VGU VHM VIA VIB VIT VJE VMD VMF VNC VPH VUG VUH VVL VVW VVX VZU WAW WAX
WBX WCM WCO WCP WEO WES WFF WFH WGK WLA WMT WOT WPJ WPP WPU WRK WTJ WTX WUG WUH WUJ WUK WUL WUN WUO WUT WUU XGG XPF YBD
YEY YGC YKL YRF YRK YYF ZLH ZLY ZLZ ZXC BABB ABC ABH AEU AHI AIK AIP AMC AXU AXV AYO AYP AZS BBC BCI BDT BJX BKA BKB
BKE BKY BNJ BTT BTZ CBX CCC CRT CTW CUH CUJ CZN DBU DFJ DFZ DOD DSL DTX DUM DUO DZC EIG ELT EOK EWP FFY
FGW FIY FLM FOG FSR FVU FWL GBI GEA HIY IFY IOC JOV LVS MBB MLX MXJ NFI OBV OIV OMN ORY OTP OUJ OUZ OVS OVT PAB PAW PAX
PCJ PEM PGB PGY PGZ PNA POS PRP PUX PWG PWM PWN RBH RJT RLR RNC RTJ SBZ SEJ SJU SJZ SKA SRC SSB SYV SYW SZU SZV TES
TGP THE TIN TSN TTE TYC UCS UCT UGG UJU UNS URH WGU WII WVL CSBM SFC DENA ENB ENC END ECBH JMG FAYE FEN INA GBLR
CNZ FLY LED HFCB FCI IVE ULL UNY IANJ NGR JWDS LUCK MABE NSTG OIDW JVH KED STY PHAA LAN SADE ALL AMZ CAT TAIL
UFLY WYMP YIII

A150 AEROBAT: G-AXRT XRU XSW XUF YBW YCF YOZ YRO ZID ZJY ZKV ZLL ZOZ ZUZ ZZX ACC ACN ACO ACP AEP AEV AEZ AII AIN AOP
APH API APJ AUY BCF BEO BKF BKU BNX BNY BTB BTK BXB CDY CFR CKU CRN CTU CUY CVG CVH DAI DEX DNR DOW DRD EIA EKN EMY
EOE EOY FGG FGX FGZ FIE FRR HRH JTB LPH MEX OFW OFX OYU PJW PRO TFS UCA UTT CLUB FMSG HFCA OISO OPIC OSND

152: G-BFEK FFC FFE FFW FHT FHU FHV FKG FKH FLU FOE FOF FSB FXH GAA GAB GAD GAE GBP GFX GGO GGP GHI GIB GLG GNT GSX HAA
HAI HAV HCP HDM HDR HDS HDU HDW HEC HFC HFI HHG HIN HNA HPX HPY HRB HRM HRN HSA HUI HWA HWB HWS HYX HZH ICG IDH IJV IJW
IJX ILR ILS IOK IOM ITF ITH IUM IXH IZG JKX JKY JNF JVJ JVT JWH JYD KAZ KFC KGW KTV KWY LJO LWV LZE LZH LZP MCN MCV MFZ
MGG MJB MJC MJD MMM MSU MTA MTB MTJ MTL MVB MXA MXB MXC MXX NAJ NDO NFR NFS NHJ NHK NID NIV NJB NJC NJD NJH NJJ NJV NKC
NKI NKP NKR NKS NKV NMC NMD NME NMF NOZ NPY NPZ NRK NRL NSI NSM NSN NSU NSV NSW NUL NUS NUT NXC NYL NYN OAI ODO OFL
OFM OGC OGG OHI OHJ OIO OIP OIR OIW OKY OLV OLW ONW OOI ORI ORJ ORO OTB OTG OYL OZR PBG PBJ PBK PEO PFZ PGM PHT PIO PIY
PJL PME PTF PTU PVJ PZX RBF RBP RND RNE RNK RNN RPV RTD RTP RUA SCP SCZ SDO SDP SFP SFR SHE SRC STO STP SWH SZI SZO SZW
TAL TCE TDW TFC TGH TGR TGW TGX TIK TVW TVX TYT UEF UEG VTM WEU WEV WNB WNC WND XGE XJM XRN XTB XUZ XVB XVY XWC XYU YFA
CHIK PFC DACF ESY RAG ENTT NTW FIGA IGB HART FCL FCT IAFT BRO RAN KAFC ATT LAMS SMI MASS OAFT AMY BAT BEN DAC FRY IMC
LEE PAM PJC SFC VMC WAC WAK WOW RICH SACB ACF HAH TAYS WACB ACE ACF ACG ACT

A152 AEROBAT: G-BFGK FKF FMK FRV FZN FZT FZU GAF GLN HAC HAD HED HEN HJA HJB HMG IHE ILJ ILK IMT LAC LAX MUO MYG OPW
OPX OSO OYB RCD BRUM FIFE LIP JEET ONI LEIC MPBH OCPC RLFI TFCI WACH ACU ALS ZOOL

170: G-AORB PVS WOU BCLS N5428C

172/SKYHAWK (excluding R172 HAWK XP/FR172 ROCKET & 172RG CUTLASS variants): G-APSZ RID RLU RMO RMR ROA RWH RWO RWR RYI
RYK RYS RZD RZE SFA SIB SMJ SNW SOK SPI SSS SUH SUP SVM SWL TAF TFY TGO TKT TKU TLM TSL TWJ VBZ VEC VHH VIC VIS VJF VJI
VKG VPI VTP VVC VZV WBW WGD WGJ WGR WLF WMP WUX WUZ WVA XBH XBJ XDI XSI XVB XWF YCT YRG YRT YUV ZDZ ZJV ZKW ZKZ ZLM ZLV
ZTK ZTS ZUM ZXD ZZV BAAL AEO AEW AEY AIW AIX ANX AOB AOS AVB AXY AZT BDH BJD BJY BJZ BKI BKZ BNZ BOA BTG BTH CCD CEC
CHK COL CPK CRB CUF CVJ CYR CZM DCE DNU DZD EBI EHV EMB ENK EUX EWR EZK EZO EZR EZV FGD FKB FMX FOV FPH FPM FRS FTH FTX
FZV GAG GBR GIU GIY GLO GMP GND GNS GRO GSV HAW HCC HCM HDX HDZ HIH HMI HPZ HSB HUG HUJ HVR HYP HYR IBW IDF IGJ IHI IIB
IIE ING IOB ITM IZF JDE JDW JGO JGY JVM JWI JWW JXZ KCE KEP KEV KHZ KII KIJ KLO KLP KRB LHJ LVW MCI MHS MIG MTS MVJ NKD
NKE NRR NST NTP NXD NYM OEN OHH OIL OIX OIY OJR OJS OLI OLX OLY OMS OMT ONO ONR ONS OOL ORW OUE OUF OVG OYP PML PRM PTL
PVA PVY PWS RAK RBI RBJ RCM RWX RZS SCR SEP SHR SNG SOG SOO SPE STM TMA TMR TRE UAN UJN ULH UOJ URD UZN WEI WJP XGV XHG
XLJ XOI XSD XSE XSF XSM XSR XXD XXK YBD YEA YEB YEN YES YET YNA ZZD ZGH
CBOR CCC FLY LUX OCO SCS URR DCKK EMH ENR ODD RAM RBG UVL ECGC NII NOA TDC WUD FNLD NLY GBLP RAY WYN YAV ZDO HILS ICOM
JFWI ONE ONZ VMD LANE AVE ICK OOK MALK ELT ICK ILA OBMS ERS FCM OLE PFT PYE RMG SII SKY TAM VFR PDSI RARB OOK OUP SWO
UIA USS SACD BAE EVE EXI HSP KAN KYH TASH OBI OBY RIO YRE WACL ACW ACY ACZ YORK TWO

172RG CUTLASS: G-BHYC ILU IXI PARI

R172 HAWK XP/FR172 ROCKET variants: G-AWCN WDR WWU WYB XBU YGX YJW BAIL ARC BKG BXH CTK DOE EZS FFZ FIG FIU FSS HYD LMX
LPF PCI PWR TMK XYY DIVA FANL JANS LOYA OMAC PJTM YBAA

175/SKYLARK variants: G-APZS RCV REB RFG RFL RML RMN ROC RRG RUZ RWS OTOW

177 CARDINAL: G-BAJE EBN FMH PSL RDO RPS TSZ UJE

177RG CARDINAL: G-AYPG YPH YPI YSX YSY ZFP ZTF ZTW ZVP BAGN AIS AJA AJB BHI BJV CUW FGF FIV LNYS OAMP TOTO

180/SKYWAGON variants: G-ARAT SIT XZO BEOD ETG MAF NCS OIA TSM UPG DAPH

182/SKYLANE variants: G-ARAW SLH SNN SRR SSF SUL SXZ TCX TLA TPT TTD VCV VDA VGY VID XNX XZU YOW YWD ZNO BAAT AFL AHD
AHX AMJ BGX BYH BYS CWB DBJ DIG EKO FOD FSA GAJ GFH GPA HDP HIB HIC HVP IRS JVH KHJ KKN KKO LEW MMK MUD NRY OPG OTH RKR
RRK SDW SRR THA UVO WMC WRR XEZ XZM YEG CBIL DOVE RGS UNC EOHL HRNT UFF IFAB OPT RPC SEH JOON KWAX LEGG SKW MISH LAS
NLEE OCJW KOS LSC PST RAY PDHJ LEE OWL OWR RITZ OWE SAAM KYL TPSL WARP HDP XLTG

R182 SKYLANE RG: G-BFZD GVT HEO HYA JDI NMO NOX OPH OWO PUM YEM EIWT GEAR OZO JENI NOCK OTRG ZOI

185 SKYWAGON/AG CARRYALL variants: G-AYNN BBEX DKC KPC LOS XRH YBP RNRM

188 AG WAGON/AG TRUCK/T.188 AG HUSKY variants: G-AZZG BHTD

190/195 variants: G-BSPK TBJ

205: G-ASNK SOX

206 SUPER SKYLANE/SUPER SKYWAGON/STATIONAIR variants: G-ASVN TCE TLT WUA YCJ ZRZ BAGV ATD FCT GED GWR JRW MHC MOF NRI
OFD PGE RID SMB SUE XDB XRO DROP EESE SEAI KYE TAT

207 SKYWAGON/STATIONAIR 8 variants: G-NJAG PARA

208 CARAVAN: G-EELS

210 CENTURION (including TURBO & PRESSURISED variants): G-ASXR BBRY ENF EYV NZM SGT VZM IKIS MANT OFLY PIIX SEEK UIT VMDE

T303 CRUSADER: G-BKXG XRI YNG CRUS RUZ YLS DOLY EDRY GAME IKAP NDC JUIN OAPE PUSI ROCH

305 BIRD DOG (L-19): G-PDOG

310: G-APNJ RBC RCI VDB XLG YGB YND ZRR ZUY ZYM BALN ARG ARV BBX BHG BXL CTJ GTT GXK HEH IFA JMR KSB MMC ODY PIL RIA TFF TGN TYK WYE WYG WYH XUY XYF EGEE GLT FFOR FWD ISH GREN IMLI MIWS PBI OBNF DLY REDB EDD IST ODD SOUL TKPZ ROP VDIR XITD

320 SKYKNIGHT: G-AZCI BKRD

335: G-FITZ

336 SKYMASTER: G-ASLL TAH PIXS

337 SUPER SKYMASTER: G-ATCU TID TSM XFG XHA ZKO ZLO ZRW BARD BBL CBZ EDL FGH FJR MJR NNG OWD TVV HIVA NYTE RGEN ORO

340: G-BISJ VES FEBE LAST IZA OPLB PUFN DMH REEN SAMM VAUN

401/402 (including BUSINESSLINER & UTILINER variants): G-AVKN WWW ZFR ZRD BXJA DACC OBN EYES NOSE ROAR

404 TITAN (including AMBASSADOR & COURIER variants): G-BWLF EXEX ILGW KIWI MIND TASK

406 CARAVAN II: G-BVJT DFLT LEAF MAFA AFB SFPA FPB URF TWIG

414/CHANCELLOR variants: G-CRML DYNE SMJJ

421/GOLDEN EAGLE variants: G-BAGO BUJ DCS DYF DZU FTT HKJ KNA LST MLZ TDK CSNA JEA EAGL FTAX WRP GILT HASI JACK DTI KWLI MUVG OOJB RCL SAL SCH PEAT RLMC SAIR HOE TAMY REC UVIP VVIP

425 CORSAIR/CONQUEST I variants: G-BNDY

441 CONQUEST II: G-FCAL PLC RAX RAZ OFHJ

500/501 CITATION 1 variants: G-CITI DJAE LOFT OEJA RHE RJB SCA TJHI ZAPI

525 CITATION JET: G-BVCM OCSB ICE RSCJ

550/551 CITATION II variants: G-BFRM JIR WOM ESTA FJET LVU JCFR ETA ETJ OCDB SPUR THCL

560 CITATION V: G-CZAR

650 CITATION III: G-HNRY

CFM
SHADOW (including STREAK SHADOW): G-BONP ROI RSO RWP RZZ SMN SOR SPL SRX SSV TDD TEL TGT TKP TZZ UGM UIL ULJ UOB UTB UVX UWR UXC VDT VFR VLF VOR VPY VTD WAI WCA WHJ WOZ WPS XFK XVD XWR XXZ XZV XZY YAZ YCI YFI
CAIN DMWW FAME GORE HLCF LYNK MEOW GDB GGT GPH GTW GUY JVF MWT NCM NER NIS NSV NTK NTP NVJ NVK NWK NWY NXX NZJ NZP NZR NZZ TBE TCA TCT TDU TDX TFU TFZ TGN TGV TGW THS THT THV TKR TMX TMY TMZ TSG TTH TWH TWK TWL TWM TWN TWP TXR VAC VAM VAN VBB VCC VCW VEI VEN VFH VHD VIG VLJ VLP VOH VPK VRE VRO VRP VRR VRT VVT VYZ WAE WDB WDN WEN WEZ WFB WIZ WJF WJZ WLD WMU WON WOW WPN WPP WRL WRY WSZ WTJ WTN WTP WUA WVG WVH WYD YAA YBC YBL YCM YDE YEP YGO YIF YIP YKE YLV YNA YNX YOH YON YOS YPL YPT YSM YTH YTY YUS YWF YWM YXY YZP ZBE ZBN ZBS ZCT ZGS ZKH ZRS ZLO ZLP ZMI ZNH ZOM ODVB LGA PIT RAF TCH PBEL RINT OTS SHIM NEV TRK TEHL TOY WESX HOG YAT

CGS HAWK (including ARROWFLIGHT): G-MWYS YTP ZGU

CH1 ATI: G-BXZN

CHAMPION (AERONCA) (including BELLANCA)
7AC/7DC CHAMPION: G-AJON KTO KTR OEH THK VDT WVN BGWV PFM PGK RAR RCV RER RFI RWA RXG TGM TNO TRH UYE VCS CHMP HAMP JTYE LEVI OTOE TECC

7BCM (L-16): G-BFAF TIMP

7EC TRAVELER: G-ARAP

7FC TRI-TRAVELER: G-APYT PYU RAS

CITABRIA/DECATHLON/SCOUT (including BELLANCA production): G-AYXU BAYZ BEN BXY CSM DBH FHP GGA GGB GGC GGD ITA IZW KBP OID OIN OLG OTO PMM RJW SLW TXX UGE VLT EXPL HUNI

CHANCE-VOUGHT - see VOUGHT

CHARGUS T.225/T.250 (Trike): G-MBEU BJG MRY

CHASLE YC-12 TOURBILLON: G-AYBV

CHICHESTER-MILES LEOPARD: G-BRNM

CHILTON DW.1/1A/1B/2: G-AESZ FGH FGI FSV FSW BWGJ DWIA WIB

CHRISLEA:
 LC.1 AIRGUARD: G-AFIN

 CH.3 SUPER ACE: G-AKUW KVF KVR

CHRISTEN
 EAGLE: G-BPZI EEGL GAL GEL GLE GUL LKA OEGL

 A-1 HUSKY: G-BUVR

CHRIS TENA MINI COUPE: G-BPDJ

CIERVA
 C.8L: G-EBYY

 C.24: G-ABLM

 C.30A AUTOGIRO (AVRO 671): G-ACUU CWM CWP

CIVILIAN CAC.1 COUPE: G-ABNT

CLUTTON-TABENOR FRED: G-BBBW DBF DSA GAH GFF GHZ ISG ITK KAF KDP KEY KVF KZT LNO MAX MMF MOO MSL NZR OLS PAV SSJ TCO VCO
 WAP FRED MANX OLVR PFAF FAL RONW USTY

COLT - see COLTING
 Airship (Gas):
 GA-42: G-MATS ZEPI ZEPY

 Airship (Hot Air) variants:
 AS-42: G-WZZZ
 AS-56: G-BNKF TXH NOVO
 AS-80: G-BORF PCF PKN ROL TSW NDRW OVAX
 AS-105: G-BNAO TFD UKV WKE WMV XEY XNV XYF RBOS
 AS-120: G-BXKU

 Balloon (Gas):
 AA-1050: G-BWVM

 Balloon (Hot Air) variants:

 12A/14A CLOUDHOPPER: G-BHKN HKR HOJ HPN IDV VKX

 17A CLOUDHOPPER: G-BIYT JWV KBO KWE KXM LHI ONV OSG PXH RBU HELP ROBY

 21A CLOUDHOPPER: G-BKIV LXG MKI NFM NPI NZJ OLN OLP OLR SAK SIG TNN TXM UEU WBJ SOOS

 25A SKY CHARIOT: G-BSOF VAO OKBT

 31A AIR CHAIR: G-BHIG LOB PGJ RKP ROJ SDV SMM VTL XXU DHLZ OWN HOUS IMAN LBCS MUTE

 42A/R: G-BJZR VHP SEAT

 56A/B/C/D: G-BGIP HEX HGX HRY ICM IFP ISX IXW JXP JYF KSD LCH LLW LOT MNX MYA PDE RVV TZY UGO VCN VOZ VUC VYL CFBI ILEE
 MERC POSH TTWO WIMP

 69A: G-BLEB LUY OSF OVW PAH SHC SHD TMO VDD COLR FZZY JBJB OABC BUD BUY DIY SNAX TCAN WEY

 77A/C: G-BGOD IGT KOW LSK LTA MYN NGP OCF OGT OHD ORA ORE ORT PEZ PFB PJK RLT RVF RVU SCI SUB SUK SZL TDS TTS
 TVH TXB TZR TZS UJH UKS ULF URG UVB UVE UVS UVT UYO UZF VAX XFN XIE YFX
 CURE DING RAW URX FLAG GGOW OBT HOME OTI OTZ RZN IMAG JONO LOWA SHI MAUK KAK OAWS BJH CAR DAD LPG NCL RON SST READ FIL
 SGAS IXX TRUX UPPP ZLE WHAT HIM OOL RIT

 90A: G-BLWE MLU OBU PUW RFF RFH RHG RRU SIU TCS TMH TPV VEI XUW EXPR FOWL HWKR IRLY JNNB OBBC LDV MMM PEGG
 HSI SAUF END TOFT

 105A: G-BLHK LMZ MBS NAG PZS RUH SBK SCC SHS SNU TAV THX URL USV WMA WRM XOV XOW DYNG HSHS OFLI PLUG RAIL TIKI USGB

 120A: G-BOJO XAI XCO XLD YDJ OBIB CPS VYGR

 180A: G-BOGR ONK SUU CUCU PICT

 210A: G-BTYZ UGN ULN UXA VSR ZEBR

 240A: G-BNAP VCZ VVT IGLA LCIO

 260A: G-HUGO

 300A: G-RAPE

 315A: G-KAUR VVBF

 2500A: G-USUK

SPECIAL SHAPES:

AGFA FILM CASSETTE	- G-OHDC		HOP	- G-MALT
APPLE	- G-BRZV		HOT DOG	- G-BVKG
ARIEL BOTTLE	- G-BNHN		HUT	- G-SMTC
BEER GLASS	- G-BNHL PUBS		ICE CREAM CONE	- G-BWBE WBF OJHB
BIBENDUM	- G-GRIP PNEU TRED		J & B WHISKEY BOTTLE	- G-JANB
BLACK KNIGHT	- G-BNMI		JUMBO JET	- G-BRDP OVAA UMBO VJIM
BOTTLE	- G-BOTL VHU OAPB		KINDERMOND	- G-BMUL
BUDWEISER CAN	- G-BUET VIO		MAXWELL HOUSE COFFEE JARS	- G-BVBJ VBK
CAN	- G-BXPR		MICKEY MOUSE	- G-BTRB
CHEESE	- G-BRZU		OLD PARR WHISKY BOTTLE	- G-PARR
CLOWN	- G-GWIZ		PANASONIC BATTERY	- G-PSON
COMPAC COMPUTERISED HEAD	- G-HEAD		PIG	- G-BUZS
DRACHENFISCH	- G-BMUJ		PIGGY BANK	- G-BVJS WBV XVW
EGG	- G-BWWL		SANTA CLAUS	- G-HOHO
FINANCIAL TIMES	- G-ETFT FTFT		SATZENBRAU BOTTLE	- G-BIRE
FIRE EXTINGUISHER	- G-CHUB		SHUTTLECOCK	- G-OOUT
FLAME	- G-BLKU		SKOL LAGER CAN	- G-BTUN
FLYING MITT	- G-WCAT		SNOWFLAKE	- G-BNBP
FLYING YACHT	- G-AXXJ		SPARKASSE BOX	- G-BXKH
GAS FLAME	- G-BGOO		STORK	- G-BRGP
GOLF BALL	- G-BJUY		UFO	- G-BMUK
GORDON'S GIN BOTTLE	- G-BUYG		WORLD	- G-DHLI
HAND	- G-BUDM			

COLTING Ax7-77: G-BLUE

COLOMBAN MC.12/15 CRI-CRI variants (including ZENAIR): G-BOUT WFO CRIC OCRI SHOG

COMMANDER - see ROCKWELL

COMMONWEALTH - see NORTH AMERICAN

COMPER CLA.7 SWIFT: G-ABTC BUS CTF LCGL

CONSOLIDATED-VULTEE - see STINSON

CONVAIR L-13A: G-BGHE

COOK ARIES P: G-MYXI

CORBEN
 BABY ACE: G-BTSB UAA

 JUNIOR ACE: G-BSDI

CORBY CJ-1 STARLET: G-BVVZ ILSE

COSMOS TRIKE: G-MVCK

COUGAR (Wing): G-MMUJ

CRANFIELD A.1 CHASE: G-COAI

CRAWFORD DHCA.1: G-DJIM

CREMER: G-BIWH JGL JLX JLY JRP JRR JRV JVB

CROSBY - see ANDREASSON

CUB PROSPECTOR - see PIPER

CULVER LCA CADET: G-CDET

CURRIE WOT (including TURNER TSW variant): G-APNT RZW SBA VEY YMP YNA BANV DFB EBO FAH FWD GES KCN LPB XMX CWBM WOT
 MINI PFAP SWOT

CURTISS
 ROBIN C.2: G-BTYY HFBM

 P-40 KITTYHAWK/TOMAHAWK variants: G-KITT TOMA

CURTISS-WRIGHT TRAVEL AIR 12Q: G-AAOK

CUTLASS - see SKYHOOK

CVJETKOVIC CA-65 SKYFLY: G-BWBG

CYCLONE - see AERIAL ARTS/CHARGUS/SOLAR WINGS
 70 (Trike): G-MMYL NMY

 AX3: G-BUTC VJG VRY MGRW YFI YFV YFW YFY YFZ YGD YHG YHH YHJ YHM YHR YIJ YIU YKA YKF YKT YME YMF YMW YMZ YOY YPM YPR
 YRO YRU YRV YSO YTM YUI YVN YXH YYL YZC YZF YZG ZDO ZDS ZELE

AX2000: G-JONY MGUN YER ZER ZFA ZFX ZGA ZGB ZGC ZGM ZGP ZHR ZIV ZJF ZJL ZJR ZKC ZLS ZLU ZMX ZOE OAJB ROMW

CYCLONE (Wing): G-MBOK

TS.440 (Wing): G-MBDU

TITAN 38 (Trike): G-MBDU BEV YZH

VORTEX (Wing): G-MJWH

CZL AERO 45/145 variants: G-APRR TBH YLZ

DALOTEL DM-165 VIKING: G-BILA

DART KITTEN: G-AEXT

DASSAULT

FALCON 20/200: G-BGOP FFRA RAD RAE RAF RAH RAI RAJ RAK RAL RAM RAO RAP RAR RAS RAT RAU RAW RBA

FALCON 900: G-EVES GSEB MLTI OPWH

FALCON 2000: G-GEDI JCBI

DAVIS DA-2: G-BPFL

de HAVILLAND - see HAWKER SIDDELEY
(AIRCO) DH.2: G-BFVH

(AIRCO) DH.6: G-EAML

(AIRCO) DH.9: G-EAQM

DH.51: G-EBIR

DH.53 HUMMING BIRD: G-EBHX EBQP

DH.60 MOTH (including DH.60G/60M/60X and MORANE & MOTH CORPN variants): G-EBLV EBWD EBZN AAAH ACD ADR AEG AHI AHY AMX AMY ANF ANL ANO ANV AOR AWO BAG BDX BEV BSD BYA TBL

DH.60GIII MOTH MAJOR: G-ABZB CXB DHD BVNG

DH.71 TIGER MOTH: G-ECDX

DH.80A PUSS MOTH: G-AAZP BLS EOA

DH.82A TIGER MOTH: (G-ABUL) CDA CDC CDI CDJ CMD DGT DGV DIA DJJ DNZ DPC DWJ DWO DXT FGZ FVE FWI GEG GHY GNJ GPK GYU GZZ HAN HIZ HLT HMN HOO HUF HUV HVU HVV IDS IRI IRK IVW IXJ JHS JHU JOA JTW JVE KUE KXS LBD LIW LJL LNA LND LRI LTW LUC LVP LWS LWW MBB MCK MCM MHF MIU MNN MTF MTK MTV MVS NCS NCX NDE NDM NDP NEH NEJ NEL NEM NEN NEW NEZ NFC NFI NFL NFM NFP NFV NFW NHK NIX NJA NJD NJK NKK NKT NKV NKZ NLD NLH NLS NLX NMO NMV NMY NNB NNE NNG NNI NNK NNN NOD NOH NOM NON NOO NOR NPC NPE NPK NRF NRM NRN NRX NSM NTE NZU NZZ OAA OBH OBO OBX ODT OEI OEL OES OET OGI OGR OHY OIL OIM OIS OJJ OJK OUR OZH PAL PAM PAO PAP PBI PCC PFU PGL PIH PJO PLU PMX PPN RAZ REH RTL SKP SPV VPJ XAN XBW XBZ XXV YDI YIT ZDY ZGZ ZZZ BAFG BRB EWN FHH HLT HUM JAP JZF MPY NDW PAJ PHR RHW STJ TOG UJY WIK WMK WMS WVT XMN DHTM EMSY RDS ISIS MOTH OOSY TIGA

DH.82B QUEEN BEE: G-BLUZ

DH.83/C FOX MOTH: G-ACCB CEJ OJH

DH.84 DRAGON: G-ACET CIT

DH.85 LEOPARD MOTH: G-ACLL CMA CMN COJ CUS IYS PKH

DH.87B HORNET MOTH: G-ADKC DKK DKL DKM DLY DMT DND DNE DOT DRH DSK DUR ELO ESE HBL HBM

DH.88 COMET: G-ACSP CSS

DH.89A DRAGON RAPIDE: G-ACYR CZE DAH EML GJG GSH GTM HAG HED HGD IDL IUL IYR JBJ KDW KIF KOE LAX LXT MAI

DH.90 DRAGONFLY: G-AEDT AEDU

DH.94 MOTH MINOR: G-AFNG FNI FOB FOJ FPN FPR

DH.98 MOSQUITO: G-ASKC WJV MOSI

DH.100 VAMPIRE (including FFW production): G-DHXX FBIX MKVI SWIS

DH.104 DOVE/DEVON variants: G-AHRI LCU LFT LFU MXT NAP NDX NOV NUW NVU PSO RBE RBH RDE REA RHW RHX RJB VVF BLRN VXR DEVN HDV VON HBBC KOOL NAVY OEWA PLC RNAS SDEV

DH.106 COMET: G-ALYW LYX OJT PAS PDB PMB PYD BDIW DIX

DH.110 SEA VIXEN: G-CVIX VIXN

DH.112 VENOM (including FFW production): G-BLID LIE LKA LSD DHSS DHTT HUU GONE VENI ICI NOM

DH.114 HERON: G-ANUO NXB ORG OTI HRON

DH.115 VAMPIRE TRAINER: G-DHAV HVV HWW HYY HZZ USK HELV OBLN VMPR TII

DH.121 TRIDENT - see HAWKER SIDDELEY

DH.125 - see HAWKER SIDDELEY

de HAVILLAND (AUSTRALIA) DHA.3 DROVER: G-APXX

de HAVILLAND (CANADA)
DHC.1 CHIPMUNK: G-AKDN LWB MUF NWB OFE OJZ ORW OSF OSK OSO OSU OSY OTD OTF OTR OTY OUO OUP OZP PLO PPA PPM PYG RGG RMB
RMC RMD RMF RMG RWB THD TVF BAPB ARS AVH BMN BMO BMR BMT BMV BMW BMX BMZ BNA BNC BND BRV BSS CAH CCX CEY CGC CHL CHV
CIH CIW CKN COI COO COU COY CPU CRX CSA CSB CSL CXN CYJ CYM CZH DBP DCC DDD DET DEU DRJ FAW FAX FDC HRD NZC PAL TWF VBT
VTX VWP VZZ WHI WJY WJZ WMX WNK WNT WOX WTG WTO WUN WUT WUV WVY WVZ XCR XCP XCT XCV XDA XDG XDH XDI XDM XDP XEC XGL XGM
XGO XGP XGX XHA XHF XIA XIM XNN YHL CHPY PMK DHCC HCI HAPY IDDY JAKE MAJR OACP PVET TRIC ULAS

DHC.2 BEAVER: G-BUCJ UVF VER

DHC.6 TWIN OTTER: G-BIHO VVK

DHC.7 DASH SEVEN: G-BRYA RYD

DHC.8 DASH EIGHT: G-BRYH RYI RYJ RYK RYM RYO RYP RYR RYS RYT RYU RYV RYW RYY RYX RYZ XPZ NVSA VSB VSC

DEMON - see HIWAY

DENNEY KITFOX: G-BNYX ONY PII PKK RCT SAZ SCG SCH SCM SDD SES SFX SFY SGG SHK SIF SIK SLJ SMO SRT SSF SUZ SVK TAT TBG
TBN TDC TDN TFA TIF TIP TIR TKD TMT TMX TNR TOL TSV TTY TVC TWB UDR UIC UIP UKF UKP ULZ UNM UOL UPW UWS UYK UZA VAH VCT
VEY VGO WAR WHV WSJ WSN WWZ WYI XCW XWH CJUD RES TOY DJNH ELIZ YAS FOXC OXD OXE OXG OXI OXS OXX OXZ HOBO UTT KAWA FOX
ITF ITY LACR EED ESJ EZJ OST OFOX PDS PHYL PPP RAYA WSS SSF WSS TFOX

DEPERDUSSIN MONOPLANE: G-AANH

DESIGNABILITY DUET - see JORDAN

DESOUTTER DESOUTTER 1: G-AAPZ

DIAMOND - see HOAC

DORNIER - see BUCKER
DO.27: G-BMFG NMK

DO.28/SKYSERVANT: G-ASUR BWCN WCO XTK

228: G-BMMR UXT MAFE AFI OMAF

328: G-BWIR WWT

DORRINGTON SKYCYCLE D2: G-BUOP

DOUGLAS
AD-4 SKYRAIDER: G-RAID

DC-3/C-47 DAKOTA: G-ALWC MCA MHJ MPO MPP MPY MPZ MRA MSN MSV MYJ NAF PML BGCG HUB VOL DAKK AKS

DC-6: G-APSA SIXC

DC-9/10 - see MCDONNELL DOUGLAS

DRAGON 77: G-BKRZ

DRAGON: G-MJSL JUZ JVY MAC MAE MAI MML MNH MPR NJF

DRAGONFLY MPA: G-BDFU

DRAGONFLY 250: G-MJLK

DRAYTON B-56: G-BITS

DRUINE
D.31 TURBULENT (including ROLLASON production): G-AJCP PIZ PNZ POL PTZ PUY PVN PVZ PWP RBZ REZ RGZ RIM RJZ RLZ RMZ RNZ
RRU RRZ SDB SFX SHT SMM SPU SSY STA TBS VPC WBM WDO WFR WMR WWT BGBF GMA KXR LTC RIZ UKH VLU WID OJJF

D.5 TURBI: G-AOTK PBO PFA

D.62 CONDOR (including ROLLASON production): G-ARHZ RVZ SEU SRB SRC TAU TAV TOH TUG TVW VAW VEX VJH VKM VMB VOH VXW WAT
WEI WFN WFO WFP WSN WSP WSS WST XGS XGU XGV XGZ YFC YFD YFE YFF YFG YZS BADM UOF OPJH YNOT

DYN'AERO MCR-01: G-BYEZ POOP GAC

EAA
 ACROSPORT: G-BJHK KCV LCI PGH PKI SHY TAK TWI VVL OJDA VCIO

 BIPLANE: G-ATEP VZW YFY BBMH PUA RUU PFAA FAY

EAGLE - see AMERICAN AEROLIGHTS

EAVES (EUROPEAN): G-BJDK JFB JFC JGF JGG JIC JJE JMI JRB JRC JRD JTW FYBP YDC YDN YEL YFA YFG YFH YFI

ECLIPSE SUPER EAGLE: G-BGWZ

EDGAR PERCIVAL EP.9 PROSPECTOR (including LANCASHIRE AIRCRAFT production): G-APWZ PXW RDG

EDGLEY OPTICA (including BROOKLANDS/FLS/OPTICA production): G-BMPF MPL OPM OPN OPO OPR TRAK

EDWARDS HELICOPTER: G-ASDF

EH INDUSTRIES EH-101: G-EHIL

EIPPER QUICKSILVER: G-MBBM BCK BFO BYM JAM JBI JBT JCL JDU JDW JFH JHU JHX JIR JJB JJK JKH JNV JPV JUJ JVP JVT JVU JZL
 MBU MCG MEG MIL MMG MNB MNC MND MSE MWC MYR MNCO MTDO WDZ YBH

EIRI PIK-20E: G-BGZL HFR HIJ HNP OCAT FJC PIK POPE SOAR

EKW C-3605: G-DORN

ELECTRAFLYER - see AMERICAN AEROLIGHTS

ELISPORT CH-7 ANGEL: G-HALO

ELMWOOD CA-05 CHRISTAVIA: G-MRED

EMBRAER
 EMB-110 BANDEIRANTE: G-BGYT FLTY JBAC LOOT OBPL CSI FLT TABS

 EMB-145: G-EMBA MBB MBC MBD MBE MBF MBG MBH

ENGLISH ELECTRIC
 WREN: G-EBNV

 CANBERRA: G-BURM VIC VXC XOD

 LIGHTNING: G-BTSY

ENSIGN CROSSLEY RACER: G-BKRU

ENSTROM
 F-28: G-BAAU AWI BIH BIN BPM BPN BPO BXO BZS DKD HAX ONG POZ PPL RZG SHX SHZ URI WOV XLV XLW XLX XXB
 DICE MHCA HCE HCJ OABO SCOX ERA NAZ WSEC

 280C SHARK/280FX: G-BEYA GWS IBJ PXE RPO SDZ SIE SLV WSK XEE XFD XRD
 CKCK OLL ECHO GKAT HDIX YST IDUP MEYO HCB HCD HCF HCG HCH HCI HCK HCL OITV PDM THE PALS BYY REFI SHAA HNN HSS HUU
 OPP TOYS VETS WRFM SKY

 480: G-BWMD GUAY HADA IGHH LIVA OGHH SKP ZAR PBTT PAH WOOF

ERCOUPE 415 (including ALON/FORNEY production variants): G-ARHB RHC RHF ROO SNF VIL VTT BKIN COUP EGHB RCO HARY ONHH

EUROCOPTER - see AEROSPATIALE/SUD AVN/MBB
 EC.120: G-BXYD

 EC.135: G-AXXV CCAU CHSU HDDP NESV WPS

EUROPA AVIATION EUROPA: G-BVGF VIZ VJN VKF VLH VLV VOS VOW VRA VUV VVH VVP VWM WCV WDP WDX WEG WFH WFX WGH WIJ WIV WJH
 WKG WNL WON WRO WUP WVS GWB WYD WRA WZT XCH XDY XEF XFG XGG XHY XII XIJ XLK XLZ XNC XOB XTD XUM YFG YIK YPM
 CHAV HEB HET HUG ROY UTY DAMY AYI AYS DXS LCB ONZ RMM EENI ESA IKY MIN MSI OFS UXS FELL LOR LOX LYT GBXS HOFC IBBS NAV
 VET JOST ULZ KITS WIP LABS ACE AMM MFHI IME KPU UZO NDOL EAT IGL OBEV DJG DTI DTW EZY GAN JHL KEV MIK PJK SMT URO WWW
 PATF ATS ATZ TAG TYE UDS RATZ BBB ICS MAC OBD ONA OOV OPA SAMY HSH MDH SGS YCO TERN VPSJ WUFF WWG XSDJ YURO ZORO TED

EUROWING GOLDWING: G-MBDG BFZ BJA BON BPM BPX BZH JAJ JAY JDP JEG JOE JPO JRL JRO JRS JRV JSY JUT JUU JUY JWB JWS MBN
 MLE MTZ MWL NNS NZU

EVANS
 VP-1: G-AYUJ YXW BAAD AJC APP BPK BXZ CTT DAH DAR DTB DTL DUL EHJ EIS EKM FAS FHX FJJ GEE GFK GLF HKA HMT HYV ICT IDD
 IFO INO KFI LCW LKK LWT MJM VAM VEL VJU VPI VUT WFJ PFAG FAH FAO FAW ROSE TEDY EI-AYY BBD BLU BRU

 VP-2: G-BCVE EFV EHX EVP EYN FFB FYL GFC GPM HUO HXL HZF JVC JZB MSC PBB TAZ THJ TSC UGI UKZ VPM XOC RASC VPII

EVERETT GYROPLANE - see CAMPBELL: G-BIPI KPK MZN MZP MZS OUU OUX SJW SRL TMV TVB UAI UZC WCK LAXY MICY OFRB GOS ULPS

EXPERIENCE TRIKE: G-MYLU

EXPERIMENTAL AVN BERKUT: G-REDX

EXTRA
 EA.230/260: G-EXTR XTRA

 EA.300: G-EXEA HIII IITI IZI MIII SIII XTRS

FAIRCHILD - see **SWEARINGEN**
 24/ARGUS: G-AIZE JOZ JPI JSN BCBH CBL FANC LEPF RGUS

FAIREY
 FLYCATCHER: G-BEYB

 FIREFLY: G-ASTL

 FULMAR: G-AIBE

 GANNET: G-BMYP

 SWORDFISH: G-AJVH BMGC

 ULTRA-LIGHT HELICOPTER: G-AOUJ PJJ

FAIRTRAVEL - see **PIEL**

FALCONAR F-9/F-11/F-12: G-AWHY XDY YEG BGHT ODEL TIMS WBTS

FARNELL TRIKE: G-MJKO

FEWSDALE TIGERCRAFT GYROPLANE: G-ATLH

FFA AS.202 BRAVO: G-BNTE NTF NTH NTI NTJ NTK NTL NTM NTN NTO

FFW - see **de Havilland**

FIAT G.46: G-BBII

FIESELER **STORCH** MS.500 - see **MORANE-SAULNIER** G-FIST

FISHER FP202U KOALA/SUPER KOALA: G-BTBF UVL MMTY

FLAGLOR SKY SCOOTER: G-BDWE

FLEET 80 CANUCK: G-FLCA

FLEXIFORM **RAPIER** 1+1 - see **MAINAIR**
 HILANDER (Wing): G-MJAN

 SEALANDER (Wing): G-MBBY BDJ BGA BIA BLO JFK MFL MGU

 STRIKER (Wing) (including DUAL STRIKER): G-MBDE BHK BPZ BWF BZO JER JFB JFI JIA JIC JIF JJO JMN JMX JTP JUM JVN JWI JWN JXX JYP JZO JZU MAL MAN MAX MBS MCJ MCZ MDK MDN MDT MEJ MFD MFE MFG MFH MFK MFV MGH MGI MHY MJG MKM MMR MMW MNT MPL MPT MRW MWG MWN MWS MYV NZY TFK

 FLS-EDGLEY SPRINT (including **TRAGO MILLS SAH-1** production): G-BVNU XWU XWV FLSI SAHI SCLX

FOCKE WULF

 FW.190: G-FOKW

FOCKE WULF PIAGGIO - see **PIAGGIO**

FOKKER
 D.VII: G-BFPL

 DR.1: G-ATJM BVGZ

 E.III: G-AVJO

 S.11 INSTRUCTOR: G-BEPV IYU

 F-27 FRIENDSHIP (including **FAIRCHILD-HILLER** production): G-BAUR CDN CDO HMW HMY MXD NCY NIZ VOB VRN XZW YBT CEXA EXB EXD EXE EXF HNL JEAD EAE EAF EAG EAH EAI EAP

 F.50 (F.27-50): G-BWZL WZM UKTA KTB KTC KTD KTE KTF KTG KTH KTI

 F.70 (F28-70): G-BVTE VTF VTG

 F.100 (F.28-100): G-BVJA VJB VJC VJD XNF XRE XWE XWF YDP UKFA KFB KFC KFD KFE KFF KFG KFH KFI KFJ KFK KFL KFM KFN KFO KFP KFR

FOLLAND GNAT: G-BVPP FRCE GNAT MOUR NAAT ATY RORI TIMM

FORNEY - see **ERCOUPE**

FOSTER-WIKNER GM.1 WICKO: G-AFJB

FOUGA CM-170 MAGISTER: G-FUGA

FOURNER
 RF3: G-ATBP YJD BCWK FZA HLU IIA IPN LXH NHT

 RF4D: G-AVHY VKD VLW VNX VNZ VWY WBJ WEK WEL WEM WGN WLZ YHY BHJN IIF UPJ XLN IVEL

 RF5/RF5B SPERBER: G-AYME ZJC ZPF ZRK ZRM BACE EVO JXK LAA PWK KCIG RFSB SSWV

 RF6B - see SLINGSBY T-67: G-BKIF LWH OLC GANJ

 RF7: G-LTRF

 RF10 - see AEROMOT AMT-200

 FRED - see CLUTTON

 FUJI FA.200: G-BBGI BNV BRC BZN BZO CFF CKS CKT CNZ DFR DFS EUK FGO FUJI HAMI KARI ARY MCOX

 GADFLY HDW-1: G-AVKE

 GAERTNER Ax4 SKYRANGER: G-BSGB

 GARDAN
 GY-20 MINICAB (including CAB & BARRITAULT JB.01 production): G-ATPV VRW WEP WUB WWM ZJE BANC BFL CER CNC CPD DGB GKO GMJ GMR RGW TATT VERA

 GY-80 HORIZON: G-ASJY SZS TGY TJT VMA VRS WAC ZAW ZRX ZYA BCVW FAA JAV KNI YBL GYBO

 GARDNER T-M SCOUT: G-MJTD TKM

 GARLAND-BIANCHI - see PIEL

 GATES LEARJET: G-GJET HUGG JETG ETN LEAR JET MURI OCFR RAFF ZENO

 GAZEBO AX6-65: G-BCGP

 GAZELLE - see SOUTHERN MICROLIGHT

 GEMINI - see MAINAIR

 GENERAL ACFTGAL.42 CYGNET: G-AGBN

 GLASER-DIRKS
 DG-400: G-BLJD LRM NCN NXL PIN PXB RTW SOM DGDG IRK HAJJ INCA LEES OAPW RTM

 DG-500M: G-BRRG SOOM

 DG-800: G-BVJK XSH XUI YEC DGIV ORIG

 GLOBE GC-1B SWIFT: G-AHUN RNN

 GLOSTER
 GLADIATOR: G-AMRK GLAD

 METEOR (including ARMSTRONG-WHITWORTH production): G-ARCX BPOA WMF JETM LOSM METE

 GOLDMARQUE GYR (Wing): G-MJKO

 GOULD Mk.1: G-OULD

 GOULD-TAYLORCRAFT - see TAYLORCRAFT

 GRANGER ARCHEOPTERYX : G-ABXL

 GRASSHOPPER GRASSHOPPER (including SERVOTEC): G-ARVN WRP XFM ZAU

 GREAT LAKES 2T-1A SPORT TRAINER - see OLDFIELD: G-BIIZ UPV

 GREEN S-25: G-BSON

 GREGA GN-1 - see PIETENPOL

 GREGORY FREE SPIRIT: G-FSII

 GRIFFITHS GH.4: G-ATGZ

 GROB
 G-109: G-BIXZ JVK JZX LMG LUV MCG MFY MGR MLK MLL MMP RCG XSP XXG CHAR DKDP IPSI KEMC LULU NDGC SAGA AMG TACK UILD WAVE

 G-115/HERON: G-BOPT OPU PKF VHC VHD VHE VHF VHG YDB YFD MERF RAFA AFB TAYI WIZB

GRUMMAN:
 F-6F HELLCAT: G-BTCC

 F-7F TIGERCAT: G-RUMT

 F-8F BEARCAT: G-RUMM

 FM-2 WILDCAT: G-RUMW

 TBM-3 AVENGER: G-BTDP

 G.44 WIDGEON: G-DUCK

 G-159 GULFSTREAM I: G-BNCE

 G-1159 GULFSTREAM II/III/IV/V: G-DNVT HARF

GRUMMAN-AMERICAN (including AMERICAN AVN/GULFSTREAM-AMERICAN production)
 AA-1 (YANKEE/TRAINER/LYNX variants): G-AYFX YHA YLP ZKS BBFC BWZ CIL CLW DLS DNW DNX ERY EXN FOJ TLP RUMN SEXY

 AA-5/AG-5 (TRAVELER/CHEETAH/TIGER variants): G-AZMJ ZVG BAFA AJN AJO AOU ASG ASH AVR AVS BBI BCZ BDL BDM BLS BRZ BSA
 BUE BUF CCJ CCK CEE CEF CEO CEP CIJ CIK CLI CLJ CPN CRR DCL DFY DLO DLR EBE EZC EZF EZG EZH EZI FIJ FIN FLW FLX FPB FTF
 FTG FVS FXW FXX FZO GCM GFG GFI GPH GPK GVV GVW GVY HKV HLX HZK HZO IAY IBT IPA IPV IVV IWW JAJ JDO KPS LFW LSF MYI NVB
 OXU OZO OZZ PIZ STR TII TUZ XCY XCZ XHH XOO XOX XTT YDX
 CCAT COL HTA DAVO INA OEA ONI ERRY STE GAJB IRY OCC IDEA FLI RIS JAZZ ENN UDY WDG KINE LSFI MALC ELD ILY OGI STC NASH
 ODE ODY ONI OABR BMW CAM DAM ECH MOG PPL PWK STC STU PAWS ENN ING ORK ROP URR RATE EEK OWL UBB TGER YGA WINK MTM ZARI
 ERO

 GA-7 COUGAR: G-BGNV GON GSY LHR OGS OOE OXR CYMA EENY FLII GABD ENN OTC HIRE OOGA OGI OGO REAT SHIV TANI

GRYPHON SAILWINGS GRYPHON - see WASP/WILLGRESS: G-MJGO MYC

GS TRIKE: G-MJHR

GUIDO: G-BJSP

GULFSTREAM-AMERICAN - see GRUMMAN-AMERICAN

GYROFLIGHT - see BROOKLAND

HADLAND WILLOW: G-MMMH

HALLAM FLECHE: G-FLCT

HANDLEY PAGE
 O/400 Rep: G-BKMG

 HP.39 GUGNUNC: G-AACN

 HP.81 HERMES: G-ALDG

 HP.137 JETSTREAM - see BAe

HANDLEY PAGE (READING) HPR.7 DART HERALD: G-APWA PWJ SKK SVO TDS TIG VEZ VPN BAZJ BXJ EYF EYK CEAS EXP GNSY SCTT TVN

HANRIOT HD.1: N75

HAPI CYGNET SF-2A: G-BRZD WFN XCA XHJ CYGI

HARKER DH/WASP: G-MJSZ

HATZ CB-1: G-BRSY XXH HATZ

HAWKER
 AUDAX: G-BVVI

 CYGNET: G-EBJI EBMB CAMM

 DEMON: G-BTVE

 FURY (Biplane): G-BKBB

 FURY/SEA FURY - see W.A.R.: G-AGHB BTTA UCM WOL EEMV

 HART: G-ABMR

 HIND: G-AENP

 HUNTER: G-BNCX UEZ VGH VMB VVC WAF WFR WFS WFT WGK WGL WGM WGN WIU WKB WKC WOU XFI XKF XNZ EGHH FFOX GAII
 HNTR PUX VIP KAXF PSST SIAL TVII VETA

 HURRICANE: G-AMAU BKTH WHA YDL HURI URR URY KAMM ROBT TDTW WTD

 NIMROD: G-BURZ WWK

SEA HAWK - see <u>ARMSTRONG-WHITWORTH</u>

TEMPEST: G-BSHW PEST TEMT HA557/RAF

TOMTIT: G-AFTA

<u>HAWKER SIDDELEY</u>
HS.121 TRIDENT: G-ARPH RPK RPO RPP RPZ VFB VFE VFG VFJ VFK VFM VYE WZI WZJ WZK WZM WZO WZS WZU WZX WZZ

HS.125 (including <u>de HAVILLAND/BAe/RAYTHEON HAWKER</u>): G-ARYB RYC SNU SSM TPD WYE XDM BGYR KBH LSM LTP MIH OCB TAB WSY YHM DBAL EZC JLW ETOM FANN GDEZ HCFR ICFR FTC FTE JETI LORI NCFR OCAA HEA JPB LDD MGD MGE WDB PLGI RCEJ SHEC UFC VLB TACE CAP CDI SAM VIPI WBPR XRMC YUGO

HS.748 - see <u>AVRO</u>

HARRIER: G-VTOL

<u>HEAD</u> Ax8-105: G-UKUK

<u>HEATH</u> PARASOL: G-AFZE

<u>HEINKEL</u> He 111 (CASA 2.111): G-AWHB

<u>HEINTZ</u> ZENITH (including <u>ZENAIR</u> <u>CH.200/250/300</u> variants): G-BIRZ PTO TXZ DUNN GFKY RAYS

<u>HELIO</u> SUPER COURIER: G-BAGT GIX

<u>HELTON</u> LARK 95: G-LARK

<u>HILL</u> HUMMER - see <u>MAXAIR</u>

<u>HILLER</u> UH-12 (360): G-APKY SAZ STP TKG BEDK

<u>HINDUSTAN</u> PUSHPAK: G-AVPO BXTO

<u>HISPANO</u> - see <u>MESSERSCHMITT</u> Bf.109

<u>HIWAY</u>
DEMON (Wing): G-MBAL BDD BEU BFK BFU BIT BPU BTE BUA BVV BXJ BZA JAV JDJ JDR JHM JHV JKF JMA JMD JMT JNK JNT JOU JPE JRP JSO JXE JXY JYX JYY JYY MEI MHD MHP MLH MNW MRH MTD NCA MNME THD WXE YBN

EXCALIBUR (Wing): G-MBAA

SKYTRIKE: G-MBAA BCI BCL BDD BFK BGP BGW BIA BIT BJF BJS BKZ BLM BPU BTE BVS BVV BXF BXJ JAN JAP JAV JCW JDJ JDR JHV JMA JMD JMS JMT JMU JNK JNT JOU JPE JPP JSO JUM JXY JYY MBJ MBS MCV MEF MEI MHK MHL MHP MLH MOO MRH MUR NME YBN

SUPER SCORPION (Wing): G-MBGW BVS JCW MEF MHK MHL

VULCAN (Wing): G-MBIZ JAP MRY

<u>HORNET</u>
Trike: G-MBCX BHJ BJL JDA JIB JWN MHD MNM

INVADER (Trike): G-MMHY MMW

DUAL TRAINER/RAVEN (Combi): G-MNRI NRJ NRK NRL NRM TDA TGX THU TJX TMP TMR TRK TRL TXE TXY VHZ

R/RS (Combi): G-MVUR VUU VYG VYH VYI VYJ VYK VYL VYM VYN VYO VZW WAH WBH WBM WBN WBP WBR WBS WBU WBW WBX WBY WBZ WCA WDE WDF WDI WEU WEV WKE WKF

<u>HOAC</u> DV-20 KATANA (including <u>DIAMOND</u>): G-BWEH WFD WFE WFI WFV WGY WGZ WIO WLP WLS WLT WLV WPY WTA WYM XBW XGH XJV XJW XMZ XOF XPB XPC XPD XPE XTP XTR XTS YFL KATA OBDA RIBS

<u>HOFFMANN</u> H-36 DIMONA/HK-36 SUPER DIMONA: G-BKPA LCV NUX XGI IMOK KOKL LIDA LIDR LYDA OMDG MRG

<u>HORIZON</u> <u>1</u>: G-DOGZ

<u>HOVEY</u>
BETA BIRD: G-BMOX

WD-II/III WHING DING: G-MBAB BTS MNVO

<u>HOWARD</u> SPECIAL T-MINUS: G-BRXS

<u>HOWES</u> Ax6: G-BDWO

<u>HUGHES</u>
269 (Srs 300) (including <u>SCHWEIZER</u> production) : G-AYLX BATT AUK AXE BIV MWA OVX OVY OXT PJB PPW PPY RFP RTT SCD SML SVR UEX WAV WDV WNJ WWJ WZJ XHI XMY XRP XTL XTM XUP GINZ IRO HFLA JHAS JMDI LEMJ MARE OCJK GOB JAE SLO ZAP PKPK LOW LPC REBL HCB IFB OCR SAND HCB HPP TEP WARK XALP

369 (Srs 500) (including <u>McDONNELL DOUGLAS</u> production): G-AYIA ZVM BPLZ RTL TRP CSPJ DADS IZZ RAR ERIS GASC EEE HSOO IDWR JETZ KBOT LIBS INC OGO MRAJ NIPY OMDH SOO TDB ROMA SIVA OOC OOE SCL TEF WEL TRUE VICE

548

HUNTING - see PERCIVAL
P.84 JET PROVOST (including BAC.145/167 STRIKEMASTER variants): G-AOBU OHD YHR BKOU VEG VEZ VSP VTC WBS WCS WDR WEB WGF
WGS WGT WOF WOT WSG WSH WUW WZE WZZ XBH XBI XBJ XDL XFP XFR XFS XFU XFV XFW XFX YED JETP PRO PTV PVA PROV RAFI SARK
TOMG ORE UNNY VIVM

HUNT WING/AVON/EXPERIENCE: G-MGTR GUX MGT NCA WPT YFG YPO YTV YUG YUR YUT YWE YWH YYE YYJ YYT ZCX ZCZ ZDZ ZFE ZFF ZGH
ZLB ZLK

HUNTAIR PATHFINDER: G-MBWG BYK BYL JBZ JDE JDH JFM JJA JOC JTY JUV JWK JXS MBV MCB MDR MWB

HYBRED - see MEDWAY

ICA IS.28B2/M2: G-BKAB KXN MMV MMX MOM ROM TODD

III SKY ARROW: G-BXGT YCY CIAO SKYG KYT UTN

IMCO - see CALLAIR

ISAACS
FURY: G-ASCM YJY BBVO CMT EER IYK KFK KZM MEU PWY TPZ WWN PFAR RODI

SPITFIRE: G-BBJI XOM

INTERAVIA 70TA: G-BUUT

JABIRU: G-BXAO XNU XSI YBM YBZ YCC YCZ YFC YIA YIF YIM CSDJ DMAC OJAB PUS ZZI MGCA PBUS THOT UJAB VJAB

JODEL - see FALCONAR & ROBIN production
D.9 BEBE (including D.92 variant): G-AVPD WFT XKJ XYU ZBL BAGF DEI DNT GFJ URE KDIX

D.11 (including D.112/D.117/D.119 & AERO D.1190S variants): G-ARDO RNY SJZ SXY TIN TIZ TJN TWB VPM WFW WMD WVB WVZ WWI
XAT XCG XCY XFN XHV XTX XWT XXW XZT YBP YBR YCP YEB YGA YHX YKJ YKK YKT YMU YWH YXP ZFF ZHC ZII ZKP ZVL BAAW AKR APR
ARF ATJ AUH AZM BPS CGW CLU DBV DDG DIH DJD DMM EDD EZZ FEH FGK FNG FXR GEF GTX GWO HCE HEL HFF HHX HKT HNL HNX IAH
IDX IEO IOU IPT ITO IVB IVC IWN IYW IZY JOT KAO KIR MIP OOH PFD RCA RVZ VEH VPS VVE BWMB DAVE

D.18: G-BODT PJN RZO SBP SYA TRZ UAG UPR WVC WVV XFC HERS SHRL TREK WIBB

D.120 PARIS-NICE (WASSMER): G-ASPF SXU TLV VLY VYV XNJ YGG YLV YRS ZEF ZGA ZLF BACJ ANU CGM DDF DEH DWX FOP GZY HGJ HNK
HPS HXD HXS HZV ICR IEN JFM JOE JYK KAE KCW KCZ KGB KJS KPX MDS MID MLB MYU OWP YBE DIZO UIDE

D.140 MOUSQUETAIRE: G-ARDZ RLX ROW RRY TKX YFP BJOB SPC WAB DCXL OBAN REES TOAD

150 MASCARET (including SUPER MASCARET variant): G-ASKL SRT VEF ZBI BACL FEB HEG HEZ HVF IDG KSS LAT LXO MEH VSS VST
DISO EDGE FARR IEJH JDLI MASC OABB TIDS

DR.100 series (DR.100/1050/M1/1051/M1 - AMBASSADEUR SICILE/SICILE RECORD/EXCELLENCE variants): G-ARFT RRD RRE RUH RXT
SXS TAG TEV TFD TGE TGP THX TIC TJA TLB TWA VGJ VGZ VHL VJK VOA WEN WUE WVE WWN WWO XLS XSM XUK XUY YEH YEJ YEV YEW
YGD YJA YKD YLC YLF YLL YUT YYO YYT YZK ZAD ZOU ZWF BAEE DMW EAB EYZ FBA GBE GRI HHE HOL HSY HTC HUE IOI KDX LKM LRJ
LUL PLH THH TIW XIO XYJ YCS YFM IOSI JODL WBB WIV SPOG

DR.200: G-AYDZ

DR.220/221 (2+2/DAUPHIN): G-AVOM BANA FHR HRW LCT LLH MKF UTH CPCD GOSS STEV

DR.250: G-ATTM BCGG JBO KPE SZF UVM XCG YEH

DR.253 REGENT: G-AWYL XWV YUB BOSM

DR.300 series (DR.315 PETIT PRINCE/DR.340 MAJOR/DR.360 CHEVALIER & KNIGHT/REMORQUEUR variants): G-AXDK YCO ZIJ ZJN BGVB
ICP LAM LGH LHH OEH OZV VYG VYM XOU DRSV RZF KIMB

JORDAN DUET: G-MBWH JTO

JUNKERS Ju.52/3m (CASA.352L): G-BFHD FHF

JURCA
MJ.2 TEMPETE: G-ASUS YTV

MJ.5 SIROCCO: G-AWKB ZOS BFXM UGC ORFC

K & S SA.102.5 CAVALIER: G-AZHH BCMJ CRK DKJ DLY JAN UNJ WSI

JUNGSTER: G-BLDC OWEN

KENSINGER KF: G-ASSV

KAY GYROPLANE: G-ACVA

KEN BROCK KB-2: G-BSEG UYT UZV VMN VUJ

KLEMM - see BA & BRITISH KLEMM
L.25: G-AAUP AXK

KL.35: G-BVXI WRD

KNIGHT - see PAYNE

KOLB TWINSTAR: G-BUZT KOLB G-MWWM YDP YIK YKB YLN YLP YMI YNY YOG YOO YOR YPC YRA YVA YWP YXS ZGJ ZKB ZZT

KRONFELD - see BAC

LA MOUETTE PROFIL (Wing): G-MVCK

LAFAYETTE HI-NUSKIE: G-MBWI

LAKE LA-4/LA-250 (including BUCCANEER RENEGADE & SKIMMER variants): G-BASO MGY OLL LAKE OSMR

LANCAIR - see NEICO

LANCASHIRE AIRCRAFT - see EDGAR PERCIVAL

LANCASHIRE MICRO-TRIKE: -MJXX JYW JZO MFG MPL

LAVERDA - see AVIAMILANO

LAVOCHKIN
 LA-9: G-BWUD

LAZAIR - see ULTRAFLIGHT

LAZER - see STEPHENS AKRO

LEDERLIN 380L LADYBUG: G-AYMR

LEOPOLDOFFL-7: G-AYKS

LET
 C-11: see YAKOLEV

 L-200A/D MORAVA: G-ASFD BNBZ

 Z-37 CMELAK: G-AVZB KDLN

LETOV LK-2M SLUKA: G-MYRP YRR YUP YVG YVT YXO ZBF ZBK ZDX ZES ZFC ZGF ZLY ZNZ ZOI ZOT ZOX XPBI

LE VIER COSMIC WIND: G-ARUL BAER

LIGHT AERO AVID FLYER/SPEEDWING/AEROBAT: G-BSPW TGL THU TKG TMS TNP TRC UFV UIR UJJ UJV ULC ULY UON USZ UZE UZM VAA
 VBR VBV VFO VHT VIV VLW VSN VYX WCI WLW WRC WZD XNA EFRY LKS FOLD IJAC MPY LAPN ORT MOTT OVID ZEE PILL SPAM

LIGHTNING - see SOUTHDOWN

LILLIPUT TYPE 1: G-HONY

LINDSTRAND
 Airship (Hot Air):
 HS-110 Airship: G-BWLH TRIB

 Balloon (Hot Air):
 LBL-9: G-BVRP

 LBL-14: G-BWBB WEO WER XAJ XEP

 LBL-21/RR-21: G-BVRL YEY OJNB UNRL

 LBL-25 CLOUDHOPPER: G-BVUI XHM OLAW OER

 LBL-31 AIR CHAIR: G-BVOJ WHD XIZ XUH ONCB

 LBL-42: G-BWCG

 LBL-56: G-COSY XWWF

 LBL-60: G-OERR

 LBL-69: G-BVDS VGG VIR WLA LBLI

 LBL-77: G-BUBS UWI UZR VPV VRR WAW WBO WEP WFK WKZ WMH WTU XDR XDX HUNK ICEY CKY MERE PATP

 LBL-90: G-BVAG VWW VXG VZT WBT WRV WTN WWE WZU XLF XXO XZF XZI YEP CLAG FLEW MRKT OLBL SUP ULLS NGE

 LBL-105: G-BUUN UYJ VDO VON VOO VRU WGA WIY WOK WRZ WSB WTB WWY XDZ XHE XHP XJG XSO XUO YFU YIY
 ENRI GULF ICOI ICOZ OAER DDY MXS PMT OICO RDMS XUK SNAK ZOOI

 LBL HS-110: G-HSTH

 LBL-120: G-BVLZ WDM WEA

 LBL-150: G-BVEW XCM

LBL-180: G-BVBM VIX WCL EVNT GVBF KNOB OTUP WIZD

LBL-203: G-BXGK

LBL-210: G-BVLL VML XNX DVBF FVBF HVBF JVBF NVBF WVBF

LBL-240: G-BVKW XBL OGAV

LBL-260: G-PVBF

LBL-310: G-SIZE TVBF

LBL-317: G-YVBF

LBL-330: G-BXVE

AM.25000: G-ORTW

AM.32000: G-GLBL

SPECIAL SHAPES:

ARMCHAIR	- G-LAZY	G144	- G-BVHN
AUDI SALOON CAR	- G-BWRU	ICE CREAM CONE	- G-YMYM
BANANAS	- G-OCAW	J & B BOTTLE	- G-OJBW
BABY BEL	- G-BXUG	LOZENGE	- G-BVID
BENZ	- G-BWTF	MOUNTAIN DEW CAN	- G-MDEW
BIRTHDAY CAKE	- G-WISH	PIG	- G-PIGG
BUDWEISER CAN	- G-BXHN	PINK PANTHER	- G-PINX
BUNNY	- G-FLUF	RACING CAR	- G-TKGR
DIET PEPSI CAN	- G-DIET	SYRUP BOTTLE	- G-BXUB
FLOWERS	- G-ODBN	TELEWEST SPHERE	- G-BXHO

LOCKHEED
10 ELECTRA: G-LIOA

18 LODESTAR: G-BMEW

414 HUDSON: G-BEOX

L.749 CONSTELLATION: G-CONI

T-33A (including CANADAIR production): G-NASA TBRD WGHB

L.188 ELECTRA: G-BYEF CEXS HNX FIJR IJV IZU LOFB OFC OFD OFE OFRT

L.1011 TRISTAR: G-BBAE BAF BAH BAI BAJ

LOEHLE 5151 MUSTANG: G-BTSD

LORIMER IOLAIRE: G-MZFI

LOVEGROVE
AV-8: G-BXXR

PL.1 - see BENSEN

TYRO GYRO mk.II: G-BVPX

LUSCOMBE 8 SILVAIRE/MASTER/RATTLER: G-AFUP FYD FZK FZN GMI HEC ICX JAP JJU JKB KPG KTI KTM KTN KTT KUF KUG KUH KUI KUJ KUK KUL KUM KUP KVP BNIO NIP POU PPO PVZ PZA PZC PZE RDJ RGF RGG RHX RHY RJA RJK RKA ROO RPZ RRB RSW RUG SHH SHI SNE SNT SOE SOX SSA STX SUD SYF SYH TCH TCJ TDF TIJ TJA TJB TJC UAO UKT UKU ULO VEP VGW VGY VMD WOB DAIR KENM LUSC USI UST NIGE OWIZ ROTI SAGE YRIL

LUTON
LA-4/A MINOR (including PARKER CA-4 & PHOENIX DUET variants): G-AFIR MAW RIF RXP SAA SEA SEB SML SXJ TCJ TCN TFW TKH TWS VDY VUO WIP WMN XGR XKH YDY YSK ZHU ZPV BANF BCY BEA CFY DJG DZY IJS KHR RWU

LA-5A MAJOR: G-ARAD SWH YXO BCKP

LUTON BETA - see ROLLASON

LVG C.VI: G-AANJ

MACAIR MERLIN: G-BTAD WEN

McCANDLESS M.4: G-ARTZ TXX XVN BIPZ VLE

McCULLOGH J.2: G-ORVB

McDONNELL-DOUGLAS DC-10: G-BEBL EBM HDH HDI HDJ YDA DCIO MCA GOKT LYON MULL NIUK

McDONNELL-DOUGLAS HELICOPTERS - see MD HELICOPTERS
MD.500N (520N): G-BXEL

MAINAIR
BLADE: G-BYCW MYRC YRD YSH YTD YTG YTL YTU YTW YUC YUM YUN YVB YVE YVH YVO YVY YVZ YXJ YXM YXN YYA YYG YYH YYW YYY ZAA
ZAB ZAD ZAE ZAF ZAG ZAI ZAJ ZAL ZAM ZAP ZAR ZAS ZAT ZAU ZAY ZAZ ZBA ZBL ZCC ZCD ZCE ZCF ZCG ZCN ZCU ZDF ZDK ZDT ZEB ZED
ZEF ZEG ZEJ ZEW ZFB ZFS ZFZ ZGI ZGW ZIH ZIR ZIS ZIT ZIW ZJA ZJD ZJK ZJV ZJX ZJZ ZKG ZKJ ZKK ZKM ZKO ZKV ZKZ ZLC ZLZ
ZMB ZMD ZMJ ZML ZMM ZMP ZMV ZMY ZMZ ZNC ZNI ZNJ ZNK ZNL ZNO ZOC ZOF ZOP ZOR ZPH ZSD ZSM ZZY OHNA YES

FLASH (Wing) - see SOLAR WINGS PEGASUS/FLASH

GEMINI/FLASH (Combi): G-MJYF JZD MDP MKL MOW MPO MSP MUE MUO MUS MUT MUW MVP MWA MXC MXD MXG MXH MXJ MXK MXL MXT MXU
MXV MZA MZB MZC MZD MZE MZF MZJ MZK MZM MZN MZV NAE NBD NBF NBG NBN NBP NBR NBS NBT NBU NBV NBW NCF NCG NCJ NDC NDF NDM
NEF NEG NEH NET NEV NEY NFE NFF NFH NFJ NFK NFM NFN NFP NGK NGL NGM NGN NGT NGU NGW NGZ NHZ NIA NID NIE NIF NIG NIH NII
NIP NIX NIZ NJU NKL NLI NLX NLY NMG NMH NMI NMJ NMO NMV NNE NNF NNI NNK NNL NNP NNR NNU NNV NPC NPG NPX NRW NRX NRY NSA
NSE NSI NSJ NSR NTI NTS NTU NTV NTW NTX NTZ NUA NUB NUF NUG NUO NUR NUV NVR NVS NVT NVU NVV NVW NWD NWI NWO NWZ NXR
NXS NXT NXU NYJ NYK NZB NZC NZD NZE NZF TAB TAC TAE TAF TAG TAH TBC TBD TBG TBH TBI TBJ TBW TBX TBY TCC TCE TCU TCW TDF
TDR TDW TDY TEH TEJ TEK TEN TEY TFF TFI TFJ TFX TGA TGH TGO THW THY THZ TIA TIB TIC TIL TIM TIN TJA TJB TJC TJD TJE TJF
TJK TJL TJM TJT TJV TJW TJY TJZ TKN TKO TKV TKW TKX TKZ TLB TLC TLD TLL TMA TMC TML TMT TMV TMW TNC TNG TNH TNI TNJ TNL
TNM TNX TNY TPA TPB TRA TRB TRF TRZ TSB TSC TTI TTM TTP TTR TTS TTW TUU TUV TVG TVH TVI TVJ TWF TWG TWR TWS TWX TXM TXP
TXS TXZ TZG TZH TZL TZM TZO TZV TZW TZX TZY TZZ VAA VAB VAD VAO VAP VBD VBF VBG VBH VBI VBK VBL VBM VBN VBO VCE VCF VCY
VDA VDT VEH VEJ VEK VEL VEO VEP VER VES VET VEV VEW VGM VHE VHF VHG VHH VIB VIC VLH VIX VIY VIZ VJA VJB VJC VJE VJL VKC
VLL VLR VMN VMO VMR VMT VMU VMV VMX VMY VMZ VNM VNW VNX VNY VNZ VOB VOF VON VOR VPA VPB VPD VPE VPI VPO VRA VRB VRC VRD
VRM VSN VSO VSP VST VSV VTC VUA VXB VXC VXR VXS VYS VZS WAB WAU WCE WCW WDJ WEL WGG WHI WHO WHR WHY WIA WIG WIH WIN WIV
WJY WLP WLT WLX WMM WMS WMT WMX WMY WNE WNS WNT WNU WOJ WOK WOL WPA WPB WPC WPD WPF WPO WRA WRB WRC WRD WRE WRF WRG WRH
WRI WRJ WRR WSB WSL WSM WTG WTH WTO WTR WTY WTZ WVN WVO WVR WVS WVT WVW WVY WVZ WWB WWC WWI WWJ WWK WWN WXA WXB WXC WXD
WXL WXN WXN WXO WXS WXU WXV WYA WYG WYH WYL WYT WYV WZC WZG WZL WZN YAO YAS YAU YBJ YCK YCR YCS YDV YEU YFP YFR YFU YGZ
YHF YHL YHN YHX YIH YIV YIY YJB YJC YJM YKC YKG YKH YKV YLG YLR YMK YMO YMV YND YOM YOW YPE YPW YRX YSJ OLJT

GEMINI (Trike): G-MBST BTF BTG JYP MAJ MAR MFC MHR MIR MIV MJT MKM MKU MLP MMD MOB MRO MRP MRW MSC MSO MTB MTG MTL MTM
MTX MUX MXW NGB NJD NMC NUM TBY WTF

MERCURY: G-MWVK WXF WXJ WXK WZA YAI YAV YCJ YCL YCN YCV YDC YGG YGJ YJN YJR YKI YKW YKX YKY YLS YML YMT YNC YNF YNJ YOB
YOF YOV YOX YPD YPV YRW YSG YSZ YTB YTK YTX YUB YUD YUE YUK YUW YVL YVS YWA YYU ZAK ZCO

RAPIER: G-BYBV MZEP ZEV ZFD ZFW ZGL ZHJ ZHL ZIL ZIM ZJE ZKN ZND ZNU ZON

SCORCHER SOLO: G-MNDD NNM NPV NPY NPZ NRE NRF NRG NRZ VBE YFT ZKI ZKN

STARLET: G-MYLT

TRI-FLYER (Trike): G-MBCJ BDJ BGA BHK BIZ BPG BPZ BUK BWF BZA BZO JEE JEY JFK JIF JJO JMN JMR JMX JRP JTP JXE JYV
JYX JZH JZU MAL MAN MCM MCZ MDK MDN MDT MEJ MFD MFE MFK MFV MJG MKR MMB MNW MTD MTO MUG MUH MWG MWN MYV NFA NFR NGB NIW
NJG NUI NXB NZY VBC

MAINAIR/FLEXIFORM RAPIER 1+1 (Combi): G-MJYV MAW

MALMO - see BOLKOW

MANNING-FLANDERS MF.1: G-BAAF

MANTA PFLEDGE (Wing): G-MBNY

MANUEL LADYBIRD: G-MJPB

MARQUART MA.5 CHARGER: G-BHBT VJX

MARTIN MONOPLANE: G-AEYY

MAVERICK: G-BYCV MZJJ ZJS ONFL

MASQUITO M.58: G-MASX ASY ASZ

MAULE
  M.4 ROCKET: G-MAWL

  M.5 LUNAR ROCKET: G-BHJK ICX IES PMB VFT VFZ FAMY KRIS NHVH OJGT RAGG AIN JWW N56643 OY-ANZ

  M.6 SUPER ROCKET: G-BKGC MOUL

  M.7 SUPER/STAR ROCKET/STARCRAFT variants: G-BSKG SKO SKT TMJ TWN TXT UEO UEP UXD VIK VIL CROL GROL HIND ITON LOFM

MAX HOLSTE MH.1521M BROUSSARD: G-BWGG WLR

MAXAIR
  DRIFTER: G-MYBB

  HUMMER: G-MJZX MAP MZZ NIM TMJ

MBA TIGER CUB: G-MBUE JRU JSP JSU JSV JUC JUF JUW JWF JWG JWJ JWW JXD JXJ JZC MAG MAK MAM MBH MBT MCX MEY MFN MFS MFT
MGF MGL MHN MIE MIH MIM MIX MJS MJV MKP MLB MLF MLM MOF MSW MUM MVG NJC NKM WFT

MBB
  Bo.105: G-AZOR BAMF ATC CXO FYA GKJ THV TKL UIB UTN UXS CDBS DCCH NLB EYNL NAAB PASB ASC ASD ASG ASX SPOL THLS WMAA YPA

  BK.117: G-DCPA

MD HELICOPTERS MD.900 EXPLORER: G-BXZK PASS WPAS

MEA MISTRAL TRAINER: G-MBET BOH

MEDWAY - see SOUTHDOWN
 HALF PINT (Trike): G-MMSZ MZI NDE NEK NEL NJV NLW NTT

 HYBRED (Trike/Combi): G-BYBJ YBO MGOM JVE MKG MKH MTK NCU NCV NEI NFW NJK NMN NWR NXN NXO TDJ TFC TJG TJP TLX TNE TNF TUX VCD VDB VDC VDJ VEE VGB VGL VGY VIF VKB VMK VPF VPG VPL VRY VRZ VSI VSR VUC VUD VVF VVG VVH VVI VVR VVV VXD VXE VXI VXJ VXM VYP VYR VZO WBJ WCX WCY WCZ WGC WGD WIK WIL WJP WJR WJX WLB WLS WRM WSS WST WSU WUJ WVU MYRI YVV YVX ZGE ZME

 PUMA SPRINT: G-MWBI

MENAVIA - see PIEL

MERCURY DART: G-BKKS

MERIDIAN ULTRALIGHTS MAVERICK: G-BXSZ MYUJ ZLE

MESSERSCHMITT - see NORD: Bf.109 (including HISPANO HA.1112): G-AWHS BOML WUE YDS SMIT

MICRO AVN B-22 BANTAM: G-BXZU MZEY ZJC ZLX

MICROFLIGHT SPECTRUM: G-MVJM VSU VWX VXH WCG WHD WKW WKX WOF WPG WPH WPI WTD WTE WWR WWX YAY

MIDLAND ULTRALIGHTS SIROCCO: G-MNDU NDV NDW NRT TEO TJN TRC VSM

MIGNET
 HM.14/HM.19 POU-DU-CIEL variants: G-ADRG DRX DRY DVU DXS DYV DZW EBB EEH EFG EGV EHM EJZ EKR EMY EOF EOH FFI BWRI MYSI

 HM.293: G-AXPG

 HM-1000 BALERIT: G-MYDZ YXL ZIX ZLI ZMW ZPB ZTA

MIKOYAN (including WSK-PZL variants)
 MiG-15 (LIM 2): G-BMZF OMIG

 MiG-17 (LIM 5): G-BWUF

 MiG-21: G-BRAM

MILES
 M.2H HAWK MAJOR: G-ADMW

 M.2L HAWK SPEED SIX: G-ADGP

 M.3 FALCON: G-AEEG

 M.5 SPARROWHAWK: G-ADNL

 M.11A WHITNEY STRAIGHT: G-AERV EUJ

 M.12 MOHAWK: G-AEKW

 M.14A HAWK TRAINER 3: G-AFBS HUJ IUA JRS KAT KKR KKY KPF NWO

 M.17 MONARCH: G-AFJU FLW FRZ

 M.18: G-AHKY

 M.38/48 MESSENGER: G-AGOY HUI IEK ILL JOC JOE JWB KBO KEZ KIN KIS KVZ LAH

 M.65 GEMINI: G-AKDK KEK KEL KER KGD KGE KHP KHZ KKB KKH

 M.75 ARIES: G-AOGA

 M.100 STUDENT: G-MIOO

MILLS MH-1: G-OMHI

MIRAGE - see ULTRAFLIGHT

MITCHELL
 WING B-10: G-MMJA NJW

 WING U-2: G-MMNS

MITCHELL-PROCTER KITTIWAKE - see PROCTER: G-ATXN WGM BBRN BUL

MONG SPORT: G-BTOA

MONNETT
 MONI: G-BMVU INOW MONI SULY TRIM

 SONERAI: G-BGEH GLK ICJ JBM JLC KDC KFA KNO LAI MIS OBY SGJ VCC CCOZ PFAT RILY

MONOCOUPE 90A: G-AFEL

MONTGOMERIE-BENSEN - see BENSEN

MOONEY M.20 (including M.252 variant): G-APVV SUB TOU WLP BCJH DTV DVU HBI HJI IBB IWP IWR JHB KMA KMB NZS PCR PFC
 PKL SXI UYR VZY WJG WTW XML YDD YEE CERT DBYE ESS EST PUK FLYA GCKI JKK TPL JAKI DIX ENA MALS OON UNI OBAL DJH EAC JAC
 JJB ONE OOO PWS SUS RAAD AFW ZZIP

MORANE-SAULNIER - see DE HAVILLAND
 TYPE N: G-AWBU

 MS.500 series - see FIESELER: G-BIRW PHZ

 MS.733 ALCYON: G-MSAL SHOW

 MS.880 RALLYE series (including GEMS/SEEMS/SOCATA & PZL-110 KOLIBER production): G-ARTT RXW SAT SAU VIN VPK VTV VVJ
 VZX WAA WKT WOA WXY WYX XAK XCL XCM XCN XGC XGE XHG XHS XHT XIT XOH XOS XOT YDG YET YFJ YRH YTA YYX ZEE ZGI ZGL ZKC ZKE
 ZMZ ZUT ZVF ZVH ZVI ZYD BAAI AOG AOH AOJ AOM BAK BED BGC BHX BLM CAC CLT COR CST CUL CVC CXB DEC DWH ECA ECB ECC EIL
 ERA ERC ETO EVB EVC EVW FAK FDF FGS FTZ GKC GKD GMT GPZ GSA GZO HWK IAC IIK IOR IPS IRB JDF KBF KGA KGT KJF KOA KVA KVB
 LGS LIY OJL PJD RDN TIU TOW TUG UDO UGX UKR VAI VAN VWA WWG XLR XLS XZT
 EXIT FARM GIGI KHRE OLI MELV OACI MIA PIGS VAJT WCEI

MOSSCRAFT MA.1/MA.2: G-AFHA FJV

MOTH CORPN - see DE HAVILLAND

MOTO-DELTA - see CENTRAIR

MOULT (Trike): G-MTFK

MOYES MEGA (Wing): G-MZCL

MSS - see EUROWING

MUDRY - see CAARP

MURPHY
 REBEL: G-BUTK VHS WCY WFZ WLL YBK DIKY LJCC YELL

 RENEGADE/SPIRIT: G-BTHN TKB WPE BYBU MGOO VZP VZX WAJ WDM WGF WKA WMW WNF WNR WOO WPS WPZ WUH WVP WWD YAM YAZ YCO YFM
 YJP YRK YUF YXR YIG MZIP ZIZ NINE RCMC ENE TBAG BMW

NANCHANG - see YAKOVLEV

NASH - see PROCTER

NAVAL ACFT FACTORY - see BOEING-STEARMAN

NEICO LANCAIR 235/320/IV variants: G-BSPX SRI UNO UST VLA FOPP PJMT UILE

NICOLLIER HN.700 MENESTREL: G-BVHL MINS

NIEUPORT
 SCOUT 17/23: G-BWMJ

 28: G-BSKS

NIMROD - see AIRWAVE

NOBLE HARDMANSNOWBIRD: G-MTRY TXL VCI VCJ VIL VIM VIN VIO VOI VOJ VOL VYT VYU VYV VYW VYX

NOORDUYN - see NORTH AMERICAN

NORD
 1002 PINGOUIN: G-ASTG SUA TBG

 1101 NORALPHA: G-ATDB THN BAYV SMD

 1203 NORECRIN: G-BAYL EDB

 3202: G-BIZK IZM PMU

 3400: G-BOSJ

 NC.854 series - see SNCAC

NORMAN
NAC-1 FREELANCE: G-NACA NACI

NDN-1 FIRECRACKER/TURBO FIRECRACKER: G-NDNI

NAC-6 FIELDMASTER/FIREMASTER: G-NACL ACO ACP RDC

NORTH AMERICAN
T-6/AT-16 HARVARD (TEXAN) (including CCF production): G-AZBN ZSC BBHK DAM GHU GOR GPB HTH ICE IWX JST KRA MJW RBC RLV
RVG RWB SBG TKI TXI UKY WUL CTKL DDMV ELMH HRVD JUDI RAIX TSIX VIJ

B-25 MITCHELL: G-BWGR YDR

P-51 MUSTANG - see LOEHLE: G-BIXL TCD HAEC LYNE MSTG UST PSIC SIRR USY

F-86 SABRE: G-SABR

NOSTALGAIR N.3 PUP: G-BVEA

NOTT-CAMERON ULD-1/2/3: G-BLJN NXK NOTT

OLDFIELD BABY LAKES: G-BBGL GEI GLS KCJ KHD MIY RKO SXY TZL WMO POND

OMEGA BALLOONS
Free Balloons (Hot Air):
O-20: G-AXMD
56: G-AXAO YAL
84: G-AXJB XVU

OPTICA - see EDGLEY

ORD-HUME - see LUTON MINOR

ORIENTAL: G-BINY

ORLICAN L-40 META-SOKOL: G-APUE PVU ROF

OSPREY (CHOWN): G-BJHP JHW JID JLE JND JNH JPL JRA JRG JSC JSD JSF JSI JTN JTY JUE JUI JUU FYAV YBD YBE YBF
YBG YBH YBI YBJ YBR YCL YCV YCZ YDF YDO YDS YDW YEV YFN

PAKES JACKDAW: G-MBOF

PANTHER - see ULTRASPORTS/SOLAR WINGS

PARKER CA-4 - see LUTON MINOR: G-AFIU

PARNALL ELF: G-AAIN

PARSONS GYROPLANE: G-BTFE UWH VOD VPH WTP IIXX

PAYNE Ax6-62: G-AZRI BFMZ

PENN-SMITH GYROPLANE: G-AXOM

PICCARD
HAFB: G-ATTN

Ax6: G-AWCR ZHR

PIXIE: G-EBJG

PIXIE - see SKYHOOK

PARTENAVIA
P.64B OSCAR: G-BMDP

P.68: G-BCDK CPO FBU GXJ HBZ HJS IFZ JRZ MOI ENCE FJMS HUBB KWIK OLMA RVR UNIT

PAYNE KNIGHT TWISTER: G-APXZ BRAX

PAZMANY
PL-1: G-BDHJ

PL-2: G-OPAZ

PL-4: G-BMMI RFX FISK PAZY LIV

PEARSON: G-BIXX

PERCIVAL - see HUNTING
P.1 GULL: G-ACGR DPR

P.6 MEW GULL: G-AEXF

P.10 VEGA GULL: G-AEZJ

P.16 Q SIX: G-AFFD

P.28/31/34/44 PROCTOR: G-AHTE HVG HWO KIU KZN LCK LJF NXR

P.40 PRENTICE: G-AOKH OKL OKO OKZ OLK OLU PIT PIU PIY PJB PPL

P.56 PROVOST: G-ASMC WPH WRY WVF BDYG GSB KFW LIW TDH KAPW MOOS TMKI

P.57/66 PRINCE/SEA PRINCE/PEMBROKE: G-AMLZ BNPH NPU RFC XES DACA GACA RACA

PEREIRA OSPREY: G-BEPB VGI GEOF

PHANTOM - see SKYRIDER

PHILLIPS ST.1 SPEEDTWIN: G-DPST EMNI GPST

PHOENIX PM-3 DUET - see CURRIE WOT/LUTON: G-AYTT

PIAGGIO
P.149 (including FOCKE WULF production): G-BPWW RKD RORY

P.166: G-APWY

PIEL CP.301/328 EMERAUDE (including COOPAVIA, MENAVIA, ROUSSEAU & SCINTEX production & including FAIRTRAVEL/BINDER variants): G-APNS RDD RRS RSJ RUV SCZ SLX SMT SVG SZR XXC YCE YEC YTR ZGY ZYS BBKL CCR DCI DDZ DKH HRR IDO IJU IVF KFR KNZ KUR LHL LRL PRT SVE XAH XYE DENS PIEL

CP.1310/5 SUPER EMERAUDE (incluing SCINTEX production): G-ASMV SNI BANW CHP GVE HEK JCF JVS LXI XRF

PIETENPOL AIR CAMPER (including GREGA): G-ADRA BBSW KVO MDE MLT NMH POL RXY SVZ UCO UXK UZO VYY WAT WVB WVF XZO YFT ECOX DFS IMBY OFFA HAL PCAF IET RAGS SILS TARN VALS

PIK - see EIRI & SIREN

PILATUS
P.2: G-BLKZ ONE CJCI PTWO

P.3: G-BTLL

PC.6 PORTER: G-WGSC

PIPER
J/2 CUB: G-AEXZ FFH JTWO

J/3C CUB (including L-4/O-59 variants): G-AFDO GAT GIV GVV HIP IIH ISS ISX JAD JAO JES KAZ KIB KRA KTH KUN SPS TKI TZM XGP XHP XHR XVV YCN YEN BAET BHJ BLH BUU BXS CNX COB COM CPH CPJ CUB CXJ DCD DEY DEZ DHK DJP DMS DOL ECN EDJ EUI FBY FDL FHI FZB GPD GSJ GTI GXA HPK HPT HVV HXY HZU IJE ILI JAF JAY JSZ JTO KHG LPA MKC OTU OXJ PCF PUR PVH PYN REB ROR SAX SBT SFD SNF STI SVH SVJ SYO TBX TET TSP TUM TZX VAF VPN WEZ
CCUB OPS UBY VIL FRAN HEWI KIRK LIVH OCH NCUB OCUB INK POOH RAMP SEED NDY TCUB

J/4A CUB COUPE: G-AFGM FWH FZA BRBV SDJ UWL

J/5A CUB CRUISER: G-BRIL RLI SDK SXT TKA WUG

PA-12 SUPER CRUISER: G-AMPG RTH WPW XUC BCAZ OWN SYG PAIZ

PA-15/PA-17 VAGABOND: G-AKTP LEH LGA LIJ MYL SHU WKD WOF WOH BCVB DVA DVB DVC IHT LMP OVB RJL RPY RSX SFW SMV SWG TBY TCI TFJ TOT UKN UXX FKNH VAGA

PA-16 CLIPPER: G-BAMR BUG IAP SVI SWF

PA-18 SUPER CUB (including L-18/L-21 variants): G-AMEN PZJ RAM RAN RAO RCT REO RGV RVO SCU TRG VOO WMF XGA XLZ YPM YPO YPP YPR YPS YPT ZRL BAFS AFT AFV AKV BOL BYB CFO CMD EOI EUA EUU FFP GPN GWH GYN HGC HOM HPM IDJ IDK IID IJB IMM IRH ITA IYJ IYR IYY IZV JBK JCI JEI JFE JIV JLH JTP JWX JWZ KET KJB KRF KTA KVM LGT LHM LIH LLN LLO LMI LMR LMT LPE LRC MAY MEA MKB NXM OOC PJG PJH PUL ROZ RRL SGC SHV TBU TDX TDY TUR UBA VIE VIW VMI VRZ WHH WOR WUB CUBB UBJ UBP FUZZ GCUB DAM HACK ELN JCUB KAMP LION NETY ICK NAC OFER ROD SPS TAN TUG PCUB IPR UDL ULL ROVE SCUB UPA TUGG WGCS LAC XCUB YCUB ZAZA

PA-20 PACER (including tailwheel PA-22 variants): G-APYI RBS RGY RNK TBX VDV BFAO FMR IYP SED TLM UOI UXV XBB GGLE PAXX

PA-22 TRI-PACER (including CARIBBEAN/COLT variants): G-APTP PUR PXR PXT PXU PYN PZL PZX RAI RAX RBV RCC RCF RDS RDT RDV REL RET REV RFB RFD RGO RHN RHP RHR RIK RIL RJC RJE RJF RJH RKK RKM RKN RKP RKR RKS RND RNE RNG RNH RNI RNJ RNL RON RSU RSW RSX RYH SSE TXA WLI ZRS BHCW MCS NED OAK RNX TIC TKV TWU UVA WWU HALL TJAY TLDK

PA-23/PA-27 APACHE/AZTEC: G-APMY RBN RCW RHL RJR RJS RJT RJU RJV RMA RTD RYF SEP SER SHH SHV SMO SMY SND SNH SRI TFF THA TJR TMU TOA VKZ XDC XOG XZP YBO YMO YSA YWY ZRG ZSZ ZXG ZYU BADI ADJ AED APL ATN ATX AUA AUI AUJ AUW AVL AVZ AXP BCC BCW BDO BEW BEY BGB BGE BHF BIF BMJ BNO BRA BRJ BTJ BTL BVG CBG CBM CCE CEX CRP EXO DAX FBB FJK FVP FWE GTG GWW HCT HNG ICY JNZ JXX KJW KVT LLM LXX MFD MOL NUV RAV SVP XPS
CALL SFT ESKU SKY FOTO HFTG JANK TCA KEYS LIZZ MLFF OLY OART BEY PME SNI XTC RVRC VRD SFHR HIP TAPE AXI USFT VSFT WSFT XSFT YSFT ZSFT

PA-24/PA-26 COMANCHE: G-APUZ PXJ RBO RDB RFH RHI RIE RLK RUO RXG RYV SEO TIA TJL TNV TOY VCM VGA XMA XTO YED ZKR ZWY
BAHG AHJ RDW RXW UTL WNI DISK KSVB MOTO

PA-25 PAWNEE: G-ASIY SKV SLK SVP TFR VPY VXA XED ZPA BAUC CBJ DDS DDT DPJ DWL EHS EII ENL EPN ETL ETM EXK FEV FEW FPS
FRX FRY FSC FSD HUU ILL LDG NZV PWL STH UXY VYP XST CMGC DSGC LYND TOWS

PA-28-140 CHEROKEE (including CHALLENGER, CRUISER & FLITE-LINER variants): G-ARUR RVS RVT RVU RVV RYR SFL SHX SII SIJ
SIL SKT SLV SPK SRW SSW SUD SVZ SWX TAS TDA TEM TEZ THI THR TIS TJF TJG TLW TMW TNB TOI TOJ TOK TOL TOM TON TOO TOP
TOR TOS TOT TPN TRO TRP TRR TTF TTG TTI TTK TTU TTV TTX TUB TUD TUL TVK TVL TVO TVS TXM TYS TZK VAX VBG VBH VBS VBT VFP
VFR VFX VFZ VGC VGD VGE VGG VGH VGI VGK VLB VLC VLD VLE VLF VLG VLH VLI VLJ VLR VLT VNN VNO VNP VNR VNS VNU VNW VOZ VPV
VRK VRP VRT VRU VRY VRZ VSA VSB VSC VSD VSE VSF VSI VSP VUS VUT VUU VUT VUU VWA VWD VWE VWG VWI VWJ VWL VWM VYL VYM VYP
VYR VZR WBE WBG WBH WBS WDP WET WEV WEX WIT WPS WSL WSM WTL WTM WXR WXS XAB XIO XJV XJX XMP XOR XSG XSZ XTA XTC XTJ XTK
XTL XTP XZD XZF YAA YAB YAR YAT YAW YEE YEF YIF YIG YJP YJR YKW YKX YMK YMN YNF YNJ YPJ YPV YRM YUH YWE ZDX ZEG ZFC ZLN
ZMX ZRH ZWB ZWD ZWE ZZO BABG AFU AGX AHE AHF AJR AKH AMM ASJ ASL ATV ATW AWK AXZ BBK BBN BBY BDB BDC BEC BEF BEV BHY
BIL BIX BKX BPY BYP BZF CDJ CGI CGU CGN CGT CJM CJN CJP CLL DGY DSH DWY EAC EEU EEV EFF EYO EYT FBF FPE FXK GAX
GPU GRC GVU HXK IFB IHG IYX ODM OFY OHM OSR OSU RBW RGI RPK RPL RWO SEF SER SGD SLM SLU SSE STZ TEX TGO TON TVR ULR
UTZ UUX UYY XJD XPL XVU XYM YCA
CGHM JBC DENE EVS IAT LTR FIAT GALA CAT HOCK KATS ERY LFSC FSI IZI TFC MATZ IDD KAS NHRH ITA
OFTI IBO KYM MAT NET SOW PAWL ETR IKK RECK SCPL MTH OOT TEFC EMP EWS IMW WOLF YULL

PA-28-151/161 CHEROKEE WARRIOR I/II/III/CADET: G-BCIE CIR CRL CTF DGM DPA DZX EBZ EFA ELP FBR FDK FMG FNI FNJ FNK FWB
FXD FXE FYB FYM FZG GKS GOG GPJ GPL GVK GYG GYH HFK HJO HOR HRC HVB ICW IEY IIT IUW JBW JBX JBY JCA JSV JYG LEJ LVL MFP
MKR MTR MUZ NCR NEL NJM NJT NMB NNO NNS NNT NNY NNZ NOE NOF NOG NOH NOI NOJ NOK NOL NOM NON NOO NOP NOR NOS NOT NOU NOV
NOW NRG NSY NSZ NTD NXE NXT NXU NZB NZZ OAH ODA ODB ODC ODD ODE ODF ODR OER OFZ OHA OHO OHR OIG OJW OJZ OKB OKK OKL OKM
OKN OKO OKP OKR OKS OKT OKU OKX OMY OPC ORK ORL OSP OTF OTI OTN OUP OUR OVH OVK OXA OXB OXC OYH OYI OZI PAC PAF PAU PBM
PCK PDT PDU PEL PFH PHB PHE PHL PID PIU PJO PJP PJR PJS PJT PJU PKM PKR PMF PMR PMV POM PPK PRN PRY PWA PWE RBA RBB RBD
RBE RDF RDG RDM RFM RJV RRM RRN RSE RSG RTM RTX RUB RXC RZP SAW SBA SCV SCY SFK SGL SGN SHP SIB SJX SLE SLK SLT SMZ SOK
SOZ SPI SPM SSC SSR SSW SSX SVF SVG SVM SXA SXB SXC SYZ SZT TAW TBC TDV TFO TGY TID TIH TIM TIV TKT TNE TNT TNV TRK TRS
TRY TSJ TUW UFH UFY UIF UIJ UIK UJO UJP UKX URT VBF VIH VJZ VTO WOH WOI WOJ XAB XJJ XJX XLY XNH XOJ XTX XTY XTZ YHI YXU
CBAL DON LAC LEA PCH PTM DENH EDGI GLD GTR KKL SFT SSX TDA FIZZ LAV LEN MAM OXA GFCA FCB FCF RRC USS HMED MES IKBP SDB
JAMP ASE AVO KART BPI DET NAP LACA ACB BMM ORC MAND AYO SFT NINA SFT OAAA ANC ANI BFC CTU DEN GCA JWS MPS ONY TYJ WAR
PSFT RIZZ SFT SKR OWS SACI ACO ACR ACS ACT ACU ACZ ARH EJW LYN SFT UZN TAGS SFT VICC WARA ARB ARC ARE ARO ARR ARS ARU
ARV ARW ARX ARY ARZ FFW XENA ZULU

PA-28-180/181 CHEROKEE ARCHER I/II/III: G-BCCF DSB EIP EMW EXW EYL FDI FMM FSY FVG GBG GTJ GVZ GWM HNO HWZ HYS HZE IIV
IUY JAG JOA KCC LFI LYY MIW MPC MSD NGT NPN NPO NRP NVE NYP OBZ OEE OJM OMP OMU OOF OPA ORS OSE OXY PAY PFI PGU POT PTE
PXA PYO RBG RBX RME RNV RUD RXD SCS SEU SIM SIZ SKW SNX SVB SXS SZJ TAM TGZ TKX TYI UMP VNS VOA WPH WUH XEX XIF XOZ XRG
XRJ XTW XWO
CHAS HIP IFR DENK IXY JJA EMAZ PJM RNI FBRN GASP IBBO LLY JACS ANA ANT CAS JAN OYT OYZ KAIR EES EMI EVB ITE LACD ORR
MALA ASF DAC ERI NIKE OTE OBFS BUS GEM ODW RAR PIPA RADI CHA EXS SARA GSE HED VEA TERY IMK SGJ WEL USSY VOAR WACP ACR
YANK

PA-28-236 DAKOTA (including TURBO DAKOTA variant): G-BGXS HTA NYB OKA PCX RKH WSX XCC FRGN WPW KOTA LEAM TART

PA-28R CHEROKEE ARROW (including PA-28RT variants): G-AVWN VWO VWR VWT VWU VWV VXF VYS VYT WAZ WBA WBB WBC WEZ WFB WFC
WFD WFJ XCA XWZ YAC YII YPU YRI ZAJ ZDE ZFI ZFM ZNL ZOG ZRV ZSF ZSH ZWS BAAZ AHS AIH AMY APW AWG AZU BDE BEB BEL BFD
BIA BZH BZV CGS CJO COP CPG EOH EWX FDO FLI FTC FZH GKU GKV GOL GVN HAY HEV HFJ HGY HIR HWY IDI IKE IZO KCB KFZ KXF LXP
MGB MHT MHZ MIV MJG MKK MLS MNL MOE MOP MPR MVE NEE NJR NNX NSG NTC NTS NVT NZG OBA OET OGM OIC OJH OJI ONC OOG OUS OWY
OYV PBO PXJ PZM REP RLG RMS RRJ SLD SNP SPN TLG TRT UND UNH UUM VDH WMI WNM XVC XYO XYP XYR XYS XYT
DAAH DAY IZY MCS NCS ONS ORA ECJM DVL MAK PTR FBWH ULL GDOG EHP HRW PMW YMM HALC ERB IBFW JOE SCA JANO EFS ESS MTT LBRC
EEM FSE MACK EAH EGA EME ERL RST ODOG JIM KAG KEN MHC MNI OTC PEP PJD RDN RACO JMS ONG UBY SABA HUG TCTC HSL TOBE UTSY
VOID WEND ILS WAL YAWW

PA-30 TWIN COMANCHE (including PA-39 C/R): G-ASMA SON SRH SRO SSB SSP SWW TET TEW TMT TSZ TWR TXD VAU VCX VJJ VKL VPR
VPS VUD VVI WBN WBT XAU XRO YAF YLB YSB YZE ZAB ZBC BAKJ AWN AWU FUF KCL LOR COMB LADI ARE OAJS GET LIN RDO PCOM SHAW
IGN JAB URG TCOM

PA-31 NAVAJO: G-AYEI BBZI EZL FIB FOM HGA IYO JLO LFZ PYR WHF EEAC FILL IKPS SFC LYDD NAVO WAC ONAV PRA WLC UMMI

PA-31-350 NAVAJO CHIEFTAIN: G-BASU MBC RFA TAX TLE VYF XKS XUV CITY EPED MAX GLTT LUG RAM TAX HTAX VRD IFIT LEA LIDE
MOHS RMR NERC EWR OAMT JIL LDB LLY NPA SGB PLAC ZAZ ZIZ VIPP YEOM

PA-31P PRESSURISED NAVAJO: G-BWDE EHJM OIEA SASK

PA-32 CHEROKEE SIX/SARATOGA: G-ATES TJV TRW TRX VFS VFU VTJ VTK VUZ ZDJ ZTD BADO AGG AXJ BFV BSM EZP GUB HGO IWL KEK
MDC RGT RNZ STV VWZ XWP DENI IGI IWY ETBY FRAG IFFR LTS KFRA NOW LADE MCAR NEAL OCPF CTI SCC SIX TBY RAYE SALA IXD TOGA
WAIR INS

PA-32R CHEROKEE LANCE/SARATOGA SP: G-BDWP EHH FUB FYC HBG JCW KMT MEV MJA NJF OGO OON OTV PVI PVN RHA SUF SYC TCA VBG
VEB DCAV CSW TCP EENA LLA GOTO HDEW ERO IHI YLT IMPW JPOT LLTT UNA MOLL OVI NIOS ROY OCCA JCW PAPS RAMS EAH HHT IGH OLF
SULL TRIP WOZA YSTT

PA-34 SENECA: G-AZIK ZOL ZOT ZVJ BABK ACB AIG AKD ANK ASM ASX ATR BLU BNH BNI BPX BXK BZJ CDB CGA CID CVY DEF DUN EAG
EHU EJV ETT EVG FKY FLH GFT GLW HFH HYE HYF HYG LWD LYK MDK MJO MNT MUT NEI NEN NRX OCG OCP OCR OCS OCT OCU OCV OCW OCX
OCY OFE OIZ OJK OPV ORH OSD OUK OUL OUM OWE BPAD PON PXX RHO RXO SDN SGK SHA SII SOY SPG SUW TGU TGV UBU VDN VEV
WDT XPV XPW XUT XXY
CAHA DAV EGA HEM LOS LUE TWW DARA CEA SID ELBC MER XEC FILE LYI GFEY FCD UYS HCSL MJB IFLP JANN LCA LORD MAIK AIR AXI
PWT RPP OACG MAR PAG WAL PEGI LUS OPS ROLA OUS VRB SENX KYZ SFC TAIR EST VASA VBK WATS IZO WAS

PA-38 TOMAHAWK: G-BFVF GBK GBN GBW GBY GEK GGE GGF GGG GGI GGL GGM GGN GIG GKY GLA GRK GRL GRM GRN GRR GRX GSH GSI GVL
GWN GWU GXB GXN GXO GZF GZJ GZW HCZ JNN JUR JUS JYN KAR KAS KCY KMK LWP MKG MML MNP MSF MTO MTP MVL MVM MXL NCO NEK NGR
NGS NHG NIM NKH NNU NPL NPM NSL NUY NVD NXV NYK NYV OBJ OBK OBL OCC ODP ODS OEC OHN OHS OHT OHU OLD OLE OLF OMO OMZ OUD
OZM PBR PER PES PHI PIK PPD PPE PPF RFL RFN RHR RHT RJR RLO RLP RMJ RML RNJ RSJ RTA SFE SKC SKK SKL SOT SOU SOV SVV SVW
SVX SVY SYK SYL SYM TAP TAR TAS TEV TFP TGC TIL TJK TJL TND TOD TOM VBL VHM VLP WNR WNU WNV WSC XET XZU DFLY TOO YOU
EDNA MMS ORG NGR GTHM JEFF LFSA FSB FSD MSFC NCFC OAAL ATS EDB LFC PSF TFT PRIM REPM VRF VRG SION UKI TOMS EI-BJT BUR
BUS BVK

PA-44 SEMINOLE: G-BGCO GSG GTF HFE HRP OHX RUI RUX DENZ FRST SFT GSFT HSI PDOC SEMI TWIN

PA-46 MALIBU: G-BMBE UPN XER CUPN DODI HYHY MICZ PALL VRST
PA-60 AEROSTAR - see TED SMITH

PIPER CP.1 METISSE: G-BVCP

PITTSS-1/S-2 SPECIAL: G-AXNZ ZCE ZPH BADW ADZ BOH ETI HSS IRD KDR KPZ KVP LAG MTU OEM OXH OXV OZS PDV PLY PRD PVP PZY
RAA RAW RBN RCE RCI RJN RRS RVL RVT RZL RZX SDB SRH TEF TOO TTR TUK TUL UAW UWJ VFN VSZ XAF XAU XFB XTI YIP YIR YJP
EWIZ FLIK OLY ORZ HISS ICAS III IIR IIT IIX TII JAWZ KITI LITZ OOP MAGG INT OGEE KAY ODI SIS WAZ PEAL ITS ITZ REAP
OLL SIIB KYD OLO PIN TUA TUB TYL WUN TIII WAZZ ILD REN YOYO

PLUMB BGP.1 BIPLANE: G-BGPI FUNN

POBER P-9 PIXIE: G-BUXO

PORTERFIELD
 CP-50: G-AFZL

 CP-65: G-BVWY

PORTSWOOD: G-FYBS YBX

POTEZ 840: F-BMCY

POTTIER P.80S: G-BTYH

POWERCHUTE
 KESTREL: G-MVRV WCI WCJ WCK WCL WCN WCO WCP WCS WFG WFI WFL WFN WGT WGU WGV WGW WGY WGZ WMA WMB WMC WMD WMG WMH WNV WNX
WNY WNZ WOC WOD WOE YCW YCX YCY YCZ YDA YDB YEX YFA YHS

 RAIDER: G-MTVZ VHB VHC VMD VNA VNB VNC VNE VNI VNK VNL VNM VVZ VWB VWD VWF VWH VWI

PRACTAVIA PILOT SPRITE: G-AXRK ZZH BALY CVF CWH ILF ROSS

PRICE
 Ax7-77: G-BLEL MDJ

 TPB.2: G-BULE

PRIVATEER - see SLINGSBY MOTOR CADET

PROCTER PETREL - see MITCHELL: G-AXSF

PROTECH PT-2C SASSY: G-EWAN

PTERODACTYL (PFLEDGLING/PTRAVELER) - see SOLEAIR: G-MBAW BHZ BKB BLN JBX JST MWJ

PUTZER ELSTER B: G-APVF BMWV LUFT

PZL
 PZL-104 WILGA: G-BKWG TNS UNC WDF XBZ XMU WILG LGA

 PZL-110 KOLIBER - see MORANE-SAULNIER RALLYE

 PZL SZD-45A OGAR: G-BEBG KTM MFI OGAR

QAC QUICKIE (including TRI-Q): G-BKFM KSE MFN MVG MZG NCG NJO OBS PMW PNL PUC SPA SSK UBC UOO UXM VYT WIT WIZ XOY KUTU
WKI RUDI

QUAD-CITY CHALLENGER: G-CAMR IBFC MGAA GRH VZK WFU WFV WFX WFY WFZ YAG YDN YDS YFH YGM YIA YIX YOZ YPZ YRH YRJ YSD YTO
YTT YUL YXC YXK YXV YYF ZAC ZBW ZBZ ZEA ZHO ZKW ZNA

R.A.F.
 BE.2E: G-BVGR

 SE-5A - see REPLICA PLANS & SLINGSBY: G-EBIA EBIB EBIC BKDT LXT

RAND ROBINSONKR.2: G-BEKR FKC LOU MFL MMD NAD NML OLZ OTT OUN PIH PRR RJX RJY RSN TGD UDF UDS URF UWT VIA VZJ WNN XXE
DGWW JCMW KISS RII OFMB RAND TIMJ UTSI WYNN XRAY

RANGO (Model Free Balloons) (including RANGO-SAFFERY): G-BHAL IAL IIX JAS JNP FYEJ YEM YEU YFT YFW YFY YGA YGB YGI YGK

 NA 24 (Model Airship): G-FYEB

 NA-36/Ax3: G-BJRH

RANS
S-4/S-5 COYOTE: G-MVPJ VPZ VRN VXW WBO WEP WES WFF WFW WGA WGN WIO WLA WLY WLZ WWP YDO YWV ZGD

S-6 COYOTE II: G-BSMU SSI STT SUA SUT TNW TXD UOK UTM UWK VCL VFM VIN VOI VPW VRK VUM VZO VZV WHK WWP WYR XCU XRZ XWK
YBR YCM YCN YCO YIB YJO YKE CHAZ IZIT MGEC GND WCH WHP WIF WRK WSC WTT WUK WUL WUN WVL WWL WYE WYN YAJ YBA YBI YDK YDX
YES YFE YFN YGH YGP YGR YHI YHK YHP YIR YIS YJD YJL YJY YKN YLA YLD YLF YLO YLW YMH YMP YMR YMS YNE YNH YOA YOI YOT YPA
YPJ YSP YSU YTE YUZ YVP YXB YXG YXP YYV YZR ZAH ZBD ZBH ZBU ZBV ZCA ZDA ZDG ZDM ZDR ZEN ZEO ZEU ZFL ZFN ZFY ZIY ZJI ZJM
ZKE ZLG ZLL ZMP ZMS ZMU ZNV ZOZ ZUB RINS SSIH

S-7 COURIER: G-BVNY WKJ WMN KATI

S-9 CHAOS: G-BPUS SEE

S-10 SAKOTA: G-BRPT RSC RZW SBV SGS SMT SNN SWB SWI TCR TGG TJX TKS TWZ UAX UGH UKB ULW VCB VFA VHI WIA WIL BYRE JSCL
OEYE RANS RANZ

RAVEN-EUROPE MFM FS-57A: G-BRUZ

RAVEN - see SOUTHDOWN

RAVEN VECTOR: G-MBTW JAZ

RAYTHEON HAWKER - see HAWKER SIDDELEY

REARWIN
175 SKYRANGER: G-BTGI RWIN

8125 CLOUDSTER: G-BVLK

8500 SPORTSTER: G-AEOF

9000L SPORTSTER: G-BGAU

REECE SKY RANGER: G-MJRR

REID & SIGRIST RS.4 DESFORD: G-AGOS

REIMS - see CESSNA

RENEGADE - see MURPHY

REPLICA PLANS SE-5A : G-BDWJ IHF KER MDB UOD UWE INNY SEVA

REPUBLIC RC-3 SEABEE: G-SEAB

REVOLUTION HELICOPTERS MINI-500: G-BWCZ HIAH MSOO OREV PDWI SWSH YEAR

RH7B TIGER LIGHT: G-MZGT

RICH PROTOTYPE GLIDER: G-BKEX

RIDOUT: G-BIRP IWF IWG JMX JMZ JNA

RIGG: G-BHLJ IAR

ROBIN
DR.400 series (including 2+2/PETIT PRINCE/EARL/KNIGHT/MAJOR/REGENT variants): G-BAEB AEM AEN AFP AFX AGC AGR AGS AHL
AJY AJZ AKM ALF ALG ALH ALI ALJ AMS AMT AMU AMV ANB APV APX AZC BAX BAY BCH BCS BDP BJU BMB CXE DUY EUP FJZ GRH GWC
HAJ HFS HJU HLE HLH HOA IHD IZI JUD KDH KDI KDJ KVL NFV NXI OGI PHG PTT PZP RBK RBL RBM RNT RNU SDG SDH SFF SLA SSP SVS
SYU SZD TRU UGJ UYS XRT YIT
CONB DUDZ EGGS HMM LEN YCO FCSP ILO TIL TIM TIN UEL GBUE HANS IEYE OOI JBDH EDH MTS UDE LARA EOS MIFF NBDD ONGC RONS
SELL TUGY UKE UAPA XLXL YOGI ZACH IGI IPI

DR.500: G-LISE MOTI

HR.100 ROYALE/SAFARI/TIARA: G-AZHB ZHK BAEC APY AWR AYR BAW BCN BIO BPW EUD GTP LHN LWF VMZ WPG XWB HRIO MPWI

HR.200/CLUB: G-BBOE CCB CCY DJN ETD FBE GXR LTM NIK UWZ VMM WFG WPG WVG XDT XGW XOR XVK

R.1180T AIGLON: G-BGHM IRT JVV GBAO DER EEP PACE ROBN VITE

R.2100/R.2112 ALPHA: G-BGBA ICS IVA KXA PLAY RAFC TOUR

R.2160: G-BLWY VYO WZG YBF MATT SACK BMO

R.3000: G-BLYP OLU PAVL

ROBINSON REDWING: G-ABNX

ROBINSON
R-22/ALPHA/BETA/MARINER: G-BJUC LDK LME LTF NKX NRZ NUZ OAM ODZ OEW OEX OEZ OVR OXX OYC OYX PGV PIT PNF PNI PTP PTZ RBY
RHN RKN RLD ROX RRY RTI RVI RWD RXV SCE SCL SEK SGF SIN SIT SXN SZS TBA TDI THI TNA TNB TOC TVU UBW UIW VCI VGS VPR WAK
WHY WTH XLA XMR XOA XRK XSG XSY XTU XUC XWJ XXN XYK YCF YCK YCU YHD YHE YTE
CHIS HYL NDY RAY DAAM EER EJL ELT ERB HGS IRE LDL MCD ODB ODR RAI EIBM LFI PAR RBL TIN VER FAGN IRS LYU OLI USI GDAY
HZM JCD SFC HBMW ERA IEL IPO RHE UMF URN VRS IBED CCL HSB IRF LYS SPL JARA BWI ERS HEW ONH RBH WFT KENN EVN ILY RAY
LAIN AND EDA IDS IPE OLO MAVI DKD FHT ICH OGY RSN UFY NHSR ICH JSH OASH BIL BIO DCS DOT EAT FAS FJS GOG HLL ICV KEY
LAU LIZ LRT MMG MSG PAL PTS RMB ROB SEE SHL SIP SMS TAC TED THL TOY VNR PACL BES PHEL IKE PLH RACH ALD ENT IAT ICE OGG
OUT SVP SWW USO SANS BUT EGO IMN OLD PEE TOY UMT TCMP GRS ILE OSH THC UNE UDAY ESY LAB NYT PMW VCJH FSI MSL WADS FOX
IRL IZA IZR IZY URL XIIX TEC YKEN MBO ZAPY

R-44 ASTRO: G-BVMC WVH XKI XPY XUK XUN YCE YKK
CHAP LKE EYET FABI LYZ ODI HALE REH RHS ICAB FTS NDY VIV JANI LATK UKY MURY NTEE ODOC FIL JRH KES LOW MEL PAO PFML OLT
OTT RET RONN OZI TWW SUNY TAND HEL PTS URUH STE WISP YMR XPTS ZONK

ROCKWELL COMMANDER 112/114 - see AERO COMMANDER: G-BDAK DFC DFW DIE DKW DLT DYD EBU EDG ENJ EPY ERI ERW FAI FPO FRA FXS
FZM GBZ HRO HSE IOJ IUO KAY LTK MJL MWR OLT PTG USW VNL CRIL DANT ASH IME ERIC FATB LPI GRIF HILO MBJ PSE ROI IMPX JILL
URG LADS IMA ITE NATT OOR OIBM LFT MUM PADS RCED DCI JCP SAAB TCSL ECH SMI WIZ VICS ZIPA

ROE
TRIPLANE: G-ARSG

ROLLASON - see DRUINE BETA: G-AWHX BADC ETE UPC

ROMAIN COBRA BIPLANE: G-MNLH

ROOSTER - see LIGHTWING

ROTEC RALLY 2B: G-MBAP BAZ BGS BMG JEH JOD JPA VRF YAL

ROUSSEAU - see PIEL

ROTARY AIR FORCE RAF 2000: G-BUYL VSM WAD WAE WHS WTK WWS XAC XEA XEB XGS XKM XMG YDW YIN IRAF TXSE

ROTORWAY SCORPION/EXEC: G-BHHZ JBZ NZL NZO PCM PNC RGX RNP SGV SRP SUR TVF UJZ URP USN VAJ VOY VTV WLY WUJ ESUS FLIT IROY
KENI LUKY MAMC PWH NEEL OJCM PILE URS REID HYS SFOX VCSI YEWS

RUSCHMEYER R90: G-TODE UAPO

RUTAN
COZY: G-BXDO XVX COZI LOAT OGJS SCUL PFX

DEFIANT: G-OTWO

LONG-EZ/VARIEZE: G-BEZE EZY IMX KST KVE KXO LLZ LMN LRH LTS LZM MHA MIM MUG NCZ NUI OOX PWP RFB SIH UPA VAY VKM EEZE
MMY ZOS HAIG IPSY LASS EZE UKE MUSO OMJT OSE PUSH RAEM AFT EZE PEZ SENA TIMB VEZE WILY

RYAN ST3KR/PT-22: G-AGYY BPUD TBH

SAAB
32 LANSEN: G-BMSG

91 SAFIR: G-ANOK BCFW KPY HRLK SAFR

SF.340: G-GNTA NTB NTC NTD NTE NTF NTG NTH NTI NTJ RUNG

SABRE - see SKYHOOK

SABRE (Wing): G-MJDA JFX JIB JMI JNY MNM

SAFFERY: G-BERN FBM HRI IHU INF INU IVT NHP FYGM

SAI KZ.VIII: G-AYKZ

SAN - see JODEL

SAUNDERS-ROE (SARO) SKEETER: G-APOI WSV BJWC KSC LIX HELI SARO

SCALLAN: G-FYEO YEZ

SCHEIBE
SF.23 SPERLING: G-BCHX

SF.24A MOTORSPATZ: G-BBKR

SF.25 FALKE (including MOTORFALKE & SUPER FALKE & SLINGSBY T-61/VENTURE variants): G-AVIZ XEO XIW XJR YBG YSD YUM YUN
YUP YUR YYK YYL YZU YZW ZHD ZHE ZIL ZMC ZMD ZPC ZYY BADH AIZ AKY AMB DZA ECF EGG FPA FUD GMV HSD IGZ KVG LCU LTR LZA
MBZ MVA ODU PIR PZU RRD RWT SEL SUO SWL SWM TDA TRW TTZ TUA TWC TWD TWE UDA UDB UDC UDT UED UEK UFG UFN UFP UFR UGL UGT
UGV UGW UGZ UHA UHR UIH UJA UJB UJI UJX UNB UXJ VKK VKU VLX WTR XAN XMV XWS XXC FEFE HAS KAOM DEY DFF FAN MFMM OWGC

SF.27MB: G-BSUM

SF.28 TANDEM FALKE: G-BARZ YEJ

SCHEMPP-HIRTH
 JANUS CM: G-BMBJ XJS LOAF

 3DM/4DM: G-BPMH MOAK ROAM
SCHLEICHER
 ASK14: G-BKSP SIY

 ASK16: G-BCHT CTI

 ASH26E: G-BWBY DAVT OPHT

SCHWEIZER - see GRUMMAN/HUGHES

SCOBLE GAZELLE - see SOUTHERN MICROLIGHT

SCINTEX - see PIEL

SCOTTISH AVIATION
 BULLDOG: G-ASAL XEH XIG BCUO CUS CUV DOG HXA HXB HZR HZS HZT PCL ULL WIB XGU CCOA

 TWIN PIONEER: G-APRS ZHJ BBVF

SCRUGGS: G-BILE ILG INI INL INM INX IPH ISL ISM ISS IST IWB IWC IWD JEN

SE.5A - see R.A.F./SLINGSBY/REPLICA PLANS

SEEMS - see MORANE-SAULNIER

SEQUOIA - see AVIAMILANO

SERVOTEC - see CIERVA

SHARP & SONS TARTAN (Trike): G-MBDE

SHAW TWIN-EZE: G-IVAN

SHEFFIELD TRIDENT: G-MBNV

SHERRY BUZZARD: G-MMNN

SHERWOOD RANGER - see TIGER CUB RL5A

SHIELD XYLA: G-AWPN

SHORT - see EMBRAER
 S.16 SCION: G-ACUX EZF

 SA.6 SEALAND: G-AKLW

 SC.5 BELFAST: G-BEPS FYU HLFT

 SC.7 SKYVAN: G-BKMD VXW PIGY

 SD.3-30: G-BDBS GNH IOE ITW JLK KIE NTX SBH DACS IOCS LEDN OATD GIL SSWT SSWU

 SD.3-60: G-BKMX LZT MAR NMT NMU NYI PFN PFR VMX CBAC EAL LAS DASI KBAC LEGS OBHD BLK JSY LAH RMCT UBAC VBAC
 ZAPD

SIKORSKY - see WESTLAND
 S-52 - see VERTICAL AVN TECHNOLOGIES

 S-61: G-ATBJ TFM YOY BBHL BHM BVA CEA CEB CLC CLD DIJ DOC EIC EJL EWM FFJ FFK FMY FRI GWJ GWK HOF HOH IMU
 PWB XSN EI-BLY CNL MES SAR

 S-76: G-BHBF HGK IBG IEJ ISZ ITR JFL JGX JVX MAL OND OYF TLA URS UXB VCX VKR WDO XZS YDF CBJB HCD DRNT EWEL HARH
 IJCB OAUS POAH SMAF SSC SSD SSE UKLS XXEA

SIAI-MARCHETTI
 S.205: G-AVEH YXS BBRX FAP VELA

 SF.260: G-BAGB MACH

SIPA 901 series (including SP.903/91): G-AMSG SXC TXO WLG BBBO BDV DAO DKM GME HMA SIPA

SIGMA - see SOUTHDOWN

SIREN PIK-30: G-BMMJ

SKY
 21: G-BYCB

 25: G-BXWX

 31: G-BWOY XVP OSVY

56: G-BWYP

65: G-BWDY WLM WUS XFZ XKO XUS DUNG

70: G-BXZJ

77: G-BWSL XHL XVG XXP CLRK LOWS RCML

80: G-BYBS

90: G-BWKR XGD XJT XJU XLP XPP XVR XWL CLOE VINO ZABC

105: G-BWDZ WJE WOA WPP WUM XCN XDV XIW XVN XXS DONG
120: G-BWIX WJR WPF WPI WYU XDW XLC XWG YEX

140: G-BWHM YKZ

160: G-BWUK WVP XZZ

180: G-BWIW WSF XVL

200: G-BWEL WST XIH

220: G-BWRW XDH EGUY SPEL

240: G-BXUE

260: G-KTKT OLYN

SPECIAL SHAPE:
 FLYING MAP - G-MAPS

SKYCRAFT SCOUT - see WHEELER

SKYFOX CA-25N GAZELLE: G-IDAY

SKYHOOK

 SAILWINGS TR1 (Trike) (including PIXIE): G-MJFX JNU JNY MVS NGH

 SAILWINGS TR2 (Trike): G-MBVW

 SAILWINGS CUTLASS (Wing): G-MBHJ BVW JNH JNU NUI

 SAILWINGS ZEUS (Wing): G-MMVS MNGH

SKYRAIDER: G-BUUS

SKYRIDER: G-BJTF

SKYRIDER AIRSPORTS PHANTOM: G-MJKX JSE JSF JTE JTX JTZ JUR JUX JVX MKX NCS TTN

SKY RANGER: G-MJKB

SKYSALES S-31: G-BDYM

SKYTRIKE - see HIWAY

SLINGSBY MOTOR CADET/TUTOR (including T.7/T.21/T.29/T.31 & CADET III variants): G-AXMB YAN ZSD BCYH DSM EMM MDD NPF ODG
 ODH OKG OOD PIP RTZ RVJ UAC VFS

 T.57 SOPWITH CAMEL replica - see SOPWITH

 T.61A FALKE - see SCHEIBE

 T.67/T.67M FIREFLY - see FOURNIER: G-BIOW IZN JIG JNG JXA JXB JZN KAM KTZ LLP LLR LLS LLV LPI LRF LRG LTT LTU LTV LTW
 LUX LVI NSO NSP NSR OCL OCM ONT ONU OXK UUA UUB UUC UUD UUE UUF UUG UUI UUJ UUK UUL WGO WXA WXB WXC WXD WXE WXF WXG WXH
 WXI WXJ WXK WXL WXM WXN WXO WXP WXR WXS WXT WXU WXV WXW WXX WXY WXZ XKW YBX DLTA EFSM HONG KONG OPUB RAFG SFTZ KYC ZEIN

 NIPPER - see TIPSY

SMAN PETREL AMPHIBIAN: G-GULL

SMD - see SOUTHERN MICROLIGHT

SMITH DSA-1 MINIPLANE: G-BTGJ

SMYTH SIDEWINDER: G-BRVH

SNCAC (AEROCENTRE) NC854/858 (including NORD production): G-BCGH DJR DXX GEW IUP JEL JLB PZD NORD

SNCAN - see NORD/STAMPE

SNIAS - see SUD/AEROSPATIALE

SOCATA - see MORANE-SAULNIER
ST.10 DIPLOMATE: G-AZIB BBTU HOLY

TB.9 TAMPICO/TB.10 TOBAGO: G-BGXC GXD GXT HDE HDT HER HGP HIT HJF HOZ IAK IBA ITE IXA IXB IZR JDT JKF KBN KBV KBW
KCR KIA KIB KIS KIT KTY KUE KVC LCG LCM LYE MEG MYC MZE NDR NIJ NRA OIT OIU PGX RIV SDL THR TIE TWX TZP
CFME ONL OCL DAND EDEN GBHI HZJ MSI OLF HALP ILT IGGL JURE MOOR RTN OFIT FLG PATN HTG OPI RENO SERL ONA TBIO EDS INA
OBA VMJM

TB.20/21 TRINIDAD (including TB.200 TOBAGO XL): G-BLXA LYD NXX PAS PFG PTI RYN SCN TEK TZO XLT XVA YJS CPMS DLOM EGHR
GJA WFN FITI IFI GDGR OOD HGPI JDEE KKDL KES OALD PEKT TRE STNO TANS BXX BZI BZO THZL OAK RIN YNE WERY

SNOWBIRD - see NOBLE HARDMAN
SOKO P-2 KRAGUJ: G-BSXD RADA SOKO

SOLAR WINGS - see ULTRASPORTS/SOLAR WINGS PANTHER
PEGASUS (including PEGASUS/FLASH, PEGASUS/PHOTON, PEGASUS QUASAR & PEGASUS QUANTUM variants): G-BYEU YIZ YDM YDZ YEW
YIS DEAN DINO EDMC MCJL GCD GDL GDM GEF GFK GFO GGG GGV GMC GMT GPD GTG MOH MTC MTR MYA NAN NAO NAR NAU NAW NAX NAY NAZ
NBA NBB NBC NDO NEM NGF NGG NHB NHC NHD NHE NHF NHH NHI NHJ NHK NHL NHM NHN NHP NHR NHS NHT NHU NHV NIK NIU NJH NJJ NJK
NJL NJN NJO NJR NKB NKC NKD NKE NKG NKH NKI NKK NKO NKP NKR NKS NKV NKW NKX NMK NND NNY NNZ NPA NPB NSH NSN NUD NUE NUJ
NUX NVB NVC NVE NVG NVH NVY NVZ NWP NWU NWV NWW NWX NXP NYA NYB NYC NYT NYU NYV NYW NYX NYZ NZA NZK NZL NZO ROC TAA TAI
TAJ TAL TAO TAT TAV TAW TAX TAY TAZ TBA TBL TCG TCH TCK TCO TCR TCX TDG TDH TDI TDP TDS TDT TDV TEB TEC TED TEE TER TES
TET TEU TEW TEX TFA TFB TFE TFM TFO TFP TFR TFT TGJ TGK TGL TGM THG THH THI THJ THN THO TIE TIH TII TIJ TIO TIP TIR TIS
TIU TIV TIW TIX TIY TIZ TJH TJR TJS TKG TKH TKI TKJ TKP TLG TLH TLI TLJ TLT TLU TLV TLW TLY TME TMF TMG TMH TMI TNO TNP
TOA TOB TOC TOD TOE TOF TOG TOH TOI TOJ TOK TOL TOM TON TOO TOP TOR TOS TOT TOU TOW TOX TOY TOZ TPO TPP TPR TPS TPZ TRM
TRN TRO TRR TRS TRU TRV TSN TSO TSP TSR TSS TSU TSV TSX TSY TSZ TTA TTB TTD TTE TTU TTX TTZ TUA TUI TUJ TUK TUL TUP TUR
TUR TUS TUT TUY TVB TVC TVK TVL TVM TVN TVO TVX TWA TWB TWC TWD TWE TXH TXI TXJ TXK TYA TYC TYD TYE TYF TYH TYI TYL TYM
TYN TYP TYR TYS TYT TYU TYY TZI TZJ TZK TZP TZR TZS TZT VAR VAS VAT VAU VAV VAW VAY VBJ VBY VBZ VCA VCB VCL VCM VCN
VCO VCP VCR VCS VCT VCV VDU VDV VDW VDX VDY VDZ VEA VEC VED VEF VEG VEX VEZ VFA VFB VFC VFD VFE VFF VFG VFP VFR VFS VFT
VFV VFW VFX VGN VGO VGP VGR VGS VGT VGU VGV VGW VGY VGZ VHO VHP VHR VHS VHT VHU VHV VHW VHX VHY VIA VJD VJN VJO VJP VJR
VJS VJT VJU VJW VKE VKF VKJ VKK VKL VKM VKN VKO VKP VKS VKT VKU VKV VKX VLM VLX VLY VMA VMB VMC VOE VPR VPS
VPU VPW VPX VPY VRH VRI VRJ VRU VRW VRX VSB VSE VSD VSW VSX VSY VSZ VTA VTG VTI VTJ VTK VUF VUG VUH VUI VUJ VUL VUM VUN
VVK VVM VVN VVO VVP VYB VYC VYD VZJ VZL VZT VZU VZV VZW WAC WAD WAF WAG WAI WAL WAT WAV WBK WBL WCB WCC WCF WCU WCV WDC WDD
WDK WDL WEE WEF WEG WEH WER WFA WFO WFP WFS WGL WGM WGR WHC WHF WHG WHJ WHL WHT WHU WHV WHW WHX WID WIE WIN WIR WIS WIT
WIU WIW WIX WIY WJD WJG WJH WJI WJJ WJK WJN WJO WJS WJT WJU WJV WKO WKP WKY WKZ WLE WLF WLG WLH WLI WLJ WLK WLL WLM WLU
WRO WRP WRT WRU WRV WRW WRX WSD WSE WSF WSG WSH WSI WSJ WSK WSO WSP WSR WTA WTB WTC WTI WTK WTL WTM WTU WUB WUC WUD WUE
WUF WUG WUO WUP WUR WUS WUU WUV WUW WUX WUY WUZ WVA WVE WVF WVM WWA WWG WWH WWO WWV WXG WXH WXI WXP WXR WYB WYC WYI WYJ
WYU WYY WZD WZE WZF WZH WZI WZJ WZO WZP WZR WZS WZT WZU WZV WZW WZX WZY WZZ YAB YAC YAD YAE YAF YAK YBD YBE YBF YBG YBO
YBP YBR YBS YBT YBV YBW YBX YBY YBZ YCE YCF YDI YDJ YEA YEC YED YEG YEH YEK YEM YFJ YFK YFL YFS YFX YGT YGL YGV
YIM YIN YIO YJJ YJK YJS YJT YJU YKP YKR YKS YLC YLE YLH YLI YLK YLL YLM YLZ YMB YMC YMD YMX YNB YNK YNL YNM YNN YNO YNP
YNR YNS YNT YNU YNV YNZ YOE YOU YPF YPG YPI YPN YPX YPY YRF YRM YRN YRS YRT YRY YRZ YSB YSC YSR YSW YSX YSY YTC YTI
YTJ YTN YTR YUH YUO YUU YUV YVC YVJ YVK YVM YVR YWG YWI YWJ YWK YWL YWO YWR YWT YWU YWW YWX YWY YXD YXE YXT YXW YXX YXZ
YYB YYC YYI YYK YYN YYX YZB YZJ YZK YZL YZM YZY ZAN ZAW ZAX ZBB ZBC ZBI ZBM ZBO ZBT ZBY ZCI ZCJ ZCM ZCP ZCR ZCV ZCW ZDB
ZDC ZDE ZDH ZDN ZDU ZDV ZDY ZEC ZEE ZEH ZEM ZET ZEX ZEZ ZFG ZFM ZFV ZGG ZGK ZGN ZGO ZGV ZHH ZHI ZHK ZHN ZHP ZIB ZIC ZIE
ZIF ZIJ ZIK ZIU ZJG ZJH ZJN ZJO ZJT ZJU ZJW ZJY ZKA ZKD ZKF ZKL ZKX ZKY ZLA ZLD ZLF ZLH ZLJ ZLN ZLR ZLT ZLV ZLW ZMA ZMC
ZMF ZMG ZMH ZMN ZMT ZNB ZNG ZNP ZNG ZNS ZNT ZRM ZOD ZOG ZOJ ZOS ZOV ZOW ZPD ZPW ZRC ZRH ZSC OHKS PRSI WHEE

PHOTON (Wing): G-MNNG NXB

STORM (Wing): G-MMUR

TYPHOON (Wing): G-MBCI BCJ BCL BGP BJS BOK BPG BUK JCU JEE JMR JPP JVE MBJ MBZ MCV MDX MKG MKH MLI MPU MTK MUG MUK NCU
NCV NEI NFA NFR NGD NSD NZI ZLK

(Unidentified Wing): G-MBTJ

SOMERS-KENDALL SK.1: G-AOBG

SOPWITH
CAMEL: G-AWYY BFCZ POB

PUP/DOVE: G-EAGA EAVX EBKY ABOX PUP BIAU

TABLOID SCOUT: G-BFDE

TRIPLANE: G-BOCK WRA

"1 1/2" STRUTTER: G-BIDW

SORCERER - see WHITTAKER

SORRELL SNS-7 HYPERBIPE: G-HIPE

SOUTHDOWN
LIGHTNING (Wing): G-MBGX BKC BLU JEY JHC JHR JHZ JIZ JRT JZH MAS MDF MEO MKR MKZ MMI

PIPISTRELLE - see AEROSTRUCTURE

PUMA/PUMA SPRINT (Combi-unit) - see MEDWAY: G-MBZJ BZN JCE JEB JHZ JRT JTR JUE JVN JYT MAO MAR MAZ MBL MCI MCM MCW
MES MGP MHE MHF MII MIR MIV MIW MJD MJM MJT MKD MKV MLV MMD MPG MPH MRN MST MSV MTH MTI MTM MTZ MUA MUJ MUV MVA MVI MVO
MVX MVZ MWH MWI MWX MWZ MXN MXO MXP MYF MYI MYJ MYO MYT MYU MYY MYZ MZR MZW MZX NAV NBE NBH NBM NCI NCK NCL NCP NDG NDP
NDZ NFB NFG NFX NFZ NGR NGS NGX NHL NJD NJG NJS NKU NMC NSB NUM TTK VAF VOS WCR

RAVEN (including MEDWAY) - see <u>HORNET</u> <u>DUAL</u> <u>TRAINER/RAVEN</u>: G-MGOD MRT MVH NFD NJB NJT NKZ NLB NLE NLK NLL NLM NLN NLO NLT NLU NLV NLZ NMD NMU NNA NNB NNC NNN NNO NRP NRS NSL NSW NSX NSY NTC NTE NTF NTG NTM NTN NTO NTY NUH NUT NUU NUW NVN NVP NWA NWG NXA NXD NXE NXF NXG NXI NYG NYI NYL NYM NYP NYS NZW TAP TBB TBK TBN TBO TBZ TCM THC TID TIK TJI TMK TMO TNB TRT TRW TSD TYV TYW TYX VOS YKL YKU YLX YLY YMJ YVU YVW YYO YYZ YZO ZBR ZDJ RAVE

SIGMA (Wing): G-MBDM BLM

SPRINT (Wing) - see <u>PUMA</u>: G-MBST BTF BTG MAJ MDP MHR MKU MLP MMB MOB MRO MRP MSO MTB MTG MTL MTO MTX MUH MUX MXW WTF

WILD CAT (Trike): G-MJUE MDF

<u>SOUTHERN</u>
AEROSPORTS SCORPION: G-MBNH

FLYER: G-MJCN

MICROLIGHT (SMD) GAZELLE (Trike): G-MMGU MPT

MICROLIGHT (SMD) VIPER: G-MMHS

<u>SOUTHERN</u> MARTLET: G-AAYX

<u>SPAD</u> XIII: G-BFYO

<u>SPARTAN</u>
ARROW: G-ABWP

CRUISER: G-ACYK

THREE-SEATER: G-ABYN

<u>SPECTRUM</u> - see <u>MICROFLIGHT</u>

<u>SPEZIO</u> DAL-1 TUHOLER/SPORT: G-NGRM NOBI

<u>SPORTAVIA</u> - see <u>FOURNIER</u>
RS.180 SPORTSMAN: G-VIZZ

<u>SQUIRES</u> LIGHTFLY: G-MNNG

<u>STAAKEN</u> Z-1 FLITZER: G-BVAW FLIZ

<u>STAMPE</u> SV.4A/B/C (including <u>SNCAN</u> & <u>AIA</u> production and <u>BETTS</u> TB.1): G-AIYG MPI SHS TIR WEF WIW WXZ XHC XNW XRP YCG YCK YDR YGE YIJ YJB YWT YZI ZCB ZGC ZGE ZNK ZSA ZTR BAKN ALK EPC EPF HFG HYI IMO KRK KSX LOL MNV NYZ PLM RXP TIO VUG WEF WRE WRS YDK EEUP FORC ORD GMAX HJSS OODE STMP VIV

<u>STARCK</u> AS.80: G-BJAE

<u>STAR-LITE</u> SL-1: G-BUZH FARO SOLA UIDA

<u>STEARMAN</u> - see <u>BOEING-STEARMAN</u>

<u>STEEN</u> SKYBOLT: G-BGRT IMN RIS UXI VXE WPJ KEST SBLT KIE TURN

<u>STEER</u> TERROR (Trike): G-MBNY

<u>STEMME</u> S-10: G-BVYZ XGZ XHR CHLT JCKT ULS OJTA STEM TEN

<u>STEPHENS</u> AKRO (including <u>LAZER</u> 200): G-BMZZ RHZ WKT LAZA RIDE VILL

<u>STERN</u> ST.80 BALADE: G-BWVI

<u>STEVENDON</u>: G-BIWA

<u>STINSON</u>
RELIANT: G-BUCH

HW-75/105 VOYAGER: G-AFYO BMSA

108 STATION WAGON: G-BHMR PTA RZK

<u>STITS</u> SA.3A PLAYBOY: G-BDRL GLZ VVR

<u>STODDARD-HAMILTON</u>
GLASAIR: G-BMIO ODI OVU SAI UBT UHS CINY IIRG KRES SIR LAIR ASR OPNH TRUK

GLASTAR: G-BYEK CBCL LAZZ EZZ STR

STOLP
 SA.100 STARDUSTER: G-BSZG

 SA.300 STARDUSTER TOO: G-BNNA OBT PCE RVB SZB TGS UPB DUST JIII KEEN OTOO UINN

 SA.500 STARLET: G-AZTV

 SA.750 ACRODUSTER TOO: G-BLES UGB

 SA.900 V-STAR: G-BLAF

STRIKER - see FLEXIFORM

STRIPLIN LONE RANGER: G-MBDL BJM

STROJNIK S-2A: G-BMPS

SUD AVIATION - see GARDAN/SOCATA
 SE.3130 ALOUETTE II series (including SA.315 LAMA): G-BSFN SFS SFU VSD LAMA

 SA.321 SUPER FRELON: F-BTRP

 SA.341 GAZELLE (including WESTLAND & SOKO production): G-BAGL CHM KLS XJK XTH XZD XZE EHUP FDAV GAZA GAZI AZZ HTPS LOYD
 MANN OGAZ PAGS YOB SFTA UTZY ZEL WDEV

 SA.365 DAUPHIN 2 (AEROSPATIALE production): G-BKXD LEZ LUM LUN TEU TNC TUX XLL XPA HEMS PLMI

SUKHOI SU-26M: G-SOOK XXVI

SUPER SCORPION - see HIWAY

SUPERMARINE - see VICKERS-SUPERMARINE

SURREY FLYING SVS AL-1: G-AALP

SUSSEX
 Balloon (Gas):
  G-AWOK

SWALLOW AEROPLANE SWALLOW B: G-MJNS

SWEARINGEN SA-227 METRO III: G-BUKA

SZD - see PZL

SZEP HFC-125: G-BCPX

TARJANI (Trike): G-MJCU

TARTAN - see SHARP & SONS

TASK SILHOUETTE: G-ZUMY

TAYLOR
 JT.1 MONOPLANE: G-APRT WGZ XYK YSH YUS BBBB BDN DAD DAG DJB DKU DNC DNG DNO EEW EHM EUM EVS EYW FBC FDZ FOU FRF GCY
 GHY ILZ JMO KEU KHY LDB MAO MET NAR RUO UXL VDE XTC YAV CDGA JIM RIS DIPS RAY SUZY WARD

 JT.2 TITCH: G-AYZH BABE ARN CSY DRG FID GCX GMS IAX IBK KWD VNI EVAN MISS OLE OJON TTAM VIVI

TAYLOR - see AEROCAR

TAYLOR-WATKINSON DINGBAT: G-AFJA

TAYLORCRAFT (AUSTER) - see AUSTER

TAYLORCRAFT - see HOWARD SPECIAL T-MINUS
 BC-12D/BL-65/DF-65/DCO-65 variants: G-AHNR KVO BIGK OLB PHO PHP PPZ PTC REY RIH RIY RPX RXE SCW SDA TFK TMF VDZ VRH VXS
 WLJ

 F-19/F-21/F-22 variants: G-BPJV RIJ VOX WBI

 PLUS C/D: G-AHCR HGW HGZ HSD HUG HWJ HXE IXA

TEAM
 HIMAX: G-MZHM ZIA

 MINIMAX: G-BVSB VSX VYK XCD XSU YBW YFV YII MVXZ WFC WFD WHH WLW WSA WWE WZM YAT YAW YBM YCT YDF YGF YGL YII YIZ YKJ
 YKZ YLB YMG YNI YRG YRL YSK YTA YXA YYR YYS YZE ZCS ZGR ZII ZMO ZNM ZNN ZPJ NADS OSCO THEO

TED SMITH AEROSTAR 601 (including PIPER production): G-MOVE PAMS RIGS TIME

TEMAN MONO-FLY: G-MMJX MPZ

THERMAL AIRCRAFT 104: G-BRAP

THORN COAL GAS BALLOON: G-ATGN

THORP
  T-18: G-BLIT SVN YBY

  T-211 (including VENTURE variant): G-BTHP XPF XPO

THRUSTER
TST: G-DRUM MNWB TGB TGC TGD TGE TGF TGP TGR TGS TGT TGU TKA TKB TKD TKE TLM TLN TLO TLR TNR TNS TNT TNU TNV TNW TPT
TPU TPV TPW TPX TPY TSH TSI TSJ TSK TSL TSM TST TUB TUC TUD TUE TUF TUG TVP TVR TVS TVT TVV TWY TWZ TXA TXB TXC TXD TZA
TZB TZC TZD TZE TZF VAG VAH VAI VAJ VAK VAL VBP VBR VBS VBT VBU VDD VDE VDF VDG VDH VFJ VFK VFL VFM VFN VFO VHI VHJ VHK
VHL VIR VIS VIU VIV VIW VME VMG VMH VMI VOT VOU VOV VOW VOX VOY VXL VYE WDP YWZ

T.300/SUPER T300: G-MGWH VUB VWN VWP VWR VWS VZA VZB VZC VZD VZE VZG VZI WAM WAN WAP WAR WAS WDS WWS WWT YAP YAR YDR
YDT YDU YJF YJG YJH YXU

T.600: G-BYFN FJCE INGE MYWD YWE ZFO ZFP ZFR ZFU ZGX ZGY ZGZ ZHA ZHC ZHD ZHE ZHF ZHS ZHU ZHV ZHW ZHX ZHY ZHZ ZKP ZKR
ZKS ZKT ZKU ZNW ZNX ZNY ZOA ZOB

THRUXTON
  JACKAROO: G-ANFY NZT OEX OIR

THUNDER
  AS-33 Airship: G-ERMS

  0.5: G-BBOD

  Ax3 SKY CHARIOT: G-BHUR JGE JVF KBD KFG KIY NEIL OFOR

  Ax4-31: G-LORY

  Ax5-42: G-BDAY EEP EMU LOV

  Ax6-56: G-BBCP BDJ BOO BOY CCH DVG EEE EJB ERD ETH FOS GPF GWY GZZ HAM HTG HXT IIL IZU JVU KUJ LWB PSJ PUF USY VRI
VUH DICK LDYS IFE RTBI THOM NTN

  Ax7-65: G-BBDJ CCG GST HEU HHH HIS HOO HZX JHT JSW JZC LCY LGX LKJ LTN LUI MHJ TAN TXK BZBH FUND NIGS PIAF RBOW VIVA

  Ax7-77: G-BAIR AWW AXK BOX CAN CAR CAS CIN CNR CSX CZI DGH DGO DMO DON EVI FIX GRS HAT HSP IGF KDK KUU LAD LAH LET LZF
MCC MJS MKV MMU MMW MMY MOG MUU MVT MYS NBL NBV NBW NCC NCU NGO NHO NMX NXZ NZK OAO OIJ ORD OSB PBZ PGF PHU PNU PVU PYK
PYZ RDC RDE RLS ROA RVN RWF RXB RZE SAV SBN SCF SCO SOJ SZH TAU THK TRR TSX TTW TVA TWS UDK UIN UKI ULB UNV UPU UYI VDB
WED GASS GGG HIN HOWE LENS YTE MLWI NEGS OFBJ JDC ONI RDY PIES UFF RAFE IGB INO OCK OSI RSG UBI SFRY OFT THOS USIL WDEB
INE

  Ax8-84: G-BOHF SPB INGA STT OGGS

  Ax8-90: G-BOTE RTT RVY SKI STK STY TJD TPX TRO UJW UXW UYD VDW VGX VKH VLS VWB WKW GEMS HAZE OPS KBKB
OMDD TEL PINE

  Ax8-105: G-BJMW PZZ SCX SFJ TBB THM TTK UBL UBY UEI UYM VGB VPA WJB PUNK THOR OOL ZEBO

  Ax9-120: G-BTMN TOZ TUJ UAT ULK VKZ VSY FABS IOAZ

  Ax9-140: G-BTJO

  Ax10-160: G-BPSI ZBRA

  Ax10-180: G-BTJF TNL TYF UNZ UVZ VUF WLX WUY

  Ax10-210: G-BWUR OLEO

  AX11-225: G-BXAD

  AX11-250: G-BXVF

SPECIAL SHAPES:
  FILM CASSETTE   - G-PHOT
  FORK LIFT TRUCK   - G-BWBH
  ICE CREAM   - G-ICES
  JUMBO JET   - G-UMBO
  WHISKY BOTTLE   - G-RARE

THURSTON TAWNEY OWL: G-APWU

THURSTON TEAL: G-OWET TEAL

TIGER: G-BIMK

TIGER CUB RL5A SHERWOOD RANGER - see MBA: G-GKFC HVAN MWND ZNF WZOL

TIPSY
 TRAINER/B/BELFAIR: G-AFJR FSC FVN FWT ISA ISC PIE POD

 JUNIOR: G-AMVP

 T.66 NIPPER (including COBELAVIA/SLINGSBY production): G-APYB RBG RBP RDY RFV RXN SXI SZV TBW TKZ TUH VKI VKJ VKK VXC
 VXD WDA WJE WJF WLR WLS XLI XZM ZBA BLMW RIK RPM WCT WHR CORD ENIE NIPA TEDZ IPS

TRAGO MILLS - see FLS

TREKKING - see AIRWAVE

TRI-FLYER - see MAINAIR SPORTS

TRI-R KIS: G-BVTA VZD XJI MANW OKIS KMA KPW SKIS TKIS

TRIDENT - see SHEFFIELD

TRION J.1: G-MWHZ

TRIPACER - see ULTRASPORTS

TROTTER Ax3-90: G-BRBT

TURLEY VECTOR - see RAVEN

TURNER SUPER T-40A: G-BRIO

TURNER TSW - see CURRIE WOT

TWAMLEY TRIKE: G-MBGF JWI

TYPHOON - see SOLAR WINGS

UAS SOLAR/STORM BUGGY (Trike): G-MJBS

ULTIMATE AIRCRAFT 10 DASH 200: G-BOFO

ULTRAFLIGHT
 LAZAIR: G-MBYI NRD TDN TFL MVGZ

 MIRAGE:G-MBRH BSX BXX BYT

ULTRAMAGIC H-77/M-77: G-BXPT DWPH VOTE

ULTRASPORTS - see SOUTHDOWN PUMA
 TRIPACER: G-MBAL BBY BDE BFU BLU BPY BTJ BZA JER JFB JFI JHC JHM JHZ JIA JIC JIZ MEO MFL MIJ MMI MMR MPU MUK NGD
 NSD THD ZCL

 ULTRASPORTS/SOLAR WINGS PANTHER (combi TRIPACER/TYPHOON): G-MBZK JIY JPU JWZ JYC MBY MDS MGS MHZ MJF MKA MLX MMN MNX
 MOK MRJ MRK MRL MRR MRZ MSA MSG MSH MTA MTC MTS MTT MUN MVC MVF MWO MYN MZG MZP NAH NAI NAJ NAK NAM NBI

ULTRAVIA
 SUPER PELICAN: G-MWRS

 PELICAN CLUB: G-BWWA

UNICORN: G-BINR INS INT IWJ JGM JLF JLG JSX FYEK

UTVA-66: YU-DMN

VALENTIN TAIFUN 17E: G-BMSE OACE TFUN

VAN'S
 RV-3: G-BVDC

 RV-4: G-BOHW ROP ULG VDI VLR VRV VUN VVS XPI XRV FTUO PIPS RMIT VMJ VRV VANS

 RV-6: G-BUEC UTD VCG VRE XJY XVM XVO XWT XYN XYX YDV YEL
 GRIN HOPY KELL NESI PKJ OJVA NUN TRV REAS IVT VAN VAW VCL VDJ VEE VET VGA VIA VIN VIT VIV VSX VVI SIXY VANZ

VARGA 2150A KACHINA: G-BLHW PVK CHTT DJCR VARG

VAN DEN BEMDEN
 Balloon (Gas): G-BBFS DTU IHP WCC

VECTOR 600/610 - see RAVEN

VENTURE - see THORP

VERTICAL AVN TECHNOLOGIES S-52-3 HUMMINGBIRD: G-BVBD VBO

VICKERS
 FB-5 GUNBUS: G-ATVP

 VIMY replicas: G-AWAU

 60 VIKING replica: (G-EBED)

 V.600 srs VIKING: G-AGRU GRW IVG
 V.668 VARSITY: G-BEDV HDD

 V.700/800 VISCOUNT: G-ALWF MOG OHL OHM OJC OJD OYR PEY PIM ZLP ZLS ZNA ZNC BAPF FZL LOA OPFI PFBT

 V.950/1 VANGUARD/MERCHANTMAN: G-APEK PEP

 VC-10: G-ARVF RVM SGC

VICKERS-SUPERMARINE
 WALRUS/SEAGULL: G-AIZG RNLI

 SPITFIRE (including SEAFIRE variant): G-AIST ISU WII WIJ BJSG KMI MSB RAF RDV RMG RRA RSF SKP UAR UOS UWA WEM XHZ XVI
 YDE CCIX CVV TIX FXII XIV HFIX VDM IXCC LFIX FVB MKIX KVB KXI XVI OXVI PMNF RXI RRGN SPIT TRIX XVIE RK858

 SWIFT: G-SWIF

VICTA AIRTOURER (including AESL production): G-ATCL TEX THT TJC WDE WMI WVG XIX YLA YMF YWM ZBE ZHI ZHT ZMN ZOE ZOF ZRP
 ZTN BANY

VIKING DRAGONFLY: G-BKPD NEV RKY DKGF

VOISIN: G-BJHV

VOLMER
 VJ.22 SPORTSMAN: .G-BAHP

 VJ-24: G-MBBZ

VORTEX - see CHARGUS

VOUGHT F4U CORSAIR: G-BXUL FGID

VPM
 M-14 SCOUT: G-BUEN

 M-16 TANDEM TRAINER: G-BUPM UZL VRD VWX XEJ XIX CVPM NANA POSA YFLY RAT

VULCAN - see HIWAY

VULTURE: G-BICC

WACO
 UPF-7: G-WACO

 YKS-7: G-BWAC

WAG-AERO
 CUBY ACROTRAINER: G-BLDD TWL

 SPORT TRAINER: G-BVMH

 WAG-A-BOND: G-BNJA

WALLBRO MONOPLANE: G-BFIP

WALLINGFORD (WMB): G-BGZN IAI IBX ILB

WALLIS
 WA.116/WA.122 (including BEAGLE-WALLIS & VINTEN): G-ARRT RZB SDY THM TTB VJV VJW XAS YVO BAHH GGU GGV GGW KLZ LIK
 MJX SCAN VIEW TEN

 WA.201: G-BNDG

W.A.R.
 FOCKE-WULF 190: G-BSLX SYFW WULF

 P-47 THUNDERBOLT: G-BTBI

WARD P45 GNOME: G-AXEI

WASP GRYPHON (Wing): G-MBPY JYW

WASSMER - see JODEL
 WA.41 SUPER BALADOU: G-ATSY TZS VEU

 WA.52 PACIFIC/EUROPA: G-AZYZ BTLB

WA.81 PIRANHA: G-BKOT

WATKINSON - see TAYLOR-WATKINSON

WEEDHOPPER
  JC-24: G-BHWH G-MBAD BPW TNK

  JC-31: G-MVXF

WEST Ax3-15: G-BCFD

WESTERN
  20: G-AYMV

  O-31: G-AZPX

  O-56: G-AZUX

  O-65: G-AZBT ZJI ZOO BBCB BUT

WESTLAND - see SUD AVIATION
  LYSANDER: G-AZWT BCWL LIZY

  WS.51 DRAGONFLY: (G-AJOV) BRMA

  WS.51/2 WIDGEON: G-ANLW OZE PTW

  WS.55 WHIRLWIND (including SIKORSKY): G-ANFH NJV ODA PWN YNP YXT YZJ BDBZ EBC JWY KHA VGE RWWW

  WG.13 LYNX: G-BEAD LYNX

  WG.30: G-BGHF IWY KGD KKI ELEC HAUL KATE OGAS

  WS.58 WESSEX: G-ATBZ VNE WOX ZBY

  SCOUT: G-BKLJ WHU WJW WLX XOE XRR XRS XSL CRUM KAXL NOTY ONEB SCTA ROE

  WASP: G-BMIR YCX RIMM

WESTLAND-AGUSTA EH.101 - see EH INDUSTRIES

WESTLAND-BELL - see BELL

WHE AIRBUGGY: G-AXYX XYZ XZA XZB

WHEELER SCOUT (including SKYCRAFT) - see FLYLITE: G-MBAR BBB BOU BRE BUZ JAL NKN NMS

WHEELER SLYMPH: G-ABOI

WHITTAKER
  MW.2B EXCALIBUR: G-BDDX

  MW.4/5/SORCERER (including AEROTECH): G-MBTH MGV NMM NXZ TAS TBP TBR TBS TBT TDK TFH TFN THB TLZ TRX VHM VNN VNO VNP
    VNR VNS VNT VNU WEK WEO WGI WGJ WGK WIC WJW WLN WSX WSY YAH YAN YDL YDW YJZ YRB ZEI ZOH

  MW.6 MERLIN/MW.6S FATBOY FLYER/MW.6T: G-BUOA G-MGCK NMW TMD TRE TTF TXO VPH VPM VPN VTD VTE VXA WAW WHM WIP WLO WOV WPR
    WSW WTS WVI YCA YCP YCU YDM YEF YET YEV YGE YIE YKO YMN YPP YPS YSN YZA YZN ZBG ZBX ZCH ZDI ZDL ZFK ZFS ZHG ZHT ZID
    ZIN ZJP ZNE ZOK ZZZ

  MW.7: G-BOKH OKI OKJ PUP REE RMW SXX TFV TUS WVN

  MW.8: G-MYJX

WILLGRESS GRYPHON - see GRYPHON: G-MBPS

WILLIAMS KFZ-1 TIGERFALCK: G-KFZI

WILLIAMS (WESTWIND): G-FYAN YAO YAU YDI YDP YFJ

WILLS AERA: G-BJKW

WINDSOR: G-BJGD

WITTMAN TAILWIND: G-BCBR DAP DBD DJC JWT MHL NOB OHV OIB PYJ CIPI JBPR PFAD ZIPY

WITTY: G-BJLV

WOLF W-II BOREDOM FIGHTER: G-BMZX NAI

WOMBAT: G-BFYP WBAT

WOOD DUET: G-DUET

WOODS - see AEROSPORT

WSK-PZL - see MIKOYAN

WSK-PZL MIELEC: TS-11 ISKRA: G-BXVZ

X'AIR 582: G-BYCL YHV

YAKOVLEV
YAK 1: G-BTZD

YAK 3: G-BTHD WOE

YAK 11 (including LET production): G-BTUB TZE DYAK IYAK KYAK OYAK

YAK 18 (including NANCHANG version): G-BMJY VFX VVF VVG VVX XZB

YAK 50: G-BTZB VVO WFM WJT WWH WWX WYK XNO FUNK IVAR VLAD YAKA

YAK 52: G-BVMU VOK VVA VVW VXK WFP WOD WSV WSW WVR WVX XAK XAV XID XJB CCCP YAKI AKS AKX AKY KSZ

YAK 55: G-YAKM

ZEBEDEE V-31: G-BXIT

ZENAIR - see HEINTZ/COLOMBAN
CH-600/CH.601/ZODIAC variants: G-BRII RJB UTG UZG VAB VAC VPL VVM VZR OANN MWE ZAIR

CH-701 STOL: G-BRDB TMW XIG YEO FAMH TTDD

ZLIN 226/326/526 TRENER/TRENER MASTER/AKROBAT variants: G-AWJX WJY WSH BEWO EZA IVW KOB LMA PNO UPO EJGO TINY ZLIN LYN

Z.242: G-BWTC WTD OZLN

Z.381 - see BUCKER Bu 181 BESTMANN

Z.50L: G-MATE

SECTION 7 - PART 2 - ALPHABETICAL TYPE INDEX - NON UK

AERO (CZECH) L-29 DELFIN: ES-YLK

AERO COMMANDER 680/685/690/900 (including ROCKWELL/GULFSTREAM production): N71VE N840LE N9143C N91384 VP-BMZ VR-BLK

AERO DYNAMICS SPARROWHAWK: N5832M N8728A

AERO SPACELINES 377GT SUPER GUPPY: F-BTGV

AERONCA
11AC CHIEF/11CC SUPER CHIEF: EI-CCF

15AC SEDAN: EI-BJJ BKC ETC

65CA: N33884

AEROSPATIALE - see SUD AVN
AS.350B ECUREUIL: EI-CGQ IRV

AS.355 TWIN SQUIRREL: N26ET N766AM

AGUSTA A.109: EI-BUX CHV ECA JBC N109TW N133H VP-BQK CCK CHJ CIZ CLA

AIR & SPACE 18A: EI-CNG

AIRBUS INDUSTRIE
A.300B: EI-CEB CJK CPC CPD CPE CPF EAA EAB EAC EAD EAT TLB TLK TLL TLM TLQ TLR TLS F-BVGB BVGC

A.320/A.321: EI-CPC CPD CPE CPF CPG CPH TLE TLF TLG TLH TLI TLJ TLO TLP

A.330: EI-CRK DUB JFK LAX ORD SHN

AMERICAN BLIMP A-60 LIGHTSHIP: N606LG

AMF CHEVVRON: EI-BVJ CAU

ANTONOV
AN-2: D-FOFM HA-MEP MKA MKE MKF LY-ABW ASA N61SL SP-FBO YL-LEU LEV LEW LEX LEY LEZ LFA LFB LFC LFD

AN-124 RUSLAN: RA-82042 82043 82044 82045 82046 82047

ATR
ATR 42: EI-CBF CBK COD CPT

ATR 72: EI-CBD CLB CLC CLD CMJ

AUSTER
5: F-BBSO

J/1 AUTOCRAT & J/1N ALPHA: EI-AGJ AMK AMY AUM F-BFUT BGRZ

J/4: EI-CPN

J/5F AIGLET TRAINER: EI-AUS

AEROMERE (including LAVERDA homebuilts) F.8L FALCO: EI-BCJ BMF

AVIATIKA MAI-890 BABY-MIG: YL-MIG 034 038 039 042 043 069

AVRO
631/643 CADET: EI-ALP ALU

652A ANSON: VH-ASM

748: EI-BSF

BA: SWALLOW 2: EI-AFF

BAC ONE-ELEVEN: EI-BWJ VR-BEA BEB 5N-AOK BAB HTC

BAe BAe 146 (all variants): EI-CLG CLH CLI CLJ CLY CMS CMY CNB CNI CNJ CNK CNQ COF COQ CPJ CPK CPL CPY CSK CSL

BEAGLE-AUSTER
A.61 TERRIER: EI-ASU

A.109 AIREDALE: EI-AYL BAL BBK

B.121 PUP: EI-ATJ HB-NAV

B.206: N181WW

BEECHCRAFT
17 TRAVELER (including UC-43 variant): N18V NC18028

18 (3TM): N96240

23 MUSKETEER/SUNDOWNER: EI-BFF CCA N6632L

24R SIERRA: N23840

33 BONANZA: N1234T

35 BONANZA ("V" tail version - see 33 & 36 variants): N20RJ N150JC N3023W OO-DOL

36 BONANZA: N36NB N36UV N250TP N836TP

T-34 MENTOR: N6251S

55/56/58 BARON: EI-CPS F-GALL N55BN N55EN N79AP N142TW N273TB N773DC N951SF N1012W N2099L N7148R N23659 N60526 OO-FAN

60 DUKE: N80RF N961EL N1024L

70 QUEEN AIR: N70AA

76 DUCHESS: EI-BUN CMX

77 SKIPPER: EI-BHT

90 KING AIR: EI-BHL F-GFLD N190RM N816RL N7775 VP-CCT 5N-ATU

200/350 SUPER KING AIR: EI-WHE N8PY N27MW N86Y N1069S VP-BBK CMA

400 BEECHJET: N79EL N709EL N1565B

BELL P-39 AIRACOBRA: N139DP

BELL HELICOPTERS
206 JET RANGER (including AGUSTA production): EI-BHI BIJ BKT BXX BYJ CAW CLT GHL HER ONE PMI N206NT

206L LONG RANGER: EI-BYR CHL CIO

212: YU-HCE

222: EI-BOR TAR

412: N126NH

430: EI-WAV VP-BKQ

BELLANCA 17-30 SUPER VIKING: N8862V

BENSEN B.7/B.8 GYROCOPTER: EI-BCF BSG

BOEING
247D: N18E

B-17G FLYING FORTRESS: F-BDRS N5237V

707: D2-TOU EL-AJT AKJ HZ-SAK1 N707KS N709PC P4-FDH YN-CCN 5N-ABJ ANO MXX 9G-SGF 9Q-CBW

727: EI-HCA HCB HCC HCD HCI LCH SKY HZ-DG1 N60FM VP-BKC CBQ MMM XT-BBE 5B-DBE

737: EI-BXA BXB BXC BXD BXI BXK BZE BZF BZJ BZL BZM BZN CDA CDB CDC CDD CDE CDF CDH CDS CHH CJC CJD CJE CJF CJG CJH CJI CKK CKP CKQ CKR CKS CLK CLO CLW CLZ CNP CNT CNV CNW CNX CNY CNZ COA COB COH COI COJ COK CON COX CPU CRC CRN TVA TVB TVN

747: EI-BZA

757: EI-CEY CEZ CJX CJY CLU

767: EI-CJA CJB CKD CKE CLS CNS CPV CRD CRF CRL

BOEING-STEARMAN 75 KAYDET (including N2S/N3N/PT-13/PT-17 variants): CF-EQS EI-RYR N75TL N707TJ N768WM N1325M N3922B N4596N N5057V N5345N N8162G N38940 N50755 N53091 N54922 N62842 N63590 N65200 N68200 N68427 N73410

BOLKOW
Bo.102: D-HMQV

Bo.208 JUNIOR (including MALMO): EI-AWR

BRISTOL
149 BOLINGBROKE (BLENHEIM): RCAF 9893 9940

170 FREIGHTER: C-FDFC

175 BRITANNIA: EL-WXA

BRITTEN-NORMAN
BN.2A/B/T ISLANDER (including IRMA production): EI-AYN BCE

BUCKER
Bu.131 JUNGMANN (CASA 1.131): D-EAZO

Bu.133 JUNGMEISTER (including CASA & DORNIER): N40BJ ES1-16

CAMERON
O-25 Airship: OO-JAT

56: EI-BBM OO-ARK

65: EI-BSN BVC

77: C-GYZI EI-CKJ

84: EI-BAY N413JB

90: D-PAMGAS OO-BDO

140: 5Y-SIL

CANADAIR CL.600/601 CHALLENGER: EI-MAS SXT HB-IVR HZ-SJP3 N417CL VP-BCC BCI BIE BLA CAM CIC CPO

CARLSON SPARROW: EI-COO

CESSNA (including REIMS [F.prefix] production)
140: N76402

150: EI-APF AST AVM AWE BAT BFE BHW BYF CDV CHM CIN CML CMV COP N4081J N4232Y N4337K N7263S N7997E N11824

A150 AEROBAT: EI-AUC AUO AYF BRX N7374A

152: EI-BGJ BIB BMM BMN CCJ CCK CCL CCM CGT

A152 AEROBAT: EI-BJM

172/SKYHAWK (excluding R172 HAWK XP/FR172 ROCKET & 172RG CUTLASS variants): EI-AOK AYK BAG BAO BAS BCK BIC BIR BKF BPL BRM N9059H N9694Q N50029

172RG CUTLASS: EI-BPC F-GDPA

R172 HAWK XP/FR172 ROCKET variants: EI-BJI BJO CCV

175/SKYLARK variants: EI-AND N6907E

177 CARDINAL: EI-POD

177RG CARDINAL: EI-BHC D-EASB N177CE

180: N36362

182/SKYLANE variants: EI-AOD BCL BPJ CDP GSM C-FJNU N735CX N735XQ N1745M N9727G OO-VPC

185: N4893K

R182 SKYLANE RG: EI-CAP

190: D-EFTH

195: N995MH

206 STATIONAIR: EI-BGK BNK

210 CENTURION (including TURBO & PRESSURISED variants); EI-AWH BUF CAX CDX CGH N210MP N1778X

T303 CRUSADER: N624TC

305 BIRD DOG (L-19): N33600

310: EI-AOS BEO N3TQ N510PS N6834L

320 SKYKNIGHT: N4173T

335: N2706X

337 SUPER SKYMASTER: EI-AVC BHM N19F N772H

340: EI-CGX CIJ N15FH N25PJ N27BG N56ME N66SW N340AS N340YP N2675Y N2668Z N8618G

401/402 (including BUSINESSLINER & UTILINER variants): N37WC N402R N9146N
414/CHANCELLOR variants: N414FZ

421/GOLDEN EAGLE variants: EI-DWN TCK N5NN N9AY N2657N N2989Q N41098 VP-CLL CPR

425 CORSAIR/CONQUEST I variants: N146GA N425TV VP-BDR BNM
441 CONQUEST II: N999DF

500/501 CITATION 1 variants: N12NM N74PM N145DF N501CF N636N VP-CAT CDM CFG CJB CMO COM CSP

525 CITATION JET: N1280A VP-BZZ CIS

550/551 CITATION II variants: EI-CIR N86BA N112JS N800LA N829CB N841WS N7070A VP-CBE CBM CJR CNM CTE CTF CWM

560 CITATION V: N46WB N311DG N560MM N966SW N2000M VH-FHJ VP-CCV CSC CSN

650 CITATION III: N141M N650J VP-CDW

CFM SHADOW (including STREAK SHADOW): EI-CHR CMF

CHAIZE CS.2200: F-GHOB

CHAMPION (AERONCA) (including BELLANCA)
7AC/7DC CHAMPION: EI-ATL AVB BJB BJC N68556

7EC TRAVELER: EI-BBE BHV

CITABRIA/DECATHLON (including BELLANCA production): EI-ANT BIV BSU BYX

CHRISTEN A-1 HUSKY: N8754J

CIERVA C.30A AUTOGIRO (AVRO 671): G-ACUU CWM CWP

COLT
AS-261: F-GHRI

77: EI-BGT

COLOMBAN MC.15 CRI-CRI: F-PYVA

CONSOLIDATED PBY-5A/6A CATALINA: VP-BPS

CURTISS P-40 KITTYHAWK/TOMAHAWK: 53 Soviet AF ZK-RMH

CVJETKOVIC CA-65 SKYFLY: G-BWBG

CYCLONE AX-3: 59-EE

DASSAULT
FALCON 10: N703JS N991RV

FALCON 50: N159M VP-BSA BSL CEZ

FALCON 100: N45JB

FALCON 900: N352AE VP-BHJ BNJ BPW CGB

de HAVILLAND
DH.80A PUSS MOTH: VH-UQB

DH.82A TIGER MOTH: EI-AHI ANN AOP AWP F-BGEQ VT-DOU DOX DOY DOZ DPA DPB DPC DPH

DH.84 DRAGON: EI-ABI VH-SNB

DH.89A DRAGON RAPIDE: CN-TTO

DH.104 DOVE/DEVON variants: EI-BJW D-IFSB JY-RJU VP-YKF

DH.112 VENOM (including FFW production): J-1626

de HAVILLAND (CANADA)
DHC.1 CHIPMUNK: N70727

DHC.2 BEAVER: OY-JRR

DHC.6 TWIN OTTER: VP-FAZ FBB FBC FBL

DHC.8 DASH EIGHT: EI-CBJ CHP

DEWOITINE D.27: F-AZJD

DOUGLAS
A-26 INVADER: N4806E

DC-3/C-47 DAKOTA: EI-AYO N47FK N47FL N4565L N9050T

DC-8: EI-BNA CGO

DRUINE D.62 CONDOR (including **ROLLASON** production): EI-BCP BXT

DUET: EI-BOX

EIPPER QUICKSILVER: EI-BKS BLE BLN BOH BPP

EKW C-3605: C-558 Sw AF

EMBRAER EMB-110 BANDEIRANTE: N97121

ENGLISH ELECTRIC CANBERRA: N2138J

ENSTROM F-28: EI-BSD N281Q

ERCOUPE 415 (including **ALON/FORNEY** production variants): EI-AUT CGG CIH N3188H

EUROPA AVIATION EUROPA: EI-COE

EUROWING GOLDWING: EI-BNF CMK

EVANS VP-2: EI-BNJ BVT

FAIRCHILD
24/ARGUS: NC1328 NC16676

PT-19/PT-23/PT-26 CORNELL: N9606H N33870 N49272

FAIRCHILD-HILLER FH-227: EI-CAZ CLF

FARMAN F.40: F-HMFI

FIRE BALLOONS GAT/HAFB: D-OPHA

FISHER FP202U KOALA/SUPER KOALA: 50-BH

FLEXIFORM RAPIER 1+1
STRIKER: EI-BPN

TRIKE: EI-BRK

FLEXIWING M17727: EI-BRT

FOCKE WULF FW.189: V7+1H

FOKKER
F-27 FRIENDSHIP (including **FAIRCHILD-HILLER** production): EI-MLA VR-BLX

F.50 (F.27-50): EI-FKA FKB FKC FKD FKE FKF

FOUGA CM-170 MAGISTER: EI-BXO

FOURNER RF-4D: F-BMKC

GARDAN GY-80 HORIZON: EI-AYB

GATES LEARJET: N2FU N12FU N17GL N31UK N125GP N139XX N331SJ N459LJ VR-CRB

GENERAL ACFT MONOSPAR ST-12: VH-UTH

GROB
G-109: EI-HCS

G-115/HERON: EI-CAC CAE CCD

GROPPINO: I-4818

GRUMMAN:
F-6F HELLCAT: N79863

F-8F BEARCAT: N800H

FM-2 WILDCAT: N909WJ

TBM-3 AVENGER: CF-KCG

G.21 GOOSE: N93GS

G-1159 GULFSTREAM II/III/IV/V: A6-HHH EI-WGV HZ-KAA N52N N52NW N252JS N90005 VP-BIS BJV BNZ BUS CBW CBX CMF CNP CRY CUB CYM

GRUMMAN-AMERICAN (including AMERICAN AVN/GULFSTREAM-AMERICAN production)
AA-1 (YANKEE/TRAINER variants): EI-CCY N5644L

AA-5/AG-5 (TRAVELER/CHEETAH/TIGER variants): EI-AYD BJS BMV BNR N31RB N666GA N2121T

GYROSCOPIC ROTORCRAFT GYROPLANE: EI-COG

HANDLEY PAGE H.P.137 JETSTREAM: N14234

HANG-GLIDER: D-NFBU

HAWKER
FURY/SEA FURY: N36SF

  HURRICANE: Z5207 Israeli/RAF

  TEMPEST: N7027E

HAWKER SIDDELEY
HS.125 (including de HAVILLAND/BAe/RAYTHEON HAWKER): EI-COV WDC N125XX N367M VP-BKK BKY BMB BPE BSI CAS CPT

HEINTZ ZENITH (including ZENAIR CH.200/250/300 variants): EI-BVY BYL F-PYOY

HELI ATLAS F-WGTX GTY

HILLER UH-12 (360): N5025J

HIWAY
DEMON (Wing): EI-BPU BRV CGE

  SKYTRIKE: EI-BMW BNH BRV

  VULCAN (Wing): EI-BMW

HOAC DV-20 KATANA: EI-CLA

HOFFMAN H.36 DIMONA: EI-CRV

HOVEY DELTA BIRD: EI-BRW

HOWARD 500: N500LN

HUGHES
269 (Srs 300) (including SCHWEIZER production): EI-LRS VIP

  369 (Srs 500): N252JP

HUNT WING/AVON/EXPERIENCE: EI-CKG

IAI 1125A ASTRA-SPX: N65TD

III SKY ARROW: EI-CPX

ILYUSHIN IL-76: RA-76401 76758 UR-78755

JABIRU: EI-JAK MAT

JODEL
D.9 BEBE (including D.92 variant): EI-BUC

  D.11 (including D.112 & AERO D.1190S variants): EI-BSB CKX EC-AOY

  D.18: EI-CKZ

  D.120 PARIS-NICE (WASSMER): EI-CJS

  DR.1050 AMBASSADEUR (SAN): EI-ARW

KAMOV KA.26: D-HOAY

LAKE LA-4/LA-250 (including BUCCANEER variant): C-FQIP EI-BUH CEX

LATULIP LM-3X: N6FL

LAVOCHKIN LA-11: 20

LEOPOLDOFF L-6: N10LC

LET
L-200A/D MORAVA: OE-FBC

L-410: UR-67199 67477 67519

LETOV LK-2M SLUKA: EI-CNA

LIGHT AERO AVID: EI-CIM

LINDSTRAND
LBL-90: EI-CRB

LOCKHEED

JETSTAR: N6NE

L.100 HERCULES: ZS-RSI

L.188 ELECTRA: EI-HCF N360Q

L.1011 TRISTAR: EI-CNN COL TF-ABP

LUSCOMBE 8 SILVAIRE: N1134K

LUTON
LA-4A MINOR: EI-ATP

LA-5A MAJOR: EI-CGF

McCANDLESS M.4: EI-ASR

McDONNELL-DOUGLAS
DC-9 (including MD-82/83/87 variants): EI-BTX BTY BWD CBO CBR CBS CBY CBZ CCC CCE CDY CEK CEP CEQ CFZ CGI CIW CKM CMM CMZ CNR CPB CRE CRH CRJ VP-BOO BOP

DC-10: EI-DLA

McDONNELL-DOUGLAS HELICOPTERS MD.500N (520N): VP-CDC

MAINAIR
GEMINI/FLASH (Combi): EI-BRH CKT

MERCURY: EI-CMU

MAULE M.7 STAR ROCKET: EI-GER N5632R N5668H

MAX HOLSTE 1521M BROUSSARD: F-GGKR

MBB Bo.105: EI-BLD

MESSERSCHMITT Bf.109 (including **HISPANO** HA.1112): 4 3579 8347 10132 C4E-88

MIKOYAN (including **WSK-PZL** variants)
MiG-15 (LIM 2): 008

MiG-23: 04 50

MiG-27: 23 71

MIL
Mi-2: CCCP-20320 SP-SAY YL-LHN LHO

Mi-24 HIND: 03 06 [3532424810853]

MILES M.38 MESSENGER: VP-KJL

MITSUBISHI
MU.2/MARQUISE: N33EW N747SY

MU.300 DIAMOND: N70XX

MONNETT SONERAI: EI-BMU

MOONEY M.20 (including M.252 variant): EI-CAY CIK N72FG N201XJ N252BH N252RM N909RM N7133J

MORANE-SAULNIER
MS.317: F-BCNL

MS.502: EI-AUY

MS.760 PARIS: N999PJ

MS.880 RALLYE series (including <u>GEMS/SEEMS/SOCATA</u> production): EI-ATS AUE AUG AUJ AUP AWU AYA AYI AYT AYV BBG BBI BBJ BBO BCH BCS BCU BCW BDH BDK BEA BEP BFB BFI BFM BFP BFR BFV BGA BGB BGC BGD BGG BGS BGU BHB BHF BHK BHN BHP BHY BIM BIT BIW BJK BKE BKN BKU BMA BMB BMH BMJ BNG BNU BOP BUJ BUT CEG CFV CHN CIA

<u>MOSKITO</u> <u>2</u>: EI-CJV

<u>NOBLE</u> <u>HARDMAN</u> SNOWBIRD: EI-BUW

<u>NORD</u> 1002 PINGOUIN: LV-RIE
<u>NORTH</u> <u>AMERICAN</u>
 T-6/AT-16 HARVARD (TEXAN) (including <u>CCF</u> production): B-163 D-FABE FAP 1513 Fr AF 114700 MM53432 LN-AMY BNM

 B-25 MITCHELL: N7614C N9089Z N9115Z
 T-28 TROJAN (including <u>FENNEC</u>): F-AZFV N14113 N99153

 P-51 MUSTANG: NL314BG N6526D

 F-86 SABRE: N196B

<u>PIASECKI</u> HUP-3 RETREIVER: N6699D

<u>PARTENAVIA</u> P.68: EI-BWH N997JB

<u>PERCIVAL</u> P.66 PEMBROKE: N46EA

<u>PIAGGIO</u> P.180 AVANTI: N220TW

<u>PIEL</u> CP.301 EMERAUDE (including <u>ROUSSEAU</u> production): EI-CFG

<u>PILATUS</u> PC.XII: N321DH VP-BLS

<u>PIPER</u>
 J/3C CUB (including L-4/O-59 variants): EI-AFE AKM BBV BCM BCN BCO BEN BFO BIO BSX BYY CCH CFO CHK COY CPP CUB N2MD

 J/5A CUB CRUISER: EI-CGV

 PA-12 SUPER CRUISER: EI-ADV CFF CFH

 PA-16 CLIPPER: N5240H N5718H

 PA-18 SUPER CUB (including L-18/L-21 variants): EI-ANY BID BIK CIG CKH MM54-2372 N4085E

 PA-20 PACER: EC-AOZ

 PA-22 TRI-PACER (including CARIBBEAN/COLT variants): EI-AWD AYS BAV UFO N2652P

 PA-23/PA-27 APACHE/AZTEC: EI-BDM BLW EEC WAC N139DB N250MC N6601Y N54211 PH-NLK VP-BBN

 PA-24/PA-26 COMANCHE: N5052P N5092P N7348P N7832P N9381P N9469P

 PA-28-140 CHEROKEE (including CHALLENGER, CRUISER & FLITE-LINER variants): EI-AOB ATK BBC BDR BSO CGP CIV CMB COZ N519MC N7

 PA-28-151/161 CHEROKEE WARRIOR I/II/III/CADET: N45CD N2273Q N2929W N4306Z N43069

 PA-28-180/181 CHEROKEE ARCHER II: N8360Y

 PA-28-236 DAKOTA: N6339U N8471Y OO-MHB

 PA-28R CHEROKEE ARROW (including PA-28RT variants): EI-BGF EDR N2CL N45AW N473BS N4647J N8153E N38273 N43230 N82507 N83196

 PA-30 TWIN COMANCHE: N502TC

 PA-31 NAVAJO: N31NB N61HB N97RJ N27495 N27850 N61422 ST-AHZ

 PA-31-350 NAVAJO CHIEFTAIN: EI-BYE CNM N27597 5N-AVC

 PA-31T CHEYENNE: N80CP N809SW

 PA-32 CHEROKEE SIX/SARATOGA: N47BK N1351H N2923N N2967N N3995W N47914

 PA-34 SENECA: EI-BSL CMT EIO N1172X N2495Q N3036A N3044B N21381 N32625 N80302 OO-JPJ

 PA-38 TOMAHAWK: N5824H N91342 N91457 SE-GVH

 PA-44 SEMINOLE: EI-CCB CHF

 PA-46 MALIBU: N88PL N295SS N666Lp N797HG N9122N

<u>PITTS</u> S-2 SPECIAL: N74DC N80BA N260QB

<u>POLARIS</u> F1B OK350: EI-BXL

<u>PTERODACTYL</u> (<u>PFLEDGLING/PTRAVELER</u>) - see <u>SOLEAIR</u>: EI-BOA

PZL PZL-101 GAWRON: SP-CHD

RAND ROBINSON KR.2: EI-BNL BOV

REARWIN 7000 SPORTSTER: NC14485

REPUBLIC
P-47 THUNDERBOLT: N47DD NX47DD N47DG

RC-3 SEABEE: N6191K

ROBIN
DR.400 series: EI-CRG VP-BNU

R.1180T AIGLON: EI-BIS

R.2112 ALPHA: EI-BIU

ATL: F-GFNO GFOR

ROBINSON
R-22/ALPHA/BETA/MARINER: EI-CFE CFX CMI CPO JWM MAC TKI WCC XMA XMC N5115C

R-44 ASTRO: EI-CPO

ROCKWELL COMMANDER 112/114: N388CA N1350J N1407J N4698W N5834N N6010Y N6039X N6107Y

ROTEC RALLY 2B: N904RE

ROTORWAY SCORPION/EXEC: EI-CMW

RUTAN LONG-EZ/VARIEZE: EI-CMR CPI F-PYYV

RYAN ST3KR/PT-22: N1344 N56421

SAAB 91 SAFIR: SE-BNN

 2000: EI-CPM CPQ CPW

SABRE (Wing): EI-BPT

SCHLEICHER
ASK 14: EI-APS

ASK 16: EI-AYR

SCOTTISH AVIATION BULLDOG: G102 G108

SHORT
S.25 SUNDERLAND/SANDRINGHAM: VH-BRC

SC.7 SKYVAN: VH-WGL

SD.3-30: EI-EXP

SD.3-60: EI-CPR

SIKORSKY
S-70/UH-60 BLACKHAWK: N4050S

S-76: N3CX VP-CHC

SIAI-MARCHETTI
SF.260: N260KH N407FD

SKYFOX CA-25N GAZELLE: VH-YOT

SLINGSBY
CADET III: EI-CJT

T.56 SE.5 replica: EI-ARH ARM

SOCATA
ST-10 DIPLOMATE: EI-BUG

TB-9 TAMPICO/TB-10 TOBAGO: EI-BMI BOE BSK BYG FLY GFC N99ET

TB-20/21 TRINIDAD (including TB-200 TOBAGO XL): EI-BSV N1FD N700S

TBM-700: N79Z N228CX N700JJ

SOKO KRAGUJ: 30151

SOLAR WINGS
 PEGASUS (including PEGASUS/FLASH, PEGASUS QUANTUM variants): EI-BSW CGJ CGM CGN CHT CKU CNU

SOUTHDOWN PUMA: EI-BPO

STAMPE SV-4A/B/C (including SNCAN & AIA production): EI-BAJ BLB CJR N12426 ZS-VFW

STEEN SKYBOLT: EI-CIZ

STINSON
 JUNIOR SR: NC2612

 108 STATION WAGON: EI-CGC

STOLP
 SA.100 STARDUSTER: N40D

 SA.300 STARDUSTER TOO: EI-CDQ N46294

SUD AVIATION
 SA.341 GAZELLE (including SOKO production): YU-HEH HEI HEK

 SA.365 DAUPHIN 2 (AEROSPATIALE production): EI-MIP

SUKHOI
 SU-17B FITTER: 35 54

 SU-26M: RA-44517

 SU-29: RA-01277 01496 01606 01607 01609 01610

 SU-31: RA-01480 01608

SUPERMARINE 228 SEAGULL: VH-ALB

TAYLOR JT.1 MONOPLANE: EI-BKK

TAYLORCRAFT
 BC-65: EI-CES

 PLUS C/D: EI-AGD ALH AMF ANA

TEAM MINIMAX: EI-CGB CNC

TECHNOAVIA
 SM-92 FINIST: RA-44485

 SM-93: RA-44488

TED SMITH AEROSTAR 601 (including PIPER PA-60 production): N60VB N70VB N3839H

THRUSTER
 TST: EI-BYA CKI

 T.300/SUPER T300: EI-CEN

THUNDER Ax8-105: EI-BAR

TRAVEL AIR MODEL 2000: N6268

UTVA-66: YU-DMN

VICKERS
 VIMY replica: NX71MY

 V.700 VISCOUNT: F-BGNR

 VC-10: A4O-AB

VICKERS-SUPERMARINE 304 STRANRAER: CF-BXO

VIKING DRAGONFLY: EI-BPE

VOUGHT F4U CORSAIR: N179PT

VULTEE BT-15 VALIANT: N58566

WESTLAND
 WS.51 DRAGONFLY: N9987Q

 WG.30: N112WG N113WG N114WG N116WG N118WG N5820T N5840T N5880T

 WS.55 WHIRLWIND: VR-BEP BEU

580

SCOUT: 5X-UUW

__WHITTAKER__
MW.4/5/SORCERER (including __AEROTECH__): EI-BUL CAN

MW.6 MERLIN/MW.6S FATBOY FLYER/MW.6T: EI-BVB CJZ CKN CLL COM

__YAKOVLEV__
YAK-11: OK-JIY

YAK-12: LY-FKD SP-FKD

YAK-18: LY-AMI AMJ AOO AOQ RA-01370 44467 44470 44480 44483 44527 00153

YAK-50: 05 05 LY-AOT SE-LBR

YAK-52: 09 20 56 LY-ABQ ABZ AFA AFB AFH AFV AFX AKW ALJ ALN ALO ALS ALT ALU ALZ AMP AMS AMU ANI AOB AOC AOK AOX AOZ
RA-01378 01493 02050 02209 02293 02622 22521 44463 44464 44508 44514 44515 44516 44518

YAK-55: RA-01333 44465 44510

__ZLIN__ 526 TRENER MASTER: EI-BIG

SECTION 7 - PART 3 - INDEX OF AIRCRAFT WEARING MILITARY, OTHER, FICTITIOUS OR NO MARKINGS

In certain circumstances the Civil Aviation Authority may permit the operation of an aircraft without the need to carry regulation size registration letters. These conditions are referred to as "exemptions". The CAA will issue to each operator an exemption certificate which is usually valid for two years. The basic requirements for the issue of an exemption certificate are that the owner undertakes to notify the CAA the markings carried and may not, without specific permission of the overseas country, fly overseas. In the case of aircraft wearing military markings the authority of the relevant department at the Ministry of Defence is required for British markings and the equivalent establishment for overseas military markings.
We set out below details of all aircraft known to be currently wearing military marks including static, BAPC and overseas registered aircraft in the UK. In addition we detail those aircraft who carry no markings at all or fictitious registrations.

Serial	Code	Regn	Type
SERVICE MARKINGS (RAF unless otherwise shown)			
168		G-BFDE	Sopwith Tabloid Scout replica (RNAS)
304		BAPC.62	Cody Biplane (RFC)
687		BAPC.181	RAF BE.2b (RFC)
1701		BAPC.117	RAF BE.2c replica (RFC)
2345		G-ATVP	Vickers FB5 Gunbus replica (RFC)
2882		BAPC.234	Vickers FB5 Gunbus replica (RFC)
3066		G-AETA	Caudron G.III (RNAS)
5964		BAPC.112	DH.2 replica (RFC)
6232		BAPC.41	RAF BE.2c replica (RFC)
A1742		BAPC.38	Bristol Scout D replica (RFC)
A4850		BAPC.176	SE.5A replica (RFC)
A7317		BAPC.179	Sopwith Pup replica (RFC)
A8226		G-BIDW	Sopwith 1+-Strutter replica (RFC)
B415		BAPC.163	AFEE 10/45 Rotabuggy replica
B595	"W"	G-BUOD	SE.5A replica (RFC)
B1807	"A7"	G-EAVX	Sopwith Pup (RFC) (Intended marks)
B2458	"R"	G-BPOB	Sopwith Camel replica (RFC)
B3459	"2"	G-BWMJ	Nieuport 17/23 Repilca (RFC)
B4863	"G"	G-BLXT	SE.5A (RFC)
B6291		G-ASOP	Sopwith Camel (RFC)
B6401		G-AWYY	Sopwith Camel replica (RFC)
B7270		G-BFCZ	Sopwith Camel replica (RFC)
C1904	"Z"	G-PFAP	SE.5A (Currie Wot) (RFC)
C3011	"S"	G-SWOT	SE.5A (Currie Wot) (RFC)
C4451		BAPC.210	Avro 504J replica (RFC)
C4918		G-BWJM	Bristol M.1C replica
C4994		G-BLWM	Bristol M.1C replica (RFC)
C9533	"M"	G-BUWE	SE.5A replica (RFC)
D276	"A"	BAPC.208	SE.5A replica (RFC)
D3419		BAPC.59	Sopwith Camel replica (RFC)
D7889		G-AANM	Bristol F2B Fighter
D8084	"S"	G-ACAA	Bristol F2B Fighter
D8096	"D"	G-AEPH	Bristol F2B Fighter
D8781		G-ECKE	Avro 504K replica (RFC)
E449		G-EBJE	Avro 504K
E2466		BAPC.165	Bristol F2B Fighter
F141	"G"	G-SEVA	SE.5A replica (RFC)
F235	"B"	G-BMDB	SE.5A replica (RFC)
F904	"H"	G-EBIA	SE.5A (RFC)
F938		G-EBIC	SE.5A (RFC)
F943		G-BIHF	SE.5A replica (RFC)
F943		G-BKDT	SE.5A replica (RFC)
F5447	"N"	G-BKER	SE.5A replica (RFC)
F5459	"Y"	G-INNY	SE.5A replica (RFC)
F5459	"Y"	BAPC.142	SE.5A replica (RFC)
F5475		BAPC.250	SE.5A replica (RFC)
F8010	"Z"	G-BDWJ	SE.5A replica (RFC)
F8614		G-AWAU	Vickers Vimy replica
H1968		BAPC.42	Avro 504K replica
H3426		BAPC.68	Hawker Hurricane replica
H5199		G-ADEV	Avro 504K
J7326		G-EBQP	DH.53 Humming Bird (Intended marks)
J9941		G-ABMR	Hawker Hart II
K1786		G-AFTA	Hawker Tomtit
K1930		G-BKBB	Hawker Fury II

Serial	Code	Regn	Type
K2050		G-ASCM	Hawker (Isaacs) Fury
K2059		G-PFAR	Hawker (Isaacs) Fury
K2060		G-BKZM	Hawker (Isaacs) Fury
K2075		G-BEER	Hawker (Isaacs) Fury
K2227		G-ABBB	Bristol Bulldog IIA
K2567		G-MOTH	DH.82 Tiger Moth
K2572		G-AOZH	DH.82A Tiger Moth
K2587		G-BJAP	DH.82A Tiger Moth
K3215		G-AHSA	Avro Tutor
K3731		G-RODI	Hawker (Isaacs) Fury
K4232		SE-AZB	Cierva C.30A (Avro Rota)
K4235	"KX-H"	G-AHMJ	Cierva C.30A (Avro Rota)
K4259	"71"	G-ANMO	DH.82A Tiger Moth
K5054		G-BRDV	Supermarine Spitfire Prototype replica
K5054		BAPC.190	Supermarine Spitfire replica
K5054		BAPC.214	Supermarine Spitfire replica
K5414	"XV"	G-AENP	Hawker Hind
K5600		G-BVVI	Hawker Audax
K5673		BAPC.249	Hawker Fury I replica
K7271		BAPC.148	Hawker Fury replica
K8203		G-BTVE	Hawker Demon I
K8303		G-BWWN	Hawker (Isaacs) Fury
K9853	"QV-H"	G-AIST	Supermarine Spitfire IA
K9926	"JH-C"	BAPC.217	Supermarine Spitfire replica
L1070	"XT-A"	BAPC.227	Supermarine Spitfire replica
L1679	"JX-G"	BAPC.241	Hawker Hurricane 1 replica
L1710	"AL-D"	BAPC.219	Hawker Hurricane replica
L2301		G-AIZG	Supermarine Walrus 1 (RN)
L6906		G-AKKY	Miles Magister
L8841	"QY-C"	G-BPIV	Bristol Blenheim IV
N500		G-BWRA	Sopwith Triplane replica (RNAS)
N546		BAPC.164	Wight Quadruplane replica
N1854		G-AIBE	Fairey Fulmar 2 (RN)
N3194	"GR-Z"	BAPC.220	Supermarine Spitfire replica
N3289	"QV-K"	BAPC.65	Supermarine Spitfire replica
N3313	"KL-B"	BAPC.69	Supermarine Spitfire replica
N5182		G-APUP	Sopwith Pup (RNAS)
N5195		G-ABOX	Sopwith Pup (RNAS)
N5492	"B"	BAPC.111	Sopwith Triplane replica (RNAS)
N6181		G-EBKY	Sopwith Pup (RNAS)
N6290		G-BOCK	Sopwith Triplane replica (RNAS)
N6452		G-BIAU	Sopwith Pup replica (RNAS)
N6466		G-ANKZ	DH.82A Tiger Moth
N6740		G-AISY	DH.82A Tiger Moth
N6797		G-ANEH	DH.82A Tiger Moth
N6847		G-APAL	DH.82A Tiger Moth
N6848		G-BALX	DH.82A Tiger Moth
N6965	"FL-J"	G-AJTW	DH.82A Tiger Moth
N6985		G-AHMN	DH.82A Tiger Moth
N9191		G-ALND	DH.82A Tiger Moth (RN)
N9192	"RCO-N"	G-BSTJ	DH.82A Tiger Moth
N9389		G-ANJA	DH.82A Tiger Moth
P2793	"SD-M"	BAPC.236	Hawker Hurricane replica
P2902	"DX-X"	G-ROBT	Hawker Hurricane I
P3059	"SD-N"	BAPC.64	Hawker Hurricane replica
P3208	"SD-T"	BAPC.63	Hawker Hurricane replica
P3386	"FT-I"	BAPC.218	Hawker Hurricane replica
P6382	"C"	G-AJRS	Miles Magister
P7350	"BA-Y"	G-AWIJ	Vickers Supermarine 329 Spitfire F.IIA
P8140	"ZF-K"	BAPC.71	Supermarine Spitfire replica
P8448	"UM-D"	BAPC.225	Supermarine Spitfire replica
R1914		G-AHUJ	Miles Magister
R4897		G-ERTY	DH.82A Tiger Moth
R4959	"59"	G-ARAZ	DH.82A Tiger Moth
S1287	"5"	G-BEYB	Fairey Flycatcher replica (FAA)
S1579	"571"	G-BBVO	Hawker Nimrod (Isaacs Fury) (RN)
T5424		G-AJOA	DH.82A Tiger Moth
T5672		G-ALRI	DH.82A Tiger Moth
T5854		G-ANKK	DH.82A Tiger Moth
T5879		G-AXBW	DH.82A Tiger Moth
T6066		G-ANJK	DH.82A Tiger Moth
T6313		G-AHVU	DH.82A Tiger Moth
T6390		G-ANIX	DH.82A Tiger Moth
T6818	"91"	G-ANKT	DH.82A Tiger Moth
T6953		G-ANNI	DH.82A Tiger Moth

Serial	Code	Regn	Type
T6991		G-ANOR	DH.82A Tiger Moth
T7230		G-AFVE	DH.82A Tiger Moth
T7245		G-ANEJ	DH.82A Tiger Moth
T7281		G-ARTL	DH.82A Tiger Moth
T7404	"04"	G-ANMV	DH.82A Tiger Moth
T7471		G-AJHU	DH.82A Tiger Moth
T7842		G-AMTF	DH.82A Tiger Moth
T7909		G-ANON	DH.82A Tiger Moth
T7997		G-AHUF	DH.82A Tiger Moth
T9707		G-AKKR	Miles Magister
T9738		G-AKAT	Miles Magister
V1075		G-AKPF	Miles Magister
V3388		G-AHTW	Airspeed Oxford 1
V7476	"LE-D"	BAPC.223	Hawker Hurricane replica
V7767		BAPC.72	Hawker Hurricane replica
V6028	"GB-D"	G-MKIV	Bristol Blenheim IV
V9441	"AR-A"	G-AZWT	Westland Lysander IIIA
V9545	"BA-C"	G-BCWL	Westland Lysander IIIA
V9673	"MA-J"	G-LIZY	Westland Lysander III
W2718	"AA5Y"	G-RNLI	Supermarine Walrus (RN)
W5856	"A2A"	G-BMGC	Fairey Swordfish II
W9385	"YG-L"	G-ADND	DH.87B Hornet Moth
Z2033	"N/275"	G-ASTL	Fairey Firefly TT.1
Z3781	"XR-T"	G-HURI	Hawker Hurricane IIB
Z5053		G-BWHA	Hawker Hurricane IIB
Z5252	"GO-B"	G-BWHA	Hawker Hurricane IIB
Z7015	"7-L"	G-BKTH	Hawker Sea Hurricane IB (RN)
Z7197		G-AKZN	Percival Proctor III
AA908	"UM-W"	BAPC.230	Supermarine Spitfire replica
AB910	"ZD-C"	G-AISU	Vickers Supermarine 349 Spitfire LF.VB
AE977		G-TWTD	Hawker Sea Hurricane X
AP507	"KX-P"	G-ACWP	Cierva C.30A (Avro Rota)
AR213	"PR-D"	G-AIST	Supermarine Spitfire IA
AR501	"NN-A"	G-AWII	Supermarine Spitfire Vc
AR614	"DU-Z"	G-BUWA	Supermarine Spitfire Vc
BB807		G-ADWO	DH.82A Tiger Moth
BE417	"AE-K"	G-HURR	Hawker Hurricane IIB
BE421	"XP-G"	BAPC.205	Hawker Hurricane replica
BL924	"AZ-G"	BAPC.242	Supermarine Spitfire VB replica
BM597	"JH-C"	G-MKVB	Supermarine Spitfire VB
BR600	"SH-V"	BAPC.222	Supermarine Spitfire replica
BR600	"JP-A"	BAPC.224	Supermarine Spitfire replica
(NOTE: Another "BR600" Spitfire replica was in open storage Dunkeswell 11.95)			
BW881		G-KAMM	Hawker Hurricane XIIA
CB733		G-BCUV	Scottish Bulldog
DE208		G-AGYU	DH.82A Tiger Moth
DE470	"16"	G-ANMY	DH.82A Tiger Moth
DE623		G-ANFI	DH.82A Tiger Moth
DE673		G-ADNZ	DH.82A Tiger Moth
DE970		G-AOBJ	DH.82A Tiger Moth
DE992		G-AXXV	DH.82A Tiger Moth
DF112		G-ANRM	DH.82A Tiger Moth
DF128	"RCO-U"	G-AOJJ	DH.82A Tiger Moth
DF155		G-ANFV	DH.82A Tiger Moth
DG590		G-ADMW	Miles Hawk Major
DR613		G-AFJB	Foster-Wikner Wicko (Warferry)
DR628		N18V	Beechcraft Traveler
EM720		G-AXAN	DH.82A Tiger Moth
EN224		G-FXII	Supermarine Spitfire XII
EN343		BAPC.226	Supermarine Spitfire replica
EN398	"WO-A"	BAPC.184	Supermarine Spitfire IX replica
EP120	"AE-A"	G-LFVB	Supermarine Spitfire VB
FB226	"MT-A"	G-BDWM	N-A Mustang (Bonsall Mustang)
FE695	"94"	G-BTXI	N-A Harvard IIB
FE905		LN-BNM	N-A Harvard IIB
FE992	"K-T"	G-BDAM	N-A Harvard IIB
FH153		G-BBHK	N-A Harvard IIB
FJ777		G-BRTK	Boeing-Stearman Kaydet
FJ992		G-BPTB	Boeing-Stearman Kaydet
FR886		G-BDMS	Piper Cub
FT239		G-BIWX	N-A Harvard IV
FT323	"GN"	FAP 1513	N-A Harvard III
FT375		G-BWUL	N-A Harvard IIB
FT391		G-AZBN	N-A Harvard IIB
FX301	"FD-NQ"	G-JUDI	N-A Harvard III
HB275		G-BKGM	Beechcraft Expeditor
HB751		G-BCBL	Fairchild Argus III
HM580		G-ACUU	Cierva C.30A (Avro Rota)

Serial	Code	Regn	Type
KB889	"NA-I"	G-LANC	Avro Lancaster X
KD345	"130"	G-FGID	Vought FG-1D Corsair (RN)
KG391	"AG"	G-BVOL	Douglas Dakota III
KJ351		BAPC.80	Airspeed Horsa II
KL161	"VO-B"	N88972	N-A B-25D Mitchell II
LB312		G-AHXE	Taylorcraft Plus D (Auster I)
LB375		G-AHGW	Taylorcraft Plus D (Auster I)
LF789		BAPC.186	DH.82B Queen Bee
LF858		G-BLUZ	DH.82B Queen Bee
LS326	"L/2"	G-AJVH	Fairey Swordfish II
LZ766		G-ALCK	Percival Proctor III
MAV467	"R-O"	BAPC.202	Supermarine Spitfire V replica
MH434	"PK-K"	G-ASJV	Supermarine Spitfire IXB
MH486	"FF-A"	BAPC.206	Supermarine Spitfire replica
MH777	"RF-N"	BAPC.221	Supermarine Spitfire replica
MJ627	"9G-P"	G-BMSB	Supermarine Spitfire T.IX
MJ730	"GZ-?"	G-HFIX	Supermarine Spitfire IXE
MJ751	"DU-V"	BAPC.209	Supermarine Spitfire replica
MJ832	"DN-Y"	BAPC.229	Supermarine Spitfire replica
MK732	"OU-U"	G-HVDM	Supermarine Spitfire IXC
MK805	"SH-B"	(see note)	Supermarine Spitfire IX replica

(This was built by TDL replica Aircraft, in 64 Sqn c/s as "SH-B/"Peter John III")

Serial	Code	Regn	Type
MK912	"MN-P"	G-BRRA	Supermarine Spitfire IX
ML407	"OU-V"/"NL-D"	G-LFIX	Supermarine Spitfire T.IX
ML417	"2I-T"	G-BJSG	Supermarine Spitfire IXC
MP425		G-AITB	Airspeed Oxford I
MT438		G-AREI	Auster III
MT928	"ZX-M"	G-BKMI	Supermarine Spitfire VIIIC
MV262		G-CCVV	Supermarine Spitfire XIV (Intended marks)
MV293	"OI-C"	G-SPIT	Supermarine Spitfire XIVE
MV370	"EB-Q"	G-FXIV	Supermarine Spitfire XIV
MW763	"HF-A"	G-TEMT	Hawker Tempest II
MW800	"HF-V"	G-BSHW	Hawker Tempest II
NH238	"D-A"	G-MKIX	Supermarine Spitfire IX
NJ673		G-AOCR	Auster V
NJ695		G-AJXV	Auster IV
NJ703		G-AKPI	Auster V
NJ719		G-ANFU	Auster V (Intended marks)
NL750		G-AOBH	DH.82A Tiger Moth
NL785		G-BWIK	DH.82A Tiger Moth
NM181		G-AZGZ	DH.82A Tiger Moth
NS519		G-MOSI	DH.98 Mosquito 35 (RAF/USAAF)
NX534		G-BUDL	Auster III
NX611	"LE-C/DX-C"	G-ASXX	Avro Lancaster B.VII
PL344	"Y2-B"	G-IXCC	Supermarine Spitfire IXE
PL965	"R"	G-MKXI	Supermarine Spitfire PR.XI
PL983		G-PRXI	Supermarine Spitfire XI
PP972		G-BUAR	Supermarine Seafire III (Intended marks)
PR772		G-BTTA	Hawker Iraqi Fury
PS853	"C"	G-RRGN	Supermarine Spitfire PR.XIX
PV202	"5R-Q"	G-TRIX	Supermarine Spitfire T.IX
PZ865	"Q"	G-AMAU	Hawker Hurricane IIc
RG333		G-AIEK	Miles Messenger
RG333		G-AKEZ	Miles Messenger
RM221		G-ANXR	Percival Proctor IV
RN201		G-BSKP	Supermarine Spitfire XIV (Intended marks)
RN218	"N"	G-BBJI	Isaacs Spitfire
RR232		G-BRSF	Supermarine Spitfire IXC
RT486	"PF-A"	G-AJGJ	Auster 5
RT610		G-AKWS	Auster 5A
RX168		G-BWEM	Supermarine Seafire L.III (Intended marks)
SM520		G-BXHZ	Supermarine Spitfire HF.IX
SM832	"YB-A"	G-WWII	Supermarine Spitfire F.XIV
SM845		G-BUOS	Supermarine Spitfire XVIIIE (Intended marks)
SM969	"D-A"	G-BRAF	Supermarine Spitfire XVIII
SX336		G-BRMG	Supermarine Seafire XVII
TA634	"8K-K"	G-AWJV	DH.98 Mosquito TT.35
TA719	"6T"	G-ASKC	DH.98 Mosquito TT.35
TA805		G-PMNF	Supermarine Spitfire IX
TB252	"GW-H"	G-XVIE	Supermarine Spitfire XVIE
TD248	"D"	G-OXVI	Supermarine Spitfire XVIE
TE184		G-MXVI	Supermarine Spitfire XVIE
TE517		G-CCIX	Supermarine Spitfire IXE (Intended marks)
TE566	"DU-A"	G-BLCK	Supermarine Spitfire IXE (Czech c/s)
TJ398		BAPC.70	Auster V
TJ565		G-AMVD	Auster V
TJ569		G-AKOW	Auster V
TJ672		G-ANIJ	Auster V

Serial	Code	Regn	Type
TJ704	"JA"	G-ASCD	Auster AOP.6 (RN)
TS291		BGA.852	Slingsby Tutor
TS423	"YS-L"	G-DAKS	Douglas Dakota III
TS798		G-AGNV	Avro 685 York C.1
TW439		G-ANRP	Auster V
TW467	"ROD-F"	G-ANIE	Auster V
TW511		G-APAF	Auster V (Army)
TW536	"TS-V"	G-BNGE	Auster AOP.6
TW591		G-ARIH	Auster AOP.6 (Army)
TW641		G-ATDN	Auster AOP.6
TX183		G-BSMF	Avro Anson C.19
VF512	"PF-M"	G-ARRX	Auster AOP.6
VF516		G-ASMZ	Auster AOP.6
VF526	"T"	G-ARXU	Auster AOP.6 (Army)
VF548		G-ASEG	Auster AOP.6
VF581		G-ARSL	Auster AOP.6
VL348		G-AVVO	Avro Anson C.19/2
VL349		G-AWSA	Avro Anson C.19/2
VM360		G-APHV	Avro Anson C.19/2
VP955		G-DVON	DH.104 Devon C.2/2
VR192		G-APIT	Percival Prentice T.1
VR249	"FA-EL"	G-APIY	Percival Prentice T.1
VR259	"M"	G-APJB	Percival Prentice T.1
VS356		G-AOLU	Percival Prentice T.1
VS610	"K-L"	G-AOKL	Percival Prentice T.1
VT871		G-DHXX	DH.100 Vampire FB.6
VX118		G-ASNB	Auster AOP.6
VX147		G-AVIL	Ercoupe 415
VX926		G-ASKJ	Auster AOP.6
VZ345		D-CATA	Hawker Sea Fury T.20 (RN)
VZ467	"A"	G-METE	Gloster Meteor F.8
VZ638	"HF"	G-JETM	Gloster Meteor T.7 (RN)
VZ728		G-AGOS	Reid & Sigrist Bobsleigh
WA591		G-BWMF	Gloster Meteor T.7 (Intended marks)
WB531		G-BLRN	DH.104 Devon C.2/2
WB533		G-DEVN	DH.104 Devon C.2/2
WB565	"X"	G-PVET	DHC.1 Chipmunk T.10 (Army)
WB571	"34"	G-AOSF	DHC.1 Chipmunk T.10
WB585	"RCU-X"	G-AOSY	DHC.1 Chipmunk T.10
WB588	"D"	G-AOTD	DHC.1 Chipmunk T.10
WB615		G-BXIA	DHC.1 Chipmunk T.10
WB652		G-CHPY	DHC.1 Chipmunk T.10
WB654		G-BXGO	DHC.1 Chipmunk T.10
WB660		G-ARMB	DHC.1 Chipmunk T.10
WB671		G-BWTG	DHC.1 Chipmunk T.10
WB697		G-BXCT	DHC.1 Chipmunk T.10
WB702		G-AOFE	DHC.1 Chipmunk T.10
WB703		G-ARMC	DHC.1 Chipmunk T.10
WB711		G-APPM	DHC.1 Chipmunk T.10
WB726	"E"	G-AOSK	DHC.1 Chipmunk T.10
WB763	"14"	G-BBMR	DHC.1 Chipmunk T.10
WD286	"J"	G-BBND	DHC.1 Chipmunk T.10
WD288		G-AOSO	DHC.1 Chipmunk T.10
WD292		G-BCRX	DHC.1 Chipmunk T.10
WD305		G-ARGG	DHC.1 Chipmunk T.10
WD310		G-BWUN	DHC.1 Chipmunk T.10
WD331		G-BXDH	DHC.1 Chipmunk T.10
WD363		G-BCIH	DHC.1 Chipmunk T.10
WD373	"12"	G-BXDI	DHC.1 Chipmunk T.10
WD379	"K"	G-APLO	DHC.1 Chipmunk T.10
WD390		G-BWNK	DHC.1 Chipmunk T.10
WD413		G-BFIR	Avro Anson C.21
WE402		G-VENI	DH.112 Venom FB.1
WE569		G-ASAJ	Beagle Terrier (Auster T.7)
WF877		G-BPOA	Gloster Meteor T.7
WG307		G-BCYJ	DHC.1 Chipmunk T.10
WG316		G-BCAH	DHC.1 Chipmunk T.10
WG321		G-DHCC	DHC.1 Chipmunk T.10
WG348		G-BBMV	DHC.1 Chipmunk T.10
WG350		G-BPAL	DHC.1 Chipmunk T.10
WG407	"67"	G-BWMX	DHC.1 Chipmunk T.10
WG422		G-BFAX	DHC.1 Chipmunk T.10
WG465		G-BCEY	DHC.1 Chipmunk T.10
WG469		G-BWJY	DHC.1 Chipmunk T.10
WG472		G-AOTY	DHC.1 Chipmunk T.10
WG719	"705"	G-BRMA	Westland Dragonfly HR.5
WG754	"912/CU"	N9987Q	Westland Dragonfly HR.5
WJ237	"113/0"	G-BLTG	Hawker (WAR) Sea Fury replica (RN)

Serial	Code	Regn	Type
WJ358		G-ARYD	Auster AOP.6
WJ680	"CT"	G-BURM	EE Canberra TT.18
WJ945	"21"	G-BEDV	Vickers Varsity T.1
WK126	"843"	N2138J	EE Canberra TT.18
WK163		G-BVWC	EE Canberra B.2(mod)
WK511		G-BVBT	DHC.1 Chipmunk T.10 (RN)
WK512	"A"	G-BXIM	DHC.1 Chipmunk T.10 (Army)
WK517		G-ULAS	DHC.1 Chipmunk T.10
WK522		G-BCOU	DHC.1 Chipmunk T.10
WK549		G-BTWF	DHC.1 Chipmunk T.10
WK586	"V"	G-BXGX	DHC.1 Chipmunk T.10 (Army)
WK590	"69"	G-BWVZ	DHC.1 Chipmunk T.10
WK609		G-BXDN	DHC.1 Chipmunk T.10
WK611		G-ARWB	DHC.1 Chipmunk T.10
WK622		G-BCZH	DHC.1 Chipmunk T.10
WK624	"M"	G-BWHI	DHC.1 Chipmunk T.10
WK628		G-BBMW	DHC.1 Chipmunk T.10
WK630		G-BXDG	DHC.1 Chipmunk T.10
WK633		G-BXEC	DHC.1 Chipmunk T.10
WK638	"83"	G-BWJZ	DHC.1 Chipmunk T.10
WK640	"C"	G-BWUV	DHC.1 Chipmunk T.10
WK642		G-BXDP	DHC.1 Chipmunk T.10
WL505		G-FBIX	DH.100 Vampire FB.9
WL505		G-MKVI	DH.100 Vampire FB.6
WL626	"P"	G-BHDD	Vickers Varsity T.1
WM167	"M"	G-LOSM	AW Meteor NF.11
WP321	"750/CU"	G-BRFC	Hunting Sea Prince T.1 (RN)
WP788		G-BCHL	DHC.1 Chipmunk T.10
WP790	"T"	G-BBNC	DHC.1 Chipmunk T.10
WP795	"901"	G-BVZZ	DHC.1 Chipmunk T.10 (RN)
WP800	"2"	G-BCXN	DHC.1 Chipmunk T.10
WP803		G-HAPY	DHC.1 Chipmunk T.10
WP808		G-BDEU	DHC.1 Chipmunk T.10
WP809	"778"	G-BVTX	DHC.1 Chipmunk T.10 (RN)
WP840		G-BXDM	DHC.1 Chipmunk T.10
WP843	"F"	G-BDBP	DHC.1 Chipmunk T.10
WP844		G-BWOX	DHC.1 Chipmunk T.10
WP851		G-BDET	DHC.1 Chipmunk T.10
WP856	"904"	G-BVWP	DHC.1 Chipmunk T.10 (RN)
WP857	"24"	G-BDRJ	DHC.1 Chipmunk T.10
WP859		G-BXCP	DHC.1 Chipmunk T.10
WP860	"6"	G-BXDA	DHC.1 Chipmunk T.10
WP896	"M"	G-BWVY	DHC.1 Chipmunk T.10
WP901		G-BWNT	DHC.1 Chipmunk T.10
WP903		G-BCGC	DHC.1 Chipmunk T.10 (Queens Flight)
WP920		G-BXCR	DHC.1 Chipmunk T.10
WP925	"C"	G-BXHA	DHC.1 Chipmunk T.10
WP928		G-BXGM	DHC.1 Chipmunk T.10
WP929	"F"	G-BXCV	DHC.1 Chipmunk T.10
WP930		G-BXHF	DHC.1 Chipmunk T.10
WP971		G-ATHD	DHC.1 Chipmunk T.10
WP977		G-BHRD	DHC.1 Chipmunk T.10
WP983		G-BXNN	DHC.1 Chipmunk T.10
WP984	"H"	G-BWTO	DHC.1 Chipmunk T.10
WR410	"N"	G-BLKA	DH.112 Venom FB.4
WR410		G-DHUU	DH.112 Venom FB.1
WR421		G-DHTT	DH.112 Venom FB.1
WT327		G-BXMO	EE Canberra B.6
WT333		G-BVXC	EE Canberra B(I).8
WT722	"878"	G-BWGN	Hawker Hunter T.8C (RN)
WV198	"K"	G-BJWY	Sikorsky Whirlwind HAR.21
WV318		G-FFOX	Hawker Hunter T.7B
WV372	"R"	G-BXFI	Hawker Hunter T.7
WV493	"29"/"A-P"	G-BDYG	Percival Provost T.1
WV494	"04"	G-BGSB	Percival Provost T.1
WV666	"O-D"	G-BTDH	Percival Provost T.1
WV740		G-BNPH	Hunting Percival Pembroke C.1
WW453	"W-S"	G-TMKI	Percival Provost T.1
WZ507		G-VTII	DH.115 Vampire T.11
WZ553	"40"	G-DHYY	DH.115 Vampire T.11
WZ589		G-DHVV	DH.115 Vampire T.11
WZ662		G-BKVK	Auster AOP.9 (Army)
WZ706		G-BURR	Auster AOP.9 (Army)
WZ711		G-AVHT	Auster AOP.9 (Army)
WZ729		G-BXON	Auster AOP.9
WZ847		G-CPMK	DHC.1 Chipmunk T.10
WZ868	"H"	G-ARMF	DHC.1 Chipmunk T.10
WZ868	"H"	G-BCIW	DHC.1 Chipmunk T.10 (wreck)

Serial	Code	Regn	Type
WZ879	"73"	G-BWUT	DHC.1 Chipmunk T.10
WZ882		G-BXGP	DHC.1 Chipmunk T.10
WZ884		G-BXGL	DHC.1 Chipmunk T.10
XA880		G-BVXR	DH.104 Devon C.2 (RAE)
XD693	"Z-Q"	G-AOBU	Percival Jet Provost T.1
XE665	"876"	G-BWGM	Hawker Hunter T.8C (RN)
XE677		G-HHUN	Hawker Hunter F.4
XE685	"861/VL"	G-GAII	Hawker Hunter GA.11 (RN)
XE689	"864/VL"	G-BWGK	Hawker Hunter GA.11 (RN)
XE920	"D"	G-VMPR	DH.115 Vampire T.11
XE956		G-OBLN	DH.115 Vampire T.11
XF114		G-SWIF	Supermarine Swift F.7
XF357	"871"	G-BWGL	Hawker Hunter T.8C (RN)
XF375	"05"	G-BUEZ	Hawker Hunter F.6A
XF515	"C"	G-KAXF	Hawker Hunter F.6A
XF516	"F"	G-BVVC	Hawker Hunter F.6A
XF597	"AH"	G-BKFW	Percival Provost T.1
XF603	"H"	G-KAPW	Percival Provost T.1
XF690		G-MOOS	Percival Provost T.1
XF836	"J-G"	G-AWRY	Percival Provost T.1
XF877	"J-X"	G-AWVF	Percival Provost T.1
XG160	"U"	G-BWAF	Hawker Hunter F.6A
XG232		G-BWIU	Hawker Hunter F.6
XG452		G-BRMB	Bristol Belvedere HC.1
XG547	"T-S/S-T"	G-HAPR	Bristol Sycamore HR.14
XG775	"VL"	G-DHWW	DH.115 Vampire T.11 (RN)
XH558		G-VLCN	Avro Vulcan B.2
XH568		G-BVIC	English Electric Canberra B.2/B.6
XJ347		G-AMXT	DH.104 Sea Devon C.20
XJ348		G-NAVY	DH.104 Sea Devon C.20 (RN)
XJ729		G-BVGE	Westland Whirlwind HAR.10
XJ763	"P"	G-BKHA	Westland Whirlwind HAR.10
XK416		G-AYUA	Auster AOP.9
XK417		G-AVXY	Auster AOP.9
XK895	"CU-19"	G-SDEV	DH.104 Sea Devon C.20 (RN)
XK896		G-RNAS	DH.104 Sea Devon C.20 (RN)
XK940		G-AYXT	Westland Whirlwind HAS.7
XL426		G-VJET	Avro Vulcan B.2
XL502		G-BMYP	Fairey Gannet AEW.3 (RN)
XL572	"83"	G-HNTR	Hawker Hunter T.7
XL573		G-BVGH	Hawker Hunter T.7
XL577		G-BXKF	Hawker Hunter T.7
XL602		G-BWFT	Hawker Hunter T.8M
XL613		G-BVMB	Hawker Hunter T.7A
XL616	"D"	G-BWIE	Hawker Hunter T.7A
XL621		G-BNCX	Hawker Hunter T.7
XL714		G-AOGR	DH.82A Tiger Moth
XL809		G-BLIX	Saro Skeeter AOP.12
XL812		G-SARO	Saro Skeeter AOP.12
XL929		G-BNPU	Hunting Percival Pembroke C.1
XL954		G-BXES	Hunting Percival Pembroke C.1
XM223		G-BWWC	DH.104 Devon C.2
XM365		G-BXBH	Hunting Jet Provost T.3A
XM370		G-BVSP	Hunting Jet Provost T.3A
XM376	"27"	G-BWDR	Hunting Jet Provost T.3A
XM378		G-BWZE	Hunting Jet Provost T.3A
XM405		G-TORE	Hunting Jet Provost T.3A
XM424		G-BWDS	Hunting Jet Provost T.3A
XM470		G-BWZZ	Hunting Jet Provost T.3
XM478		G-BXDL	Hunting Jet Provost T.3A
XM479	"54"	G-BVEZ	Hunting Jet Provost T.3A
XM553		G-AWSV	Saro Skeeter AOP.12
XM575		G-BLMC	Avro Vulcan B.2A
XM655		G-VULC	Avro Vulcan B.2A
XM685	"PO/513"	G-AYZJ	Westland Whirlwind HAS.7
XM693		G-TIMM	Folland Gnat T.1
XM697		G-NAAT	Folland Gnat T.1
XM819		G-APXW	Lancashire Acft EP.9 (Army)
XN351		G-BKSC	Saro Skeeter AOP.12 (Army)
XN441		G-BGKT	Auster AOP.9
XN459		G-BWOT	Hunting Jet Provost T.3A
XN470		G-BXBJ	Hunting Jet Provost T.3A
XN498	"16"	G-BWSH	Hunting Jet Provost T.3A
XN510		G-BXBI	Hunting Jet Provost T.3A
XN629	"49"	G-BVEG	Hunting Jet Provost T.3A
XN637	"03"	G-BKOU	Hunting Jet Provost T.3
XP242		G-BUCI	Auster AOP.9 (Army)

588

Serial	Code	Regn	Type
XP254		G-ASCC	Auster AOP.11
XP279		G-BWKK	Auster AOP.9 (Army)
XP282		G-BGTC	Auster AOP.9
XP355	"A"	G-BEBC	Westland Whirlwind HAR.10
XP672	"27"	G-RAFI	Hunting Jet Provost T.4 (Still 8458M)
XP772		G-BUCJ	DHC.2 Beaver AL.1 (Army)
XP907		G-SROE	Westland Scout AH.1
XP924		G-CVIX	DH.110 Sea Vixen D.3
XR240		G-BDFH	Auster AOP.9 (Army)
XR241		G-AXRR	Auster AOP.9 (Army)
XR246		G-AZBU	Auster AOP.9
XR267		G-BJXR	Auster AOP.9
XR486		G-RWWW	Westland Whirlwind HCC.12 (Queens Flight)
XR537		G-NATY	Folland Gnat T.1
XR595	"M"	G-BWHU	Westland Scout AH.1 (Army)
XR673		G-BXLO	Hunting Jet Provost T.4
XR724		G-BTSY	EE Lightning F.6
XR944		G-ATTB	Wallis WA.116
XR991		G-MOUR	Folland Gnat T.1 (Yellowjacks)
XR993		G-BVPP	Folland Gnat T.1 (Red Arrows)
XS101		G-GNAT	Folland Gnat T.1 (Red Arrows)
XS165	"37"	G-ASAZ	Hiller UH-12E (RN)
XS587	"252/V"	G-VIXN	DH.110 Sea Vixen FAW.2
XS765		G-BSET	Beagle Basset CC.1
XS770		G-HRHI	Beagle Basset CC.1 (Queens Flight)
XT223		G-BGZK	Westland Sioux AH.1 (Army)
XT610		G-APRS	Scottish Twin Pioneer (RAE)
XT788		G-BMIR	Westland Wasp HAS.1
XV126	"X"	G-SCTA	Westland Scout AH.1 (Army)
XV130	"R"	G-BWJW	Westland Scout AH.1 (Army)
XV134		G-BWLX	Westland Scout AH.1 (Army)
XV140		G-KAXL	Westland Scout AH.1 (Army)
XV268		G-BVER	DHC.2 Beaver (Army)
XW289	"73"	G-JPVA	BAC Jet Provost T.5A
XW293	"Z"	G-BWCS	BAC Jet Provost T.5
XW310	"37"	G-BWGS	BAC Jet Provost T.5A
XW324		G-BWSG	BAC Jet Provost T.5
XW325	"E"	G-BWGF	BAC Jet Provost T.5A
XW333	"79"	G-BVTC	BAC Jet Provost T.5A
XW355	"20"	G-JPTV	BAC Jet Provost T.5A
XW423	"14"	G-BWUW	BAC Jet Provost T.5A
XW428		G-TOMG	BAC Jet Provost T.4
XW431	"A"	G-BWBS	BAC Jet Provost T.5A
XW433	"63"	G-JPRO	BAC Jet Provost T.5A
XW635		G-AWSW	Beagle Husky
XW784	"VL"	G-BBRN	Mitchell-Procter Kittiwake (RN)
XX110		BAPC.169	BAC/Sepecat Jaguar GR.1
XX263	"263"	BAPC.152	BAe Hawk T.1A
XX297		BAPC.171	BAe Hawk T.1 (Red Arrows)
XX467		G-TVII	Hawker Hunter T.7
XX725	"GU"	BAPC.150	BAC/Sepecat Jaguar GR.1
XZ363	"A"	BAPC.151	BAC/Sepecat Jaguar GR.1A
ZA368	"AJ"/"P"	BAPC.155	Panavia Tornado GR.1
ZA634	"C"	G-BUHA	Slingsby T-61F Venture T.2
ZA663		G-BUFP	Slingsby T-61F Venture T.2
ZD472	"01"	BAPC.191	BAe Harrier GR.5
8458M	"27"	G-RAFI	Hunting Jet Provost T.4
G-17-3		G-AVNE	Westland Wessex 60
G-29-1		G-APRJ	Avro Lincoln
G-48/1	(Class "B")	G-ALSX	Bristol Sycamore
U-0247	(Class "B")	G-AGOY	Miles Messenger (Intended marks)
W-2	(Class "B")	BAPC.85	Weir W-2
215		G-HELV	DH.115 Vampire T.55
F		G-RUMW	Grumman FM-2 Wildcat (RN/FAA)

OTHER ARMED FORCES

Australia

A2-4		VH-ALB	Supermarine Seagull
A16-199	"SF-R"	G-BEOX	Lockheed Hudson IIIA
A17-48		G-BPHR	DH.82A Tiger Moth
361		N36SF	Hawker Sea Fury FB.11 (RAN)
WH588	"NW/114"	G-EEMV	Hawker Sea Fury FB.11 (RAN)

Serial	Code	Regn	Type
Belgium			
HD-75		N75 (G-AFDX)	Hanriot HD.1
Canada			
622		N6699D	Piasecki HUP-3 Retreiver (RCN)
671		G-BNZC	DHC.1 Chipmunk
920	"QN-."	CF-BXO	Supermarine Stranraer
16693	"693"	G-BLPG	Auster J/1N (Painted as AOP.6)
18013		G-TRIC	DHC.1 Chipmunk
18393		G-BCYK	Avro Canada CF.100 Canuck IV
20310	"310"	G-BSBG	N.A. Harvard IV
China			
1219	"57"	G-BVVG	Nanchang CJ-6A
2028	"69"	G-BVVF	Nanchang CJ-6A
1532008	"08"	G-BVFX	Nanchang CJ-6A
Czechoslavakia			
TE566	"DU-A"	G-BLCK	Supermarine Spitfire IXE
France			
73		G-BWRF	Morane-Saulnier MS.505 Criquet
120	"3"	G-AZGC	Stampe SV-4C
124		G-BOSJ	Nord 3400
143		G-MSAL	Morane-Saulnier MS.733 (Aeronavale)
185		G-BWLR	Max Holste Broussard
192	"44-GI"	G-BKPT	Max Holste Broussard
316/315-SN		F-GGKR	Max Holste Broussard
394		G-BIMO	Stampe SV-4C
396		G-BWRE	Stampe SV-4C
56-5395	"CDG"	G-CUBJ	Piper L-18C Super Cub (ALAT)
MS.824		G-AWBU	Morane-Saulnier N replica
1/4513		G-BFYO	SPAD XII replica
(F-GGKG)	"315-SQ"	G-BWGG	Max Holste Broussard
Germany			
3		G-BAYV	Nord 1101 (pseudo Messerschmitt)
3 (Red)		G-BOML	Messerschmitt Bf.109 (HA.1112)
4		G-BSLX	WAR FW190 Scale replica
6 (Black)		G-USTV	Messerschmitt Bf.109G-2
7		G-BWRD	Klemm Kl.35D
8 + -		G-WULF	WAR FW190 Scale replica
14		BAPC.67	Messerschmitt Bf.109 replica
14+		G-BBII	Fiat G-46
114		G-BSMD	Nord 1101 (pseudo Messerschmitt)
152/17		G-ATJM	Fokker DR.1 replica
422/15		G-AVJO	Fokker E-III replica
425/15		G-BWRJ	Fokker DR.1 replica
425/17		BAPC.133	Fokker DR.1 replica
626/8		N6268	Fokker D.VII (Travel Air 2000)
D5397/17		G-BFXL	Albatros D.VA replica
1227	"DG+HO"	G-FOKW	Focke-Wulfe FW190A-5
1480	"6"	BAPC.66	Messerschmitt Bf.109 replica
6357	"6"	BAPC.74	Messerschmitt Bf.109 replica
7198/18		G-AANJ	LVG C.VI
AM+YA		G-AMYA	Bucker (Zlin) 181 Bestmann
BU+CC		G-BUCC	Bucker (CASA) 131 Jungmann
BU+CK		G-BUCK	Bucker (CASA) 131 Jungmann
CC+43		G-CJCI	Pilatus P.2 (pseudo Arado Ar.96B)
CF+HF		EI-AUY	Fieseler Storch (MS.502)
D604		G-FLIZ	Staaken Flitzer
D692		G-BVAW	Staaken Flitzer
F+IS		G-BIRW	Fieseler Storch (MS.505)
LG+01		G-AYSJ	Bucker 133 Jungmeister
LG+03		G-AEZX	Bucker 133 Jungmeister
NJ+C11		G-ATBG	Messerschmitt Bf.108 (Nord 1002)
RJ+NP		G-BFHF	Junkers (CASA) Ju52/3m
S4+A07		G-BWHP	Bucker (CASA) 131 Jungmann
S5+B06		G-BSFB	Bucker (CASA) 131 Jungmann
TA+RC		G-BPHZ	Fieseler Storch (MS.505)
TQ+BC		LV-ZAU	Focke-Wulf FW.44J Steiglitz
2+1	"7334"	G-SYFW	WAR FW190 Scale replica

Serial	Code	Regn	Type
28+10		G-BWTT	Aero L-39ZO Albatros
6J+PR		G-AWHB	Heinkel (CASA) He.111H-16
97+04		G-APVF	Putzer Elster B
-		G-BFPL	Fokker D.VII replica (Skull & crossbones c/s)

Hungary

503		G-BRAM	Mig 21PF

Ireland

177		G-BLIW	Percival Provost T.51

Italy

MM12822		G-FIST	Fieseler Fi 156C Storch
W7		G-AGFT	Avia FL.3

Japan

24		BAPC.83	Kawasaki Ki 100-1b
2-134		114700 (French)	NA T-6G Texan

Jordan

712	"E"	G-BWKC	Hawker Hunter F.58

Netherlands

BI-005		G-BUVN	Bucker (CASA) Jungmann
E-15		G-BIYU	Fokker S.11 Instructor
R-151		G-BIYR	Piper L-21B Super Cub
R-163		G-BIRH	Piper L-21B Super Cub
R-167		G-LION	Piper L-21B Super Cub
S-9		G-BUVF	DHC.2 Beaver

New Zealand

NZ3009		ZK-AMH	Curtiss P-40E Kittyhawk
NZ5648	"648"	G-BXUL	Vought FG-1D Corsair

North Korea

01420		G-BMZF	MiG-15

Norway

321		G-BKPY	Saab Safir
423		G-AMRK	Gloster Gladiator

Portugal

85		G-BTPZ	Hawker (Isaacs) Fury
1377		G-BARS	DHC.1 Chipmunk
1747		G-BGPB	CCF Harvard 4

Spain

E3B-143		G-JUNG	CASA I.131 Jungmann
E3B-153	"781-75"	G-BPTS	CASA I.131 Jungmann
E3B-350	"97- "	G-BHPL	CASA I.131 Jungmann
E3B-369	"781-32"	G-BPDM	CASA I.131 Jungmann
-	"781-25"	G-BRSH	CASA I.131 Jungmann
-	"781-26"	G-BUOR	CASA I.131 Jungmann

Sweden

32028		G-BMSG	SAAB 32 Lansen

Serial	Code	Regn	Type
Switzerland			
A-10		G-BECW	Bucker (CASA) Jungmann
A-57		G-BECT	Bucker (CASA) Jungmann
A-806		G-BTLL	Pilatus P.3
J-1149		G-SWIS	DH.100 Vampire FB.6
J-1573		G-VICI	DH.112 Venom FB.50
J-1605		G-BLID	DH.112 Venom FB.50
J-1611		G-DHTT	DH.112 Venom FB.50
J-1614		G-BLIE	DH.112 Venom FB.50
J-1632		G-VNOM	DH.112 Venom FB.50
J-1758		G-BLSD	DH.112 Venom FB.50
J-4031		G-BWFR	Hawker Hunter 58
J-4058		G-BWFS	Hawker Hunter 58
J-4081		G-BWKB	Hawker Hunter 58
J-4083		G-EGHH	Hawker Hunter 58
J-4090		G-SIAL	Hawker Hunter 58
U-80		G-BUKK	Bucker Jungmeister
U-95		G-BVGP	Bucker Jungmeister
U-110		G-PTWO	Pilatus P.2
U-142		G-BONE	Pilatus P.2
U-1234		G-DHAV	DH.115 Vampire T.11
V-54		G-BVSD	SE.3130 Alouette II
USA			
2		G-AZLE	Boeing-Stearman Kaydet (US Army)
5		G-BEEW	Taylor Mono (Boeing P-26A) (US Army)
14		G-ISDN	Boeing-Stearman Kaydet (US Army)
23		N49272	Fairchild PT-23 Cornell (USAAC)
26		G-BAVO	Boeing-Stearman Kaydet (US Army)
27		G-AGYY	Ryan PT-21 (USAAC)
27		G-BRVG	NA SNJ-7 Texan (US Navy)
28		N8162G	Boeing-Stearman Kaydet (US Army)
33		G-THEA	Boeing-Stearman Kaydet (US Navy)
43	"SC"	G-AZSC	NA AT-16 Texan (USAAF)
44		G-BWHH	Piper L-21B Super Cub (US Army)
44		G-RJAH	Boeing-Stearman Kaydet (US Army)
49		G-KITT	Curtiss TP-40M Kittyhawk (US Army)
54		G-BCNX	Piper L-4H (USAF)
85		G-BTBI	Republic P-47 Thunderbolt Scale replica (USAF)
112		G-BSWC	Boeing-Stearman Kaydet (US Army)
118		G-BSDS	Boeing-Stearman Kaydet (US Army)
208		N75664	Boeing-Stearman Kaydet
243		G-BUKE	Boeing-Stearman Kaydet (US Army)
379		G-ILLE	Boeing-Stearman Kaydet (US Army)
441		G-BTFG	Boeing-Stearman Kaydet (US Navy)
526		G-BRWB	NA T-6G Texan (USAF)
624	"D-39"	G-BVMH	Piper L-4 (Wag-Aero Cuby) (USAAC)
669		N75TL	Boeing-Stearman Kaydet (US Army)
854		G-BTBH	Ryan PT-22 (US Army)
855		N56421	Ryan PT-22 (US Army)
897	"E"	G-BJEV	Aeronca Chief (US Navy)
985		G-ERIX	Boeing-Stearman Kaydet (US Navy)
1164		G-BKGL	Beechcraft C-45 (US Army)
1180		G-BRSK	Boeing-Stearman Kaydet (US Navy)
1411		N444M	Grumman Widgeon (US Coast Guard)
2807	"V-103"	G-BHTH	NA T-6G Texan (US Navy)
6531	"5"	G-BSKS	Nieuport 28C-1 (US AEF)
7797		G-BFAF	Aeronca L-16A (US Army)
8178	"FU-178"	G-SABR	North American F-86A Sabre (USAF)
02538		N33870	Fairchild PT-19 Cornell (USAAC)
14863	"TA-863"	G-BGOR	NA AT-6D Texan (USAAF)
16136	"205"	G-BRUJ	Boeing-Stearman Kaydet (US Navy)
18263	"822"	N38940	Boeing-Stearman Kaydet (USAAC)
28521	"TA-521"	G-TVIJ	NA T-6J Harvard (USAF)
29261		G-CDET	Culver Cadet (USAAF) (Not used as NC29261)
31145	"G-26"	G-BBLH	Piper L-4B (US Army)
31171		N7614C	NA B-25J Mitchell (US Marines)
31952		G-BRPR	Aeronca L-3C Grasshopper (US Army)
34037		N9115Z	NA B-25N Mitchell (USAAF)
38674		G-MTKM	Thomas-Morse S4 Scout Scale replica (USASC)
40467	"19"	G-BTCC	Grumman F6F Hellcat (US Navy)
41386		G-MJTD	Thomas-Morse S4 Scout Scale replica (USASC)
46214	"3-X"	CF-KCG	Grumman TBM-3E Avenger (USN)
53319	"RB/319"	G-BTDP	Grumman TBM-3R Avenger (US Navy)
54137	"69"	G-CTKL	Noorduyn Harvard IIB (US Navy)

Serial	Code	Regn	Type
67543	"KI-S"	NX3145X	Lockheed P-38J Lightning (USAAF)
80425	"4- WT"	G-RUMT	Grumman F7F-3P Tigercat (USN)
80480	"E-44"	G-BECN	Piper L-4J (USAAC)
91007	"TR-007"	G-NASA	Lockheed T-33A (USAF)
93542	"LTA-542"	G-BRLV	NA T-6 Texan (USAF)
111836	"JZ/6"	G-TSIX	NA AT-6C Texan (US Navy)
111989		N33600	Cessna L-19A Bird Dog (US Army)
115042	"TA-042"	G-BGHU	NA T-6G Texan (USAF)
115302	"TP"	G-BJTP	Piper L-18C Super Cub (US Marines)
115684		G-BKVM	Piper L-21A Super Cub (US Army)
124485	"DF-A"	G-BEDF	Boeing B-17G Flying Fortress (USAAC)
122351		G-BKRG	Beechcraft C-45G
126603		G-BHWH	Weedhopper JC-24C (US Navy)
126922	"AK-402"	G-RAID	Douglas AD-4NA Skyraider (US Navy)
151632		G-BWGR	NA TB-25N Mitchell (USAF)
21714	"201B"	G-RUMM	Grumman F8F-2P Bearcat (USN)
217786	"177"	G-BRTK	Boeing-Stearman Kaydet (USAAF)
226413	"ZU-N"	N47DD	Republic P-47D Thunderbolt (USAAF)
226671	"MX-X"	N47DD	Republic P-47D Thunderbolt (USAAF)
231983	"IY-G"	F-BDRS	Boeing B-17G Flying Fortress (USAAF)
233752	"52"	G-BVCV	Fairchild PT-19A Cornell (USAAC)
236800	"A-44"	G-BHPK	Piper L-4A (USAAF)
237123		BAPC.157	Waco CG-4A Hadrian
243809		BAPC.185	Waco CG-4A Hadrian
252983		N66630	Schweizer TG-3A
269097		G-BTWR	Bell P-63A Kingcobra (USAAF)
314887		G-AJPI	Fairchild UC-61 Forwarder (USAAF)
315509	"W7-S"	G-BHUB	Douglas C-47A Dakota (USAAF)
329405	"A-23"	G-BCOB	Piper L-4H (USAAC)
329417		G-BDHK	Piper L-4A Cub (USAAC)
329471	"F-44"	G-BGXA	Piper L-4H (USAAC)
329601	"D-44"	G-AXHR	Piper L-4H (USAAC)
329854	"R-44"	G-BMKC	Piper L-4H (USAAC)
329934	"B-72"	G-BCPH	Piper L-4H (USAAC/French)
330238	"A-24"	G-LIVH	Piper L-4H (USAAC)
330485	"C-44"	G-AJES	Piper L-4H (USAAC)
343251	"27"	G-NZSS	Boeing-Stearman Kaydet (USAAC)
413573	"B6-V"	N6526D	NA P-51D Mustang (USAAC)
436021		G-BWEZ	Piper L-4 Cub (US Army)
454467	"J-44"	G-BILI	Piper L-4J (US Army)
454537	"J-04"	G-BFDL	Piper L-4J (US Army)
461748	"Y"	G-BHDK	Boeing B-29A Superfortress (USAF)
463209	"WZ- "	BAPC.255	NA P-51D Mustang (USAAF)
463221	"G4-S"	G-BTCD	NA P-51D Mustang (USAAF)
472216	"AJ-L"	G-BIXL	NA P-51D Mustang (USAAF)
472218	"WZ-I"	G-HAEC	NA P-51D Mustang (USAAF)
472773	"AJ-C"	G-SUSY	NA P-51D Mustang (USAAF)
474008	"VF-R"	G-PSIC	NA P-51D Mustang (USAAF)
479744	"M-49"	G-BGPD	Piper L-4H (USAAC)
479766	"D-63"	G-BKHG	Piper L-4H (USAAC)
480015	"M-44"	G-AKIB	Piper L-4H (USAAC)
480133	"B-44"	G-BDCD	Piper L-4J (USAAC)
480321	"H-44"	G-FRAN	Piper L-4J (USAAC)
480636	"A-58"	G-AXHP	Piper L-4J (USAAC)
480752	"E-39"	G-BCXJ	Piper L-4J (USAAC)
483868	"N"	N5237V	Boeing B-17G Flying Fortress (USAF)
493209		G-DDMV	NA T-6G Texan (Calif ANG)
607327	"L-09"	G-ARAO	Piper (L-21B) Super Cub (US Army)
3-1923		G-BRHP	Aeronca O-58B Grasshopper (US Army)
18-2001		G-BIZV	Piper L-18C Super Cub (US Army)
41-33275	"CE"	G-BICE	NA AT-6C Texan (USAAC)
42-17786	"25"	CF-EQS	Boeing-Stearman PT-17 (US Army)
42-58678	"IY"	G-BRIY	Taylorcraft L-2A (USAAC)
42-78044		G-BRXL	Aeronca L-3F (US Army)
42-84555	"EP-H"	G-ELMH	NA AT-6D Harvard (USAAC)
44-30861		N9089Z	NA B-25J Mitchell (USAAC)
44-63507		NL51EA	NA P-51D Mustang
44-79609	"PR"	G-BHXY	Piper L-4H (USAAC)
44-80594		G-BEDJ	Piper L-4J (USAAC)
44-83184	"7"	G-RGUS	Fairchild UC-61K Forwarder (USAAC)
51-7545	Fennec No.119	N14113	NA T-28B Trojan
51-7962	Fennec No.142	F-AZFV	NA T-28B Trojan
51-11701A	"AF258"	G-BSZC	Beechcraft C-45H (USAF)
51-15227	"10"	G-BKRA	NA T-6G Texan (US Navy)
52-8543	"66"	G-BUKY	NA (CCF) Harvard IV (US Navy)
54-2447		G-SCUB	Piper L-21B Super Cub (US Army)
54-21261		G-TBRD	Lockheed T-33A (USAF)
146-11042	"7"	G-BMZX	SPAD replica (Wolf W.II) (US Army/AEF)

Serial	Code	Regn	Type
146-11083	"5"	G-BNAI	SPAD replica (Wolf W.II) (US Army/AEF)
I-492		G-BPUD	Ryan PT-22 (US Army)
-	"H-57"	G-AKAZ	Piper L-4A (USAAF)
-	"K-33"	G-BJLH	Piper L-18C Super Cub (US Army)

USSR

Serial	Code	Regn	Type
01		G-YKSZ	Yak 52
07		G-BMJY	Yak 18
09		G-BVMU	Yak 52 (DOSAAF)
15		G-BXJB	Yak 52 (DOSAAF)
26		G-BVXK	Yak 52 (DOSAAF)
27		G-OYAK	Yak 11
27		G-YAKX	Yak 52 (DOSAAF)
42			Yak 52
50		G-BWJT	Yak 50 (DOSAAF)
52		G-YAKY	Yak 52 (DOSAAF)
52		LY-AMP	Yak-52 (DOSAAF)
55		G-BVOK	Yak 52 (DOSAAF)
69		G-BTZB	Yak 50
72		G-BXAV	Yak 52 (DOSAAF)
74		G-BXID	Yak 52 (DOSAAF)
100		G-YAKI	Yak 52 (DOSAAF)
139		G-BWOD	Yak 52 (DOSAAF)
6247		G-OMIG	MiG-15 (Korean War c/s)
853007		G-BVVO	Yak 50
-		G-BTUB	Yak 11

Yugoslavia

Serial	Code	Regn	Type
30140		G-RADA	Soko Kraguj
30146		G-BSXD	Soko Kraguj
30149		G-SOKO	Soko Kraguj

Serial	Code	Regn	Type

AIRCRAFT WITHOUT EXTERNAL MARKINGS

		G-AANI	Blackburn Monoplane
		G-AANG	Bleriot XI
		G-ASPP	Bristol Boxkite replica
		G-BWJM	Bristol M.1C replica
		G-AANH	Deperdussin Monoplane
		G-EBNV	English Electric Wren
		G-BAAF	Manning-Flanders MF.1
		G-ARSG	Roe Triplane IV replica
		G-BFIP	Wallbro Monoplane

AIRCRAFT WITH FICTITIOUS MARKINGS

		Regn	Type
		K.158	Austin Whippet rep
			(See BAPC.207)
		"G-EAOU"	Vickers Vimy rep
			(See NX71MY)
		"G-EASQ"	Bristol 30/46 Babe III rep
			(See BAPC.87)
		"G-EBED"	Vickers 60 Viking IV rep
			(See BAPC.114)
		"G-AAAH"	DH.60G Moth rep
			(See BAPC.168)
		"G-AACA"	Avro 504K rep
			(See BAPC.177)
		"G-ABUL"	DH.82A Tiger Moth
			(C/n 83805) ex XL717/G-AOXG/T7291
			Fleet Air Arm Museum RNAS Yeovilton
		"G-ACDR"	DH.82A Tiger Moth
			(C/n 86536) ex N9295 Denton, Texas, USA 6.91
		"G-ACSS"	DH.88 Comet model
			(See BAPC.216)
		"G-ACSS"	DH.88 model
			(See BAPC.257)
		"G-ADRG"	Mignet HM.14 Pou-Du-Ciel
			(See BAPC.77)
		"G-ADRX"	Mignet HM.14 Pou-Du-Ciel
			(See BAPC.231)
		"G-ADRY"	Mignet HM.14 Pou-Du-Ciel
			(See BAPC.29)
		"G-ADVU"	Mignet HM.14 Pou-Du-Ciel
			(See BAPC.211)
		"G-ADYV"	Mignet HM.14 Pou-Du-Ciel
			(See BAPC.243)
		"G-ADZW"	Mignet HM.14 Pou-Du-Ciel
			(See BAPC.253)
		"G-AEFG"	Mignet HM.14 Pou-Du-Ciel
			(See BAPC.75)
		"G-AEOF"	Mignet HM.14 Pou-Du-Ciel
			(See BAPC.22)
		"G-AFAP"	CASA 352L (Junkers Ju52/3m)
			(C/n 163) ex Sp AF T2B-272 RAF Museum RAF Cosford
			(In original British Airways c/s)
		"G-AFFI"	Mignet HM.14 Pou-Du-Ciel
			(See BAPC.76)
		"G-AFUG"	Luton LA.4 Minor
			(See BAPC 97)
		"G-AJOV"	Westland WS-51 Dragonfly HR.3
			C/n WA/H/80 ex WP495 RAF Museum RAF Cosford
			(BEA c/s)
		"G-AMSU"	Douglas C-47A Dakota 3
			(See G-AMPP)
		"G-AOXL"	DH.114 Heron 2
			(See G-ANUO)
		"G-CARS"	Pitts S-2A Special
			(See BAPC.134)
		"G-CDBS"	MBB Bo.105D
			(See G-BCXO)
		"G-MAZY"	DH.82A Tiger Moth Winthorpe
			H.Hodgson "Maisie" (Cotswold Acft Restoration Grp)
			(Composite ex Newark components and G-AMBB/T6801;
			also reported as ex DE561 lost at sea in 1942;
			rebuilt for static display and on loan to
			Newark Air Museum 3.97)

SECTION 7 - PART 4 - BGA GLIDER INDEX

ABBOTT-BAYNES
SCUD I: HFZ

SCUD II: AAA

SCUD III: ACF AVA

AEROMERE M.100S - see CARMAM

ALLGAIER GEIER: EBP

ASC
FALCON: HPZ

SPIRIT: HPY

AVIA 40P: AUW

AVIALSA - see SCHEIBE:

AVIONAUTICA RIO - see CARMAM:

BAC VII replica: EQY

BIBBY G.1: HPK

BIRMINGHAM GUILD BG.135 (including SWALES SD.3-15 & YORKSHIRE SAILPLANES YS-55 CONSORT): CRF CUF CXN CXP DCY DLZ

BOLKOW PHOEBUS C: CGX CHC CHJ CJB CJJ CKC GDD HTZ JHX

BREGUET 905 FAUVETTE: CVJ DGV EGR ELJ EPN ESM

CARMAM (including AEROMERE/AVIONAUTICA RIO)
M.100S MESANGE: CBR CLU DFP DTS DUC EPG EQM ETN FCH FKV HFP HGU HQF

M.200 FOEHN: EQX EVC FXN HCN HGJ

JP.15/36A AIGLON (and 15/34 KIT-CLUB): DYL EDB FDC FQV HKF HKZ HMU HTW

CAUDRON C.801: EHF

CENTRAIR ASW 20F - see SCHLEICHER
101 PEGASE: EPK EQK ERX ESD ESH ESW ETJ ETM ETQ EVE EVM EVQ FAN FCB FCD FEH FFC FFS FGW FHJ FJK FJT FMK FNM FRD FRR FRV FRX FVM FVN FVP FVV FWG FWX FWY FXD GBU GCN GCY HDD HDW HES HKN HNY HNZ HRK HZF

201 MARIANNE: HTA

ALLIANCE SNC-34: JHR

CHARD OSPREY - see KING-ELLIOTT-STREET OSPREY

DFS
DFS/49 GRUNAU BABY - see GRUNAU BABY

KRANICH (including SCHLEICHER): BGT BQJ

OLYMPIA-MEISE - see EoN OLYMPIA & NORD 2000: AKD

108-68 WEIHE (including FOCKE-WULF WEIHE 50): AKC BKC BNC BTV BWR EDL

DWLKK PW-5 SMYK: HYM HZB JCG JDW JKB JKE

EDGLEY EA.9: HPJ

EICHELSDORFER SB.5: EHC EJH HYC

EIRI PIK-20: DFE DFK DFZ DHH DHN DHV DJN DJZ DKT DLJ DLY DMU DMV DMY DPL DQU DRT DVJ DVN DWS DYT DZT EAR EAT JBH JGK

EoN:
AP.5 OLYMPIA - see DFS/NORD 2000: AMK AMP AMR AMT AMW ANW APC APV ART AUU AVD AWU AZR AZT BBH BCK BEL BGR BGX BHC BJC BKK BKL BKS BKU BKX BLN BLP BLQ BLS BNG BPL BQQ BRL BWX CAF CAK CBS CGU CHK CPE CQG CTA CTS DBA DPU EI-115

AP.6 OLYMPIA 401/403/419: BLJ BLK BVW DAL DTR

AP.7 PRIMARY (ETON TX.1): AQQ AQY AQZ CLJ FEZ

AP.8 BABY: ASS AST G-ALRH EI-118

AP.10 460/463/465: BQM BQS BQT BRQ BSQ BTG BTN BTQ BUG BUH BUK BUV BVN BWB BWE BWG BWU BXC BXY BYE BZB BZR BZS BZV BZW CAB CAN CAT CBV ELS G-APWL

FAUVEL
AV.22S: DSM

AV.36C: ETE

FEDEROV Me-7 MECHTA: HMZ HPS HPT HUQ JFY JFZ JGA

FFA DIAMANT: CDG CDW CGM CGS HGT

FOCKE-WULF
KRANICH III: ENG

WEIHE 50: see DFS WEIHE

GINN-LESNIAK KESTREL: CJC

GLASER-DIRKS
DG-100/DG-101: DFN DHJ DHK DHL DKQ DMD DRB DUY EDN EDP EKP ENU EPU FBH FBW FFU FYU HMS HWP JEZ

DG.200/DG.202: DTA DTM DUQ DWJ DXN DYH EBR EDM EKA EME EMU EQP FQC HAT HBD HDH JAE JAJ JAW JDD JDP JHW JKF JKM EI-145 EI-147

DG.300/DG.303 ELAN: ESQ FAJ FBF FCM FDW FGT FJR FJS FJX FLC FLX FNS FPK FSR FSX FTS FUJ FUT FUU FWM FZW GAJ GBS HBE HBW HCU HCY HDR HMB HSB HVM JAB JDV GGA.312

DG-500/DG-505 ELAN: GBZ HBP HEF HGV HHJ HNA HRC HYE JDN

DG-600: FKB FNT FPW FQQ FVG

DG-800: HPU JBL JJH

GLASFLUGEL
H.201 STANDARD LIBELLE: CFS CFX CFY CKF CKY CLM CLN CLP CLR CLV CLW CMH CMQ CMR CMS CMV CMW CMX CNE CNF CNG CNH CNJ CNP CNY CPA CPF CPM CRB CRQ CRS CRV CRW CSJ CSR CTU CUJ CUK CVL CVQ CWE CWG CWN CWT CWX CWY CWZ CXK CYG CZL DCC DMS DNL ECY FLT FLU GAU GDM GEE HAA HAD HAV HCQ HHY HJR HWC HWG JAS JBF JEU JGZ JHJ

H.205 CLUB LIBELLE: DBP DEQ DKZ DVM FAR FYG GCS HAE

H.206 HORNET: DKD DKM

H.301 LIBELLE: FEV GAN HLK

H.303 MOSQUITO: DMN DPK DRN DTK DTV DTX DTY DUB DVZ DWB DWL DWO DWR DXA DXW EAK ECH ECS EDH EDJ FBN FWR HMT JEH

H.304: EHU ENT HMM

H.604: ECT

GROB - see SCHEMPP-HIRTH
G.102/G.104 (SPEED) ASTIR: DFR DJD DJQ DJX DKR DKS DKU DKV DKW DKX DLH DLM DMH DMP DMR DNC DNE DNK DPJ DPQ DPY DQB DQE DQG DQR DRK DRU DRW DSH DSN DSU DUL DUX DWQ DWU DXJ DYF DZJ DZU EAC EAF EAW EBB EBM ECQ EEQ EKF ELN EQD EVK EVL FBR FCJ FDF FEB FEF FEX FHW FGK FHT FHW FJH FJH FRL FSA FSH FSZ FTK FTR FXA GAT GBJ GBK GCL GDQ GEB HAU HBL HBM HBT HCS HFD HGB HJV HKB HKM HPM HQT HRA HSE HTD HTE HTG HTR HUN HVK HWK HXB HXM HXY HYQ HZC JAZ JBZ JCF JCR JCW JEK JFD JHE JHG JHN JKW JLR JML R8 R9 R18 R19 R57 R60 R63 R67 R77 R97 GGA.540 GGA.742 AGA.6 EI-124

G.103 TWIN ASTIR/ACRO: DRQ DSJ DSL DUU EGN EWP EWR EZE FEA FFJ FQK FWC HBH HBK HCA HCJ HQS HWW JKV JLD JLZ R50 R52 R58 R70 R71 GGA.556

GRUNAU BABY (including DFS/FOKKER/HAWKRIDGE): ABZ AQN ASC BTD CBK CMY CRM CYJ DNA DNB DUW DWF EHX EMW HJB D-8006 D-3-340

HAWKRIDGE DAGLING: ALX ALZ

HIRTH Go.III MINIMOA: CLY

HOLS-DER-TEUFEL: FHQ

HUTTER
H.17: ALW EPR HEY

H.28: HJM HPB

ICA
IS-28B2: DEG DLT DLU DZR EHS EHW EJA HMG R93

IS-29D: DAM DBG DDJ DEN DEZ FDG FFN

IS-30: FDB FDP

IS-32A: FAV

ISF MISTRAL C: JBE

ISSOIRE
 D77 IRIS: EET EJW

 E78 SILENE: EBE EEU HPA

JANSSON BJ-1B DUSTER: ETL

JASTREB STANDARD CIRRUS - see SCHEMPP-HIRTH

KING-ELLIOTT-STREET OSPREY: DCZ

LAK-12 LIETUVA: FXR GAB GCB GCJ HEG HGQ HGR HGX HHM HHW HLT HQG HRB HSR HTF JBS JBY JFW

LANAVERRE - see SCHEMPP-HIRTH

LET
 L-13 BLANIK: BVY BXR BXV BXW CAW CFD CUZ CVA CVB CYR DCL DEX DEY DGB DGP DKH DPD DVD EFX ESV EUG EVR FDV FLV FZS GAK HTY JDU JGQ EI-120

 L-23 SUPER BLANIK: FXP FYP FYR FYS

 L-33 SOLO: FZY FZZ

LETOV LF-107 LUNAK: HXL

MANUEL
 CONDOR: DJW

 WILLOW WREN: BGA.162

MARCO J-5: HKW

MAUPIN WOODSTOCK: HCG HPG

MDM-1 FOX: JCH JKC

MOLINO PIK.20 - see EIRI

MONNETT MONERAI: FAP JBV

MULLER MOSWEY III: DXY

MUNCHEN MU-13D: CZM DPG

NEUKOM STANDARD ELFE S-2: FMR JGF

NORD 2000 - see EoN OLYMPIA: EPJ

OBERLERCHNER Mg19a STEINADLER: ERZ

OBERLERCHNER STANDARD AUSTRIA - see SCHEMPP-HIRTH

PENROSE PEGASUS: HKJ

PIK-16C VASAMA: CGV

PIK.20 - see EIRI

PILATUS B4 PC-11: CSN CSP CSW CUB CUC CUQ CUT CVG CVK CVM CVV CYA CYC CYK CZD DBC DLA DND DQM DRP DSV EQU HDA HDE HLC HSY HVH EI-121

POTTIER JP15 - see CARMAM

PZL
 SZD-8 JASKOLKA: DZS

 SZD-9 BOCIAN: BJD BVS CCN CEB CHF CKN CND CNM CTW CVP DAA DBW DBX DCR DDN DNF DRS EJY ESA FLL FUD FZG HFU HPF HQU

 SZD-12A MUCHA: HDM EI-100 EI-140

 SZD-24/SZD-32 FOKA: BZP BZZ CBP CMF CPC HGY

 SZD-30 PIRAT: CBN CDX CEN CHG CHL CKD CNK CPV CPX CQC CQX CSV CTV CTX CUM CVC CVR CXL CYD CZE CZG CZJ DAN DAP DAT DAU DBD DBV DCH DCJ DDK DDW DFW DGH DHB DHZ DJA DLW DNT DTW EQB FKD

 SZD-36A COBRA 15: CQW CRD CVN CVS CVT CXH CXJ DAC DAQ DCA

 SZD-38A JANTAR-1: DAV DDE DDV DFL DFU DFV FNE

 SZD-41A/SZD-48 JANTAR-STANDARD: DFX DHC DJL DJM DVK EKK ESP ETK FDX FHV FQT FTJ HBS HUB

 SZD-42 JANTAR-2: DNU EUV HFJ

SZD-50-3 PUCHACZ: EUF EVS FBG FEN FTH FUY FWE FWT FYA FYL FZQ GBD GCK GCU GEL HAC HAF HAS HCC HCD HCF HDP HEP HFH HHA HHC HSC HYP JEC G-BTJV

SZD-51-1 JUNIOR: FFV FFY FHF FPM FTC FUS FZA FZF FZP FZX GCC HCR HCW HDB HDU HEK HHD HHE HMA HNK HQV HRG HRP JJQ JLG JMG AGA.5

SZD-55: GAX HEC HHR HRV HVD

SZD-59 ACCRO: HVA HWX

RAAB DOPPELRAAB: EVU

ROLLADEN-SCHNEIDER
LS1F: FQZ

LS3: DNQ ECP EEF EES EEX EEZ EFS EFZ EGE EVD GAD GDA GDN HWR HYH JDJ EI-137

LS4: EHK EHL EKV ELT EMB EMF EMG EMT EMY ENA ENE EQA ERV ESC ESE ESY ETG ETV ETY EUH FAQ FHL FJM FKG FLF FNU FVE FYH GBT GDJ HEL HKX HLB HMX HNV HNX HPL HVV HXF HXT HXZ HZM HZY JBX JEP JJB JKP JLH JLJ AGA.1 AGA.2

LS6: FBE FCP FMC FRA GAR GBG GBQ GBR GCM HAQ HBC HBJ HET HEW HEZ HFM HFQ HGP HHH HHT HHU HJC HJF HJP HJX HMK HPD HQL HQZ HRY HSA HUM HYA JBP JBQ JBU JCB JDG JDH JGC JLK R69 GGA.553

LS7: FMY FPD FQG FQH FTV FTY FUV FVH FVQ FWF FWJ FWU FXE FYB FYK FYW FZV GBL GBY GCZ HAY HBA HBY HDX HEH JEJ AGA.3

LS8: HQA HSZ HTL HTM HTP HTQ HTS HUG HUV HUW HVF HVL HVU HWL HWM HWS HXC HXN HXW HYF HYZ HZG HZP JBB JCL JCP JCY JDE JDK JDT JDY JEA JEG JFB JFL JFX JGS JHU JHY JJK JJU JKD JKL JKN JLN JMB JMF JMO JMR JMT JMW R4

SCHEIBE
BERGFALKE: CDR CEV EBD EPZ EVT FVD HQC

L-SPATZ (including AVIALSA/ROCHETEAU A.60 FAUCONNET): DLR DPR DPT DUH DVR DZC EFN EFR EQL FAK FHE FPF FXX HCP HWQ JHB GGA.502 EI-130

ZUGVOGEL III: EBS ELV FRS FSU FVL FVY FYE HKV HND HSH HXA EI-146

SF-26 STANDARD: DRL EDS EUM

SF-27A ZUGVOGEL V: DZV EKS EUE FHY FLZ FQF FQM FRM FUF FUQ FWH FZM GAV GBM GDW HGM HLU HMW HSG HSX HUS HVJ EI-142

SFH-34 DELPHIN: EPM FKQ

SCHEMPP-HIRTH
STANDARD AUSTRIA (including OBERLERCHNER): BPN DBT DKB

SHK/SHK-1: CAQ CAR CBU CCB CGT CGZ CJK CJL CJN CJZ CLG CVH DJS DKK DMK DTG ECG FJZ FZC

HS.2 CIRRUS & CIRRUS VTC: CDH CEA CEC CFK CGY CJR CLQ CUS CVE CVF CWL CWR CWS DDM DVY FXG GCQ HEV HTU HUL HUR JJA

HS.4 STANDARD CIRRUS (including CS-11/75, GROB/JASTREB): CKZ CLA CLH CNN CPU CQN CQR CQY CRH CRN CTB CTT CUL CYM CYP CYQ CYT DAS DDA DDR DFC DFY DGE DGX DLG DVS DXL DZF EEN EGK FBB FCN FGU FLW FMT FMU FRJ FRZ FVS FYJ FZK GAH GAL GCD GEP HAN HAX HFF HGG HJN HJU HJY HKC HKD HKR HKS HKU HMY HNM HRL HSV HVZ HWD HWF HWY HXX HZJ HZL HZU HZV JBJ JCJ JCN JCU JDS JER JEV JEY JFA JGN JGY JHA JHH JJJ JJM JLX JMH

HS.5 NIMBUS 2: CQL CQP CQQ DAJ DDD DGY DHW DKL DMM DNG DTU DYU DYZ DZK EAJ EAM EEK EFB EFF EFT EGS EHP EHT EKR EKW FCS FPP FRC FVF FVT HBF HBV HNE HNH HQN JGH JMN JMV G-BKPM

HS.6 JANUS: DTC EKB HDG HNB HSP HTB HTH HUC HUH JAA JFE JLM R2 R9 R16

HS.7 MINI NIMBUS: DPH DSE DSP DSW DXQ DXT EAV EBF EBK EDF EER EGW FHG FSL HQY HRQ JGU

NIMBUS 3/4: ENN ENP EQN ERU EVF FAM FBM FFK FGF FRP FWK FXQ HBR HCB HFX HKQ HNU HWN HYY HZA HZW JCT JDA JDZ JEQ JFQ JHF JJG

DISCUS A/B/CS: FBY FDU FEJ FER FES FFT FFX FHR FKK FKM FLE FMG FMQ FNL FNQ FNR FQY FTW FUL FUP FXM FYM FYN FYX GCT GDR GDX HCL HDF HDT HDZ HEE HEM HEN HGK HGL HGS HGZ HHP HHQ HJH HJL HKA HKL HKY HLD HLN HLQ HLS HLY HML HMP HMQ HPH HPR HPX HQJ HQM HQR HQW HRS HRX HSD HSJ HSQ HUZ HVR HWV HXH HYB HYU HZE JAH JAN JAQ JAR JBD JBN JBR JBW JCK JCX JDL JFC JFG JGL JGM JGR JHM JHT JHV JJD JJE JJZ JKR JKX JLC JLP JLW JMD JMM R6 R10 R12 R15 R17 R23 R27 R39 R53 R55 R61 R87 GGA.501 GGA.547 AGA.4 EI-138

DUO DISCUS: HNF HNN HNW HQE HRW HSW HWB JAC JEM JFF JFH JGV JJP R1 R26

VENTUS A/B/C: EHH EKH EKJ ELG ELR ENJ EPX EUJ EUS FAW FBT FCK FDE FEG FEP FHS FJJ FJQ FMN FNN FPE FPL FQN FRB FRT FUH FUR FVB FVW FWD FYC FZH GAP GAS HAJ HED HFA HFV HFY HGN HHN HUY HVE HWH HXR HYG JBG JCE JEF JET JFP JFR JFS JJY JKH JKY JLA JLU R24 R28 R30 R38 GGA.557

VENTUS 2: HSL HUP HUX HVE HVT HVY HWA HXS HYL HZS JAF JBC JEX JGP JLB

SCHLEICHER
RHONBUSSARD: AEM DFJ

RHONSPERBER: ABG

Ka2B RHONSCHWALBE: DCG DGT DJG DPP DRR ESK FBL FPU FSF HZN

Ka4 RHONLERCHE II: CTF CWV EAL EUT HQH GGA.591

Ka6/BR/CR (RHONSEGLER): BKJ BKW BND BNH BQL BTJ BTM BUZ BVR BVX BVZ BWC BXT BYL BYM BYU BZQ BZX CBM CBY CCJ CJY DAW DCF DCW DDY DEP DEV DGK DHG DJE DJR DKG DKN DLP DNW DNX DQC DQF DQJ DQS DRA DRD DRE DRF DRG DRY DSG DSR DSY DUR DVG DYC DYJ DYN DYP DYQ DZW ECC ECF EDG EEW EGL ELY EPW EQQ FBZ FDR FGJ FHZ FKA FKH FKU FKX FLS FMM FNP FNW FQL FSE FTB FTF FUB FUM FWA FZR GAC GAW GBE GCP GDE GDF GEA GEF GEM HAB HBQ HEB HFB HPQ HRE HSN HUK HZH JCZ JEW JJV EI-111 127 128

Ka6E: BYX CAC CAE CAG CAS CCA CCD CCG CCL CCR CCU CCV CDA CDB CDD CDF CDV CDZ CED CEG CEL CEM CEQ CEW CEY CFL CGB CGD CGE CGK CGN CHB CHZ CKL CLZ CPJ DGG DHM DHT DLE DMQ DQK DSB DUS DVE DVH DWC DXH EAH EFM EHM EKC EKX ETB FCR FND FPV FRE FSS FVZ FXC FXS FXU GDV HAP HJD HRF JAK JAL JHD JHL JLT JLV

Ka7 RHONADLER: BFP BKN BQK BQU BRM BVB CFC CLF CLK CLT CMG CMZ CPG CQT CRA CWJ DBF DHY DJT DKY DMF DML DQX DRM DWE DWN DXM DYB DYR EAU EDC EDK EFD ELX EMV ENC EPV ETR ETU EUQ EVB EVG FEL FGV FGZ FHU FJW FKW FLK FMD FMZ FPQ FQU FRF FTG FTU FXH GAQ HAG HCM HGC HHL HJK HNJ HSS JME EI-105

K8B: CDC CDK CFF CGH CGJ CHU CJF CJM CKW CLX CML CMN CQD CTZ CYZ DDL DFQ DGA DHA DJP DKC DLD DLS DMB DMG DMJ DNZ DQL DQP DQY DRV DRZ DSF DTN DUF DUK DVQ DWG DWH DXP EAZ EEM EFG EFP EHA EJF EJG EPT EQZ ESJ ESX FAZ FBJ FCL FCQ FDD FDL FHN FJU FKJ FKT FLH FLP FLQ FNA FQD FQE FQR FQX FTA FTM FTN FVA FWL FXB FXW GCG GDB GDK GEG HAR HCZ HDN HDY HFW HJE HKK HLH HLV HMH HNG HRJ HRT HWE HWT HYN HYV HYW HYX HZX JAT JFT JGB JGD JGX JHK JLS R42 R44 R45 R47 R75 R91 R95 R98 GGA.558 GGA.562 AGA.21 NEJSGSA?? EI-108 EI-133

Ka10: EVH

ASK13 (including Ka7s modified to ASK13 standard): CAV CBW CCE CCF CCM CCP CCT CCW CCX CCY CCZ CDJ CEJ CEX CFA CFB CFG CFM CGQ CGR CHW CJD CKR CKU CKV CMK CRL CRT CWH DDB DKE DLC DMX DNV DQA DRJ DVB DVC DVX DXV EBL EBZ EDU EKD ENY EPP EQE EQF ETS EUC EVJ EVP FAT FCW FEQ FFA FGR FHM FHU FMH FPX FSD FSQ FVC FVU FWB FWN FYY FZN GBA HAL HDC HMV HPE HSM HTJ HUD HUF HUU HVQ HVW HXJ HXP HXV JFM JGW JJC JJW JKT JLE JLF JLL JLQ JMJ JMP JMW R3 R7 R31 R34 R37 R40 R41 R46 R51 R80 R83 R86 R88 R90 GGA.509 GGA.567 AGA.14 AGA.15 EI-112 EI-113 EI-143

ASW15: CHT CJP CKP CZN DDS FBC FBD FCY FDA FJV FKE FME FML FMS FPB FQB FRK FTD FXY GCH GCR GCX GDS GDY GEH HEJ HGF HJZ HNT HQX HTC HZD JAM JCA JDM JDR JED JGG JJX EI-134

ASW17: CPD CTE EDD EGD EI-132

ASK18: DJJ DJK DLB DNJ DPA EMH EUX HRN HSU JHQ JKG JKU JMA JMK R32 R33 R36 R43 R48 R49 GGA.563 EI-136

ASW19: DPX DSX DTD DTE DVL DVP DWZ DXX DZD DZG DZY EBJ EEH EJR ELA ENZ EPE EQG FFP FGP FNH FPJ FWP FWZ GCA GDP HCE HCV HDV HER HGH HHK HKT HLM HLW HNC HUA HWZ HXE HXU JBK JBT JCQ JDQ JES JFU JHC JHS JJL JKS

ASW20 (including CENTRAIR ASW 20F): DST DTP DTQ DUT DVV DVW DXB DXK DYE DYX EAE EBN EBX ECX EDE EEC EEE EEJ EEV EFA EFE EFH EFJ EFK EFL EFV EGP EHD EHV EHZ EJK EJL EJQ EKE EKU ELU ELZ ENV ENW EPF EPS EQJ ERA ETZ EUD EUK EUY FAF FBA FBQ FCV FFH FHD FJE FKL FPH FPN FPT FRH FRW FTL FTP FTQ FUN FWS FZL HBU HCH HDJ HDL HEQ HGW HHS HJT HLZ HPC HQD HQK HRU HSK HTT HTX HUJ HUT HVP HVX HYK HZT HZZ JAG JAY JEE JEN JFJ JFK JHZ JMQ G-BSTS BUCG

ASK21: ECW ECZ EDW EGZ EHQ ELE ENK EPD EQR ERH ESB ESU ETA FBV FWQ FYF FYV GAF GAG GAM GBB GBF GBN GBP GBV HCX HLG HLP HPV HPW HRR HTV HVG HYJ HYS HYT HZR JAD JAV JAX JBM JFV JGE JGJ JJR JKA JKJ JKQ JKZ JMC JMS R20 R21 R22 R35 R73 GGA.513 GGA.514 GGA.515 GGA.521 AGA.8 AGA.11 AGA.21

ASW22: FDT FEU FGY FNF GBX HTN

ASK23: EVV EVW EVX EVY FCX GCF HKP AGA.18

ASW24/E: FLN FLY FMP FMX FNG FXJ GDT GDU GDZ HBB HBG HYD JCD JEB JEL G-BVUP

ASH25: FKN FLG FST FSY FUG FWW FXL FYD FYZ GCE HAZ HFL HLX HXQ JCV JDF JFN

ASW27: HUE HXD HYR HZQ JCM JDC JJF JJT JLY

SCHMETZ CONDOR: DQH

SCHWEIZER TG-3A: N66630

SCOTT VIKING: AHU

SHENSTONE HARBINGER: BNA

SHORT NIMBUS: ALA

SIEBERT SIE 3: EFC FRG

SLINGSBY
T.1 FALCON 1: ABN FCZ

T.6 KITE 1: AAF AAX ACH ADJ AGW AHC

T.7 CADET: AWZ BQE

T.8 TUTOR: AJW AKW ALR AZK AZQ BAA BBG BCB BCH BDW BEF CRK CRZ CSL DQD IGA.6

T.9 KING KITE REPLICA: ELK

T.12 GULL I: AGE BED

T.13 PETREL: AHW ATR

T.15 GULL III: ATH HBZ

T.21: AQE AQG AQH ARM ASB ATK AUG AUJ AUP AWD AZC BCF BCU BDA BDM BFD BFY BGB BGG BGP BGY BJF BJV BMQ BMU BQF BTH BUW BXK BZA CEK DAR DCN DDC EJJ EJP ELH ERW ETP EUN EUZ FCF FCT FEE FFG FFL FFZ FGB FGG FGM FGS FHB FHC FJA FJB FJD FJF FKP FNC FTT GEN HCK HFC HFE HFG HNS HQB HRD JAU R92

T.25 GULL 4: APZ

T.26 KITE 2: AUD AVF EI-102

T.30B PREFECT: ARK ASN AVT AZF BAN CKJ DSA DTZ EBC EHE G-ALLF

T.31B: BZY CHQ EVA FCC FCG FDQ FFQ FGA FGC FHK FJN FSJ FUW HAK HHG HVB JCS EI-139

T.34 SKY: AVB AVC AVL AVQ BLL DPZ

T.38 GRASSHOPPER: FMA FSV GDC HEA HJJ HPP HVC JAP JBA JDB JJN JJS EI-135

T.41 SKYLARK 2: AWX AXB AXP AXR AXU AYD AYY AZP AZY BAH BAM BAV BAZ BBA BBU BCX BDY BEA BFL CCS CHE CYH DCE

T.42 EAGLE: AXJ AZA BAY BBB BBQ BDF

T.43 SKYLARK 3: AXD AXE AXL AYF AYH BAC BAW BBT BCM BCP BCS BCV BCW BER BET BEX BEZ BFC BFE BFG BGD BGH BGL BHQ BHT BJB BJK BJW BKE BUT

T.45 SWALLOW: BCY BDR BEM BEY BFB BHV BJP BJY BJZ BKP BLU BML BNS BNU BPX BRC BRE BRG BSX BTA BVF BWK BXP BYB BYJ BYK BZL BZM CAX CHY DCS DHP DLX ELC EMK FRQ HBX NEJSGSA.3 R99

T.49 CAPSTAN: BJQ BNR BPD BPS BPT BPU BPV BPW BRA BRW BSE BSK BSS BST BUC BUR BZG

T.50 SKYLARK 4: BKA BLA BLE BLH BLW BLZ BMW BMX BMY BNE BNK BNM BNN BNP BNQ BPA BPB BPC BPE BPG BPJ BPK BPZ BQZ BSC BSG BSH BSR BSY BSZ BTK BUE ERB FXF

T.51 DART: BRB BRD BRT BRU BRY BSA BSL BSM BSV BSW BUF BUL BUP BVC BVE BVH BVJ BVL BVM BWJ BWM BWP BWQ BWS BWT BXE BXG BXH BXL BXM BYA BYC BYG BZC BZF BZH BZJ CAZ CBA DBB

T.53 (including YORKSHIRE SAILPLANES YS-53 SOVEREIGN): CUD CXV CXW DHR

T.59 KESTREL: CFT CNV CNW CNX CPB CQJ CQM CSA CSB CSD CSF CSG CSK CTJ CTL CTM CTN CTP CTQ CTR CVW CVX CVY CVZ CWA CWB CWD CWF CXM CYN CZQ CZR CZS CZT CZU CZV CZW CZZ DBJ DBK DBN DBQ DBR DBS DEB DXU DYG ERY

T.65 VEGA: DWT DWW DXD DXE DXF DXG DXR DZA DZB DZM DZN DZP EAD EAG EBA ECJ ECK ECL ECM ECN EDA EDV EDX EDY EDZ EEA EEG EFW EGF EGG EGH EGJ EGT EGU EGX EHG EHN EHY EJB EJC EJD EJE EJS EJT EKY ELD ELQ EMJ EML EMN EMP EMR EMS EMZ FNK G-VEGA

STANDARD AUSTRIA - see SCHEMPP-HIRTH STANDARD AUSTRIA

SWALES SD.3-15 - see BIRMINGHAM GUILD BG-135

VFW-FOKKER FK-3: HJA

VALENTIN MISTRAL: JHP

VOGT LO-100 ZWERGREIHER: ELL

WASSMER
WA21 JAVELOT II: CJG

WA22 SUPER JAVELOT: CEH

WA26P SQUALE: EEP HFN HGA HHX

WA28F ESPADON: JDX

WA30 BIJAVE: FNX HMR

WRIGHT FALCON: ECA

YORKSHIRE SAILPLANES
YS-53 SOVEREIGN - see SLINGSBY T.53

YS-55 CONSORT - see BIRMINGHAM GUILD BG-135

ZLIN 24 KRAJANEK: ATV

AIR-BRITAIN SALES

Companion publications to the United Kingdom and Ireland Registers are also available by post-free mail order from
Air-Britain Sales Department (Dept UK99)
19 Kent Road, Grays
ESSEX RM17 6DE

VISA/MASTERCARD accepted - please give full details of card number and expiry date.

* EUROPEAN REGISTERS HANDBOOK 1999 (Available June 1999) - £ 21.00
   Current registers of over 40 Western and Eastern European countries plus Middle East.
   Available in ring-bound / hardback format.

* AIRLINE FLEETS 1999 (Available May 1999) - £ 18.50
   Over 1600 fleets listed plus leasing companies and "airliners in limbo". Available in
   ring bound/hardback format.

* BUSINESS JETS INTERNATIONAL 1999 (Available June 1999) - £ 15.00
   Complete production lists of all purpose-built business jets with full 20,000+ cross-reference.

* TURBOPROP AIRLINERS AND MILITARY TRANSPORTS OF THE WORLD 1999
   (Available Autumn 1999) - £ 18.50
   Detailed production lists of 80 turboprop airliner types including Eastern Europeans
   and military transports with full cross-reference index.

* JET AIRLINERS OF THE WORLD 1949-1998 (including military transport, reconnaissance
   and surveillance types and variants) - £ 17.50
   Detailed production lists of nearly 100 jet airliner types including expanded coverage on
   Soviet built types and purely military jet transports with full cross-reference index
   containing over 47,150 registrations and serials. 528 pages.

* CIVIL REGISTERS OF GERMANY 1996 - £ 15.50
   Current registers in same format as United Kingdom & Ireland Register.

* BUSINESS TURBOPROPS INTERNATIONAL 1996 - £ 12.50
   53 production lists - in same format as Business Jets International.

* COMPLETE CIVIL AIRCRAFT REGISTERS OF FINLAND SINCE 1926 - £ 11.00
   Fully researched and detailed history of all civilian aircraft in Finland.

* BAC ONE-ELEVEN - £ 20.00
   The complete development history and comprehensive production details, 240 A4 pages,
   hard cover.

* CONVAIRLINERS - £27.00
   Convair 110-680, full aircraft & operator histories, 24 pages of colour photos, 336 pages.

* BOEING 707/720/C-135 - £37.00
   Full production histories, airline and air force operators, almost 500 pages, 200 colour
   & nearly 100 b&w photos.

* MILITARY TITLES -
   Air-Britain also publishes a comprehensive range of military titles -

      * RAF Serial Registers
      * Detailed RAF Type "Files"
      * Squadron Histories
      * Royal Navy Aircraft Histories.

   Please write for details.

IMPORTANT NOTE - Members receive substantial discounts on all of the above Air-Britain publications.
For details of membership - see overleaf.

AIR-BRITAIN MEMBERSHIP

If you are not already a member of Air-Britain why not join now ?

Members can receive -

* Discounts on Air-Britain Monographs.

* Quarterly Air-Britain Digest A4 magazine

    - containing articles of current and historical aviation interest and comprehensive black & white and colour photographic coverage.

* Monthly Air-Britain News

    - 24.5cm x 17cm size magazine with minimum of 100 pages, includes

    - complete coverage of UK civil and military aviation scene;

    - comprehensive updates on virtually all overseas registers, including USA;

    - sections on bizjets, bizprops and jet, turbine & piston commercial aircraft;

    - full coverage of air displays, UK and overseas.

* Quarterly - Archive and Aeromilitaria.

    Historical A4 magazines packed with previously unpublished information and photos.

* Access to our Information Services, Black and White Photo and Colour Slide Libraries, Air-Britain Travel to overseas airfields, museums and displays.

* Access to our expanding Branch network.

   Basic Membership fee for 1999 is £32.00 (to include 4 Air-Britain Digests and 12 Air-Britain News).
   (Visa/Mastercard accepted - please give full card details including number and expiry date.)

   To join or for more information please write to:-

   Air-Britain Membership Department (Dept UK99)
   1 Rose Cottages
   179 Penn Road
   Hazlemere
   Bucks HP15 7NE

For samples of Air-Britain Digest and News please enclose £1.00; to include samples of Aeromilitaria and Archive please forward £2.00.